KU-175-197

The Good Pub Guide 2005

The Good Pub Guide 2005

Edited by
Alisdair Aird and Fiona Stapley

Managing Editor: Karen Fick
Assistant Editor: Elizabeth Adlington
Associate Editor: Robert Unsworth
Editorial Assistance: Fiona Wright, Tim Locke

EBURY PRESS
LONDON

Please send reports on pubs to

The Good Pub Guide
FREEPOST TN1569
WADHURST
East Sussex
TN5 7BR

or contact our website:
www.goodguides.co.uk

Good Guide publications are available at special discounts for bulk purchases or for sales promotions or premiums. Special editions, including personalized covers, excerpts of existing Guides and corporate imprints, can be created in large quantities for special needs. Enquiries should be sent to the Sales Development Department, Random House, 20 Vauxhall Bridge Road, London SW1V 2SA (020 7840 8400).

This edition first published in 2004 by Ebury Press,
Random House, 20 Vauxhall Bridge Road,
London SW1V 2SA

The Random House Group Limited Reg. No. 954009

www.randomhouse.co.uk

1 3 5 7 9 10 8 6 4 2

Copyright © 2004 The Random House Group Ltd.
Maps copyright © 2004 PerrottCartographics
Cover design by Main Artery
Cover photograph © 2004 Alamy Images

All rights reserved. No part of this publication may be reproduced, stored in a retrieval system, or transmitted in any form or by any means, electronic, mechanical, photocopying or otherwise, without the prior permission of the copyright owners.

Alisdair Aird has asserted his moral right to be identified as the author of this work in accordance with the Copyright, Design and Patents Act 1988.

A CIP catalogue record for this book is available from the British Library.

ISBN 0 09 189930 3

Typeset from author's disks by Clive Dorman
Edited by Pat Taylor Chalmers
Printed and bound in Great Britain by Cox and Wyman Ltd, Reading, Berkshire

Contents

Introduction

What's new this year? (Apart from all the new entries in this *Guide*, that is – more than 120 new main entries, more than 2,000 new small print entries, several hundred of which have never figured in any of our previous 22 editions.)

We have this year spotted a number of trends, some welcome, some not so welcome.

THE RISE AND RISE OF THE PUBCOS

Two non-brewing pub-owning companies or 'pubcos', Enterprise and Punch, now dominate the pub market. In this last year they have between them now amassed another 7,000 or so pubs, and between them now control some 16,000 pubs. These two giant chains have mushroomed by raising money to buy successive blocks of leased and tenanted pubs, sometimes sold to them by other similar financiers. Effectively, they secure their borrowings against the security of the pub properties, and against the income stream from them – both rental, and sales of beer, which they buy at huge discounts from the brewers, and which their tenants are tied to buy from them in turn.

Several years ago, when the former pub empires owned by a handful of big breweries started breaking up, and falling into the hands of these new operators, we recommended that each tenant of any very large pubcos should be given the right to sell one beer bought on the open market, rather than from their pubco. We warned that otherwise it seemed likely that an effective monopoly would form, pushing up beer prices without the restraining effects of normal competition.

In our beer price survey, Enterprise and Punch both average out at exactly the same price for a pint – £2.25. This is significantly more expensive than beer prices in free houses, where the price nationally averages out at £2.16.

It is difficult to escape the conclusion that this pattern of pub ownership, by loading nearly 10p a pint extra on to the cost of a pint, is working against the interests of consumers.

It seems imperative that the effects of price competition are now brought back into play. Tenants of pubcos owning more than a certain number of pubs – say, 3,000 – should be given the legal right to buy and stock one beer from an independent supplier other than their own pubco.

MORE PUBS GO SMOKE-FREE

The number of pubs which ban smoking completely is still very small, but this year has more than doubled. Fourteen of the main entries now ban smoking, against only six last year. What's more, they span the whole range of pubs, from smart dining places to simple taverns, from bustling town and city pubs to quiet and traditional country hideaways – one of them in the same family for at least 300 years.

This brings us to a much more demanding question.

Three-quarters of the pubs in this *Guide* are at least partly no smoking. In many, the no smoking part is dominant. Generally, this is simple business sense on the part of the pubs. They know that only a minority of their customers smoke. They know that their staff and customers are increasingly worried about the health risks of 'second-hand smoking', with mounting evidence that these risks are graver than previously estimated. And they know that even smokers tend to dislike cigarette smoke wafting round them while they eat.

Pressure for a complete ban on smoking in pubs (along with restaurants and other hospitality-industry work places) is building strongly. Doctors' and nurses' organisations, and the government's Chief Medical Officer, have recently been prominent in urging a ban; the main union representing pub staff has joined these calls. A recent report on improving the nation's health, the second Wanless report (commissioned by the Treasury as groundwork towards a promised White Paper on public health), has also pointed to a workplace smoking ban, particularly in the hospitality industry, as a key step forward.

No doubt the government would prefer a voluntary no smoking scheme to something which diehard smokers could condemn as 'nanny state' – forcing people to be healthy, like it or not. The trouble is that there is simply too much resistance within the industry to real progress for the voluntary approach to give good results. In this field, the voluntary approach all too often serves simply as cover for doing little or nothing. One existing voluntary scheme, for example, even sets great store by notices saying that Smoking Is Allowed Throughout This Pub – and its champions seem unable to see the absurdity of suggesting that this is an improvement. In a similar sort of vein, one compromise target suggests aiming for no smoking areas in 80% of pubs by 2006 – not actually wildly different from the proportion of pubs having them already. Faced with what now must be the near-certainty of an eventual ban on smoking in public places, people have been suggesting following Norway's gradualist example, where no smoking areas in bars and restaurants were increased step by step over a period of 15 years from an initial one-quarter of the space available to the present total ban.

This suggestion of a lengthy delay has to be seen from the perspective of the results of a ban. In this *Guide*, we now have to recognise that non-smoking readers exposed to smoky pubs face more than the obvious discomfort. It is now known that spending much time in smoky places can increase the risk of heart disease by around 50%, that passive smoking kills at least 1,000 people each year, and that it makes many more people ill. More important, the ban on smoking in workplaces is predicted to cut the proportion of people who are smokers from 27% (there has been no drop in this figure for several years) to 23%. That is equivalent to eliminating several thousand smoking-related deaths each year – and it makes the ban powerfully attractive to the many smokers who would like additional impetus to help them give up.

Most pub-goers would prefer quicker progress towards a ban. When the Republic of Ireland followed such places as New York and California in banning smoking in bars and restaurants, in spring 2004, many people were sceptical about the ban's chances of success. Initially, there were scare stories about a sharp drop in pub takings. However, in just a few months Ireland's ban has proved to be working well, without the pub closures that some pessimists feared.

Our own liberal leanings have always inclined us towards believing that people should be allowed to make their own choice – about whether to go into a smoky pub, or not. And we have to admit to a personal fondness for an occasional cigar with a glass of good whisky. However, we now believe that a ban on smoking in pubs is so overwhelmingly in the interests of both customers and staff, that we would like to see a ban in place as soon as possible.

THE MUSIC PIPES DOWN

A lot of people complain to us about irritating background music. Two years ago, when the proportion of *Guide* pubs which had installed piped music had risen to 57%, we worried that it would eventually become almost impossible to escape. But at last the rising tide of piped music seems to be turning. In the last couple of years there has been no increase, and now the proportion may even be dropping slightly.

Certainly, pub juke boxes are nearing extinction, despite ambitious plans for new internet-linked versions which could expose pub customers to over three million tunes. At this year's count, only one in 25 pubs still has a juke box.

CHILDREN WELCOME, BUT…

More than 80% of the main entries in this *Guide* now allow children inside. This proportion has been rising year by year.

This year, we have noticed two changes.

First, the general 'Children welcome' policy adopted by many pubs in past years (and in principle strongly supported by us) has been modified, in the light of bitter experience. Publicans have told us that all too often British parents (unlike their continental counterparts) let their offspring behave badly – running around, screaming, generally spoiling other customers' enjoyment. And we do get agonised letters from readers who have walked out of pubs because they have seemed overrun by spoilt brats.

As a result, many publicans who did let them roam free are now keeping children to eating areas, sometimes adding time restrictions.

The bane of responsible parents has been the cold and unloved back Family Room – an unappealing place of banishment. Another change we have spotted this year is that these rooms are disappearing, usually turning into extra dining space. Now, only about 5 or 6% of pubs confine children to a designated family room. It looks as if the family room is headed for imminent extinction.

PUB MENUS COME DOWN TO EARTH

Over this last year, most pub chefs have got over their flirtation with fanciful concoctions and menu descriptions. Common sense has come back into pub cooking, letting good produce speak for itself. There is at least as much imagination as ever, but it is channelled into coaxing great tastes from carefully matched ingredients, instead of smothering everything under towers and stacks of conflicting flavours.

This has worked brilliantly for customers. A year or two ago all too many people told us that elaborate menus were promising much and delivering little, leading to great disappointment. Now, people feel they are getting real taste value – what those simpler menus promise, they deliver.

PUB FOOD GOES LOCAL

Two years ago we drew attention to the way pub chefs were starting to use more local produce. This trend is now snowballing. Most pubs which pride themselves on their food – however simple or elaborate – are now working hard to find local suppliers of good fresh ingredients. In particular, they are using local farms to provide their meat, big local estates for game and farmed venison, local growers for their vegetables, local fishermen too. Some even grow or catch their own. This all makes for great tastes.

British breads, however, seem to be fighting a losing battle against foreign invaders. Baguettes, panini, ciabattas, brioches and croissants are usurping straightforward rolls and breads, let alone regional variations such as stotties, baps, huffers, barm cakes, bannocks and oatcakes.

PORTION DECONTROL

A common complaint from our readers was that pubs were inflexible over the size of their food helpings. If a child or older customer didn't have the appetite for a full helping, they still had to pay for one – and see the leavings go to waste. The only alternative was the Children's Menu with its ubiquitous burgers, chicken nuggets, and chips.

More and more pubs are instead now letting people have smaller or starter-size helpings of proper food, at cut price. Full marks for this.

AN UNWELCOME ECONOMY

This year several readers have spotted a chilling new development – the log fire which stays unlit at lunchtime, even on a cold day. In winter, most good pubs put a match to the kindling before their first customer is through the door. Although we wouldn't like to assert that an unlit fire is always the sign of a cold-hearted publican, customers' comfort does deserve more consideration.

CITY BINGES BRING PEACE TO COUNTRY PUBS

The conglomeration of cut-price binge-drinking pubs in city centres, which have brought such a cost in terms of disorder, violence and vandalism, has also brought one unexpected result. Until recently, some country pubs just outside big towns tended to attract crowds of young drinkers on Friday and Saturday nights. This often made them pretty yobby – places for lovers of good pubs to avoid.

Now, the yobs home in on the big town boozers instead. Two results for the pubs outside those towns: one, the obvious riddance of those rowdy crowds. Second, those weekend drink marathons were what kept those pubs' tills full – they didn't need to bother much for the rest of the week. To replace that lost income, they are now doing their best to attract a good range of customers all through the week.

So many pubs outside those towns have now been reborn, as worthwhile places we'd all be happy to go to.

BEER PRICES – THE *GOOD PUB GUIDE* ANNUAL PRICE SURVEY

Our annual national price survey is now in its 15th year. Each year, we compare the beer prices charged in a nationwide sample of over 1,000 pubs with what each of those individual pubs was charging the previous year. This is the most accurate existing survey of how beer prices are changing.

The survey shows that once again pub beer prices have surged up more than the prices of most things you buy. The overall increase averages out at just under 4% – more than double the rise in other consumer prices.

The average price of a pint of real ale is now £2.15. This is also the average price of beers from two of the four international combines which now dominate UK brewing, Interbrew and Scottish & Newcastle – their brands include Boddingtons, Flowers, Bass, Websters, Theakstons, John Smiths, Courage and McEwans. The other two, Coors and Carlsberg, average a few pence cheaper, with their brands such as Stones, Hancocks, Worthington, M&B, Tetleys and Ansells.

The Table which follows shows how smaller brewers compare with the £2.15 national price norm. It includes only those brewers whose beers we found offered as the cheapest by at least two pubs, and excludes Channel Islands brewers, which work under a different tax regime. The number in brackets after each name shows the number of pubs we found offering their beer as its cheapest – obviously, the more pubs, the more reliable our price.

As the Table shows, less widely advertised beers from smaller independent brewers often give big savings – as well as a more distinctive taste. But some of the less common beers can be very expensive indeed – it does not seem that customers are getting their fair share of the kinder tax treatment now benefiting smaller-scale brewing.

£/pint	
£1.47	Sam Smiths (4)
£1.60	Breconshire (2), Wyre Piddle (2)
£1.70	Castle Rock (4)
£1.74	Hydes (3)
£1.75	Barnsley (2)
£1.79	Burton Bridge (3)
£1.90	Bathams (2)
£1.92	Batemans (4), Yates (3)
£1.96	Hobsons (11)
£1.97	Hawkshead (3)
£1.98	Donnington (5), Hanby (2)
£1.99	Thwaites (7)
£2.00	Goachers (3), Hop Back (3), Moorhouses (2), RCH (2), Robinsons (15)
£2.01	Burtonwood (4), Ridleys (5)
£2.02	Jennings (16)
£2.03	Cains (2), Teignworthy (6)
£2.04	Wye Valley (10)
£2.07	Cotleigh (9)
£2.08	Hardys & Hansons (6)
£2.10	Black Sheep (40), Butcombe (18), Earl Soham (2)
£2.13	Archers (9), Hopdaemon (2)
£2.14	Banks's (11), Grainstore (5), Hook Norton (49), Nethergate (4), St Austell (19)
£2.15	Bath (2), Cottage (2), Moles (3)
£2.16	Brains (5)

£2.17	Otter (18), Sharps (26)
£2.20	Gales (5), Shepherd Neame (15), St Peters (2), Uley (2), Wadworths (29)
£2.21	Belhaven (2), Palmers (7)
£2.22	Oakham (5), Charles Wells (14)
£2.23	Exmoor (11), Marstons (10), West Berkshire (7)
£2.24	Greene King (99)
£2.25	Broughton (2), Goddards (2), Ringwood (19)
£2.26	Badger (17), Caledonian (17), Timothy Taylors (7)
£2.27	Woodfordes (8)
£2.28	Cheriton (7), King (6)
£2.30	Everards (5), Vale (4), Wylam (2), Youngs (29)
£2.31	Adnams (67)
£2.32	Brakspears (16), Fullers (29)
£2.34	Larkins (6)
£2.35	Harveys (18)
£2.38	Skinners (2)
£2.43	Isle of Skye (4)
£2.45	Loddon (2)
£2.85	Pitfield (2)

Averaging £1.86 a pint, pubs brewing their own beer are also exceptionally good value. And other beers we found as cheap as that or cheaper were (starting with the cheapest) Holts, Reepham, Titanic, Clarks, York, Lees and Itchen Valley; as we found these beers in only single pubs, they do not figure in the Table.

This year Lancashire regains from Nottinghamshire its crown as the cheapest area for drinks. Our price survey shows that beer there was typically 25p a pint cheaper than the national average. The Table below shows how much extra people in other areas now have to pay for their beer:

How much extra you pay per pint

Nottinghamshire	3p
Cheshire	7p
Cumbria, Yorkshire	10p
Shropshire	11p
Staffordshire, W Midlands	12p
Herefordshire	13p
Worcestershire	14p
Northumbria	16p
Derbyshire	17p
Wales	19p
Gloucestershire	21p
Cornwall	23p
Devon	24p
Somerset, Warwickshire	25p
Wiltshire	26p
Dorset	27p
Essex, Leicestershire and Rutland, Northamptonshire	28p
Lincolnshire, Norfolk	30p
Hertfordshire, Isle of Wight, Suffolk	32p
Bedfordshire, Cambridgeshire	33p
Oxfordshire	34p
Hampshire, Kent	35p
Scotland	36p
Sussex	38p
Buckinghamshire	42p
Berkshire	44p
Surrey, London	52p

Pub prices for other drinks normally follow beer prices quite closely. So whatever you drink, pubs in London and Surrey, and in other areas towards the bottom of the Table, are penalising you very heavily indeed. A couple of rounds of drinks for half a dozen people in London or Surrey would now set you back over £6 more than it would up in Lancashire.

THE *GOOD PUB GUIDE 2005* AWARDS

Dozens of our main entries now brew their own beer, typically saving their customers 30p on each pint. Particularly notable are the Brewery Tap in Peterborough (Cambridgeshire), Brunswick in Derby, Bentley Brook at Fenny Bentley and John Thompson near Melbourne (Derbyshire), Flower Pots at Cheriton (Hampshire), Marble Arch in Manchester, entirely organic (Lancashire chapter), Exeter Arms at Barrowden and Grainstore in Oakham (Leicestershire and Rutland chapter), Swan on the Green at West Peckham (Kent), Keelman in Newburn (Northumbria chapter), Black Horse at Caythorpe (Nottinghamshire), Burton Bridge Inn in Burton upon Trent (Staffordshire), Beacon in Sedgley (Warwickshire and W Midlands chapter), New Inn at Cropton, Queens Arms at Litton and Fat Cat in Sheffield (Yorkshire), and Fox & Hounds in Houston and Moulin in Pitlochry (Scotland). In its striking building, and producing its good Big Lamp beers at bargain price, the Keelman in Newburn on the edge of Newcastle is **Own Brew Pub of the Year 2005**.

For many, good beer is the essential lifeblood of a good pub. Keeping one or two regular real ales in top condition is hard enough. So it is a tremendous achievement to keep a changing range of many different beers from interesting small breweries, all at their best. Pubs which master this hard challenge are the Bhurtpore at Aston (Cheshire), Blisland Inn at Blisland and Old Ale House in Truro (Cornwall), Watermill at Ings (Cumbria), Bridge in Topsham (Devon), Wine Vaults in Southsea (Hampshire), Taps in Lytham (Lancashire), Cow & Plough in Oadby (Leicestershire and Rutland chapter), Fat Cat in Norwich (Norfolk), Church Inn in Ludlow (Shropshire), Halfway House at Pitney (Somerset), Fat Cat in Sheffield (Yorkshire), and Guildford Arms in Edinburgh and Bon Accord in Glasgow (Scotland). Pubs in the small mainly East Midlands Tynemill group are also admirable for their beer choice and quality. The Bridge in Topsham has not just a splendid beer range, but also admirable licensees very happy to talk informatively about them, and a wonderfully old-fashioned atmosphere in which to drink them: the Bridge is **Beer Pub of the Year 2005**.

Among many exceptional brewers, the Yorkshire family firm of Timothy Taylors stands out this year, becoming a favourite in many areas far from its home base, including particularly London and Scotland. Its Landlord beer is its most widely available, but if you get the chance to try others from the range, such as Best, Golden Best or the splendid winter Ram Tam, go for it. Timothy Taylors, stocked now by more than one in ten of our main entries, is **Brewer of the Year 2005**.

In Scotland most worthwhile pubs keep a good collection of malt whiskies. Outstanding ones are to be found at the Bow Bar and Kays Bar in Edinburgh, Bon Accord in Glasgow, Fox & Hounds in Houston, George at Inveraray, Stein Inn on Skye and Ailean Chraggan at Weem. South of the border, places carrying the malt whisky flag proudly are the Bhurtpore at Aston (Cheshire), Rifle Volunteer at St Anns Chapel (Cornwall), Hardwick Inn at Hardwick Hall (Derbyshire), Nobody Inn at Doddiscombsleigh (Devon), Britons Protection in Manchester (Lancashire chapter), Fortescue Arms at Billingborough, Angel & Royal in Grantham and Wig & Mitre in Lincoln (Lincolnshire), Victoria in Beeston and Lincolnshire Poacher in Nottingham (Nottinghamshire), Manor House Inn at Carterway Heads (Northumbria chapter), Fox & Hounds at Great Wolford (Warwickshire), Marton Arms at Thornton in Lonsdale (Yorkshire), and the Glasfryn at Mold and Goose & Cuckoo at Rhyd-y-Meirch (Wales). Manchester isn't an obvious place to find a treasure-trove of rare malt whiskies: all the more praise to the friendly Britons Protection there, with its rows and rows of tempting bottles earning it the title of **Whisky Pub of the Year 2005**.

With wine taking over from beer as many pub-goers' drink of choice, most good pubs now take at least as much trouble over their wine choice as they do over their beer. In many pubs the choice and quality are now outstanding. Tops for wine are the Knife & Cleaver at Houghton Conquest (Bedfordshire), Bell at Boxford (Berkshire), Stag at Mentmore, Crooked Billet at Newton Longville and Bull & Butcher at Turville (Buckinghamshire), Punch Bowl at Crosthwaite (Cumbria), Trengilly Wartha near Constantine and Old Inn at St Breward (Cornwall), Drunken Duck near Hawkshead (Cumbria), Culm Valley at Culmstock and Nobody Inn at Doddiscombsleigh (Devon), Wykeham Arms in Winchester (Hampshire), Stagg at Titley (Herefordshire), Olive Branch at Clipsham and Red Lion at Stathern (Leicestershire and Rutland chapter), George of Stamford (Lincolnshire), Rose & Crown at Snettisham and Old Ram at Tivetshall St Mary (Norfolk), Victoria in Beeston and Caunton Beck at Caunton (Nottinghamshire), Royal Oak at Ramsden and Trout at Tadpole Bridge (Oxfordshire), Cornwallis at Brome, Crown in Southwold and Crown at Stoke-by-Nayland (Suffolk), West End Inn at West End (Surrey), White Horse at Chilgrove (Sussex), Pear Tree at Witley (Wiltshire), Talbot at Knightwick (Worcestershire), Appletree at Marton, Kings Head in Masham, Millbank at Mill Bank and White Swan in Pickering (Yorkshire), Starbank in Edinburgh (Scotland), and the Penhelig Arms in Aberdovey (Wales). Also, all the pubs in the small Brunning & Price group (mainly Cheshire and North Wales) and the even smaller Huntsbridge group (mainly Cambridgeshire) have excellent carefully chosen wines by the glass, reflecting a particular enthusiasm of their owners. Very unusually, it is an entirely new entry which takes the top award of **Wine Pub of the Year 2005**: the Crown at Stoke-by-Nayland.

In many places hotels with good welcoming bars make a first-class alternative to the area's pubs. It's not an easy trick to pull off: a bar with the easy-going pubby conviviality which brings locals in for a drink and a chat, as well as the civilised comfort which you'd want if you were staying there. Places which have succeeded include the Pheasant at Bassenthwaite Lake (Cumbria), Monsal Head Hotel at Monsal Head (Derbyshire), Eagle & Child attached to the Royalist Hotel in Stow-on-the-Wold (Gloucestershire), Feathers in Ledbury (Herefordshire), Seaview Hotel in Seaview (Isle of Wight), Inn at Whitewell (Lancashire), Angel in Grantham and George of Stamford (Lincolnshire), Mermaid in Rye (Sussex), White Swan in Pickering and Boars Head in Ripley (Yorkshire), Plockton Hotel at Plockton and Tigh an Eilean at Shieldaig (Scotland), and Harbourmaster in Aberaeron, Penhelig Arms in Aberdovey, Bear in Crickhowell and Kilverts in Hay-on-Wye (Wales). The George of Stamford takes the *Good Pub Guide* title of **Hotel Bar of the Year 2005**.

So many pubs are piling the pounds on to their menu prices that it is a delight to find ones which not only keep their prices down in the bargain basement, but also offer a tempting choice. Current favourites for pocket-friendly food are the Sweeney & Todd in Reading (Berkshire), Brewery Tap in Peterborough (Cambridgeshire), Black Dog near Dalton-in-Furness (Cumbria), Black Dog at Belmont (Lancashire), Nevill Arms at Medbourne (Leicestershire and Rutland chapter), Adam & Eve in Norwich (Norfolk), Lincolnshire Poacher in Nottingham (Nottinghamshire), Basketmakers Arms in Brighton and Six Bells in Chiddingly (Sussex), and Whitelocks in Leeds, and Fat Cat and New Barrack in Sheffield (Yorkshire). To find such splendid value at the Basketmakers Arms in trendy Brighton is a real treat: the Basketmakers Arms is **Bargain Pub of the Year 2005**.

Among the dozens of truly unspoilt pubs which figure among the main entries – not to mention the hundreds to be found in the Lucky Dip sections – some stand out for their individuality and charm: the Bell at Aldworth (Berkshire), Queens Head at Newton (Cambridgeshire), Rising Sun at Altarnun (Cornwall), Bear at Alderwasley, Olde Gate at Brassington, Barley Mow at Kirk Ireton and Three Stags Heads at Wardlow Mires (Derbyshire), London at Molland, Bridge in Topsham and Northmore Arms at Wonson (Devon), Digby Tap in Sherborne and Square & Compass at Worth Matravers (Dorset), Red Lion at Ampney St Peter and Boat at Ashleworth Quay (Gloucestershire), Flower Pots at Cheriton and Harrow at Steep (Hampshire), Carpenters Arms at Walterstone (Herefordshire), Woodman at Chapmore End (a surprise for Hertfordshire), Red Lion at Snargate (Kent), New Inn at Peggs Green (Leicestershire and Rutland chapter), Victoria in Durham (Northumbria chapter), Black Horse at Checkendon (Oxfordshire), Tuckers Grave at Faulkland and Rose & Crown at Huish Episcopi (Somerset), Yew Tree at

Cauldon (Staffordshire), Kings Head at Laxfield (Suffolk), Stag at Balls Cross (Sussex), Turf in Bloxwich, Beacon in Sedgley and Case is Altered at Five Ways (Warwickshire and W Midlands chapter), Monkey House near Defford (Worcestershire), Birch Hall at Beck Hole, White Horse in Beverley and Whitelocks in Leeds (Yorkshire), and the Cresselly Arms at Cresswell Quay and Plough & Harrow at Monknash (Wales). The Square & Compass at Worth Matravers, in the same friendly family for nearly a century, and truly one of a kind, is **Unspoilt Pub of the Year 2005**.

This year we have added over 120 new main entries to the *Guide*. Ones which made a particularly strong impression on us, and stay very vivid in our minds, are the Magpie & Parrot in Shinfield (Berkshire), Dyke's End at Reach (Cambridgeshire), Plough at Eaton (Cheshire), Rising Sun at Altarnun (Cornwall), Cock & Pullet at Sheldon (Derbyshire), Hunters Moon at Middlemarsh (Dorset), Queens Head at Fyfield (Essex), Glasshouse Inn at Glasshouse (Gloucestershire), Rhydspence at Whitney-on-Wye (Herefordshire), Hook & Hatchet at Hucking (Kent), White Hart in Lydgate (Lancashire), Jackson Stops at Stretton (Leicestershire and Rutland chapter), Crown in Wells-next-the-Sea (Norfolk), Great Western Arms near Aynho (Northamptonshire), Keelman in Newburn (Northumbria chapter), Chequers at Churchill (Oxfordshire), Bottle & Glass at Picklescott (Shropshire), Bear & Swan at Chew Magna (Somerset), Crown at Stoke-by-Nayland (Suffolk), Marneys in Esher (Surrey), Star & Garter at East Dean (Sussex), Golden Lion at Easenhall (Warwickshire), Forester at Donhead St Andrew (Wiltshire), Drapers Arms and Boathouse (London), and Harbourmaster in Aberaeron (Wales). The Hook & Hatchet at Hucking is **Newcomer of the Year 2005**.

Most good food pubs are now using top-quality fresh ingredients. This means that they are scoring on the pure quality of their food, rather than on over-fanciful recipes and descriptions. This year's top dining pubs are the Chequers at Fowlmere (Cambridgeshire), Punch Bowl at Crosthwaite (Cumbria), Drewe Arms at Broadhembury and Dartmoor Inn at Lydford (Devon), Kings Arms at Didmarton (Gloucestershire), Lough Pool at Sellack and Stagg at Titley (Herefordshire), Dove at Dargate and Bottle House near Penshurst (Kent), Olive Branch at Clipsham (Leicestershire and Rutland chapter), Crown in Wells-next-the-Sea (Norfolk), County in Aycliffe, County Durham (Northumbria chapter), Caunton Beck at Caunton (Nottinghamshire), Trout at Tadpole Bridge (Oxfordshire), Burlton Inn at Burlton (Shropshire), Bear & Swan in Chew Magna and Pilgrims Rest at Lovington (Somerset), Crown at Buxhall (Suffolk), Jolly Sportsman at East Chiltington and Griffin in Fletching (Sussex), Howard Arms at Ilmington (Warwickshire), Pear Tree at Whitley (Wiltshire), Bell & Cross at Holy Cross (Worcestershire), Tempest Arms at Elslack, Star at Harome, Millbank at Mill Bank, Three Acres at Shelley, Wombwell Arms at Wass and Sportsmans Arms at Wath in Nidderdale (Yorkshire), Applecross Inn at Applecross and Plockton Hotel at Plockton (Scotland), Penhelig Arms in Aberdovey and Clytha Arms near Raglan (Wales), and the Drapers Arms in London. It is the Howard Arms at Ilmington which is the **Dining Pub of the Year 2005**.

The country's best pubs – those deeply enjoyable places which have been inspiring the warmest praise from readers in recent months – are the Bell at Aldworth (Berkshire), Halzephron near Helston (Cornwall), Drewe Arms at Broadhembury, Duke of York at Iddesleigh and Jack in the Green at Rockbeare (Devon), Royal Oak in Cerne Abbas (Dorset), Bell at Sapperton (Gloucestershire), Chestnut Horse at Easton and Trooper near Petersfield (Hampshire), Lough Pool at Sellack (Herefordshire), Inn at Whitewell (Lancashire), Angel in Lavenham (Suffolk), Griffin at Fletching (Sussex), Howard Arms at Ilmington (Warwickshire), Horseshoe at Ebbesbourne Wake (Wiltshire), Tempest Arms at Elslack, Star at Harome, Nags Head at Pickhill, St Vincent Arms at Sutton upon Derwent and Wombwell Arms at Wass (Yorkshire), Plockton Hotel at Plockton (Scotland), and Clytha Arms near Raglan (Wales). The Lough Pool at Sellack takes the top title of **Pub of the Year 2005**.

Several of these superb pubs (notably the Halzephron, the Trooper, the Howard Arms, the Star, the Wombwell Arms, the Clytha Arms and the Plockton Hotel) are also splendid places to stay in. Among the 240 main entries which have qualified for our Place to Stay Award this year, other outstanding places are the Pheasant at Bassenthwaite Lake (Cumbria), Durant Arms at Ashprington and Masons Arms at Branscombe (Devon), Inn at Whitewell (Lancashire), Nevill Arms at Medbourne (Leicestershire and Rutland chapter), George of Stamford (Lincolnshire), White Horse at Brancaster Staithe and Crown in Wells-next-the-Sea (Norfolk), Crown in Southwold (Suffolk), Golden Lion at Easenhall (Warwickshire), Pear Tree at Whitley (Wiltshire), Sportsmans Arms at Wath in Nidderdale (Yorkshire), Stein Inn on Skye (Scotland), and the Penhelig Arms in Aberdovey (Wales). The Star at Harome stands out as an exceptionally nice place to stay in; it is **Inn of the Year 2005**.

At the pinnacle of their profession are a handful of landlords and landladies who combine great skill at running their pub really well with the gift of making all their customers feel special, and warmly welcome. Those who stand out are Angela Thomas of the Halzephron near Helston (Cornwall), Jamie Stuart and Pippa Hutchinson of the Duke of York at Iddesleigh (Devon), David and Janice Birch of the Royal Oak in Cerne Abbas (Dorset), Hassan Matini of the Trooper near Petersfield (Hampshire), Vera Watkins of the Carpenters Arms at Walterstone (Herefordshire), Pete and Elizabeth Blencowe of the Exeter Arms at Barrowden and Maria Christina Kell of the New Inn at Peggs Green (Leicestershire and Rutland chapter), Andrew Stammers of the Angel at Larling, Lucille and Barry Carter of the Woolpack at Terrington St John and Sue Prew of the Red Lion in Upper Sheringham (Norfolk), Maggie Chandler of the George at Kilsby (Northamptonshire), Peter and Assumpta Golding of the Chequers at Churchill and Josh and Kay Reid of the Chequers in Chipping Norton (Oxfordshire), Alan East of the Yew Tree at Cauldon (Staffordshire), Alan Stoneham of the Compasses at Chicksgrove and Charlie and Boo West of the Neeld Arms at Grittleton (Wiltshire), John and Trudy Greaves of the Bell at Pensax (Worcestershire), Andy and Sue Cole of the Wombwell Arms at Wass (Yorkshire), and the Key family of the Nags Head in Usk (Wales). Particularly kind and welcoming to his customers, Hassan Matini of the Trooper near Petersfield is **Landlord of the Year 2005**.

What is a Good Pub?

The main entries in this book have been through a two-stage sifting process. First of all, some 2,000 regular correspondents keep in touch with us about the pubs they visit, and nearly double that number report occasionally. We are now also getting quite a flow of reports through our **www.goodguides.co.uk** web site. This keeps us up-to-date about pubs included in previous editions – it's their alarm signals that warn us when a pub's standards have dropped (after a change of management, say), and it's their continuing approval that reassures us about keeping a pub as a main entry for another year. Very important, though, are the reports they send us on pubs we don't know at all. It's from these new discoveries that we make up a shortlist, to be considered for possible inclusion as new main entries. The more people that report favourably on a new pub, the more likely it is to win a place on this shortlist – especially if some of the reporters belong to our hard core of about 600 trusted correspondents whose judgement we have learned to rely on. These are people who have each given us detailed comments on dozens of pubs, and shown that (when we ourselves know some of those pubs too) their judgement is closely in line with our own.

This brings us to the acid test. Each pub, before inclusion as a main entry, is inspected anonymously by the Editor, the Deputy Editor, or both. They have to find some special quality that would make strangers enjoy visiting it. What often marks the pub out for special attention is good value food (and that might mean anything from a well made sandwich, with good fresh ingredients at a low price, to imaginative cooking outclassing most restaurants in the area). The drinks may be out of the ordinary (pubs with several hundred whiskies, with remarkable wine lists, with home-made country wines or good beer or cider made on the premises, with a wide range of well kept real ales or bottled beers from all over the world). Perhaps there's a special appeal about it as a place to stay, with good bedrooms and obliging service. Maybe it's the building itself (from centuries-old parts of monasteries to extravagant Victorian gin-palaces), or its surroundings (lovely countryside, attractive waterside, extensive well kept garden), or what's in it (charming furnishings, extraordinary collections of bric-a-brac).

Above all, though, what makes the good pub is its atmosphere – you should be able to feel at home there, and feel not just that *you're* glad you've come but that *they're* glad you've come. A good landlord or landlady makes a huge difference here – they can make or break a pub.

It follows from this that a great many ordinary locals, perfectly good in their own right, don't earn a place in the book. What makes them attractive to their regular customers (an almost clubby chumminess) may even make strangers feel rather out-of-place.

Another important point is that there's not necessarily any link between charm and luxury – though we like our creature comforts as much as anyone. A basic unspoilt village tavern, with hard seats and a flagstone floor, may be worth travelling miles to find, while a deluxe pub-restaurant may not be worth crossing the street for. Landlords can't buy the Good Pub accolade by spending thousands on thickly padded banquettes, soft music and menus boasting about signature dishes nesting on beds of trendy vegetables drizzled by a jus of this and that – they can only win it, by having a genuinely personal concern for both their customers and their pub.

Using the *Guide*

THE COUNTIES

England has been split alphabetically into counties, mainly to make it easier for people scanning through the book to find pubs near them. Each chapter starts by picking out the pubs that are currently doing best in the area, or are specially attractive for one reason or another.

The county boundaries we use are those for the administrative counties (not the old traditional counties, which were changed back in 1976). We have left the new unitary authorities within the counties that they formed part of until their creation in the most recent local government reorganisation. Metropolitan areas have been included in the counties around them – for example, Merseyside in Lancashire. And occasionally we have grouped counties together – for example, Rutland with Leicestershire, and Durham with Northumberland to make Northumbria. If in doubt, check the Contents.

Scotland and Wales have each been covered in single chapters, and London appears immediately before them at the end of England. Except in London (which is split into Central, East, North, South and West), pubs are listed alphabetically under the name of the town or village where they are. If the village is so small that you probably wouldn't find it on a road map, we've listed it under the name of the nearest sizeable village or town instead. The maps use the same town and village names, and additionally include a few big cities that don't have any listed pubs – for orientation.

We always list pubs in their true locations – so if a village is actually in Buckinghamshire that's where we list it, even if its postal address is via some town in Oxfordshire. Just once or twice, when the village itself is in one county but the pub is just over the border in the next-door county, we have used the village county, not the pub one.

STARS ★

Really outstanding pubs are picked out with a star after their name. In a few cases, pubs have two stars: these are the aristocrats among pubs, really worth going out of your way to find. The stars do NOT signify extra luxury or specially good food – in fact some of the pubs which appeal most distinctively and strongly of all are decidedly basic in terms of food and surroundings. The detailed description of each pub shows what its particular appeal is, and this is what the stars refer to.

FOOD AND STAY AWARDS

The knife-and-fork rosette shows those pubs where food is quite outstanding. The bed symbol shows pubs which we know to be good as places to stay in – bearing in mind the price of the rooms (obviously you can't expect the same level of luxury at £50 a head as you'd get for £100 a head). Pubs with bedrooms are marked on the maps as a square.

This wine glass symbol marks out those pubs where wines are a cut above the usual run, and/or offer a good choice of wines by the glass.

The beer tankard symbol shows pubs where the quality of the beer is quite exceptional, or pubs which keep a particularly interesting range of beers in good condition.

£

This symbol picks out pubs where we have found decent snacks at £2.50 or less, or worthwhile main dishes at £5.95 or less.

RECOMMENDERS

At the end of each main entry we include the names of readers who have recently recommended that pub (unless they've asked us not to).

Important note: the description of the pub and the comments on it are our own and not the recommenders'; they are based on our own personal inspections and on later verification of facts with each pub. As some recommenders' names appear quite often, you can get an extra idea of what a pub is like by seeing which other pubs those recommenders have approved. In the rare instances where we have discovered a good pub which has no reader recommenders, or judge that a pub deserves to stay in the main entries despite a very recent management change we include the acronym BOB (buyer's own brand) as a recommender.

LUCKY DIPS

The Lucky Dip section at the end of each county chapter includes brief descriptions of pubs that have been recommended by readers, with the readers' names in brackets. As the flood of reports from readers has given so much solid information about so many pubs, we have been able to include only those which seem really worth trying. Where only one single reader's name is shown, in most cases that pub has been given a favourable review by other readers in previous years, so its inclusion does not depend on a single individual's judgement. In all cases, we have now not included a pub in the list unless readers' descriptions make the nature of the pub quite clear, and give us good grounds for trusting that other readers would be glad to know of the pub. So the descriptions normally reflect the balanced judgement of a number of different readers, increasingly backed up by similar reports on the same pubs from other readers in previous years. Many have been inspected by us. In these cases, LYM means the pub was in a previous edition of the *Guide*. The usual reason that it's no longer a main entry is that, although we've heard nothing really condemnatory about it, we've not had enough favourable reports to be sure that it's still ahead of the local competition. BB means that, although the pub has never been a main entry, we have inspected it, and found nothing against it. In both these cases, the description is our own; in others, it's based on the readers' reports. This year, we have deleted many previously highly rated pubs from the book simply because we have no very recent reports on them. This may well mean that we have left out some favourites – please tell us if we have!

Lucky Dip pubs marked with a ☆ are ones where the information we have (either from our own inspections or from trusted reader/reporters) suggests a firm recommendation. Roughly speaking, we'd say that these pubs are as much worth considering, at least for the virtues described for them, as many of the main entries themselves. Note that in the Dips we always commend food if we have information supporting a positive recommendation. So a bare mention that food is served shouldn't be taken to imply a recommendation of the food. The same is true of accommodation and so forth.

The Lucky Dips (particularly, of course, the starred ones) are under consideration for inspection for a future edition – so please let us have any comments you can make on them. You can use the report forms at the end of the book, the report card which should be included in it, or just write direct (no stamp needed if posted in the UK). Our address is The Good Pub Guide, FREEPOST TN1569, WADHURST, East Sussex TN5 7BR. Alternatively, you can get reports to us immediately, through our web site **www.goodguides.co.uk**

MAP REFERENCES

All pubs outside the big cities are given four-figure map references. On the main entries, it looks like this: SX5678 Map 1. Map 1 means that it's on the first map in the book (see first colour section). SX means it's in the square labelled SX on that map. The first figure, 5, tells you to look along the grid at the top and bottom of the SX square for the figure 5. The third figure, 7, tells you to look down the grid at the side of the square to find the figure 7. Imaginary lines drawn down and across the square from these figures should intersect near the pub itself.

The second and fourth figures, the 6 and the 8, are for more precise pin-pointing, and are really for use with larger-scale maps such as road atlases or the Ordnance Survey 1:50,000 maps, which use exactly the same map reference system. On the relevant Ordnance Survey map, instead of finding the 5 marker on the top grid you'd find the 56 one; instead of the 7 on the side grid you'd look for the 78 marker. This makes it very easy to locate even the smallest village.

Where a pub is exceptionally difficult to find, we include a six-figure reference in the directions, such as OS Sheet 102 map reference 654783. This refers to Sheet 102 of the Ordnance Survey 1:50,000 maps, which explain how to use the six-figure references to pin-point a pub to the nearest 100 metres.

MOTORWAY PUBS

If a pub is within four or five miles of a motorway junction, and reaching it doesn't involve much slow traffic, we give special directions for finding it from the motorway. And the Special Interest Lists at the end of the book include a list of these pubs, motorway by motorway.

PRICES AND OTHER FACTUAL DETAILS

The *Guide* went to press during the summer of 2004. As late as possible, each pub was sent a checking sheet to get up-to-date food, drink and bedroom prices and other factual information. By the summer of 2005 prices are bound to have increased a little – to be prudent, you should probably allow around 5% extra by then. But if you find a significantly different price please let us know.

Breweries or independent chains to which pubs are 'tied' are named at the beginning of the italic-print rubric after each main entry. That generally means the pub has to get most if not all of its drinks from that brewery or chain. If the brewery is not an independent one but just part of a combine, we name the combine in brackets. When the pub is tied, we have spelled out whether the landlord is a tenant, has the pub on a lease, or is a manager. Tenants and leaseholders of breweries generally have considerably greater freedom to do things their own way, and in particular are allowed to buy drinks including a beer from sources other than their tied brewery.

Free houses are pubs not tied to a brewery, so in theory they can shop around to get the drinks their customers want, at the best prices they can find. But in practice many free houses have loans from the big brewers, on terms that bind them to sell those breweries' beers. So don't be too surprised to find that so-called free houses may be stocking a range of beers restricted to those from a single brewery.

Real ale is used by us to mean beer that has been maturing naturally in its cask. We do not count as real ale beer which has been pasteurised or filtered to remove its natural yeasts. If it is kept under a blanket of carbon dioxide to preserve it, we still generally mention it – as long as the pressure is too light for you to notice any extra fizz, it's hard to tell the difference. (For brevity, we use the expression 'under light blanket pressure' to cover such pubs; we do not include among them pubs where the blanket pressure is high enough to force the beer up from the cellar, as this does make it unnaturally fizzy.) If we say a pub has, for example, 'Whitbreads-related real ales', these may include not just beers brewed by the national company and its subsidiaries but also beers produced by independent breweries which the national company buys in bulk and distributes alongside its own.

Other drinks: we've also looked out particularly for pubs doing enterprising non-alcoholic drinks (including good tea or coffee), interesting spirits (especially malt whiskies), country wines (elderflower and the like), freshly squeezed juices and good farm ciders.

Bar food refers to what is sold in the bar, not in any separate restaurant. It means a place serves anything from sandwiches and ploughman's to full meals, rather than pork scratchings or packets of crisps. We always mention sandwiches in the text if we know that a pub does them – if you don't see them mentioned, assume you can't get them.

The **food listed** in the description of each pub is an example of the sort of thing you'd find served in the bar on a normal day, and generally includes the dishes which are currently finding most favour with readers. We try to indicate any difference we know of between lunchtime and evening, and between summer and winter (on the whole stressing summer food more). In winter, many pubs tend to have a more restricted range, particularly of salads, and tend then to do more in the way of filled baked potatoes, casseroles and hot pies. We always mention barbecues if we know a pub does them. Food quality and variety may be affected by holidays – particularly in a small pub, where the licensees do the cooking themselves (May and early June seems to be a popular time for licensees to take their holidays).

What we call OAP meals are usually available for all 'seniors', not only people of pensionable age.

Any separate **restaurant** is mentioned. But in general all comments on the type of food served, and in particular all the other details about bar food at the end of each entry, relate to the pub food and not to the restaurant food.

Children's Certificates exist, but in practice **children** are allowed into at least some part of almost all the pubs included in this *Guide* (there is no legal restriction on the movement of children over 14 in any pub, though only people over 18 may get alcohol). As we went to press, we asked the main-entry pubs a series of detailed questions about their rules. **Children welcome** means the pub has told us that it simply lets them come in, with no special restrictions. In other cases we report exactly what arrangements pubs say they make for children. However, we have to note that in readers' experience some pubs make restrictions that they haven't told us about (children only if eating, for example). Also, very occasionally pubs which have previously allowed children change their policy altogether, virtually excluding them. If you come across this, please let us know, so that we can clarify the information for the pub concerned in the next edition. Beware that if children are confined to the restaurant, they may occasionally be expected to have a full restaurant meal. Also, please note that a welcome for children does not necessarily mean a welcome for breast-feeding in public. If we don't mention children at all, assume that they are not welcome. All but one or two pubs (we mention these in the text) allow children in their garden or on their terrace, if they have one. In the Lucky Dip entries we mention children only if readers have found either that they are allowed or that they are not allowed – the absence of any reference to children in a Dip entry means we don't know either way.

We asked all main entries what their policy was about **dogs**, and if they allow them we say so. Generally, if you take a dog into a pub you should have it on a lead. We also mention in the text any pub dogs or cats (or indeed other animals) that we've come across ourselves, or heard about from readers.

Parking is not mentioned if you should normally be able to park outside the pub, or in a private car park, without difficulty. But if we know that parking space is limited or metered, we say so.

We now say if a pub does **not** accept **credit cards**; some which do may put a surcharge on credit card bills, as the card companies take quite a big cut. We also say if we know that a pub tries to retain customers' credit cards while they are eating. This is a reprehensible practice, and if a pub tries it on you, please tell them that all banks and card companies frown on it – and please let us know the pub's name, so that we can warn readers in future editions.

Telephone numbers are given for all pubs that are not ex-directory.

Opening hours are for summer; we say if we know of differences in winter, or on particular days of the week. In the country, many pubs may open rather later and close earlier than their details show unless there are plenty of customers around (if you come across this, please let us know – with details). Pubs are allowed to stay open all day Mondays to Saturdays from 11am (earlier, if the area's licensing magistrates have permitted) till 11pm. However, outside cities most English and Welsh pubs close during the afternoon. Scottish pubs are allowed to stay open until later at night, and the Government has announced plans to allow later opening in England and Wales too; it's just possible that the law will be changed during the currency of this edition. We'd be very grateful to hear of any differences from the hours we quote. You are allowed 20 minutes' drinking-up time after the quoted hours – half an hour if you've been having a meal in the pub.

Bedroom prices normally include full English breakfasts (if these are available, which they usually are), VAT and any automatic service charge that we know about. If we give just one price, it is the total price for two people sharing a double or twin-bedded room for one night. Otherwise, prices before the / are for single occupancy, prices after it for double. A capital B against the price means that it includes a private bathroom, a capital S a private shower. As all this coding packs in quite a lot of information, some examples may help to explain it:

£65	on its own means that's the total bill for two people sharing a twin or double room without private bath; the pub has no rooms with private bath, and a single person might have to pay that full price.
£65B	means exactly the same – but all the rooms have private bath
£50(£65B)	means rooms with private baths cost £15 extra
£35/£50(£65B)	means the same as the last example, but also shows that there are single rooms for £35, none of which have private bathrooms

If there's a choice of rooms at different prices, we normally give the cheapest. If there are seasonal price variations, we give the summer price (the highest). During the winter, many inns, particularly in the country, will have special cheaper rates. And at other times, especially in holiday areas, you will often find prices cheaper if you stay for several nights. On weekends, inns that aren't in obvious weekending areas often have bargain rates for two- or three-night stays.

MEAL TIMES

Bar food is commonly served from 12-2 and 7-9, at least from Monday to Saturday (food service often stops a bit earlier on Sundays). If we don't give a time against the *Bar food* note at the bottom of a main entry, that means that you should be able to get bar food at those times. However, we do spell out the times if we know that bar food service starts after 12.15 or after 7.15; if it stops before 2 or before 8.45; or if food is served for significantly longer than usual (say, till 2.30 or 9.45).

Though we note days when pubs have told us they don't do food, experience suggests that you should play safe on Sundays, and check first with any pub before planning an expedition that depends on getting a meal there. Also, out-of-the-way pubs often cut down on cooking during the week, especially the early part of the week, if they're quiet – as they tend to be, except at holiday times. Please let us know if you find anything different from what we say!

NO SMOKING

We say in the text of each entry what, if any, provision a pub makes for non-smokers. Pubs setting aside at least some sort of no smoking area are also listed county by county in the Special Interest Lists at the back of the book.

DISABLED ACCESS

Deliberately, we do not ask pubs questions about this, as their answers would not give a reliable picture of how easy access is. Instead, we depend on readers' direct experience. If you are able to give us help about this, we would be particularly grateful for your reports.

PLANNING ROUTES WITH *THE GOOD PUB GUIDE*

Computer users may like to know of a route-finding programme, Microsoft® MapPoint™ European Edition, which shows the location of *Good Pub Guide* pubs on detailed maps, works out the quickest routes for journeys, adds diversions to nearby pubs – and shows our text entries for those pubs on screen.

OUR WEB SITE (www.goodguides.co.uk)

Our Internet web site uses material from *The Good Pub Guide* in a way that gives people who do not yet know it at least a taste of it. The site is being continually improved and expanded, and we hope to use it to give readers extra information. You can use the site to send us reports – this way they get virtually immediate attention.

CHANGES DURING THE YEAR – PLEASE TELL US

Changes are inevitable, during the course of the year. Landlords change, and so do their policies. And, as we've said, not all returned our fact-checking sheets. We very much hope that you will find everything just as we say. But if you find anything different, please let us know, using the tear-out card in the middle of the book (which doesn't need an envelope), the report forms at the back of the book, or just a letter. You don't need a stamp: the address is The Good Pub Guide, FREEPOST TN1569, WADHURST, East Sussex TN5 7BR. As we have said, you can also send us reports by using our web site **www.goodguides.co.uk**

Authors' Acknowledgements

The *Guide* owes its unique authority largely to the extraordinarily generous help we have from the many thousands of readers who report to us on the pubs they visit, often in great detail. For the special help they have given us this year, we are deeply grateful to Ian Phillips, Michael and Jenny Back, George Atkinson, the Didler, Kevin Thorpe, Steve Whalley, Susan and John Douglas, Michael Dandy, LM, CMW and JJW, Gerry and Rosemary Dobson, Tracey and Stephen Groves, Michael Doswell, Paul and Ursula Randall, Martin and Karen Wake, Peter Meister, Paul Humphreys, Dennis Jenkin, Phyl and Jack Street, Richard Lewis, Joe Green, Pete Baker, Dr and Mrs M E Wilson, Tony and Wendy Hobden, Guy Vowles, Joan and Michel Hooper-Immins, Tom Evans, Ann and Colin Hunt, Derek and Sylvia Stephenson, John Beeken, Pamela and Merlyn Horswell, John Foord, Rona Murdoch, W W Burke, Jenny and Brian Seller, Roger and Jenny Huggins, Tom McLean, Ewan McCall, Dave Irving, E G Parish, Martin Grosberg, A P Seymour, Howard Dell, Graham Coates, Paul A Moore, Simon Collett-Jones, MDN, Mr and Mrs Colin Roberts, Mr and Mrs G S Ayrton, B and K Hypher, John Wooll, Peter and Audrey Dowsett, Val and Alan Green, Comus and Sarah Elliott, Phil and Sally Gorton, John Evans, Andy and Jill Kassube, Michael Butler, Keith and Chris O'Neill, Neil and Anita Christopher, Peter Scillitoe, Alan and Paula McCully, Margaret Dickinson, Peter F Marshall, Michael and Alison Sandy, Mike Ridgway, Sarah Miles, Dr and Mrs C W Thomas, J R Ringrose, Esther and John Sprinkle, Mike Gorton, KC, Tina and David Woods-Taylor, Bob and Margaret Holder, John and Joan Nash, Bert Newman, John Saville, Mike and Mary Carter, Richard Houghton, MLR, R T and J C Moggridge, David Crook, Bruce Bird, Joyce and Maurice Cottrell, Dick and Madeleine Brown, B and M Kendall, Fred and Lorraine Gill, J F M and M West, Phil and Jane Hodson, Brian and Anna Marsden, Pat and Tony Martin, Barry and Anne, Charles and Pauline Stride, Roy and Lindsey Fentiman, Nick Holding, Tony Hobden, Ted George, Marjorie and David Lamb, Tim and Ann Newell, Maggie and Tony Harwood, M G Hart, Pete and Rosie Flower and John and Vivienne Rice.

Warm thanks too to John Holliday of Trade Wind Technology, who built and looks after our state-of-the-art database; and above all to the thousands of devoted publicans, who give us all so much pleasure.

Alisdair Aird and Fiona Stapley

ENGLAND

Bedfordshire

Good value food is a strong point in many of the county's pubs. For reliable cooking at appealing prices, the Three Tuns at Biddenham, Chequers at Keysoe and proudly unspoilt Cock at Broom are all popular. Moving up the scale a bit, we'd pick out the Crown at Northill (a charming new entry), the Hare & Hounds at Old Warden (a smart gastropub), the rambling well run Live & Let Live at Pegsdon, the cheerful Fox & Hounds at Riseley (great for steak lovers), the stylish up-to-date Five Bells at Stanbridge (doing particularly well these last few months), and the Three Cranes at Turvey, a consistent all-rounder. Tops for a special meal out, with imaginative cooking, is the restauranty Knife & Cleaver at Houghton Conquest, our choice as Bedfordshire Dining Pub of the Year. In the Lucky Dip section at the end of the chapter, the Black Horse at Ireland and Bell at Studham are both well worth noting. Drinks prices are a shade above the national average here, with those pubs taking the trouble to get beers from small breweries some way off tending to show the smallest price increase over the last year. The county's major brewer is Charles Wells.

BIDDENHAM TL0249 Map 5

Three Tuns

Village signposted from A428 just W of Bedford

Handy if you're in the area, this thatched village pub is popular for its very good value enjoyable bar food. It can draw a crowd (particularly at lunchtime) so it's worth booking. The low-beamed lounge is fairly straightforward with wheelback chairs round dark wood tables, window seats and pews on a red turkey carpet, and country paintings. Even more down-to-earth, the green-carpeted public bar (readers have found it a bit smoky in here, but the dining area is no smoking) has photographs of local sports teams, darts, table skittles and dominoes. Work on an extension is due to start in the autumn. Just missing the threshold for our bargain award, standard but tasty, food is served in good sized helpings and includes dishes such as soup (£2.60), sandwiches (from £2.50; soup and sandwich £4.50), ploughman's (£4), home-made dishes such as quiche of the day (£6.50), steak and kidney pie, steak braised in tarragon and red wine and meat or vegetable lasagne (£7.50), steaks (from £9.50, but not served on Sunday), Sunday roast (£7), and puddings (£3). On handpump, Greene King Abbot is well kept alongside a guest such as Everards Tiger. There are seats in the attractively sheltered spacious garden, and a big decked terrace has lots of picnic-sets. The very good children's play area has swings for all ages. *(Recommended by Michael Dandy, Bob and Maggie Atherton)*

Greene King ~ Tenant Kevin Bolwell ~ Real ale ~ Bar food (12-2, 6-9; not Sun evening) ~ (01234) 354847 ~ Children in eating area of bar ~ Dogs welcome ~ Open 11.30-2.30, 6-11; 12-3, 7-10.30 Sun

BROOM TL1743 Map 5

Cock ★ £

High Street; from A1 opposite northernmost Biggleswade turn-off follow Old Warden 3, Aerodrome 2 signpost, and take first left signposted Broom

You'll appreciate this 300-year-old place if you like your pubs simple and unspoilt – its four quietly cosy rooms have survived almost untouched over the years. Original latch doors lead from one little room to another, where you'll find warming winter log fires, low ochre ceilings, stripped panelling, and farmhouse tables and chairs on antique tiles. There's no bar counter, and the very well kept Greene King IPA, Abbot and Ruddles County are tapped straight from casks by the cellar steps off a central corridor. Straightforward bar food includes sandwiches (from £2.95), soup (£3.25), ploughman's (from £4.95), scampi or vegetarian curry (£5.95), breaded plaice (£6.95), chicken balti or filled yorkshire pudding (£7.25). The restaurant is no smoking; piped (perhaps classical) music, darts, table skittles, cribbage and dominoes. There are picnic-sets and flower tubs on the terrace by the back lawn; caravanning and camping facilities are available. *(Recommended by the Didler, Quentin and Carol Williamson, Kevin Thorpe, Paul Humphreys, W W Burke, Pete Baker, Ian Phillips, Mark and Ruth Brock)*

Greene King ~ Tenants Gerry and Jean Lant ~ Real ale ~ Bar food (12-2.30, 7-9; not Sun evening) ~ Restaurant ~ (01767) 314411 ~ Children in restaurant and family room ~ Dogs allowed in bar ~ Open 12-3(4 Sat), 6-11; 12-4, 7-10.30 Sun

HOUGHTON CONQUEST TL0441 Map 5

Knife & Cleaver

Between B530 (old A418) and A6, S of Bedford

Bedfordshire Dining Pub of the Year

Dishes at this attractive 17th-c dining pub are stylishly presented, contemporary and fully flavoured, with the same care taken over ingredients and cooking in the bar as with the separate more elaborate (and pricier) restaurant menu. While some readers find it a bit too restauranty for their tastes, others are grateful to find such well prepared and fairly priced food in an area where pubs serving really good meals are a little thin on the ground. Beware that it does get very busy, and on Saturday evening and Sunday lunchtime if the restaurant is fully booked they may not serve bar meals: soup of the day such as carrot and ginger (£3.50), ploughman's (£4), filled breads such as chicken and bacon ciabatta (£5.95), salmon and shrimp fishcake or a dish of the day such as braised lamb shank with black olive mash (£6.50), thai-style seafood noodles (£6.50), caramelised onion and goats cheese pancakes (£6.95), moules marinière (£7.25) and puddings which might include apple brioche and butter pudding with calvados custard or home-made ice-cream (£3.75), and there's a proper cheeseboard (£4.95). The comfortably civilised bar has dark panelling which is reputed to have come from nearby ruined Houghton House, as well as maps, drawings and old documents on the walls, and a blazing fire in winter. The airy white-walled no smoking conservatory restaurant has rugs on the tiled floor and lots of hanging plants. There's also a no smoking family room. Service is really welcoming and efficient. Well kept Batemans XB and Fullers London Pride on handpump, Stowford Press farm cider, around 30 good wines by the glass, and over 20 well aged malt whiskies; unobtrusive piped music. There are tables on the terrace alongside a neatly kept appealing garden, and the church opposite is worth a look. *(Recommended by Phil and Heidi Cook, Peter and Anne-Marie O'Malley, Sue Forder, Karen and Graham Oddey, Mr and Mrs P L Haigh, Blaise Vyner, Michael Dandy, Ryta Lyndley, Bob and Maggie Atherton)*

Free house ~ Licensees David and Pauline Loom ~ Real ale ~ Bar food (12-2.30(2 Sat), 7-9.30; not Sun or bank hol evenings; but see text about wknds) ~ Restaurant ~ (01234) 740387 ~ Children in eating area of bar, restaurant and family room ~ Dogs allowed in bedrooms ~ Open 12-2.30(2 Sat, 3 Sun), 7-11; closed Sun evening, 27-30 Dec ~ Bedrooms: £53B/£68B

KEYSOE TL0762 Map 5

Chequers

Pertenhall Road, Brook End (B660)

Steady and reliable, this pleasant village local is usually fairly quiet at lunchtime (unless a group is in). Its two neat and simple beamed rooms are divided by an unusual stone-pillared fireplace. Comfortable seats in one room and piped local radio or music lend a homely 1960s air. The friendly licensees have been here for over 25 years but never seem to tire of making their customers feel at home. Really good value bar food includes sandwiches, plain or toasted (£2.50), home-made soup (£2.75), garlic mushrooms on toast (£3.75), ploughman's (£4), chilli (£6), home-made steak and ale pie (£6.50), chicken breast stuffed with stilton in chive sauce (£8.50), steaks (from £10) and blackboard specials such as spinach and mushroom lasagne (£6.50). The handpumps on the stone bar counter serve well kept Fullers London Pride and Hook Norton Best, and they have some malt whiskies, and mulled wine in winter; darts, shove-ha'penny and dominoes. Tables and chairs on the back terrace look over the garden, which has a play tree and swings. *(Recommended by Michael and Jenny Back, Gordon Tong)*

Free house ~ Licensee Jeffrey Kearns ~ Real ale ~ Bar food ~ (01234) 708678 ~ Children in eating area of bar ~ Open 11.30-2.30, 6.30-11; 12-2.30, 7-10.30 Sun; closed Tues and two wks in summer

NORTHILL TL1446 Map 5

Crown

Ickwell Road; village signposted from B658 W of Biggleswade

Prettily cottagey, this black and white thatched pub stands just across from the church in a green and peaceful village, with picnic-sets under cocktail parasols out in front looking over the village pond. The smallish bar has a big open fire, flagstones and low heavy beams, comfortable bow window seats, and well kept Greene King IPA and Abbot Batemans XXB on handpump from the copper-topped counter; good coffee comes with a jug of cream, and refills if you want. On the left is a carpeted side room with Leech hunting prints (from *Mr Sponge's Sporting Tour*) and reproduction brewery mirrors. On the right, the airy main dining room has elegantly laid tables on bare boards, witty contemporary fashion-hat cartoons and some appealing nude drawings and paintings, with steps up to a smaller more intimate side room. Throughout, the atmosphere is warm and relaxed, thanks particularly to the concerned and friendly service; daily papers; fairly unobtrusive piped music. Enjoyable food includes lunchtime sandwiches and baguettes (from £3.95), daily roast or sausage and mash (£7.95), ricotta and spinach cannelloni topped with provençale sauce and pie or curry of the day (£8.95), with daily specials such as grilled tuna and niçoise salad (£9.95) or duck breast and orange segment salad (£10.95); daily puddings (£4.50) are good; no smoking restaurant. Outside, a sheltered side terrace has more picnic-sets, and opens into a very large garden with a few widely spaced canopied tables, plenty of trees and shrubs, a good play area, and masses of room for children to run around. *(Recommended by Michael Dandy, Pete Baker, K Stringer)*

Greene King ~ Tenant Marian Hawkes-Blodau ~ Real ale ~ Bar food (12-2.30, 6.30-9.30; not Sun evening) ~ Restaurant ~ (01767) 627337 ~ Children in eating area of bar and restaurant ~ Dogs allowed in bar ~ Open 11.30-3, 6-11; 12-4 (maybe later in summer) Sun; closed 25 Dec evening

OLD WARDEN TL1343 Map 5

Hare & Hounds

Village signposted off A600 S of Bedford and B658 W of Biggleswade

Still fresh from its refurbishment over a year ago, this welcoming pub is popular for its thoughtfully prepared food. Breads and ice-cream are home-made, and where possible they use local ingredients – such as pork from the surrounding Shuttleworth estate. The changing bar menu might include bruchetta (£6.95), smoked haddock with macaroni cheese, pie of the day or pork sausage and red wine casserole (£8.95), and you can eat from the pricier restaurant menu in the bar: chicken liver parfait (£5.95), lamb shank with grilled mediterranean vegetables and roast garlic polenta (£10.95), roast bass with lemon and rosemary (£13.95) and puddings such as poached pear in white wine syrup, panna cotta or cheese platter (£4.95). Rambling around a central servery, and painted warmly cosy red and cream, the four beamed rooms have dark standing timbers, comfortable upholstered armchairs and sofas on stripped flooring, light wood tables and coffee tables, a woodburning stove in an inglenook fireplace and fresh flowers on the bar. Prints and photographs depict the historic aircraft in the Shuttleworth Collection just up the road. Charles Wells Eagle and Bombardier and a guest such as Greene King Old Speckled Hen are well kept on handpump, and the half a dozen or so wines by the glass include some from the local Southill estate. Service from well turned out staff is attentive and friendly, and two rooms are no smoking. The village itself is part of the Shuttleworth estate and was built about 200 years ago in a swiss style. The glorious sloping garden, which stretches up to pine woods behind the pub, dates back to the same period and style (more tables at the side on a small terrace, and a couple in front), and there are some substantial walks nearby. Though there's an ample car park, they sometimes need to commandeer the grounds of the village hall as an overflow. *(Recommended by Neil Coburn, John Redfern, Maysie Thompson, Tom Gondris, Michael Dandy, Bill Newton, Emma Watts, John Saul, Dr G and Mrs J Kelvin, Sarah Markham Flynn)*

Charles Wells ~ Lease Jane Hasler ~ Real ale ~ Bar food (12-2, 6.30-9.30; 12-4 Sun; not Sun evening) ~ Restaurant ~ (01767) 627225 ~ Children in family room ~ Dogs allowed in bar ~ Open 12-3, 6-11; 12-10.30 Sun; closed Mon except lunchtime bank hols

PEGSDON TL1130 Map 5

Live & Let Live

B655 W of Hitchin

This rambling old place has been much extended from its snugly traditional tiled and panelled core, with a big beamed dining room behind the cosier salmon-painted rooms at the front, separated by a double-sided fireplace. There are fresh flowers on the sewing machine tables, stripped brick floors, rustic pictures and gun displays on the walls, and a nice, chatty feel. In summer the big back garden has a startling array of hanging baskets and flowers, as well as tables and chairs on a terrace, and picnic-sets on the long lawn, with views of the Chiltern Hills (a track leads straight up almost opposite). There's just as much colour in the winter, when the bars are transformed by particularly good decorations at Christmas. Tasty bar food includes sandwiches (from £3.75), filled baked potatoes (from £3.95), ploughman's (£5.45), leek and potato bake (£9.35), steak and mushoom pudding (£10.95), steak (from £13.75), daily specials such as thai king prawn and mango kebab (£13.25), duck breast with fruit of the forest gravy (£14.95) and puddings such as cheesecake or home-made apple pie (£4.50): there may be a wait for meals at the busiest periods. Well kept Brakspears, Fullers London Pride, Marstons Pedigree, and a guest such as Youngs on handpump, and a comprehensive wine list with plenty by the glass. Most parts are no smoking; piped music. Though the pub's postal address is Hertfordshire, it's actually in Bedfordshire, which bulges down here almost as if it's determined just to capture this nice pub. *(Recommended by Mrs Diane M Hall, Steve and Stella Swepston, B and M Kendall, Michael Dandy, Phil and Heidi Cook)*

Free house ~ Licensees Ray and Maureen Scarbrow ~ Real ale ~ Bar food (12-2.30, 6.45-9.30) ~ Restaurant ~ (01582) 881739 ~ Children in eating area of bar and restaurant ~ Dogs allowed in bar ~ Open 12-11(10.30 Sun) ~ Bedrooms: £57.50S/£57.50S

RISELEY TL0362 Map 5

Fox & Hounds

High Street; village signposted off A6 and B660 N of Bedford

You can choose your own piece of steak from the cold counter (you're charged by the weight – say, £11.60 for 8oz rump, £12.60 for 8oz of sirloin and £14.20 for fillet) and watch it cooked on an open grill at this very welcoming pub. Other, fairly robust dishes are listed on blackboards and might include ploughman's (£6.95), spinach and ricotta cannelloni (£7.95), grilled plaice (£8.50), steak and mushroom pie (£9.50), chicken chasseur (£9.75) and beef stroganoff (£11.25). Even if you don't see anything you fancy, it's worth asking: they're very obliging here, and will try to cope with particular food requests. It's a happy bustling place that has been cheerily run by the same jovial landlord and his wife for over a decade. Service is normally very attentive, but it does get busy, and as they don't take bookings on Saturday night you may have to wait for your table and food. A relaxing lounge area, with comfortable leather chesterfields, lower tables and wing chairs, contrasts with the more traditional pub furniture spread among timber uprights under the heavy low beams; unobtrusive piped classical or big band piped music. Charles Wells Eagle and Bombardier with perhaps a changing guest such as Shepherd Neame Spitfire are kept well on handpump, alongside a decent collection of other drinks including bin-end wines and a range of malts and cognacs. An attractively decked terrace with wooden tables and chairs has outside heating, and the pleasant garden has shrubs and a pergola. *(Recommended by Michael Dandy, Margaret and Roy Randle, Sarah Flynn, Michael Sargent, JWAC)*

Charles Wells ~ Managers Jan and Lynne Zielinski ~ Real ale ~ Bar food (12-1.45, 6.30-9.30 (12-2, 7-9 Sun)) ~ Restaurant ~ (01234) 708240 ~ Children welcome ~ Dogs allowed in bar ~ Open 11.30-2.30, 6.30-11; 12-3, 7-10.30 Sun

STANBRIDGE SP9623 Map 4

Five Bells

Station Road; pub signposted off A5 N of Dunstable

This very enjoyable old country pub is smartly relaxed with a fresh, contemporary zing. Very low exposed beams are stylishly complemented by earthy colours on walls and ceilings, and careful spotlighting creates quite different moods around the various areas. Rugs on wooden floors, armchairs and sofas, and candles on the neatly polished tables all add luxury. Cream and airy, the elegant no smoking restaurant leads into a large garden with plenty of good wooden tables and chairs, and big perfectly mown lawns with fruit trees. Five real bells form the pub sign, and the cream frontage with its striking grey woodwork is an attractive backdrop to more tables nestling under a big tree. The chefs here trained at hotels such as the Lanesborough in London, and on gourmet nights really show off what they can do, while the well trained staff look good in their modern uniforms – needless to say there's always quite an emphasis on the imaginative food. The snack menu might include soup such as carrot with coriander and cumin (£3.50), penne putanesca (£6.50), roast red and yellow peppers stuffed with vegetable couscous (£7.95), oak smoked pork sausages on cheddar mash (£8.95) with dishes such as noisettes of lamb with bean salad and beetroot and orange vinaigrette (£15.50) and 8oz Aberdeen Angus sirloin (£17.50) from the restaurant menu, which you can order from in the bar. Well kept Black Sheep and Marstons Pedigree and a guest such as Hook Norton on handpump, and a good range of wines by the glass. If you ask for water for the table make sure you specify if you want tap water; piped music, dominoes. *(Recommended by Susan and John Douglas, Ian Phillips, Mel Smith, Shirl Hanlon, M and G Rushworth, Gerry and Rosemary Dobson)*

Traditional Freehouses ~ Licensee Andrew MacKenzie ~ Real ale ~ Bar food (restaurant menu only Sat evening and Sun lunchtime) ~ Restaurant ~ (01525) 210224 ~ Children in eating area of bar and restaurant ~ Open 12-11(10.30 Sun)

TURVEY SP9452 Map 4

Three Cranes

Just off A428 W of Bedford

A warm friendly atmosphere, tasty food and well kept beer combine comfortably here to make this stone-built 17th-c coaching inn well worth a visit. Neat and clean, the airy two-level carpeted bar (with piped music, and a solid-fuel stove) is quietly decorated with old local photographs and Victorian-style prints. The no smoking main dining area has sensible tables with upright seats. There are picnic-sets in a neatly kept sheltered garden with a climbing frame, and in summer, the pub frontage attractively overflows with colourful hanging baskets and window boxes. Bar food includes lunchtime sandwiches (from £4), filled baked potatoes (from £4) and ploughman's (£6), as well as sausage and mash (£7) and steak and ale pie (£8). Greene King IPA and Abbot are well kept on handpump alongside sometimes interesting guests such as Adnams Regatta, Hop Back Crop Circle and Timothy Taylor Landlord; cribbage. *(Recommended by Maysie Thompson, George Atkinson, Michael Dandy, Bill Newton, Emma Watts, Blaise Vyner, Dr P C Rea, Steve Godfrey)*

Greene King ~ Manager Adam Dowdy ~ Real ale ~ Bar food (12-8) ~ Restaurant ~ (01234) 881305 ~ Children in restaurant ~ Open 11.30-11; 12-10.30 Sun ~ Bedrooms: £40S/£50S

LUCKY DIP

Besides the fully inspected pubs, you might like to try these Lucky Dips recommended to us and described by readers (if you do, please send us reports: www.goodguides.co.uk).

BEDFORD TL0549

Castle [Newnham St]: Recently refurbished, with attractive garden, polite staff; dogs welcome *(Bill Newton, Emma Watts)*

BIGGLESWADE TL1844

Brown Bear [Hitchin St; from A6001 follow sign for Hitchin Street shops]: Local worth knowing for its wide range of real ales *(LYM, Pete Baker)*

Wheatsheaf [Lawrence Rd]: Unpretentious local, as they used to be a few decades ago; one small very friendly room, well kept Greene King ales inc Mild, darts, dominoes and cards, TV for horseracing, no food or music; terrace tables behind, open all day Fri-Sun *(Pete Baker)*

BLETSOE TL0157

Falcon [Rushden Rd (A6)]: Ex-coaching inn dating from 17th c, Charles Wells Eagle and Bombardier, several wines by the glass, food from good lunchtime sandwiches and ploughman's to steaks, pleasant service, banquettes in carpeted L-shaped main bar with flame-effect fireplaces each end, copper jugs and so forth, small snug with leather settee and armchairs, two dining areas; big riverside garden *(Michael Dandy)*

DUNSTABLE TL0221

Victoria [West St]: Comfortable and welcoming neatly kept local, well kept real ales; terrace tables, barbecue *(Richard Houghton)*

GREAT BARFORD TL1351

Anchor [High St; off A421]: Pleasantly refurbished pub by medieval bridge and church, generous food from sandwiches and baked potatoes to good puddings, wider evening choice, Charles Wells Bombardier, Eagle and a changing guest beer, good wine choice, quick friendly service, open-plan bar with small no smoking area down steps and back restaurant; piped music; bedrooms, roadside picnic-sets overlooking River Ouse *(Michael Dandy, Ryta Lyndley)*

Golden Cross [Bedford Rd]: Thriving atmosphere in main-road pub with pretty back restaurant/bar serving good chinese food (worth booking); pristine tables, white linen cloths and napkins, very attentive service *(Sarah Flynn)*

HENLOW TL1738

Engineers Arms [High St]: Hospitable village pub with nine handpumps for changing real ales from small breweries, two farm ciders, fine log fire, daily papers, rolls and pies, breweriana and whisky-water jugs, two friendly dogs, back bar with juke box, TV, games inc table football and lots of old soccer posters and photographs; piped radio, occasional live music, quarterly bank hol beer festivals; back terrace *(Kevin Thorpe, Bruce Bird, Conor Mc Gaughey)*

IRELAND TL1341

☆ *Black Horse* [off A600 Shefford—Bedford]: Busy and attractive dining pub consistently reliable for wide choice of plentiful piping hot food from good value ciabattas up, good fresh ingredients, up-to-date presentation, wider evening menu, sizeable smart lounge, two pleasant dining rooms, well kept ales such as Fullers London Pride and Greene King IPA and Old Speckled Hen, good range of wines and good coffee, attentive service from helpful friendly staff; bar can be smoky; plenty of tables in neat front garden with play area, cottage bedrooms – nice peaceful rural setting *(Anthony Barnes, Maysie Thompson, BB, Gordon Tong, Eithne Dandy, Gwyn Jones, Brian Root, Bob and Maggie Atherton, John Branston)*

KEMPSTON TL0347

Slaters Arms [Box End Rd (A5134, off A4218 W of Bedford)]: Low-beamed bar with separate eating area, wide food choice from sandwiches, baguettes and baked potatoes up, separate evening menu, Greene King ales and good choice of wines by the glass; piped music, pub games; big garden with play area *(Michael Dandy)*

LEIGHTON BUZZARD SP9225

Stag [Heath Rd]: Cosy, comfortable and relaxing, traditional home cooking inc some scottish dishes, full Fullers beer range kept well, changing guest beers, welcoming efficient service, candles at night; Tues quiz night *(MP, Tony Hobden)*

LINSLADE SP9126

Globe [off A4146 nr bridge on outskirts]: 19th-c pub nicely set below Grand Union Canal, lots of rooms, beams and flagstones, log and coal fires, well kept Greene King IPA,

Abbot and Ruddles and a guest beer, usual food (not winter Sun evening), no smoking restaurant; piped music; children welcome in eating areas, tables up on embankment and in garden, open all day *(Ian Phillips, LYM, Mrs P J Pearce)*

MAULDEN TL0538

Dog & Badger [Clophill Rd]: Attractive and friendly thatched village pub, refurbished bare-boards bar, steps down to two carpeted areas and no smoking restaurant, Fullers London Pride and Greene King IPA, good choice of wines by the glass, wide range of good value food (best to book wknds) from sandwiches to steaks, quick pleasant service; piped music; tables in front garden *(Mrs Diane M Hall, Michael Dandy)*

MELCHBOURNE TL0266

St John Arms [Knotting Rd]: Unpretentious rambling country pub with low-priced food from good chunky sandwiches to Sun lunch, Weds steak night and Fri fish bargains, well kept Greene King ales, friendly landlord, log fire, toby jugs and cigarette cards, games room with darts, pool and hood skittles; piped radio; peaceful cottagey garden *(LYM, CMW, JJW)*

MILLBROOK TL0138

Chequers: Two-room refurbished village pub opp golf club, log fire and plate collection in small low-beamed carpeted bar, Flowers IPA and Stonehenge Great Bustard, decent choice of food, quick cheerful service, back restaurant; cl Sun/Mon *(Michael Dandy)*

MILTON BRYAN SP9730

Red Lion [Toddington Road, off B528 S of Woburn]: Beamed dining bar with some stripped brickwork, boards and flagstones, well kept ales such as Hook Norton and Greene King IPA, Old Speckled Hen and Ruddles County, reasonably priced wines, friendly attentive staff, usual food inc good value OAP lunch; children welcome, plenty of tables in garden with terrace and climbing frame *(June and Malcolm Farmer, LYM, Teresa and David Waters, Mr and Mrs R A Buckler)*

ODELL SP9657

Bell [off A6 S of Rushden, via Sharnbrook; High St]: Appealing old pub under new management, several low-beamed rooms around central servery, well kept Greene King and perhaps a guest beer, mix of old settles and neat modern furniture, three log or coal fires (not always lit); usual food from sandwiches and baked potatoes up (not Sun evening); children welcome away from counter, delightful big garden backing on to River Ouse, handy for Harrold-Odell country park *(George Atkinson, Michael Dandy, LYM)*

PULLOXHILL TL0634

Cross Keys [High St; off A6 N of Barton le Clay]: Modernised early 17th-c local, lots of timbering and flower baskets, rambling front bars, very friendly long-serving landlord and family, good value usual food, children in big back no smoking dining room, Adnams Broadside and Charles Wells Bombardier and Eagle; popular jazz sessions; garden with play area, pretty part of village in nice countryside *(Phil and Heidi Cook)*

RADWELL TL0057

☆ *Swan* [Felmersham Rd]: Charming beamed and partly thatched pub, two spacious carpeted eating rooms either side of small flagstoned bar, one with woodburner, lots of prints, wide choice of good food from lunchtime sandwiches and baked potatoes up, service friendly even when very busy, well kept Charles Wells Eagle, decent wines by the glass and coffee, popular evening restaurant (must book Fri/Sat); unobtrusive piped music; pleasant small garden, attractive quiet village *(Michael Dandy)*

RAVENSDEN TL0754

Horse & Jockey [Church End]: Spotlessly kept village local with attractively priced food inc good steaks, well kept beer *(Sarah Flynn)*

RIDGMONT SP9736

☆ *Rose & Crown* [A507, 2 miles from M1 junction 13: follow Ampthill signs – High St]: Relaxed off-motorway standby, run by same unruffled landlord for many years, comfortable lounge with open fire, games in low-ceilinged public bar, no smoking dining area (children allowed), lots of Rupert Bear memorabilia and old english sheepdog china, well kept Charles Wells Eagle and Bombardier and guests such as Adnams Broadside and Everards Tiger, up to 50 malt whiskies, usual food from sandwiches up; piped music; good wheelchair access, long and attractive suntrap sheltered back garden, camping and caravanning *(LYM, Joan York)*

SHARNBROOK TL0059

Fordham Arms [SE of village]: Smallish bar with Flowers IPA, Fullers London Pride, Greene King Abbot and a monthly guest beer, pool and TV in room off, pleasantly decorated dining extension with lots of plates, copper and local paintings, wide range of enjoyable food from baguettes and baked potatoes up, quick friendly service even when busy; Sun quiz night, fortnightly live music; big garden with terrace and play area *(Michael Dandy)*

SHARPENHOE TL0630

☆ *Lynmore*: Low beams and end woodburner in traditional pub's long rambling warmly refurbished family lounge, good value food from bar snacks up with newish French chefs adding uplift to the specials board, views of The Clappers from big back no smoking dining area, well kept ales such as Greene King IPA, good service; good garden for children, big wendy house; popular with walkers *(Phil and Heidi Cook, David Gough)*

SHILLINGTON TL1234

Musgrave Arms [Apsley End Rd, towards Pegsdon and Hexton]: Low-beamed village local with settles, tables, prints and horsebrasses in friendly and civilised lounge, woodburner in comfortable public bar, small no smoking dining room, wide choice of generous home-made usual food from sandwiches, baguettes and tortillas to steak, bass and good Sun roast, Greene King IPA, Abbot and Old Speckled Hen tapped from cooled casks, cheerful service; big back garden with picnic-sets *(Barry and Marie Males, Michael Dandy)*

SILSOE TL0835

Star & Garter [High St]: Smart pub by village church, large bar and raised no smoking dining area, enjoyable usual bar food from sandwiches and baked potatoes up, low prices, efficient service, well kept ales such as Adnams, B&T Shefford and Black Sheep, evening restaurant menu, darts; piped music; nice good-sized terrace *(Michael Dandy, Dudley and Moira Cockroft, Phil and Heidi Cook)*

SOUTHILL TL1542

☆ *White Horse* [off B658 SW of Biggleswade]: Friendly and comfortable country pub with extensive eating area, wide range of enjoyable food inc lunchtime favourites, well kept Fullers London Pride, Greene King IPA and Shepherd Neame Spitfire, reasonable wine choice; lots of tables in large pleasant neatly kept garden with good play area *(LYM, Michael Dandy, Jane Ratcliff)*

STREATLEY TL0728

Chequers [just off A6 N of Luton; Sharpenhoe Rd]: Popular partly panelled open-plan L-shaped local, mix of chairs and table sizes, old-fashioned prints and old local photographs, good value food inc some inventive dishes, doorstep sandwiches and omelettes till late, Greene King IPA, Abbot, Old Speckled Hen and Ruddles County, cheerful staff, open fire in public bar; nostalgic piped music, Tues quiz night; garden with Sun lunchtime jazz *(Phil and Heidi Cook)*

STUDHAM TL0215

☆ *Bell* [Dunstable Rd]: Pretty village pub dating from 16th c, plenty of brasses and bric-a-brac in beamed and timbered dining lounge (partly no smoking), plentiful enjoyable fresh food made by landlady from big baguettes to imaginative main dishes, welcoming landlord and quick attentive service, real ales such as Adnams, Fullers London Pride and Greene King IPA and Abbot, darts and games machine in public bar; booking advised Sat, Sun lunch very popular; tables and views in big well reworked garden, good walks, handy for Whipsnade and the Tree Cathedral *(Peter and Jan Humphreys, Ron and Val Broom)*

TEMPSFORD TL1652

Wheatsheaf [Church St]: 18th-c two-bar village pub sensitively refurbished by friendly new owners, cosy fire in public bar, home-made seasonal bar food from sandwiches up, OAP lunches Mon/Tues, reasonably priced restaurant; garden tables *(John Lammie)*

TILSWORTH SP9824

Anchor [just off A5 NW of Dunstable]: Bright and airy, good value quickly served food inc Sun lunch, friendly staff, well kept Fullers; side lawn with picnic-sets on paving stones, more paddocky part with play area *(anon)*

TODDINGTON TL0128

Oddfellows Arms [Market Sq (A5120, handy for M1 junction 12)]: Small attractive bars, heavy beams and stripped pine, warm and pleasant, real ales such as Adnams Broadside and Fullers London Pride, bottled imports, occasional beer festivals, reasonably priced food, helpful landlord; terrace tables, attractive village, may be cl wkdy lunchtimes *(Conor McGaughey)*

☆ *Sow & Pigs* [Church Sq]: Quaint 19th-c pub named after carving on church opp, bare-boards front bar with old wall bench, carpeted saloon, mixed bag of furnishings inc pews, two armchairs and a retired chesterfield, lots of pig decorations, also old books and knick-knacks, friendly landlord, particularly well kept Greene King ales, good coffee, basic food (not Sun; back Victorian-style dining room can be booked for parties), two real fires, children allowed; picnic-sets in small garden, bedrooms, open all day *(Conor McGaughey)*

WESTONING SP0332

Bell [1½ miles from M1, junction 12: High St (A5120)]: Small low-beamed village local with huge inglenook fireplace in each bar (smaller public bar can be smoky), Greene King Abbot and IPA, pub food, restaurant with thai food *(Phil and Heidi Cook)*

Chequers [Park Rd (A5120 N of M1 junction 12)]: Attractive multi-gabled thatched pub with black bargeboards and low beams, newish Jamaican chef doing enjoyable food in bars and big stables restaurant; locals' bar can get smoky and noisy, with piped music and sports TV *(Phil and Heidi Cook)*

WOBURN SP9433

Bell [Bedford St]: Small bar area, longer bare-boards dining lounge up steps, good value generous food from baguettes and ploughman's to steaks, well kept Greene King IPA and Abbot, good choice of wines by the glass, efficient friendly service, good coffee, pleasant décor and furnishings inc fireplace fish tank; children welcome at lunchtime; tables outside, hotel part across road, handy for Woburn Park *(Michael Dandy)*

Birchmoor Arms [Newport Rd]: Country dining pub under same management as Black Horse at Ireland, small front bar, large eating area opening into conservatory, enjoyable food from ciabattas up, well kept Adnams Best and Fullers London Pride, good choice of wines by the glass, friendly efficient staff *(Michael Dandy)*

☆ *Black Horse* [Bedford St]: Friendly and roomy recently spruced up 19th-c food pub, wide choice from sandwiches and baked potatoes to steaks and fish cut to order and grilled in the bar, also children's and special orders, several room areas, coal fire, steps down to pleasant back restaurant; well kept Greene King ales, good choice of wines by the glass; children in eating areas, open all day, summer barbecues in attractive sheltered courtyard, bedrooms across road *(LYM, JHBS, Michael Dandy, John and Joyce Snell)*

Berkshire

Two new entries here this year show what a very wide range of pub styles Berkshire has to offer. The little Magpie & Parrot on the edge of Shinfield is an intimate and friendly home from home, most unusual, beautifully kept, no food at all (unless you count free peanuts and the like); by contrast, the Royal Oak in Ruscombe majors on the food side, with an eclectic menu and good wines. At what might be called the Magpie & Parrot end of the scale, other unspoilt pubs on top form here, both doing good simple pub food in appealing country surroundings, are the 14th-c Bell at Aldworth (a great favourite, one of Britain's very finest pubs – with splendidly low beer prices, too) and the Pot Kiln at Frilsham (brewing its own good beers). Two notable town pubs are the Sweeney & Todd in Reading (bargain imaginative pies and a good beer choice) and the friendly and interestingly decorated Two Brewers in Windsor. The civilised Bell at Boxford deserves a special mention for its remarkable range of wines by the glass, even a dozen champagnes, and the Old Boot at Stanford Dingley is doing well as a good all-rounder. For a special meal out, pubs well worth knowing include the Horns at Crazies Hill, the Dundas Arms by the canal at Kintbury, the restauranty Red House at Marsh Benham (under new French management), and the upmarket Royal Oak at Yattendon. Berkshire Dining Pub of the Year is the Dundas Arms at Kintbury; though its bar meals are nice enough, it's the restaurant which takes the award. The Lucky Dip section at the end of the chapter has plenty of fine pubs. Our current pick would be Elm Tree at Beech Hill, Swan at East Ilsley, Green Man at Hurst, Cricketers at Littlewick Green, Union in Old Windsor, Bull in Sonning, restauranty George & Dragon in Swallowfield, Bell at Waltham St Lawrence, Five Bells at Wickham and Wheelwrights Arms at Winnersh. Drinks cost far more in Berkshire than most other places, with a typical pint of beer costing some 20p more than the national average. Beer from the local West Berkshire brewery, now widely available, tends to be good value.

ALDWORTH SU5579 Map 2

Bell ★ 🍷 🍺 £

A329 Reading—Wallingford; left on to B4009 at Streatley

'If ever I lived out of the country the thought of a Sunday lunchtime summer or winter at the Bell would have me racing to the nearest airport' writes one reader, who has been coming to this 14th-c country pub for 20 years. Bewitchingly unspoilt, it's simply furnished with benches around the panelled walls, an ancient one-handed clock, beams in the shiny ochre ceiling, and a woodburning stove; rather than a bar counter for service, there's a glass-panelled hatch. What sets it apart is the genuine friendliness of the welcome: the same family have run it for over 200 years, and you are made to feel at home immediately. A convivial atmosphere is helped along by a ban on games machines, mobile phones and piped music; darts, shove-ha'penny, dominoes, and cribbage. Well priced Arkells BBB and Kingsdown are superbly kept alongside Old Tyler, Dark Mild and a monthly guest on handpump from the local West Berkshire Brewery; no draught lager. They also serve good house wines and winter mulled wine (£2). Excellent value bar food is limited to filled hot crusty rolls such as honey-roast ham, wild mushroom and port pâté, cheddar, stilton or brie (£1.90), smoked salmon, crab, tongue or salt beef (£2.20), and a variety of ploughman's (from £4); in winter they also do home-made soup (£2.95). The quiet, old-fashioned pub garden is by the village cricket ground, and behind the pub there's a paddock with farm animals. In summer morris dancers visit sometimes, while at Christmas local mummers perform in the road by the ancient well-head (the shaft is sunk 400 feet through the chalk). It tends to get busy at weekends; dogs must be kept on leads. *(Recommended by Jeremy Woods, Dick and Madeleine Brown, N Bayley, A P Seymour, Paul Hopton, the Didler, J R Reayer, Catherine Pitt, Anthony Longden, Susan and John Douglas, Kevin Thorpe, Doreen and Haydn Maddock, Derek and Sylvia Stephenson, Rob Winstanley)*

Free house ~ Licensee H E Macaulay ~ Real ale ~ Bar food (11-2.30, 6-10; 12-2.45, 7-10 Sun; not Mon) ~ No credit cards ~ (01635) 578272 ~ Children must be well behaved ~ Dogs welcome ~ Open 11-3, 6-11; 12-3, 7-10.30 Sun; closed Mon exc bank hols, 25 Dec

ASHMORE GREEN SU5069 Map 2

Sun in the Wood

NE of Newbury, or off A4 at Thatcham; off A34/A4 roundabout NW of Newbury, via B4009 Shaw Hill, then right into Kiln Road, then left into Stoney Lane after nearly 0.5 miles; or get to Stoney Lane sharp left off Ashmore Green Road, N of A4 at W end of Thatcham via Northfield Road and Bowling Green Road

Popular locally for its enjoyable food, this enthusiastically run country pub has a great setting surrounded by tall trees. The high-beamed front bar has bare boards on the left, carpet on the right, with a mix of old bucket chairs, padded dining chairs and stripped pews around sturdy tables. It opens into a big back dining area which has the same informal feel, candles on tables, and some interesting touches like the big stripped bank of apothecary's drawers. There's a small conservatory sitting area by the side entrance. Most of the bar and the restaurant are no smoking; staff are friendly and obliging. Besides fresh baguettes (£4.95, not Sunday), enjoyable lunchtime bar food could include turkey and ham pie with a crusty cheese pastry or fried trout fillets with hoisin sauce and chinese stir-fried vegetables (£6.95), along with other dishes such as home-made soup (£3.75), crispy goats cheese salad (£4.90), fried calves liver with roasted onion and potato compote with a rich port sauce (£11.75), baked cod loin with welsh rarebit on chive mash with tomato and basil sauce (£12.50), and 8oz fillet steak (£16.25); puddings such as delicious lemon curd cheesecake with raspberry coulis and vanilla ice-cream. (£4.65). They also do children's meals, with home-made chicken nuggets (£4.50), and roasts on Sundays. You'll find good house wines, with eight by the glass (they'll let you have a taste first), and well kept Wadworths IPA and 6X, with a guest such as Wadworths JCB on handpump. The big woodside garden has plenty of picnic-sets, and there's a play area with slide and climber; by the time this guide comes out work should have been completed on a 9-hole golf course. It's hard to believe the pub is only a few minutes away from the centre of Newbury. More reports please. *(Recommended by June and Robin Savage, Ian Phillips, James Goldwood, Veronica Turner)*

Wadworths ~ Tenant Philip Davison ~ Real ale ~ Bar food (12-2(3 Sun), 6-9.30; not Mon) ~ Restaurant ~ (01635) 42377 ~ Children welcome ~ Open 12-2.30(3 Sat), 5.30-11; 12-4, 6.30-10.30 Sun; closed Mon

BOXFORD SU4271 Map 2

Bell 🍷

Back road Newbury—Lambourn; village also signposted off B4000 between Speen and M4 junction 14

You can choose from a whopping 60 different wines by the glass and 12 champagnes by the flute at this civilised mock-Tudor inn. If wine is not your thing, they also stock a range of whiskies, and they've four changing beers such as Badger Best, Bass, Wadworths 6X and Shepherd Neame Spitfire well kept (under light blanket pressure) on handpump. The long-standing landlord cleverly manages to maintain a relaxed, country local atmosphere, and service is friendly and cheerful. Quite long but cosy, the bar has a nice mix of racing pictures, old Mercier advertisements, red plush cushions for the mate's chairs, some interesting bric-a-brac, and a log-effect fire at one end. Pool, cribbage, shove-ha'penny, dominoes, TV, and piped music. From an extensive menu (prices haven't changed since last year), good portions of well cooked bar food might include sandwiches and toasties (from £3.95), soup (£3.95; with a sandwich £6.25), snacks to share such as vegetable tempura (£5.25), filled baked potatoes (from £6.95), vegetarian mixed grill (£7.95), battered haddock or various curries (£8.85), home-made pies (£9.95), and fillet steak (£17.95), with puddings such as chocolate brownie with home-made vanilla ice-cream or bread and butter pudding (£4.95). Most people eat in the rather smart, no smoking restaurant area on the left, but you can also dine on the attractive covered and heated terrace (prettily lit at night). The side courtyard has white cast-iron garden furniture. More reports please. *(Recommended by Dr P J W Young, Dr Paull Khan, John and Tania Wood, Mayur Shah, Andy and Yvonne Cunningham)*

Free house ~ Licensee Paul Lavis ~ Real ale ~ Bar food (12-2(3 Sun), 7-9.45) ~ Restaurant ~ (01488) 608721 ~ Children welcome ~ Dogs allowed in bar and bedrooms ~ Open 11-11; 12-4, 7-11 Sun ~ Bedrooms: £50S/£60S

BRAY SU9079 Map 2

Crown

1¾ miles from M4 junction 9; A308 towards Windsor, then left at Bray signpost on to B3028; High Street

A friendly place with a good mix of customers, this 14th-c pub puts the emphasis on the enjoyable (though not cheap) food. Dishes are cooked to order, and could include home-made soup (£3.95), pâté of the day (£5.85), home-made chicken and tarragon pie (£9.95), moules marinière (£11.95), and steak (£15.85), with puddings such as apple strudel or spotted dick (from £4). Best to arrive early as it does get busy, and they recommend you book if you want to eat in the restaurant. Throughout, there are lots of beams (some so low you have to mind your head), and plenty of old timbers handily left at elbow height where walls have been knocked through. The partly panelled main bar has oak tables, leather-backed armchairs, and a roaring fire. One dining area has photographs of WWII aeroplanes. It's especially cosy in winter when you really feel the benefit of the three log fires; good service. Well kept Brakspears Special, Courage Best and Directors on handpump along with a decent choice of wines. There are tables and benches out in a sheltered flagstoned front courtyard (which has a flourishing grape vine), and in the large back garden. *(Recommended by Susan and John Douglas, Michael Dandy, Alison Hayes, Pete Hanlon, Dr and Mrs A K Clarke, Phyl and Jack Street)*

Scottish Courage ~ Tenants John and Carole Noble ~ Real ale ~ Bar food (not Sun or Mon evenings) ~ Restaurant ~ (01628) 621936 ~ Children in restaurant ~ Dogs allowed in bar ~ Open 11-3, 6-11; 12-3, 7-10.30 Sun; closed 25, 26 Dec

CRAZIES HILL SU7980 Map 2

Horns

From A4, take Warren Row Road at Cockpole Green signpost just E of Knowl Hill, then past Warren Row follow Crazies Hill signposts

The comfortable bars of this tiled and whitewashed cottage have rugby mementoes on the walls, exposed beams, open fires and stripped wooden tables and chairs, while the no smoking barn room is opened up to the roof like a medieval hall. The food here is popular, and it's essential to book a table at weekends if you want to eat from the bar menu (it gets particularly busy on Sunday lunchtimes). Dishes could include field mushrooms topped with provençale vegetables and toasted goats cheese (£5.95), seafood pancake (£6.95), pork and honey sausages with spring onion mash or aubergine topped with roasted mediterranean vegetables and toasted mozzarella (£8.95), and coq au vin or slow-roasted lamb shank with roasted vegetables and red wine jus (£10.95), along with fish specials from Billingsgate such as poached salmon fillet with creamy white wine and bay leaf sauce (£13.95), and whole baked bass (£14.95), while good puddings could include vanilla and raspberry cheesecake and apple and cinammon pie (£4.95); they also do lunchtime baguettes (£4.75). Well kept Brakspears Bitter, Special, and seasonal ales on handpump, a thoughtful wine list, and several malt whiskies; they make a good bloody mary. A gentrified country atmosphere is helped along by the absence of juke box, fruit machine or piped music. There's access to the large landscaped garden (which has a play area) from the garden bar with its open fire. No dogs in the evening. *(Recommended by Ian Phillips, Simon Collett-Jones, Guy Charrison, Brian England, Jeremy Woods, J and B Cressey, David Rule, John and Penny Spinks, Wombat, Michael Porter, Tracey and Stephen Groves, Stephen McCormick, Claire George)*

Brakspears ~ Tenant A J Hearn ~ Real ale ~ Bar food (not Sun evening) ~ Restaurant ~ (0118) 940 1416 ~ Children allowed in barn room ~ Dogs allowed in bar ~ Open 11.30-3 (3.30 Sat), 6-11; 12-5.30, 7-10.30 Sun; cl Sun evening in winter; closed 25 Dec

FRILSHAM SU5573 Map 2

Pot Kiln ★

From Yattendon take turning S, opposite church, follow first Frilsham signpost, but just after crossing motorway go straight on towards Bucklebury ignoring Frilsham signposted right; pub on right after about half a mile

There are plenty of opportunities for good walks near this welcoming brick pub. The three basic yet comfortable bar areas have wooden floorboards, bare benches and pews, and good winter log fires. From a hatch in the panelled entrance lobby (which has room for just one bar stool), friendly, efficient staff serve well kept Brick Kiln Bitter and a monthly guest (from the pub's own microbrewery behind) alongside Arkells BBB and Morlands Original. The public bar has darts, dominoes, shove-ha'penny and cribbage; the back room is no smoking. The atmosphere is chatty, and it does get busy, especially at weekends. Freshly prepared, tasty food includes good filled hot rolls (from £1.90), soup (£3.10), salmon and broccoli fishcake (£7.35), steak and kidney pudding or nut cutlets (£8.25), and venison and red wine casserole (£10.65), and puddings such as chocolate and orange fudge cake (£3.65); on Sundays they only serve rolls. It's in a charming rural spot, and picnic-sets in the big suntrap garden have good views of the nearby forests and meadows. *(Recommended by the Didler, Dick and Madeleine Brown, N Bayley, P Price, Brenda and Rob Fincham, Lynn Sharpless)*

Own brew ~ Licensee Philip Gent ~ Real ale ~ Bar food (not Tues) ~ (01635) 201366 ~ Well behaved children in public bar ~ Open 12-3, 6.30-11; 12-3, 7-10.30 Sun; closed Tues

INKPEN SU3864 Map 2

Crown & Garter

Inkpen signposted with Kintbury off A4; in Kintbury turn left into Inkpen Road, then keep on into Inkpen Common

Tucked away up a narrow country lane, this 16th-c brick-built pub is handy for good downland walks, and you can pick up local walks leaflets here free. Surprisingly substantial for somewhere so remote-feeling, it has an appealing low-ceilinged bar, a few black beams, and an attractive variety of mainly old prints and engravings on walls painted cream or shades of pink. The relaxed central bar serves well kept Arkells Moonlight and West Berkshire Mr Chubbs and Good Old Boy on handpump. Three areas radiate from here; our pick is the parquet-floored part by the raised log fire, which has a couple of substantial old tables, a huge old-fashioned slightly curved settle, and a neat little porter's chair decorated in commemoration of the Battle of Corunna (the cats' favourite seat – they've three). Other parts are carpeted, with a good mix of well spaced tables and chairs, and nice lighting; they've recently redecorated the no smoking restaurant. The long side garden is lovely in summer, with picnic-sets and a play area, by shrubs and a big oak tree. From an imaginative menu, dishes might be home-made soup (£3.45), wild mushroom risotto with parmesan shavings, rocket and tarragon oil (£4.50), cod and pancetta fishcakes with fresh asparagus and saffron cream sauce or chick pea burgers (£8.50), various thai curries or chargrilled chicken supreme with mild jerk sauce, sun-dried bananas and jamaican rice (£8.95), half a roast duck with orange and Grand Marnier sauce (£11.95 – highly recommended by readers), and steaks (from £12.95), with puddings such as pear crumble with cinnamon custard (£4.25). They do a popular OAP bargain lunch (Wednesday to Friday) with a choice of two or three courses (£7.95 or £9.95). In a separate single-storey building, the well equipped bedrooms form an L around a pretty garden; good breakfasts. *(Recommended by A P Seymour, Simon Cooke, Ian Phillips, John and Joyce Snell, Paul Humphreys)*

Free house ~ Licensee Gill Hern ~ Bar food (not Mon and Tues lunchtime) ~ Restaurant ~ (01488) 668325 ~ Children welcome ~ Dogs allowed in bar ~ Open 12-3, 5.30-11; 12-11 Sat; 12-3, 7-10.30 Sun; closed Mon and Tues lunchtime ~ Bedrooms: £50B/£70B

KINTBURY SU3866 Map 2

Dundas Arms

Station Road

Berkshire Dining Pub of the Year

What makes this old-fashioned pub special is its waterside setting, standing between the River Kennet and the Kennet & Avon Canal, surrounded by lots of ducks, and in spring banks of daffodils; there's a lock just beyond the hump-backed bridge. Inside, the partly panelled and carpeted bar is well liked by locals, and one of the walls has a splendid collection of blue and white plates. Enjoyable bar food made with good quality ingredients might include soup (£4), ploughman's (£5.25), spinach and red pepper lasagne (£7), fried scampi or home-baked ham, egg and chips (£7.95), steak and kidney pie (£9.95), roast duck breast with cider and apple sauce (£13), and fried monkfish with prawn sauce (£13.50), with puddings such as bread and butter pudding (£4.25); children's meals (£4.25). Their evening restaurant is a place to splash out on a treat. Four real ales such as Adnams Southwold, Butts Barbus Barbus, Greene King Old Speckled Hen, and West Berkshire Good Old Boy, and they've a good range of wines. A real pleasure in fine weather, there are seats on the canalside jetty and on the riverside terrace. The former barge-horse stables have been converted into comfortable, quiet bedrooms, which look out through french windows on to their own secluded terrace. Built for canal workers in the early 19th c, the pub takes its name from Admiral Lord Dundas who, along with his brother, was responsible for the creation of the Kennet & Avon Canal. Readers warn us you may have to wait a while at the level crossing. *(Recommended by Robin Tandy, Alan and Paula McCully, Ian Walker, Peter and Jean Hoare, Angus and Rosemary Campbell, Colin Wood, Craig Turnbull, Tom Evans, Paul Humphreys, James Morrell, Mayur Shah, J Stickland, V Brogden)*

Free house ~ Licensee David Dalzell-Piper ~ Bar food (not Sun, or Mon evening) ~ Restaurant ~ (01488) 658263 ~ Well behaved children in eating area of bar and restaurant ~ Open 11-2.30, 6-11; 12-2.30 Sun; closed Sun evening, 25 Dec ~ Bedrooms: £75B/£85B

MARSH BENHAM SU4267 Map 2

Red House

Village signposted from A4 W of Newbury

The kind of place you'd come to for a special meal, this smartly renovated thatched dining pub changed hands shortly before we went to press, so we're keen to hear from readers about the new regime. The comfortable bar has a light stripped wood floor, and a mix of Victorian and older settles. The appealing library-style front restaurant (which is no smoking) is lined with bookcases and hung with paintings. A terrace with teak tables and chairs overlooks the long lawns that slope down to water meadows and the River Kennet. They have good wines (the landlord has plans to expand the list), lots of malt whiskies, and quite a few brandies and ports along with Fullers London Pride on handpump; piped music. Dishes are innovative (though certainly not cheap), and the menu might include tomato and parmesan crumble with pesto (£6.95), cornish scallop ravioli and sautéed prawns with a light morel velouté (£8.95), grilled bass with roasted artichokes, baby fennel and a citrus reduction or seabream fillet with an almond crust, stir-fried vegetables and an orange infused sauce (£15.95), and roast rack of lamb with sweet potato mash, black pudding and lamb sweetbread fricassee with mint reduction (£17.85), with puddings such as pear parfait with poached pear and dark chocolate sauce (£5); vegetables are from £2.50. They do two courses for £14.95 (not Friday or Saturday evenings, best to check first). *(Recommended by C S Samuel, Colette Annesley-Gamester, Jonathan Harding, Neil and Karen Dignan, Michael Kaye, Brenda and Rob Fincham)*

Free house ~ Licensee Bruno Gaultier ~ Real ale ~ Bar food (not Sun evening or Mon) ~ Restaurant ~ (01635) 582017 ~ Children welcome ~ Open 12-2.15, 6-11; closed Sun and Mon evenings

READING SU7272 Map 2

Hobgoblin

2 Broad Street

The friendly landlord will be happy to help you choose if the terrific range of real ales at this basic but cheery pub leaves you confounded. Three beers from the West Berkshire Brewery are well kept alongside five rapidly changing and interesting guests: a typical selection might include Church End Poo Bear, Elgood's Black Dog and Whitby Abbey, Nottingham EPA, and RCH Steam Shower. If that isn't enough, they've also lots of different bottled beers, czech lager on tap, Weston's farm cider, and country wines. Pump clips cover practically every inch of the walls and ceiling of the simple bare-boards bar – a testament to the enormous number of brews that have passed through the pumps over the past few years (over 4,400 when we went to press). Up a step is a small seating area, but the best places to sit are the three or four tiny panelled rooms reached by a narrow corridor leading from the bar; cosy and intimate, each has barely enough space for one table and a few chairs or wall seats, but they're very appealing if you're able to bag one; the biggest also manages to squeeze in a fireplace. Although it gets very busy (especially at weekends), the atmosphere remains friendly. They don't do any food at all, and they don't allow children or mobile phones. Piped music (very much in keeping with the rough and ready feel of the place), TV and fruit machine. *(Recommended by Bernie Adams, Paul Hopton, R T and J C Moggridge)*

Community Tavern ~ Manager Rob Wain ~ Real ale ~ No credit cards ~ (0118) 950 8119 ~ Open 11-11; 12-10.30 Sun

Sweeney & Todd £

10 Castle Street

This successful cross between café and pub is an excellent place for a pie and a pint. If you can resist rump steak and stilton (the most popular choice), other delicious inventively filled pies might be chicken, honey and mustard, venison, duck and apricot or cajun chicken (all £4.20). Also on the generously served, very fairly priced menu are soup (£3), a choice of ploughman's (from £4.10), casseroles (£6.20), and roasts (£6.50). There's a nice range of seating from little nooks between the shop and bar to a large room at the back, with more seating in the basement. Behind the counter and down some stairs in the lively bar, a surprising number of tiny tables is squeezed into one long thin room; most of them are in rather conspiratorial railway-carriage-style booths separated by curtains, and each has a leather-bound menu to match the leather-cushioned pews. The period feel is enhanced by the old prints which line the walls, the colonial-style fans and the bare-boards floor. A small but well stocked bar serves Adnams Best, Badger Tanglefoot, Wadworths 6X and a changing guest well kept on handpump, as well as various wines and liqueurs. It's hidden away behind a baker's shop which sells take-away pies until 10.30pm (all £2.10). *(Recommended by Paul Hopton, CMW, JJW, Susan and John Douglas, D J and P M Taylor, Ian Phillips)*

Free house ~ Licensee Mrs C Hayward ~ Real ale ~ Bar food (served all day) ~ Restaurant ~ (0118) 958 6466 ~ Children in restaurant ~ Open 11-11; closed Sun and bank hols

RUSCOMBE SU7976 Map 2

Royal Oak

Ruscombe Lane (B3024 just E of Twyford)

One of our regular reporters who lives a few minutes' walk away tipped us off about the interesting changes here just in time for us to inspect anonymously shortly before going to press with this new edition – and confirm that this is indeed a nice find. We were struck by the immediate sense of welcome, the feeling that they really want to look after you well here, whether you want just a drink, a light snack, or a full meal. It's open plan, carpeted more or less throughout (not the cheerful side garden room), and well laid out so that each bit is fairly snug, yet keeps the overall feel of a lot of people enjoying themselves. A good variety of furniture runs from dark oak tables to big chunky pine ones, with mixed seating to match (the deeply squashy sofa we had our own eye on was bagged by another couple – inviting, though it would have meant eating off a very low table). Contrasting with the exposed ceiling joists, mostly unframed modern paintings and prints decorate the walls, mainly dark terracotta over a panelled dado; one back area has a big bright fruity cocktail mural. The eclectic blackboard food choice includes sandwiches and paninis (from £5.95), as well as dishes such as carrot and coriander soup (£3.50), asparagus in smoked salmon with saffron crème fraîche (£6.95), mackerel fillet on sauerkraut with pesto salad, fried scallops and prawns with a warm cucumber and noodle salad and thai green curry sauce (£9.50), baked cod with ginger and coriander sauce, chicken breast stuffed with sun-dried tomatoes and mozzarella wrapped in parma ham (£9.95), beef medallions with gorgonzola potato cake and a brandy and wild mushroom sauce or sirloin steak with tarragon garlic butter (£11.95); they have plans to introduce an italian food night on Mondays. Well kept Fullers London Pride and Youngs on handpump, and half a dozen nicely chosen wines in two glass sizes; the restaurant and conservatory are no smoking. Service is quick and friendly; on our visit they had 1950s/60s piped music. Picnic-sets are ranged around a venerable central hawthorn in the garden behind, which has a barbecue area. We look forward to hearing from readers who have stayed overnight. *(Recommended by Paul Humphreys)*

Enterprise ~ Tenants Jenny and Stefano Buratta ~ Real ale ~ Bar food (not Sun and Mon evenings) ~ Restaurant ~ (0118) 934 5190 ~ Children in eating area of bar, restaurant and family room ~ Dogs welcome ~ Open 12-3, 5.30-11; 12-10.30 Sun ~ Bedrooms: £35/£50

SHINFIELD SU7367 Map 2

Magpie & Parrot ¶

2.6 miles from M4 junction 11, via B3270; A327 just SE of Shinfield – heading out on Arborfield Road, keep eyes skinned for small hand-painted green Nursery sign on left, and Fullers 'bar open' blackboard

A real charmer, this unexpected combination of pub and plant nursery. They raise good value alpines, perennials and bedding plants in the glasshouses and shade house here, and unless you already knew you'd never guess that the little brick roadside cottage includes a genuine pub (as indeed it did in the early 19th c). Go in through the lobby (with its antiquated telephone equipment), and you find a cosy and inviting high-raftered room with a handful of small polished tables – each with a bowl of peanuts – and a comfortable mix of individualistic seats from Victorian oak thrones to a red velveteen sofa, not to mention the armchair with the paw-printed cushion reserved for Spencer the labrador. Everything is spick and span, from the brightly patterned carpet to the plethora of interesting bric-a-brac covering the walls: miniature and historic bottles, dozens of model cars and vans, veteran AA badges and automotive instruments, mementoes of a pranged Spitfire (ask about its story – they love to chat here). Well kept Fullers London Pride on handpump from the small corner counter, a good range of malt whiskies and of soft drinks; very hospitable landlady; a warm log or coal fire. What a nice relaxed place to while away an hour or so in the afternoon! There are teak tables on the back terrace, and an immaculate lawn beyond; the outside lavatories surely qualify for some sort of award. In the summer they have hog roasts. Note the unusual opening hours; no children inside. *(Recommended by Kevin Thorpe, Tom McLean)*

Free house ~ Licensee Mrs Carole Headland ~ Real ale ~ No credit cards ~ (0118) 988 4130 ~ Dogs allowed in bar ~ Open 12-7; 12-3 Sun

STANFORD DINGLEY SU5771 Map 2

Bull

From M4 junction 12, W on A4, then right at roundabout on to A340 towards Pangbourne; first left to Bradfield, and at crossroads on far edge of Bradfield (not in centre) turn left signposted Stanford Dingley; turn left in Stanford Dingley

Reasonably priced for the area, the six well kept real ales on handpump at this attractive 15th-c brick pub could include Bass, Brakspears Bitter, Loddon Hoppit and West Berkshire Good Old Boy, Dr Hexters Healer, and Skiff. The beamed tap room is firmly divided into two by standing timbers hung with horsebrasses. The main part has an old brick fireplace, cushioned seats carved out of barrels, a window settle, wheelback chairs on the red quarry tiles, and an old station clock; a carpeted section has an exposed wattle and daub wall. The half-panelled lounge bar reflects the motorsport and classic car interests of the licensees; on some summer Saturdays owners of classic cars and motorcycles gather in the grounds. Besides tasty lunchtime (and Sunday evening) snacks such as home-made soups (from £3.50), sandwiches and baguettes (from £3.50, toasted 25p extra), filled baked potatoes (from £5), and ham, egg and chips (£7), you can choose from tempting daily specials such as asparagus and sun-dried tomato tartlet (£4), and lamb curry or caribbean sausages and mash (£8.50). The evening menu could include seafood chowder (£5.50), bacon-wrapped chicken supreme (£10.50), and seared bass with pea mash and lime butter sauce (£14), with home-made puddings such as sticky toffee pudding (£4.95); they also do children's dishes (from £4.50), and Sunday roasts (£8). The dining room (and saloon bar at weekends) is no smoking; dominoes, ring-the-bull and piped music. In front of the building are some big rustic tables and benches, and to the side the big garden has plenty of seats. Morris men visit in August, and on St George's Day and New Year's Day. More reports please. *(Recommended by Liz and Brian Barnard, Mr and Mrs S Felstead, Mike and Sue Richardson, Neil and Karen Dignan, P Price)*

Free house ~ Licensees Robert and Kate Archard, Robin and Carol Walker ~ Real ale ~ Bar food (12-2.30, 6.30-9.30; not Sun evening Oct-Mar) ~ Restaurant ~ (0118) 974 4409 ~ Children in eating area of bar and restaurant ~ Dogs allowed in bar ~ Open 12-3, 6-11; 12-3, 7-10.30 Sun ~ Bedrooms: £60S/£75S

Old Boot

Off A340 via Bradfield, coming from A4 just W of M4 junction 12

The beamed bar of this stylish 18th-c pub has two welcoming fires (one in an inglenook) and bunches of fresh flowers. Everything is neatly kept, with fine old pews, settles, old country chairs, and well polished tables, attractive fabrics for the old-fashioned wooden-ring curtains, and some striking pictures and hunting prints. The tranquil sloping back garden and terrace have pleasant rural views, and there are more tables out in front of the pub. Enjoyable bar food from an interesting menu might include home-made soup (£3.50), filled baguettes (£4.95), cheese and spinach filo pie (£8.75), fresh battered cod and chips (£9.50), monkfish (£11.95), and calves liver and bacon or guinea fowl (£12.95), with home-made puddings (£4.50). The dining conservatory is no smoking. Three well kept beers such as Archers Best, local Loddon Hoppit and West Berkshire Good Old Boy on handpump, and good, generously poured wine; the landlord is friendly. *(Recommended by Dr P J W Young, James Woods, Martin and Karen Wake, P Price, John and Glenys Wheeler, Dick and Madeleine Brown, E M Probyn)*

Free house ~ Licensees John and Jeannie Haley ~ Real ale ~ Bar food ~ Restaurant ~ (0118) 974 4292 ~ Children in eating area of bar and restaurant ~ Dogs allowed in bar ~ Open 11-3, 6-11

WINDSOR SU9676 Map 2

Two Brewers ♀ ◖

Park Street, off High Street next to Mews

There's lots to keep your eyes occupied at this charmingly old-fashioned pub, and around the bar are a plethora of tickets, for everything from Royal Ascot to the final of *Pop Idol*. Rambling around a central servery, each of the three quaint but cosily civilised bare-board rooms has a different feel. The red room on the left is our favourite, with a big armchair, sizeable piles of magazines, and a rarely used, discreetly tucked-away TV. Chalkboards record events of the day in history, and there are distinctive old pews and tables. The back bar leading off has a champagne theme, with hundreds of corks lining the walls, particularly around a big mirror above the fireplace. The bar on the right has stripped tables, and a stack of daily papers. Their wide-ranging, fairly priced wine list has several by the glass (including champagne), and Courage Best and Fullers London Pride are well kept on handpump along with a guest such as Wadworths 6X; you can buy cigars here too. Although all the tables are given over to diners (and the friendly staff will try their best to squeeze you in), it's best to book if you want to enjoy the good bar food. The menu might include home-made soup (£3), lunchtime sandwiches (from £3), home-made liver pâté with red onion marmalade (£4.75), home-made chilli con carne with cheese and sour cream (£7.50), home-made fishcakes (£8.50), liver and bacon or smoked haddock topped with poached egg with spring onion mash (£9); they also do a choice of Sunday roasts (£8.50). Most dishes have a £1 surcharge in the evening. Bustling but pleasantly relaxed atmosphere; piped jazz throughout. There are a few tables out in front, under an array of hanging baskets; dogs are treated to a bowl of water. The pub is handily set next to the entrance to Windsor Great Park's Long Walk, and there are plenty of big car parks nearby. Please note that they don't allow children. *(Recommended by Ian Phillips, R T and J C Moggridge, Tracey and Stephen Groves, Kevin Thorpe, John Saville)*

Free house ~ Licensee Robert Gillespie ~ Real ale ~ Bar food (12-2.30, 6.30-10 Mon-Thurs; 12-2.30 Fri; 12-4 wknds) ~ Restaurant ~ (01753) 855426 ~ Dogs welcome ~ Open 11.30-11; 12-10.30 Sun; closed 25 Dec evening

WINTERBOURNE SU4572 Map 2

Winterbourne Arms

3.7 miles from M4 junction 13; A34 S, then cutting across to B4494 Newbury—Wantage from first major slip-road, and follow Winterbourne signs

We went to press shortly before this lovely countryside pub changed hands, and although we don't expect any big changes, it would be a good idea to check the opening times if you're coming from any distance. The bars are interestingly decorated with a collection of old irons around the fireplace, early prints and old photographs of the village, and a log fire; piped music. The peaceful view over the rolling fields from the big bar windows cleverly avoids the quiet road, which is sunken between the pub's two lawns. There's a decent wine list with 13 wines by the glass (served in elegant glasses), and three real ales such as Adnams Broadside, Fullers London Pride and West Berkshire Good Old Boy are well kept on handpump. Besides lunchtime sandwiches (£4.95), sausages and roasted garlic mash (£7.25), and beer battered cod fillets (£7.95), interesting dishes could include roasted vegetable terrine with citrus dressing and warm rosemary bread (£6.35), crispy duck and vegetable spring rolls on chilli noodles with coriander spring onion salad (£10.95), pork filled with caramelised apples on leek mashed potato with cherry brandy sauce (£11.50), and monkfish wrapped in parma ham on buttered savoy cabbage with leek and Pernod sauce (£13.50); puddings such as warm pear and pistachio tart with vanilla ice-cream (£5.95). The little no smoking restaurant area was once a bakery, and you can still see the original bakers' ovens. The pub is in a charming spot, and there are nearby walks to Snelsmore and Donnington. In summer, flowering tubs and hanging baskets brighten up the picnic-sets, and there's a big weeping willow in the garden. Reports on the new regime please.

(Recommended by Maysie Thompson, Bob and Maggie Atherton, Paul Humphreys, Evelyn and Derek Walter, R T and J C Moggridge, Mrs S Fry, John Hale, Sharon and Alan Corper, W W Burke, Colin Wood, Sebastian and Paris Leach, Mike Pugh, Dick and Madeleine Brown)

Free house ~ Real ale ~ Bar food (not Sun evening, or Mon) ~ Restaurant ~ (01635) 248200 ~ Children in eating area of bar and restaurant ~ Dogs allowed in bar ~ Open 12-3, 6-11; 12-3 Sun; closed Sun pm, all day Mon

WOODSIDE SU9270 Map 2

Rose & Crown

Woodside Road, Winkfield, off A332 Ascot—Windsor; coming from Windsor, take last right turn before the racecourse (from Ascot, first left turn after it), then turn right at corner in about 100 yards

The peaceful setting of this attractive white dining pub is quite a contrast to the bustle you'll find inside, especially on race days (it's handy for Ascot). The low beamed bar has been extended and refurbished giving more seating in the no smoking dining area. Although most of these tables are set for diners, it's still somewhere that regulars drop into for a drink. Well liked bar food includes lunchtime sandwiches and filled baguettes (£3.95), ploughman's (£5.95), home-made fishcakes or home-made pie of the day (£7.95), with evening dishes such as cod and chips or cumberland sausage and mash (£8.95), or you can choose more elaborate dishes from the restaurant menu such as almond crusted goats cheese with slices of duck breast and red onions (£6.95), seared scallops with chorizo sausage and sautéed new potatoes (£15.95), and rack of lamb with bubble and squeak and red wine sauce (£16.95), with puddings such as apple and blackberry crumble (£3.95); readers recommend their Sunday lunch. They serve Greene King IPA and Morlands Original on handpump, with a guest such as Wadworths 6X; piped music and fruit machine. The pub is backed by woodland; the side garden has tables and a swing. More reports please. *(Recommended by Robert Turnham, Alistair Forsyth, Bob and Margaret Holder)*

Greene King ~ Tenant Mr Morris ~ Real ale ~ Bar food (12-2.30, 7-9.30; 12-4 Sun, not Sun or Mon evening) ~ Restaurant (evening) ~ (01344) 882051 ~ Children in eating area of bar and restaurant ~ Open 11-11; 12-7 Sun; closed Sun evening ~ Bedrooms: £35/£50

YATTENDON SU5574 Map 2

Royal Oak

The Square; B4009 NE from Newbury; turn right at Hampstead Norreys, village signposted on left

In a pretty village (one of the few still privately owned), this handsome inn is an appealing place for an imaginative meal. In summer, you can eat at tables in the pleasant walled garden, and there are more in front by the peaceful village square. Inside, the panelled and prettily decorated brasserie/bar has a nice log fire and striking flower arrangements. Service is good, and the atmosphere is relaxed; piped music. Carefully prepared dishes could include soup (£4.50), smoked venison and ham hock terrine (£6.25), roast quail with boiled eggs (£8.50), and mains such as smoked haddock kedgeree with a poached egg and curry cream (£13.50), slow-roast guinea fowl with butternut and bacon risotto (£15.25) and fried beef fillet with green pak choi, oyster mushrooms and sweet chilli sauce (£17.50), with puddings such as pistachio soufflé (£4.75); vegetables are extra. It's best to book for the no smoking restaurant. They serve well kept real ales such as West Berkshire Good Old Boy and Wadworths 6X, and the wine list is good. The bedrooms are attractive and well appointed (though not cheap); some overlook the garden. The poet Robert Bridges once lived in the village. *(Recommended by the Didler, Neil and Karen Dignan, Brenda and Rob Fincham, Mr and Mrs G Swire)*

Regal-Corus ~ Manager Corinne Macrae ~ Real ale ~ Bar food ~ Restaurant ~ (01635) 201325 ~ Children over 6 at lunchtime in eating area of bar and restaurant ~ Open 11-11; 11-10.30 Sun; closed 1 Jan ~ Bedrooms: £95B/£110B

LUCKY DIP

Besides the fully inspected pubs, you might like to try these Lucky Dips recommended to us and described by readers (if you do, please send us reports: www.goodguides.co.uk).

ARBORFIELD SU7666

Swan [Arborfield Cross, A327 Eversley Rd]: Attractive small pub, good range of real ales and peaceful friendly atmosphere *(Dr and Mrs A K Clarke)*

ASTON SU7884

☆ *Flower Pot* [small signpost off A4130 Henley—Maidenhead at top of Remenham Hill]: Roomy old-fashioned two-bar pub with lots of picnic-sets giving quiet country views from nice big orchard garden (dogs allowed there), side field with chickens, ducks and guinea fowl; well kept Brakspears inc a seasonal beer, good unusual reasonably priced food from sandwiches to lots of fish and game in season, cheerful welcoming staff, endless stuffed fish and other river-inspired decorations in bright bare-boards public bar and (children allowed here) bigger blue-carpeted saloon, tiled-floor adult dining area; may be unobtrusive piped music, friendly siamese cats and spaniel, very busy with walkers and families wknds, when service can slow *(Brian England, BB, Mark Percy, Lesley Mayoh)*

BAGNOR SU4569

☆ *Blackbird* [quickest approach is from Speen on edge of Newbury]: Chatty traditional pub in very peaceful setting nr Watermill Theatre – they do a pre-show menu; friendly service, changing real ales inc West Berkshire, well prepared straightforward food, winter log fire; bar simple and unfussy with plates around walls, leaded lamps, plain wooden furnishings, old farm tools and firearms hanging from ceiling, more formal no smoking eating area opens off; tables in pleasant side garden and on green in front *(BB, Mark and Ruth Brock)*

BEECH HILL SU6964

☆ *Elm Tree* [3½ miles from M4 junction 11: A33 towards Basingstoke, turning off into Beech Hill Rd after about 2 miles]: Five carefully furnished and decorated rooms, one with dozens of clocks, Hollywood photographs and a woodburner, nice views especially from conservatory, barn-style restaurant, quick friendly staff, enjoyable and generous if not cheap food (all day wknds) from toasties and baked potatoes to alluring puddings, well kept Fullers London Pride, Greene King IPA and Old Speckled Hen and a guest beer, exemplary lavatories; children welcome away from bar, benches and tables on front terrace in nice setting, open all day *(Michael Dandy, LYM, Neil and Karen Dignan, Julia and Richard Tredgett, John and Glenys Wheeler)*

BINFIELD SU8471

Victoria Arms [Terrace Rd N]: Neat and welcoming no-frills Fullers local with good choice of seating areas, well kept real ales, good reasonably priced bar food, children's room; summer barbecues in quiet garden *(LYM, Richard Houghton)*

BRACKNELL SU8769

Golden Retriever [Nine Mile Ride (junction A322/B3430)]: Impressive new pastiche of largely thatched farmhouse-style pub, olde-worlde Vintage Inns interior, their usual food all day, Bass and Fullers London Pride, plenty of wines by the glass, super staff, log fires, daily papers; open all day *(Ian Phillips)*

BRAY SU9079

Hinds Head [High St]: Handsome Tudor beams and panelling, 1930s décor with sturdy old oak furniture, leather porter's chairs, other comfortable seating, plenty of memorabilia and nice pictures, two blazing log fires, well kept Greene King IPA and Old Speckled Hen and a guest beer, good wines, decent usual food from sandwiches, baguettes and baked potatoes up, friendly locals and staff, upstairs restaurant; tables on suntrap front terrace *(LYM, Michael Dandy, Dr and Mrs A K Clarke, Simon Collett-Jones)*

BRIMPTON SU5564

Three Horseshoes: Particularly good food, friendly local atmosphere, well kept Arkells, hard-working licensees *(R M Sparkes)*

BUCKLEBURY SU5769

Blade Bone [Chapel Row]: Large pub, warm and friendly, with plush seats and dark tables, tasteful pictures and plates on pastel walls, matching carpets, small dining room with no smoking conservatory, wide choice of good well presented food inc good puddings, children's helpings, well kept ales such as Fullers and West Berkshire; tables in big neat garden with play area *(P Price)*

COLD ASH SU5169

Spotted Dog [Gladstone Lane]: Comfortable modern pub, bright and roomy, with tempting food choice, several real ales and friendly efficient service *(Stan Edwards)*

COOKHAM SU8985

☆ *Bel & the Dragon* [High St (B4447)]: Smart old dining pub with heavy Tudor beams, open fires, thoughtful furnishings, pastel walls and modern lighting, interesting well presented if not cheap food, lunchtime sandwiches and baguettes, indoor barbecue in back room, well kept Brakspears, Courage Best and Marstons Pedigree, good choice of other drinks; children welcome, dogs allowed in bar, Stanley Spencer Gallery almost opposite, open all day *(Prof H L Freeman, LYM, David Tindal, Paul Humphreys, Colin Wood, P and E Kenyon)*

EAST ILSLEY SU4981

☆ *Crown & Horns* [just off A34; Compton Rd]: Relaxed and unpretentious racing-country pub with rambling snug beamed rooms, soft lighting, blazing log fire, tables tucked into intimate corners, no smoking snug with big oval table, no smoking dining room; lots of interesting racing prints and photographs, perhaps TV racing in the locals' bar, well kept ales such as Black Sheep, Brakspears, Fullers London Pride and Youngs Special, impressive collection of whiskies, wines by the glass, bar food from sandwiches and ciabattas up; fruit machine, piped music; children and dogs allowed, tables in pretty paved stable yard under two chestnut trees, bedrooms, open all day *(LYM, P and J Shapley, Dennis Jenkin, Colin Wood, Val and Alan Green, Dick and Madeleine Brown)*

☆ ***Swan*** [High St]: Spacious, neat and well decorated dining pub with friendly chef/landlord doing enterprising range of good bar food, civilised layout and pleasantly informal atmosphere, attentive service, well kept Greene King IPA and Abbot, good wines by the glass, daily papers; no smoking restaurant, busy with families Sun – best to book; tables in courtyard and walled garden with play area, excellent bedrooms, some in house down road *(Stan Edwards, LYM, Val and Alan Green, Philip Goddard)*

FIFIELD SU9076

Fifield Inn [just off B3024 W of Windsor]: Neatly kept and attractive old stone-built pub with good friendly atmosphere, eclectic décor, generous good fresh food inc interesting dishes and popular Sun roasts (restaurant-type meals only that day, best to book wknds), well kept Greene King, lots of wines by the glass; live jazz Sun evening; children welcome, lovely small garden *(Karen and Steve Brine)*

FINCHAMPSTEAD SU7963

Queens Oak [Church Lane, off B3016]: Relaxed and friendly country local, largely open-plan, with good mix of simple seats and tables, some in airy parquet-floored area on right, well kept Brakspears Bitter and Special, good value food, pleasant helpful staff, separate no smoking room where children allowed; picnic-sets, some sheltered, in good-sized garden with aunt sally, play area, Sun lunchtime barbecues, and perhaps wild rabbits; Weds quiz night, open all day at least in summer *(Andy and Yvonne Cunningham, Tom McLean, BB)*

GREAT SHEFFORD SU3875

Swan [2 miles from M4 junction 14 – A338 towards Wantage]: Low-ceilinged bow-windowed pub with good range of lunchtime snacks and evening meals (can have just a starter), well kept Courage Best and Wadworths 6X, good wine choice, civil attentive service, good log fire, daily papers and magazines, no smoking river-view restaurant; good wheelchair access, children in eating areas, tables on quiet waterside lawn and terrace *(Pauline and Philip Darley, Pamela and Merlyn Horswell, LYM, Mark and Ruth Brock)*

HALFWAY SU4068

☆ ***Halfway Inn*** [A4 Hungerford—Newbury]: Nicely done Badger dining pub with softly lit well divided back dining area, wide choice of enjoyable imaginative food from lunchtime ciabattas and baked potatoes up, fresh veg, good children's dishes (and children's helpings of most main ones), well kept Best and Tanglefoot, good range of wines and beers, daily papers and log fire in attractive rambling traditional bar, friendly helpful staff; may be faint piped music; picnic-sets on side terrace and neat back lawn *(Peter Scillitoe, BB)*

HAMSTEAD MARSHALL SU4165

☆ ***White Hart*** [off A4 W of Newbury]: New owners doing good enterprising food in comfortable dining pub, Hook Norton Best and Wadworths 6X, log fire; children welcome, no smoking restaurant, pretty tree-sheltered walled garden, quiet and comfortable beamed bedrooms in converted barn *(LYM, J L A Gimblett)*

HOLYPORT SU8977

☆ ***Belgian Arms*** [handy for M4 junction 8/9, via A308(M) and A330]: Good long-serving tenants left in summer 2004, so we haven't yet had a chance to assess their replacements, but this L-shaped low-ceilinged bar is cosy and cheerful, with interesting belgian military uniform prints, cricketing memorabilia and a good log fire, and has had well kept Brakspears Bitter and Special and simple but tasty bar food; children in eating areas, pleasant outlook over pond and charming green from garden; more reports please *(LYM)*

HUNGERFORD SU3368

John o' Gaunt [Bridge St (A338)]: Pleasantly refurbished town pub with good choice of usual food from cold or hot baguettes up, good service, well kept Greene King IPA, Abbot and Ruddles, decent wines, daily papers; quiet piped music, can be smoky; outside seating area with play things, open all day *(LYM, Ian Phillips, Meg and Colin Hamilton, Sue and Mike Todd)*

Plume of Feathers [High St]: Big well run open-plan pub, bare boards and lack of fabrics giving a slight brasserie feel, good food from soup and well made sandwiches up, very large helpings, well kept Greene King, friendly atmosphere, cosy fire towards the back; bedrooms *(A P Seymour)*

HURLEY SU8281

☆ ***Dew Drop*** [small yellow sign to pub off A4130 just W]: Country pub tucked away in nice rustic setting, gently refurbished and expanded (new bar in former kitchen), emphasis on popular food from sandwiches (not Sun) to enjoyable meals, good quick service, well kept Brakspears ales, quite a few malt whiskies, darts, shove-ha'penny, backgammon and dominoes; children in eating area, french windows to courtyard and attractive sloping garden with barbecue, good walks *(LYM, John and Glenys Wheeler, Jeremy Woods, Michael Dandy, Simon Collett-Jones)*

Red Lion [A4130 SE, just off A404]: Comfortable Vintage Inn with four separate areas and neat bar, two log fires, amiable service, decent food from sandwiches and generous starters up, Bass, Fullers London Pride and good wine choice, daily papers; picnic-sets in garden behind, open all day *(Michael Dandy)*

HURST SU8074

☆ ***Green Man*** [Hinton Rd, off A321 just outside

village]: Softly lit cosily old-fashioned low-beamed bar with log fires, snug little lower room with just four tables, lighter and airier no smoking area, wide range of enjoyable well prepared blackboard food, well kept Brakspears, good choice of wines by the glass, pleasant service, pub games; cast-iron tables out on heated terrace, picnic-sets in attractive garden under big oak trees, sturdy play area *(Peter Needham, BB, D J and P M Taylor, John Baish)*

INKPEN SU3564

☆ *Swan* [Lower Inkpen; coming from A338 in Hungerford, take Park St (first left after railway bridge, coming from A4)]: Rambling beamed country pub with cosy corners, three log fires, Butts, Hook Norton and organic Caledonian Golden Promise, local farm cider, organic wines and champagne, home-made sloe gin, and organic produce featuring strongly in the food, from sandwiches and pubby food to more upscale dishes – nice if pricey largely no smoking restaurant; flagstoned games room, piped music, may try to keep your credit card; well behaved children welcome in eating areas, picnic-sets out in front, small quiet garden, well equipped bedrooms, open all day in summer, and the farming owners have an organic shop next door *(Alan and Paula McCully, Alan and Jill Bull, Mrs Romey Heaton, LYM, Bill and Jessica Ritson, Mark and Ruth Brock)*

LAMBOURN SU3175

Hare & Hounds [Lambourn Woodlands, well S of Lambourn itself (B4000/Hilldrop Lane)]: Smart dining pub with several nicely individual rooms inc popular bar, sophisticated lunchtime food from filled baguettes to aberdeen angus steak, more elaborate evening menu inc seasonal local game, friendly efficient service, well kept Bass and Wadworths IPA or 6X, nice wines, exemplary lavatories; piped music; children welcome, garden behind with decent play area, cl Sun evening *(LYM, Mark and Ruth Brock, Simon and Mandy King)*

LITTLEWICK GREEN SU8379

☆ *Cricketers* [not far from M4 junction 9; A404(M) then left on to A4, from which village signed on left; Coronation Rd]: Welcoming new Dutch landlady and daughter, well kept Badger and Harveys, fine choice of wines by the glass, reasonably priced food from good range of sandwiches to some imaginative dishes and Sun roast, spick and span housekeeping, lots of cricketing pictures, cosy local atmosphere; charming spot opp cricket green *(LYM, Doreen and Haydn Maddock)*

MIDGHAM SU5566

Berkshire Arms [A4]: Large well decorated Chef & Brewer, wide choice of well priced food, Courage Directors and guest beers *(Geoff Palmer)*

Coach & Horses [Bath road (N side)]: Friendly comfortably refurbished main-road pub with good helpful service, masses of bric-a-brac from safes and brassware to maori masks and spears, wide choice of reasonably priced food from lunchtime sandwiches up, Fullers and West Berkshire ales; garden behind *(BB, Ian Phillips, R L R Nicholson)*

MORTIMER SU6464

Turners Arms [Fairfield Park, West End Rd, Mortimer Common]: Friendly open-plan L-shaped pub with Brakspears beers inc Mild, full range of good value generous bar food inc OAP special in no smoking dining area, prompt pleasant service, log fire; tables in garden *(June and Robin Savage, Andy Coleby)*

OAKLEY GREEN SU9276

Olde Red Lion [B3024 just W of Windsor]: Cosy old low-beamed dining pub with good interesting reasonably priced food from wide sandwich range up, welcoming helpful staff, Bass, Courage Best and Flowers IPA in small bar, mix of seating from homely old chairs to trendy modern ones; comfortable bedrooms, good breakfast, pleasant garden *(Susan and John Douglas, June and Robin Savage)*

OLD WINDSOR SU9874

Fox & Castle [Burfield Rd]: Attractive pub by green, central flame-effect fire in long comfortable bar, friendly staff, good value food, well kept Adnams and Charles Wells Bombardier *(R A Watson)*

☆ *Union* [Crimp Hill Rd, off B3021 – itself off A308/A328]: Friendly and comfortable old pub, well kept ales such as Courage Best, Marstons Pedigree and Theakstons, consistently good service from long-serving staff, woodburner in big fireplace, lots of black and white show-business photographs, bank notes on beams, good traditional bar food from sandwiches and omelettes up and good value attractive copper-decorated restaurant (little for vegetarians); soft piped music, fruit machine; tables under cocktail parasols on sunny front terrace (heated in cooler weather), country views; comfortable bedrooms with own bathrooms *(BB, Jeremy Woods, Ian Phillips, Susan and John Douglas, K Hutchinson)*

PALEY STREET SU8675

Bridge House: Small cottagey black and white pub with warm beamed bar, friendly landlady and helpful service even when busy, real ales such as Brakspears and Fullers, reasonably priced home-made food from good value lunchtime baguettes and baked potatoes up, pleasant no smoking back dining room; big garden *(June and Robin Savage, Paul Humphreys)*

PANGBOURNE SU6376

Swan [Shooters Hill]: Attractive pub dating from 17th c, worth knowing for its Thames-side location with picnic-sets on terrace overlooking the weir and moorings, river-view dining balcony and conservatory (food all day); Greene King ales, decent wines; piped music, sports TV *(Roger and Pauline Pearce, Adrian White)*

READING SU7272

☆ *Fishermans Cottage* [Kennet Side – easiest to walk from Orts Rd, off Kings Rd]: Friendly local in nice spot by canal lock and towpath (gasometer view), with waterside tables, lovely big back garden and light and airy conservatory; modern furnishings of character, pleasant stone snug behind woodburning range, good value lunches inc lots of hot or cold sandwiches (very busy then but service quick), full Fullers beer range kept well, small choice of wines, small darts room, SkyTV; dogs allowed (not in garden) *(R T and J C Moggridge, the Didler)*

Griffin [Church Rd, Caversham]: Reliable and roomy chain dining pub with good varied blackboard food choice, not particularly cheap but good value, Courage, Theakstons and a guest beer, good friendly service, separate areas with several log fires; tables in courtyard, beautiful spot on Thames overlooking swan sanctuary *(Chris and Jo Nicholls, Tony Hobden, D J and P M Taylor)*

REMENHAM SU7682

☆ *Little Angel* [A4130, just over bridge E of Henley]: Good atmosphere in low-beamed pub under new management, small welcoming front bar with attractive prints (dogs allowed here), well kept Brakspears PA and SB, splendid range of wines by the glass, friendly helpful unhurried service, food from good ciabatta cheese melts and other light dishes to some ambitious restaurant dishes, attractive panelled restaurant area (doubling as gallery selling local prints and paintings) with extension into roomy conservatory; pleasant floodlit terrace *(Rob Jarvis, Michael Dandy, LYM, Chris Glasson, Dick and Madeleine Brown)*

SINDLESHAM SU7769

Walter Arms [signed from B3349 or B3030]: Three comfortably traditional main rooms each with a log fire, good range of reasonably priced popular food, well kept real ales, efficient service and warm atmosphere, no smoking area; tables outside *(LYM, John Baish)*

SLOUGH SU9879

Rose & Crown [High St]: Two-bar pub, the oldest on the High St, with well kept changing ales; open all day *(Richard Houghton)*

SONNING SU7575

☆ *Bull* [off B478, by church; village signed off A4 E of Reading]: Attractive old-fashioned inn in pretty setting nr Thames, low heavy beams, cosy alcoves, cushioned antique settles and low-slung chairs, inglenook log fires, no smoking back dining area (children allowed), well kept Gales GB, HSB and Butser and a guest such as Fullers London Pride, lots of country wines, bar food from baguettes and baked potatoes to steaks, good friendly service, charming courtyard; open all day summer wknds, nice bedrooms *(Ian Phillips, LYM, DHV, Paul Humphreys, A P Seymour, Karen and Steve Brine)*

SWALLOWFIELD SU7364

☆ *George & Dragon* [Church Rd, towards Farley Hill]: Relaxed cottagey pub very popular with business diners, stripped beams, red walls, rugs on flagstones and big log fire, plenty of character and atmosphere, food using fresh seasonal produce and normally hitting the mark with good interesting recipes, well kept Adnams, Fullers London Pride and Wadworths 6X, good wines, charming friendly and relaxed young staff; piped music; well behaved children welcome, open all day *(KC, J R Reayer, LYM, Mike and Jayne Bastin, Ian Phillips, Colin Wood, Peter B Brown, John Baish, John and Glenys Wheeler, David Tindal)*

THEALE SU6471

Fox & Hounds [Station Rd, Sunnyside]: Large neatly kept pub, friendly and busy, with good range of well kept ales, welcoming staff, enjoyable food *(Dr and Mrs A K Clarke)*

Winning Hand [A4 W, opp Sulhamstead turn; handy for M4 junction 12]: Friendly pub with good service, well kept Arkells and Hook Norton, varied wine list, wide changing choice of enjoyable food from sandwiches, baguettes and light meals to very substantial dishes, restaurant; quiet piped music; bright gardens, four bedrooms *(Mike and Sue Richardson)*

TWYFORD SU7876

Duke of Wellington [High St]: Congenial pub with lively bar and quiet lounge, wide choice of lunchtime food, well kept Brakspears, friendly landlady; nice back garden with play area *(Paul Humphreys)*

UPPER BASILDON SU5976

Red Lion [Aldworth Rd]: Small Victorian pub with emphasis on upmarket food in bar and dining room, well kept Brakspears and Fullers London Pride, decent house wines; evening live music, popular with young people then *(Stan Edwards)*

WALTHAM ST LAWRENCE SU8376

☆ *Bell*: Handsome heavy-beamed and timbered village pub on good form, daily papers and log fire in compact panelled lounge, no smoking front snug, cheery local public bar, several interesting well kept changing ales inc West Berkshire Mild, plenty of malt whiskies, good wine, friendly attentive service, good value pubby bar food (not Sun evening) from good sandwich range up, big sofa (enjoyed by pub dog – other dogs welcome); children in eating areas and family room, tables in back garden with extended terrace, open all day wknds *(LYM, Paul Humphreys, Tracey and Stephen Groves, Anthony Longden, Bob and Laura Brock, Simon Collett-Jones, Mike and Sue Richardson, A P Seymour)*

WARGRAVE SU7878

☆ *Bull* [off A321 Henley—Twyford; High St]: Good friendly atmosphere in cottagey low-beamed two-bar pub popular for interesting and enjoyable food esp good value lunchtime filled baguettes and hot dishes, well kept Brakspears, good wine choice, friendly staff, good log fires; tables on neat partly covered terrace, bedrooms *(LYM, Michael Dandy, Paul Humphreys)*

WEST ILSLEY SU4782

☆ *Harrow* [signed off A34 at E Ilsley slip road]: Appealing knocked-through bar with Victorian prints on deep-coloured walls, some antique furnishings, log fire, bar food from lunchtime filled rolls (not Sun/Mon) to local game and aberdeen angus steaks, well kept Greene King

Abbot, IPA and Morlands Original, decent wines, recently extended dining room; children in eating areas, dogs allowed in bar, picnic-sets in big garden, more seats on pleasant terrace – peaceful spot overlooking cricket pitch and pond; cl Sun evening *(John Hale, David Handforth, Emma Rampton, Colin Wood, Dr D Taub, LYM, Toppo Todhunter, R M Sparkes, Susan and John Douglas)*

WHITE WALTHAM SU8477

Beehive [Waltham Rd]: Country local by cricket field, accent on enjoyable food, friendly landlord and quick service, three or four well kept changing ales such as Brakspears, Fullers London Pride and Greene King Abbot, smallish front bar, larger back saloon, no smoking dining area – roomy, light and airy; terrace and garden, open all day wknds *(Mike and Sue Richardson, D Crook)*

WICKHAM SU3971

☆ ***Five Bells*** [3 miles from M4 junction 14, via A338, B4000; Baydon Rd]: Neatly kept local in racehorse-training country, big log fire, tables tucked into low eaves, inviting good value food from generous baguettes up, well kept ales inc Greene King Old Speckled Hen and Ringwood, good choice of reasonably priced wines, friendly landlord and staff, good lunchtime mix from regulars to family groups, no smoking at bar; children in eating area, garden with good play area and rabbit hutches, good value bedrooms, interesting church nearby with overhead elephants *(LYM, Esther and John Sprinkle, G W A Pearce, Paul Humphreys)*

WINDSOR SU9675

Windsor Castle [Kings Rd]: Pleasant atmosphere, areas for drinkers and diners, decent food inc innovative specials, real ales such as Adnams, Caledonian Deuchars IPA and Courage, log fire, no music or machines; sports TV; good parking, small outside deck, handy for the Park with view over Royal Paddocks to Frogmore House *(Jeremy Woods)*

WINNERSH SU7870

☆ ***Wheelwrights Arms*** [off A329 Reading—Wokingham at Winnersh crossroads by Sainsburys, signed Hurst, Twyford; then right into Davis Way]: Traditional beamed bar with big woodburner, bare black boards and flagstones, cheerful bustling local atmosphere, well kept Wadworths IPA, 6X and guest beers, enjoyable lunchtime food from huge doorstep sandwiches up, quick friendly service, cottagey no smoking dining area; may keep your credit card, can be a bit smoky by bar; children welcome, picnic-sets in smallish garden with terrace, disabled parking and facilities *(John Baish, June and Robin Savage, BB, D J and P M Taylor)*

WOKINGHAM SU8168

Dukes Head [Denmark St]: Comfortable and well run local with well kept Brakspears, good choice of lunchtime food, skittle alley *(Richard Houghton)*

WOOLHAMPTON SU5766

☆ ***Rowbarge*** [Station Rd]: Big canalside family dining pub with good log fire in attractive beamed bar, panelled side room, small snug, large no smoking water-view conservatory, wide choice of good freshly made food from lunchtime baguettes and baked potatoes to Sun lunch and curry nights, well kept Greene King ales, plentiful pleasant staff; tables out by water and in roomy garden with fish pond, moorings not far *(LYM, Andy Coleby)*

Post Office address codings confusingly give the impression that some pubs are in Berkshire, when they're really in Oxfordshire or Hampshire (which is where we list them).

Buckinghamshire

Half a dozen new main entries here this year (some of them pubs now in new hands which were in the *Guide* some years ago) are the White Hart in Chalfont St Giles (good enterprising food, comfortable bedrooms), the stylishly updated Swan in Denham (good food and wines, with an appealing garden and attractive village surroundings), the friendly and nicely extended 16th-c Dinton Hermit at Ford (enjoyable food, nice bedrooms), the pretty Hare & Hounds just outside Marlow (interesting food and nice wines by the glass), the Crown at Penn (possibly Chef & Brewer's very best pub), and the beautifully placed Bull & Butcher at Turville (an amazing choice of wines by the glass). Other pubs on top form here include the Royal Oak at Bovingdon Green (a sister pub of the Denham Swan – a similarly stylish food place), the welcoming and individualistic Red Lion at Chenies (a fine all-rounder), the Mole & Chicken at Easington (an appealing candlelit dining pub with good restauranty food and a fine choice of malt whiskies), the friendly Green Dragon at Haddenham (good imaginative food in a thriving atmosphere), the Crown at Little Missenden (a classic proper pub with some bargain home-made food), and the welcoming and nicely set Frog at Skirmett (gains a Food Award this year, and has good bedrooms). The little Old Ship at Cadmore End is well worth knowing for properly kept beers tapped from the cask, in cheerfully unspoilt and unpretentious 17th-c surroundings, the rambling Royal Standard of England at Forty Green for its great character and sense of history, the friendly White Horse at Hedgerley for its fine choice of real ales in top condition, the Stag & Huntsman at Hambleden and Full Moon on Hawridge Common for the joy of finding nice pubs in attractive surroundings (good walks), and the Stag at Mentmore and Boot at Soulbury for their splendid choice of wines by the glass, among other virtues. The Crooked Billet at Newton Longville has dozens of interesting brandies and malt whiskies, and a choice of literally hundreds of wines by the glass. Many of the pubs we have picked out so far, as we have implied, specialise in good food, and the county is now very well served on that side. For the second year running the Green Dragon at Haddenham takes the title of Buckinghamshire Dining Pub of the Year. In the Lucky Dip section at the end of the chapter pubs which are making their mark these days include the Bull & Butcher at Akeley, Chequers at Fingest, Cross Keys in Great Missenden, Blackwood Arms on Littleworth Common, Angel in Long Crendon (really a restaurant rather than pub now), Two Brewers in Marlow, Carrington Arms at Moulsoe, Old Swan at The Lee (quite a favourite of ours – we wish more readers tried it), George & Dragon at West Wycombe, Cowpers Oak at Weston Underwood, Royal Standard on Wooburn Common and Clifden Arms at Worminghall. Drinks in the county tend to be markedly more expensive than the national average.

Anyone claiming to arrange or prevent inclusion of a pub in the *Guide* is a fraud. Pubs are included only if recommended by genuine readers and if our own anonymous inspection confirms that they are suitable.

BENNETT END SU7897 Map 4

Three Horseshoes

Horseshoe Road; from Radnage follow unclassified road towards Princes Risborough and turn left into Bennett End Road, then right into Horseshoe Road

This unpretentious old country inn is a lovely tranquil spot, with surroundings made particularly distinctive by a red phone box rising incongruously from the fenced-off duck pond. Inside you'll find old beams and original brickwork, flagstones, and a wooden floor in the bar, lots of sporting prints, wartime silk postcards, horsebrasses and copperware, a selection of old bottles, and oil lamps and antiques; high wooden corner settles, and a few seats are tucked around an antique range. Besides sandwiches, enjoyable home-made lunchtime bar food might include omelettes (£5.25), home-cooked ham, egg and chips (£6.25), home-made cottage pie or lasagne (£7.25), with other dishes such as home-made soup (£3.95), field mushrooms with tomato and goats cheese (£3.95), wild mushroom stroganoff (£8.95), chargrilled salmon supreme with a pesto crust or home-made steak and mushroom pie (£9.95), rack of roasted lamb with rosemary gravy (£13.95), and 8oz fillet steak (£14.95); best to book for Sunday lunch, when they have a choice of three roasts (£8.95, 2-courses £11.50). Adnams and Hook Norton are well kept on handpump with a guest such as Shepherd Neame Spitfire, and they've a variety of whiskies, and six wines by the glass; attentive service from the friendly licensees. There are three ensuite bedrooms, and readers tell us this is a nice place to stay; generous breakfasts. Look out for red kites circling overhead in the valley. More reports please. *(Recommended by Derek and Sylvia Stephenson)*

Free house ~ Licensee Richard Howard ~ Real ale ~ Bar food ~ Restaurant ~ (01494) 483273 ~ Children in eating area of bar and restaurant ~ Open 11.30-11; 12-10.30 Sun ~ Bedrooms: £65S/£78B

BOVINGDON GREEN SU8286 Map 2

Royal Oak

¾ mile N of Marlow, on back road to Frieth signposted off West Street (A4155) in centre

The emphasis at this stylish rambling country pub is on the high quality food. A good selection of skilfully prepared dishes, from a seasonally changing blackboard menu, might include soup (£4), goats cheese croquettes with sweet pepper relish (£5.75), warm monkfish tart with béarnaise sauce (£6.50), roast vegetable wellington with dolcelatte potatoes (£10.25), slow-cooked lamb shoulder with onion mash and minty peas (£12.50), spaghetti with tiger prawns, smoked bacon and sun-dried tomatoes (£12.75), with puddings such as sticky treacle and apple tart or caramelised bananas on pancakes (from £4.50); a good few tables may have reserved signs (it's worth booking ahead, especially on Sundays). Several attractively decorated areas open off the central bar, the half-panelled walls variously painted in pale blue, green or cream: the cosiest part is the low-beamed room closest to the car park, with three small tables, a woodburner in an exposed brick fireplace, and a big pile of logs. Throughout there's a mix of church chairs, stripped wooden tables and chunky wall seats, with rugs on the partly wooden, partly flagstoned floors, co-ordinated cushions and curtains, and a very bright, airy feel. It's a well organised and civilised place, and thoughtful extra touches set the tone, with a big, square bowl of olives on the bar, smart soaps and toiletries in the lavatories, and carefully laid out newspapers; most tables have fresh flowers or candles. A terrace with good solid tables leads to an appealing garden with plenty more, and there's a smaller garden at the side as well (all the staff get a shift looking after the garden). They serve 13 wines by the glass, and well kept Brakspears, Fullers London Pride and Marlow Rebellion on handpump; hard-working and helpful staff, piped music. The pub is part of a little group which comprises the Alford Arms in Frithsden (see Hertfordshire main entries) and the Swan at Denham (see Buckinghamshire main entries). *(Recommended by Simon Collett-Jones, DM, Howard Dell, Phil Roberts, Tracey and Stephen Groves, David Edwards, Susan and John Douglas)*

Enterprise ~ Lease Trasna Rice Giff and David Salisbury ~ Real ale ~ Bar food (12-2.30 (3 Sun), 7-10) ~ (01628) 488611 ~ Children in eating area of bar and restaurant ~ Dogs allowed in bar ~ Open 11-11; 12-10.30 Sun; closed 25-26 Dec

CADMORE END SU7892 Map 4

Old Ship

B482 Stokenchurch—Marlow

The four well kept real ales at this carefully restored 17th-c tiled cottage are tapped straight from the cask, and might be from brewers such as Brakspears, Butts, Vale and Young's. With plenty of unpretentious character and charm, the tiny low-beamed two rooms of the bar are separated by standing timbers, and simply furnished with scrubbed country tables and bench and church chair seating (one still has a hole for a game called five-farthings); cribbage, dominoes, TV, shove-ha'penny and unobtrusive piped music. Outside, there are seats in the sheltered garden with a large pergola and a terrace at the end of the bar with cushioned seats and clothed tables. Simple bar food includes home-made soup or pâté (£3.95), filled organic baguettes with chips or caramelised red onion and goats cheese tart (£4.95), local sausages and mash or local ham and eggs (£6.95), home-made steak and ale pie (£7.95), with puddings such as treacle sponge or spotted dick (£2.95); cheerful service. Parking is on the other side of the road. More reports please. *(Recommended by the Didler, Tracey and Stephen Groves, Pete Baker)*

Free house ~ Licensee Philip Butt ~ Real ale ~ Bar food (12-2, 6-9, not Mon lunch) ~ Restaurant ~ (01494) 883496 ~ Children in eating area of bar ~ Open 11-3, 5.30-11; 12-4, 7-10.30 Sun; closed Mon lunchtime

CHALFONT ST GILES SU9893 Map 4

White Hart

Three Households (main street, W)

This former community local has recently been well reworked as a good dining pub. It does still have a proper civilised front bar where drinkers are welcome, with broadsheet daily papers, bar stools, one or two pub tables and a couple of liberally cushioned dark green settees, and well kept Greene King IPA, Triumph, Morlands Original and Old Speckled Hen on handpump. However, the main emphasis is on the food side, with a spreading extended dining area, mainly bare boards (the bright acoustics make for a lively medley of chatter – sometimes rather on the noisy side when it's busy), and white walls decorated with lots of foody cartoons. The food is good, carefully cooked modern british cooking. There are two menus, with sandwiches such as warm brie and bacon (£5.50), duck salad (£6.75), and mussels or fishcakes (£7.95) on the short bar one, while the interesting main menu might include fried calves liver (£12.25), chicken wrapped in parma ham and stuffed with mozzarella and spinach (£12.75), baked salmon supreme with a herb crust (£13.95), and fillet steak with foie gras (£17.50); puddings such as sticky toffee pudding (£5.25). They do small helpings for children, and there is a good choice of wines by the glass. Service from the neatly dressed young staff is friendly, helpful and efficient. A sheltered back terrace has squarish picnic-sets under cocktail parasols, with more beyond in the garden, which has a neat play area; the comfortable newly done 11-room bedroom block is on the other side (breakfasts are good). *(Recommended by Mr and Mrs P Lally, Alison Cook, Howard Dell)*

Greene King ~ Lease Scott MacRae ~ Real ale ~ Bar food (12-2, 6.30(7 Sun)-9.30) ~ Restaurant ~ (01494) 872441 ~ Children in eating area of bar and restaurant ~ Dogs allowed in bar ~ Open 11.30-2.30, 6(5.30 Fri and Sat)-11; 12-10.30 Sun; 12-3, 7-10.30 Sun in winter ~ Bedrooms: £77.50S/£97.50S

Bedroom prices include full English breakfast, VAT and any inclusive service charge that we know of.

CHENIES TQ0198 Map 3

Red Lion ★

2 miles from M25 junction 18; A404 towards Amersham, then village signposted on right; Chesham Road

Handy for the M25, this well run pub is a good all rounder with well kept beers, a welcoming atmosphere and tasty home-made food. The bustling unpretentious L-shaped bar has comfortable built-in wall benches by the front windows, other traditional seats and tables, and original photographs of the village and traction engines; there's also a small no smoking back snug and a dining room. Benskins Best, Marlow Rebellion Lion Pride (brewed for the pub and highly recommended by readers), Wadworths 6X, and a guest beer are kept in top condition on handpump. There's a terrific choice on the inventive menu, and handily lots of the dishes come in two sizes. Good value food includes baguettes or wholemeal baps (from £3.50), baked potatoes with some unusual fillings (from £4.25), curried sausage and herb meatballs with mint and cucumber yoghurt (£5.50), mixed seafood and ratatouille gratin or lemon and pepper chicken goujons with minted mayonnaise (£5.75; main course £7.95), home-made pies such as bison in red wine or ham and parsley (from £7.25), cumberland sausage on bubble and squeak with rich red wine gravy (£9.50), and red mullet fillets with green pea guacamole with wine and horseradish cream (£11.25). The hanging baskets and window boxes are pretty in summer, and there are picnic-sets on a small side terrace. No children, games machines or piped music. *(Recommended by John Saville, Peter and Giff Bennett, Charles Gysin, LM, Mrs Pamela Quinn, Derek and Sylvia Stephenson, Tracey and Stephen Groves)*

Free house ~ Licensee Mike Norris ~ Real ale ~ Bar food (12-2, 7-10)(9.30 Sun) ~ (01923) 282722 ~ Dogs allowed in bar ~ Open 11-2.30, 5.30-11; 12-3, 6.30-10.30 Sun; closed 25 Dec

DENHAM TQ0486 Map 3

Swan 🍴 🍷

¾ mile from M40 junction 1; follow Denham Village signs

In a charming village street, among old tiled, wisteria-clad buildings, this civilised pub is a popular place for a well cooked meal. Along with lunchtime sandwiches (from £4, not weekends), you'll find high quality, beautifully presented dishes such as soup (£4), chicken, cranberry and sage terrine with fig chutney (£6), oak smoked bacon on bubble and squeak with hollandaise and poached egg (£6; £11.50 main course), slow-roasted belly pork on swede mash with roasting juices (£11.75), roast cod on wilted spinach with chorizo and new potatoes (£12.50), and calves liver on crushed beetroot and herb potatoes with rosemary gravy (£12.75), with puddings such as roasted peaches with marsala and mascarpone (£5.25). A good wine list includes over a dozen by the glass, and they keep Courage Best and Directors and Morrells Oxford Blue on handpump; excellent courteous staff, and a friendly bustling atmosphere. It's stylishly furnished, with a nice mix of antique and old-fashioned chairs, and solid tables, with individually chosen pictures on the cream and warm green walls, rich heavily draped curtains, inviting open fires (usually lit) and fresh flowers; piped music. The extensive garden is floodlit at night, and leads from a sheltered terrace with tables, to a more spacious lawn. It can get busy at weekends, and parking may be difficult. *(Recommended by Howard Dell, Mrs Ann Gray, A P Seymour, Karen Barr, Jane Pritchard, Ian Phillips, Tracey and Stephen Groves)*

Scottish Courage ~ Lease Mark Littlewood ~ Real ale ~ Bar food (12-2.30(3 Sun), 7-10) ~ (01895 832085) ~ Children welcome ~ Dogs allowed in bar ~ Open 11-11; 12-10.30 Sun; closed 26 Dec

Pubs with particularly interesting histories, or in unusually interesting buildings, are listed at the back of the book.

EASINGTON SP6810 Map 4

Mole & Chicken

From B4011 in Long Crendon follow Chearsley, Waddesdon signpost into Carters Lane opposite the Chandos Arms, then turn left into Chilton Road

An excellent choice for a special meal, this enjoyable dining pub is set in lovely countryside. The open-plan layout is cleverly done, so that all the different parts seem quite snug and self-contained without being cut off from what's going on, and the atmosphere is relaxed and sociable. The beamed bar curves around the serving counter in a sort of S-shape, and there are pink walls with lots of big antique prints, flagstones, and (even at lunchtime) lit candles on the medley of tables to go with the nice mix of old chairs; good winter log fires. Although customers do drop in for just a drink, you'll probably feel you're missing out if you're not eating; you must book to be sure of a seat. Delicious, generously served food might include sandwiches, home-made soup (£3.50), chicken satay or roasted field mushrooms with spinach and cheese (£5.95), salmon fillet wrapped in parma ham with warm green salad and yoghurt dressing, steak, Guinness and mushroom pie (£9.95), Gressingham duck with orange sauce or thai prawn curry with hot asian spices and saffron rice (£12.95), and shoulder of slow roasted lamb (£13.95), with daily specials. They serve a good choice of wines (with decent french house wines), over 40 malt whiskies, and well kept Fullers London Pride, Greene King IPA and Hook Norton Best on handpump. The garden, where they sometimes hold summer barbecues and pig and lamb roasts, has quite a few tables and chairs. *(Recommended by Michael Jones, Maysie Thompson, MP, Karen and Graham Oddey, Mr and Mrs A Stansfield, Richard Siebert, Susan and John Douglas, Jenny and Peter Lowater, Peter D B Harding, Ian Phillips, Martin and Karen Wake)*

Free house ~ Licensees A Heather and S Ellis ~ Real ale ~ Bar food ~ Restaurant ~ (01844) 208387 ~ Children welcome ~ Dogs allowed in bar ~ Open 12-3, 6-11; 12-10.30 Sun; closed 25 Dec ~ Bedrooms: £50S/£65B

FORD SP7709 Map 4

Dinton Hermit

SW of Aylesbury

Tucked away in pretty countryside, this welcoming 16th-c stone cottage has a very old print of John Bigg, the supposed executioner of King Charles I and the man later known as the Dinton Hermit. With a huge inglenook fireplace (good log fire in winter), the bar has scrubbed tables and comfortable cushioned and wicker-backed mahogany-look chairs on a nice old black and red tiled floor, with white-painted plaster on very thick uneven stone walls; the extended back dining area is very much in character, with similar furniture on quarry tiles. A nice touch is the church candles lit throughout the bar and restaurant, and there are hundreds of bottles of wine decorating the walls and thick oak bar counter. Although locals do still drop in for just a drink, there's quite an emphasis on the enjoyable food. Generously served dishes might include home-made soup (£4.95), mussels sautéed with white wine, shallots and garlic (£6.25), crispy duck salad with warm plum and star anise dressing (£6.50), grilled salmon and prawns with herbed tomato and white wine sauce or braised ham hock with butterbeans, tarragon and mature cheddar cheese (£12.50), and pot-roast guinea fowl with raisins, pine nuts, orange zest and sherry (£13.95), and home-made puddings such as bread and butter pudding (£5.50); they also do lunchtime sandwiches (from £4). Alongside well kept Fullers London Pride, and Vale Wychert on handpump, they serve a changing guest such as Adnams, and there's a decent choice of wines; friendly and attentive service, and a congenial atmosphere. As we went to press, the huge garden was being landscaped; barbecues in summer and live jazz events. The comfortable, well decorated bedrooms are in a sympathetically converted barn. *(Recommended by John and Pauline Day, Peter and Pat Branchflower, L Graham, Nigel Ward, Michael Jones)*

Free house ~ Licensees John and Debbie Colinswood ~ Real ale ~ Bar food (not Sun evening) ~ Restaurant ~ (01296) 747473 ~ Children in eating area of bar and restaurant, must be over 12 in evening ~ Dogs allowed in bar ~ Open 11-11; 12-4 Sun; closed Sun evening ~ Bedrooms: /£80B

FORTY GREEN SU9292 Map 2

Royal Standard of England

3½ miles from M40 junction 2, via A40 to Beaconsfield, then follow sign to Forty Green, off B474 ¾ mile N of New Beaconsfield; keep going through village

This ancient place is great to look round, with enormous appeal, both in the layout of the building itself and in the fascinating collection of antiques which fill it. The rambling rooms have huge black ship's timbers, finely carved old oak panelling, roaring winter fires with handsomely decorated iron firebacks, and there's a massive settle apparently built to fit the curved transom of an Elizabethan ship; you can also see rifles, powder-flasks and bugles, ancient pewter and pottery tankards, lots of brass and copper, needlework samplers, and stained glass. Outside, there are seats in a neatly hedged front rose garden, or in the shade of a tree. As well as a guest such as Wychwood Hobgoblin, they serve kept Brakspears Bitter, Fullers London Pride, Greene King Old Speckled Hen, and Marstons Pedigree on handpump, and country wines and mead; the main dining bar and one other area are no smoking. They do interesting lunchtime sandwiches (£5.75), as well as home-made soup (£3.95), garlic and sherry stuffed mushrooms with brie (£4.50), chestnut, mushroom, celeriac and squash roulade (£7.95), pork fillet with peppercorn, cream and brandy sauce with grain mustard mash or crisp battered haddock with minted pea purée (£8.25), and slow-cooked lamb marinated in mint and honey (£9.90), with home-made puddings such as gooseberry fool (£3.95). Until after the Battle of Worcester in 1651 (when Charles II hid in the high rafters of what is now its food bar), the pub used to be called the Ship. *(Recommended by the Didler, Kevin Blake, Anthony Longden, Lesley Bass, Alison Hayes, Pete Hanlon, David and Higgs Wood, John and Tania Wood, Ian Phillips, Tracey and Stephen Groves, Nigel Howard, Susan and John Douglas)*

Free house ~ Licensees Cyril and Carol Cain ~ Real ale ~ Bar food ~ (01494) 673382 ~ Children in eating area of bar ~ Open 11-3, 5.30-11; 12-3, 7-10.30 Sun; 25 Dec evening

GREAT HAMPDEN SP8401 Map 4

Hampden Arms

Village signposted off A4010 N and S of Princes Risborough

This quietly set pub is on the edge of Hampden Common (and right opposite the village cricket pitch), so there are good walks nearby. Although the emphasis is on the well prepared food, the friendly staff do make drinkers feel welcome. The enjoyable menu could include soup (£3.50), pancetta, black pudding and poached egg salad (£7.25), game pie with rich port sauce (£9.95), baked trout with horseradish butter (£12.45), half a roast duck with apple and calvados and black cherry sauce (£13.95), and steaks (from £14.95), with puddings such as bread and butter pudding (£3.50); they also do lunchtime sandwiches (£4.25). The beige-walled front room has broad dark tables with a few aeroplane pictures and country prints, and the back room has a slightly more rustic feel, with its cushioned wall benches and big woodburning stove. Well kept Adnams and Hook Norton on handpump, and Addlestone's cider from the small corner bar. There are tables out in the tree-sheltered garden. More reports please. *(Recommended by John Roots, Peter Saville, Tracey and Stephen Groves, Marjorie and David Lamb)*

Free house ~ Licensees Louise and Constantine Lucas ~ Real ale ~ Bar food ~ Restaurant ~ (01494) 488255 ~ Children welcome ~ Dogs welcome ~ Open 12-3, 6-11

The letters and figures after the name of each town are its Ordnance Survey map reference. *Using the Guide* at the beginning of the book explains how it helps you find a pub, in road atlases or large-scale maps as well as in our own maps.

HADDENHAM SP7408 Map 4

Green Dragon

Village signposted off A418 and A4129, E/NE of Thame; then follow Church End signs

Buckinghamshire Dining Pub of the Year

It's no surprise that this welcoming pub is so popular with readers, the friendly licensees and helpful staff really care that their customers have a good time, and the food is superb. On the imaginative menu you might find home-made soup (£3.95), scottish smoked halibut (£6.50), confit of duck leg glazed with local honey and black pepper with pineapple chutney (£6.95), creamed onion risotto with roasted vegetables and deep-fried brie (£9.50), braised lamb shank with parsnip mash, roasted root vegetables and tarragon jus (£10.50), whole lemon sole with lemon butter or halibut fillet on saffron and lobster mash with saffron sauce (£13), as well as daily specials such as salmon fillet on linguini with leek and dill sauce (£8.95), and pavé of spring lamb with buttered spring cabbage, clear broth and baby vegetables (£13), while puddings could be steamed chocolate pudding with mango sorbet or mouthwatering home-made Baileys cheesecake (£5.50); a discretionary 10% service charge is added to the bill. On Tuesday and Thursday evenings, they do an excellent value two-course dinner (£11.95), best to book. The main eating area is no smoking. The neatly kept opened-up bar, in colours of pale olive and antique rose, has an open fireplace towards the back of the building and attractive furnishings throughout; the dining area has a fine mix of informal tables and chairs. Well kept Deuchars IPA, Wadworths 6X and a guest from the Vale Brewery on handpump, and a sensibly priced well chosen wine list includes around eight by the glass. A big sheltered gravel terrace behind the pub has white tables and picnic-sets under cocktail parasols, with more on the grass, and a good variety of plants. This part of the village is very pretty, with a duck pond unusually close to the church. *(Recommended by MP, Tracey and Stephen Groves, Paul Coleman, Maysie Thompson, Mike and Sue Richardson, Dr R C C Ward, Tim and Ann Newell, Colin Whipp, Neil and Karen Dignan, J Woollatt, Brian Root, B H and J I Andrews, Jeff and Wendy Williams, Tim and Janet Mears, John and Claire Pettifer, Stuart Turner, Jeremy Woods, Phyl and Jack Street)*

Enterprise ~ Lease Peter Moffat ~ Real ale ~ Bar food ~ Restaurant ~ (01844) 291403 ~ Children over 7 in restaurant lunchtime only ~ Open 12-3, 6.30-11; 12-4 Sun; closed Sun evening, 1 Jan

HAMBLEDEN SU7886 Map 2

Stag & Huntsman

Turn off A4155 (Henley—Marlow Rd) at Mill End, signposted to Hambleden; in a mile turn right into village centre

This handsome brick and flint pub is set opposite a church on the far edge of one of the prettiest Chilterns villages; it's just a field's walk from the river. In fine weather you'll have to be quick if you want to bag one of the seats in the spacious and neatly kept country garden. The half-panelled, L-shaped lounge bar has low ceilings, a large fireplace, and upholstered seating with wooden chairs on the carpet. Attractively simple, the public bar serves well kept Rebellion IPA, Wadworths 6X, and a guest beer such as Loddon Hoppit on handpump, and they've farm cider, and good wines; darts, dominoes, cribbage, shove-ha'penny, and piped music. There's a dining room, and a cosy snug at the front; friendly and efficient service, and a buoyant atmosphere. Well liked, reasonably priced bar food might include home-made soup (£3.95), chicken liver and cognac pâté (£5.25), ploughman's (£5.95), vegetarian quiche (£7.25), steak, mushroom and ale pie (£8.95), battered cod and chips (£9.25), marinated pork loin with apple and cider sauce (£9.50), and sirloin steak (£12.25), while puddings could be raspberry and cherry cheesecake (£3.95). *(Recommended by John Roots, John Hale, Anthony Longden, Brian England, John and Glenys Wheeler, M Thomas, Peter Saville, Paul Humphreys, Iwan and Sion Roberts, Roy and Lindsey Fentiman, Gill and Keith Croxton, Susan and John Douglas)*

Free house ~ Licensees Hon. Henry Smith and Andrew Stokes ~ Real ale ~ Bar food (not Sun evenings) ~ (01491) 571227 ~ Children in eating area of bar and restaurant ~ Dogs allowed in bar ~ Open 11-2.30(3 Sat), 6-11; 12-3, 7-10.30 Sun; closed 25 Dec, evenings 26 Dec and 1 Jan ~ Bedrooms: £58B/£68B

HAWRIDGE COMMON SP9406 Map 4

Full Moon

Hawridge Common; left fork off A416 N of Chesham, then follow for 3.5 miles towards Cholesbury

This prettily set little country local is bustling with a friendly mix of locals, walkers and visitors. The low-beamed rambling bar is the heart of the building, with oak built-in floor-to-ceiling settles, ancient flagstones and flooring tiles, hunting prints, and an inglenook fireplace. In summer, you can sit at seats on the terrace (which has an awning and outside heaters for cooler evenings) and gaze over the windmill nestling behind; plenty of walks over the common from here. At lunchtime the enjoyable menu (with meat, poultry and game from an organic butcher) might include sandwiches (from £3.50), home-made soup (£4.50), whitby scampi and chips (£7.95), ploughman's (£8.25), pork and apple sausages and mash or lamb and mint suet pudding (£9.25), with evening dishes such as sautéed chicken liver, orange and mandarin salad (£5.75), braised lamb shank with honey and apricots and celeriac mash (£10.95), bass on sun-dried tomato couscous with lemon grass sauce or roasted pork fillet with mustard mash and Drambuie jus (£12.95), with puddings (£4). Both the restaurants are no smoking. They keep six real ales on handpump, with regulars such as Adnams, Bass, Brakspears Special, and Fullers London Pride, and weekly changing guests such as Courage Best and Wadworths 6X; piped music, and good service. *(Recommended by Andrea and Guy Bradley, Tracey and Stephen Groves, Tim Maddison, Mark Percy, Lesley Mayoh, Brian Root, Sue Rowland, Paul Mallett)*

Enterprise ~ Lease Peter and Annie Alberto ~ Real ale ~ Bar food (not Sun evening) ~ Restaurant ~ (01494) 758959 ~ Children welcome ~ Dogs allowed in bar ~ Open 12-3, 5.30-11; 12-11 Sat; 12-10.30 Sun; closed 25 Dec

HEDGERLEY SU9686 Map 2

White Horse

2.4 miles from M40 junction 2: at exit roundabout take Slough turnoff then take Hedgerley Lane (immediate left) following alongside M40. After 1.5 miles turn right at T junction into Village Lane

The fine range of seven or eight real ales at this proper country local is tapped from the cask in a room behind the tiny hatch counter. Greene King IPA and Marlow Rebellion are well kept alongside five daily changing guests from anywhere in the country, with good farm cider and belgian beers too; their regular ale festivals are very popular. The cottagey main bar has plenty of character, with lots of beams, brasses and exposed brickwork, low wooden tables, some standing timbers, jugs, ball-cocks and other bric-a-brac, a log fire, and a good few leaflets and notices about future village events. There is a little flagstoned public bar on the left. On the way out to the garden, which has tables and occasional barbecues, they have a canopy extension to help during busy periods. The atmosphere is jolly with warmly friendly service from the long-standing licensees and cheerful staff. At lunchtimes they do bar food such as sandwiches (from £3.25) ploughman's (from £4.50), coronation salmon (£5.50), and changing straightforward hot dishes such as steak and mushroom pie (£6.45). In front are lots of hanging baskets, with a couple more tables overlooking the quiet road. There are good walks nearby, and the pub is handy for the Church Wood RSPB reserve. It can get crowded at weekends. *(Recommended by the Didler, Lesley Bass, Susan and John Douglas, Anthony Longden, Tracey and Stephen Groves, Martin and Karen Wake, Stuart Turner)*

Free house ~ Licensees Doris Hobbs and Kevin Brooker ~ Real ale ~ Bar food (lunchtime only) ~ (01753) 643225 ~ Children in canopy extension area ~ Dogs allowed in bar ~ Open 11-2.30, 5-11; 11-11 Sat; 12-10.30 Sun

LEY HILL SP9802 Map 4

Swan

Village signposted off A416 in Chesham

The main bar of this charming little timbered 16th-c pub has black beams (mind your head) and standing timbers, an old working range, a log fire and a collection of old local photographs, and a cosy snug. There's a chatty mix of locals and visitors, and a nice old-fashioned pubby atmosphere; the licensees are friendly. Enjoyable lunchtime bar food might include filled baked potatoes (from £3.25), home-made soup (£3.95), filled baguettes or baked potatoes (from £4.25), home-smoked trout or goats cheese and bacon salad (£5.95), king prawns (£7.25), home-baked ham and eggs or sausages (£7.95) and home-made steak and chilli pie (£8.25), with evening dishes from the restaurant menu such as chicken liver terrine (£4.25), baked peppered salmon with lemon butter tagliatelle (£11.95), pork tenderloin wrapped in smoked bacon with black pudding, mash and sage jus or local duck breast with sweet red cabbage (£13.95), with puddings such as summer pudding (£3.50); they've recently brightened up the mostly no smoking restaurant. Well kept Adnams, Fullers London Pride, Marstons Pedigree, Timothy Taylors Landlord and Young's Ordinary on handpump, seven wines by the glass, and Addlestone's cider. In front of the pub amongst the flower tubs and hanging baskets, there are picnic-sets with more in the large back garden. There's a cricket pitch, a nine-hole golf course, and a common opposite. *(Recommended by Martin Price, Tracey and Stephen Groves, John and Glenys Wheeler, Heather Couper, Geoff and Sylvia Donald, Hunter and Christine Wright, Conor McGaughey, Susan and John Douglas)*

Punch ~ Lease David and Natalia Allen ~ Real ale ~ Bar food (bar snacks lunchtime only) ~ Restaurant ~ (01494) 783075 ~ Children in eating area of bar and in restaurant but no small children in evening ~ Open 12-3, 5.30-11; 12-11(10.30 Sun) wknds; 12-4, 7-10.30 Sun in winter

LITTLE MISSENDEN SU9298 Map 4

Crown ★ £

Crown Lane, SE end of village, which is signposted off A413 W of Amersham

With an appealingly traditional pubby feel, the spotlessly kept bustling bars of this country brick cottage are more spacious than they might first appear, with old red flooring tiles on the left, oak parquet on the right, built-in wall seats, studded red leatherette chairs, and a few small tables. You'll find darts, shove-ha'penny, cribbage, and dominoes, but no piped music or machines; a good mix of customers, including a loyal bunch of regulars, add to the cheerfully chatty (sometimes boisterous) atmosphere. Adnams, Fullers London Pride, Woodforde's Wherry and a guest or two from brewers such as Batemans and Vale are kept in top condition on handpump, and there are decent malt whiskies. Well liked home-made bar food from a very fairly priced straightforward menu includes good fresh sandwiches (from £3), ploughman's (from £4.50), buck's bite (a special home-made pizza-like dish) or steak and kidney pie (£4.95), and winter soup (£2.50). The large attractive sheltered garden behind has picnic-sets and other tables, and the interesting church in the pretty village is well worth a visit. The landlord is friendly, and the pub has been run by the same family for more than 90 years. No children. *(Recommended by Brian England, R T and J C Moggridge, Anthony Longden, Tracey and Stephen Groves, Derek and Sylvia Stephenson, DM, P Price, D C T and E A Frewer, Brian Root, Mr and Mrs John Taylor)*

Free house ~ Licensees Trevor and Carolyn How ~ Real ale ~ Bar food (lunchtime only; not Sun) ~ No credit cards ~ (01494) 862571 ~ Open 11-2.30, 6(5.30 Sat)-11; 12-3, 6.30-10.30 Sun

> 'Children welcome' means the pubs says it lets children inside without any special restriction; readers have found that some may impose an evening time limit – please tell us if you find this.

MARLOW SU8586 Map 2

Hare & Hounds 🍷

Henley Road (A4155 W)

The helpful family who have taken over this pretty creeper-covered gabled cottage – primarily a dining pub – are stimulating a lot of local interest in their food. Besides good generous lunchtime sandwiches (from £4.95) and salads (from £6.75), and other dishes such as home-made soup (£3.25), leek, asparagus and basil tartlet (£5.25), lamb and apricot stew or asparagus, brie and spinach strudel with watercress coulis (£9.95), and herb-crusted beef medallions with shallot and marsala jus (£13.95), they do enterprising specials such as fried barramundi with a fennel and rocket salad and salsa verde (£7.50), or their Monday mussels deal (as much as you can possibly eat, £8.50). The quarry-tiled cream-walled bar itself, heavily black-beamed like much of the rest of the pub, is pretty minuscule: two or three smart swivelling chrome and black leather bar stools, a brown leather sofa and a couple of housekeeper's chairs, with a winter log fire in the big inglenook, and well kept Brakspears Bitter on handpump. There is a small carpeted eating room on the left, and a much bigger dining area on the right, also carpeted and snugly divided, with one or two steps up and down here and there, and little balustrades across door-sized wall openings; this part, largely no smoking, has a warmly relaxed feel, helped along by its gentle lighting and the terracotta paintwork of some walls. They have a good choice of wines in several glass sizes, and good coffees including espresso. The front terrace has half a dozen picnic-sets under cocktail parasols (the road isn't too busy), with a few more in the little recently reworked side garden. *(Recommended by Michael Dandy, John and Glenys Wheeler)*

Enterprise ~ Lease Bryan and Barry Evans ~ Real ale ~ Bar food (12-2.30, 6-9.30; 12-5 Sun, not Sun evening) ~ Restaurant ~ (01628) 483343 ~ Under-12s welcome till 7pm in restaurant ~ Open 11.30-3, 5.30-11; 11-11 Sat; 12-10.30 Sun

MENTMORE SP9119 Map 4

Stag 🍷

Village signposted off B488 S of Leighton Buzzard; The Green

They've around 50 different kinds of wine at this pretty village pub, and they're all available by the glass. With a relaxed atmosphere, the small civilised lounge bar has low oak tables, attractive fresh flower arrangements, and an open fire; the more simple public bar leading off has shove-ha'penny, cribbage and dominoes. Well kept Wells Bombardier, Eagle and IPA and maybe a guest from Greene King on handpump, and champagne cocktails. There are seats too out on the pleasant flower-filled front terrace looking across towards Mentmore House, and a charming, well tended, sloping garden. Good, reasonably priced lunchtime bar food includes interesting sandwiches (£5.50), salads (£6), and hot meals such as smoked haddock with kedgeree and fried egg or cheese and mushroom omelette (£6), and chicken curry with rice or moules and crusy bread (£8), while in the evening the menu could include prawn cocktail (£4), macaroni cheese with poached egg (£6), seafood and saffron risotto, thai roast duck with spring onion egg fried rice or slow-cooked pork with black pudding, tomatoes and new potatoes (£8). Part of the more formal restaurant is no smoking. *(Recommended by Karen and Graham Oddey, Mrs J Ekins-Daukes)*

Charles Wells ~ Lease Jenny and Mike Tuckwood ~ Real ale ~ Bar food (not Mon evenings) ~ Restaurant ~ (01296) 668423 ~ Children in restaurant and eating area of bar but must be over 12 in evening ~ Dogs allowed in bar ~ Open 12-11(10.30 Sun); may be shorter opening hours in winter

> If we don't specify bar meal times for a main entry, these are normally 12-2 and 7-9; we do show times if they are markedly different.

NEWTON LONGVILLE SP8430 Map 4

Crooked Billet 🍷

Off A421 S of Milton Keynes; Westbrook End

Wine-lovers will find it hard to tear themselves away from this thatched dining pub (in a slightly unusual position by a modern housing estate), as there are over 400 wines by the glass to choose from, with plans to add a further 100 by the time the *Guide* comes out. Although it manages to feel like a proper pub, the focus is very much on the adventurous (though not cheap) food. At lunchtime as well as sandwiches and wraps (from £4.75), thoughtfully prepared dishes, made with lots of local ingredients, could include courgette and parmesan soup with thyme cream and deep-fried courgette (£4.75), beef and beer sausages and mash with wilted spinach (£8.50), fried lobster ravioli with fish stock, champagne and tomato cream (£9.75), lamb rack with mustard and parsley crust, swede purée, baby turnip and lamb jus (£15), and fried scallops with pea purée, crispy pancetta, rosemary and fish stock cream (£18), with unusual puddings such as honey and rosemary roasted figs with goats cheese ice-cream and sweet walnut biscuit (from £5.75); they do a good cheeseboard (£8). Reserve your table well in advance if you want to eat in the evening in the no smoking restaurant. The brightly modernised and extended bar has beam and plank ceilings, some partly green-painted walls, sporting trophies on the shelves, and usually a few chatting locals. Well kept Greene King IPA and Abbot, and a couple of guests such as Everards Tiger and Wadworths 6X on handpump, 30 malt whiskies, and 30 cognacs and armagnacs. There are tables out on the lawn. More reports please. *(Recommended by Andrea and Guy Bradley, Bob and Maggie Atherton, Mike Turner, John Saville, Karen and Graham Oddey, Mr and Mrs John Taylor)*

Greene King ~ Lease John and Emma Gilchrist ~ Real ale ~ Bar food (lunchtime only, not Mon) ~ Restaurant ~ (01908) 373936 ~ Children in restaurant ~ Dogs allowed in bar ~ Open 12-2.30, 5.30-11; 12-11 Sat; 12-4, 7-11 Sun; closed Mon lunchtime, 25-26 Dec, 1 Jan

PENN SU9193 Map 4

Crown

B474 Beaconsfield—High Wycombe

In front of this welcoming creeper-covered old dining pub, tables among pretty roses face a 14th-c church, which has a fine old painting of the Last Judgement. This is one of the best Chef & Brewer pubs we've come across, and the nicely decorated bars are unusually laid out in an old-fashioned style; one comfortable low-ceilinged room used to be a coffin-maker's workshop. The food here is popular, and the menu has a good range of enjoyable dishes. As well as changing specials (with an emphasis on fresh fish) such as crab and chilli salad (£4.35), pheasant sausages and mash (£8.15), and skate wing with citrus caper butter (£12.95), they serve beef and Theakstons pie (£6.85), thai red chicken curry (£7.95), and lentil, sweet potato and bean gratin (£8.50), and snacks (available till 6) such as generous sandwiches (from £2.95; hot baguettes from £4.10), filled baked potatoes (£3.95), and ploughman's (from £4.25), with puddings (£3.95). Well kept Courage Best and a couple of guests such as Fullers London Pride and Greene King Old Speckled Hen on handpump, and a decent short wine list (they serve all their wines by the glass); piped classical music, two roaring log fires. The staff are friendly and helpful, and there's a pleasant atmosphere; look out for Toby the pub labrador. Perched high on a ridge, the pub has relaxing views of distant fields and woodlands; they hold weekend barbecues in the gardens in summer. *(Recommended by Martin and Karen Wake, Gill and Keith Croxton, Howard Dell, Geoff Pidoux, D Reay, Mrs Ann Gray, Ian Phillips, Dr and Mrs D Woods, Sean and Sharon Pines)*

Spirit Group ~ Manager Peter Douglas ~ Real ale ~ Bar food (11-10 Mon-Sat; 12-9 Sun) ~ Restaurant ~ (01494) 812640 ~ Children away from bar ~ Open 11-11.30; 12-10.30 Sun

PRESTWOOD SP8700 Map 4

Polecat

170 Wycombe Road (A4128 N of High Wycombe)

Lovely in summer, the attractive garden of this cheerfully run pub has lots of bulbs in spring, and colourful hanging baskets, tubs, and herbaceous plants; there are quite a few picnic-sets under parasols on neat grass out in front beneath a big fairy-lit pear tree, with more on a big well kept back lawn. Opening off the low-ceilinged bar are several smallish rooms with an assortment of tables and chairs, various stuffed birds as well as the stuffed white polecats in one big cabinet, small country pictures, rugs on bare boards or red tiles, and a couple of antique housekeeper's chairs by a good open fire; the Gallery room is no smoking. The pub attracts a loyal following, and at lunchtime there tend to be chatty crowds of middle-aged diners, with a broader mix of ages in the evening; readers like the friendly, relaxed atmosphere. Enjoyable, home-made dishes from a popular menu could include soup (£3.60), kipper mousse with toasted brioche (£4.70), shepherd's pie and mash or mushroom and courgette rissoles (£8), lamb, aubergine and tomato casserole (£8.90), grilled halibut with pesto crust and tapenade dressing (£9.60), and sirloin steak with green peppercorn sauce (£11.40), with blackboard specials such as pork, prune and chestnut roulade with calvados sauce (£9.50), and grilled swordfish steak with mango and chilli coulis (£9.90), and they also do lunchtime snacks such as sandwiches (from £3.30), and filled baked potatoes (from £4.70); puddings might be chocolate torte with cherry coulis or steamed marmalade sponge pudding (£3.95). You can choose from 16 wines by the glass, and Flowers IPA, Greene King Old Speckled Hen, Marstons Pedigree and a guest are well kept on handpump at the flint bar counter; a good few malt whiskies too; piped music. Readers recommend the nearby farm shop. *(Recommended by Lesley Bass, Roy and Lindsey Fentiman, Simon Collett-Jones, Michael Dandy, Chris Hoy, M G Hart, Tracey and Stephen Groves, K H Richards)*

Free house ~ Licensee John Gamble ~ Real ale ~ Bar food (12-2, 6.30-9; not Sun evening) ~ Restaurant ~ No credit cards ~ (01494) 862253 ~ Children in family room ~ Dogs allowed in bar ~ Open 11.30-2.30, 6-11; 12-3 Sun; closed Sun evening, evenings 24 and 31 Dec, all day 25-26 Dec

SKIRMETT SU7790 Map 2

Frog

From A4155 NE of Henley take Hambleden turn and keep on; or from B482 Stokenchurch—Marlow take Turville turn and keep on

You'll find a good mix of customers and a warm welcome at this bustling country inn, set right in the heart of the Chiltern hills. A side gate leads to a lovely garden with a large tree in the middle, and the unusual five-sided tables are well placed for attractive valley views. Inside, although brightly modernised, it still has something of a local feel with leaflets and posters near the door advertising raffles and so forth. Neatly kept, the beamed bar area has a mix of comfortable furnishings, a striking hooded fireplace with a bench around the edge (and a pile of logs sitting beside it), big rugs on the wooden floors, and sporting and local prints around the salmon painted walls. The function room leading off is sometimes used as a dining overflow. You must book in advance if you want to eat the good, freshly cooked food. Served by very friendly staff, dishes could include lunchtime baguettes (£5.45), home-made soup (£3.75), caesar salad with bacon, croutons, citrus chicken and home-made caesar dressing (£5.75), smoked trout salad with capers, chives and horseradish cream or warm potato rosti, black pudding and smoked salmon with a poached egg salad (£6.75), wild mushrooms and asparagus lasagne with chervil cream sauce (£10.50), roast pork loin with whiskey cream sauce (£10.95), seared monkfish fillet with lightly curried lentils and crème fraîche (£13.50), and grilled rump steak with port and stilton sauce (£13.95); irresistible home-made puddings such as orange and Grand Marnier pancakes or banoffi pie (from £4.75). The restaurant and family room are no smoking; piped music. Three well kept real ales such as Fullers London Pride, Rebellion IPA and Young's Bitter on handpump, a good range of wines, quite a few whiskies, and various coffees. The appealing bedrooms make a nice base for the area. Henley is close by, and just down the road is the delightful Ibstone windmill; there are many surrounding hiking routes. *(Recommended by Brian England, Peter Saville, Piotr Chodzko-Zajko, Mike and Sue Richardson, Di and Mike Gillam, Tracey and Stephen Groves, Paul Humphreys, Michael Dandy, Colin McKerrow, Jeremy Woods, Howard Dell)*

Free house ~ Licensees Jim Crowe and Noelle Greene ~ Real ale ~ Bar food (12-2.30, 6.30-9.30; not winter Sun evening) ~ Restaurant ~ (01491) 638996 ~ Children in restaurant and family room ~ Dogs allowed in bar ~ Open 11-3, 6.30(6 Fri/Sat)-11; 12-4, 6-10 Sun; closed Sun evening Oct-May ~ Bedrooms: £55B/£65B

SOULBURY SP8827 Map 4

Boot 🍷

B4032 W of Leighton Buzzard

Brightly modernised, this civilised village pub is a good place to come for an interesting, well cooked meal, especially if you happen to like fish. The partly red-tiled bar has a light, sunny feel, thanks mainly to its cream ceilings and pale green walls, and there's a nice mix of smart and individual furnishings, as well as sporting prints and houseplants, and neat blinds on the windows. Behind the modern, light wood bar counter are plenty of bottles from their well chosen wine list; they do around 40 by the glass including champagne. Friendly smartly dressed staff also serve well kept Adnams Southwold, and Greene King IPA and Abbot on handpump, and they've organic fruit juices. One end of the room, with a fireplace and wooden floors, is mostly set for diners, then at the opposite end, by some exposed brickwork, steps lead down to a couple of especially cosy rooms for eating, a yellow one with beams and another fireplace, and a tiny red one. All the eating areas are no smoking; piped music. Fresh fish is listed on a daily changing blackboard, and you can choose between fillets, whole fish or shellfish, with a typical menu taking in salmon, marlin, bass, shark and trout. If fish is not your thing, the menu also includes dishes such as home-made soup (£3.95), creamy woodland mushrooms with toasted brioche (£4.95), lamb and rosemary pie and minted potatoes (£10.95), polenta crusted chicken with sweetcorn mash, banana and green tomato (£11.50), and bacon loin with mustard sauce, mash and vegetables (£12.50), with puddings such as banana and toffee mousse or lemon and ginger posset crunch or home-made ice-cream (£4.25); they also do sandwiches at lunchtime (from £4.25). Overlooking peaceful fields, there are tables behind in a small garden and on a terrace (with heaters for cooler weather), and a couple more in front. More reports please. *(Recommended by Brian Root)*

Pubmaster ~ Lease Greg Nichol, Tina and Paul Stevens ~ Real ale ~ Bar food (12-2.30, 6.30-9.30; 12-4, 6.30-9 Sun) ~ (01525) 270433 ~ Children welcome ~ Open 11-11; 12-10.30 Sun; closed 25/26 Dec

TURVILLE SU7691 Map 2

Bull & Butcher 🍷

Off A4155 Henley—Marlow via Hambleden and Skirmett

Handily open all day, this black and white timbered pub is in a lovely Chilterns valley among ancient cottages. There are seats on the lawn by fruit trees in the attractive garden which has a children's play area, and they hold barbecues in the summer. Big helpings of well presented bar food might include home-made soup (£4.95), ham with orange salad (£5.95; £9.95 main course), twice-baked cheese soufflé (£7.50), braised root vegetable lasagne or steak and kidney pudding with stout gravy and crushed root mash (£9.95), smoked haddock risotto (£10.95), and braised lamb shank with honey and rosemary (£11.50), with specials such as chargrilled provençal vegetable terrine (£5.95) or pork loin with bubble and squeak and roasting juices (£11.50), and home-made puddings (£3.95); they do children's helpings (£6.95), and readers are keen on their Sunday lunch. As well as some three dozen wines by the glass, they serve well kept Brakspears Bitter, Special, and a seasonal guest on handpump alongside Hook Norton Mild; Addlestone's cider, and a good choice of juices too; piped jazz. There are two low-ceilinged, oak-beamed rooms (the Windmill lounge is no smoking), and the bar has a deep well incorporated into a glass-topped table, with tiled floor, cushioned wall settles and an inglenook fireplace. The village is popular with television and film companies; *The Vicar of Dibley*, *Midsomer Murders* and *Chitty Chitty Bang Bang* were all filmed here. A fine place to end up after a walk (though no muddy boots), the pub does get crowded at weekends. *(Recommended by M Thomas, LM, Martin and Karen Wake, Gill and Keith Croxton, Simon Collett-Jones, Piotr Chodzko-Zajko, Bob and Margaret Holder, John and Glenys Wheeler, Ian Phillips, Susan and John Douglas, Torrens Lyster)*

Brakspears ~ Tenants Hugo and Lydia Botha ~ Real ale ~ Bar food (12-2.30(3 Sat), 7-9.45; 12-4 Sun and bank hol Mon) ~ Restaurant ~ (01491) 638283 ~ Children in eating area of bar and restaurant ~ Dogs allowed in bar ~ Open 11-11; 12-10.30 Sun; closed 25 Dec evening

WOOBURN COMMON SU9187 Map 2

Chequers

From A4094 N of Maidenhead at junction with A4155 Marlow road keep on A4094 for another ¾ mile, then at roundabout turn off right towards Wooburn Common, and into Kiln Lane; if you find yourself in Honey Hill, Hedsor, turn left into Kiln Lane at the top of the hill; OS Sheet 175 map reference 910870

Despite the fact that lots of its customers are drawn from the thriving hotel and restaurant side, the bar still manages to attract a nicely mixed crowd. They offer a sizeable wine list (with champagne and good wine by the glass), a fair range of malt whiskies and brandies, and well kept Greene King Abbot, IPA, Ruddles County and a guest on handpump. The low-beamed, partly stripped-brick bar has standing timbers and alcoves to break the room up, comfortably lived-in sofas (just right for settling into) on its bare boards, a bright log-effect gas fire, and various pictures, plates, a two-man saw, and tankards. One room is no smoking; piped music. The changing bar menu has a good choice of well prepared, interesting dishes and, besides sandwiches, could include soup (£3.95), tuna melt (£6.95), toasted muffin with scrambled egg and smoked salmon (£7.95), deep-fried squid salad with sweet chilli sauce (£8.95), tasty crab and asparagus risotto (£9.95), and chargrilled rib-eye steak with béarnaise sauce (£14.95), with puddings (£3.95). The spacious garden, set away from the road, has cast-iron tables. The attractive stripped-pine bedrooms are in a 20th-c mock-Tudor wing. *(Recommended by Chris Glasson, Lesley Bass, Mrs Ann Gray, John Saville, Edward Mirzoeff, John and Glenys Wheeler)*

Free house ~ Licensee Peter Roehrig ~ Real ale ~ Bar food ~ Restaurant ~ (01628) 529575 ~ Children in eating area of bar and restaurant ~ Open 10.30-11; 10.30-10.30 Sun ~ Bedrooms: £99.50B/£107.50B

Several well known guide books make establishments pay for entry, either directly or as a fee for inspection. These fees can run to many hundreds of pounds. We do not. Unlike other guides, we never take payment for entries. We never accept a free meal, free drink, or any other freebie from a pub. We do not accept any sponsorship – let alone from commercial schemes linked to the pub trade. All our entries depend solely on merit. And we are the only guide in which virtually all the main entries have been gained by a unique two-stage sifting process: first, a build-up of favourable reports from our thousands of reader-reporters; then anonymous vetting by one of the senior editorial staff.

LUCKY DIP

Besides the fully inspected pubs, you might like to try these Lucky Dips recommended to us and described by readers (if you do, please send us reports: www.goodguides.co.uk).

AKELEY SP7037

☆ *Bull & Butcher* [just off A413 Buckingham—Towcester]: Cheery village pub with good fires each end of long open-plan beamed bar, red plush banquettes and lots of old photographs, chatty landlord and friendly efficient service, good value food from good paninis up, well kept Fullers Chiswick, IPA and London Pride, good house wines, traditional games; may be piped radio; children allowed in eating area, tables in pleasant small back garden, handy for Stowe Gardens *(LYM, George Atkinson)*

AMERSHAM SU9597

Crown [Market Sq]: Seen in *Four Weddings and a Funeral*, small peaceful modernised hotel bar, beams and polished wood floors, neat tables set for dining, interesting 16th-c features in comfortable lounge, short choice of bar food from sandwiches up, afternoon teas, good restaurant, cheery helpful staff, Flowers Original, good range of wines by the glass; nearby parking may be difficult; attractive split-level outside seating area with cobbled courtyard and plant-filled garden, comfortable bedrooms *(John and Glenys Wheeler, BB, Derek and Sylvia Stephenson)*

Eagle [High St]: Cosy rambling low-beamed pub, landlady doing decent food, log fire, simple décor with a few old prints, quick helpful service even when busy, several well kept real ales; pleasant streamside back garden *(Sean and Sharon Pines)*

ASHENDON SP7014

Gatehangers [Lower End]: Pleasant inn with good value food; bedrooms *(Brian Root)*

ASTON CLINTON SP8811

Duck In [London Rd]: Vintage Inn with enjoyable reasonably priced generous food inc lighter lunchtime dishes, Worthington, fine choice of wines by the glass, nice variety of furnishings with flagstones and dark brown and dark cream paintwork; picnic-sets under trees in garden, bedrooms, open all day *(Matthew Shackle, Tony and Shirley Albert, Sean and Sharon Pines)*

☆ *Oak* [Green End St]: Cosy and attractively refurbished beamed Fullers pub, good bar and plenty of dining room, friendly efficient new management, enjoyable home-made food (not Sun pm) cooked to order inc good value lighter lunches, decent wines, real fire, no music or machines *(John and Glenys Wheeler, Brian Root, Sean and Sharon Pines)*

BEACHAMPTON SP7736

Bell [Main St]: Large pub with pleasant view from bar down attractive streamside village street, log fire dividing bar from lounge and attractive dining area, Bass, Greene King Abbot and Hook Norton, home-made food inc Weds steak night, pool in small separate games room; piped music; open all day, terrace and play area in big garden *(John Dorrell)*

BEACONSFIELD SU9489

Greyhound [a mile from M40 junction 2, via A40; Windsor End, Old Town]: Rambling former coaching inn, well kept ales inc Marlow Rebellion in well run two-room bar, daily papers, increasing emphasis on modern cooking in partly no smoking back bistro area *(LYM, Tracey and Stephen Groves)*

BLEDLOW SP7702

Lions of Bledlow [off B4009 Chinnor—Princes Risboro; Church End]: Low 16th-c beams, attractive oak stalls, antique settle, ancient tiles, inglenook log fires and a woodburner, and fine views from bay windows; well kept ales such as Courage Best, Marlow Rebellion and Wadworths 6X, and good value straightforward bar food from sandwiches up; no smoking restaurant; well behaved children allowed, tables out in attractive sloping garden with sheltered terrace, nice setting, good walks *(LYM, the Didler, John Roots, Richard List)*

BOLTER END SU7992

☆ *Peacock* [just over 4 miles from M40 junction 5, via A40 then B482]: Pleasantly set Chilterns pub, brightly modernised bar with nice little bolt-hole down to the left, no smoking room, good log fire, well kept Brakspears and generous food inc familiar favourites and fresh veg; picnic-sets in garden, has been cl Sun evening *(LYM, John and Glenys Wheeler, Brenda and Rob Fincham)*

BOURNE END SU8986

Garibaldi [Hedsor Rd]: 18th-c beamed local with blue and yellow décor, sofas and assorted rustic furniture on bare boards, log fire, well kept Adnams and Greene King Abbot, pleasant landlord, small no smoking conservatory; country views from garden tables *(Susan and John Douglas, Simon Collett-Jones)*

BRILL SP6513

☆ *Pheasant* [off B4011 Bicester—Long Crendon; Windmill St]: Simply furnished beamed pub in marvellous spot looking over to ancient working windmill, nearby view over nine counties, good choice of food inc sophisticated dishes, well kept Hook Norton Best and Youngs Special, good value house wines, attractive dining room up a step; piped music, no dogs; children welcome, verandah tables, superior picnic-sets in garden with terrace, bedrooms, open all day wknds *(Tim and Ann Newell, LYM, Geoff Pidoux, Ian Phillips)*

BURROUGHS GROVE SU8589

Three Horseshoes [back rd Marlow—High Wycombe]: Spacious and comfortable former coaching inn now doing well under Marlow Brewery, interesting quickly changing food choice, good range of real ales, good service *(D and M T Ayres-Regan, Richard Houghton)*

BUTLERS CROSS SP8407

Russell Arms [off A4010 S of Aylesbury, at Nash Lee roundabout; or off A413 in Wendover, passing stn; Chalkshire Rd]:

Straightforward roadside pub with proper traditional bar, well kept real ales, good speedy service, enjoyable bar food and separate restaurant (worth booking wknd evening meals); small sheltered garden, well placed for Chilterns walks *(LYM, B H and J I Andrews)*

CHACKMORE SP6835

Queens Head [Main St]: Comfortable village pub by Stowe Gardens, with nice local feel in bar, welcoming landlord, good value varied lunchtime food from toasties and baguettes up, well kept real ales, small separate dining room *(Guy Vowles)*

CHALFONT ST GILES SU9893

Fox & Hounds [Silver Hill]: Small quietly set 16th-c local with unspoilt interior, limited choice of good value food, welcoming service, open fire; no credit cards; pleasant garden behind *(Charles Gysin)*

☆ ***Ivy House*** [A413 S]: Smartly reworked 18th-c dining pub, wide range of good freshly cooked food, not cheap but generous, prompt friendly service, well kept changing ales such as Bass and Fullers London Pride, good wines by the glass, espresso coffee, attractive open-plan layout with comfortable fireside armchairs in elegantly cosy L-shaped tiled bar, lighter flagstoned no smoking dining extension; pleasant terrace and sloping garden (can be traffic noise) *(Anthony Longden, BB, Simon Collett-Jones)*

CHALFONT ST PETER TQ0090

Greyhound [High St]: Spacious beamed dining pub dating from 15th c, emphasis on enjoyable if not cheap food in bar and comfortable partly no smoking restaurant (some emphasis on fish), well kept ales, good wine list, friendly staff; small pleasant garden, well equipped comfortable bedrooms *(LYM, G McGrath)*

White Hart [High St]: Pleasantly refurbished character old low-beamed pub popular with older people and said to be haunted; well kept ales such as Everards Tiger and Fullers London Pride, wide choice of well priced food, four linked areas, nice inglenook, no music *(Conor McGaughey)*

CHEARSLEY SP7110

☆ ***Bell*** [The Green]: The welcoming hands-on licensees who made this cottagey thatched pub a real favourite left in autumn 2004, and we hope the new people may prove as good; traditional cosy beamed bar with enormous fireplace, has had well kept Fullers Chiswick, London Pride and seasonal brews and well chosen choice of wines by the glass, bar food from sandwiches up, cribbage, dominoes; children in eating area, dogs welcome, plenty of tables (and play equipment) in spacious back garden, more on a terrace, attractive play area, has been open all day in summer, cl Mon lunchtime *(LYM)*

CHICHELEY SP9045

☆ ***Chester Arms*** [quite handy for M1 junction 14]: Cosy and pretty beamed pub with rooms off semicircular bar, log fire, comfortable settles and chairs, wide choice of good popular home-made food from sandwiches to daily fresh fish (they do lobster with notice) and aberdeen angus beef, children's helpings, friendly staff, well kept Greene King IPA, decent wines, good coffee, daily papers, back dining room down steps; darts, fruit machine, quiet piped music; picnic-sets in small back garden *(Michael Dandy, David and Mary Webb, Sarah Flynn, Maysie Thompson, BB, Ryta Lyndley)*

COLESHILL SU9594

Magpies [A355]: Modern family-oriented chain dining pub with wide range of generous food all day from sandwiches and baked potatoes up inc good children's choice, staff friendly and helpful even on a busy wknd, real ales and wines by the glass; piped music; tables outside with play area, good walking country *(R M Young)*

Red Lion: Welcoming early 20th-c local quietly placed well off the road, one room with a few dining tables for wide choice of good value home-made blackboard food Mon-Sat, sandwiches too, two or three well kept changing ales such as Greene King IPA and Vale Wychert, amiable helpful licensees, real fires; picnic-sets out in front and in back garden with sturdy climbing frames outside, good walks *(Howard Dell, Jarrod and Wendy Hopkinson)*

DINTON SP7611

Seven Stars [signed off A418 Aylesbury—Thame, nr Gibraltar turn-off; Stars Lane]: Pretty pub with inglenook bar, comfortable beamed lounge and spacious dining room, well kept changing ales such as Fullers London Pride, food (not Sun evening) from sandwiches and baked potatoes to traditional puddings; cl Tues, tables under cocktail parasols in sheltered garden with terrace, pleasant village, handy for Quainton Steam Centre *(LYM, Dr R C C Ward, Marjorie and David Lamb, Richard C Morgan)*

DORNEY SU9278

☆ ***Palmer Arms*** [B3026, off A4, two miles from M4 junction 7]: Friendly and roomily extended early 20th-c pub well updated under newish licensee, smallish dark green bar and appealing stripped brick back dining room, pine and dark wood, interesting good value food from ciabattas and flatbreads up, smaller children's and OAP helpings, wider evening choice, well kept Greene King IPA, Abbot and Old Speckled Hen, ten wines by the glass, good attentive service, no smoking area; solid garden furniture in good mediterranean-feel garden behind, open all day Sat *(I D Barnett, DC, Martin and Karen Wake, Susan and John Douglas, Michael Dandy)*

Pineapple [off A4 Maidenhead—Cippenham by Sainsburys; Lake End Rd]: Old-fashioned beamery and panelling, gleaming bar, simple furniture, great range of outstanding sandwiches, other food inc Sun roasts, well kept Fullers London Pride and Tetleys, decent house wine, good friendly service even when busy; disabled access, verandah, picnic-sets in garden, good walks *(Ian Phillips, Mike and Sue Richardson)*

DRAYTON PARSLOW SP8328

Three Horseshoes [Main Rd]: Good reasonably priced food inc classic steak and kidney pie and some interesting puddings in bar and dining area (just snacks Sat lunchtime), real ales such as Everards Tiger, friendly helpful service *(Marjorie and David Lamb)*

FAWLEY SU7587

Walnut Tree [off A4155 or B480 N of Henley]: This charmingly set Chilterns dining pub, a *Guide* main entry, closed in late spring 2004, with reports that it might become a private house; news please *(LYM)*

FINGEST SU7791

☆ *Chequers* [signed off B482 Marlow—Stokenchurch]: Proper traditional Chilterns local with several rooms around old-fashioned Tudor core, roaring fire in vast fireplace, sunny lounge by good-sized charming and immaculate country garden with lots of picnic-sets, small no smoking room, interesting furniture, Brakspears full range kept well, dominoes and cribbage, wholesome lunchtime food (not Mon) from sandwiches up, good self-serve salad table, reasonable prices, quick cheerful service, attractive restaurant; children in eating area; interesting church opp, picture-book village, good walks – can get crowded wknds *(the Didler, Chris Smith, Tracey and Stephen Groves, LYM, M G Hart, Clare and Peter Pearse, Howard Dell)*

FLACKWELL HEATH SU8889

☆ *Crooked Billet* [off A404; Sheepridge Lane]: Cosily old-fashioned and comfortably worn in 16th-c pub with lovely views (beyond road) from wittily flower-filled suntrap front garden, low beams, good choice of reasonably priced tasty summer lunchtime food (not Sun) and winter evening meals, eating area spread pleasantly through alcoves, charming considerate landlord, prompt friendly service, well kept Brakspears, good open fire; juke box; good open walks *(BB, Paul Humphreys)*

FRIETH SU7990

☆ *Prince Albert* [off B482 SW of High Wycombe]: Another change of licensees for old-fashioned and cottagey Chilterns local with low black beams and joists, high-backed settles, big black stove in inglenook, big log fire in larger area on the right; has had reasonably priced bar food all day (not Sun evening) and well kept Brakspears Bitter, Old and Special on handpump; children and dogs welcome, nicely planted informal side garden with views of woods and fields, open all day *(LYM, Pete Baker, the Didler)*

FULMER SU9985

Black Horse [Windmill Rd]: Small traditional stepped bar areas with plenty of nooks and crannies, beams, woodburner, chequered tables, some sofas, well kept Greene King IPA and Abbot and Hook Norton, popular food from sandwiches and baguettes up, decent wines, friendly service, good décor; small garden, attractive village, open all day wknds *(LM, Mrs Ann Gray, G McGrath)*

GAWCOTT SP6831

Crown [Hillesden Rd]: Traditional beamed village pub with rustic bric-a-brac, Italian chef-landlord doing enjoyable often intensely flavoured food from sandwiches and home-made pasta through main dishes to exemplary tiramisu, well kept Adnams and a guest such as Marstons Pedigree, good italian wines, friendly service, pool and machine in games room, pub dog, small panelled dining area, open fire and woodburner; piped music; long back garden with swings *(BB, CMW, JJW, George Atkinson)*

GREAT BRICKHILL SP9029

☆ *Red Lion* [Ivy Lane]: Friendly two-roomed pub popular with families in school hols, simple décor and round pine tables, Flowers Original and Greene King IPA and Abbot, reasonably priced nicely presented food from baguettes up in bar and restaurant, good service, log fires; fabulous view over Buckinghamshire and beyond from neat walled back lawn *(Ian Phillips, LYM)*

GREAT HORWOOD SP7731

Crown [off B4033 N of Winslow; The Green]: Comfortable recently refurbished two-bar Georgian pub with striking inglenook fireplace, rugby photographs, Adnams, Flowers IPA and Greene King Old Speckled Hen, pleasant service, good value food from baguettes to steaks, parlour-like dining room with big wooden tables; piped music; tables on neat front lawn, pretty village, very handy for Winslow Hall *(BB, Michael Dandy)*

GREAT KIMBLE SP8206

☆ *Bernard Arms* [Risborough Rd (A4010)]: Plushly upmarket but friendly, with some nice prints (and photographs of recent prime ministers dropping in for a drink), daily papers, good imaginative food in bar and restaurant, four changing real ales, decent wines, good range of malt whiskies and bottled beer, good log fire, games room; children welcome, no dogs, attractive fairy-lit gardens, well equipped bedrooms *(K Drane, John and Glenys Wheeler, Alastair McKay)*

Swan & Brewer [Grove Lane (B4009, nr A4010)]: Attractive pub with beamed and tiled tap room, wide choice of good value fresh food from sandwiches and baked potatoes up, well kept ales such as Adnams, Fullers London Pride and Hook Norton Best, friendly staff, pleasant end dining area; well behaved children allowed, small well kept garden and tables out on village green *(B Brewer, Mel Smith, Shirl Hanlon, Marjorie and David Lamb)*

GREAT LINFORD SP8542

Nags Head [High St]: Thatched pub with big inglenook fireplace in low-beamed lounge, Greene King IPA and Tetleys, food all week, traditional games in public bar *(Tony Hobden)*

GREAT MISSENDEN SP8901

☆ *Cross Keys* [High St]: Cheerfully unspoilt beamed bar divided by standing timbers, bric-a-brac, traditional furnishings inc high-backed settle and open fire in huge fireplace, well kept Fullers Chiswick, London Pride and ESB, good wines, enjoyable and interesting modern food from tasty baguettes up, friendly attentive staff; children in attractive and spacious beamed restaurant, back terrace *(Mike Turner, LYM, David Hoare, Tracey and Stephen Groves)*

GROVE SP9122

Grove Lock: Well kept Fullers, enjoyable food and friendly staff; very clean pub in pleasant canalside location *(David Eagles)*

IBSTONE SU7593

Fox [1¾ miles from M40 junction 5, down lane S from exit roundabout]: Nicely placed newly refurbished 17th-c country inn, low beams, high-backed settles and country seats, log fires, friendly service, enjoyable sensibly priced food, well kept ales such as Brakspears and Fullers; children allowed in no smoking dining area and restaurant, tables under cocktail parasols in side garden overlooking common, pleasant bedrooms *(LYM, Gill and Keith Croxton)*

LACEY GREEN SP8201

☆ *Pink & Lily* [from A4010 High Wycombe—Princes Risboro follow Loosley sign, then Gt Hampden, Gt Missenden one]: Charming little old-fashioned tap room (celebrated sillily by Rupert Brooke – poem framed here) in much-extended Chilterns pub with airy and plush main dining bar, well presented good food; well kept Brakspears and other changing beers, good well priced wines, friendly attentive service, log fires, dominoes, cribbage, ring the bull; piped music, children over 5 welcome if eating; conservatory, big garden – and good free range eggs from next-door farm *(the Didler, LYM, K Drane, Heather Couper)*

LAVENDON SP9153

Green Man [A428 Bedford—Northampton]: Roomy and attractive thatched and beamed 17th-c pub in pretty village, closed for refurbishment as we went to press; has had decent generous food from baguettes and interesting soups up, wkdy two-for-one lunches, snacks all afternoon, relaxed open-plan bar with lots of stripped stone, woodburner and hops around bar (news of changes, please), Greene King IPA, Abbot, Ruddles County and Old Speckled Hen, good choice of wines by the glass, big restaurant with no smoking area; children welcome, may be unobtrusive piped music; open all day, tables out in neatly kept good-sized secluded garden behind *(Michael Dandy, Mike Ridgway, Sarah Miles)*

LITTLE BRICKHILL SP9029

George & Dragon [Watling St, off A5 SE of Milton Keynes]: Comfortable lounge with settees and two fires, another in L-shaped restaurant opening into back conservatory, friendly attentive service, Adnams Broadside and Greene King IPA, good choice of other drinks, daily papers, enjoyable food (not Sun evening or Mon lunchtime) inc unusual dishes; piped music, TV; heated terrace, play equipment in mature garden *(CMW, JJW)*

LITTLE HAMPDEN SP8503

☆ *Rising Sun* [off A4128 or A413 NW of Gt Missenden; OS Sheet 165 map ref 856040]: Comfortable if firmly run no smoking dining pub in delightful setting, opened-up bar with woodburner and log fire, good reasonably priced food, well kept Adnams, Brakspears Bitter and a seasonal beer from Shepherd Neame, short but decent wine list, home-made mulled wine and spiced cider in winter; piped music, and they may try to keep your credit card if you eat outside; prime walking area (but no walkers' boots), tables out on terrace, bedrooms with own bathrooms, cl Sun evening and all Mon exc bank hols *(R T and J C Moggridge, Peter Saville, Mrs J Smythe, Peter and Giff Bennett, Peter Shapland, Richard Bernholt, Julia and Richard Tredgett, Jerry Harwood, M G Hart, Mrs Ann Gray, LYM)*

LITTLE MARLOW SU8788

☆ *Kings Head* [A4155 about 2 miles E of Marlow; Church Rd]: Long low flower-covered pub with homely open-plan beamed bar, wide blackboard choice of generous reasonably priced food from substantial sandwiches to some unusual main dishes, children's menu, smart red dining room, no smoking areas, well kept ales such as Brakspears, Marlow Rebellion and Timothy Taylors Landlord, quick service, Sun bar nibbles; can get crowded wknds; big attractive garden behind popular with families, nice walk down to church *(Mike Turner, BB, Richard List, Howard Dell)*

Queens Head [Church Rd/Pound Lane; cul de sac off A4155 nr Kings Head]: Small and attractive quietly placed pub with interestingly varied good food (not Mon/Tues evening) from rabbit pie to kangaroo and unusual thai dishes, well kept ales such as Adnams and Charles Wells Bombardier, lots of books in saloon, welcoming helpful service; darts and TV in public bar, may be jazz Tues; picnic-sets in appealing cottagey front garden, a couple more tables on secluded terrace across lane – short walk from River Thames *(Paul Humphreys)*

LITTLE MISSENDEN SU9298

Red Lion: Small 15th-c local, two coal fires, well kept real ales, decent wines, generous good value standard food, preserves for sale; piped music; tables (some under awning) and busy aviary in sunny side garden by river with ducks, swans and fat trout *(John and Glenys Wheeler, Brian Root)*

LITTLEWORTH COMMON SP9386

☆ *Blackwood Arms* [3 miles S of M40 junction 2; Common Lane, OS Sheet 165 map ref 937864]: Friendly country pub with up-to-date stylish décor in cream and mulberry, dark woodwork and blinds, small bar and larger eating area with smart white linen, good home cooking from fancy open sandwiches and simple lunchtime dishes to pricier evening meals and great puddings, well kept Brakspears and a guest beer such as Batemans from handsome oak counter, prompt pleasant service, roaring log fire; quiet piped music, dogs allowed in bar; views from large pleasant garden, lovely spot on edge of beech woods – good walks *(Tracey and Stephen Groves, C and R Bromage, LYM, Nick Binns,*

Michael Dandy, Jarrod and Wendy Hopkinson)
Jolly Woodman [2 miles from M40 junction 2; off A355]: Busy pub by Burnham Beeches, Bass, Brakspears, Flowers Original, Fullers London Pride, Gales HSB and Timothy Taylors Landlord, wide food choice from sandwiches and baked potatoes up, quick attentive service, reasonable wine choice, log fire and central woodburner in rambling and cottagey beamed and timbered linked areas, farm tools and hurricane lamps, useful tourist leaflets; unobtrusive piped music, games, jazz Mon; tables out in front, picnic-sets in garden behind *(LYM, Susan and John Douglas, Michael Dandy)*

LONG CRENDON SP6808

☆ ***Angel*** [Bicester Rd (B4011)]: Partly 17th-c restaurant-with-rooms rather than pub, though still has something of the flavour of a pub, particularly in the civilised pre-meal menu-perusing lounge with sofas and easy chairs; most enjoyable interesting meals (lunchtime open sandwiches and baguettes too), fish and puddings particularly good, friendly and crisply organised service, good no smoking dining areas inc a conservatory; well kept Hook Norton and Ridleys, good house wines; may be piped music; tables in garden, good bedrooms *(LYM, Mr and Mrs A Stansfield, Bob and Maggie Atherton, Geoff Pidoux, Roger Braithwaite, Phyl and Jack Street)*
Churchill Arms [B4011 NW of Thame]: Friendly and obliging new licensees in neatly reworked village pub, long and low, with good value food in bar and thai restaurant, nice atmosphere, well kept real ales, good log fire in big fireplace; children welcome, pleasant garden overlooking cricket field *(LYM, A J Clark, Tim and Ann Newell)*

LUDGERSHALL SP6617

Bull & Butcher [off A41 Aylesbury—Bicester; The Green]: Quiet and cool little beamed country pub with good value fresh food, well kept real ales; children allowed in back dining room, tables in nice front garden, attractive setting *(Brian Root)*

MARLOW SU8486

Chequers [High St]: Attractive pub with large air-conditioned front bar, bare boards and heavy beams, leather settees, daily papers, Brakspears ales, friendly service, good food, range from basics to more exotic things in bright and pleasant back restaurant area, children welcome; piped music, games – popular with young people; homely tables on pavement, bedrooms *(Michael Dandy)*
Claytons [Quoiting Sq, Oxford Rd]: Popular trendy bar, not pub, several beer taps (inc Brakspears – not on handpump), nice wines, pleasant atmosphere, friendly staff, good tapas, smooth piped jazz – may be louder piped music evenings, and crowds of young people then even, midweek; heated terrace *(the Didler, John and Glenys Wheeler, David Tindal)*
Donkey [Station Rd]: Modernised open-plan bar with Marstons Pedigree, good choice of wines by the glass, low-priced food from baguettes and baked potatoes up, quick service; piped music, pool and games; tables on terrace *(Michael Dandy)*
Hand & Flowers [West St (A4155)]: Olde-worlde bar with brasses and old prints, wide choice of good value generous home-made food from sandwiches and baguettes up in big sympathetically lit dining area leading off; pleasant staff, well kept Greene King IPA, Morlands and Ruddles, daily papers; piped music, small garden with play area *(Michael Dandy)*

☆ ***Two Brewers*** [St Peter St, first right off Station Rd from double roundabout]: Busy low-beamed pub with plenty of atmosphere and character, most tables set for good imaginative food from baguettes and ciabattas up (may have to book Sun lunch), shiny black woodwork, nautical pictures, gleaming brassware, an unusual crypt-like area, well kept Bass, Brakspears, Fullers London Pride and Marlow Rebellion, good wines, welcoming service, relaxed atmosphere; children in eating area, unobtrusive piped music; tables in sheltered back courtyard with more in converted garage, front seats with glimpse of the Thames (pub right on Thames Path) *(Simon Collett-Jones, Michael Dandy, LYM, Charles Davey, Gerry and Rosemary Dobson, David Tindal)*

MARSWORTH SP9114

Red Lion [village signed off B489 Dunstable—Aylesbury; Vicarage Rd]: Low-beamed partly thatched village pub with cheerful service, well kept ales such as Fullers London Pride and Vale Notley, decent wines, good value food from the kitchen door, quiet lounge with two open fires, steps up to snug parlour and games area, nice variety of seating inc traditional settles, no smoking areas; sheltered garden, not far from impressive flight of canal locks *(LYM, Tony Hobden)*

MILTON KEYNES SP8739

Barge [Newport Rd, Woolstone]: Large beamed Vintage Inn in untouched corner of an original village just off central Milton Keynes, with picnic-sets on spacious tree-dotted lawns, no smoking areas inc modern conservatory, well kept Bass, lots of wines by the glass, wide food choice, daily papers friendly staff, good food service (not in garden); piped music *(Tony Hobden)*
Cross Keys [Newport Rd, Woolstone]: Pleasant old much-extended thatched and beamed pub, several rooms around central bar area, with jovial landlord, friendly service, well kept Charles Wells ales and a guest such as Greene King, good range of food (not Sun-Tues evenings), games and piano in public bar *(Tony Hobden)*

☆ ***Old Beams*** [Osier Lane, Shenley Lodge; in grounds tucked into curve of ridge-top Paxton Cresc, off Fulmer St or Childs Way]: Comfortably modernised and extended former farmhouse, relaxing flagstoned bar with through fireplace, matching chairs around handsome candlelit tables, lots of brick and wood, old photographs, paintings and brass, good choice of enjoyable food inc light dishes and Sun roasts, usually something available all day, well kept McMullens ales, friendly young staff, speciality coffees, no smoking areas; business faxes sent and received free, very popular with local office staff; piped music; children in dining area; large pleasant garden perhaps with swans and ducks in former moat – a striking oasis in vast tracts of new red-brick housing *(BB, Margaret and Roy Randle)*

MOULSOE SP9041

☆ *Carrington Arms* [1¼ miles from M1, junction 14: A509 N, first right signed Moulsoe; Cranfield Rd]: Interesting if not cheap pub majoring on meats and fresh fish sold by weight (priced per 100g) from refrigerated display then cooked on indoor barbecue, good puddings, three well kept real ales, champagnes by the glass, friendly helpful staff, comfortable mix of wooden chairs and cushioned banquettes; open all day Sun, children allowed, long pretty garden behind *(Mrs Catherine Draper, LYM, John Saville, Alan Sutton, David and Ruth Shillitoe)*

NORTH CRAWLEY SP9244

Cock [High St]: Lounge with sofa and dining area, Charles Wells ales, bar food (not Sun/Mon evenings), separate room with darts and games machine; piped music; seats out by car park *(CMW, JJW)*

OLNEY SP8851

Bull [Market Pl/High St]: Spacious, clean and tidy, two small front bar rooms, more restauranty main room, Charles Wells ales with a guest beer and flourishing Aug bank hol beer festival, popular food, good coffee, log-effect gas fires, very friendly chatty landlord; small courtyard, big back garden with big climbing frame; HQ of the famous Shrove Tuesday pancake race *(Mike Ridgway, Sarah Miles)*

☆ *Swan* [High St S]: Cosily well worn in beamed and timbered pub with good choice of excellent value generous food from baguettes and baked potatoes up, bargain daily special, well kept real ales such as Hook Norton and Shepherd Neame Spitfire, good value wines by the glass, quick helpful service; very busy and popular at lunchtime, several rooms off bar, candles on pine tables, log fires, small no smoking back bistro dining room (booking advised for this); no under-10s; marsh views from roomy bedrooms, garden with tables in courtyard, one under cover *(Michael Dandy, BB, Michael Sargent)*

OVING SP7821

Black Boy [off A413 Winslow rd out of Whitchurch]: Quietly friendly and interesting old pub nr church, more spacious inside than it looks; attractive old tables, magnificent collection of jugs, log fire, well kept real ales, enjoyable generous food esp fish, good children's choice, cheerful service (can slow at wknds), superb views from extended back dining area over pleasant terrace and big sloping garden; TV in small bar *(Karen and Graham Oddey, Brian Root)*

PENN SU9093

Red Lion [Elm Rd]: Attractive low-ceilinged traditional bar with vast log fire and plenty of bric-a-brac, no smoking area, separate games room, wide choice of generous well priced food showing imagination, five real ales, friendly landlord and efficient service; piped music may obtrude; children welcome, nice spot opp green and duck pond *(Tracey and Stephen Groves)*

PENN STREET SU9295

Hit or Miss [off A404 SW of Amersham, then keep on towards Winchmore Hill]: Well laid out low-beamed pub with own cricket ground, new tenant doing enjoyable if not cheap food inc popular Sun lunch, well kept Badger ales, decent wines, cheerful atmosphere in three clean linked rooms, log fire, charming décor inc interesting cricket and chair-making memorabilia, good-sized no smoking area; picnic-sets out in front, pleasant setting *(Tracey and Stephen Groves, LYM, Graham Chamberlain)*

PITSTONE GREEN SP9216

Duke of Wellington [Pitstone Wharf]: Unpretentious country pub with two rooms divided by log fire, mainstream real ales, reasonably priced homely food, friendly obliging landlord, black beams, brasses, copper and decorative china; nr Grand Union Canal *(Tony Hobden)*

PRESTON BISSETT SP6529

☆ *White Hart* [off A421 or A4421 SW of Buckingham; Pound Lane]: Charming little thatched and timbered 18th-c pub with helpful friendly service, enjoyable if not cheap home-made food, well kept real ales, good choice of wines by the glass, three cosily traditional rooms (the biggest is no smoking), log fire and low beams *(LYM, MJB)*

SAUNDERTON SU8198

Rose & Crown [Wycombe Rd]: Pub/hotel with nice log fires, big winged leather chairs and some quirky touches, good choice of wines and guest beers, friendly staff, smart upmarket restaurant with good food inc well presented contemporary dishes and good value set meals, comfortable coffee lounge; well placed for Chilterns walks, comfortable bedrooms *(Neil and Karen Dignan, John and Glenys Wheeler)*

STOKE GOLDINGTON SP8348

Lamb [High St]: Cosy lounge/dining area with sheepish décor, well kept ales such as Caledonian Deuchars IPA, Nethergate IPA and Old Growler and Woodfordes Wherry, good choice of good generous home-made food at appealing prices, friendly welcoming staff; sizeable garden and terrace *(George Atkinson)*

STONE SP7912

Bugle Horn [Hartwell; A418 SW of Aylesbury]: Long low 17th-c stone-built Vintage Inn family dining pub, warm and friendly series of comfortable rooms, pleasant furnishings, good choice of decent food, usual large range of wines by the glass, well kept Bass and Hook Norton, log fire and prettily planted well furnished conservatory; no under-21s unless eating; lovely trees in large pretty garden, horses grazing in pastures beyond

(Tim and Ann Newell)

STONY STRATFORD SP7840

☆ *Cock* [High St]: Comfortable old-fashioned hotel, quiet at lunchtime but lively in the evenings, with leather settles and library chairs on bare boards, decent bar food from filled baps to chargrills, friendly prompt service, well kept ales inc Greene King, interesting old local photographs and memorabilia; tables out in attractive back courtyard, barbecues; bedrooms *(LYM, David and Ruth Hollands)*

Crown [Market Sq]: Airy contemporary refurbishment, light colours and local artwork for sale, pre-meal area on left with comfortable leather sofas, more traditional bar on right (smoking allowed only here), extensive back dining area with enjoyable enterprising food from lunchtime sandwiches and light dishes up, good wine choice, real ales, friendly helpful staff; open all day, cl Sun evening *(Mrs J Groom)*

Fox & Hounds [High St]: 17th-c pub with several well kept changing ales, cheerful chef/landlord doing decent cheap lunchtime food from sandwiches and baked potatoes to bargain specials in no smoking lounge area, pictures and photographs, fresh flowers; piped radio, games area with hood skittles, darts, folk, blues or jazz Thurs, Sat and first Tues; tables in walled garden, open all day *(George Atkinson, Pete Baker, Joe Green)*

TAPLOW SU9185

Feathers [Taplow Common, opp Cliveden entrance]: Large welcoming much modernised Chef & Brewer family dining pub opp Cliveden entrance (NT), enjoyable food from sandwiches, crusty rolls and baguettes to wide blackboard choice, well kept Courage Directors, Fullers London Pride and Theakstons Old Peculier, good choice of decent wines, good coffee, quick helpful service; piped music, games; courtyard tables, play area, dogs allowed only by front picnic-sets *(Bob and Laura Brock, Michael Dandy, John and Sue Woodward)*

THE LEE SP8904

☆ *Old Swan* [Swan Bottom, back rd ¾ mile N of The Lee]: Charming civilised 16th-c dining pub with very good interesting food esp seafood cooked by long-serving landlord, good value, and sandwiches too; four simply but attractively furnished linked rooms, low beams and flagstones, cooking-range log fire in inglenook, particularly well kept Adnams and Brakspears, decent wines, friendly relaxed service; spacious prettily planted back lawns with play area, good walks *(LYM, Piotr Chodzko-Zajko, John and Glenys Wheeler)*

THORNBOROUGH SP7433

☆ *Lone Tree* [A421 4 miles E of Buckingham; pub named on OS Sheet 165]: Extended and newly refurbished with nice new tables, wide choice of gently upmarket food, helpful efficient service, well kept changing real ales, big log fire *(George Atkinson, LYM, Dave Braisted, Michael Dandy)*

TYLERS GREEN SU9093

Horse & Jockey [Church Rd]: Homely cottage-style pub with well kept Adnams and Greene King, some home-cooked specials, comfortable simple furnishings, pleasant alcoves, beams and brasses, bright tartan carpet, cheery locals *(Tracey and Stephen Groves)*

WADDESDON SP7416

☆ *Five Arrows* [High St (A41)]: Elegant and civilised series of light and airy well furnished high-ceilinged rooms with Rothschild family portrait engravings and lots of old estate-worker photographs; has been very popular with readers for good interesting food and splendid wines (well kept Fullers London Pride too), but is really now entirely a restaurant operation, with less of a personal touch; no smoking area, children allowed; appealing back garden, comfortable bedrooms, handy for Waddesdon Manor; has been cl last wknd Aug *(B N F and M Parkin, Lesley Bass, Richard and Margaret Peers, Chris Chaplin, Dr R C C Ward, Karen and Graham Oddey, Neil and Karen Dignan, Bob and Maggie Atherton, David and Ruth Hollands, Mr and Mrs John Taylor, LYM, Michael Dandy)*

WEEDON SP8118

Five Elms [Stockaway]: Cottagey low-beamed two-room pub, welcoming and homely, with well kept Adnams, old photographs and prints, australian influence on food (not Tues lunchtime or Mon) with some thai touches, separate dining room; pretty village *(MP, Monica Cockburn, Mike Jefferies)*

WENDOVER SP8607

Firecrest [A413 about 2 miles S]: Large roadside Vintage Inn, cosy and civilised eating areas with settles and brocaded chairs around polished tables, turkey carpets, old fireplace, pictures on stripped brickwork, good choice of good value quickly served food inc smaller dishes, neat efficient staff; disabled parking *(Marjorie and David Lamb)*

WEST WYCOMBE SU8394

☆ *George & Dragon* [High St; A40 W of High Wycombe]: Handsome and popular centrepiece of beautifully preserved Tudor village, thriving atmosphere in rambling bar with massive beams, sloping rust-coloured walls, interesting 1890s village picture over its big log fire, well kept Adnams, Courage Best and Charles Wells Bombardier, prompt friendly service even when busy, good food choice from fresh lunchtime sandwiches and wraps to some exotic specials, small no smoking family dining room (wknd children's menu); spacious peaceful garden with fenced play area, neatly kept character bedrooms (magnificent oak staircase) and good breakfast, handy for West Wycombe Park *(Tracey and Stephen Groves, LYM, Simon Collett-Jones, M G Hart, Piotr Chodzko-Zajko, Paul Humphreys)*

WESTON UNDERWOOD SP8650

☆ *Cowpers Oak* [signed off A509 in Olney; High St]: Charming wisteria-covered old pub, beams, dark red walls, dark panelling and some stripped stone, well kept changing ales such as Adnams Best, Cropton Two Pints, Greene King IPA and Abbot and Fullers London Pride, generous good value food (all day wknds) inc good soup and light dishes, no smoking back restaurant, nice medley of old-fashioned furnishings, log fire, good games room with darts, bar billiards, hood skittles and table football, daily papers; piped music, TV; children very welcome, dogs in main bar; small suntrap front terrace, more tables on back decking and in big attractive orchard garden (no dogs) with play area and farm animals, bedrooms, open all day wknds, pretty thatched village *(LYM, George Atkinson, John Saville, J I Davies, Mike Ridgway, Sarah Miles, Gerry and Rosemary Dobson)*

WHEELER END SU8093

☆ *Chequers* [off B482 NW of Marlow]: Neatly kept 17th-c pub with inglenook log fire in convivial low-ceilinged little bar, bigger back no smoking room, candlelit tables and hunting prints, good choice of bar food (not Sun evening) from sandwiches up using their garden herbs, well kept Fullers London Pride, ESB and a guest beer, friendly helpful service, dominoes and cribbage; children welcome in eating areas, dogs in bar, two neat gardens (M40 noise), open all day *(LYM, Tracey and Stephen Groves, Michael Dandy)*

WINCHMORE HILL SU9394

Plough [The Hill]: Chic upmarket dining place, restaurant rather than pub now, comfortable and spacious, with several interconnecting areas, enjoyable enterprising food inc good value set lunch, neat helpful staff, reasonably priced house wines, fashionable imported lagers; piped music turned off if you ask; tables on lawn with wishing well *(BB, John Faircloth)*

WING SP8822

Cock [off A418 SW of Leighton Buzzard; High St]: Partly 16th-c, with good range of well kept changing ales, decent wines, good coffee, friendly attentive service, cottage armchairs and roaring fire, lots of books, partly no smoking dining areas with good varied choice of fresh food from pubby to more restauranty things; garden with picnic-sets and play area *(Craig Turnbull)*

WINGRAVE SP8719

Rose & Crown [The Green]: Efficient friendly newish management, pleasant bar with two linked areas and beamed dining room (families particularly welcome here), usual pub food, four real ales; pleasant tables outside, attractive church and duck pond, good walks nearby *(MP)*

WINSLOW SP7627

☆ *Bell* [Market Sq]: Fine old former coaching inn with roomy modernised lounges and bar, cheerful efficient service, good value food in bar and carvery restaurant, Greene King IPA and Abbot, good coffee, no music; courtyard tables (nice to see the way the building has grown in a succession of styles), good value bedrooms *(LYM, George Atkinson)*

WOOBURN COMMON SU9387

☆ *Royal Standard* [about 3½ miles from M40 junction 2]: Thriving low-ceilinged local with friendly helpful staff, wide choice of enjoyable good value straightforward food from good value baguettes up, up to ten well kept changing ales such as Black Sheep, Everards Tiger, Hook Norton Old Hooky and Charles Wells Bombardier, well chosen wines, lots of daily papers, open fire, daily papers and crossword reference books, popular refurbished dining area; picnic-sets on pretty front terrace and in back garden, open all day *(LYM, Susan and John Douglas, Michael Dandy, Roy and Lindsey Fentiman)*

WORMINGHALL SP6308

☆ *Clifden Arms* [Clifden Rd]: Archetypal 16th-c beamed, timbered and thatched pub in pretty gardens, old-fashioned seats, rustic memorabilia and roaring log fires, attractive lounge bar leading to further no smoking dining area, interesting well priced food inc bargain wkdy lunches, well kept changing ales such as Adnams Broadside, Caledonian Deuchars IPA, Hook Norton Best and a seasonal beer, traditional games in public bar, children allowed; service priority for those who have booked; good play area, aunt sally; attractive village *(Dick and Madeleine Brown, Tim and Ann Newell, LYM)*

If a pub tries to make you leave a credit card behind the bar, be on your guard. The credit card firms and banks which issue them condemn this practice. After all, the publican who asks you to do this is in effect saying: 'I don't trust you'. Have you any more reason to trust his staff? If your card is used fraudulently while you have let it be kept out of your sight, the card company could say you've been negligent yourself – and refuse to make good your losses. So say that they can 'swipe' your card instead, but must hand it back to you. Please let us know if a pub does try to keep your card.

Cambridgeshire

Three fine pubs making their break into the main entries this year are the down-to-earth Free Press in Cambridge (bargain food and entirely no smoking), the relaxed and individual Red House at Longstowe (good all round, with a friendly horse-loving landlord) and the Dyke's End at Reach (a charmer, owned by a village consortium, with enjoyable food). All three have a good choice of well kept real ales. Other pubs on fine form here include the Cambridge Blue in Cambridge (also entirely no smoking, strong on beers and good value food), the handsome old Eagle there, the cosily traditional Black Horse at Elton (interesting tasty food), the Ancient Shepherds at Fen Ditton (fat sofas and enjoyable food), the airy and civilised White Pheasant at Fordham, the fine old Chequers at Fowlmere (quite a favourite for a special meal out – it now takes the title of Cambridgeshire Dining Pub of the Year), the cheerful Blue Bell at Helpston (lunchtime bargains for OAPs), the Queens Head at Newton (welcoming and utterly unspoilt pub, a great favourite), Charters in Peterborough (lots of real ales on this converted dutch barge), and the civilised and very friendly Anchor at Sutton Gault (imaginative food in attractive surroundings). In the Lucky Dip section at the end of the chapter, pubs to note particularly are the George at Buckden, John Barleycorn at Duxford, Crown at Elton, Oliver Twist at Guyhirn, and George in Huntingdon. Drinks prices in the county are somewhat higher than the national average. The Brewery Tap and their offshoot bar-boat Charters, both in Peterborough, score bargain points with their own good Oakham ales, and beers shipped in from small breweries in neighbouring counties such as Woodfordes, Nethergate and Adnams tend to be cheaper here than competing national brands.

CAMBRIDGE TL4658 Map 5

Cambridge Blue £

85 Gwydir Street

The rather charming collection of rowing memorabilia at this quiet back street pub includes the bow section of the Cambridge boat that famously rammed a barge and sank before the start of the 1984 boat race. Chris Lloyd the landlord rowed for Cambridge, and there's such a nice selection of rowing photographs you feel you're browsing through someone's family snaps. Two uncluttered rooms are simply decorated with old-fashioned bare-boards style furnishings, candles on the tables and a big collection of oars, and are completely no smoking; cribbage, dominoes, chess and draughts. An interesting range of seven regularly changing well kept real ales on handpump are (with the odd exception such as Fullers) picked from East Anglian breweries such as Adnams, City of Cambridge, Hobsons, Iceni, Nethergate, Potton Brewery or Woodfordes; they also have a decent choice of wines and malt whiskies and fresh orange juice. Reasonably priced straightforward bar food is served in an attractive little conservatory dining area, and includes home-made soup (from £2.95), filled ciabatta rolls (from £3.50), vegetable chilli (£5), sausage and onion gravy (£5.50), meat pudding (£6), a cold table with game or picnic pies, nut roast, and various quiches, and daily specials such as game casserole or roast mediterranean vegetable lasagne (£5.50); Sunday roast (£6.50). Children like the surprisingly rural feeling and large back garden and its wendy house. *(Recommended by the Didler, Mr and Mrs T B Staples, Paul Hopton, Rona Murdoch, Clare and Peter Pearse)*

Free house ~ Licensees Chris and Debbie Lloyd ~ Real ale ~ Bar food (12-2.30, 6-9.30; not 25 Dec) ~ (01223) 505110 ~ Children welcome in conservatory ~ Dogs welcome ~ Open 12-2.30(3 Sat), 5.30-11; 12-3, 6-10.30 Sun

Eagle 🍷 £

Bene't Street

Just what you imagine a big town pub should be, the five rambling rooms at this old stone-front coaching inn are chatty and lively with a good mix of customers, and possibly standing room only at peak times. Its interior shows many charming original architectural features from its lovely worn wooden floors to plenty of pine panelling, two fireplaces dating back to around 1600, two medieval mullioned windows, and the remains of two possibly medieval wall paintings. The creaky old furniture is nicely in keeping. Don't miss the high dark red ceiling which has been left unpainted since World War II to preserve the signatures of British and American airmen worked in with Zippo lighters, candle smoke and lipstick. There is a no smoking room. You queue at the servery for the straightforward but good value bar food which comes in generous helpings and includes filled baguettes (from £4.75), and ploughman's, vegetarian quiche, steak in ale pie, ham and eggs or lasagne (all £5.95). Prices go up a tad in the evening when dishes are a bit more substantial and served to the table by (sometimes over busy) staff: half a roast chicken (£6.75), giant battered cod (£6.95), and steaks (from £7.95); Sunday carvery roast (£6.95). Greene King IPA, Abbot, Old Speckled Hen and Ruddles County, and a guest such as Caledonian 80/- are well kept on handpump alongside just over a dozen wines by the glass. An attractive cobbled and galleried courtyard, screened from the street by sturdy wooden gates and with heavy wooden seats and tables and pretty hanging baskets, takes you back through the centuries – especially at Christmas, when they serve mulled wine and you can listen to the choristers from King's College singing here. No children inside. *(Recommended by Dr Andy Wilkinson, Mike Turner, B N F and M Parkin, Terry Mizen, John Saville, Chris Flynn, Wendy Jones, the Didler, M Borthwick, Kevin Thorpe, John Wooll, Gwyn Jones)*

Greene King ~ Managers Steve Ottley and Sian Crowther ~ Real ale ~ Bar food (12-9 (8 Fri/Sat, 4 Sun)) ~ (01223) 505020 ~ Open 11-11; 12-10.30 Sun

Free Press £

Prospect Row

Pubby and cheerful, this unspoilt old place is completely no smoking. In winter you can read a newspaper by the log fire which warms its simple but characterfully sociable bare-board rooms, and in summer the sheltered paved garden at the back is quite a suntrap. Over the years loyal customers have donated little items that are displayed in old printing trays, which are hung up amongst old newspapers, printing memorabilia and a collection of oars. Real ale lovers enjoy the well kept Greene King IPA, Abbot and Mild and a guest such as Batemans on handpump; cribbage, dominoes and shove-ha'penny. Good value tasty bar food is served in generous helpings: soup (£3.25), ploughman's (£4.50), stuffed peppers (£4.95), meatballs or fresh fish (£5.95). *(Recommended by Terry Mizen, John Wooll)*

Greene King ~ Tenant Donna Thornton ~ Real ale ~ Bar food (12-2, 6-8.30; not Sun evening) ~ (01223) 368337 ~ Children welcome ~ Dogs welcome ~ Open 12-2.30(3 Sat), 6-11; 12-3, 7-10.30 Sun; closed 25, 26 Dec, 1 Jan

Post Office address codings confusingly give the impression that some pubs are in Cambridgeshire, when they're really in the Leicestershire or Midlands groups of counties (which is where we list them).

Live & Let Live ■ £

40 Mawson Road; off Mill Road SE of centre

For entertainment value, the drink to order at this friendly old local is their speciality, a 'Brownie-Boy Shandy'. It's a mix of two farm ciders and when one is ordered the welcoming landlord rings the bell and announces 'and another'. And it's worth sticking around until last orders, for his closing speech to thank everybody for coming. He stocks a good range of real ales with regulars such as Everards Tiger and Nethergate Umbel, and guests from brewers such as Crouch Vale, Featherstone, Milton and Tring on handpump too, as well as over a dozen malts, belgian beers on tap, lots of belgian bottled beers and farm cider. Down to earth but popular, the heavily timbered brickwork rooms have sturdy varnished pine tables with pale wood chairs on bare boards, real gas lighting, lots of interesting old country bric-a-brac, some steam railway and brewery memorabilia and posters about local forthcoming events; cribbage, dominoes. The eating area of the bar is no smoking until 9pm, and simple but good value home-made food includes doorstop sandwiches (£2.50), soup (£2.95), shepherd's pie or lamb curry (£4.95), game pie (£6.95), Sunday roast (£4.95) and all-day breakfast (weekends only, £4.95). *(Recommended by Paul Hopton, Alan Dickinson, John Wooll)*

Burlison Inns ~ Lease Peter Wiffin ~ Real ale ~ Bar food (12-2(3 Sun), 6(7 Sun)-9) ~ (01223) 460261 ~ Children in eating area of bar ~ Dogs allowed in bar ~ Folk most Sat evenings ~ Open 11.30-2.30(3 Sat), 5.30(6 Sat)-11; 12-3, 7-10.30 Sun

ELTON TL0893 Map 5

Black Horse

B671 off A605 W of Peterborough and A1(M); Overend

This rather nice looking honey brick dining pub happily combines a cosy traditional interior with a good choice of tasty food. There's all you'd expect in a country inn from the welcoming atmosphere to roaring fires, hop-strung beams, a homely and comfortable mix of furniture (no two tables and chairs seem the same), antique prints, and lots of ornaments and bric-a-brac including an intriguing ancient radio set. Dining areas at each end of the bar have parquet flooring and tiles, and the stripped stone back lounge towards the partly no smoking restaurant has an interesting fireplace. Bass, Everards Tiger, Nethergate Suffolk County and a guest from a brewer such as Caledonian are well kept on handpump, alongside an extensive wine list with over a dozen wines by the glass. The enjoyable food is very popular so you may need to book. Served in generous helpings by helpful staff, the bar menu includes home-made soup (£3.95), sandwiches (from £4.50), filled baguettes (from £6.25), salads or ploughman's (from £6.95), and home-made pie of the day (£8.95), with changing blackboard specials such as cherry and tomato brie tart (£10.95), fried ostrich medallions with red onion marmalade or fried monkfish wrapped in parma ham (£14.95). The big garden is prettily divided into separate areas with super views across Elton Hall park, some tables shaded by horse chestnut trees and a couple of acres of grass for children to play. *(Recommended by Gordon Theaker, M and G Rushworth, Roy Bromell, Simon and Sally Small, Oliver and Sue Rowell, Stephen and Jean Curtis, Phil and Jane Hodson)*

Free house ~ Licensee John Clennell ~ Real ale ~ Bar food (12-2, 6-9; not Sun evening; maybe tapas summer afternoons) ~ Restaurant ~ (01832) 280240 ~ Children welcome ~ Dogs allowed in bar ~ Open 12-11; 12-5 Sun; 12-3, 6-11 winter; closed Sun evening

ELY TL5380 Map 5

Fountain ■

Corner of Barton Square and Silver Street

Very simple and traditional with no music, fruit machines or even food, this genteel, if basic, town corner pub is the type of place that's nice to come to for a chat. You'll find a real mix of age groups, and the atmosphere is pleasant and inclusive. They serve well kept Adnams Bitter and Broadside, Fullers London Pride and a changing guest such as Timothy Taylors Landlord on handpump. Old cartoons, local photographs, regional maps and mementoes of the neighbouring King's School punctuate the elegant dark pink walls, and neatly tied-back curtains hang from golden rails above the big windows. Above one fireplace is a stuffed pike in a case, and there are a few antlers dotted about – not to mention a duck at one end of the bar; everything is very clean and tidy. A couple of tables are squeezed on to a tiny back terrace. Note the limited opening times. *(Recommended by the Didler, Dr Andy Wilkinson)*

Free house ~ Licensees John and Judith Borland ~ Real ale ~ No credit cards ~ (01353) 663122 ~ Children welcome away from bar until 8pm ~ Dogs welcome ~ Open 5-11; 12-2, 6-11 Sat; 12-2, 7-10.30 Sun

FEN DITTON TL4860 Map 5

Ancient Shepherds

Off B1047 at Green End, The River signpost, just NE of Cambridge

Readers enjoy the tasty food and well kept beer at this pleasantly welcoming pub. Perhaps the nicest room is the softly lit central lounge, where you can't fail to be comfortable on one of the big fat dark red button-back leather settees or armchairs at low solid indonesian tables, by the warm coal fire, and all tucked in by heavy drapes around the window seat with its big scatter cushions. Above a black dado the walls (and ceiling) are dark pink, and decorated with little steeplechasing and riding prints, and comic fox and policeman ones. On the right the smallish convivial more pubby bar with its coal fire serves Adnams and Greene King IPA on handpump, while on the left is a pleasant no smoking restaurant (piped music in here). A decent choice of good bar food includes home-made soup (£3.95), filled baguettes (from £4.40), ploughman's (from £5.95), home-made fishcakes or sausage and mash (£7.95), spinach and ricotta cheese cannelloni (£8.95), steak and ale pie (£9.95) and braised lamb shank in minted rosemary gravy (£10.95). The licensees' new west highland terrier Billie might be around outside food service times. *(Recommended by John Saville, Robert Turnham, Mr and Mrs T B Staples)*

Pubmaster ~ Tenant J M Harrington ~ Real ale ~ Bar food (lunchtimes only) ~ Restaurant ~ (01223) 293280 ~ Children in eating area of bar and restaurant ~ Dogs allowed in bar ~ Open 12-2.30, 6-11; 12-5.30 Sun; closed Sun evening

FEN DRAYTON TL3368 Map 5

Three Tuns

Signposted off A14 NW of Cambridge at Fenstanton; High Street

Set in a particularly delightful village, it's thought that this well preserved ancient thatched building may once have housed the guildhall. Its heavy-set moulded Tudor beams and timbers certainly give the impression of solidity and timelessness. The relaxed and friendly bar has a pair of inglenook fireplaces, there are comfortable cushioned settles, and a nice variety of chairs here and in the appealing partly no smoking dining room. New licensees have reduced the price of the enjoyable bar food a little: lunchtime sandwiches (from £3), various omelettes (£4.95), home beer-battered cod, home-made steak, Guinness and mushroom pie or home-made lasagne (£5.95), and steaks (from £6.95). A new blackboard menu is planned, which might include dishes such as thai green curry, red snapper and tuna. Well kept Greene King IPA and either Greene King Abbot or Old Speckled Hen on handpump; piped music, sensibly placed darts, and a fruit machine. A well tended lawn at the back has tables under cocktail parasols, a covered dining area, a good play area and pétanque. More reports please. *(Recommended by Michael and Marion Buchanan, Wendy and Carl Dye, Michael Dandy)*

Greene King ~ Tenants Ken Culpeck and Emma Douglas ~ Real ale ~ Bar food (12-2, 7-9(9.30 Fri/Sat); not Sun evening) ~ Restaurant ~ (01954) 230242 ~ Children in restaurant ~ Open 12-2.30, 6-11; 12-10.30 Sun

FORDHAM TL6270 Map 5

White Pheasant

Market Street; B1085, off A142 and A11 N of Newmarket

The unassuming exterior of this roadside pub belies a civilised but very relaxed place. Smallish but open plan and airy, it has a mix of well spaced out big farmhouse tables and chairs on bare boards, some stripped brickwork, and a cheery log fire at one end. One or two steps lead down to a small similarly furnished but carpeted room. Woodfordes Wherry and a guest such as Wychwood Shires are well kept on handpump and a dozen carefully chosen wines by the glass are served by very friendly staff from the horseshoe bar that faces the entrance. Food here is very good, and you can choose from the bar or restaurant menu or specials board. The bar menu (not available on Sunday) includes sandwiches (from £5.50), filled focaccia (from £6.50), an imaginative choice of salads such as fried haloumi with red onion and hot tomatoes (from £7.95), sausage and mash and red onion gravy or tagliatelle carbonara (£7.95) and a huge breakfast (lunchtime only £9.50). The restaurant menu includes dishes such as chicken liver parfait (£5.95) or fried fillet steak with red wine carrot jus (£16.95), while the daily specials board lists a good choice of fish dishes: fried bass with creamed leeks and shallots or battered scallops and squid with dipping sauces (£16.95). There are seats outside in a garden. *(Recommended by John Saville, Michael Dandy, Molly and Arthur Aldersey-Williams)*

Free house ~ Licensee Elizabeth Meads ~ Real ale ~ Bar food (12-2.30, 6-9.30) ~ Restaurant ~ (01638) 720414 ~ Children in restaurant ~ Open 12-3, 6-11.30(7-10.30 Sun); closed 25-30 Dec

FOWLMERE TL4245 Map 5

Chequers (🍴) 🍷

B1368

Cambridgeshire Dining Pub of the Year

With its smart country house atmosphere and emphasis largely on dining, this civilised historical 16th-c inn stands out as something a little bit special. Warmed by an open log fire, its two comfortably furnished downstairs rooms are probably far smarter now than when Pepys dined here in 1660 – though he may have seen the priest's hole above the bar. Upstairs there are beams, wall timbering and some interesting moulded plasterwork above the fireplace. The airy no smoking conservatory overlooks white tables under cocktail parasols among flowers and shrub roses in an attractive well tended floodlit garden – in summer overhead you might see historic aeroplanes flying from Duxford. From an imaginative menu served by professionally attentive staff, very good food might include soup (£3.80), creamed mushrooms in a filo case (£5.10), country pâté (£5.60), crab claws sautéed with garlic butter (£5.90), ciabatta topped with sliced pigeon breasts with rocket and truffoil salad (£6.90), moroccan lamb and prune tagine (£10.90), calves liver on celeriac mash with cavolo nero (£12.20), baked halibut topped with mushroom duxelle, chopped tomato and basil pesto (£12.80), grilled dover sole (£24.90), puddings such as hot date sponge with sticky toffee sauce (£4.60), irish cheese platter (£5) and Sunday lunch (£12). The thoughtful selection of attractively priced fine wines by the glass includes vintage and late-bottled ports. There's also a good list of malt whiskies, well kept Adnams with a guest from a brewer such as Fullers or Oakham on handpump, freshly squeezed orange juice, just under a dozen wines by the glass and several malts and brandies. *(Recommended by Bob and Maggie Atherton, A J Bowen, Gordon Prince, Dr and Mrs D A Blackadder, SH, Dr Andy Wilkinson, Chris Flynn, Wendy Jones, Tony and Shirley Albert, Adele Summers, Alan Black, John and Enid Morris, Mike and Jennifer Marsh)*

Free house ~ Licensees Norman and Pauline Rushton ~ Real ale ~ Bar food ~ Restaurant ~ (01763) 208369 ~ Well behaved children in conservatory ~ Open 12-2.30, 6-11; 12-3, 7-10.30 Sun; closed 25 Dec

GODMANCHESTER TL2470 Map 5

Exhibition

London Road

There's an unexpectedly attractive choice of rooms (given the somewhat straightforward-looking frontage) at this bustling brick house. A particular surprise is the main bar with its walls humorously decorated with re-created shop-fronts – a post office, gallery, and wine and spirit merchant – complete with doors and stock in the windows. It's a cosy room with big flagstones on the floor, cushioned wall benches, fresh flowers and candles on each of the tables and white fairy lights on some of the plants; piped music. Very good internationally eclectic food (possibly heading for a food award) includes soup (£4.25), leek and ricotta tart with caramelised apple (£8.95), oriental roast pork with hoi sin glaze and spring onion and coriander mash (£9.75), goan fish curry (£9.95) and rump of lamb on cassoulet beans and chorizo sausage (£12.75), with one or two additional changing lunch dishes such as hot thai beef baguette or burger (£4.95), salads (from £5.95) and pasta of the day (£8.95). The dining room, with smart candelabra and framed prints, is no smoking. Well kept Fullers London Pride, Greene King IPA and a changing guest beer like Timothy Taylors Landlord on handpump, a good wine list and several malt whiskies. There are picnic-sets on the back lawn, some shaded by pergolas, and a couple in front as well, and they hold barbecues in summer. Every year the Exhibition and its sister pub, the nearby White Hart, organise a gathering of steam engines. More reports please. *(Recommended by A C English, Michael Dandy, George Atkinson)*

Free house ~ Licensee Willem Middlemiss ~ Real ale ~ Bar food ~ Restaurant ~ (01480) 459134 ~ Children in eating area of bar and restaurant ~ Monthly live jazz or blues on Tues ~ Open 11.30-3, 5-11; 11.30-11 Sat; 12-10.30 Sun

HELPSTON TF1205 Map 5

Blue Bell

Woodgate; off B1443

The very good value OAP weekday lunchtime menu (two courses £4.95), and smaller helpings of quite a few dishes draws an older set to this friendly place. Other good honest food includes sandwiches (£2.95), baguettes (£3.45), fishcakes or pâté (£3.55), home-made steak in ale pie, stilton and vegetable crumble or fresh battered fish (£7.25), chicken in tarragon (£7.45), barbecued ribs (£7.50), and puddings such as home-made crumbles (£3.45). There is plenty of red plush here, including cushions for the three oak settles, pictures on the bar's dark brown panelling-effect walls, a nice collection of antique and country prints, big china ornaments, lots of tankards, mugs and horsebrasses overhead, and an enormous brass platter above the small fireplace. The corner bar counter has well kept Adnams, Everards Tiger and Old Original and a guest such as Moles Holy Moley on handpump, and the good coffee comes with fresh cream; piped music, cribbage and dominoes. The comfortable flagstoned no smoking dining room on the right, with stripped joists and some stripped stone, gives the greatest impression of the building's age; John Clare the early 19th-c peasant poet was born next door and originally worked here. Wheelchair access; there may be faint piped pop music. A sheltered terrace has plastic garden tables under outdoor heaters. *(Recommended by Michael and Jenny Back, Des and Jen Clarke, M J Codling)*

Free house ~ Licensee Aubrey Sinclair Ball ~ Real ale ~ Bar food (not Sun, Mon evenings) ~ Restaurant ~ (01733) 252394 ~ Children welcome ~ Dogs allowed in bar ~ Open 11.30-2.30, 5-11; 11.30-11 Sat; 12-10.30 Sun

Ideas for a country day out? We list pubs in really attractive scenery at the back of the book – and there are separate lists for waterside pubs, ones with really good gardens, and ones with lovely views.

HEYDON TL4340 Map 5

King William IV

Off A505 W of M11 junction 10

The lovingly put together interior of this rambling dining pub is filled with a charming jumble of rustic implements from ploughshares, yokes and iron tools, cowbells, beer steins, samovars, brass or black wrought-iron lamps, copper-bound casks and milk ewers, harness, horsebrasses and smith's bellows, to decorative plates, cut-glass and china ornaments. In winter its beamed nooks and crannies are warmed by a hearty log fire, and in summer the wooden deck has teak furniture and outdoor heaters; there are more seats in the pretty garden. It all rather reflects the landlady's enjoyable character. Bar food includes soup (£3.95), lunchtime filled panini (£4.95), around ten vegetarian dishes such as milanese risotto or puff pastry parcel stuffed with mushrooms, leek and pesto (from £9.65), steak and kidney pudding (£9.95), whole bass baked in a bag with thai flavours (£13.95), and puddings such as strawberries in a brandy snap basket or apple crumble (from £5.25). Part of the restaurant is no smoking. Well kept real ales such as Adnams Best, Greene King IPA, Ruddles and a guest such as City of Cambridge Darwins Downfall on handpump; they also do cocktails. Fruit machine; more reports please.
(Recommended by DRH and KLH, Robert Turnham, Bob and Maggie Atherton, Dr and Mrs D A Blackadder, Andrew and Samantha Grainger, Peter and Joan Elbra, Alan Tidbury, Mrs Margo Finlay, Mr Kasprowski, Richard Siebert)

Free house ~ Licensee Elizabeth Nicholls ~ Real ale ~ Bar food (12-2, 6.30-10; 12-3, 7-10 Sun) ~ Restaurant ~ (01763) 838773 ~ Children in eating area of bar ~ Dogs allowed in bar ~ Open 11-3, 6-11; 12-3, 7-10.30 Sun

HINXTON TL4945 Map 5

Red Lion

Between junctions 9 and 10, M11; just off A1301 S of Great Shefford

There's plenty of age to this very attractive pink-washed and twin-gabled inn. The dusky mainly open-plan bustling bar (no smoking on Sundays) has leather chesterfields on wooden floors; cribbage, dominoes. Off here there are high-backed upholstered settles in an informal dining area, and the smart no smoking restaurant is filled with mirrors, pictures and assorted clocks. Food is attractively presented and tasty. Under its new licensee, the lunch menu might include sandwiches (from £3.95), filled baked potatoes (from £4.50), salads, sausage and mash or pasta with roast mediterranean vegetables (£7.50) and home-made steak and ale pie (£8.95), as well as dishes such as poached egg florentine on a garlic croûte (£5.25); chicken curry of the day or stuffed butternut squash (£8.95) and duck breast with root vegetables and black cherry and kirsch sauce (£13.95) on the main menu. Puddings run from banana and mascarpone cheesecake to apple and fruits of the forest strudel (from £4.25); Sunday roast (£7.25), Adnams, Greene King IPA, Woodfordes Wherry and perhaps a guest such as Adnams Regatta are well kept on handpump alongside just over half a dozen changing wines by the glass. In the tidy, attractive garden there's a pleasant terrace with picnic-sets, a dovecote and views of the village church. The pub is not far from the Imperial War Museum, Duxford.
(Recommended by Mrs Margo Finlay, Mr Kasprowski, Martin Webster, Sue Rowland, Paul Mallett)

Free house ~ Licensee Alex Clarke ~ Real ale ~ Bar food ~ Restaurant ~ (01799) 530601 ~ Children welcome ~ Dogs allowed in bar ~ Open 11-3, 6-11; 12-4, 7-10.30 Sun

HUNTINGDON TL2371 Map 5

Old Bridge Hotel ★

1 High Street; ring road just off B1044 entering from easternmost A14 slip road

The main emphasis at this very civilised ivy-covered Georgian hotel is on the excellent imaginative food, which you can eat in the big no smoking airy Terrace (an indoor room, but with beautifully painted verdant murals suggesting the open air) or in the slightly more formal panelled no smoking restaurant. Changing monthly, the menu might include tuscan bean soup with morello olive oil (£4.95), sandwiches (from £5), hot sandwiches such as goats cheese and chargrilled vegetables in pitta (£6), risotto of the day (£5.50/ £10), leek tart with roast turnip, spinach, red wine and celeriac sauce or sausage and mash (£9.50), slow braised pork with gnocchi, roast sweet potato and sage (£13.50), hake fillet with casserole of tomato, mussels, potato, olives and saffron (£13.75), roast fillet of aberdeenshire beef with fondant potato, spinach and fricassee of wild mushrooms (£19.95), puddings such as Valrhona chocolate and hazelnut mousse with hazelnut ice-cream (£7.50), cheese platter (£7.50), and a Monday-Saturday two-course bargain lunch for £12. They excel too in their wine list which includes a fine choice by the glass; there's also freshly squeezed orange juice, smoothies, and good coffee. The bar, with its fine polished floorboards, good log fire, and quietly chatty atmosphere, serves well kept Adnams Southwold and a couple of guests such as Nethergate Augustinian and Potton Shannon IPA on handpump. The building is tucked away in a good spot by the River Great Ouse with its own landing stage, and tables on the waterside terraces (unfortunately there may be traffic noise, too). More reports please. *(Recommended by Philip J Cooper, J F M and M West, Andy and Ali, Joe Green, Michael Sargent; also in the* Good Hotel Guide*)*

Huntsbridge ~ Licensee Martin Lee ~ Real ale ~ Bar food (12-2, 7(6.30 Sat)-10; 12-2.30, 7-9.30 Sun) ~ Restaurant ~ (01480) 424300 ~ Children welcome ~ Dogs allowed in bar and bedrooms ~ Open 11-11; 12-10.30 Sun ~ Bedrooms: £85B/£145B

KEYSTON TL0475 Map 5

Pheasant

Village loop road; from A604 SE of Thrapston, right on to B663

Immaculately kept throughout, this long low thatched white inn is known for its imaginative food and comfortably civilised atmosphere. The oak-beamed spreading bar has open fires, simple wooden tables and chairs on deep coloured carpets, guns on the pink walls, and country paintings. The excellent wine list includes an interesting choice of reasonably priced bottles and around 15 wines by the glass (plus three champagnes); fine port and sherry too. There's also well kept Adnams Bitter with changing guests such as Nethergate Suffolk County and Potton Village Bike on handpump, and freshly squeezed juices. The pub is no smoking throughout, except in the bar. Under a new chef, well prepared food, using carefully sourced ingredients, might include leek and asparagus soup (£4.95), risotto of jerusalem artichoke and ceps with parmesan cheese (£5.95/£10.95), bresaola with shredded savoy cabbage, baby leeks and baby beets (£6.25), wild boar sausages and mash (£8.95), calves liver with puy lentil casserole and garlic mash (£13.75), fried salmon with tomato and fennel compote (£13.95), steak (from £14.95), puddings such as passion fruit and vanilla mousse with almond praline (£5.95), cheese platter (£7.95), and there's a two-course lunch menu for £9.95 (Monday-Saturday). Seats out in front of the building. *(Recommended by J R Bird, Stephen, Julie and Hayley Brown, Oliver and Sue Rowell, J F M and M West, Brenda and Rob Fincham, Gerry and Rosemary Dobson, Michael Sargent, DRH and KLH)*

Huntsbridge ~ Licensees Johnny Dargue and John Hoskins ~ Real ale ~ Bar food (12-2, 6.30-9.30) ~ Restaurant ~ (01832) 710241 ~ Children welcome ~ Dogs allowed in bar ~ Open 12-3, 6-11; 12-2.30, 6.30-10.30 Sun

KIMBOLTON TL0967 Map 5

New Sun

High Street

It's worth a detour from your route to take in the lovely main street village setting of this nice old place. The low-beamed front lounge is perhaps the cosiest, with a couple of comfortable armchairs and a sofa beside the fireplace, standing timbers and exposed brickwork, books, pottery and brasses, and maybe mid-afternoon sun lighting up the wonkiest corners. This leads into a narrower locals' bar, with well kept Charles Wells Bombardier and Eagle, and a guest such as Greene King Old Speckled Hen, and over a dozen wines by the glass; fruit machine and piped music. Opening off here are a dining room and a bright, busy tiled conservatory, with wicker furniture, an unusual roof like a red and yellow striped umbrella, and plenty of tables for eating. As well as lunchtime sandwiches (from £2.75) and filled baked potatoes (from £2.95), the menu might include kiln roasted salmon with sweet mustard and dill sauce (£5.75), parma ham, rocket salad and antipasti (£5.95/£8.95), creamed parsnip risotto (£8.95), steak and kidney pudding (£7.95), osso bucco with risotto (£9.25), venison sausages and grain mustard mash (£9.75), grilled dover sole (£17.25) and puddings such as Malteser cheesecake or syrup sponge and custard (from £4.25). Service is friendly and attentive. There's a very pleasant garden behind, with plastic tables and chairs. Some of the nearby parking spaces have a 30-minute limit. More reports please, it would be a shame to drop this for want of feedback. *(Recommended by George Atkinson)*

Charles Wells ~ Tenant Stephen Rogers ~ Real ale ~ Bar food (12-2.15(2.30 Sun), 7-9.30; not Sun, Mon evenings) ~ Restaurant ~ (01480) 860052 ~ Children in eating area of bar and restaurant ~ Dogs allowed in bar ~ Open 11(11.30 Sat)-2.30, 6(6.30 Sat)-11; 12-10.30 Sun

LONGSTOWE TL3154 Map 5

Red House

Old North Road; A1198 Royston—Huntingdon, S of village

There's ample evidence at this very easy-going place as to where the friendly licensees' interest lies, from the fox mask and horse tack through quite a few good hunting prints to the rosettes mounted proudly behind the bar, you'll guess that he's into horses. Greene King IPA and three or four interesting guests such as Greene King Morland Original, Triple fff, Oldershaw Newtons Drop, a dozen wines by the glass and a good range of soft drinks are served in the bar, with its red-tiled floor. From here go round to the right, past the big log fire with its fat back kettle and a couple of tables beside it, and step down into another dark-tiled area with chintzy easy chairs and settees; a very comfortable haunt, looking out into a sheltered and attractive little garden with picnic-sets. On the left is an attractive restaurant area; daily papers, maybe piped music. As well as lunchtime sandwiches, bar food, which is served in generous helpings, includes soup (£4.25), liver and wild mushroom pâté (£5.75), fish and chips (£8.95), grilled chicken breast with herb butter or gnocchi with tomato and basil (£10.95) and steaks (from £12.95). *(Recommended by Derek and Sylvia Stephenson, Clive Jones)*

Free house ~ Licensee Martin Willis ~ Real ale ~ Bar food (12-2, 6-9.30) ~ Restaurant ~ (01954) 718480 ~ Children in eating area of bar and restaurant ~ Dogs allowed in bar ~ Open 12-2.30, 5.30-11; 12-11(10.30 Sun) Sat; closed Mon am

MADINGLEY TL3960 Map 5

Three Horseshoes

Off A1303 W of Cambridge

To be sure of a table at this very civilised white thatched place it's best to book well in advance. Being the most restauranty of this little chain of pubs, emphasis here is firmly on the innovative menu, which is served in the bar or conservatory-restaurant. It's not cheap, but they do sometimes put on a three-course special offer lunch menu for £15. Daily changing dishes might include roast chicken, tarragon and tuscan bread soup (£5.95), peppered beef carpaccio (£7.50), organic salmon with sun-dried tomato and green bean salad and artichokes (£15.50), sugar cured duck breast with fagioli beans, swiss chard, tomato, watercress, lemon and anchovy or grilled rump of beef marinated in chianti and sage with asparagus and fontina, leek and potato gratin with beer sauce (£16.50), puddings such as vanilla panna cotta with white wine poached apricots (from £6.50) and a cheese platter (£8). Not just the food but the wine list too is outstanding, with up to 20 wines by the glass, plus sweet wines and ports. The pleasantly relaxed little airy bar (which can be a bit of a crush at busy times) has an open fire, simple wooden tables and chairs on the bare floorboards, stools at the bar and pictures on the green walls. Well kept Adnams Southwold plus a guest such as City of Cambridge Hobsons Choice on handpump. *(Recommended by Terry Mizen, Maysie Thompson, Colin McKerrow, J F M and M West, Michael Dandy, Charles Cooper)*

Huntsbridge ~ Licensee Richard Stokes ~ Real ale ~ Bar food (12-2(2.30 Sun), 6.30-9) ~ Restaurant ~ (01954) 210221 ~ Children welcome ~ Open 11.30-3, 6-11; 12-4, 6.30-10.30 Sun

NEWTON TL4349 Map 5

Queens Head ★ £

2½ miles from M11 junction 11; A10 towards Royston, then left on to B1368

It's the very genuine hospitality and simple unspoilt feel of this place that seem to generate such unanimously heartfelt praise from readers, and the licensees who've been here for over 27 years extend such a cheery encompassing welcome that one or two go as far as to list this as their firm favourite in the entire *Guide*. It's so popular that you will need to get here early for a seat during busy times. The well worn main bar has a low ceiling and crooked beams, bare wooden benches and seats built into the walls, paintings on the cream walls, and bow windows. A curved high-backed settle stands on yellow tiles, a loudly ticking clock marks the unchanging time, and a lovely big log fire happily warms the place. The little carpeted saloon is similar but even cosier. Adnams Bitter and Broadside are tapped straight from the barrel, with any one of the Adnams range on as a guest, as well as Crone's organic cider and apple juice. Darts in a no smoking side room, with shove-ha'penny, table skittles, dominoes, cribbage, and nine men's morris. The pubby food here is very simple and there's only a limited range but it's very fairly priced, well liked, and comes in hearty helpings: toast and beef dripping (£2), good value lunchtime sandwiches (from £2, including things like banana with sugar and lemon or herb and garlic), a mug of their famous home-made brown soup (£2.50), and filled baked potatoes (£2.70). In the evening and on Sunday lunchtime you can get plates of excellent cold meat, smoked salmon, cheeses and pâté (from £3.50). There are seats in front of the pub, with its vine trellis. *(Recommended by Dr Emma Disley, Ian Phillips, Charles Gysin, Michael and Marion Buchanan, Tim Maddison, Howard Selina, Conor McGaughey, Mr and Mrs T B Staples, Patrick Hancock)*

Free house ~ Licensees David and Juliet Short ~ Real ale ~ Bar food ~ No credit cards ~ (01223) 870436 ~ Very well behaved children in games room ~ Dogs allowed in bar ~ Open 11.30-2.30, 6-11; 12-2.30, 7-10.30 Sun; closed 25 Dec

PETERBOROUGH TL1999 Map 5

Brewery Tap £

Opposite Queensgate car park

A two storey high glass wall running down one side of this enormous pub gives a fascinating view of the massive copper-banded stainless brewing vessels which turn out the very good Oakham beers that are produced at what is said to be one of the largest microbreweries in Europe. Bishops Farewell, Helterskelter, JHB and White Dwarf are their own Oakham beers, and they are served alongside up to eight guests from breweries scattered all over the country. There's an easy going relaxed feel to the design of the place which is a striking conversion of an old labour exchange, with blue-painted iron pillars holding up a steel-corded mezzanine level, light wood and stone floors, and hugely enlarged and framed newspaper cuttings on its light orange or burnt red walls. It's stylishly lit by a giant suspended steel ring with bulbs running around the rim, and steel-meshed wall lights. A band of chequered floor tiles traces the path of the long sculpted light wood bar counter, which is boldly backed by an impressive display of bottles in a ceiling-high wall of wooden cubes. A sofa seating area downstairs provides a comfortable corner for a surprisingly mixed bunch of customers from young to old. It gets very busy in the evening. The extensive choice of very good thai bar food is prepared by Thai chefs and includes snacks (£1.50-£3.95), stir fries (£4.95-£6.50), curries (£4.95-£5.95), and set menus (from £10.95) and buffets (from £11.95). Prices in 2005 are expected to be up a little, though it should still be very good value. The pub is owned by the same people as Charters and is sadly still under threat of being turned into a parking complex. *(Recommended by Rona Murdoch, Richard Lewis, Peter and Pat Frogley, the Didler, Pat and Tony Martin, Evelyn and Derek Walter, Steve Nye, Patrick Hancock)*

Own brew ~ Licensees Stuart Wright, Jamie Howley, Jessica Loock ~ Real ale ~ Bar food (12-2.30, 6-9.30; 12-9.30 Fri/Sat) ~ Restaurant ~ (01733) 358500 ~ Children welcome ~ Dogs welcome ~ Occasional live music ~ Open 12-11(till 1.30 am Fri/Sat); 12-10.30 Sun; closed 25/26 Dec, 1 Jan

Charters £

Town Bridge, S side

There's lots going for this lively and rather unusual pub. It makes a fascinating visit, as it's housed in a remarkable conversion of a sturdy 1907 commercial Dutch grain barge. There's plenty of seating in the well timbered sizeable nautically themed bar, which is down in the cargo holds, and above deck a glazed oriental restaurant replaces the tarpaulins that used to cover the hold; piped music and fruit machine. Real ale is a big feature. As well as their own three Oakham beers, Bass and Timothy Taylors Landlord they keep up to eight quickly changing guests from many widely spread breweries on handpump, have around 20 foreign bottled beers and monthly beer festivals. Good value asian-style bar food lunchtime includes snacks such as crispy seaweed, spring rolls, tempura prawns or salt and pepper crispy squid (from £1.95 to £4.65), pitta bread with fillings such as oriental duck or beef in black bean sauce (£3.95), and singapore chicken curry or lamb rendang curry (£5.65); credit cards are accepted in the restaurant only. Another surprising plus is the garden, possibly the biggest pub garden in the city. *(Recommended by the Didler, Peter F Marshall, Rona Murdoch, Pat and Tony Martin, Steve Nye, Patrick Hancock)*

Free house ~ Licensees Stuart Wright and James Parsonage ~ Real ale ~ Bar food (12-2.30 (restaurant only 6-11)) ~ Restaurant ~ No credit cards ~ (01733) 315700 ~ Children in restaurant ~ Dogs allowed in bar ~ Live bands Fri/Sat ~ Open 12-11(2 am Fri/Sat, 10.30 Sun)

REACH TL5666 Map 5

Dyke's End

From B1102 E of A14/A1103 junction, follow signpost to Swaffham Prior and Upware – keep on through Swaffham Prior (Reach signposted from there); Fair Green

With its weather-worn inn-sign, big front yew tree, adjacent church and charming village-green setting, this looks every inch the classic village pub. Its village character runs deep: it was bought a few years ago by a consortium of locals, to save it from being turned into a private house, and now has the happy feel inside of a co-operative endeavour that's working out well. A high-backed winged settle screens off the door, and the simply decorated ochre-walled bar has stripped heavy pine tables and pale kitchen chairs on dark boards with one or two rugs, a few rather smarter dining tables on parquet flooring in a panelled section on the left, and on the right a step down to a red-carpeted bit with the small red-walled servery, and sensibly placed darts at the back. All the tables have lit candles in earthenware bottles, and on our visit a big bowl of lilies brightened up the serving counter almost as much as the well kept Adnams and Woodfordes and three guests from brewers such as Adnams, Greene King and Elgoods on handpump, also country cider. A wide range of enjoyable food, using local and seasonal produce, includes soup (£4.50), good lunchtime sandwiches (around £4.75), sausage and mash (£6.75), roast peppers filled with ratatouille (£7.75), penne pasta of the day (£7.95), pigeon, black pudding and stilton pie (£8.25), cod in ale batter (£8.50) and baked bass on samphire with coran sauce or rib-eye steak (£8.95), with local game in season such as jugged hare. The evening restaurant is upstairs. Service is pleasant and efficient, the atmosphere chatty and relaxed, piped music (such as Bach cello suites) unobtrusive, and we gather the piano sometimes gets a hearing. The front grass has picnic-sets under big green canvas parasols. *(Recommended by Michael and Marion Buchanan, Pam and David Bailey, C J Fletcher, M and GR)*

Free house ~ Licensee Simon Owers ~ Real ale ~ Bar food (not Sun evening, Mon) ~ Restaurant ~ (01638) 743816 ~ Children in eating area of bar ~ Dogs allowed in bar ~ Open 12-2.30, 6-10.30; 12-2, 7-10.30 Sun; closed Mon lunchtime

STILTON TL1689 Map 5

Bell 🍷 🛏

High Street; village signposted from A1 S of Peterborough

A bistro extension to this elegant 16th-c stone coaching inn has been sympathetically built in materials that complement the original building. Neatly kept, this extended room and the residents' bar have bow windows, sturdy upright wooden seats on flagstone floors as well as plush button-back built-in banquettes, and there's a good big log fire in one handsome stone fireplace. The partly stripped walls have big prints of sailing and winter coaching scenes, and a giant pair of blacksmith's bellows hangs in the middle of the front bar; backgammon, dominoes and piped music. Through the fine coach arch is a very pretty sheltered courtyard with tables, and a well which supposedly dates back to Roman times. Bar food includes stilton, celery and apple soup (£3.50), crispy duck sping rolls (£4.95), mussels in a creamy garlic and thyme sauce (£4.95/£9.75), pancetta and wild mushroom risotto (£6), wild mushroom pappardelle (£8.95), scallops, crab claws and crevettes in garlic butter with mashed potato (£6.75/£13.50), braised steak and Guinness stew with stilton dumplings (£10.95), sirloin steak (£13.95) and puddings such as glazed lemon tart or sticky toffee pudding (£3.95). The eating area of the bar and lower part of the restaurant are no smoking. Well kept Greene King IPA and Abbot, Oakham JHB and a guest such as Fullers London Pride on handpump, and a decent choice of wines by the glass; attractive chintzy bedrooms. *(Recommended by Gordon Theaker, David and Betty Gittins, Barry Collett, Robert Turnham, David and Brenda Tew, Peter Abbott, Charles and Pauline Stride)*

Free house ~ Licensee Liam McGivern ~ Real ale ~ Bar food (12-2, 6.30-9.30(7-9 Sun)) ~ Restaurant ~ (01733) 241066 ~ Children in eating area of bar at lunchtime, and in bistro at any time ~ Open 12-2.30(3 Sat), 6-11; 12-3, 7-11 Sun ~ Bedrooms: £72.50B/£96.50B

SUTTON GAULT TL4279 Map 5

Anchor ★ 🍴 🍷

Village signed off B1381 in Sutton

This is a jolly nice place for an enjoyably civilised meal, and as most of its customers are here for the particularly good food, it's best to book to be sure of a table. During the week there are a handful of dishes on a light lunch menu such as a sandwich or ploughman's (£5.95) and sausage and mash (£7.50). From the main menu, changing dishes might include starters such as pea and lettuce soup (£4.95), ham hock terrine with quails egg and pineapple pickle (£6.95), main courses such as tomato and black olive tart (£11.50), roast cod on grain mustard and parsley mash (£12.50), osso bucco on saffron risotto (£14.50) and puddings such as sticky toffee pudding, lemon crème brûlée, and a cheese platter (from £4.95); three-course Sunday lunch (£19.95). Service is friendly and helpful. Four heavily timbered rooms are stylishly simple with a nice informal pubby atmosphere, three log fires, antique settles and well spaced scrubbed pine tables on the gently undulating old floors, good lithographs and big prints on the walls, and lighting by gas and candles; three of the four rooms are no smoking. Real ale from a brewer such as City of Cambridge is tapped straight from the cask, there's a thoughtful wine list (including a wine of the month and eight by the glass), winter mulled wine and freshly squeezed fruit juice. The pub is tucked away a little off the beaten track, there are pleasant seats outside, nice walks along the high embankment by the river, and the bird-watching is said to be good. *(Recommended by Gordon Theaker, O K Smyth, M and*

G Rushworth, Adele Summers, Alan Black, John Saville, David Green, Anthony Longden, Bob and Maggie Atherton, Jeff and Wendy Williams, M and GR)

Free house ~ Licensee Robin Moore ~ Real ale ~ Bar food (12-2, 7-9; 6.30-9.30 Sat) ~ Restaurant ~ (01353) 778537 ~ Children welcome ~ Open 12-3, 6.30-11(7-10.30 Sun); closed 26 Dec ~ Bedrooms: £50S(£65B)/£75S(£95B)

THRIPLOW TL4346 Map 5

Green Man

3 miles from M11 junction 10; A505 towards Royston, then first right; Lower Street

This comfortably cheery Victorian pub has a good mix of furniture – mostly sturdy stripped tables and attractive high-backed dining chairs and pews on a flowery red carpet, and shelves on strongly coloured walls with pewter mugs and decorated china. To the right of the bar a cosy little room has comfortable sofas and armchairs, while two arches lead through to a no smoking restaurant on the left. Bar food includes lunchtime sandwiches (from £5.50), home-made burger (£5.50) and sausage and mash (£6.25) and daily specials such as french onion soup (£4.50), filled baguettes such as stilton and mango (£5), goats cheese and black olive tart (£5.50), beef in beer (£6.50), cod fillet with parsley sauce (£8), pork hock with apple mash (£9.50). In the evening you can choose your own combination of sauce and meal, such as creamy mushroom or port sauce with chicken, stuffed pepper, steak and so on (from £7.50). Regularly changing real ales come from brewers such as Milton, Oldershaw, Ringwood and Woodfordes. There are tables and an outdoor heater outside. *(Recommended by Maureen and Bill Sewell, Ian Phillips, S Horsley, Roger Everett, Francis Johnston)*

Free house ~ Licensee Ian Parr ~ Real ale ~ Bar food (not Mon or Sun eve) ~ Restaurant ~ (01763) 208855 ~ Children welcome ~ Open 12-3, 6-11; closed Sun evening, all Mon

---

LUCKY DIP

Besides the fully inspected pubs, you might like to try these Lucky Dips recommended to us and described by readers (if you do, please send us reports: www.goodguides.co.uk).

ABINGTON PIGOTTS TL3044
Pig & Abbot: Thriving L-shaped bar with Adnams, Fullers London Pride and two guest beers, open woodburner in inglenook, food inc good hot beef baguettes; open all day wknds *(JHBS)*

ARRINGTON TL3250
Hardwicke Arms [Ermine Way (A1198)]: Handsome coaching inn built incrementally since 13th c (more recently shrinking to make room for a cul de sac), dark-panelled dining room, huge central fireplace, decent bar food, well kept Greene King IPA and a guest beer, good friendly service; bedrooms with own bathrooms, handy for Wimpole Hall *(LYM, Conor McGaughey)*

BABRAHAM TL5150
George [High St; just off A1307]: This popular beamed and timbered dining pub, being restored after fire damage as we go to press, is now in the hands of the family who run the good Axe & Compasses in Arkesden (see Essex main entries), so will be well worth watching; tables on front grass, attractive setting on quiet road *(anon)*

BARNACK TF0704
Millstone [off B1443 SE of Stamford, via School Lane into Millstone Lane]: Timbers, high beams and stripped stone, with well kept real ales, good friendly service, food in neatly kept bar and no smoking conservatory extension *(LYM, MJB)*

BARRINGTON TL3849
Royal Oak [turn off A10 about 3¾ miles SW of M11 junction 11, in Foxton; West Green]: Rambling thatched Tudor pub with tables out overlooking classic village green, heavy low beams and timbers, bar food from sandwiches to steak and special offers, prompt service, well kept Greene King IPA, Morlands and Old Speckled Hen, light and airy no smoking dining conservatory, children welcome; may be piped music *(P and D Carpenter, LYM, Michael Dandy)*

BOURN TL3256
☆ *Duke of Wellington* [signed off B1046 and A1198 W of Cambridge; at N end of village]: Consistently good range of generous imaginative freshly made food inc good home-made puddings in quiet and civilised relaxing bar divided by arches and so forth – where the locals come to dine out; well spaced tables, pleasant attentive staff, well kept Greene King; cl Mon *(BB)*

BOXWORTH TL3464
Golden Ball [High St]: Extensively refurbished pub/restaurant with well presented interesting food, well kept real ales, helpful service; piped

music; big well kept garden, nice setting, ten new bedrooms *(Gerard Paris)*

BROUGHTON TL2877

Crown [off A141 opp RAF Wyton; Bridge Rd]: Three changing well kept real ales and good enterprising food in bar with restaurant end, pub owned by village consortium; disabled access and facilities *(Dr and Mrs Irvine Loudon)*

BUCKDEN TL1967

☆ *George* [Old Gt North Rd]: Stylish and elegant modern revamp of handsome former coaching inn, good reasonably priced brasserie food all day inc interesting dishes, great staff, good wines (and choice of champagnes) by the glass; tables out on sheltered pretty terrace, work still proceeding on bedrooms as we go to press *(BB, Karen and Steve Brine, Michael Sargent)*

BURWELL TL5867

Anchor [North St]: Traditional bar with good value food inc enterprising special nights (such as choice of 20 english cheeses with a glass of port), affable licensees, good service, wide food choice esp seafood in restaurant, games room with big-screen sports TV; garden backing on to small river, handy for nearby campsite *(P and D Carpenter)*

BYTHORN TL0575

☆ *White Hart* [just off A14]: Attractively relaxed dining pub with good generous lunchtime food from baguettes to one-price main courses in homely bar and several smallish interestingly furnished linked no smoking rooms off, cheaper small helpings, wider evening restaurant menu; thoughtfully chosen affordable wines, well kept Greene King IPA and Abbot and a guest beer, excellent coffee, quick service, very friendly landlord, children welcome; cl Sun evening and Mon *(LYM, David and Mary Webb, Michael Dandy)*

CAMBRIDGE TL4658

Alexandra Arms [Gwydir St]: Simple front bar, artwork and plain modern wooden furnishings in dining bar with short and enjoyable lunchtime choice of mediterranean-slanted food, Greene King ales, good wines by the glass *(John Wooll)*

Anchor [Silver St]: Well laid out pub in beautiful riverside position by a punting station, fine river views from upper bar and suntrap terrace; Flowers IPA, bar lunches till 4, evening baguettes, children in eating areas, open all day *(Mark Walker, LYM, Dr and Mrs A K Clarke)*

☆ *Castle* [Castle St]: Large, airy and well appointed, with full Adnams range kept well and guests such as Wadworths, wide range of enjoyably pubby food, generous and quickly served, friendly staff, no smoking area with easy chairs upstairs; can be crowded (not many students though), may be piped pop music; picnic-sets in good garden *(P and D Carpenter, the Didler, Mark o'Sullivan, Abi Benson)*

Clarendon Arms [Clarendon St]: Quaint partly flagstoned backstreet pub with well kept Greene King IPA and Abbot and a guest such as Batemans XXXB, friendly landlord and staff, nice mix of customers, wide choice of good value food, carpeted dining area, darts, cribbage; Thurs quiz night; open all day, bedrooms simple but clean and comfortable *(Dr David Cockburn)*

Fort St George [Midsummer Common]: Picturesque pub in charming waterside position overlooking ducks, swans, punts and boathouses; extended around old-fashioned Tudor core, good value bar food inc traditional Sun lunches, well kept Greene King ales, decent wines, oars on beams, historic boating photographs, stuffed fish and bric-a-brac; lots of tables outside *(LYM, John Wooll)*

Green Dragon [Water St, Chesterton]: Attractive late medieval timber-framed building, friendly and comfortable linked areas with beams, huge inglenook fireplace and so forth, good value substantial basic lunches, well kept Everards Tiger and Greene King ales; waterside tables across quiet street, easy parking *(MLR)*

Kingston Arms [Kingston St]: Large popular U-shaped pub with ten well kept real ales inc several Lidstones brews from their own brewery over at Wickhambrook, good choice of wines by the glass, enjoyable home cooking inc sensibly priced lunches, friendly licensees, no music, machines or children inside; wkdy lunchtime free internet access; small enclosed torch-lit back garden *(Mike and Mary Carter, John Wooll, Louise Symons, JHBS, Dr David Cockburn)*

Pickerel [Magdelene St]: Spacious pub with low beams and cosy corners, friendly staff, well kept beers, limited lunchtime food inc good baguettes; heated courtyard *(M Borthwick, Dr and Mrs A K Clarke)*

Waterside [Thompsons Lane]: Well kept real ales and helpful staff in riverside pub reworked in up-to-date style, all light wood and colourful sofas; plastic beakers for verandah drinking *(Dr and Mrs A K Clarke)*

CLENCHWARTON TF5820

Victory [Main Rd]: Well kept Elgoods and other changing ales, enjoyable food inc Tues steak night and Sun lunch, summer barbecues; comfortable bedrooms, with good breakfast *(Eddie Williamson)*

CROYDON TL3149

☆ *Queen Adelaide* [off A1198; High St]: Big beamed dining area very popular for wide range of attractively priced food, well kept mainstream ales, impressive array of spirits, efficient friendly service, standing timbers dividing off part with settees, banquettes and stools; garden, play area *(Margaret and Roy Randle, Tony Brace)*

DRY DRAYTON TL3862

Black Horse [signed off A428 (was A45) W of Cambridge; Park St, opp church]: Roomy olde-worlde village pub, well kept Adnams Bitters and Broadside and Greene King IPA, enjoyable reasonably priced food inc good Sun lunch, friendly prompt service, welcoming fire in central fireplace, no smoking dining area; tables on pretty back terrace and neat lawn *(BB, Keith and Janet Morris)*

DUXFORD TL4745

☆ ***John Barleycorn*** [off A1301; Moorfield Rd, pub at far end]: Welcoming food pub in thatched and shuttered early 17th-c cottage, good home-made food all day (cooked to order, so may be a wait), Greene King IPA and Abbot and a guest beer, decent wines, helpful service, softly lit spotless but relaxed bar with old prints, decorative plates and so forth; may be piped music; tables out among flowers, open all day, pleasantly simple beamed bedrooms *(C and G Fraser, Mr and Mrs T B Staples, LYM, David Twitchett)*

ELSWORTH TL3163

George & Dragon [off A14 NW of Cambridge, via Boxworth, or off A428]: Neatly furnished restauranty pub, very popular lunch spot for older people (OAP wkdy lunchtime discount card), panelled main bar and back dining area, well kept Greene King IPA, Old Speckled Hen and Ruddles County, decent wines, friendly attentive service, open fire; disabled access (step down to lavatories), nice terraces, play area in garden, attractive village *(Michael and Jenny Back, Bill and Doreen Sawford, O K Smyth, Maysie Thompson, LYM, Gordon Theaker, Mr and Mrs T B Staples, M Borthwick)*

ELTON TL0893

☆ ***Crown*** [Duck St]: Carefully rebuilt stone pub opp green in beautiful small village, long-serving landlord and cheerful welcoming service, pleasant layout with big log fire, banknotes on beams, artwork for sale and more formal no smoking conservatory restaurant (cl Sun pm and Mon), wide choice of above-average food from good proper sandwiches (wknd baguettes instead) to enjoyable hot dishes and tempting puddings trolley, well kept Greene King IPA and a guest such as Woodfordes Wherry, well chosen wines; lavatories upstairs *(Michael and Jenny Back, H Bramwell)*

FULBOURN TL5156

Bakers Arms [Hinton Rd]: Picturesque well cared for pub in pleasant village, popular with local business lunchers and wknd families for good choice of generous enjoyable food, good service, well kept Greene King ales; roomy conservatory, good-sized garden *(Adele Summers, Alan Black, Mike and Shelley Woodroffe)*

GIRTON TL4262

☆ ***Old Crown*** [High St]: Roomy and tastefully refurbished restaurant/pub, antique pine on polished boards, good generous food (best to book wknds), well chosen menu with fish emphasis, prompt smiling service, well kept Greene King IPA, good wine choice, real fires; children welcome, disabled facilities, pleasant terrace overlooking countryside *(P and D Carpenter, Eric George)*

GRANTCHESTER TL4355

Green Man [High St]: Individual furnishings, log fire and lots of beams, new licensees doing sensibly short changing choice of enjoyable good value food, well kept Adnams Bitter and Broadside and Greene King IPA, no smoking dining room, no music; disabled facilities, tables out behind, nice village a short stroll from lovely riverside meadows *(LYM, P and D Carpenter, Pat and Roger Fereday, DC)*

Red Lion [High St]: Welcoming family food pub, comfortable and spacious, with quick friendly service, well balanced menu and good beer choice; sheltered terrace, good-sized lawn *(LYM, P and D Carpenter)*

Rupert Brooke [Broadway; junction Coton rd with Cambridge—Trumpington rd]: Cosy beamed bar with central log fire, sympathetic extension mainly for eating in, usual food from baguettes and lunchtime light dishes up (beware of 10% service charge), crisp white tablecloths, Greene King Old Speckled Hen and Charles Wells Bombardier, good choice of wines by the glass; piped music *(Michael Dandy)*

GREAT CHISHILL TL4239

☆ ***Pheasant*** [follow Heydon signpost from B1039 in village]: Welcoming new hands-on licensees and good friendly local atmosphere in split-level flagstoned bar with beams, timbering and some elaborately carved though modern seats and settles, good freshly made food, first-class service, real ales such as Adnams, Courage Best and Directors and Theakstons, good choice of wines by the glass, small no smoking dining room, darts, cribbage, dominoes; piped music; children welcome, charming back garden with small play area *(LYM, Keith and Janet Morris, E Smeeten, Ronald Sebley, Alexandra Cox)*

GUYHIRN TF3903

☆ ***Oliver Twist*** [follow signs from A47/A141 junction S of Wisbech]: Comfortable open-plan lounge with cheerful welcoming licensees, well kept sturdy furnishings, good range of home-made generous food from huge crusty warm rolls to steaks, well kept Everards Beacon and Tiger with a weekly guest beer, big open fires, restaurant; may be piped music; six new bedrooms *(BB, Barry Collett, Phil and Jane Hodson)*

HAIL WESTON TL1662

Royal Oak [High St; just off A45, handy for A1 St Neots bypass]: Picturesque 17th-c thatched and beamed pub in quiet and pretty village nr Grafham Water, unpretentious neatly kept low-beamed bar, cosy log fire, enjoyable honest food, welcoming staff, well kept Charles Wells ales and perhaps a guest beer, family room; darts, piped music and fruit machine in room off; open all day, big neat attractive garden with good play area *(Father Robert Marsh)*

HEMINGFORD GREY TL2970

☆ ***Cock*** [village signed off A14 eastbound, and (via A1096 St Ives rd) westbound; High St]: Small uncluttered bar with woodburner, darts and well kept ales such as Adnams, Elgoods Black Dog, Oakham JHB and Woodfordes Wherry, mid-Aug beer festival, steps down to more seating below black beams; stylishly simple spotless restaurant on right with pale bare boards and canary walls above powder-blue dado, good food from traditional dishes with a touch of flair to plenty of fish (must book wknds), good affordable wines, quick friendly service; tables out behind in neat garden by gravel car park, pretty village with extremely venerable manor house *(David Collins, David and Judith Stewart, BB, B N F and M Parkin, George Atkinson)*

HILDERSHAM TL5448

☆ ***Pear Tree*** [off A1307 N of Linton]: Friendly Victorian pub in picturesque thatched village, clean and bright with odd crazy-paved floor and plenty of curios, good value changing home cooking from ploughman's up, cheerful service, well kept Greene King IPA, Abbot and Ruddles Best, daily papers, board games; children welcome, tables in garden behind, aviary with canaries and finches *(Dr and Mrs D A Blackadder, BB, Michael and Jenny Back, Keith and Janet Morris)*

HOLYWELL TL3370

☆ ***Old Ferry Boat*** [signed off A1123]: Roomy and congenial old thatched low-beamed Greene King inn, sympathetically refurbished with several open fires and side areas, dozens of carpenter's tools, window seats overlooking Great Ouse, Greene King IPA, Abbot and Old Speckled Hen, decent wines by the glass, enjoyable generous food from sandwiches to full meals (all day in summer), pleasant service, good no smoking areas; quiet piped music, games, can get very busy; open all day wknds, children welcome, tables and cocktail parasols on front terrace and riverside lawn, moorings, bedrooms, conference facilities *(LYM, Michael Dandy)*

HOUGHTON TL2772

Three Jolly Butchers [A1123, Wyton]: Good atmosphere, friendly attentive service, enjoyable food (not Sun/Mon evenings) from sandwiches to restaurant dishes, well kept ales such as Fullers London Pride and Greene King IPA, Abbot and Old Speckled Hen, good house wines, beams and brasses; children and dogs allowed in one area, pool table on covered back terrace, huge back garden, play area and occasional barbecues, lovely village *(Gordon Theaker, Lucien Perring)*

HUNTINGDON TL2371

☆ ***George*** [George St]: Relaxed, friendly and comfortable hotel lounge bar, good choice of generous reasonably priced food, well kept real ales, good coffee, staff eager to please; magnificent galleried central courtyard, comfortable bedrooms *(LYM, Joe Green, Nigel Blackhall)*

NEEDINGWORTH TL3571

☆ ***Pike & Eel*** [pub signed from A1123; Overcote Rd]: Marvellous peaceful riverside location, with spacious lawns and small marina; two separate eating areas, one a well run carvery with good fresh roasts, in extensively glass-walled block overlooking water, boats and swans; easy chairs, settees and big open fire in room off separate rather hotelish plush bar, well kept Adnams, Bass, and Greene King Abbot, good coffee and wines, friendly helpful staff, children roam free; clean simple bedrooms, good breakfast *(LYM, J Stickland)*

PETERBOROUGH TL1897

Coalheavers Arms [Park St, Woodston]: Small friendly traditional flagstoned pub being refurbished by Milton Brewery, their real ales and guest beers, farm cider, good range of continental imports and malt whiskies; pleasantly reworked garden *(the Didler, Richard Houghton, Steve Nye)*

Goodbarns Yard [St Johns St; behind Passport Office]: Two-room pub with good changing real ale choice, annual beer festival, food wkdy lunchtime, big conservatory; open all day *(the Didler)*

Palmerston Arms [Oundle Rd]: 16th-c stone-built pub with well kept Batemans and guest ales tapped from the cask, good pork pies, welcoming service, old tables, chairs, benches and a sofa in carpeted lounge, tiled-floor public bar, no music or machines; step down into pub, steps to lavatory; small garden, open all day *(the Didler)*

SHEPRETH TL3947

Plough [signed just off A10 S of Cambridge; High St]: Neatly kept bright and airy local with popular generous home-made food from good sandwiches, baguettes and home-made soup up, quick welcoming service, well kept ales changing monthly such as Adnams, Greene King IPA, Tetleys and Wadworths 6X, decent wines, modern furnishings, family room, small no smoking dining room; tidy back garden with fairy-lit arbour and pond, summer barbecues and play area *(BB, Michael Stockhill)*

SOMERSHAM TL3477

Windmill [St Ives Rd (B1086)]: Good interesting if not cheap food inc lots of fresh fish and wider evening choice in attractive two-part lounge/dining area with stripped bricks and beams, panelled bar with windmill pictures, wide wine choice, Greene King IPA and Abbot, quick friendly service; garden with play area *(M and GR)*

SPALDWICK TL1372

George [just off A14 W of Huntingdon]: 16th-c village pub reopened after smart open-plan refurbishment, cool, stylish and largely no smoking; emphasis on enjoyable if pricey food with up-to-date touches in bar and larger bistro area (children allowed), lots of wines by the glass and a couple of well kept real ales *(LYM, Michael Sargent, Dr Brian and Mrs Anne Hamilton)*

ST NEOTS TL1859

Chequers [St Marys St, Eynesbury]: Charming 16th-c beamed inn, interesting antique furnishings in small bar, well kept Tetleys and interesting guest beers, good varied bar food from sandwiches and baked potatoes to steaks, friendly service, restaurant; sheltered terrace and garden *(Michael Dandy)*

STILTON TL1689

Stilton Cheese [signed off A1; North St]: Well balanced choice of tasty food inc imaginative dishes in spacious dining areas with good tables, well kept real ales, decent wines, warm atmosphere, welcoming staff, interesting old interior inc unpretentious public bar; bedrooms, big back terrace and garden

(Oliver and Sue Rowell)

STOW CUM QUY TL5160

Wheatsheaf [Stow Rd (B1102), off A1303 E of Cambridge]: Clean, bright and welcoming, with good choice of nicely cooked quickly served food in comfortable eating area, Greene King IPA, efficient service; handy for Anglesey Abbey at Lode *(Mr and Mrs Gordon Turner)*

STRETHAM TL5174

Fish & Duck [from A1123 E of Stretham turn left on to long signed track just after railway]: Excellent fenland spot at junction of two water-courses, enjoyable food, good service *(Robert Turnham)*

Red Lion [High St (off A10)]: Neat village pub with wide daily-changing choice of good generous food inc children's and Sun lunch, solid pine furniture and old village photographs, friendly attentive service, five well kept real ales, marble-topped tables in pleasant no smoking dining conservatory; children welcome, picnic-sets in garden *(Abi Benson)*

SWAVESEY TL3565

Trinity Foot [by A14 eastbound, NW of Cambridge]: Comfortably worn in pub with well spaced tables, well kept Elgoods, decent wines, food from sandwiches and light lunches to fish and reasonably priced seafood, attractive conservatory; piped music may obtrude *(LYM, R M Corlett, Peter and Jean Hoare, Adam and Joan Bunting)*

White Horse [signed off A14 (ex A604) NW of Cambridge; Market St]: Welcoming village pub with attractive traditional furnishings in public bar, more straightforward spacious lounge and no smoking dining room, well kept ales such as Adnams, Caledonian Deuchars IPA and Fenland Osier Cutter, good soft drinks choice, good value generous pub food, log fire; children allowed *(Keith and Janet Morris)*

UFFORD TF0904

Olde White Hart [back rd Peterborough—Stamford, just S of B1443]: Recently refurbished 17th-c village pub with interesting features and nice snug, good affordable bar food, well kept real ales, good short wine list, proper coffee, log fires; children welcome, big garden with extensive terrace and play area *(LYM, Martin and Helen Ball)*

WANSFORD TL0799

☆ ***Haycock*** [just off A1 W of Peterborough]: Handsome old coaching inn greatly extended as hotel and conference centre, useful if not cheap as A1 break, with enjoyable bar food all day from good sandwiches and ciabattas up, well kept Adnams and Bass, good wines, variety of attractive seating areas with plenty of character, big log fire, no smoking restaurant; attractive courtyard and garden, children in eating areas, dogs allowed in bar and comfortable bedrooms, open all day *(Mr and Mrs T B Staples, LYM, Mrs M E Mills, Phil and Jane Hodson)*

WARESLEY TL2454

Duncombe Arms [Eltisley Rd (B1040, 5 miles S of A428)]: Comfortable and welcoming old pub, long main bar, fire one end, good range of generous reasonably priced food from lunchtime sandwiches to imaginative good value main dishes and roasts, consistently well kept Greene King ales, good service, no smoking back room and restaurant; picnic-sets in garden *(Colin McKerrow, Gerry and Rosemary Dobson, JWAC)*

WHITTLESFORD TL4648

Bees in the Wall [North Rd; handy for M11 junction 10]: Comfortable timbered lounge, traditional public bar with darts and old wall settles, good food choice from sandwiches up, well kept Timothy Taylors Landlord and two interesting changing guest beers; picnic-sets in attractive garden, bees' nest visible in wall, open all day wknds *(Kevin Thorpe)*

Red Lion [Station Rd]: Handsome building dating from 16th c, character bar opening off reception area, three real ales, friendly helpful staff, enjoyable generous reasonably priced food; bedrooms, adjacent to Duxford Chapel (EH), handy for Imperial War Museum Duxford *(Keith and Janet Morris)*

WICKEN TL5670

Maids Head [High St]: Neatly kept dining pub in lovely village-green setting, friendly local atmosphere, well kept real ales such as Adnams, fair-priced wines, no smoking restaurant; quiet piped music; tables outside, handy for Wicken Fen nature reserve (NT) *(M and G Rushworth, Roger Wain-Heapy, M and GR)*

Real ale may be served from handpumps, electric pumps (not just the on-off switches used for keg beer) or – common in Scotland – tall taps called founts (pronounced 'fonts') where a separate pump pushes the beer up under air pressure. The landlord can adjust the force of the flow – a tight spigot gives the good creamy head that Yorkshire lads like.

Cheshire

Current front-runners on the county's pub scene are the Grosvenor Arms at Aldford (good food, drink and atmosphere in civilised surroundings), the Bhurtpore at Aston (great on the drinks side, enjoyable food too), the timeless old thatched White Lion at Barthomley, the interestingly converted Cholmondeley Arms near Bickley Moss (gaining a Food Award this year, and nice to stay in), the distinctively old-fashioned Albion in Chester, the Plough at Eaton (attractively updated 17th-c pub, good all round under the people who took over a couple of years ago – a new main entry), the relaxing and accommodating Ring o' Bells in the pretty village of Daresbury, the friendly Pheasant at Higher Burwardsley (terrific views, good food), the Hanging Gate up at Langley (great views in this ancient and welcoming drovers' inn, too), the rather baronial 16th-c Sutton Hall Hotel near Macclesfield (a good interesting all-rounder), the Legh Arms in Prestbury (this appealing all-rounder now has bedrooms), and the Swan at Wybunbury (another new entry, friendly, cosy and interesting, with good beers and tasty food). With nothing but praise for its cooking and good friendly service this year, the Cholmondeley Arms near Bickley Moss is Cheshire Dining Pub of the Year. Pubs that currently stand out in the Lucky Dip section at the end of the chapter are the Mill in Chester, Alvanley Arms at Cotebrook, Ring o' Bells in Frodsham (only a lack of reports from readers keeps this fine pub out of the main entries this year), Calveley Arms in Handley, Leathers Smithy up at Langley, Chetwode Arms at Lower Whitley, Spread Eagle in Lymm, Roebuck in Mobberley and Ryles Arms up at Sutton. Drinks prices here are well below the national average (and particularly appealing in the civilised Dog at Peover Heath). This is one result of keen competition on the brewing side, with long-established family brewers Robinsons of Stockport the major presence, and plenty of other firms such as Hydes of Manchester, Hanby from Shropshire, and Moorhouses and Thwaites from Lancashire jostling for trade alongside local Burtonwood (that brewery now owned independently by Thomas Hardy, and no longer by the Burtonwood pub company), and other smaller breweries such as Weetwood.

ALDFORD SJ4259 Map 7

Grosvenor Arms ★

B5130 Chester—Wrexham

Hugely popular, this very well run pub is an excellent all-rounder, with enjoyable food, a great choice of drinks, swift friendly service and if that wasn't enough, it's handily open all day too. Lovely on summer evenings, the airy terracotta-floored conservatory has lots of huge low hanging flowering baskets and chunky pale wood garden furniture, and opens on to a large elegant suntrap terrace and neat lawn with picnic-sets, young trees and a tractor. Inside, it's spacious and open plan, with a traditional feel, and a buoyantly chatty atmosphere prevails in the huge panelled library. Tall book shelves line one wall, and lots of substantial tables are well spaced on the handsome board floor. Several quieter areas are well furnished with good individual pieces. There are plenty of interesting pictures, and the lighting is welcoming; cribbage, dominoes, Trivial Pursuit and Scrabble. A tempting choice of whiskies includes 100 malts, 30 bourbons, and 30 from Ireland, and all 20 wines (largely new world) are served by the glass. Flowers IPA, Caledonian Deuchars IPA and Robinsons Best are well kept on handpump with a couple of guests from brewers such as Freeminer and Derwent. A good choice of well presented bar food might include mushroom soup (£3.75), sandwiches (from £3.95), asparagus and goats cheese tart (£5.45), ploughman's (£6.45), butternut squash and lemon grass risotto (£7.95), pork steak with black pudding, bacon and sweet potato mash (£9.95), grilled salmon with olive crushed potatoes and pesto dressing (£10.25), and duck breast with herb potato cake and sweet and sour beetroot (£11.50), with mouthwatering puddings such as sultana and cinnamon bread and butter pudding or chocolate fudge roulade with cream and fruit coulis (£4.50); best to book on weekend evenings. The pub is a favourite with families, and can get very busy. *(Recommended by Chris Flynn, Wendy Jones, Richard and Jean Phillips, Andrea and Guy Bradley, Graham and Lynn Mason, John Knighton, Revd D Glover, Mike and Wendy Proctor, Peter Abbott, Mrs P J Carroll, E S Funnell, Angie Coles, A P Seymour, Paul Boot, Mike Marsh, Mr and Mrs A H Young)*

Brunning & Price ~ Managers Gary Kidd and Jeremy Brunning ~ Real ale ~ Bar food (12-10(9 Sun and bank hols); not 25 Dec, or 26 and 31 Dec evenings) ~ (01244) 620228 ~ No children inside after 6pm ~ Dogs allowed in bar ~ Open 11.30-11; 12-10.30 Sun

ASTBURY SJ8461 Map 7

Egerton Arms

Village signposted off A34 S of Congleton

In a pretty spot overlooking an attractive old church, this village inn was originally a farmhouse, and some parts date back to the 16th c. Rambling round the bar, the brightly yellow-painted rooms have a cheery pubby feel, and around the walls are the odd piece of armour, shelves of books, and mementoes of the Sandow Brothers, who performed as 'the World's Strongest Youths' (one of them was the landlady's father). In summer dried flowers fill the big fireplace; parts of the bar and restaurant are no smoking. Robinsons Frederics, Unicorn, and Hartleys Cumbria Way are well kept on handpump; piped music, fruit machine, TV. A wide choice of straightforward dishes could include soup (£2.40), sandwiches (from £2.80), ploughman's (£4.75), sardines grilled in garlic butter (£3.95), spicy bean and vegetable pasta, steak, kidney and mustard pie, roast ham with cranberry glaze or battered cod with mushy peas (all £5.99), with puddings such as chocolate rum truffle (£2.95). They also do OAP lunches Mon-Thurs (two courses £4.50, three £5.50), as well as children's meals (£2.80). Out in front, you'll find a few well placed tables, and a play area with wooden fort; look out for the sociable pub dogs. Despite the large car park, at Sunday lunchtime you might struggle to get a place. Their ensuite bedrooms are very good value. More reports please. *(Recommended by Maurice and Della Andrew, E G Parish, Mike and Wendy Proctor)*

Robinsons ~ Tenants Alan and Grace Smith ~ Real ale ~ Bar food ~ Restaurant ~ (01260) 273946 ~ Children in eating area of bar and restaurant, no babies in restaurant in evening ~ Open 11.30-11; 12-3, 6.45-10.30 Sun ~ Bedrooms: £45S/£60S

ASTON SJ6147 Map 7

Bhurtpore ★

Off A530 SW of Nantwich; in village follow Wrenbury signpost

'Every beer-drinkers dream' according to one reader, this marvellous roadside pub serves a truly awesome range of drinks. The pub takes its unusual name from the town in India, where local landowner Lord Combermere won a battle, and the carpeted lounge bar bears some indian influences, with a growing collection of exotic artefacts (one turbaned statue behind the bar proudly sports a pair of Ray-Bans), as well as good local period photographs, and some attractive furniture. At lunchtime or earlyish on a weekday evening the atmosphere is cosy and civilised, but even on weekends, when it gets packed, the cheery staff cope superbly. Tables in the comfortable public bar are reserved for people not eating, and the snug area and dining room are no smoking; darts, dominoes, cribbage, pool, TV, and fruit machine. More than 1,000 different superbly kept real ales pass through the 11 handpumps every year, including some really unusual ones. Alongside Hanbys Drawwell, you might find Abbeydale Absolution and Belfry, Copper Dragon Dark, Dark Star Over the Moon, Gales Frolic, Moorhouses Bursting Bitter, Salopian Golden Thread, and Titanic Longitude, and they also serve continental beers such as Bitburger Pils, Pilsner Urquell and Timmermans Peach Beer, with dozens of unusual bottled beers and fruit beers. If you're not a beer-fan, there's still a great deal to choose from, with a tempting selection of farm ciders and perries, 100 different whiskies, and a good wine list (with fine wines and fruit wines). The enjoyable menu has snacks (not Friday or Saturday night) such as sandwiches (from £2.50, hot filled baguettes £3.95), baked potatoes (£4.25), and local sausages, egg and chips (£4.75), as well as other reasonably priced dishes such as cheese and leek cakes with creamy dijon sauce (£7.75), cod fillet baked with mozzarella, cherry tomatoes and basil or pork slices in apple and cider sauce (£9.50), chicken breast in stilton and smoked bacon sauce (£9.95), and 8oz rib-eye steak marinated in mild mustard (£10.95), with a choice of about six delicious home-made indian curries (£7.95-£8.25), and maybe a seasonal game dish too; puddings such as home-made apple and rhubarb crumble (£3.50). *(Recommended by Sue Holland, Dave Webster, E G Parish, Martin Grosberg, the Didler, Margaret and Allen Marsden, Mr and Mrs S Felstead, Mike and Wendy Proctor, Mrs P J Carroll)*

Free house ~ Licensee Simon George ~ Real ale ~ Bar food (12-2, 7-9; 12-9 Sun) ~ Restaurant ~ (01270) 780917 ~ Well behaved children lunchtime and early evenings ~ Dogs allowed in bar ~ Open 12-2.30(3 Sat), 6.30-11; 12-10.30 Sun; closed 25-26 Dec, 1 Jan ~ Bedrooms: £30S/£40S

BARTHOMLEY SJ7752 Map 7

White Lion ★ £

A mile from M6 junction 16; from exit roundabout take B5078 N towards Alsager, then Barthomley signposted on left

The main bar of this lovely 17th-c black and white thatched pub feels timeless, with its blazing open fire, heavy oak beams dating back to Stuart times (mind your head), attractively moulded black panelling, Cheshire watercolours and prints on the walls, latticed windows, and thick wobbly old tables. Up some steps, a second room has another welcoming open fire, more oak panelling, a high-backed winged settle, a paraffin lamp hinged to the wall, and shove-ha'penny, cribbage and dominoes; local societies make good use of a third room. Outside, seats and picnic-sets on the cobbles have a charming view of the attractive village, and the early 15th-c red sandstone church of St Bertiline across the road is well worth a visit. At lunchtime, friendly and efficient staff serve good value sandwiches (from £3.75), as well as simple dishes such as cheese and onion oatcakes with beans and tomatoes (£2.50), sausages and mash (£4.90), daily roasts or stilton and local roast ham ploughman's (£5); they have plans to refurbish the kitchen. It's best to arrive early on weekends to be sure of a table. Well kept real ales on handpump include Burtonwood Bitter and Top Hat, with a couple of guests such as Belhaven 70/- and Wadworths 6X; no noisy games machines or music. The cottage behind the pub is available to rent. *(Recommended by the Didler, John Dwane, Dr D J and Mrs S C Walker, Sue Holland, Dave Webster, S and R Gray, Paul Humphreys, MLR, Mike and Wendy Proctor, G Coates, Michael and Marion Buchanan, Richard Greaves, J B R Ashley, Edward Mirzoeff)*

Burtonwood ~ Tenant Terence Cartwright ~ Real ale ~ Bar food (lunchtime only, not Thurs) ~ (01270) 882242 ~ Children welcome away from public bar ~ Dogs welcome ~ Open 11.30-11(5-11 only Thurs); 12-10.30 Sun; closed Thurs afternoon

Post Office address codings confusingly give the impression that some pubs are in Cheshire, when they're really in Derbyshire (and therefore included in this book under that chapter) or in Greater Manchester (see the Lancashire chapter).

BICKLEY MOSS SJ5650 Map 7

Cholmondeley Arms

Cholmondeley; A49 5½ miles N of Whitchurch; the owners would like us to list them under Cholmondeley Village, but as this is rarely located on maps we have mentioned the nearest village which appears more often

Cheshire Dining Pub of the Year

This imaginatively converted Victorian schoolhouse is winning lots of praise from readers for its good food and friendly, efficient service. Generously served, well prepared bar food includes lunchtime snacks such as delicious sandwiches (£4.50), stuffed pancakes (£6.95), and lasagne (£8.25), with other dishes such as garlic mushrooms with bacon (£5.25), fish, chips and mushy peas (£10.25), and tender rib-eye steak (£12.50), and changing specials such as warm goats cheese mousse with basil, olive oil and garlic (£4.95), salmon and smoked haddock pie or chicken breast with mushroom, dijon mustard and cream sauce (£9.95), and rack of lamb with onion sauce and rosemary gravy (£10.95). They do good-sized children's meals (£4.50), and readers recommend the Sunday roast (£9.95). It's best to book at popular times such as weekends. There's lots to look at, and the cross-shaped high-ceilinged bar is filled with objects such as old school desks above the bar on a gantry, and there are masses of Victorian pictures (especially portraits and military subjects); over one of the side arches is a great stag's head; gothic windows and huge old radiators too. A medley of seats runs from cane and bentwood to pews and carved oak settles, and the patterned paper on the shutters matches the curtains. Well kept Adnams, Banks's, Marstons Pedigree and perhaps a guest such as Everards Tiger on handpump, and around ten interesting and reasonably priced wines by the glass are listed on a blackboard; they also do good coffees (liqueur ones too), and some speciality teas. There are seats outside on the sizeable lawn, and more in front overlooking the quiet road. The pub is handy for Cholmondeley Castle Gardens. *(Recommended by Joyce and Geoff Robson, E G Parish, Paul Humphreys, Mike and Wendy Proctor, Rod Stoneman, Mrs P J Carroll, Susie Symes, Ray and Winifred Halliday, J S Burn, Mike Ridgway, Sarah Miles, Mrs P Dewhurst, Jane Thomas)*

Free house ~ Licensees Guy and Carolyn Ross-Lowe ~ Real ale ~ Bar food (12-2.30, 6.30-10) ~ Restaurant ~ (01829) 720300 ~ Children in eating area of bar and restaurant ~ Dogs welcome ~ Open 11-3, 6.30-11 ~ Bedrooms: £50B/£65B

BUNBURY SJ5758 Map 7

Dysart Arms

Bowes Gate Road; village signposted off A51 NW of Nantwich; and from A49 S of Tarporley – coming this way, coming in on northernmost village access road, bear left in village centre

Tables on the terrace and in the neatly kept slightly elevated garden of this popular dining pub are lovely in summer, with views of the splendid church at the end of the pretty village, and the distant Peckforton Hills beyond. Nicely laid out spaces ramble around the pleasantly lit central bar. Under deep venetian red ceilings, the knocked-through cream-walled rooms have red and black tiles, some stripped boards and some carpet, a comfortable variety of well spaced big sturdy wooden tables and chairs, a couple of tall bookcases, some carefully chosen bric-a-brac, properly lit pictures, and good winter fires. One area is no smoking. They've lowered the ceiling in the more restauranty end room (with its book-lined back wall), and there are lots of plants on the window sills. You'll find an interesting selection of 16 wines by the glass, and Thwaites Bitter and Timothy Taylors Landlord are well kept on handpump, along with a couple of guests such as Hanby Drovers and Weetwood Eastgate. Interesting, well presented dishes from a changing menu could include soup (£3.75), sandwiches (from £4.50), ploughman's or sesame king prawns with sweet chilli dressing (£6.95), filo parcel with oriental vegetables and spicy sweet and sour sauce (£7.95), grilled bacon chop with bubble and squeak and wholegrain mustard sauce (£9.95), grilled salmon fillet with lemon and saffron sauce (£10.50), and braised shoulder of lamb with minted gravy and dauphinoise potatoes (£11.95), with puddings such as rhubarb crumble tart with vanilla ice-cream (£4.50), and a tasty cheeseboard (£5.95). *(Recommended by E G Parish, Sue Holland, Dave Webster, Mike Schofield, Revd D Glover, Kevin Blake, Brenda and Stuart Naylor, JES, Stephen Buckley, Mr and Mrs J E C Tasker, MLR, Mrs P J Carroll, E S Funnell, Brian and Anna Marsden, J S Burn, Paul Davies)*

Brunning & Price ~ Managers Darren and Elizabeth Snell ~ Real ale ~ Bar food (12-2.15, 6-9.30; 12-(9 Sun)9.30 Sat) ~ (01829) 260183 ~ No children under 10 after 6pm ~ Dogs allowed in bar ~ Open 11.30-11; 12-10.30 Sun; closed 25 Dec, evenings 26 Dec and 1 Jan

CHESTER SJ4166 Map 7

Albion ★

Park Street

Run by the same landlord for over 30 years, this old-fashioned corner pub is tucked away in a quiet part of town just below the Roman Wall. The atmosphere is peacefully relaxed and chatty, and the lack of piped music, noisy machines and children makes the pub especially popular with a loyal following of older visitors. Throughout the rooms you'll find an absorbing collection of World War I memorabilia: big engravings of men leaving for war, and similarly moving prints of wounded veterans, are among the other more expected aspects – flags, advertisements and so on. The post-Edwardian décor is appealingly muted, with floral wallpaper, appropriate lamps, leatherette and hoop-backed chairs, a period piano, a large mangle, and cast-iron-framed tables; there's an attractive side dining room too. Service is friendly, though race-goers are discouraged, and they don't like people rushing in just before closing time; it can get smoky. Well kept real ales such as Cains Bitter, Jennings Cumberland, and Timothy Taylors Landlord on handpump and maybe a guest, with over 25 malt whiskies, new world wines, and fresh orange juice; the pub cat is called Kitchener. Big portions of hearty bar food (made with lots of local ingredients) such as doorstep sandwiches (£3.50, club sandwiches £3.75), filled Staffordshire oatcakes (£3.90), haggis and tatties, cottage pie, lambs liver, bacon and onions in cider gravy with creamed potatoes or roast turkey and stuffing (all £6.95), with puddings such as home-made creamy coconut rice pudding with fresh fruit coulis (£3.30); it can get very busy at lunchtime. New bedrooms are now due to open by 2005. *(Recommended by Peter F Marshall, Sue Holland, Dave Webster, the Didler, Michael Butler, Joe Green, Patrick Hancock, Brenda and Rob Fincham, Angie Coles)*

Punch ~ Lease Michael Edward Mercer ~ Real ale ~ Bar food (12-2, 5(6 Sat)-8, not Sun evening) ~ Restaurant ~ No credit cards ~ (01244) 340345 ~ Dogs allowed in bar ~ Open 12-3, 5(6 Sat)-11; 12-11 Fri; 12-3, 7-10.30 Sun

Old Harkers Arms

Russell Street, down steps off City Road where it crosses canal – under Mike Melody antiques

Relaxing with a drink (and they've a good choice), you can watch canal and cruise boats glide past from the windows of this attractively converted early Victorian warehouse. Alongside Harkers Silver Pale Ale (brewed for the pub by Ossett), they serve up to six regularly changing guests on handpump: a typical choice might be Fullers London Pride, Interbrew Flowers IPA, Phoenix Arizona, Shepherd Neame Spitfire, Weetwood Oasthouse Gold and York Guzzler. They also do around 50 malt whiskies, and decent well described wines. The bar is nicely decorated, with attractive lamps, interesting old prints on the walls, and newspapers and books to read from a well stocked library at one end. Though the tables are carefully arranged to create a sense of privacy, the lofty ceiling and tall windows give an appealing sense of space and light; the bar counter is apparently constructed from salvaged doors. Good dishes from an interesting changing menu could include sandwiches (from £3.75, toasted from £4.25), soup (£3.75), cheese and herb fritters with chilli jam (£4.25), mushroom stroganoff on toast (£5.95), sausage and leek hash with red cabbage (£6.95), ploughman's (£7.25), chicken stir fry with noodles in spicy szechuan sauce (£7.50), steak, mushroom and ale pie (£8.95), and grilled hake with parsley sauce and new potatoes (£9.95), with puddings such as citron tart (£4.25). On Friday and Saturday evenings it gets very busy (and is popular with younger visitors). *(Recommended by Kevin Blake, Sue Holland, Dave Webster, Oliver and Sue Rowell, Simon J Barber, Simon Calvert, Andrew York, Joe Green, Roger and Anne Newbury)*

Brunning & Price ~ Managers Barbie Hill and Catryn Devaney ~ Real ale ~ Bar food (12-2.30, 5.30-9.30; 12-9.30 Sat, 12-9 Sun) ~ (01244) 344525 ~ Children till 6pm ~ Open 11.30-11; 12-10.30 Sun

COTEBROOK SJ5865 Map 7

Fox & Barrel

A49 NE of Tarporley

A traditional jazz band plays every Monday at this bar and restaurant, which is handily open all day on the weekends, and although lots of people come here to eat, you'll feel perfectly comfortable just dropping in for a drink. The snug distinct areas are interestingly furnished, with a good mix of tables and chairs including two seats like Victorian thrones, an oriental rug in front of a very big log fireplace, a comfortable banquette corner, and a part with shelves of rather nice ornaments and china jugs; silenced fruit machine, unobtrusive piped music. Beyond the bar is a huge uncluttered candlelit dining area (no smoking) with varying-sized tables, comfortable dining chairs, attractive rugs on bare boards, rustic pictures above the panelled dado, and one more extensively panelled section. Neatly uniformed staff serve well kept John Smiths, Marstons Pedigree and a couple of guests such as Bass and Jennings Cumberland through a sparkler (though you can ask for it to be taken off) by handpump; there's a decent choice of wines. As well as bar snacks (not Friday and Saturday evening) such as sandwiches or baguettes (from £4.25), ploughman's (£6.35), and chicken fajitas (£7.50), well presented dishes from a changing menu might include home-made soup (£3.50), delicious home-made smooth liver pâté (£5.25), black pudding, feta cheese and poached pear salad (£5.50), home-made lasagne (£7.95), chicken breast wrapped in bacon topped with mozzarella with crushed potatoes and white wine cream sauce (£11.50), king prawns with green thai curry (£13.75), and 8oz sirloin steak (£14.50); it's a good idea to book for Sunday lunch. *(Recommended by Olive and Ray Hebson, Kevin Blake, Simon J Barber, Mrs G Coleman, Mrs P J Carroll, MLR, E G Parish, J S Burn)*

Punch ~ Tenant Martin Cocking ~ Real ale ~ Bar food (12-2.30, 6.30(6 Sat)-9.30; 12-3, 6-9 Sun; not 25 Dec) ~ Restaurant ~ (01829) 760529 ~ Children in restaurant ~ Trad jazz band Mon evening ~ Open 12-3, 5.30-11; 12-(11 Sat)10.30 Sun; closed 25 Dec

DARESBURY SJ5983 Map 7

Ring o' Bells

1½ miles from M56 junction 11; A56 N, then turn right on to B5356

This pleasantly relaxing pub manages to cleverly combine a spacious and airy atmosphere with a cosy, homely feel, and there's a good choice of places to sit. On the right is a comfortable, down-to-earth part popular with walkers from the nearby canal, while the left has more of a library style, and some reflection of its 19th-c use as a magistrates' court; in winter the coal fire is a real bonus. The long bar counter has well kept Courage Directors, Greenalls Bitter and Theakstons, and a couple of weekly changing guests such as Charles Wells Bombardier or Mauldons Black Adder on handpump, and all their wines are available by the glass; they've a dozen malt whiskies too. Well liked bar food from an enjoyable menu could include soup (£2.95), sandwiches (from £2.95, hot baguettes from £4.10), filled baked potatoes (from £3.95), ploughman's (from £4.25), whitebait (£4.50), thai red chicken curry (£7.95), smoked chicken pesto penne (£8.50), chicken breast stuffed with camembert and wrapped in bacon (£8.35), and grilled bass (£10.95); two of the dining rooms are no smoking. Although there are plenty of tables in the long partly terraced garden, in summer you have to be quick to get a seat. This is a pretty village, and from the front of the pub you can see the church where Lewis Carroll's father was vicar – one window shows all the characters in *Alice in Wonderland*. This is a Chef & Brewer, and there's piped music and a fruit machine; all rooms have wheelchair access, and they provide highchairs for children. *(Recommended by Pat and Tony Martin, E G Parish, Graham and Lynn Mason, Roy and Lindsey Fentiman, Hugh A MacLean, Hilary Forrest, Mr and Mrs J Williams, Mrs P J Carroll, David A Hammond, Andrew York)*

Spirit Group ~ Manager Martin Moylon ~ Real ale ~ Bar food (12-(9.30 Sun)10) ~ (01925) 740256 ~ Children in eating area of bar ~ Open 11-11; 12-10.30 Sun; closed 25 Dec evening

EATON SJ8765 Map 7

Plough

A536 Congleton—Macclesfield

There's a nicely civilised feel to this handsome 17th-c village pub, a well run place where the various extensions and extra facilities have been conceived with some aplomb. The appealingly designed bedrooms are in a converted stable block, and the old raftered barn at the back – used as the restaurant – was moved here piece by piece from its original home in Wales. Smart but welcoming, the neat bar has plenty of beams and exposed brickwork, comfortable armchairs and cushioned wooden wall seats, long red curtains leading off to a cosy no smoking room, mullioned windows, and a big stone fireplace; there are a couple of snug little alcoves. The big tree-filled garden is attractive, with good views of the nearby hills, and there are picnic-sets on the lawn and a smaller terrace. Very good home-made bar food might include lunchtime sandwiches, soup (£3.20), black pudding and apple baked in a tartlet case (£4.20), steak and kidney pudding (£7.95), thai green curry (£8.50), lamb rump on parsnip mash with honey and rosemary (£9.95), and pink duck breast with plum sauce and stir-fried vegetables and egg noodles (£12.50); they do a three-course Sunday lunch for £10.95. Hydes Bitter and Jekylls Gold and Wadworths 6X on hand pump, and a decent expanding wine list; they have a happy hour between 4 and 7 (not Sun). Service is friendly and attentive. They run regular quiz and curry nights; piped music. *(Recommended by Arthur Baker, E G Parish, Jack Morley)*

Free house ~ Licensee Mujdat Karatas ~ Real ale ~ Bar food ~ Restaurant ~ (01260) 280207 ~ Dogs allowed in bar ~ Open 11-11; 12-10.30 Sun ~ Bedrooms: £50B/£70B

HAUGHTON MOSS SJ5855 Map 6

Nags Head

Turn off A49 S of Tarporley into Long Lane, at 'Beeston, Haughton' signpost

Dating back to the 16th c, this pretty black and white country pub is immaculatly kept. Black and white tiles gleam by the serving counter, with pews and a heavy settle by the fire in a small quarry-tiled room on the left, and button-back wall banquettes in the carpeted room on the right, which also has logs burning in a copper-hooded fireplace. Below the heavy black beams are shelves of pewter mugs, attractive Victorian prints and a few brass ornaments. On the right is a sizeable carpeted dining area, and an extension has a dining room conservatory with oak beams; there may be very quiet piped music. Outside, there's a big neat garden with well spaced picnic-sets, a good little adventure playground, and even a bowling green. They do a reasonably priced self-service buffet (12-2 weekdays; £5.85), and snacks such as sandwiches (£3.50), filled baked potatoes (£3.95), omelettes (£3.60) and ploughman's (£5.80), served till 4.30. Other well liked home-made bar food could include soup (£3.15), fishcakes (£4.15), mushroom stroganoff or gammon and egg (£8.20), and steak (£10.80); there's a puddings trolley and various ice-creams (£2.95). There are well chosen generous wines, and Flowers and Wadworths 6X on handpump; efficient service. The front window of the pub is full of charmingly arranged collector's dolls. More reports please. *(Recommended by E G Parish, Dr G B Carter, Mrs P J Carroll)*

Free house ~ Licensees Rory and Deborah Keigan ~ Real ale ~ Bar food (12-9; 12-10 Fri and Sat) ~ Restaurant ~ (01829) 260265 ~ Children in eating area of bar and restaurant ~ Open 12-11(10.30 Sun); closed evening 25 Dec

HIGHER BURWARDSLEY SJ5256 Map 7

Pheasant (food award)

Burwardsley signposted from Tattenhall (which itself is signposted off A41 S of Chester) and from Harthill (reached by turning off A534 Nantwich—Holt at the Copper Mine); follow pub's signpost on up hill from Post Office; OS Sheet 117 map reference 523566

Popular with walkers and motorists, this half-timbered and sandstone 17th-c pub is well placed for the Sandstone Trail along the Peckforton Hills. It's a great place if you like views: on a clear day the telescope on the terrace lets you make out the pier head and cathedrals in Liverpool, while from the well spaced tables inside you can see right across the Cheshire plain. The bar has a bright modern feel, with wooden floors and light-coloured furniture. The see-through fireplace is said to house the largest log fire in the county, and there's a pleasant no smoking conservatory. Besides lunchtime sandwiches (£3.70), and ploughman's made with freshly baked bread (£6.95), superbly cooked dishes could include soup (£3.30), mussels (£4.95), game terrine (£5.95), pork loin (£10.95), corn-fed chicken with fondant potatoes (£11.95), and rib-eye steak (£11.95), with puddings such as crème brûlée (£5.25). Good service from the friendly young staff. Four very well kept ales on handpump from the local Weetwood brewery, and over 30 malts; piped music, daily newspapers. A big side lawn has picnic-sets, and on summer weekends they sometimes have barbecues. Be warned that there's a flight of stairs to the entrance. *(Recommended by Chris Hutt, B A Jackson, F H Saint, Liz Hryniewicz, Mrs P J Carroll, E G Parish, J S Burn)*

Free house ~ Licensee Simon McLoughlin ~ Real ale ~ Bar food (12-2.30, 6.30-9.30; Sun 12-4, 6.30-8.30) ~ Restaurant ~ (01829) 770434 ~ Children welcome ~ Dogs welcome ~ Open 12-11; 12-10.30 Sun ~ Bedrooms: £65B/£80B

LANGLEY SJ9569 Map 7

Hanging Gate

Meg Lane, Higher Sutton; follow Langley signpost from A54 beside Fourways Motel, and that road passes the pub; from Macclesfield, heading S from centre on A523 turn left into Byrons Lane at Langley, Wincle signpost; in Sutton (½ mile after going under canal bridge, ie before Langley) fork right at Church House Inn, following Wildboarclough signpost, then 2 miles later turning sharp right at steep hairpin bend; OS Sheet 118 map reference 952696

This welcoming old drover's inn was first licensed around 300 years ago, but is thought to have been built long before that. The three cosy low-beamed rambling rooms are simply and traditionally furnished with some attractive old prints of Cheshire towns, and big coal fires; piped music. Down some stone steps, the recently extended airy garden room has terrific views; the appealingly snug blue room, with its little chaise longue, is no smoking. Well kept Hydes Bitter, Jekylls Gold and a guest from the brewery on handpump, and they've got quite a few malt whiskies, along with 8 wines by the glass; service is very friendly and attentive. Popular bar food could include soup (£2.95), prawns in filo parcels or deep-fried camembert (£3.95), fried cod (£7.65), steaks (from £8.95), and delicious lamb chops (£10.50), with puddings such as crème caramel (£3.45); best to book on weekends. The pub is set high on a Peak District ridge, and seats out on the crazy-paved terrace give spectacular views over a patchwork of valley pastures to distant moors, and the tall Sutton Common transmitter above them. *(Recommended by Sheila and Phil Stubbs, Mr and Mrs Colin Roberts, the Didler, Derek and Heather Manning, M and GR, Stephen Buckley, Mike and Wendy Proctor, Nick and Lynne Carter, Mandy and Simon King)*

Hydes ~ Tenants Peter and Paul McGrath ~ Real ale ~ Bar food (not Sun evening) ~ Restaurant ~ (01260) 252238 ~ Children in eating area of bar ~ Open 12-3, 7-11; 12-11 Sat; 12-10.30 Sun

LOWER PEOVER SJ7474 Map 7

Bells of Peover

The Cobbles; from B5081 take short cobbled lane signposted to church

What makes this wisteria-covered Chef & Brewer special is its beautiful setting, off the beaten track in a peaceful hamlet. In front, seats on the crazy-paved terrace overlook a fine black and white 14th-c church, while at the side a spacious lawn beyond the old coachyard spreads down through trees and under rose pergolas to a little stream. Inside the neatly kept tiled bar is cosy, with side hatches for its serving counter, and toby jugs and comic Victorian prints; the original lounge has antique settles, high-backed windsor armchairs and a spacious window seat, antique china in the dresser, and pictures above the panelling. There are two small coal fires, and two of the three rooms are no smoking; dominoes, cribbage and piped music. Courage Directors, Greenalls and Theakstons are well kept on handpump, and all their wines are available by the glass; good tea. Bar food such as sandwiches (from £2.95), filled baked potatoes (from £3.95), ploughman's (from £4.25), smoked chicken and pesto penne (£8.50) and steak (£10.50), with specials such as fried red snapper with green thai cream (£10.95), and puddings such as hot chocolate truffle pudding (£4.50). *(Recommended by Darly Graton, Graeme Gulibert, the Didler, Andrew Scarr, Revd D Glover, Steve Whalley, Brenda and Stuart Naylor, Stephen Buckley, Patrick Hancock, Catherine and Rob Dunster, Dr T E Hothersall)*

Spirit Group ~ Manager Richard Casson ~ Real ale ~ Bar food (11-10; 12-9 Sun) ~ (01565) 722269 ~ Children in family room until 9pm ~ Open 11-11; 12-10.30 Sun

MACCLESFIELD SJ9271 Map 7

Sutton Hall Hotel ★

Leaving Macclesfield southwards on A523, turn left into Byrons Lane signposted Langley, Wincle, then just before canal viaduct fork right into Bullocks Lane; OS Sheet 118 map reference 925715

Charming inside and out, this 16th-c baronial hall is a good place for a civilised meal. It stands in lovely grounds with tables on the tree-sheltered lawn, and ducks and moorhens swimming in the pond. Divided into separate areas by tall oak timbers, the bar has some antique squared oak panelling, lightly patterned art nouveau stained-glass windows, broad flagstones around the bar counter (carpet elsewhere), and a raised open fire. It's mostly furnished with straightforward ladderback chairs around sturdy thick-topped cast-iron-framed tables, but there are a few unusual touches such as a suit of armour by a big stone fireplace, a longcase clock, a huge bronze bell for calling time, and a brass cigar-lighting gas taper on the bar counter itself. There's a good relaxed atmosphere, and the staff are friendly and efficient. Enjoyable bar food might include soup (£3.25), sandwiches (from £3.75, toasties from £4.75), home-made lasagne or cheese basket filled with sautéed leeks (£6.95), grilled gammon and pineapple (£8.50), and battered cod and chips (£8.55), with changing specials such as fried pigeon breast or grilled asparagus wrapped in smoked salmon (£5.45), home-made chilli con carne (£7.25), and cajun salmon caesar salad (£8.75); puddings such as crème brûlée and sticky toffee pudding (£3.50). Well kept Bass, Greene King IPA, Marstons Best and a guest such as York Brideshead Revisited are well kept on handpump, and there are over 40 malt whiskies, decent wines, freshly squeezed fruit juice, and well prepared Pimms. If you're lucky enough to be staying here, they can arrange clay shooting, golf or local fishing; there's access to canal moorings at Gurnett Aqueduct 200 yards away. *(Recommended by the Didler, Hugh A MacLean, June and Ken Brooks, Mrs P J Carroll, Derek and Sylvia Stephenson, Mart Lawton, MLR)*

Free house ~ Licensee Robert Bradshaw ~ Real ale ~ Bar food (12-2.30, 7-10) ~ Restaurant ~ (01260) 253211 ~ Children in restaurant ~ Dogs allowed in bedrooms ~ Open 11-11; 12-10.30 Sun ~ Bedrooms: £79.95B/£94.95B

You can send us reports through our web site: www.goodguides.co.uk

PEOVER HEATH SJ7973 Map 7

Dog

Off A50 N of Holmes Chapel at the Whipping Stocks, keep on past Parkgate into Wellbank Lane; OS Sheet 118 map reference 794735; note that this village is called Peover Heath on the OS map and shown under that name on many road maps, but the pub is often listed under Over Peover instead

The pretty garden of this friendly, civilised pub is nicely lit on summer evenings, and underneath colourful hanging baskets there are picnic-sets on the peaceful lane. The main bar is very comfortable, with easy chairs and wall seats (including one built into a snug alcove around an oak table), and two wood-backed seats built in either side of a coal fire, opposite which logs burn in an old-fashioned black grate. Well kept Hydes, Moorhouses Black Cat, Weetwood Best and a guest from a brewer such as Copper Dragon on handpump, Addlestone's cider, 35 different malt whiskies, and eight wines by the glass; darts, pool, dominoes, TV, and piped music. Service is very friendly and helpful. Enjoyable, reasonably priced bar food includes soup (£2.95), sandwiches (from £3.05, hot baguettes from £4.15), black pudding (£3.95), ploughman's (from £4.55), chilli con carne (£6.55), sausage of the day and mash (£7.55), steak and kidney pie, lamb shank braised in red wine with creamy mash and root vegetables or roast of the day (£9.95), and king cod with chips and mushy peas (£10.95), with puddings such as strawberry pavlova (£3.95). The dining room is no smoking; it's a good idea to book at weekends. There are picnic-sets too out on the rear lawn. It's a pleasant walk from here to the Jodrell Bank Centre and Arboretum. *(Recommended by Arthur Baker, Mr and Mrs Colin Roberts, JWAC, E G Parish, Revd D Glover, Andy Sinden, Louise Harrington, Mrs P J Carroll, David Field, Steve Whalley, Maurice and Della Andrew, Roger and Anne Newbury)*

Free house ~ Licensee Steven Wrigley ~ Real ale ~ Bar food (12-2.30, 6-9; 12-8.30 Sun; not evenings 25, 26 Dec) ~ Restaurant ~ (01625) 861421 ~ Children in eating area of bar and restaurant ~ Dogs allowed in bar ~ Live music one Friday in month ~ Open 11.30-3, 4.30-11; 11.30-11 Sat; 12-10.30 Sun ~ Bedrooms: £55B/£75B

PLUMLEY SJ7175 Map 7

Smoker

2½ miles from M6 junction 19: A556 towards Northwich and Chester

A good haven from the M6, the three connecting rooms of this welcoming 400-year-old pub are well decorated, with dark panelling, open fires in impressive period fireplaces, military prints, and a collection of copper kettles. Comfortable furnishings include deep sofas, cushioned settles, windsor chairs, and some rush-seat dining chairs. Look out for the Edwardian print of a hunt meeting outside, which shows how little the pub's appearance has changed over the centuries. They serve a good choice of wines with around a dozen by the glass, 23 malt whiskies, and Robinsons Unicorn, Hatters Mild and Old Stockport are well kept on handpump, alongside a guest such as Young Tom; good helpful service. There are no smoking areas in the bar; piped music, fruit machine. The same menu covers the bar and restaurant, and along with sandwiches (from £3.95), you'll find bar food such as soup (£2.95), baked potatoes (£4.25), garlic chicken wings (£4.45), lamb rogan josh (£7.95), seafood pasta bake (£8.55), beef stroganoff (£8.95), and ham hock with apricot and brandy sauce (£9.95). The sizeable side lawn has roses and flowerbeds, and the extended garden has a children's play area (readers tell us the fort could do with updating). The pub is named after a favourite racehorse of the Prince Regent. *(Recommended by Karen Eliot, E G Parish, J Silcock, Martin and Jane Bailey, Mart Lawton)*

Robinsons ~ Tenants John and Diana Bailey ~ Real ale ~ Bar food (12-2.15, 6-9.30; 12-9.30 Sun) ~ Restaurant ~ (01565) 722338 ~ Children in eating area of bar and restaurant ~ Open 11.30-3, 6-11; 12-10.30 Sun

PRESTBURY SJ8976 Map 7

Legh Arms

A538, village centre

A combination of inventive food, an interesting interior and a relaxed atmosphere makes this civilised 16th-c building a good place to spend an afternoon. Skilfully prepared dishes (the landlord is a well known Manchester restaurateur) might include soup (£2.95), lunchtime sandwiches (£4.25), spicy fishcakes with sweet chilli sauce or warm goats cheese with sweet onion and apple chutney on asparagus spears (£4.75), thai mild chicken curry (£6.95), pot-roasted pheasant with bacon, shallots, mushrooms and a suet dumpling (£7.25), wild mushroom risotto with herbs, asparagus and parsnip crisps (£7.95), salmon fillet with chargrilled vegetables and tomato confit (£9.25), and grilled calves liver on champ potatoes with grilled apple juices and rich juice (£11.25), with puddings such as home-made apple pie (£4.25); you can also eat from the more elaborate restaurant menu, and they have a good value set menu (£16.95 for three courses). The restaurant is comfortable and attractive; pleasant informal service from the uniformed staff. Opened up inside, the bar is well divided, with several distinctive areas: muted tartan fabric over a panelled dado on the right, with ladderback dining chairs, good solid dark tables, elegant french steam train prints, italian costume engravings and a glass case of china and books; brocaded bucket seats around similar tables, antique steeplechase prints, staffordshire dogs on the stone mantelpiece and a good coal fire on the left; a snug panelled back part with cosy wing armchairs and a grand piano; a narrow side offshoot with pairs of art deco leather armchairs around small granite tables, and more antique costume prints, of french tradesmen. The bar, towards the back on the left, has well kept Robinsons Best and Hatters Mild on handpump and nice house wines, good coffee, and maybe genial regulars chatting on the comfortable leather bar stools; this part looks up to an unusual balustraded internal landing. There are daily papers on a coffee table, and an antique oak dresser with magazines below and menus on top; piped music. A garden behind has tables and chairs. More reports please. *(Recommended by Mrs P J Carroll)*

Robinsons ~ Tenant Peter Myers ~ Real ale ~ Bar food (12-2, 7-9(10 Fri/Sat), 12-10 Sun) ~ Restaurant ~ (01625) 829130 ~ Children welcome till 7.30 ~ Open 12-11(10.30 Sun) ~ Bedrooms: /£80B

TARPORLEY SJ5563 Map 7

Rising Sun

High Street; village signposted off A51 Nantwich—Chester

Quite a sight in summer with its mass of colourful hanging baskets and flowering tubs, this friendly bustling pub is set in a pretty village. The cosy rooms have well chosen tables surrounded by eye-catching old seats including creaky 19th-c mahogany and oak settles, and there's also an attractively blacked iron kitchen range, sporting and other old-fashioned prints on the walls, and a big oriental rug in the back room. Vegetarians can choose from around a dozen different dishes on the wide-ranging menu, with bar food such as black bean sizzler, spinach pancakes and lasagne (all £8.50), and the menu also includes a variety of tasty pies (from £6.65), poached salmon with prawn and tomato sauce (£8.25), beef stroganoff (£8.95); they also do snacks too such as soup (£2.50), sandwiches (from £2.65), toasties and filled baked potatoes (from £3.10); helpful service. Well kept Robinsons Best, Hartleys Cumbria Way and Hatters Mild on handpump. *(Recommended by F H Saint, Maurice and Della Andrew, E G Parish, the Didler, Mrs P J Carroll)*

Robinsons ~ Tenant Alec Robertson ~ Real ale ~ Bar food (11.30-2, 5.30-9.30; 12-9 Sun) ~ Restaurant (evening) ~ (01829) 732423 ~ Children lunchtime away from bar, restaurant only in the evening ~ Open 11.30-3, 5.30-11; 11.30-11 bank hols; 11.30-11 Sat; 12-10.30 Sun

WETTENHALL SJ6261 Map 7

Boot & Slipper

From B5074 on S edge of Winsford, turn into Darnhall School Lane, then right at Wettenhall signpost: keep on for 2 or 3 miles; OS Sheet 118 map reference 625613

With a relaxed welcoming atmosphere, the knocked-through beamed main bar of this pleasant old pub has three shiny old dark settles, more straightforward chairs, and a fishing rod above the deep low fireplace with its big log fire. The modern bar counter also serves the left-hand communicating beamed room with its shiny pale brown tiled floor, cast-iron-framed long table, panelled settle and bar stools; darts, dominoes, and piped music. An unusual trio of back-lit arched pseudo-fireplaces forms one stripped-brick wall, and there are two further areas on the right, as well as an attractive back restaurant with big country pictures. Bass and Tetleys on handpump, a good choice of malt whiskies and a decent wine list; the landlady and staff are friendly. Tasty lunchtime dishes could include home-made soup (£2.75), good sandwiches (from £3.40), roast of the day, braised beef in red wine with shallots and baby mushrooms or poached scottish salmon with rich butter cream parsley sauce (all £5.95), with evening dishes such as deep-fried breaded brie with tangy cumberland sauce (£4.75), leek and potato bake (£8.50), trout grilled with garlic butter and herbs (£9.95), pork fillet with black pudding and black peppercorn sauce (£10.85), and mixed grill (£14.50), with puddings such as fruit pie (£3.50); children's meals (£3.80). It's best to book on weekends. There are picnic-sets out on the cobbled front terrace by the big car park; children's play area. The bedrooms are good value. *(Recommended by E G Parish, Leo and Barbara Lionet, Alec and Joan Laurence, Mrs P J Carroll)*

Free house ~ Licensee Joan Jones ~ Real ale ~ Bar food (12-2, 6-9) ~ Restaurant ~ (01270) 528238 ~ Children in restaurant, and in eating area of bar till 8pm ~ Open 12-3, 5.30-11.30; 12-10.30 Sat and Sun ~ Bedrooms: £36S/£48S

WINCLE SJ9666 Map 7

Ship

Village signposted off A54 Congleton—Buxton

Tucked away in scenic countryside, this is said to be one of the oldest pubs in Cheshire. Great for relaxing in after a walk (there are plenty nearby to choose from), the two old-fashioned and simple little tap rooms have thick stone walls, and a coal fire; no piped music or games machines. Four well kept ales include Moorhouses Premier and Timothy Taylors Landlord with a couple of guests on handpump such as Copper Dragon Best and Storm Windgather, and they also have belgian beers, Weston's cider and fruit wines; dominoes. Tasty bar food could include home-made soup (£3.25), lunchtime sandwiches (from £3.95), oak-smoked bacon on bubble and squeak with hollandaise sauce and poached egg (£5.50), spinach, ricotta and roasted vegetable canelloni provençale (£8.95), grilled trout with tarragon and citrus butter (£9.95), lamb shank pie with rosemary mash and rich red wine gravy (11.50), and steak (£14.95), with specials such as home-made fishcakes with mushy peas (£5.25), and venison steak with rosemary mash, black pudding and red wine jus (£13.50); puddings might include home-made banoffi pie (£3.95). On Saturday evenings and Sunday lunchtimes (when it's best to book) it can get busy, and you might have to park on the steep, narrow road outside. A small garden has wooden tables. They sell their own book of local walks (£3). *(Recommended by Ian Phillips, the Didler, Peter Abbott, M and GR, Stephen Buckley, John Hillmer, Mike and Wendy Proctor)*

Free house ~ Licensee Giles Henry Meadows ~ Real ale ~ Bar food (not Mon) ~ Restaurant ~ (01260) 227217 ~ Children in family room ~ Dogs allowed in bar ~ Open 12-3, 7(5.30 Fri)-11; 12-11 Sat; 12-10.30 Sun; closed Mon (exc bank hols)

If we know a pub does summer barbecues, we say so.

WRENBURY SJ5948 Map 7

Dusty Miller

Village signposted from A530 Nantwich—Whitchurch

Charming even on a chilly, foggy winter's day, this attractively converted 19th-c mill enjoys a lovely peaceful setting by the Shropshire Union Canal. In fine weather picnic-sets on the gravel terrace, among rose bushes by the water, are a great place to sit – you get to them either by the towpath or by a high wooden catwalk over the River Weaver. Inside you get a good view of the striking counter-weighted drawbridge going up and down, from a series of tall glazed arches. The modern main bar area is comfortable, with long low-hung hunting prints on green walls, and the mixture of seats flanking the rustic tables includes tapestried banquettes, an ornate church pew and wheelback chairs; further in, a quarry-tiled part by the bar counter has an oak settle and refectory table. There's quite an emphasis on the food, and good, well presented dishes (made with mostly local ingredients) could include soup (£3.10), shropshire blue cheese pâté with fruit chutney (£4.25), staffordshire oatcake filled with courgette, tomato, peppers and coriander glazed with cheshire cheese (£7.25), chargrilled chicken fillet with peppered red cabbage and stilton sauce or jugged beef braised with red wine, onions, mushrooms, redcurrant jelly and spices served with garlic mash (£9.95), baked salmon with fresh asparagus and dill and tarragon mayonnaise or slow-roast duck breast with cumberland sauce and garlic mash (£10.25), and puddings such as profiteroles with warm chocolate sauce (£3.95); they also do sandwiches. The restaurant and five tables in the bar are no smoking; fresh flowers on tables. Friendly, eager-to-please staff serve well kept real ales such as Cwmbran Double Hop, Robinsons Hatters Mild and Unicorn Old Tom on handpump; eclectic piped music, dominoes. The pub can get very crowded in fine weather. *(Recommended by David Carr, Mike Schofield, Amanda Eames, Brenda and Stuart Naylor, Mrs P J Carroll, E G Parish)*

Robinsons ~ Tenant Mark Sumner ~ Real ale ~ Bar food (12-2, 6.30-9.30, all day Sun in summer; not Mon in winter) ~ Restaurant ~ (01270) 780537 ~ Children in eating area of bar and restaurant ~ Dogs allowed in bar ~ Open 12-3, 6-11; 11-11 Sat; 12-10.30 Sun; 12-3, 6-11 Sat/Sun in winter; closed Mon afternoon in winter

WYBUNBURY SJ6950 Map 7

Swan

B5071

This pretty pub stands next to a lovely sloping churchyard with great lime trees and an unusual leaning stone-built church tower. In winter two big fires warm the cosy two-room bar (one room divided off into different areas), which are full of bric-a-brac, with lots of copper and brass, ornate lamps and a magnificent model galleon. The comfortable seats include good bays built into the windows; the front lounge is no smoking. Enjoyable food (served by friendly staff) might be thick cut sandwiches (from £3.50, hot sandwiches from £5.95), ploughman's (£6.25), home-made soup (£2.95), creamy garlic mushrooms with melted brie (£4.50), good salmon and smoked haddock fishcakes with tomato and pesto salad (£7.95), sweet and sour vegetable and noodle stir fry (£8.25), glazed lamb shank on garlic and rosemary mash with rich redcurrant and port jus (£11.95), and steaks (from £13.95), with puddings such as warm pecan tart (£3.95); they do a two-course lunch (Tuesday to Friday) for £5.95. Well kept Jennings Cumberland and Cocker Hoop along with three guests on handpump such as Castle Rock Hemlock Best, Charles Wells Bombardier, and Greene King Abbot, and good reasonably priced wines; piped music, darts, fruit machine, cribbage and dominoes. There are picnic-sets under cocktail parasols in a neat garden, with a couple more in the sheltered back yard. *(Recommended by Mrs P J Carroll, Sue Holland, Dave Webster)*

Jennings ~ Lease Richard and Fiona Fitzgerald ~ Real ale ~ Bar food (12-2, 6.30-9.30; 12-8 Sun and bank hols) ~ (01270) 841280 ~ Children welcome ~ Dogs allowed in bar ~ Open 12-11(10.30 Sun); closed Mon until 5pm ~ Bedrooms: £40B/£65B

LUCKY DIP

Besides the fully inspected pubs, you might like to try these Lucky Dips recommended to us and described by readers (if you do, please send us reports: www.goodguides.co.uk).

ADLINGTON SJ9381
Miners Arms [Wood Lane N, by Middlewood Way and Macclesfield Canal]: Extended family dining pub, pleasant efficient service even when packed, reasonably priced food from sandwiches up inc smaller helpings, plenty of quiet corners, no smoking area, well kept Boddingtons and Theakstons; picnic-sets and play area outside, good setting by Macclesfield Canal *(Brian and Anna Marsden)*

ALPRAHAM SJ5859
Tollemache Arms [Chester Rd (A51)]: Extended family pub with country décor, interesting pictures and bric-a-brac, cheerful bar, separate dining areas, reasonably priced food all day, real ales inc Greene King Old Speckled Hen, good service, open stove; big play area outside *(E G Parish, Pete Baker)*
Travellers Rest [A51 Nantwich—Chester]: Chatty four-room country local with veteran landlady (same family for three generations), particularly well kept Tetleys Bitter and Mild, leatherette, wicker and Formica, some flock wallpaper, fine old brewery mirrors, darts, back bowling green; no machines, piped music or food (apart from crisps and nuts), cl wkdy lunchtimes *(the Didler, Pete Baker)*

ALSAGER SJ7956
Wilbraham Arms [Sandbach Rd N (B5078)]: Large open-plan pub with comfortable armchairs and banquettes, well kept Robinsons ales from long bar, good choice of food (very popular with older lunchers), helpful service, ample no smoking area, big conservatory dining area; play area, popular jazz Sun and summer Thurs *(E G Parish)*

ANDERTON SJ6475
Stanley Arms [just NW of Northwich; Old Rd]: Busy friendly local in pleasant surroundings overlooking Anderton boat lift, wide choice of good value generous food all day from toasted sandwiches and baked potatoes to Sun lunch, well kept real ales, agreeable dining area, children welcome; tables in attractive yard with grassy play area, overnight mooring *(E A Eaves)*

BELL O' TH' HILL SJ5245
Blue Bell [just off A41 N of Whitchurch]: Heavily beamed partly 14th-c country local with friendly new licensees, well kept ales, two cosy and attractive rooms, pub dogs; pleasant garden and surroundings *(LYM, John and Wendy Allin)*

BOLLINGTON SJ9377
Church House [Church St]: Small village pub with wide reasonably priced food choice from standard snacks to swordfish and tuna (can book tables for busy lunchtimes), quick friendly service, well kept ales such as Flowers, Theakstons and Timothy Taylors Landlord, good range of wines, furnishings inc pews and working sewing-machine treadle tables, roaring fire, separate dining room, provision for children; five bedrooms *(DJH, Dr W J M Gissane, Michael Doswell)*
☆ *Poachers* [Mill Lane]: Friendly stone-built village local, well kept Boddingtons, Timothy Taylors Landlord and two guest beers such as local Storm, decent wines, good home-made food with appealingly priced lunches attracting older people and more upscale evening choice, helpful and attentive young licensees; attractive secluded garden and terrace behind, pretty setting, handy for walkers, cl Mon lunchtime *(Stephen Buckley, MLR, Brian and Anna Marsden)*

BOTTOM OF THE OVEN SJ9872
☆ *Stanley Arms* [A537 Buxton—Macclesfield, 1st left past Cat & Fiddle]: Isolated moorland pub, small, friendly and cosy, lots of shiny black woodwork, plush seats, dimpled copper tables, open winter fires in all rooms inc dining room, generous well cooked traditional food, well kept Marstons and guest beers; children welcome, piped music; picnic-sets on grass behind, may close Mon in winter if weather bad *(LYM, Stephen Buckley, Mike and Wendy Proctor, Richard Waller, Pauline Smith)*

BRADFIELD GREEN SJ6859
☆ *Coach & Horses* [A530 NW of Crewe]: Doing well under new licensees, good blackboard food choice from sandwiches up in comfortable bar and nicely set restaurant section, hospitable staff, well kept real ales, good value house wine, horse-racing pictures; discreet piped music *(E G Parish)*

BRERETON GREEN SJ7864
☆ *Bears Head* [handy for M6 junction 17; set back off A50 S of Holmes Chapel]: Handsome old heavily timbered inn doing well under new management, good choice of well prepared enjoyable fresh food, good service, well kept ales and decent wines by the glass, welcoming and civilised linked rooms with old-fashioned furniture, flagstones, carpets and hop-hung low beams, cheerful log fires, daily papers; open all day, good value bedrooms in modern block *(Ian Phillips, LYM, E G Parish)*

BRIDGE TRAFFORD SJ4569
Nags Head [A52]: Comfortable and friendly, with popular food; attractive garden *(Angie Coles)*

BROOMEDGE SJ7086
Jolly Thresher [Higher Lane]: Spacious open-plan pub with country chairs and tables on stripped boards, two open fires, good value generous food from lunchtime sandwiches up, well kept Hydes, pub games and neat restaurant; piped music, occasional folk nights *(LYM, Mr and Mrs Colin Roberts)*

BROWNLOW SJ8360
Brownlow Inn [Brownlow Heath Lane, off A34 S of Congleton]: Tucked-away well furnished traditional country pub, wide choice of good value food from baguettes up (should book for the popular Sun lunch), choice of

beers, reasonably priced house wine, good friendly staff, log fire, dining room and conservatory *(Pauline and Terry James)*

BURLEYDAM SJ6042

Combermere Arms [A525 Whitchurch—Audlem]: 16th-c beamed pub being reopened by Brunning & Price (see Grosvenor Arms, Aldford main entry); should be well worth knowing for their usual blend of enjoyable food, good beers, wines and service, and appealing ambiance – reports please *(LYM)*

BUTLEY TOWN SJ9177

Butley Ash [A523 Macclesfield—Stockport]: Popular dining pub with well kept ales such as Boddingtons, Greene King IPA and Charles Wells Bombardier, wide choice of generous food, interlinked areas inc 'library', attentive staff *(LYM, Mr and Mrs P J Barlow)*

CHESTER SJ4166

☆ *Boot* [Eastgate Row N]: Down-to-earth and relaxed pub in lovely 17th-c Rows building, heavy beams, lots of dark woodwork, oak flooring and flagstones, even some exposed Tudor wattle and daub, black-leaded kitchen range in lounge beyond good value food servery, no smoking oak-panelled upper area popular with families (despite hard settles), good service, cheap well kept Sam Smiths; piped music, downstairs can be smoky, children allowed *(the Didler, Mr and Mrs Colin Roberts, Kevin Blake, LYM, Sue Holland, Dave Webster, Joe Green)*

☆ *Falcon* [Lower Bridge St]: Striking ancient building with handsome beams and brickwork, well kept Sam Smiths, good value lunches (not Sun), friendly helpful staff; piped music, fruit machine; children allowed lunchtime (not Sat) in airy and attractive no smoking room upstairs; open all day Sat (can get packed then, with lunchtime jazz), interesting tours of the vaults *(Mr and Mrs S Felstead, LYM, Sue Holland, Dave Webster, Patrick Hancock, Angie Coles, Andrew York)*

☆ *Mill* [Milton St]: A dozen or more changing well kept and well priced ales from smaller breweries inc a Mild and one brewed for them by Coach House in neat and comfortably carpeted sizeable bar to right of smart hotel reception, relaxed mix of customers from teenagers to older folk and ladies lunching (good value ciabattas and enjoyable hot dishes, till late evening), friendly efficient staff, restaurant overlooking canal (good value Sun lunch); quiet piped music, unobtrusively placed big-screen SkyTV, jazz Mon; good with children, waterside benches, boat trips; good bedrooms, open all day *(Sue Holland, Dave Webster, BB, the Didler, Edward Leetham, Joe Green, Patrick Hancock, Martin Grosberg, Colin Moore)*

☆ *Old Custom House* [Watergate St]: Traditional bare-boards bar well furnished with settles, high chairs and leatherette wall seats, lounge with cosy corners, prints, etchings, panelling and coal-effect gas fire, well kept Banks's and Marstons Bitter and Pedigree, well reproduced piped music, fruit machine; open all day *(BB, Michael Butler)*

Olde Kings Head [Lower Bridge St]: Fine old timbered building, lots of woodwork, beams and bric-a-brac, coal fires, low lighting, friendly efficient bar service, well kept real ale, lunchtime bar food; upstairs restaurant and hotel part, comfortable bedrooms *(Kevin Blake, Angie Coles)*

Pied Bull [Upper Northgate St]: Roomy open-plan carpeted bar, attractive mix of individual furnishings, divided inner area with china cabinet and lots of pictures, nice snug by pillared entrance, imposing intriguingly decorated fireplace; wide choice of generous reasonably priced food all day inc afternoon teas, real ales, attentive welcoming staff, no smoking area; fruit machines, may be piped music; open all day, handsome Jacobean stairs up to bedrooms *(Kevin Blake, BB, Michael Butler)*

Telfords Warehouse [Tower Wharf, behind Northgate St nr rly]: Converted canal building, bare brick and boards, high pitched ceiling, big wall of windows overlooking water, massive iron winding gear in bar, some old enamelled advertisements, good photographs for sale; several well kept ales such as Timothy Taylors Landlord, good wine choice, up to date freshly made generous food, efficient friendly staff, steps to heavy-beamed restaurant area with more artwork; live music Fri/Sat (very busy then), tables out by water *(BB, Martin and Rose Bonner, Sue Holland, Dave Webster, Angie Coles)*

Union Vaults [Francis St/Egerton St]: Unreconstructed corner alehouse with well kept and reasonably priced Greenalls, Timothy Taylors Landlord and a guest beer (suggestions book), friendly knowledgeable staff, bagatelle, dominoes, cards and two TV sports channels, back room with pool, two quieter upper rooms; piped music; open all day *(the Didler, Sue Holland, Dave Webster, Patrick Hancock, Martin Grosberg, Joe Green)*

CHILDER THORNTON SJ3678

☆ *White Lion* [off A41 S of M53 junction 5; New Rd]: Low two-room whitewashed proper pub, old-fashioned and unpretentious, with well kept Thwaites Bitter, Mild and Lancaster Bomber, enjoyable well priced down-to-earth wkdy lunches from good ciabattas and hot filled rolls up, welcoming staff, open fire, framed matchbooks, no music or machines (small TV for big matches); tables out in sheltered area behind, swings in nice quiet front garden *(Pete Moore, MLR, Mrs P J Carroll, Angie Coles)*

CHURCH MINSHULL SJ6660

Badger [B5074 Winsford—Nantwich; handy for Shrops Union Canal, Middlewich branch]: Roomy village pub concentrating on enjoyable blackboard food using local produce in bar and restaurant, OAP lunches Mon-Thurs, staff eager to please; street-facing windows heavily screened off; tables in garden behind, pretty village, open all day wknds *(E G Parish, LYM)*

CONGLETON SJ8663

Beartown Tap [Willow St]: Light and airy tap for nearby Beartown small brewery, their well priced beers and perhaps a guest microbrew from six handpumps, changing farm cider, bottled belgians, bare boards in friendly bar and two pleasant rooms off, no games or music; upstairs lavatories; open all day Fri-Sun *(the Didler)*

COPPENHALL MOSS SJ7058

White Lion [Warmingham Rd]: Tasteful furnishings in comfortably opened-up lounge, wide choice of reasonably priced bar food from melted cheese chip butties up, hands-on landlord and friendly helpful staff, Boddingtons and Marstons Pedigree, attractive sunny restaurant; picnic-sets on lawn, farmland just outside Crewe *(E G Parish)*

COTEBROOK SJ5765

☆ *Alvanley Arms* [A49/B5152 N of Tarporley]: Fine old sandstone inn, 16th-c behind its Georgian façade, with three attractive beamed rooms (two no smoking areas), big open fire, chintzy little hall, shire horse décor (plenty of tack and pictures – adjacent stud open in season), good generous food with extra lunchtime snack choice and good value specials, Robinsons Best and a seasonal beer, good service; garden with pond and trout, seven good bedrooms with own bathrooms *(Olive and Ray Hebson, T R Emdy, LYM, MLR, Jean and Douglas Troup, Susie Symes)*

CREWE SJ7055

Borough Arms [Earle St]: Titanic Bitter, Mild and Stout and half a dozen or more interesting guest beers from small breweries in top condition, five or six foreign beers on tap and dozens in bottle, friendly and dedicated landlord, two small plain rooms off central bar, railway theme, green décor – restaurant and basement microbrewery on the wish list; games machine, TV, cl wkdy lunchtimes *(the Didler, E G Parish, Martin Grosberg)*

Cheshire Cheese [Crewe Rd, Shavington (B5071)]: Comfortably refurbished and roomy chain family dining pub, quiet alcoves, good friendly young staff, above-average bar food inc OAP and other bargains, less sedate evenings, well kept real ales; good parking and disabled access, high chairs, baby-changing, tables outside, play area *(Mike and Mary Carter)*

Crown [Earle St]: Popular high-ceilinged refurbished local with welcoming landlady, well kept Robinsons, traditional snug with service bell pushes, back games area; handy for Railway Heritage Centre *(E G Parish, Pete Baker)*

Express [Mill St]: Comfortable local with well kept ale, a welcome for visitors; sports TV, theme nights *(E G Parish)*

Gaffers Row [Victoria St]: Spacious and attractive new Wetherspoons, decent food all day, well spaced tables, good choice of real ales from invitingly long bar counter, polite service, reasonable prices, pleasant family section; soft piped music, games machines *(E G Parish)*

Rising Sun [Middlewich Rd (A530), Wolstanwood]: Chef & Brewer comfortably done out in olde-worlde style with beamery, panelling, prints and lots of separate areas, wide choice of enjoyable food from doorstep sandwiches and melts to quite a list of specials (may take quite a while), well kept ales such as Courage and White Star, occasional beer festivals, raised eating area; children's facilities, good disabled access (inc lift), tables and play area outside, open all day, quiet countryside *(Martin Grosberg, E G Parish)*

DISLEY SJ9784

Rams Head [A6]: Enjoyable food inc good choice of Sun roasts, separate no smoking area; large enclosed garden behind *(Jane McConaghie)*

FARNDON SJ4154

Farndon Arms [High St]: Nicely decorated timbered pub in pretty village, unpretentious bar with interesting choice of well kept seasonal real ales, decent straightforward bar food from sandwiches with chips up, friendly staff, smart upstairs restaurant area with much more ambitious menu; dogs welcome *(Mrs P J Carroll)*

FRODSHAM SJ5277

☆ *Ring o' Bells* [Bellemonte Rd, Overton – off B5152 at Parish Church sign; M56 junction 12 not far]: Friendly and distinctive early 17th-c pub, little rambling rooms (one no smoking), antique seating and prints, beams, dark oak panelling and stained-glass, three changing real ales from old-fashioned hatch-like central servery, 85 malt whiskies, good value lunchtime bar food, games room, three friendly pub cats; children in eating areas, secluded back garden with pond, colourful hanging baskets *(LYM, Mike Schofield, GSB, Mike Marsh)*

GAWSWORTH SJ8969

☆ *Harrington Arms* [Church Lane]: 17th-c farm pub with two small basic rooms (children allowed in one), bare boards and panelling, fine carved oak bar counter, Robinsons Best and Hatters Mild on handpump, friendly service, pickled eggs or onions, pork pies, fresh chunky lunchtime sandwiches; Fri folk night; sunny benches on small front cobbled terrace *(LYM, the Didler, R F Grieve, MLR)*

GOOSTREY SJ7869

☆ *Olde Red Lion* [Station Rd]: Comfortable open-plan bar and restaurant with relaxed atmosphere and well presented nourishing food inc Thurs OAP lunches, friendly efficient service, real ales, winter mulled wine; children welcome, nice garden with play area *(LYM, E G Parish)*

GRAPPENHALL SJ6386

Parr Arms [nr M6 junction 20; A50 towards Warrington, left after 1½ miles; Church Lane]: Pleasant pub with several different areas off central bar, good genuine home cooking, real ales, no piped music, rugby league photographs – landlord was captain of St Helens and an international; tables out by church, picture-postcard setting *(Pete and Josephine Cropper)*

GUILDEN SUTTON SJ4468

☆ *Bird in Hand* [Church Lane]: Good enterprising well presented food in quiet civilised dining pub, friendly service, good choice of well kept beer; children welcome

(Dr R A Smye, Philip Hastain, Andrea Brown)

HANDLEY SJ4758

☆ *Calveley Arms* [just off A41 S of Chester]: Good changing food from sandwiches and baguettes to interesting specials and fish dishes in black and white beamed country pub licensed since 17th c, courteous welcoming service (they even keep a visitors' book), well kept Boddingtons and Theakstons Black Bull with occasional guest beers and interesting soft drinks, open fire, cosy alcove seating, traditional games; piped music; very well behaved children allowed, secluded garden with boules *(E G Parish, LYM, Maurice and Della Andrew, Paul and Margaret Baker, Olive and Ray Hebson)*

HARTFORD SJ6371

Coachman [A559 SW of Northwich opp station]: Simply furnished two-bar former coaching inn with John Smiths, Tetleys and a guest beer, well cooked reasonably priced food, new back conservatory; unobtrusive piped music, big-screen TV; open all day *(Martin Grosberg)*

HASLINGTON SJ7355

Fox [Crewe Rd]: Large front family dining area, back bar and further dining area, pleasant décor, wide choice of generous food inc children's, well kept mainstream ales, friendly helpful staff *(Mrs P J Carroll)*

HEATLEY SJ7088

Green Dragon [Mill Lane]: Spacious and attractive, with well kept beer and enjoyable food *(Mike Marsh)*

HIGH LEGH SJ7084

Bears Paw [Warrington Rd (A50 E of M6 junction 20)]: Comfortable, popular and welcoming, two carpeted dining rooms off bar, enjoyable food (busy even midweek lunchtimes) cooked to order so may take a while, well kept Marstons Pedigree; tables out behind *(Mr and Mrs Colin Roberts)*

HOLLINGWORTH SK0096

Gun [Market St]: Well run, with decent value food (all day wknds) from baguettes up, well kept Boddingtons and Theakstons, bright friendly service *(Gerry and Rosemary Dobson)*

HOO GREEN SJ7283

Kilton [Warrington Rd (A50, a mile NW of A556)]: Pleasant refurbished Chef & Brewer with enjoyable sensibly priced food *(Andy and Jill Kassube)*

KELSALL SJ5268

Olive Tree [Chester Rd (A54)]: Refurbished in clean spare modern style, roomy and civilised, with two bars, wine bar area and restaurant, low beams and comfortable country-style furniture, enjoyable food inc interesting dishes (service can slow on Sun), pleasant relaxing atmosphere, well kept real ales inc local ones, decent wines, log fires *(E G Parish, Roger and Anne Newbury)*

KETTLESHULME SJ9879

☆ *Swan* [Macclesfield Rd (B5470)]: 16th-c, smart and well run, with traditional beamed décor and warm-hearted atmosphere, old settles and pews, Dickens prints, log fires, three or four well kept changing ales, tempting honest lunchtime food; good walks, open all day wknds, cl Mon lunchtime *(Ian and Liz Rispin, R A K Crabtree)*

KNUTSFORD SJ7578

Lord Eldon [Tatton St, off A50 at White Bear roundabout]: Compact former coaching inn, four rooms with well kept low-priced Tetleys, open fire, friendly hands-on landlord *(David Heath)*

LANGLEY SJ9471

☆ *Leathers Smithy* [off A523 S of Macclesfield, OS Sheet 118 map ref 952715]: Isolated pub up in fine walking country, sympathetic extensions to spotless flagstoned bar and newly carpeted dining room, attractive redecoration with interesting local prints and photographs, pleasant relaxing atmosphere, new kitchen producing wide-ranging enjoyable bar food (all day Sun) from sandwiches to exotic fish, good steaks and good value Sun roasts, log fire, winter glühwein and lots of whiskies, well kept Courage Directors, Marstons Pedigree, Theakstons Best and a guest beer, farm cider, quick cheerful service; unobtrusive piped music; family room but no dogs inside *(LYM, Stephen Buckley, Michael Porter, Mr and Mrs R P Begg)*

LITTLE BOLLINGTON SJ7286

☆ *Swan With Two Nicks* [2 miles from M56 junction 7 – A56 towards Lymm, then first right at Stamford Arms into Park Lane; use A556 to get back on to M56 westbound]: Refurbished beamed village pub full of brass, copper and bric-a-brac, some antique settles, log fire, good choice of generous above-average food from filling baguettes up, well kept ales such as Boddingtons, Greene King Old Speckled Hen and Timothy Taylors Landlord, decent wines, cheerful helpful staff; tables outside, open all day, attractive hamlet by Dunham Hall deer park, walks by Bridgewater Canal *(LYM, Mr and Mrs Colin Roberts, John and Sylvia Harrop)*

LOWER WHITLEY SJ6178

☆ *Chetwode Arms* [just off A49, handy for M56 junction 10; Street Lane]: Family dining pub with traditional layout, good original home cooking in side bar and other rooms (cheaper dishes not served evenings, when it's wortrh booking), generous helpings, solid furnishings all clean and polished, friendly local atmosphere in front bar, warm coal fires, four real ales, good wines by the glass, good service; immaculate bowling green, play area, has been open all day Sat *(LYM, Simon J Barber)*

LYMM SJ7087

Barn Owl [Agden Wharf, Warrington Lane (just off B5159 E)]: Comfortably extended pub in picturesque setting by Bridgewater Canal, good value fresh food inc popular OAP bargain lunches, well kept Marstons Bitter and Pedigree and two guest beers, decent wines by the glass, friendly atmosphere, pleasant service even though busy; disabled facilities, little ferry for customers (and may be canal trips), open all day *(Mrs P J Carroll)*

☆ *Spread Eagle* [not far from M6 junction 20; Eagle Brow]: Long rambling beamed village pub, very attractive black and white façade, big comfortable two-level lounge with good value home-made food all day from sandwiches and baguettes through two-course bargains to steaks, proper drinking area by central bar, particularly well kept Lees Bitter and Red Dragon, good choice of wines, cheery atmosphere and good service, coal fire, lots of brasses, separate games room with pool; piped music; attractive village *(Derek and Sylvia Stephenson, Pete Baker, BB)*

MACCLESFIELD SJ9273

Dolphin [Windmill St, just off A523 S]: Friendly three-room pub kept traditional in sympathetic refurbishment, good home-made lunchtime food at bargain prices, well kept Robinsons, darts and cards *(Pete Baker)*

Railway View [Byrons Lane (off A523)]: Half a dozen or more unusual changing ales in pair of 1700 cottages knocked into roomy pub with lots of intimate attractively furnished areas, farm cider, good value simple food, friendly staff and locals; back terrace overlooking railway, remarkably shaped gents'; cl lunchtime Mon-Thurs, open all day Fri-Sun *(the Didler)*

Waters Green Tavern [Waters Green, opp stn]: Boddingtons and three well kept interesting quickly changing guest beers in large L-shaped open-plan carpeted bar with padded seats, home-made lunchtime food (not Sun), friendly staff and locals, pool room; open all day *(the Didler)*

MARTON SJ8568

Davenport Arms [A34 N of Congleton]: Welcoming, comfortable and spaciously modernised, with generous good value home-made food in bar and restaurant inc popular Sun lunch, well kept real ales inc a Mild, speedy service, no smoking area; nr ancient half-timbered church (and Europe's widest oak tree) *(Dr D J and Mrs S C Walker, Mr and Mrs Colin Roberts)*

MICKLE TRAFFORD SJ4470

Shrewsbury Arms [Warrington Rd (A56)]: Roomy refurbished beamed and carpeted pub (quarry-tiled around servery), with reliable quickly served food inc light dishes in decent helpings, friendly staff, around four real ales; children welcome, tables outside *(John Andrew)*

MOBBERLEY SJ8079

☆ ***Bird in Hand*** [Knolls Green; B5085 towards Alderley]: Cosy low-beamed rooms with comfortably cushioned heavy wooden seats, warm coal fires, small pictures on Victorian wallpaper, little panelled snug, good no smoking top dining area, good choice of enjoyable promptly served food, summer afternoon teas, helpful quietly friendly service, well kept Sam Smiths, lots of malt whiskies, decent house wines, pub games; occasional piped music; children allowed, open all day *(LYM, Mrs P J Carroll)*

Plough & Flail [Paddock Hill; small sign off B5085 towards Wilmslow]: Friendly and relaxed three-room pub, well kept real ales, log fire, food all day from snacks to restaurant dishes inc carvery and some lunchtime bargains, decent wines; children welcome, good garden with play area *(Mrs P J Carroll, John Wooll)*

☆ ***Roebuck*** [Mill Lane; down hill from sharp bend on B5085 at E edge of 30mph limit]: Spacious and appealing open-plan bar with brasses, pews, polished boards, panelling and alcoves; good fresh food from lunchtime sandwiches to interesting modern hot dishes, very welcoming young staff, well kept real ales, no smoking area, upstairs restaurant; children welcome, can get busy Sat night; pretty outside, with tables in cobbled courtyard and pleasant extended two-level garden behind, play area *(Mrs P J Carroll, LYM, R F Grieve)*

NANTWICH SJ6552

☆ ***Black Lion*** [Welsh Row]: Three little rooms alongside main bar, old-fashioned nooks and crannies, beams and bare floors, big grandfather clock; three well kept local Weetwood ales and Titanic White Star, farm cider, cheap sandwiches, very friendly cat, chess; occasional live music; heated marquee outside, open all day *(BB, Pete Baker, Ken Flawn, Edward Leetham, the Didler)*

Oddfellows Arms [Welsh Row]: Enlarged without losing its pleasantly rustic low-ceilinged character, real fires, friendly staff, Burtonwood and perhaps a guest beer, reasonably priced generous home-made food; unobtrusive piped music, no smoke-free area; garden tables, lovely street, antique shops *(Graham Burns, Edward Leetham)*

Red Cow [Beam St]: New licensees keeping up the strong vegetarian and vegan tradition in this well renovated low-ceilinged former Tudor farmhouse's good value home-made food, well kept Robinsons and a guest beer, smallish lounge and bar, coal fire, relaxed atmosphere, no smoking dining area; terrace with pergola and play area, bedrooms being refurbished *(Edward Leetham)*

Shakespeare [Beam St]: Roomy and comfortable town pub, reputedly the oldest here, large dining room with very reasonably priced food inc all-afternoon Sun carvery and lots of special offers, real ales, good service; occasional live music; tables outside *(E G Parish)*

Vine [Hospital St]: Dates from 17th c though sympathetically modernised inside, stretching far back with dimly lit quiet corners, well kept Hydes beers inc seasonal ones, friendly service, pub games, cheap plain food; piped music; children welcome, open all day Sat, cl Mon lunchtime *(David Carr, BB, Roger and Anne Newbury)*

NESS SJ3076

Wheatsheaf [Neston Rd]: Large Thwaites roadhouse by Ness Gardens, overlooking Dee Estuary, sturdy comfortable furnishings in open-plan L-shaped bar with spacious alcoves, 1940s stained-glass, cheerful family food from baguettes up, friendly staff; sports TVs, games; picnic-sets on lawn, play area, open all day *(Paul Humphreys)*

NESTON SJ2976

☆ *Harp* [Quayside, SW of Little Neston; keep on along track at end of Marshlands Rd]: Tucked-away country local with particularly well kept ales such as Fullers London Pride, Greene King Abbot, Holts, Ind Coope Burton, Moorhouses Black Cat Mild and Timothy Taylors Landlord, good malt whiskies, woodburner in pretty fireplace, pale quarry tiles and simple furnishings (children allowed in room on right), lunchtime food; picnic-sets up on grassy front sea wall look out over the marshes of the Dee to Wales, glorious sunsets with wild calls of wading birds; open all day from noon *(BB, MLR, Paul Davies)*

Hinderton Arms [Chester High Rd (A540)]: Large tastefully decorated bar/dining area, Courage Directors and good choice of other drinks, enjoyable middle-priced pub food and lunchtime snacks, friendly service *(Paul Humphreys)*

NORLEY SJ5772

Tigers Head [Pytchleys Hollow]: Pleasantly refurbished and cheerful 17th-c inn nr Delamere Forest, good simple sensibly priced food, well kept real ales inc Moorhouses Black Cat Mild, no smoking area *(J S Burn)*

OVER PEOVER SJ7873

Olde Park Gate [Stocks Lane; off A50 N of Holmes Chapel at the Whipping Stock]: Popular country pub with generous food from sandwiches up, Sam Smiths *(LYM, Hilary Forrest)*

Whipping Stocks [Stocks Lane]: Several neatly kept rooms, good oak panelling and fittings, solid furnishings, well kept cheap Sam Smiths, friendly smartly dressed staff, big log fire, wide choice of low-priced popular straightforward food all day; children in eating area, picnic-sets in good-sized garden with safe play area, easy parkland walks *(LYM, E G Parish, Mike Marsh)*

PARKGATE SJ2778

☆ *Red Lion* [The Parade (B5135)]: Comfortable and neatly kept local on attractive waterfront, big windows look across road to silted grassy estuary with Wales beyond, typical pub furnishings, shiny brown beams hung with lots of china, copper and brass, standard food inc sandwiches, OAP lunches and other bargain offers, well kept Adnams, Tetleys and Charles Wells Bombardier, flame-effect fire in pretty Victorian fireplace, good games room off public bar; picnic-sets out on small front terrace, open all day *(BB, MLR)*

Ship [The Parade]: Picture-window estuary views from long bar of large hotel, well kept Theakstons and a guest such as Weetwood, good value bar food inc local fish, quick friendly service, open fire, restaurant; bedrooms *(MLR)*

POYNTON SJ9483

Boars Head [Shrigley Rd N, Higher Poynton, off A523]: Welcoming Victorian country pub, very friendly and unpretentious, well refurbished with button-back leather seats (and darts) in bar, lounge with good value home-made food (all day wknds) inc speciality pies, well kept reasonably priced Boddingtons and a guest beer, coffee etc, big open fire; next to Middlewood Way (ex-railway walk and cycle route) and Macclesfield Canal, handy for Lyme Park *(Pete and Kate Holford)*

RAINOW SJ9576

☆ *Highwayman* [A5002 Whaley Bridge—Macclesfield, NE of village]: Unchanging 17th-c moorside pub with small low-beamed rooms, well kept Thwaites ales, bar food inc good sandwiches and ideal black pudding, good winter fires (electric other times), plenty of atmosphere, lovely views *(LYM, the Didler, Stephen Buckley)*

SHOCKLACH SJ4349

Bull [off A534 from Wrexham at crossrds with Farndon]: Good food inc interesting dishes and wide range of puddings, changing daily, good value house wines, conservatory; can be very busy *(Mrs P J Carroll, Rita and Keith Pollard)*

SMALLWOOD SJ7861

☆ *Legs of Man* [A50 S of Sandbach]: Good home-cooked food inc some imaginative dishes and a suggestion of spanish or portuguese influence in comfortable roadside pub with carefully matched chairs, banquettes, carpet, curtains and wallpaper, fin de siècle tall white nymphs on columns, lush potted plants, well kept Robinsons ales, good friendly service even when busy; restaurant, children truly welcome; well spaced tables on side lawn with play area *(BB, Mrs P J Carroll)*

SPURSTOW SJ5657

Yew Tree [A49 S of Tarporley]: Pleasantly extended country pub doing well under new landlord from Madeira, limited tasty and reasonably priced food inc Sat specials, well kept mainstream beers, smiling faces; may be unobtrusive piped music *(Ken Black, John Lunt)*

STOCKPORT SJ8991

Navigation [Manchester Rd (B6167, former A626)]: Fairly basic pub recently perked up by local Beartown Brewery, seven of their ales and a well kept guest beer, several farm ciders tapped from cellar casks, continental imports, friendly landlady and staff; open all day *(the Didler)*

STRETTON SJ6282

Stretton Fox [Spark Hall Cl, Tarporley Rd, just off M56 junction 10 exit roundabout]: Spacious Bass Vintage Inn in sympathetically converted farmhouse, surprisingly rural setting, interesting variety of rooms, generous well priced food, welcoming staff, real ales and good choice of wines *(Simon J Barber)*

SUTTON SJ9469

☆ *Ryles Arms* [Hollin Lane, Higher Sutton]: Carefully extended popular dining pub in fine countryside, thriving atmosphere, consistently good generous food from sandwiches and juicy home-made burgers to game and interesting dishes, well kept Worthington and local Storm, decent well priced wines, good choice of whiskies, friendly helpful service, pleasant décor and some attractively individual furnishings, no smoking hill-view dining room, no music or games; french windows to terrace, new bedrooms in converted barn *(LYM, Mr and Mrs Colin Roberts, Mrs P J Carroll)*

SWETTENHAM SJ8067

Swettenham Arms [off A54 Congleton—Holmes Chapel or A535 Chelford—Holmes Chapel]: Attractive old country pub very popular for its pretty setting next to the Quinta (scenic wildlife area), wide choice of good food in charming series of individually furnished rooms from sofas and easy chairs to no smoking dining area (must book Sun), well spaced tables, well kept ales such as Beartown, Hydes, Jennings and Tetleys, farm cider, picnic-sets on quiet side lawn; children welcome, live music Weds *(LYM, E G Parish, Brenda and Stuart Naylor, Mrs P J Carroll)*

TARPORLEY SJ5562

Swan [High St, off A49]: Tastefully modernised Georgian inn with cosy little spaces, competent straightforward food from lunchtime sandwiches and snacks to restaurant dishes, polite service, real ales and good choice of other drinks; provision for children, tables outside, charming well equipped bedrooms, good breakfast in sunny former kitchen *(LYM, Susie Symes)*

TATTENHALL SJ4959

Bear & Ragged Staff [High St]: Warm, friendly and relaxing, with changing real ales, tasty well priced food, good coal fires in dining room; children welcome, tables in good-sized back garden *(Chris Smith)*

WARRINGTON SJ6091

Winwick Quay [Woburn Rd, just off M62 junction 9]: Handy for retail park, with good value food, quick friendly service though busy *(Mr and Mrs Colin Roberts)*

WESTON SJ7352

☆ *White Lion* [not far from M6 junction 16, via A500]: Pretty black and white timbered inn, low-beamed main room divided by gnarled black oak standing timbers, fine 18th-c style settles as well as more modern seating (some tables rather low), two no smoking side rooms, generous bar food, Bass and Jennings Cumberland, sizeable wine list, pleasant atmosphere, dominoes; piped music, TV, hosts business events; children in eating areas, lovely garden with bowling green, spacious bedrooms *(Philip and June Caunt, Martin Grosberg, Brenda and Stuart Naylor, Susie Symes, Mike and Mary Carter, John and Sylvia Harrop, LYM)*

WHEELOCK SJ7559

Commercial [off new A534 bypass; Game St]: Old-fashioned local, two smaller rooms (one no smoking) off high-ceilinged main bar, unaltered décor, Boddingtons, Marstons Pedigree, Thwaites and perhaps a guest beer, real fire, firmly efficient service, no food; pool in games room, may be Thurs folk night, open from 8 evenings only, and Sun lunchtime *(the Didler, Pete Baker, Howard Selina)*

WILLASTON SJ3277

Pollards [Village Sq, off B5151 just S of B5133 junction]: Striking partly 14th-c building with cheerily comfortable beamed and flagstoned bar, unusual cushioned wall seats with some stone armrests, wide choice of enjoyable food, real ales, restaurant; dining conservatory overlooking sizeable pleasant garden, bedrooms *(Olive and Ray Hebson)*

WILLINGTON SJ5367

☆ *Boot* [Boothsdale, off A54 at Kelsall]: Enjoyable dining pub in terrific hillside setting, views over Cheshire Plain to Wales, good if pricey food (all day wknds and bank hols), well kept Bass, Cains, Timothy Taylors Landlord and a guest from Weetwood, decent wine list, plenty of malt whiskies, small unpretentiously furnished areas around central bar, woodburner, no smoking area, log fire in charming restaurant; no under-8s; garden with picnic-sets on suntrap raised stone terrace, two donkeys, golden retriever H and cat called Sooty *(E G Parish, F H Saint, Mrs P J Carroll, Olive and Ray Hebson, LYM)*

WINTERLEY SJ7557

Forresters Arms [A534]: Cosy and friendly low-beamed village local with warmly welcoming cheerful and attentive landlord, inventive good value bar lunches from open-view kitchen, well kept Tetleys ales inc Dark Mild; darts and quiz night, Weds raffle; pleasant garden with dovecote and retired tractor *(E G Parish, Sue Holland, Dave Webster)*

Holly Bush [nr Sandbach on A534]: Comfortably restored after fire damage, food from light dishes to Sunday roasts, real ales inc Tetleys, good value wines, helpful young staff, ample seating, sensible tables and picture windows; large garden, play area, handy for canal *(E G Parish)*

WORLESTON SJ6556

Royal Oak [Main Rd (B5074 N of Nantwich)]: Roomy and largely no smoking cottagey pub with Boddingtons and Tetleys, reasonably priced well prepared food, pleasant young licensees and good service, well spaced tables in varying sizes; tables in good-sized wooded garden, handy for canal walks *(E G Parish)*

WRENBURY SJ5948

Cotton Arms [Cholmondeley Rd]: Welcoming beamed and timbered pub in popular spot by canal locks and boatyard, with good value food in two large comfortable dining areas, friendly staff, well kept real ales inc a guest beer, lots of brass, open fire, side games room *(Mike Schofield, E G Parish, Mrs P J Carroll)*

We checked prices with the pubs as we went to press in summer 2004. They should hold until around spring 2005 – when our experience suggests that you can expect an increase of around 10p in the £.

Cornwall

Quite a few changes here, with several pubs leaving the main entries, and a good crop of newcomers: the warm-hearted Rising Sun near Altarnun (hearty bargain food, good beers – a great find in this remote countryside), the friendly Royal Oak at Perranwell (enjoyable often unusual food, with at least something tempting to eat throughout opening hours), the beautifully placed Slipway in Port Isaac (nice hotel with friendly little bar, yummy local lobster in season), the Rifle Volunteer at St Anns Chapel (good local atmosphere, popular interesting food, great collection of whiskies), and the thriving Crooked Inn at Trematon (another good all-rounder, lots of character, particularly appealing to families). Other pubs on top form this year include the Blisland Inn (great for beer, with tempting prices), the exceptionally well run Halzephron near Helston (a charming place to stay, with great if not cheap food), the Halfway House in Kingsand (new people settling in well, good all round), the Royal Oak in Lostwithiel (another consistent all-rounder), the Pandora in its idyllic spot near Mylor Bridge, the Roseland at Philleigh (a special favourite), the Rashleigh in its fine seaside position at Polkerris, the Port Gaverne Inn near Port Isaac (a popular place to stay), the Ship perched over Porthleven harbour, the peaceful and unchanging Turks Head in its very special island spot on St Agnes, the friendly Old Inn on the moors at St Breward, the splendidly unchanging St Kew Inn, the cheerful Springer Spaniel at Treburley (good all round), the New Inn out on Tresco (a lovely spot, and amazing to have three real ales out here), and the Old Ale House packed with atmosphere in Truro (its name nearly says it all, but there's good value food here too). Cornwall's Dining Pub of the Year is the Halzephron at Gunwalloe south of Helston: not a cheap place, and so small that you may sometimes have difficulty booking, but really special. There is no end of good often ambitious food to be had in Cornwall's pubs now. But a word of warning: considering that (even after the EU's enlargement) this is still one of Europe's poorest areas, the county's pub food prices strike us as amazingly high, especially after the price hikes of £1 or so in many dishes that we have seen this year. By contrast, beer prices tend to be around or a little below the national average. Among our readers, Sharps now seems the most popular local beer, with Skinners also favoured, and Keltek and (true to its name) Organic well worth looking out for too, alongside long-established St Austell. The Lucky Dip section at the end of the chapter has plenty of hot prospects. Ones at the top of our current notebook include the Harbour Inn at Charlestown, Crows Nest at Crows Nest, Old Quay House at Devoran, Seven Stars in Falmouth, Fishermans Arms at Golant, Blue Anchor in Helston, Church House at Linkinhorne, Top House at Lizard, White Hart at Ludgvan, Fountain in Mevagissey, Bush at Morwenstow, Admiral Benbow in Penzance, Weary Friar at Pillaton, Blue Peter and Three Pilchards in Polperro, Rising Sun at Portmellon Cove, Sloop in St Ives, White Hart at St Teath, and in the Isles of Scilly the Seven Stones on St Martin's and Bishop & Wolf on St Mary's.

ALTARNUN SX2182 Map 1

Rising Sun £

Village signposted off A39 just W of A395 junction; pub itself NW of village, so if coming instead from A30 keep on towards Camelford

In an attractive spot on the NE edge of Bodmin Moor, this cheerful 16th-c pub is likely to be full of chatty locals and their dogs on even the wettest and windiest weekday lunchtimes, with the barmaids absolutely in the thick of things. On the Land's End Trail, it's handy too for longer-distance walkers. The low-beamed L-shaped main bar has bare boards and polished delabole slate flagstones, some stripped stone, a couple of coal fires, guns on the wall, and plain traditional furnishings. The central bar has well kept Bass, Cotleigh Tawny, Greene King IPA and Marstons Pedigree on handpump, and decent house wines. The food is hearty home cooking: thick chunky soup a bargain at £2, specials such as vegetarian shepherd's pie (£3), roast beef salad (£5.50) and steak and kidney suet pudding (£7), and the regular menu which includes three sausages (made specially for the pub, £3.80), good large baguettes (from £4), home-cooked ham with two eggs (£5.50), proper home-made meat pies with 3 or 4 vegetables (£6.50), seafood pie (£7), a greek lamb dish (£7.50), steaks (from £8), and puddings like apple crumble or treacle tart (£2.50). A small back area has darts, fruit machine and a pool table, with a second pool table in the carpeted room beyond (no dogs allowed in that one). The main bar can get a bit smoky sometimes. There are tables outside; they have bedrooms, but we have had no news of these from readers yet. Screened off by high evergreens, the field opposite has space for caravans. The village itself (with its altarless church – hence the name) is well worth a look. *(Recommended by Dennis Jenkin, W F C Phillips, JP, PP, Howard Gregory, Dr and Mrs M W A Haward, Gordon Briggs, Guy Vowles)*

Free house ~ Licensee Jim Manson ~ Real ale ~ Bar food ~ Restaurant ~ No credit cards ~ (01566) 86636 ~ Dogs allowed in bar ~ Open 11-3, 5.30-11; 11-11 Sat; 12-10.30 Sun ~ Bedrooms: £20/£40

BLISLAND SX0973 Map 1

Blisland Inn

Village signposted off A30 and B3266 NE of Bodmin

Run by a knowledgeable landlord, this welcoming local stocks a fine range of eight or more perfectly kept real ales. Every inch of the beams and ceiling is covered with beer mats (or their particularly wide-ranging collection of mugs), and the walls are similarly filled with beer-related posters and memorabilia. A blackboard lists the day's range, which has a firm emphasis on brews from Cornwall. They also have a changing farm cider, fruit wines, and real apple juice. Above the fireplace another blackboard has the choice of enjoyable, hearty home-made food, which might include sandwiches, leek and mushroom bake (£5.45), home-made lasagne (£5.95), a number of good home-made pies (£6.95 – the gravy for the steak and ale is made purely from beer, without any water), simple basket meals, changing fresh fish, and a popular Sunday lunch (booking advisable); service is cheerful and friendly. The partly flagstoned and carpeted no smoking lounge has a number of clocks and barometers on one wall, a rack of daily newspapers for sale, a few standing timbers, and a good chatty atmosphere. Note children are allowed only in the separate, plainer family room (with darts, euchre, and pool), though there are plenty of picnic-sets outside; dominoes and cribbage. The Camel Trail cycle path is close by. As with many pubs in this area, it's hard to approach without negotiating several single-track roads. *(Recommended by Dr D J Groves, Sue Spencer-Hurst, JP, PP, Matthew Lidbury, DAV, Margaret Mason, David Thompson, Gordon Briggs, the Didler, Rona Murdoch)*

Free house ~ Licensees Gary and Margaret Marshall ~ Real ale ~ Bar food (12-2.30; 2 Sun, 6.30-9.30; 9 Sun) ~ (01208) 850739 ~ Children in family room ~ Dogs welcome ~ Live music Sat evening ~ Open 11.30-11; 12-10.30 Sun

BODINNICK SX1352 Map 1

Old Ferry ★

Across the water from Fowey; coming by road, to avoid the ferry queue turn left as you go down the hill – car park on left before pub

From seats on the terrace in front of this 16th-c inn, there are lovely views of the pretty Fowey river; the guest lounge has binoculars and a telescope to make the most of any water activity or birdlife. Three simply furnished little rooms have quite a few bits of nautical memorabilia, a couple of half model ships mounted on the wall, and several old photographs, as well as wheelback chairs, built-in plush pink wall seats, and an old high-backed settle; there may be several friendly cats and a dog. The family room at the back is actually hewn into the rock; piped music. Decent bar food includes home-made soup (£3.50), sandwiches (from £2.75; toasties 40p extra), quite a few dishes with chips (from £4.50; home-cooked ham and egg £5.95), home-made cream cheese and broccoli pasta bake or curry of the day (£6.95), home-made steak and kidney in ale pie (£7.50), fresh smoked haddock with scrambled egg (£8.25), puddings (from £3.25), and popular evening daily specials like home-made duck liver and orange pâté (£5.50), wild mushroom and brandy sauce puff pastry parcel (£9.25), and fresh scallops, king prawns and monkfish in garlic and herb butter (£13.75). Sharps Own on handpump, kept under light blanket pressure; darts and TV. The lane beside the pub, in front of the ferry slipway is extremely steep and parking is limited, and some readers suggest parking in the public car park in Fowey and taking the little ferry to the pub. *(Recommended by Dave Braisted, Dr and Mrs M W A Haward, Michael Dandy, Tony and Maggie Bundey, John Taylor, Brian and Rosalie Laverick, Patrick Hancock, Cathy Robinson, Ed Coombe, Michael Butler, Christopher Turner, Sue Demont, Tim Barrow, J V Dadswell, Nick Lawless, Reg Fowle, Helen Rickwood)*

Free house ~ Licensees Royce and Patricia Smith ~ Real ale ~ Bar food (12-3, 6-9; 12-2.30, 6.30-8.30 in winter) ~ Restaurant ~ (01726) 870237 ~ Children in eating area of bar and family room ~ Open 11-11; 12-10.30 Sun; 12-10.30 weekdays in winter; closed evening 25 Dec ~ Bedrooms: /£55(£65S)(£70B)

CADGWITH SW7214 Map 1

Cadgwith Cove Inn

Down very narrow lane off A3083 S of Helston; no nearby parking

Set in a working fishing cove at the bottom of a steep village (it's best to park at the top and walk down), this remains an old-fashioned and bustling thatched local. Its two snugly dark front rooms have plain pub furnishings on their mainly parquet flooring, a log fire in one stripped stone end wall, lots of local photographs including gig races, cases of naval hat ribands and of fancy knot-work, and a couple of compass binnacles. Some of the dark beams have ship's shields and others have spliced blue rope hand-holds. Well kept Flowers IPA, Greene King Abbot, Sharps Doom Bar, and Wadworths 6X on handpump. A plusher pink back room has a huge and colourful fish mural. The daily specials tend to be the things to go for in the food line: local crab soup or greek salad (£5.95), moules marinière (£5.95 or £9), smoked seafood platter or super local cod and chips (£6.95), lamb and mint casserole (£7.95), and grilled fresh mackerel (£8.95). Other dishes include sandwiches and baguettes (from £4.25; the crab are particularly good), a cheese lunch with four different choices (£7.25), home-made lasagne (£7.55), home-made curry (£7.75), steak (£11.45), and puddings like home-made blackberry and apple pie with clotted cream (£3.85); best to check food times in winter. The left-hand room has darts, dominoes and cribbage, and there may be 1960s piped music. A good-sized front terrace has green-painted picnic-sets, some under a fairy-lit awning, looking down to the fish sheds by the bay. Coast Path walks are superb in both directions. *(Recommended by Malcolm and Jennifer Perry, Di and Mike Gillam, P R and S A White, Sue Holland, Dave Webster, Ian and Liz Rispin, Sarah Trayers)*

Pubmaster ~ Lease David and Lynda Trivett ~ Real ale ~ Bar food ~ Restaurant ~ (01326) 290513 ~ Children in restaurant ~ Dogs welcome ~ Folk club Tues, Cornish singing Fri ~ Open 12-3, 7-11; 12-11 Fri and Sat; 12-10.30 Sun; closed evening 25 Dec ~ Bedrooms: £25/£50(£70S)

CONSTANTINE SW7229 Map 1

Trengilly Wartha ★

Simplest approach is from A3083 S of Helston, signposted Gweek near RNAS Culdrose, then fork right after Gweek; coming instead from Penryn (roads narrower), turn right in Constantine just before Minimarket (towards Gweek), then pub signposted left in nearly a mile; at Nancenoy, OS Sheet 204 map reference 731282

It's quite a surprise to find such an extremely popular inn tucked away on a peaceful hillside not far from the Helford River. There's a pretty landscaped garden with some tables under large parasols, an international sized piste for boules, and a lake; lots of surrounding walks. Inside, the long low-beamed main bar has a woodburning stove and attractive built-in high-backed settles boxing in polished heavy wooden tables, and at one end, shelves of interesting wines with drink-in and take-out price labels (they run their own retail and wholesale wine business). The bright no smoking conservatory is popular with families; darts, shove-ha'penny, dominoes, and cribbage. Popular bar food includes soup (£3), pasties (from £4.20), chicken liver and port pâté with home-made chutney (£5.60), king prawns in garlic and chilli oil (£5.80), lunchtime ploughman's with home-made breads and pickles (from £6.70), their own sausages with mustard mash and onion gravy (£7.20), big salads such as roast vegetable and goats cheese or thai chicken (from £7.80), cheese and herb soufflé (£8.60), ham hock with a honey glaze (£9.50), crab cakes with a rich white wine sauce £13.20), plenty of daily specials like spring onion and herbed local goats cheese tartlet with creamy oyster mushrooms (£5.90), gratin of local mussels with spinach, cream and gnocchi (£6.60), various risottos (£7.20), chump of lamb with lentil salad and dauphinoise potatoes (£9.80), monkfish fillet on a puy lentil, coriander and new potato broth (£13.95), and roast loin of local venison (£14.20), with puddings such as pear and almond tart, home-made crumble or chocolate pecan fudge cake (£3.50). You can eat the restaurant food in the bar but not vice versa; they offer many dishes in helpings for smaller people. Well kept Sharps Cornish Coaster and Skinner's Betty Stogs tapped from the cask. Over 50 malt whiskies (including several extinct ones), up to 20 wines by the glass (from a fine list of over 250), and around 10 armagnacs. The pub does get very busy at peak times and there may be a wait for a table then. *(Recommended by DRH and KLH, David Rule, Hazel Morgan, Roger and Jenny Huggins, Nigel and Olga Wikeley, Comus and Sarah Elliott, JP, PP, M A Borthwick, Tom McLean, Lyn Huxtable, Richard Seers, Mandy and Simon King, Cathy Robinson, Ed Coombe, Ian and Celia Abbott, A J Atyeo, Mike Green, David Tindal, Neal Wills, J V Dadswell, the Didler)*

Free house ~ Licensees Nigel Logan and Michael Maguire ~ Real ale ~ Bar food (12-2.15 (2 Sun), 6.30(7 Sun)-9.30; not 25 or 31 Dec) ~ Restaurant ~ (01326) 340332 ~ Children welcome ~ Dogs allowed in bar and bedrooms ~ Open 11-3, 6.30-11; 12-3, 7-10.30 Sun ~ Bedrooms: £49B/£78B

DULOE SX2358 Map 1

Olde Plough House

B3254 N of Looe

The two communicating rooms in this neatly kept and popular pub have lovely dark polished delabole slate floors, some turkey rugs, a mix of pews, modern high-backed settles and smaller chairs, foreign banknotes on the beams, and three woodburning stoves. The décor is restrained – prints of waterfowl and country scenes, and a few copper jugs and a fat wooden pig perched on window sills. Well liked and reasonably priced food at lunchtime includes home-made soup (£2.75), filled baguettes (from £3.75), a roast of the day (£5.45), ploughman's (from £5.45), local pork and garlic sausages, chips and fried egg (£5.75), vietnamese sweet chilli chicken (£6.25), lamb hotpot (£6.65), and vegetables with oriental sauce (£7.95), with evening choices such as devilled whitebait or home-made chicken liver and pistachio nut pâté with home-made chutney (£4.95), goats cheese and sunblush tomato tart or beef and stilton cobbler (£7.45), steak on hot stones (from £7.95), lamb shank with blueberry and damson sauce (£10.25), and half duckling with a spiced orange sauce (£11.25). One room is no smoking; piped music. Well kept Bass and Sharps Doom Bar on handpump, and sensibly priced wines. There is a small more modern carpeted dining room, and a few picnic-sets out by the road. The two friendly jack russells are called Jack and Spot, and the cat, Willow. *(Recommended by J M Tansey, Theocsbrian, Dr and Mrs M W A Haward, Ian Phillips, John Hale, P R and S A White, Michael Butler, John Edwards, Prof and Mrs Tony Palmer, Mr and Mrs R P Welch, Mark Flynn, Nick Lawless)*

Free house ~ Licensees Gary and Alison Toms ~ Real ale ~ Bar food (not 25 Dec) ~ Restaurant ~ (01503) 262050 ~ Children in eating area of bar ~ Dogs allowed in bar ~ Open 12-2.30, 6.30-11; 12-2.30, 7-10.30 Sun; closed evenings 25-26 Dec

EGLOSHAYLE **SX0172 Map 1**

Earl of St Vincent £

Off A389, just outside Wadebridge

At midday, when the 162 antique clocks in this pretty pub – tucked away in a narrow quiet back street behind the church – all start charming, it does get pretty noisy. They also have some golfing memorabilia, art deco ornaments, and all sorts of rich furnishings. Well kept St Austell HSD, Tinners and Tribute with a guest like IPA or Black Prince on handpump; piped music. Bar food includes soup (£3.50), sandwiches (from £4), ploughman's (from £5), mushroom and broccoli au gratin or ham and egg (£6.50), fish dishes (from £7.50), and grills (from £11.50). The snug is no smoking. In summer, there are picnic-sets in the lovely garden and marvellous flowering baskets and tubs. *(Recommended by JP, PP, Keith and Margaret Kettell, R J Herd, Canon Michael Bourdeaux, David Crook, the Didler)*

St Austell ~ Tenants Edward and Anne Connolly ~ Real ale ~ Bar food (not Sun evening) ~ Restaurant ~ (01208) 814807 ~ Children in eating area of bar ~ Open 11-3, 6.30-11; 12-3, 7-10.30 Sun

HELFORD **SW7526 Map 1**

Shipwrights Arms 🍷

Off B3293 SE of Helston, via Mawgan

Now a free house, this thatched pub looks down over the pretty wooded creek (at its best at high tide) and can be reached by foot ferry (open April to the end of October) from Helford Passage (01326) 250770 or by car, though it is quite a walk from the nearest car park. There are seats on the terrace making the most of the water views, and plenty of surrounding walks, including a long distance coastal path that goes right past the door. Inside, there's quite a nautical theme, with navigation lamps, models of ships, sea pictures, drawings of lifeboat coxswains, and shark fishing photographs. A dining area has oak settles and tables; winter open fire. Well kept Castle Eden and Sharps Doom Bar on handpump, a good wine list, and bar food such as home-made soup (£3.75), buffet lunch platters (from £5.10), summer evening barbecue dishes that include steaks (from £10.25), marinated lamb chops (£12), and monkfish marinated with chilli, lime and coriander (£12.50), and home-made puddings (£5.10); piped music. Dogs must be kept on a lead. *(Recommended by Paul Humphreys, JP, PP, Maggie and Tony Harwood, John Martin, V Banting, Andrea Rampley, Geoff Pidoux, P R and S A White, J V Dadswell, the Didler)*

Free house ~ Licensee Charles Herbert ~ Real ale ~ Bar food (not Sun or Mon evenings in winter) ~ (01326) 231235 ~ Children welcome ~ Dogs welcome ~ Open 11-2.30, 6-11; 12-2.30, 7-10.30 Sun; closed Sun and Mon evenings

Places with gardens or terraces usually let children sit there – we note in the text the very few exceptions that don't.

HELSTON SW6522 Map 1

Halzephron

Gunwalloe, village about 4 miles S but not marked on many road maps; look for brown sign on A3083 alongside perimeter fence of RNAS Culdrose

Cornwall Dining Pub of the Year

Mrs Thomas and her genuinely attentive staff make this former smugglers' haunt a really special place. There's always a good mix of regulars and visitors, and although it does get packed at the height of the season, the really friendly feeling in the bustling bar remains. It is kept spotlessly clean, and has comfortable seating, copper on the walls and mantelpiece, and a warm winter fire in the big hearth; there's also a no smoking family room. Using the best of local produce, the particularly enjoyable food might include lunchtime sandwiches (the crab are delicious), home-made soup (£4), ploughman's (from £5.10), pâté of the day with home-made toasted brioche (£5.20), local smoked fish selection (£7.60), tagliatelle bolognese (£8.50), sirloin steak (£12.95), and crab platter (£13.40), with specials like smoked duck and wild mushroom risotto with parmesan and herbs or seafood chowder (£6.50), chicken cacciatore (£9.50), mediterranean vegetables, artichokes and olives with fresh pasta (£12.50), gressingham duck breast on butternut squash purée with poached pears and juniper sauce (£15), and bass on basil potato purée with fennel confit and rosemary butter sauce (£16). All the eating areas are no smoking. Well kept Organic Halzephron Gold (this local brewer only supplies organic beers), Sharps Special, Own and Doom Bar, and St Austell Tribute on handpump, a good wine list, lots of malt whiskies, and around 25 liqueurs; darts, dominoes and cribbage. This is a smashing place to stay with sea views in some rooms and good breakfasts. There are lots of lovely surrounding unspoilt walks with fine views of Mount's Bay, Gunwalloe fishing cove is just 300 yards away, and there's a sandy beach one mile away at Church Cove. The church of St Winwaloe (built into the dunes on the seashore) is also only a mile away, and well worth a visit. *(Recommended by Pete and Rosie Flower, John and Gloria Isaacs, David Crook, R and S Bentley, Dr Phil Putwain, JMC, Maggie and Tony Harwood, Stephen Hobbs, Paul Humphreys, Sue Holland, Dave Webster, Stuart Turner, Jacquie and Jim Jones, Derek and Margaret Underwood, Dr and Mrs M W A Haward, Patrick Hancock, Derek and Heather Manning, Andrea Rampley, Karl and Julie Stamper, A J Atyeo, Susie Symes, P Hennessey, Mike Green, Tom McLean, Brian and Bett Cox, Nick Lawless)*

Free house ~ Licensee Angela Thomas ~ Real ale ~ Bar food (not 25 Dec) ~ Restaurant ~ (01326) 240406 ~ Children in family room, in restaurant if over 8 ~ Open 11-2.30, 6(6.30 winter)-11; 12-2.30, 6(6.30 in winter)-10.30 Sun; closed 25 Dec ~ Bedrooms: £45B/£80B

KINGSAND SX4350 Map 1

Halfway House

Fore Street, towards Cawsand

For a weekend break, this well run and attractive inn is just the place to be. There are plenty of chatty locals, a friendly welcome, enjoyable beer and food (including nice breakfasts), and comfortable bedrooms. There are marvellous surrounding walks, too, especially in the cliff area at Rame Head, and the picturesque village is well placed for visiting Mount Edgcumbe House and Country Park, and the new diving venue at Whitsand Bay. The simply furnished but quite smart bar is mildly Victorian in style, and rambles around a huge central fireplace, with low ceilings, and soft lighting. Popular bar food using local produce includes daily specials such as scallops in white wine, cream and tarragon sauce (£6.25), trio rack of lamb with tomato couscous and minted gravy (£10.95), chicken with stilton sauce, steaks from a local butcher (from £11.35), bass fillet (£11.95), and grilled mixed fish with paella (£13.95). Also, filled baguettes (from £3.05), home-made soup (£3.50), filled baked potatoes (from £4.85), mediterranean vegetable lasagne (£5.50), locally made pasty (£5.80), ploughman's (from £6), goats cheese and sunblush tomato tart (£6.50), home-cooked ham and egg (£7), local crab salad (£9.30), and constantly changing home-made puddings (£3.95). They open for morning coffee and serve summer afternoon teas. The restaurant is no smoking. Well kept Courage Best, Marstons Pedigree, Sharps Doom Bar, and a beer made for the pub by Sharps called Cawking on handpump kept under light blanket pressure, and decent wines. To reach the inn, you can either park in the council car park and walk through the narrow hilly streets down towards the sea, or park in the private car park next to the inn. *(Recommended by Nicholas Regam, B J Harding, Steve Whalley, John and Pat Morris, Mrs J Levinson, Chris Pelley, Richard and Anne Ansell, B Forster, Allegra Taylor)*

Free house ~ Licensees Hudi and Shauna Honig ~ Real ale ~ Bar food ~ Restaurant ~ (01752) 822279 ~ Children welcome ~ Dogs allowed in bar and bedrooms ~ Open 11-11; 12-10.30 Sun; 12-3, 7-11 in winter ~ Bedrooms: £30S/£60B

LANLIVERY SX0759 Map 1

Crown

Signposted off A390 Lostwithiel—St Austell (tricky to find from other directions)

The same company that owns the popular Springer Spaniel at Treburley have taken over this inn, and indeed, have installed the licensee from over there, too. There will be quite a few changes over the next few months including a kitchen extension and various refurbishments. But the small, dimly lit public bar still has its heavy beams, slate floor and built-in wall settles, and attractive alcove of seats in the dark former chimney. A much lighter room leads off, with beams in the white boarded ceiling, some settees in one corner, cushioned black settles, a small cabinet with wood turnings for sale, and a little fireplace with an old-fashioned fire; there's also another similar small room. No noisy games machines or music. Well liked bar food at lunchtime now includes baguettes and filled baked potatoes (from £4.50; local crab £6.95), hand-made pasty (£4.95), moules marinière (£5.50 or £8.50), meaty or vegetarian sausages of the day with caramelised onion gravy (£5.95), local cheese ploughman's (£6.50), apricot, mushroom and chestnut pie (£6.95), and steak in ale pie (£7.50), with evening dishes such as mushroom pot (£4.50), smoked haddock and avocado mousse (£5.95), local scallops in garlic and lemon butter (£6.95), fish pie (£8.50), pork chops braised in local cider (£8.95), shank of lamb (£11.95), changing local fish, steaks (from £11.95), and local crab salad (£12.95); daily specials like home-made tomato and brie soup (£3.50), calamari with sweet chilli dip (£5.95), cajun spicy mackerel fillets with yoghurt and mint (£7.50), and swordfish steak in a white wine and green peppercorn sauce (£13.95), and puddings such as sticky toffee pudding and summer fruit crumble (£4.75). Well kept Sharps Coaster, Doom Bar, and a couple of beers named for the pub, Crown and Glory, on handpump; local cider. Darts, dominoes, and cribbage. The slate-floored porch room has lots of succulents and a few cacti, and wood-and-stone seats, and at the far end of the restaurant is a no smoking sun room, full of more plants, with tables and benches. There's a sheltered garden with granite faced seats, white cast-iron furniture, and several solid wooden tables. The Eden Project is only ten minutes away. We'd be grateful for reports on the changes. *(Recommended by Dennis Jenkin, Frank Willy, John and Jackie Chalcraft, David M Cundy, M and R Thomas, David Heath, David Rule, Dr and Mrs M W A Haward, Graham and Lynn Mason, Evelyn and Derek Walter, Prof and Mrs Tony Palmer, Bill and Jessica Ritson, Martin and Karen Wake, Mrs Sally Kingsbury, Mrs Joy Griffiths, Jenny and Brian Seller)*

Wagtail Inns ~ Licensee Andrew Brotheridge ~ Real ale ~ Bar food (12-2, 6-9.15) ~ Restaurant ~ (01208) 872707 ~ Children in eating area of bar and restaurant ~ Dogs allowed in bar ~ Trad jazz every 2nd Sun of month; music nights during week in winter ~ Open 12-11; 12-10.30 Sun; 12-3, 6-11 in winter; closed 25 Dec ~ Bedrooms: £50S/£70S

LOSTWITHIEL SX1059 Map 1

Royal Oak

Duke Street; pub just visible from A390 in centre – best to look out for Royal Talbot Hotel

There's always a good mix of visitors and locals in this bustling old town centre pub – and a warm welcome for all. The six real ales are quite a draw, with well kept Bass, Fullers London Pride, and Marstons Pedigree, and changing guests such as Blue Anchor Spingo, and Keltek Royal Oak and Special on handpump – as well as lots of bottled beers from around the world. Well liked bar food includes lunchtime sandwiches (from £2.10; toasties 50p extra), ploughman's (from £4.85), and fried chicken (£5.75), as well as soup (£2.85), stuffed mushrooms (£4.45), vegetarian lasagne (£7.75), fresh local trout (£9.25), steaks (from £10.25), daily specials like curry or steak and kidney in ale pie (£8.75), fresh whole local plaice (£10.95), and barbary duck with orange and ginger sauce (£13.45), and puddings such as home-made jam sponge pudding or summer fruit terrine (£3.50); an area of the restaurant is no smoking. The neat lounge is spacious and comfortable, with captain's chairs and high-backed wall benches on its patterned carpet, and a couple of wooden armchairs by the gas-effect log fire; there's also a delft shelf, with a small dresser in one inner alcove. The flagstoned and beamed back public bar has darts, fruit machine, TV, and juke box, and is liked by younger customers; dominoes and cribbage. On a raised terrace by the car park are some picnic-sets. *(Recommended by Mrs Pam Mattinson, Graham and Lynn Mason, Alan and Paula McCully, Hazel Morgan, George Atkinson, Ron Shelton, A and B D Craig, Margaret Mason, David Thompson, John Taylor, Tom Bottinga, P R and S A White, David Crook)*

Free house ~ Licensees Malcolm and Eileen Hine ~ Real ale ~ Bar food (12-2, 6.30-9.15) ~ Restaurant ~ (01208) 872552 ~ Children in family room ~ Open 11-11; 12-10.30 Sun ~ Bedrooms: £43B/£75B

MALPAS SW8442 Map 1

Heron

Trenhaile Terr, off A39 S of Truro

To enjoy the view over the pretty creek, you must bag one of the seats on the terrace or one of the window tables inside. The spotlessly kept bar is long and narrow with several areas leading off and a raised area at one end, and it is all very light and airy with blue and white décor and furnishings throughout. Two gas fires, mainly wooden floors with flagstones by the bar, modern yacht paintings on the wood-planked walls, some brass nautical items, heron pictures and a stuffed heron in a cabinet, and a chatty brasserie-type atmosphere; half the pub is no smoking. Bar food includes lunchtime filled rolls (from £5.25), tortilla wraps (from £5.95), warm chicken caesar salad (£6.75), and hot spicy king prawns with sweet chilli dip (£6.50), as well as crab cakes (£4.95), ham and eggs (£7.20), goats cheese and red pepper cannelloni (£7.95), chicken curry (£8.95), braised lamb shank or beef bourguignon (£10.25), and local crab and smoked salmon salad (£10.50). They keep your credit card behind the bar. Well kept St Austell IPA, HSD, and Tribute on handpump, good wines by the glass, and several malt whiskies; piped music. Parking is extremely difficult at peak times. *(Recommended by Pete and Rosie Flower, Debbie and Neil Hayter, Andrea Rampley, Ian Phillips, Di and Mike Gillam, David and Sally Cullen)*

St Austell ~ Tenant F C Kneebone ~ Real ale ~ Bar food ~ (01872) 272773 ~ Children in eating area of bar ~ Open 11-4, 6-11; 12-3, 7-10.30 Sun

MITCHELL SW8654 Map 1

Plume of Feathers

Just off A30 Bodmin—Redruth, by A3076 junction; take the southwards road then turn first right

The attractive bars here have stripped old beams and an enormous open fire, pastel-coloured walls, plenty of seats for either a drink or a meal, and a natural spring well that has been made into a glass-topped table. There's a no smoking restaurant with interesting paintings, and an eating area near the main bar for the minority who want to smoke. Bar food includes lunchtime sandwiches (from £2.95; club toasted panini or ciabatta £5.95), and hand-made pasty (£5.75), as well as smooth chicken liver pâté with red onion jam (£4.50), moules marinière (£5.95), chargrilled burger with home-made chutney (£6.75), and potato gnocchi in a cheese, spinach and chive cream or green thai chicken curry (£7.25), with specials like home-made pumpkin soup (£3.50), game terrine with grilled date and walnut bread and nectarine fennel chutney (£6), seared local scallops (£7.10), grilled mackerel with pak choi and laksa curry sauce (£12.30), and roast rack of lamb with pumpkin ratatouille and wild mushroom confit (£14.60), with puddings like white chocolate, saffron and cardamom panna cotta or banoffi pie (£4.50). Well kept Barum Jester, Greene King IPA, Sharps Doom Bar and Shepherd Neame Spitfire on handpump, a comprehensive wine list, their own bottled water, and good fresh italian coffees. Piped music, juke box, fruit machine, and TV. The well planted garden areas have plenty of seats. *(Recommended by Andy Sinden, Louise Harrington, George Atkinson, Catherine and Rob Dunster, Ian Wilson, Brian and Bett Cox, Mrs Pat Crabb, Kevin Mayne, Mandy and Simon King, Callum and Letitia Smith-Burnett, B and M Kendall, Guy Vowles, Sheila Brooks, Charles Cooper, Reg Fowle, Helen Rickwood)*

Free house ~ Licensees M F Warner and J Trotter ~ Real ale ~ Bar food (12-10) ~ Restaurant ~ (01872) 510387/511125 ~ Children welcome ~ Dogs allowed in bar ~ Open 10-11; 11-10.30 Sun; closed evening 25 Dec ~ Bedrooms: £48.75S(£56.25B)/£65S(£75B)

MITHIAN SW7450 Map 1

Miners Arms

Just off B3285 E of St Agnes

New licensees have taken over this 16th-c pub but seem to have settled in quickly. Several cosy little rooms and passages are warmed by winter open fires, and the small back bar has an irregular beam and plank ceiling, a wood block floor, and bulging squint walls (one with a fine old wall painting of Elizabeth I); another small room has a decorative low ceiling, lots of books and quite a few interesting ornaments. The Croust Room is no smoking; piped music. Bar food includes home-made soup (£3.95), filled baguettes (from £3.95), sausage and mash (£6.95), steak in ale pie or a vegetarian dish (£7.95), crab salad (£9.95), rack of lamb (£10.95), and venison (£11.95), and puddings (£3.95). Well kept Morlands Old Speckled Hen and Sharps Doom Bar on handpump, and several wines by the glass. There are seats on the back terrace, with more on the sheltered front cobbled forecourt. *(Recommended by Mr and Mrs P Eastwood, JP, PP, Stephen and Judy Parish, Andrea Rampley, Ken Arthur, Ian Phillips, Stephen Buckley)*

Inn Partnership (Pubmaster) ~ Lease Mr and Mrs K Hodge ~ Real ale ~ Bar food ~ (01872) 552375 ~ Children in restaurant ~ Dogs allowed in bar ~ Open 12-2.30, 6-11; 12-11 Sat; 12-10.30 Sun

MOUSEHOLE SW4726 Map 1

Old Coastguard

The Parade (edge of village, coming in on coast road from Newlyn – street parking just before you reach the inn); village also signposted off B3315

Although this seaside hotel's main bar has an atmosphere more akin to a wine bar than a local, it does have well kept Bass and Sharps Doom Bar on handpump, and customers do drop in for just a drink. The position is lovely, and the neat and attractive sizeable garden has palms and dracaenas, marble-look tables on decking, and a path leading down to the water's-edge rock pools. Inside, it is light, airy and spacious and has been redecorated this year in blue and white giving a mediterranean feel: modern metal and wicker seats around well spaced matching tables on wood strip flooring, modern light watercolours on the walls, and palms, potted plants and fresh flowers. Its lower dining part, liked by readers, has a glass wall giving a great view out over the garden to Mounts Bay. A quiet back area is darker, with comfortable art deco leatherette tub chairs, and fair choice of wines by the glass, and a thoughtful choice of fresh juices and pressés. At lunchtime, bar food includes soup (£4), sandwiches (from £4; local crab with citrus mayonnaise £8), salmon and crab fishcakes with sweet chilli dip (£6), steamed local mussels with chilli, lime and coriander butter (£9.50), thai green chicken curry (£13), and local sirloin steak (£14); in the evening, when the tables are linen-clothed, there might be marinated smoked goats cheese with toasted pine nut pesto (£5.50), local scallops (£6.50), filo pastry and parmesan cases filled with roasted mediterranean vegetables, puy lentils, local blue cheese and roast garlic sauce (£11), roasted rack of lamb (£15.50), and honey roast duck breast and confit of duck leg (£16). Daily specials such as butternut squash and saffron ravioli (£5.50), mixed grilled fish with walnut pesto (£15.50), and whole grilled lemon sole with caper and anchovy butter (£17). The restaurant and sun lounge are no smoking. *(Recommended by Andy Sinden, Louise Harrington, E G Parish, Ian and Liz Rispin, Barry and Anne, Ken Arthur, Callum and Letitia Smith-Burnett, Dr R A Smye, David Glynne-Jones, Susie Symes, Simon J Barber, Sue Demont, Tim Barrow)*

Free house ~ Licensee Bill Treloar ~ Real ale ~ Bar food (12-2.30, 6.30-9) ~ Restaurant ~ (01736) 731222 ~ Children in restaurant ~ Open 11-11; 11-10.30 Sun; closed 25 Dec ~ Bedrooms: £48B/£85B

MYLOR BRIDGE SW8137 Map 1

Pandora ★★ 🍷

Restronguet Passage: from A39 in Penryn, take turning signposted Mylor Church, Mylor Bridge, Flushing and go straight through Mylor Bridge following Restronguet Passage signs; or from A39 further N, at or near Perranarworthal, take turning signposted Mylor, Restronguet, then follow Restronguet Weir signs, but turn left down hill at Restronguet Passage sign

On a peaceful sunny day, it would be hard to find a pub in such an idyllic position. Thatched and medieval, it faces a sheltered waterfront, and you can sit on the long floating pontoon with a drink and while away an hour or so watching children crabbing and customers arriving by boat. Inside, the several rambling, interconnecting rooms have low wooden ceilings (mind your head on some of the beams), beautifully polished big flagstones, cosy alcoves with leatherette benches built into the walls, old race posters, two large log fires in high hearths (to protect them against tidal floods); half the bar area is no smoking – as is the restaurant. Bar food includes home-made soup (£4.25), sandwiches (from £4.50, good local crab £7.95), ploughman's (from £6.95), grilled local cumberland sausages with red pepper pesto (£7.80), chargrilled sirloin steak ciabatta (£8.40), and cornish crab cakes with citrus and orange-flesh dressing (£8.95), with daily specials such as mussels in chive and creamy white wine sauce (£4.50 or £8.50), cheese and bacon quiche (£5.50), seared sea bream (£9.50), and braised lamb shank (£11.50). They also serve afternoon teas in summer. Well kept Bass, and St Austell HSD, Tinners and Tribute on handpump, several wines by the glass, and local cider. It does get very crowded in summer, and parking is difficult at peak times. Good surrounding walks. *(Recommended by DRH and KLH, Richard Dixon, JP, PP, Andy and Ali, P R and S A White, Bob and Sue Hardy, Geoff and Jan Dawson, Tim and Ann Newell, David Crook, Comus and Sarah Elliott, Paul Humphreys, Richard Fendick, David Rule, Di and Mike Gillam, Alison Hayes, Pete Hanlon, John Martin, V Banting, Kevin Thorpe, John Close, Patrick Hancock, Dr and Mrs Michael Smith, Andrea Rampley, Gene and Tony Freemantle, Ken Arthur, Geoff Pidoux, Ian and Celia Abbott, Robert Coates, A J Atyeo, Guy Vowles, Mike Green, J M Tansey, Philip and Ann Board, the Didler, Jenny and Brian Seller, Reg Fowle, Helen Rickwood)*

St Austell ~ Tenant John Milan ~ Real ale ~ Bar food (12-3, 6.30-9) ~ Restaurant ~ (01326) 372678 ~ Children in eating area of bar and restaurant ~ Dogs allowed in bar ~ Open 11-11; 12-10.30 Sun

PENZANCE SW4730 Map 1

Turks Head

At top of main street, by big domed building (Lloyds TSB), turn left down Chapel Street

As we went to press, we heard that this reliably friendly local was about to change hands. Mr Phillips (who runs the popular Roseland at Philleigh) and his partner (who will also be the chef) are not planning to make any sweeping changes, so we are keeping our fingers crossed that things will continue more or less the same here.

The bustling bar has old flat irons, jugs and so forth hanging from the beams, pottery above the wood-effect panelling, wall seats and tables, and a couple of elbow rests around central pillars; piped music. Additions to the menu will obviously appear, but popular bar food has included soup (£2.60), lunchtime sandwiches, baguettes and filled baked potatoes (from £2.95), omelettes (£4.25), cajun chicken with onions and sweet peppers (£5.75), fish pie (£6.95), steak and mushroom in ale pie (£7.95), white crabmeat salad (£9.50), steaks (from £9.75), and local bass on mediterranean roasted vegetables (£13.65). The restaurant area is no smoking. Well kept Greene King IPA, Sharps Doom Bar, Wadworths 6X, and a guest on handpump; helpful service. The suntrap back garden has big urns of flowers. There has been a Turks Head here for over 700 years – though most of the original building was destroyed by a Spanish raiding party in the 16th c. More reports on the changes, please. *(Recommended by Peter Meister, Neil and Anita Christopher, JP, PP, Helen Flaherty, Barry and Anne, Andrea Rampley, Callum and Letitia Smith-Burnett, Susie Symes, Gordon Tong)*

Pubmaster ~ Lease Colin Philips and Jonathan Gibbard ~ Real ale ~ Bar food ~ (01736) 363093 ~ Children in downstairs dining room ~ Open 11-11; 12-10.30 Sun; may close afternoons in winter

PERRANWELL SW7739 Map 1

Royal Oak

Village signposted off A393 Redruth—Falmouth and A39 Falmouth—Truro

This pretty and quietly set stone-built village pub is welcoming and relaxed, with a buoyant gently upmarket atmosphere. Its roomy carpeted bar has horsebrasses and pewter and china mugs on its black beams and joists, plates and country pictures on its cream-painted stone walls, and cosy wall and other seats around its tables. It rambles around beyond a big stone fireplace (with a good log fire in winter) into a snug little nook of a room behind, with just a couple more tables. Good, interesting bar food includes super tapas like smoked anchovies, artichoke hearts and guacamole (available at all times the bar is open), lunchtime specials such as seafood platter (£5.50 or £8.95), and smoked chicken and avocado salad or minced lamb in brown ale, ginger and worcester sauce (£6.95), and evening choices like paella valencia (£9.25), seared tuna steak (£9.95), duck breast (£10.95), and roast rack of lamb (£12.50). In summer, booking for their great value Thursday night lobster specials is essential, and they make good proper sandwiches (ask, if you don't see them on the menu). The restaurant area is no smoking. Well kept Bass, Flowers IPA, and Sharps Special on handpump from the small serving counter, good wines by the glass (the wine list is well balanced and not over-long), a particularly good landlord, and prompt friendly service; piped music and shove-ha'penny. There are some picnic-sets out by the quiet village lane. *(Recommended by David Crook, Andy Sinden, Louise Harrington, Gene and Tony Freemantle)*

Free house ~ Licensee Richard Rudland ~ Real ale ~ Bar food (12-2.30, 7-9.30) ~ Restaurant ~ (01872) 863175 ~ Children in restaurant ~ Dogs allowed in bar ~ Open 11-3, 6-11; 12-3, 6-10.30 Sun

PHILLEIGH SW8639 Map 1

Roseland ★ 🍷

Between A3078 and B3289, just E of King Harry Ferry

Despite the many holiday visitors, this busy little pub still manages to be a genuine local with plenty of cheerful banter in the small lower back bar, maybe a game of cards, and a relaxed, friendly atmosphere. The helpful and efficient staff offer a welcome to all – dogs and children included – and do their utmost at peak times to serve you as quickly as possible. The two bar rooms (one with flagstones and the other carpeted) have wheelback chairs and built-in red-cushioned seats, open fires, old photographs and some giant beetles and butterflies in glasses, and maybe the large pub cat. Good, interesting, if not cheap, bar food includes lunchtime sandwiches (from £4; local crab £7), pasty with chips and salad (£6.25), ploughman's with three cornish cheeses or beer battered cod (£7.95), wild mushroom and pesto pasta (£8.80), and daily specials such as well liked, if hot, thai green chicken curry (£10.95), rack of local lamb with liver dumplings (£12.95), and monkfish and seafood cocktail or foil-baked sea bream (£14.95); puddings (from £3). You must book to be sure of a table; the restaurant is no smoking. Well kept Bass, Greene King Old Speckled Hen, Ringwood Best and Sharps Doom Bar on handpump, a good wine list with quite a few by the glass, and several malt whiskies. Dominoes and cribbage. The pretty paved front courtyard is a lovely place to sit in the lunchtime sunshine beneath the cherry blossom, and the pub is handy for Trelissick Gardens and the King Harry Ferry. *(Recommended by J L Wedel, Geoff and Jan Dawson, Anthony Rickards Collinson, Richard Till, Jack Clark, Fred and Lorraine Gill, Mr and Mrs B J P Edwards, JP, PP, Alison Hayes, Pete Hanlon, Kevin Thorpe, Andrea Rampley, Ian and Celia Abbott, P R and S A White, Mrs Kaye Frost, Gill and Tony Morriss, Mrs Maricar Jagger, Guy Vowles, Mark Flynn, Jodie Collins, D S Jackson, the Didler, Nick Lawless, Jenny and Brian Seller)*

Authentic Inns ~ Lease Colin Phillips ~ Real ale ~ Bar food (12-2.30, 6-9.30) ~ Restaurant ~ (01872) 580254 ~ Children in eating area of bar and restaurant ~ Dogs welcome ~ Live jazz Sun ~ Open 11-11; 12-10.30 Sun; 11-3, 6-11 winter ~ Bedrooms: /£80B

POLKERRIS SX0952 Map 1

Rashleigh

Signposted off A3082 Fowey—St Austell

Seats on the stone terrace in front of this former fishermen's tavern have fine views towards the far side of St Austell and Mevagissey bays, and the splendid beach with its restored jetty is only a few steps away; there are safe moorings for small yachts in the cove. Inside, the bar is snug and cosy, and the front part has comfortably cushioned seats and half a dozen or so well kept real ales on handpump such as Sharps Doom Bar and a beer named for the pub, Timothy Taylors Landlord, and guests like Blue Anchor Spingo, Exmoor Gold, Marstons Pedigree and Ring O' Bells Dreckly; Addleston's farm cider in the summer and several wines by the glass. The more simply furnished back area has local photographs on the brown panelling, and a winter log fire; fruit machine and shove-ha'penny. From the totally refurbished kitchen, reasonably priced bar food includes soup (£2.95), sandwiches (from £2.75; open ones from £5.90), ploughman's (from £4.95), hazelnut and vegetable crumble (£5.95), home-made cottage pie (£6.50), home-made fish pie (£7.25), and seasonal fresh local fish and game. There is no restaurant menu available on Sundays. The pub's car park has been resurfaced and extended this year, but there's also a large village car park. This whole section of the Cornish Coast Path is renowned for its striking scenery. *(Recommended by David and Pauline Brenner, Kevin Flack, Mr and Mrs B J P Edwards, JP, PP, Mayur Shah, Bob and Margaret Holder, Alan and Paula McCully, Dave Braisted, Prof and Mrs Tony Palmer, M and R Thomas, Charles and Pauline Stride, Brian and Rosalie Laverick, Patrick Hancock, Val and Alan Green, Geoff Pidoux, Mrs M Granville-Edge, Sue Demont, Tim Barrow, the Didler, Reg Fowle, Helen Rickwood)*

Free house ~ Licensees Jon and Samantha Spode ~ Real ale ~ Bar food (12-2, 6-9; snacks on summer afternoons from 3pm) ~ Restaurant ~ (01726) 813991 ~ Children welcome ~ Open 11-11; 12-10.30 Sun

PORT ISAAC SX0080 Map 1

Golden Lion

Fore Street

The best place to sit here on a really balmy day is on the terrace, which looks down on the rocky harbour and lifeboat slip far below. Inside, the simply furnished rooms have a bustling local atmosphere, and the main bar has a fine antique settle among other comfortable seats (those by the window enjoy the view) and decorative ceiling plasterwork; the back room has an open fire. Bar food includes sandwiches (lunchtime only, from £2.45), filled baked potatoes (from £3.25), home-made vegetable korma (£6.95), proper fish and chips (£7.95), home-made fish pie

(£8.25), sirloin steak (£11.95), and daily specials like fresh crab sandwich (£6.25); during the summer, evening meals are also served in the no smoking bistro. Well kept St Austell Tinners, HSD and Tribute on handpump and several malt whiskies. Darts, dominoes, cribbage, a fruit machine in the public bar, and piped music. You can park at the top of the village unless you are lucky enough to park on the beach at low tide. *(Recommended by Betsy Brown, Nigel Flook, Canon Michael Bourdeaux, DRH and KLH, Mayur Shah, Karen and Graham Oddey, Margaret Mason, David Thompson, Simon Collett-Jones, Mr and Mrs John Taylor, Mrs M Granville-Edge, Michael Butler, the Didler)*

St Austell ~ Tenants Mike and Nikki Edkins ~ Real ale ~ Bar food ~ Restaurant (evening) ~ (01208) 880336 ~ Children in eating area of bar and restaurant ~ Open 11.30-11; 12-10.30 Sun; closed 25 Dec

Port Gaverne Inn

Port Gaverne signposted from Port Isaac, and from B3314 E of Pendoggett

In a lovely spot, just back from the sea and close to splendid clifftop walks, this well liked 17th-c inn remains a popular place to stay. There's a bar with a bustling atmosphere, big log fires and low beams, flagstones as well as carpeting, some exposed stone, and lots of chatty locals. In spring, the lounge is usually filled with pictures from the local art society's annual exhibition, and at other times there are interesting antique local photographs. Bar food includes sandwiches, home-made chicken liver pâté, home-made soup (£5.50), ploughman's (£5.25), creamy vegetable risotto (£6), ham and egg (£6.25), home-made seafood pie (£6.75), daily specials like home-made crab soup (£4.75), steak sandwich on ciabatta (£6.25) or crab salad (£7.95), and puddings such as chocolate and brandy mousse or summer pudding (£3.95); you can eat in the bar, the 'Captain's Cabin' – a little room where everything is shrunk to scale (old oak chest, model sailing ship, even the prints on the white stone walls) or on a balcony overlooking the sea; the restaurant is no smoking. Well kept Bass, St Austell HSD, and Sharps Doom Bar and Cornish on handpump, a good wine list, and several whiskies; cribbage and dominoes. There are seats in the garden close to the sea. *(Recommended by John and Jackie Chalcraft, Alan and Paula McCully, Peter Salmon, Keith Stevens, Betsy Brown, Nigel Flook, Charles Gysin, Hugh Roberts, P R Morley, Mrs Angela McArt, John and Vivienne Rice, A Sadler, M A Borthwick, Earl and Chris Pick, Rona Murdoch)*

Free house ~ Licensee Graham Sylvester ~ Real ale ~ Bar food ~ Restaurant ~ (01208) 880244 ~ Children in eating area of bar ~ Dogs allowed in bar and bedrooms ~ Open 12-11; 12.30-10.30 Sun ~ Bedrooms: £47.50B/£95B

Slipway

Middle Street; limited foreshore parking, or use top car park and walk down

Low dark beams, delabole slate flagstones and some stripped stone walling give something of a cellar feel to this small and friendly family-run bar. It's entirely unpretentious, not at all 'hotelish' though pleasantly civilised, with one or two nice touches like the appealing local watercolours (for sale). Service is quick and particularly helpful; they have Sharps Doom Bar on handpump, and decent wines by the glass. The lunchtime bar menu gives an attractive choice without being overlong: sandwiches (from £3.45; crab £6.50), filled baked potatoes (from £5.50), mixed bean cassoulet (£6.95), burgers (from £6.95), fresh haddock in beer batter (£7.75), and local mussels, seafood pancakes, crab brûlée or bouillabaisse (all £7.95). Readers have found them happy to modify dishes to suit children. You can also choose from the menu for the comfortable two-level beamed restaurant, which concentrates on beautifully cooked fresh local fish, particularly the abundance of lobster and crab for which the village is famous in season – around May to October. There may be piped music. The position could hardly be bettered, at the foot of this delightful steep conservation village, and just across from the slipway down to the beach where crabbing boats are pulled up for the night, and the fish and seafood sales point is located. Overlooking the cove, the crazy-paved terrace has good solid teak tables and chairs under an awning. This hotel dates from the 16th c; we have not yet heard from any readers who have stayed here, but would expect it to be a good place to stay, if you don't mind steep stairs. *(Recommended by Neil and Beverley Gardner, Mrs Sally Kingsbury, Earl and Chris Pick)*

Free house ~ Licensees Mark and Kep Forbes ~ Real ale ~ Bar food (12-6, 7-9.30) ~ Restaurant ~ (01208) 880264 ~ Children welcome ~ Dogs allowed in bedrooms ~ Open 11-11; 12-10.30 Sun; may close Mon and Tues in Jan ~ Bedrooms: £67.50B/£90B

PORTHLEVEN SW6225 Map 1

Ship

Village on B3304 SW of Helston; pub perched on edge of harbour

One reader was delighted to find that after a gap of 40 years, this old fisherman's pub really hadn't changed much. What certainly can't change is the marvellous view over the pretty working harbour and out to sea – if you are lucky, you might be able to bag a window seat inside or one of the tables out in the terraced garden; at night, the harbour is interestingly floodlit. The knocked-through bar has log fires in big stone fireplaces and some genuine character. The no smoking family room is a conversion of an old smithy and has logs burning in a huge open fireplace. Popular, if not cheap, bar food includes sandwiches, toasties and crusties (from £4.95), filled baked potatoes (from £5.50), moules marinière or grilled goats cheese on a pesto croûton with gooseberry sauce (£5.25), ploughman's (from £6.95), home-made chilli or half a barbecue chicken (£8.95), mediterranean vegetable bake (£9.95), steaks (from £10.50), crab and prawn mornay (£11.95), local crab claws (£12.95), and daily specials; the candlelit dining room also enjoys the good view. Well kept Courage Best, Greene King Old Speckled Hen and Sharps Doom Bar on handpump; good, friendly service. Dominoes, cribbage, fruit machine, and piped music. *(Recommended by Tom McLean, Vivian Stevenson, JMC, John and Gloria Isaacs, Nigel and Olga Wikeley, Clifford Blakemore, Geoff Calcott, Giles and Annie Francis, Roger and Jenny Huggins, Maggie and Tony Harwood, Brian Skelcher, Di and Mike Gillam, Andrea Rampley, Dr and Mrs M W A Haward, P R and S A White, Susie Symes, the Didler, Reg Fowle, Helen Rickwood)*

Free house ~ Licensee Colin Oakden ~ Real ale ~ Bar food (12-9 in summer) ~ (01326) 564204 ~ Children in family room ~ Dogs welcome ~ Open 11.30-11; 12-10.30 Sun

SENNEN COVE SW3526 Map 1

Old Success

Off A30 Land's End road

From the terraced garden of this well placed, old-fashioned seaside hotel, there are marvellous views of the surf of Whitesands Bay. The beamed and timbered bar has plenty of lifeboat memorabilia, including an RNLI flag hanging on the ceiling; elsewhere are ship's lanterns, black and white photographs, dark wood tables and chairs, and a big ship's wheel that doubles as a coat stand. Bar food includes lunchtime sandwiches, locally baked cornish pasty (£2.75), soup (£2.95), fresh cod in beer batter (£6.50), lasagne (£7.15), gammon and egg (£8.25), and daily specials such as chargrilled sardines (£6.95), barbecue ribs (£8.95), and 12oz T-bone steak (£13.75). Well kept Sharps Doom Bar and Special and Skinners Cornish Knocker and Heligan Honey on handpump. Service is friendly and efficient, even in the height of summer; it's less hectic out of season. The upper bar and restaurant are no smoking. Piped music, TV; quiz night most Fridays. Bedrooms are basic but comfortable, enjoying the sound of the sea; they also do self-catering suites. Land's End is a pleasant walk away, and the clean beach is very attractive – as well as a big draw for surfers. *(Recommended by Maggie and Tony Harwood, Geoff Calcott, David Crook, Keith Stevens, Anthony Barnes, Roger and Jenny Huggins, Callum and Letitia Smith-Burnett, Margaret Booth)*

Free house ~ Licensee Martin Brooks ~ Real ale ~ Bar food (12-2.30, 6-9.30) ~ Restaurant ~ (01736) 871232 ~ Children in eating area of bar and restaurant ~ Dogs allowed in bar ~ Open 11-11; 12-10.30 Sun ~ Bedrooms: £31(£44B)/£88B

ST AGNES SV8807 Map 1

Turks Head

This is the St Agnes in the Isles of Scilly; The Quay

The most south-westerly pub in Britain, this is a special place on a lovely island, and although it does get rather swamped by visitors in the summer (the hard-working licensees still cope as efficiently as ever), this is the best time to come as you can sit on the extended area across the sleepy lane or on terraces down towards the sea. There are steps down to the slipway so you can take your drinks and food and sit right on the shore; the hanging baskets are very pretty. Winter opening hours tend to be quite sporadic, given that only some 70 people live on the island. The simply furnished but cosy and very friendly pine-panelled bar has quite a collection of flags, helmets and headwear, as well as maritime photographs and model ships. The real ale arrives in St Agnes via a beer supplier in St Austell and two boat trips, and might include St Austell Dartmoor Best and a beer named for the pub, and Ales of Scilly Scuppered (from a local microbrewery) on handpump; decent house wines, a good range of malt whiskies, and hot chocolate with brandy. At lunchtime, the well liked bar food includes open rolls (from £3.25; local crab £5.95), ploughman's (£4.95), salads (from £6.50; local crab £9.75), cold ham with chips (£6.50), vegetable pasta bake (£7.25), and puddings (£3.20), with evening dishes like feta and spinach tart (£7.25), braised lamb shank (£8.50), and mixed seafood salad (£9.95). Ice-cream and cakes are sold through the afternoon, and in good weather they may do evening barbecues. The dining extension is no smoking, and the cats are called Taggart and Lacey, and the collie, Tess. Darts, cribbage, dominoes and piped music. If you wish to stay here, you must book months ahead. *(Recommended by Pete and Rosie Flower, Neil and Anita Christopher, Peter Meister, Maureen and Bill Sewell, A J Longshaw, JP, PP, Ian and Liz Rispin, David Crook, Val and Alan Green, Mr and Mrs P Dix, Michael Butler, Paul Hopton)*

Free house ~ Licensees John and Pauline Dart ~ Real ale ~ Bar food (12-2.30, 6.30-9) ~ (01720) 422434 ~ Children welcome ~ Dogs allowed in bar ~ Open 11-11; 12-10.30 Sun; best to phone for limited opening hours in winter ~ Bedrooms: /£60S

ST ANNS CHAPEL SX4170 Map 1

Rifle Volunteer

A390

Main road pubs, especially on holiday routes, are not exactly racing certainties if you are hoping to find good food. Here's one you can bank on, though. What's more, it's kept a pleasantly pubby feel in its two front bars. The main one on the left has a log fire in its big stone fireplace, cushioned pews and country kitchen chairs, a turkey rug on its parquet floor, and a relaxed ochre and green décor; on the right, the Chapel Bar has similar furnishings on its dark boards, another open fire, and motorcycle prints on its cream walls. They have well kept Sharps Doom Bar, Coaster and Special on handpump, over 70 whiskies, and decent wines by the glass; piped music, darts, pool, dominoes, TV, and skittle alley. The food changes daily, with concentration on fresh produce, and imaginative touches perking up standard menu items. It might include home-made soup (£3.95), hummous (£4.25), smoked salmon pâté (£4.75), mixed bean and coriander chilli, steak and mushroom in ale pie or a curry of the day (£8.50), honeyed pork or chicken with ginger, lemon, and peppercorns (£9.50), steaks (from £10.95), daily specials like spaghetti tossed in warm pesto (£4.95), dressed crab (£5.50) or baked bass with garlic, coriander and toasted cashew nuts (£11.95), and puddings such as apple and ginger crumble, lemon, lime and almond cheesecake and chocolate fudge cake (£3.95). Service is friendly; it can slow on busy nights. The modern back dining room has picture windows to take advantage of a very wide view that stretches down to the Tamar estuary and Plymouth. An elevated astroturf deck beside it has some tables, with more in the garden which slopes away below. A skittle alley doubles as a function room. We have not yet heard from readers who have used the bedrooms here. *(Recommended by Mark Rogers, Dave Maunder, Jacquie and Jim Jones, Paul and Sue Merrick, Alan and Paula McCully)*

Free house ~ Licensees Frank and Lynda Hilldrup ~ Real ale ~ Bar food ~ Restaurant ~ (01822) 832508 ~ Children in restaurant and family room ~ Dogs allowed in bar ~ Blues last Fri of month ~ Open 12-2.30, 6-11; 12-3, 6.30-10.30 Sun ~ Bedrooms: £30B/£50B

ST BREWARD SX0977 Map 1

Old Inn

Old Town; village signposted off B3266 S of Camelford, also signed off A30 Bolventor—Bodmin

To get here, just head for the church which is a landmark for miles around – the pub originally housed the monks who built it. There's a friendly welcome for both regulars and visitors (quite a few of our readers are on foot, cycling or with dogs), and the spacious middle bar has plenty of seating on the fine broad slate flagstones, banknotes and horsebrasses hanging from the low oak joists that support the ochre upstairs floorboards, and plates on the stripped stonework; two massive granite fireplaces date back to the 11th c. Good, straightforward bar food includes home-made soups like enjoyable leek and potato (£3.25), filled baps or sandwiches (from £3.50), filled baked potatoes (from £5.50), local ham and eggs (£6.95), ploughman's (from £6.95), lunchtime breakfast (£7.95), mixed grill (£12.50 or £15.50), and daily specials like home-made mushroom stroganoff (£6.95) or smoked haddock and spring onion fishcakes, a home-made pie of the day, and liver and bacon (all £7.95); puddings such as home-made sticky toffee pudding or hot blackberry and apple crumble (£3.50). The restaurant and family room are no smoking. Well kept Bass, and Sharps Doom Bar, Eden and Special on handpump, all their wines available by the glass, and quite a few malt whiskies; sensibly placed darts, piped music, and fruit machine. Picnic-sets outside are protected by low stone walls. There's plenty of open moorland behind, and cattle and sheep wander freely into the village. In front of the building is a very worn carved stone; no one knows exactly what it is but it may be part of a Saxon cross. *(Recommended by JP, PP, Alan and Paula McCully, A and B D Craig, Margaret Mason, David Thompson, Simon Collett-Jones, David Crook, Guy Vowles, Jacquie and Jim Jones, the Didler, Rona Murdoch, Mick and Moira Brummell, Andrea Rampley)*

Free house ~ Licensee Darren Wills ~ Real ale ~ Bar food (11-2(3 Sun), 6-9) ~ Restaurant ~ (01208) 850711 ~ Children in eating area of bar and family room ~ Dogs allowed in bar ~ Open 11-11; 12-10.30 Sun; 11-3, 6-11 Mon-Thurs in winter

ST KEW SX0276 Map 1

St Kew Inn

Village signposted from A39 NE of Wadebridge

This year, we heard from two sets of quite unrelated readers, both of whom had not visited this rather grand-looking old stone building for around 40 years, and both of whom were delighted to find it relatively unchanged. The neatly kept bar has winged high-backed settles and varnished rustic tables on the lovely dark delabole flagstones, black wrought-iron rings for lamps or hams hanging from the high ceiling, a handsome window seat, and an open kitchen range under a high mantelpiece decorated with earthenware flagons. At lunchtime, the good, popular bar food includes soups like curried sweet potato or stilton and celery (£2.75), sandwiches (from £2.75; crab £6.50), feta, gruyère, and onion tart or vegetable curry (£6.95), lasagne (£7.50), nice fresh fish pie (£8.25), steak and kidney or game pie (£8.50), local crab cakes (£10.50), and large lemon sole (£11.50). Well kept St Austell Tinners, HSD, and Tribute tapped from wooden casks behind the counter (lots of tankards hang from the beams above it), a couple of farm ciders, a good wine list, and several malt whiskies; darts, cribbage, dominoes, and shove-ha'penny. The big garden has a small summer marquee, seats on the grass and picnic-sets on the front cobbles. *(Recommended by Tracey and Stephen Groves, M A Borthwick, Bob and Sue Hardy, JP, PP, Margaret Mason, David Thompson, Bill and Jessica Ritson, Jacquie and Jim Jones, R T and J C Moggridge, J S Burn, the Didler, Rona Murdoch, Andrea Rampley)*

St Austell ~ Tenant Desmond Weston ~ Real ale ~ Bar food ~ (01208) 841259 ~

Children in dining room ~ Open 11-2.30, 6-11(all day July and Aug); 12-3, 7-10.30(all day in July and Aug) Sun; closed 25 Dec

ST MAWGAN SW8766 Map 1

Falcon

NE of Newquay, off B3276 or A3059

Set in a very pretty village, this neatly kept inn has a good bustling and friendly atmosphere. The neatly kept big bar has a log fire, small modern settles, large antique coaching prints and falcon pictures on the walls, well kept St Austell Tinners, HSD and Tribute on handpump, and a decent wine list; efficient service even when busy. Bar food includes sandwiches, garlic mushrooms (£4.50), local goats cheese salad (£4.75), vegetable pasta (£6.95), sausages (£7.45), moroccan-style lamb with orange and mint couscous (£7.95), and sirloin steak (£11.75), with fish dishes such as fresh cod in beer batter (£8.50), Fowey river mussels in cider and cream or fresh haddock with local smoked blue cheese topping (£9.95), scallops grilled in their shells with ginger and coriander (£11.95), and plain grilled whole dover sole with parsley butter (£13.95). The restaurant is no smoking and has paintings and pottery by local artists for sale; darts and euchre. Particularly when the fine wisteria is flowering, the cobbled courtyard in front, with its stone tables, is a lovely spot to relax; outside heaters for cooler evenings. The peaceful, attractive garden has plenty of seats, a wishing well, and play equipment for children. *(Recommended by Neil and Anita Christopher, Mrs A P Lee, JCW, Jane Taylor, David Dutton, A and B D Craig, Brian Skelcher, Ray and Winifred Halliday, Val and Alan Green, David Crook, David Eberlin, Bob and Margaret Holder, Robert Coates, Brian and Bett Cox, Mark Flynn)*

St Austell ~ Tenant Andy Banks ~ Real ale ~ Bar food ~ Restaurant ~ (01637) 860225 ~ Children in restaurant ~ Dogs welcome ~ Open 11-3, 6-11; 12-3, 7-10.30 Sun ~ Bedrooms: £26/£52(£72S)

TREBURLEY SX3477 Map 1

Springer Spaniel 🍴 🍷

A388 Callington—Launceston

Owned by the same company that now runs the Crown at Lanlivery, this bustling roadside pub has a new licensee, again, but readers are quick to voice their enthusiasm. There's been a little refurbishment, but the relaxed, friendly bar still has a lovely, very high-backed settle by the woodburning stove in the big fireplace, high-backed farmhouse chairs and other seats, and pictures of olde-worlde stage-coach arrivals at inns; this leads into a cosy room with big solid teak tables. Up some steps from the main bar is the beamed, attractively furnished, no smoking restaurant. Good enjoyable food now includes lunchtime sandwiches (from £4.95; crab £6.95), mushroom pot (£5.50), chicken and bacon terrine or local ham and egg (£5.95), ploughman's (£6.50), steak in ale pie (£7.50), red pepper and fennel savoury cheese tart (£8.95), and stilton beef (£11.95), with daily specials like home-made leek and potato soup (£3.50), potted local game pâté (£4.95), local venison and mushroom casserole (£8.95), fillet of local pork with jerk-style marinade and mango and pepper salsa (£10.95), and fillets of bass with saffron cream sauce (£14.95), and puddings such as minted white chocolate cheesecake or treacle and lemon tart (£5). Well kept Sharps Doom Bar, Coaster, and a beer named for the pub on handpump, a good wine list, local cider, and a few malt whiskies; cribbage and dominoes. *(Recommended by C P Baxter, Brian and Bett Cox, DRH and KLH, Mr and Mrs G M Pearson, Ryta Lyndley, A Sadler, Pamela and Merlyn Horswell, Jacquie and Jim Jones, Paul and Philippa Ward, Mary Ellen Cummings)*

Wagtail Inns ~ Licensee Craig Woolley ~ Real ale ~ Bar food (12-2, 6-9) ~ Restaurant ~ (01579) 370424 ~ Children in eating area of bar and restaurant ~ Dogs allowed in bar ~ Open 12-3, 6-11; 12-3, 7-10.30 Sun; closed 25 Dec

TREGADILLETT SX2984 Map 1

Eliot Arms

Village signposted off A30 at junction with A395, W end of Launceston bypass

New owners and a new licensee again this year for this creeper-covered inn, but luckily, little seems to have changed. The series of small softly lit rooms is still full of interest: 72 antique clocks (including seven grandfathers), 400 snuffs, hundreds of horsebrasses, old prints, old postcards or cigarette cards grouped in frames on the walls, quite a few barometers, and shelves of books and china. Also, a fine old mix of furniture on the delabole slate floors, from high-backed built-in curved settles, through plush Victorian dining chairs, armed seats, chaise longues and mahogany housekeeper's chairs, to more modern seats, and open fires; piped music. Straightforward bar food includes lunchtime baguettes and filled baked potatoes, home-made soup (£2.95), pâté or garlic mushrooms (£3.95), ploughman's (£4.95), vegetable tikka masala or ham and eggs (£6.25), a pie of the day (£6.50), chicken in barbecue sauce or sardines in garlic butter (£7.95), steaks (from £10.95), and Sunday lunch (£5.95). Well kept Butcombe Bitter, Courage Best and Sharps Eden on handpump; darts, fruit machine, and piped music. There are seats in front of the pub and at the back of the car park. *(Recommended by Janet Walters, John and Elizabeth Thomason, David Crook, Brian and Bett Cox, Duncan Cloud, Terry and Linda Moseley, JP, PP, Louise English, Charles Gysin, Di and Mike Gillam, Mr and Mrs P Dix, Dr and Mrs D Woods, Dr D Taub, Philip and Ann Board, the Didler, Dorsan Baker)*

Coast & Country Inns ~ Manager Sarah Richards ~ Real ale ~ Bar food ~ Restaurant ~ (01566) 772051 ~ Children in family room ~ Dogs allowed in bar ~ Open 11.30-11; 12-10.30 Sun ~ Bedrooms: /£60S(£50B)

TREMATON SX3959 Map 1

Crooked Inn

Off A38 just W of Saltash

A long well lit drive leads you down to this surprisingly isolated but relaxed and friendly inn. The bar is more or less open-plan, with high bar stools by the curved stone counter, mate's chairs and brocaded stools around a mix of tables in front of the big open fireplace, and a piano for impromptu entertainment. Down a step is the lower lounge with heavier stripped beams, upholstered settle seating, and another fireplace with a woodburning stove. A new conservatory leads off this, with ceiling fans, a growing vine, and doors opening out onto the new decking area which looks over the garden and valley below. For children there are swings, a slide built into the hillside, a tree house and trampoline. Sheep, ducks, a pig, pigmy goat, and two dogs roam the grounds, and a rather fine horse may be nibbling the lawn. Well kept Sharps Own and Doom Bar, Skinners Cornish Knocker and St Austell HSD on handpump, and a decent wine list; piped music. Generous helpings of bar food include sandwiches (from £2.25), home-made soup (£2.95), pâté (£4.25), ploughman's (from £4.95), lunchtime ham and eggs (£5.95), home-made curry of the day (£6.25), home-made steak and kidney pie (£6.50), fresh local cod in crispy batter (£6.75), steaks (from £10.95), and daily specials such as lambs liver and bacon (£10.25), plaice véronique (£10.95), and duck breast with crushed pineapple and black pepper sauce (£11.95). The bedrooms (which we would be grateful for reports on) overlook the courtyard where there are seats, and maybe some feathered friends. *(Recommended by Clive, David M Cundy, Esther and John Sprinkle, Laura Wilson, Michael Lamm, Ted George)*

Free house ~ Licensees Sandra and Tony Arnold ~ Real ale ~ Bar food (12-3, 6-9.30) ~ (01752) 848177 ~ Children welcome ~ Dogs welcome ~ Open 11-11; 12-10.30 Sun ~ Bedrooms: £45B/£70B

> If you stay overnight in an inn or hotel, they are allowed to serve you an alcoholic drink at any hour of the day or night.

TRESCO SV8915 Map 1

New Inn

New Grimsby; Isles of Scilly

A short stroll from the New Grimsby quay, this friendly place is, not surprisingly given such a lovely spot, very popular. The locals' bar has a good chatty atmosphere, while visitors enjoy the main bar room or the light, airy dining extension. There are some comfortable old sofas, banquettes, planked partition seating, and farmhouse chairs and tables, a few standing timbers, boat pictures, a large model sailing boat, a collection of old telescopes, and plates on the delft shelf. The Pavilion extension has plenty of seats and tables on the blue wooden floors, cheerful yellow walls, and looks over the flower-filled terrace where there's plenty of teak furniture and views of the sea. Well liked bar food includes soup (£3.50), meaty or vegetarian pasties (£5), sandwiches (from £5.50; fresh crab £9), trio of cornish sausages (£6.50), ploughman's (£7), potted local crab (£7.50), beef in ale casserole (£8), pasta with chargrilled mediterranean vegetables or fish and chips in newspaper wrapper (£9), smoked haddock and salmon fishcakes (£10), and puddings (£4); various breakfasts are available until 11am (from £6). Service does slow down when the pub is particularly busy, and it can get packed in summer. Well kept Ales of Scilly Natural Beauty, Skinners Betty Stogs Bitter and a beer brewed just for the pub by St Austell, Tresco Tipple, on handpump; interesting wines (by the large glass), up to 25 malt whiskies, and ten vodkas; real espresso and cappuccino coffee, piped music, darts, pool, cribbage, and dominoes. Note that the price below is for dinner, bed and breakfast. *(Recommended by Andy Sinden, Louise Harrington, Pete and Rosie Flower, Neil and Anita Christopher, Bernard Stradling, R J Herd, Val and Alan Green, Michael Butler, Paul Hopton, Gwyn Jones)*

Free house ~ Licensee Alan Baptist ~ Real ale ~ Bar food (12-3, 6-9) ~ Restaurant ~ (01720) 422844 ~ Children welcome ~ Open 11-11; 12-10.30 Sun; 11-3, 6-11 in winter ~ Bedrooms: /£218B

TRURO SW8244 Map 1

Old Ale House £

Quay Street

Of course the fine range of real ales is a big draw here, but there's also a tremendous local atmosphere, and a genuinely friendly welcome to all – and the food is good, too. On handpump or tapped from the cask, the well kept, regularly changing beers might come from breweries such as Bass, Butcombe, Courage, Everards, Exmoor, Greene King, Sharps, Shepherd Neame and Skinners; 21 country wines. Tasty wholesome bar food prepared in a spotless kitchen in full view of the bar includes doorstep sandwiches (from £2.75; 'hands' or half bloomers with toppings such as bacon, onions and melted cheese or tuna, mayonnaise and melted cheese, small £2.25, large £3.95), filled baked potatoes or ploughman's (from £3.25), hot meals served in a skillet pan like five spice chicken, sizzling beef or vegetable stir fry (small helpings from £4.50, big helpings from £6.25), and home-made dishes like a pie of the day or lasagne (£4.95); puddings (£2.95), Sunday lunch (£4.95), and theme nights (£6.95). The dimly lit bar has an engaging diversity of furnishings, some interesting 1920s bric-a-brac, beer mats pinned everywhere, matchbox collections, and newspapers and magazines to read. Dominoes, giant Jenga, giant Connect Four, and piped music. *(Recommended by JP, PP, B J Harding, Joyce and Maurice Cottrell, Ted George, Di and Mike Gillam, Callum and Letitia Smith-Burnett, R T and J C Moggridge, Jacquie and Jim Jones, Ian Phillips, the Didler)*

Enterprise ~ Tenant Mark Jones ~ Real ale ~ Bar food (12-2.45(5 Sat), 7-8.45; no food Sat or Sun evenings) ~ (01872) 271122 ~ Children in eating area of bar until 9 ~ Live jam sessions Mon, jazz Weds, bands Thurs ~ Open 11-11; 12-10.30 Sun; closed 26 Dec, 1 Jan

If you report on a pub that's not a main entry, please tell us any lunchtimes or evenings when it doesn't serve bar food.

LUCKY DIP

Besides the fully inspected pubs, you might like to try these Lucky Dips recommended to us and described by readers (if you do, please send us reports: www.goodguides.co.uk).

ASHTON SW6028
Lion & Lamb [A394 Helston—Penzance]: Welcoming pub with wide range of food from good sandwiches and paninis up, well kept ales such as Sharps Doom Bar, occasional mini beer festivals, obliging staff; lovely hanging baskets and flowerbeds, open all day, handy for SW Coastal Path *(Maggie and Tony Harwood, Dennis Jenkin)*

BOLVENTOR SX1876
Jamaica Inn [signed just off A30 on Bodmin Moor]: Lots of character in oak-beamed stripped stone 18th-c core, comfortable and cosy, with big log fire, well kept Sharps Doom Bar, young enthusiastic staff and plaque commemorating murdered landlord Joss Merlyn; pretty secluded garden with play area, bedrooms, properly bleak moorland setting (if you forget about the big side all-day cafeteria and souvenir shop) *(A and B D Craig, Dr and Mrs A K Clarke, David Crook)*

BOSCASTLE SX0990
Cobweb [B3263, just E of harbour]: Well used local with plenty of character, hundreds of old bottles hanging from heavy beams, two or three high-backed settles, dark stone walls, cosy log fire, real ales such as Dartmoor and St Austell, no smoking area; darts, dominoes, cribbage, pool, fruit machine and juke box, more machines and another fire in sizeable family room; live music Sat, open all day *(David Eagles, LYM, Dr D J Groves, JP, PP, Geoff Pidoux, Mayur Shah, the Didler)*

Napoleon [High St, top of village]: 16th-c pub, low beams, slate floors, different levels, log fires, interesting prints of Napoleon, bar food from snacks to steaks, well kept St Austell ales tapped from the cask, decent wines, good coffee, traditional games; piped music; dogs allowed in bar, children in eating areas, tables on covered terrace, large sheltered garden, steep climb up from harbour (splendid views on the way), open all day *(LYM, JCW, JP, PP, W F C Phillips, Keith and Margaret Kettell, Dr Martin Owton, Gill and Tony Morriss, Mike Green, the Didler)*

BOTALLACK SW3632
Queens Arms: Friendly pub with good food choice inc local fish and good Sun lunch, well kept local beers, helpful staff, log fire in unusual granite inglenook, comfortable settles and other dark wood furniture, tin mining and other old local photographs on stripped stone walls, attractive new family room; large pleasant back garden with owl refuge, wonderful clifftop walks nearby *(Helen Flaherty, Mr and Mrs Ian Davidson)*

BREAGE SW6128
Queens Arms [3 miles W of Helston]: Long thriving bar with log fire each end, beams festooned with plates, Sharps Doom Bar and several other well kept changing ales, wide range of good value food inc sausage specialities, welcoming landlord, daily papers, games area one end, no smoking dining room the other; tables and children's games room outside, another play area and garden over the lane; quiz night Weds, jazz Thurs; bedrooms, medieval wall paintings in church opp *(Alan Bowker)*

CALLINGTON SX3569
☆ *Coachmakers Arms* [A388 towards Launceston]: Imposing 18th-c pub, beams and timbers, ceilings with flags from around the world matching clock collection with differing time zones, bric-a-brac and tropical fish, well kept ales inc Sharps Doom Bar and Skinners Cornish Knocker, bar food from baguettes and baked potatoes to chargrills, restaurant; piped music, Weds quiz night; children in eating areas, bedrooms *(LYM, Howard Gregory, Val and Alan Green)*

CANONS TOWN SW5335
Lamb & Flag [A30 Hayle—Penzance; half a mile Penzance side of St Erth station]: Redecorated under newish management, decent food from baguettes and baked potatoes to good range of specials, well kept ales inc a guest such as Caledonian Deuchars IPA, evening restaurant; dogs very welcome, tables in courtyard and extended garden *(Peter Salmon)*

CAWSAND SX4350
☆ *Cross Keys* [The Square]: Unpretentious pub opp boat club, well kept ales such as Blackawton West Country Gold, Courage Best, John Smiths and Teignworthy Friendly Ferret, wide range of enjoyable generous reasonably priced food in bar and restaurant, friendly service; dogs welcome, pool, may be piped music; pleasant bedrooms *(Kathleen Henry, Pat and Derek Westcott)*

CHAPEL AMBLE SW9975
☆ *Maltsters Arms* [off A39 NE of Wadebridge]: Bright neatly kept knocked-together rooms with panelling, stripped stone and eau de nil paintwork, big open fire, oak joists, heavy furnishings on partly carpeted flagstones; friendly young staff, well kept ales inc one brewed by Sharps for the pub, good wines, food (not cheap) from nice doorstep sandwiches up in bar and restaurant; may be piped music; dogs welcome in bar, children treated well in plain upstairs family room, benches out in sheltered sunny corner *(DAV, Brian and Bett Cox, A Sadler, R and S Bentley, Bob and Sue Hardy, WINN, Jane Taylor, David Dutton, LYM, Neil and Beverley Gardner, Mrs Angela McArt, John and Vivienne Rice, Geoff Pidoux, Canon Michael Bourdeaux, David Tindal, Rona Murdoch)*

CHARLESTOWN SX0351
☆ *Harbour Inn* [part of Pier House Hotel]: Small well managed bar attached to comfortable hotel (27 bedrooms – and good value cream

teas in its restaurant), in first-class spot alongside and looking over the classic little harbour and its historic sailing ships, red plush and copper-topped cask tables, good choice of enjoyable traditional food and plenty of fresh seafood, more tables in back area (no view), well kept Bass, Sharps Own and Doom Bar and Wadworths 6X, good wines, quick service, helpful charming staff; parking away from harbour, walk down; tables out by harbour wall, interesting film-set conservation village with shipwreck museum *(David Rule, Di and Mike Gillam, John and Wendy Allin, Ken Flawn, BB, Reg Fowle, Helen Rickwood)*

Rashleigh Arms [Quay Rd]: Large bar and very big lounge well refurbished with nautical touches, wide choice of good value generous food all day, unpretentious carvery restaurant, lots of tables out on terrace (dogs allowed there) and separate garden above little harbour and heritage centre; good choice of well kept ales, good coffee, cheery quick helpful service, good canalside family room; piped music may be loud, on the coach circuit; good value bedrooms *(G W A Pearce, M Joyner)*

CHILSWORTHY SX4172

White Hart: Relaxed and unassuming, with generous enjoyable food in back dining area inc good Thurs curry night, well kept Sharps beers, lots of local activities, discreet pool table; nice steep garden, stunning views of Tamar valley and Dartmoor from back terrace *(Nigel Long, Alan and Paula McCully)*

CRACKINGTON HAVEN SX1496

Coombe Barton [off A39 Bude—Camelford]: New licensees for much-extended old inn in beautiful setting opposite splendid craggy bay popular with surfers and walkers; side terrace with plenty of tables, big modernised bar with plenty of room for summer crowds, lots of local pictures, surfboard hanging from plank ceiling, smartly uniformed young staff, wide range of food inc fresh fish and children's menu, three local real ales, no smoking restaurant and big plain family room, darts; glazed-off pool table, fruit machines, piped music, TV; dogs allowed in bar, bedrooms, open all day Sun, also Sat in school hols *(LYM)*

CRAFTHOLE SX3654

☆ ***Finnygook***: Clean and comfortable much-modernised lounge bar, light and airy, well kept St Austell beers, reasonably priced wines, wide food choice from good generous open sandwiches up, friendly staff, restaurant; discreet piped music, one car park is steep; tables in yard, good sea views from residents' lounge, low-priced bedrooms *(BB, Dennis Jenkin)*

CRANTOCK SW7960

☆ ***Old Albion*** [Langurroc Rd]: Pleasantly placed photogenic thatched village pub, low beams, flagstones and open fires, old-fashioned small bar with brasses and low lighting, larger more open room with local pictures, informal local feel despite all the summer visitors (and the souvenirs sold here), friendly staff, generous basic home-made bar lunches inc good sandwiches and giant ploughman's, well kept Sharps and Skinners ales, farm cider, decent house wines; dogs welcome, tables out on terrace, open all day *(JP, PP, Dennis Jenkin, LYM)*

CROWS NEST SX2669

☆ ***Crows Nest*** [signed off B3264 N of Liskeard; OS Sheet 201 map ref 263692]: Old-fashioned 17th-c pub with attentive cheerful staff, gleaming horsey bits hanging from bowed dark oak beams, mining pictures and some interesting and unusual furnishings, big log fire, well kept St Austell Tinners and HSD and a guest beer, decent wines, good blackboard food choice from ploughman's and pasties up (strong on puddings), two linked rooms for eating, one no smoking (children welcome and well treated here); piped music; picnic-sets on terrace by quiet lane, handy for walks on Bodmin moor *(LYM, Nigel Long, Gill and Keith Croxton, Paul and Sue Merrick, Mr and Mrs G M Pearson)*

CUBERT SW7858

☆ ***Smugglers Den*** [village signed off A3075 S of Newquay, then brown sign to pub (and Trebellan holiday park) on left]: Hugely extended open-plan 16th-c thatched pub, lots of well ordered tables, dim lighting, stripped stone and heavy beam and plank ceilings, west country pictures and seafaring memorabilia, small barrel seats, steps down to no smoking area with enormous inglenook woodburner, another step to big side family dining room; neat helpful friendly staff, fresh generous enjoyable food inc local seafood, well kept ales such as Sharps Eden, Skinners Betty Stogs and St Austell HSD and Tribute, farm cider; well lit pool area, darts; fruit machine, may be loud piped music; picnic-sets in small courtyard and on lawn with climbing frame; has been cl winter Mon-Weds lunchtime *(David Crook, JP, PP, Tim and Ann Newell, BB, Chris Reeve, the Didler)*

DEVORAN SW7938

☆ ***Old Quay House*** [Quay Rd – brown sign to pub off A39 Truro—Falmouth]: Very pleasant old local at end of coast to coast cycle way, welcoming and relaxing; two small unpretentious rooms, one with good sensibly priced food inc good baguettes, some interesting specials and strong seafood influence, the other with daily papers and big coal fire, boating bric-a-brac, well kept Fullers London Pride and Sharps Doom Bar, quick friendly service, evening restaurant; bar can be smoky; steeply terraced garden behind making the most of the idyllic spot – peaceful creekside village, lovely views, walks nearby; good value bedrooms, open all day in summer *(David Crook, David Billington, BB, Dr and Mrs M W A Haward, Andy Sinden, Louise Harrington, Guy Vowles, J V Dadswell)*

EDMONTON SW9672

☆ ***Quarryman*** [off A39 just W of Wadebridge bypass]: Welcoming service and some good individual cooking besides lunchtime snacks such as sandwiches, home-made burgers and ploughman's in unusual three-room beamed bar, partly no smoking, around courtyard of former quarrymen's quarters, and part of a small holiday complex; some interesting decorations inc old sporting memorabilia, well kept Sharps Eden, Skinners Coastliner and a couple of good guest beers; pool, cribbage and dominoes, friendly dog called Floyd (visiting dogs welcome), cosy no smoking bistro; well behaved children in eating area, open all day *(Mrs S Wiltshire, Alan and Paula McCully, DRH and KLH, Cynthia and Stephen Fisher, M A Borthwick, LYM, Andrin Cooper)*

FALMOUTH SW8132

Chain Locker [Custom House Quay]: Popular with visitors for fine spot by inner harbour with window tables and lots outside, well kept ales such as Sharps Doom Bar and Skinners, well priced generous food from sandwiches to fresh local fish, quick service, strongly nautical bare-boards décor, darts alley; fruit machine, piped music; well behaved children welcome, open all day, self-catering accommodation *(JP, PP, LYM, Joyce and Maurice Cottrell, Patrick Hancock, M Joyner, the Didler)*

Packet Station [The Moor]: Restaurant-look Wetherspoons with long bars on both floors, ten low-priced real ales and pocket-friendly food (steak night Tues, curry night Thurs); bilingual cornish/english signs *(Alan Bowker)*

☆ *Quayside Inn & Old Ale House* [Arwenack St/Fore St]: Bustling bare-boards dark-panelled bar with good range of well kept ales inc Sharps, Skinners and more distant favourites, decent wines, efficient service, reasonably priced food (all day in summer) from good value doorstep sandwiches to Sun roasts, more skillets evening, upstairs harbour-view lounge with armchairs and sofas one end; lots of pub games, juke box or piped music, TV, busy with young people evenings, esp Fri/Sat for live music; children welcome, plenty of waterside picnic-sets, open all day *(Geoff and Jan Dawson, JP, PP, LYM, Richard Fendick, John Martin, V Banting, Patrick Hancock, Callum and Letitia Smith-Burnett, David Crook, the Didler)*

☆ *Seven Stars* [The Moor (centre)]: Classic unchanging and unsmart 17th-c local with long-serving and entertaining vicar-landlord, no gimmicks (nor machines or mobile phones), warm welcome, Bass, Sharps and Skinners tapped from the cask, home-made rolls, chatty regulars, big key-ring collection, quiet back snug, corridor hatch serving tables on prime-site roadside courtyard *(JP, PP, the Didler, BB, Giles and Annie Francis, Kevin Thorpe, Patrick Hancock)*

Star & Garter [High St]: Thriving two-room local with fine high views over harbour and estuary, friendly service, reasonably priced bar food, well kept real ales, huge collection of teapots, local murals; theme and music nights *(Patrick Hancock)*

FLUSHING SW8033

Royal Standard [off A393 at Penryn (or foot ferry from Falmouth); St Peters Hill]: Trim waterfront local with veteran welcoming landlord, plenty of genuine characters, great views to Falmouth from front terrace, neat bar with pink plush and copper, alcove with pool and darts, simple well cooked food inc good baked potatoes, home-made pasties and fruit pies, well kept Bass and Sharps Doom Bar; outside gents' *(JP, PP, the Didler, Di and Mike Gillam, Debbie and Neil Hayter)*

FOWEY SX1252

☆ *Galleon* [Fore St; from centre follow Car Ferry signs]: Superb spot overlooking harbour and estuary, spotless solid pine and modern nautical décor with lots of wood, dining areas off, well kept and priced Flowers IPA, Sharps Cornish Coaster and a guest beer, generous good value food with plenty of fish, fast friendly service; pool, jazz Sun lunchtime; children welcome, disabled facilities, tables out on attractive extended waterside terrace and in sheltered courtyard with covered heated area, good estuary-view bedrooms *(Michael Dandy, George Atkinson, BB, Michael Lamm, Jim and Maggie Cowell, Nick Lawless, Mary Ellen Cummings)*

☆ *King of Prussia* [Town Quay]: Large neat upstairs bar in handsome quayside building, bay windows looking over harbour to Polruan, St Austell ales, sensibly priced wines, side family food bar with good value individually cooked food inc fish and seafood, friendly service; pool, may be piped music, occasional live; seats outside, open all day at least in summer, pleasant bedrooms *(LYM, Edward Mirzoeff, Charles and Pauline Stride, Martin and Karen Wake, Patrick Hancock, Geoff Pidoux, Sue Demont, Tim Barrow)*

Lugger [Fore St]: Spotless pub with unpretentious locals' bar, comfortable small candlelit dining area, very family-friendly but popular with older people too for wide choice of good generous food inc lots of seafood, cheap well kept St Austell ales, friendly service, big waterfront mural; piped music; pavement tables, bedrooms *(BB, the Didler, Jim and Maggie Cowell, Nick Lawless)*

☆ *Ship* [Trafalgar Sq]: Friendly, clean and tidy local, good choice of good value generous food from sandwiches up inc fine local seafood, lots of sea pictures, coal fire, pool/darts room, family dining room with big stained-glass window, well kept St Austell beers; juke box or piped music, small TV for sports; dogs allowed, old-fashioned bedrooms, some oak-panelled *(LYM, Patrick Hancock, Nick Lawless)*

GOLANT SX1155

☆ *Fishermans Arms* [Fore St (B3269)]: Current welcoming licensees doing well in partly flagstoned waterside local with lovely views across River Fowey from front bar and terrace; good value generous home-made standard food from sandwiches to curry specials and fresh local fish, all day in summer (cl Sun afternoon), well kept Sharps Doom Bar and Ushers Best, good wines by the glass, friendly service (can slow on busy days), log fire, interesting pictures, fancy goldfish, back family room; piano, TV, may be piped radio; pleasant garden *(Andy and Ali, George Atkinson, Evelyn and Derek Walter, the Didler, Martin and Karen Wake, B and M Kendall, Mrs M Granville-Edge, BB)*

GOONHAVERN SW7853

New Inn [A3075 S of Newquay]: Neatly kept roadside village pub with good choice of wines, beers and generous lunchtime food, friendly service; tables and play area outside, huge car park *(Mick and Moira Brummell)*

GUNNISLAKE SX4371

Buccaneer [Commercial St]: Local with mainly keg beers but occasional guest real ale; dogs allowed, pleasant seats out in front, small garden behind, open all day *(Alan and Paula McCully)*

☆ *Rising Sun* [lower road to Calstock, S of village]: Comfortable 17th-c pub with enjoyable straightforward food (not Sun or Mon) using seasonal produce, friendly service, well kept Bass and Sharps, beams and flagstones, pleasant furniture, lots of pictures and china, woodburners; stunning views of Tamar valley from pretty terraced garden with play area *(Alan and Paula McCully)*

Tavistock [Fore St]: Traditional old family-run coaching inn, welcoming staff, real ales such as Bass and Sharps Cornish Special, enjoyable well priced food inc good fish choice; live music, quiz nights; open all day *(Alan and Paula McCully)*

GURNARDS HEAD SW4337

Gurnards Head Hotel [B3306 Zennor—St Just]: New owners for isolated hotel in bleak NT scenery, surrounded by glorious walks, both inland and along the cliffy coast; pubby bar, log and coal fires at each end, local pictures on plank panelling, real ales such as Courage and Skinners, bar and restaurant food, no smoking family room; tables in garden behind, bedrooms with rugged moorland or sea views *(Sue Demont, Tim Barrow, Peter Salmon, LYM, Adrian Johnson)*

HARROWBARROW SX4069

Cross House [off A390 E of Callington; School Rd]: Enjoyable reasonably priced food in bar and no smoking restaurant, friendly service, plenty of old-world atmosphere (especially when the locals start on those Cornish tales), well kept ales, open fire, darts; children welcome, big garden with play area *(anon)*

HAYLE SW5335

Cornish Arms [Commercial Rd]: Attractive central pub with good value food from sandwiches to steaks, St Austell ales; dogs and children allowed, outside seating, handy for Hayle estuary bird reserve and Towans nature reserve *(anon)*

HELFORD PASSAGE SW7627

Ferry Boat [signed from B3291]: Big family bar included for its super position, about a mile's walk from gate at bottom of Glendurgan Garden (NT), by sandy beach with swimming, small boat hire, fishing trips and summer ferry to Helford, suntrap waterside terrace with covered area and barbecues; full St Austell range kept well, very good range of wines by the glass, usual food, no smoking restaurant; may be piped music, games area with pool, juke box and SkyTV, steep walk down from the overflow car park; usually open all day summer (with cream teas and frequent live entertainment); bedrooms *(John Wooll, Maggie and Tony Harwood, LYM, Roger Wain-Heapy, Michael Dandy, Patrick Hancock, David Crook)*

HELSTON SW6527

☆ *Blue Anchor* [Coinagehall St]: 15th-c basic thatched local, very popular for the Spingo IPA, Middle and specials they still brew in their ancient brewhouse; quaint rooms off corridor, flagstones, stripped stone, low beams and simple old-fashioned furniture, traditional games, family room, cheap lunchtime food (if not, they let you bring your own); seats out behind, open all day *(Tim and Ann Newell, Sue Holland, Dave Webster, Giles and Annie Francis, Tom McLean, JP, PP, Maggie and Tony Harwood, Roger and Jenny Huggins, Di and Mike Gillam, John Martin, V Banting, LYM, Patrick Hancock, Andrea Rampley, the Didler, Rona Murdoch)*

HESSENFORD SX3057

Copley Arms [A387 Looe—Torpoint]: Emphasis on good bar and restaurant food in linked areas of modernised eating area, well kept St Austell ales, nice wine choice; piped music, dogs allowed in one small area, big plain family room; sizeable and attractive streamside garden and terrace (but by road), play area, bedrooms *(Gill and Keith Croxton)*

KILKHAMPTON SS2511

London [A39 Bude—Bideford]: Village local with friendly staff, well kept Sharps Doom Bar, good value food, good atmosphere; children welcome *(Jane and Mark Hooper)*

LAMORNA SW4424

☆ *Lamorna Wink* [off B3315 SW of Penzance]: Unspoilt no-frills country local short stroll above pretty cove, with good coast walks; good collection of warship mementoes, sea photographs, nautical brassware and hats, Sharps Own and Doom Bar and Skinners Cornish Knocker, nice house wine, sandwiches and other simple lunchtime food from homely kitchen area (may not be available out of season), books for sale, coal fire, pool table; children in eating area, benches outside, open all day in summer *(Roger and Jenny Huggins, Bob and Sue Hardy, John and Vivienne Rice, LYM, Duncan Cloud, Adrian Johnson)*

LANGDON SX3091

Countryman [Boyton, B3254 N of Launceston]: Comfortably refurbished, with several well kept real ales, reasonably priced food inc good toasties and baguettes, friendly service, dining area, restaurant and family room; very busy Sun lunchtime and school hols; tables and swings outside, handy for Tamar Otter Sanctuary *(P Hennessey)*

LANNER SW7240

☆ *Fox & Hounds* [Comford; A393/B3298]: Relaxed and rambling pub under new management, low black beams, stripped stone, dark panelling, high-backed settles and cottagey chairs on flagstones, warm fires, good choice of generous reasonably priced food from sandwiches and baguettes up, well kept St Austell ales tapped from the cask, decent house wines, good service, children welcome in no smoking dining room; pub games, dogs allowed in bar, piped music; great floral displays in front, neat back garden with pond and play area, open all day wknds *(Dennis Jenkin, LYM, Charles Gysin, P R and S A White)*

LANREATH SX1757

☆ ***Punch Bowl*** [signed off B3359]: Rambling 17th-c inn with traditional flagstoned public bar and comfortable black-panelled lounge, antique settles and huge fireplace, well kept Sharps Figgys Brew and Skinners Betty Stogs or Cornish Knocker, bar food and separate striking panelled medieval restaurant with chandeliers and gargoyles; TV and games; children welcome, cl Mon lunchtime in winter, bedrooms, pleasant tucked-away village *(LYM, George Atkinson, Michael Butler)*

LELANT SW5437

Badger [village signed off A30 W of Hayle; Fore St]: Spaciously extended dining pub with wide range of food from sandwiches to fresh fish and OAP lunches, attractively softly lit modern L-shaped interior, partly no smoking, with panelled recesses, some high-backed settles, airy back conservatory, well kept St Austell ales, cheerful efficient service; may be piped music; children welcome, good value pretty bedrooms, wonderful breakfast *(Callum and Letitia Smith-Burnett)*

Old Quay House [Griggs Quay, Lelant Saltings; A3047/B3301 S of village]: Large neatly kept modern pub in marvellous spot overlooking bird sanctuary estuary, good value wholesome usual food, real ales, good service, dining area off open-plan bar; decent motel-type bedrooms *(John and Jackie Chalcraft, Alan Bowker, J V Dadswell)*

Watermill [Lelant Downs; A3074 S]: Converted mill dining pub, working waterwheel behind with gearing in dark-beamed central bar opening into brighter airy front extension and gallery restaurant area with racks of wine, quick friendly service, good choice of well kept real ales, food inc good generous baguettes, decent wines (off-sales too), good coffee; dark pink pool room, may be piped nostalgic pop music; tables out under pergola and among trees in pretty streamside garden *(Richard Fendick, BB, Mr and Mrs Jamieson, Callum and Letitia Smith-Burnett)*

LERRYN SX1457

Ship [signed off A390 in Lostwithiel; Fore St]: Lovely spot esp when tide's in, nr famous stepping-stones and three well signed waterside walks, picnic-sets and pretty play area outside; well kept ales such as Bass, Skinners and Sharps Eden, local farm cider, good wines, fruit wines and malt whiskies, wide food choice from pasties and good sandwiches up inc popular Sun carvery, no smoking area, huge woodburner, attractive adults-only dining conservatory (booked quickly evenings and wknds); games room with pool, dogs on leads and children welcome; nice bedrooms in adjoining building, wonderful breakfast *(George Atkinson, Peter and Audrey Dowsett, LYM, David Crook)*

LINKINHORNE SX3173

☆ ***Church House*** [off B3257 NW of Callington]: Neatly modernised bar, part rustic furniture and flagstones, part plush and carpet, with some decorative china etc, woodburner, darts; well kept Sharps Doom Bar and Skinners Cornish Knocker, low mark-ups on wine, welcoming service, popular home-made food inc local produce and some bargains for children, also plush no smoking restaurant (best to book wknds); piped music; nice spot opp church, has been cl Mon *(BB, Rona Murdoch, Derek and Heather Manning, Paul and Sue Merrick)*

LIZARD SW7012

☆ ***Top House*** [A3083]: Spotless well run pub particularly popular with older people, in same friendly helpful family for over 40 years; lots of interesting local sea pictures, fine shipwreck relics and serpentine craftwork (note the handpumps) in neat bar with generous good value bar food from sandwiches to local fish and seafood specials, well kept ales such as Flowers IPA, Sharps Doom Bar and Wadworths 6X, reasonably priced wines, roaring log fire, big no smoking area, no piped music (occasional live); tucked-away fruit machine, darts, pool; tables on sheltered terrace, interesting nearby serpentine shop, and handy for Goonhilly *(Mrs Roxanne Chamberlain, BB, Sue Holland, Dave Webster, E G Parish, Pat and Robert Watt, P R and S A White, B Pike)*

LONGROCK SW4931

Mexico [Riverside; old coast rd Penzance—Marazion]: Welcoming open-plan pub in former office of Mexico Mine Co, big log fire, massive stone walls, well kept Sharps and Skinners, friendly service, comfortable no smoking dining extension *(Gill and Tony Morriss)*

LOOE SX2553

Olde Salutation [Fore St, E Looe]: Good welcoming local bustle in big squarish slightly sloping beamed and tiled bar, red leatherette seats and neat tables, blazing fire in nice old-fashioned fireplace, lots of local fishing photographs, side snug with olde-worlde harbour mural and fruit machine, step down to simple family room; good value food from notable crab sandwiches to wholesome specials and Sun roasts, fast friendly service, well kept Sharps Doom Bar and Ushers Best; piped music, forget about parking; open all day, handy for coast path *(BB, Joyce and Maurice Cottrell, Ted George, Michael Butler, George Atkinson)*

Ship [Fore St, East Looe]: Pleasant beamed pub, lots of maritime pictures, good range of sensibly priced food, friendly cheerful service, decent coffee; bedrooms *(George Atkinson)*

LOSTWITHIEL SX1059

☆ *Globe* [North St]: Rambling traditional local with cheerful relaxed bustle in roomy unassuming front bar, wide choice of enjoyable local food inc fresh fish in comfortable and attractive no smoking restaurant (worth booking – locally very popular), well kept changing ales such as Cotleigh Tawny, reasonably priced wines, friendly licensees and attentive staff, open fire; may be ad lib folk music (the dancing jack russell is called Jessie); tables in small attractive courtyard garden *(P G Ashford, Bob and Sue Hardy, Neal Wills, Reg Fowle, Helen Rickwood)*

LUDGVAN SW5033

☆ *White Hart* [Churchtown; off A30 Penzance—Hayle at Crowlas – OS Sheet 203 map reference 505330]: Friendly, unpretentious and well worn in 19th-c pub with much appeal to the many readers who like things truly unspoilt; great atmosphere in small beamed rooms, paraffin lamps, masses of mugs, jugs and pictures, rugs on bare boards, two big blazing woodburners, well kept Bass, Flowers IPA and Marstons Pedigree tapped from the cask, sensibly priced home cooking (not Mon evenings exc high season) from sandwiches up, no piped music; no high chairs *(the Didler, Helen Flaherty, Keith Stevens, P R and S A White, LYM, Callum and Letitia Smith-Burnett, Pat and Roger Fereday, Andrea Rampley)*

MANACCAN SW7624

☆ *New Inn* [down hill signed to Gillan and St Keverne]: Thatched village pub in lovely setting not far from Helford or St Anthony, bar with beam and plank ceiling, traditional built-in wall seats, individually chosen chairs, well kept Flowers IPA and Sharps Doom Bar, bar food, cribbage, dominoes; children and dogs welcome, picnic-sets in rose-filled garden *(LYM, JP, PP, Paul Humphreys, Ian and Liz Rispin, John Hale, Susie Symes, the Didler, Andrea Rampley)*

MARAZION SW5230

Fire Engine [Higher Fore St]: Friendly local with well kept St Austell ales and cider, varied food choice; fantastic St Michael's Mount views from picnic-sets on suntrap sloping lawn *(Derek and Heather Manning)*

MAWNAN SMITH SW7728

☆ *Red Lion* [W of Falmouth, off former B3291 Penryn—Gweek; The Square]: Attractive old thatched pub with open-view kitchen doing wide choice of enjoyable food inc seafood (should book summer evening), friendly helpful service, fresh flowers, dark woodwork, pictures, plates and bric-a-brac in cosy softly lit interconnected beamed rooms inc no smoking room behind restaurant, lots of wines by the glass, well kept real ales, good coffee; piped music, live Sat, TV; children welcome, handy for Glendurgan and Trebah Gardens *(LYM, Cathy Robinson, Ed Coombe)*

METHERELL SX4069

☆ *Carpenters Arms* [follow Honicombe sign from St Anns Chapel just W of Gunnislake A390; Lower Metherell]: Heavily black-beamed local with huge polished flagstones and massive stone walls in cosy bar and brightly lit lounge, tasty reasonably priced honest food (may be best to book wknds), well kept Sharps ales, friendly considerate landlord, helpful efficient service; darts, may be piped radio; children welcome in the two modern carpeted eating areas (one no smoking), picnic-sets on front terrace, bedrooms, handy for Cotehele *(LYM, Alan and Paula McCully)*

MEVAGISSEY SX0145

☆ *Fountain* [Cliff St, down alley by Post Office]: Unpretentious and interesting local, low beams, slate floor and some stripped stone, with good value simple food inc good crab sandwiches, good fish in popular upstairs evening restaurant, well kept St Austell ales, lovely coal fire, lots of old local pictures, small fish tank, back locals' bar with glass-topped cellar (and fruit machine and SkyTV sports); local artist does piano sing-song Fri (may be trombone accompaniment), occasional live music other nights; dogs welcome; bedrooms, pretty frontage, open all day *(Pete and Rosie Flower, JP, PP, the Didler, Bob and Margaret Holder, Rona Murdoch, BB, David Crook, B and M Kendall, Gill and Tony Morriss, Mayur Shah, J V Dadswell)*

Ship [Fore St, nr harbour]: Lively 16th-c pub with interesting alcove areas in big open-plan bar, low ceilings, flagstones, nice nautical décor, open fire, friendly helpful staff, good range of generous quickly served food inc good crab sandwiches, full St Austell range kept well; games machines, piped music, occasional live; comfortable bedrooms, open all day *(Pete and Rosie Flower, DF, NF, Mrs Maricar Jagger, Mayur Shah)*

MORWENSTOW SS2015

☆ *Bush* [signed off A39 N of Kilkhampton; Crosstown]: One of Britain's most ancient pubs, beguiling, individual and unchanging; part Saxon, with serpentine Celtic basin in one wall, ancient built-in settles, beams and flagstones, and big stone fireplace, upper bar with interesting bric-a-brac, well kept St Austell HSD and Worthington BB tapped from the cask, Inch's cider, friendly service, darts, no piped music; limited lunchtime food (not Sun), no children or dogs, seats out in yard; lovely setting, interesting village church with good nearby teashop, great cliff walks; cl Mon in winter *(Tracey and Stephen Groves, LYM, the Didler)*

MOUNT HAWKE SW7147

Old School: Unusual building (ex 19th-c primary school), largely open-plan but with plenty of separate areas; Skinners Cornish Knocker, Tetleys, a beer brewed for the pub and a guest ale, good cheap food (landlord catches fish); live music Sat, family skittles Sun, Tues, Thurs, cl Tues/Weds lunchtime *(Gill and Tony Morriss)*

MOUSEHOLE SW4626

☆ *Ship* [Harbourside]: Bustling harbourside local very popular for its lovely setting; beams, panelling, flagstones and open fire, well kept St

Austell ales; prominent TV and machines in one part, restaurant area – busy early evening with families eating; children and dogs welcome, nice bedrooms, open all day *(Maggie and Tony Harwood, Colin Gooch, Bob Broadhurst, LYM, Keith Stevens, Alison Hayes, Pete Hanlon, Ian and Liz Rispin, Barry and Anne, Andrea Rampley, Dr R A Smye, Gill and Tony Morriss, Sue Demont, Tim Barrow)*

MULLION SW6719

☆ ***Old Inn*** [Churchtown – not down in the cove]: Extensive thatched and beamed family food pub with central servery doing generous good value food (all day Jul/Aug) from good doorstep sandwiches to pies and evening steaks, linked eating areas with lots of brasses, plates, clocks, nautical items and old wreck pictures, big inglenook fireplace, no smoking rooms, well kept Sharps Doom Bar, Skinners Cornish Knocker and John Smiths, lots of wines by the glass, friendly attentive staff; children welcome, open all day Sat/Sun and Aug; can be very busy (esp on live music nights), darts, fruit machine; open all day, picnic-sets on terrace and in pretty orchard garden, good bedrooms *(Mrs B Sugarman, LYM, Richard Fendick, Anne and Paul Horscraft, David Crook)*

NEWBRIDGE SW4231

Fountain [A3071 Penzance—St Just]: Stone-built pub with attractively old-fashioned original beamed and flagstoned core, big pine tables and cheery log fire (which the cats enjoy) in awesome fireplace, friendly efficient service, full St Austell beer range kept well (may offer tasters), wide choice of satisfying food from fresh sandwiches up, modern extension; may be piped local radio, Thurs folk night; garden tables, bedrooms, camping available *(Callum and Letitia Smith-Burnett, Di and Mike Gillam, Adrian Johnson)*

NEWLYN SW4628

Red Lion [Fore St]: Old beamed local in great spot above harbour, lovely views, nautical memorabilia, enjoyable cheap food inc fish-crammed seafood soup, Sharps real ale, darts; dogs allowed *(Martin and Anne Muers)*

Tolcarne [Tolcarne Pl]: Clean and well kept traditional pub, good value food inc good fish and vegetarian choice, friendly staff, well kept Greene King Old Speckled Hen and Sharps Doom Bar; new terrace by sea wall, good parking – useful here *(Mick and Moira Brummell)*

NEWQUAY SW8061

Lewinnick Lodge [Pentire headland, off Pentire Rd]: Attractively rebuilt and newly furnished in open uncluttered style; outstanding position built into the bluff just above the sea, with big picture windows in bar and restaurant for the terrific views, good interesting if not cheap food, friendly staff *(Brian Skelcher, Father David Cossar)*

Skinners Ale House [East St]: Open-plan bare-boards proper pub with steps up to back part, good choice of Skinners ales with some guests tapped from the cask, good value food, free peanuts; live music wknds inc trad jazz Sun night, occasional beer festivals; small front terrace, open all day *(the Didler, JP, PP)*

NORTH HILL SX2776

Racehorse [North Hill, off B3254 Launceston—Liskeard]: Two-bar beamed pub (formerly gabled village school) refurbished by friendly new owners, good sensibly priced food in bar and restaurant, attentive staff, several Sharps real ales, two coal fires; views from tables out on decking *(John and Sarah Perry, David C West)*

PADSTOW SW9175

Golden Lion [Lanadwell St]: Pleasant black-beamed front bar, high-raftered back lounge with plush banquettes against ancient white stone walls, cheerful local bustle, reasonably priced simple lunches inc very promptly served good crab and other sandwiches, evening steaks and fresh seafood, well kept Bass, Sharps Doom Bar and Skinners, friendly service, coal fire; pool in family area, piped music or juke box, fruit machines; terrace tables, bedrooms, open all day *(the Didler, JP, PP, BB, Michael Butler)*

☆ ***London*** [Llanadwell St]: Down-to-earth fishermen's local, impressive hanging baskets out in front, lots of pictures and nautical memorabilia, buoyant atmosphere, St Austell beers, decent choice of malt whiskies, wknd lunchtime bar food inc good if pricey crab sandwiches, fresh local fish, more elaborate evening choice (small back dining area – get there early for a table), great real fire; games machines but no piped music – home-grown live music Sun night; dogs welcome in bar, open all day, bedrooms good value *(JP, PP, LYM, Brian and Bett Cox, A Sadler, Margaret Mason, David Thompson, Gordon Briggs)*

Old Ship [Mill Sq, just off North Quay/Broad St]: Cheery local atmosphere in hotel's bustling open-plan bar with well kept Sharps Doom Bar and a guest such as Brains SA, good range of reasonably priced food from sandwiches to plenty of fresh fish, upstairs restaurant; back games toom with SkyTV, may be piped radio; tables in sunny (and heated) front courtyard tucked away just off harbour, open all day from breakfast on at least in summer, 15 bedrooms *(BB, Alan and Paula McCully, Margaret Mason, David Thompson, D W Stokes, George Atkinson)*

Shipwrights [North Quay; aka the Blue Lobster]: Stripped brick, lots of wood, flagstones, lobster pots and nets in big low-ceilinged quayside bar with quick popular food, St Austell ales, friendly service, upstairs restaurant; busy with young people evenings; a few tables out by water *(BB, Bob and Sue Hardy, Brian Skelcher, D W Stokes, P R and S A White)*

PAR SX0553

Britannia [corner A390 and Par Moor]: Extended pub with several bar areas inc no smoking part, enjoyable usual food using local produce, five or six real ales, wide range of wines by the glass, no smoking restaurant;

disabled facilities, large garden area *(Peter Salmon)*

PAUL SW4627

Kings Arms: Appealing beamed bar, friendly landlord, St Austell ales, popular reasonably priced food; bedrooms *(Dr R A Smye)*

PELYNT SX2054

☆ *Jubilee* [B3359 NW of Looe]: Immaculate 16th-c inn with interesting Queen Victoria mementoes and some handsome antique furnishings in relaxed beamed lounge bar and Victoria Bar, good generous food and atmosphere, well kept Skinners Betty Stogs and another local beer brewed for the pub, children welcome in eating areas; separate public bar with sensibly placed darts, pool, fruit machine, and piped music; picnic-sets under cocktail parasols in inner courtyard with pretty flower tubs, good play area, nine comfortable bedrooms, open all day wknds *(LYM, B J Harding, Prof and Mrs Tony Palmer, Michael Butler)*

PENDEEN SW3834

North: Small, friendly and interesting, with tin-mining memorabilia, well kept St Austell ales, enjoyable food; bedrooms *(Peter Salmon)*

PENELEWEY SW8240

☆ *Punch Bowl & Ladle* [B3289]: Much extended thatched dining pub in picturesque setting handy for Trelissick Gardens, cosy Victorian-feel bar with big settees and rustic bric-a-brac, wide choice of reasonably priced generous food from good sandwiches up (Thurs very popular with elderly lunchers), pleasant efficient service, Bass and St Austell ales; unobtrusive piped music; children and dogs on leads welcome, small back sun terrace, open all day summer *(David M Cundy, LYM, Mr and Mrs J Evans, Peter Salmon, P R and S A White, D S Cottrell)*

PENZANCE SW4730

☆ *Admiral Benbow* [Chapel St]: Well run pub with wonderfully nautical décor in interesting maze of areas, friendly staff and welcoming atmosphere, good value above-average food inc local fish, four well kept ales inc Sharps Doom Bar, decent wines, downstairs restaurant, pleasant view from top back room; children allowed, open all day summer *(LYM, Louise Symons, Gordon Tong)*

☆ *Dolphin* [The Barbican; Newlyn road, opp harbour after swing-bridge]: Roomy welcoming pub with attractive nautical décor, good harbour views, good value food using local produce, well kept St Austell ales, good service, great fireplace, children in room off main bar; big pool room with juke box etc, no obvious nearby parking *(the Didler, Darly Graton, Graeme Gulibert, LYM, JP, PP)*

☆ *Globe & Ale House* [Queen St]: Well kept Bass, Sharps Own and Skinners Betty Stogs and Bettys Mild with guest beers, some tapped from the cask, in small low-ceilinged tavern, lots of old pictures and artefacts, bare boards and dim lighting, enthusiastic helpful landlord, enjoyable prompt food *(the Didler, JP, PP)*

Mounts Bay Inn [Promenade, Wherry Town]: Small busy pub nr seafront, welcoming landlord, straightforward food inc local meat and fish, well kept ales inc Sharps Doom Bar and Skinners, pool; no children *(JP, PP, the Didler)*

PERRANARWORTHAL SW7738

☆ *Norway* [A39 Truro—Penryn]: Large pub with half a dozen areas, beams hung with farm tools, lots of prints and rustic bric-a-brac, old-style wooden seating and big tables on slate flagstones, open fires, tropical fish tank; big helpings of popular food with good specials board, quick welcoming service, well kept Bass and St Austell, decent wines, attractive restaurant; games machine and piped music; tables outside, open all day *(BB, David Crook, Mr and Mrs Ian Davidson)*

PERRANUTHNOE SW5329

☆ *Victoria* [signed off A394 Penzance—Helston]: Comfortable and relaxed L-shaped pub, cosy low-beamed bar, some stripped stonework and no smoking part, coastal and wreck photographs, enjoyable food from freshly baked lunchtime baguettes and doorstep sandwiches to good venison, interesting evening specials, friendly efficient service, well kept ales such as Bass and Sharps Doom Bar, nice wine choice, neat coal fire, refurbished no smoking restaurant; quiet piped music; picnic-sets outside, good bedrooms, handy for Mounts Bay *(Ann and Bob Westbrook, LYM, Neil and Anita Christopher, Peter Salmon)*

PHILLACK SW5638

Bucket of Blood [Churchtown Rd]: Welcoming bustle in traditional low-beamed village pub, thick whitewashed stone walls, sturdy stripped pine tables, enjoyable generous fresh food, low prices, well kept St Austell Tinners and HSD, gruesome ghost stories, locals' back snug; tables outside *(LYM, Val Baker)*

PILLATON SX3664

☆ *Weary Friar* [off Callington—Landrake back road]: Pretty tucked-away 12th-c pub with four spotless and civilised knocked-together rooms (one no smoking), appealing décor, comfortable seats around sturdy tables, easy chairs one end, log fire, nicely presented substantial bar food inc lunchtime sandwiches, children's helpings and good puddings, quick cheerful helpful service, well kept ales such as Bass and Sharps Eden, farm cider; big back restaurant (not Mon), children in eating area; tables outside, Tues bell-ringing in church next door; comfortable bedrooms with own bathrooms *(Ted George, LYM, Jacquie and Jim Jones, Paul and Sue Merrick)*

POLGOOTH SW9950

Polgooth Inn [well signed off A390 W of St Austell; Ricketts Lane]: Large softly lit traditional country local, modernised but unspoilt, with good big family room and (up steps) outside play area, good value generous food with helpful chef and plenty of choice (but only roasts on Sun), St Austell and guest ales, efficient friendly service, good garden, pretty countryside; fills quickly in summer (handy for nearby caravan parks) *(LYM, Margaret Dickinson, Geoff Ziola)*

POLMEAR SX0853

Ship [A3082 Par—Fowey]: Good friendly atmosphere, chatty locals and welcoming uniformed staff, good food using fresh produce, farm cider, nice shipping décor, big stove, back dining area still in keeping with dark furniture, big conservatory opening to tables in sizeable garden; nr holiday camps *(Pete and Rosie Flower, M and R Thomas, Mrs Maricar Jagger)*

POLPERRO SX2051

☆ *Blue Peter* [Quay Rd]: Dark and cosy, in great setting up narrow steps above harbour; unpretentious little low-beamed wood-floored local, well kept Sharps Doom Bar, St Austell and guest beers, farm cider, quick friendly service, log fire, may be bar food (if not you can bring you own), nautical memorabilia, traditional games, dogs and children welcome, family area upstairs with video game; can get crowded, and piped music – often jazz or nostalgic pop – can be loudish, may be live music Sat; some seats outside, open all day *(the Didler, LYM, JP, PP, P R and S A White, Christine and Phil Young, Mrs Yvette Bateman)*

☆ *Old Mill House* [Mill Hill; bear right approaching harbour]: Cheery bar with stripped pine, bare boards and flagstones, nautical décor, big log fireplace, well kept Sharps real ales, decent bar food inc low-priced crab baguettes, no smoking dining room; quiz nights, games area with darts and pool, TV, piped music (some live), no nearby parking; children in eating areas, dogs in bar, picnic-sets out in streamside garden, open all day *(LYM, Prof and Mrs Tony Palmer, Michael Butler, George Atkinson)*

Ship [Fore St]: Attractive building festooned with hanging baskets, big spotless and civilised bar, well kept ales inc Greene King Abbot, generous good value fresh food, steps down to large well furnished family room, pleasant staff; small back terrace *(Ted George, Michael Butler)*

☆ *Three Pilchards* [Quay Rd]: Welcoming fishermen's local behind the fish quay, doing well under newish licensees, good value food from baguettes to nicely cooked local fish and seafood, well kept real ales, low beams, lots of black woodwork, dim lighting, simple furnishings, open fire in big stone fireplace, regulars' photographs; piped music, can get very busy; tables on upper terrace (no sea view) up steep steps, open all day *(Mayur Shah, Esther and John Sprinkle, Prof and Mrs Tony Palmer, BB, P R and S A White, Mrs Yvette Bateman, Edward Leetham)*

POLRUAN SX1251

☆ *Lugger* [back roads off A390 in Lostwithiel, or passenger/bicycle ferry from Fowey]: Beamed waterside pub with high-backed wall settles, big model boats etc, open fires, good views from upstairs partly no smoking family room, well kept St Austell ales, bar food servery, restaurant; piped music (occasional live), sports TV, pool, games machine; children and well behaved dogs welcome, good walks, open all day *(the Didler, John Taylor, Martin and Karen Wake, Geoff Pidoux, Edward Leetham)*

Russell [West St]: Fishermen's local, friendly and lively yet relaxing, popular straightforward food, well kept St Austell beers, log fire; lovely hanging baskets *(Nick Lawless)*

PORTHLEVEN SW6225

Harbour Inn [Commercial Rd]: Large well looked-after pub/hotel in outstanding setting, tables out on big quayside terrace; good value simple food in impressive dining area off expansive lounge and bar, quick friendly service, well kept St Austell ales, comprehensive wine list, restaurant; decent bedrooms, some with harbour view *(E G Parish, Richard Fendick, Sue Demont, Tim Barrow)*

PORTHTOWAN SW6948

Blue [Beach Rd, East Cliff]: Great bare-boards beach bar with spectacular views from terrace, good value food inc lunchtime baguettes and a popular burger, good friendly staff, decent wines, Boddingtons; pool *(Andy Sinden, Louise Harrington, Dr R A Smye)*

PORTLOE SW9339

Ship: Comfortable, bright and cosy L-shaped local, plenty of interesting nautical and local memorabilia and photographs, sensibly priced generous food inc local crab sandwiches, good pasties, curries and pizzas, children's menu, well kept St Austell ales, welcoming staff; piped music; sheltered and attractive streamside garden over road, pretty fishing village with lovely cove and coast path above, open all day Fri-Sun in summer *(Pete and Rosie Flower, Christopher Wright, Fred and Lorraine Gill, Jeanne and Paul Silvestri, TB, BB, Derek and Gillian Henshaw, Jenny and Brian Seller)*

PORTMELLON COVE SX0143

☆ *Rising Sun* [just S of Mevagissey]: Particularly good food from bar lunches to upmarket dishes in pleasant evening restaurant, flagstoned bar with unusual open fire, well kept Sharps and other ales such as Caledonian Deuchars IPA, faultless service, charming cool plant-filled conservatory, big upper family/games room; tables outside, fine spot overlooking quiet sandy cove *(BB, Pete and Rosie Flower, M J Bourke, Mrs M Granville-Edge, Tom Gondris)*

PORTREATH SW6545

Basset Arms [Tregea Terr]: Very friendly village pub at end of Mineral Tramways cycle path to Devoran, enjoyable food inc fresh fish and good value Sun lunch in comfortable bar, no smoking dining room and big bright conservatory, caring service, well kept beers inc Sharps Doom Bar; unobtrusive piped music; picnic-sets on sunny terrace and grass with play area, short stroll from beach, open all day Sun and summer *(Lawrence Pearse, Brian Skelcher, David Crook)*

Portreath Arms [by B3300/B3301 N of Redruth]: Tidy hotel lounge bar with green plush seating, steps down to no smoking dining room, good choice of enjoyable food from open sandwiches to steaks, local fish and good value Sun roast, friendly helpful staff, well kept ales inc Skinners, decent house wine, separate large public bar with pool, darts etc; bedrooms, well placed for coastal walks *(Debbie and Neil Hayter, Stephen Buckley)*

PORTSCATHO SW8735

☆ ***Plume of Feathers*** [The Square]: Comfortable and cheerful largely stripped stone pub in pretty fishing village, sea-related bric-a-brac in linked room areas, side locals' bar (can be very lively in the evening), well kept St Austell and other ales, good staff, pubby bar food inc popular bargain Fri fish night, restaurant; very popular with summer visitors but perhaps at its best with really welcoming local atmosphere out of season; dogs welcome, open all day in summer (and other times if busy), lovely coast walks *(Geoff and Jan Dawson, Malcolm and Jennifer Perry, Jack Clark, Fred and Lorraine Gill, LYM, P R and S A White, Kevin Thorpe, Jenny and Brian Seller)*

PRAZE AN BEEBLE SW6336

St Aubyn Arms [The Square]: Traditional two-bar country pub that grows on you, well kept Ring O' Bells, Sharps and Skinners, wide choice of enjoyable low-priced food inc Fri steak specials and children's (who are warmly welcomed), some interesting decorations, two restaurants, one upstairs; public bar with games and piped music; picnic-sets in large attractive garden perhaps with big green marquee *(Colin Gooch, P R and S A White, Maggie and Tony Harwood, Guy Vowles)*

QUINTRELL DOWNS SW8560

Two Clomes [A392 E]: Attractive extended but largely unspoilt 18th-c former cottage with apt furnishings, friendly staff and regulars, well kept Sharps Doom Bar, reasonably priced food from good choice of soups and good baguettes up, welcoming fire, no smoking family area; garden with terrace, handy for campsites *(Peter Salmon)*

RILLA MILL SX2973

Manor House: Friendly local with wide-ranging good value food inc good choice of curries, well kept Skinners Cornish Knocker, good house wines, cheerful helpful service *(DAV, R T and J C Moggridge)*

ROSUDGEON SW5529

Falmouth Packet: Nice place with quite a history, well kept St Austell Tinners and friendly landlord; pool, juke box *(Giles and Annie Francis)*

RUAN LANIHORNE SW8942

☆ *Kings Head* [off A3078]: Attractive homely and neatly kept beamed pub opp fine old church, sofa by good log fire in front bar, no smoking eating area with plenty to look at, pleasant family room, standard food inc children's (limited choice Sun), well kept real ales inc ones brewed for the pub by Sharps and Skinners, chatty staff; piped music, traditional games – for children too; suntrap sunken garden, views over the Fal estuary, cl Mon lunchtime (and Mon evening in winter) *(Fred and Lorraine Gill, LYM, Kevin Thorpe, D J Elliott, Mr and Mrs P Hill)*

ST AUSTELL SX0152

Stag [Victoria Pl]: Small friendly bare-boards local with well kept ales such as Black Sheep, Greene King Old Speckled Hen, Sharps Doom Bar and Youngs Waggle Dance, good choice of other drinks and of good value food inc children's helpings, some Fri folk nights; piped music, TV, games machine; bedrooms *(Rev John Hibberd)*

ST DOMINICK SX4067

☆ ***Who'd Have Thought It*** [off A388 S of Callington]: Comfortable country pub with plenty of individuality and superb Tamar views, esp from no smoking conservatory; plush lounge areas with antique bric-a-brac and open fires (not always lit), helpful staff, popular food from sandwiches, baked potatoes and good pasties to steaks, children's menu, partly no smoking dining area, Bass, St Austell HSD, Skinners Betty Stogs and Worthington Best, decent wines; garden tables, handy for Cotehele (NT) *(Dennis Jenkin, LYM, John Evans, Ted George, Pamela and Merlyn Horswell, Mary Ellen Cummings)*

ST EWE SW9746

☆ *Crown* [off B3287]: Attractive cottagey dining pub, smartly traditional and up a notch from the Mevagissey norm, airy and spacious, with beams, 16th-c flagstones, church pews and a fine settle, lovely log fire, voluble parrot, St Austell ales kept well, good house wines, quick welcoming service, large back dining room up steps; outside gents', children in eating areas, picnic-sets on raised back lawn, handy for the Lost Gardens of Heligan, open all day in summer *(Pete and Rosie Flower, LYM, Patrick Renouf, Dr and Mrs M W A Haward, Christopher Wright, Dennis Jenkin, M Joyner, Gill and Tony Morriss, David Eberlin, Peter and Anne Hollindale, Andrea Rampley, Jenny and Brian Seller)*

ST ISSEY SW9272

Pickwick [Burgois, signed off A389 at St Issey]: Spacious and comfortable lounge around central bar, good reasonably priced food using fine raw materials, well kept St Austell HSD, decent wines, friendly efficient uniformed staff, log fire, Dickensian memorabilia and dark oak beams, pretty candlelit restaurant, family room; quiet piped music, pool, machines; garden with good play area, bowling green and tennis, bedrooms, lovely setting above Camel estuary *(Alan and Paula McCully, John and Penny Spinks)*

ST IVES SW5441

Castle [Fore St]: Cosy and spotless, low ceilings and lots of dark panelling in one long room, stained-glass windows, old local photographs, maritime memorabilia, well priced ample wholesome bar food, good range of well kept ales such as Greene King Abbot tapped from the cask (beer festivals), good value coffee, friendly staff; unobtrusive piped music; bustling in summer, relaxing out of season *(Roger Wain-Heapy, Ted George, Tim and Ann Newell, Pat and Roger Fereday)*

☆ ***Pedn Olva*** [The Warren]: More hotel than pub, tasteful modern mediterranean décor and some emphasis on the handsome restaurant's good modern cooking, particularly in the evenings; large bar with well kept St Austell Bitter and Tribute, good friendly service, picture-window views of sea and Porthminster beach, esp from tables on rooftop terrace; comfortable bedrooms *(E G Parish, Alan Johnson)*

☆ ***Sloop*** [The Wharf]: Low-beamed and flagstoned harbourside pub crowded all year (the friendly staff cope well), with bright St Ives School pictures and attractive portrait drawings in front bar, booth seating in panelled back bar, well cooked down-to-earth food from sandwiches and baguettes to lots of fresh local fish, well kept Bass, John Smiths, Greene King Old Speckled Hen and Sharps Doom Bar, good coffee; juke box or piped music, TV; children in eating area, a few beach-view seats out on cobbles, open all day, clean cosy bedrooms, handy for Tate Gallery *(LYM, Alan Johnson, the Didler, JP, PP, Giles and Annie Francis, James Woods, R T and J C Moggridge, Callum and Letitia Smith-Burnett, Mrs Yvette Bateman, P R and S A White, David Glynne-Jones, Peter Salmon, David Crook, Dr J Barrie Jones)*

Union [Fore St]: Spotless friendly pub, roomy but cosy dark interior, low beams, small fire, masses of old local photographs, neatly ordered tables, food from good soup and filled baguettes to local fish, well kept ales inc Bass and John Smiths, decent wines, coffee, roaring fire, broadsheet papers; piped music, can get crowded *(Alan Johnson, Dr J Barrie Jones)*

ST JUST IN PENWITH SW3631

Kings Arms [Market Sq]: Friendly local, comfortable, light and simple, with plenty of character, good local photographs, good value bar meals from tasty baguettes up, well kept St Austell ales, some tapped from the cask; popular live music nights, Sun quiz; reasonably priced bedrooms with own bathrooms, prodigious breakfast *(the Didler, Peter and Anne Hollindale)*

☆ ***Star*** [Fore St]: Harking back to the 60s in customers, style and relaxed atmosphere; interesting and informal dimly lit low-beamed local with regulars clustered around the bar, good value home-made food from sandwiches and pasties up, well kept St Austell ales, farm cider in summer, mulled wine in winter; traditional games inc bar billiards, nostalgic juke box, local male voice choir usually in late Fri; tables in attractive back yard, simple bedrooms, good breakfast *(the Didler, LYM, Barry and Anne, Callum and Letitia Smith-Burnett)*

ST KEVERNE SW7921

Three Tuns [The Square]: Relaxing village pub by church, handsome high ceilings and lots of old photographs, real ales such as Greene King Abbot and Sharps Doom Bar; picnic-sets out by square, sea-view garden, bedrooms *(Sue Holland, Dave Webster, BB, Mrs Roxanne Chamberlain, Reg Fowle, Helen Rickwood)*

ST KEW HIGHWAY SX0375

Red Lion [A39 Wadebridge—Camelford]: Newish licensees doing enjoyable food – try the fillet steak *(Gordon Briggs)*

ST MABYN SX0473

St Mabyn Inn: Cheerful bustling country pub, pleasant service, attractive décor, good choice of real ales inc Sharps and Skinners, farm cider, interesting wines, generous enjoyable restaurant food inc lots of fish, darts *(the Didler, Margaret Mason, David Thompson)*

ST MAWES SW8433

Idle Rocks [Tredenham Rd (harbour edge)]: Recently extended waterfront hotel with enjoyable lunchtime food inc good upmarket sandwiches in bar and adjoining informal brasserie, well kept Skinners Betty Stogs, good house wines, attentive welcoming service, smart leisurely evening restaurant; superb sea view from bar and terrace tables, bedrooms *(Dennis Jenkin, E G Parish)*

☆ ***Rising Sun*** [The Square]: Close-set tables in smartly modernised hotel bar with dozens of old Cornwall prints, interesting choice of reasonably priced good food here and in restaurant, great puddings, proper sandwiches and interesting seafood snacks, well kept ales inc Sharps Doom Bar, decent wines, good coffee, efficient, welcoming and helpful staff; pleasant conservatory, slate-topped tables on handsome sunny terrace just across lane from harbour wall of this pretty seaside village; dogs allowed, open all day summer, good value attractive bedrooms *(Fred and Lorraine Gill, Dennis Jenkin, R and S Bentley, Gordon Stevenson, LYM, Mr and Mrs P Hill, Jenny and Brian Seller)*

☆ ***Victory*** [Victory Hill]: Open-plan bar with darts one end, dining area the other, cheerful locals, Bass, Greene King IPA and Old Speckled Hen and Sharps Doom Bar, warm log fires, cheery local atmosphere, good no smoking area, bar food from sandwiches up, upstairs restaurant in season; piped music may be loud, occasional live music; pleasant picnic-sets outside, good value bedrooms, good breakfast, open all day *(LYM, Jack Clark, Clifford Blakemore, Michael Dandy, Richard Till, Fred and Lorraine Gill, Geoff and Jan Dawson, Peter Gondris, Alison Hayes, Pete Hanlon, David Crook, Guy Vowles, Jodie Collins, D S Jackson)*

ST MERRYN SW8874

☆ ***Cornish Arms*** [Churchtown (B3276 towards Padstow)]: Well kept St Austell ales, friendly efficient service and usual bar food at reasonable prices, also more extensive evening menu, in spotless local with fine slate floor, some 12th-c stonework, RNAS memorabilia; children over 6 may be allowed in eating area, good games room; picnic-sets out under cocktail parasols *(LYM, Alan and Paula McCully, P R and S A White)*

ST TEATH SX0680

☆ ***White Hart*** [B3267]: Unpretentious flagstoned village local with warm welcome, good value generous food from sandwiches to good steaks and good value Sun roasts, well kept Bass and Sharps Doom Bar, decent wines, friendly attentive staff, sailor hat-ribands and ship's pennants from all over the world, coal fire, neat dining room off; games bar, live music wknds; children very welcome, open all day wknds, comfortably refurbished bedrooms, good breakfast *(LYM, Tom Bottinga, Simon Collett-Jones, R T and J C Moggridge)*

STITHIANS SW7640

Cornish Arms [NE of A393 – ie opp side to Stithians]: Good value generous food, well kept local ales and friendly welcome in comfortable recently extended and refurbished village pub *(BB, J M Tansey)*

Golden Lion [Stithians Lake, Menherion]: Welcoming pub with lakeside terrace, good sensibly priced food from sandwiches and other bar food to restaurant meals (neat white linen – busy Fri and wknds), well kept St Austell ales, friendly helpful licensees, no smoking area *(Sue Rowland, Paul Mallett, David Crook)*

STRATTON SS2406

☆ ***Tree*** [just E of Bude; Fore St]: Rambling 16th-c inn with cheerful and helpful family service, interesting old furniture, great log fires; well kept ales inc Sharps Doom Bar and St Austell Tinners, enjoyable well priced generous home-made food from soup and sandwiches to Sun carvery, character evening restaurant; children welcome in back bar; dimly lit bar rooms get very busy at lunchtimes – or for big-screen sports TV; seats alongside unusual old dovecot in attractive ancient coachyard, bedrooms *(Tom Evans, BB, Ryta Lyndley)*

TREBARWITH SX0586

☆ ***Mill House*** [signed off B3263 and B3314 SE of Tintagel]: Marvellously placed in own steep streamside woods above sea, convivial black-beamed bar with fine delabole flagstones, informal mix of furnishings and interesting local pictures, good rather upmarket food, well kept ales inc Sharps Doom Bar, cheerful service, restaurant; piped music; provision for dogs and children, tables out on terrace and by stream, 12 comfortable bedrooms, open all day *(BB, M A Borthwick, D B)*

TREEN SW3824

☆ ***Logan Rock*** [just off B3315 Penzance—Lands End]: Relaxed local nr fine coast walks, low-beamed traditional bar with inglenook seat by hot coal fire, well kept if not cheap local ales, wide food choice (all day in summer) from good sandwiches up, courteous service, lots of games in family room, no smoking in small back snug with cricket memorabilia, gorgeous pub dog (others allowed on leads); may be juke box or piped music, no children inside; tables in small and pretty sheltered garden *(Anthony Barnes, David Crook, the Didler, LYM, Helen Flaherty, Lucien Perring, Celia Minoughan, Barry and Anne, Callum and Letitia Smith-Burnett, P R and S A White)*

TREGONY SW9245

☆ ***Kings Arms*** [Fore St (B3287)]: Well run 16th-c local, long chatty comfortable main bar with well kept Skinners and St Austell ales, decent wine, friendly licensees, good value quickly served standard food using local produce inc fresh fish and Sun lunch, woodburners in two smart beamed and panelled front rooms, one a no smoking dining room, the other for families, pool and juke box in back games room; tables in pleasant garden, charming village, open all day *(Christopher Wright, Kevin Thorpe, Reg Fowle, Helen Rickwood)*

TRESILLIAN SW8646

☆ ***Wheel*** [A39 Truro—St Austell]: Neatly thatched, steps between two compact main areas with plush seating, timbering, stripped stone and low ceiling joists, plenty of spotless bric-a-brac, strong local following for good value food, reliably well kept ales such as Bass and John Smiths, pleasant service; piped music, narrow entrance to car park; children welcome, play area in neat garden stretching down to tidal inlet *(BB, Phil and Jane Hodson, D S Cottrell)*

TREVAUNANCE COVE SW7251

Driftwood Spars [off B3285 in St Agnes; Quay Rd]: 17th-c inn just up from beach and dramatic cove, great coastal walks; slate, granite and massive timbers, lots of nautical and wreck memorabilia, brews its own Cuckoo Ale, plus Sharps Doom Bar, Skinners Betty Stogs, St Austell HSD and Tetleys, over 100 malt whiskies, Addlestone's cider, 15 wines by the glass, log fire, bar food (all day in summer), upstairs simple dining area and residents' areas; juke box, pool, fruit machine, TV; children welcome, dogs allowed in bar, garden tables, bedrooms, open all day *(Tim and Ann Newell, David Crook, JP, PP, DRH and KLH, LYM, John Martin, V Banting, Cathy Robinson, Ed Coombe, Mrs Yvette Bateman, R L R Nicholson, John and Vivienne Rice, Gill and Tony Morriss, Philip and Ann Board, Brian and Bett Cox, the Didler)*

TRURO SW8244

Barley Sheaf [Old Bridge St, behind cathedral]: Stretches back through linked beamed areas, lots of wood, two chesterfields by the fire, well kept Boddingtons, Sharps Doom Bar and Skinners Cornish Knocker, bargain meals, conservatory; piped music, big-screen TV; suntrap terrace *(David Crook, Patrick Hancock, Mrs Angela McArt)*

☆ ***City*** [Pydar St]: Enjoyable food inc light lunchtime dishes, well kept Courage Best, Skinners Betty Stogs, Sharps Doom Bar and a guest beer, cheerful helpful service, genuine character, cosy linked areas off big main bar, attractive bric-a-brac, pool in room off; sheltered back courtyard garden *(Tim and Ann Newell, Patrick Hancock, Ted George)*

White Hart [New Bridge St (aka Crab & Ale House)]: Good food and beer in tidy efficiently run pub, nautical theme, friendly staff *(Ted George, Di and Mike Gillam)*

William IV [Kenwyn St]: Clean and fresh panelled split-level bar with well kept St Austell beers, decent wine, wide range of food, elegantly tiled airy two-level conservatory dining room opening into small flowery garden; multi-screen TV sport, evening piped music *(David Crook)*

TYWARDREATH SX0854

New Inn [off A3082; Fore St]: Friendly and informal conversion of private house in nice village setting, busy local atmosphere, well kept Bass tapped from the cask and St Austell ales on handpump, food (till 8 evening), games and children's room; large secluded garden behind, bedrooms *(BB, the Didler, Mrs Maricar Jagger, Jim and Maggie Cowell)*

UPTON CROSS SX2772

Caradon [B3254 N of Liskeard]: Pleasant country local with built-in banquettes and dark chairs, carpet over 17th-c flagstones, woodburner, pewter hanging from joists, Castella card collection, decorative plates, fish tank; cheery friendly staff, wide choice of good value generous home-made food inc some unusual dishes, well kept Bass, Boddingtons and Sharps Own and Special, airy and comfortable public bar with pool; children welcome, some picnic-sets outside *(DAV, BB, Rona Murdoch, Paul and Sue Merrick)*

VERYAN SW9139

☆ *New Inn* [village signed off A3078]: Neat and comfortably homely one-bar beamed local with good value nourishing food inc popular Sun lunch, well kept St Austell ales, good value house wines, good coffee, leisurely atmosphere, inglenook woodburner, lots of polished brass and old pictures, no smoking dining area; friendly alsatian and burmese cat; quiet garden behind the pretty house, bedrooms, interesting partly thatched village – nearby parking unlikely in summer *(Jeanne and Paul Silvestri, Christopher Wright, John Moulder, Pauline and Philip Darley, BB, the Didler, David Crook)*

WADEBRIDGE SW9872

Molesworth Arms [Molesworth St]: Plush and friendly main bar with three areas and interesting fireplace, wide range of bar food from good hot baguettes up, good service, attractive restaurant in former back stables, locals' bar across coach entry; children welcome, bedrooms with own bathrooms *(Neil and Beverley Gardner, John Cadge)*

WIDEMOUTH SS2002

Bay View [Marine Drive]: Open-plan and unpretentious, with fine views over beach, good value food, well kept Sharps Doom Bar and Own, Skinners Betty Stogs and a beer brewed for the pub; tables on front decking, open all day in summer, bedrooms *(the Didler, A and B D Craig)*

ZENNOR SW4538

Tinners Arms [B3306 W of St Ives]: Individual country local in lovely windswept setting by church nr coast path, usually an ale or two such as Sharps Doom Bar and Wadworths 6X kept well in casks behind bar, Lane's farm cider, decent coffee, friendly licensees, dogs and cats, long plain room with flagstones, granite and stripped pine, real fires each end, back pool room (where children may be allowed), no music; limited food (all day in summer inc cream teas); tables in small suntrap courtyard, fine long walk from St Ives *(the Didler, Maggie and Tony Harwood, LYM, Guy Vowles, David Crook, Andrea Rampley)*

ISLES OF SCILLY

BRYHER SV8715

☆ *Fraggle Rock*: Tiny welcoming waterside local, unpretentious and owner-run, the only 'off-island' pub with a piano; well kept Timothy Taylors Landlord in season, good range of attractively priced bar food inc good pizzas and Fri night fish and chips, fine views from upstairs eating area, miniature juke box; attractive terrace, self-catering accommodation, campsite a field away; odd opening hours out of season *(Pete and Rosie Flower, Val and Alan Green, O G D Goldfinch)*

ST MARTIN'S SV9215

☆ *Seven Stones* [Lower Town]: Stunning location and sea-and-islands view, 11 steps up to big main bar unpretentiously reworked inside, friendly ex-HGV landlord, well kept Sharps Doom Bar and St Austell Dartmoor and Tribute, decent wines, appealing reasonably priced fresh food from baguettes through good pizzas to thai dishes, steaks and local crab, summer teas and sandwiches, bar billiards, local art for sale, nice window seats; lots of terrace tables, limited winter opening *(Pete and Rosie Flower, Peter Meister, Bernard Stradling, Andy Sinden, Louise Harrington, Michael Butler)*

ST MARY'S SV9010

Atlantic Inn [The Strand; next to but independent from Atlantic Hotel]: Spreading rather dark bar with nice little room at one end, low beams, hanging boat and lots of nautical bits and pieces, flowery-patterned seats, bar food, reasonably priced St Austell ales, friendly efficient service, mix of locals and tourists – busy evenings, quieter on sunny lunchtimes; darts, pool, fruit machines; little terrace with green cast-iron furniture and wide views, good bedrooms *(Neil and Anita Christopher, Kevin Thorpe, BB, Val and Alan Green, Michael Butler)*

☆ *Bishop & Wolf* [Hugh St/Silver St (A3110)]: Lively and friendly local atmosphere, interesting sea/boating décor with secluded corners and gallery above road, nets, lots of woodwork and maritime bric-a-brac, lifeboat photographs, friendly helpful staff, well kept St Austell Tinners and HSD, very wide choice of good generous food with plenty of seafood (should book, attractive relaxed upstairs restaurant – no bar food after 7.30), games area with pool; piped music, popular summer live music *(Pete and Rosie Flower, Neil and Anita Christopher, Peter Meister, David Crook, Michael Butler)*

Mermaid [The Bank]: Thorough-going nautical theme in unpretentious bar with ceiling flags, lots of seafaring relics, rough timber, stone floor, dim lighting, big stove; real ales such as Ales of Scilly Scuppered, Bass and Greene King IPA or Tetleys, picture-window all-day restaurant (not Tues) with views across town beach and harbour; packed on Weds and Fri when the gigs race; cellar bar with boat counter, pool table, TV and music for young people (live wknds) *(Pete and Rosie Flower, Roger and Jenny Huggins, David Crook, Michael Butler)*

Old Town Inn [Old Town]: Uncluttered wood-floor conversion of former Lock Stock & Barrel, doing well under enthusiastic new young licensee, nice local feel in smallish front bar and big dining area, well kept Ales of Scilly Scuppered and other real ales such as Courage and Sharps Doom Bar, decent food; pool, darts, double bowling alley alongside; front terrace, tables out in tidy garden behind, open all day *(Val and Alan Green, Michael Butler, Pete and Rosie Flower)*

Porthcressa [Little Porth, Hugh Town]: Former restaurant in superb position right on beach, simple décor, beers inc St Austell Tribute, takeaway food on Sun; karaoke and disco some nights; seats out on terrace *(Michael Butler)*

Several well known guide books make establishments pay for entry, either directly or as a fee for inspection. These fees can run to many hundreds of pounds. We do not. Unlike other guides, we never take payment for entries. We never accept a free meal, free drink, or any other freebie from a pub. We do not accept any sponsorship – let alone from commercial schemes linked to the pub trade. All our entries depend solely on merit. And we are the only guide in which virtually all the main entries have been gained by a unique two-stage sifting process: first, a build-up of favourable reports from our thousands of reader-reporters; then anonymous vetting by one of the senior editorial staff.

Cumbria

Of course the scenery is a big bonus here, often adding an element of the unforgettable to visiting Cumbrian pubs. But even putting that special feature aside, the area has a fine variety of top pubs, from simple locals and walkers' pubs of real character to welcoming and open-to-all bars in smart civilised hotels. It's friendly too, with cheery landlords, landladies and chefs. Places which have been giving special pleasure to readers in the last few months are the Wateredge in Ambleside (a new main entry – its superb lakeside position is what matters here), the Dukes Head at Armathwaite (back in the *Guide* after a break, nice food and a warm welcome), the smart Pheasant near Bassenthwaite Lake (lovely little bar, good interesting lunches, well liked as a place to stay), the cosy Blacksmiths Arms at Broughton Mills (new licensees doing well, tasty food), the Punch Bowl at Crosthwaite (delicious food in an idyllic setting, fine wine choice – and plenty of locals dropping in for a drink), the friendly Watermill at Ings (great beer choice), the Swinside Inn near Keswick (a new entry, making the most of its lovely setting), the Kirkstile Inn at Loweswater (now brewing its own good beers), the well run good value Newfield Inn at Seathwaite (a walkers' and climbers' favourite), the Eagle & Child at Staveley (another new entry, its food perhaps the main draw, but good beers too, and a nice place to stay), the largely no smoking Blacksmiths Arms at Talkin (a friendly and well run all-rounder, with three extra bedrooms now), and the interesting Queens Head at Troutbeck (another fine all-rounder). Half a dozen or so pubs here qualify for our Food Award, all of them most enjoyable for a special meal out. The Punch Bowl at Crosthwaite currently stands out among them for its lovely imaginative food; it is the Cumbria Dining Pub of the Year. From a fine choice of places in the Lucky Dip section at the end of the chapter, we'd pick out particularly the Sun at Bassenthwaite, Brook House at Boot, Hare & Hounds at Bowland Bridge, Hole in t' Wall in Bowness, Wheatsheaf at Brigsteer, Black Bull in Coniston, Stag at Dufton, Bower House at Eskdale Green, Prince of Wales at Foxfield, Highland Drove at Great Salkeld, White Horse at Scales, Greyhound at Shap and Brown Horse at Winster. This is a part of the world where a pint of beer more often than not still costs under £2 – well below the national norm. The Bitter End in Cockermouth, brewing its own, offers outstanding value, and quite a few other pubs here now offer their customers good savings (as well as an individual taste) by brewing their own. Besides Jennings, the dominant local brewer, beers from Yates and Hawkshead are also worth looking out for.

AMBLESIDE NY3804 Map 9

Golden Rule

Smithy Brow; follow Kirkstone Pass signpost from A591 on N side of town

It's the atmosphere and genuine welcome from both the landlord and chatty, friendly regulars that make this straightforward town local appealing to visitors. The bar has lots of local country pictures decorating the butter-coloured walls, horsebrasses on the black beams, built-in leatherette wall seats, and cast-iron-framed tables; dominoes and cribbage. There is a no smoking back room with TV (not much used), a left-hand room with darts and a fruit machine, and a further room down a few steps on the right, with lots of seats and an internet cubicle. Well kept Robinsons Hatters Mild, Hartleys XB, Cumbrian Way, and Best Bitter, and Cwmbran Double Hop on handpump; pork pies (50p or 75p), jumbo scotch eggs (£1), and filled rolls (£2). There's a back yard with benches, and especially colourful window boxes. The golden rule referred to in its name is a brass measuring yard mounted over the bar counter. *(Recommended by Mayur Shah, MLR, James Woods, Patrick Hancock, Richard and Anne Ansell, Sue Holland, Dave Webster, David A Hammond)*

Robinsons ~ Tenant John Lockley ~ Real ale ~ No credit cards ~ (015394) 32257 ~ Children welcome until 9pm ~ Dogs welcome ~ Open 11-11; 12-10.30 Sun

Wateredge

Borrans Road

It's the setting and views that earn this busy place its entry, as the sizeable garden runs right down to the edge of Windermere. It's a charming and sometimes surprisingly peaceful spot, with enough tables and garden furniture to cope comfortably with plenty of visitors, and bench swings looking past the boats on the water to the hills beyond. In the evening there may be candles on some of the tables out here. You get the same view through the big windows of the modernised bar – and from some of the bedrooms. No longer the upmarket hotel it once was, this is now more determinedly pubby, with three well kept beers usually including Coniston Bluebird and two rapidly changing guests like Roosters or Youngs Waggle Dance. Depending on when you visit they may have jugs of Pimms or mulled wine, and they're well geared up for families, with baby juices and so on. The building was originally two 17th-c cottages, though the knocked-through bar gives few clues to its age; the main part, with a mix of polished floorboards and carpet, has long curtains alongside the windows, a mix of contemporary and more traditional lighting, solid wooden tables, a long curved bar counter, and plenty of hops. Down a couple of steps is a cosier area with beams and timbers, and a sofa in front of the log fire; piped music. Service is fast, friendly and accommodating. Bar food (priced rather on the high side for what it is, and not the highlight of our stay) is mostly things like lasagne, steak and ale pie, or fish and chips (around £8–£9). Between meals you can usually get teas, scones and so on; you can't eat at the tables on the grass, but there are plenty of other outdoor tables on a gravelled terrace, or in a nicely landscaped area. There may be midges at the water's edge in summer. Some bedrooms are in an adjacent extension. *(Recommended by Margaret Dickinson, MDN, Michael Dandy, Margaret and Roy Randle, Hugh Roberts)*

Free house ~ Licensee Derek Cowap ~ Real ale ~ Bar food (12-4, 5-8.30) ~ (015394) 32332 ~ Children welcome till 9 ~ Dogs welcome ~ Contemporary folk music Mon eves ~ Open 11-11; 12-10.30 Sun; closed possibly over Christmas ~ Bedrooms: £45B/£70B

APPLEBY NY6921 Map 10

Royal Oak

B6542/Bongate is E of the main bridge over the River Eden

Despite new owners and a new licensee, this old-fashioned coaching inn remains popular with both locals and visitors. The oak-panelled public bar has a chatty, relaxed atmosphere and a good open fire, and the beamed lounge has old pictures on the timbered walls, some armchairs and a carved settle, and a panelling-and-glass snug enclosing the bar counter. Bar food at lunchtime includes filled ciabatta, granary cob or baguette (from £3.25; sausage, bacon, black pudding and tomato £3.95), and steak and mushroom pie, spinach and ricotta cannelloni or cumberland sausage ring (all £6.45), with evening dishes such as home-made soup (£2.95), home-made salmon and crab fishcakes with a sweet chilli dip (£4.95; main course £9.45), moules marinière (£5.25; main course £9.45), steak in ale pie (£7.95), chicken supreme stuffed with smoked cheese with stir-fried vegetables and a fresh basil and tomato sauce (£9.25), lamb cutlets with honey, mint and rosemary sauce

(£9.45), and steaks (from £10.25). The restaurant is no smoking. Well kept Black Sheep and John Smiths, and a couple of guests on handpump. There are seats on the front terrace, and attractive flowering tubs, troughs and hanging baskets. You can get here on the scenic Leeds/Settle/Carlisle railway (best to check times and any possible delays to avoid missing lunch). *(Recommended by Angus Lyon, David Edwards, Diane Manoughian, A and B D Craig, Jeremy Woods, J S Burn, Paul Boot, John and Wendy Allin, Tony and Betty Parker, Dr D G Twyman)*

Landmark Inns ~ Manager Nigel Duffin ~ Real ale ~ Bar food (12-2.30, 6-9; all day Sun) ~ Restaurant ~ (01768) 351463 ~ Children in eating area of bar and restaurant ~ Dogs allowed in bar ~ Open 11-11; 12-10.30 Sun ~ Bedrooms: £35B/£69B

ARMATHWAITE NY5046 Map 10

Dukes Head

Off A6 S of Carlisle

Readers have very much enjoyed their visits to this warmly welcoming village pub over the last year. The civilised lounge bar has oak settles and little armchairs among more upright seats, oak and mahogany tables, antique hunting and other prints, and some brass and copper powder-flasks above the open fire. Using as much local produce as possible, the good, popular food includes freshly made soup with croutons (£3.45), butter bean and black olive pâté with pesto dressing (£3.95), home-made pork, venison and apricot terrine (£4.50), hot potted Solway shrimps (£4.55), three cheese ploughman's (£6.95), lentil, carrot and cashew loaf with minted cucumber dip (£7.75), cold home-cooked ham with chips or home-made salmon and coley fishcakes (£7.95), fingers of pork fillet cooked in cider, brandy, cream and apple sauce (£8.85), well liked roast duckling (£11.95), and daily specials like brie in oatmeal with gooseberry sauce (£3.95), tuna fried in a spicy garlic, chilli and coriander butter (£4.75), home-made steak in ale pie (£8.25), moroccan-style braised lamb and apricots (£8.95), grilled bass fillets with prawns (£10.50), and fillet steak (£12.95). The restaurant is no smoking. Well kept Jennings Cumberland and Tetleys Mild on handpump, and home-made lemonade; dominoes, and a separate public bar with darts and table skittles. There are tables out on the lawn behind; boules. You can hire bicyles. *(Recommended by Michael Doswell, Jason Caulkin, Dr and Mrs M W A Haward, Richard J Holloway, Dr T E Hothersall, Mr and Mrs A Campbell, Greg Bridges, Alistair and Kay Butler, M Sharp, Fred and Lorraine Gill, Hugh and Susan Ellison, Mr and Mrs W D Borthwick, David and Ruth Shillitoe)*

Pubmaster ~ Tenant Henry Lynch ~ Real ale ~ Bar food ~ Restaurant ~ (016974) 72226 ~ Children in eating area of bar and restaurant ~ Dogs allowed in bar and bedrooms ~ Open 12-11; 12-10.30 Sun ~ Bedrooms: £32.50(£35.50S)/£52.50(£55.50S)

BARBON SD6282 Map 10

Barbon Inn

Village signposted off A683 Kirkby Lonsdale—Sedbergh; OS Sheet 97 map reference 628826

Our readers have enjoyed this friendly 17th-c coaching inn for many years now, and the quiet and comfortable little bedrooms are a nice place to stay; some overlook the lovely sheltered and prettily planted garden, and there are plenty of surrounding tracks and paths all around to walk along. Several small rooms lead off the simple bar with its blackened range, each individually and comfortably furnished: carved 18th-c oak settles, comfortable sofas and armchairs, a Victorian fireplace. Reasonably priced bar food includes hot and cold filled baguettes (from £3.25), morecambe bay potted shrimps (£4.95), brie wedges and cranberry sauce or home-made lasagne (£6.25), steak in ale pie or chicken and bacon salad (£6.95), and westmorland lamb pie (£7.25); the restaurant is no smoking. Well kept Theakstons Best and a guest such as Greene King Old Speckled Hen on handpump; dominoes and piped music. *(Recommended by Vivienne and Alan Morland, Margaret Dickinson, Mrs Hilarie Taylor, Lee Potter)*

Free house ~ Licensee Lindsey MacDiarmid ~ Real ale ~ Bar food ~ Restaurant ~ (015242) 76233 ~ Children welcome ~ Dogs allowed in bar ~ Open 12-2.30(3 Sat), 6.30-11(10.30 Sun) ~ Bedrooms: £40B/£65B

BASSENTHWAITE LAKE NY1930 Map 9

Pheasant ★

Follow Pheasant Inn sign at N end of dual carriageway stretch of A66 by Bassenthwaite Lake

Of course many of this civilised hotel's customers are here to enjoy the lovely comfortable bedrooms and very good food, but there are plenty of people who much enjoy their lunchtime visits for a pint or informal lunch. The little bar remains as pleasantly old-fashioned and pubby as ever, with mellow polished walls, cushioned oak settles, rush-seat chairs and library seats, hunting prints and photographs, and well kept Bass, Jennings Cumberland, and Theakstons Best on handpump; a dozen good wines by the glass and over 50 malt whiskies. Several comfortable lounges have log fires, fine parquet flooring, antiques, and plants; one is no smoking – as is the restaurant. Enjoyable lunchtime bar food includes freshly made soup with home-made bread (£3.35), open sandwiches with home-made crisps (from £5.75; prawn waldorf £6.25), their own potted silloth shrimps (£5.95), ploughman's (£6.25), pasta with sunblush tomatoes and fresh herbs, gratinated with fresh breadcrumbs (£7.95), venison sausages braised in red wine with mushrooms (£8.75), escalope of chicken on a mushroom and baby onion risotto with cider sauce or steak and mushroom pie (£8.95), poached fillet of smoked haddock with poached egg (£10.25), and puddings (£4.25). There are seats in the garden, attractive woodland surroundings, and plenty of walks in all directions. *(Recommended by Peter F Marshall, Dr D J and Mrs S C Walker, Alan Thwaite, Jack Clark, David and Ruth Shillitoe, R A K Crabtree, Andy and Jill Kassube; also in the* Good Hotel Guide*)*

Free house ~ Licensee Matthew Wylie ~ Real ale ~ Bar food (not in evening – restaurant only) ~ Restaurant ~ (017687) 76234 ~ Children in eating area of bar if over 8 ~ Dogs allowed in bar and bedrooms ~ Open 11.30-2.30, 5.30-10.30(11 Sat); 12-2.30, 6-10.30 Sun; closed 25 Dec ~ Bedrooms: £80B/£140B

BEETHAM SD5079 Map 7

Wheatsheaf

Village (and inn) signposted just off A6 S of Milnthorpe

In a quiet village close to the River Bela, this busy 16th-c coaching inn is welcoming to both locals and visitors alike. The opened-up front lounge bar has lots of exposed beams and joists, and the main bar is behind on the right, with well kept Brysons Shifting Sands, Jennings Cumberland, and a fortnightly changing guest beer on handpump, and several wines by the glass; there's also a cosy and relaxing smaller room for drinkers, and a roaring log fire. The pub is no smoking apart from the tap room. Piped music and dominoes. Good lunchtime bar food includes home-made soup (£3.20), sandwiches or feta cheese salad (£4.70), cod and prawn fishcakes with chilli, ginger and coriander (£6.25), their own recipe sausages, home-made beef in ale pie or sweet and sour vegetables (£7.95), beef madras (£8.95), daily specials, and puddings such as quince and raspberry crumble, white chocolate mousse on a chocolate genoa topped with black cherries or crème brûlée with side serving of boozy fruit (£4.95). Three-course Sunday lunch (£11.95). The 14th-c church opposite is pretty. *(Recommended by John Foord, Mr and Mrs C J Frodsham, Revd D Glover, David Carr, Tim and Judy Barker, Richard Greaves, Malcolm Taylor, Jo Lilley)*

Free house ~ Licensees Mark and Kath Chambers ~ Real ale ~ Bar food (12-2, 6-9) ~ Restaurant ~ (015395) 62123 ~ Well behaved children in family room ~ Open 11.30-3, 5.30-11; 12-3, 6-10.30 Sun; closed 25 Dec ~ Bedrooms: £55B/£67.50B

BOUTH SD3386 Map 9

White Hart

Village signposted off A590 near Haverthwaite

The bar in this traditional Lakeland inn has been extended this year and now has a no smoking area. Many customers come to enjoy the fine range of well kept real ales on handpump: Black Sheep, Jennings Cumberland, and Tetleys, and changing guests such as Brysons Shifting Sands, Foxfield Hoad Mild, and Timothy Taylors Landlord. They also have 40 malt whiskies. The sloping ceilings and floors show the building's age, and there are lots of old local photographs and bric-a-brac – farm tools, stuffed animals, a collection of long-stemmed clay pipes – and two woodburning stoves. The games room has darts, pool, dominoes, fruit machine, TV, table football, and juke box; piped music. Bar food (using local meat) includes sandwiches (from £4.25; the garnish is more of a side salad), pizzas (from £6.25), salads (from £7.25), vegetarian chilli (£7.45), sirloin steak (£10.95), daily specials like pork medallions and black pudding with a cider, apple and cream sauce (£9.25) or herdwick lamb (£9.45), and sticky ginger pudding (£3.75). The restaurant is no smoking. Seats outside, and plenty of surrounding walks. *(Recommended by Jane Taylor, David Dutton, Mr and Mrs W D Borthwick, S and R Gray, Sheila and Phil Stubbs, Karen Eliot, Margaret and Roy Randle, Margaret Dickinson, Charles and Pauline Stride, Patrick Hancock, Ron Gentry, J S Burn, Ian and Sue Wells)*

Free house ~ Licensees Nigel and Peter Barton ~ Real ale ~ Bar food (12-2, 6-8.45; not Mon or Tues lunchtime) ~ Restaurant ~ (01229) 861229 ~ Children in eating areas until 9pm ~ Dogs allowed in bedrooms ~ Live music maybe Thurs or Sun ~ Open 12-2, 6-11; 12-11 Sat; 12-10.30 Sun; closed Mon and Tues lunchtimes (exc bank hols) ~ Bedrooms: £20(£35S)(£25B)/£40(£70S)(£50B)

BROUGHTON MILLS SD2190 Map 9

Blacksmiths Arms

Off A593 N of Broughton-in-Furness

Friendly new licensees have taken over this charming little pub, and readers have been quick to voice their enthusiasm. Three of the four simply but attractively decorated small rooms have open fires, as well as ancient slate floors, and well kept Dent Aviator, Hawkshead Bitter and Jennings Cumberland on handpump, and summer farm cider. Bar food is very good and they use meat from local farms, and local game and fish: soup (£2.95), lunchtime sandwiches (from £3.50), morecambe bay shrimps (£3.85), slow cooked duck leg with braised red cabbage and port sauce (£4.35), cumberland sausage with black pudding mash and red onion gravy (£6.95), steak and mushroom in ale pie (£7.60), peppered fillet of salmon with a whisky and cream sauce (£8.50), lamb shoulder marinated in mint (£8.95), daily specials such as red onion, goats cheese and sun-dried tomato tart with red onion jam (£6.75), game pie (£9.50), and baked whole local brown trout with lemon butter (£9.95), and puddings like home-made sticky toffee pudding or raspberry crème brûlée (£3.95). There are three smallish dining rooms (the back one is no smoking). Darts, dominoes, cribbage, and children's books and games. Pretty summer hanging baskets and tubs of flowers in front of the building. *(Recommended by JES, S and R Gray, Angus Lyon, Julie and Bill Ryan, Margaret Dickinson, Derek Harvey-Piper, Richard and Anne Ansell, Peter F Marshall, Kevin Thorpe, Michael Doswell)*

Free house ~ Licensees Mike and Sophie Lane ~ Real ale ~ Bar food (12-2, 6-9; not Mon lunchtime) ~ Restaurant ~ (01229) 716824 ~ Children welcome ~ Dogs welcome ~ Open 12-11; 12-10.30 Sun; 5-11 Mon (cl winter Mon), 12-2.30, 5-11 Tues-Fri in winter; closed 25 Dec

We mention bottled beers and spirits only if there is something unusual about them – imported belgian real ales, say, or dozens of malt whiskies; so do please let us know about them in your reports.

BUTTERMERE NY1817 Map 9

Bridge Hotel

Just off B5289 SW of Keswick

When walkers and locals descend on the bar here, there's a warm, chatty and vibrant atmosphere. Crummock Water and Buttermere are just a stroll away. The flagstoned area in the beamed bar is good for walking boots, and has built-in wooden settles and farmhouse chairs around traditional tables, a panelled bar counter, and a few horsebrasses. There's a dining bar with brocaded armchairs around copper-topped tables, and brass ornaments hanging from the beams, and a no smoking restaurant and guest lounge. Tasty bar food includes lots of interesting sandwiches (from £3.25), filled baguettes (from £4.20), and toasties such as cajun chicken with garlic mayonnaise or hot cumbrian ham, dijon mustard and melted cheddar, and chicken and peppers with tomato salsa in a tortilla wrap (from £4.95), home-made burgers with different toppings (from £4.50), ploughman's (£4.95), butterbean casserole (£6.65), cumberland sausage with apple sauce and onion gravy (£6.95), and lamb hotpot (£7.20). Well kept Black Sheep, Theakstons Old Peculier, and a guest beer on handpump, several malt whiskies, and a decent wine list. Outside, a flagstoned terrace has white tables by a rose-covered sheltering stone wall. The views from the bedrooms are marvellous; please note, the bedroom prices are for dinner, bed and breakfast; self-catering, too. *(Recommended by Richard J Holloway, Rod Stoneman, A S and M E Marriott, Dr D J and Mrs S C Walker, Len Beattie, Duncan Cloud, Michael Dandy, Jarrod and Wendy Hopkinson)*

Free house ~ Licensees Adrian and John McGuire ~ Real ale ~ Bar food (12-9.30) ~ Restaurant ~ (017687) 70252 ~ Children in eating area of bar and, if over 7, in restaurant ~ Dogs allowed in bedrooms ~ Open 10.30-11; 10.30-10.30 Sun ~ Bedrooms: £75B/£150B

CARTMEL FELL SD4288 Map 9

Masons Arms

Strawberry Bank, a few miles S of Windermere between A592 and A5074; perhaps the simplest way of finding the pub is to go uphill W from Bowland Bridge (which is signposted off A5074) towards Newby Bridge and keep right then left at the staggered crossroads – it's then on your right, below Gummer's How; OS Sheet 97 map reference 413895

The view from the terrace here, overlooking the Winster Valley to the woods below Whitbarrow Scar, is stunning; there are rustic benches and tables. The new licensees seem to have made few changes, and the main bar still has plenty of character, with low black beams in the bowed ceiling, country chairs and plain wooden tables on polished flagstones, and a grandly Gothick seat with snarling dogs as its arms. A small lounge has oak tables and settles to match its fine Jacobean panelling, there's a plain little room beyond the serving counter with pictures and a fire in an open range, a family room with an old-parlourish atmosphere, and a no smoking upstairs dining room. Well kept Black Sheep, Hawkshead Bitter and Red, and Timothy Taylors Best on handpump; fruit beer, quite a range of foreign bottled beers, and locally produced damson gin. Bar food now includes home-made soup (£3.25), sandwiches (£4.95; chicken, stuffing and gravy £5.50; tortilla wraps £5.25), barbecue ribs (£5.25), ploughman's or roast vegetable lasagne (£8.25), curry of the day (£8.95), fresh haddock in home-made batter with chips (£9.95), 10oz rib-eye steak (£12.95), daily specials like breast of pheasant with redcurrant jus (£9.50) or monkfish wrapped in parma ham with a rich tomato sauce (£9.95), and puddings such as sticky toffee pudding or warmed chocolate fudge cake (£3.95). Self-catering cottages and apartments behind. *(Recommended by John Dwane, Deb and John Arthur, S and R Gray, Mr and Mrs Maurice Thompson, Anthony Rickards Collinson, Malcolm Taylor, Peter Abbott, Clive and Fran Dutson, Simon Calvert, Jo Lilley, Michael Doswell, Dr and Mrs R G J Telfer)*

Free house ~ Licensees John and Diane Taylor ~ Real ale ~ Bar food (12-2(3 Sun), 6-9 (8 Sun) ~ Restaurant ~ (015395) 68486 ~ Children in eating area of bar ~ Open 11.30-11; 12-10.30 Sun; 11.30-3, 6-11 winter

CASTERTON SD6279 Map 10

Pheasant

A683 about 1 mile N of junction with A65, by Kirkby Lonsdale; OS Sheet 97 map reference 633796

The no smoking restaurant in this family owned place has been refurbished and now has flowers and candles on crisp clothed tables. The neatly kept and attractively modernised beamed rooms of the main bar have wheelback chairs, cushioned wall settles, a woodburning stove surrounded by brass ornaments in a nicely arched oak framed fireplace, and Black Sheep, Theakstons Bitter, and a guest beer on handpump; over 30 malt whiskies and an extensive wine list. Using locally sourced produce, the bar food at lunchtime includes home-made soup (£2.95), sandwiches (from £3.25), ploughman's (£5.80), mushroom and asparagus stuffed cannelloni (£5.95), beef in ale pie (£6.25), roast chicken (£6.50), and battered haddock (£7.50), with evening choices such as poached fresh pears with stilton dressing (£3.95), home-made pâté (£4.45), prawn and apple cocktail (£4.65), pork fillet in creamy pepper sauce or fresh salmon wrapped in smoked salmon baked with butter and poppy seeds (£10.95), and beef stroganoff (£12.95); home-made puddings (£3.95). Darts, dominoes and piped music. There are some tables with cocktail parasols outside by the road, with more in the pleasant garden. The nearby church (built for the girls' school of Brontë fame here) has some attractive pre-Raphaelite stained-glass and paintings. *(Recommended by Robert Hill, Deb and John Arthur, Revd D Glover, Peter and Jean Walker, Brian and Anita Randall, Lady Freeland, G Dobson)*

Free house ~ Licensee The Dixon Family ~ Real ale ~ Bar food (12-2, 6-9) ~ Restaurant ~ (015242) 71230 ~ Children welcome ~ Open 12-3(2.30 Sun), 6-11(10.30 Sun); closed 1 wk mid Jan ~ Bedrooms: £42S/£70B

COCKERMOUTH NY1231 Map 9

Bitter End

Kirkgate, by cinema

You can view the little brewery in this bustling and friendly pub through a tiny Victorian-style window – Cuddy Luggs, Cocker Snoot and Farmers Ale; the licensee also keeps several Jennings ales, and two or three differing weekly guests on handpump, in good condition; quite a few bottled beers from around the world. The three main rooms have a different atmosphere in each – from quietly chatty to sporty, with the décor reflecting this, such as unusual pictures of a Cockermouth that even Wordsworth might have recognised, to more up-to-date sporting memorabilia, various bottles, jugs, and books, and framed beer mats. The snug is now no smoking. As well as simple lunchtime snacks, the good value bar food includes cumberland sausage (£6.15), three cheese pasta and broccoli bake or fish and chips (£6.25), chicken balti (£6.45), lasagne or steak and mushroom in ale pie (£6.45), and daily specials. Service is very welcoming; piped music. The public car park round the back is free after 7. *(Recommended by Kevin Flack, R M Corlett, David and Rhian Peters, C A Hall, Kevin Thorpe, Edward Mirzoeff)*

Own brew ~ Licensee Susan Askey ~ Real ale ~ Bar food (12-2, 6-8.30) ~ (01900) 828993 ~ Children in eating area of bar ~ Open 12-2.30, 6-11; 11-11 Sat; 12-3, 7-10.30 Sun; 11.30-3, 6-11 Sat in winter

People named as recommenders after the main entries have told us that the pub should be included. But they have not written the report – we have, after anonymous on-the-spot inspection.

CROSTHWAITE SD4491 Map 9

Punch Bowl

Village signposted off A5074 SE of Windermere

Cumbria Dining Pub of the Year

The excellent, imaginative food in this bustling 16th-c inn continues to draw warm praise from our readers, and quite a few were particularly pleased to also find plenty of locals enjoying the well kept Black Sheep, and Coniston Bluebird and XB on handpump, and a chat. There are several separate areas carefully reworked to give a lot of space, and a high-raftered central part by the serving counter with an upper minstrel's gallery on either side; much of the pub is no smoking. Steps lead down into a couple of small rooms on the right, and there's a doorway through into two more airy rooms on the left. It's all spick and span, with lots of tables and chairs, beams, pictures by local artist Derek Farman, and an open fire. As well as a popular set-price lunch Tuesdays–Saturdays (two courses £12.95, three courses £14.95), the menu might include sandwiches, cream of mushroom and smoked bacon soup (£2.75), duck liver parfait with sultana, damson and balsamic dressing, toasted pine nuts, and toasted walnut and raisin bread (£5.25), crab and prawn gateau with tomato and avocado with coconut relish and sweet chilli and lime dressing (£6.95), half a baked aubergine filled with crumbled goats cheese with a sweet pepper sauce and basil pesto (£8.95), fried fillet of bass on crushed new potatoes with queenie scallops and a creamy lemon grass, chilli and cumin sauce (£13.25), chargrilled fell bred rib-eye steak with creamy pepper sauce (£13.75), duck breast on chinese-style hoi sin and oyster mushroom sauce or roasted chump of local lamb on grain mustard mash with rosemary and thyme jus and braised white beans (£13.95), and puddings like soft chocolate and mint tart with home-made honey ice-cream and chocolate sauce, honey and Drambuie crème brûlée or tarte demoiselles tatin (for 2 people) (from £4.25). Three-course Sunday lunch £15.95; a carefully chosen wine list with 20 by the glass, and several malt whiskies. There are some tables on a terrace stepped into the hillside. This is a nice place to stay. *(Recommended by C Tranmer, W K Wood, John and Sylvia Harrop, Revd D Glover, Margaret and Roy Randle, Ron Gentry, M and GR, Richard Greaves, David Mee, Sheila Stothard, Tony Pope, Karen Bonham, Olive and Ray Hebson, Prof Keith and Mrs Jane Barber)*

Free house ~ Licensee Steven Doherty ~ Real ale ~ Bar food (12-2, 6-9; not Sun evening or Mon) ~ Restaurant ~ (015395) 68237 ~ Children welcome ~ Dogs allowed in bar ~ Open 11-11; 12-3 Sun; closed Sun evening, all day Mon, 2 wks Jan ~ Bedrooms: £37.50B/£65B

DALTON-IN-FURNESS SD2376 Map 7

Black Dog £

Holmes Green, Broughton Road; 1 mile N of town, beyond A590

A former farmhouse, this is a simple, comfortable local that's lifted out of the ordinary by the cheery licensee who runs it; access is from the terrace in the car park. The unpretentious bar has beer mats and brasses around the beams, two log fires, partly tiled and flagstoned floor, and plain wooden tables and chairs; the eating area is no smoking. Good value hearty bar food – all home-made – includes sandwiches, soup (£1.95), leek and potato bake (£4.50), cumberland sausage or chilli (£4.95), poached hake fillets with parsley sauce (£5.95), daily specials like tuna and pepper flan (£4.50), chicken pie, braised rabbit with onions in cider or tuna steak in mediterranean sauce (£4.95), and 14oz rib-eye steaks (£7.50), and puddings such as rhubarb fruit crumble or syrup and ginger sponge (£2.50). The six real ales change constantly but might include Abbeydale Absolution, Barngates Tag Lag, Copper Dragon Golden Pippin, Hart Mild, Roosters Yankee, and Charles Wells Eagle on handpump; they also have several farm ciders and perries, home-made elderflower cordial and lemonade, and children's milkshakes. Table skittles, darts, shove-ha'penny, cribbage, and dominoes. A side terrace has a few plastic tables and chairs. The pub is handy for the South Lakes Wild Animal Park. *(Recommended by Richard Gibbs, Kevin Thorpe, Harry Clegg)*

Free house ~ Licensee Jack Taylor ~ Real ale ~ Bar food (12-8 summer weekdays, 12-9 all weekends; best to phone for winter weekday lunchtime serving) ~ (01229) 462561 ~ Children welcome ~ Dogs allowed in bar ~ Open 12-11; 12-10.30 Sun; 4.30-11 weekdays in winter; may be closed winter weekday lunchtimes ~ Bedrooms: £17.50(£26S)/£42S

ELTERWATER NY3305 Map 9

Britannia

Off B5343

This is a beautiful part of Cumbria, and being close to Langdale and the central lakes, and with tracks over the fells to Grasmere and Easedale, this inn is not surprisingly very popular with walkers. As well as a small and traditionally furnished back bar, there's a front one with a couple of window seats looking across to Elterwater itself through the trees on the far side: cosy coal fires, oak benches, settles, windsor chairs, a big old rocking chair, and well kept Coniston Bluebird, Jennings Bitter, Tetleys, Timothy Taylors Landlord, and maybe Archers Bouncing Bunnies or Isle of Skye Coruisk on handpump. Quite a few malt whiskies, country wines, and winter mulled wine; the lounge is comfortable. Bar food includes lunchtime filled rolls, home-made soup (£3.10), home-made cumberland pâté (£4.40), red pesto with sweet pepper filo tart topped with cheese (£8.30), cumberland sausage with onion gravy (£8.95), home-made steak and mushroom pie with puff pastry top (£9.25), roast leg of local lamb with apricot and honey jus (£10.95), and puddings such as toffee apple flan (£4.20). There are inevitably queues and long waits at peak times. The restaurant and residents' lounge are no smoking. In summer, people flock to watch the morris and step and garland dancers. Plenty of seats outside. More reports please. *(Recommended by Roy and Lindsey Fentiman, Andy and Ali, Ian and Jane Irving, Neil and Jean Spink, John Foord, Michael Doswell, MSL Webster, Dr S Edwards, S and R Gray, Mr and Mrs Maurice Thompson, A Sadler, Richard and Karen Holt, Mayur Shah, Jane Taylor, David Dutton, Margaret Dickinson, Jonathan Shephard, Ron Gentry, Tina and David Woods-Taylor, Richard and Anne Ansell, Malcolm and Jane MacDonald, J S Burn, Andy and Ali, David A Hammond, Tim Maddison, Ewan and Moira McCall)*

Free house ~ Licensees Clare Woodhead and Christopher Jones ~ Real ale ~ Bar food (all day) ~ Restaurant ~ (015394) 37210 ~ Children welcome ~ Dogs allowed in bar and bedrooms ~ Quiz Sun evenings ~ Open 10-11; 11-10.30 Sun; closed 25 Dec ~ Bedrooms: /£84S(£76B)

ENNERDALE BRIDGE NY0716 Map 9

Shepherds Arms

Ennerdale signposted off A5086 at Cleator Moor E of Egremont; it's on the scenic back road from Calder Bridge to Loweswater

This year, the bathrooms in this splendidly placed inn have been refurbished, as have the bar areas, and there are new places to sit outside. Walkers are genuinely welcomed, however wet and miserable, and there's a detailed pictorial display of the off-road footpath plans in the porch, a daily updated weather-forecast blackboard, and a bookcase full of interest, including Wainwright books – it's on his popular coast-to-coast path. The friendly bar has its serving counter in a bare-boards inner area up three steps, with a longcase clock and a woodburning stove below a big beam hung with copper and brass objects, and over 80 pictures. Its carpeted main part has an open log fire and a homely variety of comfortable seats; it opens into a small brick-floored no smoking extension with pub tables and objets d'art. Using local produce, the well liked bar food includes home-made soup (£2.95), sandwiches (from £3), home-made chicken liver pâté (£3.95), omelettes, home-made spinach and wensleydale tart or roast vegetable pasta bake (£6.95), cumberland sausage with fried egg (£7.50), home-made steak in ale pie (£7.95), sirloin steak (£11.95), daily specials such as salmon fillet with thyme and lemon sauce (£8.95), pork hock braised in vintage cider (£10.95), and lamb shank in red wine (£12.95), and puddings like sticky toffee pudding or raspberry meringue

(£3.95); the Georgian panelled dining room, conservatory, and half the bar are no smoking. Well kept Coniston Bluebird, Jennings Bitter, Timothy Taylors Landlord, and a couple of guests like Harviestoun Bitter & Twisted and Oakham JHB on handpump, decent coffee, and a good choice of wines by the glass; a couple of daily papers, and maybe piped music. An entrance lounge has sofas, ancestral portraits, and antiques. *(Recommended by Angela and Steve Handley, Barry James, Alan Robinson, Mrs S Johnstone; also in the* Good Hotel Guide*)*

Free house ~ Licensees Val and Steve Madden ~ Real ale ~ Bar food ~ Restaurant ~ (01946) 861249 ~ Children welcome ~ Dogs allowed in bar and bedrooms ~ Open 11-11; 12-10.30 Sun; maybe 11-3, 6-11 Mon-Thurs in winter; closed 2 wks Feb ~ Bedrooms: £39.50S(£44.50B)/£64S(£74B)

HAWKSHEAD NY3501 Map 9

Drunken Duck

Barngates; the hamlet is signposted from B5286 Hawkshead—Ambleside, opposite the Outgate Inn; or it may be quicker to take the first right from B5286, after the wooded caravan site; OS Sheet 90 map reference 350013

Even at the start of this civilised place's journey from country pub to something much more restauranty, there was a school of thought that regretted those changes, feeling it didn't fit the bill for this walking area. The fact that two more rooms have now been turned into another dining area, leaving just a last tiny toehold for drinkers, means that this can hardly be considered as a pub any more – so this will probably have to be the very last year in which we can reasonably include it among the main entries. A shame for us, as we've always had a real soft spot for it. There's a good winter fire in one traditional beamed room with cushioned old settles and a mix of chairs, a newly refurbished snug, and as we've said those two rooms off the bar which have now been knocked into one, making another dining area with an oak floor and dark leather seating. Everywhere is no smoking except the little bar area. Imaginative, if pricey, food includes smoked haddock, pea and crispy air-dried ham risotto (£6.95), spring onion pancake with smoked wild salmon and baked goats cheese or deep-fried duck confit cake with watercress and sweet chilli and ginger jam (£7.95), lamb cutlets with sweet roast onion, parsnip dauphinoise and rosemary jus or duck breast pot-roast with a fennel and blueberry glaze (£14.45), venison in cocoa with chestnut polenta, caramelised figs and espresso iced pistachios (£14.95), beef fillet with honey mustard, roasted beetroot, watercress mash and fried black pepper soufflé (£18.95), and puddings such as melting dark chocolate and orange pudding with marmalade ice-cream and candied baby oranges, rhubarb compote with warm gingerbread and a vanilla sabayon or rice pudding coconut brûlée with caramelised spiced mango and coconut tuille (from £5.95). Their own Barngates Chesters Strong & Ugly, Cracker Ale, Tag Lag, and Catnap are kept on handpump with Yates Bitter as a guest, and a fine wine list has over 20 by the glass. Seats on the front verandah have stunning views and there are quite a few rustic wooden chairs and tables at the side, sheltered by a stone wall with alpine plants along its top; the residents' garden has been reworked this year. *(Recommended by A N Caldwell, Karen Eliot, Mark Kenny, A Sadler, Jim Abbott, Mike Pugh, Michael Doswell, Jack Clark, MSL Webster, Dr S Edwards, Mrs Jane Kingsbury, Jeremy Woods, Margaret Dickinson, Duncan Cloud, Mrs J A Taylar, Pat and Sam Roberts, Steve Cawthray, Pierre and Pat Richterich, Frazer and Louise Smith, Ray and Winifred Halliday, Dr Terry Murphy, Revd D Glover, Dr D G Twyman, Tim Maddison)*

Own brew ~ Licensee Steph Barton ~ Real ale ~ Bar food (12-2.30, 6-9) ~ Restaurant ~ (015394) 36347 ~ Children in eating area of bar and restaurant ~ Dogs allowed in bar ~ Open 11.30-11; 12-10.30 Sun; closed evening 25 Dec ~ Bedrooms: £86.75B/£115B

Bedroom prices are for high summer. Even then you may get reductions for more than one night, or (outside tourist areas) weekends. Winter special rates are common, and many inns cut bedroom prices if you have a full evening meal.

Kings Arms

The Square

Bustling and pleasant, this inn is set on a glorious square. There are traditional pubby furnishings, some fine original Elizabethan beams (including the figure of a medieval king holding up the ceiling, carved recently), and Black Sheep, Coniston Bluebird, Hawkshead Bitter, and Tetleys on handpump; 30 malt whiskies, summer cider, locally made damson gin, and a decent wine list. Piped music, fruit machine, shove-ha'penny, dominoes and cribbage. Enjoyable bar food at lunchtime includes soup (£2.95), filled baked potatoes (£4.25), filled foccacia, ciabatta or tortilla wraps (£4.50), and cumberland sausage, home-made steak in ale pie or home-battered fish and chips (£6.25); in the evening, there might be smoked chicken and olive salad (£8.50), chargrilled local trout on rocket and roast pepper salad (£9.50), and trio of fell bred minted lamb chops (£10.55), with daily specials such as bacon and emmenthal tart (£5.95), pheasant and honey mustard sausage (£6.95), and puddings like home-made sticky toffee pudding or banoffi pie (£4.25). The restaurant is no smoking. As well as bedrooms, they offer self-catering cottages. *(Recommended by Deb and John Arthur, John Foord, Dr and Mrs R G J Telfer, Angus Lyon, Brian and Anna Marsden)*

Free house ~ Licensees Rosalie and Edward Johnson ~ Real ale ~ Bar food (12-2.30, 6-9.30) ~ Restaurant ~ (015394) 36372 ~ Children welcome ~ Dogs allowed in bar and bedrooms ~ Open 11-11; 12-10.30 Sun ~ Bedrooms: £38(£43S)/£66(£76S)

Queens Head

Main Street

Readers very much enjoy their visits to this lovely black and white timbered pub. There's a good mix of regulars and visitors, a friendly, bustling atmosphere, and pleasant, helpful staff. The low-ceilinged bar has heavy bowed black beams, red plush wall seats and plush stools around heavy traditional tables, lots of decorative plates on the panelled walls, and an open fire; a snug little room leads off. Lunchtime food served in either the bar or no smoking restaurant includes home-made soup (£3.25), ciabatta, focaccia, baguettes, and tortillas with interesting fillings (from £4.75), chicken liver pâté (£5.25), cumberland sausage with white onion sauce (£7.25), roasted mediterranean vegetables with pasta and buffalo mozzarella (£7.50), battered haddock with home-made chips (£7.75), and seared organic orkney salmon (£9.95); in the evening, there might be warm goats cheese soufflé on roasted aubergine and tomato salad (£5.75), crispy duck confit with caramelised figs and red onion salad (£5.95), calves liver and rich onion gravy topped with pancetta or roasted herdwick lamb (£14.95), and venison fillet on an apple and celeriac purée (£15.50). Well kept Robinsons Cumbria Way, Double Hop, Best, and Young Tom on handpump, and 30 whiskies; dominoes, cribbage, and piped music. Walkers must take their boots off. As well as bedrooms in the inn, they have three holiday cottages to rent in the village. The summer window boxes are very pretty. No children. *(Recommended by John Foord, Deb and John Arthur, Michael Doswell, Andrew Crawford, Duncan Cloud, Michael Dandy, Angus Lyon, Ray and Winifred Halliday, Brian and Anna Marsden)*

Robinsons ~ Tenants Mr and Mrs Tony Merrick ~ Real ale ~ Bar food ~ Restaurant ~ (015394) 36271 ~ Open 11-11; 12-10.30 Sun ~ Bedrooms: £47.50(£57.50B)/£68(£84B)

HESKET NEWMARKET NY3438 Map 10

Old Crown

Village signposted off B5299 in Caldbeck

Despite friendly new licensees taking over this unfussy local, the own-brewed beers are as good as ever. Well kept on handpump, these include Hesket Newmarket Blencathra Bitter, Great Cockup Porter, Helvellyn Gold, Skiddaw Special Bitter, Old Carrock Strong Ale, Catbells Pale Ale, and the new Volunteer Gold. Bar food includes good home-made soup (£2.50), sandwiches (from £2.50), ham and egg

(£5), steak in ale pie (£7), and evening curries (£7.50). The dining room is no smoking. The little bar has a few tables, a coal fire, and shelves of well thumbed books, and a friendly atmosphere; piped music, darts, pool, fruit machine, cribbage and dominoes. The pub is in a pretty setting in a remote, attractive village. You can book up tours to look around the brewery; £10 and a minium of six people. *(Recommended by Gwyneth and Salvo Spadaro-Dutturi, MLR, Michael and Jennifer Wadsworth, Peter F Marshall, G Coates, Ian and Sue Wells, Maggie and Tony Harwood, Steve Nye, Patrick Hancock)*

Own brew ~ Licensees Lou and Linda Hogg ~ Real ale ~ Bar food (12-2, 6.30-8.30; not Mon or Tues, not Sun evening) ~ Restaurant ~ No credit cards ~ (016974) 78288 ~ Children in eating area of bar and restaurant ~ Dogs allowed in bar ~ Folk 1st Sun of month ~ Open 11-11; 12-10.30 Sun; closed Mon and Tues lunchtimes

INGS SD4599 Map 9

Watermill

Just off A591 E of Windermere

It is quite remarkable that the cheerful, hard-working licensee in this very popular pub manages to keep his 16 regularly changing real ales in such tip top condition. On handpump, there might be Black Sheep Best and Special, Coniston Bluebird, Hawkshead Bitter, Lees Moonraker, Moorhouses Black Cat, Theakstons Best and Old Peculier, with changing guests like Hart Retrievers Legend, Marlow Rebellion Blonde, Oakham JHB, Orkney Dark Island, Tirril Bewshers, Timothy Taylors Landlord, and York Final Whistle; also, over 60 bottled beers, farm cider, and up to 50 malt whiskies. Cleverly converted from a wood mill and joiner's shop, the bars have a friendly, bustling atmosphere, a happy mix of chairs, padded benches and solid oak tables, bar counters made from old church wood, open fires, and interesting photographs and amusing cartoons by a local artist. The spacious lounge bar, in much the same traditional style as the other rooms, has rocking chairs and a big open fire; two areas are no smoking. Generous helpings of tasty bar food include home-made soup (£3.30), lunchtime sandwiches, toasties or filled baguettes (from £3.25), home-made pâté (£4.30), ploughman's (£5.50), leek and potato crumble (£7), battered haddock, cumberland sausage or home-made chicken pie (£7.95), beef in ale pie (£8.25), 10oz sirloin steak (£14.25), and daily specials such as vegetable bake (£7), beef and ale sausage (£8.50), chicken breast stuffed with local smoked cheese and wrapped in cumbrian air-dried ham (£9), local venison casserole (£9.45), and steamed fillet of swordfish (£9.50). Darts, cribbage, and dominoes. There are seats in the front garden. Lots to do nearby. Note that even residents cannot book a table for supper. *(Recommended by Jack Morley, Mr and Mrs D W Mitchell, A N Caldwell, S and R Gray, Jim Abbott, MDN, Michael Doswell, Richard Lewis, Hugh Roberts, Mayur Shah, Mike Pugh, Mr and Mrs Maurice Thompson, A S and M E Marriott, Lee Potter, Dr D J and Mrs S C Walker, Julie and Bill Ryan, MLR, Brian and Anna Marsden, Richard and Anne Ansell, David Reid, Kevin Thorpe, M and GR, Ray and Winifred Halliday, Mrs B M Hill, Sue Holland, Dave Webster, Peter Abbott, J S Burn, Ian and Sue Wells, Tony Pope, Karen Bonham, Paul Boot, Simon Calvert, Steve Whalley)*

Free house ~ Licensee Brian Coulthwaite ~ Real ale ~ Bar food (12-4.30, 5-9) ~ (01539) 821309 ~ Children in family room ~ Dogs allowed in bar and bedrooms ~ First Tues of month storytelling club, third Tues of month folk ~ Open 12-11(10.30 Sun); closed 25 Dec ~ Bedrooms: £32S/£70B

KESWICK NY2421 Map 9

Swinside Inn

Only pub in Newlands Valley, just SW; OS Sheet 90 map reference 242217

Looking over a quiet valley to the high crags and fells around Grisedale Pike, this friendly country inn has been recently refurbished but has kept many of its original 17th-c features. The long bright public bar has traditional wheelbacks and red and cream wall banquettes, and well kept Jennings Cumberland, Theakstons Best, and a guest on handpump; a central chimney with an open fire divides off the games area, which has pool, fruit machine, TV, cribbage, and dominoes. There are two no smoking dining rooms and two further open fires. Tasty bar food includes sandwiches, home-made soup (£2.35), breaded mushrooms with garlic dip (£3.95), cod in their own beer batter or mushroom stroganoff (£6.50), lime and chilli chicken or home-made lasagne (£6.95), steaks (from £8.95), and puddings like sticky toffee pudding (£2.95). Seats in the garden and on the upper and lower terraces make the most of the view. *(Recommended by Rev John Hibberd, Margaret Dickinson, Tina and David Woods-Taylor, Mrs M Hitchings)*

Jennings ~ Lease Joyce and Jim Henderson ~ Bar food (12-2, 6-8.45) ~ (017687) 78253 ~ Children welcome ~ Dogs allowed in bar ~ Open 11-11; 12-10.30 Sun ~ Bedrooms: £45S/£60S

LANGDALE NY2906 Map 9

Old Dungeon Ghyll

B5343

This no-nonsense walkers' pub is in a marvellous position at the heart of the Great Langdale Valley, and surrounded by fells including the Langdale Pikes flanking the Dungeon Ghyll Force waterfall. The whole feel of the place is basic but cosy – and once all the fell walkers and climbers crowd in, full of boisterous atmosphere. There's no need to remove boots or muddy trousers, and you can sit on the seats in old cattle stalls by the big warming fire, and enjoy the well kept real ales such as Black Sheep Special, Isle of Skye Black Cuillin, Jennings Cumberland, Theakstons Old Peculier, Charles Wells Eagle, and Yates Bitter on handpump. Part of the bar is no smoking. Straightforward food includes sandwiches (£2.50, lunchtime), home-made soup (£2.75), filled baked potatoes (£3.75), and maybe cumberland sausage, a vegetarian dish or half chicken (from around £7); the eating areas are no smoking. Darts, cribbage and dominoes. It may get lively on a Saturday night (there's a popular National Trust campsite opposite). *(Recommended by Hugh Roberts, Mayur Shah, Thomas Day, Richard and Anne Ansell, Sarah and Peter Gooderham, Tim Maddison; also in the* Good Hotel Guide*)*

Free house ~ Licensee Neil Walmsley ~ Real ale ~ Bar food (12-2, 6-9) ~ Restaurant ~ (015394) 37272 ~ Children in eating area of bar and restaurant ~ Dogs allowed in bar and bedrooms ~ Folk first Weds of month ~ Open 11-11; 11.30-10.30 Sun; closed 21-27 Dec ~ Bedrooms: £41(£44B)/£82(£88S)

LITTLE LANGDALE NY3204 Map 9

Three Shires

From A593 3 miles W of Ambleside take small road signposted The Langdales, Wrynose Pass; then bear left at first fork

From seats on the terrace here, there are lovely views over the valley to the partly wooded hills below Tilberthwaite Fells, with more seats on a well kept lawn behind the car park, backed by a small oak wood. Inside, the comfortably extended back bar has stripped timbers and a beam-and-joist stripped ceiling, antique oak carved settles, country kitchen chairs and stools on its big dark slate flagstones, Lakeland photographs lining the walls, and a warm winter fire in the modern stone fireplace with a couple of recesses for ornaments; an arch leads through to a small, additional area. Bar food at lunchtime includes sandwiches (£3.50; soup and a sandwich £5), home-made fishcake with lime and cucumber crème fraîche or home-made terrine (£5.50), ploughman's (£6.50), and cumberland sausage or a home-made pie of the day (£7.95), with evening dishes such as spiced lamb kebab with mint and yoghurt dressing (£5.50), baked crab and ginger parcel with chilli jam (£6.25), parsnip tartlet with lemon, pine nut and poppy seed salad (£9.25), roast cod with pea purée and vanilla jus (£11.50), and venison steak with apple and wild mushroom stew and liquorice game jus (£12.95). Most of the inn is no smoking (apart from the main bar). Well kept Jennings Bitter and Cumberland, and a guest such as Coniston Old Man or Hawkshead Bitter on handpump, 40 malt whiskies, and a decent wine list; darts, cribbage and dominoes. The three shires are Cumberland, Westmorland and Lancashire, which used to meet at the top of the nearby Wrynose Pass. *(Recommended by Howard and Lorna Lambert, Mr and Mrs Maurice Thompson, DC, Jack Clark, Dr and Mrs R G J Telfer, Sarah and Peter Gooderham, Tina and David Woods-Taylor, Mr and Mrs John Taylor, Ewan and Moira McCall)*

Free house ~ Licensee Ian Stephenson ~ Real ale ~ Bar food (12-2, 6-8.45; no evening meals midweek in Dec or Jan) ~ Restaurant ~ (015394) 37215 ~ Children welcome ~ Dogs allowed in bar ~ Open 11-10.30(11 Sat); 12-10.30 Sun; 11-3, 8-10.30 midweek in winter; closed 25 Dec ~ Bedrooms: /£72B

LOWESWATER NY1421 Map 9

Kirkstile Inn

From B5289 follow signs to Loweswater Lake; OS Sheet 89 map reference 140210

The Loweswater Brewery in this 16th-c inn is now well established and produces Grassmoor and Melbreak ales on site. They also keep Coniston Bluebird, Hawkshead Bitter, and Yates Bitter on handpump. The bar is low-beamed and carpeted, with a roaring log fire, comfortably cushioned small settles and pews, and partly stripped stone walls; slate shove-ha'penny board. Well liked bar food includes home-made soup (£2.95), pâté en croûte with home-made cumberland sauce or lunchtime filled baguettes (£3.95), lunchtime filled baked potatoes (from £3.50), lunchtime ploughman's (£5.25), mushroom and lentil bake (£6.25), home-made steak and kidney pudding (£7.25), and dijon and tarragon chicken (£8.50), with daily specials such as smoked salmon parcels stuffed with crème fraîche laced with a tomato and rosemary dressing (£4.25), vegetable lasagne (£6.50), fillet of fresh breadcrumbed plaice with a tomato concasse and sour cream (£7.95), and rump steak with a stilton and brandy sauce (£9.50), and puddings like chocolate and Cointreau crème brûlée, sherry trifle or fruit crumble (£3.75); friendly staff. The restaurant, lounge, and bedrooms are no smoking. You can enjoy the view from picnic-sets on the lawn, from the very attractive covered verandah in front of the building, and from the bow windows in one of the rooms off the bar. *(Recommended by Guy Vowles, Mr and Mrs D W Mitchell, Mike and Penny Sutton, Sylvia and Tony Birbeck, Kevin Flack, John Kane, Michael and Jennifer Wadsworth, Mr and Mrs John Taylor, Jenny Ellis, Michael Jones, Edward Mirzoeff, Tim Maddison)*

Free house ~ Licensees Roger and Helen Humphreys ~ Real ale ~ Bar food (12-2, 6-9) ~ Restaurant ~ (01900) 85219 ~ Children welcome ~ Dogs allowed in bar and bedrooms ~ Jazz once a month ~ Open 11-11; 11-10.30 Sun; closed 25 Dec ~ Bedrooms: £40B/£60(£70B)

MUNGRISDALE NY3630 Map 10

Mill Inn

Off A66 Penrith—Keswick, a bit over 1 mile W of A5091 Ullswater turn-off

There are good walks nearby and some strenuous hillwalking further on, so it's useful that in high season, you can get some food all day here. The simply furnished and neatly kept main bar has a wooden bar counter with an old millstone by it, an open fire in the stone fireplace, and well kept Jennings Bitter and Cumberland, and Black Sheep on handpump; 30 malt whiskies. Bar food includes 13 varieties of home-made shortcrust pastry pies such as wild venison, pheasant and rabbit, a medley of roasted vegetables in a sweet chilli and tomato sauce, local lamb with spices and apricots, and wild venison, pheasant and rabbit (from £6.95), as well as home-made soup (£2.75), snacks like filled white rolls (from £3.25), filled toasted muffins (from £3.60), and open sandwiches (£4.60), lunchtime three-egg omelette (£4.60) or ploughman's (£5.75), and daily specials such as smoked mackerel pâté (£4.25), grilled fresh haddock in a cheese and prawn sauce (£8.65), and duck breast with a plum, red wine and redcurrant sauce (£9.95). The restaurant is no smoking; afternoon tea during the summer. The games room has darts, pool, dominoes, and piped music. There are tables on the gravel forecourt and neat lawn sloping to a little river. The bathrooms have been upgraded this year. Please note that there's a quite separate Mill Hotel here. *(Recommended by Angus Lyon, Mike and Penny Sutton, Jack Morley, Alan and Paula McCully, Paul Davies, Steve Nye, Tim Maddison)*

Free house ~ Licensees Jim and Margaret Hodge ~ Real ale ~ Bar food (12-2.30, 6-8(9 Sat)) ~ Restaurant ~ (017687) 79632 ~ Children in eating area of bar and restaurant ~ Dogs allowed in bar ~ Open 11-11; 12-10.30 Sun; closed 25-26 Dec ~ Bedrooms: /£60B

NEAR SAWREY SD3796 Map 9

Tower Bank Arms

B5285 towards the Windermere ferry

As Beatrix Potter's Hill Top Farm (owned by the National Trust) backs on to this little country inn, and it features in *The Tale of Jemima Puddleduck*, there are lots of customers at peak times. The low-beamed main bar has a fine log fire in the big cooking range, high-backed settles on the rough slate floor, local hunting photographs, postcards of Beatrix Potter, and signed photographs of celebrities on the walls, a grandfather clock, and good traditional atmosphere. Well kept Theakstons Old Peculier and Best and Charles Wells Bombardier and a couple of guests like Adnams Broadside or Barngates Tag Lag on handpump, as well as lots of malt whiskies, and belgian fruit beers and other foreign beers, Well liked food includes home-made soup (£2.60), lunchtime filled rolls (from £3.25), morecambe bay potted shrimps (£4.95), ploughman's (from £5.25), home-made cheese flan (£6.50), a vegetarian dish or cumberland sausage (£6.75), battered whitby scampi (£7.50), wild boar and pheasant pie (£8.80), and steaks (from £10.50); friendly staff. Darts, dominoes, cribbage, and piped music. Seats outside have pleasant views of the wooded Claife Heights. This is a good area for golf, sailing, bird-watching, fishing (they have a licence for two rods a day on selected waters in the area), and walking, but if you want to stay at the pub, you'll have to book well in advance. *(Recommended by Angus Lyon, John Dwane, Mr and Mrs Maurice Thompson, Jason Caulkin, Michael Doswell, David and Helen Wilkins, Dave and Sue Mitchell, Tina and David Woods-Taylor, Michael Dandy, Michael and Marion Buchanan, Catherine and Rob Dunster)*

Free house ~ Licensee Philip Broadley ~ Real ale ~ Bar food (not 25 Dec) ~ Restaurant ~ (015394) 36334 ~ Children in eating area of bar lunchtime but in restaurant only, in evenings ~ Dogs welcome ~ Open 11-3, 5.30-11; 12-3, 5.30(6 in winter)-10.30 Sun ~ Bedrooms: £40B/£57B

PENRUDDOCK NY4327 Map 10

Herdwick

Off A66 Penrith—Keswick

Run by polite, helpful staff, this well cared for cottagey inn is mainly busy in the evening. There's plenty of stripped stone and white paintwork, a good cosy atmosphere, well kept Jennings Cumberland and Bitter with summer guests like Shepherd Neame Spitfire or Robinsons Best on handpump from an unusual curved bar, and a no smoking dining room with an upper gallery (best to book, especially in the evenings); the cocktail bar is also no smoking; 23 malt whiskies. Good bar food at lunchtime includes home-made soup (£2.95), sandwiches or baguettes (£4.50), filled baked potatoes (£5), a vegetarian dish of the day or ploughman's (£5.55), and a roast of the day or cumberland sausage (£5.95); evening dishes such as black pudding in pepper cream sauce (£3.90), poached fresh pears with stilton dressing (£3.95), home-made pâté (£4.25), spinach and cheese roulade (£7.75), home-made steak in ale pie (£7.90), and herdwick spiced lamb with home-made scone (£8.45), daily specials like game casserole (£7.90) or fresh fish (from around £10.35), and home-made puddings (£3.50). Pool, piped music, juke box, darts, pool, cribbage and dominoes. Nearby Dalemain is well worth a visit. More reports please. *(Recommended by Mike and Penny Sutton, C L Clarkson, Michael Doswell, Alan and Paula McCully, Richard J Holloway)*

Free house ~ Licensees Ian and Sandra Hall ~ Real ale ~ Bar food (12-2, 6-9) ~ Restaurant ~ (017684) 83007 ~ Children in eating area of bar and restaurant ~ Open 12-2.30(2 if they are not busy), 6-11; 12-3, 7-10.30 Sun ~ Bedrooms: £30S/£60S

SANDFORD NY7316 Map 10

Sandford Arms

Village and pub signposted just off A66 W of Brough

Tucked away in a very small village by the River Eden, this neat and welcoming little inn was once an 18th-c farmhouse. The compact and comfortable no smoking dining area is on a slightly raised balustraded platform at one end of the L-shaped carpeted main bar, which has stripped beams and stonework, well kept Black Sheep and a guest like Hesket Newmarket Skiddaw Special Bitter on handpump, a good range of malt whiskies, and nice new world house wines (also ones from the Sandford Estate – no connection); dominoes, and Sunday quiz evening. The two sons do the cooking, and the food might include home-made soup (£2.75), grilled black pudding with mustard sauce (£3.50), sandwiches (from £3.95), salads or home-made pie of the day (£7.45), chicken with mushrooms and bacon in a creamy sauce or gammon with egg or pineapple (£7.95), salmon fillet with parsley sauce (£8.45), steaks (from £12.50), and puddings like sticky toffee pudding or highland trifle (from £2.95). There's also a more formal separate dining room (open if pre-booked), and a second bar area with broad flagstones, charming heavy-horse prints, an end log fire, and darts and piped music. Some picnic-sets outside. *(Recommended by Dr and Mrs R G J Telfer, Richard J Holloway)*

Free house ~ Licensee Susan Stokes ~ Real ale ~ Bar food (12-1.45, 6.30(7 Sun, Mon)-8.30; not Mon, Weds, Thurs lunchtimes, not Tues) ~ Restaurant ~ (017683) 51121 ~ Children welcome ~ Dogs allowed in bar ~ Open 12-1.45, 6.30(7 Weds, Thurs, Sun)-11(10.30 Sun); closed Mon lunchtime, all day Tues ~ Bedrooms: £50B/£60B

SANTON BRIDGE NY1101 Map 9

Bridge Inn

Off A595 at Holmrook or Gosforth

Run by a cheerful and helpful licensee, this traditional little black and white Lakeland inn has fell views and seats out in front by the quiet road. The turkey-carpeted bar has stripped beams, joists and standing timbers, a coal and log fire, and three rather unusual timbered booths around big stripped tables along its outer wall, with small painted school chairs and tables elsewhere. Bar stools line the long concave bar counter, which has well kept Jennings Bitter, Cumberland, Cocker Hoop, and Sneck Lifter, and a guest such as Marstons Pedigree on handpump; good big pots of tea, speciality coffees, and maybe well reproduced piped nostalgic pop music; darts, and dominoes. Bar food includes filled baguettes, home-made soup (£2.50), salads such as caesar or greek (from £4.20), cumberland sausage (£7.50), steak and kidney pie or whitby scampi (£7.95), vegetarian stir fry (£8.95), chicken riesling (£10.95), steaks (from £11.95), daily specials, and Sunday carvery (£6.20). The back bistro is no smoking (no children under 10 in here), the small reception hall has a rack of daily papers, and there's a comfortable more hotelish lounge (with an internet café) on the left. *(Recommended by Roger Braithwaite, Paul Davies, Maggie and Tony Harwood, Derek Harvey-Piper)*

Jennings ~ Tenants John Morrow and Lesley Rhodes ~ Real ale ~ Bar food (12-2.30, 6-9.30) ~ Restaurant ~ (01946) 726221 ~ Children in eating area of bar and restaurant ~ Dogs allowed in bar and bedrooms ~ Live music first Thurs of month ~ Open 11-11; 12-10.30 Sun ~ Bedrooms: £40(£45S)/£55(£60B)

SEATHWAITE SD2396 Map 9

Newfield Inn

Duddon Valley, near Ulpha (ie not Seathwaite in Borrowdale)

In a quieter corner of the Lakes, this is an enjoyable pub to visit. It is well run and neatly kept with a friendly welcome for both visitors and regulars. The slate-floored bar has a genuinely local and informal atmosphere, with wooden tables and chairs, and some interesting pictures, and well kept Caledonian Deuchars IPA, Hawkshead Bitter, Jennings Bitter, and York Stonewall on handpump. There's a comfortable side room and a games room with darts, bar billiards, shove-ha'penny, cribbage, and dominoes. Good value bar food includes soup (£2.45), sandwiches and filled rolls (from £2.80), filled baked potatoes (from £3.95), pasta and tomato and basil sauce (£5.95), home-made lasagne (£6.85), home-made steak pie (£6.95), salmon fillet with lime butter (£7.95), steaks (from £10.95), daily specials like home-made meat and potato pie (£5.25) or herdwick lamb (£11.50), and puddings such as home-made apple pie or pear and chocolate crumble (£2.95). The grill room is no smoking; piped music There are good walks from the doorstep so it's not surprising that walkers and climbers crowd in at weekends, and there are tables out in the nice garden with good hill views. The pub owns and lets the next-door self-catering flats. *(Recommended by David Heath, Margaret Dickinson, David Field, Maggie and Tony Harwood, Mrs J Walker, Derek Harvey-Piper)*

Free house ~ Licensee Paul Batten ~ Real ale ~ Bar food (12-9) ~ Restaurant ~ (01229) 716208 ~ Children in eating area of bar and restaurant ~ Dogs allowed in bar ~ Open 11-11; 12-10.30 Sun

SEDBERGH SD6692 Map 10

Dalesman

Main Street

Walkers enjoy this nicely modernised pub and the Dales Way and Cumbrian Cycle Way both pass the door. The various rooms have quite a mix of decorations and styles – lots of stripped stone and beams, cushioned farmhouse chairs and stools around dimpled copper tables, and a raised stone hearth with a log fire; also, horsebrasses and spigots, Vernon Stokes gundog pictures, various stuffed animals, tropical fish, and a blunderbuss. Through stone arches on the right, a no smoking buttery area serves generous helpings of bar food (with prices unchanged since last year) such as home-made soup (£2.50), home-made chicken liver pâté with plum chutney (£4), chargrilled flat mushrooms with pesto (£3), a big ploughman's, mushroom lasagne, pork and leek sausage or steak and kidney pie (all £7), omelettes (from £7), lamb shank with redcurrant (£8), popular belly of pork with crackling or fresh cod in beer batter (£9), aberdeen angus steaks (from £13), and puddings like orange crème brûlée or chocolate and Baileys terrine (£4). Well kept Tetleys Bitter, and their own Dalesman Bitter on handpump, and several malt whiskies; dominoes and piped music. Some picnic-sets out in front, and a small car park. More reports please. *(Recommended by Tony and Ann Bennett-Hughes, Clare and Peter Pearse)*

Free house ~ Licensees Michael and Judy Garnett ~ Real ale ~ Bar food (all day Sun) ~ Restaurant ~ (015396) 21183 ~ Children in eating areas and in family room ~ Monthly jazz ~ Open 11-11; 12-10.30 Sun ~ Bedrooms: £30B/£60B

STAVELEY SD4798 Map 9

Eagle & Child

Kendal Road; just off A591 Windermere—Kendal

The good home-made food has been drawing a growing number of readers to this appealingly updated small inn. Two rooms that we remember as being separate from our last visit some years ago have been carefully knocked together, to give a roughly L-shaped flagstoned area with plenty of separate parts to sit in. It has pews, banquettes, bow window seats and some high-backed dining chairs around polished dark tables, some nice photographs and interesting prints, just a few farm tools and a delft shelf of bric-a-brac, and two good log fires, one under an impressive mantelbeam. The food runs from enterprising baguettes, ciabattas and wraps with fillings such as roasted vegetables and goats cheese or spicy cajun chicken and soured cream (£4.50) to home-made soup (£2.50), warmed local black pudding with a creamy grain mustard and brandy sauce (£3.95), field mushrooms stuffed with stilton, breadcrumbed and deep fried and served with a garlic and herb dip (£4.95), cumberland sausage with rich red wine onion gravy (£7.95), home-made fresh spinach and ricotta puff pastry lattice with a creamy wild mushroom sauce or fresh trout in cider, dill and pink peppercorns (£8.50), duck in hoi sin sauce (£10.50), lamb shank with sweet redcurrant and mint jus (£10.95). Puddings (£3.50) are tempting, with the odd unexpected touch like the honey and Drambuie sauce with their bread and butter pudding. They provide thoughtfully for children, and serve a generous Sunday lunch. The licensees are welcoming and helpful, and have four well kept ales on handpump changing every week or so from breweries like Barngates, Black Sheep, Coniston, Tirril and Yates from the small bar counter; also three ciders, ten wines by the glass, and several malt whiskies; piped music, darts, TV, cribbage and dominoes. An upstairs barn-theme dining room (with its own bar for functions and so forth) doubles as a breakfast room – they do good breakfasts. There are picnic-sets under cocktail parasols in a sheltered garden by the River Kent, with more on a good-sized back terrace and second newer garden behind. *(Recommended by Jackie Moffat, S and R Gray, Mr and Mrs Maurice Thompson, Richard Lewis, MLR, Michael Doswell, Bill Braithwaite, Stephen Gibbs, Rowena Lord)*

Free house ~ Licensees Richard and Denise Coleman ~ Bar food (12-2.30, 6-9) ~ Restaurant ~ (01539) 821320 ~ Children welcome ~ Dogs allowed in bar ~ Open 11-11; 12-10.30 Sun ~ Bedrooms: £35B/£55B

STONETHWAITE NY2613 Map 9

Langstrath

Off B5289 S of Derwent Water

At its pubbiest at lunchtime, the neat and simple bar in this completely no smoking and civilised little inn has a welcoming coal and log fire in a big stone fireplace, just a handful of cast-iron-framed tables, plain chairs and cushioned wall seats, and on its textured white walls quite a few walking cartoons and attractive Lakeland mountain photographs. Well kept Black Sheep and Jennings Bitter on handpump, with a couple of guest beers such as Hawkshead Bitter or Timothy Taylors Landlord, and quite a few malt whiskies; piped music. A little oak-boarded room on the left reminded us almost of a doll's house living room in style – this is actually the original cottage built around 1590. Enjoyable bar food (they tell us prices have not changed since last year) includes home-made soup (£2.95), sandwiches (from £3.25), mushrooms in creamy garlic sauce (£4.25), morecambe bay potted shrimps (£4.95), mushroom, broccoli and stilton pasta bake (£7.95), local trout poached with tarragon (£8.95), local roast lamb with mint (£10.25), daily specials like cumberland sausage with onion gravy (£8.25), wild boar and duckling pie (£8.90), and fillet of halibut in pastry parcel with lemon butter sauce (£9.25). It is essential to book a table in advance. There is also a separate back restaurant, by the residents' lounge. Outside, a big sycamore shelters a few picnic-sets. This is a lovely spot surrounded by the steep fells above Borrowdale. *(Recommended by Mayur Shah, Kevin Flack, Tina and David Woods-Taylor, Fred and Lorraine Gill, J C Clark, Peter J and Avril Hanson, Jarrod and Wendy Hopkinson)*

Free house ~ Licensees Donna and Gary MacRae ~ Bar food (12-2, 6-8; soup served all day) ~ Restaurant ~ (017687) 77239 ~ Children in eating area of bar ~ Open 11-11; 12-10.30 Sun; closed weekdays Dec-Jan ~ Bedrooms: £27/£54(£66S)(£72B)

TALKIN NY5557 Map 10

Blacksmiths Arms

Village signposted from B6413 S of Brampton

Both locals and visitors really enjoy this well run and friendly former blacksmith's. On the right is a warm, neatly kept lounge (no smoking at lunchtime) with upholstered banquettes, tables and chairs, an open fire, and country prints and other pictures on the walls; the Garden Room is no smoking. Well kept Black Sheep, Coniston Bluebird and Hawkshead Bitter on handpump, and over 20 wines by the glass; piped music, cribbage and dominoes. As well as lunchtime sandwiches and filled baguettes, the good, enjoyable food might include home-made soup (£2.20), chicken and pistachio pâté (£3.55), fresh haddock in home-made beer batter (£5.95), steak and kidney pie or vegetable curry (£6.35), chicken curry

(£7.25), beef stroganoff (£11.25), steaks (from £12.45), and daily specials such as fishcakes (£4.45), venison in Guinness casserole (£8.25), and shoulder of lamb in mint, honey and garlic (£10.45); three-course Sunday lunch (£6.95; children £4.75), and nice breakfasts. The no smoking restaurant on the left is pretty. There are seats outside in the garden. Three more bedrooms have been added this year. *(Recommended by Dr and Mrs R G J Telfer, David and Julie Glover, Michael Doswell, Ian and Jane Irving)*

Free house ~ Licensees Donald and Anne Jackson ~ Real ale ~ Bar food (12-2, 6-9) ~ Restaurant ~ (016977) 3452 ~ Children welcome ~ Open 12-3, 6-11(10.30 Sun) ~ Bedrooms: £35B/£50B

TIRRIL NY5126 Map 10

Queens Head

3½ miles from M6 junction 40; take A66 towards Brough, A6 towards Shap, then B5320 towards Ullswater

The old brewery here has been knocked down and a new no smoking lounge has been created, with disabled and baby changing facilities. The oldest parts of the bar have low bare beams, black panelling, original flagstones and floorboards, and high-backed settles; the little back bar has a lot of character, and there are four open fireplaces including one roomy inglenook. Their own beers, brewed at Brougham Hall a couple of miles away, include Bewshers Bitter (after the landlord in the early 1800s who bought the inn from the Wordsworths and changed its name to the Queens Head in time for Victoria's coronation), Academy Ale, Brougham Ale, Old Faithful, 1823, and the new Graduate (only available in December), and a guest like Dent Rambrau on handpump. During the Cumbrian Beer & Sausage Festival during August, there are 24 local real ales. Over 40 malt whiskies, a good choice of brandies and other spirits, and a carefully chosen wine list. As well as lunchtime filled baked potatoes or baguettes (from £4.50), the menu might include home-made soup (£3.25), ploughman's (£7.50), lasagne or mushroom and hazelnut pasta (£7.95), cumberland sausage (£8.25), home-made pie of the day (£8.50), and shoulder of lamb with redcurrant gravy (£10.50), with daily specials like tuna steak with lime and ginger crust (£9.95) or red snapper on szechuan vegetables (£13.95), and puddings such as white chocolate brûlée with chocolate dipped shortbread (£3.50). The restaurant is no smoking. Pool, juke box, and dominoes in the back bar. The pub is very close to a number of interesting places, such as Dalemain House at Dacre, and is just 2½ miles from Ullswater. More reports please. *(Recommended by Darly Graton, Graeme Gulibert, John Oates, Hugh Roberts, Mike and Maggie Betton, Eric Larkham, Geoff and Angela Jaques, Christine and Neil Townend, David and Barbara Knott, Jeremy Woods, Alan and Paula McCully, Callum and Letitia Smith-Burnett, Dr and Mrs M W A Haward, Robert F Smith, Richard Houghton, John and Claire Pettifer, Richard and Anne Ansell, Paul Boot, Simon Calvert, Jo Lilley, John and Wendy Allin, Dr D G Twyman)*

Own brew ~ Licensee Chris Tomlinson ~ Real ale ~ Bar food (12-2, 6-9.30) ~ Restaurant ~ (01768) 863219 ~ Children in eating area of bar and in restaurant; under 3 or over 13 for accommodation ~ Dogs allowed in bar and bedrooms ~ Open 12-11; 12-10.30 Sun ~ Bedrooms: £40B/£70B

TROUTBECK NY4103 Map 9

Queens Head ★

A592 N of Windermere

Readers have enjoyed staying at this civilised inn over the past year, and as well as good traditional breakfasts, you might be offered something different such as field mushrooms on an oatmeal pancake with feta cheese. The big rambling original U-shaped bar has a little no smoking room at each end, beams and flagstones, a very nice mix of old cushioned settles and mate's chairs around some sizeable tables (especially the one to the left of the door), and a log fire in the raised stone fireplace with horse harness and so forth on either side of it in the main part, and a log fire in the other; some trumpets, cornets and saxophones on one wall, country pictures on others, stuffed pheasants in a big glass case, and a stag's head with a tie around his neck, and a stuffed fox with a ribbon around his neck. A massive Elizabethan four-poster bed is the basis of the finely carved counter where they serve Boddingtons, Coniston Bluebird and Jennings Bitter, with guests such as Hawkshead Bitter or Tirrell Old Faithful on handpump. The newer dining rooms (where you can also drop in for just a drink) are similarly decorated to the main bar, with oak beams and stone walls, settles along big tables, and an open fire. Popular bar food includes home-made soup with home-made bread (£2.75), baked goats cheese topped with roasted hazelnut crumb (£5.95), steak, ale and mushroom cobbler (£7.25), mixed bean and lentil strudel with tomato compote or chicken supreme filled with stilton forcemeat and wrapped in bacon with a grape compote finished with cream (£9.95), whole shank of lamb on mint mash with a redcurrant and rosemary jus (£10.50), fillet of salmon with coriander risotto (£10.95), and haunch of local venison on braised red cabbage (£14.25); proper food for children (from £3), and a three-course menu £15.50. Piped music. Seats outside have a fine view over the Trout valley to Applethwaite moors. *(Recommended by Roy and Lindsey Fentiman, Tony and Ann Bennett-Hughes, Mayur Shah, Phil and Heidi Cook, Fred and Lorraine Gill, A Sadler, Barry Robson, Jack Clark, Mike Pugh, Sarah and Peter Gooderham, David and Helen Wilkins, Ron Gentry, Revd D Glover, Richard and Anne Ansell, Malcolm and Jane MacDonald, Catherine and Rob Dunster, Sue Holland, Dave Webster, Hugh Roberts, Stephen Gibbs, Rowena Lord, J S Burn, K H Richards)*

Free house ~ Licensees Mark Stewardson and Joanne Sherratt ~ Real ale ~ Bar food ~ Restaurant ~ (015394) 32174 ~ Children welcome ~ Dogs allowed in bar ~ Open 11-11; 12-10.30 Sun; closed 25 Dec ~ Bedrooms: /£95S(£105B)

ULVERSTON SD2978 Map 7

Bay Horse

Canal Foot signposted off A590 and then you wend your way past the huge Glaxo factory

Once a staging post for coaches that crossed the sands of Morecambe Bay to Lancaster in the 18th c, this civilised and smart hotel is at its most informal at lunchtime. The bar, notable for its huge stone horse's head, has a relaxed atmosphere despite its smart furnishings: attractive wooden armchairs, some pale green plush built-in wall banquettes, glossy hardwood traditional tables, blue plates on a delft shelf, and black beams and props with lots of horsebrasses. Magazines are dotted about, there's a handsomely marbled green granite fireplace, and decently reproduced piped music; darts, shove-ha'penny, cribbage and dominoes. Good, imaginative bar food might include sandwiches (from £3.50), home-made cream of potato, leek and watercress soup (£3.95), cheese platter with home-made biscuits and soda bread (£5.95), home-made cheese and herb pâté or chicken liver pâté with cranberry and ginger sauce (£6.25), chicken strips with leeks and button mushrooms with a sweet and sour sauce (£8.50), red and green peppers stuffed with mushroom and onion pâté on a tomato provençale with garlic and chive cream and a breadcrumb and pine nut topping (£8.75), cumberland sausage with date chutney, cranberry and apple sauce (£9), fresh crab and salmon fishcakes on a white wine and fresh herb cream sauce (£9.50), and home-made puddings (£4.50). Well kept Jennings Best and Cumberland, and a guest like Bass on handpump, a decent choice of spirits, and a carefully chosen and interesting wine list with quite a few from South Africa. The no smoking conservatory restaurant has fine views over Morecambe Bay (as do the bedrooms) and there are some seats out on the terrace. Please note, the bedroom price includes dinner as well. More reports please. *(Recommended by Sylvia and Tony Birbeck, Tina and David Woods-Taylor; also in the* Good Hotel Guide*)*

Free house ~ Licensee Robert Lyons ~ Real ale ~ Bar food (lunchtime only; not Mon) ~ Restaurant ~ (01229) 583972 ~ Children in eating area of bar and in restaurant if over 12 ~ Dogs allowed in bar and bedrooms ~ Open 11-11; 12-10.30 Sun ~ Bedrooms: /£160B

Farmers Arms

Market Place

Right in the heart of Ulverston, and very much a focal part of town, this friendly 16th-c pub is attractively extended and modernised inside. The original fireplace and timbers blend in well with the more contemporary furnishings in the front bar – mostly wicker chairs on one side, comfortable sofas on the other; the overall effect is rather unusual, but somehow it still feels like the most traditional village pub. A table by the fire has newspapers, glossy magazines and local information, then a second smaller bar counter leads into a big raftered eating area, part of which is no smoking; piped music. Up to six swiftly changing well kept real ales on handpump: Greene King Ruddles County, Hawkshead Bitter, Moorhouses Bitter, St Peters Best Bitter, Theakstons Best and Timothy Taylors Landlord. They specialise in carefully chosen new world wines, with around a dozen by the glass. Good food includes lunchtime hot and cold sandwiches (from £3.95; bacon, sun-dried tomato and goats cheese £4.25) and filled baked potatoes (£6.95), plus home-made soup (£2.75), hot garlic prawns on toast (£3.95), cumberland sausage or battered cod (£6.95), chicken curry (£7.25), steaks (from £12.95), and daily specials like home-made mushroom stroganoff (£6.95), beef in chilli and ginger with stir-fried oriental vegetables (£7.95), a huge plate of mussels, squid and langoustines in garlic and chilli (£9.95), and bass with garlic butter and fresh herbs (£11.95). In front is a very attractive terrace with plenty of good wooden tables looking on to the market cross, big heaters, and lots of colourful plants in tubs and hanging baskets. If something's happening in town, the pub is usually a part of it, and they can be busy on Thursday market day. More reports please. *(Recommended by Lesley Bass, Simon Calvert)*

Free house ~ Licensee Roger Chattaway ~ Real ale ~ Bar food ~ Restaurant ~ (01229) 584469 ~ Children welcome ~ Open 11-11(10.30 Sun)

LUCKY DIP

Besides the fully inspected pubs, you might like to try these Lucky Dips recommended to us and described by readers (if you do, please send us reports: www.goodguides.co.uk).

ALSTON NY7146

Alston House [Townfoot]: Comfortable pub/hotel reopened in 2003, friendly and relaxed, with a welcome for walkers, well kept beers, decent wines by the glass, interesting well sourced food; bedrooms *(Ian Thurman)*

☆ *Angel* [Front St]: Friendly 17th-c local on steep cobbled street of charming small Pennine market town, beams, timbers, big log and coal fire, traditional furnishings, prompt service, good value generous quickly served food (not Tues evening) from well filled sandwiches to steaks, well kept Flowers IPA and Wadworths 6X, decent house wines; no dogs; children welcome in eating area, tables in sheltered back garden; cheap bedrooms *(LYM, MLR, R T and J C Moggridge)*

☆ *Turks Head* [Market Pl]: Comfortable and convivial old-world local with new licensees, good value traditional food, well kept Bass, basic low-beamed front bar allowing dogs, steps down to cosy main back lounge, log fires; at top of steep cobbled street *(Maggie and Tony Harwood)*

AMBLESIDE NY4008

☆ *Kirkstone Pass Inn* [A592 N of Troutbeck]: Splendid position and surrounding scenery – Lakeland's quaint highest inn; flagstones, stripped stone and simple furnishings, lots of old photographs and bric-a-brac, two log fires, hearty food all day from 9.30, well kept Hawkshead and Jennings ales, good coffee, hot chocolate, mulled wine, daily papers; piped music, pool room; tables outside, three bedrooms, open all day *(LYM, Kevin Thorpe, Mrs B M Hill)*

Sportsman [Compston Rd]: Worth knowing for its reasonably priced food *(Sarah and Peter Gooderham)*

ARMATHWAITE NY5045

Fox & Pheasant Cosy, comfortable and neatly kept 18th-c coaching inn overlooking River Eden, enjoyable generous food inc imaginative dishes, well kept Jennings and Hesket Newmarket ales, cafetière coffee, attractive beamed and flagstoned stripped-stone bar, shining brass, roaring fire, charming small dining room, helpful staff; picnic-sets outside, bedrooms *(Jackie Moffat, Michael Doswell)*

ARNSIDE SD4578

Albion [Promenade]: Refurbished and extended, with enjoyable food from hot and cold sandwiches and baked potatoes through some nice good value specials, well kept Thwaites Bitter and Lancaster Bomber, pleasant atmosphere, great views over estuary to Lakeland mountains from bar and terrace tables *(Michael Doswell)*

ASKHAM NY5123

☆ ***Punch Bowl*** Rambling beamed lounge bar, small snug, enjoyable food from good lunchtime sandwiches up, wider evening choice, well kept Barngates Cracker and Black Sheep, lots of whiskies, good coffee, welcoming service, two roaring log fires, arches to public bar with juke box and pool room; children really welcome, plastic tables out in front facing green, delightful village *(Stuart Turner, Christine and Neil Townend, Michael Doswell, Hugh Roberts, C M Vipond, C L Clarkson, LYM, Angus Lyon)*

BARROW-IN-FURNESS SD1969

Ambrose [Duke St]: Five well kept changing ales in welcoming well furnished pub with big recently refurbished lounge, bar and separate restaurant, fair-priced standard bar meals, live entertainment most nights; 17 bedrooms with own bathrooms *(Dr B and Mrs P B Baker)*

BASSENTHWAITE NY2332

☆ ***Sun*** [off A591 N of Keswick]: Opened-up rambling bar, homely and friendly, with wide range of quickly served good value home-made food inc three Sun roasts, friendly service, good choice of well kept Jennings ales, enterprising wines by the glass, two big log fires, low 17th-c beams, interesting local photographs, pool; provision for children, tables in pretty front yard looking up to the fells *(Christopher Tull, LYM, Mrs M Hitchings, Richard J Holloway, Simon J Barber, D F Lye)*

BOOT NY1700

☆ ***Brook House*** Converted small Victorian hotel, warm and welcoming, with obliging family service, wide choice of good generous home-made food inc some interesting dishes on solid timber tables, small no smoking plushly modernised bar, comfortable hunting-theme lounge, log fires, four well kept ales such as Black Sheep, Coniston, Timothy Taylors Landlord and Yates, decent wines, peaceful dining room, good views; handy for Ravenglass rly and great walks, eight good bedrooms with own bathrooms – and good drying room *(John Dwane, Tim and Judy Barker, Mike and Penny Sutton, Paul Davies, Annie Rosenthal)*

Burnmoor [signed just off the Wrynose/Hardknott Pass rd]: Comfortably modernised beamed bar with ever-burning fire, well kept Black Sheep, Jennings Bitter and Cumberland and a guest beer, decent wines and malt whiskies, good mulled wine all year, reasonably priced home-made lunchtime bar food from sandwiches and baked potatoes up using carefully chosen ingredients, no smoking restaurant and dining conservatory; booked minibus parties may have priority, games room with pool, TV and juke box; children welcome, seats out on sheltered front lawn with play area, open all day, bedrooms, good walks, lovely surroundings *(LYM, Tina and David Woods-Taylor)*

Woolpack [Bleabeck, midway between Boot and Hardknott Pass]: Last pub before the notorious Hardknott Pass, a whitewashed beacon for travellers and walkers with generous good value home cooking from sandwiches up, well kept Jennings and several summer guest beers, woodburner, hunting prints, brasses and fresh flowers; children welcome, nice garden with mountain views, bedrooms and bunkhouse *(John Dwane, Jean and Douglas Troup)*

BORROWDALE NY2617

Borrowdale Hotel [B5289, S end of Derwentwater]: A hotel, but very good choice of reasonably priced 'pub lunch' food from sandwiches up, roomy bar, light conservatory, pleasant staff; garden tables, bedrooms *(Kevin Flack, Guy Consterdine)*

BOWLAND BRIDGE SD4189

☆ ***Hare & Hounds*** [signed from A5074]: Spick and span country dining pub thriving under current management, roaring log fire in small bar, attractive eating areas off with polished flagstones or red carpet, some stripped stone, wide range of enjoyable food from baguettes through typical pub dishes to some tempting up-to-date specials, quick attentive service, real ales inc Black Sheep, Boddingtons and a bargain beer brewed for the pub; children welcome, picnic-sets in spacious side garden, bedrooms, quiet hamlet in lovely scenery *(LYM, Margaret and Roy Randle, Michael Doswell, Dr R C C Ward)*

BOWNESS-ON-WINDERMERE SD4096

Albert [Queens Sq]: Well kept Robinsons Hartleys, wide choice of wines and popular food from baguettes and baked potatoes in refurbished bar and dining area; piped music may be loud, live some nights; comfortable bedrooms *(Michael Dandy)*

☆ ***Hole in t' Wall*** [Lowside]: Ancient beams and flagstones, stripped stone, lots of country bric-a-brac and old pictures, lively bustle, splendid log fire under vast slate mantelpiece, upper room with attractive plasterwork (and dominoes and juke box), good value generous honest pub food from sandwiches to steak and good curries, well kept Robinsons Frederics, Best and Hartleys XB, may be home-made lemonade or good winter mulled wine; very busy in tourist season; no dogs or prams, sheltered picnic-sets in tiny flagstoned front courtyard *(David Heath, LYM, Jim Abbott, Margaret Dickinson, Peter Abbott, Tony Pope, Karen Bonham, Mrs J Walker)*

Olde John Peel [Rayrigg Rd]: Attractively refurbished lounge, panelled bar, country artefacts, good value family bar food from rolls and baked potatoes up, well kept Theakstons, mulled wine, friendly staff; upstairs games rooms with darts, pool and machines; handy for World of Beatrix Potter, open all day *(Michael Dandy)*

BRAITHWAITE NY2323

☆ ***Coledale Hotel*** [signed off A66 W of Keswick, pub then signed left off B5292]: Bustling inn perfectly placed at the foot of Whinlatter Pass, fine views of Skiddaw, winter coal fire, little 19th-c Lakeland engravings, plush banquettes and studded tables, well kept Jennings, John

Smiths and Theakstons XB, friendly staff; darts, dominoes, piped music, hearty food, no smoking dining room; garden with slate terrace and sheltered lawn, pretty bedrooms, open all day *(LYM, Don and Shirley Parrish)*

Royal Oak Welcoming staff, good value food, prompt service, well kept Jennings *(Julia and Richard Tredgett)*

BRIGSTEER SD4889

☆ *Wheatsheaf* Cosy and comfortable traditional pub well run by new landlady, comfortable atmosphere and country views, welcoming efficient staff, good food from interesting sandwiches to good fresh fish (takeaways some nights – fish and steak and kidney pie), good value Sun lunch inc splendid fish hors-d'oeuvre, well kept changing ales such as Yates, well chosen wines; quiet pretty village *(Malcolm Taylor, John and Sylvia Harrop, Michael Doswell, Maurice and Gill McMahon, A C English, Jonathan Shephard)*

BROUGHTON-IN-FURNESS SD2187

☆ *Black Cock* [Princes St]: Olde-worlde pub dating from 15th c, some emphasis on enjoyable reasonably priced food and spacious comfortable dining room, also lounge bar with convivial atmosphere and cosy fireside, good range of well kept beers, good service; games room up steps in former back stables; comfortable pleasantly decorated bedrooms *(Clifford Blakemore, Richard Houghton)*

☆ *Manor Arms* [The Square]: Outstanding choice of well kept ales, several changing award-winners from far and wide as well as regulars such as Coniston Bluebird, Timothy Taylors Landlord and York Terrier in neatly kept and comfortable open-plan pub on quiet sloping square, flagstones and bow window seats, coal fire in big stone fireplace, chiming clocks, good sandwiches, pizzas and bockwurst sausages, winter soup, pool table; children allowed, stairs down to lavatories (ladies' has baby-changing); well appointed good value bedrooms, big breakfast, open all day *(BB, Andrew Jackson, Richard Houghton)*

Old Kings Head [Church St]: Smart but relaxed old-world pub with newish licensees doing enjoyable food, friendly obliging service, well kept real ales, stone fireplace, chintz and knick-knacks, separate games area, small cosy no smoking restaurant; tables outside *(Derek Harvey-Piper)*

BURTON-IN-KENDAL SD5277

☆ *Dutton Arms* [4 miles from M6 junction 35; just off A6070 N of Carnforth (and can be reached – unofficially – from M6 northbound service area between junctions 35 and 36)]: Stylish and popular pub/restaurant keeping up standards under new licensees, small smartly comfortable pre-meal bar with two real ales, roomy two level restaurant, partly no smoking, with candlelit dark tables, log fire, grand piano, wide choice of enjoyable food inc interesting dishes, good value wines; smallish back garden with play area and view of Virgin trains; newish bedrooms, open all day Sun and summer wkdys *(BB, Glenn and Julia Smithers, Michael Doswell)*

BUTTERMERE NY1716

☆ *Fish* Spacious, fresh and airy former coaching inn on NT property between Buttermere and Crummock Water, fine views, well kept Jennings, Hesket Newmarket and Theakstons XB, friendly service, decent generous food from fresh sandwiches to delicious fish; can get crowded; tables out on terrace, bedrooms *(BB, Don and Shirley Parrish)*

CALDBECK NY3239

☆ *Oddfellows Arms* [B5299 SE of Wigton]: Modernised split-level pub with fine old photographs and woodburner in comfortable front bar, big no smoking back dining room, well cooked generous food from baked potatoes and lunchtime sandwiches to lots of blackboard specials, well kept Jennings Bitter and Cumberland and Youngers, decent wines, reasonable prices, obliging uniformed staff; piped music, games area with darts, pool, juke box and TV; children welcome, open all day Fri-Sun and summer, low-priced bedrooms, nice village *(Gwyneth and Salvo Spadaro-Dutturi, Mike and Penny Sutton, Canon David Baxter, Kevin Thorpe)*

CARLISLE NY4056

Griffin [Court Sq, nr station]: Big John Barras pub with good value food and good range of beers; handy for centre *(Richard Greenwood)*

Sportsmans [Heads Lane, nr Marks & Spencer]: Small and neatly kept, oldest pub in town, with good value food 12-7 (5 Sun) from excellent baguettes up, real ale; quiz night Mon *(David Carr)*

CARTMEL SD3879

☆ *Kings Arms* [The Square]: Picturesque and inviting, nicely placed at the head of the attractive town square – rambling and neatly kept heavy-beamed bar, mix of furnishings from traditional settles to banquettes, several well kept real ales, enjoyable generous home-made bar food inc meats from rare breeds, reasonable prices, all-day scones, cakes and so forth, good friendly service and attentive landlord, nice view from small no smoking back dining area; children welcome, sunny seats out on square and in attractive back courtyard by beck, craft and gift shop upstairs *(John Dwane, John Foord, LYM, Margaret Dickinson, Matthew Lidbury)*

Royal Oak [The Square]: Low beams and flagstones, cosy nooks, pleasant décor, generous good value food from baguettes up, well kept real ales such as Bass, Shepherd Neame Spitfire, Timothy Taylors Landlord and Tetleys Mild, decent wines, welcoming helpful staff, log fire, modern public bar with darts, pool, fruit machine, TV and piped music; nice big riverside garden, bedrooms *(Maggie and Tony Harwood, BB, Kevin Thorpe, Mrs Yvette Bateman)*

CASTLE CARROCK NY5455

Weary Sportsman Unusual reworking of 17th-c building, comfortable sofas and stylish bucket chairs on bare boards of light and airy bar with good prints and wall of glassware and objets, smart conservatory dining room, good carefully prepared upmarket food, well kept

Black Sheep, interesting wines; back japanese garden, bedrooms being upgraded *(Michael Doswell)*

CHAPEL STILE NY3205

☆ ***Wainwrights*** [B5343]: Roomy new-feeling slate-floored bar welcoming walkers and dogs, old kitchen range, cushioned settles, well kept Jennings beers, friendly staff, lots of high chairs in busy no smoking family dining area, food from sandwiches and baked potatoes up inc children's dishes, darts and dominoes; piped music, Tues quiz night; good views from front picnic-sets, good walks, open all day wknds and summer *(LYM, Michael Butler, John and Caroline, Ewan and Moira McCall)*

COCKERMOUTH NY1230

Black Bull [Main St]: Recent open-plan refurbishment with flagstones, stripped panelling and bright lighting at the long bar, Jennings ales and guest beers such as Theakstons and Woods, reasonably priced lunchtime food inc Sun roasts; piped pop music, pool, juke box, darts and TV – popular with young people; disabled facilities *(Kevin Thorpe)*

Bush [Main St]: 18th-c pub with four welcoming and cosy linked areas, two with carpets and banquettes, two with bare boards, beams and old tables, attractive décor, open fires, stripped stone and dark panelling, well kept Jennings (full range) and a guest beer, very friendly bar staff; cheap and cheerful generous lunchtime food, afternoon soup and sandwiches for walkers; children allowed, open all day *(Kevin Thorpe)*

CONISTON SD3098

☆ ***Black Bull*** [Yewdale Rd (A593)]: Good Coniston Bluebird, XB and Old Man brewed here, Theakstons XB, lots of Donald Campbell water-speed memorabilia, bustling flagstoned back area (dogs allowed), banquettes and open fire in partly no smoking lounge bar (no smoking restaurant too), friendly attentive service, simple good value food inc children's, good sandwiches and more enterprising specials, farm ciders, quite a few bottled beers and malt whiskies; children welcome in eating areas, tables out in former coachyard, bedrooms, open all day *(Michael Doswell, Jim Abbott, Peter Abbott, Angus Lyon, A N Caldwell, S and R Gray, LYM, Patrick Hancock, Andrew Crawford, John Foord, Jo Lilley, Jarrod and Wendy Hopkinson)*

☆ ***Sun*** 16th-c pub below dramatic fells, interesting Donald Campbell and other Lakeland photographs in old-fashioned back bar with beams, flagstones, good log fire in 19th-c range, cask seats and old settles, big no smoking conservatory off carpeted lounge (children allowed here), well kept Coniston Bluebird, Moorhouses Black Cat and several guest beers, decent wines, darts, cribbage, dominoes; they may ask to keep your credit card if you eat; dogs in bar, tables on pleasant front terrace, big tree-sheltered garden, simple comfortable bedrooms, good hearty breakfast, open all day *(Peter Abbott, Jim Abbott, Keith Jacob, S J Lawton, LYM, S and R Gray, Fred and Lorraine Gill, K Nicholls, Mr and Mrs Ireland, Duncan Cloud, Ron Gentry, Tina and David Woods-Taylor, Michael and Marion Buchanan, Ray and Winifred Halliday, Patrick Hancock, Tim Maddison)*

CROOK SD4795

☆ ***Sun*** [B5284 Kendal—Bowness]: Wide choice of good plentiful food (all day wknds) from unusual sandwiches to enterprising hot dishes and winter game, two comfortable no smoking dining areas off low-beamed bar, roaring log fire, fresh flowers, well kept Coniston Bluebird and Courage Directors, good value wines, cheerful helpful service *(Sue and Geoff Price, Michael Doswell, LYM, Sheila and Phil Stubbs, Deb and John Arthur, Jean and Douglas Troup, D C T and E A Frewer)*

DACRE NY4526

☆ ***Horse & Farrier*** [between A66 and A592 SW of Penrith]: 18th-c black-beamed village local with helpful staff, landlady cooks generous good value straightforward food inc proper steak pie, particularly well kept Jennings inc a Mild, small cheerful front room with elderly stove, more modern dining extension down steps on the left, darts, dominoes, bridge, quiz and gourmet nights; very popular with older people Thurs lunchtime, but children welcome too; integral post office, pretty village *(Geoff and Angela Jaques, Richard Stancomb, Kevin Flack, A H C Rainier, BB)*

DUFTON NY6825

☆ ***Stag*** Small unspoilt pub by peaceful green of lovely village on Pennine Way; friendly landlord and regulars, good value food using local meat, good lunchtime sandwiches, well kept Black Sheep Best and Flowers IPA, good coffee, sensible prices, splendid early Victorian kitchen range in main bar, room off on left, back dining room; children, walkers and dogs welcome; open all day wknds and summer (cl winter Mon lunchtime), picnic-sets in charming front garden, bedrooms in next-door cottage, big breakfast *(Mrs R Somers, Mr and Mrs Maurice Thompson, Ian Thurman)*

ESKDALE GREEN NY1300

☆ ***Bower House*** [½ mile W]: Civilised and quietly charming old-fashioned stone-built inn with good log fire in main lounge bar extended around beamed and alcoved core, well kept ales such as Hesket Newmarket, friendly staff, enjoyable generous bar food, no noisy machines (but may be piped music), no smoking restaurant; nicely tended sheltered garden by cricket field, charming spot with great walks, bedrooms, open all day *(Derek Harvey-Piper, Tina and David Woods-Taylor)*

FOXFIELD SD2185

☆ ***Prince of Wales*** [opp stn]: Friendly and simple, with half a dozen well kept and served ales inc beers brewed in the former stables here and at the Tigertops brewery down in Wakefield (same owners), bottled imports, farm cider and regular beer festivals, enthusiastic licensees, enjoyable simple home-made food inc speciality pasties, hot coal fire, maps, customer snaps and beer awards, pub games inc bar billiards, daily papers and beer-related reading matter, back room with one huge table; children very welcome, games for them; steps up to door; cl Mon/Tues, opens 5 Weds/Thurs, open all day Fri-Sun, reasonably priced bedrooms with own bathrooms *(David Heath, Dr B and Mrs P B Baker, G Coates, Richard Houghton, BB)*

GARRIGILL NY7441

☆ *George & Dragon* [off B6277 S of Alston]: Nicely set small 17th-c village inn with enjoyable food (but may stop serving at 1.30), well kept ales such as Black Sheep, good wines, great log fire in flagstoned bar and attractive stone-and-panelling dining room; pleasant bedrooms, open all day Sat *(LYM, Mrs Laurie Humble, Maggie and Tony Harwood)*

GOSFORTH NY0703

Lion & Lamb [The Square]: Thriving proper local with well kept John Smiths, Theakstons Best and guest beers, hearty generous food, darts; tables outside, open all day *(Jenny and Brian Seller)*

GRASMERE NY3307

Red Lion [Red Lion Sq]: Plush wall seats and stools and cast-iron pub tables in hotel's Lamb bar, open fire in slate fireplace, simple décor with some paintings, china and cider jugs, well kept Theakstons Best and XB, good range of malt whiskies, decent bar food inc all-day soup, good friendly service; pool and darts in back room, TV; cane-chair conservatory, well priced restaurant; comfortable bedrooms, good breakfast, lovely views, open all day *(Kevin Thorpe)*

Travellers Rest [A591 just N]: Comfortable lounge bar with settles, banquettes, upholstered armchairs and log fire, local watercolours, old photographs, suggested walks, bar food (all day in summer), Jennings real ales, family games room; they may try to keep your credit card if you eat; children in eating areas, dogs in bar, open all day, bedrooms *(LYM, Tina and David Woods-Taylor, Don and Shirley Parrish, Kevin Thorpe)*

Tweedies [Dale Lodge Hotel]: Big square bar with settles and tartan panels, prompt friendly service, real ale such as Jennings Cumberland and Theakstons, family dining room, plenty of young people, pool and TV; walkers welcome, picnic-sets out in large pleasant garden, bedrooms *(Michael Butler, Brian and Anna Marsden)*

GREAT SALKELD NY5536

☆ *Highland Drove* [B6412, off A686 NE of Penrith]: Neatly kept 18th-c inn with good food from unusual sandwiches to enterprising home cooking based on local produce, fish and game, also great vegetarian mezze; straightforward bar and plain pool room, large orthodox dining lounge, hunting-lodge style upstairs dining room with woodburner and Pennine views, well kept Black Sheep, Theakstons and a monthly guest beer, above-average house wines and good list, good whisky choice, proper soft drinks, cheerful service, welcoming helpful father-and-son licensees; nice balcony tables, stone tables out in garden with water feature, good value comfortable bedrooms with own bathrooms *(Kevin Tea, BB, JWAC, Richard J Holloway)*

GREAT STRICKLAND NY5522

Strickland Arms Comfortable and civilised old two-bar village inn, good value home-made food from sandwiches to steak, Black Sheep, Ind Coope Burton, Greene King Old Speckled Hen and Jennings, small pool room with darts; may be piped classical music *(Mr and Mrs Maurice Thompson, Michael Doswell)*

HEVERSHAM SD4983

Blue Bell [A6]: Civilised beamed and partly panelled lounge bar, warm log fire, big bay-windowed no smoking area, Sam Smiths OB, bar food (all day during hols), no smoking restaurant, long public bar (games, TV, piped music); children and dogs welcome, comfortable bedrooms, open all day *(Sylvia and Tony Birbeck, Tony and Ann Bennett-Hughes, Andy and Ali, MLR, Dr T E Hothersall, David Mee, LYM)*

KENDAL SD5392

Alexanders [Castle Green Hotel, Castle Green Lane]: Separate building off substantial hotel, medieval décor, hideaway bar, terrace tables high over town with great Lakeland views; kind bar staff, enjoyable sensibly priced food inc good home-made specials, good choice of real ales; comfortable bedrooms, separate restaurant and fitness/leisure centre with swimming pool *(Margaret Dickinson)*

Vats Bar [Brewery Arts Centre, Highgate]: Light and airy bar in good arts centre, seating in huge vats around tables, well kept Courage Directors and two other ales, enjoyable food inc good pizzas made to order here and in adjoining restaurant, relaxed atmosphere, friendly staff; terrace tables overlooking garden *(TB)*

KESWICK NY2623

Dog & Gun [Lake Rd]: Lively unpretentious town local with some high settles, low beams, partly slate floor (rest carpeted or boards), fine Abrahams mountain photographs, coins in beams and timbers by fireplace (collected for local mountain rescue), model cars, log fire; well kept Theakstons Best and Old Peculier, Yates and several guest beers from afar, open fires, generous straightforward bar food all day from sandwiches up inc speciality goulash; piped music, games machine, no dogs; children welcome, open all day *(LYM, A and B D Craig, Don and Shirley Parrish, Kevin Thorpe, MLR)*

☆ *George* [St Johns St]: Attractive traditional black-panelled side room, open-plan main bar, old-fashioned settles and modern banquettes under Elizabethan beams, pleasant staff, daily papers, well kept Jennings Bitter, Cocker Hoop, Cumberland and Sneck Lifter, bar food, no smoking restaurant; piped music, fruit machine; children welcome in eating areas, dogs in bar, bedrooms with own bathrooms, open all day *(LYM, Don and Shirley Parrish, Mrs J Walker)*

Oddfellows [Main St]: Long busy open-plan bar with masses of horse-racing memorabilia, pleasant staff, four well kept Jennings ales, plenty of food all day, upstairs dining room; piped music, live nightly; huge beer garden, open all day *(Kevin Thorpe)*

KING'S MEABURN NY6221

White Horse Small friendly family-run pub, real fire, Black Sheep, Tetleys and a guest ale, big varied menu inc lots for vegetarians and children; cl Mon-Weds lunchtimes *(Jon Hamilton)*

KIRKBY LONSDALE SD6178

Orange Tree [Fairbank]: Well stocked bar, good range of food inc speciality steaks, softly lit back restaurant, discreetly placed pool and SkyTV; comfortable new bedrooms over road *(Simon Calvert)*

Snooty Fox [B6254]: Rambling partly panelled pub with interesting pictures and bric-a-brac, country furniture, two coal fires, no smoking dining annexe, Timothy Taylors Landlord, Theakstons Best and a guest beer, several country wines, quite a choice of food; piped music, machines; children in eating areas, tables in pretty garden, bedrooms, open all day *(Angus Lyon, LYM, Dave Braisted, Brian and Anita Randall, Maggie and Tony Harwood, Simon Calvert)*

☆ *Sun* [Market St (B6254)]: Low-beamed and partly stripped-stone bar, cosy pews, two good log fires, well kept ales such as Black Sheep, Pendle Pride and Timothy Taylors Landlord, lots of malt whiskies, good value generous food, cheerful staff, attractive no smoking back dining room; quiet piped music; bedrooms *(LYM, Roger Thornington)*

KIRKBY STEPHEN NY7707

☆ *Croglin Castle* [South Rd]: Stone-built local with basic décor in large comfortable bar, remarkably good interesting food in pleasant dining room, friendly staff, good wines, Thwaites and a guest beer *(R Wilkinson)*

KIRKOSWALD NY5541

☆ *Crown* Friendly attractively renovated 16th-c coaching inn, clean and tidy, beams covered with plates, brasses around fireplace, teapots over bar, good generous reasonably priced food from big sandwiches to innovative dishes using local produce and fish (same menu in bar and small no smoking restaurant), pleasant service, well kept Jennings ales, proper coffees *(Kevin Tea, Roy Morrison, C J Sewell, Mr and Mrs P Preston, JWAC)*

LAMPLUGH NY0720

Lamplugh Tip [A5086 Cockermouth—Cleator Moor]: Well kept Jennings pub, big helpings of well priced enjoyable food, friendly staff *(Jean and Douglas Troup)*

LANGDALE NY2906

Stickle Barn [by car park for Stickle Ghyll]: Lovely views from roomy and busy café-style walkers' and climbers' bar (boots welcome), generous good value food inc packed lunches, well kept Scottish Courage beers, quick friendly service, small no smoking area, mountaineering photographs; fruit machines, TV, piped music; big pleasant terrace with inner verandah, open all day; bunkhouse accommodation, live music in loft *(Paul and Jane Walker)*

LOWICK GREEN SD3084

☆ *Farmers Arms* [just off A5092 SE of village]: Cosy public bar with heavy beams, huge slate flagstones, big open fire, cosy corners and pub games (also piped music, TV; this part may be cl winter), some interesting furniture and pictures in plusher hotel lounge bar across yard, tasty reasonably priced food in bar and restaurant inc daily roast, and good home-made puddings, well kept ales such as Theakstons and Charles Wells Bombardier; unobtrusive piped music; children welcome, open all day, comfortable bedrooms *(LYM, Margaret and Roy Randle, D and M Senior)*

MELMERBY NY6237

Shepherds [A686 Penrith—Alston]: Heavy-beamed comfortable no smoking room off flagstoned bar, spacious end room with woodburner, straightforward bar food, well kept Badger IPA, Black Sheep Riggwelter, Hesket Newmarket Blencathra and Jennings, quite a few malt whiskies, games area with pool and juke box; children welcome, open all day *(Mr and Mrs Maurice Thompson, Mike and Wendy Proctor, A and B D Craig, Alan and Paula McCully, LYM, JWAC)*

METAL BRIDGE NY3564

Metal Bridge Hotel [off A74 Carlisle—Gretna, nr Rockcliffe]: Cheerful and neatly kept, with friendly staff, enjoyable bar food, good value wines by the glass, nice river view from sun lounge *(Richard J Holloway)*

NATEBY NY7807

Black Bull [B6259 Kirkby Stephen—Wensleydale]: Peaceful and friendly old moors-edge inn, recently renovated, with roaring log fire, enjoyable bar lunches, well kept real ales, civilised landlord, pleasant layout, nice decorations and beams; five bedrooms, lovely setting *(M and GR, R Halsey)*

NENTHEAD NY7843

Miners Arms Stripped stone lounge with leather sofas among other seating, well kept changing ales such as Black Sheep, Boddingtons, Newmarket Helvellyn Gold and Tetleys, good range of coffees, good genuine home cooking, reasonable prices, friendly helpful staff, no piped music, bar billiards in partly panelled flagstoned public bar, view from big conservatory; dogs welcome, picnic-sets out in front, homely family bedrooms, filling breakfast, also bunkhouse, open all day in summer, handy for Pennine Way and cycle path *(Maggie and Tony Harwood)*

NETHER WASDALE NY1204

Screes Interesting public bar and steps up to long plush lounge, stunning views of mountains and along Wasdale, particularly well kept ales such as Black Sheep, Yates Best and Derwent Springtime, quick friendly service, good value home-made food inc lunchtime sandwiches and enjoyable vegetarian dishes, decent piped music; picnic-sets out on large front green, five bedrooms *(John Foord, Tony Hughes, Maggie and Tony Harwood)*

NEWBY BRIDGE SD3686

☆ *Swan* [just off A590]: Substantial hotel in fine setting below fells next to river with waterside picnic-sets under cocktail parasols by old stone bridge, extensive neatly kept rambling bar with all sorts of comfortable nooks and crannies inc no smoking areas, decent all-day bar snacks from sandwiches and ciabattas up, brasserie meals (all day wknds), Bass and Boddingtons, good coffee, obliging uniformed staff; piped music; children in eating areas, open all day, comfortable bedrooms with own bathrooms *(Roger Thornington, LYM)*

NEWTON SD2372

Farmers [Newton Cross Rd]: Well kept real ale, good atmosphere, food inc very popular Sun lunch *(Ron Gentry)*

OUTGATE SD3599

☆ *Outgate Inn* [B5286 Hawkshead—Ambleside]: Attractively placed, neatly kept and very hospitable country pub with three pleasantly modernised rooms, well kept Robinsons Best, Frederics and Hartleys XB, friendly licensees, popular food inc sandwiches; trad jazz Fri, open all day wknds, comfortable bedrooms, good breakfast, nice walks *(BB, Angus Lyon)*

OXENHOLME SD5390

☆ *Station Inn* [½ mile up hill, B6254 towards Old Hutton]: Spruce and roomy dining pub with good generous home-made food from hearty sandwiches and standard bar meals to interesting specials, well kept Black Sheep, Flowers and Timothy Taylors Landlord with an interesting guest beer, nice wine list, good friendly service, log fire; large garden with extensive play area, bedrooms, good walks *(Michael Doswell, John and Gillian Scarisbrick)*

PENRITH NY5130

Agricultural [A592 in from M6 junction 40]: Bustling down-to-earth Victorian pub with many original features, comfortable L-shaped beamed lounge with partly glazed panelling, plenty of seating, log fire, curved sash windows over the bar, and a thorough mix of customers; full Jennings ale range, over 30 malt whiskies, decent bar food, no smoking restaurant (children allowed), darts and dominoes; piped music; good views from side picnic-sets, bedrooms, open all day *(MLR, LYM, Michael Jones, Christopher Turner)*

POOLEY BRIDGE NY4724

Sun Down-to-earth panelled village pub with good value generous food from sandwiches and baked potatoes to nicely cooked main dishes, cheery young landlord, full Jennings range kept well, good wine choice, small no smoking lounge bar, steps past servery to bigger bar with games, TV and piped music, no smoking restaurant; bedrooms, plenty of garden tables, great views *(Hugh Roberts, David Edwards, Michael Dandy)*

RAVENGLASS SD0894

☆ *Ratty Arms* Extended former waiting room a 200-metre walk over the footbridge from the Ravenglass & Eskdale terminus and rail museum, well kept Jennings ales, interesting food, good value restaurant, service friendly and efficient even when busy; pool table in busy public bar; children very welcome, open all day wknds and summer, big courtyard *(LYM, M and GR)*

RAVENSTONEDALE SD7401

Fat Lamb [Crossbank; A683 Sedbergh—Kirkby Stephen]: Remote inn with pews in cheery bar, log fire in traditional black kitchen range, good local photographs and bird plates, friendly helpful staff, above-average hearty bar food from filled baguettes up, enjoyable restaurant meals, perhaps well kept Tetleys; facilities for disabled, children welcome; reasonably priced bedrooms with own bathrooms, tables out by sheep pastures, good walks – they have their own nature reserve *(M and GR, T Pascall, BB, M S Catling)*

SANDSIDE SD4781

☆ *Ship* [B5282]: Roomy modernised beamed pub with relaxed atmosphere, good value generous standard food from baguettes up, well kept Marstons Pedigree and Theakstons, decent reasonably priced wines, glorious view over estuary to mountains beyond; subdued piped music; children allowed, high chairs, summer barbecues, picnic-sets out on grass by good play area *(LYM, Michael Doswell)*

SCALES NY3426

☆ *White Horse* [A66 W of Penrith]: Light and airy beamed pub-restaurant now all no smoking, cosy corners, interesting farmhouse-kitchen memorabilia and good open fires, well kept Jennings ales, fairly priced wines, wide choice of good food inc some local specialities and good wknd fish, welcoming landlord; well behaved children welcome (over 5 evening), lovely setting below Blencathra *(David Cooke, Mike and Penny Sutton, LYM, Angus Lyon)*

SEDBERGH SD6592

☆ *Red Lion* [Finkle St (A683)]: Cheerful beamed Jennings local, down to earth and comfortable, with their full beer range kept well, good value generous home-made food from baguettes to bargain Sun lunch, helpful attentive staff, friendly regulars, splendid coal fire, sports TV *(BB, Malcolm Taylor, Dr D J and Mrs S C Walker, Colin McKerrow, Derek Stafford)*

SHAP NY5615

☆ *Greyhound* [A6, S end]: Bustling and unpretentious former coaching inn, good local food esp slow-cooked meats and memorable puddings in open-plan bar or restaurant (chef happy to share his recipes), hearty helpings, half a dozen well kept ales such as Greene King, Jennings, Tirril, Wadworths 6X and Youngs, good reasonably priced house wines, quick service by happy helpful staff; unobtrusive piped classical music, resident collie, dogs welcome; comfortable bedrooms, popular with coast-to-coast walkers *(Michael Doswell, David Edwards, Paul and Anita Holmes, James Snowden, Catherine and Rob Dunster, J S Burn, John and Wendy Allin)*

STAINTON NY4828

Kings Arms [village signed off A66, handy for M6 junction 40]: The long-serving licensees who made this unassuming open-plan pub such a popular stop (and a main entry) for reasonably priced traditional food and well kept ales such as Greene King, Tetleys and Charles Wells Bombardier will have retired by the time this edition is published – reports on their successors, please; tables on side terrace and small lawn *(LYM)*

TEBAY NY6104

Cross Keys [very handy for M6 junction 38]: Comfortable roadside pub with plentiful good value homely food from baguettes and baked potatoes up in separate eating area, prompt friendly service, well kept Black Sheep, decent wine, coal fire, darts, pool, cribbage; good value bedrooms *(John Leslie)*

THRELKELD NY3225

☆ *Horse & Farrier* Comfortably enlarged and refurbished 17th-c dining pub with enjoyable food from enterprising lunchtime sandwiches, light dishes and walkers' bar meals to venison, duck and steaks, three well kept Jennings ales, good house wines, good welcoming service, cosy snug, fairly close-set tables in eating area; open all day, dogs allowed when restaurant is closed, good bedrooms *(Angus Lyon, Michael Doswell)*

Salutation [old main rd, bypassed by A66 W of Penrith]: Low-beamed pub below Blencathra, padded wall seats in three areas divided by standing timbers, good coal or log fire, well kept Jennings Cumberland and Theakstons, quite a few malt whiskies, substantial food from sandwiches and baguettes up; can be smoky, darts, piped music or juke box and TV; dogs welcome, spacious upper children's room, some tables outside *(Neil and Jean Spink, LYM, Tina and David Woods-Taylor, Kevin Thorpe)*

TROUTBECK NY4103

☆ *Mortal Man* [A592 N of Windermere; Upper Rd]: Neatly kept partly panelled beamed hotel bar with big log fire, comfortable mix of seats inc a cushioned settle, copper-topped tables, well kept ales such as Jennings, John Smiths and Theakstons Best, friendly young staff, darts, dominoes, cosy eating room, no smoking picture-window restaurant; piped music,TV room, Sun folk/blues night; great views from gloriously sited tables in sunny garden, children welcome, open all day, comfortable bedrooms – lovely village *(Brian and Janet Ainscough, LYM, D W Stokes, Don and Shirley Parrish, Guy Consterdine, Ewan and Moira McCall)*

WASDALE HEAD NY1807

Wasdale Head Inn [NE of Wast Water]: Mountain hotel in marvellous fellside setting, roomy walker's bar with side hot food counter (all day in summer, may be restricted winter), well kept ales including their own Great Gable brews, decent choice of wines and malt whiskies, interesting mountain photographs, traditional games, comfortably old-fashioned residents' bar, lounge and restaurant; children welcome, dogs allowed in bar, open all day, bedrooms *(John Foord, Mike Pugh, LYM, Jason Caulkin, Thomas Day, Peter F Marshall, Alison Hayes, Pete Hanlon, Tim Maddison)*

WATERMILLOCK NY4523

Brackenrigg [A592, Ullswater]: Opened-up rustic 19th-c inn in lovely spot overlooking Ullswater, good imaginative food, friendly helpful staff, particularly well kept Black Sheep Special, Theakstons and Jennings Cumberland, friendly mix of holiday-makers and locals; comfortable bedrooms, self-catering *(Geoff and Angela Jaques, Malcolm and Jane MacDonald)*

WELTON NY3544

Royal Oak [B5299 S of Dalston]: Recently carefully extended under new owners to include appealing and comfortable dining area, village bar with real ales, friendly family service; picnic-sets outside, four comfortable bedrooms, attractive village surroundings *(anon)*

WESTNEWTON NY1344

Swan [B5301 N of Aspatria]: Attractive 18th-c inn in small village, wide range of meals and snacks and of local beers inc Jennings and Yates *(Richard Greenwood)*

WINSTER SD4193

☆ *Brown Horse* [A5074 S of Windermere]: Open-plan dining pub doing well under new management, attractive layout with roomy no smoking dining area not too cut off from bar, good generous attractively priced food inc interesting dishes and good Sun lunch, log fire, friendly helpful service, well kept Black Sheep and Jennings Bitter and Cumberland, decent wines; children and walkers welcome, handy for Blackwell Arts & Crafts House *(Michael Doswell, Malcolm Taylor, LYM, A C English, Jonathan Shephard, M and GR, Clive and Fran Dutson, Dr and Mrs R G J Telfer)*

WINTON NY7810

☆ *Bay Horse* [off A685 N of Kirkby Stephen]: Two homely low-ceilinged rooms with Pennine photographs and local fly-tying, very good generous home-cooked food inc local meat and fresh veg, well kept beers such as Black Sheep, Daleside and Rudgate, low prices, games room, children welcome; cl winter afternoons, open from 1.30 (noon wknds) summer but not till 7 Tues; comfortable modestly priced bedrooms, good breakfast, tiny peaceful moorland hamlet *(Peter Abbott, LYM, John Close, D J M Lowe)*

YANWATH NY5128

Gate Inn [off B5320, handy for M6 junction 40]: Spruced up and more straightforwardly restauranty now than in its days as a main entry, with short upmarket menu and cheaper two-course lunches; has been cl Mon evening; more reports on current regime please *(D and B M Clark, LYM, Christine and Neil Townend, Mrs B M Hill)*

If we know a pub has a no smoking area, we say so.

Derbyshire

Three newcomers to this chapter are the friendly and well located Scotsmans Pack just outside Hathersage, the bustling Royal in Hayfield (a good pubby feel and excellent beers) and the Cock & Pullet at Sheldon (its charmingly unspoilt atmosphere and all-round quality seems set to make it quite a favourite). Other pubs on top form here these days are the intriguing old Bear at Alderwasley (good imaginative food, and it gains a Place to Stay Award this year), the rather sophisticated Waltzing Weasel at Birch Vale (good food with Italian leanings), the lovely and ancient Olde Gate at Brassington (its food is enjoyed, too), the Brunswick in Derby (outstanding for the lover of good beers in a buoyant atmosphere), the friendly Miners Arms at Eyam (a fine all-rounder), the cosy and friendly Barrel up on its ridge near Foolow (interesting beers), the Plough prettily placed just outside Hathersage (a fine dining pub with good bedrooms), the charmingly unspoilt and old-fashioned Barley Mow at Kirk Ireton, the happy good value Red Lion at Litton, the cheerful and neatly kept John Thompson by the Trent near Melbourne (bargain and drink), and the big busy Monsal Head Hotel with its stunning views (a particular favourite). As we have shown, many of these top pubs have good food; prime among them is the Plough at Hathersage, which takes the title of Derbyshire Dining Pub of the Year. In the Lucky Dip section at the end of the chapter, pubs coming in for warm praise recently are the Wheel in Holbrook, Holly Bush at Makeney and Royal Oak at Ockbrook. Quite a few pubs in this section, like several of the main entries, score for bargain food pricing. Drinks prices in the area, too, are rather lower than the national average, with the Brunswick in Derby offering the cheapest beer we found – it brews its own. Other own-brew pubs are the John Thompson near Melbourne and the Bentley Brook at Fenny Bentley (its Leatherbritches beers can also be found elsewhere), and other good locally brewed beers worth looking out for include Whim and Lloyds.

ALDERWASLEY SK3153 Map 7

Bear ★

Village signposted with Breanfield off B5035 E of Wirksworth at Malt Shovel; inn ½ mile SW of village, on Ambergate—Wirksworth high back road

The several small dark rooms at this enchantingly unspoilt village pub have low beams, bare boards and ochre walls, a great variety of old tables, and seats running from brocaded dining chairs and old country-kitchen chairs to high-backed settles and antique oak chairs carved with traditional Derbyshire motifs. One little room is filled right to its built-in wall seats by a single vast table. There are log fires in huge stone fireplaces, candles galore, antique paintings and engravings, plenty of staffordshire china ornaments and no fewer than three grandfather clocks. Despite the treasures, this is a proper easy-going country local, with dominoes players clattering about beside canaries trilling in a huge Edwardian-style white cage (elsewhere look out for the talkative cockatoos, an african grey parrot, and budgerigars). The sensibly imaginative food is popular so you may need to book. Made mostly with ingredients from local farms and growers, and listed on a daily changing blackboard, dishes might include home-made soup (£2.95), beer battered haggis balls in whisky sauce (£4.50), crab claws in shallots with parsley butter (£4.95), root vegetable stew with cheddar mash, lasagne, battered cod or ham, egg and chips (£7.95), tuna steak in creamy mushroom sauce (£9.95), venison steak in roast garlic jus or lamb shank in mint jus (£12.95) and puddings such as rhubarb crumble (£3.75). Service is friendly and helpful. They have a fine range of interesting wines, and three changing real ales such as Bass, Marstons Pedigree and Timothy Taylor Landlord on handpump. There are peaceful country views from well spaced picnic-sets out on the side grass, and it's popular with walkers. There's no obvious front door – you get in through the plain back entrance by the car park. *(Recommended by Richard Cole, Kevin Blake, Derek and Sylvia Stephenson, JP, PP, Andrew Pearson, Patrick Hancock, CMW, JJW, Pat and Roger Fereday, the Didler, Michael and Margaret Slater, Cathryn and Richard Hicks, Dave and Sue Mitchell)*

Free house ~ Licensee Nicky Fletcher-Musgrave ~ Real ale ~ Bar food (12-9.30) ~ Restaurant ~ (01629) 822585 ~ Children welcome away from bar ~ Dogs welcome ~ Open 12-11 ~ Bedrooms: £35S/£70S

BEELEY SK2667 Map 7

Devonshire Arms

B6012, off A6 Matlock—Bakewell

Big log fires cheerfully warm the cosy black-beamed rooms of this handsome old stone building, which was cleverly converted from three early 18th-c cottages, to become a prosperous coaching inn by the 19th c – when Dickens is said to have been a regular. Comfortably cushioned stone seats line some of the stripped walls, and antique settles and simpler wooden chairs stand on old flagstoned floors. There's a big emphasis on the tasty bar food, which is served all day, and could include soup (£3.15), generously filled baguettes (from £4.45), starters such as duck and fig terrine (£5.85), ploughman's (£6.75), haggis and neeps (£6.95), battered haddock (£7.10), steak and ale pie (£7.70), roasted vegetable lasagne (£7.65), salmon hollandaise (£8.75), braised knuckle of lamb in rosemary sauce (£9.75) and steak (from £12.50), with puddings (from £3.25). They have a Friday fish night, and on Sundays do a Victorian breakfast (£11.50); you'll need to book for both, and at weekends. Five handpumps serve well kept Bass, Black Sheep Best and Special, Marstons Pedigree and Theakstons Old Peculier. They've also decent good value house wine, and about three dozen malt whiskies. The restaurant and cocktail bar are no smoking; shove-ha'penny, cribbage and dominoes. Beeley is a very pretty Peak District estate village, and is only about a mile away from Chatsworth House, and the Duchess of Devonshire's excellent produce shop is to be found in nearby Pilsley. *(Recommended by M G Hart, Keith and Chris O'Neill, Anne and Steve Thompson, the Didler, Ann and Colin Hunt, JP, PP, Romayne and Donald Denham, Mrs P J Carroll, Steve Whalley, Susan and John Douglas)*

Free house ~ Licensee John A Grosvenor ~ Real ale ~ Bar food (12-9.30) ~ (01629) 733259 ~ Children welcome ~ Open 11-11; 12-10.30 Sun; closed 25 Dec

BIRCH VALE SK0286 Map 7

Waltzing Weasel

A6015 E of New Mills

Home cooking (even down to the shortbread biscuits served with coffee) and sourcing of good ingredients are key to the success of the beautifully presented food at this well run dining pub. Prices are a little high for the area, but most readers feel it's very fair value. The licensees are very keen on all things Italian, and the menu includes quite a few southern european dishes: soup (£4.25), pâté of the day (£4.95), grilled ciabatta or sardine tapenade (£5.75), pizzas (£5.75–£10.75), ploughmans (£8.75), tart provençale (£8.95), moroccan vegetable casserole (£9.75), seafood tart or casserole of the day (£10.95), italian platter (£11.95) and tasty puddings such as bread and butter pudding or brandy snap baskets with fruit and ice-cream (£4.85); Sunday roast (£10.95); they may do smaller helpings for children. As well as a good choice of decent wines and malt whiskies, they've very well kept Kelham Gold, Marstons Best and perhaps a guest such as Timothy Taylors on handpump. The bar has a comfortably worn-in pubby atmosphere, with a cosy fire, plenty of houseplants on corner tables, and daily papers on sticks. The licensees' interest in antiques (they're former dealers) is reflected in some of the furnishings, with handsome oak settles and tables (and some more usual furniture), lots of nicely framed mainly sporting Victorian prints, and a good longcase clock. The bedrooms are spacious, and comfortably furnished; good breakfasts. Bess, the friendly pub dog, likes meeting visitors. *(Recommended by Kevin Blake, Graham Holden, Julie Lee, Frank Gorman, Mike and Linda Hudson, Mr and Mrs C W Widdowson, Anne and Steve Thompson, JP, PP, Alison Hanratty, Patrick Hancock, Annette and John Derbyshire, Mrs P J Carroll, Brenda and Rob Fincham, Peter F Marshall, Brian and Anna Marsden)*

Free house ~ Licensee Michael Atkinson ~ Real ale ~ Bar food ~ Restaurant ~ (01663) 743402 ~ Children in eating area of bar, restaurant and family room ~ Dogs allowed in bar and bedrooms ~ Open 12-3, 5.30-11 ~ Bedrooms: £48S/£78B

BRASSINGTON SK2354 Map 7

Olde Gate ★

Village signposted off B5056 and B5035 NE of Ashbourne

The charming interior of this lovely old ivy clad inn is an absolute treat. The timelessly relaxing public bar is traditionally furnished, with a fine ancient wall clock, rush-seated old chairs, antique settles, including one ancient black solid oak one, and roaring log fires. Gleaming copper pots sit on a 17th-c kitchen range, pewter mugs hang from a beam, and a side shelf boasts a collection of embossed Doulton stoneware flagons. To the left of a small hatch-served lobby, another cosy beamed room has stripped panelled settles, scrubbed-top tables, and a blazing fire under a huge mantelbeam. Stone-mullioned windows look out across lots of tables in the pleasant garden (boules in summer) to small silvery-walled pastures, and in fine weather, the small front yard with a few benches is a nice place to sit (listen out for the village bell-ringers practising on Friday evenings). Although the date etched on the building reads 1874, it was originally built in 1616, from magnesian limestone and timbers salvaged from Armada wrecks, bought in exchange for locally mined lead. Bar food, from a regularly changing menu, is mostly home-made and could include well presented open sandwiches and baguettes (£4.95–£6.95), ploughman's (£6.75), home-made pies such as ham, leek and stilton or salmon and asparagus (from £7.50), cheese and leek bake with mushrooms (£8.95), home-made curries (£10.50) and seafood lasagne (£11.50), with puddings such as chocolate fudge cake or (highly recommended by readers) lemon pie (£3.75). The dining room is no smoking; the back bar is prettily candlelit at night. Well kept Marstons Pedigree and a guest such as Adnams Broadside on handpump, and a good selection of malt whiskies; cribbage and dominoes. Carsington reservoir is only a five-minute drive away. *(Recommended by RWC, Phil and Heidi Cook, JP, PP, the Didler, Kevin Blake, John Saul, Anne and Steve Thompson, Patrick Hancock, Jim Abbott, Peter F Marshall, B Forster, Pat and Roger Fereday, Derek and Heather Manning)*

Marstons (W & D) ~ Tenant Paul Burlinson ~ Real ale ~ Bar food (not Sun evening or Mon) ~ (01629) 540448 ~ Children over 10 ~ Dogs welcome ~ Open 12-2.30(possibly earlier if quiet; 3 Sat), 6-11; 12-3, 7-10.30 Sun; closed Mon except bank hols

BUXTON SK1266 Map 7

Bull i' th' Thorn

Ashbourne Road (A515) 6 miles S of Buxton, near Hurdlow

Themed food nights are a feature at this rather intriguing cross between a medieval hall and a straightforward roadside dining pub, with sizzle and griddle on Monday, seafood on Tuesday, steak on Wednesday, vegetarian on Thursday (when they add ten extra dishes to a bar menu that already lists about that number) and curries on Friday night. The usual menu includes soup (£2.25), filled baguettes (from £3.75), a range of salad platters (from £7.25), steak and kidney pie, vegetable wellington or mushroom and pepper stroganoff (£7.50), salmon (£8.25), and roast lamb shank with redcurrant and rosemary (£8.75), with puddings such as spotted dick (from £3.25). There's lots to look at inside, and among the lively old carvings that greet you on your way in is one of the eponymous bull caught in a thornbush (the pub's name comes from a hybrid of its 15th-c and 17th-c titles, the Bull and Hurdlow House of Hurdlow Thorn), and there are also images of an eagle with a freshly caught hare, and some spaniels chasing a rabbit. In the hall, which dates from 1471, a massive central beam runs parallel with a forest of smaller ones, there are panelled window seats in the embrasures of the thick stone walls, handsome panelling, and old flagstones stepping gently down to a big open fire. It's furnished with fine long settles, an ornately carved hunting chair, a longcase clock, a powder-horn, and armour that includes 17th-c german helmets, swords, and blunderbusses and so forth. Stuffed animals' heads line the corridor that leads to a candlelit hall, used for medieval themed evening banquets. An adjoining room has pool, and dominoes. A simple no smoking family room opens on to a terrace and big lawn, and there are more tables in a sheltered angle in front. They serve Robinsons Best on handpump. *(Recommended by the Didler, JP, PP, Paul and Margaret Baker, Ann and Colin Hunt, A Sadler, Mike and Wendy Proctor)*

Robinsons ~ Tenant Annette Maltby-Baker ~ Real ale ~ Bar food (9.30-9) ~ Restaurant ~ (01298) 83348 ~ Children in restaurant and family room ~ Dogs welcome ~ Open 9.30-11(10.30 Sun) ~ Bedrooms: /£60B

CASTLETON SK1583 Map 7

Castle Hotel

High Street at junction with Castle Street

Staff at this neatly kept spacious historic hotel cope well with its share of the large numbers of walkers and excursionists who visit this popular village. For entertainment value it's worth visiting on 29 May, when the colourful Garland Ceremony procession that commemorates the escape of Charles II takes place. The pub itself has plenty of history, and lots of spooky tales too, including one about the ghost of a bride who, instead of enjoying her planned wedding breakfast here, died broken-hearted when she was left at the altar. The inviting bar has stripped stone walls with built-in cabinets, lovely open fires, finely carved early 17th-c beams and, in one room, ancient flagstones. They have well kept Bass and Tetleys and a guest such as John Smiths on handpump, over a dozen wines by the glass and freshly squeezed fruit juice. A good part of the pub is no smoking; piped music. Good value bar food is served all day and includes sandwiches (lunchtime and afternoon only, from £4.25), crispy bacon and warm black pudding salad (£4.25), tiger prawns in creamy white wine topped with toasted cheddar (£4.95), gammon steak (£6.50), fish and chips or mediterranean vegetable lasagne (£6.75), beef, mushroom and ale pie (£7.95), sirloin steak (£9.95), with blackboard specials such as pork calvados or coriander crumbed hake fillet (£9.75); service is very pleasant and efficient. There are good views from the heated terrace. *(Recommended by Mark Percy, Lesley Mayoh, Paul Hopton, JP, PP, Chris Smith, Mike and Wendy Proctor, Duncan Cloud, Guy Vowles)*

Vintage Inns ~ Manager Glen Mills ~ Real ale ~ Bar food (12-10(9.30 Sun)) ~ (01433) 620578 ~ Children welcome ~ Open 11-11; 12-10.30 Sun ~ Bedrooms: /£69.95B

DERBY SK3435 Map 7

Alexandra

Siddals Road, just up from station

Like the other establishments in this successful little chain, this classic Victorian town pub offers a very good range of well kept real ale. Besides Bass, Castle Rock Nottingham Gold and York Yorkshire Terrier, they have up to nine frequently changing guest beers from all sorts of small countrywide breweries such as Belvoir, Buffys, Jennings, Rebellion and Robinsons. They also have up to five continental beers on tap, country wines, cider tapped from the cask and around two dozen malt whiskies; their soft drinks are very good value too. Two simple rooms have a buoyantly chatty atmosphere, good heavy traditional furnishings on dark-stained floorboards, shelves of bottles, breweriana, and lots of railway prints and memorabilia. The lounge is no smoking; darts, dominoes and piped music. At lunchtime they serve good value rolls (from £2), and on Sundays they may do a bargain roast (£3.75, two for £7). Handily, it's just a few minutes from Derby Station. *(Recommended by David Carr, Richard Lewis, JP, PP, Paul and Ann Meyer, Paul Hopton, the Didler, C J Fletcher, Patrick Hancock)*

Tynemill ~ Manager Mark Robins ~ Real ale ~ Bar food (lunchtimes only) ~ No credit cards ~ (01332) 293993 ~ Children in eating area of bar ~ Dogs allowed in bar ~ Open 11-11; 12-3, 7-10.30 Sun; closed 25 Dec ~ Bedrooms: £25S/£35S

Brunswick £

Railway Terrace; close to Derby Midland railway station

The plain brick exterior of this railwaymen's hostelry, at the apex of a row of preserved railway cottages, gives no clue to the treasure trove of beers inside. Up to 17 real ales, on handpump or tapped from the cask, include seven which are produced in the purpose-built brewery tower which is tucked away behind the pub (Father Mikes Dark Rich Ruby, Old Accidental, Second Brew Usual, Railway Porter, Triple Hop and Triple Gold) as well as around 10 regularly changing widely sourced guests such as Batemans, Everards Tiger, Holdens Golden Glow, Marstons Pedigree, and Timothy Taylors Landlord; farm cider is tapped from the cask. You can tour the brewery (£7.50 including a meal and a pint). The welcoming high-ceilinged bar has heavy well padded leather seats, whisky-water jugs above the dado, and a dark blue ceiling and upper wall, with squared dark panelling below. The no smoking room is decorated with little old-fashioned prints and swan's neck lamps, and has a high-backed wall settle and a coal fire; behind a curved glazed partition wall is a chatty family parlour narrowing to the apex of the triangular building. Interesting wall displays tell you about the history and restoration of the building, and there are interesting old train photographs; darts, dominoes, cribbage, fruit machine and TV. Tasty good value lunchtime bar food is limited to filled rolls (from £1.75), soup (£1.95), hot beef, cheese and bacon or sausage cobs (from £2.10), and a couple of dishes such as quiche, ploughman's, chilli and a vegetarian dish (£3.75) and lasagne (£4.10); on Sunday they do rolls only. There are two outdoor seating areas, including a terrace behind. They'll gladly give dogs a bowl of water. *(Recommended by Paul Hopton, Martin Grosberg, Kevin Blake, Keith and Chris O'Neill, Paul and Ann Meyer, JP, PP, David Carr, Kevin Thorpe, the Didler, Richard Lewis, R T and J C Moggridge, Brian and Rosalie Laverick, Patrick Hancock, C J Fletcher)*

Everards ~ Licensee Graham Yates ~ Real ale ~ Bar food (12-5 Mon-Sat) ~ No credit cards ~ (01332) 290677 ~ Children in family room ~ Dogs welcome ~ Jazz Thurs evenings ~ Open 11-11; 12-10.30 Sun

Olde Dolphin £

Queen Street; nearest car park King St/St Michaels Lane

Much restored but still showing its age, this quaint old timber frame place is Derby's oldest surviving pub. The four snug old-fashioned rooms (two with their own separate street doors) have big bowed black beams, shiny panelling, cast-iron-framed tables, opaque leaded windows, lantern lights, and coal fires; there are varnished wall benches in the tiled-floor public bar, and a brocaded seat in the little carpeted snug. There's no piped music or noisy fruit machines to spoil the pleasant chatty atmosphere, and the lounge bar and restaurant are no smoking. One or two readers have felt there could be a little more attention to detail and neatness. Up to ten real ales on handpump including Adnams, Bass, Black Sheep, Caledonian Deuchars IPA, Greene King Abbot and Marstons Pedigree, along with guests from breweries such as Coach House and Lees, and there's a beer festival in the last week of July. Good value tasty bar food includes soup (£1.95), filled rolls (from £2.60), all day breakfast (£3.70), sausage and mash or tortilla wraps (£3.75), home-made pie of the day (£4), battered cod (£4.70), leek and mushroom crumble or 8oz rump

(£4.95) and puddings such as apple and blackberry crumble (£2.25). A no smoking upstairs restaurant serves reasonably priced steaks. The pub is just a stroll from the cathedral, and the terrace is a nice spot to escape the bustle of the city centre. *(Recommended by the Didler, JP, PP, Kevin Blake, Paul Hopton, Paul and Ann Meyer, David Carr, Patrick Hancock, C J Fletcher, Peter F Marshall)*

Mitchells & Butlers ~ Lease James and Josephine Harris ~ Real ale ~ Bar food (11-11; 12-6 Sun) ~ Restaurant ~ (01332) 267711 ~ Open 10.30-11; 12-10.30 Sun

EARL STERNDALE SK0967 Map 7

Quiet Woman

Village signposted off B5053 S of Buxton

Very much a countryside inn, this old-fashioned and without frills stone-built cottage is for those who enjoy a good friendly down-to-earth pub – but not if you're particularly fussy about the housekeeping. A fun time to visit is during their Sunday lunchtime folk session. It's very simple inside, with hard seats, plain tables (including a sunken one for dominoes or cards), low beams, quarry tiles, lots of china ornaments and a coal fire. There's a pool table in the family room (where you may be joined by two friendly jack russells eager for a place by the fire), cribbage, dominoes and darts. Mansfield Dark Mild and Marstons Best and Pedigree are well kept on handpump along with a couple of guests such as Archers and Tetleys. Bar food is limited to locally made pork pies. There are picnic-sets out in front, and the budgies, hens, turkeys, ducks and donkeys help keep children entertained. You can buy free-range eggs, local poetry books and even silage here; they have a caravan for hire in the garden, and you can also arrange to stay at the small campsite next door. Needless to say, it's a popular place with walkers. *(Recommended by the Didler, Barry Collett, R M Corlett, JP, PP, Ann and Colin Hunt, Rona Murdoch, Patrick Hancock, Reg Fowle, Helen Rickwood)*

Free house ~ Licensee Kenneth Mellor ~ Real ale ~ No credit cards ~ (01298) 83211 ~ Children in family room ~ Jamming sessions most Sun lunchtimes ~ Open 12-3, 7-11; 12-5, 7-10.30 Sun

EYAM SK2276 Map 7

Miners Arms

Signposted off A632 Chesterfield—Chapel-en-le-Frith

In the couple of years that the cheery licensees have been at this welcoming pub they've really brought it up to scratch. It's very well run, and the friendly owners and helpful chatty staff contribute strongly to the pleasantly relaxed and civilised atmosphere. Very cosy in winter, each of the three little neatly kept plush beamed rooms has its own stone fireplace. It gets nicely lively in the evening, when locals drop in for a well kept pint. Good home-made bar food includes soup (£3.95), sandwiches (from £3.50), ploughman's (£6.95), sausage of the day and mash or roast of the day (£7.95), pie of the day (£8.95), changing dishes such as moroccan stuffed aubergine (£7.95), fried red snapper with tapenade dressing or chicken breast marinated in lemon grass and chilli (£8.95) and puddings such as delicious trifle and bread and butter pudding (from £3.95). They have Bass, Stones and a guest such as Greene King Old Speckled Hen on handpump; cribbage, dominoes and piped music. Bedrooms are nicely decorated, and breakfasts are good. This is an excellent base for exploring the Peak District, and there are decent walks nearby, especially below Froggatt Edge. Eyam is famous for the altruism of its villagers, who isolated themselves during the plague to save the lives of others in the area. *(Recommended by the Didler, JES, R T and J C Moggridge, Ann and Colin Hunt, JP, PP, B and M Kendall, Mr and Mrs Gregg Byers, Revd John E Cooper, Betty and Cyril Higgs, Catherine and Rob Dunster)*

New Century Inns ~ Tenants John and Michele Hunt ~ Real ale ~ Bar food (12-2(3 Sat, Sun), 6-9; not Sun evening) ~ Restaurant ~ (01433) 630853 ~ Children in eating area of bar and restaurant ~ Dogs allowed in bar and bedrooms ~ Monthly jazz suppers ~ Open 12-11(10.30 Sun); closed 25 December ~ Bedrooms: /£60B

FENNY BENTLEY SK1750 Map 7

Bentley Brook

A515 N of Ashbourne

Very much a family run operation, this substantial timbered inn has been in the same capably friendly hands for just under thirty years and has a range of attractions on offer. The main bar area is traditional but with quite an airy feel, thanks to big windows, fairly high ceilings and quite a few mirrors, with well lit pictures, some brassware and decorative plates on the neat white walls, wheelback and other chairs around plenty of dark polished tables on the bare boards, and a log fire in the stone fireplace between the two linked areas. Food here is good. They use herbs, fruit and some vegetables from their own garden, and you can buy their own preserves, sausages and so forth from their little kitchen shop. A separate smarter no smoking restaurant has its own menu, while in the bar you can have quickly served sandwiches and baguettes from a blackboard, or from the menu, generous helpings of soup (£3.55), home-made black pudding (£3.95), fisherman's pie or derbyshire hotpot (£6.75), chicken breast with white wine and cream sauce (£7.75), mushroom stroganoff (£7.95), steak and ale pie (£8.50). Well worth trying are the attractively priced Leatherbritches ales they brew here, and which are increasingly available in other pubs we list. The range includes Goldings, Ashbourne, Belter, Hairy Helmet and Bespoke, and at their May bank holiday beer festival you get a chance to taste the full range (and dozens of other beers), but usually they have just a selection on handpump, alongside a guest such as Marstons Pedigree, and local Saxon farm cider; well reproduced piped music, dominoes, chess, cards, Jenga and board games. Picnic-sets under cocktail parasols on a broad flower festooned terrace look down over a pleasant lawn and proper barbecue area, and they have summer barbecues, boules, croquet, skittles and a good play area. The streamside grounds include a wildflower meadow, and room for campers, and the location is handy for Dovedale. *(Recommended by Dr R C C Ward, JP, PP, Andy and Ali, Derek and Sylvia Stephenson, Peter Meister, Michael Butler, Guy Vowles, Mr and Mrs A Campbell, the Didler, John and Wendy Allin, Cathryn and Richard Hicks, Patrick Hancock)*

Own brew ~ Licensees David and Jeanne Allingham ~ Real ale ~ Bar food (12-9) ~ Restaurant ~ (01335) 350278 ~ Dogs allowed in bar and bedrooms ~ Open 11-11; 12-10.30 Sun ~ Bedrooms: £50B/£72.50B

Coach & Horses

A515 N of Ashbourne

Woodburners at either end of the comfy flagstoned front bar make this 17th-c rendered stone house a very cosy place to relax on a chilly winter's day. Library chairs are arranged around dark tables, and there are hand-made flowery-cushioned wall settles, wagon wheels hanging from the black beams, horsebrasses, pewter mugs and prints. There are prints on the stained pine panelling in the little back room, with country cottage furnishings, and a lovely old fireplace; cribbage, dominoes and quiet piped music. Marstons Pedigree and a couple of guests such as Orkney Red MacGregor and Springhead Olivers Army are well kept on handpump alongside over 20 whiskies. From a changing menu and served by efficient uniformed staff, tasty bar food might include home-made soup (£2.95), warmed goats cheese with spicy fruit chutney (£3.50), vegetable provençale (£6.50), sausage and mash or steak and stilton shortcrust pastry pie (£6.75), poached halibut with lime and chilli jam (£9.50) and rib-eye steak (£10). The dining room and back bar are no smoking. Outside, there are views across fields from picnic-sets in the side garden by an elder tree, and wooden tables and chairs under cocktail parasols on the front terrace. *(Recommended by Peter Meister, Kevin Thorpe, Sue Holland, Dave Webster, Anne and Steve Thompson, JP, PP, R T and J C Moggridge, the Didler, M G Hart, Richard and Karen Holt, Mr and Mrs John Taylor, Chris Smith, Cathryn and Richard Hicks, Peter F Marshall, Joan and Tony Walker, Dave Braisted)*

Free house ~ Licensees John and Matthew Dawson ~ Real ale ~ Bar food (12-9) ~ (01335) 350246 ~ Children in eating area of bar and restaurant ~ Open 11-11; 12-10.30 Sun; closed 25 Dec

FOOLOW SK2077 Map 7

Barrel ★

Bretton; signposted from Foolow, which itself is signposted from A623 just E of junction with B6465 to Bakewell; can also be reached from either the B6049 at Great Hucklow, or the B6001 via Abney, from Leadmill just S of Hathersage

The very cheery licensee generates a happy welcoming atmosphere at this magnificently set old stone turnpike inn. The pub is on the edge of an isolated ridge in excellent walking country and the view from here is unparalleled – when the weather is right you can see five counties (one of the recently renovated bedrooms shares this outlook). The peacefully cosy oak-beamed bar has an old-fashioned charm, with flagstones, studded doors in low doorways, lots of pictures, antiques, and a collection of bottles and gleaming copper. Stubs of massive knocked-through stone walls divide it into several areas: the cosiest is at the far end, with a log fire, a leather-cushioned settle, and a built-in corner wall-bench by an antique oak table. Hardys & Hansons Kimberley and the very strong 6% William Clark Strong Ale, Marstons Pedigree and a guest from the Hardys & Hansons range are very well kept; also more than 25 malts. Bar food includes sandwiches (from £3.20) and hot ciabatta rolls (£5.95), starters such as home-made soup (£2.65) and brie, spinach and walnut crêpe (£4.95), main courses such as roast of the day (£7.50), beer-battered cod or steak, kidney and Guinness pie (£8.25), and 10oz rump steak (from £12.45), and puddings (£3.95). Seats out on the front terrace and a courtyard garden give good shelter from the inevitable breeze at this height; we'd like to hear from readers who have stayed here. *(Recommended by Peter F Marshall, Keith and Chris O'Neill, JP, PP, the Didler, Nick and Meriel Cox, Derek and Sylvia Stephenson, A J Law, Alan Cole, Kirstie Bruce, Richard Waller, Pauline Smith, Betty and Cyril Higgs, B and M Kendall, Jim Abbott)*

Free house ~ Licensee Paul Rowlinson ~ Real ale ~ Bar food (12-2.30, 6.30-9.30(9 Sun)) ~ Restaurant ~ (01433) 630856 ~ Children in eating area of bar ~ Dogs allowed in bar ~ Ceilidh Weds evening ~ Open 11-3, 6-11; 11-11 Sat, Sun; closed 25 Dec ~ Bedrooms: £45B/£65B

Bulls Head

Village signposted off A623 Baslow—Tideswell

There's a buoyantly friendly atmosphere in the simply furnished flagstoned bar at this neatly kept welcoming pub, with a couple of quieter areas set out for a relaxing meal. A step or two takes you down into what may once have been a stables, with its high ceiling joists, some stripped stone, and a woodburning stove. On the other side, a smart no smoking dining room has more polished tables set in cosy stalls. Interesting photographs include a good collection of Edwardian naughties. The wide range of enjoyable food is popular, so you may need to book at the weekend: lunchtime snacks such as sandwiches (from £3), hot filled baps (£4.95), ploughman's (£5.50), as well as soup (£3.25), thai fishcakes with sweet chilli sauce (£4.25), battered cod, chicken with lemon cream sauce or minted lamb casserole (£6.95), rump steak (£10.75), and three succulent roasts on Sunday. Tetleys is well kept alongside three changing guests such as Adnams, Black Sheep and Shepherd Neame Spitfire; piped music and darts. You can buy basic provisions here (milk, eggs, bread, and so forth), which is handy, as there's no shop in this upland village. It's an appealing village, surrounded by rolling stone-walled pastures – good walks nearby mean it's popular with ramblers. Picnic-sets at the back have nice views, and the small pretty green has a medieval cross and a pond. *(Recommended by Jane Taylor, David Dutton, Susan and Tony Dyer, Derek and Sylvia Stephenson, Peter F Marshall, Patrick Hancock, John Wooll, B and M Kendall, Dick and Penny Vardy, Jim Abbott)*

Free house ~ Licensees William and Leslie Bond ~ Real ale ~ Bar food (12-2, 7-9(5-8 Sun)) ~ Restaurant ~ (01433) 630873 ~ Children in eating area of bar, restaurant and family room ~ Dogs allowed in bar ~ Live folk Fri evening ~ Open 12-3(2 Sat), 6.30-11; 12-2 5-8 Sun; closed Mon ~ Bedrooms: £40S/£65S

FROGGATT EDGE SK2477 Map 7

Chequers

A625 off A623 N of Bakewell; OS Sheet 119 map reference 247761

An ideal place to visit if you want to combine a very good meal with a walk, this old country inn with its peacefully rustic garden nestles on the edge of acres of wood, through which a path leads right up to Froggatt Edge. Inside, the bar is smartly countrified, with library chairs or small high-backed winged settles on well waxed boards, an attractive richly varnished beam-and-board ceiling, antique prints on white walls and some big dark stone blocks, and a big solid-fuel stove. One corner has a nicely carved oak cupboard. It's a good idea to book if you are going for the very well prepared attractively presented bar food (not cheap but most readers feel it's worth the prices), which includes huge tasty sandwiches (from £4.75), stilton, chorizo and black pudding salad (£7.95), sausage and mash, lamb casserole or wild mushroom and cherry tomato tart (£8.95), salmon and crab cakes (£9.95), 10oz sirloin (£11.95) and frequently changing daily specials such as pork fillet wrapped in basil and parma ham with apple jus (£14.95). About half of the eating area is no smoking. On handpump, they've well kept Greene King IPA and Abbot, and there's a good range of malt whiskies and a changing wine board; piped music. Service is friendly and efficient. *(Recommended by W K Wood, Maureen and Bill Sewell, DC, Jane Taylor, David Dutton, M G Hart, A J Law, Cathryn and Richard Hicks, Patrick Hancock, Mrs Brenda Calver, D J and P M Taylor, Richard Marjoram, Peter F Marshall, Mike and Linda Hudson)*

Pubmaster ~ Lease Jonathan and Joanne Tindall ~ Real ale ~ Bar food (12-2, 6-9.30; 12-9.30(9 Sun) Sat) ~ Restaurant ~ (01433) 630231 ~ Children welcome ~ Open 12-2, 6-10; 12-10 Sat, Sun; closed 25 Dec ~ Bedrooms: /£55B

HARDWICK HALL SK4663 Map 7

Hardwick Inn

2¾ miles from M1 junction 29: at roundabout A6175 towards Clay Cross; after ½ mile turn left signed Stainsby and Hardwick Hall (ignore any further sign for Hardwick Hall); at sign to Stainsby follow road to left; after 2½ miles turn left at staggered road junction

The elegant gold stone exterior of this 17th-c inn with its stone-mullioned latticed windows is a refreshing surprise just off the M1. It's particularly handy as they serve good value food all day, and the very pleasant back garden is a useful place for children to let off steam. With plenty more tables in front they are geared for the crowds (you do need to book at the weekend). The house was originally built as a lodge for the nearby Elizabethan Hall, and is owned by the National Trust. Of the cosy but fairly old-fashioned rooms, though one has an attractive 18th-c carved settle, the carpeted lounge is the most comfortable, with its upholstered wall settles, tub chairs and stools around varnished wooden tables. The carvery restaurant and one family room are no smoking. It does get very busy (especially on weekends) but service remains friendly and efficient, and the atmosphere is cheerfully bustling. An extensive range of very generously served dishes could include beef and Guinness pie (£6.75), grilled cod with stilton and mushroom sauce (£7.75), marinated lamb steak in rosemary and garlic (£7.95), crab salad (£8.25) and half lobster and prawn mornay (£10.50); readers enjoy the Sunday carvery (£13.20) and afternoon cream teas (£3.25). As well as more than 200 malt whiskies, they've well kept Greene King Old Speckled Hen and Ruddles County, Marstons Pedigree and Theakstons XB and Old Peculier on handpump; piped music. *(Recommended by Andy and Ali, Mrs Anthea Fricker, Susan and John Douglas, Keith and Chris O'Neill, Brian and Janet Ainscough, JES, June and Ken Brooks, Dave Braisted, the Didler, Peter F Marshall, Pat and Tony Martin, JP, PP, Darly Graton, Graeme Gulibert,*

Mrs G R Sharman, M Borthwick, Patrick Hancock, Adam and Joan Bunting, Dr and Mrs A K Clarke, Gerry and Rosemary Dobson, J Stickland)

Free house ~ Licensees Peter and Pauline Batty ~ Real ale ~ Bar food (11.30-9.30; 12-9 Sun) ~ Restaurant ~ (01246) 850245 ~ Open 11.30-11; 12-10.30 Sun

HASSOP SK2272 Map 7

Eyre Arms

B6001 N of Bakewell

The atmosphere at this lovely 17th-c stone-built inn is comfortably peaceful. The beamed dining bar which has a longcase clock, cushioned settles around the walls, comfortable plush chairs, and lots of brass and copper is dominated by the Eyre coat of arms which is painted above a stone fireplace (coal fire in winter). A smaller public bar has an unusual collection of teapots, dominoes and another fire; the eating areas are no smoking. Black Sheep Special, John Smiths and Marstons Pedigree are well kept on handpump; piped classical music, darts, cribbage and dominoes. Besides lunchtime sandwiches (from £3.75) and ploughman's (from £5.55), the menu includes soup (from £3.65), thai-style crab cakes with sweet pepper sauce (£3.55), breaded plaice (£7.25), steak and kidney pie (£7.95), bulgar wheat and walnut casserole (£8.25), chicken breast with smoked bacon and mushrooms topped with cheese (£8.40), and steak (from £9.45). They also do daily specials such as rabbit pie (£10.45), and service is obliging and friendly. There's a fountain in the small garden, which has tables looking out over beautiful Peak District countryside. Colourful hanging baskets brighten up the exterior stonework in summer, and in autumn, virginia creeper. There are good walks near here. *(Recommended by JP, PP, Ann and Colin Hunt, DC, the Didler, Trevor and Sylvia Millum, M G Hart, Derek and Sylvia Stephenson, Dick and Penny Vardy, Jim Abbott, Susan and John Douglas)*

Free house ~ Licensee Lynne Smith ~ Real ale ~ Bar food (12-2, 6.30-9) ~ Restaurant ~ (01629) 640390 ~ Children in eating area of bar ~ Open 11.30-3, 6.30-11(10.30 Sun)

HATHERSAGE SK2380 Map 7

Plough

Leadmill; B6001 (A625) towards Bakewell, OS Sheet 110 map reference 235805

Derbyshire Dining Pub of the Year

The emphasis at this former farmhouse is very firmly on the excellent choice of highly imaginative food. Unfortunately drinkers may have trouble finding a seat at busy times, and it is worth booking for Sunday lunch. The menu changes every three months but usually includes some pubby staples alongside more creative dishes: home-made soup (£3.50), gravadlax (£5.95), carpaccio of beef with truffle oil and shaved parmesan (£6.25), sausage and mash (£6.95), cod and chips (£8.45), steak and kidney pudding (£8.95), roast red pepper and mascarpone risotto (£9.95), fillet of red mullet with egg noodles in a pumpkin seed and lemon grass broth or moroccan spiced lamb chump with falafel and yoghurt and mint sauce (£14.95) and poached beef fillet with horseradish rösti, spinach and shallot jus or seared scallops with pea and mint risotto (£15.95). Everything is spotlessly kept, and the attractive bar, with dark wood tables and chairs on a turkey carpet, is on two levels, with a big log fire at one end and a woodburning stove at the other. The atmosphere is pleasantly relaxed, and the service friendly and efficient; piped music and no smoking restaurant. They serve around 18 good value wines by the glass, alongside Adnams, Batemans, Theakstons Bitter and Old Peculier, and a guest such as St Georges on hand or electric pump. The pub is beautifully placed by the River Derwent with picnic-sets in the pretty secluded garden going right down to the water. Readers really enjoy staying in the very comfortable rooms, and the breakfasts are excellent. *(Recommended by Lynne and Philip Naylor, DC, Keith and Chris O'Neill, Rod and Chris Pring, Tom and Ruth Rees, R N and M I Bailey, Barry and Anne, M Sharp, Elizabeth Crabtree, Dr L Kaufman, Nigel Epsley, Mrs Brenda Calver, Jeremy Hebblethwaite, D J and P M Taylor, Mrs P J Carroll, Michael Doswell, Revd D Glover, Adrian White)*

Free house ~ Licensee Bob Emery ~ Real ale ~ Bar food (11.30-2.30, 6.30-9.30; 11.30-9.30 Sat; 12-9 Sun) ~ Restaurant ~ (01433) 650319 ~ Children in eating area of bar, and restaurant until 7.30pm ~ Open 11-11; 12-10.30 Sun; closed 25 Dec, 26 Dec evening ~ Bedrooms: £49.50B/£79.50B

Scotsmans Pack

School Lane, off A625

Well placed for walkers and close to the church where Little John is said to be buried, this welcoming local is a comfortable place for a good, quietly civilised meal. There's been a pub on the spot for centuries, though the current building dates from around 1900. The most comfortable area is on the left as you enter, with a fireplace, and patterned wallpaper somewhat obscured by a splendid mass of brasses, stuffed animal heads and the like. Elsewhere there's plenty of dark panelling, lots of mugs and plates arranged around the bar, and a good few tables, many with reserved signs (it's worth booking ahead, particularly at weekends). The wide range of food might include a good choice of sandwiches, home-made pea and ham soup, a well regarded steak pie or several vegetarian dishes like cashew nut and pine kernel stir fry (£8.50), and peppered pork fillet with smoked stilton and leek sauce (£11.95). Burtonwood Bitter and Top Hat on handpump, along with a monthly changing guest like Wadworths 6X; service remains prompt and cheery even when busy. They have regular quiz and bingo nights. One area is no smoking. Outside is a small but very pleasant patio, next to a trout-filled stream. *(Recommended by Jane Taylor, David Dutton, David Carr, Peter F Marshall, Keith and Chris O'Neill, Paul A Moore)*

Free house ~ Licensee Nick Beagrie ~ Real ale ~ (01433) 650253 ~ Children welcome till 9 ~ Dogs welcome ~ Open 11-3, 5.30-11; 11-11 Sat; 12-10.30 Sun ~ Bedrooms: £32B/£61B

HAYFIELD SK0387 Map 7

Royal

Market Street, just off A624 Chapel-en-le-Frith—Buxton

A big bustling inn at the centre of this unspoilt village, the Royal impresses with its honest welcome and genuinely pubby feel – as well as its well sourced range of beers. You'll normally find anything between six and ten well kept real ales on at once; on our visit we found Frankton Bagby Dizzy Blonde, Hydes Bitter, Marstons Pedigree, Ossett Pale Gold, RCH Pitchfork, Tetleys and York Yorkshire Terrier. They usually have a civilised beer festival in early October. A former vicarage, the 18th-c building still has many of its original features, so there's lots of dark panelling in the separate-seeming areas around the central island bar counter, as well as several fireplaces, bookshelves, brasses and house plants, and newspapers to read. It can get busy, but with plenty of room easily absorbs the crowds. Good, tasty and sensibly priced bar food includes changing specials such as supreme of chicken on black pudding with asparagus and tarragon sauce (£8.75), monkfish and mussel broth with a hint of Pernod, garlic and herbs (£10.95), and turbot and haddock with a tuna and dill crust and cream sauce (£11.95). Service is prompt and friendly – walkers are made to feel particularly welcome. On fine days drinkers spill out on to the terrace in front, which has lots of picnic-sets. The River Sett runs alongside the car park. Bedrooms are comfortable, and it's a useful base for exploring the local scenery. *(Recommended by Brian and Anna Marsden)*

Free house ~ Licensee David Ash ~ Real ale ~ Bar food (12-2.30, 5.30-9.30) ~ (01663) 742721 ~ May be jazz Sun afternoon ~ Open 11-11; 12-10.30 Sun ~ Bedrooms: £45S/£60S

By law pubs must show a price list of their drinks. Let us know if you are inconvenienced by any breach of this law.

HOGNASTON SK2350 Map 7

Red Lion

Village signposted off B5035 Ashbourne—Wirksworth

The open-plan oak-beamed bar at this well run welcoming pub has a relaxing almost bistro feel. An attractive mix of old tables (candlelit at night) and old-fashioned settles and other seats is arranged on ancient flagstones. There are three open fires, and a growing collection of teddy bears among other bric-a-brac and copies of *Country Life*; the conservatory restaurant is no smoking. The generously served, nicely presented food here is popular, and from a frequently changing, fairly priced menu, dishes could include home-made soup (£3.95), black pudding fritters with tomato and apple relish (£4.95), mushroom stroganoff or roast beef, pork or lamb (from £8.95), lamb and apricot tagine or thai green chicken curry (£9.95), whole bass with prawns and Pernod and chive sauce (£12.95) and puddings such as sticky toffee pudding (£4). They've well kept Bass, Greene King Old Speckled Hen and Marstons Pedigree, and perhaps a guest such as Whim Hartington on handpump, and you can get country wines; piped music, dominoes and cribbage. It's in a lovely peaceful spot, handy for Carsington Reservoir and bedrooms are big and comfortable. *(Recommended by R T and J C Moggridge, Mike and Maggie Betton, Anne and Steve Thompson, JP, PP, Alan Bowker, Mrs P J Carroll, Ian and Jane Irving, Annette and John Derbyshire, Jim Abbott, Cathryn and Richard Hicks)*

Free house ~ Licensee Pip Price ~ Real ale ~ Bar food (12-2, 6.30-9; not Sun evening, not Mon) ~ Restaurant ~ (01335) 370396 ~ Children in restaurant ~ Dogs allowed in bar ~ Open 12-3, 6-11.30(7-10.30 Sun); closed Mon lunchtime ~ Bedrooms: £50S/£80S

HOLBROOK SK3644 Map 7

Dead Poets £

Village signposted off A6 S of Belper; Chapel Street

Tucked into a quiet street, this low white-painted pub continues to serve a great selection of eight real ales. Alongside well kept Everards Original, Greene King Abbot, Marstons Pedigree, Timothy Taylor Landlord and Burton Bridge Golden Delicious, a couple of guests could be from brewers such as Church End, Clarks or Holdens, on handpump or served by the jug from the cellar; also farm cider and several country wines. The regular beer festivals here are very popular. It's very dark inside, with low black beams in its ochre ceiling, stripped stone walls with some smoked plaster, and broad flagstones. Candles burn on scrubbed tables, there's a big log fire in the end stone fireplace, high-backed winged settles form snug cubicles along one wall, and there are pews and a variety of chairs in other intimate corners and hide-aways. The décor makes a few nods to the pub's present name (it used to be the Cross Keys), and adds some old prints of Derby. Alongside cobs (from £2, nothing else on Sundays), bar food is limited to a few good value hearty dishes such as home-made soup (£2) and chilli con carne, casserole or chicken jalfrezi (£4.25). There's a good atmosphere, and a nice mix of customers, male and female; well reproduced piped music. Behind is a sort of verandah room, with lanterns, fairy lights and a few plants, and more seats out in the yard, with outdoor heaters. *(Recommended by the Didler, JP, PP, Derek and Sylvia Stephenson, Bernie Adams, Alan Bowker, MLR)*

Everards ~ Licensee William Holmes ~ Real ale ~ Bar food (lunchtimes Mon-Sat) ~ No credit cards ~ (01332) 780301 ~ Children in family room ~ Dogs welcome ~ Poetry night first Tues in month ~ Open 12-3, 5-11; 12-11 Fri-Sat; 12-10.30 Sun

IDRIDGEHAY SK2848 Map 7

Black Swan

B5023 S of Wirksworth

Most of the open-plan space at this very restauranty French-run place is given over to eating, but there is still a little sitting area by the big bow window on the left, with a rack of daily papers and magazines, a few bar stools, wicker armchairs and padded seats, and snapshots of some very cheery customers. Bass, Marstons Pedigree and John Smiths are well kept on handpump, there's a pleasant unhurried atmosphere, and the staff are polite and efficient. There are well spaced tables with wicker chairs comfortably cushioned in a mix of colours, and a bright and airy simple décor – white ceiling, ragged yellow walls with a few pictures of french restaurants, wine bottles and local scenes. The bare floors make for cheerful acoustics (not too clattery); fairly quiet piped light jazz. Down steps is a similarly furnished no smoking area, given a slight conservatory feel by its high pitched roof light (with rattan blinds) and two narrow floor-to-ceiling windows at the far end, looking out over the neat and pleasant garden to rolling tree-sheltered pastures. Deliciously imaginative lunchtime bar food can be taken as two courses (£15.95) or three courses (£20.95) and might include starters such as parfait of fromage blanc with pickled wild mushrooms or terrine of ham hock and main courses such as seared red mullet with artichoke risotto and red wine jus or braised blade of beef with madeira jus. In the evening prices go up (two courses £19.95, three courses £24.95) and dishes might include warm confit of duck with chinese scented red onion salad and roast pork tenderloin with rosemary jus. *(Recommended by BOB)*

Free house ~ Licensee Aaron Neale ~ Real ale ~ Bar food (12-2, 7-9.30; 12-4 Sun) ~ Restaurant ~ (01773) 550249 ~ Children welcome ~ Open 11-3, 6-11; 12-6 Sun; closed Sun evening

KIRK IRETON SK2650 Map 7

Barley Mow

Village signed off B5023 S of Wirksworth

The landlady at this unspoilt rural gem recently celebrated her 70th birthday, so it's good to know that she's well looked after by her huge newfoundland, Hector. Other than that, little changes here from year to year – the dimly lit passageways and narrow stairwells of this tall gabled Jacobean brown sandstone inn have a timeless atmosphere, helped along by traditional furnishings and civilised old-fashioned service. It's a place to sit and chat, and though the only games you'll find here are dominoes and cards it still pulls in a good crowd of youngsters and local old folk at weekends, and walkers at other times. The small main bar has a relaxed pubby feel, with antique settles on the tiled floor or built into the panelling, a roaring coal fire, four slate-topped tables, and shuttered mullioned windows. Another room has built-in cushioned pews on oak parquet and a small woodburning stove, and a third room has more pews, a tiled floor, beams and joists, and big landscape prints. One room is no smoking. In casks behind a modest wooden counter are well kept (and reasonably priced) Archers, Hook Norton Best and Old Hooky, Whim Hartington and possibly a guest from another small brewery such as Cottage or Storm; farm ciders too. Lunchtime filled rolls (85p) are the only food; the good home-made interesting evening meals are reserved for residents staying in the comfortable rooms. There's a decent-sized garden, and a couple of benches out in front, and they've opened a post office in what used to be the pub stables. Handy for Carsington Water, the pretty hilltop village is in good walking country. *(Recommended by P and S Blacksell, JP, PP, the Didler, Kevin Thorpe, Pete Baker, Jim Abbott)*

Free house ~ Licensee Mary Short ~ Real ale ~ No credit cards ~ (01335) 370306 ~ Children in a side room lunchtime only ~ Dogs allowed in bedrooms ~ Open 12-2, 7-11(10.30 Sun); closed 25 Dec and 1 Jan ~ Bedrooms: £30S/£50B

LADYBOWER RESERVOIR SK1986 Map 7

Yorkshire Bridge

A6013 N of Bamford

This big roadside hotel is a very popular stop near the Ladybower, Derwent and Howden reservoirs (immortalised by the World War II Dambusters). Service is friendly and obliging, and there's a cheerful bustling atmosphere. One area has a country cottage feel, with floral wallpaper, sturdy cushioned wall settles, staffordshire dogs and toby jugs on a big stone fireplace with a warm coal-effect gas fire, china on delft shelves, a panelled dado and so forth. Another extensive area, with another fire, is lighter and more airy with pale wooden furniture, good big black and white photographs and lots of plates on the walls. The Bridge Room has yet another coal-effect fire and oak tables and chairs, and the small no smoking conservatory gives pleasant views across a valley to steep larch woods. The bar and Bridge Room have no smoking areas too. In summer it's a good idea to arrive early, to be sure of a table. The enjoyable menu, which has lots of generously served traditional dishes, includes lunchtime sandwiches (from £3.60), filled baked potatoes (from £3.80), and ploughman's (£6.50), as well as soup (£3), prawn cocktail (£4.60), home-made steak and kidney pie (£7.25) and good steaks (from £10.25), with specials such as chicken, mushroom and asparagus pie (£7.25) or halibut steak with stir-fried vegetables (£8.50) and puddings such as lemon meringue pie (from £3.40); children's meals (£3.25). All three dining rooms are no smoking; the restaurant is for residents only. Well kept on handpump are Black Sheep, Stones, Theakstons Old Peculier and Timothy Taylor Landlord; darts, dominoes, fruit machine, and piped music; disabled lavatories. *(Recommended by Anne and Steve Thompson, John and Glenna Marlow, Michael Butler, Mike and Wendy Proctor, Patrick Hancock, Dr T E Hothersall)*

Free house ~ Licensees Trevelyan and John Illingworth ~ Real ale ~ Bar food (12-2, 6-9(9.30 Fri, Sat); 12-8.30 Sun) ~ Restaurant ~ (01433) 651361 ~ Children in eating area of bar, restaurant and family room ~ Dogs welcome ~ Open 11-11; 12-10.30 Sun ~ Bedrooms: £47B/£64B

LITTON SK1675 Map 7

Red Lion

Village signposted off A623, between B6465 and B6049 junctions; also signposted off B6049

The enjoyable local atmosphere and good value tasty food are what readers like about this welcoming 17th-c village pub, where the cheerily friendly landlord makes everyone feel like a regular. The two inviting homely linked front rooms have low beams and some panelling, and blazing log fires. There's a bigger back room (no smoking during food service) with good-sized tables, and large antique prints on its stripped stone walls. The small bar counter has well kept Barnsley Bitter, Black Sheep, Theakstons Old Peculier and Timothy Taylor Landlord on handpump, with decent wines and 30 malt whiskies; shove-ha'penny, cribbage, dominoes and table skittles. Fresh tasting bar food includes steak and kidney pudding (£6.50), rabbit casserole (£6.85), chicken and mushroom pancakes (£6.95) and beef in horseradish cream (£7.25). The peaceful tree-studded village green in front of this is pretty, and there are good walks nearby. A good time to visit is during the annual village well-dressing carnival (usually the last weekend in June), when villagers create a picture from flower petals, moss and other natural materials, and at Christmas a brass band plays carols. No children under 6. *(Recommended by the Didler, Keith and Chris O'Neill, Ann and Colin Hunt, Derek and Sylvia Stephenson, JP, PP, Barry Collett, Patrick Hancock, Mrs R McLauchlan)*

Free house ~ Licensees Terry and Michele Vernon ~ Real ale ~ Bar food (12-2, 6-8.30(not Sun evening)) ~ (01298) 871458 ~ No children under 6 ~ Dogs welcome ~ Open 12-3, 6-11; 12-11 Fri, Sat; 12-10.30 Sun ~ Bedrooms: /£48(£55S)

MELBOURNE SK3427 Map 7

John Thompson £

Ingleby, which is NW of Melbourne; turn off A514 at Swarkestone Bridge or in Stanton by Bridge; can also be reached from Ticknall (or from Repton on B5008)

Down to earth but very hospitable, this simply converted 15th-c farmhouse is worth a visit for the good value beers that the very welcoming landlord has been brewing here since 1977: JT XXX, Rich Porter and Summer Gold, which are well kept alongside a guest such as Burtons. It's a simple but comfortable place. The big modernised lounge has ceiling joists, some old oak settles, button-back leather seats, sturdy oak tables, antique prints and paintings, and a log-effect gas fire; piped music. A couple of smaller cosier rooms open off, with a piano, fruit machine, pool and a juke box in the children's room; there's a no smoking area in the lounge. The menu is very short but the food is home-made and jolly tasty: sandwiches (£1.50), soup (£2), delicious salads with cold ham or beef (£5), tasty roast beef with yorkshire puddings and gravy (£6, not Mondays), and mouth-watering puddings such as bread and butter pudding or rhubarb crumble (£2). Outside are lots of tables by flowerbeds on the well kept lawns, or you can sit on the partly covered outside terrace which has its own serving bar. *(Recommended by the Didler, Bernie Adams, Theo, Anne and Jane Gaskin, Joan and Graham Varley, Geoff and Anne Sirett)*

Own brew ~ Licensee John Thompson ~ Real ale ~ Bar food (lunchtime; sandwiches only Sun) ~ (01332) 862469 ~ Children in family room ~ Dogs allowed in bar ~ Open 11-3, 5-11(10.30 Sun)

MILLTOWN SK3561 Map 7

Miners Arms

Off B6036 SE of Ashover; Oakstedge Lane

Perhaps underlining the emphasis on the restaurant-style food, this neatly kept stone-built pub is now entirely no smoking throughout and you will need to book. Listed on a board, the (fairly straightforward) changing dishes are very good value considering the quality, and could include home-made soup (from £2.10), spinach-stuffed mushrooms (£3.65), chicken liver pâté (£3.95), pork, apple and sausage pie (£7.75), turkey escalope with herb butter (£9.95), chicken breast with mustard cream sauce or grilled cod (£9.10), and puddings such as chocolate crumble cheesecake and crème brûlée (£3.25); the vegetables are especially well cooked. Service is friendly and efficient. The layout of the building is basically L-shaped, with a local feel up nearer the door. They serve good value wines, and two constantly rotating well kept real ales such as Archers Golden and Greene King Abbot; at lunchtime there may be quiet piped classical music. Virtually on the edge of Ashover, the pub is in former lead-mining country, with vestiges of the old workings adding interest to attractive country walks right from the door. Please note their opening times. *(Recommended by the Didler, Derek and Sylvia Stephenson, Cathryn and Richard Hicks)*

Free house ~ Licensees Andrew and Yvonne Guest ~ Real ale ~ Restaurant ~ (01246) 590218 ~ Children welcome ~ Open 12-3, 7-11; 12-3 Sun; closed Weds evening except Dec in winter; closed Sun evening and Mon, Tues

MONSAL HEAD SK1871 Map 7

Monsal Head Hotel

B6465

In a marvellous spot, perched high above the steep valley of the River Wye and doing very well at the moment, this busy extended hotel has plenty on offer, from eight well kept real ales through to its jolly good solidly inventive home-cooking. It's very well run, and readers are full of praise for the friendly, helpful staff. The cosy stable bar once housed the horses that used to haul guests and their luggage from the station down the steep valley; the stripped timber horse-stalls, harness and brassware, and lamps from the disused station itself, all hint at those days. There's a big warming woodburning stove in the inglenook, and cushioned oak pews around the tables on the flagstones. Eight well kept real ales on handpump include Monsal Best (brewed for them by Lloyds), Timothy Taylors Landlord and Whim Hartington, alongside guests from breweries such as Abbeydale, and they also keep a very good choice of bottled german beers, sensibly priced wines with about a dozen by the glass. Very fairly priced given the high standard of cooking, the menu might include soup (£3.20), crispy duck spring roll (£4.50), cod in beer batter (£6.90), roast bruschetta with vegetables and halloumi (£7.20) and steak pie (£8.90), with specials such as mozzarella and parma ham salad (£4.20), grilled squid with harissa dressing (£4.40), cassoulet (£10.30), chargrilled halibut (£10.50), fried duck breast with orange and raspberry sauce (£10.50), and puddings such as hot chocolate sponge (£3.90). From 12 to 6, they do sandwiches (from £3.95). The boundary of the parishes of Little Longstone and Ashford runs through the hotel, and the spacious no smoking restaurant and smaller lounge are named according to which side of the line they sit; beer garden. The best place to admire the terrific view is from the big windows in the lounge, the garden, and from four of the seven bedrooms; good generous breakfasts. *(Recommended by Anne and Steve Thompson, Nick and Meriel Cox, the Didler, Phil and Heidi Cook, Peter F Marshall, Ann and Colin Hunt, Keith and Chris O'Neill, JP, PP, Mike and Wendy Proctor, Richard Waller, Pauline Smith, Andrew Pearson, Simon and Amanda Southwell, John and Wendy Allin, Paul and Margaret Baker, Mike and Linda Hudson, Leigh and Gillian Mellor)*

Free house ~ Licensees Christine O'Connell and Victor Chandler ~ Real ale ~ Bar food (12-9.30(9 Sun)) ~ Restaurant ~ (01629) 640250 ~ Children welcome ~ Dogs welcome ~ Open 11.30-11.30; 12-11 Sun; closed 25 Dec ~ Bedrooms: £45.75B/£50B

OVER HADDON SK2066 Map 7

Lathkil

Village and inn signposted from B5055 just SW of Bakewell

The views from this pleasantly unpretentious hotel are spectacular – the walled garden is a good place to sit and soak them in. Steeply down below the pub lies one of the quieter of the dales, Lathkil Dale – a harmonious landscape of pastures and copses. Not surprisingly the pub is very popular with walkers (who can leave their muddy boots in the pub's lobby, and they're not fussy about dress here) so it's best to arrive early in fine weather. Five reasonably priced real ales include Charles Wells Bombardier and Whim Hartington, which are well kept alongside a couple of guests from brewers such as Black Sheep, Cottage and Theakstons. They have a few unusual malt whiskies and a good range of new world wines (not cheap). The airy room on the right as you go in has a nice fire in the attractively carved fireplace, old-fashioned settles with upholstered cushions and chairs, black beams, a delft shelf of blue and white plates, original prints and photographs, and big windows. On the left, the spacious and sunny no smoking dining area doubles as a restaurant in the evenings. The changing blackboard menu could include tasty home-made soup (£2.45), filled rolls (from £2.50), smoked mackerel, fish pie or a vegetarian dish (£6), beef and ale pie (£6.50), chicken stuffed with apricot (£6.50) and venison in red wine (£7.85), with puddings (from £3). There are darts, bar billiards, shove-ha'penny, backgammon, dominoes, cribbage, and piped music. *(Recommended by JP, PP, the Didler, Hugh A MacLean, Ann and Colin Hunt, Peter Meister, Mike and Wendy Proctor, David and Helen Wilkins, Ian and Liz Rispin, Patrick Hancock, P Price, Don and Shirley Parrish, MLR, Matthew Shackle)*

Free house ~ Licensee Robert Grigor-Taylor ~ Real ale ~ Bar food (lunchtime) ~ Restaurant ~ (01629) 812501 ~ Children in restaurant and family room ~ Dogs allowed in bar and bedrooms ~ Open 11.30-3, 6.30(7 winter)-11; 11.30-11 Sat; 12-10.30 Sun ~ Bedrooms: £37.50S/£70B

SHARDLOW SK4330 Map 7

Old Crown

3 miles from M1 junction 24, via A50: at first B6540 exit from A50 (just under 2 miles) turn off towards Shardlow – pub E of Shardlow itself, at Cavendish Bridge, actually just over Leics boundary

Early feedback since Burtonwood's recent takeover of this 17th-c coaching inn suggests very little has changed, and readers have found the new landlady pleasantly helpful. Some of the former landlord's memorabilia left with him, but the bustling bar is still packed with hundreds of jugs and mugs hanging from the beams, and brewery and railway memorabilia and advertisements and other bric-a-brac still cover the walls (even in the lavatories). Half a dozen well kept real ales on handpump include Bass, Burtonwood Top Hat and Marstons Pedigree with a couple of guests such as Marston Moor Cromwell and Moorhouses Black Cat, and they have a nice choice of malt whiskies; fruit machine and piped music. Bar food might include soup (£1.70), sandwiches (from £2), a good range of baguettes (from £3.25), omelettes (from £4.25), mediterranean vegetable lasagne (£4.95), cod (£6.95), grilled ham (£7.25) and steaks (from £8.25), with good specials such as tasty beef and kidney pie (£6.55), chicken with mustard and cider sauce (£6.95) or lamb shank in red wine (£7.95), and puddings such as chocolate sponge and spotted dick (from £2.95); best to book for Sunday lunch. Handy for the A6 as well as the M1, the pub was once a deportation point for convicts bound for the colonies. *(Recommended by Kevin Blake, Marian and Andrew Ruston, Jenny and Dave Hughes, Michael and Marion Buchanan, the Didler, Joy and Simon Maisey, JP, PP, Cathryn and Richard Hicks, Derek and Sylvia Stephenson, Roger and Pauline Pearce, Alistair and Kay Butler)*

Burtonwood ~ Tenant Monique Johns ~ Real ale ~ Bar food (lunchtime) ~ Restaurant ~ (01332) 792392 ~ Children welcome ~ Dogs allowed in bar ~ Open 11-11; 12-10.30 Sun; 11-3, 5-11; 12-3, 7-10.30 Sun winter ~ Bedrooms: £35S/£45S

SHELDON SK1768 Map

Cock & Pullet

Village signposted off A6 just W of Ashford

The flagstoned bar of this popular place feels as if it's been here for centuries, so it's quite a surprise to discover that the building was converted into a pub only ten years ago. The friendly family that run it have created a proper traditional village local, taking great pains to include the sort of mismatched furnishings and features that other pubs have taken decades to amass. As well as low beams, exposed stonework, and scrubbed oak tables and pews, the small, cosy rooms have 24 fully working clocks (one for every hour of the day), whose decorous chimes further add to the relaxed, peaceful atmosphere. Well kept Bass, Black Sheep, and Timothy Taylors Landlord on handpump. As well as good sandwiches and a choice of popular Sunday roasts, favourite dishes on the shortish menu include steak and ale pie or chicken breast with local hartington stilton sauce (£5.75); the well presented meals are highly praised by readers. A fireplace is filled with flowers in summer, and around it are various representations of poultry, including some stuffed. A plainer room has pool and a TV; there's also a no smoking snug. At the back is a pleasant little terrace with tables and a water feature. The pub is a year-round favourite with walkers (it can be busy at weekends); the pretty village is just off the Limestone Way. We haven't yet heard from readers who have stayed overnight here. *(Recommended by DC, Peter F Marshall, JP, PP, Keith and Chris O'Neill, Patrick Hancock, Guy Vowles)*

Free house ~ Licensees David and Kath Melland ~ Real ale ~ Bar food (12-2.30, 6-9) ~ (01629) 814292 ~ Children welcome ~ Dogs allowed in bar ~ Open 11-11; 12-10.30 Sun; closed 25 Dec ~ Bedrooms: £30S/£55S

WARDLOW SK1875 Map 7

Three Stags Heads

Wardlow Mires; A623 by junction with B6465

One reader was delighted to find five customers, eight dogs and two blazing fires on his Sunday lunchtime visit to this simple but friendly white-painted cottage. Genuinely traditional, this is a real find if you like your pubs basic and full of character, and enjoy a chat with friendly locals at the bar. It's situated in a natural sink, so don't be surprised to find the floors muddied by boots in wet weather (and the dogs even muddier). Warmed right through by a cast-iron kitchen range, the tiny flagstoned parlour bar has old leathercloth seats, a couple of antique settles with flowery cushions, two high-backed windsor armchairs and simple oak tables (look out for the petrified cat in a glass case). Four well kept real ales on handpump are Abbeydale Absolution, Black Lurcher (brewed for the pub at a hefty 8% ABV) and Matins, and Broadstone Charter Ale, they've lots of bottled continental and english beers (the stronger ones aren't cheap), and in winter they do a roaring trade in mugs of steaming tea – there might be free hot chestnuts on the bar; cribbage and dominoes, nine men's morris and backgammon. Food is hearty and home-made, and the seasonal menu notably countrified: possibly pasta (£6.50), cold pheasant pie or chicken and aubergine curry (£7.50) steak and kidney pie (£8.50), fried pigeon breasts (£9.50) and hare pie (£10.50); the hardy plates are home-made (the barn is a pottery workshop). You can book the tables in the small no smoking dining parlour. The front terrace looks across the main road to the distant hills. Please note the opening times. *(Recommended by JP, PP, the Didler, Trevor and Sylvia Millum, Pete Baker, Mike and Wendy Proctor, Patrick Hancock, Kevin Thorpe, Jim Abbott)*

Free house ~ Licensees Geoff and Pat Fuller ~ Real ale ~ Bar food ~ No credit cards ~ (01298) 872268 ~ Dogs welcome ~ Folk music most Sat evenings and alternate Fri ~ Open 7-11 Fri; 12-11 Sat, Sun and bank hols; closed wkday lunchtimes

WOOLLEY MOOR SK3661 Map 7

White Horse

Badger Lane, off B6014 Matlock—Clay Cross

A very good play area with a wooden train, boat, climbing frame and swings, and a puzzle sheet and crayons with their meal means children are well catered for at this attractive old pub. It's in a delightful spot and picnic-sets in the well maintained garden (with its own boules pitch) have lovely views across the Amber Valley. A sign outside shows how horses and carts carried measures of salt along the toll road in front – the toll bar cottage still stands at the entrance of the Badger Lane (a badger was the haulier who transported the salt). Still very much in its original state, the bustling tap room has a pleasant chatty atmosphere, well kept Adnams Broadside and Black Sheep and a changing guest such as Fullers London Pride; decent wines too, and efficient friendly service. There is piped music in the lounge and no smoking conservatory (great views of the Ogston reservoir from here). Bar food, which is enjoyable, good value and generously served, could include soup (£2.95), sandwiches (from £4.50), spicy chinese spare ribs (£4.50), ploughman's (from £5.95), chicken, leek and ham pie (£6.95), fried lambs liver (£7.95), salmon wellington filo parcels (£8.95), roast duck breast (£10.95) and home-made puddings including a changing cheesecake and chocolate and Baileys mousse (£3.75). It's best to book for the linen laid restaurant. *(Recommended by JP, PP, Andy and Ali, Jenny Coates, the Didler, Maurice and Della Andrew, Patrick Hancock, WAH, Keith and Chris O'Neill)*

Musketeers ~ Managers Keith Hurst and Forest Kimble ~ Real ale ~ Bar food (12-2, 6-9; 12-7 Sun; not Sun evening) ~ Restaurant ~ (01246) 590319 ~ Children welcome away from tap room ~ Dogs allowed in bar ~ Live music last Fri in month ~ Open 12-3, 6-11; 12-10.30 Sun

Several well known guide books make establishments pay for entry, either directly or as a fee for inspection. These fees can run to many hundreds of pounds. We do not. Unlike other guides, we never take payment for entries. We never accept a free meal, free drink, or any other freebie from a pub. We do not accept any sponsorship – let alone from commercial schemes linked to the pub trade. All our entries depend solely on merit.

LUCKY DIP

Besides the fully inspected pubs, you might like to try these Lucky Dips recommended to us and described by readers (if you do, please send us reports: www.goodguides.co.uk).

ASHBOURNE SK1846

☆ *Smiths Tavern* [bottom of market place]: Neatly kept traditional pub, chatty and relaxed, stretching back from heavily black-beamed bar to warmly refurbished light and airy end no smoking dining room, well kept Banks's, Marstons Pedigree and a guest beer, lots of whiskies and vodkas, daily papers, traditional games; children welcome, open all day summer Sun *(R T and J C Moggridge, JP, PP, Guy Vowles, Patrick Hancock, LYM, K H Richards)*

ASHFORD IN THE WATER SK1969

Bulls Head [Church St]: Busy dining pub with cosy and homely lounge, thriving bar, well kept Robinsons Best, Old Stockport and Hartleys XB, enjoyable meals, lunchtime sandwiches, daily papers; may be piped music or radio; tables out behind and by front car park *(DJH, Dr Emma Disley, Patrick Hancock, Jennifer Banks, Annette and John Derbyshire)*

BAKEWELL SK2168

Peacock [Bridge St]: Clean, bright and cheerful, well kept Theakstons and guests such as Adnams Bitter and Broadside, popular food (not Mon-Weds evenings), good prices, friendly service *(Simon and Amanda Southwell)*

BAMFORD SK1982

Rising Sun [Hope Rd (A6187)]: Old inn with extensive lounge and bar areas, doing well under current hard-working but relaxed and warmly welcoming family, enjoyable food, good wines, lovely flower arrangements; attractively refurbished big bedrooms, has been open all day *(Kathy and Chris Armes)*

BARLBOROUGH SK4777

De Rodes Arms [handy for M1 junction 30 – A619 Chesterfield Rd roundabout]: Modernised Brewers Fayre useful for all-day food till 10pm, pleasant friendly atmosphere, two real ales, decent wine and soft drinks choice, no smoking area; piped music; children allowed, picnic-sets outside *(CMW, JJW)*

BARLOW SK3474

☆ *Old Pump* [B6051 towards Chesterfield]: Comfortable lounge and bars with valley views, good choice of enjoyable attractively priced food from well filled rolls to popular Sun lunch, well kept Everards, Mansfield and Marstons Pedigree, good value wines, good polite service, restaurant; bedrooms, good walks *(Keith and Chris O'Neill, David Carr)*

BASLOW SK2572

Devonshire Arms [A619]: Small hotel in pleasant surroundings, footpath to Chatsworth; long Victorian-theme L-shaped bar with nice mix of different-sized tables and various seats inc leather chairs, well kept Bass and Marstons Pedigree, good young staff, food from decent sandwiches and baguettes to good carvery, fish nights and evening restaurant with attractive draped ceiling, end games area; may be unobtrusive piped music; bedrooms *(M G Hart, Mrs Dilys Unsworth)*

BELPER SK3349

Bulls Head [Belper Lane End]: Smallish two-bar pub extended into large conservatory restaurant high above town, enjoyable food, well kept beers *(Theocsbrian)*

Cross Keys [Market Pl]: Two-room pub with Batemans and a guest beer, bar food, coal fire in lounge, bar billiards; summer beer festival, open all day *(the Didler)*

Queens Head [Chesterfield Rd]: Warm and cosy three-room pub with well kept Caledonian Deuchars IPA, Tetleys and guest beers, constant coal fire, local photographs; good upstairs band nights, beer festivals; terrace tables, open all day *(the Didler)*

Thorntree [Chesterfield Rd (B6013)]: Two-bar real ale local with well kept Bass and three or four guest beers from far and wide *(the Didler)*

BIRCH VALE SK0186

Sycamore [Sycamore Rd; from A6015 take Station Rd towards Thornsett]: Popular four-roomed dining pub, reasonable prices, well kept ales, friendly helpful service, fountain in downstairs drinking bar, restaurant open all day Sun; piped music; children welcome, spacious streamside gardens with good play area and summer bar, handy for Sett Valley trail *(LYM, Michael Lamm)*

BIRCHOVER SK2362

☆ *Druid* [off B5056; Main St]: Spacious and airy two-storey candlelit dining pub, largely no smoking, which has been popular for remarkably wide choice of enjoyable food inc plenty for vegetarians, but the long-serving landlord who made this such a popular main entry has now left; has had well kept Marstons Pedigree and a beer brewed for them by Leatherbritches, good choice of malt whiskies and reasonably priced wines; piped music; children welcome if eating, picnic-sets out in front, good area for walks, has been cl Mon; more reports on new regime, please *(Richard Cole, LYM, Stephen Buckley)*

BONSALL SK2858

Barley Mow [off A6012 Cromford—Hartington; The Dale]: Friendly tucked-away pub with well kept Whim Hartington and two or three guest beers, fresh sandwiches and other food, character furnishings; live music wknds inc landlord playing accordion, organises local walks; cl wkdy lunchtimes (may open Fri by arrangement, open all day Sat) *(JP, PP, the Didler)*

BRACKENFIELD SK3658

Plough [A615 Matlock—Alfreton, about a mile NW of Wessington]: Much modernised oak-beamed stone-built 18th-c former farmhouse in lovely setting, cosy and welcoming three-level bar, cheerful log-effect gas fire, several well kept ales inc Adnams and Greene King Old Speckled Hen, sensibly priced freshly made food inc children's, OAP bargain lunch and splendid puddings range, appealing stone-built lower-level restaurant extension, small but good wine choice; big beautifully kept gardens with play area *(Marian and David Donaldson)*

BROUGH SK1882

Travellers Rest [B6049/A6187 Hope—Hathersage]: Well run true country inn, plenty of character, enjoyable food inc original specials and local steaks, friendly efficient staff, well kept Stones; bedrooms, in good walking country *(Mike Turner)*

BUXTON SK0673

Old Sun [33 High St]: Well kept Banks's and Marstons Best and Pedigree, good choice of reasonably priced wines by the glass, farm cider, friendly staff, open fires, several small dimly lit traditional areas off central bar, low beams, bare boards or tiles, stripped wood screens, old local photographs, usual food from sandwiches up; piped music, TV; children in back bar, open all day *(Barry Collett, Peter F Marshall, JP, PP, Anne and Steve Thompson, the Didler, LYM, MLR, Roger and Anne Newbury)*

BUXWORTH SK0282

☆ *Navigation* [S of village towards Silkhill, off B6062]: Lively décor in cheerful extended pub by reopened canal basin, linked low-ceilinged flagstoned rooms with canalia and brassware, lacy curtains, coal and log fires, flagstone floors, well kept Marstons Pedigree, Timothy Taylors Landlord, Websters Yorkshire and a guest beer, summer farm ciders, winter mulled wine, enjoyable generous food (all day wknds), games room; quiet piped music; tables on sunken flagstoned terrace, play area and pets corner; open all day *(Anne and Steve Thompson, Keith and Chris O'Neill, Brian and Anna Marsden, Patrick Hancock, LYM, Bill Sykes)*

CALVER SK2474

Bridge Inn [Calver Bridge, off A623 N of Baslow]: Unpretentious two-room stone-built village local, welcoming if hardly quiet, short choice of good value plain food (not Mon evening or winter Sun evening), small separate eating area, particularly well kept Hardys & Hansons ales, quick friendly service, cosy comfortable corners, coal fires, bank notes on beams, local prints and bric-a-brac inc old fire-fighting equipment in lounge; picnic-sets in nice big garden by River Derwent *(DC, Ann and Colin Hunt, Patrick Hancock, John Dwane)*

CASTLETON SK1583

Olde Cheshire Cheese [How Lane]: Two communicating family-friendly beamed areas, cosy, welcoming and spotless, lots of photographs, cheery landlord, well kept real ales, back lounge set for wide choice of usual reasonably priced food all day, open fire, toby jugs and local paintings, sensibly placed darts; piped music may obtrude; bedrooms *(BB, Patrick Hancock, Simon and Amanda Southwell)*

CHELMORTON SK1170

Church Inn [between A6 and A515 SW of Buxton]: Comfortable split bar, ample space for diners, good range of reasonably priced generous food inc fresh veg and delicious puddings, friendly landlord and golden labrador, well kept Adnams and Marstons Pedigree with a guest such as Wadworths 6X; piped music, outside lavatories; tables out in pleasant sloping garden with terrace, well tended flower boxes, superb walking country, open all day summer wknds *(JP, PP, David and Helen Wilkins, Michael Lamm, Patrick Hancock, Peter F Marshall)*

CHESTERFIELD SK3871

Barley Mow [Saltergate]: Former Wards pub with original stained-glass, well kept Marstons Pedigree and John Smiths, wide choice of enjoyable food and hot drinks; very active in charity work *(Keith and Chris O'Neill)*

☆ *Royal Oak* [Chatsworth Rd]: Large friendly pub, well kept Greene King Ruddles Best, Theakstons Best and Old Peculier, Whim Hartington and Arbor Light and weekly guest beers, big-screen sports TV, jazz Sun afternoon, Weds band night *(Kevin Bloom)*

Rutland [Stephenson Pl]: Ancient L-shaped pub next to crooked spire church, well kept Badger Best, Timothy Taylors Landlord and three or more interesting guest beers, farm cider, good clear price and details boards, rugs and assorted wooden furniture on bare boards, low-priced pub food all day from sandwiches and baguettes up, no smoking eating area, friendly polite service even when busy, darts, old photographs; piped music; children welcome, open all day *(Keith and Chris O'Neill, Patrick Hancock, Tony Hobden, Andrew York)*

Woodside [Ashgate Rd]: Civilised and up to date, with plenty of sofas and wing armchairs, good value traditional food (all afternoon Sun), real ales such as Marstons Pedigree, John Smiths and Charles Wells Bombardier, good choice of wines by the glass; no children, great terrace, open all day *(Andrew Crawford)*

COMBS SK0378

Beehive: Roomy and comfortable, neatly kept by pleasant current licensee, with good generous home cooking (good wkdy lunch deals, bargain suppers Mon, Weds/Thurs steak nights, food all day wknds), well kept ales such as Black Sheep, log fire; quiet piped jazz, live music Fri, quiz night Tues; bedrooms, tables outside, by lovely valley tucked away from main road *(Anne and Steve Thompson, Mr and Mrs B C McGee)*

COXBENCH SK3743

Fox & Hounds [off B6179 N of Derby; Alfreton Rd]: Entirely no smoking village local with long partly flagstoned bar, attractive raised restaurant area, wide choice of good interesting fresh food, reasonable prices, well kept changing ales such as Fullers London Pride, Marstons Pedigree and Tetleys, good welcoming service; may be piped music *(the Didler, JP, PP)*

CRICH SK3454

Cliff [Cromford Rd, Town End]: Cosy and unpretentious two-room pub with real fire, well kept Hardys & Hansons Bitter and Mild, good value generous straightforward food inc children's; great views, handy for National Tramway Museum *(Tony Hobden, JP, PP, the Didler, Stuart Paulley)*

CROMFORD SK2956

☆ ***Boat*** [Scarthin, off Mkt Pl]: Traditional 18th-c waterside pub (though no view of water), nicely refurbished and doing well under young brother and sister, well kept Marstons Pedigree, Springhead and perhaps beers from small local breweries, friendly relaxed atmosphere, coal fire, good value food (not Sun/Mon eves), long narrow low-beamed bar with stripped stone, bric-a-brac and books, darts, cellar bar, adjacent restaurant; live music Tues; children welcome, back garden, open all day wknds *(JP, PP, C J Thompson, the Didler, BB)*

DENBY SK3847

Old Stables [Park Hall Rd, just off B6179 (former A61) S of Ripley]: Friendly tap for Leadmill microbrewery in raftered former stable barn in Park Hall grounds, their full range, some from the cask, at low prices, two or three guest beers, fresh filled cobs, bench seating and sawdust on floor, plenty of brewery memorabilia, visits of the 1800s former mill brewery opposite; open only Fri evening and all day wknds *(the Didler, B and H)*

DERBY SK3438

☆ ***Abbey Inn*** [Darley St, Darley Abbey]: Conversion of surviving part of 11th-c abbey into pub, massive stonework remnants, brick floor, studded oak doors, big stone inglenook, stone spiral stair to upper bar with handsome oak rafters and tapestries (and the lavatories with their beams, stonework and tiles are worth a look too); well kept cheap Sam Smiths, decent low-priced lunchtime bar food, children allowed; piped music; opp Derwent-side park, pleasant riverside walk out from centre *(the Didler, JP, PP, Kevin Thorpe, LYM)*

Babington Arms [Babington Lane]: Large well run open-plan Wetherspoons, usual style and comfortable seating, good welcoming service, well kept ales inc some brewed for the pub, 20 whiskies *(Richard Houghton)*

Exeter Arms [Exeter Pl]: Several comfortable areas inc super little snug with black-leaded and polished brass range, black and white tiled floor, two built-in curved settles, lots of wood and bare brick, HMS *Exeter* and regimental memorabilia and breweriana; friendly staff, well kept Banks's and Camerons Strongarm, fresh rolls and pork pies, daily papers, well reproduced piped music; open all day *(the Didler, JP, PP, Patrick Hancock)*

Falstaff [Silver Hill Rd, off Normanton Rd]: Lively and friendly basic three-room local in former coaching inn aka the Folly, brewing its own good value ales such as 3 Faze and Phoenix; right-hand bar with coal fire usually quieter; open all day *(the Didler)*

☆ ***Flower Pot*** [King St]: Extended real ale pub with great choice of well kept changing beers mainly from small breweries – glazed panels show cellarage, regular beer festivals; friendly staff, three linked rooms inc comfortable back bar with lots of books, side area with old Derby photographs and brewery memorabilia, good value food till early evening, daily papers, pub games; piped music, concert room – good live bands wknds; open all day, tables on cherry-tree terrace; same small group runs the Smithfield *(Richard Lewis, Keith and Chris O'Neill, JP, PP, Patrick Hancock)*

☆ ***Old Silk Mill*** [Full St]: Welcoming two-room 1920s pub with old prints and full-scale mural of 1833 Derby turnout, good range of beers, lots of country wines, good value cheap food from sandwiches to steaks all day from 9am on, back dining area, daily papers, real fires, big-screen sports TV; open all day, handy for cathedral and Industrial Museum *(the Didler, Kay Wheat , JP, PP, Patrick Hancock)*

Rowditch [Uttoxeter New Rd (A516)]: Good value friendly local with well kept Mansfield, Marstons Pedigree and guest beers, country wines, attractive small snug on right, coal fire, piano *(the Didler)*

☆ ***Smithfield*** [Meadow Rd]: Friendly and comfortable bow-fronted pub with big bar, snug, back lounge full of old prints, curios and breweriana, fine choice of well kept changing ales, filled rolls and hearty lunchtime meals, real fires, daily papers; piped music, pub games inc table skittles, board games, TV and games machines, quiz nights, summer blues nights; children welcome, riverside terrace, open all day *(JP, PP, C J Fletcher, the Didler, Patrick Hancock)*

☆ ***Standing Order*** [Irongate]: Imposing and echoing banking hall converted to vast Wetherspoons, central bar, booths down each side, elaborately painted plasterwork, pseudo-classical torsos, high portraits of mainly local notables; usual popular food all day (good steaks), good range of well kept ales, reasonable prices, daily papers, neat efficient young staff, no smoking area; good disabled facilities *(JP, PP, Kevin Blake, BB, the Didler, David Carr)*

Station Inn [Midland Rd, below station]: Friendly and basic local with good food lunchtime and early evening in large back lounge, particularly well kept Bass in jugs from cellar, Worthington 1744 on handpump, tiled floor bar, side room with darts, pool and TV, ornate façade; piped music, open all day Fri *(the Didler, JP, PP)*

DRONFIELD SK3378

Jolly Farmer [Pentland Rd/Gorsey Brigg, Dronfield Woodhouse; off B6056]: Spreading bar pleasantly refurbished with old pine, bare bricks, boards and carpets, bric-a-brac, alcoves and cosy corners, open fire, well kept changing ales from glazed cellarage such as Batemans, Burton Bridge, Tetleys and Charles Wells Bombardier, good wine choice, enjoyable simple food inc choice of Sun roasts, very friendly staff, daily papers, no smoking dining area; piped music, games area with pool and TV, quiz nights Tues and Sun; children allowed if eating, open all day *(Andrew Crawford, Patrick Hancock)*

EDLASTON SK1842

Shire Horse [off A515 S of Ashbourne]: Immaculate and hospitable rambling timbered pub with blazing fires in beamed bar, good food inc some interesting recipes, friendly attentive service, well kept Bass, Marstons Pedigree and a guest such as Fullers London Pride, back conservatory; tables outside, peaceful spot *(Darly Graton, Graeme Gulibert, Barrie Frost, Martin Grosberg)*

ELTON SK2261

☆ *Duke of York* [village signed off B5056 W of Matlock; Main St]: Unspoilt old-fashioned local in charming Peak District village, very long-serving friendly landlady, lovely little quarry-tiled back tap room with coal fire in massive fireplace, glazed bar and hatch to corridor, more fires in the two front ones – one like private parlour with piano and big dining table (no food, just crisps); Adnams and Mansfield, welcoming regulars, darts; lavatories out by the pig sty; open 8.30-11, and Sun lunchtime *(Kevin Thorpe, JP, PP, the Didler, Pete Baker, RWC)*

GLOSSOP SK0294

Globe [High St W]: Good choice of changing well kept ales, comfortable relaxed atmosphere, friendly licensees, now doing reasonably priced food inc vegan in bar and restaurant; frequent live music *(Charles Eaton, Sarah Hone)*

Star [Howard St]: Bare-boards alehouse opp station, up to a dozen changing real ales inc small breweries; open all day *(the Didler)*

GREAT HUCKLOW SK1878

Queen Anne: Friendly family atmosphere, beams and gleaming copper, well kept Mansfield and guest beers such as Adnams, open fire, walkers' bar, unpretentious blackboard food (may be just soup and sandwiches, winter lunchtimes); may be unobtrusive piped music; french windows to small back terrace and charming garden with lovely views, two quiet bedrooms, good walks *(the Didler, JP, PP, Patrick Hancock)*

GRINDLEFORD SK2478

Maynard Arms [Main Rd]: Keen and friendly young manager, good wholesome attractively priced blackboard food, well kept real ales and good if not cheap wines in spacious high-ceilinged hotel bar with dark panelling, local and autographed cricketing photographs, no smoking restaurant overlooking neat gardens with water feature; piped music; children in eating areas, open all day Sun, comfortable bedrooms, nice setting *(LYM, Kathy and Chris Armes)*

HATHERSAGE SK2381

Millstone [Sheffield Rd (A625 E)]: Cosy and very welcoming, with good choice of well kept beers, wines and whiskies, good generous bar meals, interesting food in side brasserie, OAP wkdy lunches, lots of knick-knacks and antiques (many for sale); tables outside with excellent Hope Valley views, bedrooms *(R A Watson, DC)*

HAYFIELD SK0388

☆ *Lantern Pike* [Glossop Rd (A624 N)]: Enjoyable fresh food inc bargain Sun lunch, welcoming service, well kept Boddingtons, Caledonian Deuchars IPA and Timothy Taylors Landlord, plush seats, lots of brass, china and toby jugs, good choice of malt whiskies, darts, dominoes, fine view from no smoking back dining room and terrace; may be piped music; children welcome, good value bedrooms (quieter at back), great spot for walkers, open all day wknds *(JE, LYM, Jack Morley, Christine Miller)*

HOLBROOK SK3644

☆ *Wheel* [Chapel St]: Friendly beamed village local with well kept Courage Directors, Marstons Pedigree, Theakstons Best, lots of guest beers, some in jugs from the cellar, and now its own back microbrewery; biannual beer festivals, interesting whiskies and brandies, good value home-made food (not Sun evening or Mon) from sandwiches and baguettes to popular Sun lunch, good log fire, cheerful attentive staff, snug, family room, attractive conservatory restaurant; pleasant secluded garden with covered terrace and barbecue, open all day Sat, cl Mon lunchtime *(Peter and Sheila Tarleton, the Didler, JP, PP, Bernie Adams, Brian and Rosalie Laverick)*

HOLLINGTON SK2238

Red Lion [off A52 Derby—Ashbourne]: Enjoyable food, good atmosphere and service, more table space with new extension *(anon)*

HOLMESFIELD SK3277

Angel [Maid Rd, by church]: Enjoyable generous food, friendly helpful staff, well kept beer *(Matthew Lidbury)*

HOLYMOORSIDE SK3469

Lamb [Loads Rd, just off Holymoor Rd]: Small, cosy and spotless two-room village pub in leafy spot, Bass, Theakstons XB and up to six guest beers, friendly service, coal fire, pub games; tables outside, cl wkdy lunchtimes *(the Didler, JP, PP, Patrick Hancock)*

HOPE SK1783

☆ *Cheshire Cheese* [off A625, towards Edale]: 16th-c village pub handy for Pennine Way and Edale Valley, three snug beamed rooms each with a coal fire, no smoking lower dining room, well kept local Edale ales with guests such as Cottage, Eccleshall and Kelham Island, good choice of house wines and malt whiskies; empty tables may have Reserved signs even early evening, piped music; children in eating areas, open all day Sat, attractive bedrooms *(JP, PP, Dr and Mrs P Truelove, LYM, the Didler, Michael Lamm, C J Fletcher)*

HULLAND WARD SK2647

Black Horse [Hulland Ward; A517 Ashbourne—Belper]: 17th-c pub with good fresh food inc interesting dishes in low-beamed quarry-tiled bar or dining room with popular Sun carvery, well kept Harviestoun Bitter & Twisted and changing guest beers, friendly licensees; children welcome, tables in garden, comfortable bedrooms, nr Carsington Water *(the Didler)*

ILKESTON SK4643

Bridge Inn [Bridge St, Cotmanhay; off A609/A6007]: Two-room local by Erewash Canal, popular with fishermen and boaters for early breakfast and sandwich lunches; low-priced well kept Hardys & Hansons Best and Best Mild, interesting photographs in lounge; well behaved children allowed, nice back garden with play area, open all day *(the Didler)*

Ilford [Station Rd]: Former club reopened as popular local, welcoming staff, well kept Whim Hartington and a guest beer or two from small breweries, pool, TV, wknd live music *(the Didler)*

KILBURN SK3845

Travellers Rest [Chapel St]: Two-room 1850s local with Greene King Abbot, Ind Coope Burton, Tetleys and a local Leadmill beer *(the Didler)*

LITTLE HUCKLOW SK1678

☆ *Old Bulls Head* [signed from B6049]: Old country pub with two neatly kept heavily low-beamed rooms (hatch service in one), well kept John Smiths and Tetleys, straightforward bar food, unusual little back 'cave' room, lots of local bric-a-brac and local photographs, coal fire, darts, dominoes; neat garden with views and unusual collection of attractively painted old farm machinery, cl wkdy lunchtimes, bedrooms *(Kevin Blake, Patrick Hancock, LYM)*

LITTLE LONGSTONE SK1971

☆ *Packhorse* [off A6 NW of Bakewell via Monsal Dale]: Rustic charm in snug 16th-c cottage with old wooden chairs and benches in two homely and appealing well worn in beamed rooms, well kept Marstons Best and Pedigree, simple food from toasties to good steak and kidney pie, welcoming informal service; pub games, Weds folk night; hikers welcome (on Monsal Trail), terrace in steep little back garden, open all day Sun *(the Didler, LYM, Peter F Marshall, JP, PP, M and H Paiba , Patrick Hancock)*

MAKENEY SK3544

☆ *Holly Bush* [from A6 heading N after Duffield, take 1st right after crossing R Derwent, then 1st left]: Unspoilt two-bar village pub, cosy and friendly, five well kept changing ales (may be brought from cellar in jugs), beer festivals, lots of brewing advertisements; three blazing coal fires (one in old-fashioned range by snug's curved settle), flagstones, beams, black panelling and tiled floors; cheap food from lunchtime rolls up inc Thurs steak night; games lobby; children allowed in rough and ready hatch-served back conservatory, picnic-sets outside, dogs welcome *(BB, the Didler, JP, PP, Bernie Adams, Alan Bowker)*

MARSTON MONTGOMERY SK1338

Crown: Bar/brasserie with interesting imaginatively presented food from excellent lunchtime sandwiches using six breads and two-course meals to enterprising evening menu, well kept Bass and Marstons Pedigree, friendly staff, cheerful atmosphere with open fire (even at breakfast), good garden; six large comfortable bedrooms *(L Elliott)*

MATLOCK SK2960

Thorn Tree [Jackson Rd, Matlock Bank]: Superb views over valley to Riber Castle from homely and immaculate 19th-c stone-built two-room local, esp from front picnic-sets; well kept Whim Hartington and several guest beers, sensibly priced enjoyable fresh lunchtime food from sandwiches up (Weds-Sun), quick friendly service, chatty licensees, interesting bric-a-brac, darts, dominoes; TV, piped nostalgic music, outside gents'; cl Mon/Tues lunchtime *(the Didler)*

MATLOCK BATH SK2958

Princess Victoria [South Parade]: Small Batemans pub with three of their beers and guest ales kept well, good value food in comfortable long beamed and panelled bar and upstairs restaurant, chatty landlady, coal fire; games machine, piped music, busy wknds; open all day *(Richard Lewis, the Didler)*

MILFORD SK3545

William IV [Milford Bridge]: Relaxing stone-built pub with beams, bare boards and quarry tiles, changing ales such as Bass, Fullers London Pride, Timothy Taylors Landlord, Charles Wells Bombardier and Whim Hartington tapped from casks in back room, blazing coal fire, good filled rolls, friendly chatty landlady *(JP, PP, the Didler)*

MILLERS DALE SK1473

Anglers Rest [just down Litton Lane; pub is PH on OS Sheet 119, map ref 142734]: Friendly creeper-clad pub in lovely setting on Monsal Trail, wonderful gorge views and riverside walks; cosy lounge, ramblers' bar and no smoking dining room, well kept Marstons Pedigree, Tetleys and a guest such as Barnsley, lots of toby jugs, plates and teapots, food from cobs up, pool room; children welcomed, attractive village *(Derek and Sylvia Stephenson, the Didler, JP, PP, Patrick Hancock)*

MONYASH SK1566

☆ *Bulls Head* [B5055 W of Bakewell]: Welcoming bustle in high-ceilinged two-room local with oak wall seats and panelled settle, horse pictures, shelf of china, mullioned windows, good value home cooking using local ingredients, sandwiches too, well kept Whim Hartington and other ales, obliging service, good log fire; two-room dining room, darts, dominoes, pool in small back bar; friendly ginger cat and elderly dog, may be quiet piped music; children and muddy dogs welcome, long pews out facing small green, simple bedrooms, attractive village *(JP, PP, D C Leggatt, BB, Rona Murdoch, Matthew Shackle)*

MUGGINTON SK2843

☆ *Cock* [back rd N of Weston Underwood]: Clean, comfortable and relaxing, with tables and settles in rambling panelled L-shaped bar, big dining area, wide choice of good value wholesome food from lunchtime sandwiches and snacks up, well kept Bass, Marstons Pedigree and a guest such as Hop Back Summer Lightning, sensibly priced wines, friendly staff; tables outside, nice surroundings, good walks *(Darly Graton, Graeme Gulibert)*

NEW MILLS SJ9886

Fox [Brookbottom; OS Sheet 109 map ref 985864]: Friendly and unchanging old country pub cared for well by long-serving landlord, well kept Robinsons, plain good value food (not Tues evening) inc sandwiches, log fire, darts, pool; children welcome, handy for walkers (can get crowded wknds); splendid tucked-away hamlet down single-track lane *(the Didler, David Hoult, Michael Lamm)*

OCKBROOK SK4236

☆ *Royal Oak* [village signed off B6096 just outside Spondon; Green Lane]: Quiet 18th-c village local run by same family for half a century, small unspoilt rooms (one no smoking), well kept Bass and several interesting guest beers (Oct beer festival), good soft drinks choice, tiled-floor tap room, turkey-carpeted snug, inner bar with Victorian prints, larger and lighter no smoking side room, nice old settle in entrance corridor, open fires, cheap popular food (not wknd evenings) from good fresh rolls and sandwiches up, OAP bargains, good value Sun lunch, traditional games inc darts, no music or machines; band night Sun; tables in sheltered cottage garden, more on cobbled front courtyard, separate play area *(the Didler, BB, JP, PP, Pete Baker, Derek and Sylvia Stephenson, CMW, JJW)*

OLD TUPTON SK3865

Royal Oak [A61 Derby Rd S of Chesterfield]: Friendly three-room pub with several real ales in lined glasses, reasonable choice of good value straightforward food all day, pleasant service; TV and pool in games room, may be piped pop music; children welcome, picnic-sets in garden with play area *(CMW, JJW)*

OWLER BAR SK2978

☆ *Peacock* [A621 2 miles S of Totley]: Warm, welcoming and attractive Chef & Brewer in moorland setting with panoramic views of Sheffield and Peak District, good food from huge sandwiches, rolls, baguettes and baked potatoes to extensive blackboard menu, big log fires, helpful attentive staff, good beer choice, large no smoking area away from central bar; open all day *(Kathy and Chris Armes, Matthew Lidbury, David and Ruth Hollands)*

PARWICH SK1854

Sycamore: Welcoming old unspoilt pub with jovial landlady, lively chat and roaring log fire in simply furnished but comfortable main bar, lots of old local photographs, hatch-served tap room with games and younger customers; plain wholesome fresh food lunchtimes and most Weds-Sat evenings, big helpings, well kept Robinsons inc seasonal Old Tom, and Theakstons; tables out in front and on grass by car park, quiet village not far from Tissington *(Pete Baker, the Didler, JP, PP)*

PILSLEY SK2371

☆ *Devonshire Arms* [off A619 Bakewell—Baslow; High St]: Welcoming tastefully refurbished local with good value generous home cooking inc interesting fish and Thurs-Sat evening carvery (may need to book), well kept Boddingtons, Mansfield and a guest beer, San Miguel on tap, appealing lounge bar with warm atmosphere and bric-a-brac, public bar area for walkers and children, open fires; service may slow at busy times, quiz and music nights; very handy for Chatsworth farm and craft shops, lovely village *(John Evans, Ann and Colin Hunt, DC, W W Burke)*

ROWARTH SK0189

Little Mill [off A626 in Marple Bridge at Mellor sign, sharp left at Rowarth sign, then pub signed]: Beautiful tucked-away setting, unusual features inc working waterwheel; cheap cheerful plentiful bar food all day, bargain midweek meals, big open-plan bar with lots of little settees, armchairs and small tables, Banks's, Marstons Pedigree and a guest beer, big log fire, busy upstairs carvery restaurant evening and Sun lunchtime (good generous local beef); pub games; children welcome, pretty garden dell across stream great for them, with good play area; vintage Pullman-carriage bedrooms, open all day *(LYM, Michael Lamm)*

ROWSLEY SK2565

Grouse & Claret [A6 Bakewell—Matlock]: Spacious and comfortable family dining pub in well refurbished old stone building, good reasonably priced food (all day wknd) from carvery counter with appetising salad bar, friendly helpful service, no smoking area, decent wines, open fires; tap room popular with walkers, tables outside; good value bedrooms, small camp site behind nr river *(P Price)*

☆ *Peacock* [Bakewell Rd]: Civilised 17th-c small country hotel with comfortable chairs and sofas and just a few antiques in spacious uncluttered lounge, interesting stone-floored inner bar, restful colours, enjoyable bar food from sandwiches up, Greene King IPA and Worthington 1744, good wines, well prepared meals in separate dining room; attractive riverside gardens, trout fishing, good bedrooms *(LYM, Kathy and Chris Armes, W W Burke)*

SANDIACRE SK4737

Blue Bell [Church St]: Friendly tucked-away 1700s former farmhouse, beams and breweriana, well kept ales inc local brews and a Mild *(the Didler)*

SHARDLOW SK4330

☆ *Malt Shovel* [3½ miles from M1 junction 24, via A6 towards Derby; The Wharf]: Old-world beamed pub in 18th-c former maltings, interesting odd-angled layout, well kept Banks's Best and Marstons Pedigree, quick friendly service, cheap lunchtime food from baguettes and baked potatoes up, good central open fire, farm tools and bric-a-brac; no small children; lots of tables out on canalside terrace, pretty hanging baskets *(JP, PP, Marian and Andrew Ruston, LYM, the Didler, MLR, John Beeken)*

SHEEN SK1160

Staffordshire Knot [off B5054 at Hulme End]: Stone-built country pub with good range of good value food from interesting snacks to full meals, flagstones, two welcoming log fires,

Marstons Pedigree and a guest beer, friendly landlord *(Mr and Mrs B C McGee)*

SMALLEY SK4044

☆ *Bell* [A608 Heanor—Derby]: Small thriving two-room village pub, well kept cheap real ales such as Mallard, Oakham JHB and Whim IPA and Hartington and one or two guest beers, good choice of wines, pots of tea or coffee, smart efficient friendly staff, dining area with good reasonably priced changing food; post office annexe, tables out in front and on big relaxing lawn with play area, beautiful hanging baskets, open all day wknds, attractive bedrooms behind *(JP, PP, Derek and Sylvia Stephenson)*

SOUTH NORMANTON SK4556

Castlewood [just off M1 junction 28, via A38; Carter Lane E]: Busy family Brewers Fayre with large friendly collection of rooms and dining nooks, good choice of beers and wines, big good value menu inc children's, quick service, huge indoor play area; piped music; comfortable attached Travel Inn *(Peter and Audrey Dowsett)*

SOUTH WINGFIELD SK3755

Old Yew Tree [B5035 W of Alfreton; Manor Rd]: Cosy and convivial local doing well under current owners, good value food esp steaks and big Sun lunch, well kept Cottage, Marstons Pedigree and a couple of interesting guest beers, log fire, panelling, kettles and pans hanging from beams, separate restaurant area *(JP, PP, Derek and Sylvia Stephenson)*

SPONDON SK3935

☆ *Malt Shovel* [off A6096 on edge of Derby, via Church Hill into Potter St]: Cheap well prepared food, well kept Bass and Highgate Saddlers Best from hatch in tiled corridor with cosy panelled and quarry-tiled or turkey-carpeted rooms off, old-fashioned décor, gas heater in huge inglenook, steps down to big games bar with full-size pool table, cheerful efficient staff; lots of picnic-sets, some under cover, in big well used back garden with rabbit pens and good play area *(the Didler, JP, PP, John Beeken, BB)*

STANTON IN PEAK SK2464

Flying Childers [off B5056 Bakewell—Ashbourne; Main Rd]: Settles by coal fire in cosy and unspoilt beamed right-hand room, well kept changing ales such as Black Sheep, Fullers London Pride, Shepherd Neame Spitfire and Slaters, friendly and chatty old-fashioned landlord and locals, good value lunchtime rolls, dominoes and cribbage; in delightful steep stone village overlooking rich green valley, good walks, cl Mon and perhapsThurs lunchtimes *(Peter F Marshall, JP, PP, the Didler, Patrick Hancock)*

STARKHOLMES SK3058

White Lion [Starkholmes Rd]: Well run village pub in exceptional location, views over Matlock Bath and Derwent valley, enjoyable imaginative food at reasonable prices, well kept Bass, Burtonwood, Marstons Pedigree, Whim Hartington and a guest beer, attentive staff, low ceilings and stripped stone, coal fire in restaurant; pleasant tables outside, boules, bedrooms *(C J Thompson, the Didler)*

STAVELEY SK4374

☆ *Speedwell* [Lowgates]: Attractively refurbished, brewing its own good keenly priced Townes beers, fine choice of bottle-conditioned belgian beers too, friendly staff, no smoking area, no juke box or machines (nor food); cl wkdy lunchtimes, open all day wknds *(Keith and Chris O'Neill, Patrick Hancock)*

STONEY MIDDLETON SK2375

Moon [Townend (A623)]: Good sensibly priced food inc OAP lunchtime bargains, well kept ales such as Black Sheep and Charles Wells Bombardier, reasonably priced wines, friendly staff, nice décor with old photographs; handy for dales walks *(Peter F Marshall, Patrick Hancock)*

SUTTON CUM DUCKMANTON SK4371

Arkwright Arms [A632 Bolsover—Chesterfield]: Friendly pub with bar, pool room and dining room, all with real fires, decent choice of lunchtime food and drinks inc two real ales; quiet piped music; garden and play area, open all day *(CMW, JJW, Patrick Hancock)*

TIDESWELL SK1575

☆ *George* [Commercial Rd (B6049, between A623 and A6 E of Buxton)]: Friendly cheerful staff in pleasantly unpretentious inn, traditional L-shaped bar/lounge inc dining area and linked no smoking room, good value generous food from bar meals to wide choice of restaurant dishes, three well kept Hardys & Hansons ales, modestly priced wines, open fires; piped music, separate bar with darts, pool, juke box and machines; children really welcome, dogs too, live 60s music Fri; by remarkable church, tables in front overlooking pretty village, sheltered back garden; five comfortable bedrooms (church clock strikes the quarters), pleasant walks *(Derek and Sylvia Stephenson, BB, Peter F Marshall, the Didler, Michael Butler, JP, PP, R T and J C Moggridge)*

TROWAY SK3979

Black-a-moor Head [B6056 Dronfield—Eckington]: Tudor-look candlelit dining pub open for food all day, good choice and big helpings, three interesting well kept real ales, good choice of other drinks, attentive service; quiet piped music; lovely views from terrace picnic-sets *(CMW, JJW)*

TURNDITCH SK2946

Cross Keys [A517 W of Belper]: Efficient friendly management, good choice of enjoyable food, pleasant setting and atmosphere *(Marian and David Donaldson)*

WALTON SK3669

Blue Stoops [A632 SW of Chesterfield]: Recently comfortably refurbished two-bar former coaching inn with well kept Fullers London Pride, Marstons Pedigree and John Smiths, good value food from sandwiches to sizzlers, good wine choice; front verandah, good view from back garden *(Andrew Crawford)*

WENSLEY SK2661

Red Lion [B5057 NW of Matlock]: Virtually a pub with no beer (may not even have bottles now), but worth a visit for its unspoilt appeal; friendly two-room no smoking farmhouse with chatty brother and sister owners, an assortment of 1950s-ish furniture, piano in main bar (landlord likes sing-songs), unusual tapestry in second room (usually locked, so ask landlady), no games or piped music, just tea, coffee, soft drinks and filled sandwiches or home-baked rolls perhaps using fillings from the garden; outside lavatories; open all day *(Pete Baker, JP, PP, the Didler)*

WHITTINGTON SK3875

Cock & Magpie [Church Street N, behind museum]: Old stone-built dining pub with no smoking dining area/conservatory (children welcome here) and good choice of good food inc sandwiches and early evening bargains for two (booking suggested for the bargain Sun lunch – they may need your table when you finish); friendly service, particularly well kept Banks's, Mansfield and Marstons Pedigree, tap room, proper snug with own servery and games room; piped music; next to Revolution House museum *(Keith and Chris O'Neill, CMW, JJW)*

WHITTINGTON MOOR SK3873

☆ ***Derby Tup*** [Sheffield Rd; B6057 just S of A61 roundabout]: Pleasantly down-to-earth Tynemill pub with lots of well kept changing real ales and good choice of other drinks inc good value soft drinks, simple furniture and lots of standing room, two small no smoking rooms (children allowed in them), daily papers and wide-ranging choice of good value straightforward bar food; can get very busy wknd evenings; dogs welcome, open all day Weds-Sat *(LYM, Keith and Chris O'Neill, the Didler, JP, PP, Patrick Hancock, David Carr, MLR)*

Donkey Derby [Sheffield Rd]: Large chain pub with usual food quickly served, good choice of beers and other drinks, hearty landlord *(Keith and Chris O'Neill)*

Red Lion [Sheffield Rd (B6057)]: Small friendly 19th-c stone-built pub tied to Old Mill, with their Bitter, Bullion and a seasonal beer kept well, thriving atmosphere, old local photographs in two rooms *(the Didler, Keith and Chris O'Neill, Patrick Hancock)*

WHITWELL SK5276

Mallet & Chisel [Hillside]: Well kept real ales inc a Mild and cheap food inc bargain Sun lunch (popular, so best to book), pleasant bar with TV and linked dining room, children welcome; pool room, quiet piped music *(Patrick Hancock)*

WINSTER SK2460

Bowling Green [East Bank, by NT Market House]: Pleasantly traditional refurbished local with friendly staff, well kept beers such as Whim Hartington, wide choice of enjoyable generous home cooking inc good Sun lunch, log fire, dining area and family conservatory; has been cl wkdy lunchtimes, open all day wknds *(JP, PP, the Didler, Reg Fowle, Helen Rickwood)*

Miners Standard [Bank Top (B5056 above village)]: Welcoming 17th-c local, friendly family service, well kept ales such as Storm, attractively priced generous food inc huge pies, big open fires, lead-mining photographs and minerals, ancient well, restaurant; children allowed away from bar, attractive view from garden, interesting stone-built village below, open all day (at least Sun) *(JP, PP, the Didler, Reg Fowle, Helen Rickwood)*

WIRKSWORTH SK2854

Royal Oak [North End]: Traditional backstreet local, small and comfortable, with key fobs, old copper kettles and other bric-a-brac, friendly licensees and locals, well kept Bass, Timothy Taylors Landlord, Whim Hartington and two guest beers, may be filled cobs, pool room; opens 8, cl lunchtime exc Sun *(the Didler)*

YOULGREAVE SK2064

Farmyard [Main St]: Comfortable low-ceilinged local, warm and welcoming, with well kept real ales, fire in impressive stone fireplace, old farm tools, cheap food, big upstairs restaurant; children, walkers and dogs welcome, TV, tables in garden *(DC)*

☆ ***George*** [Alport Lane/Church St]: Handsome yet unpretentious bare-boards stone-built 17th-c inn opp church, quick friendly service, welcoming locals, good straightforward low-priced home cooking inc game, comfortable banquettes, well kept John Smiths, Theakstons Mild and a guest such as Hartington; flagstoned locals' and walkers' side room, dogs welcome, games room, juke box; attractive village handy for Lathkill Dale and Haddon Hall, roadside tables, simple bedrooms, open all day *(JP, PP, Maggie and Tony Harwood, the Didler, Patrick Hancock, Des and Jen Clarke)*

'Children welcome' means the pub says it lets children inside without any special restriction. If it allows them in, but to restricted areas such as an eating area or family room, we specify this. Some pubs may impose an evening time limit. We do not mention limits after 9pm as we assume children are home by then.

Devon

Devon has a fine mix of all sorts of very different good pubs, from simple unspoilt places to smart dining pubs, with some really excellent modern cooking and quite a lot of fresh fish and seafood. There is a good choice of West Country real ales, and still quite a few places to find good local cider (though we get fewer reports on this than we used to – by a long way). Many of the best pubs here are in lovely countryside (or the drive to them takes you through it), and many have plenty of good walks nearby. There have been quite a few changes, too, with several pubs leaving the main entries this year, and a good crop of newcomers taking their place: the cosy thatched Sir Walter Raleigh at East Budleigh (super home-made food and a friendly licensee), the Church House at Holne (nice all round, in good walking country), the Castle Inn at Lydford (full of character, with good food and drink – back in the *Guide* on fine form again after a break), the Dolphin looking down on the water in Newton Ferrers (enjoyable food, a good choice of real ales), the Fox & Goose at Parracombe on Exmoor (nice atmosphere, virtually all local produce for its well liked food), the unpretentious ancient Tavistock Inn at Poundsgate on Dartmoor (just right for the area), and the Old Church House at Torbryan (evocative ancient core, and nice all round). Other pubs which have been giving readers special pleasure in the last few months are the Durant Arms at Ashprington (good all round, and gaining a Place to Stay Award), the unspoilt 15th-c Fountain Head in Branscombe (brewing its own beer), the smashing Drewe Arms at Broadhembury (excellent fresh fish), the cheerful Butterleigh Inn (more space inside and out, including new bedrooms), the fine old New Inn at Coleford (succeeds all round, as pub, inn and restaurant – and we're fond of that parrot), the Nobody Inn at Doddiscombsleigh (a very popular all-rounder, outstanding on the drinks side), the relaxed and slightly off-beat Turf Hotel in its lovely spot at Exminster, the cheerful Duke of York at Iddesleigh (very good unpretentious food, good wines by the glass, a nice place to stay in), the delightful thatched Cleave at Lustleigh, the restauranty Dartmoor Inn near Lydford (very much enjoyed for its food), the well run Church House at Marldon (another good all-rounder), the smart rather foody waterside Ship at Noss Mayo (good local beers, too), the Peter Tavy Inn (a busy and appealing moorland all-rounder), the particularly well run Hare & Hounds near Sidbury (big and busy, yet full of interest, with good food), the Blue Ball at Sidford (in the same family since early last century, an enjoyable pub that's nice to stay at), the Kings Arms at Stockland (an excellent balance between its thriving local side and its appeal to people wanting a more formal meal or overnight stay), the Bridge on the edge of Topsham (an exceptional unspoilt pub with lots of real ales), the Start Bay at Torcross (immensely popular for its wonderful fish straight off the beach, some caught by the landlord), the Kings Arms at Winkleigh (lively and friendly, nice all round), the cottagey local Northmore Arms at Wonson (good beer, proper home cooking), and the sizeable rather plush Rising Sun at Woodland (good food and drink, comfortable bedrooms). Many of these pubs stand out for good or even exceptional food. Our final choice for Devon Dining Pub of the Year is the Drewe Arms at Broadhembury: nothing but praise for the atmosphere and the cooking here, but bear in mind that it's not cheap, and not large (so you may have to book). In the Lucky Dip section at the end of the chapter, current favourites include the Awliscombe Inn, Ship in Axmouth, Barrel o' Beer and Dolphin in Beer, George at Blackawton, Salterton Arms at Budleigh Salterton, Exeter Inn at Chittlehamholt, Providence at East Prawle, Double Locks and Great Western in Exeter, Rock at Georgeham, Poachers at Ide, Grampus at Lee, East Dart at Postbridge, Old Ship in Sidmouth, Ridgeway at Smallridge, Millbrook at South Pool, Church House at Stokenham, Kings Arms at Tedburn St Mary, Golden Lion at Tipton St John, Passage House in Topsham, Kingsbridge Inn in Totnes, Maltsters Arms at Tuckenhay and Rising Sun at Umberleigh. Drinks prices in Devon are close to the national average. The Imperial in Exeter has much lower beer prices than elsewhere. The Fountain Head at Branscombe, brewing its own, was the next cheapest we found. Devon pubs often charge less for beers from smallish local breweries than they do for the well known national brands. Ones to look out for include Otter, Teignworthy, Princetown, Branscombe Vale, Summerskills and Mildmay, from Devon itself. We have found quite a few pubs getting their cheapest beers from just over the border: from Cornwall, St Austell (their 'Devon' brew is Dartmoor Best), Sharps, Skinners and Ring o' Bells; from Somerset, Cotleigh, Exmoor, Butcombe and Juwards; and from Dorset, Palmers.

ASHPRINGTON SX8156 Map 1

Durant Arms

Village signposted off A381 S of Totnes; OS Sheet 202 map reference 819571

Run by charming and helpful licensees who really care, this neatly kept and rather smart country inn has a new Stay Award this year. Readers have very much enjoyed their visits – as somewhere to spend a few nights, for a particularly good meal out, and as a place for a drink and a chat in a spotless bar. The beamed open-plan bar has several open fires, lamps and horsebrasses, fresh flowers, and a mix of seats and tables on the red patterned carpet; there's a lower carpeted lounge too, with another open fire. With quite an emphasis on dining and all the food cooked to order, there might be sandwiches (from £2.25), home-made soup (£3.75), home-cooked ham and eggs (£6.75), good liver and onions or spinach and mushroom lasagne (£7.95), steak and kidney pie (£8.45), scallops and tiger prawns in a cream and white wine sauce (£13.95), sirloin steak (£14.95), and home-made puddings such as blackberry and apple pie or crème brûlée (£4); best to book if you want to be sure of a table. The no smoking dining room has lots of oil and watercolours by local artists on the walls. Good, attentive service. St Austell Dartmoor Best and Tribute on handpump, and Luscombe cider; no games machines but they do have piped music. The back terrace has wooden garden furniture and there's a water feature. *(Recommended by Mike Gorton, Richard and Margaret Peers, Jay Bohmrich, Comus and Sarah Elliott, Ann and Bob Westbrook, E B Ireland, Mike and Heather Watson, Dennis Jenkin, Cathy Robinson, Ed Coombe, Richard Haw, Mrs Anne Lowe, Doreen and Haydn Maddock, John Mitchell, Keith and Margaret Kettell)*

Free house ~ Licensees Graham and Eileen Ellis ~ Real ale ~ Bar food ~ Restaurant ~ (01803) 732240 ~ Children in family room ~ Dogs allowed in bar ~ Open 11.30-2.30, 6.30-11; 12-2.30, 7-10.30 Sun ~ Bedrooms: £40B/£70B

Please tell us if the décor, atmosphere, food or drink at a pub is different from our description. We rely on readers' reports to keep us up to date. No stamp needed: *The Good Pub Guide*, FREEPOST TN1569, Wadhurst, E Sussex TN5 7BR.

BERRYNARBOR SS5646 Map 1

Olde Globe

Village signposted from A399 E of Ilfracombe

Once three cottages, this rambling old place has a series of dimly lit homely rooms as well as a sizeable no smoking family room with a play area. There are low ceilings, curved deep-ochre walls, and floors of flagstones or of ancient lime-ash (with silver coins embedded in them); old high-backed oak settles (some carved) and plush cushioned cask seats around antique tables, and lots of cutlasses, swords, shields and fine powder-flasks, a profusion of genuinely old pictures, priests (fish-coshes), thatcher's knives, sheep shears, gin traps, pitchforks, antlers, and copper warming pans; there's a partly no smoking family room with a play area, and no smoking dining room. Well kept Bass, St Austell Dartmoor Best, and a guest such as Shepherd Neame Spitfire on handpump; sensibly placed darts, pool, skittle alley, dominoes, piped music, and winter quiz nights every other Sunday evening. Bar food includes sandwiches (from £2.25), home-made soup (£2.50), filled baked potatoes or burgers (from £4), yorkshire pudding filled with sausage or beef (£5.50), home-made steak and kidney or vegetable pies (from £5.95), daily specials, and children's meals (£3.50, with an activity bag). The dining room is no smoking. The crazy-paved front terrace has some old-fashioned garden seats, and there is a children's activity house. *(Recommended by Canon Michael Bourdeaux, R and J Bateman, Dr and Mrs P Truelove, Annette Tress, Gary Smith, Maysie Thompson, David Eberlin, W W Burke, Dorsan Baker)*

Unique (Enterprise) ~ Lease Don and Edith Ozelton and family ~ Real ale ~ Bar food (12-2, 6(7 in winter)-9; not 25 Dec) ~ (01271) 882465 ~ Children in family room or in dining room if over 8 ~ Dogs allowed in bar ~ Open 12-2.30, 6-11(10.30 Sun); evening opening time 7 in winter; closed evening 25 Dec

BRANSCOMBE SY1888 Map 1

Fountain Head

Upper village, above the robust old church; village signposted off A3052 Sidmouth—Seaton, then from Branscombe Square follow road up hill towards Sidmouth, and after about a mile turn left after the church; OS Sheet 192 map reference SY188889

Once a simple cider house, this old-fashioned and unspoilt 500-year-old stone pub brews its own beers in the Branscombe Vale Brewery: Branoc, Draymans Best, Jolly Geff (named after Mrs Luxton's father, the ex-licensee), and summer Summa That, and summer guest beers like Adnams Broadside or Exmoor Fox; they also hold a midsummer weekend beer festival which comprises three days of spitroasts, barbecues, live music, morris men, and over 30 real ales; farm cider, too. The room on the left – formerly a smithy – has forge tools and horseshoes on the high oak beams, a log fire in the original raised firebed with its tall central chimney, and cushioned pews and mate's chairs. On the right, an irregularly shaped, more orthodox snug room has another log fire, white-painted plank ceiling with an unusual carved ceiling-rose, brown-varnished panelled walls, and rugs on its flagstone-and-lime ash floor; the children's room is no smoking, the airedale is called Max, another dog, Chester, and the black and white cat, Casey Jones. Bar food such as sandwiches (from £2.95), filled baked potatoes (from £4.95), sausage and mash with onion gravy (£5.50), and good ham and egg, steak and kidney pie, fresh battered cod or moussaka with greek salad (all £6.50). Darts, shove-ha'penny, cribbage, and dominoes. There are seats out on the front loggia and terrace, and a little stream rustling under the flagstoned path. They offer self-catering; pleasant nearby walks. *(Recommended by Mike Gorton, Steve Crick, Helen Preston, Roger and Pauline Pearce, the Didler, JP, PP, Maurice Ribbans, Peter Herridge, Derek and Sylvia Stephenson, Gordon Stevenson, Phil and Sally Gorton, Tom and Ruth Rees, Mrs C Lintott, Conor McGaughey, Pete Walker)*

Own brew ~ Licensee Mrs Catherine Luxton ~ Real ale ~ Bar food ~ (01297) 680359 ~ Children in restaurant at lunchtime but must be over 10 in evening ~ Dogs welcome ~ Folk/country & western/rock ~ Open 11.30-3, 6-11; 12-3, 6.30-10.30 Sun

Masons Arms

Main Street; signed off A3052 Sidmouth—Seaton, then bear left into village

This thatched 14th-c longhouse in set in a village surrounded by little wooded hills in National Trust territory, and close to the sea. At its heart is the rambling low-beamed main bar with a massive central hearth in front of the roaring log fire (spit-roasts on Tuesday and Sunday lunch and Friday evenings), windsor chairs and settles, slate floors, ancient ship's beams, and a bustling atmosphere created by a good mix of customers. The no smoking Old Worthies bar also has a slate floor, a fireplace with a two-sided woodburning stove, and woodwork that has been stripped back to the original pine. There's also the original no smoking restaurant (warmed by one side of the woodburning stove), and the newer Waterfall Restaurant, set slightly away from the pub, and with an open kitchen so you can watch the chefs at work (closed on Sunday and Monday evenings). Using as much local and organic produce as possible, the very good bar food includes lunchtime sandwiches (from £3; panini with fillings such as roasted vegetables with mozzarella and pesto or sausage, bacon, fried egg and tomato from £5.75), ploughman's (from £5.25), bisque of local crab (£4.50), basil marinated goats cheese tartlet (£5.95), confit of duck leg with spiced pickled red cabbage (£6.95), organic lamb and rosemary sausages or thai spiced sour orange vegetable curry (£8.95), steak and kidney in ale pudding (£9.50), pot-roasted local pheasant with orange, fresh herbs, redcurrants and port (£12.50), local estate steaks (from £12.95), daily specials such as smoked trout, chive and horseradish mousse with a lemon and dill dressing (£5.75), baked cod with baby capers, cherry tomatoes, basil and mozzarella (£10.95), and poached monkfish, mussels, langoustines and salmon in garlic and lemon cream (£14.95), and puddings like dark chocolate crème brûlée, raspberry torte or caramelised prune rice pudding (£3.95); children's meals (from £4.25). Well kept Bass, Otter Ale and Bitter, and a couple of guests from maybe Branscombe Vale or Cotleigh on handpump; they hold a popular beer festival in July, and keep 33 malt whiskies, 15 wines by the glass, and local farm cider. Occasional darts. Outside, the quiet flower-filled front terrace has tables with little thatched roofs, extending into a side garden. Writing so enthusiastically about this favourite pub, and making it Devon Dining Pub of the Year as we did for the 2004 *Guide*, naturally focuses a great deal of attention on it. It is clear that everyone's expectations will be very high indeed. This last year, this merciless scrutiny has shown up occasional shortcomings in service, but we should stress that the overall picture is still very positive. *(Recommended by June and Jeff Elmes, JP, PP, Alan and Paula McCully, the Didler, Richard and Margaret Peers, John and Jane Hayter, Barry Steele-Perkins, Mr and Mrs Allan Chapman, Cathryn and Richard Hicks, Lyn Huxtable, Richard Seers, Andrea Rampley, Cathy Robinson, Ed Coombe, Mrs J Poole, Richard and Anne Ansell, Brian and Bett Cox, D Stilgoe, Liz and Alun Jones, Mike Gorton, A P Seymour, John Knighton, Conor McGaughey, Pete Walker; also in the* Good Hotel Guide*)*

Free house ~ Licensees Murray Inglis, Mark Thompson and Tim Manktelow-Gray ~ Real ale ~ Bar food ~ Restaurant ~ (01297) 680300 ~ Children in eating area of bar ~ Dogs allowed in bar ~ Occasional live duo ~ Open 11-11; 12-10.30 Sun; 11-3, 6-11 in winter ~ Bedrooms: £30(£60B)/£50(£100B)

BROADHEMBURY ST1004 Map 1

Drewe Arms ★

Signposted off A373 Cullompton—Honiton

Devon Dining Pub of the Year

In the 16 years Mr and Mrs Burge have run this fine old pub, we've never had a poor report, and with their son Andrew now in charge of the kitchen, we hope this can continue. It's a civilised but friendly place and a favourite with a great many readers, and despite the emphasis on the marvellous fish dishes, the small bar area has kept its lovely local chatty atmosphere so that anyone walking in for just a drink would not feel at all out of place. The bar has neatly carved beams in its high ceiling, and handsome stone-mullioned windows (one with a small carved roundabout horse), and on the left, a high-backed stripped settle separates off a little room with flowers on the three sturdy country tables, plank-panelled walls painted brown below and yellow above with attractive engravings and prints, and a big black-painted fireplace with bric-a-brac on a high mantelpiece; some wood carvings, walking sticks, and framed watercolours for sale. The flagstoned entry has a narrow corridor of a room by the servery with a couple of tables, and the cellar bar has simple pews on the stone floor; the dining room is no smoking. Unfailingly good, the food might include open sandwiches (from £5; crab £6.95; rump steak £8.25), daily specials such as spicy crab soup (£5), warm salmon salad (£7; main course £13.50), whole langoustines (£7; main course £15.50), smoked haddock with stilton rarebit (£12.50), wing of skate with black butter (£13.50), lyme bay crab (£14), seared tuna salad (£14.50), and sea bream with orange and chilli (£15), with some meaty choices such as hot chicken and bacon salad (£7; main course £10.50), fillet of beef with mushroom sauce (£18), and excellent seasonal partridge; puddings like bread pudding with whisky butter sauce, St Emilion chocolate or hazelnut parfait (£5). Best to book to be sure of a table. Well kept Otter Bitter, Ale and Bright tapped from the cask, and a very good wine list laid out extremely helpfully – including quite a few by the glass. There are picnic-sets in the lovely garden which has a lawn stretching back under the shadow of chestnut trees towards a church with its singularly melodious hour-bell. Thatched and very pretty, the 15th-c pub is in a charming village of similar cream-coloured cottages. *(Recommended by JP, PP, John and Fiona Merritt, John and Joan Nash, John and Sonja Newberry, Andy and Jill Kassube, the Didler, Bob and Margaret Holder, Andy Harvey, P M Wilkins, J Coote, Howard and Margaret Buchanan, Mandy and Simon King, Alan and Jill Bull, Mark and Heather Williamson, Francis Johnston, Peter Burton, Mrs S Lyons, Conor McGaughey, W W Burke)*

Free house ~ Licensees Kerstin and Nigel Burge ~ Real ale ~ Bar food (not Sun evening) ~ Restaurant ~ (01404) 841267 ~ Well behaved children in eating area of bar ~ Dogs allowed in bar ~ Open 11-3, 6-11; 12-3 Sun; closed Sun evening, 25 and 31 Dec

BUCKLAND BREWER SS4220 Map 1

Coach & Horses

Village signposted off A388 S of Monkleigh; OS Sheet 190 map reference 423206

The heavily beamed bar in this 13th-c thatched house has a bustling pubby atmosphere, comfortable seats (including a handsome antique settle), a woodburning stove in the inglenook, and maybe Harding the friendly cat – who is now 18; a good log fire also burns in the big stone inglenook of the cosy lounge. A small back room has darts and pool. Bar food includes sandwiches (from £2.95), ploughman's (£4.95), home-made curries (£7.95), daily specials such as stilton, spinach and mushroom pasta bake (£6.95), steak and mushroom in ale pie (£7.95), lamb shank in red wine and rosemary (£8.95), and locally caught skate wing with capers (£11.95), and puddings like sticky toffee pudding or lemon and lime mousse (£3.75). The restaurant is no smoking. Well kept Bass, Fullers London Pride, and a guest beer on handpump; dominoes, fruit machine, skittle alley, and piped music. There are tables on a terrace in front, and in the side garden. Please note, they no longer offer bed and breakfast. *(Recommended by Ryta Horridge, Bob and Margaret Holder, John and Sonja Newberry, the Didler, R J Walden, Simon Robinson, Michael Bayne, Francis Johnston)*

Free house ~ Licensees Oliver Wolfe and Nicola Barrass ~ Real ale ~ Bar food (not 25 Dec or evening 26 Dec) ~ Restaurant ~ (01237) 451395 ~ Children welcome ~ Dogs allowed in bar ~ Open 12-3, 6-11; 12-3, 7-10.30 Sun

BUCKLAND MONACHORUM SX4868 Map 1

Drake Manor

Off A386 via Crapstone, just S of Yelverton roundabout

Near Buckland Abbey and the lovely Garden House, this charming little pub is popular with locals and visitors. The heavily beamed public bar on the left has brocade-cushioned wall seats, prints of the village from 1905 onwards, some horse tack and a few ship badges on the wall, and a really big stone fireplace with a woodburning stove; a small door leads to a low-beamed cubby hole where children are allowed. The snug Drakes Bar has beams hung with tiny cups and big brass keys, a woodburning stove in an old stone fireplace hung with horsebrasses and stirrups, a fine stripped pine high-backed settle with a partly covered hood, and a mix of other seats around just four tables (the oval one is rather nice). On the right is a small, beamed no smoking dining room with settles and tables on the flagstoned floor. Shove-ha'penny, darts, euchre, dominoes, and fruit machine. Enjoyable bar food includes lunchtime baguettes (from £3.95), ploughman's (from £4.50), and snacks like sausage and chips (£2.95), as well as soup (£3.25), crab cakes with a lemon and dill cream dressing or home-made brie and broccoli filo parcels on a sweet pepper sauce (£3.95), home-made steak and kidney pie or roasted vegetable and feta filo tart (£6.50), chicken wrapped in bacon with a three cheese, white wine and cream sauce (£8.95), and steaks (from £9.75), with daily specials such as scallops on spinach with a light mustard and chive sauce or beef medallions with a chilli, mushroom and Guinness sauce (£9.25).Well kept Courage Best, Greene King Abbot and Sharps Doom Bar on handpump, around 70 malt whiskies, and a decent wine list with nine by the glass. The floral displays at the front of the building are very attractive all year round, and the sheltered back garden – where there are picnic-sets – is prettily planted. *(Recommended by Jacquie and Jim Jones, Sheila Brooks, Gordon Stevenson, B J Harding, John Wilson, David Crook, Brian and Bett Cox, John and Elizabeth Cox)*

Innspired Inns ~ Lease Mandy Robinson ~ Real ale ~ Bar food (12-2, 7-10(9.30 Sun)) ~ Restaurant ~ (01822) 853892 ~ Children in restaurant and in small area off main bar ~ Dogs allowed in bar ~ Open 11.30-2.30(3 Sat), 6.30-11; 12-3, 7-10.30 Sun

BUTTERLEIGH SS9708 Map 1

Butterleigh Inn

Village signposted off A396 in Bickleigh; or in Cullompton take turning by Manor House Hotel – it's the old Tiverton road, with the village eventually signposted off on the left

New bedrooms have been opened up here, the snug has been extended to create a new restaurant, and there are now two gardens and a summer house. But despite all these changes and upheavals, customers have been quick to voice their enthusiasm about the friendly welcome and enjoyable food. There's plenty to look at in its little rooms: pictures of birds and dogs, topographical prints and watercolours, a fine embroidery of the Devonshire Regiment's coat of arms, and plates hanging by one big fireplace. One room has pine dining chairs around country kitchen tables, and another has an attractive elm trestle table and sensibly placed darts; two no smoking areas. Good bar food includes sandwiches (from £2.50), home-made soup (£2.95), filled baguettes (from £3.25), ploughman's (£4.95), bacon chops (£8.95), steaks (from £9.25), and daily specials such as home-made pâté (£3.50), lemon sole with prawn sauce (£8.95), local catfish or chicken with brie and bacon (£9.95), lamb shank (£10.95), and beef wellington (£12.95). Well kept Cotleigh Tawny and Otter Ale, and a guest like O'Hanlons Yellowhammer on handpump; darts, shove-ha'penny, dominoes, and piped music. *(Recommended by Dr and Mrs P Truelove, Brian Brooks, Richard and Anne Ansell, Michael and Ann Cole, Dr D E Granger, Hugh and Peggy Holman)*

Free house ~ Licensees David and Suzanne Reed ~ Real ale ~ Bar food (not Sun evening) ~ (01884) 855407 ~ Children in family room lunchtime only ~ Dogs allowed in bar ~ Open 12-2.30, 6-11(10.30 Sun) ~ Bedrooms: £30(£35S)/£45(£50S)

If a service charge is mentioned prominently on a menu or accommodation terms, you must pay it if service was satisfactory. If service is really bad you are legally entitled to refuse to pay some or all of the service charge as compensation for not getting the service you might reasonably have expected.

CHERITON BISHOP SX7793 Map 1

Old Thatch Inn

Village signposted from A30

Friendly, professional new licensees have taken over this 16th-c pub and are very keen to keep a strong emphasis on both drinks and food, and not to be thought of as a restaurant with a bar. The lounge and the rambling beamed bar (the only place where you can smoke) are separated by a large open stone fireplace (lit in the cooler months), and have Adnams Broadside, Otter Ale, Sharps Doom Bar, and a guest like Princetown Jail Ale on handpump; several wines by the glass. The daily specials are interesting and popular: home-made carrot and coriander soup (£3), gateau of fresh local crab and cucumber with lemon mayonnaise (£5.75), tagliatelle topped with mushrooms, pepper and courgettes with garlic cream (£7.95), fillet of smoked haddock on spinach with cheese sauce and topped with a poached egg (£9.50), and pheasant breast wrapped in bacon and cranberry sauce (£10.95). Also, lunchtime sandwiches or baguettes (from £3.25), lunchtime ploughman's (from £5.50), steaks (from £11.95), and home-made puddings like hot chocolate brownie or rhubarb crumble (£4.25). The family room leads on to the terrace with a thatched water well; piped music. *(Recommended by John and Vivienne Rice, A Sadler, R J Walden, Fred and Lorraine Gill, Dr and Mrs R E S Tanner, Ron Shelton, Mayur Shah, Geoff Pidoux, Michael Butler, C W Burke, Mark Flynn, Sheila Brooks, David Crook, Mick and Moira Brummell, Adrian Johnson)*

Free house ~ Licensees David and Serena London ~ Real ale ~ Bar food ~ Restaurant ~ (01647) 24204 ~ Children in eating area of bar, restaurant and family room ~ Dogs allowed in bar ~ Open 11.30-3, 6-11; 12-3, 7-10.30 Sun; closed winter Sun evenings ~ Bedrooms: £39B/£60B

CLAYHIDON ST1615 Map 1

Merry Harriers

3 miles from M5 junction 26: head towards Wellington; turn left at first roundabout signposted Ford Street and Hemyock, then after a mile turn left signposted Ford Street; at hilltop T junction, turn left towards Chard – pub is 1½ miles on right

Customers do drop into this charmingly laid out dining pub for just a drink and feel quite comfortable doing so, although there is no doubt that there is quite a strong emphasis on the good restauranty food. As well as lunchtime sandwiches (from £4), the enjoyable dishes might include home-made soup (from £3.50), somerset brie roasted in hazelnuts with a sweet pepper confit (£4), brixham scallops in thyme and garlic butter (£5; main course £9.50), hand carved ham with free range eggs (£6.50), fresh fish in beer batter (£8.50), local squash and vegetable curry (£10), free range organic chicken breast on local creamy honeyed leeks (£11.50), local steaks (from £11.50), free range pork, cider and wild mushroom casserole (£12), confit of quantock duck on onion marmalade (£14), and home-made puddings like crème brûlée or steamed chocolate pudding filled with chocolate ganache and served with chocolate sauce (£4.50). Several small linked green-carpeted areas have comfortably cushioned pews and farmhouse chairs, lit candles in bottles, a woodburning stove with a sofa beside it, and plenty of horsey and hunting prints and local wildlife pictures. Two dining areas have a brighter feel with quarry tiles and lightly timbered white walls. You can smoke only in the bar area; dominoes and chess. Well kept Juwards (Moor) Bishops Somerset Ale, Cotleigh Barn Owl, and Otter Head on handpump, 10 wines by the glass, several bottle belgian beers, 18 malt whiskies, and local Bollhaye's farm cider and apple juice. There are two dogs, Annie who likes real ale, and Nipper who has only three legs. Picnic-sets on a small terrace, with more in a sizeable garden sheltered by shrubs and the old skittle alley; this is a good walking area. No children except on Sunday lunchtimes and must be over 6. More reports please. *(Recommended by Di and Mike Gillam, B H and J I Andrews)*

Free house ~ Licensees Barry and Chris Kift ~ Real ale ~ Bar food (not Sun evening or Mon) ~ Restaurant ~ (01823) 421270 ~ Dogs allowed in bar ~ Open 12-3, 7-11; 12-3 Sun; closed Sun evening, Mon

CLYST HYDON ST0301 Map 1

Five Bells

West of the village and just off B3176 not far from M5 junction 28

Just after we had gone to press last year, new licensees took over this most attractive thatched pub – and of course there have been some changes, but readers have been quick to voice their support. The partly no smoking bar has a bustling atmosphere, and is divided at one end into different seating areas by brick and timber pillars; china jugs hang from big horsebrass-studded beams, there are many plates lining the shelves, lots of sparkling copper and brass, and a nice mix of dining chairs around small tables (fresh flowers and evening candles in bottles), with some comfortable pink plush banquettes on a little raised area. Past the inglenook fireplace is another big (but narrower) room they call the Long Barn with a series of prints on the walls, a pine dresser at one end, and similar furnishings. Well liked bar food now includes summer sandwiches and ploughman's, soup (£3.95), game terrine (£4.95), filled baked potatoes (£5.95), ham and egg or butternut squash and feta cheese risotto (£7.95), steak and kidney suet pudding or fresh cod in beer batter (£8.95), coq au vin (£9.95), and steaks (from £10.95). Well kept Cotleigh Tawny, O'Hanlon's Yellowhammer, and Otter Bitter on handpump, and half a dozen wines by the glass; piped music. The immaculate cottagey front garden is a fine sight with its thousands of spring and summer flowers, big window boxes and pretty hanging baskets; up some steps is a sizeable flat lawn with picnic-sets, a play frame, and pleasant country views. *(Recommended by Malcolm and Jennifer Perry, Martin Jennings, N and S Alcock, J C Brittain-Long, Maurice Ribbans, Andrew and Samantha Grainger, Ann and Max Cross, R J Walden, Peter Saville, John and Sonja Newberry, Alison Hayes, Pete Hanlon, Cathryn and Richard Hicks, Dr and Mrs M W A Haward, Tim Gorringe, B H and J I Andrews, Mr and Mrs W Mills, Alan and Jill Bull, Ken and Barbara Turner, John and Joan Nash, Mark and Heather Williamson, Gene and Tony Freemantle, Mike Gorton, John and Vivienne Rice, Paul Boot, Canon Michael Bourdeaux)*

Free house ~ Licensees Mr and Mrs R Shenton ~ Real ale ~ Bar food ~ (01884) 277288 ~ Children in eating area of bar ~ Open 11.30-3, 6.30-11; 12-3, 6.30-10.30 Sun; evening opening 7(6.30 Sat) in winter

COCKWOOD SX9780 Map 1

Anchor

Off, but visible from, A379 Exeter—Torbay

Even on a chilly midweek day in winter, you have to arrive early at this extremely popular fishy place to get a table – and there's usually a queue to get in. They do two sittings in the restaurant on winter weekends and every evening in summer to cope with the crowds. There are 30 different ways of serving mussels (£7.50 normal size helping, £12.25 for a large one), 14 ways of serving scallops (from £5.75 for a starter, from £13.45 for a main course), ten ways of serving oysters (from £7.25 for a starter, from £14.25 for a main course), and four 'cakes' such as crab cakes or mussel cakes (£6.25 for a starter, £10.25 for a main course), as well as salmon steak with fresh lime and ginger (£12.50), cod fillet topped with smoked halibut with a pink smoked salmon sauce (£14.75), and a shellfish selection (£16.25). Non-fishy dishes feature as well, such as home-made soup (£3.15), sandwiches (from £3.25), home-made chicken liver pâté (£4.25), cheese and potato pie (£5.25), home-made steak and kidney pudding (£7.25), rump steak (£8.50), and children's dishes (£4.50). But despite the emphasis on food, there's still a pubby atmosphere, and they keep six real ales on handpump or tapped from the cask: Bass, Fullers London Pride, Greene King Abbot and Old Speckled Hen, Otter Ale and Wadworths 6X. Also, a rather a good wine list (12 by the glass – they do monthly wine tasting evenings September–June), 30 brandies, 90 malt whiskies, and west country cider. The small, low-ceilinged, rambling rooms have black panelling, good-sized tables in various alcoves, and a cheerful winter coal fire in the snug; the cosy restaurant is no smoking. Darts, dominoes, cribbage, fruit machine, and piped music. From the tables on the sheltered verandah you can look across the road to the bobbing yachts and crabbing boats in the harbour. *(Recommended by Ken Flawn, John and Vivienne Rice, John and Sonja Newberry, Alain and Rose Foote, J F Stackhouse, John Beeken, N and S Alcock, Cathryn and Richard Hicks, John and Marion Tyrie, David Field, Pat and Robert Watt)*

Heavitree ~ Tenants Mr Morgan and Miss Sanders ~ Real ale ~ Bar food (12-3, 6.30-10(9.30 Sun)) ~ Restaurant ~ (01626) 890203 ~ Children in restaurant ~ Dogs allowed in bar ~ Open 11-11; 12-10.30 Sun; closed evening 25 Dec

COLEFORD SS7701 Map 1

New Inn

Just off A377 Crediton—Barnstaple

It is not easy to get the balance right between a proper pub, a good restaurant, and a comfortable, well equipped inn, but this 13th-c place seems to have mastered it. It's an L-shaped building with the servery in the 'angle', and interestingly furnished areas leading off it: ancient and modern settles, spindleback chairs, plush-cushioned stone wall seats, some character tables – a pheasant worked into the grain of one – and carved dressers and chests; also, paraffin lamps, antique prints and old guns on the white walls, and landscape plates on one of the beams, with pewter tankards on another. The resident parrot Captain is chatty and entertaining. Good, interesting food using local produce includes soup (£4), filled baguettes (from £4; ciabatta with honey marinated chicken and smoked bacon £7), wild boar pâté with hawthorn berry jelly or leek, smoked bacon and applewood crumble (£5), various omelettes (from £5.25), ploughman's (from £6), chive and potato cakes with mushroom sauce (£7), creamy fish pie with herb mash (£7.50), pork sausages with redcurrant gravy and red onion confit or lamb and mint meat balls with tomato sauce and lemon couscous (£8), steaks (from £8.50), lambs liver and bacon with onion gravy (£9), pork schnitzel or beef olives (£10), daily specials, and puddings. The restaurant is no smoking. Well kept Badger Best, Ring O' Bells Bodmin Boar, and a guest beer on handpump, and quite a range of malt whiskies, ports and cognacs. Fruit machine (out of the way up by the door), and piped music. There are chairs, tables and umbrellas on decking under the willow tree along the stream, and more on the terrace. *(Recommended by Mike Gorton, Richard and Margaret Peers, Mrs Joy Griffiths, Richard and Judy Winn, DRH and KLH, Mandy and Simon King, Alan and Jill Bull, Sarah and Anthony Bussy, Mike and Mary Carter, Bob and Margaret Holder, A P Seymour, W W Burke)*

Free house ~ Licensees Paul and Irene Butt ~ Real ale ~ Bar food (till 10(9.30 Sun)) ~ Restaurant ~ (01363) 84242 ~ Children in eating area of bar and in restaurant ~ Dogs allowed in bar ~ Open 12-2.30, 6-11; 12-3, 7-10.30 Sun; closed 25 and 26 Dec ~ Bedrooms: £60B/£75B

COMBEINTEIGNHEAD SX9071 Map 1

Wild Goose

Just off unclassified coast road Newton Abbot—Shaldon, up hill in village

There's a fine range of seven well kept west country ales on handpump here, from breweries such as Archers, Harveys, RCH, St Austell, Sharps, Skinners, and Teignworthy. Also, 9 wines by the glass, over 50 malt whiskies, and two local ciders. The spacious back beamed lounge has a mix of wheelbacks, red plush dining chairs, a decent mix of tables, and french windows to the garden, with nice country views beyond; the front bar has some red Rexine seats in the window embrasures of the thick walls, flagstones in a small area by the door, some beams and standing timbers, and a step down on the right at the end, with dining chairs around the tables and a big old fireplace with an open log fire. There's a small carved oak dresser with a big white goose, cribbage, dominoes, and shove-ha'penny, and also a cosy section on the left with an old settee and comfortably well used chairs; open fires in winter. Good, reasonably priced bar food includes lunchtime snacks such as filled baguettes (from £3.75); rump steak and fried onions (£5.75), hand-made pasty (£3.95), various omelettes (from £5.25), and ploughman's (£5.95), as well as home-made soup (£3.25), chicken liver pâté (£5.75), ham and egg (£6.25), stilton and vegetable crumble or steak and kidney pie (£7.75), game sausages with redcurrant gravy and mustard mash (£7.95), whole rack of ribs (£9.95), lamb shank (£10.95), and daily specials (fresh fish is delivered daily). The garden behind this bustling pub, overlooked by the 14th-c church, has plenty of seats, and there are outdoor heaters for chillier evenings. More reports please. *(Recommended by E B Ireland, JP, PP, Mr and Mrs B Hobden, the Didler)*

Free house ~ Licensees Jerry and Kate English ~ Real ale ~ Bar food (till 10(9.30 Sun)) ~ (01626) 872241 ~ Well behaved children in eating areas ~ Dogs allowed in bar ~ Open 11.30-2.30(3 Sat), 6.30-11; 12-2.30, 7-10.30 Sun

CORNWORTHY SX8255 Map 1

Hunters Lodge

Off A381 Totnes—Kingsbridge ½ mile S of Harbertonford, turning left at Washbourne; can also be reached direct from Totnes, on the Ashprington—Dittisham road

As we went to press, new licensees were on the point of taking over this well liked pub. We are keeping our fingers crossed that the new people might stay for a while as there have been several owner changes over the last few years. The small low-ceilinged bar has two rooms with an engagingly pubby feel and a combination of wall seats, settles, and captain's chairs around heavy elm tables; there's also a small and pretty cottagey dining room with a good log fire in its big 17th-c stone fireplace. Half the pub has been no smoking. Good bar food has included lunchtime sandwiches and ploughman's (£5.75), plus salmon and dill fritters (£4.95), fresh local scallops (£5.25; main course £11.95), baked avocado and crab (£5.95), roasted vegetable tortilla wrap or battered cod (£6.95), smoked ham and eggs (£7.25), moroccan lamb casserole (£8.45), seafood spaghetti in a spicy thai sauce (£9.95), calves liver with bacon and onions (£12.95), and steaks (from £12.95). Well kept Teignworthy Reel Ale and a seasonal ale, and a guest like Smiles Frolic on handpump, 60 malt whiskies, and Hogwash local cider. Dominoes, cribbage and piped music. In summer, there is plenty of room to sit outside, either at the picnic-sets on a big lawn or on the flower-filled terrace closer to the pub. *(Recommended by N and S Alcock, Mr and Mrs N Smith, Jeffrey Stackhouse, Joe and Marion Mandeville, Len Beattie, Brian and Bett Cox, OPUS)*

Free house ~ Licensees J Reen and G Rees ~ Real ale ~ Bar food ~ Restaurant ~ (01803) 732204 ~ Children in eating area of bar and in family room ~ Dogs allowed in bar ~ Open 11.30-2.30, 6.30-11; 12-3, 7-10.30 Sun

CULMSTOCK ST1013 Map 1

Culm Valley

B3391, off A38 E of M5 junction 27

Interesting and even a little quirky (the landlord's own words), this village inn at first glance looks a bit scruffy. Inside, it's actually rather civilised and run by accommodating and friendly people. The licensee and his brother import wines from smaller french vineyards, so you can count on a few of those (they offer 50 wines by the glass), as well as some unusual french fruit liqueurs, somerset cider brandies, good sherries and madeira, local ciders, and an excellent range of real ales tapped from the cask. You'll usually find between five and nine mostly local brews, such as Archers Spirit of St George, Cotleigh Cuckoo or Peregrine, Glastonbury Excalibur, O'Hanlons Yellowhammer, Otter Bright and Teignworthy Old Moggie, but the choice can swell to 17 during their occasional beer festivals. The very good bar food usually comes with a choice of helping size, and might include home-made soup (£4), sandwiches (from £4), home-made real ale sausages (£5), ploughman's (from £5), wild mushrooms with samphire (£6; main course £12), razor shell clams in garlic butter (£7; £14 main course), scallops with a pomegranate and molasses dressing (£8; main course £16), lamb braised in coriander, ginger and garlic (£9), local cracked crab (from £10.15), and puddings such as crème brûlée, sticky toffee pudding or chocolate marquise with pistachio nut sauce (£3.50); their tapas are very popular (£6; £12; £18). There's a good thriving mix of locals and visitors in the salmon-coloured bar, which has well worn upholstered chairs and stools, a big fireplace with some china above it, newspapers, and a long stripped wooden bar counter; further along is a dining room with chalkboard menu, and a small room at the front. Cribbage and dominoes. Old photographs show how the railway line used to run through what's now the car park. Outside, tables are very attractively set overlooking the bridge and the River Culm. The gents' is in an outside yard. *(Recommended by Simon Watkins, D and S Price, Brian and Li Jobson, Mrs V C Greany, June and Peter Shamash, Paul and Philippa Ward, Conor McGaughey)*

Free house ~ Licensee Richard Hartley ~ Real ale ~ Bar food (may not do food Sun evenings) ~ Restaurant ~ No credit cards ~ (01884) 840354 ~ Children welcome away from bar ~ Dogs welcome ~ Open 12-3, 6-11(10.30 Sun); maybe all day throughout the year ~ Bedrooms: £30B/£55B

DALWOOD ST2400 Map 1

Tuckers Arms

Village signposted off A35 Axminster—Honiton

A new large covered pergola with outdoor heating has been put up here which is ideal for families or customers with dogs, and in summer the hanging baskets, flowering tubs and window boxes in front of the building are lovely. Inside, the fine flagstoned bar has a lot of atmosphere, plenty of beams, a random mixture of dining chairs, window seats, and wall settles (including a high-backed winged black one), and a log fire in the inglenook fireplace. The back bar has an enormous collection of miniature bottles. Popular, well liked bar food at lunchtime includes soup (£2.95), toasted rustic bread topped with things such as spanish meat balls and chorizo sausage or bacon, black pudding and fried egg, and open sandwiches or ploughman's (from £4.95); in the evening they offer two courses for £15.95 or three courses for £18.95 with choices like grilled goats cheese with walnuts and salad, smoked salmon with citrus salad, supreme of duck with orange glaze, rack of lamb, whole monkfish tail with tarragon cream and brandy, and sirloin steak with wild mushrooms and port. The restaurant is no smoking. Well kept Courage Directors, Otter Ale and Salopian Firefly on handpump, and a dozen wines by the glass. Skittle alley and piped music. Parts of this pretty cream-washed thatched old hunting lodge date back to the 13th c, which makes it the oldest building in the parish. *(Recommended by Andy Harvey, John and Vivienne Rice, Bob and Margaret Holder, R T and J C Moggridge, James A Waller, Mrs C Lintott, Brian and Bett Cox, Mark Flynn, Pete Walker)*

Free house ~ Licensees David and Kate Beck ~ Real ale ~ Bar food ~ Restaurant ~ (01404) 881342 ~ Children in restaurant and family room ~ Open 12-3, 6.30-11; 12-3, 7-10.30 Sun; closed 26 Dec ~ Bedrooms: £36.50S/£59.50S

DARTMOUTH SX8751 Map 1

Cherub

Higher Street

This 14th-c Grade II* listed building has shown a resilient attitude to the progress of time: it survived an 1864 fire which destroyed the southern end of the street, and the World War II bombing which destroyed the north side; hence it's the oldest building around here. In summer particularly, it's a striking sight with each of the two heavily timbered upper floors jutting further out than the one below, and very pretty hanging baskets. The bustling bar has tapestried seats under creaky heavy beams, leaded-light windows, a big stone fireplace, and Cains Bitter, Sharps Doom Bar and Speical, and a guest named for the pub on handpump; quite a few malt whiskies and several wines by the glass. Upstairs is the fine, low-ceilinged and no smoking restaurant; piped music. Bar food includes soup (£3.50), sandwiches (from £3.50), smoked haddock in white wine sauce and topped with cheese (£6), steak, mushroom and Guinness pie or curry of the day (£7.95), and steak and chips (£10.95). Children over 10 may be allowed in the restaurant, but best to check ahead. It does get very crowded at peak times. *(Recommended by Nick Vernon,*

Graham and Rose Ive, Steve Whalley, JP, PP, Tony Middis, John and Laney Woods, Comus and Sarah Elliott, Ann and Bob Westbrook, DM, David Swift, Margaret and Roy Randle, Ken Flawn, Margaret and Peter Brierley, David Carr)

Free house ~ Licensee Laurie Scott ~ Real ale ~ Bar food ~ Restaurant ~ (01803) 832571 ~ Dogs allowed in bar ~ Live blues winter Sun evenings ~ Open 11-11; 12-10.30 Sun; 11-2.30, 5-11 in winter

DODDISCOMBSLEIGH SX8586 Map 1

Nobody Inn ★★

Village signposted off B3193, opposite northernmost Christow turn-off

With well kept real ales, probably the best pub wine cellar in the country, an amazing choice of whiskies, and an exceptional cheese board, it's not surprising that so many of our readers enjoy this fine old place. There are around 800 wines by the bottle and 25 by the glass kept oxidation-free, and they hold tutored tastings (they also sell wine retail, and the good tasting-notes in their detailed list are worth the £3.50 it costs – anyway refunded if you buy more than £30-worth). Well kept RCH East Street Cream, Sharps Doom Bar, and a beer named for the pub from Branscombe on handpump or tapped from the cask, 200 whiskies, and local farm ciders. The two rooms of the lounge bar have handsomely carved antique settles, windsor and wheelback chairs, benches, carriage lanterns hanging from the beams, and guns and hunting prints in a snug area by one of the big inglenook fireplaces. Bar food can be good and might include home-made soup (£3.90; their special one is very popular), duck liver pâté, thai prawn cakes with sweet chilli sauce or goats cheese roulade with courgette pickle (all £4.90), ploughman's, garlic pork sausages with onion gravy or fennel and tarragon crumble (£6.90), saffron, smoked haddock and fennel risotto (£7.50), steak and kidney suet pudding or braised lamb shank in port sauce (£9.50), bass fillets with sauerkraut and peanut oil dressing (£10.50), and puddings like orange and cardamom brûlée, stem ginger pudding with ginger sauce or marbled chocolate marquise with clotted cream (all £4.50); half a dozen good West Country cheeses from an incredible choice of around 40 (£5.90; you can buy them to take away as well). The restaurant is no smoking. There are picnic-sets on the terrace with views of the surrounding wooded hill pastures. The medieval stained-glass in the local church is some of the best in the West Country. No children are allowed inside the pub. *(Recommended by R J Walden, A Sadler, J Wedel, John and Sonja Newberry, J L Wedel, JP, PP, Steve Whalley, DRH and KLH, Fred and Lorraine Gill, Mr and Mrs Richard Hanks, Duncan Cloud, Ann and Colin Hunt, the Didler, B N F and M Parkin, Dr and Mrs Rod Holcombe, R M Corlett, Andrew Shore, Maria Williams, Stuart Turner, Betsy Brown, Nigel Flook, Terry and Linda Moseley, N and S Alcock, Lucy Bishop, Cathryn and Richard Hicks, Bill and Jessica Ritson, J P Marland, Dr Martin Owton, John Close, Patrick Hancock, Tim and Rosemary Wells, Andrea Rampley, Mr and Mrs W Mills, John Urquhart, David Handforth, Michael Butler, John and Christine Lowe, Mr and Mrs Taylor, Jim and Maggie Cowell, JHW, Nick and Meriel Cox, Canon Michael Bourdeaux, Simon Rodway, D S Jackson; also in the* Good Hotel Guide*)*

Free house ~ Licensee Nick Borst-Smith ~ Real ale ~ Bar food (till 10) ~ Restaurant ~ (01647) 252394 ~ Open 12-2.30, 6-11; 12-3, 7-10.30 Sun; closed 25 and 26 Dec, 1 Jan ~ Bedrooms: £25(£39B)/£35(£75B)

DOLTON SS5712 Map 1

Union

B3217

New licensees took over this pleasant village inn just before we went to press, so we are keeping our fingers crossed that things won't change too much. The little lounge bar has a cushioned window seat, two cushioned benches, and some dark pine country chairs with brocaded cushions, as well as dagging shears, tack, country prints, and brass shell cases. On the right, and served by the same stone bar counter, is another bar with a chatty atmosphere and liked by locals: heavy black beams hung with brasses, antique housekeeper's chairs, a small settle snugged into the wall, and various dining chairs on the squared patterned carpet; the big stone fireplace has some brass around it, and on the walls are two land-felling saws, antlers, some engravings, and a whip. Bar food includes sandwiches, home-made soup (£2.50), filled baked potatoes (from £3.95), ham and eggs (£4.25), home-made cottage pie or lasagne (£4.95), other home-made dishes (from £4.95), and steaks (£8.95); the restaurant is no smoking. Well kept St Austell Tribute and Teignworthy Reel Ale on handpump, and decent wines; piped music. Outside on a small patch of grass in front of the building are some rustic tables and chairs. More reports on the new regime, please. *(Recommended by Mrs E A Brace, A C and B M Laing, Janice and Phil Waller, Lloyd Moon)*

Free house ~ Licensees Mr P Thomas, Miss A Thomas, and Mrs D Thomas ~ Real ale ~ Bar food (not Weds) ~ Restaurant ~ (01805) 804633 ~ Children in eating area of bar and restaurant ~ Dogs allowed in bar and bedrooms ~ Open 11-3, 6-11; 12-10.30 Sun; closed Weds ~ Bedrooms: £35S/£55S(£65B)

DREWSTEIGNTON SX7390 Map 1

Drewe Arms

Signposted off A30 NW of Moretonhampstead

As we went to press, we heard that this unpretentious and friendly old thatched pub was up for sale. It's such a delightful place that we are obviously hoping the new people will make few, if any, changes. The small, unspoilt room on the left has a serving hatch and basic seats, and the room on the right with its assorted tables and chairs has a log fire, and is not much bigger. Well kept Bass, Gales HSB, Otter Bitter, and a summer guest kept on racks in the tap room behind, and local cider. At the back is a sizeable eating area, with well liked food (and unchanged prices) such as a huge bowl of soup with a loaf of bread (£3.50), good sandwiches (from £4.50), a proper ploughman's (from £5.95), pork and sage sausage with bubble and squeak, a vegetarian dish, big cod fillet in beer batter or crispy belly of pork on tatties and leeks with apple sauce (all £7.95), and shank of lamb with an orange and red wine sauce (£12). The restaurant is no smoking. Dominoes, cribbage, darts, shove-ha'penny, and skittle alley. Castle Drogo nearby (open for visits) looks medieval, though it was actually built earlier last century. It's best to phone to see if children are allowed inside. *(Recommended by DAV, Barry Steele-Perkins, Anthony Longden, JP, PP, Ann and Colin Hunt, John and Sonja Newberry, the Didler, D I Lucas, Tim and Carolyn Lowes, Di and Mike Gillam, Rose, Len Banister, Peter Craske, Mayur Shah, John Hale, Revd R P Tickle, Andy and Glenda Matheson, Mrs C Lintott, Jennifer Hutchings, Michael and Margaret Slater, OPUS, Mark Flynn)*

Enterprise ~ Real ale ~ Bar food ~ Restaurant ~ (01647) 281224 ~ Dogs allowed in bar ~ Open 11-2.30, 6-11; 12-3, 7-10.30 Sun ~ Bedrooms: /£70B

EAST BUDLEIGH SY0684 Map 1

Sir Walter Raleigh

High Street

In a pretty thatch-and-cob village, this charming pub is run by a warmly welcoming licensee. There's a low-beamed bar with lots of books on shelves, a cosily chatty atmosphere, and well kept Adnams Broadside, Otter Bitter and Charles Wells Bombardier on handpump; reasonably priced wines. The attractive restaurant down a step from the bar is no smoking. Lunchtime bar food is very good and using fresh local produce might include sandwiches (from £2.25), home-made soup (£2.95), ploughman's (£4.75), home-made sausages (£4.75 with chips, £6.95 with chive mash and onion gravy), extremely popular steak and kidney pie with a herb and suet crust or roasted vegetable pancake on plum tomatoes topped with mozzarella (£7.95), medallions of pork in a spicy cream sauce (£8.95), plenty of local fish such as sole, plaice, bass, lobster and crab (from £9.95), steaks (from £9.25), and home-made puddings like bakewell tart, belgian chocolate mousse or crème brûlée (£3.25). There's a fine church with a unique collection of carved oak bench ends, and the pub is handy for Bicton Park gardens. Raleigh himself was born at nearby Hayes Barton, and educated in a farmhouse 300 yards away. Parking is about 100 yards from the pub. No children. *(Recommended by Dr and Mrs M E Wilson, Mike and Wendy Proctor, John and Doris Couper, M G Hart)*

Enterprise ~ Lease Lindsay Mason ~ Real ale ~ Bar food (lunchtime) ~ Restaurant ~ (01395) 442510 ~ Dogs allowed in bar ~ Open 12-3, 6-11; 12-3, 7-10.30 Sun

EXETER SX9292 Map 1

Imperial £

New North Road (St David's Hill on Crediton/Tiverton road, above St David's Station)

To get the best out of this early 19th-c mansion, head for the light and airy former orangery with the huge glassy fan of its end wall lightly mirrored – when the sun streams through in the early evening, it really is quite special. The rest of the building is rather spread out with various different areas including a couple of little clubby side bars, a left-hand bar that looks into the orangery, and a fine ex-ballroom filled with elaborate plasterwork and gilding brought here in the 1920s from Haldon House (a Robert Adam stately home that was falling on hard times). One area is no smoking. The furnishings give Wetherspoons' usual solid well spaced comfort, and there are plenty of interesting pictures and other things to look at. Well kept and very cheap Bass, Courage Directors, Greene King Abbot, Shepherd Neame Spitfire, Theakstons Best, and changing guests such as Everards Tiger, Exmoor Stag and Hop Back Summer Lightning on handpump; friendly, efficient staff – even when the place is hopping with students. Standard bar food includes filled panini (£2.99), battered cod or ham and eggs (£4.55), chicken caesar salad (£5.05), mediterranean pasta bake or sausages and mash (£5.25), burgers (£5.99; after 5pm), barbecue chicken melt (£6.09), steaks (from £6.35), and puddings. The attractive cobbled courtyard in front has elegant garden furniture, and there are plenty of picnic-sets in the grounds. *(Recommended by Mike Gorton, Tim and Carolyn Lowes, Steve Crick, Helen Preston, JP, PP, the Didler, Joe Green, Jim and Maggie Cowell, Dr and Mrs A K Clarke, Roger Huggins, Tom and Alex McLean, Pete Walker)*

Wetherspoons ~ Managers Val Docherty and Paul Knott ~ Real ale ~ Bar food (all day) ~ (01392) 434050 ~ Children in family area only until 6pm ~ Open 10-11; 11-10.30 Sun

EXMINSTER SX9487 Map 1

Turf Hotel ★

Follow the signs to the Swan's Nest, signposted from A739 S of village, then continue to end of track, by gates; park, and walk right along canal towpath – nearly a mile; there's a fine seaview out to the mudflats at low tide

The cheerful, caring licensees of this isolated pub work really hard to make this the friendly place it is. On a lovely sunny day, a trip here makes a really memorable excursion. You cannot reach it by car. You must either walk (which takes about 20 minutes along the ship canal) or cycle, and there's a 60-seater boat which brings people down the Exe estuary from Topsham quay (15 minute trip, adults £3, child £2); there's also a canal boat from Countess Wear Swing Bridge every lunchtime. Best to phone the pub for all sailing times. For those arriving in their own boat there is a large pontoon as well as several moorings. The decking area with outdoor rotisserie for chicken and pig roasts and outside bar is very popular. Inside, the pleasantly airy bar has church pews, wooden chairs and alcove seats on the polished bare floorboards, and pictures and old photographs of the pub and its characters over the years on the walls; woodburning stove and antique gas fire. From the bay windows there are views out to the mudflats (full of gulls and waders at low tide). Good bar food (using as much local produce as possible) includes a big choice of sandwiches, toasties and filled baked potatoes (from £2.80; bacon and egg toastie £4.50; crab sandwich £5.50), as well as home-made soup (£3.75), hummous and cracked olives (£4.25), a tart of the day (£6.25), shepherd's pie (£7), chilli nachos (£7.50), thai green chicken and coconut curry (£8.50), and puddings like fruit crumble or treacle pudding (from £3.80). The dining room is no smoking. Well kept Otter Bitter, Bright, and Ale, and a guest beer on handpump, Green

Valley and Dragon Tears farm ciders, locally pressed apple juice, and cappuccino and espresso coffee; cribbage, dominoes, and piped music. The garden has a children's play area built using a lifeboat from a liner that sank off the Scilly Isles around 100 years ago. Please note, they no longer do bedrooms, though you could hire their Red Indian teepee. *(Recommended by Mike Gorton, JP, PP, Minda and Stanley Alexander, Jenny Perkins, the Didler, Ken Flawn, John Beeken, Mark and Heather Williamson, David Carr, Alain and Rose Foote)*

Free house ~ Licensees Clive and Ginny Redfern ~ Real ale ~ Bar food (12-2.30(3 summer), 7-9.30; not Sun evening) ~ (01392) 833128 ~ Children welcome ~ Dogs welcome ~ Open 11.30-11; 11.30-10.30 Sun; closed Nov-Feb

HARBERTON SX7758 Map 1

Church House

Village signposted from A381 just S of Totnes

Parts of this ancient village pub may in fact be Norman and some of the oldest sections have benefited from being hidden for centuries. The open-plan bar has some magnificent medieval oak panelling, and the latticed glass on the back wall is almost 700 years old and one of the earliest examples of non-ecclesiastical glass in the country. Furnishings include attractive 17th- and 18th-c pews and settles, candles, and a large inglenook fireplace with a woodburning stove; one half of the room is set out for eating. The family room is no smoking. Under the new licensee, bar food includes sandwiches, home-made soup (£3.50), garlic and cheese mushrooms (£4.50), local sausages with mustard mash and onion gravy (£6.50), a fry-up or leek, stilton and potato gratin (£7.95), salads (from £7.95), fresh fillet of plaice (£9.50), local lamb steak with a port, rosemary and redcurrant sauce (£9.75), and local rump steak (from £10.50). Well kept Butcombe Bitter, Courage Best, Marstons Pedigree, and St Austell Tribute on handpump, farm cider, 14 wines by the glass, and several malt whiskies; piped music, darts, cribbage, and dominoes. More reports please. *(Recommended by Comus and Sarah Elliott, John and Sonja Newberry, Mr and Mrs C R Little, JHW)*

Coast & Country Inns ~ Licensee Martin Ward ~ Real ale ~ Bar food ~ (01803) 863707 ~ Children in family room ~ Dogs welcome ~ Open 12-2.30(3 Sat), 6-11; 12-3, 7-11 Sat ~ Bedrooms: £30B/£60B

HAYTOR VALE SX7677 Map 1

Rock ★

Haytor signposted off B3387 just W of Bovey Tracey, on good moorland road to Widecombe

In the evening, there's no doubt that many of the customers coming to this civilised and neatly kept place are here to enjoy the very good restauranty food or are residents. But at lunchtime, readers drop in after a walk or a drive around the moors for a drink and a more informal meal. The two communicating, partly panelled bar rooms have polished antique tables with candles and fresh flowers, old-fashioned prints and decorative plates on the walls, and warming winter log fires (the main fireplace has a fine Stuart fireback); most of the pub is no smoking. At lunchtime, the well liked bar food includes home-made soup (£3.50), sandwiches (from £4.50; hand-made crisps come too), chicken liver pâté with red onion marmalade (£5.50), dartmouth smoked salmon and prawns, chicken curry or ploughman's (£7.95), steak and kidney suet pudding or wild mushroom and hazelnut risotto (£8.95), and seafood fishcakes (£9.95); evening choices such as local mussels in chilli, lemon and parsley (£6.95), beef fillet with pancetta, herb salad and hazelnut dressing (£8.50), chicken on roasted vegetables with red pepper dressing or seared fillet of bream on herb risotto with sauce vierge (£12.95), lamb shank on spring onion mash with redcurrant rosemary jus or chargrilled rib-eye steak with roquefort butter (£13.95), and puddings like treacle and walnut tart with clotted cream, chocolate and orange truffle cake or apple bread and butter pudding (from £4.50). Well kept Bass, Greene King Old Speckled Hen, and St Austell

Dartmoor Best on handpump, and several malt whiskies. In summer, the pretty, large garden opposite the inn is a popular place to sit and there are some tables and chairs on a small terrace next to the pub itself. Parking is not always easy. Although they are open all day, if it has been a particularly busy lunchtime, the licensee tells us they might occasionally stop service at standard times. To be sure, it might be best to phone ahead. *(Recommended by Mike Gorton, Alan and Paula McCully, Richard and Margaret Peers, DF, NF, J F Stackhouse, Margaret Ross, Alun Howells, N and S Alcock, Betsy Brown, Nigel Flook, Brian England, Andrea Rampley, Ron Gentry, Val and Alan Green, Neil and Beverley Gardner, John and Marion Tyrie, Mark and Heather Williamson, Peter Cole, Brian and Bett Cox, Mark Flynn)*

Free house ~ Licensee Christopher Graves ~ Real ale ~ Bar food (not 25 Dec) ~ Restaurant ~ (01364) 661305 ~ Children in family room ~ Dogs allowed in bedrooms ~ Open 11-11; 12-10.30 Sun; closed 25 Dec ~ Bedrooms: £65S/£75.50S(£85.95B)

HOLBETON SX6150 Map 1

Mildmay Colours

Signposted off A379 W of A3121 junction

In a quiet village, this is a friendly pub with a good mix of locals and holidaymakers – and a new licensee this year. The bar has various horse and racing pictures, and the framed racing colours of Lord Mildmay-White on the partly stripped stone and partly white walls, plenty of bar stools as well as cushioned wall seats and wheelback chairs on the turkey carpet, and a tile-sided woodburning stove; an arch leads to a smaller, similarly decorated family area with pool, fruit machine, TV, pinball, cribbage, dominoes, and a basket of toys. One area is no smoking; piped music. Though the brewery has moved away, they still offer Mildmay Colours and a guest beer such as Skinners Betty Stogs on handpump; local farm cider. Bar food includes sandwiches and filled baguettes (from £3.10), home-made soup (£3.20), home-made chicken liver pâté (£3.75), ham and egg (£4.10), local sausages (£4.90), ploughman's (from £4.95), and daily specials such as local smoked trout (£7.95) or grilled tuna with thai chilli noodles (£9.95). The well kept back garden has picnic-sets, a swing, and an aviary, and there's a small front terrace with lots of colourful flowers. More reports please. *(Recommended by Laura Wilson, Esther and John Sprinkle, John and Joan Calvert, John Evans, Stephen and Jean Curtis, Richard and Anne Ansell, B J Harding, Alice Harper)*

Free house ~ Licensee George Suttie ~ Real ale ~ Bar food ~ Restaurant ~ No credit cards ~ (01752) 830248 ~ Children in restaurant and family room ~ Dogs welcome ~ Open 11-3, 6-11; 12-3, 7-10.30 Sun ~ Bedrooms: £35B/£55B

HOLNE SX7069 Map 1

Church House

Signed off B3357 W of Ashburton

There are fine moorland views from the pillared porch here (where regulars tend to gather), and plenty of surrounding walks – the short quarter-hour one from the Newbridge National Trust car park to the pub is rather fine. Inside, the lower bar has stripped pine panelling and an 18th-c curved elm settle, and is separated from the lounge bar by a 16th-c heavy oak partition; open log fires in both rooms. Bar food includes lunchtime filled baked potatoes (from £4), sandwiches and baguettes (from £4.25), and ploughman's (from £5.50), as well as soup (£3.75), home-made pâté (from £4.50), and favourites like steak in ale pie or rabbit casserole (£8); more elaborate choices in the evening. The restaurant and eating area of the bar are no smoking. Well kept Butcombe Bitter, Summerskills Best Bitter and Teignworthy Reel Ale on handpump, a dozen wines by the glass, and organic cider, apple juice and ginger beer; darts. Morris men and clog dancers in the summer. Charles Kingsley (of *Water Babies* fame) was born in the village. *(Recommended by Len Banister, Neil and Beverley Gardner, Gene and Tony Freemantle, Simon and Jane Williams)*

Free house ~ Licensee J Silk ~ Real ale ~ Bar food ~ Restaurant ~ (01364) 631208 ~ Children in eating area of bar and restaurant ~ Dogs welcome ~ Open 12-2.30(3 Sat),

7-11(10.30 in winter); 12-3, 7-10.30 Sun; closed Mon in winter ~ Bedrooms: £33S/£55(£66B)

HORNDON SX5280 Map 1

Elephants Nest

If coming from Okehampton on A386 turn left at Mary Tavy Inn, then left after about ½ mile; pub signposted beside Mary Tavy Inn, then Horndon signposted; on the Ordnance Survey Outdoor Leisure Map it's named as the New Inn

This is an isolated old pub on the lower slopes of Dartmoor, with benches on the spacious lawn in front that look over dry-stone walls to the pastures and the rougher moorland above; they have their own cricket pitch. Inside, the bar has a good log fire, flagstones, and a beam-and-board ceiling; there are two other rooms plus a no smoking dining room and garden room. Well kept Palmers IPA and Copper and St Austell HSD, and a guest such as Exmoor Gold, Otter Bright or Teignworthy Beachcomber on handpump, ten wines by the glass, farm cider, and proper tea and coffee; friendly service. Enjoyable bar food includes home-made soup (£3.50), sandwiches (from £3.95), ploughman's or local cheese and biscuits (£5.25), ham and egg (£5.75), home-made sausage with onion gravy (£6.95), cajun chicken (£8.25), leek and cheese pie (£8.95), sirloin steak or duck breast with cassis sauce (£12.25), pink bream in wine and cream (£12.95), home-made puddings (£4.25), and a choice of Sunday roasts (£8.95); children's dishes (£3.50).

(Recommended by DAV, John and Marion Tyrie, Jacquie and Jim Jones, Len Banister, Oliver and Sue Rowell, Neil and Beverley Gardner, Mick and Moira Brummell, JHW)

Free house ~ Licensee Peter Wolfes ~ Real ale ~ Bar food (12-2.15, 6.30-9) ~ (01822) 810273 ~ Children in dining room only ~ Dogs allowed in bar ~ Folk music first and third Weds of month ~ Open 12-3, 6.30-11; closed Sun evening, all day Mon

HORNS CROSS SS3823 Map 1

Hoops

A39 Clovelly—Bideford

In summer, the flowering window boxes of this picturesque thatched 13th-c inn are very pretty, and there's an attractive sheltered central courtyard with lots of flowering tubs and baskets. Inside, the oak-beamed bar has an ancient well set into the floor, paintings and old photographs of the pub on the walls, cushioned window seats and oak settles, and logs burning in big inglenook fireplaces; leading off here is a small similarly furnished room with another fireplace. The restaurant and part of the bar are no smoking. Well kept Greene King Old Speckled Hen, Jollyboat Mainbrace, a beer named for the pub from Burrington Brewery, and up to three summer guest beers tapped from the cask; lots of malt whiskies. Bar food at lunchtime includes sandwiches (from £3.95), ploughman's (from £4.75), and their special ham, cheese and egg toast (£6.50) or cumberland sausages (£6.50); also, home-made soup (£3.90), chilli pasta with chargrilled king prawns, tomatoes and basil (£6.90), beer battered cod (£8.90), lambs liver with crispy bacon and onions (£9.50), pasta with smoked cheese, asparagus and sun-dried tomatoes (£9.75), half shoulder of lamb (£12.50), local cod fillet with herb crust and smoked bacon and caper sauce (£12.50), steaks (from £12.50), and daily specials like fillet of grilled brill with pesto dressing (£11.50) or rack of lamb with rhubarb compote (£12.50); service can slow down at peak times. Piped music, darts, and TV.

(Recommended by the Didler, Brian and Bett Cox, Liz Webb, Tom Evans, Ryta Horridge, David Gibbs, Dr and Mrs A K Clarke, Sebastian and Paris Leach, W W Burke)

Free house ~ Licensee Gay Marriott ~ Real ale ~ Bar food (12-3.30, 6-9.30; all day weekends) ~ Restaurant ~ (01237) 451222 ~ Well behaved children in eating area of bar until 8pm; over 12 in restaurant ~ Dogs allowed in bar ~ Open 11-11; 12-10.30 Sun; closed 25 Dec ~ Bedrooms: £60B/£90B

Pubs brewing their own beers are listed at the back of the book.

IDDESLEIGH SS5708 Map 1

Duke of York ★ 🍷 🛏

B3217 Exbourne—Dolton

This is a smashing pub and very much enjoyed by a good mix of customers. The bar is full of friendly locals (plenty of chat and no noisy games machines or piped music), the food is first rate, and it's a nice place to stay with excellent breakfasts. The bar has a lot of character, with rocking chairs by the roaring log fire, cushioned wall benches built into the wall's black-painted wooden dado, stripped tables, and other homely country furnishings, and well kept Adnams Broadside, Cotleigh Tawny and a guest such as Sharps Doom Bar tapped from the cask; freshly squeezed orange and pink grapefruit juice, and 10 wines by the glass. Generous helpings of good bar food include sandwiches, home-made soup such as pea and mint (£2.25 small, £4 large), sandwiches (from £4), chicken liver and brandy pâté (£5), grilled or battered fish and chips (£5.50; large £7.50), ham and eggs (£5), delicious scallops wrapped in smoked bacon or crab mayonnaise (£5.50 small, £9 large), cottage pie or ploughman's (£6), vegetable korma, smoked haddock or beef in Guinness (£7), steak and kidney pudding (£8.50), and double lamb chop with rosemary and garlic gravy (£9); it can get a bit cramped at peak times. Cribbage, dominoes, shove-ha'penny, and darts. Through a small coach arch is a little back garden with some picnic-sets. Fishing nearby. *(Recommended by Mike Gorton, Roy Smith, Mike Peck, M and D Toms, Steve Crick, Helen Preston, JP, PP, David and Pauline Brenner, R J Walden, Andrew and Samantha Grainger, Anthony Longden, Theo, Anne and Jane Gaskin, Ron and Sheila Corbett, Richard Till, John and Marion Tyrie, Michael and Ann Cole, JHW, Jacquie and Jim Jones, the Didler, Peter Craske)*

Free house ~ Licensees Jamie Stuart and Pippa Hutchinson ~ Real ale ~ Bar food (all day) ~ Restaurant ~ (01837) 810253 ~ Children welcome ~ Dogs welcome ~ Open 11-11; 12-10.30 Sun ~ Bedrooms: £30B/£60B

KINGSTON SX6347 Map 1

Dolphin 🛏

Off B3392 S of Modbury (can also be reached from A379 W of Modbury)

Several knocked-through beamed rooms in this quietly set 16th-c inn have a good mix of customers, and a relaxed, welcoming atmosphere – no noisy games machines or piped music. There are amusing drawings and photographs on the walls and rustic tables and cushioned seats and settles around their bared stone walls; half the bar area and the family room are no smoking. Bar food includes home-made soup (£3.25), sandwiches, (from £3.25), smoked mackerel mousse with gooseberry sauce (£4.75), ploughman's (£5.25), home-cooked smoked gammon and egg (£6.95), home-made crab bake or a pie of the day (£7.95), and daily specials such as wild venison in port or fresh lemon sole. Well kept Courage Best, Sharps Doom Bar, Ushers Founders and Wadworths 6X on handpump. Outside, there are tables and swings. Half a dozen tracks lead down to the sea and unspoilt Wonwell Beach about a mile and a half away. *(Recommended by Rod and Chris Pring, Angus Lyon, Tim and Carolyn Lowes, Mrs V Hyndman, Stephen and Jean Curtis, Richard and Anne Ansell, Mrs C Longdon, Alice Harper, Alan and Anne Driver)*

InnSpired ~ Lease Janice Male ~ Real ale ~ Bar food (12-2(2.30 Sun), 6-9; not winter Mon) ~ (01548) 810314 ~ Children welcome ~ Open 11-3, 6-11; 12-3, 6.30(7 in winter)-10.30 Sun; 12-2.30, 6-11 in winter ~ Bedrooms: £42.50S/£58S

LITTLEHEMPSTON SX8162 Map 1

Tally Ho!

Signposted off A381 NE of Totnes

This little pub is run by a father and his two daughters which gives a friendly, relaxed feel to the place. There are neatly kept and cosy rooms with low beams, an interesting mix of chairs and settles (many antique and with comfortable cushions), and fresh flowers and candles on the tables. The bare stone walls are covered with porcelain, brass, copperware, stuffed wildlife, old swords, and shields and hunting horns and so forth. Well liked bar food includes lunchtime snacks such as sandwiches (from £3.25), ploughman's or sausage and chips (£4.95), and lasagne (£6.95), plus a home-made cream soup (£2.95), spicy crab cakes (£4.25), garlic mushrooms or home-made chicken liver pâté with onion marmalade (£4.50), home-made steak and kidney pie (£7.95), gammon topped with cheese and served with egg or pineapple (£8.95), chargrilled lamb chops with redcurrant and rosemary sauce or grilled tuna steak with a crab and brandy cream sauce (£9.95), roasted chicken with butter-fried leeks and a white wine and bacon sauce (£10.95), steaks (from £10.95), and roast duck breast with raspberry sauce (£10.95) or tuna steak with a crushed black pepper crust with lemon sauce (£11.95). Two well kept changing ales like Greene King IPA or Charles Wells Bombardier on handpump; piped music. The four cats are called Monica, Thomas, Ellie and Tiggy. The terrace is full of flowers in summer. More reports please. *(Recommended by Pamela and Merlyn Horswell)*

Free house ~ Licensees P Saint, T Saint and L Saint ~ Real ale ~ Bar food ~ Restaurant ~ (01803) 862316 ~ Children in eating area of bar ~ Dogs allowed in bar ~ Open 12-2.30(3 Sat), 6-11; 12-3, 7-10.30 Sun; closed 25 Dec ~ Bedrooms: £50S/£60S

LOWER ASHTON SX8484 Map 1

Manor Inn

Ashton signposted off B3193 N of Chudleigh

Particularly at weekends, it's best to book ahead to be sure of a table in this popular creeper-covered pub. There's a good mix of customers, although the left-hand room with its beer mats and brewery advertisements on the walls is more for locals enjoying the well kept Princetown Jail Ale, RCH Pitchfork, Teignworthy Reel Ale and a constantly changing guest on handpump; ten wines by the glass and local cider. On the right, two rather more discreet rooms have a wider appeal, bolstered by the good, popular home-made food which might include sandwiches (from £2.60), home-made soup (£2.95), lots of filled baked potatoes (from £3.75), home-made burgers with various toppings (from £4.25), filled baguettes (£5.50), ploughman's (from £5.50), vegetable bake (£5.95), home-cooked ham and egg or beef and mushroom in ale (£6.95), pork steak in cider and apple sauce (£7.95), and steaks from (£9.95), with a good choice of changing specials such as vegetable and nut curry (£6.25), game sausages with creamy onion and butter sauce (£7.50), and chicken breast in smoked bacon sauce (£8.25); puddings (£3.50). Shove-ha'penny. The garden has lots of picnic-sets under cocktail parasols (and a fine tall scots pine), and pretty hanging baskets. No children inside. *(Recommended by Mr and Mrs J and S E Garrett, JP, PP, the Didler, Mike Gorton)*

Free house ~ Licensees Geoff and Clare Mann ~ Real ale ~ Bar food (12-1.30, 7-9.30; not Mon except bank hols) ~ (01647) 252304 ~ Dogs welcome ~ Open 12-2(2.30 Sat), 6.30-11; 12-2.30, 7-10.30 Sun; closed Mon (except bank hols)

LUSTLEIGH SX7881 Map 1

Cleave

Village signposted off A382 Bovey Tracey—Moretonhampstead

As this delightful thatched 15th-c pub is deservedly popular with walkers, it's best to arrive around midday to avoid a bit of a wait at the bar. The low-ceilinged no smoking lounge bar has attractive antique high-backed settles, cushioned wall seats, and wheelback chairs around the tables on its patterned carpet, granite walls, and a roaring log fire. A second bar has similar furnishings, a large dresser, harmonium, an HMV gramophone, and prints, and the no smoking family room has crayons, books and toys for children. Good bar food listed on daily changing boards might include home-made soup (£3.95), home-made smoked mackerel pâté or deep-fried brie with a sweet and sour sauce (£4.95), ploughman's (£6.50), local sausages (£6.95), popular home-made steak and kidney in stout pie (£8.95), tuna steak marinated in Pernod and herbs with a tomato and basil salsa (£10.95), steaks (from

£11.95), and half a honey-roast duckling with Grand Marnier and orange sauce (£13.95); the dining room is no smoking. Well kept Greene King Abbot, Otter Ale and Wadworths 6X on handpump kept under light blanket pressure, quite a few malt whiskies, and a dozen wines by the glass. The sheltered garden is neat and very pretty, and the summer hanging baskets and flowerbeds are lovely. Until the car parking field in the village is opened during the summer, parking can be very difficult. *(Recommended by Jacquie and Jim Jones, Mark and Amanda Sheard, David and Teresa Frost, Andrea Rampley, John and Marion Tyrie, Jim and Maggie Cowell, Alice Harper, C W Burke, Mike Turner)*

Heavitree ~ Tenant A Perring ~ Real ale ~ Bar food ~ Restaurant ~ (01647) 277223 ~ Children in family room ~ Dogs welcome ~ Open 11-3, 6.30-11; 11.30-3, 6.30-10.30 Sun; closed Mon Oct-Mar

LYDFORD SX5184 Map 1

Castle Inn

Off A386 Okehampton—Tavistock

After a walk in the beautiful nearby river gorge (owned by the National Trust; closed November-Easter), this pink-washed Tudor inn is a relaxing place for a refreshing drink. It has a lot of character and charm, and the twin-roomed bar has country kitchen chairs, high-backed winged settles and old captain's chairs around mahogany tripod tables on big slate flagstones. One of the rooms has low lamp-lit beams, a sizeable open fire, masses of brightly decorated plates, some Hogarth prints, and, near the serving counter, seven Lydford pennies hammered out in the old Saxon mint in the reign of Ethelred the Unready, in the 11th c. The bar area has a bowed ceiling with low beams, a polished slate flagstone floor, and a stained-glass door with the famous Three Hares; there's a snug with high-backed settles which is used by families. Good, enjoyable bar food includes home-made soup (£3.75), sandwiches (£4.50), stuffed mushrooms with bacon and pine nuts with a crème fraîche and mustard sauce (£4.95), ploughman's or greek salad (£5.95), home-made lasagne (£6.50), home-cooked ham with an apricot and mango sauce (£6.95), a pie of the day or lambs liver and bacon with onion gravy (£7.50), spinach pancakes with wild mushrooms, cream and white wine (£7.95), and breast of local duckling with orange sauce and leek and sweet potato mash (£13.50). Well kept Fullers London Pride, Otter Ale, and Wadworths 6X on handpump, and 11 wines by the glass; piped music, darts, cribbage and dominoes. *(Recommended by Mike Gorton, Ann and Colin Hunt, Jacquie and Jim Jones, James and Helen Read, Dr and Mrs Rod Holcombe, Guy Vowles, John and Joan Nash, DRH and KLH, David Crook, Adrian Johnson, Andrea Rampley, Mary Ellen Cummings)*

Heavitree ~ Tenant Richard Davies ~ Real ale ~ Bar food ~ Restaurant ~ (01822) 820241 ~ Children in restaurant ~ Dogs allowed in bar and bedrooms ~ Open 11.30-11; 12-10.30 Sun ~ Bedrooms: £45B/£65B

Dartmoor Inn 🍴 🍷

Downton, on the A386

There's no doubt that most customers in this well run and very popular place are here to enjoy the exceptionally good food, but locals and weekend walkers do drop into the small bar for a pint of well kept Fullers London Pride, Otter Ale or St Austell Dartmoor Best on handpump. Taken in one of the other four interestingly decorated rooms, the lunchtime bar menu might offer a bowl of tomato soup with a nutmeg cream (£4.50), smooth chicken liver pâté with peppered toasts (£6), ploughman's with apricot chutney (£6.75), cod and chips with a green mayonnaise (£8.50; large £13.75), sausages with mustard mash or omelette with smoked salmon and asparagus (£8.75), cornish crab with rocket leaves (£10.75), lambs liver with bacon and onions (£11), and chargrilled chump of lamb with wild garlic leaves and a tomato salad (£15). Also, scallops in their shells with lemon grass, chilli and green onions (£7.75), casserole of spring vegetables (£12.75), fillet of duck with fennel and saffron and celery leaf fritters (£15.75), and puddings such as jasmine scented crème brûlée with vanilla tuiles, hot chocolate pudding with chocolate sauce or bakewell pudding with clotted cream (from £4.95); two-course set lunch or dinner (£12.75). An interesting and helpfully short wine list offers six good wines by the glass. The overall feel is of civilised but relaxed elegance: matt pastel paintwork in soft greens and blues, naïve farm and country pictures, little side lamps supplemented by candles in black wrought-iron holders, basketwork, dried flowers, fruits and gourds, maybe an elaborate bouquet of fresh flowers. The whole pub is no smoking. There are tables out on the terrace, with a track straight up on to the moors. *(Recommended by Adrian and Ione Lee, Andy Sinden, Louise Harrington, Jacquie and Jim Jones, Mr and Mrs W Mills, John and Christine Lowe, Ron and Sheila Corbett, Richard and Margaret Peers, Paul Hopton, Charles Cooper, Peter Craske)*

Free house ~ Licensee Philip Burgess ~ Real ale ~ Bar food (lunchtime only; not Mon) ~ Restaurant ~ (01822) 820221 ~ Children welcome ~ Dogs allowed in bar ~ Occasional live jazz ~ Open 11.30-3, 6-11; 12-2.30 Sun; closed Sun evening, Mon

MARLDON SX8663 Map 1

Church House

Just W of Paignton

There's a genuinely warm welcome for all from the helpful and friendly staff in this attractive, charming inn. The spreading bar (half of which is no smoking) has a relaxed atmosphere and several different areas that radiate off the big semicircular bar counter. The main bar has interesting windows, some beams, dark pine chairs around solid tables on the turkey carpet, and yellow leather bar chairs; leading off here is a cosy little candlelit room with just four tables on the bare-board floor, a dark wood dado and stone fireplace, and next to this is the attractive, no smoking restaurant with a large stone fireplace. At the other end of the building, a characterful room is split into two parts with a stone floor in one bit and a wooden floor in another (which has a big woodburning stove). Extremely good, interesting bar food includes sandwiches, home-made soup (£5; tasty smoked haddock, mussel and potato chowder with a poached egg £6.50), warm asparagus and local cheese tart with cherry tomato dressing or home-made chicken liver and mushroom pâté with a cranberry and orange compote (£5.50), seared duck breast with celery and hazelnut salad and a raspberry and honey dressing (£6), broccoli and three cheese pasta (£7.50), loin of pork with sweet and sour sauce and noodles (£11.50), local sirloin steak with shallot, garlic and brandy cream sauce (£13.50), chargrilled rack of lamb, garlic and olive oil mash and mint and red wine sauce (£14), and king prawns in paprika and sour cream (£15); efficient service even when busy. Well kept Bass, Fullers London Pride, Greene King IPA, and St Austell Dartmoor Best on handpump, and 12 wines by the glass; skittle alley. There are three grassy terraces with picnic-sets behind. *(Recommended by John and Sonja Newberry, Pamela and Merlyn Horswell, Gordon Tong, Darly Graton, Graeme Gulibert, Mr and Mrs Colin Roberts, Neil and Beverley Gardner, John and Christine Lowe, Jim and Maggie Cowell, Felicity Stephens, David Fox, David M Cundy, Dr and Mrs A K Clarke, Cathryn and Richard Hicks, Adrian White, Mike and Mary Carter)*

Whitbreads ~ Lease Julian Cook ~ Real ale ~ Bar food (12-2, 7-9.30) ~ Restaurant ~ (01803) 558279 ~ Children welcome ~ Dogs allowed in bar ~ Open 11.30-2.30, 5-11; 11.30-11 Sat; 12-10.30 Sun ~ Bedrooms: /£60B

MEAVY SX5467 Map 1

Royal Oak

Off B3212 E of Yelverton

On the edge of Dartmoor in a peaceful rustic village, this partly 15th-c pub has seats on the green in front and by the building itself. Inside, the heavy-beamed L-shaped bar has pews from the church, red plush banquettes and old agricultural prints and church pictures on the walls; a smaller bar – where the locals like to gather – has flagstones, a big open hearth fireplace and side bread oven. Promptly served by friendly staff, the well liked bar food at lunchtime includes soup (£2.95), filled baked potatoes and baguettes (from £3.95; stilton and orange £5.25), ham and egg (£5.75), ploughman's (£5.95), home-made vegetable lasagne (£6.95), and home-made steak and kidney pie (£7.15); in the evening there might be garlic mushrooms (£4.25), potato, leek and stilton bake (£6.95), pork escalope with apple and cider sauce (£8.50), salmon with a caper and cream dressing (£8.95), and steaks (from £9). The lounge bar is no smoking during food times. Well kept Princetown IPA and Jail Ale, and maybe Bass and Sharps Doom Bar on handpump. The ancient oak from which the pub gets its name is just close by. No children inside. More reports please. *(Recommended by Mr and Mrs J E C Tasker, Alan and Paula McCully)*

Free house ~ Licensee Ann Davis ~ Real ale ~ Bar food ~ (01822) 852944 ~ Dogs welcome ~ Open 11-3, 6.30-11; 12-3, 6.30-10.30 Sun

MOLLAND SS8028 Map 1

London

Village signposted off B3227 E of South Molton, down narrow lanes

Although it is a little off the beaten track, this proper Exmoor inn is worth the diversion for its chatty and informal atmosphere undisturbed by piped music or noisy games machines. The two small linked rooms by the old-fashioned central servery have lots of local stag-hunting pictures, tough carpeting or rugs on flagstones, cushioned benches and plain chairs around rough stripped trestle tables, a table of shooting and other country magazines, ancient stag and otter trophies, and darts, table skittles, and dominoes; maybe working dogs from local shoots (there is a bowl of water left for them by the good log fire). On the left an attractive beamed room has accounts of the rescued stag which lived a long life at the pub some 50 years ago, and on the right, a panelled dining room with a great curved settle by its fireplace has particularly good hunting and gamebird prints, including ones by McPhail and Hester Lloyd. Honest bar food includes home-made soup (£3), sandwiches (from £3.50), ham and egg (£4.70), ploughman's (£4.95), filled baked potatoes (£5.20), savoury pancakes (£5.80), and a dish of the day (£5.80); evening choices like chicken and stilton wrapped in bacon with a white wine sauce (£9.40) or double lamb chops (£9.60). The dining room is no smoking. A small hall with stuffed birds and animals and lots of overhead baskets has a box of toys, and there are good country views from a few picnic-sets out in front. The low-ceilinged lavatories are worth a look, with their Victorian mahogany and tiling (and in the gents' a testament to the prodigious thirst of the village cricket team). And don't miss the next-door church, with its untouched early 18th-c box pews – and a spring carpet of tenby daffodils in the graveyard. *(Recommended by the Didler, JP, PP, Jeremy Whitehorn, Andrea Rampley, J C Brittain-Long)*

Free house ~ Licensees M J and L J Short ~ Real ale ~ Bar food ~ Restaurant ~ No credit cards ~ (01769) 550269 ~ Children in family room, in eating area of bar and in restaurant ~ Dogs allowed in bar and bedrooms ~ Open 11.30-2.30, 6-11; 12-2.30, 7-10.30 Sun ~ Bedrooms: /£50B

NEWTON ABBOT SX8468 Map 1

Two Mile Oak

A381 2 miles S, at Denbury/Kingskerswell crossroads

Attractive and friendly, this old coaching inn has a relaxed atmosphere, a beamed lounge and an alcove just for two, a mix of wooden tables and chairs, and a fine winter log fire. The beamed and black-panelled bar is traditionally furnished, again with a mix of seating, lots of horsebrasses, and another good log fire. Well kept Bass, Flowers IPA, Greene King Abbot and Otter Ale tapped from the cask, and decent wines. Bar food includes filled baguettes (from £4.95), ploughman's (from £5.85), and ambitious daily specials such as skate wing with capers and black butter, ostrich with seville orange sauce or wild boar with apricots (from £10.95), and lamb shank with blueberry and ginger sauce (£12.25); lots of puddings from a daily-changing choice of eight (£3.75). Part of the restaurant is no smoking; piped music, darts, and cribbage. There are picnic-sets on the terrace where they hold summer barbecues, and a lawn with shrubs and tubs of flowers. *(Recommended by Mrs A P Lee, JP, PP, B J Harding, Mr and Mrs Colin Roberts, Ian Phillips, the Didler, Joe Green, Alan and Paula McCully, Mrs Sylvia Elcoate, Dr and Mrs A K Clarke)*

Heavitree ~ Manager Melanie Matthews ~ Real ale ~ Bar food ~ (01803) 812411 ~ Children in eating area of bar, restaurant and family room ~ Dogs allowed in bar ~ Folk music Sun evening ~ Open 11-11; 11-11 Sat; 12-10.30 Sun

NEWTON FERRERS SX5447 Map 1

Dolphin

Riverside Road East – follow Harbour dead end signs

In summer the two terraces across the lane are the place to be: by day they have a grandstand view of the boating action on the busy tidal River Yealm below the cottages on these steep hillsides, and at night the floodlit church over in Noss Mayo makes a lovely focal point. Service out here is quick and friendly, as it is in the 18th-c pub itself. The L-shaped bar has a few low black beams, slate floors, some white-painted plank panelling, and simple pub furnishings including cushioned wall benches and small winged settles; chatty and relaxed out of season, it can get packed in summer. Enjoyable food includes sandwiches (from £3.90; filled baguettes from £4.95), filled baked potatoes (from £4.50), ploughman's (from £5.95), fresh cod (from £6.45), home-made vegetable lasagne (£6.95), home-made beef curry (£8.60), and daily specials such as scallops in garlic butter (£4.95), thai-style chicken (£8.60), home-made steak and mushroom in ale pie (£8.95), and honey and mustard quarter shoulder of lamb (£10.95); puddings like date and sticky toffee pudding or caramel and chocolate parfait (from £3.95). Bass, Sharps Doom Bar, and a Skinners brew for the pub are kept well on handpump, Heron Valley cider, organic apple juice, and nine wines by the glass; they have darts, a popular quiz night on Wednesdays in winter, and the pub is decorated with lots of coastal watercolours (for sale). The carpeted family area is up a few steps at the back, and there is a no smoking restaurant upstairs. Parking by the pub is very limited, with more chance of a space either below or above. *(Recommended by Esther and John Sprinkle, Ann and Bob Westbrook, Vivian Stevenson, Geoff Pidoux)*

Free house ~ Licensee Sandra Dunbar Rees ~ Bar food ~ Restaurant ~ (01752) 872007 ~ Children in eating area of bar ~ Dogs welcome ~ Open 12-2.30(3 Sat), 6-11; 12-3, 7-10.30 Sun; opens 12.30 in winter

NOMANSLAND SS8313 Map 1

Mount Pleasant

B3131 Tiverton—South Molton

This is the sort of friendly and relaxed place where you often have to step over dogs and farmers' wellies to get in. There's a new bay window extension to fit an extra four tables, and the long bar is divided into three, with huge fireplaces each end, one with a woodburning stove under a low dark ochre black-beamed ceiling, the other with a big log fire. A nice informal mix of furniture on the patterned carpet includes an old sofa with a colourful throw, old-fashioned leather dining chairs, pale country kitchen chairs and wall pews, and tables all with candles in attractive metal holders; there are country prints and local photographs including shooting parties. The bar, with plenty of bar stools, has well kept Cotleigh Tawny and Barn Owl, and Marstons Pedigree on handpump, and decent wines. Generous helpings of well liked bar food (they tell us prices have not risen since last year) using local produce, includes home-made soup (£2.95), baguettes and toasties (£4.50), filled baked potatoes (£5.50), all-day breakfast (£5.95), ham and egg (£6.50), beef stroganoff or steak and kidney pie (£6.95), pasta with mushroom and pesto cream (£7.50), fillets of bass (£8.95), steaks (from £12.95), and puddings (£3.95). On the left a high-beamed stripped stone no smoking dining room with a stag's head over the sideboard was once a smithy, and still has the raised forge fireplace. Piped music, fruit machine, TV, and darts; picnic-sets under smart parasols in the neat back garden. Samuel the spaniel comes in to say hello at closing time. More reports please. *(Recommended by Richard and Anne Ansell, Shaun and Beccy Haydon)*

Free house ~ Licensees Anne Butler, Karen Southcott and Sarah Roberts ~ Real ale ~ Bar food (all day) ~ Restaurant ~ (01884) 860271 ~ Children welcome ~ Dogs allowed in bar ~ Open 11.30-11; 12-10.30 Sun; closed evening 25 Dec, 1 Jan

NOSS MAYO SX5447 Map 1

Ship

Off A379 via B3186, E of Plymouth

The terrace in front of this rather smart pub has been refurbished this year. It's an idyllic spot in summer, and you can sit at the octagonal wooden tables and look over the inlet; visiting boats can tie up alongside – with prior permission. Parking is restricted at high tide. Inside, the two thick-walled bars have a happy mix of dining chairs and tables on the wooden floors, log fires (so hot you might not want to sit too close!), bookcases, dozens of local pictures, newspapers and magazines to read, and a friendly, chatty atmosphere. All of the first floor is no smoking; board games and dominoes. Good food (which can be eaten anywhere in the pub and features much local produce) might include curried vegetable soup (£4.25), sandwiches (from £4.25; baguettes £5.25), smooth chicken liver pâté (£4.95), smoked duck salad with coarse grain, honey and mustard dressing (£6.25), vegetable stir fry with toasted almonds, egg noodles and hoi sin sauce (£7.95), smoked haddock fishcakes (£8.25), roast loin of pork with apple sauce or sausages with mustard mash, black pudding, onions and gravy (£8.95), 8oz steak burger topped with gruyère cheese (£9.95), a tapas plate for two to share (£11.95), braised shoulder of local lamb (£12.50), and grilled lemon sole (£13.75); cheerful, helpful staff. Well kept Princetown Dartmoor IPA, Summerskills Tamar, and guests like Keltek Magik or Blackawton 44 Special on handpump, lots of malt whiskies, and eight wines by the glass. It does get very busy, particularly in fine weather. *(Recommended by John Evans, R J Walden, David and Heather Stephenson, Esther and John Sprinkle, Laura Wilson, John and Joan Calvert, Dr and Mrs M E Wilson, Charles and Pauline Stride, Margaret and Roy Randle, Ian Wilson, John and Joan Nash, Geoff Pidoux, Mrs C Sleight, B Forster, Alice Harper, Richard and Margaret Peers, Christopher Turner, Brian and Bett Cox, Vanessa Stilwell, OPUS, Mike Gorton, Alan and Anne Driver)*

Free house ~ Licensees Lesley and Bruce Brunning ~ Real ale ~ Bar food (12-9.30) ~ Restaurant ~ (01752) 872387 ~ Children allowed before 7pm ~ Dogs allowed in bar ~ Open 11.30-11; 12-10.30 Sun

PARRACOMBE SS6644 Map 1

Fox & Goose

Village signposted off A39 Blackmoor Gate—Lynton (actually a short cut, but winding and rather narrow)

The log fire, brown-varnished plank ceiling, assorted mounted antlers, horns and ex-wildlife in some variety give a proper Exmoor feel to the bar of this quietly placed late 19th-c inn. The good food relies strongly on local connections, too, with local fish and exmoor lamb and venison. Starters such as fish soup, stilton, port and walnut pâté, local crab or garlic mushrooms (£2.25–£5.25), vegetarian dishes like nut roast or cheese and onion bake (from £8.95), and meat or fish choices such as chicken stroganoff, lamb chops with minted gravy, rib-eye steak, king scallops and red mullet in a Sambuca cream sauce, cod fillet with tiger prawns and bacon butter, and lynmouth lobster thermidor (£8.95–£27.95). They are particularly proud of their steak and seaweed pie, and some of their puddings are unashamedly over-the-top, such as a 'foxy fondue' concoction of white chocolate, Malibu, marshmallow and fresh fruit. The restaurant and part of the bar are no smoking. They have Cotleigh Barn Owl and Exmoor Gold tapped from the cask, local farm cider and ten wines by the glass; service is quick and friendly, and the atmosphere relaxed and informal. Juke box and piped music. Seating is mainly wheelback carver chairs around solid tables, with more tables at a comfortable height for people eating over

on the left, and rambling around behind; there are some interesting black and white photographs. The dining room on the right looks down on a little stream, and the front verandah has a couple of picnic-sets, with hanging baskets and flower tubs. We look forward to hearing from readers who have tried the bedrooms here.
(Recommended by Paul and Ursula Randall, Annette Tress, Gary Smith, David Gibbs, Steve Godfrey)

Free house ~ Licensees S Dallyn and P J Reed-Evans ~ Bar food ~ (01598) 763239 ~ Children in eating area of bar and restaurant ~ Open 11-3, 5-11; 12-3, 7-10.30 Sun ~ Bedrooms: /£45B

PETER TAVY SX5177 Map 1

Peter Tavy Inn

Off A386 near Mary Tavy, N of Tavistock

It's best to get to this attractive old stone inn early to be sure of not only a table, but a parking space. The low-beamed bar has a good bustling atmosphere, high-backed settles on the black flagstones by the big stone fireplace (a fine log fire on cold days), smaller settles in stone-mullioned windows, a snug, no smoking side dining area, and efficient service. Popular food at lunchtime might include vegetable soup (£3.75), red lentil and sunblush tomato pâté (£4.95), ham and egg (£5.75), chicken and bacon tartlet (£6.75), roast stuffed shoulder of pork with apple sauce (£6.95), ploughman's with a choice of six local cheeses (£7.95), and chicken supreme stuffed with smoked salmon mousse (£8.95); in the evening there might be crab and avocado tian or chicken liver and orange pâté with pear chutney (£4.95), vegetable madras (£7.95), venison steak diane (£11.95), salmon with a tomato, basil and lemon risotto (£12.95), and duck breast with plum sauce (£13.45). Home-made puddings such as rich chocolate and nut tart or turkish delight and white chocolate mousse (£3.95). Well kept Princetown Jail Ale and Summerskills Tamar, and Sharps Doom Bar, with a couple of guests from breweries like Blackawton or Sutton on handpump, kept under light blanket pressure; local farm cider, 30 malt whiskies and nine wines by the glass; piped music and darts. From the picnic-sets in the pretty garden, there are peaceful views of the moor rising above nearby pastures. *(Recommended by Joyce and Maurice Cottrell, John Evans, JP, PP, Jacquie and Jim Jones, Cathryn and Richard Hicks, Guy Vowles, John and Vivienne Rice, D Hines, Richard and Anne Ansell, John and Christine Lowe, Michael and Margaret Slater, Richard and Margaret Peers)*

Free house ~ Licensees Graeme and Karen Sim ~ Real ale ~ Bar food ~ Restaurant ~ (01822) 810348 ~ Children in restaurant and family room ~ Dogs welcome ~ Open 12-3, 6-11(10.30 Sun); closed 25 Dec and evenings 24, 25 and 31 Dec

POSTBRIDGE SX6780 Map 1

Warren House

B3212 ¾ mile NE of Postbridge

This is just the place to head for after a walk on Dartmoor. The cosy bar has a fireplace at either end (one is said to have been kept almost continuously alight since 1845), and is simply furnished with easy chairs and settles under a beamed ochre ceiling, wild animal pictures on the partly panelled stone walls, and dim lighting (fuelled by the pub's own generator); there's a no smoking family room. Good no-nonsense home cooking includes home-made soup (£2.90), locally made meaty or vegetable pasties (£3), sandwiches (from £3.75), filled baked potatoes (from £4.50), good ploughman's (£5.95), home-made rabbit pie or home-made vegetable curry (£7.75), home-made steak in ale pie (£7.95), daily specials (from £6), and home-made puddings such as chocolate truffle torte (£3.95). Well kept Badger Tanglefoot, Ringwood Old Thumper, Sharps Doom Bar, and a guest like Shepherd Neame Spitfire on handpump, local farm cider, and malt whiskies. Darts, pool, cribbage, and dominoes; maybe piped music. There are picnic-sets on both sides of the road that enjoy the moorland views. *(Recommended by Andrea Rampley, Joyce and Maurice Cottrell, David Crook, Pat and Robert Watt, Peter Salmon)*

Free house ~ Licensee Peter Parsons ~ Real ale ~ Bar food (all day summer and winter weekends; more restricted in winter) ~ (01822) 880208 ~ Children in family room ~ Dogs welcome ~ Open 11-11; 12-10.30 Sun; may shut weekday afternoons in winter

POUNDSGATE SX7072 Map 1

Tavistock Inn

B3357 continuation

Sir Arthur Conan-Doyle wrote *The Hound of the Baskervilles* while staying in this picturesque, family-run 15th-c local. It's in a Dartmoor-edge village and moorland walks start and finish at the pub or pass it en route; boots and even waders are welcome, as are dogs on a lead – there's a bowl of water outside for them, and maybe if they are lucky, a dog biscuit behind the bar. Some original features include a narrow-stepped granite spiral staircase, original flagstones, ancient log fireplaces and beams, and there's a friendly atmosphere and a good mix of locals and visitors. Well kept Courage Best, Wadworths 6X and a guest such as Wychwood Hobgoblin Best on handpump, decent wines, and a few malt whiskies. Tasty traditional bar food includes filled baguettes (from £3.10; sausage and onion £3.50), filled baked potatoes (from £4), basket meals (from £4.60), locally made burger (£5.75), chicken curry (£6.10), yorkshire pudding filled with sausages, baked beans and onions or home-made lasagne (£6.20), mushroom, broccoli and pasta bake with stilton and cream (£6.20), beef in ale pie (£7.20), and steaks (from £10). Tables on the front terrace and pretty flowers in stone troughs, hanging baskets, and window boxes, and more seats in the quiet back garden with a gazebo overlooking the children's play area; lovely scenery. *(Recommended by Susan and Erik Falck-Therkelsen, JHW)*

InnSpired ~ Lease Peter and Jean Hamill and family ~ Real ale ~ Bar food (12-2, 6-9; not Mon evening Oct-Easter) ~ (01364) 631251 ~ Children allowed if over 4 ~ Dogs allowed in bar ~ Open 11-3, 6-11; 12-3, 7-10.30 Sun

RATTERY SX7461 Map 1

Church House

Village signposted from A385 W of Totnes, and A38 S of Buckfastleigh

This is one of Britain's oldest pubs, and the spiral stone steps behind a little stone doorway on your left as you come in date from about 1030. There are massive oak beams and standing timbers in the homely open-plan bar, large fireplaces (one with a little cosy nook partitioned off around it), windsor armchairs, comfortable seats and window seats, and prints on the plain white walls; the no smoking dining room is separated from this room by heavy curtains, and there's also a separate no smoking lounge area. Bar food includes soup (£3.25), sandwiches (from £3.75; toasties £4.50; filled baguettes from £4.50), devilled whitebait (£4.75), ploughman's (from £5.25), battered cod or sausages (£6.75), creamy coconut chicken curry (£6.95), steak and kidney pie (£7.25), vegetable lasagne (£7.95), citrus and olive lamb shank (£9.25), steaks (from £10.95), and puddings (£3.50). Well kept Greene King Abbot, Hook Norton Old Hooky, Otter Ale, and St Austell Dartmoor Best on handpump, several malt whiskies, and a decent wine list. The garden has picnic benches on the large hedged-in lawn, and peaceful views of the partly wooded surrounding hills. *(Recommended by Dudley and Moira Cockroft, David M Cundy, B J Harding, Ted George, Liz and Tony Colman, JP, PP, Mr and Mrs I Bell, Dr and Mrs D Woods, Ron and Sheila Corbett, Andrea Rampley, John and Christine Lowe, Simon and Jane Williams, JHW, John Evans, Jacquie and Jim Jones)*

Free house ~ Licensee Ray Hardy ~ Real ale ~ Bar food ~ Restaurant ~ (01364) 642220 ~ Children welcome ~ Dogs allowed in bar ~ Open 11-2.30, 6-11; 12-2.30, 6-10.30 Sun

Pubs staying open all afternoon at least one day a week are listed at the back of the book.

ROCKBEARE SY0295 Map 1

Jack in the Green

Signposted from new A30 bypass E of Exeter

A favourite with several readers, this consistently enjoyable dining pub is particularly well run and offers a friendly welcome from the hard-working landlord and his helpful staff. The neat and comfortable good-sized bar has wheelback chairs, sturdy cushioned wall pews and varying-sized tables on its dark blue carpet, with sporting prints, nice decorative china and a dark carved oak dresser; piped music. The larger no smoking dining side is air-conditioned but similarly traditional in style: some of its many old hunting and shooting photographs are well worth a close look, and it has button-back leather chesterfields by its big woodburning stove. Using fresh local produce, the high-standard popular food includes bar snacks such as soup (£3.95), chicken liver pâté (£4.25), toasted ciabatta topped with red pesto, buffalo mozzarella and plum tomato (£8.50), spicy pork meatballs in tomato sauce on tagliatelle with fresh parmesan (£8.95), venison sausages with parsnip mash (£9.25), and fillet of smoked haddock topped with welsh rarebit (£11.50); they also offer two-course (£19.75) and three-course (£24.25) meals with choices such as cod and pancetta fishcake with tomato and fennel salad or local crab and prawns with curry mayonnaise, celery and pineapple broth, roast chicken supreme with morel mushrooms and asparagus cream sauce, red mullet with parsley oil and garlic chips, and loin of venison with butternut squash and shallot purée. Well kept Branscombe Vale labelled as JIG for the pub, Otter Ale, and Greene King Ruddles Best on handpump, and 12 good wines by the glass. There are some tables out behind, by a back skittle alley, with more in a garden area.

(Recommended by John and Sonja Newberry, David Rule, David Jeffreys, Andy Millward, Martin and Karen Wake, Oliver and Sue Rowell, John and Vivienne Rice, John Cadge, A Sadler, Mrs Sylvia Elcoate)

Free house ~ Licensee Paul Parnell ~ Real ale ~ Bar food (12-2, 7-9 but all day Sun) ~ Restaurant ~ (01404) 822240 ~ Well behaved children in eating area of bar ~ Open 11-3, 5.30(6 Sat)-11; 12-10.30 Sun; closed 25 Dec-5 Jan

SIDBURY SY1595 Map 1

Hare & Hounds

3 miles N of Sidbury, at Putts Corner; A375 towards Honiton, crossroads with B3174

At mealtimes particularly, this very well run roadside pub is extremely full of cheerful customers, but as it is open all day, the crowds can be avoided. It is so much bigger inside than you could have guessed from outside, rambling all over the place, but despite this, the very friendly and efficient staff will make you welcome and serve you promptly. There are two good log fires (and rather unusual wood-framed leather sofas complete with pouffes), heavy beams and fresh flowers throughout, some oak panelling, plenty of tables with red leatherette or red plush-cushioned dining chairs, window seats and well used bar stools too; it's mostly carpeted, with bare boards and stripped stone walls at one softly lit no smoking end. At the opposite end of the pub, on the left, another big dining area has huge windows looking out over the garden. As you come in, the first thing you see is the good popular daily carvery counter, with a choice of joints, and enough turnover to keep up a continuous supply of fresh vegetables (lunchtime £6.85, evening £7.35, children £4.45). Other food includes sandwiches or baguettes (from £3.25), filled baked potatoes (from £4.10), home-made soup (£3.75), home-made chicken liver pâté (£4.25), nut roast (£6.50), ploughman's (£6.75), home-made pie of the day (£6.95), home-made lasagne or curry (£7.25), local steaks (from £10.75), and daily specials such as cauliflower cheese topped with crispy bacon (£5.25), liver and bacon (£6.50), beer battered cod (£7.30), and braised lamb shank with rosemary mash (£8.25). Well kept Branscombe Summa Vale and Otter Ale and Bitter tapped from the cask; side room with a big-screen sports TV. Alley skittles and piped music. The big garden, giving good valley views, has picnic-sets, a play area enlivened by a pensioned-off fire engine, and a small strolling flock of peafowl.

(Recommended by Brian and Bett Cox, Chris Ray, Alan and Paula McCully, Joyce and Maurice Cottrell, Mike and Wendy Proctor, Howard and Margaret Buchanan)

Free house ~ Licensee Peter Cairns ~ Real ale ~ Bar food (all day) ~ Restaurant ~ (01404) 41760 ~ Children welcome ~ Dogs allowed in bar ~ Live music Sun lunchtimes in marquee ~ Open 10-11.30; 12-10.30 Sun

SIDFORD SY1390 Map 1

Blue Ball ★

A3052 just N of Sidmouth

Since 1912, the same friendly family have been running this thatched 14th-c inn. The low, partly-panelled and neatly kept lounge bar has heavy beams, upholstered wall benches and windsor chairs, three open fires, and lots of bric-a-brac; the family room and part of the restaurant are no smoking. Bar food includes home-made quiches, flans and so forth from an all-day salad bar, as well as sandwiches (from £2.75; fresh local crab £4.50), home-made soup (£3.25), local sausages (£4.25), ploughman's (£5.50), omelettes (£6), cheddar, red onion and mushroom flan (£6.25), steak in ale pudding (£8.25), fresh salmon fillet with lime, chilli and ginger dressing (£8.50), steaks (from £9.50), and daily specials. Bass, Flowers IPA, Greene King Old Speckled Hen, Otter Ale and a guest such as Black Sheep on handpump, kept well in a temperature-controlled cellar; good service. A plainer public bar has darts, dominoes, cribbage, and a fruit machine; piped music. Tables on a terrace look out over a colourful front flower garden, and there are more seats on a bigger back lawn – as well as in a covered area next to the barbecue; see-saw and play house for children. This is a nice play to stay and the breakfasts are good. The large car park is across a very busy road. *(Recommended by Mike Gorton, JP, PP, Maurice Ribbans, Steve Crick, Helen Preston, Alan and Paula McCully, John and Jane Hayter, P R and S A White, Tony Radnor, Geoffrey G Lawrance, Joan and Michel Hooper-Immins, Mike and Wendy Proctor, Barry and Anne, Warham St Leger-Harris, David and Julie Glover, Mr and Mrs P B Berry, Mr and Mrs W D Borthwick, KC, Joyce and Maurice Cottrell)*

Pubmaster ~ Lease Roger Newton ~ Real ale ~ Bar food (11-2, 6.30-9.30 but they also offer breakfast between 8 and 10am) ~ Restaurant ~ (01395) 514062 ~ Children in restaurant and family room ~ Dogs allowed in bar ~ Occasional live entertainment Fri evening ~ Open 11-11; 12-10.30 Sun ~ Bedrooms: £30(£45B)/£50(£75B)

SLAPTON SX8244 Map 1

Tower ★

Signposted off A379 Dartmouth—Kingsbridge

The new licensees seem to have settled easily into this fine old place, and as the same chef stayed on, the food is as good as ever. The low-ceilinged beamed bar has armchairs, low-backed settles and scrubbed oak tables on the flagstones or bare boards, open log fires, and well kept Adnams Best, Badger Tanglefoot, and St Austell Dartmoor Best on handpump; several wines by the glass. At lunchtime, the popular food includes home-made soup (£3.75), sandwiches (from £4.25; fresh crab when available £5.25), home-made ham, asparagus and baby leek terrine with wholegrain dressing (£5.95), italian antipasto (£6.95), trio of local sausages with onion gravy (£7.95), roasted vegetables with tagliatelle and a hot tomato and basil dressing (£8.45), and beef and mushroom in ale pie (£8.95); in the evening, there might be cheddar cup filled with a warm aubergine, halloumi and cherry tomato salad (£5.75), crab and prawn tower with light basil oil (£6.25), mushroom stroganoff (£8.95), slow cooked lamb shank with a stew of peas, flageolets, garlic and parsley (£10.95), pheasant supreme on a diced potato, smoked bacon, spinach and mushroom salad (£12.95), and roast bass with glazed crab mashed potatoes and a lime and tarragon sauce (£13.95). Puddings such as double chocolate and orange truffle torte, vanilla crème brûlée with a raspberry, vanilla and lemon compote or sticky toffee pudding with toffee sauce (£4.75); piped music. The lane up to the pub is very narrow and parking can be pretty tricky. *(Recommended by BOB, Brian Kneale, Geoffrey and Karen Berrill, Richard and Margaret Peers, Richard and*

Anne Ansell, Roger Wain-Heapy, Brian Root, David Eberlin, Alice Harper, Mr and Mrs J Curtis, Lynda and Trevor Smith, Brian and Bett Cox, the Didler, DRH and KLH)

Free house ~ Licensees Annette and Andrew Hammett ~ Real ale ~ Bar food ~ Restaurant ~ (01548) 580216 ~ Children in eating area of bar ~ Dogs welcome ~ Open 12-3, 6-11; 12-3, 7-10.30 Sun ~ Bedrooms: £35S/£55S

SOUTH ZEAL SX6593 Map 1

Oxenham Arms

Village signposted from A30 at A382 roundabout and B3260 Okehampton turn-off

It's worth dropping into this marvellous building to have a drink and a look around as it is full of interest. It was first licensed in 1477 – though it has grown up around the remains of a Norman monastery, built here to combat the pagan power of the neolithic standing stone that still forms part of the wall in the family room behind the bar (there are actually twenty more feet of stone below the floor). It later became the Dower House of the Burgoynes, whose heiress carried it to the Oxenham family. And Charles Dickens, snowed up one winter, wrote a lot of *Pickwick Papers* here. The beamed and partly panelled front bar has elegant mullioned windows and Stuart fireplaces, and windsor armchairs around low oak tables and built-in wall seats. The small family room has beams, wheelback chairs around polished tables, decorative plates, and another open fire. Bar food, Cottage Southern and Sharps Doom Bar and Own on handpump or tapped from the cask, and quite a few wines. Note the imposing curved stone steps leading up to the garden where there's a sloping spread of lawn. More reports please. *(Recommended by Pete Baker, DRH and KLH, Brian and Bett Cox, Joyce and Geoff Robson, Jacquie and Jim Jones, Colin and Stephanie McFie, JP, PP, Paul Humphreys, the Didler, R T and J C Moggridge, R J Walden, Ann and Colin Hunt, John and Sonja Newberry, Betsy Brown, Nigel Flook, Dr and Mrs M W A Haward, Richard and Margaret Peers, Bernard Stradling, Phil and Sally Gorton, Andrea Rampley, Guy Vowles, Mr and Mrs W Mills, Mike Turner, John and Joan Nash, C W Burke, Jeremy Morrison, Lucien Perring)*

Free house ~ Licensee Paul Lucas ~ Real ale ~ Bar food ~ Restaurant ~ (01837) 840244 ~ Children in family room ~ Dogs allowed in bar ~ Open 11-3, 5-11; 12-2.30, 7-10.30 Sun ~ Bedrooms: £45B/£70B

STAVERTON SX7964 Map 1

Sea Trout

Village signposted from A384 NW of Totnes

Some careful refurbishment here has not changed the character of this friendly old village pub. The neatly kept rambling beamed lounge bar has a cheerful mix of locals and visitors, sea trout and salmon flies and stuffed fish on the walls, cushioned settles and stools, and a stag's head above the fireplace; the main bar has low banquettes, soft lighting and an open fire, and there's also a public bar with darts, pool, TV, bar billiards, shove-ha'penny, cribbage, dominoes, and a juke box. Enjoyable bar food includes home-made soup (£3.50), lunchtime sandwiches (from £4.50), chicken, saffron and baby leek terrine (£4.75), baked spinach and parmesan soufflé (£5.50), gammon and egg (£8.75), steak in ale pie (£8.95), and daily specials such as lamb noisettes with lyonnaise potatoes and thyme jus, seared fillets of sea trout with a lemon crab risotto and leek and tarragon dressing, wild mushroom fricassee with wild rice and parmesan biscuit, and lancashire hotpot or individual beef wellington with coarse grain mustard and wild mushroom duxelle (from £7.95). The whole pub apart from one bar is no smoking. Well kept Palmers IPA, Copper, Gold, and 200 on handpump, a decent range of wines, quite a few whiskies, and farm cider; efficient, helpful staff. There are seats under parasols on the attractive paved back garden. A station for the South Devon Steam Railway is not too far away. *(Recommended by Joyce and Maurice Cottrell, David M Cundy, Dr and Mrs Rod Holcombe, Comus and Sarah Elliott, Dennis Jenkin, the Didler, JP, PP, Brian and Bett Cox, Simon Rodway)*

Palmers ~ Tenants Nicholas and Nicola Brookland ~ Real ale ~ Bar food (12-2(2.30 Sat and Sun lunchtimes), 7-9(9.30 Fri and Sat evenings)) ~ Restaurant ~ (01803) 762274 ~ Children in eating area of bar and restaurant ~ Dogs allowed in bar ~ Open 11-3, 6-11; 12-4, 7-10.30 Sun; closed evenings 25 and 26 Dec ~ Bedrooms: £45B/£58B

STOCKLAND ST2404 Map 1

Kings Arms

Village signposted from A30 Honiton—Chard; and also, at every turning, from N end of Honiton High Street

You can be sure of a genuinely warm welcome from the helpful, friendly staff in this spotlessly kept and individually run 16th-c inn. It manages to cater for a wide mix of customers, too, which is not easy to do – young or elderly, those dropping in for a quick snack and drink, for a leisurely meal or for an overnight stay. The dark beamed, elegant Cotley Bar has solid refectory tables and settles, attractive landscapes, a medieval oak screen (which divides the room into two), and a great stone fireplace across almost the whole width of one end; the cosy restaurant has a huge inglenook fireplace and bread oven. Enjoyable bar food is served at lunchtime only (not Sunday): sandwiches (from £2.50), home-made soup (£3), omelettes (from £4), duck liver pâté (£5), ploughman's (£5.50), various pasta dishes (small £4.50, large £7.50), sausage and mash with onion gravy (£6.50), and daily specials like portuguese sardines, confit of duck with a plum sauce, steak and kidney pie, and king prawn thermidor; puddings such as apple and treacle crumbly or chocolate truffle torte (£5). In the evening, only the restaurant menu is available and diners are invited to the Cotley Bar to have the menu explained in full detail. Well kept Exmoor Ale and Otter Ale, and maybe O'Hanlons Yellowhammer and Royal Oak on handpump, over 40 malt whiskies (including island and west coast ones; large spirit measures), a comprehensive wine list, and farm ciders. At the back, a flagstoned bar has cushioned benches and stools around heavy wooden tables, and leads on to a carpeted darts area, another room with dark beige plush armchairs and settees (and a fruit machine), and a neat ten-pin skittle alley; TV, and quiet mainly classical piped music. There are tables under cocktail parasols on the terrace in front of the white-faced thatched pub and a lawn enclosed by trees and shrubs. *(Recommended by Andy Harvey, John and Fiona Merritt, Ian Wilson, John and Sonja Newberry, Douglas Allen, Brian and Anita Randall, Alan and Paula McCully, A Sadler, B H and J I Andrews, Brian and Bett Cox, Mike and Heather Watson, DRH and KLH, Andrew Shore, Maria Williams, Martin and Karen Wake, KN-R, Mr and Mrs W Mills, Mrs Angela McArt, Anthony Barnes, Richard and Margaret Peers, Bob and Margaret Holder, Comus and Sarah Elliott, MLR)*

Free house ~ Licensees Heinz Kiefer and Paul Diviani ~ Real ale ~ Bar food ~ Restaurant ~ (01404) 881361 ~ Children welcome ~ Dogs allowed in bar ~ Live music Sat and Sun ~ Open 12-3, 6.30-11; closed 25 Dec ~ Bedrooms: £40B/£60B

STOKE FLEMING SX8648 Map 1

Green Dragon

Church Road

Peter Crowther, the long-distance yachtsman, runs this very relaxed place; on the walls are cuttings about him, maps of his races, and accounts of his sinking 800 miles out in the Atlantic. The main part of the flagstoned and beamed bar has two small settles, bay window seats and stools, boat pictures, and maybe Maia the burmese cat or Rhea the german shepherd; down on the right is a wooden-floored snug with throws and cushions on sofas and armchairs, a few books (50p to RNLI), adult board games, and a grandfather clock. Down some steps is the no smoking Mess Deck with an open winter fire, and old charts and lots of ensigns and flags; piped music, darts, shove-ha'penny, cribbage, and dominoes. Enjoyable home-made bar food includes soup (£2.50), filled baguettes (£3.90), light lunches such as catalan bean and chorizo stew, shepherd's pie or venison and pork kofta on a lemon and basil couscous (from £4), as well as crab and mushroom bake (£4.40), pasta with various sauces (£4.50), bangers and mash (£5.20), a curry of the day (£5.90), and steak in ale or fish pie (£6.50); winter Sunday lunch. Well kept Bass, Flowers IPA, Otter Ale and Wadworths 6X on handpump (all except Bass kept under light blanket pressure), big glasses of good house wines, Addlestone's cider, and a decent range of spirits; you can take the beer away with you. Some seats outside and outdoor heaters on the front terrace. The church opposite has an interesting tall tower. Parking can be tricky at peak times. *(Recommended by Kim and Jerry Allen, John and Fiona Merritt, Laura Wilson, D J Elliott, OPUS)*

Heavitree ~ Tenants Peter and Alix Crowther ~ Real ale ~ Bar food (12-2.30, 6.30-9) ~ (01803) 770238 ~ Children in eating area of bar and in restaurant ~ Dogs allowed in bar ~ Open 11-3, 5.30-11; 12-3, 6-10.30 Sun

STOKE GABRIEL SX8457 Map 1

Church House

Village signposted from A385 just W of junction with A3022, in Collaton St Mary; can also be reached from nearer Totnes

Relations with the Church of England and this friendly old local go back a long way – witness the priest hole, dating from the Reformation, visible from outside. Inside, there's an exceptionally fine medieval beam-and-plank ceiling in the lounge bar, as well as a black oak partition wall, window seats cut into the thick butter-coloured walls, decorative plates and vases of flowers on a dresser, and a huge fireplace still used in winter to cook the stew; darts. The mummified cat in a case, probably about 200 years old, was found during restoration of the roof space in the verger's cottage three doors up the lane – one of a handful found in the West Country and believed to have been a talisman against evil spirits. Straightforward bar food with prices unchanged since last year includes home-made soup (£2.95), a big choice of sandwiches and toasties (from £2.95; ham, cheese, pineapple and onion toastie £3.95), filled baked potatoes (from £3.95), ploughman's (from £4.75), steak and kidney pie, turkey curry or stilton and leek bake (£6.95), and puddings (£3.75). Well kept Bass, Charles Wells Bombardier, and Worthington Best on handpump, and 20 malt whiskies. Euchre in the little public locals' bar. There are picnic-sets on the little terrace in front of the building. No children inside. The church is very pretty. More reports please. *(Recommended by Dr and Mrs M E Wilson, David A Hammond, Dr and Mrs A K Clarke)*

Free house ~ Licensee T G Patch ~ Real ale ~ Bar food (11-3, 6-9.30) ~ No credit cards ~ (01803) 782384 ~ Dogs welcome ~ Open 11-11; 12-4, 7-10.30 Sun

TOPSHAM SX9688 Map 1

Bridge

2¼ miles from M5 junction 30: Topsham signposted from exit roundabout; in Topsham follow signpost (A376) Exmouth on the Elmgrove Road, into Bridge Hill

For over 100 years, this marvellously unspoilt old favourite has been run by the same family – and you can be sure of a genuinely warm welcome from the chatty, knowledgeable licensees. The utterly old-fashioned layout and character include fine old traditional furnishings (true country workmanship) in the little lounge partitioned off from the inner corridor by a high-backed settle; log fire. A bigger, lower no smoking room (the old malthouse) is open at busy times. The cosy regulars' inner sanctum keeps up to ten real ales tapped from the cask: Adnams Broadside, Blackawton Westcountry Gold and Exhibition, Branscombe Vale Branoc or Summa That, Exe Valley Hope and Spring Beer, Moor Old Freddy Walker, O'Hanlons Yellowhammer or Royal Oak, Otter Ale, and Teignworthy Old Moggie or Maltsters. Local farm cider and elderberry and gooseberry wines; friendly service. Simple, tasty bar food such as pasties (£2), sandwiches (from £3.25; the smoked chicken with elderflower and gooseberry pickle is liked), and various ploughman's (from £5.50); the local hand-fried crisps are excellent. No noisy music or machines – just a chatty, relaxed atmosphere. Our correspondent the Didler (whose pseudonym you may have noticed among the recommenders of rather a lot of pubs – he seems to devote much of his life to the search for good beer in a warm-hearted atmosphere) puts this pub right at the top of his list of all-time favourites. Outside, riverside picnic-sets overlook the weir. *(Recommended by Pete Baker, RWC, Catherine and Rob Dunster, Tony Radnor, Michael Rowse, JP, PP, Hugh Roberts, Jenny Perkins, the Didler, Phil and Sally Gorton, Mark and Heather Williamson, Mrs C Lintott, MLR, Dr and Mrs M E Wilson, OPUS)*

Free house ~ Licensee Mrs C Cheffers-Heard ~ Real ale ~ Bar food ~ No credit cards ~ (01392) 873862 ~ Children in room without bar ~ Dogs allowed in bar ~ Occasional live music ~ Open 12-2, 6(7 Sun)-10.30(11 Fri/Sat)

TORBRYAN SX8266 Map 1

Old Church House

Most easily reached from A381 Newton Abbot—Totnes via Ipplepen

Built in 1400 on the site of a very ancient cottage, this pub once housed the workmen restoring the part-Saxon church with its battlemented Norman tower. Bustling and neatly kept, the bar on the right of the door is particularly attractive, and has benches built into the fine old panelling as well as the cushioned high-backed settle and leather-backed small seats around its big log fire. On the left there are a series of comfortable and discreetly lit lounges, one with a splendid deep Tudor inglenook fireplace with a side bread oven. Enjoyable bar food at lunchtime includes home-made soup (£3.45), sandwiches (£5.50), cauliflower cheese (£5.70), ploughman's (£5.85), cottage pie (£5.95), chicken curry (£6.25), and roast lamb or beef (£6.50); evening choices such as pâté or grilled sardines (£4.95), pork in apple and mustard sauce or beef with bacon and wild mushrooms (£12.55), cod in a prawn and white wine sauce (£14.95), and duck with an orange and brandy sauce (£15.95). Puddings like chocolate pecan torte or black cherry cheesecake (£4.75). Well kept Palmers Dorset Gold, Skinners Betty Stogs, seasonal ale from Teignworthy, and a beer named for the pub on handpump, and around 25 malt whiskies; piped music, dominoes and cribbage. Plenty of nearby walks. *(Recommended by M J Caley, Alan and Paula McCully, Ann and Bob Westbrook)*

Free house ~ Licensees Richard and Carolyn McFadyen ~ Real ale ~ Bar food ~ Restaurant ~ (01803) 812372 ~ Children in restaurant and family room ~ Dogs welcome ~ Open 12-3, 6-11; 12-3, 7-10.30 Sun ~ Bedrooms: £50S/£85B

TORCROSS SX8241 Map 1

Start Bay

A379 S of Dartmouth

There are often queues outside this extremely popular dining pub before it opens, so to be sure of a table, you must get there early. Local fishermen work off the beach right in front of the pub and deliver all kinds of fish, a local crabber drops the crabs at the back door, and the landlord enjoys catching plaice, scallops, and bass: cod (medium £4.90; large £6.70; jumbo £8.70) and haddock (medium £4.90; large £6.70; jumbo £8.70), whole lemon sole (from £6.90), skate wing in batter (£7.90), whole dover sole (in four sizes from £8.50), brill (£10.50), and whole bass (small £9.50; medium £10.50; large £11.50). Other food includes sandwiches (from £2.95), ploughman's (from £4.75), vegetable lasagne (£5.95), gammon and pineapple (£7.50), steaks (from £8.90), and children's meals (£3.95); they do warn of delays at peak times. Well kept Bass and Flowers Original or Otter Ale on handpump, and maybe Heron Valley cider and fresh apple juice, and local wine from the Sharpham Estate. The unassuming main bar is very much set out for eating with wheelback chairs around plenty of dark tables or (round a corner) back-to-back settles forming booths; there are some photographs of storms buffeting the pub and country pictures on its cream walls, and a winter coal fire; a small chatty drinking area by the counter has a brass ship's clock and barometer. The winter games room has darts and shove-ha'penny; there's more booth seating in a no smoking family room with sailing boat pictures. There are seats (highly prized) out on the terrace overlooking the three-mile pebble beach, and the freshwater wildlife lagoon of Slapton Ley is just behind the pub. *(Recommended by Laura Wilson, Tony Middis, Claire Nielsen, Esther and John Sprinkle, Jill Hummerstone, Nigel Long, Brian Kneale, Jack Clark, Michael Porter, Mrs Sylvia Elcoate, Brian and Bett Cox, Keith and Margaret Kettell, Cathryn and Richard Hicks)*

Whitbreads ~ Tenant Paul Stubbs ~ Real ale ~ Bar food (11.30-2, 6-10) ~ (01548) 580553 ~ Children in family room ~ Dogs welcome ~ Open 11.30-11; 12-10.30 Sun; 11.30 (12 Sun)-2.30, 6-11(10.30 Sun) in winter

WIDECOMBE SX7176 Map 1

Rugglestone £

Village at end of B3387; pub just S – turn left at church and NT church house, OS Sheet 191 map reference 720765

Just up the road from the bustling tourist village, this is an unspoilt and often very busy local. The small bar has a strong rural atmosphere, just four small tables, a few window and wall seats, a one-person pew built into the corner by the nice old stone fireplace, and a rudimentary bar counter dispensing well kept Butcombe Bitter and St Austell Dartmoor Best tapped from the cask; local farm cider and a decent little wine list. The room on the right is a bit bigger and lighter-feeling, and shy strangers may feel more at home here: another stone fireplace, beamed ceiling, stripped pine tables, and a built-in wall bench. There's also a little no smoking room which is used for dining; darts and dominoes. Tasty simple bar food includes filled baked potatoes (from £3.10), home-made soup (£3.50), ploughman's (£5.95), and daily specials such as a vegetarian choice (from £4.40), steak and kidney pie (£4.95), and good liver and bacon casserole; service can suffer at peak times. Outside across the little moorland stream is a field with lots of picnic-sets. Tables and chairs in the garden. *(Recommended by Mike Gorton, the Didler, JP, PP, Paul Hopton, Guy Charrison, Phil and Sally Gorton, Andrea Rampley, JHW, Steve and Liz Tilley, Patrick and Phillipa Vickery, Michael Weston)*

Free house ~ Licensees Rod and Diane Williams ~ Real ale ~ Bar food ~ No credit cards ~ (01364) 621327 ~ Children in dining room and second bar ~ Dogs welcome ~ Open 11-3, 6.30-11; 12-3, 6.30-10.30 Sun

WINKLEIGH SS6308 Map 1

Kings Arms

Village signposted off B3220 Crediton—Torrington; Fore Street

Lively and friendly, this popular, well run thatched village pub welcomes visitors and locals alike. There's an attractive main bar with beams, some old-fashioned built-in wall settles, scrubbed pine tables and benches on the flagstones, and a woodburning stove in a cavernous fireplace; another woodburning stove separates the bar from the dining rooms (one is no smoking). Well liked bar food includes home-made soup (£3.25), sandwiches (from £3.25; filled baguettes from £3.95), chicken liver and brandy pâté (£3.50), filled baked potatoes or omelettes (from £5.50), ploughman's or three sausages and two eggs (£5.95), vegetable roulade (£6.95), chicken stir fry or curry of the day (£7.50), pork medallions in cider sauce (£8.95), steaks (from £9.95), and puddings like rhubarb crumble or marmalade steamed pudding (£3.50). Well kept Butcombe Bitter, Flowers IPA and Skinners Cornish Knocker on handpump, local cider, and decent wines; darts, cribbage, dominoes, and shove-ha'penny on handpump. There are seats out in the garden. *(Recommended by M and D Toms, Comus and Sarah Elliott, R J Walden, Dr and Mrs M E Wilson, Rod Stoneman, Mark Flynn, D P and M A Miles)*

Enterprise ~ Lease Chris Guy and Julia Franklin ~ Real ale ~ Bar food (all day) ~ Restaurant ~ (01837) 83384 ~ Children welcome ~ Dogs welcome ~ Open 11-11; 12-10.30 Sun

Planning a day in the country? We list pubs in really attractive scenery at the back of the book.

WONSON SX6789 Map 1

Northmore Arms

A30 at Merrymeet roundabout, take first left on old A30, through Whiddon Down; new roundabout and take left on to A382; then right down lane signposted Throwleigh/Gidleigh. Continue down lane over hump-back bridge; turn left to Wonson; OS Sheet 191 map reference 674903

Down narrow high-hedged lanes on the north-east edge of Dartmoor, this secluded cottage is all the more remarkable in this area for being open all day. It's almost as if time has stood still here. The two small connected beamed rooms – modest and informal but civilised – have wall settles, a few elderly chairs, five tables in one room and just two in the other. There are two open fires (only one may be lit), and some attractive photographs on the stripped stone walls; darts, dominoes, and cribbage. Besides well kept ales such as Adnams Broadside, Cotleigh Tawny and Exe Valley Dobs, they have good house wines, and simple but reasonably priced food such as sandwiches (from £1.75; toasties from £2.25), garlic mushrooms (£2.65), ploughman's (£4.25), filled baked potatoes (from £4.25), ham and egg (£4.75), feta, spinach and mushroom flan (£4.75), roast lamb with garlic potatoes (£5.95), Tuesday curries (£6.95), and sirloin steak in stilton sauce (£8.25). The ladies' lavatory is up steep steps and some feel the gents' could do with some refurbishment. The steep garden has been made larger and new tables and chairs were arriving as we went to press – it's all very peaceful and rustic; excellent walking from the pub (or to it, perhaps from Chagford or Gidleigh Park). The car park is larger this year. Castle Drogo is close by. *(Recommended by Mike Gorton, JP, PP, Keith Stevens, R J Walden, Alice Harper, M A Borthwick, the Didler, Anthony Longden, Mike and Wendy Proctor, Andrea Rampley, Gordon Briggs, JHW)*

Free house ~ Licensee Mrs Mo Miles ~ Real ale ~ Bar food (all day Mon-Sat; 12-2.30, 7-9 Sun) ~ (01647) 231428 ~ Well behaved children in family room ~ Dogs allowed in bar ~ Open 11-11; 12-10.30 Sun ~ Bedrooms: /£35

WOODBURY SALTERTON SY0189 Map 1

Diggers Rest

3½ miles from M5 junction 30, off A3052 towards Sidmouth

This thatched village pub is named after a former Australian landlord. The bars have antique furniture, local art on the walls, and Fullers London Pride, and Otter Bitter and Ale on handpump; there's a cosy seating area by an open fire with an extra large sofa and armchair. Since last year, a new dining area has been opened up. Using carefully sourced fresh local produce where possible, bar food at lunchtime includes home-made soup (£3.95), sandwiches (from £4.25; fresh crab £4.95), home-made hummous (£5.25), home-cooked ham with free range egg (£6.95), local cheeses with chutney and fresh bread (£7.50), steak and kidney pie (£8.25), and fresh haddock fishcakes (£8.35); in the evening there might be chick pea fritters (£4.50), local crab crostini (£5.95), local scallops (£6.75), fresh local cod in beer batter or pasta in mushroom, parmesan and cream sauce with wilted baby spinach (£7.95), greek salad (£8.75), and steaks (from £11.50). Changing specials such as twice baked goats cheese soufflé, slow cooked lamb shanks, aubergine and red pepper moussaka or braised pheasants in cider. All the dining areas are no smoking during mealtimes; ten wines by the glass and organic local soft drinks. Piped music and darts. Contemporary garden furniture under canvas parasols in the terraced garden, and lovely countryside views. More reports please. *(Recommended by Dr and Mrs M E Wilson, Richard and Margaret Peers, Diana Brumfit, Mike Gorton, John and Vivienne Rice, Joyce and Maurice Cottrell)*

Free house ~ Licensee Stephen Rushton ~ Real ale ~ Bar food (12-2, 7-9.30; 12-2.30, 6-9.30 weekends) ~ (01395) 232375 ~ Children in restaurant ~ Dogs allowed in bar ~ Open 11-2.30, 6-11; 11-11 Sat; 12-10.30 Sun

We say if we know a pub allows dogs.

WOODLAND SX7968 Map 1

Rising Sun 🍷 🛏

Village signposted off A38 just NE of Ashburton – then keep eyes peeled for Rising Sun signposts (which may be hidden in the hedges); pub N of village itself, near Combe Cross

Although people do drop into this friendly pub for just a drink, there's quite an emphasis on the popular, frequently changing food: home-made soup (£3.50), home-made coarse pâté (£4), sandwiches (from £4.50), fried local pigeon breast with orange salad (£4.95), home-cooked ham with free range egg and home-made chips or ploughman's with four local cheeses and home-made chutney (£6.25), spiced chick pea cakes with home-made tomato sauce or home-made pies like venison with stout and juniper (£7.95), trio of local pork sausages with spring onion mash (£8.95), fillet of lemon sole with a pine nut and basil butter (£11.95), roast rack of local lamb with a lemon and pepper crust and thyme and rosemary jus (£12.95), and home-made puddings such as white chocolate marquise or rhubarb crumble (£3.50); Sunday roast (£7.95). The dining area is no smoking. There's an expanse of softly lit red plush button-back banquettes and matching studded chairs, partly divided by wooden banister rails, masonry pillars and the odd high-backed settle. A forest of beams is hung with thousands of old doorkeys, and a nice part by the log fire has shelves of plates and books, and old pictures above the fireplace. Well kept Princetown Jail Ale, Sharps Doom Bar and maybe a guest like Moor Avalon on handpump, 12 wines by the glass, and local Luscombe cider; cheerful service. The family area has various toys (and a collection of cookery books). There are some picnic-sets in the spacious garden, which has a play area including a redundant tractor. *(Recommended by John and Vivienne Rice, Graham and Rose Ive, Daphne Ross, Brian and Bett Cox, John and Marion Tyrie, David M Cundy, D S Jackson)*

Free house ~ Licensee Heather Humphreys ~ Real ale ~ Bar food (12-2.15(3 Sun), 6(7 Sun)-9.15) ~ Restaurant ~ (01364) 652544 ~ Children in restaurant and family room ~ Dogs welcome ~ Open 11.45-3, 6-11; 12-3, 7-10.30 Sun; closed Mon (except bank hols) ~ Bedrooms: £38B/£60B

LUCKY DIP

Besides the fully inspected pubs, you might like to try these Lucky Dips recommended to us and described by readers (if you do, please send us reports: www.goodguides.co.uk).

APPLEDORE SS4630

Beaver [Irsha St]: Great estuary views from raised area in thriving unpretentious harbourside pub, good value food esp fresh local fish, friendly staff, well kept Bass and local ales such as Jollyboat Mainbrace, farm cider, decent house wines, great range of whiskies; pool in smaller games room; tables on sheltered terrace, children really welcome, disabled access *(Andy and Jill Kassube, Paul and Ursula Randall)*

☆ *Royal George* [Irsha St]: Simple but good fresh food inc local fish in no smoking dining room with superb estuary views, well kept ales, decent wines, good friendly service, cosy unspoilt front bar (dogs allowed), attractive pictures (sensitive souls should steer clear of the postcards in the gents'), fresh flowers; disabled access, picnic-sets outside, picturesque street sloping to sea *(Dr and Mrs P Truelove, Rod Stoneman, Michael and Ann Cole)*

ASHBURTON SX7569

Exeter [West St]: Friendly pleasantly old-fashioned pub with bargain straightforward food from sandwiches up, good local chilled ciders as well as real ale; small outside area *(Comus and Sarah Elliott, Nick Lawless)*

ASHPRINGTON SX8156

☆ *Watermans Arms* [Bow Bridge, on Tuckenhay rd]: Busy quarry-tiled heavy-beamed pub in great waterside spot, high-backed settles and other sturdy furnishings, stripped stonework, partly no smoking eating area, log fire, chatty and helpful new landlord, friendly staff, well kept Bass, Theakstons XB and a beer brewed for the pub, decent wines, local farm cider, wide food choice inc children's, Fri/Sat evening restaurant, darts, dominoes, cribbage; piped music, TV; children and dogs welcome, pretty flower-filled garden, close-set tables over road by creek, comfortable modern bedrooms, open all day *(Ann and Bob Westbrook, Dr and Mrs M E Wilson, Tony Harwood, LYM, Comus and Sarah Elliott, Brian and Bett Cox, Mr and Mrs D Boley, John Evans, A P Seymour)*

ASHWATER SX3895

Village Inn: Roomy slate-floored bar, wide choice of enjoyable food from sandwiches and baked potatoes up, well kept Exmoor and a guest beer, welcoming licensees, no smoking dining room, pool room, no music or machines, venerable grape vine in conservatory; tables on interestingly planted terrace *(anon)*

AVONWICK SX7158

Avon [off A38 at W end of South Brent bypass]: Comfortable fairly modern dining pub with some interesting dishes and good fresh fish, well kept ales such as Badger Best and Teignworthy, woodburner; may be piped music; picnic-sets in meadow by River Avon, adventure playground *(John Evans, LYM)*

Mill [½ mile off A38 roundabout at SW end of S Brent bypass]: Good value food inc children's helpings in roomy and pretty converted mill, friendly service, well kept local real ale; reasonable disabled access, high chairs; play area in big lakeside garden *(John Evans)*

AWLISCOMBE ST1301

☆ *Awliscombe Inn* [A373 just NW of Honiton]: Comfortably refurbished big-beamed main bar with good chunky elm tables, flowery-cushioned pews and high-backed wall banquettes, attractive three-room dining extension with William Morris fabrics and no smoking rockery conservatory, good reasonably priced home cooking inc children's and carvery, friendly helpful family service, well kept Otter and decent wines; piped music, silenced fruit machine, back public bar with pool; good tables out in garden with small terrace, quiet village *(BB, Mrs J Poole, Bob and Margaret Holder)*

AXMOUTH SY2591

Harbour Inn [B3172 Seaton—Axminster]: Prettily set thatched local, beams, flagstones, traditional settles and big log fires, well kept Flowers IPA and Original, pool and big simple summer family bar, food from sandwiches up, cheerful if not always speedy service, friendly cats; children in eating area, disabled access and facilities, tables in the neat back flower garden, cl winter Sun evenings *(Gerry and Rosemary Dobson, Richard C Morgan, LYM, Mr and Mrs W Mills, Mrs C Lintott)*

☆ *Ship* [Church St]: Comfortable, civilised and very welcoming, good fresh local fish and other tasty food using their own herbs inc children's and interesting vegetarian speciality, well kept Bass and Otter, good wines and coffee, lots of embroidered folk dolls, one room devoted to Guinness memorabilia, eager-to-please staff and friendly samoyeds, computer for customers, no smoking restaurant; skittle alley full of nostalgiamenta, tables (may be candlelit) in attractive estuary-view garden with long-established owl rescue home *(LYM, Mike and Cheryl Lyons, Richard C Morgan, Perry Mills)*

BAMPTON SS9520

☆ *Exeter Inn* [A396 some way S, at B3227 roundabout]: Long low stone-built roadside pub under steep hill overlooking River Exe, several friendly and comfortable linked rooms, mainly flagstoned, huge choice of good reasonably priced food inc local crab and fish, large pleasant carvery restaurant, well kept Cotleigh Tawny and Exmoor Ale and Gold tapped from the cask, quick service, early coffee, log fire, daily papers, no piped music; tables out in front, reasonably priced bedrooms with own bathrooms, open all day, fairly handy for Knightshayes Court *(Andy and Jill Kassube, Peter and Audrey Dowsett, BB)*

BANTHAM SX6643

☆ *Sloop* [off A379/B3197 NW of Kingsbridge]: Appealing 16th-c pub with black beams, flagstones, stripped stone, woodburner and country furniture, easy chairs in quieter side area, enjoyable food using local ingredients, well kept Bass and Palmers IPA, good wines, no smoking dining room, lots of (well behaved) children now; the good long-serving landlord has now left, and the new owners failed to respond to our repeated attempts to get up-to-date price and other factual details from them, so lose their place among the main entries; dogs very welcome, seats outside, bedrooms being refurbished, plenty of surrounding walks *(LYM, Gordon Stevenson, Helen Sharpe, Mr and Mrs J Curtis, Lynda and Trevor Smith, David Eberlin, Norman and Sarah Keeping, Alan and Anne Driver)*

BEER ST2289

☆ *Anchor* [Fore St]: Neatly refurbished sea-view dining pub with good choice of well cooked food from baguettes and ciabattas to local and Brixham fish, Greene King IPA and Abbot and Otter, decent wines, neat efficient service, rambling open-plan layout with old local photographs, large no smoking eating area; may be piped pop music, live Fri-Sun; reasonably priced bedrooms, lots of tables in garden opp, balcony harbour views, delightful seaside village – parking may not be easy *(Ken Flawn, Dr and Mrs M E Wilson, Gerry and Rosemary Dobson, LYM, Maggie and Tony Harwood)*

☆ *Barrel o' Beer* [Fore St]: Welcoming and comfortably straightforward family-run pub with surprisingly good generous food using fresh local ingredients from simple dishes to upmarket recipes and good interestingly cooked and served local fish and seafood (they cure and smoke their own), well kept Exe Valley Bitter and Devon Glory, Fullers London Pride and Wadworths 6X, choice of ciders, cheerful attentive staff, log fire, very small no smoking back dining area; piped music; dogs welcome, open all day *(Chris Powell, Maggie and Tony Harwood, Miss E M Ford, Mrs L Wressel, Martin and Jane Wright, BB)*

☆ *Dolphin* [Fore St]: Friendly and lively open-plan local quite near sea, bags of atmosphere and individuality, old-fashioned décor, oak panelling, nautical bric-a-brac and interesting nooks inc marvellous old distorting mirrors and antique boxing prints in corridors leading to back antique stalls, Bass and Cotleigh ales, decent wine, popular food from good lunchtime sandwiches up; piped music, can be smoky, no credit cards; children and dogs very welcome, one or two tables out by pavement, bedrooms (booked well ahead) *(Mike Gorton, LYM, Barry and Anne, Geoff Pidoux, Meg and Colin Hamilton)*

BEESANDS SX8140

Cricket: Friendly open-plan pub in great spot by sea wall, enjoyable food inc good crab sandwiches and good choice of fresh fish, well kept real ales, log fire, interesting local photographs, family room; unobtrusive piped music; tables outside, bedrooms, at start of coast path to Hallsands and Start Point *(Tony Middis, Comus and Sarah Elliott, Brian Root, Matthew Shackle, Mike and Shelley Woodroffe)*

BELSTONE SX61293

Tors [a mile off A30]: Austere granite building popular with walkers, wide choice of good value generous food from good big baguettes up, friendly local licensees, well kept Flowers IPA, Sharps Doom Bar and Timothy Taylors Landlord, decent wines and malt whiskies, old settles nicely dividing bar; picnic-sets outside (you can make more of the view by crossing the road to sit on the moor), bedrooms, attractive N Dartmoor village *(John and Vivienne Rice, Gill and Tony Morriss)*

BICKINGTON SX8072

Dartmoor Half Way [A383 Ashburton—Newton Abbot]: Big helpings of well cooked reasonably priced food, wide range, real ale, pleasant environment; space for touring caravans, bedrooms *(Mrs B Cushion)*

BICKLEIGH SS9108

Cadeleigh Arms: Good atmosphere and plenty of character, sensibly short changing choice of good food in bar areas and restaurant, pleasant service *(Jeremy Whitehorn)*

BISHOP'S TAWTON SS5629

☆ *Chichester Arms* [signed off A377 outside Barnstaple; East St]: Friendly 15th-c cob and thatch pub with low bowed beams, large stone fireplace, old local photographs, plush banquettes, open fire, quick agreeable service, well priced good generous food from home-made soup and sandwiches to fine steaks and carvery (all meat from named local farms), well kept Dartmoor Best, Ind Coope Burton and Tetleys, decent wines, games in family room, partly no smoking restaurant; picnic-sets on front terrace and in back garden; open all day *(LYM, June and Robin Savage, Mark Flynn)*

BLACKAWTON SX8052

Forces Tavern [A3122 N]: Friendly pub of some character, enjoyable food, concerned chef/landlord, Princetown Dartmoor IPA *(Len Beattie)*

☆ *George* [signed off A3122 and A381]: Very welcoming two-bar family pub fresh from some redecoration, enjoyable reasonably priced hearty food (not Mon lunchtime) inc fresh fish and some good specials, Teignworthy Spring Tide and Marthas Mild and a guest beer, good choice of belgian beers (early May and Aug beer festivals with live bands), woodburner in cosy end lounge, traditional games; children welcome, nice views from garden picnic-sets, cottagey bedrooms *(Comus and Sarah Elliott, LYM, Len Beattie, Brian Kneale, Howard and Lorna Lambert)*

BOLBERRY SX6939

☆ *Port Light*: Alone on dramatic NT clifftop, bright, clean, spacious and busy, with superb picture-window views, well kept Dartmoor, friendly efficient eager-to-please service, interesting memorabilia of its time as a radar station, decent food, restaurant and conservatory; well behaved children and dogs welcome (they host dog wknds), tables on quiet terrace and in garden with splendid fenced play area; five bedrooms, nr fine beaches, right on the coast path *(Esther and John Sprinkle, Jack Clark)*

BRAMPFORD SPEKE SX9298

Agricultural [off A377 N of Exeter]: Dining pub with huge range of good interesting nicely presented bar food inc good Sun lunch, fair prices, their own enjoyable beer, good wine (frequent special events such as tastings), efficient service, very friendly staff and atmosphere, gallery restaurant (children allowed); picnic-sets on sheltered cobbled forecourt – often almost as many dogs there as cars *(Patrick Tolhurst, Peter Craske)*

BRENDON SS7547

☆ *Rockford Inn* [Lynton—Simonsbath rd, off B3223]: Unspoilt 17th-c inn well set for walkers (and fishermen) by East Lyn river, generous low-priced homely food from good sandwiches to fresh fish, cream teas (all day in summer), friendly staff, well kept Cotleigh Tawny and Barn Owl and a guest beer, good house wines, good choice of malt whiskies, farm cider, interesting layout, lots of local pictures, darts, pool, shove-ha'penny, cribbage, dominoes, restaurant; folk night every 3rd Sat; children in eating areas, dogs welcome, bedrooms, open all day summer *(Andy and Jill Kassube, Peter and Audrey Dowsett, Dr D J and Mrs S C Walker, LYM, Gaynor Gregory)*

☆ *Staghunters*: Family-run hotel in idyllic setting with garden by East Lyn river, warmly welcoming neat traditional bar with woodburner, enjoyable freshly prepared food from delicious filled baguettes to good Sun roast, good helpings and low prices, well kept Wadworths 6X and Addlestone's cider, family room with pool table, restaurant; can get very busy; walkers and dogs welcome, good value bedrooms *(Peter and Audrey Dowsett, Lynda and Trevor Smith)*

BRIDESTOWE SX5287

Fox & Hounds [A386 Okehampton—Tavistock]: Popular old-fashioned well worn in moors-edge local, good value generous food (all day at least in summer) inc good steaks, friendly licensees, good range of real ales; dogs welcome, bedrooms *(BB, Dr D J and Mrs S C Walker, Richard and Margaret Peers)*

BRIXHAM SX9255

Blue Anchor [Fore St/King St]: Attractive harbourside pub with well kept Dartmoor Best, Greene King Abbot and a guest such as Exmoor, good mix of locals and visitors, banquettes and plenty of nautical hardwear, usual food inc local fish in two small dining rooms – one a former chapel, down some steps; no children, piped music, live Fri/Sat; open all day *(JP, PP, Steve Whalley)*

BROADCLYST SX9995

Hungry Fox [Station Rd (was B3185), S of Dog Village – ½ mile off A30 opp airport]: Roomy, welcoming and popular mock-Tudor dining pub, good home-made food inc some imaginative dishes, pleasant atmosphere, Bass, Flowers IPA, Otter and Whitbreads, decent wines by the glass, good service *(John and Sonja Newberry)*

Red Lion [B3121, by church]: Heavy-beamed flagstoned core with cushioned pews and low tables by old woodburner, cushioned window seats, some nice chairs around a mix of oak and other tables, good food in bar and (longer menu) separate dining area, pleasant management and good service, real ales inc Bass and Fullers London Pride; picnic-sets on front cobbles below fine wisteria, more in small enclosed garden across quiet lane, nice village and church, not far from Killerton (NT – they own the pub too) *(Dr and Mrs M E Wilson, LYM, Klaus and Elizabeth Leist)*

BROADHEMPSTON SX8066

☆ *Monks Retreat* [The Square]: Friendly atmosphere, black beams, massive old walls, lots of copper, brass and china, superb log fire in huge stone fireplace, well kept Bass, Butcombe and a guest beer, good changing attractively priced food using local materials and unusual vegetables, lunchtime sandwiches and wide children's choice too, sizeable no smoking dining area a couple of steps up (best to book), congenial landlord, prompt cheerful service; by arch to attractive churchyard, a few picnic-sets out in front *(Keith and Liz Harding, BB, Mrs M Beseke)*

BUCKFASTLEIGH SX7466

☆ *Dartbridge* [Totnes Rd, handy for A38]: Big dependable family pub prettily placed opp South Devon Rly, generous popular food (all day at least in summer) inc good crab sandwiches and choice of Sun roasts, well kept Otter ales, good house wines; reasonable disabled access, tables on neatly kept front terrace, bedrooms, open all day *(John Evans, Alan and Paula McCully, Dr and Mrs D Woods, Dr and Mrs A K Clarke)*

Kings Arms [Fore St]: Friendly family-run local, Ushers ales, farm cider, cheap wholesome food; darts, pool, wknd discos and karaoke; beautiful garden, bedrooms *(Neil and Beverley Gardner)*

Watermans Arms [Chapel St]: Friendly family-run pub with cheap wholesome food, Ushers ales, darts and pool; wknd discos and karaoke; bedrooms *(Neil and Beverley Gardner)*

White Hart [Plymouth Rd]: Chattily local open-plan bar with woodburner in dining end, usual pub furnishings, well kept changing ales such as Teignworthy Amy and Beachcomber, Gales HSB and one named for the pub, Sam's local farm cider, quick service; dogs welcome, outside gents'; bedrooms, tables in back courtyard with barbecues; has been open all day Sat (all week summer but cl Sun afternoon and Mon lunchtime) *(Angus Lyon, Neil and Beverley Gardner, BB)*

BUDLEIGH SALTERTON SY0682

☆ *Salterton Arms* [Chapel St]: Spruced up under new licensees, cushioned metal chairs and new carpet, some emphasis on sensible choice of good low-priced home-made food (not Mon lunchtime), well kept Bass, Butcombe and Marstons Pedigree, quietly friendly staff, compact back restaurant and larger but still cosy upper dining gallery; can get very busy summer; children welcome, has been open all day wknds *(Dr and Mrs M E Wilson, LYM, John Beeken, John and Doris Couper, David Carr)*

BURGH ISLAND SX6444

☆ *Pilchard* [300 yds across tidal sands from Bigbury-on-Sea; walk, or take summer Tractor – unique bus on stilts]: Great setting high above sea on tidal island with unspoilt cliff walks, neatly refurbished but keeping its ancient beams and flagstones, lanterns, nautical/smuggling feel and blazing fire; decent food, real ales, good uniformed service, family room – useful for trippers by day, friendly local atmosphere at night; can be smoky; some tables down by beach, open all day all year *(Mayur Shah, the Didler, Comus and Sarah Elliott, JP, PP, Esther and John Sprinkle, Cathy Robinson, Ed Coombe, LYM, Neil and Beverley Gardner, Geoff Pidoux)*

CHAGFORD SX6987

☆ *Bullers Arms* [Mill St]: Cheery panelled local with good value food servery (very wide range inc bargain steak nights Sun and Thurs), well kept Bass, Butcombe and Courage Directors, decent coffee, very friendly efficient staff, militaria, copper and brass, darts; summer barbecues *(LYM, C A Hall)*

☆ *Ring o' Bells* [off A382 Moretonhampstead—Whiddon Down]: Old black and white pub with new licensees this year, appealing oak-panelled bar, black and white photographs of the village and local characters, copper and brass, log-effect fire, bar food, well kept Butcombe Bitter, St Austell Dartmoor Best and Teignworthy Reel Ale, Addlestone's cider, traditional games, small no smoking candlelit dining room; dogs in bar, sunny walled garden behind with seats on lawn, bedrooms *(LYM)*

CHILLINGTON SX7942

☆ *Open Arms* [A379 E of Kingsbridge]: Roomy modernised open-plan turkey-carpeted bar with good choice of inexpensive home-made food, well kept ales, good wines and choice of spirits, friendly local atmosphere, back games room with pool; tables in pleasant back garden *(BB, E B Ireland)*

CHITTLEHAMHOLT SS6521

☆ *Exeter Inn* [off A377 Barnstaple—Crediton, and B3226 SW of South Molton]: Spotless old inn with friendly staff and long-serving licensees, enjoyable food from sandwiches, baguettes and baked potatoes to good local steaks and Sun roast, no smoking restaurant, well kept Dartmoor Best, Greene King Abbot and a guest beer, farm ciders, good wine choice, open stove in huge fireplace, side area with booth seating; traditional games, piped music, dogs allowed; children in eating areas, benches out on terrace, decent bedrooms with showers *(Paula, Paul and Ella Hawkins, LYM, Crystal and Peter Hooper, Rod Stoneman, Mrs Brenda Westerman, Dr and Mrs A K Clarke)*

CHRISTOW SX8384

☆ ***Artichoke***: Pretty thatched local with comfortable open-plan rooms stepped down hill, low beams, some black panelling, flagstones, reliable food inc fish and game, lovely log fire (2nd one in no smoking end dining room), real ales tapped from the cask, welcoming helpful service; tables on back terrace, pretty hillside village nr Canonteign Waterfalls and Country Park *(BB, Ann and Colin Hunt, Nick and Meriel Cox)*

CHUDLEIGH SX8679

Bishop Lacey [Fore St, just off A38]: Quaint partly 14th-c church house with good service, well kept Branscombe Vale, Flowers IPA, Fullers London Pride and a guest such as Princetown Jail, some tapped from casks in back bar, good strong coffee, two log fires, good value food, no smoking dining room; live bands in next-door offshoot; garden tables, winter beer festival, bedrooms, open all day *(JP, PP, the Didler)*

Old Coaching House [Fore St]: Popular flagstoned country pub with good value food inc good curries and mixed grill in bar or restaurant, well kept Greene King Abbot and Teignworthy, friendly staff, local jazz Fri *(the Didler, JP, PP)*

CHURCHSTOW SX7145

☆ ***Church House*** [A379 NW of Kingsbridge]: Long character pub with heavy black beams (dates from 13th c), stripped stone, cushioned settles, quickly served generous food from sandwiches to mixed grill and (Weds-Sat nights, Sun lunch) popular carvery, well kept Bass and local ales, decent wines, nice atmosphere, back conservatory with floodlit well feature; well behaved children and dogs welcome, tables outside *(LYM, Comus and Sarah Elliott, Ann and Bob Westbrook)*

CHURSTON FERRERS SX9056

☆ ***Churston Court*** [off A3022 S of Torquay; Church Rd]: Welll converted manor house dating back to Saxon times in pretty spot next to ancient church; warren of largely no smoking candlelit rooms, suits of armour, historic portraits, faded tapestries, partly flagstoned main bar, plenty of oak beams, long wooden tables, sofas, gilt-framed mirrors, huge inglenook fireplace, Greene King Abbot, Princetown Dartmoor and Jail; carvery plus local fish, piped classical music; children welcome, lots of tables in attractive walled lawn, bedrooms, good walks nearby, open all day *(J E M Andeville, D and S Price, Neil and Anita Christopher, John and Glenys Wheeler, LYM)*

CLAYHIDON ST1615

☆ ***Half Moon***: Pretty village pub with tasteful furniture and inglenook fireplace in comfortable bar, helpful staff, good choice of reasonably priced home-made food, three well kept Cotleigh ales; children welcome, quiet views from picnic-sets in tiered garden over road *(Mike Gorton)*

CLEARBROOK SX5265

☆ ***Skylark*** [village signed down dead end off A386 Tavistock—Plymouth]: Welcoming and chatty old two-room pub in pretty cottage row tucked right into Dartmoor, well kept Bass, Courage Best and Greene King Old Speckled Hen, wide choice of good value food from sandwiches up inc good vegetarian dishes, good service, simple furnishings, log fire, plenty of locals; quite separate children's room in big back garden with plenty of picnic-sets and other seats, small adventure play area, wandering ponies *(BB, Jacquie and Jim Jones)*

CLOVELLY SS3225

New Inn [High St]: Attractive old inn halfway down the steep cobbled street, simple easy-going lower bar (front part has more character than back room), good choice of inexpensive bar food and of well kept beers inc a local one brewed for the pub; quiet piped music, dogs allowed; bedrooms *(Dr and Mrs A K Clarke)*

CLYST ST GEORGE SX9788

St George & Dragon: Spaciously extended open-plan low-beamed bar divided by timbers into smaller areas, good helpings of food, good wine list, welcoming landlord, friendly young staff, open fires *(Dr and Mrs M E Wilson)*

COCKINGTON SX8963

Drum [Cockington Lane]: Cheerfully bustling Vintage Inn in thatched and beamed tavern (designed by Lutyens to match the quaintly touristy Torquay-edge medieval village), Dartmoor Bitter and Legend, good choice of wines by the glass, roomy well divided bar with two family eating areas, quick service, decent food; open all day, tables on terrace and in attractive back garden by 500-acre park *(Alain and Rose Foote)*

COCKWOOD SX9780

Ship [off A379 N of Dawlish]: Comfortable 17th-c inn overlooking estuary and harbour, partitioned beamed bar with big log fire and ancient oven, decorative plates and seafaring prints and memorabilia, small no smoking restaurant, generous reasonably priced food from open crab sandwiches up inc imaginative evening fish dishes and good puddings (freshly made so takes time), well kept Greene King Abbot and Old Speckled Hen and Sharps Doom Bar, friendly helpful staff; piped music; good steep-sided garden *(John Beeken)*

COLYTON SY2494

Gerrard Arms [St Andrews Sq]: Friendly open-plan local with well kept Branscombe Vale Branoc and guest beers, good value home-made food inc Sun roasts; nice garden; in summer you may be able to come by tram from Seaton then a horse-drawn wagon from the station *(JP, PP, the Didler, Pete Walker)*

☆ ***Kingfisher*** [off A35 and A3052 E of Sidmouth; Dolphin St]: Village local with hearty popular food from good crab sandwiches and baked potatoes up, stripped stone, plush seats and elm settles, beams and big open fire, well kept Badger Best and Tanglefoot and changing guest beers, farm cider, low-priced soft drinks, friendly family service; pub games, upstairs family room, skittle alley, tables out on terrace, garden with water feature *(LYM, the Didler, KN-R, Pete Walker)*

COUNTISBURY SS7449

Exmoor Sandpiper [A39, E of Lynton]: Beautifully set rambling heavy-beamed pub under pleasant new licensees, several good log fires, enjoyable food in bar and restaurant, decent wines, well kept ales such as Exmoor, reasonable prices; children in eating area, garden tables, good nearby cliff walks, comfortable bedrooms, open all day *(LYM, John Saville, Beryl and Tim Dawson, J V Dadswell, Steve Godfrey)*

CROYDE SS4439

☆ *Thatched Barn* [B3231 NW of Braunton; Hobbs Hill]: Lively rambling thatched pub nr great surfing beaches, with cheerful efficient young staff, laid-back feel and customers to match (can get packed in summer); wide choice of generous food from sandwiches and baguettes up, lunchtime bargains for two, well kept ales inc Bass, morning coffee, teas; restaurant, children in eating area; piped music; open all day, bedrooms simple but clean and comfortable, tables outside *(LYM, Mark Flynn)*

DARTINGTON SX7762

Cott [Cott signed off A385 W of Totnes, opp A384 turn-off]: Picturesque long 14th-c thatched pub, cosy atmosphere boosted by heavy beams, steps, flagstones and big log fires, friendly staff, well kept Greene King IPA and Abbot and Otter, food (not cheap) from lunchtime sandwiches and baked potatoes up; summer singalongs, children welcome, picnic-sets in garden and on pretty terrace, bedrooms with own bathrooms, open all day at least in summer *(Pat and Robert Watt, Comus and Sarah Elliott, Ian Phillips, Ann and Bob Westbrook, LYM, Nigel Long, Daphne Barkhouse, Brian and Bett Cox, E B Ireland)*

White Hart Bar [Dartington Hall]: Light bright modern décor and open fires in the college's bar (open to visitors), good low-priced food here and in baronial hall, real ales such as Exmoor and one brewed for the bar; very special atmosphere sitting out in the famously beautiful grounds *(Graham and Rose Ive, Charles Cooper, Dr and Mrs A K Clarke)*

DARTMOUTH SX8751

Dolphin [Market St]: Interesting building in picturesque part of town, well kept real ales inc a guest beer tapped from the cask, cosy upstairs restaurant with good generous seafood; piped music, no children *(David Carr)*

George & Dragon [Mayors Ave]: Cosy traditional pub with naval theme, enjoyable food at sensible prices, enterprising landlord, well kept Bass and Flowers Original; children catered for, fishing parties arranged, back terrace with barbecue, good value well equipped bedrooms *(David Carr)*

☆ *Royal Castle Hotel* [the Quay]: Rambling 17th-c or older hotel behind Regency façade overlooking inner harbour, pleasant lounge-like Galleon bar on right, neatly reworked Harbour Bar on left (TV, piped music, dogs allowed – no children), Exe Valley Dobs Best, all-day bar food from sandwiches up, perhaps winter lunchtime spit-roasts from their 300-year-old Lidstone range; comfortable bedrooms with secure parking, open all day *(Tim and Carolyn Lowes, Terry and Linda Moseley, JP, PP, Tony Middis, David and Julie Glover, J E Shackleton, Joyce and Maurice Cottrell, Norman and Sarah Keeping, Keith and Margaret Kettell, LYM)*

DITTISHAM SX8654

☆ *Ferry Boat* [Manor St; best to park in village – steep but attractive walk down]: Idyllic waterside setting, big windows making the most of it, friendly landlord and family, limited good value food inc baguettes and pies, real ale; no parking, quite a walk down; nr little foot-ferry you call by bell, good walks *(Geoffrey and Karen Berrill, Graham and Rose Ive, LYM, Mrs C Lintott, Vanessa Stilwell)*

DOUSLAND SX5368

Burrator Inn: Big Victorian pub with good value if not cheap fresh food in bar and restaurant (friendly landlord is ex-Smithfields butcher and ex-farmer), real ales, pool room, lots of facilities (in and out) for children; live music some nights, good value bedrooms *(Brian and Bett Cox)*

DUNSFORD SX8189

☆ *Royal Oak* [signed from Moretonhampstead]: Relaxed village inn with good generous food (home-made so may take a while), well kept Greene King Abbot, Princetown Jail, Sharps Cornish Coaster and Doom Bar and changing guest beers, local farm ciders, friendly service, light and airy lounge bar with woodburner, steps down to games room, provision for children; quiz nights, piped music; Fri barbecues in sheltered tiered garden, good value bedrooms in converted barn *(R M Corlett, LYM, the Didler)*

EAST PRAWLE SX7836

Pigs Nose [Prawle Green]: Cheery and homely, with low beams and flagstones, well kept ales such as Golden Celebration tapped from the cask, enjoyable if limited food from good ploughman's and sandwiches up, open fire, easy chairs and sofa, interesting knick-knacks and local pictures, lots of nice dogs, jars of wild flowers and candles on tables, bird log, darts, small family area with small box of unusual toys; unobtrusive nostalgic piped music, hall for live bands; tables outside, nice spot on village green *(Mr and Mrs M Dalby, Comus and Sarah Elliott, Jill Hummerstone, Brian Kneale)*

☆ ***Providence*** [off A379 E of Kingsbridge]: Simple bare-boards pub, friendly and relaxed, with laid-back staff and regulars, enjoyable food inc fresh fish from sharply focused kitchen, well kept Dartmoor IPA, welcoming fire in interesting fireplace, chunky elm tables, a couple of armchairs and a traditional settle among other furnishings, model ship, word games; may be piped local radio or 1970s CDs;

children welcome, wrought-iron tables in nice small sea-view walled garden, good coast walks *(LYM, Fiona Eddleston, MP)*

EXETER SX9292

Chaucers [basement of Tesco Metro, High St]: Large dim-lit modern olde-worlde pub/bistro/wine bar down lots of steps, comfortable furnishings, candles in bottles, several levels inc no smoking areas, well kept Bass, good range of generous food inc adventurous dishes, quick friendly service, pleasant atmosphere; piped music *(Mr and Mrs Colin Roberts)*

Countess Wear [on B3181 ring rd roundabout]: Well run Beefeater pub/restaurant with well kept real ale, reliable food, good quick service; good value comfortable bedrooms in attached Travel Inn *(Mr and Mrs Colin Roberts)*

☆ ***Double Locks*** [Canal Banks, Alphington, via Marsh Barton Industrial Estate; OS Sheet 192 map ref 933901]: Remote retreat by ship canal, a favourite for its unspoilt character, friendly informality, laid-back atmosphere, great range of eight or so well kept ales often tapped straight from the cask (also Gray's farm cider) and good value plain home-made bar food from sandwiches and hot filled rolls up all day; refurbishment due, piped music, frequent live; children welcome in eating areas, dogs very welcome too, distant view to city and cathedral from seats out on decking, good big play area, open all day *(Mike Gorton, Laura Wilson, Esther and John Sprinkle, Barry Steele-Perkins, LYM, JP, PP, SH, the Didler, JHBS, Phil and Sally Gorton, Ian and Deborah Carrington, John Prescott, Richard and Anne Ansell, Brenda and Rob Fincham, David Carr, Andy Sinden, Louise Harrington, Mrs Sylvia Elcoate, A P Seymour, John and Vivienne Rice, Dick Ward)*

☆ ***Great Western*** [St David's Hill]: Up to a dozen or more well kept changing ales usually inc Adnams, Bass, Exmoor, Fullers London Pride and Teignworthy in large hotel's small sociable public bar, with plenty of regulars, wholesome good value bar food all day from sandwiches up (also a restaurant), daily papers, no music; bedrooms fresh and warm *(Philip Kingsbury, the Didler, Colin Gooch, JP, PP, Joe Green, Phil and Sally Gorton, Revd R P Tickle, Dr and Mrs A K Clarke)*

Hour Glass [Melbourne St, above the quay]: Handsome 19th-c city pub, beams, panelling, candles and open fire, well kept ales such as Bass, Otter and Sharps Doom Bar, good house wine, enjoyable reasonably priced bar food, friendly helpful staff, big popular cellar restaurant *(the Didler, Mike Gorton, Dr and Mrs M E Wilson)*

Mill on the Exe [Bonhay Rd (A377)]: Good spot by new pedestrian bridge over weir, heated waterside terrace, bar comfortably done out with bare boards, old bricks, beams and timbers, large airy river-view conservatory restaurant, good sensibly priced food inc good value lunchtime light dishes, well kept St Austell ales, good house wines, friendly young staff; children welcome *(John and Vivienne Rice, BB, Joe Green)*

Old Fire House [New North Rd]: Superb collection of Fire Service memorabilia in small busy flagstoned pub with Wadworths IPA and 6X and Youngs Special, enjoyable bargain food, further eating area upstairs; through high arched wrought-iron gates to block of flats or offices *(Dr and Mrs M E Wilson)*

Port Royal [Weirfield Path, off Weirfield Rd]: Low gabled waterside pavilion with sofas in neat, convivial and attractive nautical-theme lounge, real ales such as Flowers IPA, Greene King Old Speckled Hen and Wadworths 6X, wide choice of reasonably priced fresh food inc some interesting dishes, friendly service; public bar with games and piped music; river-view tables, by left bank path downstream from The Quay *(Dr and Mrs M E Wilson, John Western)*

Prospect [The Quay (left bank, nr rowing club)]: Good quayside spot, spick and span refit and modern colour-scheme and prints contrasting with the old building's beams, sensibly priced up-to-date bar food inc huge sandwiches, well kept ales inc Otter, friendly helpful young staff, raised river-view dining area; piped music – live some evenings; tables outside *(Dr and Mrs M E Wilson, Sue and Mike Todd, P F Willmer, Joe Green, Derek and Sylvia Stephenson, John and Vivienne Rice)*

☆ ***Ship*** [Martins Lane, nr cathedral]: Pretty 14th-c building with genuine dark heavy beams, done up inside in olde-worlde city pub style, well kept Bass, Greene King Old Speckled Hen and Marstons Pedigree, farm cider, speedy friendly service, generous sandwiches only down here, reasonably priced meals in comfortable upstairs restaurant *(Dr and Mrs M E Wilson, LYM, DAV, Stephen Hussey, Dr and Mrs A K Clarke, Roger Huggins, Tom and Alex McLean, Mark Flynn, Alain and Rose Foote)*

Welcome [Haven Banks, off Haven Rd (which is first left off A377 heading S after Exe crossing)]: Old two-room pub near the gasometers and little changed since the 1960s (ditto the juke box), gas lighting and flagstones, very friendly old-school landlady, well kept ales inc RCH PG Steam; a few tables out overlooking basin on Exeter Ship Canal, and can be reached on foot via footbridges from The Quay *(the Didler, Dr and Mrs M E Wilson, JP, PP)*

Well House [Cathedral Yard, attached to Royal Clarence Hotel]: Big windows looking across to cathedral in open-plan bistro-look bar with tables divided by inner walls and partitions, lots of interesting Victorian prints, good choice of well kept mainly local ales such as Blackawton, quick service, popular bar lunches inc good sandwiches and salads, daily papers; Roman well beneath (can be viewed when pub not busy) *(BB, Stephen Hussey, Derek and Sylvia Stephenson, Roger Huggins, Tom and Alex McLean, Pete Walker)*

☆ ***White Hart*** [South St]: Attractively old-fashioned largely no smoking rambling bar (heavy beams, oak flooring and nice furnishings inc antiques), charming inner cobbled courtyard, well kept Bass, good wines, efficient cheerful staff, good value bar food inc good sandwich choice, bar billiards; handy reasonably priced central place to stay, with good breakfast and free parking *(JP, PP, LYM, Susan and Nigel Wilson, Clare and Peter Pearse, Joan and Michel Hooper-Immins, Jim and Maggie Cowell, Roger Huggins, Tom and Alex McLean)*

EXMINSTER SX9587

Swans Nest [Station Rd, just off A379 on outskirts]: Huge well arranged mass-throughput food pub very popular for wide choice of reasonably priced food from sandwiches and children's dishes to extensive carvery, Otter Best and Youngs Special, helpful staff, no smoking areas; especially good for family groups, handy for M5 *(LYM, Father Robert Marsh, John Beeken, David Carr)*

EXMOUTH SX9980

Beach [Victoria Rd]: Down-to-earth old quayside local with shipping and lifeboat memorabilia and photographs, beams, posts and panelling, cast-iron framed tables, Bass, Greene King Old Speckled Hen and Otter, food, friendly landlord, staff and salty regulars *(Dr and Mrs M E Wilson)*

Grove [Esplanade]: Roomy panelled Youngs outpost set back from beach, their beers kept well, decent house wines, good coffee, good value food inc plenty of local fish and children's menu, good friendly service, simple furnishings, caricatures and local prints, 1930s replicas, attractive fireplace at back, sea views from appealing upstairs no smoking dining room and balcony; live music Fri; picnic-sets in garden (no view) with play area *(John Beeken, Dr and Mrs M E Wilson, Alain and Rose Foote)*

Powder Monkey [The Parade]: Well managed Wetherspoons with long bar, armchairs in two smaller front rooms (children allowed in one), five real ales, low prices; very popular with young people wknds; a few tables on courtyard facing roundabout *(Dr and Mrs M E Wilson, Craig Turnbull, Alain and Rose Foote)*

EXTON SX9886

Puffing Billy: Wide choice of good inventive food inc seafood in smartly reworked dining pub (more dining than pub, though has small bar and flagstoned entrance), friendly staff; close-set picnic-sets on terrace, small back garden *(Ken Flawn, Anthony Barnes)*

FILLEIGH SS6727

☆ ***Stags Head*** [off A361, via B3226 N of S Molton]: Pretty 16th-c thatched and flagstoned pub with good value home-made food from sandwiches up, well kept Barum Original, Bass and Tetleys, reasonably priced wines, welcoming landlord, friendly local bar with crack darts team, banknotes on beams, Corgi toy collection and very high-backed settle, separate lounge bar, newer and larger cottagey dining room up a couple of steps; old rustic tables out in fairy-lit honeysuckle arbour by big tree-sheltered pond with lots of ducks and fish; bedrooms comfortable and good value, good breakfast *(Tracey and Stephen Groves, BB, Mark and Amanda Sheard, Mark Flynn, D A Walker)*

FROGMORE SX7742

Globe [A379 E of Kingsbridge]: Lots of ship and yacht paintings, some built-in settles creating corner booths, mix of simple tables, generous bar food from sandwiches and good ploughman's to steak inc children's, well kept Exmoor Ale and Greene King Abbot, local farm cider in summer, good wines, fine log fire in good cosy restaurant, games and TV in flagstoned locals' bar; tables out on pretty terraces with play area and a bit of a creek view, plenty of walks, comfortable bedrooms *(LYM, Margaret Booth)*

GEORGEHAM SS4639

Kings Arms [B3231 Croyde—Woolacombe]: Cheered up by new licensees, fresh open-plan refurbishment with distinct eating area, well kept Bass and Fullers London Pride, with local Barum tapped from the cask, decent coffee, short but interesting food choice inc popular good value Sun roast *(Paul and Ursula Randall)*

☆ ***Rock*** [Rock Hill, above village]: Well restored oak-beamed pub with well kept ales such as Cotleigh Golden Eagle, Fullers London Pride, Greene King IPA and Abbot and Timothy Taylors Landlord, local farm cider, decent wines, good value generous straightforward food inc speciality baguettes and appealing puddings, quick friendly service, old red quarry tiles, open fire, pleasant mix of rustic furniture, lots of bric-a-brac, vine-adorned back family conservatory; piped music, darts, fruit machine, pool room and juke box; dogs welcome, tables under cocktail parasols on front terrace, pretty hanging baskets *(Kev and Gaye Griffiths, BB, Simon Robinson, Mark and Amanda Sheard, Paul and Ursula Randall)*

GRENOFEN SX4971

Halfway House [A386 near Tavistock]: Good choice of reasonably priced home-made food using local produce, friendly efficient licensees, good range of well kept real ales, farm cider, decent wines, lounge, restaurant and traditional bar with pool and darts; tables out overlooking Dartmoor, good value bedrooms *(Wally Parson)*

HARTLAND QUAY SS2224

☆ ***Hartland Quay Hotel*** [off B3248 W of Bideford, down toll road (free Oct—Easter); OS Sheet 190 map ref 222248]: Unpretentious and relaxed old hotel in formidable cliff scenery, real maritime-feel bar with fishing memorabilia and interesting shipwreck pictures, down-to-earth helpful staff, small no smoking room, may have well kept Sharps Doom Bar (often keg beer only), good value generous food, good mix of customers; dogs welcome, lots of tables outside (very popular with holidaymakers in season), good value bedrooms, seawater swimming pool, rugged coast walks; cl midwinter *(Mr and Mrs John Taylor, Earl and Chris Pick)*

HATHERLEIGH SS5404

☆ *George* [A386 N of Okehampton; Market St]: Timbered pub with huge oak beams, enormous fireplace, easy chairs, sofas and antique cushioned settles in original core, more modern monk-theme main bar, more settles and woodburner in L-shaped beamed back bar, Bass, St Austell Dartmoor Best and a beer named for the pub, lots of malt whiskies, farm cider, bar food from sandwiches to steaks and fresh fish, restaurant; children in eating area, dogs in bar, rustic tables in pretty courtyard and walled cobbled garden, bedrooms, open all day *(Ryta Horridge, J Simmonds, JP, PP, the Didler, LYM, John and Joan Nash)*

☆ *Tally Ho* [Market St (A386)]: Attractive heavy-beamed and timbered linked rooms, sturdy furnishings, big log fire and woodburner, decent food from lunchtime sandwiches up, good real ales brewed for them locally by Clearwater, no smoking restaurant, traditional games; piped music; tables in nice sheltered garden, three cosy and prettily furnished bedrooms *(LYM, the Didler, JP, PP, Ron and Sheila Corbett)*

HOLCOMBE ROGUS ST0518

Prince of Wales: Spacious, comfortable and friendly, enjoyable food cooked by new landlady, landlord proud of his quickly changing well kept guest beers, new restaurant *(John and Fiona McIlwain)*

HOLSWORTHY SS3408

Kings Arms [Fore St/The Square]: 17th-c inn with Victorian fittings, etched windows and coal fires in three interesting traditional bars, old pictures and photographs, 40s and 50s beer advertisements, lots of optics behind ornate counter, particularly well kept Bass and Sharps Doom Bar, friendly locals; open all day, Sun afternoon closure *(JP, PP, the Didler)*

HONITON SY1198

Greyhound [Fenny Bridges, B3177 4 miles W]: Big busy thatched family dining pub with wide food choice from good open sandwiches and baked potatoes up, quick friendly service, well kept Otter beers, heavy beams and stylish décor, attractive restaurant with no smoking area; bedrooms *(Dr and Mrs M E Wilson, LYM, Meg and Colin Hamilton)*

☆ *Red Cow* [High St]: Plain welcoming local, very busy on Tues and Sat market days, scrubbed tables, pleasant alcoves, log fires, well kept Bass, Courage Directors and local Otter, decent wines and malt whiskies, good value quickly served no-nonsense food from sandwiches up in restaurant part, lots of chamber-pots and big mugs on beams; pavement tables, bedrooms *(BB, Dr and Mrs M E Wilson, Sue and Mike Todd, Mark Flynn, Colin and Janet Roe)*

HORSEBRIDGE SX3975

☆ *Royal* [off A384 Tavistock—Launceston]: Cheerful slate-floored rooms, interesting bric-a-brac and pictures, tasty food from baguettes and baked potatoes up, Bass, Sharps Doom Bar, Wadworths 6X and guest beers, farm cider, bar billiards, cribbage, dominoes, no smoking café-style side room, no music or machines; no children in evening, tables on back terrace and in big garden *(LYM, DAV, Andrea Rampley)*

IDE SX8990

☆ *Poachers* [3 miles from M5 junction 31, via A30; High St]: Welcoming atmosphere, good generous food, both traditional and inventively individual, inc good fish choice (worth booking evenings), well kept Bass, Branscombe Vale Branoc, Otter and one brewed locally for the pub, good value house wines, friendly landlord and helpful attentive service, sofas and open fire; blues night, picnic-sets in nice garden, attractive bedrooms, small quaint village, cl Mon lunchtime *(R J Walden, John and Vivienne Rice, Mrs Deborah Phillips, John and Marion Tyrie, John and Sonja Newberry, Mrs Jill Silversides, Barry Brown, Dr and Mrs M E Wilson, the Didler)*

IDEFORD SX8977

☆ *Royal Oak* [2 miles off A380]: Cosy thatched and flagstoned village local brightened up but still unspoilt, interesting Nelson and Churchill memorabilia, welcoming service, well kept Flowers IPA and Original, bar food, log fire *(JP, PP, the Didler, Phil and Sally Gorton)*

ILSINGTON SX7876

Carpenters Arms: Unspoilt and convivial 18th-c local next to church in quiet village, friendly licensees, wholesome cheap food, well kept ales on handpump or tapped from the cask, log fire, parlour off main public bar; no music, good walks *(Neil and Beverley Gardner)*

INSTOW SS4730

Quay Inn [Marine Parade]: Friendly down-to-earth open-plan seaside pub just above quay, tables looking out over estuary, simple reasonably priced food from baguettes to lobster tails, also afternoon teas, local real ales; piped music may obtrude; disabled access, open all day *(Andy and Jill Kassube, Michael and Ann Cole, J V Dadswell)*

IPPLEPEN SX8366

Wellington [off A381 Totnes—Newton Abbot; Fore St]: Attractively furnished two-bar village pub popular for good fresh reasonably priced food inc imaginative recipes and wonderful fish choice; helpful friendly staff, good choice of beer and wines, picnic-sets outside, pleasant village *(Mr and Mrs N Ward, Gordon Tong, John and Sonja Newberry)*

KENN SX9285

☆ *Ley Arms* [signed off A380 just S of Exeter]: Extended thatched pub in quiet spot nr church, attractive inside and out, beams and polished granite flagstones, plush black-panelled lounge with striking fireplace, good wines, real ales, enjoyable bar lunches, interesting evening menu, efficient service, sizeable smartish restaurant side; piped music, no smoking family room, games area *(LYM, Tim and Rosemary Wells)*

KENTON SX9583

Devon Arms [Fore St; A379 Exeter—Dawlish]: Comfortable 16th-c beamed bar with old farm tools, animal photographs and hunting trophies, sound good value food from good filled baguettes and pasties up, well kept Bass, Scattor Rock Teign Valley Tipple and Wadworths 6X, short choice of decent wine, friendly helpful service, dining area; small back garden with play area, aviary and caged rabbits; bedrooms with own bathrooms, handy for Powderham Castle *(Dennis Jenkin, Alain and Rose Foote, Ken Flawn)*

KINGSBRIDGE SX7343

Crabshell [Embankment Rd, edge of town]: Lovely waterside position, charming when tide in, with big windows and tables out on the hard; simple bar with plainly furnished eating area, friendly staff, real ales, good farm cider, warm fire, wide choice of food from good fresh lunchtime shrimp or crab sandwiches to local fish and shellfish (this may be confined to upstairs restaurant, with good views) *(BB, B Forster)*

KINGSTEIGNTON SX8773

☆ *Old Rydon* [Rydon Rd]: Dining pub with big log fire in small cosy heavy-beamed bar with upper gallery, no smoking restaurant with pleasant vine-draped conservatory, reasonably priced food from baked potatoes and toasted muffins to chargrills, children's dishes, well kept changing ales such as Bass, Fullers London Pride and Greene King Abbot, decent wines; piped music; tables on terrace and in nice sheltered garden *(Pamela and Merlyn Horswell, Ian Phillips, LYM, Neil and Beverley Gardner, John and Sonja Newberry, Jim and Maggie Cowell)*

Ten Tors [Exeter Rd]: Large extended 1930s pub, wide choice of good value typical food from doorstep sandwiches to OAP specials, end restaurant, well kept Courage and local beers, cheerful service *(John and Sonja Newberry, Alain and Rose Foote)*

KNOWSTONE SS8223

☆ *Masons Arms*: This former favourite Exmoor pub has under its new owner turned into much more of a french restaurant – certainly enjoyable as that (and still has Cotleigh real ale and a big log fire in its nicely furnished bar); cl Sun evening, Mon lunchtime *(Patrick and Phillipa Vickery, J C Brittain-Long, LYM)*

LAKE SX5288

Bearslake [A386 just S of Sourton]: Thatched stone-built Dartmoor inn with beams, flagstones, inglenook fireplace, pews and plenty of locals in friendly character bar, enjoyable and popular home-made food, good family service; picnic-sets in sizeable garden with terrace, six olde-worlde bedrooms, filling breakfast *(A McCormick, T Powell, Francine Lee-Thompson)*

LEE SS4846

☆ *Grampus* [signed off B3343/A361 W of Ilfracombe]: Attractive unassuming 14th-c pub short stroll from sea, friendly helpful service, simple furnishings, wide range of good simple home-made food from toasties up (evening meals if booked), well kept real ales such as Exmoor Gold, woodburner, pool in family room, dogs very welcome; lots of tables in appealing sheltered garden, superb coastal walks *(BB, Lynda and Trevor Smith, R L R Nicholson, Rona Murdoch)*

LIFTON SX3885

Arundell Arms [Fore St]: Substantial and delightfully run if not cheap country-house fishing hotel in same ownership for many years, rich décor, very agreeable welcoming atmosphere, good interesting lunchtime bar food and evening restaurant, good choice of wines by the glass, sophisticated service; can arrange fishing tuition – also shooting, deer-stalking and riding; bedrooms – a pleasant place to stay *(Alain and Rose Foote, Mary Ellen Cummings)*

LUPPITT ST1606

Luppitt Inn [back roads N of Honiton]: Unspoilt little basic farmhouse pub, friendly chatty landlady who keeps it open because she (and her cats) like the company; tiny room with corner bar and a table, another not much bigger with fireplace, Otter tapped from the cask, metal puzzles made by neighbour, no food or music, lavatories across the yard; a real throwback, may be cl some lunchtimes and Sun evening *(JP, PP, the Didler, RWC, Conor McGaughey)*

LUTON SX9076

☆ *Elizabethan* [Haldon Moor]: Charming and popular low-beamed old-world pub with welcoming owners and friendly efficient staff, good well presented if not cheap food, well kept real ales such as Fullers London Pride with a local guest beer such as Teignworthy Reel, reasonably priced house wines, nice atmosphere; garden tables *(Phil and Sally Gorton, Father David Cossar)*

LYMPSTONE SX9984

Globe [off A376 N of Exmouth; The Strand]: Roomy dining area with generous food from sandwiches and bargain lunchtime fish and chips up, well kept Adnams, Bass, Fullers London Pride and Otter, decent house wines, roaring fire and individual local atmosphere in bar; children welcome, some live entertainment, open all day in summer *(LYM, Ken Flawn, Phil and Sally Gorton, Mike Turner)*

☆ *Redwing* [Church Rd]: Friendly two-bar pub with good value well prepared food inc lots of local fish and good puddings, well kept Greene King Abbot, Otter and Palmers Bitter and Dorset Gold, local farm ciders, good house wines, caring licensees and helpful efficient staff, brightly painted lounge, neat little no smoking dining area with wild flowers, open all day wknds; may be discreet piped music, quiz nights, live music most wknds, some bank hols, and jazz Tues; pretty garden behind (sometimes music here in fine weather), unspoilt village with shore walks *(the Didler, Ken Flawn, Chris Parsons, Michael Rowse, BB, Peter Burton, Dr and Mrs M E Wilson)*

LYNTON SS7249

Crown [Market St/Sinai Hill]: Good relaxed atmosphere in hotel lounge bar, friendly and chatty staff and locals, open fire, decent reasonably priced food here and in small comfortable restaurant, well kept local Clearwater Ales, farm cider, horse tack; good bedrooms *(Bruce Bird)*

Hunters [Hunters Inn well signed off A39 W of Lynton]: Superb Heddon Valley position by NT information centre down very steep hill, great walks inc one, not too taxing, down to the sea; big spreading bar with some plush banquettes and so forth, enjoyable freshly prepared generous food from soup and baguettes to local seafood (may be a wait when crowded), cheerful young helpful staff, well kept Exmoor ales, woodburner (may be a dozing boxer dog), no smoking area; piped music; bedrooms, picnic-sets on balconied terrace overlooking attractively landscaped pondside garden with peacocks, open all day *(Theocsbrian, Bruce Bird, BB)*

MAIDENCOMBE SX9268

☆ ***Thatched Tavern*** [Steep Hill]: Spotless much extended three-level thatched pub with lovely coastal views, well kept Flowers IPA and Original and a summer guest beer in pubby bar, well priced generous food inc local fish (can be a wait) and tempting puddings in two cosy eating areas, one no smoking, quick attentive service even when busy, big family room, pleasant restaurant; children allowed, no dogs inside, nice garden with small thatched huts, small attractive village above small beach *(Geoffrey and Karen Berrill, B and F A Hannam, Alan Garnett, E G Parish, E B Ireland)*

MARSH ST2510

☆ ***Flintlock*** [pub signed just off A303 Ilminster—Honiton]: Long open-plan dining pub popular for wide choice of good varied reasonably priced food inc well cooked Sun lunches, friendly landlord and staff, well kept Fullers London Pride and Otter, neat furnishings, woodburner in stone inglenook, beamery and mainly stripped stone walls, plenty of copper and brass; piped music, cl Mon *(BB, Brian and Bett Cox)*

MODBURY SX6551

Exeter Inn [Church St]: Picture-book 14th-c double-fronted inn, decent traditional food inc Sun roast, wide choice of well kept local beers, farm ciders; children welcome, tables in garden behind, well equipped bedrooms *(Ann and Bob Westbrook)*

MONKLEIGH SS4520

☆ ***Bell***: Laid-back beamed and partly thatched village local with good Civil War pictures by local artist (prints for sale), log fire, well kept changing ales such as Burrington Black Newt, Exmoor Gold and Sharps Wills, Thatcher's farm cider, bargain down-to-earth home-made food inc plenty of local produce and some interesting variations, friendly licensees and staff, woodburner, no smoking eating area beyond piano, children and dogs welcome – friendly boxer called Tasha; pleasant back room with Aga and pool table; piped music, Fri music night; attached shop with organic meats and local food, pleasant garden, good walks, low-priced bedrooms, open all day *(James Davies, Charlie Davidson, BB)*

MORCHARD BISHOP SS7707

London [signed off A377 Crediton—Barnstaple]: Open-plan low-beamed 16th-c coaching inn in picturesque village position, big carpeted red plush bar with woodburner in large fireplace, huge helpings of good traditional home-made food inc roasts in bar or small dining room, friendly engaging service, real ales inc Fullers London Pride and Sharps Doom Bar, pool, darts and skittles *(M and D Toms, Peter Craske)*

MORETONHAMPSTEAD SX7586

White Hart [A382 N of Bovey Tracey; The Square]: Reopened under new ownership after smart bright refurbishment, enjoyable bar food from toasties and hot meat sandwiches up, well kept real ales, attractive new restaurant; courtyard tables, well equipped bedrooms, well placed for Dartmoor, good walks *(LYM, Mrs S Lyons)*

MORTEHOE SS4545

Chichester Arms [off A361 Ilfracombe—Braunton]: Lots of interesting old local photographs in busy plush and leatherette panelled lounge and comfortable no smoking dining room, wide choice of good value generous food (not Sun night or Mon/Tues, at least in winter) cooked by landlord inc local fish and meat and tempting puddings (loudspeaker announcements), well kept local Barum Original and a guest beer, reasonably priced wine, speedy service even on crowded evenings; pubby locals' bar with darts and pool, no piped music; skittle alley and games machines in summer children's room, tables out in front and in small garden, good coast walks *(Joyce and Maurice Cottrell, Bruce Bird)*

☆ ***Ship Aground*** [signed off A361 Ilfracombe—Braunton]: Welcoming open-plan beamed village pub, well kept ales such as Cotleigh Tawny, Burton Bridge and Greene King Abbot, Hancock's cider in summer, decent wine, good choice of inexpensive bar food from good crab sandwiches up (may be a wait when busy), big log fires, friendly service; massive rustic furnishings, interesting nautical brassware, children allowed in big back family room, pool, skittles and other games; tables on sheltered sunny terrace with good views, by interesting church, wonderful walking on nearby coast footpath *(LYM, Dr and Mrs P Truelove, Rona Murdoch)*

NEWTON ABBOT SX8571

Dartmouth [East St]: Thriving three-room pub now brewing its own McBrides ales, with others from the area's small breweries, farm cider, decent wines, log fires, enjoyable food; children welcome till 7, tables and barbecues in nice outside area *(the Didler)*

Jolly Abbot [East St]: Olde-worlde, with beams, friendly helpful staff and cheerful customers, wide choice of good value home-made food (must book Weds market day), well kept ales inc guests, short wine list leaning to Australia *(Ken Flawn)*

☆ ***Olde Cider Bar*** [East St]: Casks of eight interesting low-priced farm ciders and a couple of perries, with more in bottles, in basic old-fashioned cider house, dark stools, barrel seats and wall benches, flagstones and bare boards; good country wines, baguettes, heated pies and venison pasties etc, very low prices; small games room with machines *(JP, PP, the Didler, Joe Green)*

NEWTON POPPLEFORD SY0889

Cannon [High St]: 16th-c two-bar inn with full-blown maritime décor, reasonably priced food inc speciality steaks and lunchtime bargain, good choice of beers tapped from the cask, log fires; good garden, bedrooms *(JP, PP, A and B D Craig)*

NEWTON ST CYRES SX8798

☆ ***Beer Engine*** [off A377 towards Thorverton]: Friendly helpful licensees in cheerful and roomy pub, well worn in and brewing its own good beers, with good home-made bar food esp fish, no smoking eating area welcoming children, traditional games; verandah and large sunny garden, popular summer barbecues, open all day *(LYM, John and Bryony Coles, J V Dadswell)*

Crown & Sceptre: Roadside pub with enjoyable food from sandwiches up, good family area, well kept Otter, pool; garden with trees, stream and good play area *(Tim Sedgwick)*

NORTH BOVEY SX7483

☆ ***Ring of Bells*** [off A382/B3212 SW of Moretonhampstead]: Attractive bulgy-walled 13th-c thatched inn, low-ceilinged bar with well kept real ales inc Butcombe, Gray's farm cider and good log fire, enjoyable freshly made bar food inc good ploughman's and notable treacle tart, restaurant, longer more functional room with pool and TV; by lovely tree-covered village green below Dartmoor, garden picnic-sets, good walks from the door, big bedrooms with four-posters *(LYM, Clare West, Dr and Mrs M E Wilson, Brian and Bett Cox)*

NOSS MAYO SX5447

Swan [off B3186 at Junket Corner]: Small two-room beamed pub right on the creek, with lovely waterside views; redecorated by new licensees but kept unpretentiously old-fashioned, with a warm welcome, plenty of beautifully cooked low-priced fresh fish, well kept Bass and a beer brewed for the pub, open fire; can get crowded, with difficult parking; dogs on leads and children welcome, tables outside *(Esther and John Sprinkle, Alice Harper)*

OAKFORD SS9121

Red Lion: 17th-c two-bar coaching inn partly rebuilt in Georgian times, well kept ales such as Cotleigh Tawny, attractively priced food inc steaks and seafood, big fireplace, cigarette cards, rifles, swords, irons, popular no smoking restaurant areas *(Andy and Jill Kassube, Guy Vowles)*

OKEHAMPTON SX5895

Plymouth [West St]: Pretty pub with friendly helpful landlord and staff, local-feel bar with enterprising food at very reasonable prices, well kept real ales from far and wide tapped from the cask (May and Nov beer festivals), no smoking area, provision for children; open all day wknds *(Mr and Mrs M Saunders, Dr and Mrs A K Clarke)*

White Hart [Fore St]: Rambling pub/hotel (quite a few steps) with St Austell Tinners, good value bar food, pleasant atmosphere; clean and comfortable bedrooms, old-fashioned plumbing *(Ron and Sheila Corbett, Dr and Mrs A K Clarke)*

OTTERTON SY0885

Kings Arms [Fore St]: Big open-plan family dining pub in charming village, good value quick food inc children's helpings and real promptly made sandwiches, well kept Otter (proper bar area), friendly service, TV and darts in lounge; dogs welcome, good skittle alley doubling as family room; bedrooms, beautiful evening view from picnic-sets in good-sized attractive back garden with play area *(Dennis Jenkin)*

PAIGNTON SX8960

☆ ***Inn on the Green*** [Esplanade Rd]: Big brightly comfortable unpubby bar open all day, useful lunchtime for enormous choice of popular keenly priced quick food, well kept Wadworths 6X, good soft and hot drinks, good welcoming service, great Christmas decorations; out-of-the-way family room, live music and dancing nightly, restaurant, big terrace looking out over green to sea *(LYM, Mr and Mrs Colin Roberts)*

Ship [Manor Rd, Preston]: Large yet homely mock-Tudor pub specialising in wide choice of cheap food (small helpings of any dish for children), bargain steaks, dining areas on three levels, comfortable furnishings inc leather settees, soft lighting, well kept Wadworths 6X from very long bar, speedy cheerful service even though busy; shame about the piped music; children welcome, a minute's walk from Preston beach *(Mr and Mrs Colin Roberts, David Carr)*

PLYMOUTH SX4755

☆ ***China House*** [Sutton Harbour, via Sutton Rd off Exeter St (A374)]: Attractively done Vintage Inn in Plymouth's oldest warehouse, super views day and night over harbour and Barbican, great beams and flagstones, bare slate and stone walls, good log fire, great choice of wines by the glass, well kept Bass and Tetleys, food all day from ciabattas and filled baguettes up, well organised welcoming service; piped music; good parking and disabled access and facilities, open all day *(Ian Phillips, LYM, Pamela and Merlyn Horswell, B J Harding)*

Dolphin [Barbican]: Well used lively and unspoilt local, good range of beers inc particularly well kept Bass and Worthington Dark tapped from the cask, coal fire; colourful green and orange décor, Beryl Cook paintings inc one of the friendly landlord; open all day *(JP, PP, the Didler)*

Lounge [Stopford Pl, Stoke]: Unspoilt open-plan backstreet pub, Bass and a guest beer from oak-panelled counter, popular lunchtime food, friendly landlord *(JP, PP, the Didler)*

Thistle Park [Commercial Rd]: Welcoming pub nr National Maritime Aquarium, good range of well kept beers inc some from next-door Sutton brewery, tasty straightforward food all day, friendly landlady, interesting décor, children welcome; open all day, live music wknds *(the Didler, JP, PP)*

PORTGATE SX4185

☆ *Harris Arms* [Launceston Rd (old A30)]: Timbered 16th-c pub under new owners, long beamed bar refurbished, with log fire and oak furniture, good meals and small choice of bar snacks, well kept Greene King Abbot and Sharps Doom Bar, interesting wines imported direct, good friendly service, wonderful view from dining room; dogs welcome, cl Tues *(DAV, David C West, Peter Craske)*

POSTBRIDGE SX6579

☆ *East Dart* [B3212]: Central Dartmoor hotel by pretty river, in same family since 1861; roomy and comfortable lightened-up open-plan bar with hands-on landlord and good friendly staff, promptly served enjoyable generous food using local ingredients from large crisp rolls up, well kept Dartmoor ale, good wines by the glass, good fire, hunting murals and horse tack, pool room; children and dogs welcome, tables out in front and behind, decent bedrooms, some 30 miles of fishing *(Dennis Jenkin, BB, David M Cundy, Nigel Long, David Swift, Mrs S Lyons)*

PRINCETOWN SX5973

☆ *Plume of Feathers* [Plymouth Hill]: Much-extended local, cheerful, welcoming and individual, with wide choice of good value generous food, quick cheerful service even with crowds, well kept ales inc Princetown Jail, good house wines, two log fires, solid slate tables, live music Fri night, Sun lunchtime; big family room with a real welcome for children, play area outside; good value bedrooms, also bunkhouse and good camp site, open all day *(Joyce and Maurice Cottrell)*

RACKENFORD SS8518

Stag [pub signed off A361 NW of Tiverton]: 13th-c low-beamed thatched pub worth a look for its ancient layout, original flagstoned and cobbled entry passage between massive walls, huge fireplace flanked by ancient settles; well kept Cotleigh Tawny and local guest beers, farm cider, cottagey dining room (children allowed), simple bedrooms *(June and Robin Savage, LYM, JP, PP, Peter Webster, Guy Vowles)*

RINGMORE SX6545

☆ *Journeys End* [signed off B3392 at Pickwick Inn, St Anns Chapel, nr Bigbury; best to park up opp church]: Ancient village inn with character panelled lounge, well kept changing ales, some tapped from casks in back room, local farm cider, decent wines, log fires, varied interesting food inc good fresh fish (lunchtime menu may be limited, but helpful about special diets), friendly locals and staff, sunny back add-on family dining conservatory; may be piped radio; pleasant big terraced garden, attractive setting nr thatched cottages not far from the sea, bedrooms antique but comfortable and well equipped *(JP, PP, LYM, the Didler, MP)*

SALCOMBE SX7438

Ferry Inn [off Fore St nr Portlemouth Ferry]: Splendid estuary position, with tiers of stripped-stone bars rising from sheltered flagstoned waterside terrace, inc top one opening off street, and middle dining bar; well kept Palmers and farm cider; piped music can be loud, can get busy, may be cl part of winter *(LYM, Jack Clark)*

☆ *Fortescue* [Union St, end of Fore St]: Sizeable but homely, popular for its enjoyable promptly served food inc hot pork rolls yet still a proper pub, popular and welcoming, nautical theme in five interlinked rooms, lots of old local black and white shipping pictures, well kept changing beers such as Banks's, Bass and Courage Directors, decent wines, pleasant service, good woodburner, restaurant, big public bar with pool, darts etc, no piped music; children welcome, picnic-sets in courtyard *(Angus Lyon, Geoff Calcott, Comus and Sarah Elliott, Keith Stevens, Ann and Bob Westbrook, Gordon Stevenson)*

Victoria [Fore St]: Extensively and comfortably refurbished busy local under welcoming new landlord, enjoyable generous food from good sandwiches and chips up, wide evening choice too, well kept St Austell ales, decent wines, good coffee, no smoking area, good housekeeping; large sheltered terrace garden behind *(Comus and Sarah Elliott, David Eberlin, Roger Wain-Heapy, P Mason, Frances Mumford)*

SAMPFORD COURTENAY SS6300

New Inn [B3072 Crediton—Holsworthy]: Attractive 16th-c thatched pub with good food, well kept Otter, hospitable landlord, pleasant décor in low-beamed open-plan bar, open fires; dogs welcome, nice garden with play area, picturesque village *(R J Walden, Peter Craske)*

SANDY GATE SX9690

Blue Ball [handy for M5 junction 30; 1st right off A376, towards Topsham]: Extended dining pub with good rather upmarket food (even the baked potatoes never see a microwave), good helpings, beams, old wood and tile floors, lovely settles, well kept Bass and well priced wine, no smoking section, friendly attentive young staff, nice village atmosphere; good gardens inc good play area *(Dr and Mrs M E Wilson, John and Vivienne Rice, Barry Steele-Perkins)*

SANDY PARK SX7087

☆ *Sandy Park Inn* [A382 S of Whiddon Down]: Thatched country pub with small low-beamed bar, stripped pine tables, built-in high-backed wall seats, big black iron fireplace, enjoyable food, two small cosy dining rooms (children allowed there), friendly staff, well kept ales such as Blackawton, Otter, Scattor Rock and Teignworthy, decent wines and farm cider; wide moor views from picnic-sets in back garden *(LYM, Len Banister, Richard and Margaret Peers)*

SHALDON SX9372

Clifford Arms [Fore St]: Cheerful young new licensee and good food from speciality baked potato up in attractive two-bar open-plan

18th-c local, well kept Bass and four guest beers from fine copper-topped bar, good wine choice, low beams, local photographs and sailing paintings, woodburner; games area with darts and pool, family room; wrought-iron furniture and colourful flowers on little front courtyard and nice back terrace, pleasant seaside village *(Margaret and Peter Brierley)*

Ferryboat [Fore St]: Cosy and quaint little waterside local, basic but comfortable, long low-ceilinged bar overlooking estuary with Teignmouth ferry and lots of boats, welcoming helpful staff, Dartmoor, Greene King IPA and Old Speckled Hen, interesting wines, big helpings of good value varied home-made food, open fires, seafaring artefacts; tables on small sunny terrace across narrow road by sandy beach *(Ken Flawn, Meg and Colin Hamilton)*

London [Bank St/The Green]: Well run village pub, enjoyable food from good sandwiches up, well kept Greene King Abbot, decent wines, pleasant landlord; children welcome, good value bedrooms with wholesome breakfast, pretty waterside village *(Ken Flawn, J D O Carter, Mike Turner)*

SIDMOUTH SY1287

☆ *Old Ship* [Old Fore St]: Partly 14th-c, with low beams, mellow black woodwork and carved panelling, sailing ship prints, good inexpensive food from huge crab sandwiches to local fish, well kept Bass, Flowers IPA and Otter, decent wine choice, prompt courteous service even when busy, chatty manager and quietly friendly atmosphere, no piped music; close-set tables but roomier raftered upstairs bar with family room, dogs allowed; in pedestrian zone just moments from the sea (note that around here parking is limited to 30 mins) *(Dr and Mrs M E Wilson, BB, Meg and Colin Hamilton, Phil and Sally Gorton, Joan and Michel Hooper-Immins)*

☆ *Swan* [York St]: Lively and convivial local, pleasant staff, decent food inc good crab sandwiches and reasonably priced fresh fish, well kept Branscombe Vale Branoc, boarded walls and ceilings, lounge bar with interesting pictures and memorabilia, bigger light and airy public bar with thriving darts team and other games, separate dining area; nice small flower-filled garden *(B H and J I Andrews, Phil and Sally Gorton, Klaus and Elizabeth Leist, Alan and Paula McCully)*

SILVERTON SS9502

☆ *Three Tuns* [Exeter Rd]: 17th-c or older, with comfortable settees and period furniture in attractively old-fashioned beamed bars, efficient friendly staff, well kept ales inc Exmoor, good range of food, cosy restaurant (where children welcome); lovely flower displays, tables in pretty inner courtyard, handy for Killerton *(Michael Rowse, Jim and Maggie Cowell, Dr and Mrs M E Wilson)*

SLAPTON SX8245

Queens Arms: Modernised village local, friendly and welcoming, with snug comfortable corners, good value straightforward food from sandwiches and chips up, well kept Bass, Exmoor and Palmers, interesting World War II pictures; lovely suntrap back garden with plenty of tables *(Angus Lyon, David Eberlin)*

SMALLRIDGE ST3000

☆ *Ridgeway* [off A358 N of Axminster]: Friendly largely no smoking country bar with fresh flowers and chunky tables, more tables in back two-lane skittle alley, raftered upstairs dining room (no under-12s) with another skittle alley, very wide choice of good value generous food inc good fish range prepared to order (so may be a wait), well kept Branscombe Vale and Otter, good wines by the glass, attentive very helpful service, woodburner, family atmosphere; piped music; ten bedrooms, pleasant two-level quiet terrace and garden, lovely views *(R T and J C Moggridge, Michael and Jenny Back, Michael Doswell, BB)*

SOURTON SX5390

☆ *Highwayman* [A386, S of junction with A30]: Marvellously eccentric décor in warren of dimly lit stonework and flagstone-floored burrows and alcoves, all sorts of things to look at and visual tricks to enjoy, even a make-believe sailing galleon; Teignworthy real ales, farm cider, organic wines, food confined to sandwiches or pasties, friendly chatty service, old-fashioned penny fruit machine, 40s piped music, no smoking at bar counters; outside has fairy-tale pumpkin house and an old-lady-who-lived-in-the-shoe house – children allowed to look around pub but can't stay inside; period bedrooms with four-posters and half-testers, bunk rooms for walkers and cyclists *(the Didler, JP, PP, Ann and Colin Hunt, R J Walden, LYM, Mayur Shah, Dr and Mrs D Woods)*

SOUTH BRENT SX6958

Woodpecker [A38]: Pleasant décor, booth tables, no smoking area, very wide choice of enjoyable good value food (should book in season), Bass and Blackawton 44, reasonably priced wines *(Dudley and Moira Cockroft)*

SOUTH POOL SX7740

☆ *Millbrook* [off A379 E of Kingsbridge]: Warmly welcoming new owners in charming little creekside pub (very busy at high tide), two happy compact bars and dining extension, tasty good value food using much local produce inc good crab sandwiches, well kept Bass, Fullers London Pride, Wadworths 6X and a changing guest beer tapped from the cask, local farm cider; children in eating area/family room, covered seating and heaters for front courtyard and waterside terrace, bedrooms *(Claire Nielsen, LYM, David and Heather Stephenson, Jack Clark, Jill Hummerstone, Richard and Anne Norris, Brian and Jean Hepworth, Mrs C Lintott, Geoffrey Townsend)*

SPARKWELL SX5857

Treby Arms: Warmly old-world atmosphere, very wide choice of good value food with some enterprising specials, friendly helpful service, good range of beers inc unusual guests and one brewed locally for the pub, decent house wines, small dining room; disabled facilities, nearby wildlife park *(John Evans)*

Key to map areas

ULLAPOOL

11

ABERDEEN

PERTH

GLASGOW ■ EDINBURGH

9 10

STRANRAER CARLISLE NEWCASTLE

LEEDS HULL

7 8

HOLYHEAD LIVERPOOL

NORWICH

6 ■BIRMINGHAM 5

4 ■CAMBRIDGE

CARDIFF OXFORD LONDON 13 12

■BRISTOL

CHANNEL 2 3

ISLANDS 1 SOUTHAMPTON

PLYMOUTH BRIGHTON

Reference to sectional maps

	Motorway		
	Trunk road	●	**Totnes** Guide entry
	Major road	◉	**Lynton** Guide entry with accommodation
-----	County boundary	■	BODMIN Place name to assist location

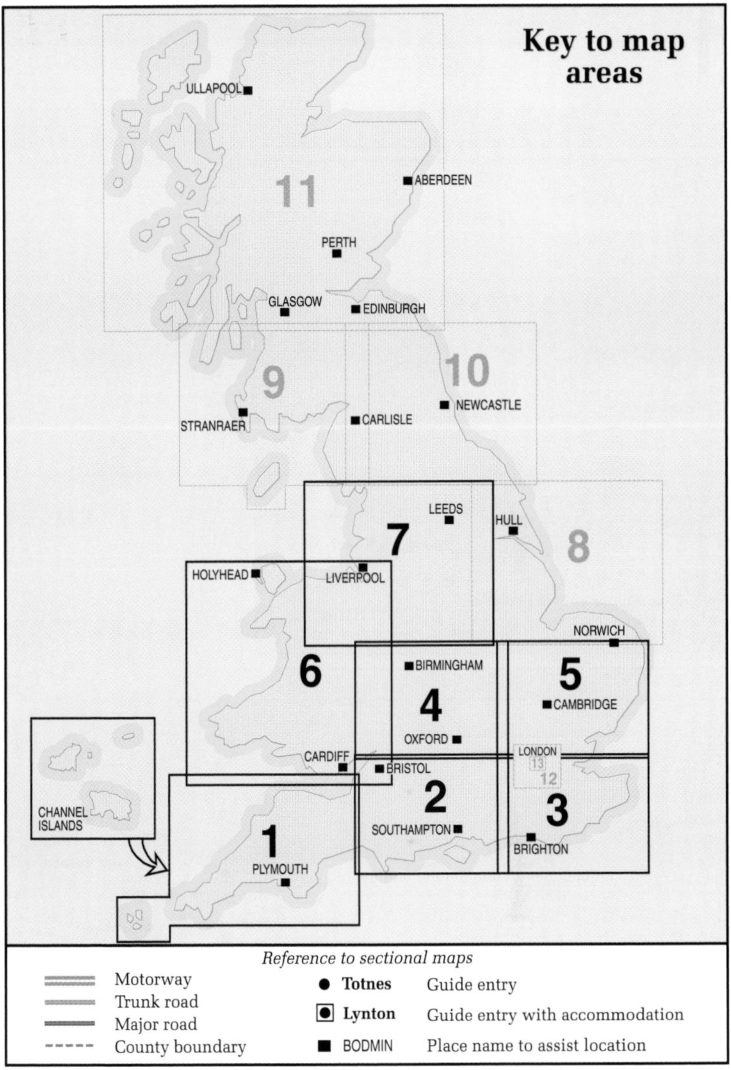

MAPS IN THIS SECTION

The South-West and Channel Islands Map 1
Southern England Map 2
The South-East Map 3
Central and Western England Map 4
Central England and East Anglia Map 5
Wales Map 6
The North-West Map 7

For Maps 8 – 13 see later colour section

1

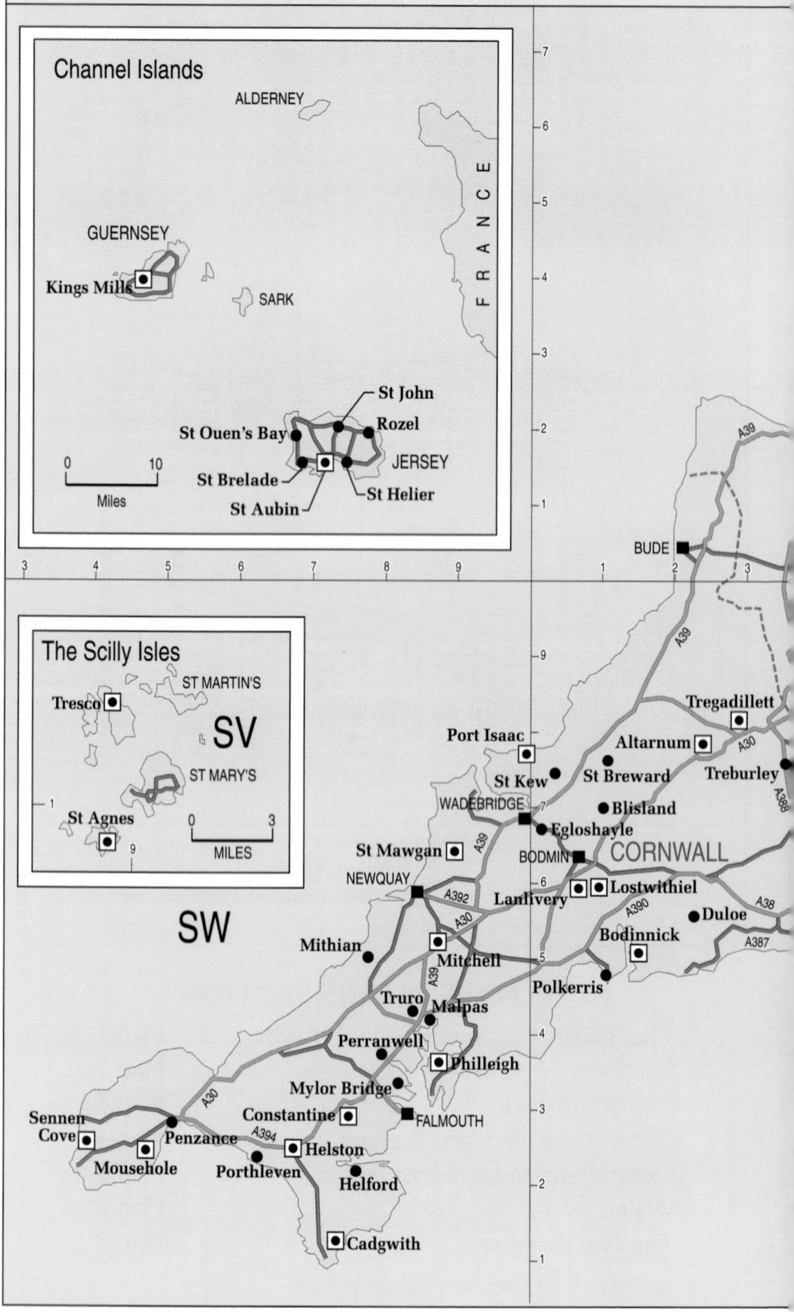

Channel Islands
ALDERNEY
GUERNSEY
Kings Mills
SARK
FRANCE
St John
Rozel
St Ouen's Bay
JERSEY
St Brelade
St Helier
St Aubin
0
10
Miles
The Scilly Isles
ST MARTIN'S
Tresco
SV
ST MARY'S
St Agnes
0
3
MILES
SW
BUDE
A39
Tregadillett
Port Isaac
Altarnum
A30
St Kew
St Breward
Treburley
A388
WADEBRIDGE
Blisland
Egloshayle
St Mawgan
BODMIN
CORNWALL
NEWQUAY
Lanlivery
Lostwithiel
A392
A390
A38
Duloe
Bodinnick
A387
Mithian
Mitchell
Polkerris
Truro
Malpas
Perranwell
Philleigh
Mylor Bridge
Constantine
FALMOUTH
Sennen Cove
Penzance
A394
Helston
Mousehole
Porthleven
Helford
Cadgwith

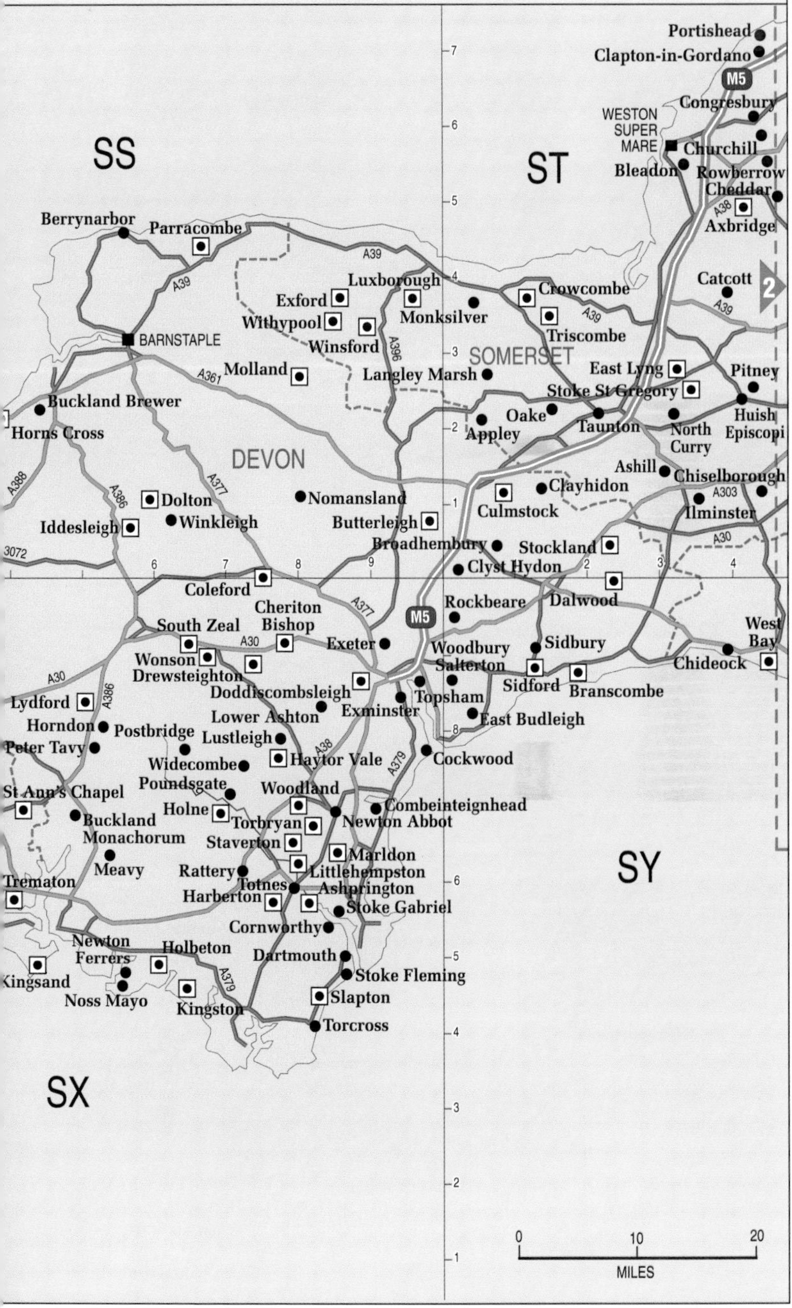
SS
ST
SX
SY
DEVON
SOMERSET
BARNSTAPLE
WESTON SUPER MARE
Portishead
Clapton-in-Gordano
Congresbury
Churchill
Bleadon
Rowberrow
Cheddar
Axbridge
Catcott
Pitney
Huish Episcopi
Berrynarbor
Parracombe
Luxborough
Exford
Withypool
Winsford
Monksilver
Crowcombe
Triscombe
Molland
Langley Marsh
East Lyng
Stoke St Gregory
Buckland Brewer
Horns Cross
Oake
Appley
Taunton
North Curry
Ashill
Chiselborough
Ilminster
Clayhidon
Culmstock
Dolton
Winkleigh
Iddesleigh
Nomansland
Butterleigh
Broadhembury
Stockland
Clyst Hydon
Coleford
Cheriton Bishop
South Zeal
Rockbeare
Dalwood
Exeter
Woodbury Salterton
Sidbury
West Bay
Chideock
Wonson
Drewsteighton
Doddiscombsleigh
Topsham
Sidford
Branscombe
Lydford
Exminster
Lower Ashton
East Budleigh
Horndon
Postbridge
Lustleigh
Peter Tavy
Haytor Vale
Widecombe
Cockwood
Poundsgate
Woodland
St Ann's Chapel
Holne
Combeinteignhead
Buckland Monachorum
Torbryan
Newton Abbot
Staverton
Marldon
Meavy
Rattery
Littlehempston
Trematon
Totnes
Ashprington
Harberton
Stoke Gabriel
Cornworthy
Newton Ferrers
Holbeton
Dartmouth
Kingsand
Noss Mayo
Stoke Fleming
Kingston
Slapton
Torcross
A39
A361
A377
A386
A388
A396
A3072
A30
A38
A379
A303
M5
2
0
10
20
MILES

2

Oldbury-on-Severn
Littleton-upon-Severn
Tetbury
GLOUCESTERSHIRE
Didmarton
Malmesbury
Brinkworth
SWINDON
M4
M5
Almondsbury
Old Sodbury
Norton
Grittleton
WILTSHIRE
Ogbourne St Andrew
BRISTOL
A420
A4
A46
Corsham
Box
Lacock
Beckhampton
A4361
Axford
MARLBOROUGH
A38
A37
Bath
Whitley
Rowde
A361
A346
Chew Magna
Holt
Seend
Devizes
Stanton Wick
Freshford
Bradford-on-Avon
Great Hinton
Poulshot
Woodborough
A345
A342
Compton Martin
Faulkland
SOMERSET
A367
Holcombe
Mells
A350
A360
A371
Wookey
Wells
A39
Doulting
A359
A36
Heytesbury
A303
Newton Tony
Berwick St James
Batcombe
Great Durnford
ST
Kilmington
Stourton
Shepton Montague
Hindon
A30
Pitton
Lovington
Chicksgrove
Salisbury
Kingsdon
A357
Donhead St Andrew
Ebbesbourne Wake
Berwick St John
A338
Sherborne
YEOVIL
Stourton Caundle
Farnham
Fritham
Sturminster Newton
North Gorley
Shroton
A352
DORSET
A354
Middlemarsh
BLANDFORD
Tarrant Monkton
Corscombe
Cerne Abbas
A356
A31
Colehill
Pamphill
Godmanstone
Piddlehinton
East Morden
Mudeford
A35
DORCHESTER
Burton Bradstock
BOURNEMOUTH
East Knighton
West Bexington
A353
East Chaldon
A351
Corfe Castle
Osmington Mills
WEYMOUTH
Church Knowle
SWANAGE
SY
Worth Matravers
1
4
5
6
7
8
9
2
3

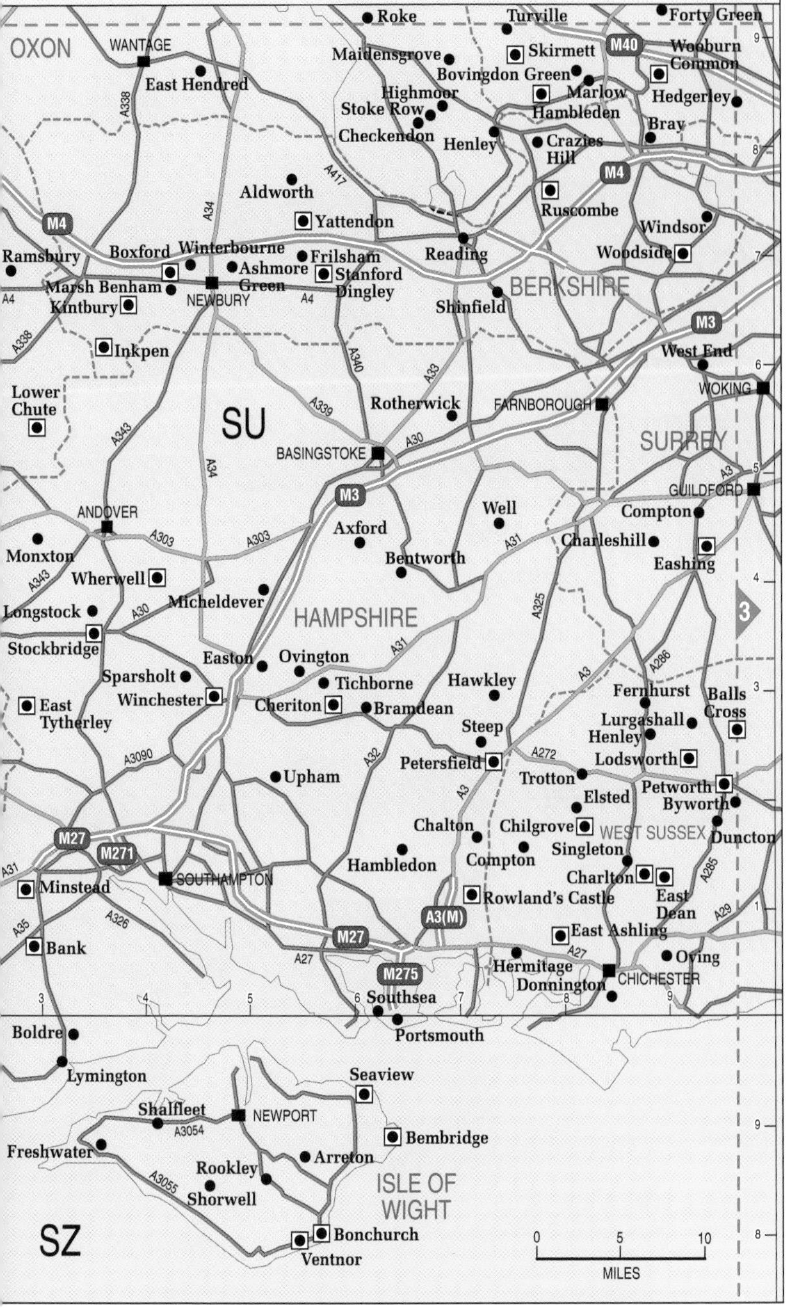
OXON
WANTAGE
East Hendred
Roke
Turville
Forty Green
Maidensgrove
Skirmett
M40
Wooburn Common
Bovingdon Green
Marlow
Highmoor
Stoke Row
Hambleden
Hedgerley
Checkendon
Henley
Bray
Crazies Hill
M4
Aldworth
Ruscombe
Yattendon
Windsor
Ramsbury
Boxford
Winterbourne
Frilsham
Reading
Woodside
Ashmore Green
Stanford Dingley
Marsh Benham
NEWBURY
BERKSHIRE
Kintbury
Shinfield
M3
Inkpen
West End
Lower Chute
WOKING
Rotherwick
FARNBOROUGH
SU
BASINGSTOKE
SURREY
GUILDFORD
ANDOVER
Well
Compton
Axford
Charleshill
Monxton
Bentworth
Eashing
Wherwell
Micheldever
Longstock
HAMPSHIRE
3
Stockbridge
Easton
Ovington
Sparsholt
Tichborne
Hawkley
Fernhurst
Balls Cross
Winchester
Cheriton
Bramdean
East Tytherley
Lurgashall
Steep
Henley
Lodsworth
Petersfield
Trotton
Upham
Petworth
Elsted
Byworth
Chalton
Chilgrove
WEST SUSSEX
Duncton
M27
M271
Singleton
Hambledon
Compton
Charlton
East Dean
SOUTHAMPTON
Minstead
Rowland's Castle
A3(M)
East Ashling
Bank
Oving
Hermitage
M275
Donnington
CHICHESTER
Southsea
Portsmouth
Boldre
Lymington
Seaview
Shalfleet
NEWPORT
Bembridge
Freshwater
Arreton
Rookley
ISLE OF WIGHT
Shorwell
SZ
Bonchurch
Ventnor
0
5
10
MILES
A338
A34
A417
A4
A340
A33
A339
A343
A30
A303
A31
A325
A3
A286
A272
A32
A3090
A35
A326
A27
A285
A29
A3054
A3055

3

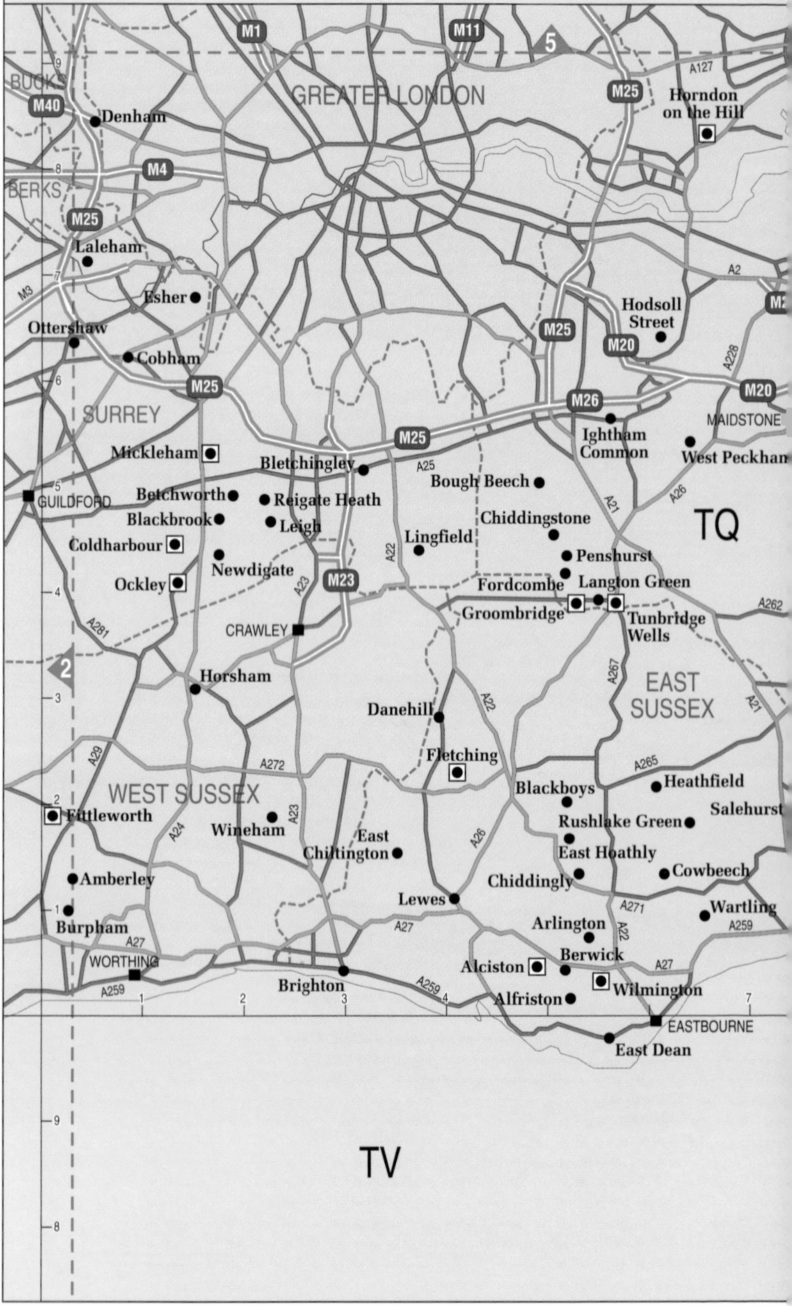
M1
M11
5
A127
GREATER LONDON
M25
Horndon on the Hill
BUCKS
M40
Denham
M4
BERKS
M25
Laleham
M3
Esher
A2
Hodsoll Street
Ottershaw
M25
M20
Cobham
A228
M25
M20
SURREY
M26
Ightham Common
MAIDSTONE
M25
West Peckham
Mickleham
Bletchingley
A25
Bough Beech
GUILDFORD
Betchworth
Reigate Heath
A26
Blackbrook
Leigh
Chiddingstone
A21
TQ
Coldharbour
Lingfield
A22
Penshurst
Newdigate
Ockley
A23
M23
Fordcombe
Langton Green
A262
Groombridge
Tunbridge Wells
A281
CRAWLEY
2
Horsham
A267
EAST SUSSEX
Danehill
A22
A21
A29
Fletching
A272
A265
Heathfield
WEST SUSSEX
Blackboys
Salehurst
Fittleworth
A23
Wineham
A24
Rushlake Green
East Chiltington
A26
East Hoathly
Cowbeech
Amberley
Chiddingly
Lewes
A271
Wartling
Burpham
A27
Arlington
A22
A259
A27
Berwick
WORTHING
Alciston
A27
Brighton
Wilmington
A259
A259
Alfriston
EASTBOURNE
East Dean
TV

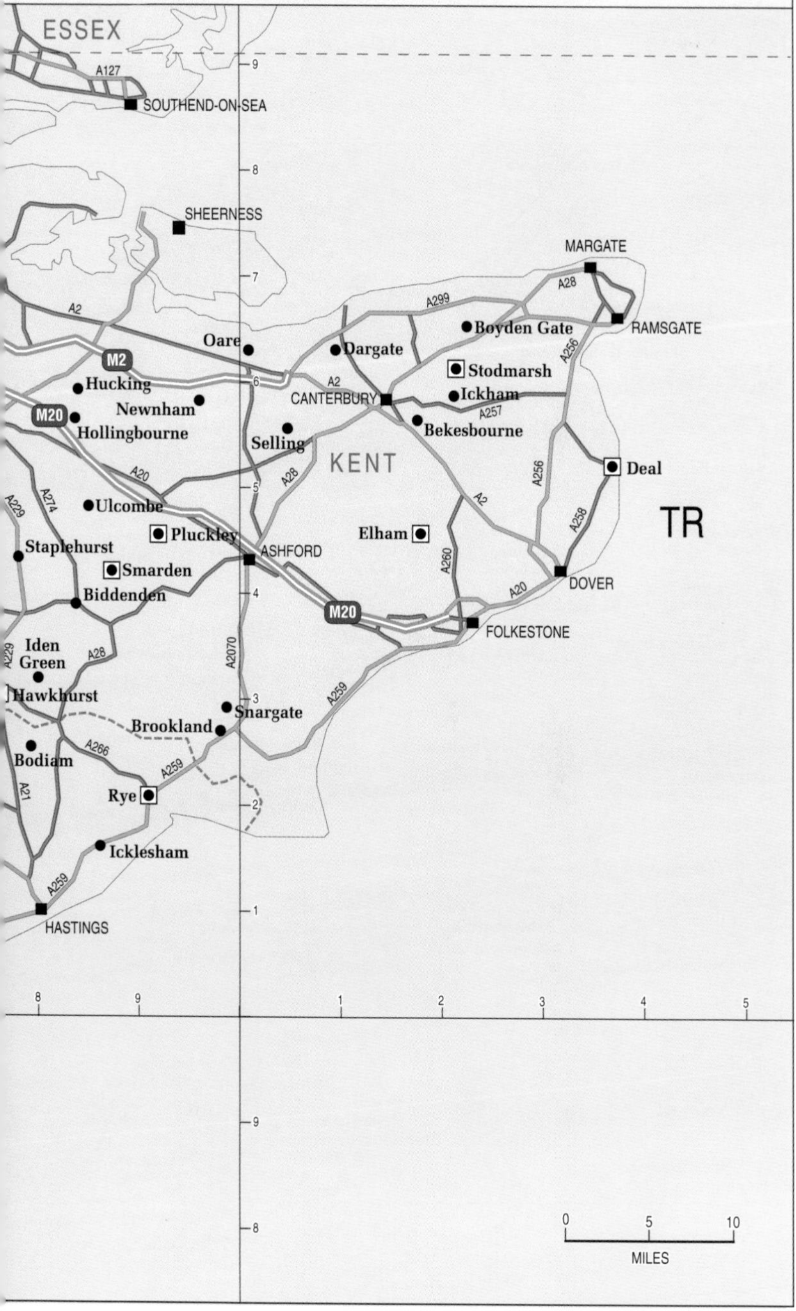
ESSEX
A127
SOUTHEND-ON-SEA
SHEERNESS
MARGATE
A28
A299
A2
Oare
M2
Boyden Gate
RAMSGATE
Dargate
Stodmarsh
A256
Hucking
A2
CANTERBURY
Ickham
A257
Newnham
M20
Hollingbourne
Bekesbourne
Selling
KENT
Deal
A20
A28
A256
A229
A274
Ulcombe
A2
A258
TR
Pluckley
Elham
Staplehurst
ASHFORD
Smarden
A260
DOVER
Biddenden
A20
M20
FOLKESTONE
Iden Green
A28
A229
A2070
Hawkhurst
Snargate
A259
Brookland
A266
Bodiam
A259
A21
Rye
Icklesham
A259
HASTINGS
0
5
10
MILES

4

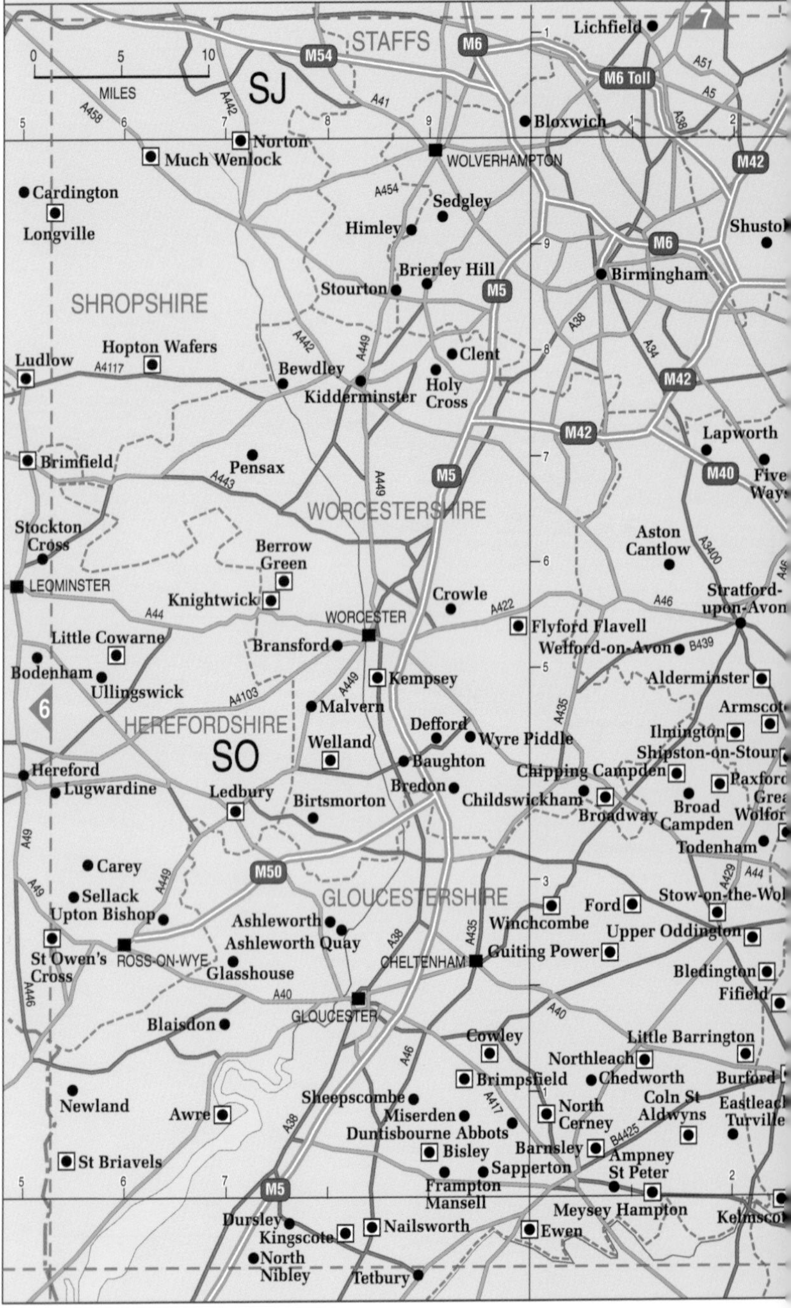

STAFFS
SJ
0 5 10
MILES
M54
M6
M6 Toll
M42
M5
M40
M50
A41
A442
A458
A51
A5
A38
A454
A4117
A443
A449
A34
A3400
A44
A422
A46
B439
A4103
A435
A429
A40
A49
A446
A417
B4425
Lichfield
Bloxwich
Norton
Much Wenlock
WOLVERHAMPTON
Cardington
Longville
Sedgley
Himley
Shustoke
Brierley Hill
Birmingham
Stourton
SHROPSHIRE
Hopton Wafers
Ludlow
Clent
Bewdley
Kidderminster
Holy Cross
Lapworth
Brimfield
Pensax
Five Ways
WORCESTERSHIRE
Stockton Cross
Aston Cantlow
Berrow Green
LEOMINSTER
Knightwick
Crowle
Stratford-upon-Avon
WORCESTER
Flyford Flavell
Welford-on-Avon
Little Cowarne
Bransford
Bodenham
Kempsey
Alderminster
Ullingswick
Malvern
Armscote
HEREFORDSHIRE
Defford
Wyre Piddle
Ilmington
SO
Welland
Shipston-on-Stour
Baughton
Hereford
Chipping Campden
Paxford
Lugwardine
Ledbury
Bredon
Childswickham
Broadway
Broad Campden
Birtsmorton
Todenham
Carey
GLOUCESTERSHIRE
Sellack
Ford
Stow-on-the-Wold
Upton Bishop
Ashleworth
Winchcombe
Upper Oddington
St Owen's Cross
ROSS-ON-WYE
Ashleworth Quay
Guiting Power
Glasshouse
CHELTENHAM
Bledington
Fifield
GLOUCESTER
Blaisdon
Cowley
Little Barrington
Northleach
Brimpsfield
Chedworth
Burford
Newland
Sheepscombe
Coln St Aldwyns
Eastleach Turville
Awre
Miserden
North Cerney
Duntisbourne Abbots
Barnsley
Bisley
Ampney St Peter
St Briavels
Sapperton
Frampton Mansell
Meysey Hampton
Dursley
Nailsworth
Kingscote
Ewen
Kelmscot
North Nibley
Tetbury

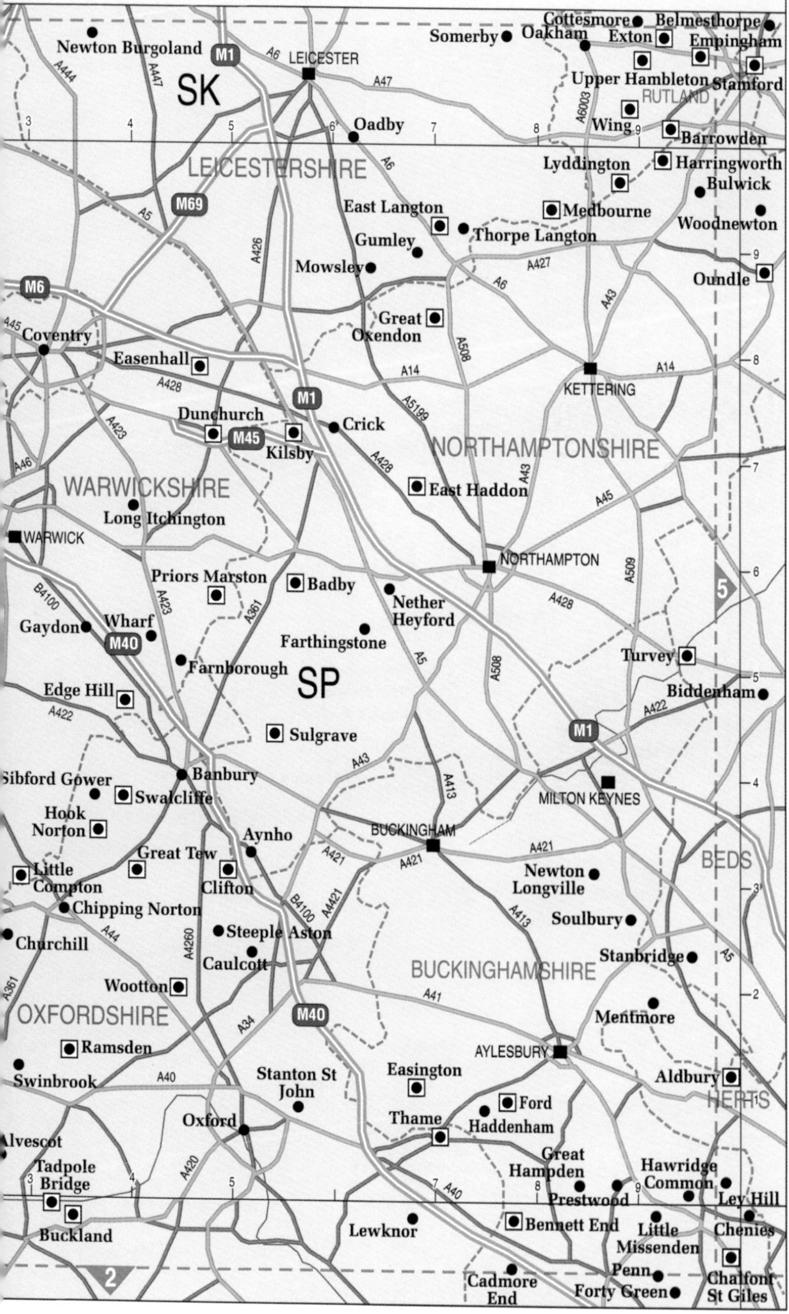
SK
SP
LEICESTERSHIRE
RUTLAND
NORTHAMPTONSHIRE
WARWICKSHIRE
BUCKINGHAMSHIRE
OXFORDSHIRE
BEDS
HERTS
Newton Burgoland
LEICESTER
Somerby
Oakham
Cottesmore
Exton
Belmesthorpe
Empingham
Upper Hambleton
Stamford
Oadby
Wing
Barrowden
Lyddington
Harringworth
Bulwick
East Langton
Medbourne
Woodnewton
Gumley
Thorpe Langton
Mowsley
Oundle
Great Oxendon
Coventry
Easenhall
KETTERING
Dunchurch
Crick
Kilsby
East Haddon
Long Itchington
WARWICK
NORTHAMPTON
Priors Marston
Badby
Nether Heyford
Gaydon
Wharf
Farthingstone
Farnborough
Turvey
Edge Hill
Biddenham
Sulgrave
Banbury
Sibford Gower
Swalcliffe
MILTON KEYNES
Hook Norton
BUCKINGHAM
Aynho
Great Tew
Little Compton
Clifton
Newton Longville
Chipping Norton
Steeple Aston
Soulbury
Churchill
Caulcott
Stanbridge
Wootton
Mentmore
Ramsden
AYLESBURY
Swinbrook
Stanton St John
Easington
Aldbury
Ford
Oxford
Thame
Haddenham
Alvescot
Tadpole Bridge
Great Hampden
Hawridge Common
Prestwood
Ley Hill
Buckland
Lewknor
Bennett End
Little Missenden
Chenies
Penn
Cadmore End
Forty Green
Chalfont St Giles
M1
M6
M69
M45
M40
A6
A47
A444
A447
A5
A426
A427
A6003
A43
A508
A14
A5199
A428
A423
A46
A45
A509
A361
B4100
A422
A413
A421
A4421
A44
A4260
A34
A41
A40
A420
2
5

5

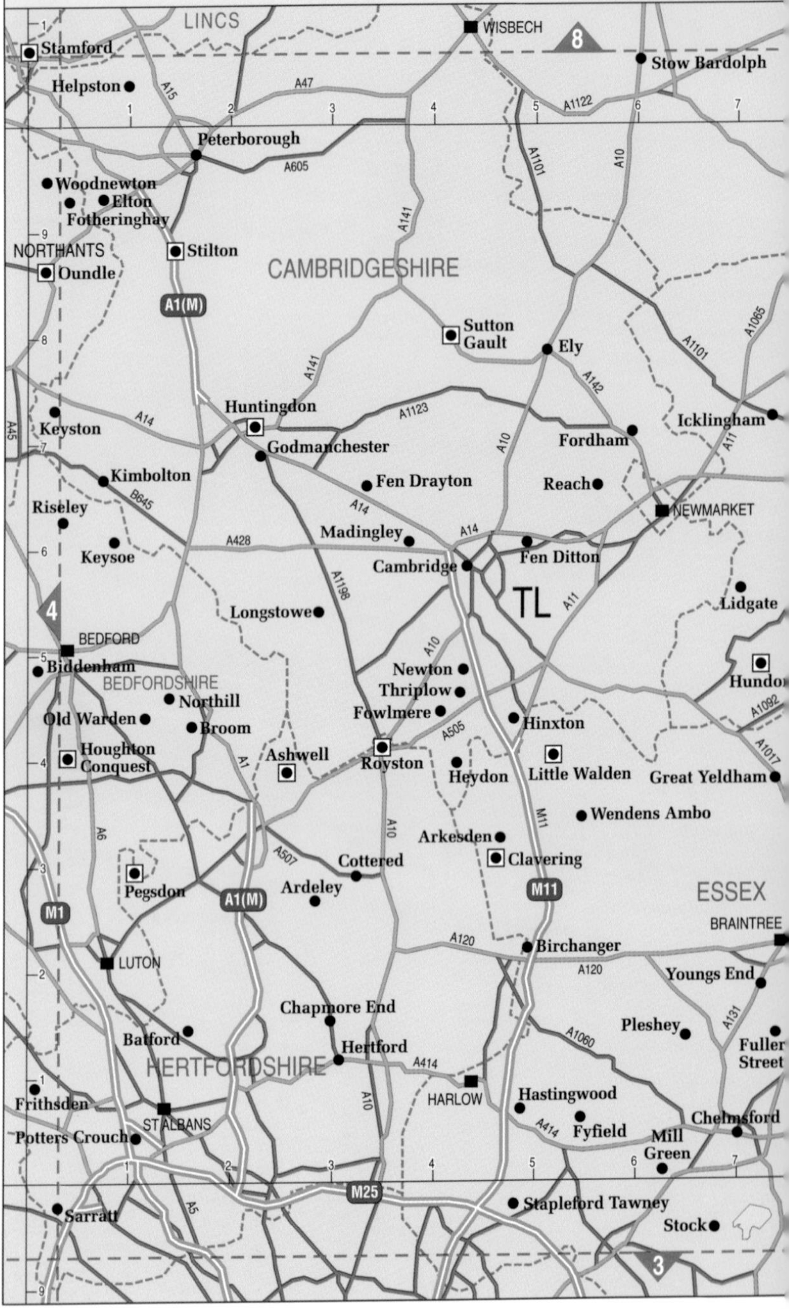
LINCS
WISBECH
8
Stamford
Stow Bardolph
Helpston
A15
A47
A1122
Peterborough
A605
A1101
A10
Woodnewton
Elton
Fotheringhay
A141
NORTHANTS
Stilton
Oundle
CAMBRIDGESHIRE
A1(M)
Sutton
Gault
Ely
A1065
A1101
A142
Huntingdon
A1123
Icklingham
A45
Keyston
A14
Godmanchester
Fordham
A11
Kimbolton
Fen Drayton
Reach
B645
A14
NEWMARKET
Riseley
Madingley
A14
A428
Keysoe
Cambridge
Fen Ditton
A1198
TL
A11
Lidgate
4
Longstowe
BEDFORD
Biddenham
A10
Newton
BEDFORDSHIRE
Thriplow
Hundon
Northill
A1092
Old Warden
Fowlmere
Broom
Hinxton
A505
A1017
Houghton
Conquest
A1
Ashwell
Royston
Little Walden
Heydon
Great Yeldham
M11
Wendens Ambo
A6
A10
Arkesden
A507
Cottered
Clavering
Pegsdon
Ardeley
A1(M)
M11
ESSEX
M1
BRAINTREE
A120
Birchanger
LUTON
A120
Youngs End
Chapmore End
A131
Pleshey
Batford
A1060
Fuller
Street
Hertford
HERTFORDSHIRE
A414
HARLOW
A10
Hastingwood
Frithsden
Chelmsford
ST ALBANS
A414
Fyfield
Mill
Green
Potters Crouch
M25
Stapleford Tawney
Sarratt
A5
Stock
3

5

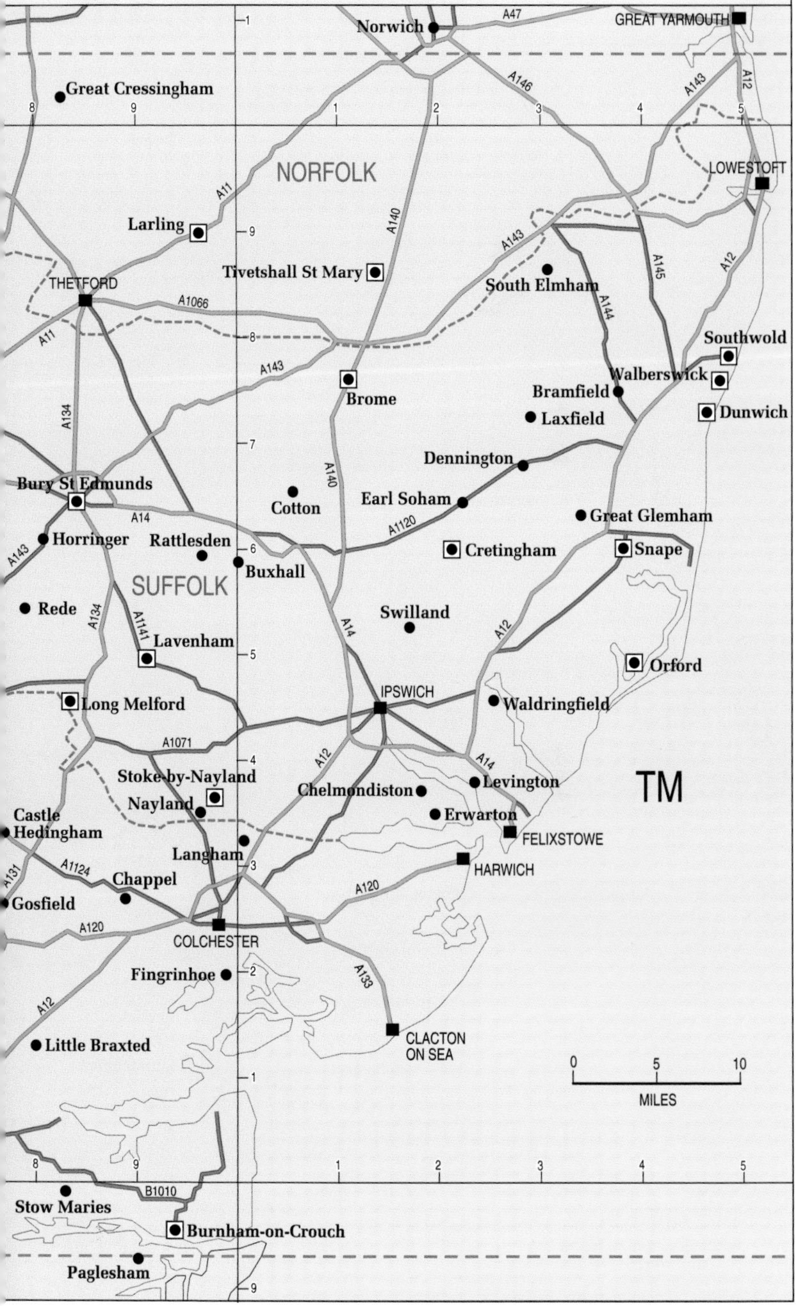
Norwich
A47
GREAT YARMOUTH
Great Cressingham
A146
A143
A12
NORFOLK
LOWESTOFT
A11
A140
Larling
A143
Tivetshall St Mary
South Elmham
A145
A12
THETFORD
A1066
A144
A11
Southwold
A143
Walberswick
Brome
Bramfield
Dunwich
A134
Laxfield
Dennington
A140
Bury St Edmunds
Cotton
Earl Soham
Great Glemham
A14
A1120
Horringer
Rattlesden
Cretingham
Snape
A143
Buxhall
SUFFOLK
Rede
Swilland
A134
A14
A12
A1141
Lavenham
Orford
IPSWICH
Long Melford
Waldringfield
A1071
A12
A14
Stoke-by-Nayland
Chelmondiston
Levington
TM
Nayland
Erwarton
Castle Hedingham
FELIXSTOWE
Langham
HARWICH
A1124
A131
Chappel
A120
Gosfield
A120
COLCHESTER
Fingrinhoe
A133
A12
CLACTON ON SEA
Little Braxted
0
5
10
MILES
B1010
Stow Maries
Burnham-on-Crouch
Paglesham

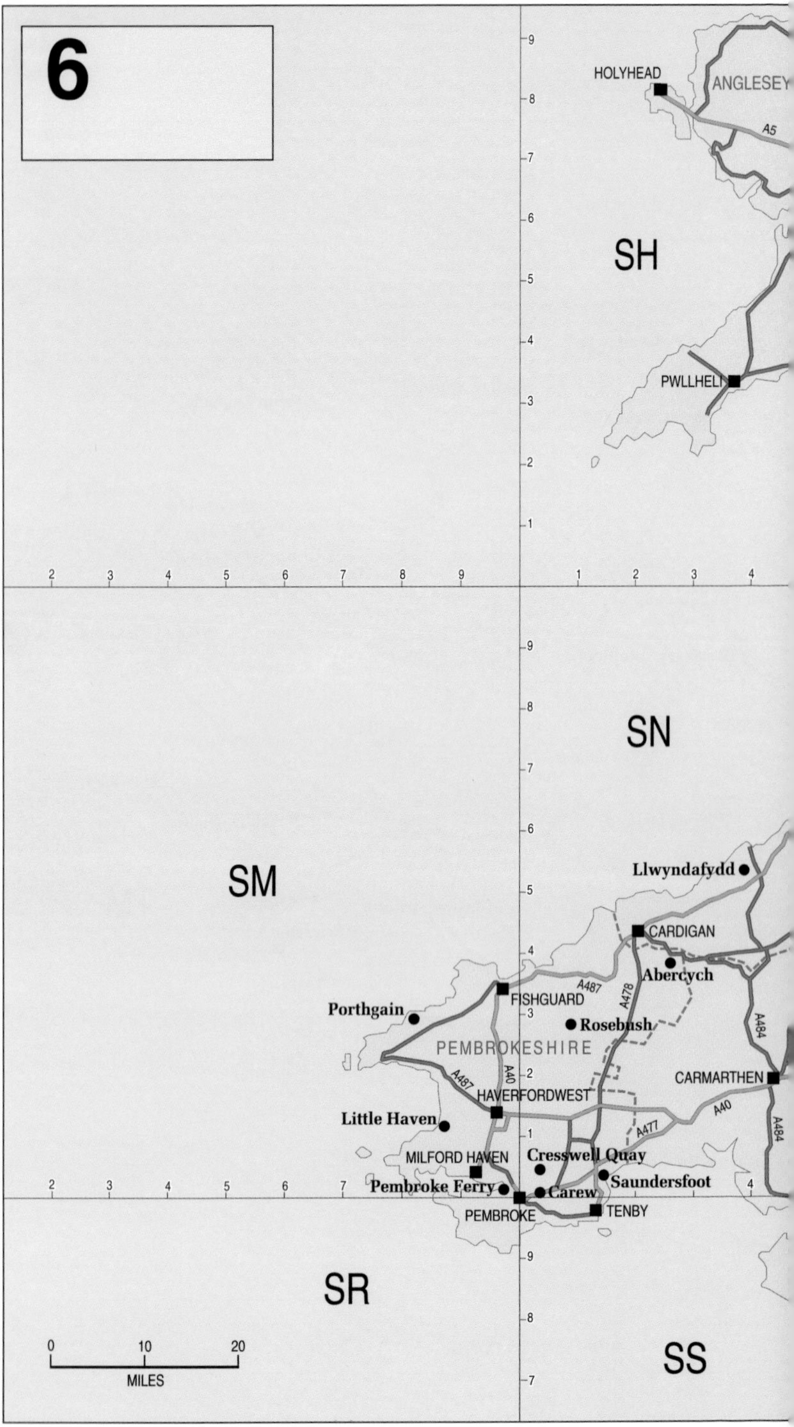

6
HOLYHEAD
ANGLESEY
A5
SH
PWLLHELI
SN
SM
Llwyndafydd
CARDIGAN
Abercych
A487
A478
FISHGUARD
Porthgain
Rosebush
PEMBROKESHIRE
A484
A40
A487
CARMARTHEN
HAVERFORDWEST
A40
Little Haven
A477
A484
MILFORD HAVEN
Cresswell Quay
Saundersfoot
Pembroke Ferry
Carew
PEMBROKE
TENBY
SR
SS
0
10
20
MILES

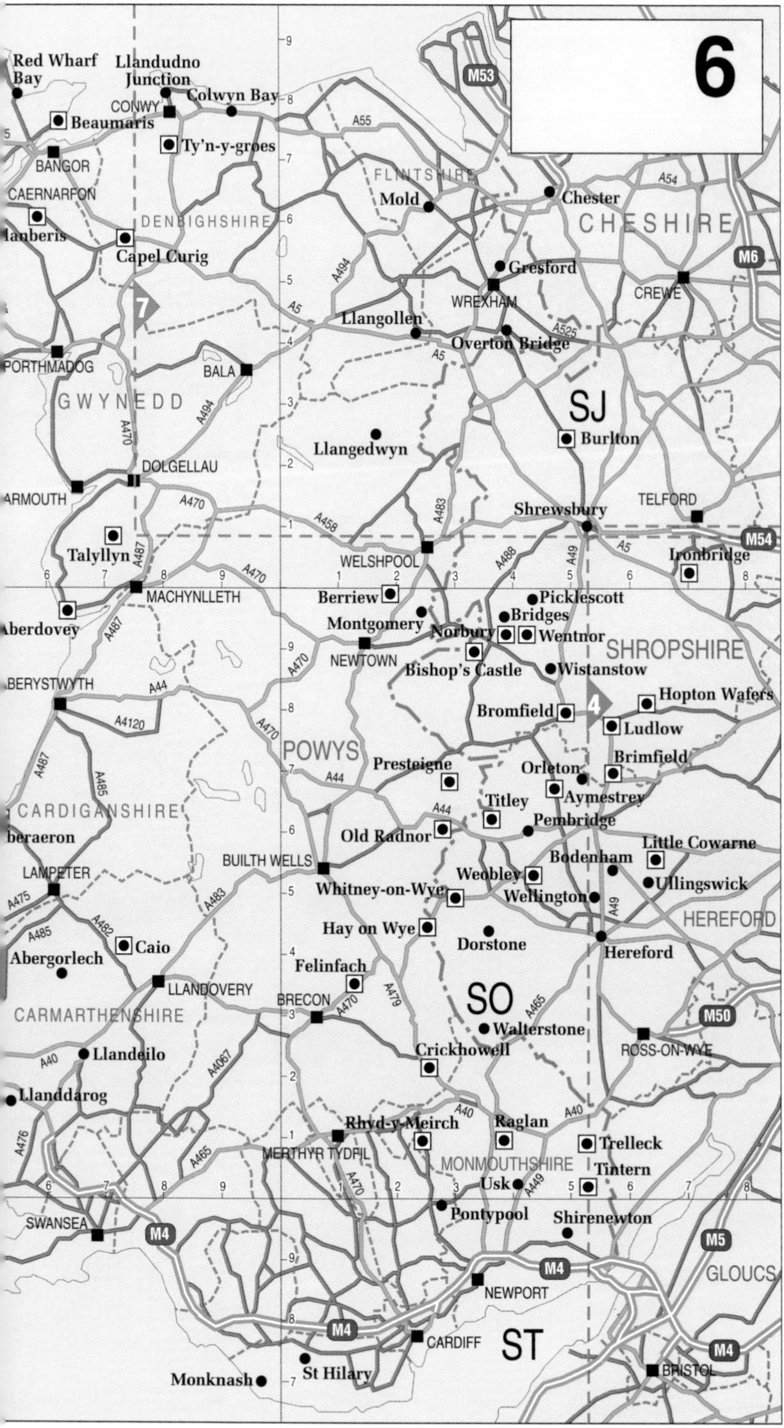
6
Red Wharf Bay
Llandudno Junction
CONWY
Colwyn Bay
Beaumaris
Ty'n-y-groes
BANGOR
CAERNARFON
Llanberis
DENBIGHSHIRE
Capel Curig
FLINTSHIRE
Mold
Chester
CHESHIRE
Gresford
WREXHAM
CREWE
Llangollen
Overton Bridge
PORTHMADOG
BALA
GWYNEDD
SJ
Burlton
Llangedwyn
DOLGELLAU
BARMOUTH
TELFORD
Shrewsbury
Talyllyn
WELSHPOOL
Ironbridge
MACHYNLLETH
Berriew
Pickelscott
Bridges
Aberdovey
Montgomery
Norbury
Wentnor
NEWTOWN
Bishop's Castle
SHROPSHIRE
Wistanstow
ABERYSTWYTH
Hopton Wafers
Bromfield
Ludlow
POWYS
Brimfield
Presteigne
Orleton
Aymestrey
Titley
CARDIGANSHIRE
Pembridge
Aberaeron
Old Radnor
Little Cowarne
Bodenham
BUILTH WELLS
LAMPETER
Weobley
Ullingswick
Whitney-on-Wye
Wellington
HEREFORD
Hay on Wye
Dorstone
Caio
Hereford
Abergorlech
Felinfach
LLANDOVERY
BRECON
SO
CARMARTHENSHIRE
Walterstone
ROSS-ON-WYE
Llandeilo
Crickhowell
Llanddarog
Rhyd-y-Meirch
Raglan
Trelleck
MERTHYR TYDFIL
MONMOUTHSHIRE
Tintern
Usk
Pontypool
Shirenewton
SWANSEA
GLOUCS
NEWPORT
CARDIFF
ST
St Hilary
Monknash
BRISTOL
M53
M6
M54
M50
M5
M4
A55
A54
A494
A5
A525
A470
A487
A458
A483
A488
A49
A44
A4120
A485
A475
A482
A479
A465
A4067
A40
A476
A449
7
4

7

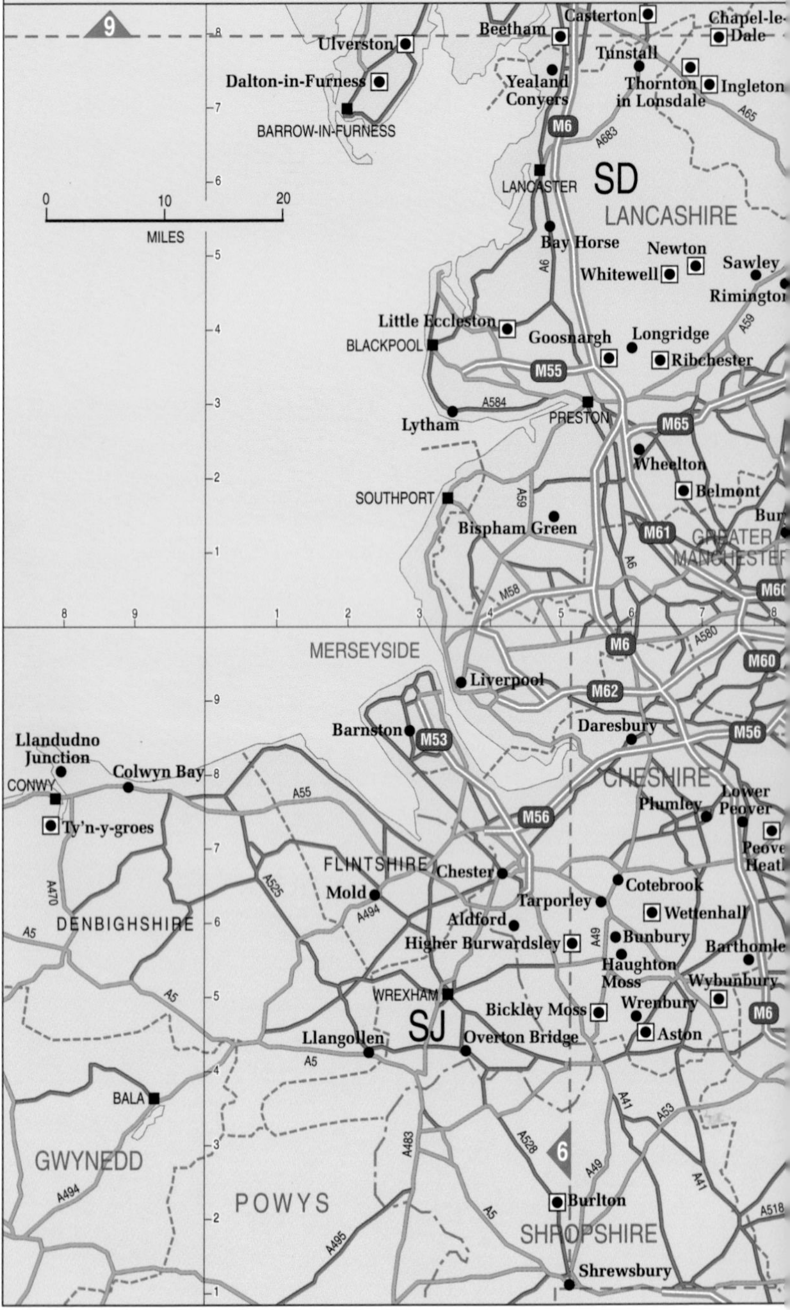

9
Ulverston
Dalton-in-Furness
BARROW-IN-FURNESS
Beetham
Casterton
Chapel-le-Dale
Yealand Conyers
Tunstall
Thornton in Lonsdale
Ingleton
A65
M6
A683
LANCASTER
SD
LANCASHIRE
0
10
20
MILES
Bay Horse
A6
Newton
Whitewell
Sawley
Rimington
Little Eccleston
BLACKPOOL
Goosnargh
Longridge
Ribchester
A59
M55
A584
Lytham
PRESTON
M65
Wheelton
Belmont
SOUTHPORT
A59
Bispham Green
M61
GREATER MANCHESTER
A6
M58
M60
MERSEYSIDE
M6
A580
Liverpool
M62
Barnston
M53
Daresbury
M56
Llandudno Junction
Colwyn Bay
CONWY
Ty'n-y-groes
A55
CHESHIRE
Plumley
Lower Peover
Peover Heath
M56
A470
FLINTSHIRE
Chester
A525
Mold
A494
Cotebrook
Tarporley
Wettenhall
DENBIGHSHIRE
A5
Aldford
Higher Burwardsley
A49
Bunbury
Barthomley
Haughton Moss
Wybunbury
A5
WREXHAM
Bickley Moss
Wrenbury
M6
SJ
Llangollen
Overton Bridge
Aston
A5
BALA
A41
A53
A483
A528
6
GWYNEDD
A49
A41
A494
POWYS
Burlton
A5
A518
A495
SHROPSHIRE
Shrewsbury

STAPLE CROSS ST0320

Staplecross Inn: Recently reopened by experienced landlord after restoration as simple country pub, well kept real ales and honest pub food *(Jeremy Whitehorn)*

STICKLEPATH SX6494

Devonshire [off A30 at Whiddon Down or Okehampton]: Unpretentious 16th-c thatched village local next to foundry museum, low-beamed slate-floored bar with big log fire, longcase clock and easy-going old furnishings, sofa in small snug, well kept Bass and St Austell ales tapped from the cask, farm cider, magazines to read, sandwiches, bookable Sun lunches and evening meals, games room with piano and bar billiards; lively folk night 1st Sun in month, open all day Fri/Sat, bedrooms, good walks *(LYM, JP, PP, the Didler)*

STOKEINTEIGNHEAD SX9170

☆ *Church House* [signed from Combeinteignhead, or off A379 N of Torquay]: 13th-c thatched pub under new management, heavy beams, inglenook fireplace, antique furnishings, ancient spiral stairs and relaxed, informal atmosphere, some emphasis on enjoyable food from good sandwiches and baked potatoes up, well kept Adnams, Bass and Greene King Old Speckled Hen, farm cider, good coffee, friendly obliging staff, smart extended no smoking dining room, simple public bar with traditional games and TV; quiet piped music; children in eating area, neat interestingly planted back garden, unspoilt village *(LYM, Comus and Sarah Elliott, Tim and Rosemary Wells, Richard and Margaret Peers)*

STOKENHAM SX8042

☆ *Church House* [opp church, N of A379 towards Torcross]: Comfortable open-plan pub under new landlord, enjoyable food from proper generous sandwiches and filled baked potatoes to fresh local seafood and good steaks, real ales inc Bass and Flowers Original, farm cider, no smoking dining room; unobtrusive piped music; attractive garden with enjoyably individual play area and fish pond *(Comus and Sarah Elliott, LYM, Mr and Mrs M Dalby, Brian Root, Roger Wain-Heapy)*

☆ *Tradesmans Arms* [just off A379 Dartmouth—Kingsbridge]: New licensees settling in well now in upmarket 15th-c thatched dining pub, enjoyable food inc wide lunchtime choice, good evening specials, lots of local fish and good puddings, choice of well kept ales such as Brakspears, local farm cider, well chosen wines, nice antique tables in beamed bar and no smoking dining room; some garden tables, open all day *(Roger Wain-Heapy, LYM, Mr and Mrs J Curtis, Keith and Margaret Kettell, Torrens Lyster)*

STRETE SX8446

Kings Arms: Pleasant service, good choice of really good food esp fresh fish, more elaborate dishes (Weds-Sat evenings) in sea-view restaurant *(Susan Pinney, DM)*

TEDBURN ST MARY SX8193

☆ *Kings Arms* [off A30 W of Exeter]: Picturesque traditional pub, open-plan but comfortable and quietly welcoming, with enjoyable varied food from good sandwiches and baguettes to tender steaks and Sun carvery, well kept Bass, Otter and Sharps Doom Bar, local farm cider, efficient friendly young staff, heavy-beamed and panelled L-shaped bar, lantern lighting and snug stable-style alcoves, big log fire, lots of brass and hunting prints, end games area, sparkling Christmas decorations, modern restaurant; may be piped pop music; children in eating area, tables on back terrace, bedrooms *(LYM, John and Vivienne Rice, Geoffrey Medcalf, Richard Purser, John and Sonja Newberry, Dennis Jenkin)*

TEIGNMOUTH SX9372

Molloys [Teign St]: Town pub notable for its short choice of good cheap food inc bargain steaks, cosy booth seating; no credit cards *(Meg and Colin Hamilton)*

☆ *Ship* [Queen St]: Upper and lower decks like a ship, good friendly atmosphere, nice mix of locals, families and tourists, good reasonably priced food (all day in summer) esp simply cooked local fish and good Sun lunch, good service from obliging staff, well kept ales inc Bass and Greene King Abbot, interesting wine list, fresh coffee, gallery restaurant; open all day, fine floral displays, lovely riverside setting, beautiful views *(David Carr)*

THELBRIDGE CROSS SS7912

Thelbridge Cross Inn [B3042 W of Tiverton]: Welcoming lounge bar with log fire and plush settees, good generous food inc some unusual dishes in extensive dining area and separate restaurant, friendly helpful service, particularly well kept Bass and Butcombe, good drinks prices; reasonable disabled access, bedrooms smallish but good breakfast *(Mr and Mrs A Forgie, BB, Mark Flynn)*

THURLESTONE SX6743

Village Inn: Busy much refurbished pub owned by neighbouring smart hotel and emphasising wide food choice (cool cabinet, open kitchen behind servery, blackboards, etc); well kept Dartmoor, Palmers and Wadworths 6X, comfortable country-style furnishings, dividers forming alcoves; children and dogs catered for, darts, quiz nights, live music, handy for coast path *(M Thomas)*

TIPTON ST JOHN SY0991

☆ *Golden Lion* [signed off B3176 Sidmouth—Ottery St Mary]: Doing well under current management, quick friendly service, good blackboard choice of enjoyable food from good sandwiches to seafood and some interesting dishes, well kept mainstream and local ales inc Otter, roaring log fire, attractive décor and mix of furnishings in spacious relaxing bar with quiet back room, no smoking restaurant; piped music; children in eating areas, open all day wknds, garden and terrace tables, two comfortable bedrooms with showers *(Mark Clezy, LYM, Mark and Heather Williamson, W Perry)*

TOPSHAM SX9688

☆ *Globe* [Fore St; 2 miles from M5 junction 30]: Substantial traditional inn dating from 16th c, solid comfort in heavy-beamed bow-windowed bar, good interesting home-cooked food from tasty sandwiches and toasties up, reasonable prices, well kept local and national beers, good value house wines, prompt friendly helpful service, plenty of locals, log-effect gas fire, snug little dining lounge, good value separate restaurant, back extension; children in eating area, open all day, good value attractive bedrooms *(LYM, Barry Steele-Perkins, the Didler, Mark and Heather Williamson, Dr and Mrs M E Wilson)*

☆ ***Lighter*** [Fore St]: Comfortably extended and refurbished, panelling and tall windows looking out over tidal flats, raised enclosed no smoking area, nautical décor, brisk staff, well kept Badger Best and Tanglefoot, food from good sandwiches and popular local cheese platter to mildly upmarket dishes and local fish, central log fire, good children's area; games machines, piped music; tables out in lovely spot on old quay, handy for big antiques centre *(Dr and Mrs M E Wilson, Minda and Stanley Alexander, Hugh Roberts, the Didler, Andy Millward, BB, Mark and Heather Williamson, David Carr, Mrs Sylvia Elcoate)*

☆ ***Passage House*** [Ferry Rd, off main street]: Attractive foody pub with new landlady settling in well, good fresh fish choice, other dishes from sandwiches up, well kept Otter and other ales, good wines, traditional 18th-c black-beamed bar and no smoking slate-floored lower bistro area (children welcome here), pleasant service; may be piped music; quiet terrace looking over moorings and river (lovely at sunset) to nature reserve beyond, open all day wknds and summer *(LYM, Ian Phillips, Tony Middis, Dr and Mrs M E Wilson, Ann and Bob Westbrook, Hugh Roberts, the Didler, John and Vivienne Rice, David Crook, Mike and Wendy Proctor, Derek and Sylvia Stephenson, Peter Burton, Louise Symons, David Carr)*

TORQUAY SX9175

Crown & Sceptre [Petitor Rd, St Marychurch]: Friendly two-bar local in 18th-c stone-built coaching inn, eight well kept changing ales, interesting naval memorabilia and chamber-pot collection, good-humoured long-serving landlord, food (not Sun) available without making a point of it, inc bar lunches and snacks any time, jazz Tues and Sun, bands Sat, monthly folk night; dogs very welcome, children too *(the Didler, JP, PP, Jim and Maggie Cowell, John Haslam, Linda Drew)*

Kent [Ilsham Rd (off B3199)]: Popular villagey local with bare boards, no smoking main bar area with banquette bays, stools and back carvery-style blackboard eating area, Bass, Boddingtons or Courage Best, Fullers London Pride, Sharps and John Smiths, public area papered with newsprint, TV in upper side room; side terrace tables *(Jim and Maggie Cowell)*

London [Strand]: Vast Wetherspoons bank conversion overlooking harbour and marina, big local ship paintings and a couple of reproduction ship's figureheads, good value food all day, bargain coffee as well as usual real ales, no piped music; small back no smoking area, family area up two flights of stairs; can be very busy *(Tim and Carolyn Lowes, Jim and Maggie Cowell)*

Willow Tree [Condor Way, The Willows]: Comfortable modern chain dining pub attractively set in residential area, decent generous food (may be two for one bargains), well kept Wadworths 6X, good friendly service, disabled access; children welcome, play area *(Mr and Mrs Colin Roberts, Pamela and Merlyn Horswell)*

TORRINGTON SS4919

☆ ***Black Horse*** [High St]: Pretty twin-gabled inn dating from 15th c, overhanging upper storeys, beams hung with stirrups, solid furniture, oak bar counter, no smoking lounge with striking ancient black oak partition wall and a couple of attractive oak seats, oak-panelled back restaurant with aquarium, good value generous straightforward food inc OAP wkdy lunchtime bargains and children's dishes, good friendly service, well kept Courage Best and Directors, John Smiths and changing guest beers, darts, shove-ha'penny, cribbage, dominoes; well reproduced piped music, friendly cat and dogs; disabled access, open all day Sat (may close slightly over-promptly other days), handy for RHS Rosemoor garden and Dartington Crystal *(LYM, D and S Price, Dr and Mrs M E Wilson, Brian Brooks, Lesley Hampson)*

TOTNES SX8060

King William IV [Fore St]: Warm, spacious and comfortably carpeted Victorian pub, popular (esp with older people) for enjoyable bargain main dishes, real ales such as Fullers London Pride, friendly service; big-screen sports TV; bedrooms with own bathrooms *(Mr and Mrs Colin Roberts)*

☆ ***Kingsbridge Inn*** [Leechwell Street]: Attractive and hospitable rambling bar, neat and tidy, with black beams, timbering and some stripped stone, combines well with eating areas inc small no smoking upper part (children allowed here); two log fires, plush seats, good home-made food (not Mon lunchtime) from lunchtime baguettes, toasted bagels and baked potatoes to some unusual hot dishes, well kept Bass, Greene King Morlands and a local beer, friendly service, leisurely atmosphere; may be piped music; children in eating area, some live music and readings *(LYM, DAV, Mr and Mrs N Ward, Adrian and Ione Lee, David Swift, Colin and Janet Roe)*

☆ ***Steam Packet*** [St Peters Quay, on W bank (ie not on Steam Packet Quay!)]: Newly refurbished, with thriving atmosphere, half a dozen well kept ales inc Otter and Theakstons, cheerful efficient staff, enjoyable food from tasty lunchtime crab and other sandwiches up, good wines and coffee, log fire, restaurant with spectacular river view from no smoking conservatory; children welcome (books and games for them in leather-seated side area), jazz Sun lunchtime, winter quiz night Mon; tables outside, bedrooms, open all day

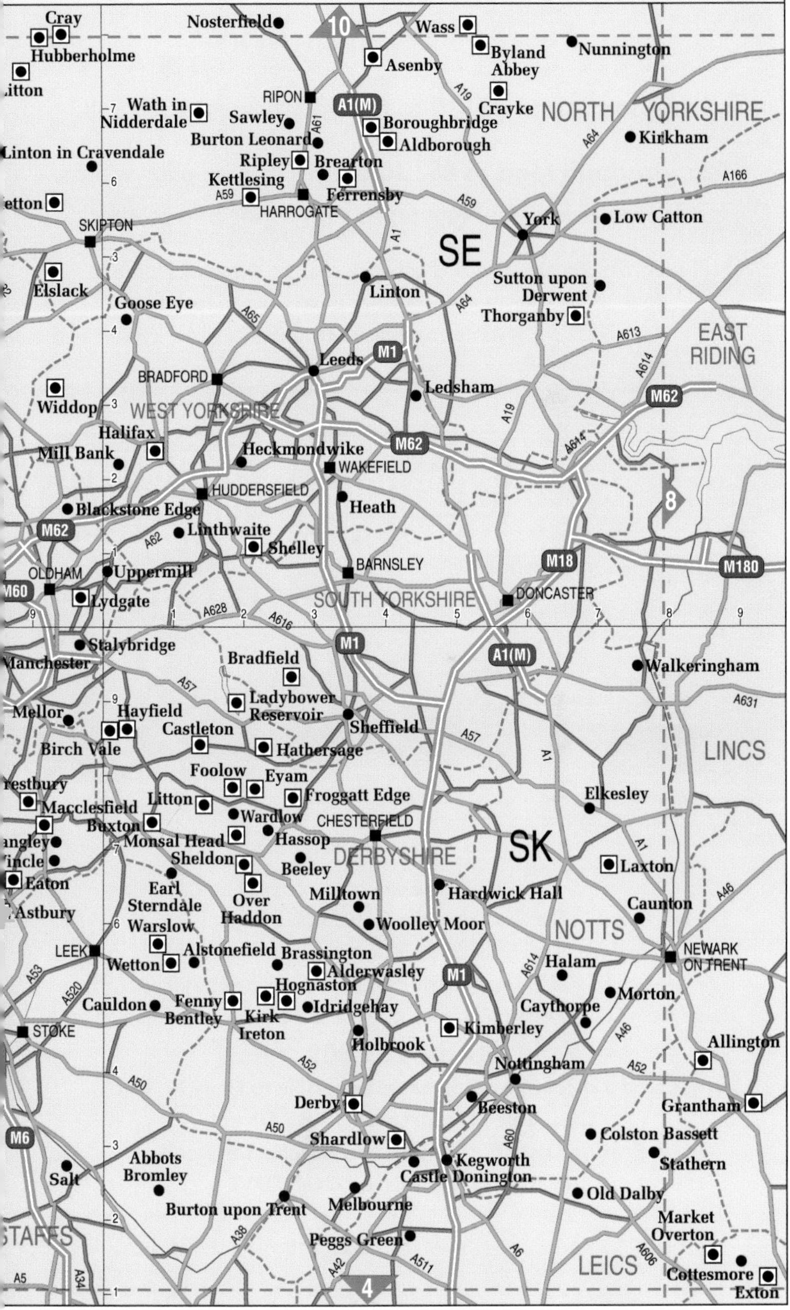

Cray
Nosterfield
10
Wass
Hubberholme
Nunnington
Byland Abbey
Asenby
Litton
RIPON
A19
Wath in Nidderdale
A1(M)
Crayke
NORTH YORKSHIRE
Sawley
A61
Boroughbridge
Burton Leonard
Aldborough
A64
Kirkham
Linton in Cravendale
Ripley
Brearton
A166
Kettlesing
A59
HARROGATE
Ferrensby
A59
Hetton
SKIPTON
York
Low Catton
A1
SE
Elslack
Linton
Sutton upon Derwent
Goose Eye
A64
Thorganby
A65
A613
EAST RIDING
M1
Leeds
A614
BRADFORD
Ledsham
Widdop
WEST YORKSHIRE
M62
A19
Halifax
M62
A614
Mill Bank
Heckmondwike
WAKEFIELD
HUDDERSFIELD
Heath
8
Blackstone Edge
M62
Linthwaite
A62
Shelley
M18
M180
OLDHAM
Uppermill
BARNSLEY
M60
DONCASTER
Lydgate
SOUTH YORKSHIRE
A628
A616
Stalybridge
M1
A1(M)
Manchester
Bradfield
Walkeringham
A57
Ladybower Reservoir
A631
Mellor
Hayfield
Sheffield
Castleton
A57
Birch Vale
Hathersage
LINCS
A1
Foolow
Eyam
Prestbury
Froggatt Edge
Elkesley
Macclesfield
Litton
Wardlow
Buxton
CHESTERFIELD
Langley
Monsal Head
Hassop
A1
SK
Wincle
Sheldon
DERBYSHIRE
Laxton
Beeley
Eaton
Earl Sterndale
Over Haddon
Milltown
Hardwick Hall
Caunton
A46
Astbury
Woolley Moor
Warslow
NOTTS
LEEK
Alstonefield
Brassington
Halam
NEWARK ON TRENT
Wetton
Alderwasley
A614
A53
M1
Hognaston
Morton
A520
Cauldon
Fenny Bentley
Idridgehay
Caythorpe
Kirk Ireton
STOKE
Kimberley
A46
Holbrook
Allington
A52
Nottingham
A52
A50
Derby
Beeston
Grantham
A50
M6
A60
Shardlow
Colston Bassett
Abbots Bromley
Kegworth
Salt
Castle Donington
Stathern
Burton upon Trent
Old Dalby
Melbourne
Market Overton
STAFFS
A38
Peggs Green
A6
A606
A511
LEICS
A42
Cottesmore
A5
A34
4
Exton

IF YOU HAVE A MOBILE PHONE, THERE'S A NEW, QUICK AND EASY WAY TO FIND A PUB NEAR YOU

Text **goodpub** to **85130** to find your nearest good pub.

Text **goodpub food** to **85130** to only include pubs where meals are served – serving times vary – ring pub to check.

(Texts cost 50p plus standard network charges. Involves a location look-up on your mobile – further details can be found at **www.goodguides.co.uk**)

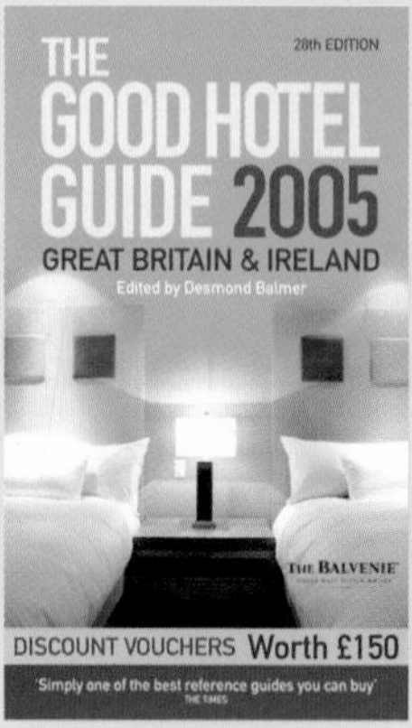

THE
28th EDITION
GOOD HOTEL GUIDE 2005
GREAT BRITAIN & IRELAND
Edited by Desmond Balmer
DISCOUNT VOUCHERS Worth £150
'Simply one of the best reference guides you can buy'

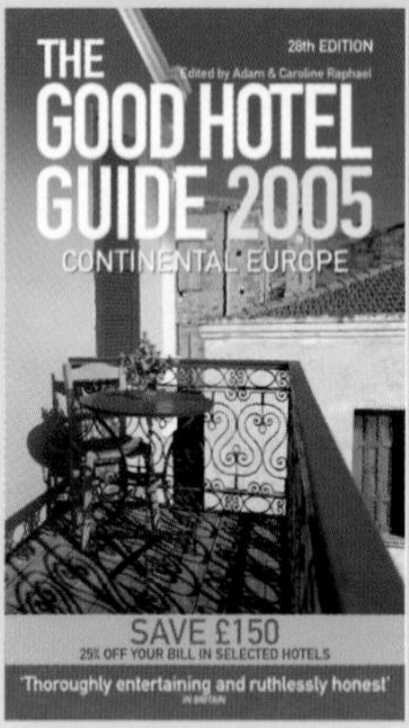

THE
28th EDITION
Edited by Adam & Caroline Raphael
GOOD HOTEL GUIDE 2005
CONTINENTAL EUROPE
SAVE £150
25% OFF YOUR BILL IN SELECTED HOTELS
'Thoroughly entertaining and ruthlessly honest'

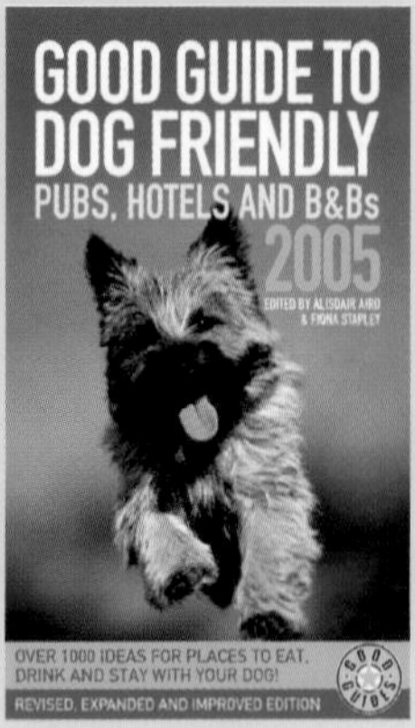

GOOD GUIDE TO DOG FRIENDLY
PUBS, HOTELS AND B&Bs
2005
EDITED BY ALISDAIR AIRD & FIONA STAPLEY
OVER 1000 IDEAS FOR PLACES TO EAT, DRINK AND STAY WITH YOUR DOG!
REVISED, EXPANDED AND IMPROVED EDITION

If you would like to order a copy of
The Good Hotel Guide 2005 (£15.99),
The Good Hotel Guide 2005 – Continental Europe (£17.99),
or the *Good Guide to Dog Friendly Pubs, Hotels and B&Bs 2005* (£9.99)
direct from Ebury Press (p&p free), please call our credit-card hotline on

01206 255 800

or send a cheque/postal order made payable to Ebury Press to
Cash Sales Department, TBS Direct,
Frating Distribution Centre, Colchester Road,
Frating Green, Essex CO7 7DW

For more information about these titles, please refer to the back of the next colour section.

(Dr and Mrs M E Wilson, Joyce and Maurice Cottrell, Alain and Rose Foote, Comus and Sarah Elliott)

TUCKENHAY SX8156

☆ *Maltsters Arms* [Ashprington rd out of Totnes (signed left off A381 on outskirts)]: Lovely spot with waterside tables out by peaceful wooded creek, enjoyable food inc good interesting dishes and real food for children, well kept Princetown Dartmoor IPA and up to three changing guest beers, lots of good wines by the glass and other good drinks, chatty atmosphere, simple up-to-date décor (a no smoking area would be appreciated), traditional games, dogs welcome in bar, compact restaurant (booking recommended; wknd barbecues with live music; children in eating areas, bedrooms (there may be a minimum wknd stay of two nights), open all day *(Mike Gorton, Lynda and Trevor Smith, LYM, Comus and Sarah Elliott, John Evans, the Didler, JP, PP, Andrew Pearson, Barry and Anne, Doreen and Haydn Maddock, Felicity Stephens, David Fox, John and Doris Couper, A P Seymour, Lorna Duff, Mrs Susan Pritchard, Alan and Anne Driver, OPUS)*

UGBOROUGH SX6755

Anchor [off A3121]: Village pub with log fire, locals and dogs in unpretentious beamed bar, well kept Bass, Shepherd Neame Spitfire and Suttons XSB, partly no smoking restaurant, food from light lunchtime things to ambitious dishes with bison, ostrich and so forth; shame about the TV; children welcome, small outside seating area, open all day wknds *(Esther and John Sprinkle, Laura Wilson, David M Cundy, John and Joan Calvert, LYM, Roger and Jenny Huggins, Mr and Mrs J E C Tasker, Dr and Mrs A K Clarke)*

UMBERLEIGH SS6023

☆ *Rising Sun* [A377 S of Barnstaple]: Comfortable and civilised fishing inn with five River Taw salmon and sea trout beats, lots of stuffed fish and fishing memorabilia in pleasant partly no smoking divided bar with woodburner and flagstones; welcoming friendly staff, good food inc lunchtime sandwiches, well kept real ales inc Cotleigh Barn Owl, good wines by the glass and farm cider; children in eating areas, tables outside, good bedrooms *(Mrs P Burvill, LYM, David Gibbs, Dr and Mrs A K Clarke)*

WEMBWORTHY SS6609

☆ *Lymington Arms* [Lama Cross]: Large dining pub, clean and bright, with wide choice of good reasonably priced food (not Mon), friendly service, well kept Sharps Doom Bar, Inch's cider, decent wines, agreeable restaurant (not Sun/Mon); children welcome, tables in garden, pleasant country setting *(R J Walden, A C and B M Laing, M and D Toms, Guy Vowles, Mark Flynn)*

WIDECOMBE SX7176

☆ *Old Inn* [B3387 W of Bovey Tracey]: Busy, friendly and comfortable, with 14th-c stonework, big log fires, olde-worlde pubby front bar, some concentration on large restaurant area with wide choice of good value hearty food from well filled granary rolls up, well kept ales inc Wadworths 6X, local farm cider, decent wines, good friendly service, family room; in pretty moorland village – get there before about 12.30 in summer to miss the tourist coaches; room to dance on music nights, attractively reworked garden with water features and pleasant terrace; great walks *(LYM, JP, PP, Ian and Nita Cooper, Ian Wilson)*

WITHERIDGE SS8014

Angel [The Square]: Bright, airy and spacious, with homely bric-a-brac, friendly licensees, well kept interesting changing beers, good range of malt whiskies, reasonably priced tasty food *(C R Cann)*

WOODBURY SY0187

White Hart [3½ miles from M5 junction 30; A376, then B3179; Church St]: Good local atmosphere, good choice of good value food, well kept Bass and Everards Tiger, decent wines, plain public bar, comfortable quieter dining lounge, log fire; attractive small walled garden with aviary, skittle alley, nice spot by church in peaceful village *(Mark Clezy, Dr and Mrs M E Wilson)*

WOOLACOMBE SS4543

Captain Jacks [West Rd]: Touristy place with dark timbering and flooring, on site of 12th-c farm building, with well kept St Austell HSD and Tribute, friendly staff, restaurant; pool, piped music may be loud, dogs allowed; suntrap terrace *(Rona Murdoch)*

Westbeach [Beach Rd]: Cool new continental bar, lots of style, bean bags and comfortable chairs around chunky tables, skinny pedestal bar stools, some emphasis on cocktails, juices and wines, also Boddingtons, Hoegaarden and Leffe, friendly service; good seafood restaurant with clean crisp décor and modern art; DJs Thurs-Sun in summer; brilliant ladies', sturdy benches on big terrace overlooking surfing beach, Sun barbecue with some interesting dishes, open all day at least in summer *(Rona Murdoch)*

WRAFTON SS4935

Williams Arms [A361 just SE of Braunton]: Modernised thatched family dining pub geared to holiday-makers and giving children free rein, two big subdivided bars, wide food choice majoring on unlimited self-service carvery, children's helpings, quick service, Bass and Worthington, decent house wines; pool, darts, piped music, discreet TV; picnic-sets outside with play area and aviary *(Joyce and Maurice Cottrell, K R Harris)*

YEALMPTON SX5851

Rose & Crown [A379 Kingsbridge—Plymouth]: Warmly welcoming, locally popular for wide range of enjoyable food inc imaginatively prepared specials (roomy enough for the summer crowds too), well kept beer, reasonable prices, efficient service; lots of theme nights *(Simon Batchelor, Margaret and Roy Randle, Peter Salmon)*

Dorset

A lot of new entries here this year, some of them back in the *Guide* after a break (often of many years): the 17th-c thatched George at Chideock (enjoyable home-made food), the very traditional old Fox in Corfe Castle (good beers), the foody thatched Fox at Corscombe, the very well run and comfortable Hunters Moon at Middlemarsh (a splendid all-rounder under its new owners), the appealingly cottagey Ship in Distress in Mudeford (good fish and seafood), the bustling and well run Smugglers at Osmington Mills, and the delightfully unspoilt and well cared for Vine at Pamphill on the National Trust's Kingston Lacy estate. Other pubs doing particularly well here these days are the Royal Oak in Cerne Abbas (an exemplary all-rounder, using a lot of local produce in its good food), the Cock & Bottle at East Morden (also strong on food and good all round), the West Bay in West Bay (imaginatively prepared fresh seafood in appealing surroundings – and a nice place to stay), the Manor Hotel at seaside West Bexington (coupling a welcoming bar side with its comfortable hotel side) and the timelessly unspoilt and rustic Square & Compass in Worth Matravers. For the second year running, the West Bay in West Bay carries off the title of Dorset Dining Pub of the Year. Pubs currently scoring highly in the Lucky Dip section at the end of the chapter are the Gaggle of Geese at Buckland Newton, Fox & Hounds at Cattistock, Blue Raddle in Dorchester, Blackmore Vale at Marnhull, Marquis of Lorne at Nettlecombe, Three Horseshoes at Powerstock, Crown at Puncknowle, Shave Cross Inn, New Inn at Stoke Abbott, Bankes Arms at Studland, Greyhound at Sydling St Nicholas and Crown at Uploders. Dorset drinks prices are generally around the national average; the county's main brewers are Palmers and Badger, though we found that many of the pubs with cheaper than average beer were getting it from small brewers outside the county.

BURTON BRADSTOCK SY4889 Map 1

Anchor 🍴

B3157 SE of Bridport

The beautifully cooked food at this bustling little seafood pub is much better than you'd expect from the rather rough and ready style of the place. As well as snacks such as filled baguettes (from £3.50), ploughman's (£5.25), barbecue chicken salad (£6.25), and baked ham and egg (£6.95), the blackboard lists other (by no means cheap) popular well presented dishes such as various curries or sizzling scallops (£7.95), shoulder of lamb with garlic and rosemary, seafood thermidore or lemon sole (£9.95), brill (£16.95), and dover sole fillets or poached salmon supreme in creamy prawn, parsley and white wine sauce (£19.95), with puddings such as sherry trifle (£3.25). It's best to book well ahead if you want a table, especially at weekends; the restaurant is no smoking. The fairly straightforward lounge bar has pink plush wall seats and some fishy décor, and the public bar (there's usually a crowd of lively locals in here) has big windows and more cushioned seats. Darts, table skittles, bar billiards, TV, shove-ha'penny, cribbage and dominoes; pleasantly relaxed service, from the welcoming Scottish landlord and his staff. There are now more than 80 different malt whiskies to choose from, as well as three or four well kept beers such as Hampshire Strong's Best, Morrells Grumpy Cow, Ringwood Best and Wychwood Hobgoblin. *(Recommended by David and Julie Glover, Graham and Rose Ive, Mrs J L Wyatt, Terry Mizen, Joan and Michel Hooper-Immins, Peter Meister, Rob Winstanley, Conor Mc Gaughey, Mrs Hilarie Taylor, Tony Beaulah, Terry and Linda Moseley, Oz and Annette, Roland and Wendy Chalu)*

Free house ~ Licensee J R Plunkett ~ Real ale ~ Bar food (12-2, 6.30-9, maybe all day in summer) ~ Restaurant ~ (01308) 897228 ~ Children in eating area of bar ~ Dogs allowed in bar ~ Open 11-11; 12-10.30 Sun ~ Bedrooms: £30S(£30B)/£55S(£55B)

CERNE ABBAS ST6601 Map 2

Royal Oak

Long Street

With delicious bar food, welcoming service and a good choice of drinks, this picturesque creeper-covered Tudor dining pub is well worth a detour. Made using good quality, mostly local ingredients (with herbs grown in the garden), well presented dishes include lunchtime sandwiches (£3.75, good open sandwiches £4.95), ham, egg and chips or battered haddock (£7.95), wild mushroom stroganoff (£8.95), and steak (from £13.50), with specials such as local venison sausage and mash or lamb and apricot pie (£9.75), chargrilled salmon (£10.95), or halibut fillet with cream, tomato and chive sauce (£15.95), and puddings such as treacle tart and wild berry crumble (£4.25), and an interesting cheese platter (£4.25); smaller portions are available for children. The three flagstoned communicating rooms have sturdy oak beams, lots of shiny black panelling, an inglenook with an oven, and warm winter log fires. The stone walls and the ceilings are packed with all sorts of small ornaments from local photographs to antique china, brasses and farm tools; candles on tables, and fresh flowers, occasional piped music. It's smoothly run by the enthusiastic licensees, and the staff are pleasant and efficient. Butcombe, Greene King Old Speckled Hen, Quay Weymouth and St Austell are served from handpumps on the uncommonly long bar counter. They also do around a dozen wines by the glass, and 15 malt whiskies; fruit teas and good coffee too. The enclosed back garden is very pleasant, with purbeck stone terracing and cedarwood decking, comfortable chairs, and tables under cocktail parasols, and outdoor heaters. On sunny summer afternoons they sometimes serve drinks and snacks out here. Readers tell us parking can be a problem at busy times. *(Recommended by Mr and Mrs Bentley-Davies, the Didler, JP, PP, W W Burke, Rosanna Luke, Julia and Richard Tredgett, Andrew Shore, Maria Williams, Terry Mizen, M G Hart, Pete Baker, Mike and Shelley Woodroffe, Dom Bradshaw, Mark Boulding, Jeff and Wendy Williams, John Coatsworth, Derek Thomas, Joan and Michel Hooper-Immins)*

Free house ~ Licensees David and Janice Birch ~ Real ale ~ Bar food ~ Restaurant ~ (01300) 341797 ~ Children in eating area of bar ~ Dogs allowed in bar ~ Open 11.30-3, 6.30(6 Sat)-11; 12-3, 7-10.30 Sun; closed 25 Dec

CHIDEOCK SY4292 Map 1

Anchor

Seatown signposted off A35 from Chideock

With new tenants since our last edition, this strikingly set pub nestles dramatically beneath the 188-metre (617-ft) Golden Cap pinnacle, just a few steps from the cove beach and very near the Dorset Coast Path. Ideally placed for the lovely sea and cliff views, there are seats and tables on the spacious front terrace; get here really early in summer if you want to bag a seat. Even out of season it's a pleasure, after a walk by the stormy sea, when the sometimes overwhelming crowds have gone. The little bars feel especially snug then, with roaring winter fires, some sea pictures and lots of interesting local photographs, a few fossils and shells, simple but comfortable seats around neat tables, and low white-planked ceilings; the family room is no smoking. Friendly, efficient staff serve well kept Palmers 200, IPA and Copper on handpump (under light blanket pressure in winter only), and there's a decent little wine list; piped, mainly classical, music. Tasty bar food such as lunchtime sandwiches (from £2.50, baguettes from £4.95) and ploughman's (from £5.75), as well as soup (£3.45), deep-fried camembert with cranberry dip (£5.75), spicy bean casserole (£6.75), minted lamb and suet pudding (£6.95), and steak and kidney pie (£7.25), and specials such as spinach and feta pie (£7.95), and whole grilled plaice (£11.75), with puddings such as apple cake and clotted cream (£3.50); children's menu (from £4.25). There are plans to upgrade the toilets in the autumn. *(Recommended by Dr and Mrs M E Wilson, Mike and Cheryl Lyons, John Beeken, John and Vivienne Rice, James Woods, Joan and Michel Hooper-Immins, Paul Morris, Peter Meister, David Thornton, Doug Sawyer, Mayur Shah, Mrs C Lintott, Rob Winstanley, John Coatsworth, Roderick and Jill Leslie, David Crook, K Hutchinson, Roland and Wendy Chalu)*

Palmers ~ Tenants Paul Wiscombe and Ben Ambridge ~ Real ale ~ Bar food (all day in summer) ~ (01297) 489215 ~ Children welcome ~ Dogs welcome ~ Open 11-11; 12-10.30 Sun; 11-3, 6-11 winter

George

A35 Bridport—Lyme Regis

In summer, you can eat out on the patio at this pretty 17th-c thatched inn, and they hold regular barbecues. Inside, the dark-beamed lounge bar has pewter tankards hanging from the mantelpiece above the big fireplace (with good winter log fires), boat drawings and attractively framed old local photographs on its cream walls, a collection of over 250 foreign banknotes donated by customers, and high shelves of bottles, plates, mugs and so forth. There are comfortable red plush stools and wall and window seats. Listed on monthly changing blackboards, freshly cooked bar food might include lunchtime bar snacks such as sandwiches or baked potatoes (from £3.95), ploughman's (£4.95), local sausages or home-cooked ham and eggs (£6.95), and irish stew (£7.95), while evening dishes might be thai green chicken curry (£7.95), mushroom stroganoff or beef stir fry and noodles (£9.95), lamb chops with rosemary and garlic or pork medallions fried in wholegrain mustard and honey sauce with fine beans and chorizo sausage (£12.95), local fillet steak (from £15.95), and fish specials such as seared salmon with baby leeks and dill (£10.95), bream and cajun seasoning and avocado dressing (£12.95), and seared scallops with smoky bacon (£13.95). The two restaurants are no smoking. Friendly staff serve well kept Palmers 200, IPA and Copper on handpump; darts, cribbage, dominoes, unobtrusive piped music. *(Recommended by Mrs Jill Silversides, Barry Brown, Oz and Annette, Terry and Linda Moseley)*

Palmers ~ Tenant Paul Crisp ~ Bar food ~ Restaurant ~ (01297) 489419 ~ Children in eating area of bar and restaurant ~ Dogs allowed in bar ~ Live Jazz and Blues fortnightly ~ Open 11-2.30, 6-11; 12-3, 6-10.30 Sun; closed 25 Dec evening

CHURCH KNOWLE SY9481 Map 2

New Inn 🍷

Village signposted off A351 just N of Corfe Castle

Serving good food (and prettily set in a nice little village), this partly thatched 16th-c inn is very restauranty in style, and not really a place to drop into for a drink. A great choice of fresh fish might include half a pint of prawns (£7.50), fruits de mer (£9.50), large haddock (£13.50), locally caught sea bream (£13.95), and bass (£14.95), with other meals such as sandwiches (from £4), popular blue vinney soup (£4.25), ploughman's (from £6.25), steak and kidney pie (£8.25), and steaks (from £12.95). The two main areas, linked by an arch, are attractively furnished with farmhouse chairs and tables, with lots of bric-a-brac, and a log fire at each end; one area is no smoking. You can choose wines from a tempting display in the wine cellar, which often includes interesting bin ends in their wine shack (they also do off sales from here), and they serve several wines by the glass (either 175 or 250 ml). Well kept Flowers Original, Greene King Old Speckled Hen and Wadworths 6X on handpump, farmhouse cider and organic apple juices, and around a dozen malt whiskies; skittle alley (private hire only) and piped music. There are disabled facilities, though there's a step down to the gents'. The good-sized garden has plenty of tables and fine views of the Purbeck hills. If you book beforehand you can camp in two fields behind. *(Recommended by William and Jenifer Ruxton, Mrs Hazel Blackburn, Pat and Robert Watt, James Woods, W W Burke, Terry and Linda Moseley, Mr and Mrs P L Spencer)*

Inn Partnership (Pubmaster) ~ Tenants Maurice and Rosemary Estop ~ Real ale ~ Bar food (12-2, 6(6.30 winter)-9) ~ (01929) 480357 ~ Children in eating area of bar and restaurant ~ Open 11-3, 6-11; 12-3, 6-10.30 Sun; closed Mon Jan-end Mar

COLEHILL SU0302 Map 2

Barley Mow

From roundabout junction of A31 Ferndown bypass and B3073 Wimborne road, follow Colehill signpost up Middlehill Road, pass Post Office, and at church turn right into Colehill Lane; OS Sheet 195 map reference 032024

The cosy low-beamed main bar of this attractive part-thatched and part-tiled former drovers' cottage has a good winter fire in the huge brick inglenook, attractively moulded oak panelling, some Hogarth prints, and a relaxed dining atmosphere. The friendly staff serve very well kept Badger Best, Tanglefoot and a seasonal ale on handpump, and they've a dozen fruit wines. The cat is called Misty; unobtrusive piped music and a fruit machine. Big helpings of home-made bar food could include soup (£2.75), sandwiches (from £3.95), salmon fishcakes or ham and egg (£5.50), ploughman's (£5.75), steak and kidney pie or mediterranean vegetable lasagne (£7.25), plaice fillet (£7.95), braised lamb steak with root vegetables in honey and mint sauce or chicken filled with brie and wrapped in bacon with cider sauce (£8.95), puddings such as tiramisu (£3.75), and they also do a Sunday roast (£6.95); an extension to the main bar is set for diners. Sheltered by oak trees, there's a big pleasant, enclosed lawn at the back with a boules pitch. The pub is specially striking in summer, when colourful flowers in tubs and hanging baskets are set off vividly against the whitewash; there are some nice country walks nearby. *(Recommended by Nigel and Sue Foster, B and K Hypher, R J Walden, W W Burke, Peter Burton, Mr and Mrs R W Allan, David Cannings)*

Badger ~ Manager Bruce Cichocki ~ Real ale ~ Bar food ~ (01202) 882140 ~ Children in family room ~ Dogs allowed in bar ~ Open 11-3, 5.30-11; 12-3, 7-10.30 Sun

CORFE CASTLE SY9681 Map 2

Fox

West Street

Full of character, this very traditional pub is beautifully set with the evocative ruins of Corfe Castle rising up behind the pleasant suntrap garden (reached through a pretty flower-hung side entrance). Much of the pub is built from the same stone as the castle – it's particularly evident in an ancient fossil-dotted alcove and in the pre-1300 stone fireplace. Tiny and atmospheric, the front bar has closely set tables and chairs, a romantic painting of the castle depicting it in its prime, and other pictures above panelling, old-fashioned iron lamps, and hatch service. An ancient well in the lounge bar has been glassed over and lit from within; no piped music or games machines. Tapped from the cask, three to six well kept real ales might include Greene King Abbot and Old Speckled Hen, Fullers London Pride, Timothy Taylors Landlord, Wadworths 6X and Worthington 1744. Big portions of tasty bar food include sandwiches (from £2.90, filled baguettes from £3.20), home-made soup (£3.25), ploughman's (£5.10), ham and egg (£5.20), battered fresh cod (£6.95), and daily specials such as chicken balti (£6.95), southern fried chicken (£7.95), and 15oz rib-eye steak (£13.95). Children are allowed only in the garden. The countryside surrounding this National Trust village is well worth exploring, and there's a local museum opposite. *(Recommended by Paul A Moore, John and Laney Woods, Chris Ferguson, Tony Brace, the Didler)*

Free house ~ Licensees Graham White and Miss Annette Brown ~ Real ale ~ Bar food ~ (01929) 480449 ~ Dogs welcome ~ Open 11-3, 6.30-11; 12-3, 7-11 Sun; closed 25 Dec

CORSCOMBE ST5205 Map 2

Fox 🍷 🍺

Outskirts, towards Halstock

In a lovely country setting, this picturesque old thatched pub (there are even roses over the door) has a very good thoughtful wine list, or if you fancy something a bit different you can choose from home-made elderflower cordial, damson vodka, and sloe gin. Along with interesting specials such as crab, bass and prawn gratin (£6.95), fish pie (£10.95), chargrilled sirloin steak with béarnaise sauce or crab risotto with asparagus (£14.95), enjoyable (though not cheap) dishes might include fish soup or wild mushroom risotto with parmesan cheese (£5.50), chicken in a creamy sauce with celery and red pepper (£8.25), rack of lamb with mustard mash and rosemary jus (£14.50), with home-made puddings such as treacle tart (£3.50); they've also lunchtime baguettes (from £4.25, not Sunday), and ploughman's (from £5.25). Exmoor Ale and Butcombe Bitter are well kept on handpump alongside an occasional summer guest such as Exmoor Fox, and they've local cider. A flagstoned room on the right has harness hanging from the beams, small Leech hunting prints and Snaffles prints, Spy cartoons of fox hunting gentlemen, a long scrubbed pine table, and two open fires with large inglenooks. In the left-hand room (partly no smoking) there are built-in settles, candles on the blue-and-white gingham tablecloths or barrel tables, an assortment of chairs, lots of horse prints, antlers on the beams, two glass cabinets with a couple of stuffed owls in each, and an L-shaped wall settle by the inglenook fireplace. The no smoking dining room (which is open when they're busy and for winter breakfast) has an Aga, pine cupboards, and a welsh dresser. In summer, breakfast is taken in the conservatory with its maturing vine, orchids, and huge oak table. There are seats across the quiet village lane on a lawn by the little stream; this is a nice area for walks.
(Recommended by Mike Gorton, Paul Morris, John Hale, Mrs H Filmer, Kim and Ann Miller, Francis Johnston, W W Burke, Conor Mc Gaughey, OPUS, Roland and Wendy Chalu)

Free house ~ Licensees Clive Webb and Margaret Hannell ~ Real ale ~ Bar food (not 25 Dec) ~ Restaurant ~ (01935) 891330 ~ Well behaved children over 5 in restaurant ~ Open 12-3, 7-11(10.30 Sun); closed 25 Dec evening ~ Bedrooms: £55B/£80B

EAST CHALDON SY7983 Map 2

Sailors Return

Village signposted from A352 Wareham—Dorchester; from village green, follow Dorchester, Weymouth signpost; note that the village is also known as Chaldon Herring; OS Sheet 194 map reference 790834

Usefully for walkers, this well extended thatched pub is open all day, and they serve six real ales on handpump: alongside Hampshire Strongs Best and Ringwood Best you might find four well kept guests such as Archers City Boy, Badger Tanglefoot, Hop Back Summer Lightning and Young's Special, and they also have country wines and several malt whiskies. The pub is set in lovely countryside, close to Lulworth Cove, and from nearby West Chaldon a bridleway leads across to join the Dorset Coast Path by the National Trust cliffs above Ringstead Bay. Picnic-sets, benches and log seats on the grass in front look down over cow pastures to the village, and you can wander to the interesting little nearby church or enjoy a downland walk from the pub. The flagstoned bar still keeps much of its original country-tavern character, while the newer part has unfussy furnishings, old notices for decoration, and open beams showing the roof above. A wide choice of straightforward bar food such as baguettes (from £3.50), ploughman's or filled baked potatoes (£5.25), chilli con carne or sausage, egg and chips (£6.95), rainbow trout or sizzling chicken (£7.95), gammon hock (£9.75), and lamb shoulder (£9.95). The no smoking dining area has solid old tables in nooks and corners; darts, cribbage, dominoes, TV and piped music. Although fairly isolated it gets very busy at weekends, especially in fine weather. *(Recommended by B and K Hypher, Marjorie and David Lamb, Simon and Jane Williams, Paul and Annette Hallett, Ian and Deborah Carrington, S P Watkin, P A Taylor, Bruce Bird, Roy and Lindsey Fentiman)*

Free house ~ Licensees Mike Pollard, Claire Kelly and David Slater ~ Real ale ~ Bar food (12-2, 6-9(9.30 Fri/Sat); 12-9(9.30 Fri/Sat)Thurs-Sun in summer) ~ Restaurant ~ (01305) 853847 ~ Children in restaurant ~ Dogs allowed in bar ~ Open 11-11; 12-10.30 Sun

EAST KNIGHTON SY8185 Map 2

Countryman

Just off A352 Dorchester—Wareham; OS Sheet 194 map reference 811857

Families are well catered for at this big bustling pub, with toys inside, play equipment in the garden, and baby-changing facilities. The neat and comfortable long main bar has a mix of tables, wheelback chairs and comfortable sofas, and fires at either end. This room opens into several other smaller areas, including a no smoking family room, a games bar with pool and darts. Courage Best, Greene King Old Speckled Hen and Ringwood Best and Old Thumper are well kept on handpump, as well as farm cider, and they do a good choice of wines; piped music, disabled lavatories. As well as around half a dozen vegetarian dishes such as chilli potato tart or tomato and lentil lasagne (£7.95), the menu might include sandwiches or filled rolls (from £2.75), filled baked potatoes or omelettes (from £4.95), ploughman's (from £5.95), whitebait (£7.95), garlic and herb chicken breast (£8.75), and gammon steak (£10.25), with daily specials such as lamb and potato moussaka or chicken curry (£7.95), and puddings such as blackcurrant pie (from £3.95); children's meals (from £4.50). They also do a carvery (readers highly recommend the beef), which is £13.25 for a roast and pudding; not Monday, nor lunchtime on Tuesday. It's a very popular place (and service can be slow at busy times), so best to book if you want to eat on Sunday, when they have two lunchtime sittings. The restaurant is no smoking. *(Recommended by Brian and Karen Thomas, OPUS, Mr and Mrs A Stansfield, Philip and Elaine Holmes, James A Waller, Alain and Rose Foote, Peter Salmon, Simon and Jane Williams, S P Watkin, P A Taylor, Jason Caulkin, Renee and Dennis Ball, Roy and Lindsey Fentiman, Richard and Margaret Peers, M G Hart)*

Free house ~ Licensees Jeremy and Nina Evans ~ Real ale ~ Bar food ~ Restaurant ~ (01305) 852666 ~ Children in eating area of bar, restaurant and family room ~ Dogs welcome ~ Open 10.30-2.30, 6-11; closed 25 Dec ~ Bedrooms: £56B/£72B

EAST MORDEN SY9195 Map 2

Cock & Bottle

B3075 between A35 and A31 W of Poole

The interesting, well cooked bar food is so popular, that it's a good idea to book if you want to eat at this particularly welcoming pub. From an interesting changing bar menu dishes might include fresh prawn bisque with crème fraîche and french brandy (£4.95), home-cured salmon gravadlax with sweet dijon mustard and dill dressing (£5.50), stuffed vine leaves with spiced vegetable risotto on mushroom and courgette tomato provençale (£8.50), braised lamb chump with creamed potato and rich vegetable, rosemary and redcurrant sauce (£11.50), steamed bass fillets on white wine, saffron and leek and potato stew with asparagus (£12.50), and barbary duck breast marinated with spices and honey, kumquat, plum and Cointreau sauce (£14.95), with puddings such as apple and cinammon suet pudding with fresh vanilla sauce or panettone bread and butter pudding with spiced rum fruits (£4.50); lunchtime sandwiches. There's a children's menu, and they'll also do half helpings of some main courses. The interior is divided into several communicating areas (mostly laid out for dining), with heavy rough beams, some stripped ceiling boards, squared panelling, a mix of old furnishings in various sizes and degrees of antiquity, small Victorian prints and some engaging bric-a-brac. There's a roaring log fire, and comfortably intimate corners each with just a couple of tables. Although the emphasis is on dining there's still a pubby wood-floored public bar with piped music, a fruit machine, and a sensibly placed darts alcove. This in turn leads on to yet another individually furnished dining room. Most of the restaurant is no smoking, and they have some disabled facilities. As well as a good choice of decent house wines (including half a dozen by the glass), they have well kept Badger Best, K&B and Tanglefoot on handpump; helpful service from the pleasant staff. There are a few picnic-sets outside, a garden area, and an adjoining field with a nice pastoral outlook. *(Recommended by Ian Phillips, Geoffrey G Lawrance, Mark Clezy, Malcolm Taylor, DJH, Mr and Mrs A Stansfield, Terry and Linda Moseley, Howard and Margaret Buchanan, Norman and June Williams, Joan and Michel Hooper-Immins, Mrs H E Cunliffe, Roy and Lindsey Fentiman, AB Mason, Tim and Rosemary Wells, Peter Neate, John and Joan Nash)*

Badger ~ Tenant Peter Meadley ~ Real ale ~ Bar food (12-2, 6(7 Sun)-9) ~ Restaurant ~ (01929) 459238 ~ Children in restaurant ~ Dogs allowed in bar ~ Open 11-2.30(3 Sat), 6-11; 12-3, 7-10.30 Sun

FARNHAM ST9515 Map 2
Museum ⊕ ♀ ■ ⇌
Village signposted off A354 Blandford Forum—Salisbury

Built in the 17th c by General Pitt Rivers to offer accommodation and refreshment for his nearby museum, this attractively extended building has been opened up into a series of appealing interconnecting rooms and bars. Cheery yellow walls and plentiful windows give the place a bright, fresh feel. The flagstoned bar has a big inglenook fireplace, light beams, good comfortably cushioned furnishings and fresh flowers on all the tables. To the right is a dining room with a fine antique dresser, while off to the left is a cosier room, with a very jolly hunting model and a seemingly sleeping stuffed fox curled in a corner. Another room feels rather like a contemporary version of a baronial hall, soaring up to a high glass ceiling, with dozens of antlers and a stag's head looking down on a long refectory table and church-style pews. It leads to an outside terrace with more wooden tables. As well as an excellent choice of wines, there are three well kept real ales from smaller breweries, such as Hop Back, Otter and Ringwood; prompt service from the antipodean staff. Using lots of local and organic produce (they make their own bread, jams, chutney and marmalades), innovative, though certainly not cheap, dishes might include soup (£4.50), roasted chestnut mushrooms on rosemary toast with sautéed duck egg, balsamic and truffle oil (£5.50), roast cornish scallops, cauliflower purée lightly spiced with curry and chilly or fried potato gnocchi, grilled vegetables, soft herbs and parmesan crisps (£9), lemon sole fillets with leeks, saffron fettuccini and butter sauce or slow-roast lamb shoulder with tomato and olive salsa (£15), and puddings such as treacle tart and custard with vanilla ice-cream (£5.50); lunchtime baguettes (£6). It's a good idea to book if you want to eat in the stylish restaurant (no smoking till 10pm), which is open only for Friday and Saturday dinner and Sunday lunch. *(Recommended by Phil Metcalfe, Phyl and Jack Street, Dr L Kaufman, Colin and Janet Roe, Dr D G Twyman, Terry and Linda Moseley, Penny Simpson; also in the Good Hotel Guide)*

Free house ~ Licensees Vicky Elliot and Mark Stephenson ~ Real ale ~ Bar food ~ Restaurant (Fri and Sat evening and Sun lunch) ~ (01725) 516261 ~ Well behaved children in eating area of bar, must be over 8 in evening ~ Dogs allowed in bar and bedrooms ~ Open 12-3, 6-11; 12-3, 7-10.30 Sun; closed 25 Dec, and evenings 26 and 31 Dec ~ Bedrooms: £65B/£75B

GODMANSTONE SY6697 Map 2
Smiths Arms £
A352 N of Dorchester

One of the smallest pubs in the whole country, this old-fashioned 15th-c thatched inn has just six tables in its one quaint bar (which measures only 12 by 4 metres). It's traditionally furnished with long wooden stools and chunky tables, antique waxed and polished small pews and an elegant little high-backed settle, all tucked against the walls. There are National Hunt racing pictures and some brass plates on the walls, an open fire, dominoes and cribbage; because of their restricted opening hours they've decided they can't keep real ale any longer. Seats and tables are very pleasantly set out on a crazy-paved terrace and on the grassy mound by the narrow River Cerne. Simple but tasty (and very reasonably priced) home-made bar food includes sandwiches (from £2.35), giant sausage (£3.95), ploughman's (from £4.35), with daily specials such as chicken salsa tortilla pie (£5.20), moussaka (£5.45), and tender ham and chips (£5.75), with puddings (from £2.45); pleasant service. There's a nice walk over Cowdon Hill to the River Piddle. Note the limited opening times. *(Recommended by the Didler, Dom Bradshaw, OPUS)*

Free house ~ Licensees John and Linda Foster ~ Bar food (12-3) ~ No credit cards ~ (01300) 341236 ~ Open 11(12 Sun)-5.30; closed mid-Oct till Easter

MIDDLEMARSH ST6607 Map 2

Hunters Moon

A352 Sherborne—Dorchester

Opened in 2002 after a thorough-going refurbishment (and renaming – it used to be the White Horse), this is now a comfortable, neatly kept and welcoming country inn with good food and drink. It rambles around through several largely no smoking linked areas, with a great variety of tables and chairs, plenty of bric-a-brac from decorative teacups, china ornaments and glasses through horse tack and brassware to quite a collection of spirits miniatures. Beams, some panelling, soft lighting from converted oil lamps, three log fires (one in a capacious inglenook), and the way that some attractively cushioned settles form booths all combine to give a cosy relaxed feel. The food (made with lots of local produce) includes lunchtime sandwiches (from £2.45), soup (£2.95), scottish smoked salmon with prawns (£4.95), home-made game pie, chargrilled vegetables and pasta, or fishcakes (all £6.95), braised lamb shank with red wine, mushrooms and shallots in rich gravy (£8.95), and puddings such as treacle tart (£2.95). On our inspection visit they had well kept Caledonian Six Nations, Palmers Dorset Gold and St Austell Tribute on handpump, with decent wines by the glass, proper coffee, and a good range of spirits and soft drinks; service was good, and the piped pop music was faint. The neat lawn has circular picnic-sets as well as the more usual ones; the new bedrooms are in what was formerly a skittle alley and stable block. *(Recommended by Joy and Arthur Hoadley, M G Hart, Peter Neate, Joan and Michel Hooper-Immins, Ian and Mary Logan)*

Free house ~ Licensees Liz and Brendan Malone ~ Real ale ~ Bar food ~ (01963) 210966 ~ Children in eating area of bar ~ Dogs allowed in bar ~ Open 11-3, 6-11; 12-3, 6-10.30 Sun ~ Bedrooms: £45S/£60S

MUDEFORD SZ1892 Map

Ship in Distress

Stanpit; off B3059 at roundabout

The décor in the bar's two cottagey rooms is good fun: well worth a close look round at quiet times, when you've room to move freely. All sorts of more or less nautical bric-a-brac spans the gamut from rope fancywork and brassware through lanterns, oars and ceiling nets and ensigns to a somewhat murky aquarium, boat models (we particularly liked the Mississippi steamboat), and the odd piratical figure. Besides a good few boat pictures, the room on the right has masses of snapshots of locals caught up in various waterside japes, under its glass tabletops. Service is friendly, and they have well kept Adnams Broadside, Bass, Brakspears Three Sheets and Ringwood Best on handpump, and good wines by the glass; darts, fruit machine, a couple of TV sets, and the sort of dated piped pop music that fits in rather well. All this cheery clutter, and the homely old leather sofas alongside more orthodox pub furnishings, might give you the idea that this is just an entertaining local. Don't be fooled. The carefully cooked fresh local fish and seafood is good and imaginative. The menu includes bar snacks (not Friday and Saturday night) such as sandwiches (from £4.50, they bake their own bread), deep-fried whitebait with smoked paprika (£4.50), half a dozen oysters (£7.50), and seafood pancakes

(£8.95), with other dishes such as brixham scallops grilled with garlic and herb butter (£7.50), lobster salad (half £12.50; whole £22), roast turbot fillet with wild mushrooms, shallots and sunblush tomato (£14.50), and grilled dover sole (£15.50), with puddings such as strawberry mousse with vodka minted strawberries (£5.50); they also do steak (£13.50), and a vegetarian dish, and you can get cream teas in summer. A spreading and appealing two-room restaurant area, as cheerful in its way as the bar, has a light-hearted mural sketching out the impression of a window open on a sunny boating scene, and another covering its dividing wall with vines. There are tables out on the back terrace; look out for the two springer spaniels. *(Recommended by A D Marsh, Michael and Robin Inskip)*

Punch ~ Tenants S Canning and Dennis Smith ~ Real ale ~ Bar food (all day in summer) ~ Restaurant ~ (01202) 485123 ~ Children in restaurant ~ Dogs allowed in bar ~ Open 10-11(10.30 Sun)

OSMINGTON MILLS SY7381 Map 2

Smugglers

Off A353 NE of Weymouth

This popular partly thatched inn is handily open all day in summer, though perhaps a better time to visit is out of season, when you can enjoy the beautiful surroundings away from the holiday-making hordes. The spacious interior has shiny black panelling and woodwork dividing the relaxing bar into cosy, welcoming areas. Soft red lantern-lights give an atmospheric hue to the stormy sea pictures and big wooden blocks and tackle on the walls, and there are logs burning in an open stove. Some seats are tucked into alcoves and window embrasures, with one forming part of an upended boat. Well kept Badger Dorset Best, Tanglefoot and a guest on handpump. Darts, pool, and the fruit machine are kept sensibly out of the way; piped music, cribbage, shove-ha'penny, dominoes and TV. As well as sandwiches (from £4.25), enjoyable bar food includes creamy garlic mushrooms (£2.95), sausage and mash (£5.95), stuffed peppers or irish stew (£6.75), lamb shank with onion marmalade mash or half a duck with orange sauce and dauphinoise potatoes (£8.95), with puddings such as spotted dick or apple and toffee crumble (£3.45); they do smaller portions of some main courses (from £4.75), and there's a children's menu (£2.95). Part of the restaurant is no smoking. Although it does get very busy in high season (there's a holiday settlement just up the lane), service remains friendly and efficient. There are picnic-sets out on crazy paving by a little stream, with a thatched summer bar, and a good play area over on a steep lawn. The four ensuite double bedrooms will have been refurbished by the time the *Guide* comes out. They have summer barbecues and hog roasts, and occasional special events such as fancy dress parties. *(Recommended by Joan and Michel Hooper-Immins, S P Watkin, P A Taylor, A J Batty, the Didler)*

Badger ~ Manager Michael Rowe ~ Real ale ~ Bar food (12-2, 6-9.30 Mon-Fri; 12-9.30 wknds and summer hols) ~ Restaurant ~ (01305) 833125 ~ Children in restaurant and family room ~ Open 11-11; 12-10.30 Sun; 11-3, 6-11 Mon-Fri in winter ~ Bedrooms: /£90B

PAMPHILL ST9900 Map 2

Vine

Off B3082 on NW edge of Wimborne: turn on to Cowgrove Hill at Cowgrove signpost, then turn right up Vine Hill

Two tiny bars make up this charmingly simple and unspoilt country pub, on the National Trust's Kingston Lacy estate. In 1991 the Trust bought the pub from Whitbreads, though it's run independently by the family who have been tenants now for three or four generations. They certainly look after it extremely well – it has that well cared-for feel that matters so much in places like this. One room with a warm coal-effect gas fire has three tables, the other just half a dozen or so seats on its lino floor, some of them huddling under the stairs that lead up to an overflow room. Local photographs (like the regular with his giant pumpkin) and notices decorate the painted panelling, with a few animal prints and decorative plates. On our weekday inspection visit, piped Classic FM mingled quietly with a blackbird's song drifting in through the french window, though at weekends and in summer it can get very busy – there are walks all around on National Trust land. In winter they have good mulled wine as well as ales such as Stonehenge Danish Dynamite and Youngs, all well kept on handpump, and simple food including fresh sandwiches (from £1.80) and ploughman's (£3.50); service is friendly. There are picnic-sets and benches out on a sheltered gravel terrace, and more share a heated and fairy-lit verandah with a grape vine. Round the back a patch of grass has a climbing frame. No children inside. *(Recommended by Phil and Sally Gorton)*

Free house ~ Licensee Mrs Sweatland ~ Real ale ~ Bar food (lunchtime only) ~ (01202) 882259 ~ Dogs welcome ~ Open 11-2.30, 7-11; 12-3, 7-10.30 Sun

PIDDLEHINTON SY7197 Map 1

Thimble £

B3143

They serve well kept Badger Best, Tanglefoot, Palmers Copper and IPA, and Ringwood Old Thumper on handpump at this partly thatched streamside pub, along with quite a few fruit wines and 15 malt whiskies. It's set in one of the county's prettiest valleys, and the flower-filled garden is floodlit at night. Inside it's simpler than the exterior suggests, and the spotlessly kept low-beamed bar is nicely spacious and airy; in spite of attracting quite a lot of people in the summer, it never feels too crowded. There are two handsome brick fireplaces, and a deep glassed-over well; darts, shove-ha'penny, dominoes, cribbage. Besides good sandwiches (from £2.55), they serve straightforward bar food such as soup (£2.75), filled baked potatoes (from £3.50), king prawn and chilli rolls with chilli mayonnaise dip (£4), mushroom and spinach lasagne (£5.85), breaded plaice (£5.95), and gammon and pineapple (£7.75), with puddings such as lemon meringue pie (£3.95); they also do children's meals (£3.05), and a Sunday roast (£6.30). *(Recommended by R Kendall, Dudley and Moira Cockroft, Dennis Jenkin, Joan and Michel Hooper-Immins, Prof Keith and Mrs Jane Barber, Norma and Noel Thomas, Tony Rose, Daphne Slater)*

Free house ~ Licensees N R White and V J Lanfear ~ Real ale ~ Bar food (not 25/26 Dec) ~ Restaurant ~ (01300) 348270 ~ Children in eating area of bar ~ Dogs allowed in bar ~ Open 12-2.30, 7-11(10.30 Sun); closed 25 Dec

SHERBORNE ST6316 Map 2

Digby Tap £

Cooks Lane; park in Digby Road and walk round corner

Handy for the glorious golden stone abbey, this down-to-earth old-fashioned ale house serves around four or five superbly kept beers on handpump. Mostly from West Country brewers such as Exmoor, Otter, Sharps and St Austell, the beers change regularly, with around 20 different types a week. Not a pub for those seeking sophistication, the interior is simple but full of character, and the flagstoned main bar is relaxed and friendly with a good mix of customers. Several small games rooms have pool, cribbage, fruit machine, TV and piped music. Large portions of reasonably priced, straightforward bar food include tasty soup (£1.95), sandwiches or baguettes (from £1.75, toasted from £1.80), filled baked potatoes (from £2.80), potato wedges (£2.95), and daily specials such as lasagne or gammon and pineapple (£3.95), and steak and chips (£4.50). There are some seats outside. *(Recommended by W W Burke, Simon and Jane Williams)*

Free house ~ Licensees Peter Lefevre and Nick Whigham ~ Real ale ~ Bar food (12-1.45, not evenings, or Sun) ~ No credit cards ~ (01935) 813148 ~ Children welcome in eating area of bar at lunchtime ~ Dogs welcome ~ Open 11-2.30, 5.30-11; 11-3, 6-11 Sat; 12-3, 7-10.30 Sun; closed 1 Jan

You can send us reports through our web site: www.goodguides.co.uk

Skippers

A352 link road, W of centre; car park, or park around corner, in Horsecastles

This comfortably extended pub is cheerfully decorated, with bright tablecloths in the dining area at the far end, scatter cushions on a window seat, a lively collection of helicopter and other mainly RNAS photographs, and puce Anaglypta walls. There's basically a line of three fairly snug rooms, partly separated by knocked-through stone walls, starting with the serving area – which has well kept Butcombe and Wadworths Henrys, IPA and 6X on handpump and maybe a guest such as Young's Special (Old Timer is tapped from a cask in the cellar in winter). Tables on the turkey carpet vary from dark pub style to sturdy varnished pine. There's a rack of daily papers and a coal-effect gas fire; fruit machine, cribbage, shove-ha'penny, dominoes, and may be unobtrusive piped radio. The landlord is sociable, and the staff are efficient. Along with lots of fish fresh from Portland and Poole, such as grilled plaice (£10.50), and lemon sole or bass (£12.95), the colourful chalk boards list a good choice of dishes such as soup (£2.70), smoked salmon and prawns (£4.95), broccoli and cream cheese bake (£8.95), steaks (from £10.50), venison with wild mushroom and port sauce (£12.95), and rack of lamb with red wine, onion and wild mushroom sauce (£13.95), with lunchtime bar snacks such as sandwiches (£2.50, toasties £2.90), ploughman's (£4.95), sausage, egg and chips (£6.95), pork and mustard casserole or cottage pie (£7.95). They do a bargain three-course OAP lunch (£5.95, not Sunday). There are tables outside. More reports please. *(Recommended by BOB)*

Wadworths ~ Tenants Sandra and Chris Frowde ~ Real ale ~ Bar food (11-2, 6.30-9.30; 12-2, 7-9 Sun) ~ Restaurant ~ (01935) 812753 ~ Children in eating area of bar and restaurant ~ Open 11-3, 6-11; 12-3, 7-10.30 Sun

SHROTON ST8512 Map 2

Cricketers

Off A350 N of Blandford (village also called Iwerne Courtney); follow signs

Secluded and attractive, the lovely garden at this warmly welcoming red brick pub has big sturdy tables under cocktail parasols and some outdoor heaters, a fairy-lit clematis arbour, well tended shrubs, and a well stocked (and well used) herb garden by the kitchen door. Inside, the bright divided bar has a big stone fireplace, alcoves and cricketing memorabilia, and well kept changing ales such as Bass, Butcombe, Charles Wells Bombardier and Everards Original are served from pumps with handles made into little cricket bats. They've also a dozen wines by the glass, and quite a few malt whiskies; good friendly service from the attentive landlord and his neatly uniformed staff. Besides filled baguettes (£5.50), good, reasonably priced dishes could include soup (£3.25), sautéed lamb kidneys with balsamic vinegar cream (£3.75), crab filo tart with coriander mayonnaise (£3.95), faggots with wholegrain mash (£6.95), smoked haddock and coriander fishcakes with lemon mayonnaise (£7.25), spinach, mushroom and goats cheese filo tart (£7.95), with puddings such as raspberry meringue roulade or chocolate torte (£3.95). The comfortable back restaurant (there's a no smoking area on the way through to here) has a fresh neutral décor, and a sizeable games area has pool, darts, cribbage, dominoes, fruit machine and piped music. The pub is prettily set facing the peaceful village green; there are good walks from here over Hambledon Hill with its fine views (though you will need to leave your boots outside). *(Recommended by Paul and Annette Hallett, Pat and Robert Watt, Peter Neate, Mrs H E Cunliffe, Terry and Linda Moseley, Colin and Janet Roe)*

Free house ~ Licensees George and Carol Cowie ~ Real ale ~ Bar food (not some Sun evenings in winter) ~ Restaurant ~ (01258) 860421 ~ Children welcome ~ Open 11.30(12 Sun)-3, 6.30-11; closed 25 Dec evening ~ Bedrooms: /£60S

> Post Office address codings confusingly give the impression that some pubs are in Dorset, when they're really in Somerset (which is where we list them).

STOURTON CAUNDLE ST7115 Map 2

Trooper £

Village signposted off A30 E of Milborne Port

Opposite Enid Blyton's former farm (better known as Finniston Farm in one of her Famous Five books), this appealing little stone-built pub now has friendly new licensees. The tiny low-ceilinged bar on the left has cushioned pews and wheelback chairs, a cabinet of sports trophies, charity bookshelves, over 80 horse bits, and lots of good horsebrasses on their leathers decorating the big stripped stone fireplace, which now has an oak pew built into it. There's another big fireplace in the stripped stone dining room on the right; cribbage, dominoes, shove-ha'penny, TV, darts, piped music, and a skittle alley. Simple lunchtime snacks (made with local produce) include good soup (£2.75), sandwiches (from £3, baguettes from £3.50) ploughman's (from £3.50), and a handful of hot meals such as cod and chips, sausage and chips, ham and egg (£4.95), and steak and kidney pie (£5.75); children's meals (£3.50). Two or three well kept real ales on handpump might include Archers Best and Hop Back Crop Circle. There are a few picnic-sets out in front and in its side garden, by a stream which is cut into a deep stone channel along the village lane. *(Recommended by Marjorie and David Lamb)*

Free house ~ Licensees Roger and Rachel Paull ~ Real ale ~ Bar food (lunchtime Tues-Sat only) ~ (01963) 362405 ~ Children welcome ~ Dogs welcome ~ Open 12-2.30, 7-11; 12-11(10.30 Sun) wknds; 12-2.30, 7-11(10.30 Sun) in winter; closed Mon lunchtime

STURMINSTER NEWTON ST7813 Map 2

Bull

A357 near junction with B3092, S of village centre

Readers recommend the crab starter at this cosily compact thatched local, run by a cheerful landlord. Other simple, but generously served home-made dishes might include sandwiches (from £2.75), ploughman's (from £5.25), chicken and broccoli lasagne (£7.95), lamb steak braised in honey and mint gravy (£8.50), smoked haddock pancakes or seafood tagliatelle (£8.75), and brie, cranberry and mushroom wellington with white wine and mushroom sauce (£8.95); home-made puddings could be syrup sponge or spotted dick (from £3.25). Friendly staff serve well kept Badger Best, Sussex Bitter and Gribble Fursty Ferret on handpump, along with good house wines. The comfortable more or less L-shaped bar has soft lighting and some low beams. The joists by the serving counter are packed with key fobs, while others have lots of decorative mugs, and the swirly cream walls have anything from country prints and bull cartoons to snaps of happy regulars; there are charity shelves of readable paperbacks at one end. They have a skittle alley; piped Classic FM and local radio. You'll find picnic-sets out in front by rather totemic wooden statuary (and the busy road), and more in a fenced garden. *(Recommended by Mike and Shelley Woodroffe, D Rossi, Colin and Janet Roe)*

Badger ~ Tenant H C Edward-Jones ~ Real ale ~ Bar food ~ (01258) 472435 ~ Children in eating area of bar ~ Dogs welcome ~ Open 11-2.30, 6.45-11; 12-3, 7-10.30 Sun

Swan

Town signposted off A357 Blandford—Sherborne, via B3092; Market Place

You can drop into this friendly 18th-c coaching inn for something to eat all day, and the reasonably priced bedrooms make a good base for exploring the area. Traditional and very neatly kept, the busy beamed bar has a particularly interesting brick fireplace at one end, its tiny grate sitting incongruously next to an old safe. Close by is a comfortable green leatherette sofa, as well as wooden corner seats, a table with newspapers to read, and the odd stuffed fish or bird in glass cases. Elsewhere there's lots of exposed brickwork, including sturdy brick pillars dividing the room, plenty of panelling, and a good number of tables leading through into a couple of eating areas (one is no smoking). Well kept Badger Best and Tanglefoot on handpump (prices at the bar are displayed with admirable clarity); fruit machine, TV, shove-ha'penny, cribbage, dominoes, board games and soft piped music. Tasty bar food includes lunchtime soup (£2.95), good sandwiches and baguettes (from £2.95), burgers (from £3.95), mediterranean pasta bake (£6.45), beef lasagne (£6.75), chicken and spinach curry (£6.95), and properly cooked sirloin steak (£8.95), with evening dishes such as gammon and egg or pork sausages (£7.45), and chicken en croûte (£8.75), and nice puddings such as raspberry and sherry trifle (from £3.45). They've refurbished the mostly no smoking restaurant. There are lots more tables out on a terrace and in the enclosed garden. *(Recommended by D P and M A Miles, Martin and Jane Wright, Paul Humphreys)*

Badger ~ Tenants Roger and Marion Hiron ~ Real ale ~ Bar food (11.30-9) ~ Restaurant ~ (01258) 472208 ~ Children over 5 in restaurant ~ Dogs allowed in bar ~ Open 10-11; 11.30-10.30 Sun ~ Bedrooms: £40S/£55S

TARRANT MONKTON ST9408 Map 2

Langton Arms

Village signposted from A354, then head for church

As we went to press, the friendly licensees were in the process of re-building part of this pretty 17th-c pub, after a fire which destroyed the thatched roof and first floor, but they hope to have fully reopened by the time this *Guide* comes out. Whether you're a family looking for a leisurely lunch or a dog-walker after a well kept pint, you can expect a cheerful welcome here. Alongside Hop Back Best and a beer from Ringwood they serve three constantly changing guests from brewers such as Cottage, Hampshire and Scattor Rock on handpump; there's an annual beer festival. The fairly simple beamed bar has a huge inglenook fireplace, settles, stools at the counter and other mixed dark furniture, and the public bar has a juke box, darts, pool, a fruit machine, TV, cribbage, and dominoes; piped music. The no smoking bistro restaurant is in an attractively reworked barn, and the skittle alley doubles as a no smoking family room during the day. With some really interesting choices, the enjoyable menu includes bar snacks such as filled baguettes (from £3.25), ploughman's (from £5.50), and pork and leek sausages and chips (£6.95), with other dishes such as deep-fried brie wedges with mixed fruit sauce (£5.50), chicken strips with home-made curry sauce or home-made broccoli, brie and mushroom lasagne (£7.50), crispy haddock goujons (£7.95), pigeon breast in cranberry and red wine sauce (£8.75), game pie (£8.95), and local steaks (from £10.95), with puddings such as home-made steamed coffee and walnut pudding or butter toffee waffles with bananas and cream or local ice-creams (from £3.75); children's meals (£3.50). There's a very good wood-chip children's play area in the garden, and your dog may be lucky enough to be offered a free sausage. Tarrant Monkton is a charming village (with a ford that can flow quite fast in wet weather), and is well located for local walks and exploring the area. The comfortable ensuite bedrooms are in a modern block at the back; good breakfasts. *(Recommended by G Coates, Tom Evans, Stephen and Judy Parish, Val and Alan Green, Pat and Robert Watt, Francis Johnston, John and Joan Nash, Dr J Puszet)*

Free house ~ Licensees Barbara and James Cossins ~ Real ale ~ Bar food (11.30-2.30 (3 Sun), 6-9; 11.30-9.30 Sat) ~ Restaurant ~ (01258) 830225 ~ Children in restaurant and family room ~ Dogs allowed in bedrooms ~ Open 11-11; 12-10.30 Sun ~ Bedrooms: £50B/£70B

A very few pubs try to make you leave a credit card at the bar, as a sort of deposit if you order food. They are not entitled to do this. The credit card firms and banks which issue them warn you not to let them out of your sight. If someone behind the counter used your card fraudulently, the card company or bank could in theory hold you liable, because of your negligence in letting a stranger hang on to your card. Suggest instead that if they feel the need for security, they 'swipe' your card and give it back to you. And do name and shame the pub to us.

WEST BAY SY4690 Map 1

West Bay

Station Road

Dorset Dining Pub of the Year

'Excellent' is a word that crops up frequently when readers are describing this superbly run seaside pub. If you've come to eat you're in for a treat (though it's so popular, booking is virtually essential even on a winter weekday), especially if you like fish. There's always at least ten fresh fish dishes to choose from: a typical selection might include skate wing with mustard butter crust or mild smoked salmon on creamy leeks with warm poached egg (£11.95), and blackened monkfish tail with sweet potato mash and lime yoghurt dressing (£15.50). Other imaginative dishes (they use local suppliers wherever possible) might be steak and kidney casserole with mustard dumplings (£8.50), chicken breast stuffed with brie and wrapped in bacon with guacamole or 10oz rump steak (£10.95), and duck breast with stir-fried vegetables and hoi sin sauce (£12.95), with lunchtime bar snacks such as sandwiches (from £3.25), ploughman's or prawn and smoked salmon salad (£5.95), and cajun prawns with sweet peppers (£5.50): they also do children's meals (from £4.25). The friendly hands-on licensees and cheerful staff help generate an enjoyably relaxed atmosphere. An island servery separates the fairly simple bare-boards front part with its coal-effect gas fire and mix of sea and nostalgic prints from a cosier carpeted no smoking dining area with more of a country kitchen feel. Well kept Palmers IPA, Copper and 200 on handpump, good house wines (with ten by the glass), and whiskies; decent piped music, and a skittles alley (the local team meets here). A dining terrace has tables outside; there's plenty of parking. Readers very much like staying in the quiet and homely bedrooms; delicious breakfasts.
(Recommended by Bob and Margaret Holder, Janet and Julian le Patourel, M G Hart, Simon and Jane Williams, Joan and Michel Hooper-Immins, John and Hazel Deacon, Peter Meister, David and Julie Glover, David Thornton, Brian Thompson, Geoffrey Leather, Mayur Shah, J P Humphery, Mrs Veronica Duggan, Roderick and Jill Leslie, Charles Gysin, Adrian White, OPUS, Roland and Wendy Chalu)

Palmers ~ Tenants John Ford and Karen Trimby ~ Real ale ~ Bar food (not Sun evening exc bank hols) ~ Restaurant ~ (01308) 422157 ~ Children in restaurant ~ Dogs allowed in bar ~ Open 11-2.30, 6-11; 12-3 Sun; closed Sun evening exc bank hols ~ Bedrooms: £50B/£65B

WEST BEXINGTON SY5387 Map 2

Manor Hotel

Village signposted off B3157 SE of Bridport; Beach Road

Mentioned in the Doomsday book, this well liked stone-built hotel is a relaxing place to spend the night. You can see the sea from the smart no smoking Victorian-style conservatory (which has airy furnishings and lots of plants), the comfortable lounge with its log fire, the bedrooms, and also the garden, where there are picnic-sets on a small lawn with flowerbeds lining the low sheltering walls; a much bigger side lawn has a children's play area. The bustling downstairs cellar bar has horsebrasses on the walls, stools and low-backed chairs (with one fat seat carved from a beer cask) under the black beams and joists, as well as heavy harness over the log fire; piped music. Enjoyable bar food might include sandwiches (from £3.15), delicious fish soup (£4.65), ploughman's (£5.65), crab and asparagus pancakes or cottage pie (£6.95), liver and bacon or mushroom stroganoff (£8.95), duck leg casserole or smoked haddock (£10.95), with puddings such as chocolate roulade (£3.95); the good restaurant is no smoking. It's well run, and the helpful staff go out of their way to make visitors feel welcome, and are kind to families with young children. Well kept Butcombe Gold and Quay Harbour Master on handpump, quite a few malt whiskies, and several wines by the glass. The pub is just a stroll from lovely if tiring walks on Chesil beach and the cliffs above; there are stunning views from the approach road. *(Recommended by R W E Farr, Peter and Giff Bennett, Gerry and Rosemary Dobson, W Seymour-Hamilton, Lawrence Pearse,*

Dennis Jenkin, Andrea Rampley, Alice Harper, Mayur Shah, A P Seymour, Anthony Rogers, Mrs A P Lee, OPUS, Roland and Wendy Chalu)

Free house ~ Licensees Peter King and Sheree Lynch ~ Real ale ~ Bar food ~ Restaurant ~ (01308) 897616 ~ Children welcome ~ Dogs allowed in bar ~ Open 11-11; 12-10.30 Sun ~ Bedrooms: £75B/£120S(£120B)

WORTH MATRAVERS SY9777 Map 2

Square & Compass ★

At fork of both roads signposted to village from B3069

This charmingly old-fashioned pub is set on a peaceful hilltop, with a fantastic view from benches out in front, looking down over the village rooftops to the sea between the East Man and the West Man (the hills that guard the coastal approach) and out beyond Portland Bill. The pub has been run by the Newman family for more than 90 years, and hardly anything has changed during that time. It's so completely unspoilt and basic that on a winter's evening with the rain lashing the windows, you wouldn't be altogether surprised if a smuggler, complete with parrot and wooden leg, suddenly materialised. Well kept Badger Tanglefoot, Ringwood Best and a guest from a brewer such as Hop Back or Palmers are tapped from a row of casks and passed to you in a drinking corridor through two serving hatches – there's no bar counter. A couple of rooms opposite have simple furniture on the flagstones, a woodburning stove, and a loyal crowd of friendly locals; cribbage, shove-ha'penny and dominoes. Bar food is limited to tasty home-made pasties and pies (£2.20, served till they run out); service is friendly. A little free museum shows local fossils and artefacts, mostly collected by the current landlord and his father; mind your head on the way out. You may find free-roaming hens, chickens and other birds clucking around your feet. There are good walks from the pub – but parking is limited, so it's usually best to park in the public car park 100 yards along the Corfe Castle road. *(Recommended by Pete Baker, A C Nugent, the Didler, Joyce and Geoff Robson, John Roots, James Woods, JP, PP, Simon and Jane Williams, Peter Meister, Bruce Bird, Richard Siebert, John and Laney Woods, Jason Caulkin, Andrea Rampley, John and Joan Nash, Chris Ferguson, MLR, Joan and Michel Hooper-Immins, Phil and Sally Gorton)*

Free house ~ Licensee Charlie Newman ~ Real ale ~ Bar food (all day) ~ No credit cards ~ (01929) 439229 ~ Children welcome away from bar ~ Dogs allowed in bar ~ Open 12-3, 6-11; 12-11 Sat; 12-4, 7-10.30 Sun; closed Sun evening winter

LUCKY DIP

Besides the fully inspected pubs, you might like to try these Lucky Dips recommended to us and described by readers (if you do, please send us reports: www.goodguides.co.uk).

ABBOTSBURY SY5785

Ilchester Arms [B3157]: Busy rambling stone inn done out as themed servants' quarters from cook's sitting room to potting shed, with old pine furniture and lots to look at inc prints of the famous swans; welcoming service, decent food from sandwiches, ciabattas or baked potatoes up, attractive no smoking conservatory restaurant, quick service, Courage-related real ales tapped from the cask, good house wines in three glass sizes, blazing log fire, darts, winter pool; piped music, TV, fruit machine; children in eating areas, nice views from suntrap terrace tables, open all day *(L Elliott, Lawrence Pearse, Gloria Bax, LYM, OPUS, P Goldman)*

ALMER SY9097

☆ *Worlds End* [B3075, just off A31 towards Wareham]: Very long and busy open-plan thatched and partly flagstoned family dining pub, beams, panelled alcoves and candles, very wide choice of food all day (you can choose generous or smaller helpings), well kept Badger ales, hard-working staff (lots of tables, even so you may have to wait), restaurant with no smoking area; open all day, picnic-sets and heaters out in front and behind, outstanding play area *(Mrs J Slowgrove, BB, Lynn Sharpless, Michael and Robin Inskip)*

ANSTY ST7603

Fox [NW of Milton Abbas]: The original home of the Hall & Woodhouse brewers (now trading under the name of Badger), more hotel than pub, with interesting family history in the high-ceilinged partly no smoking main bar; lots of toby jugs, well kept Badger Best, Tanglefoot and a seasonal beer, good wines by the glass, extremely wide food choice, children welcome in restaurant, friendly staff; piped music, separate bar with pool and TV, skittle alley; garden tables (diners allowed to use heated swimming pool), attractive countryside, open all day *(Anthony Rogers, LYM, Joan and Michel Hooper-Immins, David and Elizabeth Briggs)*

ASKERSWELL SY5292

☆ *Spyway* [off A35 Bridport—Dorchester]: Charming beamed country pub with old-fashioned high-backed settles, cushioned wall and window seats, cosy old-world décor, well kept ales such as Otter and Weymouth Best, good value food from sandwiches and baguettes to standard cooked dishes inc good fresh local fish (service can slow), friendly staff, no smoking dining area with steps down to overflow area; soft piped music; disabled access though not ideal, children in eating areas, marvellous views from back terrace and large informal garden, good walks *(David and Julie Glover, Mrs A P Lee, Graham and Rose Ive, LYM, Roland and Wendy Chalu)*

BEAMINSTER ST4801

Greyhound [A3066 N of Bridport; The Square]: Flagstones and simple furnishings on right, plusher on left, gas fires, well kept Palmers IPA and BB, wide blackboard choice of decent reasonably priced standard food, congenial service, small back family room; darts, piped music *(BB, Marjorie and David Lamb)*

Red Lion [The Square]: Relaxed 17th-c pub/hotel, small but efficient, with friendly landlord, Palmers BB, Taunton cider, substantial good value food; bedrooms pleasant, clean and comfortable – good value *(Joan and Michel Hooper-Immins)*

BERE REGIS SY8494

Drax Arms [West St; off A35 bypass]: Comfortable and welcoming village local with cheerful helpful service, well kept Badger ales and farm cider, limited choice of good generous reasonably priced home-made food from sandwiches up, esp pies and casseroles, big open fire on left, small dining area (busy in summer); good walking nearby *(R T and J C Moggridge, John and Joan Nash)*

BISHOP'S CAUNDLE ST6913

☆ *White Hart* [A3030 SE of Sherborne]: Nicely moulded dark beams, 18th-c panelling and flagstones, attractive furnishings, friendly helpful service, well kept Badger Best, K&B and perhaps a seasonal beer, wide choice of generous food from reasonably priced lunchtime sandwiches to steaks inc smaller and children's helpings, sizeable no smoking family area, darts, skittle alley; fruit machine, muted piped music; french windows to big prettily floodlit garden with fine play area and all sorts of games, reasonably priced bedrooms *(LYM, Marjorie and David Lamb, Joan and Michel Hooper-Immins)*

BLANDFORD FORUM ST8806

Crown [West St]: Best Western hotel's well furnished spacious bar areas used by locals as pub, well kept Badger beers from nearby brewery, good range of reasonably priced straightforward bar food inc light meals, separate restaurant; bedrooms *(Colin and Janet Roe, Peter Neate, J C Poley, Craig Turnbull)*

BLANDFORD ST MARY ST8805

Hall & Woodhouse: Visitor centre for Badger brewery, tours (not Sun), their full beer range in top condition, popular food from well filled baguettes up, friendly staff; spectacular chandelier made of Badger beer bottles, lots of memorabilia in centre and upper gallery *(Joan and Michel Hooper-Immins, Meg and Colin Hamilton)*

BOURNEMOUTH SZ0891

Goat & Tricycle [West Hill Rd]: Comfortable and roomy two-level local with well kept Wadworths ales and good changing range of guest beers, farm cider, inexpensive generous food, friendly staff, good coffee, coal fire, lots of bric-a-brac inc hundreds of hats and helmets *(Roger Huggins, Tom and Alex McLean, Theocsbrian, Michael and Alison Sandy)*

Porterhouse [Poole Rd, Westbourne, just off A35]: Smallish old-fashioned tavern with full Ringwood ale range kept well at sensible prices (also takeaway jugs), changing farm ciders, good choice of malt whiskies, bare boards and dark panelling, simple cheap bar lunches; disabled access *(G Coates, Michael and Alison Sandy)*

BOURTON ST7430

☆ *White Lion* [High St, off old A303 E of Wincanton]: Welcoming licensees in plushly refurbished stripped stone dining pub, nicely lit beamed bars with sporting equipment, well kept Fullers London Pride, Greene King IPA and a guest beer, well prepared and sensibly priced blackboard food using good fresh ingredients, good range of home-made puddings, friendly service, no smoking beamed restaurant; dogs welcome, well spaced tables in pleasant garden, two neat bedrooms with own bathrooms *(Michael Yeo, LYM, Colin and Janet Roe, M Benjamin)*

BRIDPORT SY4692

George [South St]: Convivial unpretentious two-bar town local, traditional dark décor, bargain home-made pub food (not Sun) cooked in sight, filling sandwiches, well kept Palmers ales, decent wines, efficient service, thriving atmosphere on Sat market day, hatch-served family room; can get smoky, piped radio; level entrance, dogs welcome, open all day, from 9am for wkdy breakfast or coffee *(LYM, Roland and Wendy Chalu, Phil and Sally Gorton, Brenda and Rob Fincham)*

Woodman [South St]: Friendly and lively, with well kept real ales, decent food even on Sun *(OPUS)*

BUCKHORN WESTON ST7524

Stapleton Arms [Church Hill]: Friendly and spacious old-fashioned village pub, wide choice of food in bar and restaurant, attentive service, Ringwood and other local beers; tables outside, pleasant countryside *(Colin and Janet Roe)*

BUCKLAND NEWTON ST6804

☆ *Gaggle of Geese* Comfortable and well run country local with good atmosphere and attractive décor, welcoming hard-working landlord, well kept Badger Best, Butcombe and Ringwood Best and Fortyniner, decent wines and spirits, good reasonably priced usual bar food, smartish restaurant, no music; goose auction May and Sept, spacious pool/snooker and skittle rooms, small garden but sizeable grounds (room for caravans) *(BB, Joan and Michel Hooper-Immins, Peter Salmon, R J Davies, OPUS)*

BURTON BRADSTOCK SY4889

☆ *Three Horseshoes* [Mill St]: Attractive thatched inn in charming village, with comfortable, homely and roomy carpeted lounge, well kept Palmers real ales, good wines, smiling helpful service, unpretentious quickly served bar food from sandwiches and baked potatoes up, separate no smoking restaurant, unobtrusive piped music (may be eclipsed by the local bellringers); Fri band night; tables out on lawn, pleasant shingle beach a few minutes' drive away (with NT car park), bedrooms *(James Woods, Pat and Tony Martin, LYM, Terry Mizen, Mrs C Lintott)*

CASHMOOR ST9713

Cashmoor Inn [A354 6 miles E of Blandford]: Well kept Badger family pub in spacious former coaching inn, wishing well in lounge bar, good range of reasonably priced bar food inc good value Sun lunch; tables in garden with play area *(Stephen and Jean Curtis)*

CATTISTOCK SY5999

☆ *Fox & Hounds* [off A37 N of Dorchester]: Tucked-away 17th-c or older pub, flagstones and nicely moulded Jacobean beams, stripped stone, log fire in huge inglenook, minimal décor, enjoyable food from baguettes up inc generous OAP meals, good friendly service, Palmers ales from attractively carved counter, Taunton cider, good reasonably priced wine choice, table skittles, pleasant side dining room, back public bar with well lit darts and TV, immaculate skittle alley; piped pop music, live some Sats; dogs allowed on back terrace, comfortable bedrooms, cl Mon lunchtime, open all day wknds *(Joan and Michel Hooper-Immins, BB, Ron Shelton, John and Joan Nash)*

CERNE ABBAS ST6601

New Inn [14 Long Street]: Handsome Tudor inn with mullioned window seats in unpretentious beamed bar, well kept ales such as Flowers IPA and Wadworths 6X, new chef perking up the food side with some interesting dishes using local ingredients alongside nicely presented traditional favourites, no smoking dining area; children welcome, tables on sheltered lawn behind old coachyard, bedrooms with own bathrooms, open all day wknds and summer *(Mr and Mrs Bentley-Davies, LYM, Joyce and Geoff Robson, Julia and Richard Tredgett, Joan and Michel Hooper-Immins)*

CHEDINGTON ST4805

☆ *Winyards Gap* [A356 Dorchester—Crewkerne]: Spectacular view from tables in front of tastefully modernised pub, very welcoming licensees, wide choice of good home-made food, well kept ales such as Exmoor Stag, Gribble (Badger) Fursty Ferret and Sharps Doom Bar in named glasses (tasters offered), no smoking dining area welcoming children, skittle alley, also darts, pool etc; pet goats, bedrooms planned, good walks nearby *(LYM, Steve Felstead)*

CHRISTCHURCH SZ1696

☆ *Fishermans Haunt* [Winkton: B3347 N]: Avon-side hotel with neat well divided partly no smoking big-windowed bar, well kept Bass, Gales HSB and GB and Ringwood Fortyniner, lots of country wines, friendly staff, generous reasonably priced standard food (all day wknds) from sandwiches and filled baked potatoes up, river-view wknd restaurant; disabled facilities, children and dogs welcome, well kept gardens, comfortable bedrooms, open all day *(Eddie Edwards, David M Cundy, Philip and June Caunt, LYM, Richard and Liz Dilnot, Richard Haw, A and B D Craig, Joan and Michel Hooper-Immins)*

Olde George [Castle St]: Bustling 17th-c character pub, low beams, cosy bar, friendly staff, well kept Ringwood Best and Fortyniner and two changing ales such as Marstons Pedigree and Charles Wells Bombardier, good choice of home-made standard food with different evening menu; some music nights, tables in large courtyard *(Joan and Michel Hooper-Immins)*

CORFE CASTLE SY9681

Greyhound [A351]: Bustling much photographed old pub in centre of tourist village, three small low-ceilinged panelled rooms, several well kept changing ales such as Gales and Hook Norton, traditional games inc purbeck long board shove-ha'penny, no smoking family room, food (all day in summer, inc wknd breakfast) from filled rolls and baked potatoes up; piped music may be loud, live Fri; garden with fine castle and countryside views, pretty courtyard opening on to castle bridge, bedrooms, open all day wknds and summer *(LYM, James Woods, Dave Braisted, JP, PP, the Didler, Darly Graton, Graeme Gulibert, Geoff Pidoux)*

CORFE MULLEN SY9798

Coventry Arms [A31 W of Wimborne; Mill St]: Two linked low-beamed bars separated by open fire, Ringwood and guest ales tapped from the cask, decent clutch of malt whiskies, good unusual food from filled baked potatoes and baguettes up, good children's dishes, reasonable prices, good service, various nooks and corners, fishing décor, board games and books to browse; quiet lunchtime but busy evenings. with weekly live music and lots of special events; tables out by small stream *(Ian and Deborah Carrington, J S Davies)*

DEWLISH SY7798

Oak [off A354 Dorchester—Blandford Forum]: Light and airy village pub with well kept ales such as Marstons Pedigree tapped from the cask or from handpump, good basic bar food at pine tables, helpful landlord *(John and Joan Nash)*

DORCHESTER SY6890

☆ *Blue Raddle* [Church St, nr central short stay car park]: Thriving unpretentious local with good very attractively priced food from generous sandwiches to game, well kept changing ales such as Otter, Palmers 200 and Sharps Doom Bar, good wines, obliging landlord, cheery pub dog, coal-effect gas fire; no credit cards, piped music may be a bit loud; disabled access, but one step *(Peter Neate, Simon and Jane Williams, Meg and Colin Hamilton, the Didler, David Swift, BB, Dr and Mrs M E Wilson)*

Kings Arms [High East St]: Hotel bar with thriving atmosphere, appealing décor, well kept Bass and Courage Directors, decent wines, enjoyable food from sandwiches up, attentive service, open fire; close associations with Nelson and Hardy's *Mayor of Casterbridge*; bedrooms (the Lawrence of Arabia suite and the Tutenkhamen are pretty striking) *(LYM, the Didler, Kathy Higley, Dr and Mrs M E Wilson)*

☆ *Poet Laureate* [Pummery Sq, Poundbury]: Substantial new building in the Prince of Wales's Poundbury development, largely no smoking light and airy L-shaped bar with lots of chandeliers, enjoyable straightforward food from baguettes to full meals (meats from named local farms), well kept Palmers 200, Gold and Best and a guest such as Wadworths 6X, short choice of decent wines, proper coffee, pleasant restaurant area, quick friendly service, daily papers and a couple of sofas, flame-effect stove and quiet unhurried feel; unobtrusive piped music, jazz Sun evening; a few picnic-sets on side terrace *(W W Burke, Terry and Linda Moseley, B and K Hypher, D P and M A Miles, Peter Neate, Ian and Deborah Carrington)*

Tom Browns [High East St]: Small plain bare-boards L-shaped bar notable for very well kept Goldfinch beers such as Tom Browns Best, Flashmans Clout or Ghost and Midnight Blinder brewed in back microbrewery, wholesome reasonably priced bar food most lunchtimes (not Sun); welcoming staff, friendly locals, traditional games; nostalgic juke box, outside lavatories; open all day Fri and Sat *(Simon and Jane Williams, Dr and Mrs M E Wilson, Bruce Bird, BB)*

Trumpet Major [Alington Ave (A352 towards Wareham, just off bypass)]: Bright and airy big-windowed modern lounge bar with easy chairs in raised area and peaceful dining conservatory, well kept Bass and Wadworths 6X, good choice of wines by the glass, uncomplicated food, second bar with games machines, TV and games room with two pool tables; handy for Max Gate (Thomas Hardy's house); children welcome, spacious tree-lined garden with aviaries and adventure play area, very busy lunchtime *(B and K Hypher, Joan and Michel Hooper-Immins)*

EVERSHOT ST5704

☆ *Acorn* [off A37 S of Yeovil]: Oak panelling, log fires, pictures by local artists, another lounge with woodburner, good bar meals, well kept beers such as Branscombe Vale and Draymans Best and Fullers London Pride, interesting wines and other drinks, games bar with pool, darts, dominoes, cribbage, backgammon, chess, juke box, skittle alley; children allowed in eating areas, dogs in bar, terrace with dark oak furniture, bedrooms, charming village, good surrounding walks, open all day *(LYM, Mike and Shelley Woodroffe, Guy Vowles, Colin and Janet Roe)*

EYPE SY4491

New Inn: Warm and friendly village pub, well kept Palmers, popular food inc children's; magnificent views from back terrace *(Marjorie and David Lamb, Cathy Robinson, Ed Coombe)*

FIDDLEFORD ST8013

Fiddleford Inn [A357 Sturminster Newton—Blandford Forum]: Good generous quickly served wknd food from sandwiches up in comfortable lounge bar, restaurant area and back family area, three linked smartly refurbished areas (can get full despite all the space), ancient flagstones, some stripped stone; unobtrusive piped music; big pleasant garden with play area safely fenced from busy road *(Tom Evans, B and K Hypher, LYM)*

FONTMELL MAGNA ST8616

Crown: Much modernised pub with newish licensees putting emphasis on reasonably priced food from bar snacks to full meals, interesting wine list, well kept beer *(Colin and Janet Roe)*

FURZEHILL SU0102

☆ *Stocks* [off B3078 N of Wimborne]: Partly thatched 17th-c dining pub interestingly extended as rambling set of snug low-beamed areas with comfortable seating, soft lighting and attractive décor strong on local pictures and bric-a-brac, friendly helpful staff, well kept Ringwood Best and Fortyniner and a guest beer, bar food inc lunchtime sandwiches and hot baguettes (not Sun) through standard dishes to some more enterprising things, largely no smoking restaurant, darts; piped music, fruit machine; children in eating areas, dogs in bar, some outside tables, open all day *(Carol Mills, A D Marsh, Dr and Mrs A K Clarke, LYM, R T and J C Moggridge)*

GILLINGHAM ST8027

☆ *Dolphin* [Peacemarsh (B3082)]: Popular dining pub with good choice of particularly good value imaginative food esp fish all freshly cooked to order (so can take a while), regular themed menus, friendly helpful staff, partly no smoking restaurant area, well kept Badger beers in pleasant beamed bar; garden with play area *(BB, Colin and Janet Roe)*

GUSSAGE ALL SAINTS SU0010

☆ *Drovers* [8 miles N of Wimborne]: Welcoming new people in attractively placed thatched pub, pleasant country furnishings in extended two-room bar, well kept Ringwood beers, good value generous food, roaring log fire; pretty village, tables on pretty front lawn with views across the Dorset hills *(LYM, David Cannings, J Stickland, Pat and Robert Watt)*

KINGSTON SY9579

Scott Arms [West St (B3069)]: Busy holiday pub with rambling warren-like rooms, panelling, stripped stone, beams, open fires and some fine antique prints, attractive room overlooking garden, decent family extension, well kept Courage Best and Ringwood Best, lots of wines, nice staff, generous if not cheap standard food (may be queues to order and pay), summer cream teas, no smoking dining area; darts, dominoes and fruit machine, piped music; attractive garden with superb views of Corfe Castle and the Purbeck Hills *(the Didler, John Roots, LYM, JP, PP, K H Frostick, Joan and Michel Hooper-Immins)*

LANGTON HERRING SY6182

☆ *Elm Tree* [signed off B3157]: Low black beams, lots of copper, brass and bellows, cushioned window seats, windsor chairs and scrubbed pine tables, inglenook, and traditionally furnished extension, good range of food from lunchtime sandwiches and ciabattas up inc some interesting dishes, mainly organic local suppliers, decent house wine, Bass and Flowers or Marstons Pedigree, friendly staff cope well even when busy; no dogs inside, can get smoky; pretty flower-filled sunken garden, track down to Coast Path which skirts Chesil lagoon *(Liz and John Soden, Lawrence Pearse, J S Davies, OPUS, LYM, S P Watkin, P A Taylor, Peter Neate, Mrs Romey Heaton)*

LITTLE CANFORD SU0400

Fox & Hounds [Fox Lane, by B3073 off A31 Wimborne—Ferndown]: Extended and much modernised beamed and thatched country pub with roomy and comfortable linked eating areas inc no smoking, reasonably priced food from wide choice of hot filled baguettes and sandwiches up, good choice of beers and wines; spacious lawns with summer barbecues and pig roasts, good play area, pleasant walks *(Ian and Deborah Carrington)*

LITTON CHENEY SY5590

☆ *White Horse*: Relaxed and unpretentious, with good home-made food using fresh local ingredients (some home-grown veg, and good vegetarian meals), well kept Palmers ales, friendly efficient staff, woodburner, pictures on stripped stone walls, some flagstones, country kitchen chairs in dining area, table skittles; good spot on quiet lane into quaint village, picnic-sets on pleasant streamside front lawn *(BB, Joan and Michel Hooper-Immins, Marjorie and David Lamb, A D Marsh)*

LODERS SY4994

Loders Arms [off A3066 just N of Bridport]: Comfortably worn in extended 17th-c stone-built local, welcoming and relaxed, quick friendly service, good value changing food from huge baguettes and baked potatoes up inc interesting starters and main dishes as well as the usual staples, Palmers real ales, good choice of wines by the glass, log fire with parrot alongside, magazines and daily papers, no smoking dining room, skittle alley; may be unobtrusive piped music; level access, children in eating areas, pleasant views from picnic-sets in small informal back garden, pretty thatched village, open all day Sun *(LYM, Marjorie and David Lamb, Roland and Wendy Chalu)*

LONGBURTON ST6412

Rose & Crown [A352 Sherborne—Dorchester]: Welcoming pleasantly modernised village pub with good value generous straightforward food from sandwiches up, Badger beers, main dining area nr inglenook fireplace, overflow in next room, skittle alley *(Francis Johnston, Marjorie and David Lamb)*

LONGHAM SZ0699

Angel [A348 Ferndown—Poole]: Refurbished and well organised beamed roadside pub with roomy bar, family room in extension, tables and chairs on wooden floors, wide choice of food all day from baguettes and light dishes to good value unpretentious piping hot dishes inc steaks and children's, choice of helping size, plenty of cheerful helpful staff, well kept Badger Best and Tanglefoot, decent wines, sensible prices; disabled facilities, big lawned garden with good play area *(John and Vivienne Rice, Barrie and Valerie Meech)*

LYME REGIS SY3391

Cobb Arms [Marine Parade, Monmouth Beach]: Spaciously refurbished, with wide range of reasonably priced generous bar food, quick service even when busy, good value cream teas, well kept Palmers ales, decent wines, interesting ship pictures and marine fish tank; popular with local young people till late; next to harbour, beach and coastal walk, children welcome, open all day, tables on small back terrace, bedrooms, good breakfast *(Bruce Bird)*

Nags Head [Silver St]: Friendly open-plan local with enormous fire, lots of bric-a-brac inc some nautical objects and an old signal box sign, changing well kept ales such as Butcombe and Otter, welcoming staff, interesting bar food, lower games area with pool; Sat live music *(Steve Felstead)*

Pilot Boat [Bridge St]: Handy all-day family food spot, nicely set nr waterfront, plenty of tables in cheery nautically themed bars with no smoking dining area, low prices, Palmers real ales, several wines by the glass, skittle alley; piped music; children and dogs welcome, tables out on terrace, open all day *(Mike and Cheryl Lyons, James A Waller, LYM, Pat and Tony Martin, Mrs C Lintott, Betsy and Peter Little, Vanessa Stilwell)*

Royal Standard [Marine Parade, The Cobb]: Right on broadest part of beach, lively bar serving area dominated by pool table and piped pop, but has some fine built-in stripped high settles, and there's a quieter no smoking area with stripped brick and pine; friendly service, well kept Palmers BB, 200 and Copper, good value food inc sensibly priced sandwiches, plenty of local crab and fish, good cream teas, darts; children welcome, suntrap courtyard (own servery and wendy house – and you can keep an eye on your children on the beach just feet away) *(BB, Joan and Michel Hooper-Immins, Marjorie and David Lamb, Howard and Lorna Lambert)*

LYTCHETT MINSTER SY9693
St Peters Finger [Dorchester Rd]: Well run beamed two-part Badger pub with good value standard food from sandwiches and baguettes up, well kept beer inc Tanglefoot, cottagey mix of furnishings in different sections and end log fire giving a cosy feel despite its size; good skittle alley, tables on big terrace, part covered and heated *(Mr and Mrs John Taylor)*

MARNHULL ST7719
☆ *Blackmore Vale* [Burton St, via Church Hill off B3092]: Kind new licensees in comfortably modernised pub with enjoyable generous food inc OAP Tues and Thurs lunches, opened-up beamed and newly flagstoned no smoking dining bar with woodburner, cosy smaller bar with settles, sofas and pub games, well kept Badger beers, good choice of reasonably priced wines, quick pleasant service; piped music, Weds quiz night; children welcome, tables in attractively reworked garden, open all day wknds *(LYM, Colin and Janet Roe, Pat and Robert Watt, Paul Humphreys)*

Crown [about 3 miles N of Sturminster Newton; Crown Rd]: Part-thatched 17th-c dining pub, generous food with nice blackboard choice, well kept Badger Best and Tanglefoot, considerate service, linked rooms with oak beams, huge flagstones or bare boards, old settles, stuffed animals amd old prints and plates, log fire in big stone hearth in oldest part, more modern furnishings and carpet elsewhere; skittle alley, may be piped music; tables in peaceful enclosed garden, children welcome *(LYM, Paul Humphreys)*

MARSHWOOD SY3799
Bottle [B3165 Lyme Regis—Crewkerne]: 16th-c thatched country local with enjoyable food inc interesting dishes, organic ingredients and a good vegetarian choice, well kept ales inc Weymouth, big inglenook log fire in attractive low-ceilinged bar, small games bar, skittle alley; good spacious garden with camp site beyond, pretty walking country *(Pat and Tony Martin, LYM, Mrs C Lintott)*

MELPLASH SY4897
Half Moon [A3066 Bridport—Beaminster]: Friendly Palmers pub with good range of well presented reasonably priced food, cheerful service, good choice of wines; garden tables, shares car park with cricket club next door *(Marjorie and David Lamb)*

MILTON ABBAS ST8001
Hambro Arms [signed off A354 SW of Blandford]: In beautiful late 18th-c thatched landscaped village, good log fire, three well kept real ales, enjoyable generous food from sandwiches to popular Sunday carvery, prompt service even when busy, bright décor; darts, pool and TV in cosy back public bar, children in restaurant; no dogs, tables out on terrace, comfortable bedrooms *(LYM, Norma and Noel Thomas)*

MOTCOMBE ST8426
Coppleridge: Former 18th-c farmhouse in good-sized grounds, well cooked and presented food from sandwiches to speciality steaks in bar/lounge and two smallish dining rooms, Boddingtons and Butcombe, decent wines, welcoming service; bedrooms big and airy *(Colin and Janet Roe)*

MUDEFORD SZ1891
☆ *Haven House* [beyond huge seaside car park at Mudeford Pier]: Much-extended and smartly refurbished, best in winter for old-fashioned feel in quaint little part-flagstoned core and lovely seaside walks (dogs banned from beach May-Sept), good value food from good crab sandwiches and winter soup up, well kept real ales, cheerful service; very popular wknds and summer for position on beach with family cafeteria, tables on sheltered terrace *(LYM, A R Hawkins)*

NETTLECOMBE SY5195
☆ *Marquis of Lorne* [off A3066 Bridport—Beaminster, via W Milton]: Smart and well run, with neat and comfortable panelled front bar, log or coal fires, enjoyable food from sandwiches to steaks and game, well kept Palmers BB, Copper and 200, decent wines, friendly service, two candlelit beamed dining areas, one no smoking, bare-boards public bar with cribbage, dominoes and table skittles; disabled access and facilities, children in eating areas, seven comfortable bedrooms with big breakfast, picnic-sets in big pretty garden with rustic-style play area *(R Clark, Keith Barker, David and Julie Glover, Paul and Annette Hallett, Anthony J Woodroffe, Simon and Jane Williams, Philip and Elaine Holmes, LYM, Michael Graubart and Valerie Coumont Graubart, Joan and Michel Hooper-Immins, Peter and Audrey Dowsett, Howard and Lorna Lambert, Conor McGaughey, Roland and Wendy Chalu)*

NORTH WOOTTON ST6514
☆ *Three Elms* [A3030 SE of Sherborne]: Warm-hearted and comfortable country pub with thousands of interesting and immaculate Matchbox and other model cars and other vehicles, well kept ales such as Butcombe, Fullers London Pride and Otter, good home cooking, sandwiches too, friendly helpful landlord; may be piped pop music, seaside postcard collection in gents'; big garden behind with sturdy play area, three comfortable bedrooms, shared bathrooms, good breakfast *(Mark Boulding, BB, Gill Elston)*

OKEFORD FITZPAINE ST8011
☆ *Royal Oak* [Lower St]: Well kept Ringwood Best, Wadworths 6X and weekly changing guest beer, farm cider, enjoyable food from traditional pub dishes to more upmarket things, huge fireplace with copper-hooded stove in small traditional beamed and flagstoned front bar, no smoking green-painted L-shaped eating area with three very small cottagey interconnected rooms off, steps up to refurbished skittle alley, pool; quiz night, beer festival first wknd in July, tables on back lawn with play area, charming village *(BB, Norma and Noel Thomas)*

PIDDLETRENTHIDE SY7099
☆ *Piddle* [B3143 N of Dorchester]: Emphasis on good food inc whole board of imaginative fish specials, most tables set for eating, but

comfortable leatherette sofas in refurbished bar; well kept Greene King ales, friendly plain-speaking landlord, children's room, dining room, end pool room with SkyTV; informal streamside garden with picnic-sets and play area, new bedrooms *(BB, Geoff Pidoux)*

Poachers [B3143 N of Dorchester]: Welcoming family service, well kept Courage Best, Theakstons Best and Websters, good atmosphere in large bar, bigger tables in nicely furnished beamed restaurant, generous food inc Sat steak night and Sun lunch; piped music, good upstairs skittle alley, dogs welcome; garden with stream at bottom, 18 comfortable good value motel-style bedrooms around residents' swimming pool *(Geoff Pidoux)*

PIMPERNE ST9009

Anvil [well back from A354]: 16th-c thatched family pub with bays of plush seating in bright and welcoming bar, neat black-beamed restaurant, enjoyable home-made food from generous lunchtime baguettes and ciabattas to piping hot main dishes, real ales such as Butcombe, Hop Back Crop Circle and Timothy Taylors Landlord, friendly hard-working young staff; fruit machine, piped music; pleasant garden, 12 bedrooms with own bathrooms, attractive surroundings *(Ron Shelton, BB, Brian Chambers)*

Farquarson Arms [A354 NE of Blandford Forum]: Neat Badger pub with decent choice of reasonably priced food, four real ales inc Best and K&B *(Val and Alan Green)*

PLUSH ST7102

☆ ***Brace of Pheasants*** [off B3143 N of Dorchester]: Handsome charmingly placed 16th-c thatched pub, airy beamed bar with good solid tables and log fire, generally good food, no smoking restaurant and family room, well kept Bass, Fullers London Pride, Ringwood Best and a guest such as Otter tapped from the cask; children and dogs welcome, decent-sized attractive garden and terrace, cl Mon *(Dr and Mrs M E Wilson, the Didler, Ann Evans, LYM, Simon and Jane Williams, S P Watkin, P A Taylor, Dave Morgan, Phil and Jane Hodson, John Coatsworth, Mrs Diane M Hall)*

POOLE SZ0090

Antelope [High St]: Good local atmosphere in former coaching inn just off quay, enjoyable food in bar and refurbished restaurant, Ringwood real ales, lots of RNLI photographs *(Nigel Howard)*

☆ ***Guildhall Tavern*** [Market St]: Largely restaurant rather than pub, French-run and good (if not cheap), mainly fish; friendly service, small front bar, well kept Ringwood and decent house wine, thorough-going bright nautical décor, thriving atmosphere *(B and K Hypher, LYM, Derek Thomas)*

☆ ***Inn in the Park*** [Pinewood Rd, off A338 towards Branksome Chine, via The Avenue]: Pleasantly decorated open-plan bar in substantial Edwardian villa (now a small hotel), popular with local residents and business people for well kept Adnams Broadside, Bass and Wadworths 6X and good value generous bar food (not Sun evening) from good 'sandwedges' (sandwiches with chips) to fresh seafood, cheerful young staff, log fire, oak panelling and big mirrors, airy and attractive restaurant (children allowed) and Sun carvery; tables on small sunny terrace, comfortable bedrooms, quiet pine-filled residential area just above sea *(Mrs V A Goulds, LYM, Michael and Alison Sandy)*

Nightjar [Ravine Rd, Canford Cliffs]: Ember Inn attractively refurbished in modern style, several separate areas, well kept Bass, Batemans and a guest beer from long bar, wide range of reasonably priced food from sandwiches up; piped music, machines, two quiz nights; tables on pleasant lawn, nice quiet spot in upmarket district *(W W Burke)*

PORTLAND SY6872

George [Reforne]: Particularly well kept Ringwood Best, Greene King Abbot and a guest beer, good value food (not Weds lunchtime) from big filled baps to cheap home-made hot dishes in 17th-c stone-built pub mentioned by Thomas Hardy and reputed to have smugglers' tunnels running to the cliffs; low beams, flagstones, small rooms, scrubbed tables, interesting prints and a case of Georgian shillings, children's room *(Joan and Michel Hooper-Immins)*

Mermaid [Wakeham]: Popular local with Adnams Best, Bass and Greene King Old Speckled Hen, honest well cooked food inc local scallops and choice of Sun carvery roasts, pleasant back restaurant with extended evening menu, real fire in stone fireplace, two chesterfields, old photographs and interesting bric-a-brac inc ship models; suntrap back terrace, lovely flower displays, three bedrooms *(Joan and Michel Hooper-Immins)*

PORTLAND BILL SY6768

Pulpit: Welcoming extended dark-beamed pub in great spot nr Pulpit Rock, short stroll to lighthouse and cliffs, picture-window views; generous quickly served food inc good fresh fish and chips and local crab (wide evening choice), well kept Bass, Fullers London Pride, Greene King Old Speckled Hen and Ringwood Best; may be piped music *(Joan and Michel Hooper-Immins, Pat and Robert Watt)*

POWERSTOCK SY5196

☆ ***Three Horseshoes*** [off A3066 Beaminster—Bridport via W Milton]: Plain country pub doing well under current landlord/chef, appealing fresh food from generous baguettes to full meals inc good fish, plenty of interest and nice presentation, well kept Palmers ales, good range of wines by the glass, friendly landlady and staff, good log fires and stripped panelling, children welcome in no smoking pine-plank dining room, no music; level access, dogs welcome, lovely views towards the sea from back terrace (steps down to this) and big sloping garden with picnic-sets and swings, open all day, three pleasant bedrooms with own bathrooms, good walks *(Chris and Ann Coy, S G N Bennett, Michael Graubart and Valerie Coumont Graubart, LYM, Philip and Elaine Holmes, Simon and*

Jane Williams, C W Burke, Peter and Audrey Dowsett, Conor McGaughey, Joan and Michel Hooper-Immins, Roland and Wendy Chalu)

PRESTON SY7082

Spyglass [Bowleaze Coveway]: Big busy bright and airy family dining pub with picture-window views over Weymouth Bay from top of Furzy Cliff, wide choice of enjoyable generous food with plenty for children, well kept ales such as Courage Directors, Ringwood Fortyniner and Quay JD1742 and Harbourmaster; piped music; tables outside, adventure play area *(Colin and Janet Roe, Joan and Michel Hooper-Immins)*

PUNCKNOWLE SY5388

☆ ***Crown*** [off B3157 Bridport—Abbotsbury]: 16th-c thatched and heavy-beamed inn facing partly Norman church, welcoming inglenook log fires, plush stripped stone lounge, neat rambling public bar (darts and table skitles) with no smoking family room, friendly cheerful staff, well kept Palmers Copper, IPA, 200 and seasonal Tally Ho, ten wines by the glass, straightforward food from sandwiches and baked potatoes up, local paintings for sale, books and magazines, family room with children's books; views from nice peaceful back garden, good walks, bedrooms *(LYM, Alan and Paula McCully, Marjorie and David Lamb, Dr Diana Terry, Tim O'Keefe, Geoffrey G Lawrance, Joan and Michel Hooper-Immins, Mike and Shelley Woodroffe, Val and Alan Green, Ian and Deborah Carrington, Colin and Janet Roe, Roland and Wendy Chalu)*

PYMORE SY4794

Pymore Inn [off A3066 N of Bridport]: Attractive Georgian beamed and stone-built pub popular with older people for good value generous food (most tables laid for eating), friendly prompt service, well kept changing ales such as Badger Best and Youngs, prints on panelled walls, woodburner, small pretty dining room; soft piped music; level access, big garden *(Roland and Wendy Chalu)*

SANDFORD ORCAS ST6220

☆ ***Mitre*** [off B3148 and B3145 N of Sherborne]: Tucked-away country local with flagstones and fresh flowers throughout, welcoming attentive service, good value attractively presented straightforward food, well kept real ales, country wines, small bar and larger pleasantly homely dining area; has been cl Mon lunchtime *(LYM, Debbie and Neil Hayter, OPUS)*

SHAFTESBURY ST8622

Mitre [High St]: Cheerfully unpretentious, with quickly served good value food inc enjoyable carvery, Blackmore Vale views from back dining room and small suntrap garden, well kept Youngs, good choice of wines, daily papers; children welcome *(M Vlassova, J Longworth, BB)*

☆ ***Two Brewers*** [St James St]: Down steep famously photogenic Gold Hill, friendly well divided open-plan plush-seated bar, lots of decorative plates, well kept Courage Best, Fullers London Pride, Gales HSB, Greene King Old Speckled Hen and a guest beer, wide choice of low-priced bar food from sandwiches up (children's helpings of any dish), good value wines, no smoking back dining room, skittle alley; children in eating areas, dogs in bar, picnic-sets in attractive good-sized garden with pretty views *(JP, PP, LYM)*

SHAVE CROSS SY4198

☆ ***Shave Cross Inn***: Charming partly 14th-c thatched pub in beautiful quiet countryside, flagstones and enormous inglenook in small bar, enjoyable food from sandwiches to traditional meals and caribbean cooking (just roasts, crab sandwiches or prawns Sun lunchtime, just meals – not cheap – evenings), friendly and chatty newish owners, nicely set out dining room, ancient skittle alley; children and dogs welcome, lovely garden with well and new play area, good walks, has been cl Mon *(LYM, Joan and Michel Hooper-Immins, Marjorie and David Lamb, J S Davies, Conor McGaughey, John and Joan Nash)*

SHERBORNE ST6316

Antelope [Greenhill]: Comfortable hotel bar, interesting choice of restaurant food, attentive staff; good bedrooms *(OPUS)*

Half Moon [Half Moon St]: Smart and relaxed, with clubby alcoves in multi-level bar, good choice of enjoyable food from sandwiches and baked potatoes up, Ansells, Bass and Tetleys, attractive bright and airy no smoking restaurant; 16 bedrooms with own bathrooms *(Joan and Michel Hooper-Immins)*

STOBOROUGH SY9286

Kings Arms [B3075 S of Wareham]: Pleasant inside and out, enjoyable food such as trout and venison, well kept Timothy Taylors Landlord, good service *(Peter Neate)*

STOKE ABBOTT ST4500

☆ ***New Inn*** [off B3162 and B3163 2 miles W of Beaminster]: 17th-c thatched pub with friendly attentive service, generous home-made food from good sandwiches, baguettes and baked potatoes to some inventive cooking, local fish and game (must book wknds), well kept Palmers IPA, Copper and 200, decent wines, good soft drinks choice; beams, flagstones and brasses, stripped stone alcoves on either side of one big log fireplace, another with handsome panelling, no smoking flagstoned dining room, no music; bar can get a little smoky; wheelchair access, children welcome, neat and attractive sizeable garden (the two gardeners are aged 98 and 101), unspoilt quiet thatched village, good walks, bedrooms *(LYM, Simon and Jane Williams, Mrs G Coleman, J S Davies, Mrs A P Lee, Tim, Ann and Polly Hunt, Joan and Michel Hooper-Immins, Roland and Wendy Chalu)*

STOURPAINE ST8609

White Horse [Shaston Rd; A350 NW of Blandford]: Small friendly country pub with good choice of reasonably priced enjoyable food from lunchtime sandwiches with salad to mediterranean-style evening dishes, well kept Badger ales, nice layout and décor, scrubbed tables, side pool room; bedrooms

(Mrs Kay Wellings)

STRATTON SY6593

☆ *Saxon Arms* [off A37 NW of Dorchester; The Square]: The good friendly licensees who launched this new but traditional thatched pub leave in autumn 2004; spacious bright open-plan bar (dogs allowed) with open fire, large no smoking dining section (children welcome) on right, part flagstones, part carpet, light oak tables and comfortable settles, friendly staff, traditional games; it's had good food, well kept Fullers London Pride, O'Hanlons Royal Oak and Palmers Best and Copper (sold here as Saxon), and very reasonably priced wines – reports on the new regime, please; tables out overlooking village green *(LYM)*

STUDLAND SZ0382

☆ *Bankes Arms* [off B3351, Isle of Purbeck; Manor Rd]: Very popular spot above fine beach, outstanding country, sea and cliff views from huge pleasant garden with masses of seating; comfortably basic, friendly and easy-going big bar with raised drinking area, very wide choice of decent food (at a price) all day from baguettes to local fish and good crab salad, half a dozen or more changing real ales (it now brews some of its own), local farm cider, good wines by the glass, efficient service, great log fire; piped music, machines, big-screen sports TV, darts and pool in side games area; children welcome, just off Coast Path; can get very busily trippery wknds and in summer, parking in season can be complicated or expensive if you're not a NT member; big comfortable bedrooms *(Ron Shelton, Betsy Brown, Nigel Flook, A C Nugent, Dr B and Mrs P B Baker, William and Jenifer Ruxton, James Woods, Dr Diana Terry, Tim O'Keefe, John and Laney Woods, Richard Fendick, Roy and Lindsey Fentiman, John Coatsworth, Terry and Linda Moseley, Phil and Sally Gorton)*

STURMINSTER MARSHALL SY9499

☆ *Red Lion* [N end of High St, opp church; off A350 Blandford—Poole]: Attractive and civilised village pub opp handsome church, old-fashioned roomy U-shaped bar, good friendly relaxed atmosphere, good value home-made food inc substantial interesting starters, bargain OAP two-course lunch, sandwiches on Sun too, smart efficient service, well kept Badger Best and Tanglefoot, log fire, team photographs and caricatures, cabinet of sports trophies, quiet end round corner, roomy no smoking restaurant/family room in skittle alley conversion *(BB, Paul and Annette Hallett, John and Joan Nash, Marjorie and David Lamb)*

SUTTON POYNTZ SY7083

☆ *Springhead* [off A353 NE of Weymouth]: New chef raising the food stakes in this appealingly placed smart pub, some innovative upmarket cooking using local ingredients, well kept Flowers IPA and Greene King Old Speckled Hen, good value wines, good range of malt whiskies, beams and dark décor, comfortable mix of furnishings, log fires, daily papers; well chosen piped music; lovely spot opp willow stream in quiet village, entertaining ducks, good play area in big garden with fruit trees, walks to White Horse Hill and Dorset Coastal Path *(Joan and Michel Hooper-Immins)*

SWANAGE SZ0278

Red Lion [High St]: Stone-built two-bar pub, low beams densely hung with hundreds of keys, usually real ales such as Flowers, Greene King Old Speckled Hen and Ringwood, Addlestone's cider, decent food, prompt friendly service; piped music; children's games in large barn, picnic-sets in extended garden with partly covered back terrace *(Peter and Audrey Dowsett, the Didler, JP, PP)*

SYDLING ST NICHOLAS SY6399

☆ *Greyhound* [High St]: Wide choice of good food from filled crusty rolls to good fish and delicious puddings, friendly family service, chatty locals, well kept Palmers and Youngs Special, long brick bar counter, some stripped stonework and flagstones, comfortable seating, pleasant bistro-style flagstoned conservatory, restaurant; pool, piped music; good tables in nice small garden with play area, very pretty village *(Anthony Barnes, Simon and Jane Williams, BB, Dr and Mrs D Woods, Peter Neate)*

SYMONDSBURY SY4493

☆ *Ilchester Arms* [signed off A35 just W of Bridport]: Friendly and chatty new chef/landlord in attractive partly thatched old inn, snugly traditional open-plan low-ceilinged bar with high-backed settle built in by big inglenook, cosy no smoking dining area with another fire, straightforward lunchtime food from sandwiches and baked potatoes up, wider evening menu strong on meat, well kept Palmers beers, Taunton cider, pub games, skittle alley; fairly quiet piped music; level entrance (steps from car park), children welcome, tables in pretty brookside back garden with play area, peaceful village, good walks nearby *(Marjorie and David Lamb, Simon and Jane Williams, LYM, Stephen, Julie and Hayley Brown, Dr Diana Terry, Tim O'Keefe, Mrs C Lintott, Roland and Wendy Chalu)*

TOLPUDDLE SY7994

Martyrs [former A35 W of Bere Regis]: Relaxed local with well kept Badger beers, wide food choice in bar and busy attractively laid out restaurant; children welcome, nice garden, open all day, quiet bypassed village *(Glenwys and Alan Lawrence, Gerald Wilkinson, Roy and Lindsey Fentiman)*

TRENT ST5818

Rose & Crown: Attractively old-fashioned ex-farmhouse pub gradually being renovated by hard-working new licensees, log fire, flagstones, oak settles, well kept ales, dining conservatory; children welcome, picnic-sets behind – lovely peaceful surroundings, good walks *(OPUS)*

UPLODERS SY5093

☆ *Crown* [signed off A35 E of Bridport]: New tenants yet again here, working out well, with prompt friendly service, wide variety of good food from snacks to full meals, sensible prices, well kept Palmers ales, ten wines by the glass, daily papers; appealing low-beamed bar with cheerful décor, flowers and candles on tables, table skittles and log fires, steps down to pretty no smoking restaurant; piped music, quiz nights; picnic-sets in small attractive two-tier garden *(Simon and Jane Williams, Brian and Bett Cox, Alan and Paula McCully, Mrs A P Lee, LYM, David Martin, Roland and Wendy Chalu)*

UPWEY SY6785

Old Ship [off A354; Ridgeway]: Quiet beamed pub with lots of alcoves and log fires each end, well kept Greene King Old Speckled Hen and a guest beer, food from lunchtime baguettes up, quick friendly service; picnic-sets in garden with terrace, interesting walks nearby *(M G Hart, Joyce and Geoff Robson, Cathy Robinson, Ed Coombe, Simon and Jane Williams, LYM, Marjorie and David Lamb)*

VERWOOD SU0808

Monmouth Ash [Manor Rd (B3082 S)]: Recently refurbished with nice pine tables and settles, good choice of well kept real ales, decent attractively priced food, quick friendly service *(anon)*

WAREHAM SY9287

Duke of Wellington [East St]: Small traditional 18th-c pub, good range of local real ales, wide choice of reasonably priced food inc interesting fish and Tues thai evening, some original features; piped music; open all day *(Dr B and Mrs P B Baker)*

WAYTOWN SY4797

Hare & Hounds [between B3162 and A3066 N of Bridport]: Peaceful 17th-c country local, two small cottagey rooms and pretty dining room, good value well presented straightforward food from sandwiches, baguettes and baked potatoes up inc popular Sun lunch, friendly landlady and staff, well kept Palmers Copper and IPA tapped from the cask, no music; step down to entrance, into bar, and into dining room; lovely Brit valley views from picnic-sets in sizeable simple garden with good play area *(Joan and Michel Hooper-Immins, Roland and Wendy Chalu)*

WEST BAY SY4690

George [George St]: Red plush banquettes, mate's chairs, masses of shipping pictures, some model ships and nautical hardware, roomy L-shaped public bar with games and juke box, separate no smoking back restaurant; food inc lots of good value local fish from prawn and crab sandwiches up, well kept Palmers IPA and Gold, cheery helpful staff; tables outside, bedrooms *(BB, Geoff Pidoux)*

WEST KNIGHTON SY7387

New Inn [off A352 E of Dorchester]: Neat biggish pub with good value food inc tempting puddings, friendly attentive staff, real ales, country wines, small restaurant, skittle alley, good provision for children; big colourful garden, pleasant setting in quiet village with wonderful views *(Simon and Jane Williams, Terry and Linda Moseley, Jason Caulkin)*

WEST LULWORTH SY8280

☆ *Castle Inn* [B3070 SW of Wareham]: Pretty thatched inn in lovely spot nr Lulworth Cove, good walks and lots of summer visitors; quaintly divided flagstoned bar concentrating on food (not cheap) from sandwiches to local crab inc children's dishes and summer salad bar, decent house wines, farm cider, Courage Best, Gales HSB and Ringwood Best, friendly chatty staff, maze of booth seating divided by ledges for board games and jigsaws, cosy more modern-feeling separate lounge bar and pleasant restaurant, splendid ladies'; piped music, video game; popular garden with terrace, giant chess boards, boules and barbecues, bedrooms *(LYM, J and B Cressey, Richard Fendick, Joan and Michel Hooper-Immins)*

WEST PARLEY SZ0898

☆ *Curlew* [Christchurch Rd]: Attractively reworked and civilised Vintage Inn with nicely mixed furnishings in half a dozen linked room areas inc no smoking ones, hops on beams, extensive wine racks and old bric-a-brac, two log fires, good food inc interesting dishes, plenty of good value wines, well kept Bass, very friendly well trained service *(David and Ruth Shillitoe)*

WEST STOUR ST7822

Ship [A30]: Old-style pub with good value very generous food cooked by landlord, proper sandwiches, low prices, friendly landlady, well kept Palmers, spotless attractive furnishings, big log fire, lovely views from chatty bright and airy bar, intimate split-level dining room; dogs allowed in bar but not garden behind, comfortable bedrooms *(Pat and Robert Watt, Colin and Janet Roe, Dennis Jenkin, Comus and Sarah Elliott)*

WEYMOUTH SY6778

Boot [High West St]: Largely 18th-c bare-boards pub nr harbour, beams and stone-mullioned windows even older, emphasis on well kept Ringwood ales with a guest beer, Cheddar Vale and Thatcher's farm cider, welcoming bearded landlord, cheap filled rolls, pork pies etc; pavement tables *(Simon and Jane Williams, Joan and Michel Hooper-Immins, the Didler)*

Dolphin [Park St]: Neatly kept alehouse tied to Hop Back, their GFB, Crop Circle and Summer Lightning and three guest beers such as Gales HSB and O'Hanlons Royal Oak, may be filled rolls; new bedrooms with own bathrooms *(Joan and Michel Hooper-Immins)*

Kings Arms [Trinity Rd]: Two-room partly 16th-c black-beamed quayside pub reopened as dining pub with enjoyable food inc plenty of local fish and seafood, well kept Ringwood Best and Fortyniner and a guest such as Bass; good view of bridge lifting every 2 hrs *(Joan and Michel Hooper-Immins, Vanessa Stilwell)*

Old Rooms [Cove Row/Trinity Rd]: Bustling low-beamed pub, large unpretentious dining room with excellent harbour view, well priced food (some all day at least in summer) from good crab baguettes to lots of fish, friendly efficient staff, changing real ales, old nautical lamps and maps; may be piped music, no nearby parking; terrace by part-pedestrianised harbourside street *(Liz and John Soden, Colin Wood, John Coatsworth, Meg and Colin Hamilton)*

Park [Grange Rd]: Comfortable and roomy open-plan local with cheap lunchtime bar food from sandwiches and baguettes up, well kept Bass and Fullers London Pride *(Joan and Michel Hooper-Immins)*

☆ ***Red Lion*** [Hope Sq]: Lively unsmart bare-boards pub with well kept Courage Best and Quay beers from smart touristy complex in former brewery opp, quickly served cheap simple lunches from good crab sandwiches up, interesting RNLI and fishing stuff all over the walls and ceiling (even two boats), coal fire, daily papers, friendly family atmosphere, good staff; plenty of tables on sunny terrace (more than inside), open all day in summer (food all day then too) *(the Didler, Simon and Jane Williams, BB, Joan and Michel Hooper-Immins)*

Wellington Arms [St Alban St]: Unpretentious panelled town pub, good value lunchtime food (all day summer wkdys) from toasted sandwiches and baguettes to sensibly priced hot dishes inc daily roasts, well kept Ind Coope Burton, Tetleys and Wadworths 6X, children welcome in no smoking back dining room *(Joan and Michel Hooper-Immins)*

WIMBORNE MINSTER SU0000

Green Man [Victoria Rd, W of town]: Splendid flower-draped façade, three linked areas with nooks and alcoves, usual pub furnishings, brasses and prints, well kept Wadworths ales from back bar, good value food inc fine ploughman's, wider evening choice, small dining area, relaxed atmosphere, efficient welcoming service; piped music (occasional live), machines, no dogs, lavatories up steps; benches out under ivy trellis *(W W Burke)*

Kings Head [The Square]: Brasserie/bar in old-established hotel, enjoyable food, plenty of room for drinkers in big reception area, fast service; comfortable bedrooms *(Geoff Pidoux)*

White Hart [Corn Market]: Busy old-fashioned low-beamed bar in pedestrian precinct a few steps from Minster, well kept real ales, wide range of good fresh reasonably priced bar food from good warm baguettes up in eating area, OAP bargains, good welcoming service *(Dr and Mrs A K Clarke, Geoff Pidoux)*

WINFRITH NEWBURGH SY8085

Red Lion [A352 Wareham—Dorchester]: Comfortable and welcoming Badger family dining pub with wide range of reliable food, their usual beers, good service, reasonably priced wines; TV room, piped music, tables in big sheltered garden (site for caravans), bedrooms *(Marjorie and David Lamb, Paul and Penny Rampton)*

WINTERBORNE WHITECHURCH ST8300

Milton Arms [A354 Blandford—Dorchester]: Good range of well cooked generous food inc some less common dishes in refurbished village local, two busy bars, one with no smoking area, pleasant atmosphere, helpful staff, good beer range inc Ringwood *(K R Harris)*

WINTERBORNE ZELSTON SY8997

Botany Bay [A31 Wimborne—Dorchester]: Spreading open-plan roadside dining pub, front part divided into areas by partly glazed partitions, back more restauranty, food from baguettes through usual pubby dishes to steaks, sensible prices, well kept Ringwood, decent house wines and coffee, quick friendly service; tables on back terrace *(Miss J F Reay, BB)*

WOOL SY8486

Ship [A352 Wareham—Dorchester]: Roomy open-plan thatched and timbered family pub, good choice of generous locally sourced food all day from baguettes and baked potatoes to seafood inc children's in low-ceilinged linked areas of long dining lounge and plush back restaurant, friendly quick service, well kept Badger Best, K&B and Tanglefoot, decent wines, good coffee; quiet piped music; picnic-sets overlooking railway in attractive fenced garden with terrace and play area, handy for Monkey World and Tank Museum, pleasant village *(Joan and Michel Hooper-Immins, Terry and Linda Moseley, M G Hart)*

Several well known guide books make establishments pay for entry, either directly or as a fee for inspection. These fees can run to many hundreds of pounds. We do not. Unlike other guides, we never take payment for entries. We never accept a free meal, free drink, or any other freebie from a pub. We do not accept any sponsorship – let alone from commercial schemes linked to the pub trade. All our entries depend solely on merit. And we are the only guide in which virtually all the main entries have been gained by a unique two-stage sifting process: first, a build-up of favourable reports from our thousands of reader-reporters; then anonymous vetting by one of the senior editorial staff.

Essex

The county's top pubs this year are the Axe & Compasses at Arkesden (excellent food, welcoming too if all you want is a drink), the Three Willows at Birchanger (good value fresh fish), the nicely set Swan at Chappel (good fish cooking here too), the Cricketers at Clavering (an immaculate upmarket dining pub), the Queens Head at Fyfield (a nice find, this new entry is a good all-rounder), the exceptionally friendly Green Man at Gosfield (good generous food), the White Hart at Great Yeldham (good food and wines in a magnificent building), the Rainbow & Dove at Hastingwood (this good value M25 refuge is back on fine form), the interesting Bell in Horndon-on-the-Hill (very good all round), the easy-going and relaxed Viper surrounded by woodland at Mill Green, and the cheerful 15th-c White Horse at Pleshey (enjoyable food and plenty of special events bring this friendly pub back into the *Guide* after quite a break). As we have shown, good food comes across as a strong point at most of these fine pubs; it is the Axe & Compasses at Arkesden which takes the top title of Essex Dining Pub of the Year. In the Lucky Dip section at the end of the chapter, current pubs to note particularly are the Theydon Oak at Coopersale Street, Sun at Dedham, Sun at Feering, Black Bull at Fyfield, Cricketers at Mill Green and restauranty Green Man at Toot Hill. Drinks prices in the county are close to the national average, with Ridleys the main local brewer often attractively priced, and Crouch Vale, Mighty Oak and Maldons other local brews to look out for.

ARKESDEN TL4834 Map 5

Axe & Compasses ★ 🍴 🍷

Village signposted from B1038 – but B1039 from Wendens Ambo, then forking left, is prettier

Essex Dining Pub of the Year

A smashing place to eat, though you'll feel just as welcome if you only want a drink, this rambling thatched country pub continues to win much praise from readers. Excellent home-made bar food might include lunchtime sandwiches (from £3.50, not Sunday), breaded plaice goujons (£4.95), home-made steak and kidney pie or chicken, leek and bacon crumble (£9.95), lamb kebabs with greek salad and pitta bread (£10.95), and around half a dozen well prepared fresh fish dishes such as grilled skate wing with butter and capers (£11.95), halibut cooked with prawns, cream and cheese (£12.95), and monkfish on roasted red pepper sauce (£13.95); on the puddings trolley you might find mouthwatering home-made puddings such as raspberry and hazelnut meringue or crème brûlée (£4). The no smoking restaurant has a more elaborate menu. The pub dates back to the 17th c, and the oldest part is the cosy carpeted lounge bar, which has beautifully polished upholstered oak and elm seats, easy chairs and wooden tables, a blazing fire, and lots of gleaming brasses. A smaller quirky public bar (which can get a bit smoky) is uncarpeted, with cosy built-in settles, and darts; bar billiards. The atmosphere is welcoming and relaxed; friendly service from the pleasant staff. You'll find a very good wine list (with 14 wines by the glass) and around two dozen malt whiskies, along with well kept Greene King Abbot, IPA and maybe Old Speckled Hen on handpump. There are seats out on a side terrace with pretty hanging baskets; parking at the back. It's in a very pretty village. *(Recommended by Angela Gorman, Paul Acton, H O Dickinson, Adele Summers, Alan Black, Philip and Elaine Holmes, B N F and M Parkin, S Horsley, Richard Siebert, Len Banister, David Barnes, Bob and Maggie Atherton, John and Claire Pettifer, John Saville, Mr and Mrs T B Staples, B and M Kendall, Mrs Margo Finlay, Mr Kasprowski, Nigel Howard)*

Greene King ~ Lease Themis and Diane Christou ~ Real ale ~ Bar food (not Sun in winter) ~ Restaurant ~ (01799) 550272 ~ Children in restaurant ~ Open 12-2, 6-11; 12-3, 7-10.30 Sun

BIRCHANGER TL5022 Map 5

Three Willows

Under a mile from M11 junction 8: A120 towards Bishops Stortford, then almost immediately right to Birchanger Village; don't be waylaid earlier by the Birchanger Services signpost!

This welcoming pub's name refers to cricket bats of the last three centuries, and above a puce dado in the roomily extended carpeted main bar, the buff and brown ragged walls have a plethora of cricketing prints, photographs, cartoons and other memorabilia. Good value and generously served, the food is a big draw, and it's best to arrive early if you want to eat. Besides a wide selection of more standard bar food such as lunchtime sandwiches (from £2.40), filled baked potatoes (from £3.50), ploughman's (£3.95), chilli con carne (£4.95), and other dishes such as steak pie (£7.95), and steaks (from £9.95), you can choose from deliciously fresh simply cooked fish specials (served with chunky chips and plain salads) such as crab salad (£7.95), haddock (£8.95), and monkfish cutlets (£9.95). Booking is a good idea if you want to eat in the restaurant. A small public bar has pool and sensibly placed darts, and there's a fruit machine. Friendly and attentive staff serve well kept Greene King IPA, Abbot and Ruddles County on handpump, and there are decent house wines. There are picnic-sets out on a terrace with heaters and on the lawn behind, with a sturdy climbing frame, swings and a basketball hoop (you can hear the motorway out here). No children are allowed inside. *(Recommended by Tina and David Woods-Taylor, Mrs J Ekins-Daukes, Leigh and Gillian Mellor, Stephen and Jean Curtis, George Atkinson, Ian Phillips, Matthew Shackle, Mr and Mrs P L Spencer, Reg Fowle, Helen Rickwood)*

Greene King ~ Tenants Paul and David Tucker ~ Real ale ~ Bar food (12-2, 6-9.30, not Sun evening) ~ Restaurant ~ (01279) 815913 ~ Dogs allowed in bar ~ Open 11.30-3, 6-11; 12-3, 7-11 Sun

BURNHAM-ON-CROUCH TQ9596 Map 5

White Harte

The Quay

It's a real pleasure to relax with a drink on a fine evening listening to the water lapping against the private jetty of this welcoming old hotel (there are seats here and out in front of the pub), and the rigging slapping against the masts of boats on moorings beyond. Throughout the partly carpeted bars, with cushioned seats around oak tables, are models of Royal Navy ships, and assorted nautical hardware such as a ship's wheel, a barometer, even a compass in the hearth. The other traditionally furnished high-ceilinged rooms have sea pictures on panelled or stripped brick walls. An enormous log fire makes it cosy in winter, and the atmosphere is cheerful. Well kept Adnams and Crouch Vale Best on handpump are promptly served by the friendly staff. From a straightforward menu, good value bar food includes sandwiches (from £2.30, toasted sandwiches from £3.20), a handful of daily specials such as chilli con carne, lamb casserole, various curries, lasagne, and steak and kidney pie (all £6.30), locally caught skate, plaice or cod (£9.30), and puddings such as apple crumble and fruit pies (£3). It's popular with boaty types in summer, and can get very busy on Friday and Saturday evenings. *(Recommended by G A Hemingway, Ian Phillips, Peter Meister, Keith and Chris O'Neill)*

Free house ~ Licensee G John Lewis ~ Real ale ~ Bar food ~ Restaurant ~ (01621) 782106 ~ Children welcome ~ Dogs welcome ~ Open 11-11; 12-10.30 Sun ~ Bedrooms: £19.80(£50B)/£37(£65B)

CASTLE HEDINGHAM TL7835 Map 5

Bell

B1058 E of Sible Hedingham, towards Sudbury

This fine old coaching inn has been run by the same welcoming family for more than 35 years. The unchanging beamed and timbered saloon bar has Jacobean-style seats and windsor chairs around sturdy oak tables, and, beyond standing timbers left from a knocked-through wall, some steps lead up to an unusual little gallery. Behind the traditionally furnished public bar, a games room has dominoes, cribbage and shove-ha'penny; piped music. Each of the rooms has a warming log fire, and one bar is no smoking; look out for Porsha, the sociable german pointer, who has quickly become a favourite with readers. Well kept Adnams, Greene King IPA and Mighty Oak Oscar Wilde Mild are tapped from the cask along with a guest such as Adnams Broadside. Tasty, good value bar food includes home-made soup (£3.25), panini (from £3.95), lamb burger or smoked prawns (£4.95), ploughman's or salmon fishcakes (£5.50), mushroom stroganoff (£7.25), turkish lamb casserole (£7.95), red thai curry (£8.50), and lamb chops (£8.75), with puddings such as apple and blackberry pie and bread and butter pudding (£3.80); children's meals (from £3). On Monday night they have a fish barbecue: mackerel (£7.25) and red mullet fillets (£7.50). The big walled garden behind is pleasant in summer, with an acre or so of grass, trees and shrubs, as well as toys for children; there are more seats on a vine-covered terrace. The village is pretty, and the 12th-c castle keep nearby is worth visiting. Dogs are welcome but you must phone first. *(Recommended by Charles Gysin, Paul and Margaret Baker)*

Grays ~ Tenants Penny Doe and Kylie Turkoz-Ferguson ~ Real ale ~ Bar food (not 25 Dec) ~ (01787) 460350 ~ Children welcome away from bar ~ Traditional jazz last Sun lunchtime of month, acoustic guitar group Fri evening ~ Open 11.30-3, 6-11; 11.30-11 Fri; 12-4, 7-10.30 Sun

CHAPPEL TL8927 Map 5

Swan

Wakes Colne; pub visible just off A1124 Colchester—Halstead

Even a 74-mile round trip isn't enough to deter one couple from coming to this deservedly popular old timbered pub. A treat for fish-lovers, there's an excellent range of superbly cooked fresh fish including scallops grilled with bacon (£6.95; large £13.95), fried rock eel (£7.95, large £10.25), haddock (£8.95, large £12.95), skate (£9.50) and fried tuna with garlic mushrooms or grilled lemon sole (£13.95). Other bar food (prices haven't gone up since last year) includes lunchtime filled baguettes or sandwiches (from £1.95), and ploughman's (from £3.95), as well as chicken curry or gammon and pineapple (£6.95), calves liver and bacon (£9.95), and sirloin steak (from £11.95), with home-made puddings such as plum crumble (from £3.45); they also do a simple children's menu (from £2.50). The pub is splendidly set, with the River Colne running through the garden on its way downstream to an impressive Victorian viaduct. Big overflowing flower tubs and french street signs lend the sheltered suntrap cobbled courtyard a continental feel, and gas heaters mean that even on cooler evenings, you can still sit outside. The spacious and low-beamed rambling bar has standing oak timbers dividing off side areas, plenty of dark wood chairs around lots of dark tables for diners, a couple of swan pictures and plates on the white and partly panelled walls, and a few attractive tiles above the very big fireplace. The central bar area keeps a pubbier atmosphere, with regulars dropping in for a drink; fruit machine, cribbage, dominoes and piped music. One of the lounge bars is no smoking. Well kept Greene King IPA and Abbot and a guest such as Morland Tanners Jack on handpump are swiftly served by the friendly staff; they've wines by the glass, and just under two dozen malt whiskies. The Railway Centre (a must for train buffs) is only a few minutes' walk away. *(Recommended by Malcolm and Jennifer Perry, John and Elspeth Howell, Bryan and Mary Blaxall, John Saville, Philip and Elaine Holmes, Richard Siebert, Mike and Mary Carter, Tom Bottinga, Pete Bennett, Colin and Dot Savill)*

Free house ~ Licensee Terence Martin ~ Real ale ~ Bar food (12-2.30, 6.30-10(10.30 Sat); 12-3, 6.30-9.30 Sun) ~ Restaurant ~ (01787) 222353 ~ Children in eating area of bar and restaurant ~ Dogs allowed in bar ~ Open 11-3, 6-11; 11-11 Sat; 12-10.30 Sun

CHELMSFORD TL7006 Map 5

Alma

Arbour Lane, off B1137 (Springfield Road)

With an attractive layout and décor and a civilised country-pub feel, this is an enjoyable place to come for an evening, and readers recommend catching one of the regular theme nights. The mainly carpeted beamed bar has a comfortable mix of tables and brocade-cushioned chairs and stools, a central brick fireplace with a club fender, a piano nearby, and a big mirror over a trompe l'oeuil flanked by bookcases. One cosy alcove has a deeply cushioned button-back leather sofa and armchair, and above a dark dado is a nice collection of old advertising posters on the puce rough-cast walls. There are bar stools on flagstones by the brick-built serving counter – look out for the another trompe l'oeuil on the wall opposite. Besides the bar dining area, a comfortable no smoking restaurant is prettily decorated in creams and blues, with an inglenook fireplace. A planned new extension will open up the bar area creating a no smoking area, and providing new lavatories. They serve decent wines (with nine by the glass), and Greene King IPA and a couple of guests such as Adnams Broadside, Crouch Vale Brewers Gold, and Shepherd Neame Spitfire are well kept on handpump; piped music and fruit machine. As well as enjoyable changing specials such as chicken supreme wrapped in parma ham filled with mozzarella and sunblush tomatoes or king prawn risotto with poppy seed snaps (£9.95), fresh cromer crab (£11.95), 8oz fillet steak with foie gras, spinach and wild mushrooms (£14.95), and venison cutlets with pancetta and thyme galette and raspberry jus (£15.95), they also serve lunchtime (not Sunday) sandwiches (from £2.95), and ploughman's (£4.50), and on Sundays there's a choice of roasts (£6.95); as the food is cooked to order, service may be slow when it's busy. They do a good value weekday two-course bargain meal: you can choose from a £5.99 or £9.99 menu (not Sunday lunch, Saturday evening or on theme nights). The pub is enthusiastically run, and there are regular special offers. You'll find picnic-sets out on a crazy-paved terrace at the front and in a small garden at the back. *(Recommended by Anthony Rogers, John Saville, Reg Fowle, Helen Rickwood)*

Free house ~ Licensees David and Sheila Hunt ~ Real ale ~ Bar food (12-2.30, 6-9.30) ~ Restaurant ~ (01245) 256783 ~ Children in restaurant ~ Dogs allowed in bar ~ Open 11-11; 12-10.30 Sun; closed 25 Dec evening, 26 Dec

CLAVERING TL4731 Map 5

Cricketers

B1038 Newport—Buntingford, Newport end of village

An enjoyable place for a treat, this immaculately modernised smart 16th-c dining pub has been run by the same licensees (parents of TV chef Jamie Oliver) for nearly 30 years. It attracts a well heeled set, prices aren't cheap, but standards are very high, and readers have nothing but praise for the imaginative food. The seasonally changing menu might include soup (£4), meatballs with rich juniper and thyme gravy and parmesan shavings (£5.75), stuffed corn-fed chicken roulade with tarragon and green peppercorn mayonnaise (£6.25), stuffed pepper rolls with artichoke and italian parsley pesto (£13), sautéed calves liver and bacon in rich red onion gravy (£15), barbury duck breast with rhubarb and juniper sauce (£16.50), chargrilled rib-eye steak with creamy blue cheese sauce (£15.75), and interesting puddings such as banana and coffee bread pudding with lemon grass and redcurrant compote and vanilla ice-cream or tangy lime and sultana cheesecake with raspberry syrup and fresh fruits (£4.75); they also do sandwiches (from £3.75). You can get half price portions of some of the main meals for children, and there's a children's menu (£4.50). The spotlessly kept and roomy L-shaped beamed bar has standing timbers resting on new brickwork, and pale green plush button-backed banquettes, stools and windsor chairs around shiny wooden tables on a pale green carpet, gleaming copper pans and horsebrasses, dried flowers in the big fireplace (open fire in colder weather), and fresh flowers on the tables; one area and the restaurant are no smoking. Adnams Broadside, Tetleys and a guest are well kept on handpump, and they've decent wines; the atmosphere can be really lively on busy lunchtimes, and the attentive staff cope well with the crowds. The attractive front terrace has picnic-sets and umbrellas among colourful flowering shrubs. The bedrooms are in the adjacent cottage. *(Recommended by Maysie Thompson, Adele Summers, Alan Black, Angela Gorman, Paul Acton, Bob and Maggie Atherton, Mike and Heather Watson, David J Bunter, David Glynne-Jones, M R D Foot, John and Claire Pettifer, John Saville)*

Free house ~ Licensee Trevor Oliver ~ Real ale ~ Bar food (12-2, 7-10) ~ Restaurant ~ (01799) 550442 ~ Children welcome ~ Open 11-11; closed 25/26 Dec ~ Bedrooms: £70B/£100B

FINGRINGHOE TM0220 Map 5

Whalebone

Follow Rowhedge, Fingringhoe signpost off A134, the part that's just S of Colchester centre; or Fingringhoe signposted off B1025 S of Colchester

A good way to start the day, you can get a tasty breakfast (10-11.30am) at this civilised and relaxing pub. The pale yellow-washed interior has been very nicely done out, its three room areas airily opened together, leaving some timber studs; stripped tables on the unsealed bare boards have a pleasant mix of chairs and cushioned settles. Roman blinds with swagged pelmets, neat wall lamps, a hanging chandelier and local watercolours (for sale) are good finishing touches. Although you'll feel welcome if you're just after a drink (the staff are friendly and courteous), the main focus is the imaginative, freshly cooked food. An enticing choice of dishes, listed on a blackboard over the small but warming coal fire, might include soup (£3.50), double baked cheese soufflé (£7.95), liver and bacon with madeira cream sauce (£8.95), seared duck breast with sloe gin and orange sauce (£10.50), steaks (from £10.50), and grilled dover sole with parsley sauce and peppered potatoes (£11.50), with puddings such as apple and cinnamon crumble with crushed almonds (£4.50); they do weekday lunchtime sandwiches and baguettes (from £3.50 – they let you choose your own fillings), and children's meals (from £3.95). Greene King IPA and Old Speckled Hen are well kept alongside a couple of guests such as Ridleys Prospect and Mighty Oak Burntwood on handpump, and there are decent house wines; piped music. Pleasant on a fine day, the back garden, with gravel paths winding through the grass around a sizeable old larch tree, has picnic-sets with a peaceful valley view; they sometimes have plays out here in summer. Readers recommend stopping off at the Fingringhoe Wick Nature Reserve. *(Recommended by Andrew Morgan, M and G Rushworth, MDN, Paul and Ursula Randall)*

Free house ~ Licensees Sam and Victoria Burroughes ~ Real ale ~ Bar food (10-2.30, 7-9.30) ~ (01206) 729307 ~ Children in family room ~ Dogs welcome ~ Open 10-3, 5.30-11; 10-11(10.30 Sun) wknds

FULLER STREET TL7416 Map 5

Square & Compasses

From A12 Chelmsford—Witham take Hatfield Peverel exit, and from B1137 there follow Terling signpost, keeping straight on past Terling towards Great Leighs; from A131 Chelmsford—Braintree turn off in Great Leighs towards Fairstead and Terling

Tuesday night is sausage and mash night at this civilised little country pub, and you can choose from around 20 different varieties of sausage (from £8.50). Along with the stuffed birds, traps and brasses which adorn the L-shaped beamed bar, there are otter tails, birds' eggs and old photographs of local characters, many of whom still use the pub. This comfortable and well lit carpeted bar has a woodburning stove as well as a big log fire; shove-ha'penny, table skittles, cribbage and dominoes; disabled lavatories. Very well kept Nethergate Suffolk County and Ridleys IPA are tapped from the cask, and they've also decent french regional wines. Besides lunchtime sandwiches (from £3.50), soup (£3.75), lasagne (£9.25) and fish pie (£10), good home-made dishes include changing specials such as beer-battered cod and chips (£10.75), tiger prawns in coconut milk and coriander (£12.50; main £19.75), seared tuna loin with sautéed potatoes (£13.75), and properly cooked rib-eye steak (£15.75), with home-made puddings such as sticky toffee pudding (from £3.50); on Sunday evenings they have a limited menu. There are gentle country views from tables outside. *(Recommended by M and GR, Philip and Elaine Holmes, Colin and Dot Savill, Sherrie Glass, Nick Mattinson, John Saville, Peter Howarth, Hazel Morgan)*

Free house ~ Licensees Howard Potts and Ginny Austin ~ Real ale ~ Bar food (12-2.30, 7-9.30(10 Sat); 12-2.30, 7-8.30 Sun; not Mon) ~ Restaurant ~ (01245) 361477 ~ Children welcome away from bar ~ Dogs welcome ~ Open 11.30-3, 6.30(7 in winter)-11; 12-3, 7-10.30 Sun; closed Mon exc bank hol Mon lunchtime

FYFIELD TL5706 Map 5

Queens Head 🍷 🍺

Corner of B184 and Queen Street

This welcoming and popular 15th-c thatched pub has low black beams and joists in its compact L-shaped bar, with some timbers in the terracotta-coloured walls, fresh flowers and pretty lamps on its nice sturdy elm tables, and comfortable seating from button-back wall banquettes to attractive and unusual high-backed chairs, some in a snug little side booth. Two facing log fireplaces have lighted church candles instead in summer. They have a splendid choice of well kept changing ales on handpump such as Adnams Bitter and Broadside, Caledonian Deuchars IPA, Crouch Vale Brewers Gold, Exe Valley Dobs Best, Hop Back Summer Lightning and Kings Red River, also Weston's Old Rosie farm cider, and good wines by the glass including champagne – most of the pictures have a humorous wine theme, including a series of Ronald Searle cartoons. Besides good lunchtime (not Sunday) sandwiches (from £3.25, toasted baguettes £4.50), and baked potatoes or ploughman's (£6.25), well prepared generous food might include avocado baked in stilton and almonds (£5.75), home-made steak and kidney pie (£8.95), bass fillets with steamed leeks and ginger or calves liver with bacon and onion cooked in sherry and cream (£10.95), scallops cooked in Pernod and cream (£11.50), and skate wing with black peppercorn butter (£12.95). The young licensees are enthusiastic and friendly; they've a cat and two dogs. At the back, a neat little prettily planted garden by a weeping willow has a teak bench and half a dozen picnic-sets under canvas parasols, and beyond a picket fence the sleepy River Roding flowing past. *(Recommended by Mr and Mrs C F Turner, Len Banister)*

Free house ~ Licensees Daniel Lemprecht and Penny Miers ~ Real ale ~ Bar food (not Sun evenings) ~ Restaurant ~ (01277) 899231 ~ Open 11-3.30, 6-11; 12-3.30, 7-10.30 Sun

GOSFIELD TL7829 Map 5

Green Man 🍴 🍷

3 miles N of Braintree

It's worth trying to catch the help-yourself cold table at this smart dining pub: you can choose from home-cooked ham and pork, turkey, tongue, beef and poached or smoked salmon, as well as game pie, salads and home-made pickles (from £7.65). If you want something hot, big portions of bar food (served with fresh vegetables and home-made chips) from a mostly traditional english menu include steak and kidney pudding (£7.65), trout baked with almonds (£7.75), calves liver and bacon or pork chops marinated in dill and mustard (£8.95), and half a roast duck with orange and red wine sauce (£12.50), or you can choose from snacks such as soup (from £3), sandwiches (from £3.45), filled baked potatoes (from £3.50), and soft roe on toast

(£4.25); puddings might be fruit pie or treacle tart (£3.50). Even midweek it's a good idea to book. The two little bars have a happy relaxed atmosphere (or you can sit outside in the garden), and the staff are exceptionally friendly. Many of the decent nicely priced wines are available by the glass, and they've very well kept Greene King IPA and Abbot on handpump; pool and a juke box. *(Recommended by David Twitchett, David and Christine Vaughton, Richard Siebert, David J Bunter, Richard and Margaret Peers)*

Greene King ~ Lease Richard Parker ~ Real ale ~ Bar food (not Sun evening) ~ Restaurant ~ (01787) 472746 ~ Children in restaurant ~ Dogs allowed in bar ~ Open 11-3, 6-11; 12-4, 7-10.30 Sun

GREAT YELDHAM TL7638 Map 5

White Hart

Poole Street; A1017 Halstead—Haverhill

One of only a handful of pubs to be Grade I* listed, this popular black and white timbered dining pub has a jazz night every Friday, and regular events such as dinner dances, steak nights and murder mystery evenings. Most people come for the inventive, well cooked food, so booking is a good idea if you want to eat here. The same menu is available in the bar or in the no smoking restaurant, and delicious (though by no means cheap), dishes could include mediterrannean fish soup (£5.50), honey-roast ham and cheddar sandwich (£5.95), bacon, black pudding and poached egg salad (£6.25), ploughman's (£7.50), fresh pasta with basil pesto and parmesan cheese (£8.50), rump steak or tuna steak (£11.95), roast rack of lamb on fondant potato, swede and carrot mash with mint jus (£16.25), and grilled bass with roasted plum tomatoes and olives with flat parsley pesto (£16.50), with puddings such as fig tart with rum and raisin cream (£5.50); you have to pay extra for vegetables. They do a lunch special (two courses £10.50, not Sunday), and smaller helpings are available for children. Cheerful service from the well trained staff. They've got a very good wine list with ten by the glass, and aside from well kept Adnams, they serve one or two continually changing guests such as City of Cambridge Boathouse Bitter and Nottingham Cock & Hoop; also a good choice of belgian bottled beers, organic fruit juices, Weston's cider, and a dozen malt whiskies. Watch your head as you come in: the door into the bar is very low. The main areas have stone and wood floors with some dark oak panelling, especially around the fireplace. In fine weather, the attractive landscaped garden is a pleasant place to sit, with well tended lawns and pretty seating. *(Recommended by RWC, Mrs Roxanne Chamberlain, Derek Thomas, M and G Rushworth, Adele Summers, Alan Black, David J Bunter, JWAC)*

Free house ~ Licensee John Dicken ~ Real ale ~ Bar food (12-2, 6.30-9.30) ~ Restaurant ~ (01787) 237250 ~ Children welcome ~ Fri night jazz and live music first Sun evening of month ~ Open 12-3, 6-11(10.30 Sun)

HASTINGWOOD TL4807 Map 5

Rainbow & Dove

¼ mile from M11, junction 7

This comfortable 17th-c rose-covered cottage is an excellent place to stop if you want a break from the motorway. There are cosy warming fires in the three homely little low-beamed rooms which open off the main bar area; the one on the left is particularly snug and beamy, with the lower part of its wall stripped back to bare brick and decorated with brass pistols and plates. A small function room is no smoking. It does get very busy, but the staff cope well with the crowds, and the atmosphere remains relaxed; when it's quiet dogs are allowed in the bar. Good value, well presented bar food includes tasty sandwiches (from £2.50, readers recommend the crab), soup (£3.30), baked potatoes (from £4), ploughman's (from £5.50), home-made steak and ale pie or spinach and red pepper lasagne (£5.95), local sausages and mash (£6.15), and steaks (from £8.95), with fresh fish dishes such as skate wing (£8.95), and bass (£9.25); puddings might be treacle sponge and

spotted dick (£3.25). Courage Directors, Greene King IPA and a guest such as Youngs Special are well kept on handpump; piped music and darts. Hedged off from the car park, a stretch of grass has picnic-sets under cocktail parasols.
(Recommended by Bob and Margaret Holder, Ian Phillips, R T and J C Moggridge, Alan and Paula McCully, John and Wendy Allin, Bob Richardson, Sean and Sharon Pines, Tony Beaulah, Colin and Janet Roe)

Punch ~ Tenants Jamie and Andrew Keep ~ Real ale ~ Bar food (12-2.30, 7-9.30) ~ (01279) 415419 ~ Children in eating area of bar ~ Open 11.30-3, 6-11; 12-4, 7-10.30 Sun

HORNDON-ON-THE-HILL TQ6683 Map 3

Bell

M25 junction 30 into A13, then left into B1007 after 7 miles, village signposted from here

Seven real ales, an outstanding choice of wines, and imaginative food make this bustling 15th-c village inn a popular choice with readers. The heavily beamed bar has some antique high-backed settles and benches, rugs on the flagstones or highly polished oak floorboards, and a curious collection of ossified hot cross buns hanging from a beam. They stock over a hundred well chosen wines from all over the world, including 16 by the glass, and you can buy very fairly priced bottles off-sales. They're keen on supporting local brewers: three swiftly rotating guests such as Mauldons Suffolk Pride, Mighty Oak Burntwood and Charles Wells Bombardier are well kept on handpump alongside Bass, Crouch Vale Brewers Gold and Greene King IPA. They hold occasional beer festivals. The ambitious menu changes frequently, and is available in the bar and no smoking restaurant; you may need to book. Beautifully presented dishes might include soup (£4.95), confit of belly pork glazed with haddock mornay, dill and watercress purée (£6.95), roast salmon with smoked salmon crust and wild garlic or roast rib of beef with caramelised onions and fennel and balsamic crème fraîche (£13.50), with puddings such as white chocolate, rhubarb and mascarpone trifle with maple marshmallows (£5.50). The separate bar menu contains dishes such as lunchtime sandwiches (£4.95), fried lambs kidneys with mustard and sage or grilled cod with white beans and watercress (£8.50), and roast sausages with parsley and truffle sauce (£9.50); they also do a popular olives, bread and butter platter (£3.95). Centuries ago, many important medieval dignitaries would have stayed here, as it was the last inn before travellers heading south could ford the Thames at Highams Causeway.
(Recommended by Malcolm and Jennifer Perry, Adrian White, Bob and Maggie Atherton, Sarah Markham Flynn, Alan Cole, Kirstie Bruce, Len Banister, John and Enid Morris, Ian Phillips, David J Bunter, Mike and Shelley Woodroffe, Richard Siebert, Bob Richardson, Nick Lawless)

Free house ~ Licensee John Vereker ~ Real ale ~ Bar food (12-2, 6.30(7 Sun)-9.45; not bank hol Mon or 25/26 Dec) ~ Restaurant ~ (01375) 642463 ~ Children in eating area of bar and restaurant ~ Dogs allowed in bar and bedrooms ~ Open 11-2.30(3 Sat), 5.30(6 Sat)-11; 12-4, 7-10.30 Sun; closed bank hol Mon, and 25-26 Dec ~ Bedrooms: /£65B

LANGHAM TM0233 Map 5

Shepherd & Dog

Moor Road/High Street; village signposted off A12 N of Colchester

The spick and span L-shaped bar of this bustling village pub embraces an engaging hotch-potch of styles, with interesting collections of continental bottled beers and brass and copper fire extinguishers. The food here is popular, and it does get busy, but the friendly staff cope well. Chalked on boards around the bar, the enjoyable menu changes regularly, but includes around ten fish specials such as chilli-glazed butterfish or tuna (£8.95), and hummous-crusted halibut or lemon sole (£9.95), with other dishes such as sandwiches (£2.30), soup (£2.95), chicken liver pâté (£3.95), ploughman's (from £4.20), scampi (£6.95), duck with curried parsnip mash (£11.95), and fillet steak (£13.95), with puddings such as apple and apricot crumble (£3.95); they do children's meals (£3.95), and a Sunday roast (£6.95). Greene King IPA, Abbot and Ruddles County, and a monthly changing guest are well kept on handpump, or you can choose from a short but carefully selected wine list; piped music, and readers tell us it can get smoky. In summer, there are very pretty window boxes, and a shaded bar in the enclosed side garden; tables outside. They hold occasional theme nights. *(Recommended by John Saville, R M Corlett, Philip Denton, Shirley Mackenzie, Charles and Pauline Stride)*

Free house ~ Licensee Julian Dicks ~ Real ale ~ Bar food (12-2.15, 6-9.30(10 Fri); 12-10 Sat; 12-9 Sun) ~ Restaurant ~ (01206) 272711 ~ Children welcome ~ Dogs allowed in bar ~ Open 11-3, 5.30-11; 11-11 Sat; 12-10.30 Sun; closed 26 Dec

LITTLE BRAXTED TL8314 Map 5

Green Man £

Kelvedon Road; village signposted off B1389 by NE end of A12 Witham bypass – keep on patiently

On a fine afternoon, picnic-sets in the pleasant sheltered garden behind this pretty brick pub are a good place to while away an hour or two. Inside the welcoming little lounge has an interesting collection of bric-a-brac, including 200 horsebrasses, some harness, mugs hanging from a beam, and a lovely copper urn; it's especially cosy in winter when you'll really feel the benefit of the open fire. The tiled public bar has books, darts, shove-ha'penny, cribbage, dominoes and a video machine. Welcoming staff serve Ridleys IPA, Rumpus and Old Bob on handpump, along with several malt whiskies. Reasonably priced, hearty bar food such as sandwiches (from £2.65), filled baguettes or baked potatoes (from £3.45), ploughman's (£5.50), cottage pie or prawn cocktail (£3.95), sausages and creamed potatoes (£4.95), lasagne (£6.75), and a couple of daily specials such as steak and ale pie (£7.25), and minted lamb shank (£7.95), while puddings might be treacle tart (£3.25). The pub is tucked away down an isolated country lane. *(Recommended by John Saville, Len Banister, G Culliford)*

Ridleys ~ Tenant Neil Pharaoh ~ Real ale ~ Bar food ~ (01621) 891659 ~ Dogs allowed in bar ~ Open 11.30-3, 6-11; 12-3.30, 7-10.30 Sun

LITTLE WALDEN TL5441 Map 5

Crown

B1052 N of Saffron Walden

The cosy low-beamed bar of this friendly 18th-c low white cottage has a good log fire in the brick fireplace, bookroom-red walls, flowery curtains and a mix of bare boards and navy carpeting. Seats, ranging from high-backed pews to little cushioned armchairs, are spaced around a good variety of closely arranged tables, mostly big, some stripped. The small red-tiled room on the right has two little tables; piped local radio. The big draw is the four or five well kept real ales tapped straight from the cask, which might include Adnams, Greene King IPA and Abbot, and a couple of changing guests such as City of Cambridge Boathouse and Mauldons Bitter. Hearty bar food includes sandwiches (from £2.95), soup (£3.95), ploughman's (from £5.75), home-made lasagne (£7.25) and steak and ale pie (£7.95), with daily specials on blackboards such as vegetable curry (£7.50), smoked haddock mornay (£8.25), chicken cacciatore (£8.95), cold seafood platter (£9.75), and beef stroganoff (£10.25); puddings might be tasty apple crumble or bread and butter pudding (from £3.95). There are tables out on a side patio. *(Recommended by B N F and M Parkin, Mr and Mrs T B Staples, Margaret and Allen Marsden, the Didler)*

Free house ~ Licensee Colin Hayling ~ Real ale ~ Bar food (not Mon evening) ~ (01799) 522475 ~ Children in eating area of bar and restaurant ~ Dogs welcome ~ Trad jazz Weds evening ~ Open 11.30-3, 6-11; 12-10.30 Sun ~ Bedrooms: £45S/£60S

Please let us know of any pubs where the wine is particularly good.

MILL GREEN TL6401 Map 5

Viper £

The Common; from Fryerning (which is signposted off north-east bound A12 Ingatestone bypass) follow Writtle signposts

This charmingly uncomplicated little pub is peacefully set in the middle of a wood, and tables on the lawn overlook a carefully tended cottage garden which is a dazzling mass of colour in summer (when the front of the pub is almost hidden by pretty overflowing hanging baskets and window boxes). The two timeless cosy lounge rooms have spindleback seats, armed country kitchen chairs, and tapestried wall seats around neat little old tables, and there's a log fire. Booted walkers are directed towards the fairly basic parquet-floored tap room, which is more simply furnished with shiny wooden traditional wall seats, and beyond that another room has country kitchen chairs and sensibly placed darts; shove-ha'penny, dominoes, cribbage. From an oak-panelled counter you can get well kept Mighty Oak Oscar Wilde Mild and Ridleys IPA, and three weekly changing guests from more or less local breweries such as Crouch Vale, Mighty Oak and Nethergate on handpump or tapped straight from the cask; farm cider too. There's an easy-going welcoming atmosphere, and it's the kind of place where you're quite likely to fall into casual conversation with the sociable locals or welcoming landlord; the friendly pub dog is called Ben. Simple but tasty bar snacks are served only at lunchtime, and might include sandwiches (from £2.50, toasted from £2.75), soup (£3.25), hawaiian toast (£3.50), chilli con carne (£3.75), and ploughman's (from £4.95). No children inside the pub. *(Recommended by Pete Baker, Kevin Thorpe, Anthony Rogers, the Didler, Nick Lawless, Reg Fowle, Helen Rickwood)*

Free house ~ Licensees Roger and Sharon Beard ~ Real ale ~ Bar food (lunchtime) ~ No credit cards ~ (01277) 352010 ~ Dogs allowed in bar ~ Open 12-3(5 Sat), 6-11; 12-5, 7-10.30 Sun

PAGLESHAM TQ9293 Map 3

Punchbowl

Church End; from the Paglesham road out of Rochford, Church End is signposted on the left

Cosy and spotlessly kept, the beamed bar of this pretty white weatherboarded pub has pews, barrel chairs and other seats, and lots of bric-a-brac. They serve four well kept real ales which, besides Adnams and Ridleys Old Bob, might include guests such as Exmoor Fox and Nethergate Old Chap on handpump; cribbage, dominoes, shove-ha'penny, and piped music (can be obtrusive). Reasonably priced bar food such as rolls, sandwiches and filled baguettes (from £2.50), soup (£2.75), filled baked potatoes (£3.50), ploughman's (£4.65), aubergine and cheese melt (£5.95), liver and bacon or battered cod (£6.25), cajun chicken (£7.25), and rump steak (from £9.95), with enjoyable daily fish specials such as skate (£7.95), and lemon sole (£9.25); puddings might be chocolate and hazelnut roulade (from £3.25). In a secluded spot down long country lanes, the pub has a peaceful outlook over the fields; there are some tables in the little garden, with a couple more out by the quiet road. Be warned that they sometimes close a few minutes early. *(Recommended by Kevin Thorpe, George Atkinson)*

Free house ~ Licensees Bernie and Pat Cardy ~ Real ale ~ Bar food ~ Restaurant ~ (01702) 258376 ~ Children in restaurant ~ Open 11.30-3, 6.30-11; 12-3, 6.30-10.30 Sun

Bedroom prices normally include full English breakfast, VAT and any inclusive service charge that we know of. Prices before the '/' are for single rooms, after for two people in double or twin (B includes a private bath, S a private shower). If there is no '/', the prices are only for twin or double rooms (as far as we know there are no singles). If there is no B or S, as far as we know no rooms have private facilities.

PLESHEY TL6614 Map 5

White Horse

The Street

They hold lots of special events at this cheerful 15th-c pub, from Tudor feasts to jazz buffets and barbecues. Inside lots of nooks and crannies are filled with a fascinating array of jugs, tankards, antlers, miscellaneous brass, prints, books, bottles – and even an old ship's bell. The rooms have a genuinely friendly feel and are furnished with wheelback and other chairs and a mix of dark wooden tables; a welcoming fireplace has an unusual curtain-like fireguard. The snug room by the tiny bar counter has brick and beamed walls, a comfortable sofa, some bar stools and a table with magazines to read. Well kept Youngs Best and maybe a guest are swiftly served by friendly and helpful staff, and there are seven wines by the glass; fruit machine and piped music. At lunchtime you can choose from enjoyable home-made bar snacks such as toasted sandwiches (from £3.50), herring roes fried in butter or prawn cocktail (£4.25), ploughman's (£6), smoked ham and eggs (£6.75), and steak and kidney pie or fried plaice (£7.50), with more elaborate evening dishes from the à la carte menu such as smoked scottish salmon (£5.75), rabbit poached in cider with rich mushroom sauce (£8.75), poached smoked haddock with cream and mushroom sauce or venison casserole (£9.50), and grilled sirloin steak (£11.50), with irresistible puddings such as lemon cream pie or home-made rhubarb crumble (£3.50); on Sunday lunchtime (when it does get busy) they do only a two-course set menu (£10). Glass cabinets in the big dining room are filled with lots of miniatures and silverware; also sturdy furniture, and flowers on tables. Doors from here open on to a terrace with a grass area with newly-planted trees and shrubs, and picnic-sets. The pub has an arts and crafts shop, and a little art gallery with paintings for sale by local artists. *(Recommended by Tony Beaulah, Anthony Rogers)*

Free house ~ Licensees Mike and Jan Smail ~ Real ale ~ Bar food (not Sun-Tues evening) ~ Restaurant ~ (01245) 237281 ~ Children in restaurant ~ Dogs allowed in bar ~ Regular Jazz bands Sat evening ~ Open 10.30-5, 6.30-11; 12-4.30 Sun; closed Sun-Tues evenings

STAPLEFORD TAWNEY TL5001 Map 5

Mole Trap

Tawney Common, which is a couple of miles away from Stapleford Tawney and is signposted off A113 just N of M25 overpass – keep on; OS Sheet 167 map reference 500013

Although it's tucked away in what seems like the back of beyond, this country pub is usually humming with customers. The smallish carpeted bar (mind your head as you go in) has black dado, beams and joists, brocaded wall seats, library chairs and bentwood elbow chairs around plain pub tables, and steps down through a partly knocked-out timber stud wall to a similar area. There are a few small pictures, 3-D decorative plates, some dried-flower arrangements and (on the sloping ceiling formed by a staircase beyond) some regulars' snapshots, with a few dozen beermats stuck up around the serving bar. It's especially cosy in winter, when you can fully appreciate the three blazing coal fires. As well as Fullers London Pride, they have three constantly changing guests such as Crouch Vale Brewers Gold, Hop Back Summer Lightning and Timothy Taylors Landlord on handpump; the piped radio tends to be almost inaudible over the contented chatter. Besides sandwiches (from £2.95, baguettes from £3.50), bar food includes lasagne, lamb curry and chilli (all £5.95), and steak or fresh daily fish such as plaice, cod or salmon (all £7.50); they do a roast on Sunday (£6.95). Outside are some plastic tables and chairs and a picnic-set, and there's a growing tribe of resident animals, many rescued, including friendly cats, rabbits, a couple of dogs, hens, geese, a sheep, goats and horses. The pub is run with considerable individuality by forthright licensees. Do make sure children behave well here if you bring them. *(Recommended by H O Dickinson, Bruce M Drew, Paul A Moore, David Twitchett, Derek Thomas, Philip and Elaine Holmes, Evelyn and Derek Walter, LM, J H Wright, the Didler, Nick Lawless)*

Free house ~ Licensees Mr and Mrs Kirtley ~ Real ale ~ Bar food (not Sun evening) ~ No credit cards ~ (01992) 522394 ~ Well behaved children in family room ~ Dogs welcome ~ Open 11.30-3, 6-11; 12-4, 6.30-10.30 Sun

STOCK TQ6998 Map 5

Hoop

B1007; from A12 Chelsmford bypass take Galleywood, Billericay turn-off

You can choose from six well kept changing ales tapped from the cask or on handpump at this refreshingly unmodern village pub. Alongside Adnams, you'll find beers from brewers such as Crouch Vale, Hop Back, Mighty Oak, Old Kent, Shepherd Neame and Young's, and they've also got changing farm ciders and perries, and mulled wine in winter; no fruit machines or piped music. With a cheerfully inclusive atmosphere, the cosily bustling bar is very popular with locals; friendly and accommodating service. There's a coal-effect gas fire in the big brick fireplace, brocaded wall seats around wooden-top tables on the left, and a cluster of brocaded stools on the right; sensibly placed darts (the heavy black beams are pitted with stray flights), dominoes and cribbage; over-21s only in the bar. The reasonably priced, mostly traditional menu includes tasty dishes such as sandwiches (from £2), soup (£3.25), filled baked potatoes (from £3), whitebait (£4.50), ploughman's (from £5), sausage pie or chicken curry (£6.50), and poached smoked haddock (£7), with around seven daily specials such as braised steak and dumplings, steak and kidney pudding or stuffed hearts (£6), and home-made puddings such as spotted dick or cherry bakewell (£3); vegetables are £1.25 extra. Prettily bordered with flowers, the large sheltered back garden has picnic-sets, a covered seating area, and in fine weather an outside bar and weekend barbecues. They hold a popular May beer festival. *(Recommended by Evelyn and Derek Walter, Kevin Thorpe, Adrian White, Peter Hagler, Mrs Roxanne Chamberlain, John and Enid Morris)*

Free house ~ Licensees Albert and David Kitchin ~ Real ale ~ Bar food (11-2.30, 6-9; 11-9 Fri-Sat; 12-8 Sun) ~ (01277) 841137 ~ Children in eating area of bar ~ Dogs welcome ~ Open 11-11; 12-10.30 Sun

STOW MARIES TQ8399 Map 5

Prince of Wales

B1012 between S Woodham Ferrers and Cold Norton Posters

As well as five interesting, frequently changing real ales on handpump from brewers such as Everards, Mauldons, Phoenix, Ridleys and Stonehenge, you'll also find four draught belgian beers at this appealingly laid-back pub; several bottled beers, farm cider, and vintage ports too. Although the cosy and chatty low-ceilinged rooms appear unchanged since the turn of the century, they've in fact been renovated in a traditional style. Few have space for more than one or two tables or wall benches on the tiled or bare-boards floors, though the room in the middle squeezes in quite a jumble of chairs and stools. Besides sandwiches or ciabattas (from £3.25), enjoyable, generously served dishes (with good fish specials) could include ham, egg and chips (£4.95), sausage and chips (£5.15), deep-fried calamari (£5.75), beer-battered cod with mushy peas (£7.95), lamb shank with raspberry beer and mash (£8.25), and baked sea bream with rosemary and garlic (£10.95), and puddings such as sticky toffee pudding (£3); one of the dining areas is now no smoking. On Thursday evenings in winter they fire up the old bread oven to make pizzas in the room that used to be the village bakery (from £4.95), while in summer on some Sundays, they barbecue unusual fish such as saupe, mahi-mahi and black barracuda (there are also steaks for the less adventurous). There are seats and tables in the back garden, and between the picket fence and the pub's white weatherboarded frontage is a terrace with herbs in Victorian chimney pots. On most bank holidays and some Sundays, there are live bands, and they've a marquee for summer weekends. *(Recommended by Adrian White, Paul A Moore, Ian Phillips, Kevin Thorpe)*

Free house ~ Licensee Rob Walster ~ Real ale ~ Bar food (12-2.30, 7-9.30, 12-9 Sun) ~ (01621) 828971 ~ Children in family room ~ Dogs welcome ~ Open 11-11; 12-10.30 Sun

WENDENS AMBO TL5136 Map 5

Bell

B1039 just W of village

The small cottagey low-ceilinged rooms of this village pub have brasses on ancient timbers, wheelback chairs around neat tables, comfortably cushioned seats worked into snug alcoves, quite a few pictures on the cream walls, and an inviting open fire. A real bonus in summer, the extensive back garden has plenty to keep children entertained, with a wooden wendy house, crazy golf (£1), a sort of mini nature-trail wandering off through the shrubs, and a big tree-sheltered lawn; they're currently landscaping the meadow at the bottom. Nicely lit up in the evenings, you can eat out on the suntrap patio; look out for Reggie and Ronnie the goats (who have a habit of escaping). Adnams Broadside and Ansells Mild are well kept on handpump, along with a couple of changing guests such as Fullers London Pride and Shepherd Neame Spitfire. Friendly service from the new landlord and his staff; cribbage, dominoes, and piped music. Tasty bar food includes sandwiches (from £3.95), sausages and mash (£6.50), steak, mushroom and ale pie (£7.85), and sirloin steak (£10.95), with puddings such as brioche and Baileys butter pudding (£4.25); the dining room is no smoking. The pub is handy for Audley End. *(Recommended by S Horsley, Mrs Margo Finlay, Mr Kasprowski, Mr and Mrs T B Staples)*

Free house ~ Licensees Martin Housen and Elizabeth Silk ~ Real ale ~ Bar food (12-2, 6-9, not Sun evenings) ~ Restaurant ~ (01799) 540382 ~ Children welcome away from bar ~ Dogs welcome ~ Open 11.30-2.30, 5-11; 11.30-11 Fri-Sat; 12-10.30 Sun

YOUNGS END TL7319 Map 5

Green Dragon

Former A131 Braintree—Chelmsford (off new bypass), just N of Essex Showground

This pleasant dining pub manages to combine enjoyable food with a good pubby atmosphere. Lunchtime dishes might include sandwiches (from £2.95, baguettes from £3.95), home-made soup (£3.50), cottage pie (£5), ploughman's (£5.25), home-cooked ham and eggs (£7.50), curry (£8.50), with other dishes such as steak and ale pie (£7.95), chicken supreme with creamy wild mushrooms and smoked garlic sauce (£9.75), and tasty seafood specials such as seafood pancake (£4.75), and tuna loin with roasted mediterranean vegetables and sweet red pepper tapenade (£10.50). The no smoking restaurant area has an understated barn theme: you'll find stripped brick walls, a manger at one end, and a 'hayloft' part upstairs. The two bar rooms have ordinary pub furnishings, and there's an extra low-ceilinged snug just beside the serving counter. Greene King Abbot, IPA and perhaps Ruddles County are well kept on handpump; unobtrusive piped jazz music. At lunchtime (not Sunday) you can have bar food in part of the restaurant, where the tables are bigger than in the bar. Now that the new A131 has been built, it's much quieter in the neat back garden, which has lots of picnic-sets under cocktail parasols, and a budgerigar aviary. *(Recommended by Adrian White, Tina and David Woods-Taylor, Evelyn and Derek Walter)*

Greene King ~ Lease Bob and Mandy Greybrook ~ Real ale ~ Bar food (12-2.30, 6-9(9.45 Fri/Sat); 12-9 Sun) ~ Restaurant ~ (01245) 361030 ~ Children in restaurant ~ Open 11.30-3, 5.30-11; 12-10.30 Sun

> Post Office address codings confusingly give the impression that some pubs are in Suffolk, when they're really in Essex (which is where we list them).

LUCKY DIP

Besides the fully inspected pubs, you might like to try these Lucky Dips recommended to us and described by readers (if you do, please send us reports: www.goodguides.co.uk).

BALLARDS GORE TQ9092
Shepherd & Dog: Beamed country pub by golf course, dark wood, rugs on parquet, lots of pictures, four well kept ales from small breweries, wide food choice in bar or nicely laid out back restaurant; piped music; pleasant tables in small back garden *(Kevin Thorpe)*

BATTLESBRIDGE TQ7894
☆ *Barge* [Hawk Hill]: White clapboarded local right by waterside antiques and craft centre, low beams and panelled dado, chatty bar on right, quieter eating areas on left (decent food all day), real ales such as Adnams, Greene King Abbot, Ind Coope Burton and Marstons Pedigree, cheery landlord; piped music; children welcome, tables out in front, open all day *(BB, George Atkinson, Kevin Thorpe)*
Lodge [Hayes Chase, just off A132]: Popular bargain lunchtime specials and good filling baguettes, plenty of food choice inc several fish dishes, Crouch Vale ales, separate restaurant; service may slow when busy; tables and chairs on terrace and big protected lawn with bouncy castles and other play things, bedrooms *(Adrian White)*

BELCHAMP ST PAUL TL7942
Half Moon [Cole Green]: Thatched pub with friendly new licensees (from the Swan in Clare), snug beamed lounge, cheerful locals' bar, enjoyable food in bar and restaurant, well kept real ales; children welcome, tables in back garden *(LYM, Mr and Mrs W E Cross)*

BILLERICAY TQ6893
Duke of York [Southend Rd, South Green]: Pleasant beamed local with some emphasis on modern restaurant, good choice of food here and in bar, well kept Greene King beers, long-serving licensees, good service, real fire, longcase clock, local photographs, upholstered settles and wheelback chairs; may be unobtrusive piped music, monthly quiz night, fortnightly ladies' darts *(John Saville, R T and J C Moggridge, Reg Fowle, Helen Rickwood)*

BOREHAM TL7509
Grange [B1137 off A12/A130 interchange]: Newish Chef & Brewer with striking crooked roof, three log fires, Adnams and Greene King Abbot, decent hot drinks, good range of usual food, cheerful manageress and enthusiastic young staff *(Tina and David Woods-Taylor, Reg Fowle, Helen Rickwood)*

BRENTWOOD TQ5993
Nags Head [A1023, just off M25 junction 28]: Wide choice of enjoyable food inc reasonably priced Sun lunch in old place refurbished as Vintage Inn dining pub, prompt friendly helpful service, good wine choice, Bass, no smoking area *(John and Enid Morris, Nick Lawless)*

BUCKHURST HILL TQ4094
Warren Wood [Epping New Rd]: Traditional friendly London/Essex local looking over Epping Forest, thriving atmosphere, well kept ales such as Adnams Old, Courage Best and Fullers London Pride and ESB, good value straightforward lunchtime food (not Sun) from baguettes up, breakfast from 8am, back eating area, friendly fast service even to picnic-sets outside; piped music, sports TV; open all day, good walks *(Ian Phillips)*

BURNHAM-ON-CROUCH TQ9596
Ship [High St]: Welcoming pub with courteous attentive staff, well cooked food using local produce; comfortable bedrooms *(Mr and Mrs L H Latimer)*

CHELMSFORD TL7006
Queens Head [Lower Anchor St]: Lively and welcoming Victorian backstreet local, well run and orderly, with three well kept Crouch Vale real ales and five changing guest beers, late Sept beer festival, summer farm cider, winter log fires, simple and substantial cheap lunchtime food (not Sun) inc filled rolls; nr county cricket ground – its popularity with players and supporters occasionally gives it rather an unusual sports-club atmosphere; open all day from noon (11 Sat) *(Keith and Janet Morris, Bruce M Drew, Kay Davy)*
Riverside [Victoria Rd]: Open-plan Youngs pub, formerly a weatherboarded watermill, with low heavy beams and some mill gearing, generous good value food, well kept ales, efficient, neat and cheerful staff, separate restaurant; small waterside garden, bedrooms *(Paul and Ursula Randall)*

CHIGNALL ST JAMES TL6709
Three Elms: Small recently renovated open-plan country dining pub with beams and big inglenook fireplace, cheerful relaxed atmosphere, enjoyable fresh food, four well kept changing ales, helpful staff *(Mark Hope)*

CHIGWELL TQ4493
Kings Head [High Rd (A113)]: Large and handsome weatherboarded 17th-c neo-Tudor Country Carvery with interesting Dickens memorabilia (features in *Barnaby Rudge*), some antique furnishings, quick friendly service, well kept Courage Directors, popular bar food and upstairs carvery restaurant, conservatory; piped music, can get very crowded wknd evenings; picnic-sets in attractive back garden *(Ian Phillips)*

COGGESHALL TL8224
Compasses [Pattiswick, signed off A120 W]: Country pub surrounded by rolling farmland, neatly comfortable spacious beamed bars, bar food from sandwiches to steaks inc plenty of main dishes, generous Sun curry night, well kept Greene King IPA, partly no smoking barn restaurant (not always open); have been rather frequent management changes; children welcome, plenty of lawn and orchard tables, adventure play area, open all day wknds and summer *(LYM, Stephen and Jean Curtis, Richard Siebert, Reg Fowle, Helen Rickwood)*
☆ *White Hart* [Bridge St]: Civilised dining pub

with lots of low 15th-c beams in cosy neatly kept front bar, antique settles among other thoroughly comfortable seats, prints and fishing trophies, prompt service even when busy, wide choice of food from sandwiches up, well kept Adnams or Greene King IPA, decent wines and coffee, restaurant; pleasant small courtyard, nicely refurbished bedrooms *(BB, B N F and M Parkin)*

COLCHESTER TL9925

Stockwell Arms [W Stockwell St]: Friendly and relaxing timber-framed local in the old dutch quarter, country feel with heavy 14th-c beams and lots of pictures and bric-a-brac, cheap bar lunches from snacks and baguettes to wide range of hot dishes, bargain Fri fish night and popular Sun lunch (must book), well kept Caledonian Deuchars IPA, Fullers London Pride, Shepherd Neame Spitfire and guest beers; landlord organises local walks *(Pete Baker)*

COLD NORTON TL8400

Norton Barge [Latchingdon Rd]: Open-plan pub with well kept Crouch Vale Gold and Greene King IPA from central bar, quite a choice of good value food inc good hot baguettes; can be smoky *(Tina and David Woods-Taylor)*

COOPERSALE STREET TL4701

☆ *Theydon Oak* [off B172 E of Theydon Bois; or follow Hobbs Cross Open Farm brown sign off B1393 at N end of Epping]: Attractive weatherboarded dining pub very popular esp with older lunchers for ample good value quickly served straightforward food from sandwiches up inc plenty of bargain specials, Sun roasts and puddings cabinet, well kept Black Sheep and Wadworths 6X, friendly staff, long convivial beamed bar with masses of brass, copper and old brewery mirrors, decorative antique tills, interesting old maps, log fire; no piped music, bookings evenings and Sun lunch only, no credit cards, no dogs; tables on side terrace and in garden with small stream (may be ducks), lots of hanging baskets, wknd barbecues and separate play area *(H O Dickinson, Robert Lester, BB, Roger and Pauline Pearce, George Atkinson, Reg Fowle, Helen Rickwood)*

DANBURY TL7704

Cricketers Arms [Penny Royal Rd]: Cheerful country local overlooking common, good family atmosphere, three beamed areas and restaurant, friendly bar staff, generous food, Shepherd Neame beers, appropriate prints and autographed bat of 2000 West Indies team (but what is Juan Pablo Montoya's signature doing on another bat?); may be piped music *(John Saville)*

☆ *Griffin* [A414, top of Danbury Hill]: Popular Chef & Brewer, spacious but charmingly divided into small homely and congenial sections,16th-c beams and some older carved woodwork, roaring log fires, thoughtful friendly service, very wide blackboard food choice, well kept Adnams Broadside, good choice of wines by the glass, soft lighting and candles at night; no bookings so get there early, subdued piped music, high chairs *(Adrian White, Oliver Hylton, Tina and David Woods-Taylor, Reg Fowle, Helen Rickwood)*

DEDHAM TM0533

☆ *Sun* [High St]: Roomy Tudor pub now back under caring private ownership and comfortably refurbished, cosy panelled rooms with big log fires in splendid fireplaces, handsomely carved beams, well kept Adnams Broadside, Crouch Vale Brewers Gold and changing ales, typically Timothy Taylors Landlord and Wadworths 6X, decent wines and soft drinks, sensibly short changing choice of good inventive food (not winter Sun evening) with a mediterranean slant using local produce and garden herbs, affordable prices, cheerful helpful attentive staff; may be well chosen piped music; picnic-sets on back lawn, car park behind reached through medieval arch, wonderful wrought-iron inn sign; four nicely redone panelled bedrooms with modern bathrooms, good walk to or from Flatford Mill *(LYM, Peter and Margaret Glenister, Mike and Mary Carter)*

DUTON HILL TL6026

☆ *Three Horseshoes* [off B184 Dunmow—Thaxted, 3 miles N of Dunmow]: Quiet traditional village local (doubling as post office) with low-priced simple pub food Thurs-Sun, Archers, Ridleys IPA and one or two guest beers, masses of bottled beers, late spring bank hol beer festival, central fire, aged armchairs by fireplace in homely left-hand parlour, friendly licensees, interesting theatrical and 1940s memorabilia, breweriana and enamel signs; darts and pool in small public bar, pleasant views and pond in garden, cl Mon-Weds lunchtime *(BB, Len Banister, Pete Baker, the Didler)*

EPPING FOREST TQ3997

Owl [Lippitts Hill, nr High Beach]: Big 1930s family pub with great views of Epping Forest from cypress-shaded terrace, pets corner with owlery and tame rabbits, picnic-sets spreading down to pony paddocks, wknd barbecues; beams and plates above bar, good cosy atmosphere, McMullens AK and Country, decent bar food inc sandwiches, rolls and baked potatoes *(Ian Phillips, LM)*

FEERING TL8720

☆ *Sun* [Feering Hill, B1024]: Friendly and easy-going, with half a dozen quickly changing interesting real ales, Biddenden farm cider, lots of malt whiskies, open-plan bar divided by standing timbers, 16th-c beams (watch out for the very low one as you enter), plenty of bric-a-brac, woodburners in huge inglenook fireplaces, daily papers, board games, food from sandwiches up; well behaved children allowed, tables out on partly covered paved terrace and in attractive garden behind, some wknd barbecues *(LYM, Kevin Mayne, Kevin Thorpe, Edmund Coan, the Didler)*

FIDDLERS HAMLET TL4701

☆ *Merry Fiddlers* [Stewards Green Rd, a mile SE of Epping]: Long low-beamed and timbered 17th-c country pub, lots of copper and brass, chamber-pots, beer mugs and plates, real ales such as Adnams, Bass and Greene King IPA and Old Speckled Hen, good helpings of reasonably priced sensible home-cooked food inc substantial Sun roast, family dining area, attentive friendly staff; may be unobtrusive piped music, occasional live sessions; big garden with good play area (motorway can be heard) *(B N F and M Parkin, H O Dickinson, Reg Fowle, Helen Rickwood)*

FINCHINGFIELD TL6832

☆ *Red Lion* [Church Hill – B1053 just E of B1057 crossroads]: Good blackboard choice of sensibly priced food from huffers to some interesting dishes and no-nonsense roast Sun lunch, well kept Adnams and Ridleys, interesting wine choice, chatty enthusiastic landlord, cosy local atmosphere and simple furnishings, Tudor beams, log fire in huge dividing chimney breast, bar billiards, dominoes and cards, small upstairs dining area; attractive garden, three good value bedrooms with own bathrooms, nice spot opp churchyard and 15th-c guild hall, open all day *(Pete Baker, Mary O'Sullivan, Craig Turnball)*

FRATING TM0923

Kings Arms [Main Rd]: Roadside pub with decent food from reasonably priced sandwiches, baked potatoes and other straightforward dishes to more expensive seafood; Fri steak night *(Pat and Robert Watt)*

FYFIELD TL5606

☆ *Black Bull* [B184, N end]: 15th-c pub under new management, heavy low beams and standing timbers, no smoking country-style dining area with wide range of enjoyable food, comfortably modernised pubby bar, well kept Fullers London Pride, Greene King Ruddles, Marstons Pedigree and John Smiths, open fire, traditional games; quiet piped music; tables outside, lots of flower-filled barrels *(LYM, Roy and Lindsey Fentiman)*

GESTINGTHORPE TL8138

Pheasant [off B1058]: Country views, wide food choice (not Sun evening or Mon) from baked potatoes and other bar food to more exotic blackboard dishes, well kept ales such as Adnams, Fullers London Pride and Greene King IPA and Old Speckled Hen, interesting old furnishings and log fire in lounge, another in low-beamed public bar, cigarette card collection; children welcome, picnic-sets in garden, cl Mon lunchtime *(LYM, Mr and Mrs W E Cross)*

GREAT HORKESLEY TL9732

Yew Tree [The Causeway (A134)]: Handy Chef & Brewer, attractive flower-covered thatched building (rebuilt in the 1970s after a fire), well kept Courage Best and Directors; tables in pleasant courtyard with fountain *(Tina and David Woods-Taylor)*

GREAT YELDHAM TL7638

Waggon & Horses [High St]: Cheerful 16th-c timbered inn with attractive oak-beamed bars, well kept Greene King IPA and three other changing ales inc a seasonal Nethergate, enjoyable generous good value food from baguettes to fish and steaks, friendly family service, popular restaurant; lacks no smoking area; bedrooms, most in modern back extension *(Maurice Young, Adele Summers, Alan Black)*

HATFIELD BROAD OAK TL5416

Cock [High St]: Character 15th-c beamed village pub with well kept Adnams Best, Nethergate IPA and changing guest beers, Easter beer festival, decent wines, friendly attentive young staff, light sunny L-shaped bar with open fire, music hall song sheets and old advertisements, good choice of enjoyable fresh food (not Sun evening) from sandwiches to interesting hot dishes, restaurant; bar billiards, juke box and darts; children in eating area *(LYM, Laurence)*

HERONGATE TQ6391

Boars Head [Billericay Rd, just off A128]: Picturesque and popular low-beamed dining pub with pleasant nooks and crannies, wide blackboard choice of reliable sensibly priced traditional food all day from good choice of lunchtime baguettes to choice of Sun roasts, up to five changing real ales, reasonably priced wines, friendly staff; can get crowded at peak times; garden tables overlooking big attractive reed-fringed pond with ducks and moorhens *(Mark Morgan, Roy and Lindsey Fentiman, Nick Lawless)*

HEYBRIDGE BASIN TL8707

Old Ship [Lockhill]: Good choice of reliable standard food and changing specials, well kept Shepherd Neame Best and Spitfire, malt whiskies, blond wooden furniture (window tables reserved for diners), more ambitious upstairs restaurant with estuary views, good friendly service, daily papers; well behaved dogs and children welcome; seats outside, some overlooking water by canal lock – lovely views of the saltings and across to Northey Island, pretty window boxes; can be very busy, esp in summer when parking nearby impossible (but public park five mins' walk) *(Peter Butterworth, Paul and Ursula Randall, Reg Fowle, Helen Rickwood)*

HIGH ONGAR TL5903

☆ *Wheatsheaf* [signed Blackmore, Ingatestone off A414 just E of Ongar]: Comfortable low-beamed pub/restaurant with emphasis on good food (not Sun evening; best to book), unusual intimate stalls in small traditional bar's big front bay window, log fires each end, friendly efficient service, Greene King IPA; children in side room, charming big back garden, plenty of play space and equipment *(LYM, H O Dickinson, Len Banister, Colin and Dot Savill)*

KIRBY LE SOKEN TM2122

Red Lion [B1034 Thorpe—Walton]: Attractive and pleasantly furnished 14th-c local, friendly helpful service, good range of bar food inc imaginative dishes and good value Sun lunch, well kept real ales, roomy bar and dining room; piped music, predominantly young people in the evenings; big garden with play area and thatched eating area *(Robert Turnham)*

LEIGH-ON-SEA TQ8385

☆ *Crooked Billet* [High St]: Homely old pub with waterfront views from big bay windows, local fishing pictures and bric-a-brac, beams and bare boards, well kept changing ales such as Adnams, Bass and Theakstons, good spring and autumn beer festivals, home-made lunchtime food (not Sun) inc seafood, friendly service, woodburner; piped music, live music nights; open all day, side garden and terrace, seawall seating over road shared with Osbornes good shellfish stall; pay-and-display parking (free Sat/Sun) by fly-over *(LYM, John and Enid Morris)*

LITTLE BADDOW TL7807

Generals Arms [The Ridge; minor rd Hatfield Peverel—Danbury]: Pleasantly refurbished and roomy, with decent food, efficient attentive service, three well kept Shepherd Neame ales, reasonably priced wines; tables on terrace and back lawn with play area, good walks nearby *(LYM, Paul and Ursula Randall, George Atkinson)*

LITTLE DUNMOW TL6521

☆ *Flitch of Bacon* [off A120 E of Dunmow; The Street]: Informal country local under friendly new licensees, simple but attractive small timbered bar, flowery-cushioned pews and ochre walls, well kept Greene King IPA and a couple of guests from brewers such as Crouch Vale and Nethergate, short choice of simple bar food from sandwiches up (not Sun evening), no smoking back eating area (children welcome here) with french windows looking out on to terrace; piped music; a few picnic-sets outside, peaceful views, bedrooms *(Mrs Margo Finlay, Mr Kasprowski, LYM)*

LITTLE TOTHAM TL8811

Swan [School Rd]: Splendid range of well kept changing real ales tapped from the cask, often local, also three farm ciders and a perry, in low-beamed bar with open fire, dining room extension with enjoyable local food, bar billiards and darts in tiled games room; welcoming landlord, music nights, morris dancers at Jun beer festival; children welcome, small terrace and picnic-sets under cocktail parasols on sizeable front lawn, open all day *(Kevin Thorpe, the Didler)*

LITTLE WALTHAM TL7314

☆ *Dog & Gun* [E of village, back rd Great Leighs—Boreham]: Long L-shaped timbered dining lounge refurbished with stripped woodwork and pastel walls, good generous food from lunch snacks to more enterprising dishes and popular Sun family lunches, friendly informal atmosphere and charming cheerful staff, well kept Ridleys IPA, decent wine, suntrap conservatory; may be piped music, may be changing hands; separate menu for picnic-sets in good-sized pretty garden with floodlit heated terrace, elegant pondside willow, tidy play area *(Adrian White)*

LITTLEY GREEN TL6917

Compasses [off A130 and B1417 SE of Felsted]: Unpretentiously quaint and old-fashioned flagstoned country pub with well kept Ridleys from nearby brewery tapped from casks in back room, lots of malt whiskies, big huffers, ploughman's and baked potatoes, no machines; tables in big back garden, benches out in front *(the Didler)*

LOUGHTON TQ4296

Kings Head [Church Hill (A121)]: Comfortable open-plan pub with Greene King Ruddles and Websters Yorkshire on handpump, good value food, good atmosphere, restaurant; wknd smart dress code *(Robert Lester)*

Victoria [Smarts Lane]: Friendly traditional local with well kept ales such as Adnams, Bass, Greene King and Harveys, wide blackboard choice of good value generous home-made food, small separate dining area, good Sun bar nibbles; pleasant neatly kept garden *(Peter Fuller, Richard Morris, J E Draper)*

MALDON TL8407

☆ *Blue Boar* [Silver St; car park round behind]: Quirkily decorated coaching inn, luxurious main lounge with gilt and chenille love-seats, seductive paintings, Canova-look marble figures, dining room with chandeliers, pewter, more paintings and antique refectory table, beams and panelling, upper room with spectacular vaulted ceiling, separate smallish rather basic bar with dark oak beams and timbers, dark pub furniture inc Jacobean carved oak dresser, woodburner, ship paintings, well kept Adnams tapped from the cask and own-brew Farmers Pucks Folly, friendly staff; open all day, parking £3 *(Oliver Hylton, George Atkinson, Barry L Sidney, LYM)*

Jolly Sailor [Church St/The Hythe]: Charming quayside timber-framed pub, three real ales, meals served; tables out overlooking barges on Thames *(John and Enid Morris)*

MARGARETTING TL6701

Red Lion [B1002 towards Mountnessing]: Busy but relaxed beamed and timbered local, all tables laid for good choice of reliable generous food inc good fish specialities, no smoking dining area, well kept Ridleys IPA, Bob and Prospect, efficient unrushed service; piped radio; good wheelchair access, pretty in summer, with picnic-sets and play area *(Roy and Lindsey Fentiman, John and Enid Morris, Reg Fowle, Helen Rickwood)*

MARGARETTING TYE TL6801

White Hart: Popular and unassuming L-shaped bar with good value unpretentious food from sandwiches up, cheerful friendly service, well kept Adnams and interesting guest beers from afar, bright and comfortable conservatory-roofed family dining room; robust play area and pets corner in attractive garden by quiet village green, good walks *(Carole and John Smith, Paul Hunkin, Paul and Ursula Randall, Reg Fowle, Helen Rickwood)*

MATCHING GREEN TL5310

Chequers: Friendly pub/restaurant, candles on plain pine tables, lounge with sofas and open fire, sparse decoration, good traditional and mediterranean-style food, american-style central bar with Greene King IPA and Old Speckled Hen and Charles Wells Bombardier, lots of lagers, shiny taps and glistening bottles (good wine choice), relaxed at lunchtime, busy evenings; jazz Tues, cl Mon; garden, quiet spot overlooking pretty cricket green *(Len Banister, Sean and Sharon Pines)*

MILL GREEN TL6301

☆ *Cricketers*: Low beams, lots of interesting cricketing memorabilia, generous and popular simple fresh bar food, nice restaurant, well kept Greene King IPA, Abbot and Old Speckled Hen tapped from the cask, decent wines, friendly attentive service, no smoking area, no music; children very welcome, picturesque setting, plenty of picnic-sets on big front terrace and in extensive garden behind, cl winter Sun evenings *(David J Bunter, Len Banister, Piotr Chodzko-Zajko, Evelyn and Derek Walter, Reg Fowle, Helen Rickwood)*

MORETON TL5307

Nags Head [signed off B184, at S end of Fyfield or opp Chipping Ongar school]: Attractive array of salvaged rustic beams and timbers still showing their wedges and dowels, comfortable mix of tables, three big log fires, country knick-knacks, wide rather adventurous blackboard choice of good value food, friendly service, full Ridleys range kept well, restaurant; children welcome, picnic-sets on side grass *(H O Dickinson, Len Banister, Sean and Sharon Pines)*

White Hart [off B184, just N of A414]: Comfortable divided L-shaped lounge bar with log fire, soft lighting, nice prints and lots of woodwork, well kept Adnams, Greene King IPA and Youngs Special, decent house wines, generous if not cheap italian food all day, attractive small timbered dining room; picnic-sets on small back terrace and in informal garden with play area *(LYM, Len Banister, Sean and Sharon Pines)*

NAVESTOCK TQ5496

Alma Arms [Horsemanside, off B175]: Enjoyable generous sensibly priced food inc Sun lunch (no bookings) in bar or side conservatory, real ales inc a guest beer; loudspeaker food announcements when it's ready to collect *(Paul and Penny Rampton)*

NEWNEY GREEN TL6506

☆ *Duck* [off A1060 W of Chelmsford via Roxwell, or off A414 W of Writtle – take Cooksmill Green turn-off at Fox & Goose, then bear right]: Quiet welcoming dining pub with attractive rambling bar full of hop-hung beams, timbering, panelling and interesting bric-a-brac, comfortable furnishings, enjoyable food inc good value set lunches, well kept Shepherd Neame real ales, decent wines by the glass, attentive polite young staff; well laid tables out on attractive terrace *(LYM, Paul and Ursula Randall, John and Enid Morris, Reg Fowle, Helen Rickwood)*

NEWPORT TL5234

Coach & Horses [Cambridge Rd (B1383)]: Well kept and friendly, with big helpings of enjoyable good value food, well kept Adnams, Greene King and a guest beer; tables outside *(Stephen and Jean Curtis)*

NORTH END TL6617

☆ *Butchers Arms* [A130 SE of Dunmow]: Small attractively unpretentious 16th-c country pub with low beams, timbers, log fire and inglenook woodburner, particularly well kept Ridleys IPA, Rumpus and Old Bob, some emphasis on good value straightforward food (not Sun/Mon evenings), satisfying OAP lunches, prompt cheerful service, no smoking dining area, games room with pool; children welcome, sheltered garden and well equipped play area, open all day wknds *(Paul and Ursula Randall, Martin Grosberg, Tony Beaulah)*

NORTH WEALD TL4903

Kings Head [B181]: Rambling timber-framed 16th-c pub done up in the usual attractive Vintage Inns style, largely no smoking, with flagstones and low beams, lots of alcoves, old timber partitions, log fires in each main area, pews and other old furnishings, plenty of pictures, decent food from good value sandwiches up, friendly efficient service, wide choice of wines by the glass, refillable coffee, Bass and Tetleys; piped music; tables out in front planted area *(George Atkinson)*

OLD HARLOW TL4711

Marquis of Granby [Market St]: Comfortable and interesting two-level local with good choice of well kept changing ales from far and wide, friendly staff, usual food, old gas cigar lighter on bar; pool, piped music, TV; attractive old tiled building *(anon)*

ORSETT TQ6481

Foxhound [High Rd]: Proper local, long-serving chef doing enjoyable food inc great Sun lunch (she sticks to fresh veg and local produce inc rare breed meats) *(Tina and David Woods-Taylor)*

Whitmore Arms [Rectory Rd]: Friendly, cosy and comfortable village pub, enjoyable acceptably priced restaurant food; good family garden *(Mrs J R Sutcliffe)*

PELDON TM0015

☆ *Rose* [on B1025 Colchester—Mersea]: Low 17th-c beams and some venerable bar furnishings contrasting with spacious airy no smoking conservatory, lots of good wines by the glass, well kept Adnams Best and Broadside, Greene King IPA and a guest beer, enjoyable home-made bar food from sandwiches to local mersea fish, children's helpings, friendly staff; children very welcome away from bar (high chairs in restaurant), roomy well furnished garden with duck pond, open all day *(LYM, Ken Millar)*

RADWINTER TL6137

☆ *Plough* [Sampford Rd (B1053/54 crossroads E of Saffron Walden)]: Friendly new management and neat new no smoking dining room extension with enjoyable food inc game, fish and steaks, red plush open-plan black-timbered beamed bar, good service, well kept Greene King IPA and a changing guest beer; children welcome, very attractive terrace and garden, open countryside; comfortable bedrooms *(DC, BB, Adele Summers, Alan Black)*

RICKLING GREEN TL5129

☆ *Cricketers Arms* [just off B1383 N of Stansted Mountfichet]: Civilised and nicely laid out dining pub reopened 2004 after sensitive updating under welcoming new owners, beams and timbers, open fires, real ales and decent wines, restaurant with interesting modern british cooking; children welcome in eating areas, tables in sheltered front courtyard, nice position on village cricket green, elegant bedrooms, open all day *(LYM, Charles Gysin)*

RIDGEWELL TL7341

☆ *Kings Head* [A1017 Haverhill—Halstead]: Much modernised unpretentious pub leaning towards dining pub under friendly current tenants, enjoyable generously priced set menus, well kept Greene King IPA, decent wines, some signs of Tudor origins, interesting local USAF World War II memorabilia; may be subdued piped music, a few tables in roadside garden *(BB, Roy and Lindsey Fentiman)*

ROCHFORD TQ8790

Golden Lion [North St (one-way)]: Small white weatherboarded 17th-c pub specialising in well kept ales – Fullers London Pride, Greene King Abbot and five changing guest beers; dim lighting, hanging hops and pump clips, darts in one side room; can be smoky, TV, juke box, live music Fri; dogs welcome, small terrace, open all day *(Kevin Thorpe)*

ROXWELL TL6508

Hare [Bishops Stortford Rd (A1060)]: Comfortable beamed panelling-effect lounge with farm tools and rustic touches, popular food inc children's, neat attentive staff, several real ales, light and airy no smoking dining room; may be piped music; attractive garden with wendy house and climber *(George Atkinson)*

SAFFRON WALDEN TL5438

Eight Bells [Bridge St; B184 towards Cambridge]: Large pub with friendly young staff, Adnams and Greene King IPA, wide choice of enjoyable food inc cheap lunch deals and good home-made puddings, linked rooms inc snug with leather chairs and flame-effect fire in big fireplace, bare-boards room with darts, pool and machines, carpeted back restaurant in handsomely raftered and timbered medieval hall; children allowed, pleasant garden tables, handy for Audley End, good walks, open all day *(LYM, John Saville, Peter Hagler, Len Banister, David and Ruth Shillitoe, W W Burke)*

Saffron Hotel [High St]: Former coaching inn recently smartly refurbished with contrasting modern and traditional décor, well kept Greene King IPA and Abbot, good house wines, wide food choice from good baguettes up, proficient smiling service, two bars with snug alcoves, restaurant; terrace tables, bedrooms *(Michael Sargent)*

SIBLE HEDINGHAM TL7535

Bottle Hall [Delvin End]: Quietly placed country pub with enjoyable reasonably priced food esp steaks, warm welcome *(Ron Deighton)*

SOUTH HANNINGFIELD TQ7497

Old Windmill [off A130 S of Chelmsford]: Attractive 18th-c beamed and timbered building opp reservoir, divided alcoves off spacious L-shaped bar, good freshly cooked bar food, well kept ales such as Adnams, Marstons Pedigree and Theakstons Best, decent wines, also carvery with armchairs and settees in anteroom; piped music turned down on request; picnic-sets on grass behind and on terrace *(BB, Tony Brace)*

SOUTHEND TQ8885

Cork & Cheese [basement of Victoria Plaza, top of High St]: Purpose-built cave specialising in quickly changing real ales (five at a time) from small breweries, often unusual or new, with cheap Nethergate IPA as a regular; cheap lunchtime sandwiches or baguettes and all-day toasties, lots of breweriana on walls and ceiling; juke box, pool table; some tables outside, open all day, cl Sun *(Kevin Thorpe)*

STISTED TL7924

☆ *Dolphin* [A120 E of Braintree, by village turn]: Well kept Ridleys tapped from the cask in heavily beamed and timbered locals' bar on right, popular well priced straightforward food (not Tues or Sun evenings) inc steak bargains Sat evening, log fire, bright eating area on left (children allowed here); tables in pretty garden, nice hanging baskets *(Pete Baker, LYM, the Didler)*

STURMER TL6944

☆ *Red Lion* [A1017 SE of Haverhill]: Attractive and nicely smartened-up thatched and beamed pub with freshly cooked food inc light lunchtime dishes in bar, dining area, pleasant conservatory and small dining room (both no smoking), well kept real ales, good service, well spaced tables with solid cushioned chairs, big fireplace; level access, large appealing garden *(Adele Summers, Alan Black, BB)*

THAXTED TL6031

Swan [Bull Ring]: Attractively renovated Tudor pub opp lovely church and windmill, well kept Adnams and Greene King, plenty of well spaced tables (but they take your credit card when you order food), good choice of well presented food, good-sized helpings, light dishes all afternoon, welcoming staff, restaurant; piped music may obtrude; open all day, bedrooms with own bathrooms *(David J Bunter, Tim and Ann Newell)*

THORPE-LE-SOKEN TM1722

Rose & Crown [High St]: Welcoming mansard-roof pub with interesting reasonably priced home-made food, several wines by the glass, Greene King and Mauldons real ales *(Adrian White)*

TILLINGHAM TL9903

Cap & Feathers [South St (B1021)]: Low-beamed and timbered 15th-c pub, attractive old-fashioned furniture, well kept Crouch Vale Best, IPA, Best Dark and an interesting guest beer, decent food (some things may run out quite quickly), pleasant service, no smoking family room with pool and table skittles; picnic-sets on side terrace; three bedrooms *(LYM, Brenda and Rob Fincham)*

TOOT HILL TL5102

☆ *Green Man* [off A113 in Stanford Rivers, S of Ongar, or A414 W of Ongar]: Simply furnished country pub in appearance though aiming more at restaurant in style and price (meals rather than bar food), with a long plush dining room alongside the colourful front terrace; very good wine list, real ales such as Crouch Vale Best, Fullers London Pride, Nethergate and Ridleys PA; may be piped music, no under-10s, tables in back garden *(LYM, Philip and Elaine Holmes, David J Bunter, Len Banister, John and Enid Morris)*

WALTHAM ABBEY TQ4199

Woodbine [handy for M25 junction 26, via A121; Honey Lane]: Friendly open-plan local with well kept Courage Directors, Greene King IPA and Tetleys from central servery, reasonably priced usual food from sandwiches and baked potatoes up, several curries, old piano, plates on walls, large conservatory; piped music may obtrude; by Epping Forest, good walks from forest car park opp *(Ian Phillips)*

WEST BERGHOLT TL9528

White Hart [2 miles from Colchester on Sudbury rd]: Pleasant no smoking village pub, former old coaching inn, with well kept Adnams, good food inc plenty of fish, comfortable dining area; children welcome, big garden *(Colin and Dot Savill)*

WEST TILBURY TQ6677

Kings Head [The Green]: Comfortable and homely local, bench seating, pleasant staff and friendly landlord, good range of good value home-made food, nice wines; pleasant setting on small green *(Tina and David Woods-Taylor, Colin and Dot Savill)*

WRITTLE TL6706

Inn on the Green [The Green]: Spacious well worn in pub on large attractive green, buoyant atmosphere, half a dozen well kept ales, neat and friendly staff, enjoyable reasonably priced bar food, old advertisements, sepia photographs; end games area popular with young people *(Bruce M Drew, Mr and Mrs C F Turner, the Didler)*

Wheatsheaf [The Green]: Good pubby atmosphere in traditional 19th-c local, well kept Greene King, Mighty Oak and a guest beer, friendly knowledgeable landlord; open all day wknds *(the Didler)*

'Children welcome' means the pub says it lets children inside without any special restriction. If it allows them in, but to restricted areas such as an eating area or family room, we specify this. Places with separate restaurants often let children use them, hotels usually let them into public areas such as lounges. Some pubs impose an evening time limit – let us know if you find this.

Gloucestershire

This county has a lot of pubs that are really good well run all-rounders, and to add spice to the variety a few unspoilt traditional gems, and some seriously foody pubs bringing plenty of imagination to their cooking (this is one of Britain's best areas for good wine in pubs). Many of these places are in lovely countryside or villages. Pubs new to this edition, or back in the *Guide* after a few years' break, are the Green Dragon near Cowley (good all round, with an appealing layout), the friendly Plough at Ford (great atmosphere, and enjoyable food in nice surroundings), and the charming old Glasshouse Inn at Glasshouse. Other current favourites include the unspoilt Red Lion at Ampney St Peter, the Boat at Ashleworth Quay (another proudly unspoilt period piece), the welcoming Bear in Bisley (kind to families), the smart restauranty Village Pub at Barnsley, the Bakers Arms in Broad Campden (a chatty proper pub), the Eight Bells in Chipping Campden (upgraded bedrooms in this attractive all-rounder) and the Volunteer there (particularly for its good beers), the New Inn at Coln St Aldwyns (clever combination of good smart food and bedrooms with well kept beers and a friendly pubby feel), the Kings Arms at Didmarton (gaining a Place to Stay Award under its new landlady, with its imaginative food a big draw), the Five Mile House at Duntisbourne Abbots (this appealing unspoilt pub gains a Food Award this year for its landlord's honest cooking), the well run civilised Hunters Hall at Kingscote (licensed continuously for five centuries – and gains a Place to Stay Award this year), the Carpenters Arms at Miserden (a friendly proper pub with enjoyable food), the Weighbridge near Nailsworth (popular all round, but particularly for its 2-in-1 pies), the cosily traditional Ostrich at Newland (an unspoilt welcoming country inn of great age, good interesting food and a fine drinks choice), the Anchor in Oldbury-on-Severn (new licensees keeping a nice balance between village pub and dining place), the Churchill at Paxford (imaginative upmarket cooking in simple surroundings – and gains a Place to Stay Award this year), the thoroughly good Bell at Sapperton (super food, a welcome for all), the tucked-away Farriers Arms at Todenham (good food and drink in a good friendly atmosphere), and the remarkably friendly Horse & Groom at Upper Oddington. Plenty of these pubs offer that little bit extra that makes for a special meal out. The food in the Kings Arms at Didmarton has been giving a great many readers special pleasure, with approval often warmer than ever since a new landlady took over last autumn: it is Gloucestershire Dining Pub of the Year. In the Lucky Dip section at the end of the chapter, quite a few pubs look really promising, as main entry candidates. Ones to note particularly include the Sherborne Arms at Aldsworth, Black Horse at Amberley, Old Passage at Arlingham (restaurant rather than pub though), Fox at Broadwell, Hare & Hounds near Chedworth, Twelve Bells in Cirencester, Tunnel House at Coates, Plough at Cold Aston, Cross House at Doynton, Fox at Great Barrington, Fox at Lower Oddington, Kings Arms at Mickleton, Butchers Arms at Oakridge Lynch, Royal Oak at Prestbury, Boat at Redbrook, Swan at Southrop, Kings Arms and Queens Head in Stow-on-the-Wold, Crown at Tolldown, Ship at Upper Framilode and Bell at Willersey. Drinks prices here tend to be a trifle below the national average. Hook Norton, brewed over the border in Oxfordshire, is often the cheapest beer you'll find in pubs here. The local beers from Donnington, Uley, Wickwar, Freeminer and Goffs often show up as good value, too.

ALMONDSBURY ST6084 Map 2

Bowl

1¼ miles from M5, junction 16 (and therefore quite handy for M4, junction 20; from A38 towards Thornbury, turn first left signposted Lower Almondsbury, then first right down Sundays Hill, then at bottom right again into Church Road

A popular break from the M5, this bustling pub is prettily set with a church next door and lovely flowering tubs, hanging baskets, and window boxes. Well kept on handpump, they serve around half a dozen real ales such as Bass, Bath Barnstormer and Gem, Courage Best, Moles Best and Smiles May Fly; piped music and fruit machine. The long beamed bar is neatly kept, with terracotta plush-patterned modern settles, dark green cushioned stools and mate's chairs around elm tables, horsebrasses on stripped bare stone walls, and big winter log fire at one end, with a woodburning stove at the other. Besides filled baguettes (from £4.50, club sandwich £7.25), enjoyable bar food includes interesting salads such as chilli beef with water chestnuts and spring onion (from £4.50 for starter helpings, and from £8.50 for a main course), ploughman's (£4.95), battered haddock and chips or faggots and mash with onion gravy (£6.95), steak and kidney pie or crispy duck noodles (£9.95), and rib-eye steak (£12.95), with specials such as thai chicken curry (£8.95), and puddings such as apple and blackberry crumble (£3.95); half helpings of some main courses are available for children under 12. They ask to keep your credit card behind the bar. In good weather, the seats outside get snapped up quickly. *(Recommended by Rod Stoneman, Neil Rose, John and Enid Morris, Mr and Mrs J E C Tasker, Meg and Colin Hamilton, Liz and Alun Jones)*

Free house ~ Licensee Miss E Alley ~ Real ale ~ Bar food (12-2.30, 6-10; 12-8 Sun, not 25 Dec) ~ Restaurant ~ (01454) 612757 ~ Children in eating area of bar and restaurant ~ Dogs allowed in bar and bedrooms ~ Open 11.30-3, 5(6 Sat)-11; 12-10.30 Sun; closed 25 Dec ~ Bedrooms: £44.50S/£71S

AMPNEY ST PETER SP0801 Map 4

Red Lion

A417, E of village

'A gem' according to readers, this delightfully unspoilt little roadside pub is the kind of place where it's easy to fall into conversation with the charming long-standing landlord and friendly locals. A central corridor, served by a hatch, gives on to the little right-hand tile-floor public bar. Here, one long seat faces the small open fire, with just one table, and behind the long bench an open servery (no counter, just shelves of bottles and – by the corridor hatch – handpumps for the well kept Hook Norton Best and Timothy Taylors Landlord, and maybe a guest such as Flowers IPA); reasonably priced wine. There are old prints on the wall, and on the other side of the corridor is a small saloon, with panelled wall seats around its single table, old local photographs, another open fire, and a print of Queen Victoria one could believe hasn't moved for a century – rather like the pub itself. There are seats in the side garden. Please note the limited opening hours. *(Recommended by Dr and Mrs A K Clarke, R Huggins, D Irving, E McCall, T McLean, Giles and Annie Francis, the Didler, Phil and Sally Gorton, Paul and Ann Meyer, Jeff and Sue Evans, RWC)*

Free house ~ Licensee John Barnard ~ Real ale ~ No credit cards ~ (01285) 851596 ~ Children and dogs in the tiny games room ~ Open 6-10(10.30 Fri); 12-2.30, 6(7 Sun)-10.30 Sat; closed weekday lunchtimes

ASHLEWORTH SO8125 Map 4

Queens Arms 🍴 ☐ ◀

Village signposted off A417 at Hartpury

They do interesting South African dishes at this immaculately kept low-beamed country dining pub: alongside specials such as roast partridge wrapped in bacon with sage and port sauce on bubble and squeak (£13.50), and gressingham duck breast with a potato, carrot and garlic rösti and spicy plum and port sauce (£13.95), you might find frikkadels (meatballs) with tomato and sherry sauce (£7.95), and tomato bredie (lamb stew) with turmeric rice (£12.50). Other home-made dishes might be chicken livers piri-piri (£4.95), grilled salmon with hot black cherries (£9.95), and delicious steaks (from £11.50), with lunchtime specials such as filled baguettes (from £5.95), pork, apple and cider casserole (£7.50), and chicken satay kebabs with peanut sauce (£7.75). Softly lit by fringed wall lamps and candles at night, the comfortably laid out and civilised main bar has faintly patterned wallpaper and washed red ochre walls, big oak and mahogany tables and a nice mix of farmhouse and big brocaded dining chairs on a red carpet. Three real ales on handpump, from a rotating choice of 20, could include Brains Rev James, Donnington BB, and Marstons Pedigree, and their thoughtful wine list (with ten by the glass) includes quite a few South African choices; 22 malt whiskies too. Piped music, shove-ha'penny, cribbage, dominoes, and winter skittle alley; Bonnie, the little black pub cat, entertains customers with her ping-pong football antics. Two perfectly clipped mushroom shaped yews dominate the front of the building. There are cast-iron tables and chairs in the sunny courtyard, and they have plans to add more when they pave part of the front lawn, so as to be able to accommodate more walkers. The pub is completely no smoking. *(Recommended by Mrs J L Wyatt, Brian and Pat Wardrobe, Neil and Anita Christopher, David Carr, James Woods, Bernard Stradling, Mike and Wendy Proctor, Jane Bailey, Ian and Nita Cooper, Jim Abbott, Andrew Shore, Maria Williams, Carl and Jackie Cranmer, Bob and Margaret Holder, Dr G and Mrs J Kelvin, Jeffrey Barber, A G Simmonds, Mark and Sarah Baldwin, Craig Jones, Ken Marshall)*

Free house ~ Licensees Tony and Gill Burreddu ~ Real ale ~ Bar food (till 10 Fri/Sat) ~ Restaurant ~ (01452) 700395 ~ Well behaved children welcome ~ Open 12-3, 7-11(10.30 Sun); closed 25/26 Dec

ASHLEWORTH QUAY SO8125 Map 4

Boat ★

Ashleworth signposted off A417 N of Gloucester; quay signed from village

Set in an idyllic spot on the bank of the River Severn, this very friendly unspoilt pub has been run by the same family ever since it was originally licensed by Royal Charter in the 17th c – we believe this is a record for continuous pub ownership. The front suntrap crazy-paved courtyard is bright with plant tubs in summer, with a couple of picnic-sets under cocktail parasols; there are more seats and tables under cover at the sides. Inside, the little front parlour has a great built-in settle by a long scrubbed deal table that faces an old-fashioned open kitchen range with a side bread oven and a couple of elderly fireside chairs; there are rush mats on the scrubbed flagstones, houseplants in the window, fresh garden flowers, and old magazines to read. The pub is no smoking throughout; shove-ha'penny and dominoes, and darts in the front room. A pair of flower-cushioned antique settles face each other in the back room where around half a dozen swiftly changing beers from breweries such as Arkells, Bath, Hereford, RCH, Slaters and Wye Valley are tapped from the cask, along with a full range of Weston's farm ciders. During the week, they usually do good lunchtime rolls (from £1.50), and sometimes cake (75p). *(Recommended by Pete Baker, Theocsbrian, David Carr, Guy Vowles, the Didler, Peter Scillitoe, James Woods, Tom McLean, Jim Abbott, Giles and Annie Francis, Derek and Sylvia Stephenson, Joyce and Geoff Robson, Dr G and Mrs J Kelvin, Ted George, R Huggins, D Irving, E McCall, T McLean)*

Free house ~ Licensees Ron, Elisabeth and Louise Nicholls ~ Real ale ~ Bar food (lunchtime only; not Mon and Weds) ~ No credit cards ~ (01452) 700272 ~ Children in eating area of bar ~ Open 11-2.30(3 Sat), 6.30(7 winter)-11; 12-3, 7-11 Sun; closed Mon and Weds

AWRE SO7108 Map 4

Red Hart

Village signposted off A48 S of Newnham

As we went to press, this tall 15th-c pub had just gained new licensees, so it might be a good idea to check the opening times if you're coming from any distance. With lots of character, the neat L-shaped bar, the main part of which has a deep glass-covered illuminated well, has an antique pine bookcase filled with cookery and wine books, an antique pine display cabinet with Worcester china, pine tables and chairs. The bottom end of the bar has old prints of the village and surrounding area, and the restaurant has some exposed wattle and daub. Freshly cooked bar food (made with lots of local ingredients) includes lunchtime sandwiches (£3.75), and ploughman's (£5.25), with other dishes such as gloucester old spot sausages with mash and coarse grain mustard, scampi, lambs liver and bacon with onions and a rich wine gravy or wild and field mushrooms with shallots, brandy, paprika and sour cream (all £7.50), with monthly changing evening specials such as chargrilled tuna steak with lime and coriander sauce (£10.05), leg of lamb steak with honey and rosemary jus (£11.25), and half a roast duck with oriental-style spring onion and ginger (£14.25), and mouth-watering puddings such as lime cheesecake with a ginger biscuit base or summer fruit pudding (£3.85); they do a children's menu (£4.50). The eating part of the bar and restaurant are no smoking. Friendly staff serve well kept Fullers London Pride, and a couple of guests such as Goffs Jouster and Wickwar BOB on handpump, and there's a varied wine list. Out in front are some picnic-sets. The pub is nicely placed in an out-of-the-way little farming village between the River Severn and the Forest of Dean. *(Recommended by David Jeffreys, Theocsbrian, Brian McBurnie, Bob and Margaret Holder)*

Free house ~ Licensees Marcia Griffiths and Martin Coupe ~ Real ale ~ Bar food (12-2.30, 6.30-9) ~ Restaurant ~ (01594) 510220 ~ Well behaved children welcome until 8pm ~ Open 12-3, 6.30-11; 12-3, 7-10.30 Sun ~ Bedrooms: /£80B

BARNSLEY SP0705 Map 4

Village Pub (🍴) 🍷

B4425 Cirencester—Burford

They make their own bread at this smart and rather civilised dining pub – a great place to come if you're in need of a treat. The menu changes twice a day, and good (but not cheap) lunchtime dishes might include sandwiches (from £6), country terrine with home-made chutney (£6.95), fish and chips (£10.75), cold beef salad (£11), and smoked haddock with fresh lava bread, poached egg and bacon (£12), with evening dishes such as steamed mussels with white wine and herbs (£6.50), roast quail with grilled courgettes and aubergine (£7), chicken and chorizo stew (£12), and fried salmon with lemon and dill rice (£12.50); puddings might be coconut tart with strawberry sorbet or banana and golden syrup bread and butter pudding (£5). Calm and relaxing, the low-ceilinged communicating rooms (one is no smoking) have oil paintings, plush chairs, stools, and window settles around polished candlelit tables, and country magazines and newspapers to read. Well kept Hook Norton Bitter and Wadworths 6X with maybe a guest such as Archers Best on handpump, local cider and apple juice, and around 14 wines by the glass; service is swift and courteous. The sheltered back courtyard has plenty of good solid wooden furniture under umbrellas, outdoor heaters and its own outside servery. *(Recommended by Mrs E V McDonald, Maysie Thompson, Dr W I C Clark, Mrs Sally Lloyd, Lesley and Peter Barrett, Mr and Mrs B Golding, Alec and Barbara Jones, Bernard Stradling, John Kane, David Glynne-Jones, A P Seymour, Geoffrey and Penny Hughes, Adrian White)*

Free house ~ Licensees Tim Haigh and Rupert Pendered ~ Real ale ~ Bar food (12-3, 7-10) ~ Restaurant ~ (01285) 740421 ~ Children in eating area of bar and restaurant ~ Dogs welcome ~ Open 11-3, 6-11; 11-11 Sat; 12-10.30 Sun ~ Bedrooms: £65S/£80S(£105B)

BISLEY SO9006 Map 4

Bear

Village signposted off A419 just E of Stroud

Readers very much like the friendly atmosphere at this elegantly Gothic 16th-c inn, and whether you're a first time visitor or a local, you can expect a genuinely warm welcome. With a pleasantly relaxed pubby atmosphere, the meandering L-shaped bar has a long shiny black built-in settle and a smaller but even sturdier oak settle by the front entrance, and an enormously wide low stone fireplace (not very high – the ochre ceiling's too low for that); the separate no smoking stripped-stone area is used for families. Flowers IPA, Marstons Pedigree, Tetleys and Wells Bombardier are well kept on handpump; dominoes, cribbage, and table skittles. Besides nicely cooked daily specials such as cottage pie or beef and Guinness sausages on new potato crush with onion and red wine gravy (£9.95), beef casserole with red wine, shallots, bacon and mushrooms or braised lamb steak with cherry tomatoes, onions, garlic and rosemary (£10.95), enjoyable home-made bar food includes soup (£3.60), goats cheese toasties (£3.95), lots of interestingly filled baguettes (mostly £5.75), provençale vegetables (£6.50), and vegetable pasty or home-made rabbit or steak, kidney and Guinness pies (from £8). A small front colonnade supports the upper floor of the pub, and the sheltered little flagstoned courtyard made by this has a traditional bench. The garden is across the quiet road, and there's quite a collection of stone mounting-blocks. The steep stone-built village is attractive. *(Recommended by Bob and Margaret Holder, R Huggins, D Irving, E McCall, T McLean, P R and S A White, Gaynor Gregory, Dick and Mary Pownall, Guy Vowles, Simon Collett-Jones, Margaret Morgan, Di and Mike Gillam, Brian McBurnie, Nick and Meriel Cox, Tim Gee)*

Punch ~ Tenants Simon and Sue Evans ~ Real ale ~ Bar food (not Sun evening) ~ (01452) 770265 ~ Children in family room ~ Dogs welcome ~ Monthly Irish music, occasional folk music ~ Open 11.30-3, 6-11; 12-3, 7-10.30 Sun ~ Bedrooms: /£40

BLAISDON SO7017 Map 4

Red Hart

Village signposted off A4136 just SW of junction with A40 W of Gloucester; OS Sheet 162 map reference 703169

The flagstoned main bar of this welcoming pub, tucked away in the Forest of Dean, has cushioned wall and window seats, traditional pub tables, a big sailing-ship painting above the log fire, and a thoroughly relaxing atmosphere – helped along by well reproduced piped bluesy music, and maybe Spotty the perky jack russell. On the right, there's an attractive beamed two-room no smoking dining area with some interesting prints and bric-a-brac, and on the left, you'll find additional dining space for families. They serve five well kept real ales such as Hook Norton Best, Otter Head, Timothy Taylors Landlord, RCH Pitchfork and Uley Bitter on handpump, and there's a decent wine list; cribbage, dominoes, shove-ha'penny and table skittles. Enjoyable bar food includes home-made soup (£3.75), sandwiches (from £3.75), breaded plaice (£6.25), chicken curry (£6.50), and sirloin steak with bubble and squeak (£10.25), with specials such as crab tartlets (£5.25), moussaka (£7.95), poached salmon with spinach and white wine sauce (£10.50), and lamb fillet with red wine and rosemary sauce (£12.95); children's meals (£3.75). There are some picnic-sets in the garden and a children's play area, and at the back of the building is a large space for barbecues. More reports please. *(Recommended by Peter Scillitoe, Hugh and Erica Swallow, P and J Shapley, Neil and Jean Spink, S P Watkin, P A Taylor, Ian Phillips)*

Free house ~ Licensee Guy Wilkins ~ Real ale ~ Bar food ~ Restaurant ~ (01452) 830477 ~ Children in eating area of bar, restaurant and family room ~ Dogs allowed in bar ~ Open 11.30-3, 6ish-11; 12-3.30, 7-10.30 Sun

BLEDINGTON SP2422 Map 4

Kings Head 🍷 🍺 🛏

B4450

The main bar of this classic-looking Cotswold pub is full of ancient beams and other atmospheric furnishings (high-backed wooden settles, gateleg or pedestal tables), and there's a warming log fire in the stone inglenook with a big black kettle hanging in it. To the left of the bar a drinking space for locals (popular with a younger crowd in the evening) has benches on the wooden floor, a woodburning stove, and darts, cribbage, TV, and piped music; on Sunday lunchtimes it's used by families. The lounge looks on to the garden. Besides an excellent wine list, with eight by the glass (champagnes too), you'll find well kept Hook Norton Best, and a couple of guests from brewers such as Burton Bridge and Goff's on handpump, and they've also over 20 malt whiskies, organic cider and perry, and local apple juice; readers warn it can get smoky. Interesting and often of award standard (though not cheap), bar food might include lunchtime soup (£3.95), sandwiches (from £4.50, toasted panini £5.95), home-made duck spring rolls with sweet chilli sauce (£5.95), haddock, salmon and prawn pie with mash or spicy lamb burger with chips (£8.95), and marinated pork skewers with stir-fried vegetables and lime and mango salsa (£10.95), with evening dishes such as seared king scallops with herb gratin (£7.25), tagliatelle with wild mushrooms and crispy leeks (£9.25), fried lamb chump with champ potatoes and red wine jus (£12.95), and home-made puddings such as treacle tart or lemon posset (£3.95); they also do a selection of interesting cheeses (three for £6.50). The dining room is no smoking. Set in a peaceful village, the pub overlooks the village green where there might be ducks pottering about; there are seats in the back garden; aunt sally. *(Recommended by Steve Harvey, Maysie Thompson, Mr and Mrs John Taylor, John and Jackie Chalcraft, John Kane, P and J Shapley, C A Hall, Walter and Susan Rinaldi-Butcher, Sally Ramsay Patrick, Hugh Spottiswoode, Jane McKenzie, Matthew Shackle, Carolyn Price, Paul Hopton, Chloe Selicourt, Angus Lyon, Ian Phillips, Dick and Mary Pownall, Ann and Colin Hunt, Stephen Buckley, Paul and Penny Dawson, Brenda and Rob Fincham, Caroline Dunstall, Edmund Coan, Richard Greaves, Tom Ewing, David and Nina Pugsley, Tracey and Stephen Groves, Mrs Pamela Fisher, Clifford Blakemore, Don and Maureen Medley, Mr and Mrs Martin Joyce)*

Free house ~ Licensees Nicola and Archie Orr-Ewing ~ Real ale ~ Bar food ~ Restaurant ~ (01608) 658365 ~ Children in restaurant and family room ~ Dogs allowed in bar ~ Open 11(12 Sat)-3, 6-11; 12-3, 6.30-10.30 Sun; closed 25-26 Dec ~ Bedrooms: £50B/£95S(£70B)

BRIMPSFIELD SO9413 Map 4

Golden Heart 🍷

Nettleton Bottom (not shown on road maps, so we list the pub instead under the name of the nearby village); on A417 after the Brimpsfield turning, northbound

This bustling pub is 'a good place for a break after a long drive'. The main low-ceilinged bar is divided into three cosily distinct areas, with a roaring log fire in the huge stone inglenook fireplace in one, traditional built-in settles and other old-fashioned furnishings throughout, and quite a few brass items, typewriters, exposed stone, and wood panelling. A comfortable parlour on the right has another decorative fireplace, and leads into a further room that opens on to the terrace; two rooms are no smoking. A good selection of bar food includes popular vegetarian specials such as mushroom stroganoff or nut roast (£8.95), and stilton, leek and walnut pie (£9.25), with other choices such as chilli and lemon chicken fillets (£4.95), malaysian beef curry (£9.25), and wild boar with orange and nutmeg (£12.95), while the bar menu includes sandwiches (from

£3.95), ploughman's (from £5.95), omelettes (from £6.95), fish and chips (£7.50), and steaks (from £10.95), with puddings such as chocolate and praline truffle (£3.95); they have a children's menu (£3.95). As well as decent wines, friendly staff serve well kept Archers Golden Best and Timothy Taylors Landlord, with a couple of guests such as Bass and Wickwar Cotswold Way on handpump; there's an August bank holiday beer festival. From the rustic cask-supported tables on the suntrap terrace, there are pleasant views down over a valley; nearby walks. If you are thinking of staying here, bear in mind that the nearby road is a busy all-night link between the M4 and M5. *(Recommended by Angus and Rosemary Campbell, Neil and Anita Christopher, R Huggins, D Irving, E McCall, T McLean, John Wheeler, Giles and Annie Francis, W W Burke, Malcolm Taylor, Simon J Barber, Guy Vowles, Mark and Ruth Brock, Ian Phillips, A P Seymour, Tony Pope, Karen Bonham, Mike and Mary Carter, R B Gardiner)*

Free house ~ Licensee Catherine Stevens ~ Real ale ~ Bar food (12-3, 6-10; 12-10 Sun) ~ (01242) 870261 ~ Children in family room ~ Dogs welcome ~ Open 11-3, 5.30-11; 11-11 Fri and Sat; 12-10.30 Sun ~ Bedrooms: £35S/£55S

BROAD CAMPDEN SP1637 Map 4

Bakers Arms

Village signposted from B4081 in Chipping Campden

Undisturbed by noisy games machines or piped music, the atmosphere at this traditional village pub is enjoyably chatty and relaxed, and you'll find a good mix of customers. The part with the most character is the tiny beamed bar with its mix of tables and seats around the walls (which are stripped back to bare stone), and inglenook fireplace at one end; there's a big framed rugwork picture of the pub. From the attractive oak bar counter you can get five well kept ales such as Donningtons BB, Hook Norton Best, Stanway Stanney Bitter, Timothy Taylors Landlord and Wells Bombardier on handpump; darts, cribbage, dominoes. Besides tasty lunchtime bar food such as sandwiches (from £3.25, baguettes from £3.95), ploughman's (£4.75), and filled yorkshire puddings (£4.95), reasonably priced dishes include smoked haddock bake or thai red vegetable curry (£6.25), and moussaka or steak and kidney suet pudding (£6.50), and daily specials such as pork and apricot or coq au vin (£6.75); the no smoking dining room has beams and exposed stone walls. A terraced area has seats by the play area behind, and there are more seats under parasols by flower tubs on other terraces and in the back garden. Broad Campden is a peaceful village. *(Recommended by Maurice Ribbans, Brian and Anna Marsden, P R and S A White, Ann and Colin Hunt, Peter and Anne Hollindale, Tracey and Stephen Groves, Di and Mike Gillam, H O Dickinson)*

Free house ~ Licensees Ray and Sally Mayo ~ Real ale ~ Bar food (12-9 in summer; 12-2(2.30 Sat-Sun), 6-9(8.30 Sun) in winter;) ~ No credit cards ~ (01386) 840515 ~ Children in eating area of bar and restaurant ~ Folk music third Tues evening of month ~ Open 11.30-11; 12-10.30 Sun; 11.30-2.30, 4.45-11 weekdays in winter; closed 25 Dec, evenings 26, 31 Dec

CHEDWORTH SP0511 Map 4

Seven Tuns

Village signposted off A429 NE of Cirencester; then take second signposted right turn and bear left towards church

This cosy little 17th-c pub is a pleasant place to drop into for a drink after a visit to the famous Roman villa nearby. A good winter log fire in the big stone fireplace warms the snug little lounge on the right, which has comfortable seats and decent tables, sizeable antique prints, tankards hanging from the beam over the serving bar, and a partly boarded ceiling. Down a couple of steps, the public bar on the left has an open fire, and this opens into a no smoking dining room with another open fire; as we went to press the upstairs skittle alley was about to be renovated and gain its own bar. Well kept Youngs Bitter and Waggle Dance, and a guest on handpump, and lots of malt whiskies; darts, cribbage, shove-ha'penny, dominoes, and piped music. There's a short choice of tasty bar food such as lunchtime sandwiches or baguettes (from £4.75), and ploughman's (£6.75), soup (£4.25), ham and eggs (£7.25), sausage and mash (£8.95), fish and chips (£9.95), seafood stir fry with prawns and monkfish (£12.95), and steaks (from £12.95), with puddings such as bread and butter pudding (£4.50); service can be slow at times. Across the road is a little walled raised terrace with a waterwheel and a stream, and there are plenty of tables both here and under cocktail parasols on a side terrace. There are nice walks through the valley. *(Recommended by Derek Carless, R Huggins, D Irving, E McCall, T McLean, Anne Morris, Neil and Anita Christopher, Tim and Carolyn Lowes, Guy Vowles, Di and Mike Gillam, M Thomas, Dennis and Gill Keen, Joyce and Geoff Robson, Richard Greaves, Nick and Meriel Cox)*

Youngs ~ Tenant Mr Davenport-Jones ~ Real ale ~ Bar food ~ (01285) 720242 ~ Children in eating area of bar and restaurant ~ Dogs welcome ~ Open 11-11; 12-10.30 Sun; 11-3, 6-11 in winter

CHIPPING CAMPDEN SP1539 Map 4

Eight Bells

Church Street (which is one way – entrance off B4035)

Doing very well at the moment, this fine old pub has large terraced garden with plenty of seats, and striking views of the almshouses and church. Inside are heavy oak beams with massive timber supports, stripped stone walls, cushioned pews and solid dark wood furniture on the broad flagstones, daily papers to read, and log fires in up to three restored stone fireplaces. Part of the floor in the no smoking dining room has a glass inset showing part of the passage from the church by which Roman Catholic priests could escape from the Roundheads. Very good food might include home-made soup (£4.25), aubergine, wild mushroom and chorizo tart with gruyere cheese (£5.50), crispy duck pancake with apple, honey and ginger chutney (£6.25), vegetable moussaka with smoked cheese sauce and grilled parmesan (£9.50), pork medallions with fondant potato and creamed cabbage and bacon (£11.75), fried bass with mediterranean vegetables, new potatoes and basil pesto (£14.25), and home-made puddings such as maple syrup sponge with custard or chocolate profiteroles with hot fudge sauce (£4.50); they also do lunchtime (not Sunday) ciabatta (from £5.25). Alongside a guest such as Marstons Pedigree, they serve Hook Norton Best and Old Hooky on handpump from the fine oak bar counter; country wines, and decent coffee. Piped music, darts, cribbage and dominoes. Handy for the Cotswold Way walk to Bath, the pub is popular with walkers. They've recently refurbished the bedrooms. *(Recommended by P R and S A White, Grahame Brooks, Mrs N W Neill, Lynda Payton, Sam Samuells, Ted George, Gillian and Les Gray, Ian Phillips, Peter Burton, Ann and Colin Hunt, Chris Smith, W W Burke, Gerry and Rosemary Dobson, Dr David Cockburn, Peter J and Avril Hanson, Peter and Anne Hollindale, Dr G and Mrs J Kelvin, Mrs C Lintott, M Joyner, Peter Coxon, Stephen Buckley, David J Austin, Simon Collett-Jones)*

Free house ~ Licensee Neil Hargreaves ~ Real ale ~ Bar food (12-2(2.30 Fri/Sat), 6.30-9.30; 12.30-3 Sun, 7-9) ~ Restaurant ~ (01386) 840371 ~ Children in restaurant and family room ~ Dogs allowed in bar ~ Open 12-3, 5.30-11; 11-11 Sat; 12-10.30 Sun; closed 25 Dec ~ Bedrooms: £50B/£85.95B

Volunteer

Lower High Street

The friendly barman at this popular local is happy to let you have a taste before you decide which of the half a dozen well kept real ales you want to choose. Besides Hook Norton Best, North Cotswold Brewery Genesis and Stanway Stanney Bitter on handpump, the three guests might include Archers Spring Blond, Wickwar Cotswold Way and Wood Shropshire Lad; they also do quite a few malt whiskies. The little bar by the street has cushioned seats in bay

windows, a good log fire piled with big logs in the golden stone fireplace with hops, helmets and horse bits above it, proper old dining chairs with sage green plush seats and some similarly covered stools around a mix of tables, old army (Waterloo and WWI) paintings and bugles on the walls, with old local photographs on the gantry, and quite a few brass spigots dotted about. The public bar (which is popular with a younger crowd) has modern upholstered wing settles, juke box, darts, pool, fruit machine, shove-ha'penny, cribbage, dominoes. Outside, there are picnic-sets in a small brick-paved ivy courtyard with an arch through to the back garden where there are more seats. Welcoming staff serve hearty, well priced bar food such as soup (£2.95), goats cheese baked on puff pastry with bacon (£4.95), home-roasted honey glazed ham with egg and chips or battered cod (£6.50), steak and kidney pie (£6.95), calves liver and bacon with balsamic gravy (£7.95), chicken breast flamed with calvados and finished with cream and almonds (£8.75), and 10oz rib-eye pepper steak (£10.75); they do Sunday roasts (£6.95). The pub is named after the men who signed up for the Volunteer Army. Readers tell us the bedrooms are spacious but basic.
(Recommended by Lawrence Pearse, Guy Vowles, Ted George, Bruce M Drew, Paul and Margaret Baker, Tracey and Stephen Groves, Dr G and Mrs J Kelvin, Peter Coxon, Tony and Betty Parker, Margaret Dickinson, Simon Collett-Jones)

Free house ~ Licensee Hilary Mary Sinclair ~ Real ale ~ Bar food (not 25 Dec) ~ (01386) 840688 ~ Children welcome ~ Dogs allowed in bar ~ Open 11.30-3, 5(6 Sat)-11; 12-3, 7-10.30 Sun ~ Bedrooms: £35B/£60B

COLN ST ALDWYNS SP1405 Map 4

New Inn

On good back road between Bibury and Fairford

A meal at this smart inn, set in a peaceful Cotswold village, is a fine reward after a pleasant riverside walk to Bibury. Spotlessly kept, the two main rooms are attractively furnished and decorated, and divided by a central log fire in a neat stone fireplace with wooden mantelbeam and willow-pattern plates on the chimneybreast; there are also low beams, some stripped stonework around the bar servery with hops above it, oriental rugs on the red tiles, and a mix of seating from library chairs to stripped pews. Down a slight slope, a further room has a coal fire in an old kitchen range at one end, and a white pheasant on the wall. Skilfully cooked (though not cheap), well presented dishes might include vine tomato and buffalo mozzarella salad with basil pesto (£5.25), mushroom gougere or chicken liver pâté with bacon and apricot chutney and melba toast (£5.95), ploughman's or tomato and mushroom risotto (£8.95), thai chicken (£9.50), bass with mediterranean vegetables, citrus cream and broccoli (£10.50), crab salad or lamb shank with tomatoes and new crushed potatoes (£11.50), and steak with green peppercorn sauce (£14.50), with puddings such as steamed chocolate and orange pudding with chocolate sauce (£4.75); they also do lunchtime sandwiches. The restaurant is no smoking. Well kept real ales such as Archers Village, Hook Norton Best and Wadworths 6X on handpump, and they've eight good wines by the glass, and several malt whiskies. The split-level terrace has plenty of seats, and you can get popular day tickets for fly fishing on the river in the water meadows.
(Recommended by Peter and Giff Bennett, George and Gill Peckham, David Rule, James Morrell, Claire George)

Free house ~ Licensee Angela Kimmett ~ Real ale ~ Bar food ~ Restaurant ~ (01285) 750651 ~ Children in eating area of bar; must be over 10 in restaurant ~ Dogs allowed in bar and bedrooms ~ Open 11-11; 12-10.30 Sun ~ Bedrooms: £90S/£120B

Please tell us if any Lucky Dips deserve to be upgraded to a main entry – and why. No stamp needed: *The Good Pub Guide*, FREEPOST TN1569, Wadhurst, E Sussex TN5 7BR.

COWLEY SO9714 Map 4

Green Dragon

Off A435 S of Cheltenham at Elkstone, Cockleford signpost; OS Sheet 163 map reference 970142

Gathering much support from readers in recent months, this attractive stone-fronted dining pub was a cider house when it first opened in 1643. Cosy and genuinely old-fashioned, the two bars have big flagstones and wooden boards, beams, two stone fireplaces (welcoming fires in winter), candlelit tables, and a woodburning stove. The furniture and the bar itself in the upper Mouse Bar were made by Robert Thompson, and little mice run over the hand-carved chairs, tables and mantelpiece; the larger Lower Bar is no smoking. The food here is good, and well presented dishes (which you can eat anywhere) could include lunchtime sandwiches (from £5, not Sunday), wilted spinach with onion welsh rarebit (£4.75), breaded lemon sole goujons with hollandaise sauce or penne pasta with chorizo, cherry tomatoes, roast peppers and cream (£5, large £10), spinach and ricotta tortellini in parmesan cream or fried black pudding with pork loin chop and sage butter (£11), calves liver or whole baked sea bream with tarragon, garlic and lemon (£13), and 10oz rib-eye steak with watercress and blue cheese butter (£13.50), with puddings such as lemon and almond pudding with raspberries or baked egg custard (£4); they also do children's meals (£3.50). The upstairs restaurant is no smoking. Good service from the friendly and helpful young staff, and a buoyant bustling atmosphere. Well kept real ales include Butcombe Bitter, Courage Directors, Hook Norton Best and a guest on handpump; piped music. Terraces outside overlooking Cowley Lake and the River Churn, and the pub is a good centre for the local walks. *(Recommended by R Huggins, D Irving, E McCall, T McLean, Guy Vowles, Bob Moffatt, Jo Rees, C Howard, Tony Pope, Karen Bonham)*

Buccaneer Holdings ~ Manager Mhari Ashworth ~ Real ale ~ Bar food (12-2.30, 6-10; 12-9.30 Sat-Sun) ~ Restaurant ~ (01242) 870271 ~ Children welcome ~ Dogs welcome ~ Open 11(12 Sun)-11 ~ Bedrooms: /£65S(£65B)

DIDMARTON ST8187 Map 2

Kings Arms

A433 Tetbury road

Gloucestershire Dining Pub of the Year

Great for a meal or just a drink, this 17th-c coaching inn has been attractively restored and decorated. Well prepared dishes (which you can eat in the bar or the no smoking restaurant) could include venison and madeira terrine with brioche toast and apple, cinnamon and sage chutney (£4.95, £8.50 large), roast shallot and tapenade tart with brie and a balsamic reduction (£9.95), lamb shank braised in moroccan spices with lemon and thyme mash (£11.95), steamed brill with mussels and prawns topped with basil and ricotta aïoli and lemon oil (£13.95), and 10oz rump steak (£17.95), with puddings such as blood orange cheesecake with curd or rich chocolate and pistachio torte with chocolate syrup (£5.10); they also do lunchtime snacks such as sandwiches (from £4.95), ploughman's (£5.95), and beer-battered haddock (£8.95). Very neatly kept, the knocked-through rooms work their way around a big central counter: deep terracotta walls above a dark green dado, a pleasant mix of chairs on bare boards, quarry tiles and carpet, hops on beams, and a big stone fireplace. Friendly staff serve well kept Uley Bitter and Wickwar Cotswold Way, along with a couple of guests such as Bath Spa Barnstormer and Butcombe Blond on handpump, and there's a good wine list with around a dozen by the small or large glass, and several malt whiskies; darts, cribbage and TV. There are seats out in the pleasant back garden, and they have self-catering cottages in a converted barn and stable block. *(Recommended by Guy Vowles, Martin Jennings, S H Godsell, Jenny and Brian Seller, Mike Pugh, Colin McKerrow, Paul Hopton, John and Gloria Isaacs, Gaynor Gregory, Mike and Mary Carter, Di and Mike Gillam, Bernard Stradling, Ian and Nita Cooper, Richard Stancomb, Simon Collett-Jones, Tom Evans, Hugh Roberts,*

Alec and Barbara Jones, Tom and Ruth Rees, Donald Godden, M G Hart, Mr and Mrs W D Borthwick, Stephen Woad, Matthew Shackle)

Free house ~ Licensee Zoe Coombs ~ Real ale ~ Bar food ~ Restaurant ~ (01454) 238245 ~ Children in eating area of bar ~ Dogs allowed in bar ~ Open 11-11 ~ Bedrooms: £45S/£70S(£80B)

DUNTISBOURNE ABBOTS SO9709 Map 4

Five Mile House

Off A417 at Duntisbourne Abbots exit sign; then, coming from Gloucester, pass filling station and keep on parallel to main road; coming from Cirencester, pass under main road then turn right at T junction

An enjoyable all-rounder, this welcoming 300-year-old coaching inn is a great place to bring visitors. The front room has a companionable bare-boards drinking bar on the right, with wall seats around the big table in its bow window and just one other table. On the left is a flagstoned hallway taproom snug formed from two ancient high-backed settles by a woodburning stove in a tall carefully exposed old fireplace; newspapers to read. There's a small cellar bar, a back restaurant down steps, and a family room on the far side; cribbage, dominoes and darts. The lounge and cellar bar are no smoking. The food here is proper pubby stuff, but the way the landlord cooks it wins such acclaim from readers that this year he gains a food award. The menu includes lunchtime open sandwiches (from £4.50), ploughman's (from £5.50), baked potatoes (from £4.50), gammon steak with egg and pineapple or scampi (£7.95), local trout with prawn and lemon butter (£8.95), and evening dishes such as home-made soup (£3.25), deep-fried butterfly prawns with garlic mayonnaise (£4.50), shoulder of lamb stuffed with redcurrant and mint or chicken breast stuffed with stilton and wrapped in bacon with mushroom and brandy cream sauce (£9.95), and steaks (£11.75), with daily specials such as home-made faggots with herby mash and onion gravy (£8.95), and pork loin with plum and orange glaze (£9.50), and puddings such as treacle tart or fruit crumble (£3.95); it's a good idea to book on weekends and in the evenings. Friendly staff serve well kept Donningtons BB, Timothy Taylors Landlord and Youngs Bitter with a local guest such as Wye Valley Butty Bach on handpump (the cellar is temperature-controlled), and they've got interesting wines (strong on New World ones). The gardens have nice country views; the country lane was once Ermine Street, the main Roman road from Wales to London.

(Recommended by John Holroyd, R Huggins, D Irving, E McCall, T McLean, Peter Scillitoe, the Didler, Dennis Jenkin, Debbie and Neil Hayter, Guy Vowles, Giles and Annie Francis, P R and S A White, Ann and Colin Hunt, Graham and Helen Eastwood, Jo Rees, Evelyn and Derek Walter, Kevin Thorpe, Nick and Meriel Cox)

Free house ~ Licensees Jo and Jon Carrier ~ Real ale ~ Bar food (12-2.30, 6-9.30; 12-2.30, 7-9 Sun) ~ Restaurant ~ (01285) 821432 ~ Children welcome if well behaved ~ Dogs allowed in bar ~ Open 12-3, 6-11; 12-3, 7-10.30 Sun

DURSLEY ST7598 Map 2

Old Spot £

By bus station

Up to eight well kept real ales on handpump and a cheerful buzzing atmosphere make this unassuming town pub worth popping into. Alongside Uley Old Ric, a typical choice of beers might include Badger Tanglefoot, Butcombe Bitter, Otter Bitter, Ringwood Old Thumper, Sharp's Doom Bar and Wadworths Henry's Original; there are several malt whiskies too; they hold four beer festivals a year. The front door opens into a deep pink little room with stools on shiny quarry tiles along its pine boarded bar counter, and old enamel beer advertisements on the walls and ceiling; there's a profusion of porcine paraphernalia. A little room on the left leading off from here has a bar billiards table, shove-ha'penny, cribbage and dominoes, and the little dark wood floored room to the right has a stone fireplace. From here a step takes you down to a cosy Victorian tiled snug and (to the right) the no smoking meeting room. Served only at lunchtime, bar food might include home-made soup (£2.75), egg and tuna salad (£3.25), fajitas (£3.75), cauliflower cheese (£4.25), cottage pie (£4.75), sausages with leek mash and onion gravy (£5.50), and they also do sandwiches. More reports please. *(Recommended by Hugh Roberts, P R and S A White, S Fysh, R Huggins, D Irving, E McCall, T McLean)*

Free house ~ Licensee Steve Herbert ~ Real ale ~ Bar food (lunchtime only) ~ (01453) 542870 ~ Dogs welcome ~ Folk and jazz Weds evenings ~ Open 11-3, 5-11; 11-11 Fri-Sat; 12-10.30 Sun

EASTLEACH TURVILLE SP1905 Map 4

Victoria 🍷

Village signposted off A361 S of Burford

Picnic-sets out in front of this thriving low-ceilinged old pub, set at the top of a delightful streamside village, look down over a steep bank of daffodils at the other stone-built houses and a couple of churches. Although it's open-plan inside, it's nicely divided, and rambles cosily around a central bar, with sturdy pub tables of varying sizes, and some attractive seats – particularly those built in beside the log fire in the stripped stone chimneybreast. There are some unusual engravings and lithographs of Queen Victoria around the back. Arkells 2B and a guest such as 3B are well kept on handpump, and they've six or seven nice New World wines by the large glass, and good cafetière coffee; may be unobtrusive piped music. The right-hand area has more of a public bar feel, with darts, shove-ha'penny, cribbage and dominoes. Nicely cooked bar food includes filled baguettes (from £4.25), moules marinière (£4.55), warm smoked chicken, bacon and brie salad (£6.95), gammon and mozzarella (£7.25), steak and mushroom pie (£7.75), delicious calves liver and bacon with red wine sauce (£9.25), organic pork chop with apple and calvados sauce (£9.25), and bass fillet with prawn and lobster sauce (£12.50), with home-made puddings such as white chocolate and Baileys mousse (£3.75); part of the restaurant is no smoking. The staff are friendly and efficient, even on warm days when it does get busy. There are also seats at the back behind the car park. *(Recommended by Peter and Audrey Dowsett, R M Corlett, M Thomas, D Reay, P R and S A White, R Huggins, D Irving, E McCall, T McLean, Richard Greaves, Dr A Y Drummond)*

Arkells ~ Tenants Stephen and Susan Richardson ~ Real ale ~ Bar food ~ Restaurant ~ (01367) 850277 ~ Children in restaurant ~ Dogs allowed in bar ~ Open 12-3(4 Sat), 7-11; 12-4, 7-10.30 Sun; closed evening 25 Dec

EWEN SU0097 Map 4

Wild Duck 🍷

Village signposted from A429 S of Cirencester

They serve more than 25 wines by the glass at this civilised 16th-c inn, which is quietly placed on the edge of a peaceful village. The high-beamed main bar has a nice mix of comfortable armchairs and other seats, paintings on the red walls, crimson drapes, a winter open fire, candles on tables, and magazines to read; overlooking the garden, the residents' lounge has a handsome Elizabethan fireplace and antique furnishings. Besides Duckpond Bitter (brewed especially for the pub), you'll find well kept real ales such as Charles Wells Bombardier, Greene King Old Speckled Hen, Sharps Doom Bar, and Theakstons Best and Old Peculier, and several malt whiskies; piped music (which can be obtrusive). Good, though not cheap, dishes from a changing menu might include soup (£3.50), chicken liver and wild mushroom parfait (£6.50), home-smoked duck breast with rocket salad and honey, mustard and dill dressing (£7.50), roast rack of pork on leek, bacon and cheese mash with a wild boar sausage and grain mustard and red wine sauce (£12.95), seared tuna steak on sweet potato mash with roast cherry tomato and rosemary sauce (£12.95), and peppered fillet steak on sweet onion marmalade with sautéed potatoes and madeira and peppercorn sauce (£17.95), with a tempting choice of puddings such as warm apple and sultana cake with vanilla sauce and chocolate ice-cream or dark chocolate and whiskey tart with coffee sauce and pistachio ice-cream (from £4.50). The service, though normally good, could perhaps sometimes do with more supervision. Pleasant in summer, the neatly kept and sheltered garden has wooden tables and seats. Beware, unless you pay in advance for your bar food, or have booked, you will be asked to leave your credit card with them. *(Recommended by M Sambidge, Roger and Jenny Huggins, Pat and Tony Martin, Graham Holden, Julie Lee, Mr and Mrs G S Ayrton, Matthew Shackle, KC, Maysie Thompson, Peter B Brown, Nick and Alison Dowson, Dr and Mrs A K Clarke, R Huggins, D Irving, E McCall, T McLean, Inga and Keith Rutter, Simon and Amanda Southwell, Gary and Jane Gleghorn)*

Free house ~ Licensees Tina and Dino Mussell ~ Real ale ~ Bar food (12-2, 6.45-10; 12-2.30, 7-9.30 Sun) ~ Restaurant ~ (01285) 770310 ~ Children in eating area of bar and restaurant ~ Dogs allowed in bar and bedrooms ~ Open 11-11; 12-10.30 Sun ~ Bedrooms: £60B/£80B

FORD SP0829 Map 4

Plough

B4077 Stow—Alderton

Opposite a well known racehorse trainer's yard, this pretty pub used to be the local courthouse, and what is now the cellar was the gaol. The beamed and stripped-stone bar has racing prints and photos on the walls, and a friendly bustling atmosphere; also, old settles and benches around the big tables on its uneven flagstones, oak tables in a snug alcove, four welcoming log fires (two are log-effect gas), and dominoes, cribbage, shove-ha'penny, darts, fruit machine, TV (for the races), and piped music. Delicious, well presented bar food includes lunchtime filled baguettes (from £4.95), baked ham and free-range eggs or liver and smoky bacon with onion gravy (£7.95), and evening dishes such as fresh halibut with shrimp and lemon butter (£10.95), half a shoulder of lamb with mint and rosemary jus or half a crispy duck with orange and Cointreau sauce (£12.95), and aberdeen angus steak with bacon and chive mash (£13.95). They offer breakfasts for travellers on the way to the Gold Cup meeting at Cheltenham, and have traditional asparagus feasts every April to June. Well kept Donnington BB and SBA on handpump, and Addlestone's cider; good efficient service. There are benches in the garden, pretty hanging baskets, and a play area at the back. The Cotswold Farm Park is nearby. *(Recommended by Neil and Anita Christopher, the Didler, Lucien Perring, Peter and Audrey Dowsett, John and Gloria Isaacs, Denys Gueroult, Paul and Annette Hallett, Roger Braithwaite, Patrick Hancock, Tracey and Stephen Groves, Geoff Pidoux, Stephen Woad, J C Brittain-Long, Val and Brian Garrod, David J Austin)*

Donnington ~ Tenant Craig Brown ~ Real ale ~ Bar food (all day wknds) ~ (01386) 584215 ~ Children in restaurant ~ Dogs allowed in bar ~ Open 11-11; 12-10.30 Sun ~ Bedrooms: £35S/£60S

FRAMPTON MANSELL SO9201 Map 4

White Horse 🍷

A491 Cirencester—Stroud

In fine weather, they plan to hold Saturday lunchtime barbecues at this smart, welcoming dining pub, and on Sunday lunchtime they do a good roast (£10.25). Alongside the pine tables, rush matting and up-to-date décor of the main part, there's a cosy bar area with a large sofa and comfortable chairs for those who want a relaxing drink. Well kept Uley Bitter and a guest such as Arkells Summer Ale or Hook Norton Best on handpump, eight wines by the glass from a well chosen wine list, and quite a few malt whiskies; they also do good tea and coffee. A typical choice of modern british dishes (made with high quality ingredients) includes lunchtime snacks such as filled baguettes (£4.95), excellent home-glazed ham, egg and chips (£7.95), beef and coriander burger with bacon and smoked

cheddar or fish pie with mashed potatoes, hard-boiled eggs and peas (£8.95), while other choices could be soup (£3.50), buffalo mozzarella with red peppers, griddled aubergine, sun-dried tomatoes and basil pesto or creamed spinach with bacon lardons, poached duck egg and parmesan shavings (£5.75), toulouse sausages with mashed potato and onion gravy (£10.95), slow-braised belly pork with celeriac mash and soy, balsamic and ginger jus (£11), several fish dishes, and puddings such as sticky toffee pudding with butterscotch sauce (£4.50). Some of the more extreme taste combinations may not always give as much pleasure as the simpler dishes (and one or two readers have been given hot food on cold plates), but when the cooking here hits the mark – as it usually does – it's very good indeed. The landscaped garden is a pleasant place for a meal or a drink.
(Recommended by Dr and Mrs C W Thomas, Tom and Ruth Rees, Mr and Mrs R Drury, Paul Hopton, Mr and Mrs G S Ayrton, John Kane, Evelyn and Derek Walter, Rod Stoneman, Anne Colley, Inga and Keith Rutter, John and Gloria Isaacs, Paul and Penny Dawson, Dr J J H Gilkes, Tim Gee)

Free house ~ Licensees Shaun and Emma Davis ~ Real ale ~ Bar food (not Sun evening) ~ Restaurant ~ (01285) 760960 ~ Children welcome ~ Dogs welcome ~ Open 11-3, 6-11; 12-4 Sun; closed Sun evening

GLASSHOUSE SO7121 Map 4

Glasshouse Inn

First right turn off A40 going W from junction with A4136; OS Sheet 162 map reference 710213

This carefully extended ancient country tavern is just the place to head to for a relaxed pint before a walk in nearby Newent Woods and up May Hill. You'll find a homely mixture of kitchen chairs, settles and old bench and plain wooden tables on the red quarry tiles and flagstones, warmed by open fires in a cavernous black hearth and a smaller cottagey Victorian fireplace; decorative plates, fish-poaching warnings, hunting and fishing prints, rugby and other memorabilia, and old advertisements cover the walls. Friendly staff serve very well kept Bass and Butcombe alongside a guest such as Archers Village tapped straight from the cask. The relaxed atmosphere is helped along by the absence of games machines and piped music; no children inside. Besides generous sandwiches (from £3, readers recommend the cold beef), hearty bar food might include ploughman's or basket meals such as half a chicken and chips (from £4.50), cauliflower cheese and bacon (£6.95), mushroom stroganoff or lasagne (£7.50), steak and kidney with Guinness and yorkshire pudding or fish pie (£8.50), and steaks (from £11); they don't take bookings. There are seats outside on a tidy fenced lawn with interesting topiary including a yew tree seat; lovely hanging baskets in summer.
(Recommended by Neil and Jean Spink, the Didler, Mike and Mary Carter, TB, Guy Vowles, Phil and Sally Gorton, Dr A Y Drummond)

Free house ~ Licensee Steve Pugh ~ Real ale ~ Bar food (not Sun) ~ (01452) 830529 ~ Open 11.30-11; 12.30-3, 7-10.30 Sun; 11.30-3, 6.30-11 Mon-Sat in winter; closed Sun evening Jan-Mar

GUITING POWER SP0924 Map 4

Hollow Bottom

Village signposted off B4068 SW of Stow-on-the-Wold (still called A436 on many maps)

The comfortable beamed bar of this friendly and relaxed 17th-c inn has lots of racing memorabilia including racing silks, tunics and photographs (it's owned by a small syndicate that includes Peter Scudamore and Nigel Twiston-Davies). There's a winter log fire in an unusual pillar-supported stone fireplace, and the public bar has flagstones and stripped stone masonry and racing on TV; newspapers to read, darts, cribbage, dominoes, Spoof, and piped music. Fullers London Pride, Hook Norton, and a guest such as Timothy Taylors Landlord are well kept on handpump, they've 15 malt whiskies, and half a dozen wines by the glass; the staff are friendly and obliging. Besides adventurous specials such as grilled red snapper with pesto and pine kernels or fried pheasant breast in port and celery sauce (£11.95), and crocodile medallions with coarse-grain mustard sauce with cream (£14.95), a wide choice of enjoyable bar food could include home-made soup (£4.25), filled baguettes (from £5.45), filled baked potatoes (from £6.45), ploughman's or home-made burger (£7.95), home-made cottage pie or lasagne (£8.50), steaks (from £14.95); they also do a Sunday carvery (£9.95). From the pleasant garden behind are views towards the peaceful sloping fields. The bedrooms are good value, and there are decent walks nearby. *(Recommended by Stuart Turner, Chris Glasson, Neil and Anita Christopher, Di and Mike Gillam, Paul and Annette Hallett, Mike and Mary Carter, Tom Bottinga, Michael and Jenny Back, Ian Arthur, Peter B Brown, Dr G and Mrs J Kelvin, David A Hammond)*

Free house ~ Licensees Hugh Kelly and Charles Pettigrew ~ Real ale ~ Bar food (12-9; snacks during the afternoon rather than meals)) ~ Restaurant ~ (01451) 850392 ~ Children in eating area of bar and restaurant ~ Dogs allowed in bar and bedrooms ~ Open 11-11; 12-10.30 Sun ~ Bedrooms: £45B/£65B

KINGSCOTE ST8196 Map 4

Hunters Hall

A4135 Dursley—Tetbury

Well run and civilised with a warmly welcoming atmosphere, this creeper-covered inn has held a continuous licence for over 500 years. There's quite a series of bar rooms and lounges with fine high Tudor beams and stone walls, a lovely old box settle, sofas and miscellaneous easy chairs, and sturdy settles and oak tables on the flagstones in the lower-ceilinged, cosy public bar. You can eat the enjoyable, freshly prepared food in the airy end room or there are more tables in the Gallery upstairs. Served by helpful and friendly staff, the well thought out menu might include lunchtime sandwiches (from £2.25, not Sunday), home-made soup (£3.75), seafood chowder (£4.75), ploughman's (£5.95), pork and leek sausages with mustard mashed potatoes and cream of mushroom sauce (£7.75), wild mushroom and baby vegetable stroganoff or grilled trout with citrus oil (£8.95), grilled pork steak with raspberry and peppercorn sauce (£10.25), and 8oz fillet steak (£14.50). The Retreat Bar and restaurant (where there is piped music) are no smoking. A back room – relatively untouched – is popular with local lads playing pool; darts, cribbage, shove-ha'penny, fruit machine, shove-ha'penny, TV and juke box. On handpump, they've well kept Greene King Abbot and Ruddles Best, and Uley Hogs Head. The garden has seats, and a wooden fortress, play house and swings for children. The bedrooms are good value, and well maintained. *(Recommended by John and Marion Tyrie, Peter and Audrey Dowsett, R Huggins, D Irving, E McCall, T McLean, Neil and Anita Christopher, Meg and Colin Hamilton, Tom and Ruth Rees, Mr and Mrs E Barnes, Steve Godfrey, Ken Marshall, Mrs Pat Crabb)*

Old English Inns ~ Tenant Stephanie Ward ~ Real ale ~ Bar food ~ Restaurant ~ (01453) 860393 ~ Children welcome ~ Dogs allowed in bar and bedrooms ~ Open 11-11; 12-10.30 Sun ~ Bedrooms: £55B/£90B

LITTLE BARRINGTON SP2012 Map 4

Inn For All Seasons

On the A40 3 miles W of Burford

Not only does this civilised old inn have a good wine list with a dozen by the glass (and 100 bin ends), but the food here is very good too. Deliciously-cooked fresh fish is their speciality, and a typical choice might include grilled sardines with garlic and parsley butter sauce (£6.25; £9.95 large), poached skate wing with baby caper and shallot butter sauce (£11.50), fried red mullet with rich rosemary and tomato butter sauce (£14.95), and grilled dover sole with lemon and parsley butter (£16.50). If you prefer meat, you can choose from well presented dishes such as smoked duck breast salad with chorizo and pine nuts (£5.50), home-made pork faggots with creamed potatoes and red wine and onion jus (£9.95), lamb steak with minted sauté potatoes and sweet garlic jus (£11.50), and chargrilled scotch rump steak with chunky chips and wild mushroom sauce (£14.95), and they do lunchtime snacks such as home-made soup (£3.75), sandwiches (£3.95), ploughman's (£6.50), and scottish oak-smoked salmon (£9.50); puddings might be chocolate brownie with chocolate sauce and double cream (£4.50). The attractively decorated, mellow lounge bar has low beams, stripped stone, flagstones, old prints, leather-upholstered wing armchairs and other comfortable seats, country magazines to read, and a big log fire (with a big piece of World War II shrapnel above it); readers tell us there can be traffic noise. Well kept Bass, Sharps Doom Bar and Wadworths 6X on handpump, and they've over 60 malt whiskies; cribbage, dominoes, TV and piped music. The pleasant garden has tables and a play area; there are walks straight from the inn. It gets very busy during Cheltenham Gold Cup Week – when the adjoining field is pressed into service as a helicopter pad. *(Recommended by Peter and Audrey Dowsett, Mr and Mrs J McAngus, Simon Collett-Jones, A Bradshaw, Mike and Heather Watson, Mr and Mrs L Hemmingway, Mr and Mrs N Ward, John Kane, James Woods, Jim Abbott, Richard and Margaret Peers, Ian Phillips, Piotr Chodzko-Zajko, Chris and Val Ramstedt, Peter Neate)*

Free house ~ Licensees Matthew and Heather Sharp ~ Real ale ~ Bar food (11-2.30, 6-9.30) ~ Restaurant ~ (01451) 844324 ~ Children welcome ~ Dogs allowed in bar and bedrooms ~ Open 10.30-2.30, 6-11; 12-2.30, 7-10.30 Sun ~ Bedrooms: £56.50B/£97B

LITTLETON-UPON-SEVERN ST5990 Map 4

White Hart

3½ miles from M4 junction 21; B4461 towards Thornbury, then village signposted

As we went to press, a new landlord had just taken over this cosy 17th-c farmhouse, so we'd very much welcome reports on the new regime. Best on a cold winter's day when the log fires are roaring away, the three atmospheric main rooms have some fine furnishings: long cushioned wooden settles, high-backed settles, oak and elm tables, and a loveseat in the big low inglenook fireplace. There are flagstones in the front, huge tiles at the back, and smaller tiles on the left, plus some old pots and pans, and a lovely old White Hart Inn Simonds Ale sign. By the black wooden staircase are some nice little alcove seats, there's a black-panelled big fireplace in the front room, and hops on beams. Similarly furnished, a family room (usually no smoking), has some sentimental engravings, plates on a delft shelf, and a couple of high chairs, and a back snug has pokerwork seats; darts, chess, backgammon and Jenga. Outside, there are picnic-sets on the neat front lawn with interesting cottagey flowerbeds, and by the good big back car park are some attractive shrubs and teak furniture on a small brick terrac; there are several enjoyable walks from the pub. Bar food includes filled baguettes (from £3.50), ploughman's (£5.50), ham and egg, battered haddock or sausage and creamy mash with onion gravy (£7.95), and puddings such as bread and butter pudding (£3.95). Youngs Bitter, Special, Waggle Dance and Winter Warmer, along with a guest such as Smiles Best are well kept on handpump. They may stay open longer in summer. Beware, they ask to retain your credit card behind the bar. *(Recommended by Dr and Mrs C W Thomas, Tom Evans, Pat and Derek Roughton, Mike and Mary Carter, Andy Sinden, Louise Harrington, Di and Mike Gillam, R Huggins, D Irving, E McCall, T McLean, Meg and Colin Hamilton)*

Youngs ~ Manager Greg Bailey ~ Real ale ~ Bar food ~ (01454) 412275 ~ Children in family room ~ Dogs welcome ~ Open 12-2.30(3 Sat), 6-11; 12-4, 7-10.30 Sun ~ Bedrooms: £55B/£75B

Post Office address codings confusingly give the impression that some pubs are in Gloucestershire, when they're really in Warwickshire (which is where we list them).

MEYSEY HAMPTON SU1199 Map 4

Masons Arms

High Street; just off A417 Cirencester—Lechlade

With a pleasantly pubby atmosphere, friendly licensees, well kept beers and reasonably priced food, this village local manages to attract a good mix of customers. The longish open-plan bar has painted stone walls, carefully stripped beams with some hops, solid part-upholstered built-in wall seats with some matching chairs, good sound tables, a big inglenook log fire at one end with fairylights, an expanding hat collection, and daily newspapers; a few steps up is the no smoking restaurant. Hook Norton Best and Wickwar Cotswold Way, and a couple of guests such as Archers Golden and Timothy Taylors Landlord are well kept on handpump, and they've got decent wines including several ports; dominoes, cribbage, TV, and piped music (which can be obtrusive). Hearty bar food includes snacks such as sandwiches (from £1.95; filled baguettes from £3.95), baked potatoes (from £4.25), and ploughman's (from £5.65), with other dishes such as home-made soup (£2.65), stilton and bacon mushrooms (£4.65), moules marinière (small £5.25; large £7.25), local sausages with mustard mash and onion gravy (£6.35), rogan josh (£6.95), vegetable cottage pie (£7.95), grilled salmon with a creamy hollandaise sauce or braised lamb shank with rosemary and red wine (£8.95), and steaks (from £9.45). *(Recommended by P and J Shapley, R T and J C Moggridge, Darly Graton, Graeme Gulibert, R Huggins, D Irving, E McCall, T McLean, Anne Morris, P R and S A White, James Woods, Di and Mike Gillam, Jeff and Sue Evans, Mr and Mrs John Taylor, Brian McBurnie, A P Seymour, Kevin Thorpe)*

Free house ~ Licensees Andrew and Jane O'Dell ~ Real ale ~ Bar food (not Sun evening) ~ Restaurant ~ (01285) 850164 ~ Children in eating area of bar and restaurant ~ Dogs welcome ~ Open 11.30-2.45(3 Sat), 6-11; 12-4, 7-10.30 Sun; closed Sun evening in winter ~ Bedrooms: £45S/£65S

MISERDEN SO9308 Map 4

Carpenters Arms

Village signposted off B4070 NE of Stroud; also a pleasant drive off A417 via the Duntisbournes, or off A419 via Sapperton and Edgeworth; OS Sheet 163 map reference 936089

Set in an idyllic Cotswold estate village, this properly run pub is as warmly welcoming to drinkers as it is to diners. The two open-plan bar areas have low beams, nice old wooden tables, seats with the original little brass name plates on the backs, and some cushioned settles and spindlebacks on the bare boards; also, stripped stone walls with some interesting bric-a-brac, and two big log fires; the small no smoking dining room has dark traditional furniture. A sizeable collage (done with Laurie Lee) has lots of illustrations and book covers signed by him. As well as lunchtime filled baguettes (from £3.95), filled baked potatoes (from £4.50), and ploughman's (£5.25), enjoyable dishes (made with lots of local produce) might include tiger prawns in filo pastry with sweet chilli sauce (£4.75), home-made cheese and pepper quiche (£7.50), fishcakes or chicken breast with honey and mustard sauce (£7.95), pie of the day, poached salmon steak in parsley sauce or lambs liver, sausage and bacon with mash and onion gravy (£8.25), with specials such as grilled shark steak and tomato and pesto sauce (£8.95), and beef wellington (£10.25); pleasant and efficient service. Well kept Greene King IPA and Wadworths 6X, and a guest such as Smiles Bitter on handpump, country wines, and darts. There are seats out in the garden; the nearby gardens of Misarden Park are well worth visiting. *(Recommended by Guy Vowles, Philip Hill, Neil and Anita Christopher, Di and Mike Gillam, Bernard Stradling, Mike and Mary Carter, Graham and Helen Eastwood, Brian McBurnie, R Huggins, D Irving, E McCall, T McLean)*

Free house ~ Licensee Johnny Johnston ~ Real ale ~ Bar food ~ Restaurant ~ (01285) 821283 ~ Children in eating area of bar and in restaurant until 9pm ~ Dogs allowed in bar ~ Occasional country music and summer morris dancing ~ Open 11.30-2.30, 6-11; 11-3, 6-11 Sat; 12-3, 7-10.30 Sun

NAILSWORTH ST8599 Map 4

Egypt Mill

Just off A46; heading N towards Stroud, first right after roundabout, then left

With a cheerful bistro-ish atmosphere, this stylish conversion of a three-floor stone-built mill still has working waterwheels and the millstream flowing through. The brick-and-stone-floored split-level bar gives good views of the wheels, and there are big pictures and lots of stripped beams in the comfortable carpeted lounge, along with some hefty yet elegant ironwork from the old mill machinery; piped music. Ideal for summer evenings, the floodlit terrace garden by the millpond is pretty, and there's a little bridge over from the car park; boules. Well prepared, but not cheap, dishes change around every two months, but a typical choice might include lunchtime sandwiches (from £4.95), omelettes (£6.50), and local sausages (£8.95), with evening dishes such as sautéed squid risotto (£5.95), mixed pepper tarte tatin with pesto and balsamic dressing (£13.50), and poached monkfish with red wine sauce (£14.50), and steaks (from £14.95), with puddings such as lemon meringue crème brûlée (£4.95). It can get quite crowded on fine weekends, but it's spacious enough to feel at its best when busy, and the cheerful staff cope well; Archers, and a changing guest beer on handpump. *(Recommended by Dr and Mrs C W Thomas, Mike and Mary Carter, Joyce and Maurice Cottrell, P R and S A White, Fred and Lorraine Gill, John Mitchell, Jenny and Brian Seller)*

Free house ~ Licensee Stephen Webb ~ Real ale ~ Bar food ~ (01453) 833449 ~ Children welcome ~ Open 11-11; 12-10.30 Sun ~ Bedrooms: £60B/£105S(£75B)

Weighbridge

B4014 towards Tetbury

The speciality at this deservedly popular and very welcoming pub (now with a new landlord) is the delicious 2-in-1 pies, which they have been serving for more than 20 years. They come in a large bowl, and half the bowl contains the filling of your choice while the other is full of home-made cauliflower cheese (or broccoli mornay or root vegetables), and topped with pastry: turkey and trimmings, salmon in a creamy sauce, steak and mushroom, roast root vegetables, pork, bacon and celery in stilton sauce or chicken, ham and leek in a cream and tarragon sauce (from £8.40; you can also have mini versions from £5.90 or straightforward pies from £7). Enjoyable bar food also includes soup (£2.75), filled baguettes (from £3.60), chilli con carne or moussaka (£7.45), and braised lamb shank with shallots and red wine with creamed potatoes (£9.95), and puddings such as banana crumble (£4.25). The relaxed bar has three cosily old-fashioned rooms (one is no smoking) with stripped stone walls, antique settles and country chairs, and window seats. The black beamed ceiling of the lounge bar is thickly festooned with black ironware – sheepshears, gin traps, lamps and a large collection of keys, many from the old Longfords Mill opposite the pub; good disabled access and facilities. Upstairs is a raftered hayloft with an engaging mix of rustic tables; no noisy games machines or piped music. Uley Old Spot and Wadworths 6X are well kept alongside a guest such as Uley Laurie Lee on handpump, they've 14 wines (and champagne) by the glass, and Weston's cider. Behind is a sheltered landscaped garden with picnic-sets under umbrellas. *(Recommended by R Huggins, D Irving, E McCall, T McLean, John and Jane Hayter, Bruce Adams, Tom and Ruth Rees, Gerald Wilkinson, Andrew Shore, Maria Williams, Mike and Lynn Robinson, Dr and Mrs C W Thomas, Paul and Penny Dawson)*

Free house ~ Licensee Howard Parker ~ Real ale ~ Bar food (12-9.30) ~ (01453) 832520 ~ Children in family room till 9pm ~ Dogs welcome ~ Open 12-11; 12-10.30 Sun; closed 25, 31 Dec

Pubs close to motorway junctions are listed at the back of the book.

NEWLAND SO5509 Map 4

Ostrich

Off B4228 in Coleford; or can be reached from the A466 in Redbrook, by the turn-off at the England-Wales border – keep bearing right

With enjoyable food, eight well kept beers, friendly service and a good pubby atmosphere, it's no wonder that this fine unspoilt country pub (an inn since 1216) is so well liked. Spacious but cosily traditional, the low-ceilinged bar has creaky floors, uneven walls with miners' lamps, window shutters, candles in bottles on the tables, and comfortable furnishings such as cushioned window seats, wall settles and rod-backed country-kitchen chairs, and a fine big fireplace; quiet piped blues, and newspapers to read. Their real ales change constantly but a typical selection might include Badger Best, Greene King Abbot, Gribble Pig's Ear, Hook Norton Old Hooky, RCH Pitchfork, Shepherd Neame Spitfire, Timothy Taylors Landlord and Wye Valley Butty Bach on handpump; the sociable pub dog is called Alfie. Popular home-made bar food could include soup (£4.95), three cheese tart with sun-dried tomatoes and basil (£7), sizzling pork ribs or steak and ale pie (£7.50), or you can eat the restaurant menu in the bar, and choose from dishes such as pigeon and foie gras terrine with sloe and crab apple jelly (£6.50), trout with chive butter sauce (£10.95), rib-eye steak and béarnaise sauce (£13.50), and rack of lamb with creamy garlic potato and caramelised shallots (£16); good puddings. There are seats in a walled garden behind, and out in front; the church opposite, known as the Cathedral of the Forest, is well worth a visit. *(Recommended by LM, Denys Gueroult, Tim and Ann Newell, R Huggins, D Irving, E McCall, T McLean, Chris and Val Ramstedt, Mike and Mary Carter, Phil and Heidi Cook)*

Free house ~ Licensee Catherine Horton ~ Real ale ~ Bar food (12-2.30, 6.30-9.30) ~ Restaurant ~ (01594) 833260 ~ Children welcome ~ Dogs allowed in bar ~ Open 12-3, 6.30(6 Sat)-11; 12-3, 6.30-10.30 Sun

NORTH CERNEY SP0208 Map 4

Bathurst Arms

A435 Cirencester—Cheltenham

The former stables at this handsome 17th-c inn have now been converted into a new restaurant, and they've also added a no smoking bar. The original beamed and panelled bar has a fireplace at each end (one quite huge and housing an open woodburner), a good mix of old tables and nicely faded chairs, old-fashioned window seats, and some pewter plates. There are country tables in a little carpeted room off the bar, as well as winged high-backed settles forming a few booths around other tables; dominoes, darts and piped music. They've a good wine list (with around ten wines and champagnes by the glass), and Hook Norton Best and Wickwar Cotswold Way are well kept alongside a guest such as Wadworths 6X on handpump, with a choice of bottled beers too. Enjoyable food includes sandwiches (from £4.95), home-made soup (£3.95), smoked haddock and spinach fishcakes (£4.95), ploughman's (£5.95), old spot sausages with bubble and squeak and red onion gravy, beer-battered haddock or beef and ale pie with a suet crust (£7.95), pork tenderloin on spring onion mash with a creamy wild mushroom, sage and apple sauce (£9.95), and sirloin steak with brandy and peppercorn sauce (£12.25), with puddings such as double chocolate mud pie (£3.95); they do a Sunday roast lunch (£8.95). The restaurant is no smoking. Running down to the River Churn, the pleasant garden has picnic-sets sheltered by small trees and shrubs; there are plenty of surrounding walks. *(Recommended by R Huggins, D Irving, E McCall, T McLean, Guy Vowles, Julia and Richard Tredgett, Howard and Lorna Lambert, P R and S A White, A R Ainslie, Oliver Richardson, Alan Strong)*

Free house ~ Licensee James Walker ~ Real ale ~ Bar food ~ Restaurant ~ (01285) 831281 ~ Children in restaurant ~ Dogs allowed in bar and bedrooms ~ Open 11(12 in winter)-3, 6-11; 12-3, 7-10.30 Sun ~ Bedrooms: /£65B

NORTH NIBLEY ST7596 Map 4

New Inn

Waterley Bottom, which is quite well signposted from surrounding lanes; inn signposted from the Bottom itself; one route is from A4135 S of Dursley, via lane with red sign saying Steep Hill, 1 in 5 (just SE of Stinchcombe Golf Course turn-off), turning right when you get to the bottom; another is to follow Waterley Bottom signpost from previous main entry, keeping eyes skinned for small low signpost to inn; OS Sheet 162 map reference 758963; though this is the way we know best, one reader suggests the road is wider if you approach directly from North Nibley

Peacefully set in lovely South Cotswold countryside, this is a splendid place to relax in before embarking on one of the many nearby walks. Well kept Bath Gem Bitter and SPA, Cotleigh Tawny, Greene King Abbot and a guest such as Burton Bridge Bitter are dispensed from Barmaid's Delight (the name of one of the antique beer engines). The friendly licensees also serve Thatcher's cider and around 50 malt whiskies, and they import their own french wines; there's a beer festival on the last weekend in June. The lounge bar has cushioned windsor chairs and varnished high-backed settles against the partly stripped stone walls, and there are dominoes, cribbage, TV and sensibly placed darts in the simple public bar. Outside, there are lots of seats on the lawn, and there's also a neat terrace; three boules pitches. A short choice of home-made bar food includes sandwiches or toasties (from £2), soup (£3), filled baguettes (from £3.30), ploughman's (from £4.20), goats cheese and red onion flan or steak and kidney pie (£7.50), lamb tagine or beef and mushroom casserole (£8), poached plaice with prawn sauce (£8.50), and rib-eye steak with garlic potatoes (£12); they've redecorated the dining areas. *(Recommended by the Didler, Phil and Jane Hodson, Guy Vowles, Lawrence Pearse, Andrew Birkinshaw)*

Free house ~ Licensees Jackie and Jacky Cartigny ~ Real ale ~ Bar food (12-2, 6-9, not Mon-Tues) ~ (01453) 543659 ~ Children welcome ~ Dogs allowed in bar ~ Open 12-2.30, 6(7 Mon)-11; 12-11 Sat; 12-10.30 Sun; closed Mon lunchtime

NORTHLEACH SP1114 Map 4

Wheatsheaf

West End; the inn is on your left as you come in following the sign off the A429, just SW of its junction with the A40

An especially good time to visit this handsomely proportioned 16th-c stone-built inn is on Monday or Tuesday, when all bottles of wine are half price with a meal. A pretty garden behind the pub is pleasant in fine weather, with picnic-sets on tiers of grass among flowering shrubs. Inside there's plenty to see (including a fascinating collection of musical boxes and clocks, polyphons and automata), and it's all light and airy, with the three big-windowed rooms lining the street now run together. The central bar part has flagstones, the dining area open to it on the right has bare boards, and both have quite high ceilings – so the acoustics are lively. The room on the left, with new chairs, tables and settees, has a less exposed atmosphere which some might prefer. Well kept Hook Norton Best, Wadworths 6X and a changing guest on handpump, and 14 wines by the glass; dominoes, piped music. Besides lunchtime sandwiches (£5), you'll find well liked bar food such as soup (£4), seared scallops with bacon and rocket (£6; £12 large), mussels in cream and white wine or tagliatelle with pesto and grilled red pepper (£8), and rib-eye steak (£14), with specials such as tasty gloucestershire old spot sausages with spring onion mash (£8), and bass fillets with vegetable provençale (£10), while puddings might include rice pudding with strawberry jam (£4); good service from the welcoming licensees and attentive staff. This is a pleasant little town. *(Recommended by H O Dickinson, David Blackburn, Michael Dandy, C Tilley, Ian and Nita Cooper, W W Burke, Gerald Wilkinson, Martin and Karen Wake, Peter and Barbara Gardiner, Mr and Mrs D Renwick, Ian Phillips, Ben Seale)*

It's against the law for bar staff to smoke while handling food or drink.

Punch ~ Lease Caspar and Gavin Harvard-Walls ~ Real ale ~ Bar food (12-3, 7-10) ~ Restaurant ~ (01451) 860244 ~ Children welcome ~ Dogs allowed in bar ~ Open 12-11; 12-10.30 Sun ~ Bedrooms: £50B/£60B

OLD SODBURY ST7581 Map 2

Dog

Not far from M4 junction 18: A46 N, then A432 left towards Chipping Sodbury

A good place to unwind after a hot sticky drive on the nearby M4, the large garden of this bustling village pub has lots of seating, and a summer barbecue area, climbing frames, swings, slides and a football net. Inside, the two-level bar and smaller no smoking room both have areas of original bare stone walls, beams and timbering, low ceilings, wall benches, cushioned chairs and open fires; arrive early to be sure of a seat. Marstons Pedigree, Wadworths 6X, Wickwar BOB, and a guest beer are well kept on handpump, and you'll find several malt whiskies and quite a few wines; fruit machine and juke box. There are masses of reasonably priced dishes to choose from (with lots for vegetarians) such as sandwiches (from £2.50), mushrooms in garlic butter (£3.95), ploughman's (£5.95), vegetarian moussaka or cheese and onion flan (£6.95), chicken pieces with japanese barbecue sauce or hungarian beef goulash (£7.95), and plenty of fish dishes such as sole, plaice, halibut, cod, trout, scallops; puddings might be hot sticky toffee butterscotch pudding or home-made fruit pie (from £3.25). There's also a children's menu (from £2.50), but they don't provide highchairs. Lots of nearby walks. *(Recommended by Roger and Jenny Huggins, Jane Taylor, David Dutton, Tom Evans, Ian Phillips, Simon and Amanda Southwell, David and Ruth Shillitoe, George Atkinson, Bob Moffatt, S Fysh, Don and Thelma Anderson, Roy and Lindsey Fentiman, Mr and Mrs A H Young, John Branston, Monica Cockburn, Mike Jefferies, Dr and Mrs C W Thomas, Fiona McElhone, Dr and Mrs A K Clarke, Andy and Yvonne Cunningham, Pamela and Merlyn Horswell)*

Enterprise ~ Lease John and Joan Harris ~ Real ale ~ Bar food (12-2.30, 6(7 Sun)-9.30) ~ (01454) 312006 ~ Children in eating area of bar ~ Dogs allowed in bedrooms ~ Open 11-11; 12-10.30 Sun ~ Bedrooms: £30(£45S)(£45B)/£45(£65S)(£65B)

OLDBURY-ON-SEVERN ST6292 Map 2

Anchor 🍷 🍺

Village signposted from B4061

Thankfully the new licensees at this welcoming pub have managed to retain the good combination of proper village local with plenty of chatty regulars, and dining pub with enjoyable food. Well priced for the area, they've Bass, Butcombe Bitter, Theakstons Old Peculier and Wickwar BOB well kept on handpump or tapped from the cask, and you'll find over 75 malts, and a decent choice of good quality wines, with a dozen by the glass. The neatly kept lounge has modern beams and stone, a mix of tables including an attractive oval oak gateleg, cushioned window seats, winged seats against the wall, oil paintings by a local artist, and a big winter log fire. Diners can eat in the lounge or bar area or in the no smoking dining room at the back of the building (good for larger groups) and the menu is the same in all rooms. Using local produce, home-made dishes might be soup (£3), sandwiches (from £3.75), and ploughman's (from £4.25), potted cornish crab (£5.25), creamy risotto with marinated artichokes (£6.25), seared chicken breast with blue cheese and grapes or salmon and asparagus bake (£7.75), shepherd's pie (£7.95), and 8oz sirloin steak (£9.25), with puddings such as sticky toffee pudding (£3.50); instead of chips they offer a choice of roast, new, sautéed, baked or dauphinoise potatoes (£1.75). In summer (when the hanging baskets and window boxes are lovely) you can eat in the pretty garden. They have wheelchair access and a disabled lavatory; darts and cribbage, and boules too. Plenty of walks to the River Severn and along the many footpaths and bridleways, and St Arilda's church nearby is interesting, on its odd little knoll with wild flowers among the gravestones (the primroses and daffodils in spring are lovely). *(Recommended by James Morrell, Dr and Mrs C W Thomas, Tom Evans, Andrew Shore, Maria Williams, Charles and Pauline Stride, John and Gloria Isaacs, R Huggins, D Irving, E McCall, T McLean, Geoff Manning)*

Free house ~ Licensees Michael Dowdeswell and Mark Sorrell ~ Real ale ~ Bar food (12-2,7(7.30 Sun)-9.30) ~ Restaurant ~ (01454) 413331 ~ Children in restaurant ~ Dogs allowed in bar ~ Open 11.30-3, 6.30-11; 11.30-11 Sat; 12-10.30 Sun

PAXFORD SP1837 Map 4

Churchill

B4479, SE of Chipping Campden; no car park (it really needs one)

This is the kind of pub where locals drop in for a glass of wine and a bowl of chips, though if you do decide to eat here, you're in for a treat. Up on blackboards, the continually changing menu includes imaginative dishes such as soup (£4), game terrine with green tomato chutney or aubergine and pine nut frittata with baby gem, parmesan and anchovies (£6), grilled flounder with sherry, rosemary and tomato (£7.50), monkfish with sweet and sour sauce and deep-fried okra (£11.50), and lamb fillet with roast fennel, ginger and sultanas or salmon supreme with onion mash and chilli oil (£12), and puddings such as maple and mascarpone cheesecake with pineapple and shortbread biscuit (£5). They don't allow advance table booking, and your name goes on a chalked waiting list if all the tables are full. The simply furnished flagstoned bar has low ceilings, assorted old tables and chairs, and a snug warmed by a good log fire in its big fireplace; there's also a dining extension. You'll find well kept Arkells Moonlight and Hook Norton, promptly served along with a guest such as Archers Golden, and they've a good choice of wines by the glass; dominoes. There are some seats outside; aunt sally. They do a really good breakfast, if you're staying. *(Recommended by Susan and John Douglas, Brian and Pat Wardrobe, Dr John Lunn, Mike and Sue Richardson, Mr and Mrs C W Widdowson, John Kane, John Evans, Dr R A Smye, Dr G and Mrs J Kelvin, Mr and Mrs Martin Joyce, Mr and Mrs G S Ayrton, Simon Collett-Jones)*

Free house ~ Licensees Leo and Sonya Brooke-Little ~ Real ale ~ Bar food ~ Restaurant ~ (01386) 594000 ~ Children welcome ~ Open 11-3, 6-11; 12-3, 7-10.30 Sun ~ Bedrooms: £40B/£70B

SAPPERTON SO9403 Map 4

Bell

Village signposted from A419 Stroud—Cirencester; OS Sheet 163 map reference 948033

This particularly well run pub continues to be a real favourite with our readers, and no wonder: whether you're a walker or a local, a day-tripping family or a couple out for a special meal, you'll be made to feel genuinely welcome. Freshly cooked with high quality ingredients, imaginative dishes change regularly but might include pigeon faggot on potato cake with white cabbage and mustard dressing (£6.95), rabbit confit with roasted celeriac and orange in sweet chilli sauce (£7.50), home-made butternut and red pepper ravioli with confit fennel and balsamic butter (£11.95), grilled guinea fowl breast with butternut squash, lime, ginger and apple dressing or braised local beef blade with sweet potato mash (£12.95), and roasted haunch of marinated venison with smoked almond risotto and fig or steamed halibut supreme with cheesy leek mash (£14.50), with puddings such as maple and mascarpone cheesecake with poached pear and nutmeg ice (£5.50); they also do an excellent lunchtime ploughman's (£6.75, with a choice of three different cheeses), and a basket of home-made bread and butter and olives comes with every meal. There are three separate, cosy rooms with stripped beams, a nice mix of wooden tables and chairs, country prints and modern art on stripped stone walls, one or two attractive rugs on the flagstones, roaring log fires and woodburning stoves, fresh flowers, and newspapers and guidebooks to browse. As well as more than a dozen wines by two sizes of glass, and champagne by the flute, they serve well kept Uley Old Spot, Wickwar Cotswold Way and Goff's Jouster, and a guest such as Hook Norton Best on handpump; Weston's cider too. A hit with children, Harry the springer spaniel is very sociable. There are tables out on a small front lawn and in a partly covered and very pretty courtyard, for eating outside. Good surrounding walks, and horses have their own tethering rail (and bucket of water). *(Recommended by Evelyn and Derek Walter, Paul Hopton, Dr and Mrs C W Thomas, Barry and Victoria Lister, Guy Vowles, John and Joan Wyatt, M A and C R Starling, Gaynor Gregory, Di and Mike Gillam, Marianne and Peter Stevens, Mr and Mrs G S Ayrton, John Kane, Andy and Jill Kassube, Mrs N W Neill, R Huggins, D Irving, E McCall, T McLean, Tom and Ruth Rees, Inga and Keith Rutter, James Morrell, Paul and Penny Dawson, Derek Thomas, Mr and Mrs P L Spencer)*

Free house ~ Licensees Paul Davidson and Pat Le Jeune ~ Real ale ~ Bar food (not 25 Dec) ~ Restaurant ~ (01285) 760298 ~ Children welcome till 6.30pm ~ Dogs welcome ~ Open 11-2.30, 6.30-11; 12-3, 7-10.30 Sun; closed 25 Dec and evenings 26 and 31 Dec

SHEEPSCOMBE SO8910 Map 4

Butchers Arms 🍷

Village signed off B4070 NE of Stroud; or A46 N of Painswick (but narrow lanes)

This bustling 17th-c pub has log fires, seats in big bay windows, flowery-cushioned chairs and rustic benches, and lots of interesting oddments like assorted blow lamps, irons and plates. With a popular policy of not reserving tables in the bar (so casual diners and drinkers have a relaxed area in which to enjoy their drinks), the pub attracts a good mix of customers. Well kept Hook Norton Best, and a couple of guests such as Moles Best and Wye Valley Dorothy Goodbodys on handpump, eight wines by the glass, country wines, and good soft drinks; darts, cribbage, and dominoes. Besides a choice of lunchtime filled rolls, bagels or wraps (from £3.50), burgers or spinach and ricotta cannelloni (£7.50), and grilled gammon steak (£7.95), you'll find straightforward dishes such as chicken breast with creamy mushroom and white wine sauce (£8.25), grilled salmon with sesame seeds and noodles (£8.50), and mixed grill (£15); readers tell us that service can be slow at times. The restaurant and a small area in the bar are no smoking. Outside there are teak seats below the building, and tables on the steep grass behind; the views are terrific. The cricket ground behind is on such a steep slope that the boundary fielders at one end can scarcely see the bowler. This pub is part of the little Blenheim Inns group. *(Recommended by R Huggins, D Irving, E McCall, T McLean, Andrew Shore, Maria Williams, R J Herd, P R and S A White, Peter Scillitoe, Di and Mike Gillam, Theocsbrian, Neil and Anita Christopher, Mike and Lynn Robinson, D Norfolk, Pat and Roger Fereday, John and Gloria Isaacs, Giles and Annie Francis)*

Free house ~ Licensees Johnny and Hilary Johnston ~ Real ale ~ Bar food ~ Restaurant ~ (01452) 812113 ~ Children in restaurant, and in eating area of bar till 9pm ~ Occasional morris dancing and folk music ~ Open 11.30-3, 6-11; 12-3.30, 7-10.30 Sun

ST BRIAVELS SO5605 Map 4

George 🛏

High Street

Seats on the flagstoned terrace behind this attractive white painted pub overlook a grassy former moat to the silvery 12th-c castle built as a fortification against the Welsh; an ancient escape tunnel connects the castle to the pub. With a welcoming, bustling atmosphere, the three rambling rooms have old-fashioned built-in wall seats, some booth seating, cushioned small settles, toby jugs and antique bottles on black beams over the servery, and a large stone open fireplace; a Celtic coffin lid dating from 1070, discovered when a fireplace was removed, is now mounted next to the bar counter. Besides lunchtime filled baguettes (£4.95), popular enjoyable home-made dishes could include soup (£3.45), prawn cocktail (£4.50), rabbit casserole (£7.95), moroccan lamb or chicken breast stuffed with apricots and brie, wrapped in bacon with a tarragon and sherry sauce (£9.95), fresh bass (£10.95), and braised lamb shoulder (£12.95), with home-made puddings such as lemon meringue and crumble (£3.45). The dining room and restaurant are no smoking; piped music. Friendly and courteous staff serve well kept Freeminer Bitter, Fullers London Pride and RCH Pitchfork, with a couple of guests from brewers such as Archers and Freeminer on handpump; also 15 malt whiskies, farm cider and country wines. Lots of walks start nearby but muddy boots must be left outside; outdoor chess. *(Recommended by Stephen and Helen Digby, Mike and Mary Carter, Jane and Graham Rooth, Neil and Jean Spink, S P Watkin, P A Taylor, Bob and Margaret Holder, Ian Phillips, JHW, Pamela and Merlyn Horswell)*

Free house ~ Licensee Bruce Bennett ~ Real ale ~ Bar food ~ Restaurant ~ (01594) 530228 ~ Children in eating area of bar and restaurant ~ Dogs allowed in bar ~ Open 11-2.30, 6.30-11; 12-2.30, 7-10.30 Sun ~ Bedrooms: £35S/£50S

STOW-ON-THE-WOLD SP1925 Map 4

Eagle & Child

Attached to Royalist Hotel, Digbeth Street

In a lovely small town, this appealing pub has flagstone floors, dark low beams and joists, terracotta pink walls with a modicum of horsey prints and old school photographs, russet curtains, and a woodburning stove. There's a nice mix of individual tables in the main part and a back conservatory, which has humorous horseracing pictures on its terracotta walls, and french windows to a small courtyard with a couple of picnic-sets and some topiary tubs. The pub is mainly 17th-c, but with some striking features and parts of great antiquity, including thousand-year-old timbers (there was some sort of inn on the site in 947). Served by smartly dressed, friendly and efficient staff, skilfully prepared dishes might include soup (£4.25), sweet potato risotto with parmesan and spinach (£4.25; £7.95 large), chicken, pepper and liver kebabs (£4.95; £8.25 large), spaghetti with creamed artichoke, baby spinach, cherry tomatoes, feta and red onion or local sausages with onion gravy and mash (£8.95), grilled chicken supreme with creamy lemon and herb pesto sauce (£11.95), and local trout with honey, sweet chilli and hazelnut (£12.25), with puddings such as sticky toffee pudding with butterscotch sauce and vanilla ice-cream (£4.50); at busy times all the tables may be reserved for diners. Along with 14 wines by the glass, they have well kept Hook Norton Best, Timothy Taylors Landlord and maybe a guest on handpump, and 50 malt whiskies. The comfortable bedrooms are in the adjacent hotel. Nearby parking is not always easy. *(Recommended by Guy Vowles, Janet and Philip Shackle, Ted George, Michael Dandy, Dr G and Mrs J Kelvin, George Atkinson, Sean and Sharon Pines, Mr and Mrs Martin Joyce, David J Austin, Peter and Jackie Barnett)*

Free house ~ Licensees Peter and Amanda Rowan ~ Real ale ~ Bar food (12-2.30, 6-9) ~ Restaurant ~ (01451) 830670 ~ Children in eating area of bar ~ Dogs allowed in bar ~ Open 11-11; 12-10.30 Sun ~ Bedrooms: £60B/£90B

TETBURY ST9195 Map 4

Trouble House

A433 towards Cirencester, near Cherington turn

Although the main focus at this pub is on the freshly prepared food, you can still drop in for just a drink, and there are 14 wines by the glass to choose from. Furnishings are mainly close-set stripped pine or oak tables with chapel chairs, some wheelback chairs and the odd library chair, and there are attractive mainly modern country prints on the cream or butter-coloured walls. The rush-matting room on the right is no smoking, and on the left there's a parquet-floored room with a chesterfield by the big stone fireplace, a hop-girt mantelpiece, and more hops hung from one of its two big black beams. In the small saggy-beamed middle room, you can commandeer one of the bar stools, where they have well kept Wadworths IPA and Henrys Original on handpump; piped music and cribbage. The ambitious menu might include soup (£4.25), fried smoked haddock and parsley dumplings (£5.75), roasted guinea fowl with pea and bacon broth or pork belly in cider with sweet and sour beetroot, apricots and prunes (£13.50), roasted monkfish with savoy cabbage, celeriac and garlic or calves sweetbreads with pea and broad bean purée and roasted garlic (£15), with puddings such as strawberry and raspberry gratin or nougat glace with bitter chocolate mousse (£5.25), and an interesting selection of cheeses (from £6); friendly service. They sell quite a few of their own preserves such as tapenade or preserved tomatoes with onions. You can also sit out at picnic-sets on the gravel courtyard behind. *(Recommended by Mrs Sally Lloyd, Derek Thomas, Guy Vowles, Richard Stancomb, John Kane, Lyn Huxtable, Richard Seers, Paul Williams, Joyce and Maurice Cottrell, Mr and Mrs A H Young)*

Wadworths ~ Tenants Michael and Sarah Bedford ~ Real ale ~ Bar food (not Sun or Mon) ~ Restaurant ~ (01666) 502206 ~ Children in restaurant ~ Dogs welcome ~ Open 11-3, 6.30(7 winter)-11; closed Sun and Mon and around 2 wks over Christmas and New Year

TODENHAM SP2436 Map 4

Farriers Arms 🍷 🍺

Between A3400 and A429 N of Moreton-in-Marsh

With a lovely welcoming atmosphere, the main bar of this tucked away pub has nice wonky white plastered walls, hops on the beams, fine old polished flagstones by the stone bar counter and a woodburner in a huge inglenook fireplace. A tiny little room off to the side is full of old books and interesting old photographs. The licensees are friendly, and nothing is too much trouble for the courteous staff. Readers very much enjoy the reasonably priced bar food, which might include home-made soup (£3.75), goats cheese and red onion tart or home-made chicken liver parfait (£4.95), filled baguettes (from £4.95), home-made lamb burger (£6.25), home-made steak and ale pie (£7.95), with daily specials such as whole grilled place (£10.95) and seared scallops (£13.75), and puddings such as banoffi pancakes (£3.95); the restaurant is no smoking. Hook Norton Best, and a couple of guests such as Timothy Taylors Landlord or Wye Valley Butty Bach are well kept on handpump, and they've eight wines by the glass; cribbage, darts, dominoes, board games and aunt sally. The pub has fine views over the surrounding countryside from the back garden, and there are a couple of tables with views of the church on a small terrace by the quiet little road. *(Recommended by Alan and Jill Bull, H O Dickinson, Neil and Anita Christopher, John Bowdler, Alun Howells, Di and Mike Gillam, Rod and Chris Pring, Pat and Roger Fereday, WAH, Mike and Mary Carter, Lloyd Moon)*

Free house ~ Licensees Thomas Young and Charlotte Bishop ~ Real ale ~ Bar food ~ Restaurant ~ (01608) 650901 ~ Children in eating area of bar and restaurant ~ Dogs allowed in bar ~ Open 12-3, 6.30-11; 12-3, 7-10.30 Sun

UPPER ODDINGTON SP2225 Map 4

Horse & Groom

Village signposted from A436 E of Stow-on-the-Wold

Handily open all day, the bar at this attractive, 16th-c Cotswold inn has pale polished flagstones, a handsome antique oak box settle among other more modern seats, dark oak beams in the ochre ceiling, stripped stone walls, and an inglenook fireplace. You'll find well kept real ales such as Bass and Hook Norton Best on handpump, and nine wines by the glass. Service is prompt and very friendly. The menu changes around every six weeks, but popular dishes might include lunchtime sandwiches (£4.50), carbonara (£8.50), and local sausages (£9), as well as home-made soup (£3.95), roast pepper and goats cheese strudel or chicken liver brandy parfait (£5.50), hazelnut and pistachio potato cakes (£11), marinated pork loin with asparagus, jerusalem artichokes, and warm basil oil (£12), swordfish steak with lime and mango salad (£14.25), with blackboard specials such as onion and tomato tarte tatin (£5.50), and monkfish in spicy tempura batter (£13), and puddings such as chocolate roulade or rhubarb and ginger crumble (£5); they've refurbished the no smoking dining room. There are seats on the terrace, and in the pretty garden, and there's a fine play area; they've also a vineyard. The bedrooms are comfortable, and breakfasts are generous. *(Recommended by Michael G Butler, Stuart Turner, Dr and Mrs James Harris, Sir Nigel Foulkes, Mr and Mrs Martin Joyce)*

Free house ~ Real ale ~ Bar food ~ Restaurant ~ (01451) 830584 ~ Children welcome ~ Open 11-11; 12-10.30 Sun; closed 25 Dec ~ Bedrooms: £49S/£65S

WINCHCOMBE SP0228 Map 4

White Hart 🍷 🛏

High Street (B4632)

Like the landlady, the friendly staff at this interesting place (more café-bar than pub) are virtually all Swedish, and this is reflected in the delicious Swedish specials. On Friday and Sunday lunchtimes and Wednesday evenings, they do a popular smorgasbord buffet (£13.95). Otherwise, big plates of well prepared food might include a delicious scandinavian seafood platter (£6.95), meatballs in creamy sauce (£8.95), and smorgasbord platter (£9.95), alongside more traditional lunchtime bar snacks such as ploughman's (from £4.95), baguettes (£5.95), and home-made burger (£7.75), and other dishes such as chargrilled steaks (from £10.95), duckling breast with balsamic red wine (£15.25), halibut steak with creamy mash and rich lobster sauce (£15.95), with puddings such as apple and cinnamon cheesecake (£4.95). There's also a pizzeria (not open Monday, pizzas from £4.65). The main area has mate's chairs, dining chairs and small modern settles around dark oak tables (candlelit at night) on black-painted boards, cream walls, and what amounts to a wall of big windows giving on to the village street – passers-by knock on the glass when they see their friends inside. A smaller no smoking back area has its kitchen tables and chairs painted pale blue-grey, and floor matting. A downstairs bar with black beams, stripped stone above the panelled dado, and pews and pine tables on the good tiles, may be open too at busy times. Well kept Greene King IPA and Old Speckled Hen, Wadworths 6X, and a changing guest such as Goff's White Knight on handpump, and a good choice of wines by the glass – brought to your table unless you're sitting at the big copper-topped counter. There's a good mix of all ages, and an enjoyably relaxed atmosphere; daily papers, laid-back piped music. The back car park is rather small. *(Recommended by Rod Stoneman, Di and Mike Gillam, Richard and Jean Phillips, Mr and Mrs D Renwick, Guy Vowles, Roy and Lindsey Fentiman)*

Enterprise ~ Lease Nicole Burr ~ Real ale ~ Bar food (all day) ~ Restaurant ~ (01242) 602359 ~ Children in restaurant, and away from bar till 9pm ~ Dogs allowed in bar and bedrooms ~ Occasional jazz evenings ~ Open 11-11; 12-10.30 Sun ~ Bedrooms: £55B/£65B

LUCKY DIP

Besides the fully inspected pubs, you might like to try these Lucky Dips recommended to us and described by readers (if you do, please send us reports: www.goodguides.co.uk).

ALDERTON SP0033

Gardeners Arms [Beckford Rd, off B4077 Tewkesbury—Stow]: Well run thatched Tudor pub with decent food from filled baps and baked potatoes to bistro dishes and fresh fish, well kept Flowers IPA, Greene King Abbot and Old Speckled Hen and guest beers, above-average wines, hospitable landlady, log fire; piped music (turned down on request); dogs and children welcome, tables on sheltered terrace, well kept garden with boules *(LYM, Andrew Wones, Theocsbrian, Geoff Pidoux, Peter Coxon)*

ALDSWORTH SP1510

☆ *Sherborne Arms* [B4425 Burford—Cirencester]: Cheerful extended wayside pub with wide choice of quickly served good old-fashioned fresh food from baked potatoes and ploughman's up esp fish; log fire, beams, some stripped stone, smallish bar, big dining area and attractive no smoking conservatory, welcoming obliging service and attentive landlord, well kept Greene King IPA, Abbot and Ruddles County, farm cider; games area with darts, lots of board games, fruit machine, piped music; dogs welcomed kindly, pleasant front garden, lavatory for disabled *(Giles and Annie Francis, BB, David Gunn, Sheila Brooks, John and Hazel Williams, Joyce and Geoff Robson, R Huggins, D Irving, E McCall, T McLean, P and J Shapley)*

AMBERLEY SO8401

☆ ***Black Horse*** [off A46 Stroud—Nailsworth; Littleworth]: Spectacular views and cheerful local atmosphere, friendly staff, well kept changing ales such as Archers Best and Golden and a seasonal Wickwar beer (special prices midweek and early evening), farm cider, interesting wines, good value usual food inc midweek bargains, open fire and daily papers, interesting murals, conservatory, large no smoking family area on left (other bar can get smoky), games room; tables on back terrace with barbecue and spit roast area, more on lawn (sometimes a parrot out here); open all day summer wknds, has been cl Mon *(R Huggins, D Irving, E McCall, T McLean, LYM, John and Gloria Isaacs, Derek and Margaret Underwood, John Davis, Guy Vowles, S Fysh)*

AMPNEY CRUCIS SP0701

Crown of Crucis [A417 E of Cirencester]: Bustling rather hotelish food pub very popular particularly with older people, pleasant lemon and blue décor, split-level no smoking restaurant, real ales; children welcome, disabled facilities, lots of tables out on grass by car park, comfortable modern bedrooms around courtyard, good breakfast, open all day *(Peter and Audrey Dowsett, LYM, Mrs Belinda Mead)*

ANDOVERSFORD SP0219

☆ ***Royal Oak*** [signed just off A40; Gloucester Rd]: Cosy, attractive and warmly welcoming beamed village pub, lots of stripped stone, nice galleried raised dining room beyond big central open fire, well kept ales inc Hook Norton Best, good reasonably priced food using much local produce inc good value light meals, prompt obliging service; can get smoky; popular quiz night, tables in garden *(BB, Guy Vowles, Dr and Mrs James Stewart, Mr and Mrs D Renwick, Brian McBurnie, Derek and Sylvia Stephenson)*

APPERLEY SO8628

☆ ***Coal House*** [Gabb Lane; village signed off B4213 S of Tewkesbury]: Light and airy bar in splendid riverside position, welcoming licensees, well kept Hook Norton Best, Charles Wells Bombardier and Whittingtons, decent wines by the glass, plenty of blackboards for enjoyable inexpensive food from baguettes and light dishes up, walkers welcome, no music; tables and chairs on front terrace and lawn with Severn views, play area, moorings *(Pete and Rosie Flower, BB, Theocsbrian, Andy and Jill Kassube, Rod Stoneman, Dave Braisted, P R and S A White, P and J Shapley)*

ARLINGHAM SO7111

☆ ***Old Passage*** [Passage Rd]: Roomy upmarket place now restaurant rather than pub (they do keep a real ale, but you can't go just for a drink), interesting choice of good food esp fish and seafood, friendly helpful staff, nice clean décor; beautiful setting, french windows to pleasant terrace and big garden extending down to River Severn *(Jane McKenzie, Michael Herman, BB, DM, Jo Rees, Guy Vowles)*

☆ ***Red Lion***: Pleasant beamed pub, good generous freshly made food (not Sun evening) from traditional to modern, well kept ales such as Black Sheep, Greene King Ruddles and Fullers London Pride, three ciders, friendly efficient service, tiled and partly carpeted bar with big fireplace, comfortable button-back seats in no smoking dining lounge on left, steps to small dining room beyond, photographs, paintings (some for sale) and a few rustic implements on uncluttered soft green or terracotta walls, pool room on right, skittle alley; picnic-sets in small courtyard, not far from Severn estuary walks, cl Mon *(Dr and Mrs C W Thomas, Mrs G P Hall, Neil and Anita Christopher)*

AUST ST5789

☆ ***Boars Head*** [½ mile from M48, junction 1, off Avonmouth rd]: Useful ivy-covered motorway break with wide choice of reasonably priced food, good helpings, well kept real ales, good house wines, nice mix of old furnishings in rambling series of linked rooms and alcoves, beams and some stripped stone, huge log fire; piped music; children in partly no smoking eating area away from bar, dogs on lead in bar, pretty sheltered garden *(LYM, Colin Moore, John and Enid Morris)*

AYLBURTON SO6101

Cross [High St]: Decent choice of good food, Flowers IPA, Greene King Abbot, Tetleys, Wadworths 6X and Worthington, flagstone floors and spruce décor; picnic-sets in pleasant orchard garden *(Ian Phillips)*

BIBURY SP1106

Catherine Wheel [Arlington; B4425 NE of Cirencester]: Open-plan main bar and smaller back rooms, low beams, stripped stone, good log fires, no smoking dining area (children allowed), well kept ales inc Adnams, reasonably priced food from sandwiches up, traditional games; picnic-sets in attractive and spacious garden with play area, famously beautiful village, handy for country and riverside walks (can be busy in summer); open all day, children welcome *(Joyce and Geoff Robson, Peter and Audrey Dowsett, LYM, Geoff Pidoux, Gloria Bax)*

Swan [B4425]: Hotel in lovely spot facing River Coln, roomy and relaxing bar used by locals, big comfortable armchairs and sofas, well kept Goffs Jouster, enjoyable bar food inc good ploughman's, good service, nice adjoining brasserie; tables out by pergola with masses of flowers, comfortable bedrooms *(Guy Vowles, David J Austin)*

BIRDLIP SO9316

Air Balloon [A417/A436 roundabout]: Much extended chain dining pub, standard value food all day from breakfast on, good-sized no smoking area with many levels and alcoves, pubbier front corner with open fire, stone walls and flagstones, real ales and friendly young staff; tables, some covered, on heated terrace and in garden with play area, open all day *(P R and S A White, Mr and Mrs G S Ayrton)*

Royal George: Big smart two-level bar beyond hotel reception, beams with chalked witticisms, small area with armchairs and low tables, extensive wine racks in lower part, wide range of reasonably priced bar and restaurant food from sandwiches up, three well kept Greene King ales, good wine choice, good service, soft lighting; piped music; fine garden, pleasant setting, bedrooms *(R Huggins, D Irving, E McCall, T McLean, Mick and Moira Brummell)*

BISLEY SO9006

Stirrup Cup [Cheltenham Rd]: Long rambling well furnished local with good modestly priced food from sandwiches and tasty baguettes to generous Sunday roasts inc children's meals, well kept real ales, decent wines, cheerful helpful landlord, friendly bustle, no piped music (occasional live folk nights); dogs welcome *(R Huggins, D Irving, E McCall, T McLean)*

BLOCKLEY SP1634

Crown [High St]: Golden stone Elizabethan inn under new management, good imaginative food in linked bar areas and two no smoking restaurants (one upstairs), well kept Hook Norton Best, decent wines, sensible prices, largely foreign bar staff; children in eating areas, tables in terraced coachyard surrounded by beautiful trees and shrubs, comfortable bedrooms *(LYM, Guy Vowles, Mike and Mary Carter, Annette and John Derbyshire)*

☆ ***Great Western Arms*** [Station Rd (B4479)]: Convivial and comfortable, with straightforward modern-style lounge/dining room, cheery landlord, wide choice of quickly served good value home-made pub food from substantial sandwiches and soups up, three well kept Hook Norton ales, no piped music, busy public bar with games room; attractive village, lovely valley view *(Alec and Barbara Jones, G W A Pearce, Paul and Sue Merrick)*

BOURTON-ON-THE-WATER SP1621

Coach & Horses [A429 Stow Rd]: A few tables in bar with settle by huge woodburner, enjoyable generous food (children well looked after), well kept Hook Norton, good friendly service, separate restaurant; good play area, pleasant bedrooms in former stables, open all day *(D P and M A Miles, Keith and Chris O'Neill)*

Kingsbridge Inn [Riverside]: Large comfortable open-plan pub popular for pleasant village/river view from tables on terrace, popular food inc two-for-one bargains, good friendly atmosphere, interesting old prints and cartoons; piped music *(Ted George)*

Old Manse [Victoria St]: Front garden and one end of long turkey-carpeted beamed bar (over-21s only) overlooking River Windrush, big log fire, attractive old prints, bookshelves, some stripped stone, friendly attentive staff, well kept Greene King ales, good choice of decent food from all-day sandwiches up inc afternoon teas and good steaks, pretty restaurant (children allowed here); piped music; good bedrooms, open all day *(BB, Richard and Margaret Peers, Ted George, Michael Dandy)*

BOX SO8500

☆ ***Halfway Inn*** [edge of Minchinhampton Common, off A46 via Amberley; OS Sheet 162 map ref 856003]: Light and airy open-plan bars with sturdy wooden furnishings on stripped wood floors, good interesting food, well kept Greene King IPA, Smiles and a couple of guest beers, decent wines, woodburner; piped music, fruit machine; children welcome in dining area and no smoking restaurant, tables in landscaped garden, cl Mon, open all day summer *(LYM, R Huggins, D Irving, E McCall, T McLean)*

BROADWELL SP2027

☆ ***Fox*** [off A429 2 miles N of Stow-on-the-Wold]: Relaxing small pub opp neat broad green in pleasant village, friendly landlord, good range of enjoyable food (not Sun evening) from baguettes up, well kept Donnington BB and SBA, Addlestone's cider, decent wines, nice coffee, stripped stone and flagstones, beams hung with jugs, log fire, darts, dominoes and chess, plain public bar with pool room extension, pleasant separate restaurant (locally popular for Sun family lunches); may be piped music; peaceful outlook, tables out on gravel, good big back garden with aunt sally, meadow behind for Caravan Club members *(BB, Alun Evans, Angus Lyon, Geoff Calcott, Roger and Maureen Kenning, Mrs N W Neill, Martin and Karen Wake, M and J Lindsay)*

BROCKHAMPTON SP0322

Craven Arms [off A436 Andoversford—Naunton]: Attractive 17th-c inn under new landlady, sizeable linked eating areas off smaller bar servery, low beams, thick roughly coursed stone walls, some tiled flooring, mainly pine funiture with some wall settles, tub chairs, log fire, popular bar food, well kept Fullers London Pride, Hook Norton Best and a weekly guest beer, shove-ha'penny; children in eating areas, sizeable garden, attractive gentrified hillside village with lovely views and walks, cl Sun evening *(LYM)*

CHARFIELD ST7292

Railway Tavern [Wotton Rd]: Cheerful bustle, well kept real ales, welcoming service, railway décor, games room *(Dr and Mrs A K Clarke)*

CHEDWORTH SP0609

☆ ***Hare & Hounds*** [Fosse Cross – A429 N of Cirencester, some way from village]: Good if not cheap inventive food in rambling stone-built dining pub interestingly furnished with modern touches, low beams, soft lighting, cosy corners and little side rooms, two big log fires, small conservatory; well kept Arkells 2B, 3B and Kingsdown, good house wines, friendly and helpful landlord, happy staff; children welcome away from bar, disabled facilities, open all day Fri-Sun *(Peter and Audrey Dowsett, Tim and Carolyn Lowes, Fred Chamberlain, LYM, Phil and Jane Hodson, P R and*

S A White, R Huggins, D Irving, E McCall, T McLean, Rod Stoneman)

CHELTENHAM SO9325

Kemble Brewery [Fairview St]: Small backstreet local with friendly atmosphere and charming Irish landlady, well kept Smiles Best, Timothy Taylors Landlord and Youngs, good value robust lunchtime food; small back garden *(Derek and Sylvia Stephenson, Giles and Annie Francis, Joe Green)*

Montpellier Wine Bar [Bayshill Lodge, Montpellier St]: Wine bar not pub, but may have a real ale such as Timothy Taylors Landlord (and a good Pimms), and worth knowing for enterprising not cheap food from sandwiches up; thriving atmosphere, friendly staff, open glass front leading out to pavement tables, interesting décor in well furnished downstairs restaurant with second bar; SkyTV sports *(Gary and Jane Gleghorn)*

Old Swan [High St]: Back to its proper name and character after a spell as O'Hagans, two levels and several areas inc conservatory, three well kept real ales, reasonably priced fresh food, bubbly individualistic staff; open all day *(David Gough)*

☆ ***Tailors*** [Cambray Pl]: Friendly pub in substantial town house, attractive flight of steps to main bar with lots of dark wood, old clocks and prints, two fireplaces and comfortable armchairs, good basic lunchtime food inc plenty of ploughman's and baked potatoes, well kept Wadworths 6X and guest ales; cosy snug, cellar bar Fri/Sat evenings; piped music, two discreet TVs; some tables outside *(M Thomas)*

Tavern in the Town [Bath Rd]: Bay-windowed local comfortably opened up under new licensees, well kept Bass, good wines by the glass, friendly landlord interested in wine, landlady cooks short choice of decent bar food; piped music, big-screen SkyTV *(Guy Vowles)*

CHIPPING CAMPDEN SP1539

☆ ***Kings Arms*** [High St]: Small lively hotel under same management as Village Pub at Barnsley, inventive modern changing food, enthusiastic young friendly staff, well kept Hook Norton beers, good log fire in charmingly refurbished bar with widened eating areas; secluded back garden, open all day Sat, bedrooms *(LYM, Peter Coxon, Annette and John Derbyshire)*

☆ ***Lygon Arms*** [High St]: Comfortably worn in stripped-stone bar with welcoming long-serving landlord, helpful staff, very wide choice of enjoyable reasonably priced food till late evening inc interesting dishes, well kept Greene King Old Speckled Hen, Hook Norton Best and Wadworths 6X and JCB (they use sparklers), lots of horse pictures, open fires, small back dining room, raftered evening restaurant beyond shady courtyard with tables; children welcome, open all day exc winter wkdys; good bedrooms *(Geoff Calcott, LYM, Lynda Payton, Sam Samuells, Peter Coxon, Gene and Kitty Rankin)*

☆ ***Noel Arms*** [High St]: Handsome old inn with polished oak settles, attractive old tables, armour, casks hanging from beams, antique prints, tools and traps on stripped stone walls, decent food from sandwiches to some interesting dishes, good service, coal fire, well kept Hook Norton Best, no smoking restaurant; piped music; children welcome, tables in enclosed courtyard, bedrooms *(Susan and John Douglas, LYM, Angus Lyon)*

Red Lion [Lower High St]: Nicely refurbished, with small comfortable locals' bar, good range of good value generous food in larger flagstoned front eating area, well kept Greene King ales, upstairs dining room *(Angus Lyon)*

CHIPPING SODBURY ST7282

Squire [Broad St]: Three large rooms (inc a big no smoking area), good range of freshly cooked food inc some interesting dishes and good value family Sun lunch, pleasant atmosphere, good welcoming service, real ales; on broad old market street *(Mr and Mrs R L Booth)*

CIRENCESTER SP0201

Somewhere Else [Castle St]: Two light and airy rooms with pastel walls and café tables, well kept Youngs, decent house wine and cheerful service – bistro-feel café/restaurant by day, with small interesting choice of quickly served food inc interesting tapas, more of a lively pub mood evenings; piped music can be rather loud; lots of tables on heated terrace, games room off with pool *(R Huggins, D Irving, E McCall, T McLean, Joyce and Maurice Cottrell)*

☆ ***Twelve Bells*** [Lewis Lane]: Cheery and recently refreshed backstreet pub with particularly well kept Abbey Bellringer and enterprising choice of five ever-changing beers, small old-fashioned low-ceilinged three-roomed bar, small back dining area with sturdy pine tables and rugs on quarry tiles, good coal fires, pictures for sale, clay pipe collection, forthright hard-working landlord, good generous fresh food inc local produce and some unusual dishes lunchtime and early evening; can get smoky, piped music may be loud; small sheltered back terrace with fountain *(R Huggins, D Irving, E McCall, T McLean, Pete Baker, Paul and Ann Meyer, Nick and Alison Dowson, BB, Mike Pugh, Edward Longley, Ian and Nita Cooper, R Michael Richards, Phil and Sally Gorton)*

Waggon & Horses [London Rd]: Stone-built pub with comfortably cottagey L-shaped bar, lots of bric-a-brac, well kept ales such as Courage, Fullers London Pride and Hook Norton, back dining room with enjoyable food lunchtime and evening *(R Huggins, D Irving, E McCall, T McLean)*

Wheatsheaf [Cricklade St]: Busy local with ales such as Fullers London Pride, Smiles IPA and Worthington 1744, wide choice of cheap and cheerful food from baguettes up until 4pm, OAP bargains some wkdys, quick invariably welcoming service, no piped music; no children in bar, big-screen TV in back room; well used skittle alley, back car park, open all day *(R Huggins, D Irving, E McCall, T McLean, Peter and Audrey Dowsett)*

CLIFFORD'S MESNE SO6922

Yew Tree [out of Newent, past Falconry

Centre]: On slopes of May Hill (NT), large open-plan divided area emphasising enterprising blackboard meals (all day Sun), well kept RCH Pitchfork and Shepherd Neame Spitfire; children welcome, tables out on sunny terrace, play area; two bedrooms with own bathrooms *(J E Shackleton)*

COALEY SO7701

Fox & Hounds [The Street]: Long bar with reasonably priced food, interesting real ales inc one brewed for them by Uley, back skittles alley *(R Huggins, D Irving, E McCall, T McLean)*

COATES SO9600

☆ *Tunnel House* [follow Tarleton signs (right then left) from village, pub up rough track on right after railway bridge; OS Sheet 163 map ref 965005]: Beamed country pub gently upgraded and extended, idiosyncratic original bar with homely and comfortable mix of chairs and settees, engaging mish-mash of unlikely bric-a-brac, log fire, extension eating area and back conservatory (fills quickly – new porch, too), well kept ales such as Archers, Wickwar Cotswold Way and Wye Valley, Stowford Press cider, enjoyable if not cheap food from sandwiches to some interesting dishes, quick friendly service, amiable ambling black labrador; juke box, smoking allowed throughout; children and dogs welcome (play area and plenty of room to run around outside, too), impressive views from tables on nice terrace, big garden sloping down to former canal (under slow restoration), Sunday barbecues, good walks *(Lawrence Pearse, LYM, David A Hammond, Guy Vowles, Mike and Lynn Robinson, R Huggins, D Irving, E McCall, T McLean, Neil and Anita Christopher, Mike and Mary Carter, Mr and Mrs G S Ayrton)*

COBERLEY SO9616

Seven Springs [Andoversford, just SW of junction with A435 Cheltenham—Cirencester]: Spacious and airy chain dining pub, huge helpings of reasonably priced food, Greene King ales, lofty ceiling, big windows, snugger side areas; piped music; children welcome, sizeable sloping pond-side garden *(LYM, Ann and Colin Hunt)*

COLD ASHTON ST7472

White Hart [A420 Bristol—Chippenham just E of A46]: Welcoming and helpful, with well kept beers and good food choice inc good ham ploughman's *(Pat and Robert Watt)*

COLD ASTON SP1219

☆ *Plough* [aka Aston Blank; off A436 (B4068) or A429 SW of Stow-on-the-Wold]: Tiny 17th-c village pub, low black beams and flagstones, old-fashioned simple furnishings, welcoming service and locals, log fire, well kept Donnington BB, Hook Norton Best and a guest beer, tables set for enjoyable usual food from baguettes up; piped music; well behaved children welcome, picnic-sets under cocktail parasols on small side terraces, good walks, has been cl Mon *(P and J Shapley, LYM, Lawrence Pearse, Di and Mike Gillam, Guy Vowles, R Huggins, D Irving, E McCall, T McLean)*

COLESBOURNE SO9913

Colesbourne Inn [A435 Cirencester—Cheltenham]: 18th-c grey stone gabled coaching inn, beams, partly panelled dark red walls and log fires, comfortable mix of settles and softly padded seats, even a chaise longue, most tables now set for the well presented food, well kept Wadworths IPA and 6X, good wine list, separate no smoking candlelit dining room; traditional games, no visiting dogs, piped music; views from attractive back garden and terrace, nice bedrooms in converted stable block *(P R and S A White, LYM, Di and Mike Gillam, Denys Gueroult, Malcolm Taylor, Guy Vowles, Carl and Jackie Cranmer)*

COMPTON ABDALE SP0616

Puesdown Inn [A40 outside village]: Rather upmarket dining pub, former coaching inn, with wide choice of good imaginative food using local supplies, from panini up (no sandwiches), pleasantly airy no smoking restaurant, smart and relaxing bar with well padded seats on polished boards, cheerful easy chairs and settees by big log fire, quick hospitable service, Hook Norton, decent wines by the glass; piped music; nice garden behind, bedrooms *(Derek Carless, Peter and Audrey Dowsett, Mrs Koffman, Guy Vowles, Jo Rees)*

COOMBE HILL SO8827

Swan [A38/A4019]: Light and airy dining pub with several rooms, polished boards and panelling, red leather chesterfields, Greene King Abbot, Uley Old Spot and a guest beer, wide choice of attractively presented freshly cooked good value food, real ales, decent house wine, welcoming landlord *(Theocsbrian, Neil and Anita Christopher)*

CRANHAM SO8912

☆ *Black Horse* [off A46 and B4070 N of Stroud]: Well worn in 17th-c pub with good log fire and high-backed wall settles in quarry-tiled public bar, cosy little lounge, well kept Archers Best, Village and Golden Rain, Hancocks HB and Wickwar BOB, massively generous home cooking (not Sun evening) from good sandwiches and omelettes using their own free range eggs to fish and duck, cheaper small helpings, shove-ha'penny, a couple of pub dogs, no smoking upstairs dining rooms; piped music; children welcome *(Pete Baker, Giles and Annie Francis, LYM, Andrew Shore, Maria Williams, Di and Mike Gillam)*

DOYNTON ST7174

☆ *Cross House* [High St]: Chattily convivial 18th-c village pub with good friendly mix of locals and visitors, well kept Courage Best, Fullers London Pride, Greene King Old Speckled Hen and John Smiths, good wholesome country food, decent wines, welcoming helpful landlord, prompt service, beams, stripped stone, old prints, inglenook log fire, darts, steps down to candlelit restaurant with small no smoking area off, no piped music; good walking country, handy for Dyrham Park *(Colin and Peggy Wilshire, Pete and Rosie Flower, Barry and Anne, Tom and Ruth Rees, Dr and Mrs C W Thomas)*

DYMOCK SO6931

Beauchamp Arms: Friendly parish-owned pub with well kept local Whittingtons ales, interesting range of reasonably priced food, welcoming obliging staff; small pleasant garden with pond, bedrooms, handy for Daffodil Trail walkers, cl Mon lunchtime *(Duncan Cloud, Martin Jennings)*

EASTCOMBE SO8904

Lamb: Much extended and refurbished pub with peaceful valley views from lovely terrace and garden, popular inexpensive food, three or four well kept ales, well priced wines, two bars and sunken conservatory-style dining room; sports TV *(Alec and Susan Hamilton)*

EBRINGTON SP1840

Ebrington Arms [off B4035 E of Chipping Campden or A429 N of Moreton-in-Marsh]: Well refurbished village pub with low beams, stone walls, flagstones and inglenooks, well kept Donnington SBA, Hook Norton Best and Charles Wells Bombardier, sensible wine range, new dining room; children welcome, no dogs at meal times, picnic-sets on pleasant sheltered terrace, handy for Hidcote and Kiftsgate, bedrooms *(John Kane, Michael and Anne Brown, LYM, Barry and Anne)*

ELKSTONE SO9610

☆ *Highwayman* [Beechpike; off northbound A417 6 miles N of Cirencester]: Rambling and relaxing 16th-c warren of low beams, stripped stone, cosy alcoves, antique settles, armchairs and sofa among more usual furnishings, big log fires, rustic decorations, welcoming staff, well kept Arkells ales, good house wines, big back eating area (wide affordable choice); may be quiet piped music; disabled access, good family room, outside play area *(the Didler, P R and S A White, LYM, John and Claire Pettifer)*

FAIRFORD SP1501

☆ *Bull* [Market Pl]: Civilised and friendly beamed hotel in charming village (church has UK's only intact set of medieval stained-glass windows), large comfortably old-fashioned timbered bar with plenty of character and local RAF memorabilia, enormous blackboard choice of good value food, happy helpful staff, well kept Arkells 2B and 3B, log fire, charming restaurant in former stables, no smoking areas, no piped music; children welcome, 22 fresh bright bedrooms, open all day *(Peter and Audrey Dowsett, Stephen and Yvonne Agar)*

FOREST OF DEAN SO6212

Speech House [B4226 nearly 1m E of junction with B4234]: Olde-worlde hotel superbly placed in centre of Forest, warm interior with lots of oak panelling, huge log fire, well kept Bass, bar food, afternoon teas, attractive plush restaurant; comfortable bedrooms, tables outside *(Tom and Ruth Rees, Alan and Paula McCully)*

FRAMPTON MANSELL SO9202

☆ *Crown* [brown sign to pub off A491 Cirencester—Stroud]: Emphasis on food, with some good unusual dishes from sandwiches up (two lunch sittings at wknds), well kept Courage Best and a guest beer, good choice of wines by the glass, nice atmosphere in heavy-beamed bar with two log fires, stripped stone and rugs on bare boards, friendly helpful staff, daily papers, turkey-carpeted restaurant; piped music; picnic-sets in sunny front garden with terrace and pretty views over village and steep wooded valley; decent bedrooms, good breakfast *(LYM, Gerald Wilkinson, R Huggins, D Irving, E McCall, T McLean)*

FRAMPTON ON SEVERN SO7407

Bell [The Green]: Georgian dining pub by huge village cricket green, well kept real ales inc Bass and interesting guests, friendly service, log fire and plush seats, steps up to L-shaped family dining room, separate locals' bar with pool; bedrooms, good small back play area, open all day *(Mrs Ann Gray, Mrs Pamela Fisher)*

FROCESTER SO7831

George [Peter St]: Traditional welcoming two-bar coaching inn owned by a village consortium, adventurous changing well kept ales such as Caledonian Deuchars IPA and Orkney Dark Island, knowledgeable chatty barman, good food, big but cosy main room with two log fires, daily papers, smaller no smoking room, no machines; courtyard with boules, huge shuttered bedrooms *(R Huggins, D Irving, E McCall, T McLean)*

GLOUCESTER SO8318

☆ *Fountain* [Westgate St/Berkeley St]: Friendly and civilised L-shaped bar, plush seats and built-in wall benches, charming helpful service, well kept ales such as Caledonian Deuchars IPA, Fullers London Pride, Greene King Abbot, Timothy Taylors Landlord and Wickwar BOB, good range of whiskies, attractive prints, handsome stone fireplace (pub dates from 17th c), log-effect gas fire; cheap usual food; tables in pleasant courtyard, good disabled access, handy for cathedral, open all day *(BB, David Carr, A and B D Craig, Roger and Jenny Huggins, Mike Pugh)*

Longford Inn [A38, by Travel Inn]: Beefeater with reliable food all day, good friendly service, well kept Greene King Old Speckled Hen; bedrooms in attached Travel Inn *(Mr and Mrs Colin Roberts)*

New Inn [Northgate St]: Lovely medieval building with galleried courtyard, restored as pub in recent years, three bars with up to six often local real ales in one, Black Rat farm cider, enjoyable inexpensive lunchtime food, coffee shop, restaurant; good value bedrooms, open all day (till 1.30 Thurs-Sat) *(Theocsbrian, the Didler)*

Royal Oak [Hucclecote Rd]: Popular main road pub with good range of real ales, food inc bargain Sun roasts; live entertainment Fri, Sun quiz night; plenty of picnic-sets on big lawns *(B M Eldridge)*

Tall Ship [Southgate St, docks entrance]: Extended Victorian pub near historic docks, raised dining area with emphasis on wide choice of enterprisingly cooked fresh fish, also good sandwiches, ploughman's and daily roasts, morning coffee and afternoon tea, well kept Wadworths and a guest beer; pool table and juke box (may be loud) on left; terrace, open all day *(David Carr, Pat Nelmes)*

GOTHERINGTON SO9629

Shutter [off A435 N of Cheltenham; Shutter Lane]: Good value pub lunches, well kept Adnams, Wadworths 6X and Wickwar Cotswold Way, decent house wines, good welcoming service; children welcome, disabled access, garden with good play area, by GWR private railway station, good walks *(Mike and Liz Nash, Martin Jennings)*

GREAT BARRINGTON SP2013

☆ ***Fox*** [off A40 Burford—Northleach; pub towards Little Barrington]: 17th-c pub in nice spot by River Windrush (swans and private fishing), low-ceilinged small bar with stripped stone and simple country furnishings, well kept Donnington BB and SBA, farm cider, friendly landlord, good choice of promptly served food (not Mon night in winter) from sandwiches (not Sun) to good seasonal pheasant casserole, river-view dining room in former skittle alley, darts, shove-ha'penny, cribbage, dominoes; juke box, fruit machine, TV, can be smoky in eating area; heated terrace, orchard with pond, children welcome, open all day, food all day Sun and summer Sat *(LYM, Neil and Anita Christopher, the Didler, R Huggins, D Irving, E McCall, T McLean, Tim and Ann Newell, Joyce and Geoff Robson, Rod Stoneman, Pete Baker, James Woods, Jim Abbott, Suzanne Miles, Mrs S Wilkinson)*

GREAT RISSINGTON SP1917

☆ ***Lamb*** [off A40 W of Burford, via Gt Barrington]: Partly 17th-c, with civilised two-room bar, well kept ales such as Hook Norton Best and Charles Wells Bombardier, decent wines, open fire, enjoyable food (can be a wait), darts, dominoes, and cribbage, no smoking olde-worlde candlelit restaurant; may be piped music; children welcome, nice sheltered hillside garden, bedrooms *(LYM, Mr and Mrs I Bell, Paul Humphreys, Tom Bottinga, James Woods, Lawrence Pearse, Suzanne Miles, David A Hammond, Guy Vowles, Mr and Mrs J Brown, Tom Evans)*

GREET SP0230

Harvest Home [Evesham Rd (B4078 by Winchcombe Station bridge)]: Well spaced tables, bay window seats, hop bines on beams, wide choice of enjoyable food inc good baguettes and wkdy OAP lunches in bar or big beamed pitched-roof barn restaurant (no smoking), real ales such as Goffs Jouster, Greene King IPA and Old Speckled Hen, Tetleys and Charles Wells Bombardier, decent house wines, log fires, entertaining landlord, friendly attentive service; sizeable garden, not far from medieval Sudeley Castle *(LYM, Mr and Mrs J Williams, Dave Braisted)*

GRETTON SP0131

Royal Oak [off B4077 E of Tewkesbury]: Appealing upmarket pub with linked bare-boarded or flagstoned rooms, beams hung with tankards, hop bines and chamber-pots, old prints, nice mixed bag of seats and tables, stripped country furnishings in no smoking dining conservatory; has had various changes of staff and management over the last year or two, but well kept Goffs and a guest ales and decent wines have been a constant theme; children and dogs allowed, fine views from flower-filled terrace, big pleasant garden with play area and tennis, GWR private railway runs past, good nearby walks, open all day summer wknds *(LYM, Brenda and Rob Fincham, Nick and Meriel Cox)*

GUITING POWER SP0924

Farmers Arms [Fosseway (A429)]: Stripped stone and flagstones, particularly well kept cheap Donnington BB and SBA, wide blackboard range of unpretentious food from sandwiches and good ploughman's up inc children's dishes, prompt service, good coal or log fire; skittle alley, games area with darts, pool, cribbage, dominoes, fruit machine; piped music; seats (and quoits) in garden, good walks; children welcome, bedrooms, lovely village *(LYM, Guy Vowles, the Didler, Lawrence Pearse)*

HAWKESBURY UPTON ST7786

Beaufort Arms [High St]: Well kept Hook Norton, Wickwar BOB and guest beers, local farm cider, friendly landlord and staff, good choice of good value home-made food in extended uncluttered dining lounge on right, darts in stripped-brick bare-boards bar, interesting local and brewery memorabilia, skittle alley; children welcome, seats outside, on Cotswold Way *(S Fysh, Matthew Shackle)*

HINTON DYRHAM ST7376

☆ ***Bull*** [2.4 miles from M4 junction 18; A46 towards Bath, then first right (opp the Crown)]: Pretty 16th-c stone-built pub, with two huge fireplaces facing each other across ancient pitted flagstones in main bar, window seat, massive built-in oak settles, pews, dark captain's chairs, big oriental rugs, wall sconces, low ceiling; stripped stone back area with unusual cushioned cast-iron chairs, family room on the left, piped music, well kept Wadworths IPA, 6X and a guest, no smoking restaurant; plenty of picnic-sets and play equipment in a sizeable sheltered upper garden, with more on sunny front terrace, enjoyable food; cl Mon lunchtime, dogs (and children till 7.30) in bar *(Michael Doswell, Brian Root, Barry and Anne, LYM)*

KEMBLE ST9897

Thames Head [A433 Cirencester—Tetbury]: Stripped stone, timberwork, softly lit cottagey no smoking back area with pews and log-effect gas fire in big fireplace, country-look dining room with another big gas fire, real log fire in front area, good value wines, Arkells 2B and 3B, helpful staff, tranquil atmosphere; skittle alley, seats outside, children welcome, good value four-poster bedrooms, nice walk to nearby low-key source of River Thames *(LYM, R Huggins, D Irving, E McCall, T McLean, David Edwards)*

KILCOT SO6925

Kilcot Inn [B4221, not far from M50 junction 3]: Recently reopened after renovation and extension, Greene King Old Speckled Hen and local Whittingtons ale, good value blackboard food in bar and no smoking eating area, stripped beams, rustic bare brick, log fires; dogs welcome, garden picnic-sets *(Theocsbrian, Neil and Jean Spink)*

KILKENNY SP0018

Kilkeney Inn [A436 W of Andoversford]: Spacious and reliable modernised dining pub with log fire and comfortable no smoking conservatory, well kept Bass and Hook Norton, pleasant relaxed surroundings; well behaved children allowed in eating areas, tables outside, attractive Cotswold views, open all day wknds *(Joyce and Geoff Robson, LYM, John and Glenys Wheeler, Brian and Pat Wardrobe, John and Joan Wyatt, Trevor and Sylvia Millum, Bernard Stradling, Mrs T A Bizat)*

LECHLADE SU2199

New Inn [Market Sq (A361)]: Very wide choice of good value generous food from good filled baguettes up, good changing range of well kept ales inc Archers, helpful staff, huge log fire in big pleasantly plain lounge with games machine and TV at one end, back restaurant; piped music; play area in big garden extending to Thames, good walks, comfortable bedrooms *(Fred Chamberlain, Peter and Audrey Dowsett, Gerald Wilkinson, Dr and Mrs A K Clarke, David Edwards)*

Trout [A417, a mile E]: Low-beamed three-room pub dating from 15th c, nice big Thames-side garden with boules, aunt sally and spill-over bar out in converted boathouse; well kept Courage Best, John Smiths and a guest such as Charles Wells Bombardier, popular if not cheap food, good log fire, flagstones, stuffed fish and fishing prints, local paintings for sale, no smoking dining room; children in eating areas, board games and magazines, jazz Tues and Sun, no piped music, fishing rights; may be long waits in summer (open all day Sat then), when very busy, with bouncy castle and fairground swings; large car park, camping *(P R and S A White, Neil and Anita Christopher, LYM, R Huggins, D Irving, E McCall, T McLean, Paul and Annette Hallett, Geoff Calcott, Giles and Annie Francis, Peter and Audrey Dowsett)*

LEIGHTERTON ST8290

Royal Oak [off A46 S of Nailsworth]: Quiet and unpretentious old stone-built pub, emphasis on good value simple food from soup and sandwiches up, three well kept ales such as Butcombe, prompt pleasant service, mullioned windows, linked carpeted rooms with pleasantly simple décor in original part and matching extension; nice garden, quiet village, good walks, quite handy for Westonbirt Arboretum *(Guy Vowles, Mrs Sally Lloyd, Peter and Audrey Dowsett)*

LONGFORD SO8320

Queens Head [Tewkesbury Rd]: Attractive open-plan bar with no smoking restaurant area, good value lunches from baguettes and baked potatoes up, slightly more upmarket evening meals, well kept ales such as Bass, Fullers London Pride, Greene King Old Speckled Hen and Hook Norton, pleasant efficient service *(Mr and Mrs J Norcott, Dr and Mrs A K Clarke, Tony Pope, Karen Bonham)*

LOWER ODDINGTON SP2326

☆ *Fox*: Spotless flagstoned pub-restaurant with interesting carefully cooked upmarket food, good well priced wines, well kept ales such as Badger Tanglefoot and Hook Norton Best, antique tables and chairs in linked rooms with inglenook fireplace, sisal mats and attractive prints; smokers not segregated; children welcome (they'll cook anything for them), tables on heated terrace with awning, pretty garden, pleasant walks, comfortable bedrooms *(Karen and Graham Oddey, Terry and Linda Moseley, Tom Evans, Maurice Ribbans, John Saville, Jay Bohmrich, Dr W I C Clark, LYM, Martin Jones, Michael and Anne Brown, Rod Stoneman, Mr and Mrs P Lally, Ann and Colin Hunt, C Tilley, Bernard Stradling, Martin and Karen Wake, Caroline Dunstall, Tracey and Stephen Groves, A P Seymour, Gary and Jane Gleghorn, Nick and Meriel Cox)*

LOWER SWELL SP1725

☆ *Golden Ball* [B4068 W of Stow-on-the-Wold]: Neat and simple stone-built beamed local with well kept Donnington BB and SBA from the pretty nearby brewery, good range of ciders and perry, very friendly landlady, well presented generous home-made food, big log fire, games area with fruit machine and juke box behind big chimneystack, small evening restaurant (not Sun evening), conservatory; no dogs or children; small garden with occasional barbecues, aunt sally and quoits; three decent simple bedrooms, pretty village, good walks *(the Didler, George Atkinson, Roger and Jenny Huggins, LYM, Giles and Annie Francis)*

MARSHFIELD ST7773

☆ *Catherine Wheel* [High St; signed off A420 Bristol—Chippenham]: Stripped stone traditional pub owned by consortium of customers, warm atmosphere, friendly staff, wide choice of well kept ales and of enjoyable food inc imaginative dishes, farm cider, decent wines, plates and prints, medley of settles, chairs and stripped tables, open fire in impressive fireplace, cottagey back family bar, charming no smoking Georgian dining room, darts, dominoes; flower-decked back yard, bedrooms, unspoilt village *(LYM, Pete and Rosie Flower, Susan and John Douglas, Dr and Mrs A K Clarke, John and Gloria Isaacs)*

MICKLETON SP1543

☆ *Kings Arms* [B4632 (ex A46)]: Well organised service with friendly staff eager to please in relaxed and civilised open-plan family lounge with no smoking area, wide choice of good locally sourced food from well filled sandwiches up (best to book at wknds), good value OAP lunches, well kept ales such as Goffs Tournament, good value wines by the glass, farm cider, nice mix of comfortable chairs, soft lighting, interesting homely décor, small log fire; piped music; small welcoming locals' bar with darts, dominoes and cribbage; tables outside, handy for Kiftsgate and Hidcote

(Ian Phillips, Martin and Karen Wake, BB, K H Frostick, Mrs Mary Walters, Martin Jones, Mrs B J Edwards, Martin Jennings, John H Franklin, Clive and Fran Dutson)

MINCHINHAMPTON SO8500

☆ *Old Lodge* [Nailsworth—Brimscombe – on common fork left at pub's sign; OS Sheet 162 map ref 853008]: Relaxed and welcoming dining pub, small snug central bar opening into eating area with beams and stripped brick, no smoking area, friendly efficient staff, well kept Youngs ales; trad jazz Sun lunchtime, tables on neat lawn with attractive flower border, looking over common with grazing cows and horses *(LYM, Bernard Stradling, Tom and Ruth Rees)*

MORETON-IN-MARSH SP2032

Black Bear [High St]: Unpretentious beamed pub, stripped stone with hanging rugs and old village pictures, well kept local Donnington XXX, BB and SBA, good coffee, good value home-made pub food inc fresh fish, large airy dining room (not Sun evening), friendly service; public bar with lots of football memorabilia, darts, sports TV and games machine; may be piped radio; tables outside, big bedrooms sharing bathrooms *(the Didler, BB, Ted George, Bernard and Marilyn Smith)*

☆ *Redesdale Arms* [High St]: Fine old coaching inn with prettily lit alcoves and big stone fireplace in solidly furnished comfortable panelled bar on right, well kept ales such as Courage Directors and Wye Valley, small but good wine list, cafetière coffee, interesting choice of generous food, good friendly service, log fires, spacious back child-friendly restaurant and dining conservatory, darts in flagstoned public bar; piped music, fruit machine, TV; tables out on heated floodlit courtyard decking, comfortable well equipped bedrooms beyond *(Joyce and Maurice Cottrell, BB, Guy Vowles, Peter Gondris, Peter Coxon)*

Swan [High St]: Good choice of low-priced generous food inc pies and children's, well kept Boddingtons and Wadworths 6X, decent wine, neat bright lounge with flowered wallpaper and old photographs, pool on public side, attractive separate dining room, quick friendly service even when coachloads roll in on Tues market day, skittle alley *(Ted George)*

NAILSWORTH ST8499

George [Newmarket]: Good valley views, attractive central bar with lounge/eating area one side, dining room the other, above-average freshly made food, four well kept ales inc Timothy Taylors Landlord and Wickwar Cotswold Way, good welcoming service *(Bruce Adams, R Huggins, D Irving, E McCall, T McLean)*

NAUNTON SP1123

☆ *Black Horse* [off B4068 W of Stow]: New tenants in neat unspoilt black-beamed bar with stripped stone and log fire, straightforward food from huge baguettes and baked potatoes up, well priced Donnington BB and SBA, darts, cribbage, dominoes, no smoking dining room; piped music; children and dogs welcome, some tables outside, bedrooms with own bathrooms, charming village, fine Cotswold walks *(A and B D Craig, Pete Baker, Dr G and Mrs J Kelvin, LYM, Martin Jennings)*

NEWENT SO7425

Travellers Rest [B4215 E]: Popular for decent pub food inc good choice of Sun roasts in two helping sizes, good range of well kept ales, personable licensees, attractive dining conservatory *(Mr and Mrs J Norcott, B M Eldridge)*

NEWNHAM SO6911

Ship [High St]: Two-bar pub with up to three real ales, local farm cider, wide choice of enjoyable fresh food using local produce, upstairs restaurant, friendly young staff; pool, piped music, live Weds/Thurs – popular with young people; tables in garden with terrace, bedrooms *(Caroline and Michael Abbey, CMW, JJW)*

NORTH NIBLEY ST7495

☆ *Black Horse* [Barrs Lane]: Friendly village pub handy for Cotswold Way, nice décor, wide range of generous good value home-made food, well kept Flowers Original and Marstons Pedigree, decent wines, good log fire, restaurant; tables in pretty garden, good value cottagey bedrooms, good breakfast *(James Morrell, LYM, Mike Green)*

NORTHLEACH SP1114

Sherborne Arms [Market Pl]: New regime with stylish and interesting fresh food in smart restaurant up a few stairs, also large lively back bar with plenty of dining tables, comfortably small front bar, cosy lounge with four wing armchairs around big stone fireplace, attentive staff, well kept Goffs Jouster and Greene King Old Speckled Hen, good wines *(Derek Carless, Claire Lymer, R Huggins, D Irving, E McCall, T McLean, W G Myatt, Gene and Kitty Rankin)*

NORTON SO8524

Kings Head [just off A38; Old Tewkesbury Rd]: Spacious simply furnished divided bar, nice atmosphere, Greene King Old Speckled Hen and Goffs Jouster, enjoyable efficiently served food; garden tables *(Neil and Anita Christopher)*

NYMPSFIELD SO7900

Rose & Crown [The Cross; signed off B4066 Stroud—Dursley]: Bright well decorated stone-built dining pub with generous food from good value baguettes to interesting restauranty dishes and things for children, well kept Butcombe, John Smiths and a guest beer, decent wines, helpful friendly staff, daily papers, log fire and beams in front part with serving bar, pews and other seats in large back area; unobtrusive piped music, children and dogs welcome, picnic-sets in side yard and on sheltered lawn with good play area; bedrooms, handy for Cotswold walks *(BB, Gordon Briggs)*

OAKRIDGE LYNCH SO9103

☆ *Butchers Arms* [off Eastcombe—Bisley rd E of Stroud]: An unpretentious welcoming favourite; rambling partly stripped stone bar, enjoyable food (not Sun evening or Mon) from hot baguettes to steak, well kept ales such as Archers Best, Goffs Jouster, Greene King

Abbot and Wickwar BOB, three open fires, no smoking restaurant; children welcome away from bar, tables on neat lawn overlooking valley, good walks by former Thames & Severn canal *(R Huggins, D Irving, E McCall, T McLean, LYM, BB, Bernard Stradling, Nick and Meriel Cox, Brian McBurnie, Mr and Mrs P L Spencer)*

OLD DOWN ST6187

Fox [off A38 Bristol—Thornbury; Inner Down]: Doing well under current landlord, locally popular now for enjoyable very varied food, particularly good vegetarian choice *(James Morrell)*

PAINSWICK SO8609

☆ *Falcon* [New St]: Sizeable old stone-built inn opp churchyard famous for its 99 yews; open-plan, relaxing and comfortable, largely panelled, with high ceilings, bare-boards bar with stuffed birds and fish, mainly carpeted dining area with lots of prints, high bookshelves and shelves of ornaments by coal-effect fire, wide range of sensibly generous food from baguettes up, lots of wines by the glass, well kept Boddingtons, Hook Norton Best and Old Hooky and Wadworths 6X, good coffee, helpful service, daily papers; big comfortable bedrooms, good breakfast *(R Huggins, D Irving, E McCall, T McLean, James Morrell, Meg and Colin Hamilton, BB, Neil and Anita Christopher, Dr L Kaufman, DC)*

☆ *Royal Oak* [St Mary's St]: Old-fashioned partly 16th-c town pub doing well under friendly new management, some attractive old or antique seats, plenty of old prints, enjoyable good value food from filled rolls to interesting main dishes, well kept Flowers Original and Hook Norton, decent wines, good service, open fire, no smoking lounge and small sun lounge by suntrap pretty courtyard; children in eating area *(R Huggins, D Irving, E McCall, T McLean, LYM, Brian McBurnie, Neil and Anita Christopher)*

PARKEND SO6208

Fountain [just off B4234]: Assorted chairs and settles, real fire, old local tools and photographs, wide choice of fresh food inc good range of curries, efficient landlord, well kept local Freeminer and one or two guest beers; children and dogs welcome *(Pete Baker, CMW, JJW)*

Miners Arms [Moseley Green]: Friendly stone-built pub in Forest of Dean with well kept Holdens and three quickly changing guest beers, local farm cider, good range of food inc fresh sandwiches, darts, board games, small no smoking room with a few toddler toys, skittle alley; tables in attractive garden, picnic-sets in paddock by Riber Lyd, boules, quiet spot *(Theocsbrian, G Harvey)*

PILNING ST5684

Plough [handy for M5 junction 17 via B4055 and Station Rd; Pilning St]: Building of character, friendly current licensees working hard on the food side, with good cooking and wide range lunchtime and evening every day, good wine choice; live music Sun evening; pleasant garden overlooking open country *(Joyce and Maurice Cottrell, James Morrell)*

POULTON SP1001

☆ *Falcon* [London Rd (A417)]: Appealing décor, good interesting modern food, well kept real ales, nice choice of wines, good friendly service, big fireplace, long dining room; children welcome, tables outside, pretty village with ancient church *(Fiona Duncan, Inga and Keith Rutter, Adrian White)*

PRESTBURY SO9624

☆ *Plough* [Mill St]: Well preserved thatched village local opp church, cosy and comfortable front lounge with panelling-look wallpaper, service from corner corridor counter in basic but roomy flagstoned back taproom, grandfather clock and big log fire, consistently friendly service, well kept Greene King Abbot and Charles Wells Bombardier tapped from the cask; lovely flower-filled back garden *(Roger and Jenny Huggins, Di and Mike Gillam)*

☆ *Royal Oak* [The Burgage]: Small comfortable village local popular for good generous freshly made restaurant food at attractive prices, good service, nice house wines, welcoming atmosphere, well kept ales such as Archers, Timothy Taylors Landlord and Wadworths 6X, Thatcher's cider and good value house wines, low-beamed bar with green plush settles, cushioned pew and other seats, brasses and fresh flowers, no machines; good-sized garden behind, open all day summer wknds *(Mr and Nrs R L Fraser, Mr and Mrs J Brown, Mrs C Lintott, Michael Sargent, Joe Green)*

PUCKLECHURCH ST6976

Rose & Crown [Parkfield Rd, NW]: Two-bar flagstoned pub with large tasteful no smoking dining extension, busy even midweek lunchtimes for enjoyable straightforward food cooked to order (get there before 8, kitchen closes promptly), friendly service, well kept Bass and Wadworths 6X and JCB; seats outside, quiet country setting *(Andrew Shore, Maria Williams, Dr and Mrs M E Wilson)*

REDBROOK SO5410

☆ *Boat* [car park signed on A466 Chepstow—Monmouth, then 100-yard footbridge over Wye; or very narrow steep car access from Penallt in Wales]: Beautifully set laid-back and congenial unsmart pub on Wye, friendly licensees, changing well kept ales such as Greene King IPA and Abbot, Robinsons Best, Stonehenge Bodyline and Wye Valley Butty Bach tapped from casks, good range of country wines and hot drinks, stripped stone walls, flagstone floors and roaring woodburner, inexpensive no-nonsense food inc good value baked potatoes, good fresh baguettes and children's dishes (can be delays if busy); live music Tues and Thurs; several cats, dogs and children welcome, rough home-built seats in informal garden with stream spilling down waterfall cliffs into duck pond, open all day *(LYM, Roger and Anne Newbury, David Carr, LM, Bob and Margaret Holder, Tim Gorringe, Donald Godden, R Huggins, D Irving, E McCall, T McLean, Ann and Colin Hunt,*

Phil and Heidi Cook)

RODBOROUGH SO8404

Bear [Rodborough Common]: Comfortably cosy and pubby beamed and flagstoned bar in smart hotel, friendly staff, pleasant window seats, welcoming log fire, hops hung around top of golden stone walls, interesting reproductions, well kept Bass and Uley, good value food (bar and restaurant) inc afternoon tea; children welcome, bedrooms *(BB, Meg and Colin Hamilton)*

SAPPERTON SO9403

Daneway Inn [Daneway; off A419 Stroud—Cirencester]: Flagstone-floored local worth tracking down for its tables on terrace and lovely sloping lawn in charming quiet wooded countryside; amazing floor-to-ceiling carved oak dutch fireplace, sporting prints, well kept Wadworths IPA, 6X and JCB, Weston's farm cider, reasonably priced generous food from filled baps up (may be a wait on busy days), small no smoking family room, traditional games in inglenook public bar; camping possible, good walks by canal under restoration with tunnel to Coates *(R Huggins, D Irving, E McCall, T McLean, LYM, Peter and Audrey Dowsett)*

SHIPTON MOYNE ST8989

Cat & Custard Pot [off B4040 Malmesbury—Bristol; The Street]: Enormous choice of good value robust food from sandwiches up, well kept Fullers London Pride, Wadworths 6X and guest beers, Thatcher's cider, neat staff and good service, hunting prints in divided bar/dining room, cosy back snug; picturesque village *(BB, Richard Stancomb)*

SIDDINGTON SU0399

☆ *Greyhound* [Ashton Rd; village signed from A419 roundabout at Tesco]: Good choice of enjoyable food from good sandwiches up in two friendly linked rooms each with a big log fire, well kept Badger Tanglefoot, Wadworths IPA and seasonal beers, public bar with slate floor, darts and cribbage, striking deep well in skittle alley/function room; piped music may be loud and service can slow on busy lunchtimes; garden tables *(LYM, R Huggins, D Irving, E McCall, T McLean, P R and S A White, Peter and Audrey Dowsett)*

SLAD SO8707

Woolpack [B4070 Stroud—Birdlip]: Small hillside village pub with lovely valley views, several linked rooms with Laurie Lee photographs, some of his books for sale, good value food (not Sun evening) from sandwiches and baguettes to enjoyable hot dishes inc generous Sun roast, well kept Bass and Uley ales, farm cider and perry, log fire and nice tables, games and cards *(R Huggins, D Irving, E McCall, T McLean, Matthew Shackle, Pete Baker)*

SNOWSHILL SP0934

Snowshill Arms: Spruce and airy carpeted bar in honeypot village, stripped stone, neat array of tables, local photographs, friendly service, well kept Donnington BB and SBA, log fire, quickly served straightforward food (fill in your own order form); skittle alley, charming village views from bow windows and from big back garden with little stream and play area, friendly local feel midweek winter and evenings, can be very crowded other lunchtimes – nearby parking may be difficult; children welcome if eating, handy for Snowshill Manor and Cotswold Way walks *(LYM, Maysie Thompson, Dr David Cockburn, Angus Lyon, Mrs Edna M Jones)*

SOMERFORD KEYNES SU0195

Bakers Arms: Pretty stone-built pub, large knocked-together stripped-stone area with lots of pine tables for decent food from baguettes and ciabattas up, well kept Charles Wells Bombardier and a beer brewed for the pub, good house wine, two log fires; children welcome, big garden, lovely Cotswold village *(Roger Huggins, Tom and Alex McLean)*

SOUTH CERNEY SU0496

Royal Oak [High St]: Sympathetically extended local, Bass, Fullers London Pride and Greene King, lively atmosphere; pleasant garden with big terrace and summer marquee *(R Huggins, D Irving, E McCall, T McLean, Philip Nicholas)*

SOUTHROP SP2003

☆ *Swan*: New chef/landlord doing particularly good generous interesting food in attractively refurbished low-ceilinged dining lounge with log fire and flagstones, well spaced tables, friendly attentive service, well kept Greene King Abbot and Hook Norton, good wines, no smoking restaurant (not Sun evening); stripped stone skittle alley, public bar; children welcome, pretty village esp at daffodil time *(Mrs M Milsom, LYM, Mrs Challiner, Dr J J H Gilkes)*

STANTON SP0734

☆ *Mount* [off B4632 SW of Broadway; no through road up hill, bear left]: Stunning spot up steep lane from golden-stone village, heavy beams, flagstones and big log fire in original core, horseracing pictures and trappings and plenty of locals, roomy picture-window extensions, one no smoking with cricket memorabilia; well kept Donnington BB and SBA, farm cider, bar food (not Sun evening) from super baguettes up; open all day Sat and summer Sun, well behaved children allowed, views to Welsh mountains from large terrace, attractive garden with pets' corner *(Richard and Karen Holt, Bruce M Drew, Tim and Carolyn Lowes, LYM, Di and Mike Gillam, Lawrence Pearse, Angus Lyon, Mrs B J Edwards, John Foord, Mr and Mrs Colin Roberts, C Howard, Ken Marshall)*

STAUNTON SO7829

Swan [Ledbury Rd (A417)]: Enthusiastic young couple have turned former skittle alley into tasteful restaurant with generous imaginative food cooked by landlord *(Mrs R Blair)*

STOKE GIFFORD ST6279

Beaufort Arms [North Rd]: Friendly pub with three real ales inc a guest such as Fullers London Pride or Timothy Taylors Landlord, belgian and czech bottled beers *(Andrew York)*

STOW-ON-THE-WOLD SP1925

Bell [Park St; A436 E of centre]: Flagstoned bar with small carpeted dining area on right, carpeted lounge bar on left, well kept Boddingtons, Flowers and Hook Norton, sensibly priced food, cheerful service; bedrooms, open all day *(Ann and Colin Hunt)*

☆ *Coach & Horses* [Ganborough (A424 N)]: Beamed and flagstoned country pub alone on former coaching road, well kept and priced Donnington BB and SBA, very wide choice of popular generous well priced food (all day summer Fri/Sat) from baguettes up, good fires, steps up to carpeted dining area with high-backed settles, no smoking area; popular skittle alley, children welcome, tables in garden, open all day Sun too *(A H C Rainier, Giles and Annie Francis, LYM, John Kane, Martin Jennings)*

Grapevine [Sheep St]: Substantial hotel with very friendly small front bar, Bass, decent wines by the glass, good coffee, bar food from generous sandwiches and baguettes to steak and bass, restaurant with live vine, good service; pavement tables, bedrooms, open all day *(Michael Dandy)*

☆ *Kings Arms* [The Square]: Reasonably priced good food inc lots of fish and real food for children in pleasant bar and charming upstairs dining room overlooking town, good choice of wines by the glass, Greene King Old Speckled Hen and Ruddles County, good coffee (opens early for this), cheerful friendly service, some Mackintosh-style chairs on polished boards, bowed black beams, some panelling and stripped stone, log fire; bedrooms, open all day *(BB, Peter Burton, Michael and Anne Brown, Mrs Angela Bromley-Martin, Pat and Roger Fereday, Michael Jones, Gary and Jane Gleghorn, Mr and Mrs Martin Joyce)*

☆ *Queens Head* [The Square]: Friendly new licensees in proper traditional unfussy local, heavily beamed and flagstoned traditional back bar with high-backed settles, big log fire, horse prints, piped music, usual games; lots of tables in civilised softly lit stripped stone front lounge, good value pub food (may be a wait), well kept Donnington BB and SBA, decent house wines, good friendly service; dogs and children positively welcome, tables in attractive garden, occasional jazz Sun lunchtime *(LYM, Paul and Sue Merrick, Gary and Jane Gleghorn, the Didler, Ian and Celia Abbott)*

☆ *Talbot* [The Square]: Light, airy and spacious modern décor, relaxed brasserie/wine bar feel, good reasonably priced continental-feel food, bright friendly service even when busy, three real ales, lots of good value wines by the glass, good coffee, big log fire, plain tables and chairs on new wood block floor, modern prints, daily papers; no children inside, may be piped radio, lavatories upstairs; bedrooms nearby, open all day *(George Atkinson, Guy Vowles, BB, W W Burke, Dave and Sue Norgate)*

STROUD SO8403

Kings Head [The Street, Kingscourt (just off A46 S)]: Interesting old-fashioned two-room rustic local below Rodborough hill fort, good views, two or three real ales, farm cider, good value basic food *(Guy Vowles)*

TETBURY ST8993

Crown [Gumstool Hill]: Large friendly 17th-c town pub, good value bar lunches, well kept ales such as Black Sheep and Hook Norton Best, long oak-beamed front bar with big log fire and attractive medley of tables, efficient service; may be unobtrusive piped music; pleasant back no smoking family dining conservatory with lots of plants, picnic-sets on back terrace, comfortable bedrooms *(R Huggins, D Irving, E McCall, T McLean, Peter and Audrey Dowsett)*

☆ *Gumstool* [at Calcot Manor Hotel; A4135 W]: Upmarket dining bar attached to good country hotel, imaginative food (small helpings of some dishes), well kept Courage Best, Wickwar BOB and changing guest beers, dozens of malt whiskies and fine choice of wines by the glass, good coffees, daily papers, stripped pine, flagstones and gingham curtains, leather armchair by big log fire, mainly no smoking restaurant; piped music; children welcome, tables in pleasant garden, comfortable well equipped bedrooms, open all day wknds *(JMC, Donald Godden, Alec and Barbara Jones, Rod Stoneman, Carol and Dono Leaman, Dr and Mrs C W Thomas, Tom and Ruth Rees, Bernard Stradling, LYM)*

Royal Oak [Cirencester Rd]: Family-run stone-built former coaching inn with good fires in friendly unspoilt bar, Courage, Fullers London Pride and John Smiths, enjoyable reasonably priced food, quick service, cosy dining areas; well equipped bedrooms with own bathrooms, by free long-stay car park *(Norman and Sheila Davies, Peter and Audrey Dowsett)*

Snooty Fox [Market Pl]: Good food both traditional and unusual in high-ceilinged hotel lounge, smart, unstuffy and relaxing, with well kept beer, good house wines, helpful staff, medieval-style chairs and elegant fireplace, charming side room and ante-room, restaurant; unobtrusive piped jazz; children welcome, bedrooms good value *(Barry and Anne, Colin and Janet Roe, David A Hammond, Dr and Mrs A K Clarke)*

TEWKESBURY SO8932

Olde Black Bear [High St]: Well worth a look for the building which houses what has now become quite a large commercial operation – the county's oldest pub, rambling rooms with heavy low beams (one with leather-clad ceiling), lots of timbers, armchairs in front of open fires, bare wood and ancient tiles, plenty of pictures and bric-a-brac; well kept beers such as Greenalls and Charles Wells Bombardier, reasonably priced wines; piped music; children welcome, terrace and play area in riverside garden, open all day *(David Carr, John Beeken, LYM, the Didler, John Foord, Paul Williams)*

TOCKINGTON ST6186

Swan: Popular roomy pub with beams, standing timbers, bric-a-brac on stripped stone walls, log fire, helpful service, reasonably priced food; piped music; good wheelchair access, tables in tree-shaded garden, quiet village *(Pamela and Merlyn Horswell, Charles and Pauline Stride)*

TOLLDOWN ST7577

☆ *Crown* [a mile from M4 junction 18 – A46 towards Bath]: Well run heavy-beamed pub reopened after extensive refurbishment (following storm damage), appealing light décor with plenty of wood and fresh flowers, good value generous interesting food from good ciabattas up, well kept Wadworths ales, good house wines, good log fire, no smoking area; children in eating area and restaurant, good garden with play area, comfortable bedrooms *(LYM, Howard and Lorna Lambert, Mike and Cherry Fann, C L Kauffmann, Dr and Mrs A K Clarke)*

TWYNING SO8737

☆ *Fleet* [off westbound A38 slip rd from M50 junction 1]: Family holiday pub in superb setting at end of quiet lane, good river views from roomy high-ceilinged bars, interesting boating-theme décor, five well kept real ales, tasty bar food, woodburner, airy back restaurant area, tearoom and tuck shop; games room with darts and bar billiards (no children in here while games are being played), piped music, fruit machines, entertainment Fri/Sat; disabled access, children welcome, picnic-sets in big waterside garden with two floodlit terraces, rockery cascade and pets corner; stop on Tewkesbury—Bredon summer boat run, even own ferry across from Worcs bank, bedrooms, open all day *(LYM)*

ULEY ST7998

Old Crown [The Green]: Unpretentious warmly rustic pub prettily set by village green just off Cotswold Way, long narrow room with settles on bare boards and step up to partitioned-off lounge area, friendly staff, enjoyable home cooking from sandwiches and baked potatoes to good fish choice, local Uley and several other well kept changing ales, small games room up spiral stairs with pool, darts etc; dogs welcome, live music Tues and Fri; attractive garden behind, bedrooms *(Di and Mike Gillam, Geoffrey Tyack, R Huggins, D Irving, E McCall, T McLean, Pete Baker)*

UPPER FRAMILODE SO7510

☆ *Ship* [Saul Rd; not far from M5 junction 13 via B4071]: Attractive and comfortable modernised dining pub doing well under current regime, wide range of above-average food inc local game and ramblers' menu (order, then walk, then eat), well kept ales such as Hook Norton, decent wines, efficient friendly service, relaxed and easy-going atmosphere in two bars and restaurant extension; good garden, tucked away by disused canalside offshoot from Severn with ducks and swans *(Peter Neate, Alec and Susan Hamilton, Mark Williamson, Betty Haynes)*

WANSWELL GREEN SO6801

Salmon: Small pleasant pub in quiet village, unobtrusive dining extension, friendly staff, varied menu inc vegetarian, real ales inc Greene King Old Speckled Hen; tables out on lawns, big front play area, nr Berkeley Castle and Severn walks *(Richard Fendick)*

WHITMINSTER SO7708

Old Forge [A38 1½ miles N of M5 junction 13]: Simple and welcoming L-shaped beamed pub with small carpeted bar, games room, good generous inexpensive food (not Sun evening or Mon) inc bargain lunch, well kept changing ales such as Butcombe, Greene King IPA and Ushers Founders and Summer Ale, happy staff, decent wines, no smoking dining room with panelled dado; children welcome, garden tables *(Tony Hobden, Roger and Jenny Huggins)*

WICK ST7072

☆ *Rose & Crown* [High St (A420)]: Well run Chef & Brewer, busy and roomy, very wide blackboard food range from good value lunchtime sandwiches and baguettes to unusual fish dishes (only main meals on Sun), efficient friendly staff, well kept Courage Best and one or two other ales, interesting wine choice, plenty of character in largely untouched linked 17th-c rooms with low beams, mixed furnishings and candlelight, daily papers; pleasant tables facing village green *(Michael Doswell, Andrew Shore, Maria Williams, Ron Shelton, Dr Louise Bawden, Dr Ed Bond, John Cook, Barry and Anne)*

WILLERSEY SP1039

☆ *Bell* [B4632 Cheltenham—Stratford, nr Broadway]: Attractive stone-built pub, open-plan and much modernised, comfortable front part impressively set for the carefully prepared interesting and unpretentious home-made food, Aston Villa memorabilia and huge collection of model cars in back area past the big L-shaped bar counter with its well kept Hook Norton Best, Tetleys and Wadworths 6X, relaxed atmosphere, quick friendly helpful service; darts, may be piped music, Thurs evening chess ladder; overlooks delightful village's green and duck pond, lots of tables in big garden, bedrooms in outbuildings *(Alec and Susan Hamilton, Miss J Brotherton, BB, John Foord)*

WINCHCOMBE SP0228

☆ *Old Corner Cupboard* [Gloucester St]: Attractive golden stone pub with generous reasonably priced food in nice back partly no smoking eating area, cheerful fast service, well kept Fullers London Pride, Hook Norton Old Hooky and seasonal local Stanway ales, decent wines, comfortable stripped-stone lounge bar with heavy-beamed Tudor core, traditional hatch-service lobby, small side smoke room with woodburner in massive stone fireplace, traditional games; children in eating areas, tables in back garden, open all day *(George Atkinson, Joyce and Geoff Robson, Norman and Sarah Keeping, LYM, Dave Braisted, Di and Mike Gillam, Ann and Colin Hunt, David and Nina Pugsley, Mrs C Lintott)*

☆ *Plaisterers Arms* [Abbey Terr]: 18th-c pub with stripped stonework, beams, Hogarth prints, bric-a-brac and flame-effect fires, two chatty front bars both with steps down to dim-lit lower back dining area with tables in stalls, enterprising cooking by landlady, good service, well kept Goffs Jouster, Greene King Old Speckled Hen and Ushers Best; dogs very welcome, good play area in charming garden, long and narrow, comfortable simple bedrooms with own bathrooms (tricky stairs), handy for Sudeley Castle *(BB, George Atkinson, Di and Mike Gillam, Joyce and Maurice Cottrell, W W Burke, David and Nina Pugsley, Ian and Celia Abbott)*

WOODCHESTER SO8403

Old Fleece [Rooksmoor; A46 a mile S of Stroud – not to be confused with Fleece at Lightpill a little closer in]: Informal bare-boards décor in open-plan line of several big-windowed room areas, largely no smoking, bar on right, restaurant on left (nice rooms), wide choice of good interesting freshly made bar food from unusual lunchtime sandwiches up, well kept Bass, Boddingtons and Greene King Abbot, good wines, local non-alcoholic drinks, big log fire, candles, daily papers, stripped stone or dark salmon pink walls; children welcome, two roadside terraces, one with heater *(BB, S Fysh)*

☆ ***Ram*** [Station Rd, South Woodchester]: Attractively priced well kept ales such as Archers Best, John Smiths, Theakstons Old Peculier, Uley Old Spot and several interesting guest beers, in relaxed L-shaped beamed bar with friendly staff, nice mix of traditional furnishings, stripped stonework, bare boards, three open fires, darts, varied menu from good value generous baguettes to steaks, restaurant; children welcome, open all day Sat/Sun, spectacular views from terrace tables *(Gill and Tony Morriss, LYM, Tom and Ruth Rees, S Fysh)*

☆ ***Royal Oak*** [off A46; Church Road, N Woodchester]: Changing well kept ales such as Archers, Bath and Wickwar, scrubbed tables and chapel chairs in several pleasant areas inc upstairs dining room with great valley view, big log fire in huge fireplace, decent food inc baguettes and some interesting specials; big-screen TV, piped music, some live; children and dogs welcome, open all day *(R Huggins, D Irving, E McCall, T McLean, LYM, Alan Bowker)*

WOOLASTON COMMON SO5900

Rising Sun [village signed off A48 Lydney—Chepstow]: Unpretentiously old-fashioned 17th-c village pub on fringe of Forest of Dean, friendly and welcoming, reasonably priced fresh food (not Weds evening) inc curries, well kept Fullers London Pride, Hook Norton and perhaps a guest beer, darts and piano in side area (folk nights alternate Tues); picnic-sets and swing outside, cl Weds lunchtime *(Pete Baker, CMW, JJW)*

Please tell us if the décor, atmosphere, food or drink at a pub is different from our description. We rely on readers' reports to keep us up to date. No stamp needed: *The Good Pub Guide*, FREEPOST TN1569, Wadhurst, E Sussex TN5 7BR.

Hampshire

This county has a satisfying variety of good pubs, from simple unspoilt places to well run civilised dining pubs, with an appealing choice of food to match from straightforward and unpretentious pub lunches to good interesting meals. The pubs which have been getting particular praise from readers in recent months reflect this variety: the bustling Oak in its attractive New Forest spot at Bank, the very well run Sun at Bentworth (a welcoming all-rounder), the Red Lion at Boldre (popular food in a good part of the New Forest for walks), the civilised Fox at Bramdean (a consistently good dining pub), the Flower Pots at Cheriton (a rustic country pub brewing its own good beers), the Star at East Tytherleigh (a good place to stay, with enjoyable food and atmosphere), the friendly and interesting Chestnut Horse at Easton (good upmarket food), the Hawkley Inn (an unpretentious real ale pub with surprisingly good food), the Peat Spade at Longstock (good food relying on local produce), the Trusty Servant at Minstead (a new entry, for its enjoyable food in a pretty New Forest spot), the thatched Black Swan at Monxton (good value food, especially its bargain OAP lunches), the attractively placed streamside Bush at Ovington (a nice all-rounder), the Trooper up above Petersfield (good food and local beers, nice bedrooms, and a top-notch landlord), the Still & West in Portsmouth (another new entry, very much liked for its great harbour views, on particularly good form under its current management), the light and airy Falcon at Rotherwick (friendly staff, enjoyable food), the chatty Wine Vaults in Southsea (great for real ales, food all day too), the friendly and well run Plough at Sparsholt (excellent food), the delightfully unspoilt and unchanging Harrow at Steep, the rather stately Grosvenor in Stockbridge (nicely reworked as a good all-rounder by its current owners – another new entry), the Brushmakers Arms at Upham (a good welcoming all-rounder), the unusual Black Boy in Winchester (lots to look at, good local beers and homely bar lunches) and the busy and civilised Wykeham Arms there (good interesting food, fine drinks choice). As we have said, good food is an important part of the appeal of many of these top Hampshire pubs. With the Trooper near Petersfield now running it very close indeed, the Plough at Sparsholt still holds on to the title which it won last year, of Hampshire Dining Pub of the Year. Pubs currently showing particularly well in the Lucky Dip section at the end of the chapter are the Milbury's at Beauworth, Bull at Bentley, Three Tuns at Bransgore, Hampshire Arms in Crondall (a hot pick now), Compasses at Damerham, Hampshire Bowman at Dundridge, Shoe at Exton, Foresters Arms at Frogham, Alverbank House in Gosport, Fur & Feathers at Herriard, John o' Gaunt at Horsebridge, Trout at Itchen Abbas, Jolly Farmer in Locks Heath, Chequers on the edge of Lymington, Bucks Head at Meonstoke, White Horse on the downs above Petersfield, Greyhound in Stockbridge, Cricketers Arms at Tangley, Red House in Whitchurch and Horse & Groom at Woodgreen. Drinks prices in Hampshire pubs tend to be 10p or so higher than the national average. The Flower Pots at Cheriton (brewing its own beer) and Chestnut Horse at Easton (stocking local Itchen Valley beer) were the only main entries here where we found real ale for under £2 a pint. The Flower Pots' Cheriton beers quite often show up as the cheapest stocked in other pubs, and besides beers from Ringwood and Gales (the county's main brewers), another local beer which we found fairly frequently is fff.

AXFORD SU6043 Map 2

Crown 🍷

B3046 S of Basingstoke

On a warm day, the suntrap terrace in the sloping shrub-sheltered garden behind this tucked-away country pub is a popular place for a drink; there are also picnic-sets out in front. Inside, the three compact rooms ramble around the central servery and open together enough to build a chatty atmosphere – each keeping its own character: appealing late 19th-c local villager photographs, cream walls, patterned carpet and stripped boards on the left, for instance, abstract prints on pale terracotta walls and rush carpeting on the right. Furnishings are largely stripped tables and chapel chairs, and each room is candlelit at night, with a small winter log fire; daily papers, piped music, and TV. Well kept Bass, Cheriton Pots Ale, Triple fff Moondance and Altons Pride on handpump, and nine wines by the glass. Bar food includes lunchtime snacks such as filled baked potatoes (£5.50), filled ciabattas (£5.95), ploughman's (£6.50), and ham and eggs (£6.75), as well as pâté (£4.50), haddock and spring onion fishcakes (£4.95), burgers (£7.95), vegetarian pasta (£8.25), home-made pie of the day (£8.95), cajun chicken (£9.50), and beer battered haddock (£9.95), with daily specials like steak and kidney pudding (£8.95), whole bass with lemon butter (£12.95), and crocodile or kangaroo kebabs (£13.50). There are lovely walks around Moundsmere, and in the woods of Preston Oak Hills (bluebells in May). More reports please. *(Recommended by Julian McCarthy, Phyl and Jack Street, J V Dadswell)*

Free house ~ Licensee Steve Nicholls ~ Real ale ~ Bar food (all day summer weekends) ~ Restaurant ~ (01256) 389492 ~ Children in eating area of bar and restaurant ~ Dogs allowed in bar ~ Open 12-3, 6-11; 12-11(10.30 Sun) Sat; 12-3, 6-11 weekends in winter

BANK SU2807 Map 2

Oak 🍺

Signposted just off A35 SW of Lyndhurst

This is a peaceful New Forest spot, but inside this welcoming place you'll find a good bustling atmosphere. On either side of the door in the bay windows of the L-shaped bar are built-in green-cushioned seats, and on the right, two or three little pine-panelled booths with small built-in tables and bench seats. The rest of the bar has more floor space, with candles in individual brass holders on a line of stripped old and blond newer tables set against the wall on bare floorboards, and more at the back; some low beams and joists, fishing rods, spears, a boomerang, and old ski poles on the ceiling, and on the walls are brass platters, heavy knives, stuffed fish, and guns. A big fireplace, cushioned milk churns along the bar counter, and little red lanterns among hop bines above the bar. Friendly staff serve well kept Hop Back Summer Lightning, Ringwood Best and a couple of guests such as Cottage Champflower Ale and Triple fff Stairway to Heaven; country wines too. Piped music. Well liked bar food includes lunchtime doorstep sandwiches (from £4.25) and ploughman's (from £5.25), as well as baked brie with almonds and honey (£3.95), various cured meats with roasted red pepper and pickles (£5.75), pork and herb sausages with rich onion gravy (£6.95), a pie of the day (£7.95), greek salad topped with sliced grilled chicken breast (£8.95), fresh cod in beer batter (£9.95), chargrilled 12oz rib-eye steak (£12.95), and daily specials such as baked crab (£8.50), whole local plaice (from £10), and duck breast (£11). The side garden has picnic-sets and long tables and benches by the big yew trees. No children inside. *(Recommended by M Joyner, J V Dadswell, R T and J C Moggridge, David M Cundy, Alan M Pring, Tom and Ruth Rees, Prof Keith and*

Mrs Jane Barber, Charles and Pauline Stride, Brian and Janet Ainscough, Gordon Stevenson, Dr Alan and Mrs Sue Holder, Roger and Pauline Pearce)

Free house ~ Licensee Karen Slowen ~ Real ale ~ Bar food (all day summer Sun) ~ Restaurant ~ (023) 8028 2350 ~ Dogs allowed in bar ~ Open 11-3, 6-11; all day during school holidays; 11-11 Sat; 12-10.30 Sun ~ Bedrooms: /£60B

BENTWORTH SU6740 Map 2

Sun

Sun Hill; from the A339 coming from Alton the first turning takes you there direct; or in village follow Shalden 2¼, Alton 4¼ signpost

This tucked away friendly pub is a thoroughly good all-rounder. It's very popular with both locals and visitors, there's a fine choice of eight real ales, food is enjoyable and promptly served, and the staff are welcoming and efficient. The two little traditional communicating rooms have high-backed antique settles, pews and schoolroom chairs, olde-worlde prints and blacksmith's tools on the walls, and bare boards and scrubbed deal tables on the left; big fireplaces with roaring winter fires and candles make it especially snug in winter; an arch leads to a brick-floored room with another open fire. Well kept Badger Fursty Ferret, Cheriton Pots Ale, Fullers London Pride, Gales HSB, Hogs Back TEA, Ringwood Best, Stonehenge Pigswill and Timothy Taylors Landlord on handpump; several malt whiskies. Good home-made bar food includes sandwiches, soup (£3.25), creamy garlic mushrooms or pork liver pâté (£3.25), yorskhire pudding with roast beef or pork and leek sausages (£6.50), avocado and stilton bake or fresh tagliatelle with smoked salmon, lemon and dill cream sauce (£7.95), home-made burger with relish, steak and kidney pie or chicken stuffed with walnuts and stilton in a mushroom and port sauce (all £8.95), salmon wrapped in parma ham with pesto (£9.95), well liked cumberland sausage with onion gravy or venison in Guinness with pickled walnuts (£10.95), steaks (from £11.95), and puddings (£3.25). There are seats out in front and in the back garden, and pleasant nearby walks. *(Recommended by Martin and Karen Wake, Lynn Sharpless, the Didler, Mr and Mrs P L Haigh, John Hale, Phyl and Jack Street, Tim and Carolyn Lowes, John Davis, Tony and Wendy Hobden, D P and M A Miles, Ann and Colin Hunt, Andrin Cooper, R Lake)*

Free house ~ Licensee Mary Holmes ~ Real ale ~ Bar food ~ (01420) 562338 ~ Children in eating area of bar ~ Dogs welcome ~ Open 12-3, 6-11; 12-10.30 Sun

BOLDRE SZ3198 Map 2

Red Lion ★ 🍷

Village signposted from A337 N of Lymington

Consistently well run, this is a bustling New Forest pub in a fine walking area. The four neatly kept black-beamed rooms are filled with heavy urns, platters, needlework, rural landscapes and so forth, taking in farm tools, heavy-horse harness, needlework, gin traps and even ferocious-looking man traps along the way. The central room has a profusion of chamber-pots, and an end room has pews, wheelback chairs and tapestried stools, and a dainty collection of old bottles and glasses in the window by the counter; most of the pub is no smoking. There's a fine old cooking range in the cosy little bar, and two good log fires. Generously served and enjoyable bar food includes sandwiches (from £3.95; club sandwich £6.50), soup (£4), pork and wild mushroom pâté with home-made crab apple jelly (£5.80), home-made salmon and crab fishcakes (£5.90), ploughman's (£6.50), broccoli and leek risotto with stilton and cream or their special pasta salad (£8.50), sausages with rich onion gravy (£8.60), home-made steak and kidney pie or salmon and prawn pasta (£9.90), calves liver and bacon (£10.20), steaks (from £10.20), home-made puddings such as whisky bread and butter pudding or raspberry crème brûlée (£4.25), and specials like beer battered haddock (£9.50), mixed seafood paella (£11.20), and half a guinea fowl with white wine, bacon, mushrooms and lemon thyme (£11.90). They have an extensive wine list with 14 by the glass, and well kept Bass and Flowers IPA on handpump. In summer, the flowering tubs and hanging baskets outside are charming, and there are tables out in the back garden. No children or dogs inside. *(Recommended by Lynn Sharpless, Phyl and Jack Street, JMC, John Davis, A D Marsh, Joan and Michel Hooper-Immins, Prof Keith and Mrs Jane Barber, Dr and Mrs A K Clarke, Glenwys and Alan Lawrence, Gordon Stevenson, Jeff and Wendy Williams, Roger and Pauline Pearce)*

Eldridge Pope ~ Tenant Vince Kernick ~ Real ale ~ Bar food (12-2.30, 6.30-9(9.30 wknds)) ~ Restaurant ~ (01590) 673177 ~ Open 11-11; 12-10.30 Sun

BRAMDEAN SU6127 Map 2

Fox

A272 Winchester—Petersfield

It's best to book to be sure of a table in this civilised 17th-c weatherboarded dining pub. Reliably good and cooked by the landlord using lots of fresh ingredients, the food at lunchtime includes sandwiches, soup (£3.50), pâté (£4.95), poached pear, blue cheese and crispy bacon salad (£6.95), cauliflower cheese with bacon or battered fillet of cod (£8.95), home-made steak and kidney pie (£9.95), and grilled lamb cutlets (£11.95), with evening choices such as deep-fried whitebait (£4.95), baked brie in filo pastry with redcurrant jelly (£5.95), scallops with smoked bacon (£6.95), chicken supreme with parma ham in Boursin sauce or rib-eye steak (£13.95), and fillet of monkfish with tarragon sauce or confit of duck with orange gravy (£14.95). The carefully modernised open-plan bar has black beams, tall stools with proper backrests around the L-shaped counter, and comfortably cushioned wall pews and wheelback chairs – the fox motif shows in a big painting over the fireplace, and on much of the decorative china. At least one area is no smoking. Well kept Greene King Ruddles County on handpump; piped music. At the back of the building is a walled-in terraced area, and a spacious lawn spreading among the fruit trees; a play area has a climbing frame and slide. No children inside. Good surrounding walks. *(Recommended by Michael and Robin Inskip, Father Robert Marsh, John Davis, Phyl and Jack Street, Meg and Colin Hamilton, Tony and Wendy Hobden, W W Burke, Betty Laker, Mr and Mrs W Mills, Mike and Heather Watson, R B Gardiner, P F Dakin)*

Greene King ~ Tenants Ian and Jane Inder ~ Real ale ~ Bar food ~ (01962) 771363 ~ Open 11-3, 6-11; 12-3, 7-10.30 Sun; 7pm opening in winter

CHALTON SU7315 Map 2

Red Lion

Village signposted E of A3 Petersfield—Horndean

The most characterful part of this county's oldest pub (first licensed in 1503) is the heavy-beamed and panelled front bar with high-backed traditional settles and elm tables, and an ancient inglenook fireplace with a frieze of burnished threepenny bits set into its mantelbeam; the lounge and extended dining room are no smoking. Popular bar food includes sandwiches (from £3.55; sausage and fried onion baguette £5.15), filled baked potatoes (from £4.85), and ploughman's (from £5.25), plus daily specials such as soup (£3.95), home-made thai fishcakes (£5.45), braised bacon hock with a honey and mustard glaze (£7.95), grilled chicken with a spiced yoghurt crust (£8.75), tuna steak with anchovy and orange butter (£9.30), slow roasted half shoulder of lamb with apricot stuffing (£9.95), and scallops in avocado cream dressing (£10.30). Well kept Gales Butser, GB, HSB, Festival Mild and a guest like Wadworths 6X on handpump, 10 wines by the glass, and a fine choice of malt whiskies; piped music. The garden is pretty in summer and the views are super; the pub is popular with walkers and riders as it is fairly close to the extensive Queen Elizabeth Country Park, and about half a mile from an Iron Age farm and settlement. The car ferry is only about 20 minutes away from here. *(Recommended by P R and S A White, Ian Phillips, Ann and Colin Hunt, Colin Christie)*

Gales ~ Managers Mick and Mary McGee ~ Real ale ~ Bar food (not Sun evening) ~ Restaurant ~ (023) 9259 2246 ~ Children in restaurant ~ Dogs allowed in bar ~ Open 11-3, 6-11; 12-3, 7-10.30 Sun; closed evenings 25-26 Dec

CHERITON SU5828 Map 2

Flower Pots ★ £

Pub just off B3046 (main village road) towards Beauworth and Winchester; OS Sheet 185 map reference 581282

It's the simple rusticity that appeals to our readers so much in this charming village local – and of course, their particularly good own brew beers from the brewhouse across the car park; well kept Pots Ale, Diggers Gold and Cheriton Best tapped from casks behind the bar. The two little rooms get an interesting mix of customers, though the one on the left is a favourite, almost like someone's front room, with pictures of hounds and ploughmen on its striped wallpaper, bunches of flowers, and a horse and foal and other ornaments on the mantelpiece over a small log fire; it can get smoky in here. Behind the servery is disused copper filtering equipment, and lots of hanging gin traps, drag-hooks, scaleyards and other ironwork. The neat extended plain public bar (where there's a covered well) has cribbage and dominoes. Very useful in fine weather (when the pub can fill up quickly), the pretty front and back lawns have some old-fashioned seats, and there's now a summer marquee; maybe summer morris dancers. Bar food from a fairly short straightforward menu includes sandwiches (from £2.60; toasties from £2.70; big baps from £3.20), winter home-made soup (£3.30), filled baked potatoes (from £4.20), ploughman's (from £4.50), and hotpots such as lamb and apricot, chilli or beef stew (from £5.50); popular curries on Wednesday evenings; friendly service. The menu and serving times may be restricted at weekend lunchtimes, or when they're busy. The pub is near the site of one of the final battles of the Civil War; it got its name through once belonging to the retired head gardener of nearby Avington Park. No children inside. *(Recommended by Lynn Sharpless, Phil and Sally Gorton, Simon Collett-Jones, the Didler, P R and S A White, Tim and Carolyn Lowes, Ann and Colin Hunt, John Davis, Leigh and Gillian Mellor, Vincent Howard, Tracey and Stephen Groves, Val and Alan Green)*

Own brew ~ Licensees Jo and Patricia Bartlett ~ Real ale ~ Bar food (not Sun evening or bank hol Mon evenings) ~ No credit cards ~ (01962) 771318 ~ Dogs welcome ~ Open 12-2.30, 6-11; 12-3, 7-10.30 Sun ~ Bedrooms: £40S/£60S

EAST TYTHERLEY SU2927 Map 2

Star

Off B3084 N of Romsey; turn off by railway crossing opp the Mill Arms at Dunbridge

A new lounge area has been created in this consistently well run inn and furnished with leather sofas and tub chairs, and the bar and restaurant have been redecorated. Most customers come to enjoy the good food: home-made soup (£3.25), sandwiches (from £3.50; toasted focaccia with mozzarella, parma ham and pesto £5.95), filled baked potatoes (from £3.90), smoked haddock terrine (£4.95), warm tomato and basil tart (£5.50; main course £10.50), steak, kidney and Guinness pudding (£8.95), lambs liver and bacon (£9.50), grilled chicken and monkfish with cumin roasted sweet potato and tempura vegetables (£14.50), trio of duck on spinach and gratin potatoes with madeira jus (£16.50), and fillet of beef with roasted shallots and garlic topped with foie gras (£18.50); vegetables are extra. They also offer a two-course (£10) or three-course (£15) menu. The bar has log fires in attractive fireplaces, horsebrasses and saddlery, and a mix of comfortable furnishings; there's a lower lounge bar, and a cosy and pretty no smoking restaurant. Ringwood Best and a guest such as Hydes Fine & Dandy are well kept on handpump, they've several malt whiskies, and a thoughtful wine list with around ten by the glass; shove-ha'penny, and a popular skittle alley for private dining. You can sit out on a smartly furnished terrace, and a children's play area has play equipment made using local reclaimed wood. The well liked bedrooms overlook the village cricket pitch (which is used every Tuesday and Saturday through the summer), and breakfasts are highly thought of. Good nearby walks. *(Recommended by Dr and Mrs W T Farrington , Phyl and Jack Street, Terry and Linda Moseley, Mrs J A Taylar, Paul Humphreys, Andy Sinden, Louise Harrington, Derek Hayman, Prof and Mrs Tony Palmer, Patrick Hall, Peter J and Avril Hanson, Trevor Moore, Jeff and Wendy Williams, Dr D G Twyman, Prof Keith and Mrs Jane Barber, Brenda and Rob Fincham)*

Free house ~ Licensees Paul and Sarah Bingham ~ Real ale ~ Bar food (not Mon except bank hols) ~ Restaurant ~ (01794) 340225 ~ Children in eating area of bar and restaurant ~ Dogs allowed in bar ~ Open 11-2.30, 6-11; 12-2.30, 7-10.30 Sun; closed Mon except bank hols; not evening 25 Dec, not 26 Dec ~ Bedrooms: £50S/£70S

EASTON SU5132 Map 2

Chestnut Horse

Village signposted off B3047 Kings Worthy—Itchen Abbas; bear left in village

In a quiet, pretty village with thatched cottages, this rather up-market 16th-c dining pub offers a friendly welcome from particularly kind and efficient staff. Although inside it's all opened together, the pub manages to retain the cosy feel of small separate rooms, with a really snug décor: candles and fresh flowers on the tables, log fires in cottagey fireplaces, comfortable furnishings, black beams and joists hung with all sorts of jugs, mugs and chamber-pots, and lots of attractive pictures of wildlife and the local area. The two restaurants are no smoking. Very good – though not cheap – food at lunchtime includes caesar salad (£4.50), deep-fried brie with fruit coulis (£4.95), toasted ciabatta sandwiches (£5.95; grilled open ones £6.95), home-made mackerel pâté (£5.95), bangers on whole grain mustard mash with deep-fried leeks and rich onion and red wine jus (£9.95), home-made lasagne (£10.95), popular beer-battered fish (£10.95; massive £13.95), and rib-eye steak (£13.95), with evening main courses such as stuffed roasted red peppers (£10.95), steak and kidney pudding (£14.50), and chicken fillet stuffed with sun-dried tomato and mozzarella wrapped in pancetta with leek and cream sauce (£14.95); fish specials like coquille saint jacques (£5.95), fresh crab cocktail (£7.95), and poached fillet of scotch salmon with watercress and cream sauce (£12.95), and two-course (£12.95) and three-course (£14.95) lunch and early evening options (not available on Sunday lunch or weekend evenings). Well kept Courage Best, Fullers London Pride and Chestnut Horse (brewed specially for the pub by Itchen Valley) on handpump, 12 wines and a champagne by the glass, and more than 50 malt whiskies; fairly unobtrusive piped music. There are good tables out on a smallish sheltered decked area with colourful flower tubs and baskets; plenty of Itchen Valley walks. *(Recommended by Tim and Carolyn Lowes, Lynn Sharpless, Norman and Sheila Sales, Martin and Karen Wake, Susan and John Douglas, Ann and Colin Hunt, Mike and Heather Watson, Vincent Howard, A J Atyeo, David Sizer, Francis Johnston, Phyl and Jack Street, Mrs J A Taylar, Ian Harrison)*

Free house ~ Licensees John and Jocelyn Holland ~ Real ale ~ Bar food (12-2, 6.45-9.30) ~ Restaurant ~ (01962) 779257 ~ Children welcome ~ Dogs allowed in bar ~ Open 11-11; 12-10.30 Sun; closed Sun evenings in winter

FRITHAM SU2314 Map 2

Royal Oak

Village signed from exit roundabout, M27 junction 1; quickest via B3078, then left and straight through village; head for Eyeworth Pond

As well as ponies and pigs out on the green, there's plenty of livestock close to this charming brick-built thatched pub as it is part of a working farm; gentle views across forest and farmland, fine surrounding walks, and a neatly kept big garden where summer barbecues are held (they have a marquee for poor weather). Inside, the three neatly kept, simple bar rooms have a proper traditional atmosphere, antique wheelback, spindleback, and other old chairs and stools with colourful seats around solid tables on the new oak flooring, and prints and pictures involving local characters on the white walls; restored panelling, black beams, and two roaring log fires. Well kept Cheriton Pots Ale, Hop Back Summer Lightning and Ringwood Best and Fortyniner, along with guests such as Archers Village Bitter, Cheriton Village Elder and Palmers Dorset Gold tapped from the cask; they hold a beer festival in September. Darts, dominoes, shove-ha'penny and cribbage, and the back bar has quite a few books. The pub attracts a good mix of customers, and the staff are friendly. Simple lunchtime food is limited to home-made soup (£3), and ploughman's with home-made pâté, home-cooked pork pie, and home-cooked gammon or cumberland sausage ring (£5). *(Recommended by Philip and Susan Philcox, David M Cundy, the Didler, Pete Baker, Tom and Ruth Rees, Andrea Rampley, Mrs C Lintott, Terry and Linda Moseley)*

Free house ~ Licensees Neil and Pauline McCulloch ~ Real ale ~ Bar food (lunchtime only) ~ No credit cards ~ (023) 8081 2606 ~ Children welcome but must be well behaved ~ Dogs welcome ~ Open 11-3, 6-11; 11-11 Sat; 12-10.30 Sun

HAMBLEDON SU6414 Map 2

Vine

West Street, just off B2150

'A first class village local' sums up this country place rather well. There's a smile and a welcome from the landlord, a nice mix of regular drinkers and older diners, and a charming pub dog called Blue who has his place on the chenille-covered sofa in one bow window (ignore his entreaties for food). The usual pub tables and chairs plus a winged high-backed settle, tankards and copper kettles (and even an accordion) hanging from old brown beams and joists, decorative plates, sporting and country prints, and some interesting watercolours of early 20th-c regimental badges on the cream or dark red walls, and quite a bit of bric-a-brac – signed cricket bats, bank notes, gin traps, a boar's head, snare drums and a sort of shell-based mandolin on the piano. A couple of log fires and a woodburning stove. They tell us bar food and prices have not changed since last year: lunchtime sandwiches (from £2.95), daily specials such as aubergine, leek and tomato bake, home-made steak and kidney pie, and breaded plaice (all £6.95), popular peppered lamb baked with ginger, coriander and red wine (£8.95), and evening dishes such as coq au vin (£8.95), fried sirloin steak with peppercorn sauce (£10.95), and bass poached with butter, dill and parsley (£11.95). The restaurant and one part of the bar are no smoking. Well kept Gales Butser, Marstons Pedigree and Ringwood Best with guests like Cheriton Village Elder and Youngs Special on handpump, and Addlestone's cider; shove-ha'penny, dominoes and cribbage. Tables in a small informal back garden. This pretty downland village has good walks nearby. *(Recommended by Ann and Colin Hunt, P R and S A White, Charles and Pauline Stride, Phyl and Jack Street)*

Free house ~ Licensee Peter Lane ~ Bar food (not Sun evening) ~ Restaurant ~ (023) 9263 2419 ~ Children may be allowed in if exceptionally well behaved; best to check beforehand ~ Dogs allowed in bar ~ Open 11.30-3, 6-11; 12-4, 7-10.30 Sun

HAWKLEY SU7429 Map 2

Hawkley Inn

Take first right turn off B3006, heading towards Liss ¾ mile from its junction with A3; then after nearly 2 miles take first left turn into Hawkley village – Pococks Lane; OS Sheet 186 map reference 746292

Cheerful and unpretentious, this country local is popular with real ale lovers as there are usually half a dozen constantly changing beers, well kept and often from small breweries: one from Downton (new to us), Itchen Valley Fat Controller, King Red River and Horsham Best Bitter, and RCH East Street Cream ; they have their own cider, too. The opened-up bar and back dining room have a simple décor – big pine tables, a moose head, dried flowers, and prints on the mellowing walls; parts of the bar can get a bit smoky when it's busy, but there is a no smoking area to the left of the bar. Besides good soups such as bacon and mushroom, stilton and celery or tomato and watercress (£4.85), swiftly served tasty bar food includes filled rolls (£3.95), ploughman's (£6.25), cottage pie or spinach and ricotta tart (£8.25), cheese, leek and potato pie, pork and cider sausages or faggots and mash (all £8.95), beef stew (£9.25), and puddings such as spotted dick (£3.75); friendly service. The pub is on the Hangers Way Path, and at weekends there are plenty of walkers; tables and a climbing frame in the pleasant garden. *(Recommended by the Didler, Martin and Karen Wake, Tony Radnor, Father Robert Marsh, JCW, Ann and Colin Hunt, Ian Phillips, H H Hellin, Phil and Sally Gorton, Sue Plant)*

Free house ~ Licensee Al Stringer ~ Real ale ~ Bar food (not Sun evening) ~ (01730) 827205 ~ Children welcome until 8pm ~ Dogs welcome ~ Open 12-2.30(3 Sat), 6-11; 12-3, 7-10.30 Sun

LONGSTOCK SU3537 Map 2

Peat Spade 🍷

Village signposted off A30 on W edge of Stockbridge, and off A3057 Stockbridge—Andover

There's no doubt that while locals do drop in for a pint and a chat, the emphasis in this well run place is very much on the good, interesting food; to be sure of a table, it is best to book in advance. The roomy and attractive squarish main bar is airy and high-ceilinged, with pretty windows, well chosen furnishings and a nice show of toby jugs and beer mats around its fireplace. A rather elegant no smoking dining room leads off, and there are doors to a big terrace. Served by helpful, pleasant staff and using local (and often organic) produce, the sensibly short menu might typically include cabbage and bacon soup (£4.50), smoked haddock mousse (£5.50), borlotti bean and tarragon casserole (£5.60), vegetable fajitas (£7.95), lamb curry (£8.95), singapore-style duck with noodles (£10.25), baked goats cheese and leek tart (£10.60), baked fillet of cod with cheese crust (£11.75), chicken goujons with neapolitan sauce (£12.50), and aberdeen angus rib-eye steak (£13.50), with puddings such as rhubarb fool, sticky toffee pudding or fresh lemon delight (£4.50). Well kept Batemans Spring Blonde, Hop Back GFB and Ringwood Fortyniner on handpump, and eight wines by the glass from a carefully chosen list. There are teak seats on the terrace, with more in the pleasant little garden, and maybe free range chickens, two cats, Cleo the cocker spaniel and Mollie the diabetic dog (who is not allowed to be fed). There are plenty of surrounding walks – along the Test Way at the end of the road and in the water meadows in Stockbridge; Longstock Water Gardens is at the end of the village, and open alternate summer Sundays. *(Recommended by Jill Franklin, Patrick Hall, Stuart Turner, Derek Harvey-Piper, John Hale, John Davis, Lynn Sharpless, Andrea Rampley, R T and J C Moggridge, B & C Perryman, Vincent Howard, Pat and Robert Watt, Ann and Colin Hunt, Catherine FitzMaurice)*

Free house ~ Licensees Bernie Startup and Sarah Hinman ~ Real ale ~ Bar food ~ Restaurant ~ No credit cards ~ (01264) 810612 ~ Children welcome ~ Dogs welcome ~ Open 11.30-3, 6.30-11; 12-3 Sun; closed Sun evening, all Mon

LYMINGTON SZ3295 Map 2

Kings Head

Quay Hill; pedestrian alley at bottom of High Street, can park down on quay and walk up from Quay Street

Rambling darkly up and down steps and through timber dividers, this 17th-c pub has tankards hanging from great rough beams, and is mainly bare boarded, though there's a rug or two here and there. Lighting is dim, and even in daytime they light the candles on the tables – a great mix from an elegant gateleg to a huge chunk of elm, with a nice old-fashioned variety of seating too; the local pictures include good classic yacht photographs. One cosy upper corner past the serving counter has a good log fire in a big fireplace, its mantelpiece a shrine to all sorts of drinking from beer tankards to port and champagne cases: they have well kept Adnams Bitter, Fullers London Pride, Gales HSB, Greene King IPA and a seasonal Ringwood ale on handpump. Enjoyable food includes home-made soup (£3.75), sandwiches (from £4.65), crispy duck salad with soy sauce, ginger and lemon grass (£7.95), pasta with smoked chicken and bacon in creamy parmesan sauce (£8.95), home-made steak and mushroom in ale pie (£9.50), and specials such as home-made chicken liver pâté (£5.25), pork and leek sausages with onion gravy (£7.95), mixed fish grill with lemon and parsley butter (£9.95), venison with shallots and redcurrant jus (£10.25), and duck breast with an orange, port and ginger sauce (£10.95). A wall rack holds daily papers; piped pop music. More reports please. *(Recommended by Derek Thomas)*

Inn Partnership (Pubmaster) ~ Lease Paul Stratton ~ Bar food (12-2.10, 6-10) ~ Restaurant ~ (01590) 672709 ~ Children welcome ~ Dogs welcome ~ Open 11-3, 5-11; 11-11 Sat; 12-10.30 Sun

MICHELDEVER SU5138 Map 2

Half Moon & Spread Eagle

Village signposted off A33 N of Winchester; then follow Winchester 7 signpost almost opposite hall

Under the friendly new licensees, this country local has remained a popular village pub. The simply decorated and beamed bar has heavy tables and good solid seats, and a woodburning stove at each end; a no smoking area leads off. Well liked bar food includes soup (£3.95), sandwiches (from £4.50), fried foie gras with apples and calvados sauce or ploughman's (£5.95), brochette of the day with salad (£7.95), sausages of the week or mushroom, pepper and parmesan risotto (£7.95), thai chicken curry (£8.95), steak and mushroom in ale pie or liver and bacon (£10.95), chargrilled duck breast with roasted tomato and sherry sauce (£11.50), wok-fried tiger prawns with garlic butter (£11.95), and puddings like orange crème brûlée, pithivier of caramel and hazelnut mousse or tarte tatin with apple custard (all £4.25). Well kept Greene King IPA and Abbot, and guests such as Caledonian 80/- or St Austell Tribute on handpump; darts, pool, fruit machine, cribbage, and piped music. There are seats on a sheltered back terrace, and picnic-sets and a play area on the recently upgraded garden. This is a good starting point for exploring the Dever Valley, and there are lots of pleasant walks nearby. *(Recommended by Phyl and Jack Street, Roy and Lindsey Fentiman, DJH, Lynn Sharpless, Ian Phillips, John Davis, Tim and Carolyn Lowes, Mary Kirman and Tim Jefferson, Francis Johnston, Charles Gysin)*

Greene King ~ Tenants Christina Nicholls, Richard Tolfree, Alex Tolfree ~ Real ale ~ Bar food ~ Restaurant ~ (01962) 774339 ~ Children welcome ~ Dogs allowed in bar ~ Open 12-3, 6-11; 12-3, 7-10.30 Sun

MINSTEAD SU2811 Map 2

Trusty Servant

2.2 miles from M27 junction 1; keep on A31 for just over a mile then turn left into village; also signposted off A337 Cadnam—Lyndhurst

Suiting this scattered and prettily wooded New Forest hamlet with its wandering ponies, this welcoming 19th-c pub has a pleasantly relaxed feel – and a bonus for walkers on warm summer days is that its big airy dining room, with plenty of open windows, is pleasantly cool then. This is a pretty room, with comfortable chairs. The two opened-together rooms of the bar area (they also open through into the dining room) have a rather more local feel, with assorted chairs, carpet and bare boards, some Victorian and sporting prints, and an old piano (some of the regulars have been known to have a strum when the mood takes them). A nicely varied choice of very good generous food, nicely presented on big plates, might include soup (£2.95), sandwiches (£3.50; filled baguettes £6.50), filled baked potatoes (£4.95), mozzarella ball on a pistachio and stuffed olive salad (£5.25), omelettes (£5.50), ploughman's (£5.75), home-made steak and kidney pie, double egg, ham and chips or liver and bacon (all £6.95), sizzling thai vegetable stir fry (£8.50), fillet of pork honey roasted with balsamic cherry tomatoes and sweet red onions (£10.95), local skate wing (£12.50), and daily specials such as whole bass with Pernod-scented provençale sauce or wild boar loin with orange and nutmeg sauce (£12.95) or medallions of beef with coriander mash and roasted baby vegetables (£14.95). In season, they do good game dishes, particularly pheasant. Service is friendly and commendably quick even when all the tables inside and in the good-sized side and back garden are full. They have well kept changing ales such as Fullers London Pride, Ringwood Best and Wadworths 6X on handpump, and decent house wines and country wines. The bedrooms are simple and pleasant, and they do a good breakfast. The nearby church is interesting for its unspoilt Georgian interior, and Sir Arthur Conan Doyle is buried in its graveyard; there are plenty of easy walks all around. *(Recommended by Dick and Madeleine Brown, Caraline and Richard Crocker, M Joyner, Phyl and Jack Street, A D Marsh, Tom and Ruth Rees, Mike and Heather Watson, R J Davies, Brian and Janet Ainscough, Mrs C Lintott)*

Enterprise ~ Lease Tony and Jane Walton ~ Real ale ~ Bar food (12-9.30) ~ Restaurant ~ (023) 8081 2137 ~ Children in restaurant ~ Dogs allowed in bar ~ Pianist alternate Fri evenings ~ Open 11-11; 11-11 Sat; 12-10.30 Sun ~ Bedrooms: £30S/£60S

MONXTON SU3144 Map 2

Black Swan

Village signposted off A303 at Andover junction with A343; car park some 25 metres along High Street

There's a friendly, bustling atmosphere in this pretty thatched pub, with plenty of customers keen to enjoy the very good food. Besides ample lunchtime sandwiches (from £4.50) and ploughman's (£6), the daily changing choices could include home-made soup such as cream of parsnip, ham and eggs (£7.50), steak in ale pie, chicken and spinach curry, gnocchi in neapolitan sauce or wild mushroom risotto (all £9.50), salmon fillet in fennel butter or 10oz rib-eye steak in wholegrain mustard sauce (£11.50), ostrich with a red wine jus (£13.50), and puddings such as rich chocolate cake or baked rum and raisin cheesecake (from £3.95). They do a good value OAP offer (£5 for two courses Monday-Thursday lunchtimes). Past a lobby with a settee and easy chairs, a couple of steps take you up to the small mansard-ceiling timbered bar with the menu boards, a log fire, a table of daily papers and just a few pub tables; well kept Fullers London Pride, Ringwood Best and Timothy Taylors Landlord on handpump, ten wines by the glass from a large list, and over 40 malt whiskies. Angling off behind here is the main action: a triangular room with floor-to-ceiling windows looking out at picnic-sets in a small sheltered garden by the little slow-flowing Pillhill Brook, and a further good-sized no smoking room, both carpeted, with country-kitchen chairs and tables set for eating. Service is quick and pleasant, with plenty of neatly dressed staff; cribbage. *(Recommended by Phyl and Jack Street, W W Burke, Mandy Barron, Justin le Page)*

Enterprise ~ Lease Matt McCann ~ Bar food (12-2, 6-10; 12-2.30, 6-10 Fri and Sat) ~ Restaurant ~ (01264) 710260 ~ Children allowed but must leave by 9pm ~ Dogs allowed in bar ~ Open 12-11; 12-10.30 Sun

NORTH GORLEY SU1611 Map 2

Royal Oak

Ringwood Road; village signposted off A338 S of Fordingbridge

As this 17th-c thatched pub (originally a hunting lodge) is on the edge of the New Forest, there are usually ponies and cattle roaming around; ducks on the big pond across the road, and a neatly kept sheltered back garden with plenty of seating and a play area for children. Inside, there's a quiet, comfortable and neatly refurbished no smoking lounge on the left, though we prefer the busier main bar on the right: carpeted too, with a corner gas stove, old copper and heavy horse decorations, and steps down to an attractive L-shaped eating area. This has a mix of dark pine tables and pleasant old-fashioned chairs on bare boards, and a further no smoking part with pine booth seating. Friendly and efficient staff serve the well liked popular food which at lunchtime includes sandwiches (from £3.95; bacon, cranberry and brie baguette £4.95), home-made lasagne or ham and eggs (£7.50), home-made sausages or seafood linguini (£7.95), home-made steak and kidney pie (£8.95), and seafood salad bowl (£9.95), with evening dishes such as moules marinière (£4.95), wild mushroom risotto (£7.95), beer battered fresh cod or whole rack of ribs glazed with hickory sauce (£8.95), chicken breast filled with apricots on cajun sauce (£9.50), and rack of lamb in mint, garlic and rosemary (£10.95). Well kept Fullers London Pride, Ringwood Best and a guest such as Adnams Broadside on handpump, decent wines, and several malt whiskies; fruit machine, TV, piped music and boules. *(Recommended by Peter and Anne Hollindale, Peter Neate, W W Burke, Mark Barker, Dr D G Twyman)*

Enterprise ~ Lease Sharon Crush and Tom Woods ~ Real ale ~ Bar food (12-2.30, 6-9, but all day during school summer holidays) ~ Restaurant ~ (01425) 652244 ~ Children welcome ~ Dogs welcome ~ Pianist alternate Fri evenings; monthly band Sun ~ Open 11-11; 12-10.30 Sun

OVINGTON SU5631 Map 2

Bush

Village signposted from A31 on Winchester side of Alresford

As this is such a lovely spot, and the back garden of this picturesquely set little cottage runs down to the River Itchen, it's not surprising to find quite a few customers on a warm sunny day; but it's well worth visiting in spring, too, when the nearby banks are covered in snowdrops and daffodils. Inside, the rooms have a nice old-fashioned décor, and the low-ceilinged bar has cushioned high-backed settles, elm tables with pews and kitchen chairs, masses of old pictures in heavy gilt frames on the walls, and a roaring fire on one side with an antique solid fuel stove opposite. Well kept Wadworths 6X, IPA, JCB and seasonal guests on handpump, and several country wines and malt whiskies; cribbage, dominoes and board games. The sociable scottish springer spaniel is called Paddy. Bar food – not cheap – includes lunchtime sandwiches (from £4.75) and ploughman's (from £6.50), soup (£4.75), home-made chicken liver pâté (£6.75), king prawns in garlic, chilli and ginger butter (£10.75), leek and mushroom cottage pie with smoked garlic mash (£10.90), beef in ale pie or local trout fillets with hazelnut and coriander butter (£11.95), and puddings such as sticky toffee pudding and chocolate and black cherry bread and butter pudding (£4.50); efficient, friendly service. Two rooms are no smoking. Please note that if you want to bring children it's best to book, as there are only a few tables set aside for families. *(Recommended by Michael and Robin Inskip, Val and Alan Green, Tim and Carolyn Lowes, Phyl and Jack Street, Mrs J V Leighton, Mrs Joy Griffiths, John Davis, Ann and Colin Hunt, Lynn Sharpless, Giles and Annie Francis, Prof and Mrs Tony Palmer, Michael and Ann Cole, John and Vivienne Rice, Lesley and Peter Barrett, M A and C R Starling, Peter F Marshall)*

Wadworths ~ Managers Nick and Cathy Young ~ Real ale ~ Bar food (not Sun evening) ~ (01962) 732764 ~ Well behaved children in small family area ~ Dogs welcome ~ Open 11-3, 6-11; 12-2.30, 7-10.30 Sun

PETERSFIELD SU7227 Map 2

Trooper

From B2070 in Petersfield follow Steep signposts past station, but keep on up past Steep, on old coach road; OS Sheet 186 map reference 726273

'A good all-rounder' is how many of our readers describe this particularly well run pub. The landlord really goes out of his way to make customers feel welcome, the beers are well kept and from local breweries, the food is extremely good, and it's a comfortable place to stay. There's an island bar, tall stools by a broad ledge facing big windows that look across to rolling downland fields, blond wheelback and kitchen chairs and a mix of tripod tables on the bare boarded or red tiled floor, little persian knick-knacks here and there, quite a few ogival mirrors, big baskets of dried flowers, lit candles all around, fresh flowers, logs burning in the stone fireplace, and good piped music; newspapers and magazines to read. The raftered restaurant is most attractive; the pub is no smoking except for around the bar counter. Very good food (best to book to be sure of a table) might include sandwiches, carrot, ginger and honey soup (£4.50), bacon and cheddar potato skins (£5), chicken and wild mushroom puff (£6), locally cured hand carved ham with free range egg or chilli con carne (£9), tuna steak (£10), thai glazed vegetable skewers with chilli and pepper noodles (£12), slow roasted half shoulder of lamb with rich honey and mint gravy (£13), free range chicken breast with kiwi fruit wrapped in parma ham and served with a vanilla vodka cream sauce (£14), and wild boar steak with calvados and apple sauce (£15); well liked breakfasts. The four well kept real ales change frequently but might include Cheriton Pots Ale, Ringwood Best and Fortyniner, and Triple fff Moondance on handpump, and they have decent house wines. There are lots of picnic-sets on an upper lawn and more on the partly covered sunken terrace which has french windows to the dining area. The horse rail in the car park ('horses only before 8pm') does get used. *(Recommended by JMC, John Davis, Ian Phillips, Paul and Penny Dawson, Tony Radnor, Paul Humphreys, John and Tania Wood, Bruce and Penny Wilkie, Simon Collett-Jones, Barry and Anne, Peter Goddard, Clare and Peter Pearse, Wendy Arnold, Dr and Mrs D Woods, Ann and Colin Hunt, John and Glenys Wheeler)*

Free house ~ Licensee Hassan Matini ~ Real ale ~ Bar food ~ Restaurant ~ (01730) 827293 ~ Children welcome ~ Dogs allowed in bar ~ Open 12-2, 6-11; 12-2, 7-10.30 Sun; closed 25 and 26 Dec, 1 Jan ~ Bedrooms: £69S(£62B)/£89S(£79B)

PORTSMOUTH SZ6299 Map 2

Still & West

Bath Square, Old Portsmouth

The wonderful views from here reach as far as the Isle of Wight, and the boats and ships fighting the strong tides in the very narrow mouth of Portsmouth harbour seem almost within touching distance. As well as seats on the terrace, the upper deck partly no smoking restaurant has fine views from all tables – best to book. The downstairs bar is decorated in nautical style, with paintings of galleons on the ceiling, ship models, old cable, and photographs of famous ships entering the harbour, and they serve well kept Gales Butser, HSB, GB, and a guest beer on handpump, and 21 country wines; piped music and fruit machine. As well as sandwiches, the food now includes home-made soup (£3.75), stilton and white wine mushrooms (£4.75), warm duck salad (£5.25), a trio of sausages with red onion gravy (£7.95), goats cheese soufflé, cod in beer batter or steak in ale pie (all £8.95), and chinese duck breast (£9.25). The pub is not far from HMS *Victory*, and can get busy on fine days. Nearby parking can be difficult. *(Recommended by Colin Gooch, Ian and Jacqui Ross, Ann and Colin Hunt, Andy and Jill Kassube, Ken Flawn, Mrs Maricar Jagger)*

Gales ~ Manager Tina Blackhall ~ Real ale ~ Bar food (12-3, 6-9) ~ Restaurant ~ (023) 9282 1567 ~ Children welcome ~ Open 10-11; 11-10.30 Sun

ROTHERWICK SU7156 Map 2

Falcon

4 miles from M3 junction 5; follow Newnham signpost from exit roundabout, then Rotherwick signpost, then turn right at Mattingley, Heckfield signpost; village also signposted from B3349 N of Hook, then brown signs to pub

There's a light and fresh open-plan layout in this quietly placed country pub, with quite a mixture of dining chairs around an informal variety of tables on its varnished floorboards, big bay windows with sunny window seats, and minimal decoration on its mainly pale mustard-coloured walls; flowers on the tables, and perhaps a big vase of lilies on the terracotta-coloured central bar counter, give colour. A rather more formal no smoking back dining area is round to the right, and on the left are an overstuffed sofa and a couple of ornate easy chairs by one log fire. Quite a range of enjoyable bar food, served by friendly staff, includes home-made soup (£3.25), interesting sandwiches (from £3.50; bacon, mushroom and cheese toasties £4.75), filled baked potatoes (from £4.50), buck rarebit (two slices of toast with special topping and two eggs £5), ploughman's (£5.25), sausage and egg (£6.95), roasted vegetable lasagne (£7.50), steak and mushroom pie or pork and apple sausages with onion gravy (£7.95), curries (£8), baked red snapper with chive and hollandaise sauce (£10.95), and steaks (from £10.95), with daily specials such as crayfish tails wrapped in smoked salmon with lime mayonnaise (£5.95), three cheese pasta with tomato, cream and parsley (£7.95), and duck breast with gooseberry glaze and crushed new potatoes (£13.95). They do stick ridgidly to the 2pm deadline for food. Well kept Adnams Best, Fullers London Pride, and a guest on handpump; maybe piped local radio. Terraces at the front and back have sturdy tables and benches, and there are picnic-sets in a sizeable informal back garden, which has a pair of swings and pasture views; easy walks nearby. *(Recommended by Howard Dell, John Davis, Norman and Sheila Sales, Ian Phillips, KC, Andy and Yvonne Cunningham, R Lake)*

Unique (Enterprise) ~ Lease Andy Francis ~ Real ale ~ Bar food ~ Restaurant ~ (01256) 762586 ~ Children in restaurant ~ Dogs allowed in bar ~ Open 11-2.30, 6-11; 12-10.30 Sun; closed 25 and 26 Dec

ROWLAND'S CASTLE SU7310 Map 2

Castle Inn

Village signposted off B2148/B2149 N of Havant; Finchdean Road, by junction with Redhill Road and Woodberry Lane

In a pleasant village with good surrounding walks, this is a cheerful and chatty pub with helpful, smart staff. There are two appealing smallish eating rooms on the left. The front one (no smoking) has rather nice simple mahogany chairs around sturdy scrubbed pine tables, one quite long, rugs on flagstones, a big fireplace, and quite a lot of old local photographs on its ochre walls; the back one is similar, but with bare boards, local watercolour landscapes by Bob Payne for sale, and cases of colourful decorative glassware from nearby Stansted Park. Popular bar food at lunchtime includes sandwiches and filled baguettes (from £3.25), filled baked potatoes (from £3.25), ham and eggs or a vegetarian dish of the day (£5.50), a pie or curry of the day or battered cod (all £6), and daily specials, with evening choices such as smoked mackerel pâté (£3.50), mushroom, garlic and mascarpone filo parcel (£3.75), seared cajun tuna steak (£7.50), leg of lamb steak with rosemary and garlic (£8.25), and 10oz rib-eye steak (£10.25). Well kept Gales Butser, GB and HSB and a seasonal guest on handpump, and country wines. There is a small separate public bar on the right; disabled access and facilities are good, and the garden behind has picnic-sets. *(Recommended by Ann and Colin Hunt, Andy and Jill Kassube)*

Gales ~ Licensees Jan and Roger Burrell ~ Bar food (12-9; not after 3pm on winter Sun and Mon) ~ Restaurant ~ (023) 9241 2494 ~ Children in eating area of bar only ~ Dogs allowed in bar ~ Open 11-11; 12-10.30 Sun ~ Bedrooms: /£30

SOUTHSEA SZ6498 Map 2

Wine Vaults

Albert Road, opposite Kings Theatre

Despite the crowds, the efficient and friendly staff remain unflustered in this enjoyably basic pub, and serve up to ten well kept real ales on handpump. They also do some good special offers too – if you arrive before 5.30 and are coming to eat, you get a free drink with selected meals, and they have a double happy hour on any night from Monday to Thursday between 5.30 and 7.30 when the beers are cheaper (in fact on Monday it's £1.30 all night). Courage Best and Directors, Fullers London Pride, Greene King Ruddles Best and Hop Back Summer

Lightning plus five guests. Popular with a good mix of age groups, the busy straightforward bar has wood-panelled walls, a wooden floor, and an easy-going, chatty feel; the raised back area is no smoking. There are newspapers for you to read, plus pool, chess, draughts, backgammon and a football table; piped music. Handily served all day, good portions of reasonably priced bar food include sandwiches (from £2.45; grilled ones £3.95), filled baked potatoes (from £3.95), steak in ale pie (£5.95), roasted vegetable and goats cheese bruschetta (£7.95), mexican vegetable burrito or various nachos (from £6.25), salads such as cajun chicken, greek or brie and avocado (from £6.50), and puddings (£3.25); the partly no smoking Vines brasserie has more elaborate dishes. There are seats in the little garden, and a wooden gazebo. *(Recommended by Tony Hobden, the Didler, Val and Alan Green, Catherine Pitt, Richard and Gaetana Carey, Mrs Maricar Jagger, M B Griffith)*

Free house ~ Licensee Mike Hughes ~ Real ale ~ Bar food (12-9) ~ Restaurant ~ (023) 9286 4712 ~ Children welcome ~ Dogs welcome ~ Open 11-11; 12-10.30 Sun; closed 1 Jan

SPARSHOLT SU4331 Map 2

Plough

Village signposted off B3049 (Winchester—Stockbridge), a little W of Winchester

Hampshire Dining Pub of the Year

With helpful, friendly staff, excellent food, good beer, and a bustling atmosphere, it's not surprising that this well run place is so popular. Everything is neatly kept, and the main bar has an interesting mix of wooden tables and chairs, and farm tools, scythes and pitchforks attached to the ceiling; two no smoking areas. On daily changing blackboards, the interesting bar food might include lunchtime sandwiches (from £3.95), chilli and chick pea cakes with an avocado salsa, loin of pork on garlic sweet potatoes with mushroom and grain mustard sauce or salmon and crab fishcakes (all £8.95), braised faggots with bubble and squeak and carrot and swede mash (£10.95), whole plaice with caper butter or bass with wilted pak choi and roasted pepper coulis (£14.95), beef fillet stuffed with goats cheese and pine nuts on a madeira sauce (£16.95), and puddings like poached pear and caramel ice-cream or pecan pie and clotted cream (£4.50); to be sure of a table or to avoid a long wait, you must book a table in advance. Well kept Wadworths IPA, JCB, 6X, a seasonal ale and maybe a guest on handpump, and an extensive wine list. There's a children's play fort, and plenty of seats on the terrace and lawn. *(Recommended by Lynn Sharpless, Patrick Hall, John and Joan Calvert, Tim and Carolyn Lowes, Eleanor and Nick Steinitz, Phyl and Jack Street, Richard and Margaret Peers, Mick Simmons, Dr and Mrs A K Clarke, Mandy Barron, Vincent Howard, Peter F Marshall, Val and Alan Green, Ann and Colin Hunt)*

Wadworths ~ Tenants R C and K J Crawford ~ Real ale ~ Bar food ~ (01962) 776353 ~ Children welcome ~ Dogs welcome ~ Open 11-3, 6-11; 12-3, 6-10.30 Sun; closed 25 Dec

STEEP SU7425 Map 2

Harrow

Take Midhurst exit from Petersfield bypass, at exit roundabout first left towards Midhurst, then first turning on left opposite garage, and left again at Sheet church; follow over dual carriageway bridge to pub

A favourite with quite a few of our readers, this old-fashioned place remains as charming and unchanging as ever. The cosy public bar has hops and dried flowers hanging from the beams, built-in wall benches on the tiled floor, stripped pine wallboards, a good log fire in the big inglenook, and wild flowers on the scrubbed deal tables; dominoes. Well kept Ballards Best, Cheriton Diggers Gold and Ringwood Best are tapped from casks behind the counter, and they've local wine. Good helpings of enjoyably unfussy home-made bar food (they tell us prices have not changed since last year) include sandwiches, home-made scotch eggs (£3), lovely generous soups such as ham, split pea and vegetable (£4.10), ploughman's, home-made cottage pie, lasagne or quiches (£7.50), and salads (£10), with mouthwatering puddings such as treacle tart or seasonal fruit pies (£3.50); staff are polite and friendly, even when under pressure. The big garden is left free-flowering so that goldfinches can collect thistle seeds from the grass. The Petersfield bypass doesn't intrude on this idyll, though you will need to follow the directions above to find it. No children inside. *(Recommended by John Davis, Ann and Colin Hunt, A D Marsh, Ian Phillips, Tony Radnor, the Didler, Lynn Sharpless, Brenda and Rob Fincham, M B Griffith, Charles and Pauline Stride, J Stickland, R B Gardiner, Phil and Sally Gorton)*

Free house ~ Licensee Ellen McCutcheon ~ Real ale ~ Bar food (limited Sun evenings) ~ No credit cards ~ (01730) 262685 ~ Dogs welcome ~ Open 12-2.30, 6-11; 11-3, 6-11 Sat; 12-3, 7-10.30 Sun; closed winter Sun evenings

STOCKBRIDGE SU3535 Map 2

Grosvenor

High Street

This handsome Georgian country-town coaching inn has been attractively restored and refurbished by its new owners. The high-ceilinged main bar's pleasantly restrained decoration is now entirely in keeping with the distinction of the building itself, with a good log fire, some sporting pictures and *Vanity Fair* caricatures of former jockeys. Well divided into separate room areas, it is comfortable and relaxing. Service is cheerful and efficient; they have well kept Greene King IPA, Abbot and Ruddles County on handpump, a dozen enjoyable wines by the glass, and decent coffee. Bar food includes soup such as sweet roasted pepper and tomato (£3.95), chicken liver and mushroom parfait with red onion marmalade (£4.25), crab cakes with sweet chilli sauce (£5.45), sandwiches and filled ciabatta (from £4.95; open smoked salmon and scrambled egg ciabatta £7.25), home-made lasagne (£5.95), sausages and mash with caramelised onions and gravy (£7.25), home-made steak in ale pie (£7.45), grilled goats cheese salad (£7.95), beer battered cod (£8.95), and braised lamb shank (£9.95). The impressive partly oak-panelled dining room has some attractive late 19th-c pictures of horse race winners from the stables of the hotel's then owner, who was Master of the Danebury Harriers. A back conservatory has more tables. A couple of pavement tables stand out beside the imposing front portico, with more tables in the good-sized back garden, prettily laid out with attractive plantings and a small lily pond. We have not heard yet from any readers who have stayed since the management changes, but would expect good value. This is an appealing small town, with good antiques shops, the National Trust Common Marsh along the River Test, and downland walks all around. *(Recommended by W W Burke, Dennis Jenkin, Geoffrey Kemp, Ann and Colin Hunt)*

Greene King ~ Managers Colin and Valerie Holman ~ Real ale ~ Bar food ~ Restaurant ~ (01264) 810606 ~ Children welcome ~ Dogs allowed in bar ~ Open 11-11; 12-10.30 Sun ~ Bedrooms: £80B/£95B

Three Cups 🍷 🍺

High Street

Visitors and locals mix easily in this inviting looking pub, helped by the enjoyably relaxed atmosphere and friendly staff. There's a settle and hall chair in a small quarry-tiled hallway, an old-fashioned leather porter's chair by the telephone in an inner lobby, and a snug low-beamed bar on the right: quite narrow and very dimly lit (candles in bottles on all the tables at night), with an engaging mix of furnishings on its turkey carpet, from high-backed settles to a button-back leather sofa, and a variety of mainly oak tables. The dark red walls are packed with old engravings, fishing gear, one or two guns and a fair bit of taxidermy, and there are daily papers and logs blazing in the woodburning stove. Well kept Fullers London Pride and Ringwood Best, along with a guest like Hampshire Ironside, and decent wines by the glass; fairly quiet piped music. Interesting freshly cooked bar food might include home-made soup (£4.95), scottish smoked salmon and scrambled eggs on toast or baked smoked haddock (£5.25), home-made game terrine set in port jelly with sweet red onion marmalade (£5.95), good filled baguettes (from £6.25), croque monsieur (£6.95), seared scallops on cauliflower purée with pink butter and crispy pancetta (£7.25), wild mushroom risotto (£7.95), ham and eggs (£8.50), chicken caesar salad (£8.95), baked local trout (£12.95), saddle of venison with fresh thyme and port jus (£14.95), and rack of lamb with wild mushroom jus (£15.95). There is a no smoking restaurant on the left. Behind the bar, there's a little cottage garden and the terrace next to the stream is a nice place to sit on a fine afternoon. *(Recommended by John Oates, Dennis Jenkin, Nigel and Sue Foster, Mr and Mrs R W Allan, Ron Shelton, David and Sheila Pearcey, Phyl and Jack Street, M A and C R Starling, Edward Mirzoeff, Dr D G Twyman, Ann and Colin Hunt)*

Free house ~ Licensee Lucia Foster ~ Real ale ~ Bar food ~ Restaurant ~ (01264) 810527 ~ Children welcome ~ Dogs allowed in bar ~ Open 12-2, 5-11; 12-2, 7-10.30 Sun ~ Bedrooms: £42.50(£52.50B)/£55(£65B)

TICHBORNE SU5630 Map 2

Tichborne Arms

Village signed off B3047

This is a proper country pub – charmingly old-fashioned and friendly. The comfortable square-panelled room on the right has wheelback chairs and settles (one very long), a log fire in the stone fireplace, and latticed windows. On the left is a larger, livelier, partly panelled room used for eating. The pictures and documents on the walls inside recall the bizarre Tichborne Case (a mystery man from Australia claimed fraudulently to be the heir to this estate); friendly golden labrador. Home-made bar food includes sandwiches (from £3), stilton mushrooms (£5.50), ploughman's (£6), coronation chicken salad (£7.50), spinach and ricotta cannelloni (£8.25), curry (£8.50), pies such as chicken, tarragon and mushroom, steak, ale and stilton or fish (from £8.75), confit of duck with red onion marmalade (£9.50), crab salad (£10.50), and lamb shank (£12.50), with puddings such as hot plum tart or rhubarb and ginger crumble (£3.50). Well kept Ringwood Best and Wadworths 6X, and a couple of guests tapped from the cask, a decent choice of wines by the glass, country wines and farm cider; sensibly placed darts, bar billiards, shove-ha'penny, dominoes, cribbage and piped music. Picnic-sets outside in the big well kept garden, and a pétanque pitch. You can expect to find quite a few walkers here during the day, as the Wayfarers Walk and Itchen Way pass close by, and many fine walks lead off in all directions. No children inside. *(Recommended by Martin and Karen Wake, Lynn Sharpless, Michael and Robin Inskip, the Didler, Michael Rowse, Ann and Colin Hunt, Phil and Sally Gorton, Stephen and Jean Curtis, Dr and Mrs D Woods, Mandy and Simon King, M B Griffith, P Hennessey, R B Gardiner)*

Free house ~ Licensees Keith and Janie Day ~ Real ale ~ Bar food (12-1.45, 6.30-9.45) ~ Restaurant ~ (01962) 733760 ~ Dogs welcome ~ Open 11.30-2.30, 6-11; 12-3, 7-10.30 Sun; closed evenings 25 and 26 Dec and evening 1 Jan

UPHAM SU5320 Map 2

Brushmakers Arms

Shoe Lane; village signposted from Winchester—Bishops Waltham downs road, and from B2177 (former A333)

Bustling and attractive old village local with a comfortable L-shaped bar divided in two by a central brick chimney – there's a woodburning stove in the raised two-way fireplace. It has comfortably cushioned wall settles and chairs, a variety of tables including some in country-style stripped wood, a few beams in the low ceiling, and quite a collection of ethnic-looking brushes; there's also a little snug. Dominoes, cribbage, fruit machine, shove-ha'penny and sensibly placed darts. Reasonably priced and well kept Ballards Best, Ringwood Best and Charles Wells

Bombardier on handpump. Unchanged since last year, bar food includes lunchtime snacks such as sandwiches (from £4.50), filled baked potatoes (£5.75), ploughman's (from £5.75), and ham and egg (£6.25), as well as sardines in garlic (£5.50), mushroom stroganoff (£6.95), steak and kidney pie (£8.95), local partridge with stilton and bacon sauce (£9.50), lamb steak with garlic and red wine or crab and sherry bake (£9.95), and steaks (from £10.95), with home-made puddings (£4.50). The big garden is well stocked with mature shrubs and trees, and there are picnic-sets on a sheltered back terrace among lots of tubs of flowers, with more on the tidy tree-sheltered lawn. Good walks nearby. *(Recommended by Richard Dixon, P R and S A White, Lynn Sharpless, Prof and Mrs Tony Palmer, Ann and Colin Hunt, Amanda Irvine, Michael and Robin Inskip, Betsy and Peter Little, A J Atyeo, Father Robert Marsh, Roy and Lindsey Fentiman)*

Free house ~ Licensee Tony Mottram ~ Real ale ~ Bar food ~ (01489) 860231 ~ Children in eating area of bar ~ Dogs allowed in bar ~ Open 11-3, 5.45-11; 11-3.30, 6-11 Sat; 12-3.30, 7-10.30 Sun

WELL SU7646 Map 2

Chequers

Off A287 via Crondall, or A31 via Froyle and Lower Froyle

This is a friendly place with a good welcome for all – best to get there soon after it opens as it fills up quickly. The low-beamed rooms have lots of alcoves, wooden pews, brocaded stools and a few GWR carriage lamps, and the panelled walls are hung with 18th-c country-life prints and old sepia photographs of locals enjoying a drink; roaring winter log fire, fruit machine, dominoes, chess and Jenga. Generous helpings of very tasty bar food include home-made soup (£3.25), sandwiches (from £4.25), duck and orange pâté with tangy fruit and cider chutney (£4.75), warm chicken and bacon salad (£4.95), home-made burger topped with bacon and brie or honey roast ham and egg with bubble and squeak (£6.95), stuffed red peppers topped with melted cheese (£7.25), feta, sunblush tomato and olive salad, steak in ale pie or pork and herb sausages on mustard mash with onion gravy (all £7.95), lamb shank with mint gravy and redcurrant mash (£9.45), and steaks (from £12.50); the restaurant is no smoking. Well kept Badger Best, Tanglefoot and Fursty Ferret on handpump, and decent wines. The vine-covered terrace is a very pleasant place to sit in summer and the spacious back garden has picnic-sets too. They provide bowls of water and biscuits for dogs. *(Recommended by Martin and Karen Wake, Mr and Mrs A Swainson, Piotr Chodzko-Zajko, Paul A Moore, M A and C R Starling, Andrin Cooper)*

Badger ~ Managers Sonia Henderson and Tim Llewellyn ~ Real ale ~ Bar food (12-3(4 Sat and Sun), 6-9.30(8.30 Sun)) ~ Restaurant ~ (01256) 862605 ~ Children in restaurant ~ Dogs allowed in bar ~ Open 12-3, 6-11; 12-11 Sat; 12-10.30 Sun

WHERWELL SU3840 Map 2

White Lion

B3420, in village itself

Run by friendly, hard-working licensees, this 17th-c village pub is deservedly popular with both regulars and visitors. The multi-level beamed bar has delft plates, sparkling brass, fresh flowers, and well kept Courage Directors and Ringwood Best on handpump. The Village bar has an open fire, and there are two dining rooms – the lower one is no smoking; piped music. Well liked bar food includes soup (£3.80), smooth pork liver pâté (£4.50), filled baguettes (£5.30), ploughman's (£5.75), curry or pie of the day (£8.25), ham and eggs (£8.50), pork steak with honey and mustard sauce (£8.75), steaks (from £12.25), daily specials such as cheese, leek and macaroni bake (£8), beef goulash (£8.25), smoked haddock and broccoli quiche (£8.40), lambs liver and bacon (£8.50), fresh seasonal crab (£8.95), and braised lamb shank (£10), and puddings (from £3.80); its a good idea to book for their Sunday roast. The chocolate labrador is called Harley. Plenty of seats in the courtyard and on the terrace. The village is pleasant to stroll through, and there's a nice walk over the River Test and meadows to Chilbolton. They may close early on quiet evenings. *(Recommended by Mike Gorton, John Davis, Leigh and Gillian Mellor, B J Harding, Tim and Carolyn Lowes, Prof and Mrs Tony Palmer, W W Burke, G W A Pearce, Ann and Colin Hunt, A J Atyeo, Phyl and Jack Street)*

Punch ~ Lease Adrian and Patsy Stent ~ Real ale ~ Bar food ~ Restaurant ~ (01264) 860317 ~ Well behaved children in restaurant ~ Dogs welcome ~ Folk first and second Thurs of month ~ Open 11-2.30(3 Sat), 6(7 Mon and Tues)-11; 12-3, 7-10.30 Sun ~ Bedrooms: £39.50/£49.50

WINCHESTER SU4828 Map 2

Black Boy

1 mile from M3 junction 10 northbound; B3403 towards city then left into Wharf Hill; rather further and less easy from junction 9, and anyway beware no nearby daytime parking – 220 metres from car park on B3403 N, or nice longer walk from town via College Street and College Walk, or via towpath

As there is so much of enjoyable interest to look at in this unsual pub with its splendidly eccentric décor, it's best to visit at a quiet time. Several different areas run from a bare-boards barn room with an open hayloft (now an evening dining room) down to an orange-painted room with big oriental rugs on red-painted floorboards; a new area has been created out of the old kitchen. There are books from floor to ceiling in some parts, lots of big clocks, mobiles made of wine bottles or strings of spectacles, some nice modern nature photographs in the lavatories and on the brightly stained walls on the way, and plenty of other things that you'll enjoy tracking down. Furnishings are similarly eclectic. Lunchtime bar food includes sandwiches (£3.50), and home-made hot meals such as sausage and mash with onion gravy, vegetarian pasta, and lamb hotpot (£6-£7.50); in the evening, there might be deep-fried whitebait with lemon mayonnaise (£5.95), liver and bacon with red wine syrup (£6.25), chicken and mushroom pie (£9.50), seared salmon fillet with noodles and an oriental sauce (£14.50), and puddings like eton mess with raspberry sauce or crème brûlée (from £4.75). On Sunday they only do roasts (£6.50). The beers on handpump are more or less local – with Cheriton Pots, Ringwood Best and Hop Back Summer Lightning alongside a couple of guests from Archers and Itchen Valley; decent wines, two log fires, and friendly staff. Well chosen and reproduced piped music; table football, shove-ha'penny, cribbage and dominoes; a couple of slate tables out in front, more tables on an attractive secluded terrace with barbecues. Children allowed at parents' liability. *(Recommended by Val and Alan Green, David and Carole Chapman, Tim and Carolyn Lowes, Phil and Sally Gorton, Ann and Colin Hunt, Len Beattie)*

Free house ~ Licensee David Nicholson ~ Bar food (lunchtime; not Sun evening, all day Mon, Tues lunchtime) ~ (01962) 861754 ~ Dogs welcome ~ Open 11-3, 5-11; 12-3, 7-10.30 Sun

Wykeham Arms ★

75 Kingsgate Street (Kingsgate Arch and College Street are now closed to traffic; there is access via Canon Street)

Even on a cold and wet winter weekday, it's best to book to be sure of a table in this rather civilised inn, and there's always a good mix of customers of all ages keen to enjoy the fine choice of drinks: Bass, and Gales Best, Butser, HSB and a couple of seasonal guests on handpump, 20 wines by the glass (including a sweet one), and quite a few brandies, armagnacs and liqueurs. A series of stylish bustling rooms radiating from the central bar has 19th-c oak desks retired from nearby Winchester College, a redundant pew from the same source, kitchen chairs and candlelit deal tables and big windows with swagged paisley curtains; all sorts of interesting collections are dotted around. A snug room at the back, known as the Jameson Room (after the late landlord Graeme Jameson), is decorated with a set of Ronald Searle 'Winespeak' prints, a second one is panelled, and all of them have a log fire. Served by neatly uniformed staff, the lunchtime menu might include good sandwiches (from £3.95; smoked salmon and prawn in a brandy and dill sauce £5.75), pork and green peppercorn pâté with bramley apple jelly (£5.50), smoked haddock topped with welsh rarebit on a tomato, rocket and chive oil salad or creamy risotto of wild mushrooms, baby spinach and roquefort cheese (£7.50), and raised chicken, lemon and thyme flavoured sausage meat pie with an apple and stem ginger chutney (£7.95), with evening choices such as thai spiced crab and coconut mousse with a sweet chilli dip or pork, stilton and hazelnut pâté with rapsberry vinaigrette (£5.50), paupiette of plaice with salmon mousse on crushed new potato and olives, and fresh asparagus with a creamy lobster sauce (£13.95), roasted breast of duck on sweet potato purée, braised red cabbage, and a rich griottine cherry sauce (£14.25), roast rack of local lamb with roasted mediterranean vegetable ratatouille and redcurrant and rosemary jus (£14.95), and puddings like chocolate nemesis with a chocolate fudge sauce or panna cotta of vanilla and lavender with a compote of mixed berries (£4.50). The eating areas are no smoking. There are tables on a covered back terrace (they will serve food at lunchtime only here), with more on a small but sheltered lawn. No children inside. *(Recommended by John Oates, P R and S A White, Lynn Sharpless, John Davis, Martin and Karen Wake, the Didler, Mr and Mrs R W Allan, John and Jane Hayter, Andy and Yvonne Cunningham, Mr and Mrs S Felstead, Penny Simpson, Tim and Carolyn Lowes, Susan and John Douglas, Di and Mike Gillam, Phil and Sally Gorton, Mrs Joy Griffiths, Vincent Howard, Brenda and Rob Fincham, Edmund Coan, Joan York, M Sharp, Ann and Colin Hunt, Dr D Taub, Derek Thomas, Dr D G Twyman, John and Vivienne Rice, Barry and Anne; also in the* Good Hotel Guide*)*

Gales ~ Managers Peter and Kate Miller ~ Real ale ~ Bar food (12-2.30, 6.30-8.45; not Sun evening) ~ Restaurant ~ (01962) 853834 ~ Dogs allowed in bar ~ Open 11-11; 12-10.30 Sun; closed 25 Dec ~ Bedrooms: £55S/£90B

LUCKY DIP

Besides the fully inspected pubs, you might like to try these Lucky Dips recommended to us and described by readers (if you do, please send us reports: www.goodguides.co.uk).

ALRESFORD SU5832

Bell [West St]: Relaxing Georgian coaching inn refurbished and doing well under new management, with extended bar, smallish dining room, several well kept beers, friendly staff, good value food, log fire, daily papers; attractive back courtyard, comfortable bedrooms (some sharing bathroom), open all day *(G W H Kerby, Ron Shelton)*

☆ *Horse & Groom* [Broad St; town signed off A31 bypass]: Warm and welcoming beamed and timbered bar, roomily open-plan but with cosy alcoves, stepped levels and good bow window seats, enjoyable reasonably priced food inc good puddings, well kept ales such as Bass, Fullers London Pride and Wadworths 6X, decent wines by the glass, quick bar service, nice back no smoking restaurant area; decent piped music, open till midnight Sat – popular then with young people; children welcome, small enclosed garden, open all day *(Ann and Colin Hunt, Lynn Sharpless, LYM, Mr and Mrs R W Allan, Peter Salmon)*

ALTON SU7139

Crown [High St]: Former coaching inn dating from 16th c, lots of old beams and stripped brick, much altered over the years – stairway to nowhere, behind bar; bargain simple lunchtime food, real ales such as Caledonian Deuchars IPA, Fullers London Pride, Greene King Old Speckled Hen and Hogs Back TEA, no smoking restaurant *(Tony Hobden)*

☆ *French Horn* [The Butts; S of centre on old Basingstoke rd, by rly line]: Relaxed and convivial under welcoming newish landlord, with mugs on beams, old photographs and inglenook fires in attractive traditional bar, good choice of well kept ales and of wines, efficient hospitable service, generous pub food, sizeable restaurant; motorcyclists not spurned, skittle alley; comfortable if not large bedrooms *(Mick Simmons, Martin and Karen Wake, E G Parish, Phil and Sally Gorton)*

ARFORD SU8336

☆ *Crown* [off B3002 W of Hindhead]: Unpretentious low-beamed bar with coal and log fires, steps up to homely eating area, well kept Adnams, Fullers London Pride, Greene King Abbot and a guest beer such as fff Moondance, decent wines by the glass, welcoming service, good food from sandwiches to seasonal game and some interesting dishes, children's menu, no smoking restaurant; piped music; children welcome in eating areas, picnic-sets out in peaceful dell by a tiny stream across the road *(Ian Phillips, LYM, Martin and Karen Wake, J D Derry, R B Gardiner)*

ASHURST SU3410
Forest [A35 Lyndhurst—Southampton]: Pleasantly refurbished main-road pub, pubby bar with Fullers London Pride, Gales HSB and Ringwood Best, country wines, good friendly service, darts and good juke box, no smoking dining area on left with snug areas off flagstoned main part, decent food; big garden *(R J Anderson, Phyl and Jack Street, BB, J A Snell)*

BARTON STACEY SU4340
Swan [just off A303]: Friendly former coaching inn with beamed front bar (smoking allowed here), smaller eating area off with good air conditioning, enjoyable food here and in back restaurant (not always open), real ales inc Wadworths 6X, good wine list; tables on front lawn – pleasant spot *(Malcolm Daisley)*

BASING SU6653
Bolton Arms [The Street]: Village local with good atmosphere and decent food *(Tony Radnor)*

BATTRAMSLEY SZ3098
Hobler [Southampton Rd (A337 S of Brockenhurst)]: Heavy-beamed pub with nice well used mix of furniture, lots of books and rustic bric-a-brac, well kept Flowers Original, Wadworths 6X and a guest such as Gales HSB, dozens of malt whiskies and country wines, traditional games, food from snacks up; piped music; spacious lawn with summer bar, very good play area and livestock paddock, good forest walks; no children or mobile phones inside, jazz Tues, blues 2nd Thurs *(LYM, Jim and Maggie Cowell)*

BEAUWORTH SU5624
☆ *Milbury's* [off A272 Winchester/Petersfield]: Warmly welcoming newish South African licensees in attractive ancient pub, beams, panelling and stripped stone, massive 17th-c treadmill for much older incredibly deep well, log fires in huge fireplaces; several well kept real ales, Addlestone's cider, country wines, bar food inc some interesting dishes and weekly barbecue; piped music; children in eating areas, garden with fine downland views, plenty of walks, open all day *(the Didler, P R and S A White, Ann and Colin Hunt, LYM, Paul A Moore, Ed and Jane Pearce, H H Hellin, Guy Vowles)*

BENTLEY SU8044
☆ *Bull* [A31 Alton—Farnham dual carriageway, not in village itself]: Good choice of good well presented food from baked potatoes and delicious sandwiches to interesting and exotic dishes, friendly welcome for drinkers as well as diners, well kept ales such as Courage Best, Fullers London Pride, Hogs Back TEA and Youngs, log fire, low beams, lots of local prints; a few picnic-sets out in front (pleasant despite the traffic noise) *(Mrs Maricar Jagger, John and Joyce Snell, LYM, J P Humphery, Ian Phillips)*

BIGHTON SU6134
Three Horseshoes [off B3046 in Alresford just N of pond; or off A31 in Bishops Sutton]: Unspoilt and peaceful village local with very friendly licensees, well kept Gales HSB and BBB and Palmers BB and Copper, decent house wines, reasonably priced standard food, Sun bar nibbles, woodburner in huge fireplace, dining room, darts and pool in bare-boards stripped-stone back public bar; may be piped music; children welcome, good walks nearby, cl Mon winter lunchtime *(the Didler, Phil and Sally Gorton, Lynn Sharpless, Ann and Colin Hunt)*

BINSTED SU7741
Cedars [The Street]: Lively high-ceilinged local with cheerful welcome, well kept ales, good simple home-made traditional food inc very fresh fish, reasonable prices, blazing fire; dogs welcome *(BB, Wendy Arnold)*

BISHOP'S WALTHAM SU5517
Barleycorn [Lower Basingwell St]: Comfortably relaxed L-shaped main area with some panelling, well kept Adnams and Ringwood Best, log fire, wide choice of good value food inc popular Sun lunch and children's dishes, log fire, TV and games on public side; small back garden and play area *(Ian Phillips, Phyl and Jack Street, Val and Alan Green)*

☆ *Bunch of Grapes* [St Peters St]: Small and simple unspoilt village local run by the same family for a century, well kept Courage Best and Ushers Best tapped from the cask, good chatty landlord and friendly locals, plenty of character, quaintly furnished snug off main room; attractive medieval street *(Val and Alan Green, the Didler, Ann and Colin Hunt)*

White Horse [Beeches Hill, off B3035 NE]: Long country pub in converted hillside cottages, unspoilt and friendly, well kept ales such as Courage Directors, Greene King Old Speckled Hen and Ringwood Best, reasonably priced fresh and imaginative food inc curry specialities and several fish dishes, long-serving landlord, log fire; picnic-sets on front terrace, small play area *(Val and Alan Green, Ian Phillips)*

BOTLEY SU5213
Railway Hotel [Station Hill, nr stn]: Warmly welcoming railway-themed pub with well kept real ales inc Greene King, decent wines, good menu and specials board inc lots of fresh fish, efficient service, large conservatory (worth booking Sun) *(Bruce and Penny Wilkie)*

BRAISHFIELD SU3725
☆ *Newport* [Newport Lane]: Basic two-bar local, unsmart and unspoilt – quite a 1950s time warp; popular with older people at lunchtime (younger people evenings) for simple huge cheap sandwiches and bargain ploughman's, particularly well kept Gales HSB, BB and Butser, country wines, decent milky coffee, down-to-earth long-serving licensees; piped music, cribbage, wknd piano singsongs; good garden with geese, ducks and chickens *(Phil and Sally Gorton, the Didler, Lynn Sharpless)*

☆ *Wheatsheaf* [Crooks Hill]: Wide choice of good enterprising food in interesting pub/restaurant, roomy woody layout with terracotta walls and stripped boards, well kept ales such as Hook Norton, Ringwood Best,

Timothy Taylors Landlord and Wadworths 6X, good wine choice, helpful staff, side pool area, huge friendly black dog; fine views over meadowland to distant woods from big garden with lots of amusements for children inc field for ball games, pleasant walks; open all day *(Lynn Sharpless, Geoff Pidoux, Cynthia Norman)*

BRAMBRIDGE SU4721

☆ *Dog & Crook* [village signed off M3 junction 12 exit roundabout, via B3335]: Lots of neat tables under hop-hung beams around central bar, emphasis on enlarged kitchen's good food choice from pub standards to some more unusual and restauranty dishes inc lovely puddings (Sun lunch booked weeks ahead), relaxing atmosphere, quick warmly welcoming young staff, well kept Fullers London Pride, Gales HSB and Ringwood Best, country wines, small smoking area; alloy tables and chairs out on deck and under fairy-lit arbour, grass beyond, nearby walks on Itchen Way *(BB, John and Joan Calvert, Ann and Colin Hunt, A and B D Craig)*

BRANSGORE SZ1997

☆ *Three Tuns* [opposite church, Ringwood Rd, off A35 N of Christchurch]: Pretty 17th-c thatched pub, wide range of above-average imaginative food from ciabattas up, cheerful efficient service, well kept Greene King IPA, Ringwood Fortyniner and Timothy Taylors Landlord, good range of wines and hot drinks, tastefully refurbished olde-worlde bar with stripped brickwork and beamery, comfortable partly no smoking dining area popular with older people at lunchtime, fresh flowers; dogs allowed, pleasant back garden with play area and open country views, large flower-decked front terrace; bedrooms *(A D Marsh, BJSM, P J French, Phyl and Jack Street, Prof Keith and Mrs Jane Barber)*

BROCKENHURST SU3002

Rose & Crown [A337]: Varied decent blackboard food inc good value OAP lunch, pleasant efficient staff *(Alan M Pring, Mrs Joy Griffiths)*

BROOK SU2713

Bell [B3079/B3078]: Really a hotel and restaurant (with thriving golf club), in same family for over 200 years; nice range of enjoyable food from sandwiches to steak in neatly kept quiet bar, helpful friendly uniformed staff, good choice of well kept ales inc Ringwood, lovely inglenook log fire; different menu in plush restaurant, big garden, delightful village, 25 comfortable bedrooms with own bathrooms *(David M Cundy, Phyl and Jack Street, Carol and Dono Leaman)*

Green Dragon [B3078 NW of Cadnam]: Big open-plan New Forest building dating from 15th c, concentrating on wide choice of reliable food yet keeping good pub atmosphere, variety of areas with scrubbed pine tables or longer refectory tables, proper bar areas too, quick smiling service, well kept Fullers London Pride, Gales HSB and Ringwood, pool room; may try to keep your credit card as you eat; big pleasant garden with good enclosed play area, picturesque village *(Dick and Madeleine Brown, Ron Shelton, JWAC)*

BROUGHTON SU3032

Tally Ho [High St, opp church; signed off A30 Stockbridge—Salisbury]: Open-plan largely tiled square bar, two open fires, hunting prints, local landscapes for sale, well kept fff Stupidly Happy and Ringwood Best and True Glory, good house wines in two glass sizes, darts, good sandwiches and straightforward hot dishes, no piped music; smoking allowed throughout, no credit cards; children welcome, tables in charming secluded back garden, good walks; has been cl Tues *(Geoffrey G Lawrance, BB, Peter Neate)*

BUCKLERS HARD SU4000

Master Builders House: Original small yachtsman's bar with beams, flagstones and big log fire attractive when not too crowded, bar food (not cheap) and real ales, garden tables; part of a substantial Best Western hotel complex in charming carefully preserved waterside village (you have to pay to enter it), good bedrooms *(LYM, Alan M Pring)*

BURGATE SU1515

Tudor Rose [A338 about a mile N of Fordingbridge]: Imposing and picturesque wisteria-covered thatched pub with very low well padded beams (and they say a ghost), wide choice of generous straightforward food, well kept Ringwood beers, friendly attentive service, log-effect gas fire in big fireplace, family rooms (one no smoking), back garden with play area; Avon Valley footpath passes the door, fine pedestrian suspension bridge *(Phyl and Jack Street)*

BURITON SU7320

☆ *Five Bells* [off A3 S of Petersfield]: Welcoming new licensees putting emphasis on food in appealing pub with fresh flowers and good atmosphere in smartened-up restaurant, big log fire in low-beamed lounge, some ancient stripped masonry and woodburner on public side, well kept Badger beers inc Gribble Fursty Ferret, good wines by the glass; fruit machine, piped music; children in eating areas, tables on informal lawn behind and more on sheltered terraces, pretty village, good walks, self-catering in converted stables *(LYM, Ann and Colin Hunt, Shirley Mackenzie, Tony Phillips, Guy Vowles)*

BURLEY SU2103

☆ *Queens Head* [The Cross; back rd Ringwood—Lymington]: Large pub dating partly from 17th c and probably earlier, several rambling rooms, good friendly atmosphere, some flagstones, beams, timbering and panelling, wide choice of good reasonably priced food, well kept Bass, Ringwood Fortyniner and Whitbreads; may be piped music, gift/souvenir shop in courtyard – pub and New Forest village can get packed in summer; children welcome *(LYM, W W Burke)*

☆ *White Buck* [Bisterne Close; ¾ mile E, OS Sheet 195 map ref 223028]: Big pleasantly refurnished bar in 19th-c mock-Tudor hotel, very wide choice of reasonably priced good generous food, Gales Butser, HSB and GB and

Ringwood Best, decent wines and country wines, cheap soft drinks, good coffee, log fire, courteous efficient staff, thriving atmosphere, smart and attractive end dining room with tables out on decking (should book – but no bookings Sun lunchtime); may be quiet piped music; dogs welcome, pleasant front terrace and spacious lawn, lovely New Forest setting, good value well equipped bedrooms, superb walks towards Burley itself and over Mill Lawn *(Caraline and Richard Crocker, BB, John and Joan Calvert)*

BURSLEDON SU4909

☆ *Jolly Sailor* [off A27 towards Bursledon Station, Lands End Rd; handy for M27 junction 8]: Has been a popular main entry, chiefly for its superb position overlooking the yachting inlet, but closed for lengthy refurbishment by Badger (possibly as a more restauranty place) through the months leading up to our going to press; news please *(LYM)*

CADNAM SU2913

Bartley Lodge [A337 Lyndhurst Rd]: Hotel in 18th-c former hunting lodge, fairly small attractive bar open to non-residents, enjoyable lunches, coffee and biscuits all day, friendly staff, children allowed till 9, and calm dogs on leads; bedrooms *(Dennis Jenkin)*

Coach & Horses [Southampton Rd]: Popular for wide choice of good value food from baguettes and baked potatoes to more imaginative dishes, OAP discounts on food and drink, efficient cheerful service *(A D Marsh)*

☆ *Sir John Barleycorn* [Old Romsey Rd; by M27, junction 1]: Picturesque low-slung thatched pub, attractive medieval core on left with dim lighting, low beams and timbers, large more modern extension on right, wide food choice from sandwiches up, not cheap but generous, afternoon cream teas, well kept ales such as Fullers London Pride and Ringwood Fortyniner, reasonably priced wines, two roaring log fires, no smoking restaurant end, prompt and friendly young staff; dogs and children welcome, can be very busy; suntrap benches in front and out in garden, eye-catching flowers, open all day *(Roy and Lindsey Fentiman, LYM, Mike and Sue Richardson, Phyl and Jack Street, Vince)*

CANTERTON SU2613

☆ *Sir Walter Tyrell* [off A31 W of Cadnam, follow Rufus's Stone sign]: Biggish pretty pub by lovely New Forest clearing often with ponies, long divided front bar, long back dining room, wide choice of popular food, good range of real ales inc Ringwood, good service; big play area, sheltered terrace, good base for walks *(W W Burke)*

CHARTER ALLEY SU5957

White Hart [White Hart Lane, off A340 N of Basingstoke]: Friendly village pub with wide range of real ales such as Timothy Taylors Landlord and West Berkshire Mild, continental beers, decent wines, wide choice of reasonably priced food in dining area, pleasant service, woodburner and no smoking area in lounge bar, skittle alley in simple public bar *(J V Dadswell)*

CHAWTON SU7037

Greyfriar [Winchester Rd]: Well run and popular 17th-c pub opp Jane Austen's house, pleasantly relaxing low-beamed bar, standing timbers studded with foreign coins, enjoyable reasonably priced generous food from very well filled home-baked bread sandwiches to game and aberdeen angus steaks, quick friendly service, well kept Fullers ales, good coffee; small garden behind with barbecue, lovely village, good walks *(Ian and Deborah Carrington, Phyl and Jack Street, R B Gardiner, Roger and Pauline Pearce, Phil and Jane Hodson)*

CHILBOLTON SU3939

☆ *Abbots Mitre* [off A3051 S of Andover]: Wide choice of tasty food inc very good value OAP special in side lounge and attractive restaurant with small log fire, reasonable helpings, well kept ales such as Boddingtons, Flowers Original, Greene King Abbot and Old Speckled Hen and Ringwood, quick smartly dressed staff, separate front public bar and games room; a bit dark, but friendly, busy and roomy; garden with pleasant covered terrace, baskets and tubs of flowers, play area; open all day Sun, attractive village, River Test and other walks *(Pat and Robert Watt)*

CHILWORTH SU4118

Clump [A27 Romsey Rd]: Busy extended chain eating place, largely no smoking; well kept Boddingtons, Fullers London Pride and Gales HSB, good choice of wines, two log fires, smart décor with sofas and easy chairs in one part, spacious conservatory; unobtrusive piped music, disabled facilities but steps at entrance; open all day, large garden *(Phyl and Jack Street)*

COLDEN COMMON SU4821

Fishers Pond: Big busy refurbished Brewers Fayre, sensibly priced generous food inc children's, decent coffee, polite friendly service; pretty setting by pond with ducks, handy for Marwell Zoo, open all day *(Ann and Colin Hunt, John and Joan Calvert)*

CRAWLEY SU4234

Fox & Hounds [off A272 or B3420 NW of Winchester]: Striking almost swiss-looking building, mix of attractive wooden tables and chairs on polished floors in neat and attractive linked beamed rooms with three log fires, real ales such as Fullers London Pride, Gales HSB, Ringwood Best and Wadworths 6X, decent wines, attentive smartly dressed staff, civilised atmosphere; tables in garden, pretty village with duck pond *(LYM, Phyl and Jack Street, Lynn Sharpless, Ann and Colin Hunt)*

CRONDALL SU7948

☆ *Hampshire Arms* [village signed off A287 S of Fleet; Pankridge St]: Enthusiastic young chef/landlord doing good sandwiches, well filled home-baked baguettes and quickly changing one-price choice of very good enterprising main dishes in snug beamed bistro-bar with candles in bottles on dining tables and a pair of leather sofas by huge log fire, well kept Greene King IPA, Abbot and Ruddles County and a guest such as Hook

Norton Old Hooky, a dozen good wines by the glass, relaxed informal atmosphere and friendly staff, wider menu for gently upmarket restaurant in back extension (book well ahead wknds, worth booking wkdy evenings too), exemplary lavatories, compact sturdily furnished public bar (dogs welcome); children welcome (high chairs available), fenced back garden with picnic-sets, heaters and floodlit boules pitch, open all day *(Martin and Karen Wake, Mike and Jayne Bastin, Andy and Yvonne Cunningham, BB, Brian and Karen Thomas, KC)*

CURDRIDGE SU5314

Cricketers [Curdridge Lane, off B3035 just under a mile NE of A334 junction]: Open-plan low-ceilinged Victorian village local with banquettes in lounge area, little-changed public part (can be smoky), rather smart dining area, friendly attentive licensees, wide choice of well presented generous food inc sandwiches and good value daily specials, Greene King Abbot and Old Speckled Hen; quiet piped music (live Thurs; tables on front lawn, two friendly dogs, pleasant footpaths *(A and B D Craig, P R and S A White)*

DAMERHAM SU1016

☆ *Compasses* [signed off B3078 in Fordingbridge, or off A354 via Martin; East End]: Appealing country inn with good affordable home cooking from sandwiches up esp soups and shellfish, marvellous cheese choice, friendly staff and caring management, five well kept ales from local brewers, good choice of wines by the glass, well over a hundred malt whiskies, neatly refurbished small lounge bar divided by log fire from pleasant dining room with booth seating (children allowed here), pale wood tables and kitchen chairs, separate locals' bar with pool and juke box; long pretty garden by quiet village's cricket ground, high downland walks, attractive bedrooms with own bathrooms *(Geoffrey G Lawrance, Ann Brown, Janet Upton, Phyl and Jack Street)*

DOWNTON SZ2793

☆ *Royal Oak* [A337 Lymington—New Milton]: Wide choice of good value food in neat partly panelled family pub, half no smoking, with well kept Whitbreads-related ales, good wine choice, jovial atmosphere, impeccable friendly service with nice touches such as good-sized napkins, small restaurant; unobtrusive piped music; huge well kept garden with good play area *(A D Marsh, L C T Cottrell, John Fairley)*

DROXFORD SU6018

White Horse [A32; South Hill]: No reports yet on new regime in rambling old inn with several small linked areas, low beams, bow windows, alcoves and log fires, two no smoking dining rooms, roomy separate public bar with plenty of games, also TV and CD juke box; has been welcoming and popular, with well kept Greene King ales and standard food from lunchtime sandwiches, baguettes and filled baked potatoes up; children and dogs welcome, tables out in sheltered flower-filled courtyard, bedrooms, open all day, rolling walking country; news please *(LYM)*

DUMMER SU5846

Queen [½ mile from M3 junction 7; take Dummer slip road]: Beams, lots of softly lit alcoves, log fire, queen and steeplechase prints, bar food and no smoking restaurant allowing children (they may keep your credit card), well kept Courage Best, Fullers London Pride and Greene King Old Speckled Hen, good service; fruit machine, well reproduced piped music, no mobile phones; picnic-sets under cocktail parasols on terrace and in extended back garden, attractive village with ancient church *(Tim and Carolyn Lowes, LYM, Geoff Palmer, P Hennessey, Ian Phillips)*

DUNDRIDGE SU5718

☆ *Hampshire Bowman* [off B3035 towards Droxford, Swanmore, then right at Bishops W signpost]: Cosy and unspoilt country local, great mix of customers (children, dogs and walkers welcome, usually some classic cars or vintage motorcycles), well kept Ringwood Best and Fortyniner, a changing Cheriton ale and up to three guest beers tapped from the cask, decent house wines, country wines, growing choice of attractively priced home-made food inc good value Sun roast, good welcoming service, some colourful paintings; tables on spacious and attractive lawn, good downland walks *(Val and Alan Green, Geoff Palmer, Ann and Colin Hunt, LYM, the Didler)*

DURLEY SU5217

Robin Hood [Durley Street, just off B2177 Bishops Waltham—Winchester]: Smart pub with good gently upmarket food in lounge and dining room, log fire, good cheerful service, well kept Greene King ales with a guest beer, reasonably priced wines, public bar with darts and two amiable labradors; back terrace and big pleasant garden with fine view and play area, good walks *(Val and Alan Green, Nigel Braithwaite)*

EAST BOLDRE SU3700

☆ *Turf Cutters Arms* [Main Rd]: Small dim-lit New Forest country local, relaxed and quite unpretentious, lots of beams and pictures, sturdy tables, rugs, bare boards and flagstones, log fire, Gales HSB, Ringwood Best and Wadworths 6X, several dozen malt whiskies, no smoking room, fish tanks, two big friendly dogs, simple food from sandwiches and basic dishes to quite a lot of game; garden tables, some good heathland walks, three big old-fashioned bedrooms, simple but comfortable, good breakfast *(BB, W W Burke)*

EAST MEON SU6822

☆ *George* [Church St; signed off A272 W of Petersfield, and off A32 in West Meon]: Rambling and relaxing rustic pub with heavy beams and inglenooks, four log fires, cosy areas around central bar counter, deal tables and horse tack; well kept Badger Best and Tanglefoot, decent wines, country wines, wide choice of good fresh substantial food from sandwiches to interesting dishes, helpful prompt service; soft piped music, quiz night Sun; children welcome, good outdoor seating arrangements, small but comfortable bedrooms (book well ahead), good breakfast, pretty village with fine church, good walks *(LYM, Dave and Lesley Walker, Ann and Colin Hunt, Nicholas and Dorothy Stephens, P R and S A White, Simon Collett-Jones)*

Izaak Walton [High St]: Friendly two-bar local in delightful village, helpful efficient service, smart lounge mainly for eaters (good value fresh food inc children's), well kept Wadworths 6X, darts and pool in public bar; nice table out by front stream, massive back garden (maybe unusual rabbits); children welcome, open all day Sun, quiz night most Weds *(R T and J C Moggridge)*

EAST STRATTON SU5339

☆ ***Northbrook Arms*** [brown sign to pub off A33 4 miles S of A303 junction]: Substantial big-windowed brick pub with log fire in unpretentious L-shaped quarry-tiled bar, carpeted dining area on left, decent food (Weds steak night, quiz and curry Tues), Gales HSB, Otter and local guest beers (usually high strength), darts, bar billiards, skittle alley; piped local radio; dogs and children welcome, picnic-sets across lane on neat lawn, bedrooms, fine walks nearby *(LYM, Lynn Sharpless, Ann and Colin Hunt, Mary Seers, David and Sheila Pearcey)*

EASTON SU5132

☆ ***Cricketers*** [off B3047]: Open-plan local with good atmosphere, well kept Otter, Ringwood Best and guests such as Archers Special and Cheriton Brandy Mount, reasonably priced wines, wide choice of good value generous food from sandwiches to piping hot dishes, prompt friendly service, pleasant well worn in mix of pub furnishings, darts and shove-ha'penny one end, small bright no smoking restaurant, good wine range; can be a bit smoky, jazz duo Weds; well cared for bedrooms *(BB, Tim and Carolyn Lowes, Lynn Sharpless, Ron Shelton, J R Ringrose, Ann and Colin Hunt, Val and Alan Green)*

EMERY DOWN SU2808

☆ ***New Forest*** [village signed off A35 just W of Lyndhurst]: Good position in one of the nicest parts of the Forest, with good walks nearby; attractive softly lit separate areas on varying levels, each with its own character, hunting prints, two log fires, good imaginative generous if not cheap food from filled baguettes up, welcoming staff, well kept Hook Norton and two Ringwood beers, wide choice of realistically priced house wines, proper coffee; children allowed, small but pleasant three-level garden *(Dick and Madeleine Brown, B and K Hypher, LYM, Kevin Flack, David Cannings, Mrs J A Steff-Langston)*

EMSWORTH SU7406

Coal Exchange [Ships Quay, South St]: Friendly bustle in comfortably compact L-shaped Victorian local, low ceilings, lots of locals and yachtsmen, cheerful landlady proud of her well kept Gales ales, good value lunchtime food inc good crab salad and popular Sun lunch (open all day then) and Tues curry night, coal fire each end; can be smoky when busy; tables outside, handy for Wayfarers Walk and Solent Walk *(Ann and Colin Hunt, Andy and Jill Kassube)*

☆ ***Kings Arms*** [Havant Rd]: Neat and tidily organised local popular for generous wholesome interesting food cooked by landlady, fresh veg and some organic dishes, good choice of wines, good service, cheerful landlord, well kept Gales ales and a guest beer, good wine choice and coffee, small restaurant area, no mobiles; no children in bar, pleasant garden behind *(Miss J F Reay, Martin and Rose Bonner, Ann and Colin Hunt)*

Lord Raglan [Queen St]: Friendly and relaxing Gales local, their ales kept well, cheerful long-serving landlord, wide choice of reasonably priced generous home-made food from sandwiches up, log fire, popular restaurant (must book summer wknds); live music Sun evening, children welcome if eating, pleasant sea-view garden behind *(Ann and Colin Hunt, Tony Hobden, Andy and Jill Kassube, Irene and Derek Flewin)*

EVERSLEY SU7861

☆ ***Golden Pot*** [B3272]: Interlinked spreading areas inc snug armchairs and sofa by log-effect gas fire, decent if not cheap food from baguettes up, well kept Greene King Abbot and Ruddles County and a guest beer, nice wines by the glass, pretty no smoking restaurant; piped music, pianist/vocalist Mon night; dogs allowed in bar, picnic-sets outside with masses of colourful flowers, cl winter Sun evening *(Mr and Mrs S Felstead, Francis Johnston, Ian Phillips, KC, LYM, Chris Sexton)*

EVERTON SZ2994

☆ ***Crown*** [pub signed just off A337 W of Lymington]: Good interesting food cooked to order (so may be a wait), attractive prices, tiled central bar, two attractive rooms with sturdy tables on polished boards off tiled-floor bar, log fires, lots of jugs and china, well kept Gales HSB, Hampshire Strongs Best and Ringwood Best, friendly attentive and helpful service; no dogs, picnic-sets on front terrace and back grass, quiet village on edge of New Forest *(David Sizer, BB, Mrs S Hayward, A D Marsh, Don and Maureen Medley)*

EXTON SU6120

☆ ***Shoe*** [village signed from A32]: Food (not Sun night) interesting and increasingly popular under good new chef, cheerful obliging staff, well kept Wadworths ales, decent house wines, neat bright décor in rustic bar, attractive light oak-panelled room off and cosy log-fire restaurant (very popular with older people, with small helpings on request); piped music; smart façade, tables in nice garden across lane (stretched down to River Meon), pretty village, good walks *(Peter B Rea, Dr and Mrs D Woods, John and Joan Calvert, Phyl and Jack Street)*

FAREHAM SU5806

Cob & Pen [Wallington Shore Rd, not far from M27 junction 11]: Pleasant pine furnishings, flagstones and carpets, Hook Norton Best and Ringwood ales, good value straightforward food, nice separate games room; large garden *(Val and Alan Green)*

Lord Arthur Lee [West St]: Large open-plan Wetherspoons, attractively priced well kept beers, good value food, provision for children; named for the local 1900s MP who presented Chequers to the nation *(Val and Alan Green, Lynn Sharpless)*

FARNBOROUGH SU8756

☆ *Prince of Wales* [Rectory Rd, nr Farnborough North stn]: Impressive range of well kept changing beers in friendly Edwardian local, small but lively, stripped brickwork, open fire and antiquey touches in its three small connecting rooms, popular lunchtime food from sandwiches to imaginative specials, good service, decent malt whiskies *(Dr Martin Owton)*

FLEET SU8155

Heron on the Lake [Old Cove Rd]: Reliable new Chef & Brewer, recently done out in pleasant old-fashioned style, good choice of decent food *(Andy and Yvonne Cunningham)*

FROGHAM SU1712

☆ *Foresters Arms* [Abbotswell Rd]: Busy and well run extensively refurbished New Forest pub, flagstones and small woodburner, good helpings of reasonably priced enjoyable blackboard food from sandwiches to very popular Sun lunch, friendly service, well kept Wadworths and guest ales, decent wines, extended no smoking dining room; children welcome, pleasant garden and pretty front verandah; small camp site adjacent, nearby ponies and good walks *(Martin and Karen Wake, J and B Cressey, LYM, John and Joan Calvert)*

GOODWORTH CLATFORD SU3642

Royal Oak: Smart and comfortable modern-looking village pub with friendly efficient service, good food from old favourites and Sun roast to more interesting dishes, well kept beer; colourful sheltered dell-like garden, large, neatly kept and safe for children, good riverside walks nearby *(Phyl and Jack Street, P R and D C Groves)*

GOSPORT SZ5998

☆ *Alverbank House* [Stokes Bay Rd, Alverstoke]: Comfortable and pleasant partly divided hotel lounge with good interesting choice of food (not cheap) inc plenty for vegetarians, Ringwood and four well kept guest beers, great choice of malt whiskies, friendly well trained staff; piped music; in woods at end of Stanley Park, over road from promenade, nice big mature garden with views of Solent and Isle of Wight; play area, bedrooms very well appointed *(Val and Alan Green, Ian Phillips, Phyl and Jack Street, Peter and Audrey Dowsett)*

Fighting Cocks [Clayhall Rd, Alverstoke]: Unpretentious local with cheap food, popular Tues folk night; piped music may be loud; big garden with play area *(Peter and Audrey Dowsett)*

Jolly Roger [Priory Rd, Hardway]: Harbour-view pub doing well under friendly current licensees, four well kept ales inc Greene King Abbot and Youngs Special, decent house wines, reasonably priced food, attractive eating area *(Peter and Audrey Dowsett, Ann and Colin Hunt)*

Queens [Queens Rd]: Bare-boards pub whose landlady expertly keeps Ringwood, Roosters Yankee, Youngs Best and two more changing strong beers, three areas off bar with good log fire in interesting carved fireplace, docile pyrenean mountain dog a general favourite now; very quick service, Sun bar nibbles, perhaps huge filled rolls and other simple food; beer festivals, sensibly placed darts, family area with TV, no piped music, quiz night Thurs; open all day Sat *(Ann and Colin Hunt)*

HAMBLE SU4806

☆ *Olde Whyte Harte* [High St; 3 miles from M27 junction 8]: Cheerful low-beamed bar, plenty of well used seats in well integrated flagstoned eating area, welcoming licensees and helpful pleasant yacht-minded staff, blazing inglenook log fire, imaginative well priced fresh food inc plenty of fish, four well kept Gales ales, lots of country wines, decent coffee, yachting memorabilia; piped music may be loud and lively (less so in no smoking area); children in eating area, some seats outside, handy for nature reserve *(LYM, Val and Alan Green)*

Victory [High St]: Three well kept real ales, enjoyable bar food, convivial staff; piped 1960s music, no youngsters – middle-aged crowd *(John E Bailey)*

HAMBLEDON SU6716

☆ *Bat & Ball* [Broadhalfpenny Down; about 2 miles E towards Clanfield]: Extended dining pub opp seminal cricket pitch (matches most summer Sundays), plenty of cricket memorabilia, comfortable modern furnishings in three rooms and panelled restaurant, log fire; good interesting food from modestly priced snacks inc baguettes and toasties to fresh fish, good service even when crowded, well kept Gales ales; children welcome, lovely downs views and walks *(Mrs P Sladen, P R and S A White, LYM, Phyl and Jack Street, Peter Salmon)*

Horse & Jockey [Hipley, pub signed well off B2150]: Smart biggish dining pub with good choice of attractively served food inc imaginative dishes, reasonably priced, friendly polite staff, well kept ales inc Fullers London Pride; large garden by stream *(David and Ruth Hollands, Carole Hall)*

HANNINGTON SU5455

Vine: Spacious and friendly country dining pub, reliable reasonably priced food inc Sun lunches, restaurant and attractive dining conservatory, real ales such as Fullers London Pride, Greene King Old Speckled Hen and Youngs Special; may be piped music; terrace, big garden, nice spot up on downs, good walks; cl Mon *(Tony and Wendy Hobden)*

HATHERDEN SU3450

☆ *Old Bell & Crown*: Picturesque old thatched village pub, roomy inside, with well kept Wadworths and guest ales, restaurant with no smoking part, enjoyable food from quick lunchtime snacks up, well kept Greene King

Ruddles County and Wadworths IPA and 6X; pretty garden *(Phyl and Jack Street)*

HAVANT SU7106

☆ *Old House At Home* [South St]: Much modernised low-beamed Tudor pub, nice rambling alcovey feel, two fireplaces in lounge, well kept Gales ales and a guest beer, quite a wide food choice, good welcoming service, smokers' area; piped music (live Sat – very popular with young people Fri/Sat night), back garden *(LYM, Ann and Colin Hunt, Tony Hobden, Mrs Maricar Jagger)*

Robin Hood [Homewell]: Relaxing old local with low ceilings in rambling open-plan bar, well kept Gales ales and a guest beer, reasonably priced lunchtime food, good service, open fire, sensibly placed darts; smoking allowed throughout *(Ann and Colin Hunt, Tony Hobden)*

HAYLING ISLAND SU7098

Inn on the Beach [Sea Front, South Hayling]: Largeish modern pub on shingle, roomy sunken bar, several real ales, friendly staff, good value food in dining area; some live music *(Mrs Maricar Jagger)*

HAZELEY SU7459

Shoulder of Mutton [Hazeley Heath]: 18th-c dining pub with friendly helpful service from long-serving licensees, entertaining menu with popular bar lunches from ploughman's to good pies and steaks (no snacks just meals on Sun, when many tables are booked), good log fire in cosy lounge, no smoking area, well kept Courage Best, Wadworths 6X and a seasonal ale; may be quiet piped music; attractive mellow-tiled building, terrace and garden *(Francis Johnston, Colin McKerrow, Ian Phillips, R Lake, Roger and Pauline Pearce)*

HERRIARD SS6744

☆ *Fur & Feathers* [pub signed just off A339 Basingstoke—Alton]: Good value generous home-made food from filled rolls and baked potatoes up in chatty open-plan pub with stripped pine tables and chairs on bare boards, friendly staff, well kept Cheriton Pots, fff Moondance and Shepherd Neame Spitfire, interesting wines of the month, log fire, lots of jockey cigarette cards; well lit pool table in carpeted area with big prints; picnic-sets out on front tarmac *(BB, Tony Radnor, Martin and Karen Wake, James Streatfeild)*

HILL TOP SU4003

Royal Oak [B3054 Beaulieu—Hythe]: Good-sized neatly kept New Forest pub with well kept Flowers Original, Gales HSB, Greene King Abbot, Ringwood Best and John Smiths, popular food; good tables and chairs in pleasant garden behind *(W W Burke)*

HORSEBRIDGE SU3430

John o' Gaunt [off A3057 Romsey—Andover, just SW of Kings Somborne]: Nicely placed in River Test village, log fire in unpretentious L-shaped bar, interesting prints in small back dining area, picnic-sets out in side arbour; has been very popular with walkers for good attractively priced home cooking, good choice of well kept ales and decent wines by the glass, but under new management and no news yet – reports please *(BB)*

HOUGHTON SU3432

Boot [S of Stockbridge]: Quiet country local with good food from top-notch bangers and mash to more unusual dishes in unpretentious bar with blazing log fire or roomy and attractive restaurant on left, Ringwood and other real ales, attentive service, pleasant long garden running down to lovely (unfenced) stretch of River Test, where they have fishing; good walks, and opp Test Way cycle path *(Phyl and Jack Street, Edward Mirzoeff)*

HYTHE SU4306

Travellers Rest [Hart Hill, off Frost Lane]: Former quiet forest-edge local trendily refurbished as restauranty pub, appealing menu, Ringwood Best and Wadworths 6X *(Dr Martin Owton)*

IBSLEY SU1409

Old Beams [A338 Salisbury—Ringwood]: Big busy black and white thatched all-day Appletons eatery, largely no smoking, redone with lots of pine furniture under aged oak beams, wide choice of food inc large help-yourself salad bar, Greene King real ales, conservatory; open all day *(the Didler, David M Cundy, LYM, D and S Price)*

ITCHEN ABBAS SU5332

☆ *Trout* [4 miles from M3 junction 9; B3047]: Smallish country pub with welcoming efficient service, enjoyable food from baguettes and bangers and mash to some interesting dishes, simple but smartish décor in quiet lounge and no smoking dining room, chatty public bar, well kept Greene King ales with a guest such as Everards, decent wines; tables in sheltered pretty side garden, good river and downland walks nearby, comfortable bedrooms *(Lynn Sharpless, Susan and John Douglas, Val and Alan Green, LYM, Tim and Carolyn Lowes, Mrs Joy Griffiths, Dr and Mrs D Woods, Diana Brumfit)*

KEYHAVEN SZ3091

Gun: Busy 17th-c pub looking over boatyard and sea to Isle of Wight, low-beamed bar with lots of nautical memorabilia and plenty of character (less in family rooms); good choice of generous food using local produce, well kept beers tapped from the cask such as Gales HSB, Greene King Old Speckled Hen, Ringwood and Wadworths 6X, well over a hundred malt whiskies, bar billiards; back conservatory, garden with swings and fish pond *(A D Marsh, M G Hart, Gordon Stevenson)*

LANGSTONE SU7104

Royal Oak [off A3023 just before Hayling Island bridge]: Charmingly placed pub overlooking tidal inlet and ancient wadeway to Hayling Island, boats at high tide, wading birds when it goes out, spacious simply furnished flagstoned bar, two linked dining areas, winter open fires, well kept Boddingtons, Flowers Original, Gales HSB and guest beer, good choice of wines by the glass, popular food inc all-day snacks; can get very busy and smoky; children in eating areas, good coastal paths nearby, open all day

(Dennis Le Couilliard, LYM, Ann and Colin Hunt, Irene and Derek Flewin, Mr and Mrs S Felstead)

☆ ***Ship*** [A3023]: Busy waterside 18th-c former grain store, smart and well cared for, plenty of tables on heated terrace by quiet quay, lovely views to Hayling Island from roomy dimly lit nautical bar with upper deck dining room, good no smoking areas, fast friendly helpful service, full Gales range kept well with a guest beer, good choice of wines by the generous glass, country wines, log fire, wide range of generous food inc fresh fish and platters for two, good no smoking areas; children's room, open all day, good coast walks *(Val and Alan Green, David and Carole Chapman, Ann and Colin Hunt, Lynn Sharpless, Geoff Pidoux, D J and P M Taylor, Dr D G Twyman)*

LASHAM SU6742

☆ ***Royal Oak***: Thriving two-bar village local, friendly and comfortable, with well kept changing ales, wide range of enjoyable home-made food, fair prices, log fire, much talk of aircraft and gliding (airfield nearby); may be quiet piped music; pleasant garden by church, attractive village, good walks *(Peter Dimmick)*

LIPHOOK SU8330

Links Hotel [Portsmouth Rd]: Spacious golf-oriented pub with subdued modern décor in small interesting rooms and alcoves, good 1880-1920s local photographs, Courage Best, Fullers London Pride and Hogs Back TEA, decent wines, enjoyable varied food from bar snacks to crab, lobster and game, good atmosphere, friendly staff; pleasant woodland and lakeside walks at Foley Manor, handy for Bohunt Manor *(Ian Phillips, Phyl and Jack Street)*

LITTLE LONDON SU6359

Plough [Silchester Rd, off A340 N of Basingstoke]: Cosy unspoilt tucked-away local with tiled floor, low beams, friendly landlord, limited food inc lots of good value baguettes, well kept Ringwood and interesting guest beers, log fire, darts, bar billiards, no piped music; attractive garden, handy for Pamber Forest and Calleva Roman remains *(Pat and Robert Watt, J V Dadswell)*

LITTLETON SU4532

Running Horse [Main Rd]: Small village pub with simple furnishings and flagstones, surprisingly good individual cooking at sensible prices; big garden with play area *(Mrs J A Taylar)*

LOCKS HEATH SU5006

☆ ***Jolly Farmer*** [2½ miles from M27 junction 9; A27 towards Bursledon, left into Locks Rd, at end T-junction right into Warsash Rd then left at hire shop into Fleet End Rd]: Appealing country-style pub with wide choice of food from filled baps to steaks and good value very popular two-sitting Sun lunch in extensive series of softly lit rooms, nice old scrubbed tables (quite close-set), a forest of interesting bric-a-brac and prints, coal-effect gas fires, no smoking area, well kept Flowers Original, Gales HSB and Fullers London Pride, decent wines and country wines, interesting landlord, good quick friendly service; two sheltered terraces, one with a play area and children's lavatories; nice bedrooms *(Peter and Audrey Dowsett, Michael and Robin Inskip, Charles and Pauline Stride, LYM, Ann and Colin Hunt, Roger and Pauline Pearce)*

LONGPARISH SU4344

Plough [B3048, off A303 just E of Andover]: Obliging new licensees in comfortable open-plan food pub divided by arches, partly no smoking restaurant, well kept Gales and Ringwood ales, decent house wines, food (may take a while) from sandwiches up; piped music; children in eating areas, tables on terrace and in nice garden, bedrooms *(LYM, KC, Dr D E Granger, Phyl and Jack Street)*

LOWER FROYLE SU7643

☆ ***Anchor*** [signed off A31]: Unassuming 14th-c traditional pub with roomy and brightly lit low-ceilinged bar and dining room, popular with older people lunchtime (esp Weds) for reasonably priced food with wide choice from sandwiches to fish, cheerful family service, well kept Courage and Timothy Taylors Landlord, decent malt whiskies; tables outside, bedrooms *(Ron Shelton, R B Gardiner)*

LYMINGTON SZ3295

Angel [High St]: Large open-plan pub spreading comfortably around central bar, panelling and black beams, enjoyable food inc children's, well kept Wadworths 6X, reasonable prices, helpful staff, no smoking area; piped music; tables in attractive inner courtyard, bedrooms, open all day *(LYM, Tim and Carolyn Lowes, A D Marsh)*

☆ ***Chequers*** [Ridgeway Lane, Lower Woodside – dead end just S of A337 roundabout W of Lymington, by White Hart]: Busy yachtsmen's local with polished boards and quarry tiles, attractive pictures, plain chairs and wall pews; generous good food inc local fish, real ales such as Bass, Ringwood and Wadworths 6X, pleasant young staff, traditional games; may be piped music; well behaved children allowed, tables and summer marquee in neat walled back family garden, attractive front terrace, handy for bird-watching at Pennington Marshes *(JMC, LYM, A D Marsh, Gordon Stevenson)*

☆ ***Fishermans Rest*** [All Saints Rd, Woodside]: Wide choice of consistently good interesting food inc very popular Sun lunch, reasonable prices, well kept Ringwood ales, decent wines, friendly staff, pleasant atmosphere, plenty of locals at bar; can get busy, wknd booking recommended *(A D Marsh, Ben Whitney and Pippa Redmond)*

LYNDHURST SU2908

Crown [Top end of High St opposite church]: Best Western hotel, cheerful log fire in attractive traditional panelled bar, pleasant and efficient young staff, well kept Ringwood Best and Porter, bar food as well as restaurant; bedrooms, fine forest walks *(Phyl and Jack Street, Brian and Janet Ainscough)*

Stag [High St]: Good smart italian restaurant attached to plush bar with well kept Greene

King IPA and Abbot, limited bar lunches, good service; bedrooms with own bathrooms, open all day *(Brian and Janet Ainscough, Joan and Michel Hooper-Immins)*

MAPLEDURWELL SU6851

☆ *Gamekeepers* [off A30, not far from M3 junction 6]: Popular dining pub with dark beams, joists and standing timbers, well spaced prettily set tables, glass-topped well with carp in flagstoned and panelled core, large no smoking dining room, well kept Badger Best and Tanglefoot, good choice of food; piped music; children welcome, picnic-sets on terrace and back grassy area, lovely thatched village with duck pond, good walks, open all day *(LYM, Ian Phillips)*

MARCHWOOD SU3810

☆ *Pilgrim* [Hythe Rd, off A326 at Twiggs Lane]: Beautiful immaculately kept thatched pub with red plush banquettes in long L-shaped bar, wide choice of consistently good value home-made food, good long-serving landlord, well kept mainstream beers, english wines, open fires, separate more expensive restaurant; can be crowded, handy for otter and owl park at Longdown; neat garden *(A and B D Craig, Phyl and Jack Street, LYM, Anthony Groves)*

MATTINGLEY SU7357

Leather Bottle [3 miles from M3, junction 5; in Hook, turn right-and-left on to B3349 Reading Road (former A32)]: Wisteria-covered tiled dining pub with good value food all day from sandwiches up, well spaced tables in linked areas, black beams, flagstones and bare boards, good inglenook log fire, efficient friendly service, well kept ales such as Courage Best, Greene King Abbot and Charles Wells Bombardier, extension opening on to covered heated terrace; piped music; picnic-sets in two pretty garden areas, one pleasantly modern *(LYM, Tracey and Stephen Groves, Dr and Mrs A K Clarke, Pat Tweed, Tom Evans)*

MEDSTEAD SU6537

☆ *Castle of Comfort* [signed off A31 at Four Marks; Castle St]: True leisurely village local, homely and cosily old-fashioned beamed lounge bar, well kept ales such as Gales HSB and Ushers Best, good basic bar lunches inc soup and sandwiches, toasties and ploughman's, warmly friendly efficient service, plush chairs, woodburner and small open fireplace, spartan public bar with darts etc; sunny front verandah, more tables in neat side garden with fairy lights and play tree, nice downland walks to the west *(BB, Phyl and Jack Street)*

MEONSTOKE SU6119

☆ *Bucks Head* [village signed just off A32 N of Droxford]: Plush banquettes, log fire, rugs on bare boards and well spaced tables in partly panelled L-shaped dining lounge looking over road to water meadows, nice public bar with leather settee by another log fire, darts and juke box, food in copious helpings, well kept Greene King IPA, Gales HSB and a seasonal beer, decent wines, cheerful service; tables and picnic-sets in small garden, lovely village setting with ducks on pretty little River Meon, good walks, bedrooms with own bathrooms, open all day *(BB, Peter Salmon, Ann and Colin Hunt)*

MINLEY SU8357

Crown & Cushion [A327, just N of M3 junction 4A]: Attractive small traditional pub with reasonably priced food from baguettes and ciabattas up, Adnams Broadside, Bass and Tetleys, coal-effect gas fire; big separate raftered and flagstoned rustic 'meade hall' behind, very popular wknds (evenings more a young people's meeting place), with huge log fire; children in eating area, heated terrace overlooking own cricket pitch *(Ian Phillips, LYM)*

MORTIMER WEST END SU6363

Red Lion [Church Rd; Silchester turn off Mortimer—Aldermaston rd]: Welcoming country dining pub with good food from generous doorstep sandwiches up, well kept Badger and other ales, lots of beams, stripped masonry, timbers and panelling, good log fire; dogs and children welcome, plenty of seats in pleasant garden with play area, and on small flower-filled front terrace, open all day, handy for Roman Silchester *(LYM, Shirley Mackenzie, J V Dadswell)*

NORTH WALTHAM SU5645

Fox [signed off A30 SW of Basingstoke; handy for M3 junction 7]: Foxy décor in comfortable village pub, bar and smoking area, bigger bright elongated dining area with log fire, well kept real ales, swift friendly service, good range of food from sandwiches and baguettes to Sun roasts; children welcome, garden responding attractively to new owners, pleasant village in nice spot (nice walk to Jane Austen's church at Steventon) *(Martin and Karen Wake, Phyl and Jack Street)*

NORTH WARNBOROUGH SU7351

Swan [Hook Rd, nr M3 junction 5]: Village local popular for its food, with well kept real ales, friendly service, beams and stripped brickwork, pubby front bar with pool, TV and fruit machine; large well equipped play area beyond back courtyard, by Basingstoke Canal and handy for Odiham Castle *(Richard Houghton)*

ODIHAM SU7451

Water Witch [signed off main st]: Chef & Brewer done out in olde-worlde style, reliable food, real ales; garden with extensive children's facilities, very busy wknds *(Andy and Yvonne Cunningham)*

OTTERBOURNE SU4623

Old Forge [Main Rd]: Pleasantly reworked and well run Vintage Inn, their usual decent food all day, good atmosphere, efficient friendly staff, Bass and Tetleys *(Phyl and Jack Street)*

OWER SU3216

Mortimer Arms [Romsey Rd, by M27 junction 2]: Recent classy refurbishment for handy motorway stop-off, enjoyable good value food inc imaginative dishes; comfortable well equipped bedrooms *(Janet Upton, Mr and Mrs Lane)*

OWSLEBURY SU5123

☆ *Ship* [off B2177 Fishers Pond—Lower Upham;

Whites Hill]: Popular family summer pub with play area, toddler zone, pets corner, lots of space to run around, wknd summer bouncy castle, and great views from both garden areas; has been good inside, too, with 17th-c black oak beams and timbers, big central fireplace, comfortable dining area and restaurant (both no smoking), well kept Cheriton Pots and Greene King IPA, Ruddles County and Morlands Original, good choice of wines by the glass, cribbage, dominoes and alley skittles, but under temporary management as we go to press (previous good tenants have left); news please *(LYM)*

PETERSFIELD SU7423

☆ ***Good Intent*** [College St]: Gales full beer range kept well with a guest such as Charles Wells Bombardier, wide choice of decent food from sandwiches and baguettes to rather pricey hot dishes inc speciality sausages, 16th-c core with low oak beams, log fire, well spaced good-sized pine tables with flowers, camera collection, cosy family area; some live music *(Ian Phillips, Tony and Wendy Hobden)*

☆ ***White Horse*** [up on old downs rd about halfway between Steep and East Tisted, nr Priors Dean – OS Sheet 186 or 197, map ref 715290]: Country pub high and isolated on the downs, a favourite for its rustic unspoilt feel in two charming and idiosyncratically old-fashioned parlour rooms (candlelit at night); attractive no smoking family dining room, open fires throughout, up to nine real ales, decent food (not Sun evening) from sandwiches and baked potatoes to steaks, quick cheerful service; children welcome, rustic tables outside *(Ann and Colin Hunt, the Didler, John Davis, Ian Phillips, Colin Gooch, Charles and Pauline Stride, LYM, Mrs Maricar Jagger, R B Gardiner)*

PILLEY SZ3298

☆ ***Fleur de Lys*** [off A337 Brockenhurst—Lymington; Pilley St]: Heavy-beamed no smoking bar with huge inglenook log fire, no smoking family room, relaxed pubby atmosphere, enjoyable changing bar food from wide choice of sandwiches and baguettes to steaks, well kept Ringwood Best and Fortyniner, decent wines and country wines; piped music, fruit machine; dogs welcome, garden tables and play area, fine forest and heathland walks nearby *(LYM, Betsy Brown, Nigel Flook, Paul A Moore, John Davis, Alan M Pring, Charles and Pauline Stride)*

PORTCHESTER SU6204

Cormorant [next to Portchester Castle]: Big smartly kept open-plan dining pub with solid 1930s feel, friendly helpful staff, reasonably priced generous home-made food all day (several blackboards), well kept ales such as Fullers London Pride, Gales GB and HSB and Marstons Pedigree, cafetière coffee, children in large raised back dining area; tables on terrace with lots of flower tubs and baskets, in pleasant close, views over Portsmouth harbour; plenty of parking *(Michael and Alison Sandy)*

PORTSMOUTH SZ6399

American Bar [White Hart Rd]: Spacious colonial-theme bar with good mix of customers, well kept Courage Directors and a guest beer, reasonably priced all-day bar food from sandwiches and baguettes up, popular restaurant (one room no smoking) with some emphasis on fresh local fish and seafood, good friendly service; garden behind, handy for IOW ferry *(Colin Moore)*

Bridge Tavern [East St, Camber Dock]: Comfortable and nicely placed, with flagstones, bare boards, lots of dark wood, maritime theme, good water views, good simple food from baguettes and baked potatoes up, full range of well kept Gales ales, country wines, smiling service; waterside terrace *(Mrs Maricar Jagger, Joan and Michel Hooper-Immins)*

Churchillian [Portsdown Hill Rd, Widley]: Smallish open-plan dining pub, oak, cream and red carpet, big windows with lovely views over Portsmouth and Solent, Bass and Gales GB and HSB, generous popular food; may be piped music; handy for Fort Widley equestrian centre and nature trail *(Val and Alan Green)*

Dolphin [High St, Old Portsmouth]: Spacious old timber-framed pub with half a dozen or more well kept ales, wide choice of food inc Sun roasts, friendly staff, good log fire, cosy snug; children welcome in eating area, small terrace *(Ann and Colin Hunt)*

Sallyport [High St, Old Portsmouth]: Comfortable spick-and-span beamed bar with leather chesterfields, soft lighting, lots of naval prints, usual bar food, decent coffee, three real ales inc Gales HSB, upstairs restaurant; bedrooms *(Ann and Colin Hunt)*

Three Crowns [St James's St, Portsea]: Small friendly local with well kept Marstons Pedigree and good value meals; pool *(Mrs Maricar Jagger)*

Toby Carvery [Copnor Rd/Norway Rd, Hilsea]: Popular family dining pub specialising in generous daily carvery, busy on Sun (no booking); quick friendly service inc drinks at tables, real ale, decent value wine, tables in garden *(Peter and Audrey Dowsett)*

Wellington [High St, off Grand Parade, Old Portsmouth]: Quietly comfortable open-plan pub with large Georgian bow window, nr seafront and historic square tower, relaxed chatty atmosphere, good bar food esp fresh fish, Wadworths 6X and a beer brewed for the pub, generous wine *(Ann and Colin Hunt)*

RINGWOOD SU1405

Inn on the Furlong [Meeting House Lane, next to supermarket]: Long flagstoned bar, stripped brick and oak timbering, simple décor, full range of Ringwood beers from nearby brewery kept well, daily papers, good friendly young staff, good value lunchtime food from low-priced soup and hot-filled sandwiches up, daytime no smoking area, conservatory dining extension; quiet piped music; open all day (cl Sun afternoon), live music Tues, Easter beer festival *(Bruce Bird, Terry and Linda Moseley, W W Burke)*

ROCKFORD SU1608

Alice Lisle: Family-friendly modernised open-plan pub attractively placed on green by New Forest (can get very busy, popular with older folk wkdy lunchtimes), emphasis on big conservatory-style family eating area, generous helpings from sandwiches up, well kept Gales and guest beers, country wines; baby-changing facilities, garden overlooking lake with peacock and other birds, ponies wander nearby, play area, separate adults-only garden, handy for Moyles Court *(BB, David M Cundy)*

ROMSEY SU3521

Abbey Hotel [Church St]: Friendly and comfortable plush and mahogany dining bar with enterprising food choice from sandwiches, home-made soup and baked potatoes to rabbit pie and guinea fowl, fast service, well kept Courage Best and Directors, risqué Victorian photographs and postcards; bedrooms, opp Abbey *(Ron Shelton)*

☆ *Dukes Head* [A3057 out towards Stockbridge]: Attractive 16th-c dining pub festooned with flowering baskets in summer, picturesque series of small linked rooms each with its own quite distinct and interesting décor, pleasant attentive staff, well kept Courage Best, Fullers London Pride and Greene King Abbot, decent house wines, good coffee, rewarding choice of popular well presented food from unusual fresh sandwiches up, big log fire; may be quiet piped music; picnic-sets out in front, nicer tables on sheltered back terrace, attractive back garden *(Ian Phillips, Prof and Mrs Tony Palmer, BB, A R Hawkins, Geoff Pidoux, Dr and Mrs Michael Smith, J V Dadswell)*

Old House At Home [Love Lane]: Attractive 16th-c thatched pub with tastefully old-fashioned décor, good freshly made food (can be a wait, no bar snacks Sun), welcoming staff, well kept Gales ales inc a seasonal one; no mobile phones *(Ian Bell, Prof and Mrs Tony Palmer, Roger and Pauline Pearce)*

ROTHERWICK SU7156

☆ *Coach & Horses* [signed from B3349 N of Hook; also quite handy for M3, junction 5]: Individual furnishings and roaring fire in two small beamed front rooms, tasty generous food from lunchtime sandwiches to steaks, fresh veg, no smoking eating areas, inner parquet-floored serving area with several Badger ales and a couple of Gribble guests, daily papers, relaxed friendly atmosphere, helpful staff, entertaining parrot; tables in back garden, pretty flower tubs and baskets *(M R Jackson, Debbie Lovely, John and Joan Calvert, Norman and Sheila Sales, Mr and Mrs S Felstead, LYM, Colin and Sandra Tann, Robin Cordell)*

ROWLAND'S CASTLE SU7310

Robin Hood [The Green]: Modern-style bar, light and airy, with quarry tiles, bare boards and some carpet, sturdy pine and other tables, nice contemporary retro artwork, enjoyable up-to-date food inc plenty of fish on most days, well kept Fullers London Pride and Hook Norton Old Hooky, good wine choice; piped music; disabled access and facilities, picnic-sets on heated front terrace, on green of pleasant village *(BB, Ann and Colin Hunt, John Evans)*

SELBORNE SU7433

☆ *Selborne Arms* [High St]: Hop-festooned village local with well kept Cheriton Pots, Courage Best, Itchen Valley Fagins and Ringwood Fortyniner, plenty of wines by the glass (three glass sizes), enjoyable fresh food using local ingredients inc lunchtime baguettes, enormous New York deli-style sandwiches and buffet, dining room off unpretentious bar (smoking in both) with old photographs, fresh flowers, log fire in fine inglenook, twinkly landlord, cheerful polite service even when very busy, good cream teas in back parlour doubling as collectables shop; plenty of tables in garden with arbour, terrace, orchard and good play area, right by walks up Hanger, and handy for Gilbert White museum *(Val and Alan Green, Ian Phillips, Martin and Karen Wake)*

SETLEY SU3000

Filly [A337 Brockenhurst—Lymington]: Close-set tables for wide choice of generous enjoyable food inc Sun carvery, well kept Flowers, Ringwood Old Thumper and Wadworths 6X, decent wines, quick service, curry and quiz nights; piped music; some tables outside, New Forest walks, open all day *(LYM, Phyl and Jack Street)*

SHAWFORD SU4724

Bridge: Roomily refurbished and well run chain pub with smart décor, several interesting rooms and cosy nooks and corners, courteous attentive staff, nice range of beers and wines and food all day; garden with play area, downland and Itchen Way walks *(Phyl and Jack Street, Jim and Janet Brown)*

SHEDFIELD SU5613

Old Forge [Winchester Rd (B2177)]: Recently opened after major restoration, coloured walls, black beams and dark oak, proper bar and dining bar, Courage Best, Gales Trafalgar and Charles Wells Bombardier, wide food choice inc quite a lot of vegetarian dishes, very friendly staff *(Val and Alan Green)*

Wheatsheaf [A334 Wickham—Botley]: Busy and friendly local with well kept Cheriton ales tapped from the cask, nice cooking, impromptu piano sessions in public bar; garden, handy for Wickham Vineyard *(Ann and Colin Hunt, Val and Alan Green)*

SOPLEY SZ1597

☆ *Woolpack* [B3347 N of Christchurch]: Pretty thatched pub with rambling candlelit open-plan low-beamed bar, rustic furniture, woodburner and little black kitchen range, friendly helpful staff, enjoyable food from sandwiches and ploughman's to steaks and Sun roasts, well kept Flowers Original, Ringwood Best and Wadworths 6X, good house wine, no smoking conservatory; piped music, bustling Fri and Sat night; open all day, children in eating areas, charming garden, picnic-sets under weeping willows, stream with ducks and footbridges *(David M Cundy, LYM, Eddie Edwards, S Horsley, John and Vivienne Rice)*

SOUTHAMPTON SU4212

Cowherds [The Common (off A33)]: Low-beamed Vintage Inn dining pub in nice setting by common, welcoming atmosphere, cosy alcoves and tables in nice little bay windows, lots of Victorian photographs, carpets on polished boards, log fires, good generous unfussy food inc fresh fish, well kept Bass and Fullers London Pride, good wine choice, cheery caring quick service; very busy with young people Sun; tables outside with tie-ups and water for dogs (50p deposit on glasses taken out) *(Mr and Mrs R W Allan, Neil Rose, Gill and Keith Croxton, Dr and Mrs Michael Smith, Val and Alan Green)*

Crown [Highcrown St, Highfield]: Bustling warmly relaxed local, well kept Archers, Flowers Original, Fullers London Pride and Wadworths 6X, good value substantial lunchtime food from baked potatoes up, helpful staff, open fires; piped music, can be packed with students and academics from nearby Uni; dogs allowed in main bar (giving country feel in the suburbs), heated covered terrace, Sun quiz night, open all day *(Phyl and Jack Street, Prof and Mrs Tony Palmer, Prof Keith and Mrs Jane Barber)*

☆ *Duke of Wellington* [Bugle St (or walk along city wall from Bar Gate)]: Ancient timber-framed building on 13th-c foundations, bare boards, log fire, friendly relaxed atmosphere, really helpful service, well kept reasonably priced ales such as Bass, Ringwood Best, Vale Best and Wadworths IPA and JCB, good choice of wines by the glass, good value home-made bar food, no smoking back dining room; front bar can get smoky; very handy for Tudor House Museum *(Val and Alan Green, Ken Flawn)*

Pensioners Arms [Carlton Pl]: Friendly Victorian-style local, well kept Greene King ales, good value food from doorstep sandwiches up, pleasant service *(R T and J C Moggridge)*

South Western Arms [Adelaide Rd, by St Denys stn]: A dozen or so real ales inc Badger, Gales and Wadworths, good friendly staff, basic food and décor (bare boards and brickwork, toby jugs and stag's head on beams, lots of woodwork, ceiling beer mats), upper gallery where children allowed; popular with students, easy-going atmosphere, juke box; picnic-sets on terrace, live jazz Sun afternoon *(Dr Martin Owton, Richard Houghton)*

Waterloo Arms [Waterloo Rd]: Small plain and comfortable 1930s local with well kept Hop Back ales, enjoyable lunchtime food, open fires, plenty of light-coloured wood, ochre walls with brewing awards, traditional games, nice conservatory and garden *(Cynthia Norman)*

White Star [Oxford St]: Attractive building recently revamped as dining place (maître d' to welcome you), red-walled bar with comfortable sofas and armchairs in one area, banquettes and open fire in the other, good if not cheap light dishes available here (veg are charged extra) but main emphasis on smart and pleasant dining area; good wine choice *(anon)*

SOUTHSEA SZ6498

5th Hampshire Volunteer Arms [Albert Rd]: Popular two-bar backstreet local, Gales beers, military memorabilia; open all day *(the Didler)*

Eldon Arms [Eldon St/Norfolk St]: Roomy rambling local with old pictures and advertisements, attractive mirrors, lots of bric-a-brac and bookcases; changing well kept ales such as Adnams Best and Greene King IPA, friendly service, lunchtime food (not Sat); sensibly placed darts, fruit machine, can get smoky; tables in back garden *(Mrs Maricar Jagger)*

Hole in the Wall [Gt Southsea St]: Small, cosy and friendly local, in old part, with several changing beers inc John Smiths and an own brew, enjoyable well presented food *(Mrs Maricar Jagger)*

Old Vic [St Pauls Rd]: Friendly local with good landlady and popular karaoke *(Mrs Maricar Jagger)*

Olde Oyster House [Locksway Rd, Milton]: Two-bar pub with four or five real ales mainly from small breweries inc a Mild, and farm cider; name recalls Langstone Harbour's oyster beds; busy wknd evenings *(the Didler)*

Red White & Blue [Fawcett Rd]: Busy open-plan local, well kept Gales, food Sat lunchtime; games nights, jazz Weds, open all day *(the Didler)*

Sir Loin of Beef [Highland Rd, Eastney]: Up to eight frequently changing well kept ales, reasonably priced bar food, helpful friendly staff, interesting submarine memorabilia *(Andy and Jill Kassube)*

SOUTHWICK SU6208

Red Lion [High St]: Low-beamed Gales dining pub, mainly no smoking, good choice from good baguettes up, BB and a seasonal beer, friendly prompt service from smart staff *(Val and Alan Green, Ann and Colin Hunt)*

STOCKBRIDGE SU3535

☆ *Greyhound* [High St]: Substantial inn reworked as upmarket restaurant-pub (you can, though not cheaply, still have a beer and a simple lunchtime ploughman's or generous sandwich at the bar), log fires each end of bow-windowed bar, old trestle tables and simple seating on woodstrip floor, dark low beams and joists with low-voltage spotlights, lots of good black and white photographs, very civilised atmosphere, good wines inc some costly stars, notable meals, Greene King IPA and Abbot and Wadworths 6X; service charge added to bills; tables in charming Test-side garden behind, children and dogs allowed, bedrooms and fly fishing *(BB, Margaret Ross, W W Burke, Terry and Linda Moseley)*

☆ *White Hart* [High St; A272/A3057 roundabout]: Friendly, roomy and welcoming divided bar, attractive décor with antique prints, oak pews and other seats, enjoyable quickly served food from sandwiches up, full range of Gales ales kept well, decent wines, country wines, cheerful service; children allowed in comfortable beamed restaurant with blazing log fire, tables in garden with terrace, bedrooms, open all day *(Stephen and Jean Curtis, Mrs E A Macdonald, Mr and Mrs S Felstead, LYM)*

STROUD SU7223

Seven Stars [A272 Petersfield—Winchester]: Large recently refurbished flint and brick pub with wide choice of good value food from good sandwiches to some exotic dishes served quickly and cheerfully, well kept Badger beers and good wine list, large restaurant extension; tables outside, comfortable bedrooms with own bathrooms, good if strenuous walking *(Father Robert Marsh)*

SWANMORE SU5816

Hunters [Hillgrove]: Much-extended family dining pub, excellent for children, with big plain family room, winding garden with secluded tables (each with a buzzer for when your food's ready) and several substantial play areas for different age groups, plenty under cover and even one for babies; long-serving live-wire landlord, well kept Gales HSB and Charles Wells Bombardier tapped from the cask, good house wine and country wines, attentive service, plush bar with lots of boxer pictures, bank notes, carpentry and farm tools, no smoking area; very busy wknds, nice walks N of village *(Phyl and Jack Street, Val and Alan Green)*

New Inn [Chapel Rd]: Village pub with Greene King ales, enjoyable food inc some adventurous dishes; plenty of local activity, sports TV, some live music *(Val and Alan Green)*

Rising Sun [Hill Pound; off B2177 S of Bishops Waltham]: Comfortably updated tile-hung pub with smart food from baguettes up (booking advised wknd), Weds theme night, well kept Adnams, Greene King Old Speckled Hen, Marstons Pedigree and Ringwood Best, good value wines, good log fires, quick polite service, low beams, scrubbed pine, well separated extended dining area; the cat's called Fritz; occasional live music, pleasant good-sized side garden with play area and perhaps summer bouncy castle, handy for Kings Way long distance path – best to head W *(Geoff Palmer, Phyl and Jack Street, Val and Alan Green, Ann and Colin Hunt)*

SWANWICK SU5109

Elm Tree [handy for M27 junction 9]: Neat and comfortable, with two bars and dining room off, several real ales, wide range of home-made food; quiet piped music; children welcome, tables in garden, handy for Hampshire Wildlife Reserve *(Val and Alan Green)*

SWAY SZ2898

Hare & Hounds [Durns Town, just off B3055 SW of Brockenhurst]: Bright and airy comfortable New Forest family dining pub, lots of children, good value enjoyable fresh food, well kept ales inc Ringwood and Wessex, cheerful and enthusiastic young staff, log fires; picnic-sets and play frame in sizeable neatly kept garden, open all day Sat *(LYM, Geoff Pidoux, J M G Clarke, Penny and Peter Keevil)*

TANGLEY SU3252

☆ *Cricketers Arms* [towards the Chutes]: Tucked away in unspoilt countryside, relaxed atmosphere, character small front bar with tiled floor, massive inglenook, roaring log fire, hospitable caring landlord, hard-working staff and friendly black labradors (Pots and Harvey), bistroish back flagstoned extension with a one-table alcove off, some good cricketing prints, good value food from fresh baguettes to enterprising light and main dishes, well kept ales such as Cheriton Pots and Hampshire Ironside tapped from the cask, bar billiards; dogs welcome, tables on neat terrace, good new nordic-style block of 10 bedrooms *(I A Herdman, LYM, Lee Matthews, Phyl and Jack Street)*

THRUXTON SU2945

George [just off A303]: Generous enjoyable food (may take a while), big eating area with well spaced tables *(Jennifer Banks)*

TIMSBURY SU3325

☆ *Bear & Ragged Staff* [A3057 towards Stockbridge; pub marked on OS Sheet 185 map ref 334254]: Useful pull-in with wide and attractive blackboard choice of enjoyable reasonably priced food all day, good-sized beamed interior, welcoming service, well kept ales such as Ringwood Best and Wadworths 6X, lots of wines by the glass, country wines; children in eating area, tables in extended garden with good play area, handy for Mottisfont, good walks *(Phyl and Jack Street, LYM, Dr and Mrs Michael Smith, Mike and Shelley Woodroffe)*

TITCHFIELD SU5406

Fishermans Rest [Mill Lane, off A27 at Titchfield Abbey]: Busy all-day chain pub/restaurant with close-set tables and no smoking family area, well kept ales such as Gales HSB, Greene King IPA and Wadworths 6X, cheerful service, two log fires (not always lit), daily papers, fishing memorabilia, no music or machines; fine riverside position opp Titchfield Abbey, tables out behind overlooking water *(LYM, Ann and Colin Hunt, Carol and Dono Leaman)*

Titchfield Mill [A27, junction with Mill Lane]: Large popular Vintage Inn catering well for families in neatly kept converted watermill, olde-worlde room off main bar, smarter dining room, upstairs gallery, stripped beams and interesting old machinery, well kept Bass and Tetleys, good choice of wines by the glass, freshly squeezed orange juice, neat attentive and friendly staff; piped music; open all day, sunny terrace by mill stream with two waterwheels – food not served out here *(Charles and Pauline Stride, Mrs Joy Griffiths, Phyl and Jack Street, Ann and Colin Hunt, Michael and Robin Inskip)*

TOTFORD SU5737

Woolpack [B3046 Basingstoke—Alresford]: Friendly and relaxing bar with well kept Gales HSB, Palmers IPA and local Cheriton Pots, stripped-brick bar, large separate dining room, decent food inc good Sun roast, open fire; may be piped radio; tables out by small pond, lovely setting in good walking country; bedrooms *(Ann and Colin Hunt)*

TURGIS GREEN SU6959

☆ *Jekyll & Hyde* [A33 Reading—Basingstoke]: Bustling rambling pub with nice mix of furniture and village atmosphere in black-beamed and flagstoned bar, larger stepped-up three-room dining area with enjoyable varied food from sandwiches up all day inc breakfast, children's helpings (they are welcome), prompt service, well kept Badger Best and IPA and Wadworths 6X, some interesting prints, blazing fire; can get smoky; lots of picnic-sets in good sheltered garden (some traffic noise), play area and various games; disabled facilities *(KC, LYM, D Crook)*

TWYFORD SU4724

Phoenix [High St]: Cheerful open-plan local with lots of prints, bric-a-brac and big end inglenook log fire, wide choice of sensibly priced generous food from sandwiches to steaks and theme nights, friendly enthusiastic landlord, well kept Greene King and guest beers, decent wines, back room with skittle alley, children allowed at one end lunchtime; quiet piped music; garden *(Val and Alan Green, Lynn Sharpless)*

UPPER CLATFORD SU3543

Crook & Shears [off A343 S of Andover, via Foundry Rd]: Homely olde-worlde thatched 17th-c two-bar pub, bare boards and panelling, small popular dining area, changing real ales such as Ringwood, back skittle alley *(the Didler)*

UPTON GREY SU6948

Hoddington Arms [signed off B3349 S of Hook; Bidden Rd]: Homely and unpretentious open-plan beamed local with dining rooms each end (one no smoking, children allowed), minimal decoration, good value food from lunchtime sandwiches to impressive specials, well kept Adnams and Greene King Old Speckled Hen and Ruddles Best, small selection of good house wines, friendly helpful service; small games room with darts and bar billiards, may be piped music; good-sized neat garden with terrace and sizeable play area, quiet pretty village *(BB, Martin and Karen Wake)*

VERNHAM DEAN SU3456

George: Rambling open-plan beamed and timbered pub, exposed brick and flint, inglenook log fire, pleasant courteous service, well kept Greene King IPA, Abbot and Ruddles County, decent wines, roomy no smoking eating area (children allowed); darts, shove-ha'penny, dominoes and cribbage; picnic-sets in pretty garden behind, lovely thatched village, fine walks *(LYM, the Didler, Phyl and Jack Street)*

WALHAMPTON SZ3396

Towles [B3054 NE of Lymington]: Refurbished Georgian-style building popular with older people for its emphasis on enjoyable restauranty food inc carvery in three roomy areas, Gales ales, pleasant atmosphere *(David M Cundy)*

WALTHAM CHASE SU5616

Chase [B2177]: Smart comfortable lounge, second room with nicely extended no smoking eating area, Greene King IPA and Ruddles, generous reasonably priced food *(Val and Alan Green)*

WEST END SU4714

Southampton Arms [Moorgreen Rd, off B3035]: Thriving local, quite big, with Ringwood ales, enjoyable reasonably priced food, no-nonsense landlady and friendly efficient service, comfortable and cosy bar, attractive conservatory restaurant; good garden *(Phyl and Jack Street)*

WEST MEON SU6424

Thomas Lord [High St]: Attractive village pub with well kept Bass, Gales GB, Greene King Old Speckled Hen and Ringwood Best, farm ciders and good selection of wines, log fire, cricket memorabilia inc club ties and odd stuffed-animal cricket match, pool table tucked around corner, pleasant and popular separate dining area, fresh flowers; soft piped music; tables in big garden with play house, good walks W of village *(Ian Phillips, Phyl and Jack Street, John Branston)*

WEYHILL SU3146

Weyhill Fair [A342, signed off A303 bypass]: Popular well run local with six well kept sensibly priced ales inc good varied guests, wide choice of daily-changing enjoyable food, spacious solidly furnished lounge with easy chairs around woodburner, old advertisements, smaller family room, no smoking area; children welcome, good-sized grounds inc caravan camping space, handy for Hawk Conservancy *(BB, J Stickland)*

WHERWELL SU3839

☆ *Mayfly* [Testcombe, outside village; A3057 SE of Andover]: Very popular for its splendid setting – get there early to bag a table on decking out by River Test; bright contemporary red walls (some original fishing pictures remain), bright lighting, new modern pine tables and new kitchen, new lavatories, Gales HSB, Marstons Pedigree, Ringwood Best and Wadworths 6X, buffet-style food all day with several hot specials; piped music; children and dogs welcome, open all day *(LYM, W W Burke, John Urquhart, Hugh Roberts, B J Harding, Angus and Rosemary Campbell, Tim and Carolyn Lowes, Susan and John Douglas, Leigh and Gillian Mellor, Joyce and Geoff Robson, Catherine FitzMaurice)*

WHITCHURCH SU4648

☆ *Red House* [London St]: Attractive dining pub with 14th-c beams and fireplaces (one an inglenook with ancient flagstones in front), family-friendly lounge with step up to no smoking restaurant, both pleasantly compact, stripped pine and bare boards, good generous cooking by landlord/chef from filled home-baked baps and baguettes to modern european hot dishes, friendly efficient service under on-the-ball landlady, well kept Cheriton Pots and a couple of guests such as Archers Golden, decent house wines, separate public bar on left; attractive terrace with play area *(Ian and*

Deborah Carrington, LYM, Mr and Mrs Robert Jamieson, Jennifer Banks, Lynn Sharpless, Irene and Derek Flewin, Val and Alan Green, Guy Consterdine)

WHITSBURY SU1219

Cartwheel [off A338 or A354 SW of Salisbury]: Tucked-away local, simple but comfortable, with decent straightforward food (not Mon evening), Adnams Broadside, Ringwood Best and guest beers, choice of ciders, pitched high rafters in one part, lower beams elsewhere, snug little room by door, another small side room with darts, pool, other games; fruit machine, TV, piped music; children and dogs welcome, garden with play area *(Phyl and Jack Street, LYM)*

WICKHAM SU5711

Greens [The Square]: Upmarket feel, with smart dining pub on upper level, Bass, Fullers London Pride and a guest such as Hop Back Summer Lightning, long-serving licensees and friendly staff, steps down to no smoking restaurant; tables out on pleasant lawn overlooking water meadows, cl Mon exc bank hols *(Val and Alan Green)*

Kings Head [The Square]: Pretty two-bar town pub with pleasant décor, good log fire, Gales ales, good coffee, no smoking restaurant nicely secluded up some steps; bar can be rather smoky; tables out on square and in back garden with play area, attractive village *(Val and Alan Green, Phyl and Jack Street)*

Roebuck [Kingsmead; A32 towards Droxford]: Well appointed, with two dining rooms (one no smoking), wide range of food from decent sandwiches to some less usual things, Fullers London Pride and a house beer, generally good helpful service, lots of prints and plates, library of books, white grand piano (friendly new ex-panto landlord sometimes plays and sings); children in no smoking area, conservatory *(A D Marsh, Mrs Maricar Jagger, Tim and Carolyn Lowes)*

WINCHESTER SU4728

Bell [St Cross Rd]: Unpretentious local with well kept Greene King ales, decent wines by the glass, welcoming obliging service, fresh usual food, liner pictures in comfortable lounge; separate plain public bar with juke box and smokers; big pleasant walled garden with swing and slide, handy for St Cross Hospital – lovely water meadows walk from centre *(Val and Alan Green, Craig Turnbull, Phil and Sally Gorton, Lynn Sharpless)*

Jolly Farmer [Andover Rd]: Neatly kept, with decent standard menu, Boddingtons, Hook Norton Old Hooky, Ringwood Best and Wadworths 6X *(Val and Alan Green)*

King Alfred [Saxon Rd, Hyde]: Welcoming Victorianised pub with unfussy traditional décor, wood and opaque glass dividers, no smoking areas, enjoyable food from lunchtime baguettes and baked potatoes through bargain standbys to imaginative blackboard dishes and popular Sun lunch, Greene King ales inc Ruddles, good wine choice, sensible prices, friendly attentive staff; TV, pool, piped music; large pleasant garden with play area *(Lynn Sharpless)*

Old Gaol House [Jewry St]: Big busy Wetherspoons pub with large no smoking area, food all day, good choice of locally brewed beers, low prices, no piped music *(Ann and Colin Hunt, Val and Alan Green)*

Queen [Kingsgate Rd]: Roomy pub in attractive setting opp College cricket ground, reasonably priced mainstream food inc Sun lunch and children's dishes, well kept Greene King ales, decent wines, cricketing and other prints, bric-a-brac on window sills, central fireplace, darts in public bar; disabled facilities, open all day, tables on front terrace and in large attractive garden *(Lynn Sharpless, the Didler)*

Royal Oak [Royal Oak Passage, off upper end of pedestrian part of High St opp St Thomas St]: Otherwise straightforward Hogshead notable for the no smoking cellar bar (not always open) whose massive 12th-c beams and Saxon wall give it some claim to be the country's oldest drinking spot; big plain partly no smoking main bar with little areas off (some raised), five or six well kept ales such as Caledonian Deuchars IPA, Greene King Abbot and Gales HSB, short choice of good value quick food; piped music, games machines, packed with young people Fri/Sat nights *(the Didler, Tim and Carolyn Lowes, Ann and Colin Hunt, LYM, Val and Alan Green)*

Willow Tree [Durngate Terr]: Warmly welcoming local, landlord/chef with an interesting repertoire, well kept Greene King beers, good wines; can get smoky; long and pleasant riverside garden *(Phil and Sally Gorton, Lynn Sharpless)*

WOLVERTON SU5658

George & Dragon [Towns End; just N of A339 Newbury—Basingstoke]: Comfortable rambling open-plan pub, beams and standing timbers, log fires, wide choice of enjoyable food, range of beers, decent wines, helpful service, no piped music, skittle alley; no children in bar; pleasant large garden with small terrace, bedrooms *(J V Dadswell)*

WOODGREEN SU1717

☆ ***Horse & Groom*** [off A338 N of Fordingbridge]: Nicely set New Forest pub doing well under current landlord, comfortable and friendly linked beamed rooms around servery, nature photographs, log fire in pretty Victorian fireplace, well kept Badger ales, good choice of good value home-cooked food; picnic-sets on front terrace and in spreading back garden *(David M Cundy, LYM, Ian Phillips, Prof and Mrs Tony Palmer, Dr and Mrs A K Clarke)*

If you know a pub's ever open all day, please tell us.

Herefordshire

This is a good part of the world for finding truly unspoilt cottagey pubs (often in unspoilt surroundings, too), and many pubs here have good beers from small local breweries, fine farm ciders and, increasingly, interesting local apple juices. There is also some excellent food to be found here these days. Pubs on particularly good form this year are the rather smart though very welcoming Roebuck Inn at Brimfield (good food and drink, and a nice place to stay), the handsome old Feathers in Ledbury (another good rather upmarket all-rounder, still with plenty of regulars popping in for a drink), the friendly and unpretentious Three Horseshoes tucked away in Little Cowarne (enjoyable food and good bedrooms), the Crown & Anchor at Lugwardine (gaining a Food Award this year, for its thoughtful and interesting cooking – a great choice of sandwiches, too), the Boot at Orleton (a most enjoyable and friendly all-rounder), the attractive Lough Pool at Sellack (emphasis on delicious food, while remaining very much a pub), the spotless Stockton Cross Inn (the landlady's home cooking is a big plus), the Stagg at Titley (marvellous food worth waiting for, and some interesting changes this year), the Three Crowns at Ullingswick (very much enjoyed for a special meal out, and keeping faith with those who just want a drink), and the homely and unspoilt Carpenters Arms at Walterstone (a bit like walking into a friend's house). Among so many pubs doing really enjoyable food, the Lough Pool at Sellack takes the award of Herefordshire Dining Pub of the Year. In the Lucky Dip section at the end of the chapter, pubs to note particularly are the Penny Farthing at Aston Crews, Crown at Colwall, Bulls Head at Craswall, Slip Tavern at Much Marcle, Newtown Inn, Saracens Head at Symonds Yat, Weston Cross Inn at Weston-under-Penyard, Butchers Arms at Woolhope and Bell at Yarpole. Drinks are generally cheaper than the national average here, with Wye Valley beers brewed locally at the Barrels pub in Hereford (see Lucky Dip entries) often turning up as good value. The Spinning Dog beer brewed and sold at the Victory in Hereford was the cheapest we found.

AYMESTREY SO4265 Map 6

Riverside Inn

A4110; N off A44 at Mortimer's Cross, W of Leominster

At the back of this idyllically placed black and white timbered inn, there are picnic-sets by a flowing river, and rustic tables and benches up above in a steep tree-sheltered garden – a beautifully sheltered former bowling green, too. Residents are offered fly-fishing (they have fishing rights on a mile of the River Lugg), and a free taxi service to the start of the Mortimer Trail; pleasant circular walks start from here. The rambling beamed bar has several cosy areas and the décor is drawn from a pleasant mix of periods and styles, with fine antique oak tables and chairs, stripped pine country kitchen tables, fresh flowers, hops strung from a ceiling wagon-wheel, horse tack, and nice pictures; you can smoke only in one specified area. Warm log fires in winter, while in summer big overflowing flower pots frame the entrances; shove-ha'penny, cribbage and piped music. Well kept Woods Shropshire Lad, Wye Valley Dorothy Goodbodys Golden Ale, and a guest such as Spinning Dog Pit Stop on handpump, local farm ciders and apple juice, 22 malt whiskies, and seven wines by the glass. The landlord likes to talk to his customers and service is good. Enjoyable bar food includes freshly made baguettes, ploughman's, lasagne, local gammon steak with parsley sauce, sausage with mustard mash and white onion gravy, and locally smoked salmon and prawn salad £4.25–£7.95), as well as starters such as fried local chicken livers and bacon on toasted brioche with a home-made rhubarb vinaigrette or gateaux of cornish crab with chive and lime and tomato dressing (£3.75-£5.25), and main courses like seared fillet of brill on summer vegetables with a saffron and mussel sauce, beetroot and orange risotto with parmesan or roasted haunch of local venison with blackcurrant jus (£8.95-£13.95). It does get busy at weekends, so booking would be wise. *(Recommended by Paul A Moore, Alan Thwaite, John Kane, Eleanor and Nick Steinitz, Stan and Hazel Allen, J E Shackleton, Di and Mike Gillam, John Hale, Richard and Margaret Peers, Guy Vowles, R M Corlett, Peter Cole, Pamela and Merlyn Horswell, Tim Frith)*

Free house ~ Licensees Richard and Liz Gresko ~ Real ale ~ Bar food ~ Restaurant ~ (01568) 708440 ~ Children in eating area of bar and restaurant ~ Dogs welcome ~ Open 11-4(3 in winter), 6-11; may open all day if busy; 11-11 Sat; 12-10.30 Sun; closed 25 Dec ~ Bedrooms: £40B/£65B

BODENHAM SO5454 Map 4

Englands Gate

Just off A417 at Bodenham turn-off, about 6 miles S of Leominster

Once an important coach stop from Wales to England, this attractively timbered black and white inn was built around 1540. It has been well opened up inside, rambling around a vast central stone chimneypiece, with a big log fire on one side and a woodburning stove on the other – there's also a coal fire near the entrance. It looks every year of its age, with heavy brown beams and joists in low ochre ceilings, well worn flagstones, sturdy timber props, one or two steps, and lantern-style lighting. One nice corner has a comfortably worn leather settee and high-backed settle with scatter cushions; a cosy partly stripped stone room has a long stripped table that would be just right for a party of eight; a lighter upper area with flowers on its tables has winged settles painted a cheery yellow or aquamarine. Decent bar food at lunchtime includes sandwiches (from £3.50; baguettes £4.55), chicken tikka skewers with salsa relish or omelette arnold bennett (£5.95), stir-fried king prawns with ginger and lime on pesto tagliatelle or spicy cumberland sausage on mustard mash with onion gravy (£6.95), and deep-fried cod in beer batter (£8.50), with evening choices such as duck liver parfait on a green bean and mushroom salad (£4.25), field mushrooms in pastry case on port and chive jus (£4.95), spinach and wild rice cakes with peppers on chilli and tomato salsa (£6.95), seared escalope of salmon with radiccio, pancetta and pine nuts (£8.95), steaks (from £11.50), and roast duck breast with parsnip mash, port and raspberries (£13.55). Well kept Marstons Pedigree, Woods Shropshire Lad and Wye Valley Hereford and Butty Bach on handpump; friendly staff; piped mellow pop music, and TV. There are tables out in an attractive garden. *(Recommended by Lucien Perring, John and Joan Wyatt, Mike and Mary Carter)*

Free house ~ Licensee Evelyn McNeil ~ Real ale ~ Bar food (12-2.30, 6-10) ~ Restaurant ~ (01568) 797286 ~ Children in restaurant until 9pm ~ Dogs allowed in bar ~ Open 11(12 Mon)-11; 12-10.30 Sun

Bedroom prices normally include full English breakfast, VAT and any inclusive service charge that we know of. Prices before the '/' are for single rooms, after for two people in double or twin (B includes a private bath, S a private shower). If there is no '/', the prices are only for twin or double rooms (as far as we know there are no singles).

BRIMFIELD SO5368 Map 4

Roebuck Inn

Village signposted just off A49 Shrewsbury—Leominster

'First class' is how several of our readers describe this well run and smart country dining pub. The friendly, cheerful landlord and his efficient staff are sure to make you welcome, the beers are well kept, and the food extremely good; it's also a comfortable place to stay. Each of the three rambling bars has a different but equally civilised atmosphere. The quiet old-fashioned snug is where you might find locals drinking and playing dominoes and cribbage by an impressive inglenook fireplace. Pale oak panelling in the 15th-c main bar makes for a quietly relaxed atmosphere, and the Brimfield Bar with a big bay window and open fire is light and airy. The brightly decorated cane-furnished airy dining room is no smoking. Absolutely everything, right down to the bread and relishes, is home-made. At lunchtime, snacks might include sandwiches (£4.75), platters with assorted cheeses, home-cooked ham, roast sirloin of beef or grilled cumberland sausages (£6.75), a large mixed salad with roast chicken breast or steamed fillet of salmon (£8), and specials such as faggots, venison casserole, cottage pie or pizza (all £8.95). More elaborate choices include a ragoût of fresh mushrooms in puff pastry with port and tarragon scented jus (£5.50), smoked chicken ravioli with a white bean cappuccino (£5.95), seared scallops (£6.50), mushroom, leek and caraway strudel (£8.95), very good fish or steak and mushroom suet pies (£9.95), glazed ginger and chilli salmon (£11.25), roast chicken breast on a crisp herb risotto cake with a smoked garlic and red wine sauce (£12.95), fillet steak (£16.50), and puddings like apricot and almond steamed pudding, three chocolate terrine or bread and butter pudding (all £4.50). They have an interesting reasonably priced wine list, a carefully chosen range of spirits and Stowford Press cider. Seats out on the enclosed terrace. *(Recommended by W W Burke, Rodney and Norma Stubington, J H Jones, KC, Neil and Anita Christopher, Rod Stoneman, Tim Field, Carole Thomas, Mr and Mrs W Mills, Dr L Kaufman, Ian Phillips, Pamela and Merlyn Horswell, Ian and Joan Blackwell, Chris Flynn, Wendy Jones)*

Free house ~ Licensees Mr and Mrs Jenkins ~ Real ale ~ Bar food ~ Restaurant ~ (01584) 711230 ~ Children in eating area of bar until 9pm ~ Dogs allowed in bar ~ Open 11.30-3, 6.30-11; 12-3, 7-10.30 Sun; closed 25 and 26 Dec ~ Bedrooms: /£70S(£70B)

CAREY SO5631 Map 4

Cottage of Content

Village signposted from good road through Hoarwithy

In fine weather, you can make the most of this out-of-the-way medieval cottage's charming position by bagging one of the picnic-sets on the flower-filled front terrace; there are also a couple of picnic-sets on a back terrace looking up a steep expanse of lawn. Inside is a pleasant mix of country furnishings – stripped pine, country kitchen chairs, long pews by one big table, and various old-fashioned tables on flagstones and bare boards; plenty of beams and prints. Bar food includes lunchtime snacks such as soup (£3.95), filled baked potatoes (from £4.50), filled pitta bread (£4.75), ploughman's (£5.25), and cauliflower cheese (£5.50), as well as ham and egg (£6.50), lasagne or curry (£6.95), steak and kidney pie or lamb casserole (£7.50), baked trout (£9.95), and sirloin steak (£11.95). Well kept Hook Norton Best and Wye Valley Bitter on handpump, and several wines by the glass; piped music and darts. *(Recommended by Ian and Denise Foster, John, Deborah and Ben Snook, Barry Collett, Di and Mike Gillam, the Didler, Christopher J Darwent, Peter B Brown)*

Free house ~ Licensee John Clift ~ Real ale ~ Bar food ~ Restaurant ~ (01432) 840242 ~ Children at landlord's discretion ~ Dogs allowed in bar ~ Live music every third Wednesday ~ Open 11.30-2.30, 6.30-11; 12-3, 7-10.30 Sun; closed Mon in winter

DORSTONE SO3141 Map 6

Pandy

Pub signed off B4348 E of Hay-on-Wye

Dating back eight centuries, this fine half-timbered building is said to be Herefordshire's oldest inn. The neatly kept homely main room (on the right as you go in) has heavy beams in the ochre ceiling, stout timbers, upright chairs on its broad worn flagstones and in its various alcoves, and a vast open fireplace with logs; a side extension has been kept more or less in character. Home-made bar food includes lunchtime sandwiches (from £3.25) and ploughman's (£7.70), as well as soup (£3.65), chicken liver pâté with cumberland sauce (£5.20), vegetarian quiche (£7.60), salmon and spinach cannelloni (£7.70), popular bobotie (£8.05), mussels in tomato and herb sauce or beer battered haddock (£8.85), steak and mushroom in ale pie (£9.40), lamb shank with redcurrant and rosemary gravy (£10.45), orange and lemon roast half duck with cider and citrus sauce (£13.20), mixed pheasant and venison pie (£15.70), and home-made puddings like ginger pudding or white chocolate and lemon cheesecake with summer berry sauce (£3.95); good service. Well kept Wye Valley Butty Bach and a guest such as Coors Hancocks HB on handpump, quite a few malt whiskies, farm cider, and decent wines; darts, quoits, a winter quiz, and piped music. The hairy persian tom is Tootsie and the ginger tom, Peanuts. There are picnic-sets and a play area in the neat side garden. *(Recommended by Mike and Mary Carter, the Didler, Caroline and Michael Abbey, A C Stone, June and Geoffrey Cox, Pam and David Bailey, Roger Thornington, R T and J C Moggridge, Jacquie and Jim Jones, Denys Gueroult)*

Free house ~ Licensees Paul and Marja Gardner ~ Real ale ~ Bar food (not Mon lunchtimes) ~ Restaurant ~ (01981) 550273 ~ Well behaved children welcome ~ Open 12-3, 6-11 Tues-Fri; 12-11 Sat; 12-3, 6.30-10.30 Sun; closed Mon lunchtime (all day winter Mon)

HEREFORD SO5139 Map 6

Victory £

St Owen Street, opposite fire station

From the Spinning Dog brewery in this down-to-earth local they produce Chase Your Tail, Mutleys Dark, Mutleys Revenge, Mutleys Springer, Pit Stop, and Mutts Nutts – there's usually a couple of guest beers well kept on handpump, too, and three farmhouse ciders. The front bar counter is like a miniature ship of the line with cannon poking out of its top, and down a companionway, the long back room is well decked out as the inside of a man o' war: dark wood, rigging and netting everywhere, benches along sides that curve towards a front fo'c'sle, stanchions and ropes forming an upper crow's nest, and appropriate lamps. With prices unchanged since last year, straightforward bar food includes sandwiches (from £2), chilli con carne or chicken curry (£4.50), ploughman's or fish of the day (£5) and 8oz steak (£5.50), with specials such as faggots, mash and peas (£5). Service is friendly and informal (they'll show you around the brewery if they're not busy). Juke box, darts, fruit machine, TV, skittle alley, table skittles, cribbage, shove-ha'penny, dominoes and a back pool table. The garden has been revamped this year and has a pagoda, climbing plants, and some seats. *(Recommended by R T and J C Moggridge, Bernie Adams, Ian Phillips, Ian and Liz Rispin, Bruce Bird, Paul Davies)*

Own brew ~ Licensee James Kenyon ~ Real ale ~ Bar food (12-3(5 weekends)) ~ Restaurant (Sun only) ~ No credit cards ~ (01432) 274998 ~ Children welcome ~ Dogs welcome ~ Live band Sat and Sun ~ Open 11-11; 12-10.30 Sun; weekday opening 12 in winter

Post Office address codings confusingly give the impression that some pubs are in Herefordshire when they're really in Gloucestershire or even Wales (which is where we list them).

LEDBURY SO7138 Map 4

Feathers

High Street, Ledbury, A417

At first glance, you might be surprised to find this elegantly striking Tudor timbered hotel in our *Guide*. But at one end of the rather civilised Fuggles bar, there's the Top Bar which at night has plenty of chatty and cheerful locals enjoying a pint quite uninhibited by those enjoying the good food and fine wines at the brasserie tables behind them. There are beams and timbers, hop bines, some country antiques, 19th-c caricatures and fancy fowl prints on the stripped brick chimneybreast (lovely winter fire), and fresh flowers on the tables – some very snug and cosy, in side bays. In summer, abundant pots and hanging baskets adorn the sheltered back terrace. Well kept Bass, Fullers London Pride and Worthington and a guest such as Timothy Taylors Landlord on handpump; lots of wines by the glass, various malt whiskies, and farm cider. As well as a 'quickies' menu with home-made soup (£3.90), sandwiches (from £4.25; rare roast beef with green peppercorn mustard £5.50), fresh cornish crab with lime, dill and ginger (£6.25), and home-cured gravadlax or fresh figs wrapped in parma ham with olives (£6.95), the good, enjoyable food includes pork and ham hock terrine with plum and apple chutney (£5.50), charcuterie with green olive bruschetta and artichoke heart salad (£5.95), home-made smoked haddock and chive fishcakes with fresh tomato sauce, pasta with broad bean, garlic and tomato olive sauce or home-made burgers (£8.50), grilled supreme of local chicken glazed with goats cheese and pancetta with a fresh herb risotto (£13.95), steaks (from £13.95), grilled fresh cornish hake fillet with garlic butter and crispy capers (£14.25), and puddings like dark chocolate and brandy pot, warm spiced fig and brandy tart with cornish clotted cream or Cointreau crème caramel with lemon sorbet (£4.50). Nice breakfasts, and friendly, helpful staff. They do fine afternoon teas in the more formal quiet lounge by the reception area, which has comfortable high-sided armchairs and sofas in front of a big log fire, and newspapers to read. *(Recommended by Bob Broadhurst, Jenny and Dave Hughes, A S and M E Marriott, Denys Gueroult, Bill and Jessica Ritson, Patrick Hancock, J E Shackleton, Dr and Mrs M W A Haward, Joan and Tony Walker, Pamela and Merlyn Horswell, David and Nina Pugsley, Dr G and Mrs J Kelvin, Annette Tress, Gary Smith)*

Free house ~ Licensee David Elliston ~ Real ale ~ Bar food (till 10pm Fri and Sat) ~ Restaurant ~ (01531) 635266 ~ Children in eating area of bar and restaurant ~ Dogs allowed in bar ~ Open 11-11; 12-10.30 Sun ~ Bedrooms: £74.50B/£99.50B

LITTLE COWARNE SO6051 Map 4

Three Horseshoes

Pub signposted off A465 SW of Bromyard; towards Ullingswick

Run by warmly friendly licensees, this bustling place is popular with locals and visitors alike. There might be a cheerful cribbage match happening, race-goers from Cheltenham reliving their wins, and residents enjoying a good meal before staying overnight in the comfortable bedrooms. The quarry tiled L-shaped middle bar has leather-seated bar stools, upholstered settles and dark brown kitchen chairs around sturdy old tables, old local photographs above the corner log fire, and hop-draped black beams in the dark peach ceiling (the walls too are peach). Opening off one side is a skylit no smoking sun room with wicker armchairs around more old tables; the other end has a games room with darts, pool, juke box, fruit machine and games machine. For the well liked bar food they use local gamekeepers and fishermen, buy local eggs and vegetables (though they grow summer salads themselves), and make their own chutneys, pickles, jams, and sloe gin. Enjoyable bar food includes sandwiches (from £2.25), garlic mushrooms with bacon and red wine or crab and lime fishcakes (£4.50), local venison and pork terrine with spiced damsons (£4.75), ploughman's (from £4.95), wild mushroom risotto (£7.95), lasagne (£8.50), steak in ale pie, cod fillet with garlic, cheese and herb sauce or chicken breast with perry and tarragon sauce (all £8.95), pheasant breast stuffed with a forcemeat of pheasant leg with a red wine and honey sauce (£11.50), and pudding such as raspberry crème brûlée, toffee and banana cheesecake or treacle sponge and custard (£3.50). Popular OAP pie lunch on Thursday. Besides well kept Greene King Old Speckled Hen, Marstons Pedigree and Wye Valley Bitter on handpump, they have decent wines (including local ones), and Oliver's local farm ciders from named apple cultivars, and perry; obliging service, and disabled access. A roomy and attractive stripped stone raftered restaurant extension has a Sunday lunchtime carvery. This is deep country indeed, and there are peaceful views from the terrace tables and chairs, or the unusual fixed tables and benches on the neat prettily planted lawn; there's a new covered barbecue and seating area. *(Recommended by Dr D J and Mrs S C Walker, Denys Gueroult, J R Ringrose, Theocsbrian, Ian Phillips, Annette Tress, Gary Smith, Maurice and Della Andrew, A S and M E Marriott, Dave Braisted, Mike and Mary Carter)*

Free house ~ Licensees Norman and Janet Whittall ~ Bar food ~ Restaurant ~ (01885) 400276 ~ Children in restaurant and family room ~ Dogs allowed in bar ~ Open 11-3, 6.30-11; 12-3.30, 7-10.30 Sun; closed Sun evening, 25 Dec, 1 Jan ~ Bedrooms: /£50S

LUGWARDINE SO5541 Map 4

Crown & Anchor

Cotts Lane; just off A438 E of Hereford

Readers enjoy their visits to this attractive black and white timbered pub. There's a friendly, relaxed atmosphere in the several smallish and charming rooms, a big log fire, newspapers to read, and usually a few locals in the bar, which is furnished with an interesting mix of pieces. Well kept Butcombe, Marstons Pedigree, Timothy Taylors Landlord and Worthington on handpump, and lots of wines by the glass. As well as a huge choice of good lunchtime sandwiches (from £2.50; hummous and avocado £3, cambozola, cucumber and kiwi £3.30, smoked trout with apple and horseradish £3.70), there might be ploughman's (£6), cold smoked ham and eggs (£7), interesting vegetarian dishes such as black-eyed bean and seaweed casserole or mushroom, and butterbean and basil stew (from £7.25), rolled fillet of plaice with muscat grapes and white wine sauce or chicken with spinach and mozzarella in a tomato and garlic sauce (£9.50), roast breast of gressingham duck with plum and port wine sauce (£12), local sirloin steak with mushroom and madeira sauce (£13), and daily specials such as terrine of venison and pistachios (£4.50), warm duck breast salad with oriental dressing (£5.50), local pork sausages with juniper and red wine sacue (£8.50), salmon, bass, mussels, prawns, cockles and monkfish in a wine and cream sauce (£10), and roast pheasant with bacon and barley and armagnac sauce (£12); two eating areas are no smoking. The garden is pretty in summer. The pub is surrounded by newish housing, but in ancient times the Lugg flats round here – some of the oldest Lammas meadows in England – were farmed in strips by local farm tenants, and meetings with the lord of the manor were held in the pub. *(Recommended by Denys Gueroult, Dr and Mrs M E Wilson, Bill and Jessica Ritson, Louise Bayly, Andy Trafford, Ian and Liz Rispin)*

Enterprise ~ Lease Nick and Julie Squire ~ Real ale ~ Bar food (till 10) ~ Restaurant ~ (01432) 851303 ~ Children welcome ~ Open 12-11; 12-10.30 Sun; closed 25 Dec

ORLETON SO4967 Map 6

Boot

Just off B4362 W of Woofferton

With welcoming licensees and locals, and super beer and food, it's not surprising that this 16th-c partly black and white timbered pub is so popular with visitors, too. The traditional-feeling bar has a mix of dining and cushioned carver chairs around a few old tables on the red tiles, one very high-backed settle, hops over the counter, and a warming fire in the big fireplace, with horsebrasses along its bressumer beam. The lounge bar is up a couple of steps, and has green plush banquettes right the way around the walls, mullioned windows, an exposed section of wattle and daub, and standing timbers and heavy wall beams. There's a small and pretty no smoking restaurant on the left. Well kept Hobsons Best and Town Crier and Black Sheep Best Bitter on handpump, and local farm cider and apple juice; cribbage and dominoes. Good, enjoyable food at lunchtime includes home-made soup (£2.75), sandwiches (from £3.25; hot baguettes from £5.45), ploughman's (£5.25), lambs liver, bacon and onion gravy (£6.95), and steak in ale pie or gammon steak with egg (£7.95), with evening choices such as home-made pâté (£3.95), breaded whitebait (£4.25), home-made lasagne (£8.25), home-made chicken and asparagus pie (£8.95), grilled duck breast with a black cherry and port sauce (£9.75), and steaks (from £10.75); specials that change every two weeks like ham and mushroom pancake (£3.95), lambs kidneys flamed in brandy (£4.25), cheese and lentil loaf with a tarragon cream sauce (£8.75), smoked haddock fillet with a mornay sauce (£9.25), pheasant casserole or sweet and sour chicken (£9.85), and crevettes in garlic and herb butter (£10.25). There are seats in the garden under a huge ash tree, a barbecue area, and a fenced-in children's play area. *(Recommended by R T and J C Moggridge, Jonathan Smith, P Hedges)*

Free house ~ Licensees Philip and Jane Dawson ~ Real ale ~ Bar food ~ Restaurant ~ (01568) 780228 ~ Children in eating area of bar and restaurant ~ Dogs allowed in bar ~ Open 12-3, 6-11; 12-3, 7-10.30 Sun

PEMBRIDGE SO3958 Map 6

New Inn

Market Square (A44)

The three simple but comfortable little beamed rooms in this ancient place ooze antiquity with their oak peg-latch doors and elderly traditional furnishings that include a fine antique curved-back settle on the worn flagstones; the log fire is the substantial sort that people needed long before central heating was reinvented. One room has sofas, pine furniture and books; the welcoming homely lounge is no smoking; darts, shove-ha'penny, cribbage, dominoes and quoits. Well kept Black Sheep and Fullers London Pride and perhaps a couple of guests such as Dunn Plowman Kingdom or Wye Valley Butty Bach on handpump, 32 malt whiskies, farm cider, and local wine and apple juice. Bar food at lunchtime includes sandwiches and ploughman's, battered fish and chips, spinach and cream cheese lasagne or hot home-baked ham with mustard mash and redcurrant sauce (all £6.95), pork, cider and apple casserole with sage dumplings (£7.50), and steak and kidney pie (£7.75); evening choices such as seafood stew (£8.50), fillet of lamb with redcurrant and mint sauce (£9.50), and duckling breast with a cherry wine sauce (£12). Tables sit on the cobblestones between the pub and the former wool market and overlook the church, which has an unusual 14th-c detached bell tower beside it. More reports please. *(Recommended by Gill and Tony Morriss, Kevin Blake, MLR, Pam and David Bailey, Bill and Jessica Ritson, R M Corlett)*

Free house ~ Licensee Jane Melvin ~ Real ale ~ Bar food ~ Restaurant ~ (01544) 388427 ~ Children in restaurant until 8pm ~ Dogs allowed in bedrooms ~ Local band occasionally ~ Open 11-3, 6-11; 12-3, 7-10.30 Sun; closed first 4 days Feb

SELLACK SO5627 Map 4

Lough Pool ★ 🍴 🍷

Back road Hoarwithy—Ross-on-Wye

Herefordshire Dining Pub of the Year

Particularly well run, this attractive black and white timbered cottage continues to serve very good food whilst firmly remaining a traditional pub. The beamed central room has kitchen chairs and cushioned window seats around wooden tables on the mainly flagstoned floor, sporting prints, bunches of dried flowers and fresh hop bines, and a log fire at one end with a woodburner at the other. Other rooms lead off, gently brightened up with attractive individual furnishings and nice touches like the dresser of patterned plates. The same interesting menu –

which changes daily – is available in the chatty bar as well as the restaurant, and might include sandwiches, cream of celeriac soup (£3.50), kipper, potato and bacon pâté (£6), a plate of spanish charcuterie or blue cheese soufflé with walnut and watercress salad (£6.50), potted prawns and brown shrimps or confit chicken and wild mushroom terrine with home-made piccalilli (£7), ploughman's with home-made chutney (£8), brixham whiting in beer batter with caper and chive mayonnaise (£11), chargrilled liver and bacon with crispy fried onions and red wine jus or pork, black pudding and sage burgers with honey, mustard and tarragon dressing (£11.50), spatchcocked poussin with yoghurt and cumin and sweet and sour sauce (£13), and pink bream with curried leeks, mussels and saffron braised potatoes (£14), with puddings such as warm chocolate fondant, lemon and elderflower panna cotta with shortbread, and warm ginger cake with treacle toffee ice-cream (£5.25); the restaurant is no smoking. Well kept John Smiths, and Wye Valley Bitter or Butty Bach on handpump, a good range of malt whiskies, local farm ciders and a well chosen reasonably priced wine list. Service is good. There are plenty of picnic-sets on its neat front lawned area, and pretty hanging baskets; plenty of bridleways and surrounding walks. *(Recommended by Pamela and Merlyn Horswell, John Kane, Guy Vowles, KN-R, Anthony Rickards Collinson, Lucien Perring, Stephen Williamson, Neil and Jean Spink, Ian and Denise Foster, Joyce and Maurice Cottrell, Di and Mike Gillam, Bernard Stradling, Michael and Jenny Back, J E Shackleton, Michael Butler, Alec and Barbara Jones, David and Nina Pugsley, Mr and Mrs J Curtis, Pat and Roger Fereday, Revd and Mrs G G Brown, Duncan Cloud)*

Free house ~ Licensee Stephen Bull ~ Real ale ~ Bar food ~ Restaurant ~ (01989) 730236 ~ Children in eating area of bar and restaurant ~ Dogs allowed in bar ~ Open 11.30-2.30, 6.30-11; 12-2, 7-10.30 Sun; closed Sun evening, all day Mon in winter

ST OWEN'S CROSS SO5425 Map 4

New Inn

Junction A4137 and B4521, W of Ross-on-Wye

The hanging baskets all around this unspoilt black and white timbered coaching inn are quite a sight, and in summer, the big enclosed garden really comes into its own; fine views stretch over rolling countryside to the distant Black Mountains. Inside, both the lounge bar (with a buoyant local atmosphere) and the no smoking restaurant have huge inglenook fireplaces, intriguing nooks and crannies, settles, old pews, beams and timbers. Lunchtime bar food includes home-made soup (£3.50), sandwiches (from £3.60), home-made chicken liver pâté (£4.95), ploughman's (£5.45), home-made lasagne (£5.95), ham and egg (£6.95), a curry of the day (£7.45), and home-made steak and kidney pie (£7.95); in the evening there might be extras such as home-made chicken liver pâté or garlic mushrooms (£4.95), trout fillets wrapped in bacon (caught by the chef, £9.45), local duckling in a chinese-style plum sauce (£11.95), and steaks (from £11.95). Midweek lunchtime two-course meal £5.99; friendly and pleasant service. Well kept Tetleys and Wadworths 6X alongside Brains Reverend James and Marstons Pedigree on handpump, local cider and perry, and a fair choice of malt whiskies; darts, shove-ha'penny, cribbage, dominoes and piped music. Be very careful if you do use the A4137 – this is England's second most dangerous road. *(Recommended by Neil and Jean Spink, Duncan Cloud, Pamela and Merlyn Horswell, Piotr Chodzko-Zajko, John and Lynn Norcliffe, Dr A Y Drummond)*

Free house ~ Licensees Nigel and Jane Donovan ~ Real ale ~ Bar food (12-2, 6.15-9) ~ Restaurant ~ (01989) 730274 ~ Children welcome ~ Dogs welcome ~ Open 12-2.30(3 Sat), 6-11; 12-4, 7-10.30 Sun ~ Bedrooms: £40S/£70S(£80B)

Stars after the name of a pub show exceptional character and appeal. They don't mean extra comfort. And they are nothing to do with food quality, for which there's a separate knife-and-fork symbol. Even quite a basic pub can win stars, if it's individual enough.

STOCKTON CROSS SO5161 Map 4

Stockton Cross Inn

Kimbolton; A4112, off A49 just N of Leominster

This is a spotlessly kept little black and white timbered pub that readers very much enjoy visiting again and again. As well as a relaxed atmosphere and a warm welcome from friendly staff, there's a comfortably snug area at the top end of the long heavily beamed bar with a handsome antique settle facing an old black kitchen range, and old leather chairs and brocaded stools by the huge log fire in the broad stone fireplace. At the far end is a woodburning stove with heavy cast-iron-framed tables and sturdy dining chairs, and up a step, a small area has more tables. Old-time prints, a couple of épées on one beam and lots of copper and brass complete the picture. Cooked by the landlady, the good, tasty bar food includes soup (£3.95), fried sardines (£5.25), pancake filled with smoked chicken, bacon and mushrooms in a creamy sauce or prawn, haddock and cheese smokie (£5.75), rack of ribs in home-made barbecue sauce (£9.50), rabbit pie (£10.50), tagine of lamb with apricots, honey and flaked almonds (£11.50), smoked haddock, cod and cheese bake (£12.80), and steaks (from £12.95), with specials like home-cooked ham and egg (£6.95), stilton and mushroom pasta (£8.50), home-made steak and kidney pie (£7.95), and venison cumberland sausage with onion gravy (£8.75); the chips and bread are really good. Puddings such as treacle tart, seasonal fruit crumble or bread and butter pudding (£4.50); half the eating area is no smoking. Well kept Brains Rev James, Teme Valley This and That, Timothy Taylors Landlord and Wye Valley Butty Bach on handpump; piped music. There are tables out in the pretty garden. *(Recommended by Rodney and Norma Stubington, R T and J C Moggridge, W W Burke, Mr and Mrs P J Fisk, Ian and Liz Rispin, Mike and Mary Carter, Dr and Mrs C W Thomas, Glenwys and Alan Lawrence, John and Lynn Norcliffe)*

Free house ~ Licensee Steve Walsh ~ Real ale ~ Bar food (snacks only Sun evening) ~ (01568) 612509 ~ Children over 6 allowed ~ Open 12-3, 7-11; 12-4.30 Sun; closed Mon evening

TITLEY SO3360 Map 6

Stagg

B4355 N of Kington

There have been several changes to this well known dining pub over the last year. Their new barn conversion, as we went to press, was virtually finished which will give them a further dining room with doors on to the terrace. This increased space should mean that the bar is freed up from people all eating, thus giving those who just want a drink and a chat a bit more space. They have also bought a Georgian vicarage four minutes away and plan to open guest accommodation; the two acre garden will also incorporate a vegetable and herb garden for the kitchen. The landlord/chef also uses local suppliers wherever possible, so you can be sure of good, fresh often organic ingredients. The pubbier blackboard menu (not available Saturday evening or Sunday lunchtime) has up to ten choices which, besides filled baguettes (from £3.50), could include three-cheese ploughman's, pasta with home-made pesto and cheese or smoked chicken and crispy bacon salad (£7.50), crispy duck leg with cider sauce (£7.90), and smoked haddock risotto or scallops on cauliflower purée with black pepper oil (£8.50). On the more elaborate restaurant menu (which can also be eaten in the bar) you might find soup (£3.50), pigeon breast on puy lentils with smoked bacon sauce (£5.70), venison carpaccio with truffled celeriac salad (£6.50), fried foie gras with apple jelly (£7.90), bass fillet with a soft parsley and lemon crust and dauphinoise potato, rack of local lamb with shepherd's pie and rosemary jus or gressingham duck breast with poached pear and perry sauce and potato fondant (all £13.90), fillet of local beef with wasabi mash and stuffed savoy cabbage (£16.90). Puddings such as dark and white chocolate mousse cake, three crème brûlées of vanilla, orange and drambuie or rum baba with local clotted cream (£4.70).

There's also a choice of around 14 british cheeses. The food can take quite a while to come and helpings can strike some people as small. The dining rooms are no smoking. A carefully chosen wine list with ten wines and champagne by the glass, well kept Hobsons Best and Town Crier, and a guest like Black Sheep or Greene King Ruddles County on handpump, a fine collection of malt whiskies, and local farm cider, perry and apple juice; cribbage and dominoes. The bar, though comfortable and hospitable, is not large, and the atmosphere is civilised rather than lively. The garden has chairs and tables on a terrace. *(Recommended by Chris Flynn, Wendy Jones, R Cross, Bernard Stradling, Terry Smith, Mr and Mrs A H Young, Guy Vowles, J E Shackleton, Christopher J Darwent, Roy and Lindsey Fentiman, George Atkinson, RJH, Mr and Mrs J Curtis, Keith Symons)*

Free house ~ Licensees Steve and Nicola Reynolds ~ Real ale ~ Bar food (not Sun evening or Mon) ~ Restaurant ~ (01544) 230221 ~ Children welcome ~ Dogs allowed in bar ~ Open 12-3, 6.30-11; 12-3.30 Sun; closed Sun evening, Mon, 25 and 26 Dec, 1 Jan ~ Bedrooms: £50B/£70B

ULLINGSWICK SO5949 Map 4

Three Crowns

Village off A465 S of Bromyard (and just S of Stoke Lacy) and signposted off A417 N of A465 roundabout – keep straight on through village and past turn-off to church; pub at Bleak Acre, towards Little Cowarne

Despite the emphasis on the particularly good food (and most customers are here for a special meal out), the landlord continues to keep a few tables free for those just popping in for a drink and a chat. The charmingly traditional interior has hops strung along the low beams of its smallish bar, a couple of traditional settles besides more usual seats, a mix of big old wooden tables with small round ornamental cast-iron-framed ones, open fires and one or two gently sophisticated touches such as candles on tables, and proper napkins; half the pub is no smoking. Using mostly local and organic products, there are starters such as grilled mullet with tomato tarte tatin and pesto, fish soup with rouille and croutons or Jersey royal and asparagus salad with fried duck egg (all £6), main courses like confit of gressingham duck with prune pommes anna and parsnip purée, grilled bass with fresh noodles, chinese greens, and tomato and ginger sauce or chargrilled beef with oxtail faggot and wild mushrooms (all £14.25), and puddings that include chocolate and blood orange pudding plate, panna cotta with roasted rhubarb compote and balsamic syrup or pear and sage tatin (£4.50). The two-course lunch is now £10.95 (three courses £12.95). Best to book to be sure of a table. They have half a dozen wines by the glass, along with well kept Hobsons Best and maybe Wye Valley Bitter on handpump, and local farm ciders and fruit juice. Nice summer views from tables out on the attractively planted lawn, and outside heaters for chillier evenings. *(Recommended by Denys Gueroult, Chris Flynn, Wendy Jones, Rodney and Norma Stubington, M S Catling, Sir Nigel Foulkes, Bernard Stradling, Jason Caulkin, Mr and Mrs A H Young, J E Shackleton, Roger White, J A Ellis, Annette Tress, Gary Smith)*

Free house ~ Licensee Brent Castle ~ Real ale ~ Bar food ~ Restaurant ~ (01432) 820279 ~ Well behaved children in eating area of bar ~ Open 12-2.30, 7-11; 12-2, 7-10.30 Sun; closed Mon

UPTON BISHOP SO6527 Map 4

Moody Cow

2 miles from M50 junction 3 westbound (or junction 4 eastbound), via B4221; continue on B4221 to rejoin at next junction

In a sleepy village, this pleasant pub has several separate snug areas that angle in an L around the bar counter, and there's a nice medley of stripped country furniture, stripped floorboards and stonework, quite a few cow ornaments and naïve cow paintings, and a lovely big log fire. On the far right is a biggish rustic and candlelit restaurant, with hop-draped rafters, and a fireside area with armchairs and sofas. The far left has a second smaller dining area (also no smoking), just five or six tables with antique pine-style tables and chairs; both rooms are no smoking. Home-made and cooked to order, the bar food might include soup (£3.75), onion tartlet topped with melted goats cheese or thai fishcakes with chilli salsa (£4.95), several pasta dishes (£3.95 starter, £6.95 main course), fresh battered cod or steak and kidney pie (£8.95), mushroom pie (£9.95), fresh fish dishes (from £10.95), duck breast with a mixed berry compote (£13.95), and puddings like bread and butter pudding or poached pears with melted belgian chocolate and vanilla ice-cream (from £4.50); they sell their home-made bread, too. Well kept Hook Norton, Wye Valley Best and a guest such as Whittingtons Cats Whiskers on handpump; piped music. *(Recommended by Guy Vowles, Mike and Mary Carter, Alain and Rose Foote, Steve Crick, Helen Preston, P and J Shapley, LM, Lucien Perring, Jo Rees, Neil and Anita Christopher, Chris Flynn, Wendy Jones)*

Free house ~ Licensee James Lloyd ~ Real ale ~ Bar food (12-2, 6.30-9.30) ~ Restaurant ~ (01989) 780470 ~ Children in eating area of bar and restaurant ~ Dogs allowed in bar ~ Open 12-2.30, 6.30-11; 12-3 Sun; closed Sun evening and Mon

WALTERSTONE SO3425 Map 6

Carpenters Arms

Village signposted off A465 E of Abergavenny, beside Old Pandy Inn; follow village signs, and keep eyes skinned for sign to pub, off to right, by lane-side barn

For many years, this charming little unspoilt stone cottage has been in the same family, and the genuine welcome from the landlady and delightful interior make you feel as though you are walking into a friend's house. The traditional rooms have ancient settles against stripped stone walls, some pieces of carpet on broad polished flagstones, a roaring log fire in a gleaming black range (complete with pot-iron, hot-water tap, bread oven and salt cupboard), pewter mugs hanging from beams, and the slow tick of a clock. The snug main dining room (which is no smoking) has mahogany tables and oak corner cupboards, with a big vase of flowers on the dresser. Another little dining area has old oak tables and church pews on flagstones; piped music. Reasonably priced and tasty, the home-made food might include sandwiches and rolls (from £2), soup, prawn cocktail, ploughman's or steak roll (all £4), home-made dishes such as cod and prawn pie, curry or beef in Guinness pie (all £8), a vegetarian choice, thick lamb cutlets with redcurrant and rosemary sauce (£9), steaks (from £9), and home-made puddings (£4). Well kept Breconshire Golden Valley and Wadworths 6X tapped from the cask; farm cider. The outside lavatories are cold but in character. *(Recommended by Dave Braisted, J Taylor, Pamela and Merlyn Horswell, Jacquie and Jim Jones, Alan and Paula McCully, Peter B Brown, Chris Flynn, Wendy Jones)*

Free house ~ Licensee Vera Watkins ~ Real ale ~ Bar food ~ No credit cards ~ (01873) 890353 ~ Children welcome ~ Open 12-3, 7-11; 12-3, 7-10.30 Sun; closed 25 Dec

WELLINGTON SO4948 Map 6

Wellington

Village signposted off A49 N of Hereford; pub at far end

The carefully refurbished bar in this red brick Victorian roadside pub has big high-backed dark wooden settles, an open brick fireplace with a log fire in winter and fresh flowers in summer, and historical photographs of the village and antique farm and garden tools around the walls. The charming candlelit restaurant is in the former stables and is no smoking. Well kept Hobsons Best, Wye Valley Butty Bach, and a couple of guests such as Shepherd Neame Best and Timothy Taylors Landlord on handpump, farm cider, and decent wines. Well liked bar food includes soup (£3.50), filled baguettes (from £4.75), sausages (made locally to their own recipe; £5), scrambled free-range eggs with smoked salmon (£5.50), ploughman's (£6), and free range chicken caesar, and steak and mushroom in ale pie or roasted vegetables in filo pastry with a rich tomato sauce (all £6.95); Sunday lunchtime carvery (no other food then). Service is friendly; darts and piped music. There are tables out in the attractive garden behind, and summer barbecues. More reports please. *(Recommended by Mr and Mrs T Lewis, Joanna Foster, Maurice and Della Andrew, Christopher J Darwent, Mike and Mary Carter)*

Free house ~ Licensees Ross and Philippa Williams ~ Real ale ~ Bar food (not Sun evening or Mon) ~ Restaurant ~ (01432) 830367 ~ Children in eating area of bar and restaurant ~ Dogs allowed in bar ~ Open 12-3, 6-11; 12-3, 7-10.30 Sun; closed Mon lunchtime

WEOBLEY SO4052 Map 6

Salutation 🍷

Village signposted from A4112 SW of Leominster; and from A44 NW of Hereford (there's also a good back road direct from Hereford – straight out past S side of racecourse)

Set in a quiet village surrounded by lovely lush countryside, this 500-year-old inn has a comfortable and partly no smoking lounge with a relaxed pubby feel. The two areas are separated by a few steps and standing timbers and are furnished with brocaded modern winged settles and smaller seats, a couple of big cut-away cask seats, wildlife decorations, and a hop bine over the bar counter; logs burn in a big stone fireplace. More standing timbers separate it from the neat no smoking restaurant area, and there's a separate smaller parquet-floored public bar with sensibly placed darts, juke box, TV and fruit machine. Well kept Fullers London Pride, Hook Norton Best Bitter and Wye Valley Butty Bach on handpump, quite a few new world wines, and several malt whiskies. Bar food includes lunchtime sandwiches (from £4.25; filled baguettes from £5.50), filled baked potatoes (from £4.25), and omelettes (£5.95), as well as home-made soup (£4.25), home-made lasagne or liver and bacon (£7.95), gammon and egg or steak in ale pie (£8.25), and 10oz rib-eye steak (£11.95); daily specials and puddings. On Sundays, they may serve only a roast (no bar snacks then). The restaurant and conservatory are no smoking. There are tables and chairs with parasols on a sheltered back terrace. More reports please. *(Recommended by the Didler, R T and J C Moggridge, Revd D Glover, Alan and Jill Bull, Mrs T A Bizat, Mike and Heather Watson, Stuart Turner, Maurice and Gill McMahon, MLR, Bernie Adams, Pam and David Bailey, George Atkinson, Keith Symons, Pat and Roger Fereday, Jacquie and Jim Jones, Nick and Meriel Cox; also in the* Good Hotel Guide*)*

Free house ~ Licensee Dr Mike Tai ~ Real ale ~ Bar food ~ Restaurant ~ (01544) 318443 ~ Children in eating area of bar and restaurant ~ Dogs allowed in bar ~ Open 11-11; 12-10.30 Sun ~ Bedrooms: £51S(£54B)/£76S(£79B)

WHITNEY-ON-WYE SO2747 Map 6

Rhydspence 🛏

A438 Hereford—Brecon

Often called the first and last pub in England, this very picturesque ancient black and white country inn is right on welsh border which follows the line of the little stream in the garden; there are seats and tables out here and fine views over the Wye valley. Inside, the rambling, neatly kept rooms have heavy beams and timbers, attractive old-fashioned furnishings; there's a log fire in the fine big stone fireplace in the central bar. What was the small dining room has been incorporated into the newer bistro-type eating area next to the bar, and this opens into the no smoking family room (which makes it less remote from the bar area for parents). The more formal restaurant is no smoking; nice breakfasts. Good bar food includes home-made soup (£3.85), home-made chicken liver pâté or lunchtime ploughman's (£5.95), vegetarian courgette and mushroom ciabatta (£7.25), lasagne (£8.50), chicken stir fry on garlic noodles (£8.95), fresh cod in lemon batter with home-made tartare sauce (£9.75), and steak and kidney pie or a spicy curry (£9.95); popular Sunday lunch (must book). Well kept Bass and Robinsons Best on handpump, local cider, and a decent wine list; darts, cribbage,

dominoes and shove-ha'penny. *(Recommended by Rodney and Norma Stubington, David and Julie Glover, Pam and David Bailey, Andrew Shore, Maria Williams)*

Free house ~ Licensee Peter Glover ~ Real ale ~ Bar food ~ Restaurant ~ (01497) 831262 ~ Children in family room ~ Open 11-2.30, 7-11; 12-2.30, 7-10.30 Sun ~ Bedrooms: £37.50S/£75B

LUCKY DIP

Besides the fully inspected pubs, you might like to try these Lucky Dips recommended to us and described by readers (if you do, please send us reports: www.goodguides.co.uk).

ASTON CREWS SO6723

☆ *Penny Farthing*: Partly 15th-c, roomy and relaxing, run well by three warmly welcoming sisters, lots of beams with horsebrasses, harness and farm tools, well in bar with skeleton at bottom; enjoyable generous competitively priced food from sandwiches, bangers and mash and good value lunches to evening fish specialities, efficient service, well kept Greene King Abbot and Wadworths 6X, decent wines, easy chairs, log fires, two restaurant areas, one with pretty valley and Forest of Dean views; subdued piped music; tables in charming garden, bedrooms *(Mike and Mary Carter, BB, Mrs R Lowth, Alastair Stevenson, Lucien Perring, Jo Rees)*

BROMYARD SO6554

Falcon [Broad St]: Attractive timbered hotel with beamed and panelled bar, leather chairs and settees in small lounge, good value food inc popular Sun roast, friendly cheerful staff; comfortable bedrooms *(George Atkinson)*

Rose & Lion [New Rd]: Welcoming local tied to Wye Valley brewery, their full range in top condition from central island servery for simple comfortable lounge and games-minded public bar with darts, cards etc; tables out in pleasant courtyard *(J A Ellis, Pete Baker)*

BROMYARD DOWNS SO6755

☆ *Royal Oak* [just NE of Bromyard; pub signed off A44]: Beautifully placed open-plan low-beamed 18th-c pub with wide views, carpeted bar with lots of pig models, dining room with huge bay window, wide range of home-made food, Hook Norton Best, friendly kind service, flagstoned bar with woodburner, pool, juke box and TV; walkers welcome (good area), picnic-sets on colourful front terrace, swings in orchard *(BB, Annette Tress, Gary Smith)*

COLWALL SO7342

☆ *Crown* [Walwyn Rd]: Welcoming and carefully refurbished, carpeted bar with step up to parquet-floor area with log fire, nice prints and lighting, good varied reasonably priced food cooked to order (so may take a while) from sandwiches, ploughman's and generous starters to popular Sun lunch, some classier dishes, friendly helpful service, well kept Shepherd Neame Spitfire, Timothy Taylors Landlord and Tetleys, decent wines, daily papers *(Dave Braisted, BB, Ian and Denise Foster)*

CRASWALL SO2736

☆ *Bulls Head* [Hay-on-Wye—Llanfihangel Crucorney Golden Valley rd]: Remote unpretentious stone-built pub, low beams, flagstones, antique settles and elderly chairs, logs burning in an old cast-iron stove, 19th-c engravings, well kept Wye Valley Butty Bach and a local beer brewed for them tapped from the cask and served from a hatch, Weston's farm cider, table skittles, cribbage and dominoes, generous filled home-baked huffers, may be some inventive hot dishes using local ingredients, partly no smoking dining area; tables outside with play area and room for camping, peaceful walking area, simple bedrooms, open all day, cl Sun evening, Mon and Tues *(Alan and Jill Bull, the Didler, LYM, Mike and Mary Carter, JWAC, Frank Willy, John Hale, MLR)*

EARDISLAND SO4258

Cross [A44]: Friendly and unpretentious family-run two-room pub with a couple of well kept ales such as Fullers London Pride, bargain lunches; open all day *(LYM, MLR)*

EWYAS HAROLD SO3828

Temple Bar: Friendly engaging landlord, well kept Hobsons and Worthington 1744, enjoyable food from baguettes to interesting range of hot platters in locals' public bar, pleasant lounge or small neat dining room *(Dr A Y Drummond)*

FOWNHOPE SO5734

Green Man: Striking 15th-c black and white inn with big log fire, wall settles, window seats and armchairs in one beamed bar, standing timbers dividing another, well kept Courage Directors, Hook Norton Best, Marstons Pedigree, John Smiths and Sam Smiths OB, Weston's farm ciders, popular well priced food from sandwiches to substantial main dishes in bar and plainer no smoking restaurant, just roasts on Sun, various special deals; children welcome, quiet garden with play area; comfortably refurbished bedrooms, good breakfast, back fitness centre *(Anne Morris, LYM, J R Ringrose, Michael and Ann Cole)*

GOODRICH SO5618

Cross Keys: Four well kept ales such as Bass, Greene King IPA and Otter, good farm cider, good value generous home-made food, barn restaurant *(Michael Edwards)*

HAREWOOD END SO5227

☆ *Harewood End Inn* [A49 Hereford—Ross]: Attractive and comfortable panelled dining lounge with enjoyable straightforward home-made food at good value prices, friendly efficient service, well kept Bass and Wye Valley Butty Bach, good value wines; nice garden, good bedrooms with own bathrooms *(T Pascall, Mike and Mary Carter)*

HEREFORD SO5139

Barrels [St Owen St]: Plain and cheery two-bar local brewing its own excellent Wye Valley Hereford and Dorothy Goodbodys ales at attractive prices (esp 5-7 happy hour), barrel-built counter also serving guest beers, farm ciders from Bulmer's, Stowford Press and Weston's, friendly efficient staff, may have sandwiches and pickled eggs, side pool room with games, juke box and TV sports, lots of modern stained-glass; piped blues and rock, live music at beer festival end Aug; picnic-sets out on cobbles by brewery, open all day *(the Didler, BB, MLR, Joe Green, Ian Phillips, Paul Davies)*

Gilbies [St Peters Cl]: Good relaxed bar and bistro, enjoyable food inc platters to share, good service, several continental beers on tap and lots of bottled beers as well as Bitter and cider, good choice of wines *(Joyce and Maurice Cottrell)*

KILPECK SO4430

Red Lion: Pleasant country pub, genial and knowledgeable landlord with good sense of humour, range of local beers, well prepared food *(Roger Allen)*

KINGSLAND SO4461

Corner [B4360 NW of Leominster]: 16th-c black and white inn, good food choice inc popular bargain steak and fish night Weds, timbered bar and restaurant in converted hay loft, Hobsons real ale; good value bedrooms with own bathrooms in converted barns *(Roy and Lindsey Fentiman)*

KINGTON SO3057

☆ *Olde Tavern* [Victoria Rd, just off A44 opp B4355 – follow sign to Town Centre, Hospital, Cattle Mkt; pub on right opp Elizabeth Rd, no inn sign but Estd 1767 notice]: Splendidly old-fashioned, and now home to the Dunn Plowman microbrewery, with their ales and guest beers; gently updated (a hatch-served side room now opening off small plain parlour and public bar), but plenty of dark brown woodwork, big windows, old settles and other antique furniture, china, pewter and curios, welcoming locals, gas fire, no music, machines or food; children welcome, though not a family pub; cl wkdy lunchtimes, outside gents' *(BB, Pete Baker, the Didler)*

LEA SO6621

Crown [A40 Ross—Gloucester]: Dark and cosy, with window seats, notable range of well kept beers, particularly welcoming landlord, good coffee, enjoyable food, daily papers *(Phil and Sally Gorton, Mike and Mary Carter)*

LEDBURY SO7137

Prince of Wales [Church Lane; narrow passage from Town Hall]: Pleasantly old-fashioned Banks's pub tucked nicely down charming narrow cobbled alley, low-beamed front bars, long back room, jovial landlord, well kept beers, tasty simple home-made food, low prices; a couple of tables in yard crammed with lovely flower tubs and hanging baskets *(John Wooll)*

☆ *Talbot* [New St]: Relaxed local atmosphere in 16th-c inn's black-beamed bar rambling around island servery, antique hunting prints, plush wall banquettes or more traditional seats, log fire in big stone fireplace, enjoyable food from baguettes to full meals, well kept ales inc a local one, good house wines, quick friendly service, smart no smoking black-panelled dining room, tales of a friendly poltergeist; fruit machine, piped music; decent bedrooms *(BB, Patrick Hancock)*

LEINTWARDINE SO4174

☆ *Sun* [Rosemary Lane, just off A4113]: Unspoilt gem, three bare benches by coal fire in red-tiled front parlour off hallway, venerable landlady brings you well kept Woods tapped from the cask in her kitchen (and may honour you with the small settee and a couple of chairs by the gas fire in her sitting room); no food exc pickled eggs and crisps *(BB, Pete Baker, RWC)*

LEOMINSTER SO4958

Black Horse [South St]: Big well run bustling bar with comfortably rustic furniture, snug lounge and eating area (no food Sun); well kept mainly local real ales, enjoyable straightforward food inc good sandwiches, traditional games *(BB, MLR)*

LINTON SO6525

Alma: Rejuvenated unspoilt local in small village, three well kept ales such as Butcombe, good fire, summer jazz festival; piped music can be loud, can be rather smoky; children very welcome, nice good-sized garden behind, cl wkdy lunchtimes *(Phil and Sally Gorton, Theocsbrian, Guy Vowles)*

MORDIFORD SO5737

☆ *Moon* [B4224 SE of Hereford]: Country pub in good spot by Wye tributary, black beams and roaring log fire, well kept Marstons Pedigree, Tetleys and Wadworths 6X, local farm ciders, reasonably priced wines, back bar popular with young locals and students out from Hereford, polite old-fashioned service; children in eating areas when food service restarts (none as we went to press), open all day wknds *(Mike and Mary Carter, LYM, Geoffrey and Penny Hughes)*

MUCH MARCLE SO6634

Royal Oak [off A449 Ross-on-Wye—Ledbury]: Superb rural spot with magnificent views, pleasant lounge with stools around small round tables and open fire, wide range of reasonably priced well prepared food from good proper sandwiches up, efficient service, Courage Directors, John Smiths and Weston's very local cider, large back dining area, bar with pool table; pleasant garden *(Jenny and Dave Hughes, K H Frostick, R M Corlett)*

☆ *Slip Tavern* [off A449 SW of Ledbury]: Unpretentious country pub with splendidly colourful gardens overlooking cider orchards (Weston's Cider Farm is close by), well kept Hook Norton Best and local farm cider, usual bar food from good value generous sandwiches and baguettes to good Sun roasts, friendly prompt service, bar popular with older people at lunchtime, with villagey local evening atmosphere, attractive no smoking conservatory restaurant; folk music first Thurs of month *(R T and J C Moggridge, Mike and Mary Carter, LYM, Ian and Denise Foster, John and Kay Grugeon, Bernie Adams, Miss M Ruse)*

NEWTOWN SO6144

☆ *Newtown Inn* [A4103 Hereford—Worcester, junction with A417]: Unassuming roadside pub transformed by enthusiastic young team doing sensibly sized helpings of good imaginative food using fresh local produce, frequent new menus, friendly service and convivial atmosphere (drinkers not squeezed out by diners), reasonable prices, decent wines *(Anthony Bradshaw, Rev Michael Vockins, S Baldwin)*

ORCOP HILL SO4727

Fountain [off A466 S of Hereford]: Small friendly village pub, simple cosy bar with daily papers, big helpings of enjoyable reasonably priced food in back dining room and restaurant, good choice inc fresh fish specials and cheap lunchtime deals, Marstons Pedigree and John Smiths; darts, piped music; tables in peaceful pretty front garden *(Ian and Denise Foster, BB)*

PETERCHURCH SO3538

Nags Head: Good helpings of good cheap home-made food in unpretentious 1960s-style pub – good value *(Christopher J Darwent)*

ROSS-ON-WYE SO5924

Mail Rooms [Gloucester Rd]: Light and airy Wetherspoons, open and modern, with busy civilised atmosphere, good value food inc Thurs curry night; pleasant terrace, open all day *(Mike and Mary Carter)*

RUCKHALL SO44539

Ancient Camp [off A465 W of Hereford]: Beautifully placed small country inn, more restaurant than pub, with friendly new landlady, comfortable furnishings in bar with Wye Valley Butty Bach from new (rather hotel-style) bar counter, decent wines, short restaurant choice of good if rather pricey food using local ingredients (can eat this in bar too, and they do summer bar snacks); smart casual dress code; tables on pretty terraces, good bedrooms, cl Mon/Tues lunchtimes *(LYM)*

SYMONDS YAT SO5615

☆ *Saracens Head* [Symonds Yat E, by ferry, ie over on the Gloucs bank]: Riverside beauty spot next to small 80p ferry, busy basic flagstoned public bar popular with canoeists, mountain bikers and hikers (lounge bar for diners only), cheerful efficient staff, good range of well presented nourishing food from good value sandwiches up, well kept Theakstons Best, XB and Old Peculier and Wye Valley, three farm ciders, pine tables, settles and window seats, cosy carpeted restaurant; pool, piped jazz and blues, SkyTV, live music Thurs, pricy parking; lots of picnic-sets out on waterside terraces, summer boat trips, super walks, nice good value bedrooms – good place to stay out of season *(David Carr, BB, Jim Abbott, John and Lynn Norcliffe)*

TILLINGTON SO4645

Bell: Traditional family-run and family-friendly local, good range of reasonably priced food in bar and restaurant from nice baguettes to generous home-made hot dishes, several real ales such as Spinning Dog Top Dog, Timothy Taylors Landlord and Wye Valley Butty Bach, comfortable banquettes in lounge extension, warm welcome; good big garden with play area *(Peter Hands)*

TRUMPET SO6639

☆ *Verzons* [A438 W of Ledbury]: Big changes afoot under new owners – sound promising; public bar and dining room to be done up, decked terrace built, bedrooms (already nice) refurbished, menus revamped along more traditional lines, music evenings planned; has had well kept Hook Norton Best and Wye Valley Butty Bach, good house wines and coffee, and pleasant layout with no smoking areas; children welcome, open all day; reports please *(LYM)*

UPPER COLWALL SO7643

☆ *Chase* [Chase Rd, off B4218 Malvern—Colwall, 1st left after hilltop on bend going W]: Great views from attractive garden and refined and comfortable lounge of genteel and friendly two-bar pub on Malvern Hills, well kept real ales inc Wye Valley Dorothy Goodbodys seasonal ones, limited choice of enjoyable lunchtime bar food inc good filled rolls, no smoking room; dogs welcome, cl Tues *(J R Ringrose, Dr D J and Mrs S C Walker)*

WELLINGTON HEATH SO7140

Farmers Arms [off B4214 just N of Ledbury – pub signed right, from top of village; Horse Rd]: Big much modernised pub in good walking country, wide food choice, decent wines, friendly staff, cosy atmosphere with plenty of comfortable plush banquettes, flame-effect gas fire, soft lighting from Tiffany-style lamps, a few big country prints *(BB, Ian and Denise Foster)*

WEOBLEY SO4151

Marshpools [SE of village; Weobley Marsh, nr Ledgemoor]: Friendly peacefully set country inn with enjoyable generous home-made food using local produce, friendly licensees, log fire; good well priced bedrooms with own bathrooms *(Mrs G Fuller, C W Foreman)*

WESTON-UNDER-PENYARD SO6323

☆ *Weston Cross Inn*: Family-run pub with good home-made food from good value bar snacks to wide choice of fine local meat and fresh fish with good fresh veg, friendly young staff, pleasantly refurbished and roomy beamed lounge/dining room (this and the bar have swapped places), Boddingtons and Tetleys, Weston's cider; walkers welcome (they have devised their own walks map), very pretty outside, with views of picturesque village from tables on front lawn, more tables and play area behind *(Guy Vowles, BB, Caroline and Michael Abbey)*

WHITNEY-ON-WYE SO2647

Boat: Spacious, quiet and neatly kept redbrick pub with lovely views of river and far beyond from big windows and picnic-sets in pleasant garden; wide choice of food (five blackboards), good friendly service, two real ales, farm cider, comfortable L-shaped lounge with no smoking dining area, games room with pool; may be piped music; children welcome, bedrooms *(CMW, JJW, Edward Leetham)*

WIGMORE SO4169

Compasses [Ford St]: Walker-friendly village inn with welcoming landlord (knowledgeable about local walks), well kept changing ales such as Hobsons, reliable and generous blackboard home cooking, old-fashioned bars; good view from garden, four bedrooms *(Roy and Lindsey Fentiman)*

WINFORTON SO2946

Sun [A438]: Two comfortably country-style beamed areas on either side of central servery, stripped stone and woodburners, no smoking area (children welcome in eating areas), sensibly sized helpings of decent food, good service, two real ales, farm cider, traditional games; piped music; garden with good play area, pleasant small campsite *(LYM, JWAC, Hugh Eagle)*

WOOLHOPE SO6135

☆ *Butchers Arms* [off B4224 in Fownhope, then beyond village]: Enjoyable food (some emphasis on this now) in 14th-c black and white timbered pub's two appealing bars, relaxing atmosphere, well kept Hook Norton Best and Shepherd Neame Spitfire, friendly helpful staff, massive low beams, log fires, french windows out to attractive terrace with teak furniture; comfortable newly refurbished bedrooms, lovely quiet valley *(LYM, MLR, John and Kay Grugeon, Patrick Hancock, Barry Collett)*

☆ *Crown*: Neatly kept lounge bar with Fullers London Pride, Smiles Best, Timothy Taylors Landlord and a guest beer, wide choice of bar food from sandwiches and baked potatoes up, straightforward comfortable furnishings, open fire, darts, timbered divider strung with hop bines, smart no smoking dining area; TV, piped music; children welcome, big garden with outdoor heaters and lighting, open all day Sat *(LYM, Lucien Perring, A H C Rainier, Geoff and Sylvia Donald, J R Ringrose)*

YARPOLE SO4664

☆ *Bell* [just off B4361 N of Leominster]: Neat and tidy picturesquely timbered ancient pub, extended into former cider mill; comfortable, bright and smart, with warmly welcoming landlady, good bar food, well kept ales such as Hook Norton, Greene King Old Speckled Hen and Timothy Taylors Landlord, decent wines, brass and bric-a-brac, more restauranty menu in country dining area; tables in sunny flower-filled garden, very handy for Croft Castle *(Mr and Mrs J Bishop, Alan Thwaite, Malcolm Taylor, Roy and Lindsey Fentiman)*

If a pub tries to make you leave a credit card behind the bar, be on your guard. The credit card firms and banks which issue them condemn this practice. After all, the publican who asks you to do this is in effect saying: 'I don't trust you'. Have you any more reason to trust his staff? If your card is used fraudulently while you have let it be kept out of your sight, the card company could say you've been negligent yourself – and refuse to make good your losses. So say that they can 'swipe' your card instead, but must hand it back to you. Please let us know if a pub does try to keep your card.

Hertfordshire

Pubs on top form here this year are the friendly Jolly Waggoner at Ardeley (good food and beer in warmly comfortable surroundings), the Woodman tucked away at Chapmore End (this unspoilt country pub makes its *Guide* debut with an immediate Beer Award – nice homely food, too), the stylish Alford Arms at Frithsden (a tempting choice of good imaginative food at fair prices), the timeless Holly Bush at Potters Crouch (a relaxing break from three motorways, this good all-rounder has some bargain food), the well run nicely updated Old Bull in Royston (another new main entry, a handsome and civilised country-town inn), and the cheerfully unspoilt Boot at Sarratt. The best pub here for a special meal out is the Alford Arms at Frithsden – for the third year running, it takes the county's top food title of Hertfordshire Dining Pub of the Year. This year, the people who run the cheerful good value Valiant Trooper in Aldbury have now taken over the attractively placed Greyhound there: an interesting and possibly exciting development. The Lucky Dip section at the end of the chapter also has quite a few places to note particularly: the Brocket Arms at Ayot St Lawrence, Crown & Sceptre near Hemel Hempstead, Woodman at Nuthampstead, Red Lion at Preston, Six Bells in St Albans, Plume of Feathers at Tewin and Fox & Duck at Therfield. Hertfordshire drinks prices tend to be a little higher than the national average. McMullens is the county's own main brewer, with the newer Tring small brewery increasingly active. This year we have also come across local Verulam beers (see Lucky Dip entry for the Farmers Boy in St Albans). Beers from Fullers of London or the big regional brewer Greene King often show up as the cheapest on offer from pubs here.

ALDBURY SP9612 Map 4

Greyhound

Stocks Road; village signposted from A4251 Tring—Berkhamsted, or reached directly from roundabout at E end of A41 Tring bypass

As we went to press we heard that a new licensee had taken over this spacious village pub (it's now owned by the Valiant Trooper up the road), so we're keeping our fingers crossed that things don't change too much. Benches outside face a picturesque village green complete with stocks and lively duck pond. The handsome Georgian façade is especially stunning in autumn when the blazing leaves of its virginia creeper provide a brilliant counterpoint to the backdrop of bronzing chiltern beechwoods (part of the National Trust's Ashridge Estate).The beamed interior shows some signs of considerable age (around the copper-hooded inglenook, for example), with plenty of tables in the two rooms off either side of the drinks and food serving areas. A big room at the back overlooks a suntrap gravel courtyard, and it's also well worth a winter visit, when the lovely warm fire and subtle lighting make it really cosy inside. Badger Best, Tanglefoot and a Badger seasonal guest such as King and Barnes Sussex are on handpump. Generous bar food from a fairly short lunchtime menu includes filled baguettes (from £5), filled baked potatoes (£5.25), ploughman's (£6.25), home-made vegetable curry (£7.75) and home-made steak and ale pie (£9.25). The evening menu includes dishes such as home-made soup (£3.50), home-made salmon fishcakes with sweet chilli sauce (£6.50), fried bream (£11.75), lamb shanks (£12) and fillet steak (£14.95); puddings £3.95. Very pleasant no smoking conservatory, piped music, cribbage and dominoes. The pub is a long-standing favourite with walkers (plastic bags are kept near the entrance for muddy boots) – there are lovely forest paths to the monument to the canal mogul, the 3rd Duke of Bridgewater, and northwards you can pick up the Ridgeway Path along the Chilterns escarpment to Ivinghoe Beacon. We have not yet heard from people who have stayed in the separate bedroom block. *(Recommended by Ian Phillips, Peter and Giff Bennett, J T Pearson, B and M Kendall, M A and C R Starling, Mike Turner, David and Ruth Shillitoe, Tim Maddison, Mr and Mrs M Dalby, Gordon Neighbour, Sean and Sharon Pines)*

Badger ~ Manager Nigel Wright ~ Real ale ~ Bar food (12-3, 6.30-9.30; not Sun or bank hol evenings) ~ Restaurant ~ (01442) 851228 ~ Children welcome ~ Dogs allowed in bar ~ Open 11-11; 12-10.30 Sun ~ Bedrooms: £55S/£65B

Valiant Trooper

Trooper Road (towards Aldbury Common); off B4506 N of Berkhamsted

On the edge of the village, this partly pink-painted and tiled pub began life as the Royal Oak, but changed its name to the Valiant Trooper in 1803 – the Duke of Wellington is said to have met his officers here to discuss tactics, and its traditional atmosphere and antique cavalry prints do well in conjuring up those days. The first room is beamed and tiled in red and black, and has built-in wall benches, a pew and small dining chairs around the attractive country tables, and a woodburning stove in the inglenook fireplace. The middle bar has spindleback chairs around the tables on its wooden floor, some exposed brickwork – and signs warning you to 'mind the step'. The far room has nice country kitchen chairs around individually chosen tables, and a brick fireplace. Generously served bar food includes filled baked potatoes or open sandwiches (£4.50), ciabatta sandwiches (£5), ploughman's (£5.50), and home-made daily specials such as soup (£3.50), crab and crayfish cocktail (£5.50), roasted vegetable and mushroom stroganoff (£8), steak and kidney pie (£9), chicken breast stuffed with feta, tomato and basil (£9.50), baked bass stuffed with garlic prawns (£11), sirloin steak with pepper or stilton sauce (£11) and fillet steak rossini (£15), with puddings such as chocolate and brandy torte (£3.75). The lounge bar is no smoking at lunchtime, and the restaurant is no smoking at all times. Well kept Fullers London Pride, Timothy Taylor Landlord and Morrells Oxford Blue, Tring Brewery and two guests from brewers such as Archer and Tring. Shove-ha'penny, dominoes, cribbage and bridge on Monday nights. The enclosed garden has a play house for children. *(Recommended by John Roots, David and Ruth Shillitoe, Brian Root, Colin McKerrow)*

Free house ~ Licensee Tim O'Gorman ~ Real ale ~ Bar food (12-2, 7-9; not Sun evening) ~ Restaurant ~ (01442) 851203 ~ Children in eating area of bar, restaurant and family room ~ Dogs allowed in bar ~ Open 11.30-11; 12-10.30 Sun

ARDELEY TL3027 Map 5

Jolly Waggoner

Village signposted off B1037 NE of Stevenage

'Lovely cosy pub, friendly staff: wish it was our local': readers continue to praise this pleasant, cream-washed dining pub, which is peacefully set in a pretty tucked-away village with thatched cottages ranged around the green. Using fresh local produce where possible, good imaginative food from the bar menu includes sandwiches (from £3), soup (£4.50), ploughman's (£6.50), home-made beefburgers topped with peppercorn sauce (£7), omelette filled with smoked haddock (£8), chicken and cashew nut salad (£10), chicken fillet with white wine, cream and garlic sauce (£12) and poached smoked haddock with cheese, spring onion and tomato sauce (£15), with changing specials such as dressed crab (£6.75/£9) and home-made steak and kidney pie (£9), wild mushroom, duck and parmesan pasta (£12), and rump steak with gorgonzola and smoked bacon sauce

(£12.50); more elaborate evening food also available. Full of nooks and crannies, the comfortable bar has a relaxed and civilised atmosphere, open woodwork and beams and a window overlooking the garden; the restaurant and (at lunchtime) the bar are no smoking, and they have darts. Decorated with modern prints, the restaurant has been extended into the cottage next door; they add a 10% service charge here, and booking is essential for their Sunday lunch. Well kept Greene King IPA tapped from the cask and Abbot on handpump, a decent range of wines and freshly squeezed orange juice in summer; the young staff are cheerful and unobtrusive. There may be piped music; £1 credit card surcharge for bills under £10. There's a pleasant garden and terrace; Cromer Windmill is nearby and Ardeley itself is a pleasant walk over fields from Benington. *(Recommended by Jill McLaren, Roger Everett, George Atkinson, Peter Shapland, Sharon and Alan Corper, Robert Turnham, Mrs Margo Finlay, Mr Kasprowski)*

Greene King ~ Tenant Darren Perkins ~ Real ale ~ Bar food (12-2, 6.30-9, not Sun evening or Mon except lunchtime bank hols) ~ Restaurant ~ (01438) 861350 ~ Children over 7 ~ Open 12-2.30(3 Sat), 6.30-11; 12-3, 7-10.30 Sun; closed Mon except lunchtime bank hols

ASHWELL TL2639 Map 5

Three Tuns

Off A505 NE of Baldock; High Street

In a delightful village full of enjoyable corners and buildings, including St Mary's church with its soaring tower, this pleasant flower-decked 18th-c hotel has a nicely old-fashioned atmosphere. It's popular with walkers at summer weekends, as the landscape around rolls enough to be interesting, and views on higher ground are far-ranging. There's an air of Victorian opulence in the cosy lounge with its relaxing chairs, big family tables, lots of pictures, stuffed pheasants and fish, and antiques. The simpler more modern public bar has pool, darts, cribbage, dominoes, a fruit machine, SkyTV, and Greene King IPA, Abbot and a guest on handpump, and there's a good choice of wines; piped light classical music. Served by friendly attentive staff, changing home-made bar food might include soup (£3.95), filled baguettes (from £3.95), chicken liver pâté (£4.50), devilled whitebait (£4.95), ploughman's (from £5.95), vegetarian pasta bake (£7.25), chicken, ham and mushroom pie (£8.95), nile perch fillet with tomato and herb sauce on rice with mixed peppers (£10.45), and roast partridge with stuffing and leek and mushroom sauce (£10.95; home-made puddings £4.55; no smoking dining room. The substantial shaded garden has boules, and picnic-sets under apple trees; lavatories are down a steep flight of steps. One of the six bedrooms has a four-poster bed, and another its own dressing room; we still have not heard from readers who have stayed here. *(Recommended by B and M Kendall, Gordon Neighbour, W W Burke, Mike Moden, Minda and Stanley Alexander)*

Greene King ~ Tenants Claire and Darrell Stanley ~ Real ale ~ Bar food (12-2.30, 6.30-9.30; all day Sat, Sun) ~ Restaurant ~ (01462) 742107 ~ Children in eating area of bar and restaurant ~ Dogs allowed in bar ~ Live entertainment Fri or Sat ~ Open 11-11; 12-10.30 Sun ~ Bedrooms: £39(£59B)/£59S(£69B)

BATFORD TL1415 Map 5

Gibraltar Castle

Lower Luton Road; B653, S of B652 junction

One area of this friendly, traditional low-beamed roadside pub on the north side of Harpenden gives way to soaring rafters and produces something of the feel of a hunting lodge. Throughout are glass cases housing an interesting collection of militaria including rifles, swords, medals, uniforms and bullets. The rest of the long carpeted bar has a pleasant old fireplace, comfortably cushioned wall benches, and a couple of snugly intimate window alcoves, one with a fine old clock. Well kept Fullers Chiswick, ESB, London Pride and a seasonal brew on handpump, a good range of malt whiskies, well made irish coffee, and a thoughtful choice of wines by the glass; board games and piped music. The tasty bar food varies according to season and might include lunchtime sandwiches (from £3.95), soup (£3.95), spinach and ricotta pancake (£5.25/£9.50), smoked salmon stuffed with prawns and seafood sauce (£5.95), steak and ale pie (£8.75), exotic fish according to availability (from £10), chicken and brie in ham with tarragon sauce (£10.25), rib-eye steak (£13.75), and home-made puddings (mostly £4.95); booking is recommended for their very popular good value Sunday roast (£8.95). There are tables and chairs on a new, safely enclosed decked back terrace, a few tables in front by the road, and pretty hanging baskets and tubs dotted around. *(Recommended by Martin and Karen Wake, Barry and Marie Males, Ian Phillips, Pat and Tony Martin, John Miles, MP)*

Fullers ~ Tenant Hamish Miller ~ Real ale ~ Bar food (12-2.30(3 Sun), 7-9, 12-4 Sun) ~ Restaurant ~ (01582) 460005 ~ Children in eating area of bar ~ Dogs welcome ~ Jam session Tues evening ~ Open 11.30-3, 5-11; 11.30-11 Sat; 12-10.30 Sun

CHAPMORE END TL3216 Map 5

Woodman

Off B158 Wadesmill—Bengeo; 300 yards W of A602 roundabout keep eyes skinned for discreet green sign to pub pointing up otherwise unmarked narrow lane; OS Sheet 166 map reference 328164

A haven of daytime tranquillity, this delightfully unspoilt early Victorian local is tucked away close to the duck pond of a small hamlet, and is popular with walkers and cyclists. The two little linked rooms have plain seats around stripped pub tables, flooring tiles or broad bare boards, log fires in period fireplaces, cheerful pictures for sale, lots of local notices, and darts on one side, with a piano (and a couple of squeeze boxes) on the other; shove-ha'penny, cribbage and dominoes. They have well kept Greene King IPA, Abbot, a house mix of the two, and a Greene King guest such as St Austell Triumph tapped from the cask, as well as five malt whiskies, and do a good choice of good value lunchtime sandwiches (from £2.35), warm baguettes (from £2.95), ciabattas (from £3.45), ploughman's (from £4.95), and a couple of daily dishes such as home-made soup, for example spicy parsnip or pea and ham (usually £3). From their very small kitchen they also manage to conjure up a simple Thursday evening meal giving one main dish such as home-made steak and kidney pudding (from £6.75) and a pudding or home-made ice-cream (from £3) – best to book ahead. Service is friendly and helpful, and in past seasons (when there's an R in the month) they've done monthly oyster nights. There are picnic-sets out in front under a couple of walnut trees; a bigger garden behind has boules and a good fenced play area; there are pet rabbits in the garden as well as a pub cat. The car park has little room. *(Recommended by Ian Arthur, Karen Horton, Gordon Neighbour)*

Greene King ~ Tenants Drs D R Davis and A C Yates ~ Real ale ~ Bar food (lunchtime and Thurs evening) ~ No credit cards ~ (01920) 463143 ~ Dogs welcome ~ Open 12-3, 6-11(5.30-11 Fri); 12-11 Sat; 12-10.30 Sun

COTTERED TL3129 Map 5

Bull

A507 W of Buntingford

Just across from this old tree-surrounded inn stands a row of pretty thatched cottages, and benches and tables in the attractive big garden make the best of the setting. The airy low-beamed front lounge is nicely laid out and well looked after, with polished antiques on a stripped wood floor, and a good fire. A second bar has darts, a fruit machine, shove-ha'penny, cribbage and dominoes; unobtrusive piped music. They have well kept Greene King IPA and Abbot on handpump, and decent wines. At lunchtime thoughtfully presented bar food includes sandwiches (from £3), home-made burgers, filled baked potatoes or ploughman's (from £6), omelettes (£6.95), steak, Guinness and stilton pie (£9), chicken in a cream, wine and garlic sauce (£12), salmon fillet with cheese and mushroom sauce (£12) and fillet of beef (£15). In the evening the same dishes are about 50p more expensive, and the menu is slightly longer; specials include dressed crab (£6/£9), home-made steak and kidney pie (£9), breast of duck with honey and mustard glaze (£12) and fresh smoked haddock in cheese, prawn and spring onion sauce (£12); puddings (£4.75); £1 surcharge for credit card bills under £10; friendly and obliging service; no smoking dining area. The church has a huge 14th-c wall painting of St Christopher. *(Recommended by Peter and Joan Elbra, Michael Dandy, Adele Summers, Alan Black, Tony Beaulah)*

Greene King ~ Tenant Darren Perkins ~ Real ale ~ Bar food (12-2, 6.30-9; closed Tues evening) ~ Restaurant ~ (01763) 281243 ~ Children over 7 ~ Open 12-2.30(3 Sat), 6.30-11; 12-3, 7-10.30 Sun

FRITHSDEN TL0110 Map 5

Alford Arms

From Berkhamsted take unmarked road towards Potten End, pass Potten End turn on right, then take next left towards Ashridge College

Hertfordshire Dining Pub of the Year

Qualifying for our Food Award for the second year, this is the county's leading food pub, so booking at the weekend is essential. It's pleasantly secluded though by no means undiscovered, by a village green and surrounded by National Trust woodland (with plenty of possibilities for walkers). Fashionably refurbished by thoughtful licensees, this is an elegantly casual place for a very good meal out. The interior has simple prints on pale cream walls, with areas picked out in blocks of Victorian green or dark red, and an appealing mix of good furniture from Georgian chairs to old commode stands on bare boards and patterned quarry tiles. It's all pulled together by luxurious richly patterned curtains. Very good and successfully innovative bar food is served by charming staff, and might include rustic bread with roast garlic and balsamic olive oil (£3.50), soup (£4), chestnut mushroom, wild garlic and ricotta tart (£5.75), oak-smoked bacon on bubble and squeak with hollandaise sauce and poached egg (£6.25/£11.50), fettuccine with asparagus and artichoke (£9.75), smoked haddock on mash with mustard sauce and poached egg (£11.75), grilled scotch rib-eye steak with chips and home-made ketchup (£13.25); extra vegetables (from £2.50), and puddings such as bread pudding with clotted cream (£4.50) and treacle and hazelnut tart (£4.75); good sweet wines. Smoking is allowed throughout. Well kept Brakspears, Flowers Original, Marstons Pedigree and Morrells Oxford Blue on handpump; piped jazz, darts. They have plenty of tables out in front. *(Recommended by Keith James, Mike Turner, Howard Dell, Bob and Maggie Atherton, Jack and Jill Gilbert, John Hale, Edmund Coan, D B)*

Enterprise ~ Lease Becky and David Salisbury ~ Real ale ~ Bar food (12-2.30(3 Sun), 7-10) ~ Restaurant ~ (01442) 864480 ~ Children in eating area of bar and restaurant ~ Dogs allowed in bar ~ Open 11-11; 12-10.30 Sun

HERTFORD TL3212 Map 5

White Horse £

Castle Street

The emphasis in this little-changed, unpretentious town-centre pub is firmly on its impressive range of perfectly kept beers. Even though it's a tied house, the choice can vary from day to day, but you can expect to find beers from brewers such as Abbey Ales, RCH, Sharps and Teignworthy, alongside the Adnams and Fullers London Pride, Chiswick and ESB – so no need to worry if you can't make it here for their May or August bank holiday beer festivals. They also keep around 20 country wines. Parts of the building are 14th-c, and you can still see Tudor brickwork in the three quietly cosy no smoking rooms upstairs. Downstairs, the two main rooms are small and homely. The one on the left is more basic, with some brewery memorabilia, bare boards, and a few rather well worn tables, stools and chairs; an open fire separates it from the more comfortable right-hand bar, which has a cosily tatty armchair, some old local photographs, beams and timbers, and a red-tiled floor. Service can be quite chatty, and though it's quite a locals' pub, visitors are made to feel welcome; bar billiards, darts, shove-ha'penny, shut the box, cribbage and dominoes. The pub faces the castle, and there are two benches on the street outside. Very good value bar food (lunchtime only) includes sandwiches (from £2.45), home-made soup (£2.50), filled baguettes (from £3.35), as well as hot dishes such as vegetarian lasagne (£4.50) and prawn thermidor or steak and kidney pie (£4.95). On Sunday they do a two-course lunch for £6.50, three courses for £7, and on Monday evenings they do a White Horse Gastronomic Tour, with one exotic dish such as curry for £5; no children's meals. More reports please. *(Recommended by Ian Arthur, Brian and Rosalie Laverick, Steve Nye, Pat and Tony Martin)*

Fullers ~ Tenant Nigel Crofts ~ Real ale ~ Bar food (lunchtime and Mon 6-8) ~ (01992) 501950 ~ Well supervised children in upstairs family room ~ Dogs welcome ~ Open 12-2.30, 5.30-11; 12-11(10.30 Sun) Fri-Sat

POTTERS CROUCH TL1105 Map 5

Holly Bush £

2¼ miles from M25 junction 21A: A405 towards St Albans, then first left, then after a mile turn left (ie away from Chiswell Green), then at T junction turn right into Blunts Lane; can also be reached fairly quickly, with a good map, from M1 exits 6 and 8 (and even M10)

On a warm day, the garden here is an idyllic spot for a drink and a light lunch. You wouldn't know it inside this welcoming and beautifully kept country pub, but it is actually surrounded (at some distance) by three motorways, so it makes a really handy place to break a journey, and relax in delightful surroundings. The meticulously furnished bar has an elegantly timeless feel, and it's not the kind of place where you'll find fruit machines or piped music. Everything is spotless, and shows unusually dedicated attention to detail. Thoughtfully positioned fixtures create the illusion that there are lots of different rooms – some of which you might expect to find in a smart country house. In the evenings, neatly placed candles cast shadows over the mix of darkly gleaming varnished tables, all of which have fresh flowers, and china plates as ashtrays. There are quite a few antique dressers, several with plates on, a number of comfortably cushioned settles, the odd plant, a fox's mask, some antlers, a fine old clock, carefully lit prints and pictures, daily papers, and on the left as you go in a big fireplace. The long, stepped bar counter has particularly well kept Fullers Chiswick, ESB, London Pride and the Fullers seasonal beer on handpump, and the sort of reassuringly old-fashioned till you hardly ever see in this hi-tech age. Service is calm and efficient even when they're busy. Straightforward, freshly prepared bar food from a fairly short menu is served lunchtimes only (not Sunday), from a menu that includes sandwiches (from £2.50), burgers (from £3.90), filled baked potatoes (from £4.40), ploughman's (from £5.30), home-made chilli or very good and generously sized platters such as meat or fish, both with salad (from £5.80), apple pie (£2.60) and chocolate fudge cake (£2.70). Behind the pretty wisteria-covered white cottagey building, the fenced-off garden has a nice lawn, handsome trees, and sturdy picnic-sets – a very pleasant place to sit in summer. No smoking at the bar counters. Though the pub seems to stand alone on a quiet little road, it's only a few minutes from the centre of St Albans, and is very handy for the Gardens of the Rose. *(Recommended by Jill McLaren, LM, Ian Phillips, Peter and Giff Bennett, John and Joyce Snell, Alan Cole, Kirstie Bruce, Brian and Rosalie Laverick)*

Fullers ~ Tenant R S Taylor ~ Real ale ~ Bar food (lunchtime only, not Sun) ~ (01727) 851792 ~ Open 11.30-2.30, 6-11; 12-2.30, 7-10.30 Sun

Post Office address codings confusingly give the impression that some pubs are in Hertfordshire, when they're really in Bedfordshire or Cambridgeshire (which is where we list them).

ROYSTON TL3540 Map 5

Old Bull

High Street, off central A10 one-way system – has own car park, or use central car park

This handsome bow-fronted early Georgian inn looks out over a sunny paved former coachyard with stylish modern tables and chairs, and outdoor heaters, tucked peacefully away from the traffic. The roomy and civilised high-beamed bar, with handsome fireplaces, big pictures and rather fine flooring, has easy chairs, a leather sofa and a table of papers and magazines (and ready-to-pour coffee) at the entrance end with the bar counter, and further in is more set out for eating. Enjoyable bar food includes sandwiches (from £2.95), soup (£3.50), roast beef in yorkshire pudding (£5.95), mushroom stroganoff or whole plaice (£6.95) and home-made puddings such as bread and butter pudding (£3.45). There is a separate more formal restaurant. They have well kept Greene King IPA, Triumph and Old Speckled Hen on handpump, and decent wines by the glass, and the atmosphere is chatty and relaxed; bar service is very professional, in the best old style, and the piped music is fairly unobtrusive; no smoking area in bar. We have not yet heard from any readers who have stayed here (the 11 bedrooms have their own bathrooms). *(Recommended by M R D Foot, Conor McGaughey)*

Greene King ~ Lease Peter Nightingale ~ Real ale ~ Bar food (12-2.30(8 Sun), 6.30-9.30) ~ Restaurant ~ (01763) 2422003 ~ Children welcome away from bar ~ Open 11-11; 12-10.30 Sun ~ Bedrooms: £75B/£85B

SARRATT TQ0499 Map 5

Boot

The Green

This delightful old tiled building faces one of the longest village greens in the country, and has an old-fashioned black wrought-iron bench and picnic-sets under a pair of pollarded century-old lime trees. The nice unspoilt feel is given a real boost by the cheery landlord and his staff, who are really out to please. Coming in generous helpings, blackboard bar meals might include soup (£3.75), good filling sandwiches (from £4.65), battered fish (£8.25), salmon and seafood bake, steak and kidney pie or navarin of lamb (£8.25), and prawn or crayfish salad (£10.25). They also have a more elaborate bistro-style restaurant menu, including fresh fish and seasonal game, on Wednesday to Saturday evenings; the supper room is no smoking. The cosy bar has a beamed ceiling, assorted traditional furniture, part-panelled walls, and a fine early 18th-c inglenook fireplace with a blazing log fire. Greene King IPA, Abbot, Speckled Hen and Ruddles County are well kept on handpump; darts, cribbage, dominoes, fruit machine and piped music. A pretty, sheltered lawn has a children's play area, and more tables among roses, fruit trees and a weeping willow. From here footpaths take you down into the Chess Valley and link the rewarding villages of Chenies and Latimer. *(Recommended by Iain and Joan Baillie, John and Glenys Wheeler, Peter Saville, Barry and Anne, Clare and Peter Pearse, Tracey and Stephen Groves)*

Free house ~ Licensee Richard Jones ~ Real ale ~ Bar food (lunchtime only) ~ Restaurant ~ (01923) 262247 ~ Children in eating area of bar and restaurant ~ Open 11.45-3, 5.30-11; 12-10.30 Sun

Cock

Church End: a very pretty approach is via North Hill, a lane N off A404, just under a mile W of A405

The latched door to this cosy cream-painted 17th-c country pub opens into a carpeted snug with a vaulted ceiling, original bread oven, and a cluster of bar stools. Through an archway, the partly oak-panelled cream-walled lounge has a lovely log fire in an inglenook, pretty Liberty-style curtains, pink plush chairs at dark oak tables, and lots of interesting artefacts and pictures of cocks; piped music, and well kept Badger Best, Sussex, Tanglefoot and a Badger guest; fruit machine and TV. Bar food includes soup (£3.50), sandwiches (from (£4.95), ham, egg and chips (£7.95), beef and ale pie (£8.75), spinach and red pepper lasagne (£9.25) with blackboard specials such as sardines in garlic and rosemary (£9.95) and bass (£10.75) and puddings such as profiteroles or crème brûlée (£3.95). The no smoking restaurant is in a nicely converted barn. In front, picnic-sets look out across a quiet lane towards the churchyard, the terrace at the back gives open country views, and a pretty, sheltered lawn has tables under parasols, with a children's play area. *(Recommended by John Hale, Stan Edwards, Peter and Giff Bennett, Ian Phillips, Jarrod and Wendy Hopkinson, Tony Radnor, Julie Ryan)*

Badger ~ Manager Nick Clarke ~ Real ale ~ Bar food (12-2.30, 6-9.30) ~ Restaurant ~ (01923) 282908 ~ Children in restaurant ~ Dogs allowed in bar ~ Open 12-11; 12-10.30 Sun

LUCKY DIP

Besides the fully inspected pubs, you might like to try these Lucky Dips recommended to us and described by readers (if you do, please send us reports: www.goodguides.co.uk).

ABBOTS LANGLEY TL0901
Compasses [Tibbs Hill Rd]: Tidy pleasantly modernised local with good choice of good value food in bar or small dining area, well kept beers, friendly efficient staff; tables on verandah-style back deck *(Stan Edwards)*

AYOT GREEN TL2213
☆ *Waggoners* [off B197 S of Welwyn]: Friendly pub with three cosy areas: low-ceilinged bar, bigger comfortably furnished extension, and nicely set out eating area with proper napkins; good enterprising food inc lunchtime bar snacks, three-course meals and Sun roasts, friendly knowledgeable service, six changing real ales; attractive and spacious suntrap back garden with sheltered terrace and play area (some noise from A1M), dogs must be on a lead, wooded walks nearby, open all day *(BB, John and Joyce Snell)*

AYOT ST LAWRENCE TL1916
☆ *Brocket Arms* [off B651 N of St Albans]: Peacefully set 14th-c pub, highly individual, two simple old-fashioned low-beamed rooms, logs blazing in big inglenook, a dozen or so wines by the glass, Greene King IPA and Abbot and others such as Hop Back Summer Lightning and Wadworths 6X, traditional games, lunchtime bar food from sandwiches to game pie (can be very long waits if busy), may be wider choice in no smoking evening restaurant, informal service; piped classical music; children welcome, nice suntrap walled garden with outside bar and play area, bedrooms, handy for Shaw's Corner, open all day *(LYM, Barry and Marie Males, Ian Phillips, Giles and Annie Francis, Alistair and Kay Butler, Tim Maddison, R F Ballinger, Peter Abbott)*

BARKWAY TL3834
Tally Ho [London Rd]: Flower-decked pub with daily papers, small open fire, clocks, brasses and pump clips in smart comfortable bar, two or three interesting changing ales from small breweries tapped from the cask, plenty to read on the walls, no music or machines, welcoming landlord, landlady doing enjoyable home-made food possibly using fruit from the tidy garden, which has picnic-sets *(Richard C Morgan, D H Burchett, Kevin Thorpe)*

BRAGBURY END TL2621
Chequers: Comfortably refurbished Vintage Inn with low-beamed rooms off central bar, Adnams and Bass, 19 wines by the glass, decent up-to-date food, quick friendly service, inglenook log fire; piped music; picnic-sets in big garden *(Michael Dandy)*

BRAUGHING TL3925
Axe & Compass [just off B1368; The Street]: Drive through a ford to reach this simple unspoilt country local; two roomy and pleasant bars (one an unusual corner-shape) and restaurant, enjoyable straightforward food, well kept beers, charming landlord, friendly service; well behaved dogs and children welcome, pretty village *(Joy Kitchener-Williams)*

BRICKET WOOD TL1502
Moor Mill [off Smug Oak Lane – turn at Gate pub]: Attractive 18th-c restored watermill, now a neatly kept two-floor chain eating pub, with decent food from baguettes up, Flowers Original and Fullers London Pride, good wine choice, central working wheel, beams, brick walls and flagstones, oak tables and comfortable chairs; piped music can be loud, queues may build up for service; plenty of octagonal picnic-sets in big waterside garden with play area, ducks and swan, stable adjoining adjacent Travel Inn, open all day *(O K Smyth, LYM, Ian Phillips)*

BROOKMANS PARK TL2504
Cock o' the North [Great North Rd (A1000, Bell Bar)]: Handy modern dining pub with wide choice of good value dependable food, quick friendly service, McMullens real ale, pleasant décor with paintings and prints, well spaced pine tables *(Robert F Smith, B and M Kendall)*

CHORLEYWOOD TQ0294
Land of Liberty Peace & Plenty [Long Lane, Heronsgate; just off M25, junction 17]: Very wide choice of modestly priced home-made food, also well kept Tring, Youngs and a guest

beer such as Shepherd Neame Early Bird, obliging service, new banquettes and bric-a-brac *(Comus and Sarah Elliott, Tracey and Stephen Groves)*

Rose & Crown [Common Rd, not far from M25 junction 18]: Cheerful unpretentious pub in cottage terrace, pretty setting facing common, well kept Fullers London Pride, sofa and oak settles in compact bar with homely old-fashioned atmosphere (labradors dozing by the log fire), good freshly made food in small no smoking dining room, pleasant staff; quiet piped music; bedrooms *(Herbert Chappell)*

Stag [Long Lane/Heronsgate Rd]: Smart pub doing well under current go-ahead management, well kept McMullens ales, wide food range inc interesting dishes, friendly attentive staff, candlelit tables, chatty civilised atmosphere, attractive open-plan layout giving feel of separate areas, large no smoking dining conservatory; tables on back lawn, play area, good walks, open all day *(Paul A Moore, Tracey and Stephen Groves)*

COLNEY HEATH TL2007

Plough [just off back rd N, between A414 St Albans—Hatfield and A1057]: Popular and reliable pleasantly refurbished 18th-c low-beamed local, warm and cosy at front with good log fire and small dining area, good value generous homely food (lunchtime Mon-Sat, and Fri/Sat evening), well kept Greene King Abbot, Fullers London Pride and Tetleys, friendly efficient staff; garden overlooking fields *(John Cadge, Brian and Rosalie Laverick, Monica Cockburn, Mike Jefferies)*

DATCHWORTH TL2717

☆ ***Horns*** [Bramfield Rd]: Appealing flower-decked weatherboarded Tudor pub facing small green, low beams and big inglenook one end, high rafters and rugs on patterned bricks the other, attractive décor, good food, friendly efficient staff, well kept real ales; tables out on crazy-paved terrace among roses *(LYM, J B Young)*

ELSTREE TQ1697

Battleaxes [Butterfly Lane]: Popular chain family dining pub with wide range of attractively priced food in bar and conservatory, well kept Marstons Pedigree; garden tables *(Stan Edwards)*

EPPING GREEN TL2906

☆ ***Beehive*** [back rd Cuffley—Little Berkhamsted]: Cosy and popular local, comfortable beamed dining area on left, huge choice of good value generous fresh food esp fish, friendly efficient staff, Greene King and a guest beer; garden seats overlooking fields *(Peter and Margaret Glenister)*

FLAUNDEN TL0100

☆ ***Bricklayers Arms*** [off A41; Hogpits Bottom]: Cottagey country pub under new owners, low beams, log fire, timbered stub walls, attractive décor, enjoyable bar food from sandwiches up lunchtime and Mon/Tues evenings, restaurant meals other evenings, good friendly atmosphere, well kept Fullers London Pride and Greene King IPA, Triumph and Old Speckled Hen, good choice of wines by the glass, no piped music; children in eating areas, nice old-fashioned garden, nearby walks *(LYM, Jill McLaren, Jarrod and Wendy Hopkinson)*

Green Dragon: Nicely refurbished, attractive and comfortable, with partly panelled extended lounge, small back restaurant area and traditional 17th-c small tap bar, good choice of food inc popular Sun lunch, well kept Greene King IPA and Abbot and guest beers, darts and shove-ha'penny; piped music may obtrude; charming well kept garden with summer-house, pretty village, only a short diversion from Chess Valley Walk *(LYM, C Galloway)*

GREAT OFFLEY TL1427

☆ ***Green Man*** [signed off A505 Luton—Hitchin; High St]: Roomy, comfortable and attractive Chef & Brewer family dining pub with peaceful country view from large flagstoned conservatory, picnic-sets on pleasant back terrace and garden; very wide choice of enjoyable food, good helpful service even when busy, well kept Courage Directors, blazing log fires; may be unobtrusive piped classical music; front play area, striking inn-sign, open all day *(LYM, Keith and Janet Morris, B and M Kendall)*

HALLS GREEN TL2728

Rising Sun [NW of Stevenage; from A1(M) junction 9 follow Weston signs off B197, then left in village, right by duck pond]: Convivial 18th-c beamed country pub with good value generous food in bar or pleasant conservatory restaurant inc special evenings (booking recommended wknds), well kept Bass, Courage and McMullens ales, friendly informal service, big log fire in small lounge; good big family garden with terrace, summer barbecues, boules and play area *(Mark Barker)*

HARPENDEN TL1413

☆ ***Carpenters Arms*** [Cravells Rd]: Cosy and welcoming, with chatty landlord, friendly efficient staff, cheap generous uncomplicated home cooking from good doorstep sandwiches up, well kept Greene King and a guest beer, open fire, lovingly collected car memorabilia inc models and overseas number-plates, special issue bottled beers; neat well planned terrace garden *(Monica Cockburn, Mike Jefferies)*

Cross Keys [High St]: Likeable compact pub with Fullers London Pride, lovely flagstones, log fire; garden *(Conor McGaughey)*

Rose & Crown [Southdown Rd]: Friendly young landlady and chef/landlord doing enjoyable lunchtime food inc omelettes and home-made pizzas, popular more inventive evening dishes, well kept Fullers London Pride, good service, woody interior; attractive conservatory, plenty of tables in garden beyond *(D L Johnson)*

Skew Bridge [Southdown Rd]: Welcoming, with no smoking area, good range of drinks and of well cooked food, no music; children welcome, nice small garden with attractive hanging baskets *(Jill McLaren)*

HEMEL HEMPSTEAD TL0411

☆ *Crown & Sceptre* [Bridens Camp; leaving on A4146, right at Flamstead/Markyate sign opp Red Lion]: Classic country pub, cheerful and cosy communicating rooms, some oak panelling, antique settles among more usual seating, good value filling food from wide range of sandwiches and baguettes up, well kept Adnams Broadside, Greene King IPA and Abbot and a guest such as Hook Norton Haymaker, friendly staff, log fires; darts and dominoes, children and dogs welcome; garden with play area, chickens, rabbits and scarecrow, heated front picnic-sets, good walks; open all day summer wknds *(LYM, R T and J C Moggridge, Ian Phillips)*

HERTFORD TL3213

Baroosh [Fore St]: Stylish modern café/bar in former bank, good conversion by McMullens the local brewery, their real ales, very good wine choice, friendly attentive young staff, good modern food *(Pat and Tony Martin)*

Hillside [Port Hill, Bengeo (B158)]: Latest reincarnation of much-changed pub, now entirely no smoking, with stripped beams and brickwork, leather sofas around log fire, two northern real ales on electric pump, side dining room with chunky scrubbed tables and simple décor, interesting modern cooking (service charge added), children welcome, barn delicatessen; open all day wknds, cl Mon *(anon)*

Salisbury Arms [Fore St]: Relaxing olde-worlde hotel lounge, well kept McMullens inc AK Mild, efficient cheerful service, reasonably priced food; splendid Jacobean staircase to nice bedrooms *(Robert F Smith)*

HEXTON TL1230

Raven [signed off B655]: Large recently refurbished 1920s family dining pub, four neat areas inc long tidy public bar (open fire, pool one end), extensive no smoking areas, plenty of dining tables, oil paintings (some for sale); wide range of good value food from baguettes and baked potatoes up, two children's menus, well kept ales inc Fullers London Pride and Greene King IPA and Old Speckled Hen, quick friendly service; piped music, bar can be rather smoky; children welcome, big garden with heated terrace, barbecue, well segregated play area *(Phil and Heidi Cook, Michael Dandy)*

HIGH WYCH TL4614

Rising Sun: Cosy unspoilt local, serving hatch to carpeted lounge with coal or log fire, central area with Courage Best and good guest beers tapped from casks behind the counter, friendly landlord and locals, bare-boards games room (children allowed) with darts and woodburner; no food, no mobile phones or pagers, no music; tables in small garden *(the Didler, Pete Baker)*

HODDESDON TL3808

Fish & Eels [Dobbs Weir]: Spacious Vintage Inn prettily placed opp weir on River Lea, flagstones, cosy corners and several open fires, usual decent food inc huge sandwiches, Bass and Tetleys, well trained attentive staff, no smoking areas; quiet piped music; garden with play area and moorings, nature reserve behind, long river walks, handy for Rye House *(Len Banister, Bill Sykes)*

KIMPTON TL1718

White Horse [High St]: Pleasantly extended around low-roofed half-timbered core, warm welcome, decent food inc seafood and fresh fish, real ales such as Bass, Courage Directors and McMullens AK Mild *(John and Joyce Snell)*

KNEBWORTH TL2320

☆ *Lytton Arms* [Park Lane, Old Knebworth]: Several spotless big-windowed rooms around large central servery, helpful friendly service, well kept Fullers London Pride, Woodfordes Wherry and half a dozen or more changing beers from small breweries, two farm ciders, good value food from sandwiches and ciabattas up, no smoking conservatory, daily papers; children welcome, picnic-sets on front terrace, back garden with play area, open all day wknds *(LYM, Bruce Bird, John Saville, Dr P C Rea)*

LILLEY TL1126

Lilley Arms [West St; off A505 NE of Luton]: Friendly attractively placed village pub with enjoyable wide-ranging home-made food in largely no smoking dining lounge, well kept Greene King IPA and Abbot, flame-effect gas fire, smaller public bar with small games room, tables in garden; bedrooms *(Phil and Heidi Cook)*

LITTLE BERKHAMSTED TL2908

Five Horseshoes [Church Rd]: Attractive Chef & Brewer nr church, 17th-c beams and stripped brickwork, two log fires, well kept Courage Best and Directors and a guest beer, decent wines, good generous food choice from sandwiches and baguettes up, quick friendly service even on busy evenings; comfortable restaurant, cosy little attic room for private dinners; garden with picnic-sets, busy in summer, attractive countryside *(Peter and Margaret Glenister)*

LITTLE HADHAM TL4322

Nags Head [Hadham Ford, towards Much Hadham]: 16th-c country dining pub with small linked heavily black-beamed rooms, three well kept Greene King beers tapped from the cask in small bar, decent house wines, freshly squeezed orange juice, no smoking restaurant down a couple of steps; children in eating areas, tables in pleasant garden *(Gordon Neighbour, LYM, B N F and M Parkin, Charles Gysin)*

LONDON COLNEY TL1803

☆ *Green Dragon* [Waterside; just off main st by bridge at S end]: Friendly and neatly kept, with good value generous food (not Sun), lots of ancient timbers, beams and brasses, soft lighting, well kept changing ales such as Adnams, Fullers London Pride and Shepherd Neame Spitfire, decent wine, woodburner, separate dining room; prettily set riverside picnic-sets *(Ian Phillips, LYM)*

MILL GREEN TL2409

Green Man: Quiet rustic-feeling pub with four well kept ales inc two guest beers, enjoyable food, two log fires; good big garden *(Don Gladstone)*

NEWGATE STREET TL3005

Crown: Attractive flower-decked building with colourful garden, cosy inside, with friendly staff, good varied food esp fresh fish, well kept Greene King IPA and Abbot, good house wine; handy for walks in Northaw Great Wood *(Peter and Margaret Glenister)*

NUTHAMPSTEAD TL4134

☆ ***Woodman*** [off B1368 S of Barkway]: Tucked-away newly extended thatched and weatherboarded village pub, welcoming and well run, sofa and other furnishings in comfortable unspoilt bar with worn tiled floor, nice inglenook log fire, another fire opposite and 17th-c low beams and timbers, old local photographs, enjoyable home-made food (not Sun evening), efficient friendly service, dining room, no music; interesting USAF memorabilia (nearby World War II airfield), inc a memorial outside; benches out overlooking tranquil lane, comfortable bedrooms, open all day Sat *(BB, M R D Foot, Kevin Thorpe, Jim and Maggie Cowell)*

PERRY GREEN TL4317

☆ ***Hoops*** [off B1004 Widford—Much Hadham]: Village pub opp Henry Moore Foundation (guided tours in summer by appt), stripped brick, terracotta walls, beams, standing timbers and inglenook, friendly attentive staff, food from sandwiches to all-day Sun lunch, Fullers London Pride, Greene King IPA and a guest beer, cosy no smoking dining area (children allowed); garden tables, some under awnings, open all day Sun *(Dr P C Rea, Hugh Roberts, LYM, M A and C R Starling, George Atkinson, Mrs Margo Finlay, Mr Kasprowski)*

PRESTON TL1824

☆ ***Red Lion*** [The Green]: Lively and popular village-owned local, very neatly kept, with enjoyable home-made food from fresh sandwiches and baguettes to game, fish and choice of Sun roasts, five well kept changing ales such as Greene King IPA and Oakham JHB, very friendly service, log fire; picnic-sets in neatly kept gardens front and back, local cricket HQ *(Barry and Marie Males, Alison Jeffers, Richard Beharrell, John and Joyce Snell, Steve Nye)*

REDBOURN TL1011

Hollybush [Church End]: Quaint white-fronted old pub in pretty spot nr medieval church, cosy old-fashioned lounge with big brick open fire, black beams, heavy wooden doors, bigger public bar with built-in settles, cask tables, well kept changing ales, bar food; pool, machines; tables in sunny garden (some M1 noise) *(Brian and Rosalie Laverick)*

REED TL3636

Cabinet [off A10; High St]: 16th-c weatherboarded pub housing attractive upmarket no smoking restaurant (enjoyable food but restaurant prices, with service charge on top), very small bar with inglenook log fire, well kept Adnams, Greene King IPA and a guest beer, attentive somewhat effusive staff; piped music; charming big garden with pond *(LYM, George Atkinson)*

SHENLEY TL1801

Black Lion [B5378]: Spick and span and welcoming, with enjoyable good value food esp sausages, Tues curry night, pleasant young staff, smoking and no smoking eating areas, conservatory, children's area; big garden, bedrooms planned *(Diana Marsh)*

ST ALBANS TL1507

Cross Keys [Chequer St]: Popular L-shaped Wetherspoons, their usual menu, eight real ales, good wine choice, great prices, helpful speedy staff, nice furnishings and décor; open all day *(Peter Abbott, Craig Turnbull)*

Farmers Boy [London Rd]: Bustling unpretentious bay-windowed pub with back brewery producing Verulam IPA, Farmers Joy and a monthly special (ask for a taster), also their own lager and ten continental bottled beers, lots of old prints on smoke-effect walls, imposing clock, real fire, back open kitchen serving straightforward food from sandwiches and baked potatoes up all day, helpful staff, two large friendly dogs; can be a bit smoky, SkyTV; open all day, plenty of suntrap tables out behind *(the Didler, Brian and Rosalie Laverick)*

Farriers Arms [Lower Dagnall St]: Plain and welcoming two-bar local where the Campaign for Real Ale started in the early 1970s, well kept McMullens inc Mild and guest beers, bar food wkdys, lots of old pictures of the pub; in no-frills old part *(the Didler, Ian Arthur, John Kearins)*

Goat [Sopwell Lane, off Holywell Hill]: Neatly modernised rambling areas around central servery, traditional wooden furnishings, open fire, cheery atmosphere, decent food, friendly staff, several real ales, good range of malt whiskies, popular darts, dominoes and quiz night; games machines, piped music; children in eating area, tables in neat back garden, open all day *(LYM, Peter Abbott)*

Lower Red Lion [Fishpool St]: Convivial two-bar local dating from 17th c, relaxing chatty atmosphere, interesting changing range of well kept beers, imported beers on tap and in bottle, May Day and Aug bank hol beer festivals, home-made food, log fire, red plush seats and carpet; open all day Sat, tables in good-sized back garden, pleasant bedrooms *(the Didler, John Kearins, Steve Nye)*

☆ ***Plough*** [Tyttenhanger Green; off A414 E]: Spacious and friendly village pub, good-humoured licensees, young staff polite and prompt even when it's packed, lovely longcase clock, good log fire, well kept changing ales, good value straightforward food, fine collection of old beer bottles, other bric-a-brac; conservatory, big garden with play area *(LYM, the Didler, Peter Abbott, Monica Cockburn, Mike Jefferies)*

☆ ***Rose & Crown*** [St Michaels St]: Busy 400-year-old beamed town pub with uneven timbered walls covered with American landlord's impressive collection of sporting memorabilia, big log fire, dominoes, cribbage and darts, Adnams, Fullers London Pride, Tetleys and a guest beer, great speciality american-style sandwiches (not cheap ones) and other pub standards (lunchtime, not Sun), family room (no smoking at lunchtime); live music Mon/Thurs evenings; lots of tables and benches outside, pretty floral and ivy-hung back yard, handy for Roman Verulam Museum *(LYM, the Didler, Ian Phillips)*

☆ ***Six Bells*** [St Michaels St]: Well kept rambling food pub, well kept ales such as Adnams, Fullers London Pride and Tetleys, cheerful helpful service even when bustling with locals, thriving civilised atmosphere, big helpings of good value freshly made food from sandwiches up, wider evening choice, low beams and timbers, log fire, quieter no smoking panelled dining room; children welcome, family room, occasional barbecues in small back garden, open all day Fri-Sun *(Mike and Jennifer Marsh, LYM, J Silverman, Ian Phillips, Michael and Alison Sandy)*

Tudor [George St]: Ancient pub with pleasant décor, mainstream ales, decent wines and food – upstairs restaurant *(J S Rutter)*

White Hart Tap [Keyfield, round corner from Garibaldi]: Small but friendly white-panelled Victorian pub, clean and tidy, with reliably well kept real ales, good value quickly served lunchtime food and Weds night special, effective air filtering; live band Tues, tables outside, open all day *(Derek Field, John Kearins)*

STEVENAGE TL2324

Marquis of Lorne [High St]: Friendly old pub in original part of town, well kept Greene King and interesting guest beers, bar food; tables outside *(Richard Houghton)*

STOCKING PELHAM TL4529

Cock: Ancient thatched village pub with enjoyable snacks and meals, good drinks choice, friendly staff *(Mr and Mrs R A Buckler)*

TEWIN TL2715

☆ ***Plume of Feathers*** [signed off B1000 NE of Welwyn; Upper Green Rd, N end of village]: Appealing country pub with hands-on chef/landlord doing consistently good fresh seasonal food and baking interesting breads, regular theme nights, friendly staff, attractive and individual layout with roomy dining area and plenty of space for drinkers, well kept Greene King ales, good coffee and decent wines; garden tables *(LYM, Frazer and Louise Smith, C S and Jane Greening)*

THERFIELD TL3336

☆ ***Fox & Duck*** [signed off A10 S of Royston; The Green]: Open-plan bow-windowed pub upgraded with country chairs and big stripped-top dark tables on new stone flooring, interesting food inc seasonal game and some thai dishes, well kept Greene King IPA, Ruddles County and Old Speckled Hen, decent wines and coffee, courteous staff, good-sized carpeted back restaurant, darts in smaller boarded area on left (with TV and fruit machine); may be piped pop music; bedrooms with own bathrooms, a few picnic-sets in garden with good play equipment, more out on front green, quiet village, pleasant walks nearby *(Pat and Tony Hinkins, Morris and Jenny Le Fleming, BB)*

TRING SP9211

Kings Arms [King St]: Green décor, pine and pews, simple wholesome home cooking (lunchtime emphasis on this, can phone order ahead) from hot baps up, ethnic and vegetarian leanings, five well kept changing ales usually inc local Tring brews and Wadworths 6X direct from the brewers, no smoking area; busy with young people evenings *(DM, Tony Hobden)*

Robin Hood [Brook St (B486)]: Olde-worlde Fullers local with wide food choice, several small drinking areas, three well kept Fullers beers, comfortable settles, lots of dark wood, slight nautical theme, dining conservatory with woodburner and random collection of prints; piped music; no children or dogs inside, tables on small pleasant back terrace, free public car park nearby *(John Branston, MP, BB, Tony Hobden, DM)*

WATTON-AT-STONE TL3019

George & Dragon [High St (B1001)]: Appealingly furnished country dining pub with interesting mix of antique and modern prints on partly timbered walls, big inglenook fireplace, well kept Greene King IPA and Abbot and a guest beer, decent wines, daily papers, wide food choice (not Sun evening) from sandwiches up; children welcome in eating areas, pretty shrub-screened garden with heaters and boules, open all day wknds *(LYM, Steve Nye, Pat and Tony Martin)*

WELWYN TL2316

White Horse [Mill Lane]: Cosy and friendly, with two log fires, enjoyable food, hospitable landlord; live music, comfortable bedrooms *(Bernadette Williams, Miss A Hardwick)*

WESTON TL2529

Cricketers [Damask Green Rd; N of Stevenage]: Friendly Victorian country pub, good food choice from baguettes and other snacks to main meals, good polite service; lovely big garden *(Tony Shepherd, Mark Barker)*

WILDHILL TL2606

Woodman [off B158 Brookmans Pk—Essendon]: Good value tucked-away country local, simple and friendly, with open-plan bar and small back parlour, well kept attractively priced Greene King, McMullens and interesting changing guest ales, darts, lunchtime food (not Sun); tables on long grassy bank above informal car park, nearby walks *(Michael and Hilary Stiffin, Tim Maddison)*

It is illegal for bar staff to smoke while handling your drink.

Isle of Wight

Four favourite pubs here are the attractive Crab & Lobster at Bembridge (good choice of fairly priced seafood, great sea views from its terrace), the very hospitable Seaview Hotel (interesting pubby bar, smart dining areas, consistently good food), the rather yachty yet unspoilt old New Inn at Shalfleet (again, good food – especially fresh local fish), and the interesting Spyglass in its prime spot by the Ventnor sea wall (a wide choice of enjoyable food all day). Of these, the bustling New Inn at Shalfleet earns the award of Isle of Wight Dining Pub of the Year. A few pubs to watch in the Lucky Dip section at the end of the chapter are the Folly outside Cowes, Fishbourne Inn, Buddle at Niton, St Lawrence Inn, and Volunteer in Ventnor. Drinks prices on the island are now close to the national average – they may have been held down to some extent by the activities of the flourishing small local breweries, Ventnor, Goddards and (from the St Lawrence Inn) Yates.

ARRETON SZ5486 Map 2

White Lion £

A3056 Newport—Sandown

A few steps away from Arreton Manor and a fine 13th-c church (home to a brass-rubbing centre) in a quiet inland village, this cosy white-painted pub has good value straightforward food, served all day. Besides sandwiches and baguettes (from £3.50) and baked potatoes (from £3.95), mostly home-made dishes include lasagne or steak and kidney pie (£5.95), wild rice and spinach bake or chilli (£6.45), battered scampi (£6.95) and steaks (from £8.95), as well as puddings with lots of cream or custard; all-you-can-eat curry night on Wednesday (£6.95, four curries including vegetarian). There's a no smoking restaurant and family room, and Badger Best and Fullers London Pride kept well on handpump. The pleasant beamed lounge bar has partly panelled walls gleaming with brass and horse tack, and cushioned wheelback chairs on the red carpet. There is very quiet piped music, and the public bar has cribbage, dominoes, darts, fruit machine and TV. You can sit out in front by the tubs of flowers, and the pleasant garden has a small play area. More reports please. *(Recommended by Nigel B Thompson, Penny and Peter Keevil)*

Whitbreads ~ Lease Chris and Kate Cole ~ Real ale ~ Bar food (all day) ~ (01983) 528479 ~ Children in family room ~ Dogs allowed in bar ~ Open 11-11; 12-10.30 Sun

BEMBRIDGE SZ6587 Map 2

Crab & Lobster (🍴)

Foreland Fields Road, off Howgate Road (which is off B3395 via Hillgate Road)

The wonderful view from the coastal bluff over the Solent alone justifies the search for this obscurely located clifftop pub, and the terrace, bedrooms and window seats make the most of its position, within strolling distance of the beach. There's more room inside than you'd expect from the frontage, which is prettily bedecked with flower baskets in summer. The attractively decorated interior has a civilised, almost parlourish style, with lots of yachting memorabilia and old local photographs. They serve a very good choice of eight or nine changing fresh local seafood specials every day, from sardines in garlic butter and lemon (£3.95), through moules marinière (from £5.95), tasty home-made crab cakes (£7.25), grilled plaice topped with olives, garlic and basil (£7.50) and bass with garlic butter and lemon (£10.50), to whole lobster (£21.95). Other very well prepared food includes sandwiches (from £3.95), soup (from £3.25), duck pâté (£4.25), baked potatoes (from £4.50), ploughman's (£5.95), home-made lasagne and fish pie (£6.95), pork steaks with mozzarella and rosemary (£8.25), spicy baked local crab in the shell (£8.95), spicy fillet steak (£10.50), local lobster salad (£10.95), seafood platter (£22.50) and puddings such as spotted dick (£3.25); due to open at Easter after refurbishment, the restaurant is no smoking. Well kept Flowers Original, Greene King IPA and a guest such as Goddards Fuggle-Dee-Dum on handpump, decent house wines, country wines from the barrel, a large selection of malt whiskies, good coffee; piped music (even in the lavatories), darts, dominoes and cribbage. It does get very popular, so best to get there early or late at lunchtime. *(Recommended by Glyn and Janet Lewis, Gordon Stevenson, Roger and Pauline Pearce, Alain and Rose Foote, Pat and Graham Williamson, Richard Dixon, Alan Skull, Trevor Moore, Phil and Heidi Cook, John and Glenys Wheeler)*

Whitbreads ~ Lease Richard, Adrian and Pauline Allan ~ Real ale ~ Bar food (12-2.30, 6-9.30) ~ Restaurant ~ (01983) 872244 ~ Children in eating area of bar and restaurant ~ Dogs allowed in bar ~ Open 11-11; 12-10.30 Sun; 11-3, 6-11 weekdays in winter ~ Bedrooms: £40B/£80B

BONCHURCH SZ5778 Map 2

Bonchurch Inn

Bonchurch Shute; from A3055 E of Ventnor turn down to Old Bonchurch opposite Leconfield Hotel

Beneath a steep and rocky slope and cut into the side of the hill, this is not at all a conventional-looking pub, with its origins as stables for the nearby manor house, hence its unusual arrangement of separate bar, restaurant, rooms and kitchens spread round a cobbled courtyard. Since it gained its licence in the 1840s, little has changed. Tables, a fountain and pergola give the courtyard a slightly continental feel on warm summer days. The furniture-packed Victorian bar has a good chatty atmosphere, and conjures up images of salvaged shipwrecks, with its floor of narrow-planked ship's decking, and seats like the ones that old-fashioned steamers used to have. A separate entrance leads to the very simple no smoking family room (a bit cut off from the congenial atmosphere of the public bar). As well as Courage Directors and a guest ale tapped from the cask, there are italian wines by the glass, a few bottled french wines, darts, bar billiards, shove-ha'penny, dominoes and cribbage. The welcoming landlord is Italian, and the menu reflects this with several good-value dishes such as lasagne (£6.50), spinach cannelloni (£6.95), seafood risotto, (£8.50) or scampi with Pernod and cream plus rice (£12.50) as well as sandwiches (from £3, toasted 30p extra), soup (£4), battered squid (£7.50), chilli chicken with rice (£7.95) and sirloin steak (£10.50); for puddings they have ice-creams and sorbets (£3); there is a £1 charge for credit cards. The no smoking restaurant is just across the courtyard (the lounge bar has also been made no smoking), and the pub owns a holiday flat for up to six people. *(Recommended by Tom and Ruth Rees, Paul Humphreys, Keith Symons)*

Free house ~ Licensees Ulisse and Gillian Besozzi ~ Real ale ~ Bar food ~ Restaurant ~ (01983) 852611 ~ Children in family room ~ Dogs welcome ~ Open 11-3, 6.30-11; 12-3, 7-10.30 Sun ~ Bedrooms: /£50B

FRESHWATER SZ3487 Map 2

Red Lion

Church Place; from A3055 at E end of village by Freshwater Garage mini-roundabout follow Yarmouth signpost, then take first real right turn signed to Parish Church

In some choice walking country near the reedy Yar Estuary and tucked well away, this red-brick pub has kept a genuine local atmosphere that visitors without smaller children tend to appreciate. It's so popular that if you want to eat here it's a good idea to book ahead. Enjoyable bar food includes sandwiches, as well as a couple of lunchtime snacks such as baguettes (from £4.25), ploughman's (from £4.75) and fish and chips (£8.50), very well prepared imaginative daily specials are listed on a big blackboard behind the bar, and might include soup such as parsnip and apple (£3.75), wild boar terrine (£4.75), herring roes on toast (£5.25), steak and kidney pie (£7.50), wild mushroom and spinach risotto (£7.95), linguini with crab (£8.75), pork cutlet with bacon mash and mustard cream (£9.25), grilled halibut with chilli and coriander sauce (£9.95), and puddings such as rhubarb crumble, home-made ice-cream or citrus cheesecake (£3.75). There's a bustling atmosphere in the comfortably furnished open-plan bar, which has open fires, low grey sofas and sturdy country-kitchen style furnishings on mainly flagstoned floors, with bare boards at one end, and lots of local pictures and photographs and china platters on the walls. Well kept Flowers Original, Fullers London Pride and Wadworths 6X, plus a guest ale such as Goddards on handpump, and the good choice of wines includes 16 by the glass; service could be friendlier at times. Fines on mobile phone users go to charity (they also collect a lot for the RNLI); there's a fruit machine but no music, and smoking is permitted throughout. There are tables on a carefully tended grass and gravel area at the back (some under cover), behind which is the kitchen's herb garden, and a couple of picnic-sets in a quiet square at the front, by the church. *(Recommended by Peter and Margaret Glenister, Sheila Stothard, June and Malcolm Farmer, John and Glenys Wheeler, Mrs Maricar Jagger, Penny and Peter Keevil, Paul Humphreys, Colin and Janet Roe, Trevor Moore, Keith Symons)*

Enterprise ~ Lease Michael Mence ~ Real ale ~ Bar food ~ (01983) 754925 ~ Children over 10 ~ Dogs allowed in bar ~ Open 11.30-3, 5.30-11; 11.30-4, 6-11 Sat; 12-3, 7-10.30 Sun

ROOKLEY SZ5183 Map 2

Chequers

Niton Road; signposted S of village

The plentiful entertainment for little people at this former customs and excise house includes a play table and giant Connect Four in the large play area outside, and a Lego table and colouring competitions in the large no smoking family room. Parents can keep an eye on children outside from the new sun lounge and bar which looks out over the garden and play area, and the pub also has a mother and baby room. The comfortable carpeted lounge bar has cottagey ornaments and in winter a good log fire; it gives inland views of rolling downland. The flagstoned public bar beyond has a good lively local character (it's popular with young farmers), with dominoes and sensibly placed darts, pool, pinball, fruit machine and TV; perhaps piped music. Five real ales include Courage Best and Directors and Gales HSB plus two guest ales such as Greene King Old Speckled Hen and Goddards on handpump. Bar food includes sandwiches (from £2.95), soup (£2.75), baked potatoes (from £5.45), ploughman's (from £5.75), vegetable lasagne (£6.95), chicken curry (£6.95), moules marinière (£8.95), half a roast duck (£9.95), steaks (from £9.95), and puddings (from £3.25). More reports please. *(Recommended by BOB)*

Free house ~ Licensees R G and S L Holmes ~ Real ale ~ Bar food (all day) ~ (01983) 840314 ~ Children in family room ~ Dogs allowed in bar ~ Open 11-11; 12-10.30 Sun

SEAVIEW SZ6291 Map 2

Seaview Hotel

High Street; off B3330 Ryde—Bembridge

With its sea views across to the mainland, nautical trappings and relaxed, comfortably bustling atmosphere, this is a civilised place to stay, with reception rooms ranging from pubby to smart dining. The airy bay-windowed bar at the front has an impressive array of naval and merchant ship photographs, as well as

Spy nautical cartoons for *Vanity Fair*, original receipts for Cunard's shipyard payments for the *Queen Mary* and *Queen Elizabeth*, and a line of close-set tables down each side on the turkey carpet. There's a more informal down to earth atmosphere in the simpler back bar, with traditional wooden furnishings on bare boards, lots of seafaring paraphernalia around its softly lit ochre walls, and a log fire. They keep Goddards on handpump, and have around 20 malt whiskies and a good wine list (the landlord used to be a director of Corney & Barrow, the wine merchants); darts, cribbage, dominoes and shove-ha'penny. Using local ingredients wherever possible and fish fresh from the sea, very good well presented and generously served bar food includes soup (£3.95), duck parfait (£5.25), hot crab ramekin that's been a long-standing favourite here (£5.95), fish pie (£8.95), aubergine with fragrant rice (£9.50) or sirloin steak (£11.95), and puddings such as iced lemon brûlée (£3.95) and chocolate roulade with marinated cherries and fresh cream (£4.95); the smart formal restaurant is no smoking. Tables on the little terraces on either side of the path to the front door look down to the sea and along the coast, and some of the attractive bedrooms also have a sea view. *(Recommended by Geoffrey Kemp, N Bayley, June and Malcolm Farmer, Dr Alan and Mrs Sue Holder)*

Free house ~ Licensee N W T Hayward ~ Real ale ~ Bar food ~ Restaurant ~ (01983) 612711 ~ Children welcome (no under 5s in restaurant after 7.30) ~ Dogs allowed in bar and bedrooms ~ Open 10.30-2.30, 6-11; 12-3, 7-10.30 Sun; closed three or four days at Christmas ~ Bedrooms: £65S(£75B)/£80S(£100B)

SHALFLEET SZ4189 Map 2

New Inn

A3054 Newport—Yarmouth

Isle of Wight Dining Pub of the Year

Just a stroll away from the quay at an inlet of the yacht-filled Newtown estuary is this welcoming 18th-c fishermen's pub that aptly specialises in fresh fish dishes. Well known for their crab or lobster salad (from £11.95) and seafood platter (£50 for two), they also have a great choice of up to 12 fresh fish dishes a day, with a daily changing menu that typically features grilled sardines in herbs and garlic (£3.95), moules marinière (£5.95/£8.95), tuna steak with lime and chives (£10.95) and bass in lemon (£13.95). A little crab shack in the garden sells potted shrimps and crab sandwiches, and there's a new decked garden area. Other dishes include smoked venison with green fig chutney (£4.95), chicken breast with honey and cream (£8.95), venison steak with rosemary butter (£11.95) and fillet steak with tiger prawns (£17.95) alongside a short menu with sandwiches (from £2.95), filled baguettes (from £3.85), ploughman's (from £5.45), sausage and mash (£6.95), home-made lasagne (£6.95), home-made pie (£7.95) and rump steak (£11.95). You will need to book, and there may be double sittings in summer. The partly panelled flagstoned public bar has yachting photographs and pictures, a boarded ceiling, scrubbed pine tables and a roaring log fire in the big stone hearth, and the carpeted beamed lounge bar has boating pictures and a coal fire. The snug and gallery (with slate floors, bric-a-brac and more scrubbed pine tables) are no smoking. Well kept Badger Best, Bass, Flowers Original, Marstons Pedigree and Ventnor Golden on handpump, and around 60 wines (six sold by the glass); piped music. *(Recommended by Tom and Ruth Rees, Peter and Margaret Glenister, Joyce and Geoff Robson, Gordon Stevenson, Pat and Graham Williamson, Vanessa Stilwell, Derek Hayman, Paul Humphreys, Brenda and Rob Fincham, Joan York, Keith Symons, OPUS)*

Whitbreads ~ Lease Mr Bullock and Mr McDonald ~ Real ale ~ Bar food (12-2.30, 6-9.30) ~ Restaurant ~ (01983) 531314 ~ Children in eating area of bar ~ Dogs welcome ~ Open 12-3, 6-11(10.30 Sun)

Pubs with outstanding views are listed at the back of the book.

SHORWELL SZ4582 Map 2

Crown

B3323 SW of Newport

Despite the holidaymakers who home in on this attractive village nestled beneath the downs, this pub still has the character of a local. In warmer months the place to sit is the tranquil tree-sheltered garden – which has closely spaced picnic-sets and white garden chairs and tables by a little stream that broadens out into a small trout-filled pool. A decent children's play area blends in comfortably. Inside, four rooms spread pleasantly around a central bar. The beamed two-room lounge has blue and white china in an attractive carved dresser, old country prints on the stripped stone walls, other individual furnishings, and a winter log fire with a fancy tile-work surround. Black pews form bays around tables in a stripped-stone room off to the left, with another log fire; it's largely no smoking. Bar food includes sandwiches (from £3.25), soup (£3.50), pâté with toast (£4.95), ploughman's (from £5.25), lasagne or fisherman's pie (£6.95), and daily specials such as steak and kidney pie (£8.95), tuna with sweet pepper salsa (£9.50) and bass with sun-dried tomato butter (£10.50), with puddings (from £3.25) and children's meals. Well kept Boddingtons, Flowers Original and Wadworths 6X, with a guest such as Badger Tanglefoot on handpump; piped music and darts. More reports please. *(Recommended by Peter and Margaret Glenister)*

Enterprise ~ Lease Mike Grace ~ Real ale ~ Bar food (12-2.30, 6-9.30) ~ (01983) 740293 ~ Children in eating area of bar and family room ~ Dogs welcome ~ Open 10.30-3, 6-11; 12-3, 6-10.30 Sun

VENTNOR SZ5677 Map 2

Spyglass

Esplanade, SW end; road down very steep and twisty, and parking nearby can be difficult – best to use the pay-and-display (free in winter) about 100 yards up the road

The location right up beside the sea wall makes the pub terrace an idyllic place to bask in the sunshine and take in the view, and there's a fascinating array of mostly seafaring bits and pieces to look at inside too. Among the memorabilia are wrecked rudders, ships' wheels, old local advertisements, rope-makers' tools, stuffed seagulls, an Admiral Benbow barometer and an old brass telescope. The bustling mainly quarry-tiled interior is snug and pubby, and the atmosphere is buoyant; fruit machine, piped music and nightly entertainment. Usefully served all day, generous helpings of good, very fairly priced bar food are promptly served and include soup (£3.95), sandwiches (from £3.75, baguettes from £4.75), filled baked potatoes (from £5.50), ploughman's (from £6.25), home-made chilli (£7.25), home-made fisherman's pie (£8.25) and sirloin steak (£11.50), with daily specials such as seafood chowder (£5), steak and kidney pie (£6.95), cauliflower cheese (£7.25) and seafood casserole (£8.75). They have well kept Badger Best, Badger Tanglefoot, Ventnor Golden and possibly several guests such as Gribble Fursty Ferret on handpump. There are strolls westwards along the coast towards the Botanic Garden as well as heftier hikes up on to St Boniface Down and towards the eerie shell of Appuldurcombe House, and the pub owners don't mind muddy boots; no smoking area. *(Recommended by Peter and Margaret Glenister, Roger and Pauline Pearce, John and Glenys Wheeler, M Joyner, Paul Humphreys, Alan Skull)*

Free house ~ Licensees Neil and Stephanie Gibbs ~ Real ale ~ Bar food (all day) ~ (01983) 855338 ~ Children in eating area of bar ~ Dogs allowed in bar ~ Live entertainment every night ~ Open 10.30-11(10.30 Sun); ~ Bedrooms: /£55B

We accept no free drinks, meals or payment for inclusion. We take no advertising, and are not sponsored by the brewing industry – or by anyone else.
So all reports are independent.

LUCKY DIP

Besides the fully inspected pubs, you might like to try these Lucky Dips recommended to us and described by readers (if you do, please send us reports: www.goodguides.co.uk).

CHALE SZ4877

☆ *Clarendon (Wight Mouse)* [off A3055/B3399]: Popular rambling family dining pub recently extensively reworked, tastefully done with flagstones here, carpet there, modern-look woody extension around traditional core with log fire, good choice of well kept Badger and other ales from long bar, imaginative well presented good value food from snacks up, attentive cheerful service, entertaining quotes chalked up, plenty to keep children occupied, no smoking dining area; extensive outdoor seating, great views out over cliffs, good bedrooms in adjoining hotel *(LYM, Alison Cook, Joan York, Mrs Maricar Jagger)*

COWES SZ5092

☆ *Folly* [Folly Lane – which is signposted off A3021 just S of Whippingham]: Splendid estuary setting with big windows and large waterside deck; very yachtie-oriented, with wind speed indicator, barometer and chronometer among the bric-a-brac and old pictures and books on the timbered walls of the opened-out bar, moorings, showers and breakfast service (call the water taxi on Channel 7); hearty reasonably priced food most of the day from sandwiches up, Flowers IPA and Original and Goddards, several wines by the glass, no smoking area; pool, TV and piped music; children welcome, garden with summer bouncy castle (very busy then), open all day *(LYM, Joyce and Geoff Robson, Eddie Edwards, Joan York, OPUS, Martin and Karen Wake)*

Union [Watch House Lane]: Small Gales local with good atmosphere, log fire, cosy side room, good choice of beers inc interesting guest, good value nicely prepared food inc fine crab sandwiches, good fish and OAP bargain lunches, farm cider and proper ginger beer shandies, dining room and conservatory; bedrooms *(Vanessa Stilwell, Penny and Peter Keevil)*

FISHBOURNE SZ5592

☆ *Fishbourne Inn* [from Portsmouth car ferry turn left into Fishbourne Lane no through road]: Hospitable, spacious and neatly kept, with comfortable wall settles in cosy bar, large dining area with good choice from ploughman's to grills and local seafood, friendly staff, real ales such as Bass, Gales and Wadworths 6X; attractive well kept outdoor area, nice setting nr ferry terminal and coast path *(Roger and Pauline Pearce, Nick and Sylvia Pascoe, June and Malcolm Farmer, Dr and Mrs A K Clarke)*

GODSHILL SZ5381

Griffin [High St]: Carefully restored old family pub in honeypot village, generous well presented standard food from hot baguettes up, friendly helpful staff, well kept beers such as Archers, Flowers and Greene King Old Speckled Hen, good wine choice; darts, pool and machines; good-sized garden with play area and maze *(Jason Reynolds)*

HAVENSTREET SZ5590

White Hart [off A3054 Newport—Ryde; Main Rd]: Cosy bar in ancient building, tidy and comfortable, well kept Badger ales, wide range of enjoyable home-made food esp pies, welcoming service, lots of locomotive prints, interesting beer-bottle collection; attractive garden *(Alan Skull)*

HULVERSTONE SZ3984

Sun [B3399]: Picture-book thatched pub, cosy bar with flagstones, stripped brickwork and woodburner, well kept real ales, sound food, no piped music or machines; smart tables under cocktail parasols in charming flower-filled garden with village stocks, peaceful setting, terrific sea views *(Nick and Sylvia Pascoe, Paul Humphreys, Pete and Kate Holford, Andy Moore)*

NEWPORT SZ5089

Bargemans Rest [Little London]: Big child-friendly pub with good value generous food all day, well kept Badger and guest beers, reminiscent of Spyglass in Ventnor (see main entries); good staff, frequent live music, quayside terrace and garden, open all day *(Alan Skull)*

NITON SZ5075

☆ *Buddle* [St Catherines Rd, Undercliff; off A3055 just S of village, towards St Catherines Point]: Pretty former smugglers' haunt, heavy black beams, big flagstones, broad stone fireplace, no smoking areas, enjoyable reasonably priced food (freshly made, so may take a while) inc generous ploughman's, seafood, griddle dishes and Sun lunches, good welcoming service, family dining room/games annexe, up to half a dozen real ales, friendly dogs; views from well cared for sloping garden and terraces, good walks; open all day, some live jazz *(Peter and Margaret Glenister, LYM, Charles and Pauline Stride, Paul Humphreys, Alan Skull)*

SHANKLIN SZ5881

Fishermans Cottage [bottom of Shanklin Chine]: Unchanging thatched cottage in terrific beach setting surrounded by boats, tucked into the cliffs, steep walk down beautiful chine, lovely beach walk to Luccombe; stripped stone and lots of bric-a-brac in low-beamed flagstoned bar, simple bar food, Courage Directors under light blanket pressure, local country wines, coffee all day; wheelchair access, children welcome, tables out on terrace, live entertainment Tues, Fri, Sat, has been cl Nov-early Mar *(LYM, Joan York)*

ST LAWRENCE SZ5376

☆ *St Lawrence Inn* [Undercliffe Drive/Steephill Rd (A3055)]: Two well kept and attractively priced Yates beers brewed in adjacent building, good choice of enjoyable food inc outstanding crab sandwich, big partly no smoking split-level dining room (former stables) with much wood, good value wines; piped music, local singer Fri; sea-view tables out on decking *(Paul Humphreys, Alan Skull)*

TOTLAND SZ3285

High Down [Highdown Lane]: Out-of-the-way refurbished pub in great spot at foot of NT Tennyson Down, popular with walkers; well kept real ale, good fresh home-made food using local produce in bar and smart little dining room, good service; piped music; dogs welcome, picnic-sets out in raised paddock area, good value bedrooms *(Paula Lyon)*

VENTNOR SZ5677

☆ ***Volunteer*** [Victoria St]: Small old-fashioned local with cheerful chatty licensees, half a dozen well kept ales such as Badger, Ringwood, Ventnor and Yates, reasonable prices, coal fire, darts, the local game of rings, perhaps sandwiches or finger buffet if you order specially, friendly cat called Rosie, no machines or juke box; no children, quiz nights, open all day *(Liz and John Soden, Jason Reynolds, M Emmerson, Dave Ellerington)*

YARMOUTH SZ3589

☆ ***Bugle*** [The Square]: Old inn with low-ceilinged panelled lounge, lively rather basic bar with nautical memorabilia and counter like galleon stern, enjoyable food from good soup and sandwiches to good fish and seafood choice, quick cheerful service, well kept Whitbreads-related ales, decent house wines, restaurant, games room with pool, children very welcome; piped music, little or no nearby parking, can be crowded Sat – get there early; sizeable garden, summer barbecues, bedrooms *(LYM, Mrs Maricar Jagger, Colin and Janet Roe)*

Kings Head [Quay St]: Cosy low-ceilinged traditional pub opp car ferry, rather dark and quaint, with well kept ales, good food till quite late evening inc well prepared local fish, plush seats, friendly staff, open fires, children's eating area; unobtrusive piped music, can get crowded, public car park some way off; bedrooms *(Dr and Mrs A K Clarke)*

☆ ***Wheatsheaf*** [Bridge Rd, nr ferry]: Well kept Goddards, Greene King Old Speckled Hen and Wadworths 6X, cheerful staff, wide choice of generous quick food all day inc fresh fish, plenty of room inc no smoking glazed extension, public bar with juke box and winter pool; children welcome in most parts, open all day, tables on back terrace *(LYM, Dr and Mrs A K Clarke)*

'Children welcome' means the pub says it lets children inside without any special restriction. If it allows them in, but to restricted areas such as an eating area or family room, we specify this. Places with separate restaurants often let children use them, hotels usually let them into public areas such as lounges. Some pubs impose an evening time limit – let us know if you find this.

Kent

Four new entries here this year, all very different from one another: the little Unicorn tucked away at Bekesbourne (fresh and simple, with enjoyable food, run by a really nice couple), the Rose & Crown in the charming village of Elham (the sort of all-round-good pub which we'd all like to have just up the road), the ancient Windmill in Hollingbourne (a pleasantly relaxed and well run dining pub) and the Hook & Hatchet all alone in lovely countryside at Hucking (another fine all-rounder, its appealing décor and layout quite new yet thoroughly in keeping with pub tradition). Other pubs doing particularly well here these days are the ancient Three Chimneys near Biddenden (good food, friendly staff), the Dove at Dargate (you have to book ahead for this relaxed dining pub, but the food quality makes that worth while), the Harrow at Ightham Common (much enjoyed for its interesting changing food), the sociable Hare at Langton Green (good food and wines), the unspoilt 17th-c Shipwrights Arms at Oare (nice Kent beers and bargain food in great surroundings), the Bottle House out in the country above Penshurst (another well liked all-rounder, with a great food choice served all day), the enterprising Dering Arms at Pluckley (good fish cooking here), the Red Lion at Snargate (hardly changed since the 19th c, with good beers), the friendly and idiosyncratic Red Lion at Stodmarsh, Sankeys in Tunbridge Wells (its new layout works well, and the beers, wines and seafood are as good as ever), and the Swan on the Green in West Peckham (imaginative modern food, and it brews its own good beers). As this impressive list shows, there is no shortage of places here for a special meal out. The well run and welcoming Bottle House near Penshurst wins the award of Kent Dining Pub of the Year – with the bonus that here you can dine at any time of day. In the Lucky Dip section at the end of the chapter, pubs that currently stand out are Yew Tree at Barfrestone, Chapter Arms at Chartham Hatch, Queens Arms at Cowden, Carpenters Arms at Eastling, Star & Eagle in Goudhurst, restauranty Plough at Ivy Hatch, newly revamped Black Robin at Kingston, Plough at Leigh, Cock at Luddesdown, Rock and Spotted Dog, both near Penshurst, Sportsman in Seasalter, Bell at Smarden, Padwell Arms at Stone Street, Grove Ferry near Upstreet and Woolpack at Warehorne. Kent pubs tend to charge a little more for drinks than the national average. Local beers from Goachers, Larkins, Hopdaemon and the county's leading brewer Shepherd Neame are the ones we found most often offered as the cheapest in the pubs we surveyed this year, and the Swan on the Green in West Peckham, brewing its own, was also good value.

BEKESBOURNE **TR1856 Map 3**

Unicorn

Coming from Patrixbourne on A2, turn left up Bekesbourne Hill after passing railway line (and station); coming from Littlebourne on A257, pass Howletts Zoo – Bekesbourne Hill is then first turning on right; turning into pub car park is at bottom end of the little terrace of houses on the left (the pub is the far end of this terrace)

Quite a surprise, this airy little place: just a few scrubbed old pine tables and bentwood café chairs on worn floorboards, canary ceiling and walls above a dark green dado, minimal décor, and a handful of bar stools against the neat counter. This gives a glimpse of the spick-and-span stainless kitchen where the kind and attentive licensees produce their enjoyable and reasonably priced food, which might include avocado and bacon salad (£3.25), avocado with grilled brie or chorizo and tomato salad (£3.50), home-baked ham and egg (£5.95), sausages and mash (£6.25), liver and bacon (£6.75), butternut curry, pies such as steak and ale or chicken and ham, or smoked cod chowder (£7.95), pork with apple in cider (£8.50), and a pudding or two such as fruit crumble (£2.95). Well kept Adnams Broadside and Shepherd Neame Best on handpump, a short but good choice of wines; perhaps piped radio, but no machines – unless you count the veteran penny-in-the-slot bagatelle machine. There's a piano in one corner, and a little Victorian fireplace. A side terrace, quite prettily planted, has teak tables and benches. *(Recommended by Ron and Sheila Corbett, Catherine and Rob Dunster)*

Free house ~ Licensees Clive and Cheryl Barker ~ Real ale ~ Bar food (12-1.45, 7-9) ~ No credit cards ~ (01227) 830210 ~ Children welcome ~ Open 11.30-2.30, 7-11(10.30 Sun); closed Sun evening in winter; closed Mon, Tues

BIDDENDEN TQ8538 Map 3

Three Chimneys 🍴 🍷

A262, 1 mile W of village

It's worth arriving early at this pretty ochre-coloured country pub for the very good food, which can be eaten in the bar or restaurant. Superbly cooked, but not cheap, dishes might include soup (£3.95), baked field mushrooms with caramelised red onions and grilled goats cheese (£5.50), thai-style crab cakes (£6.95), sautéed lambs liver and bacon with mash and port and red onion gravy (£11.95), duck leg confit on creamed potato and braised puy lentils with chorizo and bacon (£12.95), roasted venison with braised cabbage and roasted parsnip with rich port jus (£15.95), and monkfish fillets with tomato and garlic, parma ham and mozzarella (£16.95), with puddings such as strawberry and vanilla crème brûlée (£5.25); they'll also serve ploughman's in the garden (£6.50). The rambling, low-beamed series of small, very traditional rooms has plain wooden furniture and old settles on flagstones and coir matting, some harness and sporting prints on the stripped brick walls, and good log fires. The simple public bar has darts, dominoes and cribbage. French windows in the civilised candlelit bare board restaurant open on to the garden, which has picnic-sets (some nice and shady on a hot day), and a smart terrace area has tables and outdoor heaters. They've a good wine list, local Biddenden cider, several malt whiskies, and Adnams Best, Bass, Harveys Best and Shepherd Neame Bishops Spitfire are tapped straight from the cask; friendly service from the knowledgeable staff. Nearby Sissinghurst Gardens are well worth a visit; no muddy boots. *(Recommended by John Evans, Brian Wainwright, the Didler, Anthony Longden, Michael Clementson, Mrs Catherine Draper, Bob Pike, Cathryn and Richard Hicks, Bob and Margaret Holder, Mrs Sally Kingsbury, John Hendy, Mrs C Lintott, Derek Thomas, Kevin Thorpe)*

Free house ~ Licensee Craig Smith ~ Real ale ~ Bar food (12-1.50, 7-9) ~ Restaurant ~ (01580) 291472 ~ Children in eating area of bar and restaurant ~ Dogs allowed in bar ~ Open 11.30-3, 6-11; 12-3, 7-10.30 Sun; closed 25 Dec

BOUGH BEECH TQ4846 Map 3

Wheatsheaf 🍷 🍺

B2027, S of reservoir

Thoughtful touches at this enjoyably bustling pub include piles of smart magazines to read, tasty nibbles, chestnuts to roast, mulled wine in winter, and summer Pimms. Full of history, there are masses of interesting things to look at inside, and the older part of the building is thought to have been a hunting lodge belonging to Henry V. The neat central bar and the long front bar (with an attractive old settle carved with wheatsheaves) have unusually high ceilings with lofty oak timbers, a screen of standing timbers and a revealed king post; dominoes and board games. Divided from the central bar by two more rows of standing timbers – one formerly an outside wall to the building – are the snug and another bar. Other similarly aged features include a piece of 1607 graffiti, 'Foxy Holamby', thought to have been a whimsical local squire. There are quite a few horns and heads, as well as a sword from Fiji, crocodiles, stuffed birds, swordfish spears, and the only matapee in the south of England on the walls and above the massive stone fireplaces. It's appealing outside too: there are plenty of seats, and flowerbeds and fruit trees in the sheltered side and back gardens, and shrubs help divide it into various areas, so it doesn't feel too crowded even when it's full. Greene King IPA and Old Speckled Hen, Harveys and Shepherd Neame Master Brew are well kept on handpump, and they've also farm cider, a decent wine list, several malt whiskies, and a range of local fruit juices. Besides lunchtime snacks such as cheese, bacon, onion and mashed potato hash or salmon and asparagus quiche (£5.95), minced beef and onion pie with mash and gravy (£6.95), and fish platter (£7.95), the extensive menu might include soup (£4.95), poached smoked haddock with mash, spinach and citrus cream sauce or thai green chicken curry (£10.95), lamb chops with tarragon gravy (£12.95), and beef wellington with red wine gravy (£14.95), with puddings such as apple and caramel pancakes (£4.50); swift and friendly service. *(Recommended by Bob and Margaret Holder, Pamela and Douglas Cooper, Jane Cross, Debbie and Neil Hayter, A Sadler, Vanessa Stilwell, Oliver and Sue Rowell, Andrea Rampley, Derek Harvey-Piper, Mrs C Lintott, Pete Walker)*

Enterprise ~ Lease Liz and David Currie ~ Real ale ~ Bar food (12-10) ~ (01732) 700254 ~ Children in part of eating area of bar ~ Dogs welcome ~ Contemporary folk and country Weds 9pm ~ Open 11-11; 12-10.30 Sun

BOYDEN GATE TR2265 Map 3

Gate Inn ★ 🍷 £

Off A299 Herne Bay—Ramsgate – follow Chislet, Upstreet signpost opposite Roman Gallery; Chislet also signposted off A28 Canterbury—Margate at Upstreet – after turning right into Chislet main street keep right on to Boyden; the pub gives its address as Marshside, though Boyden Gate seems more usual on maps

On fine summer evenings, you can sit at the picnic-sets on the sheltered side lawn of this refreshingly old-fashioned pub and listen to the contented quacking of a multitude of ducks and geese, coots and moorhens out on the marshes (they sell food for them – 10p a bag). Inside the winter inglenook log fire serves both the well worn quarry-tiled rooms, and there are flowery-cushioned pews around tables of considerable character, hop bines hanging from the beam and attractively etched windows; the atmosphere is properly pubby. Well kept Shepherd Neame Spitfire and Master Brew, and a seasonal ale are tapped from the cask by the long-standing landlord, and you can also get interesting bottled beers, a fine range of 14 wines by the glass, and country wines; shove-ha'penny, dominoes and cribbage. From the straightforward menu, reasonably priced bar meals include a fine choice of sandwiches (from £2.75), home-made soup (£3.25), lots of filled baked potatoes (from £3.95), quite a few different ploughman's (£5.25), and salads, pasta and pesto, omelettes or spicy hotpots (from £5.95); no chips. The eating area is no smoking at lunchtime. *(Recommended by Bruce Eccles, Bob Richardson, Andrea Rampley, Alan and Paula McCully, Kevin Thorpe, B and M Kendall)*

Shepherd Neame ~ Tenant Christopher Smith ~ Real ale ~ Bar food (12-2, 6-8.45) ~ No credit cards ~ (01227) 860498 ~ Well behaved children welcome ~ Dogs welcome ~ Open 11-2.30, 6-11; 12-4, 7-10.30 Sun

Please keep sending us reports. We rely on readers for news of new discoveries, and particularly for news of changes – however slight – at the fully described pubs. No stamp needed: *The Good Pub Guide*, FREEPOST TN1569, Wadhurst, E Sussex TN5 7BR or send your report through our web site: www.goodguides.co.uk

BROOKLAND TQ9724 Map 3

Woolpack £

On A259 from Rye, about 1 mile before Brookland, take the first right turn signposted Midley where the main road bends sharp left, just after the expanse of Walland Marsh; OS Sheet 189 map reference 977244

The friendly landlord of this early 15th-c cottage plans to hold barbecues in the sheltered garden, which has recently been expanded, with plenty of picnic-sets, well developed shrubs, and pretty hanging baskets; it's all nicely lit up in the evenings. Inside, the ancient entrance lobby has an uneven brick floor and black-painted pine-panelled walls, and on the right, the simple but homely main bar has basic cushioned plank seats in the massive inglenook fireplace (a lovely log fire on chilly days), a painted wood-effect bar counter hung with lots of water jugs, and some ships' timbers that may date from the 12th c in the low-beamed ceiling. On the quarry-tiled floor is a long elm table with shove-ha'penny carved into one end, other old and newer wall benches, chairs at mixed tables with flowers and candles, and photographs of the locals on the walls. To the left of the lobby is a sparsely furnished little room, and an open-plan games room with central hearth, modern bar counter, and locals playing darts or pool; cribbage, fruit machine and piped music. Fairly priced and well kept Shepherd Neame Master Brew, Spitfire and a seasonal brew on handpump; look out for the two pub cats Liquorice and Charlie Girl. Hearty bar food from a reasonably priced menu includes sandwiches (from £2.25), good home-made soup (£3.25), baked potatoes (from £4.75), ploughman's (£5.45), home-made steak pie, chilli, lasagne or stilton and vegetable bake (all £5.95), tasty cold pies such as pork, apple and stilton (£6.95), grilled trout or salmon fillet (£7.25), and mixed grill or sirloin steak (£11.45), with changing specials, and puddings such as spotted dick and summer fruit pudding; children's menu (£3). *(Recommended by John Davis, Peter and Joan Elbra, Andrea Rampley, Paul A Moore, B and M Kendall, Christopher Turner, Conor McGaughey, Kevin Thorpe)*

Shepherd Neame ~ Tenant Barry Morgan ~ Real ale ~ Bar food (12-2, 6-9) ~ (01797) 344321 ~ Children in family room ~ Dogs welcome ~ Open 11-3, 6-11 (all day during school hols); 11-11 Sat; 12-10.30 Sun

CHIDDINGSTONE TQ4944 Map 3

Castle Inn 🍷

Village signposted from B2027 Tonbridge—Edenbridge

You can choose from an impressive list of wines at this cosy rambling old pub, an inn since 1730. The handsome, carefully modernised beamed bar has well made settles forming booths around the tables, cushioned sturdy wall benches, an attractive mullioned window seat in one small alcove, and latticed windows (a couple of areas are no smoking); darts, shove-ha'penny, dominoes and cribbage. In summer, there are tables in front of the building facing the church, with more in the pretty secluded vine-hung garden. They serve well kept Larkins Traditional (brewed in the village, and in winter they have Porter too), along with Harveys Best and a guest on hamdpump, and there's a good range of malt whiskies. Popular (though not cheap), bar food includes lunchtime open sandwiches (from £5, ciabatta £5.85), chilli con carne or curry (£5.95), and ploughman's (£7.30), with other dishes such as ham hock terrine (£7.85), mixed seafood risotto or roasted nile perch with prawn couscous (£11.45), and seared calves liver (£15.85), with puddings such as lavender panna cotta (£5.75); no chips. They do a two-course lunch on Sunday (£25), and there's a children's menu (from £3.30); afternoon tea too. It's best to avoid peak times as it gets very busy, there can be a wait and service can be variable. It's worth wandering around this National Trust village, to look at the picturesque cluster of unspoilt Tudor houses; the licensees publish three circular walks from the village. *(Recommended by Colin McKerrow, Anthony Longden, Alan and Paula McCully, Mrs Romey Heaton, Alison Hayes, Pete Hanlon, B and M Kendall, Roy and Lindsey Fentiman, Mrs C Lintott, Andrea Rampley, Mrs B M Hill)*

Free house ~ Licensee Nigel Lucas ~ Real ale ~ Bar food (11-9.30, not 25 Dec) ~ Restaurant ~ (01892) 870247 ~ Children in eating area of bar and restaurant ~ Dogs welcome ~ Open 11-11; 12-10.30 Sun

DARGATE TR0761 Map 3

Dove

Village signposted from A299

Lovely in fine weather, the sheltered garden of this tucked-away dining pub has roses, lilacs, peonies and many other flowers, picnic-sets under pear trees, a dovecote with white doves, a rockery and pool, and a swing. You have to book some time in advance if you want to enjoy the very good restaurant-style food, and at busy times (when they may finish serving food early), you may not even be able to get a lunchtime baguette unless you've booked. Well cooked, generously served dishes could include bacon, avocado and rocket salad (£5.99), salt cod with flageolet beans and chorizo (£6.90), prawns with garden herbs and pickled ginger (£7.25), plaice with capers and shallots (£14.99), chump of lamb with wild mushrooms (£15.50), and scotch beef fillet with shallots and garlic (£17.50), with puddings such as passion fruit crème brûlée or baked chocolate pudding (£5); friendly service. With a relaxed atmosphere, the charmingly unspoilt rambling rooms have photographs of the pub and its licensees throughout the past century on the walls, a good winter log fire, and plenty of seats on the bare boards; piped music. Well kept Shepherd Neame Master Brew on handpump. The pub is set down a network of narrow lanes in a quiet hamlet; a bridlepath leads up from the pub (along the quaintly-named Plumpudding Lane) into Blean Wood. *(Recommended by KN-R, Guy Vowles, John Davis, Richard Siebert, M A and C R Starling, Andrea Rampley, Ian Phillips, Philip Denton)*

Shepherd Neame ~ Tenants Nigel and Bridget Morris ~ Real ale ~ Bar food (12-2.30(1.30 Sun, Tues), 7-9; not Mon, or evenings Sun or Tues) ~ (01227) 751360 ~ Well behaved children in eating area of bar ~ Dogs allowed in bar ~ Open 12-3, 6-11; 12-3, 7-10.30 Sun; closed Mon exc bank hols, and Sun and Tues evenings

DEAL TR3752 Map 3

Kings Head

Beach Street, just off A258 seafront roundabout

A real sight in summer when it's festooned with brightly coloured hanging baskets and window boxes, this handsome three-storey Georgian inn is just across the road from the promenade and the sea; there are picnic-sets out on a broad front paved terrace. Four comfortable bar rooms work their way round a central servery, and the walls, partly stripped masonry, are decorated with marine architectural drawings, maritime and local pictures and charts, and other material underlining connections with the Royal and Merchant navies; another area has an interesting collection of cricket memorabilia. There are a couple of warming flame-effect gas fires; it can get smoky. Well kept real ales might include Bass, Fullers London Pride, Greene King IPA and Shepherd Neame Master Brew on handpump; piped music, fruit machines and TV. Generous helpings of straightforward bar food such as sandwiches and filled baguettes (from £2.75), omelettes (from £4), ploughman's (£5.95), lambs liver and bacon or chicken provençale (£7.95), and lemon sole (£9.95); two-course Sunday lunch (£8.95). In the evening, particularly Friday night, it can be crowded with young people who may be attracted by the games machines in the daytime too. Beware that traffic wardens here are vigilant during the week; there's pay-and-display (two-hour limit) parking opposite, and another (three-hour limit) just a few minutes' walk away. *(Recommended by Paul A Moore, Nigel B Thompson, Father Robert Marsh, B J Harding, Mike Ridgway, Sarah Miles, Michael Dandy)*

Courage (S & N) ~ Lease Graham Stiles and Shirley Russell ~ Real ale ~ Bar food (12-3, 6-9) ~ (01304) 368194 ~ Children in family room ~ Dogs welcome ~ Open 10-11; 12-10.30 Sun ~ Bedrooms: £45S/£59B

ELHAM TR1743 Map 3

Rose & Crown

High Street

Partly 16th-c, this pub nicely combines an easy-going atmosphere, informal and unpretentious, with the real sense of age given by its low beams, and by the inglenook fireplace on the left where a couple of low red plush settees make the most of its open woodburning stove. Soft lighting, pink walls, a homely couple of armchairs by a table with daily newspapers (there's a pile of guide books in another corner), and the friendly dogs (Frank the border terrier and Bruno the labrador – he's the talkative one) add to the relaxed feel at quiet times. There are no machines or music, and the friendly landlord is backed by keen and efficient young staff. The serving bar, in a smallish area on the right, has well kept Hopdaemon Golden Braid and a seasonal beer such as Incubus on handpump, with a couple of changing guest beers such as Harveys Best and Rother Valley Hoppers, and decent reasonably priced wines by the glass. Over on the left, not much bigger, a pleasant mix of seats and tables shares the space with the settees; it's carpeted throughout. Blackboards show the enjoyable home-made food, which includes lunchtime ciabattas (not Sunday) such as chargrilled mediterranean vegetables (£6.50) or fried cajun strips (£6.95), as well as their regular range running from soup (£3.95) and gravadlax (£5.25) through liver and bacon (£9.50) and steak and kidney pudding with proper suet pastry or salmon on samphire (£9.95) to dressed crab (£11.50) and chargrilled fillet steak (£14.95); good puddings include childhood favourites like bread and butter pudding and jam roly-poly (£4.25). Along a passage on the right is the neat no smoking restaurant, decorated with china and bookshelves. A flagstoned back terrace has teak tables, chairs and benches. We have not yet heard from readers who have stayed here; the six bedrooms have their own bathrooms. This is a charming village, with a few antiques shops and so forth, in what is perhaps Kent's prettiest valley. *(Recommended by John and Joan Calvert, Robert Coomber, GHC, Peter Meister, David Barnes, Peter Heaton, Kevin Thorpe)*

Free house ~ Licensees William and Denise McNicholas ~ Real ale ~ Bar food (12-2, 6(7 Sun)-9) ~ Restaurant ~ (01303) 840226 ~ Children welcome ~ Dogs allowed in bar ~ Open 11-3, 6-11; 12-3, 7-10.30 Sun ~ Bedrooms: £45B/£55B

FORDCOMBE TQ5240 Map 3

Chafford Arms

B2188, off A264 W of Langton Green

As this friendly tile-hung old pub is on the Wealdway walking route, the landlord doesn't mind muddy boots, and dogs are welcome too. There's plenty of room between neat tables and comfortable seats on a turkey carpet, and an uncluttered décor; the quite separate public bar, full of sporting memorabilia and trophies, often gets much busier towards the close of the evening as the dining side winds down; darts, cribbage, shove-ha'penny, dominoes, TV, and fruit machine. Larkins and a guest are well kept on handpump, and they've decent house wines. Straightforward bar food might include sandwiches (from £2.95), home-made soup (£2.45), salads (from £4.95), vegetarian quiche (£5.95), chicken or scampi and chips (£6.45), and grilled trout or gammon and pineapple (£8.45); on Tuesday evenings they do two rib-eye steaks for the price of one. In summer, the pub is covered with flowers against a backdrop of cascading creepers and carefully tended shrubs and perennials. Most of the flowers are in front but there's a pleasant sheltered lawn behind with an attractive shrubbery and arbours; just up the steepish lane is an archetypal village cricket green. Beware, they retain your credit card behind the bar if you eat in the garden. *(Recommended by Mr and Mrs H D Brierly, Peter Meister, John Davis, Geoffrey G Lawrance, Jonathan Shephard, Andrea Rampley, Gwyn Jones, Mrs C Lintott, Father Robert Marsh)*

Enterprise ~ Lease Barrie Leppard ~ Real ale ~ Bar food (not Mon evenings) ~ Restaurant ~ (01892) 740267 ~ Children welcome ~ Dogs welcome ~ Jazz third Sun evening of month ~ Open 11.45-11; 11-11 Sat; 12-10.30 Sun

GROOMBRIDGE TQ5337 Map 3

Crown

B2110

Prettily set at the end of a row of picturesque cottages overlooking the steep village green, this tile-hung old smugglers' haunt is handily placed for a visit to Groombridge Place Gardens. The snug beamed rooms (get there early if you want a seat) have a jumble of bric-a-brac including old teapots, pewter tankards and antique bottles, and there's a log fire in the big brick inglenook. The walls, mostly rough yellowing plaster with some squared panelling and timbering, are decorated with small topographical, game and sporting prints, and a circular large-scale map with the pub at its centre. The no smoking end room (normally for eaters) has fairly close-spaced tables with a variety of good solid chairs, and a log-effect gas fire in a big fireplace. Picnic-sets out in front on a brick terrace are very popular in summer. From the long copper-topped bar counter they serve Greene King Abbot and IPA, Harveys and Larkins on handpump; shove-ha'penny, dominoes, cribbage and Scrabble. Tasty bar food includes lunchtime soup (£3.95), devilled whitebait (£4.95), open sandwiches (£5.90), omelettes (£6.80), and chicken and leek pie or sausage and mash (£7.90), while in the evening you might find cod roulades with ham and spinach and creamed mash (£10.95), steaks (from £12.80), half a roast barbary duck (£12.95), and lamb rump steak (£14), with puddings such as lemon and shortbread cheesecake (£4.50). A public footpath across the road beside the small chapel leads through a field to Groombridge Place Gardens. *(Recommended by Peter Meister, John Davis, Will Watson, Joyce and Geoff Robson, Mrs J Ekins-Daukes, P and J Shapley, Andrea Rampley, Michael and Ann Cole, Mrs C Lintott, Father Robert Marsh, Liz and Tony Colman)*

Free house ~ Licensee Peter Kilshaw ~ Real ale ~ Bar food (12-3, 7-9; not Sun evening) ~ Restaurant ~ (01892) 864742 ~ Children in eating area of bar and restaurant ~ Dogs allowed in bar ~ Open 11-3, 6-11; 11-11 Sat; 12-10.30 Sun; 11-3, 6-11 Sat, 12-3, 7-10.30 Sun in winter ~ Bedrooms: £40/£45(£60S)

HAWKHURST TQ7630 Map 3

Queens

Rye Road (A268 E)

Great if you need a hearty breakfast, this civilised wisteria-covered Georgian-faced inn serves food from 8.30am. The interior has been sensitively opened up and appealingly decorated in keeping with its age (it was first recorded as an inn in the 16th c). Light filters in through creeper tendrils that threaten to cover the old sash windows of the area at the front. This used to be the more pubby part, but it has recently been converted into a piano bar, with live music in the evenings (from Wednesday to Saturday), and jazz Sunday lunchtime. Further in, the mood is like that of a wine bar: terracotta, sand or pea-green colourwashes give an airy feel despite the heavy low beams, and there's a nice mix of old pine tables on bare boards with plenty of scattered rugs, and there are sofas by the big brick inglenook fireplace. At night it's pleasantly candlelit; there are newspapers to read. Friendly staff serve well kept Fullers London Pride and Harveys Best on handpump. Tasty dishes, from a fairly traditional menu, might include sandwiches and filled baguettes or home-made soup (£4.95), ploughman's (£5.95), chicken terrine (£6.95), beer-battered haddock, spaghetti bolognese or steak and ale pie (£9.95), baked black bream (£11.95), and 8oz grilled fillet steak (£14.95), with puddings such as chocolate hazelnut meringue pie or strawberry cheesecake (£4.95); they also do a short children's menu (£5.50), and there's a Sunday carvery (£8.95). Two eating rooms are no smoking. There are outdoor heaters in the little front courtyard, and at the side there's a terrace. *(Recommended by Alan and Paula McCully, Jason Caulkin, Mike Gorton, Ann and Colin Hunt, Susan and John Douglas)*

Enterprise ~ Lease Janelle Tresidder ~ Real ale ~ Bar food (all day) ~ Restaurant ~ (01580) 753577 ~ Children in eating area of bar, restaurant and family room ~ Open 11-12(10.30 Sun) ~ Bedrooms: £55B/£85B

HODSOLL STREET TQ6263 Map 3

Green Man

Hodsoll Street and pub signposted off A227 S of Meopham; turn right in village

On Tuesday they do curry specials, Wednesday night is fish night, and on Monday evening there's a quiz at this appealingly relaxed and welcoming pub. Big airy carpeted rooms work their way round a hop-draped central bar, and neat tables are spaced tidily around the walls, with interesting old local photographs and antique plates on the walls, and a warm winter log fire; piped music. Flowers, Fullers London Pride, Youngs Ordinary and a guest such as Harveys Sussex Best are well kept on handpump, and they've decent wines; the licensees are friendly. At lunchtime tasty bar food includes sandwiches (from £3.25; good baguettes from £4), ploughman's (£4.50), and tortilla wraps or ham and eggs (£6), with other dishes such as salmon fillet with hollandaise (£11), lamb shank with red wine jus (£12), and calves liver with bubble and squeak (£13), and specials such as home-made lasagne, liver and bacon casserole or scampi and chips (all £7), and puddings. They also do a Sunday roast (£8), and children's meals (from £5.50). With pretty summer tubs and hanging baskets, the pub is next to the village green, and there are seats on a well tended lawn; look out for morris dancers who practise here regularly. The nearby North Downs have plenty of walks. They've now extended and resurfaced the car park. *(Recommended by Roger and Pauline Pearce, Annette Tress, Gary Smith, Peter Scillitoe, GHC, Peter and Joan Elbra, Ian Phillips, Bev and Jeff Brown, Ian and Barbara Rankin, Paul A Moore, Tony Brace, Gerry and Rosemary Dobson)*

Enterprise ~ Lease John, Jean and David Haywood ~ Real ale ~ Bar food (12-2, 6.30-9.30, 12-3, 6.30-9 Sun) ~ Restaurant ~ (01732) 823575 ~ Children welcome till 9pm ~ Dogs allowed in bar ~ Open 11-2.30, 6-11; 11-11 Fri and Sat; 12-10.30 Sun

HOLLINGBOURNE TQ8354 Map 3

Windmill 🍷

A mile from M20 junction 8: A20 towards Ashford (away from Maidstone), then left into B2163 – Eyhorne Street village

This dining pub, very handy for the motorway, is pretty much set for food throughout, but has a relaxed and chattily pubby atmosphere. Its island serving bar, tucked up one or two steps towards the back, with its bar stools (and fruit machine behind), makes for a welcoming core; it has well kept Flowers IPA, Greene King K&B, Shepherd Neame Masterbrew and possibly a guest in winter on handpump and eight wines by the glass. Under low heavy black beams, several small or smallish mainly carpeted areas link together around this core, sometimes partly separated by glazed or stained-glass panels; the solid pub tables have padded country or library chairs. Soft lighting, black timbers in ochre walls, shelves of books, one or two knick-knacks, and the good log fire in the huge inglenook fireplace (was that someone's leg we saw dangling down the chimney?) add up to a pleasantly old-world feel. The wide choice of enjoyable food includes good weekday lunchtime sandwiches (from £3.95, sirloin steak £5.95), baguettes or filled baked potatoes (£5.95), liver and bacon, roast red pepper salad or wild mushroom and artichoke risotto (£8.50), steaks (from £8.95), cajun spiced chicken (£9.95) and dishes of the day such as grey mullet or red snapper with a red onion and avocado salsa (£13.75) and duck confit (£13.95); vegetables are fresh and plentiful. The good choice of reasonably priced wines comes in two glass sizes. Service is friendly and punctilious, quick even at busy times – and they make young children feel really at home. A dining room behind the great fireplace is no smoking; piped music and juke box. A neatly kept sunny garden has picnic-sets under cocktail parasols, and a play area; the village has a good many handsome buildings. *(Recommended by Peter and Giff Bennett, Alison and Graham Hooper)*

Enterprise ~ Lease Graham and Deana Godmon ~ Real ale ~ Bar food (12-2.30, 6-10; 12-10(9.30 Sun) Sat) ~ Restaurant ~ (01622) 880280 ~ Children welcome ~ Open 11-3, 5-11; 11-11 Sat; 12-10.30 Sun

HUCKING TQ8458 Map 3

Hook & Hatchet 🍷

3½ miles from M2 junction 5; A249 towards Maidstone, then after a mile turn left at Hucking signpost into narrow lane; Church Road

This recently reworked isolated country pub seems all set to become a big favourite. It stands alone on the edge of the Woodland Trusts's Hucking Estate, nearly a square mile of woods, farmland and downland now open to the public (free), with plenty of interesting walks – the pub gives away a useful map. Inside, the pub is a haven of civilised comfort. Around a central chimneypiece with fireplaces each side, a variety of well spaced seats spreads over broad polished boards, from a leather armchair and low sofa covered with bright scatter-cushions to pews, cushioned stools and chairs around sturdy tables. There are one or two pictures on the smooth pink walls, varnished joists in the cream ceiling, and comfortable backed seats along the long rather smart bar counter, with its well kept Fullers London Pride and guest beers such as Adnams Broadside and Harveys Best on handpump (served in lined glasses); they have a good choice of wines by the glass. The food is enjoyable too, including soup (£2.75), filled baked potatoes (£3.95), sandwiches or baguettes (from £4.50), cottage pie or pasta (£4.95), a fry-up (£5.50), good interesting pies such as smoked haddock with turmeric and spinach, chicken with smoked devon cheese or minty aubergine and goats cheese (£5.95), children's dishes (£3) and evening restaurant dishes such as bass (£9.50). The softly lit no smoking dining room has high-backed settles forming intimate booths around some of its tables, and another side area is also no smoking. There are tables out on a heated verandah, and lots of picnic-sets in the carefully laid out garden, which has a good play area at one end, and a field with plenty of space for children to let off steam in. Two nice touches: the boot-washing tap, and what is certainly the best pub hitching rail for visiting horses that we've seen (they also encourage their horse-owning customers to debox here – with notice). *(Recommended by Rupert Reeves)*

Free house ~ Licensee Adam Silverton ~ Real ale ~ Bar food (12-2.30(3 Sun), 6.30-9.30; not Sun evening) ~ Restaurant ~ (01622) 880830 ~ Children welcome ~ Dogs allowed in bar ~ Live music Thurs ~ Open 12-11(10.30 Sun)

ICKHAM TR2257 Map 3

Duke William 🍷

Village signposted off A257 E of Canterbury

Set in a pretty village, this friendly and comfortable pub has been run by the same licensees for more than 22 years. It's bigger inside that the rather plain little street front suggests. Spotlessly kept, the open-plan carpeted bar extends on either side of the serving counter, and there's an appealingly lived-in feel in the front part, helped by the gas lighting and big inglenook fireplace hung with hops, longcase clock and all the brasses, copper, farm implements and other bric-a-brac. There's more formal seating behind, with a rather smart air-conditioned restaurant area and then a well shaded no smoking Victorian-style conservatory which overlooks the attractive neatly kept garden and fields beyond. You'll find an extensive wine list (with a dozen by the glass), and four real ales such as Adnams, Fullers London Pride, Shepherd Neame Master Brew and Wells Bombardier are well kept on handpump; freshly squeezed orange juice too. They've an african grey parrot called Nipper and a golden retriever called Harry; darts, pool, shove-ha'penny, dominoes, fruit machine and juke box. A good choice of well liked bar food might include home-made soup (£4), filled baguettes or baked potatoes (from £4.50), various pasta dishes (from £5.45), ploughman's (from £5.50), home-made burger (£6.50), baked rainbow trout, steak and kidney pie or mussels with white wine, cream, shallots and mushrooms (£7.95), with tempting puddings (£3.75). *(Recommended by Tina and David Woods-Taylor, Ian Phillips, Grahame Brooks, Peter Scillitoe, Kevin Thorpe, Glenwys and Alan Lawrence)*

We say if we know a pub has piped music.

Free house ~ Licensees Mr and Mrs A R McNeill ~ Real ale ~ Bar food (not Sun evening or Mon lunch) ~ Restaurant ~ (01227) 721308 ~ Children in restaurant and conservatory ~ Dogs allowed in bar ~ Open 11-3, 6-11; 12-4, 7-10.30 Sun; closed Mon lunch exc bank hols

IDEN GREEN TQ8031 Map 3

Woodcock

Iden Green is signposted off A268 E of Hawkhurst and B2086 at W edge of Benenden; in village at crossroads by bus shelter follow Standen Street signpost, then fork left just before the orchard down Woodcock Lane (maybe a signpost to pub here) – beware that there is an entirely different Iden Green just 10 miles away near Goudhurst

Recently taken over by new licensees, this bustling and friendly little local country pub is tucked away on the edge of Standen Wood. Snugly comfortable, the small flagstoned bar has stripped brick walls and very low ceilings bearing down heavily on a couple of big standing timbers; you'll find a comfortable sofa and armchairs by a warming woodburning stove, and chunky big old pine tables tucked snugly into little nooks; darts, shove-ha'penny, and piped local radio. Enthusiastic young staff serve well kept Greene King IPA, Abbot, and Old Speckled Hen, along with a changing guest such as Rother Valley Level Best on handpump. Generously served, enjoyable bar food such as baguettes (from £4.50), ploughman's (£5.95), burgers (from £6.95), lambs liver or garlic chicken escalope (£9.95), and puddings such as home-made crème brûlée (£3.95); you may need to book at weekends when it can get very busy. The partly panelled dining area opens on to a verandah, and there are seats in the pretty side garden. The car park is across the road. More reports please. *(Recommended by Peter and Joan Elbra, Grahame Brooks, Father Robert Marsh, Ann and Colin Hunt, Susan and John Douglas)*

Greene King ~ Lease Mark and Tracy Coxhead ~ Real ale ~ Bar food (not Sun evening) ~ Restaurant ~ (01580) 240009 ~ Children in eating area of bar ~ Dogs allowed in bar ~ Open 11-11; 12-10.30 Sun

IGHTHAM COMMON TQ5755 Map 3

Harrow

Signposted off A25 just W of Ightham; pub sign may be hard to spot

Readers very much enjoy the particularly good food at this civilised country pub, close to Ightham Mote. The interesting menu changes constantly, but might include soup (£4.95), duck and spring onion rolls with plum sauce or brie and gooseberry in filo (£5.95), wild mushroom risotto or beef and Guinness pie (£8.95), roast lamb shank with red wine jus or fried salmon with shellfish sauce and spinach (£10.95), and beef sirloin with pink peppercorn sauce (£12.95), with mouthwatering puddings such as orange and Cointreau tiramisu (£4.50). Assorted country furniture stands on nice old brick flooring or black and white squared vinyl in two simply but attractively decorated rooms, both warmed by log fires in winter. The traditional public bar is painted a cheerful sunny yellow above its dark green dado, and there is charming attention to detail – daily papers, fresh flowers, and candles on the tables. A lush grapevine grows around the delightful little antiquated conservatory which leads off an elegant no smoking dining room laid with white cloths. With plenty of rewarding wines by the glass, there's a decent sensibly priced wine list, and Greene King IPA and Abbot are well kept on handpump; piped music. Tables and chairs are out on a pretty little pergola-enclosed back terrace. *(Recommended by T Dunbar, Tim and Pam Moorey, Nigel and Olga Wikeley, Uta and John Owlett, Derek Thomas, Ian Phillips, Nicky Mayers, M and GR, Alan Cowell, Oliver and Sue Rowell, Andrea Rampley, Colin and Stephanie McFie, David Twitchett, Mrs C Lintott, Susan and John Douglas)*

Free house ~ Licensees John Elton and Claire Butler ~ Real ale ~ Bar food (12-2, 6-9; not Sun evening or Mon) ~ Restaurant ~ (01732) 885912 ~ Children in restaurant (not Sat evening) ~ Open 12-3, 6-11; 12-3 Sun; closed Sun evening and Mon

LANGTON GREEN TQ5538 Map 3

Hare

A264 W of Tunbridge Wells

A great place for a civilised summer meal, the sheltered terrace (now with lighting and heaters) at this thriving Edwardian roadside pub has picnic-sets looking out on to a tree-ringed green. With a good sociable atmosphere, the knocked-through rooms have big windows and high ceilings giving a pleasant feeling of space: dark-painted dados below light walls, oak furniture and turkey carpets on stained wooden floors, old romantic pastels, and plenty of bric-a-brac (including a huge collection of chamber-pots). Interesting old books, pictures and two big mahogany mirror-backed display cabinets crowd the walls of a big chatty room at the back, which has lots of large tables (one big enough for at least a dozen) on a light brown carpet; from here french windows lead to the terrace. The front bar (piped music here) is well liked by drinkers; shove-ha'penny, cribbage and dominoes. Service is good, and the atmosphere is pubby and sociable. A wide choice of superbly cooked food changes every day, but might include soup (£3.75), smoked chicken and roasted red pepper with cream cheese (£4.95), home-cooked ham and eggs (£7.50), potato, leek and cheddar cheese hash cakes with creamed cabbage and roasted red onions (£7.95), braised venison shank in mustard sauce with mash or crispy duck confit with white bean and chorizo ratatouille (£11.95), seared tuna with tomato and saffron risotto (£13.50), and 10oz rib-eye steak (£14.95), with tempting puddings such as treacle tart with honeycomb ice-cream or white chocolate and sultana cheesecake (£4.25); they also do snacks such as fish finger sandwich (£3.95), and hot beef granary roll (£5.95). To be sure of a table it's best to book. Greene King IPA and Abbot are well kept alongside a couple of guests such as Greene King Old Speckled Hen and Wadworths 6X on handpump, they have lots of wines by the glass, and over 50 malt whiskies. Parking is not easy at peak times unless you get here early. *(Recommended by Derek Harvey-Piper, Mrs Catherine Draper, Comus and Sarah Elliott, Derek Thomas, B J Harding, Joyce and Geoff Robson, Ian and Barbara Rankin, Gillian Rogers, M and D J Hill, Oliver and Sue Rowell, Mrs C Lintott)*

Brunning & Price ~ Tenant Christopher Little ~ Real ale ~ Bar food (12-9.30) ~ Restaurant ~ (01892) 862419 ~ Children in eating area of bar till 7pm ~ Dogs allowed in bar ~ Open 11-11; 12-10.30 Sun

NEWNHAM TQ9557 Map 3

George

44 The Street; village signposted from A2 just W of Ospringe, outside Faversham

The several atmospheric spreading rooms at this well run pub have lots for you to look at – dressers with teapots, prettily upholstered mahogany settles, dining chairs and leather carving chairs around candlelit tables, table lamps and gas-type chandeliers, and rugs on the waxed floorboards; open fires, fresh flowers, quite a few pictures, and hop bines hanging from the beams. They've a dozen wines by the glass, well kept Shepherd Neame Master Brew, Bishops Finger and Spitfire, and seasonal beers on handpump, and good coffee; piped music. Very good food, served by pleasant staff, includes lunchtime sandwiches or baguettes (from £3.50), filled baked potatoes (from £5.25) and ploughman's (from £5.75), soup (£3.50), home-made chinese fishcakes (£4.95), chicken, smoked bacon and mushroom tagliatelle, vegetable curry or steak and kidney pudding (£8.95), with changing specials such as half shoulder of lamb with redcurrant, rosemary and red wine sauce or calves liver with smoked bacon and wild mushroom and red wine sauce (£13.95), and fresh fillets of bass with fresh asparagus and hollandaise (£14.95), and home-made puddings such as cherry roly poly and banoffi pie (£4.35); the restaurant is no smoking. The spacious sheltered garden has some picnic-sets, and there are pleasant nearby walks. *(Recommended by Roger and Pauline Pearce, Philip Denton, Peter Scillitoe, Danny Nicol)*

There are report forms at the back of the book.

Shepherd Neame ~ Tenant Marc Perkins ~ Real ale ~ Bar food ~ Restaurant ~ (01795) 890237 ~ Children welcome ~ Dogs allowed in bar ~ Open 11-3, 6.30-11; 11-4, 6.30-10.30 Sun; closed evenings 26 Dec and 1 Jan

OARE TR0163 Map 3

Shipwrights Arms £

S shore of Oare Creek, E of village; coming from Faversham on the Oare road, turn right into Ham Road opposite Davington School; or off A2 on B2045, go into Oare village, then turn right towards Faversham, and then left into Ham Road opposite Davington School; OS Sheet 178 map reference 016635

They serve only Kent-brewed beers at this charmingly unspoilt 17th-c tavern: tapped straight from the cask, a typical selection might be well kept Goachers Gold Star, Mild and Shipwrecked and Hopdaemon Golden Braid and Incubus. The three simple little bars are dark and cosy, and separated by standing timbers and wood part-partitions or narrow door arches. There's a medley of seats from tapestry cushioned stools and chairs to black wood-panelled built-in settles forming little booths, pewter tankards over the bar counter, boating jumble and pictures, flags or boating pennants on the ceilings, several brick fireplaces, and a good woodburning stove. There may be piped local radio; cribbage and dominoes. Reasonably priced bar food includes sandwiches (from £2.95), filled baked potatoes (from £3.95), ploughman's (from £4.95), sausage and mash (£5.75), home-baked ham and egg or cod in crispy batter (£5.95), and smoked haddock and spring onion fishcakes (£6.25), with puddings such as cherry pancakes (£3.50); part of the eating area is no smoking. Three feet below sea level, the pub is situated in the middle of marshland, and there's plenty of surrounding birdlife. An interesting approach is a walk from the village through the tangle of boatyard; or you can moor a boat in the creek which runs just below the Saxon Shore Way (up a bank from the front and back gardens of the pub). Parking can be difficult at busy times. *(Recommended by the Didler, Keith and Chris O'Neill, Simon and Sally Small, Richard Siebert, Kevin Thorpe, Andrea Rampley)*

Free house ~ Licensees Derek and Ruth Cole ~ Real ale ~ Bar food (not Sun or Mon evenings, not Mon in winter) ~ Restaurant ~ (01795) 590088 ~ Children in dining room ~ Dogs welcome ~ Open 11-3(4 Sat), 6-11; 12-4, 6-10.30 Sun; closed Mon in winter

PENSHURST TQ5243 Map 3

Bottle House

Coldharbour Lane, Smarts Hill; leaving Penshurst SW on B2188 turn right at Smarts Hill signpost, then bear right towards Chiddingstone and Cowden; keep straight on

Kent Dining Pub of the Year

You may have trouble deciding what to eat at this very popular and welcoming pub – the range of well cooked dishes is awesome. Served all day by the friendly and obliging staff, the interesting menu could include soup (£3.75), smoked salmon mousse with lemon chutney (£4.95), vietnamese spring rolls (£5.25), chilli con carne (£7.95), vegetable nut wellington (£8.95), smoked chicken breast with wild mushroom sauce or chicken, king prawn and chorizo jambalaya (£10.95), and skate wing with capers and lemon butter, calves liver and bacon with garlic mash and caramelised red onion gravy or bass with spring onion, lemon and ginger sauce (£13.95), with around ten enticing puddings such as chocolate and pistachio parfait with chocolate sauce or kiwi pavlova with kiwi coulis (£4.50); children's meals (£4.95). On weekdays if you eat between 5 and 6.30, you get a 25% discount. Neatly kept, the low-beamed front bar has a well worn brick floor that extends behind the polished copper-topped bar counter, and big windows look on to a terrace with climbing plants and hanging baskets around picnic-sets under cocktail parasols, and beyond to views of quiet fields and oak trees. The unpretentious main red-carpeted bar has massive hop-covered supporting beams, two large stone pillars with a small brick fireplace (with a stuffed turtle to one side), and old paintings and photographs on mainly plastered walls; quite a collection of china pot lids, with more in the no smoking low-ceilinged dining room. Several cosy little areas lead off the main bar – all can be booked for private parties; one room is covered in sporting pictures right up to the ceiling, and another has pictures of dogs. Harveys and Larkins are well kept on handpump, and they have local wine; unobtrusive piped music. Good surrounding walks. *(Recommended by Tina and David Woods-Taylor, LM, Alan M Pring, Father Robert Marsh, A Sadler, Bob and Margaret Holder, Mrs C Lintott, Gwyn Jones, Humphry and Angela Crum Ewing, Sean and Sharon Pines, R B Gardiner)*

Free house ~ Licensees Gordon and Val Meer ~ Real ale ~ Bar food (12-10(9.30 Sun)) ~ Restaurant ~ (01892) 870306 ~ Children welcome ~ Dogs allowed in bar ~ Open 11-11; 12-10.30 Sun; closed 25 Dec

PLUCKLEY TQ9243 Map 3

Dering Arms

Pluckley Station, which is signposted from B2077

Fish lovers are in for a treat at this striking old dutch-gabled pub, which was originally built as a hunting lodge on the Dering estate. Skilfully cooked by the long-standing licensee, dishes might include provençale fish soup or grilled sardines with rosemary butter (£4.85), half a dozen irish oysters (£5.95), tuna steak with garlic and lemon butter (£13.95), whole crab salad (£14.95), and grilled dover sole (£15.95). If you don't like fish, other choices might be chicken livers (£4.85), ploughman's (£4.85), pie of the day (£8.45), leg of lamb with peppers, black olives, saffron and couscous (£12.95), and confit of duck (from £13.95), with puddings such as lemon posset (£4.85); they sell oysters to take away. The stylishly plain high-ceilinged main bar has a variety of good solid wooden furniture on stone floors, and a roaring log fire in the great fireplace; dominoes, cribbage and shove-ha'penny. The smaller half-panelled back bar has similar dark wood furnishings, and they've recently added a new bar with woodburning stove, comfortable armchairs and a grand piano. The extensive wine list is very good; also well kept Dering Ale (made for the pub by Goachers), home-made lemonade, local cider and quite a few malt whiskies. The big simple bedrooms have old ad hoc furnishings. Classic car meetings are held here on the second Sunday of the month, and they have regular special events such as wine tasting evenings and summer garden parties. *(Recommended by Mr and Mrs Robert Jamieson, Philip Hill, Jenny and Peter Lowater, Dick and Sue Ward, Andrea Rampley, Oliver and Sue Rowell, Mrs Sally Kingsbury, Anthony Barnes, Kevin Thorpe, Pete Walker)*

Free house ~ Licensee James Buss ~ Real ale ~ Bar food ~ Restaurant ~ (01233) 840371 ~ Children welcome ~ Dogs allowed in bar ~ Open 11.30(11 Sat)-3.30, 6-11; 12-3.30, 7-10.30 Sun; closed 26-27 Dec ~ Bedrooms: £35/£45

Rose & Crown

Mundy Bois – spelled Monday Boys on some maps – off Smarden Road SW of village centre

You can now enjoy the home-made bar food at this quietly set pub on the new terrace. Enjoyable bar snacks might include baguettes (from £4.50), chargrilled burger (£5.50), pizza (£5.75), and steak and kidney pie (£6.95), or you can choose from the restaurant menu dishes such as soup (£3.50), fried scallops with creamy hollandaise sauce (£5.25), mushroom and pepper stroganoff (£9.95), roast bass filled with tomato and onion coulis with a pesto and breadcrumb crust or calves liver with thyme and madeira jus (£13.50), and aberdeen angus fillet steak (£15.95); children's menu (£2.75). The bar menu is also available in the cosy candlelit restaurant (not Friday and Saturday evenings). The relaxed Village Bar, with its massive inglenook fireplace (favourite spot of Ted the pub labrador), leads on to a little pool room; TV, and piped music. Shepherd Neame Master Brew and a couple of guests such as Greene King IPA and Wadworths 6X are well kept on handpump, and they've a sensibly priced wine list (country wines too), plenty of malt whiskies, and farm cider; disabled facilities. There are seats in the garden, which has a children's play area. More reports please. *(Recommended by Jenny and Peter Lowater)*

Free house ~ Licensees Peter and Helen Teare ~ Real ale ~ Bar food ~ Restaurant ~ (01233) 840393 ~ Children in eating area of bar and restaurant ~ Dogs welcome ~ Open 11.30-3, 6-11; 11.30-11 Sat; 12-10.30 Sun; 11.30-3, 6-11 Sat and 12-3, 6-10.30 Sun in winter

SELLING TR0456 Map 3

Rose & Crown ★

Signposted from exit roundabout of M2 junction 7: keep right on through village and follow Perry Wood signposts; or from A252 just W of junction with A28 at Chilham follow Shottenden signpost, then right turn signposted Selling, then right signposted Perry Wood

The cottagey garden behind this welcoming 16th-c pub is something special. Charming in summer, it's attractively planted with climbers, ramblers and colourful plants, and there are plenty of picnic-sets, a neatly kept children's play area, bat and trap, and a small aviary; a new pergola (planted with vines and clematis) is fairy-lit at night, with cartwheel-back benches. The flowering tubs and hanging baskets in front are pretty too, and the terrace has outdoor heaters. Inside you'll find well kept Adnams Southwold, Goachers Mild and Harveys Best on handpump, along with a changing guest, local cider, a good range of malts and decent wines in good measures. Around the central servery there are pretty fresh flowers by each of the sturdy corner timbers, hop bines strung from the beams, and an interesting variety of corn-dolly work – more in a wall cabinet in one cosy side alcove, and much more again down steps in the comfortably cottagey no smoking restaurant. Apart from a couple of old-fashioned housekeeper's chairs by the huge fireplace (filled in summer with a colourful mass of silk flowers interlaced with more corn dollies and so forth), the seats are very comfortably cushioned, and there's a winter log fire; the walls have recently been re-painted in soft yellow and red. The licensees are friendly and attentive, and there's a pleasant atmosphere; cribbage, shove-ha'penny, dominoes and piped music. Besides tasty daily specials such as beef in mustard, caribbean chicken or stilton and asparagus pancake (all £8.50), bar food includes home-made soup (£3.75), filled rolls (from £4.25), ploughman's or whitebait (£4.95), baked potatoes from £4.95), chicken, ham and leek pie or spaghetti bolognese (£6), and chicken tikka massala, cod and smoked haddock mornay or chinese crispy chilli beef (£8.50), with lots of puddings on show in a cold cabinet down steps in a small family room (£3.50). Readers recommend the Sunday roast beef (£7.50); they do children's meals (from £2.95). The pub is surrounded by natural woodland, with good walking. *(Recommended by Peter Scillitoe, Will Watson, Guy Vowles, M and R Thomas, Alan Cowell, Mr and Mrs J Hale, Mike and Shelley Woodroffe, Ian Phillips)*

Free house ~ Licensees Richard and Jocelyn Prebble ~ Real ale ~ Bar food (not Sun or Mon evenings) ~ Restaurant ~ (01227) 752214 ~ Children in restaurant and family room ~ Dogs allowed in bar ~ Open 11-3, 6.30-11; 12-3, 7-10.30 Sun; closed evenings 25-26 Dec and 1 Jan

SMARDEN TQ8842 Map 3

Chequers 🛏

Off A20 in Charing, via Pluckley; or off A274 at Standen just under 1 mile N of its junction with A262; The Street

In an attractive village, this 14th-c inn is handily open all day. A walkway in the attractive landscaped garden leads to a pond with fish and waterfowl, and there's an arbour with climbing plants; the terrace has nice green metal tables and chairs on the york stone. With a pleasantly relaxed atmosphere and chatting locals, the cosy and comfortable bar has well kept Adnams, Bass, Harveys Best and a guest such as Kelham Island Easy Rider on handpump. They've a decent wine list, with ten wines by the glass, and several malt whiskies; piped music. Well presented bar food (not served on Saturday evening – only restaurant meals then), made with fresh local produce, could include home-made soup (£3.95), filled baguettes with chips (from £4.95), ploughman's (£5.95), gammon and eggs (£7.75), fisherman's pie or scampi (£7.95), and home-made chicken curry (£8.25), and you can also choose dishes from the restaurant menu such as tempura prawns with sweet chilli sauce (£5.50), smoked haddock with leek and bacon mash and grain mustard butter sauce (£11.95), pork tenderloin with mushroom and brandy sauce (£12.50), or chargrilled rib-eye steak with pepper and shallot mash (£12.95). There are elegant reproduction tables and chairs in the dining area, and they've added another no smoking restaurant. Readers enjoy staying here; they do good breakfasts. *(Recommended by Mr and Mrs P L Haigh, Richard and Margaret Peers, Sarah Davis, Rod Lambert, Mr and Mrs H D Brierly, Comus and Sarah Elliott, Kevin Thorpe, Conor McGaughey)*

Free house ~ Licensee Lisa Bullock ~ Bar food (12-2.30, 6-9.30(10 Sat)) ~ Restaurant ~ (01233) 770217 ~ Children in eating area of bar and restaurant ~ Dogs allowed in bar ~ Open 11-11; 12-10.30 Sun ~ Bedrooms: £40B/£70S(£70B)

SNARGATE TQ9928 Map 3

Red Lion ★

B2080 Appledore—Brenzett

In the same family for 93 years, this unusual completely unspoilt village local is a great favourite with readers. Hardly modernised since 1890, the three perfectly simple little rooms still have their original cream tongue and groove wall panelling, a couple of heavy beams in a sagging ceiling, dark pine Victorian farmhouse chairs on bare boards, lots of old photographs and other memorabilia, and a coal fire; outdoor lavatories, of course. One charming little room, with a frosted glass wall through to the bar and a sash window looking out to a cottage garden, has only two dark pine pews beside two long tables, a couple more farmhouse chairs and a nice old piano stacked with books. Cheerful groups of regulars catch up on local news and play toad in the hole; darts, shove-ha'penny, cribbage, dominoes, nine men's morris and table skittles. Goachers Light and Mild, and a couple of well kept guests from brewers such as Grand Union and Hop Back are tapped straight from casks on a low rack behind an unusual shop-like marble-topped counter (little marks it as a bar other than a few glasses on two small shelves, some crisps and half a dozen spirits bottles); you can also get Double Vision cider from nearby Staplehurst, and country wines. They don't serve food, but you're welcome to bring your own. *(Recommended by Pete Baker, R E Davidson, Richard Pitcher, Ron Shelton, the Didler, Gill and Tony Morriss, Kevin Thorpe, Phil and Sally Gorton, Andrea Rampley, Gwyn Jones, Mrs C Lintott, Pete Walker, Peter Meister)*

Free house ~ Licensee Mrs Jemison ~ Real ale ~ No credit cards ~ (01797) 344648 ~ Children in family room ~ Dogs allowed in bar ~ Open 12-3, 7-11(10.30 Sun)

STAPLEHURST TQ7847 Map 3

Lord Raglan

About 1½ miles from town centre towards Maidstone, turn right off A229 into Chart Hill Road opposite Cross at Hand Garage; OS Sheet 188 map reference 785472

You'll find no piped music or games machines at this unpretentious and simple yet quite civilised country inn, just nice little conversational nooks. The interior is quite compact, with a narrow bar – you walk in almost on top of the counter and chatting locals – widening slightly at one end to a small area with a big log fire in winter. In the other direction it works its way round to an intimate area at the back, with lots of wine bottles lined up on a low shelf. Everywhere you look on the low beams are masses of hops, and the mixed collection of comfortably worn dark wood furniture on quite well used dark brown carpet tiles and nice old parquet flooring is mostly 1930s. They serve well kept Goachers Light and Harveys Best, along with a guest from a brewer such as Woods on handpump; a good wine list too, and summer farm cider. Enjoyable bar food, up on blackboard menus, includes a few pubby staples such as sandwiches (from £2.95), filled baguettes (from £4.95), sausage, egg and chips, macaroni cheese or chilli con carne (£5.95), as well as more elaborate dishes such as smoked venison and pickled walnut (£5.50), chicken breast with white wine and mushroom sauce (£8.95), grilled lamb chops or guinea fowl breast with red wine sauce (£9.95), and grilled dover sole or fillet steak (£15.50), and home-made puddings such as treacle sponge pudding (£3.95). Small french windows lead out to an enticing little high-hedged terraced area with white plastic tables and chairs, and there are wooden picnic-sets in the side orchard; reasonable wheelchair access. More reports please. *(Recommended by Tony Hobden, John Hendy, Father Robert Marsh)*

Free house ~ Licensees Andrew and Annie Hutchison ~ Real ale ~ Bar food (12-2.30, 7-10; not Sun) ~ Restaurant ~ (01622) 843747 ~ Children welcome ~ Dogs welcome ~ Open 12-3, 6-11; closed Sun

STODMARSH TR2160 Map 3

Red Lion

High Sreet; off A257 just E of Canterbury

The genial landlord helps create a convivial and relaxed atmosphere at this memorable little pub. Full of character, several idiosyncratic rooms wrap themselves around the big island bar. You'll find hops all over the place, wine bottles (some empty and some full) crammed along mantelpieces and along one side of the bar, all manner of paintings and pictures, copper kettles and old cooking implements, well used cookery books, big stone bottles and milk churns, trugs and baskets, old tennis racquets and straw hats, a collection of brass instruments in one area with sheet music all over the walls, and some jazz records; a couple of little stall areas have hop sacks draped over the partitioning. There are green-painted, cushioned mate's chairs around a mix of nice pine tables, lit candles in unusual metal candleholders, fresh flowers on every table and big arrangements on the bars, and high bar stools with cheerful chatting locals. The large cats sit snoozily by the big log fire; piped jazz, and bat and trap. Well kept Greene King IPA, Old Speckled Hen, and a seasonal guest are tapped straight from the cask, and they've a good wine list with several by the glass, excellent summer Pimms and winter mulled wine, and cider. Made using plenty of local produce, enjoyable dishes from the regularly changing menu might include baguettes (not Sunday lunch or Saturday evening), baby spinach and streaky bacon and avocado salad (£6.25), hot asparagus with pine nuts and butter (£6.75), potted prawns with smoked wild salmon and dill (£7.25), a mixed platter of meat, fish and cheese (£7.95), pies such as chicken, pigeon breast and asparagus or oak-smoked haddock, salmon and cod with sage mash (£10.95), filo pastry parcels with thai vegetables and hoi sin sauce (£11.95), and rabbit, wild pigeon and pheasant casserole (£12.95), with puddings such as bramley apple pie or strawberry and raspberry mousse with mint (£3.95); they sell eggs and chutneys. There are picnic-sets under umbrellas in the back garden, with pretty flowerbeds; there's a rabbit called Buster, and perhaps some chickens. Although readers have really enjoyed staying overnight, please note that the bedrooms don't have bathrooms. *(Recommended by Kevin Thorpe, Barry and Patricia Wooding, Ian and Lin Gill, Tom and Ruth Rees, Mike and Linda Hudson, Sean and Sharon Pines)*

Free house ~ Licensee Robert Whigham ~ Real ale ~ Bar food (not Sun evening) ~ Restaurant ~ (01227) 721339 ~ Children welcome ~ Dogs allowed in bar ~ Live jazz first Weds in month ~ Open 10.30-11; 12-10.30 Sun ~ Bedrooms: /£60

Bedroom prices normally include full English breakfast, VAT and any inclusive service charge that we know of. Prices before the '/' are for single rooms, after for two people in double or twin (B includes a private bath, S a private shower). If there is no '/', the prices are only for twin or double rooms (as far as we know there are no singles). If there is no B or S, as far as we know no rooms have private facilities.

TUNBRIDGE WELLS TQ5639 Map 3

Beacon

Tea Garden Lane; leaving Tunbridge Wells westwards on A264, this is the left turn-off on Rusthall Common after Nevill Park

With good hillside views, the pergola-covered wooden deck at this airy Victorian pub is the perfect place to relax with a drink on a sunny afternoon. They've around nine wines by the glass to choose from, and Harveys Best, Larkins and Timothy Taylors Landlord are well kept on handpump kept under light blanket pressure. The dining area and spreading bar run freely into each other, with stripped panelling, lovely wood floors, ornately built wall units and glowing lamps giving a solidly comfortable feel. You'll usually find a nice mix of customers chatting at the sweeping bar counter with its ranks of shiny bottles, or on the comfortable sofas by the fine old wood fireplace. Besides lunchtime sandwiches (from £4.75) or baked potatoes with interesting fillings (from £5.50), enjoyable (but not cheap) bar food could be home-made soup (£4.25), moules marinière (£6.50), ale and chive-battered hake fillet (£7.50), mushroom and aubergine stroganoff with almond and raisin rice (£8), chargrilled gammon steak with champ and mild mustard sauce (£9.25), dressed crab salad (£11.50), and confit of duck with bubble and squeak and red wine jus (£10.75), with specials such as bass with clam and mussel chowder (£14.75), and grilled barracuda (£14.95), and good puddings. There's shove-ha'penny, cribbage, dominoes; in the summer volleyball, boules and (very rare for a pub these days) even rounders. The bedrooms are comfortable, and they do good breakfasts. *(Recommended by D Charry, Mrs Catherine Draper, Peter Meister, Gwyn Jones, Clare and Peter Pearse, Mrs K J Betts, Mrs C Lintott)*

Free house ~ Licensee John Cullen ~ Real ale ~ Bar food (12-2.30, 6.30-9.30; 12-9.30 in summer) ~ Restaurant ~ (01892) 524252 ~ Children in eating area of bar and restaurant ~ Dogs allowed in bar ~ Folk club second and fourth Mon of month ~ Open 11-11; 12-10.30 Sun ~ Bedrooms: £68.50S/£97B

Sankeys

Mount Ephraim (A26 just N of junction with A267)

Most people come to this thriving pub/wine bar for the delicious fresh fish. A typical choice might include seafood soup (£5), queen scallops grilled with garlic (£6.75), mussels in beer (£7), home-made salmon and cod fishcakes with parsley sauce or thai crab cakes with chilli dip (£8.50), seafood paella (£11.50), seafood thermidor (£14.50), and giant cornish spider crab (£16.50); they also do lunchtime baguettes, daily specials, and a few choices for non-fish eaters such as steaks (£17.50). With a buoyantly chatty atmosphere, the dimly lit cellar bar has pews around closely spaced sturdy old pine tables, and old mirrors, prints, enamel advertising signs, antique beer engines and other bric-a-brac (most of which has been salvaged from local pub closures); half is no smoking. French windows lead from here to a nice suntrap deck (no booking) with teak tables and chairs under cocktail parasols, and a barbecue. By comparison with the cellar bar, the new ground-floor bar is light and airy, with high ceilings and big windows, and at lunchtime at least usually quieter than downstairs; it has a good-sized serving bar, pews and wooden chairs around pubby tables on bare boards, and a rather wine-oriented décor. You need to book or arrive early if you want a table in the cellar bar; piped music and TV. Harveys Best and Larkins are well kept on handpump, and there's a very good wine list with changing offers; also interesting bottled beers, and quite a choice of unusual teas. The long-serving staff (including family) are very friendly. More reports please. *(Recommended by David and Lynne Cure, Mrs C Lintott, Dr David Cockburn)*

Free house ~ Licensee Guy Sankey ~ Real ale ~ Bar food (all day summer; 12-3, 6-10; 1-5 Sun; not Sun evening, 25-26 Dec) ~ Restaurant ~ (01892) 511422 ~ Children in eating area of bar ~ Dogs allowed in bar ~ Live bands Sun night ~ Open 12-11(10.30 Sun); closed 25-26 Dec

ULCOMBE TQ8550 Map 3

Pepper Box

Fairbourne Heath; signposted from A20 in Harrietsham, or follow Ulcombe signpost from A20, then turn left at crossroads with sign to pub, then right at next minor crossroads

Views from the terrace of this cosy old country inn stretch over a great plateau of rolling arable farmland, and if you're in the garden, with its small pond, shrubs and flowerbeds, you may be lucky enough to catch a glimpse of deer. Inside, the homely bar has standing timbers and low beams hung with hops, copper kettles and pans on window sills, some very low-seated windsor chairs and wing armchairs, and two armchairs and a sofa by the splendid inglenook fireplace with its lovely log fire. A side area, more functionally furnished for eating, extends into a snug little no smoking dining room; piped music. Well kept Shepherd Neame Bitter, Spitfire and a seasonal guest are tapped from the cask, and they've local apple juice. The tabby tom is called Fred, and there are two more cats and a couple of collies called Rosie and Molly. You can choose from bar food such as home-made soup (£3.50), sandwiches (from £3.50), ploughman's (from £4.50), local sausages and onion gravy or braised beef and onions (£8.50), or more elaborate restaurant dishes (also available in the bar) such as baked avocado with smoked bacon and stilton (£5.80), pork tenderloin with roasted oranges (£10), and fried bass with lobster bisque (£11.50); puddings might include kentish apple pie. The name of the pub refers to the pepperbox pistol – an early type of revolver with numerous barrels. No children inside. *(Recommended by Peter Scillitoe, Philip Hill, John Branston, MLR, Gordon Stevenson, Howard and Margaret Buchanan, Leo and Barbara Lionet, Father Robert Marsh, Andrea Rampley)*

Shepherd Neame ~ Tenants Geoff and Sarah Pemble ~ Real ale ~ Bar food (not Sun or Mon evenings) ~ Restaurant ~ (01622) 842558 ~ Dogs allowed in bar ~ Open 11-3, 6.30-11; 12-3, 7-10.30 Sun

WEST PECKHAM TQ6452 Map 3

Swan on the Green

Off B2016, second turning left heading N from A26 (Swanton Road)

With half a dozen own-brewed ales and well prepared food, this little tucked-away country pub has quickly become a favourite with readers. The bar is light, airy, and open-plan, with rush-seated dining chairs and cushioned church settles around an attractive mix of well spaced refectory and other pale oak tables on the wood strip floor, lovely big bunches of flowers (one placed in the knocked-through brick fireplace), hops and beams, some modern paintings at one end, black and white photographs of locals at the other end, and good aztec-patterned curtains; piped music. You'll find Bewick, Fuggles, Ginger Swan, Swan Mild, Portside, Trumpeter and Whooper Pale well kept on handpump, and a good mix of customers from suited office workers to friendly locals chatting to the amiable licensee. There's an emphasis on the enjoyable and generously served (but not cheap) bar food. From the interesting changing bar menu, dishes might include lunchtime filled ciabatta flutes (£5.50), and ploughman's (£6.50), as well as fried chicken livers with caramelised red onions (£6.45), fresh cromer crab or tagliatelle with spinach, chicken and blue cheese (£7.50), warm chicken breast and chargrilled bacon salad (£8.50), baby red mullet with minted couscous (£9.95), and steak (from £12.95), with puddings such as summer fruit pudding with raspberry coulis and clotted cream (£4.25); from January to March they do a beat the clock evening meal deal. They may add an 'optional' 10% surcharge to the bill. There are picnic-sets under parasols in front of the building, and more on the charming cricket green opposite; they take a £10 deposit for a rug if you want to eat outside. The nearby church is partly Saxon. *(Recommended by Bob and Margaret Holder, Lesley and Peter Barrett, Simon and Sally Small, Hugh Roberts, Kevin Thorpe, Paul Hopton, Gerry and Rosemary Dobson, B and M Kendall, Andrea Rampley, Richard Houghton, Mrs C Lintott, Mike Gorton, Derek Thomas)*

Own brew ~ Licensee Gordon Milligan ~ Real ale ~ Bar food (not Sun or Mon evening) ~ Restaurant ~ (01622) 812271 ~ Children welcome ~ Dogs welcome ~ Open 11-3, 6-11; 11-11 Sat; 12-10.30 Sun; 11-4, 6-11 Sat, 12-4 Sun in winter; closed 25 Dec

LUCKY DIP

Besides the fully inspected pubs, you might like to try these Lucky Dips recommended to us and described by readers (if you do, please send us reports: www.goodguides.co.uk).

ADDINGTON TQ6559

Angel [just off M20, junction 4; Addington Green]: 14th-c pub in classic village green setting, olde-worlde décor with candles in bottles on scrubbed deal tables and big fireplaces, well kept Courage Best, lots of wines by the glass, wide choice of up-to-date food from sandwiches up, Thurs pasta night, quick friendly service, stables restaurant; live music Weds *(Adam and Joan Bunting)*

ALKHAM TR2542

Marquis of Granby [Alkham Valley Rd (back rd Folkestone—Dover)]: White Georgian house with charming views, modernised inside, warm and pleasant, with no smoking areas, well kept Greene King Old Speckled Hen, Shepherd Neame ales inc seasonal one and Youngs, enjoyable food esp fish in bar and restaurant, welcoming staff; attractive garden *(Alan and Paula McCully)*

APPLEDORE TQ9529

Black Lion [The Street]: Unpretentious compact village pub with huge range of good value generous food all day esp local fish, partitioned eating area, friendly helpful staff, three or four changing ales such as Greene King; tables out by attractive village street *(J P Humphery, CJ, John Branston)*

☆ *Railway Hotel* [Station Rd (B2080 E)]: Victorian hotel with comfortable and spaciously modernised bar and lounge, woodburners, rail memorabilia, fishtank and historic newspapers, big family dining room, wide food choice from sandwiches up, two changing ales from small breweries, farm cider, late summer beer festival; garden tables, 12 bedrooms with own bathrooms in small motel wing *(Kevin Thorpe)*

BADLESMERE TR0154

Red Lion [A251, S of M2 junction 6]: Attractive and spacious partly 16th-c country pub, well kept Fullers London Pride, Greene King Abbot, Shepherd Neame and changing guests from small breweries, Johnson's farm cider from Sheppey, enjoyable food (not Sun pm) using local produce, pool and pub games; piped pop music, live Fri; pleasant garden, paddock for caravans and tents, summer beer and folk festivals, open all day Fri-Sun *(Kevin Thorpe)*

BARFRESTONE TR2650

☆ *Yew Tree* [off A256 N of Dover; or off A2 at Barham]: Chatty family-run country local tucked behind huge yew tree, hospitable licensees, good value blackboard food (not Sun evening or Mon) from baguettes, ciabattas and baked potatoes to roasts and local game, five well kept changing ales inc a Mild, farm cider, 12 good value wines by the glass, mix of old pine furniture on bare boards, small carpeted bar area, woodburner and games in family room with warm red décor; may be quiet piped music; pub serves as 'shop' for the famous next-door church with its wonderful Norman carvings, terrace tables, open all day Fri-Sun in summer, cl Mon lunchtime *(Kevin Thorpe, LYM)*

BARHAM TR2050

Duke of Cumberland [The Street]: Warm and friendly open-plan country dining pub under newish management, sensible blackboard choice of enjoyable food, three real ales such as Adnams, Flowers and Fullers London Pride, decent wines, good attentive staff, bare boards and flagstones, open fire, no smoking back room; bedrooms *(Vanessa Young, Catherine and Rob Dunster, David Barnes)*

BENOVER TQ7048

Woolpack: Pretty tile-hung and timber-framed pub with three well kept Shepherd Neame ales, flagstoned main area set for the good value tasty food, with prints on stripped brickwork, beamed and partly panelled smaller bar, friendly landlord and nice traditional atmosphere; tables on front terrace and big back lawn *(Peter Meister, LYM)*

BIDBOROUGH TQ5643

☆ *Hare & Hounds* [Bidborough Ridge]: Nicely placed smart local, recently tastefully extended, rugs on boards, stripped brick and pine, prints and old photographs, pleasant dining room, welcoming staff, wide range of enjoyable food inc both traditional and innovative dishes, well kept Harveys Best and Shepherd Neame Spitfire, cafetière coffee, no piped music; darts and pool in public bar *(Mrs C Lintott)*

BISHOPSBOURNE TR1852

☆ *Mermaid* [signed off A2]: Traditional welcoming unspoilt country local in same family for many years, simple lunchtime food (not Sun) inc good filled rolls or sandwiches and bargain hot dishes, well kept Shepherd Neame beers inc a seasonal one, friendly regulars, coal fire, darts and old books in small back public bar, no machines; may be piped local radio; dogs and walkers welcome, lovely unspoilt Kentish village nr Pilgrims Way and North Downs Way *(Peter Heaton, Guy Vowles, Kevin Thorpe)*

BOTOLPHS BRIDGE TR1233

Botolphs Bridge Inn [W of Hythe]: Edwardian local, handsome building but unpretentious and friendly, with airy chatty open-plan bar, small dining room one end (children allowed here), wide choice of enjoyable sensibly priced home-made food with real chips, big helpings, quick pleasant service, real ales such as Greene King IPA and Old Speckled Hen, two log fires; games area, occasional barbecues in small garden *(Glenwys and Alan Lawrence)*

BOUGHTON STREET TR0659

White Horse [nr M2 junction 7; The Street]: Former coaching inn comfortably refurbished as a Mulberry Inn, dark beams, tiles and bare boards, open fires and woodburner, well prepared food, well kept Shepherd Neame Bitter or Spitfire, good wine choice, daily papers, uniformed staff; piped music; children welcome, tables in garden, bedrooms, open all day *(LYM, Kevin Thorpe)*

BOXLEY TQ7758

Kings Arms [1¾ miles from M20 junction 7; opp church]: Cosy and friendly locally popular country dining pub, largely 16th/17th-c, low beams, red chesterfields by huge fireplace, well kept Adnams, Fullers London Pride and Gales HSB, good choice of sensibly priced straightforward food (all day Sun) from sandwiches and ploughman's up; may be piped music, quiet dogs allowed; appealing garden with good play area, open all day, pretty village, pleasant walks *(Julie Milton)*

BRASTED TQ4654

White Hart [High St (A25)]: Roomy largely no smoking Vintage Inn, several snug areas taking their mood from the original Battle of Britain bar with signatures and mementoes of Biggin Hill fighter pilots, beams and log fires, helpful staff, well kept Bass and Tetleys, good choice of wine and fresh orange juice; children welcome, big neatly kept garden with well spaced tables and play area; bedrooms, pretty village with several antiques shops *(LYM, Tina and David Woods-Taylor, B J Harding, Alan M Pring, GHC, Alan Kilpatrick, Conor McGaughey)*

BRENCHLEY TQ6841

Halfway House [Horsmonden Rd]: Welcoming new landlord and staff, well kept Adnams Broadside, Harveys and Larkins, plans for late May and Aug bank hol beer festivals, sensibly priced food inc steaks and Thurs night curry bargains for two *(BB, Peter Meister)*

BRIDGE TR1854

Plough & Harrow [High St]: Friendly recently extended 17th-c village local with well kept Shepherd Neame ales and good wine choice, coal fire and lots of sporting prints in open-plan brick-walled lounge, public bar with bar billiards and open fire, back games room with darts, TV and woodburner; no food, open all day Sat *(Kevin Thorpe, Roger Mardon)*

BROADSTAIRS TR3967

White Swan [Reading St, St Peters]: Low armchairs and tables in comfortable lounge, pool and darts in public bar area, well kept Adnams, Bass and four interesting changing beers from small breweries, simple food choice from cheap sandwiches up (not Sun lunchtime), modernish décor *(Kevin Thorpe)*

CANTERBURY TR1458

Millers Arms [St Radigunds St]: Welcoming pub with well kept Shepherd Neame ales, good wine choice, several pleasantly refurbished rooms, interesting pictures and sayings; unobtrusive piped music; decent bedrooms, quiet street nr river and handy for Marlow Theatre *(Richard Waller, Pauline Smith, Patrick Hancock, Keith and Janet Morris)*

New Inn [Havelock St]: Friendly bustle in unspoilt Victorian terraced local, elderly furnishings, bare boards, gas fire, good beermat collection, changing ales such as Brakspears and Greene King, simple food, modern back conservatory; juke box popular with students, nearby parking difficult *(James Woods, Patrick Hancock)*

Simple Simons [Church Lane, St Radigunds]: Step down into basic pub in 14th-c building, heavy beams, broad floorboards, flagstones and some stripped masonry, two woodburners, dim-lit upstairs banqueting hall, well kept Bass and up to five guest beers, impressive pump clip collection, simple lunchtime food inc good value sandwiches and speciality home-made pies; good piped classical music in the daytime, more studenty evening, frequent live jazz and folk; tables in courtyard, open all day *(Kevin Thorpe, Conor McGaughey)*

Three Tuns [Watling St, opp St Margaret St]: Interesting 15th-c building with nice old-fashioned décor, well kept Shepherd Neame Spitfire, friendly service, enjoyable well priced food; piped music *(Richard Waller, Pauline Smith, Patrick Hancock)*

White Hart [Worthgate Pl, opp tree-shaded square off Castle St]: Three well kept Shepherd Neame real ales, good wines by the glass, enjoyable home-made food, friendly young landlord, good prompt service, side room with open fire and SkyTV; large garden behind – one of very few in the city *(Keith and Chris O'Neill, Guy Vowles, Patrick Hancock)*

CAPEL TQ6444

Dovecote [Alders Rd; SE of Tonbridge]: Country pub recently refurbished under new licensees, beams and some stripped brickwork, pitched-ceiling no smoking dining end, friendly service, usual food from baguettes to popular Sun lunch, bargain suppers for two Mon and Thurs, several real ales such as Adnams Broadside and Larkins tapped from the cask, farm cider; picnic-sets in back garden with terrace, doves and play area *(Peter Meister)*

CAPEL-LE-FERNE TR2538

Lighthouse [Old Dover Rd]: Family-run hotel in good clifftop spot overlooking Channel, large bar and restaurant serving wide food choice from bar snacks up, good-sized area set aside for non-eaters, well kept Greene King ales, good wine choice, friendly staff, indoor play area; bedrooms *(Alan and Paula McCully)*

Valiant Sailor [New Dover Rd (B2011)]: Friendly roadside pub, open all day, with well kept Bass, popular generous straightforward food inc good value fish night (Tues), steak night (Weds) and Sun lunch, separate no smoking dining area; handy for cliff walks and Battle of Britain memorial *(Alan and Paula McCully)*

CHARTHAM HATCH TR1056

☆ *Chapter Arms* [New Town St]: Sizeable 18th-c pub overlooking orchards, flowers and candles on tables, heavily hop-hung ceiling with brass instruments and fairy lights, Harveys Best and Shepherd Neame Bitter and Goldings, decent wine, friendly service, enjoyable generous food, restaurant through doorway decorated in lilac, green and silver; quiet piped music, jazz Mon; nice teak garden furniture, lots of flower tubs etc *(Peter Dixon, BB, Bruce M Drew)*

CHILHAM TR0653

White Horse [The Square]: On prettiest village square in Kent, with a couple of tables out on the corner; comfortably modernised beamed bar with good log fire, well kept real ales, decent wines, smiling service, back eating area with separate ordering counter for food from baguettes up; piped music *(LYM, Gloria Bax)*

☆ *Woolpack* [off A28/A252; The Street]: Charming unfussy décor, pews, sofa, little armchairs, good inglenook log fires, good value food from soup and sandwiches up, cheerful welcoming service, well kept Shepherd Neame ales; children allowed in restaurant, bedrooms, delightful village *(LYM, Gloria Bax)*

CHIPSTEAD TQ4956

Bricklayers Arms [Chevening Rd]: Attractive old local overlooking lake and green, heavily beamed bar with open fire and fine racehorse painting, unpretentious larger back restaurant, good choice of appetising food (not Sun evening), full range of Harveys beers tapped from casks behind long counter, good atmosphere *(B J Harding)*

COWDEN TQ4640

☆ *Fountain* [off A264 and B2026; High St]: Attractive tile-hung country local in pretty village, steep steps to unpretentious dark-panelled bar with well kept Harveys, Larkins and guests, decent wines, friendly licensees, darts and log fire, sensibly short blackboard choice of good enterprising food inc good Sun roast, woodburner in small beamed back dining room; piped music, can get smoky, or noisy if football on TV; walkers and dogs welcome, annual flower show *(BB, Jason Caulkin, Kevin Thorpe)*

☆ *Queens Arms* [Cowden Pound; junction B2026 with Markbeech rd]: Unspoilt and warmly welcoming two-room country pub like something from the 1930s, with splendid landlady, well kept Adnams, coal fire, darts; dogs welcome, occasional folk music or morris dancers; may be cl wkdy lunchtimes but normally opens 10am *(R E Davidson, the Didler, Kevin Thorpe, Pete Baker, RWC)*

CRANBROOK TQ7736

George [Stone St]: Civilised and friendly, with well kept Harveys and guest beers, popular restaurant; nicely old-fashioned bedrooms *(John Hendy)*

CROCKHAM HILL TQ4450

Royal Oak: Cosy village local with friendly obliging landlord, well kept Shepherd Neame ales, very popular lunchtime for wide choice of enjoyable honest food from sandwiches and baked potatoes to steaks, daily papers, comfortable high-backed seats, no music or fruit machines; handy for walks *(Christopher Wright, Gwyn Jones, Len Banister, Gordon Stevenson)*

DARTFORD TQ5473

Paper Moon [High St]: Wetherspoons with well kept Courage Directors, Shepherd Neame Spitfire and three guest beers, segregated area for diners, non-smokers and children; disabled facilities *(Quentin and Carol Williamson)*

Wharf [Galleon Bvd, Crossways; just off A206 NE of centre]: Newish pub in pleasant pondside spot, usual food from sandwiches and baked potatoes up, carvery with early evening bargains Mon-Thurs, Shepherd Neame real ales; tables outside, views of Queen Elizabeth II Bridge *(Alan M Pring, Quentin and Carol Williamson)*

DEAL TR3752

Bohemian [Beach St]: Plain modern bar specialising in continental draft beers in their proper glasses, also bottled imports and Adnams Best and Regatta, friendly knowledgeable landlord, relaxed atmosphere; tables in small garden behind *(Peter Meister)*

Chequers [Golf Rd (old coast rd to Sandwich)]: Modern-look open-plan pub, airy and relaxed, well kept Adnams Broadside and Shepherd Neame Spitfire, decent food from baguettes up inc plenty of fresh fish and seafood, side eating area; adjoining chalet park *(Peter Meister)*

Port Arms [Beach St]: Seafront pub with dining tables in big carpeted front bar, nautical prints on brick walls, popular food all day inc cheap Sun lunches and massive mixed meats, Bass and Greene King IPA, Abbot and Old Speckled Hen; small back pool room, piped pop music; some tables outside *(Kevin Thorpe)*

Saracens Head [Alfred Sq]: Pleasant and well kept, with good welcoming service, well cooked reasonably priced traditional food from sandwiches up, well kept beers (landlord knowledgeable and helpful about them), side pool table; small flower-filled courtyard *(Justin MacKenzie, Valerie MacKenzie)*

Ship: Three neatly kept small linked areas, well kept Bass, Hook Norton, Hop Back Summer Lightning and two guest beers, cheap rolls, woodburner, dark wood, stripped bricks, local ship and wreck pictures, piano; piped music may obtrude a bit; small pretty garden, open all day *(Kevin Thorpe, Hywel Bevan)*

DENTON TR2147

Jackdaw [A260 Canterbury—Folkestone]: Imposing brick and flint pub serving as useful roadside all-day family eatery, comfortable open-plan bar decorated in cream and book-room red with RAF memorabilia in front area, well kept Shepherd Neame Spitfire, Tetleys Mild, Charles Wells Bombardier and a couple of guest beers, good value food, friendly young staff, large back restaurant; quiet piped music; children welcome, tables in pleasant garden, open all day *(Peter Scillitoe, Kevin Thorpe)*

DOVER TR3141

Mogul [Chapel Pl, off York St South roundabout]: Town local with three constantly changing well kept ales tapped from the cask, open-plan main bar with harbour views and raj prints, separate back public bar with woodburner and traditional pub games, basic food all day; may be piped jazz; tables outside, open all day *(Pete Baker, R E Davidson, Kevin Thorpe)*

DUNGENESS TR0916

Pilot [Battery Rd]: Small original bar, modern extension with second bar and family area, wide choice of straightforward food from sandwiches up inc good generous fish and chips, well kept Greene King IPA and Abbot *(Peter Meister)*

DUNKS GREEN TQ6152

☆ *Kentish Rifleman*: Cosy early 16th-c beamed and timbered pub (the big stone-arched vaulted cellar may even be Roman), log fire in dining lounge (the smallish room areas means there's quite a bit of coming and going), good well priced traditional menu inc plenty of sandwiches and baguettes and choice of Sun roasts, chirpy landlord and good welcoming service, well kept changing ales such as Fullers London Pride, Greene King Abbot and Youngs Special, decent wine and coffee, plenty of character, no machines, small public bar welcoming dogs (friendly pub dog); may be quiet piped music; tables in well designed garden behind, good walks *(GHC, Peter Meister, Martin Jennings, BB, K Gethin, Carl and Jackie Cranmer, Mrs Catherine Draper, Kevin Thorpe, Annette Tress, Gary Smith, Debbie and Neil Hayter)*

DUNTON GREEN TQ5156

Bullfinch [London Rd, Riverhead]: Country Carvery family dining pub, friendly service; play area in garden *(Alan M Pring)*

EAST MALLING TQ7057

King & Queen [N of stn, back rd between A20 at Larkfield and A26]: 14th-c but much altered, with big low-ceilinged dark plum rooms, some handsome panelling, wide choice of food, not cheap but imaginative, inc lots of fish, Nelson ales and changing guests such as Hook Norton Old Hooky, Ringwood Best and Wadworths 6X, separate dining room; tables in smallish garden *(BB, Kevin Thorpe)*

EASTLING TQ9656

☆ *Carpenters Arms* [off A251 S of M2 junction 6, via Painters Forstal; The Street]: Pretty, cosy and cottagey 14th-c oak-beamed pub with big log fireplaces front and back, long-serving Irish landlord and welcoming staff, decent food (not Sun evening) inc good generous Sun lunch, well kept Shepherd Neame ales, masses of bric-a-brac; children allowed in small candlelit restaurant, some tables outside, small but well equipped bedrooms in separate building, huge breakfast *(LYM, Kevin Thorpe)*

EGERTON TQ9047

George [The Street]: Friendly 16th-c timbered pub, log fire in big heavy-beamed pink-walled bar, another in big games room with darts, pool and juke box, good range of decent bar food, Fullers London Pride, Greene King Abbot and Old Speckled Hen, Shepherd Neame and Timothy Taylors Landlord, attractive candlelit restaurant, well kept Greene King, Hook Norton and Shepherd Neame ales; pretty village setting, pleasant country view *(Kevin Thorpe)*

Queens Arms [Forstal Rd]: Comfortable 200-year-old village local, simple menu, friendly staff, two Goachers, four Shepherd Neame and two small-brewery guest beers, open fire, beer-bottle collecting dog called Jess; piped music; nice garden with pond and well, open all day summer *(Kevin Thorpe)*

EYNSFORD TQ5365

☆ *Malt Shovel* [Station Rd]: Neatly kept spacious old-fashioned dining pub, child-friendly and handy for castles and Roman villa, dark panelling, good food choice from some good value straightforward pubby dishes to more costly things inc quite a few fish and seafood dishes (lobster tank), well kept Fullers London Pride and Greene King IPA, good choice of wine by the glass, quick helpful service, nice atmosphere; car park across busy road *(Jim and Maggie Cowell, GHC, LM, Pete Walker)*

FAVERSHAM TR0161

Albion [Front Brents]: New tenants for popular light and airy pub in improving waterside area, solid pine furnishings, local pictures on pale green walls, food (not Sun evening) from sandwiches up, well kept Shepherd Neame ales inc seasonal from the nearby brewery, friendly smiling staff, flowers and candles on tables; children welcome in restaurant area, disabled lavatories, picnic-sets out on riverside walkway (Saxon Shore long-distance path), open all day summer *(Tina and David Woods-Taylor, LYM, Kevin Thorpe)*

Anchor [Abbey St]: Smallish friendly two-bar local in attractive 17th-c street nr quay and station, several well kept Shepherd Neame ales, Pimms in summer, good quiet relaxed atmosphere, bare boards, open fires, settles and part-panelling, enjoyable sensibly priced food (not Sun evening or Mon), no smoking candlelit tiled eating area, piano, pub games; may be piped music, live Sun; music nights, a couple of picnic-sets outside, pretty garden, open all day, cl Mon lunchtime *(the Didler, Kevin Thorpe)*

Bear [Market Pl]: Friendly carefully refurbished local dating from 16th c (front rebuilt last century), lounge, snug and public bar off side corridor, well kept Shepherd Neame ales from the nearby brewery, basic good value lunchtime home cooking; tables outside, lively musical following, open all day Sat *(the Didler)*

Crown & Anchor [The Mall]: Friendly open-plan local dating from 19th c, wkdy lunchtime food inc Hungarian landlord's authentic goulash, Shepherd Neame real ales, games area with darts and pool *(the Didler)*

Elephant [The Mall]: Picturesque flower-decked terrace town pub doing well under newish local landlord, two-room bare-boards bar with four well kept Nelson ales inc a Mild, a changing guest beer, belgian beers, local farm cider, central log fire, darts; juke box, TV,

back pool room; suntrap terrace with fish pond, open from 3 wkdys, all day wknds *(Kevin Thorpe, the Didler, Kevin Flack, BB)*
Sun [West St]: Roomy and rambling old-world 15th-c weatherboarded town pub with good unpretentious atmosphere in small low-ceilinged partly panelled rooms, good value low-priced lunchtime food, well kept Shepherd Neame beers inc seasonal one from nearby brewery, quick pleasant service, no smoking restaurant; unobtrusive piped music; wheelchair access possible (small step), tables in pleasant back courtyard, interesting street, nine bedrooms with own bathrooms, open all day *(the Didler, Keith and Janet Morris)*

FINGLESHAM TR3353
Crown [just off A258 Sandwich—Deal; The Street]: Welcoming 16th-c country pub with wide choice of good value food in popular flagstoned inglenook dining area, well kept Courage Best and Directors, Shepherd Neame and guest beers, good service, log fire, attractive décor inc stripped brickwork; children welcome, lovely garden, summer barbecues, caravan park *(C Welland)*

FORDWICH TR1759
George & Dragon [off A28 at Sturry]: Friendly chain dining pub, huge choice of food, well kept real ales; pleasant garden leads down to River Stour, character bedrooms, handy for Stodmarsh nature reserve *(Keith and Chris O'Neill)*

FOUR ELMS TQ4748
Four Elms [B2027/B269 E of Edenbridge]: Large busy open-plan dining pub, welcoming and comfortable, wide choice of good value food (not Sun/Mon evenings) from sandwiches and baguettes to grills, may bake their own breads, rota of well kept ales inc Fullers London Pride, Greene King Abbot and Shepherd Neame Spitfire, decent wine and coffee, friendly service, several rambling rooms, two big log fires, huge boar's head, family room, no music; tables outside, handy for Chartwell *(GHC, Alan M Pring)*

GOUDHURST TQ7037
☆ ***Green Cross*** [Station Rd (A262 W)]: Good interesting food, particularly fish and seafood, well kept Harveys and Larkins, good wines, roomy and attractive back restaurant with good napkins, tablecloths etc, contrasting simple two-room bar with good fire and TV, pleasant informal service; bedrooms light and airy, good value; very handy for Finchcocks *(R D Moon, BB, Mrs Joan Hall, Peter Meister, W W Burke, Derek Thomas)*
☆ ***Star & Eagle*** [High St]: Striking medieval inn with settles and Jacobean-style seats in attractive heavily beamed open-plan areas, wide choice of generous enjoyable food from filled baguettes up, polite efficient service, well kept real ales (the bar itself seems fairly modern); children welcome, tables out behind with pretty views, lovely character bedrooms, well furnished and comfortable, open all day *(LYM, Joyce and Geoff Robson, Uta and John Owlett, Mrs J Ekins-Daukes, Leo and Barbara Lionet, Mrs C Lintott, Craig Turnbull)*

GRAVESEND TQ6473
Crown & Thistle [The Terrace]: Five changing guest beers from small breweries in small relaxed pub, can order in meals from nearby indian/chinese restaurant, brewery pictures, no juke box or machines; no children, occasional live music; open all day *(the Didler)*

GREAT CHART TQ9842
Hooden Horse [The Street]: Beamed and quarry-tiled two-roomed pub, cheerful furnishings and atmosphere, real ales such as Black Sheep and Shepherd Neame Spitfire, friendly staff, interesting food choice; may be piped music *(Peter Meister)*

GROOMBRIDGE TQ5337
☆ ***Junction Inn*** [Station Rd, off B2110]: Chattily relaxed bar, now entirely no smoking, with good generous food inc interesting dishes, friendly staff, well kept Harveys, Fullers London Pride and a guest such as Theakstons, good wines, pleasantly up-to-date décor with candles in modern wall sconces and plenty of fresh flowers, similar small room off, big airy carpeted dining room; skittle alley, picnic-sets out in front and in small pleasant back garden *(Anne Stephen, BB)*

HAWKHURST TQ7531
Great House [Gills Green, just off A229 N]: Pretty tucked-away country dining pub dating from 16th c, good often imaginative food inc good value 2-course lunches, helpful friendly French service (may be slower at lunchtime), well kept ales inc Harveys, two farm ciders, decent house wines, unusual foreign bottled beers, relaxed chatty bar, restaurant; picnic-sets under cocktail parasols in small sheltered garden *(BB)*
Kent Cricketers [Moor Hill (A229)]: 17th-c traditional country pub, inglenooks and beams, well kept real ales, good value food inc good tapas, friendly staff; well kept garden *(K West)*

HEAVERHAM TQ5758
Chequers [Watery Lane]: Cottagey old pub under new licensees, pleasantly pubby main bar and friendly locals' bar, well kept Shepherd Neame, newly refurbished kitchen and beamed restaurant; children welcome, picnic-sets in big garden *(Uta and John Owlett, Gwyn Jones)*

HERNHILL TR0660
☆ ***Red Lion*** [off A299 via Dargate, or A2 via Boughton Street and Staplestreet]: Pretty Tudor inn by church and attractive village green, densely beamed and flagstoned, log fires, pine tables, no smoking upstairs restaurant, enjoyable food, well kept Fullers London Pride and Shepherd Neame with a guest such as Marstons Pedigree, decent house wines, friendly attentive staff; children welcome, garden with boules and good play area, bedrooms *(LYM, M and R Thomas)*

HEVER TQ4743
Greyhound [Uckfield Lane]: Recently renovated under new management, food in bar and more formal dining area, popular with locals and walkers; tables in garden behind, handy for Hever Castle *(Philip J Heaps)*

HIGHAM TQ7172
Railway [Chequers St, Lower Higham]:

Friendly staff, log fire, good value Sun lunch *(Danny Nicol)*

HILDENBOROUGH TQ5549

Cock Horse [London Rd (B425)]: Comfortable and pleasant, with well kept Shepherd Neame, enjoyable food inc popular Sun lunch, attractive fire *(Tony and Katie Lewis, R E Greenhalgh)*

IDE HILL TQ4851

Cock [off B2042 SW of Sevenoaks]: Pretty village-green pub with well kept Greene King, wholesome food (not Sun evening) from sandwiches and ploughman's up, fine log fire, bar billiards; piped music, no children; some seats out in front, handy for Chartwell and nearby walks – so gets busy *(LYM, DJH, GHC, Bruce M Drew)*

IGHTHAM TQ5956

☆ *George & Dragon* [A227]: Wonky early 16th-c black and white timbered dining pub, much modernised inside with sofas among other furnishings in long sociable main bar, heavy-beamed end room, woodburner and open fires, well kept Shepherd Neame Bitter, Spitfire and seasonal ales, decent wines, good choice of fruit juices, short menu from generous snacks (all day till 6.30, not Sun) up, partly no smoking restaurant; children in family/restaurant areas, back terrace, open all day, handy for Ightham Mote (NT), good walks *(LYM, Kevin Flack, Evelyn and Derek Walter, Jenny and Brian Seller, Debbie and Neil Hayter, Susan and John Douglas)*

IGHTHAM COMMON TQ5955

Old House [Redwell, S of village; OS Sheet 188 map ref 591559]: Unspoilt and chatty two-room country local tucked down narrow lane, no inn sign, bare bricks and beams, huge log fireplace filling one wall, basic furniture, four or five changing ales from all over (some tapped from the cask), old cash register and small TV in side room; no food, music or machines, cl wkdy lunchtimes, opens 7 (later Tues) *(the Didler, BB)*

IVY HATCH TQ5854

☆ *Plough* [off A227 N of Tonbridge]: Restaurant not pub, often fully booked, with wide choice of consistently good food, fastidious french cooking, neat attentive staff, impressive range of reasonably priced wines (and well kept Greene King IPA), attractive dark candlelit décor – upmarket in a friendly informal style, and priced to match; delightful conservatory and garden *(Martin Jennings, LYM, Terence Boley, I D Greenfield, Bob and Margaret Holder)*

KINGSTON TR2051

☆ *Black Robin* [Elham valley road, off A2 S of Canterbury at Barham signpost]: Attractively reworked and extended by new owners, stylish décor and appealing layout with nice range of seating from leather armchair and chesterfield through settles, pews and chapel chairs to new thickly carpeted no smoking dining room, charming and cosy dim-lit inner room, good range of enjoyable food from hot baguettes to smart main dishes, Weds carvery, Sat brunch from 10.30am, well kept house beer (perhaps from Hopdaemon) and a guest such as Woodfordes Wherry, decent wines by the glass, Pimms, local farm apple juice, cheerful staff, candles and flowers; piped pop music; good tables on terrace with standard roses and in large garden, open all day *(Kevin Thorpe, BB)*

KNOCKHOLT TQ4658

Tally Ho [Cudham rd]: Well kept Flowers, Greene King IPA and Larkins, good coffee, wide range of good value blackboard food, welcoming efficient service even on busy lunchtimes, brown panelling and timbering, big woodburner; disabled access *(LM, Gwyn Jones)*

LAMBERHURST TQ6735

Brown Trout [B2169, off A21 nearly opp entrance to Scotney Castle]: Popular dining pub specialising in briskly served fish, biggish extension off small beamed bar, well kept ales such as Adnams, fair choice of decent wines, good log fire, children in eating areas; no no smoking area, can be very busy wknds; picnic-sets in large safe garden with play area, pretty window boxes and flower tubs in summer, open all day Sun and summer *(BB, Gordon Neighbour, Chris Pelley)*

Chequers [A21]: Low limed beams and standing timbers in fresh light open-plan main bar, parquet or flagstone floor, big leather sofa on turkey rug, nice mix of sturdy tables and dining chairs, big inglenook log fire, Shepherd Neame real ales, good house wines, daily papers, ambitious food, similar public bar; piped jazz or pop; solid tables on back deck, pretty streamside garden beyond *(BB)*

Swan [Lamberhurst Down]: Family dining pub next to Lamberhurst vineyards, lots of english wines, food inc good generous imaginative open sandwiches, friendly efficient service, three well kept real ales; children welcome, tables outside *(anon)*

LARKFIELD TQ7058

Wealden Hall [London Rd (A20, nr M20 junction 4)]: Attractive beamed and timbered 14th-c hall house with good value bar food from lunchtime sandwiches and baguettes to good evening fish choice, well kept Bass and Fullers London Pride, unpretentious furnishings, low ceilings and various levels, smarter upstairs restaurant *(Gerry and Rosemary Dobson)*

LEIGH TQ5646

☆ *Plough* [Powder Mill Lane/Leigh Rd, off B2027 NW of Tonbridge]: Attractive Tudor building opened up around big central hearth, enjoyable food from generous baked potatoes and good ciabattas to more adventurous dishes and very popular Sun carvery (often fully booked), well kept Adnams Best, Harveys and Shepherd Neame Spitfire, prompt friendly service; pleasant walks *(BB, Mark Percy, Lesley Mayoh, Peter Meister, Gillian Rodgers, Philip and Ann Board)*

LINTON TQ7550

☆ *Bull* [Linton Hill (A229 S of Maidstone)]: Enjoyable generous food (not Sun evening) running up to steak and popular Sun roast in dining pub with some carved settles and fine fireplace in nice old carpeted bar, oddly contrasting bare-boards room with café-style chrome and wood furniture, young efficient staff, well kept Shepherd Neame Bitter and Spitfire; bar snacks may not be available Fri/Sat evenings if restaurant busy; children welcome, lovely views from informal side garden, back terrace, open all day wknds *(LYM, Peter Scillitoe)*

LITTLEBOURNE TR2057

King William IV [High St (A257)]: Good fresh food from well filled sandwiches to good value Sun lunch and imaginative meals inc fish collected daily from landlord's fishing family, well kept Greene King IPA and Harveys Best, fair choice of wines by the glass, roomy straightforward bar with log fire and a frieze of dozens of varieties of beer bottles, friendly white cat; piped radio, TV, smoking allowed throughout; children welcome, a few tables outside, handy for Howletts Zoo *(Bev and Jeff Brown, Colin Goddard, BB)*

LUDDESDOWN TQ6667

☆ *Cock* [Henley Street, N of village – OS Sheet 177 map reference 664672; off A227 in Meopham, or A228 in Cuxton]: Distinctive tucked-away early 18th-c country pub, homely bay-windowed lounge, quarry-tiled bar with pews and other miscellaneous furnishings, lots of old posters, beer mats and bric-a-brac, well kept Adnams Bitter and Broadside, Goachers Mild, Harveys, Shepherd Neame and Youngs, four farm ciders, modestly priced generous food (not Sun) from sandwiches up, traditional games inc bar billiards and three types of darts board, two woodburners; no children allowed in, tables and boules in big secure garden, open all day *(LYM, Kevin Thorpe)*

LYDDEN TR2645

Hope [Canterbury Rd (B2060 NW of Dover)]: Attractive bar and cheerful restaurant, colourful plates and sea pictures, enjoyable generous food inc OAP bargains, cheerful service *(Gloria Bax)*

LYNSTED TQ9460

Black Lion: 16th-c local extended in keeping with original core, settles and old tables on bare boards, log fires, plenty of old advertisements and something of a 1950s/60s feel, freshly made honest home cooking, popular Sun lunch (always fully booked), Goachers real ales inc Mild and Crown Imperial Stout, Pawley's local farm cider, friendly forthright landlord; well behaved children welcome, garden with play area *(anon)*

MAIDSTONE TQ7656

Pilot [Upper Stone St (A229)]: Busy old roadside inn, enjoyable low-priced home-made simple food (not Sun), well kept Harveys Bitter, Mild and in season Old, whisky-water jugs hanging from ceiling, darts and pool; tables outside, boules *(Father Robert Marsh, the Didler)*

White Rabbit [A229 Sandling Rd roundabout]: Charmingly done Vintage Inn, calm and pleasant, with lots of small snugs and nooks off main bar, well kept Bass and Shepherd Neame Spitfire, good choice of wines by the glass, simple well cooked quickly served food; bedrooms in adjacent Innkeepers Lodge *(Colin Douglas)*

MARSH GREEN TQ4344

Wheatsheaf [Marsh Green Rd (B2028 SW of Edenbridge)]: Cosy and attractively renovated village pub, up to ten or so well kept ales inc Fullers, Harveys and local Larkins, special beer well kept wknds, farm cider, wide-ranging good value fresh food inc tasty lunchtime sandwiches, fresh fish and popular Sun lunch, friendly landlord and staff, roomy conservatory; tables on small terrace and in garden *(R and S Bentley)*

MOLASH TR0251

George [The Street (A251)]: Friendly low-beamed 16th-c village pub up on the downs, helpful friendly licensees and staff, enjoyable fresh bar food all day, well kept real ale, decent wines by the glass, country furnishings in spacious and airy bar, two-part restaurant; children welcome, pleasant garden with play area *(Rosamund Forester)*

NEWNHAM TQ9557

Tapster [Parsonage Farm, Seed Rd]: Long bare-boards bistro/bar reopened under new management, huge log fire one end, L-shaped bar the other with Fullers London Pride, Greene King IPA, a guest beer, freshly squeezed orange juice and good wine choice, good enterprising if not cheap blackboard lunches and evening menu, friendly staff and three welcoming dog, candles, flowers and white linens, big pot plants and ferns, popular pianists evenings, occasional hog roasts; may be piped jazz; dogs and children welcome, new picnic-sets in big garden, food all day in summer, cl Mon in winter *(Kevin Thorpe)*

PAINTER'S FORSTAL TQ9958

Alma [signed off A2 at Ospringe]: Homely and attractive timbered and weatherboarded village local, busy but neat and tidy, with good value home cooking using local ingredients (not Sun evening or Mon), well kept Shepherd Neame ales, decent wines, cheerful helpful informal service, comfortable largeish dining lounge, darts in small bare-boards public bar; may be piped classical music; picnic-sets on lawn, cl Mon evening *(Kevin Thorpe)*

PENSHURST TQ4943

☆ *Rock* [Hoath Corner, Chiddingstone Hoath; OS Sheet 188 map ref 497431]: Charmingly old-fashioned, two spartan little beamed rooms with farmers and dogs, stripped brick and timbers, wonky brick floors, woodburner in inglenook, well kept Larkins from the nearby brewery, good house wines, local farm cider, good blackboard food choice (not Sun), friendly staff, ring the bull (with a real bull's head), steps up to small dining room; children and dogs welcome, no mobile phones; front terrace, back garden, beautiful countryside nearby (handy for Eden Valley walk), cl Mon *(Mr and Mrs R P Begg, Andrea Rampley)*

☆ *Spotted Dog* [Smarts Hill, off B2188 S]: Quaint and neatly kept old tiled pub, half no smoking, with heavy low beams and timbers, antique settles and more straightforward furnishings, rugs and tiles, cosy inglenook log fire, attractive moulded panelling, well kept Harveys Best and Larkins Best and Traditional, enjoyable bar food changing daily, friendly efficient service, no smoking restaurant; may hold on to your credit card; children welcome till 7, tables out in front and on attractive tiered back terrace, open all day summer Thurs-Sun *(John Saville, Sarah Davis, Rod Lambert, Dr T E Hothersall, LYM, B and M Kendall, Father Robert Marsh, Carl and Jackie Cranmer, Mr and Mrs R Wales, C and R Bromage, Gerry and Rosemary Dobson, Mrs C Lintott)*

PETT BOTTOM TR1652

Duck [off B2068 S of Canterbury, via Lower Hardres]: Long bare-boards room with pine panelling and collectibles on delft shelves, good blackboard food choice from lunchtime sandwiches and baguettes up, popular Sun roasts, well kept Shepherd Neame Bitter and Spitfire and a guest such as Harveys, decent wines, welcoming attentive service, two log fires, friendly pub cat, restaurant; piped music; children welcome, tables in sizeable pretty garden, attractive downland spot, open all day wknds, cl Mon, bedrooms *(Kevin Thorpe, LYM)*

PLAXTOL TQ6054

☆ ***Golding Hop*** [Sheet Hill (½ mile S of Ightham, between A25 and A227)]: Secluded country pub, small and simple dim-lit two-level bar with well kept Adnams, Youngs and a couple of guest beers on handpump or tapped from the cask, four local farm ciders (sometimes even their own), basic good value bar snacks (not Mon/Tues evenings), woodburner; portable TV for big sports events, bar billiards, game machine; suntrap streamside lawn and well fenced play area over lane, open all day Sat *(the Didler, LYM, Peter Hayward, Peter Meister, Bob and Margaret Holder, Kevin Thorpe)*

PLUCKLEY TQ9245

Black Horse [The Street]: Attractive old house (said to be haunted) with open-plan bar, roomy back dining area, hops on beams, vast inglenook, plenty of old things to look at, cheery atmosphere, wide food choice from baguettes up (just roasts on Sun), well kept ales inc Fullers London Pride; piped music, big-screen TV, fruit machine; children allowed if eating, picnic-sets in spacious informal garden by tall sycamores, good walks, open all day Fri-Sun *(BB, Dr T E Hothersall, Conor McGaughey)*

Blacksmiths Arms [Smarden rd]: Quiet old pub, modern décor, hops hanging over central bar with well kept Shepherd Neame and guests such as Fullers, Robinsons and Wadworths 6X, cheerful staff, good value generous pubby food with OAP discounts, back dining area, pool and big-screen TV in front bar; garden with fine views and good facilities for children, open all day wknds *(Peter White, Kevin Thorpe)*

RAMSGATE TR3865

Artillery Arms [West Cliff Rd]: Chatty open-plan corner local with well kept Charles Wells Bombardier and four adventurous changing guest ales at sensible prices, bottled belgian beers, two farm ciders, doorstep sandwiches all day, daily papers, straightforward two-level bar with artillery prints, cannons and talking-point stained-glass windows dating from Napoleonic wars, long-established Tues lunchtime funny hat club; juke box (free on Sun) can be intrusive, fruit machine; children and dogs welcome, open all day *(Kevin Thorpe)*

Churchill Tavern [Paragon (seafront)]: Big clifftop pub rebuilt in the 1980s with old beams, bare bricks, pews and farm tools, Fullers London Pride, Ringwood Old Thumper, Charles Wells Bombardier and several changing guest beers, good value food in bar or back restaurant; live music downstairs wknds, midweek jazz and quiz nights; children welcome, open all day, harbour, marina and Channel views *(Kevin Thorpe)*

Montefiore Arms [Trinity Pl]: Busy, friendly backstreet pub, simply furnished single room, two well kept changing ales usually from small breweries, keen landlord, chatty locals; darts, TV and piped radio; children welcome away from bar, cl Weds lunchtime *(Kevin Thorpe)*

☆ ***Ramsgate Royal Harbour Brewhouse & Bakery*** [Harbour Parade]: Lively belgian-style café-bar brewing their own beers (you can look round the back brewery), also six belgian imports on tap, dozens in bottles, and Biddenden farm ciders; table service, bread, pastries and cakes baked all day, ploughman's and simple light meals too, open from 9 for tea and coffee (from 10 for alcohol), regular art shows inc sculptures; open piano, piped music; children welcome, tables out under cocktail parasols *(Peter Meister, Kevin Thorpe)*

SANDGATE TR2035

☆ ***Clarendon*** [Brewers Hill, off Sandgate—Hythe rd]: Small unpretentious Victorian local, sea-view lounge with some pubby memorabilia, right-hand locals' bar, coal fires, well kept Shepherd Neame ales, 15 wines by the glass, 20 malts, shove-ha'penny, cribbage, dominoes and backgammon; no credit cards, folk/blues Thurs; well behaved children in no smoking dining area, dogs in bar, a few benches out in front, cl from 5 Sun *(Peter Meister, John Davis, Keith Reeve, Marie Hammond, Paul A Moore, Karina Spero, Ian Phillips, LYM)*

Ship [High St]: Old-fashioned two-room local with well kept ales such as Greene King IPA, Harveys Best, Timothy Taylors Landlord and Theakstons Old Peculier tapped from the cask, farm cider, decent fairly priced wine, good value plain plentiful food, good service; simple, warm and friendly, barrel seats and tables, lots of nautical prints and posters, sea views from seats out behind; piped radio, occasional live music *(BB, Colin and Janet Roe)*

SANDWICH TR3358

Fleur de Lis [Delf St]: Comfortable 18th-c former coaching inn with old stripped pine tables in smart split-level lounge end, open fire, wide food range (all day wknds) from sandwiches to ostrich steaks, Fullers London Pride, Greene King IPA and a guest beer, pleasant uniformed staff, TV and games end, no smoking panelled back restaurant; piped music; 12 bedrooms with own bathrooms, open all day *(Kevin Thorpe)*

Kings Arms [Strand St]: Unpretentious pub with striking Elizabethan carving inside and out, welcoming service, wide choice of enjoyable food in bar and restaurant (where children allowed), well kept Shepherd Neame; traditional games and pool in public bar *(LYM, Joyce and Geoff Robson)*

Red Cow [Moat Sole; 100 yds from Guildhall, towards Woodnesborough]: Carefully refurbished open-plan pub with separate no smoking dining room, old beams and pictures, five well kept ales such as Boddingtons, Fullers London Pride, and Greene King Abbot and Old Speckled Hen, good value food, good atmosphere, friendly staff, good log fire; soft piped music; guide dogs only, picnic-tables outside with garden bar and hanging baskets *(Vanessa Young, Joyce and Geoff Robson, Keith and Janet Morris)*

SEASALTER TR0864

☆ ***Sportsman*** [Faversham Rd, off B2040]: Good busy dining pub in caravan land, just inside the sea wall; three starkly furnished linked rooms (two allowing children), wooden floor, big modern photographs, pine tables, wheelback and basket-weave dining chairs, imaginative contemporary cooking (not Sun evening or Mon), Shepherd Neame Bitter and Spitfire, well chosen wines, no smoking area; must book to get a table; perhaps outside could do with a tidy-up; open all day Sun *(Mayur Shah, Vanessa Young, Guy Vowles, Paul A Moore, LYM, Louise English, Basil Wynbergen)*

SEVENOAKS TQ5555

Bucks Head [Godden Green, just E]: Flower-decked pub with picnic-sets out on front terrace overlooking informal green and duck pond, welcoming atmosphere, neatly kept bar and restaurant area, decent blackboard food from sandwiches up, thoughtful service, full Shepherd Neame range inc a seasonal beer kept well, log fires in splendid inglenooks, no piped music; children welcome away from bar, no dogs or muddy boots; quiet enclosed back garden with bird fountain and pergola (dogs allowed in front one), attractive country behind Knole *(Eddie Edwards, Mrs J A Steff-Langston)*

Chequers [High St]: Beams and flagstones, wide changing range of well kept beers, friendly mature atmosphere (in this town of teen bars) *(Gwyn Jones)*

White Hart [Tonbridge Rd (A225 S, past Knole)]: Comfortably furnished, some old settles and fine array of prints, no smoking back conservatory, well kept Adnams and Harveys Best, decent bar food, friendly efficient service, well appointed front restaurant; pleasant lawns with well established shrubs and play area, open all day wknds *(Gerry and Rosemary Dobson)*

SHIPBOURNE TQ5952

Chaser [Stumble Hill]: Attractively and comfortably reworked hotel, stripped pine tables laid for decent pub food from sandwiches up with some up-to-date dishes as well as traditional ones, popular Sun lunch (served 12-6), friendly service, Greene King beers, good coffees, log fires, high-vaulted almost converted church-feel restaurant; tables outside, separate entrance to hotel, comfortable bedrooms, lovely spot by village church and green *(Uta and John Owlett, Bob and Margaret Holder)*

SISSINGHURST TQ7937

Bull [The Street]: Enjoyable food in bar and big pleasant dark-beamed restaurant area, Thurs bargain suppers for two, Harveys and other ales, pleasant service, log fire, shelves of books and china; may be quiet piped music; neat quiet garden *(Alan M Pring)*

SMARDEN TQ8743

☆ ***Bell*** [from Smarden follow lane between church and Chequers, then left at T-junction; or from A274 take unsignposted turn E a mile N of B2077 to Smarden]: Pretty rose-covered 17th-c inn with striking chimneys, rambling low-beamed little rooms, dim-lit and snug, nicely creaky old furnishings on ancient brick and flagstones or quarry tiles, warm inglenooks, enjoyable bar food, Flowers IPA and several Shepherd Neame real ales, local cider, country wines, winter mulled wine, no smoking room; end games area with pool, juke box and TV; picnic-sets in very pleasant mature garden, simple bedrooms *(Peter Meister, Philip Hill, the Didler, LYM, Kevin Thorpe, Andrea Rampley)*

SOUTHBOROUGH TQ5842

Weavers [London Rd (A26)]: Friendly family-run two-bar pub with big log fires, good drinks range, enjoyable food from good sandwich range through contemporary bar snacks to restaurant dishes; disabled access, big garden *(Mr and Mrs S R Dennis)*

SPELDHURST TQ5541

George & Dragon [signed from A264 W of T Wells]: Handsome partly 13th-c timbered building, panelling, massive beams and flagstones, huge log fire, high-backed settles, sofa, banquettes; well kept Harveys PA and Best and Larkins, lots of malt whiskies, friendly young staff, decent food (not Sun evening), attractive upstairs restaurant; pub games, may be piped music (live blues Sun evening); dogs welcome, provision for children, garden tables, has been open all day (not Mon-Thurs in winter) *(LYM, Gwyn Jones, Michael and Ann Cole)*

ST MARGARET'S AT CLIFFE TR3544

Smugglers [High St]: Friendly staff in compact bar, cosy welcoming atmosphere, very wide choice of enjoyable reasonably priced food from good value baguettes to good Sun lunch, well kept Greene King IPA, attractive dining room (paintings for sale) and no smoking conservatory; nice secluded garden *(W Glover, F T Cardiff, Ivan Ericsson)*

ST MARGARET'S BAY TR3744

Coastguard [The Bay]: Tremendous views to France from cheery and lively modernised seaside pub, food inc good fish and chips and more ambitious dishes, three changing real ales from small breweries; may be piped pop music; children and dogs welcome, lots of tables on balcony with pretty hanging baskets and other plants, below NT cliff and nr Pines Garden, open all day *(LYM, Kevin Thorpe, Ellen Weld, David London, John Hendy)*

STANSTED TQ6061

Black Horse [Tumblefield Rd]: Large high-ceilinged Victorian inn nicely decorated with old prints, gilded mirrors, heavy curtains and pot plants, Greene King Abbot, three Larkins ales and a guest such as Nelson, Biddenden farm cider, low-priced bar food (not Sun evening) from soup and fresh baguettes up, thai evening meals (not Sun/Mon) in handsome dining room; tables in big garden, pretty location and views, bedrooms, open all day *(Kevin Thorpe)*

STONE STREET TQ5754

☆ *Padwell Arms* [off A25 E of Sevenoaks, on Seal—Plaxtol by-road; OS Sheet 188 map ref 569551]: Chatty and spotless country local, good choice of generous home-made food inc popular Sun roast with nicely cooked fresh veg, sensible prices, efficient friendly service, well kept Badger, Hook Norton Old Hooky and lots of changing guest beers, nice wines, two local farm ciders, good coffee, red plush banquettes, airy back dining extension; long tables on front terrace (lovely flowering baskets and window boxes) overlooking orchards, more in nice back garden, plenty of shade, good walks *(John Branston, the Didler, Peter and Joan Elbra, GHC, BB, Lynn Sharpless, Geoff Pidoux, Father Robert Marsh)*

STOWTING TR1241

☆ *Tiger* [off B2068 N of M20 junction 11]: Partly 17th-c country pub with consistently good well presented food using fresh local produce, attractive unpretentious furniture, candles on tables, rugs on bare boards, good log fire, entertaining landlord, good staff and friendly atmosphere, well kept Everards Beacon and Tiger, Fullers ESB, Marstons Pedigree and Shepherd Neame Spitfire, book and games shelf, back dining room; well behaved children allowed, garden tables with occasional barbecues and hitching rail, good jazz Mon (cl Mon lunchtime), open all day wknds *(LYM, Kevin Thorpe)*

SWANLEY TQ5369

Lamb [Swanley Village Rd]: Proper traditional pub with real sandwiches and well kept beer *(Stephen Stead)*

TENTERDEN TQ8833

Eight Bells [High St]: Pleasant old inn popular with older people for lunch, young helpful and patient staff, restful traditional long bar, central courtyard glazed in as further no smoking eating area; easy wheelchair access, good value old-world beamed bedrooms, tasty breakfast *(Mike and Heather Watson)*

☆ *White Lion* [High St]: 16th-c inn, beams and timbers, masses of pictures, china and books, welcoming efficient helpful staff, wide choice of generous popular food, well kept Adnams Broadside, Bass and Greene King IPA, sensibly priced wines, big log fire, relaxed and friendly even when crowded with young people at night, smart no smoking softly lit back panelled restaurant; dogs welcome, bar can get a bit smoky; tables on heated terrace overlooking street, 15 comfortably creaky beamed bedrooms, good breakfast, open all day *(Pamela and Douglas Cooper, Pamela and Merlyn Horswell, Kevin Thorpe, Sue and Mike Todd, Peter and Jackie Barnett)*

William Caxton [West Cross; top of High St]: Cosy and friendly 15th-c local, heavy beams and bare boards, huge inglenook log fire, woodburner in smaller back bar, wide blackboard choice of enjoyable food made by licensees, well kept Shepherd Neame beers inc seasonal, pleasant small dining room; piped music may be geared to young people early evening; children welcome, tables in attractive front area, open all day, bedrooms *(Alan and Paula McCully, the Didler, Kevin Thorpe, Conor McGaughey, Peter Meister)*

THURNHAM TQ8057

Black Horse [not far from M20 junction 7; off A249 at Detling]: Popular restauranty dining pub, huge choice of enjoyable food inc lunchtime snack meals, Fullers London Pride and a beer brewed for the pub, friendly service, log fires, small bar where dogs but not children allowed; live music Weds; pleasant garden with partly covered back terrace, water features and nice views, by Pilgrims Way and handy for North Downs, bedrooms *(John and Joyce Snell, Julie Milton, Peter Meister)*

TILMANSTONE TR3051

Plough & Harrow [Dover Rd (A256)]: Small country pub with friendly staff, sensibly priced food (chef will try to meet your wishes), Shepherd Neame Bitter and Spitfire, log fire, steps down to conservatory dining room; pretty hillside garden *(Ian Phillips)*

TOYS HILL TQ47521

Fox & Hounds [off A25 in Brasted, via Brasted Chart and The Chart]: Quite different from what it was in Mrs Pelling's days here: emphasis on food now, with a changing blackboard menu (enjoyable if not cheap, not Sun evening), smart staff, extensive wine list and new carpeted dining extension; still a comfortable old tiled partly no smoking bar area with log fire, Greene King IPA and Abbot, books and guides to read; piped music, occasional live; disabled access, garden tables, open all day summer *(LYM, Kevin Flack, Kevin Thorpe)*

TUNBRIDGE WELLS TQ5839

Mount Edgcumbe Hotel [The Common]: Handsome tile-hung and weatherboarded hotel, now concentrating on malaysian and thai food (and lunchtime sandwiches), extensive wine list, well kept Harveys Best, friendly staff, small cosy bar, stripped brick and old town photographs, mini waterfall feature, tables (candlelit at night) in unusual grotto-like snug built into rock; children welcome, dogs in bar, tables out in pleasant setting with views of The Common, open all day *(LYM)*

Royal Wells [Mount Ephraim]: Well lit, friendly and civilised hotel bar with comfortable settees and padded dining chairs, cosy corners, views over T Wells, well kept Harveys Best and Shepherd Neame Bitter and Spitfire, good value relaxed brasserie with modern prints, friendly efficient staff; bar can get somewhat smoky; terrace tables, bedrooms *(BB, Peter Meister)*

UNDER RIVER TQ5551

White Rock [SE of Sevenoaks, off B245]: Pretty village pub, beams and stripped brickwork, small comfortable bar, well kept Fullers London Pride, Harveys and a guest beer, enjoyable bar snacks and some interesting main dishes, helpful landlord, no piped music, pool in larger public bar, back dining extension; children welcome, picnic-sets on big back lawn, handy for Greensand Way (walkers asked to use side door) *(Jenny and Brian Seller, Peter Meister)*

UPNOR TQ7570

Kings Arms [High St]: Old pub with three linked areas, enjoyable food, friendly service and well kept ales such as Fullers London Pride and Timothy Taylors Landlord; no no smoking area; delightful riverside village nr Upnor Castle, good walks *(Janet Box, A and B D Craig, Gerry and Rosemary Dobson)*

Ship [Upnor Rd, Lower Upnor]: Enjoyable sensibly priced home cooking inc local fish, well kept Adnams, Courage and Shepherd Neame ales, friendly staff, plenty of character; on banks of River Medway *(Derek and Heather Manning)*

UPSTREET TR2363

☆ *Grove Ferry* [off A28 towards Preston]: Open-plan refurbishment with big abstracts on cream or pink walls, variety of areas with comfortable well spaced tables (some very big), papers and magazines in front of central bar, bare-boards dining area behind with candles on tables, enjoyable food all day (not Sun evening) inc good children's choice, three or four Shepherd Neame ales from central servery, good wines by the glass, pleasant young uniformed staff, log fire in big fireplace; may be quiet piped music, fruit machine by the puddings cabinet; french windows to heated deck with tables overlooking River Stour boats, more in big side garden with play area, barbecues Sun afternoon, bedrooms, handy for Stodmarsh national nature reserve *(Keith and Chris O'Neill, Kevin Thorpe, BB)*

Royal Oak [Island Rd (A28)]: Neatly kept carpeted bar with Bass and Fullers London Pride, coal fire, comfortable newly padded settles, lots of country prints, fishing rods and flies, brasses and china, pleasant no smoking dining room, pool in back games room; sport TV, may be piped music; tables out behind overlooking fields *(Kevin Thorpe)*

WAREHORNE TQ9832

☆ *Woolpack* [off B2067 nr Hamstreet]: Big neatly kept 16th-c dining pub with very wide choice of good value generous food in rambling bar and big candlelit restaurant, no smoking area, popular carvery Weds evening (booking essential), elaborate puddings, well kept Harveys Best, decent wines, welcoming landlord, quick attentive service, huge inglenook, hops on heavy beams, plain games room; picnic-sets out overlooking quiet lane and meadow with lovely big beech trees, lots of flower tubs and little fountain, not far from the good Woodchurch rare breeds centre *(Paul and Barbara Temple, Lawrence Mitchell, BB, John Hendy, Mrs C Lintott, Glen and Debbie Carter-Parry)*

Worlds Wonder [B2067]: Neatly kept pub, two carpeted bars with clocks, bottles and books in lounge, games inc darts and pool in public bar with fine tankard collection, airy dining room, wide choice of food (not Mon evening), also cheap cornish rolls, well kept Batemans XXXB, Goachers and Harveys Best, Stowford Press cider, good collection of malt whiskies *(Kevin Thorpe)*

WEALD TQ5250

Windmill [Windmill Rd]: Quiet, unpretentious family-run local with a growing following for its good fresh home cooking (not Tues) at tempting prices, friendly service with attention to detail, well kept Greene King beers; attractive well furnished and lantern-lit terraces *(Peter and Joan Elbra)*

WEST MALLING TQ6857

Lobster Pot [Swan St]: Open fire in quiet local's carpeted main bar with old posters, nets and lobster pots, step up to pleasant small dining room, Adnams, Goachers, Larkins and three changing guest beers, enjoyable pub food from sandwiches up; darts and piped music in small dark-panelled public bar, Mon quiz night, upstairs skittle alley; open all day Fri-Sun *(Kevin Thorpe)*

☆ *Swan* [Swan St]: They no longer serve drinks unless you eat at this lively stylish brasserie/bar – a shame, as its good food and nice atmosphere brought it into the main entries last year; trendy open-plan airy décor, huge flower arrangements, flat-screen television showing old silent movies, elegant dining chairs around slate-topped tables, good wines, St Peters bottled beer; children in restaurant, open all afternoon Sun *(LYM, Derek Thomas)*

WHITSTABLE TR1064

Long Reach [Thanet Way]: Attractively built Beefeater with wide range of reasonably priced food, pleasant staff, children welcome *(M and R Thomas)*

Pearsons [Sea Wall]: What people go for is the good plain fresh fish and seafood in the tiny cheerful upstairs restaurant (with oblique sea view), where smoking is allowed; nautical downstairs bar (no view) is more run-of-the-mill, with piped pop music and sports TV, and can be smoky, but has decent wines, well kept Flowers and Greene King IPA, and a huge lobster tank in its lower flagstoned part; children welcome in eating areas, open all day wknds, just above shingle beach *(LYM, Gordon Neighbour, Keith and Chris O'Neill, Roy and Lindsey Fentiman)*

Royal Naval Reserve [High St]: Friendly, comfortable and cosy, roomier than it looks from outside, with well kept Shepherd Neame, nice house wines, good fresh local fish and other good value home cooking, spotless and attractive upstairs dining room; smoking allowed throughout, piped music (may be classical upstairs); some tables under back awning *(John and Glenys Wheeler, Keith and Janet Morris)*

WITTERSHAM TQ8927

Swan [Swan St]: Homely village local dating from 17th c, well kept Harveys Best, Goachers Light and Mild and four changing microbrews, Aug and Feb beer festivals, wide food choice (not Mon or Tues evenings) from sandwiches up inc children's, small open fire in lounge bar, public with darts, pool and juke box; garden with picnic-sets, open all day *(Kevin Thorpe)*

WORMSHILL TQ8757

Blacksmiths Arms [handy for M20 junction 8]: Attractive 18th-c low-beamed pub with big log fire, candles, old prints and well worn tiles in small bar area, smarter furnishings in upper no smoking room mainly for eating, flame-effect fire in stripped brick carpeted restaurant, decent chip-free food from baguettes to some quite expensive main dishes, changing real ales such as Archers and Black Sheep, Stowford Press cider; no children, cl Sun evening and Mon *(Kevin Thorpe)*

WYE TR0546

☆ ***New Flying Horse*** [Upper Bridge St]: Comfortably modernised 17th-c beamed inn, pleasantly light, with two or three rooms, wide choice of good interesting frequently changing fresh bar food (a regular stop for French long-distance drivers), smiling considerate service, well kept Shepherd Neame Bitter and Spitfire, decent pots of tea, inglenook log fires, bric-a-brac inc carousel horse, no smoking dining area; attractive good-sized garden with boules, pleasant bedrooms, good breakfast *(Tina and David Woods-Taylor, Jayne Robinson)*

Several well known guide books make establishments pay for entry, either directly or as a fee for inspection. These fees can run to many hundreds of pounds. We do not. Unlike other guides, we never take payment for entries. We never accept a free meal, free drink, or any other freebie from a pub. We do not accept any sponsorship – let alone from commercial schemes linked to the pub trade. All our entries depend solely on merit.

Lancashire
(with Greater Manchester and Merseyside)

A good clutch of new main entries here this year includes the Eagle & Child at Bispham Green (back in the *Guide* after a break, going great guns again since its former landlady was lured out of retirement), the Lord Raglan high over Bury (a welcoming retreat, brewing lots of good beers, with popular food, too), the upmarket White Hart in Lydgate (good brasserie food, a splendid wine list – pleasant too for just a relaxed drink), the Black Bull at Rimington (good food the main draw here too, but don't miss its amazing collection of model cars and so forth), and the Dressers Arms at Wheelton (great choice of good value beers including its own brew, bargain food too). Other pubs on fine form here are the Bay Horse at Bay Horse (good if not cheap food), the spectacular Philharmonic in Liverpool, the Taps in Lytham (a splendid quickly changing beer choice at this flourishing ale house), the Britons Protection in Manchester (a favourite city pub) and the Marble Arch there (brewing its own good beers, bargain food too), the Spread Eagle at Sawley (good food and a fine drinks choice at this civilised dining pub), the cheerful rather foody Lunesdale Arms up at Tunstall, and the Inn at Whitewell (a favourite for its food, wines, atmosphere, and as a place to stay). Food stands out as a plus at many of these top pubs. The one which gains the title of Lancashire Dining Pub of the Year is the Eagle & Child at Bispham Green: consistently good food and service in a relaxed and convivial pubby environment. In the Lucky Dip section at the end of the chapter, pubs earning particularly warm praise from readers recently are the Rams Head at Denshaw, Swan at Dobcross, Strawbury Duck at Entwistle, Hest Bank Hotel, Ship at Lathom, Doctor Duncan and Monro in Liverpool, Mr Thomas Chop House in Manchester, Royal Oak at Riley Green and Arden Arms in Stockport. Drinks prices here are well below the national average, with most pubs charging under £2 for a pint of beer – and many charging much less. We found quite a few pubs brewing their own bargain beers – always worth looking out for. And the area's thriving and highly competitive brewing industry keeps the national brands on their toes, with Boddingtons (brewed here by the giant firm Interbrew of Belgium) often very attractively priced. The main regional brewers are Robinsons and Thwaites, with Holts, Hydes and Lees particularly prominent around Manchester. There are also many good smaller breweries such as Bank Top, Cains, Moorhouses and Phoenix.

BARNSTON SJ2783 Map 7

Fox & Hounds

3 miles from M53 junction 3: A552 towards Woodchurch, then left on A551

A fine choice of drinks at this pleasant pub includes over 50 malt whiskies, around 11 wines by the glass, and half a dozen well kept real ales. Tucked away opposite the serving counter is a charming old quarry-tiled corner with an antique kitchen range, copper kettles, built-in pine kitchen cupboards, and lots of earthenware or enamelled food bins. With its own entrance at the other end of the pub, a small quarry-tiled locals' bar is worth a peek for its highly traditional layout – not to mention a collection of hundreds of metal ashtrays on its delft shelf; beside it is a snug where children are allowed. The main part of the roomy bay-windowed lounge bar has red plush button-back built-in banquettes and plush-cushioned captain's chairs around the solid tables on its green turkey carpet, and plenty of old local prints on its cream walls below a delft shelf of china, with a collection of police and other headgear; darts, shove-ha'penny and dominoes. Arrive early if you want to eat the enjoyable lunchtime bar food, which includes home-made soup (£2.75), open sandwiches (from £2.75), filled baked potatoes (from £3.75), quiche (£4.95), ploughman's (£6.50), with changing specials such as steak and kidney pie or fish and chips (£5.95), and gammon (£6.50); Sundays roasts (£6.75). Marstons Pedigree, Theakstons Best and Old Peculier, and Websters Yorkshire are swiftly served by the well groomed staff, along with a couple of guests such as Hydes Hunky Dory and Weetwood Eastgate on handpump. There are some picnic-sets under cocktail parasols out in the yard behind, below a dairy farm. More reports please. *(Recommended by Charles and Pauline Stride, Mrs P J Carroll, Mike and Linda Hudson, Paul Boot)*

Free house ~ Licensee Ralph Leech ~ Real ale ~ Bar food (lunchtime) ~ Restaurant ~ (0151) 648 1323 ~ Children in family room ~ Dogs allowed in bar ~ Open 11-11(10.30 Sun)

BAY HORSE SD4952 Map 7

Bay Horse

1¼ miles from M6 junction 33: A6 southwards, then off on left

This peacefully set, upmarket dining pub has imaginative food (made with lots of fresh local ingredients) and ten wines by the glass. Beamed and comfortable, the red-walled bar is attractively decorated, with a good log fire, cushioned wall banquettes in bays, a friendly cat, and gentle lighting including table lamps on window sills; the atmosphere is warm and cosy. As well as a decent, fairly priced wine list (fruit wines too), friendly staff serve well kept Boddingtons, Moorhouses Pendle Witches Brew and Thwaites Lancaster Bomber on handpump; good tea and coffee. There are usually fresh flowers on the counter, and may be piped music (which can be obtrusive) or perhaps cricket or racing on TV. The main emphasis though is on the food, with a series of small no smoking dining areas rambling around – the feel of a civilised country restaurant, with a red décor, another log fire, candle-flame-effect lights and nice tables, including one or two good-sized ones having an intimate corner to themselves. Delicious (but not cheap) dishes might include soup (£3.50), potted morecambe bay shrimps (£6.75), fried scallops with black pudding, sherry and black pepper caramel (£8.75), braised fennel with goats cheese, mashed potato, wild mushrooms and herb and truffle dressing (£11.95), slow-cooked goosnargh duck with potato purée and elderberry wine and honey reduction (£13.95), lamb shank slow-cooked in ale and thyme with rissole potatoes (£14.95), bass with asparagus, blush tomato and vanilla dressing (£16.95), and warm treacle, walnut and fig tart with toffee ice-cream or white chocolate and orange cheesecake with chocolate ice-cream (£4.75); they also do sandwiches (from £4.75). Arrive early or book to be sure of a table. There are tables out in the garden behind (peaceful, though the railway is not far off). *(Recommended by Mrs P J Carroll, Malcolm Taylor, Revd D Glover, Deb and John Arthur, Roy Morrison, Sarah and Peter Gooderham, Steve Whalley, Margaret Dickinson, John Kane, A C English, Pat and Sam Roberts, Vicky and Matt Wharton, Gwyn and Anne Wake, Maggie and Tony Harwood, J S Burn, Simon Calvert, Jo Lilley)*

Mitchells ~ Tenant Craig Wilkinson ~ Real ale ~ Bar food (12-2(3 Sun), 7-9; not Sun evening, not Mon; snacks only 1-2pm Sat) ~ Restaurant ~ (01524) 791204 ~ Children in restaurant ~ Open 12-3(2 Sat), 6.30-11; 12-4, 8.30-10.30 Sun; closed Mon; cl bank hol Mon evening (open lunchtime) and Tues following bank hol

BELMONT SD6716 Map 7

Black Dog £

A675

Great if you've built up a thirst walking in the area, this friendly pub serves good value Holts Bitter and Mild along with a well kept guest such as Thunderbolt. Cosy and atmospheric, the original cheery and traditional small rooms around the bar are packed with antiques and bric-a-brac, from railwaymen's lamps, bedpans and chamber-pots to landscape paintings. There are also service bells for the sturdy built-in curved seats, rush-seated mahogany chairs, and coal fires, and a plush blue banquette in the bay opposite the bar. The games room has pool, fruit machine and piped music. Outside, two long benches on the sheltered sunny side of the pub give delightful views of the moors above the nearby trees and houses. Enjoyably straightforward, generously served bar food includes chicken tikka skewers (£3.50), cajun chicken breast (£5.35), wild boar sausage and mash (£5.25), mediterranean risotto (£5.80), and grilled salmon (£6.35), and specials such as liver and onion or moussaka (£5.75), with puddings such as chocolate pudding (£2.75); until 6pm you can also get sandwiches (from £3.10) and baked potatoes (from £3), and they also do a Sunday lunch (£5.50, two courses £7.45). It tends to fill up quickly, and they don't take bookings, so get there early for a table. A small orchestra plays viennese music on New Year's Day at lunchtime, and performs on several other evenings throughout the year. A track leads from the village up Winter Hill and (from the lane to Rivington) on to Anglezarke Moor, and there are paths from the dam of the nearby Belmont Reservoir. The homely bedrooms are reasonably priced.

(Recommended by Michael and Marion Buchanan, Pat and Tony Martin, Jim Abbott, Ian Phillips, Collin and Julie Taylor, Peter Abbott, MLR, Steve Whalley, Pam and John Smith, Len Beattie, Peter Heaton)

Holts ~ Tenant Heino Chrobok ~ Real ale ~ Bar food (12-2, 6-8(not Sun-Tues evenings); 12-6 Sun) ~ (01204) 811218 ~ Children in family room ~ Open 12-11(10.30 Sun) ~ Bedrooms: £32S/£42S

BISPHAM GREEN SD4813 Map 7

Eagle & Child

Maltkiln Lane (Parbold—Croston road, off B5246)

Lancashire Dining Pub of the Year

Since the friendly former landlady came back out of retirement to run this striking red brick pub, we've had a flood of happy reports from readers. Well divided by stubs of walls, the largely open-plan bar is appealingly simple and civilised. Attractively understated old furnishings include a mix of small oak chairs around tables in corners, an oak coffer, several handsomely carved antique oak settles (the finest apparently made partly from a 16th-c wedding bed-head), and old hunting prints and engravings. There's coir matting in the no smoking snug, and oriental rugs on flagstones in front of the fine old stone fireplaces; unobtrusive piped music. You'll find quite an emphasis on the well cooked food, and besides snacks (not Saturday evening) such as sandwiches (from £3.50), fish and chips or steak and ale pie (£7.50), the friendly and helpful staff serve interesting daily changing specials such as confit duck leg with chorizo mash (£6), spiced meatballs and chilli jam (£8.50), lemon chicken kebabs with sweet chilli dressing (£10), chicken breast and chorizo (£11), grilled bass with parsley butter or baked strawberry grouper (£12), and beef medallions with brandy cream and pâté (£14), with puddings such as gooseberry cobbler or panna cotta with Cointreau (£4). A good range of well kept beers includes Moorhouses Black Cat and Thwaites, with four changing guest ales from brewers such as Hanby, Hart, Jennings and Phoenix. They also have changing farm cider, decent wines, some country wines and two dozen or more malt whiskies. The pub holds a popular beer festival in May; the dog's called Harry. You can watch players competing on the neat bowling green outside, and the pub can provide bowls for anyone who wants to try the crowns, which fool even the most experienced bowlers. A nice wild garden has crested newts and nesting moorhens.

(Recommended by Revd D Glover, John Kane, Jack Clark, Brian Kneale, Mrs P J Carroll, Mrs H Turner, A P Seymour, Pat and Roger Fereday, John and Claire Pettifer, P R Morgan, Yvonne and Mike Meadley, Mandy and Simon King, Johnny Cohen)

Free house ~ Licensee Monica Evans ~ Real ale ~ Bar food (12-2, 6-8.30(9 Fri, Sat); 12-8.30 Sun) ~ Restaurant ~ (01257) 462297 ~ Children away from main bar ~ Dogs welcome ~ Open 12-3, 5.30-11; 12-10.30 Sun

BLACKSTONE EDGE SD9716 Map 7

White House £

A58 Ripponden—Littleborough, just W of B6138

A haven for walkers (the Pennine Way crosses the road outside), this imposing 17th-c pub is high up on the bleak and moody moors with panoramic views stretching for miles into the distance. Inside the atmosphere is cheery, and the cosily bustling main bar has a turkey carpet in front of a blazing coal fire, and a large-scale map of the area. The snug Pennine Room opens off here, with brightly coloured antimacassars on its small soft settees; there's also a dining extension. A spacious room on the left has comfortable seating, and a big horseshoe window has impressive moorland views; fruit machine. Theakstons Best is promptly served by the friendly staff along with a couple of guests from brewers such as Archers and Jennings; also farm cider and malt whiskies. The reasonably priced unpretentious menu might include tasty bar food such as soup (£2), sandwiches (from £3), cumberland sausage with egg or beef curry (£4.95), steak and kidney pie (£5.25), salmon (£6.95), halibut (£7.95), and lamb henry (£8.95), with puddings such as home-made apple pie (from £2.50). Muddy boots can be left in the porch. *(Recommended by Ian Phillips, Guy Vowles, MLR, Len Beattie)*

Free house ~ Licensee Neville Marney ~ Real ale ~ Bar food (12-2, 6.30-9.30; 12-9 Sun) ~ (01706) 378456 ~ Children welcome ~ Dogs allowed in bar and bedrooms ~ Open 12-3, 6.30-11; 12-11 Sun

BURY SD8115 Map 7

Lord Raglan

Under a mile E of M66 junction 1 (use junction 2 if coming from N); Mount Pleasant, Nangreaves, along long cobbled lane

High on the moors overlooking Bury, this 18th-c pub has been run by the same family for almost 50 years. The own brew beers are a big attraction: alongside a couple of guests are well kept Leyden Black Pudding, Crowning Glory, Forever Bury, Light Brigade, Nanny Flyer and Raglan Steve on handpump. They've also 20 malt whiskies and interesting foreign bottled beers; TV, dominoes and piped music. All sorts of bric-a-brac is dotted around the snugly welcoming neatly kept beamed front bar, with lots of pewter, brass and interesting antique clocks, and there's a mix of spindleback chairs and old wooden settles. The back room has a huge open fire, china on a high delft shelf and welsh dresser, and windows giving a splendid view down the valley. A plainer but more spacious dining room on the left is panelled in light wood. Available in the bar or the restaurant, tasty dishes include open sandwiches (£2.75), baked potatoes (£4.25), chilli con carne or cumberland sausage and egg (£4.95), red thai vegetable curry or chicken balti (£6.95), poached salmon fillet or fried plaice (£7.95), chicken chasseur (£8.20), and steaks (from £8.95), with puddings such as sticky toffee pudding (£3); children's meals (£2.45). They hold a beer festival in June. *(Recommended by Gordon Tong, DJH, Steve Whalley)*

Own brew ~ Licensee Brendan Leyden ~ Real ale ~ Bar food ~ Restaurant ~ (0161) 764 6680 ~ Children in eating area of bar and restaurant ~ Dogs allowed in bar ~ Open 12-2.30, 7(5 Fri)-11; 12-11(10.30 Sun) Sat

> Post Office address codings confusingly give the impression that some pubs are in Lancashire when they're really in Yorkshire (which is where we list them).

GOOSNARGH SD5839 Map 7

Horns 🍷 🛏

Pub signed from village, about 2 miles towards Chipping below Beacon Fell

This civilised hotel, attractively set in the foothills of the Pennines, is an enjoyable place to come for a well cooked meal. Besides sandwiches (from £4.50), and ploughman's (£5.95), nicely presented dishes include soup (£4.25), hot peppered mackerel (£4.75), creamy garlic shrimps (£4.95), grilled plaice (£8.50), home-made steak and kidney pie (£8.95), roast local pheasant (£9.50), and delicious roast duckling with apple sauce (£10.25), with specials such as black pudding with mustard sauce (£5.50), halibut with prawn sauce (£9.25), and peppered sirloin steak (£12.50), and home-made puddings (£4.95); welcoming young staff. The neatly kept snug rooms have colourful flower displays and winter log fires, and a relaxing atmosphere; beyond the lobby, the pleasant front bar opens into attractively decorated middle rooms. The dining rooms are no smoking; piped music. They don't keep real ales, but there's an extensive wine list with quite a few by the glass, and a fine choice of malt whiskies. The pub is older than its brightly mock-Tudor façade suggests. *(Recommended by DJH, W W Burke, Dr T E Hothersall, Rev D E and Mrs J A Shapland, Edward Mirzoeff, K H Richards, Margaret Dickinson)*

Free house ~ Licensee Mark Woods ~ Bar food (not lunchtime Sun/Mon, or Sat evening) ~ Restaurant ~ (01772) 865230 ~ Children welcome ~ Open 11.45-3, 6.30-11(10.30 Sat-Sun); closed Mon lunchtime ~ Bedrooms: £59S(£59B)/£79S(£79B)

LITTLE ECCLESTON SD4139 Map 7

Cartford 🍺 🛏

Cartford Lane, off A586 Garstang—Blackpool, by toll bridge

Peacefully placed by a toll bridge over the River Wyre (tidal here), this handy pub serves up to seven very well kept real ales. Aside from a couple from Hart (their own good microbrewery behind the pub, with brewery tours by arrangement), you'll find Boddingtons, Fullers London Pride and up to four changing ales from interesting brewers such as Goose Eye, Moorhouses, Phoenix and Rooster; also decent house wines and several malt whiskies. The rambling interior has oak beams, dried flowers, a log fire and an unusual layout on four different levels, with uncoordinated seating areas; pool, darts, fruit machine, dominoes, TV and piped music. Two levels are largely set for dining (the upstairs part is no smoking). Straightforward bar food includes soup (£2.20), sandwiches (from £2.95), steak and mushroom pie (£4.95), lemon sole (£6.25), curries (from £6.95), and 10oz sirloin steak (£8.95), with specials. There are tables out in a garden (not by the water), with a play area; the pub has fishing rights along 1½ miles of the river. *(Recommended by Steve Whalley, David Green, Richard Lewis, Harry Gleave, Keith and Chris O'Neill, MLR, Ian and Nita Cooper, Pam and John Smith, Dr and Mrs A K Clarke, Maggie and Tony Harwood)*

Own brew ~ Licensee Andrew Mellodew ~ Real ale ~ Bar food (12-2, 6.30-9.30; 12-9 Sun) ~ Restaurant ~ (01995) 670166 ~ Children in eating area of bar and restaurant ~ Dogs welcome ~ Open 12-3, 6.30-11; 12-10.30 Sun ~ Bedrooms: £36.95B/£48.95B

LIVERPOOL SJ4395 Map 7

Baltic Fleet 🍺

Wapping

The own-brewed Wapping beers at this unpretentious pub are reasonably priced: served through a sparkler by the friendly staff, a typical choice might include Wapping Bitter, Summer Ale and Stout, alongside guests from brewers such as Charles Wells, Thwaites and Tigertops on handpump. The fairly unusual triangular end-of-terrace building has big arched windows and a bright green, burgundy and white painted exterior. An abundance of interior woodwork and stout mahogany board floors adds to its nautical feel, as do the interesting old Mersey shipping prints. There's also a good mix of old school furniture and dark wood tables; piped music. The first floor restaurant has recently been redecorated, and they've moved the lavatories in order to be able to expand the brewery. A short choice of good value lunchtime (not Sunday) bar snacks includes sandwiches and toasties (from £2.50), soup (£2.95), baked potatoes (from £3.25), salads (from £3.95), and maybe a hot dish or two such as cassoulet or scouse (£3.95); they also do Saturday brunch (£3.95). The small back room is no smoking. *(Recommended by the Didler, Mike Pugh, John Dwane, Paul Davies, Patrick Hancock)*

Own brew ~ Licensee Simon Holt ~ Real ale ~ Bar food (lunchtime, not Sun) ~ Restaurant ~ (0151) 709 3116 ~ Children in restaurant ~ Dogs allowed in bar ~ Open 12(11.30 Fri/Sat)-11; 12-10.30 Sun

Philharmonic Dining Rooms ★

36 Hope Street; corner of Hardman Street

Not only is this late Victorian gin palace worth visiting for its breathtaking opulence (from its smart marble façade to the elegant original fittings), they serve up to eight well kept real ales here too. The heart of the building is a mosaic-faced serving counter, from which heavily carved and polished mahogany partitions radiate under the intricate plasterwork high ceiling. The echoing main hall is decorated with stained-glass including contemporary portraits of Boer War heroes Baden-Powell and Lord Roberts, rich panelling, a huge mosaic floor, and copper panels of musicians in an alcove above the fireplace. More stained-glass in one of the little lounges declares 'Music is the universal language of mankind', and backs this up with illustrations of musical instruments; there are two plushly comfortable sitting rooms; two areas are no smoking. Don't miss the original 1890s Adamant gents' lavatory (all pink marble and glinting mosaics); ladies are allowed a look if they ask first. Besides well kept Bass, Cains Traditional, and Tetleys, you'll find guests such as Batemans XXXB, Caledonian Deuchars IPA, Everards Tiger, Fullers London Pride, and Timothy Taylors Landlord; fruit machine, and piped music. Straightforward lunchtime food (which can only be eaten in the table-service grand lounge dining room) could include soup (£2.75), baked potatoes (from £3.75), sandwiches (from £3.95, hot sandwiches from £4.50), ploughman's (£5.50), steak pie or fish and chips (£5.75), with puddings (from £2.50). The pub attracts a pleasant mix of customers, with theatre-goers, students, locals and tourists making up the contented bustle. No children inside. *(Recommended by R T and J C Moggridge, the Didler, John Dwane, Joe Green, MLR, Patrick Hancock, Peter F Marshall, Dorsan Baker)*

Mitchells & Butlers ~ Manager Marie-Louise Wong ~ Real ale ~ Bar food (only 12-3) ~ Restaurant ~ (0151) 707 2837 ~ Open 12-11; 12-10.30 Sun; closed bank hols

LONGRIDGE SD6039 Map 7

Derby Arms 🍷

Chipping Road, Thornley; 1½ miles N of Longridge on back road to Chipping

There's something of a hunting and fishing theme in the main bar of this pleasant old stone-built country pub, with old photographs commemorating notable catches, some nicely mounted bait above the comfortable red plush seats, and a stuffed pheasant that seems to be flying in through the wall. To the right is a smaller room with sporting trophies and mementoes, and a regimental tie collection, while off to the left are a couple of no smoking dining areas. The gents' has dozens of riddles on the wall; you can buy a sheet of them in the bar (the money goes to charity). The same welcoming family has run the pub for over 20 years (and the current licensee's great-grandmother was married from here in 1898). Along with a good range of wines including several half-bottles and a dozen or so by the glass (they're particularly strong on south african), you'll find well kept Marstons Pedigree and Theakstons on handpump. Enjoyable bar food might include sandwiches (from £3.95), soup (£3.30), ploughman's (£4.95), ham, egg and chips, spicy chicken satay or vegetarian hotpot (£7.95), seafood pasta or steak and kidney pudding (£8.95), chargrilled lamb chops (£9.95), and 10oz sirloin steak (£11.95), with puddings such as bread and butter pudding or sherry trifle (£3.75); potatoes and vegetables come in separate dishes. A few tables out in front, and another two behind the car park have fine views across to the Forest of Bowland. *(Recommended by Kevin and Barbara Wilkinson, Diane Manoughian, Ann and Bob Westbrook, Margaret Dickinson, Maurice and Gill McMahon, Norma and Noel Thomas, Jim and Maggie Cowell, Revd D Glover, Jo Lilley)*

Inn Partnership (Pubmaster) ~ Lease Mrs G M Walme ~ Real ale ~ Bar food ~ Restaurant ~ (01772) 782623 ~ Children in restaurant ~ Open 12-3.30, 6-11.30; 12-11 Sun

LYDGATE SD9704 Map 7

White Hart

Lydgate not marked on some maps so not to be confused with the one near Todmorden; take A669 Oldham—Saddleworth, and after almost 2½ miles turn right at brow of hill on to A6050 Stockport Road

A striking stone-built inn overlooking Saddleworth Moor, this is undoubtedly one of the area's finest places to eat in, and though it feels a little like a smart restaurant with rooms, it's very much a proper pub too, with a good few locals clustered round the bar, or in the two simpler rooms at the end. Many of the building's older features remain, but the overall style is more contemporary than traditional, so beams and exposed stonework are blended skilfully with deep red or purple walls, punctuated with a mix of modern paintings, black and white photographs, and stylised local scenes; most rooms have a fireplace, and fresh flowers. The main action is in the warmly elegant brasserie, the biggest of the main rooms, full of happy chat from clearly satisfied diners; it's mostly no smoking. The thoughtfully prepared meals are pricier than in most pubs around here, but the quality is consistently high; a typical menu might include open sandwiches (from £5.95), corned beef and duck liver terrine with mustard dressing (£6.50), ginger and coriander gravadlax with smoked salmon rondel and tempura oyster (£6.75), their excellent sausages (which they supply to many restaurants nearby; £6 starter, £11.75 main course), asparagus and wild mushroom tart with poached egg and mustard seed sauce (£13.75), fried guinea fowl breast with sun-dried tomatoes and smoked bacon and bean cassoulet (£14.50), roast lamb with rosemary dauphinoise potatoes and chorizo crisp (£14.95), and puddings such as carrot and marzipan sponge with amaretto ice-cream (£5); children's menu. They do a two-course lunch for £12.50 (£14.50 Sun), and as we went to press were doing a good buy-one-get-one-free set menu on Monday evenings. Well kept Lees Bitter, Timothy Taylors Landlord, Tetleys and changing guests on handpump; the wine list includes a number of half bottles. Good service from smartly dressed staff. There are picnic-sets on the lawn behind. Bedrooms are comfortable, with free internet access. They have plenty of special events based around themed menus, including wine and beer tastings and even a brass band contest. Further extensions are planned: a new function room will replace the back marquee in early 2005. The lavatories are unusually smart. *(Recommended by Andrew Crawford, Bob and Lisa Cantrell, Mrs P J Carroll, Keith Moss, John and Sylvia Harrop)*

Free house ~ Licensee Charles Brierley ~ Real ale ~ Bar food (12-2.30, 6-9.30 Mon-Sat; 1-7.30 Sun) ~ Restaurant ~ (01457) 872566 ~ Well behaved children welcome ~ Open 12-11; 12-10.30 Sun; closed evening 25 Dec ~ Bedrooms: £75B/£105B

LYTHAM SD3627 Map 7

Taps £

A584 S of Blackpool; Henry Street – in centre, one street in from West Beach

No matter how busy it gets at this thriving ale house (and with eight superbly kept real ales it does fill up quickly), service remains swift and friendly. With a good mix of visitors, the Victorian-style bare-boarded bar has a sociable unassuming feel, plenty of stained-glass decoration in the windows, depictions of fish and gulls reflecting the pub's proximity to the beach, captain's chairs in bays around the sides, open fires, and a coal-effect gas fire between two built-in bookcases at one end; you'll be lucky if you get a seat. There's also an expanding collection of rugby memorabilia with old photographs and portraits of rugby stars on the walls; shove-ha'penny, dominoes and a fruit machine. A view-in cellar lets you admire the beers, and alongside Boddingtons, regularly changing guests on handpump might include Batemans Spring Breeze, Coach House Honeypot, Phoenix Double Gold, Taps (brewed for the pub by Titanic) Best and Dark, and Woods Best and Bomber County; they also usually serve some country wines and a farm cider. There are seat belts on the bar and headrests in the gents' to help keep you out of harm's way if you have one too many. Served only at lunchtime, a few cheap, straightforward bar snacks include sandwiches (from £2.25; soup and a sandwich from £3.25), filled baked potatoes or burgers (from £2.50), and chilli or curry (£3.95). There are a few seats outside. Parking is difficult near the pub so it's probably best to park at the West Beach car park on the seafront (free on Sunday), and walk. *(Recommended by Margaret Dickinson, Maggie and Tony Harwood, Steve Whalley, Dr and Mrs A K Clarke, Simon Calvert, K H Richards)*

Hogs Head (Laurel) ~ Manager Ian Rigg ~ Real ale ~ Bar food (lunchtime only, not Sun) ~ (01253) 736226 ~ Open 11-11; 12-10.30 Sun

MANCHESTER SJ7796 Map 7

Britons Protection ♀ £

Great Bridgewater Street, corner of Lower Mosley Street

The long-standing licensees seem to take real pride in this popular city pub. The rather plush little front bar has a fine chequered tile floor, some glossy brown and russet wall tiles, solid woodwork and elaborate plastering. A tiled passage lined with battle murals leads to two cosy inner lounges, one served by hatch, with attractive brass and etched glass wall lamps, a mirror above the coal-effect gas fire in the simple art nouveau fireplace, and again good solidly comfortable furnishings. As something of a tribute to Manchester's notorious climate, the massive bar counter has a pair of heating pipes as its footrail. Although it's busy at lunchtime, it's usually quiet and relaxed in the evenings; the atmosphere is welcoming, and the staff are friendly. As well as around 235 malt whiskies, and an interesting range of spirits, they have Jennings Cumberland, Robinsons Best, Tetleys and a regularly changing guest such as Coach House Dick Turpin superbly kept on handpump, and good wines too. Straightforward bar food includes home-made soup (£1.85), sandwiches (from £2), ploughman's (£4), ham and egg (£4.50, leek and mushroom crumble (£4.75), unusual pies (£4.95), and home-made daily specials (from £4.75); piped music. There are tables out on the terrace behind. The pub is handy for Bridgewater Hall (and it is well known to many orchestral players), and the GMEX centre. *(Recommended by Stephen and Jean Curtis, Pam and John Smith, P G Plumridge, the Didler, Stephen Buckley, Patrick Hancock, Peter F Marshall, Russell Lewin)*

Punch ~ Lease Peter Barnett ~ Real ale ~ Bar food (lunchtime only) ~ Restaurant ~ (0161) 236 5895 ~ Children in family room ~ Live entertainment first Tues of month and Weds evening ~ Open 11(12 Sat)-11; 12-10.30 Sun; closed 25 Dec

Dukes 92 £

Castle Street, below the bottom end of Deansgate

What makes this tastefully converted cavernous former stables stand out is its terrific setting; it's near locks and railway arches in the rejuvenated heart of old industrial Manchester, with tables out by the canal basin which opens into the bottom lock of the Rochdale Canal. Inside, black wrought-iron work contrasts boldly with whitewashed bare plaster walls, the handsome bar is granite-topped, and an elegant spiral staircase leads to a no smoking upper room and balcony. Down in the main room the fine mix of furnishings is mainly rather Edwardian in mood, with one particularly massive table, elegantly comfortable chaises-longues and deep armchairs. As we went to press, work on the adjacent restaurant meant that they weren't able to serve any real ales, and a limited range of bar snacks was available only at lunchtime. However, by the end of 2004 they hope to have two real ales on handpump, and longer food serving times, with a wider choice of hot meals. They do an excellent range of over three dozen cheeses and several pâtés with a generous helping of granary bread (£4.50, served till 8.30), and other good value bar food includes soup (£2.80), toasties (from £3.25), filled baked potatoes or open sandwiches (from £3.95), and salads (from £5.95). They've decent wines, a wide choice of malt whiskies, and the belgian wheat beer Hoegaarden on tap; piped jazz. A function room/theatre has temporary exhibitions of local artwork. More reports please. *(Recommended by Mike and Linda Hudson, Brian and Anna Marsden, John Fiander, Stephen Buckley, Russell Lewin)*

Free house ~ Licensee James Ramsbottom ~ Bar food (12-3(6 Fri-Sun), but see text) ~ (0161) 839 8646 ~ Children welcome till 8pm ~ Open 11.30-11(12 Fri-Sat); 12-10.30 Sun

Lass o' Gowrie £

36 Charles Street; off Oxford Street at BBC

Behind its richly tiled arched brown façade, the simple big-windowed long bar of this lively and traditional Victorian pub has gas lighting, bare floorboards, lots of stripped brickwork, and hop pockets draped from the ceiling. There's a good variety of visitors: at weekends during term time, you'll find crowds of cheery university students (with the pavement outside pressed into service for extra room) and piped pop music, while at quieter times during the day, the music might be switched off to suit an older crowd of chatty locals. Black Sheep, Boddingtons, Greene King Old Speckled Hen, and Lass o' Gowrie (brewed for the pub by Titanic), are well kept alongside four or five constantly changing guests from brewers such as Hook Norton, Harviestoun and Titanic. Reasonably priced straightforward bar food such as filled baguettes (from £2.25), scampi and chips or breakfast (£3.95), veggie sausage and mash (£4.25), toad in the hole (£4.65), and rump steak (£5.95); they also do two meals for £5.95. The staff are friendly (though at busy times you may have to wait to be served). The snug is no smoking; fruit machine and satellite TV. More reports please. *(Recommended by Sue Holland, Dave Webster, Catherine Pitt, Paul Hopton, B and M Kendall, Russell Lewin)*

Laurel ~ Manager Ellie Owen ~ Real ale ~ Bar food (12-8; 12-5 Sat) ~ (0161) 273 6932 ~ Children in eating area of bar ~ Open 11-11; 12-10.30 Sun

Marble Arch £

73 Rochdale Road (A664), Ancoats; corner of Gould Street, just E of Victoria Station

The fine choice of own-brew beers, interesting décor and relaxed welcoming atmosphere, make this Victorian town pub a popular choice for readers. From windows at the back, you can look out over the brewery (tours by arrangement) where they produce the distinctive hoppy Cloudy Marble, Lagonda IPA, Manchester Bitter, N/4, Uncut Amber and Marble Ginger Ale, and they also have guests such as Bazens Riverside, Brakspear Special, and Phoenix Pale Moonlight. The interior of the pub is beautifully preserved, with a magnificently restored lightly barrel-vaulted high ceiling, and extensive marble and tiling – the frieze advertising various spirits, and the chimneybreast above the carved wooden mantelpiece, particularly stand out. The pub is furnished with leather sofas, pews, wing-back chairs, cushioned settles and deep armchairs, around a mix of tables, and all the walls are stripped back to the glazed brick; there's a collection of breweriana, and a cabinet has a display of pump clips. The sloping mosaic floor in the bar can be a bit disconcerting after a few pints; fruit machine, pinball and a juke box. They do generously filled sandwiches (from £3.95), and other good value, tasty bar food might include tortilla wraps (from £3.75), mezze plate (£4.25), irish stew, steak and ale pie or fish and chips (£4.95), and steaks (from £8.95), with specials such as mediterranean roasted vegetable pasta (£6.95), and seared salmon with caper sauce (£8.95). There's a little garden. The Laurel and Hardy Preservation Society meet here on the third Wednesday of the month and show old films. *(Recommended by Catherine Pitt, Richard Lewis, the Didler, Peter F Marshall, Revd D Glover, G Coates)*

Own brew ~ Licensee Christine Baldwin ~ Real ale ~ Bar food (12-2.30, 4.30-8, not Sun) ~ No credit cards ~ (0161) 832 5914 ~ Open 11.30-11; 12-11(10.30 Sun) Sat

MELLOR SJ9888 Map 7

Oddfellows Arms

Heading out of Marple on the A626 towards Glossop, Mellor is the next road after the B6102, signposted off on the right at Marple Bridge; keep on for nearly 2 miles up Longhurst Lane and into Moor End Road

No piped music or games machines spoil the relaxed and chatty atmosphere at this civilised old pub. What draws most customers here is the enjoyable food, and it's a good idea to get here early to be sure of a table. Served by friendly staff, a wide choice of dishes might include soup (£2.95), sandwiches (from £4.25, hot sandwiches (from £3.95), mussel chowder (£4.85), lamb rogan josh (£7.95), chick pea and apricot tagine (£8.45), hot thai chicken with lychees (£9.95), and steaks (from £10.95), with specials such as chicken satay skewers (£3.95), poached salmon with white wine and watercress sauce (£8.45), chicken tikka masala (£9.95), and cajun swordfish steak (£10.95); puddings might be rhubarb and ginger mousse or spotted dick (£3.95). The pleasant low-ceilinged flagstoned bar has nice open fires; there's a small no smoking restaurant upstairs. Served with or without a sparkler, Adnams Southwold, Marstons Best, Phoenix Arizona and a weekly changing guest such as Cottage Golden Arrow are well kept on handpump; they've eight wines by the glass. There are a few tables out by the road. It can be tricky to secure a parking space when they're busy. *(Recommended by Bob and Lisa Cantrell, David Hoult, Michael Butler, Brenda and Stuart Naylor, Brian and Anna Marsden, Mrs P J Carroll, Maurice and Della Andrew, Simon Calvert)*

Free house ~ Licensee Robert Cloughley ~ Real ale ~ Bar food (not Sun evening, Mon, or a few days over Christmas) ~ Restaurant ~ (0161) 449 7826 ~ Children allowed till 8.30pm ~ Dogs welcome ~ Open 12-3, 5.30-11(7-10.30 Sun); closed Mon, and a few days over Christmas

NEWTON SD6950 Map 7

Parkers Arms 🍷

B6478 7 miles N of Clitheroe

Not only do customers have a good time at this pretty cream and green painted pub, you get the feeling the welcoming staff do too, and there's an enjoyably buoyant atmosphere. It's comfortably furnished, with red plush button-back banquettes, a mix of chairs and tables, stuffed animals, prints, and an open fire. Beyond an arch is a similar area with sensibly placed darts, a log fire, cribbage, dominoes, fruit machine, and TV; it can get smoky. Well kept Boddingtons, and Flowers IPA on handpump along with a couple of guests from brewers such as Black Sheep or Copper Dragon, with a good range of malt whiskies and around 55 wines (nine by the glass). Enjoyable bar food includes lunchtime sandwiches (from £3.35), basket meals such as scampi or battered haddock (£4.75), and leek, ham and chicken crumble (£7.25), wild boar sausages with whisky and mustard or seafood pancakes (£8.25), kleftiko (£10.75), and halibut (£14.25), with puddings such as white chocolate and raspberry cheesecake (£3.75); the charming restaurant is no smoking. From the big front garden there are lovely unspoilt views down over the River Hodder and its valley; they keep lots of pets – pygmy goats, rabbits, guinea pigs, hens, pheasants, parrots and two playful black labradors. *(Recommended by W W Burke, Bernard Stradling, Margaret Dickinson, Martin Knowles, David Barnes, Norma and Noel Thomas)*

Enterprise ~ Lease Barbara Clayton ~ Real ale ~ Bar food (12-2.30, 6-9; 12-9 Sat/Sun, and wkdys in summer) ~ Restaurant ~ (01200) 446236 ~ Children welcome ~ Open 11-11; 12-10.30 Sun; 11-2.30, 5.30-11 Mon-Fri in winter ~ Bedrooms: £38S/£50S

Real ale to us means beer which has matured naturally in its cask – not pressurised or filtered.

RIBCHESTER SD6435 Map 7

White Bull

Church Street; turn off B6245 at sharp corner by Black Bull

Popular with locals and visitors alike, this friendly 18th-c stone dining pub has a spacious main bar with comfortable old settles, Victorian advertisements and various prints, and a stuffed fox in two halves that looks as if it's jumping through the wall. Most areas are set out for eating during the day, and well liked bar food, from a reasonably priced menu, includes home-made soup (£2.50), sandwiches (from £3.50), crispy prawns (£3.75), chilli con carne (£6.50), home-made steak and kidney pie or grilled gammon and egg (£6.95), giant battered haddock (£7.50), pork steak with creamy stilton and bacon sauce (£7.95), and steaks (from £8.50), with a changing specials board; the two dining areas are no smoking. Black Sheep, Boddingtons and a guest such as Greene King Abbot are well kept on handpump, and they've decent wines, and a good range of malt whiskies; TV, fruit machine, dominoes and piped music. In summer you can sit out in the pleasant garden behind. Ribchester is an interesting Roman village (there's a small Roman museum nearby); you'll find some remains of a Roman bath house scattered behind the pub, and the Tuscan pillars that support the entrance porch have stood here or nearby for nearly 2,000 years. *(Recommended by Pat and Tony Martin, Abi Benson, Len Beattie, Rex and Mary Hepburn, Yvonne and Mike Meadley)*

Enterprise ~ Lease Jill Meadows ~ Real ale ~ Bar food (11.30-9(9.30 Sat); 12-8 Sun) ~ Restaurant ~ (01254) 878303 ~ Children in eating area of bar and restaurant ~ Open 11.30-11; 12-10.30 Sun; closed 25 Dec evening ~ Bedrooms: /£45S(£50B)

RIMINGTON SD8045 Map 7

Black Bull

Off A59 NW of Clitheroe, at Chatburn; or off A682 S of Gisburn

This brick house is a good deal more unusual and interesting than its simple exterior suggests – not least because of the extraordinary collection of model trains, planes, cars and ships crammed into a room at the back. Entry to the little museum is by donation, and you'll need to ask the landlady to open it up for you, but it really is worth it; anyone with even the slightest interest in models of historic vehicles will be enthralled. Further exhibits are dotted around the airy, rather elegant rooms of the pub proper, where the very good, well presented food stands out as the main attraction, with a real emphasis on fresh, local ingredients. A typical menu might include local baby black puddings on a salt-roasted pork belly with a wholegrain and english mustard cream sauce (£5), hot and sour noodle broth with whole prawn tails and chorizo sausage (£5.50), linguini with sautéed wild mushrooms, roast garlic and a tarragon and white wine cream sauce (£8.50), roulade of cornfed chicken breast with foie gras and chestnut and asparagus tips on a burgundy consommé (£10), crispy duckling on stir-fried chinese vegetables with a hoi sin and plum sauce (£12), honey-roast rack of lamb with a fresh mint and redcurrant jus (£12.50), and a number of fish and seafood specials; readers have particularly praised the vegetables and the puddings. The big, old-fashioned and civilised main bar has a model locomotive in a glass case beside an attractively tiled fireplace, a plane hanging from the ceiling, various platform signs on the walls, and comfortable banquettes and window seats; a central area with leatherette chairs leads through to a quietly refined dining room, with an exhibition of wildlife art on the walls. It may all sound rather unpubby, but in the evenings it does feel very much like a village local, just as happy serving local lads a pint and a chip butty. Theakstons Best on handpump; good welcoming service. *(Recommended by JES, Mrs P J Carroll, Yvonne and Mike Meadley)*

Free house ~ Licensee Mrs Barbara Blades ~ Real ale ~ Bar food (12-2.30, 7-9.30) ~ Restaurant ~ (01200) 445220 ~ Children in eating area of bar ~ Open 12-3, 7-11(10.30 Sun); closed Mon inc bank hols

SAWLEY SD7746 Map 7

Spread Eagle

Village signposted just off A59 NE of Clitheroe

They've a terrific wine list at this well placed dining pub, with 130 bottles (10 wines by the glass), as well as more than 40 whiskies, but the main emphasis is firmly on the very good food. The short lunchtime bar menu might include sandwiches (from £3.95), grilled black pudding medallion (£4.95), and duck leg confit salad or smooth chicken liver and foie gras parfait (£5.50). In the restaurant, which overlooks the River Ribble, you can choose from dishes such as fried salmon with buttered pea stock and broad bean gnocchi (£9.95), grilled duck breast with poached pineapple, spring onions and aniseed sauce (£11.25), and slow-cooked lamb shank with tarragon sauce (£11.50); swift service from the smartly dressed and attentive staff. They have various theme and gourmet evenings, and special offers. The light and airy continental-feeling main bar (partly no smoking) has comfortable banquette seating, plenty of paintings and prints and lovely photographs of local views on the walls, a roaring winter coal fire, and well kept Black Sheep, and Swaley's Drunken Duck (brewed for the pub by local micro-brewery Bowland) on handpump. The building faces 12th-c Cistercian abbey ruins, and the pub is very handy for the Forest of Bowland. Be warned, the ladies' lavatories are upstairs. *(Recommended by K Ogden, G Hunt, Margaret Dickinson, Mrs R A Cartwright, R A K Crabtree, Adrian White, Mrs P J Carroll)*

Free house ~ Licensees Nigel and Ysanne Williams ~ Bar food (lunchtime Tues-Sat only) ~ Restaurant ~ (01200) 441202 ~ Children in restaurant ~ Open 12-3, 6-11; 12-3 Sun; closed Sun evening and all day Mon

STALYBRIDGE SJ9698 Map 7

Station Buffet £

The Station, Rassbottom Street

Not smart, but comfortably nostalgic, this classic Victorian platform bar is an enjoyable and memorable place to visit. The bar has a welcoming fire below an etched-glass mirror, newspapers and magazines to read, and old photographs of the station in its heyday and other railway memorabilia; there's a little conservatory. An extension along the platform leads into what was the ladies' waiting room and part of the station-master's quarters, with original ornate ceilings and a dining/function room with Victorian-style wallpaper; dominoes, cribbage, draughts. On a sunny day you can sit out on the platform. They serve a marvellous range of up to 20 interesting guest ales a week (and are continually being approached by microbreweries to stock their latest brew), alongside well kept Boddingtons, Flowers IPA and Wadworths 6X. You can also get farm cider, and belgian and other foreign bottled beers; beer festivals are held in early May and late November. They do cheap old-fashioned snacks such as tasty black peas (50p) and sandwiches (from £1.50), and three or four daily specials such as home-made pie with peas (£1.50), bacon casserole (£2.20) and all day breakfast (£2.25); freshly made coffee and tea by the pot. *(Recommended by Tony Hobden, the Didler, Mike and Linda Hudson, Dennis Jones, MLR, Brenda and Stuart Naylor, John Fiander)*

Free house ~ Licensees John Hesketh and Sylvia Wood ~ Real ale ~ Bar food (all day) ~ Restaurant ~ (0161) 303 0007 ~ Children welcome ~ Dogs welcome ~ Folk music Sat evenings, quiz Mon night ~ Open 11-11; 12-10.30 Sun; closed 25 Dec

We mention bottled beers and spirits only if there is something unusual about them – imported belgian real ales, say, or dozens of malt whiskies; so do please let us know about them in your reports.

TUNSTALL SD6173 Map 7

Lunesdale Arms 🍷

A683 S of Kirkby Lonsdale

The cheerful bustling atmosphere at this brightly opened-up civilised dining pub is helped along by bare boards and lively acoustics, and shades of blue and yellow. The very good food is the main focus, and they use lots of local organic produce, and meat from local farms; good home-baked bread. Enjoyable dishes might include lunchtime open sandwiches (from £3.50), soup (£3.50), welsh rarebit (£5.50), and steak and kidney pie (£8.50), with evening dishes such as chicken liver parfait (£4.25), corn-fed chicken breast with tarragon sauce (£9), lamb rump with onion mash (£9.25), and sirloin steak with gremolata sauce (£10.95), and puddings such as rhubarb fool with gingerbread biscuit or treacle tart (£3.75); Sunday lunch (from £8). They do smaller helpings of some main courses. On yellow walls the big unframed oil paintings (some for sale) are often of bluebells, some of the pews and armchairs have blue and/or yellow upholstery, and the blinds for most of the big windows are also blue and yellow. On one side of the central bar part, a white-walled area (where the pictures are framed) has a good mix of stripped and sealed solid dining tables, and sofas around a lower table with daily papers, by a woodburning stove which has a couple of orchids on the stone mantelpiece. At the other end, an airy games section has pool, table football and TV, and a snugger little flagstoned back part has another woodburning stove. Besides well kept Black Sheep and a guest such as Timothy Taylors Landlord on handpump, they have a good range of sensibly priced wines by the glass (in a choice of sizes), and summer Pimms; piped music. This pretty village in the Lune Valley has a church with Brontë associations. *(Recommended by Michael Doswell, Karen Eliot, Ray and Winifred Halliday, Malcolm Taylor, Simon Calvert, Jo Lilley, Alison Hayes, Pete Hanlon)*

Free house ~ Licensee Emma Gillibrand ~ Bar food (not Mon (exc bank hols), 25-26 Dec) ~ Restaurant ~ (01524) 274203 ~ Children welcome ~ Dogs allowed in bar ~ Live piano music most Thurs ~ Open 11-3, 6-11; 12-3.30, 6-10.30 Sun; closed Mon exc bank hols, 25-26 Dec

UPPERMILL SD9905 Map 7

Church Inn 🍺 £

From the main street (A607), look out for the sign for Saddleworth Church, and turn off up this steep narrow lane – keep on up!

Seats on a small terrace outside this ancient and isolated local look up towards the moors; more seats out in a garden – and anything from rabbits, ducks and geese to horses and a couple of peacocks. The fairly priced own-brewed Saddleworth beers are a big draw, and Saddleworth More, Ayrtons, Bert Corner, Hopsmacker, Rueben's Bitter, Shaftbender and seasonal ales are well kept alongside a couple of guests such as Boggart Hole Clough Boggart Bitter or Dark Star on handpump; several malt whiskies and farm cider too. The big unspoilt L-shaped main bar has high beams and some stripped stone; one window at the end of the bar counter looks down over the valley, and there's also a valley view from the quieter no smoking dining room. The comfortable furnishings include settles and pews as well as a good individual mix of chairs, and there are lots of attractive prints, staffordshire and other china on a high delft shelf, jugs, brasses and so forth; TV and occasional unobtrusive piped music. The horse-collar on the wall is worn by the winner of their annual gurning (or face-pulling) championship (part of the lively Rush Cart Festival, usually held over the August bank holiday), and handbells here are the church bellringers' practice set. Children and dogs are made to feel very welcome, and there's an increasing army of rescued cats. Reasonably priced bar food such as sandwiches (from £1.30), soup (£1.75), ploughman's (£3.25), steak and ale pie (£5.75), jumbo cod (£6.75), and roast beef (£5.99), with puddings such as banoffi pie (£2.25); children's meals (£2.75). *(Recommended by the Didler, MLR, Mrs P J Carroll, John Fiander)*

Own brew ~ Licensee Julian Taylor ~ Real ale ~ Bar food (12-2.30, 5.30-9; 12-9 Sat/Sun and bank hols) ~ Restaurant ~ (01457) 872415 ~ Children welcome ~ Dogs welcome ~ Open 12-11(10.30 Sun); cl from 3-7.30pm 25 Dec

WHEELTON SD6021 Map 7

Dressers Arms

2.1 miles from M61 junction 8; A674 towards Blackburn, then in Wheelton fork right into Briers Brow; 3.6 miles from M65 junction 3, also via A674

Handy from the motorway, this converted cottage row is well liked for its food and its very good range of beers, including at least one from their own microbrewery. It's much bigger than it looks from the outside, with a series of genuinely atmospheric, low-beamed little rooms that remain darkly cosy even on the sunniest of days, full of old oak and traditional features, including a handsome old woodburning stove in the flagstoned main bar. Candles on tables add to the welcoming feel, and there are newspapers, magazines and a couple of stuffed animals in glass cases; two areas are no smoking. One particularly snug room has windows overlooking the brewing equipment. They usually keep eight real ales on at once, such as their own Big Franks and possibly Annastasia, as well as the more familiar Boddingtons, Fullers London Pride, Shepherd Neame Spitfire, Tetleys, Timothy Taylors Landlord and Worthington Best; also around 20 malt whiskies, and some well chosen wines. Served all day at weekends, the good locally sourced bar food includes soup (£2.15), sandwiches (£3) and hot filled baguettes (from £5.25), several vegetarian dishes such as madras curry or cheese and broccoli bake (£5.50), steak and kidney pie or paella (£5.95), liver and onions or sausage and mash (£6.50), and blackboard specials such as green thai curry or lamb kebabs (£6.95); Sunday roasts (£8.95), and straightforward children's meals (£3.75, including an ice-cream). The licensees are great pet-lovers, and have a couple of dogs and cats. On the first floor is a cantonese restaurant. Lots of picnic-sets on a terrace in front of the pub; they have a very big car park, across the road.
(Recommended by Andy and Jill Kassube, Richard Houghton, MLR, Yvonne and Mike Meadley)

Own brew ~ Licensees Steve and Trudie Turner ~ Real ale ~ Bar food (12-2.30, 5-9; 12-9 weekends) ~ Restaurant ~ (01254) 830041 ~ Children in eating area of bar ~ Dogs welcome ~ Open 11-11; 12-10.30 Sun

WHITEWELL SD6546 Map 7

Inn at Whitewell ★★

Most easily reached by B6246 from Whalley; road through Dunsop Bridge from B6478 is also good

Set deep in the Forest of Bowland and surrounded by wooded rolling hills set off against higher moors, this superbly run inn is an excellent place to stay. Impressively furnished, the old-fashioned pubby bar has antique settles, oak gateleg tables, sonorous clocks, old cricketing and sporting prints, roaring log fires (the lounge has a very attractive stone fireplace), and heavy curtains on sturdy wooden rails; one area has a selection of newspapers and magazines, dominoes, local maps and guide books, there's a piano for anyone who wants to play, and even an art gallery. Down a corridor with strange objects like a stuffed fox disappearing into the wall, the pleasant suntrap garden has wonderful views down to the valley. In the early evening, there's a cheerful bustle but once the visitors have gone, the atmosphere is tranquil and relaxing. Their good wine list contains around 180 wines (including a highly recommended claret), and they've well kept Marstons Pedigree and Timothy Taylors Landlord on handpump. Besides lunchtime sandwiches (from £3.90), delicious, well presented food, from the mostly traditional bar menu, might include home-made soup (£3.20), grilled kipper (£6.50), cumberland sausages and champ (£7.50), fish pie (£8.50), goosnargh chicken breast wrapped with leeks and bacon, with crushed potatoes and a light jus (£12), with specials such as fried chicken livers with grilled chorizo and black pudding (£5.80), roast lamb ratatouille with champ potatoes and red wine jus (£6), fried salmon with chorizo and pepper tapas with basil pesto or roast goosnargh chicken breast with curried lentils and sweet potato scallops (£11.50), and chargrilled sirloin steak with wild mushroom ragoût and red wine jus (£12.50), with mouthwatering home-made puddings and farmhouse cheeses (from £3.80); the staff are courteous and friendly, but service can be slow at times. You can get coffee and cream teas all day; they sell jars of home-made jam. As this is such a popular place to stay, you now have to book quite a long way ahead to secure a room. There's plenty of fell walking, they own several miles of trout, salmon and sea trout fishing on the Hodder, and with notice they'll even arrange shooting; they're happy to do picnic hampers for guests. *(Recommended by Andrew Stephenson, Anthony Longden, Jim Abbott, Mike Schofield, Louise English, J F M and M West, Derek and Sylvia Stephenson, Di and Mike Gillam, Stephen Buckley, Bernard Stradling, Len Beattie, Oliver and Sue Rowell, Mrs P J Carroll, Brenda and Rob Fincham, Jo Lilley, Simon Calvert, Revd D Glover; also in the* Good Hotel Guide*)*

Free house ~ Licensee Richard Bowman ~ Real ale ~ Bar food (12-2, 7.30-9.30) ~ Restaurant ~ (01200) 448222 ~ Children welcome ~ Dogs welcome ~ Open 11-3, 6-12; 12-3, 7-11 Sun ~ Bedrooms: £69B/£94B

YEALAND CONYERS SD5074 Map 7

New Inn

3 miles from M6 junction 35; village signposted off A6

A handy place to stop if you need a break from the nearby M4, this 17th-c ivy-covered village pub is open all day. The simply furnished little beamed bar on the left has a cosy village atmosphere, with its log fire in the big stone fireplace, and cribbage and dominoes. On the right, two communicating no smoking cottagey dining rooms have dark blue furniture, shiny beams and an attractive kitchen range. Well kept Hartleys XB and Hartleys Cumbria Way on handpump, around 30 malt whiskies, winter mulled wine and maybe summer home-made lemonade; piped music. There's a bustling atmosphere with plenty of locals and visitors. The same menu runs through the dining rooms and bar, and dishes might include soup (£3.15), sandwiches or filled baked potatoes (from £3.95), cajun potato skins (£4.50), cumberland sausage or lentil and red pepper curry (£8.95), and beef in beer (£9.50), with specials such as fried duck breast with orange sauce and monkfish kebab with dill and cucumber cream sauce (from £9.95 to £12.95). A sheltered lawn at the side has picnic-sets among roses and flowering shrubs. *(Recommended by Jack Clark, Mike Schofield, David Carr, John Foord, Deb and John Arthur, Karen Eliot, Stan and Hazel Allen, Brenda and Stuart Naylor, Michael Doswell, Malcolm and Jane MacDonald, Richard Greaves, Patrick and Phillipa Vickery, Simon J Barber, Simon Calvert, Jo Lilley)*

Robinsons ~ Tenants Bill Tully and Charlotte Pinder ~ Real ale ~ Bar food (11.30(12 Sun)-9.30) ~ Restaurant ~ (01524) 732938 ~ Children welcome ~ Dogs allowed in bar ~ Open 11.30-11; 12-10.30 Sun

Several well known guide books make establishments pay for entry, either directly or as a fee for inspection. These fees can run to many hundreds of pounds. We do not. Unlike other guides, we never take payment for entries. We never accept a free meal, free drink, or any other freebie from a pub. We do not accept any sponsorship – let alone from commercial schemes linked to the pub trade. All our entries depend solely on merit. And we are the only guide in which virtually all the main entries have been gained by a unique two-stage sifting process: first, a build-up of favourable reports from our thousands of reader-reporters; then anonymous vetting by one of the senior editorial staff.

LUCKY DIP

Besides the fully inspected pubs, you might like to try these Lucky Dips recommended to us and described by readers (if you do, please send us reports: www.goodguides.co.uk).

ABBEY VILLAGE SD6422
Hare & Hounds [Bolton Rd (A675, S of M65 junction 3)]: Popular neatly kept chatty village local doing well under hard-working current licensees, big beamed main bar, roaring woodburner in snug on left, toby jugs, plates and brasses, generous sensibly priced food from baguettes up cooked by landlady, well kept Timothy Taylors Landlord and guests such as Beartown, Boddingtons and Marston Moor, friendly service; quiet piped music; dogs welcome, seats outside, good views of Darwen tower *(Steve Whalley)*

AFFETSIDE SD7513
Pack Horse [Watling St]: Attractive neatly kept moorland local on Roman road, particularly well kept Hydes ale, big helpings of lunchtime bar food, snug pool room, restaurant early evenings (not Sun); good walking country, open all day wknds *(DJH, Peter Abbott)*

ARKHOLME SD5872
Bay Horse [B6254 Carnforth—Kirkby Lonsdale]: Neatly kept and homely old three-room country pub popular for cheap generous food inc good value sandwiches, good service, well kept Boddingtons and a guest such as Everards Tiger, lovely inglenook, good pictures of long-lost London pubs; own bowling green, handy for charming Lune valley walks *(Steve Whalley, Jane Taylor, David Dutton, Margaret Dickinson)*

ASHTON-UNDER-LYNE SJ9399
Caledonia [Warrington St]: Bustling and welcoming open-plan town pub with wide choice of good value food (not Sun or Mon evenings) inc sandwiches, baked potatoes and popular pies and hotpot, some more expensive early evening dishes, well kept Robinsons inc Hatters Mild, several distinct areas inc raised no smoking section; bedrooms, open all day (cl Sun afternoon) *(Dennis Jones, Pete Baker)*
Oddfellows Arms [Alderley St, just off Kings Road]: Small, friendly and unpretentious, with several areas around single bar, log fires, well kept Robinsons, traditional games *(Pete Baker)*

BASHALL EAVES SD6943
☆ *Red Pump* [NW of Clitheroe, off B6478 or B6243]: Tucked-away partly 18th-c country pub, well refurbished and expanded, relaxed and unpretentious, with good interesting food inc good value Sun lunch, welcoming service, local Bowland ales, two roaring log fires, roomy smartly decorated restaurant, no piped music; two bedrooms, good breakfast, own fishing on River Hodder *(Richard Houghton)*

BEBINGTON SJ3385
Travellers Rest [B5151, not far from M53 junction 4; Higher Bebington]: Friendly semi-rural corner pub with several areas around central bar and separate no smoking room, all laid for enjoyable reasonably priced bar lunches from sandwiches to mixed grill (not Sun; orders stop 1.45), up to eight well kept ales inc some from small breweries, efficient staff, alcoves, beams, brasses etc; no children, open all day *(MLR)*

BIRKENHEAD SJ3289
Crown [Conway St]: Interestingly tiled alehouse with Cains and several guest beers, Weston's farm cider, good value generous food all day till 6, several rooms; open all day *(the Didler, MLR)*
Dispensary [Chester St]: Well kept Cains and guest beers, good value lunchtime food, handsome glass ceiling; handy for ferry, open all day *(the Didler)*
Stork [Price St]: Early 19th-c, carefully done up without being spoilt; Threlfalls tiled façade, four rooms around island bar, polished original floor, old dock and ferry photographs, several well kept real ales, decent food wkdy lunchtime and early evening, no smoking area; open all day (not Sun) *(the Didler)*

BLACKO SD8541
☆ *Moorcock* [A682 towards Gisburn]: Beautifully placed moorland dining pub, roomy and comfortable, with big picture windows for breathtaking views, tables set close for the huge range of popular and often enterprising food inc lamb from their own flock and excellent beef, very friendly helpful staff, decent wine, Thwaites Bitter and Mild under top pressure; tables in hillside garden with various animals, open all day for food Sun, children and dogs welcome, bedrooms *(LYM, Norma and Noel Thomas)*
Rising Sun [A682 towards Gisburn]: Traditional village pub with tiled entry, open fires in three rooms off main bar, one with sports TV, another for families with internet access, reasonably priced food, real ales such as Black Sheep, Skipton and John Smiths, warm a welcome for visitors, three well kept real ales, good low-priced food *(D J Etheridge)*

BLACKPOOL SD3136
Blue Room [Church St]: Latest name change for alehouse-theme pub with good range of changing beers, friendly staff, all sorts of pub games; handy for Winter Gardens *(Abi Benson, Dr and Mrs A K Clarke)*
Old England [Red Bank Rd]: Good food choice, easy parking *(Abi Benson)*
Pump & Truncheon [Bonny St]: Real-ale pub opp police HQ, dark bare boards, blackboards with old jokes, three well kept ales inc local Hart, basic reasonably priced lunchtime food, coal fires, occasional beer festivals; open all day *(Dr B and Mrs P B Baker)*
Ramsden Arms [Talbot Rd, opp Blackpool North stn]: Large friendly local with several panelled areas, masses of old prints and mainly beer-related bric-a-brac, helpful staff, no smoking area, well kept Boddingtons, Marstons Pedigree, Thwaites and a couple of low-priced local Blackpool brews, over 40 whiskies, may be lunchtime food; CD juke

box, pool and games; good value bedrooms *(Kevin Blake, the Didler, Richard Lewis, Abi Benson, John Dwane, Dr and Mrs A K Clarke)*

Saddle [Whitegate Dr, Marton]: Popular refurbished local dating from 18th c, two panelled rooms (one no smoking at lunchtime) off small bar, lots of old prints and photographs, well kept Bass and Worthington 1744, good value food, good atmosphere, busy Easter beer festival with marquee extension; play area *(Jim and Maggie Cowell)*

Wheatsheaf [Talbot Rd, opp Blackpool North station]: Busy but relaxed traditional pub with well kept Theakstons and good choice of guest beers, food all day, old pictures and bric-a-brac inc flags and lots of 60s pop music memorabilia; pianist Tues, tables on small terrace, barbecues, open all day *(the Didler, Abi Benson)*

BLACKROD SD6011

Thatch & Thistle [Chorley Rd (A6 N)]: Roadside pub with enjoyable food inc popular Sun lunch, reasonable prices, well kept Bank Top, welcoming efficient service *(Mr and Mrs Colin Roberts)*

BOLTON SD7109

Howcroft [Pool St]: Friendly backstreet local serving as tap for local Bank Top ales, also guest beers and Addlestone's cider; lots of small screened-off rooms around central servery with fine glass and woodwork, cosy snug with coal fire, good value lunches in lounge, plenty of games inc pinball, darts, bar billiards; bowling green, occasional folk nights, open all day *(the Didler)*

Olde Man & Scythe [Churchgate]: Interesting timbered local, largely 17th-c with cellar dating from 12th c, lively long flagstoned drinking area, two quieter rooms popular for bargain lunchtime food from sandwiches up, well kept ales such as Boddingtons, Caledonian Deuchars IPA, Flowers IPA and cheap Holts, two or more farm ciders, swift cheerful service; handy for shopping area, delightful back terrace, open all day *(Collin and Julie Taylor, Steve Whalley)*

BOLTON BY BOWLAND SD7849

Coach & Horses [Main St]: Big stone house with pleasant open-plan bar/dining area, beams, flagstones and well worn in traditional décor, good fresh food using local produce from sandwiches up, friendly licensees, well kept beers inc one or two from local Bowland, log fires, piano, darts and pool; big comfortable bedrooms with own bathrooms, good breakfast, lovely streamside village with interesting church, open all week *(BB, Hilary Forrest, Dr T E Hothersall, Richard Houghton, Ian and Sue Wells)*

BRINDLE SD5924

☆ *Cavendish Arms* [3 miles from M6 junction 29; A6 towards Whittle-le-Woods then left on B5256 (Sandy Lane)]: Extended old building, very friendly, with emphasis on enjoyable food (Italian chef), several quaint little snugs, interesting stained-glass partitions, decorative china and heraldic plasterwork, comfortable seats, well kept Burtonwood and a guest beer; children welcome, open all day wknds, tables on terrace with rockery, and on small lawn, tranquil little village with handsome stone church opposite *(LYM, Dr D J and Mrs S C Walker)*

BROUGHTON SD4838

☆ *Plough at Eaves* [A6 N through Broughton, 1st left into Station Lane just under a mile after traffic lights, then bear left after another 1½ miles]: Two linked very low-beamed mainly carpeted front rooms with coal fire, back extension toning in, consistently enjoyable fairly priced home-made food (not Mon, all day wknds) from huge sandwiches up, well kept Thwaites Bitter and a seasonal beer such as Good Elf, lots of malt whiskies, decent house wines, good uniformed staff, plenty of old-fashioned charm; small pool room, may be piped music, may refuse to serve tap water even along with meals and other drinks; picnic-sets out in front, well equipped play area in good-sized garden behind *(LYM, Steve Whalley)*

BURNLEY SD8332

Inn on the Wharf [Manchester Rd (B6240)]: Well organised pub by Leeds—Liverpool Canal, handy for centre, clean and spacious, with smart décor of beams, stripped stone and flagstones, good choice from sandwiches up at all-day food bar (busy lunchtime), well kept Hardys & Hansons, sensible prices; waterside terrace, next to little Toll House Museum *(Margaret Dickinson, Len Beattie)*

Ram [Cliviger (A646 S)]: Well kept Bass and Boddingtons, lots of wines by the glass and decent food all day in olde-worlde Vintage Inn, pleasant reconditioned pine furniture, blazing coal fire, quick service; open all day *(Steve Whalley)*

CARNFORTH SD4970

County Hotel [Lancaster Rd (A6)]: Comfortable hotel, well used by locals, reliable traditional food from good sandwiches to full meals in neat well divided informal restaurant/café off main bar, good service; bedrooms, handy for Brief Encounter visitor centre *(Margaret Dickinson)*

CATON SD5364

Ship [Lancaster Rd]: Roomy and immaculate open-plan dining pub with interesting range of nautical bric-a-brac, good fire in charming antique fireplace, good choice of reasonably priced food from sandwiches to generous fresh fish and Sun lunch, properly cooked veg, no smoking dining room, well kept Thwaites ales, interesting wines of the month, efficient friendly staff, magazines; subdued piped music, can be busy wknds; tables in garden, handy for Lune valley and Forest of Bowland *(Michael Doswell, Margaret Dickinson)*

CHEADLE HULME SJ8785

Church Inn [Ravenoak Rd (A5149 SE)]: Bustling friendly local, smart and genuinely old, with good range of well kept Robinsons ales and of good slightly unusual food lunchtime and early wkdy evenings, ordered from small hatch and served by pleasant waitresses *(Jack Clark)*

CHIPPING SD6243

☆ *Dog & Partridge* [Hesketh Lane; crossroads Chipping—Longridge with Inglewhite—Clitheroe]: Much modernised and extended neatly kept 16th-c dining pub, with eating space spreading into nearby stable, comfortable main lounge with small armchairs around fairly close-set low wood-effect tables on blue patterned carpet, brown-painted beams, winter log fire, multi-coloured lanterns, enjoyable lunchtime bar food (not Sun), decent wine list, well kept Tetleys Bitter and Mild and guest, good range of malt whiskies, no smoking dining areas; children welcome, open all day Sun *(Mike Schofield, LYM, Margaret Dickinson)*

☆ *Sun* [Windy St]: Charming stone-built country local with three small snug rooms, lots of dark oak panelling, good value hearty simple food, emphasis on bargain pies and local cheeses, well kept Boddingtons and a guest such as Coniston Bluebird or Timothy Taylors Landlord (an underground stream cools the cellar), quick friendly service, coal fire, papers and magazines, interesting local photographs and ironstone china, games room with pool and darts; very busy wknds, tables in courtyard with kiosk for families; opp church in attractive village, good walks *(BB, Mike and Alison Leyland, Margaret Dickinson)*

CHORLEY SD5819

Hartwood Hall [Preston Rd (A6, just off M61 junction 8)]: Lots of different areas each with a themed collection of bric-a-brac, good range of Henry's Table food all day inc enterprising children's menu, friendly staff, Courage Directors, good choice of wines by the glass; bedrooms in adjoining block *(Edward Leetham)*

CHURCHTOWN SD4843

Horns [A586 just W of A6]: Sizeable roadside pub with good choice of enjoyable traditional food from sandwiches and light lunches to steaks and early evening bargains, well kept real ales, no smoking areas; children welcome, tables in large garden *(Jim and Maggie Cowell)*

CLAUGHTON SD5666

Fenwick Arms [A683 Kirkby Lonsdale—Lancaster]: Recently refurbished black and white pub with enjoyable food, well kept Black Sheep and Boddingtons, good range of wines *(Simon Calvert)*

CLITHEROE SD7441

New Inn [Parson Lane]: Spotless traditional four-room pub, coal fires in both front ones, half a dozen or more interesting well kept ales inc a Mild from central bar, no smoking room *(Steve Whalley)*

COMPSTALL SJ9690

Andrew Arms [George St (B6104)]: Transformed under new licensees, welcoming landlord with remarkable memory for a name or a face, surprisingly good menu for such a small pub, Robinsons real ale, new back dining room; handy for Etherow Country Park *(Dennis Jones)*

CONDER GREEN SD4556

Stork [just off A588]: Fine spot where River Conder joins the Lune estuary among bleak marshes, cheery bustle and good fire in rambling dark-panelled rooms, generous popular standard food (all day Sun) from sandwiches up, young staff, mainstream real ales; pub games inc pool, juke box or piped music; children welcome, handy for Glasson Dock, comfortable bedrooms, open all day *(LYM, A and B D Craig, Margaret Dickinson, Mike and Linda Hudson, Dave Braisted)*

CROSTON SD4818

Wheatsheaf [Town Rd]: Convivial and chatty, nice décor, hops and fresh flowers, 19th-c Croston photographs, stripped boards and quarry tiles, alcoves, generous interesting food all day inc home-baked bread and lunchtime and early evening bargains, good friendly service, well kept weekly changing beers, no smoking area; unobtrusive piped music *(Brian Kneale, Margaret Dickinson)*

DARWEN SD7222

Old Rosins [Pickup Bank, Hoddlesden, off A6177 Haslingden—Belthorn opp Grey Mare]: Large extended open-plan moorland inn with comfortable banquettes and good log fire, mugs, jugs and chamber-pots hanging from beams, picture-window views from no smoking dining end, friendly staff, Courage Directors, John Smiths and Timothy Taylors Landlord, plenty of malt whiskies, wines strong on south african, food from sandwiches to steaks; fruit machine, piped music; children welcome, picnic-sets on big crazy-paved terrace, bedrooms with own bathrooms, open all day *(H W Roberts, LYM, Ian and Nita Cooper)*

DENSHAW SD9710

Black Horse [off M62 junction 2; Oldham Rd (A672 just N of village)]: Cosy country pub, plenty of brassware, popular sensibly priced food inc good value Sun lunches, real ales such as Boddingtons and Phoenix *(Andy and Jill Kassube)*

☆ *Rams Head* [2 miles from M62 junction 2; A672 towards Oldham, pub N of village]: Cosy and comfortable moorland dining pub with several small rooms, good meals more sophisticated than you'd expect from the location, well kept Black Sheep, Tetleys and perhaps a guest beer, reasonably priced wines, bric-a-brac on beams and panelling, log fires, traditional settles; children welcome, unobtrusive piped music; on special days eg Mothering Sunday dining room may be fully booked with no bar snacks served, but otherwise popular with walkers – lovely scenery, good walking *(BB, Julian Templeman, Mrs P J Carroll)*

DENTON SJ9395

Lowes Arms [Hyde Rd (A57)]: Smart pub brewing its own cheap LAB ales, good waitress-served food in end dining area, friendly staff, separate large games room; tables outside, open all day wknds *(Tony Hobden, Richard Houghton)*

DIGGLE SE0007

Hanging Gate [Huddersfield Rd, off A670]: Comfortably refurbished stone-built pub with well presented usual food (all day wknds), well kept Theakstons, pleasant helpful staff; pool in neat games area, Sat live entertainment *(Mrs P J Carroll)*

DOBCROSS SD9906

☆ *Swan* [The Square]: Low beams, flagstones and traditional settles, partitioned alcoves in three interesting areas (one no smoking) off small central bar, friendly atmosphere, well kept Jennings (their full range) and guest beers, some emphasis on enjoyable varied well priced home-made food inc children's, attentive young staff; Thurs folk night; tables outside, attractive village below moors *(Bill Sykes, Tony Hobden, John Fiander, Pete Baker, Richard Houghton)*

DOWNHAM SD7844

☆ *Assheton Arms* [off A59 NE of Clitheroe, via Chatburn]: Exceptionally pretty village makes this attractive pub popular at wknds; wide range of good generous food, rambling partly no smoking beamed bar with nice furniture and massive stone fireplace, Castle Eden and Moorhouses Pendle Witches Brew, 18 wines by the glass; piped music; children and dogs welcome, picnic-sets outside, open all day Sun, cl a wk in Jan *(Mike Schofield, LYM, Len Beattie, Louise English, Mrs P J Carroll, Norma and Noel Thomas, GLD, Betty and Cyril Higgs, Yvonne and Mike Meadley)*

EARBY SD9146

Red Lion: Small friendly pub with several real ales inc Skipton, simple reasonably priced bar meals *(Peter Heaton)*

ECCLES SJ7798

Grapes [Liverpool Rd, Peel Green; A57 ½ mile from M63 junction 2]: Well restored Edwardian local with superb glass, tiling and mosaic floor, lots of mahogany, brilliant staircase, cheap Holts Bitter and Mild, fairly quiet roomy lounge and smoke room, pool in classic billiards room, vault with Manchester darts (can get quite loud and smoky), drinking corridor; open all day *(the Didler, Pete Baker)*

Lamb [Regent St (A57)]: Gorgeous handsomely preserved Edwardian three-room local, splendid etched windows, fine woodwork and furnishings, extravagantly tiled stairway, admirable trophies in display case; cheap well kept Holts Bitter and Mild, bargain lunchtime sandwiches, full-size snooker table in original billiards room; popular with older people, open all day *(the Didler)*

Royal Oak [Barton Lane]: Large unspoilt Edwardian pub on busy corner, several rooms, handsome tilework and fittings, cheap Holts Bitter and Mild, good licensees, organ singalongs in back lounge; open all day *(the Didler, GLD)*

Stanley Arms [Eliza Ann St/Liverpool Rd (A57), Patricroft]: Busy mid-Victorian corner local with cheap Holts Bitter and Mild, lunchtime filled rolls, popular front bar, hatch serving two back rooms, drinking corridor *(the Didler)*

White Lion [Liverpool Rd, Patricroft, a mile from M63 junction 2]: Welcoming unchanging Edwardian local, clean, tidy and popular with older people, with great value Holts Bitter and Mild, games in lively traditional public bar, separate smoke room (wknd pianist) and quiet lounge off tiled side drinking corridor *(the Didler, Pete Baker)*

ECCLESTON SD5117

☆ *Original Farmers Arms* [Towngate (B5250, off A581 Chorley—Southport)]: Long cheery low-beamed pub/restaurant, big colourful mural at one end, wide choice of consistently good generous food all day, wkdy bargains and some unusual twists to familiar themes, tempting puddings cabinets as you go in; well decorated, keeping traditional character – black cottagey furniture, brocaded wall seats, quotations on stencilled walls, plates, pastoral prints, clocks and brasses; well kept Marstons Pedigree, Tetleys and guests such as Timothy Taylors Landlord and Youngs Special, friendly helpful service from smartly uniformed staff, darts, interesting choice of piped music; parking can be tight when busy; good value bedrooms some with own bathroom, open all day *(BB, Margaret Dickinson)*

Stanley Arms [Gillars Lane (B5203), not far from M57 junction 2]: Welcoming pub with well kept Bass, Courage Directors and Greenalls, good traditional Lancashire cooking, nice evening balance between locals and diners, pleasant no smoking conservatory *(Andrew York)*

EDGWORTH SD7316

Black Bull [Bolton Rd, Turton]: Busy three-room dining pub in moorside village, good value food from sandwiches and baguettes to bistro dishes (all day wknds), Weds night steak bargains for two, five well kept changing ales, friendly service, open fire, hill and reservoir views from light and airy restaurant extension, lovely summer floral displays; live music Thurs, Tues quiz night, good walks *(Michael and Marion Buchanan, Gordon Tong, Norma and Noel Thomas)*

☆ *Rose & Crown* [Bury Rd]: Village local recently refurbished under good new landlord, enjoyable home-made food from sandwiches, baguettes and baked potatoes up inc plenty of vegetarian options, interesting specials, Sun carvery and impressive bargain wkdy lunches and suppers, friendly efficient service in bars and flagstoned dining area, no smoking area, well kept real ales, reasonably priced wines; children welcome, good value bedrooms with own bathrooms *(Michael and Marion Buchanan, Ross and Rachel Gavin)*

ENTWISTLE SD7217

☆ *Strawbury Duck* [signed off Edgworth—Blackburn rd; by station]: Tucked-away traditional beamed and flagstoned country pub; dimly lit L-shaped bar, Victorian pictures, some bare stone, good friendly service, well kept Phoenix and other northern real ales, generous bar food all day; pool, fruit machine, TV and piped music; children welcome, tables outside, good for Pennine walks (leave muddy boots in the porch), open all day *(LYM, MLR, Michael and Marion Buchanan, Greg Yerbury, Mike and Linda Hudson, Steve Whalley, Yvonne and Mike Meadley)*

EUXTON SD5319

Plough [Runshaw Moor; a mile from A49/B5252 junction]: Charming spotless black-beamed country dining pub with good atmosphere, enjoyable food inc upmarket dishes (very popular wknds), well kept real ales, sympathetic extension; big sheltered back lawn with tables and small play area *(Margaret Dickinson)*

Travellers Rest [Dawbers Lane (A581 W)]: Open-plan main bar, real ales such as Greene King Abbot and Marstons Pedigree, enjoyable food, small separate no smoking restaurant *(Gerry and Rosemary Dobson)*

FENCE SD8237

Fence Gate [just off A6068]: Good-natured cosy traditional bar with well kept beers such as Highgate and Wychwood, bright pleasant young staff, enjoyable competitively priced fresh bar food inc speciality sausages, more expensive dishes and some lunchtime bargains in modern brasserie with topiary *(Peter Abbott)*

☆ ***Forest*** [B6248 Brierfield rd, off A6068]: Civilised Pennine-view dining pub (all day Sun) emphasising thai and oriental food, some small helpings for children, well kept ales such as Greene King Old Speckled Hen and Ruddles, Marstons Pedigree and Theakstons Best, good choice of wines, good coffee, friendly helpful service, plush banquettes in nicely lit open-plan bar, oak-panelled dining room, lots of paintings, vases, plates and books, no smoking front conservatory; unobtrusive piped music; children welcome, open all day *(LYM, Tony and Caroline Elwood, John and Sylvia Harrop)*

FLEETWOOD SD3247

☆ ***North Euston*** [Esplanade, nr tram terminus]: Big comfortably refurbished bar in massive architecturally interesting Victorian hotel with great sea and hill views, long railway connections (19th-c LMS terminal, with ferry to Scotland); a real oasis, feels like a distinct pub rather than hotel bar, with decent lunchtime food, well kept Moorhouses Black Cat Mild and Pendle Witches Brew and three other often unusual changing ales, consistently good service from smart staff, lots of separate-seeming areas inc big no smoking family room (till 7); live music Sat; hotel also has coffee bar and two restaurants, seats outside, comfortable bedrooms, open all day (Sun afternoon break) *(BB, Margaret Dickinson, Richard Lewis, Dr B and Mrs P B Baker, Keith and Chris O'Neill, Yvonne and Mike Meadley)*

GARSTANG SD4845

Royal Oak [Market Pl]: Typical small-town inn in same family for nearly 50 years, cosy yet roomy and comfortably refurbished, with attractive panelling, several eating areas inc charming snug, generous consistently above-average food (all day Sun) inc imaginative specials, small helpings for children or OAPs, pleasant staff, Robinsons real ales, good value coffee, restaurant, spotless housekeeping; food orders may stop if chef too busy; disabled access, comfortable bedrooms, open all day Sun *(Margaret Dickinson)*

☆ ***Th'Owd Tithebarn*** [off Church St]: Rustically converted barn with big flagstoned terrace overlooking Lancaster Canal, thorough-going Victorian country life theme with antique kitchen range, masses of farm tools, stuffed animals and birds, flagstones and high rafters, even waitresses in period costume and a 9-metre (30-ft) central refectory table; simple food all day from filled baguettes up, Flowers IPA and Tetleys, lots of country wines; piped music, can get very busy; children in dining room, open all day summer *(Roy Morrison, Abi Benson, LYM)*

Wheatsheaf [Park Hill Rd (one-way system northbound)]: Small and cosy neatly kept low-beamed pub with gleaming copper and brass, good range of well priced freshly cooked good food inc notable specials (esp fish), cheerful friendly service even when busy, decent malt whiskies *(BB, Peter and Jean Walker)*

GOOSNARGH SD5536

☆ ***Grapes*** [Church Lane]: Welcoming local with well kept changing ales inc some rare brews, massive helpings of food (not Mon evening) from huge doorstep sandwiches to good Sun roast and well presented more modern dishes, friendly helpful landlord, two low-beamed areas separated by big coal fire, lots of brass around this, collection of whisky-water jugs and old telephones, separate games room with darts and pool; tables outside, bowling green, open all day Thurs-Sun *(MLR)*

☆ ***Stags Head*** [B5269]: Lots of separate mainly old-world areas rambling around a central servery, plenty of nice features (even proper old-fashioned radiators), good value generous fresh food inc imaginative dishes, children's helpings, friendly well trained staff, Flowers IPA, popular restaurant (may be fully booked); well reproduced contemporary chart music, live music Fri inc frequent tribute nights; tables out in pleasant pergola with lawn *(BB, Margaret Dickinson)*

GREASBY SJ2587

Greave Dunning [Greasby Rd (off B5139)]: Smoothly refurbished extended pub with quiet alcoves in flagstoned bar, lofty main lounge with upper gallery, comfortable seating inc a sofa, enjoyable well presented food inc light dishes, polite helpful staff, well kept real ales, decent wines *(LYM, E G Parish, Mrs P J Carroll)*

GREAT ECCLESTON SD4240

Farmers Arms [Halsall Sq (just off A586)]: Locally popular, with Black Sheep, Boddingtons, Robinsons and a guest beer, real fire, new licensees building up the food side, pleasant dining room (with piped music) *(Margaret Dickinson)*

GREAT MITTON SD7138

Aspinall Arms [B6246 NW of Whalley]: Roomy dual bars with red plush wall banquettes, comfortable chairs, settees and bar stools, well kept ales such as Copper Dragon, Phoenix Arizona and Timothy Taylors Landlord, enjoyable food from good cold or hot sandwiches to fresh fish and steaks, helpful landlord, cheerful efficient service, coal fire, papers, books and magazines to read, no music or machines, small separate dining room on right; may be piped music; children welcome away from bar, nice surroundings, picnic-sets on flagstoned terrace and in big informal garden with play area just above River Ribble, bedrooms, usefully opens earlier than most pubs around here *(Derek and Sylvia Stephenson, Mike Turner, BB, Steve Whalley)*

GREENFIELD SD9904

King William IV [Chew Valley Rd (A669)]: Welcoming chatty village local, good low-priced home-made food till 7 in small eating area, separate but not cut off (best to book), well kept Bass, Lees, Tetleys and perhaps a guest beer; children and dogs welcome, no pool or darts, tables on front terrace *(Pete Baker)*

Railway Hotel [Shaw Hall Bank Rd, opp stn]: Well known for live music most nights inc Fri open mike night; well kept ales such as Timothy Taylors Landlord, Charles Wells Bombardier and guest beers, good value pizzas, chilli etc lunchtimes and early evening; pool, games bar with darts and cards, can get smoky; simple bedrooms *(Pete Baker)*

GRINDLETON SD7545

☆ *Duke of York* [off A59 via Chatburn; Brow Top]: Smart, cheery and bright old upmarket village local in attractive Ribble Valley countryside, personable landlady, husband cooks good if not cheap food from sandwiches up inc lovely puddings, well kept Boddingtons and Castle Eden, friendly attentive staff, various areas inc one with open fire, spotless dining room; tables in front, garden behind, cl Mon *(RJH, Betty and Cyril Higgs)*

HALE SJ7686

Railway [Ashley Rd, Hale (B5163)]: Warmly friendly locals, two appealingly homely rooms (one no smoking) off popular lounge, well kept Robinsons real ales, decent home-made wkdy lunches, lively proper public bar with darts, dominoes and cards; open all day *(Pete Baker)*

HAMBLETON SD3741

Shard Bridge [off A588 towards Poulton, next to toll bridge]: Attractive whitewashed pub on Wyre estuary by former toll bridge; small smartly refurbished lounge with restaurant tables beyond, wide choice of reasonably priced freshly cooked waitress-served food from soup and ploughman's up, well kept Marstons Pedigree; nice outdoor tables overlooking water *(Abi Benson)*

HAWKSHAW SD7515

Red Lion [Ramsbottom Rd]: Attractively renovated pub/hotel, good generous attractively priced home cooking in big main bar and separate particularly well run restaurant, well kept Jennings ales and local microbrew guest beers, enthusiastic friendly licensees, cheerful efficient staff; comfortable bedrooms, quiet spot by River Irwell *(Peter Abbott, Jim Abbott, Brian Wainwright)*

HELMSHORE SD7820

White Horse [Holcombe Rd]: Roomy stone-built inn, sympathetically modernised and low-ceilinged, big tables set for copious quickly served reasonably priced food, plenty of people just enjoying the well kept Boddingtons and Timothy Taylors Landlord; tables outside, Irwell valley views from the front *(Jane Taylor, David Dutton, Hilary Forrest)*

HESKIN GREEN SD5214

☆ *Farmers Arms* [Wood Lane (B5250, N of M6 junction 27)]: Cheerful sparkling clean country pub, spacious but cosy (and does get packed wknds), good range of well kept Whitbreads-related ales with guests such as Castle Eden and Timothy Taylors Landlord, heavy black beams, brasses and china, wide choice of good value home cooking (even local ostrich) inc nicely cooked veg and good vegetarian choice in two-level dining area, friendly helpful staff, public bar with darts; piped music (even outside), SkyTV; picnic-sets on big lawn, good play area, pets from pigs to peacocks (pub cat failing to catch the ducks), and tables also at front and side, comfortable pretty bedrooms, open all day wknds *(BB, Jim and Maggie Cowell)*

HEST BANK SD4666

☆ *Hest Bank Hotel* [Hest Bank Lane; off A6 just N of Lancaster]: Picturesque, welcoming and comfortable three-bar coaching inn, good for families, with wide range of good freshly made generous food all day from sandwiches up inc fresh local fish and potted shrimps, also children's dishes, bargain set menus and special food nights, well kept Boddingtons, Cains, Timothy Taylors Landlord and a monthly changing guest beer, decent wines, friendly efficient service, separate restaurant area, lively history, Weds quiz night; plenty of garden tables by Lancaster canal, attractive setting close to Morecambe Bay *(Derek and Sylvia Stephenson, BB, Stephen Gibbs, Rowena Lord, Simon Calvert)*

HOLDEN SD7749

☆ *Copy Nook* [the one up by Bolton by Bowland]: Spick-and-span roomy and well renovated stone-built ex-coaching inn, now busy dining pub with helpful staff, wide choice of good popular reasonably priced food, particularly beef, lamb and fish, and specials inc plenty of game; three dining rooms off main bar, well kept Marstons Pedigree and Tetleys, piped music; children welcome, six bedrooms with own bathrooms *(BB, W W Burke, Steve Whalley)*

HORNBY SD5868

Castle [Main St]: Small tastefully refurbished hotel, armchairs and sofas in comfortable bar with well kept changing real ale and daily papers, wide range of enjoyable local-flavoured food with imaginative touches, friendly helpful staff, handsome pricier modern restaurant (only advance ordering for this); bedrooms *(Karen Eliot, Yvonne and Mike Meadley, Margaret Dickinson)*

HURST GREEN SD6838

☆ ***Bayley Arms*** [off B6243 Longridge—Clitheroe, towards Stoneyhurst Coll]: Comfortable bar with enjoyable good value food inc children's, friendly licensees, smart staff, attractive mix of old furniture, sporting and music memorabilia, brasses, log fire, inventive menu in more formal restaurant; comfortable bedrooms, attractive Ribble valley village *(Dr and Mrs D E Awbery, Simon Calvert)*

Shireburn Arms [Whalley Rd]: Quiet comfortable 17th-c hotel in idyllic setting with panoramic Ribble valley views, good reasonably priced food, Thwaites and other ales, armchairs in beamed lounge bar, light and airy restaurant, separate tea room; lovely neatly kept back garden and terrace, safe low-key play area, bedrooms *(Margaret Dickinson)*

HYDE SJ9495

Cheshire Ring [Manchester Rd (A57, between M67 junctions 2 and 3)]: Reopened by Cheshire's small Beartown brewery, their real ales at tempting prices, warm friendly atmosphere, bargain lunchtime food from soup and filled baguettes to Sun lunch, good house wines *(Dennis Jones)*

IRBY SJ2586

Irby Mill [Irby Mill Hill, off Greasby rd]: Two low-beamed largely flagstoned rooms, one largely set for eating, well kept Cains FA and Wundshaft, Marstons Pedigree, Timothy Taylors Landlord, Theakstons and changing guest beers, decent house wines, comfortable pub furniture, coal-effect gas fire, interesting old photographs and history of the former mill, low-priced food all day (no sandwiches); can get very busy; a few tables outside *(Tony Tollitt, BB, Paul Boot)*

KING'S MOSS SD5001

Colliers Arms [Pimbo Rd (off B5205 W of Billinge)]: Traditional four-room pub very popular for good honest food from sandwiches, baguettes and baked potatoes to steaks, good friendly service, three real ales; garden tables *(John and Gillian Scarisbrick)*

LANCASTER SD4761

Brown Cow [Penny St]: Long narrow unpretentious bar, generous bargain home-made lunches in simple back dining area, well kept Thwaites Bitter and Lancaster Bomber, friendly staff *(MLR, Richard Greaves)*

John o' Gaunt [Market St]: Small unspoilt city local with great array of malt whiskies, well kept Boddingtons and Timothy Taylors Landlord, good choice of enjoyable cheap lunchtime food (inc speciality cullen skink), friendly staff, music memorabilia; piped jazz, live Sun morning; small back terrace *(Pippa and Morgan Manley, Simon Calvert, Jo Lilley)*

Sun [Church St]: Recently renovated revealing old fireplaces and original oak door, with wide range of changing real ales and bottled beers, reasonably priced healthy lunchtime food from good sandwiches up, open for imaginative breakfasts too, friendly service; nine new bedrooms with own bathrooms *(Simon Calvert, Jo Lilley)*

☆ ***Water Witch*** [parking in Aldcliffe Rd behind Royal Lancaster Infirmary, off A6]: Cheerful and attractive conversion of 18th-c canalside barge-horse stabling, flagstones, stripped stone, rafters and pitch-pine panelling, fine changing beer choice, lots of bottled beers, dozens of wines by the glass and good spirits range from mirrored bar, enjoyable stylishly cooked local food inc good cheese board, upstairs restaurant; children allowed in eating areas, tables outside, open all day *(LYM, Claire Moore, Simon Calvert, Jo Lilley)*

LANESHAW BRIDGE SD9141

Alma [Emmott Lane, off A6068 E of Colne]: Friendly new licensees, enjoyable food, well kept beer *(HP)*

Hargreaves Arms [A6068 towards Keighley]: Small open-plan pub with open kitchen doing above-average food from big open sandwiches to limited very fresh blackboard dishes, well kept John Smiths, two Timothy Taylors ales and perhaps Moorhouses, reasonably priced wines, friendly landlord, china collection, dining room; dogs welcome, no credit cards, bedrooms, cl Mon/Tues *(M S Catling, D J Etheridge)*

LATHOM SD4511

☆ ***Ship*** [off A5209 E of Burscough; Wheat Lane]: Big well run pub tucked below embankment at junction of Leeds & Liverpool and Rufford Branch canals, several separate beamed rooms, some interesting canal memorabilia and naval pictures and crests, up to nine reliably well kept changing ales from smaller breweries such as Moorhouses and Phoenix, some parts set for the good value simple home cooking from good lunchtime sandwiches up (small helpings for children), prompt friendly service even when busy; games room with pool; children welcome, tables outside, open all day *(BB, Andy and Jill Kassube, MLR, Steve Kirby, Jim and Maggie Cowell)*

LEYLAND SD5221

Dunkirk Hall [western outskirts, by bypass]: 17th-c farmhouse converted to pub, attractive and neatly kept, with interesting range of good value food, well kept Courage Directors, Greene King Abbot, John Smiths and Charles Wells Bombardier *(David Holden)*

Midge Hall [Midge Hall Lane]: Big divided open-plan room popular for wide choice of low-priced food from sandwiches and baked potatoes up, quick friendly helpful service, Tetleys; children welcome, some live music, tables out behind *(Frank Tomlinson, Margaret Dickinson)*

LIMBRICK SD6016

Black Horse [off A6 at Adlington; Long Lane]: Tastefully restored old-world up-and-down low-ceilinged stone-built pub, the first recorded in Lancs (1577); well kept Theakstons Best and XB, coal fires, friendly service, decent food; garden behind, handy for West Pennine country park, open all day *(Norma and Noel Thomas)*

LIVERPOOL SJ4395

Cains Brewery Tap [Stanhope St]: Well restored Victorian pub with Cains full beer range kept well at attractive prices, guest beers from other small breweries, friendly efficient staff, good well priced wkdy lunchtime food, nicely understated décor, wooden floors, plush raised side snug, interesting old prints and breweriana, handsome bar, flame-effect gas fire, newspapers, cosy relaxing atmosphere; popular exceptional value brewery tour ending here with buffet and singing; sports TV, open all day *(the Didler, Patrick Hancock)*

Carnarvon Castle [Tarleton St]: Neat pub next to main shopping area, long and narrow, with one main bar and comfortable back lounge, welcoming chatty atmosphere, well kept Cains Bitter and Mild and a guest such as Caledonian 80/-, lunchtime bar snacks, cabinet of Dinky toys and other eclectic collections, no music; open all day, cl Sun evening, Mon/Tues lunchtime (opens 8pm then) *(the Didler, Joe Green, Patrick Hancock)*

Cracke [Rice St]: Friendly backstreet local, bare boards and pews, lots of posters for local events and pictures of local buildings, unusual Beatles diorama in largest room, very cheap lunchtime food and Thurs curry night, well kept Cains, Marstons Pedigree, Phoenix and guest beers; juke box and TV, popular mainly with young people; open all day, sizeable garden *(the Didler, Joe Green, MLR, Patrick Hancock)*

☆ ***Dispensary*** [Renshaw St]: Small chatty local-feeling central pub with well kept Cains ales, three or four interesting guest beers, lots of bottled imports, friendly staff (may let you have tasters), good value wkdy food 12-7, polished wood and glass inc marvellous etched windows, bare boards, comfortable raised back bar, Victorian medicine bottles and instruments; open all day *(the Didler, Joe Green, Patrick Hancock, Peter F Marshall)*

☆ ***Doctor Duncan*** [St Johns Lane]: Neatly kept classic Victorian pub with full Cains range and several guest beers kept well, belgian beers on tap, convivial atmosphere, enjoyable food from sandwiches to economical main dishes till 7 (Tues curry night), pleasant helpful service, daily papers and magazines, several rooms inc impressive back area with pillared tiled ceiling, no smoking family room; may be piped music, busy wknds; open all day *(the Didler, John Dwane, Joe Green, Patrick Hancock, Peter F Marshall, Andrew York)*

Excelsior [Dale St]: Good value simple food 11-6 (and breakfast from 9), Cains Bitter and Mild and guest beers; disco and quiz nights, some live music; open all day, cl Sun lunchtime *(the Didler)*

Globe [Cases St]: Bustling well appointed comfortably carpeted local, pleasant staff, well kept Cains Bitter and Dark Mild and a guest beer, good port, lunchtime filled baps, tiny quiet sloping-floor back lounge, lots of prints of old Liverpool; may be piped 1960s music; open all day *(the Didler, Joe Green, Patrick Hancock)*

Grapes [Mathew St]: Lively and friendly, with well kept Cains and Tetleys, good value lunchtime bar food, open-plan but pleasantly well worn cottagey décor (flagstones, old range, wall settles, no two chairs the same, gas-effect lamps); open all day, can get crowded Fri/Sat, cl Sun *(the Didler, Patrick Hancock)*

Head of Steam [Lime St Station (main entrance Gt Nevill St)]: Well restored old railway buildings opp ticket hall, several rooms with diverse character, ten or so real ales from 16 handpumps, lots of lagers, interesting imported beers, railway memorabilia, impressive staff, bargain food all day from baguettes, baked potatoes, burgers and tortilla wraps up; piped music, big-screen sports TV; open all day till midnight (2am Fri-Sat) *(Joe Green, Martin Grosberg, Andrew York)*

Lion [Moorfields, off Tithebarn St]: Splendidly preserved ornate Victorian alehouse, sparkling etched glass and serving hatches in central bar, two small back lounges, unusual wallpaper, big mirrors, panelling and tilework, fine domed structure behind, friendly atmosphere and landlord interested in the history, well kept Lees, Timothy Taylors Landlord and changing guest beers, lunchtime food from cheap sandwiches and baguettes up, coal fire; open all day *(the Didler, Pete Baker, Joe Green, Patrick Hancock)*

Ma Boyles [Tower Gardens, off Water St]: Much modernised backstreet pub with good value bar food (all day Sat) from dim sum and pies to seafood specialities, well kept Hydes and guest beers, quieter downstairs bar; jazz Weds, open all day, cl Sat night and Sun *(the Didler, John Dwane)*

Midland [Ranelagh St]: Attractive and neatly kept Victorian local with original décor, ornate lounge, long corner bar, nice etched glass and mirrors; keg beers *(the Didler)*

☆ ***Monro*** [Duke St]: Wide range of good organic food from individual farms, well kept Burtonwood, fast friendly service, plenty of character *(Richard Foskett, Stephanie Lang, David Field)*

Peter Kavanaghs [Egerton St, off Catherine St]: Well kept Cains and guest beers in backstreet 19th-c local with plenty of character, interesting small rooms and bric-a-brac; open all day *(the Didler, Patrick Hancock)*

Pig & Whistle [Chapel St]: Warmly welcoming, with well kept ales inc Marstons Pedigree, good value bar food, well worn in old-fashioned seating *(Mr and Mrs John Taylor)*

Poste House [Cumberland St]: Small comfortable backstreet Victorian local, well kept Cains Bitter and Mild and guest beers, good wkdy lunches, friendly licensees, room upstairs; open all day *(the Didler)*

Roscoe Head [Roscoe St]: Three tiny unspoilt rooms, friendly, quiet and civilised, with well kept Jennings and guest beers, good value wkdy home-made lunches, amusing cartoons, tie collection, cribbage school Weds, Tues quiz night; open all day *(the Didler, Joe Green, Patrick Hancock)*

Ship & Mitre [Dale St]: Friendly gaslit local popular with university people, up to a dozen well kept changing unusual real ales served in over-sized lined glasses, imported beers, two farm ciders, good-humoured service, cheap basic food lunchtime and Fri evening, pool, occasional beer festivals, Thurs quiz night; piped music; open all day, cl Sun lunchtime *(the Didler, John Dwane, Joe Green, Paul Davies, Andrew York)*

Vernon Arms [Dale St]: Sloping-floored three-room pub with well kept Coach House Gunpowder Strong Mild and an interesting range of changing guest beers inc seasonal specials, good value bar food till 7, pleasant efficient service, plush banquettes in smarter back room; open all day, cl Sun *(the Didler, Joe Green, Paul Davies, Alyson and Andrew Jackson)*

Vines [Lime St]: Big Victorian pub, comfortable and friendly, with mosaic tilework, high-ceilinged room on right with stained-glass; may not always have real ale, can get very busy *(the Didler)*

White Star [Rainford Gdns, off Matthew St]: Welcoming traditional local with several well kept changing ales, good service, lots of woodwork, boxing prints, White Star shipping line and Beatles memorabilia, big-screen sports TV in back room; open all day *(the Didler, John Dwane, Joe Green, Patrick Hancock)*

LYDIATE SD3604

Scotch Piper [Southport Rd]: Medieval thatched pub with heavy black beams, flagstones and thick stone walls, Burtonwood beers from small bar, darts in middle room off corridor, carpeted back snug, three coal fires, no food, music or machines; picnic-sets in large garden with aviary, hens, donkey and abundant flower baskets, open all day wknds *(the Didler)*

LYTHAM SD3627

Ship & Royal [Clifton St]: Welcoming and neatly kept nautical-theme pub with well kept real ales, separate pool room; handy for shopping centre *(Dr and Mrs A K Clarke)*

MANCHESTER SJ8284

☆ ***Ape & Apple*** [John Dalton St]: Big friendly open-plan pub with low-priced Holts kept well, bargain hearty bar food, comfortable seats in bare-boards bar with nice lighting and lots of old prints and posters, armchairs in upstairs lounge; piped music, TV area, games machines; good mix on busy wknd evenings (unusually for city centre, over-25s won't feel out of place), quieter lunchtime or midweek; unusual brick cube garden, bedrooms, open all day *(Catherine Pitt, the Didler)*

Atlas [Deansgate, Castlefield end]: One of the first of the city's 'new' bars, and by now quite an institution: unique design to fit the railway arches, good modern food, usually a guest real ale, nice sitting out behind *(Chris Howarth)*

Bar Centro [Tib St]: Continental-style two-floor café-bar recently refurbished under new management, relaxed at lunchtime with well kept Hydes and a couple of local guest beers, continental draught beers, farm cider, up-to-date food, daily papers; popular with young people evenings – frequent live music and DJs, small dance floor; open all day (till 1am Thurs-Sat) *(the Didler)*

Bar Fringe [Swan St]: Café-style bare-boards bar specialising in beers from the low countries, also well kept changing ales from small breweries, farm cider, friendly staff, enjoyable food till 7, daily papers, cartoons, posters and bank notes, polished motorcycle hung above door; games inc pinball, good music; tables out behind, open all day *(the Didler, Richard Lewis)*

Beer House [Angel St, off Rochdale Rd]: Lively bare-boards open-plan pub with ten or so well kept real ales, several belgian beers on tap (each served in its proper glass), country wines, robust cheap bar food lunchtime and early evening, darts, good up-to-date CD juke box (may be loud), games machine, more comfortable upstairs bar with bar billiards, table footer and SkyTV, ceilidh band Tues; tables out in small area behind, open all day *(Catherine Pitt, the Didler, G Coates)*

Bulls Head [London Rd]: Traditional city pub, friendly staff, well kept Burtonwood Bitter and Top Hat Mild, three guest beers, enjoyable food wkdys, all-day breakfast and Sun roast lunch, lots of wood, gas fire, popular Tues quiz night *(G Coates)*

Castle [Oldham St, about 200 yards from Piccadilly, on right]: Unspoilt traditional front bar, small snug, full Robinsons range kept well from fine bank of handpumps, games in well worn back room, nice tilework outside; no food, children allowed till 7, blues Thurs, open all day (cl Sun afternoon) *(the Didler, Patrick Hancock)*

Circus [Portland St]: Two tiny rooms, back one panelled with leatherette banquettes, very well kept Tetleys from minute corridor bar, friendly landlord, celebrity photographs, no music or machines; often looks closed but normally open all day (you may have to knock) *(the Didler, P G Plumridge, Patrick Hancock)*

City Arms [Kennedy St, off St Peters Sq]: Five or six well kept changing beers, belgian bottled beers, occasional beer festivals, busy for bar lunches inc sandwiches and baked potatoes, quiet evenings; coal fires, bare boards, prints and panelling, handsome tiled façade; good piped music, TV, games machine; wheelchair access but steps down to back lounge, open all day (cl Sat lunchtime, Sun) *(P G Plumridge, the Didler)*

Coach & Horses [Old Bury Rd, Whitefield; A665 nr Besses o' the Barn Stn]: Coaching inn built around 1830, little changed and keeping several separate rooms, very popular and friendly, with well kept Holts, table service, darts, cards; open all day *(the Didler)*

Crescent [The Crescent (A6), Salford – opp Salford Univ]: Three 18th-c houses converted into beer house in 19th, unusual layout and homely unsmart décor, buoyant local atmosphere (popular with students and university staff), up to eight changing real ales, farm ciders, lots of foreign beers, good value food (not Sun), friendly staff, pool room, juke

box; small enclosed outside area, open all day *(the Didler)*
Eagle [Collier St, Salford (keep on Greengate after it leaves B6182)]: Old-fashioned basic backstreet local, well kept Holts Bitter and Mild at old-fashioned prices, friendly service, cheap filled rolls, bar servery to tap and passage with two smoke rooms, old Salford pictures; open all day *(the Didler)*
Egerton Arms [Gore St, Salford; A6 by stn]: Several rooms, chandeliers, art nouveau lamps, well kept low-priced Holts Bitter and Mild, guest beers; open all day *(the Didler)*
Grey Horse [Portland St, nr Piccadilly]: Cosy traditional Hydes local, welcoming and busy, with timbering, pictures and plates, well kept Bitter and Mild, some unusual malt whiskies; can bring in good sandwiches from next door; no juke box or machines, open all day *(P G Plumridge, the Didler, Patrick Hancock, G D K Fraser)*
Hare & Hounds [Shudehill, behind Arndale]: Long narrow bar linking front snug and comfortable back lounge (with TV), notable tilework, panelling and stained-glass, well kept Holts, Lees and Tetleys, sandwiches, friendly staff; games and machine, piano singalongs, upstairs Fri folk club; open all day *(the Didler, Pete Baker)*
Jolly Angler [Ducie St]: Plain two-room backstreet local, long a favourite, small and friendly, with well kept Hydes Bitter and a seasonal beer, coal or peat fire; darts, pool and TV, informal folk nights Thurs and Sun; open all day Sat *(BB, the Didler, Pete Baker)*
Kings Arms [Bloom St, Salford]: Big busy and friendly local refurbished in maroon and purple, new bare boards and flagstones, good range of well kept ales inc local Bazens, lunchtime food; open all day, handy for Central station *(the Didler)*
Knott Fringe [Deansgate]: Well kept Marble organic ales (see Marble Arch, in main entries), good range of continental imports, interesting if not cheap food all day inc good sandwiches *(Dennis Jones, Chris Howarth)*
Metropolitan [Lapwing Lane, Didsbury]: Huge welcoming dining pub, enjoyable generous food inc popular Sun lunch, real ales such as Timothy Taylors Landlord and Charles Wells Bombardier, impressive décor with separate areas and unspoilt airy feel, open fires, gabled roof; busy wknds; tables out on heated decking, outside summer bar *(Chris Howarth)*
☆ ***Mr Thomas Chop House*** [Cross St]: Long bustling Victorian city pub, bare boards, panelling and original gas lamp fittings in front bar with stools at wall and window shelves, back eating area with crisp tilework, interesting period features inc wrought-iron gates, good very popular traditional english lunchtime food with innovative touches, Sun lunch too now, proper waiters and waitresses, efficient and friendly, well kept Boddingtons (the new higher strength one), Timothy Taylors Landlord and guest beers, decent wines, no smoking area; open all day *(Crystal and Peter Hooper, the Didler, Susie Symes, Revd D Glover, Mr and Mrs Colin Roberts)*
Old Monkey [Portland St]: Holts showpiece recently built in traditional style, etched glass and mosaic tiling, interesting memorabilia, bargain generous tasty food, well kept cheap Bitter and Dark Mild, quick friendly service even when busy, upstairs lounge, wide mix of customers *(the Didler, C J Fletcher, John Fiander, Patrick Hancock)*
Oxnoble [Liverpool Rd]: Tempting food, well kept ales inc Timothy Taylors Landlord; bedrooms *(Stephen, Julie and Hayley Brown, Mick Miller)*
☆ ***Peveril of the Peak*** [Gt Bridgewater St]: Three very welcoming traditional rooms around central servery, lots of mahogany, mirrors and stained or frosted glass, splendidly lurid art nouveau green external tilework; busy lunchtime but friendly and homely evenings, with cheap basic lunchtime food (not Sun), family service, log fire, well kept Boddingtons, Marstons Pedigree, Charles Wells Bombardier and guest beers, sturdy furnishings on bare boards, interesting pictures, pub games inc pool, table football, Tues folk night; TV; pavement tables, children welcome, cl wknd lunchtimes *(the Didler, LYM, Patrick Hancock, Stephen Buckley)*
Plough [Hyde Rd (A57), Gorton]: Superb tiling, windows and gantry in unspoilt local, wooden benches in large public bar, two quieter back lounges, small pool room and lots of pub games, well kept Robinsons; TV; open all day *(the Didler)*
Pot of Beer [New Mount St]: Small bare-boards local with friendly licensees, four well kept interesting changing beers (some tapped from casks projecting from temperature-controlled chamber), Black Rat farm cider, good value generous polish wkdy lunchtime food (and beers), plain basic seating, stripped bricks and panelling, coal fire; music nights, tables outside, open all day, cl Sun *(Richard Lewis, the Didler, Richard Houghton, Revd D Glover)*
Prince of Wales [Lower Broughton Rd/Camp St, Salford]: Warm and welcoming local atmosphere, well kept Holts and guest beers such as Banks's *(Quentin McGraw)*
☆ ***Queens*** [Honey St, Cheetham; off Red Bank, nr Victoria Stn]: Well preserved tiled façade, well kept low-priced Phoenix Bantam and several guest beers from small breweries, lots of belgian imports, Biddenden farm cider, simple enjoyable food (all day wknds), coal fire, bar billiards, backgammon, chess, good juke box; children welcome, Tues quiz night; unexpected views of Manchester across the Irk Valley and its railway lines from large back garden with good play area, worth penetrating the surrounding viaducts, scrapyards and industrial premises; open all day *(the Didler)*
☆ ***Rain Bar*** [Gt Bridgewater St]: Appealing umbrella works conversion, lots of woodwork and flagstones, full range of Lees beers kept well, decent wines, good value food all day from 9am breakfast through panini and light meals to fish and chips etc, relaxed

atmosphere, warmly friendly service, daily papers, great canal views, large upstairs café-bar too; no under-21s, good terrace overlooking Rochdale Canal, open all day, handy for Bridgwater Hall *(the Didler, Patrick Hancock, Andy and Jill Kassube)*

Sams Chop House [Back Pool Fold, Chapel Walks]: Appealing sister pub to Mr Thomas Chop House, with identical good value food in small restaurant off bar, well kept beers, good wine choice, thriving atmosphere; formal waiters *(Ken Richards, John Fiander, Peter F Marshall, Revd D Glover)*

☆ ***Sinclairs*** [2 Cathedral Gates, off Exchange Sq]: Largely 18th-c low-beamed and timbered pub reopened after being dismantled, moved a short distance, and re-erected brick by brick, as part of the city centre reconstruction; cheap food, bargain Sam Smiths Bitter and Stout, friendly helpful staff, great atmosphere, upstairs bar with snugs and Jacobean fireplace; plastic glasses for the tables out by ultra-modern Exchange Sq *(LYM, Catherine Pitt, P G Plumridge, the Didler, Revd D Glover)*

Smithfield [Swan St]: Open-plan family-run local with well kept Phoenix and lots of interesting changing guest beers, some in jugs from the cellar, regular beer festivals, enjoyable bargain food from sandwiches up from open kitchen servery, daily papers, friendly staff and landlady; pool on front dais, games machine, juke box, sport TV in back lounge/eating area; good value bedrooms in nearby building, open all day *(Richard Lewis, the Didler, BB)*

Waldorf [Gore St]: Soft lighting, bare boards and brickwork, alcove areas off central bar, well kept Boddingtons and other real ales, busy friendly staff, wide food choice; games machines, music nights *(the Didler)*

White House [Gt Ancoats St]: Friendly local with well kept cheap Holts and two or three interesting guest beers, film star pictures in big lounge, public bar with darts and pool; cl Tues evening, opens 8 other evenings *(the Didler)*

White Lion [Liverpool Rd, Castlefield]: Busy but friendly Victorian pub, lots of dark wood, tables for eating up one side of three-sided bar, home-made food all day inc children's helpings, Phoenix ales, Timothy Taylors Landlord and a couple of changing guest beers, decent house wine, good tea, friendly service, real fire, lots of prints and Man Utd pictures, shelves of bottles and jugs; big-screen sports TV, nostalgic discos Fri-Sun; disabled access, children welcome, tables out among excavated foundations of Roman city overlooking fort gate, handy for Museum of Science and Industry and Royal Exchange Theatre, open all day *(the Didler, G Coates)*

MARPLE SJ9389

Hare & Hounds [Dooley Lane (A627 W)]: Attractive old Hydes pub with their usual beers and reasonably priced standard food, welcoming staff, pleasant relaxing atmosphere, tasteful modern extension *(Dennis Jones)*

MAWDESLEY SD4915

Black Bull [Hall Lane]: Attractive rambling village pub said to date partly from 13th c, well kept ales such as Badger Tanglefoot, Timothy Taylors Landlord and Youngs Waggle Dance, freshly made food; tables outside, boules *(Bracey Parish)*

☆ ***Robin Hood*** [Blue Stone Lane (Croston—Eccleston road, N of village – keep going)]: Spotless comfortable open-plan dining pub under same family for many years, button-back wall banquettes, reproduction Victorian prints, decorative plates, stained-glass seat dividers, some stripped stone; wide choice of good value generous home cooking (all day wknds) with cheap children's helpings in bar and small pretty upstairs evening restaurant, OAP bargain lunches, friendly staff coping well with the bustle, well kept Boddingtons, Timothy Taylors Landlord and four interesting guest ales, decent wines, children's room; may be piped music, fruit machine; picnic-sets on neat side terrace, good fenced play area, open all day *(Yvonne and Mike Meadley, Ian and Sue Wells)*

MELLOR SD6530

Traders Arms [Mellor Lane (the Mellor up near Blackburn)]: Spotless traditional décor, competitively priced typical food from sandwiches and baked potatoes up, well kept Thwaites, no smoking area; seats outside, play area *(Peter Abbott)*

MIDDLETON SD8404

Three Arrows [Middleton Rd, Rhodes]: Just off M60 junction 19, good service and enjoyable low-cost food *(Piotr Chodzko-Zajko)*

MORECAMBE SD4364

Eric Bartholomew [Euston Rd]: Wetherspoons with good value drinks and food, no smoking and family areas, plenty of wood and steel; named after Eric Morecambe *(Maggie and Tony Harwood)*

OLDHAM SD9606

☆ ***Roebuck*** [Roebuck Low, Strinesdale, off A62 NE]: Welcoming unpretentious moorland pub, a local byword for wide choice of good value generous food (often booked up even midweek); well kept Wadworths 6X, decent wines, helpful staff, log fire in front lounge, central bar, back dining room, great hillside views day and night *(Mrs P J Carroll)*

PRESTON SD5226

Black Bull [Pope Lane, Penwortham, off A582 S]: Small, spotless, cosy and civilised, with Greenalls and Theakstons Mild, enjoyable reasonably priced bar food; children welcome, open all day *(Jim and Maggie Cowell)*

Black Horse [Friargate]: Thriving friendly untouched pub in pedestrian street, full Robinsons ale range kept well, inexpensive lunchtime food, unusual ornate curved and mosaic-tiled Victorian main bar, panelling, stained-glass, two quiet cosy enclosed snugs off, upstairs 1920s-style bar; pictures of old town, lots of artefacts, good juke box; no children, open all day, cl Sun evening *(the Didler, Pete Baker, Jim and Maggie Cowell)*

RABY SJ3179

☆ ***Wheatsheaf*** [off A540 S of Heswall; Raby Mere Rd]: Attractive thatched and timbered pub with simple homely furnishings in rambling bar inc high-backed settles making a snug around fine old fireplace, splendid choice of real ales, good choice of malt whiskies, piped music in spacious evening restaurant (not Sun/Mon) and no smoking conservatory; children and dogs allowed, picnic-sets on terrace and in pleasant back garden, pretty village *(E G Parish, MLR, Paul Humphreys, Roger Thornington, LYM, Mrs B M Hill)*

RAMSBOTTOM SD7715

Hare & Hounds [Bolton Rd W, Holcombe Brook]: Nicely opened up old coaching inn, lots of well kept changing guest beers, welcoming service, reasonably priced usual food, occasional beer festivals; plenty going on, from pool and sports TVs to loud pop music some nights – heady mix from youngsters to OAPs *(Richard Houghton)*

RIBCHESTER SD6438

Halls Arms [Clitheroe Rd, Knowle Green (B6243 N of village)]: Good welcoming cottagey atmosphere, enjoyable food; pleasant garden, good position *(Rex and Mary Hepburn)*

RILEY GREEN SD6225

☆ *Royal Oak* [A675/A6061]: Cosy low-beamed three-room former coaching inn, well kept Thwaites (full range) from long back bar, friendly efficient service, ancient stripped stone, open fires, seats from high-backed settles to red plush armchairs, lots of nooks and crannies, turkey carpet, soft lighting, impressive woodwork, fresh flowers, interesting model steam engines and plenty of bric-a-brac, two dining rooms; can be packed Fri night and wknds; tables outside, short walk from Leeds & Liverpool Canal, footpath to Hoghton Tower, open all day Sun *(BB, Norma and Noel Thomas, Peter Abbott)*

ROCHDALE SD8909

Cask & Feather [Oldham Rd (A58)]: L-shaped bar with own low-priced McGuinness beers inc Mild and Porter from back brewery, good value lunches from sandwiches up, bric-a-brac inc Laurel & Hardy photographs *(MLR)*

ROYTON SD9307

Duke of York [Heyside]: Low-priced real ale and big helpings of good home cooking at bargain prices; children welcome *(T Mulvey)*

SALTERFORTH SD8845

Anchor [Salterforth Lane]: Enjoyable food, well kept real ales, friendly landlord and staff; linked to history of adjacent Leeds & Liverpool Canal, with stalactites in cellar *(Malcolm M Stewart)*

SAMLESBURY SD6229

Nabs Head Hotel [Nabs Head Lane]: Small cosy and neatly kept pub, good value home-made food inc imaginative specials and popular Sun lunch, welcoming efficient service, Thwaites ales, charming décor; lacks a no smoking area; peaceful country hamlet, handy for Samlesbury Hall *(Margaret Dickinson)*

New Hall Tavern [nr M6 junction 31; Cuerdale Lane (B6230) off A677 opp Trafalgar Hotel]: Recently refurbished, with enjoyable reasonably priced food (all day Sun), four or five quickly changing real ales, speciality coffees and teas; children welcome, live music every 2nd Thurs, open all day *(Jim and Maggie Cowell)*

SLAIDBURN SD7152

☆ *Hark to Bounty* [B6478 N of Clitheroe]: Old stone-built inn in charming Forest of Bowland village, neat rather modern décor, comfortable chairs by open fire, wide choice of good value generous food (lots of tables) inc children's and old-fashioned puddings, good hospitable service, full Theakstons range kept well, decent wines and whiskies; bedrooms, open all day, pleasant garden behind, good walks *(Diane Manoughian, LYM, Clive Gibson)*

SLYNE SD4765

Slyne Lodge [Main Rd]: Popular well run hotel, interesting décor, well kept Jennings ales, friendly helpful staff, open fire, welcoming bar, conservatory, imaginative mediterranean-style dining room; terrace tables, bedrooms with own bathrooms *(Anthony Rickards Collinson, A C English)*

SOUTHPORT SD3315

Falstaff [King St]: Roomy and fresh, with enjoyable food and well kept mainly Courage-related beers; open all day *(Keith Jacob, Patrick Hancock)*

STALYBRIDGE SJ9698

Q [Market St]: Bright and friendly one-bar pub, well kept Hydes *(Richard Houghton)*

White House [Water St]: Traditional three-room pub with low beams, pews, lots of prints, red letterbox for weekly tote, friendly staff and mix of customers, well kept Hydes, cheap meals; pool room, games machines, open all day weekdays *(Richard Houghton)*

STANDISH SD5708

Boars Head [A49/A5106 (Wigan Rd)]: Heavy low beams, log fires, cosy bays of curved wall seats, high wooden stools, sofa, two quieter rooms off; friendly helpful staff, well kept Burtonwood and guest beers, occasional home-made wines, bargain simple tasty food; well chosen piped music; tables in flower-filled garden, bowling green, open all day Sat *(Brian Kneale)*

STOCKPORT SJ8889

Alexandra [Northgate Rd]: New licensees in large backstreet local, reputedly haunted, with preserved Victorian interior, well kept Robinsons Best and Mild; pool room *(the Didler)*

☆ *Arden Arms* [Millgate St, behind Asda]: Good inventive lunchtime food and well kept Robinsons in welcoming pub with well preserved traditional horseshoe bar, old-fashioned snug through servery, two coal fires, longcase clocks; tables out in courtyard sheltered by the original stables, open all day *(John Wildman, the Didler, Pete Baker, Dennis Jones, Patrick Hancock)*

Armoury [Shaw Heath]: Comfortable lounge, small unspoilt locals' bar, Robinsons Best and Hatters Mild, perhaps Old Tom from a cask on the bar, lunchtime family room upstairs; open all day *(the Didler)*

Blossoms [Buxton Rd (A6)]: Busy traditional

main-road local, very friendly, with well kept Robinsons Best and Hatters Mild, perhaps Old Tom tapped from the cask, lunchtime food, attractive back lounge, pool room; open all day wknds *(the Didler, Bernie Adams)*

Crown [Heaton Lane, Heaton Norris]: Partly open-plan Victorian local under arch of vast viaduct, three cosy lounge areas (one no smoking) off gaslit bar, stylish décor, Bank Top, Phoenix and several other well kept ales, farm cider, good value lunchtime bar food, pool, darts; TV, some live music; seats outside, open all day Fri/Sat *(the Didler, Patrick Hancock)*

Nursery [Green Lane, Heaton Norris; off A6]: Friendly efficient service, enjoyable straightforward lunchtime food from servery on right with visible kitchen, popular set Sun lunch, big bays of banquettes in panelled front lounge, brocaded wall banquettes in back one, cheap well kept Hydes Bitter and Mild, separate games-oriented public bar, all very neat and clean; children welcome if eating, on narrow cobbled lane at E end of N part of Green Lane, immaculate bowling green behind, open all day wknds *(BB, the Didler, Pete Baker)*

Olde Woolpack [Brinksway, just off M60 junction 1 – junction A560/A5145]: Well kept Theakstons and interesting changing guest beers, good value home-made food, friendly landlord, traditional three-room layout with drinking corridor; open all day Fri-Sun *(the Didler)*

Porters Railway [Avenue St (just off M63 junction 13, via A560)]: Very cheap Porters Bitter, Dark Mild, Rossendale, Porter, Sunshine, Young Tom and Timmys Ginger Beer kept well in comfortable L-shaped bar with old Stockport prints and memorabilia, friendly staff, decent straightforward home-made food (not Sun), lots of foreign beers, farm cider, no music or machines; tables out behind, open all day *(the Didler, Richard Houghton)*

Queens Head [Little Underbank (can be reached by steps from St Petersgate)]: Long narrow late Victorian pub with delightful separate snug and back dining area; good friendly bustle, reasonable bar food, well kept Sam Smiths, daily papers, rare brass cordials fountain and old spirit lamps, old posters and adverts; no smoking area, some live jazz, open all day; famous narrow gents' *(Bernie Adams, the Didler, Patrick Hancock)*

☆ ***Red Bull*** [Middle Hillgate]: Steps up to friendly well run local, well kept Robinsons Best and Best Mild from nearby brewery, good value home-cooked bar lunches (not Sun), substantial settles and seats, open fires, impressive beamed and flagstoned bar with lots of pictures, dark panelling, brassware and traditional island servery; quiet at lunchtime, can get crowded evening, open all day (cl Sun afternoon) *(LYM, the Didler)*

Swan With Two Necks [Princes St]: Traditional panelled local, comfortable panelled bar, back skylit lounge and drinking corridor, Robinsons Mild and Bitter, friendly licensee and locals, lunchtime food; handy for shops, open all day, cl Sun *(the Didler, Patrick Hancock)*

TATHAM SD6169

Bridge Inn [B6480, off A683 Lancaster—Kirkby Lonsdale]: Cosy old pub with comfortable compact bar, well kept Dent and Jennings Cumberland, good value food, dining room along corridor *(Maggie and Tony Harwood)*

THORNTON HOUGH SJ3080

Thornton Hall Hotel [Neston Rd]: Good value light meals in bar area, good service, 18th-c features in restaurant, former grand country house in spacious grounds; bedrooms in new wing *(E G Parish)*

THORNTON-CLEVELEYS SD3242

Victoria [Victoria Rd W]: Large 1930s corner pub with roomy lounge and dining area, well kept Sam Smiths, extensive food choice all day till 7 (not Mon/Tues), roast Sun; open all day *(Dr B and Mrs P B Baker)*

TIMPERLEY SJ7789

Moss Trooper [Moss Lane]: Recently carefully renovated, open plan though keeping intimate atmosphere in distinct areas; well kept Boddingtons, Greene King and guest beers *(Mike Marsh)*

TOCKHOLES SD6621

Royal [signed off A6062 S of Blackburn, and off A675; Tockholes Rd]: Friendly and unpretentious little rooms inside, one no smoking, with big open fires, well kept beer, welcoming young landlord, old-fashioned décor, sandwiches and varied home cooking; children and walkers welcome, big garden with play area and views from sheltered terrace, good varied walks (nature trail opp), open all day Fri-Sun and summer *(LYM, Len Beattie)*

TYLDESLEY SJ6999

Cart & Horses [Manchester Rd, Astley]: Holts local, largely open-plan but keeping late Victorian décor and friendly traditional public bar with darts and cards; excellent value beer, welcoming service, good value straightforward food lunchtime and early evening inc good Sun lunch; small garden *(Collin and Julie Taylor, Pete Baker)*

Mort Arms [Elliott St]: Mature two-room pub, etched glass and polished panelling, comfortable lounge with old local photographs, well kept low-priced Holts Bitter and Mild, friendly landlord, TV horseracing Sat; open all day *(the Didler)*

WEIR SD8626

Deerplay [Burnley Rd (A671 N of Bacup)]: Country pub popular for its food; friendly service, real ales, well placed for interesting moorland walks *(Len Beattie)*

WEST KIRBY SJ2186

White Lion [A540 Chester rd]: Interesting small 17th-c sandstone pub, several small beamed areas on different levels, good value simple bar lunches inc wide choice of sandwiches, well kept Courage Directors, John Smiths, Theakstons and a guest beer, friendly staff, coal stove; no children, attractive secluded back garden *(MLR)*

WHEATLEY LANE SD8338

☆ *Old Sparrow Hawk* [Wheatley Lane Rd]: Comfortable and civilised country pub under new ownership, increasing emphasis on good fresh food from sandwiches up, good atmosphere, service and wines, well kept ales, dark oak panelling, stripped stonework, interesting furnishings; tables out on roomy terrace with views to the moors beyond Nelson and Colne; children welcome in eating areas, has been open all day *(LYM, Michael and Deirdre Ellis)*

WIGAN SD5805

John Bull [Coopers Row, The Wiend]: No-nonsense Thwaites pub said to date from 16th c, flagstones and tiles, cracking juke box; pool upstairs, no children *(Brian Kneale)*

WREA GREEN SD3931

☆ *Grapes* [Station Rd]: Busy Chef & Brewer, roomy and open-plan yet cosy and olde-worlde, with enjoyable food from good sandwiches to some imaginative specials, pleasant dining area, well kept Boddingtons, Marstons Pedigree and Theakstons, good choice of wines by the glass, good service, open fire; tables out overlooking village green, picturesque church *(M S Catling, Margaret and Roy Randle, Brian Kneale, Dr and Mrs A K Clarke)*

Villa [Moss Side Lane (B5259)]: Lots of small seating areas in smart hotel's welcoming rustic-style bar, well kept Jennings, log fire, daily papers; bedrooms, open all day *(Dr and Mrs A K Clarke)*

WRIGHTINGTON SD5011

Rigbye Arms [3 miles from M6 junction 27; off A5209 via Robin Hood Lane and left into High Moor Lane]: 16th-c moorland inn, a popular family outing for good value generous food (with good fresh veg) from straightforward favourites to some interesting specials, well kept ales inc Greene King Old Speckled Hen and Timothy Taylors Landlord, decent wines, nice relaxed atmosphere, pleasant country setting *(Andy and Jill Kassube, Nick Holding, P R Morgan)*

WRIGHTINGTON BAR SD5313

Mulberry Tree: Light and airy open-plan bar/eating area with plenty of dining tables, enjoyable and generous if not cheap imaginatively served food, good staff, roomy more formal stylish back restaurant areas *(Brenda and Stuart Naylor)*

YORK SD7133

Lord Nelson [Whalley Old Rd, just E of Langho]: Homely village pub, two small lounges with log fires, restaurant and bar area, well kept Theakstons and two guest beers, good range of well presented food, friendly new landlord and staff; unobtrusive juke box *(Jim Abbott)*

Real ale to us means beer which has matured naturally in its cask – not pressurised or filtered. We name all real ales stocked. We usually name ales preserved under a light blanket of carbon dioxide too, though purists – pointing out that this stops the natural yeasts developing – would disagree (most people, including us, can't tell the difference!)

Leicestershire and Rutland

This year five pubs here have been doing particularly well: the chatty Exeter Arms at Barrowden (good generous food, brewing its own good beers, and more welcoming than ever, now that it's entirely no smoking), the civilised and interestingly furnished Olive Branch at Clipsham (very good imaginative food, great wine choice – and good beers too), the ancient Belper Arms at Newton Burgoland (good all round, with a friendly hands-on manager), the welcoming and attractive Nevill Arms at Medbourne (another fine all-rounder), and the New Inn at Peggs Green (an unspoilt charmer, full of interest). We'd add to these two appealing newcomers to the *Guide*: the Staff of Life in Mowsley, gaining admirers for its good value food, with a splendid range of wines by the glass; and the Jackson Stops in Stretton, with its nice balance between enterprising upmarket restauranty food and a homely country bar. There's very good food to be had at quite a few other places here: the Nags Head in Castle Donnington, Old White Hart at Lyddington, Red Lion at Stathern, Bakers Arms at Thorpe Langton and Finches Arms at Upper Hambleton are all rewarding. Still top of the tree for a special meal out is the Olive Branch at Clipsham. It is Leicestershire and Rutland Dining Pub of the Year, for the third year running – a record for this part of the world. In the Lucky Dip section at the end of the chapter, we'd particularly pick out the Barnsdale Lodge at Barnsdale (a hotel, but very welcoming and relaxed), restauranty Blue Ball at Braunston, Bewicke Arms at Hallaton, Coach & Horses at Kibworth Beauchamp, Swan in the Rushes in Loughborough, Olde Red Lion in Market Bosworth, Griffin at Swithland and Pear Tree in Woodhouse Eaves. Drinks prices in the area are not far off the national average. Often the best beer deals here are to be found in pubs which brew their own; the good Grainstore beers, from the pub of that name in Oakham, are now quite widely available elsewhere, usually at attractive prices. Note that (slightly confusingly – like the Dartmoor beer which is actually brewed in Cornwall, not Devon) the excellent Oakham JHB, also quite common around here, is actually brewed by an entirely different Peterborough brewery, in Cambridgeshire. Leicestershire's main brewer is Everards.

BARROWDEN SK9400 Map 4

Exeter Arms

Main Street, just off A47 Uppingham—Peterborough

A warm generosity of spirit spreads through the unfussy (and now completely no smoking) rooms of this peaceful 17th-c coaching inn – readers couldn't be more complimentary about the welcoming licensees, enthusiastic staff and friendly locals here. Tucked away in a Rutland stone village, it's beautifully positioned, with picnic-sets on a narrow terrace overlooking the pretty village green and ducks on the pond with broader views stretching away beyond. In an old free-standing barn behind, the pub brews its own Blencowe beers. Served from up to six handpumps, these might include Beach Boys, Danny Boys, Fun Boy Four and Boys with Attitude as well as a couple of guests such as Adnams Southwold and Hook Norton Old Hooky; also about ten wines by the well filled glass. Painted a cheery yellow, the long open-plan bar stretches away either side of a long central counter. It's quite straightforwardly furnished with wheelback chairs at tables at either end of the bar, on bare boards or blue patterned carpet; there's quite a collection of pump clips, beer mats and brewery posters. The blackboard menu changes every day, but good home-made bar food served in really generous helpings might typically include sandwiches (from £3.75), sardines on toast (£4.50), mixed italian meats (£6.50), gammon steak in creamy mustard sauce (£9), chicken breast stuffed with mozzarella and wrapped in parma ham or veal escalope in breadcrumbs and anchovy sauce (£11), half a crispy duck with cumberland sauce (£12.50) and puddings such as syrup tart or banana and chocolate cheesecake (£3.50). There are more well spaced picnic-sets in a big informal grassy garden at the back. They've cribbage, dominoes, shove-ha'penny and piped music, and outside boules and horseshoe pitching. *(Recommended by John, Gwen and Reg, Tom and Ruth Rees, DC, Eric Locker, Barry Collett, Michael Doswell, Steve Whalley, Duncan Cloud, Jim Farmer, John Wooll, Dorsan Baker, Mrs Daphne White)*

Own brew ~ Licensees Pete and Elizabeth Blencowe ~ Real ale ~ Bar food (not Sun evening, Mon) ~ Restaurant ~ (01572) 747247 ~ Children welcome away from the bar till 7.30 ~ Folk club alternate Mon ~ Open 12-2.30(3 Sat), 6-11; 12-3, 7-10.30 Sun; closed Mon lunchtime ~ Bedrooms: £35S/£65S

BELMESTHORPE TF0410 Map 8

Blue Bell

Village signposted off A16 just E of Stamford

This pleasantly relaxing country dining pub was originally three cottages that have been knocked through into one. It's on two levels: so from the first little beamed cottagey room, which has gleaming brass platters, pews and settles, and an open fire in a huge stone inglenook you peer down into the bar counter. From here a slope winds down round the counter to a dining area, or you can go through to the games room. The enjoyable menu includes soup (£3.45), sandwiches (£3.50), filled ciabattas (from £5.95), home-made lincolnshire sausages and mash (£6.25), scampi and chips or gammon (£7.95), 12oz sirloin (£12.95), as well as daily specials such as chicken curry (£8.90) and puddings such as treacle sponge with custard or banoffi pie (£3.45). Well kept Bass and Hop Back Summer Lightning with guests such as Fullers London Pride and Charles Wells Bombardier on handpump, and a good choice of wines by the glass; darts, piped classical radio and pool. *(Recommended by Roy Bromell, Stephen, Julie and Hayley Brown, Bill and Sheila McLardy, Ray and Winifred Halliday)*

Free house ~ Licensees Lee Thompson and Angeline Hennessy ~ Real ale ~ Bar food (12-2, 6.30-9; not Sun evenings) ~ (01780) 763859 ~ Children welcome ~ Open 12-2.30, 6-11; 12-10.30 Sun

CASTLE DONINGTON SK4427 Map 7

Nags Head

Hill Top; A453, S end

You will probably need to book a table at this civilised low-beamed dining pub where you can watch the chefs at work through an opening to the kitchen. You order your food at the bar and are then shown to your table by the waitress when your food is ready. The little bar area as you enter is the simplest part, with quarry tiles, dark green dado and dark tables and wheelback chairs. A step takes you up into a small intimate dining room with simple pressed and punctured iron wall lamps and nice signed french prints on fresh cream walls, three chunky old pine candlelit tables on seagrass, and a little turkey rug in front of a pretty art deco slate fireplace. The other end of the bar takes you into a second much bigger and similarly decorated yellow-washed dining area, its well spaced tables giving it a more elegantly informal feel, and the view to the kitchen is from here. As well as lunchtime and early evening snacks such as sausage and mash (£5.95) and smoked salmon baguette (£6.95), the changing menu could include soup (£4.50), seared scallops (£6.95), aubergine black olive and polenta layer with sun-dried tomato dressing (£10.95), beef, mushroom and red wine casserole (£13.95), monkfish with stir-fried oriental vegetables (£15.50) and puddings such as trifle lemon cheesecake or chocolate rum torte (£3.95). Well kept Banks's Mild, Marstons Pedigree and Mansfield on handpump, around 30 malt whiskies and quite a few wines by the glass; they've pétanque outside and the pub is handy for Donnington Race Track. *(Recommended by the Didler, JP, PP, Theo, Anne and Jane Gaskin, Phil and Jane Hodson, Philip and Ann Board)*

Marstons (W & D) ~ Tenant Ian Davison ~ Real ale ~ Bar food (not Sun) ~ Restaurant ~ (01332) 850652 ~ Dogs allowed in bar ~ Open 11.30-2.30, 5.30-11; 12-2.30, 7-10.30 Sun; closed 26 Dec-3 Jan

CLIPSHAM SK9616 Map 8

Olive Branch ★ 🍴 🍷 🍺

Take B668/Stretton exit off A1 N of Stamford; Clipsham signposted E from exit roundabout

Leicestershire and Rutland Dining Pub of the Year

Still doing very well, this civilised stone-built country dining pub produces delicious food and stocks a good range of drinks to go with your meal. The friendly obliging staff are happy to help you choose from the enticing selection of blackboard wines, which includes interesting bin ends, old clarets and unusual sherries. They've also well kept Grainstore Olive Oil with a guest such as Timothy Taylors Landlord on handpump, also freshly squeezed fruit juices, home-made lemonade, good coffee, and winter mulled wine. The emphasis though is on the food, and it's worth booking or arriving early for a table, especially at lunchtime when they do a good value two-course meal (£12.50, not Sunday when they do three courses for £15). Carefully made, using lots of fresh local produce, imaginative dishes change daily, but might include soup (£3.95), sandwiches (from £4.95), game terrine with cumberland sauce (£5.50), excellent honey-roast confit of duck leg with sweet potato and spring onions (£5.95), sausage cassoulet with crispy vegetables (£9.50), braised lamb shoulder with ratatouille and herb crust (£12.50), and roast local partridge with game chips and honey-roast vegetables or fried red mullet with roasted fennel potatoes and sweet pepper sauce (£12.95), with irresistible puddings such as praline parfait or treacle tart with yoghurt ice-cream (£5.50); a nice touch is the board of home-baked bread they bring for you to slice yourself, and we liked the cheeseboard (£5.50). There are dark joists and beams in the various smallish attractive rambling room areas, a cosy log fire in the stone inglenook fireplace (they use old menus to light it), and an interesting mix of pictures, some by local artists, country furniture and books (many bought at antique fairs by one of the partners – ask if you see something you like, as much is for sale). Two of the dining rooms are no smoking; shove-ha'penny, and there may be unobtrusive piped music. Lovely in summer, there are picnic-sets out on a heated terrace, with more on the neat lawn sheltered in the L of its two low buildings. *(Recommended by Bob and Maggie Atherton, Roy Bromell, Anna and Martyn Carey, Jill Franklin, Duncan Cloud, Derek and Sylvia Stephenson, Sally Anne and Peter Goodale, Phil and Jane Hodson, Michael Rodgers, Tony and Betty Parker, Dorsan Baker)*

Free house ~ Licensees Sean Hope, Ben Jones and Marcus Welford ~ Real ale ~ Bar food ~ Restaurant ~ (01780) 410355 ~ Children welcome ~ Dogs allowed in bar ~ Open 12-3, 6-11; 12-11(10.30 Sun) Fri, Sat; closed Fri afternoon in winter

COTTESMORE SK9013 Map 7

Sun 🍷

B668 NE of Oakham

The tasty food is quite a draw at this 17th-c thatched and stone-built village pub, and as there aren't many tables in the rooms off the bar, it pays to get here early in winter, or even book; in fine weather, you can also eat out on the terrace. Meals are served by friendly efficient staff, and include soup (£2.95), baked camembert for two (£5.75), baguettes (from £4.50), calves liver or lamb shank (£9.50), and roast gressingham duck breast (£11.50), with specials such as cajun chicken caesar salad (£6.50), and salmon, cod and prawn fishcakes on chilli cream with chilli jam (£7.50), and puddings such as home-made sticky toffee pudding (£3.25). Along with stripped pine furnishings, there's a winter log fire in the stone inglenook, and pictures on the olive and terracotta walls; one dining area is no smoking; piped music, and boules outside. Besides decent wines, they serve Adnams and Everards Tiger along with a guest such as Highwood Tom Woods Bomber County on handpump; generous coffee too. *(Recommended by Barry Collett, Ruth Kitching, Anthony Barnes, Patrick Hancock, Ken and Barbara Turner, Jim Auld)*

Everards ~ Tenant David Johnson ~ Real ale ~ Bar food (not Sun evening, Mon) ~ Restaurant ~ (01572) 812321 ~ Children welcome ~ Dogs allowed in bar ~ Open 11.30-2.30, 6.30-11; 12-3, 7-10.30 Sun; closed Mon

EAST LANGTON SP7292 Map 4

Bell

The Langtons signposted from A6 N of Market Harborough; East Langton signposted from B6047

New licensees at this appealing creeper-covered country pub have continued brewing the well kept Langton ales which are produced in a converted outbuilding here: Caudle Bitter and Bowler Strong Ale are well kept alongside Greene King Abbot and IPA and served on handpump. Changing monthly, the delicious sounding bar menu but might include soup (£4.20), grilled tiger prawns (£5.20), caramelised onion, mushroom, rocket and goats cheese puff pastry tart (£9.50), beer battered cod with chips and mushy peas (£10.25), moroccan lamb kebabs on apricot and mint couscous (£11.95), baked fillet of cod and bacon with chorizo and butter bean casserole or braised lamb shank (£12.95), steak (£15.25) and puddings (£4.50). The long stripped-stone beamed bar has a good woodburning stove and fresh flowers on plain wooden tables, and the green-hued dining room is no smoking. Friendly helpful staff wear black aprons; piped music. The pub is in an attractive village in peaceful countryside, and has tables outside on the sloping front lawn. *(Recommended by JP, PP, John Cook, Howard and Margaret Buchanan, Duncan Cloud, Gerry and Rosemary Dobson, John Saville, Derek and Sylvia Stephenson, Andy Sinden, Louise Harrington, Prof and Mrs Tony Palmer, Jim Farmer, Anthony Barnes, J M Tansey, David Field, Mr and Mrs G Jibson, Laura and Stuart Ballantyne, Dorsan Baker, Patrick Hancock)*

Own brew ~ Licensee Peter Faye ~ Real ale ~ Bar food ~ Restaurant ~ (01858) 545278 ~ Children welcome ~ Open 11.30-2.30, 7(6.30 Sat)-11; 12-4, 7-10.30 Sun ~ Bedrooms: £39.50B/£55S(£59.50B)

EMPINGHAM SK9408 Map 4

White Horse

Main Street; A606 Stamford—Oakham

This big bustling old dining pub is near Rutland Water and very handily open all day. The open-plan carpeted lounge bar has a big log fire below an unusual free-standing chimney-funnel, and lots of fresh flowers, while outside are some rustic tables among urns of flowers. Under the new licensee, bar food might include soup (£3.25), moules marinière or pork, apple and calvados pâté with plum and apple chutney (£4.95), tagliatelle with creamy garlic, leek and mushroom sauce (£8.25), beef, ale and mushroom pie (£8.95), 10oz sirloin (£13.95) and specials such as venison medallions with wild mushroom and forest berry port wine sauce (£11.25). The bistro and the Orange Room are no smoking; TV, fruit machine and piped music. They've well kept Greene King Abbot and Ruddles Best, Adnams and a guest such as Charles Wells Eagle IPA on handpump, and up to ten wines by the glass – or if you prefer, they also do morning coffee and afternoon tea. Bedrooms are in a converted stable block, and in case any of their residents manage to catch anything they offer freezing facilities. They have a wheelchair for disabled visitors and a ramp makes access easy. *(Recommended by Neil Skidmore, John and Sylvia Harrop,*

Barry Collett, Mike and Wendy Proctor, Glenwys and Alan Lawrence, Jim Auld, Duncan Cloud, David and Brenda Tew)

Courage (S & N) ~ Lease Ian and Sarah Sharp ~ Real ale ~ Bar food (12-2.15, 7-9.30 (9 Sun)) ~ (01780) 460221 ~ Children welcome ~ Dogs allowed in bedrooms ~ Open 11-11; 12-10.30 Sun ~ Bedrooms: £50B/£65B

EXTON SK9211 Map 7

Fox & Hounds

Signposted off A606 Stamford—Oakham

Italian licensees at this handsome old country coaching inn add a gentle Italian lean to the good well presented bar food, and wine list (with a good range by the glass). As well as home-made soup (£3.50), sandwiches (from £3.50), fresh ciabattas or grilled panini (from £4.25) and ploughman's (£8.25), you might find mediterranean seafood salad (£5.95), tasty pasta dishes such as fusilli with gorgonzola and spinach or tagliatelle with mushrooms and parmesan (£7.95), rack of lamb with rosemary or home-made steak and kidney pie (£9.95) and grilled halibut steak with mediterranean vegetables (£12.25); excellent coffee; no smoking dining room. Quietly civilised, the comfortable high-ceilinged lounge bar has some dark red plush easy chairs as well as wheelback seats around lots of pine tables, maps and hunting prints on the walls, fresh flowers, and a winter log fire in a large stone fireplace. The separate public bar has a more pubby atmosphere, with pool, darts, dominoes and piped music. Friendly competent staff serve well kept real ales such as Grainstore Springtime, Timothy Taylor Landlord, with perhaps a guest like Greene King IPA on handpump. Seats among large rose beds on the pleasant well kept back lawn look out over paddocks, and the tranquil village green with its tall trees out in front is most attractive. Only a couple of miles away from Rutland Water, the pub is a useful stop for walkers on the Viking Way. *(Recommended by Mr and Mrs P L Spencer, Eric Locker, Barry Collett, Graham Holden, Julie Lee, Carol and Dono Leaman, Mike and Wendy Proctor, Roy Bromell, Jim Auld, Derek and Sylvia Stephenson, Patrick Hancock)*

Free house ~ Licensees Valter and Sandra Floris ~ Real ale ~ Bar food (not Sun evening) ~ Restaurant ~ (01572) 812403 ~ Children welcome ~ Dogs allowed in bar ~ Open 11-3, 6-11; 12-3, 7-10.30 Sun ~ Bedrooms: £28/£42

GUMLEY SP6790 Map 4

Bell £

Off A6 Market Harborough—Kibworth, via Foxton; or off A5199 via Laughton; Main Street

The very good value three-course Sunday lunch (£10.95), over 60s two-course menu (£4.50 – get there early for a table) and reasonably priced bar menu earn this cheerful neatly kept village pub a bargain award for the first time this year. Straightforward but tasty bar food includes sandwiches (from £2.50), home-made soup (£2.75), ploughman's (£4.95), cottage pie (£5.50), battered cod (£5.95), roast of the day (£6.95), salmon mornay (£7.95) and steaks (from £8.95), with home-made puddings such as bread and butter pudding or trifle (£2.75); small no smoking dining room. The almost L-shaped bar on the right, with typical pub furnishings, has lots of hunting prints on its cream walls, game bird plates above the bar, china jugs and mugs and horsebrasses on some of its black beams and joists, more china on a delft shelf, and ornaments on the window sills, with perhaps a big flower arrangement in the corner; darts, cribbage, dominoes and piped music (but no mobile phones). Bass, Batemans XB, Greene King IPA and a guest beer are well kept on handpump. Look out for the cricketing prints and cartoons, and the miniature bat collection in the lobby. The pretty terrace garden behind is not for children or dogs. *(Recommended by Eric Locker, John Fiander, Gerry and Rosemary Dobson, DC, G Coates, Jim Farmer, P Tailyour, George Atkinson, Lloyd Moon)*

Free house ~ Licensee David Quelch ~ Real ale ~ Bar food (not Sun or Mon evenings) ~ Restaurant ~ (0116) 2792476 ~ Children over 5 in restaurant ~ Open 11-3, 6-11; 12-5 Sun; closed Sun evening

KEGWORTH SK4826 Map 7

Cap & Stocking

A mile or so from M1 junction 24: follow A6 towards Loughborough; in village, turn left at chemists' down one-way Dragwall opposite High Street, then left and left again, into Borough Street

The three rooms of this backstreet local are an intriguing throwback to another age. The brown paint and etched glass in the right-hand room make it seem as if little has changed since the 1940s, and they serve Bass from a stainless steel jug; you'll also find Greene King IPA on handpump. The two determinedly simple but cosy front rooms both have their own coal fire and an easy-going feel, and furnishings include big cases of stuffed birds and locally caught fish, fabric-covered wall benches and heavy cast-iron-framed tables, and a cast-iron range; cribbage, dominoes, trivia and piped music. The back room has french windows to the pretty, secluded garden, where there may be floodlit boules and barbecues in summer. Straightforward bar food includes filled rolls (from £1.90), soup (£2.30), burgers (from £2.70), ploughman's and pizzas (from £5.50), beef casserole (£6.95), and daily specials such as thai chicken (£6.95). *(Recommended by the Didler, F J Robinson, Pauline and Philip Darley, J V Dadswell, Bernie Adams, Steve and Liz Tilley, Pete Baker, Alison Hayes, Pete Hanlon, Patrick Hancock, June and Ken Brooks, P Jeffries, Chris Bell, GSB, Jean and Douglas Troup, Derek and Sylvia Stephenson)*

Punch ~ Tenants Graham and Mary Walsh ~ Real ale ~ Bar food (11.30-1.45, 6.30-8.45) ~ No credit cards ~ (01509) 674814 ~ Children welcome ~ Dogs welcome ~ Open 11.30-2.30, 6.30-11; 12-2.30, 7-10.30 Sun

LYDDINGTON SP8797 Map 4

Old White Hart

Village signposted off A6003 N of Corby

This charmingly civilised old inn was originally part of the Burghley House Estate. The softly lit low-ceilinged bar has just three close-set tables in front of its glass shielded roaring log fire, and heavy bowed beams. The bar opens into an attractive restaurant, and on the other side is another tiled-floor room with some stripped stone, lots of horse pictures, cushioned wall seats and mate's chairs, and a woodburning stove. Most people come here for the excellent food, and the seasonally changing menu might include home-made soups (£3.25), cured bresaola of beef with rocket and goats cheese dressing (£5.95), sausages on bubble and squeak (£9.95), roast tenderloin of pork with pear and cinnamon glaze (£11.95), roast rack of venison with port jus (£13.95) and puddings such as white chocolate cheesecake with cherries or bread and butter pudding with crème anglaise (from £4.50). A cheaper option is their weekday early evening two-course menu (£9.95, till 7.30). Friendly and efficient staff serve well kept Greene King IPA, Abbot and a guest such as Timothy Taylors Landlord on handpump; shove-ha'penny, cribbage and dominoes, and 12 floodlit boules pitches. The pretty walled garden is very pleasant, and if you sit outside on Thursday evening you'll probably hear the church bell-ringers. Set in a picturesque village with good nearby walks, the pub is handy for Bede House. *(Recommended by Rona Murdoch, Eric Locker, Alan and Jill Bull, John Cook, Mr and Mrs G S Ayrton, Christopher Beadle)*

Free house ~ Licensee Stuart East ~ Real ale ~ Bar food (12-2, 6.30-9; not Sun evening) ~ Restaurant ~ (01572) 821703 ~ Children welcome ~ Open 12-3, 6.30-11(7-10.30 Sun); closed 25 Dec ~ Bedrooms: £55B/£80B

Pubs in outstandingly attractive surroundings are listed at the back of the book.

MARKET OVERTON SK8816 Map 7

Black Bull 🛏

Village signposted off B668 in Cottesmore

Fresh fish features quite strongly on the specials board at this friendly old thatched stone-built pub – there may be 16oz fish and chips (£10.95), bass, halibut and tilapia (£13.95). A good range of other tasty dishes (served in generous helpings) could include soup (£3.95), battered whitebait (£4.50), tiger prawns in chilli (£5.50), sweet and sour sizzling vegetables (£8.95), stilton lamb or pasta of the day (£9.95) and 16oz T-bone (£16.95). The main dining room has a no smoking area and service is friendly. With a cheerfully bustling atmosphere, the low black-beamed bar has raspberry mousse walls, red plush stools and cushioned spindleback chairs at dark wood pub tables, and flowers on the sills of its little curtained windows. They serve well kept Greene King IPA, Morlands Original and a guest such as Greene King Triumph on handpump; piped music and fruit machine. *(Recommended by Comus and Sarah Elliott, Barry Collett, Keith and Sarah Burrluck, Revd John E Cooper, Patrick Hancock, Glenwys and Alan Lawrence, Robert Turnham)*

Free house ~ Licensees John and Val Owen ~ Real ale ~ Bar food ~ Restaurant ~ (01572) 767677 ~ Children welcome ~ Dogs allowed in bar ~ Open 11-2.30, 6-11; 12-3, 7-10.30 Sun ~ Bedrooms: £35S/£48S

MEDBOURNE SP7993 Map 4

Nevill Arms ★ 🍷 £ 🛏

B664 Market Harborough—Uppingham

This enjoyable old pub is cheerily unpretentious, with a friendly welcome from the well liked longstanding licensees. The inviting main bar has a buoyant atmosphere, two log fires in stone fireplaces at either end, chairs and small wall settles around its tables, and a lofty dark-joisted ceiling; piped music. Much needed at busy times, a spacious back room by the former coachyard has pews around more tables, and some toys to amuse children. In summer most people prefer to eat at the tables out on the grass by the dovecote. Hearty home-made food from a short but reasonably priced menu includes sandwiches (from £2.50), panini with hot fillings such as mozzarella and chargrilled peppers or chicken and smoky bacon (£3.95), and blackboard specials such as pork with peppers and grain mustard and chicken with stilton and leeks (all £5.95), and steak (£7.95). They have well kept Adnams, Fullers London Pride, Greene King Abbot and two changing guests such as Bass and Wadworths 6X on handpump, and about two dozen country wines. A wide choice of games includes darts, shove-ha'penny, cribbage, dominoes, table skittles, and on request other board games and even table football; look out for Truffles the cat, and the two inquisitive great danes, Cleo and her son Bertie. The building itself is attractive, with handsome stonework and imposing latticed mullioned windows, and you get to it by a footbridge over the little duck-filled River Welland. The church over the bridge is worth a visit. The bedrooms are in two neighbouring cottages, and the first-class breakfasts are served in the pub's sunny conservatory. *(Recommended by David Carlile, John Saul, Stuart and Alison Ballantyne, Eric Locker, the Didler, Tracey and Stephen Groves, Rona Murdoch, George Atkinson, JP, PP, W W Burke, Barry Collett, CMW, JJW, R N and M I Bailey, Janet and Peter Race, Mr and Mrs Neil Draper, Patrick Hancock, Jim Farmer, David Field, John Wooll, Derek and Sylvia Stephenson, Brian and Jacky Wilson, Rod and Chris Pring)*

Free house ~ Licensees Nicholas and Elaine Hall ~ Real ale ~ Bar food (12-2, 7-9.30) ~ (01858) 565288 ~ Children welcome ~ Dogs allowed in bar ~ Open 12-2.30(3 Sat, Sun), 6-11 ~ Bedrooms: £45B/£55B

> Post Office address codings confusingly give the impression that some pubs are in Leicestershire, when they're really in Cambridgeshire (which is where we list them).

MOWSLEY SP6488 Map 4

Staff of Life 🍷

Village signposted off A5199 S of Leicester; Main Street

It's the food which is bringing increasing numbers of people to this high-gabled early 20th-c house, which from outside looks almost more like a fairly substantial private house than a pub. Inside, the roomy bar is quite traditional, with a panelled ceiling, and comfortable seating including some high-backed settles on flagstones; it does get its fair share of locals dropping in for a drink (and has darts and table skittles). It opens into a neatly kept back dining area with good tables in a roomy conservatory; piped music. The wide choice of good enterprising food is all home-made. Besides soup (£2.95) and a specials board with dishes such as fried guinea fowl with chorizo and sun-dried tomato sauce (£11.50), good value lunchtime dishes might include breaded brie with red berry dressing (£4.30), ploughman's (from £4.75), smoked chicken and bacon salad (£5.75), pie of the day or sausage and mash with black cherry gravy (£5.95), with more elaborate evening dishes such as moules marinière (£5.95), fried duck breast on olive mash with black sherry and brandy sauce (£10.50) and tiger prawns (£10.95). Their two-course OAP weekday lunch (not Mon) is a crowd-pulling bargain at £4.95, and their Sunday lunches are popular too. Well kept Greene King IPA and an interesting changing guest beer such as local Langton Caudle and an excellent choice of wines by the glass (a good many bottles are slung overhead in the bar). The young landlord and his team are friendly and efficient. The prettily planted back garden has picnic-sets, with a few more on the front terrace. *(Recommended by P Tailyour, Duncan Cloud, Michael Ward, John Coatsworth)*

Free house ~ Licensee Spencer Funnell ~ Real ale ~ Bar food (12-2.30, 7-9) ~ Restaurant ~ (0116) 240 2359 ~ Children in eating area of bar, must be over 12 in rear garden area ~ Possibly jazz Weds evening ~ Open 12-3, 6-11; 12-10.30 Sun; closed Mon lunchtime except bank hols

NEWTON BURGOLAND SK3708 Map 4

Belper Arms

Village signposted off B4116 S of Ashby or B586 W of Ibstock

The friendly landlord is very hands-on, and there's a good pubby atmosphere at this popular roadside place. Although very opened up, many ancient interior features reflect the various stages in its development (heavy beams, changing floor levels and separate areas with varying floor and wall materials) and give it an enjoyably intimate feel. Parts are said to date back to the 13th c, and much of the exposed brickwork certainly looks at least three or four hundred years old. A big freestanding central chimney has a fire one side and a range on the other, with chatty groups of captain's chairs. There are lots of interesting bits and pieces dotted around, from a suit of old chain mail, to a collection of pewter teapots, some good antique furniture and the story of the pub ghost (Five to Four Fred) which is framed on the wall. They hold a beer festival during the August bank holiday, but usually have well kept Greene King IPA, Hook Norton Best, Marstons Pedigree and a couple of guests from brewers such as J W Lees and Smiles on handpump; nine wines by the glass. Pleasant piped music and dominoes. Tasty bar food includes soup (£2.95), baguettes or ciabattas (from £4.20), smoked haddock rarebit with tomato salad (£4.75), curry of the day (£7.25), gammon steak with grilled tomato, mushrooms and a fried egg (£7.85), mediterranean vegetable lasagne (£8.25), and sirloin steak (£9.95), with specials such as salmon fillet or fish and chips (£8.95), and puddings (from £3); three-course Sunday lunch (£10.75). The restaurant is very big, and service can slow down when they get busy. A rambling garden has boules, cricket nets and children's play area, and works its way round the pub to teak tables and chairs on a terrace, and a steam-engine-shaped barbecue; there's a good campsite here too. *(Recommended by JP, PP, the Didler, I J and S A Bufton, Joyce and Maurice Cottrell, Ian and Jane Irving, Tony Rose, Daphne Slater, Joan and Tony Walker, Rona Murdoch, Derek and Sylvia Stephenson, Trevor and Sheila Sharman)*

Mercury Taverns ~ Manager Guy Wallis ~ Real ale ~ Bar food (12-2.30, 7-9.30) ~ Restaurant ~ (01530) 270530 ~ Children welcome ~ Dogs allowed in bar ~ Open 12-3, 6-11; all day Fri-Sun

OADBY SK6200 Map 4

Cow & Plough

Gartree Road (B667 N of centre)

Housed in a converted old farm and its dairy buildings, the best part of this interesting old place is undoubtedly the two dark back rooms known as the Vaults. These are packed with an extraordinary and ever-expanding collection of old brewery memorabilia lovingly assembled by the landlord. Almost every item has a story behind it, from the enamel signs and mirrors advertising long-forgotten brews, through the aged brass cash register, to the furnishings and fittings salvaged from pubs and even churches (there's some splendid stained-glass behind the counter). The pub first opened about 15 years ago with just these cosily individual rooms, but it soon tripled in size when an extensive long, light, flagstoned conservatory was added to the front; it too has its share of brewery signs and the like, as well as plenty of plants and fresh flowers, a piano, beams liberally covered with hops, and a real mix of traditionally pubby tables and chairs, with lots of green leatherette sofas, and small round cast-iron tables. One section has descriptions of all Leicester's pubs. Named after the pub jack russell *Billy*, a star feature here is the Steamin Billy beers which are brewed for the landlord under licence by Grainstore: Billy Skydiver and Steamin Billy Bitter, as well as Fullers London Pride, are well kept alongside three changing guests such as Buffys IPA, Grainstore Panther Mild and Roosters Special. They also have farm ciders and country wines. The very temptingly contemporary and freshly prepared bar food, using local and organic ingredients where possible, includes lunchtime sandwiches (£3.95), starters such as moules marinière (£4.50), grilled pigeon breast on asparagus (£4.95), poached squid stuffed with spring vegetables (£11.95), rump of lamb on lentils with whole cloves of roasted garlic and tamarind glaze (£12.95), chicken breast filled with watercress and rocket pesto mousseline with a morelle mushroom and white truffle oil sauce (£13.95), grilled fillet of beef with spiced carrots, pak choi, sweetcorn and green coconut curry sauce or sirloin of bison (£15.95) and puddings such as rhubarb fool tart with rhubarb compote, chocolate sponge pudding or chocolate meringue roulade with wild berry coulis (£5.50). The whole of the conservatory is no smoking. lots of pub games include darts, shove-ha'penny, table skittles, hood skittles, cribbage and dominoes; unobtrusive piped music. There are picnic-sets outside. *(Recommended by Rona Murdoch, Bernie Adams, Jim Farmer, the Didler)*

Free house ~ Licensee Barry Lount ~ Real ale ~ Bar food ~ Restaurant ~ (0116) 272 0852 ~ Children in eating area of bar, restaurant and family room ~ Dogs allowed in bar ~ Open 12-3, 5-11; 12-11 Sat; 12-5, 7-10 Sun; closed Mon lunchtime

OAKHAM SK8508 Map 4

Grainstore

Station Road, off A606

As soon as you arrive at this converted three-storey Victorian grain warehouse, you get the feel of a working brewery, from the bustle of deliveries leaving the building to the vats of beer which you can see through glass doors in the functional open-plan bar. The brewery is a traditional tower brewhouse, with raw materials starting on the upper floor and the finished beer coming out on the bottom floor. Laid back or lively, depending on the time of day, the interior is plain and functional, with wide well worn bare floorboards, bare ceiling boards above massive joists (and noises of the workings above) which are supported by red metal pillars, a long brick-built bar counter with cast-iron bar stools, tall cask tables and simple elm chairs. Their fine beers (Grainstore Cooking, Rutland Panther, Steamin' Billy, Triple B and Ten Fifty) are served traditionally at the left end of the bar counter, and through swan necks with sparklers on the right; the friendly staff are happy to give you samples. At lunchtimes alongside soup (£3), good baguettes (from £3.50), and ploughman's (£4.25), they serve dutchman's breakfast (three eggs, ham, cheese and bread), as well as a few reasonably priced dishes such as lasagne (£5.50) and beef and ale pie, with perhaps a special such as mushroom and mustard puff (£4.25). In summer they open huge glass doors on to a terrace stacked with barrels, and with picnic-sets; sporting events on TV, fruit machine, bar billiards, cribbage, dominoes, darts, giant Jenga and bottle-walking. Loading trucks used to pass right through the building; disabled access. You can tour the brewery by arrangement, and they do take-aways. It's very handy for the station. *(Recommended by Bernie Adams, Barry Collett, JP, PP, the Didler, Rona Murdoch, David Field, John and Wendy Allin, Peter and Jean Hoare)*

Own brew ~ Licensee Tony Davis ~ Real ale ~ Bar food (11.30-2.15, not evenings or Sun) ~ (01572) 770065 ~ Children welcome ~ Dogs allowed in bar ~ Live music once a month on Sun afternoon, Sun evening and Thurs evening ~ Open 11-11; 12-10.30 Sun

OLD DALBY SK6723 Map 7

Crown

By school in village centre turn into Longcliff Hill

Three or four intimate little rooms at this tucked-away creeper-covered former farmhouse have black beams, one or two antique oak settles, a mix of carvers and wheelback chairs, hunting and other rustic prints, and open fires; the snug is no smoking. Outside, you'll find cast-iron furniture and rustic tables and chairs on the terrace, hanging baskets and urns of flowers; steps lead down through the sheltered sloping lawn with boules. Bar food includes sandwiches (from £4.50), olives and garlic bread (£4.50), ciabattas (from £6.95), ploughman's (£7.50), sausage and mash (£7.95), pasta dishes (from £9.95) and steak and ale pie or goats cheese tart (£9.95). The dining room has paintings by a local artist and a pleasantly relaxed bistro feel. Local Belvoir Brewery, Charles Wells Bombardier, Courage Directors and three guests such as Greene King Old Speckled Hen, Marstons Pedigree or Theakstons Old Peculier are well kept on handpump or tapped straight from the cask; darts and cribbage. *(Recommended by B and J Shurmer, JP, PP, John and Sylvia Harrop, the Didler, J M Tansey, Barry and Anne, Tom Evans)*

Free house ~ Licensees Mr and Mrs Hayle ~ Real ale ~ Bar food (12-2.30, 6.30-9.30; not Mon lunchtime or Sun evening) ~ Restaurant ~ (01664) 823134 ~ Children in eating area of bar and restaurant ~ Dogs allowed in bar ~ Open 12-3, 6-11(7-10.30 Sun); closed Mon lunchtime

PEGGS GREEN SK4117 Map 7

New Inn £

Signposted off A512 Ashby—Shepshed at roundabout, then Newbold sign down Zion Hill

This delightfully alternative little gem of a pub has an incredible collection of old bric-a-brac (it'll keep you busy for ages) which covers almost every inch of the walls and ceilings of the two cosy tiled front rooms. The pub is in the second generation of the same very welcoming Irish family, who like to think of it as an extension of their home – the cluster of regulars around the old-fashioned booth bar certainly look comfortably relaxed, and no doubt you will be too. The little room on the left, a bit like a kitchen parlour, has china on the mantelpiece above a warm coal fire, lots of prints and photographs and little collections of this and that, three old cast-iron tables, wooden stools and a small stripped kitchen table. The room to the right has quite nice stripped panelling, and masses of the sort of bric-a-brac you can spend ages trawling through. The little back lounge, with a stripped wooden floor, has a really interesting and quite touching display of old local photographs including some colliery ones. They serve filled baps all day (from £1.20), but otherwise, note the limited food serving times. The short and very good value menu could include faggots and peas (£2.95), corned beef hash or two smoked haddock fillets (£3.50) with one or two specials such as stew and soda bread or steak,

Guinness and mushroom pie (£3.95). Well kept Bass, Marstons Pedigree and a weekly guest such as Caledonian Deuchars IPA on handpump; piped music, dominoes, TV, board games and various special events throughout the year. *(Recommended by the Didler, CMW, JJW, JP, PP, Bernie Adams, Mr and Mrs John Taylor, Rona Murdoch, B and M Kendall, George Atkinson)*

Enterprise ~ Lease Maria Christina Kell ~ Real ale ~ Bar food (12-2; 6-8 Mon; not Tues-Sat evenings; not Sun) ~ No credit cards ~ (01530) 222293 ~ Children welcome ~ Monthly folk sessions ~ Open 12-2.30, 5.30-11; 12-3, 6.30-11 Sat; 7-10.30 Sun

SOMERBY SK7710 Map 7

Stilton Cheese

High Street; off A606 Oakham—Melton Mowbray, via Cold Overton, or Leesthorpe and Pickwell; can also be reached direct from Oakham via Knossington

Lots of local activity, and diners in for a meal keep the atmosphere at this welcoming 16th-c pub enjoyably bustling and cheerful. The hop-strung beamed bar/lounge has dark carpets, lots of country prints on its stripped stone walls, a collection of copper pots, a stuffed badger and plenty of restful seats; shove-ha'penny, cribbage, dominoes, board games and piped music. Five handpumps serve well kept local Grainstore Ten Fifty, Marstons Pedigree, and Tetleys along with two thoughtfully sourced guests from brewers such as John O'Gaunt or Tring, and they've a good choice of wines, and about two dozen malt whiskies. Well cooked (there are three chefs in the family) and reasonably priced bar meals might include sandwiches (from £2.25), soup (£2.65), prawn cocktail (£2.90), ploughman's (£5.25), local sausages and mash or lasagne (£6.25), battered cod or chicken tikka masala (£6.75), rump steak (£9.25), and tasty specials such as stilton-stuffed mushrooms (£3.95), sliced duck breast with ginger and orange sauce or home-made venison and mushroom pie (£7.95), monkfish provençale (£8.95), and whole dover sole with lemon and parsley butter (£14.50); children's meals (£3.75). The restaurant is no smoking. The terrace has wooden seating and outdoor heaters. More reports please. *(Recommended by Eric Locker, Duncan Cloud, JP, PP, Annette and John Derbyshire, Jim Farmer, G Coates, Phil and Jane Hodson)*

Free house ~ Licensees Carol and Jeff Evans ~ Real ale ~ Bar food (12-2, 6(7 Sun)-9) ~ Restaurant ~ (01664) 454394 ~ Children in restaurant and family room ~ Dogs allowed in bedrooms ~ Open 12-3, 6-11; 7-10.30 Sun

Three Crowns £

Now that the well kept tasty Parish real ales (Special and the 11% Baz's Bonce Blower alongside Bass and Greene King IPA) served here are no longer brewed on the premises, but by the pub's former landlord Barrie Parish nearby, this popular pub has reverted to its former name. There's a friendly welcoming atmosphere in the comfortable L-shaped main bar, which has red plush stools and banquettes and plush-cushioned captain's chairs, a sofa in one corner, and a good log fire in the big stone fireplace; another bar has bays of button-back red seating. The straightforward good value bar menu includes soup (£2.25), sandwiches (from £2.95), garlic mushrooms (£3.75), ploughman's or home-made vegetable curry (£4.95), and home-made steak and Parish ale pie (£5.95), with puddings such as fruit pies (£2.50); they do a bargain two-course lunch menu (£5.95), and on Tuesday and Friday you can get two meals for £6. The dining area and part of the restaurant are no smoking. Fruit machine, darts, TV and piped music; they hold a beer festival in May. A fenced-off area by the car park has white plastic tables, and in summer they have a children's bouncy castle *(Recommended by Dave Irving, Richard Lewis, O K Smyth, CMW, JJW, JP, PP, Rona Murdoch, Bernie Adams, Barry Collett, Duncan Cloud)*

Free house ~ Licensees Wendy and Mick Farmer ~ Real ale ~ Bar food (till 9.30 Fri, Sat) ~ Restaurant ~ (01664) 454777 ~ Children welcome ~ Dogs allowed in bar ~ Live bands first Sat in month ~ Open 12-2.30, 6.30-11; 12-10.30 Sun

STATHERN SK7731 Map 7

Red Lion

Off A52 W of Grantham via the brown-signed Belvoir rd (keep on towards Harby – Stathern signposted on left); or off A606 Nottingham—Melton Mowbray via Long Clawson and Harby

The unassuming exterior of this gourmet pub is deceptive. It's run by the team behind the Olive Tree in Clipsham, and has the same enjoyable mix of good (though not cheap) food, well chosen wines, and civilised atmosphere. Like the Olive Tree, they also have a kitchen shop where you can buy produce and fully prepared dishes. Bar food ingredients are sourced locally, they smoke their own meats and make their own preserves and pickles. The twice daily changing menu offers a good choice which might include cauliflower soup (£4.95), smoked haddock and leek tart (£6), fish and chips with mushy peas (£9.50), fried calves liver with mustard mash and tarragon jus (£12.95), bass with tomato gnocchetti patsa, roasted aubergine and baby courgettes (£14.25), roast gressingham duck breast (£13.75) and puddings such as warm chocolate fondue with exotic fruits and shortbreads or rhubarb crumble with ginger ice-cream (£5.25). They also do a limited two-course set menu (£11.50). The splendid range of drinks takes in well kept Brewsters Wicked Woman from just down the road, Grainstore Olive Oil, a couple of changing guest beers such as Fullers London Pride and Caledonian Deuchars IPA, draught belgian beer, freshly squeezed orange and grapefruit, several ciders and fruit punches, and a varied wine list with just under a dozen by the glass. There's a relaxed country pub feel to the yellow room on the right, a relaxing lounge with sofas, a fireplace, and a big table with books, papers and magazines; it leads off the smaller, more traditional flagstoned bar, with terracotta walls, another fireplace with a pile of logs beside it, and lots of beams and hops. Dotted around are various oddities picked up by one of the licensees on visits to Newark Antiques Fair: some unusual lambing chairs for example, and a collection of wooden spoons. A little room with tables set for eating leads to the long, narrow main dining room in what was once the pub's skittle alley, and out to a nicely arranged suntrap garden, with good hardwood furnishings spread over its lawn and terrace, and an unusually big play area behind the car park, with swings, climbing frames and so on. *(Recommended by David and Elaine Shaw, Mr and Mrs R P Begg, Jill and Keith Wright, Derek and Sylvia Stephenson, Alan and Jill Bull, Anthony Rickards Collinson, Peter F Marshall, David Edwards, Tony and Betty Parker)*

Free house ~ Licensees Sean Hope, Ben Jones, Marcus Welford ~ Real ale ~ Bar food ~ Restaurant ~ (01949) 860868 ~ Children welcome ~ Dogs allowed in bar ~ Open 12-3, 6-11; 12-11 Fri, Sat; 12-6 Sun

STRETTON SK9415 Map 8

Jackson Stops

Rookery Road; a mile or less off A1, at B668 (Oakham) exit; follow village sign, turning off Clipsham road into Manor Road, pub on left

This thatched pub is best thought of as a dining pub (with good interesting upmarket food), though it also has an appealing and homely country bar. Down on the left, that small friendly room, with black beams and some timbering in its ochre walls, has just a couple of bar stools, a cushioned stripped wall pew and an elderly settle on its worn tile and brick floor, with a coal fire in the corner, and well kept Adnams Broadside and Oakham JHB on handpump. The main room, on the right, is airy and light, carpeted in dark blue, its stone walls mainly painted canary, and its half dozen well spaced stripped tables nicely mixing ancient and modern, with linen napkins in rings, big steel platters, and lit candles in brass sticks. This has another smokeless coal fire in its stone corner fireplace, and a couple of striking modern oils alongside a few tastefully disposed farm tools. Right along past the bar is a second dining room, older in style, with stripped stone walls, tiled floor, and an old open cooking range. The food, prettily set out in up-to-date style on big plates, includes soup of the day (£3.75), mussel and smoked bacon risotto (£5.25), seared scallops and black pudding with mash and garlic sauce (£6.50), pasta roulade of artichoke, ricotta and rocket (£9.50), roast cod fillet with dauphinoise potatoes, spinach and herb hollandaise (£12.50), roast beef fillet with braised shallots, rösti potato and red wine jus (£15.95), and cheeses fresh from Paris as well as a good puddings such as chargrilled and marinated pineapple with coconut ice-cream (£4.50). The thoughtful wine range includes around ten good wines by the glass, several enterprising half-bottles of pudding wine, and late-bottled vintage port by the glass. The unobtrusive piped music in the main dining room doesn't disturb the chatty and relaxed atmosphere. Service is efficient and attentive without being intrusive, and the lavatories are exemplary. As you might guess from the inn-sign, this used to be called the White Horse; it got its present name years ago from an estate agent's sign, when it was waiting for a buyer. In coaching days the small village itself had an even odder tag: 'Stretton in the Street, where shrews meet' – probably just rhyming nonsense to distinguish it from Stretton en le Field at the other end of the county, rather than an allusion either to sharp-tongued women or to some strange ecological phenomenon. *(Recommended by Bernie Adams, M Raworth, Mrs Margo Finlay, Mr Kasprowski)*

Free house ~ Licensee James Trevor ~ Real ale ~ Bar food (12-2, 7-10, not Sun evening) ~ Restaurant ~ (01780) 410237 ~ Children in restaurant ~ Dogs allowed in bar ~ Open 12-2.30, 6.30-11; 12-3 Sun; closed Mon exc bank hols

Ram Jam Inn 🍷 🛏

Just off A1: heading N, look out for warning signs some 8 miles N of Stamford, turning off at big inn sign through service station close to B668; heading S, look out for B668 Oakham turn-off, inn well signed on left ¼ mile after roundabout

Very handy if you're on the A1, although this popular place is not exactly a pub it certainly makes a refreshing stop. As you go in, the first part of the big stylish open-plan bar/dining area has terracotta-coloured walls decorated in one place with a spread of old breadboards, big ceramic tiles on the floor, bentwood chairs and café tables, and sofas in a cosy panelled alcove with daily papers and a standard lamp. The bar on the left here has Fullers London Pride and John Smiths on handpump, good house wines with about ten by the glass, freshly squeezed orange juice and excellent fresh-ground coffee; faint piped music. This area spreads on back to a no smoking oak-boarded part with old prints and maps, more bentwood chairs, dining chairs, and (by a woodburning stove) another sofa and some wicker armchairs. On the right is a more formal dining layout, also no smoking, with big solid tables and attractive mediterranean photoprints by Georges Meris. Swiftly served by the friendly staff, enjoyable (though not cheap) food from a menu that changes once or twice during the season might include soup (£3.50), asparagus and pecorino tartlets on spinach with spring onion oil (£7.25), open ham sandwich (£7.50), and specials such as smoked trout mousse (£4.95), pigs cheek broth with borlotti beans (£7.95), steak burger (£8.25), creamy king prawn tagliatelle or vegetarian sushi (£8.95), fried salmon with noodles and stir-fried vegetables with soy dressing (£9.75), while puddings could be iced plum soufflé mousse or white chocolate and pecan nut tartlet (£4.95). The bread is baked on the premises and comes with proper butter; they also do cream teas (£4.50), good breakfasts (from 7 to 11.30; £10.45) and Sunday roasts (from £7.95); no mobile phones. *(Recommended by John Coatsworth, Paul and Ursula Randall, Anne and David Robinson, Stuart Paulley, Eithne Dandy)*

Free house ~ Licensees Mike Littlemore and Mrs Margaret Cox ~ Real ale ~ Bar food (12-9.30) ~ Restaurant ~ (01780) 410776 ~ Children welcome ~ Dogs allowed in bedrooms ~ Open 10-11; 12-10.30 Sun; closed 25 Dec ~ Bedrooms: £57.45B/£77.90B

The letters and figures after the name of each town are its Ordnance Survey map reference. *Using the Guide* at the beginning of the book explains how it helps you find a pub, in road atlases or large-scale maps as well as in our own maps.

THORPE LANGTON SP7492 Map 4

Bakers Arms

Village signposted off B6047 N of Market Harborough

Emphasis at this unpretentiously civilised thatched pub is on the deliciously imaginative well prepared food – it's definitely the place for a special meal out rather than a quick drink – and although tables are tightly packed in, it's a good idea to book as it does get very busy. Dishes could include home-made soup (£3.95), mediterranean vegetable tartlet with goats cheese and pesto dressing (£5.50), fried scallops with black pudding and orange sauce (£7.95), baked avocado with confit of red onions and brie (£10.95), pork fillet filled with mozzarella and sage served with tomato jus (£11.95), halibut on mustard tagliatelle (£15.95) and puddings such as sticky toffee pudding or vanilla brûlée with orange in Cointreau and orange tuile biscuit (£3.95). Stylishly simple old-fashioned furnishings in the knocked-through cottagey beamed interior include stripped pine tables and oriental rugs on bare boards, and nice black and white photographs; no games or piped music. They've a good wine list (also not cheap) with around five by the glass, well kept Tetleys on handpump, and in winter they do mulled wine too; the staff are friendly and attentive. The Bakers Arms is tucked away in a little village, and has picnic-sets in the garden. It's worth checking the opening times below carefully. *(Recommended by Catherine and Rob Dunster, Eric Locker, Gerry and Rosemary Dobson, Duncan Cloud, Laura and Stuart Ballantyne)*

Free house ~ Licensee Kate Hubbard ~ Real ale ~ Restaurant ~ (01858) 545201 ~ Children over 12 ~ Open 6.30-11; 12-3, 6.30-11 Sat; 12-3 Sun; closed Mon, lunchtime Tues-Fri, Sun evening

UPPER HAMBLETON SK9007 Map 4

Finches Arms

Village signposted from A606 on E edge of Oakham

The very good attractively presented food at this stone-built dining pub is cooked fresh to order so do be prepared for a wait during busy times. The menu changes frequently but combinations tend to be robustly modern. As well as home-made soup (£3.50) and filled paninis (from £4.95), dishes might include parma ham on rocket (£5.25), home-made foie gras medallions with caramelised onions and pickled beetroots (£8.25), wild mushroom, cherry tomato, parmesan and basil pappardelle (£8.95), confit duck leg wrapped in parma ham on braised savoy and red cabbage or braised lamb gigot and crispy bacon julienne on flageolet beans and mash (£12.95), fried bass on baked beef tomato with braised fennel, pappardelle and chorizo oil (£14.95), additional side orders (£1.95), elaborate home-made puddings such as white chocolate mousse with warm rum banana and caramel sauce and coconut tuile (£3.95), and cheese (£4.50). Given that this place is doing so well it's a shame that readers feel the service is professional rather than friendly. Both the bar and modern no smoking restaurant (which has delightful views over Rutland Water) have stylish cane furniture on wooden floors. Grainstore Cooking and a couple of guests such as Greene King Abbot and Oakham JHB are well kept on handpump; piped music, dominoes and cards. In summer the suntrap hillside terrace takes in the same views as the restaurant. If you stay, they do good breakfasts. *(Recommended by John Cook, J F M and M West, Michael Doswell, Anthony Barnes, Roy Bromell, Michael Dandy, Ruth Kitching, Derek and Sylvia Stephenson, Bob and Maggie Atherton, Colin McKerrow, David Field, Robert Turnham, Dr Brian and Mrs Anne Hamilton)*

Free house ~ Licensees Celia and Colin Crawford ~ Real ale ~ Bar food (12-2, 7-9; 12-9 Sun) ~ Restaurant ~ (01572) 756575 ~ Children welcome ~ Open 11-11; 12-10.30 Sun ~ Bedrooms: £65B/£75B

WING SK8903 Map 4

Kings Arms

Village signposted off A6003 S of Oakham; Top Street

Good news is that this well liked 17th-c inn seems to being doing just as well as ever under its friendly new licensee. With a notably welcoming atmosphere, the charming bar has a traditional feel, beams, some stripped stone and a flagstone floor, pine tables, old local photographs and a collection of tankards and old-fashioned whisky measuring pots. Two large log fires, one in a copper-canopied central hearth, make it very cosy in winter; they've also a snug. Friendly, helpful staff serve well kept Grainstore Cooking and Ten Fifty, and Marstons Pedigree, and a guest such as Shepherd Neame Spitfire on handpump; piped music. The restaurant (and bedrooms) are no smoking. Caution dictates that we remove the food award until more feedback satisfies us that the menu, with its new emphasis on fish dishes, is on consistently good form: soup (£3.95), ciabatta (from £4.50), scampi (£7.50), sausage and mash, goats cheese and feta with herbs in a filo parcel or crab cakes (£7.95), a proper steak and ale pie (£10.95), pork medallions (£14.50), monkfish (£15.25) and puddings such as bakewell tart or poached pears (£4.95). Outside are colourful hanging baskets in summer, and the sunny yew-sheltered garden has seats and a small play area. There's a medieval turf maze just up the road. *(Recommended by I J and S A Bufton, David and Brenda Tew, Stephen, Julie and Hayley Brown, Robert F Smith, Duncan Cloud, Rob Powys-Smith, JP, PP, Dennis and Gill Keen, Bob and Maggie Atherton, M and G Rushworth, Barry Collett, Alan and Jill Bull, Philip and June Caunt, Colin McKerrow, Jim Farmer, Anthony Barnes, Dave Braisted, Ken Marshall, Anthony R Locke)*

Free house ~ Licensee David Goss ~ Real ale ~ Bar food (12-2, 6-9) ~ Restaurant ~ (01572) 737634 ~ No children in restaurant after 7.30pm ~ Open 11-3, 6-11; 11-11 Sat; 12-10.30 Sun ~ Bedrooms: £60B/£70B

LUCKY DIP

Besides the fully inspected pubs, you might like to try these Lucky Dips recommended to us and described by readers (if you do, please send us reports: www.goodguides.co.uk).

ASHBY PARVA SP5288
Holly Bush [Main St; off A426 N of Lutterworth, not far from M1 junction 20]: Roomy but cosily and comfortably divided, with interesting hop-draped side room, good value generous food, friendly efficient service, well kept beers inc guests, restaurant area; barbecues in garden *(J M Tansey)*

BARKBY SK6309
Brookside Inn [Brookside, towards Beeby; off A607 6 miles NE of Leicester]: Refurbished two-bar pub with well kept Burtonwood and guest beers, welcoming service, food (not Sun evening) from sandwiches and hot baguettes up, log fire in modernised lounge, extended dining area; garden tables, pretty village by little stream with intriguing footbridges to houses opposite, cl Tues lunchtime *(Rona Murdoch)*

Malt Shovel [Main St]: Thriving village local with U-shaped bar and no smoking room off, well kept Greene King Abbot, Marstons Bitter and Pedigree, Tetleys and a guest beer, good choice of food inc Mon steak night; Sun quiz night; garden and partly covered heated terrace *(CMW, JJW, Jim Farmer)*

BARNSDALE SK9008
☆ *Barnsdale Lodge* [just off A606 Oakham—Stamford]: Hotel's extensive conservatory dining bar with good food choice, inventive, generous and attractively presented (service charge added, but may be an off-menu locally advertised set lunch bargain); charming décor, plenty of friendly attentive staff, pricey real ales such as Courage Directors, Grainstore Ten Fifty and Greene King Old Speckled Hen and Ruddles, good sitting-roomish coffee lounge, cream teas; pleasant gardens, bedrooms comfortable and attractive, with good breakfast, adjacent antiques centre and handy for Barnsdale Gardens *(BB, David Coleman, George Atkinson, Gerry and Rosemary Dobson, Roy Bromell)*

BARROW UPON SOAR SK5717
Navigation [off South St (B5328)]: Extended split-level pub based on former barge-horse stabling, good value freshly made food (may be limited winter) inc interestingly filled baguettes and Sun roast, well kept Adnams, Marstons Pedigree, Timothy Taylors Landlord and a guest beer, keen friendly licensees, daily papers, central open fire, unusual bar top made from old pennies, old local photographs, darts, skittle alley, family room; piped music, SkyTV, games machine; open all day, lovely canal view from small back terrace with

moorings *(Bernie Adams, Rona Murdoch)*

BELTON SK4420

Queens Head [off A512/A453 between junctions 23 and 24, M1; Long St]: Former coaching inn attractively refurbished under new owners, two comfortable bare-boards bar areas with leather seating, up-to-date food from ciabattas to imaginative blackboard dishes in log-fire dining area, welcoming efficient service, well kept real ales, good wines and proper coffee, more formal restaurant (with tables out on decking); tables on lawn, six bedrooms, attractive village *(John and Sylvia Harrop)*

BOTCHESTON SK4805

Greyhound [Main St, off B5380 E of Desford]: Traditional two-bar village pub under welcoming new management, good freshly made food inc lunchtime and evening special deals such as enterprising Mon pie and wine night, children's food and Sun carvery roasts, well kept Burtonwood, small no smoking restaurant *(Bernie Adams, Rod Weston, Barbara Barber, Stan and Dot Garner, Michael and Pam Miller)*

BRANSTON SK8129

Wheel [Main St]: New landlord in 18th-c village pub next to church, two cosy and comfortable bars, log fires, growing reputation for enjoyable food (not Mon/Tues) inc separate grill menu, friendly atmosphere, well kept Adnams and a changing guest beer, good short reasonably priced wine choice, plans for restaurant (and for all-day summer opening); attractive garden, splendid countryside nr Belvoir castle, cl Mon/Tues lunchtimes *(Mr and Mrs R P Begg)*

BRAUNSTON SK8306

☆ *Blue Ball* [off A606 in Oakham; Cedar St]: Pretty thatched and beamed dining pub in attractive village, country pine in spotless linked rooms inc no smoking room and small conservatory, good interesting food inc children's helpings, friendly service, good range of well kept ales and wines, lovely open fire; dominoes, shove-ha'penny; children welcome, open all day Sun *(Barry Collett, LYM, R V Peel, P Tailyour)*

BRUNTINGTHORPE SP6089

Joiners Arms [Church Walk/Cross St]: More bistro restaurant than pub, with good up-to-date food in three beamed areas of open-plan dining lounge, Greene King IPA from small bar counter, short choice of decent wines, lots of china and brasses, friendly staff; cl Sun evening and Mon *(Gerry and Rosemary Dobson)*

BURROUGH ON THE HILL SK7510

Stag & Hounds [off B6047 S of Melton Mowbray; Main St]: Pleasant mix of customers, well kept real ale, attractively priced food, friendly new licensees, open fires, dining room; children allowed, garden with play area *(LYM, Duncan Cloud, Jim Farmer)*

BURTON OVERY SP6797

Bell [Main St]: Warmly welcoming and enthusiastic licensees and staff in L-shaped open-plan pub with cushioned wall seats, good open fire, honest home cooking inc bargain snacks and children's dishes, well kept Adnams, Bass, Greene King Old Speckled Hen and Marstons Pedigree, darts and fruit machine round corner, separate skittle alley; children welcome, good garden, lovely village, open all day wknds *(Rona Murdoch)*

CHURCH LANGTON SP7293

Langton Arms [B6047 about 3 miles N of Mkt Harborough; just off A6]: Extended village pub with wide choice of good value nicely presented food inc quite a lot of pasta dishes under new Italian landlord, well kept Grainstore and Greene King IPA, reasonably priced house wines, good service even when busy, no smoking restaurant; piped music; garden with play area *(Gerry and Rosemary Dobson, Jim Farmer)*

COLEORTON SK4016

Kings Arms [The Moor (off A512)]: Two-bar village pub extended into cottage next door, three real ales, good choice of other drinks and of reasonably priced fresh food inc children's and lunchtime bargains; may be piped radio; picnic-sets under cocktail parasols in front garden *(CMW, JJW)*

CROXTON KERRIAL SK8329

☆ *Peacock* [A607 SW of Grantham]: 17th-c former coaching inn with good generous home cooking in long bar and garden room (different choice in attractive restaurant), real ales, decent wines, hops on beams, real fire partitioned off at one end, some bric-a-brac, pleasant service (get the barman started on his ghost stories); well behaved children welcome, picnic-sets in garden, bedroom block with own bathrooms *(Richard and Liz Dilnot, Phil and Jane Hodson)*

DADLINGTON SP4097

Dog & Hedgehog [The Green]: Comfortably extended much restored olde-worlde 17th-c pub with minstrel's gallery, polite attentive staff, very wide choice of generous sensibly priced food inc fish and enormous grills, great views over Ashby Canal and Bosworth Field; horse tethers, cycle rack *(J A Bird, Graham Manwaring)*

ELMESTHORPE SP4696

Wentworth Arms [Station Rd]: Roomy rather modern-style pub with decent straightforward food from baguettes up, Greene King IPA, friendly service; large terrace with plenty of picnic-sets, paddock with play area *(George Atkinson)*

ENDERBY SP5399

Plough [Mill Hill]: Cosy and spacious, home-made food (they do their best to suit special wishes), good range of puddings, Marstons real ales, decent house wines, no smoking eating area *(Stuart Paulley)*

FLECKNEY SP6493

Golden Shield [Main St]: Popular two-course bargain lunches Weds-Sat, good beer range inc Greene King Abbot, successful indian restaurant Sun-Tues evenings inc take-aways *(P Tailyour)*

GLOOSTON SP7595

☆ *Old Barn* [off B6047 in Tur Langton]: Pleasant 16th-c village pub with beams, stripped kitchen tables, country chairs and log fire, well kept changing ales such as Batemans, Fullers London Pride and Woodfordes Wherry, flexible helpful service, enjoyable if not cheap food, no smoking dining area (well behaved children allowed); tables out in front, bedrooms with compact shower cabinets, good breakfast, cl Mon lunchtime *(Bernie Adams, LYM, Stephen, Julie and Hayley Brown, Duncan Cloud, Jim Farmer, David Field, Rona Murdoch)*

GREAT BOWDEN SP7488

☆ *Red Lion* [off A6 N of Mkt Harboro; Main St]: Attractively reworked with open fire, comfy sofas, well spaced tables on polished boards inc a group of ultra-tall seats at two lofty tables, deep red walls, smart dining room, up to four well kept real ales such as Greene King Abbot, Jennings Cumberland (Nov beer festival) and Charles Wells Bombardier, well chosen wines, short but interesting weekly changing menu, Sun roast; piped music; children and dogs welcome, tables in big garden, bedrooms, open all day wknds *(Stephen, Julie and Hayley Brown, Duncan Cloud, Eric George, Rona Murdoch, LYM)*

GREAT GLEN SP6597

Old Greyhound [A6 Leicester—Mkt Harboro]: Reopened after extensive renovation with increasing emphasis on the food side, Adnams Broadside and Greene King Abbot, friendly service *(David Field)*

Yews [A6]: Stylishly refurbished and roomy Chef & Brewer, spreading series of softly lit and relaxing separate areas, wide range of enjoyable freshly made food, good wine choice, Greene King Old Speckled Hen, Marstons Pedigree and a guest beer, coal fires; piped music; good disabled access and facilities, big attractive garden with terrace, open all day *(John Saville, BB, P Tailyour)*

GREETHAM SK9214

☆ *Wheatsheaf* [B668 Stretton—Cottesmore]: Comfortable and welcoming L-shaped communicating rooms, country prints and plates on dining room walls, odd pivoted clock, blazing open woodburner in stone fireplace, wide choice of good value generous food served till 11 from baguettes through bargain wkdy lunches and specials to lots of chargrills, well kept John Smiths and Tetleys, polite, cheerful speedy service, darts and pool in end room; soft piped music; wheelchair access, picnic-sets out on front lawn and in tidy garden by back car park beside pretty little stream, bedrooms in annexe *(Michael and Jenny Back, BB)*

HALLATON SP7896

☆ *Bewicke Arms* [off B6047 or B664]: Old thatched pub with sensibly priced food from sandwiches to steak, inventive specials, sensible prices, well kept beers such as Flowers IPA and Grainstore Cooking, friendly landlady, log fires, pine furnishings, orange paintwork, some interesting memorabilia about the ancient local Easter Monday inter-village bottle-kicking match; darts, shove-ha'penny, piped music; children in eating areas, stables tearoom across yard, big terrace overlooking paddock and lake, pretty spot, open all day Sun *(LYM, J M Tansey, Patrick Hancock, Jim Farmer, Pat and Roger Fereday, Mike Huysinga, Duncan Cloud)*

Fox [North End]: Comfortable country pub with good value menu, well kept Bass and Tetleys, good value wine, compact no smoking area; children welcome, sizeable attractive garden with duckpond and playthings *(O K Smyth, Gerry and Rosemary Dobson)*

HEMINGTON SK4527

Jolly Sailor [Main St]: Welcoming village local with enjoyable fresh food (not wkdy evenings or Sun), friendly service, well kept Bass, Greene King Abbot, Marstons Pedigree and two guest beers, summer farm cider, decent wines by the glass, good range of malt whiskies and other spirits; good open fire each end, big country pictures, bric-a-brac on heavy beams and shelves, candlelit back restaurant, table skittles, pub dog; quiet piped music, games machines; beautiful hanging baskets and picnic-sets out in front, open all day wknds *(Rona Murdoch, the Didler, CMW, JJW)*

HOSE SK7329

☆ *Rose & Crown* [Bolton Lane]: Unpretentious Vale of Belvoir pub with four or five well kept and well priced real ales from far and wide, friendly attentive service, pub games, generous low-priced standard food (not Sun evening) from baguettes to Sun lunch, no smoking areas in lounge and dining room (children allowed), pub games; piped music; tables on fairy-lit back terrace, fenced family area, cl lunchtimes Mon-Weds *(JP, PP, LYM, the Didler, David Glynne-Jones)*

ILLSTON ON THE HILL SP7099

☆ *Fox & Goose* [Main St, off B6047 Mkt Harboro—Melton]: Welcoming and idiosyncratic unspoilt chatty two-bar local, plain but comfortable and convivial, with interesting pictures and assorted oddments, well kept Everards ales with a guest beer, table lamps, good coal fire; no food, but bedrooms sometimes available *(LYM, JP, PP, Bernie Adams)*

KEGWORTH SK4826

Britannia [London Rd]: Newish management doing very low-priced food 12-8.30, and perhaps well kept Hardys & Hansons *(the Didler, M J Winterton)*

Red Lion [a mile from M1 junction 24, via A6 towards Loughborough; High St]: Very traditional brightly lit village local with four plainish rooms around small servery, well kept Adnams, Banks's Original and several guest beers, limited choice of good wholesome food, good prices; assorted furniture, coal and flame-effect fires, delft shelf of beer bottles, daily papers, darts and cards; picnic-sets in small back yard, garden with play area, open all day *(the Didler, JP, PP, BB, Pete Baker)*

☆ *Station Hotel* [Station Rd towards West Leake, actually just over the Notts border (and its postal address is in Derbyshire!)]: Busy well refurbished pub with bare brick and woodwork, coal fires, two rooms off small bar area, well kept Bass, Courage Directors, Worthington and guest beers, upstairs restaurant with good home cooking; big back lawn, play area, simple good bedrooms sharing bathroom *(JP, PP, the Didler)*

KIBWORTH BEAUCHAMP SP6893

☆ *Coach & Horses* [A6 S of Leicester]: Congenial turkey-carpeted local with friendly efficient staff, wide choice of good honest home-made food (mainly roasts on Sun), well kept beers such as Bass and Wadworths 6X, heartening log fire in huge end inglenook, china and pewter mugs on beams, relaxing candlelit restaurant *(Eric Locker, Duncan Cloud, Rona Murdoch, BB, Jim Farmer)*

KIRBY MUXLOE SK5104

Royal Oak [Main St]: Comfortably refurbished modernish pub with enjoyable food from wide range of baguettes through usual bar dishes to fish specialities and good value Sun lunch, early evening bargains, good friendly service, well kept Adnams and Everards, good wine list, sizeable no smoking restaurant; handy for nearby 15th-c castle ruins *(Gerry and Rosemary Dobson)*

KNOSSINGTON SK8008

Fox & Hounds [off A606 W of Oakham; Somerby Rd]: Small beamed country pub with gifted new chef/landlord doing good interesting food at reasonable prices, well kept Courage with guests such as Bass and Boddingtons, decent wines, lots of malt whiskies, coal fire in cosy comfortable lounge, small restaurant (best to book), darts, pool room for younger customers; summer barbecues in big garden *(Bernie Adams)*

LANGHAM SK8411

☆ *Noel Arms* [Bridge St]: Beams, flagstones and lots of pictures in long pleasant low-ceilinged bar/dining area, friendly service, a welcome for children, enjoyable generous fairly priced food, well kept Greene King Abbot and Tetleys, central log fire; may be piped music, well behaved dogs allowed; good tables on front terrace, new bedrooms *(JES, LYM, David and Helen Wilkins, J M Tansey)*

LEICESTER SK5804

Ale Wagon [Rutland St/Charles St]: Basic two-room 1930s interior, with changing ales inc those brewed for Hoskins & Oldfield by Tower in Burton, also Weston's perry; open all day, handy for station *(the Didler)*

Black Horse [Braunstone Gate/Foxon St]: Unspoilt two-room corner local with Everards real ale, traditional layout (with outside lavatories), darts and dominoes, character back lounge *(Pete Baker)*

Gateway [The Gateway]: Tynemill pub in old hosiery factory (ladies' underwear on show), bare boards except in no smoking area, five interesting changing ales (one at bargain price), good reasonably priced range of other drinks, sensibly priced food all day till 8 (6 Sun) inc Sun carvery and good vegetarian/vegan range, friendly knowledgeable service; piped music (may be turned down if loud), big-screen SkyTV, quiz Sun; disabled access and facilities, open all day *(the Didler, CMW, JJW)*

☆ *Globe* [Silver St]: Well refurbished early 18th-c town pub, lots of woodwork in four old-fashioned uncluttered areas off central bar, charming more peaceful upstairs dining room, wrought-iron gas lamps, well kept Everards ales, nicely priced honest food 12-7, keen young landlord and knowledgeable friendly staff, children allowed in some parts; Monopoly machine, piped pop music (not in snug), very popular with young people wknd evenings – doorman then; open all day *(the Didler, Dave Irving, Rona Murdoch, LYM, Val and Alan Green, CMW, JJW, J M Tansey)*

Hat & Beaver [Highcross St]: Basic two-room local handy for Shires shopping centre, good value well filled rolls, Hardys & Hansons real ales; TV *(the Didler, CMW, JJW)*

Marquis of Wellington [London Rd]: Splendid gold and black Edwardian exterior, open-plan but good décor, with old Leicester photographs on high panelling, bare boards, soft lighting, well kept Everards ales from long marble counter, decent usual food, good friendly service, flame-effect gas fire; piped music may be loud, big-screen TV, fruit machine; open all day, disabled access and facilities, colourful heated back courtyard with murals and attractive plants *(Duncan Cloud, J M Tansey)*

Out of the Vaults [Wellington St]: Basic concrete-floored cellar bar reopened under new name, with interesting well kept quickly changing microbrews, some tapped from the cask; low ceiling with iron pillars (can get smoky), tall settles forming booths, stripped brick walls with enamel advertising signs; may be cl Mon-Thurs lunchtime *(G Coates)*

Swan & Rushes [Oxford St/Infirmary Sq]: Well kept Oakham JHB and changing guest beers, several imported beers on tap and many dozens in bottle, farm cider, beer festivals, enjoyable food inc frequent continental theme nights; open all day *(the Didler, J M Tansey)*

LEIRE SP5290

White Horse [Main St]: Open-plan dining pub doing well under new Spanish landlord, with good choice of enjoyable fairly priced food from ciabattas and interesting snacks up, Greene King Abbot and Tetleys; children welcome, has been open all day wknds *(P Tailyour)*

LOUGHBOROUGH SK5319

Albion [canal bank, about ¼ mile from Loughborough Wharf]: Down-to-earth little old canalside local with emphasis on well kept changing ales such as Mansfield, Robinsons and local Wicked Hathern; friendly owners, cheap straightforward home-made food, coal fire; children welcome, occasional barbecues, budgerigar aviary in pleasant big courtyard *(Bernie Adams, the Didler, JP, PP)*

☆ *Swan in the Rushes* [A6]: Good range of well kept ales tapped from the cask and plenty of foreign bottled beers in cheery down-to-earth bare-boards town local; low-priced straightforward food (not Sat/Sun evenings), daily papers, traditional games, open fire, three smallish high-ceilinged rooms – can get crowded; children in eating areas, tables outside, open all day *(the Didler, LYM, BB, JP, PP, Pete Baker, Theocsbrian, Les Baldwin, Sue Demont, Tim Barrow)*

Three Nuns [Church Gate]: Traditional décor, good range of well kept ales and country wines, good value food the main lunchtime draw, popular with students at night; may be live music Sat *(Paul Horsfield)*

LUTTERWORTH SP5484

Unicorn [Church St]: Welcoming traditional town pub, banquettes in lounge and back restaurant, low-priced food from sandwiches up inc children's dishes and popular OAP bargain lunches, Sat night steak special, nice log fire, Bass, M&B Brew XI and Robinsons, more basic bar; sports TV, no credit cards *(P Tailyour, Rona Murdoch)*

MANTON SK8704

Horse & Jockey [St Marys Rd]: Unpretentious early 19th-c pub with big coal fire, good value promptly served bar food, well kept Greene King IPA; plenty of picnic-sets outside, on Rutland Water cycle route, comfortable bedrooms *(Glenwys and Alan Lawrence)*

MARKET BOSWORTH SK4003

Black Horse [Market Pl]: 18th-c, with several beamed rooms, wide choice of enjoyable plentiful food, cheerful helpful service, well kept Adnams and Greene King, good house wines and coffee, cosy local bustle, log fire, comfortable restaurant; tables outside – nice setting next to almshouses in attractive village not far from Bosworth Field *(R T and J C Moggridge, Joan and Tony Walker)*

☆ *Old Red Lion* [Park St; from centre follow Leicester and Hinckley signs]: Cheerful black-beamed split-level pub with sensibly priced food from sandwiches and baked potatoes up inc proper steak and kidney pie, plushly tidy L-shaped bar with real ales such as Banks's Bitter and Mild, Marstons Pedigree and Theakstons XB and Old Peculier, choice of ciders, good service; may be piped music; children welcome, tables and play area in sheltered courtyard, bedrooms, attractive village *(LYM, Pete Baker)*

MARKET HARBOROUGH SP7387

Sugar Loaf [High St]: Popular Wetherspoons, smaller than many (no smoking area could be expanded), good choice of real ales and good value food, no piped music; open all day *(P Tailyour, Stephen, Julie and Hayley Brown)*

☆ *Three Swans* [High St]: Comfortable and handsome coaching inn renovated as Best Western conference hotel, beams and old local prints in plush and peaceful panelled front bar, comfortable no smoking back dining lounge and fine courtyard conservatory (also no smoking) in more modern part, wide range of good value bar lunches from sandwiches up, some bar food early evenings, well kept Courage Directors and a guest beer such as Everards Tiger, decent wines, good coffee, friendly helpful staff, more formal upstairs restaurant; piped music; attractive suntrap courtyard, good bedroom extension *(George Atkinson, Michael Tack, Gerry and Rosemary Dobson)*

MELTON MOWBRAY SK7519

Anne of Cleves [Burton St, by St Mary's Church]: Basic-feel pub in former monks' chantry attached to parish church, stripped tables on flagstones, Tudor beams and stonework, cheery staff, separate snug for smokers, well kept Everards Tiger and a guest beer, popular unpretentious food, small end dining room and no smoking room; may be piped music, no under-7s; open all day, Sun afternoon closure *(Tony and Wendy Hobden, Duncan Cloud)*

Harboro Hotel [Burton St (A606 to Oakham)]: Usual sensibly priced bar food from baguettes up, pleasant welcoming service, Marstons Pedigree, restaurant; bedrooms *(Tom Evans)*

MOUNTSORREL SK5815

Waterside [Sileby Rd]: Comfortable modern split-level lounge and dining area overlooking busy lock on the Soar, four well kept Everards ales, good range of bar food from filled baps to Sun roast (to order, so may be a wait); piped music, games machine; children welcome, disabled access and facilities, picnic-sets outside *(Bernie Adams)*

MUSTON SK8237

Muston Gap [Church Lane; just off A52 W of Grantham]: Big family-oriented Brewers Fayre with large bar and several light and airy no smoking dining areas, wide choice of reliable good value family food – at busy times you get a pager to tell you when it's ready, friendly staff, well kept Flowers IPA, decent wines, good disabled access and facilities; tables outside with play area *(Richard Lewis, Phil and Jane Hodson)*

OADBY SP6399

Grange Farm [Florence Wragg Way, just off A6]: Attractive early 19th-c farmhouse sympathetically converted to roomy Vintage Inn, log fires, old local photographs, daily papers, wide food range from lunchtime sandwiches to steak, bass and Sun roast, friendly staff, well kept ales, good wine and whisky choice, good mix of customers, no smoking area; picnic-sets out in front *(Mr and Mrs D Moir)*

OAKHAM SK8508

Admiral Hornblower [High St]: Several differently decorated areas for eating or drinking, warm and inviting with three open fires, interesting menu, well kept Oakham Triple B and Cooking, polite prompt service, conservatory; outside tables *(Mike Buckingham)*

Odd House [Station Rd/Burley Rd]: Attractive old pub with good low-priced food inc gargantuan mixed grill, good service *(Robert Turnham)*

QUENIBOROUGH SK6412

Britannia: Enjoyable traditional home cooking under new management, real ales, popular weekly quiz night *(Kate Jones)*

REDMILE SK8036

Windmill [off A52 Grantham—Nottingham; Main St]: Comfortable and relaxed lounge and dining room, wide choice of enjoyable good value home-made food from baguettes to steaks and Sun roasts, well kept Boddingtons and Wadworths 6X, good house wines, friendly staff; children welcome *(Bernie Adams)*

RYHALL TF0310

Millstone [Bridge St]: Comfortably plush village local with congenial licensees, generous fresh food that's interesting without being pretentious, from baguettes to choice of Sun roasts, well kept Mansfield and Marstons ales, good short wine choice, lots of malt whiskies, proper coffee, small no smoking restaurant, separate bar with pool and juke box; well behaved children welcome *(Martin and Helen Ball, Susan Pennant Jones)*

SALTBY SK8426

Nags Head [Back St]: Friendly and attractive old small pub with good choice of enjoyable low-priced home cooking; extension planned *(R and M Tait)*

SEATON SP9098

George & Dragon [Church Lane, off B672 Caldecott—S Luffenham]: Two bars, one for dining with pine furniture and generous attractively priced food cooked to order, friendly helpful landlord, quick service, well kept Greene King IPA, Marstons Pedigree and Theakstons Best, good wine choice; juke box, pool; tables outside, unspoilt village, good views of famous viaduct *(Miss Joan Morgan, Jim Farmer)*

SHEARSBY SP6290

☆ *Chandlers Arms* [Fenny Lane, off A50 Leicester—Northampton]: Comfortable and friendly, with brocaded wall seats, wheelback chairs, flowers on tables, house plants, swagged curtains, candlemaker pictures, well kept Marstons with a guest such as Batemans, no smoking bar on left, interesting food choice (not Sun evening) with imaginative vegetarian and vegan dishes, attentive service, plenty of locals; may be piped music; tables in secluded raised garden, attractive village *(Bernie Adams, Rona Murdoch, David Coleman, BB, George Atkinson)*

SIBSON SK3500

☆ *Cock* [A444 N of Nuneaton; Twycross Rd]: Ancient picturesque black and white timbered building, low doorways, heavy black beams and genuine latticed windows, immense inglenook, three no smoking areas; well kept Bass, Hook Norton Best and a guest such as Greene King Old Speckled Hen, a dozen wines by the glass, bar food (not cheap) till 10pm; fruit machine, piped music; children welcome, tables in courtyard and small garden, handy for Bosworth Field *(Joan and Tony Walker, W and P J Elderkin, John and Wendy Allin, Leigh and Gillian Mellor, LYM)*

SILEBY SK6015

☆ *White Swan* [Swan St]: Bright, cheerful and relaxed, with imaginative attractively priced home cooking (not Sun evening or Mon lunchtime) from snacks up inc wkdy bargains and real puddings, well kept Marstons Pedigree, nice house wines, good friendly service, comfortable and welcoming dining lounge, small tasteful book-lined restaurant (booking needed) *(Joe Brown, Jim Farmer)*

SNARESTONE SK3510

Odd House [Bosworth Rd]: Former 17th-c coaching inn with enjoyable blackboard food inc some unusual dishes, fish night last Fri of month, well kept ales such as Fullers London Pride, Greene King Abbot, Marstons Pedigree and Wye Valley, traditional games in one bar, pool room, restaurant (not Sun/Mon evenings); tables outside with boules and big sturdy play area, eight good value bedrooms with own bathrooms, cl wkdy lunchtimes, open all day wknds *(Kevin and Bruna Lovelock, Derek and Sylvia Stephenson)*

SOUTH CROXTON SK6810

Golden Fleece [Main St]: Large, clean and friendly, with enjoyable fresh food from good baguettes to popular Sun lunch, proper bar with some sofas, dark corners and attractive separate restaurant, good service, well kept ales such as Bass, M&B Mild, Marstons Pedigree and Timothy Taylors Landlord, good house wine, log fire; big TV; lovely area *(David Field)*

SOUTH LUFFENHAM SK9401

Coach House [Stamford Rd A6121)]: Good-sized bar with modern upmarket décor, much scrubbed pine furniture, chef/landlord doing enjoyable bar food, changing real ales such as Greene King, quick friendly service even when busy, attractive restaurant *(Glyn and Janet Lewis)*

STAPLETON SP4398

Nags Head [A447 N of Hinckley]: Two smallish congenial rooms served by same bar, all no smoking at lunchtime (very popular then), friendly helpful service, enjoyable low-priced food from sandwiches and baguettes up, wider evening choice though still straightforward, Everards Tiger and Marstons Bitter and Pedigree, no music, restaurant; good-sized garden with play area *(Gerry and Rosemary Dobson, Stuart Turner)*

SUTTON CHENEY SK4100

☆ *Hercules* [off A447 3 miles S of Market Bosworth]: Attractive old local with darts and dominoes in cheerfully comfortable long bar, good choice of home-made bar lunches inc generous OAP meals, evening restaurant (not Mon; also Sun lunch), friendly staff (chatty obliging landlord was a Wolves footballer), well kept Bass and Tetleys, blazing log fire; piped music can be rather loud; Sun quiz night, children welcome, cl Mon lunchtime *(Bernie Adams, LYM, George Atkinson)*

SWITHLAND SK5413

☆ *Griffin* [Main St; between A6 and B5330, between Loughborough and Leicester]: Good value local, with well kept Everards, good unassuming food from sandwiches up (not Sun-Tues evenings), friendly staff, pleasant décor in two cosy arch-linked rooms with old-fashioned woodburners, separate restaurant and pool room; back skittle alley, Weds quiz night, quiet piped music; gardens by stream, nice setting, plans for bedrooms in stable block *(LYM, CMW, JJW, Pete Baker, David Glynne-Jones, Duncan Cloud)*

THORNTON SK4607
Bricklayers Arms [S of M1 junction 22; Main St]: Compact traditional village local with roaring fire and old photographs in nicely refurbished beamed bar, good value food inc bargain lunches, well kept Marstons Pedigree, friendly landlord and good staff, cosy dining room; piped radio, quiz nights; large back garden with play area, handy for reservoir walks *(Bernie Adams, W and P J Elderkin)*

THORPE SATCHVILLE SK7311
Fox [Main St]: 1930s tap for nearby John o' Gaunt brewery, three or four well kept ales, good choice of enjoyable generous food, friendly landlord, no smoking lounge/dining area, children's books and games, pool and darts in games room; quiet piped music; picnic-sets in front and in back garden with play area, small budgerigar aviary *(CMW, JJW)*

THRINGSTONE SK4217
George & Dragon [Ashby Rd]: Pleasantly refurbished, with varied bistro food at reasonable prices, young friendly efficient staff, well kept Greene King Abbot and Marstons Pedigree *(Ian and Jane Irving)*

THURCASTON SK5611
Wheatsheaf [Leicester Rd]: Cosy and clean open-plan village pub, well kept ales such as Adnams, Everards Tiger, Hook Norton Old Hooky and Marstons Pedigree, enjoyable home-made food from sandwiches to fish caught by the landlord, friendly staff, plush seating, beams and two log fires; tables on prettily planted terrace, well appointed skittle alley *(anon)*

UPPINGHAM SP8699
Falcon [High St East/Market Sq]: Civilised coaching inn with plenty of character in oak-panelled bar and comfortable lounge, light and airy, with skylights and big windows over market sq, pleasant light lunches inc sandwiches and rolls, afternoon teas, cheerful willing staff, well kept real ale, good coffee, nice open fire, daily papers; bedrooms, back barrier-exit car park *(P Tailyour)*
Vaults [Market Pl]: Attractive family-run pub next to church, well kept Marstons ales, reliable reasonably priced fresh food, comfortable banquettes; piped music; some tables out overlooking picturesque square, bedrooms *(Barry Collett, P Tailyour)*

WALCOTE SP5683
☆ *Black Horse* [1½ miles from M1 junction 20 towards Market Harborough]: Unpretentious pub noted for short choice of authentic thai food (not Mon or Tues lunchtime) cooked by the long-serving landlady, good value big helpings, friendly efficient service, half a dozen good well kept real ales inc Timothy Taylors Landlord, interesting bottled beers and country wines, no smoking restaurant; no dogs *(LYM, Mike Pugh, Rona Murdoch)*

WALTHAM ON THE WOLDS SK8024
☆ *Royal Horseshoes* [Melton Rd (A607)]: Attractive thatched stone-built inn, sturdily furnished and comfortable, with new chef doing enjoyable food, friendly staff, well kept real ales, decent wines and fair range of malts, spotless housekeeping, three open fires, interesting aquarium in dining lounge; may be piped music; children welcome in eating area, tables outside, bedrooms *(LYM, Phil and Jane Hodson)*

WHITWICK SK4316
Three Horseshoes [Leicester Rd]: Friendly and utterly unpretentious local, bar and tiny smoke room, well kept Bass and M&B Mild, darts, dominoes and cards, no food – the sort of place that has raffles, loan clubs and trips to the races; outdoor lavatories *(Pete Baker, the Didler)*

WIGSTON SP6098
Horse & Trumpet [Bull Head St]: Big friendly local, with bare boards and well kept Everards beers; spotlessly clean, good value generous lunchtime food (very popular on pensions day), skittle alley *(J M Tansey)*

WOODHOUSE EAVES SK5214
☆ *Pear Tree* [Church Hill; main street, off B591 W of Quorndon]: Attractive upper flagstoned food area with pitched roof and pews forming booths, open kitchen doing wide choice of food all day (not Sun night) from sandwiches to grills, friendly attentive staff, real ales such as Jennings Cumberland and Youngs Special, good choice of malt whiskies, decent wines, keen prices; hunting prints in simply furnished lower pub part with conservatory, log fire; piped music may obtrude; children welcome, two large friendly dogs, picnic-sets outside with summer bar, good nearby walks, open all day *(JP, PP, LYM, David Glynne-Jones, George Atkinson, Mick and Moira Brummell)*
☆ *Wheatsheaf* [Brand Hill; beyond Main St, off B591 S of Loughborough]: Busy open-plan beamed country pub with light and airy upstairs dining area, smart customers, good interesting home-cooked food from sandwiches to chargrills and other upmarket dishes, changing ales such as Greene King Abbot, Hook Norton Best, Timothy Taylors Landlord and Tetleys, good house wines, friendly landlord, attentive helpful service, log fire, motor-racing memorabilia; floodlit tables outside, dogs welcome but no motor-cyclists or children *(JP, PP, the Didler, LYM, David Field, David Glynne-Jones)*

WYMESWOLD SK6023
Three Crowns [45 Far St]: Snug 18th-c village pub with welcoming chatty atmosphere, good value lunchtime food, well kept Adnams, Marstons, Tetleys and usually a local guest beer, pleasant character furnishings in beamed bar and lounge with steps up to cosy no smoking area, darts; games machine, quiz nights; picnic-sets on small attractive terrace *(the Didler, CMW, JJW)*

WYMONDHAM SK8518
Berkeley Arms [Main St]: Welcoming and attractive old stone building, two cosy bars comfortably done up, enjoyable freshly made straightforward food from crusty bread sandwiches up, nice prices, good choice of beers such as Adnams, Marstons Pedigree and Tetleys, good coffee; restaurant *(anon)*

Lincolnshire

This year we have three new entries here: the attractively refurbished Blue Bell at Belchford (its keen young licensees serving good food in an inviting atmosphere), the splendid Angel & Royal in Grantham (a luxurious hotel now, but with a wonderful collection of malt whiskies in its hauntingly ancient bar, and a good value brasserie), and the civilised and relaxed Blacksmiths Arms at Rothwell (good all round). Other current front-runners here are the friendly Chequers at Gedney Dyke (the landlady cooks consistently good imaginative food here), the chattily unpretentious Victoria in Lincoln (excellent beers, cheap food), the interesting Blue Cow at South Witham (friendly and individual, brewing its own good beer), the extremely well run and elegant old George of Stamford (good food, fine wines and a nice place to stay), and the immaculate Mermaid at Surfleet (another consistently good all-rounder). It is the George of Stamford which for the third year running takes the title of Lincolnshire Dining Pub of the Year – certainly rewarding for a special meal out. In the Lucky Dip section at the end of the chapter, pubs to note particularly are the Bell at Halton Holegate, White Swan at Scotter, Cross Keys at Stow, Kings Head at Tealby, White Hart at Tetford and Abbey Lodge at Woodhall Spa. Drinks prices are close to the national average, with the main local brewer, Batemans, usually particularly good value. Other smaller local breweries to look out for include Oldershaws, Highwood and Newby Wyke.

ALLINGTON SK8540 Map 7

Welby Arms

The Green; off A1 N of Grantham, or A52 W of Grantham

Set in pleasant countryside, this bustling village pub is a handy place to take a break from the nearby A1. The civilised back no smoking dining lounge (where they prefer you to eat) looks out on to tables in a sheltered walled courtyard with pretty hanging baskets in summer. The large bar area is divided by a stone archway and has black beams and joists, log fires (one in an attractive arched brick fireplace), red velvet curtains and comfortable burgundy button-back wall banquettes and stools. A back courtyard formed by the restaurant extension and the bedroom block beyond has tables, with more picnic-sets out on the front lawn. Bass, John Smiths, Timothy Taylors Landlord and three guests such as Adnams Regatta, Hop Back Summer Lightning and Phoenix Wobbly Bob are well kept, but served through a sparkler. They have decent wines including ten by the glass, and a good range of country wines; dominoes, and piped music. It's advisable to book if you want to eat here, especially at weekends, and besides lunchtime filled baguettes and ploughman's (from £3.95, lunchtime only), bar food might include home-made soup (£2.95), home-made salmon fishcake with spicy salsa (£3.95), stuffed chicken with cream cheese and leek sauce or popular grimsby battered haddock (£7.95), and salmon with honey and ginger glaze or beef stroganoff (£10.95), with home-made puddings such as white chocolate cheesecake or banoffi pie (£2.95); they do Sunday roasts (£6.95). *(Recommended by Michael and Jenny Back, MJVK, Kevin Thorpe, Mrs J Caunt, the Didler, Mr and Mrs Staples, Barry Collett, P W Taylor, Michael Doswell, H Bramwell, Peter Hallinan, W and P J Elderkin, Derek and Sylvia Stephenson, JP, PP, A D Jenkins, Jenny and Dave Hughes, M and G Rushworth, John and Sylvia Harrop, Gerry and Rosemary Dobson, Patrick Hancock, Duncan Cloud, Alan and Jill Bull, Darly Graton,*

Graeme Gulibert, June and Ken Brooks, F J Robinson, P J Holt, Joyce and Geoff Robson, JMC)

Free house ~ Licensees Matt Rose and Anna Cavanagh ~ Real ale ~ Bar food ~ (01400) 281361 ~ Well behaved children in dining area at lunchtime, must be over 8 in evening ~ Open 12-2.30(3 Sat), 6-11; 12-4, 6-10.30 Sun ~ Bedrooms: £48S/£60S

BARNOLDBY LE BECK TA2303 Map 8

Ship 🍷

Village signposted off A18 Louth—Grimsby

The nostalgic collection of Edwardian and Victorian bric-a-brac at this rather genteel little pub includes half-remembered things like stand-up telephones, violins, a horn gramophone, bowler and top hats, old racquets, crops and hockey sticks, a lace dress, and grandmotherly plants in ornate china bowls. Heavy dark-ringed drapes swathe the windows, comfortable dark green plush wall benches have lots of pretty propped-up cushions, and there are heavily stuffed green plush Victorian-looking chairs on a green fleur de lys carpet. Many of the tables are booked for dining, and enjoyable (but not cheap) food could include sandwiches (from £3.50), soup (£3.95), smoked salmon and prawns (£4.95), mushroom stroganoff (£8.50), pork medallions with apricots (£11.95), chicken wrapped in bacon and stuffed with asparagus and smoked salmon, fillet steak or duck with ginger and spring onion (£12.95), and puddings such as home-made hot chocolate and brandy fudge cake (£3.95); be warned, they may stop serving early. There's an extensive wine list with quite a few by the glass, and Black Sheep and Timothy Taylors Landlord are well kept on handpump; piped music. Out behind are a few picnic-sets under pink cocktail parasols, next to big hanging baskets suspended from stands. *(Recommended by Dr D Parker, James Browne, Alan Cole, Kirstie Bruce, Alistair and Kay Butler)*

Inn Business ~ Tenant Michele West ~ Real ale ~ Bar food (12-2, 7-9; 12.30-2, 7-9.30 Sun) ~ Restaurant ~ (01472) 822308 ~ Children in restaurant ~ Open 12-3, 6-11(10.30 Sun)

BELCHFORD TF2975 Map 8

Blue Bell

Village signposted off A153 Horncastle—Louth (and can be reached by the good Bluestone Heath Road off A16 just under 1½ miles N of the A1104 roundabout); Main Road

The hard-working young couple who took over this cottagey 18th-c pub in late 2002 have made it an inviting place, with its bright window boxes, and a relaxing pastel décor in the cosy and comfortable bar. This has some armchairs and settees, as well as more upright chairs around the good solid tables; the dining room too is attractive. The real temptation here is the set of blackboards, which alongside familiar things such as soup (£2.95) and sandwiches with chips (£3.95), include more enterprising dishes like peppered goats cheese with marinated tomatoes (£4.95), tian of crab with parmesan crisp and tomato coulis (£5.95), wild mushroom and blue cheese risotto cake with poached egg, caramelised shallots and truffle oil (£10.95), roast monkfish tail wrapped in parma ham with smoked haddock cream sauce (£13.95), fried beef fillet on a mushroom stuffed with tarragon duxelle with horseradish cream and brandy jus (£17.50), puddings such as summer fruit pudding or baked white chocolate cheesecake (£3.95) and cheese platter (£3.95). The flavour combinations, never too outlandish, always work well, and presentation is a strong point, with a good deal of care taken over vegetables. Puddings are a high point. They also do popular OAP lunches on Wednesdays. They have decent reasonably priced wines by the glass, and well kept ales such as Flowers IPA, Greene King Abbot and Timothy Taylors Landlord on handpump; service is friendly and prompt. In the summer it may be wise to book. The neat garden behind, with a terrace, has picnic-sets, and the pub is well placed for Wolds walks, and the Viking Way. *(Recommended by Jill and Keith Wright, John Wall, Gordon B Thornton)*

Free house ~ Licensees Darren and Shona Jackson ~ Real ale ~ Bar food (12-2, 6.30-9) ~ Restaurant ~ (01507) 533602 ~ Children welcome ~ Open 11.30-2.30, 6.30-11; 12-4 Sun; closed Sun evening and Mon

BILLINGBOROUGH TF1134 Map 8

Fortescue Arms

B1177, off A52 Grantham—Boston

The car park at this friendly pub (good for a hearty meal) is more like the gravelled drive of a country house; on one side are picnic-sets on a lawn under apple trees, and on the other a sheltered courtyard with flowers planted in tubs and a manger. Inside, low beams, pleasant mainly Victorian prints and big log fires in two see-through fireplaces give a cosily old-fashioned feel to the line of linked turkey-carpeted rooms. There are nice bay window seats, fresh flowers and pot plants, brass and copper, a stuffed badger and pheasant with various quiz books in one place, and attractive dining rooms at each end, one with stripped stone walls, flagstones and another open fire; the restaurant is no smoking. Unusually, a long red and black tiled corridor runs right the way along behind the serving bar, making it an island. Batemans XXXB, Ind Coope Burton, and Tetley Imperial are well kept on handpump, and they've 70 malt whiskies, and decent wines. Freshly prepared food, served in generous helpings by the friendly staff, might include soup (£2.25), sandwiches (from £2.50), smoked mackerel (£3.95), lasagne (£6.95), vegetable wellington, home-made rabbit pie or baked haddock (£7.50), lamb chops (£9.50), and fillet steak (£13.95). This is a nice village. More reports please. *(Recommended by William and Elizabeth Templeton, M J Codling)*

Free house ~ Licensees John and Sharon Cottingham ~ Real ale ~ Bar food (not Mon exc bank hols) ~ Restaurant ~ (01529) 240228 ~ Children in restaurant ~ Open 11.30-3, 6-11; 12-3, 7-10.30 Sun; closed Mon exc bank hols

BRANDY WHARF TF0197 Map 8

Cider Centre

B1205 SE of Scunthorpe (off A15 about 16 miles N of Lincoln)

At this down-to-earth traditional cider tavern (one of only a handful left in Britain), they still stock a huge range of ciders with up to 15 on draught, eight tapped from casks, and the rest kept in stacks of fascinating bottles and small plastic or earthenware kegs on shelves behind the bar. There's also a good range of country wines and meads. Built in the 18th c to serve the needs of canal-building navvies and bargemen, the unpretentious main bar has wheelback chairs, brown plush wall banquettes and customer photographs. The dimly lit lounge bar has all sorts of cider memorabilia and humorous sidelights on cider-making and drinking – watch your head for the foot of 'Cyril the Plumber' poking down through the ceiling; piped music. A simple glazed verandah looks on to the river, where there are moorings and a slipway. The whole place is no smoking. Reasonably priced bar food includes sandwiches (from £2.80, £3.25 toasted), tasty pork and cider sausages (from £4.99 for two to £7.99 for six), steak and kidney pie, chicken curry or home-cured ham (£6.25); good chips. Children have lots of space to play out in the meadows (which have tables and chairs), along the water banks, or in the four acres of orchard where you can pick your own fruit when available; there's now a play area too. They hold quite a few appropriate special events. *(Recommended by Stuart Brown, Stuart Paulley, Keith and Chris O'Neill, the Didler)*

Free house ~ Licensees David and Catherine Wells ~ Bar food (12-2.30, 7-9.30; 12-9 wknds) ~ (01652) 678364 ~ Children in eating area of bar ~ Open 12-3, 7-10.30; 12-11 Sat; 12-10.30 Sun

If a service charge is mentioned prominently on a menu or accommodation terms, you must pay it if service was satisfactory. If service is really bad you are legally entitled to refuse to pay some or all of the service charge as compensation for not getting the service you might reasonably have expected.

CONINGSBY TF2458 Map 8

Lea Gate Inn

Leagate Road (B1192 southwards, off A153 E)

The pleasant interior of this welcoming 16th-c inn consists of three separate cosy, softly lit areas that are linked together around the corner bar counter, and have heavy black beams supporting ochre ceiling boards. It's attractively furnished, with a cabinet holding a collection of ancient bottles, a variety of tables and chairs, including antique oak settles with hunting-print cushions, and two great high-backed settles making a snug around the biggest of the fireplaces. Another fireplace has an interesting cast-iron fireplace depicting the Last Supper. Generously served, good value bar food includes lunchtime sandwiches (£2.65), home-made soup (£2.70), garlic mushrooms (£3.25), mushroom stroganoff (£7.25), steak and kidney pie or scampi (£7.95), chicken breast with cider, apples, bacon and herbs (£8.50), chargrilled pork steak with stilton and creamy wholegrain mustard sauce or lamb rump with rosemary and madeira jus (£8.95), and beef wellington (£10.25), and they've a good puddings trolley; children's meals (£3.50). The restaurant is no smoking. Service is very good, even when it's busy. Marstons Pedigree, Theakstons XB and possibly a guest such as Adnams are well kept on handpump; piped jazz or pop music. The appealing garden has tables and an enclosed play area. The pub once stood by one of the perilous tracks through the marshes before the fens were drained, and you can still see the small iron gantry that used to hold a lamp to guide travellers safely through the mist. Bedrooms are in a newish block. *(Recommended by the Didler, John Bailey, JP, PP, Dr John Lunn, Bill and Sheila McLardy, Pat and Tony Martin, Richard Cole, C A Hall)*

Free house ~ Licensee Mark Dennison ~ Real ale ~ Bar food ~ Restaurant ~ (01526) 342370 ~ Children in eating area of bar, restaurant and family room ~ Open 11.30-2.30, 6.30(6 Sat)-11; 12-3, 6-10.30 Sun ~ Bedrooms: £52.50B/£67.50B

DYKE TF1022 Map 8

Wishing Well

Village signposted off A15 N of Bourne; Main Street

The heavily beamed long, rambling front bar at this big bustling black and white village inn has dark stone walls, lots of shiny brasswork, a cavern of an open fireplace, and evening candlelight. They've an especially interesting choice of five real ales on handpump with well kept Everards Tiger and Greene King Abbot, alongside three regularly changing guests such as Archers Village, Hardys & Hansons Olde Trip and St Austell Tribute. Most people, though, are here for the straightforward but reasonably priced bar food. A typical choice might include soup (£2.95), sandwiches (from £2.80), prawn cocktail (£4.95), ham and egg or lincolnshire sausages (£6.50), breaded plaice (£7.95), or steaks (from £8.95), with specials such as broccoli and cheese bake (£6.95), and minted lamb chops (£8.25), and puddings such as lemon meringue (£3.50); children's meals (from £2.75). The big restaurant is no smoking. Popular with locals for a drink, the smaller and plainer public bar has sensibly placed darts, pool, fruit machine, juke box, video game and TV. The carpeted lounge area has green plush button-back low settles and wheelback chairs around individual wooden tables. There's a small conservatory, and the garden has tables and a play area. *(Recommended by JP, PP, Roy Bromell, M J Codling, Philip and Susan Philcox)*

Kelly Taverns ~ Manager Therese Gallagher ~ Real ale ~ Bar food ~ Restaurant ~ (01778) 422970 ~ Children welcome ~ Live pianist Sat evening ~ Open 11-3, 6.30(6 Sat)-11; 12-3, 6.30-10.30 Sun ~ Bedrooms: £35S/£65S

Cribbage is a card game using a block of wood with holes for matchsticks or special pins to score with; regulars in cribbage pubs are usually happy to teach strangers how to play.

GEDNEY DYKE TF4125 Map 8

Chequers

Village signposted off A17 Holbeach—Kings Lynn

Even the bread at this welcoming fenland pub (set a few feet below sea level) is home-made. Other good dishes, cooked by the landlady/chef, include bar snacks such as sandwiches (from £2.95, readers recommend the chicken club £5.50), home-made pasta with tomato and basil sauce (£5.50), and ploughman's or wild buffalo and peppercorn burger (£5.75), or you can choose from interesting blackboard specials such as pigeon breast in a white wine reduction (£4.95), guinea fowl supreme stuffed with plums and wrapped in bacon with red wine sauce (£10.50), chicken filled with goats cheese with sun-dried tomato and pesto sauce or gloucester old spot pork chop (£10.95), and good fresh fish dishes such as prawns in spicy sauce with melba toast (£5.95), salmon and smoked trout or fried cod with spring onion mash (£10.95), while home-made puddings might include strawberry pavlova (£4.95); friendly and obliging service. Spotlessly kept, it's fairly simple inside, with a welcoming open fire in the bar, and at one end a no smoking dining conservatory overlooks a garden with picnic-sets; one of the restaurants is no smoking. They've a decent wine list with around eight by the glass, and Adnams Bitter and Greene King Abbot are well kept on handpump; piped music.

(Recommended by Charles Gysin, Jamie and Sarah Allan, JP, PP, Roger Everett, Baden and Sandy Waller, Ken Marshall, Alison Hayes, Pete Hanlon, Sally Anne and Peter Goodale, Roger and Maureen Kenning, John Wooll, Bill and Marian de Bass, M J Codling, Alan and Sue Folwell)

Free house ~ Licensees Sarah Tindale and Adrian Isted ~ Real ale ~ Bar food (not Mon) ~ Restaurant ~ (01406) 362666 ~ Children welcome ~ Open 12-2, 7-11(10.30 Sun); closed Mon

GRANTHAM SK9135 Map 8

Angel & Royal

High Street

Emerging last year like a butterfly from the chrysalis of scaffolding which had hidden it during a £2 million refurbishment by its new local owners, this is now a most enjoyable combination of luxurious hotel, stylish modern bar/bistro, and some fascinating early medieval features. Its elaborately carved stone façade dates from the 14th c, when it had already been offering hospitality to kings and commoners alike for a couple of centuries, as a Commandery and Hospice of the Knights Templar. The restored gilded crown and angel over the entrance arch is thought to commemorate a visit by Edward III in the 14th c, and he and his queen Philippa may be among the other carved effigies which still watch over the street just as they did when it was the Great North Road. Through this arch, head to the left and up to the ancient Angel Bar, now refurnished evidently with no expense being spared, to see its formidable inglenook fireplace, and the charming little medieval oriel window seat jutting out over the road. The bar's pride is its collection of 200 or so malt whiskies; it also has a good range of reasonably priced wines by the glass, and well kept changing real ales such as Oldershaws High Dyke on handpump. A second high-beamed bar on the right has another massive inglenook. Downstairs, a stylish new bistro/bar with elegant modern tables and comfortable chairs on its pale oak boards, and a décor neatly combining clean lines and up-to-date pastels with some ancient stripped stonework, serves a wide choice of good modern food all day, mostly in both starter and main course sizes, such as soup (£3.25), cheese and smoked haddock (£4.95/7.95), wild salmon fishcakes (£5.50/9.50), baked Ste-Maure cheese with grilled pine nuts and elderflower syrup (£5.75/7.95), stilton, spinach and spring onion tart with quail eggs (£5.95/7.95), spiced steak strips (£6.95/11.95), liver and bacon (£8.75) and bass (£11.50), also puddings (from £4). They do a good choice of teas, coffees and soft drinks, too, and each table has a free bottle of mineral water, alongside elegant little bottles of japanese rice and balsamic vinegars, and olive oil. There is a grand-manner upstairs weekend restaurant, in the gorgeous room where Richard III may well have signed the order for the death of his treacherous cousin the Duke of Buckingham, on 19 October 1483. The lavatories are top-notch (as you might have predicted from the luxurious entrance lounge with its generous bowls of help-yourself fruit); the 26 bedrooms are in a more modern back extension, alongside the narrow flagstoned inner coachway, and they have good parking. *(Recommended by W W Burke)*

Free house ~ Licensee Diane Edwards ~ Real ale ~ Bar food (11.30-9.30) ~ Restaurant ~ (01476) 565816 ~ Children in eating area of bar ~ Open 11-2.30, 6-11; 12-2, 7-10.30 Sun ~ Bedrooms: £75B/£85B

GRIMSTHORPE TF0422 Map 8

Black Horse 🍴 🍷

A151 W of Bourne

Now with a new landlord, this handsome grey-stone coaching inn is somewhere to come for a beautifully presented meal. Made using fresh local ingredients, dishes might include sandwiches (from £3.25, baguettes from £3.75), soup (£3.95), salmon and smoked haddock fishcakes (£4.95), ploughman's (£6.95), fish and chips (£8.50), cajun chicken (£9.50), and steaks (from £12.95), or you can eat from the more elaborate (but not cheap) restaurant menu, which has choices such as confit of duck terrine (£5.25), and grilled lemon sole with lemon and herb butter (£14.95); puddings such as chocolate and brandy mousse (£5.25). There's a quietly composed eating-out mood in the neat rooms; a warming coal fire in a stripped stone fireplace, lamps, fresh flowers and patterned wallpaper create a homely feel. A cosy window seat and a nice round oak table stand on oak flooring just as you go in. The narrowish room then stretches away past the oak-timbered bar counter and bar stools down one side, and a row of tables, some of which are quite intimate in their own little booths, down the other. You'll find three changing well kept real ales from brewers such as Black Dog, Charles Wells and Newby Wyke, and they stock some decent wines, with eight by the glass. *(Recommended by Dr T E Hothersall, Derek and Sylvia Stephenson, MJB, David and Ruth Hollands, Alan and Jill Bull)*

Free house ~ Licensee Shaun Gilder ~ Real ale ~ Bar food (12-2, 6-9; 12-4 Sun) ~ Restaurant ~ (01778) 591247 ~ Children welcome ~ Open 12-2, 6-11; 12-4 Sun; closed Sun evening ~ Bedrooms: £45B/£55B

LINCOLN SK9771 Map 8

Victoria 🍺 £

Union Road

With a chatty, welcoming atmosphere, and a fine range of beautifully kept beers, this down-to-earth early Victorian local is well worth the short walk up a steep back street behind the castle. Along with Batemans XB, Castle Rock Harvest Pale and Timothy Taylors Landlord, friendly staff serve five or six guests from brewers such as Badger, Brains, Exmoor, Everards, Oakham and Oldershaws, as well as foreign draught and bottled beers, around 20 country wines, a farm cider on tap, and cheap soft drinks. They hold beer festivals in the last week in June and the first week in December. With a good mix of ages, the simply furnished little tiled front lounge has a coal fire and pictures of Queen Victoria; it's especially bustling at lunchtime and later on in the evening. Readers recommend the sausages and mash, and other good value lunchtime food, from a short menu, includes filled cobs (from £1.40, big bacon ones £2.95), toasted sandwiches (£2.10), all-day breakfast and basic home-made hot dishes such as beef stew, chilli, curry or ploughman's (from £3.95); the lounge is no smoking at lunchtime. Children are welcome in the restaurant which is open only on Sunday lunchtimes (Sunday roast £5). You can sit in the small conservatory or out in the gravelled side garden, which has good views of the castle. *(Recommended by Darly Graton, Graeme Gulibert, Andy and Jill Kassube, JP, PP, Joe Green, Patrick Hancock, Rona Murdoch, Derek and Sylvia Stephenson, David Carr, the Didler)*

Tynemill ~ Manager Neil Renshaw ~ Real ale ~ Bar food (12(11 Sat)-2.30; 12-2 Sun) ~ Restaurant (Sun) ~ (01522) 536048 ~ Dogs allowed after 3pm ~ Open 11-11; 12-10.30 Sun

Wig & Mitre ★ 🍷

Steep Hill; just below cathedral

Tremendously handy for breakfast, an afternoon snack or even a late night meal, this bustling café-style pub is open, and serving food, from 8am till midnight. They have an excellent selection of over 95 wines, many of them available by the glass, and lots of liqueurs and spirits; well kept on handpump (but not cheap), they've got Greene King Ruddles Best and Marstons Pedigree. Spreading over a couple of floors, the building itself dates from the 14th c, and has plenty of period features. The big-windowed beamed downstairs bar has exposed stone walls, pews and Gothic furniture on oak floorboards, and comfortable sofas in a carpeted back area. Upstairs, the calmer dining room is light and airy, with views of the castle walls and cathedral, shelves of old books, and an open fire. The walls are hung with antique prints and caricatures of lawyers and clerics, and there are plenty of newspapers and periodicals lying about – even templates to tempt you to a game of noughts and crosses. With prices at the higher end of the spectrum, food works its way up from the breakfast menu (full english £8.50) to a choice of caviar (from £38). Other dishes might include soup (£5.95), ham hock and field mushroom terrine (£6.95), pork medallions with parma ham, bubble and squeak and cider sauce (£13.95), fried bass with potato rösti and leek and orange beurre blanc fettuccine (£16.50), and beef fillet with foie gras (£19.50), and puddings such as iced prune and armagnac parfait with hazelnut shortbread (£4.95); also sandwiches (from £5.50). *(Recommended by Paul Humphreys, David and Ruth Hollands, Andy and Jill Kassube, Helen Whitmore, Fiona McElhone, JP, PP, Richard Jennings, Patrick Hancock, Alistair and Kay Butler, Mrs Brenda Calver, Christopher Beadle, David Carr)*

Free house ~ Licensees Valerie Hope, Toby Hope ~ Real ale ~ Bar food (8am-12pm) ~ Restaurant ~ (01522) 535190 ~ Children in eating area of bar and restaurant ~ Dogs allowed in bar ~ Open 8am-12pm

NEWTON TF0436 Map 8

Red Lion

Signposted from A52 E of Grantham; pub itself also discreetly signed off A52

When an east wind isn't blowing in thoughts of Siberia, the countryside around this friendly pub makes for pleasant walks – great for building up an appetite before enjoying one of their popular carvery roasts. A neat, sheltered back garden has some seats on the grass and on the terrace, while inside, it's comfortable and civilised, with old-fashioned seating, partly stripped stone walls covered with old farming tools, and stuffed creatures. There's a no smoking dining room; fruit machine and piped music. As well as a daily cold carvery (£7.95, £9.95 for a big plate), they do a hot carvery on Friday and Saturday evenings and Sunday lunchtime. Otherwise, reasonably priced bar food might include soup (£2.95), fried whitebait (£4.50), courgette bake (£7.95), battered haddock (£7.50), steak and ale pie (£7.95), fillet steak (£12.95), and daily specials such as chicken fillet with white wine sauce (£9.95), and rib-eye steak (£11.95), with home-made puddings such as lemon meringue or blackcurrant cheesecake. Helpful staff serve Batemans XB, Greene King Abbot and Hardys & Hansons Olde Trip on handpump. According to local tradition this village is the highest point between Grantham and the Urals. More reports please. *(Recommended by JP, PP, MJB, Gene and Kitty Rankin)*

Free house ~ Licensee Mr Blessett ~ Real ale ~ Bar food ~ Restaurant ~ (01529) 497256 ~ Well behaved children over 5 in restaurant ~ Open 12-2, 7(6 Sat)-11; 12-3, 7-10.30 Sun

Prices of main dishes usually include vegetables or a side salad.

ROTHWELL TF1499 Map 8

Blacksmiths Arms

Off B1225 S of Caistor

This long white-painted pub is a refreshing oasis in this part of the world, and handily it's open all day on the weekend. With a civilised and relaxed atmosphere, the pleasant bar is divided by a couple of arches with a warm central coal fire, a good balance between standing room and comfortable chairs and tables (with little bunches of fresh flowers), attractive wildlife prints, and heavy beams. The dining area is spacious. A typical selection of home-made dishes (with quite a few available in two sizes) might include soup (£3.35), deep-fried whitebait (£4.35), sausages and mash (£5.25, £6.25 large), grimsby haddock and chips (£6.25, jumbo size £7.95), moussaka or sweet and sour chicken (£7.25), and steaks (from £10.95), with lunchtime dishes such as baguettes (from £3.75), filled baked potatoes (from £3.95), ploughman's (£4.75), and an english breakfast (£4.95), and specials such as pork kebab with apple and cider sauce (£9.95), and roasted trout (£11.95), with home-made puddings (£3.35). They do an early evening weekday special (£7.25 for a meal and a drink from 5pm till 7pm). Batemans XB, Courage Directors, and Tom Woods Shepherds Delight are well kept along with two or three guest beers such as Daleside St George, Eccleshall Slaters Premium, and Marstons Pedigree on handpump, and they've around 16 whiskies; piped music, fruit machine, darts and dominoes. There are plenty of tables outside. Take care coming out of the car park: it's a blind bend. *(Recommended by John Branston, James Browne)*

Free house ~ Licensees Rick and Julie Sandham ~ Real ale ~ Bar food (12-2, 5-9.30; 12-9.30(9 Sun)Sat) ~ Restaurant ~ (01472) 371300 ~ Children in eating area of bar ~ Open 11.30-3, 5-11; 11.30-11 Sat; 12-10.30 Sun

SOUTH WITHAM SK9219 Map 8

Blue Cow

Village signposted just off A1 Stamford—Grantham (with brown sign for pub)

The two real ales they serve at this old stone-walled country pub are brewed by the friendly landlord in the building next door. Thirlwells Best (named after the licensees) and Witham Wobbler are available on handpump, and if the landlord is around he'll happily give you a little tour, and sell you some to take home (perhaps even in a recycled Coke bottle). With a good relaxed atmosphere, the two appealing individual bars are separated by a big central open-plan counter. One dark-beamed room has bentwood chairs at big indonesian hardwood tables, wickerwork and panelling, and prettily curtained windows. The second room has big black standing timbers and beams, partly stripped stone walls, shiny flagstones and a dark blue flowery carpet; piped music, TV, cribbage, and dominoes. Just inside the entrance lobby you pass an endearing little water feature on floodlit steps that go down to the cellar. Reasonably priced, enjoyable bar food includes sandwiches (from £3.25), tasty home-made soup (£3.50), salmon balls (£4.15, main £8.30), malaysian chicken satay (£4.50, main £9.40), chicken curry or vegetable pancake (£7.75), sweet and sour pork (£8.85), and duck breast with potato rösti and cranberry and port sauce (£11.20). The garden has tables on a pleasant terrace. *(Recommended by Paul Humphreys, Rona Murdoch, the Didler, Susan and Tony Dyer, JP, PP, Anne Harries, Stuart Paulley, Phil and Jane Hodson, David Edwards)*

Own brew ~ Licensees Dick and Julia Thirlwell ~ Real ale ~ Bar food (12-2.30, 6-9.30) ~ Restaurant ~ (01572) 768432 ~ Children in eating area of bar, restaurant and family room ~ Dogs allowed in bar and bedrooms ~ Open 12-11 ~ Bedrooms: £40S/£45S(£55B)

'Children welcome' means the pub says it lets children inside without any special restriction. If it allows them in, but to restricted areas such as an eating area or family room, we specify this. Some pubs may impose an evening time limit. We do not mention limits after 9pm as we assume children are home by then.

STAMFORD TF0207 Map 8

George of Stamford ★ 🍴 🍷 🛏

High Street, St Martins (B1081 S of centre, not the quite different central pedestrianised High Street)

Lincolnshire Dining Pub of the Year

This elegant old coaching inn is a thoroughly enjoyable place to visit, with good food, an excellent choice of wines (many of which are italian and good value, with about 18 by the glass), comfortable bedrooms, and attentive service. The atmosphere is smartly relaxed, and the labyrinth of rooms is filled with comfortably conversing customers. It was built in 1597 for Lord Burghley (though there are visible parts of a much older Norman pilgrims' hospice, and a crypt under the cocktail bar that may be 1,000 years old), and has kept its considerable character, while adding a good deal of modern style and comfort. Seats in its beautifully furnished rooms range through leather, cane and antique wicker to soft settees and easy chairs, while the central lounge has sturdy timbers, broad flagstones, heavy beams, and massive stonework. If you look hard enough, a ghostly face is supposed to appear in the wooden panelling of the London Room (used by folk headed that way in coaching days). The other front room making up the surprisingly pubby bar is the refurbished York Bar, where you can get snacks such as soup (from £4.65), sandwiches (from £4.95), ploughman's (£6.45), sausage and mash (£6.95), and a pudding of the day (£4.50). Our Food Award, though, is for the delicious (but not cheap) more elaborate meals served in the oak-panelled restaurant (jacket and tie) and less formal Garden Lounge restaurant (which has well spaced furniture on herringbone glazed bricks around a central tropical grove). Made using high quality ingredients, food in the Garden Lounge takes on a continental tilt (one of the licensees is Italian). Besides a cold buffet (£13.45), the menu includes several pasta dishes such as spaghetti with toasted walnuts and blue cheese or lasagne (£10.45), and shellfish such as oysters (£7.25 for six), and dressed crab (£12.95), as well as eggs benedict with parma ham (£8.95), home-made beef burger (£12.55), braised lamb shank with mashed potato or beef stroganoff (£12.95), and bass with cajun spices (£15.95), with puddings (£5.25); they do afternoon tea (£13.50). The staff are friendly and attentive, with waiter drinks service in the charming cobbled courtyard at the back, which has comfortable chairs and tables among attractive plant tubs and colourful hanging baskets on the ancient stone buildings. There's also a neatly kept walled garden, with a sunken lawn where croquet is often played. Adnams Broadside, Fullers London Pride and Greene King Abbot and Ruddles are well kept on handpump; freshly squeezed orange juice, and good coffees too.

(Recommended by Barry Collett, JP, PP, Charles Gysin, Tina and David Woods-Taylor, Roy Bromell, the Didler, Steve Whalley, Sherrie Glass, B and M Kendall, Gerry and Rosemary Dobson, M Sharp, W W Burke, David Glynne-Jones, Gordon Neighbour, Bob and Maggie Atherton, Martin and Anne Muers)

Free house ~ Licensees Chris Pitman and Ivo Vannocci ~ Real ale ~ Bar food (11-11) ~ Restaurant ~ (01780) 750750 ~ Children welcome ~ Dogs allowed in bar and bedrooms ~ Open 11-11; 12-11 Sun ~ Bedrooms: £78B/£78S(£110B)

SURFLEET TF2528 Map 8

Mermaid

Just off A16 N of Spalding, on B1356 at bridge

In summer, they hold regular barbecues and hog roasts at this genuinely old-fashioned dining pub, and the pretty garden has lots of seats and a terrace with thatched parasols, and its own bar; a children's play area is safely walled from the River Glen which runs beside the pub. Inside, it looks largely unchanged since the 70s, but everything is well cared for and fresh-looking. A small central glass-backed bar counter (complete with original Babycham décor) serves two high-ceilinged rooms, which have huge netted sash windows, green patterned carpets, beige Anaglypta dado, brass platters, navigation lanterns and horse tack on cream textured walls, and a mixture of banquettes and stools; cribbage, dominoes and piped music. Two steps down, the restaurant is decorated in a similar style. Besides enjoyable lunchtime snacks such as hamburgers (from £2.75), sandwiches (from £2, baguettes £1 extra), omelettes (from £2.95), and ham, egg and chips or scampi (£4.95), generous helpings of home-made food (served on hot plates) might include soup (£2.75), fried mushrooms with garlic, cream and crispy bacon (£3.25), cottage pie or aubergine and vegetable galette (£6.95), salmon and citrus cream or spicy chicken fajitas (£8.95), and steaks (from £9.50), with daily specials such as fisherman's pie (£6.95), and chicken stuffed with leeks and bacon (£8.25). Adnams Broadside, John Smiths and possibly a guest such as Charles Wells Bombardier are well kept on handpump; obliging service from the welcoming staff. *(Recommended by Michael and Jenny Back, Beryl and Bill Farmer, W M Paton, Derek and Sylvia Stephenson, Ken Marshall, M J Codling, J M Tansey, Roy Bromell)*

Free house ~ Licensee J Bell ~ Real ale ~ Bar food (12-2.30, 6.30-9.30(6-10 Fri/Sat); 12-2.30, 6.30-9 Sun) ~ Restaurant ~ (01775) 680275 ~ Children welcome ~ Dogs welcome ~ Open 11-11; 12-10.30 Sun

WOOLSTHORPE SK8435 Map 8

Chequers 🍷

The one near Belvoir, signposted off A52 or A607 W of Grantham

Up a short dead-end off the main street, this 17th-c coaching inn continues its journey into the 21st c with some subtle redecoration. Its core, the heavy-beamed main bar, is still dominated by the huge boar's head above a good log fire in the big brick fireplace, set off now by a gentle up-to-date colour scheme. Its two big tables, one a massive oak construction, have a comfortable mix of seating including some handsome leather chairs and leather banquettes. Among cartoons on the wall are some of the illustrated claret bottle labels from the series commissioned from famous artists, initiated by the late Baron Philippe de Rothschild. The lounge on the right has been smartened up with a deep red colour scheme, and new leather sofas. On the left, there are more leather seats in a dining area housed in what was once the village bakery. A corridor leads off to the light and airy main restaurant, with contemporary pictures and a newly uncovered 1920s sprung dance floor; as we went to press work was under way on a second bar, to serve this restaurant and take pressure off the main bar. As well as decent house wines (with 24 wines by the glass), and 50 single malts, they serve three or four well kept real ales on handpump such as Adnams Best, Fullers London Pride, Hardys & Hansons Best and Marstons Pedigree; also organic drinks and local fruit pressés. Bar food includes lunchtime soup (£3.75), sandwiches (from £3.95, toasted brie and parma ham £5.95), rösti potato, fried egg, smoked bacon and mushrooms (£6.95), ploughman's (£7.95), and sausages and mash (£8.50), with evening dishes such as chargrilled chicken breast with spiced coconut and carrot purée and pineapple chutney (£10.95), and stuffed rabbit leg with chorizo, spinach and wild mushrooms (£12.50), while puddings might include chocolate bread and butter pudding with chocolate sauce (£4.25; vegetables are £2.50 extra). There are nice teak tables, chairs and benches outside, and beyond some picnic-sets on the edge of the pub's cricket field; boules too, and views of Belvoir Castle. *(Recommended by JP, PP, June and Malcolm Farmer, Toppo Todhunter)*

Free house ~ Licensee Justin Chad ~ Real ale ~ Bar food ~ Restaurant ~ (01476) 870701 ~ Children welcome ~ Dogs allowed in bar and bedrooms ~ Open 12-3, 5.30-11; 12-5.30 Sun; closed Sun evening ~ Bedrooms: £40S/£50S

Please tell us if any Lucky Dips deserve to be upgraded to a main entry – and why.
No stamp needed: *The Good Pub Guide*, FREEPOST TN1569,
Wadhurst, E Sussex TN5 7BR.

LUCKY DIP

Besides the fully inspected pubs, you might like to try these Lucky Dips recommended to us and described by readers (if you do, please send us reports: www.goodguides.co.uk).

ASWARBY TF0639

Tally Ho [A15 S of Sleaford (but N of village turn-off)]: Newish management for 17th-c beamed pub in nice spot, two log fires, country prints and candles on tables (may be booked for meals) in big-windowed front bar, well kept Bass, Batemans XB and a guest beer, good house wines, daily papers, bar food from baguettes to steaks, pine-furnished restaurant; piped music; children and dogs welcome, tables out behind among fruit trees *(LYM)*

BAUMBER TF2274

Red Lion [A158 Lincoln—Skegness]: Newish licensees doing good generous food all freshly cooked inc bargain three-course wkdy lunches, decent wines at appealing prices, John Smiths and Tetleys *(Maureen and Arnold East)*

BOSTON TF3244

Eagle [West St, towards stn]: Basic cheery local with well kept Batemans, Castle Rock, Timothy Taylors Landlord and three guest beers at low prices, cheap soft drinks too, good value food, quick friendly service even when it's busy, children in eating area lunchtime; Mon folk club, live music Sat, open all day Sat *(BB, Andrew York, the Didler, JP, PP)*

Ropers Arms [Horncastle Rd]: Unassuming Batemans corner local in nice spot by river and windmill; big-screen sports TV, some live entertainment; open 2-11, all day wknds and summer *(JP, PP, the Didler)*

BOURNE TF0920

Smiths [North St]: Large extensively renovated pub, family run, with real ales, enjoyable lunchtime bar food, log fires, nooks and crannies, soft lighting; discreet piped music; large terrace with barbecues *(Martin and Helen Ball)*

CLEETHORPES TA3008

No 2 Refreshment Room [Station Approach]: Clean and comfortably updated little station bar with well kept ales inc a Mild and usually a good guest beer from a small brewery, friendly service, no food; open all day *(the Didler, Alan Cole, Kirstie Bruce)*

☆ *Willys* [Highcliff Rd; south promenade]: Open-plan bistro-style seafront pub with panoramic Humber views, café tables, tiled floor and painted brick walls; brews its own good beers, also well kept Batemans and guest beers, range of belgian beers, popular beer festival Nov, good value lunchtime home cooking, friendly staff, nice mix of customers from young and trendy to weatherbeaten fishermen; quiet juke box; a few tables out on the prom, open all day *(the Didler, JP, PP)*

EAST HALTON TA1319

Black Bull [off A160 NW of Grimsby; Townside]: Village pub with good choice of reasonably priced generous fresh food (not Mon), wide drinks choice, friendly landlady, chef and staff; handy for NT Thornton Abbey *(W Mabbott)*

EAST KIRKBY TF3362

☆ *Red Lion* [Fen Rd]: Lots of chiming clocks, jugs, breweriana and interesting old tools (some for sale behind), well kept Bass and a guest beer, good value standard food, friendly staff, open fire, family room, traditional games; wheelchair access, tables outside (and more machinery), camping; handy for Air Museum *(the Didler, JP, PP)*

EPWORTH SE7804

White Bear [Belton Rd]: Bar and three linked well furnished eating areas, enjoyable food with help-yourself veg etc, sensible prices, enthusiastic staff *(Alistair and Kay Butler)*

FROGNALL TF1610

Goat [B1525, off A16 NE of Mkt Deeping]: Log fires, low 17th-c beams, stripped stone, interesting well kept changing real ales, enjoyable food from lunchtime sandwiches up, two dining rooms (one no smoking where children welcome); may be piped music; good wheelchair access, big garden with terrace and play equipment, separate area for under-5s *(Richard Lewis, M J Codling)*

GAINSBOROUGH SK8189

Eight Jolly Brewers [Ship Court, Silver St]: Bustling unpretentious pub with beams, bare bricks and brewery posters, up to eight well kept well priced changing ales and one brewed for them by Highwood, quieter bar upstairs, simple lunchtime food (not Sun), friendly staff and locals; folk club, open all day Fri-Sun *(the Didler, JP, PP)*

GRANTHAM SK9135

☆ *Beehive* [Castlegate]: The star is for its unique living inn sign – a hive of bees up in the good-sized back garden's lime tree, the pub's sign for a couple of centuries or more; well kept ales from the nearby Newby Wyke microbrewery, unpretentious local L-shaped bar with coal fire, simple cheap food from sandwiches up (all day, not Sun evening), polite staff, friendly regulars, back room with games, juke box and TV; children welcome till 7.30, open all day *(Richard Lewis, Bernie Adams, the Didler, JP, PP, LYM, Steve Kirby)*

☆ *Blue Pig* [Vine St]: Pretty jettied Tudor pub, low beams, panelling, stripped stone and flagstones, lots of pig ornaments, friendly bustle, helpful staff, well kept changing ales such as Bass, City of Cambridge, Timothy Taylors Landlord and York Yorkshire Terrier, good simple lunchtime food, open fire, daily papers, lots of prints and bric-a-brac; piped music, juke box, games machines, no children or dogs; tables out behind, open all day *(JP, PP, BB, the Didler)*

Lord Harrowby [Dudley Rd, S of centre]: Friendly 60s-feel pub in residential part, lots of RAF pictures and memorabilia in pleasant lounge (with pianist Sat and great atmosphere then), well kept Bass, Worthington and a guest beer, games-oriented public bar; no food, cl lunchtime exc Sun *(Pete Baker)*

Nobody Inn [Watergate]: Friendly bare-boards open-plan local with five well kept changing ales inc cheap Sam Smiths OB and two or three from local Newby Wyke and Oldershaws; back games room with pool, table footer, SkyTV; open all day *(the Didler, JP, PP)*

GRASBY TA0804

Cross Keys [Brigg Rd]: Enjoyable food inc good fresh grimsby haddock on Fri, nice views from dining room *(Margaret and Roy Randle)*

GRIMSBY TA2609

Lincoln Castle [Fishermans Wharf; follow Heritage Centre signs, behind Sainsburys]: Former Humber paddle-steamer converted to friendly and pleasant bar and lower deck restaurant, good value food inc Sun carvery, engines preserved and on view, cabinet showing ship's history, real ales such as Bass and Theakstons, seats out on upper deck; games machine, piped music; handy for National Fishing Heritage Centre *(anon)*

HALTON HOLEGATE TF4165

☆ ***Bell*** [B1195 E of Spilsby]: Unchanging pretty village local, simple but comfortable and consistently friendly, with wide choice of decent generous home-made food cooked by landlord inc Sun lunches and outstanding fish and chips, tempting prices, well kept Batemans XB and Highwood Tom Woods Best or Bomber County, Lancaster bomber pictures, pub games, and Samson their nice golden labrador; children in back eating area (with tropical fish tank) and restaurant *(JP, PP, the Didler, Derek and Sylvia Stephenson, LYM, Michael and Jenny Back)*

HOLBEACH TF3626

Bulls Neck [Penny Hill (old A17, N of town)]: Beams and log fires, good choice of real ales, good value simple meals (all day Sat) inc OAP lunches Thurs and Fri, no smoking restaurant *(M J Codling)*

INGHAM SK9483

Inn on the Green [The Green]: Wide choice of quickly served good fresh home-made food from good sandwich range to steaks and venison in well modernised pub on village green; well kept changing ales such as Black Sheep, Fullers London Pride and Timothy Taylors Landlord, great wine choice, lots of brass and copper in spacious beamed lounge bar, good fire, locals' bar, downstairs and upstairs dining rooms; children welcome *(C A Hall, Keith and Chris O'Neill)*

KIRKBY LA THORPE TF0945

Queens Head [Boston Rd, backing on to A17]: Comfortably plush dining pub with good choice of reliable home-made food from well filled sandwiches and baguettes (home-baked bread) through interesting changing specials to fresh fish, very popular Thurs steak night and enjoyable puddings, good service and atmosphere, well kept Marstons, decent house wine, small cosy no smoking restaurant; easy disabled access *(Carole Hall, Henry and Jackie Lord)*

KIRKBY ON BAIN TF2462

Ebrington Arms [Main St]: Generous good value food inc cheap Sun lunch, five or more well kept changing ales from small breweries far and wide, prompt welcoming service, daily papers, low 16th-c beams, two open fires, nicely set out dining areas each side, copper-topped tables, wall banquettes, jet fighter and racing car pictures, games area with darts, restaurant, beer festivals Easter and Aug bank hols; may be piped music; wheelchair access, tables out in front, swings on side lawn, camp site behind, open all day *(JP, PP, the Didler)*

LEADENHAM SK9552

☆ ***George*** [High St; A17 Newark—Sleaford]: Enjoyable sensibly priced food from sandwiches to steaks in solid old coaching inn's pleasant neatly kept two-room bar, chatty landlady and good welcoming service, well kept real ales, good choice of wines by the glass (some direct imports), massive range of nearly 700 whiskies, good smart restaurant; side games room, may be piped music; picnic-sets out under heated pergola, good value bedrooms, good breakfast *(LYM, Phil and Jane Hodson)*

Willoughby Arms [High St; A17 Newark—Sleaford]: Comfortable bar, good food in two eating areas, friendly staff; good bedrooms *(Henry and Jackie Lord)*

LINCOLN SK9872

Golden Eagle [High St]: Cheerfully busy basic two-bar town pub, well kept and attractively priced changing ales inc Batemans, Castle Rock and Everards, good choice of country wines, cheap soft drinks, good value lunchtime food; open all day Fri/Sat *(the Didler, JP, PP, Andy and Jill Kassube)*

Morning Star [Greetwellgate]: Unpretentious well scrubbed local handy for cathedral, friendly atmosphere, enjoyable cheap lunches esp Fri specials, well kept reasonably priced ales such as Greene King Abbot and Ruddles, Marstons Pedigree and Charles Wells Bombardier, coal fire, aircraft paintings, sofas in cosy back snug; piano night Sat; nice outside area, open all day exc Sun *(the Didler, David and Ruth Hollands, JP, PP, Pete Baker, Joe Green, Patrick Hancock)*

Pyewipe [Saxilby Rd; off A57 just S of bypass]: Much extended 18th-c pub popular for wide range of good food inc good fish choice and memorable ginger pudding, well kept real ales such as Timothy Taylors Landlord, friendly atmosphere; comfortable reasonably priced bedrooms, on Roman Fossdyke Canal, pleasant walk out from centre, bedrooms *(Paul Humphreys, Gwen Kahan, Mrs Brenda Calver)*

☆ ***Queen in the West*** [Moor St; off A57 nr racecourse]: Well kept changing ales such as Bass, Marstons Pedigree, Theakstons XB and Old Peculier and reasonably priced simple bar lunches in busy and welcoming old backstreet pub below cathedral; military prints and miniatures in well decorated lounge, interesting sporting prints in public bar with TV, darts, games; open all day Fri/Sat *(JP, PP, the Didler, Joe Green, Patrick Hancock)*

Sippers [Melville St, opp bus stn]: Popular two-bar lunchtime pub with good food (not wknd evenings), Courage Directors, Greene King Old Speckled Hen, Marstons Pedigree and guest beers, friendly new landlord; has been cl Sun lunchtime *(JP, PP, the Didler)*

Strugglers [Westgate]: Small refurbished local with particularly well kept ales such as Bass, Fullers London Pride and Greene King, coal-effect fire in small back snug; terrace tables (no under-18s inside), open all day *(the Didler, David and Ruth Hollands, JP, PP, Andy and Jill Kassube, Joe Green, Patrick Hancock)*

Tap & Spile [Hungate]: Five or so well kept changing ales, farm cider and country wines from central bar, small choice of food, framed beer mats, prints and breweriana, bare boards and brickwork, stone floors, friendly atmosphere, no smoking area; open all day *(Patrick Hancock)*

LITTLE BYTHAM TF0118

☆ *Willoughby Arms* [Station Rd, S of village]: Good Newby Wyke beers from back microbrewery, interesting guest beers, Weston's farm cider, frequent beer festivals, reasonably priced substantial food from sandwiches up, friendly staff and local atmosphere, daily papers, simple bar with wall banquettes, stripped tables and coal fire, pleasant no smoking end dining room, airy games room with pool and TV; piped music; good new disabled access, children welcome, picnic-sets out behind with quiet country views, bedrooms, open all day wknds *(June and Malcolm Farmer, Bill and Sheila McLardy, JP, PP, the Didler, BB, David and Brenda Tew, Kevin Thorpe)*

LONG SUTTON TF4222

Olde Ship [London Rd]: Welcoming attractive 17th-c black and white inn, log fires, well kept real ales sometimes inc a guest beer, decent wines, good choice of home-cooked food, cosy no smoking dining room; tables out overlooking small lake *(M J Codling)*

LOUTH TF3387

Kings Head [Mercer Row]: Large unpretentious bar, well kept beer, good range of good value bar food inc roasts and traditional puddings *(the Didler, JP, PP)*

☆ *Masons Arms* [Cornmarket]: Light and airy, with plush seats, big sunny bay window, good mix of different-sized tables, panelled back bar, good friendly family service, well kept full Batemans range, Marstons Pedigree, Timothy Taylors Landlord and guest beers, farm cider, decent coffee, good home-made food from big hot sandwiches up, good upstairs dining room (remarkable art deco former masonic lodge meeting room); piped radio; good bedrooms, open all day exc Sun *(JP, PP, Roy and Lindsey Fentiman, BB, the Didler)*

Olde Whyte Swanne [Eastgate]: Ancient low beams, log fires, comfortable and relaxed front bar, good choice of enjoyable food all day, helpful friendly staff, several changing well kept real ales; children welcome, open all day, bedrooms *(JP, PP, the Didler, Peter and Sandra Cullen)*

Wheatsheaf [Westgate]: Cheerful bustle in early 17th-c low-beamed pub, coal fires in all three bars, well kept Boddingtons, Flowers and a guest beer, decent lunchtime food (not Sun); can be crowded; tables outside *(the Didler, JP, PP)*

Woolpack [Riverhead Rd]: 18th-c wool merchant's house popular for good home cooking (not Sun or Mon evenings) and Batemans ales inc a Mild, Marstons Pedigree and guest ales; bar, lounge, snug, two real fires; cl Mon lunchtime, open all day Sat *(the Didler, JP, PP)*

MESSINGHAM SE8905

Bird in the Barley [Northfield Rd (A159 S of Scunthorpe)]: Large U-shaped pub with central bar, doing well under new landlord, wholesome well presented food (not Sun evening or Mon), farmland views; cl Mon lunchtime *(Alistair and Kay Butler)*

NORTH KELSEY TA0401

Butchers Arms [Middle St; off B1434 S of Brigg]: Busy village local, opened up but not too modern, low ceilings, flagstones, bare boards, dim lighting, with five well kept Highwood beers (brewed by owner on his farm), good value cold lunches, enthusiastic cheerful service, woodburner; pub games, no juke box, tables outside, opens 4 wkdys, open all day wknds *(the Didler, JP, PP)*

NORTON DISNEY SK8859

☆ *St Vincent Arms* [Main St, off A46 Newark—Lincoln]: Welcoming village pub with well kept Batemans XXXB or Marstons Pedigree, guest beers sometimes, open fire, good cheap generous plain food from sandwiches up inc beautifully cooked veg, friendly service, appropriately decorated family room (Walt Disney's ancestors came from here) and attractive dining room; tables and big adventure playground out behind *(the Didler, M J Codling)*

SARACENS HEAD TF3426

Saracens Head [off A17 NW of Holbeach]: Recently refurbished country pub with hard-working young licensees, low-priced food from baguettes and baked potatoes to usual hot dishes cooked to order, darts and pool in public bar, hatch service to comfortable lounge, pleasant no smoking dining room *(M J Codling)*

SCAMPTON SK9579

Dambusters [High St]: Beams, hops and masses of interesting Dambusters and other World War II memorabilia, reasonably priced simple food (not Sun/Mon evenings), pleasant nostalgic atmosphere, well kept Greene King IPA, Abbot and Ruddles and guest beers, log fire, adjoining post office; very near Red Arrows runway viewpoint *(M and GR, Keith and Chris O'Neill)*

SCOTTER SE8800

☆ *White Swan* [The Green]: Expansive well kept pub comfortably laid out for dining, varied well prepared generous food inc fish board and bargain three-course special, well kept Black Sheep, John Smiths, Websters and several interesting changing guest beers, several levels inc snug panelled area by one fireplace, friendly landlady and neat cheerful staff, big-windowed restaurant looking over lawn with picnic-sets to duck-filled River Eau; piped music may obtrude; 14 comfortable bedrooms in modern extension, open all day Fri-Sun *(BB, Jenny and Dave Hughes, Mr and Mrs J R Ward, Paul and Ursula Randall)*

SKEGNESS TF5660

☆ ***Vine*** [Vine Rd, off Drummond Rd, Seacroft]: Unspoilt small hotel based on late 18th-c country house, informal unpretentious atmosphere in well run bar overlooking drive and own bowling green, imposing antique seats and grandfather clock in turkey-carpeted hall, inner oak-panelled room; well kept Batemans XB, Mild and XXB, good value food using local produce in bar and restaurant, friendly staff, welcoming fire; tables on big back sheltered lawn with swings, good reasonably priced bedrooms, peaceful suburban setting not far from beach and bird-watching *(the Didler, BB, JP, PP)*

SKENDLEBY TF4369

☆ ***Blacksmiths Arms*** [off A158 about 10 miles NW of Skegness]: Emphasis on good imaginative generous food in big busy back restaurant extension, very generous one-price main courses, also old-fashioned two-room bar, cosy and quaint, with view of cellar, deep 17th-c well, well kept Batemans XB and XXXB tapped from the cask, friendly staff, open fire *(JP, PP, the Didler)*

SLEAFORD TF0745

Carre Arms [Mareham Lane]: Hotel with sizeable pub part, good choice of light lunches and evening restaurant meals, not cheap but good, decent wines, helpful landlady; bedrooms *(Bill and Sheila McLardy)*

SOUTH ORMSBY TF3675

☆ ***Massingberd Arms*** [off A16 S of Louth]: Small welcoming refurbished 17th-c village pub, helpful and obliging landlord, well kept John Smiths Magnet and a couple of interesting guest beers, short choice of enjoyable fresh food inc game and Sun lunch, restaurant Thurs-Sun evenings; pleasant garden, good Wolds walks, cl Mon lunchtime in winter *(Derek and Sylvia Stephenson, JP, PP, the Didler, Dr John Lunn)*

SOUTH THORESBY TF4077

☆ ***Vine*** [about a mile off A16 N of Ulceby Cross]: Hard-working and welcoming new licensees in two-room village inn with small local pub part – tiny passageway servery, steps up to three-table lounge, wide choice of quickly served food, well kept Batemans XB, good value wines, nicely panelled no smoking dining room, separate pool room; bedrooms, tables in pleasant big garden *(the Didler, JP, PP, David and Ruth Hollands, R M Corlett)*

STAMFORD TF0207

Crown [All Saints Pl]: Good reasonably priced english country cooking inc wkdy two-course lunch deals, in large rambling stone-built hotel's panelled country bar and no smoking dining rooms, changing beers such as Adnams, Bass, Roosters and Timothy Taylors Landlord, decent wines and coffee, polite friendly staff; dogs welcome, comfortable quiet bedrooms, open all day *(the Didler, Roy Bromell)*

Daniel Lambert [St Leonards St]: Town local named for a prodigious 19th-c fattie (he weighed a third of a ton), with some relevant pictures and so forth; usual bar food (not Sun evening) from sandwiches to steaks, a dozen wines by the glass, Adnams, Courage Directors, Timothy Taylors Landlord, Tetleys and a guest beer, winter log fire, cribbage, dominoes, no smoking restaurant; fruit machine, piped music; children and dogs welcome, pleasant back terrace, open all day Sat *(the Didler, JP, PP, LYM)*

Green Man [Scotgate]: Comfortable L-shaped bar with good choice of well kept ales, good value food (not Sun), friendly staff, real fire, Easter beer festival; TV in raised area; garden tables, bedrooms, open all day *(Richard Lewis, the Didler)*

Lord Burghley [Broad St]: Old pub with several neat rooms, stripped stone, good atmosphere and service, well kept Bass, Fullers London Pride and Greene King IPA, farm cider, enjoyable traditional food (not Sun evening); pleasant small walled garden, open all day *(the Didler, Des and Jen Clarke, Barry Collett)*

STOW SK8881

☆ ***Cross Keys*** [B1241 NW of Lincoln]: Long-serving licensees keeping up high standards in pleasantly modernised and extended largely no smoking dining pub nr Saxon minster church, prettily presented fresh food inc lots of interesting blackboard specials and good puddings, well kept Greene King Old Speckled Hen, Highgate Cromwell and Theakstons Best and Old Peculier, good range of wines, quick friendly service, big woodburner; may be piped music, cl Mon lunchtime *(BB, David and Ruth Hollands, Nigel Clifton, Michael and Jenny Back, Mrs Brenda Calver)*

TATTERSHALL THORPE TF2159

Blue Bell [Thorpe Rd; B1192 Coningsby—Woodhall Spa]: Attractive beamed pub said to date from 13th c, good range of well kept mainly local real ales, reasonably priced food, plenty of character, small dining room, attentive service even when busy; tables in garden, impressive lavatera bushes *(Derek Smith, the Didler)*

TEALBY TF1590

☆ ***Kings Head*** [Kingsway, off B1203 towards bottom of village]: Mossy-thatched medieval beamed pub recently refurbished under new owners, wide choice of fresh food from traditional bar dishes up using local produce, well kept real ales, friendly service, local country pictures; restaurant, wheelchair access, picnic-sets in attractive garden, quiet Wolds village handy for Viking Way walk *(the Didler, Paul Humphreys, BB, JP, PP, Dominique Peckett)*

TETFORD TF3374

☆ ***White Hart*** [East Rd, off A158 E of Horncastle]: Early 16th-c pub doing well under welcoming current licensees, good choice of above-average food inc good local beef, well kept Adnams and Fullers London Pride, Stowford Press cider, interesting layout, old-fashioned curved-back settles, slabby elm tables, red tiled floor and log fire in pleasant quiet inglenook bar, no smoking snug, basic games room; unobtrusive piped music; tables on sheltered back lawn, simple bedrooms, pretty countryside *(LYM, JP, PP, the Didler, R M Corlett)*

THEDDLETHORPE ALL SAINTS TF4787

Kings Head [off A1031 N of Maplethorpe; Mill Rd]: Remote 15th-c thatched pub, very low beams, enjoyable food, usually a real ale *(J M Tansey)*

WELTON HILL TF0481

☆ *Farmers Arms* [A46 Lincoln—Market Rasen]: Well run comfortable no smoking pub with hearty helpings of good freshly made food from baguettes to popular Sun lunch, Boddingtons, Castle Rock Gold and Theakstons Mild, good house wines (with a wine theme to décor), prompt service from helpful friendly licensees and neat staff, panelling and some stripped brickwork, houseplants and fresh flowers; disabled access, very shallow steps to upper dining room *(Michael and Jenny Back, Mr and Mrs D Wellington, Mrs Brenda Calver)*

WOODHALL SPA TF1962

☆ *Abbey Lodge* [B1192 towards Coningsby]: Unchanging family-run roadside inn with bustling discreetly decorated bar, Victorian and older furnishings, World War II RAF pictures, well kept Bass, Worthington and a guest such as Greene King IPA, farm cider, friendly staff, good straightforward reasonably priced bar food from sandwiches to local-breed steak, good service; children over 10 in restaurant, may be piped Radio 1; cl Sun *(John Branston, JP, PP, Paul Humphreys, LYM, Pat and Tony Martin)*

A very few pubs try to make you leave a credit card at the bar, as a sort of deposit if you order food. They are not entitled to do this. The credit card firms and banks which issue them warn you not to let them out of your sight. If someone behind the counter used your card fraudulently, the card company or bank could in theory hold you liable, because of your negligence in letting a stranger hang on to your card. Suggest instead that if they feel the need for security, they 'swipe' your card and give it back to you. And do name and shame the pub to us.

Norfolk

Pubs which have really been catching readers' attention in recent months include the bustling Kings Arms in Blakeney (well run by its very long-serving licensees), the White Horse there (perhaps slightly smarter, though every bit as cheerful), the smartly expanded White Horse at Brancaster Staithe (very good food and drink, and a nice place to stay in), the interesting Lord Nelson at Burnham Thorpe (friendly new people settling in well now), the well run Ratcatchers at Cawston (much enjoyed for meals out, and they bake their own bread – always a good sign), the cheery Three Horseshoes at Cley next the Sea (a welcoming new landlord here too), the relaxed, civilised and individual Saracens Head near Erpingham (attractive new bedrooms, and it gains a Food Award this year), the friendly Angel at Larling (a consistently enjoyable refuge from the A11), the Adam & Eve in Norwich (very rare to find such a nice homely pub in a biggish city), the Fat Cat there (an exemplary real ale haunt), the chatty little Red Lion at Upper Sheringham (a fine all-rounder), the Crown in Wells-next-the-Sea (new owners bringing it back into the *Guide* after a break – doing really well now, with good modern food, a fine drinks choice, and charming bedrooms), the Wheatsheaf at West Beckham (another pub which hasn't been in the *Guide's* main section for some years – brought in now by keen hard-working licensees who are doing good food and keep their beers and wines well), and the friendly Fishermans Return near the beaches at Winterton-on-Sea (a nice place to stay at or just to drop into for a good pint or a pleasant bar meal). It's one of the newcomers that takes our top award for a special meal out: the Crown at Wells-next-the-Sea is Norfolk Dining Pub of the Year. Pubs which have recently been winning warm approval for the Lucky Dip section at the end of the chapter are the Kings Head at Bawburgh, Ship at Brandon Creek, Feathers near Dersingham, Crown at Gayton, Hare & Hounds near Hempstead, Recruiting Sergeant at Horstead, Blue Bell at Hunworth, Dun Cow at Salthouse, Scole Inn, Sculthorpe Mill at Sculthorpe, Goat at Skeyton, Titchwell Manor at Titchwell, Bell at Wiveton and Green Dragon in Wymondham. Drinks prices here generally tend to be a little above the national average, though the Adam & Eve in Norwich often has very attractive offers, and the Fat Cat there is reliably low-priced. Woodfordes is the local beer you are most likely to come across here, and others to look out for include Reepham, Wolf, Buffys, Chalk Hill, Fox/Heacham, Iceni, Tindalls and Blue Moon.

BLAKENEY TG0243 Map 8

Kings Arms

West Gate Street

There's always a happy throng of chatty customers in this bustling, friendly pub that has been run by the same licensees for 30 years. The three simply furnished, knocked-through pubby rooms have low ceilings, some interesting photographs of the licensees' theatrical careers, other pictures including work by local artists, and what must be the smallest cartoon gallery in England – in a former telephone kiosk. Look out for the brass plaque on the wall that marks a flood level. Two small rooms are no smoking, as is the airy garden room; darts, fruit machine, shove-ha'penny, table skittles and dominoes. Well kept Greene King Old Speckled Hen, Marstons Pedigree and a couple of changing guests often from Adnams and Woodfordes on handpump; good efficient service. Reasonably priced, well liked bar food includes sandwiches (from £1.80; toasties from £2.20), soup (£2.95), filled baked potatoes (from £4.75), ploughman's (from £5.20), grilled prawns in garlic butter (£5.25), local crab (summer only, £5.75), vegetable lasagne (£6.50), battered cod, haddock or plaice (£7.25), steaks (from £10.50), and puddings like home-made fruit crumble (£3.75). Lots of tables and chairs plus swings for children in the large garden. The pub is just a short stroll from the harbour, and there are good nearby walks. *(Recommended by Keith and Chris O'Neill, Maureen and Bill Sewell, MDN, Dr and Mrs R G J Telfer, Robert Turnham, Esther and John Sprinkle, Moira and John Cole, Sue and Graham Fergy)*

Free house ~ Licensees John Howard and Marjorie Davies ~ Real ale ~ Bar food (12-9.30(9 Sun)) ~ (01263) 740341 ~ Children welcome ~ Dogs welcome ~ Open 11-11; 12-10.30 Sun ~ Bedrooms: /£60S

White Horse

Off A149 W of Sheringham; High Street

Run by a friendly landlord, this busy little hotel has a cheerful atmosphere and a good mix of chatty locals and holiday-makers. The long main bar is predominantly green with a venetian red ceiling, and restrained but attractive décor, including watercolours by a local artist. Enjoyable tasty bar food includes lunchtime sandwiches or filled ciabattas (from £3.95), home-made soup (£3.50; home-made cockle chowder £3.95), deep-fried soft herring roes on toast (£4.95), home-made thai-style crab cakes with chilli sauce (£5.25; main course £9.25), home-made smoked haddock and prawn pie (£7.95), pork and leek sausages with onion gravy or fresh spinach and ricotta tortellini with tomato and basil sauce (£8.25), daily specials such as fresh local seasonal mussels (£5.25; main course £9.25), steak and kidney suet pudding (£8.95), and grilled skate wing with capers or whoe grilled plaice with lemon butter (£9.95), and home-made puddings like chocolate truffle torte or sticky toffee pudding. The bar is the only place you can smoke throughout the pub. Adnams Best and Broadside, and Woodfordes Nelsons Revenge and Wherry are well kept on handpump, and they have a wide choice of reasonably priced wines, and home-made elderflower cordial in summer; cribbage and dominoes. There are tables in a suntrap courtyard and a pleasant paved garden. *(Recommended by Minda and Stanley Alexander, MDN, B N F and M Parkin, Mrs J Ekins-Daukes, Eleanor and Nick Steinitz, M Thomas, M A and C R Starling, Chris and Louise Taylor, Mike and Heather Watson, Tracey and Stephen Groves, J F M and M West)*

Free house ~ Licensees Dan Goff and Simon Scillitoe ~ Real ale ~ Bar food (12-2, 6-9) ~ Restaurant ~ (01263) 740574 ~ Children in restaurant and family room ~ Open 11-3, 6-11; 12-3, 6-10.30 Sun; closed second and third wk in Jan ~ Bedrooms: £40B/£60B

BRANCASTER STAITHE TF7743 Map 8

White Horse

A149 E of Hunstanton

Cleverly, this particularly well run inn manages to appeal to a wide mix of customers. Locals tend to congregate for a chat and a pint in the front bar, those wanting to enjoy the very good, imaginative food head for the big conservatory, and the delightful, airy bedrooms attract customers all year round. It's all more-or-less open-plan. In the front bar there are good local photographs on the left, with bar billiards and maybe piped music, and on the right is a quieter group of cushioned wicker armchairs and sofas by a table with daily papers, and local landscapes for sale. This runs into the no smoking back conservatory with well spaced furnishings in unvarnished country-style wood, and some light-hearted seasidey decorations; through the big glass windows you can look over the sun deck to the wide views of the tidal marshes and Scolt Head Island beyond. Well kept

Adnams Bitter, Fullers London Pride, and Woodfordes Nelsons Revenge and Wherry on handpump from the handsome counter, manned by exceptionally friendly young staff; they also have 15 malt whiskies and about a dozen wines by the glass from an extensive and thoughtful wine list. The good menu changes twice a day, and as well as lunchtime choices such as home-made roasted tomato, garlic and basil soup (£3.95), sandwiches (£5), caesar salad with a soft-boiled egg (£6.50), chilli peanut pork belly with fine bean salad and peanut dressing (£7.50), poached salmon fishcake with spinach and sorrel sauce (£9.25), and their own sausage with white onion sauce (£9.50), there might be cured salmon and asparagus salad (£5.95), warm seafood terrine with chive butter sauce (£6.10), half a dozen oysters in tempura with julienne of vegetables and chilli sauce (£7.50), fresh home-made pasta with oven-dried tomatoes, feta cheese and herb oil (£9.95), roast loin or pork with apple crisps and sage jus (£11.15), roasted breast of corn-fed local chicken with wild mushrooms and pancetta (£12.95), and roast rib-eye steak with garlic creamed potatoes (£13.95). The coast path runs along the bottom of the garden, and if you stay they do an excellent breakfast. *(Recommended by John Wooll, Tracey and Stephen Groves, Dr T E Hothersall, M J A Switzer, Jamie and Ruth Lyons, O K Smyth, A Sadler, Comus and Sarah Elliott, Michael Dandy, Peter Rozée, M Thomas, D H Burchett, Philip and Susan Philcox, MDN, Graham and Julie Newsom, George Atkinson, Simon Rodway, Steve Nye, Mr and Mrs P L Spencer, Dr David Cockburn; also in the* Good Hotel Guide*)*

Free house ~ Licensees Cliff Nye and Kevin Nobes ~ Real ale ~ Bar food (lunchtime only) ~ Restaurant ~ (01485) 210262 ~ Children in eating area of bar and restaurant ~ Dogs allowed in bar ~ Open 11-11; 12-10.30 Sun ~ Bedrooms: /£104B

BURNHAM MARKET TF8342 Map 8

Hoste Arms

The Green (B1155)

Although this smart 17th-c inn is a civilised place, it attracts a nice variety of customers from gentry and shoppers to farmers and fishermen, and the atmosphere is welcoming. The panelled bar on the right has a series of watercolours showing scenes from local walks, there's a bow-windowed bar on the left, a nice sitting room, a little art gallery in the staircase area, and massive log fires. The lovely walled garden has dark wooden tables, chairs and benches (you can enjoy full restaurant service here), or you can eat in the airy no smoking conservatory with its comfortable sofas. A good choice of imaginative food includes sandwiches (lunchtime; from £3.75; toasted focaccia with tomato, mozzarella and parma ham £6.25), home-made soup (£4.25), caesar salad (£5.95; main course £9.95), burger with crispy bacon and cheddar (£9.25), lambs liver with horseradish mash (£10.25), fresh cromer salad (£10.95), pearl barley and spicy butternut roast with shi-itake mushrooms topped with cheese (£11.25), hoi sin pork tenderloin with thai vegetables (£12.50), fillets of bream, crushed sweet potatoes and chargrilled lemon (£12.95), chargrilled T-bone steak with tomato and mushroom compote (£16.75), and puddings such as cardamon spiced pineapple and papaya crumble, white chocolate cheesecake with raspberries and mixed berry compote (£5.50), and steamed spotted dick with vanilla custard (from £5.50). Sunday roast beef (£9.95). The good wine list has plenty of big names, and includes champagne by the glass; they also have well kept Greene King IPA and Abbot, and Woodfordes Great Eastern, Nelsons Revenge and Wherry on handpump, and a decent choice of malt whiskies. A big awning covers a sizeable eating area in the garden. *(Recommended by David Carr, B N F and M Parkin, Comus and Sarah Elliott, Mike Ridgway, Sarah Miles, Robert M Warner, Roger Wain-Heapy, Michael Sargent, David Cosham, D S Cottrell, Roy Bromell, Mike and Heather Watson, MDN, Sally Anne and Peter Goodale, George Atkinson, DF, NF, Simon Rodway, John and Claire Pettifer)*

Free house ~ Licensees Paul Whittome and Emma Tagg ~ Real ale ~ Bar food ~ Restaurant ~ (01328) 738777 ~ Children in restaurant and family room ~ Dogs welcome ~ Open 11-11; 12-10.30 Sun ~ Bedrooms: £78S/£108B

BURNHAM THORPE TF8541 Map 8

Lord Nelson

Village signposted from B1155 and B1355, near Burnham Market

As Nelson was born in this sleepy village it's no surprise to find lots of pictures and memorabilia of him lining the walls, and there are recipes for unusual rum concoctions called Nelson's Blood and Lady Hamilton's Nip. The little bar has well waxed antique settles on the worn red flooring tiles and smoke ovens in the original fireplace, and an eating room has flagstones, an open fire, and more pictures of Nelson; there are two no smoking rooms. Well kept Greene King IPA and Abbot, and Woodfordes Nelsons Revenge and Wherry tapped from the cask in a back stillroom, and 11 wines by the glass; friendly, obliging staff. Enjoyable daily changing bar food using lots of fresh local ingredients might include butternut squash and parmesan soup (£4.50), home-made salmon mousse or local cockles (£4.95), a plate of filo prawns, scampi, whitebait and squid rings (£6.95), home-made ratatouille with fragrant rice, gammon and egg or bangers and mash with onion gravy (all £8.95), smoked haddock with a wholegrain mustard cream or sugar crusted lamb cutlets with rosemary (£10.95), roast chicken breast with a bacon, mushroom and white wine cream (£11.95), 10oz rib-eye steak with aïoli (£13.95), and puddings such as crème brûlée, home-made chocolate brownies or pears poached in sangria with sweet mascarpone (all £4.75); the eating areas are no smoking. Shove-ha'penny, cribbage and dominoes. There's a good-sized play area in the very big garden, and they are kind to children. *(Recommended by the Didler, O K Smyth, Dr Andy Wilkinson, John Wooll, Derek and Sylvia Stephenson, Roy Bromell, Esther and John Sprinkle, David Boult , H O Dickinson, Maggie and Carl Van Baars, D and J Allen)*

Greene King ~ Lease David Thorley ~ Real ale ~ Bar food (not Sun evening or Mon in winter) ~ Restaurant ~ (01328) 738241 ~ Children in eating area of bar and restaurant ~ Dogs allowed in bar ~ Live bands every second Thurs Oct-June ~ Open 11(12 in winter)-2.30(3 Sat), 6-11; 12-3, 6.30-10.30 Sun; closed Mon in winter

CAWSTON TG1422 Map 8

Ratcatchers

Eastgate, S of village – on B1149 from Norwich turn left towards Haveringland at crossroads ½ mile before the B1145 Cawston turn

Usefully open all day at weekends, this well run dining pub is very popular for its interesting food, and they bake their own bread and make their own herb oils, chutneys, stocks and so forth. As well as lunchtime sandwiches and snacks (from £4.75), the menu might include a pot of mushrooms, bacon, and cambozola cheese with a puff pastry lid or locally smoked sausage with crunchy garlic bread (£4.95), sausage and mash with rich onion and red wine gravy (£7.25), omelettes (from £8.25), herb pancakes (£8.85), home-made pies such as beef in ale or chicken and mushroom (from £8.50), liver and bacon (£9.25), garlic chicken (£10.50), steaks (from £11.50; sauces £2.95 extra), duck breast with a caramelised orange and honey jus (£12.95), and home-made puddings; children's dishes (£4.95). The L-shaped beamed bar has an open fire, nice old chairs, and a fine mix of walnut, beech, elm and oak tables; there's a quieter and cosier candlelit dining room on the right, and a conservatory. Two rooms are no smoking. As well as a good wine list with eight by the glass, and 20 malt whiskies, they've well kept Adnams Bitter, Greene King IPA, and Hancocks HB on handpump; dominoes, cribbage, and piped music. The terrace has heaters for outdoor dining in cooler weather. *(Recommended by David Twitchett, Philip and Susan Philcox, Anthony Barnes, Maureen and Bill Sewell, Dr and Mrs R G J Telfer, Mr and Mrs W T Copeland, SH, Bill and Lisa Copeland, Ian Phillips, John Wooll, David Barnes, Mike and Lynn Robinson)*

Free house ~ Licensees Peter and Denise McCarter ~ Real ale ~ Bar food (12-2, 6-10; all day Sat and Sun) ~ Restaurant ~ (01603) 871430 ~ Children in eating area of bar and restaurant ~ Open 11.45-3, 6-11; 11.45-11 Sat; 11.45-11 Sun; closed 26 Dec

CLEY NEXT THE SEA TG0443 Map 8

Three Swallows

Off A149 E of Blakeney; in village, turn into Holt Road and head for church at Newgate Green

You will be warmly welcomed in this village local by the new licensee, the friendly locals, and tabby cats. The unpretentious carpeted bar on the right has a mix of pubby furnishings including long green leatherette benches around high leathered tables, a good log fire in the small fireplace at one end, and team photographs and pictures of local old boys above its dark dado; cribbage and dominoes. Well kept Adnams Best, and Greene King IPA and Abbot on handpump served from a counter richly carved with fantastical figures and faces, with a handsome carved mirror backing; a couple of steps lead up to a small family eating area. There's a second log fire in the informal no smoking stripped pine restaurant on the left. Good bar food now includes home-made soup (£3.50), sandwiches (from £3.50; fresh seasonal crab £4.25), filled baked potatoes (from £4.95), deep-fried whitebait with a creamy garlic dip (£6.25), spicy thai-style king prawns (£6.50), ham and free range eggs or spinach, tomato and mushroom lasagne (£6.95), steak in ale pie (£7.25), battered haddock or a popular daily roast (£7.50), specials like thai chicken and aubergine curry (£8.25), venison in red wine (£9.95), and honey pork with mustard (£10.95), puddings such as fruit pie or hot toffee and pecan pudding (from £3.75), and children's menu (from £4.25). Below the handsome flint church tower, the big garden has picnic-sets on two grass terraces, and is prettily planted with flowering shrubs; there's a prominent water feature with a surprisingly grandiose fountain, and a wooden climbing frame, budgerigar aviary and goat pen for children. Handy for the salt marshes, the pub is liked by bird-watchers. The bedrooms are simple and comfortable, and they do particularly good, generous breakfasts. *(Recommended by Eleanor and Nick Steinitz, Charles Gysin, Barry Collett, Tracey and Stephen Groves, John Wooll, Esther and John Sprinkle, Revd D Glover, DF, NF, Mick Martin, Wendy Fitzpatrick, Pat and Tony Martin, Pamela Goodwyn)*

Pubmaster ~ Tenant Brian Pennington ~ Real ale ~ Bar food (12-2, 6-9; 12-9 Fri-Sun) ~ (01263) 740526 ~ Children in eating area of bar and restaurant ~ Dogs allowed in bar ~ Open 11-11; 12-10.30 Sun; 11-3, 5.30-11 Mon-Thurs in winter; closed 25 Dec ~ Bedrooms: £40S/£60B

ERPINGHAM TG1732 Map 8

Saracens Head

At Wolterton – not shown on many maps; Erpingham signed off A140 N of Aylsham, keep on through Calthorpe, then where road bends right take the straight-ahead turn-off signposted Wolterton

The bedrooms in this gently civilised dining pub have been redecorated this year and two new ones added; they are still hoping to add a conservatory bar. The two-room bar is simple and stylish, with high ceilings, terracotta walls, and red and white striped curtains at its tall windows – all lending a feeling of space, though it's not actually large. There's a mix of seats from built-in leather wall settles to wicker fireside chairs as well as log fires and flowers, and the windows look out on to a charming old-fashioned gravel stableyard with picnic-sets. A pretty little five-table parlour on the right, in cheerful nursery colours, has another big log fire. Well kept Adnams Bitter and Woodfordes Wherry on handpump, an interesting wine list, local apple juice, and decent malt whiskies; the atmosphere is enjoyably relaxed, and the landlord and his daughter charming and friendly. The imaginative bar food is so popular, you must book to be sure of a table. The changing menu could have starters and snacks such as local mussels with cider and cream, deep-fried brie with apricot sauce, crispy fried aubergine with garlic mayonnaise, lamb bolognese tarts with pesto mayonnaise or red onion and goats cheese tart (from £4.50), main courses like baked cromer crab with mushrooms and sherry, baked avocado with sweet pear and mozzarella, roast local pheasant with calvados and cream, plump scallops with bacon and white wine, and pot roast leg of lamb with red and white beans (from £9.25), and puddings such as chocolate pot with orange jus, mulled wine and red fruit pudding, and treacle tart (£4.25). The Shed next door (run by Mr Dawson-Smith's daughter Rachel) is a workshop and showcase for furniture and interior pieces. *(Recommended by Comus and Sarah Elliott, M and G Rushworth, Peter and Pat Frogley, J F M and M West, Anthony Barnes, DF, NF, Wombat, M and GR, Jeff and Wendy Williams, Maggie and Carl Van Baars, Minda and Stanley Alexander)*

Free house ~ Licensee Robert Dawson-Smith ~ Real ale ~ Bar food ~ Restaurant ~ (01263) 768909 ~ Children welcome ~ Dogs allowed in bedrooms ~ Open 11.30-3.30, 6-11; 12-3.30, 7-10.30 Sun; closed 25 Dec and evening 26 Dec ~ Bedrooms: £45B/£75B

GREAT CRESSINGHAM TF8401 Map 8

Windmill

Village signposted off A1065 S of Swaffham; Water End

All sorts of rooms and side areas ramble cosily around the island servery in this carefully extended black-beamed pub, and there's a variety of pubby furniture from pews and wheelback chairs to red leatherette or plush settles, and masses of mainly rustic bric-a-brac and pictures, particularly big sentimental Victorian lithographs. The walls are mainly painted a warm terracotta pink, though there is some stripped brick and flint, and big log fireplaces are re-equipped with electric look-alikes in warmer weather. The separate more formal dining room and garden room are no smoking. Bar food includes sandwiches (from £2.55), soup (£2.65), home-made spicy steak and ale pudding (£7.25), lemon and black pepper chicken fillet (£7.95), rump steak (from £9.95), braised lamb shank with red wine and rosemary gravy (£12.95), and daily specials such as chicken satay (£3.95), vegetable lasagne (£6.95), sweet and sour chicken (£7.15), and pork in cider pie (£7.25); children's meals (from £3.25). Well kept Adnams Bitter and Broadside, Greene King IPA and Windy Miller Quixote (brewed for the pub) on handpump, with a couple of guest beers such as Batemans XXXB and O'Hanlons Royal Oak, decent sensibly priced wines, 25 malt whiskies, friendly attentive staff. Off a back corridor with a fruit machine is a neat well lit pool room, and one side snug has a big sports TV; also darts, shove-ha'penny, table skittles, cribbage, dominoes, and faint piped music. A good-sized stretch of neatly kept grass behind has picnic-sets and a well equipped play area, including a sandpit; a caravan site almost opposite is well screened by trees. It's been run by the same family for 50 years. *(Recommended by Nick and Alison Dowson, George Atkinson, Esther and John Sprinkle)*

Free house ~ Licensee M J Halls ~ Bar food (12-2, 6-10) ~ Restaurant ~ (01760) 756232 ~ Children in restaurant and family room ~ Dogs allowed in bar ~ Country and Western on Tues nights ~ Open 11-3, 6-11; 12-3.30, 6-10.30 Sun

HORSEY TG4522 Map 8

Nelson Head

Signposted off B1159 (in series of S-bends) N of Great Yarmouth

Run by a friendly landlord, this simple place has two homely unpretentious little rooms furnished with straightforward but comfortable seats (including four tractor-seat bar stools), bits of shiny bric-a-brac, and small local pictures for sale; good fire, geraniums on the window sill, and quite a mix of customers. The garden has picnic-sets and a marquee. Woodfordes Wherry, and (of course) Nelsons Revenge are well kept on handpump; cribbage, dominoes, shove-ha'penny, and piped music. Bar food includes filled baguettes, home-made soup, garlic mushrooms (£4.25), vegetable chilli (£6.25), chicken in lemon and tarragon with baby new potatoes and broccoli (£7.25), good home-made steak and kidney pie (£7.75), fresh local cod (£8.95), and fillet steak (£12.75); the restaurant is no smoking. The pub sign is often hidden by trees in summer; Horsey Windmill and the beach (pleasant walks from here to Winterton-on-Sea) are just down the road. More reports please. *(Recommended by Ian Martin, Derek and Sylvia Stephenson, Shirley Mackenzie, Jestyn Phillips, Gordon Neighbour)*

Free house ~ Licensee Reg C Parsons ~ Real ale ~ Bar food (12-2, 6.15-8.30) ~ Restaurant ~ No credit cards ~ (01493) 393378 ~ Children in family room ~ Dogs allowed in bar ~ Open 11-3, 6-11(10 on Mon-Weds evenings in winter); 12-3, 6-10.30 Sun

ITTERINGHAM TG1430 Map 8

Walpole Arms

Village signposted off B1354 NW of Aylsham

This red brick dining pub has a biggish open-plan bar with exposed beams, stripped brick walls, little windows, and a mix of dining tables. As well as snacks such as summer sandwiches, gloucester old spot pork pie (£5.95), ham and egg (£6.50), pasta with creamed mushrooms, rocket and parmesan (£7.50), and smoked mackerel and spring onion fishcakes with beetroot and crème fraîche (£8.25), the menu might include sweet and sour aubergine salad with chick pea fritters (£5.25), terrine of smoked chicken (£5.50), salad of octopus stewed in red wine with tomato bread (£5.75), risotto of mushroom with parmesan and rocket (£9.25), singapore-style rabbit (£11.95), lime roast salmon with lime pickle potatoes and curried lentils (£12.75), gigot of lamb with ratatouille and basil jus (£12.95), and puddings such as panna cotta with poached rhubarb, cheesecake with apricot purée or italian carrot and nut torta with lemon curd and yoghurt (from £4.75); the attractive restaurant is no smoking. Well kept Adnams Bitter and Broadside, and a Woodfordes beer named for the pub plus Wherry on handpump; they've also a well chosen wine list with up to 15 by the glass. Behind the pub is a two-acre landscaped garden. More reports please. *(Recommended by Anthony Barnes, Michael Williamson, O K Smyth, Wombat, John Wooll, David Twitchett, Chris and Jan Harper, Terry and Linda Moseley)*

Free house ~ Licensee Richard Bryan ~ Real ale ~ Bar food (12-2.30, 7-9; not Sun evening) ~ Restaurant ~ (01263) 587258 ~ Children welcome ~ Dogs allowed in bar ~ Open 12-3, 6-11; 12-3, 7-10.30 Sun

LARLING TL9889 Map 5

Angel

If coming along A11, take B1111 turn-off and follow pub signs

The same family have run this neatly kept pub since 1913, and both locals and visitors can expect a friendly welcome from the helpful landlord. The comfortable 1930s-style lounge on the right has cushioned wheelback chairs, a nice long cushioned and panelled corner settle, some good solid tables for eating and some lower ones, squared panelling, a collection of whisky-water jugs on the delft shelf over the big brick fireplace which houses a big woodburner, a couple of copper kettles, and some hunting prints; there are two dining rooms (one of which is no smoking). From an extensive menu, the popular bar food includes open sandwiches, soup (£3.25), home-made pâté (£4.25), welsh rarebit (£4.50), creamy mushroom pot (£4.95), omelettes (from £4.95), ploughman's (£6.25), burgers (from £6.25), ham and egg (£7.30), stilton and mushroom bake or chicken korma (£7.50), fish crumble (£7.95), lamb chops (£8.95), steaks (from £11.95), and daily specials such as poached smoked haddock mornay (£7.50), home-made steak and kidney pie (£7.95), and lamb korma (£8.25); puddings (£3.95) and children's meals (£3.25). The beers are well kept on handpump and might come from breweries like Adnams, Grainstore, Iceni, Orkney, RCH, Timothy Taylors and Wolf; around 100 malt whiskies. The quarry-tiled black-beamed public bar has a good local atmosphere, with darts, dominoes, cribbage, juke box and fruit machine, and piped music. A neat grass area behind the car park has picnic-sets around a big fairy-lit apple tree, and a safely fenced play area. Peter Beale's old-fashioned rose nursery is nearby. *(Recommended by Beryl and Bill Farmer, Steve Whalley, Stuart and Alison Ballantyne, I A Herdman, M J Caley, Tony Middis, John Saville, Ian Phillips, Catherine Pitt, Dave Braisted)*

Free house ~ Licensee Andrew Stammers ~ Real ale ~ Bar food (till 10 Fri and Sat) ~ Restaurant ~ (01953) 717963 ~ Children welcome ~ Open 10-11; 12-10.30 Sun ~ Bedrooms: £35B/£60B

LETHERINGSETT TG0538 Map 8

Kings Head

A148 just W of Holt

Children love this unpretentious pub (which is not surprisingly full of families) and the emphasis is on keeping them amused. There's a play castle, living willow tunnel, toys, bikes and games (the garden is large enough not to be overwhelmed by this), and a particularly good children's menu with plenty of choices – they even do home-made baby food. The pub is pleasantly set, in grounds well back from the road, opposite a church with an unusual round tower, and it's not far from an interesting working water mill. Inside, the bar has metal-legged tables, a couple of armchairs and log fires, with various interesting prints, pictures and other items, including a signed poem by John Betjeman. There's also a small plush lounge, and a separate games room with darts, pool, TV, shove-ha'penny, dominoes, cribbage, fruit machines, and piped music. Tasty bar food from the straightforward, reasonably priced menu includes home-made soup (£3), sandwiches, baps or baguettes (from £3), three-egg omelette (£3.95), home-made liver pâté (£4.15), filled baked potatoes (from £4.80), ploughman's and salads (from £6.20), home-cooked ham and egg (£6.80), vegetarian chilli pasta bake or home-made steak and kidney pie (£7), lamb cutlets (£7.20), and steaks (from £11.05), with daily specials, and puddings such as home-made chocolate profiteroles or apple pie (£3.15); there's also a braille menu. Friendly and efficient staff serve well kept ales from local breweries like Elgoods, Greene King Abbot, Woodfordes and Wolf; milk shakes, slush puppies, children's (and adults') cocktails, and decent wines. The pub's popularity with families does mean that housekeeping can, at busy times, become something of a lost cause. *(Recommended by Mike Ridgway, Sarah Miles, R C Vincent, John Wooll, David Cosham, Tracey and Stephen Groves, Esther and John Sprinkle, Adrian White)*

Free house ~ Licensees David and Pamela Watts ~ Real ale ~ Bar food (all day) ~ (01263) 712691 ~ Children welcome ~ Dogs welcome ~ Live bands Sat evening ~ Open 11-11; 12-10.30 Sun

NORWICH TG2308 Map 5

Adam & Eve ♀ £

Bishopgate; follow Palace Street from Tombland, N of cathedral

This is a smashing place to retreat to after shopping in the city. It's full of history and is thought to date back to at least 1249 (when it was used by workmen building the cathedral), and even has a Saxon well beneath the lower bar floor, though the striking dutch gables were added in the 14th and 15th c. The little old-fashioned bars quickly fill at lunchtime with a good mix of customers, and have antique high-backed settles (one handsomely carved), cushioned benches built into partly panelled walls, and tiled or parquet floors; the snug is no smoking, and lower bar is no smoking until 7pm. Good value and well liked straightforward bar food includes sandwiches or baguettes (from £2.85; lunchtime only and not Sunday), soup (£3.45; tasty cheese and ale soup £3.95), mushrooms stuffed with stilton or cheddar or elizabethan pork (£5.45), ploughman's, beef in ale pie or home-made chilli (all £5.95), and specials such as hot pork and apple sauce baguette (£3.25), cheese and vegetable bake (£5.45), and lasagne (£5.75). Well kept Adnams Bitter, Greene King IPA, Theakstons Old Peculier and Charles Wells Bombardier on handpump, over 60 malt whiskies, around a dozen decent wines by the glass, and Addlestone's cider; piped music. The colourful tubs and hanging baskets are really pretty in summer, and there are wooden picnic-sets out in front. *(Recommended by Peter F Marshall, Anthony Barnes, J F M and M West, the Didler, David Carr, Meg and Colin Hamilton, Alison Hayes, Pete Hanlon, John Saville, Richard Jennings, Pat and Clive Sherriff, Fred and Lorraine Gill, Tina and David Woods-Taylor)*

Unique (Enterprise) ~ Lease Rita McCluskey ~ Real ale ~ Bar food (12-7; 12-2.30 Sun) ~ (01603) 667423 ~ Children in snug until 7pm ~ Open 11-11; 12-10.30 Sun; closed 25-26 Dec, 1 Jan

Fat Cat

West End Street

With around 25 quickly changing real ales, it's not surprising that this well run classic town pub is so very popular. About half of their beers are on handpump, while the rest are tapped from the cask in a stillroom behind the bar – big windows reveal all: Adnams Bitter, Caledonian 80/-, Dark Star Red Ale, Durham White Bishop, Fullers ESB and an organic one, Honeydew, Greene King Abbot and Ruddles County, Harviestoun Bitter & Twisted, Hop Back Summer Lightning, Kelham Island Pale Rider, Leatherbritches Bespoke, North Yorkshire Flying Herbert, Oakham Bishops Farewell, RCH Old Slug Porter, a beer named for the pub from Reepham, Salopian Lemon Dream, Timothy Taylors Landlord, Tipperary Carlo Red Ale and Dwan Black Pearl Stout, and Woodfordes Norfolk Nog. You'll also find six draught belgian beers (two of them fruit), draught lagers from Germany and the Czech Republic, up to 15 bottled belgian beers, 15 country wines, and local farm cider. Open all day, with a good mix of customers, and a lively bustling atmosphere at busy times, with tranquil lulls in the middle of the afternoon. The no-nonsense furnishings include plain scrubbed pine tables and simple solid seats, lots of brewery memorabilia, bric-a-brac and stained-glass. Bar food consists of a dozen or so rolls (60p) and good pies (£1.60) at lunchtime (not Sunday). There are tables outside. *(Recommended by the Didler, Alison Hayes, Pete Hanlon, Catherine Pitt, Dr David Cockburn)*

Free house ~ Licensee Colin Keatley ~ Real ale ~ No credit cards ~ (01603) 624364 ~ Children allowed in conservatory ~ Open 12(11 Sat)-11; 12-10.30 Sun; closed 31 Dec evening

RINGSTEAD TF7040 Map 8

Gin Trap

Village signposted off A149 near Hunstanton; OS Sheet 132 map reference 707403

The well kept bar in this attractive white pained pub has beams, a woodburning stove, captain's chairs and cast-iron-framed tables, and well kept Adnams Best, Greene King Abbot, Woodfordes Norfolk Wherry and Nelson's Revenge on handpump, and half a dozen wines by the glass. The small no smoking dining room is candlelit in the evening, and the top bar is also no smoking. Bar food includes soup (£4.25), filled ciabatta or granary baps (from £4.95; ham, mustard and william pear chutney £5.25), ploughman's (£6.50), wild boar sausages with red onion gravy (£7.75), home-made gnocchi with roasted root vegetables (£8.25), steak and kidney or fish pies (£8.50), and puddings such as apple mousse with caramel sauce or dark chocolate fondant with pistachio ice-cream; you can also eat from the more elaborate dining room menu in the bar. Outside, a handsome spreading chestnut tree shelters the car park, and the neatly kept back garden has seats on the grass or small paved area, and pretty flowering tubs. There's an art gallery next door, and self-catering accommodation. The Peddar's Way is close by. *(Recommended by Mrs M A Mees, Tracey and Stephen Groves, O K Smyth, Pat and Derek Roughton, Pat and Tony Martin, David Green, Peter F Beever, Mike and Shelley Woodroffe)*

Free house ~ Licensees Margaret Greer and Susan Little ~ Real ale ~ Bar food (12-2, 6-9) ~ Restaurant ~ (01485) 525264 ~ Children in eating area of bar ~ Dogs allowed in bar ~ Open 11.30-11; 12-10.30 Sun; 11-2.30, 6-11(10.30 Sun) in winter ~ Bedrooms: /£80B

SNETTISHAM TF6834 Map 8

Rose & Crown

Village signposted from A149 King's Lynn—Hunstanton just N of Sandringham; coming in on the B1440 from the roundabout just N of village, take first left turn into Old Church Road

Extremely popular with a wide mix of customers, this pretty white cottage has a very thoughtfully put together interior, with a separate character for each of the different areas: an old-fashioned beamed front bar with black settles on its tiled floor, and a great log fire; another big log fire in a back bar with the landlord's sporting trophies and old sports equipment; a no smoking bar with a colourful but soothing décor (this room is favoured by people eating); and another warmly decorated room, lovely for families, with painted settles and big old tables, leads out to the garden. Some nice old pews and other interesting furniture sit on the wooden floor of the main dining room, and there are shelves with old bottles and books, and old prints and watercolours. All three restaurant areas are no smoking. At lunchtime, the good, interesting bar food might include chilli and mint marinated olives (£3.50), soups (£4.50), sandwiches (from £4.95; crab, lemon and dill crème fraîche £5.25), roast chicken livers with braised chicory and beetroot vinaigrette (£5.25; main course £7.50), coconut crusted chicken with fried bananas and tomato relish (£5.50; main course £7.95), fried sardines with remolata crust and tapenade (£5.75; main course £8.95), ham and eggs with red pepper ketchup (£7.50), linguini with hot paprika meatballs and crème fraîche or bratwurst sausages with sauerkraut and whole grain mustard (£8.75), and steak and kidney pudding with mustard mash (£9.50); evening choices such as crispy italian bacon, egg and rocket salad (£5.25), aromatic pork belly with sticky apples and crackling (£5.50), chicken satay terrine with chilli and mango salsa (£5.75), red mullet and king prawn tom yam and noodle broth (£10.95), crisp confit of duck leg with hash browns and pomegranate molasses (£11.75), and chargrilled marinated sirloin steak with potato and swiss cheese pie (£13.95), with puddings like roast peach melba with schnapps ice-cream, and bread and butter pudding with pistachio anglaise (all £4.50). Well kept Adnams Broadside, Bass, Fullers London Pride and Greene King IPA on handpump, 20 wines by the glass, organic fruit juices and farm cider. Smart new café-style aluminium and blue chairs with matching blue tables, cream parasols and an outdoor heater have been added this year to the colourful enclosed garden with its herbaceous borders, flowering shrubs and two spectacular willow trees; there's also a wooden fort for children. *(Recommended by Tracey and Stephen Groves, John Wooll, Jenny and Peter Lowater, Richard Cole, Jamie and Ruth Lyons, Gordon Tong, Mr and Mrs C W Widdowson, Dave Braisted, David Eberlin, Esther and John Sprinkle, Pat and Roger Fereday, DF, NF, Peter Rozee, Terry and Linda Moseley, Maggie and Carl Van Baars, Alison Hayes, Pete Hanlon; also in the* Good Hotel Guide*)*

Free house ~ Licensee Anthony Goodrich ~ Real ale ~ Bar food (12-2(till 2.30 wknds and summer holidays), 6.30-9(9.30 Fri, Sat)) ~ Restaurant ~ (01485) 540099 ~ Children in restaurant and family room ~ Dogs welcome ~ Open 11-11; 12-10.30 Sun ~ Bedrooms: £50B/£80B

STANHOE TF8036 Map 5

Crown

B1155 towards Burnham Market

Clean and bright inside, this little open-plan country local has aircraft pictures on the white walls that give a clue to the welcoming and attentive landlord's background – he's ex-RAF. There are upholstered wall seats and wheelback chairs around dark tables on the carpet, a central log fire, and beams and joists overhead – one beam densely studded with coins. Gas masks, guns and various military headgear hang behind the bar, which often has a big bunch of flowers and dispenses well kept Elgoods Greyhound and Cambridge on handpump, and decent house wines and coffee; piped music. A sensibly short choice of bar food includes sandwiches (from £3.90), sausages, chips and beans (£5.60), poached salmon, lamb chops or steak and kidney pie (£7), and puddings such as treacle sponge (£3.65). Service is friendly, and the atmosphere is good-hearted and relaxed. There are tables on a side lawn with a couple of apple trees, and a bigger lawn behind with room for caravans; fancy breeds of chicken may be running free. *(Recommended by Joyce and Maurice Cottrell, M J A Switzer, John Wooll)*

Elgoods ~ Licensees Page and Sarah Clowser ~ Bar food (not Sun evening exc bank hol wknds) ~ Restaurant ~ No credit cards ~ (01485) 518330 ~ Well behaved children welcome ~ Dogs allowed in bar ~ Open 12-3.30, 6-11; 12-3.30, 7-10.30 Sun

STIFFKEY TF9743 Map 8

Red Lion

A149 Wells—Blakeney

The new licensee doesn't seem to have made any dramatic changes to this bustling pub. The oldest parts of the simple bars have a few beams, aged flooring tiles or bare floorboards, and big open fires; also, a mix of pews, small settles and a couple of stripped high-backed settles, a nice old long deal table among quite a few others, and oil-type or lantern wall lamps. Well kept Greene King IPA and Abbot, and Woodfordes Wherry and a guest from Woodfordes on handpump, and ten wines by the glass; dominoes and cribbage. Good home-made bar food now includes sandwiches (from £3.25), soup (£3.95), thai spring rolls and sweet chilli sauce, deep-fried local whitebait, and chicken liver pâté (all £4.95), vegetable lasagne (£7.95), chicken and leek pudding with creamy leek sauce, curries, cottage pie or fish pie (all £8.50), rump steak or venison steak with plum compote (£9.95), seasonal offerings such as local moules marinière (£5.95), cromer crab salad or crab and prawn cakes (£7.95), and roast pheasant (£8.50), and puddings (£3.95); winter Sunday roasts. The back restaurant and conservatory are both no smoking. A back gravel terrace has proper tables and seats, with more on grass further up beyond; there are some pleasant walks nearby. *(Recommended by John Millwood, Maureen and Bill Sewell, Peter and Pat Frogley, MDN, Tracey and Stephen Groves, Richard Cole, Dr Andy Wilkinson, J F M and M West, the Didler, John Wooll, Fiona Wynn, Pete Stroud, Brian Haywood, M Thomas, David Cosham, Pat and Clive Sherriff, Dr B and Mrs P B Baker, P Price, Ken Arthur, Mr and Mrs I Bell)*

Free house ~ Licensee Andrew Waddison ~ Real ale ~ Bar food ~ Restaurant ~ (01328) 830552 ~ Children welcome ~ Dogs welcome ~ Open 11-11; 12-10.30 Sun

STOW BARDOLPH TF6205 Map 5

Hare Arms

Just off A10 N of Downham Market

The hard-working licensees have now run this neatly kept creeper-covered pub for 28 years and, thankfully, have no plans to move on. The friendly bar has a bustling and traditional village atmosphere, old advertising signs, fresh flowers and bric-a-brac, plenty of tables around its central servery, and a good log fire. This bar opens into a spacious heated and well planted no smoking conservatory; the restaurant is also no smoking. Enjoyable bar food includes lunchtime sandwiches (from £2.75), filled baked potatoes (from £4.75), and ploughman's (from £7.25), as well as home-made curry (£7.75), home-made lasagne (£8.25), large salads (from £8.25; avocado and cajun chicken £8.95), and daily specials such as sausages with a roast garlic mash and chive sauce (£7.25), large ravioli filled with mozzarella, goats cheese, olives and tomato coated with a creamy basil sauce, chicken breast wrapped in smoked bacon with a wild mushroom and thyme sauce or steak pie in a cream, brandy and black peppercorn sauce (all £8.25), haddock fillet topped with herb crust (£9.25), slow cooked lamb shank (£9.50), and steaks (from £12); seasonal crabs and lobsters, and Sunday roast beef (£8.25). You will be asked to leave your credit card behind the bar counter if you are running a tab. Friendly, helpful staff serve well kept Greene King IPA, Abbot and Old Speckled Hen, and a guest such as Wadworths 6X on handpump, a decent range of wines, and quite a few malt whiskies; fruit machine. There are plenty of seats in the large garden behind, and in the pretty front garden too, and chickens and peacocks roam freely. The local church contains an effigy of Lady Sarah Hare, who is reputed to have died as a consequence of sewing on a Sunday and pricking her finger. *(Recommended by Dr Andy Wilkinson, Pamela Goodwyn, John Wooll, Mike Ridgway, Sarah Miles, Mr and Mrs Richard Hanks)*

Greene King ~ Tenants David and Trish McManus ~ Real ale ~ Bar food (12-2, 7-10) ~ Restaurant ~ (01366) 382229 ~ Children in family room and conservatory ~ Open 11-2.30, 6-11; 12-2.30, 7-10.30 Sun; closed 25-26 Dec

SWANTON MORLEY TG0117 Map 8

Darbys

B1147 NE of Dereham

It's not surprising that evenings in this creeper-covered local are so busy as they keep up to eight quickly changing real ales on handpump: Adnams Best and Broadside, Badger Tanglefoot, Ringwood Old Thumper, St Peter's Organic Best, Theakstons Old Peculier, Thwaites Thoroughbred, and Woodfordes Wherry. The long bare-boarded country-style bar has a comfortable lived-in feel, with lots of gin traps and farming memorabilia, a good log fire (with the original bread oven alongside), tractor seats with folded sacks lining the long, attractive serving counter, and maybe fresh flowers on the big stripped pine tables. A step up through a little doorway by the fireplace takes you through to the no smoking dining room. The children's room (also no smoking) has a toy box and a glassed-over well, floodlit from inside; piped music. Enjoyable bar food includes filled baguettes and baked potatoes (from £4), thai fishcakes with chilli dipping sauce (£5.50), shrimp and salmon salad (£5.95), ploughman's (£6.50), beer battered haddock (£7.50), curries (from £7.50), mushroom and vegetable pesto bake (£8.95), pork steak stacked with bacon, pineapple and melted mozzarella (£9.25), steak and mushroom pudding (£10.85), baked whole bass with lemongrass and ginger (£10.95), and steaks (from £11.65). The garden has a really good play area; the two dogs are called Boots and Dylan. B&B is available in carefully converted farm buildings a few minutes away, and there's plenty to do if you're staying, as the family also own the adjoining 720-acre estate, and can arrange clay pigeon shooting, golf, fishing, nature trails and craft instruction. *(Recommended by Michael and Jenny Back, David and Ruth Hollands, Ian Phillips, MDN, Dr and Mrs R G J Telfer, Pat and Tony Martin)*

Free house ~ Licensees John Carrick and Louise Battle ~ Real ale ~ Bar food (12-2.15, 6.30-9.45; 12-9.45(9.15 Sun)) ~ Restaurant ~ (01362) 637647 ~ Children welcome ~ Dogs allowed in bar ~ Open 11.30-3, 6-11; 11.30-11 Sat; 12-10.30 Sun

TERRINGTON ST JOHN TF5314 Map 8

Woolpack

Village signposted off A47 W of King's Lynn

The warm and lively atmosphere created by the ebullient landlady is one of the reasons that this roomy and airy roadside pub is so well liked. The rooms are decorated with her bright modern ceramics and cheerful contemporary prints (she's also been elected a member of the Society of Botanical Artists), and the bar has red plush banquettes and matching or wheelback chairs around its dark pub tables, a patterned red carpet, and terracotta pink walls; the large back no smoking dining room (which looks out on to the garden) has comfortable green seating, and an art deco décor punctuated by Mondrian prints. The reliably good value food, with friendly efficient waitresses, also underpins the pub's popularity. At lunchtime you might find sandwiches and ploughman's (£3.75), along with more substantial meals such as large cod and chips or seafood medley (£7.25), lamb steak with mint gravy, pork fillet with stilton sauce and gammon and pineapple (all £7.75), salmon in lemon butter sauce (£8.50), and steaks (from £10.25), with specials such as steak and kidney pie, chicken tikka masala, sweet and sour pork, and swordfish (from £7.75); children's meals (£3.50). Puddings are a strong point, and besides a tempting display in the cold cabinet there are usually hot ones such as spotted dick or treacle sponge and custard (£3.50). Greene King IPA, and Charles Wells Eagle and Bombardier on handpump; fruit machine, piped music; good disabled access. There are picnic-sets on neat grass by a herb garden and the car park (which has recycling bins including Planet Aid clothes and shoes), and a side bowling green. *(Recommended by Michael and Jenny Back, Carole and Mick Hall, John Wooll, Sally Anne and Peter Goodale)*

Free house ~ Licensees Lucille and Barry Carter ~ Bar food ~ Restaurant ~ (01945) 881097 ~ Children in eating area of bar and restaurant ~ Open 11.30-2.30, 6.30-11; 12-7 Sun; closed evenings 25 and 26 Dec

THORNHAM TF7343 Map 8

Lifeboat

Turn off A149 by Kings Head, then take first left turn

There's plenty of atmosphere in this rambling old white-painted stone pub, and the main Smugglers bar is lit with antique paraffin lamps suspended among an array of traps and yokes on its great oak-beamed ceiling. It's cosily furnished with low settles, window seats, pews, carved oak tables and rugs on the tiled floor, and there are also masses of guns, swords, black metal mattocks, reed-slashers and other antique farm tools. A couple of little rooms lead off here, and all in all there are five open fires. No games machines or piped music, though they still play the ancient game of 'pennies' which was outlawed in the late 1700s, and dominoes. Up some steps from the bustling verdant no smoking conservatory is a sunny terrace with picnic-sets, and further back is a children's playground with fort and slide. Although it draws the crowds in summer, it's still very much a place where locals drop in for a pint. Enjoyable bar food includes home-made soup (£3.95), filled baguettes (from £5.25), chicken liver pâté with redcurrant sauce (£4.95), mushrooms in a stilton and garlic cream sauce (£5.10), mediterranean salad (£5.95; main course £8.95), ploughman's (£6.25), chargrilled burger with bacon and cheese (£8.50), spinach and mozzarella lasagne or cromer crab salad (£8.75), beer-battered fish with home-made tartare sauce or liver and bacon (£8.95), hickory pork ribs (£9.95), steaks (from £13.50), and daily specials such as local oysters (£1.40 each), home-made butternut squash, leek and potato soup (£3.95), salad of smoked duck, cherry tomatoes and pecan nuts drizzled with hoi sin sauce (£5.25), pork and apple sausages with olive mash and onion gravy (£8.25), mild, fruity chicken curry (£8.75), and seared loin of tuna with peppery noodles and sweet chilli sauce (£11.95); children's menu (from £3.75). The restaurant is no smoking. Well kept Adnams, Greene King IPA and Abbot, and Woodfordes Wherry on handpump served by friendly staff, eight wines by the glass, freshly squeezed orange juice, and Old Rosie cider. The inn faces half a mile of coastal sea flats, and there are lots of lovely surrounding walks. Most of the bedrooms have sea views. *(Recommended by Keith and Margaret Kettell, Tracey and Stephen Groves, John and Marion Tyrie, John Wooll, O K Smyth, Dr D Parker, Derek and Sylvia Stephenson, the Didler, I Louden, Mr Bishop, Dr Andy Wilkinson, Pam and David Bailey, Mr and Mrs Broadhurst, David Cosham, David Eberlin, Esther and John Sprinkle, Giles and Annie Francis, Gordon Neighbour, DF, NF, Ian Arthur, Terry and Linda Moseley, Alison Hayes, Pete Hanlon)*

Free house ~ Licensee Charles Coker ~ Real ale ~ Bar food (12-2.30, 6.30-9.30) ~ Restaurant ~ (01485) 512236 ~ Children welcome ~ Dogs allowed in bar and bedrooms ~ Open 11-11; 12-10.30 Sun ~ Bedrooms: £58B/£76B

TIVETSHALL ST MARY TM1686 Map 5

Old Ram

A140 15 miles S of Norwich, outside village

Friendly and well run, this popular place handily serves food all day. The spacious country-style main room has lots of stripped beams and standing timbers, antique craftsmen's tools on the ceiling, a huge log fire in the brick hearth, a turkey rug on rosy brick floors, and a longcase clock. It's ringed by smaller side areas, and one no smoking dining room has striking navy walls and ceiling, swagged curtains and an open woodburning stove; this leads to a second comfortable mainly no smoking dining room and gallery. A wide choice of well liked bar food includes an open sandwich of the day (£4.95; soup and a sandwich £6.50), caesar salad (£5.50), duck breast salad with parsnip crisps, honey and balsamic vinegar (£6.50), local sausages with onion gravy (£8.95), aubergine and vegetable stack with roasted sweet pepper sauce (£9.95), spaghetti with king prawns, salmon, crayfish tails, garlic and chilli (£10.95), skate with black butter (£11.95), calves liver and bacon (£13.95), and aberdeen angus steaks (from £15.50), with specials like king scallops in garlic butter (£6.95), cod with a herb crust on a rösti with creamed spinach, fried mushrooms and shallots (£11.95), and pork medallions with a mushroom and shallot cream sauce with apricot rice (£13.95), and puddings such as home-made steamed chocolate pudding with chocolate chips, belgian chocolate sauce and crème fraîche, lemon tart or crème brûlée with ginger shortbread (from £4.25). There's an OAP two-course lunch (£7.95), and a breakfast menu (7.30am-11am, from £6.95). Unobtrusive fruit machine, TV, cribbage, dominoes, and piped music. Well kept Adnams, Bass, Timothy Taylors and Woodfordes Wherry on handpump, 28 wines by the glass, fresh orange, apple, pineapple and carrot juice, milkshakes, and 20 malt whiskies. The sheltered flower-filled terrace of this much extended pub is very civilised, with outdoor heaters and big green parasols. *(Recommended by Graham Holden, Julie Lee, Mike and Wendy Proctor, Ken Millar, Martin Jennings)*

Free house ~ Licensee John Trafford ~ Real ale ~ Bar food (all day) ~ Restaurant ~ (01379) 676794 ~ Children in eating area of bar and in restaurant but under-7s must leave by 8pm ~ Dogs welcome ~ Open 11-11; 12-10.30 Sun; closed 25-26 Dec ~ Bedrooms: £60.50B/£83B

UPPER SHERINGHAM TG1441 Map 8

Red Lion

B1157; village signposted off A148 Cromer—Holt, and the A149 just W of Sheringham

This is a smashing little pub run by a cheerful landlady. There's always a buoyant atmosphere and plenty of chatty regulars, and visitors are made very welcome. The two modest but charming little bars have stripped high-backed settles and country-kitchen chairs on the red tiles or bare boards, terracotta painted walls, a big woodburning stove, and newspapers to read; the red-walled snug is no smoking. It's best to book a table if you want to enjoy the good bar food (they tell us prices have not changed since last year): home-made soup (£3.50), sandwiches (from £4), home-made pâté or stilton-stuffed mushrooms (£4.50), sweet and sour chicken (£6.50), lasagne (£7.25), vegetable curry, lambs liver in port and orange gravy (£6.75), steak and ale pie (£7.75), and around ten fresh fish dishes such as plaice, sole, cod, haddock, halibut, trout and salmon with various sauces. The restaurant gets very busy especially at weekends during the holiday season. Well kept Greene King IPA, Woodfordes Wherry and a guest on handpump, with around 12 malt whiskies and decent wines; dominoes and card games. They are still hoping to add six new bedrooms and a conservatory dining area to this traditional-looking flint cottage. *(Recommended by Shirley Mackenzie, Bruce and Penny Wilkie, Dr and Mrs R G J Telfer, David and Julie Glover, George Atkinson, John Wooll, Dr David Cockburn)*

Free house ~ Licensee Sue Prew ~ Real ale ~ Bar food (12-2, 6.30-9) ~ Restaurant ~ No credit cards ~ (01263) 825408 ~ Children in restaurant and family room ~ Dogs welcome ~ Open 11.30-11; 12-10.30 Sun; 11-3, 6.30-11 winter weekdays; 12-4 Sun in winter; closed winter Sun evenings ~ Bedrooms: /£45

WARHAM TF9441 Map 8

Three Horseshoes

Warham All Saints; village signposted from A149 Wells-next-the-Sea—Blakeney, and from B1105 S of Wells

For those who enjoy genuinely unspoilt and old-fashioned places, this cheery local is the place to head for. The simple interior with its gas lighting looks little changed since the 1920s, and parts of the building date back to the 1720s. There are stripped deal or mahogany tables (one marked for shove-ha'penny) on a stone floor, red leatherette settles built around the partly panelled walls of the public bar, royalist photographs, and open fires in Victorian fireplaces. An antique American Mills one-arm bandit is still in working order (it takes 5p pieces), there's a big longcase clock with a clear piping strike, and a twister on the ceiling to point out who gets the next round; darts, cribbage, shove-ha'penny, and dominoes. Most people choose from the specials board, but the menu offers lunchtime sandwiches (not at weekends), filled baked potatoes (from £3.60), various ploughman's (from £4.90), vegetable bake (£6.20), cod in cheese sauce (£7.50), beef in ale pie (£8.20), and puddings (£3.80). They don't take bookings, so it's a good idea to arrive early at busy times; the dining room is no smoking. Greene King IPA, Woodfordes Wherry, and a weekly guest well kept on handpump or tapped from the cask, country wines, local summer cider, and home-made lemonade. One of the outbuildings houses a wind-up gramophone museum – opened on request. There's a courtyard garden with flower tubs and a well. *(Recommended by John Wooll, I Louden, Mr Bishop, Dr Andy Wilkinson, Anthony Barnes, John Beeken, the Didler, Roger Wain-Heapy, Maureen and Bill Sewell, Anthony Longden, Pam and David Bailey, Brian Haywood, P Price, Giles and Annie Francis, Alison Hayes, Pete Hanlon)*

Free house ~ Licensee Iain Salmon ~ Real ale ~ Bar food (12-1.45, 6-8.30; not 25-26 Dec) ~ No credit cards ~ (01328) 710547 ~ Children welcome ~ Dogs welcome ~ Open 11.30-2.30, 6-11; 12-2.30, 6-10.30 Sun ~ Bedrooms: £24/£48(£52S)

WELLS-NEXT-THE-SEA TF9143 Map 8

Crown

The Buttlands

Norfolk Dining Pub of the Year

Since Chris and Jo Coubrough have taken over this 16th-c coaching inn, readers have been quick to voice their warm enthusiasm. The beamed bar is a friendly place with an informal mix of furnishings on the stripped wooden floor, local photographs on the red walls, a good selection of newspapers to read in front of the open fire, and well kept Adnams Best and Broadside and Woodfordes Wherry on handpump; 15 wines by the glass. The sunny no smoking conservatory with wicker chairs on the tiled floor, beams, and modern art is where families with well behaved children can sit, and there's a pretty no smoking restaurant; piped music. Served by friendly young staff, the very good modern bar food might include chicken and bacon terrine with chargrilled vegetables (£5.10), deep-fried fishcakes (£5.25; main course £7.50), blue cheese, mango and red onion tart (£5.50), sandwiches with home-made crisps (from £5.75; steak sandwich with garlic aïoli and tomato £7.95), dressed crab salad or a well liked tapas slate with interesting appetisers (£8.95), feta and roasted butternut squash risotto (£9.25), moroccan spiced lamb burger with butter bean and new potato salad and yoghurt dressing (£9.95), roast chicken breast with dijon and shi-itake jus (£10.50), chargrilled rib-eye steak with mustard mash and sweet onions (£13.50), and puddings such as chocolate bread and butter pudding with crème anglaise, lime crème brûlée or iced mango parfait (from £4.25). You can sit outside on the sheltered sun deck. *(Recommended by Charles Gysin, Mike and Heather Watson, Fred and Lorraine Gill, MDN, A D Cross, Alan and Sue Folwell, Terry and Linda Moseley)*

Free house ~ Licensees Chris and Jo Coubrough ~ Real ale ~ Bar food (12-2.30, 6.30-9.30) ~ Restaurant ~ (01328) 710209 ~ Children welcome ~ Dogs allowed in bar ~ Open 11-11; 12-10.30 Sun ~ Bedrooms: £60B/£95B

WEST BECKHAM TG1339 Map 8

Wheatsheaf

Off A148 Holt—Cromer; Church Road

This flint-walled village inn presents an attractive picture. It's been upgraded over the years, but kept pleasantly traditional, even homely, with its beams and cottagey doors, a roaring log fire in one part, a smaller coal one in another, comfortable chairs and banquettes, and the enormous black cat. Well kept Greene King IPA, Woodfordes Wherry, Nelsons Revenge, Norfolk Nog and Headcracker, and two guests on handpump or tapped from the cask (often at a bargain price), a good choice of wines in generous measures, and over a dozen locally produced country wines. Generous helpings of good lunchtime bar food might include sandwiches and filled baguettes (from £3.50; ciabatta with chargrilled chicken, avocado and spicy mayonnaise with salad and fries £5.50), filled baked potatoes (from £4.25), ploughman's (from £5.50), cromer crab with minted potatoes (£6.95), baby spinach, mixed bean and goats cheese strudel topped with a parsley and cheese sauce (£8.25), and home-made steak and kidney pie (£8.75), with evening choices like home-made chicken liver pâté with red onion marmalade (£4.25), potted king prawns in garlic and herb butter (£4.95), home-made lasagne (£7.50), chicken fillet in herbs and lemon on roast vegetable couscous (£9.25), and leg of lamb steak in yoghurt, mint and coriander with a mint risotto (£10.50); weekly specials such as home-made soup (£2.95), spiced sausage platter with roast basil plum tomatoes and black olives or chicken bang-bang kebabs with peanut and chilli dressing (£4.75), leek, cheddar and mozzarella filo tart (£8.50), grilled salmon fillet on creamy potato bake topped with a crab and ginger sauce (£9.25), and fillet of beef wellington filled with stilton, wilted spinach and mozzarella (£11.75). The two dining rooms are no smoking. Darts, pool, shove-ha'penny, cribbage, dominoes, fruit machine, juke box, TV and piped music. There are tables out in the partly terraced front garden, and an area for children with swings, rabbits and chickens. *(Recommended by Derek Field, Tracey and Stephen Groves)*

Free house ~ Licensees Clare and Daniel Mercer ~ Real ale ~ Bar food (not Sun evening) ~ Restaurant ~ (01263) 822110 ~ Children in eating area of bar and restaurant ~ Dogs allowed in bar ~ Open 11.30-3, 6.30-11; 12-3, 7-10.30 Sun; 12-2.30, 6.30-11 in winter

WINTERTON-ON-SEA TG4919 Map 8

Fishermans Return

From B1159 turn into village at church on bend, then turn right into The Lane

Close to good beach walks, this friendly and attractive little pub is spotlessly kept, and the cosily white-painted no smoking lounge bar has vases of fresh flowers, neat brass-studded red leatherette seats and a roaring log fire. The panelled public bar has low ceilings and a glossily varnished nautical air (good fire in here too); the family room, dining room and small bar are no smoking. It's been well run by the same hospitable licensees for almost 30 years, and the staff are friendly and courteous. The short choice of tasty bar food includes toasties (from £2.50), ploughman's (£5), fish pie (£5.75), chilli con carne or roast chicken breast (£7.25), seafood special (£8.25), and sirloin steak (£11.50), and there are regularly changing specials such as local asparagus soup (£3.50), fresh crab with granary bread or sea trout mousse (£5.75), shank of lamb in rhubarb and ginger (£10.75), and puddings such as ginger sponge custard or pineapple upside-down pudding (£3.50). Well kept Adnams Best and seasonal beers, Greene King IPA and Broadside, and Woodfordes Wherry on handpump, ten wines by the glass, around 30 malt whiskies, and farm cider; darts, piped music, dominoes, cribbage, pool, fruit machine, juke box and piped music. In fine weather you can sit on the attractive wrought-iron and wooden benches on a pretty front terrace with lovely views, or in the sheltered garden. This is a charming place to stay, and the cosy bedrooms (be careful going up the steep curving stairs) have low doors, uneven floors and individual furniture. *(Recommended by Shirley Mackenzie, Ian Martin, Keith and Chris O'Neill, Steve Whalley, Roger Everett, Colin McKerrow, Quentin and Carol Williamson, Comus and Sarah Elliott, Maggie and Carl Van Baars)*

Free house ~ Licensees John and Kate Findlay ~ Real ale ~ Bar food ~ (01493) 393305 ~ Children in family room ~ Dogs welcome ~ Open 11-2.30, 6.30-11; 11-11 Sat; 12.10.30 Sun ~ Bedrooms: £45B/£70B

WOODBASTWICK TG3315 Map 8

Fur & Feather

Off B1140 E of Norwich

It's certainly worth visiting this carefully converted thatched cottage as the Woodfordes brewery is next door and they keep all eight of their beers on handpump or tapped from the cask; readers also enjoy visiting the brewery shop. The style and atmosphere are not what you'd expect of a brewery tap as it's set out more like a dining pub and the décor is modern. Bar food includes home-made soup (£3.50), sandwiches or filled baguettes (from £3.50), filled baked potatoes (£5.50), roast pepper pasta (£7), home-baked ham and eggs (£7.50), burgers (£7.75), lambs liver and bacon (£8.50), steak and kidney pudding (£8.75), seafood medley (£10.25), sirloin steak (£12.50), and puddings (£4); children's menu (£3.50). You can smoke only in one small area of the bar; piped music. The pub forms part of a very attractive estate village and has tables out in a very pleasant garden. *(Recommended by Keith and Chris O'Neill, Geoffrey and Brenda Wilson, Simon Pyle, R C Vincent, Meg and Colin Hamilton, the Didler, Philip and Susan Philcox, Alison Hayes, Pete Hanlon, Neil and Angela Huxter, Chris Pelley, Esther and John Sprinkle, Dave Braisted)*

Woodfordes ~ Tenants Tim and Penny Ridley ~ Real ale ~ Bar food (12-2, 6-9) ~ Restaurant ~ (01603) 720003 ~ Children in eating area of bar and restaurant ~ Open 11-11; 12-10.30 Sun; 11-3, 6-11 weekdays and Sat in winter

LUCKY DIP

Besides the fully inspected pubs, you might like to try these Lucky Dips recommended to us and described by readers (if you do, please send us reports: www.goodguides.co.uk).

BACTON TG3433
Duke of Edinburgh [Coast Rd]: Enjoyable food inc good value generous Sun carvery, roomy main bar, pretty family room and dining area, Greene King IPA; big garden with particularly good play area *(Samantha Frost, Esther and John Sprinkle)*

BARFORD TG1107
Cock [B1108 7 miles W of Norwich]: Brews its own good Blue Moon Easy Life, Sea of Tranquillity, Moondance and Hingham High; attractively refurbished, with relaxed atmosphere, helpful staff, friendly landlord and chef, good interesting food – freshly made, so allow plenty of time; shove-ha'penny, occasional jazz *(Chris Pelley)*

BAWBURGH TG1508
☆ *Kings Head* [off B1108 just W of Norwich; Harts Lane]: Four comfortable and attractive linked low-beamed rooms, log fire and inglenook woodburner, wide food choice from lunchtime sandwiches to quite a few ambitious dishes, no smoking restaurant, welcoming landlord and pleasant staff, well kept Adnams, Woodfordes Wherry and a guest beer, quite a few wines by the glass; children in eating areas, back squash court, garden with rustic tables on heated terrace, open all day *(John and Elizabeth Cox, LYM, Bruce and Penny Wilkie, Tina and David Woods-Taylor)*

BINHAM TF9839
☆ *Chequers* [B1388 SW of Blakeney]: 17th-c, with prompt cheerful service, reasonably priced food using local produce, several frequently changing real ales, belgian cherry beer on tap, decent house wines, long low-beamed bar, inglenook, sturdy plush seats, good coal fires each end, some nice old local prints, small no smoking dining area; picnic-sets out in front and on grass behind, open all day, two bedrooms, interesting village with huge priory church *(BB, John Knighton)*

BLAKENEY TG0243
☆ *Manor* [The Quay]: Attractive hotel in own grounds with decorous bar, popular esp with older people for good fresh enterprising waitress-served bar food, not expensive, from well filled crab sandwiches to attractive puddings; well kept Adnams Best and Broadside, decent house wines, friendly helpful and attentive staff, conservatory; sunny tables in fountain courtyard and walled garden with bowling green, good big bedrooms; opp wildfowl reserve and sea inlet *(John Beeken, Robert M Warner, George Atkinson, BB, Rodney and Norma Stubington)*

BLICKLING TG1728
☆ *Buckinghamshire Arms* [B1354 NW of Aylsham]: Handsome Jacobean inn by gates to Blickling Hall (NT), neat pews around stripped pine tables in lounge, banquettes in small front snug, enjoyable food from baguettes and baked potatoes up, well kept Adnams Best and Broadside and Woodfordes Wherry, local cider, good range of wines, helpful service; well behaved children in restaurant, lots of tables out on big lawn with summer food servery, perhaps all-day opening in summer if busy, bedrooms with own bathrooms (two nights min wknds) *(Beryl and Bill Farmer, Maureen and Bill Sewell, Dr Andy Wilkinson, Peter and Pat Frogley, LYM, Mike and Shelley Woodroffe, Dave Braisted, John Wooll)*

BRAMERTON TG2905
Woods End [N of village, towards river]: Lovely spot with big windows overlooking bend of River Yare, wide choice of enjoyable food, well kept beer, good service, much modernised high-ceilinged lounge, roomy L-shaped extension with pool table, restaurant; terrace tables by the grassy river banks (and hordes of ducks) *(Trevor and Sylvia Millum)*

BRANCASTER STAITHE TF7944
Jolly Sailors [Main Road (A149)]: Old-fashioned pub popular with bird-watchers, three simply furnished beamed rooms, log fire, well kept Adnams and Woodfordes Wherry, decent wines and help-yourself coffee, food (all day in summer) from baguettes up, no smoking restaurant; piped music, fruit machine, TV; children in eating areas, sheltered tables in nice garden with terrace and smallish play area (best for younger children), open all day wknds and summer *(Comus and Sarah Elliott, Richard Cole, John Beeken, LYM, Neil and Angela Huxter, Esther and John Sprinkle, George Atkinson, Mr and Mrs P L Spencer)*

BRANDON CREEK TL6091

☆ *Ship* [A10 Ely—Downham Market]: Prime summer pub, in lovely spot on confluence of Great and Little Ouse, plenty of tables out by the moorings; spacious tastefully modernised bar with massive stone masonry in sunken former forge area, big log fire one end, woodburner the other, good value food, good friendly staff, real ales such as Adnams, Fullers London Pride and Timothy Taylors Landlord, interesting old photographs and prints, evening restaurant; may be piped music; bedrooms *(LYM, George Atkinson)*

BURNHAM MARKET TF8342

☆ *Lord Nelson* [Creake Rd]: Small unpretentious no smoking restaurant behind lounge bar, some Nelson memorabilia, Courage Directors, Greene King IPA and Tetleys, good choice of enjoyable generous food from baguettes to lots of fish and seafood, quick service; pool, games machine and juke box in public bar; four attractive bedrooms, two in former outbuilding *(John Wooll, LYM, A D Cross, Michael Dandy)*

CASTLE ACRE TF8115

☆ *Ostrich* [Stocks Green]: Unpretentious relaxed pub prettily placed overlooking the tree-lined green, very long-serving landlord, individual mix of utilitarian furnishings and fittings with some ancient beams, masonry and huge inglenook fireplace, well kept Greene King ales, cheap food with vegetarian emphasis, dominoes, cribbage; piped music, fruit machine, family room (but children run pretty free); jazz 2nd and 3rd Weds of month, folk last Weds; picnic-sets in sheltered informal garden with doves and aviary, cheap plain bedrooms sharing shower (good breakfast), attractive village with castle and monastery remains *(Ron and Sheila Corbett, John Wooll, LYM, Charles Gysin)*

CASTLE RISING TF6624

Black Horse: Comfortable and attractive dining pub by church and almshouses in pleasant unspoilt village, good furnishings inc sofas, L-shaped bar and back dining room, real ales such as Greene King IPA, Harviestoun Gremlin and Lees, good choice of wines by the glass, helpful manager, simple low-priced food; children welcome, no dogs, pleasant tables out under cocktail parasols, play area *(MDN, John Wooll)*

CLEY NEXT THE SEA TG0443

George [High St, off A149 W of Sheringham]: Usefully placed Edwardian inn with modern wine bar décor and emphasis on food; sizeable garden over road, bedrooms *(LYM, MDN, John Coatsworth)*

COLKIRK TF9226

☆ *Crown* [off B1146 S of Fakenham; Crown Rd]: Two-bar local with solid country furniture, rugs and flooring tiles, open fires, lots of wines by the glass, well kept Greene King IPA, Abbot, XX Mild and a guest beer, usual bar food, no smoking dining room, darts, cribbage, dominoes; fruit machine; good disabled access; children and dogs allowed, picnic-sets in garden with suntrap terrace *(R C Vincent, J V Nelson, Barry Collett, I Louden, Mr Bishop, Bill and Doreen Sawford, LYM, R Clark, Mark and Amanda Sheard, John Beeken, George Atkinson, John Wooll, Maggie and Carl Van Baars, Adrian White, Mike and Shelley Woodroffe)*

DENVER SLUICE TF6101

☆ *Jenyns Arms* [signed via B1507 off A1122 Downham Mkt bypass]: Extensive well laid out roadhouse-style pub in fine spot by spectacular hydraulic sluices controlling Great Ouse, tables out by water, generous usual food (not Sun evening) from good sandwiches to roasts and tempting puddings, friendly, helpful and efficient staff cope well with coach parties, well kept ales such as Adnams and Greene King IPA and Old Speckled Hen; children welcome, big light and airy games area with pool, piped music; bedrooms *(BB, Jestyn Phillips, Keith and Janet Morris)*

DERSINGHAM TF6930

☆ *Feathers* [B1440 towards Sandringham]: Solid Jacobean sandstone inn with two relaxed modernised dark-panelled bars, well kept Adnams, Bass and a quickly changing guest beer, log fires, wide choice of generous bar food from sandwiches up, restaurant (not Sun evening), separate games room; children welcome, can get very busy in season, some live music in barn; large family garden with elaborate play area inc wendy house and outsize snakes and ladders, attractive secluded adults' garden with pond, comfortable well furnished bedrooms *(LYM, MDN, Esther and John Sprinkle, John Wooll)*

DOCKING TF7637

Railway Inn [Station Rd]: Unpretentious local with wide choice of enjoyable home cooking from doorstep sandwiches and baked potatoes up, bargain lunches, Tues supper deals for two, quick friendly service, well kept local Buffys Bitter and Norwegian Blue, good house wines, lounge bar and panelled dining room, fresh flowers, model train chuffing along under ceiling, some rail prints and posters (station closed 50 years ago), smaller chummy public bar with pool in annexe; usually open all day *(M J A Switzer, John Beeken, John Wooll)*

EAST BARSHAM TF9133

White Horse [B1105 3 miles N of Fakenham]: Attractively done extended pub, big log fire in long beamed main bar, steps to other areas, well kept ales such as Adnams Bitter and Broadside and Charles Wells Bombardier, decent wine, good coffee, friendly attentive staff, generous reasonably priced meals (rather than snacks, no sandwiches) inc children's, OAP lunches and steak nights, two small attractive dining rooms; piped music, darts; children welcome, well priced bedrooms – a pleasant quiet place to stay *(George Atkinson, Susan and Nigel Wilson, Mike Marsh)*

EAST HARLING TL9986

Nags Head [Market St (B1111)]: Wide range of enjoyable reasonably priced food inc popular OAP bargain lunch, real ales such as Adnams and Wadworths 6X, extended comfortable no smoking dining area (children allowed), small smokers' bar; juke box; big garden, not far from Snetterton *(Meg and Colin Hamilton)*

EAST RUSTON TG3428

Butchers Arms [back rd Horning—Happisburgh, N of Stalham]: Generous enjoyable food inc bargain lunchtime specials in well run comfortable village pub with well kept real ales, lots of golf talk, restaurant; attractive garden, pretty hanging baskets *(M J Bourke)*

ERPINGHAM TG1931

Spread Eagle: Brick-built local with a true welcome for children and dogs (even from the pub's own dog), hospitable landlady and staff, snug bar with comfortable sofa, Adnams Best, Fullers London Pride, Greene King IPA and Woodfordes Nelsons Revenge, good value food, no smoking dining room, pool table; live music Sun lunchtime and Sat; neat garden *(Robert M Warner, Simon Watkins)*

GAYTON TF7219

☆ *Crown* [B1145/B1153]: Attractive flower-decked pub with some unusual old features and comfortable nooks and corners, thriving relaxed atmosphere, good choice of well cooked food from good value sandwiches through interesting specials to mixed grill, well kept Greene King IPA and Abbot, limited but good wine choice, hospitable landlady and friendly efficient staff, games room; tables in sheltered and attractive garden *(Robert M Warner, John Wooll, LYM, MDN, Mrs Ann Gray)*

GELDESTON TM3991

☆ *Locks* [off A143/A146 NW of Beccles; off Station Rd S of village, obscurely signed down long rough track]: Remote pub alone at the navigable head of the River Waveney, ancient tiled-floor core with big log fire, large extension for summer crowds, Woodfordes and very local Tindalls ales tapped from casks, friendly informal service; wknd music nights, summer evening barbecues, meadow camping; may be cl winter wkdys *(the Didler, LYM, Neil Powell)*

GREAT YARMOUTH TG5206

Red Herring [Havelock Rd]: Welcoming unpretentious backstreet alehouse with at least six well kept changing ales at attractive prices, farm ciders, good value food inc wide choice of good local sausages, may have eggs for sale, rock collection, old local photographs, books to read; can be a bit smoky *(the Didler, Comus and Sarah Elliott)*

HAPPISBURGH TG3831

Hill House [by village church]: Cheery heavy-beamed village pub with plush seats, woodburner in big inglenook, open fire other end, well kept changing ales such as Marstons Pedigree and Shepherd Neame Spitfire, wide choice of popular generous food inc good value sandwiches and original dishes, pleasant dining area, pool and children's games corner; tables outside front and back, pleasant setting *(BB, Esther and John Sprinkle)*

HARLESTON TM2483

☆ *Swan* [The Thoroughfare (narrow main st on one-way circuit, look out for narrow coach entry)]: 16th-c coaching inn, two linked lounge rooms with ancient timbers and log fire in big fireplace, snacks or meals here or in timbered restaurant (only carvery Sat night/Sun lunchtime, only bar snacks Sun evening), Adnams real ales, short choice of wines by the glass, welcoming service and atmosphere, old tools and cooking utensils, public bar with pool and SkyTV; quiet piped radio; good value comfortably worn in Georgian bedrooms *(KC)*

HEACHAM TF6737

Fox & Hounds [Station Rd]: Unpretentious spacious bar with charming friendly service, attractive choice of good generous food (not Sun evening), brewing its own good Fox Heacham Gold, also Saxon farm cider and well kept guest beers; games machines; small garden, open all day *(Peter H Stallard, Esther and John Sprinkle)*

HEMPSTEAD TG1137

☆ *Hare & Hounds* [away from village centre, over towards Baconsthorpe]: Nicely tucked away cottagey country dining pub, two beamed rooms with plenty of character and very wide blackboard choice of enjoyable food in huge helpings, from monumental baguettes to massive choice of puddings, well kept Greene King IPA and Abbot and a guest such as Hop Back Summer Lightning, helpful young hard-working staff, woodburner in one broad fireplace; lots of picnic-sets and play area on side grass by pond and rockery, open all day Sun, may be cl Mon out of season *(LYM, Anthony Barnes, John Beeken, Andrew Bayfield, Michael and Jenny Back)*

HEYDON TG1127

Earle Arms [off B1149]: Largely unchanged two-room pub in delightfully unspoilt village, nice old-fashioned décor and furnishings inc a grandfather clock, cupboards with interesting bric-a-brac, attractive prints, good log fires; usual food (not Sun/Mon evenings), well kept Adnams, Woodfordes Wherry and a guest beer, decent wines; piped music; children welcome, picnic-sets in small prettily cottagey back garden *(LYM, John Wooll, Mike and Lynn Robinson)*

HOLKHAM TF8943

Victoria [A149 near Holkham Hall]: Sumptuously refurbished small hotel (they stress that they are not a pub) with sprawling sofas, interesting pictures and good eclectic décor, well kept real ales such as Buffys, Earl Soham and Woodfordes Wherry, splendid wine choice, log fire; pricey restaurant; children and dogs welcome, picnic-sets in pretty garden with pleasant terraces, apple trees and small play area, eight luxurious bedrooms (again not cheap) – handy for coastal nature reserves, beach and Holkham Hall *(Keith and Chris O'Neill, I Louden, Mr Bishop, John Wooll, LYM, J F M and M West, Ian Arthur, M Thomas, Neil and Angela Huxter, Tracey and Stephen Groves, Esther and John Sprinkle, TW, MW, Minda and Stanley Alexander)*

HOLT TG0738

Kings Head [High St/Bull St]: Enjoyable home

cooking, specials for children and OAPs, four real ales, cheerful atmosphere, lounge bar with eating area, simple public bar *(Susan and Nigel Wilson)*

HONINGHAM TG1011

Olde Buck [just off A47]: Ancient pub with four busy beamed rooms, some emphasis on massive food choice from huge sandwiches and lunchtime bargains to adventurous dishes and popular Sun lunch, Greene King IPA and Flowers IPA, relaxing candlelit atmosphere *(M J Caley, O K Smyth, Mr and Mrs P L Spencer)*

HORNING TG3417

Swan [Lower St]: Popular Brewers Fayre by paddle-boat cruiser stop, open all day, worth knowing for its splendid views, with picnic-sets on splendid riverside terrace; reliable food, pleasant efficient service, bedrooms *(Quentin and Carol Williamson)*

HORSTEAD TG2619

☆ *Recruiting Sergeant* [B1150 just S of Coltishall]: Spacious pleasantly refurbished village pub, enjoyable generous food inc good fish choice, friendly obliging service, real ales, impressive choice of wines by the glass, big open fire, brasses and muskets, music-free smaller room; children welcome *(M J Bourke, R L Worsdall, C Galloway)*

HOVETON TG3018

Kings Head [Station Rd (B1354)]: Big riverside hotel with popular daily carvery, comfortable lounge and conservatory, friendly service; piped music may be loud; waterside garden, bedrooms *(David and Julie Glover)*

HUNWORTH TG0735

☆ *Blue Bell* [aka Hunny Bell; signed off B roads S of Holt]: Modest warmly friendly country pub with long tables and some settees in comfortable L-shaped bar, wide choice of good value well presented food from soup and sandwiches to crab salad and steak, well kept ales tapped from the cask such as Adnams, Woodfordes Wherry and one brewed for the pub by Cambrian, cheerful landlord, local pictures on red walls, china for sale in simple no smoking flagstoned family dining room; children welcome, good-sized informal garden with summer bar service, play area and pets corner *(LYM, Sally Anne and Peter Goodale, Esther and John Sprinkle)*

INGHAM TG3926

Swan: Olde-worlde low-beamed thatched inn with interesting corners in rambling rooms on two levels, scrubbed tables and fishing boat photographs, jolly atmosphere, good food from baguettes and standard pubby things to more elaborate things, five well kept ales inc Woodfordes Wherry, friendly staff, small family room; small enclosed garden and courtyard, bedrooms in detached block *(Sue Rowland, Paul Mallett)*

KING'S LYNN TF6120

Lloyds No 1 [King St/Tuesday Market Pl]: Spacious neatly kept good value Wetherspoons, two-for-one food bargains, good beer choice, decent wines, friendly helpful service; very busy at times, with doormen; attractive back garden, pleasant bedrooms *(R C Vincent, Joe Green, John Wooll)*

Wenns [Saturday Market Pl]: Extensively updated town pub with Greene King ales, decent wines, wide choice of reasonably priced simple food from baguettes and baked potatoes up, efficient friendly service *(John Wooll)*

LESSINGHAM TG3928

Star [School Rd]: Small and inviting, with two open fires, comfortable armchairs, good beer and wine choice, good side restaurant where chef/landlord uses only local produce *(Steve Toomey)*

MORSTON TG0043

Anchor [The Street]: Several pleasantly old-fashioned rooms, Greene King real ales, decent wines, food from sandwiches and rolls to quite a lot of fresh fish, daily papers, local prints and photographs *(John Wooll)*

MUNDFORD TL8093

☆ *Crown* [off A1065 Thetford—Swaffham; Crown Rd]: Unassuming heavily beamed 17th-c pub with friendly bustling lounge bar, huge fireplace, interesting local memorabilia, well kept Courage Best, Marstons Pedigree and Greene King Old Speckled Hen, dozens of malt whiskies, decent food from sandwiches up, spiral iron stairs to overflow club room and elegant restaurant, games, TV and juke box in red-tiled locals' bar; children and dogs welcome, back terrace and garden with wishing well, bedrooms with own bathrooms, open all day *(Neil Skidmore, G Coates, A Sadler, Pamela Goodwyn, SH, Anthony Barnes, Graham Findlay, LYM)*

NEEDHAM TM2281

Red Lion [High Rd]: Popular beautifully kept dining pub with wide choice of good food, welcoming landlord, Greene King IPA and Theakstons; large back garden with caravan park *(David Boult)*

NEWTON TF8315

George & Dragon [A1065 4 miles N of Swaffham]: Distinctive roadside pub, unhurried atmosphere popular with older people, good value food inc generous Sun lunch and popular puddings (advisable to book), friendly service, Black Sheep and other real ales, several small dining areas; children allowed only if eating, pleasant garden with play area, great views to Castle Acre Priory; cl Mon, at least out of season *(Mark and Amanda Sheard)*

NORTH CREAKE TF8538

Jolly Farmers [Burnham Rd]: Two cheerfully rustic small bars, good log fire in one, woodburner in the other, well kept Woodfordes Wherry, Nelsons Revenge and Admirals Reserve tapped from the cask, decent wines by the glass, good friendly service, enjoyable gently upmarket seasonal food using fresh local produce, cosy tasteful no smoking dining room with another woodburner; children in eating area, tables in sheltered garden, charming village, cl Sun evening, all Mon, Tues lunchtime *(Jim Mansfield, Mike and Shelley Woodroffe)*

NORTH ELMHAM TF9920
Railway [Station Rd]: Traditional brick and flint pub in same welcoming family for 40 years, snug L-shaped bar, settees and easy chairs by log fire at end by small restaurant, decent reasonably priced food inc bargain grill using local produce such as gloucester old spot, several well kept local ales, lots of papers, magazines and books; camping in grounds, tables in garden, open all day *(Chris Rogers, Dr B and Mrs P B Baker)*

NORWICH TG2108
Alexandra [Stafford St]: Welcoming, comfortable and efficient two-bar local, well kept real ales such as Chalk Hill (see Coach & Horses) and Exmoor Gold, cheap interesting food, open fire; pool, classic juke box *(MP, Sue Demont, Tim Barrow)*

Billy Bluelight [Hall Rd, off inner ring rd nr A11]: Friendly and roomy real ale local tied to Woodfordes, with their full beer range and interesting guests kept well, some tapped from the cask, cheapish food, real fire, bar billiards and skittles, plenty of wood and stained-glass, no music or machines; midnight supper licence *(Catherine Pitt)*

Coach & Horses [Thorpe Rd]: Light and airy tap for Chalk Hill brewery, with their own Bitter, Flint Knappers Mild, CHB, Dreadnought and Old Tackle, guests such as Boddingtons and Timothy Taylors, friendly service, good choice of generous home cooking 12-9 (8 Sun), also breakfast with limitless coffee; bare-boards L-shaped bar with open fire, lots of dark wood, posters and prints, pleasant back dining area; disabled access possible (not to lavatories), picnic-sets on front terrace, may be summer barbecues, open all day *(the Didler, Dr B and Mrs P B Baker)*

Ketts [Ketts Hill]: Several separate areas inc smart conservatory/games room, local Buffys and good choice of changing ales, frequent beer festivals, bar food using local organic meats inc evening curries and Sun roasts; tables in small garden behind, open all day *(Tony Hobden)*

☆ *Kings Arms* [Hall Rd]: Traditional woody pub with Adnams, Greene King, Wolf and 10 changing East Anglian guest beers, beer festivals, dozens of malt whiskies and plenty of wines, brewery memorabilia, good landlord and atmosphere, light and airy new garden room; unobtrusive sports TV, no food but bring your own or order out – plates, cutlery provided; vines in courtyard *(Mrs N J Howard, Catherine Pitt)*

☆ *Ribs of Beef* [Wensum St, S side of Fye Bridge]: Warm and welcoming high-ceilinged old pub, well kept ales such as Adnams, Boddingtons, Fullers London Pride and Woodfordes Wherry, farm cider, decent wine; deep leather settees and small tables upstairs, attractive smaller downstairs room with river view and some local river paintings, generous cheap reliable food (till 5 Sat/Sun), quick friendly service, long-serving licensees; can be studenty evenings *(David Carr, John Wooll, Christine and Neil Townend)*

OLD BUCKENHAM TM0691
☆ *Gamekeeper* [The Green]: Pretty 16th-c pub, good atmosphere with blazing log fire, church candles and dried hops, flavour-filled seasonal food in cosy bar or larger dining room, Sun lunch 12-5, welcoming service, well kept ales such as Adnams, local Wolf and one brewed for the pub, good wine list, no machines; children welcome *(TW, MW)*

OLD HUNSTANTON TF6842
Lodge [A149]: Comfortable main-road pub with good choice of quickly served fresh food in bar or (at higher price) restaurant, well kept Greene King IPA and Abbot, friendly staff, plenty of seats; good bedrooms *(O K Smyth)*

POTTER HEIGHAM TG4119
Falgate [A1062 Ludham Rd]: Very wide choice of well priced food, massive helpings, well kept Adnams, Greene King, John Smiths and Tetleys, friendly service, restaurant; may be piped music; handy for the river, popular with boaters *(David and Julie Glover)*

REEPHAM TG0922
☆ *Old Brewery House* [Market Sq]: Georgian hotel under new management, big log fire in no smoking high-ceilinged panelled bar overlooking old-fashioned town square, lots of farming and fishing bric-a-brac, well kept Adnams, Greene King Abbot and a guest beer, carpeted lounge, no smoking conservatory, restaurant; piped music; children and dogs welcome, tables on front terrace and back garden with pond and fountain, bedrooms with own bathrooms, open all day *(the Didler, John Wooll, LYM)*

ROUGHTON TG2136
New Inn [Norwich Rd (A140)]: Popular with locals and holiday-makers for its enjoyable very reasonably priced food and four real ales *(Susan and Nigel Wilson)*

RUSHALL TM1982
Half Moon [The Street]: Spotless extended 16th-c coaching inn popular for generous keenly priced straightforward food inc plenty of fish and big puddings, in beamed and flagstoned bar or large modern back no smoking dining room (best to book at night); well kept Adnams and Woodfordes, good friendly service, dolls and bric-a-brac for sale; bedrooms in adjacent modern chalets *(Ian and Nita Cooper, David Barnes)*

SALTHOUSE TG0743
☆ *Dun Cow* [A149 Blakeney—Sheringham]: Extensively refurbished well run airy pub overlooking salt marshes, enjoyable generous usual food all day from sandwiches and baked potatoes to fresh crab salad, local fish and steak, cheerful staff, well kept Adnams Broadside, Flowers IPA and Greene King IPA, decent wines, open fires, stripped beams and cob walls in big barn-like main bar, no smoking family bar and games room with pool; piped radio, blues nights; big attractive walled garden with sheltered courtyard, figs and apples, separate sea-view family garden with play area, good walks and bird-watching nearby (may have sightings blackboard); bedrooms *(Mrs M A Mees, Eleanor and*

Nick Steinitz, BB, David Carr, Rodney and Norma Stubington, John Wooll, Esther and John Sprinkle, George Atkinson)

SCOLE TM1579

☆ ***Scole Inn*** [off A140 bypass just N of A143; Ipswich Rd]: Stately old coaching inn of outstanding architectural interest, with relaxed atmosphere and a real sense of history, antique settles, old oak chairs and tables, two impressive inglenook log fires, old prints and collectables and other old-fashioned features in lounge and bare-boards public bar used by locals; decent bar food from baguettes to steak, more elaborate menu in large no smoking restaurant, well kept Greene King IPA and XX Mild; cribbage, dominoes; children and dogs welcome, open all day, comfortable bedrooms in former stable block *(LYM, M and G Rushworth, TW, MW)*

SCULTHORPE TF8930

☆ ***Sculthorpe Mill*** [inn signed off A148 W of Fakenham, opp village]: Rebuilt 18th-c mill conversion, comfortable beamed bar with several rooms, enjoyable food from sandwiches and snack menu to full meals, Greene King ales, decent house wines, enthusiastic young landlord and prompt attentive service; children in eating areas, spacious and appealing streamside garden, open all day wknds and summer, comfortable bedrooms, good breakfast *(LYM, Hugh and Peggy Holman, R C Vincent, John Wooll)*

SEA PALLING TG4226

Hall Inn: Roomy and pleasant old bar with low-beamed dining area off, enjoyable reasonably priced food, well kept ales inc Adnams, friendly efficient service; picnic-sets on front lawn, 10 mins from beach *(M J Bourke)*

SHERINGHAM TG1543

Lobster [High St]: Almost on seafront and doing well under friendly newish management, seafaring décor in small comfortable lounge bar, clean and tidy, with old sewing-machine treadle tables, well kept Adnams and Greene King ales, decent wines, warm fire, new Stables restaurant with enterprising choice of good attractively priced food inc crab, lobster and fish specials, also children's things; no piped music, dogs on leads allowed, enclosed courtyard and garden with summer hog roasts *(Chris and Louise Taylor, Catherine Pitt)*

SKEYTON TG2524

☆ ***Goat*** [off A140 N of Aylsham; Long Rd]: Convivial extended thatched and low-beamed pub with good reasonably priced food running up to ostrich and kangaroo in bar and attractive restaurant (best to book Sat evening), well kept Adnams and Woodfordes ales, good value wines, first-rate service by good-humoured licensees and enthusiastic cheerful staff, log-effect gas fire; pleasant terrace and good-sized garden *(Dr and Mrs R G J Telfer, Chris and Jan Harper, Philip and Susan Philcox)*

SMALLBURGH TG3324

Crown: 15th-c thatched and beamed village inn with friendly landlord, reliable fresh country cooking from immaculate kitchen in bar and small popular dining room, well kept Greene King ales with a guest such as Ridleys; no dogs or children inside; tables outside, bedrooms *(M and GR, Shaun and Diane)*

SOUTH CREAKE TF8635

Ostrich [B1355 Burnham Mkt—Fakenham]: Popular local with pine tables in long narrow bar and lounge, enjoyable food from home-made burgers to guinea fowl, well kept Greene King IPA and Abbot and Woodfordes Nelsons Revenge, good wine choice, friendly hard-working owners, side pool table; children welcome *(John Wooll, Mrs A Burton)*

SOUTH LOPHAM TM0481

White Horse [A1066 Diss—Thetford]: Cheerful beamed pub with good choice of enjoyable home-made food inc bargain OAP roast lunch with plenty of choices, good staff (holiday visitors treated like regulars), well kept Adnams, Greene King IPA and Marstons Pedigree; tables in big garden, bedrooms, handy for Bressingham Gardens *(Alan M Pring, G P V Creagh)*

SOUTH WALSHAM TG3613

Ship [B1140]: Small village pub with friendly new landlord, good fresh home cooking, well kept Adnams and Woodfordes Wherry, stripped bricks and beams; may be piped music; tables on front elevated terrace and more in back garden; children's room, play area *(Gaye Mayger)*

SOUTH WOOTTON TF6422

Farmers Arms [part of Knights Hill Hotel, Grimston Rd (off A148/A149)]: Olde-worlde conversion of barn and stables, good value tasty food all day in bar and restaurant, puddings cabinet, good changing choice of real ales, good wines, abundant coffee, friendly prompt service; children welcome, comfortable motel bedrooms, health club, open all day *(R C Vincent, MDN, John Wooll)*

STOKE HOLY CROSS TG2302

Wildebeest [Norwich Rd]: Dining pub with emphasis on good interesting bistro-style food but provision for drinkers too, good beer and wine by the glass, good service, some unusual decorations inc african wooden masks *(J Hewitson)*

THETFORD TL8782

Dolphin [Old Market St]: 17th-c pub, lots of old beams and brass, pleasant helpful licensees, well kept Greene King IPA, varied enjoyable food; quiet piped music; nice walled garden *(Judith and Edward Pearson)*

THORNHAM TF7343

Kings Head [Church St/High St (A149)]: Pretty old pub with lots of hanging baskets, roomy low-beamed bars with banquettes in well lit bays, Adnams and Greene King IPA and Abbot, enjoyable if not cheap food inc local fish, unpretentious no smoking dining room, friendly landlord and helpful staff, open fire; dogs allowed in public bar; well spaced tables on back lawn with barbecues, three homely bedrooms, pleasant walks *(George Atkinson)*

TITCHWELL TF7543

☆ ***Titchwell Manor*** [A149 E of Hunstanton]: Comfortable upmarket hotel with good food inc local fish and seafood, some imaginative dishes and all-day tapas-style wknd menu, service friendly and competent without being intrusive, well kept Greene King IPA, roaring fire in big lounge, airy no smoking restaurant, nice afternoon teas, children welcome; tables in charming walled garden, pretty bedrooms, some overlooking RSPB bird marshes towards the sea, good breakfast *(S Street, LYM, David and Ruth Hollands, Alan and Sue Folwell)*

WELLS-NEXT-THE-SEA TF9143

☆ ***Bowling Green*** [Church St]: Attractively refurbished and welcoming L-shaped bar, flagstone and brick floor, simple furnishings, hearty food at dining end (freshly made so may be a wait), friendly helpful service, two log fires, well kept Greene King IPA and Abbot and Woodfordes Wherry; tables out on back terrace *(John Beeken, Peter and Anne Hollindale, Mike and Shelley Woodroffe)*

Globe [The Buttlands]: Cheerfully unpretentious old-fashioned pub with interesting choice of good value lunchtime baguettes, well kept Greene King real ales *(Peter Rozée)*

WEST ACRE TF7815

Stag [Low Rd]: Homely village pub recently refurbished under cheerful new landlord, good value home cooking using local produce, good choice of well kept beer, welcoming service *(Mrs V A Varley, A R Clemow)*

WEST RUNTON TG1842

Village Inn [Water Lane]: Welcoming large flint pub with comfortable bar, pleasant restaurant, enjoyable varied food, well kept ales such as Adnams and Hancocks HB, decent wines; large attractive garden area, pleasant village with good beach and nice circular walk to East Runton *(Fred and Lorraine Gill)*

WEST WALTON TF4713

☆ ***King of Hearts*** [N of Wisbech; School Rd]: Comfortably refurbished beamed dining pub with wide choice of good value genuine food inc OAP lunch in smartly furnished bar and restaurant, good hot buffet (as much as you want), friendly very helpful service copes well even with big parties and special diet needs, full Elgoods range and a guest beer, lots of decorative china and brassware, no smoking area; holds key for lovely next-door church, tables in raised garden *(Sally Anne and Peter Goodale)*

WIVETON TG0342

☆ ***Bell*** [Blakeney Rd]: Big welcoming open-plan dining pub, Danish landlord cooking wide choice of enjoyable food for bar and restaurant inc some Danish dishes and interesting specials, Adnams Broadside and Bass, good wines, friendly helpful service even under pressure, no music or machines; large warmly carpeted no smoking conservatory, picnic-sets on lawn and garden behind, has been cl Mon lunchtime *(BB, John Beeken, Brian Haywood, Tracey and Stephen Groves, Pamela Goodwyn)*

WRENINGHAM TM1698

☆ ***Bird in Hand*** [just off B1113 E of Wymondham (Norwich Rd, outside village)]: Thriving dining pub, roomy and tastefully refurbished with beams and cosy alcoves, wide choice of decent reasonably priced food from sandwiches up using local fish and other fresh produce, well presented Sun lunch and OAP midweek lunches, well kept Adnams, Fullers London Pride and Woodfordes Wherry, good friendly service, local bygones and Lotus car photographs, two dining rooms, one Victorian-style with panelling, the other more country-look; quiet piped pop music; picnic-sets in neatly kept garden *(BB, Dr R C C Ward)*

WYMONDHAM TG1101

☆ ***Green Dragon*** [Church St]: Very picturesque heavily timbered jettied 14th-c inn, bulky beams, log fire (Tudor mantelpiece), well kept Adnams and Greene King, friendly relaxed service, welcoming locals, good value generous pub food from sandwiches to attractively priced main dishes, small back bar, bigger no smoking turkey-carpeted dining area, some interesting pictures; children and dogs welcome; modest bedrooms, nr glorious 12th-c abbey church *(BB, the Didler, Anthony Rogers)*

Post Office address codings confusingly give the impression that some pubs are in Norfolk when they're really in Suffolk (which is where we list them).

Northamptonshire

This year we have two new entries here: the Great Western Arms near Aynho, recently nicely reworked as a stylish and enjoyable dining pub; and the charming old stone-built Queens Head at Bulwick, good all round, with extra appeal from its food, focusing on local produce. Other pubs currently doing well here include the friendly Red Lion at Crick (generous bargain food, good beers), the civilised upmarket Falcon at Fotheringhay (very good imaginative food, and drinkers don't feel out of place), the relaxing George at Kilsby (its hard-working personable landlady is its special ingredient), and the interesting and cheerful Old Sun at Nether Heyford (a fine family-run all-rounder). The Falcon at Fotheringhay this year recaptures the title of Northamptonshire Dining Pub of the Year, which it last won two years ago: a great place for a special meal out. Pubs to target in the Lucky Dip section at the end of the chapter are the Olde Coach House at Ashby St Ledgers, Montagu Arms at Barnwell, Wharf at Bugbrooke, George & Dragon at Chacombe, White Hart at Grafton Regis, Fox & Hounds at Great Brington and Boat at Stoke Bruerne. Drinks prices here tend to be just a little above the national average; among the main entries, only the White Swan at Woodnewton and Old Sun at Nether Heyford sold real ale for under the £2 a pint barrier.

AYNHO SP5133 Map 4

Great Western Arms

Just off B4031 W, towards Deddington; Aynho Wharf, Station Road

Beside the former grey stone station buildings between the main Oxford—Banbury rail line and the Oxford Canal, this rather plain creeper-covered building gives little clue from the outside of what it's now all about. Inside, it's been recently reworked as an upmarket dining pub, striking people as 'Cotswoldy', yet keeping a very clear individuality – and still a relaxing place to drop into for a quiet drink. A rambling series of linked areas has good solid country tables and regional chairs on broad flagstones, and the golden stripped stone of some walling tones well with the warm cream and deep red plasterwork elsewhere. A good log fire warms cosy seats in two of the areas. There are candles and fresh flowers throughout, daily papers and glossy magazines, and a collection of interesting GWR memorabilia including lots of steam locomotive photographs which it had been feared might be dispersed when the pub was redeveloped; the dining area on the right is rather elegant. Quite a range of seafood and fish dishes features amongst the freshly made blackboard food which might include lunchtime sandwiches (from £5.50), soup or fish soup (£5.50), whitebait or moules marinière (£5.75), fried sardines (£5.85), mushroom stroganoff (£7.65), sausage and mash (£7.95), fish and chips (£8.75), plaice with tarragon butter (£9.25), duck breast with plum sauce (£11.95), scallops provençale (£12.95), half lobster or rack of lamb with honey and rosemary (£13.95), puddings such as lemon tart and coconut and chocolate cheesecake (£4.50) and cheese and biscuits (£5.95). They have well kept Hook Norton Best, Generation and the current Hook Norton seasonal ale on handpump, and good wines by the glass; service is welcoming and attentive. Opening out of the main bar, the former stable courtyard behind has white cast-iron tables and chairs among new plantings; there are moorings and a marina nearby. *(Recommended by Meg and Colin Hamilton, Graham Lynch-Watson, Michael Jones, Susan and John Douglas, Alan Crompton)*

Hook Norton ~ Lease Frank Baldwin ~ Real ale ~ Bar food (12-2.30, 6.30-9.30) ~ Restaurant ~ (01869) 338288 ~ Children welcome ~ Dogs allowed in bar ~ Open 12-3, 6(6.30 Sat)-11; closed Sun evening

BADBY SP5559 Map 4

Windmill

Village signposted off A361 Daventry—Banbury

Bar food at this bustling old thatched inn is popular so it is worth booking: soup of the day (£3.25), potato skins with yoghurt and mint dip (£3.95), grilled goats cheese on garlic bread with basil and tomato (£4.95), nut roast with cranberry and chilli sauce (£8.50), pie of the day (£8.95), venison burgers with creamy peppercorn sauce (£9.95), cajun chicken breast (£10.95), poached salmon with dill mayonnaise (£11.25), and puddings (from £3.50). Past Oscar, the large pub dog asleep in the corridor, two beamed and flagstoned bars have a nice country feel with an unusual white woodburning stove in an enormous white-tiled inglenook fireplace, simple country furnishings in good solid wood, and cricketing and rugby pictures. There's also a comfortably cosy lounge. The snug and the more modern-feeling, brightly lit carpeted restaurant are no smoking. Well kept Bass, Flowers Original and guests such as Fullers London Pride, Timothy Taylor Landlord and Wadworths 6X on handpump, and good fairly priced wines by the bottle; quiet piped music. The bedrooms are in an unobtrusive modern extension, well tucked away at the back, with a couple more in a pretty cottage next door. There are seats on a terrace out in front by the green, and this is a pretty village, with lots of nearby woodland walks. *(Recommended by Maysie Thompson, Anthony Barnes, Miss E J Berrill, George Atkinson, Mike and Mary Carter, Dr Martin Owton, Charles and Pauline Stride, Simon Calvert, Jo Lilley)*

Free house ~ Licensees John Freestone and Carol Sutton ~ Real ale ~ Bar food (12-2, 7-9(6.30-9.30 wknds)) ~ Restaurant ~ (01327) 702363 ~ Children in eating area of bar and restaurant ~ Dogs welcome ~ Open 11.30-3, 5.30-11; 11.30-11 Sat; 12-11 Sun ~ Bedrooms: £59.50B/£72.50B

BULWICK SP9694 Map 4

Queens Head

Just off A43 Kettering—Duddington

Gentle improvements made by the friendly country loving licensees here (they took over about two years ago) have brought this very attractive regional looking 17th-c stone pub into the running. A big draw is the changing choice of good fresh food which is cooked fresh to order, using local produce where possible. The menu runs from pubby snacks such as filled ciabattas and baguettes (from £4.95), home-made beef burger (£6.50) and pork pie and mash (£7.50) to more elaborate dishes such as cream of chicken and asparagus soup (£3.50), warm salad of black pudding and chorizo with soft poached egg (£5.25), parmesan and asparagus risotto with pancetta and parmesan (£7.95), seared salmon fillet on rocket and baby beetroot salad (£10.50), fillet of local trout with herb and lemon crust on sweet potato and red onion pureé (£10.95), pork tenderloin with roasted shallots and caramelised apple (£11.95) and puddings such as Baileys bread and butter pudding or spiced poached pear with raspberry sorbet and berry coulis (£4.25). The civilised dining area is no smoking. The ancient two-room stone floored bar has beams, and a small fire in a stone hearth at each end; darts, shove-ha'penny and dominoes. Shepherd Neame Spitfire and a couple of interesting guests from brewers such as Belvoir and Eccleshall are well kept and served from a stone bar counter by friendly efficient staff. A good wine list includes interesting bin-ends. There can be few more pleasant experiences than a summer evening on the garden terrace (with its own well) listening to swallows and martins, sheep in the adjacent field and bells ringing in the nearby church. This is an attractive bypassed village in an area where you may be lucky enough to see red kites. *(Recommended by JWAC, Anthony Barnes, John, Gwen and Reg, Fred and Lorraine Gill, Dr Carola Haigh, Cecil and Alison Chapman, William Salaman)*

Free house ~ Licensee Geoff Smith ~ Real ale ~ Bar food (12-2.30(3.30 Sun), 6-9.30(10 Fri, Sat); not Sun evening or Mon) ~ Restaurant ~ (01780) 450272 ~ Children in restaurant ~ Dogs allowed in bar ~ Open 12-3, 6-11(7-10.30 Sun)

CRICK SP5872 Map 4

Red Lion £

1 mile from M1 junction 18; A428

You can't help but be impressed by the price of the generous helpings of good home-cooked lunchtime food at this pretty stone and thatched pub: sandwiches (from £1.80), ploughman's (from £3.20), and straightforward hearty main courses such as chicken and mushroom pie, leek and smoky bacon bake, plaice or vegetable pancake rolls (all £4.20). Prices go up a little in the evening when they do a wider range of dishes that might include wild mushroom lasagne (£6.50), stuffed salmon fillet (£7.25), roast duck (£12) and steaks (from £10); puddings such as lemon meringue pie (from £2.20); Sunday roast (£4.50). Service is quick and friendly. The cosy low-ceilinged bar is relaxed and welcoming, with lots of comfortable seating, some rare old horsebrasses, pictures of the pub in the days before it was surrounded by industrial estates, and a tiny log stove in a big inglenook. The snug is no smoking. Four well kept beers on handpump include Greene King Old Speckled Hen, Hook Norton Best, Marstons Pedigree and Websters Yorkshire. There are a few picnic-sets under cocktail parasols on grass by the car park, and in summer you can eat on the terrace in the old coachyard, which is sheltered by a Perspex roof; lots of pretty hanging baskets. *(Recommended by Ian Phillips, Mrs G R Sharman, W W Burke, Humphry and Angela Crum Ewing, Ted George, Pat and Derek Roughton, F J Robinson, B and M Kendall, David and Ruth Shillitoe, Nigel Williamson, Michael Cross, Ian and Denise Foster, Keith Reeve, Marie Hammond, Ian and Nita Cooper, Patrick Hancock, R Johnson, George Atkinson, Rita and Keith Pollard)*

Wellington ~ Lease Tom and Paul Marks ~ Real ale ~ Bar food (12-2, 6.30-9; not Sun evening) ~ (01788) 822342 ~ Children welcome lunchtimes only ~ Dogs welcome ~ Open 11-2.30, 6.15-11; 12-3, 7-10.30 Sun

EAST HADDON SP6668 Map 4

Red Lion

High Street; village signposted off A428 (turn right in village) and off A50 N of Northampton

Smart and restauranty, this elegantly substantial golden stone hotel offers fairly formal dining. The neat lounge bar has some attractive antique furniture, including panelled oak settles, library chairs and a mix of oak, mahogany and cast-iron-framed tables. Little kegs, pewter, brass pots, swords and so forth are hung sparingly on a couple of beams, and there's attractive white-painted panelling with recessed china cabinets and old prints. Though a meal here might be a little more expensive than elsewhere, the good food, generous helpings and excellent service make it worth that little bit extra. The seasonally changing menu might include soup (£3.50), sandwiches (£4), greek salad (£5), smoked loch fyne salmon with whisky and horseradish dressing (£7), parsnip and onion wellington with tomato sauce (£9), lamb and black pudding casserole with boulangère potatoes or poached smoked haddock with pasta, chorizo and black olives (£11) and puddings such as bread and butter pudding or chocolate roulade (£4.50). The pretty no smoking restaurant overlooking the garden has a more elaborate menu. They serve very well kept Adnams Broadside and Charles Wells Bombardier and Eagle on handpump, and decent wines including about ten by the glass; piped music. The walled side garden is pretty, with lilac, fruit trees, roses and neat flowerbeds, and leads back to the bigger lawn, which has well spaced picnic-sets. A small side terrace has more tables under cocktail parasols, and a big copper beech shades the gravel car park. *(Recommended by Michael Dandy, Anthony Barnes, Alain and Rose Foote, Dr Brian and Mrs Anne Hamilton, Maysie Thompson, W W Burke, Lady Heath, Maurice Ribbans, Geoffrey and Penny Hughes, Gerry and Rosemary Dobson)*

Charles Wells ~ Lease Ian Kennedy ~ Real ale ~ Bar food (12.30-2, 7.30-9.30, not Sun evening) ~ Restaurant ~ (01604) 770223 ~ Children in eating area of bar and restaurant ~ Open 11-3, 6-11; 11.30-3, 7-11 Sun ~ Bedrooms: £60S/£75S

FARTHINGSTONE SP6155 Map 4

Kings Arms

Off A5 SE of Daventry; village signposted from Litchborough on former B4525 (now declassified)

The handsome gargoyled stone exterior of this traditional little 18th-c country pub is nicely weathered, and very pretty in summer, when the hanging baskets are at their best, and the tranquil terrace is charmingly decorated with flower and herb pots and plant-filled painted tractor tyres; the garden has a new pond this year. The village is picturesque, and there are good walks including the Knightley Way. Inside, there's plenty of character in the timelessly intimate flagstoned bar which has a huge log fire, comfortable homely sofas and armchairs near the entrance, whisky-water jugs hanging from oak beams, and lots of pictures and decorative plates on the walls. A games room at the far end has darts, dominoes, cribbage, table skittles and board games. Hook Norton is well kept on handpump alongside a couple of guests such as Hop Back Crop Circle and Youngs, the short wine list is quite decent, and they have a few country wines; the outside gents' has an interesting newspaper-influenced décor. It's worth ringing ahead to check the limited opening and food serving times noted below as the licensees are sometimes away. Listed on a blackboard, dishes might include winter and autumn soup (£3.95), baguettes (£2.80), steak, ale and kidney filled yorkshire pudding (£6.20), british cheese platter (£5.95) and scottish fish platter (£6.95). They also retail a few carefully sourced food items, such as cheese, wine and olive oil. *(Recommended by Pete Baker, Catherine and Rob Dunster)*

Free house ~ Licensees Paul and Denise Egerton ~ Real ale ~ Bar food (Sat, Sun lunchtime only) ~ No credit cards ~ (01327) 361604 ~ Children welcome ~ Dogs welcome ~ Open 7-11; 12-3, 7(9 Sun)-11 Sat; closed wkday lunchtimes and Mon, Weds evenings

FOTHERINGHAY TL0593 Map 5

Falcon ★

Village signposted off A605 on Peterborough side of Oundle

Northamptonshire Dining Pub of the Year

Drinkers and diners experience an equally warm welcome at this comfortably civilised pub. The buzz of contented conversation fills the neatly kept little bar, which has cushioned slatback armchairs and bucket chairs, good winter log fires in a stone fireplace, and fresh flower arrangements. The no smoking conservatory restaurant is pretty, and if the weather's nice the attractively planted garden is particularly enjoyable. A very good range of drinks includes well kept Adnams and Greene King IPA on handpump, alongside a guest, usually from Nethergate or Potton, good wines with about 15 (including champagne) by the glass, organic cordials, and fresh orange juice. Locals gather in the much smaller tap bar, which has darts. The main draw though is the very well presented, inventive food from the seasonally changing bar menu. It's not cheap, but is worth the money, particularly the very good two-course bargain lunch menu (£11.75, not Sunday): tasty home-made crisps (£1.50), soup or chicken liver pâté with brioche and red onion and apple chutney (£4.75), crispy duck spring rolls with spiced coleslaw (£6.50), warm spicy salad of chick peas, garlic, roast red onions, peppers and spinach (£9.75), pork chop with mustard mash (£12.95), sweet chilli glazed salmon fillet (£13.75), calves liver steak with red wine shallot sauce (£14.50), roast fillet of beef with courgette and beetroot salad and pesto (£18.95), and puddings such as chocolate brownie gateau or puff pastry wrapped banana with toffee crunch ice-cream and hot chocolate sauce (from £5.50). The vast church behind is worth a visit, and the ruins of Fotheringhay Castle, where Mary Queen of Scots was executed, are not far away. *(Recommended by Alan and Jill Bull, Maysie Thompson, Miss Joan Morgan, O K Smyth,*

Mr and Mrs J E C Tasker, Mrs Catherine Draper, David and Mary Webb, Michael Sargent, Oliver and Sue Rowell, Fred and Lorraine Gill, Philip and Susan Philcox, Derek Stafford, John Saul, Sally Anne and Peter Goodale, Arnold Bennett, Alan Sutton)

Free house ~ Licensees Ray Smikle and John Hoskins ~ Real ale ~ Bar food (12-2, 6.30-9.30) ~ Restaurant ~ (01832) 226254 ~ Children welcome ~ Dogs allowed in bar ~ Open 12-3, 6-11(6.30-10.30 Sun)

GREAT OXENDON SP7383 Map 4

George

A508 S of Market Harborough

This comfortable dining pub with its friendly service makes an enjoyable place for a relaxed meal out. A great deal of care has gone into the furnishings and décor, from the welcoming lobby with its overstuffed chairs, former inn-sign, and lavatories entertainingly decked out with rather stylish naughty pictures, through the attractive prints and engravings in the two opened-together rooms of the main beamed bar, to the Portmeirion plates, and the turkey-carpeted no smoking conservatory overlooking the shrub-sheltered garden. The bar is cosy and clubby, with rather luxurious dark wallpaper, panelled dark brown dado, green leatherette bucket chairs around little tables, daily papers on poles, and a big log fire; there may be piped easy-listening classical music. They put quite an emphasis on the food, which is very popular with older lunchers (you might want to book), and tends to be at its best in the bar: soup (£3.50), filled rolls (from £4.50), pork and leek sausages and mash (£7.65), beef and Guinness pie or smoked salmon and haddock fishcakes (£8.25), grilled haddock (£8.50), good honey-roast lamb shank (£9.85), and puddings such as lemon tart or chocolate truffle cake (£3.35). The evening menu is slightly more elaborate with dishes such as roast lamb with madeira sauce (£11.95). Well kept Adnams, Greene King Old Speckled Hen and possibly a guest such as Adnams Regatta on handpump, and around ten wines by the glass. *(Recommended by Duncan Cloud, G A Hemingway, David and Barbara Knott, Mike and Mary Carter, Jeff and Wendy Williams, Gerry and Rosemary Dobson, Jim Farmer, Rod and Chris Pring)*

Free house ~ Licensee Allan Wiseman ~ Real ale ~ Bar food (12-2, 7-10) ~ Restaurant ~ (01858) 465205 ~ Children welcome ~ Dogs allowed in bedrooms ~ Open 11.30-3, 6.30(7 Sat)-11; closed Sun evenings ~ Bedrooms: £55.50B/£62.50B

HARRINGWORTH SP9298 Map 4

White Swan

Seaton Road; village SE of Uppingham, signposted from A6003, A47 and A43

History has been kind to this pretty village which is famous for its magnificent 82-arch Victorian railway viaduct, and is the setting for this striking limestone Tudor inn, with its imposing gable and arched window lights (look carefully and you can also make out the blocked-in traces of its former carriage-entry). There's plenty of exposed stone inside the pub too. The neatly kept central bar area has good solid tables, a hand-crafted oak counter with a mirror base and an attractive swan carving, pictures relating to the World War II Spanhoe airfield nearby and a collection of old village photographs (in which many of the present buildings are still recognisable). An open fire divides the bar and dining area, and Greene King IPA and a guest such as Shepherd Neame Spitfire are well kept on handpump; darts and piped music. The roomy and welcoming lounge/eating area has comfortable settles, while a quieter no smoking dining room has a collection of old jugs, craft tools, dried flower arrangements and locally painted watercolours; darts, cribbage, dominoes. Bar food includes sandwiches (from £2.95), hot baguettes, soup, black pudding with stilton sauce or chicken liver and black olive pâté (£3.95), wild mushroom pasta (£7.45), steak and Guinness pie or haddock mornay (£8.45) and home-made puddings such as treacle tart or bread and butter pudding (£4.25). There are tables out on a little terrace, and Rockingham race track is just four miles away. *(Recommended by David and Mary Webb, Fred and Lorraine Gill, Jim Farmer, George Atkinson)*

Free house ~ Licensee Paul Linton ~ Real ale ~ Bar food ~ Restaurant ~ (01572) 747543 ~ Children in eating area of bar and restaurant ~ Dogs allowed in bedrooms ~ Open 12-3, 6-11(10.30 Sun) ~ Bedrooms: £45S/£65S

KILSBY SP5671 Map 4

George

2½ miles from M1 junction 18: A428 towards Daventry, left on to A5 – look out for pub off on right at roundabout

You couldn't wish for a more relaxing refuge from the motorway and A5 than this substantial inn. The hard-working landlady extends a heartwarmingly hospitable welcome, and the good value wholesome bar food is satisfying. The lighter lunch menu includes sandwiches or soup (£3), filled baguettes (from £3.75) and ploughman's (£5.95), dishes on the evening menu such as battered cod (£5.90) and steak and kidney pudding (£6.90) are more substantial; puddings such as chocolate fudge cake or a particularly good home-made bread and butter pudding (£2.50). You will need to book if you go for Sunday lunch (£6.95). A high-ceilinged bar on the right, with plush banquettes, dark panelling, a coal-effect gas stove and a big bay window, opens on the left into a cheerful and attractive no smoking dining area with solidly comfortable furnishings. A long brightly decorated back public bar has a juke box, darts, a good pool table, fruit machine, table football and a huge TV. Well kept Charles Wells Bombardier, Greene King IPA and Abbot and a guest such as St Austell Tribute on handpump, a splendid range of malt whiskies in generous measures, and decent wines in big glasses. There are wood and metal picnic-sets out in the back garden, by the car park. *(Recommended by Ian Phillips, Roger and Jenny Huggins, George Atkinson, Ted George, Mr and Mrs J Williams, Ian and Nita Cooper, CMW, JJW, B and M Kendall, Peter and Jean Hoare)*

Punch ~ Lease Maggie Chandler ~ Real ale ~ Bar food (12-2.30, 6.30-9.30; 12-4, 6-9 Sun) ~ Restaurant ~ (01788) 822229 ~ Children welcome ~ Dogs allowed in bar ~ Live music first Sat in month ~ Open 11.30-3.30, 5.30(6 Sat)-11; 12-10.30 Sun ~ Bedrooms: £30/£50

NETHER HEYFORD SP6558 Map 4

Old Sun £

1¾ miles from M1 junction 16: village signposted left off A45 westbound – Middle Street

The cheerfully welcoming family who run this 18th-c golden stone pub are genuinely hospitable and lend a jolly decent feel to its bustling bric-a-brac filled rooms. Nooks and crannies in the several small linked rooms are packed with all sorts of enjoyable curiosities, from gleaming brassware (one fireplace is a grotto of large brass animals), to colourful relief plates, 1930s cigarette cards, railway memorabilia and advertising signs, World War II posters and rope fancywork. There are beams and low ceilings (one painted with a fine sunburst), partly glazed dividing panels, steps between some areas, rugs on parquet, red tiles or flagstones, a big inglenook log fire – and up on the left a room with full-sized hood skittles, a fruit machine, darts, TV, cribbage, dominoes and sports TV. Furnishings are mostly properly pubby, with the odd easy chair; piped music. Well kept Banks's, Greene King Ruddles, Marstons Pedigree and a weekend guest such as Robinsons Young Tom are served on handpump from two counters. The old cash till is stuck at one and a ha'penny; OK, so your pint and meal won't be that cheap, but the prices here are very reasonable. Quite a lot of the cooking is done by the landlady and her son, and the very enjoyable bar food includes lunchtime sandwiches (£3.25), hot steak roll, lamb casserole or chicken in creamy sauce (£4.25). In the evening, food is served by waitresses at one end of the pub and in the restaurant only, and the menu is a little pricier: steak pie (£8.75), cod and peas (£8.95), ricotta cannelloni with spinach and goats cheese (£9.25); Sunday lunch (£7.50). A fairy-lit front terrace has picnic-sets behind a line of blue-painted grain kibblers and other antiquated hand-operated farm machines, some with plants in their hoppers. They may stay open all day at weekends. *(Recommended by George Atkinson,*

Ian Phillips, B and M Kendall, June and Ken Brooks, Val and Alan Green, Ann Price, Gerry and Rosemary Dobson, Simon Calvert, Leigh and Gillian Mellor, Catherine and Rob Dunster)

Free house ~ Licensees Geoffrey and James Allen ~ Real ale ~ Bar food (not Mon evening or Sun) ~ Restaurant ~ (01327) 340164 ~ Children in eating area of bar and restaurant ~ Open 12-3, 6-11; 12-4, 6-11 Sat; 12-5, 7-10.30 Sun

OUNDLE TL0388 Map 5

Ship

West Street

The constant comings and goings of local characters and buzz of happy chat fill the rooms of this easy going community pub. Comfortably battered at the edges, it's a nice old building, made special by the cheerful bustle and friendly smiling service. The licensees have an interest in real ale so make an effort to source interesting and quickly rotated guest beers from brewers such as Abbeydale and Glentworth, which are then well kept alongside Bass and Oakham JHB, and a good range of malt whiskies. Enjoyable bar food in generous helpings is home-made where possible, and might include soup (£3.50), steak in ale pie, lemon chicken, stilton burger or pies (£7), and puddings (£3.50). The heavily beamed lounge bar is made up of three rooms that lead off the central corridor, one of them no smoking at lunchtime. Up by the street there's a mix of leather and other seats, with sturdy tables and a log fire in a stone inglenook, and down one end a charming little panelled snug has button-back leather seats built in around it. The wood-floored public side has darts, dominoes, fruit machine and a juke box. The friendly black and white pub cat you might see lounging around is called Midnight. The wooden tables and chairs out on the series of small sunny but sheltered terraces are lit at night. *(Recommended by George Atkinson, Tom and Ruth Rees, B N F and M Parkin)*

Free house ~ Licensees Andrew and Robert Langridge ~ Real ale ~ Bar food (12-3, 7-9) ~ (01832) 273918 ~ Dogs welcome ~ Jazz last Sun in month ~ Open 11-11; 12-10.30 Sun ~ Bedrooms: £25(£30S)/£50S(£60B)

SULGRAVE SP5545 Map 4

Star

E of Banbury, signposted off B4525; Manor Road

Although the menu at this lovely old creeper-covered stone-built inn is fairly upmarket (with prices to match), they've deliberately maintained a relaxed and welcoming pubby atmosphere in the beamed farmhouse-style interior. Furnishings include small pews, cushioned window seats and wall benches, kitchen chairs and cast-iron-framed tables, with polished flagstones in an area by the big inglenook fireplace, and red carpet elsewhere. Look out for the stuffed back end of a fox, seeming to leap into the wall. Framed newspaper front pages record memorable events such as Kennedy's assassination and the death of Churchill; alley skittles (by arrangement), Jenga, cribbage and dominoes. Well kept Hook Norton Best, Old Hooky, a Hook Norton seasonal beer and a monthly changing guest such as Everards Perfick on handpump. From a seasonally changing menu you can expect bar snacks such as scotch beef burger or sausage and mash (£6.95), starters such as leek and pearl broth barley (£4.25), four cheese risotto with roasted red pepper (£5.75) and tasty fried scallops with sweet chilli dipping sauce (£7.95), main courses such as roast pork belly with black pudding and apple sauce (£8.25) and beef fillet with wild mushrooms and truffle oil (£16.75) and daily specials such as bass fillet with chive beurre blanc (£15.50). Puddings might include caramelised apple tart with chantilly cream or chocolate brownie with chocolate sauce (£3.95); no smoking back restaurant. In summer you can eat outside at wooden tables under a vine-covered trellis, and there are benches out the front, and in the back garden. The pub is a short walk from the ancestral home of George Washington, and is handy for Silverstone. *(Recommended by Mrs J Poole, Morris Bagnall, Malcolm Taylor, Mrs A Cardwell, Michael Sargent, Theocsbrian, Michael Jones)*

Hook Norton ~ Tenants Jamie and Charlotte King ~ Real ale ~ Bar food (12-2(3 Sun), 6.30-9; not Mon except bank hols) ~ Restaurant ~ (01295) 760389 ~ Children in restaurant ~ Dogs allowed in bar ~ Open 11-2.30, 6-11; 12-5 Sun; closed Mon lunchtime, Sun evening ~ Bedrooms: £40S/£70S

WOODNEWTON TL0394 Map 5

White Swan £

Main Street; back roads N of Oundle, easily reached from A1/A47 (via Nassington) and A605 (via Fotheringhay)

The very enthusiastic new licensees who recently took over this stone-built pub have lived in the village for over twenty years so you can expect some real local character here – it's their friendly welcome that brings the fairly simple but spacious beamed bar and restaurant to life. Adnams, Batemans XXXB and Fullers London Pride are well kept alongside a changing guest from brewers such as Butcombe and Oakham; piped music. The licensees are not here to make a killing but to provide a good village pub, so you'll find that with most dishes priced in under our bargain award price limit the bar food is particularly good value: soup (£3.25), smoked mackerel with horseradish and rocket (£4.25), curry of the day or chilli (£5.25), battered cod (£5.50), wild mushroom stroganoff (£5.75), pie of the day or scampi (£5.95), one or two daily specials such as duck with raspberry sauce (£9.95), and home-made puddings including their speciality cheesecakes which come in unusual but tempting flavours including Cointreau and white chocolate (£3.50). The back lawn has tables and a boules pitch (league matches Tuesday evenings).
(Recommended by Oliver and Sue Rowell)

Free house ~ Licensees Jenny Chalkley and Andrew Downing ~ Real ale ~ Bar food (12-2, 6-9; 12-4 Sun; not Sun evenings or Mon) ~ Restaurant ~ (01780) 470381 ~ Children in restaurant ~ Open 12-2.30, 5.30-11; 12-11 Sat; 12-10.30 Sun

---

LUCKY DIP

Besides the fully inspected pubs, you might like to try these Lucky Dips recommended to us and described by readers (if you do, please send us reports: www.goodguides.co.uk).

ASHBY ST LEDGERS SP5768

☆ *Olde Coach House* [off A361]: Rambling softly lit linked rooms with high-backed winged settles and old kitchen tables, flagstones or polished black and red tiles, harness and hunting pictures, a couple of woodburners, lots of atmosphere, real ales such as Ind Coope Burton and Tetleys, good choice of decent wines (generous measures), friendly service, wide food choice, front games room; big-screen TV, piped music; tables out among fruit trees and under a fairy-lit arbour, barbecues, play area, interesting church nearby – see the skeleton; children welcome, disabled access, comfortable bedrooms, open all day in summer *(LYM, M J Caley, Bruce Bird, Howard and Margaret Buchanan, Susan and John Douglas, Ian Phillips, Patrick Hancock, Mike Marsh, George Atkinson)*

ASHTON TL0588

Chequered Skipper [the one NE of Oundle, signed from A427/A605 island]: Handsomely rebuilt thatched pub in classic setting on chestnut-tree green of elegant estate village, helpful and friendly young staff, changing ales such as Adnams, Newby Wyke Bear Island, Oakham JHB and Tetleys, reasonably priced food (not Mon) from baked potatoes and ciabattas to restauranty main courses, light and airy open-plan layout with tables left and right *(Oliver and Sue Rowell, Michael and Jenny Back)*

☆ *Old Crown* [the one off A508 S of M1 junction 15]: 18th-c beamed stone-built dining pub, rather upmarket choice and prices, modern cooking, roomy no smoking area, Charles Wells Eagle and Bombardier with a guest beer, good wines, particularly good staff; tables out on lawn *(George Atkinson, Alan Sutton, Gerry and Rosemary Dobson)*

BADBY SP5659

Maltsters [The Green]: Stone-built pub with light wood furniture in long beamed room, roaring fire each end, good reasonably priced food inc unusual dishes (several small blackboards), well kept ales inc interesting guest beers, good soft drinks choice, friendly attentive service; may be quiet piped music, darts, hood skittles, fruit machine, TV; garden with terrace, well placed for walks on nearby Knightley Way, bedrooms *(CMW, JJW)*

BARNWELL TL0484

☆ *Montagu Arms* [off A605 S of Oundle, then fork right at Thurning, Hemington sign]:

Attractive unspoilt stone-built pub in pleasant streamside village, two bars with low beams, flagstones or tile and brick floors, not smart but warm, cosy and welcoming; good interesting food running up to swordfish, hearty helpings, well kept Adnams Bitter and Broadside, Flowers IPA and a guest beer, decent wines, helpful cheerful staff, log fire, neat back dining room; games room off yard, big garden with good well equipped play area, barbecue and camping; open all day wknd *(George Atkinson, Ryta Horridge, G A Hemingway, BB, Oliver and Sue Rowell, David Treherne-Pollock)*

BRACKLEY SP5837

Bell [High St]: Lots of Formula One memorabilia, barbecues in lead-up to Silverstone Grand Prix, Shepherd Neame Spitfire and Theakstons; live bands Fri; open all day *(Mick Furn)*

Fox [Banbury Rd]: Well kept Greene King IPA and a frequently changing attractively priced guest beer; landlady cooks a good Sun lunch (week's notice required, no other food) *(Mick Furn)*

Manor [Manor Rd]: Well staffed tucked-away local with well kept Adnams and Greene King IPA, bar snacks *(Mick Furn)*

Red Lion [Market Pl]: Enjoyable well priced food, inc the pub's own sausages, hams etc *(Mick Furn)*

BRACKLEY HATCH SP6441

Green Man [A43 NE of Brackley]: Large Chef & Brewer dining pub on busy dual carriageway nr Silverstone, comfortable old-look beamed lounge area and conservatory, big no smoking family restaurant, wide range of reliable food all day from baguettes and baked potatoes to steaks and mixed seafood grill, fresh veg, relaxed atmosphere, quick, friendly and helpful service, Courage beers, good wines, log fires; tables on lawn, bedrooms in Premier Lodge behind, open all day *(JHBS, Mr and Mrs G S Ayrton, BB, R C Vincent, Phil and Jane Hodson, Andy and Yvonne Cunningham)*

BRAFIELD-ON-THE-GREEN SP8258

Red Lion [A428 5 miles from Northampton towards Bedford]: Reworked bistro-style Chef & Brewer, up-to-date brasserie food from fancy sandwiches up in two main rooms (one no smoking), modern décor and furnishings, small drinking area with a couple of settees, Courage Best, Greene King Old Speckled Hen and Charles Wells Bombardier; garden tables front and back *(Michael Dandy, Gerry and Rosemary Dobson)*

BRAUNSTON SP5465

Admiral Nelson [Dark Lane, Little Braunston, overlooking Lock 3 just N of Grand Union Canal tunnel]: Warmly welcoming 18th-c ex-farmhouse in peaceful setting by Grand Union Canal Lock 3 and hump bridge, with lots of tables in pleasant waterside garden over bridge; cosy tiled-floor part by bar, longer dining end, well kept real ales with a guest such as Youngs, good cheery service, enjoyable food with interesting as well as basic dishes, games room with skittles; bedroom overlooking lock, towpath walks *(Mike Roberts, Ted George, George Atkinson)*

BRAYBROOKE SP7684

Swan [Griffin Rd]: Refurbished thatched pub with thriving local feel in bar, good value restaurant food inc Sun lunch, good service, Everards beers, long wine list *(Drs T D and E A Hall)*

BRIXWORTH SP7470

Coach & Horses [Harborough Rd, just off A508 N of Northampton]: Welcoming 17th-c stone-built inn nr Pitsford Water, good helpful staff, generous and enjoyable if not cheap food from wide choice of good sandwiches to fresh fish, seasonal game and popular Sun lunches, well kept ales such as Adnams, Banks's Original and Marstons Pedigree, decent house wines, friendly helpful service, beams and lots of pictures, small no smoking restaurant; piped music; children welcome, attractive village with famous Saxon church *(CMW, JJW, Gerry and Rosemary Dobson)*

BUCKBY WHARF SP6066

☆ ***New Inn*** [A5 N of Weedon]: Neatly redecorated 17th-c pub with plenty of picnic-sets out on pleasant terrace by busy Grand Union Canal lock, several rooms radiating from central servery, inc small dining room with nice fire, big-screen TV in back room, lively cockatiel and parakeet; good range of decent sensibly priced food from baguettes and baked potatoes up, well kept Greene King IPA and local Frog Island Best and Natterjack, friendly licensees and attentive young staff; live music Sat, quiz Sun, open all day *(LYM, George Atkinson, CMW, JJW)*

BUGBROOKE SP6757

☆ ***Wharf Inn*** [The Wharf; off A5 S of Weedon]: Spotless pub in super spot by canal, plenty of tables on big lawn with moorings and summer boat trips; emphasis on big water-view restaurant, also bar and lounge with pleasant informal small raised eating area on either side, lots of stripped brickwork, wide choice of good generous food from good value baguettes up (people like the proper steak and kidney pie), four or five well kept ales inc Courage Best, Greene King Old Speckled Hen and local Frog Island Best, farm cider, helpful friendly service, nice fire; weekly quiz and music night; children very welcome, garden with boules *(George Atkinson, Hilary Edwards, BB, Ann Price, Howard and Margaret Buchanan)*

CHACOMBE SP4943

☆ ***George & Dragon*** [2½ miles from M40 junction 11: A361 towards Daventry, then village signposted on right; Silver Street]: Good M40 respite (interesting church in pretty village), beams, flagstones and log fire in massive fireplace, wide (though not cheap) range of enjoyable food from baguettes and baked potatoes up, good friendly service, Everards real ales, no smoking area in restaurant; darts, dominoes, TV and piped music; children in eating areas, bedrooms, open all day *(Bob and Laura Brock, Rod Stoneman, Gordon Prince, Derek Tynan, Klaus and Elizabeth Leist, Roger and*

Anne Newbury, Jean and Douglas Troup, Susie Symes, Chris Glasson)

CHAPEL BRAMPTON SP7266

☆ ***Brampton Halt*** [Pitsford Rd, off A5199 N of Northampton]: Red brick former stationmaster's house on Northampton & Lamport Railway (possibly wknd train rides), Victorian-style décor, woodburner, lots of railway memorabilia, straightforward bar food (not Sun evening), well kept Adnams, Everards Old Original and Tiger, Fullers London Pride and Greene King IPA, decent wines, old farm tools in a high-raftered dining area, small sun lounge; trivia, may be piped music; children welcome, garden tables and play area, Nene Valley Way walks, open all day wknds *(Steve Kirby, Simon and Mandy King, Ted George, George Atkinson, LYM)*

Spencer Arms [Northampton Rd]: Big busy beamed Chef & Brewer family dining pub, plenty of stripped tables in long timber-divided L-shaped bar, huge blackboard food choice, pleasant service, Courage Best and Directors, two log fires; piped music *(Eithne Dandy, Gill and Keith Croxton)*

CLIPSTON SP7181

☆ ***Bulls Head*** [B4036 S of Market Harboro]: Restful décor in heavily beamed dim-lit village pub (some coins in the cracks date from World War II, put there by airmen who never made it back for their next drink); still a wonderful collection of whiskies gathered by previous landlords – pub now owned by Everards, with their Tiger, Beacon, a seasonal beer and perhaps a guest brew such as Hook Norton Old Hooky, good wine choice, decent food inc good curry specials, calm staff; children welcome in no smoking areas, tables out on terrace, bedrooms, has been cl Mon lunchtime; more reports on new regime please *(LYM, Catherine and Rob Dunster)*

COLLINGTREE SP7555

Wooden Walls of Old England [1¼ miles from M1 junction 15; High St]: Low-beamed thatched stone-built village pub, model galleon and some other nautical memorabilia (underlining the meaning of the name), two to four well kept ales, freshly cooked food (not Sun evening or Mon lunchtime) from good value wraps up, good service, open fire; quiet piped music in lounge, TV in bar; children welcome, lots of picnic-sets and play area in nice back garden *(BB, CMW, JJW)*

COSGROVE SP7843

☆ ***Navigation*** [Castlethorpe Rd]: Lovely canalside setting, bustling rambling open-plan bar up steps with chesterfield and armchairs around open fire, lots of canal prints and memorabilia, friendly helpful service, real ales such as Archers, Everards Tiger and Greene King IPA, sandwiches, baguettes and enjoyable meals cooked to order (so may be a wait at busy times), no smoking restaurant; can be very busy wknds and school hols; children welcome, lots of tables out by water, moorings *(BB, Tony Hobden, Ann Price)*

DENFORD SP9976

Cock [High St, S of Thrapston]: Neatly kept Elizabethan pub, cosy L-shaped bar with log fire, bare boards, dark beams and plank ceilings, woodburner in long restaurant (not Sun-Tues nights), wide lunchtime choice of good value food (not Mon), freshly made so may be a wait, five well kept ales, good soft drinks choice, chatty landlord, attentive service, darts, hood skittles; quiet piped music, games machine; picnic-sets in garden, River Nene walks nearby *(CMW, JJW)*

ECTON SP8263

Worlds End [A4500 Northampton—Wellingborough]: Extended 17th-c pub with two or three real ales, good choice of other drinks, reasonably priced food (inc times when few other pubs serve), steps down to partly no smoking dining room; piped music; garden with terrace and play area *(CMW, JJW)*

EVENLEY SP5834

☆ ***Red Lion*** [The Green]: Small beamed local now taken over by group of villagers keen to keep up its cricketing traditions (attractive village cricket green opposite, cricketing books and other memorabilia); has been very popular lunchtime for good value food from good sandwiches to plenty of grills, fish and vegetarian, also Sun lunches, Banks's, Marstons Pedigree and a guest such as Morrells Varsity, decent coffee and choice of wines, quick cheerful service, inglenook, some flagstones; tables out on lawn, one or two seats out in front *(George Atkinson)*

EYDON SP5450

☆ ***Royal Oak*** [Lime Ave; village signed off A361 Daventry—Banbury, and from B4525]: Old-fashioned extended late 17th-c local, several rooms with stripped stone and assorted old furnishings on polished flagstones, thriving informal atmosphere, enjoyable meals (not Sun evening or Mon, no snacks), Greene King IPA and Hook Norton Best, friendly young South African staff, nice inglenook log fire, daily papers, games room with darts, hood skittles and TV; piped music may be rather loud; children and dogs welcome, tables out in partly covered back courtyard, picnic-sets on front terrace *(Alan Sutton, CMW, JJW, Lady Heath, LYM, Michael Jones, George Atkinson, Sue and Keith Campbell)*

FARTHINGHOE SP5339

Fox [just off A422 Brackley—Banbury; Baker St]: Quiet village local with stone fireplace, floors part tiled and part carpet, big helpings of enjoyable food from good baguettes up, friendly licensee happy to do smaller ones for elderly, Charles Wells ales; garden *(Hugh Spottiswoode, Arnold Bennett)*

GAYTON SP7054

Queen Victoria [High St]: Spotless and comfortable village pub, four areas off central bar (two no smoking), light panelling, beams, lots of pictures, books and woodburner, wide choice of decent food from baguettes up, Charles Wells Eagle or Bombardier and guests such as Everards Tiger and Wadworths 6X, good wine choice, attentive friendly staff; piped music *(LYM, George Atkinson, Tony Hobden, Gerry and Rosemary Dobson)*

GRAFTON REGIS SP7546

☆ *White Hart* [A508 S of Northampton]: Thatched dining pub in thatched village, several linked rooms, good home-made bar food (not Sun evening) inc lots of splendid winter soups and fine range of baguettes, also bookings-only restaurant with open fire – very popular for flamboyant chef/landlord's good imaginative cooking; well kept Greene King IPA and Abbot, many decent wines by the glass, friendly hard-working helpful staff, pensive african grey parrot, pub dog; piped music; good-sized garden (food not served there) with terrace tables, cl Mon exc bank hols *(George Atkinson, BB, CMW, JJW, Gerry and Rosemary Dobson, Alan Sutton)*

GREAT BILLING SP8162

Elwes Arms [High St]: Thatched stone-built 16th-c village pub, two bars, wide choice of good value food inc tempting Sun lunch, pleasant no smoking dining room (children allowed here), three or four well kept ales, good soft drinks choice; may be piped pop music, Sun quiz night, no dogs; wheelchair access to top level, garden with covered terrace and play area *(CMW, JJW)*

GREAT BRINGTON SP6664

☆ *Fox & Hounds/Althorp Coaching Inn* [off A428 NW of Northampton, nr Althorp Hall]: Charming thatched stone-built pub with fine log fires in quaint low-beamed flagstoned bar with lots of atmosphere and bric-a-brac, well kept Greene King ales with Fullers London Pride and lots of interesting changing beers, decent wines, attentive friendly staff, wide choice of enjoyable traditional and mediterranean food from separate bar and restaurant menus, two small no smoking dining rooms, one in basement; children and dogs welcome, open all day wknds and summer, tables in attractive courtyard and side garden with play area, nice setting *(James Beeby, Mrs I Jones, LYM, George Atkinson, Gerry and Rosemary Dobson, Trevor and Judy Pearson, Ted George)*

GREAT DODDINGTON SP8864

Stags Head [High St (B573 S of Wellingborough)]: Old stone-built pub with bar and split-level lounge/dining room, three real ales, good choice of soft drinks and of enjoyable food; picnic-sets out in front and in garden *(CMW, JJW)*

HACKLETON SP8054

White Hart [B526 SE of Northampton]: Comfortable welcoming 18th-c country pub with no smoking dining area down corridor, stripped stone, beamery and brickwork, illuminated well, brasses and artefacts, soft lighting, fresh flowers, good value generous fresh food inc local produce, well kept Fullers London Pride and Greene King ales, split-level flagstoned bar with flame-effect fire, pool and hood skittles; quiz Sun; children welcome, garden with picnic-sets and goal posts, open all day *(Mike Becker, CMW, JJW)*

HARLESTONE SP7064

☆ *Dusty Fox* [A428, Lower Harlestone]: Attractive and relaxed Vintage Inn, small front bar and lounge, tasteful old-world furnishings, hops on beams, local photographs, mainly no smoking dining area and conservatory-style barn; enjoyable food all day from separate servery, well kept Bass and Tetleys Bitter and Imperial, decent wines, good soft drinks choice, prompt friendly attentive service, two log fires, no piped music; children welcome, tables in nice garden, open all day, handy for Harlestone Firs walks *(David Blackburn, David and Julie Glover, Michael Dandy, Mr and Mrs Bentley-Davies, Ted George, CMW, JJW, George Atkinson)*

HELLIDON SP5158

☆ *Red Lion* [Stockwell Lane, off A425 W of Daventry]: Good popular Tues/Weds OAP lunch in small wisteria-covered inn, wide choice of other good value food too inc some interesting dishes, softly lit no smoking low-ceilinged stripped stone dining area with lots of hunting prints, well kept Greene King IPA and Abbot and Hook Norton Best, two farm ciders, long-serving licensees, helpful cheerful staff, cosy and comfortable lounge, two friendly labradors by woodburner in bar, hood skittles and pool in back games room; piped music; picnic-sets in front, beautiful setting by green of unspoilt village, good bedrooms, windmill vineyard and pleasant walks nearby *(George Atkinson, CMW, JJW, Di and Mike Gillam, Arnold Bennett)*

KINGS SUTTON SP4936

Butchers Arms [Whittall St]: Well run village pub with buoyant local atmosphere, full range of well kept Hook Norton ales, decent reasonably priced food, aunt sally; in neat sandstone village easily spotted by spire *(Giles and Annie Francis, Mick Furn)*

White Horse [The Square]: Prettily positioned traditional building with contemporary twist to knocked-through rooms: low beams, timbers, exposed brickwork, cream walls, chunky tables and rugs on light wood floors, modern lighting, some good pictures, flagstoned floors in two no smoking back dining rooms (one with high rafters, old stove and red walls), piped music, well kept changing real ales such as Shepherd Neame Spitfire and Theakstons XB on handpump, carefully chosen wine list with around ten by the glass, bar food; picnic-sets in front overlook village green and striking church; children and dogs welcome *(B H and J I Andrews, Mike Carter, Meg and Colin Hamilton, LYM, Michael H Heath)*

LITTLE BRINGTON SP6663

☆ *Old Saracens Head* [4½ miles from M1 junction 16, first right off A45 to Daventry; also signed off A428; Main St]: Appealingly individual pub, entirely no smoking now, roomy U-shaped lounge with good log fire, flagstones, alcoves and lots of old prints, book-lined eating room off and extended restaurant, enjoyable food from soup or baguettes to full meals with plenty of choice and interesting dishes, well kept Fullers London Pride, Greene King IPA and Timothy Taylors Landlord, telephone in genuine red kiosk; tables in neat back garden, handy for Althorp House and Holdenby House *(BB, R M Corlett, George Atkinson)*

LODDINGTON SP8178

Hare [Main St]: 17th-c stone-built dining pub, wide choice of enjoyable good value food inc game specialities in two eating areas, one no smoking, good-sized helpings, tablecloths and fresh flowers, well kept Adnams, Greene King IPA and Fullers London Pride or Youngs Special in small bar, good wine and soft drinks choice, good coffee, polite service; piped light classics; picnic-sets on front lawn *(Gerry and Rosemary Dobson, CMW, JJW)*

LOWICK SP9780

☆ *Snooty Fox* [signed off A6116 Corby—Raunds]: Attractive pub under new ownership, pleasantly refurbished two-room lounge with handsome 16th-c beams, log fire in huge stone fireplace, dining tables on neat new flagstones, enjoyable food, well kept Fullers London Pride and Greene King IPA and Abbot, warm friendly service, restaurant; piped music, live Fri, Mon quiz night; children welcome, disabled access, floodlit picnic-sets out on front lawn *(Michael and Jenny Back, Judith Stobart, LYM)*

MAIDWELL SP7477

☆ *Stags Head* [A508 Northampton—Mkt Harboro]: Thriving pubby atmosphere in small, spotless and comfortable beamed front bar with log fire and well kept Greene King IPA and a guest such as Adnams or Fullers London Pride, friendly and very attentive service, well chosen pictures, emphasis on freshly cooked good value food in three attractively light and airy further sections – two no smoking; tables on terrace (dogs on leads allowed here) by back lawn with paddock beyond, bedrooms, not far from splendid Palladian Kelmarsh Hall in its parkland *(P Tailyour, Gerry and Rosemary Dobson, George Atkinson)*

MEARS ASHBY SP8466

☆ *Griffins Head* [Wilby Rd]: Comfortably refurbished country pub with half a dozen or so well kept ales such as Adnams, Boddingtons, Greene King IPA and Abbot, Loddon Ferrymans Gold and Bamboozle and Timothy Taylors Landlord, wide food choice from sandwiches, baguettes, baked potatoes and substantial OAP bargain wkdy lunches to much more ambitious dishes, smart front lounge, pleasant views and hunting prints, log fire in huge fireplace, small dining room with no smoking area; piped music, often soft jazz; children welcome, new seats out in neat flower-filled garden, on edge of attractive thatched village, open all day *(CMW, JJW, George Atkinson, Ben Harrison)*

MIDDLETON CHENEY SP5041

New Inn [Main Rd, off A422]: Well kept real ales, enjoyable food *(Mick Furn)*

MILTON MALSOR SP7355

☆ *Greyhound* [2¼ miles from M1 junction 15, via A508]: Big busy Chef & Brewer, well refurbished in olde-worlde mode, lots of cosy corners, 15th-c beams, old pictures and china, pewter-filled dresser, candlelit pine tables, good log fire, well kept John Smiths, Theakstons Best and Old Peculier, good range of wines, wide choice of food all day from filled rolls to good fish choice, prompt friendly service; piped jazz or classical music; well behaved seated children welcome, spreading front lawn with duck/fish pond, open all day *(George Atkinson, LYM, Ted George, Tim Keenan, CMW, JJW, Roy and Lindsey Fentiman)*

MOULTON SP7866

Telegraph [West St]: Traditional friendly village pub with well kept Greene King Old Speckled Hen, Shepherd Neame Spitfire and a guest beer *(M Warren)*

NEWNHAM SP5759

Romer Arms [The Green]: Pine panelling, mix of flagstones, quarry tiles and carpet, log fire, light and airy back conservatory, friendly attentive service, good generous home cooking inc some unusual dishes, Mon-Sat lunchtime bargains, popular Sun lunch (no snacks then), Courage Directors and Greene King IPA and Abbot, good soft drinks choice, public bar with darts and pool; piped music, opens noon or so, picnic-sets in back garden looking over fields, small attractive village *(CMW, JJW)*

NEWTON BROMSWOLD SP9965

Swan [E of Rushden; Church Lane]: Quiet village pub with roomy mock-Tudor lounge, food (not Sun pm or Mon) inc good lunchtime sandwiches, friendly chatty licensees, well kept Greene King ales, good soft drinks choice, real fire, games room with darts and hood skittles, conservatory dining room, two dogs, two cats; garden tables *(CMW, JJW)*

NORTHAMPTON SP7759

Britannia [3¾ miles from M1 junction 15; Old Bedford Rd (off A428)]: Big modernised Chef & Brewer with massive beams, mix of flagstones and carpet, 18th-c 'kitchen', Courage Best and Directors, wide food choice all day from baguettes up, no smoking area, conservatory; may be piped jazz or light classics, Tues quiz night; picnic-sets by River Nene, open all day *(LYM, Michael Dandy, Gerry and Rosemary Dobson)*

Clicker [Collingdale Rd/Silverdale Rd, Weston Favell]: Wide choice of sensibly priced food inc Sun lunch, three real ales, old local photographs; separate bar with pool, darts and machines, piped pop music; garden with play area *(CMW, JJW)*

☆ *Malt Shovel* [Bridge St (approach rd from M1 junction 15); best parking in Morrisons opp back entrance]: Long pine and brick bar, well kept Banks's, Frog Island Natterjack, Fullers London Pride, Tetleys and several interesting changing guests inc a Mild, Rich's farm cider, belgian bottled beers, over 50 malt whiskies, country wines, good soft drinks choice, occasional beer festivals, daily papers, good value lunchtime light dishes and more substantial meals (not Sun), breweriana inc some from Carlsberg Brewery opposite, open fire, darts; piped music sometimes (live Weds); picnic-sets on small back terrace, back disabled access, *(CMW, JJW, Martin Grosberg, Bruce Bird, Tony Hobden, the Didler)*

Moon on the Square [The Parade, Market Pl]: Well run Wetherspoons, some café-style furnishings, masses of books, around nine real ales from long bar, good value prompt food all day inc bargains, good coffee, efficient helpful staff, steps up to partly no smoking back conservatory (and stairs up to lavatories); no music, open all day *(Michael Tack, W W Burke)*

OLD SP7873

White Horse [Walgrave Rd, N of Northampton between A43 and A508]: Enjoyable sensibly priced blackboard food from good low-priced baguettes to interesting main dishes and popular Sun lunch, thriving atmosphere in cosy and comfortable lounge with good log fire, hunting prints and china, friendly service, well kept Banks's and Marstons Pedigree, decent wines, good coffee, restaurant, unusual theme nights; quiet piped music, TV; attractive garden overlooking 13th-c church *(CMW, JJW, Pat and Derek Roughton)*

ORLINGBURY SP8572

Queens Arms [off A43 Northampton—Kettering, A509 Wellingborough—Kettering; Isham Rd]: Stone-built pub with large airy lounge, comfortable banquettes, stools, neat décor and beamery, side no smoking area, half a dozen changing ales, wide food choice from sandwiches up in bar and evening/wknd restaurant; may be piped music, service can slow if busy; nice garden with play area, open all day wknds *(Anthony Barnes, Howard Dell, O K Smyth, CMW, JJW)*

OUNDLE TL0386

☆ *Mill* [Barnwell Rd, S (just off A605 bypass)]: Star is for this converted mill's great setting on the River Nene; stripped-stone bar (may be cl wkdy lunchtimes in winter), huge choice of generous tex-mex and other food in no smoking upstairs low-beamed Trattoria, top-floor no smoking granary restaurant (not always open), well kept Theakstons and a couple of guest beers; children welcome, picnic-sets under cocktail parasols on front terrace and side grass *(H W Roberts, Michael Tack, LYM, Jane Walker)*

Rose & Crown [Market Pl]: Armchairs and sofas in friendly stripped-stone beamed front bar overlooking busy Thurs market, Banks's, Mansfield and Marstons Pedigree, quick friendly service, back public bar, lots of old prints, photographs, brasses and plates, good imaginative food in conservatory beyond; fine view of superb church from this and suntrap terrace *(Steve Whalley, George Atkinson)*

PITSFORD SP7567

☆ *Griffin* [off A508 N of Northampton]: Two-bar pub with food side now run separately and well by young chef and partner, good lunchtime choice from baguettes and baked potatoes up, inventive and rewarding modern evening menu, pleasant no smoking restaurant extension; well kept Adnams, Fullers London Pride, Greene King IPA and Abbot and guest beers, reasonably priced wines; pretty village nr Pitsford Water/Brixworth Country Park *(Gerry and Rosemary Dobson)*

RAVENSTHORPE SP6670

☆ *Chequers* [Chequers Lane]: Refurbished and extended beamed pub locally popular for wide range of good value generous food from baguettes and baked potatoes to steaks, well kept Greene King IPA, Flowers Original, Fullers London Pride and a guest beer, good soft drinks choice, friendly attentive staff, open fire, lots of bric-a-brac, mainly no smoking dining room, games room, may have free range eggs for sale (and Fri meat raffle); TV, games machine, piped music, monthly quiz night; children welcome, open all day Sat, small secluded garden with terrace and play area *(CMW, JJW, Michael Tack, Gerry and Rosemary Dobson, George Atkinson)*

RINGSTEAD SP9875

Axe & Compass [Carlow Rd]: Extended stone-built village pub, bar and restaurant with flagstones and lots of bric-a-brac, enjoyable fresh food, attentive service, Banks's and Marstons Pedigree; piped music; cl lunchtimes Mon-Thurs; garden and play area *(CMW, JJW)*

ROADE SP7551

Cock [just off A508 S of M1 junction 15]: Friendly family-run village pub with enjoyable well presented reasonably priced bar food (all day Fri-Sun, not Mon night), Marstons Pedigree, Theakstons and guest beers, good soft drinks choice, cheerful staff, plates, horsebrasses, flame-effect gas fire, restaurant (not Mon); piped music, games machine, TV; children in lounge bar, dogs on leads allowed in garden, open all day *(CMW, JJW, Alan Ruddle)*

ROCKINGHAM SP8691

Sondes Arms [Main St]: Nicely set beamed pub with emphasis on enjoyable food in bar and large separate no smoking dining area, well kept Adnams Broadside and Charles Wells Bombardier, good friendly service; super views, tables out on terrace, lovely village (except for the traffic) *(Peter Scillitoe, Mike and Mary Carter)*

SHUTLANGER SP7249

Plough [Main Rd, off A43 N of Towcester]: Out-of-the-way 17th-c pub popular for good value food (freshly made, so may be a wait) esp good fish fresh from Cornwall, small no smoking restaurant area, simple bar with lots of hanging jugs, mugs and tankards, stuffed animals, horse pictures and brasses, nice atmosphere, well kept Charles Wells Eagle and Bombardier, darts and hood skittles, friendly dog called Fred; piped music; garden with picnic-sets, play area and boules, nearby walks *(R M Corlett, Hilary Edwards, CMW, JJW)*

SIBBERTOFT SP6782

Red Lion [Welland Rise, off A4303 or A508 SW of Mkt Harboro]: Cosy and civilised extended dining pub, lounge tables set for dining (new chef's menu shaping up nicely), well kept Everards Tiger and guest beers such as Adnams and Bass, decent wines, welcoming landlord, good service, magazines, comfortably cushioned wall seats, some dark panelling, attractive no smoking beamed dining room; covered tables outside, two holiday flats, cl Mon/Tues lunchtimes *(Gerry and Rosemary Dobson)*

SILVERSTONE SP6643

Royal Oak [Brackley Rd, just off A43 bypass]: Smart good-sized bar with bare-boards public area and cosier lounge part, central coal-effect fire, Grand Prix memorabilia, Fullers London Pride, decent food, friendly service; may be piped music; children welcome *(Val and Alan Green)*

SLIPTON SP9579

Samuel Pepys [Slipton Lane]: 16th-c pub attractively remodelled by new owners, beams and some stripped stone, long airy bar with another beyond, neat restaurant and dining conservatory, wide choice of freshly made food from good sandwiches and ciabattas to old favourites and some interesting dishes, friendly service (helpful with special diet needs), Frog Island BB and changing ales such as Oakham Bishops Farewell and JHB, five well kept ales, decent wines, good tea and coffee; disabled access, provision for children, country views from garden with play area *(Judith Stobart, Michael and Jenny Back)*

STOKE BRUERNE SP7449

☆ ***Boat*** [3½ miles from M1 junction 15 – A508 towards Stony Stratford then signed on right; Bridge Rd]: Picturesque spot by beautifully restored lock opp British Waterways Museum and shop, tables out by towpath, hood skittles in appealing two-part flagstoned bar by canal though main focus is modernised central-pillared back lounge without the views (children allowed in this bit); well kept ales such as Adnams, Banks's, Marstons Pedigree and a guest such as Mansfield Mild or Thwaites, reasonably priced bar snacks, OAP wkdy bargain lunches, no smoking restaurant and all-day tearooms; busy and rather trippery, but cheerful landlord and friendly helpful staff cope promptly; bar open all day summer Sats, canal boat trips *(LYM, Tony Hobden, W W Burke, R C Vincent)*

SYWELL SP8167

Horseshoe [off A43 NE of Northampton; Overstone Rd]: Large open-plan stone-built dining pub with blackboard food choice, three real ales, prompt service; games area with pool, darts and machines; children welcome, largish garden with picnic-sets and play area *(CMW, JJW)*

THORNBY SP6675

☆ ***Red Lion*** [Welford Rd; A5199 Northampton—Leicester]: Friendly old pub with old pictures and decorative china, pews, leather settee and armchairs, no smoking areas, flourishing houseplants, log fire, well kept ales inc Greene King, good soft drinks choice, enjoyable food from sandwiches to steaks inc Sun roasts and children's helpings, beamed dining area, good range of traditional games; quiet piped radio, no dogs; children welcome, open all day wknds and bank hols *(LYM, CMW, JJW)*

THORPE MANDEVILLE SP5344

Three Conies [off B4525 E of Banbury]: Attractive 17th-c stone-built pub with unspoilt two-room bar, beams, some stripped masonry, flagstones and bare boards, log fires each end, mix of old dining tables, enjoyable honest food, well kept Hook Norton Best and perhaps Old Hooky, friendly new chef/landlord and wife, large family dining room; piped music; tables out on grass *(LYM, Ted George, George Atkinson)*

THORPE WATERVILLE TL0281

Fox [A605 Thrapston—Oundle]: Pleasantly extended old stone-built pub with efficient friendly service, wide range of decent straightforward food, well kept Charles Wells ales with a guest beer, several wines by the glass, log-effect fire, lots of fox pictures, light and airy no smoking dining area; piped music, children allowed, no dogs, small garden with play area *(Anthony Barnes, John Wooll)*

TOWCESTER SP6654

☆ ***Peggottys*** [Foster's Booth (A5 3m N)]: Bar/restaurant rather than pub, but has well kept changing ales such as Batemans XB and Gales Robins Revenge, good choice of enjoyable food from sandwiches and light dishes to good value Sun lunch and fuller meals at slightly higher price in no smoking restaurant, genial landlord and quick attentive service even when busy, light and airy flagstoned room with settees and armchairs as well as table seating and conservatory; acceptable piped music *(George Atkinson, Gerry and Rosemary Dobson, Peter and Jean Hoare)*

Plough [Watling St E]: Well kept Charles Wells Eagle and Bombardier, decent food from simple basic snacks to good steaks, helpful landlady, cheerful efficient service, darts in back lounge section *(Pete Baker, Joe Green)*

Red Lion [Foster's Booth (A5 3m N)]: Attractive 16th-c former posting inn nicely tidied up by warm-hearted new licensees, dark wood furniture in carpeted lounge bar with big inglenook fireplace, lots of bric-a-brac, copper and brass, another fire in chatty quarry-tiled public bar, Fullers London Pride, good value blackboard food from good sandwiches and light dishes up, quick service, carpeted games room with hood skittles and darts, restaurant; piped music turned down on request, TV, lacks a no smoking area; garden picnic-sets *(CMW, JJW)*

WADENHOE TL0083

☆ ***Kings Head*** [Church Street; village signposted (in small print) off A605 S of Oundle]: Beautifully placed two-bar 17th-c country pub with picnic-sets on sun terrace and among trees on big stretch of grass by River Nene, pretty village, good walks; solid pine furniture, enjoyable food (mains come with a complimentary starter – usually good home-made soup), well kept Adnams Best and Broadside, Black Sheep and guest beers such as Fullers London Pride and Woodfordes Wherry, welcoming service, good selection of books, no smoking areas, beamed dining room, games

Please use this card to tell us which pubs *you* think should or should not be included in the next edition of *The Good Pub Guide*. Just fill it in and return it to us – no stamp or envelope needed. Don't forget you can also use the report forms at the end of the *Guide*, or report through our web site: www.goodguides.co.uk

ALISDAIR AIRD

In returning this form I confirm my agreement that the information I provide may be used by The Random House Group Ltd, its assignees and/or licensees in any media or medium whatsoever.

YOUR NAME AND ADDRESS (BLOCK CAPITALS PLEASE)

☐ *Please tick this box if you would like extra report forms*

REPORT ON *(pub's name)*

Pub's address

☐ **YES Main Entry** ☐ **YES Lucky Dip** ☐ **NO don't include**

Please tick one of these boxes to show your verdict, and give reasons and descriptive comments, prices etc

☐ Deserves FOOD award ☐ Deserves PLACE-TO-STAY award

REPORT ON *(pub's name)*

Pub's address

☐ **YES Main Entry** ☐ **YES Lucky Dip** ☐ **NO don't include**

Please tick one of these boxes to show your verdict, and give reasons and descriptive comments, prices etc

☐ Deserves FOOD award ☐ Deserves PLACE-TO-STAY award

By returning this form, you consent to the collection, recording and use of the information you submit, by The Random House Group Ltd. Any personal details which you provide from which we can identify you are held and processed in accordance with the Data Protection Act 1998 and will not be passed on to any third parties. The Random House Group Ltd may wish to send you further information on their associated products. Please tick box if you do not wish to receive any such information. ☐

THE GOOD PUB GUIDE

2

The Good Pub Guide
FREEPOST TN1569
WADHURST
E. SUSSEX
TN5 7BR

room with skittles; children in eating areas, has been cl Mon lunchtime *(LYM, Michael Tack, Ben and Helen Ingram)*

WALGRAVE SP8072

Royal Oak [Zion Hill, off A43 Northampton—Kettering]: Old ironstone pub with well kept ales such as Adnams Bitter and Broadside, Fullers London Pride and Greene King Old Speckled Hen, good value straightforward food (not Sun evening) inc some interesting dishes, bar split into smaller areas, part no smoking, no smoking dining room too; children welcome, tables outside, play area *(Gerry and Rosemary Dobson)*

WEEDON SP6359

Crossroads [3 miles from M1 junction 16; A45 towards Daventry; High St, on A5 junction]: Plush and spacious Chef & Brewer, enjoyable sensibly priced food in well divided beamed bar and dining area, friendly staff, real ales such as Timothy Taylors Landlord, good log fires, no smoking areas; piped jazz or classical music; picnic-sets in attractive gardens down to river, comfortable Premier Lodge bedroom block *(LYM, George Atkinson)*

☆ *Narrow Boat* [Stowe Hill (A5 S)]: Very popular in summer for spacious terrace and big garden running down to canal, barbecues; plain décor with canal prints, low bar tables, high-raftered back restaurant extension with canal views, two no smoking rooms, decent food from ciabatta sandwiches to popular good value Sun lunch (all afternoon) and tempting puddings, friendly helpful service, well kept Charles Wells ales, some good value wines, open fire; fruit machine, skittles, quiet piped music; bedrooms in back motel extension, narrowboat hire next door *(LYM, George Atkinson, B Allen, Gerry and Rosemary Dobson)*

WELLINGBOROUGH SP8866

Priory [Bourton Way, by A45/A509 roundabout]: Large brightly modern chain eatery useful enough for all-day family food inc Mon-Thurs bargains, good choice of beers, side children's playroom *(Michael Tack, R C Vincent, Meg and Colin Hamilton)*

WOLLASTON SP9062

Wollaston Inn [off A509 S of Wellingborough; London Rd (B569)]: Former Nags Head, reopened as restauranty pub (still has proper entrance bar, with Marstons Pedigree), chef/landlord doing wide choice of good if not cheap up to date food in main dining room with two smaller offshoots, particularly good service under friendly NZ manageress, decent wines, good soft drinks choice *(Michael Jefferson)*

WOODFORD SP9677

Dukes Arms [High St]: Family-run 18th-c pub opp village green, four real ales, fairly wide choice of decent food inc some less common dishes, no smoking beamed dining lounge with fresh flowers, bar with hood skittles, pool and games machine; piped music; children welcome, garden with small play area, may be barbecue Sat evening, walks nearby *(CMW, JJW)*

WOOTTON SP7656

Yeomen of England [High St]: Big reasonably priced dining pub, horseshoe bar with three or four real ales, good soft drinks choice, comfortable settees and armchairs, flame-effect fire in no smoking area; piped music, games machines; children welcome if eating, disabled access and facilities, heated terrace with decking, picnic-sets on back lawn *(CMW, JJW)*

YARDLEY HASTINGS SP8656

☆ *Red Lion* [High St, just off A428 Bedford—Northampton]: Pretty thatched stone-built local with good value food (not Sun/Mon evenings) from sandwiches up, wider evening choice, well kept Charles Wells Eagle, Bombardier and perhaps a seasonal beer, good range of soft drinks, friendly staff (and cat), cosy lounge with beams and stripped stone, lots of pictures, plates and interesting brass and copper, step up to tiled-floor bar with games and small no smoking carpeted dining area; quiet piped music, no dogs; tables in nicely planted sloping garden, and in front *(George Atkinson, BB, Michael Dandy, CMW, JJW)*

'Children welcome' means the pub says it lets children inside without any special restriction. If it allows them in, but to restricted areas such as an eating area or family room, we specify this. Some pubs may impose an evening time limit. We do not mention limits after 9pm as we assume children are home by then.

Northumbria
(County Durham, Northumberland and Tyneside)

Occasionally local residents take us to task for grouping together three such diverse areas. However, we feel that visitors have so much to gain from this very diversity that it's well worth linking all this into a single chapter. And there's certainly a good deal of diversity among the individual pubs which make up Northumbria's current top tier. Four of these are newcomers to this edition of the *Guide*: the 18th-c Errington Arms near Corbridge, an appealing family-run dining pub; the Tankerville Arms at Eglingham, a rewarding all-rounder; the isolated Carts Bog Inn up above Langley on Tyne, with its warm welcome and good value food; and the Keelman in Newburn, a pub with a difference, brewing its own splendid beers for a building of some distinction. Other pubs on particularly good form these days are the Allenheads Inn (such a friendly place, with a fascinating clutter of bric-a-brac), the County in Aycliffe (very much enjoyed for its good food), the Manor House Inn at Carterway Heads (food a very strong point here too – they serve all day, and now even have a deli), the Victoria in Durham (a splendid period piece), the Queens Head at Great Whittington (imaginative food in a civilised atmosphere), the Cook & Barker Arms at Newton-on-the-Moor (good value food in a buoyantly cheerful atmosphere), the Rose & Crown at Romaldkirk (good imaginative food and newly refurbished bedrooms in this well run inn), and the Olde Ship at Seahouses (great for its nautical memorabilia). There is certainly no shortage of good pub food in Northumbria. For a special meal out, we'd narrow the choice to the County, the Manor House Inn, and the Rose & Crown. Just pipping the other two at the post, the County in Aycliffe takes the title of Northumbria Dining Pub of the Year for the second year running. Pubs to note particularly in the Lucky Dip section at the end of the chapter are the Angel in Corbridge, Cottage at Dunstan, Northumberland Arms at Felton, Black Bull in Haltwhistle, Apple at Lucker, Shiremoor Farm in New York, Bridge Hotel in Newcastle, Magnesia Bank in North Shields, Badger at Ponteland, Horseshoes at Rennington and Boathouse at Wylam. Drinks prices here are below the national average, with plenty of good interesting local breweries such as Mordue, Hadrian & Border, Wylam, Big Lamp, Durham, Hexhamshire, Darwin and Jarrow.

Please keep sending us reports. We rely on readers for news of new discoveries, and particularly for news of changes – however slight – at the fully described pubs. No stamp needed: *The Good Pub Guide*, FREEPOST TN1569, Wadhurst, E Sussex TN5 7BR or send your report through our web site: www.goodguides.co.uk

ALLENHEADS NY8545 Map 10

Allenheads Inn £

Just off B6295

It's not just the amazing collection of bric-a-brac that makes this pub special, but also the warmly welcoming atmosphere, and friendly landlord and locals. There's certainly lots to keep your eyes occupied while you're here, as the walls, ceilings and counter are covered with thousands of interesting collectables. In any of the loosely themed rooms you might find stuffed animals, mangles, old radios, typewriters, long-silenced musical instruments, an engine-room telegraph, brass and copper bygones, a plastic lobster, local photographs, aeroplane propellers, brooms, birdcages and even shoes – the list is endless, and it's all very neatly kept. The games room (with darts, pool, cribbage and dominoes) has perhaps the most effervescent collection, and the car club discs and number plates on the panelling echo the efforts by members of a classic car club to try to persuade their vehicles to wend their way up here. Tables outside are flanked by more hardware – the sort of machinery that wouldn't fit inside. Black Sheep and Greene King Abbot are well kept along with a couple of guests such as Archers Best and Timothy Taylors Landlord on handpump; decent coffee, real fire, TV and piped music. Enjoyable hearty food from the straightforward pubby menu includes toasted sandwiches (from £1.75), pizzas (from £4), vegetable curry (£4.75), scampi or chicken pie (£5.75), and puddings such as rice pudding or bread and butter pudding (from £2.25); children's meals (£3.25). The Forces room and the dining room are no smoking. The pub is on the Sustrans C2C cycle route; it's particularly peaceful here in winter. They do good breakfasts. *(Recommended by Mrs K H Clark, Michele D'Lemos, Comus and Sarah Elliott, Paul Davies, A G Taylor, The Popplewells, Tracey and Stephen Groves, Colin Wakeling, Steve and Liz Tilley)*

Free house ~ Licensee Stephen Wardle ~ Real ale ~ Bar food ~ No credit cards ~ (01434) 685200 ~ Children in eating area of bar ~ Open 12-4, 7-11; 12-11 Fri/Sat; 12-10.30 Sun; closed 25 Dec ~ Bedrooms: £23(£27.50B)/£48B

ANICK NY9665 Map 10

Rat

Village signposted NE of A69/A695 Hexham junction

Tables out on the terrace and in the charming garden (with dovecote, statues and even flowers sprouting unexpectedly from boots), of this unspoilt country pub have lovely views of the North Tyne valley. Inside, a coal fire blazes invitingly in the blackened kitchen range, and soft lighting gently illuminates lots of interesting knick-knacks: antique floral chamber-pots hanging from the beams, china and glassware, maps and posters, framed sets of cigarette cards, and quite a lot of Laurel and Hardy memorabilia, from figurines to a signed photograph. Furnishings keep up the cosily relaxed traditional mood, with brocaded chairs around old-fashioned pub tables; piped music, daily papers and magazines. Besides the two small eating areas, the no smoking conservatory has pleasant valley views. From a changing blackboard menu, generous helpings of tasty pubby food might include soup (£2.70), hot sandwiches (from £3.50), ploughman's (£3.95), lamb in mint gravy or sweet and sour pork (£6.30), beef and ale pie or burger (£6.50), chicken stir fry (£8.95), and tuna steak (£9.95), with enjoyable puddings such as apple and raspberry crumble pie (£3.25). Well kept on handpump, real ales include John Smiths, Greene King Ruddles County and Old Speckled Hen, along with guests from brewers such as Adnams and Caledonian. Service is friendly, and the landlord is happy to chat about the beers. Parking is limited. *(Recommended by Kevin Thorpe, C A Hall, A D Jenkins, Andy and Jill Kassube, John Foord, Peter Burton, Mike and Lynn Robinson, Paul Davies)*

Free house ~ Licensees Joan and Donald D'Adamo ~ Real ale ~ Bar food (not Sun evening) ~ Restaurant ~ (01434) 602814 ~ Children in restaurant and family room ~ Open 11-3, 6-11; 12-3 Sun; closed Sun evening

AYCLIFFE NZ2722 Map 10

County

The Green, Aycliffe village; just off A1(M) junction 59, by A167

Northumbria Dining Pub of the Year

Readers thoroughly enjoy coming to this stylish pub for the imaginative food. Cooked by the talented chef/landlord using mostly local produce, pubby bar food (served at lunchtime and in the early evening only) includes soup (£3.90), open sandwiches (from £4.50), smoked salmon and scrambled egg toasted muffin (£5.95, £7.95 large), lambs liver and bacon with mash or cajun-spiced chicken with salsa (£7.50), and battered scampi (£8.40). Otherwise you can also eat from the more elaborate bistro menu, which might include confit duck and pork terrine with red wine jelly (£6.95), smoked haddock risotto with spinach and poached egg (£7.25), vegetable moussaka (£10.45), fried red mullet with saffron mash and lemon syrup (£12.80), roast lamb chump with braised puy lentils and smoked bacon in red wine and thyme jus (£14.20), and mouthwatering puddings; children's menu (£4.95). As dishes are freshly cooked, there might be a bit of a wait, and booking is a good idea. Furnishings in the extended bar and no smoking bistro are light and modern, definitely geared to dining, and the minimalist décor gives a fresh feel. Good service from the friendly young staff and landlord, and a welcoming civilised atmosphere. As well as a good choice of wines by the glass, they've well kept Charles Wells Bombardier and Greene King IPA on handpump, and a couple of guests such as Greene King Abbot and Caledonian Deuchars IPA; there may be piped music. The green opposite is pretty. *(Recommended by Jenny and Dave Hughes, Liz and Brian Barnard, Brian and Anna Marsden, M Borthwick, Gerry and Rosemary Dobson, Philip and June Caunt, Peter and Jean Hoare, Christine and Phil Young)*

Free house ~ Licensee Andrew Brown ~ Real ale ~ Bar food (12-2, 6-7; not Sat or Sun evening) ~ Restaurant ~ (01325) 312273 ~ Children in eating area of bar and restaurant ~ Open 12-3, 5.30(6.30 Sat)-11, 12-4 Sun; closed Sun evening, 25-26 Dec, 1 Jan

BLANCHLAND NY9750 Map 10

Lord Crewe Arms

B6306 S of Hexham

Dating back to the 13th c, when the Premonstratensians built this remote village robustly enough to resist most border raiding parties, this fine inn is still separated from the rest of the world by several miles of moors, rabbits and sheep. Originally part of the monastery guest-house, and then home to several distinguished families after the dissolution in 1536, its tremendous age is evident everywhere. The narrow bar is housed in an unusual stone barrel-vaulted crypt, its curving walls being up to eight feet thick in some places. Plush stools are lined along the bar counter and next to a narrow drinks shelf down the opposite wall. Upstairs, the Derwent Room has low beams, old settles, and sepia photographs on its walls, and the Hilyard Room has a massive 13th-c fireplace once used as a hiding place by the Jacobite Tom Forster (part of the family who had owned the building before it was sold in 1704 to the formidable Lord Crewe, Bishop of Durham). Bar food includes soup (£2.50), filled rolls (from £3.45), ploughman's (from £5), wild mushrooms in creamy sauce (£6.50), cumberland sausage with black pudding and mash (£6.75), smoked salmon, prawn and tuna salad (£6.85), and puddings (£3.50); children's meals (£2.50). Well kept Wylam Gold Tankard on handpump. The lovely walled garden was formerly the cloisters. *(Recommended by Rona Murdoch, Alan Cole, Kirstie Bruce, Andy and Jill Kassube, Anthony Longden, David and Betty Gittins, John Hale, Bill and Jessica Ritson, Paul Davies, Tracey and Stephen Groves, Michael Butler)*

Free house ~ Licensees A Todd, Peter Gingell and Ian Press, Lindsey Sands ~ Real ale ~ Bar food ~ Restaurant ~ (01434) 675251 ~ Children welcome ~ Dogs allowed in bar and bedrooms ~ Open 11-11.30; 12-10.30 Sun ~ Bedrooms: £80B/£120B

If we know a pub has an outdoor play area for children, we mention it.

CARTERWAY HEADS NZ0552 Map 10

Manor House Inn

A68 just N of B6278, near Derwent Reservoir

Superbly run by welcoming licensees, this bustling slate-roofed stone house continues to impress readers with its very good food, and they've now opened a deli, where you can buy local produce, as well as chutneys, puddings and ice-cream made in the kitchens. The delicious food is served in generous helpings, and might include soup (£2.75, £3.60 large), sandwiches (from £2.95), creamy garlic mushrooms baked with a herb crust (£4.40), locally smoked kippers or crayfish and mushroom crêpes (£4.75, £9.25 large), sausage, black pudding and mushrooms with bubble and squeak (£6.50), corn-fed chicken with asparagus, spinach and tarragon cream (£11.50), lamb cutlets with port and cranberry jus and garlic and rosemary mash (£13), and mouthwatering puddings such as sticky toffee pudding (from £3.60), with a local cheese platter (£4.95); smiling service by the helpful young staff. There are good views from the partly no smoking restaurant. The locals' bar has an original boarded ceiling, pine tables, chairs and stools, old oak pews and a mahogany counter. The comfortable lounge bar has a woodburning stove, and picture windows give fine views over moorland pastures; darts, dominoes, TV and piped music (only in the bar). They've around 70 malt whiskies to choose from, farm cider, and decent wines (with about eight by the glass), along with well kept Courage Directors, Theakstons Best, Charles Wells Bombardier and a guest from a local brewer such as Mordue on handpump. There are rustic tables out on a small side terrace and lawn; great views. Good breakfasts. *(Recommended by Andy and Jill Kassube, Liz and Brian Barnard, Brian and Anna Marsden, Andrew and Samantha Grainger, Dr and Mrs P Truelove, J F M and M West, Pat and Derek Roughton, John Oddey, John Foord, Michael E Bridgstock, Tracey and Stephen Groves, Alistair and Kay Butler, Prof and Mrs Tony Palmer, Mike and Linda Hudson, J C Poley, Michael Doswell)*

Free house ~ Licensees Moira and Chris Brown ~ Real ale ~ Bar food (12-9.30(9 Sun)) ~ Restaurant ~ (01207) 255268 ~ Children in eating area of bar and restaurant ~ Dogs allowed in bar ~ Open 11-11; 12-10.30 Sun; closed 25 Dec evening ~ Bedrooms: £38B/£60B

CORBRIDGE NY9868 Map 10

Errington Arms

About 3 miles N of town; B6318, just off A68 roundabout

Reopened a couple of years ago under a new father-and-son team, this 18th-c stone-built inn has been attractively reworked as a good dining pub. It has a relaxed atmosphere, and a nice mix of mainly pine candlelit tables under its oak beams, on stripped boards here, quarry tiles there, with a log fire, some plank panelling, some ochre paintwork, and some stripped stonework; there is a modicum of bric-a-brac, on window sills and so forth. The food, which comes in big helpings, includes lunchtime snacks such as good sandwiches (from £3.50), ploughman's or cumberland sausage and onion mash (£4.95), and spaghetti bolognese (£5.95), with a wide range of other enjoyable dishes such as soup (£2.95), jambalaya (£7.50), wild boar and pheasant pie (£7.95), cod baked with ouzo, tomato and olives (£12.50), roasted duck with leeks (£12.95), various steaks (from £12.95), and monkfish and prawns or bass (£13.95). This is all cooked to order – worth waiting for. The puddings such as blackberry crumble and banoffi pie (£3.95) are ready to serve; on Sundays they concentrate mainly on roasts. Service is friendly; they have two or three real ales on handpump such as Black Sheep and Jennings Cumberland, and make good coffee; there may be quiet piped music. Out on the front terrace are some sturdy metal and teak tables under canvas parasols. *(Recommended by Michael Doswell, Mr and Mrs Broadhurst, Dr and Mrs S Donald)*

Punch ~ Lease Nicholas Shotton ~ Real ale ~ Bar food (12-2.30, 6-9.30; not Sun evening, Mon; 25-26 Dec) ~ Restaurant ~ (01434) 672250 ~ Children welcome ~ Open 11-3, 6-11; 12-3 Sun; closed Sun evening, Mon; 25-26 Dec

COTHERSTONE NZ0119 Map 10

Fox & Hounds

B6277 – incidentally a good quiet route to Scotland, through interesting scenery

In a pretty spot overlooking the village green, this 200-year-old country inn is a good place to tuck into a hearty meal, after returning from one of the pleasant walks nearby. With a good winter log fire, the simple but cheery beamed bar has comfortable furnishings such as thickly cushioned wall seats, and local photographs and country pictures on the walls in its various alcoves and recesses. Don't be surprised by the unusual lavatory attendants – an african grey parrot called Reva and his new companion, a red fronted conure called Charlie. Made with mostly local ingredients, lunchtime dishes could include tasty wensleydale and hazelnut pâté (£3.90, £5.20 large), ploughman's (£5.40), sausages with mustard mash and onion gravy (£5.75), and chicken, ham and mushroom pie or battered whitby cod (£6.30), while the evening menu might include grilled black pudding and crispy bacon with apple and garlic purée (£4.20), roast mediterrannean vegetables with sun-dried tomato couscous (£7.50), grilled bass with garlic and herb butter (£9.60), and rack of lamb with cranberry, orange and rosemary sauce (£12.15), with puddings such as sticky toffee pudding or vanilla meringue with chocolate and hazelnut sauce (£3.75), and local cheeses (£4.30); efficient service from the friendly staff. Both of the dining rooms are no smoking. They've 11 wines by the glass, 15 malt whiskies, and Black Sheep Best, Hambleton Bitter and possibly a guest are well kept on handpump. *(Recommended by Lesley and Peter Barrett, Tim and Carolyn Lowes, R M Corlett, Michael Doswell, Derek and Sylvia Stephenson)*

Free house ~ Licensees Nichola and Ian Swinburn ~ Real ale ~ Bar food ~ Restaurant ~ (01833) 650241 ~ Children in restaurant and family room ~ Open 12-3, 6.45-12; 12-3, 7-11.30 Sun ~ Bedrooms: £42.50B/£65B

DIPTONMILL NY9261 Map 10

Dipton Mill Inn £

Just S of Hexham; off B6306 at Slaley, Blanchland and Dye House, Whitley Chapel signposts (and HGV route sign); not to be confused with the Dipton in Durham

The neatly kept, snug bar of this appealing little two-roomed pub has dark ply panelling, red furnishings, a dark red carpet and two welcoming open fires. The cheery landlord is a brewer in the family-owned Hexhamshire Brewery, and Hexhamshire Shire Bitter, Devils Water, Devils Elbow, Old Humbug and Whapweasel are all well kept on handpump, along with a guest such as Hambleton Nightmare. You can also get 15 wines by the glass (in two different sizes), two dozen malt whiskies, and Weston's Old Rosie cider. The back games room has darts, bar billiards, shove-ha'penny and dominoes. Great for cheese-lovers, they offer a dozen northumbrian cheeses which you can choose from to make up your ploughman's (from £4.50) or have after your meal. Other straightforward bar food might include sandwiches (from £1.70), salads (from £5.25), ratatouille with couscous or tomato, bean and vegetable casserole (£5), haddock baked with tomatoes and basil or turkey, bacon and mushroom pie (£5.90), and chicken breast in sherry sauce (£6.75), with puddings such as fruit crumble (from £1.65). In fine weather it's pleasant to sit out on the sunken crazy-paved terrace by the restored mill stream, or in the attractively planted garden with its aviary. The pub is tucked away in a peaceful wooded valley hamlet and surrounded by steep hills, with plenty of easy-walking footpaths nearby. *(Recommended by Karen and Graham Oddey, Andy and Jill Kassube, Jenny and Brian Seller, Michael Doswell, Paul Davies, Stephen Woad, Tracey and Stephen Groves, Mike and Lynn Robinson, Mart Lawton)*

Own brew ~ Licensee Geoff Brooker ~ Real ale ~ Bar food (12-2, 6.30(7.30 Sun)-8.30) ~ No credit cards ~ (01434) 606577 ~ Children welcome ~ Open 12-2.30, 6-11; 12-3, 7-10.30 Sun; closed 25 Dec

Pubs with attractive or unusually big gardens are listed at the back of the book.

DURHAM NZ2742 Map 10

Victoria

Hallgarth Street (A177, near Dunelm House)

Run with considerable individuality, this cosily down-to-earth neatly kept local has been in the same family for almost 30 years. Built in the closing years of Queen Victoria's reign (and little altered since), the pub celebrates her life with lots of period prints and engravings, and staffordshire figurines of her and the Prince Consort. A very traditional layout means three work-a-day rooms lead off a central bar, with mahogany, etched and cut glass and mirrors, colourful William Morris wallpaper over a high panelled dado, some maroon plush seats in little booths, some worn leatherette wall seats, long narrow drinkers' tables, handsome iron and tile fireplaces for the coal fires, a piano, and some photographs and articles showing a very proper pride in the pub. Five well kept real ales mighty typically include local Darwins Ghost, Durham Magus, Jarrow Swinging Gibbet, McEwans 80/- and Mordue Five Bridge Bitter on handpump; also good cheap house wines, around 50 malts and a remarkable collection of 36 irish whiskeys. They've dominoes, fruit machine, a veteran space invaders game, a Trivial Pursuit machine and a TV; at lunchtime they do toasties (from £1). The good value bedrooms are simple but pleasant; a hearty breakfast (good vegetarian one too) is served in the upstairs dining room. *(Recommended by Andy and Jill Kassube, the Didler, Barry Collett, Pete Baker, Steve Barrett, Patrick Hancock)*

Free house ~ Licensee Michael Webster ~ Real ale ~ (0191) 386 5269 ~ Children welcome ~ Dogs welcome ~ Open 11.40-3, 6-11; 12-2, 7-10.30 Sun ~ Bedrooms: £44B/£56B

EGLINGHAM NU1019 Map 10

Tankerville Arms

B6346 Alnwick—Wooler

With coal fires at each end, this pleasant long stone pub is especially warm and cosy in winter. There are black joists, some walls stripped to bare stone and hung with brassware, and plush banquettes and captain's chairs around cast-iron-framed tables on the turkey carpet. The snug lounge is no smoking; dominoes, darts and piped music. Well presented, enjoyable bar food might include a choice of soups (£3.50), sandwiches (£3.95), smoked chicken and brie tart (£6.95), scampi and chips or provençale bean cassoulet (£8.50), duck, orange and apricot sausage with thyme sauce (£9), cannon of venison on a red onion tart with rich port sauce (£12.50), and tasty puddings such as sticky toffee pudding (£3.95). Well kept on handpump, under light blanket pressure, they serve three or four real ales such as Black Sheep, Jennings Cumberland and Hadrian & Border Farne Islands and Secret Kingdom; decent selection of wines and malt whiskies. It's in an attractive village, and picnic-sets in the pleasant garden have fine views. *(Recommended by Tim and Sue Halstead, Dr and Mrs R G J Telfer, Lynne and Philip Naylor, Robert M Warner, GSB)*

Free house ~ Licensee J E Blackmore ~ Real ale ~ Bar food (maybe not Mon in winter) ~ Restaurant ~ (01665) 578444 ~ Children in eating area of bar and restaurant ~ Open 12-2, 6.30(7 winter)-11; 12-3, 6.30(7 winter)-11(10.30 Sun) Sat

GREAT WHITTINGTON NZ0171 Map 10

Queens Head

Village signposted off A68 and B6018 just N of Corbridge

Cooked using local meat and fish fresh from the quay, the imaginative menu is the main attraction at this attractive old pub. Modern furnishings alongside some handsome carved oak settles and log fires give its two fairly simple beamed rooms a stylishly comfortable feel; the atmosphere is civilised, and the staff are attentive and well trained. The room nearest the bar counter has a mural over its fireplace. Besides lunchtime sandwiches, imaginative bistro food (which you can eat in the bar) might include soup (£4.50), fried king scallops with bacon and green bean salad (£7.95), roast vegetable kebabs with spiced noodles and sweet and sour sauce (£9.95), salmon with ratatouille and tomato and herb coulis (£10.95), pork tenderloin with black pudding fritters and cider and sage jus (£11.95), and delicious herb-crusted rack of lamb with rosemary and redcurrant jus (£14.95), with well presented puddings such as baked vanilla cheesecake or iced nougatine (£4.50). They do a good value two-course lunch (£10). The restaurant is no smoking. Hambleton Bitter and Queens Head (brewed for them by Hambleton) are very well kept on handpump, and they've 30 malt whiskies, and an extensive wine list; perhaps unobtrusive piped music. The small front lawn has half a dozen picnic-sets. The pub is in a smart stone-built village, surrounded by partly wooded countryside. *(Recommended by Barry Robson, R Macfarlane, KN-R, Stephen Woad, Michael Doswell, John Foord)*

Free house ~ Licensee Ian Scott ~ Real ale ~ Bar food (not Mon, or Sun evening) ~ Restaurant ~ (01434) 672267 ~ Children in eating area of bar till 7pm ~ Open 12-3, 6-11; 12-3 Sun; closed Mon except bank hols, Sun evening

GRETA BRIDGE NZ0813 Map 10

Morritt Arms

Hotel signposted off A66 W of Scotch Corner

The charming pubby bar of this civilised hotel is named after Charles Dickens, who stayed here in 1838 on his way to start his research for *Nicholas Nickleby*, and a jolly larger-than-life Dickensian mural runs round its walls. It was painted in 1946 by J V Gilroy – more famous for his old Guinness advertisements, six of which are displayed on the walls here too. Big windsor armchairs and sturdy plush-seated oak settles cluster around traditional cast-iron-framed tables, and big windows look out on the extensive lawn; flowers brighten up the rooms, and there are nice open fires. The attractively laid out garden has some seats, with teak tables in a pretty side area looking along to the graceful old bridge by the stately gates to Rokeby Park, and swings, a slide and a wendy house at the far end. Black Sheep, Timothy Taylors Landlord and Jennings Cumberland are well kept on handpump, and they've quite a few malt whiskies, and an extensive wine list with about two dozen by the glass; good service from the pleasant and professional staff. There's a proper old shove-ha'penny board, with raisable brass rails to check the lie of the coins, cribbage and dominoes, and a TV. Freshly prepared and beautifully presented, bar food includes soup (£3.50), sandwiches (from £4.50), chicken liver parfait with pear and saffron chutney (£5), breaded king prawns with sweet chilli jam (£6, £10 large), lobster, brie and asparagus spring rolls with red pepper jam (£7, £10 large), home-made steak and kidney pie (£8.50), and fish mixed grill with pesto mash (£13.50), with puddings such as champagne-poached peaches with vanilla panna cotta (£5); they bake their own bread (which you can buy to take away). With a more elaborate menu, the no smoking bistro has wood floors and wrought iron, and is densely hung with paintings and prints by local artists (which you can buy). The building looks a little like a grand country house, and is an excellent place to stay. *(Recommended by Darly Graton, Graeme Gulibert, Barry Collett, Susan and John Douglas, Alistair and Kay Butler, Janet and Peter Race, Michael Doswell, Derek and Sylvia Stephenson)*

Free house ~ Licensees Peter Phillips and Barbara Johnson ~ Real ale ~ Bar food (12-9) ~ Restaurant ~ (01833) 627232 ~ Children welcome ~ Dogs allowed in bar and bedrooms ~ Open 11-11; 12-10.30 Sun ~ Bedrooms: £59.50B/£87.50B

HALTWHISTLE NY7166 Map 10

Milecastle Inn

Military Road; B6318 NE – OS Sheet 86 map reference 715660

In a famously bleak and scenic part of the county, this welcoming 17th-c pub is usually filled with a good mix of families, walkers and visitors. The snug little rooms of the beamed bar are decorated with brasses, horsey and local landscape prints and attractive dried flowers, and have two winter log fires; at lunchtime the small comfortable restaurant is used as an overflow. It pays to get here early if you want to eat the enjoyable bar food. Served in generous helpings, the menu includes lunchtime sandwiches (£3.50), home-made soup (£2.50), wild boar pie or chicken tikka (£7.95), and gammon steak (£8.75), with specials such as venison casserole, fresh trout or pheasant in orange and brandy (all £7.95), with puddings such as apple and blackberry crumble (£3.95); good fresh salads. The friendly hard-working staff serve two well kept real ales on handpump such as Big Lamb and Prince Bishop, and they have a fair collection of malt whiskies, and a good wine list; no games or music. The tables and benches out in a pleasantly sheltered walled garden with a dovecote are popular in summer; there's a large car park. On the old Roman road from Newcastle, the pub is very handy for Hadrian's Wall. *(Recommended by Tom McLean, Peter Scillitoe, A Sadler, Brenda Peery, R F Ballinger, Michael Doswell, Alistair and Kay Butler)*

Free house ~ Licensee Clare Hind ~ Real ale ~ Bar food (12-3, 6-9; 12-9 summer) ~ Restaurant ~ (01434) 321372/320682 ~ Children in eating area of bar ~ Open 12-11 (10.30 Sun); 12-3, 6-11(10.30 Sun) in winter

HEDLEY ON THE HILL NZ0859 Map 10

Feathers 🍴

Village signposted from New Ridley, which is signposted from B6309 N of Consett; OS Sheet 88 map reference 078592

Although the emphasis at this attractive old stone pub is on the reasonably priced home-made food, there's still an appealing pubby atmosphere in the three well kept turkey-carpeted traditional bars, with beams, open fires, stripped stonework, solid brown leatherette settles and old black and white photographs of local places and farm and country workers. Changing every week, the interesting menu might typically include good vegetarian dishes such as spicy bean cakes with salsa or goats cheese and red pepper pancake (£7.50), with other choices such as soup (£3.50), prawns with thai dressing (£4.50), cumberland sausage with cider and onion gravy (£7.75), and organic salmon fillet with lemon and dill butter or braised beef in red wine and brandy with shallots and mushrooms (£9.95), while puddings could be lemon and lime tart or rich chocolate, rum, raisin and nut slice (£4.50); it's a good idea to book. They've well kept John Smiths, and a couple of guest beers from brewers such as Fullers, Mordue and Yates on handpump; also decent wines (they've recently increased the choice), and around 30 malt whiskies. Shove-ha'penny, table skittles, pool, cribbage and dominoes. They hold a mini beer festival at Easter with over two dozen real ales and a barrel race on Easter Monday. Picnic-sets in front are a nice place to sit and watch the world drift by. They accept debit cards only. *(Recommended by Andrew and Samantha Grainger, David Lowes Watson, Jenny and Brian Seller, Mr and Mrs W R Bolton, Paul Davies)*

Free house ~ Licensee Marina Atkinson ~ Real ale ~ Bar food (not wkdy lunchtimes or Mon exc bank hols) ~ No credit cards ~ (01661) 843607 ~ Children in eating area of bar and side room ~ Open 6-11; 12-3, 6-11 Sat; 12-3, 7-10.30 Sun; closed wkdy lunchtimes exc bank hols

LANGLEY ON TYNE NY8160 Map 10

Carts Bog Inn

A686 S, junction B6305

The welcoming neatly kept main black-beamed bar at this isolated moorside pub has a blazing log fire in the central stone fireplace, local photographs and horsebrasses, and windsor chairs and comfortably cushioned wall settles around the tables. It rambles about, with flagstones here, carpet there, mainly white walls with some stripped stone. A side lounge (once a cow byre) with more wall banquettes has pool, darts, dominoes and piped music; quoits pitch. Enjoyable reasonably priced bar food, in generous helpings, includes sandwiches (from £2.50), soup (£2.95), baked avodaco with stilton (£6.50), green thai lamb, peppercorn pork, steak and ale pie or beer-battered cod (£7.50), and sirloin steak (£8.95), with tasty puddings such as chocolate fudge cake and apple crumble (£2.75). Friendly staff serve well kept Jennings Cumberland, Yates and a guest such as Timothy Taylors Landlord on handpump, and they've around 30 malt whiskies. There are views over the silvery dry stone walls of high hilly sheep pastures from tables in the garden. *(Recommended by Andy and Jill Kassube, GSB, John Oddey, R T and J C Moggridge, A H C Rainier, Di and Mike Gillam, Adam and Joan Bunting, Mart Lawton)*

Free house ~ Licensee Richard Bainbridge ~ Real ale ~ Bar food ~ Restaurant ~ (01434) 684338 ~ Children in restaurant and pool room ~ Dogs allowed in bar ~ Open 12-2.30, 5-11; 12-11(10.30 Sun) Sat

NEWBURN NZ1665 Map 10

Keelman

Grange Road: follow Riverside Country Park brown signs off A6085 (the riverside road off A1 on Newcastle's W fringes)

This unusual and rather distinguished-looking granite pub, very popular with families in summer, is the tap for the good Big Lamp Brewery, on the same site. It was built originally in 1854 as a pumping station, and converted in 1996. As the photographs around the bar show, the 'keelmen' had nothing to do with shipbuilding, but were the coal-heavers who took coal down the river. The high-ceilinged bar's lofty arched windows make it light and airy, and it's not too crowded with tables (access for wheelchairs is easy). There are more tables in an upper gallery, and in the newly opened all-glass conservatory dining area – nice at sunset. The bar counter's impressive array of handpumps dispenses the full Big Lamp beer range, in top condition and at attractive prices: Bitter, MM, Stout, Prince Bishop, Premium, Embers, Blackout (beware, it's very strong) and one or two seasonal beers. Service, by plenty of neatly dressed and attentive staff, is first-class; the hands-on landlord is quick to help out when needed, and the whole place is kept spick and span. Decent quickly served food includes sandwiches (from £3.20), baked potatoes (from £3.60), beef and ale pie or large fish and chips (£5.75), trout (£5.95), and 10oz sirloin steak or a big mixed grill (£8.95), with puddings such as apple pie and custard (£3.40); they do an early evening special on weekdays from 5 till 7 (£4.50 for a main course). Piped music, fruit machine. There are plenty of picnic-sets, tables and benches out on the terraces, among flower tubs and beds of shrubs; this is a great base for walks along the Tyne. We have not yet heard from readers staying in the six up-to-date bedrooms, in an adjoining block. *(Recommended by John Foord, Karen and Graham Oddey, John Oddey, Andy and Jill Kassube, Roger and Kathleen Lucas)*

Own brew~ Licensee George Story ~ Real ale ~ Bar food (12-9; not 25 Dec) ~ Restaurant ~ (0191) 267 0772 ~ Children welcome ~ Open 11-11; 12-10.30 Sun; closed 25 Dec ~ Bedrooms: £36B/£47.50B

NEWCASTLE UPON TYNE NZ2563 Map 10

Crown Posada

The Side; off Dean Street, between and below the two high central bridges (A6125 and A6127)

Quite apart from being a friendly place to come for a drink, this unspoilt pub (the second oldest in the city) is architecturally fascinating, and well worth visiting if you're in Newcastle. A golden crown and magnificent pre-raphaelite stained-glass windows add grandeur to an already imposing carved stone façade, while inside highlights include the elaborate coffered ceiling, stained-glass in the counter screens, a line of gilt mirrors each with a tulip lamp on a curly brass mount matching the great ceiling candelabra, and Victorian flowered wallpaper above the brown dado. Fat low level heating pipes make a popular footrest when the east wind brings the rain off the North Sea. It's a very long and narrow room, making quite a bottleneck by the serving counter; beyond that, a long soft green built-in leather wall seat is flanked by narrow tables. There's a fruit machine, and an old record player in a wooden cabinet provides mellow background music when the place is quiet; dominoes. From half a dozen handpumps Bass and Jennings and Timothy Taylors

Landlord are kept in top condition alongside continually changing guests such as Big Lamp Prince Bishop, Mordue Radgie Gadgie and Pictish Summer Solstice. The atmosphere is easy-going and chatty, and a good time to visit is during the week when regulars sit reading the papers in the front snug; at the weekend it's usually packed, but even then you'll get a warm welcome from the barmen. They don't do food, but at lunchtime you can get a sandwich with a packet of crisps for £1. It's only a few minutes stroll to the castle. *(Recommended by Andy and Jill Kassube, the Didler, Karen and Graham Oddey, Pete Baker, Mike and Lynn Robinson)*

Free house ~ Licensee Derek Raisbeck ~ Real ale ~ No credit cards ~ (0191) 232 1269 ~ Open 11(12 Sat)-11; 7-10.30 Sun; closed Sun lunchtime

Head of Steam @ The Cluny

Lime Street (which runs between A193 and A186 E of centre)

This unusual pub shares an impressively refurbished early 19th-c former bonded whisky warehouse with several dozen artists and craftsmen who have studios here. Its back area functions as an interesting gallery for changing exhibitions of their paintings, sculptures and pottery, and for work by visiting artists. The friendly L-shaped bar is trendy and gently bohemian-feeling despite its minimalist décor, with slightly scuffed bare boards, some chrome seating and overhead spotlights. Around seven well kept real ales include a good choice of local beers (they pride themselves in having a relationship with every North East independent brewer), and on handpump you might find well kept Caledonian Deuchars IPA, Hadrian & Border Farne Island, Hexhamshire Shire Bitter, Mordue Workie Ticket, Robinsons Unicorn, Timothy Taylor Landlord and Wylam Bitter; also rotating continental beers on tap, lots of bottled world beers, a good range of soft drinks, and a fine row of rums. Besides popular soup (£2.50), simple bar food, served by cheerful staff, might include sandwiches or toasties (from £2.50), chicken tikka kebab, chilli or burger and chips (£4), deep-fried brie with pitta bread (£5), and puddings such as fudge cake (£2); it's all home-made so there may be a wait. A raised area looking down on the river (with much redevelopment work afoot) has comfortable seating including settees, with daily papers and local arts magazines. A separate room has a stage for live bands and comedy nights; disabled access and facilities, fruit machine and well reproduced piped music. To get here – opposite the Ship on Lime Street look out for a cobbled bank leading down to the Ouseburn, by the Byker city farm, and stretching down here, the pub (known to everyone locally as the Cluny) is below the clutch of bridges. *(Recommended by Kevin Thorpe, Eric Larkham, Mike and Lynn Robinson, Russell Lewin)*

Head of Steam ~ Manager Dave Campbell ~ Real ale ~ Bar food (12-9, snacks till close) ~ (0191) 230 4475 ~ Children welcome ~ Frequent live bands ~ Open 12-11(1 Sat); closed 25 Dec

NEWFIELD NZ2033 Map 10

Fox & Hounds ♀

Turn off A688 at 'Willington, Newfield' signpost, or off A690 in Willington, into aptly named Long Lane; Newfield signposted off this, then turn left at Queens Head into Stonebank Terrace

The good food is what draws people here, but you'll be welcomed even if you just want a drink. It still keeps a pub layout with a serving bar in the single main room, and a cosy carpeted ante-room with a three-piece suite in brown velour by an old cream-coloured kitchen stove in a high stone fireplace (good fires in winter). The comfortable and gently lit no smoking main area has a polished wood-strip floor, with candles and flowers on the neatly laid tables all around its sides, big brass platters on its dark pink timbered walls, and mugs, tankards and whisky-water jugs hanging from beams skeined with fairy-lights. Big windows look down over steeply rolling countryside. The lighter lunch menu is good value, and might include soup (£3.25), chilli con carne, mushroom stroganoff or turkey spring roll with chilli sauce (£5.50), with more elaborate evening dishes such as smoked salmon with black pepper, lemon and olive oil (£4.95), mushroom, pistachio and toasted almond wellington (£8.95), salmon with sesame seeds and lemon butter or slow-roasted lamb shank with red wine, redcurrant and thyme jus (£10.50), home-marinated chicken breast with caramelised red onion and orange sauce (£12.95), and puddings such as raspberry and blueberry white chocolate cheesecake (£3.75); Sunday lunch (£5.95). Saturday night gets fully booked well ahead. Although they may not always have one, they do aim to keep a real ale such as Tetleys on handpump, and the house wines are good; friendly service. More reports please. *(Recommended by BOB)*

Free house ~ Licensee William Thompson ~ Real ale ~ Bar food (not Mon, or Sun evening) ~ Restaurant ~ (01388) 662787 ~ Children over 12 in restaurant wkdys till early evening ~ Open 12-3, 7-11; 12-3 Sun; closed Sun evening, Mon

NEWTON-BY-THE-SEA NU2424 Map 10

Ship

Village signposted off B1339 N of Alnwick; Low Newton – paid parking 200 metres up road on right, just before village (none in village)

Tucked into the top corner of a National Trust courtyard of low white-painted stone cottages, this charmingly simple refuge looks down over the sloping grassy square to the broad beach, and beyond to off-shore rocks packed with seabirds and sometimes seals. The plainly furnished bare-boards bar on the right has nautical charts on its dark pink walls, beams and hop bines. Another simple room on the left has some bright modern pictures on stripped stone walls, and a woodburning stove in its stone fireplace. It's very quiet here in winter (when opening times are complicated), when they have just one or two real ales including Black Sheep. In contrast, queues can quickly build up on hot summer days, when the beer range extends to two or three guests from local brewers such as Border, Mordue and Wylam; also decent wines, an espresso machine (colourful coffee cups, good hot chocolate), and good soft drinks. Made with fresh local ingredients, enjoyable lunchtime snacks could include toasties (from £2), local crab sandwiches (£3.25), warm ciabattas with enterprising fillings (around £3.75), kippers (£3.95), fishcakes and salad (£4.35), and ploughman's with local cheddar cheese (from £4.95), while in the evening (when you must book), dishes might be crab salad (£8.50), venison rump steak with red wine and peppercorn sauce (£10.50), scallops (£14.50), or local lobster (around £22.50, from June to October). Out in the corner of the square are some tables among pots of flowers, with picnic-sets over on the grass. There's no nearby parking. *(Recommended by Pat and Tony Martin, Keith and Janet Morris, Comus and Sarah Elliott, A C English, Tracey and Stephen Groves, John Knighton, Michael Doswell)*

Free house ~ Licensee Christine Forsyth ~ Real ale ~ Bar food (please ring) ~ No credit cards ~ (01665) 576262 ~ Children welcome ~ Dogs welcome ~ Open all day in summer hols, otherwise please ring

NEWTON-ON-THE-MOOR NU1605 Map 10

Cook & Barker Arms

Village signposted from A1 Alnwick-Felton

With a buoyant bustling atmosphere, good food and a great choice of wines, this stone inn is a popular choice for a meal. Well cooked changing bar food could include sandwiches (from £2.75), broccoli and stilton soup (£2.95), rocket, pear and goats cheese salad (£3.95), moules marinière (£4.95), smoked salmon (£5), wild mushroom risotto (£6.50), steak and onion pie (£6.95), grilled sardines with tomato ragoût (£7.50), duck confit (£7.95), braised lamb shank with mustard mash (£8.95), and puddings such as summer pudding (£3.95). Though most people are here for the generously served food, the relaxed and unfussy long beamed bar is cheerfully pubby, with stripped stone and partly panelled walls, brocade-seated settles around oak-topped tables, brasses, a highly polished oak servery, and a coal fire at one end with a coal-effect gas fire at the other. A no smoking eating area has tables, chairs, an old settle, scrubbed pine furniture, and french windows leading on to the terrace; the top bar area is also no smoking; piped music. Three or four well kept rotating ales on handpump might include Black Sheep, Fullers London Pride, Timothy Taylors Landlord and a local guest such as Mordue Workie Ticket; their extensive wine list includes a dozen by the glass, and they've also local bottled beer, and quite a few malt whiskies. *(Recommended by Mike and Wendy Proctor, Jill and Keith Wright, Malcolm Taylor, Peter and Jean Hoare, R M Corlett, Dr and Mrs R G J Telfer, David J M Taylor, Tony and Wendy Hobden, Dave and Sue Mitchell, Jenny and Dave Hughes, C A Hall, Michael Doswell, Alison Hayes, Pete Hanlon, Clare and Peter Pearse, Mrs J Ekins-Daukes, Prof and Mrs Tony Palmer, Keith and Margaret Kettell, Richard Cole, Mike Green, Michael and Margaret Slater, John and Sylvia Harrop)*

Free house ~ Licensee Phil Farmer ~ Real ale ~ Bar food (12-2, 6-9) ~ Restaurant ~ (01665) 575234 ~ Children welcome ~ Open 12-3.30, 6-11(10.30 Sun); closed 25 Dec evening ~ Bedrooms: £45B/£65B

RENNINGTON NU2119 Map 10

Masons Arms

Stamford Cott; B1340 NE of Alnwick

Well placed for exploring the nearby coast, the bedrooms at this immaculately well cared for pub are in an adjacent stable block and annexe; they've a kennel for dogs. The thoughtfully modernised and comfortable beamed lounge bar has wheelback and mate's chairs around solid wood tables on a patterned carpet, plush bar stools, and plenty of brass, pictures (some may be for sale) and photographs. The dining rooms (one is no smoking) have pine panelling and wrought-iron wall lights. Well kept on handpump, they've one or two changing real ales such as Hadrian & Border Gladiator and Secret Kingdom; shove-ha'penny, cribbage, dominoes, and piped music (which can be obtrusive). Generously served bar food, from a straightforward menu, includes lunchtime sandwiches (from £2.75), soup (£2.95), craster kipper pâté (£4.75), deep-fried haddock (£6.95), vegetable bake (£7.35), game casserole (£7.95), and steak (from £12.95), with specials such as lamb, lemon and peppercorn casserole (£7.50), and salmon and asparagus mornay (£8.25), with puddings such as lemon meringue pie (£3.15). There are sturdy rustic tables on the little front lavender surrounded terrace, and picnic-sets at the back. Only children over five are allowed to stay overnight. *(Recommended by W K Wood, H D Whitham, Mr and Mrs W D Borthwick, Mike and Wendy Proctor, Adam and Joan Bunting, Derek Stafford, Prof and Mrs Tony Palmer, Michael Doswell, Richard Cole, Christine and Malcolm Ingram)*

Free house ~ Licensees Paul and Carol Forster ~ Real ale ~ Bar food (12-2(2.30 Sun), 6.30-9) ~ Restaurant ~ (01665) 577275 ~ Children in two no smoking dining rooms; must be over 5 in bedrooms ~ Open 12-2, 6.30-11; 12-2.30, 6.30-10.30 Sun ~ Bedrooms: £40B/£60B

ROMALDKIRK NY9922 Map 10

Rose & Crown ★

Just off B6277

This 18th-c coaching inn is as popular as ever with readers, for its superbly cooked food, and welcoming service. The traditional cosy beamed bar has old-fashioned seats facing a warming log fire, a Jacobean oak settle, lots of brass and copper, a grandfather clock, and gin traps, old farm tools, and black and white pictures of Romaldkirk on the walls. Black Sheep and Theakstons Best are well kept on handpump alongside about a dozen wines, all of which you can have by the glass. The smart brasserie-style Crown Room (bar food is served in here) has large cartoons of French waiters on dark red walls, a grey carpet and smart high-back chairs. The hall has farm tools, wine maps and other interesting prints, along with a photograph (taken by a customer) of the Hale Bopp comet over Romaldkirk church. There's also a no smoking oak-panelled restaurant. You'll need to book if you want to eat here, and imaginative bar food, from a changing menu, might include lunchtime baps (from £3.95), and ploughman's (£6.95), with other dishes such as home-made corned beef (£4), scallop, prawn and bacon risotto (£6.25), wild boar sausage with onion and tomato gravy and champ (£8.95), steak, kidney and mushroom pie (£9.75), smoked haddock kedgeree or braised poussin with bacon, woodland mushrooms and puy lentils (£10.75), and chargrilled venison rump with mushrooms, marsala and cream (£11.95), and puddings such as apple and cinnamon crumble or dark chocolate tart (£3.50). The enthusiastic licensees put lots of effort into getting things just right, and they even make their own marmalades, jams, chutneys and bread. Lovely in summer, tables outside look out over the village green, still with its original stocks and water pump. The village is close to the excellent Bowes Museum and the High Force waterfall, and has an interesting old church. By the end of 2004, all the bedrooms should have been refurbished; they do good breakfasts. *(Recommended by Alan Thwaite, Margaret and Roy Randle, Tim and Carolyn Lowes, Barry Robson, Jill and Keith Wright, Michael Doswell, Mr and Mrs W D Borthwick, Di and Mike Gillam, Alison Hayes, Pete Hanlon, Mike Green, Lynda and Trevor Smith; also in the* Good Hotel Guide*)*

Free house ~ Licensees Christopher and Alison Davy ~ Real ale ~ Bar food (12-1.30, 6.30-9.30) ~ Restaurant ~ (01833) 650213 ~ Children welcome, must be over 6 in restaurant ~ Dogs allowed in bar and bedrooms ~ Open 11-3, 5.30-11; 12-3, 7-10.30 Sun; closed 24-26 Dec ~ Bedrooms: £75S(£75B)/£110S(£110B)

SEAHOUSES NU2232 Map 10

Olde Ship ★

Just off B1340, towards harbour

The entire bar of this fascinating stone harbour hotel is a tribute to the sea and seafarers – even the floor is scrubbed ship's decking, and, if it's working, an anemometer takes wind speed readings from the top of the chimney. Besides lots of other shiny brass fittings, ship's instruments and equipment, and a knotted anchor made by local fishermen, there are sea pictures and model ships, including fine ones of the North Sunderland lifeboat, and Seahouses' lifeboat the *Grace Darling*). There's also a model of the *Forfarshire*, the paddle steamer that Grace Darling went to rescue in 1838 (you can read more of the story in the pub), and even the ship's nameboard. The bar is gently lit by stained-glass sea picture windows, and it has an open fire in winter. One clear window looks out across the harbour to the Farne Islands, and as dusk falls you can watch the Longstones lighthouse shine across the fading evening sky. The low-beamed Cabin Room is no smoking; piped music, dominoes, putting and quoits. The choice of well kept ales on handpump – Bass, Black Sheep, Courage Directors, Greene King Old Speckled Hen and Theakstons Best – increases in summer months with up to three guests such as Greene King Ruddles County, Hadrian & Border Farne Island, and Hydes Fine and Dandy; also around 30 malt whiskies and a good choice of wines. Along with well liked crab sandwiches, tasty bar food could include soup (£3.50), mushroom risotto (£4), chicken and mushroom casserole or spicy lamb stew (£7.50), grilled lemon sole (£8), and fillet steak (£8.50), with puddings such as chocolate trifle or apple crumble (£4). The pub is not really suitable for children though there is a little family room, and along with walkers, they are welcome on the battlemented side terrace (you'll even find fishing memorabilia out here). This and a sun lounge look out on the harbour. You can book boat trips to the Farne Islands Bird Sanctuary at the harbour, and there are bracing coastal walks, particularly to Bamburgh, Grace Darling's birthplace. *(Recommended by Brian England, Rona Murdoch, the Didler, David and Ruth Hollands, Keith and Janet Morris, KN-R, Anna and Martyn Carey, Paul and Ursula Randall, Comus and Sarah Elliott, Ian and Nita Cooper, Michael and Hilary Stiffin, Adam and Joan Bunting, Brian and Janet Ainscough, Alan Cole, Kirstie Bruce)*

Free house ~ Licensees Alan and Jean Glen ~ Real ale ~ Bar food (12-2, 7-8.30; not 25 Dec) ~ Restaurant ~ (01665) 720200 ~ Children in family room, over 10 in bedrooms ~ Open 11-11; 12-10.30 Sun ~ Bedrooms: £48S/£96S

STANNERSBURN NY7286 Map 10

Pheasant

Kielder Water road signposted off B6320 in Bellingham

Just up the road from Kielder Water, this homely old village pub is in a peaceful valley, with quiet forests all around; the streamside garden is pleasant in summer, with picnic-sets, and a pony paddock behind. Inside everything is spotlessly kept, with gleaming polished brass and wood. The comfortable traditional lounge has stools ranged along the counter, and lots of old local photographs on stripped stone and panelling. A separate public bar is similar but simpler, and opens into a further cosy seating area with beams; panelling. The evening sees a good mix of visitors and locals, when the small no smoking dining room can get quite crowded. Building up from one to four in the summer months, real ales might include well kept Black Sheep, Timothy Taylors Landlord and Wylam Gold Tankard and Bohemia Pilsner on handpump; they've around 35 malt whiskies, and a decent reasonably priced wine list. Home-made bar food could include lunchtime sandwiches (from £2.40) and ploughman's (£5.95), garlic chicken breast salad (£6.75), and game and mushroom pie or roast lamb with redcurrant jus (£6.95). In the evening (when prices for the same dishes go up by a couple of pounds), you can also choose from a couple more elaborate dishes such as grilled bass with lemon and parsley butter (£11.50), and confit of duck breast with port and raspberry glaze (£12.50), and puddings might be lemon and lime cheesecake (£3.50); roast Sunday lunch (£7.25). *(Recommended by Prof and Mrs Tony Palmer, David and Elizabeth Briggs, Jean and Douglas Troup)*

Free house ~ Licensees Walter and Robin Kershaw ~ Real ale ~ Bar food (not Mon-Tues Nov-Easter) ~ Restaurant ~ (01434) 240382 ~ Children welcome ~ Dogs allowed in bedrooms ~ Open 11.30-3, 6.30-11; 12-3, 7-11 Sun; 12-2.30, 7-11 in winter; closed Mon-Tues Nov-Easter ~ Bedrooms: £40S/£70S

STANNINGTON NZ2279 Map 10

Ridley Arms

Village signposted just off A1 S of Morpeth

Extended and more or less open-plan, this big dining pub is cleverly laid out in a way that gives the feel of several separate relaxing areas, each slightly different in mood and style from its neighbours; even when it's busy it doesn't feel crowded. The front is a proper bar area, with darts and a fruit machine, and stools along the counter. The beamed dining areas, largely no smoking, lead back from here, with a second bar counter, comfortable armchairs and upright chairs around shiny dark wood tables on polished boards or carpet, with portraits and cartoons on cream, panelled or stripped stone walls, careful lighting and some horsey statuettes. Black Sheep and Timothy Taylors Landlord are well kept along with four guests from brewers such as Harviestoun, Hill Island, Kelham Island and Mordue on handpump, and they've ten wines by the glass. Generously served tasty bar food such as soup (£3.25), sandwiches (£3.95), grilled field mushrooms (£4.25), sausage and mash (£6.95), haddock (£7.25), steak and ale casserole or salmon (£8.50), with puddings such as lemon tart (£3.95); Sunday lunch (£7.50). Disabled access is good; unobtrusive piped music, and dominoes. There are tables outside, and work on a new garden was about to be completed as we went to press. The pub is run by the Sir John Fitzgerald pub group, a smallish group, based in the North East but extending from there. *(Recommended by Tony and Wendy Hobden, Paul and Ursula Randall, John Foord, Gerry and Rosemary Dobson, Adam and Joan Bunting, Dr Peter D Smart)*

Sir John Fitzgerald ~ Managers Lyn and Gary Reilly ~ Real ale ~ Bar food (12-9.30(9 Sun and bank hols)) ~ (01670) 789216 ~ Children in eating area of bar ~ Open 11.30-11; 12-10.30 Sun

It's very helpful if you let us know up-to-date food prices when you report on pubs.

THROPTON NU0302 Map 10

Three Wheat Heads

B6341

Well positioned in the heart of Coquetdale, this comfortable stone-built 17th-c village hotel has an attractive garden with lovely views towards the Simonside Hills, a play area and a dovecote. Inside, there's a fairly sedate dining atmosphere, and it's locally popular with older folk for meals out. The carpeted bar on the right and the pleasant and roomy flock-wallpapered dining area have good coal fires (one in a fine tall stone fireplace), which you might find lit even when it's not that cold, wheelback chairs around neat rows of dark tables, more heavily cushioned brocaded seats, comfortable bar stools with backrests, and an elaborate longcase clock. The emphasis is on the generously served food, and the bar menu includes soup (£2.95), baked potatoes (from £3.50), sandwiches (from £3.95), vegetarian choices such as roasted vegetable and chick pea casserole or linguini with sun-dried tomatoes, olives and basil (£8.95), and steak and vegetable casserole or fried king prawns with garlic (£8.95), with more elaborate dishes on the à la carte menu such as monkfish with asparagus or seared bass fillet (£12.95); they do a couple of puddings such as bread and butter pudding (£3.95), and you can get children's meals (£3.95). The restaurant is no smoking. Friendly staff serve well kept Marstons Pedigree and Theakstons on handpump; dominoes, TV and piped music. More reports please. *(Recommended by Tony and Wendy Hobden, A and B D Craig, Derek Stafford, Keith and Margaret Kettell)*

Pubmaster ~ Lease Danny and Elke Scullion ~ Real ale ~ Bar food (12-2, 6-9; 12-9 wknds) ~ Restaurant ~ (01669) 620262 ~ Children welcome ~ Dogs allowed in bar and bedrooms ~ Open 11-3, 6-11; 11(12 Sun)-11 Sat ~ Bedrooms: £45B/£65B

WARENFORD NU1429 Map 10

Warenford Lodge

Off A1 3 or 4 miles S of Belford

They make good use of fresh local ingredients at this slightly quirky stone house, and the menu changes regularly: enjoyable dishes might include ploughman's (from £4.95), red onion flan (£5.20), home-made fish soup (£5.60, £9.90 large), lamb hotpot or smoked salmon kedgeree (£7.50), thai green curry with monkfish and prawns (£10.50), with puddings such as lemon pudding (£3.40). They do an interesting local cheese platter (£5.75). The quite simple 60s décor makes the partly stripped stone bar look more modern than it actually is. It has cushioned wooden seats around pine tables, and a warm fire in the big stone fireplace; steps lead up to an extension with comfortable dining tables and chairs, and a big woodburning stove; dominoes. They have a decent selection of wines and 17 malt whiskies, farm-pressed fruit juices, a good choice of teas, and keg John Smiths; friendly service. You'll need to keep your eyes open to find the pub as there's no sign outside, and do check their limited opening times before you set out. More reports please. *(Recommended by Sam and John Pallett)*

Free house ~ Licensees Ray and Marion Matthewman ~ Bar food (Sun lunchtime only; 7-9.30) ~ Restaurant ~ (01668) 213453 ~ Children in eating area of bar and restaurant ~ Open 7-11; 12-2, 7-11(10.30 Sun) wknds; closed Sun evening, Mon/Tues in winter; closed Mon, Tues-Fri lunchtimes, 25-26 Dec, and Jan

WELDON BRIDGE NZ1399 Map 10

Anglers Arms

B6344, just off A697; village signposted with Rothbury off A1 N of Morpeth

The obliging landlord and his wife, and the friendly young staff, go out of their way to make sure that visitors enjoy coming to this substantial hotel. Nicely lit and comfortable, the traditional turkey-carpeted bar is divided into two parts: cream walls on the right, and oak panelling and some shiny black beams hung with copper pans on the left, with a grandfather clock and sofa by the coal fire, staffordshire cats and other antique ornaments on its mantelpiece, old fishing and other country prints, some in heavy gilt frames, a profusion of other fishing memorabilia, and some taxidermy. Some of the tables are lower than you'd expect for eating, but their chairs have short legs to match – different, and rather engaging. The no smoking side restaurant in a former railway dining car is more formal but light and airy, with crisp white linen and a pink carpet. Make sure you're hungry if you eat here – the enjoyable bar food comes in huge portions: dishes might include soup (£2.95), sandwiches (£5.95), steak and ale pie or scampi (£7.95), lime and coriander chicken (£8.75), and mixed grill (£12.95), with puddings such as sticky toffee pudding and strawberry pavlova (£4.25). Timothy Taylors Landlord is well kept on handpump alongside a couple of guests such as Black Sheep Bitter and Charles Wells Bombardier, also decent wines and an espresso machine; there may be almost imperceptible piped music. There are tables in the attractive garden with a good play area; they have rights to fishing on a mile of the River Coquet just across the road. *(Recommended by John and Sylvia Harrop, Anne Evans, Mart Lawton, H Bramwell, Dr and Mrs S Donald)*

Free house ~ Licensee John Young ~ Real ale ~ Bar food ~ Restaurant ~ (01665) 570271 ~ Children welcome ~ Dogs allowed in bedrooms ~ Open 11-3, 6-11; 12-3, 6-10.30 Sun ~ Bedrooms: £35S/£55S

LUCKY DIP

Besides the fully inspected pubs, you might like to try these Lucky Dips recommended to us and described by readers (if you do, please send us reports: www.goodguides.co.uk).

ACOMB NY9366
Miners Arms [Main St]: Charming small 18th-c country pub with good friendly atmosphere, well kept Durham Magus, Jennings Cumberland, Yates and a guest beer, bargain simple home cooking by landlady (not wkdy lunchtimes) from sandwiches to good value Sun lunch, comfortable settles, huge fire in stone fireplace, children in dining room; small garden behind, has been open all day Sun and summer *(Michael Doswell, Len Beattie, Andy and Jill Kassube)*

ALLENDALE NY8355
☆ *Kings Head* [Market Pl (B6295)]: Early 18th-c former coaching inn with lemon walls, navy curtains, tartan carpet, spacious bar/lounge with blazing log fire, interesting bric-a-brac, small upstairs no smoking dining room; from three to seven well kept Jennings and guest ales, around 80 malt whiskies, reasonably priced bar food from sandwiches up, darts; TV, piped pop music; children welcome, open all day *(Peter F Marshall, CMW, JJW, Prof and Mrs Tony Palmer, Mike and Lynn Robinson, JWAC)*

ALNMOUTH NU2410
Red Lion [Northumberland St]: Friendly 16th-c inn, well kept local real ale, good value food from good sandwiches to local fish and other restaurant dishes (pasta is a favourite), log fire in bar full of theatre bills and memorabilia; children and dogs welcome, quiet and appealing coastal village *(Dr and Mrs P Truelove, Bill and Sheila McLardy)*

☆ *Saddle* [Northumberland St (B1338)]: Unpretentious and hospitable stone-built hotel rambling through several areas inc spacious dining area, wide choice of good attractively priced generous pubby food inc particularly good cheeseboard, popular Sun lunch (small or large helpings), pleasant service even when busy, well kept real ales such as Greene King Old Speckled Hen and Theakstons Best, games room with ping pong as well as pool etc, no smoking restaurant; unobtrusive piped music; children welcome, open all day Sat, tables outside, comfortable bedrooms, attractive beaches, good coastal walks *(A and B D Craig, Alan Melville, Myke and Nicky Crombleholme, Mrs M Granville-Edge, LYM, Bill and Sheila McLardy)*

ALNWICK NU1912
Oaks [South Rd (A1068, off A1)]: Small hotel locally popular for well kept Jennings real ales in linked rooms of neat lounge bar with period furniture and fittings, and for enjoyable interesting food here and in charming dining room; pleasant attentive staff, bedrooms *(Paul Boot)*

BEAMISH NZ2153
Beamish Mary [off A693 signed No Place and Cooperative Villas, S of museum]: Friendly down-to-earth 1960s pub, quiet lunchtime, with Durham NUM banner in games room, very assorted furnishings and bric-a-brac in bar with Aga; interesting choice of good value very generous bar food and Sun lunch, up to seven well kept changing ales, annual beer festival; piped music, children allowed until evening, live music in converted stables concert room; bedrooms *(Richard Houghton)*

BELFORD NU1033
☆ *Blue Bell* [off A1 S of Berwick; Market Pl]: Welcoming old-fashioned lounge bar in substantial and attractive old coaching inn, decent bar and buttery food from good local

crab sandwiches up inc children's meals, good service, log fire, extensive wine list, around 20 malt whiskies, no smoking restaurant; may be only keg beers, piped music, games in public bar, can be smoky; children welcome, big neatly kept garden, bedrooms *(LYM, Mrs J Ekins-Daukes, John and Sylvia Harrop, John Hale, GSB, R J Herd, Brian and Janet Ainscough)*

BERWICK-UPON-TWEED NT9952

☆ ***Barrels*** [Bridge St]: Convivial pub, homely feel despite bistro style, with thorough-going nautical décor in bar, car memorabilia, Beatles pictures and interesting pine furniture inc old school desks in lounge, attractive prices, well kept Boddingtons, Marstons Pedigree and interesting guest beers, lunchtime filled rolls, imaginative evening food (perhaps not Mon) inc tapas, munchies, snacks and main dishes, friendly accommodating staff; varying live music downstairs, good juke box; open all day *(David Field)*

Foxtons [Hide Hill]: Cheerful two-floor bar with casual and lively bistro atmosphere, wide choice of good imaginative food, well kept changing ales such as Caledonian 80/- and Timothy Taylors Landlord (happy hour 5.30-6.30), good range of wines and whiskies, good coffee, impressive friendly service; side restaurant; busy, so worth booking evenings *(Paul and Ursula Randall, Ian and Nita Cooper, David Field, Joe Green, John and Sylvia Harrop)*

BOWES NY9913

☆ ***Ancient Unicorn***: Substantial stone inn with some 17th-c parts and interesting *Nicholas Nickleby* connection; spacious, welcoming and comfortable open-plan bar, friendly chatty licensees, good honest generous food from sandwiches to steak, two real ales, coffee shop; good-sized clean bedrooms in converted stables block around big cobbled courtyard *(LYM, Ian Thurman)*

CAMBOIS NZ3085

Buccaneer: Interesting old building converted to large hospitable nautical-theme pub in good position above Wansbeck estuary, great coast views, warm welcome, good value specials nights (curry Weds, chicken Thurs, steak Fri, sizzling platters Sat), wide range of well kept beers *(Mike and Lynn Robinson, John Oddey)*

CHATTON NU0528

Percy Arms [B6348 E of Wooller]: Stone-built inn with neat lounge bar extending through arch, generous bar food from lunchtime filled baguettes and baked potatoes up, Theakstons and plenty of malt whiskies, attractive panelled dining room, cheerful efficient staff, public bar with games, juke box or piped music; children in family area and dining room, picnic-sets on small front lawn, bedrooms (12 miles of private fishing) *(LYM, Bob Ellis, Mark and Cath Caley, Prof and Mrs Tony Palmer, R J Herd)*

CHESTER-LE-STREET NZ2649

Chester Moor Inn [Chester Moor, A167 just S]: Wide range of good value food in unpretentious bar or pleasant no smoking dining room, well kept beer, cheerful efficient staff *(M Borthwick)*

Church Mouse [A167 S, Chester Moor]: Filling food, good drinks choice, log fire, olde-worlde décor *(Jenny and Dave Hughes, M Borthwick)*

CHOPPINGTON NZ2583

Swan: Enjoyable food in big plain square room with island bar and attractive side restaurant *(John Oddey)*

CONSETT NZ1151

Grey Horse [Sherburn Terr]: Well run two-bar beamed 19th-c pub brewing its own Derwent Rose beers in former back stables, inc Paddy named for the pub dog, and Red Dust, Steel Town and The Works recalling the former steel works here; also a guest beer, lots of malt whiskies, occasional beer festivals, very friendly licensees, cheap bar lunches inc toasties, baguettes and all-day breakfast (may be evening toasties too), good range of customers, pool; pavement tables, open all day *(Brian and Anna Marsden, Richard Houghton)*

CORBRIDGE NY9964

☆ ***Angel*** [Newcastle Rd]: Small 17th-c hotel with good fresh food (not cheap by northern standards) from sandwiches to imaginative blackboard dishes in large bar with attractively simple décor and adjoining plush panelled lounge, three well kept ales such as Black Sheep, good wines and coffees, friendly service, carefully refurbished restaurant; bedrooms, nr lovely bridge over River Tyne *(Michael Doswell, Peter and Jean Hoare, Jenny and Dave Hughes, Robert M Warner, LYM, GSB, Jenny and Brian Seller, Andy and Jill Kassube)*

Dyvels [Station Rd]: Unassuming, informal and relaxing, warm welcome, good range of real ales such as Derwent and Yates, wide choice of reasonably priced usual food from toasties up (only snacks Mon); may be piped music; tables in pleasant area outside, decent bedrooms, open all day *(Andy and Jill Kassube)*

Wheatsheaf [Watling St/St Helens St]: Big refurbished stone-built village hotel, popular esp with older lunchers for wide choice of generous food (all day summer wknds) from sandwiches to seasonal game and tender Sun roasts, cheerful helpful staff, well kept Jennings Cumberland and Marstons Pedigree, good choice of wines and malt whiskies, pleasant Victorian décor in dining lounge and big warm conservatory restaurant with distant hill views; pub games, piped music, some picnic-sets outside; bedrooms *(John Foord, LYM)*

COTHERSTONE NZ0119

Red Lion: Traditional beamed 18th-c local with good value food (not Mon-Thurs) in bar and no smoking restaurant from sandwiches through familiar things to some interesting dishes, Jennings and a guest beer, log fire, snug; children, boots and dogs welcome, garden tables, bedrooms *(Peter and Eva Lowes, R M Corlett)*

CRAMLINGTON NZ2373

Snowy Owl [Blagdon Lane]: Large relaxing Vintage Inn, beams, flagstones, hop bines, stripped stone and terracotta paintwork, soft lighting and an interesting mix of furnishings and decorations, good choice of wines, well kept Bass, friendly efficient service, daily papers; may be piped music; bedrooms *(Michael Doswell, Dr Peter D Smart)*

CRASTER NU2620

Jolly Fisherman [off B1339, NE of Alnwick]: Simple take-us-as-you-find-us local, still enjoyed by many for its crab sandwiches, crab soup and picture-window harbour and sea views, with well kept ales such as Caledonian Deuchars IPA and Marstons Pedigree; can get smoky, and service can suffer, when it's very busy; games area with pool and juke box; children and dogs welcome, picnic-sets on grass behind, lovely clifftop walk to Dunstanburgh Castle, open all day in summer *(the Didler, Anna and Martyn Carey, Barry Collett, Keith and Janet Morris, KN-R, A and B D Craig, LYM, Pat and Tony Martin, Michael Doswell, David Field)*

CRAWCROOK NZ1363

Rising Sun [Bank Top]: Roomy and well refurbished, bright and welcoming, with huge choice of hearty popular food in dining area and conservatory, well kept ales such as Black Sheep, Mordue Workie Ticket and Timothy Taylors Landlord from long bar, cheerful staff, steps up to lounge, pool room; neatly kept garden, open all day *(John Foord, John Oddey)*

DARLINGTON NZ2814

Quaker Coffee House [Mechanics Yard, High Row (narrow passage by Binns)]: Small, narrow and cheerful, with cellar-bar feel from dim lighting and bare bricks, half a dozen well kept and interesting changing real ales, friendly staff, daily papers and magazines, upstairs daytime restaurant with good choice of food and wines; lively bands Weds, open all day (not Sun lunchtime) *(Andrew York)*

DINNINGTON NZ2073

White Swan [Prestwick Rd]: Bar and pleasant no smoking lounge locally very popular for bargain lunchtime and early evening specials, even cheaper for OAPs, Black Sheep and Greene King Old Speckled Hen, coffee in variety *(Michael Doswell)*

DUNSTAN NU2419

☆ ***Cottage*** [off B1339 Alnmouth—Embleton]: Big family dining pub with low beams, some stripped brickwork, banquettes and dimpled copper tables, usual lunches and evening meals, all-day sandwiches and snacks inc good local kippers, well kept Belhaven, Wylam and a guest beer, neat friendly young staff, no smoking conservatory, medieval-theme restaurant, games area; children welcome, tables out on flowery terrace and lawn, good adventure play area, modern bedrooms *(W K Wood, Tim and Sue Halstead, Mike and Wendy Proctor, LYM, A and B D Craig, Michael Doswell, Ian and Barbara Rankin, GSB, Prof and Mrs Tony Palmer, Mike and Lynn Robinson)*

DURHAM NZ2743

Bridge [North Rd, off A690]: Attractive pub below railway viaduct, enjoyable food from baguettes to bargain beef stew or chilli, well kept ales inc Theakstons; open all day *(Andy and Jill Kassube)*

Colpitts [Colpitts Terr/Hawthorn Terr]: Basic friendly two-bar local with particularly cheap Sam Smiths, sandwiches, open fires, pool, TV and machines; perhaps the country's smallest beer garden in yard, open all day *(the Didler, Patrick Hancock)*

Court Inn [Court Lane]: Good generous home-made food all day from sandwiches to steaks and late-evening bargains in unpretentious traditional town pub's extensive no smoking stripped brick eating area, real ales such as Hancocks HB and Worthington 1744, no mobile phones; bustling in term-time with students and teachers, piped pop music; seats outside, open all day *(BB, Pete Baker, Tim and Ann Newell)*

☆ ***Dun Cow*** [Old Elvet]: Unsmart and very welcoming traditional town pub in pretty 16th-c black and white timbered cottage, tiny chatty front bar with wall benches, corridor linking it to long narrow back lounge with machines etc (can be packed with students), real ales inc particularly well kept Castle Eden, cheap soup and sandwiches etc, friendly staff; piped music; children welcome, open all day Mon-Sat, Sun too in summer *(the Didler, LYM, Pete Baker, Patrick Hancock)*

Old Elm Tree [Crossgate]: Big busy pub on steep hill opp castle, two-room main bar and small lounge, prompt cheerful service, open fires, several real ales, farm cider; TV, machines, juke box; seats outside, open all day wknds *(the Didler)*

Swan & Three Cygnets [Elvet Bridge]: Comfortably refurbished Victorian pub in good bridge-end spot high above river, city views from big windows and picnic-sets out on terrace, bargain food from hot filled baguettes up, cheap well kept Sam Smiths OB; open all day *(BB, Dave Braisted, Mike and Lynn Robinson)*

EBCHESTER NZ1055

☆ ***Derwent Walk*** [Ebchester Hill (B6309 outside)]: Friendly pub by the Gateshead—Consett walk for which it's named, walkers welcome, fine Derwent Valley views from character bar, conservatory and pleasant heated terrace, wide range of satisfying home-made food from interesting sandwiches to steaks inc enterprising specials, full Jennings range kept well and a guest such as Everards Tiger, good wine range, good log fire, appealing old photographs *(Andy and Jill Kassube, Michael Doswell)*

EGGLESTON NY9924

Moorcock [Hill Top]: Congenial atmosphere, pleasant unpretentious décor, enjoyable fresh reasonably priced food inc local lamb and interesting dishes, log fire in lounge, games room with darts, pool and TV, small dining room, great Teesdale views; dogs welcome, tables out on front terrace, comfortable bedrooms, good walks *(Prof and Mrs Tony Palmer)*

ELLINGHAM NU1625

☆ *Pack Horse* [signed off A1 N of Alnwick]: Compact stone-built country pub, quietly welcoming spotless bar, some emphasis on good value fresh food using local produce from ciabattas and two-round sandwiches up, big helpings, wider evening choice, beams with a forest of jugs, well kept Black Sheep, good coffee, quick friendly attentive service, pretty dining room, neat pool room; bedrooms, peaceful village *(Michael Doswell)*

EMBLETON NU2322

☆ *Sportsman*: Large newly renovated bar and dining room (plans for extension) with good individual evening cooking mainly using local produce, fish and game at reasonable prices, good value lunchtime baguettes, small well chosen wine list, well kept Hadrian & Border real ales, friendly cheerful service, stunning views to Dunstanburgh Castle; frequent wknd live music; big terrace, bedrooms, not far from beach *(Michael Doswell, Mr and Mrs J Hale)*

ETAL NT9339

Black Bull [off B6354 SW of Berwick]: Pretty white-painted cottage, the only thatched pub in Northumberland, spacious unpretentious open-plan lounge bar with glossily varnished beams, two well kept real ales, 30 malt whiskies, farm cider, quick friendly service, decent food inc good fish and steaks; children in eating area, games room with darts, dominoes, pool, TV, juke box and piped music; open all day Sat, a few picnic-sets out in front; nice spot nr castle ruins and light railway *(LYM, Michael and Hilary Stiffin, Michael and Anne Brown, Mike and Lynn Robinson)*

FELTON NU1800

☆ *Northumberland Arms* [village signed off A1 N of Morpeth]: Good generous food all day from bargain Tues lunch to interesting specials, also children's dishes; roomy and comfortable open-plan bar with beams, stripped stone and good coal fires, nice mix of furnishings inc big blue settees, elegant small end restaurant; pleasant atmosphere, well kept Bass and Black Sheep Best, good coffee and wines, laid-back service; well reproduced piped music, esp in conservatory pool room, monthly live music 1st Weds; five bedrooms, steps down to bench by River Coquet, open all day *(Michael Doswell, BB, Mike and Lynn Robinson, John Oddey)*

GATESHEAD NZ3061

Green [White Mare Pool, Wardley; W of roundabout at end of A194(M)]: Fitzgerald pub with large nicely decorated modern lounge, light and airy, separate bar, restaurant area, half a dozen or more reasonably priced ales inc local Mordue, regular beer festivals, huge helpings of good value freshly prepared food, friendly helpful staff, picture-window outlook on golf course; light piped music, very busy wknds *(Gerry and Rosemary Dobson)*

Lambton Arms [Rockcliffe Way, Eighton Banks]: Recently comfortably refurbished in appealing up-to-date style and now entirely no smoking, with good range of reasonably priced enjoyable food in bar and restaurant, well kept real ales such as Black Sheep, Caledonian Deuchars IPA and Greene King Ruddles, good wine choice, friendly helpful staff; children welcome, quiz night Tues, open all day *(Christine and Phil Young, M Borthwick)*

Ship [Eighton Banks, quite handy for A1(M)]: Extended open-plan pub popular at lunchtime for good blackboard food choice, large ornate Victorian-style no smoking dining room with model ships and marine artefacts, well kept real ale; south-facing garden with play area, great moor views *(M Borthwick)*

Waggon [Galloping Green Rd, Eighton Banks]: Extended refurbished pub locally popular for good value generous straightforward food (can be ordered ahead) from sandwiches and baked potatoes to Sun lunch, comfortable airy eating areas inc no smoking conservatory overlooking old Bowes Railway, well kept changing beers, friendly prompt service *(M Borthwick)*

GREENHEAD NY6665

Greenhead [just off A69 Haltwhistle—Brampton]: Friendly village pub with well kept beer and enjoyable food; bedrooms, handy for Pennine Way and new Hadrian's Wall Path *(Len Beattie)*

HALTWHISTLE NY7064

☆ *Black Bull* [just off Market Sq, behind Indian restaurant]: Four or more particularly well kept changing ales inc ones brewed at the pub, welcoming landlord and locals, brasses on low beams, stripped stone with shelves of bric-a-brac, log fire in both rooms, darts and monthly quiz night; no music or food, limited disabled access, cl Mon-Weds lunchtimes *(Michele D'Lemos, Andy and Jill Kassube, G Coates, Richard Houghton)*

HART NZ4634

White Hart [just off A179 W of Hartlepool; Front St]: Interesting two-room pub with old ship's figurehead outside, nautical theme (inc unusual collection of shroud knots); popular for wide choice of reasonably priced home-made food, one changing real ale, usually a singer guitarist Sun night *(JHBS)*

HARTLEPOOL NZ5032

Causeway [Stockton Rd, Stranton]: Victorian pub with panelled bare-boards bar, two carpeted snugs, Banks's Bitter and Original, Camerons Bitter and Strongarm and a guest beer, enjoyable lunchtime food (not Sun), low prices; live folk and jazz five nights a week, sometimes Sun afternoon too; open all day *(JHBS)*

White House [Wooler Rd]: Ember Inn in converted school, half a dozen or more rooms, some with leather armchairs, two log fires and one flame-effect, six changing real ales, a dozen wines by the glass, attractively priced food all day; open all day *(JHBS)*

HAWTHORN NZ4145

Stapylton Arms [off B1432 S of A19 Murton exit]: Carpeted bar with lots of old local photographs, well kept changing ales such as Shepherd Neame Spitfire, chatty ex-miner landlord and wife – she produces enjoyable food from sandwiches to steaks and Sun roasts; dogs on leads allowed, may be open all day on busy wknds, nice wooded walk to sea (joins Durham Coastal Path) *(JHBS)*

HAYDON BRIDGE NY8364

☆ *General Havelock* [A69]: Civilised and individually furnished dining pub with good food from interesting baguettes to imaginative hot dishes using fresh local ingredients prepared in open-view kitchen, well kept changing real ales, good wines by the glass and coffee, welcoming service and relaxing atmosphere, open fires, more upmarket evening set menus in smart Tyne-view stripped stone restaurant; children welcome, tables on terrace *(Michael Doswell, LYM, Andy and Jill Kassube)*

HEXHAM NY9464

Tap & Spile [Battle Hill/Eastgate]: Congenial and cosy open-plan bare-boards pub with half a dozen quickly changing well kept ales from central bar, country wines, good filling low-priced food from hot filled stotties up, warm coal fire, expert smiling service; children welcome, no dogs, regular live music, open all day *(John Foord, Andy and Jill Kassube)*

HIGH FORCE NY8728

High Force Hotel [B6277 about 4 miles NW of Middleton-in-Teesdale]: Beautifully placed high-moors hotel, named for England's highest waterfall nearby and doubling as mountain rescue post; well kept real ales inc some brewed for them by Darwin, bar food, mixed décor; usually open all day summer (when it can get busy) but may be cl quiet lunchtimes out of season; children welcome, comfortable bedrooms, pleasant garden *(LYM, Tracey and Stephen Groves, Mike and Lynn Robinson)*

HIGH HESLEDEN NZ4538

Ship [off A19 via B1281]: Half a dozen real ales, real fire and lots of sailing ship models inc big one hanging from bar ceiling, enjoyable food here or in capacious restaurant; yacht and shipping views from car park, cl Mon *(JHBS)*

HOLY ISLAND NU1241

Crown & Anchor: Comfortable pub/restaurant with emphasis on enjoyable quickly served food though bar much used by locals, well kept Caledonian Deuchars IPA, good fresh coffee, friendly staff, pleasant décor inc interesting rope fancy-work, spotless bright modern dining room; three bedrooms *(Paul and Ursula Randall, Mrs Ann Gray)*

HORSLEY NZ0966

Lion & Lamb [B6528, just off A69 Newcastle—Hexham]: Plentiful reasonably priced decent food (not Sun evening) from sandwiches to daily roast, Mon steak night, bargains for two Tues-Weds, up to eight well kept changing ales inc local ones, cafetière coffee, two main rooms, small smart restaurant, no smoking area, stripped stone, flagstones, panelling, untreated tables and chairs; Tyne views from attractive garden with roomy terrace and particularly good adventure play area, open all day *(John Oddey, Gerry and Rosemary Dobson)*

HOUGHTON GATE NZ2950

Smiths Arms [Castle Dene; off A183 Chester-le-Street—Sunderland via A1052 then Forge Lane]: Classic friendly traditional bar with open fire in old black kitchen range, three real ales with a guest most weeks, comfortable lounge with two log or coal fires, games room with another, purple walls and gilded mirrors in upstairs restaurant (Weds-Sat evenings) with good interesting food, lunchtime bar food; cl Mon-Thurs lunchtime *(Tom and Alison Lynn)*

HURWORTH-ON-TEES NZ2814

Bay Horse [Church Row]: Two cosy lounge bars, welcoming staff and wide choice of home-made food and of drinks; reasonable prices, big public bar, charming village by River Tees *(Peter Hacker)*

HUTTON MAGNA NZ1212

Oak Tree [off A66 SE of Greta Bridge]: Enjoyable food, well kept Timothy Taylors Landlord *(Tim Wellock)*

KENTON BANKFOOT NZ2068

☆ *Twin Farms* [Main Road]: Good Fitzgerald pub in elegant period rustic style, recycled stone, timbers etc, several areas, nooks and crannies off central bar, decent food from good value sandwiches through unusual snacks to interesting main dishes and meals in well run restaurant, well kept ales inc local ones such as Darwin and Mordue, well chosen wines, real fire, quick friendly service, families welcome; piped music, machines; disabled facilities, open all day *(anon)*

LAMESLEY NZ2557

Ravensworth Arms [minor rd S of Gateshead western bypass, A1, Team Valley junction]: Largely no smoking stone-built Chef & Brewer, stripped brick and recycled timber dividers, competitively priced popular fresh food from sandwiches and baked potatoes to steak, fish and game, cheerful helpful service even when busy (food can slow then), good wine choice; may be piped music; children welcome, play area and picnic-sets outside, open all day *(Jenny and Dave Hughes, Alan Thwaite, M Borthwick)*

LANCHESTER NZ1647

Kings Head [Station Rd (B6296)]: Newly refurbished, with pleasant décor and feel in large dining area, well presented usual food; bedrooms *(John Coatsworth)*

LOWICK NU0139

☆ *Black Bull* [Main St (B6353, off A1 S of Berwick-upon-Tweed)]: Friendly bustle in nicely decorated country pub with comfortable main bar, small back bar, big back dining room locally very popular for good choice of plentiful good value food (take-aways too), well kept Marstons Pedigree, good welcoming service; children welcome, three attractive bedrooms, on edge of small pretty village *(KN-R, Michael and Hilary Stiffin)*

LUCKER NU1631

☆ *Apple* [village (and pub) signed off A1 N of Morpeth]: Nicely refurbished village pub under new licensees, pleasant service, good choice of enjoyable food from soup, baguettes and light lunches up, separate evening menu, stripped stone, bare boards or carpet, solid pub furnishings, woodburner, pleasantly fresh and airy décor in roomy and popular side dining-room extension; keg beers; has been cl Mon lunchtime *(John and Sylvia Harrop, BB, C A Hall, R J Herd, Bill and Sheila McLardy)*

MARSDEN NZ4164

Grotto [Coast Rd; passage to lift in A183 car park, just before Marsden from Whitburn]: Pub/restaurant uniquely built into seaside cliff caverns, with 10p lift (or dozens of steps) down to two floors – upper pink plush, lower brown varnish; Black Sheep and another real ale, food in bar and restaurant with good fish choice, summer barbecue lunches, good sea views, step straight out on to beach *(JHBS)*

MIDDLESTONE NZ2531

Ship [Low Rd]: Half a dozen well kept and interesting often local real ales, welcoming licensees, good choice of food inc Sun lunch, good fire, great view, beer festivals and lots of other events; piped music; cl wkdy lunchtimes, open all day Fri-Sun *(Nigel Sharman, Ann and Brian Denton)*

MITFORD NZ1785

Plough [just off A1 Morpeth bypass]: Roomy and welcoming family-friendly pub in small village, well kept ales inc a weekly guest, enjoyable food from baguettes and baked potatoes up, restaurant; small playground *(Christopher and Jo Barton)*

NETHERTON NT9807

Star [off B6341 at Thropton, or A697 via Whittingham]: Unchanging local in superb remote countryside, almost a place of pilgrimage for searchers after the unspoilt, spartan but clean, many original features, well kept Castle Eden tapped from cellar casks and served in small entrance lobby, large high-ceilinged room with panelled wall benches, charming landlady and welcoming regulars; no food, music or children; open evenings and Sun lunchtime *(the Didler, Kevin Thorpe, RWC)*

NEW YORK NZ3269

☆ *Shiremoor Farm* [Middle Engine Lane/Norham Rd, off A191 bypass]: Relaxed and civilised dining pub in stylishly converted former derelict farm buildings, vast choice of enjoyable computer-ordered food all day, good helpings, well kept very local Mordue Workie Ticket, Timothy Taylors Landlord, Theakstons Best and a guest beer, decent wines by the glass, mildly ironic modern take on rustic décor, good lighting, no smoking granary extension; children welcome away from main bar, heated covered terrace, open all day *(Michael Doswell, LYM, Keith and Margaret Kettell, Mart Lawton)*

NEWCASTLE UPON TYNE NZ2464

Barcule [St Peters Wharf]: Great sitting outside this bar/bistro on a warm summer's night – fine setting *(Mike and Lynn Robinson)*

Bob Trollopes [Sandhill]: Enjoyable entirely vegetarian food, vegan too if you want, in superb 17th-c quayside building; appealing prices, Ind Coope Burton, Tetleys and guest beers, friendly staff *(Norma and David Hardy)*

Bodega [Westgate Rd]: Edwardian drinking hall, colourful walls and ceiling with two magnificent original stained-glass domes (has been a mosque), boards, tiles and a handsome rug, cosy alcove banquettes; well kept Big Lamp Prince Bishop, Durham Magus, Mordue Geordie Pride (sold here as No 9) and three guest beers tapped from the cask, lunchtime food, table football; juke box or piped music, machines, TV, Tues quiz night, busy evenings; open all day, next to Tyne Theatre *(Eric Larkham, the Didler)*

☆ *Bridge Hotel* [Castle Sq, next to high level bridge]: Big cheery high-ceilinged room divided into several areas leaving plenty of space by the bar with replica slatted snob screens, particularly well kept Black Sheep, Boddingtons, Mordue Workie Ticket and three guest beers, decent lunchtime food and Sun afternoon teas, magnificent fireplace, great views of river and bridges from raised back no smoking area; sports TV, piped music, fruit machines, very long-standing Mon folk club upstairs; tables on flagstoned back terrace overlooking section of old town wall, open all day *(John Foord, LYM, the Didler, Eric Larkham, CMW, JJW, Mike and Lynn Robinson)*

☆ *Cooperage* [The Close, Quayside]: One of city's most ancient buildings, great atmosphere in stripped stone bar and cosy beamed lounge, good waterfront setting, well kept Bass, Fullers London Pride, Timothy Taylors Landlord and one from Mordue (good prices Mon-Thurs and till 9 Fri-Sat), hearty fresh sensibly priced lunchtime food; upstairs night club Mon (student night) and Thurs-Sat, pool, juke box, quiz night Tues; disabled facilities, cl Sun lunchtime, open all day Fri *(LYM, Eric Larkham, the Didler)*

Egypt Cottage [City Rd]: Small pleasantly refurbished pub, well kept real ales, new landlord doing more inventive food with plans for restaurant *(anon)*

Free Trade [St Lawrence Rd, off Walker Rd (A186)]: Chattily friendly atmosphere in artfully basic split-level pub with big windows for grandstand river and bridge views, well kept ales (usually two each) from Hadrian & Border, Mordue and Wylam, guest beers too, good wkdy early lunchtime sandwiches, real fire, original Formica tables; cricket radio, eclectic free CD juke box, quiz Weds, Sun open mike night, steps down to back room and lavatories (high-standard gents' graffiti); tables out on terrace (or sit on grass overlooking Tyne), open all day *(Eric Larkham, Kevin Thorpe, Mike and Lynn Robinson)*

Hotspur [Percy St]: Cheerful open-plan Victorian pub with big front windows and decorated mirrors, well kept Courage Directors, McEwans 80/-, Theakstons Best and Old Peculier and three guest beers, farm cider, lots of bottled belgian beers, good value wine, sandwiches and hot snacks all day; piped music, machines, big-screen sports TV, can get packed, esp pre-match, upstairs ladies'; open all day *(John Foord, Eric Larkham, Michael Doswell)*

Ship [Stepney Bank]: Unchanging traditional local by Byker city farm, particularly well kept Boddingtons and Castle Eden Bitter and

Nimmos XXXX, unusual toasted sandwiches (normally all day), very friendly locals, pool and juke box in lounge, darts and TV in bar; seats outside and picnic-sets on green opp, open all day *(Eric Larkham, Mike and Lynn Robinson)*

Tyne [Maling St]: Busy single-room pub at confluence of Ouseburn and Tyne, plastered with band posters and prints – frequent live music upstairs; Black Sheep, Durham Magus, a Mordue beer and a guest, exotic hot or cold sandwiches all day, free interestingly stocked CD juke box; fruit machine, sports TV, stairs up to lavatories; usefully placed at end of quayside walk, fairy-lit garden (loudspeakers out here too) under an arch of Glasshouse Bridge, barbecues Sun lunch, early Fri evening; open all day *(Eric Larkham, Kevin Thorpe, Mike and Lynn Robinson)*

NORTH BITCHBURN NZ1732

☆ ***Red Lion***: Friendly 17th-c beamed village local, enjoyable food from good value hot beef sandwiches to wider restaurant menu, two well kept interesting local beers, log fires *(Alyson and Andrew Jackson)*

NORTH SHIELDS NZ3470

☆ ***Magnesia Bank*** [Camden St]: Lively well run refurbished Victorian pub, roomy bar with raised eating areas, half a dozen or more well kept ales inc Black Sheep, Durham, Jarrow and Mordue in lined glasses, good wines and coffee, vast choice of cheerful home-made lunchtime food from cheap toasties to hot dishes using local meats, good value all-day breakfast from 8.30am, attentive friendly uniformed staff, intriguing mix of customers, open fire, no smoking side restaurant (same menu); quiet piped pop music, TV, machines, upstairs comedy nights, live music Thurs and Sun; children welcome, tables outside, open all day *(Michael Doswell, Kevin Thorpe, Mike and Lynn Robinson, D J Etheridge, John and Gloria Isaacs)*

☆ ***Wooden Doll*** [Hudson St]: Bird's-eye view of fish quay and outer harbour – get there early for a table in the largely no smoking glass-fronted extension; new management doing enjoyable food from good sandwiches up to fresh local fish, full Jennings range kept well, helpful welcoming service, informal mix of furnishings in bare-boards bar, lots of paintings by local artists for sale; disabled facilities, children welcome till 8, some live music, open all day Sat *(LYM, Robert M Warner, Mike and Lynn Robinson, J H Bescoby)*

OVINGTON NZ1314

Four Alls [off B6274, S of A67]: Friendly local with changing real ales such as Banks's or Tetleys, wide food choice running up to duck in black cherry sauce and some unusual vegetarian dishes; impressive garden *(Andrew York)*

PIERCEBRIDGE NZ2115

George [B6275 just S of village, over bridge]: Attractively placed rambling old inn, more hotel than pub, with a useful range of decent quickly served food in pleasant bar with adjoining pool room, river-view dining room; provision for children, lots of tables out in garden with bridge to small island (not easy for disabled people), bedrooms, open all day *(LYM, DC, Alistair and Kay Butler, Paul and Ursula Randall)*

PONTELAND NZ1871

☆ ***Badger*** [Street Houses; A696 SE, by garden centre]: Well done and warmly hospitable Vintage Inn, more character than most pubs in the area, relaxing rooms and alcoves, old furnishings and olde-worlde décor, flagstones, carpet or bare wood, timbered ceilings, stripped stone, brick and timbering, real fires, Bass, Tetleys and Fullers London Pride, good choice of wines by the glass and good hot drinks, generous reasonably priced food all day inc imaginative good value light dishes and interesting lunchtime sandwiches (most people here to eat – can get busy Sun lunchtime), friendly attentive uniformed staff; quiet piped music; open all day *(Michael Doswell, BB, A H C Rainier)*

RENNINGTON NU2118

☆ ***Horseshoes***: Neat and comfortable flagstoned pub doing well under current sociable and helpful landlord, well kept Bass, Black Sheep and John Smiths, good friendly service, simple bar with lots of horsebrasses, enjoyable fresh food in spotless compact restaurant with blue and white china; children welcome, tables outside, attractive quiet village nr coast *(Tom McLean, Robert M Warner, G Dobson)*

RIDING MILL NZ0161

☆ ***Wellington*** [A695 just W of A68 roundabout]: Reliable 17th-c Chef & Brewer, carefully refurbished in tune with its age, beams and candlelight, two big log fires and mix of tables and chairs, some upholstered, some not; vast good value blackboard food choice from hot ciabatta sandwiches to nice puddings, Courage Directors and Theakstons Bitter and Black Bull, good choice of wines by the glass, friendly service; piped classical music, can get busy; disabled access, children welcome, play area and picnic-sets outside, pretty village with nearby walks and river *(Peter Burton, R J Herd, Andy and Jill Kassube, Dr Peter D Smart)*

ROKER NZ4058

Roker Hotel [Roker Terr (A183)]: On pleasant seaside promenade, well kept Darwin Sunderland Best in bright comfortable Tavern Bar, good value soup and sandwiches, pleasant service; bedrooms *(R T and J C Moggridge)*

ROTHBURY NU0501

☆ ***Newcastle Hotel***: Small solid Victorian hotel in imposing spot at end of green, comfortably refurbished lounge with separate dining area, second bar, friendly service and entertaining locals (can be quite noisy wknd afternoons, when piped music may be loud), good plentiful carefully prepared food inc substantial Sun lunch from well organised kitchen, cheap high teas 3.30-5.30 Apr-Oct, toasties only winter Sun pm, real ales such as Caledonian Deuchars IPA and Greene King Abbot and Old Speckled Hen, no smoking upstairs dining room; good value comfortable bedrooms with own bathrooms, open all day, handy for Cragside (NT) *(Patrick Hancock, Mrs M Granville-Edge)*

SEATON CAREW NZ5130

Schooner [Warrior Dr]: Newish two-level bar with decent food all day, Camerons Strongarm, coal-effect gas fire; pool, SkyTV for sports; children welcome, garden with play area *(JHBS)*

SEDGEFIELD NZ3528

Dun Cow [Front St]: Large village inn where the Prime Minister took President Bush in 2003, two bars and comfortable dining room, wide changing choice of food from well filled sandwiches to game, fresh whitby fish and unusual puddings, attentive landlord, prompt service, Castle Eden and several guest beers, good range of whiskies; children welcome; good bedrooms sharing bathrooms *(Malcolm M Stewart, Peter Hacker)*

SLAGGYFORD NY6754

Kirkstyle [Knarsdale]: Attractive pleasantly refurbished old inn, with wide range of good plain food, well kept beer and decent wines, nice spot looking over South Tyne valley to hills beyond; comfortable bedrooms, handy for Pennine Way *(Dr Robin Stephenson)*

SOUTH SHIELDS NZ3567

Alum Ale House [Ferry St (B1344)]: Stylish and relaxed 18th-c pub handy for ferry, big bars with polished boards, coal fire in old inglenook range, pictures and newspaper cuttings, well kept Banks's, Camerons, Marstons and guest beers such as Northumberland (tea and coffee too), good beer festivals, good value basic lunchtime bar food inc toasties and filled stotties; piped music, machines, some live music; children welcome, open all day *(Mike and Lynn Robinson, Andy and Jill Kassube)*

Steamboat [Mill Dam/Coronation St]: Masses of interesting nautical bric-a-brac esp in split-level back room, friendly landlord, well kept Black Sheep, Timothy Taylors Landlord and local guest beers such as Jarrow, Mordue and Whitby, cheap sandwiches, pool in central area; usually open all day, nr river and market place *(Brian and Anna Marsden, Andy and Jill Kassube)*

STAMFORDHAM NZ0772

Bay Horse [off B6309]: Cheery and comfortable long beamed bar with wide range of good value food, three well kept ales, good coffee, friendly hard-working new licensees; dogs welcome, doubles as shop and post office, at end of green in attractive village *(Mike and Lynn Robinson)*

STANLEY NZ1753

Harperley Hotel [Harperley Country Park, 1½ miles W]: Good home cooking inc bargain three-course restaurant lunch and evening carvery, well kept Courage Directors and Jennings or Greene King; extensive grounds, good walks *(Mike and Lynn Robinson)*

STOCKTON-ON-TEES NZ4217

☆ *Masham* [Hartburn, southern outskirts]: Four small rooms each with its own character, from black and gold flock wallpaper to panelling, with showy chandeliers; well kept Black Sheep Special, good cheap baps, sandwiches and hot meals (not Sat-Sun evenings), keen dominoes players, occasional live music; garden with aviary and play area backing on to paddock, open all day, nr end of Castle Eden walkway *(JHBS)*

Sun [Knowles St]: Friendly town local specialising in particularly well kept Bass, well served at tempting price; folk night Mon, open all day *(the Didler)*

SUNDERLAND NZ3857

Kings Arms [Beach St, Deptford]: Chatty early 19th-c pub with several areas around central high-backed bar, well kept Timothy Taylors Landlord and half a dozen changing ales from small breweries, two coal fires, easy chairs and lots of dark wood, food Weds-Sun evenings *(Tom and Alison Lynn, Martin Grosberg)*

Saltgrass [Hanover Pl, Deptford]: Relaxed Victorian pub opp former James Laing shipyard, enjoyable interesting food in dining lounge on left, well kept changing ales such as Bass, Greene King Abbot, Marstons Pedigree and Timothy Taylors Landlord, decent wines, nautical-theme bar with good coal fire; open all day Fri-Sun *(Tom and Alison Lynn, Martin Grosberg)*

TYNEMOUTH NZ3668

Tynemouth Lodge [Tynemouth Rd (A193), ½ mile W of Tynemouth Metro station]: Genuine-feeling little Victorian-style pub (actually older), very popular for particularly well kept Bass, Belhaven 80/-, Caledonian Deuchars IPA and a guest beer, farm cider, decent wines, cheap lunchtime filled rolls, coal fire; quiet on wkdy afternoons, can be packed and smoky evenings, and is very decidedly a local; no dogs or children; open all day, tables in back garden *(LYM, Kevin Thorpe)*

WARDEN NY9166

Boatside [½ mile N of A69]: Extended dining pub decorated in light warm colours, good range of bar food using fresh ingredients from soup, filled rolls and steak pie to steaks, friendly attentive service, Courage Directors and Theakstons, interesting bric-a-brac and World War II memorabilia, restaurant and smaller dining room; small neat enclosed garden, arractive spot by Tyne bridge *(Bruce Field, Mart Lawton)*

WARKWORTH NU2506

Masons Arms [Dial Pl]: Thriving village pub, quick friendly helpful service, good value generous home-made food inc fish and bargain lunch, well kept beers, good coffee and wine choice, local pictures; dogs welcome, attractive back flagstoned courtyard *(Robert M Warner, A and B D Craig, A C English)*

WEST AUCKLAND NZ1726

Eden Arms [Staindrop Rd (A688/A68)]: Generous food from wide sandwich choice to promptly served straightforward hot dishes in large neatly kept bar and dining area, welcoming staff, Camerons and a guest beer, pale wood furnishings; nice spot at top of pretty village's green *(Edward and*

Deanna Pearce)

WEST BOLDON NZ3561

Black Horse [Rectory Bank, just off A184]: Locally popular dining pub with good range of tasty food in bar and big restaurant inc good Sun lunch, a couple of well kept ales such as Darwen Ghost, cheerful attentive staff, Victorian décor with beamery, lots of brass, large tiles, log-effect gas fire, pictures and ornaments *(John Foord)*

WHALTON NZ1281

Beresford Arms: Attractive creeper-clad dining pub particularly popular with older people for genuine straightforward home cooking at reasonable prices, friendly helpful staff, well kept real ales, three linked rooms, antlers and stags' heads; keg beers; pretty village *(Michael Doswell)*

WHORLTON NZ1014

Bridge Inn: Comfortable and individual old stone-built pub, well kept changing guest beers such as Greene King Ruddles County and Theakstons Old Peculier, friendly service, interesting menu, comfortable couches and settles in bar, separate back barn restaurant *(Andrew York)*

WYLAM NZ1265

☆ *Boathouse* [Station Rd; across Tyne from village, handy for Newcastle—Carlisle rail line]: Warm and comfortable riverside pub, friendly and well run, with local Wylam and lots of other reasonably priced changing ales from small northern breweries, always one at great bargain price, good choice of malt whiskies, cheap lunchtime sandwiches, early evening pizzas, kebabs, curries etc, clean bright low-beamed lounge with roaring woodburner, evening dining room (and for popular Sun lunch); poor disabled access; children welcome, Sat afternoon impromptu folk/blues sessions, small garden, open and busy all day *(John Foord, Mr and Mrs Maurice Thompson, Michael Doswell, Jenny and Brian Seller, Clare and Peter Pearse, Richard Houghton, G Coates)*

WYNYARD NZ4126

Stables: Looks old but in fact late 20th-c, two wood-floored rooms with sporting pictures, enjoyable food in bar and (evenings and wknds) restaurant, Courage Directors and Marstons Pedigree; handy for Castle Eden Walkway, open all day *(JHBS)*

Real ale may be served from handpumps, electric pumps (not just the on-off switches used for keg beer) or – common in Scotland – tall taps called founts (pronounced 'fonts') where a separate pump pushes the beer up under air pressure. The landlord can adjust the force of the flow – a tight spigot gives the good creamy head that Yorkshire lads like.

Nottinghamshire

Pubs on top form here these days are the chatty Victoria in Beeston (good food and a great range of drinks), the Caunton Beck in Caunton (good food all day in this civilised dining pub), the Black Horse going its own distinctive way at Caythorpe (enjoyable food with its own Caythorpe beers, also available elsewhere), the cheerful Waggon & Horses in Halam (good often inventive cooking at very approachable prices), the cheerfully family-run Nelson & Railway opposite Hardys & Hansons brewery in Kimberley (quite a favourite all-rounder, good value), and the Dovecote at Laxton (gaining a Stay Award this year, alongside its good food and friendly service). There's a splendid choice of good pubs in Nottingham itself, which is a great place for good beer and cheap food. For a special meal out the Caunton Beck at Caunton is – for the third year running – still unchallenged as Nottinghamshire Dining Pub of the Year. In the Lucky Dip section at the end of the chapter, this year's favourites are the Horse & Plough in Bingham, Beehive at Maplebeck, Red Lion at Thurgarton, French Horn at Upton, Stratford Haven in West Bridgford and Star at West Leake. Drinks prices in the county are generally far lower than the national average, with half the pubs in our survey still charging under £2 a pint for beer. Pubs brewing their own, particularly Fellows Morton & Clayton in Nottingham, offer outstanding value here, and Castle Rock (supplied to all the pubs in the small local Tynemill group, among others) is a bargain beer. The main local brewer to look out for is Hardys & Hansons, and others you may easily come across include Mallard, Springhead, Nottingham, Alcazar and Maypole.

BEESTON SK5338 Map 7

Victoria

Dovecote Lane, backing on to railway station

'Well worth missing a few trains for' is what one reader said about this down to earth but welcoming converted railway hotel, which carries an impressive choice of drinks and serves very enjoyable food. The lounge and bar back on to the railway station, and a covered heated area outside has tables overlooking the platform, with trains passing just a few feet away. Three unpretentious downstairs rooms have kept their original long narrow layout, and have simple solid traditional furnishings, very unfussy décor, stained-glass windows, stripped woodwork and floorboards (woodblock in some rooms), newspapers to read, and a chatty atmosphere; dominoes, cribbage. A lively time to visit is during their two-week beer and music festival at the end of July. There's usually an impressive range of 12 very well kept real ales, including Bass, a Batemans beer, Castle Rock Hemlock and Nottingham Gold and Everards Tiger, alongside widely sourced changing guests from brewers such as Adnams, Cotleigh, Exmoor, Newby Wyke, Oakham and St Austell; they've also continental draught beers, farm ciders, over 100 malt whiskies, 20 irish whiskeys, and even over two dozen wines by the glass. Very fairly priced and really tasty dishes (the landlord does the cooking) are listed on a daily changing blackboard, and might include filled rolls (from £1.80), pâté (£4.75), shepherd's pie or very tasty lincolnshire sausages (£6.50), roast pork, vegetable burritos or pasta (£6.95) and home-made puddings from (£2.95). Parking is limited and readers have warned us about active parking wardens in the area. *(Recommended by Michael Doswell,*

Sue Holland, Dave Webster, Darly Graton, Graeme Gulibert, the Didler, Paul and Ann Meyer, JP, PP, Andy and Jill Kassube, Andy and Ali, C J Fletcher, Tony Hobden, David Eberlin, John and Wendy Allin, P and E Kenyon, Andy and Ali)

Free house ~ Licensees Neil Kelso and Graham Smith ~ Real ale ~ Bar food (12-8.45(7.45 Sun)) ~ (0115) 925 4049 ~ Children in dining area till 8pm ~ Dogs allowed in bar ~ Live music Sun and jazz Mon evenings Sept-May ~ Open 11-11; 12-10.30 Sun

CAUNTON SK7460 Map 7

Caunton Beck

Main Street; village signposted off A616 Newark—Ollerton

Nottinghamshire Dining Pub of the Year

Almost new, but not new-looking, this delightfully civilised dining pub was reconstructed using original timbers and reclaimed oak, around the skeleton of the old Hole Arms. Scrubbed pine tables, clever lighting, an open fire and country-kitchen chairs, low beams and rag-finished paintwork in a spacious interior make for a relaxed atmosphere. With lots of flowers and plants in summer, the terrace is a nice place to sit when the weather is fine. Its main focus is on the good well presented (though not cheap) food, which is served all day. As well as delicious sandwiches (from £5.50) and a hearty english breakfast (£7.95), the fairly elaborate monthly changing menu might include starters such as soup (£4.50), oatmeal crusted sardines with truffle wilted rocket and parmesan (£5.95), confit of duck wrapped in parma ham with red onion marmalade (£6.95), main courses such as lemon and thyme chicken breast (£11.95), rib-eye steak with parsley crust or roast red mullet with sesame egg noodles, bok choi and plum sauce (£13.95) and puddings such as orange panna cotta or chocolate brownie with maple syrup anglaise (£4.75). They also do reasonably priced two- and three-course set menus (£11/£13.95, not Saturday evenings or lunchtime Sunday); no smoking restaurant. About half the wines on the very good wine list are available by the glass, and they've well kept Greene King Ruddles Best, Springhead, Marstons Pedigree and a guest such as Castle Rock on handpump; also espresso coffee. Service is pleasant and attentive; daily papers and magazines, no music. *(Recommended by Derek and Sylvia Stephenson, Stephen Woad, David and Ruth Hollands, JP, PP, June and Malcolm Farmer, Fred and Lorraine Gill, Richard Cole, Michael Doswell, Alison Hayes, Pete Hanlon, Comus and Sarah Elliott, David and Helen Wilkins, Ray and Winifred Halliday, R F Ballinger, Richard Marjoram, Joyce and Geoff Robson, Adrian White)*

Free house ~ Licensees Julie Allwood and Toby Hope ~ Real ale ~ Bar food (8am-10.30pm) ~ Restaurant ~ (01636) 636793 ~ Children in eating area of bar and restaurant ~ Dogs allowed in bar ~ Open 8am-12 midnight

CAYTHORPE SK6845 Map 7

Black Horse

Turn off A6097 450 metres SE of roundabout junction with A612, NE of Nottingham; into Gunthorpe Road, then right into Caythorpe Road and keep on

Unchanging from one edition of the *Guide* to the next, this quaint little 300-year-old country local has been run by the same family for many years. The timelessly uncluttered carpeted bar has just four tables, with brocaded wall banquettes and settles, a few bar stools hosting cheerful evening regulars, a warm woodburning stove, decorative plates on a delft shelf and a few horsebrasses on the ceiling joists. The landlady herself serves the tasty Caythorpe Dover Beck which is brewed here and is well kept alongside two changing guest beers such as Brewsters Hop Head and Greene King Abbot. Off the front corridor is a partly panelled inner room with a wall bench running right the way around three unusual long copper-topped tables, and quite a few old local photographs; down on the left an end room has just one huge round table, and a cabinet of sports trophies. Food is very enjoyable (you may need to book in the evening), and there's a fair emphasis on fresh fish. Dishes might include soup (£2), prawn cocktail (£3.25), dim sum (£3.50), king prawns in garlic and cream sauce (£4.75), fried cod, haddock or plaice (£6 at lunchtime, £7 in the evening), seafood salad (£8.85), fillet steak (£11.50) and puddings such as banana ice-cream cake and sticky toffee pudding (from £2.50). There are some plastic tables outside, and the River Trent is fairly close, for waterside walks. *(Recommended by the Didler, JP, PP, R and M Tait, Derek and Sylvia Stephenson, W M Paton)*

Own brew ~ Licensee Sharron Andrews ~ Real ale ~ Bar food (not Sat evening, Sun or Mon) ~ Restaurant ~ No credit cards ~ (0115) 966 3520 ~ Dogs allowed in bar ~ Open 12-2.30, 5(6 Sat)-11; 12-4 7(8 winter)-10.30 Sun; closed Mon exc bank hols

COLSTON BASSETT SK7033 Map 7

Martins Arms 🍷 🍺

Village signposted off A46 E of Nottingham; School Lane, near market cross in village centre

The elaborate food at this smart country dining pub is not cheap but readers are happy with the quality and feel it's worth the prices. Service is formal and neatly uniformed, and it's the sort of place where they expect you to pay for bottled water rather than have tap water. If you choose to eat in the elegant no smoking restaurant, which is smartly decorated with period fabrics and colourings, you really are getting into serious dining. As well as lunchtime sandwiches (from £4.75), imaginative dishes served in the bar could include starters such as soup (£4.75), confit of pheasant leg with olives, tarragon and game liquor (£7.95) or seared scallops, braised leek and smoked bacon tartlet with minted pea purée (£8.95) and main courses such as ploughman's or salad of black figs with halloumi cheese and tomato confit (£9.75), tagliatelle with white crab, lemon spinach and pesto (£12), venison pie (£16.95), roast cod with truffled stew of haricot beans (£18.95), side orders of vegetables (£4.50) and puddings such as chocolate and orange soufflé cake (£5.50). Antique furnishings, hunting prints and warm log fires in the Jacobean fireplaces give an upmarket air to the comfortable bar, and there's a proper no smoking snug. Seven well kept real ales on handpump include Adnams, Bass, Greene King IPA, Marstons Pedigree and Timothy Taylors Landlord alongside guests from brewers such as Black Dog and St Austell; they've a good range of malt whiskies and cognacs and an interesting wine list; cribbage and dominoes. The sizeable attractive lawned garden backs on to estate parkland, but you might be asked to leave your credit card behind the bar if you want to eat out here. You can play croquet in summer, and they've converted the stables into an antiques shop. Readers recommend visiting the church opposite, and Colston Bassett Dairy just outside the village, which sells its own stilton cheese. *(Recommended by JP, PP, A C Nugent, the Didler, Gerry and Rosemary Dobson, Ian and Nita Cooper, Annette and John Derbyshire, Hugh Roberts, Tony and Betty Parker)*

Free house ~ Licensees Lynne Strafford Bryan and Salvatore Inguanta ~ Real ale ~ Bar food (12-2, 6-10; not Sun evenings) ~ Restaurant ~ (01949) 81361 ~ Children welcome ~ Open 12-3, 6(7 Sun)-11

ELKESLEY SK6975 Map 7

Robin Hood

High Street; village well signposted just off A1 Newark—Blyth

The good value set menu (two-course £10, three-course £12) at this friendly village local is good enough reason to take a break from the nearby A1. The pub's appearance is fairly low key but the neatly kept roomy carpeted dining room and lounge area are cheery with yellow walls between red ceilings and dado, and a pleasant mix of dark wood furniture; unobtrusive piped music. Good changing bar food might include sandwiches (from £3) and ploughman's (£5.80), starters such as caesar salad (£5.50) and salmon fishcakes (£6), main courses such as chicken curry (£8), mediterranean vegetable tart (£8.50), sausage and mash (£9) and grilled beef fillet with red wine sauce (£15.50) and puddings such as crème brûlée with raspberries or chocolate nut sundae (£4.30). One bar and the dining room are no smoking. Staff are friendly and efficient. Boddingtons, Flowers IPA and Marstons Pedigree are well kept on handpump. The garden (which is moderately well screened from the A1) has picnic-sets and a play area. *(Recommended by Peter Scillitoe, Fred and Lorraine Gill, D and M T Ayres-Regan, Gordon Tong, Stuart Paulley, Rita and Keith Pollard, Mrs Anthea Fricker, G A Hemingway, Jenny and Brian Seller, Mr and Mrs J E C Tasker, Mr and Mrs Broadhurst, Kevin Thorpe, Martin and Jane Bailey, A J Bowen, MJVK, Derek and Sylvia Stephenson, Joyce and Geoff Robson, Alison Hayes, Pete Hanlon)*

Enterprise ~ Lease Alan Draper ~ Real ale ~ Bar food (not Sun evening) ~ Restaurant ~ (01777) 838259 ~ Children welcome ~ Dogs allowed in bar ~ Open 11.30-2.30, 6.30-11; 12-3, 7-10.30 Sun

HALAM SK6754 Map 7

Waggon & Horses

Off A612 in Southwell centre, via Halam Road

This heavily oak-beamed dining pub is well liked for its wide choice of enjoyable and often inventive food: lunchtime rolls or baked potatoes with unusual fillings such as ham hock, stilton and apricot (from £3.95) and ploughman's (£6.50), as well as starters such as wild mushroom and fennel soup with crème fraîche and blue cheese croûton (£3.50), fried squid with parma ham and rocket and pesto salad (£5.50) and main courses such as broad bean, cherry tomato and rocket risotto (£8), battered cod loin stuffed with prawn and garlic butter with pea purée (£12), rib-eye steak topped with stilton with port and shallot sauce (£12.50). The bright and cheery open-plan area is well divided into smallish sections (an appealing black iron screen dividing off the no smoking part is made up of tiny african-style figures of people and animals). Good sturdy high-back rush-seat dining chairs are set around a mix of solid mainly stripped tables, there are various wall seats, smaller chairs and the odd stout settle too, with lots of pictures ranging from kitten prints to Spy cricketer caricatures on walls painted cream, brick red and coffee; candles throughout give a pleasant night-time glow. Well kept Thwaites Original Bitter, Thoroughbred and Lancaster Bomber well kept on handpump; piped jazz. Out past a piano and grandfather clock in the lobby are a few roadside picnic-sets by the pretty window boxes. *(Recommended by Colin Fisher, Derek and Sylvia Stephenson, Alan Thwaite, B Clayton, CMW, JJW, Phil and Jane Hodson, W M Paton)*

Thwaites ~ Tenants Rebecca and William White ~ Real ale ~ Bar food (12-2.30, 6-9.30; not Sun evening) ~ Restaurant ~ (01636) 813109/816228 ~ Children welcome ~ Dogs welcome ~ Open 12-3, 5.30-11; 12-11 Sat; 12-10.30 Sun

KIMBERLEY SK5044 Map 7

Nelson & Railway £

1¾ miles from M1 junction 26; at exit roundabout take A610 towards Ripley, then signposted Kimberley, pub in Station Road

As popular and cheery as ever, this spotlessly kept two-roomed Victorian pub has been in the same family for over 30 years. Chatty locals enjoy the snugly beamed bar and lounge (recently freshened up) which have a mix of Edwardian-looking furniture, with interesting brewery prints and railway signs on the walls. At one time there were two competing stations within yards of the pub, and its name comes from a shortening of its original title the Lord Nelson Railway Hotel. The Hardys & Hansons brewery is directly opposite, and they've well kept Kimberley and Olde Trip and a seasonal ale on handpump; darts, alley and table skittles, dominoes, chess, cribbage, Scrabble, fruit machine, juke box and piped music. Good value straightforward but satisfying bar food includes soup (£1.60), sandwiches (from £1.50), hot rolls (from £1.70), breaded chicken goujons (£2.90), cottage pie (£3.40), ploughman's (£4.90), steak and kidney pie (£5.20), mushroom stroganoff (£5.30), scampi (£5.70) and puddings such as fruit crumble or chocolate fudge cake (£1.90); the area adjacent to the lounge is no smoking. There are tables and swings out in a good-sized cottagey garden and this is a handy break from the M1. *(Recommended by Roger and Jenny Huggins, Bernie Adams, JP, PP, Roger Noyes,*

Derek and Sylvia Stephenson, Pat and Derek Roughton, Pete Baker, Dr and Mrs A K Clarke, Brenda and Rob Fincham, Ian Phillips, Andrew York, Patrick Hancock)

Hardys & Hansons ~ Tenants Mick and Harry Burton ~ Real ale ~ Bar food (12-2.30, 5.30-9; 12-6 Sun) ~ Restaurant ~ (0115) 938 2177 ~ Children in restaurant ~ Dogs allowed in bar ~ Open 11.30-11; 12-10.30 Sun ~ Bedrooms: £29.95S/£46.95S

LAXTON SK7267 Map 7

Dovecote

Signposted off A6075 E of Ollerton

You will need to book a table if you want to eat at this very welcoming redbrick free house, which manages to maintain a pubby atmosphere, despite the popularity of the food. The very friendly courteous service, buzzing atmosphere and honestly priced enjoyable food are what make it such an agreeable place – and it's usefully close to the A1. Served in big helpings, bar food includes soup (£3.25), sandwiches and baguettes (from £3.50), steak and kidney pie (£6.99), mushroom stroganoff (£7.50) and sweet and sour battered chicken (£8.99), with specials such as chicken and mushroom cream pie (£7.99), battered cod (£8.99) and bass stuffed with prawns (£9.99). The puddings, such as cheesecake (£3.25), are made by Aunty Mary, the landlord's aunt, who lives in the village. The central lounge has dark wheelback chairs and tables on wooden floors, and a coal-effect gas fire. This opens through a small bay (the former entrance) into a carpeted no smoking dining area. Around the other side, another little lounge leads through to a pool room with darts, fruit machine, pool, dominoes and piped music. They have well kept Marstons Pedigree and a couple of guests from brewers such as Charles Wells and Wychwood on handpump and around ten wines by the glass. There are wooden tables and chairs on a small front terrace by a sloping garden, which has a disused white dovecote. As well as the two bedrooms, they have a site and facilities for six caravans. The pub stands next to three huge medieval open fields as Laxton is one of the few places in the country still farmed using the traditional open field system. Every year in the third week of June the grass is auctioned for haymaking, and anyone who lives in the parish is entitled to a bid – and a drink. You can find out more at the visitor centre behind the pub. *(Recommended by Keith and Chris O'Neill, JP, PP, Derek and Sylvia Stephenson, Dave and Sue Mitchell, Dr Michael Denton, Patrick Hancock, Richard Cole, W and P J Elderkin, Mr and Mrs D W Mitchell)*

Free house ~ Licensees Stephen and Betty Shepherd ~ Real ale ~ Bar food (12-2, 6.30 (7 Sun in winter)-9) ~ Restaurant ~ (01777) 871586 ~ Children in eating area of bar and restaurant ~ Dogs allowed in bar ~ Open 11.30-3, 6.30(6 Sat, 7 winter Sun)-11.30(10.30 Sun) ~ Bedrooms: £35B/£50B

MORTON SK7251 Map 7

Full Moon

Pub and village signposted off Bleasby—Fiskerton back road, SE of Southwell

As it's tucked away in a remote hamlet not far from the River Trent, arriving at this friendly dining pub makes a very pleasant little surprise. L-shaped and beamed, the main part has pink plush seats and cushioned black settles around a variety of pub tables, with wheelback chairs in the side dining area, and a couple of fireplaces. Fresh flowers and the very long run of Christmas plates on the walls add a spot of colour; look out for the two sociable pub cats. Charles Wells Bombardier, Dover Beck, Greene King Ruddles (which they call Full Moon) and a changing guest are well kept on handpump, and service is friendly; may be piped music. Lots of effort has gone into the garden which comprises a peaceful back terrace with picnic-sets, with more on a sizeable lawn, and some sturdy play equipment. Enjoyable food includes soup (£2.75), home-made pâté with cumberland sauce (£3.95), caesar salad (£7.50), steak and kidney pie or parsnip and chestnut bake (£8.25), salmon fillet with prawns (£9.25), lamb tagine (£9.50), mixed grill (£11.25) and puddings such as lemon brûlée or treacle sponge pudding (£3.95); two-course OAP bargain lunch (£6.50). *(Recommended by JP, PP, Derek and Sylvia Stephenson, the Didler,*

Andrew Stephenson, W W Burke, Ian and Nita Cooper, Patrick Hancock, Paul and Margaret Baker, David Glynne-Jones)

Free house ~ Licensees Clive and Kim Wisdom ~ Real ale ~ Bar food (12-2; 6.30-9.30 (10 Fri, Sat); 12-2.30, 7-9.30 Sun) ~ Restaurant ~ (01636) 830251 ~ Children welcome ~ Open 11-3, 6-11; 12-3, 7-10.30 Sun

NOTTINGHAM SK5640 Map 7

Bell £

Angel Row, off Market Square

Eight real ales at this quaint 15th-c pub (dwarfed by the office tower next door) include Hardys & Hansons Kimberley Bitter, Mild, Olde Trip and one or two of their seasonal brews, and a couple of guests from thoughtfully sourced brewers such as Bullmastiff and Mallard. These are well kept alongside about eight wines by the glass and quite a few malt whiskies; fruit machine and piped music. The building's venerable age is clearly evident throughout – some of the original timbers have been uncovered, and in the front Tudor bar you can see patches of 300-year-old wallpaper (protected by glass). This room is perhaps the brightest, with french windows opening (in summer) to tables on the street, and bright blue walls. The room with the most historical feel is the very pubby and sometimes quite smoky low-beamed Elizabethan Bar, with its half-panelled walls, maple parquet floor, and comfortable high-backed armchairs. Upstairs, at the back of the heavily panelled Belfry (usually open only at lunchtime, when it functions as a family restaurant), you can see the rafters of the 15th-c crown post roof, and you can look down on the busy street at the front. The cellars are about ten metres down in the sandstone rock – groups may be able to arrange tours. Reasonably priced straightforward bar food includes soup (£1.80), burgers (from £1.99), ploughman's (£3.99), breaded plaice or steak and kidney pudding (£4.99), red pepper and mushroom lasagne (£5.99) and puddings such as jam roly poly (£2.99) and lots of ice-cream sundaes (£3.79). *(Recommended by C J Fletcher, the Didler, Maggie and Tony Harwood, JP, PP, Ian and Nita Cooper, Doug Christian, Geoff Pidoux, Patrick Hancock)*

Hardys & Hansons ~ Manager Brian Rigby ~ Real ale ~ Bar food (10.30-8; 12-6 Sun) ~ Restaurant ~ (0115) 947 5241 ~ Children in restaurant ~ Dogs allowed in bar ~ Jazz Sun lunchtime, Mon, Tues evening ~ Open 10.30-11; 12-10.30 Sun

Fellows Morton & Clayton £

Canal Street (part of inner ring road)

This former canal warehouse was converted to a spacious pub over 30 years ago – the large decked terrace overlooking the water at the back is a great place for a relaxing drink. Inside, there's a buzzy town atmosphere in the softly lit bar, which has dark red plush seats built into alcoves, wooden tables, more seats up two or three steps in a side gallery, and bric-a-brac on the shelf just below the glossy dark green high ceiling; a sympathetic extension provides extra seating. Piped pop music, fruit machine, big TV, and a rack of daily newspapers; service is prompt and friendly. From a big window in the quarry-tiled glassed-in area at the back you can see the little brewery where they brew the tasty Samuel Fellows and Post Haste, which are served alongside Boddingtons, Castle Eden, Fullers London Pride, Timothy Taylor Landlord and a couple of guests such as Deuchars IPA and Mallard. Popular reasonably priced bar food might include soup (£2.75), bean and vegetable hotpot with herb dumplings (£5.90), fish and chips (£5.95), beef burger (£6.95), lamb and vegetable stew (£7.45) and salmon with peppercorns and spiced yoghurt (£10.50); no smoking restaurant. At lunchtime it's popular with local workers, while in the evenings (when it can get smoky) you'll find a younger set. *(Recommended by JP, PP, C J Fletcher, Rona Murdoch, Derek and Sylvia Stephenson, the Didler, Patrick Hancock)*

Own brew ~ Licensees Les Howard and Keely Willans ~ Real ale ~ Bar food (12-9) ~ Restaurant ~ (0115) 950 6795 ~ Children in restaurant ~ Live music Friday ~ Open 11 (12 Sun)-11(12 Sat)

Lincolnshire Poacher £

Mansfield Road; up hill from Victoria Centre

Typical of the inns in this great little chain, this popular two room pub has a bustling atmosphere, stocks an impressive range of drinks and serves good value tasty food. About a dozen real ales include Batemans XB and XXXB, Castle Rock Poachers Gold and Harvest Pale and Oakham JHB, which are well kept alongside guests from a wide range of brewers such as Anglo Dutch Buffys, Newby Wyke, Oldershaws and Wye Valley, continental draught and bottled beers, good farm cider, around 80 malt whiskies and ten irish ones, and very good value soft drinks. Bar food includes hummous and olives (£2.95) ploughman's (£3.25), goats cheese bruschetta (£3.75), potato and halloumi roast (£4.95), sausage and mash or pork in cream and cider (£5.50), warm chicken salad (£5.75), a couple of daily specials such as moroccan lamb tagine (£5.50) and lamb madras (£5.75). Also Friday evening fish specials such as italian baked cod (£5.25) and Sunday roast (£6.25). The traditional big wood-floored front bar has wall settles, plain wooden tables and breweriana. It opens on to a plain but lively room on the left, with a corridor that takes you down to the chatty panelled back snug, with newspapers, cribbage, dominoes, cards and backgammon; piped music; no smoking area. It can get very busy in the evening, when it's popular with a younger crowd. A conservatory overlooks tables on a large terrace behind. *(Recommended by JP, PP, Doug Christian, the Didler, Patrick Hancock)*

Tynemill ~ Manager David Whitaker ~ Real ale ~ Bar food (12-3(4 Sun); 5-8(7 Fri, Sat); not Sun evening) ~ (0115) 941 1584 ~ Children in conservatory till 8pm ~ Dogs allowed in bar ~ Open 11-11; 12-10.30 Sun

Olde Trip to Jerusalem ★ £

Brewhouse Yard; from inner ring road follow The North, A6005 Long Eaton signpost until you are in Castle Boulevard, then almost at once turn right into Castle Road; pub is up on the left

Probably quite unlike any other pub you'll visit (and people do make a crusade of coming here), parts of this ancient pub are built into caverns burrowed into the sandstone rock below the castle. The siting of the current building is attributed to the days when a brewhouse was established here to supply the needs of the castle above, and the name is a reference to the 12th-c crusaders who used to meet on this site on their way to the Holy Land. The panelled walls of the unusual upstairs bar (thought to have served as cellarage for that earlier medieval brewhouse) soar narrowly into a dark cleft above and, also mainly carved from the rock, the downstairs bar has leatherette-cushioned settles built into dark panelling, tables on flagstones, and snug banquettes built into low-ceilinged rock alcoves; there's also a no smoking parlour/snug, and two more caves open to visitors. Staff cope well with the busy mix of tourists, conversational locals and students. They keep their real ales in top condition, and you'll find Hardys & Hansons Kimberley Best and Mild and Olde Trip alongside guests such as Kelham Island Pale Rider and York Yorkshire Terrier on handpump. Attractively priced straightforward bar food includes soup (£1.20), a very good chip butty (£1.80), sandwiches (from £1.99), burgers (from £2.29), giant filled yorkshire pudding, liver and bacon, steak and ale pie or cod and chips (£4.99), scampi (£5.29) and rump steak (£5.99), with puddings (from £1.99). They've ring the bull and a fruit machine, and there are some seats in a small courtyard. *(Recommended by Richard Fendick, Kevin Blake, Rona Murdoch, the Didler, CMW, JJW, Peter F Marshall, JP, PP, Joe Green, Hugh Roberts, Bernie Adams, Doug Christian, Mike and Mary Carter, Geoff Pidoux, John and Wendy Allin, Patrick Hancock)*

Hardys & Hansons ~ Manager Karen Ratcliffe ~ Real ale ~ Bar food (10-6) ~ (0115) 9473171 ~ Children allowed until 7pm ~ Live music and storytelling nights monthly ~ Open 10-11(10.30 Sun); 11-11; 12-10.30 Sun winter

Tipping is not normal for bar meals, and not usually expected.

Pit & Pendulum

Victoria Street

This theatrical theme place is worth seeing for its entertaining gothic horror-film décor. Dark and dramatic, it's lit by heavy chandeliers and (electronically) flaring torches, with flashes of colour from an overhead tangle of Frankenstein-laboratory glass tubing and wiring. Dark seating runs from gothick thrones to spooky red-padded side booths with a heavy bat's-wing hint, tables are inset with ancient documents and arcane jewellery – even the cups and saucers have a spider's web design (the coffee is good). There is plenty of ghoulish carving and creeping ivy, and old horror movies run in silence on the TV above the bar counter – where a tortuous web of piping replaces the usual beer taps. Good wheelchair ramps add cleverly to the design, with their curves and heavy black balusters, and the disabled lavatory is through a false bookcase. Downstairs (and that is indeed a shackled skeleton looming through the distorted glass) there's more of the same, with clearly separated areas, and some more conventional seating; well reproduced piped music, fruit machine and friendly staff. Bar food includes pizza ciabatta (£2.80), frogs legs (£3.75), burgers (from £4.50), coriander chicken or brie and broccoli bake (£6.40) and puddings such as apple pie or cinnamon waffles (£2.75); more reports please. *(Recommended by Kevin Blake)*

Scottish Courage ~ Tenant Ian Povey ~ Bar food (during full opening hours) ~ (0115) 950 6383 ~ Open 11-11; 12-10.30 Sun

Vat & Fiddle £

Queens Bridge Road, alongside Sheriffs Way (near multi-storey car park)

Down to earth, chatty and relaxed, the fairly functional open-plan interior of this plain brick pub has quite a strong 1930s feel, with cream and navy walls and ceiling, varnished pine tables and bentwood stools and chairs on parquet and terrazzo flooring, patterned blue curtains, and some brewery memorabilia. Also magazines and newspapers to read, piped music some of the time, a quiz machine and sports events on terrestrial TV. The three or four Castle Rock beers here are kept in very good condition (as one would expect given that the pub is right next to the brewery) and served alongside interesting guests from brewers such as Abbeydale, Big Lamp, Kelham Island, Newby Wyke and Oakham; occasional beer festivals. They also have around 65 malt whiskies, farm cider, continental bottled beers and several polish vodkas; good value soft drinks too. Bar food consists of rolls (from £1.60), chilli (£3.75) and sausage and mash (£4.25). A back terrace has picnic-sets, with more out in front by the road; the train and bus stations are both just a short walk away. *(Recommended by Richard Lewis, JP, PP, the Didler, C J Fletcher, Tony and Wendy Hobden, Joe Green, Patrick Hancock)*

Tynemill ~ Manager Bob Gregory ~ Real ale ~ Bar food (12-3, 6-8, not Sun evening) ~ (0115) 985 0611 ~ Dogs allowed in bar ~ Open 11-11; 12-10.30 Sun

WALKERINGHAM SK7792 Map 7

Three Horse Shoes

High Street; just off A161, off A631 W of Gainsborough

The astonishing floral displays that envelop the exterior of this white painted pub are regular award winners. In summer the green-fingered landlord uses thousands of plants to put on a spectacular show of blazing hanging baskets and tubs. The japanese-style garden up by the top car park is well worth a look too. Inside is simple with old-fashioned décor, and well kept Bass, Stones, Worthington Best and a guest beer such as Wychwood Hobgoblin on handpump; also darts, dominoes, fruit machine, video game, and piped music. Served by cheerfully welcoming staff, a good choice of enjoyable food is listed on blackboards, and could include sandwiches (£1.95), soup (£2.50), fried mushrooms stuffed with garlic cheese or pâté (£3.75), steak pie or mushroom, cheese, leek and nut pie (£6.95), gammon and pineapple (£7.50), chicken with indian spices or salmon marinated in mint with pink peppercorn and mint glaze (£6.75), sirloin steak (£9.50) and puddings such as sticky toffee pudding (£2.50). *(Recommended by JP, PP, Derek and Sylvia Stephenson, Stephen Woad)*

Free house ~ Licensee John Turner ~ Real ale ~ Bar food (till 9.30 Fri, Sat; not Sun evening or Mon) ~ Restaurant ~ (01427) 890959 ~ Children welcome ~ Open 11-3, 6-11; 12-4, 7-10.30 Sun

LUCKY DIP

Besides the fully inspected pubs, you might like to try these Lucky Dips recommended to us and described by readers (if you do, please send us reports: www.goodguides.co.uk).

ARNOLD SK5845
Burnt Stump [Burntstump Hill]: Large Mansfield pub with food emphasis, good wide choice, lots of deals, two real ales, no smoking area; pool, piped music, machines; children welcome, picnic-sets on terrace *(CMW, JJW)*

AWSWORTH SK4844
Gate [Main St, via A6096 off A610 Nuthall—Eastwood bypass]: Friendly old traditional local with Hardys & Hansons Best and Mild, coal fire in lounge, small pool room; nr site of once-famous railway viaduct – photographs in passage *(the Didler, JP, PP)*

BAGTHORPE SK4751
Dixies Arms [2 miles from M1 junction 27; A608 towards Eastwood, then first right on to B600 via Sandhill Rd, then first left into School Rd; Lower Bagthorpe]: New licensees doing well in quaint 18th-c beamed and tiled-floor local, three well kept real ales, entrance bar with tiny snug next to bar, small part-panelled parlour with fine fireplace, longer narrow room with toby jugs and darts; unobtrusive fruit machine, rarely used juke box; big garden with play area and football pitch, own pigeon, gun and morris dancing clubs; open 2-11, all day wknds *(the Didler, JP, PP)*

BINGHAM SK7039
☆ *Horse & Plough* [off A52; Long Acre]: Low beams, flagstones and stripped brick, prints and old brewery memorabilia, comfortable open-plan seating inc pews, good value generous lunchtime baguettes, melts, baked potatoes and three or four hot dishes, landlord happy to discuss his well kept Caledonian Deuchars IPA, Charles Wells Bombardier and four guest beers inc a Mild (tasters offered), good wine choice, popular upstairs grill room (Tues-Sat, and Sun lunch – bargain steaks Tues-Weds) with polished boards, hand-painted murals and open kitchen; piped music may be loud; open all day *(the Didler, JP, PP, BB, Hugh Roberts, Andrew Crawford)*

BLEASBY SK7149
Waggon & Horses [Gypsy Lane]: Comfortable banquettes in country pub's carpeted lounge, coal fire in character bar, Banks's and Marstons Pedigree, good value fresh lunchtime food from snacks up, Fri fish and chips night, chatty landlord; piped music; back lobby with play area and comfortable chairs to watch over it, tables outside, small camping area behind *(JP, PP, the Didler)*

BRINSLEY SK4649
☆ *Yew Tree* [Cordy Lane]: Large well appointed pub with good choice of nicely presented food inc good Thurs fresh fish, well kept Hardys & Hansons ales, good friendly service, lots of copper and brass and coal fire in attractive lounge, restaurant *(Derek and Sylvia Stephenson)*

CHILWELL SK5135
Cadland [High Rd]: Comfortably relaxed well divided open-plan pub with well kept Bass, M&B Mild, Worthington 1744 and guest beers, good value enjoyable food all day, open fires, friendly staff; Mar beer festival, quiz night; open all day *(the Didler)*

CLAYWORTH SK7288
Blacksmiths Arms [Town St]: Neat, bright and well furnished, with good choice of beers and wines, enjoyable bar food, open fire, big comfortable restaurant *(Stephen Woad)*

COLLINGHAM SK8362
Grey Horse [Low St]: Enjoyable reasonably priced food inc children's all week; tables outside with play area *(David and Ruth Hollands)*

COSSALL SK4843
Gardeners [Awsworth Lane]: Neatly kept open-plan local with cheap well kept Hardys & Hansons Bitter, Mild and seasonal beers, good value lunchtime food, end games area with pool and sports TV, quiz nights *(the Didler)*

CROPWELL BISHOP SK6835
Wheatsheaf [off A46 E of Nottingham]: Comfortable village local with two neat lounge areas, well kept Banks's ales such as Riding and Mansfield Cask, simple snacks; public bar with darts (also TV and juke box), pool in games room beyond *(Tony and Wendy Hobden)*

EASTWOOD SK4846
Foresters Arms [Main St, Newthorpe]: Village local with Hardys & Hansons on electric pump, cosy lounge with piano sing-along wknds, old local photographs in bar with darts, dominoes and TV; nice garden, occasional barbecues *(the Didler)*

EDWINSTOWE SK6266
Forest Lodge [Church St]: Friendly, with an open fire and good range of reasonably priced home-made food *(R and M Tait)*

EPPERSTONE SK6548
Cross Keys [Main St]: Recently refurbished

two-bar village pub, comfortable lounge/eating area, reasonably priced home-cooked food (not Sun evening) inc bargain OAP wkdy lunch, prompt careful service, well kept Hardys & Hansons beers, good value house wine; pretty village, pleasant countryside *(Colin Fisher, David Glynne-Jones)*

FARNSFIELD SK6456

Plough [E end]: Attractive L-shaped beamed lounge, good value lunchtime and (not wknds) early evening food inc good Sun roasts, well kept Mansfield beers with a guest Mild, good fireplace; may be quiet piped music, darts, pool, TV and video games, Mon quiz night; garden with play area, open all day wknds *(Kevin Blake, CMW, JJW, Gerry and Rosemary Dobson)*

GRANBY SK7436

Marquis of Granby [Dragon St]: Reopened 18th-c pub with two cosy rooms, beams and flagstones, half a dozen quickly changing guest beers alongside its regular local Brewsters Marquis, regular beer festivals, enjoyable fresh food from open kitchen; wheelchair access, open all day wknds, lovely village *(R Wilkins, the Didler)*

GUNTHORPE SK6843

Unicorn [Trentside]: Picturesque riverside setting, several family-oriented rooms inc smart panelled restaurant, well kept ales, wide range of good value food; busy with summer river trade; bedrooms *(Peter and Audrey Dowsett)*

HOVERINGHAM SK6946

Reindeer [Main St]: Comfortable low-beamed pub recently taken over by Tynemill, friendly and unpretentious, well kept changing real ales inc Castle Rock, decent fairly priced food, coal fires in bar and lounge, back restaurant; hatch for back cricket pitch *(the Didler)*

KIMBERLEY SK5044

Stag [Nottingham Rd]: Friendly 16th-c traditional local run by devoted landlady, two cosy rooms, small central counter and corridor, low beams, dark panelling and settles, well kept Adnams, Boddingtons, Marstons Pedigree, Timothy Taylors Landlord, Tetleys Mild and a guest beer, occasional beer festivals, vintage working penny slot machines and Shipstones brewery photographs; attractive back garden with play area, cl wkdy lunchtime (opens 5; 1.30 Sat, 12 Sun) *(B and H, JP, PP, the Didler)*

KIRKBY IN ASHFIELD SK5056

Countryman [Park Lane (B6018 S)]: New licensees still doing good value generous bar food (not Sun, Mon evening), with well kept Bass, Theakstons and usually guest beers, in thriving traditional pub with decorative plates, mining memorabilia and attractive bas relief shooting murals in cottagey beamed lounge bar; public bar with pool, live bands wknds; popular with walkers, play area, open all day *(Kevin Blake, JP, PP, the Didler)*

LINBY SK5351

Horse & Groom [Main St]: Friendly staff, four well kept local ales and wide choice of decent straightforward food (not Sun-Thurs evenings) in unpretentious pub with no piped music or mobile phones; big play area, attractive village nr Newstead Abbey *(Richard Naish, CMW, JJW)*

LOWDHAM SK6646

☆ ***Old Ship*** [nr A612/A6097; Main St]: Friendly beamed country pub with above-average imaginative blackboard food in extended lounge/bar, several areas up and down steps, comfortable furnishings from traditional built-in settles to plush banquettes, some big round tables, well kept John Smiths and a guest beer, friendly service, coal fire, lots of pictures, plates, copper and brass, separate public bar; quiz nights; picnic-sets on neat sheltered back lawn, bedrooms, pleasant walks nearby *(W M Paton, BB)*

Worlds End [Plough Lane]: Small beamed village pub under new licensee, up to five well kept ales, good soft drinks choice, popular reasonably priced food inc OAP lunches, log fire at one end, dining area the other, some original features; piped music, smoking allowed throughout; children welcome, good window boxes, picnic-sets in garden *(David and Phyllis Chapman, Alan Bowker, CMW, JJW)*

MANSFIELD SK5260

Bold Forester [Botany Ave/A38 junction]: Welcoming landlord in big 1930s pub with ten or so well kept ales such as Black Sheep, Boddingtons, Castle Eden, Greene King Abbot and Thwaites, good value food all day, no smoking area; terrace tables, open all day *(Tony Hobden)*

Nell Gwynne [A38 W of centre]: Former gentlemen's club, two changing ales, welcoming landlord, homely lounge with log-effect gas fire, old colliery plates and mementoes of old Mansfield pubs, games room; sports TV, 1960s piped music, Weds quiz night; cl Mon-Thurs lunchtimes, nearby parking can be difficult *(the Didler)*

Railway Inn [Station St; best approached by viaduct from nr market pl]: Friendly traditional pub with long-serving licensee, well kept attractively priced Batemans XB and a guest beer, bargain home-made lunches, divided main bar and separate room; handy for Robin Hood Line stn, normally open all day, cl Sun evening *(Pete Baker, the Didler)*

MANSFIELD WOODHOUSE SK5463

Greyhound [High St]: Quietly friendly two-room village local with Banks's Mansfield, Courage Directors, Everards Home, Theakstons Mild and a guest beer, darts, dominoes and pool; quiz nights Mon and Weds *(the Didler)*

MAPLEBECK SK7160

☆ ***Beehive*** [signed down pretty country lanes from A616 Newark—Ollerton and from A617 Newark—Mansfield]: Cosy and unspoiled beamed country tavern in nice spot, chatty landlady, tiny front bar, slightly bigger side room, traditional furnishings, coal or log fire, free antique juke box, well kept local Maypole and guest ales; tables on small terrace with flower tubs and grassy bank running down to little stream, play area with swings, barbecues;

no food, may be cl wkdy winter lunchtimes, very busy wknds and bank hols *(LYM, JP, PP, the Didler, Molly and Arthur Aldersey-Williams, Keith and Janet Morris)*

NEWARK SK7953

Castle & Falcon [London Rd]: Former coaching inn with local atmosphere, John Smiths and guest beers (may offer tasters), two bars and family conservatory, spacious games area with darts and pool; skittle alley, evening opening 7 *(the Didler)*

Fox & Crown [Appleton Gate]: Comfortably unpretentious Tynemill pub, separate areas inc no smoking back family part, stone or wood floors, big brewery mirrors and other breweriana, five well kept changing real ales, continental draught and bottled beers, Inch's cider, dozens of malt whiskies, flavoured vodkas, good coffee and choice of wines, fresh food from sandwiches up, friendly efficient staff; good wheelchair access, occasional live music, open all day *(the Didler, JP, PP)*

☆ *Mail Coach* [London Rd, nr Beaumond Cross]: Friendly open-plan Georgian local, relaxing at quiet times, with attractive décor in three candlelit separate areas, lots of chicken pictures, hot coal fires and comfortable chairs, well kept Boddingtons, Flowers IPA and Original and two or more local guest beers, enjoyable home-made lunchtime food (not Mon) inc some unusual dishes, pleasant staff; May beer festival, pub games, frequent live music Thurs, upstairs ladies'; tables on back terrace *(Kevin Blake, JP, PP, the Didler, Keith and Janet Morris)*

Navigation [Mill Gate]: Lively open-plan bar in converted warehouse, Everards Tiger and bar food, big windows on to River Trent, bare boards and iron pillars, nautical decorations *(David and Ruth Hollands)*

Old Malt Shovel [North Gate]: Welcoming and comfortably opened-up, with enjoyable food from doorstep sandwiches to some portuguese restaurant dishes, well kept Adnams Broadside, Caledonian Deuchars IPA, Timothy Taylors Landlord, Charles Wells Bombardier, Worthington 1744 and guest beers, open fire, choice of teas, lots of books and bottles on shelves, cheerfully laid-back atmosphere and service; pub games, skittle alley, wheelchair access, terrace tables *(the Didler)*

NEWSTEAD SK5252

Station Hotel [Station Rd]: Busy basic red-brick village local opp station on Robin Hood rail line, bargain well kept Barnsley Bitter and Robinsons Old Tom Mild, fine old railway photographs; no food Sun *(JP, PP, the Didler)*

NOTTINGHAM SK5139

Canal House [Canal St]: Big conversion of wharf building, bridge over indoors canal spur complete with narrowboat, lots of bare brick and varnished wood, huge joists on studded steel beams, long bar recently emphasising lagers (at least a couple of real ales too), good choice of house wines (two glass sizes), lots of standing room; good upstairs restaurant and second bar, masses of solid tables out on attractive waterside terrace; piped music (live Sun), popular with young people at night; open all day – till midnight Thurs, 1am Fri/Sat *(the Didler, JP, PP, BB)*

Coopers Arms [Porchester Rd, Thornywood]: Solid Victorian local with three unspoilt rooms, Theakstons real ales; small family room in skittle alley; cl Weds lunchtime *(JP, PP, the Didler)*

Falcon [Canning Circus/Alfreton Rd]: Two small rooms with old pictures and flame-effect fire in attractive fireplace, particularly well kept Adnams Bitter and Broadside and Charles Wells Bombardier, good choice of wines, enjoyable fresh food inc some interesting specials in pleasant upstairs restaurant; pavement tables and barbecues, open all day *(the Didler, JP, PP, Patrick Hancock)*

Forest [Mansfield Rd]: Tynemill pub with lots of belgian beers plus well kept Castle Rock Hemlock, Greene King Abbot, Woodfordes Wherry and a guest such as Batemans XB, enjoyable varied food all day, two smallish rooms knocked together, prints and beer posters on tiled and panelled walls; live music in back Maze lounge with late night licence; cl Mon-Tues lunchtime *(the Didler)*

Fox & Crown [Church St/Lincoln St, Old Basford]: Open-plan pine-décor local nr new tram stop, window to back microbrewery producing its own Alcazar Ale, Black Fox Mild, Nottingham Nog, New Dawn, Brush and Vixens Vice, brewery tours Sat, perhaps a guest from another pub brewery, good continental bottle choice; enjoyable fresh food from sandwiches to wide choice of early evening pizzas, helpful staff and Canadian landlord; good piped music, games machines, Tues quiz night, frequent beer festivals, big-screen sports TV; disabled access possible (lavatories difficult), tables out behind, open all day *(the Didler, JP, PP)*

Gladstone [Loscoe Rd, Carrington]: Thriving two-room local, four or five well kept ales inc a changing guest, cosy comfortable lounge with reading matter, basic bar with darts and sports TV; upstairs folk club Weds, quiz Thurs *(B and H, the Didler)*

Globe [London Rd]: Bright and airy roadside pub with enjoyable fresh food all day, consistently well kept Mallard, Nottingham, Oakham JHB and three changing guests, farm cider, coal fire; handy for cricket or football matches, open all day *(the Didler, Des and Jen Clarke)*

Horse & Groom [Radford Rd, New Basford]: Popular and well run partly open-plan local nr new tram stop and next to former Shipstones brewery, with their name over door and other memorabilia; well kept Bass, Belvoir Star, Courage Directors, Charles Wells Bombardier and guest beers from all over, nice snug, good value fresh food from sandwiches to Sun lunches, daily papers; jazz, folk, blues or skiffle nights Fri in converted back stables, midweek open mike night; open all day *(JP, PP, the Didler, Malcolm Taylor)*

☆ ***Lion*** [Lower Mosley St, New Basford]: Three or four Batemans ales and half a dozen interesting changing guest beers kept well in one of city's deepest cellars (glass viewing panel – and can be visited at quiet times), Broadstone farm cider, ten wines by the glass, wide choice of good value wholesome home-made food inc doorstep sandwiches and children's helpings; open plan but the feel of separate areas, bare bricks and polished dark oak boards, coal or log fires, daily papers; live music Fri-Sat, jazz Sun lunchtimes; nr new tram stop, well behaved children welcome, pleasant terrace with summer barbecues, open all day *(the Didler, JP, PP, Andrew Crawford)*

News House [Canal St]: Friendly two-room Tynemill pub with attractive blue exterior tiling, eight well kept changing ales inc bargain Castle Rock, belgian and czech imports on tap, Weston's Old Rosie farm cider, lots of flavoured vodkas, enjoyable fresh food inc Sun lunch, mix of bare boards and carpet, one room filled with local newspaper front pages spanning years of events and personalities; open all day *(C J Fletcher, JP, PP, the Didler)*

Old Moot Hall [Carlton Rd, Sneinton]: Newish pub with ten well kept and priced ales from small breweries, czech Budvar on tap, foreign bottled beers, farm cider, good wine choice, enjoyable wholesome food from fresh cobs up, polished boards, nice pictures, wooden furniture, coal-effect gas fire, upstairs bar; big-screen sports TV, Sun quiz night; open all day *(the Didler)*

Pitcher & Piano [High Pavement]: Remarkable lofty-roofed well converted church with enjoyable food, decent wines, well kept Marstons; the stained-glass windows show best in daylight (and it's very busy at night); open all day *(Geoff Pidoux)*

Playhouse Café Bar [Wellington Circus, nr Playhouse Theatre]: Pleasantly refurbished bar, restaurant and all-day deli attached to Playhouse theatre, reopened under new name (was the Limelight), good choice of well kept changing ales such as Adnams, Fullers London Pride, Mallard, Marstons Pedigree, Nottingham and Oakham (the handpumps hide below the counter), enjoyable fresh food (children allowed in restaurant area – the blue seats are no smoking), pleasant efficient staff, occasional live music; attractive continental-style outside seating area, open all day *(JP, PP, the Didler, G Coates)*

☆ ***Plough*** [St Peters St, Radford]: Unpretentious two-room local brewing its own interesting Nottingham ales, also a guest beer and farm ciders, good bargain food inc fresh rolls and popular Sun lunch (live jazz then), bargain curries Tues evening, may be free chilli Thurs evening, two coal fires, traditional fittings and nice windows, bar billiards and other traditional games (competitions Weds), Thurs irish music night; open all day Thurs-Sun *(the Didler, B and H, JP, PP)*

Royal Children [Castle Gate]: Open-plan, busy but relaxed, three basic but comfortable areas with bare boards, lots of panelling, old pictures, bric-a-brac inc whale shoulder-blade, converted gas lamps, brass water fountains on bar, four or five well kept ales such as Banks's Mansfield, Greene King Ruddles County and Youngers No 3, food inc baguettes, baked potatoes and speciality sausages, friendly staff *(Doug Christian, Martin Grosberg)*

Stick & Pitcher [University Boulevard, Dunkirk]: Tynemill pub next to city tennis courts and overlooking Highfields hockey club; comfortable upstairs modern bar with highly polished woodwork, three Castle Rock ales and usually two guests, enjoyable food, SkyTV sports; open all day *(the Didler)*

OLLERTON SK6567

Rose Cottage [Old Rufford Rd (A614)]: Attractive pub handy for Rufford Country Park, good range of beers inc Banks's Mansfield and Marstons Pedigree *(Richard Greenwood)*

ORSTON SK7741

Durham Ox [Church St]: Welcoming country local opp church, well kept Everards Home, Marstons Pedigree, John Smiths, Theakstons and a guest beer, good soft drinks choice, wine fresh from sensible small bottles, good value filled rolls (no hot food), comfortable split-level open-plan bar with roaring fire, interesting RAF/USAF memorabilia, collection of whisky bottles; may be piped music or TV; terrace tables, nice garden *(the Didler, JP, PP, CMW, JJW)*

PAPPLEWICK SK5450

Griffins Head [B683/B6011]: Main bar with log fire and cottagey room off, locals' bar, attractive candlelit raftered dining area with well, wide choice of decent food inc Sun carvery, three or four well kept ales inc Theakstons, daily papers; smoking allowed throughout, piped pop music (turned down on request), games machine in lobby; picnic-sets outside, barbecues, handy for Newstead Abbey *(CMW, JJW)*

RADCLIFFE ON TRENT SK6439

Black Lion [A52]: Good choice of good value food all day from beef cobs to full meals, well kept Courage Directors, Everards Home and three changing guest ales, Black Rat cider, reasonably priced soft drinks, big comfortable lounge, half no smoking, with small TVs, games machine and coal fire, friendly bar with pool and big-screen sports TV; Weds jazz upstairs twice a month, beer festivals; big enclosed garden, barbecues and play area, open all day *(the Didler, CMW, JJW, David Glynne-Jones)*

RAVENSHEAD SK5554

Hutt [A60 Nottingham—Mansfield]: Chef & Brewer with character softly lit rooms, alcoves and intimate areas, very wide choice of enjoyable food, well kept Courage Directors, Theakstons XB and an occasional guest beer; open all day *(David Glynne-Jones)*

RUDDINGTON SK5733

Victoria [off A60 S of Nottingham; Wilford Rd]: Pleasant village local with reasonably priced food from interesting baguettes to enjoyable sizzle dishes, well kept Bass and two guest beers such as Adnams, friendly and enthusiastic young licensees *(Derek and Sylvia Stephenson)*

SELSTON SK4553

Horse & Jockey [handy for M1 junctions 27/28; Church Lane]: Three carefully refurbished main rooms on three levels, cosy snug off lower bar area, low beams, flagstones and coal fire in cast-iron range, well kept Bass, Greene King Abbot, Timothy Taylors Landlord and other ales on handpump or in jugs direct from the cellar, good value bar lunches (not wknds) inc good fresh cobs and roasts, darts, bar billiards and pool in top room; open all day Sat *(the Didler, JP, PP, Derek and Sylvia Stephenson)*

SOUTH CLIFTON SK8270

Red Lion: Well kept Everards Home, John Smiths and two guest beers, reasonably priced food inc good pies and steaks, friendly licensees and atmosphere; juke box, sports TV, pool, quiz night, some live music; small garden *(David and Ruth Hollands)*

SOUTH LEVERTON SK7881

Plough [Town St]: Tiny pub doubling as morning post office, basic trestle tables and benches, real fire, Greene King Ruddles Best and a guest beer, traditional games, tables outside; open 2-11 (all day Sat, 12-4, 7-10.30 Sun) *(JP, PP, the Didler)*

SOUTHWELL SK6953

Bramley Apple [Church St (A612)]: Good value enjoyable food (not Sun evening) from simple lunch choice to more elaborate evening dishes, well kept Springhead and changing guest ales, farm cider, friendly attentive service, light and airy long bar with front room off; may be live music wknds, open all day Sat-Sun *(John Bramley, BB, the Didler, JP, PP, Richard Jennings, Tony and Wendy Hobden, W W Burke)*

Old Coaching House [Easthorpe]: Up to six changing well kept ales (with tasters) inc a Mild, summer farm cider, welcoming service, three roaring coal or log fires, bar billiards, shove-ha'penny and other traditional games, beams, old-world alcoves; terrace tables, cl wkdy lunchtimes, open all day wknds, handy for Minster and Workhouse *(the Didler, JP, PP, Joan and Tony Walker, Dr Brian and Mrs Anne Hamilton)*

Wheatsheaf [King St]: Two-bar pub with good value pubby food, well kept Greene King Ruddles and Marstons Pedigree; may be old piped music *(Keith and Janet Morris)*

STOKE BARDOLPH SK6441

Ferry Boat [off A612 in Burton Joyce; Riverside]: Large family dining pub in lovely spot overlooking River Trent, waterside picnic-sets, sheep, ducks, geese and swans opposite, several comfortable largely no smoking areas, lots of wood, copper, brass and ornaments, good choice of good value food inc wkdy lunchtime loyalty discounts for OAPs, two real ales, fair choice of wines, attentive service, daily papers (inc framed sheets in gents'); fruit machine, quiet piped music, Tues quiz night; open all day *(Peter and Jean Hoare)*

SUTTON IN ASHFIELD SK4757

Snipe [A38 bypass, towards Mansfield]: Roomy, convivial and well furnished family pub, good choice of reasonably priced food inc OAP discounts some days, quick service, well kept Hardys & Hansons Kimberley and Olde Trip, good coffee; unobtrusive piped music; play areas inside and out *(Nigel and Sue Foster)*

TEVERSAL SK4761

Teversal Grange [Carnarvon St/Skegby Rd]: Friendly upgraded former miners' welfare, now popular family pub with big restaurant and entertainment stage, family room with pool, other spacious rooms, good range of cheap food inc good baps and a roast of the day, well kept real ale, quick service; quiet piped music; nearby nature trails *(Peter and Audrey Dowsett)*

THURGARTON SK6949

☆ *Red Lion* [Southwell Rd (A612)]: Cheery 16th-c inn with consistently good freshly cooked food (all day Sat, Sun and bank hols) inc fresh fish and some adventurous dishes in brightly decorated split-level beamed bars and restaurant, lots of nooks and crannies, comfortable banquettes and other seating, smart friendly service, well kept ales inc Black Sheep and Mansfield, flame-effect fire, big windows to attractive good-sized two-level back garden with well spaced picnic-sets (dogs on leads allowed here); unobtrusive fruit machine, steepish walk back up to car park; children welcome, comfortable bedrooms *(Andrew Crawford, BB, David and Ruth Hollands, Phil and Jane Hodson)*

UNDERWOOD SK4751

Red Lion [Church Lane; off B600, nr M1 junction 27]: Character 17th-c split-level beamed village pub, spacious open-plan quarry-tiled bar with open fire, some cushioned settles, pictures and plates on dressers, good value family food inc OAP lunches, well kept Boddingtons, Marstons Pedigree and an interesting local guest beer, good friendly service, penny arcade machine, no piped music; children welcome, picnic-sets and large adventure playground in big garden with terrace and barbecues, attractive setting; open all day wknds *(JP, PP, the Didler, Kevin Blake)*

UPTON SK7354

☆ *French Horn* [A612]: Neatly comfortable open-plan dining pub with wall banquettes and glossy tables, wide choice of good interesting generous food (all day Sun), lunchtime sandwiches, baguettes and baked potatoes too, friendly service, well kept Charles Wells Bombardier; piped music; children welcome, picnic-sets in big sloping back paddock, open all day *(W M Paton, LYM, Phil and Jane Hodson)*

WATNALL CHAWORTH SK5046

☆ *Queens Head* [3 miles from M1 junction 26: A610 towards Nottingham, left on B600, then keep right; Main Rd]: Cosy and tastefully extended three-room old pub with wide range of good value food (all day summer), well kept

Everards Home, Greene King Ruddles Best, Theakstons and a local guest beer, efficient friendly service; intimate snug, dining area, beams and stripped pine, coal fire; fruit machine, piped music; picnic-sets in spacious and attractive back garden with big play area, open all day Fri-Sat *(the Didler, JP, PP)*

Royal Oak [Main Rd; B600 N of Kimberley]: Friendly nicely restored beamed village local with interesting plates and pictures, well kept Hardys & Hansons Best, Olde Trip and a seasonal beer, fresh cobs, woodburner, back games room and pool room, upstairs lounge open Fri-Sun; monthly live 60s night in back cabin; open all day *(the Didler)*

WELLOW SK6766

☆ ***Olde Red Lion*** [Eakring Rd, just off A616 E of Ollerton]: Friendly low-beamed and panelled 16th-c pub by green with towering maypole, three well kept changing beers, quick service, low-priced food from sandwiches to bargain Sun roasts, no smoking restaurant and dining area, no piped music; children welcome, picnic-sets outside *(DC, LYM, Howard Selina, Peter and Jean Hoare)*

WEST BRIDGFORD SK5838

Southbank [Trent Bridge]: Bright and lively well run sports bar with polished wood floors, sofas, real ales such as Boddingtons, Fullers London Pride, Timothy Taylors Landlord and local Mallard and Nottingham, wide choice of lagers and soft drinks, coffee, good all day food choice from baguettes, pittas, chilli nachos and burgers to mixed grills, Mon curry night, friendly efficient staff; several big screens and lots of other sports TVs; big garden overlooking river, handy for cricket ground and Notts Forest FC, open all day till midnight (10.30 Sun) *(the Didler, Andrew Crawford)*

☆ ***Stratford Haven*** [Stratford Rd, Trent Bridge]: Busy and chatty Tynemill pub, bare-boards front bar, well kept changing ales such as Batemans XB, Caledonian Deuchars IPA, Castle Rock, Everards Tiger, Hook Norton Old Hooky and Marstons Pedigree, exotic bottled beers, farm ciders, good choice of whiskies and wines, relaxed local atmosphere in airy and skylit carpeted yellow-walled back part, good value simple home-made food all day, daily papers; some live music, can get crowded, quieter midweek afternoons; handy for cricket ground and Nottingham Forest FC; tables outside, open all day *(Andy and Ali, JP, PP, the Didler, Andrew Crawford, BB, John and Wendy Allin)*

WEST LEAKE SK5226

☆ ***Star*** [Melton Lane, off A6006]: Comfortable oak-panelled lounge with good central log fire, pewter mugs, china, pictures, attractive table lamps and side eating area, traditional beamed and quarry-tiled country bar on left with wall settles, plenty of character and traditional games, good value home-made food (not Sun-Mon evenings) from substantial baps to cheap steaks, well kept Bass and up to three changing guest beers, several malt whiskies, good coffee, jovial landlord, helpful service, ginger cat called Cracker, no piped music or machines; children in eating area, picnic-sets on front terrace (quiet spot) and in garden with play area, bedrooms *(Michael and Jenny Back, LYM, the Didler, JP, PP)*

WEST MARKHAM SK7273

Mussel & Crab [Sibthorpe Hill; B1164 nr A1/A57/A638 roundabout N of Tuxford]: Expanding pub/restaurant specialising in fish and seafood fresh daily from Brixham, other enjoyable dishes on vast array of blackboards, two roomy dining areas (beams and stripped stone, or more flamboyant pastel murals), welcoming attentive staff, wide choice of wines in racks around the room, Tetleys, good coffee; good disabled access, picnic-sets on terrace, play area, views over wheatfields *(Rita and Keith Pollard, Gerry and Rosemary Dobson)*

WIDMERPOOL SK6429

Pullman [1st left off A606 coming towards Nottingham from A46 junction; Kinoulton Lane]: Thriving family dining pub in well converted and extended station building, train-look lounge with separate areas (one no smoking), friendly efficient service, generous above-average food inc good vegetarian dishes, fish nights and Sun carvery, two real ales, good wine choice; piped pop music may obtrude; tables and picnic-sets outside *(John and Sylvia Harrop, CMW, JJW)*

WILFORD SK5637

Ferry [off B679 S of Nottingham]: Attractive split-level Chef & Brewer partly dating from 14th c, small rooms, low beams and bare boards, candlelit tables, bays of comfortable banquettes, chesterfield by one of the open fires, pictures, two snugs, restaurant with pitched roof and imposing fireplace, vast choice of food, well kept Theakstons; piped pop music; tidy back terrace, pleasant garden with play area, view over River Trent to Nottingham Castle *(J M Tansey, Richard Greenwood)*

WORKSOP SK5879

Mallard [Station, Carlton Rd]: Friendly local feel in idiosyncratic station building, quickly changing beers from small breweries, wide range of foreign bottled beers, coal fire, traditional games; beer festivals, wheelchair access, seats outside, parking in station pay-and-display, open all day Sat, cl wkdy lunchtimes and Sun evening *(the Didler, JP, PP)*

ZOUCH SK5023

Rose & Crown [Main St (A6006)]: Particularly welcoming and helpful service in two-bar pub with smart dining room, Badger Tanglefoot, Greene King Abbot, M&B Mild, John Smiths and Timothy Taylors Landlord, good wine list, reasonably priced enjoyable food inc bargain Mon curry night; garden with play area, canalised River Soar behind *(Michael and Jenny Back, Jayne Arnold)*

Pubs brewing their own beers are listed at the back of the book.

Oxfordshire

This is a very interesting county for the lover of good pubs. There are certainly plenty to enjoy, but what comes as a rather unexpected and most welcome surprise is that alongside the many places offering good food in civilised surroundings are just as many with a really good unpretentious atmosphere and appealingly unspoilt feel. And these qualities often combine together in one and the same pub – so that an upmarket inn of great distinction may come across as delightfully unspoilt, while a cheerfully pubby place may serve food that is stylishly modern. Pubs which have stood out in recent months for their overall appeal include the 17th-c Plough at Alvescot (a well run and enjoyable proper pub), the friendly Horse & Groom at Caulcott (a well run all-rounder), the Black Horse at Checkendon (a family-run unspoilt classic), the bustling Chequers in Chipping Norton (good landlord, good beer, interesting food), the well liked Duke of Cumberlands Head at Clifton, the Merrymouth at Fifield (enjoyable food in this nice family-run country pub), the lovely old Falkland Arms in Great Tew (one of England's prettiest villages), the Gate Hangs High near Hook Norton (good food, and its new bedrooms and courtyard garden look set to be new plus points here), the Kings Arms in Oxford (a favourite with students, their dons, and passing visitors), the Royal Oak at Ramsden (a proper village pub, with popular food and a direct line to some good french wines), the Trout at Tadpole Bridge (very good all round, in an enviable spot), and the Swan in Thame (another enjoyable all-rounder, its décor and furnishings adding a nice touch of the unusual). To these we'd add a handful of new entries: the Chequers at Churchill (recently saved from near-dereliction and reopened in such splendid shape that it comes straight in with a Star), the Eyston Arms in East Hendred (a thoroughly worthwhile downland village dining pub), the Rose & Crown in Oxford (a decidedly individual place, bags of character); the Red Lion in Steeple Aston (good food and wines now, alongside the more traditional appeal which won it an entry under a former landlord some years ago); and the attractive Swan in its alluring spot at Swinbrook in the Windrush valley. With its landlord/chef's keen eye for the best local produce (he's a local farmer's son), the Trout at Tadpole Bridge is now serving such delicious meals that it surpasses all these other fine pubs, to take the title of Oxfordshire Dining Pub of the Year. Prize pubs in the Lucky Dip section at the end of the chapter include the Rose & Crown at Ashbury, Bottle & Glass on Binfield Heath, Golden Pheasant in Burford, Tite at Chadlington, Crown at Church Enstone, Bat & Ball at Cuddesdon, Bear & Ragged Staff in Cumnor, Deddington Arms in Deddington, Bell at Ducklington, Trout at Godstow, Jersey Arms at Middleton Stoney, Crown at Pishill, Crown at Play Hatch, Bell at Shenington, Lamb at Shipton-under-Wychwood, George & Dragon at Shutford, Crown at South Moreton, Perch & Pike at South Stoke, Peyton Arms at Stoke Lyne, restauranty Crooked Billet at Stoke Row, Boat at Thrupp, Three Horseshoes in Witney and Killingworth Castle at Wootton. Drinks tend to cost more here than the national norm; the local Hook Norton beers are always attractively priced, and very widely available. By the time this edition is published, Brakspears should again be brewed here in Oxfordshire (at a new brewery in Witney – their main beers have recently been in exile, brewed up in Cheshire). And Loddon, just inside the Oxfordshire boundary on the edge of Reading, is a good new small brewery whose beers are becoming quite widely available here already.

ALVESCOT SP2704 Map 4

Plough

B4020 Carterton—Clanfield, SW of Witney

Very well run and popular, this partly 17th-c village pub has a proper pubby atmosphere. The carpeted bar has a new collection of aircraft prints and a large poster of Concorde's last flight, as well as plenty of cottagey pictures, china ornaments and house plants, a big antique case of stuffed birds of prey, an old harmonium, sundry bric-a-brac, and a good log fire. Comfortable seating includes cushioned settles, a nice armchair, and of course the bar stools bagged by cheerful regulars in the early evening. There's a two-part no smoking dining area – snug and intimate at night. As well as bar snacks like soup (£3.35), warm crusty rolls (from £3.20), filled baked potatoes (from £3.50), and ploughman's (from £4.80), the well liked food might include garlic mushrooms (£3.95), combination starters for two people (from £5.25), spinach and ricotta cannelloni, ham and eggs, chicken kiev or liver and bacon casserole (all £6.95), steak and kidney suet pudding (£7.25), salmon steak with watercress sauce (£7.75), a full rack of barbecue ribs (£9.75), steaks (from £10.25), half a roast duck with orange and Cointreau sauce (£11.25), half lamb shoulder with minted gravy (£11.75), and daily specials such as seafood platter (£6.95) or honey and mustard chicken breast (£7.25). On weekday lunchtimes, they offer two meals for £10. Well kept Wadworths IPA, 6X, and a seasonal beer on handpump, and hot chocolate with marshmallows; helpful, efficient service. A proper public bar has pool and a fruit machine (and rather surprisingly a big needlework of tropical birds on its patterned green wallpaper); darts, TV, bar billiards, alley skittles and piped music. The friendly black cat is called Dino. Two picnic-sets stand out in front below particularly colourful hanging baskets by the quiet village road, with more behind under trees, by a bird table and play area; aunt sally. *(Recommended by Marjorie and David Lamb, Peter and Audrey Dowsett, KN-R, Mrs Challiner)*

Wadworths ~ Tenant Kevin Robert Keeling ~ Real ale ~ Bar food ~ Restaurant ~ (01993) 842281 ~ Children in eating area of bar and in restaurant until 8.30pm ~ Dogs allowed in bar ~ Open 11-3, 6-11; 12-3, 7-10.30 Sun

BANBURY SP4540 Map 4

Reindeer £

Parsons Street, off Market Place

There's plenty of interest to look at in this friendly old place. The pubby front bar has heavy 16th-c beams, very broad polished oak floorboards scattered with rugs, a magnificent carved overmantel for one of the two roaring log fires, and traditional solid furnishings. What is definitely worth seeing is the handsomely proportioned Globe Room, which has wonderfully carved 17th-c dark oak panelling; this is where Cromwell held court before the Battle of Edgehill. Served only at lunchtime, straightforward bar food in generous helpings might include soup (£2.50), sandwiches (from £2.80), omelettes or good filled baked potatoes (from £4), all day breakfast (£4.10), shepherd's pie, bubble and squeak or mushroom florentine (£4.50–£7), and rump steak (£6.50), with puddings (£2.80). Well kept Hook Norton Best, Mild, Old Hooky, Copper Ale, and a guest like Everards Perfick on handpump, country wines, several whiskies, and even snuffs and clay pipes for the more adventurous; skittle alley, cribbage, dominoes and piped music. A smaller back room up steps is no smoking at lunchtime. The little back courtyard has tables and benches under parasols, aunt sally, and pretty flowering baskets. No under-21s (but see below). *(Recommended by the Didler, Jennie Hall, Arnold Bennett, Ted George,*

Geoff Pidoux, Tony and Wendy Hobden, Ian Phillips, Mrs P J Pearce, Klaus and Elizabeth Leist, George Atkinson)

Hook Norton ~ Tenants Mr and Mrs Puddifoot ~ Real ale ~ Bar food (11-2.30, not Sun) ~ (01295) 264031 ~ Children in family room ~ Open 11-11; 12-3, 7-10.30 Sun

BUCKLAND SU3497 Map 4

Lamb 🍷 🛏

Village signposted off A420 NE of Faringdon

In a tranquil village, this is a smart 18th-c stone dining pub. Opening off a hallway, and divided in two by dark painted timbers, the neatly kept little bar has blue plush furnishings, potted plants around the windows, and a few carefully chosen sheep and lamb pictures and models around the cream-painted walls. On a piano are newspapers to read, and examples of their own chutneys and jams; it's popular with older visitors at lunchtime, when the well liked food might include sandwiches (from £3.30; sausage with grain mustard and tomato £4.95), soup (£4.20), sautéed herring roes on toast (£4.50), confit of duck (£4.95; main course £8.95), omelettes (from £5.95), ploughman's (£6.95), home-cooked ham and eggs (£8.95), and smoked haddock and prawn kedgeree (£9.95); evening choices such as baked goats cheese in filo pastry with a roasted red pepper and rocket salad (£7.95), warm scallop, bacon and endive salad (£8.95), risotto with gorgonzola, marscarpone and parmesan (£10.95), salmon fillet with chive beurre blanc or steak and kidney in Guinness pie (£12.25), rack of lamb with mint and sorrel (£17.95), and fillet of local venison with roasted shallots and braised red cabbage (£18.95), with puddings like orange crème caramel, baked banana and rum, and chocolate and brandy mousse (from £4.25). The restaurant is no smoking. Hook Norton Best on handpump, quite a few wines by the glass, and proper Pimms; piped music. The very pleasant tree-shaded garden has quite a few picnic-sets, with a couple of terrace tables; good walks nearby. More reports please. *(Recommended by the Didler, John Hale, Richard and Margaret Peers, Peter B Brown, J F M and M West, Mr and Mrs G S Ayrton, Betsy and Peter Little, Gordon Tong)*

Free house ~ Licensees Paul and Peta Barnard ~ Real ale ~ Bar food (not Sun evening, not Mon) ~ Restaurant ~ (01367) 870484 ~ Children welcome ~ Open 11-3, 5.30-11; 12-4 Sun; closed Sun evening, Mon, 2 wks over Christmas and New Year ~ Bedrooms: £70B/£95B

BURFORD SP2512 Map 4

Lamb ★ 🍷 🍺 🛏

Village signposted off A40 W of Oxford; Sheep Street (B4425, off A361)

Although this civilised 500-year-old stone inn is perhaps more of a hotel these days, the bustling and popular proper bar remains a meeting place for those who want just a drink and a chat. The roomy beamed main lounge is charmingly traditional, with distinguished old seats including a chintzy high winged settle, ancient cushioned wooden armchairs, and seats built into its stone-mullioned windows, bunches of flowers on polished oak and elm tables, oriental rugs on the wide flagstones and polished oak floorboards, and a winter log fire under its fine mantelpiece. The pictures are quite striking, they have shelves of plates and other antique decorations, and one corner has a writing desk, and a grandfather clock. The public bar has plenty of character, high-backed settles and old chairs on flagstones in front of its fire, and well kept Hook Norton Best, Wadworths 6X, and a changing guest like Charles Wells Bombardier dispensed from an antique handpump beer engine in a glassed-in cubicle; there's also an extensive wine list with quite a few by the glass, and a good range of soft drinks. It's best to get there early if you want a table in the bar where staff serve daily changing food that could include crab mayonnaise, gazpacho and home-made bread (£6), rillette of pork, pickles, walnut and sultana bread (£6.50), hot sausage and onion sandwich with mustard mayonnaise, ploughman's or toasted crumpet, seared smoked salmon and egg mayonnaise (£7.50), pasta with smoked chicken, new potatoes and peas

(£10.50), stuffed roast duck leg on sweetcorn mash or grilled tuna, crayfish, peas, mint and hard-boiled egg (£13), grilled aged fillet of beef and chips (£15.50), and puddings like strawberry cheesecake, chocolate roulade with cherry fool or banana custard (all £4.95); you can eat the restaurant menu in the bar (but not the other way round) – two courses £25, three courses £29.50. On Sunday they do a set menu only. The Top Lounge and restaurant are no smoking. A pretty terrace with teak furniture leads down to small neatly kept lawns surrounded by flowers, flowering shrubs and small trees, and the garden itself is a real suntrap, enclosed as it is by the warm stone of the surrounding buildings. More reports on the new regime, please. *(Recommended by the Didler, A P Seymour, Stuart Turner, Martin and Karen Wake, David J Austin; also in the* Good Hotel Guide*)*

Free house ~ Licensees Bruno and Rachel Cappuccini ~ Real ale ~ Bar food (12-2.30 (3 weekends), 7-9.30) ~ Restaurant ~ (01993) 823155 ~ Children in eating area of bar and restaurant ~ Dogs allowed in bar and bedrooms ~ Open 11.30-3, 5.30-11; 11.30-11 Sat; 12-10.30 Sun ~ Bedrooms: £80B/£130B

CAULCOTT SP5024 Map 4

Horse & Groom

Lower Heyford Road (B4030)

You can be sure of a warm welcome from the friendly, hard-working licensees at this creeper-covered and partly thatched cottage, and although they have a very loyal local following, there's a wide mix of visitors too. It's not a huge place and an L-shaped red-carpeted room angles around the servery, with plush-cushioned settles, chairs and stools around a few dark tables at the low-ceilinged bar end, a polo cap collection, framed racehorse cigarette cards, and a blazing fire in the big inglenook, with masses of pump clips under its long bressumer beam; shove-ha'penny and cribbage. The far end, up a shallow step, is set for dining (and is no smoking; best to book), with lots of decorative jugs hanging on black joists, and some decorative plates. There are some lovely watercolours and original drawings dotted around, including a charming one of Harvey the west highland terrier who greets everyone on arrival; look out too for the nice old poster of the auction of the pub in 1899. Three quickly changing interesting guest beers from brewers such as Burton Bridge, Cottage and Jennings are well kept alongside Hook Norton Best on handpump; decent house wines. They serve a good selection of O'Hagan speciality sausages and you can choose from flavours such as chorizo, pork and red wine, somerset scrumpy, creole, and drunken duck (all £7.50); also, sandwiches and toasties (from £3.40), home-made soup (£3.95), filled baked potatoes (from £3.90), ham and egg (£6.25), daily specials such as a pint of prawns (£7.95), chicken breast (£8.75), steaks (from £10.95), and beef wellington (£13.95), with puddings (£4.25); food service does slow down at peak times. There is a small side sun lounge, with picnic-sets under cocktail parasols on a neat side lawn. *(Recommended by Paul and Ann Meyer, Peter Neate, Dave Braisted, Simon Collett-Jones, Peter and Jean Hoare, David Barnes, D C T and E A Frewer, Barbara and Peter Kelly)*

Free house ~ Licensees Chris and Celestine Roche ~ Real ale ~ Bar food ~ Restaurant ~ (01869) 343257 ~ Children in restaurant lunchtime only ~ Open 11-3, 6-11; 12-3, 7-10.30 Sun

CHECKENDON SU6684 Map 2

Black Horse

Village signposted off A4074 Reading—Wallingford; coming from that direction, go straight through village towards Stoke Row, then turn left (the second turn left after the village church); OS Sheet 175 map reference 666841

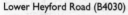

The same family has run this classic country local for decades. It's tucked away in fine walking country (and popular with walkers and cyclists) and won't disappoint those who like their pubs unspoilt and basic. There's a refreshingly relaxed atmosphere in the back stillroom, where three changing West Berkshire beers are tapped from the cask. The room with the bar counter has some tent pegs ranged above the fireplace, a reminder that they used to be made here; a homely side room has some splendidly unfashionable 1950s-look armchairs, and there's another room beyond that. They keep pickled eggs and usually do fresh filled rolls (from £1.70). There are seats out on a verandah and in the garden. *(Recommended by the Didler, Pete Baker, Ian Phillips, Dick and Madeleine Brown, Richard Greaves)*

Free house ~ Licensees Margaret and Martin Morgan ~ Real ale ~ No credit cards ~ (01491) 680418 ~ Children allowed but must be well behaved ~ Open 12-2(2.30 Sat), 7-11; 12-3, 7-10.30 Sun; closed evening 25 Dec

CHIPPING NORTON SP3127 Map 4

Chequers

Goddards Lane

This is a smashing place with an unpretentious, friendly and bustling atmosphere and run by a landlord who really cares about his customers. The three softly lit beamed rooms have no frills, but are clean and comfortable, with low ochre ceilings, plenty of character, and blazing log fires. Friendly efficient staff serve very well kept Fullers Chiswick, London Pride, ESB and seasonal brews from handpump – unusual to have the full Fullers range around here – and they have good house wines (with 16 by the glass), espresso and cappuccino coffee. Good bar food at lunchtime includes sandwiches (from £2.75), soup with garlic bread (£3.95), wild mushroom and parmesan torte (£4.50), red onion tart topped with crispy duck garnished with sweetened plum tomatoes (£4.75), ploughman's (£4.95), home-cooked honey and cider roast ham with free range egg (£6.95), pork and leek sausage with port wine gravy or mixed bean thai curry (£7.50), fresh fillet of cod in beer batter (£7.95), and chargrilled 10oz rib-eye steak (£10.95); in the evening, main courses such as butternut squash risotto (£8.95), free range chicken breast on spiced sweet potato and wilted spinach with red pepper coulis (£9.75), sea trout with peach, pink peppercorn and honey dressing (£10.25), lamb steak with leek purée (£10.50), and barbary duck breast with a rich cider sauce and apple fritters (£10.95). The no smoking restaurant at the back was converted from an old barn adjacent to the courtyard. It's very handy for the town's Victorian theatre. *(Recommended by Chris Glasson, the Didler, Steve Dark, Mike and Jennifer Marsh, Robert Gomme, Paul and Ann Meyer, Andy and Jill Kassube, Paul Hopton, Charles and Pauline Stride, Graham Gage, Simon Collett-Jones, Brian and Rosalie Laverick, Richard Greaves, A Sadler, Mrs Joy Griffiths, Mrs N W Neill)*

Fullers ~ Tenants Josh and Kay Reid ~ Real ale ~ Bar food (12-2.30, 6-9.30; 12-5 Sun; not Sun evening) ~ Restaurant ~ (01608) 644717 ~ Children in restaurant if over 12 ~ Dogs allowed in bar ~ Open 11-11; 12-10.30 Sun; closed 25 Dec

CHURCHILL SP2824 Map 4

Chequers ★

B4450 Chipping Norton—Stow (and village signposted off A361 Chipping Norton—Burford); Church Road

The delightfully friendly licensees who've transformed and reopened this 18th-c village pub are no strangers to the *Guide* – until recently they ran the Horse and Groom at Upper Oddington in Gloucestershire, where their warmly welcoming approach earned them the title of Licensees of the Year in our 2003 edition. You can expect the same reception here: one reader was impressed when the landlady remembered the names of all her grandchildren, despite not having seen them for seven months. The rest of the hard-working staff are just as charming and attentive, on our visit taking care to chat to everyone in between serving the meals. Closed for the last few years, the building has been totally refurbished, and is now a light and airy open-plan dining pub, with the big surprise the new extension at the back; a little like a church with its soaring rafters, it fits in so well that some customers have been surprised to learn that the beams aren't original and in fact are brand new. At one end is an unusual dresser with lots of wine bottles. The front bar has enjoyed a similar facelift, but has a more traditional feel, with a pale flagstoned floor, a couple of old timbers, modern oak furnishings, some exposed stone walls around a big inglenook (with a good winter log fire), and country prints on the pale yellow walls; newspapers are laid out on a table. Promptly served and attractively presented, the very popular bar food might include lunchtime sandwiches (£4.50), soup (£3.50), spinach and feta in puff pastry (£8.50), pies such as a good beef and mushroom (£9), tenderloin of pork with black pudding (£9.50), changing specials, and on Sundays a choice of roasts (from £8.50); helpings are big, and they'll bring delicious fresh bread to your table. On Wednesday nights they do roast beef (£10), and on Thursday nights half a crispy duck on a bed of mash with pink peppercorn sauce and spring onions (£13.50). Well kept Hook Norton Best and a changing guest like Greene King Old Speckled Hen on handpump. The pub has been open for only a few months, but has caught on fast, so though there's lots of space it can get busy; it may be worth booking. A couple of readers have felt that the acoustics, what with hard walls and floors and high ceilings, are a bit too lively; it's quieter in a cosy but easily missed area upstairs which, like the restaurant, is no smoking. The pub's outside has been cleaned up too: it's Costwold stone at its most golden. The village church opposite is impressive. *(Recommended by Stuart Turner, Richard Greaves, P and J Shapley, Christopher White, David Glynne-Jones, Matthew Shackle)*

Free house ~ Licensees Peter and Assumpta Golding ~ Real ale ~ Bar food (12-2 (3 Sat), 7-9.30) ~ Restaurant ~ (01608) 659393 ~ Children welcome ~ Irish music once every two months; quiz nights ~ Open 11-11; 12-10.30 Sun; closed 25 Dec

CLIFTON SP4831 Map 4

Duke of Cumberlands Head 🍷 🛏

B4031 Deddington—Aynho

Just a short walk from the canal, this small, peaceful pub is a popular place – especially on Sunday lunchtimes. The low-beamed turkey-carpeted lounge has a good log fire in a vast stone fireplace, attractive paintings by the landlord's mother of lilies and rhododendrons grown by her on the west coast of Scotland, and mainly sturdy kitchen tables, with a few more through in the little yellow-painted no smoking dining room, which has some stripped stone – none of the walls or ceilings is straight. The well liked bar food might include cullen skink (smoked haddock soup £4), chicken liver pâté or herrings marinated in dill and madeira (£4.50), sausages with onion gravy (£9; small helping £6), beef bourguignon, chicken korma, pork normandy or mushroom stroganoff (all £10; small helping £7), grilled smoked salmon with lemon butter (£11), steaks (from £14), and puddings such as white chocolate and raspberry torte, crème caramel or summer pudding (£4); two-course Sunday lunch (£15). Good-natured service, with well kept Black Sheep and Hook Norton Best on handpump, alongside a guest such as Adnams Southwold or Caledonian Deuchars IPA. Plenty of wines to choose from and more than 30 malt whiskies too. Picnic-sets out on the grass behind. *(Recommended by Marcelle Bowman, Sir Nigel Foulkes, Hugh Spottiswoode, Mr and Mrs J A Phipps, Gerry and Rosemary Dobson, William and Jenifer Ruxton, Peter Shapland, Mrs J Groom, Phoebe and Duncan Thomas, Richard Marjoram, Trevor and Judy Pearson)*

Free house ~ Licensee Nick Huntington ~ Real ale ~ Bar food (not Mon lunchtime) ~ Restaurant ~ (01869) 338539 ~ Children in eating area of bar ~ Dogs welcome ~ Open 12-2.30(3 Sat), 6.30-10.30(11 Sat); 12-3, 6.30-10 Sun; closed Mon lunchtime ~ Bedrooms: £50S/£65B

> The Post Office makes it virtually impossible for people to come to grips with British geography, by using a system of post towns which are often across the county boundary from the places they serve. So the postal address of a pub often puts it in the wrong county. We use the correct county – the one the pub is actually in. Lots of pubs which the Post Office alleges are in Oxfordshire are actually in Berkshire, Buckinghamshire, Gloucestershire or Warwickshire.

EAST HENDRED SU4588 Map 2

Eyston Arms

Village signposted off A417 E of Wantage; High Street

Recently attractively refurbished, this nicely set village pub is now much more of a gastropub, but still has the air of a thriving local. The several separate seeming areas have neat new tables and chairs, stripped timbers, flagstoned floors, and particularly low ceilings and beams; there's an attractive inglenook (with logs blazing in winter), some cushioned wall-seats, and a piano. There are olives to pick at on the bar counter, where even on a sunny day the candles may be lit. Popular for business lunches, the food can be very good indeed, including lunchtime ciabattas such as roast vegetables, goats cheese and pesto (£5), grilled king prawns (£5.75 starter, £11.75 main course), chilli prawn and smoked salmon linguini with wilted rocket (£8.95 – a nice touch is the chunk of parmesan so you can grate your own), unusual variants of caesar salads such as one with haloumi (£8.95), plenty of fresh fish, and good steaks – their beef is hung for three weeks for fuller flavour. A two-course set lunch is £12.95, three courses £14.95. The restaurant is no smoking. Service on our summer inspection was friendly and efficient. Adnams and Wadworths 6X on handpump; piped easy-listening music. A couple of outside tables overlook the pretty village lane. *(Recommended by Dick and Madeleine Brown)*

Free house ~ Licensee George Dailey ~ Real ale ~ Bar food (12-2, 6.30-10) ~ Restaurant ~ (01235) 833320 ~ Dogs allowed in bar ~ Open 11.30-3, 6.30-11

FIFIELD SP2318 Map 4

Merrymouth

A424 Burford—Stow

Friendly and family run, this 13th-c country inn is popular for its good food. The simple but comfortably furnished L-shaped bar has nice bay-window seats, flagstones, horsebrasses and antique bottles hanging from low beams, some walls stripped back to the old masonry, and an open fire in winter. Except for five tables in the bar, the pub is no smoking; piped classical music. Served by efficient and attentive staff, the enjoyable bar food might include home-made soup (£3.95), lunchtime baguettes (from £5.50), smoked mackerel pâté (£4.75), creamy leek and prawn tart (£5.25), cold home-baked ham (£7.75), sausages with onion gravy (£7.95), chicken pieces with bacon, mushrooms, cheese and cream (£8.95), steaks (from £10.95), and rack of lamb with port and redcurrant sauce (£11.95), and daily specials such as pasta with smoked cheese and tomato sauce (£7.50), steak and kidney pie (£8.50), and hake with a cheese and herb crust (£10.95), and home-made puddings like raspberry marshmallow meringue, chocolate chunk walnut pie or bread pudding with whisky sauce (all £4.25). Well kept Adnams Broadside and Hook Norton Best on handpump, and decent wines. There are tables on a terrace and in the back garden (there may be a little noise from fast traffic on the road). The quaint bedrooms are well cared for. The Domesday Book mentions an inn on this site, and its name comes from the Murimuth family, who once owned the village. *(Recommended by KN-R, Susan and John Douglas, Martin Jones, George Atkinson, Gill and Keith Croxton, A Sadler, Peter and Audrey Dowsett, Bernard Stradling, Martin Jennings, Tom Bottinga, Suzanne Miles, Colin McKerrow)*

Free house ~ Licensees Andrew and Timothy Flaherty ~ Real ale ~ Bar food ~ Restaurant ~ (01993) 831652 ~ Children welcome ~ Dogs welcome ~ Open 11-2.30, 6-10; 12-2.30, 7-10 Sun; closed Sun evening in winter ~ Bedrooms: £45S/£65B

GREAT TEW SP3929 Map 4

Falkland Arms

Off B4022 about 5 miles E of Chipping Norton; The Green

It does get extremely busy in this picturesque inn, but given that this is a charming and peaceful village full of untouched golden-stone thatched cottages, that's not surprising. The partly panelled bar has high-backed settles and a diversity of stools around plain stripped tables on flagstones and bare boards, one, two and three-handled mugs hanging from the beam-and-board ceiling, dim converted oil lamps, shutters for the stone-mullioned latticed windows, and a fine inglenook fireplace with a blazing fire in winter. Along with well kept Wadworths IPA, 6X and a seasonal ale such as Summersault, they serve up to four guests like Coach House Squires Gold, Orkney Red MacGregor, Skinners Cornish Knocker, and Thwaites Thoroughbred on handpump; they hold an annual summer beer festival. The counter is decorated with tobacco jars and different varieties of snuff which you can buy, and you'll also find 60 malt whiskies, 16 country wines, and farm cider; darts, cribbage and dominoes. Lunchtime bar food (they tell us prices have not changed since last year) includes soup (£3.50), filled baguettes (from £3.95), ploughman's (£5.95), and steak and kidney pie, bangers and mash or a vegetarian dish (from £6.50), with more sophisticated evening restaurant meals (you must book); home-made puddings might include sticky toffee pudding (£4.25). The dining room is no smoking. You have to go out into the lane and then back in again to use the lavatories. There are tables out in front of the pub, and picnic-sets under cocktail parasols in the garden behind. Small good value bedrooms (no under-14s). *(Recommended by the Didler, John and Gloria Isaacs, Kevin Blake, Guy Vowles, Patrick Hancock, Mrs P Sarson, Angus Lyon, Geoff Pidoux, Brenda and Rob Fincham, Keith Jacob, Dr David Cockburn)*

Wadworths ~ Managers Paul Barlow-Heal and S J Courage ~ Real ale ~ Bar food (12-2, 7-8; not Sun evening) ~ Restaurant ~ (01608) 683653 ~ Children in restaurant lunchtimes only ~ Dogs allowed in bar ~ Live folk Sun night, other live music last Fri/Sat of month ~ Open 11.30-2.30, 6-11; 11.30-11 Sat; 12-10.30 Sun; wknd afternoon closure in winter ~ Bedrooms: £50S/£75S(£100B)

HENLEY SU7882 Map 4

Anchor

Friday Street; coming in over bridge, first left towards A4155 then next right

In contrast to the rest of this rich little town, it's refreshing to find such an old-fashioned and homely local. The landlady is helpful and friendly, and in the two main rooms, you'll find a well worn-in mix of elderly traditional pub furnishings, with throw rugs, scatter cushions, chintz curtains, some venerable wall boarding and dim lighting adding to the cottagey feel. The beams in the dark ochre ceiling are thickly hung with chamber-pots, steins, whisky-water jugs, copperware and so forth, and there are interesting pictures: mainly local river photographs in the left room, a mix of antique sporting, ship and comical prints on the right, which has a piano and TV; shove-ha'penny, backgammon, cribbage, dominoes, and winter darts. A simply furnished no smoking back dining room has lots of rowing photographs, and a cage with a chatty cockatiel; behind is a charming informal terrace surrounded by lush vegetation and hanging vines. Besides an impressive choice of sandwiches (from £3.50), generously served bar food includes baked potatoes (from £5), baguettes, ciabattas or ploughman's (£5.50), and winter stews and hotpots, game or steak and kidney pies, summer salads and pasta dishes (all £7.50). Well kept Brakspears Bitter and Special with a seasonal ale on handpump, and a good range of malt whiskies and New World wines by the glass. The friendly chocolate labrador is called Ruger. *(Recommended by the Didler, Roy and Lindsey Fentiman, Jim Abbott, Mike and Sue Richardson, David Edwards)*

Brakspears ~ Tenant G A Ion-Savage ~ Bar food (not Sun or Mon evenings Oct-May) ~ (01491) 574753 ~ Well behaved children in restaurant until 8.30 ~ Open 11-11; 12-10.30 Sun

Anyone claiming to arrange or prevent inclusion of a pub in the *Guide* is a fraud. Pubs are included only if recommended by genuine readers and if our own anonymous inspection confirms that they are suitable.

HIGHMOOR SU6984 Map 2

Rising Sun

Witheridge Hill, signposted off B481; OS Sheet 175 map reference 697841

New licensees have taken over this pretty black and white pub but don't seem to have made any drastic changes. There are seats around a few simple tables in a smallish carpeted area on the right, by the bar, with some bar stools too, and a log-effect stove in a big brick inglenook fireplace. The main area spreading back from here has shiny bare boards and a swathe of carpeting, with well spaced tables, attractive pictures on the walls, and a side bit with a leather settee, piped music, dominoes, and cribbage. At lunchtime, the menu could include filled baguettes or baked potatoes (£6.95), ploughman's (from £6.95), pork-and-leek sausage and egg (£7.50), home-made vegetarian lasagne or chicken stir fry (£7.95), home battered cod (£8.50), and chicken tikka masala (£9.95); also, home-made soup (£3.75), roasted mushrooms in a creamy white wine sauce (£4.95), caesar salad (£5.95), chicken breast with a tomato flavoured white sauce (£9.95), lamb steak in red wine and rosemary sauce or spicy tiger prawns (£11.95), calves liver (£12.95), and steaks (from £12.95). Well kept Brakspears Bitter and Special on handpump, and eight wines by the glass. In fine weather the fairy-lit terrace is a pleasant place to sit and there are also tables on the grass among the trees. More reports please.
(Recommended by Ian Phillips, John Hale, Bob and Margaret Holder, Chris Glasson, Julia and Richard Tredgett, P Tailyour)

Brakspears ~ Licensees Haydyn Duffy and Melissa Jones ~ Real ale ~ Bar food (12-2.30, 7-9.30; 12-4 Sun; not Mon evening) ~ Restaurant ~ (01491) 641455 ~ Children welcome ~ Dogs allowed in bar ~ Open 12-3, 6-11; 12-11 Sat; 12-4 Sun; 12-3, 6.-11 Sat in winter; closed Sun evening

HOOK NORTON SP3533 Map 4

Gate Hangs High

Banbury Road; a mile N of village towards Sibford, at Banbury—Rollright crossroads

The new courtyard garden is now open though there are still seats on the broad lawn behind this tucked-away country pub, with holly and apple trees, and fine views; the flower tubs and wall baskets are very colourful. The bedrooms in the converted barns are up and running, too; we'd be grateful for any feedback. The bar has joists in the long, low ceiling, a brick bar counter, stools and assorted chairs on the carpet, baby oil lamps on each table, a gleaming copper hood over the hearth in the inglenook fireplace, and hops over the bar counter. Well kept Hook Norton Best, Old Hooky and Copper Ale on handpump, bottled beers, and decent wines; piped music and dominoes. Well liked bar food might include sandwiches, pork crackling with apple sauce (£2.95), home-made soup (£3.75), duck liver and brandy pâté with melba toast (£3.95), black pudding and bacon rösti with a poached egg (£5.95), braised rabbit in cider and mustard (£9.95), winter jugged hare or tuna steak with horseradish sauce (£12.95), rack of lamb with garlic butter (£13.50), and home-made puddings such as banoffi pie or apple and blackberry crumble (£4.25); they have a good children's menu (from £3.50), and do a two-course weekday set menu (£10.95; three courses £12.95). You'll need to book for Saturday evening and Sunday lunch, in the slightly chintzy no smoking side dining extension. *(Recommended by Andy and Jill Kassube, Andrew MacLeod, Malcolm Taylor, Martin Jones, Sir Nigel Foulkes, Stuart Turner, Mike and Sue Richardson, Matthew Shackle, JHBS, Alan Scaife, Des and Jen Clarke, Trevor and Judy Pearson, David J Austin)*

Hook Norton ~ Tenant Stephen Coots-Williams ~ Real ale ~ Bar food (12.30-2.30, 6-10; all day summer Sun) ~ Restaurant ~ (01608) 737387 ~ Children in eating area of bar and restaurant ~ Dogs allowed in bar ~ Open 12-3(4 Sat), 6-11.30; 12-10.30 Sun; 12-5, 7-10.30 Sun in winter ~ Bedrooms: £40B/£60B

The symbol shows pubs which keep their beer unusually well, have a particularly good range or brew their own.

Pear Tree

Village signposted off A361 SW of Banbury

There's a lively pubby atmosphere and good friendly service in this popular pub. And as they are barely 100 yards away from the Hook Norton brewery, you'll find the full range of their ales well kept on handpump: Hook Norton Best, Old Hooky, Generation, Mild, and seasonal ales; they do country wines too. The chatty knocked together bar area (partly no smoking) has country-kitchen furniture on the nicely timbered floor, some long tables, a well stocked magazine rack, and a welcoming log fire. A short choice of simple bar food includes sandwiches, soup (£3.25), filled baked potatoes (from £5.25), ploughman's (from £6), home-cooked ham and eggs (£6.95), beef in ale or fish pie (£7.25), and puddings such as lemon meringue pie (£3.25). It does get busy at weekends; dominoes, and Jenga. The attractive, sizeable garden has plenty of seating as well as an outdoor chess set, a wendy house, swings and slides. *(Recommended by Chris Glasson, the Didler, Michael Jones, Barry Collett, Guy Vowles, Robert Gomme, MP, Andy and Jill Kassube, JHBS, Theocsbrian, Angus Lyon, Des and Jen Clarke, D C T and E A Frewer, Stuart Turner)*

Hook Norton ~ Tenant J Sivyer ~ Real ale ~ Bar food (not Sun) ~ (01608) 737482 ~ Children in eating area of bar ~ Dogs allowed in bar ~ Open 11.30-3, 6-11; 12-4, 7-10.30 Sun ~ Bedrooms: £38S/£55S

Sun

High Street

This bustling place is opposite the church and has tables on the street in front (as well as on a back terrace) that give a pleasantly continental feel on summer evenings. Inside, the flagstoned front bar has relaxed local atmosphere, a huge log fire, flagstones, hop-strung beams, well kept Hook Norton Best, Mild, Old Hooky and a seasonal ale on handpump, and seven wines by the glass; dominoes, cribbage, and alley skittles. Behind the central servery, a cosy newly carpeted room with comfortable banquettes and other seats leads into the attractive no smoking restaurant. Under the new licensee, bar food now includes filled baguettes, soup (£3.50), marinated mozzarella with tomato and parma ham salad (£5.25), deep-fried king prawns with a tomato and chilli jam (£5.95), mushroom and goats cheese stack on roasted peppers (£8.95), chicken stuffed with Oxford Blue cheese and leeks wrapped in parma ham with a port wine jus (£9.95), calves liver on caramelised onion mash with bacon and red wine jus (£10.25), pork fillet medallions with fried black pudding on a potato cake with a creamy grain mustard sauce (£10.55), good named-breed sirloin steak (£12.95), daily specials like green chicken curry or lasagne (£7.95), and seafood pasta with scallops, monkfish and prawns (£10.25), and puddings such as vanilla panna cotta, chocolate and rum pots, and summer pudding. Good wheelchair access and disabled facilities. *(Recommended by Susan and John Douglas, Pete Baker, Brian Wainwright, Martin Jones, John Bowdler, Dick and Madeleine Brown, Sir Nigel Foulkes, Martin Jennings, MP, Jennie Hall, JHBS, Chris Glasson, Pam and David Bailey, Gill and Tony Morriss, Tim and Ann Newell, George Atkinson)*

Hook Norton ~ Tenant Stuart Rust ~ Bar food ~ Restaurant ~ (01608) 737570 ~ Children in eating area of bar and restaurant ~ Dogs allowed in bar ~ Open 11.30-3, 6-11; 12-3, 7-10.30 Sun ~ Bedrooms: £40S/£60S(£65B)

KELMSCOTT SU2499 Map 4

Plough

NW of Faringdon, off A417 or A4095

Not far from the Thames and the former summer home of William Morris, this is a rather pretty little inn. The small traditional beamed front bar has ancient flagstones and stripped stone walls, a good log fire, and the relaxed chatty feel of a real village pub with a good mix of customers. The pleasant dining area has attractively plain and solid furnishings, and bar food (often served in small and

large helpings) such as sandwiches (£4.50), home-made soup (£3.50/£5.50), roast ham and eggs (£5.50/£7.50), home-made lasagne, vegetable stir fry or ploughman's (£5.50/£7.95), devilled kidneys (£7.50), and T-bone steak (£12.95); evening choices such as home-made chicken and duck pâté with red onion jam (£5.50), moules marinière (£5.95), grilled tiger prawns with sweet chilli sauce (£6.50), slow braised rump of lamb with celeriac purée or roast duck breast with carrot and ginger purée and brandy and thyme jus (£12.50), whole lemon sole with prawns and capers (£14.50), and puddings like baked apple pie, vanilla crème brûlée or sticky toffee pudding (£4.50). Well kept Hook Norton Best and maybe Nethergate Old Growler or Timothy Taylors Landlord on handpump, and Black Rat farm cider; piped music, pool, TV, and darts. The garden is pretty, with seats among plantings of unusual flowers and aunt sally, and there are picnic-sets under cocktail parasols out in front. The Oxfordshire cycleway runs close by. More reports please.
(Recommended by R Huggins, D Irving, E McCall, T McLean, Eleanor and Nick Steinitz, JCW, Sue Dyson, Robert and Anne Dillon, Geoff Pidoux)

Free house ~ Licensee Martin Platt ~ Real ale ~ Bar food (12-2.30, 7-9; all day weekends) ~ Restaurant ~ (01367) 253543 ~ Children in eating area of bar and restaurant ~ Dogs allowed in bar ~ Live entertainment Sat evening ~ Open 11-11; 12-10.30 Sun; closed Mon ~ Bedrooms: £45S/£75B

LEWKNOR SU7198 Map 4

Olde Leathern Bottel

Under a mile from M40 junction 6; just off B4009 towards Watlington

This pleasant country pub is often used as a break from the M40 and so can get busy at lunchtimes.The two bar rooms have heavy beams in the low ceilings, rustic furnishings, open fires, and an understated décor of old beer taps and the like. The no smoking family room is separated only by standing timbers, so you won't feel segregated from the rest of the pub. Well liked bar food (with prices unchanged since last year) includes lunchtime filled baguettes or ploughman's (from £4.95), ham and eggs or all-day breakfast (£5.95), and daily specials such as beef and Guinness pie with suet topping or chicken and bacon caesar salad (£6.95), and wok-fried king prawns (£9.95), with home-made puddings such as apple and mincemeat pie or chocolate cake (£2.95). Well kept Brakspears Bitter and Special on handpump, and eight wines by the glass. The attractive sizeable garden has plenty of picnic-sets under parasols, and a children's play area. *(Recommended by John and Glenys Wheeler, Jack Clark, Stuart Turner, Colin and Sandra Tann, Alec and Joan Laurence, Howard Dell, Tracey and Stephen Groves, Ian Phillips, Mrs B M Hill)*

Brakspears ~ Tenant L S Gordon ~ Real ale ~ Bar food (12-2, 7-9.30; 12-2, 6-10 Fri/Sat) ~ (01844) 351482 ~ Children in restaurant and family room ~ Dogs welcome ~ Open 11-2.30(3 Sat), 6-11; 12-3, 7-10.30 Sun

MAIDENSGROVE SU7288 Map 2

Five Horseshoes 🍷

W of village, which is signposted from B480 and B481; OS Sheet 175 map reference 711890

This is a friendly country dining pub set on a lovely common high up in the chiltern beechwoods and close to good local walks. The rambling main bar is furnished with mostly modern wheelback chairs around stripped wooden tables (though there are some attractive older seats and a big baluster-leg table), and there's a proper log fire in winter; the low ceiling in the main area is covered in bank notes from all over the world, mainly donated by customers. Enjoyable bar food under the new licensee includes home-made soup (£4.85), baked filo parcel of goats cheese with red onion marmalade (£5.95), rustic salad of smoked tuna, crab and papaya (£6.45), king prawn and scallop tart with lemon and tarragon crème fraîche (£6.75), chilli and garlic sausages with parsley mash and caramelised onion gravy (£8.75), lambs liver with bacon and onions and a creamy gravy or thai spiced vegetables with coriander rice and a sweet chilli and coconut cream (£8.95), steaks (from £11.95), medallions of pork fillet cooked in a white stilton and apricot sauce with buttered green vegetables (£12.95), grilled bass fillets with a honey and mustard glaze on a strawberry, basil and king prawn salad (£13.25), and rosemary roasted duck breast with crisp wok-fried vegetables and a sweet plum sauce (£13.95); there's also a barbecue menu with dishes such as minted lamb and mozzarella burger (£9.95), thai chicken kebabs with a sweet peanut and coconut satay sauce (£10.95), and tuna steak marinated in a citrus and sweet basil oil topped with mango salsa (£12.95). The airy dining conservatory is no smoking. Well kept Brakspears Bitter, Special and a seasonal ale on handpump, and a good wine list. The three areas outside have a peaceful wooded outlook, and you often see red kites here. *(Recommended by Tracey and Stephen Groves, Tony Harwood, Paul Hopton, John Hale, Michael Porter, Jim Abbott, Alistair Forsyth, Bob and Maggie Atherton, Brian Root, Martin and Karen Wake)*

Brakspears ~ Tenant Greg Fitzpatrick ~ Real ale ~ Bar food (not winter Sun evening) ~ Restaurant ~ (01491) 641282 ~ Children welcome ~ Dogs allowed in bar ~ Open 11-3, 6-11; 11-11 Sat; 12-10.30 Sun; 11-3, 6-11 winter Sat; 12-6 Sun in winter

OXFORD SP5106 Map 4

Kings Arms £

Holywell Street

There's always a good, bustling atmosphere and quite a mix of customers in this 16th-c pub. Apart from the big rather bare main room, with a no smoking coffee room just inside the Parks Road entrance, there are several cosy and comfortably worn-in side and back rooms, each with a different character and customers. An extra back room has a sofa and more tables, with a further tiny room beyond. They keep a dictionary for crossword buffs in the Dons Bar, with its elderly furnishings and tiled floor, mix of old prints and photographs of customers, and sympathetic lighting; daily newspapers and fruit machine. The hardworking staff are friendly and obliging, and there's a nice relaxed atmosphere. Well kept Youngs Bitter, Special and Waggle Dance, and three changing guest beers on handpump, 20 wines by the glass, and a respectable selection of malt whiskies. Bar food includes soup (£2.25; lunchtime mug of soup and filled baked potato £3.75), sandwiches (£2.95), ploughman's or sausages and beans (£4.25), burgers (from £4.25), a wedge of toast topped with bacon, beans and egg or spinach, black olives, tomato and sliced mozzarella (£5.25), tuna fishcakes (£6.25), and steak in stout pie or vegetable moussaka (£6.95). A few tables outside. *(Recommended by R Huggins, D Irving, E McCall, T McLean, the Didler, Mrs E A Macdonald, Kevin Blake, Tracey and Stephen Groves, DRH and KLH, Dick and Madeleine Brown, Derek and Sylvia Stephenson, Arnold Bennett, Paul Hopton)*

Youngs ~ Manager David Kyffin ~ Real ale ~ Bar food (11.30-2.30, 5.30-9.30) ~ (01865) 242369 ~ Children in eating area of bar ~ Open 11-11; 12-10.30 Sun

Rose & Crown

North Parade Avenue; very narrow, so best to park in a nearby street

Bearded and sharp-witted Mr Hall and his wife have been running this congenial and chatty place in their distinctive way for quite a while now, giving what would otherwise be a fairly ordinary neighbourhood pub a great deal of atmosphere and individuality. While he keeps his Adnams Bitter and Broadside, and Hook Norton Old Hooky (on handpump) particularly well, produces almost a work of art in the five minutes or so that he takes to pour a pint of Guinness, and keeps around 25 malt whiskies and a large choice of wines, she looks after the kitchen. This produces traditional lunchtime food, straightforward but much enjoyed, such as sandwiches (from £3.45), tortilla wraps (£4.25), baked potatoes (from £4.25), ploughman's (£5.75), gammon and egg (£6.75), whole trout or 10oz rump steak (£7.45), daily specials like cottage pie or warm chicken salad (from £5.95), and puddings like sticky toffee or apple pie (£3.95). The front door opens into little more than a passage by the bar counter, with a piano in the small room on the left

(Mr Hall enjoys people playing if they're good – but quick to give his opinion if not). The panelled back room, with traditional pub furnishings and decorated with pennants, hockey sticks and the like, is slightly bigger, and you'll find reference books for crossword buffs; one room is no smoking. Unusually, you can buy a tumbler of pistachio nuts, from a bulk dispenser. There's a blessed freedom from mobile phones (though not always from smoke), as well as from piped music and machines – and not too many undergraduates, though graduate students from St Anthony's like it. The pleasant walled back yard (no children – unless with friends of the landlord) can be completely covered with a huge motorised awning, and was one of the first places in Britain to have belgian-style outdoor heaters, well over ten years ago; at the far end is a little overflow eating room. The lavatories are pretty basic. No children inside. *(Recommended by R Huggins, D Irving, E McCall, T McLean, Geoff Pidoux, Torrens Lyster, Robert Lorimer)*

Punch ~ Tenants Andrew and Debbie Hall ~ Bar food (12-2.15, 6-9; not 25, 26 or 31 Dec) ~ No credit cards ~ (01865) 510551 ~ Open 10.30-3, 5-11; 12-4, 6-10.30 Sun

Turf Tavern

Tavern Bath Place; via St Helen's Passage, between Holywell Street and New College Lane

Although it's cut off from the modern bustle of the city by the high stone walls of some of its oldest buildings (including part of the ancient city wall), this lively pub is usually overflowing with quite a mix of customers, and you may have difficulty bagging a seat. The little rooms are dark-beamed and low-ceilinged, and the cellar is open to the public. Up to 11 real ales are well kept on handpump and might include Adnams Broadside, Batemans Combined Harvest, Brains Bitter, Butcombe Gold, Caledonian Deuchars IPA and Golden Promise Organic Ale, Everards Perfick, Greene King Old Speckled Hen, Kelham Island Easy Rider, Smiles April Fuel, and Thwaites Thoroughbred; they also have Hoegaarden on tap, Weston's Old Rosie cider, and in winter mulled wine. On long summer evenings it's especially nice to sit outside in the three attractive walled-in flagstoned or gravelled courtyards (one has its own bar); in winter, they have coal braziers, so you can roast chestnuts or toast marshmallows, and there are canopies with lights and heaters. Straightforward bar food includes baguettes (from £3.75), caesar salad (£4.95), sausage and mash (£5.75), steak and ale pie (£7.25), fish and chips (£7.45), with puddings such as apple and blackberry crumble (£3.25); the top food area is no smoking. This does get very busy with students, which can over-stretch both the service and the lavatories. *(Recommended by the Didler, Paul Hopton, Tina and David Woods-Taylor, Tracey and Stephen Groves, Kevin Blake, Paul and Ann Meyer, R Huggins, D Irving, E McCall, T McLean, Derek and Sylvia Stephenson)*

Laurel ~ Manager Darren Kent ~ Real ale ~ Bar food (12-7.30) ~ (01865) 243235 ~ Children in eating area of bar ~ Dogs welcome ~ Acoustic music in back garden most weekends ~ Open 11-11; 12-10.30 Sun

RAMSDEN SP3515 Map 4

Royal Oak

Village signposted off B4022 Witney—Charlbury

Despite quite a bit of emphasis on the enjoyable food, this unpretentious inn remains very firmly a proper village pub with good beers and a fine mix of customers. There's a genial relaxing atmosphere, and the basic furnishings are comfortable, with fresh flowers, bookcases with old and new copies of *Country Life* and, when the weather gets cold, a cheerful log fire; service is friendly and attentive, and the licensees are welcoming. The dining room is no smoking. Well kept Adnams Broadside, Hook Norton Best, and a guest like Butts Barbus Barbus or West Berkshire Good Old Boy on handpump, and as Mr Oldham has joined forces with a wine producer in France, there's a splendid choice of wines from Languedoc and Roussillon (many by the glass); several armagnacs and farm cider. Using mostly local suppliers (and organic when possible), the popular bar food might include lunchtime ploughman's (£5.25), special club sandwich (£5.75), and sausages and mash (£6.95), as well as home-made soup (£3.25), smoked haddock cooked with whisky and cream, topped with cheddar cheese (£4.95; main course £9.50), a vegetarian dish of the day, a pie of the week (£7.25), home-made burgers (from £7.25), chicken curry (£7.50), mediterranean-style lamb casserole (£10.95), steamed steak and mushroom suet pudding (£11.50), sirloin steak (£12.50), daily specials, puddings (£3.95), and a Thursday evening steak, pudding and glass of wine for £13.50; three-course Sunday lunch (£15.50). There are tables and chairs out in front and on the terrace behind the restaurant (folding back doors give easy access); outdoor heaters. The bedrooms are in separate cottages. *(Recommended by John Kane, MP, Neil Woodcock, Simon Collett-Jones, Rainer Zimmer, Chris Wood, Guy Vowles, Nigel and Sue Foster, Andrew Shore, Maria Williams, Derek and Sylvia Stephenson, Mr Ronald, Mr and Mrs P Dolan, Stephen Buckley, Di and Mike Gillam, J P Marland, John Hale, Pat and Graham Williamson, B Edgar, David Barnes, Peter Green, Michael Jones)*

Free house ~ Licensee Jon Oldham ~ Real ale ~ Bar food (12-2, 7-10) ~ Restaurant ~ (01993) 868213 ~ Children in restaurant ~ Dogs allowed in bar ~ Open 11.30-3, 6.30-11; 12-3, 7-10.30 Sun; closed 25 Dec ~ Bedrooms: £40S/£60S

ROKE SU6293 Map 2

Home Sweet Home

Village signposted off B4009 Benson—Watlington

Andrew Hearn who also runs another of our popular main entries, the Horns at Crazies Hill in Berkshire, has now taken over this rather smart pub. He has redecorated throughout inside, re-carpeted the restaurant and uncovered the original floor in the bar and snug area. There are two smallish bar rooms with a pleasantly relaxed atmosphere, a lovely big log fire, heavy stripped beams, and traditional furniture, and on the right, a carpeted room with low settees and armchairs that leads through to the no smoking restaurant. Bar food now includes soup (£4.25), lunchtime filled baguettes (from £4.25; brie and mango £4.50), ploughman's or smoked chicken and avocado salad (£5.50), pasta of the day (£7.25), pork-and-leek sausages with spring onion mash and onion gravy (£7.50), beef in ale pie (£7.95), tuna and chilli fishcakes with a red thai cream sauce (£8.95), half a duckling with cranberry and redcurrant gravy (£12.95), chargrilled fillet steak with green peppercorn sauce (£13.95), specials such as potted shrimps on toast (£4.95), vegetable lasagne (£6.95), beef curry (£7.95), chicken breast filled with parma ham and mozzarella with a light chilli cream (£9.95), and chargrilled swordfish steak with a caper, parsley and lemon butter (£12.50), and puddings such as treacle tart or plum frangipane (£4.50). Well kept Adnams Best, Fullers London Pride, and Loddon Brewery Hoppit on handpump, ten wines by the glass (champagne as well), and several malt whiskies. There are lots of flowers around tables out by the well and a low-walled front garden. *(Recommended by John and Glenys Wheeler, C A Hall, Doreen and Haydn Maddock, Tracey and Stephen Groves)*

Free house ~ Licensee Andy Hearn ~ Real ale ~ Bar food (not Sun evening) ~ Restaurant ~ (01491) 838249 ~ Children in restaurant ~ Dogs allowed in bar ~ Open 11.30-2.30, 6-11; 12-3, 7-10.30 Sun; closed Sun evening; 25 and 26 Dec

SIBFORD GOWER SP3537 Map 4

Bishop Blaize

Village signposted just off B4035 W of Banbury; Burdrop

From the pub itself and from plenty of seats out in the attractively planted garden, there's a splendid view down over the sheep-strewn hillside and across the surrounding fields – on a clear day it stretches into Gloucestershire and Warwickshire; swings in one corner. Inside, the heavily beamed partly tiled bar has big windows overlooking the garden, some panelling, cosy and comfortable country furnishings, a few framed cartoons, and leaflets advertising local concerts and events. There's an unusual curved wooden counter, opposite which is a very snug inglenook, once used for wakes, but now squeezing in a couple of tiny tables and chairs by an ancient stove. Friendly staff serve good value sraightforward bar food such as sandwiches, soup (£2.95), deep-fried camembert with cranberry jelly (£3.95), haddock and chips (£5.75), ham and eggs (£6.25), chicken curry or pasta with sun-dried tomatoes and roasted garlic in a creamy sauce (£6.75), home-made steak and kidney or chicken and leek pies (£6.95), and fillet steak (£11.50). Well kept Vale Best and a couple of guests like Adnams Broadside and Vale Grumpling on handpump, and several wines by the glass; piped music and darts. There's a new level entrance on to the lawn and into the pub with a ramp on to a small terrace. Occasional summer morris dancers, and good nearby walks. *(Recommended by Arnold Bennett, Dave Braisted, K H Frostick, George Atkinson)*

Free house ~ Licensees Sam and Sheila Merchant ~ Real ale ~ Bar food (not Sun or Tues evenings Oct-April) ~ (01295) 780323 ~ Open 12-2.30, 6-11; 12-3, 7-10.30 Sun

STANTON ST JOHN SP5709 Map 4

Star

Pub signposted off B4027; village is signposted off A40 heading E of Oxford (heading W, you have to go to the Oxford ring-road roundabout and take unclassified road signposted to Stanton St John, Forest Hill etc); bear right at church in village centre

This pleasant old pub has an attractive extension on a level with the car park. There are old-fashioned dining chairs, an interesting mix of dark oak and elm tables, rugs on flagstones, pairs of bookshelves on each side of an attractive inglenook fireplace (good blazing fires in winter), shelves of good pewter, terracotta-coloured walls with a portrait in oils, and a stuffed ermine; down a flight of stairs are little low-beamed rooms – one has ancient brick flooring tiles and the other quite close-set tables. Decent bar food includes sandwiches (£3.75, soup and sandwich £5.45), chicken liver pâté (£4.50), ploughman's (from £4.95), venison pie or moussaka (£7.95), red thai chicken curry (£9.50), and fillet of beef wellington (£11.95), with puddings such as spotted dick or banoffi pie (£3.75). Well kept Wadworths IPA and 6X on handpump. The rather straightforward family room and conservatory are no smoking; piped music, darts, shove-ha'penny, and dominoes. The walled garden has seats among the rockeries and children's play equipment. *(Recommended by Susan and John Douglas, Matthew Shackle, Paul Humphreys, George Atkinson, Martin Jones, Keith Reeve, Marie Hammond, Geoff Pidoux, Mr and Mrs John Taylor, Simon Collett-Jones, Gordon Tong)*

Wadworths ~ Tenant Michael Urwin ~ Real ale ~ Bar food (not Sun evening) ~ No credit cards ~ (01865) 351277 ~ Children in family room ~ Dogs welcome ~ Open 11-2.30, 6.30-11; 12-2.30, 7-10.30 Sun

STEEPLE ASTON SP4725 Map 4

Red Lion 🍷

Off A4260 12 miles N of Oxford

In order to keep the bar as pubby as possible, the enthusiastic licensee of this rather civilised little stone place has added an oak framed and stone-walled extension to the 18th-c dining room. The comfortable partly panelled bar has beams, an antique settle and other good furnishings, well kept Hook Norton Best with guests such as Everards Tiger, Smiles IPA, Wadworths 6X and Youngs Special on handpump, a carefully chosen wine list, quite a few whiskies, single estate cognacs, and farm cider. Good bar food at lunchtime includes pork and chicken liver pâté with caramelised red onions (£4.95), shellfish gratin (£5.25; main course £9.95), filled baguettes or rolls (from £5.25; grilled chicken and bacon with cheese, lettuce, tomato and mayonnaise £6.95), good cheeses with biscuits (£6.50), cottage pie (£7.25), wild mushroom risotto topped with smoked salmon (£8.25), coq au vin (£8.95), and steak frites (£9.50), with evening choices such as mousse of smoked salmon and prawns (£5.50), sautéed chicken livers with sage and madeira and red onion confit (£5.50), chargrilled lamb rump steak with sweet potato and rosemary mash or roast duckling with morello cherry sauce (£12.95), and escalope of veal with parma ham and pecorino (£14.95), and puddings like tarte au chocolat with blackcurrant coulis, crèpes suzette or treacle sponge with proper custard (£4.95). The dining areas are no smoking; piped music in restaurant, cribbage. The suntrap front terrace has lovely flowers and shrubs and is a fine place to relax in summer. *(Recommended by Bruce and Penny Wilkie, Mrs Jill Silversides, Barry Brown, J A Ellis)*

Free house ~ Licensee Derek Dowsett ~ Real ale ~ Bar food (not Sun evening, not Mon except bank hols) ~ Restaurant ~ (01869) 340225 ~ Children in restaurant ~ Dogs allowed in bar ~ Open 12-3, 6-11; 12-3, 7-10.30 Sun; closed Mon lunchtime, 1 Jan

STOKE ROW SU6982 Map 2

Grouse & Claret

Village signposted from B481 S of Nettlebed; from village centre follow signpost to Kingwood Common, a mile S; OS Sheet 175 map reference 692825

Everything in this Chilterns hideaway seems geared to comfort and relaxation, with a good deal of red velvet, perhaps a huge bunch of flowers, a table of magazines and daily papers, a variety of comfortable seats around the well mixed tables, a leather elbow-rest along the serving counter, and good unobtrusively helpful service; also, low black beams, dark ceilings, red and black carpet, and plenty of candles. There are two softly lit small side rooms, one decorated virtually in black. The main dining area, nicely divided, is on the left. A wide range of good freshly made food runs from lunchtime filled baguettes and club sandwiches (£5.50), to dishes such as home-made soup (£4.50), trout fillets with courgettes, rocket and a light lime and coriander dressing (£4.50), smoked duck stir fry (£5.50; main course £7.50), filo parcels with mushrooms and peppers in stilton sauce (£6.50), fresh salmon and dill fishcakes (£8.95), roast corn-fed chicken or poached salmon with minted couscous (£9.50), beer battered cod, steak and kidney log or rib-eye steak and mozzarella burger (all £9.75), and mixed seafood platter (£11.50); no bar snacks Saturday night or Sunday lunchtime. They have a well chosen wine list, and a beer from both Adnams and Loddon Brewery on handpump. The sweet little garden, with a terrace and green plastic garden furniture, is surrounded by woodland. More reports please. *(Recommended by Colin Wood, John Mitchell, David and Helen Mitchell)*

Free house ~ Licensee Robin Gladman ~ Real ale ~ Bar food (12-2.30, 7-9.30) ~ Restaurant ~ (01491) 628359 ~ Children in restaurant ~ Open 12-3.30, 6-11; 12-6 Sun; closed Sun evening

SWALCLIFFE SP3737 Map 4

Stags Head 🍷

Bakers Lane, just off B4035

Behind this charmingly picturesque thatched pub is a series of neatly terraced gardens with palm trees, a small fountain, several tables under a pergola, and a sensibly segregated play area. Inside, the low-beamed bar has a big woodburning stove at one end, a standard lamp beside it, and high-backed wooden pews and cushioned seats along the stone walls. Lots of little jugs hang from the ceiling, and the 'head' of a master of foxhounds rather than the fox. A lighter room has lots more tables, and a tiled fireplace, along with newspapers to read, plenty of books, and lists of various local events and activities; at night all the tables have candles. Half the pub is no smoking. Bar food includes duck and green peppercorn terrine with apricot dressing or baked goats cheese on field mushroom with marinated roasted peppers (£5.75; main course £10.50), chicken and bacon caesar salad (£9.25), prawn stir fry with egg noodles (£10.95), mediterranean pork ribs (£11.95), and specials like hot smoked fish and prawn tartlet (£5.50; main course £9.50) and chicken, leek and spring onion risotto (£9.95); children's menu (from £4.95). Well kept Black Sheep, Brakspears Bitter, and Wye Valley St George's Ale on handpump, and several wines by the glass; piped easy listening music, shove-ha'penny, cribbage, dominoes, and Tuesday evening bridge. A letting bedroom has its own kitchenette. They've two cats, a dog, a couple of chickens, and two ducks. More reports please. *(Recommended by Martin Jones, John and Janet Davey, John Bowdler,*

Andrew Kerr, Clive and Fran Dutson)

Free house ~ Licensees Ian and Julia Kingsford ~ Real ale ~ Bar food (12-2.15, 7-9.30; 12-4 Sun; not Sun evening, Mon, Tues lunchtime) ~ Restaurant ~ (01295) 780232 ~ Children welcome ~ Dogs welcome ~ Open 11-2.30(3 Sat), 6.30-11; 12-5 Sun; closed Sun evening, all day Mon, Tues lunchtime ~ Bedrooms: £35S/£60S

SWINBROOK SP2811 Map 4

Swan

Back road 1 mile N of A40, 2 miles E of Burford

This 17th-c country pub is in a lovely spot close to the River Windrush and its bridge, and there are old-fashioned benches outside by the fuchsia hedge. The tiny interior is cosy, peaceful, and dimly-lit, with simple antique furnishings and a woodburning stove in the flagstoned tap room and the back bar; darts, dominoes and cribbage. Well kept Archers Village Bitter, Greene King IPA and Old Speckled Hen, and Wadworths 6X on handpump, a choice of good coffees, and herbal teas. Tasty bar food at lunchtime includes home-made soup (£3.95), filled baguettes (from £4.95), goats cheese salad (£5.95; main course £7.50), pasta with seafood or with sun-dried tomatoes and parmesan (£7.50), home-made steak and kidney pie (£8.95), and chicken filled with brie, wrapped in bacon and topped with pesto sauce (£9.95); in the evening, there might be wild mushrooms in garlic butter (£4.95), a starter for two people with smoked salmon, whitebait, breaded camembert, onion rings and garlic bread (£7.95), pork tenderloin with apricot, sage and cashew nut pâté and stem ginger jus (£11.95), barbary duck breast on parsnip and potato mash or salmon fillet with a champagne, shrimp and chive sauce (£12.95), and puddings such as home-made apple crumble, summer fruit pudding or chocolate fudge cake (£4.25). *(Recommended by David Handforth, Klaus and Elizabeth Leist, Michael and Ann Cole, Carol Mills, R Huggins, D Irving, E McCall, T McLean)*

Free house ~ Licensee Bob Shepherd ~ Real ale ~ Bar food (not Sun evening) ~ (01993) 822165 ~ Well behaved children welcome away from bar ~ Dogs allowed in bar ~ Open 11.30-3, 6.30-11; 12-3, 7-10.30 Sun; closed 25 Dec

TADPOLE BRIDGE SP3300 Map 4

Trout

Back road Bampton—Buckland, 4 miles NE of Faringdon

Oxfordshire Dining Pub of the Year

Although drinkers do drop into this bustling place, most customers come to enjoy the particularly good, imaginative food. It's also a nice place to stay with some rooms overlooking the Thames (a new suite has its own terrace and overlooks both the garden and river). The L-shaped bar has plenty of seats and some rugs on flagstones, a modern wooden bar counter with terracotta wall behind, some stripped stone, and a large stuffed trout. Friendly and efficient staff serve well kept Brakspears Bitter, Youngs Bitter and a guest beer on handpump, and there are 12 wines by the glass, home-made sloe gin, cherry plum brandy and elderflower cordial; darts, dominoes, cribbage, backgammon and piped music. As well as filled baguettes, the attractively presented dishes might include bacon and game terrine filled with cream compote served with a poached pear (£4.95), carpaccio of tuna with rocket and parmesan (£5.25), scallops with veal sweetbreads, black pudding and apple jus (a delicious dish) or tomato and black olive risotto with roasted vegetables (£8.95), chicken breast with linguini and sauce vierge (£11.95), marinaded then seared and caramelised pork fillet with roasted garlic mash, braised cabbage and creamy whole grain mustard sauce (£12.95), roast local lamb with a puy lentil and bacon casserole (£14.95), roast venison (from Blenheim) with fig tatin, mustard galette and apple jus (£15.95), and daily specials such as almond-crusted red mullet fillet on a lightly curried cauliflower purée or grilled lemon sole with lemon and herb butter (£14.95). Their well hung beef is normally charollais or aberdeen angus, and they do use a lot of good local produce – some from Mr Green's father's nearby farm. The restaurant is no smoking. The well kept garden is

a lovely place to sit in summer, with small fruit trees, attractive hanging baskets, and flower troughs. They sell day tickets for fishing on a two-mile stretch.
(Recommended by Mr and Mrs E Mason, J F M and M West, Matthew Shackle, Tina and David Woods-Taylor, Di and Mike Gillam, Adrian Savage, Georgina Courtenay-Evans, David and Hazel Lee, Mrs June Wilmers, Derek and Sylvia Stephenson, D R Ellis, Martin and Karen Wake, Robert Southgate, David and Ruth Hollands, Bob and Margaret Holder)

Free house ~ Licensee Chris Green ~ Real ale ~ Bar food (not Sun evening) ~ Restaurant ~ (01367) 870382 ~ Children welcome ~ Dogs welcome ~ Open 11.30-3, 6-11; 12-3 Sun; closed Sun evening; evening 25 Dec, all day 26 Dec, 31 Dec and 1 Jan, first wk Feb ~ Bedrooms: /£80B

THAME SP7005 Map 4

Swan

Upper High Street

As we went to press, this friendly, civilised 16th-c hotel was possibly up for sale, so by the time this *Guide* is published, there may be some changes. We are keeping our fingers crossed that those changes will not be too drastic. It overlooks the market square in the centre of town, and although nothing seems to match, the interesting mix of furnishings all blends together perfectly: the tables in the main bar are either chests, trunks or a butcher's block, and assorted well worn armchairs and comfortable old sofas include several grouped together around the stone fireplace. Brightly painted tiles cover the bar counter and the wall behind, and there are beams, timbers, faded rugs, old-fashioned saucy seaside postcards and a handsome clock. Cushioned sofas meander along a passageway, then down a step is an odd but cosy low-ceilinged room with paintings of erstwhile locals on the walls. Well kept Archers Spring Ale, Hook Norton Best, Shepherd Neame Spitfire, and Timothy Taylors Landlord on handpump, and quite a few wines by the glass; piped classical music (which can be quite loud), newspapers to read, dominoes, and cribbage. Enjoyable bar food includes sandwiches (£2.95; baguettes £4.25), home-made soup (£3.95), ploughman's, smoked salmon and scrambled eggs, ham and egg or cheese and tomato omelette (all £6.95), halibut and lobster fishcakes or chargrilled chicken breast with greek salad (£7.50), and lamb and mushroom hotpot, braised liver with onion gravy or baked halibut with stir-fried vegetables (£7.95). The upstairs restaurant still has its medieval ceiling. There are a few tables at the back, in a small shopping arcade. It can get very busy in the evening, and parking is quite tricky on market days – the Farmers' Market is held on Tuesdays.
(Recommended by Torrens Lyster, Giles and Annie Francis, Susan and John Douglas, Tracey and Stephen Groves, Sue Demont, Tim Barrow)

Free house ~ Licensee Sue Turnbull ~ Real ale ~ Bar food (12-2.30, 7-9; not 25 or 26 Dec) ~ Restaurant ~ (01844) 261211 ~ Children in eating area of bar and in restaurant until 8pm ~ Dogs allowed in bar and bedrooms ~ Open 11-11; 12-10.30 Sun ~ Bedrooms: £50S(£65B)/£90S(£90B)

WOOTTON SP4419 Map 4

Kings Head

Chapel Hill (which is near the church and marked by a wooden triangle in the road covering the old well); off B4027 N of Woodstock

This attractive and rather civilised 17th-c cotswold stone house is now completely no smoking. It's not really the sort of place people drop into for a quick pint, and the spacious and formal no smoking restaurant is pretty much the focal point, although you can choose to eat in the bar or garden instead. Good, enjoyable food includes soup (£3.95), warm gressingham duck salad with spicy plum sauce or szechuan pigeon breast on shallots caramelised in sesame oil and shredded ginger with a blackbean and oyster sauce (£4.95), rosette of muscovado and lime cured scottish salmon with a coriander and tomato vinaigrette (£5.50), wild mushroom risotto (£9.25), chargrilled medallions of pork fillet on red onion marmalade with an orange and juniper berry sauce (£11.25), cantonese braised leg and pink roasted breast of duck with a duck sherry gravy (£14.95), tower of orkney steak with potato rösti and wild mushrooms with a smooth black pepper dressing (£16.50), daily specials like steak and kidney pie (£8.25), warm fish salad (£12.95), and fillets of bass on roasted tomatoes (£15.95), and puddings such as caramelised citrus tart with raspberry sauce, délice of white chocolate in a chocolate cage or bread and butter pudding (£4.95). The civilised and relaxing beamed no smoking lounge bar has a nice mix of old oak settles and chairs around wooden tables, comfortable armchairs and chintzy sofas, an open log fire, and old prints and ceramics on the pale pink walls. Well kept Greene King Ruddles County and Hook Norton Old Hooky on handpump, and seven wines by the glass. Although they are allowed in the restaurant, this is not really a place geared towards children, and they don't do children's meals. *(Recommended by Sir Nigel Foulkes, Arnold Bennett, Di and Mike Gillam, DRH and KLH, Geoff Pidoux, Simon Collett-Jones)*

Free house ~ Licensees Tony and Amanda Fay ~ Real ale ~ Bar food (not Sun evening or Mon) ~ Restaurant ~ (01993) 811340 ~ Children over 12 and only if very well behaved ~ Open 12-2.45(3 Sat), 6.45(6.30 Sat)-11; 12-3 Sun; closed Sun evening and Mon (except bank hols) ~ Bedrooms: /£80B

LUCKY DIP

Besides the fully inspected pubs, you might like to try these Lucky Dips recommended to us and described by readers (if you do, please send us reports: www.goodguides.co.uk).

ABINGDON SU5098

Boundary House [Oxford Rd]: Roomy chain dining pub with good choice of well prepared and presented fresh food, huge helpings, friendly efficient service, Greene King real ales, decent wines, two buzzers on each table – one to get a waiter, the other for the bill; three steps up to main dining area, but OK for walking disabled (some tables at lower level); unobtrusive piped music; lots of tables outside *(Tony Beaulah)*

Broad Face [Bridge St]: Good spot nr Thames for dining pub with thoughtful choice of freshly made modern food all day inc plenty for vegetarians, lunchtime menu with sandwiches, baked potatoes, pasta and so forth, Greene King Morlands and Abbot and Wadworths 6X, good wine range, lively atmosphere; small side terrace *(Tim and Ann Newell)*

Kings Head & Bell [E St Helen St]: Attractive 16th-c building, softly lit linked beamed areas with stripped stone, flagstones and assorted wooden furniture, Adnams ales, decent wines, good soft drinks choice, reasonably priced food all day, upstairs games room; service may slow if busy, smoking allowed throughout, piped pop music or juke box, occasional live music; children welcome till 6, tables in coach yard *(CMW, JJW)*

ADDERBURY SP4735

Plough [Aynho Rd]: Upgraded medieval thatched pub with attractive furnishings and friendly cottagey atmosphere, popular for enjoyable food from wide choice of sandwiches and baguettes to good fresh home-made pub food; helpful staff, well kept Charles Wells Bombardier, restaurant area *(Colin Gooch)*

☆ *Red Lion* [The Green; off A4260 S of Banbury]: Congenial pub with big inglenook, panelling, high stripped beams and stonework, Victorian and Edwardian pictures, well kept Greene King ales, good wine range, quick friendly service, daily papers, popular blackboard food in bar and cosy rooms off behind, games area on left; piped music; children in eating area, picnic-sets out on well kept terrace, comfortable bedrooms, open all day summer *(Paul and Penny Rampton, George Atkinson, LYM, Meg and Colin Hamilton, Geoff Pidoux, John and Claire Pettifer)*

ARDINGTON SU4388

☆ *Boars Head* [signed off A417 Didcot—Wantage]: Enjoyable restauranty food at one end of low-beamed pub with attractively simple country décor (bar seats ex Salisbury cathedral) and plainer no smoking extension, good wines; more local atmosphere at the other end, with well kept Arkells 3B, Brakspears and a guest beer, darts, shove-ha'penny, cribbage, dominoes, board games, TV and piped music; children welcome, cl Sun evening, peaceful attractive village *(Dick and Madeleine Brown, LYM, Michael Launchbury)*

ARDLEY SP5427

Fox & Hounds [B430 (old A43), just SW of M40 junction 10]: Old stone pub with long opened-up low-beamed dining lounge, big fireplaces each end, lots of horsebrasses, pictures and old glassware, goldfish tank, flowers and candles on tables, sound choice of simple food from ploughman's to steaks and Sun lunch, barbecue and curry nights, well kept Fullers London Pride and Greene King Old Speckled Hen, decent house wines, another open fire in cosy carpeted bar *(J Stickland)*

ASHBURY SU2685

☆ *Rose & Crown* [B4507/B4000; High St]: Relaxing, roomy and comfortable open-plan beamed bar, part of old-fashioned hotel, with highly polished woodwork, traditional pictures, chesterfields, deep armchairs and pews, lovely view down pretty village street of thatched cottages, raised section with further oak tables and chairs, lots of wines, well kept Arkells 2B and 3B, good range of wines by the glass and other drinks, friendly helpful staff, enjoyable blackboard food, charming roomy restaurant, separate public bar with pool and juke box; tables out in front; 11 bedrooms, attractive village nr Ridgeway *(Marjorie and David Lamb, BB, Gerald Wilkinson)*

ASTHALL SP2811

☆ *Maytime* [off A40 at W end of Witney bypass, then 1st left]: Comfortably genteel dining pub with very wide food choice from sandwiches up (just set lunch on Sun), slightly raised plush dining lounge neatly set with tables (best ones down by fire may be booked for overnight guests), airy conservatory restaurant (children allowed behind screen), two Greene King or Wadworths ales, decent wines, prompt service, interesting pictures, small bar with flagstones and log fire; piped music; in tiny hamlet, nice views of Asthall Manor and watermeadows from garden, attractive walks, quiet comfortable bedrooms around charming back courtyard *(BB, Mike Vince)*

BANBURY SP4640

Bell [Middleton Rd]: Well run local popular for its good choice of well kept real ales; open all day Sat *(Mick Furn)*

Easington [Bloxham Rd (A361 S)]: Ember Inn with four real ales, L-shaped bar and several comfortable separate areas, welcoming fires (one with real logs), enjoyable food all day *(JHBS)*

BECKLEY SP5611

Abingdon Arms [signed off B4027; High St]: Handsome old pub with a variety of seating inc pews, bare boards, lots of beams and stripped stone, two real fires, well kept Brakspears sold metrically, enjoyable food from sandwiches up, friendly staff, separate dining room, board games; floodlit terrace, extensive pretty garden dropping away into orchard, good walks *(LYM, Geoff Pidoux)*

BESSELS LEIGH SP4501

Greyhound: Roomy family dining pub, comfortable and cheerful, with lots of no smoking rooms, varied good value food from baguettes to Sun carvery inc some imaginative dishes, well kept beers, decent wines, friendly helpful staff, open fires, children's room with toys; piped music; open all day, play area outside *(Geoff Pidoux, Colin and Janet Roe)*

BINFIELD HEATH SU7478

☆ *Bottle & Glass* [off A4155 at Shiplake; between village and Harpsden]: Lovely thatched black and white timbered Tudor cottage, scrubbed wooden tables, low beams and flagstones, fine fireplace, black squared panelling, welcoming landlord, three well kept Brakspears ales, tasty if not cheap blackboard bar food from sandwiches to big Sun lunch, no smoking dining area, shove-ha'penny, dominoes; no children or dogs inside; big attractive garden with tables under little thatched roofs *(the Didler, Anthony Longden, Michael Dandy, Peter B Brown, Mike and Sue Richardson, LYM, Wombat, D J and P M Taylor)*

BLADON SP4414

White House [Park St (A4095)]: Relaxed and cheerful, with good value traditional home-made food all day, Greene King IPA and Abbot or Old Speckled Hen, good service, rocking chair by good log fire, individual old-fashioned décor with lots hanging from ceiling; darts, weekly quiz, aunt sally, occasional live music; handy for back gate of Blenheim Park (beautiful walks), in village where Churchill is buried *(Geoff Pidoux, Mark Percy, Lesley Mayoh)*

BLETCHINGDON SP5017

Blacks Head [Station Rd; B4027 N of Oxford]: Cosy neatly kept stripped-stone lounge with woodburner, enjoyable food here and in extended upmarket dining area with conservatory, well kept Greene King ales, games room; pleasant garden, good value simple bedrooms *(Geoff Pidoux, Jo Morley)*

BLOXHAM SP4335

☆ *Elephant & Castle* [off A361, fairly handy for M40 junction 1; Humber St]: Relaxed and unchanging, with striking 17th-c stone fireplace in simple but elegant bare-boards public bar, big winter log fire in comfortable lounge; well kept Hook Norton ales, farm cider (guests in summer), around 30 malt whiskies, decent coffee, promptly served lunchtime food at very low prices, friendly service, traditional games inc antique shove-ha'penny board; children welcome, open all day Sun, sunny flower-filled courtyard and garden, may be wknd barbecues; imposing Cotswold village *(LYM, George Atkinson)*

BOARS HILL SP4901

Fox [between A34 and B4017; Fox Lane]: Well run and attractive Chef & Brewer in pretty wooded countryside, interesting rambling rooms on different levels, huge log fireplaces, poems on the wall, wide choice of reasonably priced food, well kept ales, decent wine, polite service, day's paper framed in gents'; may be soft piped classical music or jazz; children welcome, pleasant raised verandah, charming big sloping garden with play area, open all day *(Geoff Pidoux)*

BODICOTE SP4537

☆ *Plough* [Goose Lane/High St; off A4260 S of Banbury]: Well worn 14th-c pub in same family for 50 years, usually brewing its own cheap ales such as Bodicote Bitter, No 9, Porter and Life Sentence, guests such as Greene King IPA and Worthington, country wines, wide choice of well cooked straightforward food from good value sandwiches and baguettes to steaks and Sun roast (cooking as well as service may be by the friendly landlord); low heavy beams, stripped stone, hops, pictures and brasses, no music, small open fire; darts, TV and fruit machine in public bar, children and dogs welcome (pub retriever called Daisy), twice-yearly beer festivals; no credit cards *(the Didler,*

Pete Baker, BB, Dr B and Mrs P B Baker, Kevin Thorpe)

BRITWELL SALOME SU6793

Goose [B4009 Watlington—Benson]: Emphasis on limited choice of good fresh home-made food in two small back dining rooms, good sandwiches in the bar too, reasonably priced wines, good coffee; garden tables *(anon)*

BRIZE NORTON SP3007

Chequers [Station Rd]: Roomy open-plan pub with wide choice of proper pub food inc enjoyable and generous OAP lunches, friendly staff, real ales, pleasant atmosphere, RAF theme *(Dr and Mrs A K Clarke)*

BROADWELL SP2504

Five Bells [off A361 N of Lechlade]: Closed for several weeks as we went to press, while new tenants moved in; has been popular for its pleasant series of rooms with two big log fires, mix of flagstones and carpet, low beams, sizeable dining room and conservatory, with good real ales and bar food, but there has been talk of major changes afoot – even perhaps a name change; spacious flower-filled garden, aunt sally; news please *(LYM)*

BUCKNELL SP5525

Trigger Pond [handy for M40 junction 10; Bicester Rd]: Welcoming stone-built pub opp the pond, good range of popular food (must book Sun lunch), nice atmosphere, full Wadworths beer range kept well; pleasant terrace and garden *(Marjorie and David Lamb)*

BURCOT SU5695

Chequers [A415 Dorchester—Abingdon]: Attractive thatched pub under expert new licensees, enjoyable good value food in bar and upper no smoking dining gallery, smartly comfortable spacious beamed lounge, well kept ales, good wine range, open fire; shove-ha'penny, cribbage, dominoes; children welcome, wheelchair access, tables out on floodlit terrace and on lawn among flowers and fruit trees *(LYM, Mr and Mrs T Wright)*

BURFORD SP2512

Angel [Witney St]: Long heavy-beamed dining pub in attractive ancient building, good brasserie food *(LYM, Geoff Pidoux, David and Ruth Hollands)*

Cotswold Arms [High St]: Cosy bar with welcoming log fire, good sensibly priced food in busy dining area, beautiful stonework, pleasant efficient service; jazz nights Mon and Weds *(Peter and Audrey Dowsett, Geoff Pidoux)*

☆ *Golden Pheasant* [High St]: Small early 18th-c hotel with sofas and armchairs among more usual lounge bar furnishings in cosy front bar, enjoyable imaginative food from interesting sandwiches to wide choice of restaurant dishes, well kept Greene King IPA and Old Speckled Hen, good wine range, daily papers, stuffed pheasant above fire, flagstoned dining room down some steps, coffee and cream teas; regular live music; pleasant seats on back terrace, comfortable bedrooms, open all day *(BB, Michael Dandy, Derek and Sylvia Stephenson, W W Burke, R Huggins, D Irving, E McCall, T McLean, David and Ruth Hollands)*

☆ *Mermaid* [High St]: Handsome jettied Tudor dining pub with attractive long narrow bar, beams, flagstones, panelling and stripped stone, bay seating around the row of tables, well kept Greene King ales, food from good lunchtime baguettes up, airy dining room and no smoking upstairs restaurant, efficient service; piped music, fruit machine; children in eating areas, picnic-sets under cocktail parasols outside, open all day *(LYM, Jim Abbott, Geoff Pidoux, P R and S A White, Comus and Sarah Elliott, Mike and Mary Carter, Peter and Audrey Dowsett)*

Old Bull [High St]: Handsome building well reconstructed a decade or so ago with beams, panelling and big fireplaces, smartly refurbished in wine bar/bistro style, Greene King Ales, decent wines; piped music; children welcome, open all day, tables out in front or back through old coach entry, comfortable bedrooms *(LYM, Jim Abbott, Geoff Pidoux)*

☆ *Royal Oak* [Witney St]: Neat 17th-c stripped stone local with Wadworths IPA and 6X, wide range of simple food, efficient friendly service, masses of beer mugs and steins hanging from beams, antlers over warm log-effect gas fire, some settles, pine tables and chairs, more in back dining room, bar billiards; tables out on terrace, sensibly priced bedrooms off garden behind *(Stan Edwards, Geoff Pidoux, R Huggins, D Irving, E McCall, T McLean)*

CHADLINGTON SP3222

☆ *Tite* [off A361 S of Chipping Norton, and B4437 W of Charlbury; Mill End, slightly out of village – at garage turn towards Churchill, then left at playground]: Civilised and welcoming food-oriented local with good if not cheap home-made food from sandwiches to lovely puddings, some unusual dishes, vine-covered back restaurant evenings and Sun lunchtime, well kept Youngs, a Wadworths-like beer brewed for the pub and a guest beer and stout, good house wines, cheerful long-serving traditional landlord, friendly efficient service, big log fire in huge fireplace, settles, wooden chairs, prints, rack of guide books, daily papers and magazines, pink-painted walls; piped classical music, children welcome, cl Mon exc bank hols; superb garden full of shrubs, some quite unusual, with stream running under pub – path from car park winds through it; plenty of tables outside, good walks nearby *(BB, Guy Vowles, Richard Greaves)*

CHALGROVE SU6397

Red Lion [High St (B480 Watlington—Stadhampton)]: New licensees in this pleasantly restored beamed village pub, owned by local church trust since 1640; so more reports on the new regime at this former main entry, please *(LYM)*

CHARLBURY SP3519

☆ *Bell* [Church St]: Attractive civilised two-room bar in small olde-worlde 17th-c hotel, flagstones, stripped stonework and huge open fire, welcoming service, short choice of good interesting bar lunches (not Sun) from sandwiches up, well kept Hook Norton and Wadworths, wide choice of malt whiskies, pleasant restaurant; children in eating area, comfortable quiet bedrooms, good breakfast *(LYM, Geoff Pidoux)*

CHAZEY HEATH SU6979

Pack Horse [just off A4074 Reading—Wallingford by B4526]: Well kept and attractive 17th-c pub with big log fire in panelled lounge bar, friendly service, wide choice of reasonably priced home-made food from traditional basics to imaginative dishes, good choice of well kept ales, decent wines, family room; sizeable back garden with play area and barbecue terrace *(BB, David and Louise Tansley, Lydia Roberts, Mark Wyeth)*

Pack Saddle [A4074 Reading—Wallingford]: Cheerful pub with warm friendly atmosphere, eclectic bric-a-brac, good changing choice of sensibly priced food with appealing puddings (worth booking wknds), helpful friendly staff, well kept real ales, good choice of wines *(BB, Mrs Liz Turner, Neil Skidmore)*

CHESTERTON SP5521

Red Cow [The Green]: Welcoming new licensees in pleasantly updated softly lit village pub with two log fires, lunchtime food, well kept Greene King ales, small dining area *(Marjorie and David Lamb)*

CHINNOR SU7698

☆ ***Sir Charles Napier*** [Spriggs Alley, up on the ridge above Chinnor]: More good smart upmarket restaurant than pub, but does have small, friendly and traditional bar with sofas, log fire and (at a price) Wadworths IPA or 6X as well as champagne on draught and good choice of other drinks; nice service, good piped music; charming crazy-paved back courtyard, croquet lawn and paddocks, Chilterns and red kite views; cl Sun evening and Mon *(LYM, Bob and Maggie Atherton)*

CHRISTMAS COMMON SU7193

☆ ***Fox & Hounds*** [off B480/B481]: New licensees for this well liked Chilterns dining pub, but too late for us to assess for this edition; in lovely countryside, a popular lunch stop for walkers and cyclists, cosy beamed bar with two compact rooms, simply but comfortably furnished, bow windows, red and black tiles and big inglenook, snug little back room, extension barn restaurant, Brakspears real ales; children and dogs have been allowed, rustic benches and tables outside *(LYM)*

CHURCH ENSTONE SP3724

☆ ***Crown*** [Mill Lane; from A44 take B4030 turn off at Enstone]: Current licensees doing well in popular and attractive old pub with congenial and cottagey bar, log fire in brass-fitted stone fireplace, beams and stripped stone, good fresh food (not Mon night) from tasty lunchtime baguettes up, good-sized light modern dining area and roomy conservatory, welcoming service, well kept Hook Norton Best, Shepherd Neame Spitfire and Wadworths 6X, decent wines by the glass, plenty of atmosphere; may be piped music, may be cl Mon lunchtime; garden tables *(Chris Glasson, Andy and Jill Kassube, LYM, Guy Vowles, J A Ellis, Geoff Pidoux, Stuart Turner, Richard Marjoram)*

CHURCH HANBOROUGH SP4212

☆ ***Hand & Shears*** [opp church; signed off A4095 at Long Hanborough, or off A40 at Eynsham roundabout]: Newly updated open-feeling pub/restaurant, long gleaming bar, steps down into roomy back eating area, another small dining room, agreeable modern atmosphere, wide food choice, attentive young staff, well kept real ales, decent wines, open fires *(Tim Brierly, BB, Dick and Madeleine Brown)*

CLIFTON HAMPDEN SU5495

Barley Mow [towards Long Wittenham, S of A415]: Interesting thatched Chef & Brewer dining pub, very low ancient beams, oak-panelled family room, well kept ales such as Fullers London Pride and Gales Sweet & Sour, good choice of wines by the glass, efficient friendly service, relaxed atmosphere, log fire, pleasant décor, food all day from sandwiches up, restaurant; piped music; tables on pleasant terrace and in well tended waterside garden, short stroll from the Thames; open all day *(Chris Glasson, LYM, Catherine and Rob Dunster)*

COMBE SP4115

Cock [off A4095 at Long Hanborough; The Green]: Spick and span classic country pub facing green in charming village, two congenial bars, friendly landlord and helpful staff, real ale, enjoyable food from good home-made soup and baguettes up *(J A Ellis, Geoff Pidoux, DC)*

CROPREDY SP4646

☆ ***Red Lion*** [off A423 N of Banbury]: Rambling old thatched stone-built pub charmingly placed opp pretty village's churchyard, low beams, inglenook log fire, high-backed settles, brass, plates and pictures; friendly staff, well kept changing ales such as Greene King Old Speckled Hen, food from sandwiches and baguettes up (two rooms set for eating, children allowed in restaurant part), games room; piped music, limited parking, picnic-sets under cocktail parasols on back terrace by car park *(LYM, Kevin Blake, Meg and Colin Hamilton, John Saville)*

CROWELL SU7499

☆ ***Shepherds Crook*** [B4009, 2 miles from M40 junction 6]: Honest traditional pub facing common, pleasantly refurbished with stripped brick, timber and flagstones, imaginative changing food inc good fresh fish on Fri and local meat and game, carpeted raftered dining area, well kept Bathams, Hook Norton Best, Timothy Taylors Landlord and interesting guest beers such as Loddon, decent wines, friendly straight-talking landlord, no music or machines; views from comfortable canopied tables out in front *(Torrens Lyster, Tim and Ann Newell, David Oakley)*

CUDDESDON SP5902

☆ ***Bat & Ball*** [S of Wheatley; High St]: Walls covered with cricketing programmes, photographs, porcelain models in well lit cases, score books, cigarette cards, pads, gloves and hats, and signed bats, bails and balls; low beams, some flagstones, Banks's LBW, Marstons Pedigree and a guest beer, decent wines, well liked food from baguettes to elaborate dishes (evening concentration on this, big no smoking dining extension); cribbage, dominoes, piped music; children welcome, pleasant back terrace with good views, aunt sally, comfortable annexe bedrooms (some small), open all day *(Ian Phillips, LYM, Pam and John Smith, Richard Marjoram, Sean and Sharon Pines)*

CUMNOR SP4503

☆ ***Bear & Ragged Staff*** [signed from A420; Appleton Rd]: Busy comfortably rambling dining pub with lots of kitsch bric-a-brac in romantically dim-lit partly flagstoned small rooms, good choice of enjoyable food inc popular Sun roasts and enterprising vegetarian dishes, well kept real ales from varying breweries (there's a proper drinking area), efficient attentive staff, two big log fires, no smoking area; children in eating areas, open all day Sun in summer *(LYM, Geoff Pidoux, Sue Demont, Tim Barrow)*

Vine [Abingdon Rd]: Restauranty pub with wide choice of enjoyable food from good baguettes to Sun family lunches (must book these), good friendly service despite wknd bustle, three well kept guest ales, good wine range, back dining extension, no smoking area in conservatory; picnic-sets in attractive back garden *(Colin and Janet Roe, Geoff Pidoux)*

CURBRIDGE SP3208

Lord Kitchener [Lew Rd (A4095 towards Bampton)]: Comfortably refurbished, with good value food inc generous Sun lunch in smart no smoking multi-mirror end dining area, old local photographs, big log fire, well kept real ales, happy atmosphere, quick efficient service by chirpy NZ family; piped music may be obtrusive; garden with play area *(Peter and Audrey Dowsett, Richard Marjoram)*

DEDDINGTON SP4631

☆ ***Deddington Arms*** [off A4260 (B4031) Banbury—Oxford; Horse Fair]: Welcoming and relaxed beamed and timbered hotel with mullioned windows in cosy bar, some emphasis on enjoyable food from good sandwiches and light dishes up, sizeable more modern back eating area (allowing children), smart restaurant with more elaborate menu, well kept ales such as Caledonian Deuchars IPA, Greene King IPA and Wadworths 6X, good choice of wines by the glass, good log fire, friendly attentive young staff, rather modern décor with much ochre paintwork; unobtrusive piped music; open all day, comfortable chalet bedrooms around courtyard, good breakfast, attractive village with lots of antiques shops *(LYM, Gill and Keith Croxton, George Atkinson, Paul and Penny Rampton, Michael Dandy, M Sharp, Hugh Spottiswoode, Trevor and Judy Pearson)*

☆ ***Unicorn*** [Market Pl]: Busy 17th-c inn taken over late 2003 by helpful new licensees, enjoyable generous food (not Sun evening) in pleasant modernised bar or beamed restaurant (no smoking areas in both), well kept Hook Norton and Fullers London Pride, good choice of wines by the glass, proper coffee, quick friendly service, inglenook fireplace; cobbled courtyard leading to lovely walled back garden; dogs welcome in bar, open all day (from 9 Sat for farmers' market), bedrooms *(BB, R C Vincent)*

DORCHESTER SU5794

☆ ***Fleur de Lys*** [High St]: Carefully preserved coaching inn opp abbey, dating from 16th c, comfortably traditional two-level interior, wide choice of good value home cooking, all fresh, well kept Greene King and Ushers ales, good hands-on licensees and friendly helpful staff, interesting old photographs of the pub; children very welcome, unobtrusive piped music; picnic-sets on front terrace and in back garden *(R Michael Richards, Len Banister)*

☆ ***George*** [just off A4074 Maidenhead—Oxford; High St]: Handsome well cared-for timbered hotel, good choice of enjoyable bar food, well kept Brakspears, good wines, cheerful landlord, well organised service, roaring log fire and fine old furnishings in smart beamed bar; open all day, children in restaurant, bedrooms, lovely village *(LYM, Mrs E A Macdonald, Dick and Madeleine Brown, Colin Wood)*

DUCKLINGTON SP3507

☆ ***Bell*** [off A415, a mile SE of Witney; Standlake Rd]: Pretty thatched local with wide choice of enjoyable reasonably priced home-made food (not Sun eve) inc particularly good sandwiches, well kept Greene King ales, good house wines, friendly service; big stripped stone and flagstoned bar with scrubbed tables, log fires, glass-covered well, old local photographs, farm tools, hatch-served public bar, roomy and attractive well laid out back restaurant, its beams festooned with bells; cards and dominoes, no piped music; folk night 1st Sun of month, events such as morris dancing or raft races; small garden behind with play area, colourful hanging baskets, nine bedrooms – and the nearby village pond does indeed have ducks *(Peter and Audrey Dowsett, BB, Pete Baker, Comus and Sarah Elliott)*

Strickland Arms [off A415 SE of Witney; Witney Rd]: Welcoming and cosy old-world pub, low beams and flooring tiles in smart bar partly set for dining, enjoyable traditional food, well kept Adnams and Wadworths 6X, good value wines, compact no smoking restaurant, no music or machines; small pretty garden with skittles and aunt sally *(Geoff Pidoux, Mr and Mrs P Lally)*

DUNS TEW SP4528

☆ ***White Horse*** [off A4260 N of Kidlington]: New licensees doing well in unspoilt 16th-c beamed pub, enjoyable food in main area with stripped bricks and stonework, rugs on flagstones, oak timbers and panelling, enormous inglenook, settles and homely candlelit stripped tables, well kept beers inc Hook Norton Best and Wadworths 6X, decent wine list, two cosy side areas; disabled access, bedrooms in former stables, attractive village *(LYM, Neil and Jenny Dury)*

ENSLOW SP4818

Rock of Gibraltar [A4095 about 1½ miles SW of Kirtlington]: Tall pub under friendly new licensees, three well kept changing ales such as Hook Norton, well prepared reasonably priced food (not wkdys last winter), beams, stripped stone, bright narrowboat paintwork, modern dining extension overlooking canal, upper conservatory with even better view; popular Thurs folk night; lots of picnic-sets under cocktail parasols in pretty waterside garden *(Pete Baker)*

EXLADE STREET SU6582

☆ *Highwayman* [just off A4074 Reading—Wallingford]: Two beamed bar rooms, mainly 17th-c (parts older), with interesting rambling layout and variety of furniture, good if not cheap food, good service, well kept Fullers London Pride and Wadworths 6X, decent wines, airy no smoking conservatory dining room overlooking the garden (fine views); piped music; children welcome, comfortable bedrooms *(the Didler, LYM, Canon Michael Bourdeaux)*

FARINGDON SU2895

☆ *Bell* [Market Pl]: Appealing old pub with 17th-c carved oak chimney-piece for inglenook fireplace, red leather settles, interesting faded mural in inner bar, well kept Wadworths ales, wide choice of enjoyable generous food inc interesting dishes and plenty of fish in bar and restaurant, friendly staff and customers; children and dogs allowed, tables out among flowers in heated cobbled back coachyard, character beamed bedrooms *(Dave Irving, LYM, Rona Murdoch, Tom and Ruth Rees)*

FYFIELD SU4298

☆ *White Hart* [off A420 Oxford—Faringdon]: Impressive medieval hall with soaring eaves, huge stone-flanked window embrasures and attractive no smoking upper gallery, inglenook fireplace in low-ceilinged side bar, well kept ales such as Brakspears, Loddon, West Berkshire and Wychwood, enjoyable inexpensive food from sandwiches up, good-natured staff; may be piped music; children welcome and dogs allowed in the bar, rambling back garden *(LYM, Andy and Yvonne Cunningham, Ian Phillips)*

GARSINGTON SP5802

Three Horseshoes [The Green; off B480 SE of Oxford]: Nicely set out lounge and restaurant area, friendly staff, wide range of popular food all day, Greene King ales, decent wines; TV in separate public bar with pool room; lovely views *(Geoff Pidoux)*

GODSTOW SP4809

☆ *Trout* [off A34 Oxford bypass northbound, via Wytham, or A40/A44 roundabout via Wolvercote]: Olde-worlde Vintage Inn in genuinely medieval creeper-covered building, several linked rooms (all but one no smoking), log fires in three huge hearths, hop-hung beams, carvings and shiny ancient flagstones, attractive pictures and country bric-a-brac, decent food all day inc good lunchtime sandwiches, well kept Bass and Fullers London Pride, good choice of wines by the glass, friendly young well trained staff; can be very busy, quiet piped music; charming in summer with lovely flagstoned heated terrace by a stream full of greedily plump perch, long restored footbridge to island (owned by pub) with ducks and peacocks, abbey ruins opp; in winter they may serve mulled wine and hand out blankets for roasting chestnuts out here *(LYM, Alicia Coates, Eleanor and Nick Steinitz, Roger and Pauline Pearce, P R and S A White, Geoff Pidoux, George Atkinson, Peter and Audrey Dowsett)*

GORING SU6080

☆ *Catherine Wheel* [Station Rd]: Well run pub (Barleycorn's former landlord) with good informal atmosphere, friendly helpful service, good choice of well priced home-made food in two neat and cosy bar areas and restaurant (children welcome here), Brakspears full range kept well, Stowford Press cider, decent wine, good inglenook log fire; notable door to gents'; nice courtyard and garden, handy for Thames Path, attractive village *(the Didler, Rob Winstanley)*

John Barleycorn [Manor Rd]: Low-beamed cottagey local under efficient new management, prints in cosy little lounge bar, pleasant adjoining eating area, well kept Brakspears, pool in end room; children welcome, clean and simple bedrooms *(the Didler, Fiona McElhone, Rob Winstanley)*

GOZZARD'S FORD SU4698

Black Horse: Ancient village pub with dining areas giving good choice of enjoyable generous food esp fish, decent wines, cheerful service *(T R and B C Jenkins)*

GREAT HASELEY SP6301

Plough [handy for M40 junction 7; Rectory Rd]: Small friendly thatched pub with new chef/landlady doing good inventive food from bar snacks up, buoyant pubby atmosphere with thriving darts and cribbage teams, well kept Shepherd Neame Spitfire, helpful staff; garden with aunt sally, quiet area *(Tim Lumb, BB)*

HAILEY SU6485

☆ *King William IV* [the different Hailey nr Ipsden, off A4074 or A4130 SE of Wallingford]: Attractive 16th-c pub in charming peaceful countryside, some concentration on wide choice of good generous mainly traditional food, friendly landlord and helpful staff, thriving atmosphere, full Brakspears range kept well, beams, bare bricks and tiled floor (carpet in middle room), big inglenook log fire, clean fresh décor and well kept traditional furnishings, extended dining room; outstanding views from pub and tables on front terrace *(Susan and John Douglas, the Didler, LYM, J A Ellis)*

HEADINGTON SP5407

Butchers Arms [Wilberforce St]: Welcoming backstreet local with long narrow seating area, good value wkdy lunchtime food, well kept Fullers beers, lots of sports trophies and memorabilia, games corner with darts, bar billiards and sports TV; pleasant garden with barbecues *(Pete Baker)*

Chequers [Beamont Rd, Headington Quarry]: Good value food, real ales inc Wadworths 6X, may have bargain offers on beers and wines; pool, SkyTV *(Geoff Pidoux)*

HENLEY SU7882

☆ *Three Tuns* [Market Pl]: Heavy-beamed front bar with old-fashioned seating inc traditional settles, coal-effect gas fire, well kept Brakspears and decent wines; back dining area crisply rustic with cream-painted panelling and neat table linen, fresh imaginative cooking, friendly young staff; may be piped music; civilised cane furniture under awning in attractively reworked back courtyard *(Susan and John Douglas, the Didler, LYM, Jim Abbott)*

ISLIP SP5214

Red Lion [High St (B4027)]: Relaxed linked areas with decent food from fresh generous sandwiches up, three changing guest beers such as Adnams and Hook Norton, quick friendly service, conservatory; disabled facilities, good garden with play area *(D C T and E A Frewer)*

KIDLINGTON SP4914

Squire Bassett [A4260]: Big pub with good value food, good service *(Geoff Pidoux)*

KINGSTON BAGPUIZE SU4098

Hinds Head [Witney Rd]: Small country pub, welcoming and relaxed, two unpretentious rooms with good range of attractive good value meals in no smoking bar and restaurant from toasties and baguettes up, well kept Greene King Morlands Original and Abbot, quick service; plenty of picnic-sets in good-sized garden with two water features and play area *(Marjorie and David Lamb, Mr and Mrs G S Ayrton, Ian Phillips)*

KIRTLINGTON SP4919

Oxford Arms [Troy Lane, Kirtlington]: Newly refurbished oak-beamed village pub with interesting food inc lots of fish and seafood, friendly young staff, fresh wood furniture, open fire, no smoking area; small sunny back garden *(Phoebe and Duncan Thomas)*

LEWKNOR SU7198

Lambert Arms [London Rd (A40), a mile from M40 junction 6 via B4009]: Former coaching inn recently refurbished in simple style, careful colour scheme in extended bar, enjoyable food here and in idiosyncratically decorated restaurant; adjacent film-set lighthouse *(Torrens Lyster)*

LITTLE COXWELL SU2792

Plough [A420 just SW of Faringdon]: Nice old stone-built core with big log fire, good blackboard choice of reasonably priced food, quick kind friendly service, two or three well kept ales, daily papers, large back dining extension; pool, games machines, piped music; children allowed in conservatory with bowls, swings in big garden, no dogs *(Gill and Keith Croxton, Peter and Audrey Dowsett, Marjorie and David Lamb)*

LONG WITTENHAM SU5493

Plough [High St]: Enjoyable sensibly priced food (all day wknds, with OAP bargains Mon-Thurs lunchtimes) in friendly low-beamed refurbished lounge with lots of brass, no smoking dining room and room, games in public bar, inglenook log fires, Greene King IPA, Abbot and Ruddles, good value coffee, good service; Thames moorings at bottom of long spacious garden, bedrooms *(Tony and Wendy Hobden)*

LONGWORTH SU3899

☆ *Blue Boar* [Tucks Lane]: Cosy beamed and thatched country local with plenty of character, firmly wooden furnishings inc scrubbed tables and traditional settle by one of the two good log fires, good value food inc good puddings and evening and wknd specials, well kept Morrells Oxford Blue, friendly quick service, charming Australian landlady; may be piped music; quiet village *(Franklyn Roberts, M Grieve)*

Lamb & Flag [off W end of A420 Kingston Bagpuize bypass]: Good choice of good value food inc all-day carvery in big smart restaurant area with unusual wattle ceiling, good-sized bar area with open fire, friendly service; children welcome, tables outside *(Peter and Audrey Dowsett, Marjorie and David Lamb)*

LOWER ASSENDON SU7484

Golden Ball [B480]: Attractive 16th-c beamed pub, cosily rustic traditional interior, wide-ranging good food, exemplary service, well kept Brakspears, good choice of house wines, log fire; children welcome, big garden behind, vietnamese pot-bellied pig called Rosie *(Charles van der Lande, Mr and Mrs G Swire)*

LOWER HEYFORD SP4824

Bell [Market Sq]: Charming creeper-clad building in small village square of thatched cottages, uncluttered refurbished rooms around central beamed bar, cheerful helpful staff, good range of generous enjoyable food inc some interesting dishes, well kept Adnams Broadside, Bass and Greene King Abbot; disabled access and facilities, bedrooms, nearby Oxford Canal walks *(Mrs Roxanne Chamberlain, Meg and Colin Hamilton)*

MARSTON SP5208

Bricklayers Arms [Church Lane, Old Marston]: Good value food in attractively neo-Victorian two-level pub, good service, well kept ales, good wine choice; children welcome, pleasant garden with climbing frames *(Geoff Pidoux)*

Victoria Arms [Mill Lane]: By River Cherwell with spacious terrace, good play area, punt moorings and hire; full Wadworths range and guest beers kept well, enjoyable food (not Sun evening in winter) concentrating on massive choice of sandwiches and baked potatoes, friendly attentive staff, lots of tables in civilised main room and smaller ones off, real fires; very busy wknd lunchtimes and summer, soft piped music; children and dogs allowed, lavatory for disabled *(BB, Geoff Pidoux, Margaret and Roy Randle)*

MIDDLETON STONEY SP5323

☆ *Jersey Arms* [Ardley Rd (B430/B4030)]: Successful combination of small 19th-c stone-built country hotel with friendly pub; relaxing atmosphere in pleasantly 'rusticated' bar, beams, oak flooring and some stripped stone, nice tables, sofa and daily papers, good inglenook log fire, interesting if not cheap home-made fresh food from well filled baguettes up, friendly owner and staff, efficient service, a well kept mainstream real ale, good wine list and coffee, attractive largely no smoking two-level dining room; piped music, popular for business lunches, car park across road; tables in courtyard and garden, comfortable bedrooms *(BB, Maysie Thompson, Simon J Barber, D C T and E A Frewer)*

MILCOMBE SP4034

☆ ***Horse & Groom*** [off A361 SW of Banbury]: Bustling beamed and flagstoned village local with cheerful Australian licensees, nice atmosphere with settee and pub dog and parrot, landlady does short choice of good reasonably priced bar food from sandwiches to steaks, well kept Adnams Broadside and Hook Norton Best, good largely australian wine choice, separate coffee menu, inglenook woodburner, restaurant; occasional live music; children welcome, lots of picnic-sets out in front, bedrooms (they can organise fishing), handy for Wigginton Heath waterfowl and animal centre *(Chris Glasson, BB, George Atkinson)*

MINSTER LOVELL SP3211

Old Swan [just N of B4047 Witney—Burford]: Interesting old building with variety of secluded seating areas, deep armchairs and rugs on flagstones, well kept Hook Norton ales, log fire, enjoyable lunchtime snacks and light meals, restaurant; piped music, and more an adjunct to the adjacent Old Mill Conference Centre than an individual pub; tables in lovely garden, bedrooms, idyllic village *(LYM, Nigel and Sue Foster, Sean and Sharon Pines)*

MOULSFORD SU5983

☆ ***Beetle & Wedge*** [Ferry Lane]: Hotel/restaurant rather than pub, but has well kept real ales, kind service and good filled baguettes as well as good if far from cheap leisurely meals in chatty Boathouse bar/restaurant by the Thames, good wines, pleasant waterside garden; well behaved children welcome, charming comfortable bedrooms *(LYM, C S Turner)*

NEWBRIDGE SP4001

Maybush [A415 7 miles S of Witney]: Low-beamed dining pub in lovely Thamesside setting, good food choice, well kept Greene King Abbot, no piped music; service can come under pressure on busy summer wknds; children welcome, good moorings, pretty and neatly kept waterside garden with tables in verandah too *(LYM, Peter and Giff Bennett)*

NORTH LEIGH SP3813

Woodman [New Yatt Rd]: Roomy and welcoming stone-built village local with interesting choice of inexpensive freshly prepared food, real ales such as Hook Norton Best, Greene King IPA and Wadworths 6X, Easter and bank hol beer festivals, decent wines, proper coffee, attentive staff, daily papers, darts; big garden, comfortable bedrooms, open all day Sun *(C and R Bromage)*

NORTH NEWINGTON SP4139

Blinking Owl [Main St]: Relaxing ivy-covered stone-built village local, well kept Bass and Hook Norton, cheery helpful landlord, good choice of fresh home cooking by landlady inc good vegetarian dishes, beams, sturdy tables, some sofas, log or coal fires, small family dining area; piped music; back garden, two bedrooms *(Alistair Kirkwood)*

NORTHMOOR SP4202

Red Lion [B4449 SE of Stanton Harcourt]: Refurbished 15th-c stone-built village pub with thriving local atmosphere, good choice of enjoyable low-priced down-to-earth food inc popular Sun lunch, well kept ales such as Batemans XXXB, friendly landlord and locals, heavily beamed bar and small dining room off, welcoming log fire; walkers welcome, no dogs, no credit cards, Thurs morning post office; garden *(Geoff Pidoux, Dick and Madeleine Brown, Marjorie and David Lamb)*

NUFFIELD SU6787

Crown [A4130/B481]: Neatly kept beamed lounge bar with country furniture and inglenook log fire, friendly young licensees, enjoyable inexpensive food from sandwiches up, well kept Brakspears ales; children in small family room, tables outside front and back, good walks *(LYM, D C T and E A Frewer)*

OXFORD SP5106

☆ ***Bear*** [Alfred St/Wheatsheaf Alley]: Intimate low-ceilinged and partly panelled 16th-c rooms, not over-smart and often packed with students; thousands of vintage ties on walls and beams, simple lunchtime food most days inc sandwiches (kitchen may be cl Weds), well kept changing ales such as Adnams, Fullers London Pride and Hancocks HB from centenarian handpumps on recently renewed pewter bar counter, no games machines; upstairs ladies'; tables outside, open all day summer *(the Didler, LYM, R Huggins, D Irving, E McCall, T McLean)*

☆ ***Eagle & Child*** [St Giles]: Pleasant panelled front bar, intimate mid-bars full of actors' and Tolkien/C S Lewis memorabilia, tasteful stripped-brick modern back dining extension with no smoking conservatory, well kept Greene King Abbot and Old Speckled Hen, Ind Coope Burton, Marstons Pedigree and Wadworths 6X, newspapers, events posters; busy at lunchtime, nice for a quiet afternoon drink; piped music *(R Huggins, D Irving, E McCall, T McLean, Meg and Colin Hamilton, BB, GHC, Chris Glasson, Richie V)*

Fox & Hounds [Abingdon Rd (A4144)]: Good friendly service even when very busy, decent wines, enjoyable reasonably priced food *(MJB)*

Grapes [George St]: Traditional pub, some original features, lots of theatrical posters and memorabilia, decent food, well kept Morrells, pleasant service *(Kevin Blake, Peter Neate)*

☆ ***Isis Tavern*** [off Donnington Bridge Rd; no car access]: Early 19th-c former farmhouse in charming waterside spot, log fire, lots of mainly nautical bric-a-brac hanging from high ceiling and covering the walls; well kept real ales, hearty food all day, daily papers, sensibly placed darts and bar billiards in one corner, other traditional games; may be piped pop music, TV; children in eating areas, bowling alley, picnic-sets out on heated terrace and in garden, swings, slide, aunt sally by arrangement, open all day (unless winter weather poor), short walk to Iffley Lock and nearby lavishly decorated early Norman church *(LYM, Anthony Longden)*

Marsh Harrier [Marsh Rd, Cowley]: Friendly neatly kept pub with enjoyable food from wide choice of sandwiches and baguettes up, well kept Fullers ales, good wines by the glass, pleasant staff, good solid tables on bare boards, daily papers and books, darts, good-natured retriever; quiz nights; big garden with barbecue *(Simon and Sally Small, Paul Dunphy)*

Old Tom [St Aldates]: Light pine panelling and lots of mirrors for a sense of space, well kept Greene King IPA and Abbot, pubby food from sandwiches and baked potatoes up, prompt efficient service, collection of old beer bottles; tables in secluded back garden *(Martin Grosberg)*

Three Goats Heads [Friars Entry, St Michaels St]: Steps up to charming little upper bar, sparkling clean, with light panelling, ceiling plasterwork and booths of elegant bench seats, political prints and architectural drawings showing details of the work, well kept cheap Sam Smiths, good choice of quick generous food, friendly helpful service; cheery downstairs bar (cl afternoons) with bare boards, TV, fruit machine and piped music *(Kevin Blake, Sean and Sharon Pines)*

Watermans Arms [South St, Osney]: Unpretentious riverside pub nr Osney Lock, well kept Greene King ales, good value home cooking, tables outside *(Alan Kilpatrick)*

Wharf House [Butterwyke Pl/Speedwell St]: Fine range of half a dozen or so well kept changing real ales in bare-boards early Victorian local with knowledgeable, friendly and helpful landlord, two farm ciders, masses of bottled german and belgian beers with their proper glasses, rickety old tables and chairs, darts, cards, elderly bull terrier; occasional vinyl records played, old TV brought out for sports, some impromptu singing; open all day Sat *(Pete Baker)*

☆ ***White Horse*** [Broad St]: Bustling and studenty, squeezed between bits of Blackwells bookshop; single small narrow bar with snug one-table raised back alcove, mellow oak beams and timbers, ochre ceiling, beautiful view of the Clarendon building and Sheldonian, good lunchtime food (the few tables reserved for this), good range of beers, Addlestone's cider, friendly licensees *(R Huggins, D Irving, E McCall, T McLean, BB, Giles and Annie Francis)*

White House [Botley Rd]: Friendly staff, comfortably local feel, enjoyable food; charming garden *(C R Harrison)*

PISHILL SU7389

☆ ***Crown*** [B480 Nettlebed—Watlington]: Wisteria-covered ancient building, tidy and highly polished, with black beams and timbers, log fires and candlelight, good wholesome home-made food from filled baguettes up inc carefully chosen ingredients and local venison, well kept ales such as Fullers London Pride and Hook Norton; children welcome in restaurant, pleasant bedroom in separate cottage, picnic-sets on attractive side lawn, pretty country setting – lots of walks *(Susan and John Douglas, the Didler, LYM, Tracey and Stephen Groves)*

PLAY HATCH SU7476

☆ ***Crown***: Good choice of enjoyable generous food (some small helpings available) in rambling olde-worlde 16th-c pub, spacious, civilised and very popular with families (though no high chairs); two bars and several rooms inc barn extension restaurant and big no smoking conservatory, thriving atmosphere, well kept Brakspears ales tapped from the cask, decent wines, log fires, well organised welcoming service with hi-tech aids (wireless computer food orders to kitchen); pleasant garden with play area *(J and B Cressey, Betty Laker, John Baish, A P Seymour)*

Shoulder of Mutton: Country pub with small low-ceilinged bar and large conservatory restaurant, good food choice from hot filled rolls to main dishes inc interesting pies and Sun lunch (must book), fine oak settle screening fire, Greene King ales; well kept garden with old-fashioned roses, real well *(Peter B Brown)*

RADCOT SU2899

Swan [A4095 2½ miles N of Faringdon]: Welcoming Thames-side pub with enjoyable food from generous baguettes up, friendly landlord, log fire, Greene King ales, lots of stuffed fish; children in eating area; piped music; pleasant waterside garden, summer boat trips (lift to bring wheelchairs aboard), four good value bedrooms *(LYM, P Michelson, Alan Kilpatrick)*

SATWELL SU7083

☆ ***Lamb*** [2 miles S of Nettlebed; follow Shepherds Green signpost]: Cosy and attractive 16th-c low-beamed cottage, very small, with tiled floors, pine furniture, family photographs, friendly licensees, huge log fireplace, fresh generous lunchtime food from filled baguettes up, well kept Brakspears, traditional games, small carpeted family room; tables outside, nice spot, occasional barbecues *(Susan and John Douglas, LYM, Mr and Mrs M Renton)*

SHENINGTON SP3742

☆ ***Bell*** [off A422 W of Banbury]: 17th-c two-room village pub in style and mood (heavy beams, part with flagstones, some stripped stone and pine panelling, coal fire, friendly dogs and informal service), with emphasis on the landlady's good reasonably priced home cooking – often booked solid on Sun; good sandwiches too, low-priced Hook Norton Best, good wine choice, relaxed atmosphere, cribbage, dominoes; children in eating areas, tables out in front, small attractive back garden, bedrooms, good surrounding walks, cl Mon lunchtime *(LYM, Karen and Graham Oddey, John Kane, Don and*

Val Brace, Sir Nigel Foulkes, Dr John West, Theocsbrian, David and Helen Wilkins, Amanda Newcomb, Hugh Spottiswoode)

SHIPLAKE ROW SU7478

White Hart [off A4155 W of Shiplake]: Three friendly linked rooms mainly set for good unchanging choice of food (just roasts Sun lunchtime), cheerful staff, well kept Brakspears, decent house wines, log fires; interestingly planted back garden, nice location, fine views, boules, good walks *(Wombat, June and Robin Savage)*

SHIPTON-UNDER-WYCHWOOD SP2717

☆ *Lamb* [off A361 to Burford]: Peaceful and stylish dining pub with enterprising food (not cheap) from light dishes to daily fresh Brixham fish, charming service, Greene King ales and perhaps a guest beer, some stripped stone and log fire, exotic flower displays and elegant candle holders, no smoking restaurant in Elizabethan core; piped music, jazz Sun night; children and dogs welcome, tables outside, attractive bedrooms, good breakfast *(John Bowdler, Mrs Citroen, Chris Glasson, Arnold Bennett, Maysie Thompson, LYM, G and R Cartey)*

☆ *Shaven Crown* [High St (A361)]: New licensee for this memorable ancient building with its hall's magnificent lofty medieval rafters and imposing double stairway; separate beamed bar with more modern décor and booth seating, decent bar food, real ales, several wines by the glass and traditional games, no smoking restaurant; piped music; children and dogs welcome, peaceful courtyard with outside heaters, bowling green, character old-fashioned bedrooms *(LYM, A P Seymour)*

SHRIVENHAM SU2488

☆ *Prince of Wales* [High St; off A420 or B4000 NE of Swindon]: Convivial 17th-c stone-built pub doing well under enthusiastic young licensees, spotless low-beamed lounge, pictures, lots of brasses, log fire and candles, wholesome generous food (not Sun evening) inc Sun roasts, small dining area, well kept ales inc Wadworths and Charles Wells Bombardier, good soft drinks choice; children welcome, side bar with darts, board games and machines, may be quiet piped music, no dogs, busy Tues quiz night; picnic-sets and heaters in secluded back garden *(CMW, JJW, A P Seymour)*

Victoria [Station Rd (B4000 S)]: Large log fire in L-shaped bar, wide choice of reasonably priced food, Arkells 2B and 3B, good soft drinks choice, charming no smoking conservatory restaurant (can get hot); quiet piped music; picnic-sets in garden with play area *(CMW, JJW)*

SHUTFORD SP3840

☆ *George & Dragon* [Church Lane]: Ancient stone-built pub with welcoming service, good reasonably priced home-made food with flexible menu and Sun lunches, well kept Hook Norton Best and changing guests like Hopback Crop Circles and Timothy Taylor Landlord, fine choice of wines by the glass, comfortable flagstoned L-shaped bar with impressive fireplace, oak-panelled beamed dining room; children and dogs welcome, small garden, pretty village, cl Mon, open all day Sun *(BB, Mr and Mrs G Olsson, JHBS, Mrs E Widdowson, Graham Pearson)*

SIBFORD GOWER SP3537

☆ *Wykham Arms* [signed off B4035 Banbury—Shipston on Stour; Temple Mill Rd]: Pretty and cottagey thatched and flagstoned dining pub, largely no smoking, with good interesting food under new owners, comfortable open-plan low-beamed stripped-stone lounge, nice pictures, table made from glass-topped well, inglenook tap room, friendly efficient staff, well kept real ales, good house wines and coffee; children welcome; country views from big well planted garden, lovely manor house opp; has been cl Mon lunchtime *(LYM, Chris Glasson)*

SOUTH MORETON SU5588

☆ *Crown* [off A4130 or A417 E of Didcot; High St]: Rambling old open-plan village pub, bustling and convivial, with friendly licensees, well kept Badger Tanglefoot, Wadworths 6X and a guest beer, decent wines and coffee, wide range of good fresh home-made food from sandwiches up (OAP discounts), good service; piped music, Mon quiz night; children allowed, small garden *(Marjorie and David Lamb, DMH, Dudley and Moira Cockroft, Dick and Madeleine Brown)*

SOUTH NEWINGTON SP4033

Duck on the Pond: Smart recent refurbishment, popular for wide choice of usual current food from wraps, melts and other light dishes through lasagne and so forth to steak and mixed grill, old-fashioned tables and chairs, some flagstones, step up to linked eating areas; piped music may be rather loud; lots of tables out on terrace and lawn *(Stuart Turner, Ted George)*

SOUTH STOKE SU5983

☆ *Perch & Pike* [off B4009 2 miles N of Goring]: Relaxing brick and flint dining pub just a field away from the Thames, keeping proper cottagey low-beamed bar with open fires and well kept Brakspears and a guest beer, as well as sizeable timbered restaurant extension where children allowed; wide choice of good enterprising food, many dishes available in starter-size helpings, friendly staff; may be piped music; tables out on terrace and flower-bordered lawn *(Franklyn Roberts, LYM, John Hale, Dave Braisted, Peter B Brown, Rob Winstanley)*

SOUTHMOOR SU3998

Waggon & Horses: Enjoyable honest food, well kept Archers, friendly staff *(Dudley and Moira Cockroft)*

SPARSHOLT SU3487

☆ *Star* [Watery Lane]: Comfortable 16th-c country pub under friendly new management, same cook still doing short choice of good freshly made food, two well kept real ales, daily papers, log fire, attractive pictures, horse-racing talk; may be subdued piped music; back garden, pretty village – snowdrops fill churchyard in spring *(Marjorie and David Lamb, John Brightley)*

STANTON HARCOURT SP4105
Harcourt Arms [Main Rd]: Well run restauranty pub, roomy and pleasantly informal, with huge fireplaces in attractive simply furnished linked dining areas, well kept real ales, decent wines; children welcome *(Franklyn Roberts, Peter and Audrey Dowsett, LYM, Arnold Bennett)*

STANTON ST JOHN SP5709
Talk House [Wheatley Rd (B4027 just outside)]: Peacefully placed 17th-c pub under temporary management as we went to press, various big rooms with lots of oak beams, flagstones, tiles and stripped original stonework, simple but solid rustic furnishings, pleasant area by fireplace, well kept Hook Norton Best, Wadworths 6X and a guest beer, bar food, children welcome in restaurant; open all day in summer, tables in sheltered courtyard, comfortable bedrooms *(Jane Taylor, David Dutton, Mrs Catherine Draper, M E C Comer, Robert Turnham, Mike and Mary Carter, LYM)*

STEVENTON SU4791
Cherry Tree [B4017 (High St); village signed off A34 S of Abingdon via A4130]: Quiet 18th-c pub with well kept Wadworths IPA, JCB and 6X, perhaps a guest beer, decent wines, generous quickly served well priced food inc sophisticated dishes and good vegetarian choice, open-plan beamed areas around island bar, flagstones and bare boards, mix of furniture inc heavily carved settles and brocaded dining chairs, dark green walls, open fires, old prints and stuffed creatures; fruit machine, may be unobtrusive piped music in public bar; tables out on terrace, open all day Fri-Sun *(Marjorie and David Lamb, BB, W W Burke)*

North Star [Stocks Lane, The Causeway, central westward turn off B4017]: Interesting village pub now reopened after being carefully put back together (it had been partly destroyed in a bizarre incident involving a JCB digger); its original Grade I listed layout virtually unchanged, with tiled entrance corridor, built-in settles, parlourish lounge and simple dining room, Greene King real ales, plans for wkdy lunchtime bar food; tables on side grass, front gateway through living yew tree *(the Didler, LYM, Giles and Annie Francis)*

STOKE LYNE SP5628
☆ *Peyton Arms* [from minor road off B4110 N of Bicester fork left into village]: Largely unspoilt ochre-walled stone-built pub with friendly chatty licensees, simple lunchtime food such as rolls and pork pies, well kept Hook Norton beers (full range) tapped from casks behind small corner bar in sparsely decorated front snug, tiled floor, inglenook log fire, hops on beam, bigger refurbished room with darts, dominoes and cribbage, charity book store, good new lavatories; well behaved children and dogs welcome, no mobile phones, pleasant garden with aunt sally; cl Mon/Tues lunchtimes *(Susan and John Douglas, the Didler, Paul and Ann Meyer, Pete Baker, Conor McGaughey, Jeremy Morrison)*

STOKE ROW SU6784
☆ *Crooked Billet* [Nottwood Lane, off B491 N of Reading – OS Sheet 175 map ref 684844]: Rustic pub layout with heavy beams, flagstones, antique pubby furnishings and great inglenook log fire, but in practice a restaurant – good, with wide choice of well cooked interesting meals inc good value lunch, attentive welcoming service, well kept Brakspears tapped from the cask (no bar counter), decent wines, relaxed homely atmosphere – like a french country restaurant; children welcome, occasional live music, big garden by Chilterns beechwoods *(the Didler, LYM, John Hale, Gerald Hughes)*

STRATTON AUDLEY SP6026
Red Lion [off A421 NE of Bicester; Church St]: Thatched village local with particularly friendly quick service, plentiful well priced food inc notable burgers and more restauranty dishes, good atmosphere, real ales, big inglenook log fire, stripped stone and low beams, antique sale posters, old varnished wooden furniture; may be piped music; tables out by road and on terrace in small colourful garden, pretty village *(Paul and Jane Walker)*

SUNNINGWELL SP4900
Flowing Well [just N of Abingdon]: Good plentiful enterprising food from baguettes to restaurant meals, real ales, good choice of wines by the glass, remarkable collection of rare rums, good young staff; garden with picnic-sets under cocktail parasols *(Geoff Pidoux)*

SUTTON COURTENAY SU5094
☆ *Fish* [Appleford Rd]: Civilised well run restaurant rather than pub, small front bar opening into attractive three-part dining room, nice prints toning in with the dark green décor, good fresh-cooked food with some emphasis on fish, starters that can double as interesting bar snacks, good value two-course lunch, good fairly priced house wines, cheerful landlord and pleasant well trained staff, stylish back conservatory; children welcome, tables out in terrace arbour and on neat lawn *(BB, Peter B Brown, P E and M Hart)*

SWERFORD SP3731
☆ *Masons Arms* [A361 Banbury—Chipping Norton]: Smartly refurbished dining pub doing well under welcoming new management, friendly young staff, interesting choice of enjoyable food from reasonably priced sandwiches and baguettes to some ambitious main dishes, well kept Hook Norton Best, decent wines, brightly modernised bar with rugs on pale boards and comfortable blue armchairs around big tables, steps down to plank-walled room with chunky tables, roomy back candlelit dining room with great views; small terrace and picnic-sets on neat lawn with good views *(LYM, Arnold Bennett, John and Sue Woodward)*

SWINFORD SP4308
Talbot [B4044 just S of Eynsham]: Roomy recently refurbished beamed pub with very wide changing choice of good value generous fresh food inc good ciabattas and quite a few

authentic thai dishes, four well kept ales inc Arkells 3B, friendly landlord and staff, long attractive bar with some stripped stone, cheerful log-effect gas fire, games room; tables in garden (some traffic noise), pleasant walk along lovely stretch of the Thames towpath *(Chas Reed, Dick and Madeleine Brown)*

TACKLEY SP4720

Gardeners Arms [Medcroft Rd, off A4260]: Comfortable 17th-c beamed village pub with usual food, well kept Greene King, coal-effect gas fire in inglenook, prints, brasses, old photographs and cigarette cards; separate public bar with darts, TV and fruit machine, piped music, bookable skittle alley; picnic-sets on sunny terrace, handy for Rousham House *(Marjorie and David Lamb)*

TETSWORTH SP6801

Red Lion [A40, not far from M40 junction 7]: Friendly bistro-feel pub with enough candles to colour the paintwork (and crack one of the mirrors), young chef doing enjoyable food inc imaginative dishes, good beer choice inc well kept Greene King IPA, decent wines, log fire; kitchen being enlarged, and new upstairs restaurant in hand *(Torrens Lyster, B Allen)*

Swan [A40, not far from M40 junction 7]: Lively and welcoming bar and restaurant as part of antiques centre in rambling 15th-c coaching inn, well kept Brakspears, good upmarket food inc lots of fish *(B H and J I Andrews)*

THAME SP7005

Bird Cage [Cornmarket]: Quaint 15th-c black and white beamed and timbered pub refurbished in bistro style, three or four bare-boards rooms sharing flame-effect fire in central hearth, good if not cheap food choice from breakfast on, well kept ales, good coffees, friendly staff, daily papers; piped music, no children or dogs inside, can be smoky evenings; pavement tables *(LYM, Tim and Ann Newell)*

Old Trout [High St]: Attractive timbered and thatched building, upmarket restaurant not pub, but it does have a small bar with ancient flooring tiles and big inglenook log fire, and something of a pubby atmosphere in its nice collection of small higgledy-piggledy heavily beamed dining rooms; French chef doing good food inc good value light lunches with home-baked bread, good choice of wines and coffee; young Canadian staff, keg beer, piped pop music; six bedrooms *(Richard and Margaret Peers, BB, Dr and Mrs R E S Tanner)*

Six Bells [High St]: Recently reworked, with gently upmarket open-plan bar, cosier no smoking back rooms, interestingly varied food, well kept Fullers ales; large terrace *(Tim and Ann Newell)*

THRUPP SP4815

☆ *Boat* [off A4260 just N of Kidlington]: Stone-built pub particularly popular in summer for its lovely surroundings by Oxford Canal, nice safely fenced garden behind with plenty of tables, some in shade; good value decent food from good baguettes up, well kept Greene King ales, decent wine, coal fire, old canal pictures and artefacts, bare boards and stripped pine, restaurant, no piped music; good folk night 2nd Sun, occasional theatre *(Geoff Pidoux, Pete Baker, Sue Demont, Tim Barrow)*

Jolly Boatman [Banbury Rd (A4260)]: Big canalside pub open all day for enjoyable cheap food, Greene King Abbot and Old Speckled Hen, pleasant staff, converted barn eating area and conservatory overlooking canal; children welcome, plenty of outside tables *(Geoff Pidoux)*

WANTAGE SU3988

Lamb [Mill St, past square and Bell; down hill then bend to left]: Low beams, timbers and soft lighting, attractive and comfortable furnishings with cosy corners, unpretentious atmosphere, well kept ales such as Greene King Abbot and Hook Norton, wide choice of generous good value food from baked potatoes to steak, duck and salmon, quick smiling service, log fire; good play area *(LYM)*

☆ *Royal Oak* [Newbury St]: Welcoming two-bar local with lots of ship photographs and naval hatbands, particularly well kept ales such as Bass or Marstons Pedigree, Wadworths 6X and two beers brewed for the pub by West Berkshire, lunches Fri-Sat; table football, darts, cribbage; has been cl wkdy lunchtimes, bedrooms *(the Didler, BB)*

Shoulder of Mutton [Wallingford St]: Friendly and chatty local, coal fire and racing TV in bar, passage to two small snug back rooms, well kept Greene King and guest beers, popular food; tables outside, bedrooms *(the Didler, Pete Baker)*

WARBOROUGH SU5993

Cricketers Arms [Thame Rd (off A329)]: Welcoming neat local with pleasant décor, good value fresh usual food, well kept real ale, proper bar and dining area, good service; tables outside *(Margaret and Roy Randle)*

WATLINGTON SU6894

Chequers [3 miles from M40 junction 6, via B4009; Love Lane]: Attractive rambling bar with good atmosphere, character seating and a few good antique oak tables, low beams and candles, well kept Brakspears PA, SB and a seasonal beer, very wide choice of nicely presented food from sandwiches to steaks and popular Sun lunch, steps down to further eating area, vine-hung conservatory (children allowed here); picnic-sets in pretty garden, nice walks nearby *(LYM, Wombat, Colin Wood, Alistair Forsyth)*

WEST HANNEY SU4092

☆ *Plough* [Church St]: Unspoilt and pretty thatched local with attractive timbered upper storey, original timbers and uneven low ceilings, homely and welcoming panelled lounge with good log fire in stone fireplace, genial landlord, reasonably priced food inc good value Sun lunch, real ales, interesting whiskies, darts in public bar; tables in back garden, children welcome *(Brian Root)*

WHITCHURCH SU6377

☆ *Greyhound* [High St, just over toll bridge from Pangbourne]: Pretty 16th-c cottage with neat relaxed low-beamed L-shaped bar, bric-a-brac inc signed miniature cricket bats, good value fresh food from wide sandwich choice to usual hot dishes, well kept Flowers, Greene King, Marstons Pedigree and Charles Wells Bombardier, polite service, flame-effect fire, no music or machines; dogs on leads allowed, pleasant garden; on Thames Path, in attractive village *(Dick and Madeleine Brown)*

WITNEY SP3509

Angel [Market Sq]: Wide choice of bargain food from good sandwiches up inc OAP specials in comfortably bustling 17th-c town local, extended but unchanging, well kept ales such as Courage Best, Hook Norton Best and Charles Wells Bombardier, daily papers, welcoming homely surroundings and hot coal fire, quick friendly service even when packed; pool room, coffee bar; parking nearby can be difficult *(Peter and Audrey Dowsett, Ian Phillips)*

☆ ***Three Horseshoes*** [Corn St, junction with Holloway Rd]: Attractive 16th-c stone-built pub, friendly atmosphere and simple comfort, heavy beams, flagstones, log fires, well polished old furniture, consistently good home-made food from filled baguettes, ciabattas and other pubby lunchtime food to more imaginative restauranty dishes, well kept Greene King Abbot and Morlands Original and a guest beer, decent house wines, separate dining room *(LYM, John and Janet Davey, Patrick Hancock, Ian Phillips, Comus and Sarah Elliott)*

WOLVERCOTE SP5009

Plough [First Turn/Wolvercote Green]: Lots of comfortably well worn in pubby linked areas, warm and friendly, with bustling atmosphere, armchairs and Victorian-style carpeted bays in main lounge, well kept real ales, decent wines, varied inexpensive food in flagstoned ex-stables dining room and library (children allowed here), traditional snug, woodburner; picnic-sets on front terrace looking over rough meadow to canal and woods *(Franklyn Roberts, BB)*

Red Lion [Godstow Rd]: Big no smoking dining extension, good value food, friendly landlady, older part with lots of photographs, prints and memorabilia, five coal fires; quiet piped music; garden with play area *(Geoff Pidoux)*

WOODSTOCK SP4417

Black Prince [Manor Rd (A44 N)]: Subtly lit timbered and stripped-stone 18th-c pub with old-fashioned furnishings, armour, swords, big fireplace, good value food from traditional to Tex-Mex in bar and dining room, mainly roasts Sun, well kept ales such as Theakstons Old Peculier, fast friendly service, children allowed; may be soft piped music, and may try to keep your credit card while you eat; tables out in attractive streamside garden, nearby right of way into Blenheim parkland *(Geoff Pidoux, A C English, Patrick Hancock)*

Crown [High St (A44)]: Busy and comfortable pub with enjoyable food, well kept beer, roomy dining area with pleasant conservatory; sports TV in one area, very popular with young people some evenings *(Geoff Pidoux)*

Duke of Marlborough [A44 2 miles N]: Large attractive pub/restaurant with dark oak, chintz and log fire, wide choice of good value food, well kept Wadworths 6X, friendly staff *(Geoff Pidoux)*

☆ ***Feathers*** [Market St]: Not a pub but a formal Cotswold hotel with attractive period furnishings, no smoking restaurant and nice bedrooms; included for its old-fashioned back Courtyard Bar, very small and old-fashioned, with relaxed unstuffy atmosphere, good stylish bar food (not Sat evening) and good wines by the glass, swift service and log fire, opening on to charming sunny courtyard garden; children welcome, piped music *(LYM, Ian Phillips, W W Burke, G and R Cartey)*

Kings Arms [Market St/Park Lane]: Good value food, pleasant furnishings and friendly helpful staff in roomy pub/hotel with several different areas, well kept Theakstons; bedrooms *(Geoff Pidoux)*

Star [Market Pl]: Big cheerful beamed town pub, decent food all day from good filled baguettes up, lunchtime salad bar and popular family Sun lunch, well kept beers inc Wadworths 6X, good value wines, bare boards, some stripped stone, daily papers, open fires; piped music, quiz machine, TV; pavement tables, more in back courtyard, bedrooms clean and spacious, good breakfast *(Geoff Pidoux, BB, Ian Phillips, Sean and Sharon Pines, Dick and Madeleine Brown)*

Woodstock Arms [Market St]: 16th-c heavy-beamed stripped-stone local with long narrow bar, separate dining area, good value straightforward home-made food inc good vegetarian choice, friendly prompt service, warm lively atmosphere, well kept Greene King IPA, Abbot and Old Speckled Hen, decent wines, log-effect gas fires in splendid stone fireplaces; tables out in yard, bedrooms *(Geoff Pidoux, R Huggins, D Irving, E McCall, T McLean)*

WOOLSTONE SU2987

☆ ***White Horse*** [village signed off B4507]: Plushly refurbished partly thatched 16th-c pub with steep Victorian gables, two big open fires in spacious beamed and part-panelled room with quite a variety of décor styles, wide choice of decent quickly served bar food, friendly relaxed staff and black labrador, well kept ales such as Arkells 2B and Moonlight, decent wines, lots of whiskies, good coffee, log fire, evening restaurant; quiet piped music, no visiting dogs; children allowed in eating area, sheltered garden, four charming good value bedrooms, big breakfast, secluded interesting village handy for White Horse and Ridgeway walkers *(BB, Darly Graton, Graeme Gulibert)*

WOOTTON SP4320

☆ ***Killingworth Castle*** [Glympton Rd; B4027 N of Woodstock]: Striking three-storey 17th-c coaching inn, lively local atmosphere, pleasant service, well kept Greene King ales, decent house wines, wide choice of generous food, long narrow main bar with pine furnishings, parquet floor, candles, lots of brasses and log fire with books above it, daily papers, bar billiards, darts and shove ha'penny in smaller games end, attractive garden; soft piped music, Fri folk night, jazz 1st and 3rd Weds, music some other nights too; bedrooms *(BB, Pete Baker, JHBS, Simon Collett-Jones, Stuart Turner, R Huggins, D Irving, E McCall, T McLean)*

WROXTON SP4141

☆ *North Arms* [Mills Lane; off A422 at hotel, pub at back of village]: Pretty thatched stone pub with good fresh well prepared food from generous snacks up, well kept Greene King, quick friendly service, log fire, nice wooden furnishings, character restaurant; may be unobtrusive piped music; attractive quiet garden in peaceful part of lovely village, walks in abbey gardens opposite during term time *(LYM, K H Frostick, Paul Humphreys)*

WYTHAM SP4708

White Hart [off A34 Oxford ring rd]: More restaurant than pub, modern rather pricey food all day, busy no smoking dining area (children allowed here), log fire in gently updated bar with settles, handsome panelling and flagstones, young efficient staff, well kept Fullers London Pride and Hook Norton, good value house wines; open all day, pretty garden with big tables and solid fuel stove in covered eating area, may be summer barbecues, unspoilt preserved village *(Mark and Maggie Selinger, LYM, Di and Mike Gillam)*

YARNTON SP4812

Turnpike [A44 N of Oxford]: Large Vintage Inn pub/restaurant with good atmosphere in spacious low-ceilinged bar areas, wide range of promptly served food all day, well kept Bass, helpful staff, log fire *(Nigel and Sue Foster, Geoff Pidoux)*

Several well known guide books make establishments pay for entry, either directly or as a fee for inspection. These fees can run to many hundreds of pounds. We do not. Unlike other guides, we never take payment for entries. We never accept a free meal, free drink, or any other freebie from a pub. We do not accept any sponsorship – let alone from commercial schemes linked to the pub trade. All our entries depend solely on merit. And we are the only guide in which virtually all the main entries have been gained by a unique two-stage sifting process: first, a build-up of favourable reports from our thousands of reader-reporters; then anonymous vetting by one of the senior editorial staff.

Shropshire

With an interesting choice of good local beers, and a great variety of pub styles from ancient to modern and from simple to sophisticated, Shropshire has a lot to offer the pub lover. Two bonuses are the scenery (often, the trip to a pub here is part of the pleasure), and the fact that pub food here can be very good indeed – often relying strongly on the county's splendid range of local produce. Prices tend to be modest, with beer prices comfortably below the national average – beers brewed locally by Hobsons often show as good value, and Hanby, Woods and Salopian are other local beers well worth looking out for. Bishop's Castle makes a particularly good stop, with three fine pubs, all on fine form these days – and good news is that the Three Tuns here is now again brewing its own beer in that glorious Victorian tower brewhouse. Other pubs attracting special note these days are the Burlton Inn (good interesting food, and its careful enlargement has worked out really well), the nicely set Royal Oak at Cardington (Shropshire's oldest pub), the Crown at Hopton Wafers (good all round, with particularly good friendly staff), the Church Inn in Ludlow (a new entry, with a notable choice of real ales – a fine town pub, bedrooms too), the Sun quietly set in Norbury (elegant and civilised, with good food and bedrooms), the Bottle & Glass at Picklescott (another new entry, a good warmly welcoming all-rounder under its new licensees), and the Armoury in Shrewsbury (good imaginative food, a great range of drinks, and a very good feel). The Burlton Inn at Burlton, most enjoyable for anything from an interesting bar snack to a special restaurant meal out, takes the title of Shropshire Dining Pub of the Year. In the Lucky Dip section at the end of the chapter, pubs to note particularly are the Railwaymans Arms in Bridgnorth, restauranty Pheasant in Broseley, Boat in Coalport, Sun at Corfton, Inn at Grinshill, Bear in Hodnet and George & Dragon in Much Wenlock.

BISHOP'S CASTLE SO3289 Map 6

Castle Hotel

Market Square, just off B4385

This substantial early 18th-c stone coaching inn is a smashing place to stay, and the pleasant staff and friendly licensees make their customers feel genuinely welcome. Especially lovely in summer, when the pub is festooned with pretty hanging baskets, and there are picnic-sets in the splendidly reworked back garden, which has two terraces with green chairs on either side of a large formal raised fish pond, pergolas and climbing plants, and stone walls; it looks out over the town rooftops to the surrounding gentle countryside. Neatly kept and attractively furnished, the clubby little beamed and panelled bar, glazed off from the entrance, has a good coal fire, old hunting prints and sturdy leather chairs on its muted carpet. It opens into a much bigger room, with maroon plush wall seats and stools, big Victorian engravings, and another coal fire in an attractive cast-iron fireplace. The lighting in both rooms is gentle and relaxing, and the pub tables have unusually elaborate cast-iron frames; shove-ha'penny, dominoes, cribbage, board games, and no piped music. Hobsons Best and Mild, local Six Bells Big Nevs and Simpsons Finest (brewed for the pub by Six Bells) are well kept on handpump, they've decent wines, and over 30 malt whiskies. Made with good quality ingredients, a short choice of enjoyable bar food might include lunchtime baguettes (£5.25), battered haddock (£6.25), and steak and kidney pie (£7.45), with other dishes such as soup (£3.50), tasty chicken liver and mushroom pâté (£4.95), cheese, leek and mushroom sausages with sun-dried tomato sauce or salmon poached in white wine with tarragon and cream (£8.95)), lamb fillet sautéed with mint and redcurrant gravy (£9.75), and good steaks (from £11.95), with puddings such as raspberry cheesecake (£4.25). The handsome no smoking panelled dining room is open in the evening and on Sunday lunchtime. The old-fashioned bedrooms are spacious, and they do good breakfasts. *(Recommended by Paul A Moore, Steve Whalley, Kevin Thorpe, the Didler, Mrs S Butcher, Maggie and Tony Harwood, Pat Bradbury, John Wooll, Greta and Christopher Wells)*

Free house ~ Licensees David and Nicky Simpson ~ Real ale ~ Bar food (12-1.45, 6-8.45) ~ Restaurant ~ (01588) 638403 ~ Children in restaurant ~ Dogs allowed in bar ~ Open 12-2.30, 6-11; 12-2.30, 7-10.30 Sun ~ Bedrooms: £37.50B/£65S

Six Bells

Church Street

A great hit with readers for its excellent beer and cheerful chatty atmosphere, this unpretentious former coaching inn is filled with a good mix of customers (you may even find yourself sitting next to the local priest). Perhaps the main attraction, though, is the excellent beer brewed here. Big Nevs is most people's favourite, and you'll also find Marathon, Cloud Nine and Duck & Dive; you can arrange a tour of the brewery, and they have a beer festival once a year. They also keep a wide range of country wines. The pub consists of just two simple no-frills rooms. One bar is really quite small, with an assortment of well worn furniture and old local photographs and prints; this is no smoking at meal times. The second, bigger room has bare boards, some stripped stone, a roaring woodburner in the inglenook, plenty of sociable locals on the benches around plain tables, darts and lots of board games (they have regular Scrabble nights). The licensees are chatty and service is very friendly. Generously served tasty bar food such as soup (£3), hearty sandwiches (from £2.50, baguettes from £3), ploughman's (£5), fidget pie (£7), vegetable pattie or pork loin with wholegrain mustard and cheddar (£8), and grilled plaice with lemon and parsley butter (£8.50), and home-made puddings. It can be packed here on the weekend. *(Recommended by J Taylor, Kevin Thorpe, Steve Whalley, the Didler, Ron and Val Broom, Maggie and Tony Harwood, Glenwys and Alan Lawrence, Tracey and Stephen Groves)*

Own brew ~ Licensees Neville and Colin Richards ~ Real ale ~ Bar food (12-2(2.30 Sun), 6.30-9; not Sun evening or Mon) ~ Restaurant ~ No credit cards ~ (01588) 630144 ~ Children in eating area of bar ~ Folk third Sun in month and live music first Mon in month ~ Open 12-2.30, 5-11; 12-11(10.30 Sun) Sat; closed Mon lunchtime

Three Tuns

Salop Street

The four-storied Victorian brewhouse across the yard once again supplies this friendly pub with well kept beers: you'll find John Roberts XXX, Castle Steamer, Clerics Cure and Toddly Tom served from old-fashioned handpumps by the friendly staff. They do carry-out kegs, and there are sales by the barrel; a popular annual beer festival takes place in July, with morris dancers in the yard. The no-frills beamed rooms are very simply furnished with low-backed settles and heavy walnut tables, and there are newspapers, cribbage, dominoes, and cards; they hope to re-open the little museum. The pub is well liked by locals, and the sociable atmosphere is undisturbed by piped music. Tasty bar food (made with locally grown vegetables) might include sandwiches from (£3.75), duck breast salad (£4.25), beer-battered cod (£6.95), tian of mediterrannean vegetables with pesto and goats cheese (£7.95), beef and ale pie (£8.50), grilled bass with dill cream (£12), and good organic steaks (from £13), with home-made puddings such as orange and Cointreau cheesecake or gooseberry pie (£4). There's a small garden and terrace. The outside gents' is not suitable for disabled people. As we went to press, the pub was about to be taken over by the owners of the John Roberts Brewing Company, so some of the details may change. *(Recommended by the Didler, Kevin Thorpe, Pat and Tony Martin, G Coates, Karen and Graham Oddey, Tracey and Stephen Groves, R and H Fraser, John Fiander, Steve Whalley)*

Free house ~ Licensees John Russell and Bill Bainbridge ~ Real ale ~ Bar food (not evenings Sun or Mon) ~ Restaurant ~ (01588) 638797 ~ Well behaved children in eating area of bar and restaurant till 9pm ~ Dogs allowed in bar ~ Open 12-11(10.30 Sun); may be shorter opening hours in winter ~ Bedrooms: £45B/£75B

BRIDGES SO3996 Map 6

Horseshoe

Near Ratlinghope, below the W flank of the Long Mynd

In a picturesque streamside setting among deserted hills, this country pub (now with new licensees) is in good walking country, and handy for the Stiperstones. It's popular with walking groups, though you'll find locals here too. Warmed by a cosy fire, the down-to-earth yet comfortable bar has interesting windows, lots of pictures and toby jugs, and well kept Adnams Bitter, Bass and a changing guest such as Greene King Old Speckled Hen on handpump, and they've also farm cider. A small dining room leads off from here; winter darts and dominoes, and piped music. Tasty bar food such as soup (£2.95), sandwiches (from £3.50), lasagne (£5.50), local sausages (£6.50), home-made steak and kidney pie (£6.75), grilled trout (£7.25), half a duck (£9.50), and rump steak (£9.95), with puddings such as apple pie (£2.95). Tables are placed out by the little River Onny; the Long Mynd rises up behind. They have plans to turn the outbuildings into a restaurant, and maybe bedrooms. *(Recommended by Karen and Graham Oddey, Kevin Thorpe, Gloria Bax, John and Jenny Pullin, MLR, Dave Braisted, Ian Phillips)*

Free house ~ Licensees Bob and Maureen Macauley ~ Real ale ~ Bar food (12-3, 6-9; 12-9 Sat-Sun) ~ (01588) 650260 ~ Children welcome ~ Dogs welcome ~ Open 11-11; 12-10.30 Sun; closed 25 Dec

BROMFIELD SO4877 Map 6

Cookhouse Café Bar 🍷

A49 2 miles NW of Ludlow

The above name is our shortened version of the current title which is the Clive Restaurant with Rooms and Cookhouse Café Bar. Inside this handsome and immaculately kept Georgian brick house is an interesting contemporary take on the traditional inn. The front section has been brightly modernised in minimalist city style, but the back part is more traditional – though still with a modern edge. During the day the focus is on the dining room, café bar in style, with modern light wood tables, and a big open kitchen behind the end stainless steel counter. A door leads through into the bar, sparse but neat and welcoming, with round glass tables and metal chairs running down to a sleek, space-age bar counter with fresh flowers, newspapers and spotlights. Then it's down a step to the Clive Arms Bar, where traditional features like the huge brick fireplace, exposed stonework, and soaring beams and rafters are appealingly juxtaposed with wicker chairs, well worn sofas and new glass tables. Some areas are no smoking; piped jazz, daily papers. Besides sandwiches, good bar food includes soup (£3.95), smoked haddock rarebit (£5.95), croque monsieur (£6.95), cornish mullet with piccalilli or roast chicken breast with ratatouille with chargrilled polenta (£7.95), spinach and feta tart (£8.95), and roast duck breast with orange, rosemary and shallot sauce (£11.95). They do two courses for £11.50. The good wine list includes eight by the glass, and Hobsons Best and Town Crier are well kept on handpump; they also have a good choice of coffees and teas. An attractive secluded terrace has tables under cocktail parasols and a fish pond. They now have 15 bedrooms, and we'd imagine this would be a nice place to stay. *(Recommended by Kevin Thorpe, George Atkinson, John Whitehead)*

Free house ~ Licensee Paul Brooks ~ Real ale ~ Bar food (12-3, 6-10; 11-10 Sat-Sun) ~ Restaurant ~ (01584) 856565 ~ Children in eating area of bar and restaurant ~ Open 11-11; 12-10.30 Sun; closed 25-26 Dec ~ Bedrooms: £50B/£70B

BURLTON SJ4626 Map 6

Burlton Inn

A528 Shrewsbury—Ellesmere, near junction with B4397

Shropshire Dining Pub of the Year

The kind of place it's hard to tear yourself away from, this attractively restored old pub is well run by welcoming licensees. The food here is very good, and besides interesting specials such as mackerel with gooseberry and orange sauce (£9.95), honey-glazed chicken breast stuffed with goats cheese (£11.25), and duck stir fry (£12.50), an enticing choice of home-made bar food could include soup (£3.50), filled baguettes or baked potatoes (from £5.75), crab and asparagus tartlet or potted smoked trout (£5.95), chicken, bacon and brie lasagne (£11.50), fried pork with goats cheese (£12.95), and halibut with salmon gravadlax sauce (£13.95), with home-made puddings such as raspberry, pear and amaretto trifle or chocolate rum slice (£4.25); readers recommend the Sunday roasts. There may be two set-time evening sittings in the restaurant. Everything seems meticulously arranged and well cared for, from the pretty flower displays in the brick fireplace or beside the neatly curtained windows, to the piles of *Country Living* and interior design magazines in the corner; there are a few sporting prints, spurs and brasses on the walls, open fires in winter and dominoes and cribbage. French windows lead from the new garden dining room to the pleasant terrace, with its smart wooden furniture; the snug has comfortable seats, great for sinking into with a drink. There are eleven wines by the glass (in two sizes), and along with well kept Banks's, you'll find three continually changing guests from brewers such as Hop Back, St George's and Wye Valley. They now have disabled facilities. There are tables on a small lawn behind, with more on a strip of grass beyond the car park. *(Recommended by Mr and Mrs F Carroll, Mike and Mary Carter, S Horsley, Maurice and Della Andrew, I D Greenfield, R N and M I Bailey, Jason Caulkin, M Thomas, Stan Edwards, H Wardlaw, Roger Thornington, John and Caroline, Howard and Lorna Lambert, J S Burn, Ray and Winifred Halliday, Derek and Sylvia Stephenson)*

Free house ~ Licensee Gerald Bean ~ Real ale ~ Bar food (12-2, 6.30-9.45(7-9.30 Sun)) ~ Restaurant ~ (01939) 270284 ~ Well behaved children in eating area of bar and restaurant ~ Dogs welcome ~ Open 11-3, 6-11; 12-3, 7-10.30 Sun; closed bank hol Mon lunchtimes; 25-26 Dec and 1 Jan ~ Bedrooms: £50B/£80B

CARDINGTON SO5095 Map 4

Royal Oak

Village signposted off B4371 Church Stretton—Much Wenlock, pub behind church; also reached via narrow lanes from A49

Tucked away in a lovely spot, this friendly ancient place has been licensed for longer than any other pub in Shropshire. It's especially worth visiting in summer, when the frontage is ablaze with hanging baskets, and tables in the rose-filled front courtyard have lovely views over hilly fields. Inside, the rambling, low-beamed bar has a roaring winter log fire, cauldron, black kettle and pewter jugs in its vast inglenook fireplace, the old standing timbers of a knocked-through wall, and red and green tapestry seats solidly capped in elm; darts, dominoes, and maybe piped music. A comfortable no smoking dining area has exposed old beams and studwork. The welcoming and efficient waitresses help create a relaxed atmosphere. Big helpings of tasty good value bar food include soup (£2.50), garlic mushrooms (£3), baguettes (from £3.25), filled baked potatoes (from £3.50), ploughman's (from £4.50), chicken tikka masala or spinach and mascarpone lasagne (£7.50), grilled trout or excellent fidget pie (£8), and steaks (from £9); children's meals (£3). Hobsons and a couple of guests such as Salopian Heaven Sent and Six Bells Duck Dive are well kept under light blanket pressure. A mile or so away – from the track past Willstone (ask for directions at the pub) – you can walk up Caer Caradoc Hill, which has great views. *(Recommended by Mike and Heather Watson, TOH, Alison and Graham Hooper, George and Gill Peckham, Jim and Maggie Cowell, Derek and Sylvia Stephenson, John Whitehead, J S Burn, A H Gordon Clark)*

Free house ~ Licensee Michael Carter ~ Real ale ~ Bar food (12-2, 7-8.30; not Sun evening or Mon) ~ (01694) 771266 ~ Open 12-3, 7-11(10.30 Sun); closed Mon except bank hols

HOPTON WAFERS SO6476 Map 6

Crown

A4117 Kidderminster—Ludlow

Readers are full of praise for the friendly and attentive staff at this attractive creeper-covered inn, an enjoyable place to eat or stay. The emphasis is on the good, freshly prepared food, and the changing menu might include soup (£3.50), chicken liver pâté (£4.50), vegetable and mixed bean cassoulet (£7.95), home-made pie (£8.75), steaks (from £11.75), with blackboard specials (including good fresh fish dishes) such as crab and mussel chowder (£4.50), pork and stilton sausages with apricot gravy (£7.95), and salmon and asparagus fishcakes (£8.95), and mouth-watering home-made puddings (£4.25); they do smaller portions of some dishes for children. Neatly kept with an understated atmosphere, the cosy cream-painted beamed bar has a large inglenook fireplace, dark wood furniture, oil paintings, and fresh flowers. The restaurant (with a more elaborate menu) has another impressive inglenook and pretty table settings, and is no smoking; piped music. Outside, the streamside garden is lovely in summer, with tubs of bright flowers and a duck pond, and pleasant terrace areas with tables under cocktail parasols. Hobsons Best and Woods Shropshire Lad are well kept alongside a guest such as Timothy Taylors Landlord on handpump, and they've ten wines by the glass, and 30 malt whiskies. *(Recommended by Gill and Tony Morriss, Ian and Nita Cooper, Paul and Margaret Baker, Ian Phillips, Gerry and Rosemary Dobson, A P Seymour, Mike and Mary Carter, Prof Keith and Mrs Jane Barber, Dave Braisted)*

Free house ~ Licensee Howard Hill-Lines ~ Real ale ~ Bar food (12-2.30, 6.30-9.30) ~ Restaurant ~ (01299) 270372 ~ Children in eating area of bar and restaurant ~ Open 12-3, 6-11; 12-11(10.30 Sun) Sat; 12-3, 6-11(10.30 Sun)Sat in winter ~ Bedrooms: £49.50B/£85B

IRONBRIDGE SJ6704 Map 6

Malthouse

The Wharfage (bottom road alongside Severn)

The lobby and stairwell at this big lively place are exhibition spaces for interesting local artists – the only criteria for showing here is that the owner likes the pictures and that the artist helps hang the paintings. A nice touch is that they don't charge the artist a commission. Spotlessly kept, the spacious bar is broken up by pine beams and concrete pillars, and has lots of scrubbed light wooden tables with candles; piped music. Appropriately informal, the bar menu includes dishes such as pesto and parmesan pasta (£3.75), minute steak and blue cheese baguette (£5.50), egg noodles with various flavours (from £6.50), cheeseburger or steamed salmon salad (£7.95), and rib-eye steak (£9.95), with puddings such as chocolate cake with Baileys (£4); they have a good children's menu (£3.50). The atmosphere is quite different in the mostly no smoking restaurant, which has a much more elaborate menu. Boddingtons, Flowers Original, John Smiths and a guest such as Jennings Cumberland are well kept on handpump, and they've a wide choice of wines including ten by the glass; flexible and friendly service. There are a few tables outside in front (beware, they retain your credit card if you eat here). They hold live music nights from Wednesday to Saturday. *(Recommended by Mr and Mrs G S Ayrton, Ron and Val Broom, Mike and Wendy Proctor, Michael and Alison Sandy, Kevin Thomas, Nina Randall)*

Free house ~ Licensees Alex and Andrea Nicoll ~ Real ale ~ Bar food (12-2.30, 5.30-9.30) ~ Restaurant ~ (01952) 433712 ~ Children in eating area of bar and restaurant ~ Live jazz and world music Weds-Sat evenings ~ Open 11-11; 12-10.30 Sun; 11-3, 5-11 wkdys in winter; closed 25 Dec, 26 Dec evening ~ Bedrooms: £59B/£69B

LONGVILLE SO5393 Map 4

Longville Arms

B4371 Church Stretton—Much Wenlock

A terraced side garden at this pleasant pub (handily open all day on the weekends) has picnic-sets next to two big trampolines in a fun children's play area. Neatly kept, the two spacious bars have stripped beams and original stone, and the lounge bar on the left has stone walls, cushioned chairs and some nice old tables. The room on the right has oak panelling, and a large no smoking restaurant overlooks the terrace. The three well kept ales can vary from week to week, but might include Courage Directors, Theakstons Best and Woods Pot of Gold on handpump; also several malt and irish whiskies. A games room (no children in here) has a juke box, darts, pool and dominoes, and there's piped music; disabled facilities. The reasonably priced bar menu includes home-made soup (£2.50), baguettes (from £3.25), fried garlic mushrooms (£3.75), baked potatoes (from £4.20), breaded plaice (£6.25), moussaka or beef lasagne (£6.50), and cajun chicken breast (£7.95), with specials such as chicken breast wrapped in bacon (£9.95), and rib-eye steak with pepper sauce (£10.50). The countryside around here is really quite beautiful. *(Recommended by John Whitehead)*

Free house ~ Licensee Jill Livingstone ~ Real ale ~ Bar food (12-2.30, 7-9.30) ~ Restaurant ~ (01694) 771206 ~ Children in eating area of bar and restaurant ~ Dogs allowed in bar and bedrooms ~ Open 12-3, 7(6 Fri)-11; 12-11(10.30 Sun) Sat ~ Bedrooms: £30S/£50S

LUDLOW SO5174 Map 4

Church Inn

Church Street, behind Butter Cross

We've recently had a flood of happy reports on this enjoyable old inn. They serve eight well kept real ales including Hobsons Mild and Town Crier, Hook Norton Best and Old Hooky, Weetwood Eastgate, Wye Valley Bitter, and a couple of swiftly changing guests on handpump; also 14 malt whiskies, and country wines. In summer you can get three different types of Pimms, while in winter there's mulled wine and hot toddy, and they do a roaring trade in tea and coffee too. Appealingly decorated and carefully lit, with hops hanging from heavy beams, comfortable banquettes in cosy alcoves off the eye-catching island bar (part is a pulpit), and pews and stripped stonework from the church, the interior is divided into three areas. There are church pews, displays of old photographic equipment, plants on windowsills, and church prints in the no smoking side room; a long central area with a fine stone fireplace (good winter fires) leads to new lavatories. The more basic side bar has old black and white photographs of the town. The civilised no smoking upstairs lounge has vaulted ceilings, and long windows overlooking the church; it has display cases of glass, china and old bottles, and musical instruments on the walls, along with a mix of new and old pictures. Service is friendly and relaxed, the pub is popular with locals (the landlord is the town's former mayor), and there's a cheerful atmosphere; daily papers, piped music. Enjoyable sensible food (they make good use of local suppliers) could include lunchtime snacks such as sandwiches (from £3.50, baguettes from £3.95), and filled baked potatoes (£4.95), with other dishes such as soup (£3.50), garlic mushrooms with melted brie (£3.75), tomato and chive tart (£6.25), sweet thai chilli chicken (£6.95), grilled salmon with hollandaise sauce and pasta (£7.95), and rack of lamb with garlic and rosemary (£8.25), with a short choice of puddings such as caramel parfait (£3.95); children's meals (£3.25). The restaurant is no smoking. The bedrooms are simple and comfortable; good breakfasts. Car parking is some way off. *(Recommended by Kevin Thorpe, MLR, Joe Green, Tracey and Stephen Groves, Mark Rogers, Christopher J Darwent, Pam and John Smith, Ian Phillips, Kerry Law, Simon Smith, John Whitehead, J C Poley, Chris Flynn, Wendy Jones)*

Free house ~ Licensee Graham Willson-Lloyd ~ Real ale ~ Bar food (12-2, 6.30-9; 12-9(8.30 Sun) Fri/Sat in winter; not 25 Dec, evenings 24 or 31 Dec) ~ Restaurant ~ (01584) 872174 ~ Children welcome ~ Dogs welcome ~ Singer/guitarist second Weds in month ~ Open 11-11; 12-10.30 Sun; closed 25 Dec evening ~ Bedrooms: /£60S(£80B)

Unicorn

Corve Street – the quiet bottom end, beyond where it leaves the main road to Shrewsbury

Tables outside this 17th-c inn, built in a row of black and white cottages, shelter pleasantly among willow trees on the pretty little terrace right next to the modest River Corve. The solidly beamed and partly panelled bar with its huge log fire in a big stone fireplace gives a real feel of age, and there's often a pleasant mix of locals and visitors; cribbage and dominoes. Three real ales such as Greene King Abbot, Hancocks HB and Timothy Taylors Landlord are well kept on handpump; it can get smoky. Generously served bar food could include home-made soup (£3.75), sandwiches (from £3.75), garlic mushrooms (£4.50), beer-battered cod (£7.75), greek-style lamb (£7.95), and gammon and egg (£8.25), or you can eat from the restaurant menu in the bar, dishes such as bass or moroccan lamb (£13.95), with tasty puddings such as apple crumble and banoffi pie (£3.50); service can be slow at times. The timbered candlelit restaurant is no smoking. Parking in this picturesque town may be tricky. *(Recommended by Dr John Henderson, Mark Rogers, Joe Green, Chris Flynn, Wendy Jones)*

Free house ~ Licensees Mike and Rita Knox ~ Real ale ~ Bar food (12-2.15, 6(7 Sun)-9.15) ~ Restaurant ~ (01584) 873555 ~ Well behaved children in eating area of bar and restaurant ~ Dogs allowed in bar ~ Open 12-3, 6-11; 12-3.30, 6.30-10.30 Sun; closed 25 Dec

MUCH WENLOCK SO6299 Map 4

Talbot

High Street

At this ancient inn (once part of Wenlock Abbey), a flower-festooned coach entry leads off the High Street to a little courtyard with green metal and wood garden furniture and pretty flower tubs. Popular with locals, the bar has two big log fires in inglenooks – great on a miserable wet day. The several neatly kept areas have low ceilings, and comfortable red tapestry button-back wall banquettes around their tables. The walls are decorated with prints of fish and brewery paraphernalia, and there are art deco-style lamps and gleaming brasses. Bass is well kept alongside a guest from Enville or Woods on handpump, and they've several malt whiskies, and half a dozen wines by the glass; quiet piped music. The lunchtime menu might include tasty, generously served bar food such as soup (£3.25), sandwiches (from £3.75, baguettes from £4.25), filled baked potatoes (from £4.75), goulash, smoked haddock pasta bake, lamb and leek pie or caribbean chicken (all £7.95), while the more elaborate (and not as cheap) evening menu includes dishes such as pork calvados or chicken breast stuffed with leeks in blue cheese sauce (£12.95); the dining area is no smoking. It's in a lovely town; there's a cheap car park. *(Recommended by John Oates, Andrea and Guy Bradley, Nigel B Thompson, Gill and Tony Morriss, Mike and Heather Watson, Mike and Wendy Proctor, Margaret Dickinson, Tracey and Stephen Groves, Jim and Maggie Cowell, Derek and Sylvia Stephenson, John Whitehead, Kevin Thorpe, M Joyner, Brian and Jacky Wilson)*

Free house ~ Licensees Mark and Maggie Tennant ~ Real ale ~ Bar food (12-2.30, 7-9.30) ~ Restaurant ~ (01952) 727077 ~ Children welcome ~ Open 10.30-3, 6-11; 10.30-11 Sat; 12-10.30 Sun; 10.30-3, 6.30-11 Sat winter; 12-3, 7-10.30 Sun winter; closed 25 Dec ~ Bedrooms: £37.50B/£75B

> If you know a pub's ever open all day, please tell us.

NORBURY SO3692 Map 6

Sun

Off A488 or A489 NE of Bishop's Castle; OS Sheet 137 map reference 363928

This immaculately kept civilised dining pub is tucked away in a quiet Shropshire village in remote walking country below the Stiperstones. A proper tiled-floor bar has settees and Victorian tables and chairs, cushioned stone seats along the wall by the flame-effect stove, and a few mysterious implements (the kind that it's fun to guess about) on its neat white walls. Alongside is a tiled pool room with shove-ha'penny; gentle piped music. Well kept Wye Valley Hereford and maybe a guest such as Woods Shropshire Lad on handpump, and decent house wines. The restaurant side has a charming lounge with button-back leather wing chairs, easy chairs and a chesterfield on its deep-pile green carpet. The log fire, nice lighting, comfortable seats, willow-pattern china on the dark oak dresser, fresh flowers, candles and magazines quickly make you feel at home; service is friendly. The elegantly furnished dining room serves a shortish choice of good food. The blackboard bar menu (also fairly short) might typically include baguettes (from £3.95), cumberland sausage or vegetable samosa (£6.50), smoked trout (£7.50), scampi (£7.50), and readers recommend the rump steak (£8.50). There are tables outside by a pond; there's a good unusual route up the Stiperstones from here. *(Recommended by Dr T E Hothersall, Kevin Thorpe, David Field)*

Free house ~ Licensee Carol Cahan ~ Real ale ~ Bar food (7-9; 12-2 Sun, and summer Sats) ~ Restaurant ~ (01588) 650680 ~ Dogs allowed in bar ~ Open 7-11; 12-3, 7-11 Sat-Sun; cl Sat lunchtime in winter; closed Mon exc bank hol lunchtimes, Tues-Fri lunchtimes ~ Bedrooms: £50S/£60S(£120B)

NORTON SJ7200 Map 4

Hundred House

A442 Telford—Bridgnorth

The gardens at this immaculately restored old brick pub have old-fashioned roses, trees, herbaceous plants, and a big working herb garden that supplies the kitchen – you can buy bags of their herbs for £1 and the money goes to charity. Inside bunches of fresh flowers brighten the tables and counter in the neatly kept bar, and there are hops and huge bunches of dried flowers and herbs hanging from beams; there's a good chatty atmosphere. Handsome fireplaces have log fires or working coalbrookdale ranges (one has a great Jacobean arch with fine old black cooking pots), and a variety of interesting chairs and settles with some long colourful patchwork leather cushions set out around sewing-machine tables. Steps lead up past a little balustrade to a partly panelled eating area, where the stripped brickwork looks older than that elsewhere. The main dining room is no smoking; shove-ha'penny, pinball, dominoes, and piped music. They've a good range of drinks. Heritage Bitter and Mild (brewed especially for them by a small brewery) are well kept on handpump alongside a couple of guests such as Everards Tiger and Robinsons Unicorn, and they've also an extensive wine list with house wines by the carafe, half carafe and big or small glass; also farm cider, lots of malt whiskies, and good liqueur coffees. Good (but not cheap) bar food includes soup (£3.95), greek salad (£4.95), lasagne or local pork sausages and mash (£7.95), roast butternut squash with sweet pepper chutney and a mushroom and chestnut filo (£8.95), and 10oz sirloin steak (£13.95), with specials such as local asparagus with lemon, butter and black pepper (£6.95), mild thai chicken curry (£12.95), and roast ling with asparagus and butterbean casserole (£13.95), with puddings such as hot treacle tart (£4.95), and white and dark chocolate mousse (£5.95). You must book for the restaurant, though you can eat from its menu in the bar: roast rack of lamb with mediterranean vegetable casserole, cumin purée and gremolata (£17.95), or roast beef fillet with chargrilled mediterranean vegetables, mushroom pasta and balsamic sauce (£18.95). *(Recommended by Lynda and Trevor Smith, Alun Howells, Oliver and Sue Rowell, Patrick and Phillipa Vickery, A P Seymour, John H Franklin)*

Free house ~ Licensees Henry, Sylvia, Stuart and David Phillips ~ Real ale ~ Bar food (12-2.30, 6-10; 12-2.30, 7-9 Sun) ~ Restaurant ~ (01952) 730353 ~ Children welcome ~ Dogs allowed in bedrooms ~ Open 11-3, 5.30-11; 11-11(10.30 Sun) Sat ~ Bedrooms: £85B/£125B

PICKLESCOTT SO4399 Map 6

Bottle & Glass

Village signposted off A49 N of Church Stretton

In a delightful spot below the north end of the Long Mynd, this nicely unspoilt 17th-c former farmhouse changed hands shortly before we went to press, with the new licensees well known to the *Guide* from several years of running the Masons Arms at Knowstone in Devon. The jovial old-school landlord is about to celebrate his 40th year in the trade, and his 30th as a licensee; he works hard to make sure everyone is happy, and on our visit effortlessly ran the bar while striking up conversations with various customers, many of whom were soon chatting to each other as if they were old friends. The nicest part of the pub is the small beamed and quarry-tiled candlelit bar, so it's good news that over the next few months the lounge will be refurbished in a similar style; a third room will be opened up off the bar too, and each will have its own inglenook (logs in the huge one in the bar blaze away every day of the year). Very good home-made bar food (promptly served, in hearty helpings) might include lunchtime baguettes, soup (£2.95), stilton, pork and celery pâté (£4), sausage and mash (£6.50), steak, kidney and Guinness pie (£7.50), fresh fish, and crusted rack of lamb with honey, port and redcurrant sauce (£14). Well kept Woods Parish and Shropshire Lad and a changing guest beer on handpump; unobtrusive piped music. After the changes are complete (expected to be not long after this edition hits the shops), around half the pub will be no smoking. Their two cats and two dogs have moved with them from Devon. There are a few picnic-sets in front. *(Recommended by Sean Mulholland, J C Brittain-Long)*

Free house ~ Licensees Paul and Jo Stretton-Downes ~ Real ale ~ Bar food (12-2, 7-9; not Sun evening, or 25 Dec) ~ (01694) 751345 ~ Children in eating area of bar ~ Dogs allowed in bar ~ Open 12-2.30, 6-11

SHREWSBURY SJ4912 Map 6

Armoury

Victoria Quay, Victoria Avenue

With a great choice of drinks, good food and friendly and adept staff, this handsome 18th-c warehouse is a thoroughly enjoyable all-rounder. Long runs of big arched windows in the uniform red brick frontages have views across the broad river at the back, and are interspersed with brick columns, hanging baskets and smart coach lights at the front. Spacious and light, the appealing open-plan interior has a mix of wood tables and chairs on expanses of stripped wood floors, a dominating display of floor-to-ceiling books on two huge walls, a grand stone fireplace at one end, and masses of old prints mounted edge to edge on the stripped brick walls. Colonial fans whirr away on the ceilings, which are supported by occasional green-painted standing timbers, and glass cabinets display collections of explosives and shells. The long bar counter has a terrific choice of drinks, and besides well kept Armoury (brewed by Hanby), Wadworths 6X, and Woods Shropshire Lad, they've up to five changing guest beers from brewers such as Phoenix, Roosters and Thwaites on handpump. If beer is not your thing, you can also choose from a tempting wine list (with 15 by the glass), around 50 malt whiskies, a dozen different gins, lots of rums and vodkas, a variety of brandies, and some unusual liqueurs. Superbly cooked bar food, from an interesting menu, includes sandwiches with unusual fillings (from £3.95), tasty soup (£3.45), ploughman's (£6.95), local sausages and mash (£7.95), staffordshire black bacon chop with fried egg (£8.25), sweet potato and spinach curry (£8.45), lemon and black pepper chicken with ratatouille and tagliatelle (£10.25), and braised lamb shank with redcurrant gravy (£11.25), with puddings such as rhubarb and apple crumble and sticky toffee pudding (from £3.95). Tables at one end are laid out for eating. It gets busy here in the evening, particularly at weekends – there may even be queues outside. The pub doesn't have its own parking, but there are plenty of places nearby. *(Recommended by Dave Irving, I D Greenfield, Mrs Jean Clarke, Michael Butler, Kevin Blake, Mike and Mary Carter, Geoffrey and Penny Hughes, Tracey and Stephen Groves, Ian Phillips, Simon and Mandy King, Derek and Sylvia Stephenson, Steve Whalley, M Joyner)*

Brunning & Price ~ Manager Andy Barker ~ Real ale ~ Bar food (12-9.30(9 Sun)) ~ (01743) 340525 ~ Children welcome ~ Open 12-11(10.30 Sun); closed 25-26 Dec

Three Fishes

Fish Street

Just around the corner from the ancient Bear Steps area, this timbered and flagstoned pub town has been an inn since the 16th c. Although it's been extensively refurbished, you can feel its age in the slope of the flagstones under its carpeting; the bar has hops on its profusion of heavy beams, white walls, dark wood tables and chairs and brocaded wall banquettes. They serve well kept Caledonian Deuchars IPA, Fullers London Pride and Timothy Taylors Landlord, alongside a couple of guest beers from brewers such as Cottage and Oakham; decent house wines. Simple hearty bar food includes soup (£2.95), baguettes or filled baked potatoes (from £3.90), cod, chips and mushy peas (£5.95), steak and ale pie (£6.35), hunters chicken (£6.95), and 8oz sirloin steak (£9.70), with puddings such as treacle sponge (£3.45); friendly service. At lunchtime the pub is popular with an older set enjoying the smoke-free atmosphere (the new landlord has continued with the pub's complete ban on smoking). *(Recommended by Michael Butler, Kevin Thorpe, John Lunt, the Didler, Stan Edwards, Martin Grosberg, M Joyner)*

Enterprise ~ Lease David Moss ~ Real ale ~ Bar food (12-2.15, 6-8.30; not Sun evening) ~ (01743) 344793 ~ Open 11.30-3, 5-11; 11.30-11 Fri-Sat; 12-4, 7-10.30 Sun

WENTNOR SO3893 Map 6

Crown

Village and pub signposted (not very clearly) off A489 a few miles NW of junction with A49

Beams and standing timbers testify to the age of this fine building, which has been an inn since it was built in 1640. Much of the main bar area is laid for eating; one end has a snug area with pictures and two sofas, and there are good log fires. Hobsons Best and Mild, and a couple of changing guests such as Salopian Shropshire Gold, and Woods Shropshire Lad are well kept on handpump (under light blanket pressure in winter), and they have decent wines, along with a good choice of malt whiskies; piped music, dominoes, and cribbage. Tasty bar food such as sandwiches (from £2.75), soup (£2.40), smoked salmon and dill quiche (£5.50), home-made steak and ale or pork and apple pie made with good pastry (£7.25), chicken with leek and stilton sauce or cod (£6.95), and home-made puddings such as lemon cheesecake or chocolate and ginger truffle slice (£3.50); pleasant service. The cosy beamed restaurant is no smoking. It's set in lovely countryside, and there's a fine view of the Long Mynd from seats on the neat back lawn. The location and the good value pretty bedrooms make this a nice place for a night's stay. There's plenty of space for parking. *(Recommended by Mike and Shelley Woodroffe, Collin and Julie Taylor, Mrs P Antlett, John and Brenda Bensted, Ian Phillips, Kevin Thorpe)*

Free house ~ Licensees Mike and Chris Brown ~ Real ale ~ Bar food (all day wknds) ~ Restaurant ~ (01588) 650613 ~ Children welcome ~ Open 12-3, 6-11; 12-11 wknds ~ Bedrooms: £30S/£53S

Waterside pubs are listed at the back of the book.

WISTANSTOW SO4385 Map 6

Plough

Village signposted off A49 and A489 N of Craven Arms

Woods beers are brewed next door to this pleasant pub, so the Woods Parish, Plough Special, Shropshire Lad and seasonal ales are very well kept on handpump (you can buy bottles of Woods beer to take away). A bonus is that the food is enjoyable too. Making good use of local suppliers, mostly english dishes from the seasonally changing menu might include soup (£3.50), welsh rarebit (£5.20), fresh baguettes (£5.60), terrine with home-made chutney (£5.80), local sausages with mash and onion gravy (£7.65), steak and kidney suet pudding (£9.10), sweet chilli chicken with lemon and coriander and herby couscous (£9.40), and organic salmon with local asparagus (£11.50), with home-made puddings such as white chocolate rice pudding with blackcurrant sauce or rich chocolate tart with bitter orange ice-cream (£3.90). On Sundays, the menu is limited to two roasts (£7.25), a fish and a vegetarian option. Spotlessly kept, the pub is simply furnished with high rafters and cream walls, and a russet turkey carpet, oak or mahogany tables and chairs and welsh dressers to give the modernised bar a more homely feel. The games area has darts, pool, dominoes, fruit machine and piped music. Friendly staff serve Addlestone's and Weston's cider and about 15 wines by the glass, including a rosé. There are some tables under cocktail parasols outside. *(Recommended by Debbie and Neil Hayter, Revd D Glover, C R Harrison, Keith Berrett, MLR, Tracey and Stephen Groves, John Evans, Stan Edwards, John Whitehead, J C Poley)*

Own brew ~ Licensee Denis Harding ~ Real ale ~ Bar food (12-1.30, 6.30-8.30; not Mon, or Sun evening) ~ Restaurant ~ (01588) 673251 ~ Children in eating area of bar and family room ~ Dogs allowed in bar ~ Open 11.30-2.30, 6.30-11; 12-2.30, 7-10.30 Sun; closed Mon

LUCKY DIP

Besides the fully inspected pubs, you might like to try these Lucky Dips recommended to us and described by readers (if you do, please send us reports: www.goodguides.co.uk).

ALL STRETTON SO4595

Yew Tree [Shrewsbury Rd (B4370)]: Comfortable neatly kept beamed bars and dining room, houseplants and lots of interesting watercolours, well kept Hobsons Best and Wye Valley Butty Bach, good log fire, pleasant licensee, bookable dining room, lively public bar; children welcome, small village handy for Long Mynd, cl Tues *(TOH, Margaret Dickinson)*

ASTON MUNSLOW SO5187

Swan: Ancient pub with several rambling linked areas in varying styles, refreshingly old-fashioned and unmodified, good choice of good value food (inc seven types of sausage), Hobsons and Timothy Taylors Landlord, log fires; garden with shady areas *(Margaret Dickinson)*

ASTON ON CLUN SO3981

Kangaroo [Clun Rd]: Large open-plan country pub with well kept Roo (brewed for them by Six Bells in Bishop's Castle) and Charles Wells Bombardier, friendly service, food lunchtime and evening, central fireplace in main bar, front public bar with railway memorabilia inc a large model train over the fireplace, side games room with darts and pool, annual beer festival; juke box; open all day Fri-Sun, tables in large back garden *(Kevin Thorpe, Richard Houghton)*

ATCHAM SJ5409

Mytton & Mermaid: Comfortable and friendly, with good traditional food in bar and relaxed easy-going restaurant, well kept Greene King Ruddles and Woods Shropshire Lad, good wine choice, helpful staff, some theme nights; pleasant Severn-view bedrooms, nice setting opp entrance to Attingham Park (NT) *(Revd D Glover, Mr and Mrs P Lally, Joan and Tony Walker)*

BRIDGNORTH SO7193

Golden Lion [High St]: Pleasantly decorated friendly traditional two-bar pub with well kept Banks's Bitter and Mild and a guest beer, decent coffee, hearty helpings of good value bar food from low-priced basic sandwiches up; saucy pictures in gents', no music *(Gill and Tony Morriss, D W Stokes)*

Habit [E Castle St]: New owners keeping up standard, good unusual generous food with enterprising children's choice, keenly priced wines by the glass, fresh bistro atmosphere and modern décor, welcoming staff, nice fireplace on upper level, clearly marked smoking area; piped music; nr top of Cliff Railway *(Mr and Mrs G S Ayrton, M Joyner)*

☆ *Railwaymans Arms* [Severn Valley Stn, Hollybush Rd (off A458 towards Stourbridge)]: Well kept Bathams, Hobsons and interesting changing guest beers in old-fashioned converted waiting-room at Severn Valley steam railway terminus, bustling on summer days; coal fire, station nameplates, superb mirror over fireplace, tables out on platform; may be simple summer snacks and sandwiches, children welcome, wheelchair access; the train to Kidderminster (another bar there) has an all-day bar and bookable Sun lunches *(Kerry Law, Simon Smith, the Didler, Gill and Tony Morriss, LYM, Tracey and Stephen Groves)*

BROOME SO4081

☆ *Engine & Tender*: Homely bar with well kept Woods from art deco servery, railway memorabilia and other bric-a-brac, cosy corners with tables for eating, also quite extensive restaurant with interesting collection of pottery inc teapots and shelves of jugs, good freshly made food (not Mon) inc generous Sun roast and lovely puddings, good value wines, cheerful helpful unhurried service, forest of good-sized plants in conservatory, games room with pool and glassed-over well; caravan site with hook-up points and showers, nice countryside *(Mr and Mrs Robert Cooper, Mrs J Wood)*

BROSELEY SJ6701

☆ *Pheasant* [Church St]: Appealing dining pub smartly done up in shabby-chic style, small choice of good imaginative restauranty food inc seasonal game, welcoming individualistic licensees, good wines (no list, just what they have at the moment), real ales, small friendly bar, two rooms with sturdy seats, big stripped tables on oak boards, large oil paintings, coal-effect fire, fresh flowers, candles and gas lamps; tasteful bedrooms, good breakfast; cl lunchtimes exc Sun, also Sun/Mon evenings *(Mr and Mrs P Lally, Mike and Natasha Coussens, John and Lynn Norcliffe)*

BURWARTON SO6185

Boyne Arms [B4364 Bridgnorth—Ludlow]: Imposing Georgian coaching inn, generous good value home cooking, friendly helpful staff, changing well kept ales such as Bass and local Hobsons and Woods, cheerfully unassuming local atmosphere, public bar with pool; tables in large garden with good timber adventure playground, bedrooms *(Theo, Anne and Jane Gaskin, DC)*

CHETWYND ASTON SJ7517

Three Fishes: Roomy Edwardian pub recently taken over by the good small Brunning & Price group and not seen by us (being refurbished and possibly renamed, and will not open before late 2004), but if it's up to their usual standard will be well worth knowing; reports please *(BOB)*

CLEOBURY MORTIMER SO6775

Kings Arms [A4117 Bewdley—Ludlow]: Warmly decorated open-plan bar with pews, bare boards and well spaced tables (some rather bright chairs, too), good log fire, enjoyable food using fresh local produce from sandwiches and baguettes up, welcoming hard-working young staff, well kept Bathams Best and two from Hobsons, beamed dining area stretching beyond island servery; piped music, very popular with young people evenings; open all day, children welcome, garden with water feature, reasonably priced comfortable bedrooms *(Earl and Chris Pick, LYM, Joe Green, Ian Phillips)*

Royal Fountain [Church St]: Friendly pub doing well under hard-working young licensees, well kept real ale, home-made food using some local produce, sensibly short wine list; garden tables *(Joe Green)*

CLUN SO3081

☆ *Sun* [High St]: Beamed and timbered Tudor pub doing well under current charming Irish landlady, some sturdy antique furnishings, modern paintings and older prints, enormous open fire in lively flagstoned public bar with darts, cards and dominoes, good value generous blackboard food in larger carpeted lounge bar, well kept Banks's Bitter and Original and Hobsons Best; children allowed in eating area, tables in sheltered well planted back garden with terrace; lovely village, nice bedrooms, cl Weds lunchtime *(A H C Rainier, Kevin Thorpe, BB, the Didler)*

White Horse [Market Sq]: Well laid out, friendly and neatly kept beamed local with inglenook and open woodburner, helpful service, good value food, well kept changing ales, farm cider, good coffee, books and pub games near front, pool table and games machine far end; children welcome, tables in front and small back garden, bedrooms *(Tracey and Stephen Groves, Martin Lewis, Ian and Joan Blackwell)*

CLUNTON SO3381

Crown: Cosy old village local with log fire in small flagstoned bar, Worthington 1744 and changing guest beers such as Greene King Old Speckled Hen and Hobsons, dining room with good choice of popular food inc oriental sizzlers and Sun lunch, good service, small games room with pool and juke box *(Gill and Keith Croxton)*

COALBROOKDALE SJ6704

☆ *Coalbrookdale Inn* [Wellington Rd, opp Museum of Iron]: Long flight of steps up to handsome dark brick 18th-c pub, simple, cheerful and bustling tiled-floor bar with local pictures, six well kept quickly changing ales from square counter also serving rather smaller room set more for the huge platefuls of good value often imaginative food (not Sun) from sandwiches to steaks; good log fire, farm ciders, country wines, good mix of people, piano, remarkable bottled beer collection and amusing pub bric-a-brac, no piped music, naughty beach murals in lavatories; dogs welcome, a few tables outside, opens noon *(DC, BB, the Didler, Michael and Alison Sandy)*

COALPORT SJ6903

☆ *Boat* [Ferry Rd, Jackfield; nr Mawes Craft Centre]: Long but cosy 18th-c quarry-tiled bar, coal fire in lovely range, reasonably priced good food inc meat, game and cheeses and good value Sun lunch, well kept Banks's Bitter and Mild and related beers, Weston's farm cider, dining room, darts; summer barbecues on big tree-shaded lawn, in delightful if floodable part of Severn Gorge, footbridge making it handy for Coalport China Museum *(BB, the Didler, G A and G V M A Taylor, Michael and Alison Sandy)*

Shakespeare [High St]: Simple cream-washed timbered pub by pretty Severn gorge park, handy for china museum, with three well kept ales such as Everards Tiger as well as local brews in bar with small round brass tables, friendly service, large quantities of good value quickly served home-made food from inventive sandwiches to mexican specialities (separate dining area may be booked a week ahead for evenings); picnic-sets in tiered garden with play area *(BB, Michael and Alison Sandy, Gill and Tony Morriss)*

Woodbridge: Lovely setting with widely spaced tables on steepish tiered Severnside lawns giving great view of world's second-oldest iron bridge, more on side terrace with barbecue; softly lit beamed and bow-windowed bar with lots of copper and brass, Victorian prints, good open fire, sensibly priced food inc fresh fish, well kept Greene King Old Speckled Hen and Tetleys, good service, no smoking restaurant; children in eating areas, coarse fishing, open all day Sat, bedrooms *(LYM, Michael and Alison Sandy)*

CORFTON SO4985

☆ ***Sun*** [B4368 Much Wenlock—Craven Arms]: Unpretentious two-bar country local with well kept Corvedale ales such as Normans Pride, Dark & Delicious, Junior, Secret Hop and Divine Inspiration from brewery behind (takeaways and tours available), a guest beer too, friendly chatty landlord, ample sensibly priced food using local produce from generous baguettes to bargain Sun lunch, children's dishes, a mass of breweriana throughout, dining room with no smoking area and covered well, public bar has internet access as well as darts and pool; tables on terrace and in good-sized garden with good play area; piped music; tourist information, particularly good disabled access throughout *(BB, Pete Yearsley, Michael and Jenny Back, MLR, John Whitehead, Kevin Thorpe)*

CRESSAGE SJ5904

Riverside [A458 NW, nr Cound]: Spacious pub/hotel, light and airy, with lovely Severn views from roomy conservatory and tables in big terraced garden, pleasant mix of furnishings inside, relaxed atmosphere, short well rounded menu from lunchtime baguettes to salmon and steak, interesting wine choice, two or three real ales such as Salopian Shropshire Gold; open all day wknds *(Mr and Mrs G S Ayrton, Mr and Mrs M Stratton, Dave Irving, LYM, Mrs Susan Pritchard, Michael and Alison Sandy)*

ELLESMERE SJ3934

☆ ***Black Lion*** [Scotland St; back car park on A495]: Good value simple cheap substantial food all day inc popular OAP bargains (also for children), pleasantly relaxed and well run beamed bar with interesting décor and some nice unusual features such as the traditional wood-and-glass screen (so rare nowadays) along its tiled entrance corridor, quiet and comfortable roomy dining room, prompt civil service, well kept Marstons Bitter, restaurant; piped music; bedrooms, handy car park, not far from canal wharf *(BB, John Andrew, Pamela and Merlyn Horswell)*

GRINSHILL SJ5223

☆ ***Inn at Grinshill*** [off A49 N of Shrewsbury]: Early Georgian inn, comfortably and attractively refurbished, good choice of beers and of enjoyable interesting food, four real ales, well thought out selection of reasonably priced wines, good service, no piped music or machines, bistro and smart restaurant with evening pianist and kitchen view; dogs welcome in bar, great views from terrace and garden, plans for bedrooms, pretty village in popular walking/riding area; Jan-Easter may be cl Sun evening and Mon-Tues *(Mr and Mrs P Lally, Noel Grundy, John and Jenny Pullin)*

HALFWAY HOUSE SJ3411

Seven Stars [A458 Shrewsbury—Welshpool]: Spotless and utterly unspoilt, like a private house; very small bar with two high-backed settles by the gas fire, well kept cheap Burtonwood Best and Mild tapped from casks in the friendly owner's kitchen area, no food or music *(the Didler, RWC)*

HAMPTON LOADE SO7486

River & Rail: Enjoyable food and attentive service in modern surroundings; real ale *(Dr and Mrs James Stewart)*

HARLEY SJ5901

Plume of Feathers [A458 NW of Much Wenlock]: Spacious and popular beamed pub with big open fire, good range of reasonably priced well cooked food, well kept changing ales, good welcoming service even when busy, restaurant; darts, piped music (Sun evening live); pleasant tables outside, bedrooms with own baths, good walks *(M Joyner)*

HIGHLEY SO7483

Bache Arms [High St]: Unpretentious pub with cheap lunchtime sandwiches, Tetleys and Theakstons; walks down to Severn and steam railway *(Dave Braisted)*

HODNET SJ6128

☆ ***Bear*** [Drayton Rd (A53)]: Relaxing refuge from the busy road, small beamed quarry-tiled bar with log fire and Courage Directors, Theakstons Best and Youngs Special, broad arch to rambling open-plan carpeted main area with blond seats and tables set for the good range of reasonably priced well presented food from sandwiches up, well filled puddings cabinet, snug end alcoves with heavy 16th-c beams and timbers, friendly helpful staff, decent wines; may be faint piped radio; open all day, children welcome (high chairs and child-size cutlery), six good value bedrooms, opp Hodnet Hall gardens and handy for Hawkstone Park *(D L Mayer, BB, Mrs B M Needham, Neil Skidmore, Anthony Barnes)*

IRONBRIDGE SJ6703

Bird in Hand [Waterloo St (B4373 towards Broseley)]: Lovely position above wooded gorge, building older than the iron bridge;

plush banquettes and well spaced tables, wide food choice from interesting starters to good steaks, friendly helpful licensees, two well kept changing ales, brasses, mirrors and prints; steps up from road, tables on terrace and lawn, comfortable bedrooms *(Michael and Alison Sandy)*

Golden Ball [Newbridge Rd/Wesley Rd, off Madeley Hill]: Smart and interesting partly Elizabethan local at the top of the town, with good atmosphere, helpful landlord and friendly staff, well kept Everards, Timothy Taylors Landlord and guest beers, good blackboard choice of competitively priced substantial food from sandwiches and baguettes to Sun roasts in bar or restaurant, real fire, quietish lunchtime, more lively evenings; TV corner; children welcome, sheltered picnic-sets with more out in front, pleasant terraced walk down to river, comfortable bedrooms *(Gill and Tony Morriss, Michael and Alison Sandy)*

Horse & Jockey [Jockey Bank, off Madeley rd]: Cosy and welcoming, with emphasis on enjoyable sensibly priced proper food inc real steak and kidney pie, good bass and steaks, plenty of atmosphere, well kept ales such as Marstons Pedigree and Robinsons Young Tom; should book evenings; open 12-2, 7-9.30 *(Pat and Sam Roberts, Michael and Alison Sandy)*

Robin Hood [Waterloo St]: Popular Severnside pub, five comfortable and attractive linked rooms with various alcoves inc barrel-vaulted dining room, lots of gleaming brass and old clocks, well kept interesting mainly local changing ales, Stowford Press and Weston's Old Rosie ciders, wide choice of usual food from sandwiches to Sun carvery, helpful staff; attractive seating area out in front, nice setting handy for museums, bedrooms, good breakfast *(DC, Mike and Wendy Proctor, Michael and Alison Sandy)*

Swan [Wharfage]: Same management as neighbouring Malthouse, more traditional in style; pleasant atmosphere, well kept beer, decent food *(M Joyner)*

KNOWLE SANDS SO7191

Swan [off B4555 just S of Bridgnorth, nr Eardington]: Cheerful and attractive dining pub, good choice of sensibly priced bar food from standard dishes to sizzlers, prompt helpful service, good beer choice, separate restaurant; comfortable bedrooms *(David Cosham)*

LEEBOTWOOD SO4798

☆ ***Pound*** [A49 Church Stretton—Shrewsbury]: Thatched 16th-c pub, extensively modernised inside, with banquettes and log-effect gas fire in roomy carpeted main bar, good value blackboard food from sandwiches to fresh fish, big no smoking restaurant area (good local roasts for Sun carvery), well kept ales such as Black Sheep, Greene King Old Speckled Hen and Timothy Taylors Landlord, Addlestone's cider, good wine list (occasional tastings), friendly efficient staff, pool and juke box in brightly lit public bar, well reproduced piped pop music; tables in garden *(Dave Irving, BB, G S R Cox)*

LEIGHTON SJ6105

Kynnersley Arms: Simple Victorian building built on the remains of a corn mill, armchairs and settees in back area with glass panel showing mill machinery in cellar (which now has platform showing recently excavated furnace), coal fire in main area, separate dining alcove, pool table, very friendly landlady, cheap simple food with crêpes a speciality; good walks nearby *(DC)*

LEINTWARDINE SO4175

Jolly Frog [Toddings, out towards Ludlow]: Distinctive yellow-green pub/bistro with emphasis on enjoyably imaginative food esp fish, sensible prices and early evening bargains, cosy rural atmosphere, mix of table sizes (high chairs for small children), log fire, a beer brewed for them, good wine list, relaxed friendly and informative service, individualistic décor, no smoking restaurant; may be unobtrusive piped jazz *(Pete Yearsley, Rodney and Norma Stubington, Peter and Jean Hoare)*

LONGDEN SJ4304

Red Lion [Longden Common]: Unpretentious three-room pub with landlady cooking sensibly limited blackboard choice of imaginatively done local food, friendly landlord, two or three changing real ales, front games bar; tables outside *(Norma and Cedric Hart)*

LUDLOW SO5174

Bull [Bull Ring]: Solidly traditional 15th-c timbered building with long bustling rambling low-beamed bar, well kept Banks's and Marstons Pedigree, sizeable back seating area; popular evenings with young locals; courtyard through side arch *(D W Stokes, Ian and Joan Blackwell)*

Charlton Arms [Ludford Bridge]: Well worn former coaching inn overlooking River Teme and the town, popular for its super range of well kept beers mostly from small local breweries, good value food, good service; lacks a no smoking area; waterside garden, bedrooms, open all day *(Geoffrey and Penny Hughes)*

Feathers [Bull Ring]: Superb timbered building, striking inside too with Jacobean panelling and carving, fine period furnishings, pleasant service and nice bedrooms; for a snack or drink you'll probably be diverted to a less distinguished side café-bar (good sandwiches and other decent bar food, Woods real ale); good parking, comfortable bedrooms, not cheap *(the Didler, LYM, Dr and Mrs A K Clarke)*

Rose & Crown [Church St, behind Buttercross]: Small unpretentious pub useful for decent reasonably priced home-made food all day, real ales such as Adnams and Tetleys, attractively laid dining room, poster designs for Shakespeare at Ludlow Castle; picnic-sets behind, pretty spot *(Gloria Bax)*

Wheatsheaf [Lower Broad St]: Welcoming traditional 17th-c beamed pub spectacularly built into medieval town gate, spotless housekeeping, generous usual food, good service, well kept ales inc Woods Shropshire

Lad, choice of farm cider, restaurant; attractive bedrooms, warm and comfortable *(Karen and Graham Oddey, Joe Green)*

MADELEY SJ69034

All Nations [Coalport Rd]: One-bar 18th-c pub up steps from road, back to brewing its own cheap distinctive Dableys ale (until a recent sale had been brewing under the same family since the 1930s); simple new furniture, fresh cream paintwork and fires each end, guest beers such as Goldthorn and Hobsons Mild, Bulmer's farm cider, may be pork pies or filled rolls; picnic-sets on restored heated terrace, open all day Fri-Sun, handy for Blists Hill *(Michael and Alison Sandy, Kevin Thorpe)*

MARSHBROOK SO4489

☆ *Station Hotel* [Marshbrook Industrial Estate signed over level crossing by B4370/A49, S of Church Stretton]: Solidly refurbished and comfortably traditional bar on right with well kept Boddingtons, Flowers Original and Salopian Shropshire Gold from high-gloss counter, prompt attentive service, log fire, some stripped stone; extensive and popular eating areas on left, centred on separate modern glass-fronted café-bar with elegant metal-framed furniture on limestone flooring and good value food counter with a good choice from warm baguettes through interesting light dishes up; piped music *(BB, John Whitehead, Gloria Bax)*

MORVILLE SO6793

Acton Arms [A458 Bridgnorth—Shrewsbury]: Neatly kept two-bar pub, relaxed and pleasantly furnished, with good value food, well kept Banks's and Marstons Pedigree, sensibly priced wines, friendly staff; big attractive garden *(M Joyner)*

MUCH WENLOCK SO6299

Gaskell Arms [High St (A458)]: 17th-c beams, brasses, interesting prints and big brass-canopied log fire dividing the two comfortable rooms; well kept Courage Directors and John Smiths, ample food using local produce from generous baked potatoes and ploughman's to good Sun lunch in busy bars and civilised old-fashioned restaurant, good friendly service, banknote collection; subdued piped music, fruit machine in lobby; immaculate roomy garden, bedrooms *(Gloria Bax, John Whitehead)*

☆ *George & Dragon* [High St]: Smallish popular bar with snug old-fashioned no smoking rooms leading back past inglenook, lots of pictures, even a mural, timbering and beams with hundreds of jugs, antique settles among more conventional seats, promptly served generous food (not Sun or Weds evenings) from sandwiches up inc Sun roast, welcoming landlord and friendly staff, four well kept changing ales, country wines and fruit pressés; well behaved children welcome away from bar, open all day in summer *(LYM, Pete Yearsley, Sarah and Peter Gooderham, Steve Whalley, Mike and Wendy Proctor, Ian and Nita Cooper, David and Sally Cullen, Michael and Alison Sandy, Mr and Mrs J R Shrimpton)*

MUNSLOW SO5287

Crown [B4368 Much Wenlock—Craven Arms]: Tudor beams, broad flagstones and cosy nooks and crannies in split-level dining lounge and stripped stone eating area, some emphasis on good value imaginative fresh food from baguettes up, using local produce, friendly staff, good log fire, another in traditional snug, real ales; may be piped music; children welcome, attractive bedrooms, tables outside *(LYM, Debbie and Neil Hayter, Christopher Woodward)*

NEENTON SO6387

Pheasant [B4364 Bridgnorth—Ludlow]: Charming village pub where the licensees do everything themselves – well kept real ale, short choice of good reasonably priced food, quick friendly service, open fires in panelled lounge, plenty of regulars; restaurant *(Joyce and Geoff Robson, DC)*

NESSCLIFFE SJ3819

Old Three Pigeons [off A5 Shrewsbury—Oswestry (now bypassed)]: 16th-c pub with quaint and appealing dining area, wide blackboard choice of enjoyable good value meals (freshly made so may be quite a wait) inc bargains for two, plenty of fish and good puddings, well kept Moles real ale, good choice of wines by the glass, warm log fires, brown sofas and close mix of tables in two well worn in bar areas; children welcome, some tables outside, opp Kynaston Cave, good cliff walks *(David Heath, Graham and Lynn Mason, LYM, R Michael Richards, Mike and Jayne Bastin, David Gordon, Malcolm Avery, Miss J E Edwards)*

NEWCASTLE SO2482

☆ *Crown* [B4368 Clun—Newtown]: Pretty village pub under new ownership, settees and woodburner in smart stripped stone lounge with some well spaced tables in two dining areas, well kept Hobsons Bitter and Town Crier and a bargain guest such as Tetleys Champion, good coffee, attractively priced food from sandwiches to steak, two friendly dogs and a cat, locals' bar and games room under refurbishment; piped music; tables outside, charming well equipped bedrooms, attractive views and walks, open all day Sat *(LYM, A N Bance, Kevin Thorpe)*

NORTON IN HALES SJ7038

Hinds Head [Main Rd]: Comfortably extended three-room country pub under pleasant new licensees, four real ales inc Timothy Taylors Landlord, good choice of food from bar snacks to restaurant meals, friendly locals, open fire, conservatory; disabled access, beautiful village setting by church *(Margaret and Allen Marsden)*

OSWESTRY SJ2929

Black Gate [Salop Rd]: Extended 17th-c pub with friendly licensees, well kept ales inc guest beers, lunchtime meals; SkyTV *(Howard Martin)*

Fox [Church St/Cross St]: Ancient black and white timbered façade, little local entrance bar down a step, attractive low-beamed and panelled main room with dark oak furniture, good plain décor, fox theme, enjoyable food, good licensees, well kept Marstons Pedigree, log fire, no smoking area, no TV or juke box *(Keith Reynolds)*

PONTESBURY SJ4005

Plough [Chapel St, just off A488 SW of Shrewsbury]: By the ford, the village's oldest building and a reminder of what a real pub used to be; good choice of ales, friendly staff and atmosphere *(Rowan Chattaway, Paul Smith)*

PORTH-Y-WAEN SJ2623

☆ *Lime Kiln* [A495, between village and junction with A483, S of Oswestry]: Neatly opened up pub with stripped pine woodwork, pews and big pine tables, well kept Banks's, Marstons Pedigree and a guest beer, good value wines; has had good inventive blackboard food, but no reports since recent change of management (news please); children in eating areas, picnic-sets out in side garden with boules and terraced lawn, open all day wknds *(LYM)*

QUEENS HEAD SJ3326

☆ *Queens Head* [just off A5 SE of Oswestry, towards Nesscliffe]: Emphasis on wide choice of good value food (all day Fri and wknds) from speciality sandwiches inc good steak baguettes to lots of fish and steaks, well kept reasonably priced Theakstons Best, XB, Old Peculier and a guest beer, prompt helpful service, two dining areas with roaring coal fires, one no smoking with nice roomy conservatory (may need to book); picnic-sets under cocktail parasols in suntrap garden by restored Montgomery Canal, country walks *(Mike Schofield, Bill Sykes, John Andrew, Mike and Jayne Bastin, Clare and Peter Pearse)*

RYTON SJ4803

Fox [the one nr Dorrington, S of Shrewsbury]: Smart but relaxed brick-built hill-view country pub with well kept Banks's and Marstons, very welcoming licensees and good range of tasty home-made blackboard food using local produce, wider choice evenings; bright comfortable lounge bar, no smoking beamed restaurant *(David and Sally Cullen)*

SHIFNAL SJ7407

Old Bell [Church St]: Softly lit old pub with good value home-made food running up to good steaks and Sun lunch, restaurant; tables out on cheerful terrace *(A H Gregory)*

SHREWSBURY SJ4812

Bellstone [Bellstone]: Friendly minimalist modern bar/restaurant with good wine list, a couple of real ales, good value food inc good ciabattas; courtyard tables *(Mr and Mrs F Carroll, Howard and Lorna Lambert)*

Coach & Horses [Swan Hill/Cross Hill]: Welcoming unspoilt Victorian local, panelled throughout, with main bar, cosy little side room and back dining room, good value food (not Mon-Weds) inc daily roasts and some unusual dishes, well kept Bass, Goodalls Gold (brewed for pub by Salopian) and a guest beer, relaxed atmosphere, prompt helpful service even when busy, interesting prints; pretty flower boxes outside *(the Didler, Pete Baker, Jeff and Sue Evans)*

Cromwells [Dogpole]: Good affordable fresh food from baguettes to world-wide variety of dishes inc inventive puddings in smallish dim-lit bar, warm, clean, cosy and friendly; well kept ales inc Hobsons and Slaters, good house wines, pleasant staff, attractive panelled restaurant (same menu); well chosen piped music; raised garden and attractive heated terrace behind, open all day Sat, six nice bedrooms now with own bathrooms, good breakfast *(Dennis and Gill Keen, Jeff and Sue Evans)*

Dolphin [A49 ½ mile N of stn]: Well worn early Victorian pub with its own Dolphin ales from back brewhouse, changing guest beers, foreign bottled beers and perhaps farm ciders, two small gas-lit rooms; cl lunchtime Mon-Sat but opens 3 Fri-Sat *(the Didler)*

☆ *Loggerheads* [Church St]: Small old-fashioned pub, panelled back smoke room with flagstones, scrubbed-top tables, high-backed settles and real fire, three other rooms with lots of prints, flagstones and bare boards, quaint linking corridor and hatch service of Banks's Bitter and Mild, related beers and a guest beer, friendly staff and locals, bargain lunchtime food (not Sun) inc doorstep sandwiches and baked potatoes; darts, dominoes, poetry society, occasional live music; open all day *(Kevin Thorpe, Pete Baker, the Didler, Martin Grosberg)*

STIPERSTONES SJ3600

Stiperstones Inn [signed off A488 S of Minsterley; OS Sheet 126 map ref 364005]: New management but low prices still, for well kept ales such as Woods Parish and the simple fresh food all day inc local whinberry pie, small modernised lounge bar with comfortable leatherette wall banquettes, lots of brassware on ply-panelled walls, decent wine, real fire, darts in plainer public bar; may be unobtrusive piped music; restaurant, tables outside; clean basic cheap bedrooms (small dogs welcome), good breakfast, good walking – they sell maps *(BB, Edward Leetham)*

STOTTESDON SO6782

Fighting Cocks [High St]: Delightful old half-timbered pub in unspoilt countryside, good substantial home cooking using local produce (not Mon-Tues, nor winter wkdys), warm welcome, well kept Hobsons, local farm cider, log fire, low ceiling, equestrian pictures, no smoking dining room; doubles as village vegetable and bread shop, open all day wknds, may be cl winter lunchtimes *(Sue and Pete Murray)*

STREET DINAS SJ3338

Greyhound [B5069 St Martin's—Oswestry]: Comfortable bar profusely decorated with pictures, bric-a-brac and masses of chamber-pots hanging from beams, Banks's Best, Bass, Greene King Abbot, John Smiths and Theakstons, welcoming, ebullient and efficient landlord, good value food from good sandwiches and baguettes up, dining room and back games room; tables on big lawn with busy dovecote *(Michael and Jenny Back)*

UPPER FARMCOTE SO7792

☆ *Lion o' Morfe* [off A458 Bridgnorth—Stourbridge]: Country pub with good very reasonably priced food, well kept beer, log fire in plush lounge, carpeted pool room, conservatory, dogs welcome in traditional back public bar with coal fire; attractive garden spreading into orchard *(Theo, Anne and Jane Gaskin, LYM, Lynda and Trevor Smith)*

WALL UNDER HEYWOOD SO5092

Plough [B4371]: Huge helpings of reliable food in large, clean and comfortable bars and separate restaurant extension, service friendly and efficient despite the bustle, good range of well kept beers such as Salopian; tables in garden *(Gordon Tong, John Whitehead)*

WELLINGTON SJ6511

Cock [Holyhead Rd (B5061 – former A5)]: Former coaching inn popular for its friendly real ale bar, with six or seven well kept beers usually from small breweries and often changing from day to day, farm ciders, good pork pies, large pine tables and big fireplace, also comfortable no smoking lounge; open all day Thurs-Sat, bedrooms *(Michael and Alison Sandy, David Field)*

WENLOCK EDGE SO5796

Wenlock Edge Inn [B4371 Much Wenlock—Church Stretton]: Charmingly placed country dining pub, pleasant two-room bar (dogs allowed) with open fire and inglenook woodburner, more modern no smoking dining extension, home-made food from baguettes up, well kept local Hobsons Best and Town Crier; children welcome in eating areas, tables out on terraces, cosy attractive bedrooms, lots of walks; may be cl winter wkdy lunchtimes *(LYM, B and H, Alan and Jill Bull, A Sadler, Ron and Val Broom, Paul and Margaret Baker, R Michael Richards, M Thomas, David Field)*

WOOFFERTON SO5168

Salwey Arms [A456/B4362 S of Ludlow]: Pleasant old-fashioned pub with no smoking area in lounge, good value tasty standard food, well kept changing ales, pool in separate public bar *(Martin Lewis)*

WOORE SJ7342

Falcon [The Square (A51)]: Wide choice of good if not cheap home-made food inc lots of fish (best to book restaurant, esp wknds), well kept Marstons, quick welcoming service, two comfortable cottagey bars, pristine copper-topped tables, interesting prints, lots of flowers inside and out; nr Bridgemere Garden World *(E G Parish)*

YORTON SJ5023

Railway: Same family for over 60 years, friendly and chatty mother and daughter, unchanging atmosphere, simple tiled bar with hot coal fire, hard settles and a modicum of railway memorabilia, big back lounge with fishing trophies, well kept Woods Bitter and Shropshire Lad and other ales, mainly local, such as Archers, Goldthorn, Holdens, Salopian or Slaters, simple sandwiches if you ask, darts and dominoes – no piped music or machines; seats out in yard *(the Didler, Martin Grosberg)*

We checked prices with the pubs as we went to press in summer 2004. They should hold until around spring 2005 – when our experience suggests that you can expect an increase of around 10p in the £.

Somerset

In this chapter we include Bristol, as well as Bath. The classic good Somerset pub is a friendly and unpretentious place, lifted out of the ordinary by the dedication of the people running it, with no superficial airs and graces and with a real welcome for strangers. Though there's certainly good food to be found, out-and-out smart gastropubs have not made much of a mark here. And there is plenty of good beer, and some local farm cider to be found here too. The five new entries we have tracked down for this new edition show the pleasing diversity behind this general picture: the comfortably modernised Gardeners Arms in Cheddar, given real uplift by its cheerful hard-working landlord; the civilised old Bear & Swan in Chew Magna, with its nice modern food and relaxed atmosphere; the Inn at Freshford, a lovely spot in fine weather, with popular food; the George in Ilminster, rather a smart little place and perhaps the exception that proves the rule – we liked it a lot; and the Masons Arms in Taunton, a very well run town local. Other current favourites in this big county include the unchanging Old Green Tree in Bath (good local beers, enjoyable food and great atmosphere), the Cat Head at Chiselborough (friendly licensees, good food, attractive traditional bar and lovely garden), the well worn and unaffected Crown at Churchill (a fine beer range, good value home cooking), the unpretentious and chatty Black Horse at Clapton-in-Gordano, the Crown at Exford (a smart yet friendly coaching inn, good food and bedrooms), the Ring o' Roses at Holcombe (very good food, helpful service), the Rose & Crown at Huish Episcopi (a step back in time, yet thoroughly perky under its splendid veteran landlady), the friendly and relaxed Bird in Hand at North Curry (an enjoyable well run all-rounder), the Halfway House at Pitney (very popular for its great range of well kept beers), the Carpenters Arms at Stanton Wick (a fine all-rounder, gaining its Food Award this year), the City Arms in Wells (an interesting old place, with well liked food and good beer), the Royal Oak at Withypool (nice staff, plenty of atmosphere, and food that's nudging the Award level), and the chatty and unassuming Burcott at Wookey. As you can see from all this, plenty of pubs here stand out for their food. Another which very few readers have yet discovered is the Pilgrims Rest tucked away at Lovington. The landlord's careful cooking of good local ingredients wins the title of Somerset Dining Pub of the Year for this little hideaway. This year's stars in the Lucky Dip section at the end of the chapter include the Coeur de Lion and Salamander in Bath, Woolpack in Beckington, White Horse at Bradford-on-Tone, Brewery Tap and Commercial Rooms in Bristol, George at Brompton Regis, Wheatsheaf at Combe Hay, Luttrell Arms in Dunster, Faulkland Inn, Bull at Hardway, Old Crown at Kelston, Phelips Arms at Montacute, Royal Oak at Over Stratton and Slab House at West Horrington. Drinks prices here average out very close to the national norm. Butcombe, Exmoor and Cotleigh are good Somerset brews which we found in a lot of pubs here. Other local beers to look out for include RCH, Bath, Blindmans, Abbey, Cottage and Smiles; Otter and Teignworthy, both from Devon, are also often offered at attractive prices here, particularly over in the west.

APPLEY ST0621 Map 1

Globe

Hamlet signposted from the network of back roads between A361 and A38, W of B3187 and W of Milverton and Wellington; OS Sheet 181 map reference 072215

This 15th-c country pub is a friendly place and liked by both locals and visitors. The simple beamed front room has GWR bench seats and a built-in settle, bare wood tables on the brick floor, and 1930s railway posters; there's a further room with easy chairs and other more traditional ones, open fires, and a collection of model cars, art deco items and *Titanic* pictures; skittle alley. A stone-flagged entry corridor leads to a serving hatch from where Cotleigh Tawny and a couple of guest beers are well kept on handpump; Heck's farm cider. Tasty bar food includes filled rolls (from £1.75; 4oz fillet steak with battered onion rings and mushrooms £6.95; not Sunday), home-made soup (£3.25), chicken liver pâté (£5.50), ploughman's (from £5.75), seafood pancakes (£7.95), vegetarian pasta (£8.50), home-made steak and kidney pie (£8.95), thai chicken curry (£9.50), steaks (from £10.50), half a crispy duckling with madeira sauce (£11.95), daily specials such as whole lemon sole or fillet steak with stroganoff sauce (£11.95), and puddings like sticky ginger pudding with steam ginger ice-cream or chocolate and Bailey's brûlée (from £3.25); Sunday roast (£6.50) and children's meals (£4.75). The restaurant and one room in the bar are no smoking. Seats, climbing frame and swings outside in the garden; the path opposite leads eventually to the River Tone. *(Recommended by Glenwys and Alan Lawrence, RWC, Fred and Lorraine Gill, the Didler, Michael Rowse, Richard and Anne Ansell, Paul Hopton, Brian and Anita Randall, Bob and Margaret Holder)*

Free house ~ Licensees Andrew and Liz Burt ~ Real ale ~ Bar food (till 10) ~ Restaurant ~ (01823) 672327 ~ Children in eating area of bar and restaurant ~ Open 11-2.30, 6.30-11; 12-3, 7-10.30 Sun; closed Mon except bank hols

ASHILL ST3116 Map 1

Square & Compass

Windmill Hill; off A358 between Ilminster and Taunton; up Wood Torad for 1 mile behind Stewley Cross service station; OS Sheet 193 map reference 310166

Despite its nicely remote setting, you'll often find this unassuming country pub rather busy in the evenings with chatty locals – it's the sort of place that farmers turn up to on their tractors. There's an open fire and simple, comfortable furnishings in the bar, perhaps Beth the dog or the pub cats Daisy and Lilly, and well kept Exmoor Ale, St Austell HSD, and Windmill Hill Bitter on handpump. Generous helpings of enjoyable bar food includes sandwiches and soup, and daily specials such as grilled goats cheese with a pear and toasted pine nut dressing (£4.75), cauliflower cheese topped with mushrooms or bacon (£6.50), trio of local sausages with onion gravy (£6.95), tagliatelle carbonara, steak in ale pie or beef casserole (all £7.95), and chicken with a creamy stilton sauce or breast of duck with a port and cranberry sauce (£9.95). Piped classical music at lunchtimes. There's a terrace outside and a garden with picnic-sets, views over the Blackdown Hills, and a children's play area. A new self-contained barn extension for weddings and parties has been opened in the grounds and will also act as a local arts centre. More reports please. *(Recommended by Mr and Mrs Colin Roberts, Mark Clezy, Graham and Rose Ive, Mrs Sally Lloyd, Malcolm Taylor, Kevin Thorpe)*

Free house ~ Licensees Chris, Janet and Beth Slow ~ Real ale ~ Bar food (not Tues, Weds or Thurs lunchtimes) ~ (01823) 480467 ~ Children welcome ~ Dogs welcome ~ Open 12-2.30, 6.30-11; 12-2.30, 7-10.30 Sun; closed Tues, Weds and Thurs lunchtimes

Looking for a pub with a really special garden, or in lovely countryside, or with an outstanding view, or right by the water? They are listed separately, at the back of the book.

AXBRIDGE ST4255 Map 1

Lamb

The Square; off A371 Cheddar—Winscombe

As this ancient place is right on the market square, it's a popular meeting place for shoppers and locals. The big rambling bar is full of heavy beams and timbers, cushioned wall seats and small settles, an open fire in one great stone fireplace, and a collection of tools and utensils including an unusual foot-operated grinder in another. Well kept Butcombe Bitter and Gold, and a couple of guests like Ridleys Rumpus and Shepherd Neame Spitfire on handpump from a bar counter built largely of bottles, and local cider; shove-ha'penny, cribbage, dominoes, table skittles and skittle alley. Reasonably priced bar food includes lunchtime sandwiches and filled baguettes (from £2.95), as well as home-made soup (£2.50), chicken liver pâté with fruit chutney (£3.95), deep-fried brie with redcurrant jelly (£4.25), filled baked potatoes (from £4.50), home-cooked ham and eggs (£5.95), mediterranean roasted vegetable pancakes in a creamy stilton sauce (£6.50), home-made curry or beef in ale pie (£7.25), steaks (from £8.50), daily specials such as chicken breast stuffed with mushrooms and bacon (£8.25), leg of lamb steak with honey and mint sauce (£8.95), and whole bass with mediterranean vegetables and couscous (£11.25), Friday night steaks (£5.75), OAP two-course lunch (Tuesday and Thursday, £5.95), and Sunday roast (£5.50). A couple of areas are no smoking; efficient rather than friendly service. Though the sheltered back garden is not big, it's prettily planted with rock plants, shrubs and trees. The National Trust's medieval King John's Hunting Lodge is opposite. *(Recommended by Mike Gorton, Hugh Roberts, S H Godsell, P M Wilkins, J Coote, Francis Johnston, Tom Evans, Frank Willy)*

Butcombe ~ Manager Alan Currie ~ Real ale ~ Bar food (12-2.30, 6.30-9; not Sun evenings) ~ (01934) 732253 ~ Children in eating area of bar ~ Dogs allowed in bar ~ Open 11.30-3, 6-11; 11.30-11 Fri and Sat; 12-10.30 Sun ~ Bedrooms: £30S/£40S(£50B)

BATCOMBE ST6838 Map 2

Three Horseshoes (food award)

Village signposted off A359 Bruton—Frome

As we went to press, the licensees were about to leave this honey stone pub, so we are keeping our fingers crossed that the new people will continue along the same vein. The chef is staying so there's no doubt that the good interesting food will remain quite a draw. As well as bar meals like ploughman's (£4.95), filled ciabattas (from £4.95), ham and eggs (£6.95), roasted mediterranean vegetable pasta (£7.95), and moules marinière and frites, salad of warm chicken and bacon with grain mustard dressing or pork and leek sausages (all £8.95), there might be tian of fresh cornish crab and prawns with dill crème fraîche or warm tart of local brie and avocado with blush tomato salsa (£5.25), filo parcel of spinach, chick peas and aubergine on a tomato provençale coulis (£12.50), roast half duck with apricot and walnut stuffing, gratin potatoes and red wine jus (£14.75), and grilled fillets of devon turbot with prawn beurre blanc sauce on crushed olive potatoes (£15.95); puddings such as white and dark chocolate rum cappuccino mousse, crème brûlée with morello and black cherries, and banana and mango honey pancake (£4.50). The longish narrow main room has cream-painted beams and planks, local pictures on the lightly ragged dark pink walls, built-in cushioned window seats and solid chairs around a nice mix of old tables, and a woodburning stove at one end with a big open fire at the other; there's a plain tiled room at the back on the left with more straightforward furniture. The no smoking, stripped stone dining room is pretty. Well kept Butcombe and a changing guest on handpump, ten wines by the glass, and a dozen malt whiskies. The back terrace has picnic-sets, with more on the grass. The pub is on a quiet village lane by the church which has a very striking tower. Reports on the new regime please. *(Recommended by Mrs Sally Lloyd, Steve Dark, David Gough, Paul and Annette Hallett, Paul Hopton, Guy Vowles, Peter Craske)*

Free house ~ Real ale ~ Bar food ~ Restaurant ~ (01749) 850359 ~ Children in restaurant ~ Dogs allowed in bar ~ Open 12-3, 6.30-11; 12-3, 7-10.30 Sun

BATH ST7464 Map 2

Old Green Tree

12 Green Street

Although this smashing little pub is constantly busy, there's always a friendly, relaxed atmosphere, and no noisy games machines or piped music. Of course one of the draws is the six very well kept real ales on handpump – Abbey Ales Mild, Hop Back Summer Lightning, RCH Pitchfork, Wickwar Brand Oak and Mr Perretts Traditional Stout, and a beer named for the pub. Also, up to 35 malt whiskies, a nice little wine list with helpful notes (and a dozen by the glass), winter hot toddies, a proper Pimms, and good coffee. The three little oak-panelled and low wood-and-plaster ceilinged rooms include a comfortable lounge on the left as you go in, its walls decorated with wartime aircraft pictures in winter and local artists' work during spring and summer, and a no smoking back bar; the big skylight lightens things up attractively. Popular lunchtime bar food includes soup and sandwiches (£4), tasty salads or bangers and mash with cider or beer and onion sauce (£5.50), and daily specials such as enjoyable roast beef baguette (£4), ploughman's with home-made chutney (from £4), home-made pâté (£5.50), and roast duck breast with blueberry salad or mussels in wine and cream (£6.50); if you get there when the pub opens, you should be able to bag a table. Chess, backgammon, shut the box, Jenga. The gents', though good, is down steep steps. No children.

(Recommended by Dr and Mrs M W A Haward, Rona Murdoch, Clive Hilton, Gill and Tony Morriss, Bruce Bird, Paul Hopton, Mike Pugh, Jack Taylor, Tim Harper, Jenny and Brian Seller, the Didler, Dr and Mrs M E Wilson, M V Ward, Pete Baker, Nigel Long, Richard Pierce, TonyHobden, Simon and Amanda Southwell, Patrick Hancock, Dr and Mrs A K Clarke, R Huggins, D Irving, E McCall, T McLean, John and Gloria Isaacs, David Carr, Emma Hughes)

Free house ~ Licensees Nick Luke and Tim Bethune ~ Real ale ~ Bar food (lunchtime until 2.45) ~ No credit cards ~ Dogs allowed in bar ~ Open 11-11; 12-10.30 Sun

Star

23 Vineyards; The Paragon (A4), junction with Guinea Lane

An honest drinkers' pub and handy for the main shopping area, this old pub (with a new licensee this year) gives a strong sense of the past. It is set in a quiet steep street of undeniably handsome if well worn stone terraces, and the four (well, more like three and a half) small linked rooms are served from a single bar, separated by sombre panelling with glass inserts. They are furnished with traditional leatherette wall benches and the like – even one hard bench that the regulars call Death Row – and the lighting's dim, and not rudely interrupted by too much daylight. With no machines or music, chat's the thing here – or perhaps cribbage, dominoes, table skittles, and shove-ha'penny. Particularly well kept Bass is tapped from the cask, and they have Abbey Bellringer, and guests such as Hop Back Summer Lightning, and Timothy Taylors Landlord on handpump, and quite a few malt whiskies. Filled rolls only (from £1.60; served throughout opening hours during the week), and Sunday lunchtime bar nibbles; friendly staff and customers. No children inside.

(Recommended by Clive Hilton, the Didler, Catherine Pitt, Paul Hopton, Dr and Mrs M E Wilson, David and Christine Vaughton, R Huggins, D Irving, E McCall, T McLean, Pete Baker, David Carr, Di and Mike Gillam, Patrick Hancock)

Punch ~ Lease Paul Waters ~ Real ale ~ Bar food (see text) ~ (01225) 425072 ~ Dogs welcome ~ Acoustic singers and folk Sun evenings ~ Open 12-2.30, 5.30-11; 12-11 Sat; 12-10.30 Sun

We accept no free drinks, meals or payment for inclusion. We take no advertising, and are not sponsored by the brewing industry – or by anyone else.
So all reports are independent.

BLEADON ST3357 Map 1

Queens Arms

Village signposted just off A370 S of Weston; Celtic Way

Butcombe Brewery have taken over this 16th-c pub and installed new licensees but early reports from readers are very positive. It's opened up inside but with carefully divided separate areas that still let the comfortably chatty and convivial atmosphere run right through. Plenty of distinctive touches include the dark flagstones of the terracotta-walled restaurant and back bar area (both no smoking), candles in bottles on sturdy tables flanked by winged settles, old hunting prints, a frieze of quaint sayings in Old English print, and above all, the focal servery where up to half a dozen well kept changing ales are tapped from the cask: Bass, Butcombe Bitter, Gold, and Blond, Palmers IPA, and Ringwood Old Thumper; eight wines by the glass. Bar food now includes soup (£3.50), sandwiches (£3.95), filled baked potatoes (from £4.25), home-made port and duck terrine with red onion and sultana chutney (£5), ciabatta with toppings like mozzarella, avocado and tomato or strips of sirloin steak, peppers, mushrooms and onions (from £5), honey roasted ham and egg (£5.25), vegetable lasagne (£5.95), trio of sausages on spring onion mash with onion gravy or home-made pie of the day (£7.50), beer battered cod with home-made tartare sauce (£7.95), steaks (from £10.95), fillet of lime marinated bass on warm mango, potato and french bean salad or maple glazed gressingham duck breast with an orange and Cointreau sauce (£12.95), and puddings like home-made sticky toffee pudding or home-made lemon tart (£4.50). The restaurant is no smoking. There is a big cylindrical solid fuel stove in the main bar, with another woodburning stove in the stripped-stone back tap bar; TV, skittle alley, and piped music. Some benches and picnic-sets out on the tarmac by the car park entrance. No children. *(Recommended by R F Hedges, Gaynor Gregory, Anne and David Robinson, Guy Wilkins, Ken Jones, P M Wilkins, J Coote, Comus and Sarah Elliott, B I Evans, David Biggins, Michael Doswell, Mr and Mrs D Boley, Alan and Paula McCully, Canon Michael Bourdeaux, Tom Evans, Susan and John Douglas)*

Butcombe ~ Managers Daniel Pardoe, Jessica Perry, Guy Newell ~ Real ale ~ Bar food (12-2, 6.30-9.30; 12-3, 6.30-9 Sun) ~ Restaurant ~ (01934) 812080 ~ Open 11-2.30, 5.30-11; 11-11 Fri and Sat; 12-10.30 Sun

CATCOTT ST3939 Map 1

Crown

Village signposted off A39 W of Street; at T junction turn left, then at war memorial turn off northwards into Brook Lane and keep on

Not easy to find at the end of a maze of little roads, this is a tucked away former cider house. To the left of the main door is a pubby little room with built-in brocade-cushioned settles, a church pew and red leatherette stools around just four rustic pine tables, a tall black-painted brick fireplace with dried flowers and a large cauldron, and working horse plaques; around the corner is a small alcove with a really big pine table on its stripped stone floor. Most of the pub is taken up with the roomy, more straightforward dining area with lots of wheelback chairs around tables, and paintings on silk of local views by a local artist on the cream walls. From the menu, there might be sandwiches and toasties (from £1.95), soup (£2.50), stuffed mushrooms (£3.90), filled baked potatoes (from £3.95), ploughman's (from £4.50), cauliflower bake with smoked bacon and sweetcorn (£5.50), ham and egg (£5.95), fruit and vegetable curry (£6.25), nice trout topped with toasted almonds or beef stroganoff (£8.95), steaks (from £9.85), daily specials, and puddings such as apple crumble or banoffi pie (£3.60); children's meals (from £1.95). Well kept Butcombe Bitter and Smiles Best, and a guest such as Badger Tanglefoot on handpump, and piped old-fashioned pop music; fruit machine and skittle alley. The original part of the pub is white-painted stone with black shutters and is pretty with window boxes and tubs. Out behind are picnic-sets and a play area for children with wooden equipment. More reports please. *(Recommended by D Thomas, Dr and Mrs C W Thomas, Theo, Anne and Jane Gaskin, the Didler, KC, Peter Craske)*

Free house ~ Licensees C R D Johnston and D Lee ~ Real ale ~ Bar food (11.30-2, 6 (7 Sun)-10) ~ (01278) 722288 ~ Children welcome ~ Open 11.30-2.30, 6-11; 12-3, 7-10.30 Sun; closed 25 Dec

CHEDDAR ST4653 Map 1

Gardeners Arms

Silver Street, reached off B3135 via Upper North Street or Orchard Way

Dating from the 16th c though much modernised, this comfortable village pub is doing well under its current cheerful and hard-working landlord. Though it's handy for the gorge and all the tourist attractions here, it's tucked quietly away in the old part of the town. The carpeted bar has cushioned high-backed wall settles and other settles around cast-iron-framed tables, a coal-effect gas fire, and some fine recent local photographs by Lewis Whyld; well kept Bass, Butcombe and Courage Best on handpump. They bring in big-screen TV for some sporting events. On the right an attractive two-room beamed dining room has various sizes and types of table, with a similar variety of seating; one table is tucked into an imposing former inglenook. Enjoyable food includes home-made soup (£3.25), smooth chicken liver pâté (£4.45), filled ciabattas (£4.95), smoked salmon roulade, filled baguettes or ploughman's (£5.95), salami antipasto platter (served all day), omelettes or local ham and eggs (all £6.95), lambs liver and bacon with mustard mash or stilton and hazelnut loaf (£7.95), steak and stout pie (£9.95), steaks (from £10.95), veal escalope topped with mozzarella and parmesan with a tomato dressing (£13.95), and puddings like lemon posset with shortbread biscuit, chocolate rum cup or bread and butter pudding (£3.95); Sunday roast (£7.95). The restaurant is no smoking. There are picnic-sets with playthings and a wendy house in the back garden, with more out in front by pretty hanging baskets and an appealing gardening inn-sign. *(Recommended by Bob and Margaret Holder, P R and D C Groves, Brian Brooks, Rod and Chris Pring)*

InnSpired ~ Lease Will and Mary Nicholls ~ Real ale ~ Bar food (12-2, 6-9.15(8 Sun) but some food is available all day) ~ Restaurant ~ (01934) 742235 ~ Children in eating area of bar and restaurant ~ Dogs allowed in bar ~ Occasional live music ~ Open 11-11; 12-10.30 Sun

CHEW MAGNA ST5763 Map 2

Bear & Swan

B3130 (South Parade), off A37 S of Bristol

Good interesting food at sensible prices is the main draw here. Changing every day, with a manageably short and interesting blackboard choice, it might include sandwiches, courgette and red pepper soup (£3.50), griddled breast of pigeon and plum with smoky bacon and raspberry dressing (£6), griddled scallops on couscous with sugar snaps and vanilla dressing (£7.50), fresh ravioli filled with spinach and ricotta with baby tomatoes, pesto sauce and rocket (£10), confit of duck with borlotti beans, rosemary and merguez sausage (£13), baked smoked haddock on chive mash with peppered french beans (£13.50), chargrilled fillet mignons on slow roasted mediterranean vegetables with sweet potato crisps (£17.25), and puddings such as profiteroles with warm chocolate sauce, tarte au citron or crème brûlée (£4). The pub has an appealingly up-to-date feel, which comes as something of a surprise in such an austerely traditional-looking building. It's entirely open-plan, and includes an L-shaped no smoking restaurant end on the left, beyond a piano, with stripped stone walls, dark dining tables, a woodburning stove, bare boards and an oriental rug. The other half, also bare boards with the odd oriental rug, has various sizes of pine tables, pews and raffia-seat dining chairs. In this part a relaxed and civilised mix of customers runs from young men chatting on the bar stools through smart lunching mums sipping champagne to older people reading the racing form. Décor is minimal, really just plants in the windows with their heavy dark blue curtains, and some china above the huge bressumer beam over a splendid log fire; a wide-screen TV may be on with its sound turned down; cribbage. The long bar counter has a good choice of enjoyable wines by the glass, well kept Bath Gem, Butcombe, and Courage Best on handpump, and local somerset apple brandy, and service is friendly and attentive without being intrusive. The car park is small, and street parking needs care (this road is rather a lorry rat-run). *(Recommended by John Urquhart, Ken Marshall, Gaynor Gregory, Jacqueline Healy, Dr Diana Terry, Tim O'Keefe, Mr and Mrs Johnson-Poensgen, JCW)*

Free house ~ Licensees Nigel and Caroline Pushman ~ Real ale ~ Bar food (till 10pm; not Sun evening) ~ Restaurant ~ (01275) 331100 ~ Children allowed but must be well behaved ~ Open 11-11; 12-10.30 Sun ~ Bedrooms: £50S/£80S

CHISELBOROUGH ST4614 Map 1

Cat Head

Take the slip road off A303 at Crewkerne A356 junction

Run by especially friendly people, this spotlessly kept and relaxing country pub is very popular with our readers. The neatly traditional flagstoned rooms have plenty of flowers and plants, a woodburning stove, light wooden tables and chairs, some high-backed cushioned settles, and curtains around the small mullioned windows. A carpeted area to the right is no smoking. The pub often gets busy in the evenings (particularly at weekends), but at lunchtime you may have its peaceful charms almost to yourself. Very good food at lunchtime might include cream of leek and potato soup (£3.40), peppered smoked mackerel pâté and oatcakes or ploughman's (£4.20), sirloin steak and onion filled ciabatta with fries (£7.20), braised oxtail in Guinness (£7.80), baked lamb shank with red onion gravy (£8.20), specials like mixed bean, tomato and chorizo cassoulet (£5.80), aubergine and sweet pepper tart (£5.90), and steak, kidney and mushroom pie (£6.80), and puddings such as chocolate and pecan pie or sticky toffee pudding (£3.60); evening specials like fish chowder with garlic croûtons (£3.80), grilled bass fillets with shrimps and lime (£11.80), duo of monkfish and salmon with a fennel cream sauce (£11.90), baked sole with stir-fried vegetables (£12.40), and seasonal game. Well kept Butcombe, Otter and Marstons Pedigree on handpump, a good wine list, and Thatcher's cider; soft piped music, darts, alley skittles, cribbage, dominoes. Behind is a very attractive award-winning lawned garden with picnic-sets and colourful summer plants; nice views over the peaceful village. *(Recommended by Mr and Mrs J B Pritchard, Kate Francis, Michael Hasslacher, Mrs A P Lee, J V Dadswell, Brenda and Tony Morgan, Mary Ellen Cummings)*

Enterprise ~ Lease Duncan and Avril Gordon ~ Real ale ~ Bar food (till 10pm) ~ Restaurant ~ (01935) 881231 ~ Children in eating area of bar ~ Open 12-3, 6(7 Sun)-11; closed evening 25 Dec

CHURCHILL ST4560 Map 1

Crown £

The Batch; in village, turn off A368 into Skinners Lane at Nelson Arms, then bear right

Apart from the marvellous range of around ten well kept real ales, an important part of this unspoilt little cottage's appeal to its enthusiastic supporters is its far from neat-and-clean style. The small and local stone-floored and cross-beamed room on the right has a wooden window seat, an unusually sturdy settle, and built-in wall benches; the left-hand room has a slate floor, and some steps past the big log fire in a big stone fireplace lead to more sitting space. Tapped from the cask, the real ales might include Bass, Bath SPA, Hop Back GFB and Chimera Red, Palmers Copper Ale, Gold, 200 and Tally Ho, and RCH Hewish and PG Steam. Straightforward lunchtime bar food includes good soup (£2.90 small; £3.50 large), sandwiches (from £2.90), filled baked potatoes (from £3.55), ploughman's (from £4.95), salads (from £6.50), daily specials like cauliflower cheese or chilli (£4.50), and beef casserole (£5.95), and puddings such as well liked treacle pudding or hot chocolate fudge cake (£2.50). Outside lavatories. They do get busy at weekends, especially in summer. There are garden tables on the front and a smallish back lawn, and hill views; the Mendip Morris Men come in summer. Good walks nearby. *(Recommended by John Urquhart, P M Wilkins, J Coote, the Didler, Chris Flynn, Wendy Jones, Jane and Graham Rooth, Paul Hopton, Kerry Law, Simon Smith, R J Walden, Peter Herridge, Jacqueline Healy, S Fysh, Alan and Paula McCully, Dr and Mrs A K Clarke)*

Free house ~ Licensee Tim Rogers ~ Real ale ~ Bar food (12-2.30(3 weekends); not evenings) ~ No credit cards ~ (01934) 852995 ~ Children welcome ~ Dogs welcome ~ Occasional live band Sun ~ Open 12-11; 12-10.30 Sun

CLAPTON-IN-GORDANO ST4773 Map 1

Black Horse

4 miles from M5 junction 19; A369 towards Portishead, then B3124 towards Clevedon; in N Weston opposite school turn left signposted Clapton, then in village take second right, maybe signed Clevedon, Clapton Wick

Particularly in the evening or on sunny days, this unspoilt and interesting old place is packed with a good mix of locals and visitors. There's a welcoming atmosphere and plenty of character, and the partly flagstoned and partly red-tiled main room has winged settles and built-in wall benches around narrow, dark wooden tables, window seats, a big log fire with stirrups and bits on the mantelbeam, and amusing cartoons and photographs of the pub. A window in an inner snug is still barred from the days when this room was the petty-sessions gaol; high-backed settles – one a marvellous carved and canopied creature, another with an art nouveau copper insert reading East, West, Hame's Best – lots of mugs hanging from its black beams, and plenty of little prints and photographs. There's also a simply furnished room just off the bar (where children can go), with high-backed corner settles and a gas fire; piped music, darts, cribbage and dominoes. Straightforward bar food (lunchtime only) includes tasty filled hot and cold baguettes (from £3.60), ploughman's (£4.95), and a few hot dishes like corned beef hash, fish pie or chilli (from £4.95). Well kept Bass, Brains SA, Courage Best, Shepherd Neame Spitfire, Smiles Best, and Websters Green Label on handpump or tapped from the cask; friendly, chatty staff. In summer, the flower-decked building and little flagstoned front garden are exceptionally pretty; there are some old rustic tables and benches, with more to one side of the car park and a secluded children's play area. Paths from the pub lead up Naish Hill or along to Cadbury Camp. *(Recommended by the Didler, Tom Evans, George Atkinson, Gaynor Gregory, Ian Phillips, Susan and John Douglas)*

Inntrepreneur ~ Tenant Nicholas Evans ~ Real ale ~ Bar food (not evenings, not Sun lunchtime) ~ No credit cards ~ (01275) 842105 ~ Children in family room ~ Dogs welcome ~ Live music Mon evening ~ Open 11-2.30, 5-11; 11-11 Fri and Sat; 12-4, 7-10.30 Sun

COMPTON MARTIN ST5457 Map 2

Ring o' Bells £

A368 Bath—Weston

Even when this cheerful country pub is at its busiest, the landlord and his staff remain friendly and helpful. The cosy, traditional front part of the bar has rugs on the flagstones and inglenook seats right by the log fire, and up a step is a spacious carpeted back part with largely stripped stone walls and pine tables; the lounge is partly no smoking. Reasonably priced bar food includes sandwiches (from £1.95; toasties from £3.25), soup (£2.95), stilton mushrooms (£3.95), filled baked potatoes (from £3.95), omelettes (£4.25), ploughman's (from £4.75), ham and eggs (small £4.50, large £5.25), lasagne, mushroom, broccoli and almond tagliatelle or beef casserole (from £6.25), generous mixed grill (£11.50), daily specials (from £6.25), and puddings (£2.95); best to get here early to be sure of a seat. Well kept Butcombe Bitter, Blond, and Gold, and guests like Bass and Robinsons Young Tom on handpump; darts in the public bar. The family room is no smoking, and has blackboards and chalks, a Brio track, and a rocking horse; they also have baby changing and nursing facilities, and the big garden has swings, a slide, and a climbing frame. Blagdon Lake and Chew Valley Lake are not far away, and the pub is overlooked by the Mendip Hills. *(Recommended by Tom Evans, Leigh and Gillian Mellor, John and Gloria Isaacs, Brian McBurnie)*

Butcombe ~ Manager Roger Owen ~ Real ale ~ Bar food ~ Restaurant ~ (01761) 221284 ~ Children in family room ~ Dogs allowed in bar ~ Open 11.30-3, 6.30-11; 12-3, 7-10.30 Sun

CONGRESBURY ST4464 Map 1

White Hart

Wrington Road, which is off A370 Bristol—Weston just E of village – keep on

Although the names of the licensees are new, Paul and Rebecca worked for the Taylors for quite a few years here. It's a pleasant companionable country pub, and the L-shaped carpeted main bar has a few heavy black beams in the bowed ceiling of its longer leg, country-kitchen chairs around good-sized tables, and a big stone inglenook fireplace at each end, with woodburning stoves and lots of copper pans. The short leg of the L is more cottagey, with wooden games and other bric-a-brac above yet another fireplace and on a delft shelf, lace and old-gold brocaded curtains, and brocaded wall seats. A roomy family Parlour Bar, open to the main bar, is similar in mood, though with lighter-coloured country-style furniture, some stripped stone and shiny black panelling, and big bright airy conservatory windows on one side; the restaurant is no smoking. Tasty bar food includes home-made soup (£3.25), deep-fried cheese with cranberry sauce (£4.50), ham and eggs (£6.25), vegetarian dishes like cauliflower cheese or stilton, leek and walnut pie (£6-£7.50), home-made lasagne (£7.50), feta cheese and couscous stuffed peppers (£7.95), home-made steak pie (£8.25), chicken in stilton or tomato sauce (£9.25), and puddings such as home-made fruit crumbles (£3.75). Well kept Badger Best, Tanglefoot, and King & Barnes Sussex on handpump; perhaps faint music. There are picnic-sets under an arbour on the terrace behind, and the garden has been landscaped; the hills you see are the Mendips. *(Recommended by Anthony Barnes, James Morrell, Comus and Sarah Elliott, Andy Sinden, Louise Harrington, J H Bescoby, Susan and John Douglas, Bob and Margaret Holder)*

Badger ~ Tenants Paul Merrick and Rebecca North ~ Real ale ~ Bar food ~ (01934) 833303 ~ Children in family room ~ Dogs welcome ~ Open 11.30-2.30, 6-11; 12-3, 7-10.30 Sun; closed 25 Dec

CROWCOMBE ST1336 Map 1

Carew Arms

Village (and pub) signposted just off A358 Taunton—Minehead

There's some emphasis on the food in this 17th-c beamed inn, and the smart, newly bare-boarded dining room has doors to one side leading to an outside terrace where you can eat in fine weather. The front bar has long benches and a couple of old long deal tables on its dark flagstones, a high-backed antique settle and a shiny old leather wing armchair by the woodburning stove in its huge brick inglenook fireplace, and a thoroughly non-PC collection of hunting trophies to remind you that this is the Quantocks. A back room behind the bar is a carpeted and gently updated version of the front one, and on the right is a library, and residents' lounge. Well kept Otter Bitter, and Exmoor Ale and either Fox, Gold or Hart on handpump, eight wines by the glass, Lane's strong farm cider, and a dozen malt whiskies; dominoes, cribbage, darts, skittle alley, and piped music (only in the Garden Room). Bar food at lunchtime includes home-made soup (£3.95), sandwiches (from £3.95), home-made vegetable samosas with minted yoghurt (£4.50), potted brown shrimps (£5.25), ploughman's (£5.75), local sausages with red wine gravy (£7.25), gnocchi pasta with tomato dressing and baked aubergine (£7.95), honey roasted pork with buttered beans and parsnip crisps (£8.50), and roast cod with puy lentils, bacon and mustard sauce (£10); evening dishes such as deep fried goats cheese with red pepper marmalade (£5.75), seared king scallops with mango coulis and chilli oil (£7.95), chicken breast with creamed leeks and black pudding (£11.50), sirloin steak (£12.95), rump of lamb with rösti and madeira wine gravy (£13.50), and steamed whole bream with white wine and lemon grass (£15). Picnic-sets out on the back grass look over rolling wooded pasture, and the attractive village at the foot of the hills has a fine old church and church house. *(Recommended by P M Wilkins, J Coote, the Didler, Andy and Jill Kassube, Tom Evans, Catherine Pitt, Jeremy Whitehorn, June and Peter Shamash, Dennis and Gill Keen)*

Free house ~ Licensees Simon and Reg Ambrose ~ Real ale ~ Bar food ~ Restaurant ~ (01984) 618631 ~ Children welcome ~ Dogs allowed in bar ~ Live jazz Sun afternoon ~ Open 11-4, 6-11; 11-11 Sat; 12-10.30 Sun ~ Bedrooms: £25(£47B)/£50(£72B)

DOULTING ST6445 Map 2

Waggon & Horses 🍷

Doulting Beacon, 2 miles N of Doulting itself; eastwards turn off A37 on Mendip ridge N of Shepton Mallet, just S of A367 junction; the pub is also signed from the A37 at the Beacon Hill crossroads and from the A361 at the Doulting and Cranmore crossroads

Particularly when the enthusiastic Mr Cardona is in, you can be sure of a genuine welcome to the wide mix of customers here. The rambling bar has studded red leatherette seats and other chairs, a homely mix of tables including antiques, and well kept Greene King IPA and a guest on handpump, a small, carefully chosen wine list, and cocktails. Two rooms are no smoking. Bar food includes sandwiches (from £3.75), filled baguettes (from £5), spicy bean casserole or ham and eggs (£8.50), salmon fishcakes with dill mayonnaise (£9.50), chicken breast topped with ham, cheese and tomato (£12.50), ambitious daily specials, and puddings such as sticky toffee pudding with pecan nut sauce or crème brûlée (£4.50); good winter stews and game dishes. The big walled garden (with summer barbecues) is lovely: elderly tables and chairs stand on informal terracing, with picnic-sets out on the grass, and perennials and flowering shrubs intersperse themselves in a pretty and pleasantly informal way. There's a wildlife pond, and a climber for children. Off to one side is a rough paddock with a horse and various fancy fowl, with pens further down holding many more in small breeding groups – there are some really quite splendid birds among them, and the cluckings and crowings make a splendidly contented background to a sunny summer lunch. They often sell the eggs, too. During the spring and autumn, there are some remarkable classical music and other musical events, and exhibitions of local artists' work that take place in the big raftered upper gallery to one side of the building. *(Recommended by Colin and Janet Roe, Jacquie and Jim Jones, Nigel Long, Prof Keith and Mrs Jane Barber, John Urquhart, Adam and Joan Bunting, MRSM, Mrs Pat Crabb)*

InnSpired ~ Lease Francisco Cardona ~ Real ale ~ Bar food ~ Restaurant ~ (01749) 880302 ~ Children tolerated but must be well behaved and quiet ~ Dogs allowed in bar ~ Classical concerts and some jazz ~ Open 11.30-2.30, 6-11; 12-3, 7-11 Sun

EAST LYNG ST3328 Map 1

Rose & Crown

A361 about 4 miles W of Othery

Very little changes in this well liked ex-coaching inn. There's an open-plan beamed lounge bar with a winter log fire (or a big embroidered fire screen) in the stone fireplace, a corner cabinet of glass, china and silver, a court cabinet, a bow window seat by an oak drop-leaf table, copies of *Country Life*, and impressive large dried flower arrangements. Reasonably priced, popular bar food includes sandwiches (from £2.35), soup (£2.95), ploughman's (from £4.75), ham and egg (£5.25), omelettes (from £5.75), steaks (from £10.50), roast duckling with orange sauce (£12.75), daily specials such as vegetable and brie bake, good pork chop with mustard sauce, liver and bacon casserole or home-made chilli (all £6.75), and puddings like fresh fruit crumble, rum and chocolate biscuit cake or home-made treacle tart (£3.45); the dining room is no smoking. Well kept Butcombe Bitter and Gold, and Palmers 200 on handpump; skittle alley and piped music. There are lots of seats in the pretty back garden (largely hedged off from the car park) and lovely rural views. *(Recommended by G Coates, Bob and Margaret Holder, Ian Phillips, Comus and Sarah Elliott, Mrs A P Lee, D P and M A Miles)*

Free house ~ Licensee Derek Mason ~ Real ale ~ Bar food ~ (01823) 698235 ~ Open 11-2.30, 6.30-11; 12-3, 7-10.30 Sun ~ Bedrooms: £32S/£54S

EXFORD SS8538 Map 1

Crown

The Green (B3224)

Readers enjoy their visits to this comfortably upmarket Exmoor coaching inn. You can expect a friendly welcome from the licensees and their staff, the food and beer is good, and it's a nice place to stay, too. The two-room bar has a very relaxed feel, plenty of stuffed animal heads and hunting prints on the cream walls, some hunting-themed plates (this is the local hunt's traditional meeting place at New Year), and a good mix of chatty customers. There are a few tables fashioned from barrels, a big stone fireplace (with a nice display of flowers in summer), old photographs of the area, and smart cushioned benches; piped music and TV. Well kept Exmoor Ale and Gold and a guest such as Archers Best or Cotleigh Tawny on handpump; decent wine list (with some available by the half-carafe). To be sure of a table, it's best to book beforehand: sandwiches, soup (£3.95), warm salad of chicken liver and shallots or sun-dried tomato and coriander risotto (£4.75; main course £7.95), parma ham and avocado salad (£5.50; main course £9.75), leek and wild mushroom tagliatelle with blue cheese (£7.50), toasted focaccia bread with mediterranean vegetables (£7.95), braised lamb shank with herb mash or roast pork fillet with rissole potatoes (£9.75), and daily specials such as chicken liver parfait with pear chutney (£4.95), artichoke with feta cheese and olive salad (£5.95), courgette and red onion fritatta (£6.95), salmon, green bean and new potato salad (£8.50), and chicken with sage and prosciutto with olive mash or bass with salsa verde (£12.95); good Sunday lunch (two courses £12.95, three courses £16.95). The rather smart dining room is no smoking. There's a delightful water garden behind – a lovely summer spot with a trout stream threading its way past gently sloping lawns, tall trees and plenty of tables. A smaller terraced garden at the side overlooks the village and the edge of the green. They have stabling for horses. *(Recommended by Brian and Anita Randall, Patrick and Phillipa Vickery, F J M and E M Cornock, Richard and Anne Ansell, John and Joan Nash)*

Free house ~ Licensee Hugo Jeune ~ Real ale ~ Bar food ~ Restaurant ~ (01643) 831554 ~ Children in eating area of bar ~ Dogs allowed in bar and bedrooms ~ Open 11-3, 6-11; 11-11 Sat; 12-11 Sun ~ Bedrooms: £65B/£95B

White Horse

B3224

Even mid-week out of season, this sizeable creeper-covered inn is always busy, but there's a friendly welcome for all customers from the helpful staff; it does get packed on Sunday lunchtimes. The more or less open-plan bar has windsor and other country kitchen chairs, a high-backed antique settle, scrubbed deal tables, hunting prints, photographs above the stripped pine dado, and a good winter log fire. Well kept Exmoor Ale and Gold, Greene King Old Speckled Hen, and a couple of guests like Exmoor Fox or Tetleys on handpump, and over 150 malt whiskies. Straightforward bar food includes home-made soup (£1.95), sandwiches (from £1.95; filled baguettes from £2.95), filled baked potatoes (from £2.95), breaded haddock (£4.15), smoked ham and egg (£4.55), home-made venison pie (£6.25), local trout (£8.25), steaks (from £8.95), and home-made puddings (£2.95); three-course Sunday lunch (£10.95). The restaurant and eating area of the bar are no smoking; fruit machine. The village green with children's play equipment is next to the pub. This is a pretty village set beside the River Exe in the heart of the Exmoor National Park. Exmoor safaris start from here. *(Recommended by Tracey and Stephen Groves, Dr and Mrs P Truelove, Bob and Margaret Holder, Lynda and Trevor Smith, Roger and Jenny Huggins, Andy and Jill Kassube, John Brightley, Mike and Mary Carter,*

Patrick Hancock, Dr and Mrs A K Clarke, Anne and Paul Horscraft, P and J Shapley, Lloyd Moon)

Free house ~ Licensees Peter and Linda Hendrie ~ Real ale ~ Bar food (12-2.30, 6-9.30) ~ Restaurant ~ (01643) 831229 ~ Children in eating area of bar and restaurant ~ Dogs allowed in bar and bedrooms ~ Open 11-11; 12-10.30 Sun ~ Bedrooms: £50B/£100B

FAULKLAND ST7354 Map 2

Tuckers Grave ★ £

A366 E of village

Still claiming the title of Smallest Pub in the *Guide*, this is a very special place and held dear in the hearts of a great many people. It's an unchanging and warmly friendly basic cider house, and the flagstoned entry opens into a teeny unspoilt room with casks of well kept Bass and Butcombe Bitter on tap and Thatcher's Cheddar Valley cider in an alcove on the left. Two old cream-painted high-backed settles face each other across a single table on the right, and a side room has shove-ha'penny. There's a skittle alley and tables and chairs on the back lawn, as well as winter fires and maybe newspapers to read. Food is limited to sandwiches and ploughman's at lunchtime. There's an attractive back garden. *(Recommended by the Didler, Pete Baker, MLR, Dr and Mrs A K Clarke, Roger Huggins, Tom and Alex McLean, Tom McLean)*

Free house ~ Licensees Ivan and Glenda Swift ~ Real ale ~ Bar food ~ No credit cards ~ (01373) 834230 ~ Children welcome ~ Open 11-3, 6-11; 12-3, 7-10.30 Sun; closed evenings 25 and 26 Dec

FRESHFORD ST7960 Map 2

Inn at Freshford

Off A36 or B3108

Particularly in fine weather, this is a lovely spot, and the pretty garden – looking across the road to the bridge by the River Frome – has plenty of seats; walks to the Kennet & Avon Canal. Inside is comfortable modernised, and the bar has plenty of atmosphere, interesting decorations, and well kept Butcombe, Courage Best, Wadworths 6X, and a guest on handpump. Popular bar food includes home-made soup (£3.45), sandwiches (from £3.65; filled baguettes from £4.75), home-made pâté (£4.25), filled baked potatoes (from £4.45), ploughman's (£6.75), mediterranean tart, battered cod, steak in ale pie or chicken curry (all £6.95), steaks (from £8.50), and daily specials such as stilton and cherry tomato tartlet (£6.95) or local sausages with bubble and squeak (£7.25). The restaurant is no smoking; piped music. *(Recommended by Meg and Colin Hamilton, B and K Hypher, Andrew Shore, Maria Williams, Martin and Karen Wake)*

Latona Leisure ~ Manager David Brown ~ Real ale ~ Bar food (12-2, 6-9) ~ Restaurant ~ (01225) 722250 ~ Children in eating area of bar and restaurant ~ Dogs allowed in bar ~ Live Irish music Sun, jazz Thurs evening ~ Open 11-3, 6-11; 12-3, 7-10.30 Sun

HOLCOMBE ST6649 Map 2

Ring o' Roses

Village signposted off A367 by War Memorial in Stratton-on-the-Fosse, S of Radstock

The bar in this quietly placed, extensively modernised country pub has been refurbished this year, and there are now flagstones and two woodburning stoves; also, a handsome counter facing attractively cushioned window seats and some orthodox cushioned captain's chairs around cast-iron-framed pub tables, and behind is a gently lit parlourish area with sofas and cushioned chairs around low tables. There are more easy chairs in a pleasant panelled lounge on the right, and a good-sized dining area is nicely divided by balustrades and so forth, and has blue and white plates and some modern prints on the walls. Bar food is served lunchtimes only and includes home-made soup or pâté (£3.50), deep-fried breaded brie with raspberry dressing (£4.50), filled baguettes or king prawns in filo pastry with a lime and ginger dip (£4.75), mushroom and roast cashew nut stroganoff or gammon and eggs (£6.95), rainbow trout (£7.25), sirloin steak (£9.50), and daily specials such as omelettes (£6.25), plaice goujons with lemon mayonnaise (£7.95), pigeon breasts with thyme and juniper jus (£9.75), and whole dover sole (£12.50). The restaurant is no smoking. Blindmans Golden Spring and Otter Ale on handpump, Thatcher's cider, several wines by the glass, daily papers, and perhaps faint piped radio. There are peaceful farmland views from picnic-sets on a terrace and on the lawn around the side and back, with nice shrub plantings and a small rockery. The chocolate labrador is called Sam. More reports please. *(Recommended by M G Hart, DRH and KLH, Angela Gorman, Paul Acton, Jack Taylor, Michael Doswell)*

Free house ~ Licensee Richard Rushton ~ Real ale ~ Bar food ~ Restaurant ~ (01761) 232478 ~ Children welcome ~ Dogs allowed in bar ~ Open 11.30-11; 11.30-2.30, 7-11 Sat; 12-2.30, 7-10.30 Sun ~ Bedrooms: £65B/£85B

HUISH EPISCOPI ST4326 Map 1

Rose & Crown

A372 E of Langport

Known locally as 'Eli's' after the friendly landlady's father, this unspoilt thatched pub has been run by Mrs Pittard's family for well over 135 years, and Mrs Prittard was actually born in the pub (as was her mother). It's like a real step back in time with the atmosphere and character remaining as determinedly unpretentious and welcoming as ever. There's no bar as such – to get a drink (prices are very low), you just walk into the central flagstoned still room and choose from the casks of well kept Teignworthy Reel Ale or guests such as Butcombe Blond or Glastonbury Mystery Tor; also, several farm ciders (and local cider brandy). This servery is the only thoroughfare between the casual little front parlours with their unusual pointed-arch windows; genuinely friendly locals. Food is home-made, simple and cheap and uses local produce (and some home-grown fruit): generously filled sandwiches (from £2), home-made soup (£2.80), filled baked potatoes (from £3), ploughman's (£4.40), cottage pie or stilton and broccoli tart (£5.95), chicken breast in a creamy white wine and tarragon sauce, pork, apple and cider cobbler or steak in ale pie (£6.25), and puddings such as sticky toffee pudding or chocolate torte (£2.95); good helpful service. Shove-ha'penny, dominoes and cribbage, and a much more orthodox big back extension family room has pool, darts, fruit machine, and juke box; skittle alley and popular quiz nights. One room is no smoking at lunchtimes and early evening. There are tables in a garden, and a second enclosed garden with a children's play area. The welsh collie is called Bonny. Summer morris men, good nearby walks, and the site of the Battle of Langport (1645) is close by. *(Recommended by the Didler, A C Nugent, Comus and Sarah Elliott, Leigh and Gillian Mellor, Esther and John Sprinkle, Pete Baker, MLR, Bill and Jessica Ritson, Douglas Allen, Dr and Mrs A K Clarke, OPUS, Nick and Lynne Carter)*

Free house ~ Licensee Mrs Eileen Pittard ~ Real ale ~ Bar food (12-2, 6-7.30; not Sun evening) ~ No credit cards ~ (01458) 250494 ~ Children welcome ~ Dogs welcome ~ Folk singers every third Sat; Irish night once a month in winter ~ Open 11.30-2.30, 5.30-11; 11.30-11 Fri and Sat; 12-10.30 Sun

ILMINSTER ST3614 Map 1

George

North Street, opposite central butter market

This is a pub with a decided difference. The neat and relaxed tiled-floor bar is small and very civilised, just a short row of tables along the wall, each with a lit candle, vase of flowers and cushioned dining chairs, a rug at one end, and on the canary wall above the creamy yellow-painted panelled dado a series of big late Victorian prints showing the Beaufort Hunt in action. The lighting is gentle, and the piped music unobtrusive. On the bar counter a fine carving of a family of ducks is a sign of Mrs Phelps's soft spot for them; many readers will also remember fondly the duck pond outside the Strode Arms at Cranmore, which saw its heyday when she ran it with her late husband. The contrast with that pub, so very busy in their days there, must have seemed quite a culture-shock to Mrs Phelps and her daughter, now ensconced in this much smaller and quieter hideaway. We predict however that it won't be quiet for long: the virtues which made the Strode Arms so popular are all to be found here – good smiling service, good food at sensible prices, and a streak of real individuality. They have good wines by the glass and a decent choice of soft drinks as well as well kept Otter Bitter and St Austell Tribute on handpump. A neat blackboard lists a changing choice of food which might include fresh soup (£4), sandwiches (from £4), home-made game pâté with cranberry sauce (£4.50), ploughman's (£5.50), home-baked ham with eggs and sauté potatoes (£6.25), broccoli and stilton tart or a trio of farm sausages with onion gravy (£6.75), cod loin steak with lemon and parsley butter sauce (£7.50), steak and kidney pie or pot-roasted silverside (£7.75), roast bacon-wrapped pork tenderloin with stilton sauce (£8.25), fillet mignons with a mushroom, brandy and cream sauce (£14.50), and puddings such as fresh plum sponge pudding, cappuccino mousse or blackcurrant bakewell (£4). The no smoking main dining area, furnished similarly to the bar (and with plenty more ducks), is curtained off at the back. Prudes should perhaps avoid looking at the antique french cartoons in the gents'. *(Recommended by Douglas Allen)*

Free house ~ Licensee Dora Phelps ~ Real ale ~ Bar food (12-2.30, 7-9.30; no evening food Mon, Weds, Thurs, Sat or Sun; Sun lunch first Sun of month only) ~ Restaurant ~ (01460) 55515 ~ Children welcome ~ Dogs welcome ~ Open 11.30-3, 7-11; 12-3 Sun; closed Sun evening

KINGSDON ST5126 Map 2

Kingsdon Inn

At Podimore roundabout junction of A303, A372 and A37 take A372, then turn right on to B3151, right into village, and right again opposite post office

Most customers come to this pretty thatched cottage to enjoy the good and very popular food served quickly by attentive staff. There are four charmingly decorated, low-ceilinged rooms. On the right are some very nice old stripped pine tables with attractive cushioned farmhouse chairs, more seats in what was a small inglenook fireplace, a few low sagging beams, and an open woodburning stove with colourful dried and artificial fruits and flowers on the overmantel; down three steps through balustrading to a light, airy room with cushions on stripped pine built-in wall seats, curtains matching the scatter cushions, more stripped pine tables, and a winter open fire. Another similarly decorated room has more tables and another fireplace. At lunchtime, good, reasonably priced food includes filled baguettes, home-made soup (£3.60), wild boar pâté (£4.60), deep-fried whitebait or ploughman's (£4.80), and smoked haddock and prawn mornay, cottage pie, sausages with onion gravy and lambs liver, bacon and onions (all £6.90), with evening dishes like mushrooms filled with cambozola and stilton (£4.90), home-made fishcakes with pepper and chilli mayonnaise (£5.20), grilled goats cheese with onion marmalade (£5.40), mushroom parcel with wild mushroom sauce (£8.90), wild rabbit in a dijon mustard and white wine sauce (£10.90), trio of cod, salmon and sole in prawn sauce (£11.90), half a roast duck in scrumpy cider sauce (£13.40), rack of lamb with port and redcurrant sauce (£13.90), and daily specials such as smoked saddle of venison salad (£5.80), pigeon breasts in port and wild mushroom sauce (£11.90) or seafood risotto (£13.90). Two areas are no smoking. Well kept Butcombe Bitter, Cotleigh Barn Owl, and Otter Bitter on handpump, nine wines by the glass, farm cider, and over 20 malt whiskies; piped music. Picnic-sets on the grass. The Lytes Cary (National Trust) and the Fleet Air Arm Museum are nearby. *(Recommended by Terence Boley, JCW, R and S Bentley, Tom Evans, Paul Hopton, Theo, Anne and Jane Gaskin, Dr and Mrs M E Wilson, Mike and Heather Watson, Pat and Robert Watt, Robert Coates, J Stickland, J D O Carter, R T and J C Moggridge, OPUS, Julie Walton)*

Free house ~ Licensees Leslie and Anna-Marie Hood ~ Real ale ~ Bar food ~ Restaurant ~ (01935) 840543 ~ Well behaved children in eating area of bar; under-10s must leave by 8pm ~ Open 12-3, 6.30-11; 12-3, 7-10.30 Sun

LANGLEY MARSH ST0729 Map 1

Three Horseshoes

Village signposted off B3227 from Wiveliscombe

This red sandstone pub is a proper traditional local. The back bar has low modern settles and polished wooden tables, dark red wallpaper, planes hanging from the ceiling, bank notes papering the wall behind the bar counter, a piano, and a local stone fireplace. Well kept Harveys, Otter Bitter, Palmers IPA, and Youngs Bitter tapped from the cask, and farm cider. Genuinely home-made, good value food includes sandwiches (£3.75; soup and a sandwich £4.75), chicken liver pâté (£3.95), scrambled egg and smoked salmon (£4.25), filled baked potatoes (£4.75), baguette-style pizzas (from £4), steak and kidney pie (£6.75), fish pie (£7.75), steaks (from £9.75), daily specials like fried scallops with a warm red pepper and cumin dressing (£4.75), lambs liver, bacon and mushrooms or spicy vegetable, fruit and nut stir fry (£6.25), and pheasant breast with rosemary, smoked bacon and cream (£7.75), and puddings such as creamy white chocolate and strawberry shortcake tower or Guinness pudding with whisky sauce (from £3.25). The no smoking dining area has antique settles, tables and benches; dominoes, cribbage, separate skittle alley, and piped music. Part of the bar area is no smoking. You can sit on rustic seats on the verandah or in the sloping back garden, with a fully equipped children's play area; in fine weather there are usually vintage cars outside. They offer self-catering (and maybe bed and breakfast if they are not already booked up). *(Recommended by Tom Evans, M G Hart, the Didler, Lyn Huxtable, Richard Seers, Mrs Romey Heaton, Richard and Anne Ansell)*

Free house ~ Licensee John Hopkins ~ Real ale ~ Bar food (not winter Sun evening or winter Mon) ~ (01984) 623763 ~ No children under 8 inside ~ Open 12-2.30, 7-11(10.30 Sun; 9 winter Sun); closed winter Mon; 2 weeks early July

LOVINGTON ST5930 Map 2

Pilgrims Rest

B3153 Castle Cary—Keinton Mandeville

Somerset Dining Pub of the Year

There's no doubt that most visitors to this quietly placed and civilised country bar/bistro come to enjoy the very good food, but there are a few bar stools (and a frieze of hundreds of match books) by a corner counter with nice wines by the glass and well kept Cottage Champflower on handpump, from the nearby brewery. There's a chatty, relaxed feel, and a cosy little maroon-walled inner area has sunny modern country and city prints, a couple of shelves of books and china, a cushioned pew, a couple of settees and an old leather easy chair by the big fireplace. With flagstones throughout, this runs into the compact eating area, with candles on tables, heavy black beams and joists, and some stripped stone; piped music. The landlord cooks using all fresh ingredients including local meat and cheeses and daily fresh fish: sandwiches on home-baked bread (sautéed chicken breast and bacon or goats cheese with pesto and sunblush tomatoes £5), anchovy soldiers or potted smoked chicken (£5), smoked salmon, trout and eel (£7), asparagus and spring vegetable risotto (£11), lemon sole with a dash of Noilly Prat (£12), calves liver and bacon (£16), bass fillet on roasted fennel with Pernod sauce (£17), fillet steak in a light dijon sauce (£18), and puddings such as crème brûlée or a special chocolate pudding (£5). Perhaps better value are the fixed course meals (two-course lunch £12, two-course evening meal £15); there is also a separate more formal carpeted no smoking dining room. The landlady's service is efficient and friendly, and there's a rack of daily papers. Picnic-sets and old-fashioned benches on the side grass, and the car park exit has its own traffic lights – on your way out line your car up carefully or you may wait for ever for them to change. *(Recommended by OPUS, Anne Westcott, B and M Kendall, Brenda and Stuart Naylor)*

Free house ~ Licensees Sally and Jools Mitchison ~ Real ale ~ Bar food (see opening hours) ~ Restaurant ~ (01963) 240597 ~ Children welcome ~ Dogs allowed in bar ~ Open 12-3, 7-11; closed Sun evening, Mon, Tues lunchtimes; last 2 wks Oct

LUXBOROUGH SS9837 Map 1

Royal Oak

Kingsbridge; S of Dunster on minor roads into Brendon Hills – OS Sheet 181 map reference 983378

As we went to press, the back bar and four of the dozen bedrooms in this 14th-c country inn were being refurbished; they plan to refurbish the others, too. The atmospheric bar rooms have beams and inglenooks, good log fires, flagstones in the front public bar, a fishing theme in one room, and a real medley of furniture; the three characterful dining rooms are no smoking. Well kept Cotleigh Tawny, Exmoor Gold, and Palmers IPA and 200 on handpump, local farm cider, and country wines. Lunchtime bar food includes filled baguettes (£4.50), spicy potted prawns (£6.95), cep and artichoke gratin with a truffle cream (£11.25), roast fillets of sardines with a lemon and dill mayonnaise (£11.95), sirloin steak (£11.95), grilled escalopes of pork with a marjoram and tomato salsa (£13.25), five spice roasted duck breast with spicy plum sauce (£13.95), daily specials such as goats cheese salad (£5.75), steak in ale pie (£6.95), and whole roasted bass (£13.95), and home-made puddings (£4.25). Shove-ha'penny, dominoes and cribbage – no machines or music. Tables outside, and lots of good surrounding walks. *(Recommended by Kev and Gaye Griffiths, G F Couch, J M Hill, Ken and Jenny Simmonds, the Didler, Andy and Jill Kassube, Lynda and Trevor Smith, Anthony Barnes, Steve Whalley, Dr Paull Khan, R and J Bateman, Dr and Mrs P Truelove, Mike and Mary Carter, Tracey and Stephen Groves, Norman and Sarah Keeping, Gaynor Gregory, MLR, Jay Smith, Patrick Hancock, Terry and Dot Mitchell, Andrea Rampley, Brian Root, Peter and Jane Mawle, John Yardley, Richard and Anne Ansell)*

Free house ~ Licensees James and Sian Waller and Sue Hinds ~ Real ale ~ Bar food ~ Restaurant ~ (01984) 640319 ~ Children in restaurant (no under-10s evening) ~ Dogs allowed in bar ~ Monthly folk night second Fri ~ Open 12-2.30, 6-11(10.30 Sun); closed 25 Dec ~ Bedrooms: £55S/£60(£65B)

MELLS ST7249 Map 2

Talbot

W of Frome; off A362 W of Buckland Dinham, or A361 via Nunney and Whatley

Mr Elliott has commissioned a 14ft high mural behind the bar in the 15th-c tithe barn here which depicts the history of Mells from medieval times to the present day; the barn is open in the evenings and at weekends. The pub is an interesting building and there are a couple of bars where drinkers are welcome to drink the Butcombe and Fullers London Pride tapped from the cask. Taken in the no smoking restaurant, the lunchtime food might include home-made soup (£4.50), chicken liver parfait with spiced apple chutney (£5.50), ploughman's (£7.50), open ciabatta sandwich with roast chicken, grilled bacon, and melted brie (£8.50), ham and free range eggs (£8.65), cottage pie (£8.95), and brixham plaice with chilli and herb dressing (£12.50), with evening choices such as baked breadcrumbed goats cheese with sun-dried tomatoes, basil and olives (£5.95; main course £11.95), moules marinière (£6.25; main course £11.50), steaks (from £12.95), steak, mushroom and Guinness pie (£13.65), roasted corn-fed chicken breast with wild mushrooms and madeira sauce (£14.65), and breast and confit leg of gressingham duck with peppercorn sauce (£15.95). The attractive main room has stripped pews, mate's and wheelback chairs, fresh flowers and candles in bottles on the mix of tables, and sporting and riding pictures on the walls, which are partly stripped above a broad panelled dado, and partly rough terracotta-colour. A small corridor leads to a nice little room with an open fire; piped music, darts, TV, shove-ha'penny, cribbage and dominoes. There are seats in the cobbled courtyard and a vine-covered pergola. The village was purchased by the Horner family of the 'Little Jack Horner' nursery rhyme and the direct descendants still live in the manor house next door. More reports please. *(Recommended by Gaynor Gregory, John Coatsworth, Jack Taylor, Dr M Mills, David and Christine Vaughton, Neil and Angela Huxter)*

Free house ~ Licensee Roger Stanley Elliott ~ Real ale ~ Bar food ~ Restaurant ~ (01373) 812254 ~ Children welcome ~ Dogs allowed in bedrooms ~ Open 12-3, 6.30-11; 12-3, 7-10.30 Sun ~ Bedrooms: £55B/£85B

MONKSILVER ST0737 Map 1

Notley Arms

B3188

New Zimbabwean licensees have taken over this bustling pub and Mr Deary welcomes fellow Springboks with biltong, ostrich fillet and bobotie. But there are plenty of locals and visitors too which creates a friendly, unpretentious atmosphere. The beamed and L-shaped bar has small settles and kitchen chairs around the plain country wooden and candlelit tables, original paintings on the ochre-coloured walls, fresh flowers, and a couple of woodburning stoves; to be sure of a table you must arrive promptly as they don't take reservations. Generous helpings of reasonably priced food include sandwiches or filled pitta breads, home-made soup (£3.25), country-style pâté (£4.75), home-made tagliatelle with bacon, mushrooms and cream (£5.95), aubergine tagine with dates and almonds with couscous (£7.25), bacon, leek and cider pudding (£7.50), teriyaki-style chicken (£7.95), lamb chops with rosemary and red wine, beef and Guinness pie or fresh cod fillet with lemon and parsley butter (£8.50), locally reared sirloin steak (£8.95), and puddings such as treacle tart with clotted cream, lemon tart or fresh fruit crumble (from £3.50); winter Sunday lunch. Well kept Exmoor Ale, Smiles Best, and Wadworths 6X on handpump, farm cider, and country wines; cribbage, dominoes, and alley skittles; there's a bright no smoking little family room. Seats outside in the immaculate garden which runs down to a swift clear stream. This is a lovely village. *(Recommended by Anne and Paul Horscraft, Louise English, P and J Shapley, Paul Hopton, the Didler, Brian and Bett Cox)*

Unique (Enterprise) ~ Lease Russell and Jane Deary ~ Real ale ~ Bar food ~ (01984) 656217 ~ Children in family room if well behaved ~ Dogs welcome ~ Open 11.30-2.30, 6.30-11; 12-2.30, 7-10.30 Sun

NORTH CURRY ST3225 Map 1

Bird in Hand

Queens Square; off A378 (or A358) E of Taunton

This is a well run village pub with a good welcome from the friendly landlord and a very pleasant, cheerful atmosphere. The bustling but cosy main bar has some nice old pews, settles, benches, and old yew tables on the flagstones, original beams and timbers, and some locally woven willow work; cricketing memorabilia, and a log fire in the inglenook fireplace. From an interesting menu, the well liked meals might include sandwiches (from £2.95), baked garlic field mushrooms topped with grilled goats cheese (£5.25), ploughman's (£5.50), moules marinière (£6.50), pasta carbonara or very good fishcakes (£6.95), winter steak in Guinness pie (£7.25), winter game casserole (£7.95), steaks (from £11.95), fresh fish from Brixham and Plymouth twice a week such as salmon with hollandaise sauce (£12.95), and halibut fillet with seafood sauce or moroccan-style bass (£14.95), venison in port and orange sauce (£14.95), and home-made puddings such as ginger and lime crunch pie with stem ginger ice-cream (£4.50); Sunday roast lunch. More formal dining is available in the separate no smoking restaurant area. Well kept Otter Ale and a couple of guests like Butcombe Gold and Exmoor Gold on handpump, Rich's farm cider, and half a dozen wines by the glass; good service. Piped music and fruit machine. *(Recommended by JCW, Dr and Mrs A J Edwards, Ian Phillips, Dr Martin Owton, Michael Butler, John and Gloria Isaacs)*

Free house ~ Licensee James Mogg ~ Real ale ~ Bar food ~ Restaurant ~ (01823) 490248 ~ Children in eating area of bar and restaurant ~ Dogs allowed in bar ~ Open 12-3(4 Sat), 6(7 Sat)-11; 12-3, 7-10.30 Sun

OAKE ST1526 Map 1

Royal Oak

Hillcommon, N; B3227 W of Taunton

You're quite likely to find customers waiting in the car park for this neatly kept country pub to open, so it's best to arrive early to be sure of a seat. The spacious bar has several separate-seeming areas around the central servery; on the left is a little tiled fireplace, with a big woodburning stove on the other side. The windows have smart curtains, there are plenty of fresh flowers, and lots of brasses on the beams and walls. At the back is a long dining area which leads out to a pleasant sheltered garden. Tables are candlelit in the evenings. Most of the pub is no smoking and on carvery days, it is totally no smoking. Well kept Archers Village Bitter, Badger Tanglefoot, and Exmoor Gold on handpump and six wines by the glass; cheerful service. At lunchtime, bar food includes sandwiches (on brown or white bread, in a tortilla wrap or a ciabatta roll, from £3.25), filled baked potatoes (from £3.25), ploughman's (£5.95), and ham and eggs or four-egg omelettes (£6.95), with evening choices such as home-made soup (£3.50), brandied chicken liver pâté (£4.50), king prawns in filo pastry (£5.50), a curry of the day (£7.25), steak and mushroom in ale pie (£7.50), good sausages with spring onion crushed potato (£8.75), lemon and pink peppercorn chicken (£9.75), steaks (from £9.95), and lots of home-made daily specials such as bacon-wrapped chicken fillet with fresh parmesan, home-cooked ham and a roasted cherry tomato and basil pesto (£12.75), seared haunch of venison in a port, summer berry and caramelised orange sauce (£13.95), and hand-dived scallops and fillets of john dory poached in a white wine, cucumber, tarragon and cream sauce (£14.95); there's a lunchtime carvery on Sunday, Tuesday and Thursday (£6.95; OAP £5.95 including a free pudding). Skittle alley in winter, and piped music. No children inside. More reports please. *(Recommended by Bob and Margaret Holder, Andy and Jill Kassube)*

Free house ~ Licensees John and Judy Phripp ~ Real ale ~ Bar food (12-2.30, 6.30-9.30 (10 Fri and Sat)) ~ (01823) 400295 ~ Open 11-2.30(3 Sat), 6-11; 12-3, 6.30-10.30 Sun; closed 25 Dec

PITNEY ST4428 Map 1

Halfway House

Just off B3153 W of Somerton

Although often packed out and perhaps a bit smoky, this old-fashioned pub has a really good friendly atmosphere, quite a mix of customers, and a fine range of up to ten real ales. The three rooms all have roaring log fires and a homely feel underlined by a profusion of books, maps, and newspapers. As well as six regular ales tapped from the cask such as Butcombe Bitter, Cotleigh Tawny, Hop Back Summer Lightning, and Teignworthy Reel Ale, there might be guests like Archers Golden, Hop Back Crop Circle, and RCH Pitchfork. They also have 20 or so bottled beers from Belgium and other countries, Wilkins's farm cider, and quite a few malt whiskies; cribbage and dominoes. Good simple filling food includes sandwiches (from £2.95; smoked salmon and cream cheese £3.95), soup (£3.25), filled baked potatoes (from £2.95), and a fine ploughman's with home-made pickle (from £4.95). In the evening they do about half a dozen home-made curries (from £7.95). There are tables outside. *(Recommended by Paul Hopton, Theo, Anne and Jane Gaskin, the Didler, Brian Pearson, Andrea Rampley, Guy Vowles, Sarah and Anthony Bussy, Bruce Bird, Alan and Paula McCully, OPUS)*

Free house ~ Licensees Julian and Judy Lichfield ~ Real ale ~ Bar food (not Sun) ~ (01458) 252513 ~ Children in eating area of bar and restaurant ~ Dogs welcome ~ Open 11.30-3, 5.30-11; 12-3.30, 7-10.30 Sun; closed evening 25 Dec

PORTISHEAD ST4777 Map 1

Windmill

3.7 miles from M5 junction 19; A369 into town, then follow 'Sea Front' sign off left and into Nore Road

This is quite different from most of the pubs in this book, and started life as a golf club-house but re-opened as a three-level all-day family dining pub. One of its big pluses is that in fine weather there's a marvellous view over the Bristol Channel to Newport and Cardiff (with the bridges on the right), from the wall of picture windows on the top and bottom floors. The bottom floor is a simple easy-going no smoking family area, the top one a shade more elegant with its turkey carpet, muted green and cream wallpaper and dark panelled dado. The middle floor, set back from here, is quieter and (with its black-painted ceiling boards) more softly lit. A third of the building is no smoking; fruit machine. To eat, you find a numbered table, present yourself at the order desk (by a slimline pudding show-cabinet), pay for your order, and return to the table with a tin (well, stainless-steel) tray of cutlery, condiments and sauce packets. It works well: the good value generous food then comes quickly, and might include home-made soup (£3.25), grilled goats cheese with chilli jam (£3.45), sandwiches (from £3.50), filled baked potatoes (from £3.95), ploughman's (£4.95), chicken, ham and leek suet pudding (£6.95), spinach and red pepper lasagne (£7.50), home-made steak and mushroom in ale pie (£7.75), steaks (from £11.65), and puddings such as fruit crumble or belgian chocolate torte (£3.75); there are dishes for smaller appetites (from £3.25) and early bird offers. Unexpectedly, they have six quickly changing real ales on handpump, such as Bass, Butcombe Gold, Courage Best, RCH Pitchfork, and two guest beers on handpump; Thatcher's cider. Out on the seaward side are picnic-sets on three tiers of lantern-lit terrace, with flower plantings and a play area. *(Recommended by S H Godsell, Dr and Mrs M E Wilson, W R Miller, Tom Evans, Dr and Mrs A K Clarke, John A Barker, S Fysh, Ian Phillips, Emma Kingdon, J H Bescoby, Comus and Sarah Elliott, P Price)*

Free house ~ Licensee J S Churchill ~ Real ale ~ Bar food (all day) ~ (01275) 843677 ~ Children in eating area of bar and family room ~ Dogs allowed in bar ~ Open 11-11; 12-10.30 Sun

ROWBERROW ST4558 Map 1

Swan

Village signposted off A38 ¾ mile S of junction with A368

After enjoying one of the surrounding walks, it's pleasant to sit with a drink by the pond in the attractive garden of this sizeable olde-worlde pub; tethering post for horses. Inside, there are low beams, some stripped stone, warm red décor, comic hunting and political prints, an ancient longcase clock, and huge log fires. Lunchtime sandwiches (from £2.45; baguettes from £4.40), ploughman's (from £4.95), and filled baked potatoes (from £5.50), as well as more substantial dishes such as ham and eggs (£6.50), vegetable casserole (£7.45), pesto chicken (£8.25), beef in ale pie (£8.45), and steaks (from £12.25). Well kept Bass, and Butcombe Bitter, Blond and Gold on handpump, eight wines by the glass, and Thatcher's cider. Note that they are very firm about keeping children out. More reports please. *(Recommended by Bob and Margaret Holder, Gaynor Gregory, Matthew Shackle, K H Frostick, Michael Doswell, Lucien Perring, Alan and Paula McCully, Comus and Sarah Elliott, MRSM)*

Butcombe ~ Managers Elaine and Robert Flaxman ~ Real ale ~ Bar food ~ (01934) 852371 ~ Dogs welcome ~ Open 12-3, 6-11; 12-3, 7-10.30 Sun; closed evenings 25 and 26 Dec and 1 Jan

'Children welcome' means the pubs says it lets children inside without any special restriction; readers have found that some may impose an evening time limit – please tell us if you find this.

SHEPTON MONTAGUE ST6731 Map 2

Montague Inn

Village signposted just off A359 Bruton—Castle Cary

The rooms in this popular little country pub are simply but tastefully furnished with stripped wooden tables, kitchen chairs and a log fire in the attractive inglenook fireplace, and there's a no smoking candlelit restaurant – which has french windows overlooking the gardens. Using fresh organic produce where possible, the interesting food might include home-made soup or chicken liver pâté (£5), good antipasto (£7), king prawns in garlic butter or spinach, mushroom and brie lasagne (£8), halibut steaks with salsa verde, pork medallions with aubergine caviar and a shallot and bacon cream sauce or chicken breast stuffed with mozzarella, wrapped in parma ham and served on wilted spinach (all £12), duck breast with cherry and brandy sauce (£13), roast local lamb with port and redcurrant sauce (£15), and puddings (from £4); friendly service. If you do not pre-book a table, you may not get served. Well kept Greene King IPA and a guest tapped from the cask, a few wines by the glass, and local cider; shove-ha'penny. The pretty back garden and terrace have good views. *(Recommended by S G N Bennett, DF, NF, Brian and Anita Randall, Paul and Annette Hallett, John A Barker, John Close, Colin and Janet Roe, Des and Olga Hall)*

Free house ~ Licensees Julian and Linda Bear ~ Bar food (not Sun evening, Mon) ~ Restaurant ~ (01749) 813213 ~ Children in eating area of bar and restaurant ~ Dogs allowed in bedrooms ~ Open 11-2.30, 6-11; 12-2.30 Sun; closed Sun evening, Mon ~ Bedrooms: /£70S

STANTON WICK ST6162 Map 2

Carpenters Arms

Village signposted off A368, just W of junction with A37 S of Bristol

Run by a friendly and helpful licensee, this long and low tile-roofed inn is neatly kept and popular. The no smoking Coopers Parlour is on the right and has one or two beams, seats around heavy tables, and attractive curtains and plants in the windows; on the angle between here and the bar area there's a fat woodburning stove in an opened-through corner fireplace. The bar has wood-backed built-in wall seats and some leather fabric-cushioned stools, stripped stone walls, and a big log fire. Diners are encouraged to step down into a snug inner room (lightened by mirrors in arched 'windows'), or to go round to the sturdy tables angling off on the right. Enjoyable bar food includes sandwiches, home-made soup (£3.95), chicken liver and mushroom pâté with spiced apple chutney (£5.50), daily specials such as salad of warm spiced sausages and new potatoes dressed with thyme scented oil (£4.95), mussels in red thai curry sauce or smoked salmon with chive crème fraîche (£5.95), beer battered cod or seared fillet of local trout with chervil butter (£10.95), and roasted guinea fowl on casserole of root vegetables and ale (£12.95), and puddings like apple and plum crumble or honey, vanilla and rosemary crème brûlée (£4.25). Well kept Bass, Butcombe Bitter, Courage Best, and Wadworths 6X on handpump, ten wines by the glass, and a dozen malt whiskies; fruit machine and TV. The inn is set in peaceful countryside with pretty flowerbeds, lovely hanging baskets and tubs, and picnic-sets on the front terrace. *(Recommended by Ken Flawn, Dr T E Hothersall, Tom Evans, Julia and Richard Tredgett, Dr and Mrs A K Clarke, David and Wendy Puttock, Mr and Mrs Johnson-Poensgen, John Mitchell, M G Hart, Mr and Mrs R J Weller)*

Buccaneer Holdings ~ Manager Simon Pledge ~ Real ale ~ Bar food (till 10) ~ Restaurant ~ (01761) 490202 ~ Children in eating area of bar and restaurant ~ Dogs allowed in bar ~ Pianist Fri/Sat evenings ~ Open 11-11; 12-10.30 Sun; closed evenings 25 and 26 Dec and 1 Jan ~ Bedrooms: £64.50B/£89.50B

The knife-and-fork award distinguishes pubs where the food is of exceptional quality.

STOKE ST GREGORY ST3527 Map 1

Rose & Crown

Woodhill; follow North Curry signpost off A378 by junction with A358 – keep on to Stoke, bearing right in centre, passing church and follow lane for ½ mile

Bustling and friendly, this popular country pub has been in the same family for 26 years. The cosy bar is decorated in a pleasant stable theme: dark wooden loose-box partitions for some of the interestingly angled nooks and alcoves, lots of brasses and bits on the low beams and joists, stripped stonework, a wonky floor, and appropriate pictures including a highland pony carrying a stag; many of the wildlife paintings on the walls are the work of the landlady, and there's an 18th-c glass-covered well in one corner. The two rooms of the dining area lead off here with lots of country prints and paintings of hunting scenes, animals, and birds on the walls, more horsebrasses, jugs and mugs hanging from the ceiling joists, and candles in bottles on all tables. Generous helpings of enjoyable bar food (slightly more expensive in the evenings) include home-made soup (£3.50), lunchtime sandwiches (from £3.75) and ploughman's (from £4.50), local home-cooked smoked ham and eggs (£5.50), home-made steak and kidney pie (£6.50), salmon fishcakes (£7.50), lambs liver and bacon or scrumpy chicken (£8), vegetable stroganoff (£8.50), steaks (from £10), grilled brixham plaice fillets (£12.50), grilled skate wings (£13.50), and puddings such as rhubarb crumble or banoffi pie (£3.25). Plentiful breakfasts, and Sunday roast (£6.75); speedy, cheerful service, even when busy. The restaurants are no smoking. Well kept Exmoor Ale and Gold, and a guest such as Archers Village Bitter on handpump, and decent wines. Under cocktail parasols by an apple tree on the sheltered front terrace are some picnic-sets; summer barbecues. The pub is in an interesting Somerset Levels village with willow beds still supplying the two basket works. *(Recommended by Mike Gorton, Richard and Margaret Peers, Mrs J L Wyatt, Ian Phillips, Alan and Jill Bull, Mark and Amanda Sheard, Theo, Anne and Jane Gaskin, Mrs A P Lee, John and Fiona Merritt, Bob and Margaret Holder, JWAC, DRH and KLH, Michael Doswell, Michael Rowse, Rev D E and Mrs J A Shapland, Liz and Alun Jones, P and J Shapley, Mr and Mrs Colin Roberts)*

Free house ~ Licensees Stephen, Sally, Richard and Leonie Browning ~ Real ale ~ Bar food ~ Restaurant ~ (01823) 490296 ~ Children in restaurant ~ Dogs allowed in bar ~ Open 11.30-3, 6.30-11; 12-3, 7-10.30 Sun; closed evening 25 Dec ~ Bedrooms: £36.50(£46.50B)/£53(£73B)

TAUNTON ST2224 Map 1

Masons Arms

Magdalene Street, facing St Mary's church

This early 19th-c town pub owes its appeal to its genial long-serving chef/landlord – a proper guv'nor of the best traditional school. He keeps his Otter real ale well, with a couple of guest beers on handpump such as Exe Valley Dob's Best Bitter and Gribble Fursty Ferret, and has decent wines by the glass, and some interesting spirits. His food from the front servery is tempting, too, and might include filled rolls (£1.90), soups like spiced red lentil or local brie and broccoli (£2.95), home-made pâté or game terrine, hot home-made dishes such as lambs kidneys in rich port sauce, beef in ale, fish pie or baked monkfish on creamed parsnip potato (£5.50-£7.50), well liked winter curries, and steaks that customers cook themselves on a hot stone placed in front of them (from £9). The long room is divided in two by a big brick chimney-breast with a coal-effect gas fire (there's a second fire at the far end), is furnished in the usual pubby way, and has attractive prints and photographs of Taunton as well as some sporting ephemera, trophies and decorations including a huge cricketing painting (a veteran TV may emerge for cricket or rugby matches). The atmosphere is relaxed and chatty, and a wall rack holds broadsheet dailies; cribbage, dominoes and skittle alley. The pub is in a quiet and pleasant spot opposite an attractive church, and the public car park beyond is useful, if the nearby street parking spaces are all taken. They have a self-catering holiday flat. No children inside. *(Recommended by Brian and Li Jobson, Douglas Allen, Bob and Margaret Holder, Darrell Bendall, Joe Green, Guy Vowles)*

Free house ~ Licensee Jeremy Leyton ~ Bar food (12-2.15, 5.30-9.15; not Sun or bank hols) ~ (01823) 288916 ~ Dogs allowed in bar ~ Open 10.30-3, 5-11; 10.30-11 Sat; 12-4 Sun; closed Sun evening, 25 Dec

TRISCOMBE ST1535 Map 1

Blue Ball

Village signposted off A358 Crowcombe—Bagborough; turn off opposite sign to youth hostel; OS Sheet 181 map reference 155355

New licensees have taken over this rather smart place and opened up a couple of bedrooms – one has an inglenook fireplace. The inn is on the first floor of a lovely 15th-c thatched stone-built former coaching stables. The long, low building slopes gently down on three levels, each with its own fire, and cleverly divided into seating by hand-cut beech partitions. Well kept Cotleigh Tawny, and guests such as Exmoor Gold, St Austell HSD, and Sharps Doom Bar on handpump, and eight house wines by the glass. There's quite an emphasis on the interesting food which might include lunchtime filled crusty rolls or white onion and smoked haddock soup (£4.50), duck and pigeon terrine with apricot chutney (£6.50), baked goats cheese and fig parcel with port and walnut oil dressing (£5.95), ploughman's with local cheeses (£6.95), cod in beer batter (£8.50), grilled mediterranean vegetables with mozzarella and balsamic dressing (£9.95), chicken breast with wild mushroom and asparagus risotto (£12.95), duck breast and confit leg with onion marmalade and orange butter sauce (£14.50), wild bass fillet with niçoise vegetables and chorizo dressing (£16.95), and puddings like chocolate and pistachio bleeding heart, italian lemon tart or bread and butter pudding (£4.50). All dining areas are no smoking. They have two friendly springer spaniels and two pure white cats. The decking at the top of the woodside, terraced garden makes the most of the views, and there's a new terrace as well. More reports on the new regime, please.
(Recommended by Jay Smith, Gaynor Gregory, Basil and Sylvia Walden, Anne and Paul Horscraft)

Free house ~ Licensees Sharon Murdoch and Peter Alcroft ~ Real ale ~ Bar food (not 25 Dec or evening 26 Dec) ~ Restaurant ~ (01984) 618242 ~ Children in eating area of bar and restaurant ~ Dogs allowed in bar ~ Open 12-3, 7-11; 12-11 Sat; 12-10.30 Sun; 12-3, 7-11 winter Sat, 12-3, 7.10.30 Sun in winter ~ Bedrooms: /£60B

WELLS ST5545 Map 2

City Arms

High Street

To get to this pub, you walk through a lovely cobbled courtyard with metal seats and tables, trees and flowers in pots, and attractive side verandah. It's a bustling place with a good mix of both locals and visitors and the staff are efficient and cheerful. They keep six real ales on handpump: Butcombe Bitter, Gold, and Blond, Greene King Abbot, Sharps Doom Bar, and Wadworths IPA. Also, a dozen wines by the glass, 25 malt whiskies, and maybe farm cider. Rather like a cellar bar, there are arched doorways, cushioned mate's chairs, a nice old black settle, and a Regency-style settee and a couple of sofas; up a step is a room with big tables and solid chairs, and beyond that, a separate bar with neat sturdy settles forming booths around tables; plenty of Victorian and Victorian-style engravings. One area is no smoking; the fine open-beamed restaurant is upstairs. Good bar food includes sandwiches, vegetable soup (£2.95), chicken liver pâté (£3.95), fresh pasta with toppings such as tomato, basil or parmesan or carbonara (£4.95; large £6.95), salmon and spinach fishcakes (£4.95; large £7.95), ham and eggs or meaty or vegetarian burgers (£6.95), chicken curry (£7.95), fillet of pork stuffed with prunes with an apricot liqueur sauce (£9.25), calves liver with bacon and onions, organic salmon and leek in puff pastry with a white wine and dill sauce or 10oz aberdeen angus rump steak (£9.95), and puddings (£3.25); piped music. It does get crowded at peak times. *(Recommended by Sarah Money, Paul Hopton, Roger and Anne Newbury, Jane Taylor, David Dutton, Darly Graton, Graeme Gulibert, Geoff Calcott, Gwyn Jones,*

Dr and Mrs A K Clarke, Mr Williams, Richard and Margaret Peers, David Carr, Joyce and Maurice Cottrell, OPUS)

Free house ~ Licensee Jim Hardy ~ Real ale ~ Bar food (all day until 10(9 Sun) ~ Restaurant ~ (01749) 673916 ~ Children in family room ~ Dogs allowed in bar ~ Open 9-11; 9-10.30 Sun

Crown

Market Place

Despite this former coaching inn's age, the various bar areas have a very clean, contemporary feel, with the walls painted white or blue, light wooden flooring, and plenty of matching chairs and cushioned wall benches; up a step is a comfortable area with a sofa, and newspapers. A sunny back room (where children tend to go) has an exposed stone fireplace, GWR prints, and a couple of fruit machines and TV; it opens on to a small courtyard with a few tables. It's a useful place to pop in for coffee, lunch or afternoon tea. Reliable food at lunchtime includes soup (£3.75), sandwiches and panini (from £3.75), battered cod (£5.75), and ham, egg and rösti, lasagne or greek salad (£5.95), with evening choices such as chicken liver and mushroom pâté with caramelised onion jam (£4.95), mussels steamed with coconut cream, lemon grass, lime and mild chillis (£5.95), thai red vegetable curry (£8.95), supreme of corn-fed chicken stuffed with wild mushroom mousse (£9.95), and chargrilled 10oz rib-eye steak (£14.50); puddings like steamed walnut, date and stem ginger pudding or double chocolate torte with Kahlua (£4.25). B&T Dragonslayer, Butcombe Bitter, and Moles Best Bitter on handpump, and eight wines by the glass. Part of the restaurant and part of the Penn Bar are no smoking; piped music. Though there are usually lots of tourists (William Penn is said to have preached from a window here), there are generally a few young locals too. More reports please. *(Recommended by Mr and Mrs Richard Hanks, David Carr)*

Free house ~ Licensee Adrian Lawrence ~ Real ale ~ Bar food ~ Restaurant ~ (01749) 673457 ~ Children welcome ~ Dogs allowed in bedrooms ~ Open 11-11; 12-10.30 Sun ~ Bedrooms: £50S/£80B

WINSFORD SS9034 Map 1

Royal Oak

In Exmoor National Park, village signposted from A396 about 10 miles S of Dunster

There's usually a good mix of customers in this civilised and rather smart thatched inn which creates a pleasant, chatty atmosphere. The attractively furnished lounge bar has a cushioned big bay-window seat from which you can look across the road towards the village green and foot and packhorse bridges over the River Winn, tartan-cushioned bar stools by the panelled counter (above which hang horsebrasses and pewter tankards), armed and cushioned windsor chairs set around little wooden tables, and a gas-fired stove in the big stone hearth. Another similar bar offers more eating space with built-in wood-panelled seats creating booths, fresh flowers, and country prints; there are several pretty and comfortable lounges, and three no smoking rooms. Served by friendly staff, bar snacks might include lunchtime sandwiches (one and a half rounds with salad and crisps from £4.50) and ploughman's (from £6.50), as well as home-made soup (£3.95), home-made chicken liver pâté with red onion marmalade or baked potato filled with cheese and onion (£5.50), lambs liver with onion gravy (£8.50), aubergine and courgette lasagne glazed with goats cheese or braised lamb shank (£8.95), steak and kidney pudding in rich ale sauce (£9.25), fillet of scottish salmon with cherry tomatoes and a fresh coriander and herb oil (£9.95), daily specials like smoked salmon and prawn tian with citrus dressing (£6.25) or pork steak with a rich cider and apple sauce (£9.75), and home-made puddings such as treacle tart or banoffi pie (£3.75). Well kept Brakspears Bitter and Butcombe Bitter on handpump; piped music. *(Recommended by Tracey and Stephen Groves, Andy and Jill Kassube, Mike and Mary Carter, Peter Abbott, Jay Smith, Patrick and Phillipa Vickery, Michael and Margaret Slater, Lloyd Moon)*

Free house ~ Licensee Charles Steven ~ Real ale ~ Bar food ~ Restaurant ~ (01643) 851455 ~ Children in eating area of bar and restaurant ~ Dogs allowed in bar ~ Open 11-2.30, 6.30-11; 12-3, 7-11 Sun ~ Bedrooms: /£116B

WITHYPOOL SS8435 Map 1

Royal Oak 🍷 🛏

Village signposted off B3233

Even when this popular place is really busy (which it often is) the staff remain helpful and friendly. The beamed lounge bar has a fine raised log fireplace, comfortably cushioned wall seating and slat-backed chairs, and stags' heads, stuffed fish, several fox masks, sporting prints and paintings, and various copper and brass ornaments on its walls. The locals' bar (named after the barman Jake who has been here for over 26 years) has some old oak tables, and plenty of character. Good bar food includes nice lunchtime sandwiches (tuna and red onion mayonnaise, honey roast ham with home-made tomato chutney or prawn and smoked salmon with lime mayonnaise £4.95), duck liver parfait with caramelised figs (£6.25), seared scallops with chorizo and chive oil (£7.25), pasta with free range chicken breast, asparagus and cherry tomatoes in a cream and white wine sauce (£11.75), wild mushroom risotto with rocket pesto (£12.95), and fillet of beef with sweet potato wedges, green beans and tarragon jus (£16.25), with daily specials such as savoy cabbage and bacon soup (£3.95), sautéed duck fillet and orange salad with an orange and mustard dressing (£4.95), home-cooked honey roast ham with free range fried eggs (£8.25), and whole torbay sole with lemon butter (£11.95). The restaurant is no smoking. Well kept Exmoor Ale and Gold on handpump, quite a few malt whiskies, and a decent wine list. There are wooden benches on the terrace, and just up the road, some grand views from Winsford Hill. The River Barle runs through the village itself, with pretty bridleways following it through a wooded combe further upstream. R. D. Blackmore stayed here while writing *Lorna Doone*. *(Recommended by Bob and Margaret Holder, John Brightley, Colin and Stephanie McFie, Tracey and Stephen Groves, P R Morley, Jay Smith, Patrick and Phillipa Vickery, C S McVeigh, Andrea Rampley, Brian and Anita Randall)*

Free house ~ Licensee Gail Sloggett ~ Real ale ~ Bar food (12-2, 6.30-9.30) ~ (01643) 831506 ~ Children in bottom bar and restaurant ~ Dogs allowed in bar and bedrooms ~ Open 11(12 Sun)-11 ~ Bedrooms: /£100B

WOOKEY ST5145 Map 2

Burcott

B3139 W of Wells

Set in a pretty village opposite Burcott Hill historic water mill, this is an old-fashioned, neatly kept little roadside pub with chatty locals and two simply furnished small front bar rooms that are connected but different in character. There's a square corner bar counter in the lounge, fresh flowers at either end of the mantelpiece above the tiny stone fireplace, Parker-Knollish brocaded chairs around a couple of tables, and high bar stools; the other bar has beams (some willow pattern plates on one), a solid settle by the window and a high backed old pine settle by one wall, cushioned mate's chairs and fresh flowers on the mix of nice old pine tables, old-fashioned oil-type wall lamps, and a hunting horn on the bressumer above the fireplace. A little no smoking room on the right has darts, shove-ha'penny, cribbage and dominoes, neat built-in wall seats, and small framed advertisements for Schweppes, Coke, Jennings and Oakhill, and there's a roomy back no smoking restaurant with black joists, stripped stone walls and sea-green check tablecloths; piped music. Tasty bar food includes filled baked potatoes (from £3.95), creamy garlic mushrooms (£4.25), sandwiches (from £4.25 for one and a half rounds), ploughman's (£5.25), ham and eggs (£6.25), vegetable and cashew nut bake (£6.75), home-made steak in ale pie (£7.45), roasted duck breast flamed in whisky with a fresh orange marmalade sauce (£10.45), steaks (from £10.95), and daily specials such as rack of lamb with juniper sauce (£9.95), grilled trio of fish in horseradish sauce (£11.95), king prawns in garlic butter (£14.45). Well kept Hop Back Summer Lightning, RCH Pitchfork, and Burcott Ale brewed for the pub by Sharps on handpump, and several wines by the glass. The window boxes and tubs in front of the building are pretty in summer, and the sizeable garden is well spread and has picnic-sets, plenty of small trees and shrubs, and Mendip Hill views; there's a paddock beyond. *(Recommended by Comus and Sarah Elliott, Hugh Roberts, Phil and Sally Gorton, Mrs Louise Wilkes, Ian and Nita Cooper, Tom Evans, Alan and Paula McCully)*

Free house ~ Licensees Ian and Anne Stead ~ Real ale ~ Bar food (12-2, 6.30-9.30; not Sun or Mon evenings) ~ Restaurant ~ (01749) 673874 ~ Children in straightforward family room ~ Open 11.30-2.30, 6-11; 12-3, 6-11 Sat; 12-3, 7-10.30 Sun; closed 25 and 26 Dec, 1 Jan

LUCKY DIP

Besides the fully inspected pubs, you might like to try these Lucky Dips recommended to us and described by readers (if you do, please send us reports: www.goodguides.co.uk).

ABBOTS LEIGH ST5473

☆ *George* [A369, between M5 junction 19 and Bristol]: Main-road dining pub currently doing well, tidy and comfortable, with attractively presented reasonably priced food from snacks up, plenty of blackboard specials, well kept ales inc Marstons Pedigree, friendly staff, two log fires; no children, good-sized enclosed garden *(LYM, Rex Miller, Donald Godden)*

ALCOMBE SS9845

Britannia [Manor Rd]: Busy friendly local with Courage Bitter and Best and a guest beer, wide food choice reasonably priced, cosy lounge, pool in public bar, dining room; skittle alley, enclosed garden, four bedrooms with own bathrooms *(Jim Abbott, R M Corlett)*

ASHCOTT ST4336

Ashcott Inn [A39 W of Glastonbury]: Stripped-stone beamed bar, mix of old-fashioned and newer furniture, woodburner in big inglenook, usual food from sandwiches up (all day in summer), partly no smoking restaurant, real ales such as Butcombe, Fullers London Pride and Otter, decent wines; quiet piped music; skittle alley, tables on terrace and in garden with adventure play areas, open all day summer *(LYM, Dr and Mrs C W Thomas, MRSM)*

☆ *Pipers* [A39/A361, SE of village]: Reliable dining pub with large welcoming beamed lounge, well kept ales such as Greene King Old Speckled Hen, Smiles, John Smiths, Tetleys, Wadworths 6X and Youngers, Addlestone's cider, wide choice of decent reasonably priced food from sandwiches to steaks inc children's, prompt helpful friendly service, woodburner, leather armchairs, pictures for sale and potted plants, prettily set no smoking beamed dining area; unobtrusive piped music; pleasant roadside garden *(Dr and Mrs C W Thomas, Anne and David Robinson)*

ASHILL ST3217

Ashill Inn: Family pub with enjoyable bar food, well kept beers, popular carvery Fri night and Sun lunchtime, welcoming licensees; comfortable bedrooms *(Mrs B Larcombe, A J and C D Stodgell, B Kent)*

BATH ST7564

Ale House [York St]: Cosy and relaxed city-centre local with big windows to street, well kept Courage, Fullers London Pride and Charles Wells Bombardier, flame-effect fire, food in cellar bar, more seating upstairs, Bath RFC memorabilia *(Dr and Mrs M E Wilson, Dr and Mrs A K Clarke, Colin and Peggy Wilshire)*

Bell [Walcot St]: Long narrow studenty pub, new landlord keeping up tradition of over half a dozen well kept changing ales mainly from small breweries, dark ceiling, lots of pump clips and notices, good value baguettes, bar billiards; calm at lunchtime, packed and lively with loud piped music evenings, frequent live music *(R Huggins, D Irving, E McCall, T McLean, Dr and Mrs A K Clarke)*

Boathouse [Newbridge Rd]: Large unpubby but attractive riverside establishment nr Kennet & Avon marina on outskirts, rugs on wooden floor, apple-theme and riverside decorations, good value food from filled ciabattas to steaks and restaurant dishes, efficient courteous service, decent house wines, Greene King IPA and Old Speckled Hen; children very welcome, wicker furniture and potted plants in conservatory on lower level, picnic-sets out in neat garden with labelled herbs and steps up to waterside balcony *(Anne and David Robinson, Dr and Mrs M E Wilson, Dr and Mrs A K Clarke)*

☆ *Coeur de Lion* [Northumberland Pl; off High St by W H Smith]: Tiny single-room pub, not smart but perhaps Bath's prettiest, cosy and friendly, with well kept ales such as Adnams and Jennings, candles and log-effect gas fire, good mulled wine at Christmas, lunchtime filled rolls in summer; may be piped music, can get a bit smoky, stairs to lavatories; open all day, tables out in charming flower-filled flagstoned pedestrian alley *(LYM, Rona Murdoch, the Didler, Dr and Mrs*

M E Wilson, Patrick Hancock, Dr and Mrs A K Clarke, R Huggins, D Irving, E McCall, T McLean, Mike Pugh)

☆ ***Cross Keys*** [Midford Rd (B3110)]: Well refurbished dining lounge with smarter end restaurant (best to book, high chairs for children), good cheap food cooked to order from good sandwiches (home-baked bread), home-made burgers and sausages up inc popular pies and great choice of puddings, real ales such as Everards, friendly service, locals' bar; big garden with prettily populated aviary – great attraction for children *(Meg and Colin Hamilton, Francis Johnston)*

Garricks Head [Theatre Royal, St Johns Pl]: Turning out well all round under expert new licensees *(Richard Stancomb)*

George [Bathampton, E of Bath centre, off A36 or (via toll bridge) off A4; Mill Lane]: Big Chef & Brewer dining pub reopened after extensive internal reworking, lots of separate largely no smoking areas up and down, tables overlooking water inside and out on good-sized well organised terraces, wide generally enjoyable blackboard food choice at reasonable prices, well kept Courage and Greene King Old Speckled Hen, good log fires; may be quiet piped jazz *(Dr and Mrs A K Clarke, James Morrell, Meg and Colin Hamilton, Dr and Mrs M E Wilson)*

☆ ***Hop Pole*** [Albion Buildings, Upper Bristol Rd]: Bustling Bath Ales pub, their beers and a guest kept well, farm cider and decent wines by the glass, good if not cheap food (not Sun evening, just popular roasts Sun lunchtime) from sandwiches to steak in bar and former skittle alley restaurant, traditional settles and other pub furniture on bare boards in tastefully reworked rambling linked areas inc no smoking area, no juke box or pool; pleasant back garden with boules, opp Victoria Park with its great play area, open all day Fri-Sun *(Mark o'Sullivan, Colin and Peggy Wilshire, Pamela and Merlyn Horswell, OPUS)*

Olde Farmhouse [Lansdown Rd]: Pleasant setting on hill overlooking Bath, well kept Abbey Bellringer (from neighbouring microbrewery), Butcombe and Wadworths, real fire, perhaps filled cobs, L-shaped parquet-floor bar with wall seats, panelling, stained-glass lamps and bar gantry, big jazz pictures; juke box, big-screen TV; jazz some evenings, open all day *(the Didler, David Carr)*

Pig & Fiddle [Saracen St]: Lively pub with several well kept sensibly priced real ales inc Abbey and Bath, two big open fires, clocks set to different time zones, bare boards and cheery red and yellow walls and ceiling, good value home-made food, steps up to darker bustling servery and little dining area, takeaways too, games area and several TVs; lots of students at night, good piped trendy pop music then; picnic-sets on big heated front terrace *(BB, Dr and Mrs M E Wilson, Dr and Mrs A K Clarke)*

Pulteney Arms [Daniel St/Sutton St]: Small, with well kept Bass, Smiles, Wadworths 6X and a guest tapped from the cask, capacious three-sided bar counter, food inc good big chip baps, jug collection, lots of rugby posters and Bath RFC memorabilia; unobtrusive piped music; pavement tables *(Pete Baker, Dr and Mrs A K Clarke, Patrick Hancock)*

Richmond Arms [Richmond Pl, off Lansdown Rd]: Small 18th-c house converted into two-room pub off the tourist track, bare boards, clean mellow colours, pine tables and chairs, good imaginative food, well kept Bass and Butcombe, good wine choice, friendly staff, uncluttered décor inc some aboriginal artefacts and pictures; tables in enclosed pretty front garden *(David Carr)*

☆ ***Salamander*** [John St]: Traditional pub tied to Bath Ales, their full range and guest beers kept well, good friendly service, bare boards and black woodwork, three rooms inc no smoking, no pool, juke box or machines; upstairs is open-kitchen restaurant with good sensibly priced fresh food, decent wines *(Dr and Mrs M E Wilson, Geoff and Jan Dawson, Clive Hilton, Dr and Mrs A K Clarke, James Morrell, Barry and Anne)*

Sam Weller [Upper Borough Walls]: Recently cleaned up under friendly and enthusiastic young management, tasty generous food, well kept changing ales, improved wine choice at sensible prices, no smoking area *(Colin and Peggy Wilshire, Dr and Mrs M E Wilson, Jennifer Collings)*

BATHFORD ST7866

Crown [Bathford Hill, towards Bradford-on-Avon, by Batheaston roundabout and bridge]: Cheerful family pub, several distinct but linked areas inc no smoking garden room, good log fire, interesting fairly priced food, frequent bargains, well kept real ales, decent wines; piped music may obtrude, bar on right with games and machines; tables on terrace, nice garden *(Dr and Mrs A K Clarke, LYM, Meg and Colin Hamilton)*

BECKINGTON ST8051

☆ ***Woolpack*** [off A36 Bath—Warminster]: Well refurbished old inn with imaginative and well prepared if not cheap food, well kept Greene King ales, decent wines, helpful staff, big log fire and candlelit tables in flagstoned bar, smarter attractive no smoking dining room and conservatory; children welcome, comfortable period bedrooms with own bathrooms (but avoid the attic), open all day *(Lady Heath, Dr Diana Terry, Tim O'Keefe, LYM, Dr and Mrs M E Wilson, M and D J Hill, Guy Vowles)*

BICKNOLLER ST1139

Bicknoller Inn [Church Lane]: Charming traditional thatched pub nestling below Quantocks, simple flagstoned walkers' bar, lounge and restaurant, enjoyable food from generous baguettes to interesting meals (Tues evening is good fish and chips only – can take away), Palmers BB and Wadworths 6X, local farm cider, friendly staff; attractive village *(Dr D J and Mrs S C Walker)*

BISHOP'S WOOD ST2512

Candlelight [off A303/B3170 S of Taunton]: Roomy yet cosy, wide choice of popular reasonably priced food from sandwiches to bargain wkdy lunches, pleasant dining room, cheerful staff, spotless housekeeping, Butcombe and Otter, no smoking areas *(Bob and Margaret Holder)*

BLAGDON ST5058

New Inn [off A368; Park Lane]: Old-fashioned beamed pub with some comfortable antique settles among more modern furnishings, two inglenook log fires, enjoyable bar food from filled rolls up, no smoking bar and dining area, well kept Butcombe and Wadworths IPA and 6X; piped music, no mobile phones, children or dogs; nice views from tables outside looking down to Blagdon Lake and beyond *(Jane and Graham Rooth, LYM, Stuart Paulley, S H Godsell)*

BLUE ANCHOR ST0243

Smugglers [end of B3191, off A39 E of Minehead]: Mellow building in spectacular clifftop setting, well run split-level hotel bars inc a small beamed and flagstoned cellar, airy flagstoned ground-floor dining room, civilised upper restaurant, good range of food from sandwiches, ciabattas and baked potatoes to steaks (choice depends on which bit you are in), real ales inc Otter, chatty and obliging licensees and pleasant staff, comforting log fires; piped music; children welcome (not in cellar), big trim sheltered garden, comfortable pretty bedrooms, site for touring caravans *(Jenny and Peter Lowater, Derek Whitehouse)*

BRADFORD-ON-TONE ST1722

☆ *White Horse* [fairly nr M5 junction 26, off A38 towards Taunton]: Neatly kept and comfortable stone-built local in quiet village, welcoming newish management, wide choice of enjoyable reasonably priced food in straightforward bar eating area and cheerfully decorated dining room, well kept Badger Tanglefoot and Cotleigh Tawny, decent wines, armchairs by ornate woodburner, hunting cartoons, bar billiards; piped pop music may obtrude; back garden with fairy-lit arbour and picnic-sets on lawn, skittle alley *(Pamela and Merlyn Horswell, Christine and Neil Townend, Bob and Margaret Holder, Frank Willy, BB, Nick and Lynne Carter, Peter and Jean Hoare)*

BRADLEY GREEN ST2438

Malt Shovel [off A39 W of Bridgwater, nr Cannington]: Welcoming beamed main bar with straightforward furniture and woodburner, little beamed snug, no smoking restaurant and family room, well kept Butcombe Bitter, Exmoor Fox and two guest beers, wines by the glass, decent bar food, traditional games and sizeable skittle alley; piped music; children in eating areas, picnic-sets in garden *(LYM, Bruce Bird, Hugh Roberts)*

BRENDON HILLS ST0334

Raleghs Cross [junction B3190 with declassified Elsworthy—Winsford rd]: Isolated upland inn, views to Wales on clear days, good walking country; huge comfortably modernised bar with rows of plush banquettes, back restaurant, wide choice of popular generous food (some tables no smoking), real ales such as Courage Best and Exmoor, efficient service; children in restaurant and family room, no dogs; open all day summer, plenty of tables outside with play area, 17 bedrooms *(LYM, Jim Abbott, Geoff Calcott)*

BRIDGETOWN SS9233

Badgers Holt: Neat simply furnished bar, Badger ales, open fire, friendly landlord, quick service even when busy, well served food from enjoyable baked potatoes to cheap Sun roast, restaurant; tables on small terrace *(Mike Green)*

BRISTOL ST5772

Bag o' Nails [St Georges Rd, Hotwells]: Popular real ale pub so far going on much as before under new landlord, several well kept changing ales such as Bass, Burton Bridge, Wye Valley and Smiles, lots of bottled beers, long bare-boards panelled bar lined with benches and small tables, soft gas lighting, inglenook seat by gas fire, glazed portholes into cellar, old local pictures, good soup and cheeses; piped music *(the Didler, Simon and Amanda Southwell, Ian and Nita Cooper)*

Bar 155 [St Michaels Hill]: Small simple one-room bar/bistro, personal service from friendly licensees, generous good value straightforward pub lunches inc bargain steak; well chosen unobtrusive piped music, can be a bit smoky *(J H Bescoby, James Morrell)*

☆ *Brewery Tap* [Upper Maudlin St/Colston St]: Tap for Smiles brewery (may be moving in 2005), their beers kept well and sensibly priced, also unusual continental bottled ones, interesting unpretentious décor with panelling and bare boards, good chattily relaxed atmosphere even when packed, log fire in no smoking half, good value simple lunches food from filled rolls up, no piped music, popular evening brewery tours; tables on good-sized heated terrace, open all day *(Simon and Amanda Southwell, the Didler, Neville and Anne Morley, Stephen and Jean Curtis, S Fysh, Dr and Mrs A K Clarke, Joan and Michel Hooper-Immins)*

Bridge Inn [Passage St]: Neat little one-bar city pub nr floating harbour, good friendly service, lots of film stills and posters, well kept Bath ales, popular lunchtime snacks *(the Didler)*

Chateau [Park St]: Big busy pub, light and airy, with lots of pictures, open fires, enjoyable home-made lunchtime food (many tables reserved Sat), more limited evening, well kept Smiles and Youngs, good coffee range, roomy back conservatory *(Emma Kingdon)*

☆ *Commercial Rooms* [Corn St]: Good Wetherspoons conversion of impressive former merchants' club, big hall with lofty domed ceiling and snug cubicles along one side, gas lighting, comfortable quieter no smoking room with ornate balcony; wide changing choice of good real ales, food all day inc super granary bread sandwiches, tempting prices, friendly chatty bustle, wind indicator; good location, very busy wknd evenings, side wheelchair access *(Peter Scillitoe, Dr and Mrs A K Clarke, the Didler, Andrew Shore, Maria Williams,*

Tony and Wendy Hobden, Ian and Nita Cooper, Alan and Paula McCully, David Carr)

Cornubia [Temple St]: 18th-c backstreet pub hidden away in concrete jungle, well kept ales such as local Nursery and RCH, interesting bottled beers, farm cider, good value home-cooked food inc Sun roasts, small woody seating areas in oranges, browns and reds; benches outside *(Catherine Pitt, the Didler, Simon and Amanda Southwell, Mike Pugh)*

Cottage [Baltic Wharf, Cumberland Rd]: Attractively converted stone-built and panelled harbour master's office nr Maritime Heritage Centre, fine views of Georgian landmarks and Clifton suspension bridge; comfortable, roomy and civilised, with big helpings of wholesome plain home-made food (can take a while) all day from sandwiches up, well kept ales such as Archers, Flowers IPA and Smiles IPA; can be smoky when busy, piped music; terrace tables, open all day, access through sailing club, on foot along waterfront, or by round-harbour ferry *(Ian Phillips, Peter Scillitoe, Colin and Peggy Wilshire, Roger and Jenny Huggins, Ian and Nita Cooper)*

Highbury Vaults [St Michaels Hill, Cotham]: Nice series of small rooms with old-fashioned furniture and prints, well kept Youngs and Smiles, cheap bar food (not Sat-Sun evenings), bar billiards, dominoes, cribbage; busy with Univ students and teachers, steep steps to lavatories; children welcome, attractive back terrace with heated arbour, open all day *(LYM, Simon and Amanda Southwell, Ian Phillips, the Didler)*

Hope & Anchor [Jacobs Wells Rd, Clifton]: Bare-boards 18th-c pub with large shared pine tables, well kept changing ales from small breweries, fast pleasant service, reliable substantial cheap food inc lots of sandwiches, interesting dishes and sumptuous ploughman's – very popular lunchtime; piped music may be loud, occasional live music, can get crowded late evening; disabled access, summer evening barbecues on good back terrace with interesting niches *(Simon and Amanda Southwell, David Carr, Donald Godden)*

☆ ***Kings Head*** [Victoria St]: Narrow 17th-c pub lightened by big welcoming front window and splendid mirrored bar back, corridor to cosy panelled back snug with serving hatch, well kept Bass, Courage Best and Smiles, toby jugs on joists, old-fashioned local prints and interesting gas pressure gauge, friendly relaxed atmosphere, generous reasonably priced food inc filling toasties and good yorkshire puddings wkdy lunchtimes; pavement tables, cl Sat lunchtime, open all day Weds-Fri *(the Didler, BB, Pete Baker, Di and Mike Gillam, Dr and Mrs A K Clarke)*

Llandoger Trow [off King St/Welsh Back]: By docks, interesting as the last timber-framed building built here, and making the most of its picturesque past with its impressive flower-decked façade and very cosy collection of cleverly lit small alcoves and rooms with original fireplaces and carvings; reasonably priced bar food, friendly staff, good mix from students to tourists; bedrooms in adjacent Premier Lodge *(Richard Pierce, Mike and Mary Carter)*

Myrtle Tree [Hotwells]: Single unspoilt room, barrels of well kept Bass one end of bar (pub too small for a separate cellar) *(the Didler)*

Nova Scotia [Baltic Wharf, Cumberland Basin]: Unspoilt old pub on S side of Floating Harbour, views to Clifton and Avon Gorge, good changing real ale range, good value blackboard food inc filling baguettes, wooden seats, nautical charts as wallpaper *(Emma Kingdon)*

Old Fish Market [Baldwin St]: Imposing red and cream brick building converted to roomy and airy pub, good mural showing it in 1790s along one wall, lots of wood inc rather ornate counter, parquet floor, relaxed friendly atmosphere, good value lunchtime food from sandwiches through home-baked pies to Sun lunch, well kept Fullers London Pride, ESB and seasonal and guest beers, good coffee, daily papers; quiet piped music, unobtrusive sports TV *(Simon and Amanda Southwell, Richard Pierce, Dr and Mrs A K Clarke)*

Palace [West St/Old Market St]: High-backed settles, fancy chandelier, sloping floor, intricate plasterwork and paint, spiral columns, interesting photographs; real ales such as Bath Spa and Gem and Hop Back Summer Lightning *(the Didler)*

Penny Farthing [Whiteladies Rd, Clifton]: Bright panelled pub with half a dozen or more real ales such as Adnams Broadside, Badger Tanglefoot, Bass, Butcombe and Wadworths IPA and 6X racked behind bar, late Victorian bric-a-brac inc penny-farthing, armchairs opp bar, lots of table seating, very reasonably priced home-made food lunchtime and evening, friendly helpful staff; can get very busy evenings, with doorman *(Emma Kingdon)*

Prince of Wales [Gloucester Rd, Bishopston, opp Redland turn]: Warm and friendly atmosphere, comfortable seats well divided (some nice stained-glass), well kept Bath SPA, Butcombe and Courage Best, good value organic food, pleasant staff; suntrap terrace *(anon)*

Robin Hood [St Michaels Hill]: Welcoming local with well kept Wadworths beers, food from baguettes and baked potatoes up lunchtime and Mon-Thurs early evening, rock star photographs especially Elvis; small heated garden *(Simon and Amanda Southwell)*

White Lion [Quay Head, Colston Ave]: Small simple bare-boards bar with very friendly licensees, well kept Wickwar and interesting guest ales, tasters offered and one of the beers at bargain price, wide choice of sandwiches, log fire; a couple of tables out by road, garden with wrought-iron furniture *(BB, Simon and Amanda Southwell)*

BROMPTON REGIS SS9531

☆ *George*: 17th-c ex-farmhouse in quiet remote village, warmly welcoming and attentive chef/landlord, very wide choice of reasonably priced home-made food inc imaginative dishes and good Sun roast, Cotleigh Tawny and/or Barn Owl and Exmoor, organic wines, woodburners, no juke box or machines, skittle alley; may be quiet piped music; children and dogs welcome, Exmoor views from pleasant garden by churchyard, good walks, cl Mon *(Peter Abbott, Richard and Anne Ansell)*

BUCKLAND DINHAM ST7551

Bell [High St]: 16th-c pub with narrow beamed main bar, pine furnishings inc booth settles, interesting décor, woodburner in huge inglenook; wide choice of generous straightforward food, well kept ales inc Butcombe, quite a few malt whiskies, children allowed in partly no smoking two-level dining room; cribbage, dominoes, piped music; sheltered garden with side terraces *(LYM)*

CHEW STOKE ST5661

Stoke Inn [Bristol Rd]: Large straightforward family pub with good value food from sandwiches to good steaks, well kept Bass, local Butcombe, Courage, Smiles and Youngers, good fresh coffee, friendly and helpful smartly dressed staff, no smoking restaurant; piped music, side garden *(John Cook)*

CHIPPING SODBURY ST7381

Bell [Badminton Rd]: Enjoyable home-made food at attractive prices, tasteful restaurant set with linen, good choice of wines by the glass *(Shelly Janes)*

CLEVEDON ST4071

Campbells Landing [The Beach]: Good position opp restored Victorian pier, roomy lounge done up like old Campbells steamer with nautical items inc coastal charts and old local photographs, sofas, banquettes and wheelback chairs, good choice of well kept Bass, Fullers London Pride and guests, wide range of food, big restaurant, views to Wales; bedrooms *(Alan and Paula McCully)*

Little Harp [Elton Rd (seafront)]: Renovated high-throughput promenade pub, views towards Exmoor and the Welsh hills from terrace and two dining conservatories, pleasant no smoking family area with mezzanine floor, decent reasonably priced food all day from sandwiches and light dishes up (fetch your own cutlery, condiments etc), Greene King IPA and Old Speckled Hen or Abbot, friendly if not always speedy service *(W R Miller)*

COMBE FLOREY ST1531

Farmers Arms [off A358 Taunton—Williton, just N of main village turn-off]: Neatly rebuilt bustling dining pub, picturesquely thatched and beamed, four real ales, manageable choice of interesting food, cheerful staff, good log fire; plenty of tables outside *(BB, Bob and Margaret Holder)*

COMBE HAY ST7359

☆ ***Wheatsheaf*** [off A367 or B3110 S of Bath]: Pleasantly old-fashioned low-beamed rooms, rustic furnishing and décor, big log fire, friendly attentive service, enjoyable generous food, well kept Courage Best, Greene King Old Speckled Hen and John Smiths tapped from the cask, spiced hot winter drinks; children in eating areas, tables on spacious terraced lawn overlooking church and steep valley, dovecotes built into the walls, plenty of good nearby walks, open all day in summer *(LYM, Mark and Heather Williamson, Brian and Bett Cox, Mr and Mrs W D Borthwick, Rev Michael Vockins, Dr and Mrs A K Clarke)*

CONGRESBURY ST4363

Ship & Castle [High St (just off A370 from lights at W end of bypass)]: Hungry Horse budget dining pub with generous daily bargains and vast mixed grills, well kept Greene King IPA, Abbot and Old Speckled Hen, friendly staff, big family area inc no smoking room, oldish wooden furniture and couple of big settles; good play area *(John A Barker)*

CORFE ST2319

White Hart [B3170 S of Taunton]: Keen new landlord, enjoyable food from sandwiches up (chef's day off is Tues), good choice of real ales, lounge with small stools, attractive small no smoking dining room; children welcome *(Bob and Margaret Holder, John Close)*

CRANMORE ST6643

Strode Arms [off A361 Frome—Shepton Mallet]: Homely dining pub, largely no smoking, with friendly newish licensees, good service, decent generous food, well kept Wadworths real ales, good wine, attractive country furnishings in linked rooms of former farmhouse, log fire; piped music; children in restaurant, tables on front terrace and in back garden, handy for East Somerset Railway *(LYM, Chris Barker, Susan and Nigel Wilson, Annie Barratt)*

CROSCOMBE ST5844

George [Long St]: Friendly and unpretentiously refurbished village local with Canadian landlord, enjoyable reasonably priced home-made food freshly made by landlady from sandwiches up, good service, real ales, three local farm ciders, good short choice of sensibly priced wines, reopened log fire, darts, unusual table games, back skittle alley, new no smoking dining room; bar can get a bit smoky *(Sylvia and Tony Birbeck, David Barnes)*

DONYATT ST3314

George: Well run friendly pub with relaxing décor, well kept beer and interesting choice of reasonably priced enjoyable food; games machine in smaller side room *(Dr and Mrs M E Wilson)*

DOULTING ST6443

☆ ***Poachers Pocket*** [Chelynch Rd, off A361]: Cheerful and popular modernised black-beamed local, log fire in stripped-stone end wall, lots of stripped pine, gundog pictures, welcoming efficient staff, plentiful good value food from sandwiches through good specials to Sun roasts, well kept Butcombe, Wadworths 6X and a guest beer, local farm cider (a spring cider festival, as well as an autumn beer one), pub games, children in eating area and large family room/skittle alley, friendly cat and dog, back garden with country views *(Mrs Hazel Blackburn, LYM, Susan and Nigel Wilson)*

DOWLISH WAKE ST3712
New Inn [off A3037 S of Ilminster, via Kingstone]: Neatly refurbished village local popular with wkdy older lunchers for good value food from sandwiches and baked potatoes up, friendly helpful new management, dark beams and woodburner in stone inglenook, well kept Butcombe and Otter, local farm cider, games area and family room; pleasant garden, attractive village *(LYM, Warham St Leger-Harris, Stephen and Jean Curtis, Dr and Mrs M E Wilson, David and Sally Cullen)*

DULVERTON SS9127
Lion [Bank Sq]: Rambling and comfortably old-fashioned two-bar country-town hotel popular with locals from Exmoor villages, big log fire, well kept ales inc Bass and Exmoor, decent wine and coffee, helpful service, no music, sensibly priced pub food; children welcome away from main serving bar, 14 bedrooms with own bathrooms, pleasant setting *(Geoff Calcott)*

DUNSTER SS9943
Dunster Castle Hotel [High St]: Popular hotel bar with modern light oak furnishings, well kept Courage Best and Smiles, sensibly priced enjoyable food in eating area and dining room from good sandwiches to Sun lunch; bedrooms with own bathrooms, useful car park *(David Carr)*

☆ *Luttrell Arms* [High St; A396]: Privately owned hotel in 15th-c timber-framed abbey building, high beams hung with bottles, clogs and horseshoes, stag's head and rifles on walls above old settles and more modern furniture, big log fires, good welcoming service, interesting fairly priced bar menu from baguettes up, well kept Bass and Exmoor Gold; ancient glazed partition dividing off small galleried and flagstoned courtyard, upstairs access to quiet attractive garden with Civil War cannon emplacements and great views, comfortable bedrooms *(Colin and Janet Roe, LYM, H O Dickinson, R Michael Richards, Dr D J and Mrs S C Walker, Gordon Stevenson)*

EAST COKER ST5412
☆ *Helyar Arms* [off A37 or A30 SW of Yeovil; Moor Lane]: Good fresh well presented food with a strong local flavour in spotless and roomy open-plan low-beamed lounge and old-fashioned high-raftered dining room, good welcoming service, well kept real ales, local farm cider, reasonably priced wines, woodburner, lots of brass and pictures, dark-stained traditional furnishings, world map with pushpins for visitors; no dogs, comfortable bedrooms with own bathrooms, attractive setting *(Anthony J Woodroffe, Mary Ellen Cummings)*

EAST WOODLANDS ST7944
☆ *Horse & Groom* [off A361/B3092 junction]: New licensees in small country pub handy for Longleat, flagstoned bar with pews and settles, comfortable lounge with woodburner, well kept Archers Golden, Branscombe Vale Branoc and Butcombe Bitter tapped from the cask, reasonably priced bar food, traditional games, big no smoking dining conservatory; dogs welcome away from restaurant, children in eating areas, picnic-sets in nice front garden with more seats behind *(LYM, Jack Taylor, Martin and Karen Wake, Dr and Mrs M E Wilson, the Didler)*

EASTON-IN-GORDANO ST5175
Rudgleigh Inn [A369 a mile from M5 junction 19]: Two-bar roadside pub popular for welcoming service, enjoyable promptly served food from baguettes up, well kept Courage and Smiles, extension restaurant suiting families; big well tended enclosed garden with willows, tamarisks, play area and cricket-field view, open all day wkdys *(Tom Evans, LYM, Donald Godden)*

ENMORE ST2434
Tynte Arms: Doing well under current management, with well kept real ales, good food choice, low beams, open fires and pleasant dining areas *(Bob and Margaret Holder)*

FAILAND ST5171
Failand Inn [B3128 Bristol—Clevedon]: Simply furnished old coaching inn, popular for good straightforward reasonably priced food in ample helpings, friendy efficient service, well kept ales such as Websters Green Label, comfortable dining extension; may be piped music *(Rex Miller, Tom Evans)*

FARLEIGH HUNGERFORD ST7957
Hungerford Arms [A366 Trowbridge—Norton St Philip]: Relaxed local atmosphere, well kept Butcombe, Otter and Wadworths 6X, farm cider, enjoyable generous sensibly priced food, bargains Tues and Thurs, snug alcoves, stained-glass and hunting prints, heavy dark beams, carved stone fireplaces, steps down to brighter no smoking family restaurant with nice country view inc Hungerford Castle ruins; darts, fruit machine; back terrace with same view, open all day wknds *(LYM, Roger Wain-Heapy, Nigel Long, Dr and Mrs A K Clarke)*

FARMBOROUGH ST6660
Butchers Arms [Timsbury Rd]: Comfortable two-bar village pub with friendly staff and atmosphere, three well kept real ales, varied restauranty food inc bargain Sun lunch; popular Tues night quiz, children and dogs welcome *(Mandy and Phil Jones, Meg and Colin Hamilton, Dr and Mrs A K Clarke)*

New Inn [Bath Rd (A39)]: Roomy pub/restaurant under new management, well kept real ale, friendly staff, limited bar snacks, interesting food choice in restaurant *(Dr and Mrs A K Clarke)*

FAULKLAND ST7354
☆ *Faulkland Inn*: Friendly country pub doing well after refurbishment under new young couple, new dining area on left of L-shaped bar, contemporary colour scheme alongside beams, flagstones and some stripped stone, enjoyable food from interesting hot or cold filled sandwiches to wider evening choice inc modern starter/light dishes and good carefully cooked fresh fish, well trained staff, real ales, decent wines, games area in public end; piped

music; children welcome, small back garden, four good value bedrooms, pretty village *(BB, Jack Taylor)*

GLASTONBURY ST5039

☆ *Who'd A Thought It* [Northload St]: Old-fashioned country furnishings, coal fires, mellow pine panelling, stripped brick, beams and flagstones, lots of pictures and bric-a-brac, well kept Palmers IPA, Gold and 200, good choice of wines by the glass, bar food from lunchtime sandwiches to duck and quite a few fish dishes, daily papers; children and dogs welcome, open all day *(J M Hill, Ken Flawn, H O Dickinson, Patrick Hancock, Dr and Mrs A K Clarke, LYM)*

HARDWAY ST7234

☆ *Bull* [off B3081 Bruton—Wincanton at brown sign for Stourhead and King Alfred's Tower; Hardway]: Pretty and welcoming beamed country dining pub, popular locally esp with older people wkdy lunchtimes for wide choice of reliably good generous food in comfortable bar and character dining rooms, pleasant long-serving licensees, friendly obliging service, well kept Butcombe and a guest beer, farm cider, log fire; unobtrusive piped music, sell paintings and meringues; tables and barbecue in rose garden over road, bedrooms *(Charles Gysin)*

HASELBURY PLUCKNETT ST4511

Haselbury Mill [Merriott Rd; off A30 E of Crewkerne towards Merriott, away from village]: Very modernised country dining pub in quiet spot, big picture windows looking over duck pond, good inexpensive food inc carvery and OAP bargains, well spaced tables in comfortable light and airy dining lounge, snug low-ceilinged bar on right; tables out on informal lawn by pretty stream, open all day exc Sun afternoon, bedrooms *(BB, Bob and Margaret Holder)*

HINTON BLEWETT ST5956

☆ *Ring o' Bells* [signed off A37 in Clutton]: Charming low-beamed stone-built country local opp village green, very friendly landlord, good value fresh home cooking (not Sun evening) from sandwiches to some interesting main dishes, huge helpings, well kept Abbey Bellringer, Wadworths 6X and guest beers, good cafetière coffee, log fire; children welcome, pleasant view from tables in sheltered front yard *(LYM, Stuart Paulley)*

HINTON CHARTERHOUSE ST7758

Rose & Crown [B3110 about 4 miles S of Bath]: Roomy partly divided pub with well kept Bass, Butcombe and Smiles tapped from casks, wide choice of good value generous home-made food inc plenty of fish, nice panelling, ornate stone fireplace, rugby memorabilia, restaurant, skittle alley; open all day Sat *(BB, Meg and Colin Hamilton)*

☆ *Stag* [B3110 S of Bath; High St]: Attractively furnished ancient pub popular for good sensibly priced home-made food in bar and stripped-stone dining area, well kept ales such as Bass and Butcombe, smiling helpful service even when busy (can be hard to get a table even midweek Feb), log fire, provision for children, no piped music; tables outside, has been open all day *(Meg and Colin Hamilton, Dr and Mrs M E Wilson, LYM)*

HOLFORD ST1541

Plough [A39]: Busy village pub popular for enjoyable food inc good value Sun roasts and good steaks, well kept real ale, good service; handy for wonderful Quantocks walks *(Mike Vince)*

HUTTON ST3458

Old Inn [Main Rd]: Several linked rooms off large central bar, efficient cheerful service even when busy, good value food inc good Sun roast, well kept real ales, friendly local evening bustle *(Mr and Mrs D Brookes)*

KELSTON ST7067

☆ *Old Crown* [Bitton Rd; A431 W of Bath]: Four small convivial traditional rooms with hops on beams, carved settles and cask tables on polished flagstones, logs burning in ancient open range, two more coal-effect fires, well kept ales such as Bass, Bath Gem, Butcombe Gold and Blonde and Wadworths 6X tapped from the cask, Thatcher's cider, well priced wines, friendly barmaids, cheap wholesome bar food (not Sun or Mon evenings), small restaurant (not Sun), no machines or music; dogs welcome (biscuit tub behind bar), children in eating areas, open all day wknds, picnic-sets under apple trees in sunny sheltered back garden *(LYM, Meg and Colin Hamilton, Mandy and Phil Jones, Dr and Mrs A K Clarke, Michael Doswell, Barry and Anne, Dr and Mrs M E Wilson)*

KEYNSHAM ST6568

☆ *Lock-Keeper* [A4175]: Lovely spot on Avon island with big garden, lock, marina and weir; small room by bar, arches to main divided room with rust and dark blue décor, black beams and bare boards, barrel-vaulted lower area, well kept Youngs and Smiles, wide range of decent food from baguettes and baked potatoes to more upmarket dishes, friendly helpful young staff, three nicely decorated yet unpretentious areas; boules *(M G Hart, Dr and Mrs M E Wilson, Nigel Long, Dr and Mrs A K Clarke)*

KILVE ST1442

☆ *Hood Arms* [A39 E of Williton]: Doing well under former landlord now back in harness, friendly attentive service, enjoyable and attractive bar food cooked to order (no sandwiches), fair prices, well kept ales such as Exmoor, cosy little plush lounge, woodburner in bar, no smoking restaurant; skittle alley, tables on sheltered back terrace by pleasant children's garden, nice bedrooms – back are quietest *(LYM, Bob and Margaret Holder)*

KINGSBURY EPISCOPI ST4320

Wyndham Arms: Attractively unspoilt flagstoned country pub with roaring log fire, attentive helpful licensees, good range of enjoyable attractively priced home-made food inc good big steaks and impressive choice of puddings, well kept Bass and Fullers London Pride, farm cider; popular folk nights; tables in garden, two nearby self-catering cottages *(Theo, Anne and Jane Gaskin, OPUS)*

LANGPORT ST4227
Seed House [A372 towards Huish Episcopi]: Converted two-level Victorian seed warehouse with well kept ales tapped from the cask and enjoyable food, spacious flagstoned lower area *(Dr and Mrs A K Clarke)*
LANSDOWN ST7268
Blathwayt Arms: Big reliable all-day pub with well kept ales, good value generous food, attentive service; racecourse view from garden *(Frank Willy)*
MARK ST3747
Pack Horse [B3139 Wedmore—Highbridge; Church St]: Varied well cooked food inc good Sun roast and delicious puddings, good friendly service *(Mr and Mrs D Brookes)*
MARSTON MAGNA ST5922
Red Lion [Rimpton Rd]: New licensees doing enjoyable food, relaxed wine bar feel, Salisbury real ale, pleasant staff; good garden *(OPUS)*
MARTOCK ST4619
George [Church St]: 16th-c, with welcoming licensees, enjoyable food inc popular Sun carvery, Bass, Fullers London Pride, Shepherd Neame Spitfire and occasional local guest beers; opp fine church *(William Duncan)*
Nags Head [East St]: Two or three well kept ales such as Otter, good popular food (not Mon) inc good value lunches, local steaks and early-evening bargains, coal-effect gas fire, games room with pool and juke box; bedrooms in self-contained flat *(Miss N J Wild, MLR)*
MIDFORD ST7660
☆ *Hope & Anchor* [Bath Rd (B3110)]: Good attractively presented interesting food from light dishes to ostrich, barbary duck and imaginative puddings in bar and separate flagstoned restaurant end, well kept changing ales such as Bath Gem, Butcombe and Otter, good house wines, proper coffee, friendly service, candles and soft lighting, log fire; tables outside, pretty walks along canals and River Frome *(Michael Doswell, Gaynor Gregory, Roger Wain-Heapy, M G Hart)*
MIDSOMER NORTON ST6654
White Hart [The Island]: Chatty Victorian local with several rooms, Bass and Butcombe tapped from the cask; open all day *(the Didler, Dr and Mrs A K Clarke)*
MINEHEAD SS9746
Old Ship Aground [Quay West]: Old-fashioned pub with pleasant harbour views, ample menu esp fish, friendly staff, well kept Greene King Ruddles County, good coffee *(D Whateley)*
Queens Head [Holloway St]: Nicely modern interior with alcove seating, thriving atmosphere, well kept Adnams, Exmoor Gold and Greene King IPA, friendly professional service, wide choice of decent food, bar billiards; may be quiet piped music, nearby parking difficult *(Peter and Audrey Dowsett, R Michael Richards)*
MONKTON COMBE ST7761
Wheelwrights Arms [just off A36 S of Bath; Church Cottages]: Small country inn with attractively laid-out bar, wheelwright and railway memorabilia, candles and big log fire, friendly service, wide choice of good reasonably priced straightforward home-made food, well kept ales such as Adnams, Butcombe and Wadworths 6X, decent house wines, tiny darts room at end; fruit machine, quiet piped music, no children or dogs; garden with valley view, well equipped cosy bedrooms in separate block, good breakfast *(LYM, J F M and M West, Jeff and Sue Evans, Dr and Mrs M E Wilson)*
MONTACUTE ST4916
☆ *Kings Arms* [Bishopston]: Extended partly 16th-c hotel with pleasantly furnished stripped stone lounges (one no smoking), blazing log fires, enjoyable reasonably priced food from interesting light dishes up, a well kept real ale, good wines by the glass and coffee, magazines and broadsheet papers, no smoking restaurant; children welcome, pleasant garden, comfortable bedrooms *(Dennis Jenkin, A C Nugent, LYM, Colin and Janet Roe, Theo, Anne and Jane Gaskin, Mary Ellen Cummings, Peter B Brown)*
☆ *Phelips Arms* [The Borough; off A3088 W of Yeovil]: New owners emphasising good choice of interesting fresh food from filled crusty rolls to elaborate restauranty main dishes in roomy and airily refurbished open-plan bar and smart yet relaxed restaurant, friendly efficient service even when busy, well kept Palmers ales, farm cider, good coffee and carefully chosen wines; children and dogs welcome, skittle alley, tables in attractive garden, comfortable bedrooms, next to Montacute House *(Aubrey and Janet Gibson, Mary Ellen Cummings, Mr and Mrs D J Fugler, Mrs J Duke, A D Neale, Brian and Bett Cox)*
NAILSEA ST4670
Blue Flame [West End]: Small well worn 19th-c unspoilt farmers' local (though changes may be in the wind), mixed furnishings in several rooms, well kept Abbey, Bass, Bath, RCH and three guest beers tapped from the cask, Thatcher's farm cider, filled rolls and doorstep sandwiches, coal fires; folk and Thurs cards and pasties nights, pub games and cards, children's room, sizeable informal garden with barbecue *(Catherine Pitt, the Didler, Phil and Sally Gorton)*
NETTLEBRIDGE ST6448
Nettlebridge Inn [A367 SW of Radstock]: Wide choice of good value generous food, some meat from local farms, Bass and local ales, friendly landlord and staff, good atmosphere; bedrooms *(John Jordan)*
NEWTON ST LOE ST7064
☆ *Globe*: Roomy bar attractively split into smaller areas by dark wood partitions, pillars and timbers giving secluded feel, good atmosphere, friendly efficient service (can slow when very busy), enjoyable food all day, well kept beer, large no smoking area *(Dr and Mrs M E Wilson, Dr and Mrs A K Clarke)*
NORTON FITZWARREN ST1925
Cross Keys [A358 roundabout NW of Taunton]: 19th-c stone-built pub extended as above-average Chef & Brewer, big chalkboard

of enjoyable well prepared food inc good hot baguettes, staff friendly and cheerful even under pressure, Courage Best and Directors, Theakstons XB and a guest such as Smiles Slap & Tickle, generous coffee, good wine choice, roaring log fire in big hearth *(Andy and Jill Kassube, Bob and Margaret Holder, Jane McConaghie, Ian Phillips)*

NORTON ST PHILIP ST7755

☆ ***Fleur de Lys*** [High St]: 13th-c stone cottages joined centuries ago, steps and pillars giving cosy feel of separate rooms in the beamed and flagstoned areas around the central servery, unspoilt chatty local atmosphere, good value home-made food from baguettes through sausages and mash etc to steak, well kept Wadworths beers, friendly landlord, huge fireplace; car park can be awkward; children very welcome, skittle alley *(Colin McKerrow, the Didler, Dr and Mrs M E Wilson, BB, Dr and Mrs A K Clarke)*

☆ ***George*** [A366]: The star is for the fine layout of this exceptional building, an inn for over 700 years, with plenty of high beams, timbering, stonework and panelling, some distinctive furnishings, an appealing flagstoned courtyard, and character bedrooms (with own bathrooms) to match; well kept Wadworths IPA, 6X and a guest beer, a good wine choice by the glass, usual bar food inc lunchtime sandwiches, no smoking dining room (children welcome); dogs allowed in bar, open all day Sat *(LYM, Dr and Mrs A K Clarke, the Didler)*

OVER STRATTON ST4315

☆ ***Royal Oak*** [off A303 via Ilminster turn at S Petherton roundabout]: Welcoming well run thatched family dining pub, attractive line of linked rooms, flagstones and thick stone walls, prettily stencilled beams, scrubbed and bleached kitchen tables, pews, settles etc, log fires and rustic décor; good choice of competitively priced enjoyable food, no smoking restaurant, well kept Badger ales, efficient friendly service; open all day Aug, tables outside with barbecues and good play areas for toddlers and older children inc an assault course with trampolines *(LYM, Ian and Lin Gill, Oliver and Sue Rowell)*

PORLOCK SS8846

☆ ***Ship*** [High St]: Picturesque thatched partly 13th-c pub with welcoming service, well kept Cotleigh and guest beers, farm cider, food from good sandwich range to familiar hot dishes with good children's choice, low beams, flagstones and big inglenook log fires, small locals' front bar, back dining room, pub games and pool; children very welcome, attractive split-level sunny garden with decking, nearby nature trail to Dunkery Beacon, bedrooms *(LYM, Andy and Jill Kassube, Tracey and Stephen Groves, Anne and Paul Horscraft, Gordon Stevenson)*

PORLOCK WEIR SS8547

Ship [separate from but run in tandem with neighbouring Anchor Hotel]: Prettily restored old inn in wonderful spot by peaceful harbour, with tables in terraced rose garden and good walks (but no views to speak of from bars); nets and chalked beams in busy Mariners Bar with friendly relaxed atmosphere, well kept ales at a price, Taunton cider, huge log fire, usual food inc generous baked potatoes; piped music, little free parking but pay & display opposite, dogs welcome, back family room; attractive bedrooms *(H O Dickinson, LYM, John and Joan Calvert)*

PORTBURY ST4975

Priory [Station Rd, ½ mile from A369 (just S of M5 junction 19)]: Spotless much extended Vintage Inn dining pub, several beamed rooms with nice mix of solid furnishings in alcoves, good wide food choice inc some light dishes, well kept Bass, good range of house wines; piped music; bedrooms, open all day *(Comus and Sarah Elliott, James Morrell, Tom Evans, Dr and Mrs C W Thomas)*

PORTISHEAD ST4777

Poacher [High St]: Large dining pub popular with older lunchers for wide range of freshly cooked low-priced food with real veg, changing well kept ales such as Courage Best and Smiles (a proper part for village beer-drinkers, with a big fireplace), friendly staff, no smoking restaurant area; quiz nights, cl Sun pm *(Tom Evans, Emma Kingdon)*

Ship [the one on Down Rd (coast rd to Walton in Gordano)]: Quiet and relaxing modern pub, good value usual lunchtime food, Bass, Butcombe and Flowers IPA, lots of Royal Navy memorabilia, superb views across to Newport and Cardiff esp at sunset *(Tom Evans, S Fysh, Ian Phillips)*

PURITON ST3141

Puriton Inn [just off M5 junction 23; Puriton Hill]: Friendly character pub, clean and tidy, with good value straightforward food, well kept beer, warmly welcoming service even when busy; good disabled access, large garden *(B and F A Hannam, Brian and Rosalie Laverick, Dr and Mrs A K Clarke)*

RICKFORD ST4859

☆ ***Plume of Feathers*** [very sharp turn off A368]: Unspoilt cottagey and partly flagstoned pub with new management (three young sisters) hotting up the food side – one to watch, with relaxed atmosphere, friendly service, well kept real ale, table skittles and log fire; rustic tables on narrow front terrace, pretty streamside hamlet *(John Urquhart, BB)*

RIDGEHILL ST5363

Crown [Crown Hill/Regis Lane; off B3130 2 miles S of Winford]: Deep in the country, large pub pleasantly redone in rustic style with attractive furniture inc upholstered settles in small comfortably cluttered beamed rooms, nice painting of regulars in their corner; enjoyable generous usual food from good sandwiches up, well kept Bass and Wadworths IPA and 6X, friendly staff, family area, log fire in delightful old fireplace; lovely valley views from window tables and tables on pleasant terrace *(Stan Edwards)*

RODE ST8053

Bell [Frome Rd (A361)]: Comfortable, spotless and roomy, friendly new landlady putting some emphasis on nicely balanced choice of

good value food, well kept Butcombe and Courage, good atmosphere in busy no smoking restaurant and sparely decorated bar; garden tables *(Dr and Mrs M E Wilson)*
Mill: Pleasantly refurbished mill in lovely setting, manageable choice of freshly made food from unpretentious things to up-to-date main dishes inc quite a few modern pasta ones and nice salads, upstairs no smoking area, children's room with impressive games; some wknd live music; gardens and terrace overlooking river *(anon)*

RODNEY STOKE ST4850
Rodney Stoke Inn [A371 Wells—Weston]: Plush banquettes and dimpled copper tables, reception corner with candles and leather sofa, bigger nicely set back no smoking restaurant with plants in airy new high-beamed extension, good imaginative well presented and well priced food, good wine list, well kept Bass and Butcombe, cheery landlord, efficient service; well lit pool table, fruit machine and juke box or piped pop music, skittle alley, very busy holidays and wknds; picnic-sets out on roadside terrace and back lawn, camp site *(BB, John A Barker, Colin and Janet Roe, Alan and Paula McCully, Joyce and Maurice Cottrell)*

RUDGE ST8251
☆ *Full Moon* [off A36 Bath—Warminster]: Black-beamed 17th-c inn with well kept Butcombe Bitter, Timothy Taylors Landlord and Wadworths 6X, local ciders, good service, some emphasis on food (simple at lunchtime, more elaborate evenings), nice mix of furnishings in cottagey front bars, inglenook fireplace, flagstoned tap room, back no smoking restaurant extension, traditional games and skittle alley; children welcome, pretty gardens with plenty of seats, bedrooms and self-catering cottages, open all day *(Dr and Mrs M E Wilson, LYM, Mr and Mrs A H Young, Dr and Mrs A K Clarke, Mike Gorton)*

RUMWELL ST1923
Rumwell Inn [A38 Taunton—Wellington, just past Stonegallows]: Good comfortable atmosphere, old beams, lots of tables in several areas, interesting choice of well presented good value food inc lots of fish and local meat and other produce, children's dishes, well kept changing ales such as Bass and Wadworths 6X, friendly efficient service, roaring log fire, restaurant (best to book), family room; tables outside, handy for Sheppy's Cider *(Francis Johnston)*

SALTFORD ST6867
Bird in Hand [High St]: Lively local, comfortable and friendly, with lots of bird pictures, popular locally for good value fresh food inc daily roast, huge omelettes and whitby fish, attractive conservatory dining area, quick service even when quite a queue for food, small family area, good range of beers such as Abbey Bellringer, Bass and Courage Bitter; live entertainment; picnic-sets down towards river, handy for Bristol—Bath railway path *(Meg and Colin Hamilton)*

SHIPHAM ST4457
Penscot Farmhouse Hotel [The Square]: Refurbished as pub, with well kept Greene King Old Speckled Hen, enjoyable food in cosy lounge bar, dining area and restaurant, pleasant helpful service; pretty back courtyard garden, front seating on village green, bedrooms *(Alan and Paula McCully)*

SOMERTON ST4828
☆ *Globe* [Market Pl]: Chatty and bustling old stone-built local with log fire, good interesting reasonably priced home-made bar food, attentive landlord and friendly staff, well kept ales inc Bass, Boddingtons and Butcombe, good choice of wine, two spacious bars, dining conservatory, back pool room; no music, skittle alley, tables in garden *(Joyce and Geoff Robson, Theo, Anne and Jane Gaskin, Frank Willy)*

SOUTH PETHERTON ST4316
Brewers Arms [St James St]: Substantially refurbished 17th-c stone-built inn with generous enjoyable food from hearty favourites to interesting dishes at pine tables in elegant russet-walled dining lounge, prompt attentive service, good choice of several well kept changing real ales, decent wines, games in big public bar; picnic-sets in neat garden, useful A303 diversion *(Dr and Mrs M E Wilson, D P and M A Miles)*

SOUTH STOKE ST7461
☆ *Pack Horse* [off B3110, S edge of Bath]: Intriguing medieval pub, a former priory (central passageway still a public right of way to the church); heavy beams, handsome inglenook log fire, antique settles, well kept Courage Best, Ushers Best and Wadworths 6X, farm cider, shove-ha'penny tables, very wide food choice; piped music, winter quiz nights; children welcome, tables in spacious back garden, boules, open all day wknds *(Ian Phillips, LYM, Dr and Mrs A K Clarke)*

SPARKFORD ST6026
☆ *Sparkford Inn* [just W of Wincanton; High St]: Some internal changes under present regime, keeping rambling layout of softly lit low-beamed rooms (inc no smoking restaurant) with pleasant mix of furnishings; popular lunchtime carvery alongside other usual bar food and good puddings choice, Bass and Butcombe, smartly dressed staff who cope well with coach parties; children and dogs welcome, tables and decent play area outside, bedrooms with own bath or shower, open all day *(Guy Consterdine, B J Harding, B and M Kendall, Richard and Anne Ansell, Sarah and Anthony Bussy, LYM, Peter Salmon, Reg Fowle, Helen Rickwood)*

STAR ST4358
Star [A38 NE of Winscombe]: Reliable extended roadside pub with tasty food, well kept Bass, friendly service and cheery regulars, good log fire in huge inglenook fireplace, nice mix of tables, big fish tank, enthusiastic Sun lunchtime raffle (bar nibbles then); country views from picnic-sets in field behind *(Tom Evans, Alan and Paula McCully)*

STOGUMBER ST0937

☆ *White Horse* [off A358 at Crowcombe]: Little whitewashed village pub settling down well again under welcoming current landlord, nice value food choice from good sandwiches to proper Sun roasts, well kept Cotleigh Tawny, Greene King Old Speckled Hen and Marstons Pedigree, long neat bar, old village photographs with more recent ones for comparison, good log fires, no smoking dining area, games room and skittle alley; children welcome away from bar, quiet garden, bedrooms, open all day wknds and summer *(LYM, Dr D J and Mrs S C Walker, Peter F Marshall)*

STOKE SUB HAMDON ST4717

Prince of Wales [Ham Hill]: Ham Hill pub (worth the climb for its superb views), enjoyable food from hearty brunch to interesting blackboard dishes using local produce, well kept ales; may be wknd lunchtime jazz; children, dogs and muddy boots welcome *(OPUS)*

TARR SS8632

Tarr Farm [Tarr Steps; OS Sheet 181 map ref 868322]: Beautifully set for river walks, lovely views from gardens front and back, cosy inside with four smallish rooms, huge tables made from slabs of wood, well kept Exmoor and other ales, nice wine, good value food from sandwiches to fresh fish and Sun roast, good cream teas (log fires in tea room), charming evening restaurant, no piped music; nice bedrooms, self catering too, has been open all day *(Peter Abbott)*

TAUNTON ST2525

☆ *Hankridge Arms* [Hankridge Way, Deane Gate (nr Sainsbury); very handy for M5 junction 25]: 16th-c former farm reworked as well appointed old-style dining pub in modern shopping complex, buoyant atmosphere and quick friendly service, good value generous food from interesting soups and sandwiches up in bar and largely no smoking restaurant, Badger Best, K&B and Tanglefoot, decent wines, big log fire; piped music, can be hard for older people to get to when surrounding shops busy; plenty of tables outside *(Gill and Keith Croxton, Joe Green, Dr and Mrs A K Clarke, Pamela and Merlyn Horswell)*

☆ *Vivary Arms* [Middleway, Wilton; across Vivary Park from centre]: Quiet and pretty pub dating from 18th c, good value distinctive freshly made food from good soup and baked potatoes to plenty of fish, in snug plush lounge and small dining room; prompt helpful young staff, relaxed atmosphere, well kept ales such as Smiles Best, John Smiths and Charles Wells Bombardier, decent wines, interesting collection of drinking-related items, no music; bedrooms with own bathrooms in Georgian house next door, easy street parking *(Joe Green, Jacquie and Jim Jones)*

White Lodge [Bridgwater Rd, handy for M5 junction 25]: Comfortable modern Beefeater around older core, welcoming service, well kept ales such as Wadworths 6X, decent food; adjacent Travel Inn *(Mr and Mrs Colin Roberts)*

THURLOXTON ST2730

Maypole [A38 Taunton—Bridgwater]: Attractively refurbished beamed pub with several traditional areas, well kept real ales, log fire, biggish no smoking area, wide food choice; soft piped music, no dogs, skittle alley; enclosed garden with play area, lovely flowers, peaceful village *(Bob and Margaret Holder)*

TIMBERSCOMBE SS9542

Lion [Church St]: New licensees in Exmoor-edge former coaching inn dating from 15th c, she cooks well (limited lunchtime menu, wider evening choice), three rooms off comfortable flagstoned main bar,woodburner, well kept Exmoor and Sharps Doom Bar tapped from the cask, Addlestone's cider, friendly service; bedrooms *(Jenny and Peter Lowater)*

TRULL ST2122

Winchester Arms [Church Rd]: Cosy and welcoming local under helpful new young licensees, good varied food, well kept Bass, small dining room; bedrooms *(Bob and Margaret Holder)*

TYTHERINGTON ST7645

Fox & Hounds: 17th-c, with roomy and tidy L-shaped stripped-stone bar, small no smoking dining area, generous interesting food (not Mon) inc unusual curries and Sun roasts, well kept Bass, Butcombe and a guest beer tapped from the cask, farm ciders, welcoming landlord and atmosphere; tables outside, comfortable bedrooms with own bathrooms, good breakfast *(Natalie and Paul Burton, MRSM)*

UPTON NOBLE ST7139

Lamb [Church St; off A359 SW of Frome]: Small appealing 17th-c village local with welcoming Yorkshire chef/landlord and efficient staff, well kept Butcombe, Flowers and Fullers London Pride, wide blackboard choice of good home-made food inc better than usual vegetarian range, comfortable lounge bar, beams, stripped stone, brasses and ornaments, lovely view from no smoking restaurant; darts, pool etc in public bar, two dogs; big garden, cl Mon lunchtime, perhaps other wkdy lunchtimes *(Michael Doswell)*

VOBSTER ST7049

Vobster Inn [Lower Vobster]: Roomy old stone-built village inn transformed into dining pub particularly popular with older people (children welcomed too), good food choice from sandwiches and range of local cheeses to fish fresh daily from Cornwall and far eastern dishes in three comfortable open-plan areas, friendly licensees and staff, well kept Fullers London Pride, good new world wines by the glass; tables on side lawn with boules, peaceful views, adventure playground behind *(Edward Mirzoeff, BB, J Burke)*

WAMBROOK ST2907

☆ *Cotley Inn* [off A30 W of Chard; don't follow the small signs to Cotley itself]: Smartly unpretentious stone-built pub, good reasonably priced food attractively presented inc generous small-helpings choice, friendly efficient staff, Otter and Wadworths 6X, simple flagstoned entrance bar opening on one side into small plush bar, several open fires, popular two-room no smoking dining area (best to book, children allowed here); pool, piped music, skittle alley; seats and play area in nice garden, well refurbished bedrooms, quiet spot with plenty of surrounding walks *(Nigel and Teresa Traylen, Bob and Margaret Holder, LYM, Mike and Jenny Beacon)*

WATCHET ST0743

Bell [Market St]: Snug and friendly well decorated local, well kept Bass and Hancocks HB, good value simple food, pleasant licensees *(John A Barker)*

WATERROW ST0525

Rock [A361 Wiveliscombe—Bampton]: Well kept ales such as Cotleigh Tawny and Exmoor Gold, wide choice of enjoyable food, log fire in smallish scrupulously clean bar exposing the rock it's built on, couple of steps up to dining room; good well equipped bedrooms, charming setting in small valley village *(Tom Evans, Bob and Margaret Holder)*

WELLINGTON ST1320

Cottage Inn [Champford Lane]: Friendly and cosy local with Courage Best, Fullers London Pride, Otter and a beer brewed for the pub *(Dr and Mrs M E Wilson)*

WELLOW ST7358

Fox & Badger [signed off A367 SW of Bath]: Cheery bustle in flagstoned bar with snug alcoves, small winged settles, three log fires, flowers on the tables, well kept Badger, Bass, Butcombe and Wadworths 6X, Thatcher's farm cider, decent cheap bar food (try the ploughman's), good service, restaurant; games and piped music in cosy bare-boards public bar; children in eating areas, courtyard with barbecues, open all day Fri-Sun *(LYM, Roger and Jenny Huggins)*

WELLS ST5545

☆ ***Fountain*** [St Thomas St]: Comfortable dining pub dating from 16th c, good wholesome sensibly priced choice from filled baguettes and wkdy lunchtime bargains to fresh fish and interesting dishes in homely downstairs bar with roaring log fire, or popular more formal restaurant up steep stairs (worth booking wknd, good Sun lunch); quick pleasant service, well kept ales such as Butcombe, Courage Best and Greene King IPA, good choice of wines, good coffee; can get very full wknd lunchtimes, may be piped music; children welcome, right by cathedral and moated Bishop's Palace – popular with choir, and you may even be served by a Vicar Choral *(Rebecca Davidson, Alan and Jill Bull, Mr and Mrs Richard Hanks, Colin and Janet Roe, Roger and Anne Newbury, Gaynor Gregory, John Coatsworth)*

WEST BAGBOROUGH ST1733

☆ ***Rising Sun***: Welcoming pub in tiny village below Quantocks, neatly rebuilt after 2002 fire, attractive décor inc quite an art gallery, well kept Butcombe, Cottage and Exmoor, enjoyable generous freshly made food from ciabattas up, good service, wide choice of wines *(Alannah Hunt, Hugh Roberts)*

WEST BUCKLAND ST1621

Blackbird [nr M5 junction 26; A38 Wellington—Taunton]: Clean, quiet and homely partly 16th-c inn, good value home-cooked food from sandwiches to Sun lunch, two well kept real ales, friendly service, skittle alley, large restaurant; pleasant garden, well equipped bedrooms *(Bob and Margaret Holder)*

WEST CAMEL ST5724

☆ ***Walnut Tree*** [off A303 W of Wincanton; Fore St]: Extended upmarket dining pub/hotel, comfortable grey plush banquettes and red plush cushioned wicker chairs, enjoyable food (not Sun evening or Mon lunchtime) esp fresh fish and puddings, friendly efficient uniformed staff nicely flexible over menus, well kept Bass and Butcombe; neatly kept garden, good bedrooms, pretty village *(Theo, Anne and Jane Gaskin, A Thorpe)*

WEST HATCH ST2719

Farmers Arms [W of village, at Slough Green; from A358 head for RSPCA centre and keep past]: Spacious 16th-c beamed pub with bleached wood furniture and unassumingly modern décor moved further up market by new restaurateur licensees (out go the quiz night, skittle alley and pool table, in come the damask napkins), with emphasis now on changing enterprising modern food in a friendly atmosphere; two well kept Otter ales tapped from the cask, open fires, no smoking restaurant; children welcome, garden with small terrace and play area *(A J and C D Stodgell, Andy Harvey, R A Spencer, Bob and Margaret Holder)*

WEST HORRINGTON ST5948

☆ ***Slab House*** [B3139 Wells—Emborough, NE of village]: Pretty open-plan country dining pub, smallish partly flagstoned bar area with welcoming staff, cosy corners, old engravings, lots of cottagey bric-a-brac and quite a clock collection, roaring log fire in big fireplace, extensive dining area, wide choice of good generous food from sandwiches to imaginative dishes, good quick service, nice relaxed atmosphere, well kept real ales; discreet piped music; spotless lavatories, tables out on floodlit nicely planted sunken terrace and on big neat lawns, play area *(BB, David Barnes)*

WEST HUNTSPILL ST3044

☆ ***Crossways*** [A38 (between M5 exits 22 and 23)]: Friendly and comfortably worn in, with several seating areas inc a family room, interesting decorations, beams and log fires, good choice of well kept real ales and local farm cider, decent wines, enjoyable piping hot sensibly priced food, quick attentive service, no piped music; skittle alley and pub games, picnic-sets among fruit trees in sizeable informal garden *(LYM, Tom Evans, B J Harding, Rona Murdoch)*

WEST PENNARD ST5438

Lion [A361 E of Glastonbury; Newtown]: Enjoyable quickly served food using some local ingredients in three neat dining areas opening off small flagstoned and black-beamed core with settles and woodburner in big stone inglenook, log fire in stripped-stone family area, well kept Ushers ales, reasonable prices, pool in back room; tables on big forecourt, bedrooms comfortable and well equipped, in neatly converted side barn *(K H Frostick, BB, Peter and Audrey Dowsett)*

WESTON-IN-GORDANO ST4474

White Hart [B3124 Portishead—Clevedon, between M5 junctions 19 and 20]: Cheerful highly polished bar with lots of old photographs in lower room, large pleasant dining area, wide choice of decent food cooked to order (so may be a wait), pleasant staff, Courage and John Smiths; Gordano valley views from fine back lawn with play area *(B Weeks, Mrs M E Hutchison)*

WESTON-SUPER-MARE ST3261

Claremont Vaults [Birnbeck Rd; seafront, N end]: Large well used low-priced dining pub included for wonderful views down the beach or across the bay, well kept Bass, decent wine, cheerful friendly service; pool, quiet piped music, no food Mon *(Comus and Sarah Elliott, David Carr)*

Windsor [Upper Bristol Rd]: Friendly service and atmosphere, good value home cooking, full beer range *(Oliver Marshall)*

Woolpack [St Georges, just off M5, junction 21]: Firmly run olde-worlde 17th-c coaching inn with good varied well priced food inc some sophisticated dishes and lots of fresh fish, pleasant window seats and library-theme area, several well kept changing beers such as Greene King Old Speckled Hen and Palmers, good house wines, small but attractive restaurant, conservatory; starters mean starters (must be followed by main courses), they stick rather too rigidly to the menu (and the food service cut-off times), and forbid children and dirty workmen; skittle alley *(Comus and Sarah Elliott, Alan and Paula McCully)*

WILLITON ST0741

Masons Arms [on outskirts via B3191 for Watchet; pub on corner]: Recently refurbished thatched pub with convivial atmosphere, good value standard food in bar and restaurant, well kept ales such as Fullers London Pride and Palmers, pleasant landlord, well trained staff; small well fenced play area, bedrooms *(Ian and Sharon Shorthouse, John A Barker)*

WINSCOMBE ST4257

Woodborough [Sandford Rd]: Extensively refurbished as dining pub, popular for good range of reasonably priced food inc Sun roasts, Bass, Butcombe and Courage, comfortable restaurant *(Bob and Margaret Holder)*

WINSLEY ST7960

Seven Stars [off B3108 bypass W of Bradford-on-Avon (pub just over Wilts border)]: Cheerful new young landlord bringing welcoming pubby feel back to big stripped-stone open-plan pub with low beams, soft lighting, snug alcoves, log-effect gas fires, well kept Bass, Butcombe, Wadworths 6X and a guest beer, good wine choice, good value food inc good vegetarian choice, friendly attentive service, no smoking dining area; discreet piped music; picnic-sets out on pleasant terrace, attractive village *(Dr and Mrs M E Wilson, MRSM, Jenny Brand)*

WITHAM FRIARY ST7440

Seymour Arms [signed from B3092 S of Frome]: Welcoming unspoilt local, two simple rooms off hatch-service corridor, one with darts, the other with central table skittles; well kept Ushers Best, Rich's local farm cider, cards and dominoes – no juke box or machines; good-sized attractive garden by main rail line *(the Didler, Adam Manolson, Pete Baker, Edward Mirzoeff)*

WIVELISCOMBE ST0827

Bear [North St]: Good range of well priced home-cooked food from burgers and good sandwiches up, well kept local Cotleigh and other west country ales (wknd brewery visits, beer festival with music and morris dancers), farm ciders, very attentive friendly landlord; play area, good value bedrooms *(the Didler, Andy and Jill Kassube, Francis Johnston)*

WOOKEY ST5145

Ring o' Bells [High St]: Dark wood tables and settles, big log fire each end, well kept Butcombe ales, new licensees doing generous sensibly up-to-date food in bar and dining room; may be piped music *(Alan and Paula McCully)*

WOOKEY HOLE ST5347

Wookey Hole Inn: Usefully placed family pub with unusual cool and trendy décor, relaxed atmosphere, four changing real ales and several belgian beers, enjoyable and innovative realistically priced food, nice staff; jazz Sun lunchtime, pleasant garden, comfortable bedrooms *(Mr and Mrs G Taylor, Christopher Stott)*

WRANTAGE ST3022

Canal Inn [A378 E of M5 junction 25]: Welcoming recently reopened three-room pub with well kept real ales, farm cider, log fires, enjoyable fresh food in bar and dining room, helpful staff; garden with play area *(A J and C D Stodgell)*

WRAXALL ST4971

New Battleaxes [Bristol Rd]: Large neatly kept rambling pub with good value food inc daily carvery bargain, well kept real ale; handy for Tyntesfield (NT) *(W R Miller, Norman and Sarah Keeping)*

Old Barn [just off Bristol Rd (B3130)]: Rustic gabled barn conversion with scrubbed tables, school benches and soft sofas under the oak rafters, stripped boards, flagstones and festoons of dried flowers; welcoming atmosphere, wide choice of good home-made food, five well kept beers inc Bass and local brews tapped from the cask, friendly service; two TV screens, Sun quiz night; garden with good play area and barbecues on cobbled terrace *(the Didler, R W Broomfield, Alan and Paula McCully, Richard Houghton)*

WRINGTON ST4662

Golden Lion [Broad St]: Small comfortable village coaching inn with well kept Bass, Butcombe and Flowers IPA, plenty of regulars, lunchtime rolls, open fire in recently revealed fireplace, pool room, occasional Sat piano sing-songs; small back courtyard with wknd

barbecues, open all day *(John A Barker, Alan and Paula McCully)*
Plough [2½ miles off A370 Bristol—Weston, from bottom of Rhodiate Hill]: Large friendly beamed pub rambling around central servery with well kept Smiles and Youngs and interesting wine list, quarts of cocktails, popular good value food (all Sun afternoon) inc tapas, traditional pubby décor, step up to long no smoking dining area, several coal or log fires; two TVs, fruit machine and cash machine; lots of picnic-sets out on sloping grass, more under cover on heated terrace, open all day *(John Urquhart, John A Barker, BB, Bob and Margaret Holder)*

YARLINGTON ST6529

☆ ***Stags Head***: Two-bar country pub under new young licensees, good upscale cooking using fresh fish and local produce and game, well kept real ales, rustic décor; cl Sun evening and Mon *(Steve Culverhouse, Neville and Anne Morley, Richard Wyld)*

If a pub tries to make you leave a credit card behind the bar, be on your guard. The credit card firms and banks which issue them condemn this practice. After all, the publican who asks you to do this is in effect saying: 'I don't trust you'. Have you any more reason to trust his staff? If your card is used fraudulently while you have let it be kept out of your sight, the card company could say you've been negligent yourself – and refuse to make good your losses. So say that they can 'swipe' your card instead, but must hand it back to you. Please let us know if a pub does try to keep your card.

Staffordshire

The county's two pubs which this year score highest in readers' approval could hardly be more different from each other: the unashamedly basic old Yew Tree at Cauldon, going its own eccentric way under its charming landlord – good cheap beer and snacks, but the main thing is the amazing mass of seriously interesting collectables here; and the stylishly modern and very smoothly run Boat near Lichfield, with good food in up-to-date comfort. Indeed, the Boat near Lichfield keeps its title of Staffordshire Dining Pub of the Year, for the second year running. In most of the other pubs we include as main entries here, good value food is a strong point. Drinks too tend to be cheaper than the national average. Burton upon Trent is still England's brewing capital, housing Marstons (the main regional brewer), and producing well known beers like Bass and Worthington for their foreign owners Interbrew and Coors. It's home too to the craft brewers Burton Bridge, Old Cottage and Tower; beers from other small Staffordshire breweries to look out for include Enville, Eccleshall and Leek. In the Lucky Dip section at the end of the chapter, pubs of special note are the Coopers Tavern in Burton, George at Eccleshall, White Swan at Fradley, Bluebell at Hardings Wood, Meynell Ingram Arms at Hoar Cross, Plough at Huddlesford and Horseshoe at Tatenhill.

ABBOTS BROMLEY SK0824 Map 7

Goats Head

Market Place

This black and white timbered pub is comfortably relaxed, with some heavy Tudor beams in the three linked parts of its main lounge bar and dining area. Furniture runs from traditional oak settles to solid dining tables and chairs on turkey carpet, and a big inglenook has a small coal and log fire. The licensee's mother is Dutch so the changing menu might include a couple of continental dishes such as frikandell and shashlick alongside lunchtime sandwiches (from £2.95), soup (£3.25), ginger and chilli chicken goujons with mango chutney (£3.95), cottage pie (£5.95), filo pastry filled with roast vegetables and sweet and sour sauce (£7.50), poached chicken breast in creamy stilton sauce (£8.15), braised lamb shank in redcurrant and mint gravy (£8.50), sirloin steak (£10.15) and puddings (£3.50); Sunday roast (£6.95). They have a good range of wines by the glass (from Tanners of Shrewsbury), and well kept Greene King Abbot and Marstons Pedigree on handpump; service is friendly and efficient; cribbage, darts, and maybe piped radio. A panelled public bar on the right has darts, and out on a neat sheltered lawn picnic-sets and teak tables and seats look up to the church tower behind – this is a charmingly unspoilt village, famous for its annual horn dance. *(Recommended by Guy Vowles, Gordon Oakes, David J Austin)*

Punch ~ Tenant Kristian Hine ~ Real ale ~ Bar food (not Mon lunchtime, Sun evening) ~ Restaurant ~ (01283) 840254 ~ Children in eating area of bar ~ Open 12-3 6-11; 12-4, 7-10.30 Sun; closed Mon lunchtime

If we know a pub does summer barbecues, we say so.

ALSTONEFIELD SK1355 Map 7

George

Village signposted from A515 Ashbourne—Buxton

This welcoming stone-built Peak District pub makes a delightful place for a break, and all sorts of people, from sightseers and campers, to cyclists and walkers (though no muddy boots) enjoy its charming simplicity and cheery local atmosphere. It's in a peaceful farming hamlet by the green, and in fine weather it's a real pleasure to sit out on the stone seats beneath the inn-sign and watch the world go by, or in the big sheltered stableyard behind the pub which has picnic-sets by a pretty rockery. For a longer stay you can arrange with the landlord to camp on the croft. The unchanging straightforward low-beamed bar has pewter tankards hanging by the copper-topped bar counter (well kept Burtonwood Bitter and a guest such as Wadworths 6X on handpump), a collection of old Peak District photographs and pictures, a roaring coal fire on chilly days, darts, cribbage and dominoes. The spacious no smoking family/dining room has plenty of tables and wheelback chairs. Tasty no nonsense home-made food is good value and includes sandwiches (from £2.40), soup (£2.65), ploughman's (from £5.10), meat and potato pie (£6.20), chicken breast, lasagne or breaded plaice (£6.50), a couple of daily specials, and delicious home-made puddings such as fudge and walnut pie and meringue glaze (£2.85); you order food from the friendly staff at the kitchen door. *(Recommended by Matthew Shackle, John Beeken, Peter F Marshall, Sarah Day, Mark Timms, the Didler, Richard Cole, Mrs Julie Thomas, Mark Percy, Lesley Mayoh, Nigel Long, Mike and Wendy Proctor, P Price, Paul Robinshaw, Colin Buckle, Pauline and Terry James, W W Burke)*

Burtonwood ~ Tenants Richard and Sue Grandjean ~ Real ale ~ Bar food ~ (01335) 310205 ~ Children in family room ~ Open 11-3, 6-11; 11-11 Sat; 12-10.30 Sun

Watts Russell Arms £

Hopedale

Very handy for Dovedale and the Manifold (it can get busy at weekends), this 18th-c shuttered stone house is prettily set on a little lane in a deep leafy valley just outside the village. The cheerful beamed bar has brocaded wall banquettes and wheelback chairs and carvers, an open fire below a copper hood, a collection of blue and white china jugs hanging from the ceiling, bric-a-brac around the roughcast walls, and an interesting bar counter made from copper-bound oak barrels; the tap room is no smoking. You'll find well kept Black Sheep, Timothy Taylors Landlord and an occasional guest such as Deuchars IPA on handpump, over a dozen malts, and a decent range of soft drinks; darts, table skittles and dominoes. Outside there are picnic-sets under parasols on the sheltered tiered terrace, and in the garden. Under new licensees, good value tasty bar food now includes lunchtime sandwiches (£3.50), pancake wraps (from £3.75), lasagne or chicken and mushroom casserole (£5.95), puddings such as apple nut crumble (£3.50), and a handful of additional evening dishes such as tomato and tarragon soup (£3.50) and confit of duck with honey and orange glaze (£9.95). *(Recommended by the Didler, Dave Braisted, Peter and Jackie Barnett, W W Burke)*

Free house ~ Licensees Christine Corcoran and Bruce Elliott ~ Real ale ~ Bar food ~ (01335) 310126 ~ Children welcome ~ Open 12-3, 7-11(10.30 Sun); cl Sun evening winter; closed Mon except bank hols

Stars after the name of a pub show exceptional quality. One star means most people (after reading the report to see just why the star has been won) would think a special trip worth while. Two stars mean that the pub is really outstanding – many that for their particular qualities cannot be bettered.

BURTON UPON TRENT SK2423 Map 7

Burton Bridge Inn £

Bridge Street (A50)

Readers enjoy the genuinely friendly atmosphere at this straightforward, bustling old brick local. It's the tap for Burton Bridge Brewery (out in the long old-fashioned yard at the back) which produces the Bitter, Festival, Golden Delicious, Gold Medal, Porter and Top Dog Stout that are well kept and served on handpump here. They also keep around 25 whiskies and over a dozen country wines. The simple little front area leads into an adjacent bar, separated from a no smoking oak-panelled lounge by the serving counter. The bar has wooden pews, plain walls hung with notices, awards and brewery memorabilia, and the lounge has oak beams, a flame-effect fire and old oak tables and chairs. Simple but hearty bar snacks include cobs (from £1.50), toasties (£2.20), filled yorkshire pudding (from £3.30) and ploughman's (£3.60); the panelled upstairs dining room is open only at lunchtime. A blue-brick patio overlooks the brewery. *(Recommended by David Carr, C J Fletcher, the Didler, Suzanne Miles, Bernie Adams, Theo, Anne and Jane Gaskin, Pete Baker, Patrick Hancock, P Price, Dr and Mrs A K Clarke)*

Own brew ~ Licensees Kevin and Jan McDonald ~ Real ale ~ Bar food (lunchtime only, not Sun) ~ No credit cards ~ (01283) 536596 ~ Children in eating area of bar ~ Dogs welcome ~ Open 11.30-2.15, 5-11; 12-2.15, 7-10.30 Sun; closed bank hol Mon lunchtime

CAULDON SK0749 Map 7

Yew Tree ★★ £

Village signposted from A523 and A52 about 8 miles W of Ashbourne

Don't deny yourself this fascinating treat if you're travelling in the area, and don't be put off by the plain exterior, or the fact that the pub is tucked unpromisingly between enormous cement works and quarries and almost hidden by a towering yew tree. Inside is a veritable museum's-worth of curiosities all lovingly collected by the charming landlord himself. The most impressive pieces are perhaps the working Polyphons and Symphonions – 19th-c developments of the musical box, often taller than a person, each with quite a repertoire of tunes and elaborate sound-effects; take plenty of 2p pieces to work them. But there are also two pairs of Queen Victoria's stockings, ancient guns and pistols, several penny-farthings, an old sit-and-stride boneshaker, a rocking horse, swordfish blades, a little 800 BC greek vase, and even a fine marquetry cabinet crammed with notable early staffordshire pottery. Soggily sprung sofas mingle with 18th-c settles, plenty of little wooden tables and a four-person oak church choir seat with carved heads which came from St Mary's church in Stafford; above the bar is an odd iron dog-carrier (don't ask how it works!). As well as all this there's an expanding choir of fine tuneful longcase clocks in the gallery just above the entrance, a collection of six pianolas (one of which is played most nights) with an excellent repertoire of piano rolls, a working vintage valve radio set, a crank-handle telephone, a sinuous medieval wind instrument made of leather, and a Jacobean four-poster which was once owned by Josiah Wedgwood and still has his original wig hook on the headboard. The drinks here are very reasonably priced (so no wonder it's popular with locals), and you'll find well kept Bass, Burton Bridge and Grays Dark Mild on handpump or tapped from the cask, along with some interesting malt whiskies; piped music (probably Radio 2), darts, shove-ha'penny, table skittles, dominoes and cribbage. Simple good value tasty snacks include hot pork pies (70p), meat and potato pies, chicken and mushroom or steak pies (85p), big filled hot baps and sandwiches (from £1.50), quiche, smoked mackerel or ham salad (£3.50), and home-made puddings (£1.50). *(Recommended by D C Leggatt, the Didler, Sarah Day, Mark Timms, Graham and Lynn Mason, Ann and Colin Hunt, Kevin Thorpe, Bernie Adams, MLR, Mike and Wendy Proctor, Mr and Mrs John Taylor, David J Austin, Patrick Hancock, W W Burke, Rona Murdoch)*

Free house ~ Licensee Alan East ~ Real ale ~ Bar food ~ No credit cards ~ (01538) 308348 ~ Children in Polyphon room ~ Dogs welcome ~ Folk music first Tues in month ~ Open 10-3, 6-11; 12-3, 7-10.30 Sun

LICHFIELD SK0705 Map 4

Boat

Walsall Road, Muckley Corner (A461 SW)

Staffordshire Dining Pub of the Year

Going from strength to strength, this very well run modern pub is proving to be a successful growing venture, with its very good value, well presented and imaginative food at the forefront of the operation. Lunchtime snacks include sandwiches (from £3.50), pizza (£4.50), home-baked ham and egg (£4.95) and steak and mushroom pie (£6.95), alongside starters such as soup (£2.95), crayfish terrine with lemon dressing (£4.50), fried scallops with rocket salad (£6.95), main courses such as filo parcel of goats cheese with walnut and watercress (£7.50), pork fillet on sweet potato mash with crispy parma ham (£9.25), red snapper fillet with roast vegetables and lime dressing (£10.50) and puddings such as toffee and banana crumble and crème brûlée (£3.95). Well lit from above by a big skylight, the first area as you enter is the most contemporary, with bright plastic flooring, views straight into the kitchen, striking photoprints, blue and russet café furniture and potted palms, all of which is dominated by huge floor-to-ceiling food blackboards. To the left a newly converted dining area has views on to the canal (currently undergoing restoration), and to the right the solid light wood bar counter has three constantly changing thoughtfully sourced real ales such as Brakspears Bitter, Church End Hop Gun and Timothy Taylors Landlord on handpump. Further round to the right a plainer area has sturdy modern pale pine furniture on pink carpets and prints on white walls; faint piped music. It's all immaculately kept, and staff are cheerful and attentive. The newly landscaped area outside is paved with a central raised decking area. Readers tell us there is good wheelchair access throughout. *(Recommended by John and Penny Spinks, Colin Fisher, Roy and Lindsey Fentiman, Maggie and Tony Harwood, Simon and Mandy King, Brenda and Rob Fincham, Brian and Jacky Wilson)*

Free house ~ Licensee Ann Holden ~ Real ale ~ Bar food (12-2.30, 6.30-9.30; 12-8 Sun) ~ Restaurant ~ (01543) 361692 ~ Children in eating area of bar ~ Open 12-3, 6-11; 12-11 Sat

SALT SJ9527 Map 7

Holly Bush

Village signposted off A51 S of Stone (and A518 NE of Stafford)

The oldest part of this lovely white-painted thatched house dates back to the 14th c, and has a heavy beamed and planked ceiling (some of the beams are attractively carved), a salt cupboard built in by the coal fire, and other nice old-fashioned touches such as an antique pair of clothes brushes hanging by the door, attractive sporting prints and watercolours, and an ancient pair of riding boots on the mantelpiece. Several cosy areas spread off from the standing-room serving section, with comfortable settees as well as more orthodox seats. A modern back extension blends in well, with beams, stripped brickwork and a small coal fire. Notably cheerful and helpful staff serve well kept Boddingtons, Marstons Pedigree and a guest such as Adnams Broadside on handpump, and sensibly priced food which comes in generous helpings, using local supplies where possible: grilled black pudding on spinach with a poached egg (£3.45), duck and pear salad on rocket (£4.50), sausage and mash or salmon with perry and chive sauce (£7.95), seafood and white wine sauce with pasta (£8.50), baked pork fillet stuffed with sage, onion and apricots and wrapped in smoked bacon (£9.50), collops of beef in whisky sauce (£10.50) and grouse casserole (£10.25); arrive early for a table if you want to eat. The big back lawn has rustic picnic-sets, and they may have traditional jazz and a hog roast in summer and a fireworks display on 5 November. *(Recommended by Michael and Jenny Back, Collin and Julie Taylor, Graham and Lynn Mason, Bob and Laura Brock, Brenda and Stuart Naylor, Alec and Joan Laurence, Roger Braithwaite, Karen Eliot, Richard and Anne Ansell, Alan and Paula McCully, Roy and Lindsey Fentiman)*

Free house ~ Licensees Geoffrey and Joseph Holland ~ Real ale ~ Bar food (12-2, 6-9.30;

12-9.30 Sat, Sun) ~ (01889) 508234 ~ Children in eating area of bar ~ Open 12-3, 6-11; 12-11 Sat; 12-10.30 Sun

STOURTON SO8485 Map 4

Fox

A458 W of junction with A449, towards Enville

Don't let the unassuming exterior of this lonely roadside pub put you off. Once inside, it quickly grows on you, thanks largely to the atmosphere generated by the warmly friendly family who run it. Several cosily small areas ramble back from the small serving bar by the entrance, with its well kept Bathams Best and Enville on handpump (and a noticeboard of hand-written travel offers). Tables are mostly sturdy and varnished, with pews, settles and comfortable library or dining chairs; there is green carpet here, dark blue there, bare boards beyond, with a good positive colour scheme picked up nicely by the curtains, and some framed exotic menus and well chosen prints (jazz and golf both feature). The woodburning stoves may be opened to give a cheery blaze on cold days. They put out big bunches of flowers, and the lighting (mainly low voltage spots) has been done very carefully, giving an intimate bistro feel in the areas round on the right. A smart conservatory has neat bentwood furniture and proper tablecloths. Good value lunchtime snacks include hot baguettes (from £3.95), sausage and mash (£5.25), steak and mushroom pie (£6.50), scampi (£6.75), with more elaborate evening dishes such as goats cheese bruschetta or chicken tikka with filo pastry and mint yoghurt (£5.50), salmon on watercress risotto (£11.95), pork fillet stuffed with apple and sage with calvados and mustard sauce (£12.95) and fillet steak on horseradish mash with red wine jus (£15.95); it's a good idea to book if you want to come to one of their fortnightly fish evenings; no smoking dining area, piped music. A big stretch of sloping grass has well spaced picnic-sets, and the pub is surrounded by woodland; it is well placed for Kinver Country Park walks. *(Recommended by Theo, Anne and Jane Gaskin)*

Free house ~ Licensee Stefan Caron ~ Real ale ~ Bar food (12-2.15, 7-9.30; 12.30-5.30 Sun; not Mon) ~ Restaurant ~ (01384) 872614 ~ Children welcome ~ Open 10.30-3, 4.30-11; 11-11 Sat; 12-10.30 Sun

WARSLOW SK0858 Map 7

Greyhound

B5053 S of Buxton

This very welcoming slate and stone-built pub is surrounded by pretty countryside and is handy for the Manifold Valley, Dovedale and Alton Towers. The side garden has picnic-sets under ash trees, with rustic seats out in front where window boxes blaze with colour in summer. Straightforward but cosily comfortable inside, the beamed bar has long cushioned antique oak settles (some quite elegant), houseplants in the windows, cheerful fires and a no smoking area. Reasonably priced home-made bar food includes lunchtime sandwiches (from £2.25, baguettes from £3.25), filled baked potatoes (from £3.50), sausage, egg and chips (£4.50) and gammon and pineapple (£7.50), as well as soup (£2.95), thai-style fishcakes (£5), vegetarian stuffed peppers (£7.45), big battered cod or moroccan lamb (£7.95), sirloin steak (£9.50) and puddings such as chocolate fudge cake or blackberry and apple crumble (£2.95); Wednesday night curries (£4.50). They serve well kept Black Sheep, Marstons Pedigree and a couple of changing guests such as Everards Perfick and Wadworths 6X on handpump, as well as 20 malt whiskies; TV, fruit machine, pool, darts, dominoes and piped music. Bedrooms are basic but good value with a tasty breakfast. *(Recommended by Derek and Sylvia Stephenson, Doug Christian, D C Leggatt, Susan and Tony Dyer, Matthew Shackle, Michael Butler, Bernard Stradling, Mike and Wendy Proctor, Ken and Barbara Turner, David Field, Mr and Mrs A Campbell)*

Free house ~ Licensees Jan and Andy Livesley ~ Real ale ~ Bar food (12-3, 6.30-9) ~ Restaurant ~ (01298) 84249 ~ Children in eating area of bar and family room ~ Dogs allowed in bar ~ Soft rock most Sats ~ Open 12-3, 6.30-11; 12-11(10.30 Sun) Sat; 12-3, 6.30-11(10.30 Sun) Sat, Sun in winter ~ Bedrooms: £17.50/£35

WETTON SK1055 Map 7

Olde Royal Oak

Village signposted off Hulme End—Alstonefield road, between B5054 and A515

This aged white-painted and shuttered stone-built village house nestles in the heart of lovely National Trust countryside, so not surprisingly the pub is popular with walkers. Behind the pub is a croft suitable for caravans and tents, and Wetton Mill and the Manifold Valley are nearby. There's a good convivial atmosphere in the bar, which has golf clubs hanging from black beams with white ceiling boards above, small dining chairs around rustic tables, a piano surrounded by old sheet music covers, an oak corner cupboard, and a coal fire in the stone fireplace. The bar extends into a more modern-feeling area, which in turn leads to a carpeted sun lounge looking out over the small garden; piped music, darts, TV, shove-ha'penny, cribbage and dominoes. The family room is no smoking. You can choose from more than 40 whiskies, and they've well kept Black Sheep, Greene King Ruddles County, Jennings Cumberland and a guest such as Leek Stafffordshire Gold on handpump. Served in generous helpings, reasonably priced bar food includes soup or staffordshire oatcakes filled with cheese (£2.85), brie wedges with redcurrant sauce (£3.85), ploughman's (£5.85), battered haddock or mediterranean vegetable lasagne (£7.25), local rainbow trout (£7.45), steaks (from £10.25) and puddings such as ginger sponge pudding or cherry cheesecake (from £2.75); Sunday roasts (£6.45). Service is good, and the landlord is friendly. *(Recommended by Rona Murdoch, the Didler, Nigel Long, Mike and Wendy Proctor, Brian and Anna Marsden, K H Richards, Peter and Jackie Barnett, W W Burke)*

Free house ~ Licensees Kath and Brian Rowbotham ~ Real ale ~ Bar food ~ (01335) 310287 ~ Children in family room ~ Live entertainment Sat evening ~ Open 12-3, 7-11(10.30 Sun); closed Weds ~ Bedrooms: /£55S

LUCKY DIP

Besides the fully inspected pubs, you might like to try these Lucky Dips recommended to us and described by readers (if you do, please send us reports: www.goodguides.co.uk).

ABBOTS BROMLEY SK0824
Coach & Horses [High St]: Comfortable Tudor village pub with decent food in refurbished beamed bar and restaurant, well kept real ales, friendly staff; pleasant garden, good value bedrooms *(David J Austin)*
Royal Oak [Bagot St]: Traditionally furnished old inn, popular generous food from sandwiches to steaks with imaginative blackboard dishes, well kept Marstons-related ales, decent wine, efficient friendly service, open fire, comfortable and attractive dining lounge *(David J Austin)*

ACTON TRUSSELL SJ9318
Moat House [signed from A449 just S of Stafford; handy for M6 junction 13]: Busy timbered food place by Staffs & Worcs Canal, partly dating from 1320 but now with 50-room hotel attached; comfortable oak-beamed bar with big open fireplace and armchairs, nice décor, lots of efficient young staff, enjoyable bar food (only restaurant meals Sun lunchtime), good wine list, no smoking restaurant; fruit machine, piped music, bar can be smoky; children welcome, open all day wknds, attractive grounds with picnic-sets overlooking charming duck pond *(Karen Eliot, LYM, Roz Lowrie, Pauline and Terry James, Derek and Heather Manning)*

ALREWAS SK1714
William IV [William IV Rd, off main st]: Friendly backstreet pub with Marstons Pedigree and monthly guest beers, enjoyable reasonably priced honest food (all day Fri-Sun), two for one lunchtime bargains (not Sun), good service, partly no smoking raised eating area (busy wknds, best to book then); music nights, sports TV; tables in garden with aviary and chipmunks, short walk from Grand Trunk Canal *(Glenwys and Alan Lawrence, Bob and Laura Brock, C J Fletcher)*

ANSLOW SK2024
☆ *Burnt Gate* [Hopley Rd]: Pleasant country pub, comfortable lounge with well kept Bass and Marstons Pedigree, good fresh home-made food with strong local slant inc popular Sun lunch in separate restaurant *(C J Fletcher, Paul Baxter)*

ARMITAGE SK0716
Plum Pudding [Rugeley Rd (A513)]: Canalside pub and brasserie with modern warm colour scheme, real ales, friendly efficient service, enjoyable contemporary food; waterside terrace *(Alan Cole, Kirstie Bruce)*

BARTON-UNDER-NEEDWOOD SK1818
Middle Bell [Main St]: Several areas off central bar, plenty of comfortable settees and alcoves, gas fire, up-to-date style, decent food inc

notable vegetarian bake, attentive staff, good value wine *(Maggie and Tony Harwood)*

BLYTHE BRIDGE SJ9640

Black Cock [Uttoxeter Rd (A521)]: Warmly welcoming and helpful, with enjoyable freshly made food making the most of good local produce *(L and R Powys-Smith)*

BRANSTON SK2221

Bridge Inn [off A5121 just SW of Burton; Tatenhill Lane, by Grand Trunk Canal Bridge 34]: Simple canalside pub with good basic home-made food inc lots of veg, well kept Marstons Pedigree tapped from the cask, warm log fire; tables in waterside garden, good moorings, basic supplies for boaters and caravanners *(Paul Baxter)*

BREWOOD SJ8808

Bridge Inn [High Green; by Shrops Union Canal Bridge 14]: Welcoming pub doing well under current management, enjoyable food inc good value authentic italian dishes and good fresh fish, well kept Burtonwood and guest beers *(Bob and Laura Brock, Susan and Erik Falck-Therkelsen)*

BURSTON SJ9330

Greyhound [just off A51 Sandon—Stone]: Friendly family-run pub, largely no smoking, wide choice of enjoyable standard food (all day Sun) and interesting blackboard dishes in rambling bar and larger back restaurant, efficient service, well kept Bass, Tetleys Imperial and Titanic *(Ian and Sue Wells)*

BURTON UPON TRENT SK2423

Alfred [Derby St]: Tied to local small Burton Bridge brewery, their full range and guest beers kept well from central bar serving two plain rooms, good beer-oriented food too; friendly landlord, lots of country wines, no smoking area, pool in back games room, beer festivals Easter and early Nov; open all day, cheap bedrooms *(the Didler, Bernie Adams, Patrick Hancock)*

Burton Bar [part of Bass Museum, Horninglow St]: Reconstructed Edwardian bar, comfortable, with well kept unusual real ales; the brewing museum is an interesting outing *(Maggie and Tony Harwood)*

☆ *Coopers Tavern* [Cross St]: Splendidly traditional pub taken over by Tynemill, with new landlord and their Castle Rock Burton Gold and a changing guest beer alongside the well kept locally brewed Bass, Marstons Pedigree and Worthington 1744, tapped from an imposing row of casks in the counterless back room; barrel tables, cheap nourishing lunchtime food (not Sun) from hot filled cobs to a bargain curry, homely no smoking front parlour with piano and coal fire, friendly staff; impromptu folk nights Tues *(Bernie Adams, LYM, the Didler, C J Fletcher, Pete Baker, Patrick Hancock)*

Derby Inn [Derby Rd]: Unspoilt friendly local with well kept Marstons Pedigree, long-serving landlord, local produce for sale wknd, brewery glasses collection in cosy panelled lounge, lots of steam railway memorabilia in long narrow bar; sports TV; open all day Fri-Sat *(Bernie Adams, C J Fletcher, the Didler)*

Devonshire Arms [Station St]: Tied to Burton Bridge, with a good range of their ales and of continental bottled beers, also country wines, decent lunchtime food, lots of snug corners – some no smoking; pleasant back terrace, open all day Fri-Sat *(the Didler, Patrick Hancock, C J Fletcher)*

Old Cottage Tavern [Rangemoor St/Byrkley St]: Tied to local small brewery Old Cottage, three of their beers such as Oak, Halcyon Daze and Stout, also guest beers, four rooms inc no smoking room, games room and cosy back restaurant – good value food inc bargain specials; open all day *(the Didler, C J Fletcher)*

Roebuck [Station St]: Comfortable Victorian-style alehouse with several well kept changing real ales inc a bargain beer brewed for the pub, enjoyable cheap lunchtime food inc add-it-up dishes (you choose the ingredients), friendly staff, prints and artefacts; piped music; open all day wkdys, decent bedrooms *(the Didler)*

Thomas Sykes [Anglesey Rd]: In former stables and wagon shed of ex-Everards brewery (latterly Heritage Brewery Museum), two friendly high-ceilinged rooms with stable fittings and breweriana, wood benches, cobbled floors, well kept Bass and Marstons Pedigree on handpump and interesting guest beers tapped from the cask, fine pump clip collection, good cheap basic food such as filled cobs, small snug; outside gents'; seats out in yard, children welcome till 8ish, open all day Fri *(Bernie Adams, the Didler, C J Fletcher, Richard Houghton)*

BUTTERTON SK0756

Black Lion [off B5053]: Low-beamed traditional 18th-c stone inn in Peak District conservation village, log fire, kitchen range in inner room, some banquette seating, enjoyable bar food from filled rolls up, well kept ales such as Everards Tiger, Marstons Pedigree, Theakstons Best and Charles Wells Bombardier, reasonable prices, traditional games and pool room; piped music; children in eating areas, tables on terrace, tidy bedrooms, cl Mon lunchtime *(LYM, the Didler, Mike and Wendy Proctor, David and Thelma Taylor)*

CHEADLE SK0342

☆ *Queens at Freehay* [Counslow Rd, SE]: Enjoyable dining pub with arch to neat and airy no smoking dining area (children welcome here) from comfortable lounge, mainly familiar bar food, well kept Bass and Worthington, swift attentive service *(Dr T E Hothersall, Mike and Wendy Proctor, Jean and Douglas Troup, LYM)*

CONSALL SK0049

☆ *Black Lion* [Consall Forge, OS Sheet 118 map ref 000491; best approach from Nature Park, off A522, using car park ½ mile past Nature Centre]: Traditional take-us-as-you-find-us tavern tucked away in rustic old-fashioned canalside settlement by restored steam railway station, enjoyable generous unpretentious food freshly cooked by landlord inc good fish choice, good coal fire, well kept Marstons Best and Pedigree; piped music, no muddy boots; busy wknds, good walking area *(the Didler,*

LYM, Bob and Laura Brock, Mike and Wendy Proctor, Paul Robinshaw, Colin Buckle, L Elliott)

CRESSWELL SJ9739

☆ *Izaak Walton* [off A50 Stoke—Uttoxeter; Cresswell Lane]: Wide food choice all day from sandwiches and filled rolls to steaks and mixed grill in pleasant dining pub with prints and panelling, several small rooms and larger upstairs area, well kept Adnams Best and Fullers London Pride, good wines by the glass, friendly staff; well behaved children welcome, disabled facilities (but some steps), attractive back garden *(LYM, Catherine and Rob Dunster)*

DOVEDALE SK1450

☆ *Izaak Walton* [follow Ilam sign off A52, or Thorpe off A515, NW of Ashbourne]: Relaxing, informal and pleasantly individual low-beamed bar in sizeable hotel, walkers welcome, some distinctive antique oak settles and chairs, good log fire in massive central stone chimney; well kept Everards Tiger and Leatherbritches Bitter, decent wines by the glass, ample food in bar and restaurant, morning coffee and afternoon tea; very tranquil spot – seats on two spreading well kept lawns by sheep pastures, superb views; bedrooms comfortable *(LYM, W W Burke)*

ECCLESHALL SJ8328

Badger [Green Lane]: Neat and comfortable, with huge helpings of good food, quick service, well kept sensibly priced ales such as Marstons Pedigree, no smoking conservatory dining room; tables outside, well maintained comfortable bedrooms, quite handy for M6 *(Mr and Mrs Colin Roberts)*

☆ *George* [A519/B5026]: Good Slaters beers brewed by the licensees' son, such as Bitter, Original, Premium, Ecky Thump, Shining Knight and Supreme, beamed town-pub bar with well worn in unassuming furnishings, coal fire in big central inglenook, some flagstones, cosy alcoves, good wines by the glass, quick friendly service, interesting food choice from side restaurant (all day wknds), reasonable prices; may be piped music; children in eating areas, dogs welcome, open all day *(Sue Holland, Dave Webster, LYM, Derek and Sylvia Stephenson, Guy Vowles, Kevin Thorpe, Alec and Joan Laurence, Patrick Hancock, Dr and Mrs A K Clarke, Stan and Hazel Allen, PL, John Tavernor)*

ENVILLE SO8286

☆ *Cat* [A458 W of Stourbridge]: 17th-c, with heavy beams, timbers and log fire in two appealingly old-fashioned rooms on one side of servery, plush banquettes on the other, well kept local Enville Ale, White and seasonal Phoenix, other beers such as Tetleys, Wicked Hathern and Wychwood Goliath (landlord helpful with the choice), mulled wine, quickly served generous food from imaginative sandwiches to unusual specials, popular upstairs restaurant, tabby cat and quiet collie; nice yard with picnic-sets, popular with walkers (on Staffordshire Way), cl Sun *(BB, the Didler, Lynda and Trevor Smith)*

FORTON SJ7521

Swan [A519 Newport—Eccleshall]: Long main room opening into another big room that extends into conservatory, as does restaurant; four well kept real ales (they may offer tasters), vast blackboard choice of reasonably priced food, consistently good welcoming service; handy for Shrops Union Canal walks *(Guy Vowles)*

FOXT SK0348

☆ *Fox & Goose*: Three-room pub with short choice of good reasonably priced generous bar food, pre-film *Titanic* memorabilia and lots of sewing machines, four well kept ales inc one brewed for the pub, Addlestone's cider, friendly chatty service and regulars, upmarket restaurant *(HP)*

FRADLEY SK1414

☆ *White Swan* [Fradley Junction]: Perfect canalside location, very popular summer wknds; wide choice of quickly served usual food from sandwiches to good value Sun carvery, well kept Marstons Pedigree, efficient friendly staff, cheery traditional public bar, quieter plusher lounge and lower vaulted back bar (where children allowed), lots of malt whiskies, real fire, cribbage, dominoes; waterside tables, good canal walks *(LYM, Bob and Laura Brock, Ian and Jane Irving)*

FROGHALL SK0247

Railway Inn: Well kept Banks's, Marstons and Wychwood Hobgoblin, good value standard food, quick friendly service, lots of railway memorabilia; bedrooms, handy for Caldon Canal and Churnet Valley steam railway *(Dave Braisted)*

GNOSALL SJ8220

Boat [Gnosall Heath, by Shrops Union Canal Bridge 34]: Small welcoming pub in quiet village, first-floor bar with curved window seat overlooking barges, warm welcome, well kept Marstons Bitter and Pedigree, bargain food from OAP specials to wide range of good value evening meals, real fire, darts, dominoes, pool; tables out by canal, open all day from noon *(John and Lynn Norcliffe, Len Beattie)*

Navigation [Newport Rd]: Pleasant two-bar pub with dining conservatory overlooking Shrops Union Canal, friendly chatty landlord, well kept Greene King Old Speckled Hen, reasonably priced usual food *(Len Beattie)*

Royal Oak [Newport Rd]: Small, civilised and friendly, with nice atmosphere and well kept ales inc a weekly guest such as Shepherd Neame Bishops Finger *(Len Beattie)*

HANLEY SJ8847

Chaplins [Lichfield St]: Thriving recently renamed bar (was Lloyds), pleasant décor, friendly staff, enjoyable food; late licence, tables out on new terrace *(anon)*

HARDINGS WOOD SJ8354

☆ *Bluebell*: Traditional boaters' tavern between Macclesfield and Trent & Mersey Canals, welcoming and unpretentious, half a dozen well kept changing ales from small breweries, belgian beers, farm ciders, helpful staff, filled rolls, busy front bar, quieter back room;

impromptu music sessions; may be cl wkdy lunchtimes, very popular wknds *(Paul and Ann Meyer, Sue Holland, Dave Webster, Mike and Wendy Proctor)*

HARTSHILL SJ8745

Jolly Potters [Hartshill Rd (A52)]: Welcoming and gently updated local popular for its particularly well kept Bass, central bar, corridor to public bar (with TV) and three small homely lounges *(the Didler, Pete Baker)*

HIGH OFFLEY SJ7725

Anchor [off A519 Eccleshall—Newport; towards High Lea, by Shrops Union Canal, Bridge 42; Peggs Lane]: Little changed in the century or more this family have run it, two small simple rooms behind partition, well kept Marstons Pedigree and Wadworths 6X in jugs from cellar, Weston's farm ciders, may be lunchtime toasties; on Shrops Union Canal, outbuilding with small shop and semi-open lavatories, lovely garden with great hanging baskets, caravan/campsite; cl Mon-Thurs winter *(Bob and Laura Brock, the Didler)*

HOAR CROSS SK1323

☆ *Meynell Ingram Arms* [Abbots Bromley Rd, off A515 Yoxall—Sudbury]: Beamed country pub's friendly newish landlord turning it into more of a gastropub, neat minimalist décor keeping old-fashioned touches inc log fires in no smoking main lounge and in public side, separate little front snug; enjoyable and inventive if not cheap bar food from sandwiches up, plenty of local produce, formal restaurant meals, well kept Marstons Pedigree and Timothy Taylors Landlord, keen young staff; courtyard tables, attractive spot in summer *(Jackie Faker, Maggie and Tony Harwood, David Martin, Pete Baker)*

HOPWAS SK1705

Red Lion [Lichfield Rd]: Recently refurbished canalside pub with comfortable lounge, small dining room, good choice of low-priced decent food, pleasant landlord, prompt efficient service, well kept Marstons Pedigree and Charles Wells Bombardier; waterside garden, moorings *(Bob and Laura Brock)*

Tame Otter [A51 Tamworth—Lichfield]: Much extended Vintage Inn with cosy rustic feel, lots of beams, nooks and alcoves, three log fires, easy chairs, settles, dining chairs, old photographs and canalia, friendly well trained staff, reasonably priced food all day, good choice of wines, well kept Bass; huge car park *(Colin Gooch, DC)*

HUDDLESFORD SK1509

☆ *Plough* [off A38 2 miles E of Lichfield, by Coventry Canal]: Waterside dining pub extended from 17th-c cottage, wide choice of good unusual bar food from sandwiches to enterprising main dishes and good puddings, four neat and pleasant eating areas, well kept ales such as Greene King Old Speckled Hen and Marstons Pedigree, good range of wines, friendly and attentive landlord and young staff; attractive hanging baskets, canalside tables, hitching posts *(Emma and Simon Kelsey, Paul and Margaret Pryce)*

KINVER SO8483

Plough & Harrow [High St (village signed off A449 or A458 W of Stourbridge); aka the Steps]: Old split-level local tied to Bathams with their Best, Mild and XXX kept very well, good choice of ciders and malt whiskies, cheap plain bar food (filled rolls even Sun lunchtime), low prices, film star pictures; proper public bar with darts, dominoes etc, lounge with nostalgic juke box, SkyTV and fruit machine, folk nights 1st and 3rd Weds; children allowed in some parts, tables in back courtyard, open all day wknds *(the Didler, Gill and Tony Morriss, Pete Baker)*

LEEK SJ9856

Bulls Head [St Edward St]: Narrow three-level town pub with two low-priced Leek Brewery real ales, Weston's Old Rosie cider; popular with young people – pool, juke box; open all day *(Kevin Thorpe, the Didler)*

☆ *Den Engel* [St Edward St]: Belgian-style bar in high-ceilinged former bank, over 130 beers from there inc six on tap, three or four changing british real ales, three dozen genevers, upstairs restaurant with continental dishes inc flemish beer-based specialities (Fri-Sat lunch, Thurs-Sat night, bar food Sun night); piped classical music, very busy Fri-Sat evening, cl Sun-Thurs lunchtime *(the Didler, Kevin Thorpe, Mike and Wendy Proctor)*

Red Lion [Market Pl]: Large town-centre pub with well kept Hydes, good choice of wines by the glass, enjoyable food, friendly staff; nice room upstairs with lots of panelling and sofas *(Bob Richardson)*

☆ *Swan* [St Edward St]: Bustling old three-room pub popular with all ages for its cheap lunchtime food from sandwiches and baguettes up, quick helpful service even when busy, well kept changing ales such as Bass, Fullers London Pride and Jennings Sneckliſter, occasional beer festivals, lots of malt whiskies, choice of coffees, several rooms around central servery inc no smoking lounge; downstairs wine bar, folk club, seats in courtyard *(the Didler, Peter Abbott, Mike and Wendy Proctor, Rona Murdoch)*

☆ *Wilkes Head* [St Edward St]: Convivial unspoilt three-room local dating from 18th c (still has back coaching stables), tied to Whim with their ales and a guest such as Oakham JHB kept well; welcoming regulars and dogs, friendly landlord happy to chat, lunchtime rolls, home-made stilton for sale, good choice of whiskies, farm cider, pub games, gas fire, lots of pumpclips; juke box in back room, Mon music night; children allowed in one room (but not really a family pub), fair disabled access, tables outside, open all day *(Kevin Thorpe, the Didler, Pete Baker, John Wooll)*

LICHFIELD SK1010

Hedgehog [Stafford Rd (A51)]: Large Vintage Inn with lots of tables in every nook and cranny, good choice of well prepared food, Marstons Pedigree, friendly attentive staff; children welcome, picnic-sets outside, bedrooms *(Colin Gooch, Maggie and Tony Harwood)*

☆ *Queens Head* [Queen St]: Done up in quaint old-fashioned alehouse style with aged furniture on stripped boards, all thoroughly comfortable; self-choice counter of unusual cheeses in huge helpings (doggy bags provided) at very reasonable prices with free pickles, onions and gherkins, short but interesting range of bargain home-made hot dishes, well kept Marstons Pedigree and a guest such as Timothy Taylors Landlord, friendly staff *(S P Watkin, P A Taylor, David Barnes, Emma and Simon Kelsey)*

LONGNOR SK0965

Olde Cheshire Cheese: Friendly and enthusiastic new young licensees in 14th-c building, a pub for 250 years, well kept Robinsons, traditional main bar and two attractive dining rooms with their own separate bar; hikers welcome, bedrooms *(Bernie Adams, Derek and Heather Manning)*

MUCKLEY CORNER SK0806

Olde Corner House [A5/A461]: New owners keeping up pleasantly relaxed atmosphere in comfortable well decorated hotel-cum-pub, good generous sensibly priced food in two restaurants (the smarter one is no smoking), well kept Marstons Pedigree and Wadworths 6X, wide choice of modestly priced wines, friendly service; good value bedrooms *(Colin Fisher)*

ONNELEY SK7543

Wheatsheaf [Bar Hill Rd (A525 W of Newcastle)]: Roomy and sympathetically restored 18th-c country inn, friendly bar with real ales inc Black Sheep, leather chairs in alcoves and good log fire, appealing food choice, candlelit restaurant; play area, bedrooms, attractive countryside, open all day wknds *(E G Parish)*

PENKRIDGE SJ9214

Littleton Arms [St Michaels Sq/A449]: Substantial Vintage Inn done out in olde-worlde style, particularly well kept Bass, John Smiths and Tetleys, enjoyable food all day, friendly efficient staff; children welcome *(Colin Gooch, Roy and Lindsey Fentiman, Gerry and Rosemary Dobson)*

☆ *Star* [Market Pl]: Charming open-plan local well preserved under new licensees, lots of low black beams and button-back red plush, well kept Banks's ales, limited lunchtime bar food from chip butties to cheap main dishes, friendly prompt service, open fires; piped music, sports TV; open all day, terrace tables *(BB, Colin Gooch)*

RANTON SJ8422

Yew Tree: Bistro-style dining pub with good brasserie food using lots of local produce, friendly atmosphere, no smoking restaurant; pond in pleasant garden behind *(Paul and Margaret Baker, John and Lynn Norcliffe)*

RAWNSLEY SK0311

Rag [Ironstone Rd]: Unassuming woods-edge country pub transformed by friendly new licensees, enjoyable food inc interesting dishes, four real ales, good value wine list, warm pleasant décor, no smoking lounge and restaurant, locals' bar; tables out on grass with summer evening barbecues, handy for Castle Ring and Cannock Chase walks *(Alan Cole, Kirstie Bruce)*

REAPS MOOR SK0861

Butchers Arms [off B5053 S of Longnor]: Isolated moorland pub, lots of atmosphere in several distinct areas, good value food inc Sun lunch, Marstons Pedigree and a guest beer; free camping for customers *(the Didler)*

ROLLESTON ON DOVE SK23427

Spread Eagle [Church Rd]: Well run and friendly Vintage Inn dining pub with well kept Bass, good value food all day inc fresh fish and popular Sun carvery, speedy attentive service; pleasant garden, nice village, bedrooms *(Dr T E Hothersall)*

SHENSTONE SK1004

Plough & Harrow [Pinfold Hill, off A450]: Country local with cosy bar and larger divided lounge, well priced Bathams beer from long counter, friendly service even at busy times, enjoyable food, log fire; picnic-sets out on front grass *(Gill and Tony Morriss)*

STAFFORD SJ9123

Stafford Arms [Railway St; turn right at main entrance outside station, 100 yards down]: Unpretentious nautical-theme beamed real ale pub, well kept changing ales mainly from Titanic, farm cider, cheap simple food (all day wkdys, not Sun evening or Sat), daily papers; pool, bar billiards, table skittles, juke box; bedrooms with own bathrooms, open all day exc Sun afternoon *(Peter F Marshall)*

TAMWORTH SK2004

Tweedale Arms [Albert Rd/Victoria Rd]: Substantial building with modern airy atmosphere, daily papers, restaurant with good steaks and attentive service; games machines *(Colin Gooch)*

TATENHILL SK2021

☆ *Horseshoe* [off A38 W of Burton; Main St]: Civilised tiled-floor bar, cosy no smoking side snug with woodburner, two-level restaurant and back family area, good value food (all day Sat) from sandwiches to steaks and more ambitious dishes, proper children's food, well kept Marstons ales, good wine range, quick polite service; pleasant garden, good play area with pets corner *(C J Fletcher, Graham and Lynn Mason, LYM, S P Watkin, P A Taylor)*

THORNCLIFFE SK0158

Red Lion: Comfortable and attractive old-world pub with good choice of enjoyable food from sandwiches up, Thurs steak night, hard-working licensees, good atmosphere, no smoking dining room, games area with pool; children welcome *(Pauline and Terry James)*

TRYSULL SO8594

Bell [Bell Rd]: Extended red brick village pub, Holdens Bitter, Special and Golden Glow, Bathams Best and a guest beer, interesting bar and restaurant food from sandwiches up at fair prices, many original features in cosy bar with brasses and locomotive number-plates *(Gill and Tony Morriss)*

WALL SK0906

Trooper [Watling St, off A5]: Small refurbished pub with wide choice of fairly priced bar food from baguettes and panini up, pleasant efficient service, Ansells and Marstons Pedigree, separate no smoking restaurant; terrace tables, open all day *(Michael Dandy)*

WATERHOUSES SK0850

George [Leek Rd (A523)]: Large three-room 1930s roadside dining pub, good sensibly priced generous food from sandwiches and pubby things to restaurant dishes inc fresh fish and nice puddings, Greene King IPA and Marstons, play area; particularly friendly, if not full of character; handy for Manifold cycle trail, local bike hire *(Elaine Wintle)*

WESTON SJ9726

☆ ***Woolpack*** [off A518; The Green]: Linked low-beamed areas with secluded corners, well polished brassware and antique furniture inc high-backed settle, good varied fresh food, well kept Banks's, Marstons Pedigree and a guest beer, smart efficient service, extended dining room with no smoking areas; well tended garden *(Bill Sykes)*

YOXALL SK1418

Golden Cup [Main St (A515)]: Refurbished village inn dating from early 18th c, appealing homely feel, attentive service, enjoyable home-made food from sandwiches up, well kept Marstons Pedigree and a guest beer, games in public bar; waterside garden, bedrooms, open all day wknds *(Maggie and Tony Harwood)*

Several well known guide books make establishments pay for entry, either directly or as a fee for inspection. These fees can run to many hundreds of pounds. We do not. Unlike other guides, we never take payment for entries. We never accept a free meal, free drink, or any other freebie from a pub. We do not accept any sponsorship – let alone from commercial schemes linked to the pub trade. All our entries depend solely on merit.

Suffolk

Three pubs storm into the main entries here this year: the Old Cannon in Bury St Edmunds, an unusual pub away from the centre, relaxed and individual, brewing its own good beers; the prettily placed Bell at Cretingham, its good food specialising in fish caught from the landlord's own boat; and the recently opened Crown at Stoke-by-Nayland, straight in with both Food and Wine Awards, and even a Star, and looking all set to become a real favourite. Other top-rank pubs here include the Crown at Buxhall (good imaginative food, nice new garden), the Angel in Lavenham (now completely no smoking, and very much enjoyed for its food, drink, atmosphere, and as a place to stay), the delightfully unspoilt Kings Head at Laxfield, the St Peters Brewery at South Elmham (a gorgeous set of medieval buildings here, and splendid beers brewed on site), the smart Crown in Southwold (very popular for its good food and beer, and first-class changing wines by the glass), and the friendly Moon & Mushroom tucked away at Swilland (a fine all-rounder). It is the 17th-c Crown at Buxhall which is awarded the title of Suffolk Dining Pub of the Year – popular already, so to be sure of a table you'd be wise to book. Pubs coming forward strongly in recent months in the Lucky Dip section at the end of the chapter include the Cross Keys in Aldeburgh, Parrot & Punchbowl at Aldringham, Ship at Blaxhall, Cock at Brent Eleigh, Oyster at Butley, Froize at Chillesford (really a restaurant now, though), Ferry Boat at Felixstowe Ferry, Fox & Goose at Fressingfield (another restauranty place), Swan at Hoxne, Admirals Head at Little Bealings, Ramsholt Arms, Plough & Sail at Snape, and (great appeal here) Lord Nelson in Southwold. Drinks prices here tend to be rather above the national average – in our main entries, we found no real ales under £2 a pint. Greene King, with a huge and growing national chain of pubs, is the region's main brewer, though you are as likely to find beers from the much smaller Adnams brewery. Other good local brewers to look out for include Nethergate, Mauldons, St Peters and Earl Soham.

BRAMFIELD TM4073 Map 5

Queens Head (food award)

The Street; A144 S of Halesworth

They hold various special events such as wine tasting and spanish evenings at this bustling pub, and they do a popular pauper special menu (from £10.95 for three courses). Despite the concentration on food, you'll still see plenty of drinking locals, and the atmosphere is relaxed. The high-raftered lounge bar has scrubbed pine tables, a good log fire in its impressive fireplace, and a sprinkling of farm tools on the walls; a separate no smoking side bar has light wood furnishings (one side of the pub is no smoking). They've well kept Adnams Bitter and Broadside, and a good wine list, including lots of organic ones and half a dozen wines by the glass, home-made elderflower cordial, and organic apple juices and cider. Much of their food is cooked using ingredients from small local traditional organic farms: a typical choice might include sandwiches (with home-made bread), soup (£3.55), local asparagus wrapped in pancetta roasted with olive oil or mushroom omelette (£5.95), and rump steak with rich burgundy sauce (£13.95), with daily changing specials such as seafood crumble or filo parcel with spinach, cream cheese, sun-dried tomatoes, pine nuts and garlic (£9.95), plaice with crab, lemon and almond stuffing and herb butter sauce (£12.95), with a good choice of puddings such as bitter chocolate and marmalade tart or tasty lemon and lime cheesecake (£4.25) or home-made ice-cream (£3.75). You can buy their home-made preserves. There are seats in the pretty garden, a dome-shaped bower made of willow, and a family of bantams. *(Recommended by Tina and David Woods-Taylor, Pat and Tony Martin, Evelyn and Derek Walter, MJVK, Deborah Trentham, Philip and Susan Philcox, Comus and Sarah Elliott, Pat and Tony Hinkins, J F M and M West, Neil Powell, Tracey and Stephen Groves, Fred and Lorraine Gill, David Treherne-Pollock, Rob Winstanley)*

Adnams ~ Tenants Mark and Amanda Corcoran ~ Real ale ~ Bar food (12-2, 6.30-10; 12-2, 7-9 Sun) ~ (01986) 784214 ~ Children welcome ~ Dogs welcome ~ Open 11.45-2.30, 6.30-11; 12-3, 7-10.30 Sun; closed 26 Dec

BROME TM1376 Map 5

Cornwallis 🍷 🛏

Rectory Road; after turning off A140 S of Diss into B1077, take first left turn

In summer, they have jazz concerts and Shakespeare plays out on the lawn of this rather civilised largely 19th-c country hotel, which has a tree-lined drive and 20 acres of grounds. At the heart of the building is a beamed and timbered 16th-c bar where a step up from the tiled-floor serving area takes you through heavy timber uprights to a stylishly comfortable carpeted area; this is attractively furnished with a good mix of old and antique tables, some oak settles alongside cushioned library chairs, a glazed-over well, and a handsome woodburning stove. They've an extensive carefully chosen wine list with over 14 by the glass, organic local juices, bottled beers and champagne, and Adnams, St Peters Best and a guest such as Greene King IPA on handpump. Interesting bar food might include soup (£5.50), flavoured linguini with sweet pimento, chorizo and parmesan (£7, £8.95 large), crispy belly pork with japanese coleslaw and star anise reduction (£7.50), huge club sandwich (£8.50), mussels with thai curry broth and seaweed focaccia or battered haddock with lime juice and mushy peas and chips (£10), and venison bourguignon or roasted sea bream with chorizo mash and wilted spinach (£12.50), with puddings such as minted shortbread with seasonal fruits and strawberry and black pepper coulis (from £4). A nicely planted Victorian-style side conservatory has coffee-lounge cane furniture, and there's an elegant no smoking restaurant; piped music and board games. *(Recommended by J F M and M West, Mike and Wendy Proctor, M A and C R Starling, Charles Gysin, TW, MW, Sean and Sharon Pines, Adrian White)*

Swallow Group ~ Managers Peter Bartlett and Paul Beard ~ Real ale ~ Bar food ~ Restaurant ~ (01379) 870326 ~ Children welcome ~ Open 11-11; 12-10.30 Sun ~ Bedrooms: £94.50S(£94.50B)/£112S(£112B)

BURY ST EDMUNDS TL8564 Map 5

Nutshell

The Traverse, central pedestrian link off Abbeygate Street

Quaint and attractive, this tiny bare-boards pub is incredibly small. It dates from the 17th c, and has been selling beer since 1873, though a precursor is said to have been first licensed by Charles II (and there are tales of a tunnel to the abbey). There's a short wooden bench along its shop-front corner windows, one cut-down sewing-machine table, an elbow rest running along its rather battered counter, and well kept Greene King IPA and a guest on handpump – and that's it, in terms of creature comforts. There's no room to swing a cat – this thought prompted by the mummified cat (found walled up here) that hangs from the dark brown ceiling, along with stacks of other bric-a-brac from bits of a skeleton through vintage bank notes, cigarette packets and military and other badges to spears and a great metal halberd; piped music, cribbage and dominoes. The modern curved inn sign is appealing. More reports please. *(Recommended by the Didler)*

Greene King ~ Tenant Martin Baylis ~ Real ale ~ No credit cards ~ (01284) 764867 ~ Children allowed till 9pm ~ Open 11-11; 12-10.30 Sun; closed Sun evenings in winter

Old Cannon

Cannon Street, just off A134/A1101 roundabout N end of town

From outside, this square-cut and solidly built early Victorian yellow brick building looks more like a stylish private town house than a pub, and the inside makes a pleasant change from the usual pub style. For a start, there are plain signs in the bar on the right that this has special interest for the beer lover – in the shape of those two gleaming stainless steel brewing kettles, often gently burbling, that produce the pub's own good reasonably priced Old Cannon Best, Gunners Daughter, in winter their Black Pig Porter, and in summer their refreshing and light-tasting (but by no means weak) Blonde Bombshell. They also have well kept Adnams and a changing guest beer on handpump, and good wines by the glass. This room has miscellaneous chairs around a few tables on dark bare boards, dark pink or ochre walls, one with a big mirror, and plenty of standing space; a fanciful touch is that where you'd expect a ceiling there is instead a sort of floorless upper room complete with radiator, table and chairs. On the left, another dark pink-walled and bare-boards room has neat slat-backed dining chairs around tables, and opens at the back into the neat kitchen, which produces enjoyable generous lunchtime bar food such as home-made soup (£3.75), sandwiches (from £3.95, baguettes from £4.75), toad in the hole, ham, egg and chips, venison burger, roasted stuffed peppers or cod and chips (all £6.95), with puddings such as lime and chocolate cheesecake or cappuccino mousse (£3.75); the menu for the smarter restaurant is more elaborate. Service is quick, friendly and attentive, and the sociable licensees get a good buoyant atmosphere going; it can get pretty busy on Friday and Saturday nights. Behind, through the old side coach arch, is a good-sized cobbled courtyard neatly set with planters and hanging baskets, with rather stylish metal tables and chairs in bays at the back. We have so far had only secondhand recommendations for the bedrooms in a separate building across this courtyard, but these suggest that as more reports come in this is likely to qualify for one of our Place to Stay Awards. *(Recommended by RWC, Wendy and Carl Dye, Derek and Sylvia Stephenson, C W Dix, MLR, Clare Phillips)*

Free house ~ Licensee Carole Locker ~ Real ale ~ Bar food (lunchtime only, not Mon) ~ Restaurant ~ (01284) 768769 ~ Open 12-3, 5-11; 12-3, 7-11 Sun; closed Mon lunchtime ~ Bedrooms: £44S/£54S

BUXHALL TM0057 Map 5

Crown

Village signposted off B1115 W of Stowmarket; fork right by post office at Gt Finborough, turn left at Buxhall village sign, then second right into Mill Road, then right at T junction

Suffolk Dining Pub of the Year

Given the quality of the imaginative food, it's not surprising that this welcoming 17th-c timber framed country pub is so popular, and to be sure of a table, you must book. Skilfully cooked with fresh seasonal ingredients, monthly changing dishes might include soup (£4.25), fresh crab filo tart with sour cream and cucumber dressing (£5.45), duck and vegetable pancakes with ginger and lemon (£6.25), mushrooms stroganoff (£8.95), grilled skate wing with brown shrimps, capers, garlic and rosemary (£11.45), roasted pork loin with crispy crackling on a black pepper potato cake with tarragon and brandy cream (£11.95), and scottish lamb with grilled black pudding, scallion mash and thyme-infused jus (£13.95), with home-made puddings such as rum truffle cake or chocolate pecan tart (£4.25); they also do lunchtime bar snacks such as chips with cheese, chicken dippers and anchovy fillets (all £2.95), and sandwiches (from £3.50). Good service from the friendly landlord and pleasant staff. All the wines on their carefully chosen wine list are available by the glass, and they've also well kept Greene King IPA, Mauldons

Bitter, Tindalls Best, and Woodfordes Wherry on handpump; smart coffees. The intimate little bar on the left has an open fire in a big inglenook, a couple of small round tables on a tiled floor, and low hop-hung beams. Standing timbers separate it from another area with pews and candles, and flowers in summer on big stripped oak or pine tables, and there's a further light and airy room which they call the Mill Bar. Plenty of seats and picnic-sets under parasols on the heated terrace, and they've a pretty garden, with nice views over gently rolling countryside. As we went to press, they'd nearly finished adding another enclosed side garden, with wooden decking, and raised flowerbeds. *(Recommended by J F M and M West, Derek Field, MDN, M and GR, A Cowell, Dom Bradshaw, C W Dix, Mr and Mrs M Hayes, Mike and Mary Carter, Pamela Goodwyn)*

Greene King ~ Lease Trevor Golton ~ Real ale ~ Bar food (not Sun evening) ~ Restaurant ~ (01449) 736521 ~ Well behaved children in restaurant ~ Dogs allowed in bar ~ Occasional live jazz ~ Open 12-3, 6.30-11; 12-3 Sun; closed Sun evening

CHELMONDISTON TM2038 Map 5

Butt & Oyster

Pin Mill – signposted from B1456 SE of Ipswich

This staunchly simple old bargeman's pub is lovely in summer, when you can sit outside on the suntrap terrace and watch life on the water (ships coming down the River Orwell from Ipswich and lines of moored black sailing barges), and cosy in winter when you can enjoy the same view through the bay windows. Pleasantly worn and unfussy, the half-panelled timeless little smoke room has model sailing ships around the walls and high-backed and other old-fashioned settles on the tiled floor; ferocious beady-eyed fish made by a local artist stare at you from the walls. Well liked bar food from the reasonably priced straightforward menu might include soup (£3.65), deep-fried camembert (£4.95), burgers (from £4), vegetable crumble (£7.25), greek-style lamb or chilled poached salmon (£7.95), and steaks (from £8.95); they also serve sandwiches at lunchtime (till 6pm wknds). As space is limited, you might need to arrive early on the weekend to get a seat. Adnams Best and Broadside, and Greene King IPA are well kept on handpump or tapped from the cask, and there are decent wines; shove-ha'penny, cribbage, and dominoes. The annual Thames Barge Race (end June/beginning July) is fun. *(Recommended by the Didler, Peter Meister, Alistair and Kay Butler, Pamela Goodwyn, Derek and Sylvia Stephenson, MLR, David Stokes, Pat and Clive Sherriff, Mrs A Chapman, JDM, KM)*

Pubmaster ~ Tenant Steve Lomas ~ Real ale ~ Bar food (12-2.30, 6.30-9.30; all day wknds and bank hols) ~ Restaurant ~ (01473) 780764 ~ Children in restaurant ~ Dogs allowed in bar ~ Open 11-11; 12-10.30 Sun

COTTON TM0467 Map 5

Trowel & Hammer

Mill Road; take B1113 N of Stowmarket, then turn right into Blacksmiths Lane just N of Bacton

The enticing menu at this civilised, wisteria-covered pub (with a newly thatched roof) changes every day, but a typical choice of well cooked dishes might include home-made soup (£3.25), home-made creamy salmon mousse (£5.75), roast beef with yorkshire pudding or fried chicken breast with thyme and garlic cream sauce (£8.95), red snapper on creamy thai noodles (£9.95), home-made steak and ale pie (£9.25), venison and apricot sausages on spring onion mash with cranberry gravy or grilled lemon sole with lemon and parsley butter (£10.95), and braised lamb shank with rosemary gravy (£11.95). Although there is quite a lot of emphasis on the food, there's a nice informal atmosphere, and they serve well kept Adnams, Greene King IPA and Abbot, and a guest, usually from Mauldons or Nethergate on handpump or tapped from the cask; also lots of unusual spirits, and an interesting wine list. The spreading series of quiet rooms has fresh flowers, lots of beamery and timber baulks, a big log fire (as well as an ornate woodburning stove at the back), and plenty of wheelbacks and one or two older chairs and settles around a variety of tables. The staff are pleasant and friendly; pool, fruit machine and piped music. The back garden is pretty with lots of roses and hollyhocks, neat climbers on trellises, picnic-sets, and even a swimming pool. *(Recommended by Comus and Sarah Elliott, Mr and Mrs W T Copeland, Francis Johnston, Glenwys and Alan Lawrence, M and GR, Dom Bradshaw, Mrs A Chapman, Alan Cole, Kirstie Bruce)*

Free house ~ Licensees Simon and Jonathan Piers-Hall ~ Real ale ~ Bar food (12-2, 6-9) ~ Restaurant ~ (01449) 781234 ~ Children in eating area of bar ~ Dogs allowed in bar ~ Open 12-3, 6-11; 12-11(10.30 Sun) Sat

CRETINGHAM TM2260 Map 5

Bell

The Street

The enjoyable food at this neatly kept village pub (converted from four cottages) is very popular, and booking is advisable, especially on weekends. Fresh fish is the speciality – the landlord has his own fishing boat, so dishes (and prices) can vary every day according to the catch. As well as lunchtime snacks such as baguettes (from £5 – crayfish is popular), ploughman's (from £5.50), and hot flaked sea trout salad (£6.50), the interesting, reasonably priced menu might include lobster salad (around £4 per 100 grams), wilted rocket, black olive, red onion and parmesan tart (£4.50), sole (£6.50), leek, white onion and cheese risotto (£8.50), braised lamb shoulder with pease pudding (£10), crispy bass (£11), and rib-eye steak with horseradish mash and veal jus (£13), with puddings such as date and pistachio bread and butter pudding (£3.75); good service. The restaurant is no smoking. The comfortably modernised lounge bar has exposed beams, standing timbers of a knocked-through wall, a large old fireplace, and a big hunting scene tapestry. You'll find well kept Adnams Bitter and Greene King Abbot on handpump, along with a couple of changing guests from brewers such as Archers and Earl Soham, good wines, and 20 malt whiskies. The quarry-tiled public bar has shove-ha'penny, dominoes and chess. Sitting outside is pleasant, with rustic tables on the sheltered grass in front and more on the lawn by the rose bushes and fine old oak tree. *(Recommended by Francis Johnston, Ian and Nita Cooper, John F Morton, Comus and Sarah Elliott, Tracey and Stephen Groves)*

Free house ~ Licensee Lee Knight ~ Bar food (12-2, 6-9(8.30 Sun); not Mon lunchtime, or Tues) ~ Restaurant ~ (01728) 685419 ~ No children wknd evenings ~ Dogs allowed in bar ~ Folk band one Weds a month ~ Open 11-2.30(3 Sat), 6-11; 12-3, 7-10.30 Sun; closed Tues ~ Bedrooms: /£65B

DENNINGTON TM2867 Map 5

Queens Head

A1120

Gorgeously picturesque, this Tudor pub is prettily set in gardens alongside the church. The pub backs on to Dennington Park, which has swings and so forth for children, and there are seats on a side lawn, attractively planted with flowers, and sheltered by some noble lime trees, with a goldfish pond. The main neatly kept L-shaped room has carefully stripped wall timbers and beams, a handsomely carved bressumer beam, and comfortable padded wall seats on the partly carpeted and partly tiled floor. Adnams Bitter and a guest such as Fullers London Pride are well kept on handpump and served from the brick bar counter; piped music, cribbage, dominoes. Quite a choice of bar food might include around five vegetarian dishes such as moroccan vegetable curry or fennel and courgette bake (£6.95), as well as home-made soup (£3.25), deep-fried whitebait (£3.95), sausage pie (£7.50), chicken satay (£8.25), swordfish marinated in orange and lemon juice with garlic and basil (£8.75), and steaks (from £10.20), with home-made puddings such as fruit and nut pudding or pineapple cheesecake (£3.50); children's meals (£2.95). With new tables and chairs, both dining areas are no smoking. *(Recommended by Comus and Sarah Elliott, J F M and M West, Francis Johnston, Neil Powell, Edmund Coan, David Boult, M and GR)*

Free house ~ Licensees Hilary Cowie, Peter Mills ~ Real ale ~ Bar food (12-2, 6.30-9) ~ Restaurant ~ (01728) 638241 ~ Well behaved children in family room, must be over 12 in restaurant ~ Open 11-2.30, 6(6.30 winter)-11; 11-3, 6(6.30 winter)-10.30 Sun; closed 25-26 Dec

DUNWICH TM4770 Map 5

Ship

St James Street

The cosy welcoming main bar of this deceptively large old brick pub is traditionally furnished with benches, pews, captain's chairs and wooden tables on its tiled floor, a woodburning stove (left open in cold weather) and lots of sea prints and nautical memorabilia. From the handsomely panelled bar counter, you can get well kept Adnams Bitter and Broadside and a changing beer from Mauldons served with antique handpumps; fruit machine, shove-ha'penny, dominoes and cribbage. A simple conservatory looks on to an attractive sunny back terrace, and the large garden is very pleasant, with its well spaced picnic-sets, two large anchors, and enormous fig tree. Besides simple fresh fish from Lowestoft harbour, and home-made chips (£6.85 lunchtime, £8.65 in the evening), a quite short choice of tasty bar food at lunchtime includes home-made soup (£2.20), sausage and chips (£4.95), ploughman's (from £5.25 – available till 6pm, readers recommend the crab £6.55), and a hot dish of the day (£6.55), while in the evening there might be spinach flan or gammon and pineapple (£7.95), fishcakes (£9.45), and steak and ale casserole (£9.25), with home-made puddings (£4.25); children's meals (from £5.50). The restaurant is no smoking. Dunwich is such a charming little place today, it's hard to imagine that centuries ago it was one of England's busiest ports. There's plenty to do or look at around here – lots of surrounding walks, lovely coastal scenery, the RSPB reserve at Minsmere, and the nearby Dunwich Museum. *(Recommended by Nigel and Olga Wikeley, Sue Holland, Dave Webster, Steve Whalley, Tina and David Woods-Taylor, Derek and Sylvia Stephenson, J F M and M West, Steve and Liz Tilley, Comus and Sarah Elliott, Neil Powell, Penny and Fraser Hutchinson, Peter Meister, Pat and Clive Sherriff, Ian and Jane Irving, Fred and Lorraine Gill, MJVK, Stephen and Jean Curtis, David Field, A Sadler, Tracey and Stephen Groves)*

Free house ~ Licensee David Sheldrake ~ Real ale ~ Bar food ~ Restaurant (evening only) ~ (01728) 648219 ~ Children in restaurant and family room ~ Dogs allowed in bar and bedrooms ~ Open 11-11; 12-10.30 Sun ~ Bedrooms: £50S/£68S

EARL SOHAM TM2363 Map 5

Victoria £

A1120 Yoxford—Stowmarket

It's no wonder the Earl Soham beers at this unpretentious little village pub are so well kept – the brewery is right across the road: on handpump, you might find Victoria Bitter, Albert Ale, Edward Ale and Empress of India Pale Ale, and they've local farm cider too. There's an appealingly easy-going local atmosphere in the bar, which is fairly basic and sparsely furnished, with stripped panelling, kitchen chairs and pews, plank-topped trestle sewing-machine tables and other simple scrubbed pine country tables with candles, tiled or board floors, an interesting range of pictures of Queen Victoria and her reign, a piano, and open fires; cribbage and dominoes. Readers enjoy the home-made puddings (£3), while other very reasonably priced bar food could include sandwiches (from £2.50), soup (£3), ploughman's (from £4.25), popular corned beef hash (£4.95), vegetarian pasta dishes (£5.25), meat or vegetable lasagne (£5.75), pork and pineapple or lamb curry (£6.50), feta and onion tart, beef casserole or winter Sunday roast (£7.50); service is very friendly (but can be slow at times). There are seats on the raised back lawn, with more out in front. The pub is quite close to a wild fritillary meadow at Framlingham, and a working windmill at Saxtead. *(Recommended by Glenwys and Alan Lawrence, Pat and Tony Martin, J F M and M West, Comus and Sarah Elliott, Pam and David Bailey, Mark and Amanda Sheard, Judith and Edward Pearson, TW, MW, Mrs A Chapman, Tom Gondris, Pete Baker)*

Free house ~ Licensee Paul Hooper ~ Real ale ~ Bar food (till 10) ~ Restaurant ~ No credit cards ~ (01728) 685758 ~ Children in eating area of bar ~ Dogs welcome ~ Open 11.30-3, 6-11; 12-3, 7-10.30 Sun

ERWARTON TM2134 Map 5

Queens Head

Village signposted off B1456 Ipswich-Shotley Gate; pub beyond the attractive church and the manor with its unusual gatehouse (like an upturned salt-cellar)

It's a good idea to get to this relaxed 16th-c pub early if you want to bag a table by the window, which looks across fields to the Stour estuary. The friendly bar has bowed black oak beams in its shiny low yellowing ceiling, comfortable furnishings, a cosy coal fire, and several sea paintings and photographs. The no smoking conservatory dining area is pleasant. Adnams Bitter and Broadside and Greene King IPA are well kept on handpump, they have a decent wine list, and several malt whiskies. Along with specials such as home-made sausage and walnut pie with cranberry gravy or spinach and red lentil curry (£7.95), or crab salad (£8.95), tasty bar food includes home-made soup (£3.25), ploughman's (£5.75), chicken breast with peach and almond sauce, gammon and egg or home-made lasagne (£7.95), and stuffed lemon sole with crabmeat (£8.95); puddings might be sticky toffee pavlova or lemon meringue pie (£3.95). It can get busy at the weekends; darts, bar billiards, shove-ha'penny, cribbage, and dominoes, and maybe piped music. The gents' has quite a collection of navigational charts. There are picnic-sets under summer hanging baskets in front. More reports please. *(Recommended by Pamela Goodwyn, Adele Summers, Alan Black, Alistair and Kay Butler, Mrs A Chapman, Colin and Dot Savill)*

Free house ~ Licensees Julia Crisp and G M Buckle ~ Real ale ~ Bar food ~ Restaurant ~ (01473) 787550 ~ Children in restaurant ~ Open 11-3, 6.30-11; 12-3, 7-10.30 Sun; closed 25 Dec

GREAT GLEMHAM TM3361 Map 5

Crown

Between A12 Wickham Market—Saxmundham and B1119 Saxmundham—Framlingham

Nothing is too much trouble for the helpful staff or friendly licensees at this immaculately kept smart pub. It's worth booking for the popular bar food, which comes in generous helpings. Enjoyable dishes might include sandwiches (from £3.25), soup (£3.75), baked potatoes (from £4.50), crispy whitebait (£4.75), ploughman's (£5.50), sausage, egg and chips (£5.75), scampi and chips or gammon and pineapple (£7.95), with daily specials such as cottage pie (£7.95), leek and goats cheese tart (£8.25), lamb casserole (£8.95), and fried rainbow trout with almonds (£9.25); children's menu (£3.95). Past the sofas on rush matting in the big entrance hall, an open-plan beamed lounge has wooden pews and captain's chairs around stripped and waxed kitchen tables, local photographs and interesting paintings on cream walls, fresh flowers, and some brass ornaments; log fires in two big fireplaces. Well kept Greene King IPA and Old Speckled Hen are served from old brass handpumps; they've seven wines by the glass, and good coffee. A tidy, flower-fringed lawn, raised above the corner of the quiet village lane by a retaining wall, has some seats and tables under cocktail parasols; disabled access. The pub is in a particularly pretty village. *(Recommended by Mr and Mrs T B Staples, Michael and Jenny Back, David and Gilly Wilkins, Comus and Sarah Elliott, Neil Powell, Tracey and Stephen Groves, Leigh and Gillian Mellor, Alison Style, David Field, Edmund Coan, J F M and M West, Pamela Goodwyn)*

Free house ~ Licensees Barry and Susie Coote ~ Real ale ~ Bar food (not Mon) ~ (01728) 663693 ~ Children welcome ~ Dogs welcome ~ Open 11.30-3, 6.30-11; 12-3, 7-10.30 Sun; closed Mon

Pubs brewing their own beers are listed at the back of the book.

HORRINGER TL8261 Map 5

Beehive

A143

As they've refrained from pulling walls down to create the usual open-plan layout, the rambling little rooms of this civilised pub have a welcoming cottagey feel. Despite some very low beams, good chalky wall colours keep it light and airy; there are carefully chosen dining and country kitchen chairs on coir or flagstones, one or two wall settles around solid tables, picture-lights over lots of 19th-c prints, and stripped panelling or brickwork. If you want to eat here, you must arrive early. The menu changes every day, but might typically include soup (£3.95), country pâté (£4.95), spinach and parmesan tart (£7.95), polenta with roast vegetables and goats cheese (£8.95), home-made pork, tomato and paprika sausages on creamy mash (£9.50), and lamb shank with tomato herb sauce or roast pork with bubble and squeak (£11.95), and puddings such as orange bread and butter pudding (£4.25). They've decent changing wines with half a dozen by the glass, and Greene King IPA, and a changing Greene King guest are well kept on handpump. An attractively planted back terrace has picnic-sets and more seats on a raised lawn. Their friendly, well behaved dog Muffin is a great hit with readers; other dogs are not really welcome. *(Recommended by J F M and M West, John Saville, Liz Webb, Michael and Marion Buchanan, Dave Braisted, Tony Brace, Ken Millar, D S Cottrell)*

Greene King ~ Tenants Gary and Dianne Kingshott ~ Real ale ~ Bar food (not Sun evening) ~ Restaurant ~ (01284) 735260 ~ Children welcome ~ Open 11.30-2, 7-11; 12-2, 7-10.30 Sun

HUNDON TL7246 Map 5

Plough

Brockley Green – nearly 2 miles SW of village, towards Kedington

As it's set on top of one of the few hills around here, this remote pub has fine views over the Stour valley. The neatly kept knocked-through bar has soft red brickwork, old oak beams and plenty of old standing timbers, cushions on low side settles, pine kitchen chairs and sturdy low tables, and plenty of horsebrasses. Outside, there are five acres of lovely landscaped gardens, and a pleasant terrace with an ornamental pool and good wooden furniture under a wisteria-covered pergola; croquet. Cheerful staff serve Greene King IPA, Woodfordes Wherry, and a guest such as Charles Wells Bombardier on handpump, and they've a carefully chosen wine list with a dozen by the glass, and 30 malt whiskies. Besides lunchtime sandwiches (from £3.25), tasty bar food might include soup (£3.25), cajun chicken (£5.75), steak pie or sun-dried tomato and goats cheese tart (£7.95), smoked chicken and avocado salad (£8.25), and fried king scallops with lime butter (£10.75); on Friday evenings they have seafood specials such as monkfish thermidor poached in white wine (£11.95), and fried bass with lemon batter (£12.25). Part of the bar and all the restaurant are no smoking. *(Recommended by Adele Summers, Alan Black, Mr and Mrs M Hayes, Derek and Sylvia Stephenson, Pam and David Bailey, A Sadler)*

Free house ~ Licensees David and Marion Rowlinson ~ Real ale ~ Bar food ~ Restaurant ~ (01440) 786789 ~ Children in eating area of bar ~ Dogs welcome ~ Live jazz bank hol Mon lunchtime ~ Open 11-2.30, 6-11; 12-3, 7-10.30 Sun ~ Bedrooms: £45S(£50B)/£65S(£75B)

ICKLINGHAM TL7872 Map 5

Red Lion

A1101 Mildenhall—Bury St Edmunds

On Saturday nights, they serve up to up to 24 different fish dishes at this civilised 16th-c thatched dining pub, a handy place for a meal after a visit to nearby West Stow Country Park or the Anglo-Saxon Village. Well presented, but not cheap, bar food includes soup (£4.25), pâté (£6.95), lambs liver and bacon (£9.95), pork chops with apple and cider sauce (£12.95), and barnsley lamb chops with mint and redcurrant (£13.95), with fish dishes such as king prawns in garlic butter (£9.95), cromer crab salad (£14.95), and bass with chilli and paprika butter (£15.95), and home-made puddings such as eton mess or sticky toffee pudding with butterscotch sauce (£4.65); good baguettes (from £4.25). Be warned that they do sometimes finish serving food early. The pub has plenty of character – the best part is the beamed open-plan bar with its cavernous inglenook fireplace, attractive furnishings, and nice mixture of wooden chairs, big candlelit tables and turkey rugs on the polished wood floor. Another area behind a knocked-through fireplace has closely spaced dark wood pub tables on carpets. Well kept Greene King IPA and Abbot on handpump, and lots of country wines. There are picnic-sets with colourful parasols on a lawn in front (the pub is well set back from the road), and more behind on a raised terrace facing the fields, with Cavenham Heath nature reserve beyond; in fine weather they have giant outside Jenga. *(Recommended by Comus and Sarah Elliott, Pamela Goodwyn, Jamie and Ruth Lyons, Ian Phillips, Esther and John Sprinkle)*

Excalibur ~ Lease Jonathan Gates ~ Real ale ~ Bar food (12-2.30, 7-10) ~ Restaurant ~ (01638) 717802 ~ Children welcome ~ Open 12-3, 6-11; 12-2.30, 7-10.30 Sun

LAVENHAM TL9149 Map 5

Angel ★ (food award) (wine award) (beer award) (bedroom award)

Market Place

Readers very much enjoy drinking, eating and staying at this smoothly run Tudor inn, which is now completely no smoking. A friendly mix of visitors and locals (who may be enjoying a game of dominoes) fills the light and airy long bar area, which has plenty of polished dark tables, a big inglenook log fire under a heavy mantelbeam, and some attractive 16th-c ceiling plasterwork – even more elaborate pargeting in the residents' sitting room upstairs. Round towards the back on the right of the central servery is a further dining area with heavy stripped pine country furnishings. They have shelves of books and lots of board games; cribbage, and classical piped music. You can eat the delicious, popular food in the bar or the restaurant. Good lunchtime dishes could include ploughman's (£5.95), penne pasta with mixed seafood (£6.25), local pork sausages with mash and onion gravy or tomato, mozzarella and basil tart (£6.75), with other dishes such as soup (£3.75), smoked salmon and trout with lemon mayonnaise (£6.75), chicken, leek and bacon pie (£8.50), butternut squash, roast pepper and mushroom strudel (£8.75), grilled halibut with lime and herb butter (£10.95), roast lamb with apricots and rosemary (£11.95), and venison steak with wild mushroom and tarragon sauce (£12.95), with puddings such as apricot and passion fruit syllabub or steamed syrup sponge (£3.75). Very friendly and helpful staff serve well kept Adnams Bitter, Greene King IPA and Abbot, and Nethergate Suffolk County on handpump, they've nine decent wines by the glass or part bottle (you get charged for what you drink), and 20 malt whiskies. Picnic-sets out in front overlook the former market square, and there are tables under cocktail parasols in a sizeable sheltered back garden; it's worth asking if they've time to show you the interesting Tudor cellar. *(Recommended by Charles Gysin, Matthew Pexton, Stuart Manktelow, Chris Flynn, Wendy Jones, the Didler, Mr and Mrs C Quincey, Michael and Ann Cole, Maysie Thompson, Harry Gleave, M Sharp, Tina and David Woods-Taylor, A Sadler, Mr and Mrs C W Widdowson, Derek and Sylvia Stephenson, Virginia Greay, Marianne and Peter Stevens, David J Bunter, Pam and David Bailey, Len Banister, Derek and Maggie Washington, Julian Templeman, Des and Jen Clarke, Jeff and Wendy Williams, Mrs A Chapman, Lady Freeland, Tracey and Stephen Groves, Neil Skidmore, Charles Cooper, J C Poley, Stephen and Jean Curtis, Alan Cole, Kirstie Bruce, Pamela Goodwyn)*

Free house ~ Licensees Roy Whitworth and John Barry ~ Real ale ~ Bar food (12-2.15, 6.45-9.15) ~ Restaurant ~ (01787) 247388 ~ Children in eating area of bar and restaurant ~ Classical piano Fri evenings ~ Open 11-11; 12-10.30 Sun; closed 25-26 Dec ~ Bedrooms: £50B/£75B

LAXFIELD TM2972 Map 5

Kings Head ★ £

Behind church, off road toward Banyards Green

There's no bar at this bewitchingly unspoilt thatched 15th-c house – the well kept Adnams Best, Broadside and a seasonal ale are tapped straight from the cask in a cellar along with Fullers London Pride. Full of character, the three charmingly old-fashioned rooms have a welcoming atmosphere. Lots of people like the front room best, with a high-backed built-in settle on the tiled floor, and an open fire. Two other equally unspoilt rooms – the card and tap rooms – have pews, old seats, scrubbed deal tables, and some interesting wall prints; shove-ha'penny, cribbage and dominoes. Outside, the garden has plenty of benches and tables, there's an arbour covered by a grape and hop vine, and a small pavilion for cooler evenings. Simple good value bar food such as sandwiches (from £2.50, toasted sandwiches £3.50), home-made soup or garlic mushrooms (£3.50), baguettes (£4.50), ploughman's (£5), cottage pie or sausages and mash (£5.50), good fresh crispy bacon salad (£6.95), and grilled plaice (£8), with puddings such as apple and rhubarb crumble (£3.50). *(Recommended by A Sadler, the Didler, Pete Baker, Pam and David Bailey, Comus and Sarah Elliott, Ian and Nita Cooper, Mr and Mrs T B Staples, John and Enid Morris, David Carr, Tracey and Stephen Groves, G P V Creagh, Dennis and Gill Keen)*

Adnams ~ Tenants George and Maureen Coleman ~ Real ale ~ Bar food ~ Restaurant ~ No credit cards ~ (01986) 798395 ~ Children in restaurant ~ Dogs allowed in bar ~ Open 12-3, 6-11; 12-3, 7-10.30 Sun

LEVINGTON TM2339 Map 5

Ship

Gun Hill; from A14/A12 Bucklesham roundabout take A1156 exit, then first sharp left into Felixstowe road, then after nearly a mile turn right into Bridge Road at Levington signpost, bearing left into Church Lane

Inside this charming old pub there's quite a nautical theme, with lots of ship prints and photographs of sailing barges, a marine compass under the serving counter in the middle room, and a fishing net slung overhead. Along with benches built into the walls, there are comfortably upholstered small settles (some of them grouped round tables as booths), and a big black round stove. The flagstoned dining room has more nautical bric-a-brac and beams taken from an old barn; two no smoking areas. You must arrive early if you want to eat here, as the food is very popular, and there can be quite a wait for tables. Freshly prepared dishes might include soup (£3.50), dressed crab (£5.95), liver and bacon with madeira sauce (£7.25), individual joint of lamb with mint and honey glaze (£8.95), quite a few fresh fish dishes like griddled skate (£9.95) and seared scallops with wild mushroom risotto (£11.95), with puddings such as white chocolate and summer berry mousse or pear and cinnamon strudel with vanilla sauce (£4.25). Main courses can be a couple of pounds dearer in the evening. Well kept under light blanket pressure Adnams Bitter and Broadside and Greene King IPA are served by electric pumps; there are decent wines, with eight by the glass. Surrounded by lovely countryside (with good nearby walks), the pub is attractive placed by a little lime-washed church; if you look carefully enough, there's a sea view from the picnic-sets in front. No children inside. *(Recommended by Pamela Goodwyn, J F M and M West, Ian Phillips, Bill and Lisa Copeland, Ian and Nita Cooper, Edward Mirzoeff, Mr and Mrs M Hayes, Mike and Mary Carter, Charles and Pauline Stride, Tony and Shirley Albert)*

Pubmaster ~ Tenants Stella and Mark Johnson ~ Real ale ~ Bar food (12-2, 6.30-9.30; 12-3 Sun, not Sun evening) ~ Restaurant ~ (01473) 659573 ~ Open 11.30-2.30, 6-11; 12-3 Sun; closed Sun evening

> Post Office address codings confusingly give the impression that some pubs are in Suffolk when they're really in Norfolk or Cambridgeshire (which is where we list them).

LIDGATE TL7257 Map 5

Star

B1063 SE of Newmarket

With an easy-going mix of traditional english and mediterranean influences, this little village pub is a relaxing place to stop for a meal or a drink. With lots of pubby character, the cosy main room has handsomely moulded heavy beams, a good big log fire, candles in iron candelabra on good polished oak or stripped pine tables, bar billiards, dominoes, darts and ring the bull, and some antique catalan plates over the bar; piped music. Besides a second similar room on the right, there's a cosy little dining room on the left. The interesting (but not cheap) menu might include mediterranean fish soup (£4.50), grilled squid or catalan salad (£5.90), paella, roast lamb in garlic and wine or lambs kidneys in sherry (£14.50), cod in garlic mousseline, wild boar in strawberry sauce or monkfish marinière (£15.50), and puddings such as strawberry cream tart and chocolate roulade (£4), or an unusual cheeseboard (£4.50). They also do a two-course lunch (£10.50). They've enjoyable house wines, and Greene King IPA, Abbot and Old Speckled Hen are well kept on handpump; the Spanish landlady is friendly. Tables are out on the raised lawn in front, and in a pretty little rustic back garden. *(Recommended by Mrs J Hanmer, Hywel Bevan, M and GR, Tony and Shirley Albert)*

Greene King ~ Lease Maria Teresa Axon ~ Real ale ~ Bar food (not Sun evening) ~ Restaurant ~ (01638) 500275 ~ Children in eating area of bar and restaurant ~ Open 11-3, 5(6 Sat)-11; 12-3, 7-11 Sun; closed 26 Dec, 1 Jan

LONG MELFORD TL8646 Map 5

Black Lion

Church Walk

This comfortable hotel is somewhere you'd come for a civilised meal, rather than just a quick drink. One side of the oak serving counter is decorated in ochre, and, besides bar stools, has deeply cushioned sofas, leather wing armchairs and antique fireside settles, while the other, in shades of terracotta, has leather dining chairs around handsome tables set for the good bar food. The interesting changing menu could include soup (£4.25), baked brie with red onion chutney (£5.50), crispy fried ham hash cakes on grain mustard and chive sauce (£4.50), cauliflower cheese charlotte on roasted vegetables (£9.75), steamed beef and suet pudding (£10.95), lamb steak with wild mushroom sauce (£11.95), and bass on a leek, spinach and potato pie with Pernod sauce (£13.95), with puddings such as chocolate brownie with honeycomb ice-cream (£4.25). The restaurant is no smoking. Big windows with swagged-back curtains have a pleasant outlook over the green, and there are large portraits, of racehorses and of people. Service by neatly uniformed staff is friendly and efficient; the piped Radio Suffolk can be obtrusive. You'll find well kept (but not cheap) Adnams, and maybe Nethergate Suffolk County on handpump, and they've a fine range of wines by the glass, including champagne, 20 malt whiskies, and generous cafetière coffees; tortilla chips are set out in bowls. The Victorian walled garden is appealing. *(Recommended by Michael and Ann Cole, Mr and Mrs M Hayes, Tracey and Stephen Groves, MDN, Sarah Markham Flynn, Adele Summers, Alan Black)*

Ravenwood Group ~ Manager Lahsen Ighaghai ~ Real ale ~ Bar food (12-2, 7-9.30 (10 Fri/Sat)) ~ Restaurant ~ (01787) 312356 ~ Children welcome ~ Dogs welcome ~ Open 11-11; 12-10.30 Sun ~ Bedrooms: £85B/£109.50B

Please let us know what you think of a pub's bedrooms. No stamp needed: *The Good Pub Guide*, FREEPOST TN1569, Wadhurst, E Sussex TN5 7BR.

NAYLAND TL9734 Map 5

Anchor 🍷

Court Street; just off A134 – turn off S of signposted B1087 main village turn

They sell wines from their own vineyard at this carefully refurbished pub, and they've got their own smokehouse too. Even though there's quite an emphasis on the good food, they've managed to kept a warmly local feel in the bare-boards front bar. It's light and sunny inside, with interesting old photographs of pipe-smoking customers and village characters on its pale yellow walls, farmhouse chairs around a mix of tables, and coal and log fires at each end. Behind, a carpeted room with similar furniture, another fire, and cheerful seaside pictures for sale, leads into a small carpeted sun room. The interesting lunchtime menu might include soup (£3.50), sandwiches (from £4.95), poached smoked haddock rarebit with mashed potato and minted leeks (£6.95, £8.95 large), potato, goats cheese, pea and mint tart (£6.95), and herb-battered cod and chips (£8.25), with evening dishes such as pancake with chinese-style barbecue pork, spring onions and mushrooms (£5.50, £7.50), seafood risotto with lemon juice and mascarpone (£7.45), pine nut-crusted chicken supreme stuffed with basil butter (£9.95), and chargrilled rib-eye steak with lemon-roasted greek potatoes (£10.95), with puddings such as waffles with poached rhubarb and orange curd cream (£3.95). The separate no smoking restaurant, similarly light and airy, is up quite steep stairs. Served in elegant beer glasses, by friendly enthusiastic staff, Adnams and Greene King IPA are well kept on handpump, along with a couple of guests such as Greene King Old Speckled Hen and Triumph; piped music, but not too intrusive. A gravel terrace behind has picnic-sets looking across to the peaceful River Stour and its quacking ducks. Next to the pub is an ongoing Heritage Farming Project. The farmland is being worked throughout the season by suffolk punch horses using traditional farming methods. The suffolk punch is one of the most endangered species in the world – even rarer than the giant panda. Visitors are welcome to watch or to try their hand at the reins. *(Recommended by Derek Thomas, John Saville, MDN, Reg Fowle, Helen Rickwood)*

Free house ~ Licensee Daniel Bunting ~ Real ale ~ Bar food (12-2.30, 6.30-9; 12-9(8 Sun)Sat) ~ Restaurant ~ (01206) 262313 ~ Children in eating area of bar and restaurant ~ Open 11-2.30, 5-11; 11-11 Sat; 12-10.30 Sun

ORFORD TM4250 Map 5

Jolly Sailor £

Quay Street

A good base for walkers, fishermen and bird-watchers, this unspoilt 17th c brick pub is built mainly from wrecked ships' timbers. The several snugly traditional rooms have lots of exposed brickwork, and are served from counters and hatches in an old-fashioned central cubicle. There's an unusual spiral staircase in the corner of the flagstoned main bar – which also has 13 brass door knockers and other brassware, local photographs, two cushioned pews and a long antique stripped deal table, and an open woodburning stove in the big brick fireplace (with nice horsebrasses above it); a small room is popular with the dominoes and cribbage players. Adnams Bitter and Broadside are well kept on handpump. A short choice of straightforward food in generous helpings could include good battered local cod, skate, rock eel or flounder with chips, home-made steak pie or home-cooked ham and egg, chilli con carne, and daily roasts (all £5.50), with a couple of evening specials such as local cod mornay and chicken stir fry (£7.50); no sandwiches. There are lovely surrounding coastal walks and plenty of outside pursuits; several picnic-sets on grass at the back have views over the marshes. No children. *(Recommended by Dave Braisted, Michael and Ann Cole, David and Gilly Wilkins, Comus and Sarah Elliott, Pat and Clive Sherriff, Mr and Mrs John Taylor, Klaus and Elizabeth Leist, David Carr, Simon Rodway, Ken Millar, Stephen and Jean Curtis)*

Adnams ~ Tenant Philip Attwood ~ Real ale ~ Bar food (12-2, 7.15-8.45; not Mon evening, nor Mon-Thurs evenings Nov-Easter) ~ No credit cards ~ (01394) 450243 ~ Dogs allowed in bar ~ Open 11.30-2.30, 7-11; 12-2.45, 7-10.30 Sun; closed evenings 25-26 Dec ~ Bedrooms: /£50S

RATTLESDEN TL9758 Map 5

Brewers Arms

Signposted on minor roads W of Stowmarket, off B1115 via Buxhall or off A45 via Woolpit

Inside this solidly built 16th-c village local, the pleasantly simple beamed lounge bar on the left has book-lined walls, individually chosen pictures and bric-a-brac. It winds back through standing timbers to the main eating area, which is partly flint-walled, and has a magnificent old bread oven and more comfortable seating. French windows open on to the garden. Greene King Abbot, IPA, and Old Speckled Hen are well kept along with maybe a guest such as Tanners Jack on handpump, and you'll find 30 malt whiskies. An extensive menu might include soup (£3.25), lunchtime (not Sunday) sandwiches (from £3.75) and filled baked potatoes (from £4.95), roasted pepper and olive tart or steak and kidney pie (£7.95), barracuda steak with herb and mushroom risotto (£11.95), pork fillet with orange and basil (£10.95), and mixed grill (£13.95), with lots of puddings such as plum and almond tart or white chocolate mousse (£3.95); Sunday roast (£6.95). The restaurant is no smoking; piped music, cribbage, dominoes, shove-ha'penny. *(Recommended by Derek Field, Maureen and Gerry Whittles, Helen and Ian Jobson, Ian and Nita Cooper, Mike Bell)*

Greene King ~ Tenants Mr and Mrs Davies ~ Real ale ~ Bar food (12-2, 6(7 Sun)-9) ~ Restaurant ~ (01449) 736377 ~ Well behaved children in eating area of bar and restaurant ~ Open 11.30-2.30, 6-11; 12-3, 7-10.30 Sun

REDE TL8055 Map 5

Plough

Village signposted off A143 Bury St Edmunds—Haverhill

There are picnic-sets in front, and a sheltered cottagey garden at the back of this peacefully set thatched pink-washed pub. The food here is interesting and well cooked, and you may need to book to be sure of a table. The changing menu might include stuffed pigeon with green lentils, fried salmon with balsamic vinegar or rabbit wrapped in bacon with mustard sauce (£9.95), calves liver and mash (£10.95), and grilled bass with pesto and herb stuffing or venison braised with red wine and shallots, with bacon and wild mushrooms (£12.50), and puddings (£3.95). Simple and traditional, the bar has copper measures and pewter tankards hanging from low black beams, decorative plates on a delft shelf and surrounding the solid fuel stove in its brick fireplace, and red plush button-back built-in wall banquettes. Served from electric pumps by the friendly staff, Greene King IPA, Abbot and Ruddles are well kept under light blanket pressure alongside a guest such as St Austells Tribute, and they've a decent choice of wines; piped pop music. More reports please. *(Recommended by Philip and Susan Philcox, Mrs Jane Kingsbury, Mrs M Grimwood, M and GR, Adele Summers, Alan Black)*

Greene King ~ Tenant Brian Desborough ~ Real ale ~ Bar food (not Sun evening) ~ Restaurant ~ (01284) 789208 ~ Children in eating area of bar ~ Open 11-3, 6.30-11; 12-3 Sun; closed Sun evening

SNAPE TM3959 Map 5

Crown

B1069

A good place to stay, this bustling inn has a thoughtful wine list, with 14 wines by the glass (including champagne). Most people come here to eat, and regularly changing (but not cheap) dishes from the blackboard menu might include soup (£3.95), home-made pork, liver and rosemary terrine (£4.95), battered king prawns with tomato chilli dip (£7.50), home-made steak and kidney suet pudding (£10.25), chicken thai red curry (£10.50), and monkfish wrapped in parma ham with roasted peppers, capers and chips (£12.95), with puddings such as pear and almond flan or home-made ice-cream (£3.95). The dining room is no smoking; in the Festival they do a useful pre-concert short menu. The attractive bar is furnished with striking horseshoe-shaped high-backed settles around a big brick inglenook with a woodburning stove, spindleback and country kitchen chairs, and nice old tables on some old brick flooring; an exposed panel shows how the ancient walls were constructed, and there are lots of beams in the various small side rooms. At busy times the tables may all be reserved for diners; Adnams Bitter, Broadside and a seasonal ale are well kept on handpump. There's a pretty roadside garden with tables under cocktail parasols. The bedrooms, up steep stairs, are quaint, with beamed ceilings, sloping floors, and doorways that you may have to stoop through; good breakfasts. *(Recommended by Pamela Goodwyn, Bryan and Mary Blaxall, Philip and Elaine Holmes, D S Cottrell, Phil and Heidi Cook, MDN, DF, NF, Catherine and Rob Dunster, A Sadler, Gordon Prince, Alistair and Kay Butler, Brian and Pam Lamb, Comus and Sarah Elliott, Neil Powell, Peter and Pat Frogley, Ian and Jane Irving, David and Gilly Wilkins, Fred and Lorraine Gill, Mr and Mrs R W Glover, Simon Rodway, Dr Peter D Smart, Mrs A Chapman, Adrian White)*

Adnams ~ Tenant Diane Maylott ~ Real ale ~ Bar food ~ Restaurant ~ (01728) 688324 ~ Open 12-3, 6-11; 12-3, 7-10.30 Sun; closed 25 Dec, 26 Dec evening ~ Bedrooms: £60B/£70B

SOUTH ELMHAM TM3389 Map 5

St Peters Brewery

St Peter S Elmham; off B1062 SW of Bungay

The own-brew beers at this bewitching medieval manor are made using water from a 60-metre (200-ft) bore hole, in brewery buildings laid out around a courtyard; they do tours on the hour between 12 and 4pm, and there's a gift shop. On handpump they serve well kept St Peters Organic Best, Golden Ale and Ruby Red, while the rest of their ales are available by the bottle. The building is another huge draw – the hall dates back to the late 13th c, but was much extended in 1539 using materials from the recently dissolved Flixton Priory. Genuinely old tapestries and furnishings make having a drink in the small main bar feel more like a trip to a historic home than a typical pub outing, but the atmosphere is civilised and welcoming, with candles and fresh flowers on the dark wooden tables, and comfortable seats – from cushioned pews and settles to a 16th-c french bishop's throne; piped music. A highlight is the dramatic high-ceilinged dining hall (no smoking in here), with elaborate woodwork, mullion windows, a big flagstoned floor, and an imposing chandelier, as well as a couple of other appealing old rooms reached up some steepish stairs: one is no smoking, while the other is a light, beamed room with comfortable armchairs and nice big rug. It's best to book for the short choice of enjoyable waitress-served food. The lunchtime menu might include home-made soup (£3.65), baguettes (from £4.25), various salads (£5.95), and steak and ale pie or pork-and-leek sausages with wholegrain mustard mash (£8.50), with evening dishes such as roasted vegetables with mozzarella and basil (£10.50), and salmon fillet with pecorino and pesto crust or fried sirloin steak with red wine jus (£13.50), and mouthwatering puddings such as chocolate and orange pudding or caramelised pear tart (£5); they do a two-course Sunday lunch (£14.95). Outside, tables overlook the original moat. *(Recommended by Mike and Wendy Proctor, David Barnes, Peter Meister, Esther and John Sprinkle, M and GR, Dennis and Gill Keen, J F M and M West)*

Own brew ~ Licensees John Murphy and Janet Fogg ~ Real ale ~ Bar food (12-2, 6-9) ~ Restaurant ~ (01986) 782322 ~ Children in restaurant and family room ~ Open 11-11; 12-10.30 Sun

SOUTHWOLD TM5076 Map 5

Crown ★

High Street

Whether you're after an enjoyable drink or a superbly cooked meal, this rather smart old hotel is a smashing choice. With an appealingly relaxed atmosphere and a good mix of customers, the extended elegant beamed main bar has a stripped curved high-backed settle and other dark varnished settles, kitchen chairs and some bar stools, pretty flowers on the mix of kitchen pine tables, a carefully restored and rather fine carved wooden fireplace, and newspapers to read. The smaller back oak-panelled locals' bar has more of a traditional pubby atmosphere, with red leatherette wall benches and a red carpet; shove-ha'penny, dominoes and cribbage. There's a separate no smoking restaurant, too. Arrive very early if you want to eat here, as the imaginative bar food is very popular: well presented dishes might include soup (£3.75), baked goats cheese mousse (£4.95), trout tapenade (£6), roast vegetables with cumin and couscous (£9.15), lamb fillet with lentils and roast beetroot (£10.95), seared salmon with citrus salad or roast cod with salsa (£12.50), and puddings such as chocolate truffle tart (£4.50). Friendly and efficient staff serve Adnams beers in top condition on handpump, and they've a splendid wine list, with a monthly changing choice of 20 interesting varieties by the glass or bottle, and quite a few malt whiskies. Tables out in a sunny sheltered corner are very pleasant. *(Recommended by Francis Johnston, Comus and Sarah Elliott, the Didler, Sue Holland, Dave Webster, MJVK, Tina and David Woods-Taylor, D S Cottrell, Richard Siebert, Christopher and Jo Barton, Derek and Sylvia Stephenson, Glenwys and Alan Lawrence, Pat and Tony Hinkins, Pam and David Bailey, M and GR, Leigh and Gillian Mellor, John and Enid Morris, Brenda and Rob Fincham, Michael Dandy, Anthony Rickards Collinson, David Boult, David Carr, Simon Rodway, Rob Winstanley, Steve Nye, Charles Cooper)*

Adnams ~ Tenant Michael Bartholomew ~ Real ale ~ Bar food ~ Restaurant ~ (01502) 722275 ~ Children in eating area of bar and family room ~ Open 11-11; 12-10.30 Sun; 11-3, 6-11 in winter; 12-3, 6.30-10.30 Sun in winter ~ Bedrooms: £80B/£116B

Harbour Inn

Blackshore, by the boats; from A1095, turn right at the Kings Head, and keep on past the golf course and water tower

There's still plenty of genuine nautical character at this appealing old waterside pub, and the friendly landlord is a lifeboatman. In the old days the lifeboat station was next door, and the lifeboat telephone, and needless to say quite often the lifeboat men, were housed in the pub. The tiny, low-beamed, tiled and panelled front bar has antique settles, and in the back bar which has a wind speed indicator, model ships, a lot of local ship and boat photographs, smoked dried fish hanging from a line on a beam, a lifeboat line launcher, and brass shellcases on the mantlepiece over a stove. This room has rustic stools and cushioned wooden benches built into its stripped panelling. Behind here, the dining area is no smoking. Freshly prepared tasty bar food includes soup (£3.25), filled baguettes (from £4.60), half a pint of prawns (£5.25, a pint £8.95), beer-battered haddock or ploughman's (£7.95), fried lambs liver or home-made lasagne (£8.95), and smoked haddock and prawn gratin (£10.25), with fresh fish specials. Superbly kept Adnams Broadside and Southwold, and a seasonal guest on handpump; piped music. It's a good idea to arrive early in good weather, so you can bag a seat at the front of the building and watch all the activity in the bustling quay. On former marshland, the back garden has lots of tables, and a little terrace; look out for the 1953 flood level marked on the outside of the pub. *(Recommended by Sue Holland, Dave Webster, Comus and Sarah Elliott, Tracey and Stephen Groves, Peter Meister, Pat and Clive Sherriff, Fred and Lorraine Gill, Simon Rodway, Neil and Lorna Mclaughlan, Louise English, Richard Waller, Pauline Smith, Pete Baker)*

Adnams ~ Tenant Colin Fraser ~ Real ale ~ Bar food (12-2.30, 6-9) ~ (01502) 722381 ~ Children in bottom bar and restaurant till 9pm ~ Dogs allowed in bar ~ Live rock/folk/blues Sat, monthly Fri jazz ~ Open 11-11; 12-10.30 Sun

STOKE-BY-NAYLAND TL9836 Map 5

Angel (food award) (wine award)

B1068 Sudbury—East Bergholt; also signposted via Nayland off A134 Colchester—Sudbury

They offer quite a choice of seafood at this elegant pub, and the interesting menu might include seared scallops (£6.95, large £13.95), griddled skate wing (£10.95), and fresh dressed crab (£12.50). Non-fishy choices might be home-made soup (£3.25), chicken liver parfait with cumberland sauce (£4.25), chargrilled suffolk back bacon with apple mash and cider sauce, provençale stuffed peppers with stilton or chinese-style stir-fried duck with egg noodles and oriental vegetables (£7.75), with evening dishes such as pork tenderloin stuffed with apricots and wrapped in ham (£9.95), and chargrilled sirloin steak (£14.25), and home-made puddings such as baked rum and raisin cheesecake (£4.25). The restaurant is no smoking. The comfortable main bar area has handsome Elizabethan beams, some stripped brickwork and timbers, a mixture of furnishings including wing armchairs, mahogany dining chairs, and pale library chairs, local watercolours, modern paintings and older prints, attractive table lamps, and a huge log fire. Round the corner is a little tiled-floor stand-and-chat bar; neatly uniformed staff serve well kept Greene King IPA and Abbot and a guest such as Fullers London Pride on handpump, and there's a decent wine list. Another room has a low sofa and wing armchairs around its woodburning stove, and mustard-coloured walls. There are cast-iron seats and tables on a sheltered terrace. *(Recommended by Ian and Jane Irving, SH, Sherrie Glass, Philip and Elaine Holmes, Francis Johnston, MDN, Philip J Cooper, Richard Siebert, Maysie Thompson, A Sadler, David J Bunter, John and Enid Morris, David Twitchett, Alan and Jill Bull, J F M and M West, Jeff and Wendy Williams, Ken Millar, Derek Thomas)*

Horizon Inns ~ Manager Neil Bishop ~ Real ale ~ Bar food ~ Restaurant ~ (01206) 263245 ~ Children in eating area of bar, restaurant and family room ~ Dogs allowed in bar ~ Open 11-2.30, 6-11; 12-10.30 Sun; closed 25-26 Dec, 1 Jan ~ Bedrooms: £60S(£70B)/£75S(£85B)

Crown ★ (food award) (wine award)

Park Street (B1068)

Reopened towards the end of 2003 after complete refurbishment by a former landlord of the nearby Angel, in partnership with a director of Lay & Wheelers the noted wine merchant, this has quickly proved a winner. It typifies the best sort of contemporary reinterpretation of what makes a good if rather upmarket pub. The careful interior design has a lot to do with this. There is plenty of room for either drinking or eating, most of it directly open to the three-sided bar servery, yet well divided, and with two or three more tucked-away areas too. The main area, with a big woodburning stove, has quite a lot of tables, in a variety of shapes, styles and sizes. Elsewhere, several smaller areas each have just three or four tables. Seating varies from deep armchairs and sofas to elegant dining chairs and comfortable high-backed woven rush seats – and there are plenty of bar stools. This all gives a good choice between conviviality and varying degrees of cosiness and privacy. With a subtle colour scheme of several gentle toning colours, cheerful wildlife and landscape paintings, quite a lot of attractive table lamps and carefully placed gentle spotlighting, low ceilings (some with a good deal of stripped old beams), and floors varying from old tiles through broad boards or dark new flagstones to beige carpet, the overall feel is of relaxation. There is a table of daily papers. The drink, food and service are all very good. They have Adnams Bitter and Explorer and Greene King IPA and Morlands Original on handpump, good nicely served coffee (typically doing well over 100 cups a day), and take care with other drinks such as Pimms. The choice of wines is rewarding – an unusual feature is the glass-walled 'cellar' in one corner. They sell wines by the half-case to take away too, and suggest a different wine by the glass to go with each of their two dozen or so menu choices. The food is enterprising without being outlandishly unusual, taking care with ingredients (local free range chicken, pork, lamb, game and vegetables, crab from East Mersea, wild scotch salmon), and might include bouillabaisse with rouille (£4.25), salmon and scallop terrine, ham and mozzarella tart or citrus-marinated king prawns (£6.95), baby vegetable risotto (£9.75), calves liver and bacon with their own good chutney (£10.35), charcuterie with home-baked bread (£10.95), barbecued pork chop with roasted peach (£11.50), grilled chicken with fig salad (£11.95), specials such as sausage and mash (£8.50) and lemon sole or bass (£10.95), and nice seasonal puddings such as peach and blueberry tart with ice-cream (£4.95). They are happy to do small helpings if you want. Service is good, prompt and thoughtful – and given a slightly continental touch by the wrap-around white aprons worn by all the friendly young staff. A sheltered back terrace has cushioned teak chairs and tables under big canvas parasols with heaters, looking out over a neat lawn to a landscaped shrubbery that includes a small romantic ruined-abbey folly. There are many more picnic-sets out on the front terrace. Disabled access is good, and the car park is big. *(Recommended by David Twitchett, John Prescott, Keith Sale, MDN, J F M and M West, H Jones)*

Free house ~ Licensee Richard Sunderland ~ Real ale ~ Bar food (12-2.30(3.30 Sun), 6-9.30(10 Fri, Sat; 9 Sun)) ~ Restaurant ~ (01206) 262001 ~ Children in restaurant ~ Dogs allowed in bar ~ Open 11-11; 12-10.30 Sun

SWILLAND TM1852 Map 5

Moon & Mushroom

Village signposted off B1078 Needham Market—Wickham Market, and off B1077

You approach this enjoyably idiosyncratic, cosy old place through an archway of grapevines and creepers, and a little terrace in front has retractable awnings and heaters (so you can still eat outside even in cooler weather), flower containers, trellis and nice wooden furniture under parasols. The cheerful, helpful licensees only keep independent East Anglian beers – Buffys Hopleaf, Crouch Vale Brewers Gold, Norwich Terrier, Nethergate Umbel, and Woodfordes Norfolk Nog and Wherry, which are tapped straight from casks functionally racked up behind the long counter. They also serve 17 decent wines by the glass, and around 25 malt whiskies. With a good mix of locals and visitors, the homely interior is mainly quarry-tiled, with a small coal fire in a brick fireplace, old tables (with lots of board games in the drawers) arranged in little booths made by pine pews, and cushioned stools along the bar. An unusual touch is the four hearty hotpots in the no smoking dark green and brown-painted cottagey dining room, through a small doorway from the bar. These are served to you from Le Creuset dishes on a warming counter and might include beef cooked in beer with dumplings, venison in red wine and pork loin with stilton sauce (all £8.95), and you then help yourself to a choice of half a dozen or so tasty vegetables. Another few dishes might include a good ploughman's (£4.95), summer lunchtime salads (from £6.95), and fillet of cod mornay or mediterrannean vegetable bake (£8.95), with proper home-made puddings such as raspberry and apple crumble, and toffee and ginger pudding with butterscotch sauce (£3.75). It's still a real local (with an enjoyable bustling but relaxed atmosphere), and food service does end quite early. No children inside. *(Recommended by Philip and Susan Philcox, Dr and Mrs Michael Smith, M and GR, J F M and M West, Pam and David Bailey, Mrs P Sarson, Charles Gysin, Ian and Nita Cooper, Pamela Goodwyn)*

Free house ~ Licensees Clive and Adrienne Goodall ~ Real ale ~ Bar food (12-2, 6.30-8.15; not Sun-Mon) ~ (01473) 785320 ~ Dogs allowed in bar ~ Open 11-2.30, 6-11; 12-2.30, 7-10.30 Sun; closed Mon lunchtime

Bedroom prices are for high summer. Even then you may get reductions for more than one night, or (outside tourist areas) weekends. Winter special rates are common, and many inns cut bedroom prices if you have a full evening meal.

WALBERSWICK TM4974 Map 5

Bell

Just off B1387

Charming inside (and in a lovely setting), this busy old pub has brick floors, well worn flagstones and oak beams that were here 400 years ago when the sleepy little village was a flourishing port. The rambling traditional bar has curved high-backed settles, tankards hanging from oars above the counter, and a woodburning stove in the big fireplace; a second bar has a very large open fire. The best time to visit is out of season, when it's less busy; as they don't take bookings for bar food, at peak times there are usually queues. Good well presented dishes, from a changing menu, might include sandwiches (from £3.75), home-made soup (£3.95), shredded sticky pork belly with apple chutney (£4.95), ploughman's (£5.50), home-made red onion, mushroom and blue cheese tart (£7.25), home-made shepherd's pie or cajun chicken and vegetable stir fry with noodles (£7.95), with fresh fish dishes such as home-made fishcakes with hollandaise sauce (£7.95), and grilled skate wing with herb, lime and caper butter (£8.25), and home-made puddings such as tiramisu (£3.95); they've a children's menu (from £3.50). They call out your number when your food is ready. Adnams Bitter, Broadside and a seasonal ale are well kept on handpump, and they've 11 wines by the glass, and a dozen malt whiskies; piped music, shove-ha'penny, cribbage, dominoes, and boules outside. The pub is close to the beach, and most of the bedrooms look over the sea or river; tables on the sizeable lawn are sheltered from the worst of the winds by a well placed hedge. You can take the little ferry from Southwold and walk here. *(Recommended by Blaise Vyner, J F M and M West, the Didler, DF, NF, Comus and Sarah Elliott, MJVK, Peter Meister, Pat and Clive Sherriff, Tina and David Woods-Taylor, Rob Kelvey, Julie Scarsbrook, Fred and Lorraine Gill, Roy and Lindsey Fentiman, Simon Rodway, TW, MW, Neil and Lorna Mclaughlan, Phil and Helen Holt)*

Adnams ~ Tenant Sue Ireland Cutting ~ Real ale ~ Bar food (12-2(2.30 Sun and bank hols), 7-9(6-9 school summer hols), 12-2, 6-9 Fri-Sat) ~ Restaurant ~ (01502) 723109 ~ Children away from bar ~ Dogs allowed in bar and bedrooms ~ Open 11-3, 6-11 (11-11 in school summer hols); 11-11 Sat; 12-10.30 Sun ~ Bedrooms: £60S/£75S

WALDRINGFIELD TM2844 Map 5

Maybush

Off A12 S of Martlesham; The Quay, Cliff Road

The setting is what makes this busy family pub stand out, so a good time to visit is in the summer when you can sit on the verandah and enjoy a drink overlooking the River Deben; there are dozens of well arranged outside tables too. The spacious bar has quite a nautical theme, with lots of old lanterns, pistols and so forth, as well as aerial photographs, an original Twister board, and fresh flowers; though it's all been knocked through, it's divided into separate areas by fireplaces or steps. A glass case has an elaborate ship's model, and there are a few more in a lighter, high-ceilinged extension. A number of the dark wooden tables are set for eating, and though it can fill quickly at lunchtime (particularly in summer), service remains swift and friendly. Adnams Best and Broadside, and Greene King IPA are well kept on handpump, and they've a good range of wines, with around nine or ten by the glass. Besides lunchtime sandwiches, straightforward bar food includes soup (£3.25), prawn cocktail (£4.45), cheese and vegetable pie or stilton beefburger (£6.95), tiger prawns in filo pastry or steak and Guinness pie (£7.95), grilled plaice with lemon and tarragon butter (£8.45), and steaks (from £10.95), with daily specials and puddings listed on blackboards. The dining rooms are no smoking. River cruises are available nearby; fruit machine, piped music, dominoes and cribbage. *(Recommended by Bill and Lisa Copeland, Francis Johnston, Pamela Goodwyn, Mike and Wendy Proctor, David Carr, Mrs A Chapman)*

Punch ~ Tenants Steve and Louise Lomas ~ Real ale ~ Bar food (12-2.30, 6.30-9.30; all day wknds and bank hols) ~ Restaurant ~ (01473) 736215 ~ Children in eating area of bar and restaurant ~ Dogs allowed in bar ~ Open 11-11; 12-10.30 Sun

LUCKY DIP

Besides the fully inspected pubs, you might like to try these Lucky Dips recommended to us and described by readers (if you do, please send us reports: www.goodguides.co.uk).

ALDEBURGH TM4656

☆ *Cross Keys* [Crabbe St]: Busy 16th-c pub extended from low-beamed core with antique settles, Victorian prints, woodburners, well kept Adnams ales (the full range) and wines, brisk friendly service, ample enjoyable food, Sunday papers; loudspeaker food announcements, fruit machine; open all day July-Aug, children in eating areas, picnic-sets in sheltered back yard which opens on to promenade and beach; elegant bedrooms with own bathrooms *(LYM, Gordon Theaker, Tony Middis, Comus and Sarah Elliott, Tracey and Stephen Groves, MDN)*

Mill [Market Cross Pl, opp Moot Hall]: Homely 1920s corner pub nr Moot Hall and beach, friendly and relaxing, with good value food cooked to order from sandwiches, baguettes and baked potatoes to steak and local fish, good service (humorous landlord), well kept Adnams ales, decent coffee, locals' bar, lots of pictures, cosy no smoking beamed dining room with *Gypsy Queen* model, sea view and strong RNLI theme, cream teas July-Aug; fruit machine; open all day Fri-Sat and July-Aug, bedrooms *(Comus and Sarah Elliott, David and Gilly Wilkins, Colin and Janet Roe)*

Wentworth [Wentworth Rd]: Hotel not pub, but its welcoming bar has enjoyable reasonably priced food, well kept Adnams and a good choice of wines by the glass; conservatory, terrace tables, bedrooms *(Pam and David Bailey)*

ALDRINGHAM TM4461

☆ *Parrot & Punchbowl* [B1122/B1353 S of Leiston]: Neat and tidy beamed pub with new chef doing good fairly priced food inc local fish and speciality prime steaks, pleasant atmosphere, good wine choice, well kept Adnams and Greene King IPA, decent coffee, two-level restaurant, no piped music or machines; children welcome; nice sheltered garden, also family garden with adventure play area, good craft centre opp *(BB, Francis Johnston, Simon Rodway, Comus and Sarah Elliott)*

BACTON TM0467

Bull [Church Rd]: Friendly good-humoured family service, enjoyable food inc sandwiches, light dishes and some good turkish food, well kept Adnams Broadside and Greene King IPA and Abbot, wheelchair access to dining room; busy wknds *(John F Morton)*

BARHAM TM1251

Sorrel Horse [Old Norwich Rd]: Cheerful and attractive pink-washed pantiled 17th-c country pub, nicely refurbished bar with magnificent log fire, lots of beams, lounge and two dining areas off, ample wholesome home cooking inc interesting specials, prompt friendly service, particularly well kept Ridleys Tolly and Cobbold IPA, decent wines; children welcome, good garden with big play area, summer bouncy castle and barbecue, stables opp; comfortable bedrooms in converted barn, well placed for walks *(J F M and M West, G Coates)*

BARNBY TM4789

Swan [off A146 Beccles—Lowestoft; Swan Lane]: Plush beamed dining pub with emphasis on excellent choice of good fresh fish in restaurant – not cheap but good value; well kept Adnams, good house wines, fishing décor *(David Boult)*

BILDESTON TL9949

☆ *Crown* [B1115 SW of Stowmarket]: Picturesque if not smart 15th-c timbered country pub, neat beamed main bar with inglenook and comfortable banquettes, smaller more modern bar, good value food from soup and sandwiches up, good puddings choice, no smoking dining room, well kept Adnams and Broadside and a guest beer tapped from the cask, obliging pleasantly informal service; may be piped music; children and dogs welcome, nice tables out in courtyard, more in large attractive garden with pet owl, quiet bedrooms *(Eddie Edwards, I D Greenfield, Mike Moden, O K Smyth, LYM, Patrick Hancock, Colin and Janet Roe)*

BLAXHALL TM3656

☆ *Ship* [off B1069 S of Snape; can be reached from A12 via Little Glemham]: Low-beamed 18th-c village pub with wide choice of good if not cheap food cooked by ex-diver landlord inc local fish, enterprising vegetarian dishes, small helpings for children, unassuming dining lounge, well kept Adnams and Woodfordes Wherry and Nelsons Revenge, friendly architect/artist landlady, woodburner; piped music, pool in public bar, live folk nights; children in eating area, self-catering cabins available, attractive country setting; cl Mon and Tues (exc by arrangement), four bedrooms with own bathrooms *(LYM, Comus and Sarah Elliott, Jenny and Brian Seller, Christopher and Jo Barton, Brenda Crossley)*

BLYFORD TM4276

☆ *Queens Head* [B1123 Blythburgh—Halesworth]: Thatch, very low beams, a well they still use, some antique settles alongside more modern conventional furnishings, huge fireplace, popular and nicely priced generous food inc bargain lunches (but no sandwiches), well kept Adnams Bitter, Mild, and Broadside, friendly tenant; children allowed in no smoking restaurant, tables outside with good play area, bedrooms *(LYM, Mr and Mrs J V Brooks)*

BLYTHBURGH TM4575

☆ *White Hart* [A12]: Friendly and roomy open-plan family dining pub with fine ancient beams, woodwork and staircase, full Adnams range kept well, good range of wines in two glass sizes, good coffee, charming efficient service, robust pocket-friendly blackboard food inc game and fish; may be piped music;

children in eating area and restaurant, open all day, spacious lawns looking down on tidal marshes (barbecues), magnificent church over road, bedrooms *(M A and C R Starling, Comus and Sarah Elliott, LYM, Tracey and Stephen Groves, Fred and Lorraine Gill)*

BRANDESTON TM2460

☆ *Queens Head* [The Street, towards Earl Soham]: Unpretentiously attractive open-plan country local, leather banquettes and old pews, well kept Adnams ales, good wines by the glass, enjoyable food (not Sun evening) inc some interesting dishes, particularly good vegetarian choice and good puddings, friendly relaxed atmosphere with two open fires and pub dogs and cats, family room, light and airy restaurant section; shove-ha'penny, cribbage, dominoes, piped music; bedrooms, campsite, big neat garden with good play area *(LYM, Pat and Tony Martin, Mike and Wendy Proctor, Comus and Sarah Elliott, TW, MW, Mrs A Chapman)*

BRENT ELEIGH TL9447

☆ *Cock* [A1141 SE of Lavenham]: Relaxed and unspoilt thatched local with piano in clean and cosy snug, benches, table and darts in second small room, antique flooring tiles, lovely coal fire, ochre walls with old photographs of local villages (the village church is well worth a look), well kept Adnams and Greene King IPA and Abbot, good organic farm cider, obliging landlord, no food beyond crisps and pickled eggs; picnic-sets up on side grass with summer hatch service, attractive inn-sign, bedrooms *(BB, the Didler, Giles and Annie Francis, MLR, Tracey and Stephen Groves)*

BROMESWELL TM3050

☆ *Cherry Tree* [Orford Rd, Bromeswell Heath]: Comfortably modernised neat beamed lounge, very popular wknds for good value and enjoyable wide-ranging food with plenty for vegetarians, well kept Adnams and Greene King Old Speckled Hen, well spaced tables, open fire; tables outside, big adventure playground, charming inn-sign *(Christopher and Jo Barton, BB, Gloria Bax, Pamela Goodwyn)*

BURY ST EDMUNDS TL8864

Flying Fortress [Mount Rd, Gt Barton (out towards Thurston, parallel to A143)]: Much enlarged former HQ of USAF support group, on edge of housing estate now covering Rougham ex-airfield – the original for the classic war film *Twelve o'Clock High*, with World War II bomber models and evocative black and white pictures; comfortable modern lounge area, well kept Adnams and a house beer brewed by Mauldons from long bar, quick friendly service, good value food inc carvery (big echoing restaurant area); tables outside, old fire-engine for children to play on *(Pam and David Bailey)*

Rose & Crown [Whiting St]: Unassuming town local, fairly spartan and spoilt by seeming to encourage smoking throughout, but comfortable and spotless, with simple excellent value lunchtime food, particularly well kept Greene King ales and a guest beer, pleasant lounge with lots of piggy pictures and bric-a-brac, good games-oriented public bar with darts, cards and dominoes, rare separate off-sales counter; may be piped local radio *(Pete Baker, Keith and Janet Morris)*

BUTLEY TM3650

☆ *Oyster* [B1084 E of Woodbridge]: Informal traditional country local, well kept Adnams Bitter and Broadside, enjoyable bar food (not Sun evening) from good sandwiches and baguettes up, good wine by the glass, helpful staff, stripped pine tables and pews, high-backed settles and more orthodox seats on bare boards, good coal fires; may be piped music; children and dogs welcome *(Mike and Sue Richardson, LYM, Mrs Romey Heaton, J F M and M West, Tracey and Stephen Groves, Pamela Goodwyn)*

CAVENDISH TL8046

Bull [A1092 Long Melford—Clare]: Attractive 16th-c pub, open plan, with heavy beams and timbers and fine fireplaces, Adnams Bitter, Broadside and a seasonal ale, wide food choice; may be piped music; children in eating areas, tables in garden, summer barbecues, car park (useful in this honeypot village) *(LYM, I J and S A Bufton, Adrian White, MDN)*

☆ *George* [The Green]: Beautifully updated attractive inn, now more restaurant-with-rooms than pub, good inventive modern food from interesting lunchtime sandwiches and light dishes to enterprising main dishes, some lower-price two- and three-course meals, beamed no smoking room, further large eating area with bar, cheerful efficient service, nice wines, good coffees and teas; bedrooms *(Adele Summers, Alan Black, Marianne and Peter Stevens, MDN)*

CHILLESFORD TM3852

Froize [B1084 E of Woodbridge]: Good country cooking in largely no smoking dining pub's pleasantly decorated bar and restaurant, wide choice inc local pork, game and venison, good value two-course buffet-style lunch (not Mon), more elaborate evening meals Thurs-Sat, popular Sun lunch (generous helpings, and you can go back for more), original puddings, well kept Adnams, good wines in choice of glass sizes, warmly welcoming service; may be cl Feb for hols *(DF, NF, Mrs P J Pearce, LYM, Pamela Goodwyn, Tony and Shirley Albert, Mrs Hilarie Taylor, David Boult)*

CLARE TL7645

☆ *Bell* [Market Hill]: Large timbered inn with comfortably rambling bar, splendidly carved black beams, old panelling and woodwork around the open fire, side rooms (one with lots of canal and other prints), well kept Nethergate ales inc Mild (this is the brewer's local), also others such as Greene King IPA, decent wines and food from sandwiches up inc children's in dining conservatory opening on to terrace; darts, pool, fruit machine; nice bedrooms off back courtyard (very special village, lovely church), open all day Sun *(Derek and Sylvia Stephenson, Angela Gorman, Paul Acton, LYM, Helen and Ian Jobson, Patrick Hancock)*

Globe [Callis St]: Well run, with attractively priced enjoyable food; handy for the church *(Ron Deighton)*

☆ *Swan* [High St]: Much modernised early 17th-c village pub under friendly new management, lots of copper and brass and huge log fire in main room, public bar with World War II memorabilia and another fire (dogs allowed here), no smoking refurbished dining room, reasonably priced food, well kept Greene King and guest ales; big-screen sports TV; smart new tables out behind among lovely flower tubs *(BB, Patrick Hancock, MLR, Adele Summers, Alan Black)*

COCKFIELD TL9152

Three Horseshoes [Stows Hill (A1141 towards Lavenham)]: Village local dating from 14th c, cosy and friendly, with well kept Greene King IPA and a guest beer, reasonably priced generous food, simple décor, dining conservatory; children welcome, outdoor summer pool table *(Des and Jen Clarke)*

COWLINGE TL7154

Three Tuns: Enjoyable home-made food from baguettes and baked potatoes through wide choice of freshly made pubby favourites to some more elaborate dishes, smaller children's helpings, efficient pleasant staff, well kept beer, comfortable bar (can get smoky);dining room *(anon)*

CREETING ST MARY TM1155

Highwayman [A140, just N of junction with A14]: Much modernised two-bar pub with pleasant Suffolk-barn style extension, relaxed atmosphere, welcoming staff, emphasis on good value food inc interesting dishes and popular Sun lunch, Adnams, Fullers London Pride and Woodfordes Wherry, decent wines, gallery overflow; unobtrusive piped music; tables on back lawn with small pond, cl Mon and Tues-Weds lunchtime *(Ian and Nita Cooper, Comus and Sarah Elliott, Pamela Goodwyn)*

DEBENHAM TM1763

Angel [High St]: Current licensees doing enjoyable food in bar and restaurant, plenty of local produce, good choice of real ales inc Earl Soham, Aspall's farm cider; three comfortable bedrooms *(David Sadler-Bridge, Tony Cook)*

EAST BERGHOLT TM0734

☆ *Kings Head* [Burnt Oak, towards Flatford Mill]: Well kept attractive beamed lounge with comfortable sofas, interesting decorations, dining area off, widening range of good value home-made blackboard food, well kept Greene King and guest ales, decent wines and coffee, quick pleasant service, friendly atmosphere; piped classical music, juke box in plain public bar; lots of room in pretty garden, flower-decked haywain, baskets and tubs of flowers in front *(Tony and Shirley Albert, Alistair and Kay Butler, Mike and Mary Carter, Pamela Goodwyn)*

EASTBRIDGE TM4566

☆ *Eels Foot* [off B1122 N of Leiston]: Simple cheerful country pub, well kept Adnams Best, Broadside and Regatta, light modern furnishings, darts in side area, wide choice of food from good value hot-filled rolls up, neat back dining room; walkers, children and dogs welcome, pleasant garden with tables and swings, pretty village handy for Minsmere bird reserve (nice 2½-mile walk from sluice); open all day in summer, Tues Suffolk sing-song – as for the last 60 years *(LYM, David and Rhian Peters, Fred and Lorraine Gill)*

FELIXSTOWE FERRY TM3237

☆ *Ferry Boat*: Relaxed and cottagey 17th-c pub tucked between golf links and dunes nr harbour, Martello tower and summer rowing-boat ferry, great for walks by sea; extended and much modernised as family pub, impressive blackboard choice of good value food from snacks to fresh fish, well kept Adnams Best and Greene King IPA and Old Speckled Hen, warmly friendly licensees, helpful staff, good log fire; piped music; dogs welcome, tables outside, busy summer wknds – can be very quiet other times *(LYM, Giles and Annie Francis, David Carr, John Prescott, TW, MW)*

Victoria: Child-friendly riverside pub, substantial straightforward food inc local fish, well kept Adnams and Greene King ales, good log fire in snug, briskly efficient service, sea views from no smoking upstairs dining area *(Pamela Goodwyn, J F M and M West, Mike and Mary Carter, Giles and Annie Francis)*

FRAMLINGHAM TM2863

Castle Inn [Castle St]: Small and smartly decorated, next to the castle, with well kept Adnams and Greene King IPA, wide range of decent food from baguettes and baked potatoes up; children welcome, front picnic-sets overlooking duck pond, more on back terrace *(Stephen Bennett)*

☆ *Station Hotel* [Station Rd (B1116 S)]: High-ceilinged big-windowed bar with pine tables and chairs on stripped boards, interesting generous proper home cooking inc good fish dishes (an emphasis on smoked), four well kept Earl Soham ales and a guest beer, good choice of house wines, welcoming service, informal relaxed atmosphere, plenty of train pictures, small tiled-floor back snug; children welcome, picnic-sets in good-sized pleasant garden *(George and Sarah Saumarez Smith, BB, Pete Baker)*

FRESSINGFIELD TM2677

☆ *Fox & Goose* [B1116 N of Framlingham; Church St]: Restaurant rather than pub now, in beautifully timbered 16th-c building owned by the church; good kindly priced food, creative without being pretentious, inc light lunches and perhaps two-for-one bargains, comfortable armchairs and sofas in lounge for pre-dinner drinks (no bar counter), Adnams Best and Regatta tapped from the cask, fine wines, impressive personal service, two no smoking dining rooms, one with beams and modern art, the other cosy with a high-backed settle and log fire; children welcome, cl Mon *(Comus and Sarah Elliott, LYM, KC, TW, MW)*

HALESWORTH TM3877

Angel [Thoroughfare]: Civilised and comfortable 16th-c Adnams coaching inn with their beers very well kept and reasonably priced, obliging service, enjoyable bar food from soup and sandwiches up, good range of coffees and cakes, good italian restaurant, nice wines, great log fire; interesting inner courtyard with 18th-c clock and vines, seven well equipped bedrooms, open all day *(Guy Morton, TW, MW)*

HARTEST TL8352

☆ *Crown* [B1066 S of Bury St Edmunds]: Pink-washed pub by church behind pretty village green, refurbished in smartly minimalist style, good fire in impressive fireplace, very wide choice of enjoyable food inc fish and grills in two no smoking dining rooms and conservatory, well kept Greene King IPA, Abbot and Old Speckled Hen, decent house wines, quick service; piped music; children in eating areas, tables on big back lawn and in sheltered side courtyard, play area *(LYM, Adele Summers, Alan Black, Des and Jen Clarke)*

HESSETT TL9361

Five Bells [The Street]: Increasingly popular locally for its well kept beers, attractively varied home cooking inc good family Sun lunch, and friendly efficient service *(Derek Field)*

HITCHAM TL9851

White Horse [The Street (B1115 Sudbury—Stowmarket)]: Friendly local with fine choice of good home cooking in bar (dogs welcome) and restaurant, obliging service, well kept Greene King Abbot; cl Mon-Tues *(Mike and Lynn Robinson)*

HOLBROOK TM1636

Compasses [Ipswich Rd]: Tranquil old place, clean, tidy and roomy, well kept Adnams, Greene King IPA and a guest, friendly attentive staff, big log fire, fairly priced food in bar and restaurant; garden with play area, nice spot on Shotley peninsula *(Pamela Goodwyn)*

HOXNE TM1877

☆ *Swan* [off B1118, signed off A140 S of Diss; Low St]: Outstanding well restored late 15th-c thatched building, broad oak floorboards, handsomely carved timbering in the colour-washed walls, armchairs by deep-set inglenook fireplace, no smoking snug, another fireplace in dining room; two huge log fires, candles, well kept Adnams Bitter and Broadside and guest beers such as Black Sheep and Smiles tapped from the cask, bank hol beer festivals, good food from baguettes and light dishes to fresh fish, friendly landlord, hard-working cheerful staff; children welcome, sizeable attractive garden behind, summer barbecues *(Sue Anderson, Phil Copleston, Nick and Alison Dowson, LYM, TW, MW, Mrs A Chapman, Comus and Sarah Elliott, David Barnes)*

HUNTINGFIELD TM3473

Huntingfield Arms [The Street]: Neat and unpretentious, overlooking green, light wood tables and chairs, beams and stripped brickwork, decent home cooking inc good salads, fresh fish and great pudding choice, well kept Adnams and Greene King, friendly attentive service, restaurant, games area with pool beyond woodburner *(Peter Bush, Edmund Coan)*

IPSWICH TM1844

☆ *Fat Cat* [Spring Rd, opp junction with Nelson Rd]: Neatly kept reconstruction of basic bare-boards pub with 15 or more well kept interesting ales mainly from small breweries, belgian imports, farm ciders, helpful friendly service and cheery regulars, snacks such as scotch eggs, filled rolls and pasties (or bring your own food), lots of enamel beer advertisements, no music or machines; very little daytime parking nearby; back conservatory and terrace with summer thai barbecues, open all day *(Ian Phillips, the Didler, Diane Manoughian, BB, Ian and Nita Cooper)*

Greyhound [Henley Rd/Anglesea Rd]: Comfortable Victorian décor, well kept Adnams and guest ales, good substantial home cooking (even the burgers are good, and plenty for vegetarians), quick service, young staff helpful even when it's crowded; children welcome, quiet back terrace *(Paul Turner)*

Milestone [Woodbridge Rd]: Open-plan pub with up to a dozen or so real ales, farm ciders, several dozen whiskies, home-made food lunchtime and Mon-Weds evening; live bands, large front terrace *(the Didler)*

IXWORTH TL9370

☆ *Pykkerel* [High St; just off A143 Bury—Diss]: Several rooms off central servery, Elizabethan beams, attractive brickwork, panelling and paintings, big fireplaces, antique tables and comfortably well worn settles, oriental rugs on gleaming boards, small back sun lounge; friendly staff, well kept Greene King ales, good value food (not Sun evening) from sandwiches to interesting local fish choice in bar and restaurant; children and dogs welcome, comfortable bedrooms *(LYM, Derek Field, George Cowie, TW, MW)*

IXWORTH THORPE TL9173

Royal Oak: Small cheerfully comfortable village pub with changing guest beers such as Adnams, Jennings Cumberland, Tetleys, Tyndalls and Youngs, proper home cooking inc bargain lunchtime specials, welcoming landlady, no smoking areas *(BB, George Cowie)*

KERSEY TM0044

Bell [signed off A1141 N of Hadleigh; The Street]: Quaint flower-decked Tudor building in notably picturesque village, recently tastefully modernised low-beamed bar with log fire, two dining rooms, cheerful efficient service, well kept Adnams and Greene King IPA, decent house wines, good value enjoyable food from sandwiches and bar lunches to more elaborate evening dishes; children allowed, open all day, sheltered back terrace with fairy-lit side canopy *(LYM, David Biggins, Paul and Ursula Randall, Pamela Goodwyn)*

KETTLEBURGH TM2660

Chequers [The Street]: Riverside pub with enjoyable food from snacks to stylish meals, changing real ales, open fire, cosy panelled dining room; large formal garden with terrace and trees *(Comus and Sarah Elliott)*

KIRTLING TL6856

Red Lion [The Street]: Locally popular for food in bar and evening/Sun lunch restaurant, real ales too; is HQ for local cricket club *(anon)*

LAVENHAM TL9149

Cock [Church St]: Comfortable and attractive thatched village pub with generous and nicely prepared food from baguettes up, plush lounge, separate family dining room, basic bar (popular with young people wknds), Adnams and Greene King ales, good wine choice, quick friendly service, attentive and helpful; seats out in front and back garden, nice view of church *(Wendy and Carl Dye, the Didler, Des and Jen Clarke, MLR, Neil Skidmore, Adele Summers, Alan Black)*

Greyhound [High St]: Good pubby mix of old and young locals in 14th-c two-bar pub, good value food, well kept Greene King IPA and Abbot (happy hour 7-8), friendly service, snug no smoking dining area; busy wknds; tables out on terrace *(Des and Jen Clarke, Stephen and Jean Curtis, Alan Cole, Kirstie Bruce)*

LAYHAM TM0340

☆ *Marquis of Cornwallis* [Upper St (B1070 E of Hadleigh)]: Homely beamed 16th-c local popular lunchtime for enjoyable generous food inc good ploughman's and fresh veg, plush lounge bar, friendly atmosphere, well kept Adnams and Greene King, good wines and coffee, warm coal fire; good valley views, popular bird table and picnic-sets in extensive riverside garden, open all day Sat in summer; bedrooms handy for Harwich ferries *(Giles and Annie Francis, Tom Gondris)*

LITTLE BEALINGS TM2247

☆ *Admirals Head* [off A12 SW of Woodbridge; Sandy Lane]: Stylish and comfortable, with handsome beams, good choice of home-made food inc interesting dishes using good mainly local ingredients such as traditionally hung aberdeen angus beef, well kept ales inc Adnams Bitter and Broadside, decent changing house wines, friendly chatty service, upper-level candlelit raftered dining room, intriguing little cellar room down steps with trap door to one of the pub's two wells, nice Beeken yachting photographs, no music or machines; picnic-sets out on terrace *(J L Wedel, BB, Pamela Goodwyn)*

LITTLE GLEMHAM TM3458

Lion [Main Rd]: Wide food choice from baguettes, baked potatoes and light dishes up in roomy no smoking recently redecorated bar, dining areas and conservatory, cheerful service, well kept Adnams Bitter and Broadside and a guest beer, decent wines by the glass, big woodburners; sheltered back garden with heated deck *(Mr and Mrs T B Staples)*

LONG MELFORD TL8645

☆ *Bull* [Hall St (B1064)]: Medieval great hall, now a hotel, with very friendly helpful staff, well kept Greene King IPA and Abbot, daily papers, beautifully carved beams in old-fashioned timbered front lounge, antique furnishings, blazing log fire in huge fireplace, more spacious back bar with sporting prints; good range of bar food from good filled huffers to one-price hot dishes inc imaginative salads and fresh fish, no smoking restaurant; children welcome, courtyard tables, comfortable bedrooms, open all day Sat-Sun *(Chris Flynn, Wendy Jones, LYM, Sean and Sharon Pines, Richard Waller, Pauline Smith)*

Scutchers [Westgate St]: Good food and service, pleasant gently sophisticated layout, good choice of drinks *(MDN)*

MARKET WESTON TL9777

☆ *Mill* [Bury Rd (B1111)]: Opened-up pub with good staple food using local produce inc popular Sun lunch, well kept Adnams, Greene King IPA, Woodfordes Wherry and an Old Chimneys beer from the village brewery, enthusiastic effective service; children welcome, theme night *(Derek Field)*

MARTLESHAM TM2446

Black Tiles [off A12 Woodbridge—Ipswich]: Spotless and spacious family pub with pleasantly decorated bistro-style garden-room restaurant (children allowed here), big woodburner in appealing old bar, wide choice of good inexpensive generous quick home-made food, quick service from smart helpful staff, well kept Adnams Bitter and Broadside and a guest beer; garden tables, open all day *(LYM, David Carr)*

MARTLESHAM HEATH TM2445

Douglas Bader [The Square]: Helpful cheerful staff, very wide choice of reasonably priced enjoyable food inc OAP bargains, three eating areas; tables outside with play area overlooking green *(Jacqueline Deale)*

MELLIS TM1074

Railway Tavern [The Common]: Warmly friendly local, well kept Adnams and guest beers, open fires, occasional enjoyable food, quaint railway theme, very relaxed licensees; monthly R&B night, monthly curry and folk night; open all day *(Trevor Moore)*

MELTON TM2850

Wilford Bridge [Wilford Bridge Rd]: Light, roomy and well organised, with emphasis on good value food from good sandwiches to local fish in two spacious bars and restaurant, steak nights Mon-Tues, takeaways, well kept Adnams and Greene King Old Speckled Hen, good wines by the glass, prompt friendly service even when busy; nearby river walks *(Comus and Sarah Elliott, Pamela Goodwyn, Mrs A Chapman)*

MILL GREEN TL9542

White Horse [just E of Edwardstone]: Down-to-earth local atmosphere, long-serving character landlord, basic food such as burgers, well kept Adnams and two interesting guest beers, one always a Mild, motorcyclist-friendly *(Giles and Annie Francis)*

MONKS ELEIGH TL9647

☆ *Swan* [B1115 Sudbury—Stowmarket]: Proper pub under enterprising chef/landlord, good freshly made food inc bargain early supper, real ales inc Adnams and Greene King, good value wines, welcoming efficient service, comfortably modernised lounge bar, open fire, two dining areas; bedrooms *(Derek Thomas)*

NEWBOURNE TM2643

Fox [The Street]: Pleasant 17th-c pub, enjoyable food using fresh local produce, OAP wkdy lunchtime special, well kept Tolly tapped from the cask, cosy unspoilt oak-beamed drinking area around log fire, nice golden retriever (Hector), separate family room, dining extension; beware, they may try to keep your credit card while you eat; pretty hanging baskets, lots of tables out in attractive garden with pond, musical evenings *(Wendy and Carl Dye, Pamela Goodwyn)*

NEWMARKET TL6463

Bushel [Market St]: Good choice of enjoyable reasonably priced home-made food, good-sized helpings, comfortable partly no smoking bar *(Ian and Denise Foster)*

Wagon & Horses [High St]: Unpretentious local with five real ales, low-priced standard food from sandwiches and wraps up, daily papers *(Nigel and Sue Foster)*

ORFORD TM4249

Crown & Castle: Well established hotel with interesting if not cheap bar food inc good ploughman's and fresh crab, friendly relaxed atmosphere in bar with squashy sofa by the inviting log fire, well kept Greene King IPA, good wines by the glass, welcoming service, busy dining room; comfortable bedrooms in garden block *(J F M and M West, Comus and Sarah Elliott, TW, MW)*

Kings Head [Front St]: Bright and airy lounge bar overlooking churchyard, well kept Adnams ales, good coffee, good range of reasonably priced food inc sandwiches and the noted local smokery products, decent wines, friendly efficient staff, pleasant restaurant; live music Fri, attractive character bedrooms with own bathrooms, lots of flowers outside *(LYM, Neil and Lorna Mclaughlan, Gloria Bax)*

OTLEY TM1852

White Hart [Helmingham Rd (B1079)]: Friendly recently renovated pub with decent food from baguettes up, helpful attentive service, Woodfordes ale; sizeable pretty garden with tiling draughts board *(Esther and John Sprinkle)*

PAKENHAM TL9267

Fox [signed off A1088 and A143 S of Norwich]: Friendly beamed village local doing well after refurbishment under newish licensees, well kept Greene King IPA and Abbot, wide choice of enjoyable reasonably priced pub food with wkdy OAP discounts, small neat dining room, games room and quiz nights; children welcome, tables in streamside garden with ducks *(Derek Field)*

POLSTEAD TL9938

☆ *Cock* [signed off B1068 and A1071 E of Sudbury, then pub signed; Polstead Green]: Black beams and timbers, dark pink walls, woodburner and open fire, random mix of unassuming furniture, plenty of locals, interesting reasonably priced food (not Sun evening) from good value big lunchtime rolls up, well kept ales such as Adnams Broadside, Greene King IPA and Woodfordes Wherry, good choice of wines and malt whiskies, good coffee, light and airy barn restaurant; piped music; children welcome, picnic-sets out overlooking quiet green, side play area, cl Mon *(BB, Hazel Morgan, John Prescott, Pamela Goodwyn)*

RAMSHOLT TM3041

☆ *Ramsholt Arms* [signed off B1083; Dock Rd]: Lovely isolated spot, with picture-window nautical bars overlooking River Deben, handy for bird walks and Sutton Hoo; good wholesome food inc plenty of seafood and seasonal game, children's dishes, well kept Adnams Best and Broadside and local guest beers, several wines by the glass, winter mulled wine, easy-going contented bar (one of the dogs can let himself in) with good log fire, quick friendly service even when busy, no smoking restaurant; longish steep walk down from car park, busy summer wknds, can be a bit smoky; children very welcome, tables outside with summer afternoon terrace bar (not Sun), roomy bedrooms with stunning view, yacht moorings nearby *(LYM, Pamela Goodwyn, J F M and M West, Tracey and Stephen Groves, Mrs Hilarie Taylor, Peter Meister, Comus and Sarah Elliott)*

ROUGHAM TL9063

Ravenwood Hall: Country house hotel with elaborate restaurant, and worth knowing for its charming lounge bar with good blackboard bar meal choice inc sandwiches, sausages and mash and fish and chips, good service, open fires, lots of interesting touches, well kept Adnams Bitter and Broadside and St Peters Best, good wines by the glass, mulled wine at Christmas; children welcome, tables outside, wooded grounds, goats and geese by the car park, 14 bedrooms *(J F M and M West, Comus and Sarah Elliott)*

SAXON STREET TL6759

Reindeer [The Street]: Good choice of well kept real ales, friendly service, enjoyable generous food *(M and GR)*

SHOTTISHAM TM3144

Sorrel Horse [Hollesley Rd]: Simple thatched two-bar Tudor pub in tucked-away village, well kept Adnams, Greene King and a guest beer tapped from the cask, good value straightforward home cooking lunchtime and early evening (Sun lunch often completely booked even in winter), popular Thurs OAP bargain lunch, friendly helpful service, good log fire; quiz nights some Sats, tables out on green *(Mrs Roxanne Chamberlain, the Didler, Brenda Crossley, Pamela Goodwyn)*

SNAPE TM3959

Golden Key [Priory Lane]: The Kissick-Joneses, Adnams' longest-serving tenants – who made this low-beamed inn a real favourite with many readers – are due to retire in Nov 2004; a hard act to follow, so fingers crossed that the new people make the most of their great opportunities here, with the nice combination of traditional features and more up-to-date comfort, Adnams' good beers and wines, a no smoking dining room and good disabled access; children and dogs have been allowed, tables on front terrace, sheltered flower-filled garden, bedrooms; reports on the new regime, please *(LYM, Comus and Sarah Elliott)*

☆ ***Plough & Sail*** [the Maltings]: Much extended, light and airy, more enjoyable eating place than a pub, with good modern choice from snacks to full meals; original part with log fires, sofas, settles and bar with well kept Adnams Bitter, Broadside and a seasonal ale, decent wines; teak tables out in big enclosed flower-filled courtyard, open all day in summer, lovely surroundings with good walks *(LYM, Tracey and Stephen Groves, Klaus and Elizabeth Leist, Comus and Sarah Elliott, Pamela Goodwyn)*

SOMERSHAM TM0848

☆ ***Duke of Marlborough*** [off A14 just N of Ipswich; Main Rd]: Sturdy pine tables on fresh stripped boards in big open room with appealing country prints and 16th-c inglenook, light and airy turkey-carpeted dining room, good service and atmosphere, good fresh food from lunchtime baguettes and baked potatoes to some interesting hot dishes, well kept Greene King IPA and Old Speckled Hen, decent wines, good coffee with fresh cream, quick friendly service by neat staff *(BB, Pamela Goodwyn)*

SOUTH COVE TM4982

Five Bells [B1127 Southwold—Wrentham]: Friendly, well run and spacious creeper-covered pub with stripped pine, three Adnams ales, nicely cooked good value meals in bar and restaurant inc generous Sun lunch; tables out in front, play area, caravan site in back paddock *(David and Gilly Wilkins)*

SOUTHWOLD TM5076

☆ ***Lord Nelson*** [East St]: Vibrant and convivial easy-going seaside local with Adnams full range perfectly kept, decent wines, wholesome plain generous lunchtime food from sandwiches up, low prices, ever-present landlord and quick attentive service, daily papers, air cleaner; low ceilings in three small linked rooms, panelling and tiled floor, spotless light wood furniture, roaring fire, lamps in nice nooks and crannies, interesting local and Nelson memorabilia inc fine model of the *Victory*, no music; no credit cards; disabled access (not perfect, but they help), children welcome away from the bar, nice seats out in front and in sheltered back garden, open all day *(Sue Holland, Dave Webster, David and Gilly Wilkins, Derek and Sylvia Stephenson, Colin and Dot Savill, the Didler, Derek Field, Dr Andy Wilkinson, BB, DM, Pam and David Bailey, Tracey and Stephen Groves, Gloria Bax, Michael Dandy, David Field, David Carr, Neil and Lorna Mclaughlan, Pat and Tony Martin, Pete Baker, Comus and Sarah Elliott)*

Red Lion [South Green]: Big windows looking over green to sea, pale panelling, ship pictures, lots of brassware and copper, warm friendly prompt service, well kept Adnams Bitter and Broadside, popular reasonably priced food inc good fish and chips, no smoking dining room; children and dogs welcome, tables outside, right by the Adnams retail shop; bedrooms small but comfortable *(BB, Sue Holland, Dave Webster, Derek and Sylvia Stephenson, Pam and David Bailey, M and GR, Robert Turnham, Colin and Janet Roe)*

Sole Bay [East Green]: Bleached café/bar décor and light wood furnishings combined with cheerful local atmosphere, well kept Adnams, friendly service, good simple food from sensibly priced doorstep sandwiches up, conservatory; live music Fri; tables on side terrace, moments from sea and lighthouse *(P G Plumridge, Dr Andy Wilkinson, Chris Flynn, Wendy Jones, Sue Holland, Dave Webster, LYM, MDN, David Carr, Mrs A Chapman, Comus and Sarah Elliott)*

☆ ***Swan*** [Market Pl]: Smart hotel not pub, but has relaxed comfortable back bar with well kept Adnams and Broadside, full range of their bottled beers, fine wines and malt whiskies, good bar food (not cheap, but worth it) from enormous open sandwiches and ciabattas to ten or so main dishes, teas and coffee in chintzy and airy front lounge; good bedrooms inc garden rooms where (by arrangement) dogs can stay too *(LYM, Michael Dandy)*

SUDBURY TL8741

☆ ***Waggon & Horses*** [Church Walk]: Comfortable and welcoming, with well kept interesting changing real ales from compact bar, good choice of well presented fresh food inc good sandwiches even Sun afternoon, prompt courteous service, decent house wine, interesting décor, log fire; pleasant walled garden with picnic-sets, handy for Gainsborough House *(MLR)*

THORINGTON STREET TM0135

Rose: This appealing place, a favourite with many readers and a landlady who won our top award in the 2004 edition, closed down in February *(LYM)*

THORNDON TM1469

☆ ***Black Horse*** [off A140 or B1077, S of Eye; The Street]: Friendly and individual country pub with beams, lots of timbering, stripped brick, big fireplaces, ancient floor tiles in small bar areas, roomy dining areas for good well presented food inc unusual main dishes and popular Sun lunch, several well kept ales; well behaved children in eating areas, tables on spacious lawn with country views *(LYM, Alan Cole, Kirstie Bruce)*

THORNHAM MAGNA TM1070

Four Horseshoes [off A140 S of Diss; Wickham Rd]: Thatched pub open all day and much bigger inside than you'd expect, with dim-lit rambling well divided bar, drastically low heavy black beams, mix of chairs and plush banquettes, country pictures and farm tools, logs burning in big fireplaces, inside well, no smoking areas; Greene King IPA, Abbot and Old Speckled Hen, quick friendly service, wide food choice inc Sun lunch; piped music, games machine; bedrooms, picnic-sets on big sheltered lawn, handy for Thornham Walks and thatched church with ancient frescoes and fine retable *(Linda Crisp, LYM, Ian and Nita Cooper, Michael Dandy, David Barnes)*

THORPENESS TM4759

Dolphin: Attractive almost scandinavian décor, light and bright, with good choice of enjoyable food (a restauranty feel, but good lunchtime sandwiches too), well kept Adnams, good wine range; service relaxed and helpful, dogs welcome in public bar, interesting photographs of this quaint purpose-built seaside holiday village with its boating lake; three comfortable bedrooms with own bathrooms, sizeable and attractive garden with summer bar and barbecue *(Mrs Romey Heaton, Wendy and Carl Dye, Pamela Goodwyn)*

TOSTOCK TL9563

Gardeners Arms [off A14 or A1088]: New licensees in village local with warm fire in low-beamed lounge, well kept Greene King IPA and Abbot and a guest beer, games in tiled public bar, enlarged no smoking dining area and refurbished kitchen; picnic-sets in nicely planted sheltered garden *(Ian and Nita Cooper, LYM, Mrs A Chapman)*

UFFORD TM2952

White Lion [Lower St]: Charming unspoilt 16th-c village pub tucked away not far from quiet stretch of River Deben, good value home cooking using local produce, sandwiches to steaks, Adnams tapped from the cask, good log fire in central fireplace, flagstone floors, friendly service, no music; tables out on grass *(Brian and Pam Lamb, Mrs Hilarie Taylor, Pamela Goodwyn)*

WALBERSWICK TM4974

Anchor [The Street]: Comfortably modern hotel bar, roomy, airy and bright, with pine furnishings, decent food inc good range of seafood, well kept Adnams tapped from the cask, good wines, friendly landlord, no smoking bar, cosy log fires, bargain pool table, no mobile phones (RNLI 'fines'); dogs welcome, neat garden behind, bedrooms *(Julie Scarsbrook, Eddie Edwards)*

WANGFORD TM4779

Plough [A12 N]: Welcoming stop with reasonably priced home-cooked food inc fresh sandwiches, well kept Adnams *(Tina and David Woods-Taylor)*

WESTLETON TM4469

☆ *Crown* [B1125 Blythburgh—Leiston]: Extended coaching inn with some nice old settles and a big log fire, ales such as Adnams, Greene King IPA and Abbot and St Peters, dozens of malt whiskies, carefully chosen wine list, traditional games, enjoyable bar lunches, some serious restaurant cooking, carpeted no smoking dining conservatory; piped music; charmingly landscaped gardens with pets corner, good walks nearby *(LYM, David and Gilly Wilkins, Michael and Ann Cole, DF, NF, B and M Kendall, Steve and Liz Tilley, Comus and Sarah Elliott, Judith and Edward Pearson, Peter and Pat Frogley, Tracey and Stephen Groves, Simon Rodway)*

WINGFIELD TM2277

De La Pole Arms [off B1118 N of Stradbroke; Church Rd]: This appealing old-fashioned pub, previously tied to St Peters Brewery and a popular main entry, changed hands in early 2004 and as we went to press was due to close later that year; news please *(LYM)*

WOODBRIDGE TM2748

☆ *Anchor* [Quay St]: High-ceilinged plainly furnished bar with quick friendly service even when busy, good value prompt usual food inc sandwiches, good pies and well priced fresh local fish, well kept Greene King IPA and Abbot, lots of nautical character, nice mix of boating and local paintings (some for sale), separate eating area *(Mike and Mary Carter)*

Deben Seal [Ipswich Rd]: Recently built of reclaimed timber, bricks and tiles – looks as if it's been there for ever; welcoming, with good choice of good food from sandwiches and baked potatoes to restaurant-quality dishes; open all day *(anon)*

WOOLPIT TL9762

Bull [The Street]: Neat and friendly local, pleasant licensees, good range of reasonably priced food, well kept beer, prompt service even when busy; pool and darts; garden with play area, bedrooms *(Des and Jen Clarke)*

WORLINGTON TL6973

Worlington Hall [B1102 SW of Mildenhall]: Attractive country hotel with friendly and very pretty pub part, well kept Adnams and Greene King, enjoyable food; bedrooms *(Esther and John Sprinkle)*

WORTHAM TM0877

Dolphin [Bury Rd]: Good balance between welcoming local atmosphere and varied range of imaginative food; Adnams, friendly staff *(Abi Benson)*

YOXFORD TM3968

☆ *Griffin* [High St]: 14th-c village pub with log fire and nice corner sofa in appealingly laid out main bar, good value generous food using local supplies inc generous bargain lunch and children's, Adnams and changing guest beers, decent reasonably priced wines, friendly attentive staff, medieval feasts in charming log-fire restaurant decorated to match; notable music nights (the landlord is an early music specialist), quiz night Thurs, two pub cats; comfortable beamed bedrooms, good breakfast *(Comus and Sarah Elliott, Stephen and Jean Curtis)*

The letters and figures after the name of each town are its Ordnance Survey map reference. *Using the Guide* at the beginning of the book explains how it helps you find a pub, in road atlases or large-scale maps as well as in our own maps.

Surrey

Several good new entries here this year: Marneys in Esher, a very unexpected and relaxing countrified find, good all round; the Three Horseshoes in Laleham, back among the main entries after a break of nearly ten years; the smart and comfortable Kings Arms at Ockley, a charmingly decorated civilised inn; and the cheerful Castle at Ottershaw, with great real ales. Other pubs on fine form here this year are the unspoilt good value Dolphin at Betchworth, the attractive and buoyant old Cricketers on its green near Cobham, the welcoming Plough at Coldharbour (brewing their own beer, decent food, nice surroundings), the civilised Withies at Compton with its good smart restaurant, the Plough at Leigh (a nice all-rounder in an attractive setting), and the King William IV at Mickleham (huge helpings of good food, a lovely spot in summer). There are other places here where the food justifies a special trip (most notably perhaps the Hare & Hounds on the edge of Lingfield, the Inn at West End, and the Skimmington Castle on Reigate Heath), but our final choice of Surrey Dining Pub of the Year is the Withies at Compton – its restaurant with splendidly old-fashioned service is just right for a special meal out. In the Lucky Dip section at the end of the chapter, pubs to note particularly include the Abinger Hatch on Abinger Common, Rams Nest at Chiddingfold, Thurlow Arms at Cox Green, Kings Arms in Dorking, Woolpack at Elstead, Fox & Hounds in Englefield Green, Parrot at Forest Green, White Horse at Hascombe, Hautboy at Ockham, Old School House in Ockley and Punchbowl nearby, and Bulls Head at West Clandon. Surrey drinks prices are staggeringly high – as an example, the cheapest beer we found here cost nearly twice as much as the cheapest we found up in Lancashire. This may be partly because there are so few successful small breweries here to inject a serious note of price competition; Hogs Back is the main local beer to look out for.

BETCHWORTH TQ2149 Map 3

Dolphin 🍷

Turn off A25 W of Reigate opposite B2032 at roundabout, and keep on into The Street; opposite the church

This surprisingly unspoilt 16th-c village pub is usually busy with a good mix of locals, walkers and visitors and has a lovely welcoming atmosphere. The neat and homely front room has kitchen chairs and plain tables on the 400-year-old scrubbed flagstones, and the carpeted back saloon bar is black-panelled, with robust old-fashioned elm or oak tables. There are three warming fires, a nice chiming longcase clock, silenced fruit machine, darts, shove-ha'penny, cribbage and dominoes. As well as up to 18 wines by the glass, friendly staff serve well kept Youngs Bitter, Special, Waggle Dance and maybe a seasonal guest on handpump. It's best to arrive early, or book a table beforehand if you want to enjoy the generously served, good value bar food, which includes sandwiches (from £2.65), home-made soup (£2.95), ploughman's (from £5.45), very popular breaded plaice and chips (£6.95), beef or vegetable lasagne (£7.15), and steaks (from £9.90), with daily specials such as steak and mushroom pie or smoked haddock and chips (£7.95), and dressed crab salad (£8.45); puddings might be spotted dick or chocolate fudge cake (from £3.35). There are some seats in the small laurel-shaded front courtyard, and behind are picnic-sets on a terrace and lawn by the car park, opposite the church. Parking can be very difficult in summer. No children inside. *(Recommended by Mike Gorton, B and M Kendall, Geoffrey Kemp, DWAJ, M and N Watson, Pam and John Smith, the Didler, Debbie and Neil Hayter, Paul A Moore, Gordon Neighbour, A Sadler, John Ecklin)*

Youngs ~ Managers George and Rose Campbell ~ Real ale ~ Bar food (12-2.30, 7-10) ~ (01737) 842288 ~ Dogs allowed in bar ~ Open 11-3, 5.30-11; 11-11 Sat; 12-10.30 Sun

BLACKBROOK TQ1846 Map 3

Plough 🍷

On by-road E of A24, parallel to it, between Dorking and Newdigate, just N of the turn E to Leigh

Children are catered for thoughtfully at this neatly kept pub, which has a better than average children's menu and a little swiss playhouse furnished with little tables and chairs in the secluded garden. Welcoming and enjoyable, the no smoking red saloon bar has fresh flowers on its tables and on the window sills of its large windows (which have new green and gold curtains). Down some steps, the public bar has brass-topped treadle tables, old saws on the ceiling, and bottles and flat irons. Bar food includes lunchtime snacks such as sausage and chips (£4.75), nice bagels with inventive toppings such as warm chargrilled vegetables, mozzarella and pesto (£5.95), ploughman's (£5.75), steak sandwich (£7.75), and blackboard specials such as lentil, pea and ham soup (£3.95), celeriac, smoked chicken, peach and walnut salad (£5.45), battered cod (£7.45), chicken and lime curry (£8.25) and herb crusted roast rack of lamb (£12.95). Well kept Badger Best, K&B Sussex and Tanglefoot, and a guest such as Gribble Fursty Ferret on handpump, 16 wines by the glass, and several ports; shove-ha'penny, and cribbage. The countryside around here is particularly good for colourful spring and summer walks through the oak woods, and the pub's white frontage is covered in pretty hanging baskets and year round window boxes. There are tables and chairs outside on the terrace. *(Recommended by Jeff Hollingworth, B and M Kendall, John Davis, Cathryn and Richard Hicks, Father Robert Marsh, C and R Bromage, John Ecklin, Susan and John Douglas, John Evans)*

Badger ~ Tenants Chris and Robin Squire ~ Real ale ~ Bar food (not Mon evening) ~ (01306) 886603 ~ Children welcome ~ Dogs allowed in bar ~ Open 11-3, 6(7 Sun)-11.30

BLETCHINGLEY TQ3250 Map 3

Prince Albert

Outwood Lane

The very welcoming bar at this bustling old local has a couple of very low bar stools favoured by regulars, a side part with hatch service and some cushioned chairs around tables, half-panelled walls, and a little brick fireplace. To the right of the bar are a couple of charming rooms, one with lovely panelled walls and a step down to a half-panelled one – cushioned dining chairs around straightforward pubby tables, vintage car photographs and pictures, and another tiny brick fireplace. To the left of the bar are several little partitioned off rooms that run into one another, with similar furnishings and décor; the bottom room has a glass cabinet filled with Guinness memorabilia, and a fish tank. Well kept Carlsberg-Tetley Ansells, Itchen Valley Fagins and a guest such as Hogs Back TEA on handpump. Decent bar food, served by friendly and enthusiastic young staff, includes home-made soup (£3.50), filled baguettes (from £3.50), pâté (£3.95), ploughman's (from £3.95), whitebait (£4.65), macaroni cheese (£5.50), ham and egg (£5.95), cumberland sausage (£6.25), steak and Guinness pie (£8.25), daily specials such as seafood chowder (£4.95) and curried lamb shank (£10.95), and Sunday roast (£7.50); piped pop music (can be loud), cribbage and dominoes. The back garden (some traffic noise) is pretty with a terraced and lawned area, lots of mature plants and trees in pots, flowering borders, koi carp in a pond, and green plastic furniture under cocktail parasols. A couple of benches in front of the pub catch the evening sun. *(Recommended by B and M Kendall, Mrs Diane Amis,*

C and G Fraser, Dick and Madeleine Brown, John Ecklin, Quentin and Carol Williamson, Mrs B M Hill)

Free house ~ Licensees Patrick and Cathy Egan ~ Real ale ~ Bar food (12-2.30, 6.30-9.30) ~ Restaurant ~ (01883) 743257 ~ Children in eating area of bar ~ Dogs allowed in bar ~ Open 12-11(10.30 Sun); 12-3, 6-11 Mon, Tues; 12-3, 6-11 Mon-Sat winter

CHARLESHILL SU8944 Map 2

Donkey

B3001 Milford—Farnham near Tilford; coming from Elstead, turn left as soon as you see pub sign

Emphasis at this beamed cottagey pub is on the enjoyable (though not cheap) food. Friendly staff serve starters such as soup (£3.75), liver and brandy pâté (£5.95) and thai-style fishcakes (£7.95) and main courses such as hot and sour mushrooms on stir fry vegetables (£9.95), steak and Guinness pie (£10.95), mango stuffed chicken breast in coconut with curry sauce (£12.95), roast duck with apricot marmalade (£14.95) and bass fillet with king prawns on saffron cream (£16.95). The bright saloon has lots of polished stirrups, lamps and watering cans on the walls, and prettily cushioned built-in wall benches, while the lounge has a fine high-backed settle, highly polished horsebrasses, and swords on the walls and beams; the dining conservatory is no smoking. All their wines are available by the glass, and you'll also find well kept Greene King IPA, Abbot and Old Speckled Hen on handpump; piped music. The garden is very attractive, with a terrace, plenty of seats, and a play area with a wendy house for children; the two friendly donkeys are called Pip and Dusty. *(Recommended by Simon and Sally Small, Mike and Heather Watson, John and Joyce Snell)*

Greene King ~ Lease Lee and Helen Francis ~ Real ale ~ Bar food (12-2.30, 6-9) ~ Restaurant ~ (01252) 702124 ~ Children welcome ~ Dogs allowed in bar ~ Open 12-3, 6-11(11.30 Sat); 12-10.30 Sun; 12-3, 6-10.30 Sun in winter

COBHAM TQ1060 Map 3

Cricketers

Downside Common; 3¾ miles from M25 junction 10; A3 towards Cobham, first right on to A245, right at Downside signpost into Downside Bridge Road, follow road into its right fork – away from Cobham Park – at second turn after bridge, then take next left turn into the pub's own lane

It's worth arriving early (especially on Sunday) to be sure of a table at this welcoming pub. If you like salads, you'll be especially happy here, as they do a tremendous variety from smoked mackerel and coachman's pie (£6.50), and coronation chicken or avocado, tomato and mozzarella (£7.95) to mixed seafood (£7.95). Other enjoyable, freshly prepared bar food, all listed on blackboards and served by friendly young staff, could include vegetable spring rolls and rice or battered cod (£5.95), pork and leek sausages with onion gravy (£7.65) and steak, mushroom and Guinness pie (£7.95). The roomy open-plan interior has a bustling atmosphere, with a blazing log fire, and crooked standing timbers – creating comfortable spaces – supporting heavy oak beams so low they have crash-pads on them. In places you can see the wide oak ceiling boards and ancient plastering laths. Furnishings are quite simple, and there are horsebrasses and big brass platters on the walls; the stable bar is no smoking. Well kept Fullers London Pride, Greene King Old Speckled Hen, Theakstons Best and Youngs on handpump, and a good choice of wines including several by the glass; piped music. White painted metal tables on a terrace with outdoor heaters, and in the delightful neatly kept garden (with standard roses, magnolias, dahlias, bedding plants, urns and hanging baskets) have views over the village green, where riders may have tethered their horses while they stop for a drink. *(Recommended by Dr P J W Young, Mrs Angela Bromley-Martin, Mrs Sally Lloyd, Geoffrey Kemp, Ian Phillips, Gerry and Rosemary Dobson, Mr and Mrs A H Young, LM, John Saville, Vanessa Stilwell)*

Inntrepreneur ~ Tenant Wendy Luxford ~ Real ale ~ Bar food (12-2, 6.30-10; 12-9.30

(5 winter) Sun) ~ Restaurant ~ (01932) 862105 ~ Children in restaurant and family room ~ Dogs allowed in bar ~ Open 11-2.30, 6-11; 12-10.30(7 in winter) Sun

COLDHARBOUR TQ1543 Map 3

Plough

Village signposted in the network of small roads around Leith Hill

The charming licensee couple here clearly enjoy running this friendly old coaching inn.The two bars (each with a lovely open fire) have stripped light beams and timbering in the warm-coloured dark ochre walls, with quite unusual little chairs around the tables in the snug red-carpeted games room on the left (with darts), and little decorative plates on the walls; the one on the right leads through to the no smoking candlelit restaurant. From the pub's own Leith Hill Brewery, they serve Crooked Furrow and Tallywacker on handpump, along with three or four well kept real ales such as Ringwood Old Thumper, Shepherd Neame Masterbrew and Ringwood Bold Forester; also Biddenden farm cider; piped music, darts, TV, shove-ha'penny, cribbage and dominoes. Enjoyable (though not cheap) bar food includes soup (£3.95), fried baby squid with herb and garlic butter (£5.95), roast beef or roasted vegetables in tomato sauce and melted goats cheese on fettuccine pasta (£8.95), chicken, bacon and avocado salad (£9.95), baked cod fillet with herb crust (£11.95), confit of duck with zesty orange jus (£12.95), fillet steak (£14.95) and puddings such as mascarpone and lemon cheesecake or crumble of the day (£5.25). This is a peaceful setting in a hamlet high in the Surrey hills (good walks), and there are picnic-sets by tubs of flowers in front and in the terraced garden with its fish pond and water-lilies. *(Recommended by A J Longshaw, Kevin Thorpe, Susan and John Douglas, Barry Steele-Perkins, C and R Bromage, Jason Reynolds, Simon and Mandy King, Anthony Rogers, Philip and Ann Board, Paul Humphreys)*

Own brew ~ Licensees Richard and Anna Abrehart ~ Real ale ~ Bar food (12-3, 6-9.30 (9 Sun)) ~ Restaurant ~ (01306) 711793 ~ Children in eating area of bar and also in barn on Sun ~ Dogs allowed in bar ~ Open 11.30-11; 12-10.30 Sun ~ Bedrooms: £54S/£65S(£80B)

COMPTON SU9546 Map 2

Withies

Withies Lane; pub signposted from B3000

Surrey Dining Pub of the Year

Usually busy, this very civilised 16th-c pub is very attractive, with low beams in the little bar, some fine 17th-c carved panels between the windows, and a splendid art nouveau settle among the old sewing-machine tables; you'll find a good log fire in a massive inglenook fireplace; piped music. They do good straightforward pubby bar food such as soup (£3.75), filled baked potatoes (from £4), smoked salmon pâté (£4.50), sandwiches (from £4.50), ploughman's (from £4.75), cumberland sausages with mash and onion gravy (£5.25), and seafood platter (£9.50). The restaurant is more formal, with an elaborate, and expensive menu, and is very popular with a well heeled local set. Even when it's busy, the pleasant uniformed staff remain helpful and efficient. Badger K&B Sussex, Fullers London Pride, Greene King IPA and Hogs Back TEA are well kept on handpump. The neat lawn in front of the steeply tiled white house is bordered by masses of flowers, and the immaculate garden, overhung with weeping willows, has tables under an arbour of creeper-hung trellises (part of the no smoking restaurant), more on a crazy-paved terrace, and others under old apple trees. Polsted Manor and Loseley Park are a pleasant walk up the lane from here. *(Recommended by Mrs Maricar Jagger, John Davis, Ian Phillips, John Saville, Debbie and Neil Hayter, John Evans, Martin and Karen Wake, Mrs Ann Saunders, Mrs G R Sharman, Alan Cowell, John Braine-Hartnell, Bob and Margaret Holder, Guy Consterdine, Gene and Kitty Rankin)*

Free house ~ Licensees Brian and Hugh Thomas ~ Real ale ~ Bar food (12-2.30, 7-10) ~ Restaurant ~ (01483) 421158 ~ Children welcome ~ Open 11-3, 6-11; 12-3 Sun; closed Sun evening

EASHING SU9543 Map 2

Stag

Lower Eashing; Eashing signposted off A3 southbound, S of Hurtmore turn-off; or pub signposted off A283 just SE of exit roundabout at N end of A3 Milford bypass

Also known as the Stag on the River, this attractive pub has a millstream running past the garden, making this a great place to be in summer's day. Tucked down a narrow lane, the building itself has a Georgian brick façade, but dates back in part to the 15th c. Its opened up interior has a charming old-fashioned locals' bar on the right with red and black flooring tiles by the counter and well kept Courage Best, Fullers London Pride and Shepherd Neame Spitfire on handpump, about 14 wines by the glass and good coffee. A cosy gently lit room beyond has a low white plank ceiling, a big stag print and stag's head on the dark-wallpapered walls, some cookery books on shelves by the log fire, and sturdy cushioned housekeeper's chairs grouped around dark tables on the brick floor. An extensive blue-carpeted area rambles around on the left, with similar comfortable dark furniture, some smaller country prints and decorative plates on pink Anaglypta walls, and round towards the back a big woodburning stove in a capacious fireplace under a long mantelbeam. It's all rather smart yet cosily traditional, the thriving atmosphere helped along by attentive and chatty neatly dressed staff; there is a table of conservative daily papers, and they are kind to visiting dogs. Tasty lunchtime and early evening bar snacks include soup (£3.75), open ciabatta sandwiches (from £6.15), burgers (£8.95) and sausage and mash (£9.95), while a big blackboard lists food such as moules marinière (£6.50), lamb shank in red wine and tomato sauce or tuna steak with niçoise salad and soft poached egg (£11.95), venison steak on butterbean and thyme cream sauce (£14.95) and puddings such as lemon cheesecake with berry fruits or sticky toffee pudding (£3.95); no smoking restaurant. The riverside garden has picnic-sets and other tables under cocktail parasols among mature trees, and a terrace with some teak furniture, and more picnic-sets in a lantern-lit arbour. *(Recommended by Susan and John Douglas, Vicky Whitfield, Ian Phillips, Carlos Acuna, Sally Waterfall, Martin and Karen Wake, Gordon Stevenson, R B Gardiner)*

Punch ~ Lease Marilyn Lackey ~ Real ale ~ Bar food (12-2.30(3 Sun), 6-9.30; not Sun, Mon evenings) ~ Restaurant ~ (01483) 421568 ~ Children in eating area of bar and restaurant ~ Dogs allowed in bar ~ Open 11-11; 12-10.30 Sun ~ Bedrooms: /£55S

ESHER TQ1566 Map 3

Marneys 🍷

Alma Road (one way only), Weston Green; heading N on A309 from A307 roundabout, after Lamb & Star pub turn left into Lime Tree Avenue (signposted to All Saints Parish Church), then left at T junction into Chestnut Avenue

Turning off the busy trunk road, it's a real surprise to find this cottagey little pub, in such a pleasant spot right on the edge of a well wooded common, beside an attractive church and close to a lively duck pond. There's not much room in the chatty low-beamed bar with its black and white plank panelling, shelves of hens and ducks and other ornaments, small blue-curtained windows, and perhaps horse racing on the corner TV. On the left, past a little cast-iron woodburning stove, a dining area (somewhat roomier but still small) has big pine tables, pews and pale country kitchen chairs, with attractive goose pictures. Well kept Bass, Courage Best and Flowers Original on handpump, just over a dozen wines by the glass (even pink champagne on our summer visit), enterprising soft drinks, norwegian schnapps and good coffee. The sensibly small choice of good interesting food has a scandinavian lean, and runs from baguettes (from £5.50) to meatballs and red cabbage (£8), frikadillen (danish meatcakes) or good soused herring fillets (£8.25), and puddings such as almond and pear tart (£3.75); they are happy to cater for small appetites. Service by friendly uniformed staff is quick and efficient; and they have daily papers on sticks. The pleasantly planted sheltered garden has black picnic-sets under purple canvas parasols, and the front terrace has dark blue cast-iron tables and chairs under matching parasols, with some more black tables too. *(Recommended by Ian Phillips, Ian Wilson, Nigel Williamson, Alec and Barbara Jones)*

Free house ~ Licensee Henrik Platou ~ Real ale ~ Bar food (12-2.15; not evenings or Sun) ~ (020) 8398 4444 ~ Children welcome till 6pm ~ Dogs allowed in bar ~ Open 11-11; 12-10.30 Sun

LALEHAM TQ0568 Map 3

Three Horseshoes 🍷

B376 (Shepperton Road)

This busy stone-flagged tavern dates from the 13th c, and in the past has served as a coroner's court, post office and parish vestry. Under new licensees since it last appeared in the *Guide*, the recently upgraded bar is now airier with gentle lighting, cream walls, farmhouse tables, comfortable settees, newspapers to read, a fireplace with an open fire and some intimate little corners. A feng shui consultation determined the placing of the red, blue and green carpets. Reasonably priced bar food is served in generous helpings and includes soup (£3.95), sandwiches (from £3.95), ham, egg and chips (£6.75), steak and ale pie (£7.50), grilled cajun chicken with caesar salad (£7.95), chicken breast stuffed with onion and cheese (£9.95) and puddings (£4.25). The conservatory and two restaurants are no smoking. Efficient bar staff serve well kept Courage Best, Fullers London Pride, Youngs Special and a couple of guests such as Adnams Broadside and Bass on handpump and over a dozen wines by the glass; piped music. Just a short walk away is a grassy stretch of the Thames popular with picnickers and sunbathers; it can get very busy on warm summer days. *(Recommended by Mayur Shah, Tom McLean, John Mitchell)*

Unique (Enterprise) ~ Lease Sean Alderson ~ Real ale ~ Bar food (12-2.30, 6-9.30(10 Fri); 12-10(9 Sun) Sat) ~ Restaurant ~ (01784) 455014 ~ Children welcome if eating ~ Open 11-11; 12-10.30 Sun

LEIGH TQ2246 Map 3

Plough

3 miles S of A25 Dorking—Reigate, signposted from Betchworth (which itself is signposted off the main road); also signposted from South Park area of Reigate; on village green

Helpful notices inside this tiled and weatherboarded cottage warn you not to bump your head on the very low beams in the cosy timbered dining lounge on the right, which is decorated with lots of local prints on white walls. On the left, a simpler more local pubby bar has a good bow window seat, lots of different games including darts, shove-ha'penny, dominoes, table skittles, cribbage, Jenga, backgammon and shut-the-box; there's also piped music, an alcove fruit machine and occasional TV. Well kept real ales are Badger Best, Tanglefoot, Sussex, and a guest such as Gribble Fursty Ferret on handpump, and you can have a glass of anything on the decent wine list. The wide-ranging menu includes enjoyable snacks such as soup (£3.95), a big selection of sandwiches (from £3.95), baked potatoes (from £4.50), and ploughman's (from £5.95), along with blackboard specials such as creamy garlic mushrooms (£4.95), liver and bacon (£7.95), steak pie (£8.50), roast trout with lemon and thyme on sweet potato mash (£8.95), roasted vegetable mexican-style tortilla wrap or bacon wrapped chicken (£9.95), and steaks (from £11.75), with puddings such as pavlova or apple pie (from £3.75); you may need to book at the weekend. The pub is attractively placed by the village green, and picnic-sets under cocktail parasols in a pretty side garden (fairy-lit in the evening), and colourful hanging baskets make this especially pleasant in summer; nearby parking is limited. *(Recommended by M G Hart, Michael Butler, Mike Snelgrove, David Twitchett, John Davis, John Braine-Hartnell, A Sadler, David Crook)*

Badger ~ Tenant Sarah Bloomfield ~ Real ale ~ Bar food (12-10(9.30 Sun)) ~ Restaurant ~ (01306) 611348 ~ Children in eating area of bar and restaurant ~ Dogs allowed in bar ~ Open 11-11; 12-10.30 Sun

LINGFIELD TQ3844 Map 3

Hare & Hounds

Turn off B2029 N at Crowhurst, Edenbridge signpost, into Lingfield Common Road

Don't let the unassuming exterior put you off this country pub which is popular for its very well prepared food, and relaxed low key atmosphere. The smallish open-plan bar, light and airy by day, has soft lighting and nightlights burning on a good mix of different-sized tables at night – when it's full of the chatter of happy customers, some drinking, some eating, all mixing comfortably. Partly bare boards and partly flagstones, it has an eclectic variety of well worn scatter-cushioned dining chairs and other seats from pews to a button-back leather chesterfield, black and white pictures of jazz musicians on brown tongue-and-groove panelling, and perhaps unobtrusive piped jazz. It opens into a quieter dining area with big abstract-expressionist paintings. They make their own soda bread, ice-cream and pasta, and the well presented, daily changing bar food (not cheap) might include soup (£3.95), artichoke and parmesan tart with chilli smashed courgettes (£5.95), seared salmon with an onion cake, grilled cos and hollandaise or grilled pork chop with chilli roast parnsips, cider, sage and mascarpone (£8.50), mezze plate (£11.50), roast baby chicken with dates, preserved lemon, almond and couscous (£11.95), roast rack of lamb with fried aubergine, tomato, lentil, coriander and spinach dhal (£14.50) and light and delicious puddings. Friendly efficient staff serve well kept Flowers Original, Greene King IPA and Old Speckled Hen on handpump, and they have decent wines. There are tables out in a pleasant split-level garden, some on decking, This is good walking country near Haxted Mill; walkers can leave their boots in the porch, guarded by a life-size great dane statue. They hold irish theme nights around every two months. *(Recommended by Dennis Le Couilliard, B and M Kendall, Derek Thomas, Jill Dyer, Cathryn and Richard Hicks, W W Burke, R and S Bentley, John Saville)*

Pubmaster ~ Lease Fergus Greer ~ Real ale ~ Bar food (12-2.30, 7-9) ~ Restaurant ~ (01342) 832351 ~ Dogs allowed in bar ~ Open 11.30-11; 12-8 Sun

MICKLEHAM TQ1753 Map 3

King William IV

Byttom Hill; short but narrow steep track up hill just off A24 Leatherhead—Dorking by partly green-painted restaurant – public car park down here is best place to park; OS Sheet 187 map reference 173538

The lovely terraced garden at the back of this creeper-swathed brick pub (which is cut into the steep hillside) is neatly filled with sweet peas, climbing roses and honeysuckle, and plenty of tables (some in an extended open-sided wooden shelter with gas heaters) and good views over pretty Surrey countryside. A path leads from the garden straight up through woods behind. Needless to say, such an idyllic spot does draw the crowds on a sunny day and as they don't take bookings during the summer you will need to get here early to secure a table, and be aware that you will have to queue to place your order, but service should be quick enough after that. The snug plank-panelled front bar shares the same panoramic views as the garden. The more spacious back bar is quite brightly lit, with kitchen-type chairs around its cast-iron-framed tables, log fires, fresh flowers on all the tables, and a serviceable grandfather clock. There's a friendly atmosphere throughout. Very enjoyable bar food in huge helpings might include filled baked potatoes or ploughman's (from £6.25), aubergine and vegetable lasagne (£8.75), steak and kidney pie or seafood pie (£9.50), grilled catch of the day on stir-fried vegetables and pak choi with lemon rice (£12.75), tournedos rossini on a bread croûton with pâté and madeira sauce (£15.75), tapas platter (£15.75 for two) and puddings such as hot chocolate fudge cake or treacle, ginger and apple tart (£4.10). The choice is more limited on Sundays and bank holidays, and they don't do sandwiches at weekends. Very well kept Adnams Best, Badger Best, Hogs Back TEA and a monthly changing guest such as Hoggs Back Spring Call on handpump; light piped music. Parking can be difficult on the lane, so you may have a character-forming walk up from the public car park at the bottom of the hill. *(Recommended by Sarah Davis, Rod Lambert, A Sadler, John Davis, Joyce and Geoff Robson, John and Joan Nash, T R and B C Jenkins, Andrea Rampley, John Ecklin, C and R Bromage)*

Free house ~ Licensees Chris and Jenny Grist ~ Real ale ~ Bar food (12-2, 7-9.30; 12-5 Sun) ~ (01372) 372590 ~ Open 11-3, 6-11; 12-10.30 Sun; closed 25 Dec

Running Horses 🍷

Old London Road (B2209)

Picnic-sets on a terrace in front of this smartly substantial white painted inn with its big sash windows, and lovely flowering tubs and hanging baskets take in a peaceful view of the old church with its strange stubby steeple, just across the quiet lane, and are a delightful place to pass a summer evening. Inside, the two calmly relaxing rooms of the bar are neatly kept and spaciously open plan with fresh flowers (in summer) in an inglenook at one end, lots of race tickets hanging from a beam, some really good racing cartoons, hunting pictures and Hogarth prints, dark carpets, cushioned wall settles and other dining chairs around straightforward pubby tables and bar stools. Adnams, Fullers London Pride, Shepherd Neame and Youngs are well kept on handpump alongside good, if pricey wines by the glass, from a serious list. As well as a tempting choice of bar food (not cheap) such as soup (£4.50), lunchtime chunky sandwiches (from £4.50), ciabatta toasties like seared chicken with coriander and lime or devilled kidneys and wild mushrooms on toast (£6.95), smoked salmon and mussel linguini (£8.95), tempura fish with chips and sweet chilli dip (£9.50), sausage and mash (£9.75), steak, Guinness and mushroom pudding (£12.50), there's also a more elaborate restaurant menu (which you can eat from in the bar), which might include carpaccio of peppered venison with balsamic fig vinaigrette (£7.25), braised lamb shank with rosemary and burgundy on shallot mash (£12.95) and fried bass with roast pear and almonds (£18.75), as well as puddings such as sticky date and sultana pudding with butterscotch sauce and toffee ice-cream or bramley apple and vanilla crème brûlée with cinnamon crust (£5.25). The restaurant area leads straight out of the bar and although it is set out quite formally with crisp white cloths and candles on each table, it shares the thriving atmosphere of the bar; piped music and professional staff. *(Recommended by Susan and John Douglas, Howard Dell, Gerald Wilkinson, Stephen and Judy Parish, Norma and Noel Thomas, John Ecklin, Debbie and Neil Hayter)*

Punch ~ Lease Steve and Josie Slayford ~ Real ale ~ Bar food (12-2.30, 7-9.30) ~ Restaurant ~ (01372) 372279 ~ Children in restaurant ~ Dogs welcome ~ Open 11.30-11; 12-10.30 Sun ~ Bedrooms: £94(£94S)(£105.75B)/£105.75(£105.75S)(£141B)

NEWDIGATE TQ2043 Map 3

Surrey Oaks

Off A24 S of Dorking, via Beare Green; Parkgate Road

The landlord at this attractive 16th-c country pub (once a wheelwright's cottage) is keen on real ale and serves two quickly rotating guest beers, from brewers such as Crouch Vale and Harveys, alongside well kept Harveys Sussex Best, Ringwood Best and Timothy Taylor Landlord on handpump; they also do belgian and dutch bottled beers and farm cider. The pub is interestingly divided into four areas; in the older part locals gather by a coal-effect gas fire in a snug little beamed room, and a standing area with unusually large flagstones has a woodburning stove in an inglenook fireplace. Rustic tables are dotted around the light and airy main lounge to the left, and there's a pool table in the separate games room; fruit machine, TV, and piped classical music. The atmosphere is pubby, and families feel particularly welcome here. Reasonably priced tasty bar food includes filled baguettes (from £4), ploughman's (from £5), ham, eggs and chips or battered cod (£6.50), with specials such as home-made chicken and ham or steak and ale pie, and a fish dish such as red mullet or bass (all £8.50), and rib-eye steak (£11); children's meals (£5). The pleasant and quite elaborate garden has a terrace, and a rockery with pools and a waterfall – the play area, two goats and aviary help keep children amused.

(Recommended by Kevin Thorpe, DWAJ, Mike Gorton, C and R Bromage, Father Robert Marsh, Mike and Heather Watson)

Punch ~ Lease Ken Proctor ~ Real ale ~ Bar food (12-2(2.15 Sat, Sun), not Mon evening, Sun) ~ Restaurant ~ (01306) 631200 ~ Children welcome ~ Dogs allowed in bar ~ Open 11.30-2.30, 5.30-11; 11.30-3, 6-11 Sat; 12-3, 7-10.30 Sun

OCKLEY TQ1439 Map 3

Kings Arms

Stane Street (A29)

This 17th-c country inn has been most attractively rearranged as a comfortable and civilised dining pub – one where you feel perfectly at ease just dropping in for a drink. The heavily black-beamed and timbered bar, cosy and very softly lit, has three more or less distinct areas with turkey carpet throughout, button-back wall banquettes and cushioned captain's chairs, antique prints of racehorses, country scenes and so forth massed two or three deep on the wall, some nice examples of antique wood carving, and plenty of other highly polished bric-a-brac, among the rather Victorian houseplants in the heavy draped windows. Good carefully cooked food (here, a rare steak really does come rare), generous, imaginative and using well chosen fresh ingredients, might include sandwiches (from £2.95), soup (£3.95), ploughman's or scampi and chips (£6.95), crab and prawn salad (£8.95), pies or roast mediterranean vegetable quiche (£9.95), steamed salmon with a dill and cucumber sauce (£10.95), 16oz gammon steak (£11.95), shoulder of lamb roasted with honey and mustard (£13.95) and scallops wrapped in bacon (£14.95). They have champagne by the glass among a good choice of other wines, and well kept Bass, Flowers IPA, Greene King Old Speckled Hen and Marstons Pedigree on handpump (no smoking at bar counter); polite service with a pleasantly individual touch by neatly uniformed staff; a good inglenook log fire. The small restaurant (on the right as you come in from the car park) has crisp white table linen; its game soup is a hot tip. A back terrace has teak tables and chairs, with a few picnic-sets among neatly clipped shrubs on immaculate grass beyond; there may be summer barbecues out here. *(Recommended by Mike and Heather Watson, Richard Fedrick, John Ecklin, Keith and Jenny Grant)*

Free house ~ Licensee Vinda Wolf ~ Real ale ~ Bar food (12-2(2.30 Sun), 7-10.) ~ Restaurant ~ (01306) 711224 ~ Open 11-2.30, 6-11; 12-3, 7-10.30 Sun ~ Bedrooms: £50B/£70B

OTTERSHAW TQ0263 Map 3

Castle

2.6 miles from M25 junction 11; heading S on A320, after A319 roundabout pass church on right, then after another 350 yards or so take sharp left turn into Brox Road

The current licensee has brought a cheerfully thriving atmosphere to this appealing pub – with a warm welcome for strangers. Under quite an armoury of venerable guns, the servery between the two separate bars has half a dozen well kept changing ales such as Adnams, Black Sheep, Fullers London Pride, Greene King Abbot, Hop Back Summer Lightning and Shepherd Neame Spitfire on handpump, and Addlestone's cider. Good winter log fires, horse tack on the walls, rustic paraphernalia on the black ceiling joists, small pictures and some stripped brickwork (including little stub walls making two or three snugly cushioned side booths) add to the relaxed country feel; the bar on the right opens into a no smoking dining area and small side conservatory. A wide range of popular home-made food runs from good value sandwiches (from £1.85) and soup (£3.15) to other pubby dishes such as cheese and potato pie (£5.75), salads (£7.25), fish pie (£7.45), steak and ale pie (£7.95) and puddings such as apple strudel (£3.15); Sunday roast (£8.95). In the left-hand bar a low table made from a smith's bellows has a good collection of upmarket magazines. The sheltered garden has tables with rustic benches in pleasant creeper-hung booths, and picnic-sets on the front terrace are set well back from the fairly quiet road. *(Recommended by Ian Phillips, Gwyn Jones, R T and J C Moggridge, Father Robert Marsh)*

Punch ~ Lease John Olorenshaw ~ Real ale ~ Bar food (12-2, 6.30-9.15; 12-4 Sun) ~ (01932) 872373 ~ Dogs allowed in bar ~ Open 11-2.30, 5.30-11; 11-11 Sat; 12-10.30 Sun

REIGATE HEATH TQ2349 Map 3

Skimmington Castle

3 miles from M25 junction 8: through Reigate take A25 towards Dorking, then on edge of Reigate turn left past Black Horse into Flanchford Road; after ¼ mile turn left into Bonny's Road (unmade, very bumpy track); after crossing golf course fork right up hill

Readers are fond of this quaint old country pub. The bright main front bar leads off a small room with a central serving counter, with dark simple panelling and lots and lots of keys hanging from the beams. There's a miscellany of chairs and tables, shiny brown plank panelling, a brown plank ceiling, well kept Adnams, Greene King Old Speckled Hen, Youngs Special and a guest such as Sharps Eden on handpump, with over a dozen wines by the glass, farm cider and even some organic spirits. The cosy back rooms are partly panelled too, with old-fashioned settles and windsor chairs; one has a big brick fireplace with its bread-oven still beside it – the chimney is said to have been used as a highwayman's look-out. Steps take you down to just three tables in a small but pleasant no smoking room at the back; shove-ha'penny, cribbage, dominoes, ring-the-bull, board games and piped music. The bar food is good and popular, so you need to get here early for a table as they don't take bookings. Swiftly served dishes could include sandwiches (from £3.10), soup (£3.25), ploughman's (from £4.95), mushroom and spinach stroganoff, home-made fish or steak and kidney pie (£6.95), breaded haddock (£7.50), herb crusted salmon (£7.95), lamb steak with thyme jus (£9.95) and rib-eye steak (£10.50), with irresistible puddings (£3.75). In fine weather you can enjoy lovely views from the crazy-paved front terrace and tables on the grass by lilac bushes; more tables at the back overlook the meadows and the hillocks (though you may find the views blocked by trees in summer). The pub is remotely placed up a track, handy for the Greensand Way and there's a hitching rail outside for horses. No children.

(Recommended by J F M and M West, Gordon Stevenson, Geoffrey Kemp, Ian Phillips, Derek and Maggie Washington, Brian and Karen Thomas, Colin McKerrow, C and R Bromage, Conor McGaughey)

Punch ~ Tenants Anthony Pugh and John Davidson ~ Real ale ~ Bar food (12-2.15(2.30 Sun), 7-9.30(9 Sun)) ~ (01737) 243100 ~ Dogs welcome ~ Folk jam session second Tues in month ~ Open 11-3, 5.30(6 Sat)-11; 12-10.30 Sun

WEST END SU9461 Map 2

Inn at West End

Just under 2½ miles from M3 junction 3; A322 S, on right

Very much at the heart of the local community, there's always plenty going on at this cheery roadside pub. They hold regular wine tastings (the landlord is a wine merchant), as well as other special events such as golf days, portuguese evenings and quiz nights. There's an emphasis on the good (though not cheap) food, which could include soup (£4.75), sandwiches (from £5), chicken liver salad (£7.25), smoked haddock kedgeree with poached egg (£11), sausage and mash, poached salmon salad or risotto with butternut squash, red onions and sage (£12.50), fish of the day (£17.25) and beef fillet medallions with braised bok choi and stir-fried vegetables (£17.50); no smoking dining room and conservatory. The licensees are helpful, and the staff are friendly and efficient. Appealingly up-to-date, the pub is open-plan, with bare boards, attractive modern prints on canary yellow walls above a red dado, and a line of dining tables with crisp white linen over pale yellow tablecloths on the left. The bar counter, straight ahead as you come in, is quite a focus, with chatting regulars on the comfortable bar stools, well kept Courage Best and Fullers London Pride on handpump, good house wines including good value champagne by the glass (they can also supply by the case), seasonal drinks such as Pimms, bucks fizz and kir royale, and good coffee. The area on the right has a pleasant relaxed atmosphere, with blue-cushioned wall benches and dining chairs around solid pale wood tables, broadsheet daily papers, magazines and a row of reference books on the brick chimneybreast above a woodburning stove. This opens into a terracotta-tiled garden room, with a blue overhead awning, which in turn leads to a pergola-covered (with grapevine and clematis) terrace; boules.

(Recommended by Shirley Mackenzie, Martin and Karen Wake, Nigel and Sue Foster, Susan and John Douglas, Guy Consterdine, Ian Phillips, A Sadler, Edward Mirzoeff)

Free house ~ Licensees Gerry and Ann Price ~ Real ale ~ Bar food (12-2.30, 6-9.30; 12-3, 6-9 Sun) ~ Restaurant ~ (01276) 858652 ~ Well behaved children welcome if able to eat at the table ~ Dogs allowed in bar ~ Open 12-3, 5-11; 12-11 Sat; 12-10.30 Sun

LUCKY DIP

Besides the fully inspected pubs, you might like to try these Lucky Dips recommended to us and described by readers (if you do, please send us reports: www.goodguides.co.uk).

ABINGER COMMON TQ1146

☆ *Abinger Hatch* [off A25 W of Dorking, towards Abinger Hammer]: Beautifully placed pub with heavy beams and flagstones, log fires, pews forming booths around oak tables in carpeted side area, popular changing food (not Sun evening) from generous sandwiches and baked potatoes up, around five real ales, young helpful staff; dogs welcome, very busy in summer, piped music, children allowed only in plain extension; nr pretty church and pond in clearing of rolling woods, tables and friendly ducks in nice garden, summer barbecues, open all day *(Ian Phillips, Ian and Barbara Rankin, LYM, Dick and Madeleine Brown, M and GR, P and J Shapley, Mrs Sylvia Elcoate, Philip and Ann Board)*

ALBURY TQ0547

☆ *Drummond Arms* [off A248 SE of Guildford; The Street]: Comfortably worn in civilised pub with traditional bar and attractive dining room, conservatory (children allowed here) overlooking pretty streamside back garden with duck island, tables by willows, fountain, covered terrace and barbecue, popular food, well kept ales such as Brakspears, Courage Best, Gales HSB and Greene King Old Speckled Hen, attentive helpful staff; piped music; bedrooms, attractive village, pleasant walks nearby *(LYM, Barry Fenton, Ian Phillips, William and Jenifer Ruxton, Jason Reynolds, MDN, Gordon Stevenson)*

ASH VALE SU8952

Swan [Hutton Rd, off Ash Vale Rd (A321) via Heathvale Bridge Rd]: Big homely Chef & Brewer on the workaday Basingstoke Canal, cheerful helpful staff, huge blackboard choice of decent food, well kept ales such as Hogs Back TEA, Wadworths 6X and Youngs, good wines by the glass; can be very busy, piped classical music; children welcome, garden, well kept terraces and window boxes, open all day *(Dr Martin Owton, Peter and Jackie Barnett)*

BANSTEAD TQ2659

Mint [Park Rd, off High St towards Kingswood]: Comfortably opened up with several nicely decorated areas, good value food (not Sun evening) from sandwiches and ciabattas up, prompt service, good choice of well kept ales inc Bass and Fullers London Pride; garden with play area *(Jenny and Brian Seller)*

BETCHWORTH TQ2150

Red Lion [Old Rd, Buckland]: Light and airy dining pub with emphasis on good range of food from lunchtime sandwiches up, steps down to stylish long flagstoned room and no smoking rather Tuscan-seeming candlelit dining room, modern furnishings, well kept Adnams Broadside and up to three guest beers; may be piped music; children welcome, picnic-sets on lawn with play area and cricket ground beyond, dining terrace, bedroom block, open all day *(LYM, Mrs G R Sharman, Cathryn and Richard Hicks, John Evans, Gordon Neighbour)*

BLETCHINGLEY TQ3251

William IV [3 miles from M25 junction 6; Little Common Lane, off A25 on Redhill side of village]: Quaint and peaceful old country pub down pretty lane, tile-hung and weatherboarded, three bar rooms and comfortably old-fashioned little back no smoking dining room, wide choice of food from sandwiches and baguettes to enjoyable Sun roasts (extended hours Sun) and of well kept ales such as Fullers London Pride, Greene King Old Speckled Hen, Harveys Best and Youngs Special, friendly unforced service, good wines, lots of bric-a-brac; two-level garden with summer barbecues *(LYM, Debbie and Neil Hayter)*

BLINDLEY HEATH TQ3645

Blue Anchor [Eastbourne Rd]: Large well laid out main road pub with good value food inc home-made specials, friendly mainly young staff; tables in front garden *(Alan M Pring)*

BRAMLEY TQ0044

☆ *Jolly Farmer* [High St]: Welcoming rambling pub, very popular for wide choice of generous food inc some unusual dishes (freshly made so may be a wait), five changing well kept ales inc Hogs Back TEA, czech beers on tap, proper coffee, good service by nice staff, two log fires, beer mat and bank note collections, big restaurant; comfortable bedrooms *(Mike and Heather Watson, LYM, Colin McKerrow)*

CATERHAM TQ3254

Harrow [Stanstead Rd, Whitehill]: Reasonably priced enjoyable food; tables in garden, open country by North Downs Way *(Mike Walters)*

CHERTSEY TQ0566

Boathouse [Bridge Rd]: Roomy and comfortably modern family chain pub, fresh and attractive, in good Thames-side spot, efficient friendly staff, reasonably priced food, Courage Best and Fullers London Pride; waterside tables, quay and moorings, multi-storey parking, bedrooms in adjoining Bridge Lodge *(Ian Phillips)*

Crown [London St (B375)]: Relaxed traditional Youngs pub with button-back banquettes in spreading high-ceilinged bar, tall and very sonorous longcase clock, well kept ales, fine choice of wines by the glass, nicely presented no-nonsense food from doorstep sandwiches and baked potatoes up, courteous attentive staff; neatly placed darts, discreet fruit machines; no cheques, and they may try to keep your card while you eat; children and dogs welcome, garden bar with conservatory, tables in courtyard and garden with pond; smart 30-bedroom annexe *(A C Nugent, Shirley Mackenzie)*

Kingfisher [Chertsey Bridge Rd]: Vintage Inn pastiche of traditional pub using old materials, beautifully placed by busy bridge and Thames lock, warm medley of furnishings in spreading series of small intimate areas, subtle lighting, well kept Bass and Fullers London Pride, good wine choice, good log fires, daily papers, reasonably priced food; soft piped music; families welcome if eating (otherwise no under-21s), riverside garden by road, open all day *(Ian Phillips)*

CHIDDINGFOLD SU94323

☆ *Rams Nest* [Petworth Rd (A283 S)]: Relaxed country inn with welcoming fire in huge inglenook, old-fashioned prints and furnishings inc antique settles in rambling panelled bar, light and airy by day, candlelit at night, couple of steps down to appealing carpeted dining area with more big prints, sofas by second back log fire with magazines and sizeable paperback library, enjoyable food from sandwiches and baguettes up, well kept Greene King IPA and Hogs Back TEA, good value wines, friendly attentive staff; may be unobtrusive piped music; tables on covered verandah, picnic-sets among fruit trees on neat lawn with wendy house and play area, well equipped bedrooms in separate block, open all day wknds *(BB, Ian Phillips, Dr H V Hughes)*

☆ *Swan* [A283 S]: Cheerful country inn comfortably refurnished after repair of 2003 fire damage, good choice of good value food in light and airy bar and compact dining room, several well kept ales, thoughtful wine choice, friendly attentive staff, no smoking area; comfortable attractive bedrooms *(LYM, Mr and Mrs M Pattinson)*

CHILWORTH TQ0347

☆ *Percy Arms* [Dorking Rd]: Smart partly 18th-c Greene King pub well run by welcoming new landlord, lots of helpful young staff, well kept real ales, enjoyable fresh food from baguettes to steaks cut to your chosen weight, popular Sun carvery, roomy, comfortable and well lit main area, smaller public bar, restaurant; no dogs; children welcome, pretty views over vale of Chilworth to St Martha's Hill from big pleasant back conservatory and picnic-sets in extensive tidy garden, good walks *(Carolyn Graham, Philip and Ann Board)*

CHIPSTEAD TQ2757

Well House [Chipstead signed with Mugswell off A217, N of M25 junction 8]: Partly 14th-c, cottagey and comfortable, with lots of atmosphere, decent straightforward food (not Sun evening, and may take a time) from good value hefty sandwiches up, efficient friendly staff, log fires in all three rooms (one bar is no smoking), well kept ales such as Adnams, Everards Tiger, Fullers London Pride, Hogs Back Hair of the Hog and Wadworths 6X; dogs allowed; attractive garden with well reputed to be mentioned in Domesday Book (loudspeaker food announcements though), delightful setting *(LYM, Jenny and Brian Seller, Ian Phillips)*

CHOBHAM SU9761

Sun [4 miles from M3 junction 3]: Low-beamed and timbered genuine pub, pleasant and friendly, with Bass, Fullers London Pride and Courage Directors, lots of daily papers, log fire and shining brasses *(LYM, Ian Phillips)*

CHURT SU8538

Crossways: Small friendly village pub with interesting choice of up to seven or eight changing well kept ales at reasonable prices, good value usual food, two distinct bar areas, July beer festival *(R B Gardiner)*

CLAYGATE TQ1563

Foley Arms [Hare Lane]: Thriving Victorian two-bar Youngs local, their well kept ales, real fires, good reasonably priced lunches from proper sandwiches through omelettes to mixed grill; good folk club; open all day, attractive garden with play area *(anon)*

COBHAM TQ1059

☆ *Plough* [Plough Lane, towards Downside]: Cheerful black-shuttered upmarket local with comfortable low-beamed lounge bar partly divided by L-shaped settles, huge log fire separating it from very popular restaurant area, real ales such as Hogs Back TEA and Charles Wells Bombardier, decent house wines, helpful international staff, pine-panelled snug with darts, limited good value quickly served lunchtime food from sandwiches up; tables outside *(Ian Phillips, LYM, John Ecklin, Sue and Mike Todd)*

COMPTON SU9546

☆ *Harrow* [B3000 towards Godalming off A3]: Popular upmarket country local, enjoyable though not cheap home-made food, well kept ales such as Greene King IPA, Hogs Back TEA and Youngs Special, good house wines, pleasant staff, farm décor; children welcome, a few picnic-sets outside, bedrooms, open all day, cl Sun evening *(Ian Phillips, Brian and Genie Smart, LYM, R B Gardiner)*

COX GREEN TQ0734

☆ *Thurlow Arms* [Baynards signposted off A281 W of Rudgwick or B2128 N]: Tucked-away erstwhile station hotel in peaceful countryside, easy-going bare-boards bar with big windows, lots of interesting railway, farm and more random bric-a-brac on walls and high ceilings, back games area with pool, darts and juke box, plush banquettes in side dining lounge, friendly staff, well kept Badger Best, Hogs Back TEA and Ringwood Best and Fortyniner, good if not cheap food from baguettes up, no music, dogs welcome; picnic-sets on lawn by rose trellis, meadow beyond with timber play fort – by former railway, now Downs Link Path; simple bedrooms by prior arrangement *(BB, Ian Phillips)*

DORKING TQ1649

☆ *Cricketers* [South St]: Hard-working new licensees in bustling and chatty little Fullers local with solidly comfortable furniture, cricketing memorabilia on stripped brick walls, cheap no-nonsense food, well kept Chiswick, London Pride and ESB, relaxed atmosphere and helpful friendly service; nice suntrap back terrace with barbecues, open all day *(LYM, C Whittington)*

☆ *Kings Arms* [West St]: Olde-worlde rambling 16th-c pub in antiques area, masses of timbers and low beams, nice lived-in old furniture in part-panelled lounge, warm relaxed atmosphere, good choice of popular low-priced home-made food from sandwiches up, friendly efficient service, well kept Bass, Fullers London Pride, Greene King IPA and Wadworths 6X, attractive old-fashioned back dining area; piped music; open all day *(Mike and Heather Watson, Conor McGaughey)*

EAST CLANDON TQ0651

☆ *Queens Head* [just off A246 Guildford—Leatherhead; The Street]: Rambling dining pub popular with older people for home-made blackboard food from good baguettes and baked potatoes up, few dishes cheap but helpings generous, relaxed atmosphere in small, comfortable and spotless connecting rooms, big inglenook log-effect fire, fine old elm bar counter, well kept ales such as Badger K&B, Hogs Back TEA and Youngs, quick attentive service; may try to keep your credit card as you eat, no dogs, boots or overalls; children welcome, picnic-sets on pretty front terrace and in quiet side garden, handy for two NT properties, cl Mon *(LYM, John Evans, LM, DWAJ, Sue and Mike Todd, Ian Phillips, C and R Bromage)*

EFFINGHAM TQ1153

☆ *Plough* [Orestan Lane]: Friendly and well run Youngs pub with consistently well kept ales from traditional bar with handbag hooks, honest home cooking inc enjoyable Sun lunch, good wine choice, welcoming staff and relaxed atmosphere, two coal-effect gas fires, beamery, panelling, old plates and brassware in long lounge, no smoking extension; attractive garden with play area, handy for Polesden Lacey (NT) *(Gordon Stevenson, Sue and Mike Todd)*

ELSTEAD SU9043

☆ *Woolpack* [B3001 Milford—Farnham]: Wide range of temptingly enjoyable food from familiar favourites to the exotic, generous helpings, well kept ales such as Fullers London Pride, Greene King Abbot and Youngs, high-backed settles in long airy main bar, open fires each end, second big room, country décor; children allowed, garden with picnic-sets, open all day wknds *(R Lake, LYM, Joan and Tony Walker, Ian Phillips, A D Neale)*

ENGLEFIELD GREEN SU9971

Barley Mow [Northcroft Rd]: Pretty pub in nice spot with café tables out in front overlooking cricket green (summer steam fairs); good value food from good reasonably priced sandwiches up, well kept Courage Best and Directors, Fullers London Pride, Greene King Old Speckled Hen and Marstons Pedigree, friendly service and local regulars, usual refurbished interior, back dining area with no smoking section, darts, quiet piped music; pleasant back garden with play area *(Roy and Lindsey Fentiman, Ian Phillips, KN-R)*

☆ *Fox & Hounds* [Bishopsgate Rd; off A328 N of Egham]: Friendly and popular pub in good setting on edge of Windsor Great Park, short walk from Savill Garden, tables on pleasant front lawn and back terrace; well kept Brakspears and Fullers London Pride, good wines by the glass, good if not cheap food from baguettes up in bar and restaurant, good polite service even when busy, two handsome log fires, daily papers; piped music, no children; open all day wknds and July-Sept *(Martin and Karen Wake, LYM, Mike and Jennifer Marsh)*

EPSOM TQ2158

☆ *Derby Arms* [Downs Rd, Epsom Downs]: Comfortably updated dining pub opp racecourse grandstand (yet surprisingly little racing memorabilia), very popular lunchtimes with older people for wide choice of reasonably priced food from good sandwich range up, decent wines, well kept Fullers London Pride and Shepherd Neame Spitfire, log fires, no smoking area; open all day Sun, nice tables outside, good views *(Mrs G R Sharman, R T and J C Moggridge, Gordon Neighbour)*

Driftbridge [Reigate Rd]: Bargain carvery lunchtime and evening (more expensive on Sun), generous helpings and good veg, welcoming service; bedrooms *(Klaus and Elizabeth Leist)*

Rising Sun [Heathcote Rd]: Friendly and sensitively restored Victorian town pub owned by Reigate's Pilgrim brewery, up to four of their beers kept well and a good range of continental beers, good value traditional food, pleasant staff, log fire, daily papers, games, pine tables on bare boards; nice garden *(Julian Templeman)*

ESHER TQ1364

Bear [High St]: Two landmark life-size bears behind roof parapet of former coaching inn, now a thriving Youngs pub with their full range kept well, good choice of wines by the glass, popular food from sandwiches to fish and steak in bar and no smoking dining end; bedrooms *(Tony Hobden)*

Prince of Wales [West End Lane; off A244

towards Hersham, by Princess Alice Hospice]: Popular Victorian Chef & Brewer dining pub favoured for its fresh fish and steaks, attractive period décor, cosy candlelit corners, open fires, turkey carpets, old furniture, prints and photographs, well kept Courage Best, Fullers London Pride, Theakstons Best and a guest beer, good wine choice, daily papers; big shady garden, nr green and pond *(Ian Phillips, Derek and Heather Manning)*

Wheatsheaf [The Green]: Open-plan bar with lots of nooks and crannies, open fire, reasonably priced food from snacks up, well kept Adnams Broadside, Fullers London Pride and Youngs Special; lacks a no smoking area; picnic-sets out overlooking green *(Tony Hobden)*

EWELL TQ2262

Star [Cheam Rd]: Well kept Badger K&B and Tanglefoot, guest beers and good choice of wines, some food choice, quiet alcoves and low ceilings giving good old-fashioned atmosphere in front bar; long back room with frequent live music, SkyTV sports; nice garden behind *(Jason Reynolds)*

EWHURST TQ0940

Bulls Head [The Street]: Rambling village pub busy wkdy lunchtimes with good value OAP specials; attractive garden, opp village green *(Mike and Heather Watson)*

FARLEIGH TQ3659

☆ *Harrow* [Farleigh Common, off B269 Limpsfield—Warlingham]: Big welcoming Vintage Inn, busy lunchtimes even midweek (get there early Sun for a table), reliably enjoyable reasonably priced food from sandwiches up, well kept Bass and lots of wines by the glass from large horseshoe bar, pleasant well trained staff, log fires, several areas inc roomy and attractive no smoking barn, old farm tools and machinery; children welcome, plenty of good outside tables in large neatly kept area backing on to fields *(Jim Bush, Mrs J A Steff-Langston)*

FARNHAM SU8742

Duke of Cambridge [Tilford Woods, Tilford Road]: Very rural, with pleasant country views, good play area in long tree-shaded garden, picnic-sets on high grassy terrace at one end – so you can keep an eye on the children; neatly renovated with mix of chairs around pine tables, pleasant staff, several well kept real ales, decent wine by the glass, wide food choice; piped music *(Malcolm Sutcliffe, Mr and Mrs D Boley)*

Shepherd & Flock [Moor Park Lane, off A31/A324/A325 roundabout]: Good atmosphere, half a dozen well kept ales inc Hogs Back TEA and Ringwood Old Thumper, enjoyable pub lunches, service good even when busy; nicely tucked away from the roundabout traffic *(Dr Martin Owton, Richard Houghton)*

Spotted Cow [Bourne Grove, Lower Bourne (towards Tilford)]: Plain and welcoming country local with good home-made food from sandwiches to lots of fresh fish, well kept ales such as fff Moondance, attentive friendly service, reasonable prices; no under-7s inside, play area in big attractive garden, nice surroundings *(Ian Phillips, John and Joyce Snell)*

FICKLESHOLE TQ3960

☆ *White Bear* [Featherbed Lane/Fairchildes Lane; off A2022 Purley Rd just S of A212 roundabout]: Rambling interestingly furnished partly 15th-c family country pub, popular even midweek lunchtimes for good value food from fat fresh sandwiches up inc some interesting dishes, lots of small rooms, beams and flagstones, friendly service, well kept Bass, good coffee, restaurant; fruit machine, video game, piped music; children welcome, play area in pleasant sizeable garden, lots of picnic-sets on front terrace, open all day Sat *(LYM, Jenny and Brian Seller)*

FOREST GREEN TQ1241

☆ *Parrot* [nr B2126/B2127 junction]: Rambling beamed country pub with attractive furnishings and secluded extended restaurant, a well kept ale brewed for them by Hogs Back and several others such as Courage Directors, Fullers London Pride and Wadworths 6X, good generous food from good value baguettes up, helpful landlady and prompt friendly service, end bar with inglenook log fire, interesting bric-a-brac and pool; piped music; children and walkers welcome, open all day, plenty of tables in garden by cricket green, good walks nearby *(LYM, C and R Bromage, Jenny and Brian Seller)*

FRIMLEY GREEN SU8856

Old Wheatsheaf [Frimley Green Rd (B3411, was A321)]: Friendly and informal proper pub, wheelback chairs, banquettes and country prints in its opened-together bar, Greene King ales, lots of sensibly priced sandwiches as well as baguettes, ploughman's and a few substantial bargain daily specials, evening restaurant; terrace tables *(KC)*

GODALMING SU9643

Red Lion [Mill Lane, High St S end]: Lively pub formed from several old properties inc mayor's lodging and courthouse (cellar was gaol); two big friendly bars (one with games), well presented food (not Sun-Mon evenings), well kept interesting ales, good coffees and service; fair-sized garden, open all day *(Richard Houghton)*

GRAYSWOOD SU9134

Wheatsheaf [A286 NE of Haslemere]: Civilised much modernised pub, light and airy, with enjoyable food in bar and restaurant (they bake their own bread), good range of well kept ales such as Ringwood and Timothy Taylors Landlord, friendly helpful service; conference/bedroom extension *(Phil and Sally Gorton, Ruth Nixon)*

HAMBLEDON SU9639

Merry Harriers [off A283]: Homely and quietly old-fashioned country local popular with walkers, huge inglenook log fire, dark wood with cream and terracotta paintwork, pine tables, impressive collection of chamber-pots hanging from beams, well kept Greene King IPA and Abbot, Hogs Back TEA and Hop Back Crop Circle, farm cider, decent wines and coffee, daily papers and classic motorcycle magazines, reasonably priced fresh simple food from sandwiches up; pool room, folk night 1st Sun of month; big back garden in attractive countryside, picnic-sets in front and over road – caravan parking *(Phil and Sally Gorton)*

HASCOMBE TQ0039

☆ *White Horse* [B2130 S of Godalming]: Picturesque old rose-draped pub, expensive but a favourite of many and very busy even midweek, in a pretty village on the Greensand Way; attractively simple beamed public bar, traditional games and quiet small-windowed alcoves, more restauranty dining bar (children allowed), good bar food from sandwiches and baguettes up, well kept Adnams and Harveys, quick cheerful service, good wine list, log fires or woodburners; small front terrace, spacious sloping back lawn, handy for Winkworth Arboretum, open all day wknds *(Martin and Karen Wake, John Davis, LYM, T R and B C Jenkins, John Hale, Susan and John Douglas, John and Tania Wood, Jenny and Brian Seller, Gordon Stevenson)*

HOLMBURY ST MARY TQ1144

Royal Oak: Well run and relaxing low-beamed 17th-c coaching inn in pleasant spot by green and church, generous consistently well prepared usual food from sandwiches and baked potatoes up, good choice of well kept ales such as Greene King IPA, decent wines by the glass, quick friendly service, log fire; tables on front lawn, bedrooms, good walks *(R Lake, P and J Shapley, Barry Steele-Perkins)*

HORSELL COMMON TQ0160

Bleak House [Chertsey Rd, The Anthonys; A320 Woking—Ottershaw]: Welcoming, cheerful and neatly kept, with wide choice of generous quickly served reasonably priced food, real ales such as Marstons Pedigree, Tetleys and Youngs, comfortable seats; picnic-sets and barbecues in pleasant back garden merging into woods with good shortish walks to sandpits which inspired H G Wells's *War of the Worlds (Ron South)*

KINGSWOOD TQ2456

☆ *Kingswood Arms* [Waterhouse Lane]: Attractive old pub, big and busy, with enjoyable generous food inc good sandwiches and buffet bar, helpful friendly staff, good range of beers inc Fullers London Pride, Shepherd Neame Spitfire and Theakstons Old Peculier, hanging plants in pleasant light and airy conservatory dining extension; spacious rolling garden with play area *(Mrs G R Sharman, Tony Brace)*

LALEHAM TQ0568

☆ *Anglers Retreat* [B376 (Staines Rd)]: Big foody well appointed family pub, pale panelling, big tropical aquarium set into wall, even larger one in smart no smoking restaurant area extended into conservatory, wide choice of food (all day wknds) inc lots of fresh fish, two bright coal fires, Brakspears and a guest beer, decent wines; Sun quiz night, unobtrusive piped music, fruit machine, no dogs; children welcome, seats out in front, play area in back garden, open all day *(Mr and Mrs S Felstead, LYM, Susan and John Douglas, Tom McLean)*

LIGHTWATER SU9262

Red Lion [Guildford Rd]: Refurbished under new licensees and doing well, Fullers London Pride and Hop Back Summer Lightning, pub food; pleasant outside area *(Dr Martin Owton)*

LITTLE BOOKHAM TQ1254

Olde Windsor Castle: Spacious well extended Chef & Brewer family dining pub with lots of timbers, old-style country furniture and log fire, good choice of food from sandwiches to full meals, lots of decent wines by the glass, Courage Best, Hogs Back TEA and a guest beer, friendly staff, no smoking area; pleasantly quiet lunchtimes, can be busy evenings; tables in huge garden with terrace and popular play area *(John Ecklin)*

MARTYRS GREEN TQ0857

Black Swan [handy for M25 junction 10; off A3 S-bound, but return N of junction]: Much enlarged, with a dozen or more well kept ales inc bargains, simple furnishings, well used back bar, usual food (queue to order), friendly staff, log fires, restaurant; SkyTV, can get crowded with young people evenings, piped pop music may be loud then, frequent discos and theme nights; plenty of tables in big woodside garden with barbecues and good play area – bouncy castle, playground-quality frames, roundabouts etc; dogs welcome, handy for RHS Wisley Garden, open all day *(A C Nugent, Jason Reynolds)*

MERSTHAM TQ3051

Inn on the Pond [from A25 W of Godstone, follow Nutfield Church, Merstham signpost]: Lots of tables in engagingly furnished and decorated back family conservatory, sheltered back terrace; front area rambles around central fireplace, with settles, pews, shelves of old books, decent prints; half a dozen well kept real ales, good choice of well prepared food from big crusty sandwiches up, friendly licensees; views over scrubland (and the small pond and nearby cricket ground) to the North Downs *(BB, Mike Walters)*

MILFORD SU9542

Refectory [Portsmouth Rd]: Chef & Brewer pub-restaurant in former partly 18th-c manor house, succulent carvery roasts (cheaper wkdys), helpful considerate staff, good wheelchair access *(Klaus and Elizabeth Leist)*

MOGADOR TQ2453

Sportsman [from M25 up A217 past 2nd roundabout, then Mogador signed; edge of Banstead Heath]: Interesting, relaxed and welcoming low-ceilinged local, quietly placed on Walton Heath, a magnet for walkers and riders; well kept ales, enjoyable popular food, dogs welcome if not wet or muddy; tables out on common, on back lawn, and some under cover *(Conor McGaughey)*

NEWDIGATE TQ1942

Six Bells: Good atmosphere in popular recently refurbished local with good range of well kept ales, good value food, well kept Bass and

Kings, friendly service and entertaining shorts-wearing landlord, a welcome for children; plenty of tables in pleasant garden, lovely outlook over wooden-towered church *(Marc Hadley)*

NUTFIELD TQ3050

Queens Head [A25 E of Redhill]: Congenial pub with tiled bar and carpeted restaurant, enjoyable nicely presented food, helpful staff, good wine list *(C S Turner)*

OCKHAM TQ0756

☆ *Hautboy* [Ockham Lane – towards Cobham]: Remarkable red stone Gothick folly, crypt bar with four well kept ales such as Adnams, Fullers London Pride and Greene King Old Speckled Hen, friendly efficient young staff, emphasis on upstairs brasserie bar like a 19th-c arts & crafts chapel, darkly panelled and high-vaulted, with oil paintings and minstrels gallery, imaginative choice of enjoyable food from snacks up, entertaining parrot; children welcome, tables on cricket-view terrace and in secluded orchard garden with play area, bedrooms; currently the best lunch place within easy reach of RHS Wisley *(LYM, John Evans, O K Smyth, Howard and Lorna Lambert, E S Funnell, MDN)*

OCKLEY TQ1440

Inn on the Green [Billingshurst Rd (A29)]: Quiet and pleasantly refurbished open-plan pub on green of attractive village, wide choice of enjoyable food from generous toasted baguettes to restaurant dishes, well kept Greene King IPA, interesting cricket memorabilia, easy chairs and sofa by one fireplace, nice mix of tables in no smoking dining area leading to conservatory; picnic-sets in garden, bedrooms *(Mike and Lynn Robinson, BB, Jenny and Brian Seller, DWAJ)*

☆ *Old School House* [Stane St]: Very popular dining place (it's also signed as Bryce's Fish Restaurant), thriving atmosphere in pubby eating area around small bar counter with well kept Gales BB and Butser, good wines by the glass inc champagne, good value generous food from sandwiches through fresh pasta to steaks and of course seafood, good value two-course lunch, prompt attentive young staff, wonderful log fire, smarter carpeted restaurant area; picnic-sets under cocktail parasols on sunny terrace with flowers around car park *(Bob and Maggie Atherton, C and R Bromage, Barry Steele-Perkins, Gordon Stevenson, Terry Buckland, BB, Tom and Ruth Rees, Jeremy Woods)*

☆ *Punchbowl* [Oakwood Hill, signed off A29 S]: Cosy country pub, smart and clean, with cheerful relaxed atmosphere, several rooms, huge inglenook log fire, polished flagstones, lots of low beams, well kept Badger Best and Tanglefoot and a Gribble guest, good food choice from unusual ciabattas up, friendly service, daily papers and traditional games; children allowed in dining area, picnic-sets on side terrace and in pretty front garden, quiet spot with good walks inc Sussex Border Path *(LYM, Tony Adlard, C and R Bromage, Ian Phillips, Mike and Heather Watson)*

OUTWOOD TQ3246

Bell [Outwood Common, just E of village; off A23 S of Redhill]: Attractive extended 17th-c country dining pub, olde-worlde beamed bar and sparser restaurant area, good choice of well kept ales such as Flowers IPA, Harveys Best and Wadworths 6X, log fires, usual food; children and dogs welcome, piped music; summer barbecues and cream teas, pretty fairy-lit garden with country views, handy for windmill, has been open all day *(LYM, Simon Rodway)*

Castle [Millers Lane]: Welcoming panelled and carpeted pub with well kept ales inc Adnams and Harveys, short interesting choice of lunchtime food from ciabattas up, log fire and old wooden tables; large terrace *(John Ecklin)*

OXTED TQ3852

Old Bell [High St, Old Oxted]: Beamed and panelled pub/restaurant with welcoming staff and reasonably priced food inc all-day Sun carvery, decent beers and wine; good wheelchair access, disabled facilities and a welcome for children, garden *(Matthew Croxford, Simon Rodway)*

Oxted Inn [Hoskins Walk]: Spacious airy Wetherspoons, light and clean, with their usual sensibly priced food and good beer choice, no smoking area, no piped music *(Tony and Wendy Hobden)*

Royal Oak [Caterfield Lane, Staffhurst Wood, S of town]: Good choice of real ales inc Larkins in comfortable and unchanging traditional bar, good range of bar food, more in added back dining room with country views, emphasis on fish, choice of Sun roasts *(Christopher Wright, Simon Rodway)*

PEASLAKE TQ0844

☆ *Hurtwood* [off A25 S of Gomshall; Walking Bottom]: Homely pre-war country hotel in fine spot for walkers (no muddy boots inside, though), comfortable bar and lounge with well kept Fullers London Pride, Greene King IPA and local Hogs Back TEA, good range of wines by the glass, coffee and malt whiskies, good well priced bar food from sandwiches up, friendly helpful service, daily papers and magazines, two flame-effect fires, sizeable interesting restaurant; bedrooms *(BB, Ian Phillips)*

PIRBRIGHT SU9454

☆ *Royal Oak* [Aldershot Rd; A324 S of village]: Relaxed and cottagey old Tudor pub under newish management, heavily beamed and timbered rambling side alcoves, ancient stripped brickwork, three real fires, good choice of well kept ales inc Bass, Greene King IPA and Hogs Back TEA and Hair of the Hog, good range of wines by the glass, no smoking dining area and family room; disabled facilities, extensive colourful fairy-lit gardens, good walks, open all day *(Mr and Mrs S Felstead, Mr and Mrs A Swainson, KC, LYM, Ian Phillips, R T and J C Moggridge)*

PUTTENHAM SU9347

☆ *Good Intent* [signed off B3000 just S of A31 junction; The Street/Seale Lane]: Friendly efficient staff in beamed village local with good range of reasonably priced generous fresh food (not Sun-Mon evenings) from sandwiches and baked potatoes up, well kept Courage Best, Youngs Special and guests such as Hogs Back TEA and Theakstons Old Peculier, farm cider, decent wine choice, handsome log fire, pool, old photographs of the pub; dogs allowed, no children, picnic-sets in small sunny garden, good walks, open all day wknds *(Michael Sargent, Ian Phillips, Sally, Andy and Oscar de la Fontaine, BB)*

RIPLEY TQ0556

☆ ***Anchor*** [High St]: Tudor inn with interesting old-fashioned cool dark low-beamed connecting rooms, wide choice of enjoyable promptly served food with some emphasis on thai dishes (charming Thai staff), well kept Bass and Courage Best, smart coffee, nautical memorabilia and photographs of Ripley's cycling heyday, coal-effect stove, two dozing labradors, games in public bar; disabled facilities, tables in coachyard *(BB, C and R Bromage, Ian Phillips)*

Seven Stars [Newark Lane (B367)]: Neatly kept 1930s pub with lots of blackboards showing good value generous food from sandwiches and baked potatoes to plenty of seafood and good Sun lunches, well kept Fullers London Pride, Greene King IPA, Abbot and Old Speckled Hen and Tetleys, decent wines, nice efficient service, no smoking area; piped music; large secluded garden behind *(LM, Ian Phillips, Jason Reynolds, Shirley Mackenzie)*

Ship [High St]: Welcoming and comfortable olde-worlde 16th-c local with low beams and flagstones in small bar with scrubbed tables and benches and cosy nooks, log fire in vast inglenook, well kept ales such as Brakspears and Hogs Back, good value sensible food from sandwiches up, restaurant; small raised games area with bar billiards; small high-walled terrace *(Phil and Sally Gorton)*

Talbot [High St]: Substantial beamed coaching inn with roomy traditional bars each side of two big fireplaces, welcoming helpful staff, enjoyable food from generous baguettes up, Greene King IPA and Shepherd Neame Bitter, Best and Spitfire, decent wine, nice atmosphere, minimalist back brasserie; may be piped music; bedrooms, tables in back courtyard, antiques centre in outbuildings *(Andy Sinden, Louise Harrington, Ian Phillips)*

RUNFOLD SU8747

Jolly Farmer [off A31 just NE of Farnham]: Wide choice of interesting well cooked food, reasonable prices, welcoming staff, well kept Greene King Abbot, good wine choice, family restaurant; pleasant garden with good play area – nice retreat from trunk road *(Dr and Mrs B T Marsh, LYM, A D Marsh)*

Princess Royal [off A31 just NE of Farnham]: Large comfortable 1920s pub recently reopened under experienced new licensees, enjoyable food, well kept Gales ales, friendly service, inglenooks, dining conservatory – busy with families Sun lunchtime; picnic-sets and play area behind *(Mike Taylor)*

SENDMARSH TQ0455

Saddlers Arms [Send Marsh Rd]: Low-beamed local with creeper-covered porch, well kept Adnams, Fullers London Pride and Youngs, enjoyable standard food inc good snacks, friendly service, open fire, no smoking area, toby jugs, brassware etc; well behaved dogs welcome, picnic-sets out front and back *(Gordon Stevenson, Ian Phillips, Shirley Mackenzie)*

SHACKLEFORD SU9345

☆ ***Cyder House*** [Peper Harow Lane]: Roomy and civilised country pub rambling around central servery, interesting blackboard choice of reasonably priced food from ciabattas to imaginative starters and hot dishes, smaller helpings available, chatty friendly staff, well kept Badger ales and Hogs Back TEA, decent house wines, log or coal fires, pleasantly bright and airy layout with lots of mellow pine, dining room and separate children's room with toys and small furniture; fruit machine and sports TV in side room, may be piped pop music; picnic-sets on terrace and back lawn, nice leafy village setting, open all day wknds *(Mr and Mrs S Felstead, BB, Martin and Karen Wake)*

SHALFORD TQ0047

Sea Horse [A281 S of Guildford]: Warm and hospitable Vintage Inn with local memorabilia in cosy nooks and corners, good range of reasonably priced food all day, well kept Bass and Fullers London Pride, good choice of wines by the glass, several log fires, plenty of friendly attentive staff; children welcome *(C L Kauffmann, Jason Reynolds)*

SHAMLEY GREEN TQ0343

☆ ***Red Lion*** [The Green]: Smartly done-up dining pub with neat décor, dark polished furniture, rows of books, open fires, local cricketing photographs, enjoyable food all day from sandwiches and good ploughman's to steaks, children's helpings and unusual puddings, well kept Flowers, Greene King Abbot, Youngs and farm cider, good choice of wines, cafetière coffee, friendly staff, smart restaurant; open all day, children welcome, sturdy tables in nice garden, bedrooms *(LYM, Shirley Mackenzie)*

SHEPPERTON TQ0866

Red Lion [Russell Rd]: Roomy and welcoming old wisteria-covered local across rd from Thames, well kept Brakspears, Courage Best, Fullers London Pride and Greene King Abbot, generous food from baked potatoes up inc very popular good value all-day Sun lunch, quick attentive service, interesting prints in cosy front bar, back bar for sports TV, restaurant; plenty of tables on terrace among fine displays of shrubs and flowers, more on lawn over road (traffic noise) with lovely river views and well run moorings *(Ian Phillips, Mayur Shah)*

Thames Court [Shepperton Lock, Ferry Lane; turn left off B375 towards Chertsey, 100yds from Square]: Huge Vintage Inn well placed by Thames, generous usual food from snacks up all day, good choice of wines by the glass, cool Bass, Fullers London Pride and Tetleys, galleried central atrium with separate attractive panelled areas up and down stairs, two good log fires, daily papers; children welcome, large attractive tree-shaded and heated terrace *(Mayur Shah, Alan Kilpatrick, Ian Phillips)*

SHERE TQ0747

☆ *White Horse* [signed off A25 3 miles E of Guildford; Middle St]: Striking half-timbered pub extensively enlarged as Chef & Brewer, still full of character, with several rooms off the small busy bar, uneven floors, massive beams, Tudor stonework, oak wall seats, two log fires, one in a huge inglenook, reliable food all day from chunky sandwiches up, well kept beers such as Courage Best and Hogs Back TEA, lots of wines by the glass, good-sized children's area; tables outside, beautiful village, open all day *(LYM, Mrs G R Sharman, John Ecklin)*

SOUTH GODSTONE TQ3549

☆ *Fox & Hounds* [Tilburstow Hill Rd/Harts Lane, off A22]: Nicely refurbished and pleasantly rural, with racing prints and woodburner in cosy low-beamed bar, welcoming staff, tasty food from pubby staples to good seafood, well kept Greene King IPA, Abbot and Ruddles County from tiny bar counter, evening restaurant (not Sun-Mon evenings); may be piped music; children in eating area *(Bill Fillery, LYM, Geoffrey Kemp, Mike and Heather Watson)*

STAINES TQ0371

Bells [Church St]: Comfortable and relaxed genuine local, well kept Youngs ales, decent wines, prompt home-made lunchtime food from good sandwiches to popular good value Sun lunch, friendly staff, cosy furnishings, central fireplace; may be piped music – not evenings; plenty of seats in big garden with terrace *(anon)*

SUNBURY TQ1068

Magpie [Thames St]: Lovely Thames views from upper bar and small terrace by boat club with pleasant tables under parasols and heaters, steps up from moorings; bare boards and panelling inside, reliable standard food from sandwiches up, well kept Greene King IPA and Abbot or Old Speckled Hen, decent wines, efficient antipodean service, no smoking areas; jazz in lower bar Mon; bedrooms *(Ian Phillips, Mayur Shah, Joyce and Geoff Robson, Dr Martin Owton)*

SUTTON ABINGER TQ1045

Volunteer [Water Lane; just off B2126 via Raikes Lane, 1½ miles S of Abinger Hammer]: Three friendly low-ceilinged olde-worlde linked rooms, well kept ales such as Badger Best and Harveys Best, decent wines, roaring fire, homely medley of furnishings, big rugs on bare boards or red tiles, no smoking area, restaurant (food may take a while); children welcome away from bar, nice setting by clear stream, good tables out on flowery terrace and sun-trap lawns stepped up behind, has been open all day summer wknds, good walks *(LYM, Ian Phillips, Carla Francis, Robin Cordell)*

TADWORTH TQ2354

Blue Anchor [Dorking Rd (B2032)]: Busy, warm and homely pub in nice woodland setting, stone floors, log fires and candles, cheerful helpful staff, popular if not cheap food, well kept real ales, good wine choice; piped music *(Mrs G R Sharman, Gordon Neighbour)*

Dukes Head [A217 opp Common and woods]: Very popular at lunchtime for wide range of low-priced enjoyable food (not Sun evening) from formidable sandwiches up, attentive service, good choice of real ales and of wines by the glass, two big inglenook log fires; garden, open all day *(DWAJ)*

THAMES DITTON TQ1567

Albany [Queens Rd, signed off Summer Rd]: Back to its proper name after a spell as Fox on the River, with kitchen extended and furnishings upgraded; spacious and cosy, enjoyable food from sandwiches and ploughman's to more inventive dishes, Bass and Gales HSB, good choice of wines by the glass, friendly helpful staff, log fire, daily papers, river pictures, lively mix of customers, popular restaurant; delightful spot, lots of tables on attractive Thamesside terrace and lawn overlooking Hampton Court grounds, moorings, open all day *(Tom and Ruth Rees, Gordon Stevenson)*

☆ *Olde Swan* [Summer Rd]: Large riverside pub under new management with good carefully cooked food, well kept Greene King IPA and Abbot, cosy Victorian-style décor, one long bar with three good-sized areas inc civilised black-panelled upper bar overlooking quiet Thames backwater, restaurant *(BB, Tom and Ruth Rees)*

TILFORD SU8743

☆ *Barley Mow* [The Green, off B3001 SE of Farnham; also signed off A287]: Snug little low-ceilinged traditional bar on right with woodburner, nice scrubbed tables in two small rooms set for food on left, interesting cricketing prints and old photographs, good food inc late Sun lunch (bar snacks earlier till 2 that day), wknd afternoon teas, charming friendly service, well kept Courage Best, Fullers London Pride, Greene King Abbot and Youngs, imaginative wine list; darts, table skittles, no children; pretty setting opposite cricket green, tables in good-sized back garden fenced off from small stream *(John and Mary Ling, BB, R B Gardiner)*

WALLISWOOD TQ1138

Scarlett Arms [signed from Ewhurst—Rowhook back rd, or off A29 S of Ockley]: Unspoilt three-room country cottage, low black oak beams, flagstones, simple furniture, two log fires – one in huge inglenook, well kept Badger ales, bar food, welcoming staff, traditional games; fruit machine, piped music, no children; peaceful benches in front and old-fashioned seats and tables under cocktail parasols in informal garden *(LYM, Gavin Robinson)*

WALTON ON THE HILL TQ2255

Blue Ball [not far from M25 junction 8; Deans Lane, off B2220 by pond]: Facing common nr duck pond, cosily refurbished, with wide choice of good value food, good atmosphere, prompt friendly service, several real ales, decent wines, restaurant (open all day Sun) overlooking big garden with barbecue; good walking area *(C and R Bromage, Gordon Stevenson)*

Chequers [Chequers Lane]: Pleasant mock-Tudor Youngs pub with several rooms rambling around central servery, well kept ales, good value quick lunchtime bar food inc impressive sandwiches, restaurant (children allowed here), friendly service; terrace and neat sheltered garden with good summer barbecues *(LYM, Gordon Stevenson)*

WALTON-ON-THAMES TQ0966

Swan [Manor Rd, off A3050]: Three-bar riverside Youngs pub, several linked rooms, decent reasonably priced food in bar and attractive restaurant, well kept ales and good wine choice, good service; dogs welcome, lots of tables and chairs in huge pretty garden leading down to Thames, wknd barbecues, moorings, riverside walks *(A C Nugent, Gordon Prince, Mayur Shah)*

WARLINGHAM TQ3955

☆ ***Botley Hill Farmhouse*** [Limpsfield Rd (B269)]: Busy more or less open-plan dining pub, low-ceilinged linked rooms up and down steps, soft lighting, spreading turkey carpet, quite close-set tables, big fireplace with copper and blacked pans above the log fire in one attractive flagstoned room, restaurant with overhead fishing net and seashells, small no smoking area; good if not cheap food inc lots of fish and seafood, well kept ales such as Greene King and Shepherd Neame Spitfire, good house wines; children welcome away from bar, cream teas, wknd entertainments (may be loud live bands outside), tables in courtyard, neat garden with play area and toddlers' park, ducks and aviary *(BB, Alan M Pring)*

WEST BYFLEET TQ0460

Yeoman [Old Woking Rd]: Big nicely decorated Harvester family dining room, quick inexpensive food a treat for pre-teens, same food available in child-free bar, friendly staff *(Shirley Mackenzie)*

WEST CLANDON TQ0452

☆ ***Bulls Head*** [A247 SE of Woking]: Friendly and comfortably modernised 16th-c country local, very popular esp with older people lunchtime for good value generous homely food from sandwiches, ploughman's and baked potatoes through reliable home-made proper pies (suspend the diet for a day) to steak, small lantern-lit beamed front bar with open fire and some stripped brick, old local prints and bric-a-brac, steps up to simple raised back inglenook dining area, efficient service, well kept Courage Best, Greene King Old Speckled Hen and Marstons Pedigree, good coffee, no piped music, games room with darts and pool; no credit cards; children and dogs on leads welcome, lots of tables and good play area in garden, convenient for Clandon Park, good walking country *(R Lake, DWAJ, Susan and John Douglas, John Ecklin, Sue and Mike Todd)*

Onslow Arms [A247 SE of Woking]: Rambling partly 17th-c country pub with dark nooks and corners, heavy beams and flagstones, warm seats by inglenook log fires, lots of brass and copper; well kept ales such as Courage Directors, Fullers London Pride and Charles Wells Bombardier, decent wines, enjoyable food (not Sun evening), partly no smoking dining room (popular Sun lunches); children welcome (and dogs in bar), great well lit garden, open all day *(LYM, Shirley Mackenzie, Ian Phillips, John Ecklin)*

WEYBRIDGE TQ0764

☆ ***Old Crown*** [Thames St]: Friendly and comfortably old-fashioned three-bar pub, very popular lunchtime for good platefuls of good value food from sandwiches and baked potatoes up esp fresh grimsby fish (served evening too), good specials; well kept Courage Best and Directors, John Smiths, Youngs Special and a guest beer, service good even when busy, no smoking family lounge and conservatory, no music or machines but may be sports TV in back bar; children welcome, suntrap streamside garden *(DWAJ, A C Nugent)*

☆ ***Prince of Wales*** [Cross Rd/Anderson Rd off Oatlands Drive]: Congenial and attractively restored, with relaxed country-local feel at lunchtime (may be busier evenings), reasonably priced generous blackboard food inc interesting dishes and Sun lunch with three roasts, well kept ales such as Adnams, Boddingtons, Fullers London Pride, Tetleys and Wadworths 6X, ten wines by the glass, friendly service, log fire in one room, daily papers, stripped pine dining room down a couple of steps (candlelit bistro feel there at night); big-screen TV for major sports events *(Ian Phillips, Minda and Stanley Alexander)*

WINDLESHAM SU9464

☆ ***Brickmakers*** [Chertsey Rd (B386, W of B383 roundabout)]: Busy dining pub with flagstones, pastel colours and different areas for bistro feel, wide range of freshly made food from good filled baguettes up, thai fishcakes a favourite, room off with sofas and low tables, well kept Brakspears, Courage Best, Fullers London Pride and Marstons Pedigree, good choice of wines by the glass, nice coffee, welcoming service, log fire, conservatory, no music; well behaved children allowed, attractive garden with boules and barbecues (live music some summer Suns), lovely hanging baskets *(Mr and Mrs A Swainson, A C Nugent, Martin and Karen Wake, Dr and Mrs M E Wilson)*

Half Moon [Church Rd]: Extended pub with tables laid for reliable food inc family Sun lunch and fresh veg, great range of well kept changing ales too such as fff I Can't Remember, Fullers London Pride, Hogs Back TEA, O'Hanlons Myrica, Ringwood Fortyniner, Timothy Taylors Landlord and Weltons Horsham Old, Weston's farm cider, cheerful service, log fires, interesting World War II pictures, modern furnishings; piped music, silenced fruit machine; children welcome, picnic-sets in huge well kept garden *(Mr and Mrs S Felstead, Ian Phillips, Guy Consterdine)*

WITLEY SU9439

☆ ***White Hart*** [Petworth Rd]: Tudor beams, good oak furniture, log fire in cosy panelled inglenook snug where George Eliot drank, nice local atmosphere and welcoming new mother-and-daughter licensees, well kept Shepherd Neame Best and Spitfire, fairly priced home-made food, daily papers, games in public bar, restaurant; piped music; tables on cobbled terrace, lots of pretty hanging baskets etc, lower meadow with picnic-sets and play area *(Gordon Stevenson, LYM, Phil and Sally Gorton, Mike and Heather Watson)*

WOKING SU9956

Mayford Arms [Guildford Rd, Mayford (A320)]: Limited choice of good value generous food, friendly staff, no smoking dining area; garden with play area *(Roger and Pauline Pearce)*

Star [Wych Hill]: Roomy open-plan 1930s pub kept spotless, enjoyable food, wide wines and spirits choice, prompt friendly service *(Charlotte Pearce)*

Wetherspoons [Chertsey Rd]: Lots of intimate areas and cosy side snugs, good range of food all day, reasonably priced beers inc three or four interesting guest ales *(Tony Hobden)*

WOOD STREET SU9550

White Hart [White Hart Lane; off A323 just W of Guildford]: Country local dating from 16th or 17th c, good range of plentiful wholesome food from sandwiches up in big dining area, well kept Adnams, Fullers London Pride, Greene King IPA and Old Speckled Hen and Shepherd Neame Spitfire, good range of malt whiskies, helpful service; picnic-sets in garden, peaceful spot tucked away off green, bedrooms *(Ian Phillips)*

WOTTON TQ1247

☆ ***Wotton Hatch*** [A25 Dorking—Guildford]: Attractive and neatly kept Vintage Inn family dining pub, welcoming largely no smoking rambling rooms around 17th-c core, interesting furnishings, good generous reasonably priced food (all day Thurs-Sun and summer) from hearty sandwiches up, well kept Bass and Fullers London Pride, good choice of decent wines, generous soft drinks inc freshly squeezed orange juice, pleasant Italian manager and keen young staff, daily papers, conservatory; gentle piped music, no dogs; impressive views from neat garden, open all day *(Gordon Prince, M G Hart, LYM, John Ecklin, Mrs J A Steff-Langston)*

WRECCLESHAM SU8344

☆ ***Bat & Ball*** [approach from Sandrock Hill and rough unmade Upper Bourne Lane then narrow steep lane to pub]: Close-set numbered tables in neatly kept secluded valley-bottom pub recently reworked in a plethora of different wood finishes, emphasis on wide range of enjoyable food (small helpings available) from ploughman's, baked potatoes and light dishes through typical favourites to more upmarket dishes, cabinet of salads and tasty puddings, up to half a dozen or more well kept ales such as Bass, Hop Back TEA, Ringwood Fortyniner, Timothy Taylors Landlord, Youngs Special and a beer brewed for them by Hampshire, good choice of wines by the glass, no smoking areas; beware, they may try to keep your credit card while you eat, sports TV; disabled facilities, dogs and children allowed in one area with games machines, tables out on terrace and in garden with substantial play fort, open all day wknds *(R Lake, BB, KC, Sue Plant)*

Sandrock [Sandrock Hill Road]: New chef doing decent reasonably priced food from huge lunchtime sandwiches, pittas and ciabattas through pubby standards to steaks and good fish and vegetarian choice, in basic real ale tavern with well kept Bathams Best, Enville White, Holdens Special and five interesting changing ales from all over, good choice of sensibly priced wines by the glass, friendly knowledgeable staff, real fire, bar billiards in games room, annual beer festival; children and dogs welcome, garden *(Jim Miller, Martin and Karen Wake)*

Post Office address codings confusingly give the impression that some pubs are in Surrey when they're really in Hampshire or London (which is where we list them). And there's further confusion from the way the Post Office still talks about Middlesex – which disappeared in 1965 local government reorganisation.

Sussex

There have been a lot of changes here this year. We have lost one popular main entry, the Woodmans Arms at Hammerpot, to a catastrophic fire, and various other changes and developments have meant that quite a few other pubs have moved from the main entries to the Lucky Dip section. However, we have a good many new finds to replace them: the Stag at Balls Cross, a delightfully unspoilt little country pub; the White Horse at Chilgrove, a stylish inn in lovely surroundings – good food and excellent wines; the Merrie Harriers at Cowbeech, with good food using local produce, and well kept beers; the Star & Garter at East Dean, charmingly reworked by the people who made the Fox Goes Free at Charlton so popular; the Foresters Arms at East Hoathly, enterprising food in a gently updated village pub; the Swan at Fittleworth, another well run country inn, good all round; the Sussex Brewery at Hermitage, good beers and splendid sausages in a nicely old-fashioned atmosphere; the Welldiggers Arms near Petworth, enjoyable food in what looks like a very rustic traditional local but feels quite a cut above that; and the Ypres Castle in Rye, a fine all-rounder, back in these pages under new owners, after a bit of a break. Other pubs on fine form here are the Rose Cottage at Alciston (a classic country pub lovingly run by a caring landlord), the Cricketers Arms at Berwick (another good country all-rounder), the Blackboys Inn (great atmosphere, and nice garden), the Basketmakers Arms in Brighton (this super little corner local has good cheap home-made food and nice house wines), the Fox Goes Free at Charlton (the change of ownership here had us crossing our fingers, but it has worked out really well), the Six Bells at Chiddingly (bargain food in this interesting and cheerful country local), the Coach & Horses at Danehill (good imaginative food in a friendly relaxed atmosphere), the Horse & Groom at East Ashling (a good appealingly laid out all-rounder, more bedrooms this year), the beautifully placed Tiger at East Dean (a great favourite), the Three Horseshoes at Elsted (another favourite all-rounder), the civilised Griffin at Fletching (something for nearly everyone here), the Star at Old Heathfield just outside Heathfield itself (enjoyable food and beer in this friendly old local, and a lovely garden), the Queens Head at Icklesham (good honest food and nice beers in this bustling pub), and the Giants Rest at Wilmington (so well run that what could be quite an ordinary pub appeals immensely). There are plenty of good pubs for an enjoyable special meal out here. Currently top among them is the Griffin at Fletching, our Sussex Dining Pub of the Year. In the Lucky Dip section at the end of the chapter, pubs showing particularly well these days include the Bell in Burwash, Royal Oak at Chilgrove, Hatch at Colemans Hatch, George & Dragon near Coolham, Elsted Inn, Shepherd & Dog at Fulking, Anglesey Arms at Halnaker, Unicorn at Heyshott, George & Dragon at Houghton, Half Moon at Kirdford, Lamb at Lambs Green, Rising Sun at Milland, Cock at Ringmer, Lamb at Ripe, Chequers at Rowhook, Inkerman Arms at Rye Harbour, Crab & Lobster at Sidlesham, Hare & Hounds at Stoughton, Best Beech near Wadhurst and Lamb at West Wittering. Drinks prices here are noticeably higher than the national average. The main local brewer is Harveys, and other local beers you are quite likely to come across here are Ballards, Kings and Arundel, and perhaps Dark Star, Rother Valley, Weltons or Whites. The beer labelled K&B Sussex is brewed for Badger of Dorset by their Gribble pub at Oving (the name recalls King & Barnes, the Horsham brewery bought and closed by Badger a few years ago).

ALCISTON TQ5005 Map 3

Rose Cottage

Village signposted off A27 Polegate—Lewes

After a bracing walk on the South Downs, this bustling country cottage is just the place to head for. It's popular with lots of locals too, and has been owned by the same family for more than 40 years. There are cosy winter log fires, half a dozen tables with cushioned pews under quite a forest of harness, traps, a thatcher's blade and lots of other black ironware, and more bric-a-brac on the shelves above the stripped pine dado or in the etched-glass windows; in the mornings you may also find Jasper the parrot (it can get a little smoky for him in the evenings). Best to arrive early to be sure of a seat. There's a lunchtime overflow into the no smoking restaurant area. Using a local butcher, a fishmonger on the beach at Eastbourne, and as much organic produce as possible, the bar food at lunchtime might include home-made soup (£3.25), farmhouse pâté (£5.75), ploughman's (£5.50), lincolnshire pork sausages with tomato chutney (£5.75), salads (from £5.95), and honey-roast ham and poached egg (£6.25), with evening extras such as scotch steaks (from £10.25), and half a roast duckling with a changing sauce (£13.95); daily specials like hummous with toasted pitta bread (£4.25), vegetarian pancakes topped with tomato sauce, thai chicken curry or wild local rabbit casserole in cream and coarse-grain mustard (all £7.95), whole local plaice with lemon and herb butter (£8.95), and roasted monkfish wrapped in parma ham with a red pepper relish (£10.50). Sunday roast (£7.50). They also sell local eggs, honey and seasonal game. Well kept Harveys Best and a guest such as King Horsham Best on handpump, a good little wine list with good value house wines and a few nice bin ends, and local farm cider; the landlord, whom we have known now for many years, is quite a plain-speaking character. Dominoes, cribbage, darts, and maybe piped classical music. There are gas heaters outside for cooler evenings, and the small paddock in the garden has ducks and chickens. Nearby fishing and shooting. The charming little village (and local church) are certainly worth a look. They only take bedroom bookings for two nights. *(Recommended by R and S Bentley, Trevor and Sylvia Millum, Brian and Andrea Potter, the Didler, Susan and John Douglas, Jane Basso, Richard Haw, Jenny and Peter Lowater, Dr D G Twyman)*

Free house ~ Licensee Ian Lewis ~ Real ale ~ Bar food ~ Restaurant ~ (01323) 870377 ~ Children allowed if over 10 ~ Dogs allowed in bar ~ Open 11.30-3, 6.30-11; 12-3, 6.30-10.30 Sun; closed 25 and 26 Dec, 1 Jan ~ Bedrooms: /£50S

ALFRISTON TQ5203 Map 3

George

High Street

In a lovely village, this 14th-c timbered inn oozes age. The long bar has massive low beams hung with hops, appropriately soft lighting, and a log fire (or summer flower arrangement) in a huge stone inglenook fireplace that dominates the room, with lots of copper and brass around it. Sturdy stripped tables have settles and chairs around them, and there's well kept Greene King IPA, Abbot, and Old Speckled Hen, and maybe a guest beer on handpump; decent wines, dominoes and piped music. Bar food at lunchtime includes deep-fried brie with cumberland sauce (£4.50), vegetable risotto (£5.95), ploughman's or pork-and-leek sausages (£6.50), and steak, mushroom and Guinness suet pudding or ham and free range eggs (£7.50), with evening choices such as warm wild mushroom tartlet (£4.50), salmon fishcakes with a sweet chilli dipping sauce (£4.95), slow braised knuckle of lamb on rosemary and potato mash (£11.95), vodka marinated salmon on hot beetroot (£12.75), and pork loin with ginger and honey on braised fennel (£12.95). Besides the cosy candlelit no smoking restaurant, there's a garden dining room – or you can sit out in the charming flint-walled garden behind. You can escape the crowds on a fine riverside walk down to Cuckmere Haven, and two long-distance paths (South Downs Way and Vanguard Way) cross in the village. *(Recommended by John Davis, E G Parish, Richard and Margaret Peers, A Sadler, Ann and Colin Hunt, Philip and Ann Board, Dr David Cockburn, Len Beattie)*

Greene King ~ Lease Roland and Cate Couch ~ Real ale ~ Bar food (12-2.30, 7-9 (10 Fri-Sat)) ~ Restaurant ~ (01323) 870319 ~ Children in eating area of bar and restaurant ~ Dogs allowed in bar ~ Open 12-11; 12-10.30 Sun; closed 25 and 26 Dec

AMBERLEY SO8401 Map 3

Black Horse

Off B2139

After a walk along the South Downs Way, the garden of this very pretty pub is a restful place to enjoy a drink or lunch, and the views are lovely. The main bar has high-backed settles on flagstones, beams over the serving counter festooned with sheep bells and shepherd's tools (hung by the last shepherd on the Downs), and walls decorated with a mixture of prints and paintings. The lounge bar has many antiques and artefacts collected by the owners on their world travels; there are log fires in both bars and two in the no smoking restaurant. Well liked bar food includes home-made vegetable soup (£3.25), home-made chicken liver pâté (£3.95), deep-fried brie and camembert with cumberland sauce (£4.55), sandwiches with salad and chips or ploughman's (£4.95), lasagne or broccoli and pasta bake (£7.95), steak in ale pie (£8.95), and various curries or chicken with sauces such as bacon and stilton or prawn and lobster (£9.95). Well kept Charles Wells Bombardier and Greene King IPA on handpump, and several malt whiskies; piped music. The garden is a restful place. More reports please. *(Recommended by A Sadler, Brian and Andrea Potter, Ian and Barbara Rankin, Jane Basso, John Davis, Liz and Tony Colman)*

Pubmaster ~ Tenant Gary Tubb ~ Real ale ~ Bar food (12-3, 6-9(10 Fri-Sat); all day Sun) ~ Restaurant ~ (01798) 831552 ~ Children in eating area of bar and in restaurant (must be over 6) ~ Dogs welcome ~ Open 11-11; 12-10.30 Sun

ARLINGTON TQ5407 Map 3

Old Oak

Caneheath, off A22 or A27 NW of Polegate

These 17th-c former almshouses became a public house in the early 1900s and it was first used as an ale and cider house for local agricultural and brick-making workers. Today, as well as locals, there's quite a mix of customers including walkers and their dogs who enjoy sitting in the peaceful garden. The open-plan, L-shaped bar has heavy beams, well spaced tables and comfortable seating, log fires, and a calm, relaxed atmosphere. Well kept Badger Best, Harveys Best, and a guest such as Adnams Broadside or Fullers London Pride tapped from the cask, and several malt whiskies; piped music, darts, chess, draughts, and dominoes. Straightforward bar food includes home-made soup (£3.25), coarse pâté (£4.95), pasta or curry of the day (£6.95), home-made pie of the day or gammon and egg (£7.25), and daily specials like fresh dressed crab or lamb shank in rich minty gravy. The dining area is no smoking. More reports please. *(Recommended by J H Bell, R J Walden, Tony and Wendy Hobden, Jenny and Peter Lowater, Michael and Ann Cole, Father Robert Marsh)*

Free house ~ Licensees Mr J Boots and Mr B Slattery ~ Real ale ~ Bar food (12-2.30, 6.30-9.30; all day weekends) ~ Restaurant ~ (01323) 482072 ~ Children welcome ~ Dogs allowed in bar ~ Live music first Fri of month ~ Open 11-11; 11-10.30 Sun

BALLS CROSS SU9826 Map 2

Stag

Village signposted off A283 at N edge of Petworth, brown sign to pub there too

Charmingly unspoilt, chatty and convivial, this rustic little 16th-c pub stands between the small village and the woods, by a former coaching route. The tiny flagstoned bar has a good winter log fire in its huge inglenook fireplace, just a couple of tables, a window seat, and a few chairs and leather-seated bar stools; on the right a second room with a rug on its bare boards has space for just a single table. Beyond is an appealing old-fashioned dining room, carpeted, with a great many more or less horsey pictures. There are yellowing cream walls and low shiny ochre ceilings throughout, with soft lighting from little fringed wall lamps. On the left a separate carpeted room with a couple of big Victorian prints has table skittles and a good darts alley. Service is welcoming and committed, and they have well kept Badger Best, K&B and Tanglefoot on handpump, decent wines by the glass, summer cider, and some nice malt whiskies. A wide choice of good value food using meat from a local butcher and game caught by the landlord includes filled rolls (from £3), ploughman's (from £5), filled baked potatoes (£5.25), mediterranean vegetable lasagne, macaroni cheese or ham and egg (£6.75), full breakfast (£7.50), seasonal pheasant casserole (£8.25), venison casserole (£8.50), calves liver and bacon (£8.75), and fish pie (£9). The good-sized garden behind, divided by a shrubbery, has teak or cast-iron tables and chairs, picnic-sets, and in summer a couple of canvas awnings; there are more picnic-sets out under green canvas parasols in front, and the hitching rail does get used. The veteran gents' is outside. *(Recommended by J A Snell, John Beeken, Phil and Sally Gorton, R B Gardiner)*

Badger ~ Tenant Hamish Barrie Hiddleston ~ Real ale ~ Bar food (not Sun evening) ~ Restaurant ~ (01403) 820241 ~ Children in restaurant and family room ~ Dogs welcome ~ Open 11-3, 6-11; 12-3, 7-10.30 Sun ~ Bedrooms: £30/£60

BERWICK TQ5105 Map 3

Cricketers Arms

Lower Road, S of A27

At peak times this little country pub – in a tranquil village close to the downs – can get very busy, but if you catch it on a peaceful summer's afternoon, you can sit in the old-fashioned cottagey front garden, and enjoy a meal or a drink amongst the flowering shrubs and plants; there are more seats behind. Inside, the three small similarly furnished rooms (one is no smoking) have simple benches against the half-panelled walls, a pleasant mix of old country tables and chairs, burgundy velvet curtains on poles, a few bar stools, and some country prints; quarry tiles on the floors (nice worn ones in the middle room), two log fires in little brick fireplaces, a huge black supporting beam in each of the low ochre ceilings, and (in the end room) some attractive cricketing pastels; some of the beams are hung with cricket bats. Good straightforward bar food includes garlic mushrooms on sun-dried tomato bread (£5.25), local pâté (£5.50), ploughman's or local sausage and egg (£6.25), warm salads (from £7.50), sirloin steak (£10.95), and daily specials like filo prawns with sweet chilli dip (£4.95), spinach and mushroom lasagne (£6.95), and local cod in batter (£7.50); best to get here early to be sure of a seat as it does fill up quickly. Well kept Harveys Best and two seasonal ales tapped from the cask, and decent wine; shove-ha'penny, cribbage, dominoes, and an old Sussex coin game called toad in the hole. *(Recommended by Peter and Joan Elbra, Ann and Colin Hunt, the Didler, Peter Meister, B and M Kendall, M and R Thomas, Derek Hayman, LM, Guy Vowles, John Beeken, Sue Demont, Tim Barrow, Alan Cowell, Father Robert Marsh)*

Harveys ~ Tenant Peter Brown ~ Real ale ~ Bar food (12-2.15, 6.30-9; all day in summer and winter weekends) ~ (01323) 870469 ~ Children in family room ~ Dogs welcome ~ Open 11-11; 12-10.30 Sun; 11-3, 6-11 weekdays but all day weekends in winter

You can send us reports through our web site: www.goodguides.co.uk

BLACKBOYS TQ5220 Map 3

Blackboys Inn

B2192, S edge of village

In fine weather, there are always lots of customers sitting outside this pretty 14th-c pub at the many rustic tables that overlook the pond in the big garden; more seats on the front lawn under the chestnut trees. Inside, the bustling locals' bar has a chatty and properly pubby atmosphere, and there's a string of old-fashioned and unpretentious little rooms with dark oak beams, bare boards or parquet, antique prints, copious curios (including a collection of keys above the bar), and usually, a good log fire in the inglenook fireplace. Enjoyable food includes snacks like filled baked potatoes and ploughman's, as well as home-made soup (£3.50), roast confit of duck with hoi sin dressing (£6.75), scallop and fine herb risotto (£7.50), breast of corn-fed chicken with vanilla jus and spring greens (£12.95), whole bass with sea salt, olive, lemon juice and salsa verde or chargrilled rib of beef with forestière sauce (£14.95), roast rump of south down lamb with puy lentils and baby vegetables (£15.75), fillets of brill with bouillabaisse reduction, asparagus and vermicelli (£15.95), and puddings such as soft fruit crème brûlée or chocolate and Grand Marnier steamed pudding (from £3.50). The restaurant and dining areas are no smoking; obliging, efficient service even when busy. Well kept Harveys Best, Pale Ale, and a couple of guests like Armada or Porter on handpump, eight wines by the glass, and Addlestone's cider; darts, fruit machine, juke box, cribbage, and dominoes. *(Recommended by Robert M Warner, the Didler, John Davis, J H Bell, Tony and Wendy Hobden, Louise English, Michael and Ann Cole, John Hendy, Len Beattie)*

Harveys ~ Tenant Edward Molesworth ~ Real ale ~ Bar food (not Sun evenings) ~ Restaurant ~ (01825) 890283 ~ Children welcome ~ Dogs allowed in bar ~ Open 11-3, 5(6 Sat)-11; 11-11 Fri; 12-10.30 Sun; closed 1 Jan

BODIAM TQ7825 Map 3

Curlew

B2244 S of Hawkhurst, outside village at crossroads with turn-off to Castle

Just a few minutes from the lovely National Trust castle, this dining pub is popular with both drinkers and diners. There's a relaxed, informal atmosphere, and the main bar has a heavily carved bar counter with bar stools in front of it (and locals enjoying a pint of well kept Harveys Best or Youngs Bitter on handpump), a woodburning stove, and hops along the beams. Off to the right is a smaller room mainly used for dining, with timbered red walls, mirrors that give an impression of more space, and a piano. The restaurant has black timbers, more hops on beams, and pictures that are mainly trompe-l'oeuil ones of life-size wine bottles looking as if they are in wood-framed alcoves; some sunny watercolour landscapes, too, and interesting photographs in the gents'. All eating areas are no smoking. Good attractively presented lunchtime bar food might include home-made soup (£4.25), sandwiches or filled baguettes (from £5.95; all come with chips), a cheese plate with fresh baguette, biscuits and butter (£6.95), confit of duck leg or fresh pasta with tomato and basil sauce (£9.95), chicken curry with coconut cream (£10.95), fish and chips in light batter with garlic mayonnaise (£11.95), and calves liver and bacon with garlic mash and caramelised onion gravy (£12.95); you can also choose from the restaurant menu (no bar food in the evening) with dishes such as wild mushrooms on home-made toasted brioche with wild mushroom and truffle cream sauce (£7.95), tortellini of lemon sole and chives with fresh asparagus, deep-fried carrots and leeks and a fish cream froth (£8.50), pressed beetroot and thyme risotto cake with fresh spinach and a ratatouille of mediterranean vegetables (£13.95), and breasts of pigeon and fried foie gras with savoy cabbage and smoked bacon, fondant potato, and madeira sauce (£14.95). Daily specials, and super puddings like caramelised vanilla panna cotta with raspberries and oranges soaked in Grand Marnier, sticky toffee and treacle pudding with sticky toffee sauce and warm vanilla custard, and a pudding of the day (£6.95). You can eat outside on the pretty terrace in fine weather, surrounded by flowering baskets and troughs. More reports please. *(Recommended by Alan Cole, Kirstie Bruce, Susan and John Douglas, Gene and Kitty Rankin)*

Free house ~ Licensee Andy Blyth ~ Bar food (not Sun evening or Mon) ~ Restaurant ~ (01580) 861394 ~ Children in eating area of bar and restaurant ~ Dogs allowed in bar ~ Open 11.30-3, 6(6.30 Sat)-11; 12-5 Sun; closed Sun evening, Mon

BRIGHTON TQ3105 Map 3

Basketmakers Arms £

Gloucester Road – the E end, near Cheltenham Place; off Marlborough Place (A23) via Gloucester Street

As there's not a lot of space in this bustling little corner pub, it's best to get here early, especially at weekends. There's a really cheerful, chatty atmosphere, and both the locals and staff behind the bar are friendly and welcoming. The two small rooms have brocaded wall benches and stools on the stripped wood floor, lots of interesting old tins all over the walls, cigarette cards on one beam with whisky labels on another, beermats, and some old photographs and posters; quiet piped music. Good value enjoyable bar food includes lots of sandwiches (from £2.25; chicken and avocado £2.95; hot salt beef on granary £3.25), particularly good home-made meaty and vegetarian burgers (£2.60), baked potatoes with fillings such as beef, chilli and yoghurt (£3.35), ploughman's (£3.75), and specials such as steak in ale pie, local sausages with red onion and wine gravy, fajitas topped with melted cheese, salsa and salad, and lasagne (all £4.50), swordfish steak with garlic and lemon mayonnaise (£5.25), and summer niçoise salad (£5.75). Well kept Gales Bitter, GB, HSB, and seasonal ales, and a guest such as Charles Wells Bombardier; good wines (house wines come in three different glass sizes), and over 80 malt whiskies. *(Recommended by R J Walden, Ann and Colin Hunt, the Didler, Tony and Wendy Hobden, MLR, B and M Kendall, LM)*

Gales ~ Tenants P and K Dowd, A Mawer, J Archdeacon ~ Real ale ~ Bar food (12-3, 5.30-8.30; 12-3.30 Sat; 12-4 Sun; not Sat-Sun evenings) ~ (01273) 689006 ~ Children welcome until 8pm ~ Dogs welcome ~ Open 11-11; 12-10.30 Sun; closed 26 Dec

BURPHAM TQ0308 Map 3

George & Dragon

Warningcamp turn off A27 outside Arundel: follow road up and up

There's quite an emphasis on dining here and most customers do come to eat, though there is still a small bar area where drinkers enjoy the well kept beers from Arundel, Fullers, Harveys, and Kings on handpump. Bar food includes sandwiches, seafood platter (£5.25; main course £10.50), lambs liver and bacon or mushroom tortellini with cream, basil and tomato sauce (£8.95), and steak and horseradish pie (£9.95), with puddings like white chocolate mousse, sticky toffee pudding or raspberry crème brûlée (£5.25). The neatly kept, spacious open-plan bar has good strong wooden furnishings, lots of interesting prints, and a decent wine list; piped music. A short walk away are splendid views down to Arundel Castle and the river – plenty of pretty surrounding walks, too. The Norman church has some unusual decoration. More reports please. *(Recommended by Terry and Linda Moseley, A Sadler, Karen Eliot, Keith Stevens, John Davis, A and B D Craig, Mike and Gill Gadsden, J P Humphery, John Hendy, R T and J C Moggridge)*

Free house ~ Licensees James Rose and Kate Holle ~ Real ale ~ Bar food (not Sun evening) ~ Restaurant ~ (01903) 883131 ~ Well behaved children over 8 in restaurant ~ Open 11-2.30, 6-11; 12-3, 7-10.30 Sun; closed Sun evening Oct-Easter

The symbol shows pubs which keep their beer unusually well, have a particularly good range or brew their own.

BYWORTH SU9820 Map 2

Black Horse

Off A283

As we went to press new licensees were about to take over this charming old country pub. The simply furnished though smart bar has pews and scrubbed wooden tables on its bare floorboards, pictures and old photographs on the walls, large open fires, and newspapers to read; no noisy music or games machines to spoil the chatty atmosphere. The back dining room has lots of nooks and crannies, and there's an upstairs restaurant with lovely views of the downs. Good interesting bar food now includes sandwiches, soup like pepper and tomato (£2.95), duck, orange and mango salad with honey and ginger dressing or smoked salmon and dill pâté with melba toast (£4.95), moules marinière (£5.95), steak and kidney pudding or thai crab cakes with sweet chilli dressing (£8.95), roasted guinea fowl stuffed with pork and apple with an orange and red onion marmalade (£9.95), whole bass with butter and fresh herbs (£12.95), and puddings such as sticky chocolate pudding or treacle tart (£4.95). Well kept Cheriton Pots Ale and Village Elder, Courage Best, and Hogs Back TEA on handpump. The particularly attractive garden has tables on a steep series of grassy terraces sheltered by banks of flowering shrubs that look across a drowsy valley to swelling woodland. *(Recommended by Tom and Rosemary Hall, Cathy Robinson, Ed Coombe, David Cosham, John Beeken, Tony and Wendy Hobden, H H Hellin, John Davis, R B Gardiner, John Evans)*

Cockerel Inns ~ Tenants Robert Carter and Lorraine Kimber ~ Real ale ~ Bar food ~ Restaurant ~ (01798) 342424 ~ Children welcome ~ Dogs welcome ~ Open 11-3, 5-11; 11-11 Sat; 11-10.30 Sun

CHARLTON SU8812 Map 3

Fox Goes Free

Village signposted off A286 Chichester—Midhurst in Singleton, also from Chichester—Petworth via East Dean

Under its new licensee, this place is doing very well and readers have been quick to voice their enthusiasm. It's a cheerful, well run old pub with a good mix of customers and a buoyant atmosphere. The first of the dark and cosy series of separate rooms is a small bar with three tables, a few very mixed chairs and an open fireplace. Standing timbers divide a larger beamed bar which has old and new elm furniture, a huge brick fireplace with a woodburning stove, a couple of elderly armchairs, red tiles and carpet, and brasses and old local photographs on the yellowed walls. A dining area with hunting prints looks over the garden and the South Downs beyond. The family extension is a clever conversion from horse boxes and the stables where the 1926 Goodwood winner was housed; darts, cribbage, dominoes and fruit machine. Well kept Arundel Stronghold, Ballards Best, Fox Goes Free (brewed for the pub by Arundel), and Ringwoods Boondoggle on handpump, and several wines by the glass. As well as snacks like home-made chilli (£7.50), honey roast ham with free range eggs (£8), and curry (£9), the attractively presented, very good food might include summer salads of warm chorizo, red onion and goats cheese or bacon, avocado and pine nut (£7.95), starters like popular baked brie and almonds with redcurrant jelly (£4.95), local crab and cheese bake (£5.50), and king prawns in garlic butter (£6.50), main courses such as mushroom and parmesan risotto (£8.50), well liked steak and kidney pie (£8.75), venison with creamed mushroom and spinach or bream with a rhubarb and pear salad (£13.50), and fillet steak with peppercorn sauce and rocket salad (£15.95), and puddings like sticky toffee pudding with toffee sauce or baked american raspberry cheesecake (£4.50). Best to book to be sure of a table. The attractive garden has several terraces, plenty of picnic-sets among fruit trees, and a notable downland view; the barbecue area can be booked. Goodwood Racecourse is not far away (on race days it does get very busy), it's also handy for the Weald and Downland Open Air Museum, and there are some fine surrounding walks. *(Recommended by Susan and John Douglas, Keith Stevens, Martin and Karen Wake, Robert M Warner, Neil Rose,*

W W Burke, Felicity Stephens, David Fox, John Davis, Michael and Ann Cole, P R and S A White, Ian Wilson, Ann and Colin Hunt, Richard Haw, M B Griffith, Gordon Neighbour, Philip and Ann Board, R B Gardiner, Mrs Sheela Curtis, Gene and Kitty Rankin)

Free house ~ Licensee David Coxon ~ Real ale ~ Bar food (12-2.30, 6.30-10) ~ (01243) 811461 ~ Children welcome ~ Dogs allowed in bar and bedrooms ~ Live music fortnightly Weds evening ~ Open 11-11; 12-10.30 Sun ~ Bedrooms: £40S/£60S

CHIDDINGLY TQ5414 Map 3

Six Bells ★ £

Village signed off A22 Uckfield—Hailsham

There's always a chatty, bustling atmosphere in this happily old-fashioned pub, and you can be sure of a genuinely friendly welcome from the cheerful, long-standing landlord. As well as log fires, the bars have solid old wood furnishings including pews and antique seats, lots of fusty artefacts and interesting bric-a-brac, and plenty of local pictures and posters. A sensitive extension provides some much needed family space; dominoes and cribbage. Particularly for this part of the country, the bar food is a bargain: straightforward but tasty, there might be french onion soup (£2.50), filled baguettes, steak and kidney pie (£3.50), baked potatoes (from £4.20), ploughman's (from £4.75), ravioli in spicy sauce, spare ribs in barbecue sauce, tuna pasta bake or chicken curry (all £5.50), and puddings like treacle tart or banoffi pie (£3). Well kept Courage Directors, Harveys Best, and a guest such as John Smiths on handpump. Outside at the back, there are some tables beyond a big raised goldfish pond, and a boules pitch; the church opposite has an interesting Jefferay monument. Vintage and Kit car meetings outside the pub every month. This is a pleasant area for walks. *(Recommended by David and Pam Wilcox, Guy Vowles, B and M Kendall, Humphry and Angela Crum Ewing, Tony and Wendy Hobden, Michael and Ann Cole)*

Free house ~ Licensees Paul Newman and Emma Bannister ~ Real ale ~ Bar food (12-2.30, 6-10; 12-10 Sat, 12-9 Sun) ~ (01825) 872227 ~ Children in family room ~ Dogs allowed in bar ~ Live music Fri-Sat evenings and Sun lunchtime; jazz and folk Tues evening ~ Open 11-3, 6-11; 11-12 Sat; 12-10.30 Sun

CHILGROVE SU8214 Map 2

White Horse 🍷

B2141 Petersfield—Chichester

From outside, this former 18th-c coaching inn certainly looks the part, with its tiled roof and long white-painted façade covered with wisteria. Inside, it has a much more up-to-date feel, civilised and quietly upmarket – certainly more inn than pub, though service is so helpful and friendly that you do feel immediately welcome. The bar counter is made up from claret, burgundy and other mainly french wooden wine cases, and good wines by the glass, with an impressive range by the bottle, are a big plus here; they also have well kept Ballards on handpump. Dark brown deco leather armchairs and a sofa are grouped on dark boards here, and on either side are three or four well spaced good-sized sturdy tables with good pale spindleback side and elbow chairs on lighter newer boards; a feeling of freshness is accentuated by the big bow window, uncluttered cream walls and ceiling, and clear lighting. There may be piped music, well reproduced. Besides a good range of sandwiches, Spanish staff prepare enjoyable if not cheap light lunchtime dishes such as air-dried ham with melon or pigeon breast salad or mediterranean fish soup (£7.95), seared scallops (£11.95) and crab, avocado and prawn salad (£13.95), and sturdier dishes such as liver and pancetta (£12.95), lemon sole or baked crab from Selsey (£13.95), pork fillet with apple compote and port sauce (£14.95), and turbot or veal with truffles and shallots (£16.95). The bar has a woodburner on one side, and a log fire on the other. Past here, it opens into a similarly fresh-styled restaurant with comfortable modern seats and attractively laid tables – as in the bar, generously spaced out. Outside, one neat lawn has white cast-iron tables and chairs under an old yew tree, and another has wooden benches, tables and picnic-sets under a tall flag mast; completely no smoking. This is a lovely downland valley with lots of fine walks nearby, and the road through is a good one, and fairly quiet. We have not yet heard from readers who have stayed in the eight bedrooms here, but would expect this to be a nice place to stay in. *(Recommended by RDK, Ian Phillips, John Davis)*

Free house ~ Licensee Charles Burton ~ Real ale ~ Bar food (12-2, 6-10) ~ Restaurant ~ (01243) 535219 ~ Children welcome ~ Dogs welcome ~ Open 10-3, 6-10; closed Sun evening, Mon ~ Bedrooms: £47.50B/£95B

COMPTON SU7714 Map 2

Coach & Horses

B2146 S of Petersfield

With half a dozen real ales and good food, it's not surprising that this 17th-c village local is popular with both regulars and visitors. There's an open fire in the roomy front public bar, and the Village Bar has pine shutters and panelling, and the original pitched pine block floor has been restored; an open fire in the roomy front public bar. It is here that the enjoyable food, cooked by the landlord, is served: sandwiches or filled baguettes (from £3.95), home-made soup (£3.10), black pudding, bacon and poached egg salad or lamb sweetbreads on spinach (£5.25), chicken and mushroom pie (£8.95), baked aubergine with chargrilled peppers and brie (£9.25), and chicken breast with grain mustard and almond sauce (£9.75). The charming little plush beamed lounge bar serves as a relaxing ante-room to the attractive restaurant. Well kept Ballards Best, Triple fff Moondance, Fullers ESB, Hepworth Old Cocky, Palmers 200, and Stonehenge Sign of Spring on handpump; old-fashioned juke box, bar billiards and fruit machine. There are tables out by the square in front; it's not far from Uppark (NT). *(Recommended by Ian Phillips, John Evans, John Davis, Ann and Colin Hunt, Andy and Jill Kassube, Paul A Moore, Tracey and Stephen Groves, R T and J C Moggridge)*

Free house ~ Licensees David and Christiane Butler ~ Real ale ~ Bar food ~ Restaurant ~ (023) 9263 1228 ~ Children in eating area of bar and restaurant ~ Dogs allowed in bar ~ Open 11.30-2.30(3 Sat), 6-11; 12-3, 7-10.30 Sun; closed one week late Feb

COWBEECH TQ6114 Map 3

Merrie Harriers

Village signed from A271

Once a farmhouse, this is a white-clapboarded village inn in the heart of the Weald. The beamed and panelled bar has a log fire in the brick inglenook, quite a mix of tables and chairs, beers from Adnams and Harveys on handpump, and several wines by the glass. Using fresh local produce, the well liked bar food at lunchtime includes seasonal vegetable soup (£4.25), sandwiches (from £4.25; poached salmon and watercress £4.95), potted brown shrimps (£4.95), salad of buffalo mozzarella, rocket and vine tomatoes (£5.50), ploughman's (£6.95), honey roast gammon with home-made piccalilli and sautéed potatoes (£7.95), pork, honey and mustard sausages with apple sauce or fillet of local cod in breadcrumbs (£8.95), and steak in ale pie (£9.95); in the evening there might be locally smoked duck breast with parmesan shavings and a balsamic dressing (£5.95), carpaccio of beef fillet with beetroot salad and horseradish sauce (£6.95), salmon fishcakes with parsley sauce (£9.95), corn-fed chicken breast with sunblush tagliatelle and tarragon dressing (£12.95), sliced gressingham duck breast with plum chutney (£13.95), rack of lamb with thyme jus (£15.95), and whole dover sole with lemon and parsley butter (£16.95), with puddings like warm chocolate brownie with white belgian chocolate ice-cream, ginger scented pavlova with poached rhubarb, and raspberry crème brûlée with raspberry ice-cream and shortbread; regular gourmet evenings. The brick-walled and oak-ceilinged back restaurant is no smoking. There are rustic seats amongst colourful shrubs and pots in the terraced garden, and country views. *(Recommended by PL, Rob Winstanley)*

Free house ~ Licensees Roger Cotton and Lesley Day ~ Real ale ~ Bar food ~ Restaurant ~ (01323) 833108 ~ Children in eating area of bar and restaurant ~ Dogs allowed in bar ~ Jazz first Thurs of month ~ Open 11.30-3(4 Sat), 6-11; 12-4, 6-10.30 Sun

DANEHILL TQ4128 Map 3

Coach & Horses 🍴 🍷

From A275 in Danehill (S of Forest Row), take School Lane towards Chelwood Common

You can be sure of a warm welcome from the friendly staff in this well run cottagey pub, set in attractive countryside. There's a little public bar to the right with half-panelled walls, simple furniture on highly polished wooden floorboards, a small woodburning stove in the brick fireplace, and a big hatch to the bar; darts, cribbage and dominoes. The main bar is on the left with plenty of locals crowding around the wooden bar counter or sitting at the high wooden bar stools enjoying the well kept Harveys Best, and guests like Badger Horsham Best and Robinsons Best on handpump; good wines by the generous glass, and summer champagne-method cider. Leading from this bar is a terrace (adults only) under a huge maple tree which catches the evening sun. Drinks are stacked in a nice old-fashioned way on shelves behind the bar, and there's just one table on the stripped wood floor here. A couple of steps lead down to a half-panelled area with a mix of wheelbacks and old dining chairs around several characterful wooden tables on the fine brick floor, a large lantern in the tiny brick fireplace, and some large Victorian prints; candles and flowers on the tables. Down another step to the no smoking dining area with stone walls, a beamed vaulted ceiling, hops hanging from other beams, and a woodburning stove; through a lovely arched doorway is a small room with just a couple of tables. The food is very good and might include sandwiches on open granary, ciabattas or white french bread (from £3.95; pesto, mozzarella and tomato £4.95; grilled roasted pepper and goats cheese £5.25), fried chicken livers with puy lentils on toasted brioche (£5.95), pressed rabbit and foie gras terrine or sautéed scallops with beetroot salad and horseradish crème fraîche (£6.75), potato and herb gnocchi with shaved parmesan and basil oil (£8.95), chargrilled chicken breast with pearl barley and bacon (£10.25), fillet of bass with herb risotto (£12.75), and rib-eye steak (£13.50), with puddings such as caramel vanilla panna cotta with orange segments, peanut parfait with marinated grapes, and white chocolate mousse with ginger sponge (£4.25). The big attractive garden has plenty of seats. *(Recommended by Tony and Wendy Hobden, Mrs J R Sillitoe, Peter Meister, RDK, Neill Barker, Derek and Maggie Washington, Debbie and Neil Hayter, Dominic Morgan, B J Harding, Ron Gentry, A Sadler, Pete Walker, Alan Cowell)*

Free house ~ Licensee Ian Philpots ~ Real ale ~ Bar food (till 9.30 Fri and Sat; not Sun evening exc bank hol wknds) ~ Restaurant ~ (01825) 740369 ~ Well behaved, seated children welcome ~ Dogs allowed in bar ~ Open 11.30(4 Sat)-3, 6-11; 12-4, 7-10.30 Sun; closed evening 25 Dec, 26 Dec and evening 1 Jan

DONNINGTON SU8502 Map 2

Blacksmiths Arms

Turn off A27 on to A286 signposted Selsey, then almost immediately left on to B2201

Although many customers do come to this little white roadside cottage to enjoy the food, there's plenty of provision for those dropping in for just a drink, and several real ales to choose from. The small low-ceilinged rooms have Victorian prints on the walls, solid, comfortable furnishings, and a relaxed atmosphere; the back no smoking restaurant is very airy and pleasant. Well liked bar food includes soup (£4.25), sandwiches (£4.25; filled baguettes £5.25; ciabattas £5.95), filled baked potatoes (£5.25), roasted ham with bubble and squeak and a poached egg (£6.75), good steak, kidney and ale pie, fishcakes, sun-dried tomato, courgette and aubergine lasagne or curry (all £6.95), daily specials like calves liver (£10.25), beef stroganoff (£10.95), and chargrilled tuna (£11.95), and evening choices such as home-made duck liver, foie gras and armagnac pâté (£4.95), apricot and thyme pork chop with herby potatoes, parsnip and pears (£9.95), corn-fed chicken with baby ratatouille and goats cheese croquettes (£11.95), and scotch rib-eye steak (£12.95); there's also a fish menu with dishes like fillets of red mullet and shrimp with lemon and herb caesar salad (£13.95), and two-course Sunday lunch (£10.95).

Well kept Fullers London Pride, Greene King Abbot, Oakleaf Bitter and Squirrel's Delight on handpump; piped music. The big garden has a play area with swings, a climbing frame, two rabbits called Barnham and Blu, two dogs (Tess and Cleo), a cat (Amber), and four tortoises (only allowed in the garden on special occasions), and plenty of picnic-sets. *(Recommended by Paul A Moore, Bob and Margaret Holder, Bruce Bird, A and B D Craig, Ann and Colin Hunt, Tracey and Stephen Groves, Martin and Karen Wake, Tony and Wendy Hobden)*

InnSpired ~ Tenant Lesley Ward ~ Real ale ~ Bar food ~ Restaurant ~ (01243) 783999 ~ Children welcome ~ Dogs welcome ~ Open 11.30-3, 5.30-11; 11.30-11 Sat; 12-10.30 Sun

DUNCTON SU9617 Map 3

Cricketers

Set back from A285

Another new licensee has taken this pretty little white pub, and as we went to press was about to open what had been the function room into a no smoking restaurant with quite an emphasis on fish. The bar has a few standing timbers giving the room an open-plan feel, there's an inglenook fireplace at one end with a good winter fire, cricketing pictures and paintings and bats on the walls, and a mix of country chairs around scrubbed wooden tables; down a couple of steps a similarly furnished no smoking room is set for eating – piped music here. Bar food now includes sardine bruschetta (£4.50), chicken liver pâté or black pudding and crispy bacon with cinammon apple compote (£4.95), filled baguettes or tortilla wraps (from £4.95), ploughman's (from £5.50), pasta of the day (£7.95), peppered beef, mushroom and Guinness pie (£8.50), fisherman's bag (mixed fish and shellfish baked in a bag £9.25), popular fresh fish in beer and citrus zest batter (£9.95), and puddings such as popular chocolate brownie or a daily cheesecake (£4.50). Well kept Youngs Bitter and a couple of guests from Ballards on handpump, and several decent wines by the glass; shove-ha'penny, cribbage and dominoes. The charming garden behind the building has a proper barbecue, picnic-sets, and an attractive little creeper-covered seating area, and the flowering baskets and tubs at the front are very lovely. More reports on the new regime please. *(Recommended by Tracey and Stephen Groves, Felicity Stephens, David Fox, Nigel Williamson, J A Snell, Jason Caulkin, A and B D Craig, David Cosham, Roger Endersby)*

Inn Company ~ Tenant David Mcaree ~ Real ale ~ Bar food (12-9.30) ~ Restaurant ~ (01798) 342473 ~ Children welcome ~ Dogs allowed in bar ~ Open 11-11; 12-10.30 Sun

EAST ASHLING SU8207 Map 2

Horse & Groom

B2178 NW of Chichester

Six bedrooms in a newly built wing have been added to this bustling and friendly country pub, and there's also a new conservatory restaurant extension overlooking the garden. With a good mix of customers, the front part is a proper bar with old pale flagstones and a woodburning stove in a big inglenook on the right, a carpeted area with an old wireless set, nice scrubbed trestle tables, and bar stools along the counter serving well kept Brewsters Hophead, Harveys Best, Hop Back Summer Lightning, and Youngs on handpump. They also have eight wines by the glass and Addlestone's cider. A couple of tables share a small light flagstoned middle area with the big blackboard that lists changing dishes such as parsnip soufflé with cheddar cheese (£5.30), steak in ale pie (£9.35), calves liver and bacon or chicken breast in plum and hoi sin sauce (£10.20), rack of lamb with honey and rosemary jus (£12.95), and steaks (from £13.95); also, snacks such as sandwiches and filled baguettes (from £3), filled baked potatoes (from £3.95), ploughman's (from £5.45), and home-cooked ham and eggs (£6.25). The back part of the pub, entirely no smoking and angling right round behind the bar servery, with a further extension beyond one set of internal windows, has solid pale country-kitchen furniture on neat bare boards, and a fresh and airy décor, with a little bleached pine panelling and long white curtains. French windows lead out to a garden with picnic-sets under cocktail parasols. Always popular with local people in the know, the pub gets extremely busy on Goodwood race days. *(Recommended by P R and S A White, Ann and Colin Hunt, Jane Basso, Andy and Jill Kassube, J Wakeling, Roger Endersby, Cynthia McKinley, Mrs A P Lee, Bruce Bird, Richard Waller, Pauline Smith)*

Free house ~ Licensee Michael Martell ~ Real ale ~ Bar food (12-2.15, 6.30-9.15; not Sun evening) ~ Restaurant ~ (01243) 575339 ~ Children in eating area of bar and restaurant ~ Dogs allowed in bar and bedrooms ~ Open 12-3, 6-11; 12-6 Sun ~ Bedrooms: £40S/£60B

EAST CHILTINGTON TQ3715 Map 3

Jolly Sportsman

2 miles N of B2116; Chapel Lane – follow sign to 13th-c church

Even when this tucked away and civilised Victorian dining pub is at its busiest, service remains friendly and helpful. The food is imaginative and extremely good, and includes a fixed price menu (two courses £12.85, three courses £16.60), as well as cockle, tomato and saffron pasta (£5.75), sicilian-style sardine fillets with couscous (£5.85), serrano ham with pickled figs (£6.85), fresh herb omelette (£8.75), wild mushroom linguini (£9.50), cornish hake fillet with fresh chanterelles, wine and cream (£13.25), chargrilled peppered aberdeen angus rib-eye steak or free range chicken breast with artichokes, salsify and wild mushrooms (£15.85), best end of local lamb, dijon mustard and herb crust (£16.85), and puddings such as chocolate and griotte cherry loaf with coffee sauce, raspberry champagne jelly with grappa panna cotta or coconut tart with rum and raisin ice-cream (from £5.25). A couple of chairs by the fireplace are set aside for drinkers in the chatty little bar with stripped wood floors and a mix of furniture, but most people head for the smart but informal no smoking restaurant with contemporary light wood furniture, and modern landscapes on green painted walls. Two well kept ales from breweries such as Brewsters, Dark Star or Mauldons are tapped from the cask, there's a remarkably good wine list with nine wines by the glass, farm cider, 68 malt whiskies, and quite a few natural fruit drinks. There are rustic tables and benches under gnarled trees in a pretty cottagey front garden with more on the terrace and the front bricked area, and the large back lawn with a children's play area looks out towards the South Downs; good walks nearby. *(Recommended by John Hale, A C English, Michael and Ann Cole, Cathy Robinson, Ed Coombe, Margaret and Anthony D'Arcy, Pamela Goodwyn)*

Free house ~ Licensee Bruce Wass ~ Real ale ~ Bar food (till 10 Fri and Sat) ~ Restaurant ~ (01273) 890400 ~ Children welcome ~ Dogs welcome ~ Open 12-2.30, 6-11; 12-4 Sun; closed Sun evening, all day Mon

EAST DEAN SU9012 Map 2

Star & Garter

Village signposted with Charlton off A286 in Singleton; also signposted off A285; N of Chichester – OS Sheet 197 map reference 904129

This quietly set brick and flint pub is a new venture by the people who made the Fox Goes Free over at Charlton so popular. They have made a fine job of converting it (we knew it before, too – it's altogether nicer now). Inside, it is more or less one roomy square area, with sturdy and individual mainly stripped and scrubbed tables in various sizes and an interesting variety of seating from country-kitchen chairs through chunky modern dining chairs to cushioned pews and some handsome 17th-c or 18th-c carved oak seats, broad stripped boards, a few stripped beams, some stripped panelling and masonry. The high ceiling, big windows and uncluttered walls give a light and airy feel, and tables over on the right-hand side can be booked. The bar counter (with a few bar stools) is over on the left, with a dozen or so well chosen wines by the glass, well kept Ballards Trotton, Best and Nyewood Gold tapped from casks in a back stillroom, a couple of farm ciders such as Weston's and Mr Whitehead's, good malt whiskies, and an espresso machine. The owners and staff are friendly, concerned and relaxed, making for a good easy-going atmosphere; there is a rack of daily papers by the entrance; piped music. The food includes a good range of baguettes (from £4.50), omelettes (from £5), ploughman's (£6), chicken, chorizo and red onion salad (£9.50), roast pigeon breast with braised red cabbage and red wine reduction (£12), and plenty of fish and seafood such as garlic prawns (£6.50), dressed crab or smoked wild-caught salmon (£8.50 – so much better than the ubiquitous farmed stuff), smoked haddock topped with a poached egg (£10.50), baked crab (£11), lobster from Selsey (£12 for a half), seared scallops with roasted pepper risotto (£15.50) and john dory with stir-fried vegetables and noodles (£16.50). The sheltered terrace behind has teak tables and chairs with big canvas parasols and heaters; steps go up to a walled lawn with picnic-sets (there are also a few steps up to the front door). We have not yet heard from readers who have used the three bedrooms here since the conversion, but would expect this to qualify for a Place to Stay Award. It is well placed for walks, and on the South Downs Way. *(Recommended by Jason Caulkin, Jeremy and Angela Williams)*

Free house ~ Licensee Oliver Ligertwood ~ Real ale ~ Bar food (12-2.30, 6.30-10) ~ Restaurant ~ (01243) 811318 ~ Children in eating area of bar ~ Dogs allowed in bar ~ Live music Tues evening ~ Open 11-3, 6-11; 11-11 Sat; 12-10.30 Sun ~ Bedrooms: £45S(£50B)/£70S(£90B)

EAST DEAN TV5597 Map 3

Tiger 🍷

Pub (with village centre) signposted – not vividly – from A259 Eastbourne—Seaford

This is a smashing old pub and a favourite with a great many customers. It's in an idyllic spot by a secluded sloping village green lined with similar low cottages, and the outside is brightened up with lovely flowering climbers and window boxes in summer. Inside, there are just nine tables in the two smallish rooms (candlelit at night) so space at peak times is very limited – particularly in winter when you can't stand outside or sit on the grass; they don't, in the best pub tradition, take bookings so you do have to arrive early for a table. There are low beams hung with pewter and china, polished rustic tables and distinctive antique settles, and old prints and so forth. Well kept Harveys Best with guests such as Adnams Best or Broadside, and Brakspears Bitter on handpump, and a good choice of wines with a dozen by the large glass; cribbage and dominoes. They get their fish fresh from Hastings, their lamb from the farm on the hill, all vegetables and eggs from another local farm, and meat from the local butcher. From a sensibly short but ever changing menu, the imaginative food at lunchtime might include a choice of 20 different ploughman's (£5.95), home-made potato, leek and cheddar tart (£6.95), home-made tuna fishcakes with lemon mayonnaise or a bowl of feta, hummous, black olives and cherry tomato salad (£7.95), fresh local crab salad or casseroles of pork in cider or rich beef burgundy (£8.95), and fresh large whole prawns (£9.95); in the evening, there might be locally smoked breast of duck salad, locally cured gravadlax with walnut bread or local rabbit stew with bacon and cream (£7.95), chargrilled breast of chicken on home-made salsa of local asparagus, rocket, toasted pine nuts and new potatoes (£8.95), and fresh grilled fillets of bass on pak choi with soy dressing (£9.95). At lunchtimes on hot days and bank holidays they usually have only cold food. The South Downs Way is close by so it's naturally popular with walkers, and the lane leads on down to a fine stretch of coast culminating in Beachy Head. No children inside. *(Recommended by Father Robert Marsh, Susan and John Douglas, Tony and Vivien Smith, John Davis, Karen Eliot, Ann and Colin Hunt, Uta and John Owlett, Phyl and Jack Street, Jennifer Fisher, Andrea Rampley, John Beeken, Jenny and Peter Lowater, Miss Valerie Eckl, M B Griffith, Sebastian and Paris Leach, Michael and Ann Cole, Mike Gorton, Philip and Ann Board, Sue Demont, Tim Barrow)*

Free house ~ Licensee Nicholas Denyer ~ Real ale ~ Bar food ~ No credit cards ~ (01323) 423209 ~ Dogs welcome ~ Open 11-3, 6-11; 11-11 Sat; 12-10.30 Sun

Planning a day in the country? We list pubs in really attractive scenery at the back of the book.

EAST HOATHLY TQ5116 Map 3

Foresters Arms

Village signposted off A22 Hailsham—Uckfield (take south-easternmost of the two turn-offs); South Street

The new young licensees have refreshed this village pub, giving it a bit of an emphasis on good reasonably priced food without losing its simplicity and relaxed local atmosphere. The bar has two small linked rooms, with just a handful of tables on its parquet floor (one in a bow window), simple pub seating including a sturdy winged settle, eau de nil wallpaper and dark woodwork; the one on the right has a small art nouveau fireplace under a big mirror, and its ceiling is papered with sheet music, from J S Bach to 'Yes! We Have No Bananas!' and French songs of a similar vintage. Back from here is a bigger room with mulberry walls and ceiling over a panelled dado, a collection of musical instruments on one wall, a piano, and some sturdy cushioned oak settles; darts, cribbage, dominoes and shove-ha'penny. The food, all freshly cooked, might include fresh oysters (£1 each), mushroom soup (£2.95), sandwiches such as beef, crab or crayfish (£3.95, with soup £4.95), parma ham with roasted peppers and peanuts, a pint of shell-on prawns, game pâté or hot sautéed prawns with teriyaki sauce (all £4.95), filo-wrapped king prawns with a chilli dip (£5.95; main course £7.95), home-baked ham and egg or a choice of ploughman's (£5.95), mussels steamed with cream (£5.95, main course £7.95 – something of a speciality here), very popular beer-battered fish (£7.95), mint-marinated local lamb chops, steak and kidney pudding, smoked haddock and chive fishcakes or crispy duck confit (all £8.95), steaks (rib-eye £11.95), puddings such as sticky toffee or summer puddings (£3.95), and local cheeses with biscuits and fruit (£4.95). With 24 hours' notice and for at least two people, they do a special paella (£10 each) – and more humbly, evening take-away fish and home-made chips or thai curry (£5, not Sunday). On the left, a charming library-style no smoking carpeted dining room, not cut off from the rest of the pub, has just five candlelit tables. Under high beams, hop bines and copper pans, the mahogany bar counter has well kept Harveys Best on handpump, decent wines by the glass, and good coffee. There may be unobtrusive piped music. Service is informal, helpful and friendly, and there is good wheelchair access. A few picnic-sets with cocktail parasols stand out in front. *(Recommended by BOB)*

Harveys ~ Tenants Gary Skipsey and Lindsay Coates ~ Real ale ~ Bar food (12-2.30, 6.30-9.15) ~ Restaurant ~ (01825) 840208 ~ Children welcome if eating ~ Dogs welcome ~ Live music Thurs evening ~ Open 11-3, 5-11; 12-10.30 Sun

ELSTED SU8119 Map 2

Three Horseshoes

Village signposted from B2141 Chichester—Petersfield; also reached easily from A272 about 2 miles W of Midhurst, turning left heading W

In summer, the lovely garden here with free-roaming bantams, plenty of tables, pretty flowers, and marvellous downland views, is quite a draw. But it's just as nice in winter as the snug little rooms have ancient beams and flooring, antique furnishings, lovely log fires, fresh flowers on the tables, attractive prints and photographs, candlelight, and a very congenial atmosphere. Popular, enjoyable bar food includes home-made soup (£3.95), a generous ploughman's with a good choice of cheeses (£6.50), mozzarella and bacon salad or avocado and stilton with mushroom sauce and topped with bacon (£6.95), chicken in dijon mustard or tomato and goats cheese tart (£8.95), cottage pie with leeks and melted cheese (£9.50), steak, kidney and Guinness pie (made by Joan for 23 years now) or braised lamb with apples and apricots in a tomato chutney sauce (£9.95), fresh seasonal crab and lobster, and delicious home-made puddings such as treacle tart, fruit crumble or summer pudding (£4.95). The dining room is no smoking. Well kept changing ales racked on a stillage behind the bar counter might include Ballards Best, Cheriton Pots Ale, and Timothy Taylors Landlord with guests like Fullers London Pride or Hop Back Summer Lightning; summer cider; dominoes.

(Recommended by P R and S A White, RDK, John Davis, Tony Radnor, Paul and Penny Dawson, Ann and Colin Hunt, Phil and Sally Gorton, Tony and Wendy Hobden, John Evans, Martin Edwards, William and Jenifer Ruxton, John Hale, Roger Endersby, R B Gardiner)

Free house ~ Licensee Sue Beavis ~ Real ale ~ Bar food ~ (01730) 825746 ~ Well behaved children in eating areas ~ Dogs allowed in bar ~ Open 11-2.30, 6-11; 12-3, 7-10.30 Sun

FERNHURST SU8926 Map 2

Kings Arms

A286 towards Midhurst

Perhaps not very special looking from the outside, this 17th-c dining pub is charming and civilised inside and offers a warm welcome and good, popular food. The no smoking main area, on the left, is all set for eating, but keeps a traditional feel, especially at the far end with its cushioned wall benches and big log fire under a long low mantelbeam. Past here is a smaller room, with a display of often intriguing bottle openers, as well as the main concentration of the wine-oriented pictures which form the pub's decorative theme. Its choice of wines is good and interesting, with plenty by the glass. People dropping in just for a drink feel entirely at home, with friendly service, a table of local newspapers, and a pleasantly chatty seating area on the right, including one long table with a big vase of flowers, by the bar counter, which has five well kept changing real ales on handpump, such as Hogs Back Hop Garden Gold, King Horsham Best Bitter, Ringwood Fortyniner, Timothy Taylors Landlord, and Ventnor Golden Bitter; ten wines by the glass, and several whiskies. Well presented and interesting, the bar food at lunchtime includes home-made soup (£5), sandwiches with home-made chips and home-made coleslaw (from £5.50), scottish smoked salmon with quails egg salad (£6.25), smoked duck and duck tartare with ratatouille chutney (£6.45), warm salad of lobster with baby spinach and mango (£7), beer battered cod (£9), fillet of bass with crushed jersey royals and tomatoes with balsamic dressing (£13.95), and fried scallops wrapped in pancetta with rocket and parmesan salad (£14); in the evening there might be warm chicken mousse with wild mushroom cream sauce (£6.75), pasta with chervil cream and caviar (£7), roast guinea fowl with broad beans and asparagus (£12.95), roast loin of monkfish with buttered spinach and rosemary and tomato butter (£13.95), and puddings like hot chocolate fondant with ginger ice-cream, pear tarte tatin, and raspberry brûlée (£5.25). They have a nice line in english cheeses, and do espresso coffees and so forth. As they warn, because everything is cooked to order your food may take some time to come. The lavatories are exemplary, and a fair-sized garden has green picnic-sets under cocktail parasols, or shaded by a weeping willow; though it is completely screened from the road, there is some traffic noise. If you are heading S, take particular care leaving the car park. *(Recommended by C S Samuel, Mr and Mrs Gordon Turner, Martin and Karen Wake, Andy and Jill Kassube, Wendy Arnold)*

Free house ~ Licensees Michael and Annabel Hirst ~ Real ale ~ Bar food (not Sun evening) ~ Restaurant ~ (01428) 652005 ~ Children in eating area of bar ~ Dogs allowed in bar ~ Open 11.30-3, 5.30(6.30 Sat)-11; 12-3 Sun; closed Sun evening

FITTLEWORTH TQ0118 Map 2

Swan

Lower Street

Dating from 1382, this old coaching inn is popular with both those popping in for a pint and a chat and with customers wanting an enjoyable meal. The beamed main bar is comfortable and relaxed with windsor armchairs and bar stools on the part stripped wood and part carpeted floor, there are wooden truncheons over the big inglenook fireplace (which has good winter log fires), and well kept Fullers London Pride, Greene King Old Speckled Hen, and Wadworths 6X on handpump. There's an attractive panelled room – part of the no smoking restaurant – that's decorated with landscapes by Constable's brother George; piped music. Well liked bar food includes lunchtime ploughman's (£5.95) and sandwiches (£6.25, with chips and salad), as well as home-made soup (£4.25), chicken liver parfait with cumberland sauce (£5.75), home-made thai crab cakes with pineapple chutney (£5.95; main course £9.95), pie of the day or sausages with onion gravy (£8.95), sunblush tomato risotto with roasted red pepper sauce (£9.95), pork fillet in oriental spices with chilli plum sauce or calves liver on parnsip mash with onion compote and red wine vinegar sauce (£10.95), sirloin steak (£14.95), and home-made puddings like profiteroles, crème brûlée or sticky toffee pudding (£4.50); friendly, swift service. Perhaps the nicest place to sit in summer is at one of the well spaced tables on the big back lawn, sheltered by flowering shrubs and a hedge sprawling with honeysuckle; there are also benches by the village lane in front of this pretty tile-hung inn. Good nearby walks in beech woods. *(Recommended by John Evans, Irene and Derek Flewin, Jenny and Brian Seller, Barry Collett, Brenda and Rob Fincham)*

Enterprise ~ Lease Robert Carey ~ Real ale ~ Bar food (not winter Sun evening) ~ Restaurant ~ (01798) 865429 ~ Children in eating area of bar and restaurant ~ Dogs allowed in bar ~ Open 11-3, 5(6 Sat)-11; 12-4, 7-10.30 Sun ~ Bedrooms: £35B/£70B

FLETCHING TQ4223 Map 3

Griffin ★

Village signposted off A272 W of Uckfield

Sussex Dining Pub of the Year

This civilised and very well run old inn appeals to a wide mix of customers – not always an easy thing to do. It's very popular locally with plenty of chatty regulars enjoying the well kept real ales or the live jazz twice a week, there are lots of customers who drive some distance to have an imaginative meal (or residents staying overnight in the comfortable bedrooms), and they allow well behaved children and dogs, too. The beamed and quaintly panelled bar rooms therefore have a good bustling atmosphere, as well as blazing log fires, old photographs and hunting prints, straightforward furniture including some captain's chairs, and china on a delft shelf. There's a small bare-boarded serving area off to one side, and a snug separate bar with sofas and TV. As well as filled ciabattas, the extremely good food might include a tuscan vegetable soup, pork and chicken terrine with olives and onion confit or bruschetta with roasted pepper, red onion and goats cheese (£5.50), grilled lemon-scented sardines with fresh tomato sauce (£5.95), sweet potato, oyster mushrooms and taleggio tart (£7.95), organic veal meatballs with tomato salsa on tagliatelle or crab cakes with ginger and spring onion mayonnaise (£8.50), haddock in beer batter with home-made tartare sauce or slow roasted lamb shanks in red wine with herb mash (£8.95), free range chicken with rosemary potatoes, olives, fennel and white wine (£9.50), and chargrilled sirloin steak with home-made chips and béarnaise sauce (£13.95), with puddings such as chocolate brownie with chocolate sauce and crème fraîche, vanilla and grappa panna cotta with spiced apricot and almond compote or raspberry and vanila crème brûlée (£4.95). It does get particularly busy on Sunday lunchtimes. Well kept Badger Tanglefoot, Harveys Best, and King Horsham Best Bitter on handpump, and a fine wine list with a dozen (including champagne and sweet wine) by the glass, and fresh apple juice. The two acres of garden behind the pub look across fine rolling countryside towards Sheffield Park, and there are plenty of seats here and on a sheltered gravel terrace. *(Recommended by Mrs J R Sillitoe, Mrs J Potter, Paul A Moore, Dr Paull Khan, M B R Savage, Walter and Susan Rinaldi-Butcher, Mrs Jane Kingsbury, Michael Porter, Peter Meister, JMC, Simon Rodway, A P Seymour, Christopher Turner, Leigh Lain Walker, Liz and Tony Colman; also in the* Good Hotel Guide*)*

Free house ~ Licensees N Pullan and J Pullan ~ Real ale ~ Bar food (12-2.30, 7-9.30; not 25 Dec or evening 1 Jan) ~ Restaurant ~ (01825) 722890 ~ Children in eating area of bar and restaurant ~ Dogs allowed in bar ~ Jazz Fri evening and Sun lunchtime ~ Open 12-3, 6-11; 7pm opening Sun evening in winter; closed 25 Dec ~ Bedrooms: /£85B

Soup prices usually include a roll and butter.

HEATHFIELD TQ5920 Map 3

Star

Old Heathfield – head E out of Heathfield itself on A265, then fork right on to B2096; turn right at signpost to Heathfield Church then keep bearing right; pub on left immediately after church

This is a lovely pub, both in summer and winter, and you can expect a warm welcome from the friendly staff. It's very popular locally but there are plenty of visitors as well, and the L-shaped beamed bar has a relaxed, chatty atmosphere, a fine log fire in the inglenook fireplace, panelling, built-in wall settles and window seats, and just four or five tables; a doorway leads into a similarly furnished smaller room. The tables are candlelit at night. Chalked up on boards, there's a wide choice of good food that might include home-made soup (£4.75), home-made smoked salmon, white crab meat and dill pâté or stilton, courgette and tomato tartlet (£5.75), large bowl of greek salad or smoked ham and two free range eggs (£7.95), home-made steak and kidney pie or locally caught fish and chips (£8.75), pasta arrabiata (spicy tomato and sausage sauce, £9.95), stuffed supreme of chicken (£11.95), half a shoulder of lamb in rosemary, garlic and redcurrant (£13.50), and 10oz sirloin steak with green peppercorn sauce (£16.95); efficient, courteous service. You must book to be sure of a table. Well kept Harveys Best, Shepherd Neame Best Bitter, and a guest such as Hop Back Summer Lightning on handpump, half a dozen wines by the glass, Pimms by the jug, and a good bloody mary; piped music, shove-ha'penny, cribbage and bar billiards. The prettily planted sloping garden with its rustic furniture has lovely views of rolling oak-lined sheep pastures – Turner thought it fine enough to paint. *(Recommended by Uta and John Owlett, Mrs P E Brown, E G Parish, Robert M Warner, Matthew Lidbury, Alan Cowell, Marc Hadley, John Hendy, Susan and John Douglas)*

Free house ~ Licensees Mike Chappell and Fiona Airey ~ Real ale ~ Bar food (12-2.15, 7-9.30) ~ Restaurant ~ (01435) 863570 ~ Children in eating area of bar ~ Dogs allowed in bar ~ Open 11.30-3, 5.30-11; 12-4, 7-10.30 Sun; closed evenings 25 and 26 Dec

HENLEY SU8925 Map 2

Duke of Cumberland Arms

Village signposted just off A286 S of Fernhurst, N of Midhurst; if coming from Midhurst, take first turn into village, then keep bearing right; OS Sheet 186 map reference 894258

In fine weather, the three-and-a-half acre garden here is just the place for a sunny lunchtime. It's on a slope, and lush and quite big, with lilacs and other shrubs, and willows by a stream running down through a series of three ponds stocked with trout – you can watch the staff catching them for someone's meal. Gnarled old benches and more modern seats out here give lovely views over Black Down and the wooded hills south of Haslemere. Inside this 15th-c cottage, there are just two unpretentious little low-ceilinged rooms – each with a log fire; also, gas lamps on white-painted panelled walls, simple seats around scrubbed rough oak tables, and a few wood carvings, plates and old framed documents. Decent bar food includes soup (£3.75), crab cakes (£5.25), sandwiches (from £5.75), home-made burgers (from £6.75), all-day breakfast (£8.95), braised lamb shank (£10.95), their own trout (£11.95), and puddings such as home-made rice pudding or bread and butter pudding (from £3.75); their speciality english roasts need 24 hours' notice: from £12.95. Well kept Adnams Broadside, Hook Norton, and Shepherd Neame Spitfire, with guests like Charles Wells Bombardier, and Youngs tapped from the cask, and Rich's farm cider; no piped music or games. The red and white bulldog is called Jasper and his sister, Sasha. *(Recommended by Mike and Sue Richardson, Mrs Romey Heaton, Mrs Ann Gray, Roger Endersby, Martin and Karen Wake, Torrens Lyster)*

Free house ~ Licensees Gaston Duval and Christina Duval ~ Real ale ~ Bar food (12-2.30, 7-9.30; not Sun evening) ~ Restaurant ~ (01428) 652280 ~ Children welcome till 9pm ~ Dogs welcome ~ Open 11-11; 12-10.30 Sun

HERMITAGE SU7505 Map 2

Sussex Brewery

A259 just inside Sussex boundary, by Thorney Island turn just W of Emsworth

Just a stroll from the waterside, this cheerful place has a strong following among readers for its speciality sausages, about 50 different and often unusual varieties such as chicken, orange and walnut, mushroom and tarragon, hot and spicy beef, wild boar and juniper berries, moroccan lamb, and pork with apricots, herbs, and cognac (from £6.80). These are clearly the main event, though there is also plenty of other choice, such as home-made soup (£3.95), filled baked potatoes (from £4.25), ploughman's (from £5.95), steak and mushroom in ale pie or sweet and sour chicken (£7.25), fish such as bass, salmon or crab from Selsey (from £9.50), and sirloin steak (£14.50). The bar is quite small, with sawdust (yes, real sawdust) on bare boards, an old wing armchair by the huge brick fireplace (with a good winter log fire – there's a second little blue-tiled Victorian fireplace opposite it, also used), simple seats, four tables (two painted as inn signs, one as thrown-down playing cards), and small brewery mirrors on yellowing walls. Well kept Youngs Bitter, Special and Waggle Dance and a guest beer on handpump from the dark brick counter, and up to ten wines by the glass; friendly helpful staff; no machines or piped music. At the end of the bar, a little flagstoned snug with small polished pews around just two tables is kept food-free at night. Down a flagstoned passage, a snug pink-walled carpeted back no smoking dining room has comfortable plush chairs. There are picnic-sets in a small enclosed back courtyard, with one or two more out by the side. *(Recommended by RWC, Keith Stevens, Bruce Bird, Tony Hobden, Andy and Jill Kassube, J Metcalfe, Ann and Colin Hunt)*

Youngs ~ Tenant David Roberts ~ Real ale ~ Bar food (12-2.30, 7-10) ~ Restaurant ~ (01243) 371533 ~ Children in eating area of bar and restaurant ~ Dogs allowed in bar ~ Open 11-11; 12-10.30 Sun

HORSHAM TQ1730 Map 3

Black Jug 🍷

31 North Street

Even when it's really busy, the staff here remain cheerful and friendly. There's a lively, bustling atmosphere in the airy open-plan turn-of-the-century-style room, and a large central bar, a nice collection of heavy sizeable dark wood tables, comfortable chairs on a stripped wood floor, cream walls crammed with interesting old prints and photographs above a dark wood panelled dado, and a warm terracotta ceiling. A spacious no smoking conservatory has similar furniture and lots of hanging baskets; piped music. Well kept Greene King Abbot, King Horsham Best Bitter, Marstons Pedigree, and Wadworths 6X, with a guest such as Weltons on handpump, 40 malt whiskies, a good wine list with 20 by the glass, and eight chilled vodkas from Poland and Russia. Good bar food includes soup (£3.90), open sandwiches or filled baguettes (from £3.95; chicken, bacon, tomato and lettuce in a flour tortilla £5.50), home-made duck liver and orange pâté with rhubarb and red onion marmalade (£4.95), ploughman's (£5.95), smoked haddock and salmon fishcakes with lemon chutney (£6.95), home-baked ham and egg (£7.25), spinach, ricotta and mushroom pasta bake (£7.95), home-made steakburger with bacon and cheese or steak in ale pie (£8.95), fried cod in beer batter with home-made tartare sauce (£10.95), mediterranean spiced chicken on roasted vegetables (£11.95), scotch rib-eye steak with red wine and mushroom sauce (£13.95), and puddings like white and dark chocolate truffle mousse or sticky toffee pudding (£4.50). The pretty flower-filled back terrace has plenty of garden furniture by outside heaters. More reports please. *(Recommended by Mr Bannon, Wombat, Guy Vowles, Martin and Karen Wake)*

Brunning & Price ~ Manager Myles Abell ~ Real ale ~ Bar food (all day) ~ (01403) 253526 ~ Children in restaurant until 6pm ~ Dogs allowed in bar ~ Open 11-11; 12-10.30 Sun

ICKLESHAM TQ8716 Map 3

Queens Head 🍷 🍺

Just off A259 Rye—Hastings

Bustling and friendly, this handsome pub is liked by a wide mix of customers; dogs, too, are welcome but must be kept on a lead. The open-plan areas work round a very big serving counter which stands under a vaulted beamed roof, the high beamed walls and ceiling of the easy-going bar are lined with shelves of bottles and covered with farming implements and animal traps, and there are well used pub tables and old pews on the brown patterned carpet. Other areas (two are no smoking and popular with diners) have big inglenook fireplaces, and the back room is now decorated with old bicycle and motorbike prints. Well kept Courage Directors, and Greene King IPA and Abbot, with guests like Grand Union Special, Whites 1066 Country Bitter, and Woodfordes Wherry on handpump; Biddenden cider, and quite a few wines by the glass. Reasonably priced, decent bar food includes sandwiches (from £2.45), home-made lentil and bacon soup (£3.50), filled baked potatoes (from £3.95), home-made chicken liver pâté (£4.50), ploughman's (from £4.95), home-cooked ham and eggs (£5.95), home-made roasted vegetable and lentil gratin (£7.25), home-made steak and kidney pudding (£8.50), steaks (from £9.95), fresh fish dishes (from £6.95), and daily specials; prompt service from efficient staff. Shove-ha'penny, dominoes, cribbage, darts, and piped music. Picnic-sets look out over the vast, gently sloping plain of the Brede valley from the little garden, and there's an outside children's play area, and boules. Good local walks. *(Recommended by Kevin Thorpe, S and R Gray, John Davis, Peter Meister, Bob and Margaret Holder, Pamela and Merlyn Horswell, E G Parish, V Brogden, Peter and Joan Elbra, B and M Kendall, Wombat, Colin McKerrow, Brian Root, John Hendy, Paul A Moore)*

Free house ~ Licensee Ian Mitchell ~ Real ale ~ Bar food (12-2.30, 6.15-9.30; all day Sat and Sun; not 25 or 26 Dec) ~ (01424) 814552 ~ Well behaved children in eating area of bar until 8.30pm ~ Dogs welcome ~ Live jazz/blues/folk Tues evening ~ Open 11-11; 12-10.30 Sun

LEWES TQ4110 Map 3

Snowdrop 🍺

South Street; off Cliffe High Street, opposite S end of Malling Street just S of A26 roundabout

Readers continue to enjoy the lively atmosphere here and the bustle of adults, children and the odd dog. There are two spacious areas (extra seating outside) with the cliffs as a spectacular backdrop, and an interesting maritime theme with figureheads, ship lamps and other objects of interest; the corner by the spiral staircase is cosy and sunny, and a small part is no smoking. Upstairs there are more seats and a pool table. Enjoyable good value food includes soup (£3.45), filled wraps or focaccias (with fillings like hummous and roast vegetables or roast lemon chicken from £3.75), mezze plate (£5.95; large £7.95), marinated local organic tofu skewers with oriental rice and satay sauce or vegetarian sausages with spring onion mash and cider gravy (£7.95), marinated crayfish tail skewers with spicy noodles and sweet chilli dressing (£8.25), and beef and onion pie (£8.50); pizza and child menus too. Well kept Adnams Broadside, Harveys Best, and guests like Hydes Jekyll's Gold Premium Ale and Smiles Slap & Tickle on handpump; good service. Piped music and dominoes. *(Recommended by John Davis, Keith Stevens, Ann and Colin Hunt, A J Bowen, Tracey and Stephen Groves, Dom Bradshaw, LM, Tony and Wendy Hobden, Father Robert Marsh)*

Free house ~ Licensee Tanya Gander ~ Real ale ~ Bar food (12-3, 5-9) ~ (01273) 471018 ~ Children in eating area of bar and restaurant ~ Dogs welcome ~ Local bands Sat evening ~ Open 11-11; 12-10.30 Sun

> The details at the end of each main entry start by saying whether the pub is a free house, or if it's tied to a brewery or pub group (which we name).

LODSWORTH SU9223 Map 2

Halfway Bridge Inn ★

Just before village, on A272 Midhurst—Petworth

The three or four bar rooms in this smartly civilised inn have a nice bustling atmosphere, and are comfortably furnished with good oak chairs and an individual mix of tables, and they use attractive fabrics for the wood-railed curtains and pew cushions. Down some steps, the charming no smoking country dining room has a dresser and longcase clock; one of the log fires is contained in a well polished kitchen range, and paintings by a local artist line the walls. Well kept Cheriton Pots Ale and Village Elder, Gales HSB, Harveys Best, and Kings Spring Ale on handpump, a rather special local cider, and a thoughtful little wine list with a changing choice by the glass; friendly service, even when busy. Dominoes, cribbage, and shove-ha'penny, and papers to read. Good interesting bar food includes lunchtime sandwiches such as chicken satay in warm ciabatta (£6.50), rice and peanut cakes with spicy dipping sauce (£4.95), mussels steamed with a spicy thai sauce or goats cheese baked in puff pastry with onion marmalade (£5.95), local organic sausages with grain mustard mash and onion gravy (£7.95), ham hock with bacon sautéed potatoes and dill pickles or thai aubergine and coconut curry (£9.50), steak, kidney and Guinness pudding (£10.50), sesame baked red snapper with hot ginger marinade (£12.50), and good roast half shoulder of lamb with garlic and rosemary sauce (£15.50), with puddings such as banana toffee pie, mango rice pudding or walnut and treacle tart (from £3.95); big breakfasts. The friendly jack russell is called Ralph, and the jack-russell cross, Chip (they wear obligatory 'please don't feed me' badges). At the back there are seats on a small terrace. *(Recommended by Cathy Robinson, Ed Coombe, Peter and Audrey Dowsett, John Davis, Kate Hillaby, John Evans, Martin and Karen Wake, Jane Basso, JCW, Mrs Ann Saunders, John Cooper, Mrs Sheela Curtis, Basil Wynbergen, Irene and Derek Flewin, Bruce Bird)*

Free house ~ Licensees Simon and James Hawkins ~ Real ale ~ Bar food (12-2 (2.30 wknds), 7-10) ~ Restaurant ~ (01798) 861281 ~ Children over 10 in restaurant ~ Dogs allowed in bar ~ Open 11-3, 6-11; 12-3, 7-10.30 Sun ~ Bedrooms: £45B/£75B

LURGASHALL SU9327 Map 2

Noahs Ark

Village signposted from A283 N of Petworth; OS Sheet 186 map reference 936272

On the edge of a quiet village green, this charming 16th-c pub is run by friendly people. The two neatly furnished bars have warm log fires (one in a capacious inglenook), well kept Greene King IPA, Abbot and Old Speckled Hen on handpump, and several well polished trophies. The family room is decorated like the inside of an ark; darts. From a sensibly short menu, bar food includes sandwiches, filled baked potatoes (£4.75), ploughman's (£5.25), hot wraps with fillings like crispy duck, spring onion, cucumber and hoi sin (£6.45), salads such as chicken satay or parma ham and artichoke (£6.50), savoury sausage, fresh cod in cider batter or gammon and pineapple (all £6.95), chicken curry (£7.25), steak and mushroom pie (£7.50), and puddings such as dark chocolate brandy torte or sticky toffee pudding; Sunday lunch main course (£9.95). In summer, the flowering baskets are splendid, there's a back garden with seating, and picnic-sets on the grass in front ideally placed for watching the local cricket team play. More reports please. *(Recommended by Mark Percy, Lesley Mayoh, John Beeken, M B Griffith, Klaus and Elizabeth Leist)*

Greene King ~ Tenant Bernard Joseph Wija ~ Real ale ~ Bar food (not Sun evening) ~ Restaurant ~ (01428) 707346 ~ Children in restaurant and family room ~ Dogs allowed in bar ~ Open 11-3, 6-11; 12-3, 7-10.30 Sun; closed Sun evening in winter

OVING SU9005 Map 2

Gribble Inn

Between A27 and A259 just E of Chichester, then should be signposted just off village road; OS Sheet 197 map reference 900050

There's certainly a fine choice of drinks at this 16th-c thatched pub including their own-brewed real ales, and as the pub is owned by Badger, you can often find them in other pubs owned by the brewery: Gribble Ale, Pigs Ear, Plucking Pheasant, Reg's Tipple, Slurping Stoat, and winter Wobbler, plus Badger Tanglefoot on handpump. Also decent wine, 20 country wines, and farm cider. There's a cottagey feel in the several linked rooms, and the chatty bar has lots of heavy beams and timbering, and old country-kitchen furnishings and pews. Half the dining room is no smoking, and all of the family room. Reasonably priced bar food includes lunchtime sandwiches (from £4.95), ploughman's (£5.75), ham and eggs (£7.25), red pepper and spinach lasagne (£7.95), beer-battered fish or steak and mushroom pie (£8.50), steaks (from £11.95), and puddings (£4.50). Sunday lunch is extremely busy. Fruit machine, cribbage, dominoes and a separate skittle alley. There's a covered seating area, and more chairs in the pretty garden with apple and pear trees. *(Recommended by Nigel Williamson, Ann and Colin Hunt, John Davis, P R and S A White, Howard Dell, Susan and John Douglas, Andy and Jill Kassube, J A Snell, David H T Dimock, R B Gardiner, Vanessa Stilwell)*

Own brew ~ Managers Brian and Cynthia Elderfield ~ Real ale ~ Bar food (12-2.30, 6-9.30) ~ Restaurant ~ (01243) 786893 ~ Children in family room ~ Dogs allowed in bar ~ Open 11-3, 5.30-11; 11-11 Fri and Sat; 12-10.30 Sun; 11-3, 5.30-11 winter Fri and Sat, 12-3.30, 7-10.30 Sun in winter

PETWORTH SU9719 Map 2

Badgers 🍷

Coultershaw Bridge; just off A285 1½ miles S

Although there is a small chatty drinking area here with a couple of tables, bar stools and an attractive antique oak monk's chair by the entrance, most customers do come to eat. The space around the island bar servery is devoted to dining tables – well spaced, with an attractive mix of furniture from old mahogany to waxed stripped pine, and there are white walls that bring out the deep maroon colour of the high ceiling, charming wrought-iron lamps, winter log fires, stripped shutters for the big Victorian windows, and a modicum of carefully chosen decorations including a few houseplants and dried flower arrangements. Changing regularly, the bar food might include sandwiches or home-made soup (£4.65), pasta with stir-fried vegetables and fresh herbs (£5.95), seafood tapas or sausage and mash (£7.95), chicken with spinach, bacon and three-cheese sauce or marinated fresh tuna with oriental salsa (£8.95), baked cod with breadcrumbs, coriander, lime and parmesan or half a shoulder of lamb with garlic and rosemary (£14.95), rib-eye steak with champ (£15.95), and puddings such as marbled milk and white chocolate torte or raspberry cheesecake (£4.95). Well kept Badger Best and K&B on handpump, and quite a range of wines; maybe faint piped music (the dominant sound is quiet conversation). A terrace by a water-lily pool has stylish metal garden furniture under parasols, and some solid old-fashioned wooden seats. More reports please. *(Recommended by Cathy Robinson, Ed Coombe, John Evans, Alison Crooks, Dave Heffernan, Martin and Karen Wake, David H T Dimock, Roger Endersby, Arnold Bennett)*

Free house ~ Licensee Miss Arlette ~ Real ale ~ Bar food (not winter Sun evenings) ~ Restaurant ~ (01798) 342651 ~ Children in eating area of bar if over 5 ~ Open 11-3, 5.30(6.30 Sat)-11; 12-3, 7-10.30 Sun; closed winter Sun evenings ~ Bedrooms: /£80B

> Children – if the details at the end of a main entry don't mention them, you should assume that the pub does not allow them inside.

Welldiggers Arms

Low Heath; A283 towards Pulborough

This interestingly combines good generous fresh food (not that cheap, but really good value for this part of the world) with the unassuming style and appearance of an ancient country pub as it might have been in the 1930s. The result is a thoroughly civilised atmosphere, chatty and relaxed. The smallish L-shaped bar has low beams, a few pictures (Churchill and gun dogs are prominent) on shiny ochre walls above a panelled dado, a couple of very long rustic settles with tables to match, and some other stripped tables; a second rather lower side room has a somewhat lighter décor. They have well kept Youngs on handpump, and decent wines. The changing food, all home-made, might include bacon and egg baps (£3.50), crab tartlet (£4.95), french onion soup (£5.50), smoked salmon pâté (£5.95), salad niçoise (£6.50), fishcakes (£7), home-baked ham and egg (£7.50), vegetarian wellington (£8.50), steak, Guinness and stilton pie, bass, garlic king prawns or a rich oxtail casserole (all £9.50), duck with apple sauce (£14.50), good steaks (from rump, £14.50), and puddings like bread and butter pudding or rapsberry meringue (£4.50); their speciality is seafood royale (£48 for two with lobster, king prawns, crab, oysters and so forth). Under the eye of the long-serving hands-on landlord, service is friendly and informal yet efficient; no music or machines. Outside, screened from the road by a thick high hedge, are plenty of tables and chairs on pleasant lawns and a terrace, looking back over rolling fields and woodland. *(Recommended by Martin and Karen Wake, Gerry and Rosemary Dobson, John Davis)*

Free house ~ Licensee Ted Whitcomb ~ Real ale ~ Bar food ~ (01798) 342287 ~ Children welcome ~ Dogs welcome ~ Open 11-3, 6-11; closed Mon; closed Tues, Weds and Sun evenings

RUSHLAKE GREEN TQ6218 Map 3

Horse & Groom

Village signposted off B2096 Heathfield—Battle

With a strong local following – though there are plenty of visitors, too – this attractively set pub has a good thriving atmosphere. On the right is the heavily beamed dining room with guns and hunting trophies on the walls, plenty of wheelback chairs around pubby tables, and a log fire. The little L-shaped bar has more low beams (watch your head) and is simply furnished with high bar stools and bar chairs, red plush cushioned wall seats and a few brocaded cushioned stools, and a brick fireplace with some brass items on the mantelpiece; horsebrasses, photographs of the pub and local scenes on the walls, and fresh flowers. A small room down a step has jockeys' colours and jockey photographs and watercolours of the pub. Listed on boards by the entrance to the bar, the large choice of popular bar food might include soup (£4.25), mushrooms topped with brie and finished with truffle oil (£5.50), scallops lightly fried in tempura batter with chilli dressing (£7.95), steak, kidney and Guinness suet pudding or toad in the hole with proper cumberland sausages and onion gravy (£9.95), organic salmon topped with Jack Daniels and sugar and lightly grilled and served with crushed chive potatoes or chicken breast coated in sesame seeds with stir-fried noodles and pak choi (£10.95), fried bass on black spaghetti with sautéed artichokes and a lemon butter sauce (£13.95), and puddings such as squidgy chocolate meringue, orange brûlée cheesecake or bread and butter pudding with custard (£4.95). Well kept Harveys Best and Shepherd Neame Master Brew and Spitfire on handpump, and several wines by the glass. The village green is just across the lane, and there are oak seats and tables (made by the landlord) in the cottagey garden with pretty country views. More reports please. *(Recommended by Jason Caulkin, J H Bell, John Davis, Colin McKerrow, P W Taylor)*

Free house ~ Licensees Mike and Sue Chappel ~ Real ale ~ Bar food (12-2.30, 7-9.30 (9 Sun)) ~ Restaurant ~ (01435) 830320 ~ Children welcome ~ Dogs welcome ~ Open 11.30-3, 5.30-11; 12-3, 7-10.30 Sun

RYE TQ9220 Map 3

Mermaid

Mermaid Street

The sign outside this lovely black and white timbered hotel says 'rebuilt in 1472', and the cellars are two or three centuries older than that. The little bar is where those in search of a light lunch and a drink tend to head for, and there's a mix of quite closely set furnishings such as Victorian gothic carved oak chairs, older but plainer oak seats and more modern ones in character, and a massive deeply polished bressumer beam across one wall for the huge inglenook fireplace; three antique but not ancient wall paintings show old English scenes. Well kept (if not cheap) Courage Best and Greene King Old Speckled Hen on handpump, a good wine list, and a short choice of bar food such as freshly made filled baguettes (from £6), open goats cheese and spinach omelette or spaghetti bolognese (£7.50), moules marinière (£8), minute steak glazed with red onions (£9), seafood platter for two (£27), and puddings (£5.50). The smart (expensive) restaurant is no smoking; piped music (bar only), dominoes and cribbage. Seats on a small back terrace overlook the car park – where there are morris dancers on bank holiday weekends.
(Recommended by D J Penny, the Didler, E G Parish, Mr and Mrs S Felstead, John Davis, Nicky Mayers, Michael Dandy, Alan Cole, Kirstie Bruce, Ann and Colin Hunt, Jason Reynolds, Sean and Sharon Pines, Sue Demont, Tim Barrow, Andrea Rampley)

Free house ~ Licensees Robert Pinwill and Mrs J Blincow ~ Real ale ~ Bar food (not Sat evening or if restaurant is busy) ~ Restaurant ~ (01797) 223065 ~ Children welcome ~ Open 12-11(10.30 Sun) ~ Bedrooms: £80B/£160B

Ypres Castle

Gun Garden; steps up from A259, or down past Ypres Tower

Set at the base of the 13th-c Ypres Tower and museum and the even older St Mary's Parish Church, this friendly pub has lovely views from the windows and from the large, sheltered garden looking over the River Rother with its working fishing fleet, and on further to the Romney Marsh and the sea. Inside, the bars are traditionally furnished with antique furniture and rugs and there's a big eclectic art collection, and a winter log fire surrounded by comfortable chairs. You can eat in the large no smoking room, the more informal bar area or the comfortable no smoking restaurant, and although bar food is served at lunchtime only, in the evening you can enjoy the restaurant food in the bar. From the lunchtime menu, there might be wild mushroom soup (£3.75), filled baguettes (from £3.95), filled baked potatoes (from £5.25), ploughman's (£5.95), home-cooked ham and egg (£6.50), game pâté (£6.95), caramelised onion and goats cheese quiche (£7.95), prosciutto, fig and rocket salad (£8.95), and daily specials; in the evening there are main courses such as roast vegetable lasagne (£7.25), whole local plaice with fresh herbs or whole cracked local crab (£9.95), 10oz sirloin steak with brandy and peppercorn sauce (£11.95), roast duck breast with port and orange sauce, rack of local lamb with redcurrant and mint sauce or gloucester old spot pork steak with cider and apple sauce (all £12.50), and roast fillet of cod wrapped in prosciutto and stuffed with lemon and garlic parsley butter (£12.95). Vegetables are £1.95 extra. Well kept Harveys Best and White 1066 Country Bitter with guests like Adnams Broadside, Fullers London Pride, and Charles Wells Bombardier on handpump, ten wines by the glass, Weston's cider, and local fresh apple juice; shove-ha'penny, cribbage, dominoes, and piped music. During the September arts festival, several events are held here. Locals tend to call the pub 'Wipers' in true WWI style.
(Recommended by Tina and David Woods-Taylor, Alan Cole, Kirstie Bruce, Sue Austin, Gwyn Jones, Sue Demont, Tim Barrow)

Free house ~ Licensees Tom Cosgrove and Michael Gagg ~ Real ale ~ Bar food (12-2.30, 7-9; not Sun evening or winter Tues) ~ Restaurant ~ (01797) 223248 ~ Children allowed if eating but must be gone by 9pm ~ Dogs allowed in bar ~ Live music Fri evening ~ Open 11.30-3, 6-11; all day during school hols; 11.30-11 Sat; 12-4 Sun; closed Sun evening, winter Tues

SALEHURST TQ7424 Map 3

Salehurst Halt ⚲

Village signposted from Robertsbridge bypass on A21 Tunbridge Wells—Battle

Handy for the busy A21 and close to the church, this well liked little pub has a good bustling evening atmosphere; it tends to be quieter at lunchtime. The L-shaped bar has plain wooden tables and chairs on flagstones at one end, a cushioned window seat, beams, a little open brick fireplace, a time punch clock and olde-worlde pictures, and maybe fresh flowers; lots of hops on a big beam divide this from the beamed carpeted area with its mix of tables, wheelback and farmhouse chairs, and a half wall leads to a no smoking dining area. Listed on boards, the bar food at lunchtime (with prices almost unchanged since last year) includes sandwiches (from £3.95), ploughman's (£5.50), home-made burgers or home-baked ham and egg (from £7), and beef and mushroom pie (£8.50), with evening dishes such as good country pâté flavoured with oranges and Cointreau (£3.95), sizzling tiger prawns in garlic and parsley butter (£4.95), chicken in cream and red peppercorn sauce with brandy or spicy vegetable jambalaya (£8.95), rump steak (£9.95), monkfish in a tomato, garlic, oregano and olive oil sauce topped with mozzarella or roasted duck breast in a bitter orange and port sauce (£10.95), and puddings like banoffi pie or treacle pudding (£3.25). Well kept Harveys Best and a guest like Rother Valley Organic Bitter on handpump, and good wines. It can get very busy at weekends, so best to book in advance; piped music. The charming and pretty back garden is a suntrap in summer, and has terraces and picnic-sets for outside meals, and the front window boxes and tubs are most attractive.
(Recommended by Bryan R Shiner, Derek and Maggie Washington, John Saville, Kevin Thorpe)

Free house ~ Licensees Claire and Hossein Refahi ~ Real ale ~ Bar food (12-2.30, 6.30-9.30; not Sun evening or Mon) ~ Restaurant ~ (01580) 880620 ~ Children welcome ~ Dogs allowed in bar ~ Open 12-3, 6.30-11(10.30 Sun); closed Mon except bank hols

SINGLETON SU8713 Map 2

Fox & Hounds

Just off A286 Midhurst—Chichester; heading S into the village, the main road bends sharp right – keep straight ahead instead; if you miss this turn, take the Charlton road, then first left

Cosy and comfortable, this pretty 16th-c pub is run by friendly people. The partly panelled main bar has cream paintwork, a polished wooden floor, daily papers and books to borrow, and a good winter log fire. There's a second bar with red settles and another fire, a third flagstoned room on the left, and a further seating area off a side corridor; much of the pub is no smoking. Generous helpings of bar food at lunchtime include home-made soup (£4.50), pâté (£5.50), open sandwiches (from £5.50), cheese platter with pickles (£6.95), pasta of the day (£8.75), steak in ale pie or lambs liver and bacon (£8.95), gammon with mustard, mushrooms and melted cheese (£9.25), well liked shank of lamb in garlic and rosemary (£9.95), and steaks (from £9.95), with more elaborate evening dishes such as pork loin coated with french mustard and sugar with creamy mustard and cider sauce (£9.95), and seared marlin with a warm potato and basil salad or game pie using local game (£10.50); puddings (£4.50), and Sunday roast (£9.50). Well kept Fullers London Pride, Greene King IPA, and Ringwood Best on handpump, and decent wines by the glass; no music or machines. There are tables on an attractive small back terrace, and beyond that a big walled garden with colourful flowerbeds and fruit trees. The Weald & Downland Open Air Museum is just down the road, and Goodwood Racecourse is not far away. *(Recommended by Ann and Colin Hunt, John Davis, Glen and Nola Armstrong, Karen Eliot, Jane Basso, B J Harding, Derek and Maggie Washington, Ellen Weld, David London, Susan and John Douglas, PL)*

Enterprise ~ Lease Tony Simpson ~ Real ale ~ Bar food (all day summer weekends; not winter Sun evening) ~ (01243) 811251 ~ Children in family room ~ Dogs allowed in bar ~ Open 11.30-3, 6-11; 11.30-11 Sat; 12-10.30 Sun; 11.30-3, 6-11 Sat in winter

TROTTON SU8323 Map 2

Keepers Arms 🍴

A272 Midhurst—Petersfield; pub tucked up above road, on S side

The interesting décor here is worth a visit for that alone, and the walls throughout are decorated with some unusual pictures and artefacts that reflect Jenny's previous long years of travelling the world. The beamed L-shaped bar has timbered walls and some standing timbers, sofas by the big log fire, and ethnic rugs scattered on the oak floor. Elsewhere, there are a couple of unusual adult high chairs at an oak refectory table, two huge Georgian leather high-backed chairs around another table, an interesting medley of old or antique seats, and dining tables decorated with pretty candelabra, and bowls of fruit and chillis. There's also a North African-style room with a cushioned bench around all four walls, with a large central table, rare ethnic fabrics and weavings, and a big moroccan lamp hanging in the centre. The popular restaurant is no smoking. Interesting piped music (which they change according to the customers) ranges from Buddha bar-type music to classical. From a sensibly slimmed-down menu, bar food might include a lunchtime platter for two (£6 per person), hot chicken, bacon and mayonnaise panini (£6.50), cumberland sausage or hot ham and egg (£7), home-made pie of the day (£10.50), and fresh seafood platter (Fridays only and must be ordered by Wednesday lunchtime, £21); they also offer several dishes in starter and main course sizes: chargrilled chicken with thai vegetables and noodles and sweet chilli sauce (£6 and £10.50), fresh crab with asparagus and hollandaise sauce (£6 and £11.50), and calves liver and bacon with tapenade style butter (£6.50 and £13.50). Well kept Ballards Best and Nyewood Gold, and Cheriton Pots on handpump, farm cider, and decent wines. Plenty of seats on the attractive, almost mediterranean-feeling front terrace. Dogs lunchtime only. More reports please. *(Recommended by Paul and Penny Dawson, Michael and Ann Cole, John Davis, J A Snell, Martin and Karen Wake, J P Humphery, R T and J C Moggridge, Nigel Clifton)*

Free house ~ Licensee Jenny Oxley ~ Real ale ~ Bar food (not Sun evening, Mon) ~ Restaurant ~ (01730) 813724 ~ Children in restaurant ~ Dogs allowed in bar ~ Open 12-3, 6.30-10.30(11 Sat); 12-3 Sun; closed Sun evening, all Mon

WARTLING TQ6509 Map 3

Lamb 🍷

Village signposted with Herstmonceux Castle off A271 Herstmonceux—Battle

Although most customers do come to this bustling and attractive country pub to enjoy the good food, there's a little entrance bar where locals popping in for a drink and a chat tend to gather: brocaded settles and stools and just a few tables on the green patterned carpet, a big blackboard with specials of the day, and a woodburning stove with logs stacked to one side. A narrow tiled floor area runs along the carved bar counter, and leads to the no smoking snug (mind your head on the low entrance beam) with a mix of cushioned chairs and more brocaded settles around straightforward pubby tables, beams and timbering, big church candles on every table, and fresh flowers above the brick fireplace. The lounge has been refurbished this year but still has a mix of sofas and armchairs around low tables by the fireplace, and lots more big candles and fresh flowers. The no smoking restaurant has also been newly refurbished; piped music. Doors from here lead up steps to a back terrace with green picnic-sets, climbers on the gazebo, and flowering tubs and pots. Well kept Badger Best, Harveys Best, and King Horsham Best Bitter on handpump, good wines (and champagne) by the glass, and genuinely friendly, helpful staff. From an interesting menu, the very popular bar food might include soup with herb croûtons and home-made bread (£3.95), local goats cheese, toasted almond and fresh sage pâté (£5.50), fried local scallops, brioche and chorizo or local sausages and mash (£6.95), home-made pie of the day (£8.75), home-made vegetarian wellington of the day (£9.50), braised lamb shank with rosemary mash (£10.95), local cod on parsley mash with asparagus and roasted pepper coulis (£11.50), and chicken breast stuffed with mozzarella, beef tomato and basil sauce

(£11.95), with home-made puddings such as iced dark chocolate and Kahlua parfait, raspberry and vanilla crème brûlée or lemon bread and butter pudding (£4.95); best to book to be sure of a table as they are always busy, particularly in the evening. Freddie the golden retriever is an old softie. There are seats out in front. *(Recommended by Ian Dowding, Barry and Victoria Lister, Julian Petley, Mike Gorton, David Thompson)*

Free house ~ Licensees Robert and Alison Farncombe ~ Bar food ~ Restaurant ~ (01323) 832116 ~ Children in eating area of bar ~ Open 11-3, 6-11; 12-3 Sun; closed Sun evening and Mon (but this may change)

WILMINGTON TQ5404 Map 3

Giants Rest

Just off A27

Particularly well run, this comfortable Victorian pub has a really good bustling atmosphere and you can be sure of a warm welcome from the charming licensees. The long wood-floored bar and adjacent open areas, one with a log fire, are simply furnished with old pews and pine tables (each with their own bar game or wooden puzzle and much enjoyed by readers), and have well kept Harveys Best, Hop Back Summer Lightning, and Timothy Taylors Landlord on handpump; decent wines. Well liked and generously served, the bar food might include soup (£3.50), stilton and walnut pâté (£4.50), garlic king prawns with lemon mayonnaise (£5), filled baked potatoes or ploughman's (from £5.50), beef in ale pie, warm smoked duck and bacon salad or savoury vegetable crumble (£8), salmon fishcakes or home-cooked ham with bubble and squeak and home-made chutney (£8.50), lamb in red wine with thyme and orange (£9), and puddings like sticky date pudding or apple and blackberry pie (£4). Sunday lunchtime is especially busy and there may not be much space for those just wanting a drink as most of the tables are booked by diners. There's a sizeable no smoking area, and smoking at tables is banned at weekends (it is allowed at the bar then); piped music. Plenty of seats in the front garden, and the pub is watched over by the impressive chalk-carved Long Man of Wilmington at the foot of the South Downs. Elizabeth David the famous cookery writer is buried in the churchyard at nearby Folkington; her headstone is beautifully carved and features mediterranean vegetables and a casserole. *(Recommended by Gill and Tony Morriss, Dr P J W Young, Alan J Miller, Tony and Wendy Hobden, John Beeken, Mr and Mrs S Felstead, Jenny and Peter Lowater, John Hendy, Anthony Longden, Mike Gorton, Philip and Ann Board)*

Free house ~ Licensees Adrian and Rebecca Hillman ~ Real ale ~ Bar food ~ (01323) 870207 ~ Children in eating area of bar and in restaurant ~ Dogs allowed in bar ~ Open 11-3, 6-11; 11-11 Sat; 12-10.30 Sun ~ Bedrooms: £40B/£45B

WINEHAM TQ2320 Map 3

Royal Oak £

Village signposted from A272 and B2116

Popular locally, this unchanging, simply furnished and old-fashioned pub has been in the same family for over 50 years. It still has no fruit machines, piped music or even beer pumps. Logs burn in an enormous inglenook fireplace with a cast-iron Royal Oak fireback, and there's a collection of cigarette cards showing old English pubs, a stuffed stoat and crocodile, a collection of jugs, ancient corkscrews decorating the very low beams above the serving counter, and racing plates, tools and a coach horn on the walls; maybe a nice tabby cat, and views of quiet countryside from the back parlour. Well kept Harveys Best with a guest such as Shepherd Neame Spitfire or Wadworths 6X tapped from the cask in a stillroom; darts, shove-ha'penny, dominoes, cribbage. Bar snacks are limited to home-made winter soup (£2.50), simple sandwiches (from £2.25), and ploughman's (from £4.50). There are some picnic-sets outside – picturesque if you are facing the pub. No children inside. More reports please. *(Recommended by Ron Shelton, John Davis, RWC, Brenda and Rob Fincham)*

Inn Business ~ Tenant Tim Peacock ~ Real ale ~ Bar food (served during opening hours) ~ No credit cards ~ (01444) 881252 ~ Children allowed away from main bar ~ Dogs welcome ~ Open 11-2.30, 5.30(6 Sat)-11; 12-3, 7-10.30 Sun

LUCKY DIP

Besides the fully inspected pubs, you might like to try these Lucky Dips recommended to us and described by readers (if you do, please send us reports: www.goodguides.co.uk).

ALFOLD BARS TQ0333

Sir Roger Tichbourne [B2133 N of Loxwood]: Outstanding play area with 70-metre aerial runway, two trampolines and lots of climbing equipment; olde-worlde charm inside, enjoyable food from baguettes up), friendly service, Badger Best, K&B and Gribble Fursty Ferret *(Ian Phillips)*

ALFRISTON TQ5203

Olde Smugglers [Waterloo Sq]: Olde-worlde low-beamed white-panelled bar with big inglenook, plenty of bric-a-brac and smuggling mementoes, good value bar food from sandwiches to steaks, good choice of well kept real ales and of wines by the glass, good friendly service; can get crowded as this lovely village draws many visitors; children allowed in eating area and conservatory, garden tables *(LYM, Ann and Colin Hunt)*

☆ *Star* [High St]: Fascinating fine painted medieval carvings outside, heavy-beamed bar (busy lunchtime, quiet evenings) with chain-pub feel but some interesting features inc medieval sanctuary post, antique furnishings and big log fire in Tudor fireplace, some no smoking areas, bar food from sandwiches and baked potatoes up, well kept Bass, Fullers London Pride and Harveys Best, decent wines by the glass, good coffee, daily papers and magazines, easy chairs in comfortable lounge, restaurant; good modern bedrooms in up-to-date part behind, open all day summer *(Richard and Margaret Peers, LYM, Mr and Mrs S Felstead, the Didler, Tony and Wendy Hobden, Michael and Ann Cole)*

AMBERLEY TQ0313

Sportsmans [Crossgates; Rackham Rd, off B2139]: Pleasant atmosphere in three bars and pretty little back conservatory (with terrific views, shared by terrace tables), well kept changing real ales, lots of wines by the glass, friendly licensees and well organised neatly uniformed staff, food (somewhat pricey) from sandwiches through sausage and mash, cottage pie and so forth to steaks; piped music may obtrude; children welcome *(Norma and Noel Thomas, LYM, Martin and Karen Wake)*

ANGMERING TQ0704

☆ *Spotted Cow* [High St]: Appealing pub with good generous food (very popular wkdy lunchtimes with older people) from imaginative sandwiches up, well kept Fullers London Pride, Harveys Best, Ringwood Best and a guest beer, good choice of wines by the glass, friendly and enthusiastic chef/landlord, smuggling history, sporting caricatures, cool and roomy in summer, two log fires winter, no piped music; children welcome, restaurant, no smoking conservatory, big garden with boules and play area; open all day Sun, afternoon jazz sometimes then, lovely walk to Highdown hill fort *(Cathy Robinson, Ed Coombe, Tony and Wendy Hobden, Bruce Bird, John Davis, Andy and Jill Kassube, John Beeken)*

APULDRAM SU8401

☆ *Black Horse* [A286 SW of Chichester]: Comfortable open-plan pub dating from 18th c, very wide and reasonably priced blackboard food choice running up to good seafood inc huge lobsters, small bar with Courage Directors, Fullers London Pride and Greene King Old Speckled Hen, more tables in neat no smoking dining area opening on to covered terrace, friendly enthusiastic landlady and well trained staff, decent wines; terrace tables outside, picnic-sets in big orchard garden with slide and swings *(Keith Stevens, BB, Jane Basso, Brian Root)*

ARDINGLY TQ3429

Ardingly Inn [Street Lane, off B2028]: Spacious and comfortable brightly lit bar, big central log fire (not always lit), well kept Badger ales with Gribble guests, attractively presented plentiful food from sandwiches and bar snacks to interesting restaurant dishes and Sun lunch, attentive service, traditional games; piped music may be loud: dogs allowed, reasonably priced bedrooms *(Susan and John Douglas, C and R Bromage)*

☆ *Gardeners Arms* [B2028 2 miles N]: Olde-worlde pub divided by standing timbers, with inglenooks, farm tools, horsebrasses, hunting horns and old local photographs, a mix of tables inc some nice old ones, popular food from good baguettes to some interesting hot dishes (need a table number before you queue to order), well kept Badger Best and Harveys; may be piped pop music, no children inside; attractive wooden furniture on pretty terrace, with lots of picnic-sets in side garden; open all day at least wknds, opp S of England show ground and handy for Borde Hill and Wakehurst Place *(Nigel Williamson, Susan and John Douglas, BB, Alec and Joan Laurence)*

ARLINGTON TQ5407

☆ *Yew Tree* [off A22 nr Hailsham, or A27 W of Polegate]: Neatly modernised two-bar Victorian village local popular for hearty home cooking (can ask for smaller helpings) from hot filled rolls to wild boar, well kept Harveys Best, log fires, efficient cheery service, darts, no smoking conservatory; children welcome, good big garden and newly reworked play area, by paddock with farm animals *(BB, John Beeken)*

ARUNDEL TQ0208

☆ ***Black Rabbit*** [Mill Rd, Offham; keep on and don't give up!]: Long nicely refurbished riverside pub very popular with families – lovely spot nr wildfowl reserve, lots of tables outside, timeless views of water meadows and castle; enjoyable food range, Badger ales with Gribble guests, good choice of decent wines by the glass, friendly service, log fires; open all day, doubling as summer tea shop, very busy then, with summer boat trips, good walks *(Paul and Penny Rampton, LYM, Mrs Romey Heaton, Ian and Jane Irving, Susan and John Douglas)*

Kings Arms [Tarrant St/Kings Arms Hill]: Compact two-bar local with good fire in quiet lounge, well kept ales such as Fullers London Pride, Hop Back Summer Lightning and Youngs, good value lunchtime sandwiches, baguettes and baked potatoes (not Sun), friendly staff; darts and piped music in public bar, third small room up a step; small back yard, open all day wknds *(Tony Hobden)*

Red Lion [High St]: Well run and cheerful, with good choice of beers such as Fullers and Youngs, charming service, good value food *(John Davis)*

☆ ***Swan*** [High St]: Smart open-plan L-shaped bar with attractive woodwork and matching fittings, friendly efficient young staff, good choice of well presented food from baguettes and baked potatoes to restaurant meals, Gales Butser, GB and HSB and a guest beer, beaten brass former inn-sign on wall, restaurant; piped music; good bedrooms, open all day *(LYM, Mr and Mrs S Felstead, John Davis)*

ASHURST TQ1716

Fountain [B2135 S of Partridge Green]: New licensees for this 16th-c country pub, neatly kept, rustic tap room on right has high-backed wooden cottage armchairs by log fire in brick inglenook, some antique polished trestle tables, and fine old flagstones, with more in opened-up snug with heavy beams, simple furniture, and another inglenook fireplace; bar food (not Sun or Mon evenings), Fullers London Pride, Harveys and Kings Horsham; prettily planted garden with duck pond; children over 10, dogs in bar *(Cathy Robinson, Ed Coombe, Brenda and Rob Fincham, LYM)*

BALCOMBE TQ3033

Cowdray Arms [London Rd (B2036/B2110 N of village)]: Roomy main-road pub popular lunchtime for sensibly priced food from sandwiches up, well kept ales such as Greene King IPA and Abbot and Harveys, L-shaped bar and no smoking restaurant with conservatory; bar can be smoky; children welcome, large garden with good play area *(Eamonn and Natasha Skyrme, Mr Bannon, DWAJ)*

Half Moon [Haywards Heath Rd]: Villagey local with well kept Harveys, good generous sandwiches and usual hot dishes; tables in narrow front garden, good walking area *(Jenny and Brian Seller)*

BARCOMBE TQ4416

Anchor [Barcombe Mills]: Nice for summer, with lawn tables by winding River Ouse (boat or canoe hire) and lots of quiet walks; two beamed bars with well kept Badger Best and Tanglefoot and Harveys Best, unpretentious food, restaurant (bookings only), traditional games, small front conservatory; open all day *(LYM, Peter Meister)*

BARNHAM SU9604

☆ ***Murrell Arms*** [Yapton Rd]: Unspoilt and old-fashioned pub with very long-serving licensees, main room with masses of interesting bric-a-brac, nice old farmhouse chairs, very high-backed settle, mix of tables, candles in bottles, and huge polished half-barrel bar counter, cheerful public bar and simple tiny snug, Gales HSB, BBB and a changing guest, two open fires, darts, shove-ha'penny, straightforward bar food (not Thurs evening); no children or dogs; pretty flower-filled courtyard with big cider press and ancient wooden furniture under grape vine, picnic-sets in cottagey little enclosed garden up some steps, open all day wknds *(Fred Chamberlain, LYM)*

BILLINGSHURST TQ0830

☆ ***Blue Ship*** [The Haven; hamlet signposted off A29 just N of junction with A264, then follow signpost left towards Garlands and Okehurst]: Unpretentious pub in quiet country spot, beamed and brick-floored front bar with blazing fire in inglenook fireplace, scrubbed tables and wall benches, and hatch service dispensing Badger Best and Tanglefoot, and Gribble Fursty Ferret on handpump; corridor leads to a couple of small carpeted rooms (one no smoking), darts, bar billiards, shove-ha'penny, cribbage, dominoes, reasonably priced traditional bar food (not Sun or Mon evenings); children in one back room, seats by trees or tangle of honeysuckle around front door *(Phil and Sally Gorton, Mrs Romey Heaton, John Davis, the Didler, LYM)*

Olde Six Bells [High St (A29)]: Picturesque partly 14th-c flagstoned and timbered pub, newly refurbished to include roomy modern air-conditioned no smoking dining area, enjoyable straightforward food, well kept Badger ales, inglenook fireplace; big-screen sports TV and giant Connect Four, popular with young people evenings; pretty roadside garden and heated terrace *(LYM, Rebecca Davis)*

BIRDHAM SZ8199

Bell [B2198 towards Somerley]: Cheerfully and brightly refurbished open-plan pub with some stripped brick, plates, pictures and copperware, enjoyable food from sandwiches and ploughman's through pubby favourites to some interesting dishes inc local crab, friendly service, changing real ales such as Adnams, Courage Best, Fullers London Pride and Shepherd Neame Spitfire; piped music, games machine; picnic-sets and play area in good-sized garden behind *(Mrs Brenda Calver, Father Robert Marsh)*

BIRLING GAP TV5596

Birling Gap: Hotel's nicely decorated separate bar on picturesque Seven Sisters cliffs just above seashore, old thatching and carpentry tools, pleasant atmosphere, useful bar food, Courage Directors; bedrooms with own bathrooms *(E G Parish)*

BLACKHAM TQ4839

Sussex Oak [A264 towards E Grinstead]: Friendly and unpretentious, with well kept Shepherd Neame ales, good choice of food; country views from peaceful garden *(LYM, Bruce Bird)*

BOARSHEAD TQ5332

Boars Head [Eridge Rd, off A26 bypass]: Good friendly service, well kept beer and good value fresh food in attractive old unspoilt pub with separate restaurant; bar can be smoky; quiet spot *(C Whittington, Richard May)*

BOGNOR REGIS SZ9398

Elizabeth II [The Steyne]: Friendly staff, good atmosphere, reasonable prices; pool, piped music and satellite TV, karaoke Fri, disco Sat *(David Gould)*

Hatters [Queensway]: Friendly staff and atmosphere, enjoyable food *(David Gould)*

Regis [Esplanade]: Friendly and cosy, with enjoyable reasonably priced food *(David Gould)*

Steyne Bar [The Steyne, Esplanade]: Good friendly atmosphere, reasonable prices; karaoke Sat *(David Gould)*

Unicorn [High St]: Friendly reasonably priced pub with karaoke or disco every night *(David Gould)*

BOLNEY TQ2623

Bolney Stage [off old A23 just N of A272]: Neat and comfortably olde-worlde timbered dining pub locally popular for wide range of good handsomely presented bar and restaurant food, friendly expert service, relaxed atmosphere, choice of beers, large log fire; handy for Sheffield Park and Bluebell Railway *(Anne and Michael Bogod)*

BOSHAM SU8003

Anchor Bleu [High St]: Listed for its lovely waterside position in a charming village – sea and boat views, little terrace outside massive wheel-operated bulkhead door to ward off high tides (cars parked on seaward side often submerged); plenty of potential inside, open all day *(LYM, Karen Eliot, Susan and John Douglas, Ann and Colin Hunt, Brenda and Rob Fincham)*

BRAMBER TQ1810

Castle Hotel [The Street]: Pleasant and roomy olde-worlde quiet lounge, wide choice of reasonably priced food from baguettes and filled baked potatoes up, Adnams, Bass and Fullers London Pride, good friendly service; appealing back garden, bedrooms, charming village and views *(John Branston, M and R Thomas)*

BRIGHTON TQ3104

Bath Arms [Union St/Meeting House Lane, The Lanes]: Several high-ceilinged rooms with panelling and old fireplaces, lots of old photographs and cartoon prints, half a dozen real ales inc Harveys, decent coffee, New World wines, attentive staff, good value bar food from sandwiches up; pavement tables *(Val and Alan Green, John A Barker)*

Bugle [St Martins St]: Lively three-room local with Irish licensees, posters and live music, Harveys, Timothy Taylors Landlord, Youngs and a guest beer, real fire; picnic-sets out in front and on nice quiet back terrace *(MLR)*

☆ ***Colonnade*** [New Rd, off North St; by Theatre Royal]: Small nicely preserved late Victorian bar, with red plush, shining brass and mahogany, gleaming mirrors, interesting pre-war playbills and lots of signed theatrical photographs, white gloves and canes in top hats peaking over velvet drapes, good friendly service even when very busy, particularly well kept Bass, Boddingtons and Harveys (early evening wkdy happy hour), good choice of good value wines, tiny front terrace; internal stairs to Theatre Royal, they take interval orders – and performers like it *(Val and Alan Green, BB, John A Barker)*

☆ ***Cricketers*** [Black Lion St]: Cheerful down-to-earth town pub, very well run, with ageing Victorian furnishings and loads of interesting bric-a-brac – even a stuffed bear; well kept Greene King Old Speckled Hen, Harveys, Charles Wells Bombardier and Youngs tapped from the cask, good coffee, friendly bustle, usual well priced lunchtime bar food with fresh veg in upstairs bar, restaurant (where children allowed) and covered ex-stables courtyard bar; piped music; open all day *(LYM, Ann and Colin Hunt, Richard Waller, Pauline Smith)*

Druids Head [Brighton Pl]: Genuine pub with Tudor origins, flagstoned floor, sensibly priced well kept Harveys *(John A Barker)*

☆ ***Evening Star*** [Surrey St]: Chatty and appealingly unassuming tap for good Dark Star microbrewery, with several well kept changing beers from other small breweries; enthusiastic landlord (may let you sample before you buy), changing farm ciders and perries, lots of country wines, good simple food (not evenings Sat-Mon or Thurs), well worn but clean bare boards, plain furnishings, good mix of customers; unobtrusive piped music, live music nights, tables outside, open all day *(Tracey and Stephen Groves, MLR, R Tranter)*

☆ ***Greys*** [Southover St, Kemp Town]: Thriving atmosphere in compact nicely designed open-plan pub with friendly newish licensees (he's an actor), well kept real ales such as Harveys and Timothy Taylors Landlord, belgian beers, good wines by the glass, popular food (may take a while on busy evenings and wknds); may be quiet piped folk music, some live singers or entertainers; another room and lavatories upstairs, a couple of tables out behind *(BB, Richard Houghton, Val and Alan Green)*

Hand in Hand [Upper St James's St, Kemptown]: Busy idiosyncratic local brewing its own unusual Kemptown beers and lagers, also Badger Best and Tanglefoot, Stowford Press cider, good value wkdy lunchtime snacks such as sandwiches, pies and pizzas, Sun roast potatoes, cheerful service, dim-lit bar with tie collection and newspaper pages all over walls, nice photographs on ceiling, colourful mix of customers; veteran fruit machine, TV, good

piped music; open all day wknds, from mid-afternoon wkdys *(MLR, R T and J C Moggridge)*
King & Queen [Marlborough Pl]: Medieval-style lofty main hall with well kept Theakstons Best and XB from long bar, generous good value food inc good Sun roasts, friendly service, pool table; flagstoned courtyard, open all day Sun *(LYM, Ann and Colin Hunt)*
Lord Nelson [Trafalgar St]: Friendly central pub with good value lunchtime food from sandwiches to fresh fish, well kept Harveys ales inc Mild, farm cider, log fire, back conservatory; pub games, sports TV *(Jackie Jones)*
Rose Hill Tavern [Rose Hill Terrace, off A23]: Good local with attractive tiled façade, well kept Gales, Greene King Old Speckled Hen and Harveys Best *(MLR)*
Sussex Cricketer [Eaton Rd, by cricket ground]: Warm and comfortable Ember Inn with welcoming layout, well priced standard food all day from sandwiches to nice puddings, well kept ales such as Harveys, decent wines by the glass, plush seating *(Tony Hobden, Andy and Jill Kassube)*

BURWASH TQ6724

☆ ***Bell*** [A265 E of Heathfield]: Pretty tile-hung village pub opp church, picnic-sets out by colourful flower baskets and tubs, well used L-shaped bar with interesting bric-a-brac and good log fire, well kept Greene King Morlands Original and Ruddles Best and a guest such as Wadworths 6X, friendly service, decent house wines, pub games, generous home-made food (not Sun evening) from sandwiches to steaks, cosy and attractive no smoking dining room; music quizzes, TV, piped music, children and dogs welcome; roadside picnic-sets facing Norman church, bedrooms sharing bathrooms, charming village, open all day wknds *(Peter Meister, LYM, D S Cottrell, Glenwys and Alan Lawrence, Kevin Thorpe)*
Rose & Crown [inn sign on A265]: New tenants and chef for low-beamed timbered local tucked away down lane in pretty village, well kept Harveys IPA and Best, fine log fire, pleasant restaurant area with two-course Sun carvery from heated counter, decent wines, good service; music quiz nights, tables out in small quiet garden, bedrooms, limited nearby parking *(BB, Tony and Wendy Hobden)*

BURY TQ0113

☆ ***Squire & Horse*** [Bury Common; A29 Fontwell—Pulborough]: Sizeable roadside pub with wide range of popular generous home-made food inc some interesting blackboard dishes, well kept ales such as Brakspears, Harveys and Shepherd Neame, Sun bar nibbles, neatly kept partly divided U-shaped open-plan bar areas, heavy beams, pink plush wall seats, hunting prints and ornaments, flame-effect stove, flourishing two-level beamed restaurant with fresh flowers and another stove; green tables and chairs on pretty terrace; cl Sun evening, Mon *(BB, Mr and Mrs Gordon Turner, John Evans, Bruce and Pat Anderson)*

BUXTED TQ4923

White Hart [Station Rd (A272)]: Well run roadside pub with well kept Greene King Old Speckled Hen and Harveys, friendly efficient service and quite a few locals, almost too wide a choice of interesting food, cheery chatty main bar divided by timbering, big brick fireplace, hops and some horsebrasses, red leatherette seats, left-hand dining bar, big light and airy dining conservatory with fairy-lit plants and light wooden furniture on wood-strip floor; may be piped pop music; pleasant garden with plenty of seats *(Michael and Ann Cole, Sue and Mike Todd)*

CHAILEY TQ3919

☆ ***Five Bells*** [A275 9 miles N of Lewes]: Attractive rambling roadside pub, spacious and well appointed, with lots of different rooms and alcoves leading from low-beamed bar area with fine old brick floor, brick walls and inglenook, candles and fresh flowers, leather sofa by the log fire with another under window, dining extension, well kept Fullers London Pride, Greene King Old Speckled Hen and Harveys Best, decent wine choice, smallish but interesting range of well liked food inc OAP lunch discounts, good service, nice old greyhound called Bentley; Fri jazz nights; picnic-sets in pretty garden with play area *(BB, C and R Bromage, Michael Hasslacher, Tony and Wendy Hobden, Glenn and Gillian Miller)*

CHICHESTER SU8605

Bell [Broyle Rd]: Well kept changing ales such as Arundel Gold, Boddingtons and Flowers IPA, interesting wines, good food from separate counter inc super puddings, friendly attentive service, no smoking dining area (bar can get smoky); handy for theatre *(Tony Hobden, Jane Basso, Ann and Colin Hunt, Richard Waller, Pauline Smith)*
Coach & Horses [St Pancras]: Comfortable and friendly open-plan local, choice of well kept real ales, good lunchtime bar food from open side kitchen, quick service; quiet piped music; attractive back terrace *(Ann and Colin Hunt)*
George & Dragon [North St]: Bustling uncluttered bare-boards bar nicely smartened up under good new licensees, well kept real ales, decent house wines, wholesome plentiful food, pleasant service, conservatory; tables out on quiet back terrace, bedrooms *(anon)*
Globe [Southgate]: Roomy and friendly, with enjoyable food, reasonable prices; DJ competition Weds, disco Fri/-Sat *(David Gould)*
Mainline [Whyke Rd]: Large friendly pub with good value food; younger crowd evenings *(David Gould)*
Nags Hotel [St Pancras]: Lots of panelling and old books, log fires, substantial good food in bar and large pleasant eating area inc evening and Sun lunch carvery, friendly staff, thriving local atmosphere, good choice of well kept real ales *(Ann and Colin Hunt)*
Old Cross [North St]: Open-plan chain dining pub in building dating from 16th c, wide

blackboard food choice inc speciality pies, Courage Best and Directors and Charles Wells Bombardier, good choice of wines by the glass, friendly efficient service, no smoking areas; open all day *(Ann and Colin Hunt, Tony and Wendy Hobden)*

☆ ***Park Tavern*** [Priory Rd, opp Jubilee Park]: Comfortable newly refurbished pub in attractive spot opp Priory Park, enjoyable lunchtime food using fresh local produce and the day's fish, also baguettes, sandwiches and some thai dishes (may be authentic thai evening banquets), helpful licensees and cheerful service, well kept Gales BB, HSB, a seasonal beer and a guest such as Wadworths 6X, relaxing smallish front bar (no smoking on right, with huge mirrors) and extensive back eating area with crisp white tablecloths *(Ann and Colin Hunt, Jane Basso, BB, Richard Waller, Pauline Smith)*

Smith & Western [Station Approach]: Roomy pub with enjoyable food, friendly staff and free bar nibbles *(David Gould)*

Toad [West St]: Former church nicely converted into real ale pub, multi-level seating around big central bar, good value straightforward food till 6, real ales, decent coffee, friendly staff, reasonable prices; music and constant videos, good mix of customers inc lively young people at night; open all day, opp cathedral *(Jane Basso, David Gould)*

Vestry [Southgate]: Good quiet atmosphere, friendly staff, reasonable prices *(David Gould)*

CHILGROVE SU8116

☆ ***Royal Oak*** [off B2141 Petersfield—Chichester, signed Hooksway down steep single track]: Charmingly tucked-away two-room country tavern, beams, brick floors, smartly simple country-kitchen furnishings, huge log fires; well kept ales inc Timothy Taylors and a distinctive one brewed for the pub by Hampshire, chatty landlord, inexpensive no-nonsense food inc lunchtime ploughman's, games, provision for children; some live music Fri in summer; tables out in pretty garden, good walks, cl Mon and winter Sun evening *(Torrens Lyster, Ann and Colin Hunt, Martin and Karen Wake, J A Snell, LYM, Prof and Mrs S Barnett, John Davis, M B Griffith, R B Gardiner)*

CLAYTON TQ2914

Jack & Jill [A273 N of Brighton]: Friendly country pub with good range of enjoyable food from ploughman's to steak, good service, well kept changing beers *(Father Robert Marsh, Mary M Grimshaw)*

COLEMANS HATCH TQ4533

☆ ***Hatch*** [signed off B2026, or off B2110 opp church]: Quaint and attractive weatherboarded Ashdown Forest pub dating from 1430, big log fire in quickly filling beamed bar, small back dining room with another log fire, good generous food from sandwiches, baked potatoes, giant ploughman's and filled ciabatta bread through imaginative salads to bass and steak, well kept Harveys Best, Larkins Best and one or two guest beers, friendly quick young staff, good mix of customers inc families and dogs; picnic-sets on front terrace and in beautifully kept big garden, open all day Sun and summer Sat *(Pamela and Douglas Cooper, LYM, Robert M Warner, Peter Meister, John Davis, Simon and Sally Small)*

COOLHAM TQ1423

☆ ***George & Dragon*** [pub signed just off A272, about 1½ m E of village; Dragons Lane]: Friendly and chatty new landlord in appealing very low-beamed ancient pub, unpretentiously comfortable, with good fire in enormous inglenook fireplace, well kept Badger ales, sensibly priced home-made bar food from baked potatoes up, small restaurant, back games room with bar billiards; can get pretty busy; children allowed in games or eating areas, dogs allowed in bar, well spaced tables out in big attractive orchard garden, open all day wknds *(Mike and Heather Watson, John Beeken, LYM)*

Selsey Arms [A272/B2139]: Two linked areas, well kept Fullers London Pride and Harveys, chatty atmosphere, friendly considerate service even when quite busy, blackboard food from filled rolls and baked potatoes up, cheerful fire, elderly labrador (likes snacks); garden fenced off from road in front, another behind *(Terry Buckland)*

COUSLEY WOOD TQ6533

Old Vine [B2100 Wadhurst—Lamberhurst]: Attractive dining pub with lots of old timbers and beams, wide range of generous decent food inc good fish, good house wines, four well kept ales; rustic pretty restaurant on right, pubbier bare-boards or brick-floored area with woodburner by bar; credit cards impounded if you run a bar bill; a few tables out behind *(BB, Oliver and Sue Rowell)*

COWFOLD TQ2122

Hare & Hounds [Henfield Rd (A281 S)]: Welcoming refurbished pub, part flagstoned, with real ales such as Harveys, Hepworths, Kings and Tetleys, amiable landlord, good choice of well cooked food, decent wine list, darts, no smoking family area *(Tony and Wendy Hobden)*

CUCKFIELD TQ3025

☆ ***White Harte*** [South Street; off A272 W of Haywards Heath]: Pretty partly medieval pub, comfortable beamed and timbered lounge with polished floorboards and ancient brick flooring, sturdy furnishings in public bar with blazing inglenook log fire and traditional games, straightforward bar lunches, well kept Badger Best, K&B and Tanglefoot on handpump; piped music, TV; dogs in bar, children welcome, fine downland views from pretty back garden, cl Mon lunchtime in winter *(Robert M Warner, R T and J C Moggridge, Jeremy Woods, LYM, Terry Buckland, Ron Gentry, Klaus and Elizabeth Leist)*

DALLINGTON TQ6619

☆ ***Swan*** [Woods Corner, B2096 E]: Appealing low-beamed country local with good choice of food inc fish specialities, well kept Harveys Best and a guest beer, decent house wines, good coffee, friendly staff, warm log fire in bare-boards bar, small comfortable back dining room with far views to Beachy Head; steps down to smallish garden *(BB, Mike Gorton)*

DELL QUAY SU8302

☆ ***Crown & Anchor*** [off A286 S of Chichester]: Modernised 15th-c pub in splendid spot overlooking Chichester Harbour on site of Roman quay, can be packed at wknds; well kept Courage Directors and Theakstons Best or John Smiths and Charles Wells Bombardier, very wide choice of wines by the glass, enjoyable middle-priced all-day food servery (can be a queue, but service is then prompt); marina views from comfortable bow-windowed lounge bar and terrace picnic-sets, panelled public bar with unspoilt fireplace (dogs welcome), dining room; nice walks *(Ann and Colin Hunt, BB, Martin and Karen Wake, Father David Cossar)*

DENTON TQ4502

Flying Fish [Denton Rd]: Pretty and neatly kept 17th-c village local with hops and brassware, good reasonably priced home cooking, comfortable no smoking dining room, well kept Shepherd Neame ales, friendly prompt service; attractive garden behind, tables out in front too *(the Didler)*

DITCHLING TQ3215

Bull [High St (B2112)]: Beamed 14th-c inn with attractive antique furnishings in main bar, old pictures, good inglenook log fire, well kept Harveys and Timothy Taylors Landlord, enjoyable home-made food, helpful efficient staff, comfortable family room, popular restaurant; wheelchair access, picnic-sets in garden and on suntrap concrete terrace, charming old village just below downs *(LYM, Terry Buckland)*

DURRINGTON TQ1104

Farmhouse [Fulbeck Ave/Titnore Way]: Newly converted farmhouse joined by conservatory to no smoking barn pastiche, sensibly priced food all day from sandwiches up, Courage Best and Directors and Harveys Best; piped music may obtrude; tables out on decking *(Tony and Wendy Hobden)*

EARTHAM SU9409

☆ ***George*** [signed off A285 Chichester—Petworth, from Fontwell off A27, from Slindon off A29]: Popular pub smartly refurbished in light wood, comfortable lounge, attractive pubbier public bar with games, old farm tools and photographs, welcoming helpful service and hands-on landlord, enjoyable home-made food at sensible prices, well kept real ales, log fire, no smoking restaurant; piped music; easy disabled access, children welcome in eating areas, large pretty garden, attractive surroundings, open all day summer wknds *(Peter D B Harding, Jane Basso, LYM, Christine Crowther)*

EASEBOURNE SU8922

White Horse [off A272 just NE of Midhurst]: Cosy beamed village local, large mainly bare-boards bar with several distinct areas inc fireside armchairs and small no smoking dining area, convivial landlord, traditional food from baked potatoes up (worth booking wknds), well kept Greene King IPA and Abbot, two open fires; tables on back grass and in courtyard *(LYM, John Beeken)*

EAST LAVANT SU8608

☆ ***Royal Oak*** [signed off A286 N of Chichester; Pook Lane]: Upscale dining pub too restauranty now for the main entries, but still has well kept Badger ales and country wines alongside its good house wines; prompt friendly service, good relaxed atmosphere, candlelight and scrubbed tables, rugs on bare boards and flooring tiles, two open fires and a woodburner, racing prints; attractively planted gardens inc secluded terrace with bookable tables (quiet except for wknd light planes using Goodwood airfield), good walks; comfortable bedrooms, cl Sun pm, Mon *(Ron Shelton, Gerald Wilkinson, John Freestone, Sally Burn, LYM, Christopher and Elise Way)*

EASTBOURNE TV6198

Buccaneer [Compton St, by Winter Gardens]: Popular open-plan bar shaped like a galleon, raised no smoking side, Ind Coope Burton, Marstons Pedigree, Tetleys and three guest beers, theatre memorabilia; no food Sun, open all day *(the Didler)*

Pilot [Holywell Rd, Meads; just off front below approach from Beachy Head]: Bustling, comfortable and friendly local, ample enjoyable food, pleasant prompt service, well kept Harveys, good ship and aeroplane photographs, log and coal fires, nice adjoining restaurant area; garden tables *(Bob Richardson)*

Ship [Meads St]: Recently tastefully refurbished with big leather sofas and slightly colonial feel, good value food inc fresh local fish; nicely planted garden with huge new decked area and barbecue *(Marcus and Lienna Gomm)*

ELSTED SU8119

☆ ***Elsted Inn*** [Elsted Marsh]: Appealing two-bar country pub on good form, enjoyable home-cooked food, well kept ales such as Ballards, Cheriton Pots and Timothy Taylors Landlord, nice country furniture, wooden floors, original shutters, old railway photographs, traditional games, log fires; lovely enclosed downs-view garden with big terrace and summer barbecues, well appointed adjacent bedroom block *(LYM, David Cosham, John Davis)*

ERIDGE STATION TQ5434

Huntsman: Two-bar country pub under new management, good choice of reasonably priced food (not Sun evening) from sandwiches up, well kept Badger Best, K&B and Tanglefoot, farm cider, good range of wines; lacks a no smoking area; walkers and dogs welcome, big garden, cl Mon *(Paul A Moore, Father Robert Marsh, Tony and Wendy Hobden, Peter Meister)*

EWHURST GREEN TQ7924

White Dog: Extensive and attractive partly 17th-c pub/restaurant in fine spot above Bodiam Castle, cheerful unpretentious atmosphere, wide choice of reasonably priced enjoyable food (maybe not Mon), friendly helpful service, log fire, well kept ales, evening restaurant (and locals around the bar); walkers and children welcome, bedrooms, tables in big garden making the most of the view *(LYM, Alan Cole, Kirstie Bruce, Vincent Board)*

FAIRWARP TQ4626

Foresters Arms [B2026]: Welcoming Ashdown Forest local handy for Vanguard Way and Weald Way, comfortable lounge bar, enjoyable food from baguettes to steak and popular Sunday lunch, efficient smiling service, well kept Badger ales and farm cider, woodburner; piped music; children in eating area, tables out on terrace and in garden with some interesting plants, has been open all day summer *(Michael and Ann Cole, RDK, LYM)*

FERNHURST SU9028

☆ *Red Lion* [3m S of Haslemere; The Green, off A286 via Church Lane]: Wisteria-covered 15th-c pub tucked quietly away by green nr church, friendly attentive staff, good value food from interesting sandwiches and snacks to fresh fish, well kept Fullers ales, good wines, heavy beams, attractive layout and furnishings, good relaxed atmosphere, no smoking restaurant; children welcome, pretty gardens front and back *(BB, Gerry and Rosemary Dobson, H H Hellin, Mrs Maricar Jagger, Roy and Lindsey Fentiman)*

FERRING TQ0901

Tudor Close [Ferringham Lane, S Ferring]: Thatched former barn under new management, imposing intricately carved fireplace, ornate lamp stands, high rafters, no smoking restaurant end and new conservatory, upper gallery overlooking bar the other end, well kept Badger and Greene King ales with Wadworths 6X, some emphasis on enjoyable reasonably priced home-made food from sandwiches and baked potatoes up, very popular with older people at lunchtime; open all day Fri-Sun *(Tony and Wendy Hobden)*

FIRLE TQ4607

☆ *Ram* [village signed off A27 Lewes—Polegate]: Unpretentious and comfortably worn 17th-c village pub, very welcoming to families and booted walkers; big plain tables, log fires, traditional games, no smoking snug, good-sized family room, several well kept ales such as Harveys Best and RCH Pitchfork, farm cider, usual food (all day) from baguettes and baked potatoes up, with three sizes of children's meals and cream teas; play equipment and nicely segregated table area in walled garden behind, open all day *(LYM, the Didler, Peter Meister, LM, Dominic Morgan, John Davis)*

FISHBOURNE SU8304

Bulls Head [Fishbourne Rd (A259 Chichester—Emsworth)]: Interesting, relaxing and welcoming old village pub with pretty window boxes, fair-sized main bar, full Gales range kept well with guest beers such as Fullers London Pride, good varied quickly served food often using local produce (not Sun evening – Sun lunch very popular), children's helpings, friendly neatly dressed staff, log fire, children's area, restaurant with no smoking area; skittle alley, picnic-sets on terrace *(J A Snell, Ann and Colin Hunt, Jane Basso, David H T Dimock, MRSM)*

Woolpack [Fishbourne Rd W; just off A27 Chichester—Emsworth]: Big comfortably refurbished open-plan pub under new landlord, nice variety of seats inc settees, smart no smoking dining area, enjoyable food, well kept Greene King Abbot, Youngs Special and two guest beers; dogs welcome, big garden with barbecues and spit-roasts, various events inc live music *(Tony and Wendy Hobden, Ann and Colin Hunt)*

FOREST ROW TQ4235

Brambletye [A22]: Long bar at side of hotel with full range of Gales ales kept well, friendly staff, open fire, no smoking dining room with good value carvery and other dishes; children welcome, tables in colourful courtyard with fountain and bedrooms off *(Tony and Wendy Hobden)*

FRANT TQ5835

Abergavenny Arms [A267 S of T Wells]: Friendly mock-Tudor main-road pub, two bars, log fire, well kept ales inc Fullers London Pride and Harveys Best, wide choice of reasonably priced popular food from ploughman's and baked potatoes up, bar billiards; children welcome, bedrooms *(Peter Meister)*

FULKING TQ2411

☆ *Shepherd & Dog* [off A281 N of Brighton, via Poynings]: Charming partly panelled low-ceilinged country pub beautifully placed below downs, antique or stoutly rustic furnishings around log fire, attractive bow windows, well kept Badger ales, wide food choice (all day wknds) from sandwiches and baked potatoes up inc lots of ploughman's and summer salads, no piped music; can be packed out; dogs and children welcome, pretty streamside garden with upper play lawn (loudspeaker food announcements out here), open all day *(LYM, Sarah and Huw, C L Kauffmann, Jeremy Woods, M and R Thomas, John and Tania Wood, Ron Gentry, John Hendy)*

FUNTINGTON SU7908

Fox & Hounds: Much refurbished beamed pub with wide food choice inc popular Sun roasts, cottagey rooms, comfortable and attractive dining extension, welcoming service, well kept Badger Best and Tanglefoot, reasonably priced wines, good coffee, huge log fire, no music; garden behind *(Ann and Colin Hunt, R B Gardiner)*

GATWICK TQ2841

Village Inn [South Terminal]: Typical Wetherspoons, useful cross between pub, coffee shop and restaurant; first floor nr check-in and shops *(Alan M Pring)*

GLYNDE TQ4508

Trevor Arms: Well kept Harveys ales and enjoyable low-priced food from ploughman's and baked potatoes to good Sun roasts, small bar with corridor to no smoking room and big dining room, Glyndebourne posters and photographs; tables in large garden with downland backdrop – busy wknds *(A J Bowen, Tony Hobden, John Davis, John Beeken)*

GODDARDS GREEN TQ2820

Sportsman: Efficient family dining pub with wide choice of popular usual food from open sandwiches and baked potatoes up, waitress service, well kept Badger real ales, decent house wines, no smoking restaurant extension *(Tony and Wendy Hobden, Terry Buckland, Ron Gentry)*

GORING-BY-SEA TQ1004

Swallows Return [Titnore Lane, off A259/A2032 Northbrook College roundabout]: Vintage Inns barn conversion, decent food all day inc sandwiches till 5, Bass and Harveys Best, good choice of wines by the glass, no smoking end and upper gallery; open all day *(Tony and Wendy Hobden)*

GRAFFHAM SU9217

☆ *White Horse*: Spotless family pub with good food, well kept Badger Best and Tanglefoot, friendly licensees, log fires, good South Downs views from conservatory, small dining room, terrace and big garden; walkers welcome, open all day Sun in summer *(John Davis)*

HALNAKER SU9008

☆ *Anglesey Arms* [A285 Chichester—Petworth]: Charmingly unpretentious bar with well kept ales, friendly service, reasonably priced food and traditional games, simple but smart candlelit dining room with stripped pine and flagstones (children allowed), decent wines; garden tables *(John Davis, Keith Stevens, LYM, Ian Wilson, R B Gardiner)*

HAMMERPOT TQ0605

Woodmans Arms: This appealing 16th-c pub just off the A27, a main entry in the 2004 edition and a real favourite with many readers, burned down in February 2004; we hope for news of its rebuilding *(LYM)*

HANDCROSS TQ2629

Red Lion [High St]: Large bar nicely divided with plenty of tables, no smoking area, emphasis on huge blackboard food choice from snacks to fish, lively atmosphere, quick friendly service, Courage-related real ales, good wine list *(Fred Chamberlain, Amanda Eames)*

Royal Oak [Horsham Rd (A279, off A23)]: Friendly low-beamed local, two smallish rooms divided by big log-effect gas fire, welcoming staff and Harvey the dog, good range of well crafted food from light dishes to adventurous substantial dishes and seasonal game, well kept beers, winter mulled wine, old photographs and curios; tables in sunny forecourt, small garden behind *(Fred Keens, Edward and Pat Wolfe)*

Wheatsheaf [B2110 W]: Well kept Badger ales, good range of generous good value food from sandwiches to steaks inc children's, friendly service, two bars with lots of horse tack and farm tools, no smoking dining area; big garden with piped music and play equipment *(C and R Bromage, Ron Gentry)*

HARTFIELD TQ4735

☆ *Anchor* [Church St]: Welcoming 15th-c local with heavy beams and flagstones, little country pictures and houseplants, inglenook log fire and a woodburner, comfortable dining area, well kept Adnams, Bass, Flowers IPA and Harveys Best, generous reasonably priced food from sandwiches, toasties and baked potatoes up, long-serving licensees, darts in lower room; piped music; children welcome, seats out on front verandah, garden with play area, open all day *(LYM, Mike Gorton, Alan Kilpatrick)*

HASSOCKS TQ3015

Pilgrims Goose [A273 N]: Big Vintage Inn with their usual food all day, generous well served coffee and tea as well as good choice of wines by the glass, several welcoming areas, log fires; pleasant garden, open all day *(Tony and Wendy Hobden, Pamela Goodwyn)*

HASTINGS TQ8209

First In Last Out [High St, Old Town]: Congenial and chatty beer-drinkers' local brewing its own good value beers, a couple of well kept guest ales, farm cider, open-plan bar divided by settles, pews forming booths, posts and central raised log fire, simple lunchtime food (not Sun) inc decent sandwiches, character cat presiding in central armchair, no games or juke box; gents' down a few steps, parking nearby difficult; small covered back terrace *(Peter Meister, MLR, John and Wendy Allin, Gwyn Jones)*

Pig in Paradise [seafront]: Very wide bargain-priced food choice from sandwiches up, Courage Best and Directors also well priced, sturdy stripped tables; piped music may be loud *(Father Robert Marsh)*

Stag [All Saints St]: Early 17th-c former smugglers' pub among crooked Tudor buildings on high pavement (up a few steps), low beams, bare boards, stout furniture, lots of pictures, no frills; Shepherd Neame ales, plenty of malt whiskies, friendly long-serving staff, some fascinating stories – ask about the mummified cats; wknd bar food inc occasional bargain barbecues, folk nights Weds, steeply terraced garden behind *(the Didler, MLR)*

HEYSHOTT SU8918

☆ *Unicorn* [off A286 S of Midhurst]: Very friendly small country local in charming downland setting by village green, good choice of well kept ales inc ones from small local breweries, good interesting generous bar food from lunchtime sandwiches and baguettes up, may be free bar nibbles, cheerful service even when busy, comfortably cushioned bar, attractive dining area; children allowed, reasonable disabled access, downs view from pretty garden with barbecue, handy for South Downs Way *(Alan Cowell, John Davis, Cathy Robinson, Ed Coombe)*

HOLTYE TQ4538

White Horse [Holtye Common; A264 East Grinstead—Tunbridge Wells]: Ancient gently refurbished village inn with new landlord doing sensibly limited choice of good food, well kept real ales, good service, illuminated aquarium set into floor; good facilities for the disabled, marvellous view from back lawn, bedrooms *(Mr and Mrs J French, R and S Bentley)*

HOOE TQ6708

Lamb [A259 E of Pevensey]: Prettily placed Vintage Inn, extensively refurbished in their olde-worlde rustic style, arches and lots of stripped brick and flintwork, one snug area around huge log fire and lots of other seats, big tables, well kept Bass and Harveys, good range of house wines, quick friendly young staff, very wide food choice from sandwiches and baguettes up *(R and M Thomas, E G Parish)*

HORSHAM TQ1730

Malt Shovel [Springfield Rd]: Traditional flagstoned pub with up to nine well kept quickly changing real ales, Biddenden farm cider, enjoyable home cooking; open all day *(Robin Pine)*

HORSTED KEYNES TQ3828

Crown [The Green]: As we went to press this appealing 16th-c pub was being rebuilt, much as before, after serious fire damage, and should be open again around the time this edition is published – good news for the many readers who have so enjoyed its well kept beer and enjoyable food in its attractive no smoking dining bar/restaurant; children welcome, tables out in front with pretty flowers and window boxes, and behind looking over cricket green *(anon)*

Green Man [The Green]: Traditional village local in attractive spot facing green, spotless but not too modernised, with bare boards and hop bines, young genial staff, well kept Greene King IPA and Old Speckled Hen and Harveys Best, generous home-made food from ploughman's and baguettes to restaurant dishes, bistro dining room (no children in bar); lots of tables on forecourt, handy for Bluebell Line *(C and R Bromage, Michael and Ann Cole, Neil Hardwick)*

HOUGHTON TQ0111

☆ *George & Dragon* [B2139 W of Storrington]: Elizabethan beams and timbers, attractive old-world bar rambling up and down steps (so not good for disabled people), great views from back extension with no smoking restaurant (popular and generous wkdy bargain lunch for over-50s), well kept Fullers London Pride, Harveys Best and Timothy Taylors Landlord, decent wines, smartly dressed staff; may be piped classical music; children welcome, panoramic Arun valley views too from terraces of charming smartly furnished sloping garden, good walks, open for food all day wknds *(LYM, J H Bell, Jane Basso, John Beeken, David Cosham, A D Marsh, David R Crafts)*

ISFIELD TQ4516

☆ *Halfway House* [Rose Hill (A26)]: Welcoming rambling pub, low beams and timbers, dark pub furniture inc a couple of high-backed settles on turkey carpet, well kept Harveys ales inc a seasonal beer, enjoyable good value home cooking inc Sun lunch and local game in season, chatty helpful staff, busy restaurant; outside gents', children welcome, picnic-sets in small back garden *(BB, Michael and Ann Cole, Jenny and Brian Seller)*

Laughing Fish: Simply modernised village local with four or five well kept Greene King and other ales, good honest home-made food inc wkdy OAP discounts and popular Sun lunch, welcoming licensees; children welcome, tables in small garden with entertaining enclosed play area, right by Lavender Line *(BB, RDK, the Didler)*

JEVINGTON TQ5601

☆ *Eight Bells*: Busy and neatly kept, fast friendly service, good value hearty home-made food (all day Sun) from good unusual lunchtime filled rolls and baked potatoes up, well kept Adnams Broadside, Flowers Original and Harveys Best, simple furnishings, beams, bare floors, flame-effect fire in inglenook; piped music, fruit machine; walkers welcome, South Downs Way, Weald Way and 1066 Trail all nearby, quiet village with interesting church; tables under cocktail parasols on front terrace, secluded downs-view garden with some sturdy tables under cover, open all day *(BB, John Beeken, John Davis, Pam Adsley, Ann and Colin Hunt)*

KINGSTON NEAR LEWES TQ3908

Juggs [village signed off A27 by roundabout W of Lewes]: Quaint old rose-covered cottage with interesting furnishings, layout and décor, with well kept Shepherd Neame ales, good wine list, bar food from ploughman's and baked potatoes up, no smoking family room, log fires, dominoes and shove-ha'penny; nice seating areas outside, compact well equipped play area *(Kevin Flack, LYM, A J Bowen, Ian Phillips)*

KIRDFORD TQ0126

Half Moon [opp church, off A272 Petworth—Billingshurst]: Smart and attractively refurbished 17th-c tile-hung bar/restaurant, pretty and charmingly set, good interesting british cooking (may be 10% service charge), well kept Fullers London Pride from the curved counter in the partly quarry-tiled bar, good wines by the glass, log fire, friendly attentive staff, immaculate roomy and rambling largely no smoking low-beamed dining area; tables in pretty back garden and out in front *(Jeremy Woods, Mrs S Park, C and R Bromage, LYM, Gerry and Rosemary Dobson, John Davis, John Hale, Arnold Bennett)*

LAMBS GREEN TQ2136

☆ *Lamb*: Quaint old beamed pub gently smartened up without being spoiled, tied to Kings of Horsham with their good beers inc a seasonal one kept well, wide range of enjoyable food inc interesting dishes, friendly helpful young staff, nice log fire, restaurant; pleasant walks *(BB, C and R Bromage)*

LAUGHTON TQ5013

Roebuck [Lewes Rd]: Simple and welcoming, with short choice of good well prepared food (their beef and venison pie is good), well kept Harveys, chatty regulars *(A J Bowen)*

LEWES TQ4110

Brewers Arms [High St]: Neatly kept pub dating from 16th c, back lounge bar, good choice of attractively priced food, interesting range of well kept ales, games room, 260-year list of landlords in public bar *(the Didler, Dom Bradshaw, John Davis)*

Dorset Arms [Malling St]: Pleasant much refurbished local, clean and airy, with good well kept Harveys range, helpful friendly staff, generous bar food from sandwiches to fresh fish Fri lunchtime, well equipped family room, restaurant; terrace tables, comfortable bedrooms *(Dom Bradshaw)*

Gardeners Arms [Cliffe High St]: Traditional small local, light, airy and quiet, with well kept Harveys and several changing ales, good value lunchtime sandwiches and ploughman's, good friendly service (with helpful opinions on the beers), plain scrubbed tables on bare boards around three sides of bar, daily papers and magazines, Sun bar nibbles *(Tony Hobden, Dom Bradshaw)*

☆ *John Harvey* [Bear Yard, just off Cliffe High St]: Tap for nearby Harveys brewery (with separate good brewery shop), all their beers inc seasonal kept perfectly, some tapped from the cask, low-priced well prepared food from lunchtime sandwiches, baked potatoes and ciabattas up, helpful service, basic dark flagstoned bar with machines and piped pop music, a great vat halved to make two towering 'snugs' for several people, lighter room on left; a few tables outside, open all day, breakfast from 10am *(BB, Anne and Tim Locke, Sue and Mike Todd, Keith Reeve, Marie Hammond, Dom Bradshaw, Tracey and Stephen Groves, Bruce Bird)*

Kings Head [Southover High St]: Friendly corner pub with Harveys Best and Fullers London Pride from central bar, generous reasonably priced food from ploughman's and baked potatoes up, raised no smoking area with flame-effect fire, monarch portraits and china displays, board games; back garden, bedrooms, handy for Southover Grange and Anne of Cleves House *(John Beeken)*

☆ *Lewes Arms* [Castle Ditch Lane/Mount Pl – tucked behind castle ruins]: Chatty unpretentious corner local built into castle ramparts, small front bar with larger lounge, eating area off, and hatchway, well kept Greene King and Harveys ales, good orange juice, very reasonably priced simple lunchtime food from good baguettes and baked potatoes up, friendly service, daily papers, local pictures, toad in the hole, no music; small terrace *(John Beeken, Anne and Tim Locke, Dom Bradshaw, Sue Demont, Tim Barrow)*

LINDFIELD TQ3425

Linden Tree [High St]: Traditional bar with welcoming staff, real ales such as Gales HSB, Harveys, Marstons Pedigree and Ringwood Old Thumper, restaurant *(E G Parish)*

LITLINGTON TQ5201

☆ *Plough & Harrow* [between A27 Lewes—Polegate and A259 E of Seaford]: Attractive neatly extended beamed flint pub with dining area done up as railway dining car (children allowed here), quick friendly service, good home cooking, well kept ales inc Badger and Harveys, decent wines by the glass; little suntrap front garden, attractive back lawn with children's bar, aviary and pretty views *(M and R Thomas, Robert M Warner, LYM)*

LITTLEHAMPTON TQ0202

☆ *Arun View* [Wharf Rd; W towards Chichester, opp railway station]: Roomy and comfortable 18th-c inn in lovely spot right on harbour with river directly below windows, well kept ales like Ringwood Best and Old Thumper and Youngs Special, good wine list, friendly helpful service, fairly limited but interesting menu from sandwiches to good fresh fish (very popular lunchtime with older people, a younger crowd evenings), flagstoned back bar with lots of drawings and caricatures, large no smoking conservatory and flower-filled terrace both overlooking busy waterway and pedestrian bridge; disabled facilities, summer barbecues evenings and wknds, winter live music, bright and modest good value bedrooms *(Mrs D W Privett, Caroline and Gavin Callow, Sue and Mike Todd)*

LITTLEWORTH TQ1921

Windmill [pub sign on B2135; village signed off A272 southbound, W of Cowfold]: Small spotless local with log fires in panelled flagstoned public bar and compact cosy beamed lounge/eating area (smoking allowed), enjoyable sensibly priced generous food, well kept Badger beers, good hospitable service, bric-a-brac large and small inside and out, darts, dominoes, cards and bar billiards, no music; children welcome, peaceful and attractive side garden *(Bruce Bird)*

LODSWORTH SU9223

☆ *Hollist Arms* [off A272 Midhurst—Petworth]: Cheerful open-plan village pub overlooking small green, well kept Kings Horsham Best, Timothy Taylors Landlord and Youngs, good wines by the glass and coffee, good range of generous enjoyable bar food inc fresh fish and popular Sun lunch, relaxed atmosphere, lively landlord and friendly service, sofas by log fire, interesting books and magazines, country prints, another fire in separate restaurant area; may be piped classical music; children welcome, nice tree-lined back garden, good walks *(Ron Shelton, Nicholas and Dorothy Stephens, John Beeken, Martin and Karen Wake, Bruce Bird)*

LOXWOOD TQ0331

Onslow Arms [B2133 NW of Billingshurst]: Well refurbished local with pleasant staff, well kept Badger Best, K&B, Tanglefoot and a Gribble guest, good house wines, plenty of coffees and teas, lovely old log fireplaces, enjoyable food inc light dishes and smaller helpings, daily papers; dogs welcome, picnic-sets in good-sized pleasant garden sloping to river and nearby newly restored Wey & Arun canal, good walks and boat trips *(Tony and Wendy Hobden, Ian Phillips)*

LYMINSTER TQ0204

Six Bells [Lyminster Rd, Wick]: Flint-faced dining pub with good-sized helpings of unusual and enjoyable elegantly presented food from sandwiches and baguettes up, hospitable attentive service, well kept Greene King Abbot and Youngs Special, no smoking more expensive – and more expansive – restaurant area; best to book at wknds

(Tony and Wendy Hobden, John Davis)

MAPLEHURST TQ1924

White Horse [Park Lane]: Peaceful beamed country local, four seating areas inc homely cosy corners and sun lounge (no smoking at lunchtime) with redundant church furniture and lots of plants, well kept Harveys Best, Weltons Pride & Joy and interesting guest beers, farm cider, bargain coffee, good value sandwiches, toasties, baked potatoes and one or two simple hot dishes, friendly efficient staff, lots of traditional games, no music or machines; children welcome, pleasant garden with play area, beautiful wisteria in front, car enthusiasts' evenings *(C and R Bromage, Tony and Wendy Hobden, Bruce Bird)*

MAYFIELD TQ5525

Five Ashes Inn [Five Ashes (A267 SW)]: Small unpretentious friendly local, wide choice of decent generous pubby food, Harveys, Shepherd Neame Spitfire and guest beers, good wine choice; picnic-sets outside *(Sarah Hotchkiss)*

☆ *Rose & Crown* [Fletching St]: Pretty weather-boarded old inn, good choice of enjoyable fresh food with international touches, cosy little low-beamed front rooms and pleasant restaurant, big inglenook, well kept Greene King Abbot and Old Speckled Hen and Harveys Best, good friendly service; shove-ha'penny Mon and Fri, piped music; children welcome, four attractive bedrooms, good breakfast, tables outside; open all day Sat *(LYM, Roger Noble)*

MIDHURST SU8821

Bricklayers Arms [Wool Lane/West St]: Two cosily welcoming olde-worlde bars, good local atmosphere, good value generous home-made food inc Sun roast, well kept Greene King IPA and Abbot, quick and friendly helpful service, sturdy old oak furniture, 17th-c beams, old photographs and bric-a-brac *(Roger Endersby)*

Wheatsheaf [Wool Lane/A272]: Attractive and relaxing low-beamed and timbered 16th-c local with good value generous food inc good sandwich choice, quick friendly service, well kept Badger and Ballards beers; big-screen sports TV; open all day *(David and Higgs Wood, A and B D Craig)*

MILLAND SU8328

☆ *Rising Sun* [Iping Rd junction with main rd through village]: Recently comfortably redecorated largely open-plan big-windowed pub, light and airy, with friendly newish licensees and staff, french landlady cooking generous enjoyable food, all fresh, inc some recipes from Normandy and good french country puddings, well kept Gales Butser, BB and HSB with a seasonal guest such as Wadworths Summersault, sports TV, pool and fruit machine in separate games end; picnic-sets in good-sized neatly kept garden, good walking area *(BB, M B Griffith, Jean and Roy Benson)*

NETHERFIELD TQ7118

☆ *Netherfield Arms* [just off B2096 Heathfield—Battle]: Friendly low-ceilinged country pub with wide choice of enjoyable home-made food, well kept ales such as Fullers London Pride, decent wines, inglenook log fire, no smoking area, cosy restaurant, no music; lovely back garden *(BB, Father Robert Marsh)*

White Hart [B2096]: Two-bar pub, sofas in lounge, wide choice of well prepared food with plenty of fresh veg, well kept Harveys and Shepherd Neame Spitfire, good friendly service, two dining rooms, one with long views – shared by terrace tables *(C and R Bromage, Peter Meister)*

NEWPOUND COMMON TQ0626

Bat & Ball [just off B2133 Loxwood Rd]: Open-plan country pub dating partly from 16th c, bay windows, lots of beams and pillars, good range of tasty bar food from baked potatoes to interesting puddings in large dining area, well kept Badger ales, open fires; big pleasant orchard garden with pond and play area *(John Beeken)*

NORTH CHAILEY TQ3921

Kings Head [A275/A272]: Enjoyable usual food in long busy bar and adjoining restaurant, reasonable prices, obliging staff *(John and Wendy Allin)*

NORTHIAM TQ8224

Hayes Arms [Church Lane]: Civilised Georgian-fronted hotel under new landlord, well kept real ales in comfortable heavy-beamed Tudor bar, log fire in big brick inglenook, bistro-type tables for the new chef's enjoyable food, small back restaurant; bedrooms *(V Brogden)*

NUTBOURNE TQ0718

Rising Sun [off A283 E of Pulborough; The Street]: Friendly old pub doing well these days, good choice of well kept beers such as Skinners Betty Stogs, amiable landlord, some interesting food; children and dogs allowed; tables on small back terrace under apple tree *(Peter D B Harding)*

NUTHURST TQ1926

☆ *Black Horse* [off A281 SE of Horsham]: Convivial 17th-c country pub with low black beams, flagstones, inglenook log fire and plenty of character in its several small rooms, well kept Harveys Best, King, Timothy Taylors Landlord and a guest beer, good range of wines by the glass, friendly staff, no smoking snug and restaurant; may be piped music; children and dogs welcome, attractive woodland streamside back garden, more seats on front terrace, open for food all day wknds and bank hols *(William and Jenifer Ruxton, Jeremy Woods, LYM, Pam and John Smith, Mike and Heather Watson, Mr Bannon, Tony and Wendy Hobden, Ron Gentry, R Yates, John Davis)*

NUTLEY TQ4426

☆ *Nutley Arms* [Fords Green (A22)]: Carefully refurbished and freshly modern inside, with sofas as well as comfortable bucket dining chairs, snug yet airy garden room, imaginative changing menu and frequent free tapas (Greek landlord and French landlady), well kept Greene King Old Speckled Hen and Harveys Best, efficient unobtrusive service, about a dozen decent wines by the glass; piped music turned down on request, back TV; picnic-sets out on extensive decking, more on grass below with play area *(BB, Michael and Ann Cole)*

OFFHAM TQ3912

☆ ***Blacksmiths Arms*** [A275 N of Lewes]: Friendly new owners and a bit of a facelift for open-plan pub with huge inglenook one end, airy dining area the other (most of the close-set tables laid for eating), reasonably priced food inc good fresh fish and seafood, well kept Harveys Best, restaurant, french windows to terrace with picnic-sets; more reports please *(LYM, Brendan Vaughan, D J Evans, Jem Cooper)*

Chalk Pit [A275 N of Lewes]: Pleasant brightly lit bar, well kept Harveys, good range of reasonably priced food all day, good Sun roasts, friendly staff, no smoking restaurant; bedrooms, open all day *(Ann and Colin Hunt)*

PATCHING TQ0705

Fox [signed off A27 eastbound just W of Worthing]: Emphasis on no smoking dining area, enjoyable reasonably priced generous food freshly made from imaginative sandwiches, baguettes and baked potatoes up, popular Sun roasts (book ahead for these), well kept Harveys Best, Shepherd Neame Spitfire and a seasonal guest beer, friendly attentive service, daily papers, lots of panelling; quiet piped music, nice big tree-shaded garden with play area, open all day wknds *(Tony and Wendy Hobden, Bruce Bird)*

PEASMARSH TQ8823

Cock Horse [Main St]: Warm welcome, pleasing bar with log fire, well priced food from good sandwiches to home-made puddings, good choice of well kept beers inc Harveys; tidy garden *(Ann and Colin Hunt)*

PETT TQ8714

Two Sawyers [Pett Rd; off A259]: Country local with meandering low-beamed rooms, stripped tables on bare boards, tiny low-ceilinged snug, passage sloping down to low-beamed no smoking restaurant allowing children, Harveys Best, Whites 1066 Country and a couple of guest beers (pub's own brewery has closed), wide range of well priced wines, bar food; fruit machine, piped music, may try to keep your credit card if you run a tab; dogs allowed, pretty suntrap front brick courtyard and quiet back garden with shady trees and a few well spaced picnic-sets, has been open all day at least in summer *(LYM)*

PLAYDEN TQ9121

Peace & Plenty [A268/B2082]: Unpretentious welcoming pub with emphasis on enjoyable food all day in two dining areas off attractively homely small bar, roaring open woodburner in big inglenook, well kept Shepherd Neame, good coffee, good service with long-serving landlady, friendly cat; children allowed, tables in pretty garden (some traffic noise), open all day *(Adrian White, Paul and Penny Rampton, LYM, Alan Cole, Kirstie Bruce, Peter Meister)*

Playden Oasts [Rye Rd]: Converted oast house with comfortable bar and restaurant, friendly homely atmosphere, good choice of food inc lots of fish, well kept real ale *(Robin Dealhoy)*

PLUMPTON TQ3613

Half Moon [Ditchling Rd (B2116)]: Long welcoming bar with lots of beams and timbering, well kept Harveys Best, Shepherd Neame Spitfire and a guest such as Exmoor Gold, good range of bar food from baked potatoes and baguettes up, good log fire with unusual flint chimneybreast, jug collection and painting of regulars; bar billiards in games room, well behaved children welcome, tables in wisteria front courtyard and big back garden with South Downs view and play area, good walks *(John Beeken)*

POYNINGS TQ2611

Royal Oak [The Street]: Large beamed bar with well kept Courage Directors, Greene King Old Speckled Hen and Harveys from three-sided servery, efficient helpful staff, good range of popular if not cheap food, no smoking area, woodburner, no piped music; big attractive garden with barbecue, play area and country/downs views *(John Beeken)*

PUNNETTS TOWN TQ6320

☆ ***Three Cups*** [B2096 towards Battle]: Friendly and relaxed beamed country local with log fire in big fireplace, small partly no smoking back dining room, decent food from good snacks up, well kept Greene King beers with a good guest beer, traditional games; children and dogs welcome (the amiable pub bulldog is called Wilf), tables outside, great walks, has been open all day wknds *(LYM)*

RINGMER TQ4412

☆ ***Cock*** [Uckfield Rd – blocked-off section of rd off A26 N of village turn-off]: Heavy 16th-c beams and flagstones in bar with big inglenook log fire, great blackboard choice of good value food, welcoming efficient staff, well kept Fullers London Pride, Harveys Best and Mild and Youngs Waggle Dance, good wines by the glass, modernised rooms off inc no smoking lounge and back restaurant; children allowed in overflow eating area; quiet piped music; tables on small terrace and in big sloping fairy-lit garden with shrubs, fruit trees and lots of spring flowers *(LYM, John Beeken, Robert M Warner, P W Taylor, A J Bowen)*

RIPE TQ5010

☆ ***Lamb*** [signed off A22 Uckfield—Hailsham, or off A27 Lewes—Polegate via Chalvington; Church Lane]: Interestingly furnished partly panelled rooms around central servery, masses of attractive antique prints and pictures, nostalgic song-sheet covers, automotive memorabilia, Victorian pin-ups in gents'; sound choice of generous home-made food from sandwiches and baked potatoes up, children's menu, well kept Harveys Best and a couple of interesting guest beers, good range of reasonably priced wines, several open fires, small dining room set out as farmyard stalls; bar billiards, TV; pleasant sheltered back garden with play area and barbecues *(John Beeken, BB, Tony and Wendy Hobden)*

ROBERTSBRIDGE TQ7323

Ostrich [Station Rd]: Cheerful open-plan former station hotel, enjoyable food, Adnams, Harveys Best and a guest beer, games room;

tables in attractive garden, bedrooms *(the Didler)*

ROWHOOK TQ1234

☆ *Chequers* [off A29 NW of Horsham]: Attractive 16th-c pub, relaxing beamed and flagstoned front bar with portraits and inglenook fire, step up to low-beamed lounge, well kept Harveys, Youngs and two guest beers, decent wines by the glass, good coffee, friendly helpful staff, young chef/landlord doing up-to-date food from panini and light dishes up, separate restaurant menu – Sun lunch particularly enjoyed by readers; piped music; children and dogs welcome, tables out on terraces and in pretty garden with good play area, attractive surroundings *(LYM, Martin and Karen Wake, A Sadler, Frances Mumford)*

RUDGWICK TQ0936

Wheatsheaf [Ellens Green (B2128 N)]: High prices, but what you get is good – enjoyable fresh food, considerate service, neat housekeeping *(Derek and Maggie Washington, Mike and Heather Watson)*

RUSPER TQ2037

Plough [signed from A24 and A264 N and NE of Horsham]: Nicely worn in country local dating from 16th c, padded very low beams, panelling and big inglenook with lovely log fire, well kept changing ales such as Fullers London Pride and ESB, Harveys Best, Kings Best and Summer Ale and Theakstons Old Peculier, good value food, quick pleasant service, dining area; children welcome, bar billiards and darts in raftered room upstairs; pretty front terrace, fountain in back garden, occasional live music *(C and R Bromage, LYM, W W Burke, Brian Root)*

RUSTINGTON TQ0503

Windmill [Mill Lane (B2187)]: Several areas, wide choice of sensibly priced quickly served food ordered from separate counter inc Thurs OAP lunches, separate smoking area, Arundel, Fullers London Pride, Gales, Harveys and Hepworths; plenty of garden tables, play area *(Tony and Wendy Hobden)*

RYE HARBOUR TQ9220

☆ *Inkerman Arms* [Rye Harbour Rd]: Cosy and welcoming unpretentious local nr nature reserve, wide choice of good food inc lots of fresh local fish, fine home-made pies and old-fashioned puddings, well kept ales such as Harveys Best and Rother Valley Wealden and Level Best, pleasantly decorated main bar with secluded eating areas; tables in small garden; cl Mon evening and winter Mon lunchtime *(V Brogden, Gill and Tony Morriss, Alan Cole, Kirstie Bruce, John Davis, R C Livesey, Hywel Bevan, Pete Taylor)*

SCAYNES HILL TQ3824

Sloop [Freshfield Lock]: Named for the boats on the adjacent former Ouse Canal, attractively opened up yet keeping feel of interesting areas inc no smoking section, well kept Greene King ales with one or two guest beers, decent wines, bar billiards and traditional games; may be piped music; children in eating areas, lots of tables in sheltered garden, open for food all day Sun *(R J Walden, LYM, Joyce and Geoff Robson, Richard May, Ron Gentry, Susan and John Douglas)*

SEAFORD TV5199

Golden Galleon [Exceat, A259 E]: This handsomely placed big pub, handy for the walk down the valley to the sea, with plenty of tables outside, was taken over by the Harvester family dining pub chain in late 2003, and no longer brews its own beers *(LYM, Philip and Ann Board, Dr David Cockburn)*

Seven Sisters [Alfriston Rd]: Tasty reasonably priced home-made food, open fire, comfortable well spaced tables, hospitable licensees; children's room *(anon)*

SELHAM SU9320

Three Moles: Small old-fashioned pub tucked away in woodland village, quietly relaxing atmosphere, friendly landlady, well kept Skinners Betty Stogs and guest beers collected direct from small breweries (one always a Mild), farm cider, daily papers, darts, bar billiards, plenty of board games, no mobile phones; no food or children, monthly singsongs, occasional beer festivals; garden tables, nice walks, open all day wknds *(Peter D B Harding, Bruce Bird)*

SELMESTON TQ5006

Barley Mow [A27 Eastbourne—Lewes]: Neatly kept roadside pub useful for wide blackboard range of reasonably priced pubby food all day inc children's dishes, well kept Adnams Broadside and Harveys Best, good pleasant service, partly no smoking eating areas on both sides of central bar area, flowers on tables; unobtrusive piped music; large garden with sturdy timber play area *(BB, Paul A Moore, Father Robert Marsh, David Cosham, D Marsh)*

SELSEY SZ8692

Lifeboat [Albion Rd, nr seafront]: Traditional unpretentious bar (dogs allowed) with dining extension, wide choice of low-priced food from sandwiches to local crab salad, Courage Directors, Fullers London Pride and Shepherd Neame Spitfire, friendly helpful staff; tables out on big verandah – only main courses served at hatch here *(J A Snell, Tony and Wendy Hobden)*

SHIPLEY TQ1321

Countryman [SW of village, off A272 E of Coolham]: Early 19th-c, wide choice of enjoyable food from warm baguettes and baked potatoes through tapas and paella to rabbit casserole, well kept ales such as Bass, Kings Horsham Best and Youngs Special, friendly efficient staff, lounge bar, large carpeted dining area, welcoming timbered and flagstoned bar with inglenook log fire, darts and bar billiards; may be piped music; picnic-sets and play equipment in pretty garden, horse park, handy for Shipley windmill and D-Day Airfield at Coolham *(C and R Bromage, John Beeken)*

George & Dragon [Dragons Lane]: Low beams and huge fireplace, well kept Badger K&B, Best, Tanglefoot and Gribble guest, hearty good value home-made food, small dining room, bar billiards; tables and barbecue in orchard garden, handy for Shipley windmill (which is open wknds) *(John Beeken)*

SHOREHAM-BY-SEA TQ2005

Fly Inn [signed off A27, A259]: Not a pub, but this small bar in 1930s art-deco airport building has well kept changing ales such as Dark Star and Greene King IPA, enjoyable low-priced bar food from baked potatoes up, a congenial relaxed atmosphere, and friendly obliging staff; terrace tables, uninterrupted views all round (downs views, plenty of light aircraft action); children welcome, small airport museum *(John Beeken)*

☆ *Red Lion* [Upper Shoreham Rd, opp church]: Modest dim-lit low-beamed and timbered 16th-c pub with settles in snug alcoves, good value well presented individual food, well kept changing ales, post-Easter beer festival, decent wines, farm cider, friendly efficient staff, log fire in unusual fireplace, another open fire in no smoking dining room, further bar with covered terrace; piped music; pretty sheltered garden, good downs views and walks *(MLR, Bruce Bird)*

SHORTBRIDGE TQ4521

Peacock [Piltdown; OS Sheet 198 map ref 450215]: Neatly rebuilt beamed and timbered bar, comfortable and welcoming, with big inglenook, very generous nicely presented bar food served piping hot inc good fish (10% service charge), well kept Harveys and Wadworths 6X, restaurant; piped music (they will turn it down), children welcome; sizeable garden *(BB, John Davis, Richard May)*

SIDLESHAM SZ8697

☆ *Crab & Lobster* [Mill Lane; off B2145 S of Chichester]: Individualistic old country local currently on fine form, log fire in chatty traditional regulars' bar, side dining lounge, pretty back garden looking over to the bird-reserve of silted Pagham Harbour; limited choice of good home-made food (not wkdy evenings in winter) inc fresh seafood, reasonable prices, quick genial service, well kept ales such as Ballards Best, Cheriton Pots and Weltons Horsham Old, decent wines, country wines, log fire, traditional games; dogs welcome, no children, music or machines *(LYM, Phil and Sally Gorton, Tony and Wendy Hobden, Val and Alan Green, Andy and Jill Kassube, John Coatsworth, Tracey and Stephen Groves)*

SLINDON SU9708

☆ *Spur* [Slindon Common; A29 towards Bognor]: Popular, roomy and attractive 17th-c pub, welcoming atmosphere, two big log fires, pine tables, good choice of upmarket but good value food changing daily, well kept Courage Directors and Greene King Ruddles, cheerful efficient staff, large elegant restaurant, children welcome; games room with darts and pool (for over-18s), friendly dogs; pretty garden (traffic noise) *(John Evans, John Davis, John and Valerie Barnett)*

SMALL DOLE TQ2112

Fox & Hounds [Henfield Rd]: Open-plan village local with raised dining areas, good choice of usual food from sandwiches and baked potatoes up, well kept Harveys Best and Charles Wells Bombardier; piped music may obtrude; tables on terrace, handy for downland walks *(John Beeken)*

SOUTH HARTING SU7819

Ship [North Lane (B2146)]: Welcoming, unpretentious and dependable 17th-c pub, informal atmosphere, good choice of good value food inc sandwiches on request in dimly lit main bar, fine log fire, old photographs, well kept real ales, friendly staff and dogs, simpler locals' bar (dominoes, perhaps chestnuts to roast by its log fire); unobtrusive piped music; nice setting in pretty village *(John Evans, Ann and Colin Hunt, John and Tania Wood)*

SOUTHWATER TQ1427

Hen & Chicken [former A24 S of Horsham]: Ancient friendly roadside pub, four areas, one laid out as restaurant, another with armchairs, welcoming service, Courage Best and Kings Horsham, usual food from bar snacks to Sun lunch; monthly jazz 1st Mon *(Tony and Wendy Hobden)*

STAPLEFIELD TQ2728

☆ *Jolly Tanners* [Handcross Rd, just off A23]: Spotless and comfortable, good honest home-made food, well kept Fullers Chiswick and London Pride, Harveys Best, John Smiths and a guest Mild, prompt helpful service even under pressure, two good log fires, lots of china, brasses and old photographs, no smoking room (bar can be smoky); piped music; attractive garden with lots of space for children, terrace tables under cocktail parasols and picnic-sets on grass, by cricket green, quite handy for Nymans (NT) *(Bruce Bird, Jason Caulkin, Terry Buckland, Roy and Lindsey Fentiman)*

STEDHAM SU8522

Hamilton Arms [School Lane (off A272)]: Proper English local but decorated with Thai artefacts and run by friendly Thai family, basic pub food but also good interesting thai bar snacks and popular restaurant (cl Mon); pretty hanging baskets, tables out by village green and quiet lane, village shop in car park, good walks nearby *(Wendy Arnold, Roger Endersby)*

STEYNING TQ1711

Star [High St]: Rambling old pub with unpretentious front area, back dining areas, cosy alcove full of old farm tools, good value simple pub food, real ales such as Fullers London Pride and Youngs; live music Fri; streamside garden with huge cask tables *(Mark Percy, Lesley Mayoh, Tony and Wendy Hobden)*

STOPHAM TQ0318

White Hart [off A283 E of village, W of Pulborough]: Interesting old heavily timbered, beamed and panelled pub with log fire and sofas in one of its three snug rooms, well kept beers such as Flowers IPA, Fullers London Pride and Weltons Kid & Bard, wide food choice from baguettes to venison, young enthusiastic staff, no smoking restaurant; piped music; children welcome, play area over road, tables out by River Arun *(LYM, John Beeken, Tony and Wendy Hobden, Roger Endersby)*

STOUGHTON SU8011

☆ *Hare & Hounds* [signed off B2146 Petersfield—Emsworth]: Comfortable country pub with huge open fires in airy pine-clad bar and dining area, some emphasis on generous reasonably priced food inc good value Sun roast, four well kept real ales such as Timothy Taylors Landlord and Youngs Special, good helpful service; children in eating areas, tables on pretty front terrace and in back garden, lovely setting nr Saxon church, good walks nearby *(LYM, Keith Stevens, Ann and Colin Hunt, John Davis, J A Snell, Cathy Robinson, Ed Coombe)*

SUTTON SU9715

☆ *White Horse* [The Street]: Charming small and civilised country pub with island servery separating bare-boards bar from two-room barrel-vaulted dining area with stylishly simple furnishings and Rowlandson prints, good food from bar dishes to enterprising restaurant meals inc local game and fish; Courage Best, Fullers London Pride, Shepherd Neame Spitfire and Youngs Special (may have only two of these on), short interesting wine choice, log fire; tables in garden up behind, good value bedrooms with excellent breakfast, quiet little hamlet nr Bignor Roman villa *(BB, Anne and Jeff Peel, John Davis)*

THAKEHAM TQ1017

White Lion [off B2139 N of Storrington; The Street]: Appealing heavily beamed two-bar 16th-c village pub with big log fire, bare boards and basic traditional furnishings inc corner settles, well kept Fullers London Pride, Greene King Abbot or Old Speckled Hen and a couple of good guest beers, friendly informal service, food from open kitchen inc thai specialities and variety of fillings for open sandwiches, potato skins or omelettes; piped music may obtrude; terrace tables, small lawn *(Tony and Wendy Hobden, John Beeken, Bruce Bird)*

TICEHURST TQ6930

Cherry Tree [B2087 towards Flimwell, by Dale Hill golf club]: Chef-landlord doing enjoyable food with some enterprising dishes as well as pubby favourites, neat beamed bar with a chesterfield as well as dark wood pub furniture, cheerful service; pleasant tables out on terrace and in small roadside garden *(BB)*

TURNERS HILL TQ3435

☆ *Crown* [East St]: Spacious pleasantly decorated dining pub, different levels inc attractive restaurant with pitched rafters, wide choice of consistently enjoyable reasonably priced food, well kept ales such as Fullers and Harveys, good wine choice, log fire; soft piped music; tables outside, pleasant valley views from back garden; children welcome, two bedrooms *(Dr P J W Young, BB)*

Red Lion [Lion Lane, just off and parallel with B2028]: Convivial traditional local with well kept Harveys PA, Best and seasonal beers, good choice of wines by the glass, good value food from filled rolls through lasagne, liver and bacon, goats cheese quiche and so forth to good reasonably priced Sun roast, properly pubby atmosphere, narrow high-beamed bar with small fire, three steps up to smallish low-ceilinged dining area with inglenook log fire, cushioned pews and built-in settles; live music Fri; children and well behaved dogs welcome, picnic-sets in quiet side garden *(BB, Peter Taylor, Mike Gorton, Klaus and Elizabeth Leist)*

UCKFIELD TQ4720

Alma Arms [Framfield Rd]: Neatly kept open-plan pub with Harveys full range kept well from central bar, generous simple pub lunches, small no smoking family area at end of lounge part *(Tony and Wendy Hobden)*

UDIMORE TQ8519

Kings Head: Traditional village pub with much character, open fires, low beams, bare boards, well kept Harveys and Youngs from long bar, low-priced food in bar and dining room *(anon)*

Plough [B2089 W of Rye]: Recently reopened, with friendly local atmosphere, Greene King IPA, Abbot and Old Speckled Hen, woodburner, books for sale, open fire and country prints in small dining area; tables on good-sized suntrap back terrace *(Kevin Thorpe)*

WADHURST TQ6131

☆ *Best Beech* [Mayfield Lane (B2100 a mile W)]: Appealing dining pub with enjoyable food using some local produce and including some interesting modern dishes in cosy eating area with lots of pictures, bar on left with wall seats, plenty of comfortable sofas, coal fire, well kept Adnams, Harveys and Youngs, good choice of wines by the glass, good coffee, quick pleasant service; back restaurant, tables outside, good value bedrooms, good breakfast *(BB, Robert M Warner, Richard Siebert)*

WALBERTON SU9705

Holly Tree [The Street]: Two bars, one no smoking with wide good value food choice from baguettes and baked potatoes up, Fullers London Pride and Charles Wells Bombardier *(Tony and Wendy Hobden)*

WALDERTON SU7910

Barley Mow [Stoughton rd, just off B2146 Chichester—Petersfield]: Spacious flagstoned U-shaped bar popular for good choice of good generous food and well kept Ringwood ales, quick cheerful service even on busy wknds, two log fires, country bric-a-brac, no music; children welcome, skittle alley, nice furniture in big pleasant streamside garden with fish pond, aviary and swings, good walks, handy for Stansted House *(Ann and Colin Hunt, R B Gardiner)*

WALDRON TQ5419

Star [Blackboys—Horam side road]: Lively village local with big inglenook log fire in panelled bar, fair range of standard pub food with some interesting specials, well kept Harveys Bitter and seasonal Old, friendly helpful staff, no music, separate dining room; pleasant garden, seats out in front overlooking pretty village *(BB, Phil and Sally Gorton)*

WARBLETON TQ6018

☆ ***Warbil in Tun*** [S of B2096 SE of Heathfield]: Pretty dining pub with good choice of good value food esp meat (helpful ex-butcher landlord), nice puddings, well kept reasonably priced Harveys Best, good coffee, welcoming and cosily civilised atmosphere, beams and red plush, huge log fireplace, no music; tables on roadside green, attractive tucked-away village *(Michael and Ann Cole)*

WARNHAM TQ1533

Greets [Friday St]: 15th-c beamed pub under friendly new management, good value food inc special price Mon-Sat lunches, charming gimmick-free décor with stripped pine tables on uneven flagstones, inglenook log fire, lots of nooks and corners, good choice of well kept real ales, decent wines, attentive staff, convivial locals' side bar; tables in garden *(R A Watson)*

☆ ***Sussex Oak*** [just off A24 Horsham—Dorking; Church St]: Cheery linked areas with big inglenook log fireplace, mix of flagstones, tiles, wood and carpeting, heavy beams and timbers, sofas and bar billiards, well kept Adnams, Fullers London Pride, Timothy Taylors Landlord, Youngs and a guest beer from carved servery, plenty of wines by the glass, popular food (not Sun-Mon evenings) from sandwiches and baked potatoes to steaks, high-raftered no smoking restaurant; piped music; children and dogs welcome, garden picnic-sets, open all day *(Ian Phillips, John Davis, Mike and Heather Watson, Mrs Romey Heaton, Tony and Wendy Hobden, LYM)*

WEST ASHLING SU8107

Richmond Arms [just off B2146; Mill Rd]: Tucked-away unassuming village local in pretty setting nr mill pond, four Greene King and guest ales, enjoyable food from sandwiches and baguettes to steaks, open fire, darts, pool and a skittle alley; can get a bit smoky; children allowed, picnic-sets out by pergola, open all day Sun and summer Sat *(Ian Phillips, Ann and Colin Hunt, Tracey and Stephen Groves, LYM)*

WEST CHILTINGTON TQ0916

Five Bells [Smock Alley, off B2139 SE]: Four well kept real ales inc a Mild from Badger or Harveys, annual beer festival, farm cider, good value fresh food (not Sun evening) inc good ploughman's with named cheesemakers, nice puddings, log fire, friendly locals, beams and panelling, old photographs, unusual brass bric-a-brac, distinctive conservatory dining room; no piped music, peaceful garden with terrace, bedrooms *(Bruce Bird, John Evans)*

WEST DEAN SU8512

Selsey Arms [A286 Midhurst—Chichester]: Large welcoming late 18th-c dining pub with plentiful enjoyable food, well kept Greene King IPA and Fullers London Pride, decent wines, roomy no smoking area, log fire, separate public bar *(Ann and Colin Hunt, Jane Basso, Sue and Mike Todd, John Davis, R B Gardiner)*

WEST ITCHENOR SU8001

Ship [The Street]: Large panelled pub in good spot nr Chichester Harbour, tables outside, good long walk to W Wittering or foot ferry to Bosham Hoe; generous changing food from good baguettes to restaurant dishes inc local fish, good friendly service, well kept Ballards, Gales, Itchen Valley and Ringwood, two log fires, lots of bric-a-brac inc many chamber-pots, seats made from old boat, children in pleasant eating area with well spaced tables; open all day, said to be able to get supplies for yachtsmen (nearest shop is 2 miles away) *(Val and Alan Green, William and Jenifer Ruxton, Ralph and Jean Whitehouse, Richard Waller, Pauline Smith)*

WEST MARDEN SU7713

Victoria [B2146 2 miles S of Uppark]: Cosy in winter, with good value home-made food inc interesting dishes and good sandwiches in pleasant rustic surroundings, three well kept real ales, decent house wines, friendly staff, small dining room; good walks nearby *(J A Snell, Ann and Colin Hunt, Richard Waller, Pauline Smith)*

WEST WITTERING SZ8099

☆ ***Lamb*** [Chichester Rd; B2179/A286 towards Birdham]: Several rooms (some no smoking) neatly knocked through with clean smart furnishings, rugs on tiles, blazing fire, well kept Badger ales, decent wines, good choice of good value food from separate servery inc generous Sun roast, friendly efficient service; dogs on leads allowed, pleasant outside with tables out in front and in small sheltered back terrace – good for children; busy in summer *(BB, P R and S A White, Ian and Jane Irving, Martin and Karen Wake)*

Old House At Home [Cakeham Rd]: Roomy and attractively renovated, with good reasonably priced food inc fish and good Sun lunches, log fires, blue and white tables on tiles and wooden floor, main bar, garden bar and dining area; nice spot *(Michael and Robin Inskip)*

WHATLINGTON TQ7619

Royal Oak [A21]: Steps between two long welcoming beamed rooms with stripped pine tables and chairs, log fire, nooks and corners, feature well edged with flowers, generous enjoyable food with good veg, decent wine, friendly service; tables in back garden *(BB, Pamela and Douglas Cooper, Vincent Board, Veronica Ford)*

WHITEMANS GREEN TQ3025

Ship: Relaxed and welcoming, five well kept real ales, blackboard food, two log fires, some comfortable sofas, friendly pub dalmatian; no children *(Ron Gentry)*

WISBOROUGH GREEN TQ0526

Cricketers Arms [Loxwood Rd, just off A272 Billingshurst—Petworth]: Very low beams, bare boards and timbering in attractive open-plan old pub, two big woodburners, pleasant mix of country furniture, five or six real ales, no smoking stripped brick dining area on left, cheerful staff; piped music; tables out on terrace and across lane from green *(LYM, Mrs Romey Heaton, M and R Thomas, Roger Endersby)*

Three Crowns [Billingshurst Rd (A272)]: Big neat pub, warm and welcoming, very popular lunchtime for wide choice of fairly priced food from sandwiches, baguettes and big ploughman's up inc children's and small-appetite meals, good Sun lunch, open-plan bar stretching into no smoking dining room, stripped bricks and beams, well kept real ales, quick attentive service, games room; sizeable back garden *(DWAJ, David Coleman)*

WITHYHAM TQ4935

☆ *Dorset Arms* [B2110]: Bustling yet relaxed 16th-c pub in pleasant countryside, recently redecorated bar with sturdy tables and simple country seats on wide oak floorboards (sometimes a bit uneven – beware of wobbles), good log fire in Tudor fireplace, well kept Harveys PA, Best and a seasonal beer, decent wines inc local ones, attentive friendly service; bar snacks from fresh filled rolls up, best to book for landlady's consistently good home cooking at appealing prices, pretty no smoking restaurant; dogs welcome, darts, dominoes, shove-ha'penny, cribbage, fruit machine, piped music; white tables on brick terrace by small green, handy for Forest Way *(Robert M Warner, A J Holland, LYM, Peter and Joan Elbra, Peter Meister, Debbie and Neil Hayter)*

WOODMANCOTE SU7707

Woodmancote Arms [the one nr Emsworth]: Cheerful and relaxing village pub with friendly locals and their dogs, simple generous reasonably priced bar food, well kept Wadworths ales, decent wines, log fire in eating area, pretty and unpretentious restaurant; large games room for pool and darts *(Ann and Colin Hunt)*

WORTHING TQ1105

Coach & Horses [Arundel Rd, Clapham (A27 W)]: Former 17th-c coaching inn with rather 1970s feel, wide choice of bar food in extended dining area, well kept Fullers London Pride, Greene King Abbot, Harveys Best and a guest beer, quick friendly service, decent coffee, log fire, lots of brass and china, second back bar and family room; piped music; children welcome, Tues quiz night, jazz first Mon, well kept garden with lots of tables and play area *(Tony and Wendy Hobden, Quentin and Carol Williamson, Bruce Bird)*

George & Dragon [High St, Old Tarring]: Extended 17th-c pub under new licensees, four areas inc airy lounge and no smoking restaurant, good lunchtime food, well kept Harveys Best, Hop Back Summer Lightning, Charles Wells Bombardier, Youngs and an interesting guest beer, friendly efficient service, beams and panelling, bric-a-brac, brass platters and old photographs, no piped music; dogs allowed (not in attractive garden), now open all day *(Bruce Bird)*

Hare & Hound [Portland Rd, N of Marks & Spencer]: Friendly bustling extended local with well kept ales such as Badger K&B, Fullers London Pride, Greene King Old Speckled Hen and Ringwood Best from central brass and oak bar, good value promptly served straightforward food (not Fri-Sun evenings) from sandwiches and baked potatoes up, helpful staff, wide range of customers inc plenty of regulars, canopied courtyard, occasional jazz; no car park but three multi-storeys nearby *(Tony and Wendy Hobden, R T and J C Moggridge, Craig Turnbull)*

Selden Arms [Lyndhurst Rd, between Safeway and hospital]: Friendly local with half a dozen handpumps for the area's top changing beer range, interesting and well kept, lively landlady, limited generous food (not Sun evening) inc popular doorstep sandwiches, real fire, lots of old pub photographs; can get smoky; open all day *(Tony and Wendy Hobden, Bruce Bird)*

Sir Timothy Shelley [Chapel Rd]: One of the smaller Wetherspoons, no smoking area and internal conservatory, well kept beer with bargain guests, decent economical food, friendly efficient service; children welcome in family area till 6, handy for Connaught theatre, open all day *(Tony and Wendy Hobden, B and M Kendall)*

Vine [High St, W Tarring]: Neatly kept local in nice spot away from the day trippers, well kept Badger and guest beers, farm cider, jovial new landlord and friendly staff, enjoyable home-made food (not Sat-Sun evenings); occasional live music; tables in back courtyard, open all day wknds *(Bruce Bird)*

YAPTON SU9702

Lamb [Bilsham Rd (B2132)]: Child-friendly olde-worlde pub with good welcoming service, well kept Greene King Abbot, Harveys Best and a guest beer, log fire, good value food from good sandwich range to Sun roast and bargains for two, attractive no smoking dining room with fine collection of aircraft or railway decorative plates; plenty of picnic-sets in big garden with wonderful play area and pets corner *(Andy and Jill Kassube)*

Maypole [signed off B2132 Arundel rd; Maypole Lane]: Recently refurbished local with chatty landlord and regulars, well kept Ringwood Best, Skinners Betty Stogs and several changing guests inc a local Mild, enjoyable generous sandwiches and simple hot dishes lunchtimes and Fri-Sat evenings, good value Sun roasts, two log fires, friendly cat; can be smoky; skittle alley, seats outside, open all day Fri-Sun *(Bruce Bird, Tony and Wendy Hobden)*

If you have to cancel a reservation for a bedroom or restaurant, please telephone or write to warn them. You may lose your deposit if you've paid one.

Warwickshire
(with Birmingham and West Midlands)

The three new main entries we have here this year show the diversity you can find among this area's good pubs. The Turf in Bloxwich is a classic uncontrived and old-fashioned town local, unchanging over many decades – with good beers. The Golden Lion at Easenhall shines as a place to stay in, and has a pleasantly relaxed traditional bar – as we went to press, it was planning to go entirely no smoking. And the Holly Bush at Priors Marston shows how well an ancient pub can preserve its charm and character while moving into the rather more food-oriented style that so many customers now prefer. Other pubs doing particularly well here are the Bell at Alderminster (imaginative food and good wines by the glass in this well run dining pub), the Fox & Goose at Armscote (stylish, welcoming and now completely no smoking, with interesting food and highly individual bedrooms), the Kings Head at Aston Cantlow (good food in this handsome old pub), the immaculate upmarket Inn at Farnborough (sophisticated food and very good wines by the glass), the unspoilt and very welcoming old Case is Altered at Five Ways, the Howard Arms at Ilmington (a favourite, chiefly for its food – lovely bedrooms, too), and the charming old Bell at Welford-on-Avon (a fine all-rounder). It's clear from this that food is a major part of the appeal in many of the area's best pubs: currently prime among them is the Howard Arms at Ilmington, our Warwickshire Dining Pub of the Year. In the Lucky Dip section at the end of the chapter, pubs to note particularly these days are the Bear in Berkswell, Bartons Arms in Birmingham, Whitefriars in Coventry, George at Lower Brailes, Old Swan in Netherton, Rose & Crown at Ratley, Green Dragon at Sambourne, Windmill in Stratford, Blue Boar at Temple Grafton and Plough at Warmington. In the Warwickshire countryside drinks prices tend to be closely in line with the national average. In the adjoining West Midlands urban areas, though, pubs generally charge much less than the national norm; this is a part of the world where it's still easy to find a pint at well below £2. Banks's of Wolverhampton is the main regional brewer, and Bathams' very good value beers crop up quite often. Other local beers to look out for include Beowulf, Holdens and Highgate, and we found that two beers from across the county boundary – Donnington and, particularly, Hook Norton – were the cheapest on offer in some Warwickshire pubs.

ALDERMINSTER SP2348 Map 4

Bell 🍴 🍷

A3400 Oxford—Stratford

The glow of lovingly polished wood warms the interior of this civilised dining pub. The neatly kept communicating rooms of the spacious bar have stripped slatback chairs around wooden tables on flagstones and wooden floors, little vases of flowers, small landscape prints and swan's-neck brass-and-globe lamps on cream walls and a solid fuel stove in a stripped brick inglenook. It's run with enthusiastic verve by cheery licensees, and has a good menu which might include soup (£3.95),

filled lunchtime baguettes (from £4.25, not Sun), starters such as spinach and parmesan soufflé (£5.50) or seafood cocktail with green bean salad (£6.25), and main courses such as cashew, mushroom and apricot roast with leek and onion cream (£8.50), fishcakes on creamed spinach with leek and parsley sauce (£9.75), steak and kidney pudding (£10.95), braised lamb shank with candied shallots and thyme jus (£13.95), and home-made puddings such as fruit crumble, steamed pudding of the day or chocolate, brandy and almond torte (from £4.25). Do make it clear if you want to eat in the bar, as one or two readers have been unwittingly ushered into the restaurant. The licensees put great effort into keeping the atmosphere flourishing by putting on lots of parties, food festivals, and classical and light music evenings. Well kept Greene King IPA and Abbot on handpump, alongside a good range of around a dozen wines and champagne by the glass, freshly squeezed juice, cocktails and various teas. Other than the bar, the pub is no smoking. They have high chairs, and readers with children have felt particularly welcome. A conservatory and terrace overlook the garden and Stour Valley.
(Recommended by K H Frostick, Carol and David Havard, John Bowdler, Maysie Thompson, Mr and Mrs P Lally, Keith and Margaret Kettell, Paul and Annette Hallett, Catherine and Rob Dunster, Annette and John Derbyshire, Roy Bromell, Jane Legate, Susie Symes, Ian Phillips, Paul Humphreys)

Free house ~ Licensees Keith and Vanessa Brewer ~ Real ale ~ Bar food ~ Restaurant ~ (01789) 450414 ~ Children welcome ~ Dogs allowed in bar and bedrooms ~ Open 12-2.30, 7-11(10.30 Sun); closed evening 24-27 Dec, 1 Jan ~ Bedrooms: £27(£45S)(£52B)/£48(£70S)(£70B)

ARMSCOTE SP2444 Map 4

Fox & Goose

Off A3400 Stratford—Shipston

This stylishly transformed blacksmith's forge – hovering comfortably somewhere between bistro and upmarket pub – is now entirely no smoking. Walls are painted a warm red in the small flagstoned bar and cream in the larger eating area, with bright crushed velvet cushions plumped up on wooden pews, a big gilt mirror over a log fire, polished floorboards and black and white etchings. In a quirky tableau above the dining room's woodburning stove a stuffed fox stalks a big goose; piped jazz. Listed on a daily changing blackboard, the food puts together some imaginative and successful combinations of ingredients. As well as sandwiches (£4.25), there might be grilled garlic sardines (£5), home-cured gravadlax on buckwheat blinis with dill crème fraîche (£5.50), home-made tagliatelle with goats cheese, roasted peppers, pesto and parsnip crisps (£9.50), fried fillets of red mullet on pak choi with chilli and ginger dressing (£11.50), roast lamb shoulder with rosemary and redcurrant jus (£12.50), rib-eye steak with onions, tomato and chips (£14) and home-made puddings (£4.25). Service is charming and helpful. Well kept Ansells and a guest such as Adnams Broadside on handpump, mulled wine in winter, jugs of Pimms in summer, and well chosen wines including a choice of dessert wines. Bedrooms, which are named after characters in Cluedo, are mildly quirky, stylishly decorated and comfortable. Outside, the garden has an elegant vine-covered deck area overlooking a big lawn with tables, benches and fruit trees, and several of the neighbouring houses boast splendid roses in summer.
(Recommended by John Bowdler, Jennie Hall, Maurice Ribbans, Arnold Bennett, Nigel and Sue Foster, Will Watson, Brian and Bett Cox, Bob and Maggie Atherton, Keith and Margaret Kettell, John and Gloria Isaacs, Roger Braithwaite, Susan and John Douglas, Janet and Peter Race, Dr David Cockburn, Mr and Mrs G S Ayrton, David Handforth, Fred and Lorraine Gill, Paul Humphreys, Lee Potter, Roger and Maureen Kenning, Ian Phillips, W W Burke; also in the Good Hotel Guide*)*

Free house ~ Licensee Rachel Hawkins ~ Real ale ~ Bar food (12-2.30, 7-9.30) ~ Restaurant ~ (01608) 682293 ~ Children in restaurant ~ Dogs allowed in bar ~ Open 12-3, 6-11(10.30 Sun) ~ Bedrooms: £45B/£90B

The knife-and-fork award distinguishes pubs where the food is of exceptional quality.

ASTON CANTLOW SP1359 Map 4

Kings Head 🍴 🍷

Village signposted just off A3400 NW of Stratford

This lovely old black and white timbered Tudor pub is a real picture in summer, with wisteria and colourful hanging baskets. There's particular praise from readers for the good often inventive food and the high standard of enthusiastic service from attentive young staff – it is popular, so you will need to book. The creative menu changes very regularly and meals are freshly prepared: maybe fried brie with raspberry vinaigrette (£5.75), chicken, bacon and avocado salad with garlic croutons (£5.95), whisky and honey orange cured salmon with grain mustard dressing (£6.25), gorgonzola, spinach and mushroom cannelloni (£10.75), braised lamb shank with baked goats cheese and herb potato or lemon sole with caper and lemon butter (£13.95), confit and breast of duck with red cabbage and plum sauce (£14.25) and puddings such as warm chocolate brownie or lime leaf and cardamom panna cotta (£4.95). The clean and comfortable village bar on the right is a nice mix of rustic surroundings with a civilised gently upmarket atmosphere: flagstones, low beams, and old-fashioned settles around its massive inglenook log fireplace. The chatty quarry-tiled main room has attractive window seats and oak tables. Three well kept real ales on handpump include Greene King Abbot, M&B Brew XI and a guest such as Hook Norton Old Hooky, also decent wines; piped jazz. The garden is lovely, with a big chestnut tree. The pub is not far from Mary Arden's house in Wilmcote, and Shakespeare's parents are said to have married in the church next door. *(Recommended by Maysie Thompson, James Murphy, Glenys and John Roberts, John and Hazel Williams, Trevor and Sylvia Millum, Susan and John Douglas, Martin Jones, Howard and Margaret Buchanan, Di and Mike Gillam, Brenda and Stuart Naylor, Mrs Ann Gray, Steve Cawthray, Simon and Sally Small, Karen Eliot, Richard Marjoram, Stan and Hazel Allen, Stephen Woad)*

Furlong Leisure ~ Manager David Brian ~ Real ale ~ Bar food (12-2.30, 7-10; 12-3, 7-9 Sun) ~ Restaurant ~ (01789) 488242 ~ Children welcome ~ Dogs allowed in bar ~ Open 11-3, 5.30-11; 11-11 Sat; 12-10.30 Sun

BIRMINGHAM SP0686 Map 4

Old Joint Stock

Temple Row West

Opposite the cathedral, the sober exterior of this romanesque building gives little indication of the flamboyance within: chandeliers hang from the soaring pink and gilt ceiling, gently illuminated busts line the top of the ornately plastered walls, and there's a splendid if well worn cupola above the centre of the room. Drinks are served from a handsome dark wood island bar counter, and big portraits and smart long curtains create an air of unexpected elegance. Around the walls are plenty of tables and chairs, some in surprisingly cosy corners, with more on a big balcony overlooking the bar, reached by a very grand wide staircase. It can get busy (it's a lunchtime favourite with local office workers), but effortlessly absorbs what seem like huge numbers of people. A separate room with panelling and a fireplace has a more intimate, clubby feel. This is the only pub we know of N of Bristol to be owned by the London-based brewer Fullers, and it stocks their Chiswick, ESB, London Pride and one of their seasonal beers, which are well kept alongside a guest from the local Beowulf, and they have a decent range of about a dozen wines by the glass; helpful friendly service, teas, coffees. Usefully served all day, very fairly priced bar food includes soup (£3.25), sandwiches (from £3.95), ploughman's (£6.50), fish and chips (£7.90), steak and ale pie (£7.95) and three or four daily specials such as gammon steak with pineapple salsa (£6.75) and puddings such as treacle sponge with custard (£3.25). Daily papers, perhaps big-screen TV for major sporting events, and piped music (which can be quite loud). A small back terrace has some cast-iron tables and chairs. At busy times there might be a bouncer on the doors. *(Recommended by Joan and Terry O'Neill, John Dwane, Richard Lewis, Paul and Ann Meyer, Dr R C C Ward, C J Fletcher, Susan and John Douglas, Catherine and Rob Dunster)*

Fullers ~ Manager Alison Turner ~ Real ale ~ Bar food (12-9) ~ (0121) 200 1892 ~ Open 11-11; closed Sun and bank hols

BLOXWICH SJ9902 Map 4

Turf

Wolverhampton Road, off A34 just S of A4124, N fringes of Walsall; aka Tinky's

In the same family for over 130 years, and little changed during that time, this utterly uncontrived old-fashioned local is a fascinating reminder of how pubs used to be. What's particularly nice is that even though the unspoilt rooms are Grade II listed, it's far more than just a museum piece: there's a particularly impressive changing range of beers, always very well kept, which draw in a wider range of customers than just the locals you might expect. From the outside you could be forgiven for thinking it's no longer in business, as it appears to be a rather run-down terraced house. Once through the front door it still doesn't immediately look like a pub, but more like the hall of a 1930s home; the public bar is through a door on the right. Reminiscent of a waiting room, it has wooden slatted benches running around the walls, with a big heating pipe clearly visible underneath; there's a tiled floor, three small tables, and William Morris curtains and wallpaper around the simple fireplace. The bar counter has four changing real ales, on our visit taking in Bathams Bitter, Burton Bridge Golden Delicious, RCH Pitchfork and Titanic Iceberg; service is friendly and chatty. There's hatch service out to the hall, on the other side of which is the smoking room, slightly more comfortable, with unusual padded wall settles with armrests. There's also a tiny back parlour with chairs around a tiled fireplace. It almost goes without saying that there's no music or machines, but that does mean conversations here do carry; it may not be the best place to come for a sensitive discussion. The pub's basic charms won't appeal to those who like their creature comforts; the no-frills lavatories are outside, at the end of a simple but pleasant garden, and they don't do food. *(Recommended by Pete Baker, Mike Begley, RWC, Kerry Law, Simon Smith, the Didler)*

Free house ~ Licensees Doris and Zena Hiscott-Wilkes ~ Real ale ~ No credit cards ~ (01922) 407745 ~ Open 12-3, 7-11(10.30 Sun)

BRIERLEY HILL SO9187 Map 4

Vine £

Delph Road; B4172 between A461 and (nearer) A4100

Truly West Midlands in character, this genuine no-nonsense pub is warmly welcoming with a friendly down-to-earth landlord and staff. Known locally as the Bull & Bladder in reference to the good stained-glass bull's heads and very approximate bunches of grapes in the front bow windows, it's a popular place, full of local characters. It can get crowded in the front bar, which has wall benches and simple leatherette-topped oak stools. The extended and refurbished snug on the left has solidly built red plush seats, and the back bar has brass chandeliers – as well as darts, dominoes, big-screen TV and fruit machine. As it's the tap for the next-door Bathams brewery, the Bitter and Mild, and perhaps Delph Strong in winter, are in top condition and most appealingly priced. Very good value simple but tasty fresh lunchtime snacks are limited to samosas (65p), sandwiches (from £1), and curry, faggots and peas, or steak and kidney pie (£2.50). Car park opposite. *(Recommended by Theocsbrian, the Didler, Theo, Anne and Jane Gaskin, Gill and Tony Morriss)*

Bathams ~ Manager Melvyn Wood ~ Real ale ~ Bar food (12-2 Mon-Fri) ~ No credit cards ~ (01384) 78293 ~ Children in family room ~ Dogs allowed in bar ~ Open 12-11; 12-10.30 Sun

COVENTRY SP3379 Map 4

Old Windmill £

Spon Street

Known locally as Ma Brown's after a former landlady, this timber-framed 15th-c inn is probably not the sort of building that first springs to mind when you think of Coventry. Unlike the rest of the buildings in its street (which are an interesting collection of evacuee survivors from the blitz) this friendly unpretentious place stands on its original site. In the nicely battered interior, one of the series of tiny rambling old rooms is little more than the stub of a corridor, another has carved oak seats on flagstones and a woodburner in a fine ancient inglenook fireplace, and another has carpet and more conventionally comfortable seats. There are exposed beams in the uneven ceilings, and a back room preserves some of the equipment used when Ma Brown brewed here. Half a dozen well kept real ales include Courage Directors, Greene King IPA and Old Speckled Hen, Theakstons Old Peculier, Wychwood Hobgoblin and a frequently changing guest such as Greene King Abbot, all kept under light blanket pressure; fruit machine and juke box. Straightforward good value food, passed out straight from the kitchen door, includes filled toasties (£2.10), filled baked potatoes (from £1.85) and steak and onion pie or chicken curry (£3.95); part of the restaurant is no smoking. The pub is popular with students, extremely busy on Friday and Saturday evenings, and handy for the Belgrade Theatre; more reports please, we'd be sorry to drop this pub for want of feedback. *(Recommended by BOB)*

Unique (Enterprise) ~ Tenant Robin Addey ~ Real ale ~ Bar food (12-2.30) ~ No credit cards ~ (0247) 625 2183 ~ Children in eating area of bar ~ Open 11-11; 12-10.30 Sun

DUNCHURCH SP4871 Map 4

Dun Cow

A mile from M45 junction 1; on junction of A45 and A426

The spotlessly kept and handsomely oak-beamed interior of this large bustling chain pub has two no smoking areas, lots of traditional features, including welcoming log fires, rugs on the wooden and flagstone floors, country pictures and bric-a-brac, and farmhouse furniture; fruit machine. In the heyday of the coaching era up to 40 vehicles a day might have passed through this pretty village on their way to and from London, and the stables at this mainly Georgian coaching inn might have housed 20 pairs of coach horses and up to 40 post horses. These days the coachyard is filled with tables and is a delightful spot to sit out on a sunny day (there are more seats on a sheltered side lawn). The reasonably priced food is served all day, but it's worth arriving early for a table during normal meal times. Ordered from a food counter and served by friendly staff, dishes might include soup (£2.95), breaded mushrooms (£3.25), lunchtime sandwiches (from £4.25), tiger prawns in creamy white sauce (£4.95), fish and chips or mediterranean vegetable lasagne (£6.75), beef and ale pie (£7.95), stilton and mushroom stuffed chicken breast in prosciutto ham (£8.95) and mixed grill (£12.95); Sunday roast (£7.25). Well kept Bass, Hancocks and a guest such as Marstons Pedigree on handpump, and a good choice of wines by the glass; piped music. *(Recommended by Ian Phillips, Chris Glasson, Anthony Barnes, Roger and Jenny Huggins, Roger and Pauline Pearce, Joy and Simon Maisey, George Atkinson, Dr and Mrs R G J Telfer, P Tailyour, Alain and Rose Foote)*

Vintage Inns ~ Manager Florrie D'Arcy ~ Real ale ~ Bar food (12-10(9.30 Sun)) ~ Restaurant ~ (01788) 810305 ~ Children in eating area of bar, restaurant and family room ~ Open 11-11; 12-10.30 Sun ~ Bedrooms: /£59.95S

Anyone claiming to arrange or prevent inclusion of a pub in the *Guide* is a fraud. Pubs are included only if recommended by genuine readers and if our own anonymous inspection confirms that they are suitable.

EASENHALL SP4679 Map 4

Golden Lion

Village signposted from B4112 Newbold—Pailton, and from B4455 at Brinklow; Main Street

In a peaceful village, this comfortable 16th-c inn is a particularly nice place to stay at. The licensees – the third generation of their family to run it – have put a lot of effort into building up this side of the business, so that though it has many of the amenities of a hotel, it's still very much a pub, with a good atmosphere and well liked food. Traditional and cosy in a nicely unforced way, the refurbished tiled and flagstoned bar still has many of its original features, including low beams, timbers and a fine carved settle; the lower level has a brick fireplace, while a slightly raised area has a comfortable little alcove with padding overhead. The yellow walls have occasional stencilled lion motifs or Latin phrases. By the time this edition is published, the pub will be entirely no smoking. Well kept Greene King IPA, Abbot and Ruddles County on handpump; service is efficient and welcoming, even when busy. Bar food might include lunchtime sandwiches, local sausages in red wine and onion gravy with mustard grain mash (£8.95), penne with tomato, chilli and garlic topped with melted cheese (£9.35), and lamb cutlets (£11.50); the two-roomed back restaurant has a separate menu. They do a good, generously served Sunday lunch (two courses, £12.95). There are tables at the side, and a good few picnic-sets on a spacious lawn. In a sympathetic back extension, the comfortable bedrooms are modern, individual and well equipped. *(Recommended by Eleanor and Nick Steinitz, Gerry and Rosemary Dobson)*

Free house ~ Licensee James Austin ~ Bar food (12-2.15(4 Sat), 6-9.30; 12-9 Sun) ~ Restaurant ~ (01788) 832265 ~ Children in eating area of bar ~ Open 11-11; 12-10.30 Sun ~ Bedrooms: £52B/£71.50B

EDGE HILL SP3747 Map 4

Castle

Off A422

At its best by far on a sunny day when you can sit outside, and worth a look at the building itself, this beautifully positioned crenellated octagon tower (also known as the Round Tower or Radway Tower) is a folly that was built in 1749 by an 18th-c Gothic Revival enthusiast to mark the spot where Charles I raised his standard at the start of the Battle of Edge Hill. The big attractive garden (with aunt sally) has lovely glimpses down through the trees of the battlefield, and it's said that after closing time you can hear ghostly sounds of battle – a phantom cavalry officer has even been seen galloping by in search of his severed hand. Inside, there are arched doorways, and the walls of the lounge bar, which has the same eight sides as the rest of the main tower, are decorated with maps, pictures and a collection of Civil War memorabilia. Straightforward bar food includes soup (£3.15), sandwiches (£3.50), ploughman's (£4.95), bean casserole (£5.95), breaded cod (£6.40), mixed grill (£7.75), and puddings (£3.50). Hook Norton Best, Old Hooky, one of their seasonal beers, and a guest such as Shepherd Neame Spitfire are well kept on handpump; also country wines, farm cider and around 30 malt whiskies. The public bar, with old farm tools for decoration, has darts, pool, cribbage, dominoes, fruit machine and piped music. Upton House is nearby on the A422, and Compton Wynyates, one of the most beautiful houses in this part of England, is not far beyond. *(Recommended by Susan and John Douglas, C D Watson, Nigel Williamson, Keith Jacob, Alison Crooks, Dave Heffernan, Maggie and Tony Harwood, Karen and Graham Oddey, Brenda and Stuart Naylor, W M Paton, Martin Jennings, Jill Bickerton)*

Hook Norton ~ Lease N J and G A Blann ~ Real ale ~ Bar food (12-2, 6-9) ~ (01295) 670255 ~ Children in eating area of bar ~ Dogs allowed in bar ~ Open 11.15-2.30, 6.15-11(11.30-11 wknds) ~ Bedrooms: /£70B

If we know a pub has a no smoking area, we say so.

FARNBOROUGH SP4349 Map 4

Inn at Farnborough

Off A423 N of Banbury

The immaculately kept interior at this stylishly refurbished and civilised golden stone house is a pleasant mix of the traditional and contemporary, with plenty of exposed stonework, and thoughtful lighting. The emphasis however is very much on the quite sophisticated changing blackboard menu. Very well prepared dishes, using local produce where possible, might include wild mushroom risotto with parmesan crisps and rocket salad (£5.95), pork and herb sausages with caramelised onion and juniper jus (£8.95), seared king scallops and oyster mushrooms with crispy pancetta and truffle oil dressing (£9.95), baked goats cheese cheesecake with tomato and sweet pepper chutney (£10.95), fishcakes with buttered spinach and mushrooms, saffron and chive beurre blanc (£12.95), roast rump of lamb with chorizo and moroccan spiced cassoulet with red wine and rosemary (£14.95). A plus for many readers recently has been the good value two- and three-course lunchtime and early evening menu (£10.95/£12.95; not Sat evening or Sun). Service is usually cheerfully attentive but can be slow. The beamed and flagstoned bar has neat blinds on its mullioned windows, a chrome hood in the old stone fireplace, plenty of fresh flowers on the modern counter, candles on wicker tables, and smartly upholstered chairs, window seats and stools. A stable door leads out to chic metal furnishings on a decked terrace. The dining room has a comfortably roomy seat in a fireplace, nice wooden floors, a good mix of mismatched tables and chairs, and well chosen plants. Well kept Greene King Abbot and a couple of guest beers such as Highgate Davenports and Charles Wells Bombardier on handpump, and a good extensive wine list with about 17 by the glass. A machine dispenses Havana cigars; piped music. The landscaped garden is really delightful with a lovely sloping lawn, plenty of picnic-sets (one under a big old tree) and wandering hens. A string of white fairy lights around the roof gives the exterior an elegant appearance at night. *(Recommended by Arnold Bennett, George Atkinson, Jennie Hall, Andrew MacLeod, John Bowdler, Michael Jones, Mrs E Widdowson, Karen Eliot, Michael and Anne Brown, Humphry and Angela Crum Ewing, Catherine and Rob Dunster, Gerry and Rosemary Dobson)*

Free house ~ Licensee Tony Robinson ~ Real ale ~ Bar food (12-3, 6-10.30) ~ Restaurant ~ (01295) 690615 ~ Children welcome ~ Dogs allowed in bar ~ Open 11-11

FIVE WAYS SP2270 Map 4

Case is Altered

Follow Rowington signposts at junction roundabout off A4177/A4141 N of Warwick, then right into Case Lane

Definitely somewhere to get away from it all, this delightful white cottage is peacefully old-fashioned with no food, children, dogs, games machines or piped music – just a very warm welcome from the cheery staff and regulars. With so much focus on their four real ales it does mean they are very well kept: Greene King IPA, Hook Norton Old Hooky and a guest ale from a microbrewery such as St Austell are all served by a rare type of handpump mounted on the casks that are stilled behind the counter. A door at the back of the building leads into a modest little room, usually empty on weekday lunchtimes, with a rug on its tiled floor and an antique bar billiards table protected by an ancient leather cover (it takes pre-decimal sixpences). From here, the simple little main bar has a fine old poster showing the old Lucas Blackwell & Arkwright brewery (now flats) and a clock with its hours spelling out Thornleys Ale – another defunct brewery; there are just a few sturdy old-fashioned tables, with a couple of stout leather-covered settles facing each other over the spotless tiles. The homely lounge (usually open only weekend evenings and Sunday lunchtime) is reached through the front courtyard or back car park. Behind a wrought-iron gate is a little brick-paved courtyard with a stone table under a chestnut tree. *(Recommended by Paul and Ann Meyer, John Dwane, Kevin Blake, Bernie Adams, the Didler, Pete Baker, R J Herd, Ted George)*

Free house ~ Licensee Jackie Willacy ~ Real ale ~ No credit cards ~ (01926) 484206 ~ Open 12(11.30 Sat)-2.30, 6-11; 12-2, 7-10.30 Sun

GAYDON SP3654 Map 4

Malt Shovel

Under a mile from M40 junction 12; B4451 into village, then left and right across B4100; Church Road

Very handy if you're looking for a break from the M40, this busy pub has a good relaxed atmosphere and quite an unusual layout. A sort of pathway in mahogany-varnished boards runs through bright carpeting to link the entrance, the bar counter on the right and the log fire on the left. This central area has a high pitched ceiling, with milk churns and earthenware containers in a loft above the bar, where Adnams Best and Broadside, Castle Eden, Fullers London Pride, Greene King Abbot, Wadworths 6X and possibly a guest such as Everards Tiger are well kept on handpump alongside decent wines by the glass, and filter coffee. Three steps take you up to a snug little space with some comfortable sofas overlooked by a big stained-glass window and reproductions of classic posters. At the other end is a busy lower-ceilinged dining area with flowers on the mix of kitchen, pub and dining tables. Enjoyable food, cooked by the chef-landlord, includes lunchtime sandwiches (from £3.15) and ploughman's or breakfast (£4.95), as well as soup (£3.15), stilton and port mushrooms (£3.95), battered haddock (£5.95), roast pepper, mozzarella and olive salad (£7.15), three-cheese vegetable lasagne (£7.95), wild boar and apple sausages braised in calvados and cider with garlic mash (£8.45) and puddings such as Amaretti iced nougat or warm chocolate brioche (from £3.50); Sunday roast. Service is friendly and efficient; on our inspection visit, 1970/80s piped music; darts, fruit machine. The springer spaniel is Rosie, and the jack russell is Mollie. *(Recommended by Anna and David Pullman, William and Jenifer Ruxton, R T and J C Moggridge, Jennie Hall, M Joyner, Peter and Audrey Dowsett, Ian Phillips, Jill Bickerton)*

Enterprise ~ Tenants Richard and Debi Morisot ~ Real ale ~ Bar food (12-2, 6.30-9) ~ Restaurant ~ (01926) 641221 ~ Children in eating area of bar and restaurant ~ Dogs allowed in bar ~ Open 11-3, 5-11; 11-11 Sat; 12-10.30 Sun

GREAT WOLFORD SP2434 Map 4

Fox & Hounds

Village signposted on right on A3400 3 miles S of Shipston-on-Stour

You do need to book a table if visiting this inviting 16th-c stone inn for a meal as they reserve tables throughout the pub. The cosy low-beamed bar has a nice collection of chairs and old candlelit tables on spotless flagstones, antique hunting prints, and a roaring log fire in the inglenook fireplace with its fine old bread oven; piped music, darts (Sunday evening) and cribbage (Wednesday evening). An old-fashioned little tap room serves well kept Hook Norton and a couple of guests such as Bass and Timothy Taylor Landlord on handpump, and over 170 malt whiskies. Under new licensees since the last edition of the *Guide*, bar food might include cream of parsnip soup with parsnip crisps (£3.75), seared king scallops with rocket and tomato and garlic butter (£5), roast figs with parma ham (£5.50), baked field mushrooms with spinach and leek and gruyère or spaghetti with cockles, clams, sun-dried tomatoes and garlic cream sauce (£10.50), crispy duck leg on fried asian greens and peppers with egg noodles (£13.50), grilled swordfish with black olive tapenade (£13.75) and puddings such as orange and almond cake with greek yoghurt and caramelised oranges or sticky toffee pudding (£4.25); no smoking section. A terrace has green plastic furniture and a well. *(Recommended by P and J Shapley, Pat and Roger Fereday, WAH, Val and Brian Garrod, Sir Nigel Foulkes)*

Free house ~ Licensees Paul and Veronica Tomlinson ~ Real ale ~ Bar food (not Sun evening) ~ Restaurant ~ (01608) 674220 ~ Children in eating area of bar ~ Dogs welcome ~ Open 12-2.30(3 Sat, Sun), 6-11(10.30 Sun); closed Mon ~ Bedrooms: £45B/£70B

HIMLEY SO8791 Map 4

Crooked House ★

Pub signposted from B4176 Gornalwood—Himley, OS Sheet 139 map reference 896908; readers have got so used to thinking of the pub as being near Kingswinford in the Midlands (though Himley is actually in Staffs) that we still include it in this chapter – the pub itself is virtually smack on the county boundary

This wonky old pub is well worth a look-in for its novelty value. When subsidence caused by mine workings underneath threw the pub 15 degrees out of true they propped it up, rehung the doors and straightened the floors. The result leaves your perceptions spinning in a way that can really feel like being at sea. On one table a bottle on its side actually rolls 'upwards' against the apparent direction of the slope, and for a 10p donation you can get a big ball-bearing from the bar to roll 'uphill' along a wainscot. There's a friendly atmosphere throughout, and at the back is a large, level and more modern extension with local antiques. Very reasonably priced Banks's Bitter and Original and a guest such as Caledonian Deuchars IPA are well kept on handpump alongside a farm cider; piped music. Good value bar food includes soup (£2.10), filled baguettes (£3.25), jalapeno pepper battered chicken balls with sour cream and chive dip (£3.25), mediterranean wellington (£6.25), beef and red wine pie (£6.50), daily specials such as roast perch wrapped in bacon with mint and apple (£7.50), lamb cutlets with white wine and lemon sauce (£8.25) and puddings such as apple and caramel cooking dough pie (£3.50). The conservatory is no smoking at food times, and there's a spacious outside terrace. It can get busy here in summer, with coach trips. *(Recommended by Joyce and Geoff Robson, the Didler, Patrick Hancock, Ian Phillips, Pam and John Smith, Phil and Jane Hodson, Dr and Mrs A K Clarke)*

Banks's (W & D) ~ Tenants Amanda Stevens and David Shotton ~ Real ale ~ Bar food (12-9(9.30 Fri, Sat; 8 Sun), no food 2.15-5.30 winter weekdays) ~ (01384) 238583 ~ Children welcome ~ Dogs allowed in bar ~ Open 11.30-11; 12-10.30 Sun; 11.30-2.30, 5.30-11 weekdays winter

ILMINGTON SP2143 Map 4

Howard Arms 🍴 🍷 🛏

Village signposted with Wimpstone off A3400 S of Stratford

Warwickshire Dining Pub of the Year

It's always risky to describe a place as faultless, but readers' reports suggest that this beautifully kept golden-stone inn comes pretty close. The stylishly simple interior is light and airy, with a few good prints on attractively painted warm golden walls, rugs on broad polished flagstones, and a nice mix of furniture from hardwood pews to old church seats. A snug area and upper bar are no smoking. A nice choice of beers includes well kept Everards Tiger, North Cotswold Genesis and a guest from a brewer such as Wyre Piddle, as well as organic juices and about a dozen wines by the glass. The emphasis here is on the imaginative menu which changes two or three times a week and is carefully written on boards above a huge stone inglenook (with a log fire that burns most of the year). Given the quality of the freshly prepared food prices are fair: soup (£3.75), pea and asparagus risotto (£5.50), smoked salmon with warm potato cake, sour cream and chives (£6.50), brie, tomato and spinach puff pastry pie with roast tomato and red pepper sauce (£9), beef, ale and mustard pie (£9.50), spicy grilled pork belly with stir-fried chinese greens or grilled lamb burger with crushed cannellini beans and mint dressing (£10.50), grilled halibut with niçoise salad (£15.50), puddings such as iced gingerbread parfait with white chocolate sauce and poached pears or moist almond and apricot cake with caramelised oranges and mascarpone (£5) and cheeses (£5.50); service is good-humoured and efficient and you will need to book. The garden is lovely in summer with fruit trees sheltering the lawn, a colourful herbaceous border, and a handful of tables on a neat York stone terrace. The pub is nicely set beside the village green, and there are lovely walks on the nearby hills (as well as strolls around the village outskirts). *(Recommended by Maurice Ribbans,*

Martin Jennings, Arnold Bennett, Terry and Linda Moseley, Martin Jones, Janet and Peter Race, MP, John Bowdler, John Kane, P and J Shapley, Maysie Thompson, Andrew MacLeod, Roy Bromell, Susan and John Douglas, Hugh Spottiswoode, Di and Mike Gillam, Ian and Jane Irving, Paul and Annette Hallett, Dr David Cockburn, Michael and Jenny Back, David Handforth, Peter Saville, Elaine and Tony Barker, Paul Humphreys, Clive and Fran Dutson, Norman and Sarah Keeping, Mr and Mrs G S Ayrton, Nicholas and Dorothy Stephens; also in the Good Hotel Guide*)*

Free house ~ Licensees Rob Greenstock and Martin Devereux ~ Real ale ~ Bar food (12-2(2.30 Sun), 7-9(9.30 Fri, Sat; 6.30-8.30 Sun)) ~ Restaurant ~ (01608) 682226 ~ Children in eating area of bar till 7.30pm and restaurant ~ Open 11-2.30(3 Sat), 6-11; 12-3.30, 6-10.30 Sun ~ Bedrooms: £75B/£95B

LAPWORTH SP1970 Map 4

Navigation

Old Warwick Road S of village (B4439 Warwick—Hockley Heath); by Grand Union Canal, OS Sheet 139 map reference 191709

The success and appeal of this bustling local is very much down to the sanguine character of the friendly landlord – now in his 22nd year here. Filled with the happy chatter of merry locals and canal-users, the beamed bar is genuinely rustic, with an undulating flagstoned floor, high-backed winged settles, seats built in around its window bay, a coal fire in a high-manteled inglenook, one or two bits of brightly painted canal ware, and cases of stuffed fish. The fish theme is developed in the lounge, which has more cases of stuffed fish, oak and carpet floors, and pews. The quieter no smoking dining room at the back has a fresher contemporary feel with modern art on light mushroom walls, high-backed leather chairs on oak floors, and wooden venetian blinds. This room has a pleasant outlook over the sheltered flower-edged lawn, and on down to the busy canal behind. This is a great place in summer when hatch service to aluminium and wicker chairs on the terrace lets you make the most of its pretty canalside setting; they do ice-creams then too, and the pub and gardens are prettily lit at night. Served by friendly staff, bar food in generous helpings includes sandwiches (from £3.50), vegetarian quiche or goats cheese salad (£7.50), chicken balti (£7.95), tasty battered cod or beef and ale casserole (£8.50), pork loin with mustard and cider sauce (£8.95), salmon and crab fishcakes with white wine and dill sauce (£9.25), fillet steak with pepper sauce or redcurrant jus (£13.50), and puddings such as chocolate bread and butter pudding (£3.50). Very well kept Bass, M&B Brew XI and a guest from an interesting microbrewery such as Cottage on handpump, alongside a changing farm cider such as Biddenden Dry, and around 30 malt whiskies; fruit machine and TV (rarely on). *(Recommended by Lady Freeland, June and Malcolm Farmer, Arnold Bennett, Kevin Blake, DJH, Dave Braisted, Dr and Mrs A K Clarke, David Edwards, John Saville, Mrs B M Hill)*

Unique (Enterprise) ~ Lease Andrew Kimber ~ Real ale ~ Bar food (12-2(3 Sun), 6-9) ~ Restaurant ~ (01564) 783337 ~ Children welcome ~ Dogs allowed in bar ~ Open 11-3, 5.30-11; 11-11 Sat, Sun

LITTLE COMPTON SP2630 Map 4

Red Lion

Off A44 Moreton-in-Marsh—Chipping Norton

The simple but comfortably old fashioned low-beamed plush lounge at this 16th-c stone local has snug alcoves and a couple of little tables by the log fire. The plainer public bar has another log fire, Donnington BB and SBA on handpump and an extensive wine list; darts, pool, cribbage, dominoes and fruit machine. It does get busy here so you may need to book, especially at weekends. Bar food includes soup (£3.50), very good filled baguettes (from £4.25), ploughman's (£5.25), scampi (£7.50), tagliatelle niçoise with greek salad (£7.95), and daily specials such as marinated anchovies (£4.95), smoked salmon and prawn parcels with dill mustard dressing (£5.95), chicken breast with spicy tomato, mushroom and pepper sauce and melted mozzarella (£9.95), grilled fillets of red mullet on noodle and vegetable stir fry (£10.50) and roast lamb shank with rosemary, garlic and red wine on spring onion potato cake (£11.95); the restaurant is no smoking. The well maintained garden is pleasant, and this is a handy base for exploring the Cotswolds. *(Recommended by M and GR, K H Frostick, H O Dickinson, John Bowdler, Bob Broadhurst, Roger and Jenny Huggins, Guy Vowles, Brenda and Stuart Naylor, John and Johanne Eadie, Dr and Mrs R G J Telfer, Ann and Colin Hunt, Brian Root)*

Donnington ~ Tenant David Smith ~ Real ale ~ Bar food (12-2.30, 7-9.30) ~ Restaurant ~ (01608) 674397 ~ Children in restaurant and eating area of bar, over 8 if staying ~ Open 12-2.30, 6-11; 12-3, 7-10.30 Sun ~ Bedrooms: £45B/£55B

LONG ITCHINGTON SP4165 Map 4

Duck on the Pond

Just off A423 Coventry—Southam; The Green

The surprisingly eclectic interior of this spacious pub is vaguely reminiscent of a 1970s French bistro. The central bar has dark pine ceiling planks, royal blue banquettes, some barrel tables, bacchanalian carvings around its coal fire and a few big wading bird decoys. Wicker panels provide frontage to the bar counter, which has Charles Wells Bombardier and a guest such as Greene King Old Speckled Hen on handpump and about eight wines by the glass. On each side of the bar is a sizeable dining area (both no smoking) with pine furniture (some tables painted in light red chequers), a wall of wine bottles, big Edwardian prints on sienna red walls, a crystal chandelier and a grandfather clock. Service is friendly and the atmosphere warmly relaxing. The piped pop or jazzy soul music may be loud but is well reproduced; TV. Enjoyable food includes soup (£3.95), chicken pesto and walnut terrine with tomato chutney or fried sardines with tomato and basil concasse (£4.95), cajun pork fillet with sautéed sweet potato, chorizo and sweet peppers or seared tuna steak on niçoise salad (£12.95) and a good choice of delicious puddings such as mulled wine poached pears with lemon sorbet and raspberry ripple cheesecake (£4.50). Tables and chairs in front look down on a pond, which does indeed have ducks; the main road is quite busy. *(Recommended by Suzanne Miles, Catherine and Rob Dunster, Claire Procter)*

Charles Wells ~ Lease Andrew and Wendy Parry ~ Real ale ~ Bar food (12-2, 6-10; 12-10(9 Sun) Sat) ~ Restaurant ~ (01926) 815876 ~ No children Fri, Sat evenings ~ Open 11-2.30, 5-11; 12-11(10.30 Sun) Sat

PRIORS MARSTON SP4857 Map 4

Holly Bush

Village signposted from A361 S of Daventry (or take the old Welsh Road) from Southam); from village centre follow Shuckburgh signpost, then take first right turn by phone box

This golden stone 13th-c inn, once the village bakehouse, has recently been refurbished by a new owner. This has kept and even enhanced the considerable character of the interesting old building. The main part is divided into small beamed rambling rooms by partly glazed timber dividers, keeping a good-sized bar as well as the main dining area, and there are flagstones, some bare boards, a good deal of stripped stone, and good sturdy tables in varying sizes. A log fire blazes in the big stone hearth at one end, and the central lounge area has a woodburning stove. Beside a second smaller and smarter no smoking dining area is a back snug with temptingly squashy leather sofas. Good bar food includes soup (£3.95), baguettes (£4.95), game pie or mushroom and spinach lasagne (£6.95), roast salmon with mediterranean stuffing (£7.95), rump steak (£8.95), and puddings such as baked rhubarb and vanilla cheesecake (£2.95); you can also eat from the impressive restaurant menu; friendly informal service from amiable staff. They have Fullers London Pride, Hook Norton Best and a guest such as Timothy Taylors Landlord well kept on handpump from the copper-topped bar counter, alongside a farm cider, and decent wines by the glass; there may be piped music. The sheltered garden behind has tables and chairs on the lawn, and this is an attractive village.

We have not yet heard from readers who have stayed here, and look forward to reports on this aspect. *(Recommended by Di and Mike Gillam, Jane Legate, Arnold Bennett)*

Free house ~ Licensee Richard Saunders ~ Real ale ~ Bar food (12-2, 6.30-9.30; 12-2.30, 7-9 Sun) ~ Restaurant ~ (01327) 260934 ~ Children welcome in lounge area ~ Dogs welcome ~ Open 12-2, 5.30-11; 12-3, 6-11.30(7-10.30 Sun) Sat ~ Bedrooms: £40S/£45B

SEDGLEY SO9193 Map 4

Beacon ★

Bilston Street (no pub sign on our visit, but by Beacon Lane); A463, off A4123 Wolverhampton—Dudley

Lovers of unspoilt traditional pubs will be delighted with this plain-looking old Victorian brick house. When you arrive it's worth ignoring the side entrance and walking round from the car park to the front. Up a couple of steps, the front door opens into a plain quarry-tiled drinking corridor where you may find a couple of locals leaning up against the walls going up the stairs, chatting to the waistcoated barman propped in the doorway of his little central serving booth. Go through the door into the little snug on your left and you can easily imagine a 19th-c traveller tucked up on one of the wall settles, next to the imposing green tiled marble fireplace with its big misty mirror, the door closed for privacy and warmth and a drink handed through the glazed hatch. The dark woodwork, turkey carpet, velvet and net curtains, heavy mahogany tables, old piano and little landscape prints all seem unchanged since those times. Another simple snug on the right has a black kettle and embroidered mantel over a blackened range, and a stripped wooden wall bench. The corridor then runs round the serving booth, past the stairs and into a big well proportioned dark-panelled smoking room with sturdy red leather wall settles down the length of each side, gilt-based cast-iron tables, a big blue carpet on the lino, and dramatic sea prints. Round a corner (where you would have come in from the car park) the conservatory is densely filled with plants, and has no seats. Alongside a couple of guests from brewers such as Abbeydale and Mauldons, the beautifully aromatic Sarah Hughes beers served here – Dark Ruby, Pale Amber and Surprise Bitter – are brewed in the traditional Victorian brewery at the back, which you can arrange to look round. The only food served is cheese and onion cobs (£1). A children's play area in the garden has a slide, climbing frame and roundabout. *(Recommended by the Didler, Theocsbrian, Bernie Adams, Pete Baker, Keith Jacob, Ian Phillips)*

Own brew ~ Licensee John Hughes ~ Real ale ~ No credit cards ~ (01902) 883380 ~ Dogs allowed in bar ~ Open 12-2.30, 5.30-10.45(11 Fri); 11.30-3, 6-11 Sat; 12-3, 7-10.30 Sun

SHIPSTON-ON-STOUR SP2540 Map 4

White Bear

High Street

Tucked behind the fine brick Georgian frontage of this old coaching inn is the bustle of a lively town local. The long narrow front bar on the left has massive stripped settles, attractive lamps and interesting pictures (charming pen and wash drawings of Paris café society, and sporting and other cartoons from Alken through Lawson Wood to bright modern ones by Tibb) on the rag-rolled walls. The back lounge is more plainly furnished and decorated, with comfortable modern furniture, and big Toulouse-Lautrec and other prints of French music-hall life. A separate bar on the right has a woodburning stove in a big painted stone fireplace. Well kept Adnams, Bass, Hook Norton Old Hooky and a guest beer on handpump, with eclectically chosen wines, including bin ends and a good selection of ports and wines by the glass; polite, knowledgeable service; daily papers. Food from a well balanced menu is served in the bar and restaurant, and might include asparagus soup with croûtons (£2.90), cheese and tarragon fritters with pepper salad (£4.50), lambs kidneys and chorizo with grain mustard sauce (£4.90), aubergine filled with mushroom couscous or home-made burger and chunky chips (£7.95), steak, onion and Guinness pie (£8.25), bass fillets on leeks with vermouth sauce (£11.90), duck breast with juniper berries, red wine and honey (£12.50); part of the restaurant is no smoking. They have darts, dominoes and cribbage; also juke box, TV and fruit machine. *(Recommended by Paul and Ann Meyer, JHBS, Des and Jen Clarke, Ian Phillips, W W Burke)*

Punch ~ Lease George Kruszynskyi ~ Real ale ~ Bar food (12-2(2.30 Sat-Sun, 6.30-9.30 (10 Fri-Sat); not Sun evening) ~ Restaurant ~ (01608) 661558 ~ Children welcome ~ Dogs welcome ~ Live music Sun evening ~ Open 11-11; 12-10.30 Sun ~ Bedrooms: £30B/£50B

SHUSTOKE SP2290 Map 4

Griffin £

5 miles from M6 junction 4; A446 towards Tamworth, then right on to B4114 and go straight through Coleshill; pub is at Church End, a mile E of village

Almost always bustling with a cheery crowd, the low-beamed L-shaped bar at this unpretentious country local has two stone fireplaces (one's a big inglenook) with warming log fires. Besides one nice old-fashioned settle the décor is fairly simple, from cushioned café seats (some quite closely packed) to sturdily elm-topped sewing trestles, lots of old jugs on the beams, beer mats on the ceiling and a fruit machine. One reader found it a bit smoky. The finest feature here is the interesting range of up to ten real ales. From a servery under a very low heavy beam, Banks's Original and Marstons Pedigree are well kept alongside guests from small brewers such as Bathams, Everards, Exmoor, Hook Norton, Theakstons and Timothy Taylor, also country wines, farm cider, mulled wine and hot punch in winter. As well as a choice of 20 warwickshire cheeses (you can buy them to take away), good value straightforward lunchtime bar food, served by friendly efficient staff, includes pie and chips, broccoli bake, lasagne and cod, chips and mushy peas (£5.50–£5.75); you may need to arrive early to get a table. There are old-fashioned seats and tables outside on the back grass, a play area and a large terrace with plants in raised beds. *(Recommended by Roy and Lindsey Fentiman, Kevin Blake, Dr B and Mrs P B Baker, John Dwane, Mike Turner, Brian and Anita Randall, Keith Jacob, Derek and Sylvia Stephenson, Brian and Jacky Wilson)*

Free house ~ Licensee Michael Pugh ~ Real ale ~ Bar food (12-2; not Sun or evenings) ~ No credit cards ~ (01675) 481205 ~ Children in conservatory ~ Dogs welcome ~ Open 12-2.30(2.45 Sun), 7-11(10.30 Sun)

STRATFORD-UPON-AVON SP2055 Map 4

Garrick 🍷

High Street

Joining a small but growing number of pubs in the *Guide*, this ancient place is now completely no smoking. Although much altered over the years, the small but high-beamed, heavily timbered and often irregularly shaped rooms are still fairly characterful, with secluded little nooks and wonky walls that are either stripped back to bare stone or heavily plastered. Simple furnishings include long upholstered settles and stools made from barrels on bare boards. A small dining room at the back is air-conditioned. Flowers Original, Greene King Abbot, Hook Norton Old Hooky and Wadworths 6X are well kept on handpump, and attractively priced for this tourist town. Bar food is served in generous helpings and includes soup (£2.95), potted crab (£4.25), mozzarella and cheddar risotto (£5.95), spinach and mushroom cannelloni (£6.45), cold poached salmon (£7.45), battered cod or steak and ale pie (£7.95), roast rack of lamb with port and redcurrant jus (£11.95) and puddings such as apple and blackberry crumble or sticky toffee pudding (from £2.95). Staff remain good-natured even when it gets busy (and perhaps a bit cramped for some readers). Fruit machine, piped music and a TV. The name of the pub commemorates David Garrick, the actor-manager, who inaugurated the Stratford Festival in 1769. *(Recommended by Val and Alan Green, Maggie and Tony Harwood, Arnold Bennett, Kevin Blake, Duncan Cloud, Patrick Hancock, Bob and Margaret Holder, Sue Dibben)*

Laurel (Enterprise) ~ Licensee Vicky Leng ~ Real ale ~ Bar food (12-9) ~ (01789) 292186 ~ Children in restaurant ~ Live entertainment Fri monthly ~ Open 11-11; 12-10.30 Sun

WELFORD-ON-AVON SP1452 Map 4

Bell

Off B439 W of Stratford; High Street

Readers really enjoy this very well run 17th-c brick pub, its main emphasis on the very good imaginative bar food. Using local produce where possible, it's served by charmingly efficient staff and might include soup (£2.95), avocado and smoked bacon salad (£4.95), whitebait (£4.50), sandwiches (from £4.25), lasagne (£8.25), battered cod with crushed minted peas (£8.95), beef and tomato casserole (£9.95), daily specials such as leek and blue cheese tart or salmon and caper fishcakes with tarragon mayonnaise (£5.25), courgette and asparagus kedgeree with spiced nuts (£8.95), fennel roasted duck breast on crushed peas and potatoes with orange sauce (£12.50), roast plaice fillet with asparagus on blue cheese risotto (£12.95) and puddings such as apple and berry crumble or chocolate pot (£4.75); several no smoking areas. The very attractive interior is divided into five comfortable areas, each with its own character, from the cosy terracotta-painted bar to the light and airy terrace room with its peach and terracotta wash. Flagstone floors, stripped, well polished antique or period-style furniture, and three real fires (one in an inglenook) give it quite a pubby feel. Well kept Flowers, Hook Norton Old Hooky, Wadworths 6X and a guest such as Enville and Hobsons on handpump, malt whiskies and a wide choice of wines including local ones; piped music. In summer the creeper-covered exterior is hung with lots of colourful baskets, and there are seats in the pretty secluded garden area (lovely with blossom in spring) and back courtyard. The riverside village has an appealing church and pretty thatched black and white cottages. *(Recommended by Angus Lyon, Hugh Roberts, Arnold Bennett, Brenda and Stuart Naylor, John and Johanne Eadie, Oliver Richardson, Martin Jennings, Glenwys and Alan Lawrence, Peter Coxon, Margaret Dickinson, Susan and John Douglas)*

Laurel (Enterprise) ~ Lease Colin and Teresa Ombler ~ Real ale ~ Bar food (11.45-2.30, 6.45-9.30(6-10 Fri, Sat); 12-4, 7-9.30 Sun) ~ Restaurant ~ (01789) 750353 ~ Children in eating area of bar and restaurant ~ Open 11.30-3, 6.30(6 Fri/Sat)-12; 12-4, 7-10.30 Sun

WHARF SP4352 Map 4

Wharf Inn

A423 Banbury—Southam, near Fenny Compton

This open-plan pub by Bridge 136 of the South Oxford Canal very usefully serves food all day. They serve breakfast (full english £5.50) first thing, and later into the day, the bar menu (which changes four times a year) might include soup (£3.50), sandwiches (from £4), mussels in creamy white wine sauce (£4.50), vegetarian penne pasta (£7.50) and braised blade of beef with dumplings (£9); friendly efficient service, and good freshly ground coffee. A smart tall-windowed dining area on the left has plain solid tables and high-backed chairs on mainly wood strip or tiled floors, a big oriental rug, cream walls, modern artwork, and end windows so close to the water that you feel right by it. A small central flagstoned bar has Adnams, Charles Wells Bombardier, Hook Norton Best and a guest on handpump. On the right is a pair of soft white leather settees by a feature coffee table, a few more tables with deco armed chairs, a modern woodburning stove, and some appealing mainly water-related pictures; a little snug beyond has a pile of children's books. Lighting throughout is good; disabled access and facilities; faint piped pop music. The slightly sloping waterside garden has picnic-sets and a playhouse on high stilts. They have moorings, and space for caravans. *(Recommended by Arnold Bennett, Ted George, Roger and Debbie Stamp, Carol and David Havard, Meg and Colin Hamilton, Catherine and Rob Dunster)*

Punch ~ Lease Kevin Partridge ~ Real ale ~ Bar food (8-9.30) ~ Restaurant ~ (01295) 770332 ~ Children welcome ~ Dogs allowed in bar ~ Open 8.30(10 in winter)-11(10.30 Sun)

LUCKY DIP

Besides the fully inspected pubs, you might like to try these Lucky Dips recommended to us and described by readers (if you do, please send us reports: www.goodguides.co.uk).

ALCESTER SP0957
Holly Bush [Henley St]: Warren of unpretentious panelled rooms off central bar, just right for this time-warp town; well kept Cannon Royall Fruiterers Mild, Uley and several guest beers, reasonably priced straightforward food, hard-working landlady; pleasant back garden *(Jill Bickerton, Pete Baker)*
Turks Head [High St]: Welcoming traditional town pub with old country furnishings on bare boards, well kept Hook Norton, Timothy Taylors Landlord and Wye Valley Hereford, enjoyable food, coal fire, happy atmosphere, daily papers, corridor to mirrored back lounge; tables in walled garden, cl Mon lunchtime, open all day wknds *(Robert Yarwood)*

ALLESLEY SP2980
White Lion [just off A45 nr Browns Lane Jaguar; Hawkes Mill Lane]: Well run Vintage Inn with pleasant softly lit separate areas, central log fires, photographs and bric-a-brac, decent food all day inc smaller dishes and lunchtime sandwiches, good wine choice, Bass and Tetleys, cheerful prompt service; piped music; children welcome, tables in garden, open all day *(Alan Johnson)*

ANSTY SP3983
☆ *Rose & Castle* [B4065 NE of Coventry]: Tidy low-beamed pub with cheerful friendly service, wide choice of good value food, four well kept ales inc Bass, some canal-theme decoration; not big, fills up quickly; children welcome, lovely canalside garden with play area *(Alan Johnson, R A K Crabtree)*

ARDENS GRAFTON SP1153
Golden Cross [off A46 or B439 W of Stratford, OS Sheet 150 map ref 114538; Wixford rd]: Dining pub with attractive décor, light wood and good lighting, generous food from lunchtime baguettes up in flagstoned bar or comfortable dining room with well spaced tables, well kept Hook Norton and Timothy Taylors Landlord, log fire; wheelchair access, tables in charming garden, nice views *(Dave Braisted)*

AVON DASSETT SP4049
Avon [off A41 Banbury—Warwick; aka the Avon]: Pleasant décor, friendly and relaxing atmosphere, enjoyable if not cheap freshly cooked bar food, Courage, Hook Norton and a guest beer, several wines by the glass, Civil War memorabilia, nice restaurant with plenty of fish; wet and muddy walkers welcome – bar's flagstones cope well; attractive small village *(Martin and Karen Wake)*

BAGINTON SP3375
☆ *Old Mill* [Mill Hill]: Appealing Chef & Brewer conversion of old watermill nr airport (and Lunt Roman fort), smart and well run, with heavy beams, timbers and candlelight in roomy rustic-theme main bar, good food range, good wine choice, real ales, neat uniformed staff, restaurant; lovely terraced gardens leading down to River Sower, 28 bedrooms *(Susan and John Douglas, LYM, Joan and Terry O'Neill, Duncan Cloud)*

BARSTON SP2078
☆ *Bulls Head* [from M42 junction 5, A4141 towards Warwick, first left, then signed down Barston Lane]: Unassuming partly Tudor village local, comfortable lounge with pictures and plates, dining room, friendly efficient service, enjoyable food inc good fresh fish, well kept real ales, oak-beamed bar with log fires and a little Buddy Holly memorabilia; good-sized secluded garden alongside, hay barn behind *(Susan and John Douglas, Mike Begley, Pete Baker, Geoffrey and Penny Hughes)*

BARTON SP1051
☆ *Cottage of Content* [pub signed off B4085, just S of Bidford-on-Avon]: Cosy and quaint traditional flagstoned low-beamed bar with solid fuel stove in inglenook, easy-going atmosphere and plenty of locals, good simple home-cooked bar food from baguettes up, three well kept ales inc Bass, restaurant; piped music; picnic-sets in front of the pretty house, touring caravan site with good play area behind, day fishing on River Avon but no nearby moorings *(BB, Catherine and Rob Dunster)*

BERKSWELL SP2478
☆ *Bear* [off A452 W of Coventry; Spencers Lane, junction with Coventry Rd, Meriden Rd and Lavender Hall Lane]: Rambling timbered 16th-c Chef & Brewer all-day dining pub in attractive setting near interesting church (locked these days), different cosy areas decorated in their current style – bric-a-brac, log fires and mottoes chalked on beams; lots of blackboard specials, real ale, good service, bustling atmosphere, rarely used games bar upstairs; children welcome, tables on pleasant tree-sheltered back lawn, Crimean War cannon in front, open all day *(Kevin Blake, Alun Howells, Roger Thornington, Simon and Amanda Southwell, Roger Braithwaite, LYM, John Saville, Dr and Mrs A K Clarke, Geoffrey and Penny Hughes, Trevor and Sheila Sharman)*

BILSTON SO9496
Trumpet [High St]: Holdens and guest beers, good free jazz bands; trumpets and other instruments hang from ceiling, lots of musical memorabilia and photographs *(the Didler, Paul and Ann Meyer)*
White Rose [Temple St]: Friendly and lively traditional town pub with focus on up to a dozen or so well kept interesting ales from small breweries, also belgian beers and unusual lagers; reasonably priced food all day inc Sun roasts, long narrow bar, no smoking eating area; children welcome, tables outside, open all day, Sun afternoon break *(Paul and Ann Meyer, Ian and Liz Rispin)*

BIRMINGHAM SP0788

☆ *Bartons Arms* [High St, Aston (A34)]: Magnificent specimen of Edwardian pub architecture in rather a daunting area, reopened by Oakham Brewery after two-year closure and restoration, imposing series of richly decorated rooms from the palatial to the snug, original tilework murals, stained-glass and mahogany, sweeping stairs and ornate fireplaces; well kept Oakham and guest beers from ornate island bar with snob screens in one section, interesting imported bottled beers, good value thai food (not Mon), hard-working managers and young staff; open all day *(BB, Mark Rogers, Dr B and Mrs P B Baker, Matthew Ford, Theocsbrian, John Dwane, Kerry Law, Simon Smith, the Didler)*

Bennetts [Bennetts Hill]: Attractively converted bank like ballroom with egyptian/french theme, big mural, high carved domed ceiling, side library and board room with lots of old pictures, ironwork and wood, relaxed atmosphere, comfortable seats inc armchair and leather settee, dining area with usual food inc sensibly priced specials, well kept ales inc Banks's and Marstons Pedigree, decent house wines, good coffee, friendly staff; piped music may be rather loud; good wheelchair access *(Richard Lewis, Matthew Shackle, Pamela and Merlyn Horswell)*

Black Eagle [Factory Rd, Hockley]: Friendly late 19th-c pub with small bare-boards bar, three-part lounge inc one section with banquettes, bay window and old pictures, some original Minton tilework, generous popular home-made food, good traditional landlord, particularly well kept Ansells Mild, Marstons Pedigree and good changing real ales, summer beer festival with live music; shaded plastic garden tables, open all day Fri, cl Sun evening *(John Dwane, G Coates)*

Charlie Hall [Barnabas Rd, Erdington]: Large Wetherspoons conversion of former bingo hall, their usual good value food and ale range; back terrace *(John Dwane)*

Hamstead [Green Lane, Hamstead]: Good service, good choice of food and of beers such as Fullers London Pride, Marstons Pedigree and Shepherd Neame Spitfire *(Steve Jennings)*

Lord Clifden [Gt Hampton St]: Popular food from sandwiches to steaks and Sun lunch, well kept beers such as Timothy Taylors Landlord, good service; plenty of tables out behind *(anon)*

Prince of Wales [Alcester Rd, Moseley]: Chatty unspoilt local with well kept Ansells Bitter and Mild, Greene King, Ind Coope Burton and Charles Wells Bombardier, quick service even when packed, bare boards and ochre walls, tiled corridor, hatch service to snug, two quiet and comfortable back parlours (one frozen in 1900); tables out behind, on the Tolkien trail (he courted here), open all day *(Nigel Epsley)*

Utopia [Church St]: Innovative design in bar with good atmosphere, enjoyable food and beers *(Tony Green)*

Woodman [Albert St]: Victorian pub with friendly and lively L-shaped main bar, hatch service to relaxing back smoke room with original tiling and coal fire, good fresh warm baguettes, well kept Ansells Mild, Tetleys and a guest beer, friendly unhurried service, interesting juke box *(the Didler, Pete Baker)*

BISHOP'S TACHBROOK SP3161

Leopard [nr M40 junction 13, via A452]: Relaxing upmarket country pub/restaurant with enjoyable generous food from bar snacks to more sophisticated dishes in spacious back dining room (children welcome here), well kept Greene King IPA and Abbot and Marstons Pedigree, friendly service *(Arnold Bennett, Nigel and Sue Foster)*

BLOXWICH SK0002

Stag [Field Rd]: Welcoming two-bar estate pub with up to half a dozen or so well kept ales such as Adnams and Banks's, plenty of room; tables outside, open all day *(Richard Houghton)*

BRINKLOW SP4379

Bulls Head [A427, fairly handy for M6 junction 2]: Good family atmosphere, decent food from fresh sandwiches up inc plenty of vegetarian and children's dishes, well kept ales such as Badger Best, Flowers Original, Hook Norton Best and Marstons Pedigree, particularly friendly bar staff; collection of old pub signs, no smoking area, shove-ha'penny and table skittles; play areas indoors and outdoors *(Duncan Cloud, Alan Johnson, Bernie Adams)*

BUBBENHALL SP3672

Three Horseshoes [Spring Hill]: Enjoyable food in refurbished and extended old village pub *(Joan and Terry O'Neill, Geoffrey and Penny Hughes)*

CHURCH LAWFORD SP4576

Old Smithy [Green Lane]: Much extended thatched and beamed 16th-c dining pub with dark woodwork in L-shaped lounge on various levels, good range of food cooked to order from separate servery, well kept Bass, Greene King IPA and Abbot, Judges and (brewed next door) Frankton Bagby, good friendly service; games room, conservatory; no dogs, children welcome, garden with slide *(Alan Johnson)*

CORLEY MOOR SP2885

Bull & Butcher [Common Lane]: Low-beamed homely country pub, small tidy front lounge and bar with hot log fires and tiled floor, good cheap food, Hook Norton real ale, back dining room; garden with play area, walks nearby *(Ian Blackwell)*

COUGHTON SP0760

Throckmorton Arms [Coughton Hill]: Roomy and friendly open-plan bar with cosy corners, attractive wooden furniture and carvings, some comfortable settees, four real ales inc local microbrews, generous varied reasonably priced food inc adventurous specials; handy for Coughton Court *(David Oakley)*

COVENTRY SP3379

Town Wall [Bond St, among car parks behind Belgrade Theatre]: Busy Victorian town local with unspoilt basic (and sometimes smoky) front bar and famously tiny and clubby snug, Adnams Bitter and Broadside, Bass and M&B Brew XI, farm cider, good generous lunchtime doorstep sandwiches, filled rolls and cheap hot dishes, engraved windows and open fires, back lounge with photos of actors and playwrights (it's behind Belgrade Theatre), big-screen sports TV; open all day *(BB, Brian and Anita Randall, Martin Smith, Martin Bache, Alan Johnson)*

☆ ***Whitefriars*** [Gosford St]: Pair of well preserved medieval town houses, restored 2000 – three genuinely old-fashioned and dark historic rooms on both floors, the nicest downstairs at the front, with lots of ancient beams, timbers and furniture, flagstones, cobbles and real fires; up to nine well kept changing ales (more during beer festivals) – Church End prominent, basic sensibly priced food from sandwiches, ploughman's and baked potatoes up, daily papers; frequent live music Sun, folk on Weds, quiz nights, special offers for students (university nearby); no children (but shelter on good-sized terrace behind), open all day *(BB, Alan Johnson)*

DORRIDGE SP1575

Drum & Monkey [Four Ashes Rd]: Comfortable extended family dining pub with wide choice of reliable food, good beer and wine choice at sensible prices, polite efficient staff, no smoking area; big garden with play area *(Stan and Hazel Allen)*

Railway [Grange Rd (A4023, ¾ mile from station)]: Small friendly family-run local with some emphasis on good value food (10p extra for thick-sliced sandwiches), well kept M&B Brew XI and two changing guest beers, airy carpeted two-part lounge, coal fire and darts in public bar, no music or machines; small garden overlooking village green *(G Coates)*

DUDLEY SO9487

Park [Chapel St]: Welcoming and pleasantly refurbished in up-to-date style, tap for adjacent Holdens brewery, their beers well kept and so cheap it almost pays for the petrol getting here, good low-priced lunchtime food inc hot beef, pork and chicken sandwiches – very busy then; attractive octagonal conservatory *(Theocsbrian, Colin Fisher)*

FENNY COMPTON SP4152

Merrie Lion [Brook St]: Friendly little low-beamed two-bar village pub, old, neatly kept if not smart, and with plenty of cosy character; quick friendly service, well kept beers inc Banks's and Bass, reasonably priced usual food inc good sandwiches; handy for Burton Dassett country park *(John Brightley, Arnold Bennett)*

GRANDBOROUGH SP4966

Shoulder of Mutton [off A45 E of Dunchurch; Sawbridge Rd]: Well refurbished creeper-covered dining pub with attractive pine furnishings, beams and panelling, well priced fresh food (should book Fri-Sat evening and Sun lunch), cheerful helpful licensees, relaxed atmosphere, Adnams Broadside, Fullers London Pride and Greene King IPA, good coffee, no music; garden with play area, cl Mon *(Catherine and Rob Dunster)*

HALESOWEN SO9683

Hawne Tavern [Attwood St]: Well worn in sidestreet local, several well kept ales, good value cheap food inc big baguettes, good staff, quiet lounge, bar with games *(Gill and Tony Morriss, the Didler)*

Somers Club [The Grange, Grange Hill (B4551 S)]: Early Georgian mansion, now a sports and social club – visitors can sign in; comfortable bar with half a dozen or more well kept real ales from long counter, filled rolls, pies and pasties, friendly regulars; bowling green in grounds behind *(the Didler)*

Waggon & Horses [Stourbridge Rd]: Unpretentious welcoming gently refurbished bare-boards local, well kept Bathams, a house beer and up to a dozen or so interesting changing ales from small independent brewers – staff well informed about them; snacks, TV, Tues music night, open all day *(the Didler, Paul and Ann Meyer)*

HARBOROUGH MAGNA SP4779

Old Lion [3 miles from M6 junction 1; B4122]: Three-room village local with Greene King ales, food from sandwiches, baguettes and baked potatoes up inc OAP lunches, dining room, games bar with pool etc; children welcome, family events, open all day wknds *(Alan Johnson)*

HARBURY SP3660

☆ ***Shakespeare*** [just off B4451/B4452 S of A425 Leamington Spa—Southam; Mill St]: Comfortable dining pub with linked low-beamed areas, stripped stonework, big central inglenook log fire, horsebrasses, freshly cooked sensibly priced food (not Sun-Mon evenings) inc some adventurous dishes, well kept Flowers IPA, Timothy Taylors Landlord and one or two guest beers, good hospitable service (landlady has great memory for customers), proper flagstoned locals' bar area with TV, games room off with darts and pool, pleasant conservatory; children welcome, tables in back garden with aviaries *(Pete Baker, Nigel and Sue Foster, BB)*

HENLEY-IN-ARDEN SP1568

Bird in Hand [A34 towards Solihull]: Open-plan dining pub, bright and cheerful with plenty of tables and chairs off small bar area, good choice of food inc sandwiches, baguettes and bargain lunches, well kept real ales and good wine list, good service *(Gill and Keith Croxton)*

Black Swan [High St]: Former coaching inn with bay seating, pews and big fireplace in main beamed bar area, nice range of sensibly priced bar food, good service; tables out behind outdoor seating area at the back *(Margaret Dickinson)*

Blue Bell [High St]: Impressive beamed and timber-framed building with fine coach entrance; small bar, split dining area, good range of home-made food, well kept ales such as Adnams, Fullers London Pride and Timothy Taylors Landlord, pleasant staff, log fire; some courtyard tables *(Nigel and Sue Foster)*

HIMLEY SO8791

Himley House [Stourbridge rd (A449)]: Big Chef & Brewer dining pub in handsome building, plenty of character and odd corners, friendly staff, wide choice of food from sandwiches, rolls and baked potatoes to blackboard main meals *(David Green)*

ILMINGTON SP2143

Red Lion [Front St]: Stone-built village local, flagstoned bar and smarter lounge, traditional furnishings, well kept Hook Norton Best and Old Hooky, enjoyable simple good value food, friendly helpful newish licensees; may be lots of walkers Sun lunchtime; delightful neatly kept secluded garden *(Michael and Jenny Back)*

KENILWORTH SP2872

☆ *Clarendon Arms* [Castle Hill]: Busy traditional pub opp castle, huge helpings of attractively priced food in several rooms, some no smoking, off long partly flagstoned bar, largish upstairs dining room, plenty of atmosphere, efficient and friendly obliging staff, good range of well served beers, wines and other drinks; best to book wknds *(Carol and David Havard, Alan Johnson, Bob and Margaret Holder)*

☆ *Clarendon House* [High St]: Ancient timber building containing relaxed modern bar/brasserie, long serving counter, sofas, cane furniture, contemporary prints and daily papers in softly lit warmly painted areas, well kept Greene King ales and a guest, decent wines, wide choice of snacks (all day) and meals nicely served with linen napkins, and interesting wider brasserie menu, jokey complaints dept (well with paper skeleton 'complainer'); TV, piped music; comfortable bedrooms, open all day *(Andy and Jill Kassube, Joan and Tony Walker)*

KNOWLE SP1876

☆ *Herons Nest* [Warwick Rd S]: Vintage Inn dining pub in former hotel, dining tables in several individual rooms inc no smoking areas, some flagstones and high-backed settles, hops on beams, interesting décor, open fires, wide choice of sensibly priced food inc children's helpings, plenty of good value wines by the glass, well kept Bass and Tetleys, friendly staff; tables in garden by Grand Union Canal, moorings, bedrooms, open all day *(R J Herd, David Green)*

LAPWORTH SP1670

Boot [B4439, by Warwickshire Canal]: Waterside dining pub in trendy modern upmarket rustic style, raised dining area (food confined to here on busy Sat night, but may take up all tables at other times), roaring fire, good bistro atmosphere, enjoyable food (not cheap) from good baguettes to steaks and fish, well kept beers such as Greene King Old Speckled Hen and Wadworths 6X, decent wines (big glasses), good service by smart young staff, daily papers, lots of board games, cartoons; piped nostalgic pop music; good lavatories, nice garden, pleasant walks *(Arnold Bennett, Geoffrey and Penny Hughes, R A K Crabtree)*

LEAMINGTON SPA SP3165

Hogshead [Warwick St]: Good range of well kept changing ales, neat modern wooden flooring and bare brickwork, raised no smoking area with sofas as well as dining tables, good value straightforward food, helpful staff; can get busy wknds *(Ted George, Dr and Mrs A K Clarke)*

LEEK WOOTTON SP2868

Anchor [Warwick Rd]: Neat and well run bookable dining lounge very popular (esp with older people) for unusually wide choice of generous fresh hot food (all day Sat, not Sun) inc cheaper lunchtime specials, veg extra though; well kept Bass, Hook Norton Old Hooky and M&B Brew XI, decent wine, good soft drinks choice, lots of close-set tables, overflow into smaller bar with darts, TV and machines; may be piped pop music; picnic-sets in sizeable pleasant garden behind *(Alan Johnson, George Atkinson)*

LONG COMPTON SP2832

Red Lion [A3400 S of Shipston-on-Stour]: Stripped stone, bare beams, panelling, flagstones, old-fashioned built-in settles among other pleasantly assorted old seats and tables, old prints and team photographs, good value food from sandwiches and baked potatoes up in bar and restaurant, children's helpings, well kept Adnams, Hook Norton, Websters and a guest such as Courage Directors, log fires and woodburners, simple public bar with pool; pub dog and cat, unobtrusive piped music; dogs and children welcome, big back garden with picnic-sets and climber, bedrooms *(LYM, Susan and John Douglas, Theocsbrian, Phil and Jane Hodson)*

LONG ITCHINGTON SP4165

Blue Lias [Stockton Rd, off A423]: Well placed on Grand Union Canal, with friendly efficient staff, wholesome reasonably priced food, well kept ales such as Everards Tiger, snug eating booths; plenty of tables in waterside grounds, also a separate outbuilding bar with tables under a dome *(Steve and Liz Tilley, Ted George, Bernie Adams)*

Harvester [off A423 S of Coventry; The Square]: Old-fashioned two-bar village local, neat and tidy, with cheap food from sandwiches to good steaks, three well kept Hook Norton beers and a guest ale, friendly efficient service, fish tank in lounge bar, cosy relaxed restaurant; nothing to do with the chain of the same name *(Pete Baker, Bernie Adams)*

Two Boats [A423 N of Southam, by Grand Union Canal]: Lively canal views from waterfront terrace and alcove window seats, well kept Hook Norton and changing ales, cheerful staff, generous well priced food, rather a social club feel (even to the pleasant 60s piped music, live music Fri-Sat); moorings, open all day *(BB, Meg and Colin Hamilton)*

LOWER BRAILES SP3039

☆ *George* [B4035 Shipston—Banbury]: Handsome old stone-built inn under new licensees, cheerful local feel in roomy flagstoned front bar, dark oak tables, nice curtains and inglenook log fire, darts, panelled oak-beamed back bar with soft lighting and green décor, full Hook Norton range kept well, freshly made food inc game in season, smart country-style flagstoned wknd restaurant; provision for children, live music most Sat and

Mon evenings and Sun afternoon; aunt sally in sizeable neatly kept sheltered garden with terrace and covered area, six comfortable bedrooms, lovely village, open all day *(JHBS, LYM, Chris Glasson, Pete Baker, Theocsbrian, Steve Jennings)*

LOWER GORNAL SO9291

Black Bear [Deepdale Lane]: Local with plenty of character (18th-c former farmhouse), Shepherd Neame and four guest beers, good choice of whiskies *(the Didler)*

Fountain [Temple St]: Two-room local with keen and helpful landlord and staff, well kept Enville, Everards, Holdens and up to six changing ales (beer festivals Easter and Oct), two farm ciders, country wines, enjoyable inexpensive food, pigs-and-pen skittles *(the Didler, Theocsbrian)*

LOWER QUINTON SP1847

College Arms [off A46 Stratford—Broadway]: Spacious open-plan lounge in interesting building, stripped stone and heavy beams, unusual highly polished tables on partly carpeted parquet floor inc one in former fireplace, leather seats, bric-a-brac, cosy well furnished eating area, enterprising choice of well prepared reasonably priced food, friendly efficient service, good range of well kept ales; piped music, games in roomy public bar; on green of pretty village *(K H Frostick)*

LOWSONFORD SP1868

Fleur de Lys [off B4439 Hockley Heath—Warwick; Lapworth St]: Prettily placed old canalside pub, recently refurbished and largely no smoking, with log fires, lots of beams, several well kept real ales, decent wines inc many by the glass, enjoyable food esp pies in bar and dining room (may sometimes stop serving earlier than stated); waterside garden, open all day *(LYM, Roger Braithwaite)*

LOXLEY SP2552

☆ *Fox* [signed off A422 Stratford—Banbury]: Cheerful pub, very neat and clean, with wide blackboard range of good value fresh home-made food from ciabattas and other light dishes up, well kept ales such as Bass and Hook Norton, quick welcoming service, partly divided lounge with panelling, a few pictures and plates, settles and brocaded banquettes, pleasant dining area; piped music; tables in good-sized garden behind, sleepy village handy for Stratford *(Janet and Peter Race, Joan and Tony Walker)*

MANCETTER SP3296

Plough [Mancetter Rd (B4111 just SE of Atherstone)]: Very popular for bargain food from sandwiches to huge mixed grill using good local meat, beamed lounge with small inglenook, settles, plenty of plants, brass and copper, four real ales inc very cheap house Bitter; picnic-sets in garden with play area *(Ian and Joan Blackwell)*

MERIDEN SP2482

Bulls Head [Main Rd]: Very wide choice of good value generous home-made food all day in big Vintage Inn dating from 15th c, three log fires, beams, bare boards and flagstones, lots of nooks and crannies with plenty of interest, well kept Bass and Tetleys, ancient staircase to restaurant; can get busy evenings, esp wknds, but still prompt welcoming service; disabled facilities, 13 bedrooms *(Bernie Adams, M Joyner)*

MONKS KIRBY SP4682

☆ *Bell* [just off B4027 W of Pailton]: Open-plan dark-beamed and timbered bar divided into separate areas, flagstoned and cobbled floor, yet despite this classic English look and well kept Bass and Flowers Original the long-serving Spanish landlord makes it rather different – wide (almost too wide) choice of largely spanish food inc starters doubling as tapas, relaxed informal service, great choice of spanish wines, good range of brandies and malt whiskies, no smoking dining area; piped music; children welcome, dogs allowed in bar, streamside back terrace with country view, may be cl Mon *(Susan and John Douglas, D C Leggatt, Mr and Mrs J E C Tasker, R T and J C Moggridge, Sally Randall, Ian and Nita Cooper, Brian and Pat Wardrobe, LYM, Barbara and Peter Kelly, Mrs B Dalby)*

☆ *Denbigh Arms* [Main St]: 17th-c beamed pub opp church, old photographs and interesting 18th-c pew seating, no smoking family room, big helpings of enjoyable straightforward food inc bargain Tues steak night, Greene King real ales, friendly service even when busy; upstairs folk club 2nd Sun of month; play area *(Ian and Nita Cooper, Alan Johnson, Bernie Adams)*

NETHERTON SO9387

☆ *Old Swan* [Halesowen Rd (A459 just S of centre)]: Friendly and traditional, brewing its own good cheap Original, Dark, Entire and occasional other beers, lots of whiskies, wide choice of good cheap food inc some imaginative twists and Sun lunches in no smoking room on left (worth booking well ahead), airy front room with fine mirrors and open fire, steps down to comfortable back snug with nice old solid fuel stove, decorative swan ceiling, cards and dominoes; no children, regular sing-alongs, open all day *(Theocsbrian, LYM, the Didler, Alan Cole, Kirstie Bruce, Pete Baker, Martin Grosberg, Nigel Epsley, Richard Houghton)*

NEWBOLD ON STOUR SP2446

☆ *Bird in Hand* [A3400 S of Stratford]: Neatly kept traditional U-shaped bar with fresh flowers on comfortable well spaced tables, bow windows, good log fire, well kept Hook Norton Best and Old Hooky, good tea and coffee, well presented varied food at low prices inc good value Sun lunch, good friendly service, pool in side bar *(BB, Trevor and Sheila Sharman)*

NORTON LINDSEY SP2263

New Inn: Small unpretentious village pub, cleanly modernised inside, very popular locally for landlady's good reasonably priced home cooking featuring fresh fish and strong on local produce (may be largely booked up even midweek lunchtime); friendly staff, Ansells Mild, Greene King Old Speckled Hen, Hook Norton and Marstons Pedigree, choice of wines *(John Bramley, Brian Skelcher)*

NUNEATON SP3790

Attleborough Arms [Highfield Rd, Attleborough]: Large recently rebuilt pub, completely refurbished and attractively open and modern, with great access for disabled people and helpful service; enjoyable cheap food, real ales *(Kevin Rumble, Ian Blackwell)*

Camp [Camp Hill Rd]: Good disabled access, helpful service, good atmosphere; no food *(Kevin Rumble)*

OLD HILL SO9685

Waterfall [Waterfall Lane]: Down-to-earth good value local, friendly staff, well kept Bathams, Enville and other changing ales, farm cider, country wines, plain home-made food from filled rolls to Sun lunch, tankards and jugs hanging from boarded ceiling; piped music; children welcome, back garden with play area, open all day wknds *(the Didler, Theocsbrian)*

PRESTON BAGOT SP1765

☆ *Crabmill* [B4095 Henley-in-Arden—Warwick]: Comfortably upmarket timbered dining pub with sofas and coffee tables in stylish two-level lounge, real ales such as Wadworths 6X from steely modern bar, decent wines, elegant table settings in roomy candlelit low-beamed dining area, lots of nooks and crannies, food from bar meals to modern restaurant cooking, quick cheerful young staff; very busy wknd evenings; rows of picnic-sets in big garden with play area, open all day *(LYM, Peter Evans, Denise Greenhalgh)*

PRINCETHORPE SP3870

Woodhouse [B4453 towards Cubbington]: Pleasantly placed hotel with consistently good food inc carvery some days, cold table, exquisite puddings; real ales, proper coffee, decent wines, good service; lawns with play area, bedrooms *(Elaine and Tony Barker)*

PRIORS HARDWICK SP4756

☆ *Butchers Arms* [off A423 via Wormleighton or A361 via Boddington, N of Banbury; Church End]: Upmarket old-fashioned restaurant in pleasantly reworked 14th-c building, oak beams, flagstones, panelling, antiques and soft lighting (soft voices, too – a refined low murmur); huge choice of food (not cheap) inc fixed price lunches, small bar with inglenook log fire used mainly by people waiting for a table (also simple public bar); keg beer but good wines, very friendly Portuguese landlord, punctilious smartly uniformed staff, country garden *(Hugh Spottiswoode, Arnold Bennett, BB)*

RATLEY SP3847

☆ *Rose & Crown* [off A422 NW of Banbury]: Cosy and charming ancient golden stone beamed local, well kept Charles Wells Eagle and Bombardier, decent honest pub food inc good sandwiches, carefully prepared fish and nice sensibly priced puddings, friendly helpful easy-going service, woodburner in flagstoned area on left, big log fireplace in carpeted area on right; dogs and children welcome (children's meals), tables in small gravel garden, nr lovely church in small sleepy village *(Guy Vowles, Derek and Sylvia Stephenson, Joan and Terry O'Neill, Steve and Liz Tilley, Brian and Anita Randall, T Walker, BB)*

RUGBY SP5075

Alexandra Arms [James St]: Friendly traditional two-bar local with well kept Ansells, Greene King Abbot, Marstons Pedigree and two guest beers, farm cider, enjoyable straightforward home-made food lunchtime and evening, bare-boards back games room, summer beer festivals; tables in good-sized garden, open all day Fri-Sat *(G Coates)*

Three Horseshoes [Sheep St]: Friendly hotel with new management worth watching, leather sofas and armchairs in comfortable olde-worlde lounge bar, well kept real ales, decent coffee, log fire, interesting food from sandwiches and good soup up, two pleasant dining areas; 35 bedrooms *(P Tailyour)*

SAMBOURNE SP0561

☆ *Green Dragon* [village signed off A448]: Three low-beamed rooms, rugs on flagstones, interesting pictures and old bric-a-brac, open fires, enjoyable food from light dishes and lots of sandwiches up, well kept M&B and guest beers, new landlord settling in well, pleasant efficient staff; children in eating area, picnic-sets and teak seats in pretty courtyard, bowls, comfortable bedrooms, nice spot on green *(Martin Jones, LYM, Dr and Mrs A K Clarke, David and Barbara Davies)*

SHUSTOKE SP2290

Plough [B4114 Nuneaton—Coleshill]: Rambling pub cosily done up in olde-worlde style, good food, lunchtime bargains, pleasant dining room, proper bar for drinking and chatting, well kept Bass, a local Mild and a changing guest beer, good friendly service, plenty of gleaming brass *(Mrs M P Owen, Geoffrey and Penny Hughes)*

SHUTTINGTON SK2505

Wolferstan Arms [Main Rd]: Charming family pub, lots of beams and pewter tankards, friendly locals and long-serving staff, enjoyable food from wide sandwich choice to good value main dishes, well kept real ales, farm cider; well behaved children welcome, rolling country views from restaurant and big garden with play area *(Colin Gooch)*

SNITTERFIELD SP2159

Foxhunter [Smiths Lane/School Rd; off A46 N of Stratford]: Cheerful and attractive small village pub, well kept Hook Norton Best and M&B Brew XI, friendly landlord, wide range of well presented and reasonably priced food cooked to order from tasty baguettes up, banquettes and hunting pictures in L-shaped bar/lounge with simple white décor; can be smoky; children allowed, tables outside *(Catherine and Rob Dunster, T Parr)*

STOCKTON SP4363

Barley Mow [off A426 Southam—Rugby; School St]: Unpretentious and welcoming early 19th-c pub, huge helpings of enjoyable food inc wkdy bargain lunches, friendly attentive service, Greene King IPA and Abbot, bar and lounge/diner with steepish steps down to comfortable bottom dining area, stripped brick, lots of brasses and pictures, coal-effect fire, upstairs evening restaurant; pretty hanging baskets, attractive spot by green opp church *(George Atkinson, Ted George)*

STONNALL SK0703

Royal Oak [just off A452 N of Brownhills; Main St]: A proper pub, popular and welcoming, well kept Hook Norton, Charles Wells Bombardier and changing guest beers, farm cider, jovial attentive landlord, enjoyable evening food in beamed bar and dining room, also Sun lunch; no music *(Clifford Blakemore)*

STRATFORD-UPON-AVON SP2055

Dirty Duck [Waterside]: 16th-c pub nr Memorial Theatre, lots of signed RSC photographs in bustling bar, Flowers IPA, Greene King Old Speckled Hen and Wadworths 6X, open fire, modern conservatory restaurant suiting larger parties; children allowed in dining area, attractive small terrace looking over riverside public gardens – which tend to act as summer overflow; properly the Black Swan *(LYM, Maggie and Tony Harwood, Kevin Blake, David Glynne-Jones, Stephen Buckley)*

Falcon [Chapel St]: Substantial hotel extended back from timbered Tudor core and fine façade, big inglenook fireplace and furnishings reflecting its tavern origins in quiet panelled bar, other rooms inc lighter more modern ones, well kept Flowers Original and a guest such as Bass from small servery, wide range of enjoyable bar food from sandwiches up, cheery helpful staff, restaurant; may be piped music, car park fills quickly; cloistered back garden, bedrooms (quieter but more functional in modern wing) *(Ted George, George Atkinson)*

Jester [Avonbridge Wharf, Bridgefoot]: Part of Cox's Yard tourist complex and useful for families: long light and airy modern bar with friendly staff, fairly priced panini, salads and other modern food, well kept ales inc Jesters from its own brewery (tours available); summer live music brings the crowds; good disabled facilities, play area, roomy riverside terrace for watching the swans, open all day *(John Whitehead, the Didler, David Glynne-Jones, Mr and Mrs G S Ayrton, Colin Fisher)*

Pen & Parchment [Bridgefoot, by canal basin]: Shakespeare theme in L-shaped split-level lounge and snug, rustic-style beams, balusters, bare boards and tiles or flagstones, small alcoves and no smoking area, big open fire in old fireplace, decent reasonably priced food, wide wine choice, four well kept real ales, prompt helpful service; tables out among shrubs and ivy, pretty hanging baskets, good canal basin views; busy road *(Ted George, Alain and Rose Foote)*

West End [Bull St]: Attractively modernised old pub in quiet part of old town, friendly staff and thriving atmosphere, good value nicely presented seasonal food, good wine choice, changing guest beers, interesting soft drinks range, nice film star photographs; well chosen piped music; appealing terrace *(Maurice Ribbans, Sue Dibben)*

☆ ***Windmill*** [Church St]: Cosy and relaxing old pub with town's oldest licence, beyond the attractive Guild Chapel; unpretentious but civilised, with low black beams, cosy and attractive carpeted front room, varnished boards in main one, big log fire, wide choice of good value food from sandwiches to substantial Sun lunch and some unusual main dishes, well kept sensibly priced Flowers Original and Greene King IPA, friendly efficient staff, carpeted dining area; piped music; tables outside, open all day from noon *(Neil Rose, Ted George, Kevin Blake, Derek and Sylvia Stephenson)*

STRETTON-ON-FOSSE SP2238

☆ ***Plough*** [just off A429]: Olde-worlde 17th-c village pub doing well under attentive current management, lively cheerful mix of drinkers and diners, Ansells Bitter and Mild, Shepherd Neame Spitfire and a guest beer, happy staff, wide choice of generous home-made food from baguettes through OAP lunches to wknd spit roasts on the inglenook log fire (chain drive from windscreen wiper motor), small bar and larger lounge, stripped stone and some flagstones, jugs and mugs on oak beams, small attractive candlelit dining room on right; darts, a few tables outside, cl Mon lunchtime *(BB, JHBS, K H Frostick, Geoffrey and Penny Hughes)*

SUTTON COLDFIELD SP1094

Bishop Vesey [Boldmere Rd, Boldmere]: Open-plan Wetherspoons with six real ales, good choice of other drinks, their usual food all day, several areas inc no smoking and upstairs tables, no piped music; games machines *(CMW, JJW)*

TANWORTH-IN-ARDEN SP1170

Bell [The Green]: Roomy lounge recently well fitted with comfortable modern furniture and good graphics, well kept Black Sheep, Boddingtons, Hook Norton Best and Fullers London Pride, good choice of wines by the glass, enjoyable well served food inc popular business lunches; also houses a deli and back post office; children in eating areas, outlook on peaceful green and lovely 14th-c church, back terrace with alloy planters, bedrooms – good base for walks *(LYM, Martin Jennings, Dave Braisted)*

TEMPLE GRAFTON SP1255

☆ ***Blue Boar*** [a mile E, towards Binton; off A422 W of Stratford]: Extended country dining pub with beams, stripped stonework and log fires, quick cheerful service, well kept ales such as Brakspears, Greene King Old Speckled Hen, Hook Norton and Theakstons XB, good wine choice, enjoyable generous food from sandwiches and baked potatoes through traditional favourites to more imaginative dishes and good value Sun lunch, comfortable dining room (past glass-top well with golden carp) with good no smoking section and attractive farmhouse-kitchen mural, traditional games in flagstoned side room; children welcome, open all day summer wknds, picnic-sets outside, pretty flower plantings; comfortable well equipped bedrooms

(Rick Baker, Martin Jennings, LYM, Brenda and Stuart Naylor, R J Herd, Susan and John Douglas)

TIPTON SO9492

Pie Factory [Hurst Lane, Dudley Rd towards Wednesbury; A457/A4037]: Mildly zany décor and quirky food (their cow pie comes on a shovel – very Desperate Dan), good value hearty stuff (all day Sun) inc children's and lots of other pies, well kept ales inc Enville; piped music, pool, TV; some live music, children welcome, open all day, bedrooms 'almost en suite' *(LYM, Ian Phillips)*

Rising Sun [Horseley Rd (B4517, off A461)]: Welcoming pub with three well kept changing ales in lined glasses, farm cider, friendly locals' bar, back room with coal fire, alcoves and original bare boards and tiles, lunchtime food; tables outside *(the Didler, G Coates)*

TREDINGTON SP2543

White Lion [A3400]: Ancient pub doing well under current management, enjoyable food inc speciality sausages, two real ales, comfortably refurbished lounge; open all day *(JHBS, K H Frostick)*

UFTON SP3762

☆ *White Hart* [just off A425 Daventry—Leamington, towards Bascote]: Friendly old pub with big L-shaped lounge, beams, brasses and stripped stone, pictures and polo equipment, good choice of usual food inc bargain OAP wkdy lunches (several steps down to no smoking back dining part), well kept Adnams Best, Tetleys and Charles Wells Bombardier, quick cheery attentive service; unobtrusive piped radio; hatch service to hilltop garden with boules and panoramic views (can be breezy, Tannoy food announcements out here) *(DC, George Atkinson)*

UPPER GORNAL SO929921

Britannia [Kent St]: Reworked Bathams local still keeping much of its 19th-c features inc tiled floors, corridor to no smoking back room originally laid out for table drinks service; their cheap Best and Mild kept superbly, friendly regulars; tables in nice flower-filled back yard, open all day Sat *(the Didler)*

Jolly Crispin [Clarence St]: Several interesting well kept changing ales in snug 18th-c local, lunchtime bar food; open all day *(the Didler)*

WALSALL SP0198

Wharf Bar 10 [Gallery Sq/Wolverhampton St]: Light and airy building next to New Art Gallery at end of the cut, lots of pine and scrubbed wood, big windows, good choice of well kept local Highgate beers from central bar, good value tasty sandwiches, ciabattas and other snacks, pleasant atmosphere *(Dave Braisted, C J Fletcher, Jean and Richard Phillips)*

WARMINGTON SP4147

☆ *Plough* [just off B4100 N of Banbury]: Welcoming newish licensees in traditional village pub, enjoyable food inc speciality pie, well kept ales inc Marstons Pedigree, friendly service, unpretentious bar with big fireplace, ancient settle and nice chairs, extended dining room; children in eating area, delightful village with interesting church *(Arnold Bennett, Jennie Hall, LYM, Klaus and Elizabeth Leist)*

WARWICK SP2764

Old Fourpenny Shop [Crompton St, nr racecourse]: Cosy and comfortable split-level pub with up to five well kept changing beers, welcoming licensees, good value food in bar and heavily beamed restaurant, cheerful service, no piped music; pleasant reasonably priced bedrooms *(Andy and Jill Kassube, Jill Bickerton, Ian and Nita Cooper, Trevor and Sheila Sharman)*

Racehorse [Stratford Rd]: Large comfortable family dining pub with generous good value food inc children's and OAP bargains, well kept Everards Tiger and guest beers, pleasant service, no smoking areas inc conservatory (children welcome); open all day *(Michael Lamm, Ian and Nita Cooper, Trevor and Sheila Sharman)*

☆ *Rose & Crown* [Market Pl]: Up-to-date uncluttered refurbishment with bare boards and wine bar/brasserie feel in big open-plan L-shaped room, emphasis on interesting food at sensible prices from sandwiches up in bar and restaurant, relaxed atmosphere, two well kept ales such as Charles Wells Bombardier and plenty of fancy keg dispensers, good wines, good strong coffee, friendly efficient service, leather sofa by open fire; tables out under parasols, comfortable good-sized bedrooms *(Damian Dixon, June and Malcolm Farmer, LYM, Vanessa Stilwell, Trevor and Sheila Sharman)*

☆ *Zetland Arms* [Church St]: Cosy town pub with short choice of good cheap bar food (not wknd evenings) with fresh veg, well kept Marstons Pedigree and Tetleys, decent wines in generous glasses, friendly quick service, neat but relaxing small panelled front bar with toby jug collection and sports TV, comfortable larger L-shaped back eating area with small conservatory, fascinating eavesdropping when the nearby court adjourns for lunch; provision for children, interestingly planted sheltered garden, bedrooms sharing bathroom *(LYM, Suzanne Miles, Roger and Pauline Pearce)*

WELLESBOURNE SP2755

Kings Head: Vintage Inn dining pub with contemporary furnishings in high-ceilinged lounge bar, log fire and smaller areas leading off, lively public bar with games room, well kept Bass, wide choice of keenly priced wines, friendly staff; piped music; picnic-sets in garden facing church, bedrooms (handy for Stratford but cheaper), open all day *(Maggie and Tony Harwood, LYM, G W A Pearce, J F M and M West)*

WHATCOTE SP2944

☆ *Royal Oak*: Dating from 12th c, quaint low-beamed small room with Civil War connections and lots of knick-knacks and curios, wide choice of good value fresh food from nice sandwiches to venison and good steaks, cheery landlord, three well kept Hook Norton ales, decent wines, good log fire in huge inglenook, restaurant; children welcome, picnic-sets in informal garden *(Mrs Mary Walters, LYM, JHBS, George Atkinson)*

WHICHFORD SP3134

Norman Knight: Welcoming flagstoned pub with well kept Hook Norton Best and changing beers from its back Wizard brewery, nicely priced food (lunchtime and Fri-Sat evening) inc good Sun roasts; regular live music; dogs welcome, tables out by attractive village green, cl Mon/Tues *(JHBS)*

WILLENHALL SO9698

Falcon [Gomer St W]: Traditional two-bar backstreet local with half a dozen or more real ales, basic lunchtime snacks, black pub cat; wheelchair access possible *(G Coates)*

Malthouse [New Rd]: Wetherspoons, lighter and brighter than most, reminiscent of 1920s cruise ship upper deck outside, with art deco interior, well kept ales inc guests such as Everards Equinox and York Terrier, usual well thought-out menu all day till 10, exemplary lavatories; busy with young people Sat night; good disabled access and facilities, open all day *(G Coates)*

WILMCOTE SP1658

Masons Arms [Aston Cantlow Rd]: Attractive ivy-clad local handy for Mary Arden's House but off the tourist trail, generous home cooking from sandwiches to good value hot dishes in bar or good-sized dining conservatory, well kept Black Sheep and Hook Norton Best, good log or coal fires, friendly regulars and informal service, snug family area; pleasant garden *(Val and Alan Green)*

WITHYBROOK SP4384

☆ *Pheasant* [B4112 NE of Coventry, not far from M6, junction 2]: Big busy dining pub with very wide choice of generous food inc good value specials and good vegetarian choice, real ales, good coffee, big log fires, lots of dark tables with plush-cushioned chairs; piped music; children welcome, tables under lanterns on brookside terrace *(Mr and Mrs J E C Tasker, LYM, Alan Johnson, Bernie Adams)*

WOLLASTON SO8884

Unicorn [Bridgnorth Rd (A458)]: Cosy traditional Bathams pub, their Bitter and Mild well kept and cheap, unpretentious L-shaped bar and unspoilt back parlour, lots of brasses and knick-knacks, sandwiches; tables outside, open all day, Sun afternoon break *(Gill and Tony Morriss)*

WOLVERHAMPTON SO9198

☆ *Great Western* [Corn Hill/Sun St, behind BR station]: Well run and down to earth, tucked interestingly in the hinterland between the GWR low-level and current railway stations, with particularly well kept Bathams, Holdens Bitter, Golden Glow, Special and perhaps Sham Rock Stout, winter mulled wine (no tea or coffee), friendly no-nonsense service, cheap hearty lunchtime food (not Sun) from baguettes up served incredibly promptly, interesting railway and more recent motorcycle photographs, traditional front bar, other rooms inc separate no smoking bar and neat dining conservatory; SkyTV; picnic-sets in yard with good barbecues, open all day *(BB, Martin Grosberg, the Didler, Gill and Tony Morriss, Pete Baker, Joe Green)*

WOOTTON WAWEN SP1563

Bulls Head [just off A3400 Birmingham—Stratford]: Attractive black and white dining pub recently reopened under new management, welcoming traditional bare-boards bar, low Elizabethan beams and timbers, four real ales, good house wines, enjoyable food inc good Sun lunches, friendly young staff, roomy restaurant with rich colours, brocaded seats and tapestries; children welcome (small helpings available for them), garden tables, handy for one of England's finest churches and Stratford Canal walks *(LYM, Elizabeth and Bart Sheehan, Anthony R Locke)*

'Children welcome' means the pub says it lets children inside without any special restriction. If it allows them in, but to restricted areas such as an eating area or family room, we specify this. Places with separate restaurants often let children use them, hotels usually let them into public areas such as lounges. Some pubs impose an evening time limit – let us know if you find this.

Wiltshire

New entries here this year are the attractive and prettily set Forester at Donhead St Andrew (good food, thriving atmosphere), the solid old Lamb at Hindon (a nice all-rounder, usefully open all day), the civilised Wheatsheaf at Ogbourne St Andrew (enjoyable food from this attractive dining pub's open kitchen) and the Bell in the attractive village of Ramsbury (a friendly and spotless dining pub, with plans for bedrooms now). Other pubs on great form here are the Red Lion in Axford (fine choice of reliably good food, particularly fish), the Three Crowns at Brinkworth (another foody place, and not cheap, but keeping a good pubby atmosphere), the friendly and cheerful Compasses at Chicksgrove (nice all round, with good food one of its pluses), the Horseshoe at Ebbesbourne Wake (a splendid friendly all-rounder), the Black Horse at Great Durnford (enjoyable food, and a friendly helpful landlord), the ancient and very welcoming George in lovely Lacock, the interesting and nicely set Malet Arms at Newton Tony (its imaginative cooking earns it a Food Award this year), the canalside Barge at Seend (with a nice waterside garden), and the Pear Tree at Whitley (food, drink and bedrooms all first-class). It is the Pear Tree which takes the top title of Wiltshire Dining Pub of the Year. Prominent in the Lucky Dip section at the end of the chapter this year are the Beehive near Bradford-on-Avon, Black Dog at Chilmark, Lamb at Edington, Crown at Giddeahall, Royal Oak at Great Wishford, Ivy at Heddington, Who'd A Thought It at Lockeridge, Wheatsheaf at Lower Woodford, Lamb at Nomansland, Lamb at Semington, Carriers at Stockton, Bridge Inn at Upper Woodford and White Horse at Winterbourne Bassett. Drinks prices here tend to be close to the national average, with Wadworths of Devizes dominating the local beer scene; other smaller local brewers to look out for are Hop Back, Archers, Moles and Stonehenge.

AXFORD SU2370 Map 2

Red Lion

Off A4 E of Marlborough; on back road Mildenhall—Ramsbury

A wide choice of delicious food and friendly service make this pretty flint-and-brick pub a reliable bet for an excellent meal. Besides lunchtime (not Sunday) filled rolls (from £4.95), and baked potatoes (from £5.25), bar snacks (not Saturday evening or Sunday lunchtime) might include home-made soup (£4.25), home-made turkey and ham pie or chicken, mushroom and brandy fricassee (£7.95), poached salmon with white wine and cream sauce or gammon steak (£8.25), or you can choose more elaborate dishes from the à la carte menu such as spinach, dolcelatte and mascarpone tartlet (£10.50), roast local partridge with cranberry, thyme and balsamic sauce (£12.25), and lots of interesting fish dishes such as spiced crispy mackerel with sweet paprika oil (£11.95), and fried gurnard fillets with brown shrimp buter (£12.75); food is cooked freshly to order, so there may be a wait. The restaurant and bar eating area are no smoking. The beamed and pine-panelled bar has a big inglenook fireplace, and a pleasant mix of comfortable sofas, cask seats and other solid chairs on the parquet floor; the pictures by local artists are for sale. There are lovely views over a valley from good hardwood tables and chairs on the terrace outside the restaurant, and you get the same views from picture windows in the restaurant and lounge. Welcoming service from the attentive staff and landlord. Along with 18 sensibly priced wines by the glass, and around two dozen malt whiskies, you'll find well kept Hook Norton, Fullers London Pride and an occasional guest from a brewer such as Cottage on handpump. The sheltered garden has picnic-sets under parasols and swings. *(Recommended by Alec and Barbara Jones, R Huggins, D Irving, E McCall, T McLean, Dick and Penny Vardy, Andrew Kerr, Evelyn and Derek Walter, Sheila and Robert Robinson, Bernard Stradling, Karen Comber, Mr and Mrs B Thorne, Derek and Sylvia Stephenson, David Heath, J Stickland, Sir Nigel Foulkes)*

Free house ~ Licensee Seamus Lecky ~ Real ale ~ Bar food ~ Restaurant ~ (01672) 520271 ~ Children welcome ~ Dogs allowed in bar ~ Open 12-3, 6.30-11; 12-3, 7-10.30 Sun; closed 25 Dec

BECKHAMPTON SU0868 Map 2

Waggon & Horses

A4 Marlborough—Calne

For many years this handsome old pub was a cheering sight to coachmen coming in from what was notorious as the coldest stretch of the old Bath road. Nowadays you can choose from a dozen wines by the glass, and the friendly staff serve well kept Wadworths IPA, JCB, 6X and a couple of guests such as McMullen Country Best and Youngs Waggle Dance on handpump or tapped straight from the cask; piped music, darts, pool, dominoes, fruit machine, and TV. The relaxing open-plan bar has beams in the shiny ceiling where walls have been knocked through, shiny wood floors, mustard walls, an old-fashioned high-backed settle on one side of the room with a smaller one opposite, leatherette stools, and comfortably cushioned wall benches. Generous helpings of straightforward bar food include soup (£2.25), sandwiches (from £3.25), spicy thai crab cake (£3.75), chilli or breaded cod (£5.95), tasty fillet steak (£9.95), and specials such as mushroom stroganoff (£6.50), and lamb and spinach curry (£6.95), with puddings such as hot chocolate fudge cake (£3.25); it's especially popular with older visitors, and they do a good value OAP weekday lunch special (£3.95). The dining area is no smoking. Silbury Hill (a vast prehistoric mound) is just towards Marlborough from here, and Avebury stone circle and the West Kennet long barrow are very close too. *(Recommended by Brian and Pat Wardrobe, Gill and Tony Morriss, Esther and John Sprinkle, Pat and Tony Martin, Andrew Shore, Maria Williams, Sheila and Robert Robinson, John and Glenys Wheeler, Dr and Mrs A K Clarke, R C Livesey, Susan and Nigel Wilson, David Crook, Frank Willy)*

Wadworths ~ Manager Doug Shepherd ~ Real ale ~ Bar food (not Sun evening) ~ (01672) 539418 ~ Children in eating area of bar ~ Open 11-2.30, 5.30(6 Sat)-11; 12-3, 7-10.30 Sun

BERWICK ST JAMES SU0639 Map 2

Boot

B3083, between A36 and A303 NW of Salisbury

The partly carpeted flagstoned bar of this flint and stone pub has a contented cosy atmosphere, a huge winter log fire in the inglenook fireplace at one end, sporting prints over a smaller brick fireplace at the other, and houseplants on its wide window sills. A charming small back no smoking dining room has a nice mix of dining chairs around four tables, and deep pink walls with an attractively mounted collection of celebrity boots. Wadworths IPA and 6X along with a changing guest such as Young's Best are well kept on handpump, and they have a few well chosen house wines, half a dozen malts and farm cider; piped jazz. The blackboard menu lists a good choice of reasonably priced food, made using lots of local produce (vegetables may even come from the garden), such as tasty baguettes (from £4.95), and ploughman's (£5.50), soup (£4.25), breaded brie with raspberry coulis (£5.75), chilli con carne (£8.95), red thai chicken curry (£9.95), slow-roast shoulder of lamb or bass with ginger, spring onion and soy sauce (£10.95), and steaks (from £13.95), with puddings (£4.25), and they do children's meals; service can be slow when it's busy. Very neatly kept, the sheltered side lawn has pretty flowerbeds, and some well spaced picnic-sets. *(Recommended by Alan and Paula McCully, Sam and Sally Shepherd, Gerry and Rosemary Dobson, Joyce and Geoff Robson, Esther and John Sprinkle, Peter and Audrey Dowsett, Michael Doswell, Fiona Eddleston, John A Barker, David and Wendy Puttock, W W Burke, Sarah and Anthony Bussy, M G Hart, DC, Sebastian and Paris Leach)*

Wadworths ~ Tenant Kathie Duval ~ Real ale ~ Bar food (12-2.30, 6.30-9.30; not Mon) ~ Restaurant ~ (01722) 790243 ~ Children welcome ~ Dogs welcome ~ Open 12-3, 6-11; 12-3, 7-10.30 Sun; closed Mon lunchtime exc bank hols

BERWICK ST JOHN ST9422 Map 2

Talbot

Village signposted from A30 E of Shaftesbury

This attractive old pub is set in a peaceful and pretty village, with thatched old houses. The single long, heavily beamed bar is simply furnished with cushioned solid wall and window seats, spindleback chairs, a high-backed built-in settle at one end, and tables. The huge inglenook fireplace has a good iron fireback and bread ovens, and there are nicely shaped heavy black beams and cross-beams with bevelled corners; seats outside too. Reasonably priced bar food includes lunchtime ploughman's (£4), baguettes (from £4.25), sausage and mash with onion gravy or cheese and mushroom omelette (£4.25), as well as home-made lasagne (£6.25), tasty breaded scampi (£6.50), and grilled cajun chicken or salmon and broccoli mornay (£6.95), with daily specials such as steak and ale pie, battered hake, chicken balti or pork with apple and cider (£6.95). Bass, Ringwood Best, Wadworths 6X and a guest such as Shepherd Neame Spitfire are well kept on handpump, and they've farm cider; darts, cribbage. More reports please. *(Recommended by Colin and Janet Roe, D P and M A Miles)*

Free house ~ Licensees Pete and Marilyn Hawkins ~ Real ale ~ Bar food ~ (01747) 828222 ~ Children in eating area of bar ~ Dogs welcome ~ Open 12-3, 6.30-11; 12-4 Sun; closed Sun evening, Mon exc bank hol lunchtime

BOX ST8369 Map 2

Quarrymans Arms

Box Hill; coming from Bath on A4 turn right into Bargates 50 yards before railway bridge, then at T junction turn left up Quarry Hill, turning left again near the top at grassy triangle; from Corsham, turn left after Rudloe Park Hotel into Beech Road, then third left on to Barnetts Hill, and finally right at the top of the hill; OS Sheet 173 map reference 834694

With a warmly welcoming atmosphere, this unpretentious low stone pub was once the local of the Bath stone miners, so there are quite a lot of mining-related photographs and memorabilia dotted around the interior (they now run interesting guided trips down the mine itself). One modernised room with an open fire is entirely set aside for drinking, and Butcombe, Moles Best and Wadworths 6X are very well kept on handpump, they've good wines, over 60 malt whiskies, and ten or so old cognacs; they've now added a coffee machine too. Beautifully sweeping views from big windows in the dining area are usually enough to distract visitors from the mild untidiness, and the tasty bar food is a big draw. The fairly priced menu might include snacks such as sandwiches (£2.50), macaroni cheese (£5.25), scampi, ham, egg and chips or all day breakfast (£5.95), with other dishes such as moules marinière (£5.25; £8.25 main), spaghetti carbonara (£7.95), various stir fries (£8.25), and beef fillet with red wine and mushroom sauce (£12.95); pleasant informal service. The pub is ideally placed for cavers, potholers and walkers, and the atmosphere is easy-going; cribbage, dominoes, shove-ha'penny, fruit machine, and piped music. An attractive outside terrace has picnic-sets, and they play boules here (with football and cricket teams, too). Getting here involves a sinuous drive down a warren of lanes. *(Recommended by Paul Hopton, Catherine Pitt, N Bayley, Gill and Tony Morriss, Dr and Mrs C W Thomas, Susan and John Douglas, Dr and Mrs M E Wilson, Dr and Mrs A K Clarke, Guy Vowles, Tom Bottinga, Gene and Kitty Rankin)*

Free house ~ Licensees John and Ginny Arundel ~ Real ale ~ Bar food (12-3, 6-9, bookings till 9.30) ~ Restaurant ~ (01225) 743569 ~ Children welcome ~ Dogs allowed in bar ~ Open 11-3, 6-11; 11-11 Fri-Sat; 12-10.30 Sun ~ Bedrooms: £35B/£65B

BRADFORD-ON-AVON ST8261 Map 2

Dandy Lion

35 Market Street

A good place to spend an afternoon with a drink and the papers, this thriving town pub has an enjoyably continental feel, and a good mix of customers. Big windows, either side of the door, look out on to the street, and have a table and cushioned wooden armchair each. Working in, the pleasantly relaxed long main bar has nice high-backed farmhouse chairs, old-fashioned dining chairs, a long brocade-cushioned settle on the stripped wooden floor (there's a couple of rugs, too), sentimental and gently erotic pictures on the panelled walls, an overmantel with brussels horses, and fairy-lit hops over the bar counter. Up a few steps at the back, a snug little bare-boarded room has a lovely high-backed settle and other small ones around sturdy tables, a big mirror, mulberry walls and a piano; piped jazz. The upstairs restaurant is candlelit at night, and has an area with antique toys and baskets of flowers. Butcombe, Wadworths IPA, 6X and a seasonal ale are well kept on handpump, they've ten wines by the glass, and they do good coffees; friendly service. Served only at lunchtime, straightforward bar food includes soup (£3.95), sandwiches or baguettes (from £3.95), baked potatoes (from £4.95), and stuffed pepper or fish and chips (£6.25), with specials such as sweet and sour pork or chicken breast with tomato sauce and mashed potato (£6.95). In the evening, the pub is popular with a young crowd (especially weekends, when parts can get smoky). They have evening poetry readings, and occasional jazz. *(Recommended by Dr and Mrs M E Wilson, Richard Pierce, P R and S A White, Dr and Mrs A K Clarke, Sue Demont, Tim Barrow, David and Pam Wilcox)*

Wadworths ~ Tenant Jennifer Taylor ~ Real ale ~ Bar food (lunchtime; not 25 Dec) ~ Restaurant ~ (01225) 863433 ~ Children welcome ~ Open 10.30-3(3.30 Sat), 6-11; 11.30-3.30, 7-10.30 Sun

BRINKWORTH SU0184 Map 2

Three Crowns 🍷

The Street; B4042 Wootton Bassett—Malmesbury

Readers are full of praise for the way this popular place manages to remain 'a real pub that serves great food'. The elaborate menu (with prices at the top end of the pub range) covers an entire wall, and all main courses are served with half a dozen fresh vegetables. Besides lunchtime snacks such as filled rolls (from £5.75), filled baked potatoes (from £6.95), sausages and mash or chilli (£8.45), and crab cakes (£9.95), other dishes might be home-made steak and kidney pie (£13.45), locally smoked chicken with sherry and cream sauce and dijon mustard (£16.45), salmon and monkfish in cream and Pernod sauce (£17.45), crocodile (£18.45), and rack of lamb topped with garlic breadcrumbs, with red wine and cream sauce (£18.95), with puddings such as sticky toffee pudding (£5.25). Get here early if you want a table as it can get very crowded, and you may have to wait a long time. Most people choose to eat in the no smoking conservatory. The bar part is more traditional, with big landscape prints and other pictures, some horsebrasses on dark beams, a dresser with a collection of old bottles, tables of stripped deal, and a couple made from gigantic forge bellows, big tapestry-upholstered pews and blond chairs, and log fires; sensibly placed darts, shove-ha'penny, dominoes, cribbage and chess; fruit machine and piped music. There's a light and airy no smoking garden room and a terrace with outdoor heating to the side of the conservatory. Drinkers have a good range of real ales to choose from including Castle Eden Bitter, Fullers London Pride, Greene King Old Speckled Hen, Wadworths 6X and a guest such as Archers Village on handpump, and they have a long wine list, with at least ten by the glass, and mulled wine in winter. The garden stretches around the side and back, with well spaced tables and a climbing frame, and looks over a side lane to the church, and out over rolling prosperous farmland. *(Recommended by Andrew Shore, Maria Williams, Nigel and Sue Foster, Peter and Audrey Dowsett, Dr and Mrs A K Clarke, Brian and Pat Wardrobe, Mrs J Smythe, Tom and Ruth Rees, KC, Brenda and Rob Fincham, Gordon Neighbour, James Morrell, Veronica Turner, Mrs Pat Crabb)*

Whitbreads ~ Lease Anthony Windle ~ Real ale ~ Bar food (12-2(3 Sun), 6-9.30; not 25-26 Dec) ~ Restaurant ~ (01666) 510366 ~ Children allowed till 6pm, unless by arrangement ~ Dogs allowed in bar ~ Open 11-3(4 Sat), 6-11; 12-5, 6-10.30 Sun; closed 25-26 Dec

CHICKSGROVE ST9729 Map 2

Compasses ★

From A30 5½ miles W of B3089 junction, take lane on N side signposted Sutton Mandeville, Sutton Row, then first left fork (small signs point the way to the pub, in Lower Chicksgrove; look out for the car park)

This pleasantly relaxed old thatched house is 'always a delight to visit' according to readers, with tremendously welcoming service and good food. The bar has old bottles and jugs hanging from beams above the roughly timbered counter, farm tools and traps on the partly stripped stone walls, and high-backed wooden settles forming snug booths around tables on the mainly flagstoned floor; there's a cheerful atmosphere. Four real ales on handpump include well kept Bass, Chicksgrove Churl (brewed for the pub by Wadworths), Wadworths 6X and a guest, they also have six wines by the glass; cribbage, dominoes, bagatelle and shove-ha'penny. Besides snacks such as filled onion bread (from £3.95), ham, egg and chips or 6oz rib-eye steak (£6.45), ambitious dishes (served with a good choice of vegetables) from the daily-changing menu might include baked red pepper with garlic and anchovies (£5.25), and smoked duck and red onion tartlet (£5.45), steak and kidney pie with suet (£8.95), wild mushrooms with vinny, apple and cider sauce with caper risotto (£9.95), duck breast wrapped in bacon with chinese jus or monkfish steak marinated in thai spices (£12.95), or lamb fillet with mint and redcurrant jus (£14.95), with irresistible puddings such as chocolate, orange and Cointreau cheesecake or raspberry, lemon, ginger and coriander tart (£4.25), and they do good children's meals; service can be slow when it's busy. The quiet garden and flagstoned farm courtyard are very pleasant places to sit; they've a new enclosed garden behind, and two terraces with outdoor heaters. There's a nice walk to Sutton Mandeville church and back along the Nadder Valley. *(Recommended by Mr and Mrs Staples, J F Stackhouse, Paul Boot, Dr and Mrs C W Thomas, Peter J and Avril Hanson, Howard and Margaret Buchanan, Bill and Jessica Ritson, Ian Wilson, Colin and Janet Roe, Helen and Brian Edgeley, Roger and Pauline Pearce, Edmund Coan, Dr D E Granger, Phyl and Jack Street, Sebastian and Paris Leach, Ken and Sylvia Jones, Edward Mirzoeff, Mrs Belinda Mead, David and Ruth Hollands)*

Free house ~ Licensee Alan Stoneham ~ Real ale ~ Bar food (not Sun evenings, or Mon exc bank hols, then not Tues) ~ Restaurant ~ (01722) 714318 ~ Children welcome ~ Dogs welcome ~ Open 12-3, 6-11(7-10.30 Sun); closed Mon exc bank hols, then cl Tues ~ Bedrooms: £45B/£65B

CORSHAM ST8670 Map 2

Two Pigs

A4, Pickwick

Always chatty and friendly, the atmosphere at this admirably eccentric traditional little beer lover's pub is at its headiest on Monday nights, when live blues draws a big crowd into the narrow and dimly lit flagstoned bar. Amassed by the individualistic landlord, you'll find a zany collection of bric-a-brac including enamel advertising signs on the wood-clad walls, pig-theme ornaments, and old radios. A good mix of customers gathers around the long dark wood tables and benches, and friendly staff serve well kept Hop Back Summer Lightning and Stonehenge Pigswill, along with a couple of changing guests from small independent brewers such as

Church End, O'Hanlon's and Teignworthy; piped blues. A covered yard outside is called the Sty. Beware of their opening times – the pub is closed every lunchtime, except on Sunday; no food (except crisps), no under-21s. *(Recommended by Catherine Pitt, Dr and Mrs A K Clarke, R Huggins, D Irving, E McCall, T McLean, Mr and Mrs P R Thomas)*

Free house ~ Licensees Dickie and Ann Doyle ~ Real ale ~ No credit cards ~ (01249) 712515 ~ Blues Mon evening ~ Open 7-11; 12-2.30, 7-10.30 Sun

DEVIZES SU0061 Map 2

Bear 🍷 🛏

Market Place

This old coaching inn has provided shelter to distinguished guests as diverse as King George III and Dr Johnson. These days you'll find a choice of 15 different wines by the glass, along with well kept Wadworths IPA, 6X and a seasonal guest on handpump, and they've a good choice of malt whiskies, and freshly squeezed juices. Cosier after a recent refurbishment (including the restaurant and Lawrence Room too), the big main carpeted bar has log fires, black winged wall settles and muted cloth-upholstered bucket armchairs around oak tripod tables; the classic bar counter has shiny black woodwork and small panes of glass. Separated from the main bar by some steps, a room named after the portrait painter Thomas Lawrence (his father ran the establishment in the 1770s) has dark oak-panelled walls, a parquet floor, a big open fireplace, shining copper pans, and plates around the walls; it's partly no smoking. As we went to press they had plans to change their menu, but bar food might include home-made soup (£2.95), sandwiches (from £2.75), ploughman's (from £4.95), lasagne (£6.95), fish and chips (£7.95), chargrilled chicken (£8.95), and steak (£10.95), with home-made puddings (£2.95); prices for the same dishes go up in the evenings. There are buffet meals in the Lawrence Room, and you can eat these in the bar too. It's only a stone's throw from here to Wadworths brewery, where you can buy beer in splendid old-fashioned half-gallon earthenware jars. *(Recommended by the Didler, Blaise Vyner, Joyce and Maurice Cottrell, Mike Gorton, Richard Pierce, Bill and Jessica Ritson, Dr and Mrs A K Clarke, A Sadler, Tina and David Woods-Taylor)*

Wadworths ~ Tenant Andrew Maclachlan ~ Real ale ~ Bar food (11.30-2.30, 7-9.30) ~ Restaurant ~ (01380) 722444 ~ Children welcome ~ Dogs welcome ~ Open 11-11; 12-10.30 Sun; closed 25-26 Dec ~ Bedrooms: £50B/£75B

DONHEAD ST ANDREW ST9124 Map 2

Forester 🍷

Village signposted off A30 E of Shaftesbury, just E of Ludwell; Lower Street

This 14th-c thatched pub, in a charming village, looks well in line for a Food Award under the chef who took over not long before this edition went to press. The pub has also changed ownership recently, but the resident manager who has built up its reputation over the last year or so is staying on in charge; there are no plans to alter the present very successful operation. The pub is well organised inside, with stripped tables in the welcoming and appealing bar, which usually has a few local regulars around the servery, and a log fire in its big inglenook fireplace. Here, a big blackboard lists the changing food. Very nicely cooked, this might include lunchtime filled ciabattas or ploughman's (from £4.95), popular warm chicken salad (£5.50), crab cakes (£6.25), broad bean, asparagus, pea and parmesan risotto (£9), smoked haddock or rib-eye steak (£12), liver and bacon (£13.95), and fried lamb rump (£16), with delicious puddings such as poached apricots with shortbread (£4.95). They have well kept Flowers Original, Ringwood Best and perhaps a guest beer such as Bass on handpump; the choice of wines by the glass is very good, and the atmosphere is warmly welcoming. The comfortable main dining room has more country-kitchen tables in varying sizes, nicely laid out with linen napkins, and attractive wrought-iron candlesticks – they sell these, if you like the design. A second smaller and cosier dining room is, like the first, no smoking.

Service is pleasant and helpful, and there are no machines or piped music. Tables out on the good-sized recently reworked terrace have fine country views, and there are good walks nearby. The neighbouring cottage used to be the pub's coach house. *(Recommended by Colin and Janet Roe, Peter Salmon, Ian Cox, Edmund Coan, Bill and Sally Imeson, Penny Simpson)*

Free house ~ Licensee Darren Morris ~ Real ale ~ Bar food ~ Restaurant ~ (01747) 828038 ~ Children welcome ~ Dogs allowed in bar ~ Open 11-3, 6-11(10.30 Sun)

EBBESBOURNE WAKE ST9824 Map 2

Horseshoe ★

On A354 S of Salisbury, right at signpost at Coombe Bissett; village is around 8 miles further on

Doing very well at the moment, this charmingly unspoilt old country pub is tucked away in fine downland, and there are pleasant views over the steep sleepy valley of the River Ebble from seats in its pretty little garden; look out for the three goats in a paddock at the bottom of the garden, and a couple of playful dogs. Inside, there are fresh home-grown flowers on the tables in the beautifully kept bar, with lanterns, a large collection of farm tools and other bric-a-brac crowded along its beams, and an open fire; a conservatory extension seats 10 people. Well kept Adnams Broadside, Ringwood Best, Wadworths 6X and a guest such as Palmers Best are tapped from the row of casks behind the bar, and they also stock farm cider, country wines and several malt whiskies. Nothing is too much trouble for the friendly landlord and welcoming, attentive staff. Served with plenty of well cooked seasonal vegetables (and good chips), enjoyable bar food includes lunchtime ham and eggs (£6.75), curry (£8.95), steak and kidney pie or faggots (£9.50), lambs liver and bacon (£9.75), and evening dishes such as lamb cutlets in port sauce (£12.95), and fillet steak or half a honey-roasted duckling in gooseberry sauce (£15); good puddings might include treacle tart (£3.95). Booking is advisable for the small no smoking restaurant, especially at weekends when it can fill quite quickly. There are good walks nearby. *(Recommended by John and Jane Hayter, the Didler, Richard Harris, Penny Simpson, Colin and Janet Roe, Bill and Jessica Ritson, Andrea Rampley, Dr D G Twyman, David Kirkcaldy, Terry and Linda Moseley)*

Free house ~ Licensees Anthony and Patricia Bath ~ Real ale ~ Bar food (not Sun evenings or Mon) ~ Restaurant ~ (01722) 780474 ~ Children in restaurant ~ Open 12-3, 6.30-11; 12-4, 7-10.30 Sun; closed Mon lunchtime exc bank hols, 26 Dec ~ Bedrooms: £45B/£60B

GREAT DURNFORD SU1338 Map 2

Black Horse

Follow signpost to the Woodfords off A345, Amesbury—Devizes at High Post traffic lights

With good food and a helpful landlord, it's no wonder that this cheerful pub is such a lively bustling place at lunchtime. Colourful changing menu boards list a tempting choice of dishes such as garlic mushrooms (£4.50), breaded plaice (£7.75), liver, onions and bacon, vegetable moussaka or lasagne (£7.95), and home-made steak and kidney pie (£7.25), with specials such as chicken breast with stilton cream sauce (£8.50), lamb chops in redcurrant sauce (£8.95), and bass (£11.95), with puddings such as spotted dick and hot treacle sponge (£3.50); they also do baguettes (from £5.50, not Sunday), and children's meals (£5.75 including ice-cream). The brick serving counter has a line of bar stools (and a great line in funny hats), and opposite it, across a narrow brick floor, another row of bar stools facing a shelf wide enough to hold plates, with an entertaining collection of bric-a-brac above this. At one end of this central spine is an alcove with sensibly placed darts, and another with a single long table; at the other, a snug flag-draped area with three tables and a high-backed settle. Steps take you up to a couple of no smoking rooms, one with ship pictures, models and huge ensigns, the other with a big woodburning stove in a big brick inglenook. Well kept Ringwood Best, a slightly lighter house beer brewed for them by Ringwood, and a guest such as Hop Back

Crop Circle on handpump; piped Blues and Jazz, darts, shove-ha'penny, table skittles, pinball, cribbage, dominoes and ring the bull. There are picnic sets on grass leading down to the River Avon, past a timber climbing fort, gondola and tyre swings, and a small wendy house; they have pétanque, and hold summer barbecues. Readers have enjoyed spending the night here, and for breakfast they do good croissants. *(Recommended by Graham Chamberlain, Mark Flynn, Dr D G Twyman)*

Free house ~ Licensee Mike Skinner ~ Real ale ~ Bar food (not Sun evening, or winter Mon) ~ Restaurant ~ (01722) 782270 ~ Children away from bar ~ Dogs allowed in bar ~ Open 12-2, 6-9; 12-2.30, 6-11 Fri-Sat; 12-3, 6-9 Sun; closed Sun evening and Mon in winter ~ Bedrooms: £35/£45(£55S)

GREAT HINTON ST9059 Map 2

Linnet

3½ miles E of Trowbridge, village signposted off A361 opposite Lamb at Semington

Everything from bread and sausages to ice-cream is home-made at this attractive brick pub – very much somewhere to come for an imaginative meal, rather than just a drink. The set lunch (£10.75 for two courses; £13.25 for three courses) is excellent value, and to be sure of a table on the weekend, it's best to book a few weeks in advance. Well cooked by the dedicated chef/landlord, and served in the little bar or restaurant, the changing menu might include at lunchtimes filled focaccia or salads (from £6.50), smoked salmon and cod fishcakes (£7.25), and grilled rib-eye steak with blue cheese and bacon fritters in port sauce (£9.95), with evening dishes such as steamed salmon with roasted pepper, baby sweetcorn and lemon risotto with prawn sauce (£11.50), pork tenderloin filled with apple, red onion and truffles with honey and mustard sauce (£11.95), and fried rib-eye steak with braised calves kidneys stuffed with fried onions and herbs in thyme sauce (£14.50), with puddings such as lemon meringue cheesecake (£4.60). The bar to the right of the door has a cream carpet and lots of photographs of the pub and the brewery, and there are bookshelves in a snug end part. The cosy restaurant is candlelit at night. As well as more than two dozen malt whiskies, and quite a few wines (with eight by the glass), they serve well kept Wadworths 6X, and maybe a seasonal guest on handpump; piped music. In summer, the flowering tubs and window boxes with seats dotted among them are quite a sight. *(Recommended by Denise Drummond, M G Hart, Lady Heath, Mr and Mrs J Ken Jones, Andrew Shore, Maria Williams, Dr and Mrs A K Clarke, Danielle Nay, Ken and Sylvia Jones, Mike Gorton, Mr and Mrs A H Young)*

Wadworths ~ Tenant Jonathan Furby ~ Real ale ~ Bar food (not Mon) ~ Restaurant ~ (01380) 870354 ~ Children welcome ~ Dogs allowed in bar ~ Open 11-2.30, 6-11; 12-3, 7-10.30 Sun; closed Mon

GRITTLETON ST8680 Map 2

Neeld Arms

Off A350 NW of Chippenham; The Street

The friendly licensees help generate a particularly convivial atmosphere at this 17th-c black-beamed pub. It's largely open-plan, with some stripped stone, a log fire in the big inglenook on the right and a smaller coal-effect fire on the left, flowers on tables, and a pleasant mix of seating from windsor chairs through scatter-cushioned window seats to some nice arts and crafts chairs and a traditional settle. The parquet-floored back dining area has yet another inglenook, with a big woodburning stove (even back here, you still feel thoroughly part of the action). From the substantial central bar counter, you can get well kept beers such as Bath Gem, Hook Norton, Hop Back Crop Circle and Wadworths 6X on handpump, with guests from brewers such as Hop Back and Wychwood; they've also a good choice of reasonably priced wines by the glass. Enjoyable food from changing blackboards might include lunchtime (not Sunday) ciabattas (from £4.50), ploughman's (£4.95), fish, chips and mushy peas (£6.95), salmon and dill fishcakes (£7.25), and sausages or pie of the week (£7.50), with evening dishes such as salmon with parma ham (£8.95), venison with redcurrant jus (£10.50), sirloin steak (£10.95), lamb shank with mint and rosemary sauce (£11), and bass (£12), with puddings (£4.25); they do Sunday roast with local beef (£7.25). It gets tremendously busy when the Badminton horse trials are on (and service can be slow). As we went to press, the terrace was gaining a pergola; look out for Soaky, the golden retriever who likes slops. *(Recommended by Richard Stancomb, Simon Mays-Smith, Richard Pierce, Michael Doswell, Peter Neate, Anthony Barnes, Simon and Mandy King, Mike Pugh, Stephen Woad, R Huggins, D Irving, E McCall, T McLean)*

Free house ~ Licensees Charlie and Boo West ~ Real ale ~ Bar food ~ Restaurant ~ (01249) 782470 ~ Children welcome ~ Dogs welcome ~ Open 12-3, 5.30-11; 11.30-3.30, 5.30-11 Sat; 12-3.30, 6.30-11 Sun ~ Bedrooms: £40S(£40B)/£60S(£70B)

HEYTESBURY ST9242 Map 2

Angel

High Street; just off A36 E of Warminster

In a quiet village just below the Salisbury Plain, this enjoyable 16th-c inn has been completely refurbished under its new landlord. With a good open fire and plenty of comfortable armchairs and sofas, the spacious homely lounge on the right opens into the stylish restaurant with high-back leather chairs and wooden tables. This in turn opens on to an attractive secluded courtyard garden. On the left, a long beamed bar has a convivial evening atmosphere, open fire, some attractive prints and old photographs, and straightforward tables and chairs; piped music. Good bar food includes hot rolls (from £3.95), ploughman's (£5.45), tasty lemon sole goujons (£6.25), pork sausages, mash and onion gravy (£6.95), smoked haddock and salmon fishcake with sorrel hollandaise (£7.95), and scottish beef burger (£8.95). The restaurant has award-standard food; they specialise in steaks (from £14.95). There's a relaxed atmosphere, and service is efficient. Nine wines are available by the glass, and beers include Greene King IPA, Morland Original, Old Speckled Hen and Ruddles County on handpump. *(Recommended by Edward Mirzoeff)*

Greene King ~ Lease Tim Etchells ~ Real ale ~ Bar food ~ Restaurant ~ (01985) 840330 ~ Children welcome ~ Dogs allowed in bar ~ Open 11-11; 12-10.30 Sun ~ Bedrooms: £60B/£75B

HINDON ST9132 Map 2

Lamb

B3089 Wilton—Mere

The best place to sit in this civilised solid hotel (handily open all day) is probably in the two slate-floored lower sections of the roomy long bar. There's a long polished table with wall benches and chairs, blacksmith's tools set behind a big inglenook fireplace, and at one end a window seat (overlooking the village church) with a big waxed circular table, spindleback chairs with tapestried cushions, a high-backed settle and brass jugs on the mantelpiece above the small fireplace; there are lots of tables and chairs up some steps in a third bigger area. Enjoyable (but not cheap) bar food might include sandwiches (from £3.50), soup (£3.95), ploughman's (£5.50), lasagne (£6.95), steak and kidney pie (£7.95), calves liver with apple and calvados mash or corn-fed chicken with mushroom sauce (£9.95), tuna loin with thai sauce (£12.50), and rib-eye steak (£12.95), with puddings such as bread and butter pudding (£3.95); they do a Sunday roast (£7.95), and you can usually get cream teas throughout the afternoon. Pleasant staff serve four well kept Youngs beers on handpump (though this may change as the pub is due to be bought by another pub group), and a good choice of wines by the glass; the range of whiskies includes all the malts from the Isle of Islay. There are picnic-sets across the road (which is a good alternative to the main routes west); parking is limited. *(Recommended by Mike Gorton, W W Burke, Colin and Janet Roe, John Evans, Phil and Sally Gorton)*

Youngs ~ Tenant Nick James ~ Real ale ~ Bar food ~ (01747) 820573 ~ Children welcome away from bar ~ Dogs welcome ~ Open 11-11; 12-10.30 Sun ~ Bedrooms: £55B/£80B

HOLT ST8561 Map 2

Toll Gate

Ham Green; B3107 W of Melksham

Furnished and decorated with real flair, this enjoyable foody pub caters well for both drinkers and diners. One leg of the relaxed L-shaped bar has cosy settees and a log fire watched over by big stone cats (there are also two pub cats). The other leg is more adapted to eating (one lovely table gleaming in the corner was put together for the pub from three salvaged flooring planks); there are plenty of hunting prints on pinkish walls, some willow-pattern plates on black panelling, one or two beams in the venetian red ceiling, rugs on old quarry tiles, and soft lighting including table lamps. The high-raftered restaurant, up a few steps, is eclectically decorated with bright cushions on sturdy pews and other country furniture, and attractive bric-a-brac including lots of japanese parasols, all interestingly lit through church windows – this part used to be a workers' chapel, when the main building was a weavers' shed. Five well kept changing beers on handpump are bought directly from a good range of interesting mostly smaller brewers such as City of Cambridge, Exmoor, Glastonbury, Robinsons, Roosters and York; they also do nine wines by the glass, and there's farm cider and good strong coffee. Freshly cooked food includes lunchtime snacks such as soup (£4), corned beef hash with egg or hot mediterranean vegetable and mozzarella sandwich (£6.50), with more elaborate dishes such as cornish mussels with garlic, white wine and cream (£5.50), roasted pigeon with creamed leeks and juniper and rosemary sauce (£12.50), local lamb shank braised with rosemary, honey and cumin (£13.75), and bass with shallot and chive dressing (£14.50); home-made puddings such as hot chocolate and fondant pudding with orange ice-cream or apple crumble with crème anglaise (from £4.50); extra vegetables are £2.50. They name their suppliers (eggs come from the pub's own flock of chickens), and make their own bread and ice-cream. The set lunch is very good value (£9.95 two courses; £11.95 three courses). Service is friendly and attentive; piped music. The gents' is worth a look for its colourful murals. There are picnic-sets out on the back terrace; look out for the four rescued goats.

(Recommended by Dr and Mrs M E Wilson, Andrew Shore, Maria Williams, M G Hart, Dr and Mrs A K Clarke, John and Penny Spinks, Sharon and Nick Mather, Sue Demont, Tim Barrow)

Free house ~ Licensees Alison Ward-Baptiste and Alexander Venables ~ Real ale ~ Bar food (not Sun evening or Mon) ~ Restaurant ~ (01225) 782326 ~ No children under 10 ~ Dogs allowed in bar ~ Open 11.30-2.30, 5.30-11; 12-2.30 Sun; closed Sun evening, Mon ~ Bedrooms: /£75S

KILMINGTON ST7736 Map 2

Red Lion £

B3092 Mere—Frome, 2½ miles S of Maiden Bradley; 3 miles from A303 Mere turn-off

This down-to-earth 15th-c ivy-covered country inn is popular with walkers; you can buy locally made walking sticks, and a gate gives on to the lane which leads to White Sheet Hill, where there is riding, hang gliding and radio-controlled gliders. With a good local pubby atmosphere (particularly in the evenings), the snug low-ceilinged bar is pleasantly furnished with a curved high-backed settle and red leatherette wall and window seats on the flagstones, photographs of locals pinned up on the black beams, and a couple of big fireplaces (one with a fine old iron fireback) with log fires in winter. A newer big-windowed no smoking eating area is decorated with brasses, a large leather horse collar, and hanging plates. Dogs are allowed in the bar – but not at lunchtime; sensibly placed darts, dominoes, shove-ha'penny and cribbage. Butcombe, Butts Jester and a regularly changing guest such as Wye Valley Butty Bach are well kept on handpump, and they've farm cider, pressés, and monthly changing wines. Served only at lunchtime, the straightforward bar menu (prices haven't gone up since last year) includes soup (£1.80), sandwiches (from £2.80, toasted from £3.25), ploughman's (£3.95), pasties (£4), salads (£4.75), meat or vegetable lasagne (£6.75), and perhaps a couple of daily specials.

There are picnic-sets in the big attractive garden (look out for Kim the labrador).The pub is owned by the National Trust, and Stourhead Gardens are only a mile away. *(Recommended by Roger and Jenny Huggins, Edward Mirzoeff, Mike Gorton, Andrea Rampley, Colin and Janet Roe, D M Tyley)*

Free house ~ Licensee Chris Gibbs ~ Real ale ~ Bar food (12-1.50; not 25-26 or 31 Dec) ~ No credit cards ~ (01985) 844263 ~ Children welcome till 8.30pm ~ Open 11.30-2.30, 6.30-11; 12-3, 7-10.30 Sun ~ Bedrooms: £25/£35

LACOCK ST9168 Map 2

George ★

West Street; village signposted off A350 S of Chippenham

Readers very much enjoy coming to this unspoilt homely old pub, which has been licensed continuously since the 17th c. The long-serving landlord and his family are very friendly, and the atmosphere is warmly welcoming. Comfortable and relaxing, the low-beamed bar has upright timbers in the place of knocked-through walls making cosy rambling corners, candles on tables (even at lunchtime), armchairs and windsor chairs, seats in the stone-mullioned windows, and flagstones just by the counter; piped music (which can be quite loud). The treadwheel set into the outer breast of the original great central fireplace is a talking point – worked by a dog, it was used to turn a spit for roasting. Outside, there are picnic-sets with umbrellas in the lovely back garden (which has plenty of space to run round), and they've recently updated the play area; a bench in front overlooks the main street. It gets busy, so booking is a good idea if you want to enjoy the good generously served bar food. Served with fresh vegetables and tasty chips, the menu could include good vegetarian dishes such as wild mushroom lasagne, parsnip and cheese roulade or lemon and thyme risotto (£7.95), home-made steak and ale pie (£7.95), breaded scampi (£8.95), chicken breast stuffed with wild mushrooms wrapped in bacon with red wine sauce (10.95), and salmon with asparagus sauce (£11.50), with lunchtime snacks such as sandwiches (from £2.85), and baguettes and ploughman's (from £4.95); home-made puddings might be bread and butter pudding and raspberry and hazelnut roulade (£4.50). The barn restaurant is no smoking. There's a decent choice of good value wines, and reasonably priced Wadworths IPA, JCB and 6X are well kept on handpump. Dating back in part to 1362, the pub is one of the oldest buildings in the village. *(Recommended by R Huggins, D Irving, E McCall, T McLean, P R and S A White, Dr and Mrs M E Wilson, Mr and Mrs R W Allan, Richard Fendick, Andrew Shore, Maria Williams, Dr and Mrs A K Clarke, Penny and Peter Keevil, Fiona Eddleston, Edward Mirzoeff, Sue and Mike Todd, Meg and Colin Hamilton, Brian Root, Nicholas and Dorothy Stephens, Kevin Thorpe, Roger and Jenny Huggins, Louise English)*

Wadworths ~ Tenant John Glass ~ Real ale ~ Bar food ~ Restaurant ~ (01249) 730263 ~ Children in eating area of bar and restaurant ~ Open 10-3, 5-11; 10-11 Fri-Sat; 10-10.30 Sun; 10-3, 5-11 Fri in winter

Red Lion

High Street

Owned by the National Trust, this imposing Georgian inn is handy for a visit to nearby Lacock Abbey or the Fox Talbot Museum. The atmosphere is pubby and lively, especially towards the end of the evening, when the pub is popular with younger visitors, but service remains prompt and friendly. Divided into cosy areas by open handrails, the long and airy pink-painted bar has distressed heavy dark wood tables and tapestried chairs. There are turkey rugs on the partly flagstoned floor, a fine old log fire at one end, aged-looking paintings, and branding irons hanging from the ceiling. The cosy snug has comfortable leather armchairs. Wadworths IPA, JCB, 6X and one of their seasonal beers are well kept on handpump, and they've several malt whiskies; fruit machine and piped music. A short selection of tasty pubby bar food includes a couple of daily specials such as beef and stilton pie or lamb and apricot casserole (£7.25), with lunchtime snacks such as soup (£2.95), sandwiches (from £3.95), scampi (£4.95), baked potatoes (£4.50), and ploughman's (£5.50), with evening dishes such as salmon and prawns or steaks (£10.95); home-made puddings might include chocolate fudge cake or sticky toffee pudding (£4.25); one area is no smoking. In fine weather, seats outside are a pleasant place for a drink. *(Recommended by George Atkinson, Tony and Mary Pygott, Michael Doswell, R Huggins, D Irving, E McCall, T McLean, Frank Willy, Dr and Mrs A K Clarke, Betsy and Peter Little)*

Wadworths ~ Managers Chris and Sarah Chappell ~ Real ale ~ Bar food (12-2, 6-9; not 24-26 or 31 Dec) ~ (01249) 730456 ~ Children in eating area of bar and restaurant ~ Dogs allowed in bar ~ Open 11.30-2.30, 6-11; 11.30-11 Sat; 12-10.30 Sun; 11.30-2.30, 6-11(10.30)Sat-Sun in winter ~ Bedrooms: £55B/£75B

Rising Sun

Bewley Common, Bowden Hill – out towards Sandy Lane, up hill past Abbey; OS Sheet 173 map reference 935679

This cheerily unpretentious pub is a marvellous place to enjoy the sunset with a well kept beer – views from the big two-level terrace extend around 25 miles over the Avon valley. Popular with chatting locals, the three welcoming little rooms have been knocked together to form one simply furnished area, with a mix of old chairs and basic kitchen tables on stone floors, stuffed animals and birds, country pictures, and open fires. Welcoming staff serve the full range of Moles beers on handpump (and if you can't decide which one to have you'll probably be offered a taster): Moles Tap Bitter, Best, Molecatcher, Molennium and one of their seasonal ales are well kept, and they stock farm cider too. There's darts, cribbage, dominoes, board games, and unobtrusive piped music. Good helpings of enjoyable bar food include lunchtime snacks such as baguettes (from £3.75), baked potatoes (from £4.50), breaded chicken or fish platter (£6.95), with other dishes such as tempura vegetables with honey and ginger sauce (£6.95), sizzling chicken tortillas (£7.95), and salmon steak with prawn and dill sauce or lamb chops in minted gravy (£8.45), with specials such as good home-made pie or faggots (£7.95). They do children's meals, and there's a children's play area. *(Recommended by R Huggins, D Irving, E McCall, T McLean, Pat and Tony Martin, Dr and Mrs M E Wilson, Mike Gorton, Richard Pierce, Peter Meister, Dr and Mrs A K Clarke, Roger and Jenny Huggins)*

Moles ~ Managers Roger Catte, Peter and Michelle Eaton ~ Real ale ~ Bar food (12-2, 6-9; not Sun evening, or Mon lunch) ~ (01249) 730363 ~ Children in eating area of bar ~ Dogs allowed in bar ~ Live entertainment every Weds evening, and alternate Sun afternoons ~ Open 12-3, 6-11; 12-11 Sat-Sun; 12-3, 6-11 Sat in winter; closed Mon lunchtime

LOWER CHUTE SU3153 Map 2

Hatchet

The Chutes well signposted via Appleshaw off A342, 2½ miles W of Andover

A real stunner (you'll wish you'd brought your camera), this 16th-c thatched cottage is one of the county's most attractive pubs. They serve well kept Adnams, Otter and Timothy Taylors Landlord on handpump, along with a guest such as Ringwood Best, and there are ten wines by the glass to choose from, and a range of country wines. With an unchanging, friendly local atmosphere, the very low-beamed bar has a mix of captain's chairs and cushioned wheelbacks around oak tables, and a splendid 17th-c fireback in the huge fireplace (which has a roaring log fire in winter); cribbage, dominoes and piped music. Thursday night is curry night, when you can eat as much as you like (£6.95). Other tasty bar food includes around half a dozen vegetarian dishes such as jambalaya, aubergine and two-cheese ravioli, and spinach and red pepper lasagne (£3.95), mushrooms in port with mozzarella (£4.75), and ploughman's (£6.25), as well as lamb tagine or thai green chicken curry (£7.25), and tiger prawns in filo pastry or smoked salmon salad (£7.50), with daily specials; they do a good value Sunday roast. The restaurant is no smoking. There are seats out on a terrace by the front car park, or on the side grass, and there's a children's sandpit. They have only twin bedrooms. More reports please. *(Recommended by Phyl and Jack Street, James Woods, Bill and Jessica Ritson, Lynn Sharpless, J Stickland)*

Free house ~ Licensee Jeremy McKay ~ Real ale ~ Bar food (12-2.15, 6.30-9.30) ~ Restaurant ~ (01264) 730229 ~ Children in restaurant and family room ~ Dogs allowed in bar ~ Open 11.30-3, 6-11; 12-3.30, 7-10.30 Sun ~ Bedrooms: £55S/£60S

MALMESBURY ST9287 Map 2

Smoking Dog

High Street

At this double-fronted mid-terrace 17th-c pub you'll find seven real ales tapped straight from the cask or on handpump: alongside well kept Brains Revd James, Buckleys Best and SA, changing guests might include Archers Best, Greene King Old Speckled Hen, Shepherd Neame Spitfire and Wadworths 6X. They also do nine wines by the glass. The two smallish front bars have a sociable local atmosphere (with a younger crowd on some evenings), with flagstones, dark woodwork, cushioned bench seating, big pine tables and a blazing log fire. A flagstoned corridor with local notices on the walls leads to a bare-boards back bistro. The garden has pleasant views out over the town. As well as tasty bar food such as good baguettes and ciabattas (from £4.95), ploughman's (£5.75), potato, broccoli and leek galette with cream, garlic and cheese (£7.25), and home-made chicken jalfrezi (£8.75), you can choose more elaborate dishes from the restaurant menu such as grilled smoked haddock with ale and cheese (£10.50), calves liver with bacon, onions and basil gravy (£10.95), and sirloin steak (£12.25), with puddings such as mascarpone cheesecake with lemon and ginger (£4.25); on Sunday they do roasts (£7.50), and the menu is more limited. *(Recommended by Jenny and Brian Seller, R Huggins, D Irving, E McCall, T McLean, Dr and Mrs A K Clarke, Lesley and Peter Barrett)*

Brains ~ Manager Martin Bridge ~ Real ale ~ Bar food (not Fri-Sat evenings) ~ Restaurant ~ (01666) 825823 ~ Children in eating area of bar and restaurant ~ Dogs allowed in bar ~ Accoustic guitarist every 6 wks ~ Open 12-11(10.30 Sun); closed 25 Dec evening

NEWTON TONY SU2140 Map 2

Malet Arms

Village signposted off A338 Swindon—Salisbury

Happy reports from readers in the last few months have won this tiled flintstone pub, peacefully placed in a quiet village, a new food award. The imaginative blackboard menu changes regularly, but might typically include beautifully presented smoked trout pâté with whisky and horseradish (£5.75), salmon fishcakes (£8.25), home-baked smoked ham, pickles and chips (£8.95), popular rump steak sandwich (£9.50), tuna steak with lime juice and coriander (£13.50), and roast duck breast with spiced potato rösti (£14), with home-made puddings – readers recommend the cheesecake (£4.50). In winter they do Sunday roasts (£8.25), and in summer you'll find tasty locally smoked food. Nice furnishings include a mix of different-sized tables with high winged wall settles, carved pews, chapel and carver chairs, and there are lots of pictures mainly from Imperial days. The main front windows are said to have come from the stern of a ship. There's a log and coal fire in a huge fireplace (as the paintwork between the black beams suggests, it can smoke a bit if the wind's strongly in the east). There's an attractive and homely back dining room on the right. The welcoming landlord (who loves cricket) serves a couple of changing guests, usually from fairly local brewers, such as Ballards and Triple fff, alongside well kept Stonehenge Heelstone and Wadworths 6X on handpump. As well as decent wines and farm cider, they've 15 malt whiskies, and an espresso machine. The two pub jack russells are called Badger and Piper, and there's an african grey parrot called Steerpike. There are old-fashioned garden seats on the small front terrace, with some picnic-sets on the grass there, and more in a back garden which has a wendy house; there's also a little aviary. With a playing field opposite, and chickens and a horse paddock out behind, the pub looks over a chalk stream that you ford to arrive – it's best to use an alternative route in winter, when it can be quite deep. *(Recommended by Colin Moore, Mike Gorton, David and Elizabeth Tyzack, Kevin Thorpe, John Coatsworth, Bob and Margaret Holder, J Stickland, Mark Barker, Glen and Nola Armstrong, Dr D G Twyman)*

Free house ~ Licensee Noel Cardew ~ Real ale ~ Bar food (12-2.30, 6.30-10) ~ (01980) 629279 ~ Children in restaurant and family room ~ Dogs allowed in bar ~ Open 11-3, 6-11; 12-3, 7-10.30 Sun; closed 26 Dec, 1 Jan

NORTON ST8884 Map 2

Vine Tree (food award) (wine award)

4 miles from M4 junction 17; A429 towards Malmesbury, then left at Hullavington, Sherston signpost, then follow Norton signposts; in village turn right at Foxley signpost, which takes you into Honey Lane

In an attractively converted 18th-c mill house, this civilised dining pub is a popular place for a well cooked meal. Three beautifully kept little rooms open together, with limited edition and sporting prints, a mock-up mounted pig's mask (used for a game that involves knocking coins off its nose and ears), lots of stripped pine, big church candles on the tables (the lighting's very gentle), and some old settles; look out for the friendly pub dog Clementine. There are picnic-sets in a two-acre garden which includes a pretty walled terrace with a lion fountain and urns of flowers, and a good well fenced separate play area; two boules pitches. It's best to book if you want to eat here, especially at weekends. Besides baguettes made with home-baked bread (from £5.75, not Friday or Saturday evenings), a wide choice of imaginative (but not cheap) seasonally changing dishes might include foie gras and chicken liver terrine or oak-smoked salmon and prawns (£5.95), woodland mushroom and feta risotto (£8.50), shepherd's pie (£9.50), braised lamb shoulder with irish stew and herb dumplings (£10.95), gilt head bream with lemon grass and sweet basil broth or marinated yellow fin tuna medallion with seaweed and chinese egg noodles (£12.95), and roast pork wrapped in prosciutto (£13.50), with puddings such as white and dark chocolate torte (£4.95); they do a choice of three good Sunday roasts. One dining area is no smoking. Although the emphasis is on eating, there's a buoyant atmosphere, and drinkers do pop in; helpful attentive staff serve well kept Archers or Butcombe Bitter and, from an impressive list, around 16 wines are available by the glass. It's not the easiest place to find, so it feels more remote than its proximity to the motorway would suggest. *(Recommended by R Huggins, D Irving, E McCall, T McLean, Andrew Shore, Maria Williams, Esther and John Sprinkle, Jane Legate, Mrs Sally Lloyd, Simon and Mandy King, M G Hart, Dr and Mrs A K Clarke, Alice Harper, John and Joan Nash, Miss A G Drake, J Stickland, Betsy and Peter Little, Richard Stancomb)*

Free house ~ Licensees Charles Walker and Tiggi Wood ~ Real ale ~ Bar food (12-2(2.30 Sat), 7-9.30(9.45 Fri-Sat); 12-3, 7-9.30 Sun) ~ Restaurant ~ (01666) 837654 ~ Children welcome ~ Dogs welcome ~ Open 12-3, 6-11; 12-10.30 Sun

OGBOURNE ST ANDREW SU1974 Map 2

Wheatsheaf

A345 N of Marlborough

With an attractive décor, this roadside pub (heavily interlined curtains keep out the traffic noise at night) is a civilised place to stop for a meal. A central bar servery has a dining area on one side and a more informally mixed area on the other, with varying sizes and styles of table, and all sorts of different types of seating; a back extension adds even more space for diners. A cheerful sprinkling of scatter cushions, subtle wall lighting and several gently shaded table lamps give a relaxed and cosy feel, and the chalky grey walls have a profuse and interesting variety of mainly black and white pictures – especially show business, horse trials or steeplechasing, with some striking modern Ostrer prints on the way to the lavatories. As you come in from the back car park, the spotlessly kept kitchen is in plain view on your left, doing enjoyable, generously served dishes such as soup (£4), baguettes with chips (£6), tuna cakes, butterfly prawns or caesar salad (£6; £10 large), vegetable stroganoff (£9.95), half shoulder of roast lamb or duck (£13.50), and sirloin steak (£15), with puddings such as chocolate brownie with hot chocolate sauce (£5); swift service. Well kept Bass and Wadworths 6X on handpump, and decent wines. There are tables out on a pretty back terrace and in a scented garden; no muddy boots inside. They don't do cooked breakfasts, but the bedroom price includes a continental breakfast which you find in the room fridge. *(Recommended by Ann and Colin Hunt, Darly Graton, Graeme Gulibert, Brian and Janet Ainscough, Mr and Mrs D Renwick)*

Free house ~ Licensee Lesley Gallagher ~ Real ale ~ Bar food (12-2.30, 7-9.30; not Sun evening) ~ (01672) 841229 ~ Well behaved children ~ Open 11-3, 7-11; 12-3 Sun; closed Sun evening ~ Bedrooms: /£60B

PITTON SU2131 Map 2

Silver Plough 🍷

Village signposted from A30 E of Salisbury (follow brown tourist signs)

Well placed for good downland and woodland walks, this pleasant country dining pub has plenty to keep your eyes busy: the comfortable front bar has hundreds of antique boot-warmers and stretchers, pewter and china tankards, copper kettles, toby jugs, earthenware and glass rolling pins, painted clogs, glass net-floats, and coach horns and so forth hang from the black beams. Seats on the turkey carpet include half a dozen red-velvet-cushioned antique oak settles (one elaborately carved, beside a very fine reproduction of an Elizabethan oak table), and the timbered white walls are hung with Thorburn and other game bird prints, original Craven Hill sporting cartoons, and a big naval battle glass-painting. The back bar is simpler, but still has a big winged high-backed settle, cased antique guns, substantial pictures, and – like the front room – flowers on its tables. There's a skittle alley next to the snug bar; cribbage, shove-ha'penny, and piped music. Badger Best, Sussex Bitter, Tanglefoot and a guest are well kept on handpump under light blanket pressure; they've a fine wine list including eight by the glass, and some well priced and carefully chosen bottles, a good range of country wines, and a worthy choice of spirits. Generously served bar food includes baguettes (from £4.95), ploughman's (£5.50), various salads (from £5.50), beef lasagne (£8.25), and vegetable balti (£9.95), with evening dishes such as salmon with pink peppercorn sauce (£10.95), and half a roast shoulder of lamb with mint and garlic gravy (£13.25), and home-made puddings (£3.95); children's meals (£3.95). On Sunday the menu is more limited, and they do a choice of roasts. The restaurant is no smoking. A quiet lawn has picnic-sets and other tables under cocktail parasols. *(Recommended by W W Burke, Dennis Jenkin, Susan and John Douglas, Keith and Margaret Kettell, Phyl and Jack Street, Brenda and Rob Fincham, Liz and Tony Colman, J P Humphery, Dr D G Twyman, Father Robert Marsh)*

Badger ~ Tenant Hughen Riley ~ Real ale ~ Bar food (12-2, 7-9; 12-2.30, 6.30-8.30 Sun) ~ Restaurant ~ (01722) 712266 ~ Children in eating area of bar ~ Open 11-3, 6-11; 12-3.30, 6.30-10.30 Sun ~ Bedrooms: /£50S

POULSHOT ST9559 Map 2

Raven

Village signposted off A361 Devizes—Seend

Prettily placed across from the village green, this is a classic country pub, with well kept Wadworths IPA, 6X and maybe a seasonal ale tapped straight from the cask. Two intimate black-beamed rooms are well furnished with sturdy tables and chairs and comfortable banquettes; the attractive dining room is no smoking. Well cooked by the landlord, generously served bar food might include specials such as hungarian goulash, home-made salmon and fishcakes with lemon butter sauce or lamb and apricots (£8.80), with other dishes such as home-made soup (£3.35), filled ciabatta (from £5.20), devilled whitebait (£4.65), vegetable curry (£7.80), home-made lasagne (£8.60), haddock pie (£9.65), and pork stroganoff (£11.80);

puddings might include bread and butter pudding (£3.55). The gents' is outside. More reports please. *(Recommended by Mr and Mrs J Brown, John Beeken)*

Wadworths ~ Tenants Philip and Susan Henshaw ~ Real ale ~ Bar food (not Mon) ~ Restaurant ~ (01380) 828271 ~ Children in restaurant ~ Dogs allowed in bar ~ Open 11-2.30, 6.30-11; 12-3, 7-10.30 Sun; closed Mon except bank hol lunchtime

RAMSBURY SU2771 Map 2

Bell

Signed off B4192 NW of Hungerford, or A4 W

This spotlessly kept dining pub is nicely positioned in a smartly attractive village. Comfortably modernised, the airy bar has exposed beams, cream-washed walls, and two woodburning stoves; fresh flowers on polished tables add a welcome touch of colour. Victorian stained-glass panels in one of the two sunny bay windows look out on to the quiet village street. There's a pleasantly relaxed chatty atmosphere, and the friendly landlord and his staff are welcoming. Good bar food might include sausages and mash, fish and chips, burger, and beef stir fry (£8), or you can eat from the more elaborate à la carte menu in the bar, with dishes such as smoked duck salad or black pudding with scallops and shallot jus (£7), bass with cherry tarte tartin and vermouth cream or lamb chump with potato purée, ratatouille and rosemary coulis (£12), with delicious puddings such as treacle tart (£6); they do two courses for £17.50. Tables can be reserved in the restaurant. Wadworths IPA, 6X and an occasional guest beer are well kept on handpump. There are picnic-sets on the raised lawn; roads lead from this quiet village into the downland on all sides. The landlord has plans to add bedrooms in 2005. *(Recommended by Mark and Ruth Brock, Michael Gray, Peter B Brown)*

Free house ~ Licensee Jeremy Wilkins ~ Real ale ~ Bar food (not Sun evening) ~ Restaurant ~ (01672) 520230 ~ Children welcome ~ Dogs allowed in bar ~ Open 12-3, 6-11; 12-3, 7-10.30 Sun

ROWDE ST9762 Map 2

George & Dragon (🍴) 🍷

A342 Devizes—Chippenham

Fish-lovers can choose from a great selection of seafood, delivered fresh from Cornwall, at this attractive old dining pub. The seasonally changing menu (with the quality and price of an upmarket restaurant) might typically include grilled sardines (£4.50), grilled lemon sole or thai curry with hake, salmon and squid (£14), and steamed bass with ginger, soy sauce and spring onion or roast razor clams with garlic and olive oil (£16), with non-fishy choices such as guinea fowl and lentil soup (£3.50), cheese soufflé (£5, £9 main course), and fillet steak (£17); puddings such as pecan tart with crème fraîche (£5), and they do a selection of cheeses (£7). No smoking dining room; if Ralph the ginger tom is around he may try and help you finish your meal. The bar is tastefully furnished, with plenty of dark wood, and a log fire with a fine collection of brass keys by it; the bare-floored dining room has quite plain tables and chairs, and is close enough to the bar to keep a pleasant chatty atmosphere. A couple of changing well kept real ales on handpump are from breweries such as Archers and Butcombe, and they've organic cider, and continental beers and lagers; shove-ha'penny, cribbage and dominoes. A pretty garden at the back has tables and chairs; the Kennet & Avon Canal is nearby. *(Recommended by Jane and Graham Rooth, Richard Pierce, Mike Gorton, Tina and David Woods-Taylor)*

Free house ~ Licensees Tim and Helen Withers ~ Real ale ~ Bar food (not Sun or Mon) ~ Restaurant ~ (01380) 723053 ~ Children in eating area of bar and restaurant ~ Dogs allowed in bar ~ Open 12-3, 7-11(10.30 Sun); closed Mon lunchtime, 25 Dec, 1 Jan

Real ale to us means beer which has matured naturally in its cask – not pressurised or filtered.

SALISBURY SU1429 Map 2

Haunch of Venison

Minster Street, opposite Market Cross

Worth popping into for a drink if you're in Salisbury, this cosy pub was constructed over 650 years ago to house craftsmen working on the cathedral spire. The two tiny downstairs rooms are quite spit-and-sawdust in spirit, with massive beams in the white ceiling, stout oak benches built into the timbered walls, black and white floor tiles, and an open fire. A tiny snug opens off the entrance lobby. They serve only lunchtime light snacks such as wraps with various fillings, chips, and sausage sandwich (all £2.50). If you want something more substantial, you can also eat in the cosy panelled no smoking upstairs restaurant, which has a small-paned window looking down on to the main bar, and a splendid fireplace that dates back to the building's early years; behind glass in a small wall slit is the smoke-preserved mummified hand of an 18th-c card sharp still clutching his cards. Courage Best, Wadworths 6X and a guest such as Hop Back Summer Lightning are served on handpump from a unique pewter bar counter, with a rare set of antique taps for gravity-fed spirits and liqueurs. They've also 55 malt whiskies, decent wines, and a range of brandies; chess, dominoes and piped music. *(Recommended by Andrea Rampley, Peter and Anne Hollindale, Ann and Colin Hunt, Dr and Mrs A K Clarke, the Didler, Dr D G Twyman)*

Scottish Courage ~ Lease Anthony Leroy, Rupert Willcocks ~ Real ale ~ Bar food (lunchtime only, light snacks) ~ Restaurant ~ (01722) 322024 ~ Children in restaurant ~ Dogs allowed in bar ~ Open 11-11; 12-10 Sun; closed 25 Dec, 1 Jan

SEEND ST9461 Map 2

Barge

Seend Cleeve; signposted off A361 Devizes—Trowbridge, between Seend village and signpost to Seend Head

The bar at this popular attractive canalside pub has an unusual barge-theme décor, and intricately painted Victorian flowers cover the ceilings and run in a waist-high band above the deep green lower walls. A distinctive medley of eye-catching seats includes milk churns, unusual high-backed chairs (made from old boat-parts), a seat made from an upturned canoe, and the occasional small oak settle among the rugs on the parquet floor, while the walls have big sentimental engravings. The watery theme continues with a well stocked aquarium, and there's also a pretty Victorian fireplace, big bunches of dried flowers, and red velvet curtains for the big windows; fruit machine and piped music. Outside, the neatly kept waterside garden is an excellent place to watch the bustle of boats on the Kennet & Avon Canal – old streetlamps let you linger there after dark, and moorings by the humpy bridge are very useful for thirsty bargees. Butcombe, Wadworths IPA and 6X are well kept on handpump, and they've lots of malt whiskies, around half a dozen wines by the glass, and mulled wine in winter; good coffee too. Uniformed staff serve generous well liked lunchtime bar food such as good sandwiches (£3.95; soup and a sandwich £5.95), and filled baked potatoes (from £5.25), with other enjoyable dishes such as home-cooked ham and eggs (£8.50), roasted vegetable and feta strudel (£9), tasty steak, mushroom and ale pie (£9.50), rump steak (£9.95), and chicken breast with smoked cheese and wrapped in bacon (£10.50), with puddings (£4.25). The restaurant extension is no smoking. They recommend booking for meals, especially at weekends; it gets extremely busy when the weather's fine. *(Recommended by Clifford Payton, Pat and Robert Watt, Joyce and Maurice Cottrell, P R and S A White, W F C Phillips, Dr and Mrs M E Wilson, Brian and Anita Randall, Kevin Thorpe, Keith and Margaret Kettell, Dr and Mrs A K Clarke, Michael Doswell, Peter and Audrey Dowsett, Norman and Sheila Davies)*

Wadworths ~ Tenant Christopher Moorley Long ~ Real ale ~ Bar food (12-2(2.30 Sun and bank hols), 7-9.30 (10 Fri-Sat)) ~ Restaurant ~ (01380) 828230 ~ Children welcome ~ Dogs allowed in bar ~ Open 11-2.30, 6-11 (all day in school summer hols); 12-11(10.30 Sun) Sat

STOURTON ST7734 Map 2

Spread Eagle

Church Lawn; follow Stourhead brown signs off B3092, N of junction with A303 just W of Mere

The attractively decorated interior of this civilised and welcoming old pub has antique panel-back settles, a mix of new and old solid tables and chairs, handsome fireplaces with good winter log fires, smoky old sporting prints, prints of Stourhead, and standard lamps or brass swan's-neck wall lamps. One room by the entrance has armchairs, a longcase clock and a corner china cupboard. There's a welcoming atmosphere, and service is very friendly. The pub is owned by the National Trust, and has a delightful setting among other elegant National Trust stone buildings at the head of Stourhead Lake. The enjoyable, reasonably priced bar menu includes sandwiches (from £1.95), soup (£2.95), ploughman's (from £4.95), salads (£5.95), spaghetti bolognese (£5.95), steak and kidney pie (£6.50), and there are a couple of daily specials such as greek-style salad (£4.95), and chicken and mushroom pie (£6.50). In the evening the à la carte menu (which you can also eat from in the bar) might include dishes such as wild mushroom and cashew stroganoff (£10.45), swordfish steak (£10.95), and rack of lamb with ratatouille and rösti potatoes (£14.95); tasty puddings such as sticky toffee pudding (£3.25). Butcombe Best and Courage Best are well kept on handpump; dominoes, scrabble and piped music. There are benches in the courtyard behind. More reports please. *(Recommended by Geoffrey G Lawrance, John and Jane Hayter, John and Joan Nash, Colin and Janet Roe, S P Watkin, P A Taylor, R Michael Richards, John Doe, Dr and Mrs M E Wilson)*

Free house ~ Licensee Andy Martin ~ Real ale ~ Bar food (12-3, 6-9; cold dishes 12-9) ~ Restaurant (evening) ~ (01747) 840587 ~ Children welcome ~ Open 11-11; 12-10.30 Sun ~ Bedrooms: £60B/£90B

WHITLEY ST8866 Map 2

Pear Tree

Off B3353 S of Corsham, at Atworth 1½, Purlpit 1 signpost; or from A350 Chippenham—Melksham in Beanacre turn off on Westlands Lane at Whitley 1 signpost, then left and right at B3353

Wiltshire Dining Pub of the Year

This honey-coloured stone farmhouse continues to charm readers with its imaginative food, tempting choice of drinks, excellent service and comfortable bedrooms. Although you'll be made to feel welcome if you just want a drink, you'll probably feel left out if you don't have something to eat as the food is delicious. The menu might include penne pasta with chicken liver, sage and parsley sauce or crispy pork belly with shaved fennel, rocket, lemon and capers (£5.50), home-made pork, tomato and basil sausages with creamed mash and red wine sauce (£10.50), grilled aubergine and chick pea cakes with toasted hazelnuts, pecans, oregano and mint (£11.50), braised lamb shoulder with mash potato and grilled aubergine (£14.95), poached lemon sole with lemon risotto and tarragon butter sauce (£16), with puddings such as iced lemon meringue pie (£5); you can also get sandwiches (from £5.50), and they do a two-course Sunday lunch (£12.50, £15 for three courses); 25 or so decent wines are available by the glass (including champagne), and Wadworths 6X, and a couple of changing guests such as Palmers Copper Ale and Stonehenge Pigswill are well kept on handpump; lots of speciality teas too. The front bar has quite a pubby feel, with cushioned window seats, some stripped shutters, a mix of dining chairs around good solid tables, a variety of country pictures and a Wiltshire Regiment sampler on the walls, a little fireplace on the left, and a lovely old stripped stone one on the right. Candlelit at night, the popular but unhurried big back restaurant (you may need to book) has green dining chairs, quite a mix of tables, and a pitched ceiling at one end with a quirky farmyard theme – wrought-iron cockerels and white scythe sculpture. A bright spacious garden room opens on to a terrace with good teak furniture and views over the carefully maintained gardens, which are prettily lit at night to show features like the ruined pigsty; they've recently added a new terrace; boules. Half of the eight well equipped bedrooms are in a courtyard block behind, and the rest are above the pub; excellent breakfasts. *(Recommended by Richard and Judy Winn, Mrs Sally Lloyd, John and Jane Hayter, Alistair Caie, Di and Mike Gillam, Paul and Annette Hallett, Bill and Jessica Ritson, Andrew Shore, Maria Williams, Lyn Huxtable, Richard Seers, Dr and Mrs A K Clarke, Paul Humphreys, Danielle Nay, Inga and Keith Rutter, Gwen Griffiths, David Boult, A Sadler, Mike Pugh, Joyce and Maurice Cottrell)*

Free house ~ Licensees Martin and Debbie Still ~ Real ale ~ Bar food (12-2(2.30 Sun), 6.30-9.30(10 Fri-Sat)) ~ Restaurant ~ (01225) 709131 ~ Children welcome ~ Dogs allowed in bar ~ Open 11-3, 6-11; 12-10.30 Sun; closed 25-26 Dec, 1 Jan ~ Bedrooms: £75B/£90B

WOODBOROUGH SU1159 Map 2

Seven Stars

Off A345 S of Marlborough: from Pewsey follow Woodborough signposts, then in Woodborough bear left following Bottlesford signposts

There's plenty to keep wine drinkers happy at this pretty thatched red brick house (a good blend of traditional English pub with a strong gallic influence): the wine list is exemplary, with about ten wines by the glass (including plenty of french), and interesting bin ends. Although locals do drop in for a drink, food is the big draw, and it's a good idea to book as there can be a long wait when they are busy. Well cooked dishes from a changing menu (they receive regular deliveries from France) might include fried pigeon breast (£5.95), mixed smoked fish platter (£6.75), cassoulet or spicy crab cakes with sweet chilli sauce (£12.75), seared scallops with bacon, spring onions and hoi sin sauce or roast lamb with garlic and rosemary (£14.75), with puddings such as lemon soufflé and raspberry crème brûlée (£3.95), and a french cheeseboard (£5.95); they do smaller helpings for children, and on Sundays you can get two courses for £12.50. The dining room is no smoking. The bar is traditionally furnished, with polished bricks by the bar counter, hunting prints, attractively moulded panelling, a hot coal fire in the old range at one end, a big log fire at the other, a pleasant mix of antique settles and country furniture, cast-iron-framed tables, and cosy nooks here and there. You'll find Badger Best, Fullers London Pride and Wadworths 6X on handpump; sophisticated piped music. There are seven acres of riverside gardens; they've a black cat (who may try and get at milk left on tables). *(Recommended by Dr and Mrs M E Wilson, Adam and Joan Bunting, Roger and Eileen Crosby, Babla Sen, Leo Horton, J Stickland, Dr D G Twyman)*

Free house ~ Licensees Philippe and Kate Cheminade ~ Real ale ~ Bar food (see opening times) ~ Restaurant ~ (01672) 851325 ~ Well behaved children ~ Dogs allowed in bar ~ Open 12-3, 6-11; 12-3 Sun; closed Sun evening, all day Mon except bank hol lunchtime, then cl Tues

LUCKY DIP

Besides the fully inspected pubs, you might like to try these Lucky Dips recommended to us and described by readers (if you do, please send us reports: www.goodguides.co.uk).

ALDBOURNE SU2675

Crown [The Square]: Friendly local prettily facing village pond, enjoyable imaginative home cooking using seasonal produce, good service, well kept Greene King IPA and Wadworths 6X, comfortable two-part beamed lounge, oak bar furnishings and interesting bric-a-brac, unusual huge log fireplace linking to public bar, small nicely laid out dining room; may be quiet piped music; tables under cocktail parasols in neat courtyard *(Mrs Jill Silversides, Barry Brown)*

ALVEDISTON ST9723

☆ *Crown* [off A30 W of Salisbury]: 15th-c thatched inn in a pretty spot, three cosy very low-beamed partly panelled rooms, deep pink paintwork, two inglenook fireplaces, no smoking dining area, well kept Ringwood Best and guest beers, enjoyable food running up to steaks, darts, cribbage, dominoes; piped music; children welcome, dogs allowed in bar, neatly kept attractive garden, good bedrooms *(Dr Sally Hanson, Dave Braisted, LYM)*

AVEBURY SU0969

Red Lion [A361]: Much-modernised and substantially extended from pretty thatched front part, in the heart of the stone circles; quick friendly service even when packed, well kept ales such as Stonehenge and Wadworths 6X, open fires, well run food bar, no smoking area and restaurant extension – huge choice inc Sun carvery; may be piped music; children welcome *(LYM, Richard Pierce, T R and B C Jenkins, Mary Kirman and Tim Jefferson)*

BADBURY SU1980

Plough [A346 just S of M4 junction 15]: Handy for Swindon's new hospital, large friendly rambling bar area, light and airy no smoking dining room (children allowed) looking over road to Vale of the White Horse with pianola and papers to read, well kept Arkells 2B, 3B and Kingsdown, decent wines, wide blackboard choice of usual food inc afternoon snacks, friendly efficient service; darts, piped music; children welcome, play area in sunny garden above, open all day *(Kevin Thorpe, Michael and Alison Sandy, Mark and Ruth Brock, Dr and Mrs A K Clarke, Mrs Pat Crabb)*

BARFORD ST MARTIN SU0531

☆ *Barford Inn* [A30/B3098 W of Salisbury]: The Israeli landlord who gave this pleasantly old-fashioned 16th-c coaching inn such a distinctive touch is moving to the Pembroke Arms in Wilton; panelled front bar with big log fire, other chatty interlinking rooms and bars, no smoking restaurant; has had friendly staff, enjoyable bar food and well kept Badger Best; disabled access and lavatories, children welcome, dogs allowed in bar, terrace tables, more in back garden, good bedrooms, open all day (cl Sun afternoon); reports on new regime please *(LYM, Edward Mirzoeff, Dr D G Twyman)*

BLUNSDON SU1385

Crown [Ermin St (A419), just N of Swindon]: Much refurbished Arkells pub, pleasant and comfortable, with good wine range, Arkells JRA and 3B from heavily carved bar counter, button-back sofas and armchair in beamed and flagstoned corner with log fire, plank panelling and stripped stone, good choice of food from baguettes to red mullet and steak, neat panelled and carpeted dining area with lots of pewter and china; 21 bedrooms *(Ian Phillips)*

BOX ST8268

Bear [High St]: 18th-c, with friendly staff, welcoming atmosphere, log fires, enjoyable reasonably priced food, well kept Bass, Wadworths 6X and changing guest beers; bedrooms *(Colin Hobbs)*

BRADFORD LEIGH ST8362

Plough [B2109 N of Bradford]: Emphasis on good food choice in extended and smartened up dining area, efficient service, Moles and Wadworths 6X, log fire; darts and pool; children welcome, nice seats outside, play area *(Susan and Nigel Wilson, Mark Flynn)*

BRADFORD-ON-AVON ST8359

☆ *Beehive* [A363 out towards Trowbridge]: Simple cheerful old-fashioned L-shaped pub nr canal on outskirts, half a dozen interesting well kept ales on handpump or tapped from the cask, good service, huge helpings of traditional food esp substantial sandwiches (some hot) with baskets of chips, good range of wines, 19th-c playbills, cricketing prints and cigarette cards, darts; children and dogs welcome, resident cats; attractive good-sized informal back garden, play area, barbecues *(BB, Dr and Mrs M E Wilson, Pete Baker, Dr and Mrs A K Clarke, Sue Demont, Tim Barrow, Mike Gorton)*

Bunch of Grapes [Silver St]: Dim-lit wine-bar style décor, cask seats and rugs on bare boards in small front room, bigger tables on composition floor of roomier main bar, well kept Smiles and Youngs ales, good range of wines and malt whiskies, good choice of interesting reasonably priced food in bar and upstairs eating area *(BB, Dr and Mrs A K Clarke)*

Cross Guns [Avoncliff, outside town]: Listed for its position, with floodlit gardens steeply terraced above the bridges, aqueducts and river; stripped-stone low-beamed bar with 16th-c inglenook, upstairs river-view restaurant, well kept Bass, a house beer, Worthington and a guest beer, lots of malt whiskies and country wines; loudspeaker food announcements, piped music, and the pub can get very busy indeed, when service and housekeeping can come under pressure; children welcome, open all day *(LYM, Andrew Shore, Maria Williams, Paul Hopton, Richard Pierce, Gloria Bax, Michael Bayne, Dr and Mrs A K Clarke)*

Riverside [St Margarets St]: Old stone-built riverside pub, huge fireplace in big beamed bar, Badger Tanglefoot, Butcombe and Wadworths 6X, food inc decent baguettes, pool in large games room; tables out on gravel terrace hedged off from river *(Neil and Anita Christopher, Dr and Mrs A K Clarke)*

Three Horseshoes [Frome Rd, by station car park entrance]: Cosy and chatty grown-up pub doing well under current management, well kept mostly local beers, good substantial food, friendly service, plenty of nooks and corners, small restaurant; tables on terrace *(Ted George, Dr and Mrs A K Clarke, Dr and Mrs M E Wilson)*

BRATTON ST9152

Duke [B3098 E of Westbury]: Comfortable, neat and civilised open-plan pub with dining area, very good generous food (freshly cooked, so may take a while) inc lunchtime bargains, well kept ales inc Moles, quick pleasant service, exemplary lavatories; darts and fruit machine in public area, piped music; ancient whalebone arch to enclosed side garden, bedrooms *(BB, Bryan Simmons)*

BREMHILL ST9772

Dumb Post [Hazeland, just NW of Calne]: Pleasantly basic old country local with welcoming landlord, staff and parrot, well kept ales such as Archers Blackjack and Wadworths 6X, good cheap home-made bar food (not Weds) from soup and sandwiches up, woodburner, old guns and farm tools; attractive views, garden, great walking country *(Dick and Madeleine Brown)*

BROAD HINTON SU1076

Crown [off A4361 about 5 miles S of Swindon]: Open-plan slightly old-fashioned village inn, decent food from baguettes to some interesting dishes (freshly made, so may be a wait) in roomy and comfortably plush eating area, well kept Arkells ales, good range of wines and good coffee, welcoming helpful uniformed staff, no smoking area; may be piped music; unusual gilded inn sign, attractive and sheltered spacious garden with fishpond and play area; bedrooms *(LYM, Francis Johnston)*

BROMHAM ST9764

Oliver Cromwell [A342]: Neatly kept pub with good value quickly served home-made bar food (should book for lunch – you can even order lobster), Sun lunch in restaurant, Wadworths real ales, farm ciders, decent wines, friendly landlord, flowers on tables; fine view over Roundway Down Civil War battlefield – good small museum in bar *(Richard Pierce)*

BROUGHTON GIFFORD ST8764

Bell on the Common: Picturesque stone-built local on huge village green, traditional furnishings, friendly service, well kept Wadworths from handpumps on back wall, big coal fire, dining lounge full of copper and old country prints, bar with local photographs old and new, small pool room with darts and juke box, quiz night; children welcome, charming garden (occasional pig roasts and live music), bowls club next door *(Dr and Mrs M E Wilson, Dr and Mrs A K Clarke)*

BURCOMBE SU0631

Ship: Cosy two-level dining pub with unpretentious bistro atmosphere, low beams, panelling and window seats, two log fires, pleasant décor, candles and soft lighting, young chef/landlord doing good choice of good value fresh food inc enterprising dishes and children's menu, friendly efficient service, decent wines, no smoking area; unobtrusive piped music; children welcome, tables on front terrace and in peaceful riverside garden, beautiful village *(David Cuckney)*

CALNE ST9971

Lansdowne Strand [The Strand]: Hotel with two welcoming bars, one with comfortable sofas, the other with panelling and seating reflecting the building's 16th-c origins, roaring fires, good helpings of varied sensibly priced enjoyable home-made food here and in good-sized restaurant; bedrooms *(Diane Thompson)*

CASTLE COMBE ST8379

Salutation [The Gibb; B4039 Acton Turville—Chippenham, nr Nettleton]: Roomy old pub with plenty of beamery, choice of seating areas inc comfortable lounge and locals' bar, huge handsome fireplace, separate raftered thatched and timbered restaurant, welcoming landlord, well kept ales such as Abbey Bellringer, Fullers London Pride, Moles and Wadworths 6X, good choice of wines, enjoyable promptly served food from big baguettes up, children's dishes; open all day, pretty garden with pergola *(MRSM)*

White Hart [signed off B4039 Chippenham—Chipping Sodbury]: Attractive ancient stone-built pub, beams, panelling, flagstones, seats in stone-mullioned window, lots of old local photographs; Wadworths IPA, Farmers Glory and 6X and a guest such as Adnams, nice staff, log fires, smaller lounge, family room, games room; walkers welcome (handy for Macmillan Way), tables in sheltered courtyard; in centre of this honeypot village, so can be very busy *(LYM, Richard Stancomb)*

CHARLTON ST9588

☆ *Horse & Groom* [B4040 towards Cricklade]: Friendly stone-built inn with smart but relaxing bar, old firearms, farm tools and log fire, simpler right-hand bar with hops on beams, friendly and considerate staff, wide choice of good food inc some interesting specials and good value Sun lunch, well kept Archers and Wadworths, farm cider, decent wines, restaurant; dogs welcome, tables outside, comfortable bedrooms *(LYM, Margaret and Roy Randle, Dr and Mrs A K Clarke)*

CHERHILL SU0370

Black Horse [Main Rd (A4 E of Calne)]: Popular beamed oak-panelled dining pub, linked areas crowded with tables for wide range of good value generous standard food, prompt service, friendly landlord, no smoking area, huge fireplace, well kept Wadworths 6X; children welcome, good walking country *(David Crook)*

CHILMARK ST9632

☆ *Black Dog* [B3089 Salisbury—Hindon]: Comfortably modernised and attractive 15th-c beamed pub with good food (but orders may stop very early if chef busy), well kept ales inc local brews, good value house wines, friendly helpful staff, several smallish relaxing rooms with a log fire in each (armchairs by one and fossil ammonite in another's fireplace), good local atmosphere (regulars turn up on horseback); dogs welcome, tables out in good-sized roadside garden with terrace *(Arthur Baker, LYM, Julie and Bill Ryan, Douglas and Ann Hare)*

CHIPPENHAM ST9273

Four Seasons [Market Pl, by Buttercross]: Lively and friendly, with fine range of well kept sensibly priced ales, also farm ciders and malt whiskies, enjoyable bar food from sandwiches up inc sports event specials, attractive pictures and decorations inc quaintly recast proverbs and prayers *(Richard Pierce)*

Kingfisher [Hungerdown Lane]: Lively local with well kept Wadworths 6X, interesting malt whiskies and brandies, good lunchtime sandwiches and salads, fine old prints; soft piped music, board games, frequent music and good quiz nights; tables outside *(Richard Pierce)*

Old Road Tavern [Old Rd, by N side of station]: Traditional games-oriented public bar, two-part lounge, well kept Courage Best, Fullers London Pride, Greene King Old Speckled Hen and a guest beer, cheap lunchtime food from sandwiches up; frequent wknd live music; pleasant secluded little back garden *(Pete Baker)*

CHITTERNE ST9843

Kings Head [B390 between Heytesbury and Shrewton]: Quiet Salisbury Plain oasis, decent food inc good fish menu, woodburner, lovely hanging baskets in summer; bedrooms, pretty village, good walks *(Richard and Liz Dilnot, Meg and Colin Hamilton)*

CHOLDERTON SU2242

Crown [A338 Tidworth—Salisbury roundabout, just off A303]: Cheery new landlady in cosily worn-in thatched low-beamed cottage, nice local feel in L-shaped bar, simple food from sandwiches up, well kept Ringwood ales, efficient service, nice open fire, small family dining area; tables outside, handy for rare breeds farm *(Edward Mirzoeff, Pat and Robert Watt)*

CHRISTIAN MALFORD ST9679

☆ *Mermaid* [B4069 Lyneham—Chippenham, 3½ miles from M4 junction 17]: Long cheerful bar divided into areas, copious sound food from sandwiches and bar snacks to wide choice of main dishes and good Sun lunch, well kept Wadworths 6X, decent whiskies and wines, some attractive pictures, fresh flowers, pleasant service; bar billiards, darts, fruit machine, subdued piped music; garden tables, bedrooms *(BB, Michael Doswell)*

CLYFFE PYPARD SU0776

Goddard Arms: Unpretentious 16th-c village pub with log fire and raised dining area in split-level main bar, small sitting room with another fire and two old armchairs, down-to-earth chatty and welcoming licensees, well kept Wadworths 6X and guest beers, good value straightforward fresh food, back skittle alley with prints, paintings, sculptures, second-hand books and records for sale (busy music nights, and pool room off, with darts, cribbage etc); no cards taken; open all day wknds, sculpture garden, bedrooms, tiny pretty thatched village in lovely countryside *(Guy Vowles, Pete Baker, Mrs Pat Crabb)*

COATE SU1882

Sun [A4259]: Large pub with partly no smoking bar/lounge, family dining room with conservatory extension, three Arkells ales, good soft drinks choice, wide choice of food; piped music, games machines, quiz night Mon; garden with terrace and play area *(CMW, JJW)*

CODFORD ST9639

George [High St]: Talented new chef/landlord doing good food at attractive prices *(anon)*

COLERNE ST8171

Six Bells [High St]: Compact and cheerful local with friendly enthusiastic landlord, consistently well kept beers, good value restaurant-quality food in four-table dining area, good service; skittle alley, video games, sensible piped music, folk club Thurs *(David Carty, Dr and Mrs A K Clarke)*

COLLINGBOURNE KINGSTON SU2355

Barleycorn [A338]: Welcoming smartly kept village pub with several well kept ales such as Hook Norton Old Hooky, Charles Wells Bombardier and Wadworths, wide blackboard choice of affordable food from fresh sandwiches to massive steaks, decent wines, quick friendly service, pool room, attractive restaurant, exemplary lavatories; piped music; tables outside *(Peter and Audrey Dowsett, J Stickland)*

COMPTON BASSETT SU0372

White Horse: Good choice of food inc good value two-course wkdy lunch, efficient cheerful service, well kept Wadworths 6X and guest beers *(Mr and Mrs G Ives, Tony Beaulah)*

COOMBE BISSETT SU1026

☆ *Fox & Goose*: Spacious neatly kept open-plan pub by delightful riverside village green, good value food (small helpings available) inc fine puddings, Badger Best, K&B and Tanglefoot, reasonably priced soft drinks, decent coffee, welcoming attentive staff, rustic refectory-style tables, coal fires, large no smoking area, old prints, hanging chamber-pots, evening restaurant; can be very busy wknds, piped music (classical at lunchtime); children catered for, picnic-sets on covered terrace and in garden with play area, good wheelchair access *(Peter and Audrey Dowsett)*

CORSHAM ST8770

Flemish Weaver [High St]: New name and appealing new décor for picturesque building, friendly attentive service, enjoyable food from good ploughman's up, decent wines *(Gloria Bax)*

Hare & Hounds [Pickwick (A4 E)]: Cosy traditional local, cheerful welcoming landlord, well kept ales such as Greene King Old Speckled Hen, Hop Back Summer Lightning and Moles, enjoyable straightforward food up to steaks, several rooms inc comfortable and attractive panelled lounge with log fire; unobtrusive piped music and sports TV in busy main bar, another room with alcove seating and pool; open at lunchtimes when the Two Pigs (see main entries) is not *(Dr and Mrs A K Clarke, Gloria Bax)*

CORSLEY ST8246

Cross Keys [Lyes Green]: Welcoming new licensees, good log fires in quarry-tiled bar and partly no smoking dining area, good if not cheap food, well kept Wadworths ales, good wine choice, old scrubbed tables, darts, bar billiards and cribbage, skittle alley upstairs *(Ken and Sylvia Jones, Mr and Mrs A H Young)*

CORTON ST9340

☆ *Dove* [off A36 at Upton Lovell, SE of Warminster]: Cottagey country pub in lovely valley, attractively furnished partly flagstoned main bar with huge central log fire and good pictures, enjoyable food from baguettes to fresh fish and steaks, well kept real ales, good wines by the glass, friendly landlord and attentive staff, daily papers, no smoking conservatory; piped music; children welcome, tables on neat back lawn, comfortable wheelchair-friendly bedrooms, good fishing available *(LYM, Andrea Rampley, John Hale, Dr and Mrs M E Wilson, Rex Martyn)*

CRICKLADE SU1093

Red Lion [High St]: Welcoming and relaxed partly 16th-c former coaching inn, half a dozen or more well kept real ales, farm cider, good choice of malt whiskies, pleasant staff, interesting bric-a-brac on walls and ceilings, no music or mobile phones; neat garden *(CMW, JJW, R Huggins, D Irving, E McCall, T McLean, Richard Houghton)*

Vale [High St]: Pleasant winebar-style décor in reworked bar adjoining Georgian hotel, beams and stripped bricks and timbers, well kept ales such as Batemans, Greene King IPA, Abbot and Ruddles County, Smiles and Wadworths 6X, up-to-date food from lunchtime sandwiches, panini, baguettes and wraps to good blackboard restaurant dishes, friendly owners and efficient young staff, two dining areas with woodburners and local art for sale; newly modernised bedrooms *(Mr and Mrs G S Ayrton, R Huggins, D Irving, E McCall, T McLean)*

White Lion [High St]: Two-bar pub with three real ales such as Wychwood, good choice of soft drinks, reasonably priced food (not Sun), pleasantly relaxed restaurant, games room with pool, darts and machine; tables out under cocktail parasols behind *(CMW, JJW, David Edwards)*

CRUDWELL ST9592

Plough [A429 N of Malmesbury]: Nice timeless local feel, friendly service, quiet lounge, dining area with comfortable well padded seats and more in elevated part; well kept ales such as Archers Best and Timothy Taylors Landlord, wide range of good value food, open fires, bar with darts and pool room; can be smoky; pleasant side garden *(Dr and Mrs A K Clarke, R Huggins, D Irving, E McCall, T McLean)*

DERRY HILL ST9570

☆ ***Lansdowne Arms*** [Church Rd]: Striking and stately stone-built pub opposite one of Bowood's grand gatehouses, several civilised areas with relaxed period flavour, hearty log fire and candles in bottles, well kept Wadworths IPA, JCB, 6X and Red Shoot Forest Gold, good value wines by the glass, wide choice of interesting reasonably priced food in bar and restaurant, prompt attentive cheerful service; faint piped music; fine views, picnic-sets in neat side garden, good play area *(BB, Richard Pierce, Simon and Amanda Southwell, Sheila and Robert Robinson, Dr and Mrs A K Clarke)*

DEVIZES SU0061

Black Horse [Bath Rd (A361 by bridge)]: Pleasant canalside pub with standard reasonably priced food, Wadworths ales *(Dave Braisted)*

Moonraker [A342 Nursteed Rd]: Imposing and comfortable 1930s mock-Tudor pub with enjoyable food inc massive mixed grill, well kept Wadworths IPA and 6X, farm cider, good whiskies (expert Scottish landlord), friendly service *(Richard Pierce)*

Royal Oak [New Park St]: Plenty of dark oak, alcoves and shelves of memorabilia, well kept Fullers London Pride, open all day wknds *(Dr and Mrs A K Clarke)*

Southgate Inn [Southgate]: Recently restored by Hop Back Brewery as warm-hearted alehouse, at least three of their real ales and farm cider, continental beers on tap, welcoming landlord, a profusion of hops, thriving atmosphere; live blues nights *(Graham Brown)*

DOWNTON SU1721

Bull [A338 Salisbury—Fordingbridge]: Large friendly pub/hotel with long bar and comfortable and attractive eating area, well kept local Hop Back ales, cheery staff, dogs allowed; bedrooms *(LYM, K H Frostick)*

White Horse [The Borough]: Appealing pub doing well under newish landlord and chef, enjoyable food, good atmosphere following internal reworking, decent wines and beers *(Peter Clapperton, Dr and Mrs Michael Smith)*

Wooden Spoon [High St]: Convivial family-run local with friendly licensees, enjoyable good value food from sandwiches and baguettes to wide choice of hot dishes using local produce, inc good steaks, casseroles and Sun lunch, real ales such as Fullers, Ringwood and Youngs; children welcome *(Tony Shepherd, Mark Barker)*

EAST KNOYLE ST8830

☆ ***Seymour Arms*** [The Street; just off A350 S of Warminster]: Roomy creeper-covered stone-built black-beamed pub, Swiss chef/landlord doing good freshly made generous food inc interesting specials, well kept Wadworths IPA, 6X and JCB, cheerful service, quietly welcoming and comfortable rambling bar areas, cosy part with high-backed settle by log fire; tables in garden with play area, good value bedrooms *(BB, John and Joan Nash, Dr and Mrs A K Clarke)*

EASTERTON SU0255

Royal Oak [B3098]: Attractive comfortably renovated 16th-c thatched pub, low beams, flagstones, alcoves and soft lighting, two dining areas and separate simpler locals' bar, welcoming landlord taking pride in his Wadworths ales, good blackboard food choice inc interesting vegetarian options, good choice of wines by the glass, cafetière coffee, log fires; tables in small front garden *(Joyce and Maurice Cottrell, Michael Doswell, Andy and Jill Kassube, J Stickland)*

EASTON ROYAL SU2060

Bruce Arms [Easton Rd]: Nicely basic 19th-c local, scrubbed antique pine tables, brick floor, well kept Butts, Wadworths 6X and guest ales, Pewsey organic cider, good filled rolls; open all day Sun *(the Didler)*

EDINGTON ST9353

☆ ***Lamb*** [Westbury Rd (B3098)]: Cheerful open-plan beamed village pub with assorted pine furniture on bare boards, good log fire, reasonably priced food from soup, hot panini and ploughman's through some modern dishes to local steaks and game (young landlady's husband does the cooking, chatty father runs the bar), popular Sun lunch, well kept ales such as Otter and Ringwood Fortyniner, good changing wine choice at attractive prices, daily papers, dining room; piped music; children and dogs welcome, pleasant garden tables (access to pretty village's play area beyond), great views, good walks, cl Sun evening and Mon lunchtime *(Matthew Shackle, Alec and Susan Hamilton, Mike Gorton, Pete and Lynda Russell, Dr and Mrs A K Clarke, Meg and Colin Hamilton, Father Robert Marsh, Dr and Mrs M E Wilson)*

ENFORD SU14351

Swan [Long St, off A345]: Thatched village-owned dining pub, relaxed and friendly, with wide choice of enjoyable food, welcoming licensees, well kept local beers; dogs welcome *(D-J Gent)*

FARLEIGH WICK ST8064

Fox & Hounds [A363 Bath—Bradford, 2½ miles NW of Bradford]: Well extended low-beamed rambling pub with real ales such as Butcombe, Courage and Marstons Pedigree, some emphasis on interesting choice of enjoyable food; attractive garden *(Dr and Mrs A K Clarke, MRSM)*

FONTHILL GIFFORD ST9232

Beckford Arms [Off B3089 W of Wilton at Fonthill Bishop]: Civilised, smartly informal country house, on the edge of parkland estate, with light airy rooms, stripped bare wood, parquet floor, pleasant mix of tables, church candles, lounge bar with big log fire leading into back garden room with a high pitched plank ceiling, picture windows looking on to terrace, locals in straightforward public bar, darts, fruit machine, pool, TV, piped music, restaurant, well kept Greene King Abbot, Milk Street Gulp, Timothy Taylors Landlord and guest; good (if not cheap) bar food (12-2, 7-9), well behaved children welcome, dogs allowed in bar and bedrooms, open 12-11; 12-10.30 Sun, comfortable bedrooms *(LYM, B J Harding, Stuart Litster, Colin and Janet Roe, Dr D G Twyman, A Rees, Paul and Ursula Randall)*

FORD ST8474

White Hart [off A420 Chippenham—Bristol]: Comfortable heavily black-beamed stone-built country inn in attractive stream-side grounds, perhaps best seen as a restaurant with rooms, though it does have a good range of well kept real ales, bar food such as ploughman's, and good log fire in its ancient fireplace; good choice of wines by the glass, wide choice of restaurant food (all day Sun); piped music may obtrude; children in restaurant, pleasant bedrooms, open all day wknds *(LYM, Richard Pierce, John Close, Andrew Shore, Maria Williams, Oliver and Sue Rowell, Dr and Mrs A K Clarke, Brian and Karen Thomas, John Coatsworth, Dr Brian and Mrs Anne Hamilton, D S Cottrell, Veronica Turner, Matthew Shackle)*

GIDDEAHALL ST8574

☆ *Crown* [A420 Chippenham—Ford; keep eyes skinned as no village sign]: Interesting Tudor pub under new local owners, attractive rambling beamed and flagstoned bar, several small rooms off, tempting food, friendly staff, well kept changing ales such as Adnams Broadside, Fullers London Pride and Shepherd Neame Spitfire; some live music; comfortable bedrooms *(LYM, Roger Huggins, Tom and Alex McLean, Pete and Rosie Flower, Dave Irving, Ewan McCall)*

GREAT BEDWYN SU2764

Cross Keys [High St]: Cheerful relaxed village pub with comfortable chairs and settles, good range of generous attractively priced bar food inc good vegetarian choice, Wadworths ales, decent wines, friendly service; tables in garden with terrace, bedrooms – nr Kennet & Avon Canal and Savernake Forest *(Alette and Russell Lawson, Betsy and Peter Little, Mrs Pat Crabb)*

Three Tuns [High St]: Enterprising cooking by welcoming newish chef/landlord (former soap actor) in thriving biggish bare-boards village pub, helpful staff, well kept Flowers Original, Fullers London Pride and Wadworths 6X, traditional old-fashioned atmosphere *(Steve Price, Alette and Russell Lawson, Derek and Sylvia Stephenson)*

GREAT CHEVERELL ST9854

Bell [off B3098 Westbury—Mkt Lavington]: Quietly welcoming dining pub with comfortable chairs and settles, cosy little alcoves, enjoyable generous home-made food, well kept Courage Best and Marstons Pedigree, upstairs dining room, skittle alley; attractive village *(Richard and Liz Dilnot)*

GREAT WISHFORD SU0735

☆ *Royal Oak* [off A36 NW of Salisbury]: Friendly new licensees fresh from the Bell at Wylye, doing wide choice of enjoyable food in appealing two-bar pub with big family dining area and restaurant, pleasant décor with beams, panelling, rugs on bare boards and log fires, well kept real ales, decent wines; pretty village *(LYM)*

HANNINGTON SU1793

Jolly Tar [off B4019 W of Highworth; Queens Rd]: Relaxing beamed bar with big log fire, steps up to flagstoned and stripped stone dining area, lots of decorative china, wide food choice, well kept Arkells ales, good soft drinks choice, reasonable prices, quick friendly service, no piped music; children welcome, picnic-sets on front terrace and in big garden with play area, bedrooms, pretty village *(BB, Peter and Audrey Dowsett, CMW, JJW)*

HEDDINGTON ST9966

☆ *Ivy*: Picturesque thatched 15th-c village pub with good inglenook log fire in plain L-shaped bar, heavy low beams, timbered walls, assorted furnishings on parquet floor, brass and copper, jovial landlord and chatty locals, well kept Wadworths IPA and 6X tapped from the cask, good simple freshly prepared home-made food (not Sun-Weds evenings) from great lunchtime club sandwiches up, back family eating room, sensibly placed darts, piano, dog and cat; may be piped music; disabled access, open all day wknds, picnic-sets in front garden, attractively set hamlet *(the Didler, LYM, Pete Baker, Nigel Long, Michael Doswell)*

HIGHWORTH SU2092

☆ *Saracens Head* [High St]: Civilised and relaxed rambling bar, friendly tenants, wide choice of enjoyable blackboard food inc children's and four Sun roasts, up to six well kept ales inc Arkells 2B and 3B tapped from casks in bar area, good soft drinks choice, comfortably cushioned pews in several interesting areas around great four-way central log fireplace, timbers and panelling, no mobile phones; quiet eclectic piped music; children in eating area, tables in sheltered courtyard, open all day wkdys; comfortable bedrooms *(Peter and Audrey Dowsett, LYM, R Huggins, D Irving, E McCall, T McLean, CMW, JJW)*

HINDON ST9132

Angel [B3089 Wilton—Mere]: 18th-c flagstoned coaching inn under new management, the miscellaneous character furnishings replaced by standard chunky tables and chairs, well kept Bass and Wadworths IPA and 6X from chrome bar counter, decent wines, big fireplace (but may not have a fire going), no smoking lounge, long cream dining room with huge window showing kitchen; piped music; children in eating area, dogs allowed in bar and bedrooms, tables outside, open all day in summer, has been cl Sun evening *(KC, Andrea Rampley, LYM)*

HORTON SU0363

☆ *Bridge Inn* [off A361 Beckhampton rd on edge of Devizes]: Sturdy pale pine country-kitchen furniture on carpet or reconstituted flagstones, bargee and other photographs on red walls, log fire, end no smoking room, cheerful efficient service, good range of food from filled rolls, baguettes and bar meals to restaurant dishes, Wadworths IPA and 6X tapped from the cask, decent wines, pub cat; quiet piped pop music; disabled lavatories, picnic-sets and doves in garden fenced off from Kennet & Avon canal below *(BB, John Beeken, Dr and Mrs A K Clarke)*

HURDCOTT SU1633

Black Horse [signed off A338 N of Salisbury]: Pretty black and white pub with reliable generous food inc good Sun roasts (best to book at wknds), Wadworths 6X, quick welcoming service, attractive décor, new no smoking extension; no machines, dogs on leads and children allowed away from bar, tables in pretty garden *(David and Elizabeth Briggs)*

KINGTON LANGLEY ST9277

Hit or Miss [handy for M4 junction 17, off A350 S; Days Lane]: Olde-worlde cottage on little green in attractive village, emphasis on left-hand restaurant with good log fire, also small rather plush cricket-theme bar with no smoking area, appetising food from baguettes through familiar pub dishes to stir-fried locusts, ostrich and zebra, well kept Highgate Davenports, Timothy Taylors Landlord, Tetleys and Youngs, chatty interested landlady and friendly service, darts and pool in room off; tables outside *(Dick and Madeleine Brown, Mark and Joanna)*

KINGTON ST MICHAEL ST9077

Jolly Huntsman [handy for M4 junction 17]: Roomy stone-built pub with scrubbed tables, old-fashioned settees, good log fire, pleasant rather dark décor, friendly helpful staff, well kept Greene King IPA, Abbot, Old Speckled Hen and Ruddles and Wadworths 6X, dining end with enjoyable fresh-cooked food inc some interesting dishes; may be sports TV; six well equipped bedrooms in separate block *(Dr and Mrs A K Clarke, Francis Johnston)*

LACOCK ST9268

Bell [back rd, bottom of Bowden Hill]: Friendly open-plan pub with wide choice of food (all day wknds) from sandwiches to steaks, changing ales such as Archers, Robinsons, Wadworths 6X and Wickwar (take-out containers), Bulmer's cider, good wine list, lots of malt whiskies, helpful staff, brocaded banquettes, pretty blue and white restaurant; piped music, bar can be smoky, Sun quiz night; well kept sizeable garden with good play house and climbers *(BB, Esther and John Sprinkle, Kevin Thorpe)*

LEA ST9586

Rose & Crown: Smart Victorian dining pub with red and white tiles by bar, some rather individual decorations, comfortable sofas by big open fire, two small attractive dining areas off with old prints and dark red walls, helpful family-friendly staff, well kept Arkells 2B, 3B and a seasonal ale, decent wines choice, daily papers; may be unobtrusive piped music; tables outside *(Mr and Mrs G S Ayrton)*

LIMPLEY STOKE ST7861

☆ *Hop Pole* [off A36 and B3108 S of Bath]: Largely panelled 16th-c stone-built two-bar pub with log fire, well kept Bass, Butcombe, Courage Best and a guest beer, wide choice of bar food, welcoming service, traditional games; TV, piped music; children in eating areas, nice enclosed garden behind *(LYM, Dr and Mrs M E Wilson, Paul Morris, Dr and Mrs A K Clarke, Susan and Nigel Wilson)*

Rose & Crown [A36]: Large beamed main-road pub with log fires and cosy alcove seating, well kept Smiles, good food choice from big sandwiches to hearty main dishes in bar and restaurant inc good local meat and sensible children's choices; picnic-sets out on terrace and in garden with steep valley views, open all day wknds and bank hols *(Meg and Colin Hamilton, Christopher and Jo Barton, Dr and Mrs A K Clarke)*

LITTLE CHEVERELL ST9853

☆ *Owl* [just off B3098 Westbury—Upavon; Low Rd]: Cosy little village pub, bar and snug back room with black beams and pleasant jumble of furnishings, food here and in attractive back dining area overlooking garden, lots of wines by the glass, well kept Brakspeare, Hook Norton, Ringwood Best, Wadworths 6X and a guest beer; unobtrusive piped music; big raised deck in charming tree-sheltered back garden with rustic picnic-sets on long split-level lawn running down to brook, children and dogs welcome, bedrooms, open all day summer wknds *(Dennis Jenkin, Michael Doswell,*

Dr and Mrs A K Clarke, Nicholas and Dorothy Stephens, LYM)

LITTLE SOMERFORD ST9784

☆ *Saladin* [signed off B4042 Malmesbury—Brinkworth]: Recently refurbished modern dining pub, big leather seats around bar's log fire, some café tables and chairs, larger restaurant area with open kitchen, good food all home-made inc inventive dishes and splendid roasts, well kept ales such as Archers Best and Wadworths 6X, decent wines, friendly staff; may be piped music, has been open all day wknds *(BB)*

LOCKERIDGE SU1467

☆ *Who'd A Thought It* [signed just off A4 Marlborough—Calne just W of Fyfield]: Friendly pub with interesting well illustrated and annotated collection of cooperage tools in two main linked rooms set for good sensibly priced well presented food inc very popular OAP lunch, small side drinking area, well kept Hook Norton Old Hooky and Wadworths IPA and 6X, good choice of decent wines by the glass, caring landlord, coal or log fire, family room – good for children; shame about the piped pop music; pleasant back garden with play area, delightful quiet scenery, lovely walks *(Jenny and Brian Seller, BB, Jane Basso, J Stickland, Tim and Rosemary Wells)*

LONGBRIDGE DEVERILL ST8640

George [A350/B3095]: Extended village pub, spacious and relaxed even when busy, good reasonably priced food inc popular Sun carvery, well kept Gales, good service, restaurant *(Sue Plant)*

LOWER WOODFORD SU1136

☆ *Wheatsheaf* [signed off A360 just N of Salisbury]: Prettily set and well run 18th-c dining pub, big helpings of enjoyable reasonably priced food, well kept Badger Best, IPA and Tanglefoot, log fire, comfortable furnishings on oak floor with miniature footbridge over indoor goldfish pool; piped music; children welcome, good disabled access, baby-changing, good big tree-lined garden with play area *(I D Barnett, LYM, Mary and David Richards, Peter B Brown)*

LUCKINGTON ST8384

☆ *Old Royal Ship* [off B4040 SW of Malmesbury]: Rambling 17th-c country pub very popular lunchtime for good range of rather sophisticated food inc some bargains, welcoming service, well kept Archers Village, Bass, Wadworths 6X and Youngs Waggle Dance, farm cider, decent wines (two glass sizes), good coffee, individual décor, darts; may be piped music, jazz nights – a favourite with the young farmers, and massively busy over Badminton horse trials; attractive garden with boules, play area with big wooden fort, bedrooms *(BB, Dr and Mrs A K Clarke, Richard Stancomb, KN-R)*

LUDWELL ST9022

Grove Arms [A30 E of Shaftesbury]: Hotel's attractive, bright and roomy bar with linked dining area, three well kept changing beers inc interesting ones from small breweries, good varied food inc small selecion of lunchtime snacks such as generously garnished sandwiches, welcoming service, spotless housekeeping, restaurant; children welcome, bedrooms *(Gloria Bax, Alan M Pring)*

MAIDEN BRADLEY ST8038

Somerset Arms [Church St]: Relaxed, welcoming and child-friendly village pub, nicely restored and decorated without being spoilt, helpful caring licensees, good honest attractively priced food, well kept Wadworths and a guest such as Butcombe, tempting whiskies, daily papers and magazines; bedrooms *(Neville and Anne Morley, Edward Mirzoeff, Rachel Manolsen)*

MALMESBURY ST9287

Kings Arms [High St]: 16th-c town pub with two thriving friendly bars, good value well presented food from sandwiches and other bar snacks to interesting full meals, Flowers IPA and a guest beer, decent choice of wines by the glass, pleasant restaurant; nice courtyard garden, large well used function room inc jazz last Sat of month, comfortable bedrooms *(Margaret and Roy Randle, K H Frostick, Dr and Mrs A K Clarke)*

☆ *Suffolk Arms* [Tetbury Hill, S of junction with B4014]: Good value generous food and cheerful efficient service in knocked-through bar and big no smoking panelled dining room; well kept Wadworths IPA and 6X and a changing guest beer, log fire; children welcome *(LYM, Dr and Mrs A K Clarke)*

MARDEN SU0857

Millstream: Pleasantly refurbished and extended bar/restaurant with enjoyable changing fresh food inc their own bread and ice-creams, well kept Wadworths ales and good wines inc champagne by the glass, beams, flagstones, open fires and woodburners, good staff; children and well behaved dogs welcome, pleasant garden, cl Mon *(anon)*

MARLBOROUGH SU1869

Bear [High St]: Rambling refurbished Victorian inn with helpful enthusiastic landlord, well kept Arkells 2B, good wine choice, generous interesting food inc huge baguettes and good fish in old-fashioned side bar, impressive central log fire, steps between main bar and lounges, evening restaurant; medieval-style banqueting hall for special occasions, skittle alley, tables in small back courtyard *(Derek and Sylvia Stephenson)*

Castle & Ball [High St]: Grand old coaching inn at the heart of this nice town, great atmosphere, interesting choice of generous food inc speciality pie in pleasant eating area, well kept Greene King IPA and Abbot, good range of well listed wines by the glass, young enthusiastic staff; good value bedrooms, good breakfast *(Derek and Sylvia Stephenson, Dr and Mrs A K Clarke, Tim and Rosemary Wells)*

MERE ST8132

☆ *George* [The Square]: Comfortably modernised 16th-c inn, good enterprising cooking, welcoming landlady, quick helpful service, well kept Badger IPA and Best, open fire, well spaced tables in attractive restaurant, reasonable prices; good bedrooms *(BB, Mrs Roxanne Chamberlain, Colin and Janet Roe, Julian Snell)*

MILDENHALL SU2169

☆ *Horseshoe*: Relaxed and neatly kept traditional 17th-c thatched pub with appealing sensibly priced bar and restaurant menus, well kept ales such as Archers and Wadworths, good value wines, efficient courteous service even when busy, three attractive partly partitioned beamed rooms, small no smoking dining room; bedrooms, picnic-sets out on grass, pleasant village setting, good Kennet Valley and Savernake Forest walks *(Phyl and Jack Street)*

MONKTON FARLEIGH ST8065

☆ *Kings Arms* [signed off A363 Bradford—Bath]: Imposting 17th-c building in lovely village, good choice of home-made food in beamed lounge and no smoking tapestried restaurant with huge inglenook, pewter and panelling, well kept Bass, Courage Directors and Wadworths 6X, farm cider, unusual wines, quick service; darts, bar billiards, good live music Fri; rustic tables in front partly flagstoned courtyard, aviaries and guinea-pigs in well tended two-level back garden, open all day summer wknds *(Mr and Mrs T Bennett, Dr and Mrs M E Wilson, Keith Berrett, Michael Doswell, Dr and Mrs A K Clarke)*

NETHERHAMPTON SU1129

☆ *Victoria & Albert* [just off A3094 W of Salisbury]: Cosy black-beamed bar in simple thatched cottage under obliging new landlord, nicely cushioned old-fashioned wall settles on ancient floor tiles, real ales such as Butcombe and Moles Molecatcher and Barley Mole, Black Rat farm cider, reasonably priced food, friendly licensees, no smoking restaurant; children welcome, hatch service for sizeable garden behind, handy for Wilton House and Nadder Valley walks *(Susan and John Douglas, LYM, Richard Fendick, Dr and Mrs A K Clarke, Colin and Janet Roe)*

NOMANSLAND SU2517

☆ *Lamb* [signed off B3078 and B3079]: Pretty, old-fashioned and neatly kept, in lovely New Forest village-green setting with friendly donkeys and ponies, attentive welcoming service, good reasonably priced homely cooking inc lots of puddings in small no smoking dining room and long bar, Hampshire Strongs, Ringwood, Wadworths and Whitbreads ales, short sensible wine list, end pool table; good walks *(Prof and Mrs Tony Palmer, Phyl and Jack Street, Catherine Kelly)*

NORTH WROUGHTON SU1482

Check Inn [Woodland View (A4361 just S of Swindon)]: Busy extended local with glossy pine furniture, various comfortable areas inc children's, up to ten well kept interesting changing ales in oversized lined glasses, lots of bottled imports, farm cider, good soft drinks choice, tasty straightforward food, log fire, large no smoking area; traditional games and machine; disabled access, heated front terrace, garden bar (can pitch tent, motorway noise), open all day Fri-Sun *(CMW, JJW, James Woods, Richard Houghton)*

NUNTON SU1526

☆ *Radnor Arms* [off A338 S of Salisbury]: Pretty ivy-clad village pub very popular for enjoyable food inc fish and local game, friendly helpful staff, well kept Badger inc Tanglefoot; three pleasantly decorated and furnished linked rooms inc cheerfully busy yet relaxing bar and staider restaurant, log fires, very friendly labrador; can get rather crowded, booking essential at wknds; attractive garden popular with children *(R J Anderson, Dr and Mrs Michael Smith, Dr D G Twyman)*

ODSTOCK SU1426

Yew Tree [off A338 S of Salisbury; Whitsbury Rd]: Pretty thatched and low-beamed country dining pub with big blackboard choice of freshly made food, friendly staff, well kept rotating beers and decent wines, log fire, raised seating area at one end; small garden, good walks *(John Wheeler, Jeffrey Easton)*

OGBOURNE ST GEORGE SU2074

☆ *Old Crown* [A345 Marlboro—Swindon]: 18th-c pub in small village off Ridgeway path, enjoyable and individualistic food from crusty bread lunchtime sandwiches to restaurant meals, deep glass-covered well, well kept Wadworths 6X, cosy small bar with very mixed furniture, piano, pleasant décor and pictures; quiet well chosen piped music; children welcome, picnic-sets by car park, comfortable bedrooms, cl Mon lunchtime *(Barbara Ogburn, A H C Rainier, Francis Johnston, James Morrell, Mrs Pat Crabb)*

PEWSEY SU1561

☆ *French Horn* [A345 towards Marlborough; Pewsey Wharf]: Pleasantly refurbished old pub popular for food, entirely home-made (from bread to ice-cream), well kept Wadworths IPA and 6X, good choice of wines by the glass, good welcoming service, two-part back bar divided by log fire open to both sides, steps down to pleasant and rather smart flagstoned front dining area (children allowed here); piped music; picnic-sets on back terrace, many more in well fenced wood-chip area with robust timber play area above barges moored on Kennet & Avon Canal *(BB, K H Frostick)*

SALISBURY SU1429

Cloisters [Catherine St/Ivy St]: Roomy city pub done up to look old and homely, with low beams and bare boards; good value food, Gales HSB Bitter, helpful staff; open all day *(Geoff Pidoux)*

New Inn [New St]: Ancient pub with massive beams and timbers, quiet cosy alcoves, inglenook log fire, well kept Badger beers, decent house wines, food from sandwiches and chips up; shame about the piped music; children welcome, walled garden with striking view of nearby cathedral spire, open all day summer wknds *(Adam and Joan Bunting, Ian Phillips, Douglas and Ann Hare, LYM, JCW, Mrs Maricar Jagger)*

Old Ale House [Crane St]: Long open-plan bare-boards pub with hotch-potch of old sofas, seats and tables, cosy lighting, entertainingly cluttered décor, inexpensive generous lunchtime food (not Sun), well kept ales such as Courage Best, Ringwood Best and Wadworths 6X tapped from the cask, efficient cheerful service; darts, cribbage, dominoes, big-screen TV, fruit machines, loud juke box; children welcome away from the bar till 5, picnic-sets in small back courtyard, open all day *(Dr and Mrs M E Wilson, LYM, Ann and Colin Hunt)*

Old Mill [Town Path, W Harnham]: Charming 17th-c pub/hotel doing well under new management, pleasant beamed bars with prized window tables, friendly staff, well kept real ales, good wines and malt whiskies, decent bar food from sandwiches up, good value restaurant lunch; children welcome, lovely tranquil setting, picnic-sets in small floodlit garden by duck-filled millpond, a stroll across water-meadows from cathedral (classic view of it from bridge beyond garden), bedrooms *(Martin and Karen Wake, LYM, Dr D G Twyman)*

Ox Row [Ox Row]: Comfortable pub overlooking market square, good service, real ales *(Ann and Colin Hunt)*

Red Lion [Milford St]: Best Western hotel with mix of old-fashioned seats and modern banquettes in two-roomed nicely local-feeling panelled bar opening into other spacious and interesting areas, well kept Bass and Ringwood, elegant food room with good lunchtime range from sandwiches up, medieval evening restaurant; children in eating areas, loggia courtyard seats, comfortable bedrooms *(LYM, Colin and Janet Roe)*

Wyndham Arms [Estcourt Rd]: Modern corner pub, tap for reasonably priced good Hop Back beers (now brewed over at Downton), with two rooms off long bar, friendly atmosphere, country wines, simple bar food *(the Didler)*

SEMINGTON ST9259

☆ ***Lamb*** [The Strand; A361 Devizes—Trowbridge]: Busy dining pub with consistently good fresh food in attractive linked rooms, carefully chosen wines, well kept Butcombe, Ringwood Best and a guest such as Titanic, good coffee, buoyant atmosphere, helpful friendly service, woodburner and log fire; children in eating area, helpful to wheelchairs, attractive walled garden; cl Sun evening *(LYM, Mr and Mrs F J Parmenter, Mr and Mrs J Ken Jones, Dr and Mrs A K Clarke, Ken and Sylvia Jones, Dr and Mrs M E Wilson)*

SEMLEY ST8926

☆ ***Benett Arms*** [off A350 N of Shaftesbury]: Character village inn across green from church, nicely worn-in mix of furnishings and log fire, good relaxed atmosphere, well kept ales such as Brakspears, Ringwood Best and Youngs, decent wines and good range of other drinks, traditional games, no music; children and well behaved dogs allowed, restaurant, pleasant tables outside; long-serving licensee may be changing – news please *(P Tailyour, Roger and Pauline Pearce, Colin and Janet Roe, MP, Dr and Mrs A H Young, OPUS, LYM)*

SHAW ST8765

Golden Fleece [A365 towards Atworth]: Former coaching inn with good atmosphere in low-ceilinged L-shaped bar and long sympathetic front dining extension, real ales such as Butcombe, Fullers London Pride, Greene King and Smiles, good range of food inc generous bargain lunches – very popular with older people; garden tables *(Dr and Mrs M E Wilson, K R Harris, Dr and Mrs A K Clarke)*

SHERSTON ST8586

Carpenters Arms [Easton (B4040)]: Cosy small-roomed low-beamed local under new management, settles and shiny tables, log fire, well kept beers, decent wines, good choice of reasonably priced food, modern conservatory and dining rooms; TV in locals' bar, no piped music; tables in pleasant garden with play area *(Ian Rushton, Richard Pierce, Dr and Mrs A K Clarke)*

Rattlebone [Church St (B4040 Malmesbury—Chipping Sodbury)]: Oddly rambling beamed and stone-walled 17th-c village pub, pews, settles and country-kitchen chairs, log fire, decent wines, Youngs beers, partly no smoking dining area (no food Sun evening), public bar with pool, table football and other games, also TV and juke box – can be a bit loud; children in restaurant, skittle alley, picnic-sets in back garden, open all day *(Alec and Barbara Jones, P R and S A White, Andrew Shore, Maria Williams, R Huggins, D Irving, E McCall, T McLean, LYM, James Woods, Dr and Mrs A K Clarke, Richard Stancomb, Betsy and Peter Little)*

SOUTH MARSTON SU1987

Carpenters Arms [just off A420 E of Swindon]: Popular and roomy, with good value generous food in bar and separate restaurant inc OAP wkdy lunch and popular Sun roasts, well kept Arkells beers, friendly staff, pleasant olde-worlde décor; pool room, quiz night Mon; children welcome, play area and animals in big back garden, up-to-date bedrooms, open all day *(Peter and Audrey Dowsett, Mrs Pat Crabb)*

Village Inn: Smart and spacious bar, part of hotel and leisure complex; real ales such as Boddingtons and Fullers London Pride, popular sensibly priced bar food, old Hollywood film posters; piped music may obtrude; children welcome, separate restaurant, bedrooms, open all day Sun *(Peter and Audrey Dowsett)*

SOUTH WRAXALL ST8364

Long Arms [Upper S Wraxall, off B3109 N of Bradford on Avon]: Cosily refurbished country local with friendly landlord, wide-ranging popular food inc good Sun lunch and OAP lunches Tues-Fri, well kept Wadworths, good range of wines by the glass, log fire; pretty garden *(Dr and Mrs A K Clarke)*

STIBB GREEN SU2262

☆ ***Three Horseshoes*** [just N of Burbage]: Friendly and spotless old-world local, warmly welcoming, with good simple home-made food (not Sun evening) cooked by landlady, sensible prices and quick service, well kept Wadworths ales, farm cider, inglenook log fire in comfortable beamed front bar, second no smoking bar, dining room with railway memorabilia and pictures (landlord is an enthusiast); attractive garden, cl Mon *(Geoff Palmer, James Woods, Mrs Anthea Post)*

STOCKTON ST9738

☆ *Carriers* [just off A36 Salisbury—Warminster, or follow Wylye sign off A303 then turn right]: Attractive thatched village pub with another change of management but still lots of golf memorabilia and doing well, well kept Fullers London Pride, Hop Back GFB and Ringwood Best and Bold Forester, enjoyable food from good baguettes up, pleasant service, soft lighting, log fire and pretty dining extension; sunny roadside seats, quiet Wylye valley village *(Charles Moncreiffe, David R Crafts, BB, Dr Jack Barrow, Edmund Coan, Neil and Anita Christopher)*

STUDLEY ST9671

Soho [New Rd (A4 W of Calne)]: Former coaching inn, with well kept Wadworths, local farm cider, well priced wines, enjoyable food inc good fish and popular Sun lunch, airy dining conservatory; may be entertainer on Sun *(Richard Pierce)*

SUTTON BENGER ST9478

Vintage [Seagry Rd]: Friendly colourful dining pub in former home of Fry's chocolate, now run by Spanish family, wide choice of generous food in bar and stylish art gallery restaurant, from straightforward dishes inc good meats and traditional puddings to spanish specialities, well kept Archers and Wadworths, interesting wines *(Richard Pierce, Richard Stancomb)*

Wellesley Arms [handy for M4 junction 17, via B4122 and B4069; High St]: Attractively furnished beamed Cotswold stone country pub with several Duke of Wellington pictures, new licensees doing good food using local organic supplies, well kept Archers and Wadworths ales, farm cider, separate dining room *(Richard Pierce, Richard Stancomb)*

SWINDON SU1584

Duke of Wellington [Eastcott Hill; off Commercial Road at Regent Circus]: Honest unspoilt local with particularly well kept Arkells 2B and 3B tapped from the cask, coal fire, tiny snug off main bar with darts, dominoes and cribbage *(Pete Baker)*

Kingsdown [Kingsdown Rd, Upper Stratton; opp Arkells Brewery]: Much extended and comfortably refurbished tap for Arkells Brewery with 2B, 3B and Kingsdown, friendly helpful staff, reasonably priced food; good-sized garden *(Ian Phillips)*

TROWBRIDGE ST8557

Sir Isaac Pitman [Castle Pl]: Useful Wetherspoons well done out in elm-coloured wood, comfortable alcoves and different levels below cupola, the shorthand Sir Isaac invented along the beams, no smoking area, good value beer and food, pleasant staff *(Dr and Mrs M E Wilson, Dr and Mrs A K Clarke, Mike Gorton)*

UPPER WOODFORD SU1237

☆ *Bridge Inn*: Good sensibly priced food from ploughman's with lots of bread (handy for ducks in attractive riverside garden across road) to wide menu and blackboard choice, rather spruce feel with country-kitchen tables on expanse of new wooden flooring and big flower prints on eau de nil walls, quick friendly service, well kept Bass and a beer brewed for the pub, good house wines, log fire, broadsheet dailies, rather smart games room with pool and leather chesterfields; best to book wknds *(BB, Howard and Margaret Buchanan)*

UPTON LOVELL ST9441

Prince Leopold: Imaginative food from interestingly filled ciabattas up, well kept Ringwood ales, decent good value wines, cheerful staff, dark Victorian bar décor, airy new dining extension; tables in small attractive riverside garden, pretty Wylye Valley thatched village, comfortable quiet bedrooms *(Dr and Mrs M E Wilson)*

UPTON SCUDAMORE ST8647

Angel [off A350 N of Warminster]: Big dining pub with bustling modern feel, contemporary pictures for sale in long two-part dining room, good choice of food from open kitchen, well kept Butcombe, Wadworths 6X and a guest beer, good changing wine choice, traditional games; piped music, TV; sheltered flagstoned back terrace with big barbecue, bedrooms in house across car park *(Ron Shelton, Mike Gorton, Matthew Shackle, Dr and Mrs A K Clarke, LYM)*

WANBOROUGH SU2083

Cross Keys [Burycroft, Lower Wanborough]: Welcoming much extended village pub with solid wood floor, alcoves and individual décor inc lots of bric-a-brac, well kept ales, good choice of food, good service, back restaurant *(Dr and Mrs A K Clarke)*

☆ *Harrow* [3 miles from M4 junction 15; Lower Wanborough signed off A346]: Pretty thatched pub with long low-beamed stepped bar, big log fire, pine panelling, candles in bottles, settles and bay window alcoves, well kept ales such as Greene King Old Speckled Hen, Hook Norton Old Hooky and Youngs Special, friendly staff, good fresh food (not Sun evening), daily papers, no piped music, simple beamed and flagstoned stripped stone dining room with another open fire; live music Sun night, cast-iron tables and picnic-sets outside *(BB, Dr and Mrs A K Clarke)*

Plough [High St, Lower Wanborough]: Thriving down-to-earth atmosphere in long low thatched stone pub with three old-world rooms, huge centrepiece log fire in one, another more or less for evening dining, well kept ales such as Archers Village, Bass and Wadworths 6X, good interesting home-made food (not Sun), friendly efficient staff; open all day Sat *(R Huggins, D Irving, E McCall, T McLean)*

WEST LAVINGTON SU0052

Bridge Inn [Church St]: Enterprising new licensees, long relaxing family dining bar, big log fire, pleasant country pictures and the like, wide choice of good value home-cooked food in bar and restaurant, well kept real ales, decent wines, good welcoming service; piped music; pretty flower-filled garden *(J H Bescoby, Richard Stancomb)*

Churchill Arms [High St]: Comfortable country local with Wadworths IPA and 6X and enjoyable food from baguettes to popular bargain wkdy lunches and restaurant dishes, conference facilities, big car park *(Francis Johnston)*

WESTWOOD ST8159

New Inn [off B3109 S of Bradford-on-Avon]: Country pub recently pleasantly freshened up, beams, stripped stone, good fire and new slate floor, several linked rooms, emphasis on enjoyable food, generous helpings, attentive cheerful staff *(D P and M A Miles)*

WINGFIELD ST8256

☆ ***Poplars*** [B3109 S of Bradford-on-Avon (Shop Lane)]: Attractive and friendly country local very popular for good value interesting food, especially with older people at lunchtime; well kept Wadworths ales, friendly fast service even when busy, enjoyable atmosphere, no juke box or machines, light and airy no smoking family dining extension overlooking own cricket pitch *(Dr and Mrs M E Wilson, LYM, Dr and Mrs A K Clarke)*

WINTERBOURNE BASSETT SU0975

☆ ***White Horse*** [off A4361 S of Swindon]: Wide choice of good fresh generous food inc several fish dishes, popular bargain lunches Mon-Sat and good Sun roast, in neat and well cared for open-plan big-windowed pub, comfortable dining room and warm conservatory, chatty efficient service, well kept Wadworths, good wine list and coffee, huge goldfish; quiet piped music; tables on good-sized side lawn, pleasant setting *(BB, James Woods, Evelyn and Derek Walter, Mrs Pat Crabb)*

WOOTTON BASSETT SU0682

Five Bells [Wood St]: Friendly little local with great atmosphere, up to five well kept ales, enjoyable food with some interesting notions like their Weds sausage night; can get smoky, and parking here is no fun *(James Woods, Tim and Rosemary Wells, Dr and Mrs A K Clarke)*

Prince of Wales [Coped Hall roundabout (A3102/B4042)]: Open all day, with several good value food blackboards (not Sun-Mon evenings), real ales, good choice of soft drinks, dining room and conservatory; piped music, machines, darts; picnic-sets out on terrace and in garden with play area, may be Sat lunchtime car cleaning service *(Dr and Mrs A K Clarke)*

WOOTTON RIVERS SU1963

☆ ***Royal Oak*** [off A346, A345 or B3087]: 16th-c beamed and thatched pub, wide range of food, popular though not cheap, from lunchtime sandwiches, ciabattas and baguettes to plenty of specials and full meals (for which they add a 10% service charge), friendly L-shaped dining lounge with woodburner, timbered bar with small games area, well kept Fullers London Pride, Wadworths 6X and perhaps a guest beer, good wine list; children welcome, tables out in yard, pleasant village, bedrooms in adjoining house *(Phyl and Jack Street, LYM, Simon Watkins, James Woods, Andrew Shore, Maria Williams, Ann and Colin Hunt, Geoff Pidoux, Nigel Howard)*

WYLYE SU0037

Bell [just off A303/A36; High St]: Peacefully set 14th-c village pub under new management, neat bar, log fire, sturdy rustic furnishings, black beams, timbered masonry, great bell collection, bar food from sandwiches up, four well kept changing ales, no smoking restaurant; may be piped music; pleasant walled terrace and attractive back garden, fine downland walks nearby, bedrooms; more reports on new regime, please *(LYM)*

Please tell us if the décor, atmosphere, food or drink at a pub is different from our description. We rely on readers' reports to keep us up to date. No stamp needed: *The Good Pub Guide*, FREEPOST TN1569, Wadhurst, E Sussex TN5 7BR.

Worcestershire

The two new entries here this year have both figured in the *Guide* in the past: the Walter de Cantalupe in Kempsey, with enjoyable food cooked by its friendly and chatty landlord, and good bedrooms too; and the very individual Talbot at Knightwick, using local produce for both its food and its own good value Teme Valley microbrewery – it too is a nice place to stay. Other pubs earning warm praise in recent months are the Jockey at Baughton (a wider menu including lots of fish under its new landlord), the Bear & Ragged Staff at Bransford (helpful service, good food and wines in its cheerful linked rooms), the Childswickham Inn (a surprise to find such a trendy bistroish pub in this quiet village), the Old Chequers at Crowle (good food and very helpful staff, handy for the motorway), the Boot at Flyford Flavell (good all round, with a particularly warm welcome), the Bell & Cross at Holy Cross (imaginative food in this civilised and interesting small-roomed pub), and the Bell at Pensax (another fine welcoming all-rounder). The award of Worcestershire Dining Pub of the Year goes to the Bell & Cross at Holy Cross, for its interesting changing food in appealingly intimate surroundings. A favourite main entry, the Fleece at Bretforton, is being rebuilt after a disastrous fire in March 2004; we look forward to its reopening, possibly as soon as spring 2005. Other pubs to note in the Lucky Dip section at the end of the chapter include the Plough & Harrow at Drakes Broughton, Peacock at Forhill, Three Kings at Hanley Castle, and Bellmans Cross at Shatterford. Drinks tend to be a bit cheaper in Worcestershire than in the country generally; the beer at the King & Castle in Kidderminster is a real bargain (not much more than £1 a pint). The county's particular specialities are local farm ciders and apple juices. Locally brewed beers worth looking out for include Wyre Piddle, Cannon Royall and St Georges.

BAUGHTON SO8741 Map 4

Jockey

4 miles from M50 junction 1; A38 northwards, then right on to A4104 Upton—Pershore

Open-plan but partly divided by stripped brick and timbering, this neatly kept dining pub has candles alight on the mix of good-sized tables and fresh flowers, a few horse-racing pictures on the butter-coloured walls, and a cream Aga in one brick inglenook. The new landlord has expanded the menu, which now contains unusual specials such as kangaroo (£15.95), and up to half a dozen fish dishes such as king prawns in garlic and chilli oil (£5.95), and red snapper (£14.95). Other enjoyable dishes might include battered brie (£4.95), home-made lasagne (£9.95), steak and ale pie (£10.50), slow-roast lamb shank (£12.50), duck breast with orange and Grand Marnier sauce (£12.95), with puddings such as home-made treacle and orange pudding (£3.95); they also do lunchtime sandwiches (from £4.95), and ploughman's (£5.95). Attentive staff serve three changing real ales such as Robinsons Cumbria Way, Hartleys XB and Wyre Piddle Piddle in the Hole, and they've decent wines. There are picnic-sets out in front, by an antique pump that's the centrepiece of a water feature (out here, but not inside, you can hear the motorway in the distance). *(Recommended by Alan and Paula McCully, Mike and Mary Carter, Andrew and Amanda Rogers, Paul and Annette Hallett,*

Derek and Sylvia Stephenson, Geoffrey and Penny Hughes, Ron and Val Broom, Denys Gueroult, Nigel Long, Mrs S Lyons)

Free house ~ Licensee Mark Welsh ~ Real ale ~ Bar food (12-2(3 Sun), 6-9; not Mon) ~ Restaurant ~ (01684) 592153 ~ Open 12-3, 6-11(10.30 Sun); closed Mon

BERROW GREEN SO7458 Map 4

Admiral Rodney

B4197, off A44 W of Worcester

On Sundays they do a choice of three roasts at this civilised country inn. Attractively light and roomy throughout, the bare-boards entrance bar, with high beams and a sunny bow window, has big stripped kitchen tables and cushioned chairs, a traditional winged settle, and a woodburning stove in a fireplace that opens through to the comfortable no smoking lounge area. This has some carpet on its slate flagstones, dark red settees, a table of magazines and rack of broadsheet newspapers, quite a few board games, and prints of the Battle of the Saints, where Lord Rodney obliterated the french fleet in the Caribbean. A separate skittle alley has pool; also darts, Jenga, cribbage, dominoes, and perhaps piped music. It's popular with older crowds at lunchtime, and in the evening you'll find locals dropping in for a chatty drink. Besides a couple of tasty fresh cornish fish specials such as mackerel with damson fruit coulis (£10.50), and john dory fillets with white wine and prawn sauce (£12.50), enjoyable dishes include lunchtime sandwiches (£3.50), and baked potatoes (from £5.95), tortilla wraps (from £5.25), home-made pie, pizza or curry (£6.95), and lamb shank with creamed potato (£7.25), along with restaurant dishes (which can also be eaten in the bar) such as roast pigeon breast salad (£4.50), and pork fillet with apple, calvados and sage cream sauce or rack of lamb with herb crust and sweet mixed berry, port and redcurrant sauce (£13.95), with home-made puddings such as coffee and almond bavarois (£4.25). A rebuilt barn stepping down through three levels forms a charming end restaurant (mostly no smoking). Alongside well kept Wye Valley Bitter, they've three changing guests such as Cottage Hop n Drop, RCH East Street Cream and Woods Quaff, and you'll find a tempting choice of wines, and good bloody marys; cheerful service from the hands-on licensees. Out on a terrace and neat green, solid tables and chairs look over the Lower Teme valley (two of the three bedrooms share the views), and this is good walking territory. The friendly pub dog is called Penny.
(Recommended by Austin and Jean Dance, Roy and Lindsey Fentiman, Lynda and Trevor Smith, Guy Vowles, Nick and Lynne Carter, Annette Tress, Gary Smith, Denys Gueroult)

Free house ~ Licensees Gillian and Kenneth Green ~ Real ale ~ Bar food (not Mon lunchtime exc bank hols) ~ Restaurant ~ (01886) 821375 ~ Children welcome ~ Dogs allowed in bar and bedrooms ~ Open 11-3, 5-11; 11-11 Sat; 12-10.30 Sun; closed Mon lunchtime exc bank hols ~ Bedrooms: £40S/£55B

BEWDLEY SO7875 Map 4

Little Pack Horse

High Street; no nearby parking – best to park in main car park, cross A4117 Cleobury road, and keep walking on down narrowing High Street; or park 150 yards away at bottom of Lax Lane

Nestling into the peaceful back streets of this interesting riverside town, this ancient low-beamed heavily timbered pub has lots of intriguing bric-a-brac, old photographs and advertisements to look at inside. Cosily pubby and bustling, with a pleasant mix of old furnishings, it's nicely warmed by a woodburning stove in winter; the atmosphere is welcoming, and service is cheerful and efficient. You'll find a wide choice of bar food, and lots of dishes come in two sizes. The reasonably priced menu includes sandwiches (from £3.20), chicken and spinach terrine with cumberland sauce (£4.25), moroccan vegetable and chick pea couscous (£4.30, £5.60 large), tasty pies (from £5.20), scampi and chips (£5.85, £7.25 large), cajun chicken breast (£6.90), and minted lamb steak with redcurrant glaze (£8.90), with puddings such as plum and cinnamon suet pudding (£3). Alongside Greene King

IPA, they have a couple of guests such as Marstons Pedigree and Wadworths 6X; there may be piped music. It's best to leave your car in the public car park near the river and walk up. *(Recommended by Lawrence Pearse, David Cosham, John and Gloria Isaacs, T R and B C Jenkins)*

InnSpired ~ Lease Michael Stewart Gaunt ~ Real ale ~ Bar food (12-2.15, 6-9.30; 12-9.30 wknds) ~ Restaurant ~ (01299) 403762 ~ Children allowed in restaurant till 9pm ~ Dogs allowed in bar ~ Open 12-3, 6-11; 12-11(10.30 Sun) Sat

BIRTSMORTON SO7935 Map 4

Farmers Arms £

Birts Street, off B4208 W

Food prices at this pretty black and white timbered village pub have hardly changed since last year. Good value simple dishes might include sandwiches (from £1.70), soup (£2), ploughman's (from £3), well cooked macaroni cheese (£3.50), fish and chips (£4.75), chicken and vegetable curry (£4.70), lasagne (£5.15), steak and kidney pie (£5.70), gammon (£6.95), and steak (£8.25), with good puddings such as apple pie or spotted dick (from £2.20). Service is very welcoming, and there's a friendly bustling atmosphere. The neatly kept big room on the right, which has a no smoking area, rambles away under very low dark beams, with some standing timbers, and flowery-panelled cushioned settles as well as spindleback chairs; on the left an even lower-beamed room seems even cosier, and in both the white walls have black timbering; darts in a good tiled area, shove-ha'penny, cribbage and dominoes. Sociable locals gather at the bar for Hook Norton Best and Old Hooky well kept on handpump, and there's also a changing guest from a brewer such as Wye Valley. You'll find seats out on the large lawn, and the pub is surrounded by plenty of walks. Please treat the opening hours we give below as approximate – they may vary according to how busy or quiet things are. *(Recommended by the Didler, Jenny and Dave Hughes, Pam and David Bailey, Ian and Nita Cooper, Derek and Sylvia Stephenson)*

Free house ~ Licensees Jill and Julie Moore ~ Real ale ~ Bar food (12-2, 6.30-9.30) ~ No credit cards ~ (01684) 833308 ~ Children welcome ~ Dogs allowed in bar ~ Open 11-4, 6-11; 12-4, 7-10.30 Sun

BRANSFORD SO7852 Map 4

Bear & Ragged Staff

Off A4103 SW of Worcester; Station Road

Delicious food and welcoming helpful service make this civilised dining pub a smashing place for a meal. They've a good range of wines to choose from too, lots of malt whiskies, quite a few brandies and liqueurs, and Robinsons Best and a guest such as St Georges Best are well kept on handpump. The cheerful interconnecting rooms give fine views over rolling country, and in winter you'll find an open fire; cribbage, and piped music (which can be obtrusive). In fine weather, the garden and terrace are enjoyable places to sit (pleasant views from here too). The tempting changing bar menu might typically include mushroom and roasted pepper risotto (£8.25), beer-battered haddock, thai green chicken curry or beef stroganoff (£9.95), lamb shank with pesto mash (£10.95), and chargrilled rib-eye steak (£12.50), with around four fresh fish specials such as fried salmon with white wine butter sauce (£12.95), and chargrilled tuna loin (£13.50), and puddings such as steamed date and banana sponge and excellent bread and butter pudding (£4.25); they also do lunchtime sandwiches (not Sunday). There are proper tablecloths, linen napkins, and fresh flowers on the tables in the no smoking restaurant. Good disabled access and facilities. *(Recommended by Jay Bohmrich, John and Lucy Taylor, Rodney and Norma Stubington, Brenda and Rob Fincham, Mr and Mrs Donald Bostock, Jeff and Wendy Williams, Ray and Winifred Halliday)*

Free house ~ Licensees Lynda Williams and Andy Kane ~ Real ale ~ Bar food (not Sat evening) ~ Restaurant ~ (01886) 833399 ~ Children in eating area of bar and restaurant till 9pm ~ Open 12-2, 6(6.30 Sat)-11; 12-2.30, 7-10.30 Sun

BREDON SO9236 Map 4

Fox & Hounds

4½ miles from M5 junction 9; A438 to Northway, left at B4079, then in Bredon follow signpost to church and river on right

Comfortably modernised, this bustling thatched pub is attractively placed next to a church by a lane leading down to the river. The carpeted bar has hop-hung beams, stone pillars and stripped timbers, a central woodburning stove, upholstered settles, a variety of wheelback, tub and kitchen chairs around handsome mahogany and cast-iron-framed tables, dried grasses and flowers, a toy fox dressed in hunting scarlet, and elegant wall lamps. There's a smaller side bar, and the restaurant and part of the bar are no smoking. Friendly efficient staff serve Banks's Bitter and Greene King Old Speckled Hen along with a guest on handpump, several malt whiskies and wines by the glass; piped music. Besides baguettes (from £4.95), popular bar lunches might include home-made soup (£3.95), ploughman's (from £5.95), home-baked ham and eggs (£7.50), breaded plaice (£7.95), and curry (£8.75), with other dishes such as japanese prawns (£6.95), mushrooms in creamy garlic sauce with stilton (£7), caramelised onion tartlet (£8.75), marinated chicken supreme with lime and coriander (£11.25), and half a crispy gressingham duck with black cherry and cinnamon glaze (£14.95), with puddings (from £3.95); on Sunday they do a choice of roasts. The pub is especially pretty in summer, when it's decked with brightly coloured hanging baskets; some of the picnic-sets are under Perspex.
(Recommended by Ian and Denise Foster, John and Laney Woods, Jack Clark, Felicity Stephens, David Fox, JHW, Dr and Mrs A K Clarke, Ken Millar, David J Austin, Chris Flynn, Wendy Jones)

Enterprise ~ Lease Mike Hardwick ~ Real ale ~ Bar food (12-2(2.30 Sun), 6.30-9.30; not evenings 25-26 Dec) ~ Restaurant ~ (01684) 772377 ~ Children welcome ~ Dogs allowed in bar ~ Open 11.30-2.30, 6.30(6 summer)-11; closed evenings 25-26 Dec

BROADWAY SP0937 Map 4

Crown & Trumpet

Church Street

Readers like the contrast that this cheerfully easy-going golden stone pub provides to the rest of this smartly attractive, very touristy village. You can choose from a good range of games including darts, shove-ha'penny, cribbage, dominoes, ring-the-bull and Evesham quoits, and they've also a fruit machine, TV and piped music. The relaxed beamed and timbered bar has antique dark high-backed settles, good big tables and a blazing log fire; outside hardwood tables and chairs among flowers on a slightly raised front terrace are popular with walkers – even in adverse weather. Well kept on handpump they've Greene King Old Speckled Hen, Hook Norton Old Hooky and Timothy Taylors Landlord, along with a seasonal beer brewed for the pub by the local Stanway Brewery; they also do five wines by the glass, hot toddies and mulled wine in winter, and summer Pimms and kir. Straightforward bar food such as tortilla wraps (from £2.95), various pies (from £6.95), seafood mornay (£7.95), and puddings (£2.95); they do Sunday roasts.
(Recommended by Graham Holden, Julie Lee, George Atkinson, Di and Mike Gillam, James Woods, Tracey and Stephen Groves, Dr G and Mrs J Kelvin, Ted George, M Joyner, David J Austin)

Laurel (Enterprise) ~ Lease Andrew Scott ~ Real ale ~ Bar food (12-2, 6-9) ~ (01386) 853202 ~ Children in eating area of bar ~ Live music Sat evening, blues every second Thurs ~ Open 11-2.45, 5-11; 11-11(10.30) Sat ~ Bedrooms: /£58S(£65B)

Post Office address codings confusingly give the impression that some pubs are in Worcestershire, when they're really in Gloucestershire, Herefordshire, Shropshire, or Warwickshire (which is where we list them).

CHILDSWICKHAM SP0738 Map 4

Childswickham Inn 🍷

Village signposted off A44 just NW of Broadway

Particularly popular with older folk at lunchtime (in the evenings and at weekends you'll find a broader mix), this thoughtfully run place is surprisingly modern, even trendy, for a country pub in a peaceful village. It's been carefully expanded, and the main area, largely no smoking, is for eating in, with a mix of chairs around kitchen tables, big rugs on boards or broad terracotta tiles, more or less abstract contemporary prints on walls painted cream and pale violet or mauve, candlesticks in great variety, a woodburning stove and a piano. Skilfully cooked imaginative restaurant food changes daily but might include chilled duo of melon with home-made passion fruit sorbet (£4.95), whole roast stuffed quail (£5.25), bruschetta with tiger prawns and red pepper and chilli sauce (£5.95), asparagus, saffron and wild mushroom risotto (£13.25), côte de boeuf with café du paris butter (£16.25), and whole lobster salad (£21.90), with traditional puddings such as bread and butter pudding or date and syrup sponge (£4.95). Off to the right is a proper bar (no food in here), light and airy, with Hook Norton Best and Old Hooky on handpump (from a counter that seems made from old doors), Bulmer's cider, a short but good choice of sensibly priced wines, and good coffee in elegant cups; service is friendly and attentive. This small carefully lit room has a similarly modern colour-scheme moderated by some big horse pictures, a couple of leather armchairs by a log-effect gas fire, just four sturdy tables, a few kitchen and housekeeper's chairs, and another oriental rug on bare boards. The entrance lobby has the biggest doormat we have ever seen – wall to wall – with good disabled access and facilities. A large sunny deck outside has tables. *(Recommended by Miss J Brotherton, Martin Jones, Martin Jennings, A S and M E Marriott, Roger Braithwaite, David and Sue Sykes)*

Punch ~ Lease Guy Justin Brookes ~ Real ale ~ Restaurant (not Sun evening or Mon lunch) ~ (01386) 852461 ~ Children in restaurant ~ Dogs allowed in bar ~ Open 12-2.30, 6-11; 12-10.30 Sun; closed Mon lunch

CLENT SO9279 Map 4

Fountain

Off A491 at Holy Cross/Clent exit roundabout, via Violet Lane, then turn right at T junction; Adams Hill/Odnall Lane

Handy for refuelling after a walk in the surrounding Clent Hills, this thriving tucked-away pub does a great choice of interesting lunchtime sandwiches (from £4.25, not Sunday). Other swiftly served enjoyable bar food might include lunchtime specials such as liver and bacon (£7.95), and herb-roasted salmon or pork with peppercorn and cream sauce (£8.95), with other dishes such as home-made soup (£3.95), asparagus and parma ham (£4.95), duck and orange terrine (£4.25), goats cheese and mushroom filo (£10.95), and steaks with around half a dozen sauces (from £12.50), while puddings might be chocolate and caramel parfait or chocolate and kumquat truffle (from £3.75); there are also various Sunday roasts (from £8.95, children's portions from £5.95). The food is popular (especially with an older set at lunchtime), so booking is a good idea. With a buoyant atmosphere, the long carpeted dining bar – four knocked-together areas – is filled mainly by sturdy pine tables (mostly no smoking) and country-kitchen chairs or mate's chairs, with some comfortably cushioned brocaded wall seats. There are nicely framed local photographs on the ragged pinkish walls above a dark panelled dado, pretty wall lights, and candles on the tables. Banks's Mild and Bitter, and a couple of guests such as Hydes Jekyll's Gold Premium Ale and Marstons Pedigree are very well kept on handpump, and they've decent wines served in cut glass, and ten malts; also a choice of speciality teas and good coffees, and freshly squeezed orange juice; alley skittles. There are a few picnic-sets out in front. They have plans to add bedrooms. More reports please. *(Recommended by Mike and Mary Carter, Malcolm Taylor, Margaret Drazin)*

Union Pub Company ~ Lease Richard and Jacque Macey ~ Real ale ~ Bar food (12-2.15, 6-8.30(9 Fri); 12-2, 6-9 Sat, 12-4 Sun; not Sun-bank hol Mon evening) ~ Restaurant ~ (01562) 883286 ~ Children in restaurant ~ Open 11-11; 12-6 Sun

CROWLE SO9256 Map 4

Old Chequers

2½ miles from M5 junction 6; A4538 towards Evesham, then left after ½ mile; then follow Crowle signpost right to Crowle Green

This dining pub is an excellent place to stop if you're on the motorway: the staff are exceptionally obliging and cheerful, and the food is very good. Much modernised, the pub rambles extensively around an island bar, with plush-seated mate's chairs around a mix of pub tables on the patterned carpet, some brass and copper on the swirly-plastered walls, lots of pictures for sale at the back, and a coal-effect gas fire at one end (there's central heating too). A big square extension on the right, with shinily varnished rustic timbering and beamery, has more tables. Generously served, well cooked food might include lighter dishes such as soup (£2.95), pasta bolognese, smoked haddock and prawns in cheese sauce, delicious sautéed chicken livers and bacon with cream and brandy (£6.50), with more substantial meals such as thai chicken curry (£10.95), seared tuna with pink peppercorn sauce (£11.50), lamb with redcurrant, orange and mint sauce (£12.95), and scottish rib-eye steak with port and stilton sauce (£15.50). Banks's Bitter and Woods Quaff are well kept on handpump with a guest such as Adnams Broadside, and they've good value house wines. Disabled access; piped music. Outside, there are picnic-sets on the grass behind, among shrubs and small fruit trees – a pleasant spot, with pasture beyond. *(Recommended by M G Hart, Mrs Sally Lloyd, Roger and Pauline Pearce, Martin Jennings, Stuart Paulley, M Joyner, Karen Eliot, Ian and Jo Argyle, Pat and Tony Martin, Joan and Tony Walker, John and Wendy Allin, Mike and Mary Carter, Christopher Turner, Dave Braisted)*

Free house ~ Licensees Steven and Ian Thomas ~ Real ale ~ Bar food (12-1.45, 7-9.45; not Sun evening) ~ (01905) 381275 ~ Children in eating area of bar and restaurant, must be over 10 in evening ~ Open 12-2.30, 7-11; 12-3 Sun; closed Sun evening

DEFFORD SO9143 Map 4

Monkey House

A4104 towards Upton – immediately after passing Oak public house on right, there's a small group of cottages, of which this is the last

You won't find anywhere else quite like this fascinating throwback – a completely traditional cider-house, which has been in the landlord's wife's family for over 150 years. The only clue from the outside that this pretty black and white thatched cottage is actually a pub is a notice by the door saying 'Licensed to sell cider and tobacco'. Very cheap Bulmer's Medium or Special Dry cider is tapped from barrels, poured by jug into pottery mugs (some locals have their own), and served from a hatch beside the door. As a concession to modern tastes, beer is sold too, in cans. Apart from crisps and nuts they don't do food, but you can bring your own. In the summer you could find yourself sharing the garden with the hens and cockerels that wander in from an adjacent collection of caravans and sheds; there's also a pony called Mandy, Tapper the jack russell, and Marie the rottweiler. Alternatively you can retreat to a small and spartan side outbuilding with a couple of plain tables, a settle and an open fire. The pub's name comes from the story of a drunken customer who, some years ago, fell into bramble bushes and swore that he was attacked by monkeys. Please note the limited opening times. *(Recommended by the Didler, Pete Baker, Derek and Sylvia Stephenson, Dr G and Mrs J Kelvin, Dr and Mrs A K Clarke, David J Austin)*

Free house ~ Licensee Graham Collins ~ No credit cards ~ (01386) 750234 ~ Children welcome ~ Open 11-2 Fri, Sat, Mon; 6-10 Weds-Sat; 12-2, 7-10 Sun; closed Mon evening, Weds-Thurs lunchtime, all Tues

FLYFORD FLAVELL SO9754 Map 4

Boot

½ mile off A422 Worcester—Alcester; sharp turn into village beside Flyford Arms, then turn left into Radford Road

The friendly landlady and courteous staff are quick to make customers feel at home in this convivial Georgian-fronted country pub. With parts dating back to the 13th c, the heavily beamed and timbered back area is mainly for dining now, with fresh flowers on tables, a log fire in the big fireplace, and plates on its walls; part is no smoking. The lower end, divided by a timbered part wall, has a glass-topped well, and leads into a modern conservatory with brocaded dining chairs and swagged curtains. A little beamed front bar has hunting prints, antique chairs, and inglenook seats by the small log fire; on its left is a well lit pool table; also piped music, cards, and fruit machine. Up to half a dozen real ales on handpump include Fullers London Pride, Greene King IPA and Old Speckled Hen, St Austell Tribute, Worthingtons and an interesting changing guest such as St Georges Enigma; they've also ten malt whiskies, and a good range of liqueurs. Reasonably priced dishes, served on big white plates, include lunchtime sandwiches (from £3.75), and bar snacks such as duck spring rolls, thai fishcakes, chicken satay and filo-wrapped king prawns (£6.25), with other dishes such as beer-battered cod or various home-made pies (£8.50), chicken curry (£9.50), grilled bass (£10.95), duck breast with orange and brandy sauce (£11.95), and rack of lamb (£12.95); the home-made puddings might include banoffi pie or brandy snap basket (£3.75). It's very popular with older people at lunchtime. Pretty and very neatly kept, the garden has smart furniture, outdoor heating and lighting, and attractive big planted pots. Readers enjoy staying here; big breakfasts. *(Recommended by Theo, Anne and Jane Gaskin, M Joyner, Martin Jennings, Rod Stoneman, David and Barbara Knott, John and Johanne Eadie, Mr and Mrs W D Borthwick, Richard Evans, Moira and John Cole, George Atkinson)*

Free house ~ Licensee Sue Hughes ~ Real ale ~ Bar food (12-2, 7-9; 12-5, 7-9.30 Sun) ~ Restaurant ~ (01386) 462658 ~ Children in restaurant ~ Dogs allowed in bar ~ Open 12-3, 5-11; 12-11 Sun ~ Bedrooms: £50S/£60S

HOLY CROSS SO9278 Map 4

Bell & Cross

4 miles from M5 junction 4: A491 towards Stourbridge, then follow Clent signpost off on left

Worcestershire Dining Pub of the Year

The imaginative food is the big attraction at this comfortably civilised pub, although it's also popular with locals just out for an evening drink. Enticing dishes, from a changing menu, include lunchtime snacks (not Sunday) such as sandwiches (from £4.25, baguettes from £4.50), toasted muffin with potted chicken liver and port parfait (£5.50), smoked haddock with scrambled egg and chive cream (£6.25), and oregano, tomato and beef ragoût with tagliatelle (£5.75; £8.50 large), with other dishes such as pea and dolcelatte risotto with confit tomato (£10.25), pot-roasted chicken and parma ham with macaroni cheese and basil pesto (£10.95), and grilled calves liver with bubble and squeak, glazed shallots and smoked bacon (£12.50), with a few daily specials such as roasted cornish brill with spinach and ricotta ravioli and lobster and herb broth or confit pork belly wrapped in parma ham with braised leek and black pudding (£13.50); puddings might include sticky chocolate brownies and chantilly cream (from £4.95). The Sunday menu includes traditional roasts; they do children's meals (£5.25). With a classic unspoilt early 19th-c layout, the five small rooms and kitchen open off a central corridor with a black and white tiled floor: they give a choice of carpet, bare boards, lino or nice old quarry tiles, a variety of moods from snug and chatty to bright and airy, and an individual décor in each – theatrical engravings on red walls here, nice sporting prints on pale green walls there, racing and gundog pictures above the black panelled dado in another room. Two of the rooms have small serving bars, with well kept Banks's Bitter, Marstons Pedigree and maybe a guest such as Timothy

Taylors Landlord on handpump. You'll find decent house wines, a variety of coffees, daily papers, coal fires in most rooms, perhaps regulars playing cards in one of the two front ones, and piped music. The pub cat is called Pumba. There's a terrace in the pleasant garden; fine views. *(Recommended by Karen Eliot, Richard and Karen Holt, Dave Braisted, David and Ruth Shillitoe, Gill and Tony Morriss, Mr and Mrs C R Little, Nigel Long, Pete Baker, Margaret Drazin, Stuart Paulley, Drs E J C Parker, Brenda and Rob Fincham)*

Enterprise ~ Tenants Roger and Jo Narbett ~ Real ale ~ Bar food (not 25 Dec, evening 26 Dec) ~ Restaurant ~ (01562) 730319 ~ Children in restaurant ~ Dogs allowed in bar ~ Open 12-3, 6-11; 12-4, 7-10.30 Sun; closed 25 Dec

KEMPSEY SO8548 Map 4

Walter de Cantelupe

A38, handy for M5 junction 7 via A44 and A4440

Readers highly recommend the tasty ploughman's at this welcoming and unpretentious roadside inn and, to go with it, there's a good choice of wines by the glass (they have regularly changing bin ends, and english wines from a local vineyard). Boldly decorated in red and gold, the bar area has an informal and well worn in mix of furniture, an old wind-up HMV gramophone and a good big fireplace. The dining area has various plush or yellow leather dining chairs, an old settle, a sonorous clock, and candles and flowers on the tables. Cooked by the friendly landlord, using lots of local produce, enjoyable well presented dishes might be lunchtime sandwiches (from £3), home-made soup (£3.60), glamorgan sausages with mushroom gravy and mashed potato (£5.90), chicken balti (£7.50), and gammon, egg and chips (£7.60), with specials such as grilled field mushrooms with garlic butter (£4), beef and ale pie (£8.50), and cajun-spiced salmon (£8.75), with puddings such as marmalade bread and butter pudding (£3.75); you can buy jars of home-made chutney. Well kept real ales on handpump such as Hobsons Best, Cannon Royall Kings Shilling and Timothy Taylors Landlord; good service. The dining area is no smoking; cribbage, dominoes and table skittles. There's a pretty suntrap walled garden at the back; the sociable labrador is called Monti. *(Recommended by Michael and Janice Gwilliam, Dr and Mrs W T Farrington, R and J Bateman, Christopher Garrard, Mrs L Mills, George Atkinson, Denys Gueroult, C P Gill, Jack Clark, JWAC, Pat and Tony Martin, Dr and Mrs A K Clarke, David and Christine Vaughton, P R Morgan)*

Free house ~ Licensee Martin Lloyd Morris ~ Real ale ~ Bar food (12-2(2.30 Sat), 6-9.30; 12-2.30, 7-8; not Mon exc bank hols) ~ Restaurant ~ (01905) 820572 ~ Children in restaurant ~ Dogs allowed in bar and bedrooms ~ Open 12-2(2.30 summer), 5.30-11; 11-2.30(3 summer), 6-11 Sat; 12-3.30(4 summer), 7-10.30 Sun; closed Mon except bank hols, 25-26 Dec, 1 Jan ~ Bedrooms: £38.50S(£49.50B)/£49.50S(£77B)

KIDDERMINSTER SO8376 Map 4

King & Castle £

Railway Station, Comberton Hill

You can take your pint out on to the platform and watch the trains steam by at this memorable re-creation of a classic station refreshment room, right at the heart of the Severn Valley Railway terminus. Inside you get the feeling of a better-class Edwardian establishment that has let its hair down to embrace more informal modern ways. You'll find a good mix of customers, and the atmosphere is lively and sometimes noisily good-humoured; it can get rather smoky. Furnishings are solid and in character, and there's the railway memorabilia that you'd expect. Bathams, Enville Nailmaker Mild and Wyre Piddle Royal Piddle are superbly kept alongside a couple of changing guests from brewers such as Hobsons, and Wye Valley on handpump (with at least one at bargain price), and they've ten malt whiskies; piped music. The reasonably priced straightforward menu includes toasties (from £2.25), basket meals such as scampi or sausage and chips (£2.95), ploughman's (£4.50), vegetable kiev, gammon and egg or breaded plaice (£4.95), and traditional puddings such as chocolate pudding (£2.50); they also do Sunday roasts (£4.75), and children's meals (£2.50). The cheerful landlady and friendly staff cope well with the bank holiday and railway gala day crowds (you'd be lucky to find a seat then); dogs are very welcome. You can use a Rover ticket to shuttle between here and the Railwaymans Arms in Bridgnorth (see Shropshire chapter). More reports please. *(Recommended by Gill and Tony Morriss)*

Free house ~ Licensee Rosemary Hyde ~ Real ale ~ Bar food (12-2(2.30 Sat-Sun), 6-8 Fri-Sat, 7-9 Sun; not Mon-Thurs evenings) ~ No credit cards ~ (01562) 747505 ~ Children welcome in eating area of bar till 9pm ~ Dogs welcome ~ Open 11-3, 5-11; 11-11 Sat; 12-10.30 Sun

KNIGHTWICK SO7355 Map 4

Talbot

Knightsford Bridge; B4197 just off A44 Worcester—Bromyard

Well kept on handpump and fairly priced, This, That, Wot and T'Other ales (they also have Hobsons Bitter) are brewed at this 15th-c coaching inn from locally grown hops; wine drinkers are not neglected either, and there are 25 different wines by the glass to choose from. With a good log fire in winter, the heavily beamed and extended lounge bar opens on to a terrace and an arbour with roses and clematis. There are a variety of interesting seats from small carved or leatherette armchairs to the winged settles by the tall bow windows, and a vast stove squats in the big central stone hearth. The well furnished back public bar has pool on a raised side area, darts, fruit machine, video game and juke box; dominoes and cribbage. Freshly prepared with local ingredients (some of the vegetables are grown in the pub's organic garden), good bar food includes a couple of lunchtime snacks such as rolls (£1.75), ploughman's (£6), pea and tomato quiche or sausage, egg and chips (£7), with other well presented (though not cheap) dishes such as soup (£4), pork, orange and cognac pâté or tagliatelle with tomato and basil sauce (£5.50), pasta carbonara (£12), and asparagus and fennel risotto, halibut with citrus dressing, braised lambs hearts with sautéed leeks or beef shin in ale with garlic chilli potatoes (all £14), with puddings such as bread pudding or local cheeses (£5); cheerfully attentive service. There are some old-fashioned seats in front of the pub, with more on a good-sized lawn over the lane by the river (they serve out here too). Some of the bedrooms are above the bar. They hold a farmers' market here on the second Sunday in the month. *(Recommended by Mr and Mrs P J Fisk, Martin Jennings, Guy Vowles, Gill and Tony Morriss, Dick and Madeleine Brown, Alan and Jill Bull, Kevin Thorpe, Di and Mike Gillam, Cathryn and Richard Hicks, O K Smyth, JHW, George Atkinson, Dave Braisted)*

Own brew ~ Licensees Wiz and Annie Clift ~ Real ale ~ Bar food ~ Restaurant ~ (01886) 821235 ~ Children welcome ~ Dogs allowed in bar ~ Open 11-11; 12-10.30 Sun; closed evening 25 Dec ~ Bedrooms: £40S/£75B

MALVERN SO7845 Map 4

Nags Head

Bottom end of Bank Street, steep turn down off A449

In a pleasant spot between the great mass of hill swelling up behind and the plain stretching out below, this cheerfully bustling traditional tavern serves up to 11 beers on handpump. Along with well kept Greene King IPA, Marstons Pedigree and Woods Shropshire Lad, you'll find changing guest beers from brewers such as Banks's, Bathams, Cottage, Holdens, Timothy Taylors and Wye Valley. They also have a fine range of malt whiskies, and decent wines by the glass; friendly young staff. A good variety of places to sit rambles through a series of snug individually decorated rooms with one or two steps between some, all sorts of chairs including some leather armchairs, pews sometimes arranged as booths, a mix of tables with some sturdy ones stained different colours, bare boards here, flagstones there, carpet elsewhere, and plenty of interesting pictures and homely touches such as house plants and shelves of well thumbed books; there's a coal fire opposite the central servery. The pub attracts a good mix of customers (with plenty of locals),

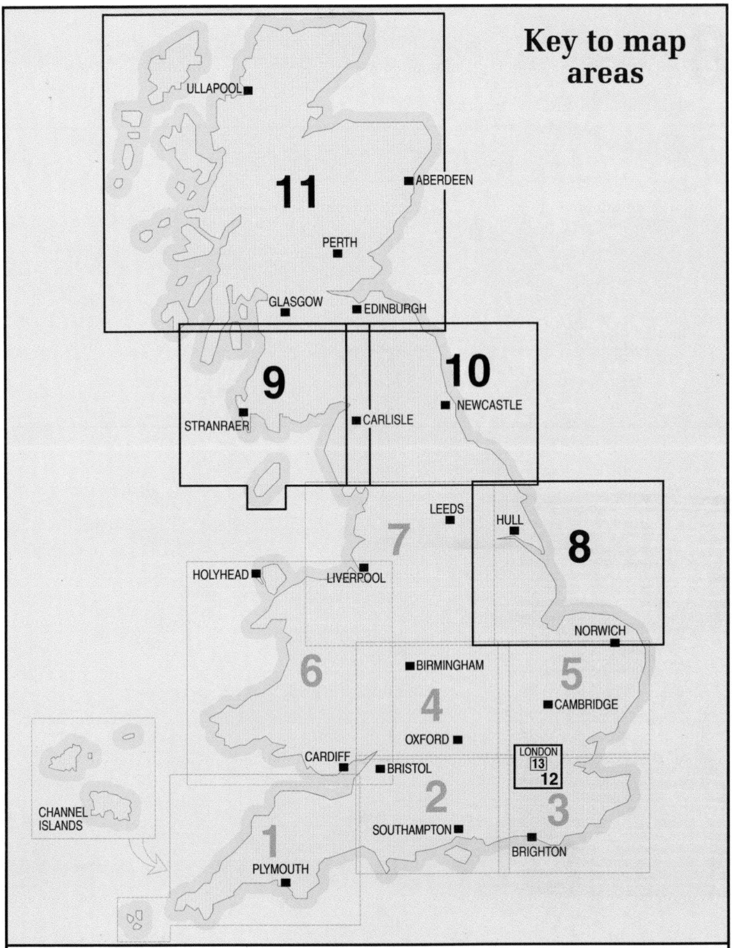

Reference to sectional maps

Motorway		● **Totnes**	Guide entry
Trunk road		⦿ **Lynton**	Guide entry with accommodation
Major road		■ BODMIN	Place name to assist location
County boundary			

MAPS IN THIS SECTION

For Maps 1 – 7 see earlier colour section

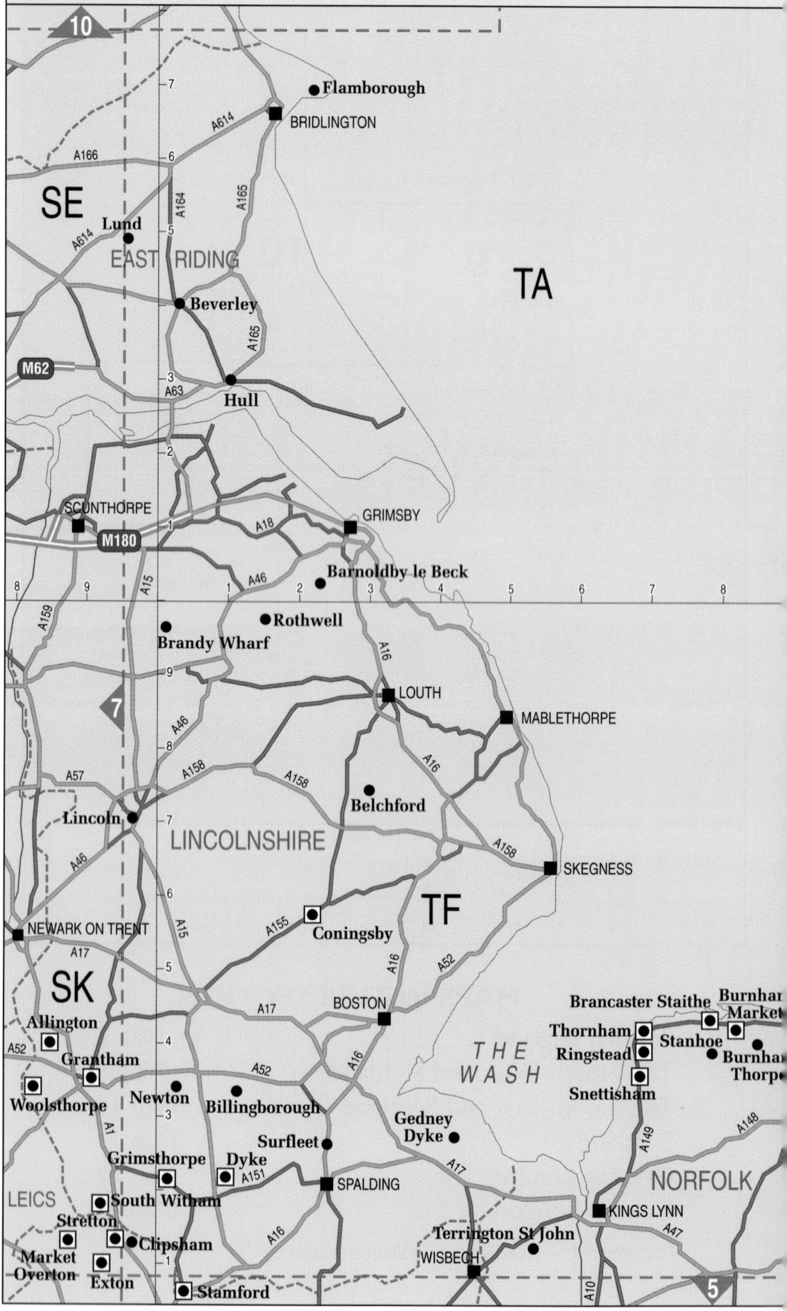
10
SE
TA
TF
SK
Flamborough
BRIDLINGTON
A614
A166
A164
A165
Lund
EAST RIDING
Beverley
M62
A63
Hull
SCUNTHORPE
M180
A18
GRIMSBY
A46
Barnoldby le Beck
A15
A159
Rothwell
Brandy Wharf
A16
LOUTH
MABLETHORPE
7
A57
A158
Belchford
Lincoln
LINCOLNSHIRE
SKEGNESS
A155
Coningsby
NEWARK ON TRENT
A17
A52
BOSTON
Allington
Grantham
Woolsthorpe
Newton
Billingborough
A1
Surfleet
Gedney
Dyke
Grimsthorpe
Dyke
A151
SPALDING
LEICS
South Witham
Stretton
Clipsham
Market
Overton
Exton
Stamford
Terrington St John
WISBECH
THE
WASH
Brancaster Staithe
Thornham
Ringstead
Snettisham
Stanhoe
A149
A148
NORFOLK
KINGS LYNN
A47
A10
5

8

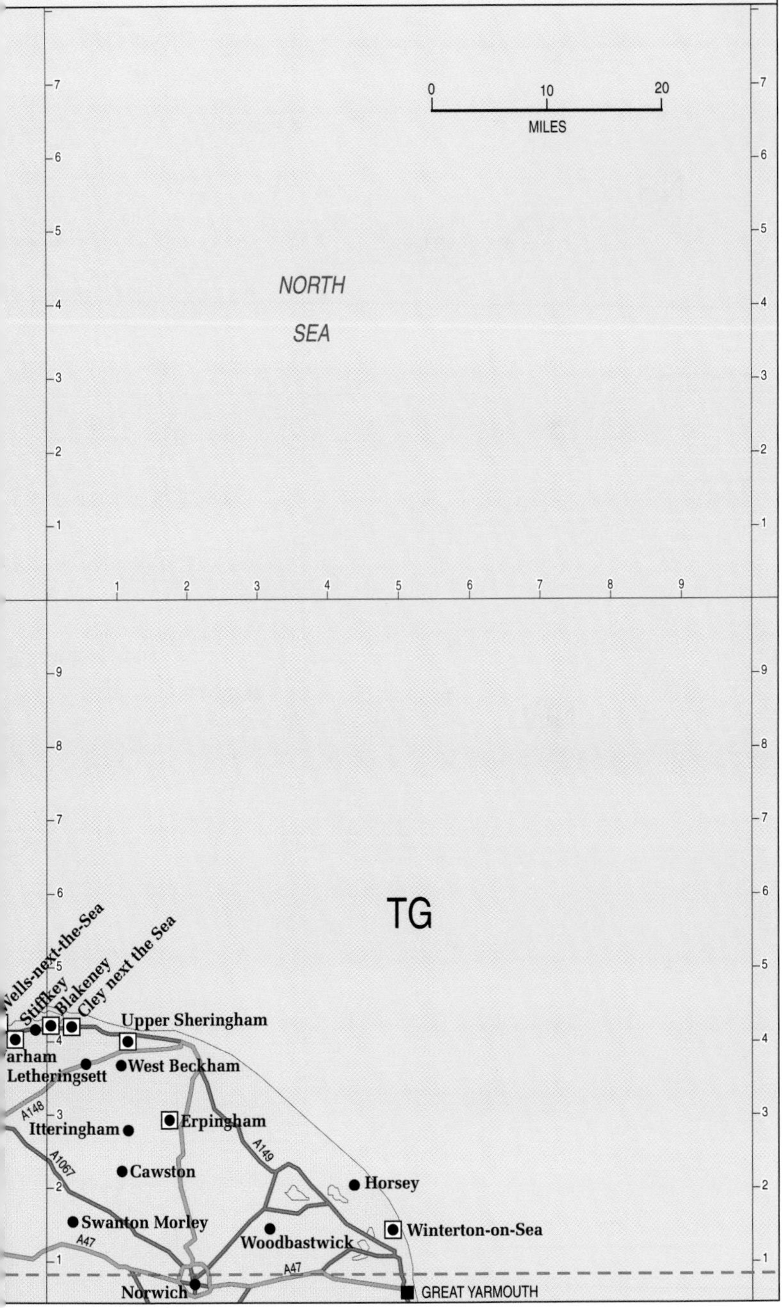
0
10
20
MILES
NORTH
SEA
TG
Wells-next-the-Sea
Stiffkey
Blakeney
Cley next the Sea
Upper Sheringham
arham
Letheringsett
West Beckham
A148
Itteringham
Erpingham
A149
A1067
Cawston
Horsey
Swanton Morley
Winterton-on-Sea
Woodbastwick
A47
A47
Norwich
GREAT YARMOUTH

9

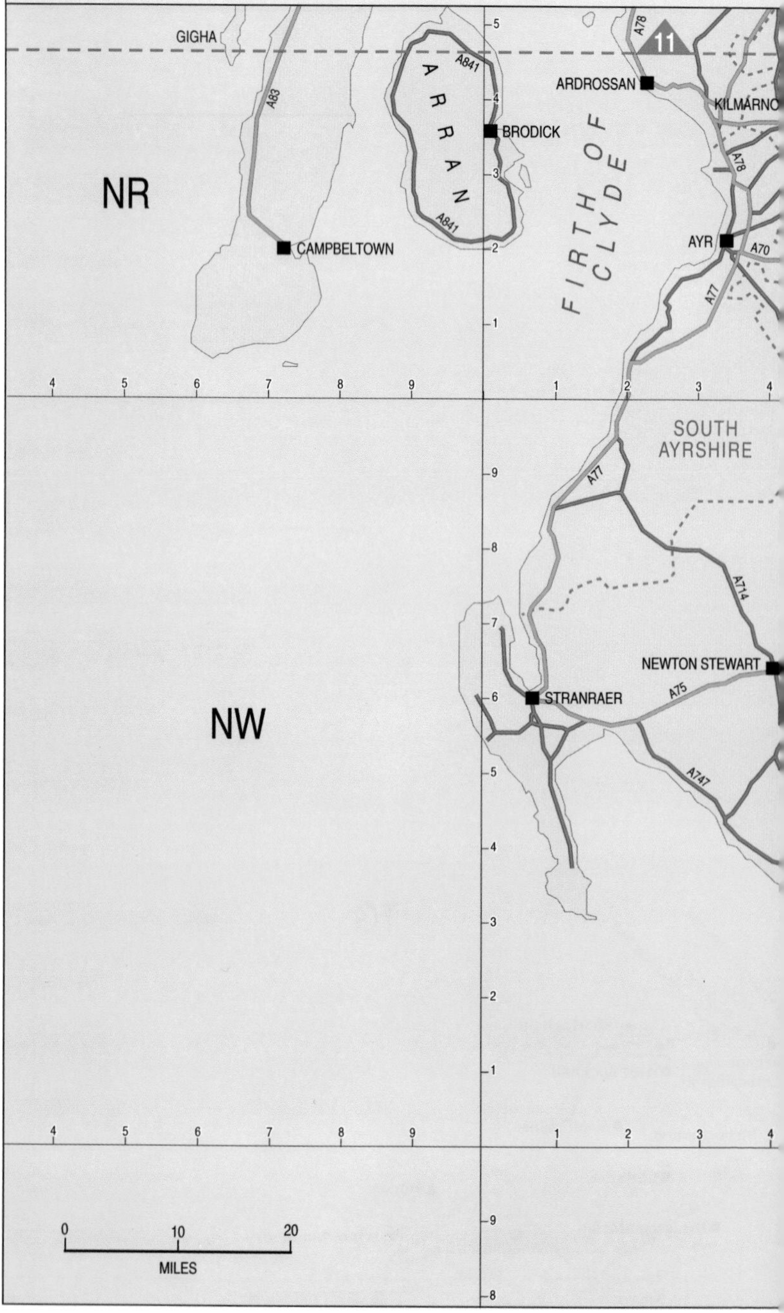

GIGHA
A83
CAMPBELTOWN
NR
A841
ARRAN
BRODICK
FIRTH OF CLYDE
A78
11
ARDROSSAN
KILMARNO
AYR
A70
A77
SOUTH AYRSHIRE
A714
NEWTON STEWART
STRANRAER
A75
A747
NW
0
10
20
MILES

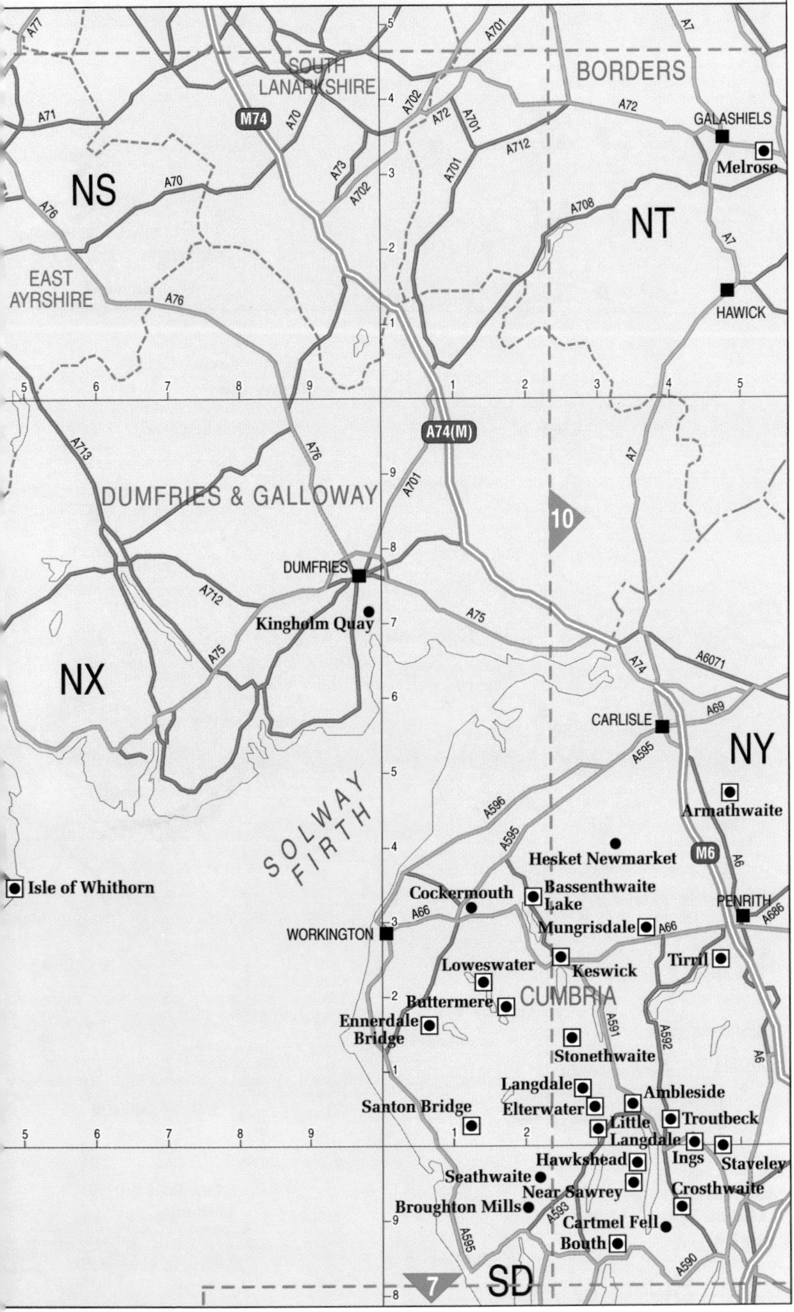
NS
NT
NX
NY
SD
SOUTH LANARKSHIRE
BORDERS
EAST AYRSHIRE
DUMFRIES & GALLOWAY
CUMBRIA
SOLWAY FIRTH
GALASHIELS
Melrose
HAWICK
DUMFRIES
Kingholm Quay
CARLISLE
Armathwaite
Hesket Newmarket
Isle of Whithorn
Cockermouth
Bassenthwaite Lake
PENRITH
WORKINGTON
Mungrisdale
Keswick
Tirril
Loweswater
Buttermere
Ennerdale Bridge
Stonethwaite
Langdale
Elterwater
Ambleside
Santon Bridge
Little Langdale
Troutbeck
Ings
Staveley
Hawkshead
Seathwaite
Near Sawrey
Crosthwaite
Broughton Mills
Cartmel Fell
Bouth
M74
A74(M)
M6
A77
A71
A70
A76
A73
A702
A72
A701
A712
A708
A7
A713
A75
A74
A6071
A69
A595
A596
A66
A686
A6
A591
A592
A593
A590
10
7

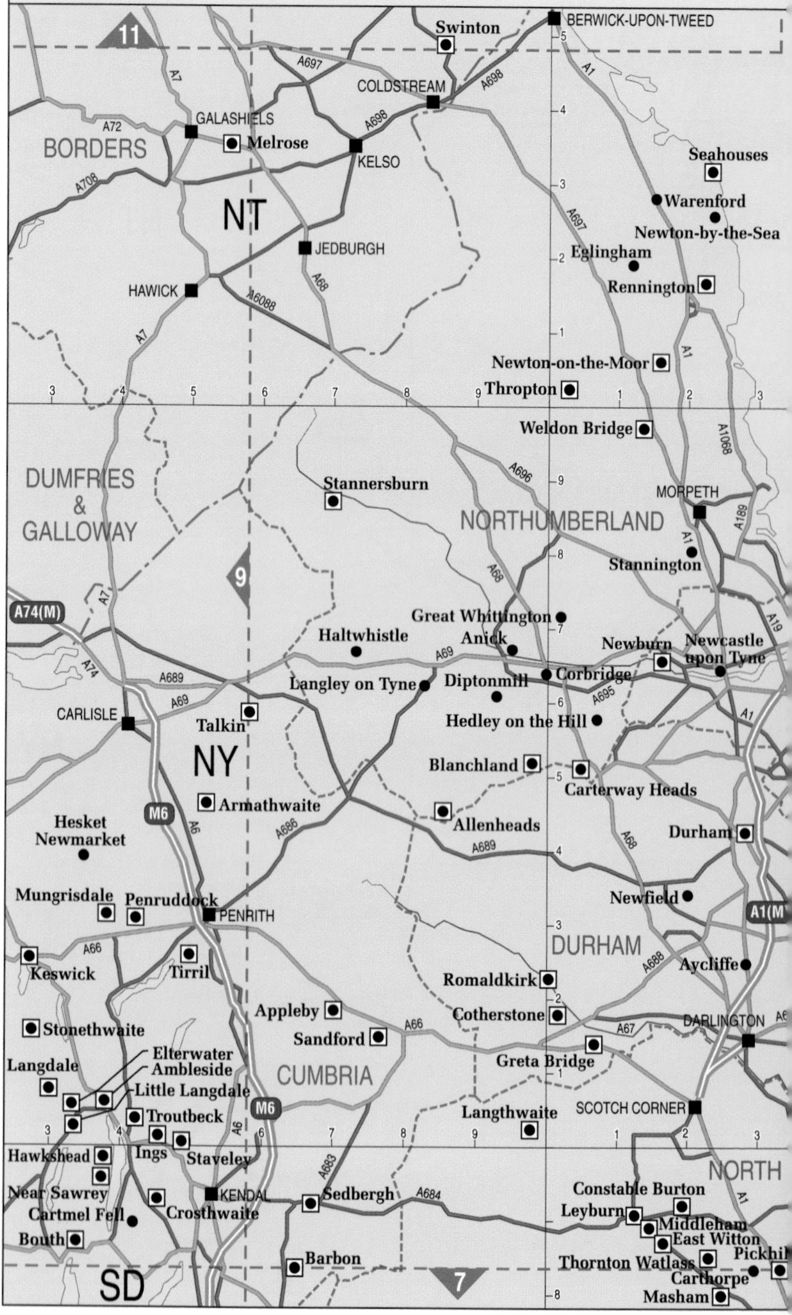
11
Swinton
BERWICK-UPON-TWEED
A697
A7
COLDSTREAM
A698
A1
GALASHIELS
A72
Melrose
BORDERS
KELSO
A708
Seahouses
Warenford
NT
A697
Newton-by-the-Sea
JEDBURGH
Eglingham
A68
HAWICK
A6088
Rennington
A7
A1
Newton-on-the-Moor
Thropton
Weldon Bridge
A1068
DUMFRIES
&
GALLOWAY
Stannersburn
A696
MORPETH
NORTHUMBERLAND
A189
A1
Stannington
9
A68
A7
A74(M)
Great Whittington
A19
Haltwhistle
Anick
Newburn
Newcastle upon Tyne
A74
A69
A689
Langley on Tyne
Diptonmill
Corbridge
A69
A695
CARLISLE
Talkin
Hedley on the Hill
A1
NY
Blanchland
Carterway Heads
M6
Armathwaite
Allenheads
Hesket Newmarket
A6
A686
A689
Durham
A68
Mungrisdale
Penruddock
PENRITH
Newfield
A1(M)
A66
DURHAM
Keswick
Tirril
A688
Aycliffe
Romaldkirk
Stonethwaite
Appleby
Cotherstone
DARLINGTON
Sandford
A66
A67
Elterwater
Ambleside
Greta Bridge
Langdale
CUMBRIA
Little Langdale
M6
Troutbeck
Langthwaite
SCOTCH CORNER
A6
Hawkshead
Ings
Staveley
NORTH
Near Sawrey
A683
KENDAL
Sedbergh
A684
Constable Burton
A1
Cartmel Fell
Crosthwaite
Leyburn
Middleham
Bouth
East Witton
Barbon
Thornton Watlass
7
Carthorpe
SD
Masham

0
10
20
MILES
NU
NORTH SEA
NZ
SOUTH SHIELDS
SUNDERLAND
HARTLEPOOL
MIDDLESBROUGH
A19
A66
A174
A171
A172
A169
A170
A165
Whitby
Robin Hood's Bay
Egton Bridge
Beck Hole
Osmotherley
YORKSHIRE
SE
Blakey Ridge
Lastingham
Fadmoor
Cropton
Appleton-le-Moors
Sinnington
Felixkirk
Kirkbymoorside
Scawton
Pickering
Harome
Marton
Scarborough
TA
8

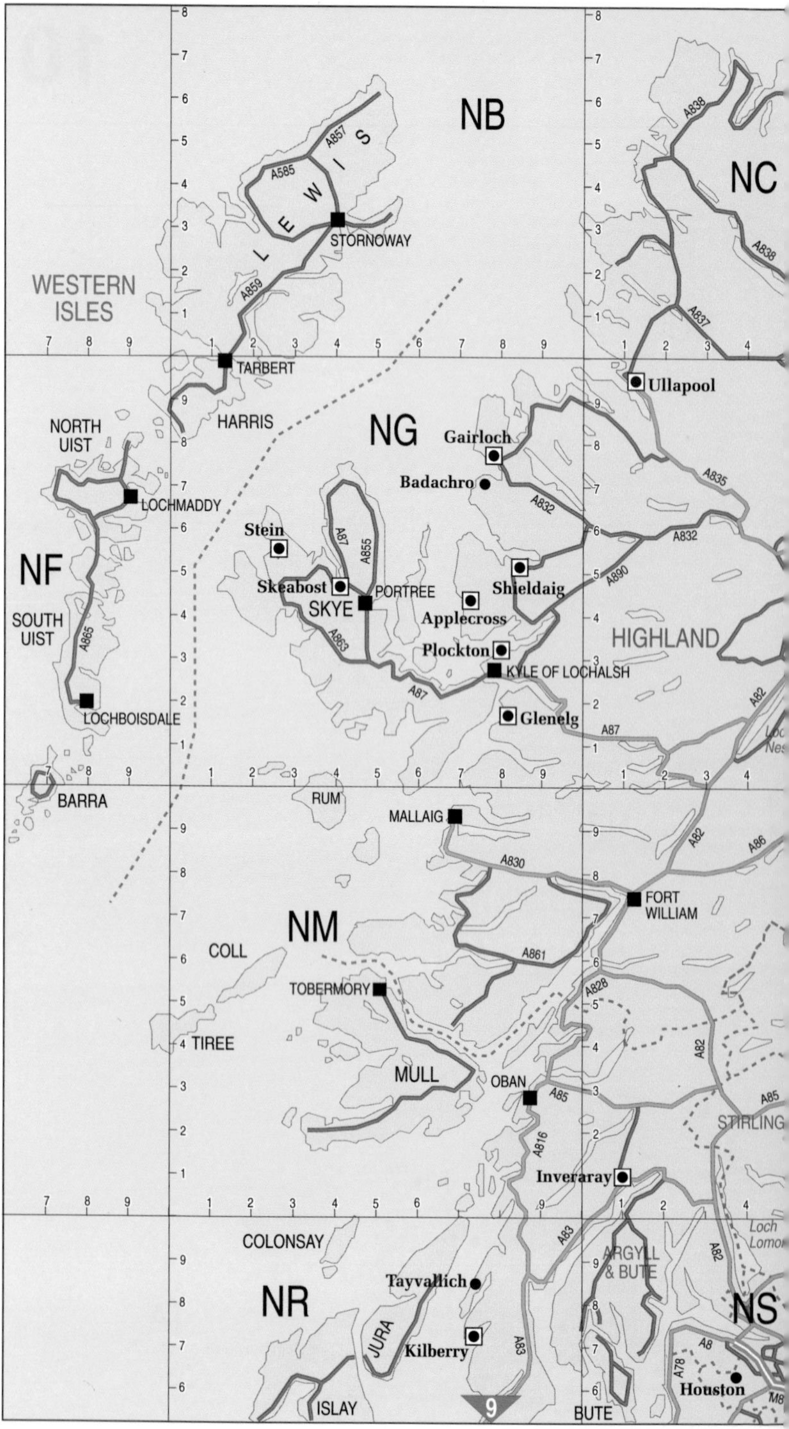
NB
NC
LEWIS
A857
A585
STORNOWAY
A859
WESTERN ISLES
A838
A837
TARBERT
HARRIS
NORTH UIST
LOCHMADDY
NF
SOUTH UIST
A865
LOCHBOISDALE
BARRA
NG
Ullapool
Gairloch
Badachro
A835
A832
Stein
A87
A855
Skeabost
SKYE
PORTREE
Shieldaig
A890
Applecross
HIGHLAND
A863
Plockton
KYLE OF LOCHALSH
A87
Glenelg
A82
RUM
MALLAIG
A830
A86
FORT WILLIAM
NM
COLL
A861
TOBERMORY
A828
TIREE
MULL
OBAN
A85
A82
STIRLING
A816
Inveraray
COLONSAY
A83
ARGYLL & BUTE
Loch Lomond
Tayvallich
NR
NS
JURA
Kilberry
A8
A78
Houston
ISLAY
BUTE
9

11

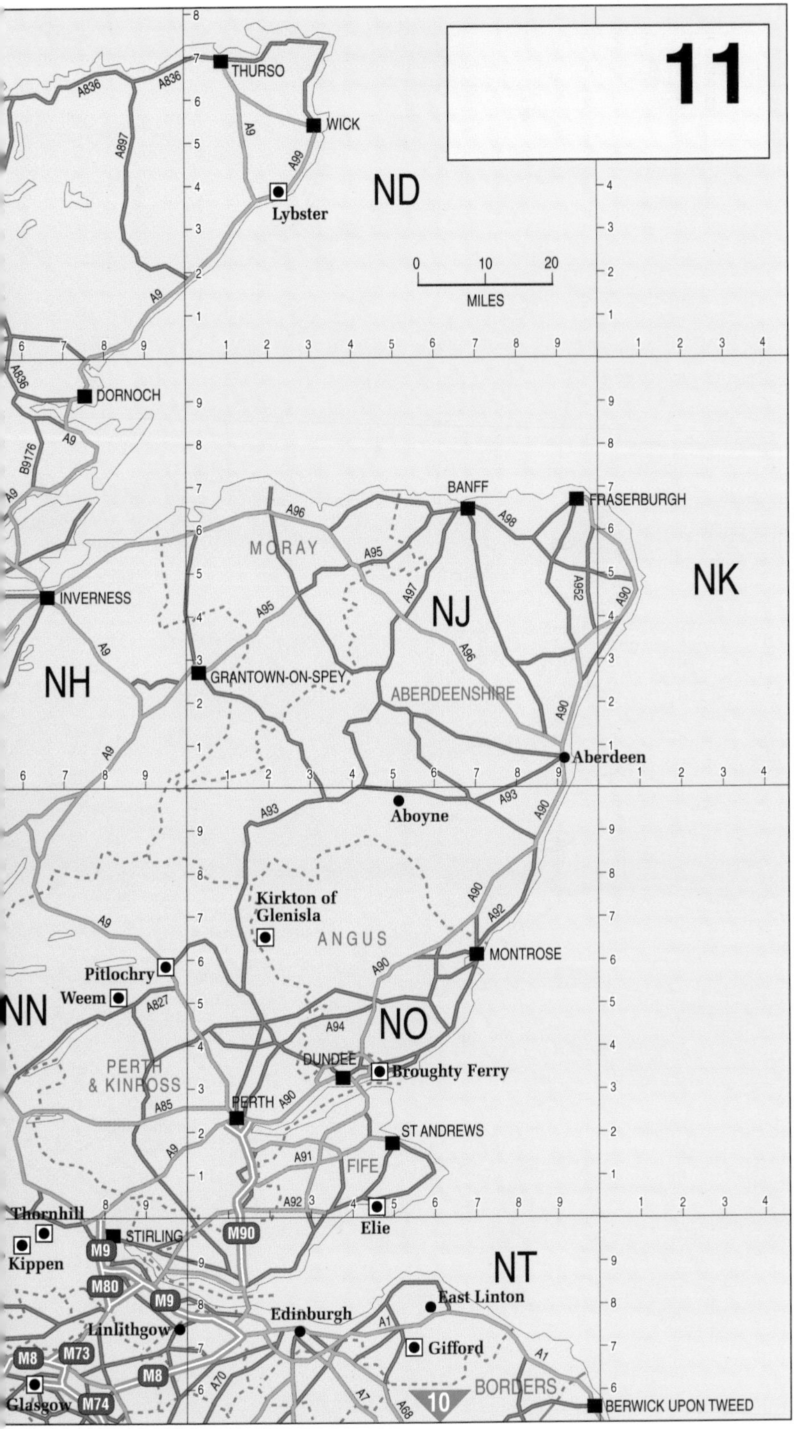
ND
NH
NJ
NK
NN
NO
NT
0 10 20
MILES
THURSO
WICK
Lybster
DORNOCH
BANFF
FRASERBURGH
MORAY
INVERNESS
GRANTOWN-ON-SPEY
ABERDEENSHIRE
Aberdeen
Aboyne
Kirkton of Glenisla
ANGUS
MONTROSE
Pitlochry
Weem
PERTH & KINROSS
DUNDEE
Broughty Ferry
PERTH
ST ANDREWS
FIFE
Elie
Thornhill
Kippen
STIRLING
East Linton
Edinburgh
Linlithgow
Gifford
Glasgow
BORDERS
BERWICK UPON TWEED
10
A836
A897
A9
A99
B9176
A96
A95
A97
A98
A952
A90
A93
A92
A94
A827
A85
A91
A1
A70
A7
A68
M90
M9
M80
M8
M73
M74

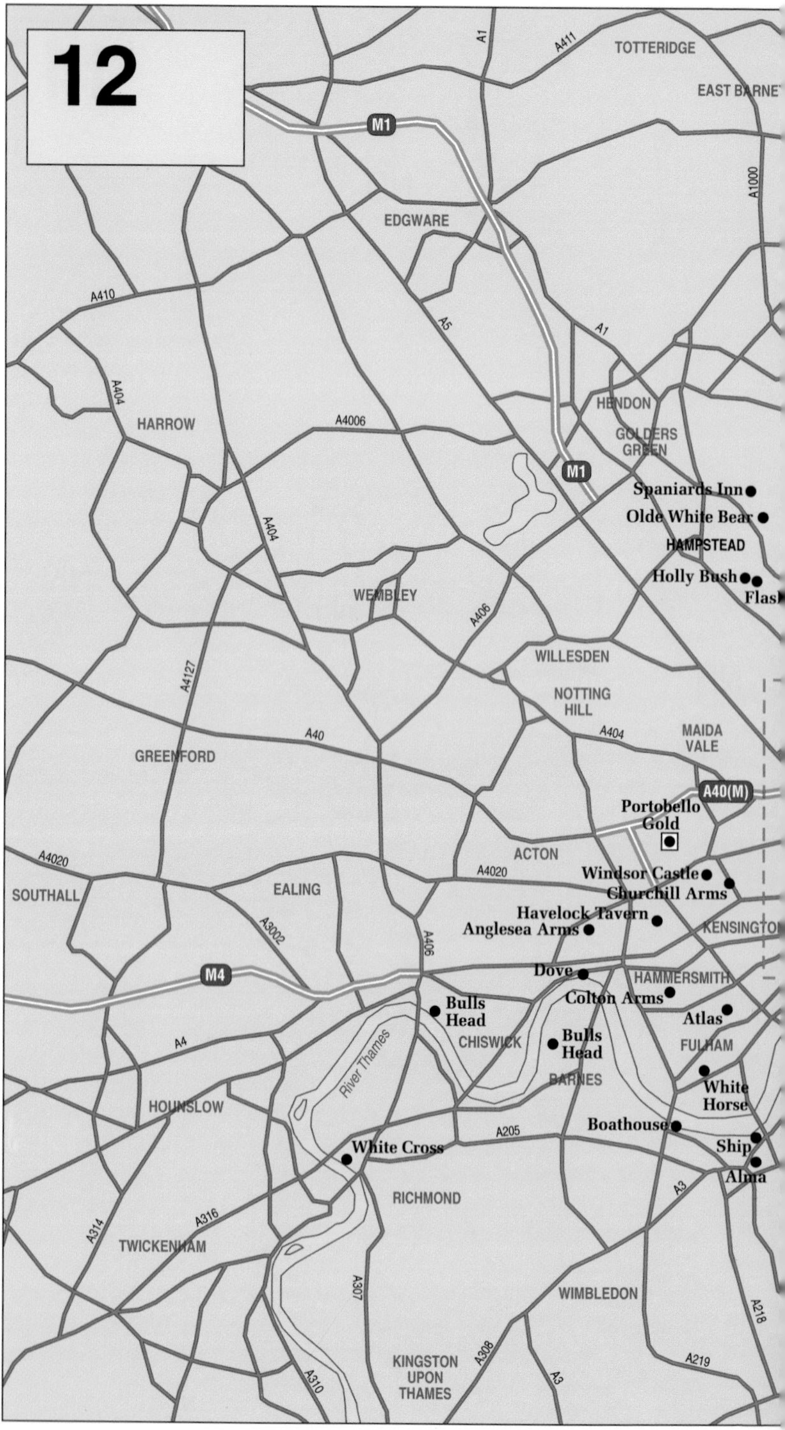
12
TOTTERIDGE
M1
A1
A411
A1000
EDGWARE
A410
A5
A1
A404
HARROW
A4006
HENDON
GOLDERS GREEN
M1
Spaniards Inn
Olde White Bear
HAMPSTEAD
Holly Bush
A404
WEMBLEY
A406
WILLESDEN
A4127
NOTTING HILL
A40
A404
MAIDA VALE
GREENFORD
A40(M)
Portobello Gold
ACTON
A4020
A4020
Windsor Castle
Churchill Arms
SOUTHALL
EALING
Havelock Tavern
Anglesea Arms
A3002
A406
M4
Dove
HAMMERSMITH
Colton Arms
Bulls Head
Atlas
A4
CHISWICK
Bulls Head
River Thames
FULHAM
BARNES
White Horse
HOUNSLOW
Boathouse
A205
White Cross
Ship
Alma
A3
RICHMOND
A316
A314
TWICKENHAM
A307
WIMBLEDON
A218
A308
A219
KINGSTON UPON THAMES
A310
A3

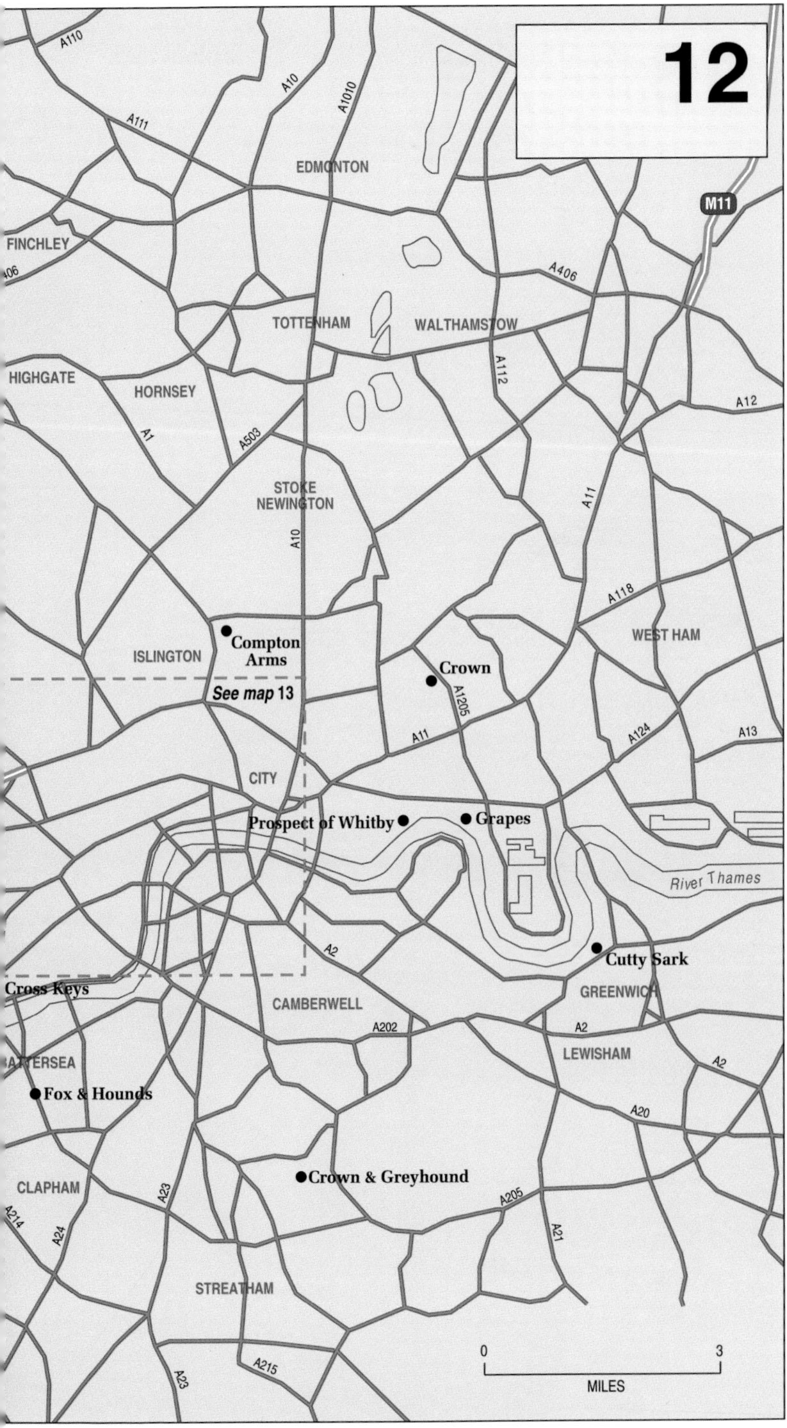
12
A110
A10
A1010
A111
EDMONTON
M11
FINCHLEY
A406
TOTTENHAM
WALTHAMSTOW
HIGHGATE
HORNSEY
A112
A12
A1
A503
STOKE
NEWINGTON
A11
A10
A118
WEST HAM
Compton
Arms
ISLINGTON
Crown
See map 13
A1205
A11
A124
A13
CITY
Prospect of Whitby
Grapes
River Thames
A2
Cutty Sark
Cross Keys
CAMBERWELL
GREENWICH
A202
A2
LEWISHAM
BATTERSEA
A2
Fox & Hounds
A20
CLAPHAM
Crown & Greyhound
A205
A23
A214
A24
A21
STREATHAM
0
3
A215
A23
MILES

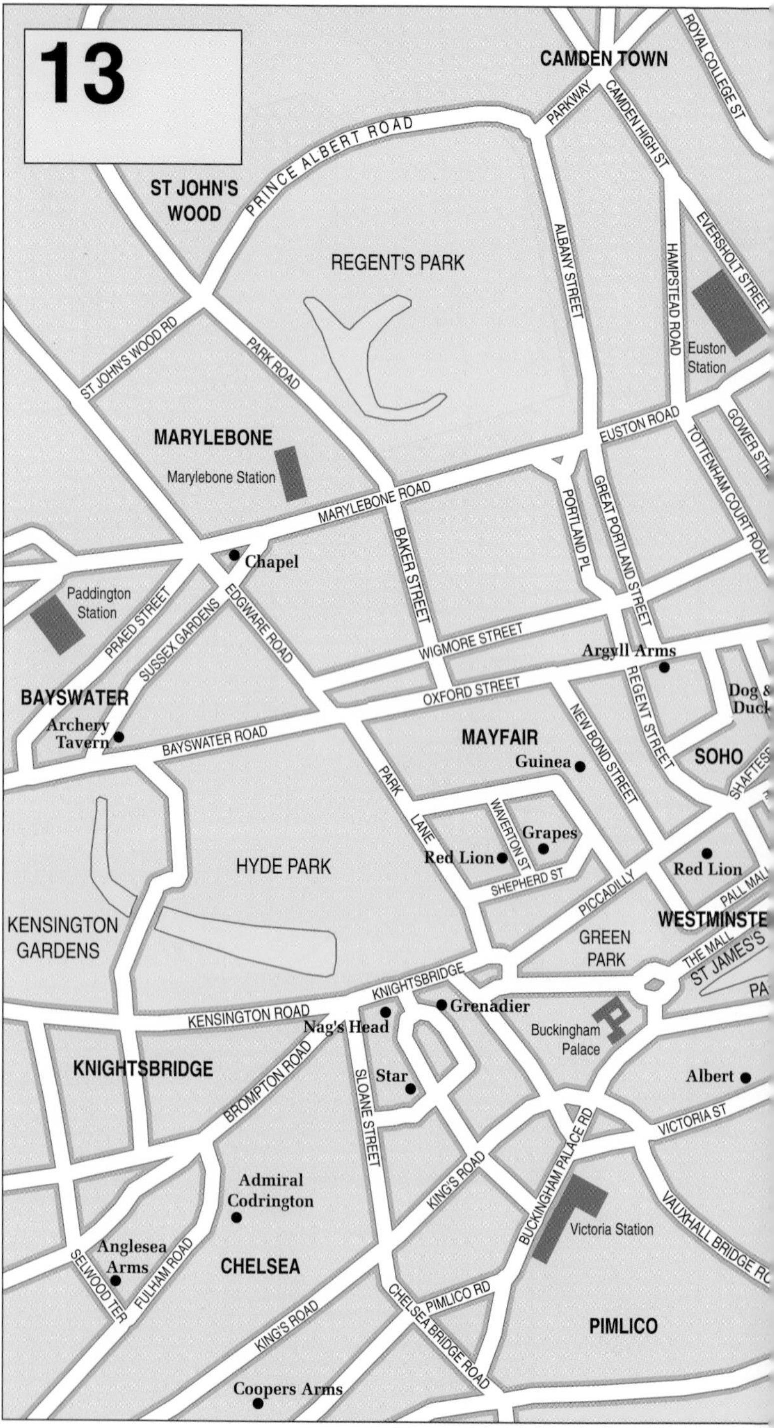
13
CAMDEN TOWN
ROYAL COLLEGE ST
PARKWAY
CAMDEN HIGH ST
PRINCE ALBERT ROAD
ST JOHN'S WOOD
REGENT'S PARK
ALBANY STREET
HAMPSTEAD ROAD
EVERSHOLT STREET
Euston Station
ST JOHN'S WOOD RD
PARK ROAD
MARYLEBONE
Marylebone Station
EUSTON ROAD
GOWER ST
TOTTENHAM COURT ROAD
MARYLEBONE ROAD
PORTLAND PL
GREAT PORTLAND STREET
BAKER STREET
Chapel
Paddington Station
PRAED STREET
SUSSEX GARDENS
EDGWARE ROAD
WIGMORE STREET
Argyll Arms
BAYSWATER
OXFORD STREET
REGENT STREET
NEW BOND STREET
Dog & Duck
Archery Tavern
BAYSWATER ROAD
MAYFAIR
Guinea
SOHO
PARK LANE
WAVERTON ST
Grapes
Red Lion
SHEPHERD ST
Red Lion
HYDE PARK
PICCADILLY
PALL MALL
KENSINGTON GARDENS
WESTMINSTE
GREEN PARK
THE MALL
ST JAMES'S
KNIGHTSBRIDGE
Grenadier
KENSINGTON ROAD
Nag's Head
Buckingham Palace
KNIGHTSBRIDGE
BROMPTON ROAD
Star
SLOANE STREET
Albert
VICTORIA ST
BUCKINGHAM PALACE RD
KING'S ROAD
Admiral Codrington
Victoria Station
VAUXHALL BRIDGE RO
Anglesea Arms
SELWOOD TER
FULHAM ROAD
CHELSEA
PIMLICO RD
CHELSEA BRIDGE ROAD
KING'S ROAD
PIMLICO
Coopers Arms

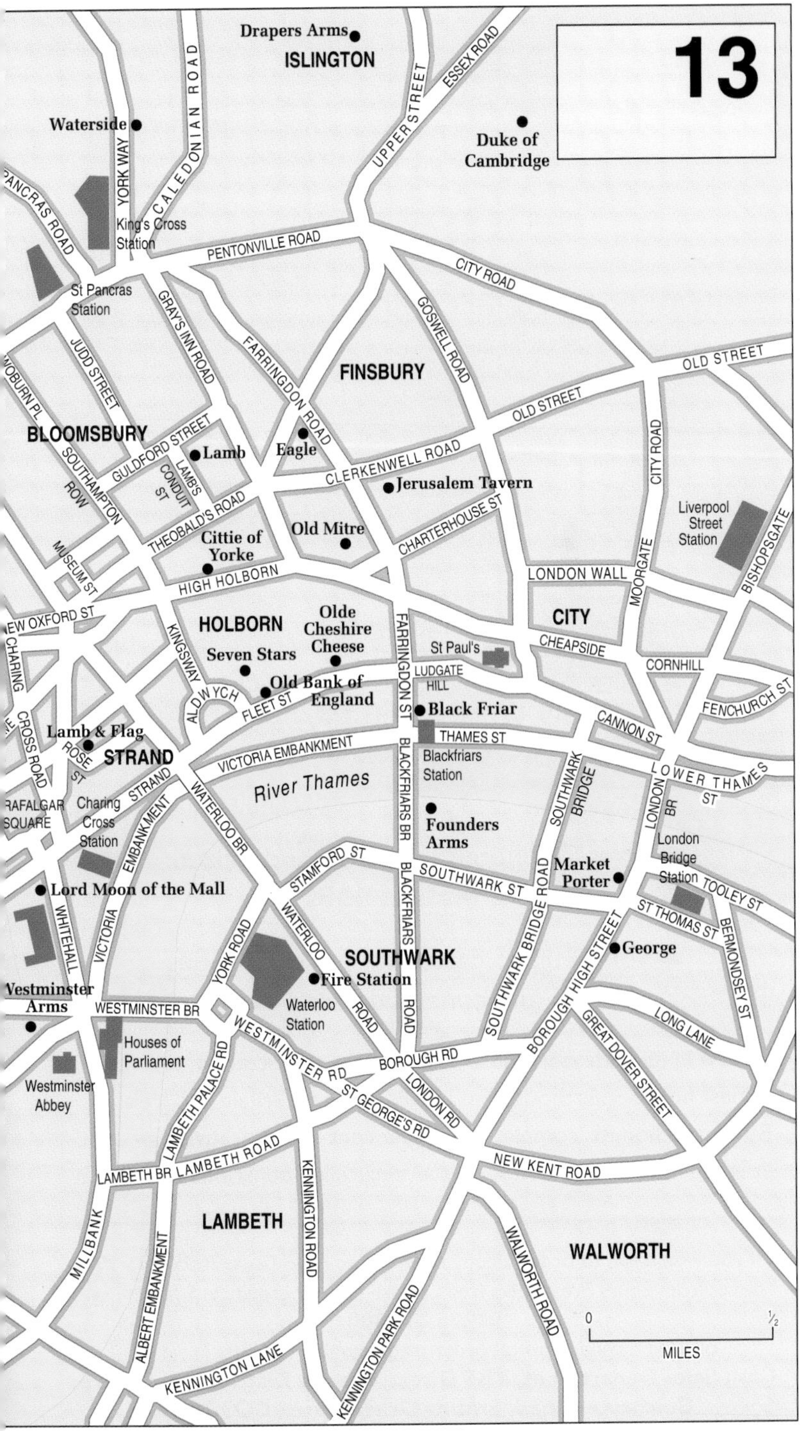
13
Drapers Arms
ISLINGTON
ESSEX ROAD
UPPER STREET
Duke of
Cambridge
Waterside
CALEDONIAN ROAD
YORK WAY
PANCRAS ROAD
King's Cross
Station
PENTONVILLE ROAD
CITY ROAD
St Pancras
Station
GRAY'S INN ROAD
GOSWELL ROAD
FARRINGDON ROAD
FINSBURY
JUDD STREET
WOBURN PL
OLD STREET
OLD STREET
BLOOMSBURY
GUILFORD STREET
Lamb
Eagle
LAMB'S
CONDUIT
ST
CLERKENWELL ROAD
CITY ROAD
SOUTHAMPTON
ROW
Jerusalem Tavern
THEOBALD'S ROAD
Liverpool
Street
Station
Old Mitre
Cittie of
Yorke
CHARTERHOUSE ST
BISHOPSGATE
MUSEUM ST
HIGH HOLBORN
LONDON WALL
MOORGATE
NEW OXFORD ST
HOLBORN
Olde
Cheshire
Cheese
CITY
CHARING
KINGSWAY
FARRINGDON ST
St Paul's
CHEAPSIDE
Seven Stars
LUDGATE
HILL
CORNHILL
Old Bank of
England
ALDWYCH
FLEET ST
Black Friar
FENCHURCH ST
CANNON ST
Lamb & Flag
THAMES ST
CROSS ROAD
ROSE
ST
STRAND
VICTORIA EMBANKMENT
Blackfriars
Station
LOWER THAMES
ST
SOUTHWARK
BRIDGE
River Thames
BLACKFRIARS BR
LONDON
BR
TRAFALGAR
SQUARE
Charing
Cross
Station
STRAND
EMBANKMENT
WATERLOO BR
Founders
Arms
London
Bridge
Station
Market
Porter
STAMFORD ST
SOUTHWARK ST
TOOLEY ST
Lord Moon of the Mall
ST THOMAS ST
WHITEHALL
VICTORIA
YORK ROAD
WATERLOO
BLACKFRIARS
SOUTHWARK
SOUTHWARK BRIDGE ROAD
BOROUGH HIGH STREET
George
BERMONDSEY ST
Westminster
Arms
Fire Station
WESTMINSTER BR
Waterloo
Station
ROAD
ROAD
LONG LANE
Houses of
Parliament
WESTMINSTER RD
GREAT DOVER STREET
BOROUGH RD
LAMBETH PALACE RD
LONDON RD
Westminster
Abbey
ST GEORGE'S RD
LAMBETH BR
LAMBETH ROAD
NEW KENT ROAD
KENNINGTON ROAD
LAMBETH
WALWORTH ROAD
WALWORTH
MILLBANK
ALBERT EMBANKMENT
KENNINGTON PARK ROAD
KENNINGTON LANE
0
½
MILES

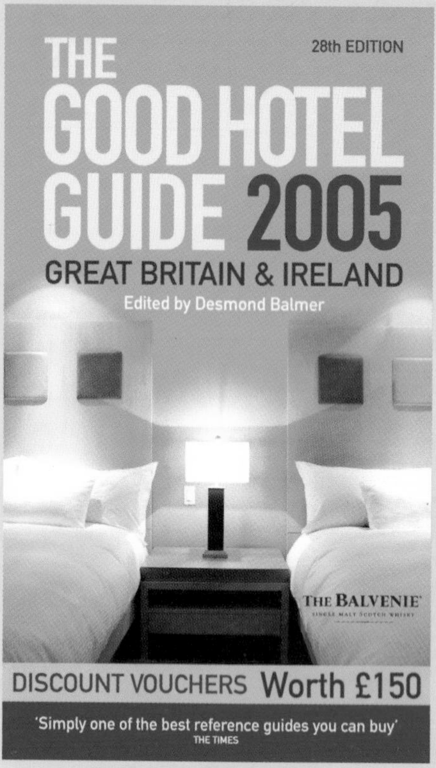
THE
28th EDITION
GOOD HOTEL
GUIDE 2005
GREAT BRITAIN & IRELAND
Edited by Desmond Balmer
THE BALVENIE
DISCOUNT VOUCHERS Worth £150
'Simply one of the best reference guides you can buy'
THE TIMES

'Refreshingly honest'
Daily Express

'The most independently-minded of all hotel publications'
The Times

'Wickedly incisive characterisation'
Daily Telegraph

'A one-stop source of ideas and special hotels'
Marie-Claire

* Over 750 hotels in the UK and Ireland, plus the best B&Bs

* Totally up to date, with prices, facilities and contact details

Now in its 28th year, the *Guide* presents a selection of the very finest hotels, guesthouses and B&Bs in Great Britain and Ireland. Ruthlessly honest, completely independent and evocatively written, it is the ideal companion for discerning, value-conscious travellers.

If you would like to order a copy of *The Good Hotel Guide 2005* (£15.99) direct from Ebury Press (p&p free), please call our credit-card hotline on
01206 255 800
or send a cheque/postal order made payable to Ebury Press to
Cash Sales Department, TBS Direct, Frating Distribution Centre, Colchester Road, Frating Green, Essex CO7 7DW

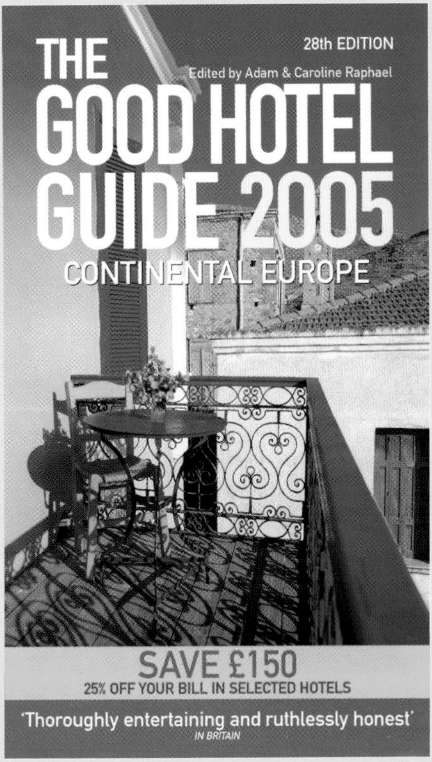
THE
28th EDITION
Edited by Adam & Caroline Raphael
GOOD HOTEL GUIDE 2005
CONTINENTAL EUROPE
SAVE £150
25% OFF YOUR BILL IN SELECTED HOTELS
'Thoroughly entertaining and ruthlessly honest'
IN BRITAIN

'The eminently reliable *Good Hotel Guide*'
Traveller

'Highly respected and authoritative'
Evening Standard

'Indispensable'
Scotland on Sunday

* Annually updated with full information on prices, opening times, credit cards and facilities

* Includes colour maps to help you plan your journey

In its 28 years of reporting on the best hotels in Continental Europe, *The Good Hotel Guide* has established an unrivalled reputation for accuracy and independence, devoting itself to discovering Europe's most beautiful, enjoyable and best-value hotels.

If you would like to order a copy of *The Good Hotel Guide 2005 – Continental Europe* (£17.99) direct from Ebury Press (p&p free), please call our credit-card hotline on **01206 255 800**
or send a cheque/postal order made payable to Ebury Press to
Cash Sales Department, TBS Direct, Frating Distribution Centre, Colchester Road, Frating Green, Essex CO7 7DW

GOOD GUIDE TO DOG FRIENDLY
PUBS, HOTELS AND B&Bs
2005
EDITED BY ALISDAIR AIRD & FIONA STAPLEY
OVER 1000 IDEAS FOR PLACES TO EAT, DRINK AND STAY WITH YOUR DOG!
REVISED, EXPANDED AND IMPROVED EDITION
GOOD GUIDES

* Over 1000 places to eat, drink and stay with your dog
* Compiled by the editors of *The Good Pub Guide* with the same commitment to accuracy and independence
* Includes completely up-to-date information on opening hours, prices and facilities

From the editors of the UK's No. 1 travel guide comes the *Good Guide to Dog Friendly Pubs, Hotels and B&Bs.* A hit in pocket format, the *Good Pub Guide* editors have now expanded and updated the book to produce the definitive travel guide for dog owners.

If you would like to order a copy of the *Good Guide to Dog Friendly Pubs, Hotels and B&Bs 2005* (£9.99) direct from Ebury Press (p&p free), please call our credit-card hotline on **01206 255 800** or send a cheque/postal order made payable to Ebury Press to **Cash Sales Department, TBS Direct, Frating Distribution Centre, Colchester Road, Frating Green, Essex CO7 7DW** and the mood is chatty and easy-going; broadsheet newspapers and a good juke box. Bar food might include sandwiches (from £3, goats cheese ciabatta £4.50), soup (£4), ploughman's (£6.50), sausages and mash (£6.80), moroccan vegetable tagine (£7), fish pie (£8), and vegetable stir fry (£8.60), with puddings (£4). In the evenings they only do meals in the extension barn dining room; they don't take bookings, and it fills up quickly so get there early. Outside are picnic-sets and rustic tables and benches on the front terrace and in a garden, there are heaters, and umbrellas for wet weather. *(Recommended by Dr and Mrs Jackson, Guy Vowles, Ian and Nita Cooper, Ray and Winifred Halliday, Chris Flynn, Wendy Jones, Mike Pugh)*

Free house ~ Licensee Duncan Ironmonger ~ Real ale ~ Bar food (12-2, 6.30-8.30) ~ Restaurant ~ (01684) 574373 ~ Children welcome ~ Dogs welcome ~ Open 11-11; 12-10.30 Sun

PENSAX SO7269 Map 4

Bell

B4202 Abberley—Clows Top, SE of the Snead Common part of the village

Picnic-sets in the back garden of this homely and welcoming roadside mock-Tudor pub look out over rolling fields and copses to the Wyre Forest; you get the same views from some tables inside. Along with Hobsons, you'll find at least four well kept changing real ales from brewers such as Cannon Royall, Hook Norton, Woods and Wye Valley on handpump, and they've farm cider too; dominoes, shove-ha'penny. The particularly friendly licensees and sociable locals help create an enjoyably pubby atmosphere, and the pub attracts a nice mix of customers. The L-shaped main bar has a restrained traditional décor, with long cushioned pews on its bare boards, good solid pub tables, and a woodburning stove. Beyond a small area on the left with a couple more tables is a more airy dining room, with french windows opening on to a wooden deck that on hot days can give a slightly californian feel; the pub has a log fire for our more usual weather. Besides good value lunchtime weekday specials such as steak and ale pie, cornish pasty or sausage, mash and gravy (all £4.95), hearty enjoyable dishes could include generous sandwiches (£3.50), faggots, chips and mushy peas or liver, bacon and onions (£6.50), and they do a popular Sunday roast (£6.50). *(Recommended by DAV, Edmund Coan, Gill and Tony Morriss, Roy and Lindsey Fentiman, Colin Fisher, Lynda and Trevor Smith)*

Free house ~ Licensees John and Trudy Greaves ~ Real ale ~ Bar food (12-2, 6-9; 12-4 Sun; not Mon lunchtime exc bank hols) ~ (01299) 896677 ~ Children in eating area and family room ~ Dogs allowed in bar ~ Open 12-2.30, 5-11; 12-10.30 Sun; closed Mon lunch except bank hols

WELLAND SO7940 Map 4

Anchor

A4104 towards Upton (Drake Street)

There are lots of different dishes to choose from at this pretty Tudor cottage, a great place to stay, and handy for the Three Counties show ground. Up on blackboards, the enjoyable changing menu might include baguettes or baked potatoes (£4.25), mackerel with horseradish or deep-fried whitebait (£3.99), steak, kidney and ale pie (£7.35), spicy chicken with noodles (£8.99), halibut with mild creamy leek and lemon sauce or lamb rump with korma sauce (£9.99), and beef fillet stroganoff (£12.65), with puddings such as strawberry shortbread cheesecake (£5.50); service can be slow. The welcoming L-shaped bar has country prints on the walls, some armchairs around chatty low tables, and more sitting-up chairs around eating-height tables. Beyond is a spreading, comfortably furnished no smoking dining area, nicely set with candles, pink tablecloths and napkins (fine views from here). Five or six well kept real ales on handpump include Hook Norton, Smiles Anchor and Best, Woods Shropshire Lad, and a guest such as Timothy Taylors Landlord, all their wines (not cheap) are available by the glass. In summer the front is festooned with colourful hanging baskets, with a passion flower and roses climbing the walls. There are picnic-sets on the lawn, with flower borders and a big old apple tree, and behind is a field for tents or caravans, with electric hook-up points. A new beer garden was due to open as we went to press (no children); shove-ha'penny, dominoes, chess, Jenga, and perhaps unobtrusive piped music. *(Recommended by Chris Flynn, Wendy Jones, Alan and Paula McCully, Jenny and Dave Hughes, Brian and Anita Randall, Bernard Stradling, Steve Whalley, Joyce and Maurice Cottrell, Mike and Mary Carter, David Green, G S R Cox, Martin Jennings, Mike Green, Dr J Puszet, Keith Trainer)*

Free house ~ Licensees Colin and Caroline Barrett ~ Real ale ~ Bar food (not Sun evening) ~ Restaurant ~ (01684) 592317 ~ Children in restaurant ~ Open 12-2.30, 6.45-11; 12-3 Sun; closed Sun evening ~ Bedrooms: £45B/£70S(£60B)

WYRE PIDDLE SO9647 Map 4

Anchor

Village signposted off A4538 WNW of Evesham

The best time to visit this 17th-c pub (once a row of boatsmen's cottages) is in summer, when you can sit out on the spacious back lawn, which runs right down to the water; views reach out over the Vale of Evesham as far as the Cotswolds, the Malverns and Bredon Hill. Good river views too (though only if you arrive early) from the big airy back bar, where they serve Banks's Bitter, Marstons Pedigree, Timothy Taylors Landlord, local Wyre Piddle and a monthly guest such as Hook Norton Old Hooky under light blanket pressure, seven wines by the glass, ten malt whiskies, country wines, and summer Pimms; fruit machine and piped music. The friendly and neatly kept little lounge has a good log fire in its attractively restored inglenook fireplace, comfortably upholstered chairs and settles, and two beams in the shiny ceiling. The dining area has an open fire, rugs on stripped wood floors and wooden tables and chairs. Big helpings of swiftly served bar food might include home-made soup (£3.25), lunchtime sandwiches (from £3.60, not Sunday), local asparagus (£4.25), mushroom stroganoff, beef vindaloo or pork and cider casserole (£7.50), gammon and pineapple or half a roast chicken with bacon (£8.75), and poached salmon with herb butter (£9.50), with puddings (£3.25); they also do a children's menu (from £3.25). *(Recommended by Brian and Anna Marsden, Roy and Lindsey Fentiman, Ian and Denise Foster, Brenda and Stuart Naylor, KN-R, Dr L Kaufman, Mr and Mrs Colin Roberts, Mr and Mrs A J Edwards)*

Enterprise ~ Lease Nigel and Hilary Green ~ Real ale ~ Bar food ~ Restaurant ~ (01386) 552799 ~ Children welcome ~ Dogs allowed in bar ~ Open 12-3, 6-11; 12-11(10.30 Sun) Sat; 12-3, 6-11 Sat in winter

---

LUCKY DIP

Besides the fully inspected pubs, you might like to try these Lucky Dips recommended to us and described by readers (if you do, please send us reports: www.goodguides.co.uk).

ABBERLEY SO7567

Manor Arms: Good food esp steaks and lots of puddings in comfortable country inn nicely tucked away in quiet village backwater, façade emblazoned with coats of arms; two bars and restaurant, interesting collection of toby jugs, Courage Directors and Fullers London Pride; ten reasonably priced bedrooms *(Edmund Coan, Simon Lawson)*

ASTON FIELDS SO9669

Ladybird [Finstall Rd (B184 just S of Bromsgrove)]: Good-sized light and airy pub with panelled bar and comfortable lounge, good value standard pub food, well kept Bathams Best, Hobsons Best and a guest beer, good service, no smoking dining area; bedrooms planned *(Dave Braisted)*

BELBROUGHTON SO9177

☆ *Queens* [Queens Hill (B4188 E of Kidderminster)]: Bustling 18th-c traditional village pub by Belne Brook, good value food inc enjoyable specials, well kept Banks's, Marstons Pedigree and guest beers such as Caledonian Deuchars IPA and Wadworths 6X, friendly efficient service, comfortable alcove seating, bigger tables in no smoking family area, fresh flowers; picnic-sets on small roadside terrace, pleasant village *(John and Laney Woods, Roy and Lindsey Fentiman)*

BEWDLEY SO7875

Black Boy [Wyre Hill, off A456]: Traditional timbered inn dating from 17th c or earlier, well kept changing beers inc Enville, interesting good value food from low-priced sandwiches up, long bar/lounge with cosy drinking area, caring service; tables outside, handy for River Severn *(Gill and Tony Morriss)*

BOURNHEATH SO9474

☆ *Gate* [handy for M5 junction 4, via A491 and B4091; Dodford Rd]: Attractive country dining pub with wide choice of attractively priced good food inc lots of vegetarian, lunchtime and early evening bargains, good value Sun lunch, well kept Highgate Saddlers Best, long-serving licensees and quick friendly service even though busy, no smoking conservatory area; nice garden *(Gerry and Rosemary Dobson, Trevor and Sheila Sharman)*

Nailers Arms [4 miles from M5 junction 4; Doctors Hill]: Stylishly modern and open-plan, comfortable light wood chairs and tables on stripped floors, good food from lunchtime sandwiches through up-to-date starters, main dishes and puddings to hefty Sun lunch, Enville White, Greene King Old Speckled Hen and two changing guest beers, country wines, friendly helpful staff, daily papers, more traditional locals' back bar; children really welcome, some tables out by car park *(Simon, Jo and Benjamin Cole, Trevor and Sheila Sharman)*

BRETFORTON SP0943

☆ *Fleece* [just off B4035 E of Evesham]: This wonderful 15th-c former farmhouse, full of beautifully preserved antique furniture and a great favourite with readers, suffered a disastrous fire in March 2004; the National Trust, its owners, are taking great care over its rebuilding (with pub service continuing in the interim from the barn), and plan to reinstate nearly all its contents, which were saved – they hope it may reopen by spring 2005 *(LYM)*

BROADWAY SP0937

☆ *Lygon Arms* [High St]: Stately top-rank Cotswold hotel, strikingly handsome, with interesting old rooms rambling away from attractive oak-panelled bar; adjoining bar/brasserie has good imaginative food, quick attentive service, nice wines; children welcome, tables in prettily planted courtyard, well kept gardens, smart comfortable bedrooms, open all day in summer *(LYM, Bernard Stradling, Peter Coxon)*

BUTTONOAK SO7578

Button Oak [B4194 NW of Bewdley]: Small pub, neatly kept and friendly, with well prepared food; tables in garden with terrace *(G Drinkwater)*

CHADDESLEY CORBETT SO8973

Talbot [off A448 Bromsgrove—Kidderminster]: Spotless comfortably refurbished late medieval timbered pub in quiet village street, well kept ales inc Banks's, good choice of bar food; comfortable outside area, attractive village and church *(I D Greenfield, John Whitehead)*

COLWALL SO7440

Wellington [A449 Malvern—Ledbury]: Neat and popular two-level bar and bright largely no smoking dining area, good food inc light dishes, fish and lots of italian recipes, Sun lunch cheaper the earlier you start, sensible wine list, good friendly service, well kept ales such as Greene King Abbot *(Stephen Williamson, Ian and Denise Foster, Neil and Anita Christopher)*

CONDERTON SO9637

Yew Tree: Pleasant beamed and flagstoned pub on S slope of Bredon Hill, with well kept Wadworths IPA and 6X, decent food, friendly atmosphere; good walks *(Derek and Sylvia Stephenson)*

CUTNALL GREEN SO8768

☆ *Chequers* [Kidderminster Rd]: Comfortable beamed country dining pub with comprehensive choice of enjoyable food inc some good italian dishes; pleasant atmosphere, scrubbed tables, stylish green and cream décor, Boddingtons and Marstons Pedigree, good wine choice *(W H and E Thomas, P B Venables, Emily Taylor)*

DRAKES BROUGHTON SO9248

☆ *Plough & Harrow* [A44 NW of Pershore]: Popular dining pub with partly no smoking extended and refurbished restaurant area, comfortable and attractive rambling lounge, reliable sensibly priced food inc cut-price small helpings for the elderly, good friendly helpful service, mainstream beers and a well kept guest ale, log fire; may be two sittings on busy days; good disabled access, pleasant terrace, big orchard-side garden with play area, open all day *(Caroline and Michael Abbey, Jason Caulkin, DMT, George Atkinson, Mr and Mrs M Pearson, P B Venables, Mr and Mrs F E Boxell, Mr and Mrs J C Lodge, Chris Flynn, Wendy Jones)*

DUNHAMPSTEAD SO9160

☆ *Firs* [just SE of Droitwich, towards Sale Green – OS Sheet 150 map ref 919600]: Smart and pretty country dining pub doing well under new licensees, good bar food from enterprisingly filled baguettes and baked potatoes up, well kept Banks's and Marstons, welcoming service, flowers on tables, comfortable no smoking dining conservatory; booking advised wknd; dogs allowed in side bar, good new tables on flower-filled terrace and in small grassy garden, nice spot not far from canal – good walks *(Lynda and Trevor Smith, LYM)*

EARLS CROOME SO8642

Yorkshire Grey [A38, N of M50 junction 1]: Bustling pub with short fair-priced choice of straightforward lunchtime food inc good fish and chips, wider evening choice, well kept Bass and good house wines, candlelit restaurant *(Caroline and Michael Abbey, C Howard)*

EGDON SO9053

Nightingale [A4538]: Well decorated and furnished beamed pub with good food choice inc light meals, good beer range, good value wines *(Caroline and Michael Abbey, Martin Jennings)*

ELDERSFIELD SO8131

☆ *Greyhound* [signed from B4211; Lime St (don't go into Eldersfield itself), OS Sheet 150 map ref 815314]: Unspoilt country local with welcoming young licensees, good inexpensive country cooking (not Mon) by landlord, well kept Bass, Butcombe and Woods Parish tapped from the cask, big woodburner and friendly tabby cat in appealing black-beamed ochre-walled public bar, horse-racing pictures in candlelit carpeted no smoking room, lively skittle alley, strikingly modern lavatories with interesting mosaic in gents'; picnic-sets in small front garden, swings and dovecote out behind *(the Didler, BB)*

ELMLEY CASTLE SO9841

☆ *Old Mill* [signed off A44 and A435, not far from Evesham]: Interesting layout and attractive bar in former mill house with lovely secluded garden looking over village cricket pitch to Bredon Hill, well kept Bass and Woods Best, comfortable dining area with wide food choice from hearty sandwiches and good value lunchtime specials to lots of fish, good choice of wines, helpful friendly staff; children allowed in eating area, comfortable well equipped bedrooms in converted granary, good walks *(LYM, Keith Jacob, Dr A Y Drummond)*

EVESHAM SP0343

Orchard [Twyford; N end of A46 bypass]: Newish Brewers Fayre with popular food, quick service, cheerful and helpful, usual keg beers; bedrooms in adjoining Travel Inn, handy for Evesham Country Park *(Mr and Mrs Colin Roberts)*

FLADBURY SO9946

Chequers [Chequers Lane]: Pretty and warmly welcoming upmarket dining pub dating from 14th c, huge old-fashioned range with log fire at end of long bar, lots of local prints, good generous food from sandwiches to steaks, well kept Fullers London Pride, Hook Norton Best and Wyre Piddle Piddle in the Hole at reasonable prices, quick friendly service, charming beamed back restaurant with carvery; children welcome, large pleasant garden with play area, peaceful pretty village, comfortable well equipped bedroom extension *(Brian and Anna Marsden, Mr and Mrs G S Ayrton)*

FORHILL SP0575

☆ *Peacock* [handy for M42, junctions 2 and 3; pub at junction Lea End Lane and Icknield St]: Appealing, quietly placed and well run Chef & Brewer with wide range of generous enjoyable food, plenty of tables in comfortably fitted knocked-through beamed rooms, woodburner in big inglenook, five or six well kept real ales inc Hobsons; children welcome, picnic-sets on back terrace and front grass, open all day *(LYM, Dennis and Gill Keen, P J Holt, David Edwards, Stan and Hazel Allen)*

GREAT WITLEY SO7566

Hundred House [Worcester Rd]: Busy much-modernised hotel (former coaching inn and magistrates' court), friendly quick service, well kept Banks's, long choice of moderately priced food from good sandwiches up; bedrooms, handy for ruined Witley Court and remarkable church *(D Reay)*

GUARLFORD SO8245

Plough & Harrow [B4211 W of Malvern]: Small friendly village local, cottagey and chintzy, with comfortable settles around the few small round tables, enjoyable home cooking inc wkdy OAP lunches, helpful attentive landlord, well kept Bass and M&B Brew XI, no smoking restaurant (may be fully booked even out of season); can get crowded in summer *(Mr and Mrs B Higgins)*

HADLEY SO8662

Bowling Green [Hadley Heath; off A4133 Droitwich—Ombersley]: Large cheerful bar in quaint pleasantly refurbished 16th-c inn, wide range of good value food from enterprising filled baguettes to popular Sun carvery (packed with families then), well kept Banks's Bitter and Mild, Marstons Pedigree and Hook Norton, good value wines, big log fire, hops on beams, attractive restaurant; children welcome, dogs welcome in back bar, tables out overlooking its bowling green (UK's oldest), comfortable bedrooms, pleasant walks nearby *(Lynda and Trevor Smith, Denys Gueroult)*

HANLEY CASTLE SO8341

☆ *Three Kings* [Church End, off B4211 N of Upton upon Severn]: Unchanging classic country local, friendly and well worn-in, with huge inglenook and hatch service in little tiled-floor tap room, consistently well kept Butcombe, Thwaites and great choice of changing beers from small breweries usually inc a Mild, farm cider, dozens of malt whiskies, two other larger rooms, one with fire in open range, low-priced homely food (not Sun evening – singer then; be prepared for a possibly longish wait other times), seats of a sort outside; family room, bedroom *(Gill and Tony Morriss, LYM, Alan and Paula McCully, the Didler, Pete Baker)*

HOLT HEATH SO8263

Holt Fleet [off A4133]: Picturesque and comfortable 1930s mock Tudor pub and restaurant overlooking River Severn, big helpings of usual food from sandwiches up, keg beers *(Ian Phillips)*

INKBERROW SP0157

☆ *Old Bull* [off A422 – note that this is quite different from the nearby Bulls Head]: Photogenic Tudor pub smartened up in last three years, lots of Archers memorabilia (it's the model for the Ambridge Bull), friendly service, well presented pubby food, well kept real ales, big log fire in huge inglenook, bulging walls, flagstones, oak beams and trusses, and some old-fashioned high-backed settles among more modern furnishings; children allowed in eating area, tables outside *(LYM, Angus Lyon, Martin Jennings)*

KINGTON SO9855

Red Hart [Cockshot Lane]: Recently reopened after renovation, with good value food, attentive young staff *(Mike and Mary Carter)*

LEIGH SINTON SO7850

☆ *Royal Oak* [Malvern Rd]: Well run dining pub with cheerful cartoons in low-beamed bar, careful service by relaxed and responsive staff, reliably enjoyable food inc notable Sun lunch and bargain Mon buffet, reasonably priced wines, plenty of locals, attractive restaurant; flower-filled garden with covered seating *(JCW, JHW, Mrs G P Hall)*

LULSLEY SO7455

Fox & Hounds [signed a mile off A44 Worcester—Bromyard]: Recently refurbished tucked-away country pub, decent food from enjoyable sandwiches and baguettes to good Sun lunch, well kept real ale, pleasant wines, smallish parquet-floored bar stepping down into neat dining lounge, pretty little restaurant on left, nice new conservatory, open fire; dogs welcome, newly furnished quiet and colourful enclosed side rose garden *(Lynda and Trevor Smith, BB)*

MALVERN SO7745

Great Malvern Hotel [Graham Rd, just off B4211]: Friendly and handy for theatre, Bass, Woods and a guest beer, bar food *(Julian Cox)*

Red Lion [St Anns Rd]: Well kept Marstons ales, wide choice of good value food inc pizzas, asiatic specialities and fresh fish; well placed for walks *(Mike Pugh)*

MALVERN WELLS SO7742

Railway Inn [Wells Rd (A449 towards Ledbury)]: Tidy pub with wide choice of enjoyable food, Banks's, Marstons Pedigree and a guest beer such as Jennings Sneck Lifter, restaurant, separate skittle alley and pool table; terrace tables, fine views *(Chris Flynn, Wendy Jones)*

MAMBLE SO6971

☆ *Sun & Slipper* [just off A456 Bewdley—Tenbury Wells]: Friendly, attractively decorated and well run 16th-c inn in small village, good food inc sandwiches, some imaginative dishes, set lunches and fish specialities, well kept Hobsons, prompt willing service; village has interesting church and superior craft centre; picnic-sets outside, bedrooms *(BB, Guy Vowles)*

OMBERSLEY SO8463

Cross Keys [A449, Kidderminster end]: Friendly efficient service, enjoyable attractively presented food from light bar meals up, well kept beers such as Adnams Broadside and Timothy Taylors Landlord, neat and comfortable beamed front bar, conservatory restaurant specialising in fish *(Chris Flynn, Wendy Jones, Nigel Long, Mrs B J Edwards)*

☆ *Crown & Sandys* [A4133]: Big popular open-plan bistro pub with imaginative if not cheap food from lunchtime sandwiches up, fine choice of wines by the glass inc champagnes, six real ales, uniformed staff, airy modern décor but keeping beams, flagstones and settles, limestone-floor conservatory leading to terrace with fountain and sizeable garden beyond; piped music; children welcome, smartly refurbished bedrooms, open all day wknds *(Mike and Mary Carter, Alun Howells, Lawrence Pearse, Ian and Jacqui Ross, Alan Cole, Kirstie Bruce, LYM, Alec Whitfield, B A and D Marsh, JHW, Chris Flynn, Wendy Jones)*

☆ *Kings Arms* [A4133]: Imposing black-beamed and timbered Tudor pub with comfortable rambling rooms, cosy wood-floored nooks and crannies with rustic bric-a-brac, one room with Charles II's coat of arms decorating its ceiling, four open fires; quite restauranty atmosphere and food, well kept Banks's Bitter, Marstons Pedigree and a guest beer, good coffee, friendly leisurely service; good disabled access, children welcome, colourful tree-sheltered courtyard, open all day Sun *(Pamela and Merlyn Horswell, Glenys and John Roberts, John Urquhart, JCW)*

PERSHORE SO9545

Angel [High St]: Nice mix of locals and visitors in comfortably old-fashioned panelled hotel lounge, friendly attentive service, wide choice of bar food inc very generous baguettes, well kept real ales; bedrooms *(Peter Shapland)*

☆ *Brandy Cask* [Bridge St]: Plain high-ceilinged bow-windowed bar, back courtyard brewery producing their own attractively priced real ales, well kept guest beers too, Aug beer festival, coal fire, enjoyable fresh food from sandwiches to steaks, quaintly decorated no smoking dining room, quick friendly helpful service; well behaved children allowed; long attractive garden down to river (keep a careful eye on the children), with terrace, vine arbour and koi pond *(BB, the Didler, Derek and Sylvia Stephenson)*

POUND GREEN SO7578

New Inn [B4194 NW of Bewdley]: Attractive pub rambling out from beamed central core, quiet nooks and corners, friendly efficient young staff, good atmosphere, good reasonably priced food in bar and well laid out dining room, two well kept local real ales; dominoes, darts, live music nights; pleasant front garden, picturesque area handy for Arley steam railway station *(David Cosham)*

SHATTERFORD SO7981

☆ *Bellmans Cross* [Bridgnorth Rd (A442)]: Dining pub popular with business people at lunchtime, interesting and attractively presented bar food from baguettes up, smart tasteful restaurant, French chefs and bar staff, pleasant service with finesse, neat timber-effect bar with well kept Bass, Greene King Old Speckled Hen and a guest beer, good choice of wines by the glass inc champagne; picnic-sets outside, handy for Severn Woods walks *(Theo, Anne and Jane Gaskin, Martin Jennings, Alan Cole, Kirstie Bruce, BB, Lynda and Trevor Smith)*

SHENSTONE SO8673

Plough: Secluded and unspoilt two-bar country local in pleasant surroundings, particularly well kept Bathams ales at attractive prices, friendly regulars, no food; bedrooms *(Colin Fisher)*

STOKE WHARF SO9468

Navigation [Hanbury Rd (B4091)]: Friendly good value pub nr Worcester & Birmingham Canal, popular for good food inc Thurs paella night and (by prior arrangement) fantastic seafood platter, real ale inc a guest beer *(Dave Braisted, Geoffrey and Penny Hughes)*

STOURPORT ON SEVERN SO8171

Bird in Hand [Holly Rd]: Good-sized two-bar canalside pub with enjoyable food and well kept ales inc Enville; peaceful waterside tables, good start or finish for canal walk *(Gill and Tony Morriss)*

Holly Bush [Mitton St]: Proper pub under welcoming new management, well kept local Batham, Enville and Hobsons, imaginative menu inc several home-made pies and fresh fish, restaurant (opens 10 for breakfast), pool room off main bar *(Dr B and Mrs P B Baker)*

TENBURY WELLS SO6168

☆ *Peacock* [Worcester Rd, Newnham Bridge (A456 about 1½ miles E – so inn actually in Shrops)]: Attractive and relaxed 14th-c dining pub with good attractively presented food from baguettes to enterprising light and main dishes, good friendly service, well kept ales such as Hobsons and Timothy Taylors Landlord, good wines by the glass, charming service; several separate rooms, heavy black beams, big log fire in panelled front lounge, comfortable kitchen chairs and ex-pew settles, back family room, attractive bistro; terrace picnic-sets, lovely setting by River Teme, good bedrooms *(LYM, Ian and Joan Blackwell)*

UPHAMPTON SO8464

Fruiterers Arms [off A449 N of Ombersley]: Homely country local (looks like a private house with a porch) brewing its own Cannon Royall Arrowhead, Kings Shilling, Muzzle Loader and seasonal brews, also farm cider; simple rustic Jacobean panelled bar serving lounge with beamery, log fire, lots of photographs and local memorabilia, comfortable armchairs; inexpensive fresh lunchtime sandwiches, no music, plain pool room, garden, some seats out in front *(Gill and Tony Morriss, Pete Baker, MLR)*

UPTON SNODSBURY SO9454

☆ *French House* [A422 Worcester—Stratford]: Extensive series of linked carpeted rooms, high-spirited frenchified décor with masses of pictures and bric-a-brac, a lot of it quirkily interesting, ceilings wicker or entirely wine bottles, two grandfather clocks, balustraded no smoking area up three steps, mix of seating from dining tables to leather chesterfields, nice cheerful staff, enjoyable food, well kept Tetleys and a couple of guest beers, cheapish wines; piped music; tables out on terrace and grass, bedrooms, open all day Sun *(M A and C R Starling, LYM, Martin Jones, Ian and Denise Foster, Pat and Tony Martin, Barry Collett)*

UPTON UPON SEVERN SO8540

Olde Anchor [High St]: Picturesque black and white 16th-c pub, rambling linked rooms with black timbers propping low beams, good fire in unusual central fireplace, tidy old-fashioned furnishings; helpful service, well kept Courage Directors, Theakstons and Charles Wells Bombardier, cheap usual food; piped music and games machines; small back terrace, some tables out in front, open all day summer, can get crowded evenings then *(LYM, Patrick Hancock)*

WEATHEROAK HILL SP0674

☆ *Coach & Horses* [Icknield St – coming S on A435 from Wythall roundabout, filter right off dual carriageway a mile S, then in village turn left towards Alvechurch; not far from M42, junction 3]: Roomy and cheery country pub brewing its own good Weatheroak beers, also good well kept choice of others from small breweries; plush-seated low-ceilinged two-level dining bar, tiled-floor proper public bar, bar food inc lots of baguettes and bargain fish and chips (they shout your number when it's ready), also modern restaurant with well spaced tables; plenty of seats out on lawns and upper terrace; piped music; children allowed in eating area *(Theocsbrian, LYM, the Didler, Pete Baker, Mike and Mary Carter, Geoffrey and Penny Hughes)*

WORCESTER SO8455

Dragon [The Tything]: Lively simply furnished open-plan alehouse with half a dozen or so well described unusual changing microbrews inc a Mild and Porter, local Saxon farm cider, welcoming helpful staff, baguettes and light meals wkdy lunchtimes; piped pop music; folksy live bands, partly covered back terrace, open all day wknds *(Kevin Thorpe, Martin Grosberg, Richard Houghton)*

Farriers Arms [Fish St]: Busy but relaxed city pub rambling through pleasantly furnished lounge and basic public bar, interesting decorations, wide choice of good value food, good cheerful service, well kept ales such as Courage Directors, Fullers London Pride and Charles Wells Bombardier, good house wines; very handy for cathedral *(LYM, Mr and Mrs Colin Roberts)*

Plough [Fish St]: Friendly local, two rooms (one with sports TV) off entrance lobby, simple wkdy bar lunches, four well kept changing ales such as Cannon Royall Kings Shilling and Hop Back Summer Lightning, character Spanish landlord; small pleasant back courtyard, cl Mon *(Pete Baker)*

Ideas for a country day out? We list pubs in really attractive scenery at the back of the book – and there are separate lists for waterside pubs, ones with really good gardens, and ones with lovely views.

Yorkshire

Quite a lot of changes here this year, with new licensees putting a slightly different slant on things at several old favourites, and giving an interesting boost to several other places. This has contributed to the increasingly interesting picture on the Yorkshire pub food front, with some delicious really innovative cooking to be found, alongside Yorkshire's traditional strengths in very good homely country cooking at sensible prices – and often in hearty helpings. With so much going on, it looks as if the coming year's inspections will be very interesting: we are building up a substantial shortlist of the most promising places. For this edition, we do have some notable new entries, or pubs returning to the *Guide* under go-ahead new management, after a break of several years. The newcomers are the aptly named Hill Inn at Chapel le Dale (warmly welcoming, with very good unflighty food – a walkers' favourite), the picturesquely set Fountaine in Linton in Craven (a nice bustling place, good all round), and the stylish and restauranty Millbank in great walking country at Mill Bank (food so good that it comes straight in with a Food Award, and nice wines by the glass). The Fox & Hounds at Sinnington also makes it back into these pages, after just one year's break, forced not by any drop in standards but simply by a lack of readers' reports: clearly this friendly all-rounder, with very good food and comfortable bedrooms, has not been 'over-discovered' yet. Other pubs on top form this year are the Lion up on Blakey Ridge (a walkers' favourite), the welcoming Malt Shovel at Brearton (consistently good all round), the Fox & Hounds at Carthorpe (good food, great wine policy), the Wyvill Arms at Constable Burton (great enthusiasm from readers for its food, beer and service), the friendly White Lion up at Cray (this most enjoyable place is extending this year), the Tempest Arms at Elslack (a favourite all round nowadays), the Carpenters Arms at Felixkirk (friendly and attractive, with good imaginative food), the well run General Tarleton at Ferrensby (imaginative modern cooking), the cheery Turkey at Goose Eye (brewing its own good beers), the interesting Shibden Mill by its leafy ravine on the edge of Halifax (great food, nice just for a drink, too), the Star at Harome (one of Britain's top pubs, exceptional all round), the Angel at Hetton (hugely popular for its food), the Charles Bathurst near Langthwaite (much enjoyed for its landlord's good cooking, its beers, and its comfortable bedrooms), Whitelocks in Leeds (an old-world city classic), the Sandpiper in Leyburn (good food, popular locals' bar), the Queens Arms in its lovely setting at Litton (brews its own good beers, proper home cooking), the Gold Cup at Low Catton (the friendly helpful staff give this place such a lift), the Wellington at Lund (very good food, and in the evening they keep one bar aside for drinkers), the Appletree at Marton (splendid modern cooking, friendly service and good drinks in this updated pub), the Nags Head at Pickhill (this consistently enjoyable all-rounder seems to get better and better over the years the Boynton brothers have been running it – they've been there for 30 years now), the Fat Cat in Sheffield (cheap proper food and great real ales), the well run welcoming St Vincent Arms at Sutton upon Derwent (good food, great beers), the Wombwell Arms at Wass (delicious food relying entirely on local produce, lovely for an overnight stay, keeping a thriving local atmosphere in its bar), the

Sportsmans Arms in Wath in Nidderdale (a classy all-rounder in a great walking area), and the chatty and lively Maltings in York (fine choice of beers, good value simple food). For a special meal out, there is a splendid variety of rewarding places – with more than two dozen pubs here now qualifying for our Food Award, Yorkshire is Britain's current pub food hot-spot. Our final choice whittles down to the Tempest Arms at Elslack, Star at Harome, Charles Bathurst near Langthwaite, Wellington at Lund and Nags Head at Pickhill. It is the Star at Harome which wins the top title of Yorkshire Dining Pub of the Year, for its remarkably imaginative cooking, in delightful surroundings. The Lucky Dip section at the end of the chapter includes a great many notable pubs. As this section now has well over 300 entries, we group this year's stars in their areas. Most are in North Yorkshire: the Falcon at Arncliffe, Buck at Buckden, Falcon at Cloughton, Bolton Arms at Downholme, Coverbridge Inn at East Witton, Crown at Great Ouseburn, Bridge Inn at Grinton, Roasted Pepper at Husthwaite, Blind Jacks in Knaresborough, Black Sheep Brewery (not a pub, but all sorts of pubby virtues) in Masham, Black Swan in Middleham, Beehive at Newholm, Greyhound at Saxton, Castle Arms at Snape, and in York the Black Swan, Blue Bell, Royal Oak and Three Legged Mare. In West Yorkshire, we'd pick out the Fleece at Addingham, Boat at Allerton Bywater, restauranty Kaye Arms at Grange Moor (a favourite), Gray Ox at Hartshead, Victoria in Leeds, Waggon & Horses in Oxenhope and Old Bridge at Ripponden; in the East Riding, the Crown & Anchor at Kilnsea, Tiger at North Newbald and Ferguson-Fawsitt Arms at Walkington; and in South Yorkshire, the Fountain at Ingbirchworth. Yorkshire drinks prices are well below the national average, with most pubs here still charging £2 or less for a pint of beer. Besides quite a lot of pubs brewing their own beer, Yorkshire has literally dozens of flourishing small breweries. The two you are much the most likely to come across are Black Sheep and Timothy Taylors, both very good indeed, and another great name here (generally at bargain price) is Sam Smiths. Others we have found in several of Yorkshire's best pubs, in rough order of frequency, are Hambleton, Daleside, York, Cropton, Copper Dragon, Clarks and Malton, and occasionally Abbeydale, Brown Cow, Goose Eye, Kelham Island, North Yorkshire, Old Mill, Roosters, Rudgate, Salamander, Shipton, Wentworth and Wold Top.

ALDBOROUGH SE4166 Map 7

Ship

Village signposted from B6265 just S of Boroughbridge, close to A1

As we went to press, we heard that the licensees of this creeper-clad village pub would shortly be leaving, but it's so handy for the A1 that we will keep it in the main section of the *Guide* with our fingers crossed. The heavily beamed bar has some old-fashioned seats around heavy cast-iron tables, lots of copper and brass on the walls, and a coal fire in the stone inglenook fireplace. Decent bar food has included sandwiches (from £2.75), soup (£3.25), filled baked potatoes (from £3.50), ploughman's (from £6), steak and kidney pudding (£6.50), and daily specials. The restaurant is no smoking. Well kept Greene King Ruddles Best, John Smiths, and Theakstons Best on handpump, a decent wine list, and quite a few malt whiskies; piped music and dominoes. There are seats on the front terrace. The Roman town with its museum and Roman pavements is nearby. More reports on the new regime, please. *(Recommended by David and Iris Hunter, Simon Turner, Carolyn Dixon, John Knighton, Alan Thwaite, Janet and Peter Race, Jim Auld, Clare and Peter Pearse, Peter and Jean Hoare, Roger and Kathleen Lucas, Andy and Jill Kassube)*

S&N ~ Lease Terry Monaghan ~ Real ale ~ Bar food (12-2 6-9; 12-2.30, 5.30-7.30 Sun) ~ Restaurant ~ (01423) 322749 ~ Children welcome ~ Open 11.45-2.30, 5.30-11; 11.45-11 Sat; 12-10.30 Sun ~ Bedrooms: £35S/£49S

APPLETON-LE-MOORS SE7388 Map 10

Moors

Village N of A170 just under 1½ miles E of Kirkby Moorside

Appropriately named, this unassuming little stone-built pub has tables in the walled garden with quiet moors views, and there are moors walks straight from here to Rosedale Abbey or Hartoft End. Inside, it is almost totally no smoking, strikingly neat and fresh, and surprisingly bare of the usual bric-a-brac. Sparse decorations include just a few copper pans and earthenware mugs in a little alcove, a couple of plates, one or two pieces of country ironwork, and a delft shelf with miniature whiskies; the whiteness of walls and ceiling is underlined by the black beams and joists, and the bristly grey carpet. It's a perfect place for a cold winter evening, with a nice built-in high-backed stripped settle next to an old kitchen fireplace, and other seating including an unusual rustic seat for two cleverly made out of stripped cartwheels; plenty of standing space. To the left of the bar, where you'll probably find a few regulars chatting on the backed padded stools, there's a games room with a pool table (the one place you can smoke) and darts; dominoes. Well kept Black Sheep and Theakstons Black Bull on handpump, and quite a few malt whiskies; efficient service. The wide choice of food in the no smoking dining room could include home-made soup (£2.95), home-made chicken liver pâté (£3.95), pork and tuna rissoles in cream and caper sauce on tagliatelle or mushroom quiche (£8.50), local trout (£8.75), chicken breast stuffed with cheese, wrapped in bacon and served with a leek sauce (£9.50), lamb shoulder with apricot stuffing (£9.75), sirloin steak (£11.95), daily specials such as lamb casserole (£8.50), game pie (£8.95), and guinea fowl in port (£9.50), and home-made puddings like bilberry flan or sticky toffee pudding (£3.50). The bedrooms are in what used to be a barn behind. More reports please. *(Recommended by Colin and Dot Savill)*

Free house ~ Licensee Janet Frank ~ Real ale ~ Bar food (not lunchtimes exc Sun (will offer food to residents on Mon)) ~ Restaurant ~ No credit cards ~ (01751) 417435 ~ Children welcome ~ Dogs allowed in bar ~ Open 7-11; 12-3, 7-10.30 Sun; closed Mon ~ Bedrooms: £30S/£50B

ASENBY SE3975 Map 7

Crab & Lobster 🍷 🛏

Village signposted off A168 – handy for A1

Handy for the A1, this interesting place has a rambling, L-shaped bar with an interesting jumble of seats from antique high-backed and other settles through settees and wing armchairs heaped with cushions, to tall and rather theatrical corner seats; the tables are almost as much of a mix, and the walls and available surfaces are quite a jungle of bric-a-brac, with standard and table lamps and candles keeping even the lighting pleasantly informal. There's also a no smoking dining pavilion with big tropical plants, nautical bits and pieces, and Edwardian sofas. Well liked bar food includes pressed terrine of potted beef, ham hock and foie gras with red onion and beetroot marmalade (£6.90), moules marinière (£7), natural cured haddock with poached egg, black pudding, cheese and bacon potatoes or slowly braised moroccan spiced lamb shank, dried fruit, couscous and cucumber yoghurt (£15), goan fish curry with coconut rice (£15.50), and puddings like iced white chocolate and raspberry parfait with macerated strawberries and basil syrup or sticky toffee pudding with butterscotch sauce (£5.75); side dishes £3.25. Well kept Courage Directors and John Smiths on handpump, and good wines by the glass from an interesting wine list; piped music. The gardens have bamboo and palm trees lining the paths, there's a gazebo at the end of the walkways, and seats on a mediterranean-style terrace. The opulent bedrooms (based on famous hotels around the world) are in the surrounding house which has three acres of mature gardens, and 180-metre golf hole with full practice facilities. More reports please. *(Recommended by Regine Webster, Alistair and Kay Butler, Charles and Pauline Stride, Mr and Mrs J E C Tasker, Mr and Mrs Allan Chapman, Janet and Peter Race, Patrick and Phillipa Vickery, Dr and Mrs R G J Telfer, Edward and Deanna Pearce, Alan Jones)*

Free house ~ Licensee Mark Spenceley ~ Real ale ~ Bar food ~ Restaurant ~ (01845) 577286 ~ Children in eating area of bar and restaurant ~ Dogs welcome ~ Live entertainment Sun lunchtime ~ Open 11.30-2.30, 6.30-11; 12-3, 7-10.30 Sun ~ Bedrooms: /£150B

BECK HOLE NZ8202 Map 10

Birch Hall

Signed off A169 SW of Whitby, from top of Sleights Moor

Time has stood still in this unique and charming pub-cum-village shop. There are two rooms with the shop selling postcards, sweeties and ice-creams in between, and hatch service to both sides. Furnishings are simple – built-in cushioned wall seats and wooden tables (spot the one with 136 pennies, all heads up, embedded in the top) and chairs on the floor (flagstones in one room, composition in the other), some strange items such as French breakfast cereal boxes and a tube of Macleans toothpaste priced 1/3d, and well kept Black Sheep Bitter, and Cropton Honey Gold Bitter and Yorkshire Moors Bitter on handpump; several malt whiskies. Bar snacks like locally-made pies (£1.40), butties (£2), and home-made scones and cakes including their lovely beer cake (from 90p); friendly, welcoming staff; dominoes and quoits. Outside, an ancient oil painting of the view up the steeply wooded river valley hangs on the pub wall, there are benches out in front, and steep steps up to a little steeply terraced side garden with a moorland view. This is a lovely spot with marvellous surrounding walks – you can walk along the disused railway line from Goathland; part of the path from Beck Hole to Grosmont is surfaced with mussel shells. *(Recommended by Pete Baker, the Didler, JP, PP, Roger and Jenny Huggins, Rona Murdoch, B and H, Alison Hayes, Pete Hanlon, David and Helen Wilkins, Patrick Hancock, M Borthwick, David and Ruth Hollands, Colin and Dot Savill, John Fiander)*

Free house ~ Licensee Colin Jackson ~ Real ale ~ Bar food (available during all opening hours) ~ No credit cards ~ (01947) 896245 ~ Children in small family room ~ Dogs welcome ~ Open 11-11; 12-10.30 Sun; 11-3, 7.30-11 in winter, 12-3, 7.30-10.30 Sun in winter; closed Mon evenings

BEVERLEY TA0340 Map 8

White Horse £

Hengate, close to the imposing Church of St Mary's; runs off North Bar

For those who love determinedly traditional and unspoilt old pubs, this fine old place – quite without frills – is quite a find. The basic but very atmospheric little rooms are huddled together around the central bar, with brown leatherette seats (high-backed settles in one little snug) and basic wooden chairs and benches on bare floorboards, antique cartoons and sentimental engravings on the nicotine-stained walls, a gaslit pulley-controlled chandelier, a deeply reverberating chiming clock, and open fires – one with an attractively tiled old fireplace. They now hold a licence for civil ceremonies to take place here. Well kept and very cheap Sam Smiths OB on handpump. Cheap, simple food includes sandwiches, bangers and mash or pasta provençal (£3.95), steak in ale pie (£4.50), lasagne (£4.95), gammon with parsley sauce (£5.50), lamb shanks (£6.95), and puddings like spotted dick and custard (£2). A separate games room has darts, TV, fruit machine, trivia, juke box, and two pool tables – these and the no smoking room behind the bar are the only modern touches. John Wesley preached in the back yard in the mid-18th c. *(Recommended by Michael Butler, Paul and Ursula Randall, the Didler, Mark Walker, JP, PP, Pete Baker, Alison Hayes, Pete Hanlon, Marlene and Jim Godfrey)*

Sam Smiths ~ Manager Anna ~ Real ale ~ Bar food (11-3 Mon-Sat; 12-3 Sun) ~ No credit cards ~ (01482) 861973 ~ Children welcome away from bar until 8pm ~ Dogs welcome ~ Live folk Mon, jazz Weds and last Tues of month ~ Open 11-11; 12-10.30 Sun

BLAKEY RIDGE SE6799 Map 10

Lion

From A171 Guisborough—Whitby follow Castleton, Hutton le Hole signposts; from A170 Kirkby Moorside—Pickering follow Keldholm, Hutton le Hole, Castleton signposts; OS Sheet 100 map reference 679996

After pounding over the fells you'll find this bustling pub just the place to enjoy a pint. There are lots of surrounding hikes and the Coast to Coast Footpath is close by; stunning views. The beamed and rambling bars have warm open fires, a few big high-backed rustic settles around cast-iron-framed tables, lots of small dining chairs, a nice leather settee, and stone walls hung with some old engravings and photographs of the pub under snow (it can easily get cut off in winter). Generous helpings of good basic bar food include giant yorkshire pudding and gravy or soup (£2.25), sandwiches (from £2.75), ploughman's (£4.95), home-cooked ham and egg, and vegetarian nut roast or chicken curry (all £7.50), with daily specials such as steak and kidney pudding or a roast (£7.50), and 10oz fillet steak (£12.25), and puddings like profiteroles with chocolate sauce or spotted dick and custard (£2.95). Three restaurants are no smoking. Well kept Greene King Old Speckled Hen, John Smiths, and Theakstons Best, Old Peculier, Black Bull and XB on handpump; piped music, dominoes, and fruit machine. The pub does get very busy in summer, and the popular bedrooms are booked up several weeks ahead. *(Recommended by Walter and Susan Rinaldi-Butcher, Rona Murdoch, Sue Wheeler, DRH and KLH, Tim Newman, R M Corlett, JHBS, Dr J Barrie Jones, Mrs P Hall, Dr David Cockburn)*

Free house ~ Licensee Barry Crossland ~ Real ale ~ Bar food (12-10) ~ Restaurant ~ (01751) 417320 ~ Children welcome ~ Dogs allowed in bar ~ Live music every third Thurs ~ Open 10.30-11; 12-11 Sun ~ Bedrooms: £17.50(£36.50B)/£50(£58B)

BOROUGHBRIDGE SE3966 Map 7

Black Bull

St James Square; B6265, just off A1(M)

The hanging baskets in front of this attractive 13th-c town centre inn are lovely in summer; the pub was due to be decorated outside as we went to press. The main bar area has a relaxed, friendly atmosphere, a big stone fireplace and brown leather seats, and is served through an old-fashioned hatch; there's also a cosy and attractive snug with traditional wall settles. The restaurant and part of the bar area are no smoking. Enjoyable bar food includes soup (£2.85), sandwiches (from £2.85; hot roast loin of pork topped with bramley apple compote £4.25), home-made pie of the day or smoked salmon and scrambled eggs on toasted brioche (£6.75), gammon and egg (£6.95), pasta with smoked ham and mushrooms in white wine and dijon mustard sauce glazed with double cheese melt (£7.25), thai beef strips stir-fried with vegetables and noodles (£7.50), sizzling platters (from £10.95), steaks (from £12.95), daily specials, and home-made puddings such as banana bread and butter pudding with toffee sauce or strawberry cheesecake (from £2.85); three-course Sunday lunch (£10.95). Well kept Black Sheep Bitter, John Smiths, and a guest such as Fullers London Pride or Timothy Taylors Landlord on handpump, enjoyable wines (with 12 by the glass), and quite a few malt whiskies; dominoes. Service is friendly and attentive, the two borzoi dogs are called Charlie and Sadie, and the two cats Mimi and Cyny; the local mummers perform here three or four times a year. Bedrooms are in a more modern wing. *(Recommended by the Didler, JP, PP, Nigel Williamson, Tom McLean, Michael Dandy, Margaret and Roy Randle, Charles and Pauline Stride, Dr Peter D Smart)*

Free house ~ Licensees Anthony and Jillian Burgess ~ Real ale ~ Bar food (12-2(2.30 Sun), 6-9(9.30 Fri-Sat)) ~ Restaurant ~ (01423) 322413 ~ Children welcome ~ Dogs allowed in bar ~ Open 11-11; 12-10.30 Sun ~ Bedrooms: £40.50S/£54S

Please let us know of any pubs where the wine is particularly good.

BRADFIELD SK2392 Map 7

Strines Inn

From A57 heading E of junction with A6013 (Ladybower Reservoir) take first left turn (signposted with Bradfield) then bear left; with a map can also be reached more circuitously from Strines signpost on A616 at head of Underbank Reservoir, W of Stocksbridge

After a visit to this isolated moorland inn – set in an area known as Little Switzerland – there are plenty of rambles all around to walk off a hearty good value meal; fine views from the picnic-sets, a safely fenced in children's playground, and some rescued animals. The main bar has a welcoming atmosphere, black beams liberally decked with copper kettles and so forth, quite a menagerie of stuffed animals, homely red-plush-cushioned traditional wooden wall benches and small chairs, and a coal fire in the rather grand stone fireplace; there's a good mixture of customers. A room off on the right has another coal fire, hunting photographs and prints, and lots of brass and china, and on the left is another similarly furnished room; two rooms are no smoking. Under the new licensee, bar food includes home-made soup (£2.65), sandwiches (from £1.95; hot panini bread with hot roast beef £3.55), filled baked potatoes (from £3.25), garlic mushrooms (£3.95), liver and onions (£6.25), mediterranean vegetable hotpot (£6.95), filled giant yorkshire puddings or popular pie of the day (£6.95), mixed grill (£9.75), daily specials such as cajun chicken (£6.95), lamb steak (£7.95), and T-bone steak (£13.95), and puddings like home-made apple pie or treacle sponge (£3.30). Well kept Adnams Broadside, Bank's Riding Bitter, and Marstons Pedigree on handpump, and several malt whiskies; piped music. The bedrooms have four-poster beds (one has an open log fire), and there's a self-catering cottage. *(Recommended by the Didler, David and Heather Stephenson, Peter F Marshall, David and Ruth Hollands, JP, PP, Matt Waite, R T and J C Moggridge, Greta and Christopher Wells)*

Free house ~ Licensee Bruce Howarth ~ Real ale ~ Bar food (12-2.30, 5.30-9 winter weekdays; all day in summer) ~ (0114) 285 1247 ~ Children welcome ~ Dogs welcome ~ Open 10.30-11; 10.30-10.30 Sun; 10.30-3, 5.30-11 weekdays and all day weekends in winter ~ Bedrooms: £45B/£67.50B

BREARTON SE3261 Map 7

Malt Shovel

Village signposted off A61 N of Harrogate

There's always a friendly welcome and a good relaxed atmosphere in this deservedly popular 16th-c village pub. As they don't take bookings, you do need to arrive early, but there is a waiting list system. Several heavily-beamed rooms radiate from the attractive linenfold oak bar counter with plush-cushioned seats and a mix of tables, an ancient oak partition wall, tankards and horsebrasses, an open fire, and paintings by local artists (for sale) and lively hunting prints on the walls; nearly half the pub is no smoking. Reliably good and reasonably priced bar food might include sandwiches, mussels steamed in white wine with garlic and cream (£3.95 or £6.95), goats cheese and leek tart or ploughman's (£5.50), roast pork belly with crackling and apple sauce or honey baked ham with honey and mustard sauce (£6.50), steak in ale or game pie (£6.75), liver, bacon and black pudding with red wine gravy (£6.95), haddock in beer batter (£7.25), thai chicken curry (£7.95), bass with herb butter (£8.95), chargrilled steaks (from £9.50), and puddings such as apple and bramble crumble, sticky toffee pudding or lemon tart (£2.95). Well kept Black Sheep Bitter, Daleside Bitter, and Theakstons Best with a couple of guests such as Durham Magus or North Yorkshire Golden Ale on handpump, quite a few malt whiskies, and a small but interesting and reasonably priced wine list. Darts, shove-ha'penny, cribbage, and dominoes. You can eat outside on the small terrace on all but the coldest of days as they have outdoor heaters; there are more tables on the grass. This is an attractive spot off the beaten track, yet handy for Harrogate and Knaresborough. *(Recommended by Andrew and Samantha Grainger, Chloe and Robert Gartery, Robert and Susan Whitehead, Jill and Keith Wright, Michael Doswell,*

Alison Hayes, Pete Hanlon, G Dobson, Tim and Ann Newell, Ken Black, Paul Boot, Jo Lilley, Simon Calvert)

Free house ~ Licensee Leslie Mitchell ~ Real ale ~ Bar food (not Mon) ~ No credit cards ~ (01423) 862929 ~ Children welcome ~ Dogs welcome ~ Open 12-2.30, 6.45-11(10.30 Sun); closed Mon

BURTON LEONARD SE3364 Map 7

Hare & Hounds

Village signposted off A61 Ripon—Harrogate (and easily reached from A1(M) exit 48)

The flowering tubs and window boxes outside this well organised country pub are very pretty all year round; seats in the back garden. Inside, there's been some refurbishment, but the bustling and friendly atmosphere remains, as does the good mix of customers. The large turkey-carpeted main area is divided by a two-way stone fireplace with a log fire, and the traditional furnishings include flowery-cushioned captain's chairs, wall pews, grey plush stools and so forth; the restaurant and lounge are no smoking. The ceiling has a couple of beech branches strung with white fairy lights, there are some olde-worlde prints and decorative plates, and an eye-catching long bar counter, under gleaming copper and brass pans and measures; well kept Black Sheep, Tetleys, Timothy Taylors Landlord, and John Smiths with guests like Greene King Old Speckled Hen and Theakstons Best on handpump, up to 15 wines by the glass, and 30 malt whiskies; dominoes. Enjoyable bar food includes lunchtime sandwiches and filled baguettes (from £3.95), as well as home-made soup (£4.50), creamy garlic mushrooms (£5.85), cajun vegetable curry or home-made steak and kidney pie (£8.95), chicken with a leek, bacon, cream and white wine sauce (£9.75), smoked haddock and broccoli mornay or gammon and egg (£9.95), breast of duck with a port, orange and summer berry sauce (£12.95), rack of lamb with mint and redcurrant sauce (£13.95), steaks (from £13.95), and daily specials such as spicy moroccan lamb with apricots and fresh orange (£7.95) and thai-style salmon and monkfish fishcakes (£4.95 or £8.95). On the left as you go in, a bright little room has a pink sofa and easy chairs, and local village prints and old postcards. *(Recommended by B and M Kendall, Janet and Peter Race, DC, R J Herd)*

Free house ~ Licensees Sarah and Tony Porter ~ Real ale ~ Bar food (12-2, 6-9; not Tues) ~ Restaurant ~ (01765) 677355 ~ Children in eating area of bar and restaurant ~ Open 12-3, 5.30-11; closed Tues

BYLAND ABBEY SE5579 Map 7

Abbey Inn

The Abbey has a brown tourist-attraction signpost off the A170 Thirsk—Helmsley

As we went to press, we heard that this very well run inn was up for sale, so it's possible that by the time the *Guide* is published, there might be new owners at the helm. We are therefore keeping our fingers crossed that not too much will change. What obviously cannot change is the lovely position overlooking the hauntingly beautiful abbey ruins opposite, which was at one time the largest ecclesiastical building in Europe. The two no smoking characterful front rooms have big fireplaces, oak and stripped deal tables, settees, carved oak seats, and Jacobean-style dining chairs on the polished boards and flagstones; there have been various stuffed birds, little etchings, and china cabinets, and some discreet stripping back of plaster to show the ex-abbey masonry. The Library has lots of bookshelves and a large single oak table (ideal for a party of up to 10 people), and the big back room has lots of rustic bygones; piped music. The menus change lunchtime and evening but some examples of the imaginative food might include home-made soup (£4.50), peppered tuna carpaccio on niçoise salad with lemon and chive vinaigrette, french brie and red onion tart with baby poached figs in syrup or breaded sweet potato and watercress cakes with chilli dressing (all £7.25), ploughman's terrine with honey and sunflower bread (£7.95), home-made chicken and mushroom pie (£8), roasted suckling pig with cider gravy and caramelised apple (£9), chicken breast stuffed with smoked mozzarella, wrapped in parma ham with roasted mediterranean vegetables and red pepper coulis (£9.25), calves liver on champ potato with rich onion gravy and crispy bacon (£10), seared red snapper on green pepper, mange tout and coriander salad (£12.50), mustard and herb rump of lamb on boulangère potato with minted jus (£14), and puddings such as a duo of chocolate mousse with glazed baby pears and griottine cherries, espresso brûlée with tuile curls, and strawberry and mascarpone roulade with vanilla pod ice-cream (£4.95). Well kept Black Sheep Bitter and Tetleys on handpump, and an interesting wine list with 20 (plus champagne) by the glass. Plenty of room outside on the terrace and in the garden. More reports on any changes, please.

(Recommended by Mr and Mrs J Holroyd, John Knighton, J Goodwin, Mrs D Fiddian, Peter and Anne-Marie O'Malley, Mrs Bramah, A S and M E Marriott, Stephen Buckley, Michael Ward, Mike and Lynn Robinson, Edward and Deanna Pearce, A and B Myers, Marlene and Jim Godfrey, Peter Burton)

Free house ~ Licensees Jane and Martin Nordli ~ Real ale ~ Bar food (not Sun evening or Mon lunchtime) ~ Restaurant ~ (01347) 868204 ~ Children welcome ~ Open 11-3, 6.30-11; 12-4 Sun; closed Sun evening and Mon lunch ~ Bedrooms: /£90B

CARTHORPE SE3184 Map 10

Fox & Hounds 🍴 🍷

Village signposted from A1 N of Ripon, via B6285

You can be sure of a friendly welcome and an especially good meal in this neatly kept and well run extended dining pub, but you must book a table in advance – especially at weekends. The cosy L-shaped bar has quite a few mistily evocative Victorian photographs of Whitby, a couple of nice seats by the larger of its two log fires, plush button-back built-in wall banquettes and chairs, plates on stripped beams, and some limed panelling; piped light classical music. There is some theatrical memorabilia in the corridors, and an attractive high-raftered no smoking restaurant with lots of neatly black-painted farm and smithy tools. Served by attentive staff, the imaginative food might include home-made soups (£3.45), grilled black pudding with caramelised apple and onion marmalade (£4.75), smoked salmon pâté (£4.95), good fresh crab tartlet (£5.25), chicken filled with coverdale cheese in a creamy sauce (£9.95), pheasant breast with a pear and thyme stuffing wrapped in bacon with a red wine sauce (£10.95), rack of lamb on a blackcurrant crouton with redcurrant gravy or fried bass on potato rösti with red pepper sauce (£12.95), half a roasted gressingham duckling with orange sauce and parsley and thyme stuffing (£13.95), and grilled fillet steak with mango and horseradish relish (£14.95), with delicious puddings such as white chocolate and irish cream cheesecake, champagne and summer fruit jelly with home-made vanilla shortbread or raspberry and almond tart (£4.95); daily specials like fresh salmon fishcakes (£4.75), moules marinière (£4.95), steak and kidney pie (£9.25), and baked haddock with crispy crumb topping and cream sauce or half a roast guinea fowl (£9.95), and on Tuesdays to Thursdays they also offer a two-course (£11.95) and three-course (£13.95) set meal. Well kept Black Sheep on handpump, and from their extensive list they will open any wine for you just to have a glass.

(Recommended by Tim and Carolyn Lowes, Ian Cameron, Austin and Marjorie Tushingham, Mr and Mrs C Cameron, Mr and Mrs D Cummings, Mr and Mrs J E C Tasker, Janet and Peter Race, Wendy and Carl Dye, R N and M I Bailey, Mr and Mrs I G Templeton, Adam and Joan Bunting, Michael Doswell, JWAC)

Free house ~ Licensees Howard and Bernie Fitzgerald ~ Real ale ~ Bar food (not Mon) ~ Restaurant ~ (01845) 567433 ~ Children welcome ~ Open 12-2.30, 7-11(10.30 Sun); closed Mon and first full week of New Year

All *Guide* inspections are anonymous. Anyone claiming to be a *Good Pub Guide* inspector is a fraud, and should be reported to us with name and description.

CHAPEL LE DALE SD7477 Map 7

Hill Inn

B5655 Ingleton—Hawes, 3 miles N of Ingleton

With views to Ingleborough and Whernside, this friendly inn is in a wonderful, remote walking spot. It's run by extremely welcoming and helpful licensees, there's a relaxed and informal atmosphere, and a good mix of locals, walkers and mountain bikers. There are old pine tables and benches on the stripped wooden floors, nice pictures on the walls, stripped-stone recesses, a warm log fire, and up to half a dozen well kept real ales on handpump: Black Sheep Best, Special, and Riggwelter, Dent Aviator and Best, and Theakstons Best. The dining room is no smoking, and there's a well worn-in sun lounge. Good, enjoyable food cooked by the licensees, might include lunchtime sandwiches (from £4.60) and sausage and mash with red wine and onion gravy (£8.25), as well as more elaborate evening meals such as blue cheese and polenta tart with sautéed vegetables and a home-made tomato sauce (£9.25), grilled salmon on chive mash with a light thai curry sauce (£9.85), beef in ale casserole or chicken provençale (£9.95), lamb shank with home-made mint sauce or confit of duck with herb mash and apple sauce (£10.95), and super puddings such as warm chocolate pudding with white chocolate sauce and home-made vanilla ice-cream, sticky toffee pudding, lemon tart with raspberry sauce and home-made lemon and mascarpone ice-cream, or crème brûlée with orange salad and home-made orange and yoghurt ice-cream (£4.65); the home-baked bread is very good. The popular bedrooms are attractively furnished, and we expect that as more reports on these come in from readers the pub will qualify for one of our Place to Stay Awards. It is essential to phone ahead to check their opening hours, especially if you plan to end up here after a long walk. *(Recommended by John and Sylvia Harrop, Jane Taylor, David Dutton, Richard and Anne Ansell, Richard Mason, Maggie and Tony Harwood, Karen Eliot, Helen Pollard, Mike Turner)*

Free house ~ Licensee Sabena Martin ~ Real ale ~ Bar food ~ Restaurant ~ (015242) 41256 ~ Children in eating area of bar ~ Dogs allowed in bar ~ Open 6.30-11; 12-11 Sat; 12-10.30 Sun; closed all Mon, also Tues-Fri lunchtimes ~ Bedrooms: /£60S

CONSTABLE BURTON SE1791 Map 10

Wyvill Arms

A684 E of Leyburn

After an upstairs flood, much of this inn has been carefully redecorated and refurbished, and readers have been quick to voice their enthusiasm. The bar is still decorated with teak and brass, with mirrors along the back of the bar, ornate shelving, and a bar counter which came from a bank 30 years ago. There's a mix of seating, a finely worked plaster ceiling with the Wyvill family's coat of arms, and an elaborate stone fireplace. The second bar, where food is served, has semi-circled, upholstered alcoves, a seventies juke box with music for all ages, hunting prints and a mounted stag's head, and old oak tables; the reception area of this room includes a huge chesterfield which can seat up to eight people, another carved stone fireplace, and an old leaded church stained-glass window partition. Both rooms are hung with pictures of local scenes, and the restaurant is no smoking. Consistently good, enjoyable food served by friendly, helpful staff includes light lunches such as soup (£3.50), filled baguettes (from £3.95), scrambled egg and smoked salmon (£5.45), and exotic mushroom lasagne (£8.95), as well as three-cheese and smoked ham terrine (£4.60), rarebit and smoked haddock with roast cherry tomatoes (£4.95), super steak and onion pie (£9.15), tasty chicken breast on leeks with stilton sauce (£10.95), lamb shank (£12.95), suckling pig (£14.65), monkfish wrapped in parma ham with a red wine and mushroom sauce or magret of duck with roasted shallots and a cranberry compote (£14.95), and delicious puddings like chocolate torte with an orange sorbet and three different brûlées (from £4.95); the breakfasts and chips come in for special praise. Well kept Black Sheep, John Smiths Bitter, and Theakstons Best with a guest like Charles Wells Bombardier on handpump, and a thoughtful wine list; cribbage, dominoes, darts and piped music. The white bull terrier is called Tricky. There's a herb and vegetable garden behind the pub, and several large wooden benches with large white parasols for outdoor dining. Constable Burton Gardens are opposite and worth a visit. *(Recommended by Richard and Anne Ansell, Ian and Nita Cooper, Andrew Shore, Maria Williams, John Close, Mrs J Doherty, Ben and Helen Ingram, Anna Cooper, E D Fraser)*

Free house ~ Licensee Nigel Stevens ~ Real ale ~ Bar food ~ Restaurant ~ (01677) 450581 ~ Children welcome ~ Dogs allowed in bar ~ Open 11-3, 6-11; 12-3, 7-10.30 Sun ~ Bedrooms: /£66B

CRAY SD9379 Map 7

White Lion

B6160, Upper Wharfedale N of Kettlewell

Damp walkers are made most welcome in this former drovers' hostelry (the highest pub in Wharfedale) with a warm open fire, a pint of well kept beer, and helpful advice from the friendly landlord about local wildlife, the weather and other hikes. The simply furnished bar has a traditional atmosphere, seats around tables on the flagstone floor, shelves of china, iron tools and so forth, and a high dark beam-and-plank ceiling; there's also a no smoking dining room. As well as lunchtime filled yorkshire puddings (from £2.95), filled baguettes (from £3.50), and ploughman's (£4.75), the enjoyable bar food might include home-made soup (£2.95), home-made smoked trout pâté (£3.95), king prawns in garlic butter (£4.50), home-made steak and mushroom pie or home-made vegetable lasagne (£7.95), cashew nut and mushroom loaf with mushroom and sherry sauce (£8.50), home-made venison casserole, duck breast with a raspberry and redcurrant sauce or three local lamb chops with rosemary and garlic (£9.95), steaks (from £10.95), puddings, and children's meals. If you eat between 5.45 and 6.15pm you get a 20% discount on some items. Well kept Moorhouses Bitter and Pendle Witches Brew, Timothy Taylors Landlord, and maybe Copper Dragon Golden Pippin on handpump, nine wines by the glass, and around 20 malt whiskies; dominoes, cribbage, shove-ha'penny, ring the bull and giant Jenga. In fine weather, you can sit at picnic benches above the very quiet steep lane or on the great flat limestone slabs in the shallow stream which tumbles down opposite. As we went to press, they were in the process of building an extension to house a new kitchen, new guest accommodation, and an additional dining room; campers in the garden will have access to showers. *(Recommended by Malcolm and Jennifer Perry, Susan and Tony Dyer, Bill Sykes, Tony and Ann Bennett-Hughes, Mike and Kathryn Budd, the Didler, Blaise Vyner, W A Evershed, Di and Mike Gillam, Stephen Buckley, Eddie Edwards, Ben Whitney and Pippa Redmond, Kevin Thorpe, MDN, B and M Kendall, Tony and Betty Parker, Kerry Law, Simon Smith)*

Free house ~ Licensees Kevin and Debbie Roe ~ Real ale ~ Bar food (12-2, 5.45-8.30) ~ (01756) 760262 ~ Children in family room ~ Dogs allowed in bar ~ Open 11-11; 12-10.30 Sun ~ Bedrooms: /£60S

CRAYKE SE5670 Map 7

Durham Ox

Off B1363 at Brandsby, towards Easingwold; West Way

As there is no shop in the village, the enterprising landlord here has started a little shop and fitted a small area by the door with shelves, a fridge, and scales and baskets for vegetables. The old-fashioned lounge bar has venerable tables and antique seats and settles on the flagstones, pictures and photographs on the dark red walls, interesting satirical carvings in its panelling (which are Victorian copies of medievel pew ends), polished copper and brass, and an enormous inglenook fireplace with winter log fires (flowers in summer). In the bottom bar is a framed illustrated acount of the local history (some of it gruesome) dating back to the 12th c, and a large framed print of the original famous Durham Ox which weighed 171 stones. As well as daily specials, the tasty (if not cheap) bar food includes home-made soup (£3.75), crispy belly of pork with sweet soy dressing and asian-style salad (£5.75), wild mushroom tortellini with roast peppers and salsa verde (£6.50), gnocchi with slow-roasted tomato and aubergine (£13.95), grilled free range chicken breast (£14.25), rib-eye steak or local lamb rump with minted new potato cake and greek salad salsa (£16.25), grilled red snapper with a light shellfish chowder (£16.50), and king prawn, pancetta and mango kebab (£18.95); there's an early bird menu on Sundays through to Thursdays, two courses (£12.95), three courses (£14.95), and Friday evening fish and chips (best to book in advance). The restaurant is no smoking. Well kept Caledonian Deuchars IPA, John Smiths, Theakstons XB, and Charles Wells Bombardier on handpump, and 12 wines by the glass; piped music and dominoes. There are seats outside on a terrace and in the courtyard, and the comfortable bedrooms are in converted farm buildings. The tale is that this is the hill which the Grand Old Duke of York marched his men up; the view from the hill opposite is marvellous. More reports please. *(Recommended by Mike Schofield, Mr and Mrs C Cameron, Pat and Graham Williamson, Ian S Morley, Edward and Deanna Pearce)*

Free house ~ Licensee Michael Ibbotson ~ Real ale ~ Bar food (12-2.30, 6-9.30(8.30 Sun)) ~ Restaurant ~ (01347) 821506 ~ Children allowed but not in restaurant ~ Dogs allowed in bedrooms ~ Folk/easy listening live music Thurs evenings ~ Open 11-3, 6-11.30; 12-13, 7-10 Sun; closed 25 Dec ~ Bedrooms: £60B/£80B

CROPTON SE7588 Map 10

New Inn

Village signposted off A170 W of Pickering

Close to the North Yorkshire Moors National Park, this comfortably modernised village inn remains particularly popular for its own brewed beers – you can arrange a tour of the brewery: Two Pints, Monkman's Slaughter, Endeavour, and Yorkshire Moors Bitter, which they keep well on handpump, and a guest such as Theakstons. Eight wines by the glass, too. The traditional village bar has Victorian church panels, terracotta and dark blue plush seats, lots of brass, and a small fire. A local artist has designed historical posters all around the no smoking downstairs conservatory. Decent bar food includes soup (£3.25), sandwiches (from £2.95), chorizo salad (£4.50), ploughman's or vegetable hotpot (£7.25), home-made steak in ale pie or home-made lasagne (£7.95), crab cake with a cream, paprika and prawn sauce (£8.75), gammon topped with pineapple and cheese (£9.50), and chicken stuffed with wensleydale cheese, wrapped in bacon with a red wine sauce (9.65); children's menu (£3.49). The elegant no smoking restaurant is furnished with genuine Victorian and early Edwardian pieces. Darts, pool, juke box, fruit machine, and piped music. There's a neat terrace, a garden with a pond, and a brewery shop. *(Recommended by Fred and Lorraine Gill, Tracey and Stephen Groves, Christine and Neil Townend, Colin and Dot Savill, Marlene and Jim Godfrey, Dr David Cockburn)*

Own brew ~ Licensee Philip Lee ~ Real ale ~ Bar food (12-2, 6-9) ~ Restaurant ~ (01751) 417330 ~ Children in family room ~ Open 11-11; 12-10.30 Sun ~ Bedrooms: £39B/£66B

EAST WITTON SE1586 Map 10

Blue Lion

A6108 Leyburn—Ripon

This busy dining pub, set on the edge of the green in a pretty village, places quite an emphasis on its popular food. The big squarish bar has high-backed antique settles and old windsor chairs on the turkey rugs and flagstones, ham-hooks in the high ceiling decorated with dried wheat, teazles and so forth, a delft shelf filled with appropriate bric-a-brac, several prints, sporting caricatures and other pictures on the walls, a log fire, and daily papers; the friendly labrador is called Archie. Restaurant-quality meals (with prices to match – some find them too steep for a Dales pub) might include hot roast beef sandwich with horseradish (£5.25), lemon chicken, leek and sage risotto with gruyère cheese (£5.55), creamed garlic mushrooms and tarragon with home-made brioche or terrine of duck and orange with grain mustard salad (£5.75), warm salad of sautéed king scallops with crispy bacon (£7.75), home-made tagliatelle carbonara (£8.90), beef and onion suet pudding with dark onion sauce or confit of duck leg with chorizo and choucroute (£12.50), slow braised lamb shank with spring onion mash (£12.95), poached fillet of smoked haddock on new potatoes topped with poached egg, leek and mushroom sauce (£13.95), and chargrilled steak with gratin of wild mushrooms and red wine sauce (£17.75). Well kept Black Sheep Bitter and Riggwelter, and Theakstons Best, and an impressive wine list with quite a few by the glass. Picnic-sets on the gravel outside look beyond the stone houses on the far side of the village green to Witton Fell, and there's a big, pretty back garden. More reports please. *(Recommended by Jenny and Dave Hughes, Mrs T C Sweeney, the Didler, Angus Lyon, Anthony Longden, Tim and Carolyn Lowes, Lynda and Trevor Smith, JP, PP, Margaret and Roy Randle, Barry and Patricia Wooding, Brian England, Louise English, J Goodwin, Mike and Maggie Betton, Ian Arthur, Bernard Stradling, Gerry and Rosemary Dobson, John Close, Ian and Nita Cooper, Pat and Sam Roberts, Mrs Yvette Bateman, Alison Hayes, Pete Hanlon, Jane Taylor, David Dutton, Neil Whitehead)*

Free house ~ Licensee Paul Klein ~ Real ale ~ Bar food ~ (01969) 624273 ~ Children welcome ~ Dogs allowed in bar and bedrooms ~ Open 11-11; 12-10.30 Sun ~ Bedrooms: £53.50S/£69S(£79B)

EGTON BRIDGE NZ8005 Map 10

Horse Shoe

Village signposted from A171 W of Whitby; via Grosmont from A169 S of Whitby

There's always a good mix of customers in this friendly place drawn by the lovely surroundings and fine walks. The attractive gardens have pretty roses, mature redwoods, and geese and bantams, and there are comfortable seats on a quiet terrace and lawn beside a little stream (where there are ducks). Fishing is available on a daily ticket from Egton Estates. Inside, the bar has old oak tables, high-backed built-in winged settles, wall seats and spindleback chairs, a big stuffed trout (caught near here in 1913), pictures on the walls, and a warm log fire; the restaurant is no smoking. Well liked food using fresh seasonal produce might include home-made soup (£2.95), sandwiches (from £3.80; filled baguettes from £4.20), wild mushroom risotto (£3.80, main course £7.50), crispy duck leg with plum sauce (£4.20; main course £9.20), a pie of the day (£7.50), gammon and egg (£8), and red snapper with coriander and ginger (£10.50). Well kept Tetleys and Theakstons Best with guests like Durham Magus and Hook Norton Best on handpump, and around 24 malt whiskies; darts, dominoes, and piped music. A different way to reach this beautifully placed pub is to park by the Roman Catholic church, walk through the village and cross the River Esk by stepping stones. Not to be confused with a similarly named pub up at Egton. *(Recommended by Ian Piper, Pete Baker, Dr and Mrs R G J Telfer, Sarah Davis, Rod Lambert, Blaise Vyner, Jarrod and Wendy Hopkinson, Peter and Anne-Marie O'Malley, Mr and Mrs P Dix, Patrick Hancock, Joyce and Maurice Cottrell, Tracey and Stephen Groves, Clare and Peter Pearse, Greta and Christopher Wells)*

Free house ~ Licensees Tim and Suzanne Boulton ~ Real ale ~ Bar food ~ Restaurant ~ (01947) 895245 ~ Children in restaurant and family room ~ Dogs allowed in bar ~ Open 11.30-3, 6.30-11; 12-3, 7-10.30 Sun; closed 25 Dec ~ Bedrooms: /£45(£55B)

ELSLACK SD9249 Map 7

Tempest Arms

Village signposted just off A56 Earby—Skipton

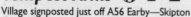

A Union Jack fluttering above the car park is your first sight of this 18th-c stone pub as it's tucked away below a grassy bank and quite difficult to spy from the road. Inside, the friendly licensees make all visitors welcome, and there's a good, bustling atmosphere, and a cosy feel in winter with three log fires (one in a dividing fireplace) to warm you up. The series of quietly decorated areas has comfortable plum or chocolate plush cushioned armchairs, cushioned built-in wall seats, and stools, and lots of tables; there's also quite a bit of stripped stonework, nice prints on the cream walls, and perhaps Molly the friendly black labrador. The Snug and dining rooms are no smoking; piped music in one area only, and winter darts and dominoes. Well kept Black Sheep, Goose Eye Wharfedale, Timothy Taylors Best, Shipton Brewery Copper Dragon, and a couple of guests on handpump, 10 wines by big or small glass from a good list, and several malt whiskies. Very good food from a menu that can be used for both the bar and restaurant, might include nibbles such as unleavened garlic bread (£1.99) or marinated olives (£2.85), home-made soup (£3.25), sandwiches (from £4.25; open sandwich of smoked salmon, cream cheese, lemon and sweetened glaze £5.25; very popular club sandwich £6.50), sticky ribs (£4.50), breast of local wood pigeon wrapped in bacon with a tapas of black pudding, chorizo, sautéed potatoes, a hint of chilli, and game jus or yorkshire blue mushrooms (£4.99), mediterranean fish soup (£6.50), smoked haddock on mashed potato topped with a swiss cheese and prawn sauce and poached egg (£9.45), crispy pork belly with crackling, apple compote and thyme-roasted potatoes (£9.95), three curries (£9.99), and their famous lamb shoulder (£10.50), with changing specials like crisp yorkshire pudding with onion gravy (£2.95), wild mushroom and lentil stroganoff (£8.50), seafood pancake or home-made chicken and ham pie (£8.95), and beef suet pudding (£9.95), and puddings such as warm lemon sponge with tangy lemon sauce served with red orange ice-cream, sticky toffee pudding, and raspberry and rhubarb frangipane (£3.95); good local and regional cheeses, too, with crackers, fruitcake and celery (£4.95). Tables outside are largely screened from the road by a raised bank. The bedrooms have been refurbished this year, and we look forward to hearing what readers think of them – this should be a nice place to stay in. *(Recommended by Karen Eliot, J Taylor, Jim and Maggie Cowell, Robert Hill, Dudley and Moira Cockroft, Patrick Hancock, Steve Whalley, B and M Kendall, Simon Calvert, Jo Lilley, Fred and Lorraine Gill)*

Free house ~ Licensees Martin and Veronica Clarkson ~ Real ale ~ Bar food (12-2.30, 6-9; 12-7.45 Sun) ~ Restaurant ~ (01282) 842450 ~ Children in eating area of bar and restaurant ~ Open 11-11; 12-10.30 Sun ~ Bedrooms: £59.95B/£74.95B

FADMOOR SE6789 Map 10

Plough

Village signposted off A170 in or just W of Kirkbymoorside

This neatly kept and friendly pub remains as popular as ever for its first rate food. The elegantly simple little rooms have rugs on seagrass, richly upholstered furnishings, and yellow walls, well kept Black Sheep and Tetleys on handpump, and an extensive wine list. Changing all the time, the imaginative meals might include home-made soup like cream of mushroom and madeira (£3.75), smooth chicken liver and brandy pâté topped with a rustic tomato and garlic chutney (£4.95), fresh steamed shetland mussels (£7.25), seared king scallops with a medley of wild mushrooms, spring onion and sweet chilli (£7.95), home-made game pie (£8.50), home-made salmon fishcakes with a lemon, dill, white wine and cream sauce (£10.50), cumberland sausage ring on cherry tomato mash with a creamy spring onion sauce (£10.95), calves liver on beetroot risotto rice with thyme sauce (£12.95), escalopes of venison steak on a potato, garlic and parsley rösti with a redcurrant gravy (£13.50), and steaks (from £14.95), with puddings such as chocolate fudge brownies with hot chocolate sauce, caramelised lemon tart with mixed berry compote, and ginger and syrup sponge with hot vanilla custard (£4.50); two-course meal (not Saturday evening, £12.75). The dining areas are no smoking; dominoes. There are seats on the terrace. More reports please. *(Recommended by Walter and Susan Rinaldi-Butcher, Mr and Mrs Maurice Thompson, Alison Hayes, Pete Hanlon, I D Barnett, Peter Burton)*

Holf Leisure Ltd ~ Licensee Neil Nicholson ~ Real ale ~ Bar food ~ Restaurant ~ (01751) 431515 ~ Children welcome ~ Open 12-2.30(3 Sat), 6.30-11; 12-3, 7-10.30 Sun; closed 25 and 26 Dec, 1 Jan

There are report forms at the back of the book.

FELIXKIRK SE4785 Map 10

Carpenters Arms

Village signposted off A170 E of Thirsk

Genuinely friendly people run this warmly inviting place, and its quiet setting in a little Yorkshire village is most appealing. There are three or four cosy areas that ramble around the bar counter (made partly from three huge casks), with dark beams and joists hung with carpentry tools and other bric-a-brac, comfortable seats around tables with check tablecloths and little lighted oil burners, and a couple of huge Japanese fans by the stone fireplace; one area is no smoking. Good, enjoyable food includes home-made soups like cream of vegetable and thyme or lightly spiced parsnip and pear (£3.25), quite a few sandwiches (from £4.50; BLT £4.95; chargrilled thai burger £6.50), warm chicken liver salad (£4.50), moules marinière (£5.50), baked queen scallops with herbs and gruyère (£6.25), pork and leek sausages with onion gravy (£6.95), home-made steak, ale and mushroom pie (£8.25), crisp fillet of scottish salmon with baby spinach, mussels and fish cream sauce (£11.95), pork fillet with rocket and red onion salad and dijon and peppercorn sauce (£12.50), and honey-glazed duck breast with stir-fried vegetables, crispy noodles and plum sauce (£13.95); daily specials, puddings such as warm treacle tart (£4.25), and three-course Sunday lunch (£14.50). Well kept Black Sheep, Greene King Old Speckled Hen, John Smiths, and Timothy Taylors Landlord on handpump, and a good wine list with eight by the glass. There are two dalmatians, George and Lloyd. The church is prettily floodlit at night. *(Recommended by H Bramwell, Margaret and Mike Iley, Michael Ward, Christine and Phil Young, Anna Cooper, P S Hoyle, Peter Burton)*

Free house ~ Licensee Karen Bumby ~ Real ale ~ Bar food ~ Restaurant ~ (01845) 537369 ~ Children welcome ~ Open 11.30-3, 6.30-11; 12-3, 7-10.30 Sun; closed 25 Dec, evening 31 Dec

FERRENSBY SE3761 Map 7

General Tarleton

A655 N of Knaresborough

Even when this rather smart and comfortable old coaching inn is very busy – which it usually is – service remains helpful and courteous. Although many customers do come to enjoy the good modern cooking, there are plenty of locals popping in for a drink and a chat. The beamed and carpeted bar has brick pillars dividing up the several different areas to create the occasional cosy alcove, some exposed stonework, and neatly framed pictures on the red walls; there's a mix of country kitchen furniture and comfortable banquettes, a big open fire, and a door leading out to a pleasant tree-lined garden with smart green tables. From the menu, the interesting bar food includes thai spiced chicken, prawn and coconut soup (£4.95), queenie scallops (£5.95; main course £8.85), grilled chicken sandwich with avocado and aïoli (£6.95), terrine of duck with cumberland sauce (£7.25), fresh pasta rolled in a garlic, tomato and almond pesto (£7.50), steak in ale pudding (£10.95), slow braised shoulder of lamb in a garlic, thyme and tomato jus (£12.50), and crisped 24-hour pork and seared tiger prawns in spicy dressing (£13.95), with daily specials such as baked salmon en croûte with lobster butter sauce (£10.95), roast red-legged partridge (£13.95), and spiced sea salt crusted halibut with roasted fennel and balsamic reduction (£14.50), puddings like steamed treacle pudding with vanilla crème anglaise, chocolate soufflé or warm apple cobble pudding (from £4.75), and children's menu (from £4.25); good breakfasts. Well kept Black Sheep Best and Timothy Taylors Landlord on handpump, over 20 good wines by the glass, and quite a few coffees. The courtyard eating area (and restaurant) are no smoking. *(Recommended by Regine Webster, Janet and Peter Race, Malcolm and Jennifer Perry, Mrs M Blundell, Kate Arscott, B and M Kendall, H Bramwell, David and Iris Hunter, Robert and Susan Whitehead, Revd D Glover, David and Ruth Hollands, Alison Hayes, Pete Hanlon, Brian Kneale, DC, M Sharp, Edward and Deanna Pearce, Patrick Hancock)*

Free house ~ Licensee John Topham ~ Real ale ~ Bar food (12-2, 6-9.15) ~ Restaurant ~ (01423) 340284 ~ Children welcome ~ Dogs allowed in bedrooms ~ Open 12-3, 6-11(10.30 Sun) ~ Bedrooms: /£84.90B

FLAMBOROUGH TA2270 Map 8

Seabirds

Junction B1255/B1229

Close to the Chalk Cliffs and lighthouse at Flamborough Head (where there are many spectacular walks) or the seabird colonies at Bempton Cliffs, this village pub is a welcoming, friendly place, and has been refurbished inside and outside this year. The public bar has quite a shipping theme, and leading off here the comfortable lounge has pictures and paintings of the local landscape, and a woodburning stove. The no smoking restaurant has been extended and re-designed. Good bar food includes sandwiches, soup (£2.50), home-made chicken liver and orange pâté (£3.95), omelettes using free range eggs (from £5.10), nice battered haddock (£6.25), pasta and stilton bake (£6.50), chicken, bacon and pineapple in barbecue sauce (£8.75), lamb shank with red wine and rosemary (£10.25), steaks (from £10.95), and daily specials such as a roast of the day (£6), home-made chicken korma (£6.25), and marlin steak with creamy prawn sauce (£9.50). Well kept John Smiths and a guest like Wold Top Falling Stone on handpump, and a decent wine list; dominoes, fruit machine, TV, and piped music. There are seats in the sizeable garden, and you can eat out here in fine weather. More reports please. *(Recommended by Paul and Ursula Randall, DC, M Borthwick, Tim and Claire Woodward)*

Free house ~ Licensee Philip Jones ~ Real ale ~ Bar food ~ Restaurant ~ (01262) 850242 ~ Children welcome if eating ~ Dogs allowed in bar ~ Open 12-3, 6.30(6 Sat)-11; 12-3, 7-10.30 Sun

GOOSE EYE SE0340 Map 7

Turkey

Just S of Laycock on road to Oakworth and Haworth, W of Keighley; OS Sheet 104 map reference 028406

This busy place is full of character with friendly licensees and locals, popular own-brew ales, and roaring winter log fires. There are various cosy and snug alcoves, brocaded upholstery, and walls covered with pictures of surrounding areas; the restaurant is no smoking. You can visit the microbrewery – they ask for a donation for Upper Wharfedale Fell Rescue: Turkey Bitter, Chris Camm, and No-Eyed Deer, and changing guest beers on handpump. Over 40 whiskies. Generous helpings of decent, straightforward bar food (they tell us prices have not changed since last year) include home-made soup (£2.10), sandwiches (from £3.50), vegetable lasagne (£5.80), home-made pie (£6), steaks (from £7.20), home-made daily specials (from £6), and puddings (from £2.40); Sunday lunch (£6). Piped music, and a separate games area with pool, fruit machine, and TV. *(Recommended by Matt Waite, Geoffrey and Brenda Wilson, Mr and Mrs P Eastwood, DC, Mrs J Doherty, Greta and Christopher Wells)*

Own brew ~ Licensees Harry and Monica Brisland ~ Real ale ~ Bar food (not Mon or Tues lunchtimes) ~ Restaurant ~ (01535) 681339 ~ Children welcome ~ Dogs allowed in bar ~ Open 12-3, 5.30-11; 12-11 Fri and Sat; 12-10.30 Sun; closed Mon and Tues lunchtimes

HALIFAX SE1026 Map 7

Shibden Mill

Off A58 into Kell Lane at Stump Cross Inn, near A6036 junction; keep on, pub signposted from Kell Lane on left

Run by helpful, sociable licensees, this hidden away restored mill is much enjoyed as somewhere to pop in for a drink, to have a leisurely meal, and to stay overnight in the comfortable bedrooms. The rambling bar has cosy side areas with enticing banquettes heaped softly with cushions and rugs; tables and chairs are well spaced, but candles in elegant iron holders give a feeling of real intimacy. There are old hunting prints, country landscapes and so forth, and a couple of big log fireplaces. They offer a dozen wines by the glass served in nice glasses, and have John Smiths, a softly flavoured golden beer brewed for them by Moorhouses, Theakstons XB, and a couple of guests kept well on handpump. Good, imaginative bar food includes home-made soup (£3.75), sandwiches on home-made bread with pickles and salad (hot cajun chicken and mint yoghurt or chunky egg mayonnaise with watercress, £5.25), scrambled egg, smoked salmon and capers (£6.50), smoked haddock topped with spring onion mash (£6.95), macaroni with ham fritter or ploughman's with scotch egg, local cheeses, ham and their own preserves and bread (£8), lambs liver with mash and onion jus (£8.50), fillet of beef with slow roasted tomatoes and chips (£14.50), and puddings such as home-made blackberry jelly with honey madeleine, peanut butter ice-cream with chocolate chip cookie, and almond and rhubarb tart with ginger custard (£4.25); british cheeses with home-made chutney and walnut bread (£5.75). Vegetables and salads are £1.95 extra; piped music. The restaurant is upstairs. There are plenty of good teak tables and chairs out on an attractive terrace, with lots of heaters; the building is prettily floodlit at night. *(Recommended by Geoffrey and Brenda Wilson, Derek and Sylvia Stephenson, Pat and Tony Martin, Andy and Jill Kassube, Ian and Nita Cooper, Kate Charman, R and P A Mitchell, Mrs J Doherty, Greta and Christopher Wells)*

Free house ~ Licensee Glen Pearson ~ Real ale ~ Bar food (12-2, 6-9.30) ~ Restaurant ~ (01422) 365840 ~ Children welcome ~ Open 12-2.30, 5.30-11; 12-11 Sat; 12-10.30 Sun ~ Bedrooms: £65B/£80B

HAROME SE6582 Map 10

Star ★

Village signposted S of A170, E of Helmsley

Yorkshire Dining Pub of the Year

This is an exceptional place for any occasion. It's a pretty, thatched 14th-c inn run with flair and imagination by very friendly, young licensees and their courteous and helpful smartly dressed staff. Much emphasis is placed, not surprisingly, on the first rate food, but there's a proper pubby atmosphere in the bar, and it's a super place to stay overnight in the lovely bedrooms. The no smoking bar has a dark bowed beam-and-plank ceiling, well polished tiled kitchen range, plenty of bric-a-brac, interesting furniture (this was the first pub that 'Mousey Thompson' ever populated with his famous dark wood furniture), a fine log fire, and daily papers and magazines; as they don't take bar reservations, it's best to arrive early to get a seat. There's also a private dining room and a popular coffee loft in the eaves, and a separate restaurant. Changing daily, the inventive food uses fish that is delivered daily from Hartlepool, local hen, duck, and guinea fowl eggs, three types of honey from the village, and their own herbs and vegetables; lots of british cheeses, too. Changing daily, there might be bubble and squeak soup with crushed pepper cream (£3.50), freshly steamed shetland mussels (£5.95), sandwiches or buns (from £6.50; seared steak with blue wensleydale £7.50), risotto of rievaulx partridge with braised chestnuts, black trumpet mushrooms and roast hazelnut pesto (£6.95; main course £11.95), dressed whitby crab with green herb mayonnaise, plum tomato and basil salad and bloody mary vinaigrette (£7.25; main course £13.50), grilled black pudding with fried foie gras, apple and vanilla chutney and scrumpy reduction (£8.95), posh ploughman's (£9.50), duck sausages with curly kale colcannon and home-baked beans (£9.95), seared scallops with deep-fried scarborough woof, pea purée and plum tomato ketchup (£13.95), and roast tail fillet of local beef with braised shin, fresh horseradish risotto, dark ale, and root vegetable juices (£16.95), and specials such as bresaola of home-cured devon red beef with elderberry balsamic, ox tongue and pickled onion and watercress salad (£7.25; main course £11), braised neck of ryedale lamb with a purée of celeriac, green lentil, and sweet cicely juices (£16.95), and local fallow dear steak with gin poached gooseberries, creamed cabbage, york ham lardons, and juniper juices (£18.95); lovely puddings like Pimms No 1 jelly with spearmint water ice, steamed ale cake with Theakstons ice-cream and dark muscovado sauce or banana bread and butter pudding with local clotted cream (from £6.50). Well kept Black Sheep, John Smiths, and a guest like Cropton Two Pints or Charles Wells Bombardier on handpump, home-made fruit juices and ten wines by the glass from a fairly extensive wine list; piped music. There are some seats and tables on a sheltered front terrace with more in the garden with fruit trees. Eight superbly equipped, stylish bedrooms in converted farm buildings plus three suites in a thatched cottage, and there's a private dining room, too. Their bakery/delicatessen is called The Corner Shop and sells take-away meals and snacks as well as all manner of delicious goodies from cakes and tarts to fresh truffles and wild mushrooms, local game and fish, and home-made terrines and pies. They have a village cricket team. *(Recommended by Terry Mizen, Mr and Mrs C Cameron, Peter and Anne-Marie O'Malley, Derek and Margaret Underwood, Mike Schofield, Tim Newman, Marian and Andrew Ruston, J Goodwin, Alison Hayes, Pete Hanlon, Comus and Sarah Elliott, Michael Butler, A C English, Mrs Yvette Bateman, Tracey and Stephen Groves, W W Burke, Edward and Deanna Pearce, Dr and Mrs S Donald, G Dobson; also in the* Good Hotel Guide*)*

Free house ~ Licensees Andrew and Jacquie Pern ~ Real ale ~ Bar food (11.30-2, 6.30-9.30; 12-6 Sun; not Sun evening, not Mon) ~ Restaurant ~ (01439) 770397 ~ Children in eating area of bar and restaurant ~ Open 11.30-3, 6.30(6.15 Sat)-11; 12-6 Sun; closed Sun evening and Mon lunchtime ~ Bedrooms: £90B/£120B

HEATH SE3519 Map 7

Kings Arms £

Village signposted from A655 Wakefield—Normanton – or, more directly, turn off to the left opposite Horse & Groom

In fine weather you can sit at seats along the front of this old-fashioned pub and make the most of the village green setting opposite and the surrounding 19th-c stone merchants' houses; there are picnic-sets on a side lawn, and a nice walled flower-filled garden. Inside, the gas lighting adds a lot to the atmosphere, and the original bar has a fire burning in the old black range (with a long row of smoothing irons on the mantelpiece), plain elm stools and oak settles built into the walls, and dark panelling. A more comfortable extension has carefully preserved the original style, down to good wood-pegged oak panelling (two embossed with royal arms), and a high shelf of plates; there are also two other small flagstoned rooms, and the conservatory opens on to the garden. Good value bar food includes sandwiches (from £1.80; hot sausage and onion £2.70), home-made soup (£2.50), mushroom stroganoff (£4.75), liver and onions in rich gravy or beef in ale pie (£5.95), rump steak (£7.45), and puddings like treacle sponge and custard (£2.75). Well kept Clarks Classic Blonde, Timothy Taylors Landlord, and a guest like Clarks Rams Revenge on handpump; quiz night Tuesdays. The landlord tell us that with four exits to the pub, customers do leave without paying which is why they say they keep your credit card in the till until the bill is paid; their credit card machine does not yet have the facilitity to swipe cards. *(Recommended by the Didler, JP, PP, M and GR, Mike and Maggie Betton, Pat and Derek Roughton, Geoffrey and Brenda Wilson, Steve Kirby, Ian Phillips, Patrick Hancock, Greta and Christopher Wells)*

Clarks ~ Manager Alan Tate ~ Real ale ~ Bar food (12-2(2.30 weekends), 6-9.30) ~ (01924) 377527 ~ Children in eating area of bar and restaurant ~ Open 11.30-11; 12-10.30 Sun; 11.30-3, 5.30-11 weekdays in winter

HECKMONDWIKE SE2223 Map 7

Old Hall

New North Road; B6117 between A62 and A638; OS Sheet 104 map reference 214244

As ever, it's the historic building itself that is the main interest here. It dates from 1470, and was once the home of Nonconformist scientist Joseph Priestley. Although it was built in the 15th c, the outer walls were replaced by stone in the 16th c, and inside there are lots of old beams and timbers, latticed mullioned windows with worn stone surrounds, and brick or stripped old stone walls hung with pictures of Richard III, Henry VII, Catherine Parr, and Joseph Priestley; new furnishings this year. Snug low-ceilinged alcoves lead off the central part with its high ornate plaster ceiling, and an upper gallery room, under the pitched roof, looks down on the main area through timbering 'windows'; one area is no smoking. Bar food is straightforward, with unchanging dishes like curry, a pie of the day or three-cheese pasta bake (£5.25). Well kept (and cheap) Sam Smiths OB on handpump; fruit machine, piped music, darts, TV, and dominoes. More reports please. *(Recommended by Ian Phillips)*

Sam Smiths ~ Lease Robert Green ~ Real ale ~ Bar food (12-2, 6-8; 12-3 Sun; not hot food Mon, Tues, Weds) ~ (01924) 404774 ~ Children welcome ~ Open 11.30-11; 12-10.30 Sun

HETTON SD9558 Map 7

Angel ★ 🍴 🍷

Just off B6265 Skipton—Grassington

Particularly well run and always very busy, this extremely popular dining pub is the sort of place customers come back to on a regular basis. You must book to be sure of a table. The four timbered and panelled rambling rooms have lots of cosy alcoves, comfortable country-kitchen chairs or button-back green plush seats, Ronald Searle wine snob cartoons and older engravings and photographs, log fires, and in the main bar, a Victorian farmhouse range in the big stone fireplace; the bar lounge is no smoking. From an interesting menu, bar food might include little moneybags (seafood baked in filo with lobster sauce, £5.75), chicken liver and foie gras terrine with grape chutney or roasted butternut squash and sage risotto topped with crispy parnsip (£5.75), pork sausages with rich red onion gravy (£8.25), vegetarian pasta (£8.95), free range crispy pork belly with black pudding and whole grain mustard mash (£9.25), confit shoulder of lamb on thyme mash with a tomato and black olive lamb sauce (£10.95), goosnargh duck breast with braised red cabbage and prunes (£13.95), daily specials, and puddings like sticky toffee pudding with caramel sauce, chocolate delice with crème anglaise, and poached pear in spiced red wine with cinnamon ice-cream (from £4.25). The early bird menu (until 6.45pm) is well liked: two courses (£13.20), three courses (£16.50). Three-course Sunday lunch (£20.90). The restaurant is no smoking. Well kept Black Sheep Bitter, Copper Dragon Best Bitter, Timothy Taylors Landlord, and Wharfedale Folly from a new nearby brewery on handpump, 300 wines (with around 25 by the glass, including champagne), and 25 malt whiskies. Wooden seats and tables under colourful sunshades on the terrace. *(Recommended by Robert Hill, Sherrie Glass, Jim Abbott, Janet and Peter Race, John and Sylvia Harrop, Bernard Stradling, Pat and Clive Sherriff, Keith and Margaret Kettell, Brenda and Rob Fincham, Mrs M E Mills, P J Holt, John Mitchell, Revd D Glover, Linda Somers, M and GR, J S Burn, Jack Morley, Simon Calvert, Jo Lilley, Fred and Lorraine Gill, Stephen Buckley, Marlene and Jim Godfrey, A Darroch Harkness)*

Free house ~ Licensees Denis Watkins and John Topham ~ Real ale ~ Bar food (12-2.15, 6-9) ~ Restaurant ~ (01756) 730263 ~ Children in eating area of bar and restaurant ~ Dogs allowed in bedrooms ~ Open 12-3, 6-11(11.30 Sat; 10.30 Sun); 12-3, 6-9.30 Sun in winter; closed 1 week Jan ~ Bedrooms: /£120B

HUBBERHOLME SD9178 Map 7

George

Village signposted from Buckden; about 1 mile NW

Seats and tables look up to the moors which rise all around this remote old place – and on to a lovely swirly stretch of the River Wharfe where they have fishing rights. Inside, the two neat and cosy rooms have genuine character: heavy beams supporting the dark ceiling-boards, walls stripped back to bare stone and hung with antique plates and photographs, seats around shiny copper-topped tables on the flagstones, and an open stove in the big fireplace. Under the new licensee, bar food at lunchtime includes home-made soup (£3.50), sandwiches (£4.50), vegetable cheese melt (£5.50), a daily quiche (£6.50), and gammon and egg (£8), with evening choices such as breadcrumbed king prawns (£4), steak in ale pie (£7.80), chicken fillet with herby tomato sauce (£8), sirloin steak (£11), and local lamb chops with red wine gravy (£12). Well kept Black Sheep Bitter and Special, and a guest like Copper Dragon Best Bitter on handpump; dominoes. The little village here has just this inn, the ancient church (where J B Priestley's ashes are scattered – this was his favourite pub), a bridge and a handful of stone-built houses. More reports on the new regime, please. *(Recommended by Maggie and Tony Harwood, B and M Kendall, Walter and Susan Rinaldi-Butcher, John Hale, Jane Taylor, David Dutton, Mr and Mrs Staples, Tony and Ann Bennett-Hughes, D W Stokes, Dr and Mrs D Woods, Tim Newman, Di and Mike Gillam, Sarah Berthelemey, John and Enid Morris, Neil and Angela Huxter, Ben Whitney and Pippa Redmond, Eddie Edwards, Tony and Betty Parker, Kerry Law, Simon Smith)*

Free house ~ Licensee Barry Roberts ~ Real ale ~ Bar food (12-2, 6.30-8.30) ~ (01756) 760223 ~ Children welcome ~ Open 12-4, 6-11; 12-2.30, 6.30-10.30 in winter; closed Mon in winter; closed first 2 weeks Dec, mid 2 weeks Jan ~ Bedrooms: /£60B

HULL TA0927 Map 8

Minerva

Park at top of pedestrianised area at top of Queen's Street and walk over Nelson Street or turn off Queen's Street into Wellington Street, right into Pier Street and pub is at top; no parking restrictions weekends, 2-hour stay Mon-Fri

From the seats out in front of this busy pub and on the piers on each side, you can watch the passing boats in the Hull estuary; it's also a handy spot for the nearby The Deep (Europe's deepest aquarium). Inside, several rooms ramble all the way round a central servery, and are filled with comfortable seats, quite a few interesting photographs and pictures of old Hull (with two attractive wash drawings by Roger Davis) and a big chart of the Humber; one room is no smoking during mealtimes. A tiny snug has room for just three people, and a back room (which looks out to the marina basin) houses a profusion of varnished woodwork; two coal fires in winter. They hold three beer festivals a year – at Easter, mid-July, and whenever the Sea Shanty Festival is on – August/September. Otherwise, they keep Tetleys with guests like Shepherd Neame Spitfire, Springhead Bare Bones, Wadworths Summersault, and Charles Wells Eagle IPA on handpump. Straightforward bar food such as filled baked potatoes (from £2.50), baguettes (from £2.95), ploughman's (£4.50), steak in ale pie (£4.55), battered haddock (£5.25), and puddings (£2.50). The lounge is no-smoking when food is being served. Dominoes, cribbage, fruit machine, TV, and piped music. *(Recommended by the Didler, Fred and Lorraine Gill, Alistair and Kay Butler, JP, PP, Roger and Pauline Pearce, Peter F Marshall, Di and Mike Gillam, Paul and Ursula Randall, Alison Hayes, Pete Hanlon, J R Ringrose, Patrick Hancock)*

Spirit Group ~ Manager Richard Semper ~ Real ale ~ Bar food (11.30-2.30, 6-9; 12-4 Sun) ~ (01482) 326909 ~ Children in eating area of bar if eating ~ Open 11-11; 12-10.30 Sun; closed 25 Dec

Olde White Harte ★

Off 25 Silver Street, a continuation of Whitefriargate; pub is up narrow passage, and should not be confused with the much more modern White Hart nearby

This ancient inn is tucked away in a cosy courtyard amongst narrow alleyways – and, despite its heritage, remains very much a bustling working pub. The three bars have some fine features. The downstairs one has attractive stained-glass windows that look out above the bow window seat, carved heavy beams support black ceiling boards, and there are two big brick inglenooks with a frieze of delft tiles. The curved copper-topped counter serves well kept Caledonian Deuchars IPA, McEwans 80/-, and Theakstons Best and Old Peculier on handpump, and straightforward bar food; the restaurant is no smoking. It was in the heavily panelled room up the oak staircase that in 1642 the town's governor Sir John

Hotham made the fateful decision to lock the nearby gate against Charles I, depriving him of Hull's arsenal; it didn't do him much good, as in the Civil War that followed, Hotham, like the king, was executed by the parliamentarians. There are seats in the courtyard, and outside heaters. *(Recommended by the Didler, Roger and Pauline Pearce, JP, PP, Paul and Ursula Randall, Peter F Marshall, Alison Hayes, Pete Hanlon, Patrick Hancock, Matt Waite)*

Scottish Courage ~ Lease Bernard Copley ~ Real ale ~ Bar food (12-2, 5-10; not Fri or Sat evenings) ~ Restaurant ~ (01482) 326363 ~ Children in restaurant ~ Open 11-11; 12-10.30 Sun

INGLETON SD6973 Map 7

Wheatsheaf

High Street

Jovial, attentive licensees run this pleasant 17th-c coaching inn, and there's plenty to do and see in the attractive village and wonderful surrounding countryside. The long open-plan bar has, at one end, a pool table overlooked by various stuffed birds and animals; at the other, past the good big log fire, there's a family area with an aquarium. Reasonably priced bar food includes home-made soup (£2.60), garlic mushrooms (£4.25), home-roasted ham with eggs and home-made chips (£6), a roast of the day (£7), home-made cheese, onion and potato pie, beef and mushroom in ale pie or sausages of the day with yorkshire pudding (all £7.25), shoulder of lamb with mint and redcurrant sauce or trout fillet with a pesto crust (£8.75), 10oz sirloin steak (£10.95), and puddings like chocolate cheesecake or banoffi pie (£3.35). The restaurant is no smoking. Well kept Black Sheep Bitter and Special, Tetleys, and Timothy Taylors Golden Best on handpump, quite a few whiskies, and piped music. The back garden (keep an eye open for Laurel and Hardy on your way out) has picnic-sets by an aviary with hawks; the black labradors are called Tia and Bella. They now have holiday cottages for rent. More reports please. *(Recommended by Gerry and Rosemary Dobson, Maggie and Tony Harwood)*

Free house ~ Licensees Jeremy and Hayley Thompson ~ Real ale ~ Bar food (12-2.30, 6-9) ~ Restaurant ~ (015242) 41275 ~ Children in eating area of bar ~ Dogs allowed in bar ~ Open 12-11(10.30 Sun) ~ Bedrooms: £45S/£64S(£74B)

KETTLESING SE2256 Map 7

Queens Head 🍷 🛏

Village signposted off A59 W of Harrogate

A good place to stop on a barren stretch of the A59, this stone-built pub has seats in the neatly kept suntrap back garden, and benches in front by the lane. The L-shaped, carpeted main bar is decorated with Victorian song sheet covers, lithographs of Queen Victoria, little heraldic shields, and a delft shelf of blue and white china. There's also a quietly chatty atmosphere, and lots of quite close-set elm and other tables around its walls, with cushioned country seats. Nicely presented food, very popular on weekday lunchtimes with older people, includes home-made soup (£2.95), filled yorkshire puddings (from £2.95), sandwiches (from £2.95), omelettes (£5.95), cottage pie or beef stew and dumplings (£7.50), and home-made battered haddock (£7.95), with evening dishes such as chicken liver pâté with port and smoked bacon (£4.25), home-made chicken and ham pie or liver and bacon (£7.95), home-made seafood bake (£8.25), fish dishes (from £8.95), minted lamb shoulder (£10.95), and steaks (from £11.50); three-course Sunday lunch (£10.95). Coal or log fires at each end and maybe unobtrusive piped radio. A smaller bar on the left, with built-in red banquettes, has cricketing prints and cigarette cards, coins and banknotes, and in the lobby there's a life-size portrait of Queen Elizabeth I. The lounge is no smoking. Well kept Black Sheep Bitter, Theakstons Old Peculier and a quickly changing guest from maybe Daleside or Rudgate on handpump, eight wines by the glass, and efficient service. *(Recommended by Graham Holden, Julie Lee, Hugh A MacLean, Mr and Mrs Staples, M and GR, DC, John and Sylvia Harrop)*

Free house ~ Licensees David and Fran Croft ~ Real ale ~ Bar food ~ (01423) 770263 ~ Children in restaurant and family room ~ Open 11-11; 11-3, 6-11 Sat; 12-3.30, 7-10.30 Sun ~ Bedrooms: £55B/£65B

KIRKBYMOORSIDE SE6987 Map 10

George & Dragon

Market Place

Perhaps one of the best days to visit this 17th-c coaching inn is on Wednesday when there's a good bustling atmosphere, as this pretty, small town has its market day then. The pubby front bar has leather chesterfields as well as the brass-studded solid dark red leatherette armchairs set around polished wooden tables, burgundy and cream walls and panelling stripped back to its original pitch pine, horsebrasses hung along the beams, newspapers to read, and a blazing log fire; piped music. There's also an attractive beamed bistro, and a no smoking restaurant. Generously served, the enjoyable bar food includes lunchtime sandwiches (from £2.95; roast chicken with cajun mayonnaise £3.95), home-made soup (£3.25), ploughman's (£5.95), chicken liver pâté with plum chutney (£4.50), pasta topped with smoked bacon, mushrooms and creamy mature cheddar sauce (£6.95), deep-fried whitby haddock in beer batter (£7.25), steak in ale pie or home-made salmon and dill fishcakes (£7.50), daily specials such as grilled goats cheese (£5.95), moules or quiche (£6.95), mexican lamb (£8.95), and duckling (£13.95), and puddings like walnut and caramel tart, chocolate terrine, and ginger syrup sponge with custard (£3.95); two courses (£9.95). Well kept Black Sheep Bitter, Tetleys, and Timothy Taylors Landlord on handpump, ten wines by the glass, and 25 malt whiskies. This is a comfortable place to stay (the bedrooms are in a converted cornmill and old vicarage at the back of the pub), there are seats under umbrellas in the back courtyard and a surprisingly peaceful walled garden for residents to use. More reports please. *(Recommended by Geoff and Angela Jaques, Alison Hayes, Pete Hanlon, I D Barnett, Dr David Cockburn)*

Free house ~ Licensee Elaine Walker ~ Real ale ~ Bar food (12-2.15, 6.30-9.15) ~ Restaurant ~ (01751) 433334 ~ Children allowed away from bar ~ Dogs allowed in bar and bedrooms ~ Open 11-11; 12-10.30 Sun ~ Bedrooms: £49S/£79B

KIRKHAM SE7466 Map 7

Stone Trough

Kirkham Abbey

As well as a friendly welcome from the attentive licensees, what readers continue to enjoy in this country inn is the fact that it manages to be both a proper pub and a restaurant. The several beamed and cosy rooms have warm log fires, well kept Black Sheep Bitter, Tetleys, Timothy Taylors Landlord, and a couple of guests such as Malton Golden Chance, and Theakstons Old Peculier on handpump, and an extensive wine list with ten by the glass; the restaurant are no smoking. From an imaginative menu, the very good bar food might include home-made soup (£3.95), sandwiches (from £3.95; popular hot steak and sautéed onion baguette £5.25), terrine of confit duck and leek wrapped in parma ham with a pear and apricot chutney (£5.25), queen scallops topped with herb breadcrumbs and glazed with gruyère cheese (£5.50), local pork sausages on a sage and onion rösti with real ale gravy (£7.25), rocket and tomato beignets with a feta cheese and olive salad (£7.95), chicken, chorizo and tarragon pasta with a fine herb salad (£8.95), baked chunk of scarborough cod on parsley mash with a lemon velouté and a poached egg (£10.25), braised lamb shank on roast garlic mash with rosemary and redcurrant jus (£10.75), daily specials such as baked langoustines with a lemon and roast garlic butter, wild mushroom and purple potato tart with herb salad, roast bread and confit leg of pheasant with a red onion tart and damson sauce, and fried fillet of bass with a truffle ravioli on buttered spinach, and puddings such as a pyramid of marbled chocolate filled with a dark chocolate and kirsch mousse with black cherries, passion fruit and orange crème brûlée, and treacle tart (£4.25); good coffees, teas, and hot chocolate with whipped cream (£1.95). The cat is called Crumble. Pool, fruit machine, dominoes, cribbage, shove-ha'penny, and piped music; TV in the no smoking pool room. From the seats outside, there are lovely views down the valley, and the inn is handy for Kirkham Abbey and Castle Howard. *(Recommended by Mr and Mrs J Powell, Christopher Turner, Mike Ridgway, Sarah Miles, Dr D Parker, Pat and Graham Williamson, Alison Hayes, Pete Hanlon, Edward Leetham, Marlene and Jim Godfrey)*

Free house ~ Licensees Sarah and Adam Richardson ~ Real ale ~ Bar food (12-2, 6.30-8.30; not Mon except bank hols) ~ Restaurant ~ (01653) 618713 ~ Well behaved children in eating areas until 9pm ~ Open 12-2.30, 6-11; 11.45-10.30 Sun; closed Mon except bank hols; 25 Dec

LANGTHWAITE NY9902 Map 10

Charles Bathurst

Arkengarthdale, a mile N towards Tan Hill; generally known as the CB Inn

As well as refurbishing the kitchen in this well run inn, a new dining room has been built with wooden floors and views of Scar House, a shooting lodge owned by the Duke of Norfolk. The inn looks appropriately stolid from the outside, and is knocked through inside to make a long bar with light pine scrubbed tables, country chairs and benches on stripped floors, plenty of snug alcoves, and a roaring fire. The island bar counter has well kept Black Sheep Bitter and Riggwelter, John Smiths, and Theakstons Best on handpump, and a short but interesting list of wines; piped music, darts, pool, TV and dominoes. Using local ingredients and cooked by the licensee, the very popular food might include lunchtime filled baguettes, carrot and coriander soup with sun-dried tomato bread (£3.85), lamb kofta with spicy tomato salsa (£4.50), asparagus, chicken and smoked bacon tartlet (£4.95), mediterranean roast vegetables on couscous (£8), loin of salmon with tagliatelle carbonara (£8.80), slow roasted pork belly with wilted spinach and wild mushrooms (£9.95), boned guinea fowl stuffed with a ham and lime duxelles with madeira jus (£11.25), and puddings such as sticky toffee pudding with caramel sauce and lime cheesecake with winter berries (£3.75). Best to book to be sure of a table; the dining room is partly no smoking. The bedrooms are pretty and comfortable, and there are fine views over Langthwaite village and Arkengarthdale. *(Recommended by Jim Abbott, Lynda and Trevor Smith, Bill and Sheila McLardy, Walter and Susan Rinaldi-Butcher, M S Catling, B and M Kendall, Adrian Savage, Pam Stacey, Anthony Barnes, David Field, David Reid, Janet and Peter Race, Ben and Helen Ingram)*

Free house ~ Licensees Charles and Stacy Cody ~ Real ale ~ Bar food ~ (01748) 884567 ~ Children welcome ~ Dogs welcome ~ Open 11-11; 12-10.30 Sun; 3-11 Mon-Thurs in winter ~ Bedrooms: /£70B

LASTINGHAM SE7391 Map 10

Blacksmiths Arms

Off A170 W of Pickering at Wrelton, forking off Rosedale road N of Cropton; or via Appleton or Hutton-le-Hole

Situated at the foot of the moors, this neatly kept stone inn is not surprisingly popular with walkers. There's a cosily old-fashioned beamed bar with a log fire in an open range, traditional furnishings, and well kept Hop Back Summer Lightning, Phoenix Tennis Elbow, Theakstons Best, and a beer named for the pub brewed for them by nearby Bob's Brewing Company on handpump. Under the new licensee, the enjoyable, genuinely home-made bar food includes soup (£2.95), deep-fried brie with cranberry dip or black pudding and red onion risotto (£3.85), terrine with tomato relish (£4.25), large filled baguettes or wholemeal rolls (from £4.50), lamb and mint pie, broccoli pancake mornay, good seasonal game dishes, cumberland sausage in yorkshire pudding, and whitby cod in beer batter (all £7.95), fresh salmon in a white wine sauce (£8.95), chicken with a sage and onion stuffing and creamy stilton sauce (£9.25), daily specials, and puddings such as old-fashioned treacle tart, rum and raisin cheesecake or strawberry cream dream (£3.65); they serve soup and sandwiches all afternoon, and the chef caters for anyone with special dietary needs. The restaurant is no smoking. There are seats in the back garden and the village is very pretty. It's worth a visit to the church as it has a unique Saxon crypt built as a shrine to St Cedd in 1078. *(Recommended by S D and J L Cooke, John Hale, Angus and Rosemary Campbell, Alison Hayes, Pete Hanlon, Colin and Dot Savill, Dr David Cockburn)*

Free house ~ Licensee Peter Trafford ~ Real ale ~ Bar food ~ Restaurant ~ (01751) 417247 ~ Children welcome ~ Open 11.30-11(10.30 Sun); 12-2.30, 6-11 weekdays in winter; closed winter Tues lunchtime ~ Bedrooms: /£60B

LEDSHAM SE4529 Map 7

Chequers

Claypit Lane; a mile W of A1, some 4 miles N of junction M62

Being so handy for the A1, this bustling and friendly stone-built village pub tends to get customers who return again and again. The old-fashioned little central panelled-in servery has several small, individually decorated rooms leading off with low beams, lots of cosy alcoves, a number of toby jugs, log fires, and well kept Brown Cow Bitter and Simpsons No 4, John Smiths, Theakstons Best and Timothy Taylors Landlord on handpump; dominoes. Popular bar food includes snacks such as filled baguettes (from £4.95; steak and onions in a large breadcake £5.85), smoked salmon with scrambled eggs (£6.85), and steak and mushroom pie (£9.85), plus more fancifully described dishes such as chorizo, chicken strips and bacon lardons in a bowl of fancy leaves (£5.95), roast mushrooms and leeks towered and topped with creamed potatoes sat amongst pools of tomato and basil coulis (£12.95), chicken breast encasing pieces of mango presented across caramelised apples and drizzled with plum syrup (£13.45), and halibut loin baked whilst sheeted with smoked mozzarella atop thyme and lemon steeped courgettes splashed with a sweet chilli dressing (£15.95); daily specials like baked goats cheese slab balancing on an italian bread croûte then masked with a garlicky cream (£6.55), monkfish tail wrapped in smoked bacon with roast beef tomatoes and balsamic vinegar dressing (£15.95), and whole grilled dover sole with tomato, caper and dill butter (£17.95), and puddings such as orange and ginger cheesecake or chocolate brownie mousse cake (from £4.45). A sheltered two-level terrace behind the house has tables among roses, and the hanging baskets and flowers are very pretty. More food reports please. *(Recommended by Mrs Anthea Fricker, Peter Burton, Andy and Jill Kassube, the Didler, MDN, K M Crook, Blaise Vyner, Michael Doswell, M Borthwick, Alison Hayes, Pete Hanlon, David and Helen Wilkins, Darly Graton, Graeme Gulibert, Philip and June Caunt, Ray and Winifred Halliday, Joyce and Geoff Robson, Matt Waite, Paul Boot)*

Free house ~ Licensee Chris Wraith ~ Real ale ~ Bar food (12-2.15, 6-9.15; 12-9.15 Sat; not Sun) ~ Restaurant ~ (01977) 683135 ~ Children welcome ~ Dogs allowed in bar ~ Open 11-3, 5-11; 11-11 Sat; closed Sun

LEEDS SE3033 Map 7

Whitelocks ★ £

Turks Head Yard; alley off Briggate, opposite Debenhams and Littlewoods; park in shoppers' car park and walk

Hardly changed since 1886, this remarkable and beautifully preserved place is thought of as a national treasure by many people. There's always a bustling atmosphere and a good mix of customers (it does get packed at peak times), and the long and narrow old-fashioned bar has polychrome tiles on the bar counter, stained-glass windows and grand advertising mirrors, and red button back plush banquettes and heavy copper-topped cast-iron tables squeezed down one side. Good, reasonably priced bar food includes giant yorkshire puddings (from £1.95), sandwiches and filled baguettes (from £3.45), and tasty shepherds's pie or home-made steak and potato pie (from £4.95); friendly, efficient staff. Well kept John Smiths, Theakstons Best and Old Peculier, Wentworth Needles Eye, and four quickly changing guest beers on handpump. *(Recommended by JP, PP, Ian Phillips, the Didler, David Carr, Alison Hayes, Pete Hanlon, Joe Green, Dr and Mrs A K Clarke, Jo Lilley)*

Scottish Courage ~ Manager Nicholas James ~ Real ale ~ Bar food (11-7 Mon-Sat, 12-4 Sun) ~ Restaurant ~ (0113) 245 3950 ~ Children in restaurant and family room ~ Open 11-11; 12-10.30 Sun; closed 25 Dec, 1 Jan

LEYBURN SE1191 Map 10

Sandpiper

Just off Market Place

There's no doubt that most customers come to this 17th-c stone cottage to enjoy the first class food, although there is a small bar used by locals for a pint and a chat. The bar has a couple of black beams in the low ceiling, antlers, and a few tables and chairs, and the back room up three steps has attractive dales photographs. Down by the nice linenfold panelled bar counter there are stuffed sandpipers, more photographs and a woodburning stove in the stone fireplace; to the left is the no smoking restaurant. At lunchtime, the enjoyable food might include good sandwiches (from £4; tomato, mozzarella, red onion and avocado toastie £6; fish club with smoked salmon and crab £6.25), potted chicken and duck (£5), devilled chicken livers with bacon and mushroom (£5.50), black pudding with a mustard and leek velouté (£6.50), sausage and mash with onion gravy or omelette arnold bennett (£6.95), fish and chips in real ale batter (£7.95), roasted salmon on creamed leeks and pasta (£8.95), breast of chicken on lentils and smoked bacon (£10.50), and grilled rib-eye steak (£11.50); evening choices such as warm goats cheese on rocket and beetroot salad (£5.25), crab and salmon cake with a red pepper mayonnaise (£5.75), smoked salmon and gravadlax (£6.50), a vegetarian dish of the day (£9.50), crispy duck leg with plum and orange sauce (£10.50), whitby cod with prawns and fennel (£12.75), local lamb with spinach, tomato and basil (£13.50), venison loin with crispy pancetta and green beans (£14.50), and puddings like sticky toffee pudding with butterscotch sauce, terrine of three chocolates with cappuccino sauce or blackcurrant vacherin (from £4). Well kept Black Sheep Bitter and Special, and a guest such as Archers Spring Ale on handpump, around 100 malt whiskies, a decent wine list with eight by the glass, and friendly, cheerful staff. There are green cast-iron tables on the front terrace amidst the lovely hanging baskets and flowering climbers. *(Recommended by Maureen and Bill Sewell, K M Crook, Brian England, Jim Abbott, Alan Cowell, Richard and Anne Ansell, Margaret and Roy Randle, B and M Kendall, Ben and Helen Ingram, Anna Cooper, M S Catling, Janet and Peter Race, John Coatsworth)*

Free house ~ Licensees Jonathan and Michael Harrison ~ Real ale ~ Bar food (12-2.30 (2 Sun), 6.30-9(9.30 Fri and Sat); not Mon) ~ Restaurant ~ (01969) 622206 ~ Children in eating area of bar but must leave restaurant by 8pm at weekends ~ Dogs allowed in bar ~ Open 11.30-3, 6.30-11; 12-3, 7-10.30 Sun; closed Mon and maybe 2 weeks Jan ~ Bedrooms: £55S(£60B)/£65S(£70B)

LINTHWAITE SE1014 Map 7

Sair

Hoyle Ing, off A62; 3½ miles after Huddersfield look out for two water storage tanks (painted with a shepherd scene) on your right – the street is on your left, burrowing very steeply up between works buildings; OS Sheet 110 map reference 101143

In summer, there are plenty of seats and tables in front of this unspoilt and old-fashioned pub that have a striking view across the Colne Valley. But it remains the large choice of own-brewed beers on handpump that customers come to enjoy: Linfit Bitter, Dark Mild, Special, Swift, Gold Medal, Autumn Gold, Old Eli, English Guineas Stout, Leadboiler, Enochs Hammer, and occasional brews like Smoke House Ale, Springbok Bier, Xmas Ale, and Ginger beer. Weston's farm cider and a few malt whiskies; weekend sandwiches. The four rooms are furnished with pews or smaller chairs on the rough flagstones or stripped wooden floors, and there are log fires in every room; one room is no smoking. The room on the left has dominoes, a juke box, shove-ha'penny, and cribbage; piano players welcome. The Huddersfield Narrow Canal is now restored through to Ashton; in the 3½ miles from Linthwaite to the highest, deepest, and longest tunnel in Britain, are 25 working locks and some lovely countryside. More reports please. *(Recommended by the Didler, Tony Hobden; JP, PP, J R Ringrose)*

Own brew ~ Licensee Ron Crabtree ~ Real ale ~ No credit cards ~ (01484) 842370 ~ Children welcome in 3 rooms away from bar ~ Dogs allowed in bar ~ Open 7(5 Fri)-11; 12-11 Sat; 12-10.30 Sun

LINTON SE3946 Map 7

Windmill

Leaving Wetherby W on A661, fork left just before hospital and bear left; also signposted from A659, leaving Collingham towards Harewood

Even when this dining pub is really busy – which it usually is – the staff remain helpful and efficient. The small beamed rooms have walls stripped back to bare stone, polished antique oak settles around copper-topped cast-iron tables, pots hanging from the oak beams, a high shelf of plates, and log fires; the restaurant is no smoking. Well liked and attractively presented, the bar food at lunchtime includes sandwiches on granary bread, baguette or folded flat naan and served with salad and potato crisps (from £3.95; prawn and lime fromage frais £4.50; hot smoked bacon with melted swiss cheese £5.75), chicken liver parfait with plum and apple chutney (£4.95), and moules marinière or filled baked potatoes (£5.95), with evening dishes such as fresh white crabmeat with redcurrant and mint syrup or foie gras with caramelised oranges (£4.95), goats cheese croquette with spiced mediterranean vegetables (£7.95), chicken with apple mash and grain mustard sauce (£8.95), bass with nut brown caper butter (£9.95), chargrilled veal escalope with swiss cheese and mushroom sauce (£11.95), and puddings such as dark chocolate tart with stem vanilla ice-cream, crepe suzette, and lemon meringue pie (£3.95). Well kept John Smiths, Theakstons Best and a couple of guests like Daleside Bitter and Jennings Cumberland on handpump, and several wines by the glass; piped music, fruit machine, and TV. The pear tree outside was planted with seeds brought back from the Napoleonic Wars, and there are seats in the sheltered garden and on the sunny terrace at the back. *(Recommended by B and M Kendall, Joyce and Geoff Robson, R A K Crabtree, Dr Peter D Smart, Michael Butler)*

Scottish Courage ~ Lease Janet Rowley and John Littler ~ Real ale ~ Bar food ~ Restaurant ~ (01937) 582209 ~ Children in eating area of bar and restaurant ~ Dogs allowed in bar ~ Open 11-3, 5-11; 11-11 Sat; 12-10.30 Sun

LINTON IN CRAVEN SD9962 Map 7

Fountaine

Just off B6265 Skipton—Grassington

With new management again, this traditional pub in a charming hamlet looks down over the village green to a little stream. The original small rooms are furnished with stools, benches and other seats, and they now keep Black Sheep Bitter, John Smiths, Tetleys Bitter, and Timothy Taylors Landlord on handpump; six wines by the glass and a dozen malt whiskies. Bar food includes home-made soup (£3.25; large £3.85), lunchtime sandwiches (from £3), pork pie with mushy peas (£3.95), and ploughman's or coarse pork terrine with black pudding and bacon and home-made chutney (£4.95), confit of duck with red onion marmalade and cassis sauce (£5.25), gammon and egg (£7), pork, apple and thyme sausages with parmesan mash and red onion gravy or home-made steak and mushroom in ale pie (£7.25), king prawn risotto (£9.25), daily specials such as scallops (£5.25), tuscan chicken (£9.50), seafood bake (£10), guinea fowl (£10.95), and lamb shank (£12.95), and puddings like sticky toffee pudding, glazed orange tart with dark chocolate sauce or raspberry bakewell tart (£3.95). The restaurant is no smoking. Darts, dominoes, and piped music. The pub is named after the local lad who made his pile in the Great Plague – contracting in London to bury the bodies.

(Recommended by Gill Honeyman, S and N McLean, Jim Abbott, Mr and Mrs D J Nash, Pat and Clive Sherriff, R L Gorick, Michael Butler, Lynda and Trevor Smith, Graham and Doreen Holden)

Free house ~ Licensee George Knight ~ Real ale ~ Bar food (all day) ~ Restaurant ~ (01756) 752210 ~ Children in eating area of bar and restaurant ~ Dogs allowed in bar ~ Open 11-11; 12-10.30 Sun

LITTON SD9074 Map 7

Queens Arms

From B6160 N of Grassington, after Kilnsey take second left fork; can also be reached off B6479 at Stainforth N of Settle, via Halton Gill

This is a smashing little inn in a lovely setting with a friendly welcome, fine own brewed ale and proper home cooking. The main bar on the right has a good coal fire, stripped rough stone walls, a brown beam-and-plank ceiling, stools around cast-iron-framed tables on the stone and concrete floor, a seat built into the stone-mullioned window, and signed cricket bats. The left-hand room is an eating area with old photographs of the Dales around the walls. Well kept Litton Ale and Potts Beck Ale on handpump from their own microbrewery; the family room is no smoking. Good, popular bar food includes home-made soup (£2.60), sandwiches (from £3.50), filled baked potatoes (from £4.50), home-made rabbit pie (£7.95), gammon and egg (£7.95), home-made game pie (£9.50), daily specials such as local blue cheese, onion, mushroom and black olive tart or vegetable pie (£7.50), roast lamb (£7.95), stilton chicken (£8.95), halibut steak in seafood sauce (£10.90), and a massive mixed grill (£16.50), and puddings like rhubarb crumble, bread and butter pudding or syrup tart (£3.50). Darts, dominoes, cribbage and piped music. There are seats and a safe area for children in the two-level garden, and the views over the fells are stunning. Plenty of surrounding walks – a track behind the inn leads over Ackerley Moor to Buckden, and the quiet lane through the valley leads on to Pen-y-ghent. Walkers enjoy staying here very much – and there is a walkers' room (price on request). *(Recommended by Liam McGreevy, Tony and Ann Bennett-Hughes, Gill Honeyman, DAV, JAE, Alison Hayes, Pete Hanlon, Jim Abbott, Lawrence Pearse, MDN, Richard Houghton, Fred and Lorraine Gill, Kerry Law, Simon Smith, A and B Myers, Dr and Mrs D Woods, Greta and Christopher Wells)*

Free house ~ Licensees Tanya and Neil Thompson ~ Real ale ~ Bar food (12-2, 6.30-8; not Mon; no food Jan) ~ (01756) 770208 ~ Children in family room ~ Dogs allowed in bar ~ Open 12-3, 7-11; 11.30-3, 6.30-11(10.30 Sun) Sat; Sat opening 7 in winter; closed Mon (except bank hols) ~ Bedrooms: /£66S

LOW CATTON SE7053 Map 7

Gold Cup

Village signposted with High Catton off A166 in Stamford Bridge or A1079 at Kexby Bridge

You can be sure of a friendly welcome from the helpful staff in this comfortable and popular white-rendered house, even when the pub is really busy. There are neatly kept communicating rooms with a fire at one end, plush wall seats and stools around good solid tables, some decorative plates and brasswork on the walls, and a relaxed atmosphere; the back bar has a woodburning stove in a brick fireplace. Good value, tasty bar food using local produce (and with prices little changed since last year) includes lunchtime sandwiches, home-made soup (£2.75), creamed stilton mushrooms (£3.50), home-made chicken liver pâté with cumberland sauce (£3.75), cod and salmon fishcakes with tangy tomato and basil sauce, cajun chicken, home-baked cider ham with wholegrain mustard sauce or home-made fish pie (from £6.50), roast beef and yorkshire pudding or roast lamb (£6.75), seared salmon steak with lemon and dill hollandaise (£7), and puddings such as lemon posset with home-made shortbread and berries or chocolate swirls with strawberries and cream (£3); children are offered half helpings of adult meals, there are small appetite dishes for older customers, a well liked candlelit Thursday and Friday evening menu, and three-course Sunday lunch (£9.75). The comfortable no smoking restaurant has solid wooden pews and tables, said to be made from a single oak tree, and pleasant views of the surrounding fields. Well kept John Smiths and Tetleys Bitter on handpump; piped music, pool, fruit machine, TV, and dominoes. The garden has a timber climbing frame and grassed area for children, and the back paddock houses Billie the goat and Polly the shetland who are kept in check by Candy the horse; they also own Boris and Marilyn (retired greyhounds), and have fishing rights on the adjoining River Derwent. *(Recommended by Roger A Bellingham, Sheila Brudenell, H Bramwell, M Mennell, Debbie Reynolds)*

Free house ~ Licensees Pat and Ray Hales ~ Real ale ~ Bar food (12-2.30, 6-9.30; all day wknds; not Mon lunchtime) ~ No credit cards ~ (01759) 371354 ~ Children in eating area of bar and restaurant ~ Dogs allowed in bar ~ Open 12-2.30, 6-11; 12-11(10.30 Sun) Sat; closed Mon lunch

LUND SE9748 Map 8

Wellington

Off B1248 SW of Driffield

There may be quite a few people queueing outside this very well run and smart pub before the doors open, so it's best to get here early. Many customers do come to eat, and as well as the restaurant, there is a back dining area where you cannot reserve a table; they've sensibly kept the main bar a haven for drinkers only in the evening. The most atmospheric part is the cosy Farmers Bar, a small heavily beamed room with an interesting fireplace and some old agricultural equipment; the neatly kept main bar is much brighter, with a brick fireplace and bar counter, well polished wooden banquettes and square tables, dried flowers, and local prints on the textured cream-painted walls; two areas are no smoking. Off to one side is a plainer flagstoned room, while at the other a york-stoned walkway leads to a room with a display case showing off the village's Britain in Bloom awards. Good enjoyable bar food at lunchtime includes soup of the day (£3.50; with half a sandwich £5.50), smoked haddock fishcakes with mild curried apple sauce or chicken liver parfait with redcurrant and orange sauce (£4.95), beer battered local haddock or sunblush tomato, smoked mozzarella and pesto filo parcels (£8.95), fresh tuna on caesar salad (£9.95), and fresh local crab with herb mayonnaise or calves liver with sage and onion mash and real ale gravy (£10.95), with evening choices such as grilled sardines with garlic butter or a trio of pâtés (£4.95), smoked chicken with chorizo, bacon and pine nuts or fresh crab and avocado with bloody mary dressing (£6.50), chicken breast stuffed with mild irish blue cheese on chargrilled vegetable ratatouille (£12.95), baked fillet of local bass on a sweetcorn and fresh crab fritter with a roast red pepper sauce (£14.95), loin of english lamb with minted hollandaise and an asparagus and goats cheese salad (£16.95), and medallions of beef fillet with cracked pepper and garlic (£17.95); puddings like sticky orange and apricot pudding with Grand Marnier custard, rum and raisin crème caramel, and warm chocolate and pear frangipane tart with vanilla bean ice-cream (from £4.25). Well kept Black Sheep, John Smiths, and Timothy Taylors Landlord with a changing local guest on handpump, and a good wine list with a helpfully labelled choice by the glass; welcoming, helpful staff. Piped music, darts, dominoes, pool, TV and fruit machine. A small courtyard beside the car park has a couple of benches. *(Recommended by Barrie and Valerie Meech, Dr D Parker, Roger A Bellingham, Mark and Cath Caley, Paul and Ursula Randall, Paul Boot, C A Hall, Alison Hayes, Pete Hanlon)*

Free house ~ Licensees Russell Jeffery and Sarah Jeffery ~ Real ale ~ Bar food (not Sun or Mon) ~ Restaurant (Tues-Sat evenings) ~ (01377) 217294 ~ Children in eating area of bar ~ Open 12-3, 6.30-11; 12-3, 7-10.30 Sun; closed Mon lunchtime

Though we don't usually mention it in the text, most pubs will now make coffee or tea – always worth asking.

MARTON SE7383 Map 10

Appletree

Village signposted off A170 W of Pickering

Throughout this spotlessly kept and stylish dining pub there are carefully co-ordinated colour schemes and lighting, and service by keen young staff is friendly and personal. The relaxed beamed lounge bar has comfortable settees in red or blue around polished low tables, an open fire in the stone fireplace, and a modicum of carefully placed decorations on the eau de nil walls. The main emphasis is on the terracotta-walled dining room, which has well spaced farmhouse tables, fresh flowers, and masses of candles at night. Meals (using top quality local produce) start with a free bottle of mineral water, and warmly fragrant savoury breads. The food is first rate, and at lunchtime might include summer sandwiches, creamed spinach and rocket soup (£3), grilled goats cheese with wild garlic and tomato salad (£4.50), crab fishcake on orange salad with sweet chilli sauce (£5), minted lamb pie (£7.90), spiced suckling pig sausages with red onion marmalade (£8.50), chicken and asparagus and parmesan tagliatelle (£9), fillet of gurnard with onion, lentils and smoked bacon (£10), and venison steak on truffled mash with wild mushrooms and chocolate jus (£13); evening choices such as tian of prawns with cucumbers, crème fraîche and avruga caviar (£5.50), foie gras and duck liver parfait with quince jelly and vanilla (£6), grilled mediterranean vegetables with pesto and aged balsamic (£9), chicken, pancetta and capers with ox tongue and redcurrant jus (£11), and salmon fillet with herb crushed potato and saffron velouté (£13); puddings like sticky toffee pudding, mini banoffi pie with coffee cream, and marbled chocolate pyramid with Baileys chocolate mousse (from £3.90), and a Sunday evening 'pie and pea' bar supper (£6.50). They grow their own herbs and vegetables, and produce their own flavoured breads, chutneys, preserves, flavoured oils and butters and so forth; in one corner what might elsewhere have been a small bar counter turns out to be a popular sales counter for their own and some other kitchen produce. Well kept John Smiths, and guests such as Archers Spirit of St George, Jennings Cumberland, and Charles Wells Bombardier on handpump, and 18 wines by two sizes of glass from a thoughtful list. Despite the emphasis on good food, regulars do drop in for a drink, and perhaps a game of dominoes, giving the bar a properly local atmosphere. There are cast-iron tables and chairs out on a sheltered flagstoned terrace behind, with plant pots and a small water feature, and looking out through young silver birches to an orchard garden with fruit trees.
(Recommended by Dr and Mrs P S Fox, Brian and Pat Wardrobe, John Knighton, I D Barnett, Michael Doswell, Alan Cowell, Peter Burton, A and B Myers)

Free house ~ Licensees Melanie and T J Drew ~ Bar food (12-2(2.30 Sun), 6.30-9; not Mon lunchtime, Tues) ~ Restaurant ~ (01751) 431457 ~ Children in eating areas but not in main dining room in evening ~ Open 12-2.30, 6.30-11; 12-3, 7-10.30 Sun; closed Mon lunchtime, Tues

MASHAM SE2381 Map 10

Kings Head

Market Square

This handsome stone inn is set opposite the broad partly tree-shaded market square, and in summer, the hanging baskets and window boxes in front of the building are very pretty; seats on the back terrace with a few in front, too. The two opened-up rooms of the bar have traditional pine tables and chairs on the wood-stripped floor, a roaring fire in the imposing fireplace, a big clock (from Masham Station), and well kept Theakstons Best, Black Bull, XB, and Old Peculier, and a couple of guests on handpump, and an extensive wine list with over 20 by the glass. Good, enjoyable bar food includes sandwiches, home-made soup (£3.45), black pudding and bacon stack with a creamy dijon and leek sauce (£4.25), chicken skewers with apple chutney (£4.45), home-made salmon fishcake with tarragon crème fraîche (£5.25), sausage and mash with red onion gravy (£5.95), steak and kidney pudding (£6.75), chicken caesar salad (£7.45), brie and broccoli parcel with red pepper sauce (£7.95), glazed pork loin with baked apple and ratatouille (£10.75), steaks (from £10.75), and cod on lemon and chardonnay risotto (£10.95); helpful, friendly service. The restaurant is no smoking; piped music, darts, fruit machine, TV and dominoes. The new bedrooms in the back courtyard area are now up and running with rooms for disabled customers and for families; they hold a civil wedding licence. *(Recommended by I J and S A Bufton, Janet and Peter Race, Jim Abbott, Angus Lyon, Jenny and Dave Hughes, Dave Braisted, Richard and Anne Ansell, John Coatsworth, Peter F Marshall, Edward and Deanna Pearce, David and Ruth Shillitoe)*

S&N ~ Manager Philip Capon ~ Real ale ~ Bar food (12-2.45, 6-9.45; all day Sat-Sun) ~ Restaurant ~ (01765) 689295 ~ Children in eating area of bar and restaurant ~ Dogs allowed in bedrooms ~ Open 11-11; 12-10.30 Sun ~ Bedrooms: £50B/£65B

MIDDLEHAM SE1288 Map 10

White Swan

Market Place

In a rather steep and pretty village, this pleasant coaching inn is set in the cobbled market place. It has a relaxed pubby atmosphere and is tastefully decorated in an understated way. The beamed and flagstoned entrance bar has a long dark pew built into the big window overlooking the sloping market square, and a mix of chairs around a handful of biggish tables. Well kept Black Sheep Best, Special and Riggwelter and John Smiths on handpump from the curved counter, 13 wines by the glass, and a couple of dozen malt whiskies, with friendly attentive service and a good inglenook log fire. A second beamed room on the right has a variety of tables and dining chairs, a red oriental rug on its black boards, and like the first is candlelit. There's a third broadly similar room behind and a no smoking restaurant. Modestly priced bar food includes sandwiches, home-made soup (£2.75), black pudding and bacon risotto (£4.25), local sausages with grain mustard mash and gravy (£6.95), vegetarian shepherd's pie (£7.50), battered fish and chips (£8), confit of duck leg with braised red cabbage or steak in ale pie (£8.95), chargrilled chicken breast (£9.75), chargrilled sirloin steak (£11.75), and daily specials. *(Recommended by Angus Lyon, Mr and Mrs Maurice Thompson, Comus and Sarah Elliott, Ian and Nita Cooper, Michael Doswell)*

Free house ~ Licensees Andrew Holmes and Paul Klein ~ Real ale ~ Bar food (12-2.15, 6.30-9.15) ~ Restaurant ~ (01969) 622093 ~ Children welcome ~ Dogs welcome ~ Open 11-11; 12-10.30 Sun ~ Bedrooms: £47.50B/£59(£69B)

MILL BANK SE0321 Map 7

Millbank

Mill Bank Road, off A58 SW of Sowerby Bridge

In deeply folded countryside close to the old mill towns of Calderdale, just off the main road through the Ryburn Valley, this is a notable country dining pub that draws people in from far around. Cottagey and traditionally Pennine from the outside, it has a calm, clean-cut minimalist modern décor with local touches such as chapel chairs and local photographs for sale. The interior is divided into the tap room, bar and no smoking restaurant, with well kept Adnams Broadside, Tetleys and Timothy Taylors Landlord on handpump, and 21 wines by the glass including champagne, port and pudding wines; it also has a specialised gin list. Discreet background music of a jazzy flavour. Outside is a terrace with a glass roof and fold-away windows that makes the most of the glorious setting overlooking an old textile mill. Below this is a garden adorned with metal sculptures made from old farm equipment. It has interesting cooking successfully combining European and Yorkshire elements. Sandwiches (from £4.95) are available along with the fixed-price menu (£10.95 for two courses and coffee), and dishes such as butternut squash soup (£4.50), chicken liver parfait with apple and grape chutney and toasted brioche (£5.95), brandade of salted whiting with aubergine crisps and chorizo with saffron mayonnaise (£5.95), venison and juniper sausages with cabbage and bacon (£8.95), beer battered haddock with pea purée (£9.95), fresh tuna niçoise (£10.95), roast suckling pig with black pudding, hash brown, roast carrot, and oriental sauce or braised shoulder of lamb with white beans, smoked bacon, pine nuts and basil (£12.95), and bass fillet with mushroom and celeriac purée lasagne with fennel cream (£14.50). Puddings are similarly innovative, and feature chocolate fondant cake with poached pear and vanilla ice-cream (£5.95), orange bread pudding with carrot and ginger ice-cream (£5.50), and poached peach with almond sponge and praline ice-cream (£5.95), in addition to a plate of selected vegetarian-suitable yorkshire cheeses (£6.50). The fixed-price Sunday lunch menu (two courses for £13.25, three courses for £16.95) is particularly good value. They're hoping to have accommodation by 2005. The former industrial hamlet of Mill Bank nearly disappeared under the bulldozers in the early 1970s, but was saved after a campaign by local residents and has now been wholeheartedly revived as a community. There is superb walking country nearby with the Calderdale Way easily accessible from the pub. *(Recommended by Anne and Tim Locke, Dr and Mrs Guy Cocker, Mike and Melanie Powell)*

Timothy Taylors ~ Licensee Joe McNally ~ Real ale ~ (01422) 825588 ~ Children in eating area of bar ~ Dogs allowed in bar ~ Open 12-3, 5.30-11; 12-10.30 Sun; closed Mon except bank hols; closed 2 wks Oct, 1 wk Jan

NOSTERFIELD SE2780 Map 7

Freemasons Arms

B6267

There's lots to look at in this chatty, friendly pub – the low black beams are hung with gas masks, steel helmets, miner's lamps, pewter tankards and so forth, there are big prints of Queen Victoria, many old enamel advertising signs, and Union flags propped in corners; the cosy feel boosted by the warm lighting, the candles on the tables, and the hot coal fires. Using only local produce, the well liked bar food includes sandwiches (from £3.50), black pudding with caramelised red onions or battered mushrooms stuffed with cream cheese (£4.95), fresh scottish mussels (£5; main course £9.50), arctic char in lemon cream sauce (£10.95), breast of gressingham duck with sweet chilli sauce (£11.45), trio of wood pigeon breasts with black pudding and apple tart (£12), aberdeen angus sirloin steak (£13), and rack of lamb with redcurrant sauce or 10oz grass fed heifer fillet (£14). The main bar area has just two or three tables with close wooden booth seating on its flagstones; there are more tables with pews and settles in the carpeted room on the left. Well kept Black Sheep, John Smiths, Theakstons Best, and Wadworths 6X on handpump, ten wines by the glass, and piped music; dominoes. There are a few picnic-sets out in front, with pretty flower tubs and baskets. No children. *(Recommended by Susan and John Douglas, Rona Murdoch, Janet and Peter Race, Pete Baker, Michael Doswell)*

Free house ~ Licensee Kris Stephenson ~ Real ale ~ Bar food (not Mon or Fri) ~ (01677) 470548 ~ Dogs allowed in bar ~ Open 12-3, 6(7 Sun)-11; closed Mon

NUNNINGTON SE6779 Map 7

Royal Oak

Church Street; at back of village, which is signposted from A170 and B1257

You can be sure of a genuinely friendly welcome from the attentive staff in this neatly kept and attractive little pub. The bar has carefully chosen furniture such as kitchen and country dining chairs or a long pew around the sturdy tables on the turkey carpet, and a lectern in one corner; the high black beams are strung with earthenware flagons, copper jugs and lots of antique keys, one of the walls is stripped back to the bare stone to display a fine collection of antique farm tools, and there are open fires; the dining room is no smoking. Popular bar food (they tell us prices have not changed since last year) includes sandwiches, vegetable soup with lentil and bacon (£4.15), chicken liver pâté with home-made chutney (£4.75), mushrooms stuffed with garlic butter and stilton (£5.25), seafood hors d'oeuvres (£5.75), ploughman's (£7.95), lasagne or sweet and sour vegetables (£9.50), steak and kidney casserole with herb dumpling or pork fillet in barbecue sauce or chicken breast in cheese and mustard sauce (£9.95), fisherman's pot (£10.50), crispy roast duckling with orange sauce (£12.50), and 12oz sirloin steak (£13.95). Well kept Tetleys, and Theakstons Best and Old Peculier on handpump. Handy for a visit to Nunnington Hall (National Trust). *(Recommended by R Macfarlane, Christopher Turner, J M Pitts, Geoff and Angela Jaques, Robert and Susan Whitehead, Michael Dandy, Peter Burton, Edward and Deanna Pearce, Simon J Barber)*

Free house ~ Licensee Anthony Simpson ~ Real ale ~ Bar food (not Mon) ~ Restaurant ~ (01439) 748271 ~ Children in family room ~ Open 12-2.30, 6.30-11; 12-2.30, 7-10.30 Sun; closed Mon

OSMOTHERLEY SE4499 Map 10

Golden Lion

The Green, West End; off A19 N of Thirsk

There's no doubt that most customers come to this old stone-built dining pub to enjoy the particularly good, interesting food, and as it is so busy (especially at weekends) you must book to be sure of a table. The roomy beamed bar on the left, simply furnished with old pews and just a few decorations on its white walls, has a pleasantly lively atmosphere, candles on tables, well kept Hambleton Bitter, Timothy Taylors Landlord, and maybe Jennings Cumberland or John Smiths on handpump, a decent wine list and 40 malt whiskies; one side of the pub is no smoking. On the right, a similarly unpretentious eating area, brightened up with fresh flowers, has good value generous food which might include sandwiches, soups such as leek, potato and lentil or french onion with gruyère cheese croûton (£3.95), creamy lemon risotto with caramelised onion (£4.95), rough pâté with onion and apricot relish or spicy pork ribs (£5.50), home-made spicy chilli chicken burger (£6.50), spaghetti with fresh baby clams or deep-fried soft shell crab with lime mayonnaise (£6.95), home-made vegetable lasagne (£7.50), steak and kidney pie (£8.95), salmon with creamy basil sauce or chargrilled poussin with rosemary and garlic (£9.95), pork and parma ham with sage and marsala wine sauce (£10.95), calves liver and onions (£11.95), and puddings such as middle eastern orange cake with marmalade cream, raspberry ripple cheesecake or poached pear in wine with hot chocolate sauce (£3.95); several teas and coffees. There's also an airy no smoking dining room, mainly open at weekends. Benches out in front look across the village green to the market cross. As the inn is the start of the 44-mile Lyke Wakes Walk on the Cleveland Way, and quite handy for the Coast to Coast Walk, it is naturally popular with walkers. *(Recommended by Peter and Jean Hoare, Jill Franklin, Geoff and Angela Jaques, David and Ruth Shillitoe, JHBS, Rona Murdoch, Tim Newman, Michael Doswell, Dr and Mrs R G J Telfer, Blaise Vyner, Tracey and Stephen Groves, Dr Peter D Smart)*

Free house ~ Licensee Christie Connelly ~ Real ale ~ Bar food (12-3, 6-9.30) ~ Restaurant ~ (01609) 883526 ~ Children welcome ~ Dogs allowed in bar ~ Open 12-3.30, 6-11; 12-11 Sat; closed evening 25 Dec

PICKERING SE7983 Map 10

White Swan ★

Market Place, just off A170

Although this is a smart old coaching inn, there is still a relaxed bar with a charming country atmosphere, panelling, a log fire and just three or four tables. Opposite, a no smoking bare-boards room with a few more tables has another fire in a handsome art nouveau iron fireplace, a big bow window, and pear prints on its plum-coloured walls. The no smoking restaurant has flagstones, a fine open fire, rich tweed soft furnishings, comfortable settles and gothic screens. Good, attractively presented lunchtime food includes soup with home-made bread (£3.95), ploughman's (from £4.95), sandwiches (from £4.95; crab and watercress £5.25), baby spinach with marinaded yorkshire feta cheese and black olive salad (£5.95; main course £9.95), seared king scallops with coverdale cheese, sweet cured bacon and parsley gratin (£8.95; main course £16.95), whitby fish and proper chips with mushy peas and home-made ketchup or chargrilled courgettes with lemon and basil risotto (£10.95), and braised ham shank with mustard mash and butterbeans (£12.50), with evening dishes such as black pudding and york ham salad with a free range poached egg, carpaccio of harome beef or potted whitby crab (£6.25), pot-roasted herbed free range chicken breast with black pudding sausage, bubble and squeak, and thyme gravy (£12.95), slow cooked venison shoulder with roast garlic mash, spring greens and bacon (£13.25), peppered harome duck breast with honey glazed apples and celeriac purée (£13.95), and grilled bass fillets with sea asparagus and beurre blanc (£14.95); puddings like chocolate cake with clotted cream and macerated cherries, peach melba fool with fruit and nut biscotti or sticky toffee pudding with caramel sauce (£4.95); good coffee. Well kept Black Sheep Bitter and Special and guests such as Cropton Yorkshire Moors Bitter or Hambleton Goldfield on handpump, good house wines (by two sizes of glass; pudding wines and superb list of old St Emilions), and quite a few malt whiskies. The old coach entry to the car park is very narrow. *(Recommended by Anthony Barnes, Di and Mike Gillam, Peter Burton, Mrs Yvette Bateman, Joyce and Maurice Cottrell, David Carr, Mrs Hannah Colton; also in the* Good Hotel Guide*)*

Free house ~ Licensees Marion and Victor Buchanan ~ Real ale ~ Bar food ~ Restaurant ~ (01751) 472288 ~ Children in restaurant ~ Dogs allowed in bar and bedrooms ~ Open 10.30-3, 6-11; 10-11 Mon and Sat; 12-5, 7-10.30 Sun ~ Bedrooms: £75B/£120B

PICKHILL SE3584 Map 10

Nags Head

Take the Masham turn-off from A1 both N and S, and village signposted off B6267 in Ainderby Quernhow

Several of our readers have been coming to this extremely popular place for many years and have never felt let down. It's been professionally run for over 30 years by the enthusiastic Boynton brothers, and you can be sure of a friendly welcome from the polite, obliging staff. The busy tap room on the left has beams hung with jugs, coach horns, ale-yards and so forth, and masses of ties hanging as a frieze from a rail around the red ceiling. The smarter lounge bar has deep green plush banquettes on the matching carpet, pictures for sale on its neat cream walls, and an open fire. From a varied menu, the enjoyable food might include sandwiches, home-made asparagus, tomato and vegetable soup (£3.50), marinated squid and mussel salad or assorted dim sum with sweet chilli and sour dips (£4.95), roasted red pepper stuffed with feta cheese, cucumber and greek minted yoghurt (£5.50), sizzling king prawns with garlic, chilli or lemon (£5.95; main course £11.95), locally smoked salmon with scrambled egg (£6.95), tagliatelle with mixed salami, sun-dried red peppers and tomato sauce (£7.50), cottage pie topped with leek and cheese mashed potato (£7.95), beef, venison and rabbit pie (£12.50), supreme of chicken filled with camembert and fresh sage wrapped in parma ham (£12.95), seared bluefin tuna with sesame seeds, ginger mash and garlic pesto (£13.50), fried duck breast with lime, ginger and honey marinade and a crispy roast leg (£13.95), sirloin steak (£14.95), and puddings such as rhubarb crème brûlée, caramelised banana tart with vanilla custard or sticky toffee and pecan pudding with butterscotch sauce (£3.95). The library-themed restaurant is no smoking. Well kept Black Sheep Bitter and Special, Hambleton Bitter, and Jennings Cumberland on handpump, a good choice of malt whiskies, vintage armagnacs, and a carefully chosen wine list with several by the glass. One table is inset with a chessboard, and they also have cribbage, dominoes, and shove-ha'penny. There's a front verandah, a boules and quoits pitch, and 9-hole putting green. *(Recommended by Mr and Mrs C Cameron, Angus Lyon, Mrs Roxanne Chamberlain, Trevor and Sylvia Millum, SH, Michael Butler, M Whitfield, G A Hemingway, Blaise Vyner, Stephen Buckley, Alison Hayes, Pete Hanlon, R F Ballinger, Oliver Richardson, R N and M I Bailey, Adam and Joan Bunting, Phil and Helen Holt; also in the* Good Hotel Guide*)*

Free house ~ Licensees Edward and Raymond Boynton ~ Real ale ~ Bar food (12-2, 6-9.30) ~ Restaurant ~ (01845) 567391 ~ Children in restaurant ~ Dogs allowed in bedrooms ~ Open 11-11; 12-10.30 Sun ~ Bedrooms: £45S(£50B)/£70B

RIPLEY SE2861 Map 7

Boars Head

Off A61 Harrogate—Ripon

Although part of a smart and comfortable hotel, the friendly bar here has a relaxed and proper pubby feel and is still very much used by locals – they also keep a fine range of real ales. It's a long flagstoned room with green checked tablecloths and olive oil on all the tables, most of which are arranged to form individual booths. The warm yellow walls have jolly little drawings of cricketers or huntsmen running along the bottom, as well as a boar's head (part of the family coat of arms), an interesting religious carving, a couple of cricket bats, and well kept Black Sheep, Daleside Old Leg Over, Theakstons Best, XB and Old Peculier, Village (Hambleton) White Boar and Premier Bull, and a beer called Crackshot brewed for them by Daleside but following the Ingilby family's own 17th-c recipe on handpump; an excellent wine list (with ten or so by the glass), and around 20 malt whiskies. Particularly good, interesting bar food includes very nice sandwiches, soup (£3.75), warm salad of smoked duck and chorizo with oriental dressing or confit of chicken and wild mushroom terrine with gribiche sauce (£6.50, main course £12.50), mediterranean vegetable, rocket and parmesan tartlet (£9.95), pork and leek sausages with dijon mustard mash or chicken tikka with herb salad and mint yoghurt (£10.95), roast duck breast with roasted butternut squash (£11.95), grilled fillet steak with parsnip purée and red wine jus (£15.95), daily specials such as pressed terrine of goats cheese and real ale beef (£5), pot roasted venison sausages with red onion gravy (£9), and seared fillets of trout with horseradish mash (£9.95), and puddings like sticky toffee pudding with butterscotch sauce, cherry and frangipane tart with banana ice-cream and raspberry sauce or baked vanilla and chocolate fudge brownie cheesecake (£4.50); efficient staff even when very busy. One room is no smoking; piped music. Some of the furnishings in the hotel came from the attic of next door Ripley Castle, where the Ingilbys have lived for over 650 years. A pleasant little garden has plenty of tables. *(Recommended by Regine Webster, Kate Arscott, Jim Abbott, M and GR, A S and M E Marriott, John and Wendy Allin, Tim and Ann Newell, Marlene and Jim Godfrey, Andrew and Samantha Grainger, Stephen R Holman; also in the* Good Hotel Guide*)*

Free house ~ Licensee Sir Thomas Ingilby ~ Real ale ~ Bar food (12-2, 6.30-9.30) ~ Restaurant ~ (01423) 771888 ~ Children in eating area of bar and restaurant ~ Dogs allowed in bedrooms ~ Open 11-11; 11-3, 5-11 in winter ~ Bedrooms: £105B/£125B

ROBIN HOOD'S BAY NZ9505 Map 10

Laurel

Village signposted off A171 S of Whitby

This delightful little pub is in one of the prettiest and most unspoilt fishing villages on the North East coast. It's at the bottom of a row of fishermen's cottages, and the landlord will welcome visitors as warmly as he does his locals. The beamed and welcoming main bar is neatly kept, and is decorated with old local photographs, Victorian prints and brasses, and lager bottles from all over the world; there's a roaring open fire. They only serve sandwiches (which are good). Well kept Adnams Broadside, Jennings Cumberland, and Tetleys on handpump; darts, shove-ha'penny, dominoes, cribbage, and piped music. In summer, the hanging baskets and window boxes are lovely. They have a self-contained apartment for two people. More reports please. *(Recommended by Margaret Whalley, JP, PP, Roger and Jenny Huggins, Alison Hayes, Pete Hanlon)*

Free house ~ Licensee Brian Catling ~ Real ale ~ Bar food ~ No credit cards ~ (01947) 880400 ~ Children in snug bar only until 9pm ~ Dogs welcome ~ Open 12-11; 12-10.30 Sun

The knife-and-fork award distinguishes pubs where the food is of exceptional quality.

SAWLEY SE2568 Map 7

Sawley Arms 🍷

Village signposted off B6265 W of Ripon

Mrs Hawes has been firmly at the helm of this rather smart and spotlessly kept no smoking dining room for 35 years now. It's not the place for a quick drink and a chat as the emphasis is on the deservedly popular food. The small turkey-carpeted rooms have log fires and comfortable furniture ranging from small softly cushioned armed dining chairs and settees, to the wing armchairs down a couple of steps in a side snug; maybe daily papers and magazines to read, piped music. The conservatory is much liked by customers. Super home-made bar food includes soup with croûtons (£3.50), lunchtime sandwiches (from £5), salmon mousse or stilton, port and celery pâté (£5.50), home-made steak pie (£7.70), corn-fed chicken breast in a creamy mushroom sauce (£8), plaice mornay (£8.95), daily specials such as smoked haddock on spinach with a cheese glaze, braised lamb shank or fish pie (all £9.70), and puddings like crème caramel or home-made apple pie (from £3.95); good house wines. In fine weather there are tables and chairs in the pretty garden, and the flowering tubs and baskets are lovely; two stone cottages in the grounds for rent. Fountains Abbey (the most extensive of the great monastic remains – floodlit on late summer Friday and Saturday evenings, with a live choir on the Saturday) – is not far away. *(Recommended by Maysie Thompson, Alan Thwaite, Howard and Margaret Buchanan, H Bramwell, Blaise Vyner, Janet and Peter Race, Hugh A MacLean, Jim Abbott, JHBS, John Branston, Walter and Susan Rinaldi-Butcher, Margaret Dickinson)*

Free house ~ Licensee Mrs June Hawes ~ Bar food (not Mon evening) ~ Restaurant ~ (01765) 620642 ~ No children under 9 ~ Open 11.30-3, 6.30-11; 12-3 Sun; closed Mon evening

SCARBOROUGH TA0489 Map 10

Hole in the Wall £

Vernon Road; covered car park at top of road, may be free parking at bottom

Handy for the main shopping street, this Victorian pub has three easy-going and down-to-earth rooms. The bottom one has bare boards and darts, with stools around its cast-iron-framed tables, while the others have carpets and softer seating, with a few brewery advertisements and old local photographs and prints; the overall impression is red. Well kept Greene King IPA, John Smiths, and Charles Wells Bombardier on handpump; lunchtime sandwiches. Juke box, darts, new pool table, fruit machine, TV, dominoes, and piped music. More reports on the new regime, please. *(Recommended by the Didler, Kevin Blake, Mark Walker, Andrew York, David Carr)*

Free house ~ Licensee John Langley ~ Real ale ~ Bar food ~ No credit cards ~ (01723) 373746 ~ Children in eating area of bar until 7.30 ~ Dogs allowed in bar ~ Open 11-11; 12-3, 7-10.30 Sun; 11-3, 5-11 Mon-Thurs in winter

SCAWTON SE5584 Map 10

Hare

Village signposted off A170 Thirsk—Helmsley, just E of Sutton Bank

A new licensee has taken over this low-built pub and preliminary reports from readers are positive. The bars are comfortably modernised without losing their cosy and unspoilt feel, and have stripped pine tables and seats on the flagstones and carpet, an old-fashioned range and a woodburner, lots of bric-a-brac, simple wall settles, a seat in the bow window, and comfortable eating areas; in the innermost part there's a heavy old beam-and-plank ceiling. Well kept Black Sheep, Jennings Cumberland, and John Smiths on handpump. At lunchtime, bar food includes home-made soup (£3.95), a plate of sandwiches with chips (£5.95), thai salmon fishcakes with lemon and caper dressing (£6.50), herb pancakes filled with celeriac, leeks and blue cheese cream sauce or chicken curry (£7.95), home-made pie of the day or leek and garlic sausages with horseradish mash and onion gravy (£8.50), and battered whitby haddock with mushy peas (£8.95); evening dishes like roast shark with curried potatoes or chilli marinated chicken breast with soy, honey and lemon sauce (£8.95), minted lamb rump steak with herby couscous (£9.95), a trio of duck with blackcurrant jus (£11.50), and chargrilled sirloin steak with wild mushroom cream sauce (£14.95). The restaurant and part of the bar are no smoking; piped music. The pub is attractive with roses against its cream walls and green woodwork, and its pair of inn-signs with naïve hare paintings; handy for Rievaulx Abbey. More reports please. *(Recommended by Christine and Phil Young)*

Free house ~ Licensee Stephen Sproson ~ Real ale ~ Bar food (not Mon) ~ Restaurant ~ No credit cards ~ (01845) 597289 ~ Children in restaurant ~ Open 12-11(10.30 Sun); 12-3, 6-11(10.30) in winter; closed Mon

SHEFFIELD SK3687 Map 7

Fat Cat £

23 Alma Street

With up to ten real ales on handpump, it's not surprising that this pub is so popular, and they have a Brewery Visitor's Centre (you can book brewery trips (0114) 249 4804) with framed beer mats, pump clips, and prints on the walls. As well as their own-brewed and cheap Kelham Island Bitter, Pale Rider, Easy Rider, and another Kelham Island beer, there are six guests on handpump like Durham White Bullet, Leyden Crowning Glory, Phoenix May Fly, Salamander Axoloti, Timothy Taylors Landlord, and Wellington Conviction, plus belgian bottled beers, two belgian draught beers, fruit gin, country wines and farm cider. Incredibly cheap, enjoyable bar food includes sandwiches, lentil soup (£2), ploughman's (£3), beef casserole, cheese and onion quiche, cheese and broccoli pasta, chicken and leek pie, and spicy mushroom and red bean casserole (from £3), and puddings such as rhubarb crumble or jam roly poly (£1.50); well liked Sunday lunch (£3.50). There's always a good, chatty bustle, and the two small downstairs rooms have brewery-related prints on the walls, coal fires, simple wooden tables and cushioned seats around the walls, and jugs, bottles, and some advertising mirrors; the one on the left is no smoking; cribbage and dominoes, and maybe the pub cat wandering around. Steep steps take you up to another similarly simple room (which may be booked for functions) with some attractive prints of old Sheffield; there are picnic-sets in a fairylit back courtyard. *(Recommended by JP, PP, the Didler, W W Burke, Patrick Hancock, David Carr, B and M Kendall, Simon Calvert, Jo Lilley)*

Own brew ~ Licensee Stephen Fearn ~ Real ale ~ Bar food (12-2.30, 6-7.30; not Sat or Sun evening) ~ No credit cards ~ (0114) 249 4801 ~ Children in no smoking room ~ Dogs welcome ~ Open 12-3, 5.30-11; 12-11 Fri and Sat; 12-3, 7-10.30 Sun; closed 25 and 26 Dec

New Barrack £

601 Penistone Road, Hillsborough

The regular live music and choice of up to nine real ales continue to draw customers to this sizeable but friendly pub. Well kept on handpump there are four regulars such as Abbeydale Moonshine, Barnsley Bitter, Castle Rock Harvest Pale, and John Smiths Magnet, and up to five constantly changing guests; also, real cider, seven continental draught lagers, lots of continental bottled beers, and a wide range of malt whiskies. The comfortable front lounge has red leather banquettes, old pine floors, a woodburning stove, and collections of decorative plates and of bottles, and there are two smaller rooms behind – one with high ceilings and benches, stools and tables around the edges, and the third room (no smoking) is more set up for eating; TV, darts, cribbage, dominoes, and piped music. Under the new licensee, the wholesome home-made food includes sandwiches (from £1.60), ploughman's with home-made chutney, mushroom and chick pea stroganoff, and various hotpots and casseroles (all £4.50), and puddings like fresh fruit flan (£2); good value Sunday lunch. Daily papers and magazines to read; maybe quiet piped radio. There's a small walled back garden. Local parking is not easy. *(Recommended by Stuart Paulley, Anne and Paul Horscraft, the Didler, JP, PP, Patrick Hancock, G Coates)*

Tynemill ~ Manager Mark Swift ~ Real ale ~ Bar food (12-2.30, 6-8(8.30 Thurs and Fri); not Sat or Sun evening) ~ (0114) 234 9148 ~ Children welcome ~ Dogs welcome ~ Live music Sat evening, occasional folk Mon and Tues evenings, Dizzy Club last Sun of month ~ Open 12-11; 12-10.30 Sun

SHELLEY SE2112 Map 7

Three Acres

Roydhouse (not signposted); from B6116 heading for Skelmanthorpe, turn left in Shelley (signposted Flockton, Elmley, Elmley Moor) and go up lane for 2 miles towards radio mast

For 35 years, the same licensees have been in charge at this civilised and very well run former coaching inn, and it certainly remains a special place to enjoy the excellent food. The roomy lounge bar is being extended this year but still has a relaxed, friendly atmosphere, tankards hanging from the main beam, button-back leather sofas, old prints and so forth, and maybe a pianist playing light music. To be sure of a place, it's best to book (quite a way ahead) – try to get a table with a view. The particularly good, interesting bar food includes pea soup with smoked haddock rarebit and pancetta crisp (£4.50), a huge choice of interesing sandwiches or filled baguettes (from £4.95; vegetarian club with mozzarella, sun-blush tomatoes, basil, rocket, avocado and pine nuts dressed with sun-dried tomato pesto; open steak on toasted onion bread with rocket, caramelised onions topped with blue cheese £7.95), chicken liver parfait with cherry tomato and onion chutney (£5.95), potted shrimps with hot buttered toast or warm salad of seared fresh tuna and jersey royals with niçoise dressing and wasabi crème fraîche (£6.95), six rock oysters (£7.50), leek cannelloni with lemon, thyme and provolone piccante au gratin (£11.95), steak, kidney and mushroom pie with home-made brown sauce or lunchtime roast of the day (£12.95), fresh mackerel fishcakes with a sorrel and spiced ratatouille salsa or crisp chinese roast belly pork with oriental vegetables and plum and black bean sauce (£13.95), roast rack of yorkshire lamb with apricot and onion jam and mint and fresh pea jus (£14.95), prime aged rib-eye steak with pepper sauce (£15.95), and puddings such as sunken chocolate pudding with hot chocolate sauce, griottine cherries and clotted cream, roasted rhubarb and almond pithivier with rhubarb compote or honey toasted bananas with soft goats cheese (£5.50). There's a specialist delicatessen next door. Well kept Black Sheep, Tetleys, and Timothy Taylors Landlord on handpump, over 40 whiskies, and an exceptional (if not cheap) choice of wines, with 13 by the glass; helpful, welcoming service, even when really pushed. There are fine views across to Emley Moor.
(Recommended by Regine Webster, W K Wood, Mr and Mrs P Eastwood, P and S Blacksell, R N and M I Bailey, Roger Everett, Ian Phillips, Dr and Mrs M W A Haward, Liz Webster, J R Ringrose, Charles Eaton, Brenda and Stuart Naylor, Mrs Yvette Bateman, Mrs R A Cartwright, Brenda and Rob Fincham, Simon Calvert, Jo Lilley)

Free house ~ Licensees Neil Truelove and Brian Orme ~ Real ale ~ Bar food (12-2, 6.30-9.30) ~ Restaurant ~ (01484) 602606 ~ Children welcome ~ Open 12-3, 6-11; closed 25 Dec-2 Jan ~ Bedrooms: £60B/£80B

SINNINGTON SE7485 Map 10

Fox & Hounds

Just off A170 W of Pickering

As well as being a nice place to stay, this neat 18th-c coaching inn draws in customers for its good, enjoyable food and friendly welcome. The nicely kept beamed bar has various pictures and old artefacts, a woodburning stove, and comfortable wall seats and carver chairs around the tidy tables on its carpet. The curved corner bar counter has well kept Black Sheep Special and Camerons on handpump, seven wines by the glass, and some rare malt whiskies. At lunchtime, bar food might include home-made soup (£3.45), sandwiches (from £4.50; flatbreads with toppings like chargrilled vegetables and taleggio cheese £6.95), chicken livers sautéed with lardons of bacon, shallots, flamed with brandy and finished with cream (£5.25), salad niçoise (£6), battered fresh haddock (£7.45), steak and Guinness pie (£7.95), leek risotto with red onion, pepper, chestnut mushrooms in chilli oil, and fresh parmesan (£8.25), and slow roast belly of pork with a fricassee of broad beans, butter beans, asparagus, sage and thyme (£8.75), with evening choices like peking pancakes with crispy duck, chilli jam and dipping sauce (£6.25), queen scallops sautéed with julienne of leek and garlic with cream and cheese (£7.25), roast supreme of chicken with a ratatouille of chorizo and fresh basil (£11.75), seared lamb cutlets with apples and red cabbage, sultanas and cider and vanilla and juniper jus (£12.25), and roast fillet of halibut with orange and garlic salad (£13.25). The lounge bar and restaurant are no smoking; piped music, dominoes, and darts. Picnic-sets out in front. The village is pretty. *(Recommended by David and Ruth Hollands)*

Free house ~ Licensees Andrew and Catherine Stephens ~ Real ale ~ Bar food ~ Restaurant (evening) ~ (01751) 431577 ~ Children in eating areas until 8pm ~ Dogs allowed in bar ~ Open 12-2.30, 6(6.30 in winter and on Sun)-11(10.30 Sun) ~ Bedrooms: £49S(£59B)/£80S(£90B)

SUTTON UPON DERWENT SE7047 Map 7

St Vincent Arms

B1228 SE of York

Warmly welcoming and friendly, this is a well run, unchanging local popular with regulars as well as visitors. The parlour-like panelled front bar has traditional high-backed settles, a cushioned bow-window seat, windsor chairs and a gas-effect coal fire; another lounge and separate no smoking dining room open off. To be sure of a seat, it's best to get here early. Well liked food includes sandwiches, home-made soup (£3.50), smoked haddock rarebit (£4.80), confit of duck with hoi sin sauce (£5), home-made lasagne (£7.50), steak and kidney pie or battered haddock (£7.90), chicken stir fry (£8.50), steak au poivre (£14.95), daily specials like asparagus wrapped in serrano ham with risotto (£6), chicken breast stuffed with black pudding and apple and calvados sauce (£10.50), hot shellfish platter with garlic butter (£11), breast of duck with Grand Marnier sauce (£12), and roast rack of lamb with rosemary jus and mini shepherd's pie (£14), and puddings such as home-made tiramisu or black and white chocolate pudding with crème anglaise (£4). Up to ten real ales on handpump or tapped from the cask: Adnams Broadside, Fullers Bitter, Chiswick, London Pride and ESB, Old Mill Bitter, John Smiths, Timothy Taylors Landlord, Charles Wells Bombardier, and York Yorkshire Terrier; a dozen wines by the glass, and 15 malt whiskies. There are seats in the garden. The pub is named after the admiral who was granted the village and lands by the nation as thanks for his successful commands – and for coping with Nelson's infatuation with Lady Hamilton. Handy for the Yorkshire Air Museum. *(Recommended by Peter and Anne Hollindale, Paul and Ursula Randall, Hugh A MacLean, Pat and Graham Williamson, W W Burke, Dr D Parker, John Evans, Tim and Liz Sherbourne, Derek and Sylvia Stephenson)*

Free house ~ Licensees Phil, Simon and Adrian Hopwood ~ Real ale ~ Bar food ~ Restaurant ~ (01904) 608349 ~ Children in eating area of bar, restaurant and family room ~ Dogs allowed in bar ~ Open 11.30-3, 6-11; 12-3, 7-10.30 Sun

THORGANBY SE6942 Map 7

Jefferson Arms

Off A163 NE of Selby, via Skipwith

Before setting out to visit this rather bistro-style dining pub, it's worth noting the restricted opening hours. There's a relaxed, stylish atmosphere, iron-framed marble-topped tables and bentwood chairs, grey and chrome colours, and large metal bar counter with big urns at either end; away from the bar are comfortable sofas and chairs, open fires, heavy draped curtains, and ornate candlesticks. As well as two attractively laid out conservatories, several areas are no smoking, and the bedrooms have been newly refurbished. With quite an emphasis on the generous helpings of good food, the menu might include home-made soup (£3.95), home-made chicken liver pâté or fresh salmon and crab fishcakes with spicy tomato salsa (£4.95), vegetable curry (£7.95), steak and kidney pie (£8.95), gammon and egg (£9.95), chicken wellington with orange sauce or fresh salmon with lime and cream sauce (£11.95), half a roast duck with apple and cider sauce (£12.95), mixed grill (£14.95), and daily specials such as caramelised onion and cheese tartlet (£4.95), wild mushroom stroganoff (£8.95), chicken supreme filled with haggis wrapped in bacon with a whisky, mushroom and cream sauce (£12.95), and calves liver with peppered mash and madeira sauce (£14.95); Sunday roast (£7.95). Well kept John Smiths and Theakstons Black Bull on handpump; piped music. The garden has a terrace with a fountain and fish pond. More reports please. *(Recommended by Walter and Susan Rinaldi-Butcher, Dr T E Hothersall, Michael Dandy, Roy Hamnett, Brenda and Stuart Naylor, Pat and Roger Fereday, Paul Boot)*

Free house ~ Licensees Clive Bland and Steven Wiper ~ Real ale ~ Bar food (12-2, 6-9) ~ Restaurant ~ (01904) 448316 ~ Children in restaurant ~ Dogs allowed in bedrooms ~ Open 6-11; 12-2, 6-11 Fri and Sat; 12-3, 7-10.30 Sun; closed Mon, Tues, Weds and Thurs lunchtimes ~ Bedrooms: £50S/£70S

THORNTON IN LONSDALE SD6976 Map 7

Marton Arms

Off A65 just NW of Ingleton (or can be reached direct from Ingleton)

Although there's a new licensee at the helm here, few changes have been made, and the exceptional choice of real ales remains. Well kept on handpump, they might include Black Sheep Bitter, Broughton Greenmantle Original, Caledonian Deuchars IPA, Cropton King Billy, Dent Bitter, Enville Bitter, Freeminer Bitter, Orkney Dark Island, Sharps Doom Bar, Theakstons, and Timothy Taylors Golden Best; four-pint take-aways, too. Also, Stowford Press and Weston's farm cider, well over 300 malt whiskies, all sorts of unusual spirits, a decent choice of wines, and an enterprising range of soft drinks, as well as proper tea and coffee. Service is friendly and attentive. The beamed partly no smoking bar is inviting, with stools on black boards by the long counter, and lots of stripped pine tables, pews and built-in wall seats in the carpeted main part – light and airy, with biggish black and white local photographs; some train memorabilia. A curtained-off flagstoned public bar has bar billiards, and both seating areas have open log fires. Bar food now includes home-made soup (£3.75), sandwiches (from £4.65; sirloin steak with onion rings and mushrooms £10.25), lots of home-made pizzas (from £6.50), cumberland sausage (£7.25), vegetable lasagne (£8.25), minted lamb shoulder (£8.90), steak and kidney pudding (£9.45), and daily specials; they offer a take-away service for pizzas and burgers. There are picnic-sets out on the front terrace, with more behind. Two of the bedrooms are equipped for disabled people; good breakfasts, which suit this great walking country. The 13th-c church opposite is where Sir Arthur Conan Doyle was married. *(Recommended by Mr and Mrs Maurice Thompson, Graham Patterson, Peter F Marshall, Patrick Hancock, Maggie and Tony Harwood, Michael Doswell, Simon Calvert, Steve Whalley)*

Free house ~ Licensee Graham Wright ~ Real ale ~ Bar food (12-3, 6-9; all day weekends and bank hols; not 25 Dec) ~ Restaurant ~ (0152 42) 41281 ~ Children welcome ~ Open 11-11; 12-10.30 Sun; closed evening 25 Dec ~ Bedrooms: £33S/£66S

THORNTON WATLASS SE2486 Map 10

Buck

Village signposted off B6268 Bedale—Masham

The newly refurbished no smoking dining room in this genuine local now has new tables and chairs, and different pictures – the large prints of old Thornton Watlass cricket teams, signed bats, cricket balls and so forth have been moved to the Long Room (which overlooks the cricket green). The place to head for is the pleasantly traditional right-hand bar with upholstered old-fashioned wall settles on the carpet, a fine mahogany bar counter, a high shelf packed with ancient bottles, several mounted fox masks and brushes, a brick fireplace, and a relaxed atmosphere; piped music. Lunchtime bar food includes home-made soup (£3.25), sandwiches (from £3.50; scrambled egg and smoked salmon baguette £4), smoked haddock fishcakes (£4.25), ploughman's (£5.75), omelettes (£5.95), vegetable and pasta stir fry (£6.95), steak and kidney pie (£7.25), deep fried whitby cod (£7.50), and large gammon and egg (£7.95), with evening dishes such as home-made chicken liver pâté (£4.25), goats cheese and tomato tartlet (£4.50), tandoori king prawns (£5.75), chick pea and potato curry (£7.95), stir-fried chicken with black bean sauce (£9.50), fresh salmon fillet with a cream and tarragon sauce (£9.75), roast breast of spicy duck in honey and soy sauce (£10.95), mixed grill (£11.25), sirloin steak (£12.50), and home-made puddings (£3.95). Well kept Black Sheep Bitter, John Smiths, Theakstons, and a couple of guests like Durham Invincible or Hambleton Mild Mannered Mare on handpump, over 40 malt whiskies, and half a dozen wines by the glass; occasional piped music, darts, cribbage, and dominoes. The sheltered garden has an equipped children's play area and summer barbecues, and they have their own cricket team; quoits. More reports please. *(Recommended by Mr and Mrs J E C Tasker, Steve Whalley, Oliver Richardson, Walter and Susan Rinaldi-Butcher)*

Free house ~ Licensees Michael and Margaret Fox ~ Real ale ~ Bar food (12-2, 7-9.15; 12-9.15 Sun) ~ Restaurant ~ (01677) 422461 ~ Children welcome ~ Dogs allowed in bedrooms ~ Jazz Sun lunchtimes ~ Open 11-11; 12-10.30 Sun; closed evening 25 Dec ~ Bedrooms: £50S/£60(£70B)

WASS SE5679 Map 7

Wombwell Arms

Back road W of Ampleforth; or follow brown tourist-attraction sign for Byland Abbey off A170 Thirsk—Helmsley

Although this particularly well run and deservedly popular pub comes in for enthusiastic praise from a great many of our readers as somewhere for a delicious meal or very comfortable overnight stay, it is still a proper village local, and the hard-working staff continue to offer a genuinely warm and friendly welcome – even when the entire cast and audience of the village pantomime pour in. The little central bar, to the left, is spotlessly kept and cosy and has a large inglenook fireplace, and the two low-beamed no smoking dining areas are comfortable and inviting and take in a former 17th-c granary. They use only fresh produce from local suppliers and producers for the exceptionally good food: sandwiches, delicious soups like pea and ham or mushroom (£3.95), salmon fishcake on spinach with pink hollandaise (£4.75), black pudding with wild mushrooms and bacon on a garlic croûte (£5.65), chicken and pork pâté (£5.95), moules marinière (£7.95), chilli con carne with dark chocolate or lambs liver with onion gravy (£8.95), tagliatelle with smoked salmon, cream and herbs or venison and red wine, lamb and mint, and pork and stilton sausages with grain mustard mash (£9.45), chicken strips with wild mushrooms, cream, dijon mustard, tarragon and button onions (£10.95), local rabbit cooked with cider and apples (£11.45), local game casserole in a real ale and port sauce (£11.85), whitby cod fillet with crispy breadcrumbs and cheese (£12.35), local lamb shank with onions, apricots, honey, treacle and ginger (£13.45), steaks (from £13.45), and puddings like super home-made rum truffle (from £4.25); Sunday roast (£8.45), and first class breakfasts. Well kept Black Sheep Bitter, Timothy Taylors Landlord, and a guest such as Malton Double Chance on handpump, up to 22 malt whiskies, and a carefully chosen wine list with eight by the glass. The two friendly and well trained black labradors, Jasper and Leo, may be allowed in after food service has ended. *(Recommended by RJH, Susan and John Douglas, Tim Newman, Walter and Susan Rinaldi-Butcher, Edward and Deanna Pearce, Robert Gartery, Fergus and Jackie O'Connor, Jeff and Wendy Williams, Jeff and Cindy Copland, Russell Burr, Janet and Peter Race, Dr and Mrs R G J Telfer, Nigel Epsley, Mike and Lynn Robinson, Michael Doswell, Richard and Karen Holt, Steve Whalley)*

Free house ~ Licensees Andy and Sue Cole ~ Real ale ~ Bar food (11.30-2, 6.30-9.30) ~ Restaurant ~ (01347) 868280 ~ Children in restaurant and family room ~ Open 11.30-2.30(3.30 Sat), 6.30-11; 12-4, 6.30-10.30 Sun; closed Sun evening and Mon in winter ~ Bedrooms: £42B/£70B

WATH IN NIDDERDALE SE1467 Map 7

Sportsmans Arms

Nidderdale road off B6265 in Pateley Bridge; village and pub signposted over hump bridge on right after a couple of miles

You can be sure of a genuinely warm welcome from the courteous, friendly staff in this civilised restaurant-with-rooms – whether you are popping in for a quick drink, a more leisurely meal, or staying overnight in the very comfortable bedrooms. Using the best local produce – game from the moors, fish delivered daily from Whitby, and nidderdale lamb, pork and beef – the carefully presented and prepared delicious food might include fresh soup (£3.75), warm camembert on red onions and roasted peppers (£5.25), really excellent lunchtime sandwiches (£5.50), their special salad with bacon, croûtons, olives, anchovies, and parmesan and pecorino cheeses on mixed leaves (£5.25), locally smoked trout fillets (£6.80), grilled stuffed peppers (£9.50), crumbed loin of pork on roasted apples with a creamy plum and calvados sauce or chicken breast with white wine, chive and mushroom sauce (£10.50), baked cod with creamy bacon mash and garlic butter (£11.20), fillets of plaice stuffed with crabmeat and prawns in a chive and tomato sauce (£13.50), sirloin steak with yorkshire blue cheese and green peppercorn sauce (£13.95), and puddings like sticky toffee pudding or popular summer pudding (from £4.10). The whole place is no smoking apart from the bar and the lounge. Well kept Black Sheep on handpump, a very sensible and extensive wine list, a good choice of malt whiskies, and several russian vodkas; open fires. Benches and tables outside. Seats outside in the pretty garden. As well as their own fishing on the River Nidd, this is an ideal spot for walkers, hikers, and ornithologists, and there are plenty of country houses, gardens and cities to explore. *(Recommended by Keith Moss, Di and Mike Gillam, P R Morley, Peter Abbott, Lynda and Trevor Smith, Anne Walford, Barry and Patricia Wooding, John Close, R A K Crabtree, H Bramwell, Michael Jones, Marlene and Jim Godfrey; also in the* Good Hotel Guide*)*

Free house ~ Licensee Ray Carter ~ Real ale ~ Bar food ~ Restaurant ~ (01423) 711306 ~ Children welcome ~ Dogs allowed in bar ~ Open 12-2.30, 6.30-11; 12-3, 7-10.30 Sun; closed 25 Dec ~ Bedrooms: £50B/£90B

WHITBY NZ9011 Map 10

Duke of York

Church Street, Harbour East Side

There's a splendid view over the harbour entrance and the western cliff from this busy pub; it's also close to the famous 199 Steps that lead up to the abbey. The welcoming and comfortable beamed lounge bar has plenty of atmosphere and decorations that include quite a bit of fishing memorabilia – best to arrive early to be sure of a table. The good value fresh local fish remains quite a draw; delicious fresh crab or prawn sandwiches (£3.75) or large fillet of fresh cod or fresh crab salad (£6.95), as well as other sandwiches (from £2.95), vegetable lasagne or chilli (£6), steak in ale pie (£6.50), and puddings (£3). Well kept Courage Directors, John Smiths, and maybe a changing guest on handpump, decent wines, quite a few malt whiskies, hot winter mulled wine, and chilled summer sangria; piped music (which some customers feel is unnecessary), darts, dominoes, TV and fruit machine. Try to get a bedroom overlooking the water – it's also quieter. *(Recommended by Colin and Dot Savill, Roger and Jenny Huggins, Rona Murdoch, W A Evershed, JP, PP, C J Fletcher, Janet and Peter Race, the Didler, David Carr, Michael Butler, Mrs Yvette Bateman, Tracey and Stephen Groves, Derek and Sylvia Stephenson, Edward and Deanna Pearce, Dr J Barrie Jones, David and Ruth Hollands, John Fiander)*

Unique (Enterprise) ~ Lease Lawrence Bradley ~ Real ale ~ Bar food (all day) ~ (01947) 600324 ~ Children in eating area of bar until 9.30pm ~ Live music Sun ~ Open 11-11; 11-10.30 Sun ~ Bedrooms: /£50B

It's against the law for bar staff to smoke while handling food or drink.

WIDDOP SD9333 Map 7

Pack Horse

The Ridge; from A646 on W side of Hebden Bridge, turn off at Heptonstall signpost (as it's a sharp turn, coming out of Hebden Bridge road signs direct you around a turning circle), then follow Slack and Widdop signposts; can also be reached from Nelson and Colne, on high, pretty road; OS Sheet 103 map reference 952317

A real oasis for travellers on the Pennine Way and Pennine Bridleway (leave your boots and backpacks in the porch), this traditional pub has a good, bustling atmosphere. The bar has warm winter fires, window seats cut into the partly panelled stripped stone walls that take in the moorland view, sturdy furnishings, and well kept Black Sheep Bitter, Greene King Old Speckled Hen, Thwaites Bitter, and a guest like Thwaites Lancaster Bomber on handpump, around 130 single malt whiskies, and some irish ones as well, and decent wines; efficient service. Bar food includes home-made pâté (£2.95), sandwiches or baps (from £3.50), home-made steak and kidney pie or mushroom stroganoff (£5.95), steaks (from £8.95), roast rack of lamb (£10.95), and specials such as italian-style beef and herb pancakes (£6.95), liver and bacon with sizzling onions (£7.95), fresh salmon fillet on dill mash with parsley sauce (£8.95), and aberdeen angus beef on horseradish mash (£9.95). The restaurant is only open on Saturday evenings. The friendly golden retrievers are called Paddy and Murphy. Seats outside and pretty summer hanging baskets. *(Recommended by Dr T E Hothersall, Ian and Nita Cooper, Len Beattie, Nigel Epsley, MJVK, Greta and Christopher Wells)*

Free house ~ Licensee Andrew Hollinrake ~ Real ale ~ Bar food (not Mon or weekday winter lunchtimes) ~ Restaurant ~ (01422) 842803 ~ Children in eating area of bar ~ Dogs allowed in bar ~ Open 12-3, 7-11; 12-11 Sun; closed Mon except bank hols ~ Bedrooms: £39S/£44B

YORK SE5951 Map 7

Maltings £

Tanners Moat/Wellington Row, below Lendal Bridge

Of course the fine choice of interesting real ales is quite an attraction, but this lively small pub has a good mix of customers, and a bustling and chatty atmosphere, and the good value lunchtime food is popular, too. The tricksy décor is entirely contrived and strong on salvaged, somewhat quirky junk: old doors for the bar front and much of the ceiling, enamel advertising signs for the rest of it, what looks like a suburban front door for the entrance to the ladies', partly stripped orange brick walls, even a lavatory pan in one corner. There are six or seven particularly well kept changing ales on handpump with Black Sheep and Roosters, and five changing guests, with frequent special events when the jovial landlord adds many more. He also has two or three continental beers on tap, up to four farm ciders, a dozen or so country wines, and more irish whiskeys than you normally see. In generous helpings, the food might include sandwiches (from £2.85), extremely good, truly home-made chips (£2.50) with chilli or curry (£3.50), filled baked potatoes (from £3.75), haddock (£4.95), and beef in ale pie or stilton and leek bake (£5.25); get there early to be sure of a seat. The day's papers are framed in the gents'; fruit machine. Nearby parking is difficult; the pub is very handy for the Rail Museum. *(Recommended by Richard Lewis, Peter F Marshall, JP, PP, M Benjamin, the Didler, David Carr, Tony Hobden, Mark Walker, Alison Hayes, Pete Hanlon, Patrick Hancock, Martin Grosberg, Nick Holding, Fred and Lorraine Gill, Andy and Jill Kassube, Dr and Mrs A K Clarke)*

Free house ~ Licensee Shaun Collinge ~ Real ale ~ Bar food (12-2 weekdays, 12-4 weekends; not evenings) ~ No credit cards ~ (01904) 655387 ~ Children allowed after food service and must be well behaved ~ Jazz Mon, blues Tues ~ Open 11-11; 12-10.30 Sun; closed 25 Dec

LUCKY DIP

Besides the fully inspected pubs, you might like to try these Lucky Dips recommended to us and described by readers (if you do, please send us reports: www.goodguides.co.uk).

ADDINGHAM SE0749

☆ *Fleece* [Main St]: 18th-c pub locally popular for food from good hearty sandwiches and generous well priced blackboard meals using fresh local meat, fish and smoked fish, popular Sun roasts (all day then), pleasant service, well kept Black Sheep, Timothy Taylors Landlord and Tetleys, good choice of wines by the glass, low ceilings, flagstones, candles and log fire, no smoking dining area, tap room with darts and dominoes; very busy wknds; children welcome, tables outside *(Dr and Mrs S Donald, Sarah McGillivary, Tina and David Woods-Taylor, C A Hall, Marlene and Jim Godfrey)*

AINDERBY QUERNHOW SE3480

Black Horse: Good variety of food in spacious bar with coal fire and pleasant service *(Janet and Peter Race)*

ALDBROUGH ST JOHN NZ2011

☆ *Stanwick Arms* [off A1 signed to Piercebridge, then signed off to left]: Attractive country dining pub in good spot with seats out on pretty village green, huge helpings of moderately priced good interesting food with Barbados influence in bistro and bar (bar food may stop if restaurant busy), happy staff, well kept Black Sheep and John Smiths Magnet, good coffee, log and coal fires in both bars, traditional décor, all clean and tidy; children welcome, bedrooms, cl Mon lunchtime *(Michael Doswell, Rob Western)*

ALLERTON BYWATER SE4227

☆ *Boat* [Main St]: Busy recently extended pub brewing its own refreshing and interesting well priced Boat ales, others such as Tetleys, good value food for the heartiest appetites (even their 'small' helpings are jolly generous) inc some interesting specials, friendly staff (landlord an ex Rugby League player for Castleford and England, appropriate mementoes), good helpful service even when busy; play area, lots of tables out by Aire & Calder Canal, open all day Sun and (not Mon-Tues afternoons) summer *(Eric Larkham, Pat and Tony Martin, JHBS, Geoffrey and Brenda Wilson, Mrs M Marshall)*

ALNE SE4965

☆ *Blue Bell* [Main St]: Dining pub with wide choice of good enterprising food in comfortable bar and pleasant barn restaurant, well kept beer *(Walter and Susan Rinaldi-Butcher, John Knighton, Marlene and Jim Godfrey)*

AMPLEFORTH SE5878

☆ *White Swan* [off A170 W of Helmsley; East End]: Three separate interestingly furnished and decorated rooms, sporting prints, comfortable squashy seating, public bar with darts and dominoes, John Smiths and Tetleys, blazing log fires, enjoyable food from sandwiches up in bar and no smoking candlelit restaurant; children welcome, attractive back terrace *(LYM, Dr and Mrs R G J Telfer)*

APPLETON ROEBUCK SE5542

Shoulder of Mutton [Chapel Green]: Cheerful and attractive unpretentious bar overlooking village green, wide choice of enjoyable bargain food inc cheap steaks in bar and restaurant, well kept cheap Sam Smiths on all four handpumps, prompt friendly service even on a busy Sun lunchtime (can be crowded with caravanners summer); bedrooms *(Alan Vere, Peter Coxon)*

APPLETREEWICK SE0560

New Inn: Stone-built country local, unpretentious bar with pool table in main sitting area, eccentric décor and interesting photographs (HQ of local soi-disant dangerous sports club), good value simple wknd food inc good sandwiches, real ales such as Daleside, John Smiths and Theakstons, helpfully described bottled imports, family room; machines and piped music, may be cl Mon lunchtime; in fine spot, lovely views, garden, good walking; bedrooms *(LYM, Stefanie and Christian Mohr, Pat and Graham Williamson)*

ARNCLIFFE SD9473

☆ *Falcon* [off B6160 N of Grassington]: Ideal setting on moorland village green for basic very conservatively run country tavern, same family for generations, no frills, open fire in small bar with elderly furnishings and humorous sporting prints, well kept Timothy Taylors Landlord tapped from cask to stoneware jugs in central hatch-style servery, generous plain lunchtime and early evening sandwiches and snacks (from old family kitchen with range and big table that looks used to having a dog tied to its legs), airy back sunroom (children allowed here lunchtime) looking on to pleasant garden; cl winter Thurs evenings; plain bedrooms (not all year), good breakfast and evening meal *(JAE, the Didler, JP, PP, Tony and Ann Bennett-Hughes, LYM, Jim Abbott, Richard and Anne Ansell, Neil and Angela Huxter, Ben Whitney and Pippa Redmond, MDN, Kerry Law, Simon Smith)*

ASKRIGG SD9591

Crown [Main St]: Neatly kept open-plan local, helpful friendly staff, several separate areas off main bar with blazing fires inc old-fashioned range, relaxed atmosphere, cheap generous home-cooked food inc cut-price small helpings, fine ploughman's, good value Sun lunch and good puddings choice, well kept Black Sheep and Theakstons XB; children and walkers welcome, tables outside *(Jim Abbott, Michael Butler, John and Enid Morris, David Field, John Fiander, Julia and Richard Tredgett)*

☆ *Kings Arms* [signed from A684 Leyburn—Sedbergh in Bainbridge]: Early 19th-c coaching inn in popular James Herriot village, thriving pubby atmosphere in flagstoned main bar with roaring log fire, interesting traditional furnishings and décor, well kept ales such as Black Sheep, John Smiths, Theakstons Best and Old Peculier, good choice of wines by the glass and of malt whiskies, wide food choice, friendly service, no smoking waitress-served grill room and set-priced restaurant, pool in barrel-vaulted former beer cellar; bedrooms run as part of Holiday Property Bond complex behind – pub side managed separately *(I J and S A Bufton, LYM, Michael Butler, Gerry and Rosemary Dobson, John and Enid Morris, Roger and Anne Newbury, John Fiander)*

AUSTWICK SD7668

Game Cock [just off A65 Settle—Kirkby Lonsdale]: Prettily placed below the Three Peaks, good fire in homely old-fashioned beamed back bar to suit wet walkers, good choice of food, well kept Thwaites, friendly staff, two dining rooms; dogs welcome, tables out in front with good play area, neat bedrooms, good walks all round *(BB, Maggie and Tony Harwood)*

Traddock: Comfortable bar in lovely old country house hotel, attractive lounge and dining room, sensibly priced good food; bedrooms *(R A K Crabtree)*

AYSGARTH SE0088

George & Dragon [just off A684]: 17th-c coaching inn under new ownership, small attractive bar, log fire, beams and panelling, well kept Black Sheep Bitter, John Smiths and Theakstons Best, polite service, polished hotel lounge with antique china, no smoking dining areas; children welcome, tables in paved garden, lovely scenery, open all day, compact bedrooms with own bathrooms *(LYM, Alec and Joan Laurence, Andrew Shore, Maria Williams, J A Snell, Julia and Richard Tredgett)*

BARDSEY SE3643

Bingley Arms [Church Lane]: Ancient smartly decorated stone-built pub with good value fresh food inc interesting dishes, two-course lunch and early-supper bargains, welcoming efficient service, well kept Black Sheep, John Smiths and Tetleys, good wines by the glass, spacious lounge divided into separate areas inc no smoking, huge fireplace, smaller public bar, picturesque upstairs brasserie; children welcome, lots of tables in attractive terraced garden, lovely Saxon church nearby *(LYM, Pat and Tony Hinkins, Marvin Hurst)*

BARKISLAND SE0416

Brown Cow: Stone-built pub in lovely Pennine setting, nicely refurbished by new licensees in smart but simple rustic style, good reasonably priced blackboard food inc interesting dishes (best to book Fri-Sun), well kept changing guest beers, good choice of wines by the glass, relaxed atmosphere, three open fires, rugged moorland views from lively flagstoned bar's front bay window, cosy no smoking dining rooms in pink or green, some unusual artwork; tables out on teak deck, cl Mon and lunchtime Tues-Sat, open all day Sun *(Mrs Yvette Bateman)*

New Rock: Modest hilltop pub popular for incredibly cheap good food esp bargain steaks – well worth booking; well trained staff, beautiful labradors, keg beers; children welcome (not late evening); cl wkdy lunchtimes *(Herbert and Susan Verity)*

BARKSTON ASH SE4936

Boot & Shoe [Main St]: Traditional welcoming local with well kept Tetleys, open-plan lounge, games room *(Les and Sandra Brown)*

BEVERLEY TA0339

☆ *Corner House* [Norwood]: Warm and welcoming, attractive pastel décor, pews, easy chairs and sofas, friendly staff, good fresh restauranty food from baguettes up (no puddings), big good value wknd breakfast from 10, Timothy Taylors and other well kept beers, good wines, wide range of fresh fruit juices, hot beverages, daily papers, air conditioning; tables outside *(Fred and Lorraine Gill)*

Woolpack [Westwood Rd, W of centre]: Small welcoming local in former 19th-c cottage pair, good value lunchtime snacks and bar lunches, generous early evening meals cooked to order now too, also Mon curry night and Fri steak night, well kept Burtonwood and guest beers such as Brains SA and Moorhouses Pendle Witches Brew, decent wines by the glass, cheerful welcoming service, cosy snug, real fires, simple spotless furnishings, no pretentions, brasses, teapots, prints and maps; subdued piped music *(Paul and Ursula Randall)*

BINGLEY SE1039

☆ *Brown Cow* [Ireland Bridge; B6429 just W of junction with A650]: Genuine and unpretentious, open-plan but snugly divided, with coal fires, easy chairs, toby jugs, lots of pictures, panelling; well kept Timothy Taylors ales with an unusual guest beer, good reasonably priced food from sandwiches to steaks, no smoking restaurant, friendly staff; may be piped music; children welcome, tables on sheltered terrace, pleasant spot *(LYM, Jane Taylor, David Dutton)*

Dick Hudsons [Otley Rd, High Eldwick]: Comfortable and appealingly old-world Vintage Inn, with popular food, Bass and Tetleys, good choice of wines by the glass; tables out by cricket field, tremendous views and good walks, open all day *(Pat and Graham Williamson, Anne and David Robinson)*

Fisherman [Wagon Lane]: Good range of good value food, quite strong on fish *(Anne and David Robinson)*

BIRSTALL SE2126

☆ *Black Bull* [Kirkgate, off A652; head down hill towards church]: Medieval stone-built pub opp part-Saxon church, dark panelling and low beams in long row of five small linked rooms, traditional décor complete with stag's head and lace curtains, lively local atmosphere, good cheap home-made food inc bargain early meals and good value Sun lunch, good service, well kept mainstream ales, upstairs former courtroom (now a function room, but they may give you a guided tour); no no smoking area; children welcome, quiz night Mon *(BB, Michael Butler)*

BISHOP MONKTON SE3266

Masons Arms [St Johns Rd]: Pretty streamside pub with lovely flower tubs and baskets, cosy carpeted bar, open fire and dark wood furnishings, well kept Black Sheep and (brewed by landlord's son) Rudgate Viking, nice choice of hearty home-made food from interesting baguettes up, neat restaurant; attractive village *(anon)*

BISHOP WILTON SE7955

☆ *Fleece* [just off A166 York—Bridlington; Pocklington Rd]: Partly panelled open-plan village inn under new licensees, generous good value food cooked to order, well kept Black Sheep and John Smiths, moderately priced wines, efficient friendly service, several areas off flagstoned entrance hall, attractive décor with lots of pictures and bric-a-brac, a longcase clock, even a hanging penny-farthing; may be subdued piped light classics; four compact comfortable bedrooms across courtyard with own bathrooms, nice spot on the edge of the Wolds nr interesting church *(Paul and Ursula Randall, Marian and Andrew Ruston)*

BISHOPDALE SD9985

Street Head [B6160 W Burton—Cray]: 17th-c coaching inn comfortably modernised inside, three pleasant linked rooms, Black Sheep, John Smiths and Theakstons, nicely laid out dining room, pool in end bar; bedrooms *(Kevin Thorpe)*

BISHOPTHORPE SE5947

Ebor [Main St]: Popular and welcoming local nr main entrance to Archbishop of York's Palace (hence name), bar and big lounge opening into dining area, helpful attentive staff, Sam Smiths, generous traditional food; children welcome, beautiful hanging baskets and big well planted back garden *(Pat and Graham Williamson, Edward Leetham)*

BOROUGHBRIDGE SE3966

Malt Shovel [St James Sq]: Bright and attractively modernised, with enjoyable interesting food from filled baguettes up, caring service, well kept Black Sheep *(Rita and Keith Pollard, Janet and Peter Race)*

Three Horseshoes [Bridge St]: Spotless unspoilt 1930s pub/hotel run by same family from the start, character landlord, friendly locals, huge fire in lounge, darts, dominoes and cards in public bar (not always open), original features inc slide-down snob screens, good plain home cooking from sandwiches to steaks in bars and restaurant, well kept Camerons Strongarm and Tetleys, splendidly tiled ladies'; bedrooms, open all day Sun *(the Didler, JP, PP, Pete Baker)*

BRADFORD SE1938

Stansfield Arms [Apperley Lane, Apperley Bridge; off A658 NE]: Neatly kept pub popular for wide choice of enjoyable food, real ales such as Black Sheep and Timothy Taylors Landlord; pleasant setting *(Richard and Karen Holt, Geoffrey and Brenda Wilson)*

Symposium [Albion Rd, Idle]: Part of Market Town Taverns, with good choice of ales, foreign bottled beers, food inc popular Sun lunch and wkdy bargains, and wines; open all day Fri-Sun *(Andy and Jill Kassube)*

BRADWAY SK3280

Old Mother Redcap [Prospect Rd]: L-shaped open-plan lounge with good value food lunchtime and Thurs-Fri evening inc good Sun roast, cheap Sam Smiths OB; smoking allowed in dining area; picnic-sets on back terrace *(CMW, JJW)*

BRAMHAM SE4242

Swan [just off A1 2 miles N of A64]: Unspoilt country local with engaging long-serving landlady, super mix of customers, well kept John Smiths and Theakstons, no food or music *(Les and Sandra Brown)*

BRANDESBURTON TA1147

Dacre Arms [signed off A165 N of Beverley and Hornsea turn-offs]: Brightly modernised comfortably bustling pub popular for wide choice of good value food (all day Sun) from lunchtime sandwiches (not wknds) to steaks, inc OAP specials and children's; friendly service, well kept Black Sheep, Courage Directors, Tetleys and Theakstons Old Peculier tapped from the cask, darts, restaurant; children welcome *(Brian and Janet Ainscough, LYM, Fred and Lorraine Gill)*

BRIGHOUSE SE1323

Red Rooster [Brookfoot; A6025 towards Elland]: Stone-built alehouse with well kept changing ales such as Caledonian Deuchars IPA, Roosters Yankee and Timothy Taylors Landlord, brewery memorabilia, open fire, separate areas inc one with pin table, no food or machines *(JP, PP, the Didler, J R Ringrose)*

BROOM HILL SE4102

Old Moor [B6273 N of Brampton]: Good value fresh home-made food inc teatime bargains, Tues-Weds supper deals, OAP wkdy lunches and (exc Sun) cheap children's dishes, Sun food all day till 8, no smoking dining room, about five well kept real ales; Mon quiz night *(G Gleadall)*

BUCKDEN SD9477

☆ *Buck* [B6160]: Attractive creeper-covered stone pub with modernised and extended open-plan bar, log fire and flagstones in snug original core, local pictures and hunting prints; huge choice of good value hearty food from lunchtime sandwiches and baguettes up, well kept ales such as Black Sheep, Copper Dragon, Timothy Taylors Landlord and Theakstons Old Peculier, plenty of malt whiskies, several wines by the glass, neat and competent young staff; children and dogs welcome, terrace with good surrounding moorland views, popular walking spot, open all day, bedrooms with own bathrooms *(LYM, John Close, Eddie Edwards, MDN, Lynda and Trevor Smith, Brian and Janet Ainscough, Tony and Betty Parker)*

BURGHWALLIS SE5311

☆ *Burghwallis* [signed off A1 southbound, S of Pontefract; Scorcher Hills Lane]: Bargain hot food counter inc carvery and a few fresh hot dishes in comfortable former village social club pleasantly refurbished with leather chesterfields, nice china on mahogany sideboards, well kept nicely priced Old Mill and Tetleys, good choice of wines by the glass, friendly licensees, full-sized pool table, conservatory; very popular with older lunchers *(Andrew Crawford)*

BURLEY WOODHEAD SE1544

Hermit: Neat and tidily renovated beamed pub, oak panelling and comfortable built-in seats, splendid Wharfedale views from bay window seat, well kept Greene King Ruddles County and Tetleys, good value food inc enterprising specials, restaurant, no piped music or machines; good walks nearby *(Tim Newman, Fiona Pacey, R A K Crabtree)*

BURN SE5928

Wheatsheaf [A19 Selby—Doncaster]: Welcoming landlord, good value usual food (not Sun-Weds evenings) inc notable fish and chips, well kept John Smiths, Timothy Taylors Landlord, Tetleys and a guest microbrew, fine whisky choice, eclectic décor inc assorted saws, hops, model lorries, galleon, big rocking horse; pool room, small garden, open all day *(J A Ellis, Matt Waite)*

BURNISTON TA0193

Three Jolly Sailors [A171 N of Scarborough; High St]: Very popular for good value generous lunches inc local fish, roomy fresh bright lounge with eating area, public bar and conservatory, interesting décor, real ales *(Janet and Peter Race)*

BURNSALL SE0361

☆ ***Red Lion*** [B6160 S of Grassington]: 16th-c inn by River Wharfe, looking across village green to Burnsall Fell, tables out on front cobbles and on big back terrace, attractively panelled sturdily furnished front area with log fire now opened through into large back area with a second new serving bar, several well kept ales inc Timothy Taylors Landlord, interesting wine choice by glass or bottle (they import direct), imaginative bar food, no smoking in dining room, bar parlour and conservatory; they may try to keep your credit card while you have a bar meal; children welcome, bedrooms (dogs allowed in some and bar), open all day, fishing permits *(Michael Butler, Mr and Mrs M Porter, B and M Kendall, LYM, Mrs P J Carroll, Jim Abbott, Dudley and Moira Cockroft, Greta and Christopher Wells)*

BURTON SALMON SE4927

Plough [just off A162 N of Ferrybridge]: Much modernised village pub with good reasonably priced home-made food (cooked to order, so will be a wait) inc good value Sun lunch, three well kept changing ales, log fire, side restaurant; nice walled back garden with picnic-sets, open all day Fri-Sun, has been cl other lunchtimes in winter *(Matt Waite)*

CADEBY SE5100

Cadeby Inn [Main St]: 18th-c building with minimalist décor, up-to-date and appealing; stripped stone, pale carpet and polished beams, modern furniture in three linked areas and dining area, Batemans XB, John Smiths, Tetleys and Wentworth Bluebell, first-rate service, well priced food mixing modern and traditional, daily papers, open fires; tables out in sunny garden *(Graham Dobson, LYM, WAH)*

CALDER GROVE SE3217

Red Kite [Denby Dale Rd (A636, by M1 junction 39)]: Recently built Vintage Inn in style of a Georgian house adjoining a cottage row, pleasant inside, with their usual food and wide range of wines by the glass, Bass and Tetleys, log fire, daily papers; bedrooms in adjacent Holiday Inn *(Ian Phillips)*

CALDWELL NZ1613

Brownlow Arms: Appealing small pub surrounded by flower boxes, good range of quality food, friendly service, dining area and pool area; isolated village, good walks *(Andrew York)*

CARLTON SE0684

☆ ***Foresters Arms*** [off A684 W of Leyburn]: Settling down well again after several landlord changes, welcoming new people brewing their own Wensleydale ales, good choice of enjoyable food inc unusual dishes, helpful service, decent wines by the glass, log fires, low beams, no smoking restaurant, darts and dominoes; children welcome, bench seats out among tubs of flowers, pretty village at the heart of the Yorkshire Dales National Park, comfortable bedrooms, lovely views, has been cl Mon *(LYM, Steve and Barbara Bamford, Michael T Swallow)*

CAWOOD SE5737

☆ ***Ferry*** [King St (B1222 NW of Selby), by Ouse swing bridge]: Unspoilt neatly kept 16th-c inn, several comfortable areas, well kept ales such as Black Sheep, Mansfield, Timothy Taylors Landlord and a couple of local beers tapped from the cask in corner bar, friendly helpful staff, limited good value food inc bargain steak baguette and lots for children, massive inglenook, stripped brickwork, bare boards; tables out on flagstone terrace and grass by interesting River Ouse swing bridge, good value modest bedrooms with bathrooms, open all day Fri-Sun, cl Mon-Tues lunchtime *(Matt Waite, Pete Baker, JP, PP)*

CHURCH FENTON SE5136

Fenton Flyer [Main St]: Homely village local with popular nicely served home-made food inc bargain Sun lunch, Mansfield and Sam Smiths real ale, friendly staff, L-shaped bar with lots of old photographs and memorabilia of the RAF base opposite, small comfortable no smoking dining room; TV, darts, Fri music night, no credit cards, basic lavatories; garden with play area *(Kevin Thorpe, Robert Johnson)*

CLIFTON SE1622

☆ ***Black Horse*** [Westgate/Coalpit Lane; signed off Brighouse rd from M62 junction 25]: 17th-c pub with pleasant décor majoring on racing, golf and football, front part focused on wide choice of popular generous food from interesting ciabattas and other snacks to restaurant meals inc good value set dinners, smaller back area by bar counter mainly just standing room, beam and plank ceiling, open fire, well kept ales such as Boddingtons, Timothy Taylors Landlord and Whitbreads Trophy, decent wines; 21 comfortable bedrooms, pleasant village *(BB, Michael Butler, Howard Martin)*

CLOUGHTON SE9798

☆ *Falcon* [pub signed just off A171 out towards Whitby]: Big dependable open-plan bar, neatly kept and well divided, light and airy, with comfortable banquettes and other seats on turkey carpet, good value honest food in quantity (no booking, but worth the wait for a table), well kept John Smiths and Theakstons Best and XB, good friendly family service, log fire in big stone fireplace, distant sea view from end windows; piped music; picnic-sets on walled lawn, good bedrooms with own bathrooms *(Geoff and Angela Jaques, BB, Patrick Renouf)*

CLOUGHTON NEWLANDS TA0195

☆ *Bryherstones* [Newlands Rd, off A171 in Cloughton]: Several interconnecting rooms inc pink-décor dining room up on right and cosy flagstoned stable-theme room on left, lighter bare-boards back room with pool and interesting see-through woodburner, good reasonably priced generous food inc two- and three-course bargains, well kept real ale, over 50 whiskies, friendly efficient service; children welcome (dogs too, it seems), picnic-sets in sheltered back garden; has been cl Mon-Weds off season *(BB, M Borthwick)*

Hayburn Wyke Hotel [just N of village, which is off A171]: Down very long steep zigzag drive, great spot nr NT Hayburn Wyke, spectacular Cleveland Way coastal path and Scarborough—Whitby path/bicycle trail; bar pleasantly brightened up with lighter colours and higher ceiling, efficient cheerful service, good value food inc popular Sun carvery, well kept Black Sheep Special and Tetleys, coal fire, big café-style dining area, pool, table football and video game in bare-boards games area, monthly karaoke; well behaved children welcome, picnic-sets out on terrace and grass, play areas, comfortably refurbished bedrooms, good breakfast *(BB, M Borthwick)*

COLDEN SD9628

New Delight [just N of Blackshaw Head]: Flagstoned pub with friendly young licensees, enjoyable food, well kept Thwaites, low prices, small games room; handy for interesting Colden Water walks, Pennine Way and Calderdale Way, camping in next field *(Len Beattie)*

CONISTON COLD SD8856

Coniston Hotel [A65 W of Gargrave]: Substantial hotel in two square miles of grounds, good bar food from reasonably priced baguettes to freshly caught trout in appealing bar (children and dogs welcome), well kept Black Sheep, log fire, restaurant; 40 comfortable bedrooms, good breakfast *(Andy and Jill Kassube)*

CONONLEY SD9846

New Inn [Main St/Station Rd]: Busy smallish village pub with good value food inc bargain mixed grill (worth booking evenings), well kept Timothy Taylors real ales *(Dudley and Moira Cockroft)*

COXWOLD SE5377

☆ *Fauconberg Arms* [off A170 Thirsk—Helmsley]: Attractive old pub in delightful unchanging village, well kept John Smiths and Theakstons Best with a guest such as Black Sheep Special, log fire and pleasant atmosphere in attractively furnished lounge bar, back locals' bar with pub games and TV, bar food from sandwiches to some successfully inventive dishes, no smoking restaurant (Weds-Sat evening and Sun lunch) with own comfortable pre-meal drinks area; dogs and children welcome, open all day in summer *(John Knighton, John Hale, Marian and Andrew Ruston, Andrew and Samantha Grainger, LYM, June and Ken Brooks, Peter and Jean Walker, Ian and Nita Cooper, Mike and Lynn Robinson)*

CRACOE SD9760

Devonshire Arms [B6265 Skipton—Grassington]: Olde-worlde pub with good value food in bar and restaurant, well kept Jennings beers, solidly comfortable furnishings, old pictures, polished flooring tiles with rugs here and there, low shiny black beams supporting creaky white planks; darts, dominoes, cribbage, piped music; children in eating areas, picnic-sets on terrace with well kept flowerbeds, more seating on lawn, comfortably refurbished bedrooms, open all day *(LYM, Dudley and Moira Cockroft)*

CRATHORNE NZ4407

Crathorne Arms: Large relaxed dining pub with good range of sensibly priced generous food from straightforward lunchtime dishes to more adventurous evening specials, well kept Black Sheep and Hambleton, friendly staff; pleasant village *(Michael Doswell)*

DACRE BANKS SE1961

☆ *Royal Oak* [B6451 S of Pateley Bridge]: Solid and comfortable stone-built pub with Nidderdale views, interesting old photographs, no smoking area with open fire, well kept Rudgate ales and Tetleys, good wine choice, friendly staff, generous food from sandwiches up (they help with individual dietary requirements), no smoking restaurant; pool, dominoes, cribbage, TV and piped music; children in eating areas, terrace and garden tables, three good value bedrooms, good breakfast *(M and N Watson, S D and J L Cooke, Susan and Tony Dyer, Alison Hayes, Pete Hanlon, Andrew Shore, Maria Williams, Peter J and Avril Hanson, Ben Whitney and Pippa Redmond, LYM, Mrs Diane M Hall, Paul and Ursula Randall)*

DARLEY SE1959

Wellington: Comfortable family-run country inn with real ales, log fires, cosy friendly atmosphere, wide choice of traditional and imaginative food; 12 good reasonably priced bedrooms with own bathrooms, good breakfast *(Mr and Mrs J D Anthony)*

DEWSBURY SE2420

Leggers [Robinsons Boat Yard, Savile Town Wharf, Mill St E (SE of B6409)]: Friendly if basic wharfside hayloft conversion, low-beamed upstairs bar with two egyptian beers brewed downstairs, and up to four guest beers inc Roosters, snacks and sandwiches or filled rolls all day, real fire, helpful staff, daily papers, lots of old brewery and pub memorabilia; open all day, and they do Calder boat trips *(JP, PP, the Didler)*

☆ ***West Riding Licensed Refreshment Rooms*** [Station, Wellington Rd]: Busy three-room early Victorian station bar on southbound platform, well kept changing ales from small breweries, farm ciders, good value interesting wkdy lunchtime food on scrubbed tables, pie night Tues, curry night Weds, daily papers, friendly staff, coal fire, no smoking area till 6, lots of steam memorabilia inc paintings by local artists; juke box may be loud, jazz nights; disabled access, open all day *(JP, PP, the Didler, Joe Green, Jim and Maggie Cowell)*

DONCASTER SE5703

Corner Pin [St Sepulchre Gate W, Cleveland St]: Well kept John Smiths and two interesting changing guest beers, plushly refurbished beamed lounge with old local pub prints, welsh dresser and china, good value traditional food from fine hot sandwiches to cheap Sun roast, friendly landlady and locals, cheery bar with darts, games machine and TV; open all day *(Richard Lewis, the Didler, Patrick Hancock)*

Hare & Tortoise [Parrots Corner, Bawtry Rd, Bessacarr (A638)]: Former surgeon's house redone as relaxed and civilised Vintage Inn pub/restaurant suiting all ages, varying-sized antique tables in eight small rooms off bar, sensibly priced food all day, friendly efficient young staff, Bass and well chosen wines, log fire *(W W Burke, Stephen Woad)*

Leopard [West St]: Lively and friendly, with superb tiled façade, well kept John Smiths, one or two local Glentworth beers and an occasional guest, cheap basic lunchtime food; lounge with lots of bric-a-brac, children's games and nostalgic juke box, basic bar area with pool, darts, TV and machine; open all day, disabled access, good live music upstairs; can get very busy, close to railway stn *(the Didler, Patrick Hancock)*

Plough [W Laith Gate, by Frenchgate shopping centre]: Old-fashioned small local with well kept cheap Barnsley and Bass, old town maps, friendly staff, bustling front room with darts, dominoes and sports TV, quieter back lounge; tiny central courtyard, open all day Tues, Fri, Sat *(the Didler, Patrick Hancock, Pete Baker)*

Railway [West St]: Well kept John Smiths Magnet and Tetleys in large popular corner local with comfortable lounge, railway paintings, pool in separate games area; open all day exc Sun afternoon *(Patrick Hancock)*

Salutation [South Parade, towards race course]: Bustling divided open-plan alehouse-theme bar with plenty of beams, stone floor and bare boards, several well kept changing ales inc rarities, low-priced food all day, friendly staff; side games area, big-screen sports TV at back, quiet juke box, Tues quiz night; tables on back terrace, open all day *(Richard Lewis, Patrick Hancock)*

DORE SK3081

Dore Moor Inn [A625 Sheffield—Castleton]: Busy extended Vintage Inn on edge of Peak District looking down on Sheffield, popular for early evening family meals; good value ample food, fine choice of wines by the glass, good coffee with refills, Bass and Tetleys, hard-working friendly staff, superb central log fires, lots of stripped pine, nice flower arrangements *(Kathy and Chris Armes, Michael Butler)*

DOWNHOLME SE1197

☆ ***Bolton Arms*** [off A6108 Leyburn—Richmond]: Consistently good interesting blackboard food cooked to order by landlord in cosy country dining pub, two good-sized rooms divided by smallish entrance bar, lots of pictures, log fire, steps up to attractive conservatory dining room with great views, well kept Black Sheep and Theakstons, good short wine choice; best to book evenings, esp wknds; two spacious bedrooms sharing bathroom *(Anna Cooper)*

DRIFFIELD TA0257

Bell [Market Pl]: Elegant and well run 18th-c coaching inn with good bar food inc good value imaginative lunchtime buffet, friendly staff and well kept beer from small breweries such as Daleside and Hambleton in long spaciously comfortable red plush bar, former Corn Exchange used as stripped-brick eating area with lots of leafy-looking hanging baskets, delightful old-fashioned restaurant; comfortable bedrooms *(Derek and Sylvia Stephenson)*

EASINGWOLD SE5270

George [Market Pl]: Trim and cheerful market town hotel popular with older people, comfortable quiet corners even when busy, well kept Black Sheep, Theakstons and guest beers, good food in bar and restaurant, pleasant staff; bedrooms *(Janet and Peter Race)*

EAST KESWICK SE3545

Travellers Rest [A659 N of Leeds]: Lightened up by new management, with comfortable new settles, deep armchairs and stools in separate tiled or carpeted areas, food from good sandwich range and ciabattas to steaks and other substantial dishes, Tetleys, upstairs restaurant *(Ray and Winifred Halliday)*

EAST MARTON SD9050

☆ ***Cross Keys*** [A59 Gisburn—Skipton]: Roomy and comfortable pub attractively set back behind small green nr Leeds & Liverpool Canal (and Pennine Way), abstract prints on canary walls contrasting with heavy beams, antique oak furniture and big log or coal fire, good range of generous food at tempting prices inc fine salads, well kept ales such as Black Sheep, Copper Dragon Bitter and Orange Pippin, Timothy Taylors Landlord and Theakstons Cool Cask, decent wines, quick friendly helpful service, more restauranty dining room; quiet piped music; tables outside *(LYM, Malcolm M Stewart, Steve Whalley)*

EAST WITTON SE1487

☆ ***Coverbridge Inn*** [A6108 out towards Middleham]: Homely and welcoming unspoilt 16th-c Dales local with two small character bars, good home-made food from tasty sandwiches to massive meals and prime local steak in eating area, well kept Black Sheep, John Smiths, Theakstons Best and three changing guest beers, log fires; open all day, bedrooms – handy for walkers *(LYM, Ian Arthur, David Varney, Kevin Thorpe, Tom and Alison Lynn)*

ELLAND SE1121

☆ *Barge & Barrel* [quite handy for M62 junction 24; Park Rd (A6025, via A629 and B6114)]: Large welcoming pub with up to ten or more well kept ales inc its own Eastwood & Sanders, farm cider, pleasant staff, huge helpings of low-priced tasty lunchtime food (not Weds), real fire, family room (with air hockey); piped radio, live music some Suns; seats by Calder & Hebble Canal, limited parking, open all day *(the Didler, JP, PP, J R Ringrose, JHBS)*

Oddfellows [Elland Lane]: Appealing little tap for Eastwood & Sanders, with their Nettlethrasher, First Light and usually two others, also three guest beers, sandwiches, baked potatoes and a few simple hot dishes *(Pat and Tony Martin, the Didler)*

EMBSAY SE0053

☆ *Elm Tree* [Elm Tree Sq]: Popular well refurbished open-plan beamed village pub little changed under new licensees, good honest hearty home-made food lunchtime and from 5.30 inc good-sized children's helpings, modest prices, friendly helpful service, well kept Goose Eye No-Eyed Deer and three or four changing guest beers, settles and old-fashioned prints, log-effect gas fire, no smoking dining room, games area; busy wknds esp evenings; comfortable good value bedrooms, handy for steam railway *(M S Catling, Margaret Dickinson, Ian and Nita Cooper, Dudley and Moira Cockroft)*

ESCRICK SE6442

Black Bull [E of A19 York—Selby]: Neat and bustling open-plan pub divided by arches and back-to-back fireplaces, flagstones one side, mix of wooden tables with benches, stools and chairs (in winter the ones near the good fires are at a premium), well kept John Smiths, Tetleys and a guest beer, back dining room, efficient staff (but too many management do and don't rules) *(Joyce and Maurice Cottrell, Roger A Bellingham, Dr and Mrs R G J Telfer, A and B Myers)*

FENWICK SE5916

Baxter Arms: Popular neatly kept traditional village pub with interesting bric-a-brac, good range of bargain sandwiches, welcoming landlord; picnic-sets on big lawn with good play area *(Stephen Woad)*

FEWSTON SE2054

Sun [Norwood; B6451 5 or 6 miles N of Otley]: Large 18th-c inn with enjoyable food (inc summer afternoon teas, and may have Fri-Sat evening barbecues), good friendly service even on busy Sun lunchtime, well kept Black Sheep and Theakstons, good wines by the glass, several rooms, open fires, games room; tables on balcony and in garden, play area, good walks *(David Coleman, Geoffrey and Brenda Wilson)*

FILEY TA1180

Imperial [Hope St]: Consistently well kept Tetleys, Woldtop and one or two guest beers in friendly stripped-down local not far from sea front, pool and juke box in public bar, stripped wood, flagstones, low lighting; dogs welcome, busy wknds *(Fred and Lorraine Gill)*

FINGHALL SE1889

Queens Head [off A684 E of Leyburn]: Warm and comfortable, with friendly helpful young management, reasonably priced good food, well kept Johns Smiths and Theakstons with a guest such as Marstons Pedigree, short interesting choice of well priced wines, low beams, good log fire, elegant roomy back Wensleydale-view restaurant; wheelchair access, disabled facilities, no dogs, open all day *(Anna Cooper)*

GIGGLESWICK SD8164

☆ *Black Horse* [Church St]: Quaint 17th-c village pub crammed between churchyard and pretty row of cottages, spotless cosy bar with lots of bric-a-brac and gleaming brasses, good simple reasonably priced food in bar or intimate dining room (but they may insist on your having a main course), well kept Tetleys, Timothy Taylors and a guest beer, hands-on landlord and son, coal fire; three comfortable bedrooms *(Margaret Dickinson, MJVK, R A K Crabtree)*

GILLAMOOR SE6890

☆ *Royal Oak* [off A170 in Kirkbymoorside]: Well run traditional stone-built village inn with some emphasis on the good value food side, roomy turkey-carpeted bar, heavy dark beams, log fires in two tall stone fireplaces (one with a great old-fashioned iron kitchen range), generous home-made food inc enterprising specials, well kept Black Sheep Bitter and Riggwelter, John Smiths and Tetleys, good coffee and reasonably priced wines, efficient service and friendly hands-on landlady, flowers and candles throughout, no music; comfortable bedrooms, good breakfast, attractive village handy for Barnsdale Moor walks *(BB, Michael Doswell)*

GLUSBURN SD9944

Dog & Gun [Colne Rd (A6068 W)]: Newly refurbished busy traditional pub with good choice of enjoyable reasonably priced food, well kept Copper Dragon and Timothy Taylors Landlord *(Dudley and Moira Cockroft)*

GOLCAR SE0815

☆ *Golcar Lily* [Slades Rd, Bolster Moor]: Attractive and unusual building (former Co-op and manager's house), small pastel-shades bar area with comfortable pink wall seats and stools, swagged curtains, good value interesting food using local produce in bar and big no smoking restaurant leading off, welcoming licensees, well kept Mansfield, Timothy Taylors and a quickly changing guest beer, decent wines, pleasant atmosphere, fine valley views; Sun quiz night, luxurious lavatories upstairs; has been cl Mon-Thurs lunchtimes *(John Hillmer, Stuart Paulley, Nigel Howard)*

GRANGE MOOR SE2215

☆ *Kaye Arms* [A642 Huddersfield—Wakefield]: Very good family-run eating place, too restauranty for the main entries but certainly well up to that standard: civilised, friendly and busy, enterprising proper food bringing back the regulars time and again, sandwiches too (they bake their own bread), courteous efficient staff, exceptional value house wines from imaginative list, hundreds of malt whiskies, no smoking room; handy for Yorkshire Mining Museum, cl Mon lunchtime *(Michael Butler, Dr and Mrs S Donald, LYM, Pierre and Pat Richterich, David and Catherine Whiting)*

GRANTLEY SE2369

Grantley Arms [off B6265 W of Ripon]: Attractive beamed stone pub in quiet Dales village, welcoming coal fires, good food (all day Sun, not Tues lunchtime or Mon) running up to steaks, well kept Black Sheep and John Smiths, paintings by landlady, music-free no smoking restaurant; children welcome if eating *(Tony and Wendy Hobden, Mr and Mrs R K Blackman)*

GRASSINGTON SE0064

☆ *Devonshire* [The Square]: Handsome small hotel with good window seats and tables outside overlooking sloping village square, good range of well presented generous food from sandwiches to good Sun lunch in big popular restaurant, interesting pictures and ornaments, beams and open fires, pleasant family room, cheerful chatty staff and buoyant mix of locals and visitors, well kept ales inc Black Sheep Best and Timothy Taylors Landlord, decent wines; comfortable bedrooms, open all day Sun *(LYM, JAE, R Gibson, Jim Abbott, Fred and Lorraine Gill, Mr and Mrs A J Edwards)*

Foresters Arms [Main St]: Locally popular opened-up old coaching inn with friendly efficient staff, well kept Black Sheep, Tetleys Mild, Timothy Taylors Landlord and changing guest beers, good value straightforward food, pool, sports TV, dining room; children welcome, reasonably priced bedrooms, open all day *(the Didler, JAE, B and M Kendall, Fred and Lorraine Gill)*

GREAT BROUGHTON NZ5405

Bay Horse [High St]: Big comfortably refurbished dining pub in attractive village, enjoyable straightforward food inc appealing puddings, Camerons Strongarm, Castle Eden and Marstons Pedigree, friendly welcome *(Michael Doswell)*

GREAT HABTON SE7576

☆ *Grapes*: Quaint, homely and cosy village pub with fine cooking by chef/landlord, fresh local fish, game and tender meat, delicious imaginative puddings, warm-hearted service, relaxing atmosphere, appealing old-world dining room with interesting bric-a-brac; attractive country walks *(Laura Grant)*

GREAT OUSEBURN SE4562

☆ *Crown* [off B6265 SE of Boroughbridge]: Cheerful country pub emphasising wide choice of good generous elegantly presented food (all afternoon Sat-Sun) from baguettes to some interesting dishes and big steaks, restaurant quality at sensible prices, early evening bargains, well kept Black Sheep, John Smiths, Theakstons and a local guest beer, good friendly service, lots of Edwardian pictures and assorted bric-a-brac, largely no smoking eating areas; may be piped music; well behaved children welcome, tables in garden with sunny terrace and play area, cl wkdy lunchtimes, open all day wknds and bank hols *(Alison Crooks, Dave Heffernan, LYM, Mr and Mrs C Cameron, Alison Hayes, Pete Hanlon, Mrs A Fletcher, Michael T Swallow)*

GREEN HAMMERTON SE4656

☆ *Bay Horse* [just off A59 York—Harrogate]: New family doing well in village pub with plenty of snug areas, some emphasis on enjoyable food (cooked by the son) from wkdy lunchtime bar snacks to good choice of meals inc several fish dishes, two dining rooms (one no smoking), sensibly priced wines; children in eating areas, garden tables, bedrooms in separate block behind, open all day Sun and summer Sats *(LYM, June and Ken Brooks, D Restarick)*

GRENOSIDE SK3394

Cow & Calf [3 miles from M1 junction 35; Skew Hill Lane]: Three connected rooms, one no smoking, high-backed settles, stripped stone and beams, reasonably priced lunchtime food, well kept low-priced Sam Smiths OB, tea and coffee; quiet piped music, music quiz nights; children welcome, family room in block across walled former farmyard with picnic-sets, splendid views over Sheffield, disabled access *(CMW, JJW, LYM)*

GRINTON SE0598

☆ *Bridge Inn* [B6270 W of Richmond]: Well run riverside inn, reasonably priced food inc good filled yorkshire puddings and all-day baguettes, prompt friendly service, warm intimate atmosphere and appealing décor with well spaced tables, well kept Jennings ales inc Dark Mild and a guest such as Adnams, pleasant restaurant area, pool in second bar; children and dogs welcome, attractive tables outside front and back, lovely spot opp Cathedral of the Dales, good walks, bedrooms with own bathrooms, open all day *(Mr and Mrs Maurice Thompson, David Field, David Reid, Matthew Shackle, Tony and Betty Parker, Andrew York)*

HACKFORTH SE2493

Greyhound: Clean, comfortable and attractive bar and separate dining room, enjoyable lunchtime food under new licensee *(R J Herd, Anna Cooper)*

HACKNESS SE9788

Everley: Comfortable lounge bar in stone-built hotel, well kept beers such as John Smiths and Greene King Ruddles County, landlady (who taught at catering college) cooks good food specialising in puddings, beautiful views from restaurant; bedrooms *(Colin and Dot Savill)*

HALIFAX SE0924

☆ *Shears* [Paris Gates, Boys Lane; OS Sheet 104 map ref 097241]: Down steep cobbled lanes among tall working textile mill buildings, roomy locals' bar with bays of plush banquettes and plenty of standing space, well kept Timothy Taylors Best, Golden Best, Landlord and Ram Tam and a guest beer, expert landlord (not

Tues); very popular for good cheap generous lunchtime food from hot-filled sandwiches to home-made pies, curries, casseroles etc; local sports photographs, big-screen sports TV; seats out above the Hebble Brook *(the Didler, BB, Tony Hobden, J R Ringrose)*

HALSHAM TA2727

Halsham Arms [B1362 Hedon—Withernsea]: Neat carpeted beamed dining room with banquettes, comfortable chairs and feature fireplace, opening into large pleasantly divided conservatory, good choice of enjoyable reasonably priced food, well kept Tetleys, respectable wines by the glass, cheerful enthusiastic well turned out staff, small locals' bar with darts and pool (also machines and piped music) *(Paul and Ursula Randall)*

HARDROW SD8691

Green Dragon: Traditional recently renovated Dales pub, well kept real ales inc Timothy Taylors Landlord and Theakstons XB, decent food, quick service, big main bar, beamed snug with big coal fire in old iron range; gives access (for a small fee) to Britain's highest single-drop waterfall; children welcome, bedrooms *(LYM, Jane Taylor, David Dutton, Andrew Stephenson, Kerry Law, Simon Smith)*

HARPHAM TA0961

St Quintin Arms [Main St]: Roomy old white-painted village pub, welcoming staff, wide choice of enjoyable beautifully presented food, well kept John Smiths and good range of other drinks; attractive garden with lawn and trellis, comfortable good value bedrooms *(Donald and Margaret Wood)*

HARROGATE SE3157

Gardeners Arms [Bilton Lane (off A59 either in Bilton itself or on outskirts towards Harrogate – via Bilton Hall Dr)]: Small 16th-c stone-built house converted into friendly old-fashioned local, totally unspoilt with tiny bar and three small rooms, tiled floors, panelling, old prints and little else; very cheap well kept Sam Smiths OB, decent bar lunches, coal fire in big stone fireplace; tables in good-sized surrounding streamside garden, lovely peaceful setting *(the Didler, D W Stokes)*

Old Bell [Royal Parade]: Relaxing pub with up to eight well kept ales such as Black Sheep, Copper Dragon, Daleside and Timothy Taylors Landlord from handsome bar counter, lots of continental bottled beers, friendly staff, enjoyable food, no smoking bar (former Farrahs toffee shop), upstairs no smoking evening restaurant; no children, music or machines, open all day *(Mr and Mrs P Eastwood, Patrick Hancock, Ben Whitney and Pippa Redmond, D W Stokes, Dr and Mrs A K Clarke, Jo Lilley, Simon Calvert, Andy and Jill Kassube)*

Winter Gardens [Royal Baths, Crescent Rd]: Amazing Wetherspoons transformation of former ballroom in landmark building, cheap well kept real ale; very busy late evening, open all day *(Dr and Mrs A K Clarke)*

HARTSHEAD SE1822

☆ *Gray Ox* [not very far from M62 junction 25]: Thriving relaxed atmosphere in stone-built moorland dining pub, great views, beams, flagstones and latticed windows, comfortable carpeted areas off inc no smoking room, good choice of generous tasty food from good sandwiches to upmarket main dishes and very popular Sun lunch (all afternoon), well kept Black Sheep, Timothy Taylors Landlord, Tetleys and Theakstons, long wine list, exemplary service – friendly, helpful and attentive; open all day Sun, picnic-sets outside *(Pat and Tony Martin, BB, Derek Earnshaw, Geoffrey and Brenda Wilson)*

HAWES SD8789

☆ *White Hart* [Main St]: Old-fashioned local bustling wknds and Tues market day, quieter on left, wide choice of good value generous food from sandwiches to some interesting hot dishes in bar and dining room, hot fire, well kept Black Sheep and John Smiths, decent carafe wines, welcoming brisk service, daily papers, darts and dominoes, juke box; occasional craft fairs upstairs, good value bedrooms, good breakfast *(BB, Don and Shirley Parrish)*

HAWNBY SE5489

Hawnby Hotel [off B1257 NW of Helmsley]: Attractive pub with good choice of consistently enjoyable generous food inc imaginative up-to-date dishes in spotless inn, well kept ales inc Black Sheep and John Smiths, unhurried service, owl theme in lounge, darts in tap room; views from pleasant garden tables, lovely village in picturesque remote walking country *(Dr and Mrs R G J Telfer, Derek and Sylvia Stephenson)*

HAWORTH SE0337

Fleece [Main St]: Open bar and small lounge, some panelling and flagstones, coal fires in stone fireplaces, full range of Timothy Taylors ales kept well, reasonably priced food, *Railway Children* film stills, restaurant *(Jim Abbott)*

Old White Lion [West Lane]: Good value home-made food, well kept Tetleys and Theakstons, friendly service, good restaurant (popular wknds, all day Sun); warm and comfortable, with plush banquettes and pleasant timber-effect décor; children welcome, very handy for museum, open all day, spotless comfortable bedrooms *(Jack and Rosalin Forrester, Karen Hands)*

HEBDEN BRIDGE SD9927

☆ *White Lion* [Bridge Gate]: Solid stone-built inn with comfortable bar and country-furnished bare-boards dining lounge, good choice of sound reasonably priced home cooking all day (just lunchtime Sun), fish specialities, well kept Boddingtons, Timothy Taylors Landlord and a guest beer, pleasant service; attractive secluded riverside garden, comfortable bedrooms *(Derek and Sylvia Stephenson, MJVK, John Fiander)*

HELMSLEY SE6184

☆ *Royal Oak* [Market Pl]: Two-bar inn recently stylishly refurbished in mildly Victorian mode, plenty of breweriana, well kept Camerons Strongarm and Marstons Pedigree from impressive central servery, good value simple substantial food from sandwiches to Sun lunch, different evening menu, welcoming landlord, quick service even though busy; pool in bare-boards back games area, piped music, TV; picnic-sets out behind, open all day, good bedrooms, big breakfast *(Michael Dandy, Richard Jennings, Michael Butler, Steve Whalley)*

HEMINGFIELD SE3901

Elephant & Castle [not far from M1 junction 36; Tingle Bridge Lane]: Friendly 17th-c waterside stone-built village local with lovely hanging baskets, well kept ales such as Black Sheep, good value food freshly made so may take a while, small helpings for children, large bar with piano, jugs on beams and delft shelf of teapots, step up to no smoking dining area; piped pop music, games machine; children welcome, benches around small fountain in front, picnic-sets and swing on grass by car park (which has CCTV), nearby walks *(CMW, JJW, Derek and Sylvia Stephenson, R T and J C Moggridge)*

HIGH HOYLAND SE2710

Cherry Tree [Bank End Lane; 3 miles W of M1 junction 38]: Clean and attractive stone-built village pub, low beams, brasses, cigarette card collections, friendly staff, well kept Eastwood & Sanders Bargee and Best, enjoyable simple lunchtime bar food and small popular restaurant (best to book, esp Sun lunch), open fire; lovely views over Cannon Hall Country Park from front *(DC)*

HIRST COURTNEY SE6124

Royal Oak [Main St]: Unpretentious local, friendly and relaxed, with well kept Tetleys, Easter beer festival, good value fresh lunchtime sandwiches and bargain evening meals, helpful friendly staff; children welcome, comfortable bedrooms, handy for Trans-Pennine cycle/walk route – they do packed lunches *(Ian and Sue Wells)*

HOLMFIRTH SD1408

Old Bridge [Market Walk]: Roomy and comfortable modernised beamed bar in small hotel, well kept Batemans XB, Black Sheep and Timothy Taylors Landlord, extensive wine list, wide choice of usual food all day from sandwiches and hot baguettes up, good service; bedrooms *(Peter Dandy, R T and J C Moggridge)*

Rose & Crown [aka The Nook; Victoria Sq]: Friendly family-run stone-built local with half a dozen well kept ales such as Black Sheep, Jennings, Moorhouses Black Cat Mild and Timothy Taylors Landlord, several rooms, real fire, tiled floor, low beams; occasional folk nights, tables outside, open all day *(the Didler, JP, PP)*

HORBURY SE3018

Boons [Queen St]: Lively, chatty and comfortably unpretentious, with well kept local Clarks, John Smiths and three or four quickly changing guest beers, simple lunchtime food, some flagstones, bare walls, Rugby League memorabilia, back tap room with pool and TV; very popular, can get crowded; no children, courtyard tables *(Michael Butler)*

Bulls Head [Southfield Lane]: Large relaxed pub well divided into more intimate areas, panelling and wood floors, library room, no smoking snug, popular food in bar and restaurant (busy wknds), Black Sheep and John Smiths, lots of wines by the glass; big car park *(Michael Butler)*

HORNSEA TA2047

Victoria [Market Pl]: Just refurbished, with stripped pine in bar, elegant dining room, enjoyable and interesting varied food (inc breakfast and tea), several real ales; pleasant seating area *(Fred and Lorraine Gill)*

HORSFORTH SE2438

Town Street Tavern [Town St]: New Market Town Taverns pub, largely no smoking, with well kept Black Sheep, Caledonian IPA, Timothy Taylors Landlord and four or five well kept changing guest beers, Erdinger wheat beer and an imported guest beer on tap, lots of continental bottled beers, friendly knowledgeable staff; upstairs bistro *(Andy Hemingway)*

HORTON IN RIBBLESDALE SD8172

☆ ***Crown*** [B6479 N of Settle]: Pretty pub by river, well placed for walkers (Pennine Way goes through car park, short walk from Settle—Carlisle line station), dark woodwork and lots of brass in cheerful low-ceilinged locals' bar with good fire and larger lounge, good value home cooking, well kept Black Sheep and Theakstons, welcoming helpful staff, restaurant; big garden behind, good value comfortable bedrooms *(R L Johnson, Guy Vowles, A H C Rainier, Joyce and Maurice Cottrell, Peter Heaton)*

HUDDERSFIELD SE1416

Head of Steam [Station, St Georges Sq]: Railway memorabilia, model trains, cars, buses and planes for sale, pies, sandwiches, baked potatoes and good value Sun roasts, four rooms inc no smoking eating area, hot coal fire, long bar with several well kept changing ales, lots of bottled beers, farm ciders, Gales fruit wines; jazz nights, can be very busy; platform tables to see the real trains pass, open all day *(JP, PP, Andy and Jill Kassube, Tony Hobden, J R Ringrose, Christine and Neil Townend)*

Slubbers Arms [Halifax Old Rd]: Warmly welcoming landlord in chatty V-shaped traditional pub with four excellently kept Timothy Taylors ales and a guest beer, a dozen good malt whiskies, and good range of simple wkdy lunchtime food (no chips); darts and dominoes *(CMW, JJW)*

Star [Albert St, Lockwood]: Well kept Eastwood & Sanders, Timothy Taylors and several changing beers inc a Mild in a friendly atmosphere, continental beers, farm cider, occasional well organised beer festivals, no juke box, pool or machines – or food (pie and peas some nights); growing bric-a-brac collection, customers' paintings; cl Mon, and lunchtime Tues-Thurs *(J R Ringrose, Andy and Jill Kassube)*

HULL TA0927

Bay Horse [Wincolmlee]: Popular unassuming corner local tied to Batemans, their beers kept well, good value basic food inc good home-made pies, pleasant licensees, open fire, raftered extension lounge/dining room, interesting brewery memorabilia; open all day *(JP, PP, the Didler)*

Olde Black Boy [High St, Old Town]: Appealing little black-panelled low-ceilinged front smoke room with carved fireplace, lofty 18th-c back vaults bar with leather seating, interesting Wilberforce-related posters etc, good value food lunchtime (not Sun) and late afternoon (not wknds), also Sun breakfast, friendly service, well kept real ales, country wines, old jugs and bottles, upstairs pool room and overflow wknd bar; darts, piano (live music Thurs), games machine; children allowed, open all day *(BB, the Didler)*

Olde Blue Bell [alley off Lowgate; look out for huge blue bell over pavement]: Friendly traditional 17th-c local with well kept cheap Sam Smiths OB, good value simple lunchtime food, three rooms off corridor, remarkable collection of bells, real fire; open all day exc Sun afternoon *(the Didler, BB)*

Spring Bank Tavern [Spring Bank]: Nice pub with long history, well kept interesting guest beers such as Archers Golden and Brains *(Giles and Annie Francis)*

HUSTHWAITE SE5275

☆ *Roasted Pepper* [Low St]: Former Blacksmiths Arms, more restaurant than pub now, imaginative spanish-flavour interior with warm cream and brown décor, stylish dark square tables on quarry tiles or sunken bare bricks, friendly staff, up-to-date food inc small helpings, tapas, sandwich bar and elaborate sandwiches, John Smiths and Theakstons, good choice of wines by the glass; terrace tables, cl Mon *(Janet and Peter Race, Mike and Lynn Robinson, JHBS, Dr and Mrs R G J Telfer)*

HUTTON RUDBY NZ4606

Bay Horse [North Side]: Comfortable low-beamed bar and larger main bar, enjoyable food from sandwiches and good value generous warm ciabattas to more substantial dishes here and in restaurant, well kept ales such as Black Sheep and Castle Eden, friendly helpful young staff; tables in immaculate big garden with lovely views over Leven Valley and church, pretty setting on village green *(Michael Doswell)*

ILKLEY SE1147

Bar t'at [Cunliffe Rd]: In small Market Town Taverns group, six real ales, decent wines and good helpings of good value brasserie food lunchtime and (not Tues or Sun) early evening, daily papers, cheerful efficient staff, spiral stairs down to light and airy no smoking bar; tables on back terrace *(David Coleman, Andy Hemingway)*

Cow & Calf [Hangingstone Rd (moors rd towards Hawksworth)]: Vintage Inn in stunning spot with lovely views over Ilkley and Wharfedale, well kept Bass and Tetleys, their usual reliable food, old-world décor and fine choice of wines by the glass; good bedrooms *(R M and M J Smith, R A K Crabtree)*

INGBIRCHWORTH SE2106

☆ *Fountain* [off A629 Shepley—Penistone; Welthorne Lane]: Emphasis on generous good value varied bar food inc exotic salads and superb puddings, very good lunchtime and early evening meal deals; well kept Black Sheep and John Smiths, good friendly service, neat and spacious red plush turkey-carpeted lounge, cosy front bar, comfortable family room, lots of beams, open fires; well reproduced piped music; tables in sizeable garden overlooking reservoir with pretty walks, comfortable bedrooms *(BB, Michael Butler, Patrick Hancock, G Dobson, Christine and Neil Townend)*

KEIGHLEY SE0641

Boltmakers Arms [East Parade]: Split-level open-plan local with particularly well kept Timothy Taylors Landlord, Best, Golden Best and guest beers, good value basic food all day, affable landlord, coal fire, nice brewing pictures; open all day, short walk from Worth Valley Rly *(the Didler)*

Globe [Parkwood St]: Refurbished local by Worth Valley steam railway track, wkdy lunches, Timothy Taylors ales; open all day *(the Didler)*

Roebuck [Skipton Rd, Utley (B6265 just N)]: Popular for very cheap good food lunchtime and early evening, pleasant friendly atmosphere, three real ales *(Dudley and Moira Cockroft)*

KETTLEWELL SD9672

☆ *Bluebell* [Middle Lane]: Roomy knocked-through 17th-c pub with snug simple furnishings, low beams and flagstones, cosy welcoming atmosphere, friendly landlord and regulars, well kept Greene King Ruddles County and Theakstons Old Peculier, good value food from sandwiches up in bar and attractive restaurant, children's room; pool room, piped music; seats out in front facing Wharfe bridge, more on good-sized back terrace, decent bedrooms, mainly in annexe *(Maggie and Tony Harwood, LYM, Michael Butler)*

☆ *Kings Head*: Cheerful old local away from centre, lively flagstoned main bar with log fire in big inglenook, comfortable snug around corner, discreet dining room, well kept Black Sheep, Littondale and Tetleys, reliable good value straightforward food, friendly service; bedrooms *(BB, Dr and Mrs D Woods, Lawrence Pearse, Michael Butler)*

☆ *Racehorses* [B6160 N of Skipton]: Comfortable and civilised, with generous good value food inc lunchtime rolls and baguettes and local game, well kept Black Sheep Best and Special and Theakstons Old Peculier, good wine choice, neat friendly staff, log fires; dogs welcome in front bar, picnic-sets (tops rather low, relative to seats) on attractive terrace, well placed for Wharfedale walks, good bedrooms with own bathrooms, open all day *(BB, D H Ford, DAV, Maggie and Tony Harwood, MDN, Michael Butler)*

KILBURN SE5179

☆ *Forresters Arms* [between A170 and A19 SW of Thirsk]: Next to Thompson furniture workshops (visitor centre opp) in pleasant village, handsomely furnished by them; big log fire, good home-made food from good value baguettes up, friendly staff, well kept real ales, side eating area, bar with TV and pool room, restaurant; well behaved children welcome, suntrap seats out in front, good value cheerful bedrooms, open all day *(LYM, Sue Wheeler, Mr and Mrs John Taylor)*

KILNSEA TA4015

☆ *Crown & Anchor* [Kilnsea Rd]: Great remote location overlooking eroding Spurn Point nature reserve and Humber estuary, with picnic-sets in back garden and out in front facing Humber estuary; single bar opening into two beamed lounges and linen-set restaurant, prints and bric-a-brac, friendly staff, well kept Tetleys and perhaps a guest beer such as Timothy Taylors Landlord, low-priced wines, above-average reasonably priced generous pub food inc good fresh fish; piped music; four bedrooms with own bathrooms, open all day *(Susan and Les Hornby, Paul and Ursula Randall, DC)*

KILNSEY SD9767

☆ *Tennants Arms*: Dramatic setting in good Wharfedale walking area, views of spectacular overhanging crag from restaurant, good range of good food, well kept Black Sheep, Tetleys and Theakstons Best and Old Peculier, log fire, prompt friendly service, several rooms, interesting decorations; piped music; comfortable immaculate bedrooms all with private bathrooms, good value *(JAE, David Findel-Hawkins, David and Pam Wilcox)*

KIRK DEIGHTON SE3950

Bay Horse [B6164 N of Wetherby]: Newly refurbished as dining pub by former Boston Spa restaurateurs, well kept Tetleys and/or a guest beer in newly flagstoned bar, enjoyable meals, reasonably priced wines *(Les and Sandra Brown)*

KIRK ELLA TA0229

Wheatsheaf [Packman Lane]: Roomy, pleasant and comfortable, with wide range of sensibly priced home-made food, Mansfield and guest beers, delightful floral displays *(Gordon B Thornton)*

KIRKBURTON SE1813

Foxglove [Penistone Rd (A629 SE of Huddersfield)]: Vintage Inn with enjoyable good value food all day, good lunchtime/afternoon sandwiches, wraps and ciabattas, good choice of wines by the glass; reasonably priced bedrooms *(Andy and Jill Kassube)*

KIRKBY OVERBLOW SE3249

Shoulder of Mutton [Main St]: Attractive pub with open fire each end of large bar, lots of sheep-related decorations, good range of real ales inc Timothy Taylors Landlord, several wines by the glass, no smoking end, enjoyable well priced food inc popular Sun lunch, upstairs restaurant; children welcome, tables in pleasant garden behind *(Andrew and Samantha Grainger)*

Star & Garter [off A61 S of Harrogate]: Roomy but cosy and relaxing old-fashioned pub, very popular lunchtime with older people for generous good value food inc imaginative specials, good vegetarian choice and Sun lunch, cheerful service, well kept Tetleys, decent wines, huge log fires, separate dining room; open all day, nice village setting *(Martin and Anne Muers)*

KIRKBYMOORSIDE SE6986

Kings Head [High Market Pl]: 16th-c inn with well priced food all home-made inc local fish, game and meat, interesting vegetarian menu, friendly service (newish licensees much in evidence), well kept beer, cosy lounge opening into sheltered courtyard and attractive garden, good log fire, unpretentious flagstoned walkers' bar (boots allowed); children welcome, bedrooms *(Sarah Davis, Rod Lambert, I D Barnett)*

KNARESBOROUGH SE3557

☆ *Blind Jacks* [Market Pl]: Charming and friendly multi-floor traditional tavern in 18th-c building, simple but attractive furnishings, brewery posters etc, well kept changing ales inc Black Sheep, Daleside, Rooster and Timothy Taylors, farm cider and foreign bottled beers, bubbly atmosphere downstairs, quieter up; well behaved children allowed away from bar, open all day wknds, cl Mon till 5.30 *(LYM, the Didler, Patrick Hancock, David Carr, Jo Lilley, Simon Calvert)*

Mother Shipton [Low Bridge; end of riverside Long Walk, by Beech Ave]: Charming spot with big terrace overlooking river (Easter tug-of-war with Half Moon on opp bank), beams, panelling, antique furnishings inc 16th-c oak table and interesting prints, good low-priced food inc good sandwiches, pleasant efficient service, well kept John Smiths and Theakstons; piped music *(Janet and Peter Race)*

LEEDS SE3033

Adelphi [Hunslet Rd]: Well restored handsome Edwardian mahogany screens, tiling and cut and etched glass, several rooms, impressive stairway; particularly well kept Tetleys Bitter, Mild and Imperial (virtually the brewery tap), prompt friendly service, good spread of lunchtime cheap food from hot baguettes up, crowded but convivial then; live jazz Sat *(the Didler, Ian Phillips, C J Fletcher)*

Duck & Drake [Kirkgate, between indoor market and Parish Church]: Two-bar pub with a dozen or more well kept reasonably priced ales inc plenty of Yorkshire ones, farm cider, good coal fires, basic furniture, bare boards and beer posters and mirrors; simple substantial low-priced lunchtime food from sandwiches to Sun lunches, friendly staff, games room with Yorkshire doubles dartboard as well as pool etc; juke box, big-screen sports TV, quiz nights, jazz nights Mon and Thurs; open all day *(the Didler, Pete Baker, C J Fletcher)*

Garden Gate [Whitfield Pl, Hunslet]: Down-to-earth local, ornate Victorian survivor in sea of modern housing, various rooms off central drinking corridor, intricate glass and woodwork, well kept Tetleys Bitter and Mild, farm cider, no food; open all day, can be lively evenings *(BB, the Didler)*

Grove [Back Row, Holbeck]: Well preserved 1930s-feel local, four rooms off drinking corridor, up to eight changing ales inc a Mild; live music nights; open all day *(the Didler)*

Palace [Kirkgate]: Well kept Ind Coope Burton, Tetleys and good changing guest beers in pleasantly uncityfied pub, polished wood, unusual lighting from electric candelabra to mock street lamps, lots of old prints, friendly helpful staff, good value lunchtime food from sandwiches up inc two-for-one bargains in no smoking dining area, may be bargain wine offers; games end with pool, TV, good piped music; tables out in front and in small heated back courtyard, open all day *(C J Fletcher)*

Viaduct [Lower Briggate]: Peaceful pleasantly furnished long narrow bar, lots of wood, well kept Tetleys and guest ales, popular lunchtime food, friendly helpful staff, no smoking area; actively caters for disabled customers, attractive back garden, open all day exc Sun afternoon *(the Didler)*

☆ ***Victoria*** [Gt George St, just behind Town Hall]: Opulent bustling early Victorian pub with grand cut and etched mirrors, impressive globe lamps extending from the majestic bar, imposing carved beams, booths with working snob-screens in lounge, smaller rooms off; well kept Black Sheep, Tetleys Best and Mild and three good changing guest beers, friendly efficient service by smart bar staff, reasonably priced food all day till early evening from sandwiches and light dishes up in luncheon room with end serving hatch, no smoking room; open all day *(Ian Phillips, the Didler, C J Fletcher)*

LEVISHAM SE8391

Horseshoe [off A169 N of Pickering]: Traditional neat local in delightful unspoilt village a steep walk up from station, brocaded seats, log fire in stone fireplace, bar billiards, well kept Theakstons Best, XB and Old Peculier, decent bar food, dominoes, no smoking restaurant; TV, piped music; children and dogs welcome, picnic-sets on attractive green, plenty of good walks, bedrooms, campsite behind, cl Sun evening and Mon in winter *(Fred and Lorraine Gill, Roger and Jenny Huggins, Joyce and Maurice Cottrell, LYM)*

LOFTHOUSE SE3325

Castle [Leeds Rd (the one nr Wakefield)]: Enjoyable lunchtime food, friendly staff and atmosphere, wide range of beers and spirits *(Ian Cowan)*

LOW MARISHES SE8278

School House: Fine isolated pub, beams hung with all sorts of unusual bric-a-brac, well kept local Hambleton, Tetleys and guests such as Elgoods and Thwaites, welcoming landlord and big pub dog, enjoyable simple blackboard food, eating area, games room with pool (doubles as locals' computer room), conservatory, no music; children and dogs welcome, charming garden, well on front terrace, interesting church opp, open all day Sun *(Kevin Thorpe)*

MALHAM SD9062

Buck [off A65 NW of Skipton]: Attractive and popular country inn, wide range of quickly served enjoyable generous home-made food from reasonably priced sandwiches up, well kept Black Sheep, Tetleys, Theakstons Best and (may be pricey) a guest beer, good value wines, good service, big log fire in plush panelled lounge, big basic hikers' bar, elegant candlelit dining room; picnic-sets in small garden, picture-book village, many good walks from the door, ten decent well equipped bedrooms *(DAV, Guy Vowles, Andy and Jill Kassube)*

Listers Arms [off A65 NW of Skipton]: Grand creeper-covered stone-built inn with easy-going open-plan lounge, busy wknds, good value wholesome traditional food inc enterprising sandwiches, well kept changing ales inc Black Sheep, lots of continental beers and malt whiskies, good service, roaring fire, friendly cat, restaurant famous for steaks (good wine list), games area; children and dogs welcome, seats out overlooking small green, more in back garden – nice spot by river, ideal for walkers; comfortable modern bedrooms *(Anna Graham)*

MALTON SE7871

Crown [Wheelgate]: In same family for generations, chatty basic town bar with strong horse-racing links (and racing TV on bar), good Malton Crown Double Chance (low price), Golden Chance and a seasonal beer from their back brewhouse, well kept guest beers, popular food (not Sun, sandwiches only Tues, bookings only evenings), daily papers; lots of local notices, beer festivals Jun and Dec; children welcome in back courtyard nicely redone as conservatory (occasional live music here), good value bedrooms *(BB, Mr and Mrs Maurice Thompson, Kevin Thorpe)*

Wentworth Arms [Town St, Old Malton]: Enjoyable food from well filled baguettes up in bar and big dining room, sensible helpings, well kept ales inc guests such as Daleside and Wold, decent wines, friendly local atmosphere, quick service and good housekeeping; children welcome *(Pat and Tony Martin, Brian and Janet Ainscough, C A Hall, Marlene and Jim Godfrey)*

MANFIELD NZ2213

Crown [Vicars Lane]: Friendly and old-fashioned village local with Village White Boar and Bull, several interesting changing guest beers, enjoyable food from good sandwiches up; pool, unobtrusive juke box, Tues quiz night *(Tim Wellock, Andrew York)*

MARSDEN SE0412

Railway [Station Rd]: Recently refurbished, with enjoyable reasonably priced food from filled baked potatoes to steak, good carvery Sun lunch, bargain wkdy early suppers; well kept Burtonwood and other ales such as Brains SA and Moorhouses Pendle Witches Brew *(Pam and John Smith)*

☆ ***Riverhead*** [Peel St, next to Co-op; just off A62 Huddersfield—Oldham]: Busy basic pub in converted grocer's, spiral stairs down to microbrewery (tours available) producing good range of interesting beers named after local reservoirs, the higher the reservoir, the higher the strength, inc Mild, Stout and Porter, farm cider, thriving friendly atmosphere in big ground-floor bar, enjoyable food upstairs, unobtrusive piped music, no food or machines; wheelchair access, streamside tables, cl wkdy lunchtimes, open from 4pm, all day wknds, nice stop after walk by Huddersfield Broad Canal or on the hills *(the Didler, Guy Vowles, Tony Hobden)*

Swan [Station Rd]: Well kept Thwaites Bitter and Mild and guest beers in neat and friendly town pub with good value bar food, dining room with waitress service (Sun lunch popular) *(Tony Hobden, the Didler)*

Tunnel End [Reddisher Rd (off A62 via Peel St)]: Four big rooms (one no smoking) refurbished but keeping quietly homely feel, big log fire in back room, well kept ales, decent food at fair prices inc Sun roasts; overlooks mouth of recently restored Standedge Canal Tunnel – at three miles under the Pennines, the UK's longest *(Bill Sykes, Clifford Payton)*

MARTON CUM GRAFTON SE4263

Olde Punch Bowl [signed off A1 3 miles N of A59]: Comfortable and attractive, with well kept Black Sheep and Timothy Taylors Landlord, decent wines, cheerful staff, good if not cheap food from imaginative sandwiches to interesting lunchtime blackboard choice, even more ambitious evening menu, roomy heavy-beamed open-plan bar, open fires, brasses, framed old advertisements and photographs, restaurant, no piped music; children welcome, good play area and picnic-sets in pleasant garden *(Michael Doswell, LYM, John Knighton, F J Robinson, Bill and Lisa Copeland)*

MASHAM SE2381

☆ ***Black Sheep Brewery*** [Crosshills]: Not exactly a pub, but well worth a visit; alongside the brewery (interesting tours), this cavernous mill shed has a great atmosphere despite its size, with good imaginative mediterranean-leaning food all day inc nice puddings in a thriving modern bistro-style café-bar and upper gallery, plenty of friendly enthusiastic staff, a sales area with some worthwhile beery tourist trinkets, and on the left the Baa'r with Black Sheep's full ale range kept well and a good choice of wines; good family facilities inc play area; cl 5 Mon and late winter Sun evenings, can be very busy *(Tim and Carolyn Lowes, Dr and Mrs Jackson, Steve Whalley, H Bramwell, Ian and Nita Cooper, Gerry and Rosemary Dobson, Paul and Ursula Randall, M and GR)*

☆ ***White Bear*** [Wellgarth, Crosshills; signed off A6108 opp turn into town]: Appealing and carefully restored old two-room stone-built pub full of interesting bric-a-brac, lively atmosphere, well kept Theakstons, pleasant attentive staff, bar food; attractive terrace, open all day *(the Didler, LYM, Janet and Peter Race)*

MEXBOROUGH SK4799

Concertina Band Club [Dolcliffe Rd]: Friendly pubby club welcoming visitors, brewing its own good changing ales, also well kept guest beers; large bar with stage and small games area with pool, other games and SkyTV; cl Sun lunchtime *(the Didler)*

MIDDLEHAM SE1288

☆ ***Black Swan*** [Market Pl]: Welcoming ivy-covered 17th-c stone-built inn with high-backed settles by the heavy-beamed bar's big stone fireplace, racing memorabilia on stripped stone walls, well kept Black Sheep Bitter, John Smiths and Theakstons Best, Old Peculier and XB, convivial landlord, wide choice of food from lunchtime sandwiches and baked potatoes to restaurant meals and popular Sun carvery, family room with TV and children's videos; tables out in front and in sheltered back garden, good bedrooms with own bathrooms, nice breakfast, good walking country *(Angus Lyon, Michael Butler, LYM, Ian and Nita Cooper, Blaise Vyner, Mike and Margaret Newton, Greta and Christopher Wells, Michael Tack)*

MIDDLETON SE7885

Middleton Arms [Church Lane]: Refurbished by new owners and now entirely no smoking pub, with good food at sensible prices, good value wines, nice coffee *(Peter and Anne-Marie O'Malley)*

MIDDLETON TYAS NZ2205

Shoulder of Mutton [just E of A1 Scotch Corner roundabout]: Friendly warren of small rooms and different-level nooks, dark woodwork, wide choice of enjoyable generous quickly served bar food inc reasonably priced light lunches and good specials (best to book wknds – serves Sun evening too), well kept Black Sheep and Marstons Pedigree, good coffee, agreeable service *(D G Bayley, Richard Cole, Michael Doswell)*

MIDHOPESTONES SK2399

Old Mustard Pot [Mortimer Rd, off A616]: Enjoyable reasonably priced bar food at nice tables, welcoming atmosphere and fast friendly unobtrusive service, open fire in beamed bar area, domestic memorabilia; separate lounge with easy chairs and settees for Tues-Sat evening restaurant, and good Sun lunch with pianist; three bedrooms with own bathrooms *(anon)*

MILLINGTON SE8351

☆ ***Gate***: Mix of old and newer furnishings inc high-backed screening settle and unusual yew-wood tables and chairs in friendly 16th-c beamed village pub run by ex-farming family, big inglenook log or coal fire, good homely food from sandwiches to good Sun lunch, well kept John Smiths, pool in back games room; Weds country & western night; children and dogs welcome, unspoilt village in good Wolds walking country *(LYM, Sheila and Don Sanders)*

MIRFIELD SE2017

Hare & Hounds [Liley Lane (B6118 2m S)]: Wide choice of good value food from enterprising lunchtime sandwiches to interesting main dishes, friendly efficient service, welcoming atmosphere, decent wines, no smoking eating area; can get very busy; tables outside, views towards Huddersfield *(Andy and Jill Kassube)*

MOULTON NZ2303

☆ ***Black Bull*** [just off A1 nr Scotch Corner]: Interesting black-beamed bar with individual comfortably worn in furnishings and big log fire, some good substantial and unusual lunchtime bar dishes, side dark-panelled seafood bar with high seats at marble-topped counter, evening restaurant meals (Brighton Belle dining car as well as polished conservatory), good wines, sherries and spirits (keg beers), jolly waitresses; no under-7s; courtyard seats under trees, cl Sun *(David and Iris Hunter, Mr and Mrs J E C Tasker, LYM, Mrs A Widdup, David Field, Alison Hayes, Pete Hanlon, Alan Cole, Kirstie Bruce, Marlene and Jim Godfrey, Greta and Christopher Wells)*

MUKER SD9097

☆ ***Farmers Arms*** [B6270 W of Reeth]: Basic friendly local in beautiful valley village, well placed both for rewarding walks and interesting drives, warm open fire, friendly landlord, real ale such as Black Sheep, darts and dominoes; gents' long due for an upgrade; children welcome, self-catering studio flat *(A H C Rainier, LYM, Jane Taylor, David Dutton, Tony and Ann Bennett-Hughes, Richard and Anne Ansell, Ben Whitney and Pippa Redmond, Matthew Shackle, Rona Murdoch)*

NEWHOLM NZ8610

☆ ***Beehive*** [signed off A171]: Long and attractive 16th-c pub with low black beams in its two snug bar rooms, enterprising good value cooking inc local seafood for bar and restaurant, well kept Rudgate, John Smiths Magnet and Theakstons Old Peculier, log fire, friendly landlord; children allowed in back room, tables outside, reasonably priced bedrooms with own bathrooms *(LYM, Catherine Poole, Robert Farley)*

NEWTON-ON-OUSE SE5160

Dawnay Arms [off A19 N of York]: Attractive comfortably worn in 18th-c inn nr Beningbrough Hall, lots of beamery, brass and copper, good log fire, bar food from sandwiches up inc early-evening bargains, well kept Greene King IPA, Old Speckled Hen and Tetleys, dozens of malt whiskies, no smoking river-view restaurant; piped music, no dogs; children in eating area, neat lawn running down to moorings on River Ouse, tables on terrace, play area *(Roger A Bellingham, Edward Leetham, LYM, Mr and Mrs J E C Tasker, Michael Dandy, Dr and Mrs R G J Telfer)*

NORLAND SE0522

Hobbit [Hob Lane, West Bottom]: Wide choice of good value filling food, Tetleys and guest beers such as Adnams and Greene King Old Speckled Hen, decent wines, helpful friendly staff, restaurant and separate bistro; lots of events and theme nights from karaoke to murder mysteries and medieval (k)nights – possibly intrusive if you're staying and don't want to join in the fun; not easy to reach (steeply up hill from Sowerby Bridge police stn); open all day, comfortable bedrooms, great views *(Nigel Epsley)*

NORTH GRIMSTON SE8467

Middleton Arms: Comfortable locally popular dining pub, cheery service, good value usual food from sandwiches and baked potatoes up, well kept Stones and Tetleys; lovely garden, nice Wolds-edge spot *(Colin and Dot Savill)*

NORTH NEWBALD SE9136

☆ ***Tiger*** [off A1034 S of Mkt Weighton; The Green]: Proper village pub of considerable character, on big green surrounded by rolling hills, handy for Wolds Way walking; roaring fire, short choice of good home-made food from fine sandwiches up, OAP lunches, consistently well kept ales such as Black Sheep, John Smiths, Timothy Taylors Landlord, Tetleys and York, games room; open all day *(LYM, Derek and Sylvia Stephenson)*

NORTHALLERTON SE3794

Tithe Bar [Friarage St]: Four quickly changing well kept real ales, masses of continental bottled beers, friendly staff, traditional settle and armchairs in one area, two rooms with tables and chairs on bare boards – in small Market Town Taverns group; restaurant upstairs; open all day *(Tim and Carolyn Lowes, Anna Cooper)*

OAKWORTH SE0138

☆ ***Grouse*** [Harehills, Oldfield; 2 miles towards Colne]: Comfortable, interesting and spotless old pub in undisturbed hamlet, lots of bric-a-brac, gleaming copper and china, prints, cartoons and caricatures, dried flowers, attractively individual furnishings; locally very popular for huge range of well presented good generous home-made lunchtime bar food (not Mon) from soup and baguettes up, charming evening restaurant, well kept Timothy Taylors, good range of spirits, entertaining landlord; fine surroundings and Pennine views *(Andy and Jill Kassube, JAE, Geoffrey and Brenda Wilson)*

OSMOTHERLEY SE4597

Queen Catherine [West End]: Good family pub, welcoming atmosphere, roomy modern décor with old local prints, popular reasonably priced hearty food inc good Sun lunch with proper yorkshire puddings and fresh veg, Tetleys and a well kept guest beer such as Hambleton, friendly service; simple but comfortable bedrooms with own bathrooms, good breakfast *(Geoff and Angela Jaques, C A Hall)*

OSSETT SE2719

☆ ***Brewers Pride*** [Low Mill Rd/Healey Lane (long cul-de-sac by railway sidings, off B6128)]: Warmly friendly basic local brewing its own good beers, four well kept guest beers, cosy front room and bar both with open fires, brewery memorabilia, small games room, enjoyable lunchtime food (not Sun) and pie or curry night Weds; quiz night Mon, popular folk club Thurs; big back garden with local entertainment summer wknds, nr Calder & Hebble Canal, open all day Fri-Sun *(JHBS, JP, PP, the Didler)*

OSWALDKIRK SE6278

☆ ***Malt Shovel*** [signed off B1363/B1257 S of Helmsley]: Attractive former small 17th-c manor house with heavy beams and flagstones, fine staircase, simple traditional furnishings, huge log fires, two cosy bars, family room, interestingly decorated dining room, well kept Sam Smiths OB, friendly landlord, enjoyable food; views from good unusual garden *(LYM, David Butterworth)*

OTLEY SE2045

☆ ***Rose & Crown*** [Bondgate]: Convivial and comfortable stone-built pub with lots of prints in cosy olde-worlde beamed bar, interesting range of good value fresh generous home-made food (not Fri-Sat evenings) from baguettes up, well kept ales inc guests, decent wines, good friendly service, small restaurant; can be busy lunchtime; pleasant terrace *(D Hamilton, Sally Corcoran)*

OTTRINGHAM TA2624

White Horse [A1033]: Comfortable and pleasantly divided open-plan local, beams and bare bricks, carpets and banquettes, bar food and wknd upstairs carvery, well kept John Smiths and Tetleys, friendly service, collection of hurricane lamps, brassware and jugs; small TV, unobtrusive piped music, games machine *(Paul and Ursula Randall)*

OXENHOPE SE0335

☆ ***Waggon & Horses*** [Dyke Nook; A6033 Keighley—Hebden Bridge]: Welcoming well run stripped-stone moorside pub brewing its own Oxenhope ales such as HoHoHo, Dark Mild and Old Tower, a Timothy Taylors guest, good range of generous food and good wine choice, open fires, pleasant simple décor, separate dining room; children welcome, good views *(LYM, Richard Houghton, D J Etheridge)*

PATRINGTON TA3122

Hildyard Arms [Market Pl]: Cheerful and friendly old coaching inn, two tastefully refurbished bars, appealing pictures and china in no smoking dining room, wide range of reasonably priced generous food inc children's and Fri steak bargain for two, well kept Bass, Tetleys and a guest such as Adnams; piped music *(Alan Thwaite, Paul and Ursula Randall)*

PENISTONE SE2402

Cubley Hall [Mortimer Rd, out towards Stocksbridge]: Handsome and rather grand, in big garden with plenty of tables, good playground and distant views; panelling, elaborate plasterwork, mosaic tiling and plush furnishings, roomy conservatory, wide choice of bar food all day, well kept Greene King Abbot and Old Speckled Hen, Marstons Pedigree and Charles Wells Bombardier, decent wines, no smoking room; piped music, fruit machine, TV; children welcome, bedrooms with own bathrooms, open all day *(Graham Holden, Julie Lee, Derek and Sylvia Stephenson, Graham Dobson, LYM, Charles Harvey, Trevor and Judy Pearson)*

POOL SE2546

Hunters [A658 towards Harrogate]: Split-level country pub with up to nine well kept ales from locals like Daleside and Roosters to far-flung novelties, Saxon farm cider, helpful staff, simple lunchtime food (not Tues) from sandwiches to popular Sun lunch, balcony for warm weather, open fires for cold, pool, dominoes, table skittles; a popular young meeting place; open all day *(Mr and Mrs Maurice Thompson, Richard Dixon, Andy and Jill Kassube)*

☆ ***White Hart*** [Just off A658 S of Harrogate, A659 E of Otley]: Popular and relaxing Vintage Inn family dining pub, four mainly no smoking and flagstoned olde-worlde rooms with assorted farmhouse furnishings, two big log fires and country décor, friendly service even when busy, well kept Bass and Tetleys, good choice of wines by the glass, their usual food from lunchtime sandwiches to steaks and Sun roasts; piped music; children welcome, pleasant tables outside, good walking country, open all day *(Marian and Andrew Ruston, Hugh A MacLean, LYM, Ray and Winifred Halliday, Roy and Lindsey Fentiman, Michael Butler)*

PUDSEY SE2131

Bankhouse [Scholebroke Lane]: Cosy Tudor-style pub charmingly decorated with lots of china and brass, several nooks and alcoves, warm lighting and comfortable chairs, popular wkdy baguettes, Black Sheep and changing guest beers, restaurant with substantial Sun roast; front terrace picnic-sets *(anon)*

Worlds End [Wesley Sq]: Thriving atmosphere, with the feel of an authentic irish bar, well kept Daleside, Theakstons Old Peculier and guest beers, popular Sun roasts; frequent live folk and jazz *(anon)*

RAINTON SE3675

Bay Horse [under a mile from A1 Boroughbridge—Leeming Bar, N of A168]: Enjoyable up-to-date food under friendly new young owners in low-beamed pub, three rooms off quaint central bar area with cooking memorabilia, open fires, particularly good service, well kept John Smiths, Theakstons and so forth *(David and Ruth Shillitoe)*

RAMSGILL SE1171

☆ ***Yorke Arms*** [Nidderdale]: Upmarket small hotel, small bar with some heavy Jacobean furniture and log fires, well kept Black Sheep Special, a fine wine list, good choice of spirits and fresh juices, good if pricey full meals (they've been insisting on at least two courses) in smart no smoking restaurant; piped music, cribbage and dominoes, no under-12s even in restaurant; good quiet moorland and reservoir walks *(Lynda and Trevor Smith, LYM, Howard and Margaret Buchanan, Keith Moss)*

REDMIRE SE0491

Bolton Arms: Traditional yorkshire village pub with small neat bar and dining room, good value generous main dishes and puddings inc popular Sun lunch, well kept Black Sheep, John Smiths, Theakstons and a seasonal beer, friendly helpful staff, exemplary lavatories;

popular with walkers, handy for Bolton Castle *(Mr and Mrs Maurice Thompson, Jim Abbott, Carol and Dono Leaman)*

REETH SE0499

Buck: Comfortably modernised and well run, with good varied food in bar and restaurant, sensible prices and good helpings, well kept Black Sheep Bitter, Best and Special and Theakstons Old Peculier, welcoming atmosphere, efficient, friendly and obliging service even when busy – it's very popular with hikers; a few tables out in front, beautifully placed village, bedrooms, good breakfast *(Revd J S B Crossley, Bill and Sheila McLardy, R Halsey, Tim and Ann Newell)*

Kings Arms [Market Pl (B6270)]: Popular beamed dining pub by green, pine pews around walls, huge log fire in 18th-c stone inglenook, quieter room behind; good reasonably priced food inc adventurous dishes, well kept Black Sheep, full Theakstons range and a guest beer, friendly efficient service; may be piped music; children very welcome, tables outside, bedrooms *(Gerry and Rosemary Dobson, David Reid)*

RILLINGTON SE8574

Coach & Horses [Scarborough Rd]: Unpretentious village local with vast china cat collection in spotless lounge, generous straightforward food at bargain prices inc proper pies and Sun roast, friendly landlord, well kept Tetleys *(Colin and Dot Savill)*

RIPON SE3171

Turf [Ripon Spa Hotel, Park St]: Comfortable bar with reliable bar food, good range of real ales; bedrooms in parent hotel *(Janet and Peter Race)*

Unicorn [Market Pl E]: Cheerful and popular traditional bar with good mix of customers and comfortable seating, enjoyable bar meals; hotel bedrooms *(Janet and Peter Race)*

RIPPONDEN SE0319

Beehive [Hob Lane, off Cross Wells Rd]: Well run small open-plan hillside pub with well kept ales such as Greene King Old Speckled Hen, Moorhouses and Timothy Taylors Landlord, flagstones and open fires, three steps up to dining area, consistently good modestly priced food from good range of bar snacks through early evening tapas to fresh fish and other restaurant dishes *(Herbert and Susan Verity)*

☆ *Old Bridge* [off A58; Priest Lane]: Civilised 14th-c pub in lovely setting by medieval packhorse bridge, great atmosphere, oak settles in thick stone walls, rush-seated chairs, a few well chosen pictures and a big woodburner, no smoking areas, good selection of tasty sandwiches and short choice of rather bistroish food (not Sat-Sun evening), good friendly service, well kept Timothy Taylors ales, 30 malt whiskies, a good choice of foreign beers and interesting wines by the glass; children in eating areas, seats outside, open all day wknds *(LYM, Mrs Yvette Bateman, Roger and Anne Newbury, James Storey)*

RISPLITH SE2468

Black-a-Moor: Dining pub with good atmosphere and enjoyable food *(Janet and Peter Race)*

ROSEDALE ABBEY SE7295

☆ *White Horse* [300 yds up Rosedale Chimney Bank – entering village, first left after Coach House Inn]: Farm-based and dog-friendly country inn in lovely spot above the village, well worn in character bar, well kept Black Sheep, John Smiths and Timothy Taylors Landlord, quite a few wines and good choice of malt whiskies, friendly service, good log fire, generous bar food from sandwiches and ploughman's up, great views from terrace (and from restaurant and bedrooms); TV, piped music; children allowed if eating, occasional jazz nights, open all day Sat; bedrooms, good walks *(LYM, R M Corlett, Joyce and Maurice Cottrell)*

ROTHERHAM SK4792

Brush & Easel [Fleming Way]: Doing well after reopening under friendly new management, well kept beer and good entertainment *(Suzie)*

SALTAIRE SE1438

Boathouse [Victoria Rd]: Looks more like converted tearooms than pub but has all the right virtues: well kept Black Sheep, John Smiths and Timothy Taylors Landlord, good wine choice, wide-ranging enjoyable food, open fire; nice spot looking across park by River Aire, handy for this World Heritage Site *(Mrs Dilys Unsworth, Roy and Lindsey Fentiman)*

SALTBURN-BY-THE-SEA NZ6621

☆ *Ship* [A174 towards Whitby]: Beautiful setting among beached fishing boats, sea views from tasteful nautical-style black-beamed bars and big plainer summer dining lounge with handsome ship model; wide choice of reasonably priced usual food, quick friendly service, evening restaurant (not Sun), children's room and menu, Theakstons, seats outside; busy at holiday times, smuggling exhibition next door *(LYM, Mike and Lynn Robinson)*

SANCTON SE9039

Star [King St (A1034 S of Mkt Weighton)]: Newly modernised, new young chef/landlord doing good blackboard food listing sources, bar with two real ales, good wines by the glass, small restaurant *(C A Hall)*

SAWDON TA9484

Anvil [Main St]: Former smithy in small village, relaxed family-friendly atmosphere, well kept Black Sheep and southern guest beers unusual for the area, good hearty food *(Patrick Renouf)*

SAXTON SE4736

☆ *Greyhound* [by church in village, 2½ miles from A1 via B1217]: Charming unchanging medieval stone-built local by church in attractive quiet village, well kept cheap Sam Smiths OB tapped from the cask, three small unspoilt rooms on linking corridor, old prints, open fires and settles, masses of china plates; TV in room on right, no food; a couple of picnic-sets in side yard with attractive hanging baskets, open all day wknds *(LYM, Kevin Thorpe, Len Beattie)*

SCALING DAM NZ7412

Grapes [Guisborough Rd (A171, opp reservoir)]: Large open-plan pub with beamed original core, red plush banquettes, open fire, spacious restaurant, decent food inc fresh fish, Tetleys, prompt friendly service; bedrooms *(Andrew York)*

SCARBOROUGH TA0488

Angel [North St]: Friendly and neatly kept; pleasant courtyard *(Margaret and Roy Randle)*

Highlander [Esplanade]: Magnificent collection of whiskies (tartan curtains and carpet too), well kept Tetleys and guest beers such as Black Sheep, Greene King and Jenkinsons, good value pub food from generous sandwiches up, friendly obliging service, civilised mature atmosphere, sea views from front bar; front courtyard tables, bedrooms, handy for South Bay beach *(C J Fletcher, Fred and Lorraine Gill)*

Lord Rosebery [Westborough]: Large handsome Wetherspoons in former Co-op (and once the local Liberal HQ), in traffic-free central shopping area; galleried upper bar, well kept cheap beers inc interesting guests, enjoyable food inc Sun roast, obliging staff; disabled facilities, open all day, very busy and lively evenings *(C J Fletcher, David Carr, Derek and Margaret Underwood)*

Tap & Spile [Falsgrave Rd]: Three rooms, bare boards or flagstones, changing well kept ales, farm cider, efficient good-humoured staff, home-made food inc barbecues, no smoking room; frequent live music *(the Didler)*

SCRUTON SE3092

Coore Arms [off A1 via A684; Station Rd]: Old family-run inn with friendly helpful staff, enjoyable reasonably priced food, particular care over vegetables (and plenty for vegetarians) *(Sheila Stothard)*

SETTLE SD8163

Royal Oak [Market Pl (B6480, off A65 bypass)]: Large market-town inn with lots of highly waxed ornate oak panelling in spotless roomy and congenial partly divided open-plan bar, well kept real ales inc local ones, comfortable seats around brass-topped tables, restaurant, no smoking area; children welcome, bedrooms with own bathrooms, open all day *(LYM, Paul Davies)*

SHEFFIELD SK3089

Admiral Rodney [Loxley Rd (B6077 W)]: Friendly, roomy pub above Rivelin Valley, wide choice of enjoyable food inc carvery restaurant, good choice of real ales *(Matthew Lidbury)*

Bankers Draft [Market Pl]: Good value Wetherspoons bank conversion, clean, tidy and very popular, bars on two roomy floors, standard food all day, good range of real ales, decent wines, friendly staff, lots of old prints, no smoking areas; good disabled facilities, open all day *(P G Topp, Patrick Hancock)*

Bath [Victoria St, off Glossop Rd]: Cosy local, two small well restored rooms with nice woodwork, local Barnsley, Kelham Island and Wentworth with changing guest beers *(the Didler)*

Carlton [Attercliffe Rd]: Tiny one-roomed traditional pub, warm welcome, well kept John Smiths Magnet, pool and darts in small back room *(Patrick Hancock)*

☆ ***Cask & Cutler*** [Henry St; Shalesmoor tram stop right outside]: Convivial and cheery alehouse, six or seven good often rare changing ales, occasional Port Mahon beers from its own back microbrewery, interesting dutch and belgian bottled beers, farm ciders and perry, coal fire in no smoking lounge on left, friendly licensees, cat and lovable dog, appropriate posters, occasional hot snacks or cobs, daily papers, pub games, good Nov beer festival; wheelchair access, open all day Fri-Sat, cl Mon lunchtime, tables in nice back garden *(the Didler, JP, PP, Patrick Hancock, Andrew York)*

Castle [Twentywell Rd, Bradway]: Stone-built two-bar pub in attractive spot, sensibly priced food (not Sun evening) inc OAP lunches, Boddingtons, Tetleys and Timothy Taylors Landlord, good soft drinks choice, friendly service and atmosphere, books to read, restaurant; quiet piped music, games machines; children welcome *(CMW, JJW)*

Cocked Hat [just off Attercliffe Common (A6178)]: Largely open-plan, tasteful dark colours, brewery memorabilia, well kept Marstons Pedigree, good value lunchtime food *(Patrick Hancock)*

☆ ***Devonshire Cat*** [Wellington Street]: Bright and airy contemporary café/bar with plenty of room inc no smoking area, polished light wood, some parquet, big flower pictures, friendly staff knowledgeable about the dozen well kept mainly yorkshire real ales, more tapped from the cask in glazed stillage (Kelham Island brew one for the pub), masses of bottled beers, two farm ciders, tea and coffee, good value food from end servery, plenty of board games; air conditioning, well reproduced piped music, TV, live music Weds, quiz night Mon; open all day *(the Didler, David Carr, Patrick Hancock, Richard Houghton)*

Fagans [Broad Lane]: Warm and welcoming old pub with long bar, fresh lunchtime food, friendly staff, well kept Barnsley IPA and Tetleys, plenty of malt whiskies, no juke box; good folk night Fri *(Patrick Hancock)*

Fulwood [Tapton Park Rd]: Stone-built private house converted to large pub, lots of wood and some original features, old Sheffield pictures, Thwaites real ales, good soft drinks choice, food all day inc carvery, raised no smoking dining area, pool and games machine at other end; piped music; disabled access, children welcome, picnic-sets on terrace *(CMW, JJW)*

Gardeners Rest [Neepsend Lane]: Well kept Timothy Taylors and several guest beers (often the full range from one microbrewery), farm cider, continental beers on tap and in bottle, friendly beer-enthusiast landlord, no smoking lounge with old brewery memorabilia, lunchtime food, daily papers, games inc bar billiards (free Mon), changing artwork; frequent live music, poetry/story-telling nights, quiz Sun; disabled access and facilities, conservatory and tables out behind overlooking River Don, open all day *(JP, PP, the Didler, Patrick Hancock)*

☆ ***Hillsborough*** [Langsett Rd/Wood St; by Primrose View tram stop]: Pub-in-hotel with well kept Edale ales at attractive prices, also lots of guest beers, friendly staff, bare-boards bar, lounge, no smoking room with fire, views to ski slope from attractive back conservatory and terrace tables, daily papers; good filled rolls and plans for hot food, TV, Sun music night; good value bedrooms with own bathrooms, covered parking, real ale bar open only Thurs-Sun evenings, from 4.30 *(the Didler, JP, PP, CMW, JJW, Patrick Hancock)*

☆ ***Kelham Island Tavern*** [Kelham Island]: Well run comfortable and relaxed backstreet local with well kept Pictish Brewers Gold at bargain price, half a dozen or more beers from other small brewers, continental imports, farm cider, lunchtime food from filled cobs up (not Mon), no smoking room planned; Sun folk night, open all day exc Mon lunchtime and Sun afternoon *(the Didler, Richard Houghton, Patrick Hancock)*

Kings Head [Poole Rd, off Prince of Wales Rd, Darnall; not far from M1 junctions 33/34]: Low-priced food from sandwiches up, real ales such as Courage Directors and Tetleys, tabloid dailies, comfortable lounge (part no smoking); big-screen TV, may be quiet piped music; children welcome, covered heated tables in small back floodlit yard with barbecue, lots of plants and small water feature, bedrooms *(CMW, JJW)*

Lord Nelson [Arundel St]: Corner local known locally as Fanny's, well kept Hardys & Hansons and a guest beer; busy before Sheffield United home games *(Patrick Hancock)*

Noahs Ark [Crookes]: Well kept Flowers IPA, John Smiths Magnet, Tetleys and two to five guest beers, huge range of simple cheap filling food (not Sun evening) all freshly prepared, so may be a wait, inc bargains, dedicated long-serving landlord and pleasant staff, good soft drinks choice; dominoes, pool, games machine, TV, unobtrusive piped music, Weds quiz night; disabled facilities, open all day *(Peter F Marshall, CMW, JJW)*

Peacock [Stannington Rd]: Large stone-built Thwaites pub open all day for quite a wide choice of low-priced food inc OAP bargains – service may slow a bit when very busy; four real ales inc a Mild, good soft drinks choice, no smoking area; events most nights, disabled access *(CMW, JJW)*

Red Deer [Pitt St]: Lively backstreet local surrounded by Univ buildings, plenty of well kept popular real ales from central bar, wide choice of good value simple lunchtime food, extended lounge with pleasant raised back area; open all day wkdys *(the Didler, Patrick Hancock, Michael Ward)*

Red House [Solly St]: Small backstreet pub with well kept ales such as Adnams, Greene King IPA and Jennings, charming licensees (and big dog), panelled front room, back snug, comfortable chairs and banquettes, delft shelf of china, good value wkdy lunchtime food, pool, darts and cards in main bar; occasional folk music *(DC, the Didler, Pete Baker, Patrick Hancock)*

Red Lion [Charles St, nr stn]: Traditional local, comfortable rooms off welcoming central bar, ornate fireplaces and coal fires, attractive panelling and etched glass, good simple lunchtime food, small back dining room, pleasant conservatory, usually have well kept Stones and Theakstons *(the Didler, Patrick Hancock, Pete Baker)*

Rutland Arms [Brown St/Arundel Lane]: Convivial pub handy for the Crucible (and station), sensibly priced well kept changing ales such as Adnams, Black Sheep, Greene King, Jennings, Marstons Pedigree and Wentworth, also bottle-conditioned Wentworth, good wine and soft drinks, plentiful good value home-made food early evening and wknd lunchtimes from cheap basic snacks to more substantial meals, handsome façade; piped music; bedrooms, tables in prettily kept compact garden *(the Didler, Patrick Hancock)*

Sheaf View [Gleadless Rd, Heeley Bottom]: Friendly and busy alehouse with wide range of well kept changing ales inc local Abbeydale, Barnsley and Wentworth, farm cider, spotless unusually shaped bar, pleasant staff; disabled facilities, tables outside, open all day wknds, cl Mon lunchtime *(Peter F Marshall, Patrick Hancock, the Didler)*

Stag [Psalter Lane]: Big busy three-room pub with three real ales, food lunchtime and evening, conservatory; picnic-sets in garden with play area, open all day *(CMW, JJW)*

Union [Union Rd, Netheredge]: Well run, with hearty food, real ales such as Greene King Abbot and Old Speckled Hen *(Patrick Hancock)*

Walkley Cottage [Bole Hill Rd]: Chatty 1930s pub popular for good value generous freshly made food (not Sun evening) inc bargain OAP lunch Mon-Thurs and good Sun roast, no smoking dining area, half a dozen or so well kept real ales, farm cider, good coffee and soft drinks choice, daily papers; quiet piped music, games room; children and dogs welcome (pub dog called Max), views from picnic-sets in small back garden with swings, lovely hanging baskets, open all day *(CMW, JJW, Patrick Hancock)*

White Lion [London Rd]: Various small lounges and snugs, at least half a dozen real ales *(Patrick Hancock)*

SHERIFF HUTTON SE6566

Highwayman [The Square]: Cosy old coaching inn nr Castle Howard, welcoming landlord, enjoyable food from good sandwiches to good value Sun lunch, well kept beers, log fires, oak beams in lounge and dining room, homely snug bar; good wheelchair access, big garden, attractive village with 12th-c church *(Walter and Sue Anderson)*

SILSDEN SE0445

Grouse [Keighley Rd]: Restauranty pub with enjoyable food, Timothy Taylors ales, lots of belgian and german bottled beers *(Anthony Henderson)*

SKEEBY NZ1902

☆ *Travellers Rest* [Richmond Rd (A6108)]: Friendly local atmosphere and cheerfully welcoming service in neatly kept long bar with copper and pewter on beams, coal fire, good well priced fresh food from bargain breakfast, baguettes and other substantial lunchtime dishes to more ambitious evening meals, well kept Black Sheep, Greene King Old Speckled Hen and John Smiths; walking parties welcome, garden tables *(Trevor and Sylvia Millum, Michael Doswell)*

SKIPTON SD9851

☆ *Narrow Boat* [Victoria St; pub signed down alley off Coach St]: Town pub nr canal in small Market Town Taverns group, up to half a dozen well kept ales from mainly Yorkshire small breweries inc a Mild, belgian beers too, good variety of fairly priced food (not Fri-Sat evening), good wine choice, welcoming staff, smoke-free dark wood bar – smokers confined to upper gallery; no children, jazz Tues, quiz Weds; tables outside, open all day *(John Foord, D J Etheridge, MLR)*

☆ *Woolly Sheep* [Sheep St]: Full Timothy Taylors range kept well and a Skipton guest beer in two beamed bars off flagstoned passage, exposed brickwork, stone fireplace, lots of sheep prints and old photographs, old plates and bottles, prompt friendly service, cheap generous plain food inc plenty for children, roomy comfortable lunchtime dining area; spacious pretty garden, six good value bedrooms, good breakfast *(Steve Whalley, Lindsay Travis, MLR)*

SLAPEWATH NZ

Fox & Hounds [A171 E of Guisborough]: Welcoming pub with Black Sheep, John Smiths and Tetleys, good value interesting baguettes, reasonable range of hot dishes; bedrooms *(Derek and Sylvia Stephenson)*

SLEIGHTS NZ8606

Plough [Coach Rd]: Pleasantly furnished two-bar stone-built pub with sensibly short choice of good value locally sourced food, well kept John Smiths and Theakstons, good staff, back dining area allowing smoking; tables in small back garden, good views *(DC, M Borthwick)*

SNAITH SE6422

Brewers Arms [Pontefract Rd]: Converted mill brewing its own good range of distinctive beers, decent quickly served food, bright friendly open-plan bar, carpeted conservatory-style dining area; piped music; children in eating areas, bedrooms *(LYM, Roger A Bellingham, Derek and Sylvia Stephenson)*

SNAPE SE2684

☆ *Castle Arms* [off B6268 Masham—Bedale]: Spotless comfortably updated low-ceilinged pub with good fresh enterprising food from interesting sandwiches up in flagstoned bar with big inglenook log fire, second flagstoned room and attractive small carpeted dining room, friendly licensees and considerate helpful service, well kept Black Sheep. Hambleton Best and John Smiths Magnet, decent wines, good coffee, country prints; unobtrusive piped music; children and dogs welcome, tables in charming courtyard, pretty village very handy for Thorp Perrow, comfortable bedrooms *(Edward and Deanna Pearce, Tim and Carolyn Lowes, Alistair Stead, Michael Doswell)*

SNEATON NZ8907

Wilson Arms [Beacon Way]: Sparkling clean and shiny, with good value filling food (not wkdy lunchtime out of season) from sandwiches up, well kept Barnsley (the welcoming licensees come from S Yorks), Black Sheep, John Smiths and Theakstons Best and XB, two good fires, neat staff, pleasant small no smoking dining room one end, large family room with pool table the other end; back garden and bedrooms with fine views towards Whitby Abbey *(M Borthwick)*

SOUTH CAVE SE9231

Fox & Coney [Market Pl]: Pleasant pub with well kept ales such as Caledonian Deuchars IPA, Timothy Taylors Landlord and Woodfordes Admirals Reserve, modestly priced food from baguettes and burgers through pasta to steaks, comfortable main bar and dining areas, friendly staff; bedrooms in adjoining hotel *(Paul and Ursula Randall)*

SPROTBROUGH SE5302

☆ *Boat* [3½ miles from M18 junction 2, less from A1(M) junction 36 via A630 and Mill Lane; Nursery Lane]: Roomy stone-built ex-farmhouse thoroughly refurbished as Vintage Inn early in 2004, keeping the feel of several separate flagstoned areas, log fires in big stone fireplaces, latticed windows, dark beams, sensibly priced food all day till 10, well kept Black Sheep, John Smiths and Tetleys, 15 wines by the glass, prompt helpful service; piped music, fruit machine, no dogs; tables in big sheltered prettily lit courtyard, River Don walks, open all day *(LYM, JHBS, GSB)*

STAINTON SK5593

Three Tuns [Scotch Spring Lane]: Tidy dining pub with roomy bar, good choice of freshly made food (so may be a wait) inc blackboard specials and carvery, two real ales; may be quiet piped music or TV, discreet games machine; attractive flower tubs and baskets out in front *(CMW, JJW)*

STAMFORD BRIDGE SE7055

Three Cups [A166 W of town]: Spacious Vintage Inn family dining pub in timbered country style, glass-topped 20-metre well in bar, sound food all day, good range of wines by the glass, well kept Bass and Tetleys, welcoming manager and staff; particularly good disabled access, children welcome, good play area behind, bedrooms, open all day *(LYM, Guy Charrison, Walter and Sue Anderson)*

STANBURY SE0037

☆ *Old Silent* [Hob Lane]: Neatly rebuilt moorland dining pub near Ponden reservoir, friendly atmosphere, reasonably priced fresh food inc particularly good meat, friendly attentive staff, well kept ales inc Timothy Taylors Landlord and Tetleys, attentive helpful service, character linked rooms with beams, flagstones, mullioned windows and open fires, games room with juke box, restaurant and conservatory; children welcome, bedrooms *(BB, Len Beattie, Peter Heaton)*

STARBOTTON SD9574

Fox & Hounds [B6160]: Small inn in pretty and very popular Dales village (so it gets busy, and there may be quite a wait for a meal), big log fire in beamed and flagstoned traditional bar, small no smoking dining room, well kept Black Sheep and guest beers, usual bar food, eager-to-please licensees; may be piped music, dogs allowed in bar; children welcome, cl Mon *(the Didler, LYM, M and N Watson, Maggie and Tony Harwood, Blaise Vyner)*

STILLINGTON SE5867

White Bear [Main St]: Pleasantly olde-worlde village local, good value food (not Sun evening) inc lunchtime and early evening bargains, friendly service, well kept Black Sheep, John Smiths, Timothy Taylors Landlord and Porter and Tetleys; cl Mon *(Tim and Ann Newell, Alan and Rosina Smith)*

STOCKTON ON THE FOREST SE6556

Fox [off A64 just NE of York]: Attractive village pub with three cosy and comfortable linked rooms and separate dining room, good proper home cooking to order with some adventurous dishes and good value puddings, well kept Tetleys, unusually wide choice of wines by the glass, quick friendly attentive service; tables outside with lots of hanging baskets *(Pat and Graham Williamson, Keith and Margaret Kettell, John Foord)*

STOKESLEY NZ5209

☆ *White Swan* [West End]: Friendly, smart and attractive, with good Captain Cook ales brewed at the pub and interesting changing guest beers, great range of cheeses, home-made pickle and several pâtés for ploughman's, welcoming staff, three seating areas, top one no smoking, lots of brass on elegant dark panelling, lovely bar counter carving, hat display, unusual clock *(Blaise Vyner, Tracey and Stephen Groves, Derek and Sylvia Stephenson)*

STUTTON SE4841

☆ *Hare & Hounds* [Manor Rd]: New people keeping up standards in pleasantly refurbished stone-built pub with cosy low-ceilinged rooms, wide choice of enjoyable food (not Sun evening) with some new dishes alongside old favourites, quick pleasant service even when busy, well kept cheap Sam Smiths OB, decent wine, well behaved children in restaurant; has been cl Mon, tables, some under marquee, in long prettily planted sloping garden with playthings *(Geoffrey and Brenda Wilson, Pat and Derek Roughton, LYM, M J Codling)*

SWAINBY NZ4702

Black Horse [High St]: Pleasant spot by stream in nice village, appealing beamed bar with plenty to look at, wide range of generous appetising home-made food from substantial doorstep sandwiches to good value Sun roasts, well kept Camerons Strongarm and John Smiths, service friendly and efficient even when busy; well spaced picnic-sets in good-sized attractive garden with play area *(Michael Doswell)*

TAN HILL NY8906

☆ *Tan Hill Inn* [Arkengarthdale rd Reeth—Brough, at junction Keld/W Stonesdale rd]: Old stone pub in wonderful setting on Pennine Way – Britain's highest, and second most remote, nearly five miles from the nearest neighbour, basic, bustling and can get overcrowded, full of bric-a-brac and pictures inc interesting old photographs, simple sturdy furniture, flagstones, ever-burning big log fire (with prized stone side seats); well kept Theakstons Best, XB and Old Peculier (in winter the cellar does chill down – whisky with hot water's good then), help-yourself coffee, generous food from good sandwiches to usual hot dishes and hearty yorkshire puddings, pool in family room; often snowbound, with no mains electricity (juke box powered by generator); swaledale sheep show here last Thurs in May; children and dogs welcome, bedrooms, inc some in extension with own bathrooms, open all day *(LYM, Jim Abbott, Richard Robinson, David Reid, Rona Murdoch)*

TERRINGTON SE6571

Bay Horse [W of Malton]: Country pub in unspoilt village with cosy lounge bar, good log fire, handsome dining area and back family conservatory with old farm tools, well kept Theakstons Black Bull, Timothy Taylors Landlord and a guest beer, over 100 whiskies, well liked bar food, traditional public bar with darts, shove-ha'penny, cribbage and dominoes, no smoking restaurant; piped music; children welcome in eating areas, garden tables *(Roger and Jenny Huggins, Pat and Tony Martin, LYM)*

THIRSK SE4382

Blacksmiths Arms [Market Pl]: Sociable and attractive timbered front lounges overlooking market sq, well kept John Smiths *(Steve Whalley)*

THIXENDALE SE8461

Cross Keys [off A166 3 miles N of Fridaythorpe]: Unspoilt welcoming country pub in deep valley below the rolling Wolds, cosy L-shaped bar with fitted wall seats, relaxed atmosphere, well kept changing Jennings and Tetleys, sensible home-made blackboard food; large pleasant garden behind, popular with walkers, handy for Wharram Percy earthworks *(the Didler)*

THORGANBY SE6942

Ferryboat: Welcoming family-run pub with well kept Roosters and a rotating guest such as Brown Cow, Durham, Old Mill or Rudgate, good wknd sandwiches, friendly service, children allowed in conservatory; lovely garden, idyllic setting by River Derwent *(David Butterworth)*

THORNTON SE0933

☆ *Ring o' Bells* [Hill Top Rd, off B6145 W of Bradford]: Spotless 19th-c moortop dining pub very popular for wide choice of well presented good home cooking inc fresh fish, speciality pies, superb steaks, good puddings, bargain early suppers, separate-sittings Sun lunch (best to book), well kept Black Sheep, Courage Directors and Websters Green Label, crisp efficient service, pleasant bar, popular air-conditioned no smoking restaurant and pleasant conservatory lounge; wide views towards Shipley and Bingley *(Andy and Jill Kassube, Nigel and Sue Foster)*

THORNTON-LE-CLAY SE6865

☆ *White Swan* [off A64 York—Malton; Low St]: Comfortably old-fashioned beamed dining pub, homely and peaceful, with friendly attentive long-serving landlord, good fresh food, big helpings and reasonable prices, well kept Black Sheep and a local guest beer, good value wines, fine log fire, shining brasses, children welcome, plenty of board games, good view from impeccable ladies'; well chosen piped music; neatly kept grounds with terrace tables, duck pond, herb garden and rescued donkeys, attractive countryside nr Castle Howard; cl Mon lunchtime *(John Knighton, Mr and Mrs P Bland, Graham and Doreen Holden)*

THRESHFIELD SD9863

Old Hall Inn [B6160/B6265 just outside Grassington]: Newish management and olde-worlde atmosphere in three knocked-together rooms, high beam-and-plank ceiling, cushioned wall pews, tall well blacked kitchen range, log fires, limited choice of enjoyable sensibly priced food in bar and restaurant, well kept Marstons Pedigree, Timothy Taylors Landlord and Theakstons; children in eating area, neat garden *(LYM, Susie Symes)*

THURSTONLAND SE1610

Rose & Crown [off A629 Huddersfield—Sheffield, via Thunder Bridge and Stocksmoor]: Spacious and friendly open-plan village pub, banquettes and some stripped stone, attractively priced enjoyable home-made food (all day Sun), five real ales, good soft drinks choice; some tables out in front, exhilarating countryside *(CMW, JJW, Trevor and Judy Pearson)*

THWING TA0570

Falling Stone [off B1253 W of Bridlington; Main St]: Newly refurbished as comfortable dining pub, keeping pubby bar; first pub tied to Hunmanby's Wold Top brewery, their three changing ales kept well, enjoyable food from whitby crab soup, unusual hot sandwiches and ciabattas up, civilised and friendly atmosphere, good choice of reasonably priced wines, separate pool room; attractive Wolds village surroundings *(Marlene and Jim Godfrey, Fred and Lorraine Gill)*

TICKHILL SK5992

Millstone [Westgate (A631)]: Large roadside pub with two real ales, good choice of other drinks, emphasis on good value food inc carvery and children's; piped music *(CMW, JJW)*

TODMORDEN SD9223

Masons Arms [A681/A6033, S of centre]: Welcoming traditional local with particularly well kept Barnsley, Tetleys and one or two guest beers, two knocked-together rooms with darts, cards and pool in popular games end; impromptu folk night Thurs *(Pete Baker)*

TOPCLIFFE SE4076

Angel [off A1, take A168 to Thirsk, after 3 miles follow signs for Topcliffe; Long St]: Big bustling place carefully and comfortably done up in separately themed areas inc an attractive and softly lit stripped-stone faux-Irish bar, also billiards room and two dining rooms, wide choice of reasonably priced enjoyable food, pleasant helpful service, John Smiths, Tetleys and Theakstons, decent wines; unobtrusive piped music; tables outside *(Janet and Peter Race)*

TOTLEY SK3080

Crown [Hillfoot Rd]: Old-fashioned country inn with friendly landlord and good staff, five well kept ales such as Fullers London Pride and Tetleys, short choice of good home-cooked food; no children *(DC)*

UPPER POPPLETON SE5553

Red Lion [A59 York—Harrogate]: Good value food and good service in comfortably refurbished olde-worlde bars and dining areas; pleasant garden, bedroom extension *(Janet and Peter Race)*

White Horse [off A59 York—Harrogate]: Lovely setting in charming village, hotel with friendly relaxed bar, pleasant landlord and staff, good choice of well kept beers, enjoyable food; can be a bit smoky when it's busy; good value bedrooms *(Mr and Mrs John Taylor)*

WAINSTALLS SE0428

Cat i' th' Well: Picturesque country pub in fine spot towards the top of Luddenden Dean, three snug linked areas, fresh and untwee, with 19th-c panelling from nearby demolished hall, nice balance between drinking and dining, above-average reasonably priced food from good sandwich choice up, Timothy Taylors Best and Landlord and interesting guest beers, quick friendly service, no smoking area; walkers welcome, handy for Calderdale Way *(Pat and Tony Martin, Anne and Tim Locke, Carol Jones)*

WAKEFIELD SE3320

Fernandes Brewery Tap [Avison Yard, Kirkgate]: Top floor of 19th-c malt store converted to tap for Fernandes microbrewery, their beers and interesting guests kept well, Biddenden farm cider, good breweriana and inn-sign collection, friendly atmosphere, bare boards and rafters; cl Mon-Thurs lunchtime, open all day Fri-Sun with lunchtime soup and sandwiches then, brewery shop *(the Didler, JP, PP, Patrick Hancock)*

Henry Boons [Westgate]: Well kept Clarks (from next-door brewery), and Black Sheep, Timothy Taylors and Tetleys, in two-room bare-boards local, friendly staff, barrel tables and breweriana; side pool area, juke box, machines, live bands; open all day (till 1am Fri-Sat) *(the Didler, JP, PP, Patrick Hancock)*

Jolly Sailor [Thornes Lane Wharf]: Ancient cream-coloured pub in former industrial area by River Calder wharf opp Wakefield flood lock, bargain food, U-shaped panelled bar around servery with brass and glass, cosy seats in window alcoves, friendly staff, one wall devoted to 1757 plan for making river navigable upstream *(JHBS)*

Redoubt [Horbury Rd, Westgate]: Busy and friendly traditional pub, four smallish rooms off long corridor, well kept Tetleys Bitter and Mild and Timothy Taylors Landlord, Rugby League photographs and memorabilia, pub games; family room till 8, open all day *(JP, PP, the Didler, Michael Butler)*

Wagon [Westgate End]: Busy friendly local specialising in well kept ales mainly from interesting small breweries, lunchtime food, reasonable prices, log fire; side pool room, juke box; benches outside, open all day *(JP, PP, the Didler)*

Wakefield Labour Club [Vicarage St]: Red wooden shed rather like a works canteen inside, small and inviting – it is a club, but visitors can just sign in; wide changing choice of keenly priced real ales from small breweries, farm cider, belgian beers; picnic-sets outside, cl lunchtime Mon-Thurs and Sun evening *(JP, PP, the Didler)*

WALES SK4782

☆ ***Duke of Leeds*** [Church St]: Comfortable 18th-c stone-faced village pub kept spotless by chatty 3rd-generation landlord, well kept Boddingtons, Castle Eden, Greene King Abbot and a guest beer, good value generous food (not Mon-Tues lunchtimes; may be a wait when busy) inc choice of fresh fish, good soft drinks range, long no smoking dining lounge (fills quickly evenings – get there by 7) and smaller room where smoking allowed, lots of brass and copper, pictures for sale, table fountains, flame-effect gas fire; may be piped music, no credit cards; nearby walks *(CMW, JJW)*

WALKINGTON SE9937

☆ ***Ferguson-Fawsitt Arms*** [East End; B1230 W of Beverley]: Doing well under current management, with good value food inc good carvery and blackboard dishes from airy no smoking flagstone-floored food bar, very popular lunchtime with older people, helpful cheerful service, real ale, decent wine, interesting recently extended mock-Tudor bars; tables out on terrace, delightful village *(June and Ken Brooks, LYM, Mr and Mrs G Ives)*

WEAVERTHORPE SE9670

Blue Bell: Attractive dining pub, warm and friendly, with good food in front bar area and intimate back restaurant, welcoming professional service *(P R Morley)*

Star [village signed off A64 Malton—Scarborough at Sherburn]: Friendly new licensees, good atmosphere in two neat rooms with comfortable maroon plush banquettes and log fires, enjoyable food inc bargain Fri steak night, well kept Wold Top and a weekly guest beer, good coffee, restaurant; children welcome, no piped music, Weds quiz night; nice clean bright bedrooms, hearty breakfast, peaceful village setting *(Colin and Dot Savill, BB, S A Crumpton, Roger A Bellingham)*

WELBURN SE7168

Crown & Cushion [off A64]: Spaciously refurbished yet cosy village local with good home cooking from well made sandwiches and ploughman's up, good service, cheerful landlord, well kept Camerons and Tetleys, decent wine, games in public bar, restaurant, children in eating areas, amusing pictures in gents'; piped music; attractive small back garden with terrace, handy for Castle Howard *(LYM, Christopher Turner)*

WELTON SE9527

Green Dragon [signed from A63 just E of Hull outskirts]: Spacious and comfortable family dining pub, good value food, Mansfield and Marstons Pedigree, friendly staff; notable as the real-life scene of the unglamorous arrest of Dick Turpin *(LYM, Norma and David Hardy)*

WENSLEY SE0989

Three Horseshoes: Short frequently changing choice of good freshly made attractively priced food, well kept Black Sheep ales, good wines, friendly staff; dogs welcome *(Terry Mizen, Lucien Perring)*

WENTWORTH SK3898

☆ ***George & Dragon*** [3 miles from M1 junction 36; Main St]: Friendly rambling split-level bar, half a dozen well kept ales such as Kelham Island, Timothy Taylors Best and Landlord and local Wentworth ones, flagstones and assorted old-fashioned furnishings, ornate stove in lounge, generous good value food inc traditional puddings in bar and restaurant, good service; high chairs provided; may be piped music, small back games room with darts and machine; benches in front courtyard, tables out on big back lawn, crafts and antiques shop – pleasant village *(LYM, Patrick Hancock, Derek and Sylvia Stephenson, Pat and Tony Martin, R T and J C Moggridge)*

Rockingham Arms [3 miles from M1 junction 36; B6090, signed off A6135; Main St]: Welcoming Steak & Ale pub with comfortable traditional furnishings, open fires, stripped stone, rooms off inc a no smoking dining/family room, good food choice all day (freshly made so can take a while), five real ales, good choice of other drinks, no smoking room; quiet piped music, TV; dogs welcome (meals available for them), tables in attractive garden with own bowling green, bedrooms, open all day *(BB, CMW, JJW)*

WEST BURTON SE0186

☆ ***Fox & Hounds*** [on green, off B6160 Bishopdale—Wharfedale]: Friendly local on long green of idyllic Dales village, wide choice of good value generous unpretentious home-made food inc children's and good puddings, well kept Black Sheep and Tetleys, residents' dining room; nearby caravan park; children and dogs welcome, good modern bedrooms, lovely walks and waterfalls nearby *(W A Evershed, Abi Benson)*

WEST WITTON SE0688

Fox & Hounds [Main St (A684)]: Much modernised 17th-c pub, central coal fire dividing bar from dining and games area, another nicely laid out room, Black Sheep, Cains, John Smiths and Tetleys Imperial, farm ciders such as Addlestone's and North Yorkshire Pipkin, home-made food, lots of wildlife pictures, darts, pool; piped music, juke box, piano; bedrooms *(Kevin Thorpe)*

WESTOW SE7565

Blacksmiths Arms [Main St]: Traditional local in attractive village, tastefully renovated by new management, decent food in bar and restaurant, John Smiths real ale; good new bedroom extension *(Giles and Annie Francis, Christopher Turner)*

WHISTON SK4489

Golden Ball [nr M1 junction 33, via A618; Turner Lane, off High St]: Pleasant bustle in extended old pub remodelled as Ember Inn, meticulously clean, wide food choice inc good value mixed grill, real ales such as Badger Tanglefoot, Bass, Caledonian Deuchars IPA, Stones, Timothy Taylors Landlord and Tetleys, several wines by the glass, log fire, no smoking room; piped music, machines, no children inside; picnic-sets outside, open all day *(Derek and Sylvia Stephenson, Peter F Marshall, CMW, JJW)*

WHITBY NZ8911

Tap & Spile [New Quay Rd]: Three-room bare-boards alehouse, small no smoking room, four or so well kept changing ales such as Greene King Old Speckled Hen, country wines, farm ciders, good value bar food inc good local fish and chips noon-7, traditional games; frequent live music, open all day *(the Didler, Damian Dixon, Roger and Jenny Huggins, JP, PP, Dr J Barrie Jones)*

White Horse & Griffin [Church St]: More restaurant than pub (you can't have just a drink), but worth knowing for good value lunches esp local fresh fish and a notable cassoulet – they do breakfasts for non-residents too, and more expensive evening meals; very tall narrow front part, low-ceilinged open back area with big fireplace, corner bar, some long tables and cosy candlelit ambiance; bedrooms *(M Borthwick)*

WHITWOOD SE3924

Rising Sun [Whitwood Common Lane; nr M62 junction 31 – A655 towards Castleford]: New owners focused on food – good range, generous helpings, adventurous specials; long pleasant bar, no smoking restaurant with front sun lounge as overflow, Timothy Taylors Landlord and Tetleys, decent house wines, afternoon teas; back terrace tables *(Peter and Jackie Barnett)*

WHIXLEY SE4457

Anchor [New Rd]: Family-friendly pub just outside village, traditional food inc bargain lunchtime sliced roasts particularly popular with OAPs, cheery efficient service, well kept John Smiths and Tetleys, several rooms, coal fire in small lounge, eccentric teapots on every surface, sunny conservatory *(Janet and Peter Race, H Bramwell, Donald and Margaret Wood)*

WIGGLESWORTH SD8056

☆ *Plough* [B6478, off A65 S of Settle]: Friendly dining pub with wide range of good reasonably priced bar food inc good Sun lunch, well kept Black Sheep and Tetleys, attractive bar with log fire, little rooms off, some simple yet cosy, others more plush, inc no smoking panelled dining room and snug, also smarter conservatory restaurant with panoramic Dales views; attractive garden, homely and comfortable bedrooms also with views *(Peter F Marshall)*

WORRALL SK3092

Shoulder of Mutton [Top Rd]: Extended open-plan stone-built pub dating from 17th c, popular and friendly, with enjoyable food (Sun roast half price for children, high chair available), three real ales, good choice of other drinks, no smoking room, woodburner; TV, may be quiet piped music *(CMW, JJW)*

WORTLEY SK3099

Wortley Arms [A629 N of Sheffield]: 16th-c stone-built coaching inn with big lounge, no smoking area, tap room and dining room, panelling and large inglenook, good value food (not Sun evening), well kept Barnsley, Bass, Timothy Taylors and guest beers, good soft drinks choice, darts; no dogs, may be piped music; children welcome, open all day, bedrooms *(R A Watson)*

WORTON SD9589

Victoria Arms: Small traditional bar with a couple of settles, well kept Black Sheep and Theakstons, long-serving landlord with dry sense of humour; no food, outside lavatories *(Ben Whitney and Pippa Redmond)*

WRAGBY SE4117

Spread Eagle [A638 nr Nostell Priory]: Popular traditional local with four homely low-beamed rooms, good bargain lunches, well kept low-priced Sam Smiths and guest beers, friendly helpful staff, photographs of regulars as youngsters in tap room, evening restaurant; quiz night, popular wknds; tables in back garden with play area *(Geoffrey and Brenda Wilson)*

YORK SE5951

☆ *Ackhorne* [St Martins Lane, Micklegate]: Fine changing range of well kept ales from small brewers, four farm ciders, perry, country wines, foreign bottled beers and good coffee; beams and bare boards, leather wall seats, Civil War prints, bottles and jugs, carpeted snug one end, good value home-made food (not Sun) from good choice of sandwiches up, friendly landlord and family, open fire, daily papers, traditional games, silenced games machine; Sun quiz night; appealing small garden behind, open all day *(Richard Lewis, the Didler, Patrick Hancock, Alison Hayes, Pete Hanlon, Roger A Bellingham, Dr David Cockburn)*

☆ *Black Swan* [Peaseholme Green (inner ring road)]: Marvellous timbered and jettied Tudor building, serving hatch to compact panelled front bar, crooked-floored hall with fine period staircase, black-beamed back bar with vast inglenook, cheerful service, low-priced usual food from baked potatoes and baguettes up, well kept Worthington Best and guests such as Bass and York Broadcaster or Yorkshire

Terrier, decent wines; piped music, jazz and folk nights; useful car park *(the Didler, Paul and Ursula Randall, LYM, David Carr, Alison Hayes, Pete Hanlon, Patrick Hancock, Peter Coxon)*

☆ ***Blue Bell*** [Fossgate]: Classic little Edwardian pub with well kept ales such as Camerons Strongarm, Caledonian Deuchars IPA, Greene King Abbot, John Smiths, Timothy Taylors Landlord and Charles Wells Bombardier, tiny tiled-floor front bar with roaring fire, panelled ceiling, stained glass, bar pots and decanters, corridor to back smoke room not much bigger, hatch service to middle bar, good friendly service, lively local atmosphere (given its size, can get crowded), good value sandwiches on counter 11-6, pub games; open all day *(RWC, the Didler, JP, PP, Richard Lewis, Nick and Alison Dowson, Pete Baker, Patrick Hancock, Paul and Ursula Randall, Nick Holding, Peter Coxon, Alison Hayes, Pete Hanlon)*

Dormouse [Shipton Rd, Clifton Park]: Purpose-built Vintage Inn, well designed and given plenty of character and atmosphere, with their usual reliable food, fairly priced wines, friendly efficient staff; good disabled access *(John Knighton, Walter and Sue Anderson)*

Fox & Roman [Tadcaster Rd, opp racecourse]: Large, rambling and welcoming Vintage Inn, lots of nooks and crannies, good value well prepared food, good choice of wines by the glass, quick cheerful helpful service, two log fires, unrushed atmosphere *(Michael Dandy, Duncan Smart, Peter Coxon)*

Golden Ball [Cromwell Rd/Bishophill]: Unspoilt 1950s local feel in friendly and well preserved four-room Edwardian pub, enjoyable straightforward wkdy lunchtime food, well kept Marstons Pedigree, John Smiths and a guest beer, bar billiards, cards and dominoes; TV, can be lively evenings, live music Thurs and Sun; small walled garden *(Pete Baker, the Didler, Alison Hayes, Pete Hanlon)*

Golden Fleece [Pavement]: Timothy Taylors Landlord and guest beers often from York Brewery, bar food all day (till 5 Sun), long corridor from bar to back lounge (beware the sloping floors – it dates from 1503), lots of ghost stories and pictures; bedrooms *(Eric Larkham, Nick Holding, Peter Coxon)*

Golden Slipper [Goodramgate]: Dating from 15th c, renovated carefully to keep distinctively old-fashioned almost rustic local feel in its neat unpretentious bar and three small rooms, good cheap plain food from sandwiches, baguettes and baked potatoes to tender roast beef, well kept Greene King Old Speckled Hen, John Smiths and Charles Wells Bombardier, friendly cheerful staff; tables in back courtyard *(Pat and Graham Williamson, Karen Eliot, Peter Coxon)*

Hole in the Wall [High Petergate]: Rambling much modernised open-plan pub handy for Minster, beams, stripped masonry, lots of prints, turkey carpeting, lots of low plush stools, well kept Banks's, Mansfield and Marstons Pedigree, good coffee, very busy lunchtime for good value food noon onwards inc generous Sun lunch, friendly service; juke box, games machines, piped music not too loud, live some nights; open all day *(Alan Vere, LYM, Martin Lewis, Mr and Mrs John Taylor)*

Last Drop [Colliergate]: Former law office dating from 17th c, restored by York Brewery in basic traditional style, several of their own beers and one or two well kept guests, decent wines and country wines, friendly staff, bare boards, big barrels and comfortable seats, big windows overlooking pavement, no music, machines or children, food served 12-4 from sandwiches and panini up (local cheeses recommended); attic lavatories; tables out behind, open all day, can get very busy lunchtime *(Richard Lewis, June and Ken Brooks, Martin Grosberg, Patrick Hancock, Nick Holding, Fred and Lorraine Gill, Peter Coxon, Dr David Cockburn)*

☆ ***Lendal Cellars*** [Lendal]: Cheerful bustling split-level alehouse down steps in broad-vaulted 17th-c cellars carefully spotlit to show up the stripped brickwork, stone floor, interconnected rooms and alcoves, very well kept changing ales such as Boddingtons, Caledonian Deuchars IPA, Marstons Pedigree and Theakstons at fair prices, farm cider, decent coffee, good choice of wines by the glass, foreign bottled beers, daily papers, cheerful staff, children allowed for good plain food 11.30-7(5 Fri-Sat), two-for-one bargains; good piped music, popular with students; open all day *(Peter F Marshall, the Didler, JP, PP, LYM, Patrick Hancock, Joyce and Maurice Cottrell, Peter Coxon)*

Olde Starre [Stonegate]: City's oldest licensed pub, and a magnet for tourists, with 'gallows' sign across York's prettiest street, original panelling and prints, green plush wall seats, several other little rooms off porch-like lobby, well kept changing ales such as Caledonian Deuchars IPA, John Smiths, Theakstons Best and York Yorkshire Terrier from long counter, cheerful young staff; piped music may be loud, fruit and games machines; open all day, children welcome away from bar, flower-filled back garden and front courtyard with Minster glimpsed across the rooftops *(Dr and Mrs Jackson, Janet and Peter Race, Rona Murdoch, LYM, Patrick Hancock, Nick Holding, Peter Coxon)*

Phoenix [George St]: Old-fashioned, unpretentious and friendly, with dominoes in proper front public bar, quietly comfortable and sensitively refurbished back horseshoe-shaped lounge, well kept ales such as Caledonian Deuchars IPA and Charles Wells Bombardier; handy for Barbican *(Pete Baker, Fred and Lorraine Gill)*

Punch Bowl [Stonegate]: Bustling family-run local with masses of hanging baskets, friendly helpful service, wide range of good generous food (12-2 and 3-6.45) from sandwiches up, no smoking area by servery, small panelled rooms off corridor, TV in interesting beamed one on left of food servery, well kept Bass,

Worthington and York Yorkshire Terrier; unobtrusive piped music, games machines; open all day *(Rona Murdoch, Joyce and Maurice Cottrell, Mrs Edna M Jones, Nick Holding)*

☆ ***Red Lion*** [Merchantgate, between Fossgate and Piccadilly]: Low-beamed rambling rooms with plenty of atmosphere, some stripped Tudor brickwork, relaxed old-fashioned furnishings, well kept real ales, decent bar lunches, good juke box or piped music; children welcome to eat at lunchtime, tables outside *(Mark Walker, LYM, Nick Holding, Peter Coxon)*

Rook & Gaskill [Lawrence St]: York Brewery's third pub, with all their beers kept well and lots of guests; refurbished in thoroughly traditional style with dark wood tables, banquettes, chairs and high stools, cheerful knowledgeable service, limited bar food; jazz and folk nights *(Eric Larkham, Paul and Ursula Randall)*

☆ ***Royal Oak*** [Goodramgate]: Comfortably worn in three-room black-beamed 16th-c pub remodelled in Tudor style 1934, warm welcoming atmosphere, cosy corners with blazing fires, good value generous homely food (limited Sun evening) inc fresh veg and home-baked bread served 11.30-8, no sandwiches till 3, speedy service from cheerful bustling young staff, reliably well kept Greene King Abbot,Timothy Taylors Landlord, Tetleys and a guest beer, decent wines, good coffee; prints, swords, busts and old guns, no smoking family room; piped music, can get crowded, outside gents'; handy for Minster, open all day *(Dr and Mrs Jackson, Paul and Ursula Randall, BB, CMW, JJW, Joyce and Maurice Cottrell, Pat and Tony Martin, Patrick Hancock, Nick Holding, Peter Coxon)*

Snickleway [Goodramgate]: Snug and interesting little open-plan pub, cosy nooks and crannies, lots of antiques, copper and brass, good coal fires, cheerful landlord, well kept Greene King Old Speckled Hen and John Smiths, good value fresh well filled doorstep sandwiches and light snacks lunchtimes, prompt service, splendid cartoons in gents', exemplary ladies'; unobtrusive piped music *(Paul and Ursula Randall, Tim and Sue Halstead)*

Swan [Bishopgate St]: Unspoilt 1950s feel, friendly, chatty and grown-up; main bar with hatch service to lobby for two small rooms off, well kept Timothy Taylors Landlord and other changing ales such as Greene King Abbot and Tetleys, helpful staff; small walled garden, nr city walls *(Pete Baker, Fred and Lorraine Gill, the Didler, Alison Hayes, Pete Hanlon)*

☆ ***Tap & Spile*** [Monkgate]: Friendly recently redecorated late Victorian two-bar pub with around eight well kept real ales, farm cider and country wines, games in raised back area, cheap straightforward lunchtime bar food (not Mon); children in eating area, tables on heated terrace and in garden, open all day *(the Didler, Richard Lewis, LYM, JP, PP, David Carr, Patrick Hancock, Peter Coxon, Paul and Ursula Randall)*

☆ ***Three Legged Mare*** [High Petergate]: Bustling open-plan light and airy café-bar with York Brewery's full beer range and guests such as Castle Rock kept well, good range of belgian Trappist beers, quick cheerful service (staff know about beers), reasonably priced lunchtime snacks inc generous interesting sandwiches and baked potatoes, some comfortable sofas, back conservatory; no children, disabled facilities (other lavatories down noisy spiral stairs); tables in back garden, with replica of the original three-legged mare – a local gallows used for multiple executions *(Andy and Jill Kassube, Richard Lewis, D W Stokes, Mark Walker, Andrew York, Peter Coxon, Paul and Ursula Randall, Pat and Tony Martin, Dr David Cockburn)*

☆ ***York Arms*** [High Petergate]: Snug and cheerful little basic panelled bar (beware the sliding door), big modern back lounge, cosier partly panelled no smoking parlour full of old bric-a-brac, prints, brown-cushioned wall settles, dimpled copper tables and an open fire; quick helpful service, well kept Sam Smiths OB, good value simple food lunchtime to early evening (not Sun-Tues), no piped music; by Minster, open all day *(BB, Patrick Hancock)*

York Brewery Tap [Toft Green, Micklegate]: Upstairs lounge at York Brewery, their own full cask range in top condition, also bottled beers, nice clubby atmosphere with friendly staff happy to talk about the beers, lots of breweriana and view of brewing plant, comfortable settees and armchairs, magazines and daily papers; no food, brewery tours by arrangement, shop; open 11.30-7, cl Sun, annual membership fee £3 unless you live in York or go on the tour *(the Didler, Michael Dandy, JP, PP, Peter F Marshall)*

Real ale to us means beer which has matured naturally in its cask – not pressurised or filtered. We name all real ales stocked. We usually name ales preserved under a light blanket of carbon dioxide too, though purists – pointing out that this stops the natural yeasts developing – would disagree (most people, including us, can't tell the difference!)

LONDON
SCOTLAND
WALES
CHANNEL ISLANDS

London

The three new main entries here this year are all well away from the centre: the laid-back Crown in East London, all its food and drink organic, all its furnishings recycled; the civilised Drapers Arms in North London, reworked as an open-plan dining pub with top-notch food; and the Boathouse in South London, bustling and thoroughly up-to-date, in a nice building and great position. In Central London, pubs pleasing a particularly wide range of readers in recent months have been the Argyll Arms (surprisingly unspoilt given its position, with some unusual good points), the art nouveau Black Friar, the Cittie of Yorke (great atmosphere in its classic long booth-lined bar), the friendly Coopers Arms (a most enjoyable all-rounder), the bustling little Dog & Duck in Soho (new manager settling in well), the Jerusalem Tavern (lovely atmosphere and good unusual beers in this clever pastiche of an antique alehouse), the Lamb (an old favourite, good all round), the Lamb & Flag (lively atmosphere, good beers, tremendous character), the relaxed and unspoilt Nags Head, the Old Bank of England (fabulous building), the ancient rambling Olde Cheshire Cheese, the tucked-away Olde Mitre (its friendly new licensees are proving popular), the Red Lion in Duke of York Street (a little gem of a building), and the Seven Stars (current licensees doing nice food, and bringing more of a sense of fun to this interesting building). In North London, the Chapel is a favourite for its food, and the Holly Bush for its atmosphere. In South London, the bustling and friendly Market Porter is on top form these days. West London has quite a clutch of top pubs: the Anglesea Arms in Wingate Road, W6 (excellent food), its namesake the altogether more traditional Anglesea Arms in Selwood Terrace, SW7 (a good all-rounder), the Atlas (another lively gastropub with innovative food), and the nicely un-Londonish Windsor Castle. For a special meal out, it's one of our new entries which takes the top award of London Dining Pub of the Year: the Drapers Arms in North London. The Lucky Dip section at the end of the chapter has over 200 entries this year. We have listed them by postal district, and separated off the outer London suburbs. These come last, after the Central, East, North, South and West numbered postal districts. In this section, particularly notable Central London pubs include the Buckingham Arms (SW1), Audley and Toucan (W1), Duke and Princess Louise (WC1), and Chandos, Porterhouse and Salisbury (WC2). In North London, ones to note include the House (N1), Flask (N6), and Head of Steam (NW1). South London's current pubs to watch are the Royal Oak (SE1), Mayflower (SE16) and Jolly Gardeners (SW15). In West London, make a note of the Brook Green (W6). Average London beer prices have now passed the £2.40 a pint mark – so particular praise for the Yorkshire brewery Sam Smiths (which holds prices at its London pubs down to about two-thirds of the normal London going rate) and for Wetherspoons (which also sells beer for well under £2 a pint in its London pubs). Beers from London's two main brewers, Fullers and Youngs, tend to be a little cheaper than many others here.

Our new pocket London guide, published earlier in 2004, besides including many of the pubs in this chapter (a few of them described in more detail), adds another 150 places which are not listed here: *Best London Pubs and Bars*, Ebury Press, £5.99.

CENTRAL LONDON Map 13

Admiral Codrington

Mossop Street, SW3; ⊖ South Kensington

The sunny back dining room is the chief draw at this busy Chelsea pub, mainly because of the very good food, but also because of its design – particularly impressive in fine weather when the retractable glass roof slides open. Offering a fresh approach to familiar dishes, the meals in this part might include salmon and smoked haddock fishcakes (£10.25), cod baked with tomatoes and mushrooms in a soft herb crust (£11.75), and lamb chops or steak (£13.75); good puddings. It's worth booking, particularly at weekends. The more pubby bar was elegantly reworked by designer Nina Campbell; it's an effective mix of traditional and chic, with comfortable sofas and cushioned wall seats, neatly polished floorboards and panelling, spotlights in the ceiling and lamps on elegant wooden tables, a handsome central counter, sporting prints on the yellow walls, and houseplants around the big bow windows. There's a model ship in a case just above the entrance to the dining room. A separate lunchtime bar menu might include soup (£3.95), goats cheese and red peppers on ciabatta (£6.25), steak sandwich (£6.95), fish pie (£8), and rib-eye burgers (£8.95); Sunday roasts. At weekends they serve brunch from 11. Well kept Charles Wells Bombardier and Greene King Old Speckled Hen on handpump, and an excellent wine list, with a decent choice by the glass; various coffees, and a range of Havana cigars, friendly service from smartly uniformed young staff. There may be piped pop or jazz – though in the evenings especially it will be drowned out by the sounds of animated conversation; the dining room is quieter. At the side is a nice little terrace with tables, benches and heaters. *(Recommended by Simon and Jane Williams, BJL, Ian Phillips, Andrew York)*

Punch ~ Lease Langlands Pearse ~ Real ale ~ Bar food (12-2.30 (11-3.30 weekends), 7-11) ~ Restaurant ~ (020) 7581 0005 ~ Children in restaurant ~ Dogs allowed in bar ~ Open 11.30-11; 12-10.30 Sun; closed 25-26 Dec

Albert

Victoria Street, SW1; ⊖ St James's Park

Always busy – especially on weekday lunchtimes and after work – the huge open-plan bar of this bustling 19th-c pub has a surprisingly airy feel, thanks to great expanses of original heavily cut and etched windows along three sides. There's also some gleaming mahogany, an ornate ceiling, and good solid comfortable furnishings. A wonderfully diverse mix of customers takes in tourists, civil servants and even the occasional MP: the division bell is rung to remind them when it's time to get back to Westminster. Service from the big island counter is efficient and friendly (particularly obliging to people from overseas), with Charles Wells Bombardier, Courage Best and Directors, Fullers London Pride, and perhaps a more unusual guest like Oakham Bishops Farewell on handpump. Served from a counter, good value bar food includes sandwiches (from £4.25), salads (from £4) and several hearty home-cooked hot dishes such as turkey casserole, fish and chips, sweet and sour chicken and vegetable lasagne (all £5.50); usefully, there's something available all day. The upstairs restaurant has a better than average carvery (all day inc Sunday, £16.50 for three courses and coffee); it may be worth booking ahead. The handsome staircase that leads up to it is lined with portraits of former prime ministers. The back bar is no smoking; other areas can feel smoky at times. Sometimes loudish piped music, fruit machine. Handily placed between Victoria and Westminster, the pub was one of the few buildings in this part of Victoria to escape the Blitz, and is one of the area's most striking sights (though it's now rather dwarfed by the surrounding faceless cliffs of dark modern glass). *(Recommended by Kevin Blake, Mark Walker, Ian Phillips, Tracey and Stephen Groves, Val and Alan Green)*

Spirit Group ~ Manager Liz Cairns ~ Real ale ~ Bar food (11(12 Sun)-10) ~ Restaurant ~ (020) 7222 5577 ~ Open 11-11; 12-10.30 Sun; closed 25 Dec

Archery Tavern

Bathurst Street, W2, opposite the Royal Lancaster hotel; ⊖ Lancaster Gate

A useful stop for visitors to this side of Hyde Park, this welcoming and nicely kept Victorian pub is next to a little mews housing some riding stables, so you can sometimes hear the sound of hooves clopping past the door. Taking its name from an archery range that occupied the site for a while in the early 19th c, it has several comfortably relaxing, pubby areas around the central servery. On the green patterned walls are a number of archery prints, as well as a history of the pub and the area, other old prints, dried hops, and quite a few plates running along a shelf. Well kept Badger Best, King & Barnes Sussex and Tanglefoot on handpump. A big back room has long tables, bare boards, and a fireplace; darts, TV, a big stack of board games, fruit machine, piped music (loudish at times). Bar food typically includes sandwiches, soup, and daily specials such as chicken, leek and stilton pie (£5.75), and 8oz rump steak (£6.95); they may do breakfasts on weekend mornings. There's lots more seating in front of the pub, under hanging baskets and elaborate floral displays, and some nicely old-fashioned lamps. *(Recommended by Ian Phillips, Jarrod and Wendy Hopkinson, Len Banister, Brian and Rosalie Laverick, Dr and Mrs A K Clarke, Thomas Agosti, Joe Green, the Didler)*

Badger ~ Manager Mac Mac Glade ~ Real ale ~ Bar food (12-3, 6-9.30) ~ (020) 7402 4916 ~ Children welcome ~ Dogs welcome ~ Open 11-11; 12-10.30 Sun

Argyll Arms

Argyll Street W1; ⊖ Oxford Circus, opposite tube side exit

Much more distinctive than its Oxford Circus location might lead you to expect, this bustling Victorian pub has three particularly unusual and atmospheric cubicle rooms at the front, essentially unchanged since they were built in the 1860s. All oddly angular, they're made by wooden partitions with very distinctive frosted and engraved glass, with hops trailing above. Because they're so secluded, and slightly cut off from the bar, the new manager has been experimenting with table service for drinks; there's usually someone on the floor taking orders between 12 and 9. A long mirrored corridor leads to the spacious back room, with the food counter in one corner. Served all day, bar food includes doorstep sandwiches (from £3.90), an all-day breakfast (£5.25), fish and chips (£6.95, or £9.95 for an especially big helping), a daily roast (£6.95), and beef and ale pie (£7.50). Well kept Fullers London Pride, Timothy Taylor Landlord, and two rapidly changing guests such as George Gale Crowning Glory and Hopback Crop Circle; also several malt whiskies. Service is generally prompt and friendly; newspapers to read, two fruit machines. Now open till midnight Thurs-Sat (and serving food through to the end of the evening), the quieter upstairs bar overlooks the pedestrianised street – and the Palladium theatre if you can see through the impressive foliage outside the window; divided into several snugs with comfortable plush easy chairs, it has swan's-neck lamps, and lots of small theatrical prints along the top of the walls. The piped music is always quieter up here – indeed it's quieter altogether under the new regime, though still a bit louder on Friday and Saturday nights. The pub can get very crowded (and can seem less distinctive on busier evenings), but there's space for drinking outside. *(Recommended by Dr and Mrs M E Wilson, Ian Phillips, the Didler, John Saville, DC, Patrick Hancock, Andrew York, R T and J C Moggridge)*

Mitchells & Butlers ~ Manager Tony Morris ~ Real ale ~ Bar food (11-10 (11.30 Thurs-Sat); 12-10 Sun) ~ (020) 7734 6117 ~ Children allowed in upstairs bar ~ Open 11-11(midnight Thurs-Sat); 12-10.30 Sun; closed 25 Dec

People named as recommenders after the main entries have told us that the pub should be included. But they have not written the report – we have, after anonymous on-the-spot inspection.

Black Friar

Queen Victoria Street, EC4; ⊖ ⇌ Blackfriars

Described by readers this year as 'a must see', this distinctive old favourite stands out for its unique décor, which includes some of the best Edwardian bronze and marble art nouveau work to be found anywhere. The inner back room has big bas-relief friezes of jolly monks set into richly coloured florentine marble walls, an opulent marble-pillared inglenook fireplace, a low vaulted mosaic ceiling, gleaming mirrors, seats built into rich golden marble recesses, and tongue-in-cheek verbal embellishments such as Silence is Golden and Finery is Foolish. See if you can spot the opium-smoking hints modelled into the fireplace of the front room. Well kept Adnams, Fullers London Pride and Timothy Taylor Landlord on handpump, and a decent range of wines by the glass; fruit machine. Usually served all day, bar food includes sandwiches (from £3.95), soup (£3.95), a good steak sandwich (£5.50), pork and herb sausages with mash and onion gravy (£5.75), a vegetarian dish of the day (£5.95), and battered cod and chips or smoked haddock fishcakes (£6.95); Sunday roasts (£6.95). An area around the bar is no smoking. The pub does get busy, and in the evenings lots of people spill out on to the wide forecourt, near the approach to Blackfriars Bridge; there's some smart new furniture out here. If you're coming by Tube, choose your exit carefully – it's all too easy to emerge from the network of passageways and find yourself on the wrong side of the street, or marooned on a traffic island. *(Recommended by Mike Gorton, Karen and Graham Oddey, the Didler, Keith Jacob, Ian Phillips, Alison Hayes, Pete Hanlon, Andrew York, Dr and Mrs A K Clarke, John and Gloria Isaacs, Sue Demont, Tim Barrow)*

Mitchells & Butlers ~ Manager David Tate ~ Real ale ~ Bar food (12-9 (may vary in winter)) ~ (020) 7236 5474 ~ Open 11-11; 12-11(10.30 Sun) Sat; 11.30-11 winter

Cittie of Yorke

High Holborn, WC1 – find it by looking out for its big black and gold clock; ⊖ Chancery Lane

A favourite with lawyers and City types, the back bar of this unique old place is like a vast baronial hall, so though it does get busy in the evenings, there's plenty of space to absorb the crowds – and indeed it's at the busiest times that the pub is at its most magnificent. Vast thousand-gallon wine vats rest above the gantry, big bulbous lights hang from the soaring high-raftered roof, and an extraordinarily extended bar counter stretches off into the distance. Most people tend to congregate in the middle, so you may still be able to bag one of the intimate, old-fashioned and ornately carved booths that run along both sides. The triangular Waterloo fireplace, with grates on all three sides and a figure of Peace among laurels, used to stand in the Hall of Grays Inn Common Room until less obtrusive heating was introduced (thanks to the readers who sent us more thorough notes on its history). Well kept Sam Smiths OB on handpump (appealingly priced at around a pound less than the typical cost of a London pint); friendly service from smartly dressed staff, fruit machine and piped music in the cellar bar. A smaller, comfortable panelled room has lots of little prints of York and attractive brass lights, while the ceiling of the entrance hall has medieval-style painted panels and plaster York roses. Served all day from buffet counters in the main hall and cellar bar, bar food includes sandwiches (from £3.25), and half a dozen daily-changing hot dishes such as steak and kidney pie or lasagne (£4.95). A pub has stood on this site since 1430, though the current building owes more to the 1695 coffee house erected here behind a garden; it was reconstructed in Victorian times, using 17th-c materials and parts. *(Recommended by Richard Austen-Baker, BJL, Rona Murdoch, Peter Meister, Ian Phillips, the Didler, Barry Collett, Alison Hayes, Pete Hanlon, Patrick Hancock, Dr and Mrs A K Clarke, Darren Le Poidevin, Paul Boot, Joe Green)*

Sam Smiths ~ Manager Stuart Browning ~ Real ale ~ Bar food (12-9) ~ (020) 7242 7670 ~ Children in eating area of bar ~ Open 11.30(12 Sat)-11; closed Sun, bank hols

Coopers Arms

Flood Street; ⊖ Sloane Square, but quite a walk

A recent refurbishment has given this spacious open-plan pub a fresh new look described by one reader as an artfully disorganised cross between a bar and a front room. It's a splendidly enjoyable place to visit, with well liked food, beer and wine, and a particularly good atmosphere, notably relaxed and friendly. Interesting furnishings include kitchen chairs and some dark brown plush chairs on the floorboards, a mix of nice old good-sized tables, and a pre-war sideboard and dresser; also, LNER posters and maps of Chelsea and the Thames on the walls, an enormous railway clock, a fireplace with dried flowers and a tusky boar's head, and tea-shop chandeliers. Well kept Youngs Bitter and Special and Smiles IPA on handpump. The bar food mixes familiar favourites with modern tastes to excellent effect, and might typically include mediterranean vegetable soup (£3.95), smoked mackerel pâté (£4.95), seared king scallops with chargrilled chorizo, crème fraîche and sweet chilli sauce (£6.95), bangers and mash (£7.95), shepherd's pie (£8), seared sea bass fillet or aberdeen angus rib-eye steak (£12), and puddings such as raspberry and white chocolate cheesecake (£3.50); pleasant helpful staff. *(Recommended by BJL, Derek Thomas, Ian Phillips, Tracey and Stephen Groves, Jarrod and Wendy Hopkinson)*

Youngs ~ Tenants Caroline and Simon Lee ~ Real ale ~ Bar food (12.30-3, 6.30-9.30 (not Sun evening)) ~ (020) 7376 3120 ~ Children allowed until 7pm ~ Dogs allowed in bar ~ Open 11-11; 12-10.30 Sun; closed Good Fri, 25-6 Dec, 1 Jan

Cross Keys

Lawrence Street; ⊖ Sloane Square, but some distance away

This bustling Victorian pub is attractive outside with its foliage and flowers, but it's the décor inside that really impresses, with an unusual array of brassware hanging from the rafters, including trumpets and a diver's helmet. The roomy high-ceilinged flagstoned bar also has an island servery, a roaring fire, lots of atmosphere, and a good mix of customers; there's a light and airy conservatory-style back restaurant, with an ironic twist to its appealing gardening décor. Enjoyable bar food includes soup (£4.95), half a dozen rock oysters with shallot vinegar and rustic bread (£7.50), toulouse sausages with mash and lentil jus (£8.90), salmon fishcake with sorrel sauce or charcuterie platter (£9.90), and daily specials. Courage Directors and John Smiths on handpump (not cheap, even for this area), and a good choice of wines by the glass. Attentive young staff; piped music. Like most pubs in the area, it can be busy and lively on Saturday evenings. *(Recommended by Richard Lippiett, Ian Phillips, Andrea Rampley, Tracey and Stephen Groves, Derek Thomas)*

Free house ~ Licensee Oliver Delestrade ~ Bar food (12-3, 6-8) ~ Restaurant ~ (020) 7349 9111 ~ Children in restaurant ~ Dogs allowed in bar ~ Open 12-11; 12-10.30 Sun; may be closed some bank hols and Christmas

Dog & Duck

Bateman Street, on corner with Frith Street, W1; ⊖ Tottenham Court Road/Leicester Square

This pint-sized corner-house packs a lot of atmosphere into a small space – the main bar really is tiny, but at times manages to squeeze in an extraordinary number of people. Essentially unchanged for 40 years, it's a real Soho landmark, friendly and welcoming, with some interesting detail and individual touches. On the floor near the door is an engaging mosaic showing a dog with its tongue out in hot pursuit of a duck; the same theme is embossed on some of the shiny tiles that frame the heavy old advertising mirrors. There are some high stools by the ledge along the back wall, and further seats in a slightly roomier area at one end. The unusual little bar counter serves very well kept Bass, Fullers London Pride, Timothy Taylors Landlord, and maybe a guest like Adnams; also Addlestone's cider, and decent wines by the glass. There's a fire in winter; piped music. Served all day, good value bar snacks include cornish pasties (£2.75), sausage sandwiches (£4.50), and fish and chips (£6.95); staff are friendly and welcoming. In good weather especially, most people tend to spill on to the bustling street, though even when the pub is at its busiest you may find plenty of space in the rather cosy upstairs bar. The pub is said to be where George Orwell celebrated when the American Book of the Month Club chose *Animal Farm* as its monthly selection. Ronnie Scott's jazz club is near by. *(Recommended by Mike Gorton, BJL, Betsy Brown, Nigel Flook, George Atkinson, LM, Patrick Hancock, Dr and Mrs A K Clarke, Ian Phillips, Darren Le Poidevin, R Huggins, D Irving, E McCall, T McLean, Joe Green, Tim Maddison, Dr and Mrs M E Wilson)*

Mitchells & Butlers ~ Manager Jon Angeloni ~ Real ale ~ Bar food (12-9) ~ (020) 7494 0697 ~ Open 12-11; 12-10.30 Sun; closed 25 Dec

Eagle

Farringdon Road, EC1; opposite Bowling Green Lane car park; ⊖ ⇄ Farringdon/Old Street

Despite the emphasis on the distinctive mediterranean-style meals, this busy place always feels chatty and pubby, with a buzzing informality that belies the quality of the cooking. Made with the finest ingredients, and served from an open kitchen that dominates the single room, typical dishes might include an andalucian gazpacho (£5), courgette and saffron risotto (£8), bruschetta with spiced aubergines, roast cherry tomatoes and buffalo mozzarella or marinated rump steak sandwich (£8.50), roast spring chicken with preserved lemons, potatoes, mustard leaves and aïoli or sardines stuffed with breadcrumbs, capers, pine nuts and raisins (£10.50), and cuttlefish stew with chilli, garlic, parsley onions and broad beans or grilled swordfish with peppers, mint, new potatoes and balsamic vinegar (£12.50); they also do unusual spanish, sardinian or goats milk cheeses (£6.50), and portuguese custard tarts (£1.20). On weekday lunchtimes especially, dishes from the blackboard menu can run out or change fairly quickly, so it really is worth getting here as early as you possibly can if you're hoping to eat. Furnishings are basic but stylish – school chairs, a random assortment of tables, a couple of sofas on bare boards, and modern paintings on the walls (there's an art gallery upstairs, with direct access from the bar). Quite a mix of customers, but it's fair to say there's a proliferation of young media folk (the *Guardian* is based just up the road). During the week it's generally very busy indeed around meal times (and can occasionally be slightly smoky then), so isn't the sort of place you'd go for a quiet dinner, or a smart night out; it's generally quieter at weekends. Well kept Charles Wells Eagle and Bombardier on handpump, good wines including a dozen by the glass, good coffee, and properly made cocktails; piped music (sometimes loud). The Eagle was London's first gastro-pub, and its continued success does mean you may have to wait for a table, or at least not be shy about sharing. *(Recommended by Richard and Karen Holt, Andrew Stephenson, Richard Siebert, Patrick Hancock, Darren Le Poidevin, Ian Phillips, Simon Calvert, Jo Lilley, Tim Maddison, Dr and Mrs M E Wilson)*

Free house ~ Licensee Michael Belben ~ Real ale ~ Bar food (12.30-3(3.30weekends), 6.30-10.30) ~ (020) 7837 1353 ~ Children welcome ~ Dogs allowed in bar ~ Open 12-11(5 Sun); closed Sun evening, bank hols

Grapes

Shepherd Market, W1; ⊖ Green Park

Atmospheric and engagingly old-fashioned, this characterful pub is in the heart of Shepherd Market, one of central London's best-kept secrets. The dimly lit bar has a nicely traditional feel, with plenty of plush red furnishings, stuffed birds and fish in glass display cases, wooden floors and panelling, a welcoming coal fire, and a snug little alcove at the back. A good range of six or seven well kept beers on handpump (as in most Mayfair pubs fairly pricey), usually taking in Boddingtons, Bass, Flowers IPA, Fullers London Pride, Marstons Pedigree and Timothy Taylor Landlord; fruit machine. No food, but, very appealingly, they say that customers are welcome to bring in their own. It can get very busy indeed in the evenings (and may be smoky then), but though service can sometimes slow down at peak times, the cheery bustle rather adds to the allure; you'll generally see smart-suited drinkers spilling on to the square outside. It's much quieter at lunchtimes. *(Recommended by Betsy Brown, Nigel Flook, Roger and Jenny Huggins, Kevin Blake, Ian Phillips, Dr and Mrs M E Wilson, Barry and Anne, Patrick Hancock, J F M and M West, Thomas Agosti, the Didler)*

Free house ~ Licensees Gill and Eric Lewis ~ Real ale ~ Open 11(12 Sat)-11; 12-10.30 Sun

Grenadier

Wilton Row, SW1; the turning off Wilton Crescent looks prohibitive, but the barrier and watchman are there to keep out cars; walk straight past – the pub is just around the corner; ⊖ Knightsbridge

It doesn't take many people to fill up this very snug and individual place, but despite its well known charms it rarely gets too crowded, so you should generally be able to plonk yourself on one of the stools or wooden benches in the tiny bar. Patriotically painted in red, white and blue, the pub was once the mess for the officers of the Duke of Wellington. His portrait hangs above the fireplace, alongside neat prints of Guardsmen through the ages. Well kept Charles Wells Bombardier, Courage Best, Fullers London Pride, and Youngs from handpumps at the rare pewter-topped bar counter. On Sundays especially you'll find several of the customers here to sample their famous bloody marys, made to a unique recipe. As we went to press the new manager was planning a few changes, particularly to the menu: bar food has included bowls of chips (£2) and nachos (£3.50) – very popular with after-work drinkers – ploughman's (£5.95), sausage and mash (£6.75) and fish and chips (£7.45); Sunday roasts. At the back is an intimate restaurant. There's a single table outside in the peaceful mews. Thanks to the active poltergeist this is said to be London's most haunted pub. *(Recommended by Kevin Blake, Dr and Mrs M E Wilson, Jason Reynolds, Ian Phillips, Alison Hayes, Pete Hanlon)*

Spirit Group ~ Manager Cellan Williams ~ Real ale ~ Bar food (12-2.30, 6-9.30) ~ Restaurant ~ (020) 7235 3074 ~ Children in restaurant ~ Dogs allowed in bar ~ Open 10-11(10.30 Sun)

Guinea

Bruton Place; ⊖ Bond Street, Green Park, Piccadilly, Oxford Circus

Pretty much standing room only, this handily-positioned little pub dates back in part to the 17th c, when it catered for the servants and stable hands of the big houses in Mayfair. Like the Grenadier above, it's hidden away in a smart mews, which even on winter evenings can serve as an overflow for drinkers. The main draw for many is their award-wining steak and kidney pie (Mon-Fri lunchtimes, £6.95), which easily lives up to the hype; their elaborate grilled ciabattas (£6.50) have won prizes too. Well kept Youngs Bitter, Special, and seasonal brews from the striking bar counter, which has some nice wrought-iron work above it. The look of the place is appealingly simple, with bare boards, yellow walls, old-fashioned prints, and a red-planked ceiling with raj fans, but the atmosphere is chatty and civilised, with plenty of suited workers from Mayfair offices. Three cushioned wooden seats and tables are tucked to the left of the entrance to the bar, with a couple more in a snug area at the back, underneath a big old clock; most people tend to prop themselves against a little shelf running along the side of the small room. Take care to pick the right entrance – it's all too easy to walk into the quite separate upscale Guinea Grill which takes up much of the same building; uniformed doormen will politely redirect you if you've picked the door to that by mistake. *(Recommended by Ian Phillips, the Didler, Mayur Shah, R Huggins, D Irving, E McCall, T McLean)*

Youngs ~ Manager Carl Smith ~ Real ale ~ Bar food (12-3 Mon-Fri only) ~ Restaurant ~ (020) 7409 1728 ~ Open 11-11; 6.30-11 Sat; closed Sat lunchtime, all day Sun, bank hols

Please let us know of any pubs where the wine is particularly good.

Jerusalem Tavern ★

Britton Street, EC1; ⊖ ⇌ Farringdon

A good few readers now describe this carefully restored old coffee house as their favourite London pub, and it's one of ours, too. Particularly inviting when it's candlelit on a cold winter's evening, the pub is a vivid re-creation of a dark 18th-c tavern, seeming so genuinely old that you'd hardly guess the work was done only a few years ago. The current building was developed around 1720, originally as a merchant's house, then becoming a clock and watchmaker's. It still has the shop front added in 1810, immediately behind which is a light little room with a couple of wooden tables and benches, a stack of *Country Life* magazines, and some remarkable old tiles on the walls at either side. This leads to the tiny dimly lit bar, which has a couple of unpretentious tables on the bare boards, and another up some stairs on a discreetly precarious-feeling though perfectly secure balcony – a prized vantage point. A plainer back room has a few more tables, as well as a fireplace, and a stuffed fox in a case. For many the highlight is the collection of delicious St Peters beers; half a dozen are tapped from casks behind the little bar counter: depending on the season you'll find St Peters Best, Fruit Beer, Golden Ale, Grapefruit, Strong, Porter, Wheat Beer, Winter, and Spiced Ales. The rest of the range are usually available in their elegant, distinctively shaped bottles (you may already have come across these in supermarkets); if you develop a taste for them – and they are rather addictive – they sell them to take away. There's a relaxed, chatty feel in the evenings, even though these days it's getting harder to bag a seat here then, and it can feel crowded at times. Blackboards list the simple but well liked lunchtime food: soup, good big sandwiches in various breads (from £4.50), and a couple of changing hot dishes such as bangers and mash (£6.50) or lamb shank (£7.50); in the evenings food is limited to a cheese plate, pâté or charcuterie. Ingredients all come from local markets such as Smithfield. The brewery also has two main entries in our Suffolk chapter, at Wingfield, and their headquarters at South Elmham. *(Recommended by Mike Gorton, the Didler, Alison Hayes, Pete Hanlon, Brian and Rosalie Laverick, Ian Phillips, Anthony Longden, R Huggins, D Irving, E McCall, T McLean, Paul Hopton, Dr and Mrs A K Clarke, Sue Demont, Tim Barrow, Patrick Hancock)*

St Peters ~ Manager John Murphy ~ Real ale ~ Bar food (11.30-3; limited evening snacks) ~ (020) 7490 4281 ~ Children welcome ~ Dogs allowed in bar ~ Open 11-11; 5-11 Sat; 11-5 Sun; closed bank holidays

Lamb ★

Lamb's Conduit Street, WC1; ⊖ Holborn

Very highly praised by readers again this year, this is one of the capital's most famous old pubs, best known for its unique Victorian fittings and atmosphere. The highlight is the bank of cut-glass swivelling 'snob-screens' all the way around the U-shaped bar counter, but sepia photographs of 1890s actresses on the ochre panelled walls, and traditional cast-iron-framed tables with neat brass rails around the rim, all add to the overall effect. It's especially nice after lunch when the crowds have gone and you can better appreciate its timeless charms. Consistently well kept Youngs Bitter, Special and seasonal brews on handpump, along with a guest such as Smiles Best, and around 40 different malt whiskies; convivial, thoughtful service. Reliable lunchtime bar food includes a popular hot ham baguette, with the meat carved on the counter (weekdays only, £4.35), as well as ploughman's (£4.75), vegetable curry (£5.75), sausage and mash (£5.95), fish and chips (£6.35), good pies such as beef and ale or pork and cider (£6.95), and lemon and tarragon chicken (£8.50); Sunday roasts (£6.75). Shove-ha'penny, cribbage, dominoes; no machines or music. A snug room at the back on the right is no smoking. There are slatted wooden seats in front, and more in a little courtyard beyond. It can get very busy, especially in the evenings. Like the street, the pub is named for the Kentish clothmaker William Lamb who brought fresh water to Holborn in 1577. Note they don't allow children. *(Recommended by the Didler, Derek Thomas, Barry Collett, Joel Dobris, John and Gloria Isaacs, Laura Wilson, Alison Hayes, Pete Hanlon, Patrick Hancock, Darren Le Poidevin, C J Fletcher, Ian Phillips, Paul Boot, Joe Green, Mike Gorton)*

Youngs ~ Manager Michael Hehir ~ Real ale ~ Bar food (12-2.30, 6-9(not Sun evening)) ~ (020) 7405 0713 ~ Open 11-11; 12-4, 7-10.30 Sun

Lamb & Flag

Rose Street, WC2, off Garrick Street; ⊖ Leicester Square

Another of our best-loved London entries, this ever-popular old place has a splendidly enjoyable atmosphere, and a lively and well documented history: Dryden was nearly beaten to death by hired thugs outside, and Dickens made fun of the Middle Temple lawyers who frequented it when he was working in nearby Catherine Street. Unspoilt and in places rather basic, it's enormously popular with after-work drinkers and visitors; it can be empty at 5pm and heaving by 6, and even in winter you'll find an overflow of people drinking and chatting in the little alleyways outside. Access throughout has been improved in recent years; the more spartan front bar now leads easily into the back, without altering too much the snug feel of the place. The low-ceilinged back bar has high-backed black settles and an open fire, and in Regency times was known as the Bucket of Blood from the bare-knuckle prize-fights held here. Half a dozen well kept real ales include Courage Best and Directors, Charles Wells Bombardier, Youngs Special and a changing guest on handpump; as in most pubs round here, the beer isn't cheap, but on weekdays between 11 and 5 you should find at least one offered at a substantial saving. Also, a good few malt whiskies. The bar food – lunchtimes only – is simple but very good value, including soup (£1.95), filled baked potatoes (£3.50), ploughman's or good doorstep sandwiches (£3.95), several main courses such as cottage pie or spicy cumberland sausages (£4.25), and a choice of roasts (£6.50; pleasant service. The upstairs Dryden Room is often quieter than downstairs, and has jazz every Sunday evening; there's a TV in the front bar. *(Recommended by Mike Gorton, the Didler, LM, BJL, Ian Phillips, David Tindal, Peter Scillitoe, Karen and Graham Oddey, Peter Meister, Dr and Mrs A K Clarke, Andrea Rampley, Jarrod and Wendy Hopkinson, R T and J C Moggridge, Jo Lilley, Roger and Jenny Huggins)*

Free house ~ Licensees Terry Archer and Adrian and Sandra Zimmerman ~ Real ale ~ Bar food (11-3.30 weekdays, 11-5 Sat, 12-5 Sun) ~ No credit cards ~ (020) 7497 9504 ~ Children in eating area of bar ~ Jazz Sun evenings ~ Open 11-11(10.45 Fri, Sat); 12-10.30 Sun; closed 25 Dec, 1 Jan

Lord Moon of the Mall £

Whitehall, SW1; ⊖ ⇌ Charing Cross

A useful pit-stop for families and visitors touring the nearby sights – not least because the food is far cheaper than you'll find anywhere else in the area – this well converted former bank is more individual than many Wetherspoons pubs. The impressive main room has a splendid high ceiling and quite an elegant feel, with smart old prints, big arched windows looking out over Whitehall, and a huge painting that seems to show a well-to-do 18th-c gentleman; in fact it's Tim Martin, founder of the Wetherspoons chain. Once through an arch the style is more recognisably Wetherspoons, with a couple of neatly tiled areas and bookshelves opposite the long bar; silenced fruit machines, trivia and now a cash machine. They usually have seven or eight real ales, with the regulars Courage Directors, Fullers London Pride, Greene King Abbot, and Shepherd Neame Spitfire; the guests can be quite unusual, and the prices always much less than the London norm – even more so during their Afternoon Club, between 3 and 6 on weekdays, when the guest beers are only £1.49. They also keep Weston's cider. The good value bar food – served all day – is from the standard Wetherspoons menu: sandwiches (from £2.25), bangers and mash (£5.15), five bean chilli (£5.65), aberdeeen angus steak pie (£5.85), and children's meals; after 2pm (all day weekends) they usually have a 2-for-1 meal offer for £6.79. The terms of the licence rule out fried food. Service can slow down at lunchtimes, when it does get busy. The back doors (now only an emergency exit) were apparently built as a secret entrance for the bank's account holders living in Buckingham Palace (Edward VII had an account here from the age of three); the area by here is no smoking. As you come out, Nelson's Column is immediately to the left, and Big Ben a walk of ten minutes or so to the right. *(Recommended by Ian Phillips, Paul Hopton, Barry Collett, Dr and Mrs M E Wilson, Len Banister, Dr and Mrs A K Clarke, Piotr Chodzko-Zajko, Sue Demont, Tim Barrow, Roger and Jenny Huggins)*

Wetherspoons ~ Manager Mathew Gold ~ Real ale ~ Bar food (10-10; 12-9.30 Sun) ~ (020) 7839 7701 ~ Children welcome till 5pm if eating ~ Open 10-11; 10-10.30 Sun

Nags Head

Kinnerton Street, SW1; ⊖ Knightsbridge

One reader says this quaint little gem is where he'd take visitors to see the sort of pub that was common in his boyhood. It's one of the most unspoilt pubs in London, genuinely characterful and atmospheric, and with the feel of an old-fashioned local in a sleepy country village. Hidden away in an attractive and peaceful mews, it's hard to believe you're only minutes from Harrods. It rarely gets too busy or crowded, and there's a snugly relaxed and cosy feel in the small, panelled and low-ceilinged front room, where friendly regulars sit chatting around the unusual sunken bar counter. There's a log-effect gas fire in an old cooking range (seats by here are generally snapped up pretty quickly), then a narrow passage leads down steps to an even smaller back bar with stools and a mix of comfortable seats. The well kept Adnams Best, Broadside and seasonal brews are pulled on attractive 19th-c china, pewter and brass handpumps, while other interesting old features include a 1930s what-the-butler-saw machine and a one-armed bandit that takes old pennies. The piped music is rather individual: often jazz, folk or 1920s-40s show tunes. There are a few seats and sometimes a couple of tables outside. Bar food (usefully served all day) includes sandwiches (from £4), ploughman's or plenty of salads (from £6.50), sausage, mash and beans, chilli con carne, steak and mushroom pie, daily specials, and a choice of roasts (£6.95); there's a £1.50 surcharge added to all dishes in the evenings and at weekends. Service is friendly and efficient. Many readers will be delighted to learn they have a fairly hard-line policy on mobile phone use. *(Recommended by Tracey and Stephen Groves, Kevin Blake, John and Gloria Isaacs, GHC, George Atkinson, the Didler, Pete Baker, Dr and Mrs M E Wilson, Andrea Rampley, Ian Phillips, Derek Thomas, Sue Demont, Tim Barrow)*

Free house ~ Licensee Kevin Moran ~ Real ale ~ Bar food (11-9) ~ No credit cards ~ (020) 7235 1135 ~ Children in eating area of bar ~ Dogs allowed in bar ~ Open 11-11; 12-10.30 Sun

Old Bank of England

Fleet Street, EC4; ⊖ Temple

The conversion of this former branch of the Bank of England into a pub by Fullers was one of the most spectacular such transformations we've ever seen. The brewery was about to start a big face-lift as we went to press, promising new furniture throughout, and a change in the overall colour scheme from green to red. But the main features and sheer opulence of the spacious bar will remain: three gleaming chandeliers hang from the exquisitely plastered ceiling high above the unusually tall island bar counter, and the walls are liberally dotted with old prints, framed bank notes and the like. Screens between some of the tables create a surprisingly intimate feel, and there are several cosier areas at the end, with more seats in a quieter galleried section upstairs. The mural that covers most of the end wall looks like an 18th-c depiction of Justice, but in fact features members of the Fuller, Smith and Turner families. Well kept Fullers Chiswick, ESB, London Pride and seasonal brews on handpump, and around a dozen wines by the glass. Available all day, the good generously served bar food includes soup (£3.25), welsh rarebit and poached egg (£4.50), pies such as mushroom, asparagus and brie or chicken, ham and leek (£6.95), beer-battered cod (£7.95), and rosemary chicken and bacon (£8.50). At lunchtimes the piped music is generally classical or easy listening; it's louder and livelier after work, when the pub can get busy. In winter the pub is easy to spot by the Olympic-style torches blazing outside the rather austere Italianate building. Note they don't allow children, and are closed at weekends. Pies have a long if rather dubious pedigree in this area; it was in the vaults and tunnels below the Old Bank and the surrounding buildings that Sweeney Todd butchered the clients destined to provide the fillings in his mistress Mrs Lovett's nearby pie shop. *(Recommended by Ian Phillips, Barry Collett, Dr and Mrs A K Clarke, Kevin Blake, Paul Boot, the Didler)*

Fullers ~ Manager Mark Maltby ~ Real ale ~ Bar food (12-9) ~ Restaurant ~ (020) 7430 2255 ~ Open 11-11; closed wknds, bank hols

Olde Cheshire Cheese

Wine Office Court, off 145 Fleet Street, EC4; ⊖ ⇌ Blackfriars

However many times you've been to this atmospheric 17th-c former chop house, on each visit you're bound to come across a room or corner you've never noticed before. Exploring the warren of dark, historic little rooms is a delight, and despite the fact that this is one of London's most famous old pubs, it doesn't feel as if it's on the tourist route. Over the years Congreve, Pope, Voltaire, Thackeray, Dickens, Conan Doyle, Yeats and perhaps Dr Johnson have called in, and many parts hardly appear to have changed since. The unpretentious rooms have bare wooden benches built in to the walls, sawdust on bare boards, and, on the ground floor, high beams, crackly old black varnish, Victorian paintings on the dark brown walls, and big open fires in winter. A particularly snug room is the tiny one on the right as you enter, but the most rewarding bit is the Cellar Bar, down steep narrow stone steps that look as if they're only going to lead to the loo, but in fact take you to an unexpected series of cosy areas with stone walls and ceilings, and some secluded alcoves. There's plenty of space, so even though it can get busy during the week (it's fairly quiet at weekends), it rarely feels too crowded. Well kept Sam Smiths OB on handpump, as usual for this brewery, extraordinarily well priced (almost £1 less than beers in some other London pubs). Usually served all day, bar food includes sandwiches or hot panini (from £3.25), good value straightforward dishes like shepherd's pie or pasta (£5), and some more expensive specials. Some of the Cellar Bar is no smoking at lunchtimes. *(Recommended by Barry Collett, LM, Ian Phillips, Dr and Mrs M E Wilson, Alison Hayes, Pete Hanlon, Patrick Hancock, Dr and Mrs A K Clarke, Jason Reynolds, Richard Marjoram, Dr J Barrie Jones, Steve Kirby, the Didler)*

Sam Smiths ~ Manager Gordon Garrity ~ Real ale ~ Bar food (12-9 Mon-Fri; 12-5 Sat; 12-2 Sun) ~ Restaurant (Sunday) ~ (020) 7353 6170/4388 ~ Children in eating area of bar and restaurant ~ Open 11-11; 12-3 Sun; closed Sun evening

Olde Mitre £

Ely Place, EC1; the easiest way to find it is from the narrow passageway beside 8 Hatton Garden; ⊖ Chancery Lane

There's a new manager at this delightful old tavern, but happily he's running things exactly as before, right down to the toasted sandwiches; the only change is the addition of a guest beer. A real hidden treasure, the pub can be notoriously difficult to find; it's best approached from Hatton Garden, where an easily missed sign points the way down a narrow alley. The cosy dark-panelled small rooms have antique settles and – particularly in the back room, where there are more seats – old local pictures and so forth. It gets good-naturedly packed between 12.30 and 2.15, filling up again in the early evening, but in the early afternoons and by around nine becomes a good deal more tranquil. An upstairs room, mainly used for functions, may double as an overflow at peak periods. Well kept Adnams, Tetleys and a changing guest on handpump. No music, TV or machines – the only game here is darts. Served all day, bar snacks are limited to scotch eggs or pork pies (£1), and really good value toasted sandwiches with cheese, ham, pickle or tomato (£1.50). There are some pot plants and jasmine in the narrow yard between the pub and St Ethelreda's church. Note the pub doesn't open weekends. The iron gates that guard one entrance to Ely Place are a reminder of the days when the law in this district was administered by the Bishops of Ely. *(Recommended by BJL, the Didler, Alison Hayes, Pete Hanlon, Ian Phillips, R Huggins, D Irving, E McCall, T McLean, Dr and Mrs A K Clarke, Dr J Barrie Jones, Patrick Hancock, Steve Kirby)*

Spirit Group ~ Manager Eamon Scott ~ Real ale ~ Bar food (11.30-9.30) ~ (020) 7405 4751 ~ Open 11-11; closed wknds, bank hols

Red Lion

Waverton Street, W1; ⊖ Green Park

Even though this is one of Mayfair's quietest and prettiest corners, the sudden appearance of what appears to be a smart village local is a real but welcome surprise. Comfortably civilised, it stands out for its very relaxed and distinctly un-London atmosphere; on some evenings after work it can be very busy indeed, but it always keeps its warmly cosy feel. The main L-shaped bar has small winged settles on the partly carpeted scrubbed floorboards, and London prints below the high shelf of china on its dark-panelled walls. Well kept beers such as Charles Wells Bombardier, Fullers London Pride, Greene King IPA and Youngs Ordinary on handpump, and they do rather good bloody marys (with a daunting Very Spicy option); also a dozen malt whiskies. Bar food, served from a corner at the front, includes sandwiches (from £3), ploughman's (£4.50), cod and chips, half rack of grilled pork ribs or cajun chicken (all £6.95), and specials such as mushroom stroganoff. The gents' usually has a copy of *Private Eye* at eye level (it used to be the *Financial Times*). On Saturday evenings they generally have a pianist. *(Recommended by Roger and Jenny Huggins, Betsy Brown, Nigel Flook, Ian Phillips, BJL, Kevin Blake, Dr and Mrs M E Wilson, Simon and Amanda Southwell, Thomas Agosti, Dr and Mrs A K Clarke)*

Spirit Group ~ Manager Greg Peck ~ Real ale ~ Bar food (12-3 (not Sat), 6-9.30) ~ Restaurant ~ (020) 7499 1307 ~ Children welcome ~ Dogs allowed in bar ~ Piano Sat evening ~ Open 11.30-11; 6-11 Sat; 12-3, 6-10.30 Sun; closed Sat am, all day 25-26 Dec, 1 Jan

Red Lion

Duke of York Street, SW1; ⊖ Piccadilly Circus

Warmly praised by readers again this year, this is perhaps central London's most perfectly preserved Victorian pub, with mirrors so dazzling, and gleaming mahogany so warm, that it's hard to believe they weren't put in yesterday. Other notable architectural features squeezed into the very small rooms include the crystal chandeliers and cut and etched windows, and the striking ornamental plaster ceiling. There's a good, bustling atmosphere, and it fills up very quickly: it's worth getting there at opening time to appreciate the building's charms more peacefully. Simple lunchtime snacks such as sandwiches (£3), filled baguettes (£4), and sausage and chips (£6); diners have priority on a few of the front tables, and there's a minuscule upstairs eating area. Well kept Adnams, Bass, Fullers London Pride, Greene King Old Speckled Hen and Tetleys on handpump; friendly efficient service. It can be very crowded at lunchtime (try inching through to the back room where there's sometimes more space); many customers spill out on to the pavement, in front of a mass of foliage and flowers cascading down the wall. No children inside. *(Recommended by BJL, the Didler, Ian Phillips, P G Plumridge, Dr and Mrs M E Wilson, Alison Hayes, Pete Hanlon, Roger and Jenny Huggins, Mayur Shah, Sue Demont, Tim Barrow)*

Mitchells & Butlers ~ Manager Michael Brown ~ Real ale ~ No credit cards ~ (020) 7321 0782 ~ Open 11.30(12 Sat)-11; closed Sun and bank hols

Pubs with particularly interesting histories, or in unusually interesting buildings, are listed at the back of the book.

Seven Stars

Carey Street, WC2; ⊖ Holborn (just as handy from Temple or Chancery Lane, but the walk through Lincoln's Inn Fields can be rather pleasant)

Facing the back of the Law Courts, this cosy little pub is doing well under its current licensees, who as well as introducing a greater emphasis on food have brought a real sense of bonhomie to the place. Long a favourite with lawyers and reporters covering notable trials nearby, it has two unspoilt rooms with a few tables set for eating, plenty of caricatures of barristers and judges on the red-painted walls, posters of legal-themed British films, big ceiling fans, and a relaxed, intimate atmosphere; checked table cloths add a quirky, almost continental touch. A third room is planned, similar in size and style, which will help free up space; it can fill up very quickly, and on busy evenings customers sometimes spill on to the quiet road in front. It generally quietens down after 8. Well kept Adnams Best and Broadside, Harveys Sussex and a changing guest on handpump; service is prompt and very friendly. Served all day, the blackboard menu might include things like half a dozen oysters (£6), extra mature cheddar with relish, salad and oatcakes (£6.50), Country Scramble (a chunk of sourdough with smoked pork, sliced potato, onion, parsley and thyme in eggs, £7.50), caesar salad with poached egg or charcuterie with artisanal bread and onion relish (£8), fresh dressed crab (£8.50), and plenty of seasonal game; at times you may also find vintage port with fruit cake. The pub cat may take umbrage if you move the newspaper he likes to sleep on. The Elizabethan stairs up to the lavatories are rather steep, but the licensees tell us that with the addition of a good strong handrail and some light grey rubber, the trip is now 'a safe and bouncy delight'. *(Recommended by the Didler, LM, B and M Kendall, Ian Phillips, Patrick Hancock, Jarrod and Wendy Hopkinson, R Huggins, D Irving, E McCall, T McLean, Sue Demont, Tim Barrow)*

Free house ~ Licensee Roxy Beaujolais ~ Real ale ~ Bar food (12-9) ~ Restaurant ~ (020) 7242 8521 ~ Children in eating area of bar but no pushchairs ~ Dogs allowed in bar ~ Open 11-11; 12-11.30 Sat; closed Sun, and some bank hols (usually inc Christmas)

Star

Belgrave Mews West, SW1, behind the German Embassy, off Belgrave Square; ⊖ Knightsbridge

A nicely traditional pub with good value food and particularly well kept beer, this timeless place is said to be where the Great Train Robbery was planned. Outside peak times it has a pleasantly quiet and restful local feel, and it always impresses in summer with its astonishing array of hanging baskets and flowering tubs outside, much more impressive than average. The small entry room, which also has the food servery, has stools by the counter and tall windows; an arch leads to a side room with swagged curtains, well polished wooden tables and chairs, heavy upholstered settles, globe lighting, and raj fans. The back room has button-back built-in wall seats, and there's a similarly furnished room upstairs. Well kept Fullers Chiswick, ESB, London Pride and seasonal brews on handpump. Bar food might include sandwiches (from £3.25), warm roast chicken, bacon and avocado salad, sausage and mash or pasta with sun-dried tomatoes, olives, garlic and cream (£6.25), and rib-eye steak (£10.95); service is prompt and efficient. *(Recommended by the Didler, Kevin Blake, Richard Dixon, Ian Phillips, Sue Demont, Tim Barrow)*

Fullers ~ Manager T J Connell ~ Real ale ~ Bar food (12-2, 7-9) ~ (020) 7235 3019 ~ Children welcome ~ Dogs allowed in bar ~ Open 11-11; 12-10.30 Sun

Westminster Arms

Storey's Gate, SW1; ⊖ Westminster

This unpretentious and friendly Westminster local is the handiest for the Abbey and the Houses of Parliament, so the friendly regulars that readers have struck up conversations with have sometimes turned out to be MPs. If you hear something a bit like a telephone bell, it's the Division Bell, reminding them to go back across the road to vote. The pub can be packed after work with government staff and researchers, but the turnover of customers is usually quite quick, and there's an appealing mix of people. A good range of seven well kept real ales takes in Adnams Best and Broadside, Ansells, Fullers London Pride, Youngs and a couple of guests like Greene King Abbot or Hogs Back Tea; they also do decent wines, and a dozen or so malt whiskies. The plain main bar has simple old-fashioned furnishings, with proper tables on the wooden floors, and a good deal of panelling; there's not a lot of room, so come early for a seat. The food is served in the downstairs wine bar (a good retreat from the ground-floor bustle), with some of the tables in cosy booths; typical dishes include soup (£3.75), various salads or ploughman's (£6.95), cottage pie (£6.95), steak and kidney pie (£7.95), fish and chips (£8.95), and daily specials. Piped music in this area, and in the more formal upstairs restaurant, but not generally in the main bar; fruit machine. There are no smoking areas and a couple of tables by the street outside. *(Recommended by the Didler, Paul Hopton, Stephen, Julie and Hayley Brown, Dr and Mrs A K Clarke, Mayur Shah, Ian Phillips, Tracey and Stephen Groves, Sue Demont, Tim Barrow)*

Free house ~ Licensees Gerry and Marie Dolan ~ Real ale ~ Bar food (12-8 weekdays, 12-4 Sat, Sun) ~ Restaurant (weekday lunchtimes (not Weds)) ~ (020) 7222 8520 ~ Children in eating area of bar and restaurant ~ Open 11-11; 11-6 Sat; 12-5 Sun; closed 25 Dec

EAST LONDON Map 12

Crown 🍷

Grove Road/Old Ford Road, E3; ⊖ Mile End

On quite a busy roundabout facing Victoria Park with its popular boating lake, this idiosyncratic pub is notable for its organic food and drinks, and its proudly recycled furnishings. Despite the big windows, it's dim inside, thanks to the very dark ceiling, some dark brown walls, and soft lighting (evidently powered by solar or wind generation) from lamps that include some big retirees from a hospital operating theatre. There is an easy-going jumble of mainly stripped tables in all sorts of sizes on the dark floorboards, with a similar mix of chairs; a couple of corners have well worn easy chairs, and big abstracts decorate the walls. Good freshly cooked food makes its entrance down broad stairs below a crystal chandelier; the big blackboard might include squash and coconut soup (£4.50), smoked mackerel terrine (£7), salt cod with croquettes and rocket, squash and tarragon risotto or asparagus with egg and hollandaise (£8), grilled rare breed pork chop with mustard mash and savoy cabbage (£13.50), and rib-eye steak with root vegetable chips (£14.50), with puddings such as banoffi and almond tart (£5), or english cheeses (£6.50); children's helpings. They may have special weekday lunch offers, and open early for breakfast at weekends. A fine choice of organic wines and other drinks (the only non-organic tipples are the single malt whiskies) includes on handpump the local Pitfield beers Eco Warrior and Singhboulton (named after the pub's hands-on joint owners) and St Peters Organic Best. Part of the bar and all of the restaurant are no smoking. The relaxed mix of customers may include the odd friendly dog, and there are some pleasant courtyard tables. *(Recommended by Derek Thomas, Catherine Cronin)*

Free house ~ Licensee Geetie Singh ~ Real ale ~ Bar food (12.30-4 (not Mon), 6.30-10.30; 10.30-4, 6.30-10.30 Sat-Sun) ~ Restaurant ~ (020) 8981 9998 ~ Children welcome ~ Dogs allowed in bar ~ Open 12-11; 12-10.30 Sun; closed till 5pm Mon, all 25 Dec

Grapes

Narrow Street, E14; ⊖ Shadwell (some distance away) or Westferry on the Docklands Light Railway; the Limehouse link has made it hard to find by car – turn off Commercial Road at signs for Rotherhithe tunnel, then from the Tunnel Approach slip road, fork left leading into Branch Road, turn left and then left again into Narrow Street

'A tavern of dropsical appearance,' was how Dickens summed up this warmly welcoming 16th-c tavern when he used it as the basis of his Six Jolly Fellowship

Porters in *Our Mutual Friend*, and not much has changed since. In a peaceful spot well off the tourist route, it's today one of London's most engaging riverside pubs, but in Dickens's day frequent visitors weren't always so well rewarded: watermen would row out drunks from here, drown them, and sell the salvaged bodies to the anatomists. The back part is the oldest, with the small back balcony a fine place for a sheltered waterside drink; steps lead down to the foreshore. The partly panelled bar has lots of prints, mainly of actors, and old local maps, as well as some elaborately etched windows, plates along a shelf, and newspapers to read. Well kept Adnams, Bass and Ind Coope Burton on handpump, a choice of malt whiskies, and a good wine list. Good bar food includes soup (£3.25), sandwiches (from £3.25), ploughman's (£4.75), a pint of shell-on prawns (£5.25), bangers and mash (£6.25), home-made fishcakes with caper sauce (£6.50), dressed crab (£7.75), and a highly regarded, generous Sunday roast (no other meals then, when it can be busy, particularly in season). They do an excellent brunch on Saturday lunchtimes. Booking is recommended for the upstairs fish restaurant, which has fine views of the river (the pub was a favourite with Rex Whistler, who used it as the viewpoint for his rather special river paintings). Shove-ha'penny, table skittles, cribbage, dominoes, chess, backgammon; there may be piped classical or jazz. *(Recommended by Tim and Pam Moorey, Bob and Sue Hardy, LM, Joan E Hilditch)*

Spirit Group ~ Manager Barbara Haigh ~ Real ale ~ Bar food (not Sun evening) ~ Restaurant ~ (020) 7987 4396 ~ Dogs allowed in bar ~ Open 12-3, 5.30-11; 12-11 Sat; 12-10.30 Sun; closed 25-26 Dec, 1 Jan

Prospect of Whitby

Wapping Wall, E1; ⊖ Wapping

Claiming to be the oldest pub on the Thames (it dates back to 1543), this entertaining pub was for a long while better known as the Devil's Tavern, thanks to its popularity with smugglers and other ne'er-do-wells. The river views can hardly be bettered, so over the centuries it's been a favourite with some of the capital's best-known figures. Pepys and Dickens were both frequent callers, Turner came for weeks at a time to study the scene, and in the 17th c the notorious Hanging Judge Jeffreys was able to combine two of his interests by enjoying a drink at the back while looking down over the grisly goings-on in Execution Dock. With such a lively history it's no wonder they do rather play on it; the tourists who flock here lap up the colourful tales of Merrie Olde London, and only the most unromantic of visitors could fail to be carried along by the fun. The pub is an established favourite on the evening coach tours, but is usually quieter at lunchtimes. Plenty of bare beams, bare boards, panelling and flagstones in the L-shaped bar (where the long pewter counter is over 400 years old), and a river view towards Docklands from tables in the waterfront courtyard. Well kept Charles Wells Bombardier, Fullers London Pride and Greene King Old Speckled Hen on handpump, and quite a few malt whiskies. Bar meals are served all day, from a menu including sandwiches and filled baked potatoes (from £3.25), various burgers, ploughman's (£5.25), beef goulash (£5.95), and jamaican jerk spiced chicken (£9.75); readers report big helpings. One room (with good river views) is no smoking; fruit machine, golf game. *(Recommended by Roy and Lindsey Fentiman, GHC, Alison Hayes, Pete Hanlon, Piotr Chodzko-Zajko, Bill Sykes, the Didler)*

Spirit Group ~ Manager Christopher Reeves ~ Real ale ~ Bar food (12-9.30) ~ Restaurant ~ (020) 7481 1095 ~ Children welcome ~ Dogs welcome ~ Open 11.30-11; 12-10.30 Sun

NORTH LONDON Map 13

Chapel (🍴) 🍷

Chapel Street, NW1; ⊖ Edgware Road

The food at this much-modernised, child-friendly gastropub has long been a draw, and regular visitors say it 'just keeps getting better and better'. The choice of imaginative and well served and presented meals changes every day, but might include soups such as courgette, lemon and mint (£3.50) or cream of vegetable, bacon and sweetcorn (£4), sun-dried tomato, olive and jarlsberg cheese tartlet (£4.50), ragoût of seabass, red snapper and oysters with baby corn and lime (£5), stuffed globe artichoke with risotto, smoked cheddar and tomato coulis (£8.50), roasted chicken breast stuffed with salami milano and green pepper cheese (£10.50), pan-fried guinea fowl with french beans, passion fruit and marjoram jus (£11.50), baked monkfish with serano, aubergine, tomato and anchovy dressing or chargrilled T-bone steak with bok choi and portabello mushroom cream (£13), and puddings like banana crème brûlée (£3.50). Prompt, charming service from friendly staff, who may bring delicious warm walnut bread to your table while you're waiting. Light and spacious, the cream-painted rooms are dominated by the open kitchen; furnishings are smart but simple, with plenty of plain wooden tables around the bar, a couple of comfortable sofas at the lounge end, and a big fireplace. It can fill up quite quickly, so you may have to wait to eat during busier periods. The atmosphere is always cosmopolitan – perhaps more relaxed and civilised at lunchtime, then altogether busier and louder in the evenings. There are more tables on a terrace outside, popular with chic local office workers on fine lunchtimes. Well kept Adnams and Greene King IPA on handpump, a good range of interesting wines (up to half by the glass), cappuccino and espresso, fresh orange juice, and a choice of tisanes such as peppermint or strawberry and vanilla. In the evening trade is more evenly split between diners and drinkers, and the music can be quite noticeable then, especially at weekends. *(Recommended by Ian Phillips, Sebastian and Paris Leach, Mayur Shah, Sue Demont, Tim Barrow)*

Punch ~ Lease Lakis Hondrogiannis ~ Real ale ~ Bar food (12-2.30, 7-10) ~ (020) 7402 9220 ~ Children welcome ~ Dogs allowed in bar ~ Open 12-11(10.30 Sun); closed some bank hols, and maybe over Christmas

Compton Arms 🍷 £

Compton Avenue, off Canonbury Road, N1; ⊖ ⇄ Highbury & Islington

Feeling like a very appealing village local, this tiny, well run pub is hidden away up a peaceful mews. An unexpected bonus is the terrace behind, with tables among flowers under a big sycamore tree; there may be heaters in winter, and occasional barbecues in summer. Inside, the unpretentious low-ceilinged rooms are simply furnished with wooden settles and assorted stools and chairs, with local pictures on the walls; there's a TV, but the only games are things like chess, Jenga and battleships. Well kept Greene King Abbot, IPA and Ruddles and a weekly changing guest on handpump, and around a dozen wines by the glass; friendly service. Decent bar food such as sandwiches and baguettes (£3.95), filled baked potatoes (£3.95), various burgers (£4.95), fish and chips or steak and ale pie (£5.95), and eight different types of sausage served with mashed potato and home-made red onion gravy (£5.95); their Sunday roasts come in two sizes, normal (£4.95) and large (£5.95). The pub is deep in Arsenal country, so can get busy on match days. *(Recommended by Ian Phillips, Tim Maddison, Darren Le Poidevin)*

Greene King ~ Managers Scott Plomer and Eileen Shelock ~ Real ale ~ Bar food (12-2.30, 6-8.30; 12-4 Sat-Sun) ~ (020) 7359 6883 ~ Children welcome in back bar and garden till 8pm ~ Open 12-11(10.30 Sun)

Drapers Arms 🍴 🍷

Barnsbury Street; ⊖ ⇄ Highbury & Islington

London Dining Pub of the Year

In a quiet residential street away from Islington's main drag, this striking Georgian townhouse is a top-notch gastropub, very highly regarded for its outstanding, thoughtfully prepared food. A meal here isn't exactly cheap, but the fresh carefully judged flavours and tempting presentation make it a particularly rewarding and memorable experience. The choice might include portabello mushroom and flat leaf parsley soup (£5), steamed mussels with cider, bacon and tarragon (£5 starter, £9.50 main course), lunchtime sandwiches such as tomato, basil and mozzarella (£5.20) or smoked salmon and caesar (£6.20), ballantine of sea trout with horseradish remoulade (£6), smoked haddock bubble and squeak with a poached egg and dill hollandaise (£6.50), linguini with crab and fresh herbs (£11.50), duck confit with warm potato salad and spiced apple jus (£13.50), roast maize-fed chicken with lentil vinaigrette and aïoli or venison cottage pie (£14), and 10oz sirloin with chips and sauce béarnaise (£15.50); the puddings (all £5.50) include a first-class sticky toffee. Service is helpful and unobtrusive. Big colourful bunches of flowers, inset shelves of paperbacks and board games, and a couple of groups of sofas and armchairs offset what might otherwise seem rather a severe open-plan layout and décor, with high-backed dining chairs or booths on dark bare boards, high ceilings, a few big drapery prints on dusky pink walls, and a pair of large fireplaces and mirrors precisely facing each other across the front area; the overall effect is not unlike a bright, elegant wine bar. The choice of wines by the glass (including champagne) is first-rate, and they have Courage Best and Greene King Old Speckled Hen on handpump, along with maybe a guest like Shepherd Neame Spitfire. On our inspection the piped music was jazz and swing. *(Recommended by Aidan Wallis)*

Free house ~ Licensees Mark Emberton and Paul McElhinney ~ Real ale ~ Bar food (12-3, 7-10; not Sun evening) ~ Restaurant ~ (020) 7619 0348 ~ Children welcome till 8pm ~ Dogs allowed in bar ~ Open 11-11; 12-10.30 Sun; closed 24-27 Dec, 1-2 Jan

Duke of Cambridge

St Peter's Street, N1; ⊖ Angel, though some distance away

London's first organic pub, this well refurbished corner house is worth tracking down for its excellent range of impeccably sourced drinks and food. Prices for both are higher than you'd pay for a non-organic meal, but it's usually worth the extra to enjoy choices and flavours you won't find anywhere else. Changing twice a day, the blackboard menu might include things like celeriac, chick pea and cabbage soup (£4.50), pumpkin, pear and celery soup (£4.50), bruschetta with chicken livers, dandelion leaves, sherry and crème fraîche (£6), roast vegetable parmigiana with parmesan and hazelnut crust (£9), bacon-wrapped scallops with tartare potato cake and basil crème (£10.50), linguini with fried red mullet, lemon and chilli sauce (£12), home-smoked lamb fillet with potato, aubergine and feta gratin (£13), and white chocolate and berry cheesecake (£4.50); children's helpings. A note explains that though they do all they can to ensure their game and fish have been sourced from suppliers using sustainable methods, these can't officially be classed as organic. They make all their own bread, pickles, ice-cream and so on. On handpump are four organic real ales: from London's small Pitfield Brewery Eco Warrior and Singhboulton (named for the pub's two owners), St Peters Best, and a guest such as East Kent Goldings or Shoreditch Organic Stout. They also have organic draught lagers and cider, organic spirits, and a very wide range of organic wines, many of which are available by the glass. The full range of drinks is chalked on a blackboard, and also includes good coffees and teas, and a spicy ginger ale. The big, busy main room is simply decorated and furnished, with lots of chunky wooden tables, pews and benches on bare boards, a couple of big metal vases with colourful flowers, daily papers, and carefully positioned soft lighting around the otherwise bare walls. The atmosphere is warmly inviting, with the sound of civilised chat from a steady stream of varied customers; no music or games machines. A corridor leads off past a few tables and an open kitchen to a couple of smaller candlelit rooms, more formally set for eating; there's also a small side terrace. Some areas are no smoking. The licensees run the Crown in Victoria Park (see East London main entries) along similar lines. *(Recommended by Darren Le Poidevin)*

Free house ~ Licensees Geetie Singh and Esther Boulton ~ Real ale ~ Bar food (12.30-3(3.30 Sat-Sun), 6.30-10.30(10 Sun)) ~ Restaurant ~ (020) 7359 3066 ~ Children welcome ~ Dogs allowed in bar ~ Open 12-11(10.30 Sun); closed 25-26 Dec

Tipping is not normal for bar meals, and not usually expected.

Flask 🍷

Flask Walk, NW3; ⊖ Hampstead

Very much in tune with its neighbourhood, this properly old-fashioned local has a rather villagey feel, and is a popular haunt of Hampstead artists, actors and characters. The snuggest and most individual part is the cosy lounge at the front, with plush green seats and banquettes curving round the panelled walls, a unique Victorian screen dividing it from the public bar, and an attractive fireplace. A comfortable orange-lit room with period prints and a few further tables leads into a rather smart dining conservatory, which with its plants, prominent wine bottles and neat table linen feels a bit like a wine bar. A couple of white iron tables are squeezed into the tiny back yard. Particularly well kept Youngs Bitter, Special and seasonal brews on handpump, around 20 wines by the glass, and decent coffees – they have a machine that grinds the beans to order. Bar food might include sandwiches, soup, daily changing specials like chicken casserole, lamb curry or spiced minced beef pie with a cheese and leek mash topping (from £5.50), and fish and chips (£6.50). A plainer public bar (which you can get into only from the street) has leatherette seating, cribbage, backgammon, lots of space for darts, fruit machines, trivia and big-screen Sky TV. Service is generally friendly, from sociable young staff. There are quite a few tables out in the alley. One reader this year found it rather smoky. The pub's name is a reminder of the days when it distributed mineral water from Hampstead's springs *(Recommended by Ian Phillips, the Didler, Tracey and Stephen Groves, Patrick Hancock, MDN, Simon Calvert)*

Youngs ~ Manager John Cannon ~ Real ale ~ Bar food (12-3(4 Sun), 6-8.30; not Sun-Mon evening) ~ Restaurant ~ (020) 7435 4580 ~ Children in eating area of bar and restaurant ~ Dogs allowed in bar ~ Open 11-11; 12-10.30 Sun

Holly Bush

Holly Mount, NW3; ⊖ Hampstead

Reached by a delightful stroll along some of Hampstead's most villagey streets, this old favourite is on top form at the moment. The service, food and drink all win praise, but as ever it's the timeless atmosphere that most stands out, particularly in the evenings, when a good mix of chatty locals and visitors fills the old-fashioned and individual front bar. One reader's visit was plunged into darkness after a powercut, but the unfazed staff simply lit the pub with candles, which with the glowing coal fire seemed to create something of an 18th-c feel; our correspondent says it wouldn't have surprised him if Dick Turpin had strode in. Under the dark sagging ceiling are brown and cream panelled walls (decorated with old advertisements and a few hanging plates), open fires, bare boards, and cosy bays formed by partly glazed partitions. Slightly more intimate, the back room, named after the painter George Romney, has an embossed red ceiling, panelled and etched glass alcoves, and ochre-painted brick walls covered with small prints; piped music, darts. Bar food includes welsh rarebit (£5), stuffed courgette (£7.50), various sausages with cheddar mash and gravy (£8.50), pies like chicken, mushroom and London Pride (£9) or beef and Harveys (£9.50), and rabbit in mustard and pilsner sauce or roasted free-range chicken in smoked paprika sauce (£10.50). Well kept Adnams Bitter and Broadside, Fullers London Pride, Harveys Sussex and an unusual guest like Cains Formidable or Hook Norton Generation on handpump, some unusual bottled beers, plenty of whiskies, and a seasonally changing wine list; friendly service. The upstairs dining room (with table service Weds-Sun) is no smoking. There are tables on the pavement outside. *(Recommended by Ian Phillips, the Didler, Tracey and Stephen Groves, Derek Thomas, Paul Boot, Simon Calvert, Jo Lilley, Tim Maddison)*

Punch ~ Lease Nicolai Outzen ~ Real ale ~ Bar food (12.30-4 (not Mon), 6.30-10 wkdays; 12.30-10 Sat, 12.30-9 Sun) ~ Restaurant ~ (020) 7435 2892 ~ Children in eating area of bar ~ Dogs allowed in bar ~ Open 12-11(10.30 Sun)

Olde White Bear

Well Road, NW3; ⊖ Hampstead

Notably friendly and very close to the Heath, this neo-Victorian pub has a wonderfully clubby feel that attracts a splendidly diverse mix of customers. The dimly lit knocked-through bar has three separate-seeming areas: the biggest has lots of Victorian prints and cartoons on the walls, as well as wooden stools, cushioned captain's chairs, a couple of big tasselled armchairs, a flowery sofa, a handsome fireplace and an ornate Edwardian sideboard. A brighter section at the end has elaborate brocaded pews and wooden venetian blinds, while a central area has Lloyd Loom furniture, dried flower arrangements and signed photographs of actors and playwrights. Bar food is served all day, from a range including soup (£4), good elaborate sandwiches (from £4.50), skewered tempura prawns (£5.50), burgers (from £6.75), spicy spanish sausages or gammon and pineapple (£7.50), cod in beer batter (£8), beef and Guinness pie (£8.50), and sirloin steak (£10.50); Sunday roasts (£7.50). Adnams, Fullers London Pride, Greene King Abbot, and Youngs on handpump; over a dozen wines by the glass, and a decent range of whiskies. There are a few tables in front, and more in a courtyard behind. Soft piped music, cards, chess, TV and excellent Thursday quiz nights. Parking may be a problem at times – it's mostly residents' permits only nearby (there are no restrictions on Sundays). *(Recommended by the Didler, Patrick Hancock, Sue Demont, Tim Barrow, Simon Calvert, Jo Lilley)*

Punch ~ Lease Christopher Ely ~ Real ale ~ Bar food (12-9) ~ (020) 7435 3758 ~ Children welcome ~ Dogs allowed in bar ~ Open 11-11; 12-10.30 Sun

Spaniards Inn

Spaniards Lane, NW3; ⊖ Hampstead, but some distance away, or from Golders Green station take 220 bus

Tales of hauntings and highwaymen continue to draw the crowds to this busy former toll house, which now has a more practical claim to fame: they recently introduced the world's first automatic dog-wash, perfect for cleaning canines who've enjoyed themselves a little too enthusiastically on the Heath. Dating back to 1585, the low-ceilinged oak-panelled rooms of the attractive main bar are full of character, with open fires, genuinely antique winged settles, candle-shaped lamps in shades, and snug little alcoves. But for many visitors the highlight is perhaps the charming garden, nicely arranged in a series of areas separated by judicious planting of shrubs. A crazy paved terrace with slatted wooden tables and chairs opens on to a flagstoned walk around a small lawn, with roses, a side arbour of wisteria and clematis, and an aviary. You may need to move fast to bag a table out here in summer. Served all day, bar food includes ciabattas (from £4.95), cottage pie (£6), greek salad (£6.50), mushroom and leek risotto (£6.95), home-made cumberland sausages (£7.50), and steak and kidney pudding (£8.50); they do a paella on Saturdays (£7.50), and a choice of roasts on Sundays. The food bar is no smoking at lunchtimes; upstairs, the Georgian Turpin Room is no smoking all day. Well kept Adnams, Charles Wells Bombardier, Marstons Old Empire, Shepherd Neame Spitfire and a guest like Everards Tiger on handpump – though in summer you might find the most popular drink is their big jug of Pimms; newspapers, fruit machine. The pub is believed to have been named after the Spanish ambassador to the court of James I, who had a private residence here. It's fairly handy for Kenwood. Parking can be difficult. *(Recommended by Tracey and Stephen Groves, Ian Phillips, R T and J C Moggridge, Simon Calvert, Jo Lilley)*

Mitchells & Butlers ~ Manager Matthew O'Keefe ~ Real ale ~ Bar food (11-10;12-9 Sun) ~ (020) 8731 6571 ~ Children welcome ~ Dogs welcome ~ Open 11-11 (12 Sat during July-Aug Kenwood concerts); 12-10.30 Sun

If we know a pub does sandwiches we always say so – if they're not mentioned, you'll have to assume you can't get one.

Waterside

York Way, N1; ⊖ ⇌ Kings Cross

Much nicer than you might expect from the surrounding area, this is a useful place to know if passing through Kings Cross, particularly in summer, when it benefits from an unexpectedly relaxed and peaceful outside terrace overlooking the Battlebridge Basin, usually busy with boats. Heaters keep it pleasant all year round. Refurbished this year to create a brighter feel, the inside is a nicely done pastiche of a 17th-c cider barn, with stripped brickwork, latticed windows, genuinely old stripped timbers in white plaster, spinning wheels, milkmaids' yokes, and horsebrasses and so on, with dimly lit alcoves and plenty of rustic tables and wooden benches. Well kept Adnams, Fullers London Pride and a changing guest such as Charles Wells Bombardier on handpump, with cocktails in summer. Promptly served bar food (available all day exc Sunday) still has something of an emphasis on fairly formidable pizzas (from £4.95), but they also do sandwiches (from £4.75), and hot dishes like fish and chips or steak pie (£6.45). The bar staff are eager to please. Live jazz Wednesday evenings. Pool, fruit machine, and sometimes loudish juke box. *(Recommended by Ian Phillips, Darren Le Poidevin, Tracey and Stephen Groves, Mrs Jane Kingsbury)*

Laurel (Enterprise) ~ Manager Alastair Calvey ~ Real ale ~ Bar food ~ (020) 7713 8613 ~ Open 11-11; 11 Sat; 12-10.30 Sun; closed 25-26 Dec, 1 Jan

SOUTH LONDON Map 12

Alma 🍷

York Road, SW18; ⇌ Wandsworth Town

In the same group as two other London main entries, the Coopers Arms in Chelsea and the Ship close by, this relaxed and comfortable corner pub feels rather like a welcoming local, if a rather smart one – and the distinctive food lifts it well out of the ordinary. Light and airy, the bar's furnishings are mostly quite simple: a mix of chairs and cast-iron-framed or worn wooden tables around the brightly repainted walls, and a couple of sofas, with gilded mosaics of the 19th-c Battle of the Alma and an ornate mahogany chimney-piece and fireplace adding a touch of elegance. Youngs Bitter, Special and seasonal brews from the island bar counter (about to be replaced as we went to press), and good house wines (around 20 by the glass); also freshly squeezed juices, and coffee, tea or hot chocolate. The popular but less pubby dining room has a fine turn-of-the-century frieze of swirly nymphs, and a window overlooking an ornamental garden; there's waitress service in here, and you can book tables. The imaginative and generously served bar food might include very good sandwiches (from £3.75), soups such as roasted fennel and parsnip (£3.75), spaghetti with english asparagus, salmon and lemon cream (£8.50), and seared lamb with ginger lentils and bok choi (£9.50); the menu is a little different on Sundays, when they do various roasts. Much of the meat is organic, and comes from their own farm in Dorking. Even when it's very full – which it often is in the evenings – service is careful and efficient. If you're after a quiet drink don't come when there's a rugby match on the television, unless you want a running commentary from the well heeled and voiced young locals. Pinball, dominoes. Travelling by rail into Waterloo you can see the pub rising above the neighbouring rooftops as you rattle through Wandsworth Town. *(Recommended by Dr Martin Owton, the Didler, Ian Phillips, Brenda and Rob Fincham)*

Youngs ~ Tenant Charles Gotto ~ Real ale ~ Bar food (12-4, 6-10) ~ Restaurant ~ (020) 8870 2537 ~ Children welcome ~ Open 11-11; 12-10.30 Sun; closed 25 Dec

Boathouse

Brewhouse Lane, Putney Wharf; ⊖ Putney Bridge, then cross the Thames – from the bridge you can see the pub on your left

Though it's been open for only a few months, this strikingly converted former vinegar factory has quickly become one of the area's most popular pubs, thanks to its splendid setting beside the river and Putney Bridge. There are plenty of tables on the busy terrace in front (snapped up quickly on fine days), but the view is just as good from the comfortable bar in the building's glazed front extension, and even better from the balcony of the upstairs dining room. As well as its huge walls of glass – creating a very light, spacious feel – the bar has several sofas and low, modern tables on rugs on the polished wooden floors; also fresh flowers and newspapers, a large, slightly incongruous candelabrum, and a big plasma TV screen for sports. Well kept Youngs Original, Special and seasonal brews on handpump from the long counter, and a good choice of wines by the glass; piped music. Up some steps is a cosier galleried room, more traditional, with panelling, a mix of leatherette and upholstered armchairs, a couple of discreet rowing oars, and another sofa tucked under the stairs. Around the walls is a variety of water- or boating-themed artwork – most interesting are the period Underground posters advertising the Boat Race (the race starts near here), many of which line the warren of corridors leading to the gents'. Served all day, good bar food might include sandwiches (from £4), curried parsnip soup (£3.50), half a pint of shell-on prawns (£4.95), various salads and platters like roasted mediterranean vegetables, olives and feta cheese or chicken liver and pork terrine with cranberry chutney (£5.50), and around three main courses such as chilli con carne (£6.95), sausage and mash (£7.25), or beef curry (£7.95). The airy restaurant has a wider choice, with fish and chips (£8), steak, and changing specials like moules marinière; it's no smoking up here, and there's another bar. The pub can be busy with under-30s in the evening (though the dining room usually has a wider mix of customers then), but quieter and rather relaxing during the day. They were about to start experimenting with table service for food and drinks as we went to press. *(Recommended by Susan and John Douglas)*

Youngs ~ Managers Elizabeth and Andrew Ford ~ Real ale ~ Bar food (12-10 (12-3, 6-10 in restaurant)) ~ Restaurant ~ (020) 8789 0476 ~ Children in eating area of bar and restaurant ~ Dogs allowed in bar ~ Open 11-11; 12-10.30 Sun

Crown & Greyhound

Dulwich Village, SE21; ⇄ North Dulwich

A highlight of this big Victorian pub is its very pleasant garden, recently spruced up with new furniture and parasols. Some of the tables are shaded by a chestnut tree, and they've added french boules; there may be barbecues out here in summer. Refurbished but retaining many of its original features, the roomy main bar area at the front is pleasantly furnished, with some quite ornate plasterwork and lamps over on the right, and a variety of nicely distinct seating areas from traditional upholstered and panelled settles to stripped kitchen tables on stripped boards, with a coal-effect gas fire and some Victoria prints. A big back dining room and conservatory opens into the garden. As well as Fullers London Pride they have three changing real ales (very much at central London prices), often including some unusual brews; they have occasional beer festivals. The lunchtime menu might include big ciabattas (from £4.75), soup (£3.80), well liked burgers, and specials such as chicken in mustard sauce, lamb in red wine or cod mornay (all £6.95). Best to arrive early for their popular Sunday carvery (£8.70, or £7.20 for the vegetarian version), as they don't take bookings; the pub can be popular with families then. Known locally as the Dog, it was built at the turn of the century to replace two inns that had stood here previously, hence the unusual name. Busy in the evenings, but quieter during the day, it's handy for walks through the park, and for the Dulwich picture gallery. *(Recommended by Tim and Jane Charlesworth, Ian Phillips, Piotr Chodzko-Zajko, Mrs Maricar Jagger, Pete Walker)*

Mitchells & Butlers ~ Manager Duncan Moore ~ Real ale ~ Bar food (12-10(9 Sun)) ~ Restaurant (evenings only) ~ (020) 8299 4976 ~ Children in eating area of bar and restaurant ~ Open 11-11; 12-10.30 Sun

We say if we know a pub allows dogs.

Cutty Sark

Ballast Quay, off Lassell Street, SE10; ⇌ Maze Hill, from London Bridge; or from the river front walk past the Yacht in Crane Street and Trinity Hospital

About to enjoy a fresh lick of paint as we went to press, this attractive late 16th-c white-painted house has a lovely old-fashioned feel, and boasts splendid views of the Thames and the Millennium Dome, both from the busy terrace across the narrow cobbled lane, or, better still, from the upstairs room with the big bow window (itself striking for the way it jetties over the pavement). It's hard not to imagine smugglers and blackguards with patches over their eyes in the flagstoned bar, which also has rough brick walls, wooden settles, barrel tables, open fires, low lighting and narrow openings to tiny side snugs; there's an elaborate central staircase. Fullers London Pride and four changing beers such as Black Sheep, Everards Tiger, Greene King IPA, and Hardys and Hansons Old Trip on handpump, with a good choice of malt whiskies, and a new organic wine list; fruit machine, juke box. Served in a roomy eating area (and available all day during the week), bar food includes sandwiches, hot dishes such as steak and ale pie, fish and chips or sausages and mash (£6.95), and changing specials (around £8.95). The pub is alive with young people on Friday and Saturday evenings, but can be surprisingly quiet some weekday lunchtimes. They have jazz festivals two or three times a year, and morris dancers occasionally drop by. Parking is limited nearby. *(Recommended by the Didler, Kevin Flack, Roger and Jenny Huggins, Tracey and Stephen Groves, Tony Brace, Michael Butler)*

Free house ~ Licensees Mark and Tina Crane ~ Real ale ~ Bar food (12-9) ~ Restaurant ~ (020) 8858 3146 ~ Children upstairs till 9pm ~ Dogs allowed in bar ~ Open 11-11; 12-10.30 Sun

Fire Station

Waterloo Road, SE1; ⊖ ⇌ Waterloo

Vibrantly busy after work, when it's popular with both diners and drinkers, this is a splendid conversion of the former LCC central fire station. It still has many of its original features, but now looks something like a cross between a warehouse and a schoolroom, with plenty of wooden pews, chairs and long tables (a few spilling on to the street), some mirrors and rather incongruous pieces of dressers, and brightly red-painted doors, shelves and modern hanging lightshades; the determinedly contemporary art round the walls is for sale, and there's a table with newspapers to read. It can get very noisy indeed, which does add to the atmosphere – though if you're after a quiet drink you could find it overpowering; it's calmer at lunchtimes and at weekends. Well kept Adnams, Charles Wells Bombardier, Fullers London Pride, Shepherd Neame Spitfire and Youngs on handpump, as well as a number of European bottled beers, variously flavoured teas, several malt whiskies, and a good choice of wines (up to a dozen by the glass). They serve a range of bar meals between 11 and 5.30, which might include several interestingly filled panini (£5.95) and ciabattas (£6.50), but it's worth paying the extra to eat from the main menu, served from an open kitchen in the back dining room. Changing daily, this has things like soup (£4.25), warm red lentil salad with poached egg (£6.50), baked pear and blue cheese tart (£9.95), saffron and wild mushroom risotto with truffle oil, wild rocket and parmesan or pan-fried cajun spiced pork fillet with a rich red wine jus (£10.95), red snapper stir-fried with rice and vegetables (£11.95), and venison Guinness stew with horseradish mash, button mushrooms and braised savoy cabbage; some dishes can run out, so get there early for the best choice. They also do a set menu at lunchtimes and between 5.30 and 7, with two courses for £10.95, or three for £13.50. You can book tables. There may be a cover charge for the bread, and they'll add a 5% service charge for groups of five or more. Piped modern jazz and other music fits into the good-natured hubbub; there's a TV for rugby matches. It's very handy for the Old Vic and Waterloo Station. *(Recommended by Keith and Chris O'Neill, Peter Meister, Ian Phillips, Michael Butler, Dr and Mrs M E Wilson)*

Wizard ~ Manager Philippe Ha Yeung ~ Real ale ~ Bar food (11-10.30.; 12-9.30 Sun) ~ Restaurant ~ (020) 7620 2226 ~ Children in eating area of bar and restaurant ~ Open 11-11; 12-10.30 Sun; closed 25-6 Dec

Founders Arms

Hopton Street (Bankside); ⊖ ⇌ Blackfriars, and cross Blackfriars Bridge

Open from 9am for breakfast, this big, modern place (rather like a huge conservatory) benefits from one of the finest settings of any pub along the Thames, particularly in the City, with fine views of the river, St Paul's, and the Millennium Bridge. Picnic-sets out on the big waterside terrace share the panorama. If you're inside, the lighting is nice and unobtrusive so that you can still see out across the river at night. Also handy for Shakespeare's Globe and the Tate Modern, it can get busy, particularly on weekday evenings, when it's popular with young City types for an after-work drink. Well kept Youngs Bitter, Special and seasonal brews from the modern bar counter angling along one side; also, coffee, tea and hot chocolate. Served pretty much all day, the promptly served bar food includes sandwiches (from £3.95), panini (from £4.75), soup (£3.95), sausages and mash (£7.45), fresh fish in beer batter (£7.60), sweet potato and spinach curry (£7.85), steak pie with minted peas (£8.45), and daily specials; Sunday roasts. Good, neat and cheerful service. One raised area is no smoking; piped music, fruit machine. Like many City pubs, it may close a little early on quieter nights. *(Recommended by Keith and Chris O'Neill, Mike Turner, Ian Phillips, Gordon Prince, the Didler, D J and P M Taylor, Patrick Hancock, Meg and Colin Hamilton, Michael Butler, John Wooll, John Coatsworth)*

Youngs ~ Managers Mr and Mrs P Wakefield ~ Real ale ~ Bar food (12-8.30(8 Sun)) ~ (020) 7928 1899 ~ Children in eating area of bar until 8.30pm ~ Open 11-11; 12-10.30 Sun

Fox & Hounds 🍴 🍷

Latchmere Road, SW11; ⇌ Clapham Junction

The garden has been extensively refurbished at this big Victorian local, with plenty of new planting and the addition of big parasols and heaters for winter. It's the second of the small group run by the two brothers who transformed the Atlas (see West London, below), so there's a similar emphasis on the excellent mediterranean food. But it's still very much the kind of place where locals happily come to drink – and they're a more varied bunch than you might find filling the Atlas. Changing every day, the bar food might include lunchtime sandwiches, spinach and nutmeg soup with yoghurt (£4), a good antipasti (£7), spaghetti with field mushrooms, chilli, thyme and parmesan (£7.50), grilled italian sausages with sicilian braised vegetables and tomato sauce (£9), pan-fried cod fillet with spiced black beans, coriander and chorizo (£10.50), roast lamb chops with jerusalem artichoke and baby spinach salad (£12.50), lemon, sultana and almond cake (£4), and creamy italian cheeses with pear and grilled bread (£5). The pub can fill quickly, so you may have to move fast to grab a table. The spacious, straightforward bar has bare boards, mismatched tables and chairs, two narrow pillars supporting the dark red ceiling, photographs on the walls, and big windows overlooking the street (the view partially obscured by colourful window boxes). There are fresh flowers and daily papers on the bar, and a view of the kitchen behind. Two rooms lead off, one rather cosy with its two red leatherette sofas. Well kept Adnams Broadside, Fullers London Pride and Harveys Sussex on handpump; the carefully chosen wine list (which includes a dozen by the glass) is written out on a blackboard. The appealingly varied piped music fits in rather well. The same team have another two similarly organised pubs: the Cumberland Arms near Olympia, and the Swan in Chiswick. *(Recommended by Russell Lewin, Sue Demont, Tim Barrow, Pete Walker)*

Free house ~ Licensees Richard and George Manners ~ Real ale ~ Bar food (12-2.30, 7-10.30 (10 Sun); not Mon lunchtime) ~ (020) 7924 5483 ~ Children welcome in eating area till 7pm ~ Dogs welcome ~ Open 12-2.30 (not Mon), 5-11 Mon-Thurs; 12-11 Fri, Sat; 12-10.30 Sun; closed Mon lunchtime; 24 Dec-1 Jan; Easter Sat-Sun

> You are allowed 20 minutes after 'time, please' to finish your drink – half-an-hour if you bought it in conjunction with a meal.

George ★

Off 77 Borough High Street, SE1; ⊖ ⇌ Borough or London Bridge

Noted as one of London's 'fair inns for the receipt of travellers' as early as 1598, this splendid-looking place is perhaps the country's best examples of a historic coaching inn, and is preserved by the National Trust. The tiers of open galleries look down over a bustling cobbled courtyard with plenty of picnic-sets, and maybe morris men and even Shakespeare in summer. Inside, the row of no-frills ground-floor rooms and bars all have square-latticed windows, black beams, bare floorboards, some panelling, plain oak or elm tables and old-fashioned built-in settles, along with a 1797 'Act of Parliament' clock, dimpled glass lantern-lamps and so forth. The snuggest refuge is the room nearest the street, where there's an ancient beer engine that looks like a cash register. Two rooms are no smoking at lunchtimes. In summer they open a bar with direct service into the courtyard. Well kept (though not cheap) Bass, Fullers London Pride, Greene King Abbot, a beer brewed for the pub by Adnams, and a changing guest on handpump; mulled wine in winter, tea and coffee. Lunchtime bar food might include filled baked potatoes (from £3), soup (£3.25), baguettes (from £3.75), ploughman's (£4.95), sausage and mash or steak, mushroom and Guinness pie (£5.75), and fish and chips (£5.95); evening meals in the restaurant are broadly similar, but a little more expensive. A splendid central staircase goes up to a series of dining rooms and to a gaslit balcony; darts, trivia. Their music nights can be quite jolly – anyone can join in the monthly cajun jam sessions. Incidentally, what survives today is only a third of what it once was; the building was 'mercilessly reduced' as E V Lucas put it, during the period when it was owned by the Great Northern Railway Company. Unless you know where you're going (or you're in one of the many tourist groups that flock here in summer) you may well miss it, as apart from the great gates and sign there's little to indicate that such a gem still exists behind the less auspicious-looking buildings on the busy high street. *(Recommended by Paul Hopton, I Louden, Mr Bishop, BJL, the Didler, Alison Hayes, Pete Hanlon, Andrea Rampley, Ian Phillips, CMW, JJW, Simon Collett-Jones, Joe Green, Mike Gorton)*

Laurel (Enterprise) ~ Manager Scott Masterson ~ Real ale ~ Bar food (12-3 (4 wknds)) ~ Restaurant ~ (020) 7407 2056 ~ Children welcome ~ Folk first Mon, Cajun third Mon ~ Open 11-11; 12-10.30 Sun

Market Porter

Stoney Street, SE1; ⊖ ⇌ London Bridge

Opening between 6.30 and 8.30 every morning to serve the workers and porters from Borough Market, this busily pubby place has perhaps London's best range of real ales. The range changes by the day, but they always have between six and eight at a time, including Courage Best and Harveys Best, and a good few brews you probably won't have heard of before – let alone come across in this neck of the woods. Among those particularly enjoyed by readers in recent months are Harviestoun Gremlin, Helligan Honey, and King Alfreds Hampshire, along with beers from the nearby London Bridge Brewery, all perfectly kept and served. The only criticism voiced this year is that sometimes there are so many people around the bar that you can't read which beers are available; it does get busy, particularly at lunchtimes (when it can be noisy with the chatter), but is usually quieter in the afternoons. The main part of the long U-shaped bar has rough wooden ceiling beams with beer barrels balanced on them, a heavy wooden bar counter with a beamed gantry, cushioned bar stools, an open fire, and 20s-style wall lamps. Sensibly priced lunchtime bar food includes sandwiches (from £2.95), and panini (from £3.95), caesar salad (£4.95), sausages and mash (£5.75), a changing home-made pie (£6.25), and sirloin steak (£7.95); good Sunday roasts. Obliging, friendly service; darts, fruit machine, TV and piped music. A cosy partly panelled room has leaded glass windows and a couple of tables. The restaurant usually has an additional couple of real ales. The company that own the pub have various others around London; ones with similarly unusual beers (if not quite so many) can be found in Stamford Street and Seymour Place. *(Recommended by BJL, Paul Hopton,*

Catherine Pitt, the Didler, Tracey and Stephen Groves, Brian and Rosalie Laverick, Patrick Hancock, Ian Phillips, Ted George, Derek Thomas, Joe Green, Mike Gorton)

Free house ~ Licensee Nick Turner ~ Real ale ~ Bar food (12-2.30 (not Sat)) ~ Restaurant ~ (020) 7407 2495 ~ Children in restaurant ~ Open 6.30am-8.30am, then 11-11; 12-10.30 Sun

Ship 🍷

Jews Row, SW18; ⇌ Wandsworth Town

Laid-back and chatty, this friendly riverside pub is tremendously popular in summer, when it's well known for its excellent barbecues (usually available on winter weekends, too). Serving very good home-made burgers and sausages, marinated lamb steaks, goats cheese quesadillas, and even cajun chicken and lobster, it's all-weather, with plenty of covered areas if necessary. The extensive terrace has lots of picnic-sets, pretty hanging baskets and brightly coloured flowerbeds, small trees, and an outside bar; a Thames barge is moored alongside. The food stands out inside as well: as at the Alma above (under the same management) it relies very much on free-range produce, much of it from Mr Gotto's farm. The menu changes daily, but might include leek and spring onion soup (£3.60), chicken liver and foie gras parfait (£4.95), moules marinière (£5.25 starter, £8.25 main course), sausages with grain mustard mash and onion gravy (£8.50), artichoke tortellini with roasted cherry tomatoes (£8.75), sautéed calves liver with bacon and bubble and squeak (£9.75) and lamb steak with savoy cabbage, celeriac crisps and red wine jus (£13.50). You can book tables (except at Sunday lunchtimes), and there's something available all day. Only a small part of the original ceiling is left in the main bar – the rest is in a light and airy conservatory style, with wooden tables, a medley of stools, and old church chairs on the floorboards. One part has a Victorian fireplace, a huge clock surrounded by barge prints, an old-fashioned bagatelle board, and jugs of flowers around the window sills. The basic public bar has plain wooden furniture, a black kitchen range in the fireplace, and a juke box. It's a great favourite with smart local twenty-somethings. Well kept Youngs Bitter, Special and seasonal brews on handpump, with freshly squeezed orange and other fruit juices, a wide range of wines (a dozen or more by the glass), and a good choice of teas and coffees. Helpful service from pleasant staff. Parking is not always easy. *(Recommended by BOB)*

Youngs ~ Tenant Charles Gotto ~ Real ale ~ Bar food (12-10.30 (9.30 Sun)) ~ Restaurant ~ (020) 8870 9667 ~ Children welcome ~ Dogs allowed in bar ~ Open 11-11; 12-10.30 Sun

White Cross 🍷

Water Lane; ⊖ ⇌ Richmond

On fine days the busy paved garden in front of this perfectly-set Thames-side pub can feel rather like a cosmopolitan seaside resort; plenty of tables overlook the water, and in summer there's an outside bar. Though it can get crowded, it's a delightful spot, with a certain wistful charm in winter as well. Inside, the two chatty main rooms have something of the air of the hotel this once was, with local prints and photographs, an old-fashioned wooden island servery, and a good mix of variously aged customers. Two of the three log fires have mirrors above them – unusually, the third is below a window. A bright and airy upstairs room has lots more tables, and a pretty cast-iron balcony opening off, with a splendid view down to the river, and a couple more tables and chairs. From a servery at the foot of the stairs, lunchtime bar food includes good sandwiches (from £2.60), salads (from £5.75), a variety of sausages (£6.75), and plenty of daily-changing specials, including a roast. Well kept Youngs Bitter, Special and seasonal beers on handpump, and a dozen or so carefully chosen wines by the glass; service is friendly and civilised, even when the pub is at its busiest. Fruit machine, dominoes. It pays to check the tide times if you're leaving your car by the river; one reader discovered just how fast the water can rise when on returning to his vehicle he found it marooned in a rapidly swelling pool of water, and had to paddle out shoeless to retrieve it. It's not unknown for the water to reach right up the steps into the bar, completely covering anything that gets in the way. Boats leave from immediately outside for Kingston and Hampton Court. *(Recommended by Mayur Shah, Martin Brunt, the Didler, David and Nina Pugsley)*

Youngs ~ Managers Ian and Phyl Heggie ~ Real ale ~ Bar food (12-3) ~ (020) 8940 6844 ~ Dogs welcome ~ Open 11-11; 12-10.30 Sun; closed 25 Dec (exc 12-2)

WEST LONDON Map 13

Anglesea Arms

Selwood Terrace, SW7; ⊖ South Kensington

In summer the place to be at this genuinely old-fashioned pub is the leafy front patio (with outside heaters for chillier evenings), but it's really rather nice in winter, when the elegant and individual bar seems especially enticing. Feeling both cosy and smart at the same time (much of the smartness due to the well heeled young locals), it's particularly friendly and chatty, with a mix of cast-iron tables on the bare wood-strip floor, panelling, and big windows with attractive swagged curtains; at one end several booths with partly glazed screens have cushioned pews and spindleback chairs. The traditional mood is heightened by some heavy portraits, prints of London, and large brass chandeliers. On busy days you'll need to move fast to grab a seat, but most people seem happy leaning on the central elbow tables. A good choice of real ales takes in Adnams Bitter and Broadside, Fullers London Pride, Greene King IPA, Youngs and a weekly changing guest; also a few bottled belgian beers, around 20 whiskies, and a varied wine list, with everything available by the glass. Downstairs is a separate eating area, with a Victorian fireplace. The lunchtime menu typically includes elaborate sandwiches (from £5.25), soup (£3.75), welsh rarebit with crispy bacon topping (£4.25), scallops with a sweet chilli dressing (£6.95), stuffed peppers with couscous ratatouille topped with goats cheese and tomato coulis (£7.25), cumberland sausage and mash (£7.95), chicken breast stuffed with spinach in a creamy tarragon sauce (£8.25), pan-fried seabass fillet or mussels in provençale or white wine sauce (£8.95), and daily specials; it's worth booking in advance for their good all-day Sunday roasts (from £7.95). Service is friendly and helpful. *(Recommended by Tracey and Stephen Groves, the Didler, BJL, J R Ringrose, Ian Phillips, T Fry, Mrs B M Hill)*

Free house ~ Licensee J Podmore ~ Real ale ~ Bar food (12-3, 6.30-10; 12-10 Sat, 12-9.30 Sun) ~ Restaurant ~ (020) 7373 7960 ~ Children in eating area of bar and restaurant ~ Dogs allowed in bar ~ Open 11-11; 12-10.30 Sun

Anglesea Arms

Wingate Road, W6; ⊖ Ravenscourt Park

One reader tells us he's been to this superior gastropub for dinner over 20 times since he first read about it in the *Guide*. It's rather off the beaten path, but deserves tracking down for its imaginative, well presented meals. Other regular visitors have detected a rise in prices this year, but say it's worth the increase. Changing every lunchtime and evening, the menu might include starters such as soup (£3.95), pigeon and duck foie gras terrine (£5.95), and moroccan stuffed squid with couscous, raisins and cumin (£5.50), a short choice of main courses like whole roast quail with chorizo, peppers, and saffron rice (£12.50), or chargrilled wild venison with dauphinoise potatoes, rosemary and red wine (£13.95), caramelised apple and calvados cake (£4.25), and some unusual farmhouse cheeses (£4.95); they usually do a set menu at lunchtimes, with two courses for £9.95. The bustling eating area leads off the bar but feels quite separate, with skylights creating a brighter feel, closely packed tables, and a big modern painting along one wall; directly opposite is the kitchen, with several chefs frantically working on the meals. You can't book, so best to get there early for a table, or be prepared to wait; it gets very busy after around 7.30. It feels a lot more restauranty than, say, the Eagle (in Central London), though you can also eat in the bar: rather plainly decorated, but cosy in winter when the roaring fire casts long flickering shadows on the dark panelling. Neatly stacked piles of wood guard either side of the fireplace (which has a stopped clock above it), and there are some well worn green leatherette chairs and stools. Fullers London Pride, Green King IPA and a guest like Adnams Broadside on handpump, with a wide range of carefully chosen wines listed above the bar. Several tables outside overlook the quiet street (not the easiest place to find a parking space). *(Recommended by John Chute, David Edwards, Simon Rodway, Richard Siebert)*

Enterprise ~ Lease Fiona Evans and Jamie Wood ~ Real ale ~ Bar food (12.30-2.45, 7-10.30) ~ Restaurant ~ (020) 8749 1291 ~ Children welcome ~ Dogs allowed in bar ~ Open 11-11; 12-10.30 Sun; closed 24-31 Dec

Atlas

Seagrave Road, SW6; ⊖ West Brompton

The excellent, innovative food here continues to impress. Influenced by recipes from North Africa, Turkey and Italy, the menu changes twice a day but might include things like sweet potato and carrot soup with coriander, orange zest and sour cream (£4), very good antipasti (£7), roast field mushroom and slow roast plum vine tomato risotto with mascarpone, rosemary, garlic and parmesan (£7.50), delicious grilled tuscan sausages with cannellini beans, thyme, white wine, tomato and leeks (£9), catalan beef casserole with thyme, red wine, wild mushrooms and chocolate (£10), braised pork chop with port, plums and ginger and grilled horseradish polenta (£10.50), and rare grilled tuna steak or chargrilled leg of lamb with cumin and paprika and couscous salad (£12.50); they usually have a good cake like chocolate and almond (£4), or soft italian cheese with pear and grilled bread (£5). It's a particularly rewarding place to eat, the one downside simply the place's popularity – tables are highly prized, so if you're planning a meal, arrive early, or swoop quickly. With a pleasantly bustling feel in the evenings (it's perhaps not the place for a cosy quiet dinner), the long, simple knocked-together bar has been well renovated without removing the original features; there's plenty of panelling and dark wooden wall benches, a couple of brick fireplaces, a mix of school chairs, and well spaced tables. Smart young people figure prominently in the mix, but there are plenty of locals too, as well as visitors to the Exhibition Centre at Earls Court (one of the biggest car parks is next door). Well kept Adnams Broadside, Deuchars Caledonian IPA, and Fullers London Pride on handpump, and a very good, carefully chosen wine list, with plenty by the glass; big mugs of coffee. Friendly service. The piped music is unusual – on various visits we've come across everything from salsa and jazz to vintage TV themes; it can be loud at times. Down at the end is a TV (though big sports events are now shown in a room upstairs), by a hatch to the kitchen. Outside is an attractively planted narrow side terrace, with an overhead awning; heaters make it comfortable even in winter. This was the first of a small chain of pubs set up by two brothers; another of the group, the Fox & Hounds, is a main entry in the South London section. *(Recommended by Martin and Karen Wake, Ian Phillips, Brenda and Rob Fincham, Evelyn and Derek Walter)*

Free house ~ Licensees Richard and George Manners, James Gill ~ Real ale ~ Bar food (12.30-3, 7-10.30(10 Sun)) ~ (020) 7385 9129 ~ Children in eating area of bar till 7pm ~ Open 12-11(10.30 Sun); closed 23 Dec-2 Jan, Easter, and second Mon in Aug

Bulls Head

Strand-on-the-Green, W4; ⇄ Kew Bridge

In a fine spot by the narrow towpath, this riverside Chef & Brewer remains an atmospheric place for a cosy drink. Though they've been comfortably refurbished, there's still a traditional feel to the series of pleasant little rooms that ramble up and down steps; old-fashioned benches are built into the simple panelling, and small windows look past attractively planted hanging flower baskets to the river. Black-panelled alcoves make useful cubby-holes, much enjoyed by readers on chilly autumn days. Lots of empty wine bottles are dotted around, and there's plenty of polished dark wood and beams. Served all day, the big menu takes in everything from good sandwiches and filled baguettes (£4.99), through fish and chips (£6.25) and beef and ale pie (£6.95) to green thai curry (£11.25); fresh fish is delivered daily, and there's a separate blackboard with fish specials. Popular Sunday roasts. A good-sized area is no smoking. Well kept Fullers London Pride and a combination of Charles Wells Bombardier and Greene King IPA or Old Speckled Hen on handpump; pleasant service from uniformed staff. Newspapers are laid out for customers. The original building served as Cromwell's HQ several times during the Civil War. *(Recommended by Alan and Paula McCully, Ian Phillips, Russell Lewin, R T and J C Moggridge, John Saville)*

Spirit Group ~ Manager Andy Cockran ~ Real ale ~ Bar food (11-10; 12-9.30 Sun) ~ (020) 8994 1204 ~ Children in eating area of bar ~ Open 11-11; 12-10.30 Sun

Churchill Arms

Kensington Church Street, W8; ⊖ Notting Hill Gate/Kensington High Street

This bustling old favourite stands out for its wonderfully cheery atmosphere; it feels like a friendly local, so that even at its busiest, you can quickly feel at home. That's mainly down to the genial Irish landlord, very much in evidence, and delightedly mixing with customers as he threads his way though the evening crowds. One of his hobbies is collecting butterflies, so you'll see a variety of prints and books on the subject dotted around the bar. There are also countless lamps, miners' lights, horse tack, bedpans and brasses hanging from the ceiling, a couple of interesting carved figures and statuettes behind the central bar counter, prints of American presidents, and lots of Churchill memorabilia. Well kept Fullers Chiswick, ESB, London Pride, and seasonal beers on handpump, with a good choice of wines. Even early in the week this isn't really a place for a quiet pint; it can get a bit smoky too. The spacious and rather smart plant-filled dining conservatory may be used for hatching butterflies, but is better known for its big choice of excellent authentic thai food, such as a very good, proper thai curry, or various rice, noodle or stir-fried dishes (all £5.85); it's no smoking in here. They do food all day, with other choices including lunchtime sandwiches, and a Sunday roast. Fruit machine, TV; they have their own cricket and football teams. There can be quite an overspill on to the street, where there are now some chrome tables and chairs. Look out for special events and decorations around Christmas, Hallowe'en, St Patrick's Day and Churchill's birthday (30 November) – along with more people than you'd ever imagine could feasibly fit inside. *(Recommended by LM, Ian Phillips, Derek Thomas, Darren Le Poidevin, Tracey and Stephen Groves, Pete Walker)*

Fullers ~ Manager Jerry O'Brien ~ Real ale ~ Bar food (12-9.30 (8 Sun)) ~ Restaurant ~ (020) 7727 4242 ~ Children in restaurant ~ Dogs allowed in bar ~ Open 11-11; 12-10.30 Sun; closed evening 25 Dec

Colton Arms

Greyhound Road, W14; ⊖ Barons Court

Kept exactly the same by its dedicated landlord for the last 40 years, and very much a family concern, this genuinely unspoilt little gem is like an old-fashioned country pub in town. The main U-shaped front bar has a log fire blazing in winter, highly polished brasses, a fox's mask, hunting crops and plates decorated with hunting scenes on the walls, and a remarkable collection of handsomely carved 17th-c oak furniture. That room is small enough, and the two back rooms are tiny; each has its own little serving counter, with a bell to ring for service. Well kept Caledonian Deuchars IPA, Fullers London Pride and Shepherd Neame Spitfire on handpump (when you pay, note the old-fashioned brass-bound till); the food is limited to sandwiches (weekday lunchtimes only, from £2.60). Pull the curtain aside for the door out to a charming back terrace with a neat rose arbour. The pub is next to the Queens Club tennis courts and gardens. *(Recommended by Susan and John Douglas, Ian Phillips)*

Enterprise ~ Tenants N J and J A Nunn ~ Real ale ~ Bar food (12-2 weekdays only) ~ No credit cards ~ (020) 7385 6956 ~ Dogs welcome ~ Open 12-3, 5.30-11 Mon-Fri; 12-3.30, 7-11(10.30 Sun) Sat; Sun 1-4 winter

Dove

Upper Mall, W6; ⊖ Ravenscourt Park

Said to be where 'Rule Britannia' was composed, this old-fashioned tavern is one of London's most famous riverside pubs, and if you're lucky enough to secure a spot on the delightful back terrace it's hard not to consider it one of the nicest. The main flagstoned area, down some steps, has a few highly prized teak tables and white metal and teak chairs looking over the low river wall to the Thames reach just above Hammersmith Bridge, and there's a tiny exclusive area up a spiral staircase. You'll often see rowing crews out on the water. By the entrance from the quiet alley, the front bar is cosy and traditional, with black panelling, and red leatherette cushioned built-in wall settles and stools around dimpled copper tables; it leads to a bigger, similarly furnished room, with old framed advertisements and photographs of the pub. They stock the full range of Fullers beers, with well kept ESB, London Pride and seasonal beers on handpump: no games machines or piped music. Bar food (currently winning more praise than it has in the past) includes sandwiches, soup (£3.50), thai fishcakes with sweet chilli sauce (£5.25), greek salad (£6.95), grilled sausages and mash or steak and ale pie (£8.25), fish and chips or peppered mackerel niçoise (£8.95), chargrilled calves liver with crispy bacon and red wine gravy (£10.25), pan-fried duck breast with black cherry sauce (£11.50), and daily specials. The pub isn't quite so crowded at lunchtimes as it is in the evenings. A plaque marks the level of the highest-ever tide in 1928. *(Recommended by the Didler, David Edwards, Patrick Hancock, R T and J C Moggridge, Simon Rodway)*

Fullers ~ Manager Alison Juliff ~ Real ale ~ Bar food (12-2.30, 5-9 Mon-Sat; 12-4 Sun) ~ (020) 8748 9474 ~ Dogs welcome ~ Open 11-11; 12-10.30 Sun

Havelock Tavern 🍴 🍷

Masbro Road, W14; ⊖ Kensington (Olympia)

In an unassuming residential street, this ordinary-looking blue-tiled cornerhouse is an excellent gastropub, busy and informal, with very classy food. Changing every day, the menu might include things like fennel, parsley and chilli soup (£4), pork, chicken liver, duck and parma ham terrine with gherkins, toast and chutney (£6), steamed mussels with white wine, tomato, bacon and mint or half a dozen pacific oysters with shallot relish (£7.50), warm leek, spinach and dolcelatte tart (£8), steamed fillet of smoked haddock with spiced red lentil, tomato and coconut dhal or chargrilled leg of lamb steak with pilaff rice, red onion, tomato and parsley salad and tzatziki (£10), and some unusual cheeses served with apple chutney (£6); you can't book tables. Until 1932 the building was two separate shops (one was a wine merchant, but no one can remember much about the other), and it still has huge shop-front windows along both street-facing walls. The L-shaped bar is plain and unfussy: bare boards, long wooden tables, a mix of chairs and stools, a few soft spotlights and a fireplace. A second little room with pews leads to a small paved terrace, with benches, a tree and wall climbers. Well kept (though not cheap) Brakspears, Fullers London Pride and Marstons Pedigree on handpump from the elegant modern bar counter, and a good range of well chosen wines, with around a dozen by the glass; mulled wine in winter, and in May and June perhaps home-made elderflower soda. Service is friendly and attentive. No music or machines, but backgammon, chess, Scrabble and other board games. Plenty of chat from the varied range of customers – at busy times it can seem really quite noisy. You may have to wait for a table in the evenings (when some dishes can run out quite quickly), but it can be quieter at lunchtimes, and in the afternoons can have something of the feel of a civilised private club. On weekdays, nearby parking is mostly residents only (there's a multi-storey a short walk away in Shepherd's Bush). *(Recommended by Jack Clark, Paul Hopton, Simon Rodway, Mandy and Simon King)*

Free house ~ Licensees Peter Richnell, Jonny Haughton ~ Real ale ~ Bar food (12.30-2.30, 7-10) ~ No credit cards ~ (020) 7603 5374 ~ Children welcome ~ Dogs welcome ~ Open 11-11; 12-10.30 Sun; closed second Mon in Aug, 22-26 Dec

Portobello Gold 🍷

Portobello Road, W11; ⊖ Notting Hill Gate

With a cheerfully relaxed, almost bohemian atmosphere, this enterprising place is an unusual combination of pub, restaurant, hotel and even internet café. Our favourite part is the exotic-seeming back dining room, with a profusion of enormous tropical plants, some up to 25 years old; comfortable wicker chairs, stained wooden tables, and a cage of vocal canaries add to the outdoor effect, and there's an impressive wall-to-wall mirror. In the old days – when we remember this being a Hells Angels hangout – this was the pub garden, and in summer they still open up the sliding roof. The walls here and in the smaller, brightly painted front bar are covered with changing displays of art and photography; the bar also has a nice old fireplace, cushioned pews, daily papers, and, more unusually, several Internet terminals (some of which disappear in the evening). The Gold was the first place in the UK to serve oyster shooters (a shot glass with an oyster, parmesan, horseradish, crushed chillies, Tabasco and lime), and the good bar food still has something of an emphasis on oysters and seafood. There's an almost bewildering number of menus, but you might typically find big toasted ciabattas (from £4.85), soup (£3.95), cajun jumbo shrimp (from £4.95), half a dozen irish rock oysters (£6.95), mexican fajitas or sausage and parsley mash with red onion and tomato gravy (£7.55), lamb cutlets in cumberland sauce (£9.95), and seafood and pasta specials; the puddings come in two sizes. At lunchtime they offer two courses for £10 and three for £14, and in the evenings, two rather more elaborate courses for £15.50, and three for £20. You can eat from the same menu in the bar or dining room (part of which is no smoking). Opening at 10 for coffee and fresh pastries, the bar has well kept Shepherd Neame Spitfire and Youngs, as well as a couple of draught belgian beers, Thatcher's farm cider, a good selection of bottled beers from around the world, and a wide range of interesting tequilas and other well sourced spirits; the wine list is particularly good (the landlady has written books on matching wine with food). They also have a cigar menu and various coffees. Polite, helpful young staff; piped music, TV (used only for cricket), chess, backgammon. There are one or two tables and chairs on the pretty street outside, which, like the pub, is named in recognition of the 1769 Battle of Portobello, fought over control of the lucrative gold route to Panama. A lively stall is set up outside during the Notting Hill Carnival. Parking nearby is metered; it's not always easy to bag a space. We've yet to hear from readers who have stayed overnight here; the bedrooms all have free Internet access. *(Recommended by Ian Phillips, Sue Demont, Tim Barrow, Stephen R Holman)*

Unique (Enterprise) ~ Lease Michael Bell and Linda Johnson-Bell ~ Real ale ~ Bar food (12-10.30 Mon-Fri; 12-5, 7-10.30 Sat; 1.30-9.30 Sun) ~ Restaurant ~ (020) 7460 4910 ~ Children in eating area of bar and restaurant till sundown ~ Dogs allowed in bar ~ Open 10am-11pm; 11-10.30 Sun ~ Bedrooms: £45(£60S)/£55(£85S)(£150B)

White Horse 🍷 🍺

Parsons Green, SW6; ⊖ Parsons Green

Few pubs can boast as extraordinary a range of carefully selected drinks as this bustling, well organised place. Six perfectly kept real ales might include Adnams Broadside, Fullers ESB, Harveys Sussex, Oakham JHB, Roosters Yankee, and Shepherd Neame Spitfire; they also have five well-chosen draught beers from overseas such as Sierra Nevada Pale Ale or Alaskan Smoked Porter, as well as 15 trappist beers, around 50 other foreign bottled beers, a dozen malt whiskies, and a constantly expanding range of good, interesting and reasonably priced wines. They're keen to encourage people to match the right drink to their food (and particularly to select beers as they might wines), so every item on the menu, whether it be scrambled egg or raspberry and coconut tart, has a suggested accompaniment listed beside it, perhaps a wine, perhaps a bottled beer. The good bar food might include sandwiches (£4.50), ploughman's (with some unusual cheeses, £5), roast pumpkin salad with rocket, pine nuts and goats cheese (£6.75), pork sausages and mash with spiced red cabbage and beer onion gravy (£8.25), salt and pepper squid with sweet chilli and lime, chicken caesar salad, or beer battered line-caught cod, fried in ground nut oil with chips and tartare sauce (£8.75), steak sandwich in focaccia with a tomato and jalapeno salsa and wedges (£10.50), king prawn and mussels in a fragrant thai laksa broth with rich noodles and coconut (£11.75), and daily specials. There's usually something to eat available all day; at weekends they do a good brunch menu, and in winter they do a popular Sunday lunch. The stylishly modernised U-shaped bar has plenty of sofas, wooden tables, and huge windows with slatted wooden blinds, and winter coal and log fires, one in an elegant marble fireplace. The pub is usually busy (and can feel crowded at times), but there are enough smiling, helpful staff behind the solid panelled central servery to ensure you'll rarely have to wait too long to be served. All the art displayed is for sale. The back restaurant is no smoking. On summer evenings the front terrace overlooking the green has something of a continental feel, with crowds of people drinking al fresco; in spring and summer you'll usually find an excellent barbecue out here Fri-Sun, when the pub's appeal to smart young people is more apparent than ever. They have quarterly beer festivals, often spotlighting regional breweries. *(Recommended by the Didler, LM, Paul Hopton, Jack and Jill Gilbert)*

Mitchells & Butlers ~ Manager Mark Dorber ~ Real ale ~ Bar food (12(11 wknds)-10.30) ~ Restaurant ~ (020) 7736 2115 ~ Children welcome ~ Dogs allowed in bar ~ Open 11-11; 12-10.30 Sun; closed 25-26 Dec

Windsor Castle

Campden Hill Road, W8; ⊖ Holland Park/Notting Hill Gate

The big tree-shaded garden at this atmospheric Victorian pub had just been refurbished as we went to press, with lots more tables and chairs on the flagstones, and an improved garden bar for summer. Although on fine days it's always busy out here (it's one of London's nicest pub gardens), there's quite a secluded feel thanks to the high ivy-covered sheltering walls. The pub's appeal is just as strong in winter, when the series of tiny unspoilt rooms, with their time-smoked ceilings and dark wooden furnishings, seems especially cosy and inviting. Each has to be entered through a separate door, so it can be quite a challenge finding the people you've arranged to meet – more often than not they'll be hidden behind the high backs of the sturdy built-in elm benches. A cosy pre-war-style dining room opens off, and soft lighting and a coal-effect fire add to the appeal. Served all day, bar food includes things like sandwiches (from £4.95), steamed mussels or fish and chips (£7.95), and various sausages with mash and onion gravy (£9); they do a choice of roasts on Sunday (£9.95), when the range of other dishes may be more limited. Adnams, Fullers London Pride and a guest like Greene King IPA on handpump (not cheap, even for this area), along with decent house wines, various malt whiskies, and perhaps mulled wine in winter. No fruit machines or piped music. Usually fairly quiet at lunchtime – when several areas are no smoking – the pub can be packed some evenings, often with (as they think) Notting Hill's finest. *(Recommended by Giles and Annie Francis, Tracey and Stephen Groves, Susie Symes, Jo Lilley)*

Mitchells & Butlers ~ Manager Richard Bell ~ Real ale ~ Bar food (12-10) ~ (020) 7243 9551 ~ Open 12-11(10.30 Sun)

A very few pubs try to make you leave a credit card at the bar, as a sort of deposit if you order food. They are not entitled to do this. The credit card firms and banks which issue them warn you not to let them out of your sight. If someone behind the counter used your card fraudulently, the card company or bank could in theory hold you liable, because of your negligence in letting a stranger hang on to your card. Suggest instead that if they feel the need for security, they 'swipe' your card and give it back to you. And do name and shame the pub to us.

LUCKY DIP

Besides the fully inspected pubs, you might like to try these Lucky Dips recommended to us and described by readers (if you do, please send us reports: www.goodguides.co.uk).

CENTRAL LONDON

EC1

☆ ***Bishops Finger*** [W Smithfield, opp Bart's]: Comfortable and smartly civilised, with yellow walls, big windows and elegant tables on polished boards, particularly well kept Shepherd Neame ales, plenty of wines by the glass, several ports and champagnes, daily papers, lunchtime food from open kitchen inc ciabattas, speciality sausages, a few dishes such as lamb chops and Thurs-Fri fish and chips, friendly service; children welcome, a couple of tables outside, open all day, cl wknds *(Ian Phillips, Dr and Mrs A K Clarke, LYM, Jarrod and Wendy Hopkinson)*

Bleeding Heart [Bleeding Heart Yard, off Greville St]: Airy one-room bar with neat staff, well kept Adnams Bitter, Broadside and a seasonal beer from ornate mahogany-and-mirrors bar, good choice of wines by the glass, café tables on scrubbed boards, red ceiling; emphasis on good french-style food in downstairs open-kitchen candlelit restaurant; breakfast from 7, cl wknds *(BB, Sue Demont, Tim Barrow)*

Butchers Hook & Cleaver [W Smithfield]: Spotless converted bank, attractive décor, nice mix of chairs inc some button-back leather armchairs, wrought-iron spiral stairs to pleasant mezzanine, decent fairly priced waitress-served food inc lots of pies and wkdy breakfast from 7.30am, full Fullers range kept well, friendly staff, good mix of customers, relaxed atmosphere; big-screen sports TV; open all day *(BB, Ian Phillips)*

Chequers [Old St/Timber St]: Small very welcoming corner pub with well kept Adnams Bitter and Broadside; bring your own sandwiches *(Ian Phillips)*

Masque Haunt [Old St/Bunhill Row]: Impressive long Wetherspoons with some alcoves in open-plan back no smoking area, lots of books in raised section, their usual food all day, efficient friendly staff, eight well kept ales most from small breweries; open all day *(Ian Phillips)*

Old Red Lion [St John St]: Theatre bar, simple and atmospherically dark; well kept Adnams Broadside *(Tracey and Stephen Groves, Dr and Mrs A K Clarke)*

Sekforde Arms [Sekforde St]: Small and comfortably simple corner Youngs local with friendly licensees, well kept beers and wide range of well priced straightforward food, with nice pictures inc Spy caricatures, upstairs restaurant; pavement tables *(Tracey and Stephen Groves, the Didler, C J Fletcher)*

Sutton Arms [Carthusian St]: Bare boards and traditionally spartan furnishings and décor, Fullers London Pride and Ridleys IPA and Old Bob, unusual lagers, upstairs dining room *(Ian Phillips)*

EC2

City House [Bishopsgate]: Civilised Youngs pub with some emphasis on food, mainly the usual pub or wine bar staples but eel and good fish dishes too; prices not unreasonable, even for champagne by the glass *(Charles Gysin)*

☆ ***Dirty Dicks*** [Bishopsgate]: Re-creation of traditional City tavern with barrel tables in bare-boards bar, interesting old prints inc one of Nathaniel Bentley, the original Dirty Dick, Youngs full beer range kept well, enjoyable food inc open sandwiches, baguettes and reasonably priced hot dishes, pleasant service, cellar wine bar with wine racks overhead in brick barrel-vaulted ceiling; loads of character – fun for foreign visitors *(LYM, Ian Phillips, Stephen and Jean Curtis, the Didler)*

☆ ***Fox*** [Paul St]: Basic well worn furnishings in bare-boards bar notable for its good enterprising lunchtime food (same small group as Eagle in Farringdon Rd – see main entries), well kept Charles Wells Bombardier, decent wines, good coffee, smarter upstairs dining room with friendly helpful service and appealing canopied terrace; may be piped jazz; dogs welcome, open all day, cl wknds *(Dr and Mrs M E Wilson, LYM, Richard Siebert, Simon Calvert, Jo Lilley)*

☆ ***Hamilton Hall*** [Bishopsgate; also entrance from Liverpool St station]: Big busy Wetherspoons showpiece, flamboyant Victorian baroque décor, plaster nudes and fruit mouldings, chandeliers, mirrors, good-sized no smoking mezzanine (can get crowded and smoky downstairs), comfortable groups of seats, reliable food all day from well filled sandwiches and baked potatoes to steaks and good curry nights, well kept real ales inc interesting guest beers, decent wines, good prices; silenced machines, no piped music; tables outside, open all day *(LYM, Ian Phillips, Kevin Blake)*

Old Dr Butlers Head [Masons Ave]: 17th-c beamed City pub with more seating than usual, bare boards, dark wood, cream paint, small-paned windows, small tables around big irregularly shaped main room, raised back area with more tables, Shepherd Neame Bitter, Best, Spitfire and Bishops Finger, quick service, enjoyable traditional food such as roasts in panelled upstairs lunchtime dining room *(Ian Phillips, Derek Thomas, Susan and John Douglas)*

Princess Royal [Paul St]: Classic corner pub with Adnams, Fullers London Pride and Shepherd Neame Bitter and Spitfire, bar snacks from pasties and sandwiches up (good salt beef), pleasant staff, upstairs restaurant *(Ian Phillips)*

EC3

Crosse Keys [Gracechurch St]: Attractive Wetherspoons in former bank, light and bright with lots of marble, domed ceiling, pillars, ornate wood and plasterwork, panelling, upper gallery, well kept ales inc lots of guest beers from big oval central bar, their usual menu and helpful prices, friendly staff, silenced games machine, no music; no smoking back children's area, open all day but cl 4pm Sat and all Sun *(Richard Lewis, Val Baker, Craig Turnbull, John Saville)*

Lamb [Grand Ave, Leadenhall Mkt]: Old-fashioned stand-up bar with spiral stairs to light and airy upper no smoking carpeted lounge bar overlooking market's central crossing, vibrant atmosphere (can get very busy), plenty of tables and corner servery doing good hot carvery rolls, well kept Youngs ales, engraved glass, plenty of ledges and shelves; also basement bar with shiny wall tiling and own entrance *(Val Baker)*

EC4

Blue Anchor [Rolls Passage, off Chancery Lane]: Buoyant atmosphere, Greene King Old Speckled Hen, Charles Wells Bombardier and Youngs, popular food; a few tables out in yard *(Ian Phillips)*

Old Bell [Fleet St, nr Ludgate Circus]: Fine old traditional tavern with brass-topped tables, stained-glass bow window, well kept changing ales such as Adnams, Fullers London Pride, Timothy Taylors Landlord and Charles Wells Bombardier from island servery, friendly service, good value standard food, coal fire, lively atmosphere, some tables tucked away to give a sense of privacy *(BB, the Didler, Ian Phillips, Jarrod and Wendy Hopkinson)*

St Brides Tavern [Bridewell Pl]: Comfortable banquettes and stools, buoyant and relaxed atmosphere, friendly staff, Greene King IPA and Abbot, upstairs dining room *(Ian Phillips)*

SW1

☆ ***Antelope*** [Eaton Terr]: Stylish panelled local, civilised and friendly; bare-boards elegance in main bar, tiny snug, lots of interesting prints and old advertisements, real ales such as Adnams, Fullers London Pride, Marstons Pedigree and Tetleys, good house wines, sandwiches, baked potatoes, ploughman's and one-price hot dishes; quiet and relaxed upstairs wkdy lunchtimes, can get crowded evenings; open all day, children in eating area *(LYM, the Didler)*

Bank Westminster [Buckingham Gate]: Stylish opulent front bar, enjoyable food, good english wine *(Tracey and Stephen Groves)*

☆ ***Buckingham Arms*** [Petty France]: Chatty and welcoming Youngs local with elegant mirrors and woodwork, unusual long side corridor fitted out with elbow ledge for drinkers (and SkyTV for motor sports), well kept ales, good value food lunchtime and evening, reasonable prices, service friendly and efficient even when busy, no music; dogs welcome, handy for Buckingham Palace, Westminster Abbey and St James's Park, open all day *(LYM, the Didler, Tracey and Stephen Groves, A Boss, Dr and Mrs A K Clarke)*

Feathers [Broadway]: Large comfortable pub, a Scotland Yard local, bar food downstairs, restaurant up, well kept real ales; rock DJs 2nd and 4th Sats till 1am *(BB, Ben Anderson)*

☆ ***Fox & Hounds*** [Passmore St/Graham Terr]: Small cosy bar with well kept ales such as Adnams, Bass, Greene King IPA and Harveys, bar food, friendly landlady and staff, wall benches, big hunting prints, old sepia photographs of pubs and customers, some toby jugs, hanging plants under attractive skylight in back room, coal-effect gas fire and organ; can be very busy Fri night, quieter wkdy lunchtimes *(the Didler, Dr and Mrs A K Clarke)*

Golden Lion [King St]: Rather distinguished bow-fronted building opp Christies auction rooms, well kept ales inc Fullers London Pride, decent wines by the glass, good value food inc bargain platters for two, friendly atmosphere; if downstairs bar busy, seats and tables usually available both in passageway alongside or upstairs in theatre bar *(J F M and M West, Dr and Mrs M E Wilson)*

Horse & Groom [Groom Pl]: Smart friendly mews-corner pub with plush seats on stripped boards, particularly well kept Shepherd Neame, personable service *(Tracey and Stephen Groves, Paul Morris)*

Jugged Hare [Vauxhall Bridge Rd/Rochester Row]: Fullers Ale & Pie pub in converted colonnaded bank with balustraded balcony, chandelier, prints and busts; their ales kept well, friendly efficient service, decent food, no smoking back area; fruit machine, unobtrusive piped music; open all day *(BB, the Didler, Sue Demont, Tim Barrow)*

☆ ***Morpeth Arms*** [Millbank]: Roomy and comfortable nicely preserved Victorian pub, the local for Tate Britain, some etched and cut glass, old books and prints, photographs, earthenware jars and bottles, well kept Youngs ales inc Waggle Dance, good range of food from sandwiches up, good choice of wines, helpful well organised service even when it's packed at lunchtime (may be lots of smokers then), quieter evenings; seats outside (a lot of traffic) *(BB, Tracey and Stephen Groves, the Didler, Craig Turnbull, Dr and Mrs A K Clarke)*

Red Lion [Parliament St]: Interesting pub nr Houses of Parliament, with Division Bell – used by MPs and Foreign Office staff; parliamentary cartoons and prints, well kept Tetleys, good range of snacks and meals, small narrow no smoking upstairs dining room; also cellar bar *(Craig Turnbull, Dr and Mrs A K Clarke)*

☆ ***Red Lion*** [Crown Passage, behind St James's St]: Nice unpretentious early Victorian local tucked down narrow and increasingly smart passage nr Christies, panelling and leaded lights giving a timeless feel, relaxed atmosphere, friendly helpful licensees, decent lunchtime food inc fresh proper sandwiches, well kept ales such as Adnams and Courage Directors, reasonable prices; unobtrusive piped music *(BB, DC)*

Wilton Arms [Kinnerton St]: Pleasant and comfortable civilised local with good choice of reasonably priced food, well kept varied ales, good friendly service even when busy; back conservatory, open all day *(BB, Joyce and Geoff Robson)*

SW3

Builders Arms [Britten St]: Smart bistro-style pub, part of a small London chain, with good food (drinkers welcomed too); attractive street *(Derek Thomas)*

Bunch of Grapes [Brompton Rd]: Splendid early Victorian local with some robust wood carving, glittering glass and effusive Victorian decoration; prompt and friendly helpful service, comfortable seats, good if not cheap food from filled rolls and baked potatoes up, well kept Fullers London Pride and Youngs, very cosmopolitan customers; may be piped radio; handy halfway point between Harrods and the V&A *(John Saville, Ian Phillips, Dr and Mrs M E Wilson)*

☆ ***Henry J Beans*** [Kings Rd]: Spacious bar in ornate mock-Tudor building, decent wines, Shepherd Neame Spitfire, pricey but splendid range of whiskies, other spirits, lagers and bottled beers, good value US-flavour bar food; well spaced tables, fine collection of enamelled advertising signs, keen young staff, the biggest sheltered courtyard garden of any central London pub, with its own summer bar; open all day, provision for children *(LYM, Ian Phillips)*

Hour Glass [Brompton Rd]: Small pub handy for V&A and other nearby museums, well kept Fullers, freshly squeezed fruit juice, good value food (not Sun), welcoming landlady and quick young staff; sports TV; pavement tables *(LM)*

☆ ***Surprise*** [Christchurch Terr]: Friendly, eclectic and enjoyably unassuming late Victorian pub with well kept ales inc Fullers London Pride, decent food, and cheerful broad-spectrum mix of locals; often surprisingly quiet evenings (this is a hidden corner of Chelsea), cosy and warm; not overly done up considering location, attractive stained-glass lanterns, 1970s mural around top of bar, leaded lights, bar billiards in back corner; well behaved dogs on leads, some tables outside *(A Rees, Tracey and Stephen Groves)*

W1

☆ ***Audley*** [Mount St]: Classic civilised Mayfair pub, opulent red plush, rich mahogany and engraved glass, clock hanging in lovely carved wood bracket from ornately corniced ceiling, well kept Courage Directors and Youngs from long polished bar, good food (reasonably priced for the area) and service, good coffee, upstairs panelled dining room; open all day *(LYM, Kevin Blake, Dr and Mrs A K Clarke)*

Barley Mow [Dorset St]: Built in 1791, a pub when Marylebone was still a village; attractive, unspoilt and cosy, with Greene King IPA, Marstons Pedigree and Tetleys, spotless housekeeping, panelling, old pictures, three unusual 19th-c cubicles opening on to serving counter, in which the poor old farmers could pawn their watches to the landlord in private; pavement café tables *(Ian Phillips)*

☆ ***Clachan*** [Kingly St]: Lovely wooden bar, ornate plaster ceiling supported by two large fluted and decorated pillars, comfortable screened leather banquettes, smaller drinking alcove up three or four steps, Adnams, Fullers London Pride and Greene King IPA, good service from hard-working smart staff, above-average food inc endangered pub species such as scotch eggs and pork pies; can get busy, but very relaxed in afternoons *(John Harcourt, BB, Dr and Mrs M E Wilson, Sue Demont, Tim Barrow)*

Cock [Great Portland St]: Large corner local with enormous lamps over picnic-sets outside, florid Victorian/Edwardian décor with tiled floor, handsome woodwork, some cut and etched glass, high tiled ceiling and mosaic floor, ornate plasterwork, velvet curtains, coal-effect gas fire, well kept cheap Sam Smiths OB from all four handpumps, popular lunchtime food in upstairs lounge with two more coal-effect gas fires; needs a no smoking area *(Ian Phillips, the Didler, Dr and Mrs M E Wilson)*

Dover Castle [Weymouth Mews]: Simple yet quite elegant and comfortable, with some panelling and old prints, charming back snug, cheap Sam Smiths OB; can be quiet, but piped music may obtrude *(Dr and Mrs A K Clarke)*

Fitzrovia [Goodge St/Whitfield St]: Attractively priced food from soup and sandwiches up, Fullers London Pride, Greene King IPA and Charles Wells Bombardier, nice atmosphere and interesting mix of customers; picnic-sets outside *(Ian Phillips)*

Fitzroy [Charlotte St]: Tidy pub with photographs of customers Augustus John, Dylan Thomas and the young Richard Attenborough, George Orwell's NUJ card and so forth, carpeted downstairs bar with white-painted brickwork, wooden settles and a couple of snugs, comfortable upstairs bar, low-priced Sam Smiths OB, good value food inc filled baguettes, expert friendly staff; may be piped music; plenty of tables out under cocktail parasols, popular in summer *(Ian Phillips)*

Hope [Tottenham St]: Cosy two-floor traditional local with well kept Fullers London Pride, Timothy Taylors Landlord and Charles Wells Bombardier, lunchtime sausages; pavement tables, next to Pollock's Toy Museum *(Tim Maddison)*

☆ ***O'Conor Don*** [Marylebone Lane]: Enjoyable and civilised family-run bare-boards pub, genuinely and unobtrusively Irish, with pubby tables and chairs on dark bare boards, elbow shelf right around frosted glass windows, high plastered ceiling, good baguettes and other freshly made bar food, waitress drinks service (to make sure the Guinness has settled properly), warm bustling atmosphere, daily papers; may be piped 1970s pop music; good upstairs restaurant with daily fresh galway oysters, folk music Sat; handy for the Wallace Collection *(Ian Phillips, BB)*

☆ ***Old Coffee House*** [Beak St]: Civilised and welcoming pub with wide choice of decent lunchtime food (not Sun) in upstairs food room full of prints and pictures, well kept Courage Best, Marstons Pedigree and Youngs, still some interesting bric-a-brac though less than there used to be; fruit machine, piped music; children allowed upstairs 12-3, open all day exc Sun afternoon; very popular with wknd shoppers and tourists *(LYM, Tracey and Stephen Groves, Patrick Hancock, Ian Phillips)*

Pillars of Hercules [Greek St]: Pleasantly old-fashioned, with dark wood and ornate heavily painted plasterwork, three distinct areas, good changing beer choice, cheerful staff *(Tracey and Stephen Groves)*

Red Lion [Kingly St]: Narrow front bar with deep leather banquettes, back bar with darts, well kept low-priced Sam Smiths, short realistically priced lunchtime food choice from baguettes up in comfortable upstairs lounge *(DC, BB, Ian Phillips)*

☆ ***Toucan*** [Carlisle St]: Charming small Guinness pub, five taps for it in relaxed dark and cosy basement bar with toucan paintings and vintage Guinness advertisements, lots of whiskeys and good Irish piped music, enjoyable food (11-5) such as Guinness pie, irish stew, galway oysters; lighter plainer upstairs bar overflows on to pavement when busy; quiet TV in both bars; open all day, cl Sun *(Tim Maddison, BB)*

Waxy O'Connors [Rupert St]: Small ordinary street entry to surprising 3D maze of communicating areas on several levels, entertaining and varied largely gothic décor; lagers and stouts, friendly young staff, food (12-7) good if not cheap, keg beers; can be packed at night with young up-front people (good piped rock music), quiet daytime; open all day *(Dr and Mrs M E Wilson, BB, Sue Demont, Tim Barrow)*

W2

Cow [Westbourne Park Rd]: Small, friendly and busy, with short choice of good mainly modern food, upstairs dining room *(Dr and Mrs S Donald)*

☆ ***Mad Bishop & Bear*** [Paddington station]: Up escalators from concourse, classic city-pub décor in cream and pastels, ornate plasterwork, etched mirrors and fancy lamps inc big brass chandeliers, parquet, tiles and carpet, booths with leather banquettes, lots of wood and prints, a guest beer and full Fullers beer range kept well from long counter, good wine choice, friendly smartly dressed staff, wide choice of good value food from breakfast (7.30 on) and sandwiches to Sun roasts, big no smoking area, train departures screen; soft piped music, fruit machine; open all day, tables out overlooking concourse *(Simon Collett-Jones, BB, Ian Phillips, Dr and Mrs A K Clarke, Susan and Nigel Wilson)*

☆ ***Victoria*** [Strathearn Pl]: Interesting and well preserved corner local, lots of Victorian Royal and other memorabilia, *Vanity Fair* cartoons and unusual little military paintings, two cast-iron fireplaces, wonderful gilded mirrors and mahogany panelling, brass mock-gas lamps above attractive horseshoe bar, bare boards and banquettes, relaxed atmosphere, friendly attentive service, full Fullers range kept well, good choice of wines by the glass, well priced food counter; upstairs has leather club chairs in small library/snug (and, mostly used for private functions now, replica of Gaiety Theatre bar, all gilt and red plush); quiet piped music, TV (off unless you ask); pavement picnic-sets *(LYM, Dr and Mrs A K Clarke, Tracey and Stephen Groves)*

WC1

Calthorpe Arms [Grays Inn Rd]: Consistently well kept Youngs Bitter, Special and seasonal beer at sensible prices in relaxed and unpretentious corner pub with plush wall seats, big helpings of popular food upstairs lunchtime and evening; nice pavement tables, open all day *(the Didler, C J Fletcher, Patrick Hancock)*

Dolphin [Red Lion St]: Small, cosy and welcoming, high stools and wide shelves around the walls, old photographs, horsebrasses, hanging copper pots and pans and so forth inside, simple wkdy lunchtime food, and real ales such as Bass, Boddingtons, Brakspears and Fullers London Pride; seats and flower-filled window boxes outside, open all day wkdys, plus Sat lunchtime *(Ian Phillips, the Didler)*

☆ ***Duke*** [Roger St]: Quietly placed and unpretentious, with emphasis on surprisingly good distinctive modern food at reasonable prices; real ales such as Greene King Old Speckled Hen and Ind Coope Burton, helpful staff, cool and welcoming young atmosphere (big Andy Warhol-style pictures), Formica-top tables and café chairs on patterned lino in main room, fresh colours, daily papers and relaxed village-local atmosphere in back room with log-effect gas fire, upstairs dining room *(Joel Dobris, BB, Ian Phillips, Tracey and Stephen Groves)*

Kings Arms [Northington St/John St]: Immaculate pub doing well under entertaining newish landlord, Adnams, Greene King IPA and Timothy Taylors Landlord, mainly thai food (Thai kitchen staff), also reasonably priced sandwiches, baguettes and conventional hot dishes *(Ian Phillips)*

Museum Tavern [Museum St/Gt Russell St]: Traditional high-ceilinged Victorian pub facing British Museum, busy lunchtime and early evening, but can be quite peaceful other times – easier then to imagine Karl Marx or J B Priestley drinking here, as they used to; well kept ales such as Courage Directors, Fullers London Pride, Theakstons Old Peculier and Youngs Bitter and Special, several wines by the glass, good hot drinks, straightforward food from end servery; one or two tables out under gas lamps, open all day *(Peter Meister, Nick Holding, Barry Collett, Ian Phillips, LYM)*

Old Crown [New Oxford St]: Now a sort of frenchified bistro/café/pub, enormous wire crowns hanging, green leathercloth tablecloths, yellow napkins and candles, good choice of wines by the glass, Bass, imported and other lagers, baguettes and salads; pavement tables *(Ian Phillips)*

Pakenham Arms [Pakenham St]: Relaxed unspoilt split-level local, quiet at lunchtime and wknds, well kept real ales, friendly staff, generous food, big open doors making it light and airy in summer; picnic-sets outside, lots of flowers *(Esther and John Sprinkle, C J Fletcher, Patrick Hancock)*

Plough [Museum St/Little Russell St]: Neatly kept two-bar Bloomsbury local with well kept beer, daily papers; upstairs no smoking room with food such as baked potatoes, ploughman's, salad, sausage and mash and pasta *(Ian Phillips)*

☆ ***Princess Louise*** [High Holborn]: Etched and gilt mirrors, brightly coloured and fruity-shaped tiles, slender portland stone columns, lofty and elaborately colourful ceiling, quiet plush-seated corners, low-priced Sam Smiths from the long counter, good friendly service, reasonably priced baguettes and upstairs lunchtime buffet; noble Victorian gents'; crowded and lively during the week, with great evening atmosphere – usually quieter late evening, or Sat lunchtime; open all day, cl Sun *(the Didler, LYM, Tracey and Stephen Groves, Dr and Mrs A K Clarke, Ian Phillips, Patrick Hancock)*

Rugby [Great James St]: Sizeable corner pub with well kept Shepherd Neame ales inc their seasonal beer, usual food, good service; tables outside *(the Didler, Joel Dobris)*

WC2

☆ ***Chandos*** [St Martins Lane]: Busy downstairs bare-boards bar with snug cubicles, more comfortable upstairs lounge with opera photographs, low wooden tables, panelling, leather sofas, orange, red and yellow leaded windows; well kept cheap Sam Smiths OB, prompt cheerful mainly Antipodean service, decent sensibly priced food from sandwiches to Sun roasts, air conditioning, darts and pinball; can get packed early evening, piped music and games machines; note the automaton on the roof (working 10-2 and 4-9); children upstairs till 6, open all day from 9 (for breakfast) *(Ian Phillips, LYM, Patrick Hancock, Susan and Nigel Wilson)*

Coal Hole [Strand]: Pleasant and comfortable, downstairs bar with carefully revamped high ceiling (may be piped music), airy and quieter upper bar; good range of beers, decent house wine, well priced sandwiches, baked potatoes, good sausages and mash etc; handy for Raymond Gubbay's opera *(BB, Gloria Bax)*

☆ ***Cross Keys*** [Endell St/Betterton St]: Friendly and cosy, refreshingly un-Londonish, with masses of photographs and posters inc Beatles memorabilia, brassware and tasteful bric-a-brac on the dark dim-lit walls, relaxed chatty feel; impressive range of lunchtime sandwiches at sensible prices and a few hot dishes then, well kept Courage Best, Fullers London Pride and Shepherd Neame Spitfire, decent wines by the glass, quick service even at busy times; small upstairs bar, often used for functions; fruit machine, gents' down stairs; picnic-sets out on cobbles tucked behind a little group of trees, pretty flower tubs and hanging baskets, open all day *(the Didler, LYM, Ian Phillips, John and Gloria Isaacs)*

Knights Templar [Chancery Lane]: Elaborately decorated Wetherspoons in big-windowed former bank, marble pillars, handsome fittings and plasterwork, good bustling atmosphere on two levels, up to nine well kept real ales from mainstream to rare, good wine choice, good all-day menu inc bargains, friendly staff, no smoking areas; remarkably handsome lavatories; open all day inc Sun *(Brian and Rosalie Laverick)*

Montagu Pyke [Charing Cross Rd]: Former Moon Under Water (and before that the Marquee Club), now rebranded by Wetherspoons as a Lloyds No 1 bar (aimed younger and livelier than the core Wetherspoons); worth knowing particularly at quieter times of day for its bargain prices, for food and drinks inc coffee, and what is that those times a very spacious and leisurely spread of different brightly modern comfortable areas; open all day *(LYM)*

Olde White Horse [St Clement's Lane]: Friendly and comfortable, with good range of real ales such as Caledonian Deuchars IPA from bar counter in raised area, burgundy décor – walls, lamps, carpets *(Tracey and Stephen Groves)*

Opera Tavern [Catherine St, opp Theatre Royal]: Cheerful bare-boards pub, not too touristy, real ales such as Adnams, Fullers London Pride and Tetleys, reasonably priced snacks from sandwiches and baked potatoes up *(Ian Phillips, Dr and Mrs A K Clarke)*

☆ ***Porterhouse*** [Maiden Lane]: London outpost of Dublin's Porterhouse microbrewery, shiny three-level maze of stairs, galleries and copper ducting and piping, some nice design touches, their own interesting if pricey unpasteurised draught beers inc Porter and two Stouts (they do a comprehensive tasting tray), also their TSB real ale and a guest, lots of bottled beers, good choice of wines by the glass, reasonably priced food 12-9 from soup and open sandwiches up with some emphasis on rock oysters, sonorous openwork clock, neatly cased bottled beer displays; piped music, Irish bands Weds-Fri and Sun, big-screen sports TV (repeated in gents'); open all day, tables on front terrace *(BB, Rona Murdoch, Patrick Hancock, Dr and Mrs A K Clarke, Tandor Claassens, Darren Le Poidevin)*

☆ ***Salisbury*** [St Martins Lane]: Floridly Victorian with plenty of atmosphere, theatrical sweeps of red velvet, huge sparkling mirrors and cut and etched glass, glossy brass and mahogany; wide food choice from simple snacks to long-running smoked salmon lunches and salad bar (even doing Sun lunches over Christmas/New Year), well kept changing ales (can be pricey) such as Courage Directors, Fullers London

Pride, Charles Wells Bombardier and Youngs Special, decent house wines, friendly helpful staff, no smoking back room *(BB, Ian Phillips, the Didler, Dr and Mrs A K Clarke, Mike Gorton, Derek Thomas, Paul Boot)*

Sans Culottes [Endell St]: Friendly, light and airy brewpub visibly producing its own good unfiltered and unpasteurised draught beer, stout and lagers, decent wines, espresso machine, french café food, stylish black and white prints on grey-blue walls, glossy bare boards, silent TV, daily papers, helpful French staff; open all day from 9.30 (from 1 Sun) *(Richard Houghton)*

Sherlock Holmes [Northumberland St; aka Northumberland Arms]: Fine collection of Holmes memorabilia, inc complete model of his apartment, also silent videos of black and white Holmes films; Boddingtons, Flowers IPA, Fullers London Pride and Wadworths 6X, usual furnishings, lunchtime pub food from doorstep sandwiches up, young staff, upstairs restaurant; busy lunchtime *(LM, BB, Dr and Mrs A K Clarke)*

Ship & Shovell [Craven Passage, off Craven St]: Two bars facing each other across passage under Charing X station, four Badger real ales kept well, reasonably priced food from baguettes, bloomers and ciabattas up, welcoming service and civilised atmosphere, warm fire, bright lighting, pleasant décor inc interesting prints, mainly naval (to support a fanciful connection between this former coal-heavers' pub properly called Ship & Shovel with Sir Cloudesley Shovell the early 18th-c admiral), cosy back section; TV *(Tracey and Stephen Groves, the Didler, Ian Phillips, Patrick Hancock, Dr and Mrs M E Wilson)*

Spice of Life [Cambridge Circus]: Ornate open-plan bare-boards Victorian pub with well kept McMullens County Best and AK Mild and a guest such as Greene King Old Speckled Hen, usual food from doorstep sandwiches and melts up, friendly staff; piped music may be loud, games machine; children welcome, open all day *(Ian Phillips)*

Welsh Harp [Chandos Pl]: Unpretentious and friendly, with some interesting if not always well executed star portraits on its red walls, lovely front stained-glass, congenial seating layout with nice high benches around back tables and along wall counter, unusual well kept ales such as Elgoods, Harveys and York, good collection of whiskeys and whiskies *(Tracey and Stephen Groves, BB, Tim Maddison)*

EAST LONDON

E1

Dickens Inn [Marble Quay, St Katharines Way]: Outstanding position above smart docklands marina, oddly swiss-chalet look from outside with its balconies and window boxes, interesting stripped-down bare boards, baulks and timbers interior, wide choice of enjoyable food, well kept Theakstons Old Peculier, friendly prompt service, several floors inc pizza/pasta restaurant; popular with overseas visitors, tables outside *(the Didler, LYM, John Saville)*

Half Moon [Mile End Rd]: Well done Wetherspoons conversion of former music hall with up-to-date bar, great drinks offers *(Giles and Annie Francis)*

E2

Anda de Bridge [Kingsland Rd]: Genuinely caribbean, with Jamaican landlord, attractively priced speciality food from interesting snacks to curried goat and proper jerk dishes (take-aways too), Red Stripe among other lagers on tap, prodigious range of rums, two rooms with rustic furniture; live music wknds *(Ian Phillips)*

☆ ***Approach Tavern*** [Approach Rd]: Imposing high-ceilinged Victorian tavern restored as good unpretentious food pub, comfortable seating, fairly priced enjoyable food inc good Sun roasts and delicious puddings, well kept Fullers and Ridleys ales, considerate service, upstairs art gallery; outstanding non-contemporary juke box; children welcome, railed and heated front terrace *(Tim Maddison, Catherine Worsley, Catherine Cronin, BB)*

E3

Palm Tree [Haverfield Rd]: Lone survivor of blitzed East End terrace, by Regents Canal and beside windmill and ecology centre in futuristic-looking Mile End Park; horseshoe bar, Edwardian décor, Bass and Timothy Taylors Landlord, sandwiches made to order, thriving local atmosphere; jazz twice a week *(Catherine Cronin, Ian Phillips)*

E8

Baxters Court [Mare St, opp Hackney Town Hall]: Large new Wetherspoons with heated open-sky lobby, dark and calm inside, with back bar and lots of comfortable seating, good range of real ales, bargain coffee, their good value food from sandwiches and baked potatoes up; open all day *(Ian Phillips)*

E9

Alex [Victoria Park Rd/Lauriston Rd]: Clean and fresh family-friendly mix of pub, pizza parlour and café, good wine range, Boddingtons and Tetleys, lots of lagers, broadsheet papers, big comfortable sofas one end, large Queen Alexandra portrait, monthly art gallery *(Ian Phillips)*

E10

William IV [High Rd Leyton]: Large friendly open-plan pub, well kept beer (it has recently started brewing its own) and good range of food *(Richard Houghton)*

E11

Duke of Edinburgh [Nightingale Lane]: Comfortably unspoilt two-bar local, warm and friendly, with good plain cheap lunchtime food (all home-made), well kept Adnams and guest beers, decent wine, cheerful service, plenty of

prints and plates, even an aquarium; garden tables, open all day *(Robert Lester)*
George [High St Wanstead]: Large 18th-c coaching inn, now a Wetherspoons, always busy but never crowded, good range of changing ales, their usual reasonably priced food all day, plenty of books to read, pictures of famous Georges down the ages *(Robert Lester)*

E12
Ruskin Arms [High St N]: Local with big back music room behind – live bands Fri, DJs Sat *(Ben Anderson)*

E14
Narrow Street Pub & Dining Room [Narrow St]: Former Barley Mow, completely reworked as trendy minimalist lager bar with pastel décor, pale floors, stainless bar and open kitchen doing food for bar and more expensive restaurant; still worth knowing for its great Thames views; children welcome, big heaters for picnic-sets on spacious if breezy terrace, open all day *(K Hutchinson)*

E17
Nags Head [Orford Rd]: Old-fashioned traditional refurbishment, with cosy fire, well kept Adnams, Fullers London Pride and a guest ale, lots of belgian beers; plenty of terrace tables *(Matt Bennett)*

NORTH LONDON

N1
Albion [Thornhill Rd]: Cosy local feel in several distinct traditional areas rambling around central bar, old prints and soft lighting (some gas lamps), small comfortable no smoking back restaurant area (front can get a bit smoky), reasonably priced straightforward food from sandwiches and baked potatoes to plenty of specials, well kept Fullers London Pride and changing guest beers such as Coniston Bluebird and Mordue Workie Ticket, interesting Victorian gents'; piped music, TV, fruit machine, games machine; flower-decked railed front courtyard, big heated back terrace with lots of close-set tables under huge parasol, weeping willow and vine bower *(BB, Tim Maddison)*
Alma [Newington Green Rd]: Relaxed local bar with sofas, big tables and open fire, candlelit restaurant area with deep red and mulberry décor, up-to-date food with wkdy lunch deals, cheerful staff; children and dogs welcome, small sheltered garden, open all day, cl Mon lunchtime *(anon)*
Angel [High St, opp Angel tube station]: Large, light and airy open-plan Wetherspoons with feel of a comfortable continental bar, busy but relaxing, friendly staff, good choice of well kept beers (some bargains), their usual food all day; no smoking areas, silenced games machine, no music, open all day *(Darren Le Poidevin)*
Camden Head [Camden Walk]: Well preserved Victorian pub very handy for the antiques market, spacious and comfortably elegant circular room, well kept Charles Wells Bombardier from island servery with decorative glass, enjoyable food inc good specials; tables out on fairly quiet terrace *(Esther and John Sprinkle, Tracey and Stephen Groves)*
Crown [Cloudesley Rd]: Good food and atmosphere in bright and airy gastropub with helpful friendly staff, well kept Fullers and interesting guest beers from impressive central servery, plenty of light oak panelling and cut and etched glass; tables out on small railed front terrace *(Aidan Wallis, Tim Maddison)*
☆ ***House*** [Canonbury Rd]: Stylish gastropub with carefully crafted tables and unusual chairs around deco central servery, sofas and daily papers by a couple of fireplaces, back partly no smoking dining area (you can eat anywhere), good mainly modern food inc good value lunchtime and early evening set meals, wide choice of wines, pricey Adnams Broadside, quite a selection of hot drinks, smiling service; piped music; children welcome, roadside terrace, open all day, cl Mon lunchtime *(BB, Peter and Jean Hoare)*
Kings Head [Upper St]: Green décor and large mirrors in big-windowed high-ceilinged Victorian pub in good spot, well kept Adnams, Tetleys and Youngs or Wadworths 6X from horseshoe bar with fine old cash register, hot solid fuel fires, theatre lighting, even some pensioned-off row seats, and lots of dated theatre photographs, bar food (via ancient dumb waiter) and popular bistro, decent coffee; an oasis of calm on wkdy lunchtimes, can get packed evenings and wknds; singer most nights, good theatre in back room (but hard seats there) *(Tracey and Stephen Groves, BB)*
Lincoln Arms [York Way]: Unusual easy-going arts pub, book exchange, art shows; well chosen piped music, some live or cabaret nights; tables outside, opens 4 (7 Sat), cl lunchtimes and Sun *(anon)*

N4
Salisbury [Grand Parade, Green Lanes]: Grandiose late Victorian former hotel reopened after careful refurbishment of its spacious richly ornamented bars, dark velvet, leather and mahogany, intricate tiling and mirrors, well kept Fullers London Pride and Ridleys ales, czech lagers on tap, food in bar and dining room (not Sun evening); open all day, till 1am Thurs-Sat *(Dr and Mrs M E Wilson, Tim Maddison)*

N6
☆ ***Flask*** [Highgate West Hill]: Comfortable Georgian pub, mostly modernised but still has intriguing up-and-down layout, sash-windowed bar hatch, panelling and high-backed carved settle tucked away in snug lower area with nice log fire, enjoyable changing all-day food (limited Sun) from soup and sandwiches up, changing beers such as Adnams Broadside, Fullers Chiswick, Harveys

Best and Timothy Taylors Landlord, Addlestone's cider, several continental beers on tap, friendly service; very busy Sat lunchtime, well behaved children allowed, close-set picnic-sets out in attractive heated front courtyard, handy for strolls around Highgate village or Hampstead Heath *(LYM, Jasmeet Fyfe, Ian Phillips)*

N20

☆ ***Orange Tree*** [Totteridge]: Attractive light and airy décor in rambling largely no smoking Vintage Inn, good value standard food from sandwiches to fish served efficiently even on busy wknds (good Sun roasts), well kept Bass and Fullers London Pride, good choice of wines by the glass, freshly squeezed orange juice and coffee, friendly efficient staff, inglenook log fires; welcoming to children (and walkers, who leave boots in porch), tables out in pleasant surroundings by duck pond (still a village feel), open all day *(LM, LYM, John Wooll, Jasmeet Fyfe)*

NW1

Albert [Princess Rd]: Welcoming split-level pub with interesting food such as quail and seafood brochettes, well kept Greene King IPA and Fullers London Pride, obliging friendly staff, roomy and appealing bar free from music and machines; dogs welcome, attractive back garden with summerhouse *(LYM, John and Hiro Charles)*

Crown & Anchor [Drummond St]: Friendly bare bricks pub with well kept beers and tasty low-priced food; tables outside *(Colin Gooch)*

Euston Flyer [Euston Rd, opp British Library]: Spacious and comfortable open-plan pub opp British Library, full Fullers range kept well at sensible prices, decent food from big well filled fresh sandwiches up, plenty of light wood, tile and wood floors, smaller more private raised areas, flying machines with Latin tags as décor, big doors open to street in warm weather; piped music may obtrude, big-screen TVs, can get packed early evening, then again later; open all day, cl 8.30 Sun *(Nigel Epsley)*

Globe [Marylebone Rd]: Handsome and neatly kept L-shaped pubby bar, good variety of intimate seating on polished boards, real ales such as Courage Best and Directors, Ridleys Rumpus, Charles Wells Bombardier and Youngs Special, foreign bottled beers, sensibly priced food from baked potatoes up; seats outside (a mass of flowers in summer), handy for Mme Tussauds *(Ian Phillips, Tracey and Stephen Groves)*

☆ ***Head of Steam*** [Eversholt St]: Large friendly and unpretentious Victorian-look bar up stairs from bus terminus and overlooking it, no smoking area, lots of railway nameplates, other memorabilia and enthusiast magazines for sale, also Corgi collection, unusual model trains and buses; nine interesting well kept ales (also take-away) changing from session to session, most from little-known small breweries, monthly themed beer festivals, Weston's farm cider and perry, lots of bottled beers and vodkas, kind service, simple cheap bar lunches, downstairs restaurant; TV, bar billiards, games machine, security-coded basement lavatories; open all day *(R T and J C Moggridge, BB, the Didler, Richard Lewis, Dr D J and Mrs S C Walker, Nigel Brown, Brian and Rosalie Laverick, Dr and Mrs A K Clarke, Darren Le Poidevin, C J Fletcher, Dr J Barrie Jones, Sue Demont, Tim Barrow)*

Hobgoblin [Balcombe St]: Interesting changing guest beers such as Timothy Taylors Ram Tam, congenial layout and sober furnishings, popular thai food in appealing cellar bar *(Tracey and Stephen Groves)*

Man in the Moon [Chalk Farm Rd]: Civilised Wetherspoons with mezzanine and lower back family area overlooking back terrace, good beer choice, good coffee and reasonable food all day from panini up, low prices, young friendly efficient staff *(Ian Phillips)*

Queens [Regents Park Rd]: Typically Victorian long narrow bar with mahogany, stained-glass windows, secluded corners inc quiet enclosed area up a few steps, ornate end mirrors; well kept Youngs, innovative food, pleasant service, upstairs restaurant; dogs welcome *(John and Hiro Charles)*

Royal George [Eversholt St, by Euston Station]: Roomy and tidily kept, with well kept beers and enjoyable cheap food inc bargains for two *(Ted George)*

NW3

Duke of Hamilton [New End]: Attractive family-run Fullers local, good value, with good range of seating, well kept London Pride, ESB and a seasonal beer, Biddenden farm cider; open all day, suntrap terrace, next to New End Theatre *(Tracey and Stephen Groves, the Didler, Patrick Hancock)*

NW8

☆ ***Crockers*** [Aberdeen Pl]: Magnificent original Victorian interior, full of showy marble, decorated plaster and opulent woodwork; relaxing and comfortable, with well kept Brakspears and Greene King, friendly service, decent food inc good Sun roasts; tables outside *(the Didler, LYM, M Thomas)*

New Inn [Allitsen Rd/Townsend Rd]: Cheerful 19th-c local with good atmosphere, honest straightforward food, Greene King ales; TV, juke box and fruit machine; dogs welcome, bedrooms *(John and Hiro Charles)*

Ordnance Arms [Ordnance Hill]: Roomy and rambling early 19th-c pub, low-priced Sam Smiths OB, decent food, militaria inc design drawings of guns and cannons, some leather chesterfields, conservatory; leafy back terrace *(LYM, John and Hiro Charles)*

NW10

Astons [Regent St, Kensal Green]: Big 1930s pub, comfortable sofas and coal-effect gas fire in back lounge, dining other side of central bar, keg beers but good choice of wines, enjoyable food (all day Sun); back terrace with sliding roof, pavement picnic-sets *(Ian Phillips)*

SOUTH LONDON

SE1

☆ ***Anchor*** [Park St, Bankside]: Historic beamed and black-panelled riverside pub, much refurbished and opened up but still with traces of its former creaky little rooms and passageways, Courage Best and Directors, a dozen wines by the glass, jugs of Pimms, winter mulled wine, various teas and coffees, ready-made baguettes, all-day simple low-priced hot dishes in upstairs bar, some parts no smoking; great Thames views from outside tables, summer barbecues, children in top restaurant and family room, new bedrooms in Premier Lodge behind, open all day *(BJL, Kevin Flack, the Didler, Ian Phillips, LYM, Roger Cox, Esther and John Sprinkle, Craig Turnbull)*

Anchor & Hope [The Cut]: Friendly and busy newish gastropub in the same group as the Eagle in Farringdon St (see Central London main entries), real ales such as Charles Wells Eagle and Bombardier, decent food inc some interesting dishes, though prices a bit high especially considering the far-from-smart furniture and bare boards *(Ian Phillips, Dr and Mrs M E Wilson)*

Duke of York [Borough Rd]: Smart and sympathetic Victorian refurbishment in burgundy and cream, panelling and period lighting, Shepherd Neame real ales; picnic-sets and floral displays outside *(Susan and John Douglas)*

☆ ***Hole in the Wall*** [Mepham St]: Well kept changing ales such as Adnams, Everards Tiger, Youngs Bitter and Special and their own Battersea Power Station, plenty of lagers, and good malts and irish whiskeys, in welcoming no-frills drinkers' dive, in railway arch virtually underneath Waterloo – rumbles and shakes with the trains; small front bar, nice medley of tables set well back from long bar in back room; loudish juke box, pinball and games machines, basic food such as sandwiches, ploughman's and salads all day (cl wknd afternoons) *(LYM, Ian Phillips, Tracey and Stephen Groves)*

☆ ***Horniman*** [Hays Galleria, off Battlebridge Lane]: Good stop on Thames walks, spacious, bright and airy, with lots of polished wood, comfortable seating inc a few sofas, no smoking area, Adnams, Fullers London Pride and Greene King IPA, choice of teas and coffees at good prices, lunchtime bar food from soup and big sandwiches up, snacks other times; unobtrusive piped music; fine Thames views from picnic-sets outside, open all day *(Ian Phillips, LYM, Patrick Hancock)*

Kings Arms [Roupell St]: Bustling and friendly well preserved pub, two distinctive curved rooms with attractive prints and fresh flowers *(Tracey and Stephen Groves)*

Lord Clyde [Clennam St]: Unpretentious panelled L-shaped main bar, small hatch-service back public bar with darts, real ales inc Fullers London Pride, Shepherd Neame Spitfire and Youngs, good value straightforward home-made food wkdy lunchtimes and early evenings, may do toasties etc on request at other times (worth asking), welcoming service; striking tiled façade *(Pete Baker)*

☆ ***Old Thameside*** [Pickfords Wharf, Clink St]: Good 1980s pastiche of ancient tavern, two floors, hefty beams and timbers, pews, flagstones, candles; splendid river view upstairs and from charming waterside terrace; well kept Tetleys and Marstons Pedigree with guests such as Adnams and Fullers, friendly staff, fresh baguettes from salad bar, lunchtime hot buffet; pool down spiral stairs, piped music; open all day but cl 3 at wknds *(LYM, Esther and John Sprinkle)*

Pineapple [Hercules Rd]: Friendly flower-decked pub with low-priced honest food from toasties and baked potatoes up, Bass, Fullers London Pride and Youngs, interesting maps of the area in the late 18th c, games room on right; picnic-sets out in front *(Ian Phillips)*

☆ ***Royal Oak*** [Tabard St]: Victorian corner pub carefully refurbished by Harveys as cosily old-fashioned two-room alehouse, period sheet music on red walls, full range of consistently well kept Harveys ales from central servery with fine clock, thriving chatty atmosphere, bargain lunchtime home cooking, no music or machines; dogs welcome, open all day, cl wknds *(Jarrod and Wendy Hopkinson, Nigel Brown, Sue Demont, Tim Barrow, the Didler, BB)*

Shipwrights Arms [Tooley St]: Nautical theme, well kept changing beers such as Adnams, Courage Best and Charles Wells Bombardier, good choice of bargain food, comfortable seats, friendly landlady and staff; quiet piped music; open all day, handy for London Dungeon and HMS *Belfast* *(Ian Phillips)*

Studio Six [Gabriel's Wharf, Upper Ground]: Bustling South Bank bar/bistro in two linked timber-framed buildings, glazed all round, picnic-sets on two terraces (one heated), good well priced blackboard food choice all day inc lots of fish, good choice of belgian beers on tap, decent wines, Boddingtons, efficient service; soft piped music; children welcome, great location opp cycle rickshaw base, open all day *(Gillian Rodgers, BB, Michael Butler)*

Wellington [Waterloo Rd, opp Waterloo station]: Comfortably refurbished late Victorian pub with large high-ceilinged linked rooms, light wood panelling, enormous stirring Battle of Waterloo murals on wall and ceiling, Adnams, Brakspears, Courage Directors, Youngs and a beer labelled for the pub from ornate bar counter, food all day, plenty of comfortable chairs and sofas, attractive tables, friendly service; piped music may obtrude, can get smoky and very crowded despite its size, sports TV; has had deaf people's night every other Fri, bedrooms, open all day *(Dr and Mrs M E Wilson)*

Wheatsheaf [Stoney St]: Simple bare-boards Borough Market local, Youngs and a guest ale from central servery, decent wine choice, lunchtime food, friendly staff, some brown panelling; sports TV in one bar, piped music, games machine; tables on small back terrace and on pavement by market, open all day, cl Sun *(Kevin Flack, the Didler)*

SE10

Greenwich Union [Royal Hill]: Tied to small Meantime brewery in nearby Charlton, with their own interesting keg and bottled beers and one real ale, friendly relaxing atmosphere, enjoyable fresh food (not Sun evening) inc two-sitting Sun lunch, up-to-date yellow décor, flagstones, some button-back leather chairs and settees, daily papers; well reproduced piped music (live Tues and fortnightly Weds); partly covered back terrace, open all day *(Richard Houghton, the Didler)*

☆ *Richard I* [Royal Hill]: Quietly old-fashioned pubby atmosphere in friendly no-nonsense traditional two-bar local with well kept Youngs, good staff, no piped music, bare boards, panelling; tables in pleasant back garden with barbecues, busy summer wknds and evenings *(Robert Gomme, the Didler)*

☆ *Trafalgar* [Park Row]: Attractive and substantial 18th-c building with four elegant rooms inc pleasant end dining room and central bar with lovely river-view bow window, careful colour schemes, oak panelling, helpful young staff welcoming even when busy (can get packed Fri-Sat evenings, may have bouncer then), good atmosphere, well prepared usual food inc speciality whitebait and good fresh veg, real ales inc Theakstons, good house wines; piped music in river-view room; handy for Maritime Museum, may have jazz wknds *(Dr and Mrs R E S Tanner, Tracey and Stephen Groves, Roger and Jenny Huggins)*

Yacht [Crane St]: Friendly, neatly kept and civilised, with enjoyable food inc particularly good fish and chips, well kept Adnams, Fullers London Pride, Greene King and Charles Wells Bombardier, good river view (Dome too) from spacious room up a few steps from bar, cosy banquettes, light wood panelling, portholes, yacht pictures *(Roger and Jenny Huggins, John Walker)*

SE11

Prince of Wales [Cleaver Sq]: Nicely placed traditional pub in quiet Georgian square, with well kept Shepherd Neame ales, pictures of notorious Londoners *(BB, Giles and Annie Francis)*

SE16

☆ *Mayflower* [Rotherhithe St]: Friendly and cosy old riverside pub with thriving local atmosphere despite growing emphasis on enjoyable and generous food (not Sun night) from ciabattas up, black beams, high-backed settles and coal fires, good Thames views from calm upstairs restaurant (cl Sat lunchtime), well kept Greene King IPA and Old Speckled Hen and a guest beer, good coffee and good value wines, efficient friendly service; unobtrusive nostalgic piped music; children welcome, tables out on nice jetty/terrace over water, open all day, in unusual street with lovely Wren church *(Susan and John Douglas, LYM, the Didler, M A and C R Starling, Roy and Lindsey Fentiman, David Edwards)*

Ship & Whale [Gulliver St]: Neatly kept opened-up pub with pleasant bar-style décor and distinct areas, full Shepherd Neame range kept well, friendly young staff, enjoyable well presented fresh food from sandwiches to round-the-world dishes, choice of teas and coffees, lots of board games; dogs welcome, small garden behind with aviary and barbecue *(LM, Susan and John Douglas)*

SE17

Beehive [Carter St]: Unpretentious bare-boards pub/bistro with well kept Courage Best and Directors and Fullers London Pride from island bar, cushioned pews, bric-a-brac on delft shelf, modern art in candlelit dining room, good choice of home-made food all day from sandwiches to steaks, wide range of wines, friendly service from neat staff; piped music, two TVs; tables outside *(BB, Pete Baker)*

SE26

☆ *Dulwich Wood House* [Sydenham Hill]: Well refurbished and extended Youngs pub in Victorian lodge gatehouse complete with turret, well kept ales, decent wines, attractively priced straightforward food cooked to order popular at lunchtime with local retired people, friendly service; steps up to entrance; lots of tables in big pleasant back garden (no dogs) with old-fashioned street lamps and barbecues *(Alan M Pring, Ian and Nita Cooper, Vanessa Stilwell)*

SW8

Canton Arms [South Lambeth Rd]: Recently refurbished large airy modern bar, comfortable traditional furniture, cheery efficient service, Fullers London Pride and Greene King IPA, decent wines, enjoyable generous proper pub food, sofa and daily papers in one quiet corner; picnic-sets out in front *(Hannah Bowler, Ian Phillips)*

Priory Arms [Lansdowne Way]: Friendly country atmosphere in town, complete with lazy dog, packed old corner bookshelf and committed regulars, good beer range inc Harveys Best, belgian and german beers on tap and in bottle, enjoyable food from ploughman's to Sun roasts *(David Barnes)*

SW11

Dovedale House [Battersea Park Rd]: New incarnation as gastropub with mismatched chairs and tables, good lunchtime menu and wine list, good coffee, limited beers on tap *(Gillian Rodgers)*

Eagle [Chatham Rd]: Attractive and friendly old backstreet local, well kept ales such as Flowers IPA, Fullers London Pride and Timothy Taylors Landlord, helpful landlord, leather sofas in fireside corner of L-shaped bar; big-screen sports TV; back terrace with marquee, small front terrace too *(Sue Demont, Tim Barrow)*

Falcon [St Johns Hill]: Edwardian pub with remarkably long light oak bar snaking through several rooms, period partitions, cut glass and mirrors, friendly service, well kept Adnams *(R T and J C Moggridge)*

Northcote [Northcote Rd]: Well kept Fullers London Pride, good range of bar food, friendly enthusiastic service *(R T and J C Moggridge)*

SW12

Grove [Oldridge Rd]: Bright and comfortably refurbished Youngs pub with their beer kept well, friendly staff, part with sofas and armchairs, upper bar for dining (imaginative menu), no smoking area; unobtrusive piped music *(Sue Demont, Tim Barrow)*

☆ ***Nightingale*** [Nightingale Lane]: Welcoming, comfortable and civilised early Victorian local, small woody front bar opening into larger back area and attractive hop-girt family conservatory, good bar food, well kept Youngs, sensible prices, friendly staff; can get a bit smoky; small secluded back garden *(BB, Sue Demont, Tim Barrow)*

SW13

☆ ***Bulls Head*** [Lonsdale Rd]: An old favourite for good live jazz nightly and Sun afternoon in its well equipped music room; big relaxed well worn in bar with Youngs real ales from central servery, fine collection of malt whiskies and plenty of wines by the glass, sandwiches, ciabattas and a few simple sensibly priced hot dishes virtually all day, friendly service, table and board games, no smoking family room; TV; dogs welcome, open all day *(LYM, Russell Lewin)*

☆ ***Idle Hour*** [Railway Side (off White Hart Lane between Mortlake High St and Upper Richmond Rd)]: Out of the way small local transformed into friendly organic gastropub, very good individually cooked food inc choice of Sun roasts, splendid bloody mary, good range of organic soft drinks, Flowers IPA; nice chunky old tables on bare boards, relaxed atmosphere, daily papers and magazines, a profusion of wall clocks, comfortable sofa by small fireplace; chill-out piped music, cl wkdy lunchtimes, no children; tables with candles and cocktail parasols out in small pretty yard behind, elaborate barbecues; if driving, park at end of Railway Side and walk – the road quickly becomes too narrow for cars *(Edward Mirzoeff, BB)*

Sun [Church Rd]: Attractive spot with tables over road overlooking green and duck pond; several areas around central servery, sofas as well as lots of tables and chairs, tuscan wall colours and tracked spotlights, real ales, enjoyable food from good if pricey sandwiches and panini up, prompt cheerful service even though busy; piped music may be loud *(Peter Rozée, Gloria Bax, Jenny and Brian Seller)*

SW14

Victoria [West Temple Sheen, SW14; [BR] Mortlake]: Comfortable bar with low chairs, good choice of wines by the glass, good interesting and elegantly presented if not cheap food in restaurant with white-painted boards, sunny conservatory, friendly young staff, games; service charge added even if you order food and get drinks at the bar; picnic-sets on back terrace with good-sized play area, bedrooms *(Martin and Karen Wake)*

SW15

☆ ***Dukes Head*** [Lower Richmond Rd]: Classic Victorian pub, spacious and grand yet friendly, light and airy civilised lounge with big ceiling fans, tables by window with great Thames view, well kept Youngs, 20 wines by the glass, good value fresh lunchtime food, pleasant service, coal fires, smaller more basic locals' bar; plastic glasses for outside *(Susan and John Douglas, BB, R T and J C Moggridge)*

☆ ***Jolly Gardeners*** [Lacy Rd]: Stylishly redecorated cool bar with two changing real ales, quite a range of draught belgian beers, good wine list, interesting choice of enjoyable food from ciabattas to grilled tuna, very friendly accommodating service, lots of sofas, trendy artwork, chill-out music; nice tables out on front terrace, one at the back *(BB, R T and J C Moggridge)*

SW18

Cats Back [Point Pleasant]: Packed with eccentric mix of the sort of things that might have ended up unsold at a collectables auction, motley furnishings from pews and scrubbed pine tables to gilt three-piece suite, dimmed chandeliers and lots of lit candelabra, well kept and interesting changing ales such as Adnams, O'Hanlons and Ringwood, lunchtime food from sandwiches up, Sun roasts, good service, blazing fire in big fireplace, lively yet relaxing atmosphere; well chosen piped music, can get smoky; open all day, in up-and-coming area near nice riverside park *(Susan and John Douglas, Guy Vowles)*

Pig & Whistle [Merton Rd (A218)]: Well maintained Youngs pub, their usual beers, enjoyable bar food, smart bar staff under no nonsense amiable landlord, pleasant décor *(Bracey Parish)*

SW19

Crooked Billet [Wimbledon Common]: Popular olde-worlde pub by common, lovely spot in summer, open all day; full Youngs range kept well, pleasant helpful service, generous sensibly priced food, lots of old prints, nice furnishings on broad polished oak boards, soft lighting, daily papers, restaurant in 16th-c barn behind *(Susan and John Douglas, R T and J C Moggridge)*

Princess of Wales [Morden Rd]: Traditional well run cream and brown Youngs pub with their full beer range kept well, enjoyable traditional food from sandwiches up, friendly landlord and efficient young staff, two boxer dogs, Princess of Wales photographs *(Derek and Heather Manning)*

Rose & Crown [Wimbledon High St]: Recently refurbished Youngs pub with their beers kept well, roomy bar and conservatory, enjoyable food, good friendly staff; tables in former coachyard, new bedrooms *(LYM, John Coatsworth, MRSM)*

WEST LONDON

SW5

Blackbird [Earls Court Rd]: Big comfortable bank conversion, dark panelling, plenty of nooks and corners, decent lunchtime food esp home-made pies and freshly carved roasts in barm cakes, full range of Fullers ales kept well, interesting pictures; open all day *(the Didler)*

Kings Head [Hogarth Pl/Fenway St]: Bass and Fullers London Pride and food such as sandwiches, caesar salad, risotto and aberdeen angus burger in corner pub with horseshoe bar and dining chairs and tables on bare boards *(Ian Phillips)*

SW6

Southern Cross [New Kings Rd]: Smartly refurbished and unfussy, with comfortable leather tub chairs, Greene King IPA and Old Speckled Hen, bar food from sandwiches to pasta, melts, fish and chips and so forth; discreet TV screens for rugby, upstairs pool room, stairs down to lavatories *(Ian Phillips)*

SW10

☆ *Chelsea Ram* [Burnaby St]: Lively yet relaxed feel in unusually winebar-like Youngs pub with pleasant décor, shutters, artwork for sale and eclectic books, pine tables, lovely fire, great mix of customers, some emphasis on good if not cheap bistro-type food changing daily, helpful friendly service, well kept Youngs, interesting wines inc good choice by the glass, outstanding bloody mary, good Pimms, no music, quiet back part; dogs welcome, open all day Fri *(BB, Humphry and Angela Crum Ewing)*

W3

Churchfield [Churchfield Rd]: Nicely reworked former station building, quite a grand upstairs dining room with attractively priced good food and good wine choice, proper bar with wide range of beers, helpful friendly staff; tables outside *(Jennifer Watts)*

W4

☆ *City Barge* [Strand on the Green]: Small panelled riverside bars, not over-modernised and with nice original features, in picturesque and welcoming partly 15th-c pub (this original part reserved for diners lunchtime), also airy newer back part done out with maritime signs and bird prints; sensibly priced bar food (not Sun) from sandwiches up, well kept Fullers London Pride and Charles Wells Bombardier, back conservatory, winter fires, some tables on towpath – lovely spot to watch sun set over Kew Bridge *(LYM, Ian Phillips, R T and J C Moggridge)*

W5

Ealing Park Tavern [South Ealing Rd]: Sensibly short blackboard choice of enjoyable frequently changing modern dishes from end kitchen in large open-plan dining room, large bar too, well kept Youngs, decent wines, pleasant service *(Jennie George, R T and J C Moggridge)*

North Star [The Broadway]: Busy suburban pub little changed since 1930s, thriving atmosphere in three big rooms, particularly well kept Youngs and other ales such as Caledonian Deuchars IPA, prompt enthusiastic service, good blackboard food choice *(R T and J C Moggridge)*

W6

☆ *Black Lion* [South Black Lion Lane]: Welcoming and civilised cottagey pub, helpful landlord and staff, Courage Best and Directors, decent generous food from baguettes and baked potatoes up, dining area behind big log-effect gas fire; large pleasant heated terrace *(Susan and John Douglas, Ian Phillips, BB, G R Butler)*

Brook Green [Shepherds Bush Rd]: Victorian hotel enlivened by enterprising current management, lofty open-plan bar rambling around sizeable central servery, ornate paintwork, plasterwork and mirrors, comfortable banquettes, coal fire in big fireplace, enjoyable changing bar food, well kept Youngs Bitter, Special and seasonal brews, over two dozen wines by the glass, friendly service; big-screen sports TVs, entertainment Thurs-Fri in downstairs wine bar; children welcome away from bar, small back terrace, good bedrooms, open all day (from 7 for breakfast) *(Pete Baker, Hywel Bevan, BB)*

Latymers [Hammersmith Rd]: Big bustling café/bar with minimal décor, lots of steel and glass inc ornate mirrored ceiling, well kept Fullers ales and friendly bar staff; three TV screens, may be unobtrusive piped music; good authentic thai food in comfortable and spacious back restaurant with cheerful attentive staff in thai dress *(Susan and John Douglas)*

Queens Head [Brook Green]: Attractive pub dating from early 18th c, lots of cosy rooms, beams, candlelight, fires, country furniture and pictures in keeping with period, wide food choice with unusual dishes alongside favourites, good wines by the glass, well kept Courage Directors; tables out in front overlooking green with tennis courts, secret garden behind *(Gloria Bax)*

☆ *Stonemasons Arms* [Cambridge Grove]: Excellent changing food from open kitchen in trendy Hammersmith gastropub, plenty of invention, some exotic ingredients, and fair prices; plain décor, basic furnishings, lots of modern art, ceiling fans, mostly young customers evenings; loudish piped music *(BB, Adrian White)*

Thatched House [Dalling Rd]: Spacious dining pub under new management, generous enjoyable food, stripped pine, modern art, big armchairs, well kept Youngs and good wine list, good service, conservatory; open all day wknds *(Susan and John Douglas, BB)*

W8

☆ *Britannia* [Allen St, off Kensington High St]: Friendly civilised local opened into single

L-shaped bar, relaxed and peaceful, with good value fresh home-cooked lunches, well kept Youngs and no music; attractive indoor back 'garden' (no smoking at lunchtime), open all day *(Susan and John Douglas, the Didler)*

W9

Grand Union [Woodfield Rd]: Victorian pub doing traditional food to top gastropub standards without the pretentious crowd and décor, well kept Adnams Broadside and seasonal beers, decent wines; attractive canalside terrace (covered in winter) and garden, open all day *(C S McVeigh)*

W10

Earl Percy [Ladbroke Grove]: Civilised three-room late Victorian pub with Greene King IPA and Abbot and Boddingtons, lots of english and continental keg beers on tap, and of wines and champagnes *(Ian Phillips)*

W11

☆ *Ladbroke Arms* [Ladbroke Rd]: Smartly chatty dining pub with good food on big plates, esp pasta, Adnams, Fullers London Pride and Greene King IPA and Abbot, pleasant staff, daily papers; tables on front terrace *(Ian Phillips, LYM)*

W14

Albion [Hammersmith Rd]: Popular and homely, with well kept Courage Directors, Theakstons Best and interesting guest beers, decent wines, good food choice from baked potatoes up, friendly staff, warm pine tables and chairs, real fire, prints, panelling and beams, spiral stairs to comfortable upper lounge; open all day *(Gloria Bax)*

Cumberland Arms [North End Rd]: Varied reasonably priced food, different evening menu, efficient friendly service, good wine choice; unobtrusive piped music, TV rarely on *(Neil Bull)*

Warwick Arms [Warwick Rd]: Early 19th-c, with lots of old woodwork, comfortable atmosphere, friendly regulars (some playing darts or bridge), good service, well kept Fullers beers from elegant Wedgwood handpumps, limited tasty food (not Sun evening), sensible prices, no piped music; open all day, tables outside, handy for Earls Court and Olympia *(the Didler, Giles and Annie Francis)*

OUTER LONDON

BARKINGSIDE TQ4490

New Fairlop Oak [Fencepiece Rd (A123), Fulwell Cross]: Former Berni Inn, now a pleasant Wetherspoons, with Courage Directors, Theakstons and guest beers, good value food *(Robert Lester)*

BARNET TQ2195

Gate at Arkley [Barnet Rd (A411, nr Hendon Wood Lane)]: Efficient friendly service, good value lunchtime baguettes and wide choice of other enjoyable food, well kept Adnams, Greene King Abbot and Wadworths 6X, reasonably priced wines, several comfortable areas with three blazing log fires, small no smoking conservatory; attractive sheltered garden *(Charles Harvey, BB, Brian and Rosalie Laverick)*

☆ *King William IV* [Hadley Highstone, towards Potters Bar]: Snug old-fashioned local, nooks and corners, some antique Wedgwood plates over fireplaces (real fires), good atmosphere and friendly service, good home-made lunchtime food inc fresh fish Fri (back restaurant), well kept ales such as Hook Norton and Tetleys; flower-framed front terrace *(Brian and Rosalie Laverick)*

BEXLEYHEATH TQ4975

Kings Arms [Broadway]: Lively pub with friendly staff; juke box, rock DJs Thurs *(Ben Anderson)*

BIGGIN HILL TQ4159

☆ *Old Jail* [Jail Lane]: Neatly kept ancient and interesting building which was a mainstay for Battle of Britain RAF pilots, with lots of interesting RAF pictures and books, cabinet of Battle of Britain plates, beams, some painted brickwork, oak floorboards, two large welcoming bar areas, one with a snug and vast inglenook fireplace, friendly efficient service, good sensibly priced quickly served food from sandwiches and baguettes to blackboard dishes, well kept Fullers London Pride, Greene King IPA, Harveys Best and Shepherd Neame Spitfire; picnic-sets in attractive shaded garden behind, good play area *(Ian Phillips, GHC, Alan M Pring, LM)*

CHEAM TQ2363

Bell [Ewell Rd (A232)]: Friendly local with welcoming licensees, enjoyable home-made food, darts matches; big-screen sports TV *(Ian Francis)*

CHELSFIELD TQ4963

☆ *Bo-Peep* [Hewitts Rd]: Small traditional pub dating from 16th c, magnificent Tudor fireplace, lots of brasses, wide choice of popular food from good soup and sandwiches to huge tender steaks, Courage and Tetleys, friendly service, no smoking sheep-theme beamed dining room; lots of tables outside *(Tony Brace)*

CHISLEHURST TQ4570

Sydney Arms [Old Perry St]: Friendly atmosphere, brisk service even when busy, good range of good value food even on Sun, well kept real ales, big conservatory; may try to keep your credit card while you eat; pleasant garden good for children, almost opp entrance to Scadbury Park, country walks *(B J Harding, Martin Jennings)*

Tigers Head [Watts Lane/Manor Park Rd, opp St Nicholas Church]: 18th-c, overlooking church and common, now pleasantly airy Chef & Brewer, nicely divided for feeling of intimacy; service efficient even when quite busy, wide food choice inc variety of fish and Sun lunch, considerable wine list, well kept beers inc Charles Wells Bombardier; smart casual dress code, no under-21s; terrace tables *(R T and J C Moggridge)*

ENFIELD TQ2994

Moon Under Water [Chase Side]: One of the oldest Wetherspoons conversions (1988 – once a chapel), with real ales inc Greene King IPA and Abbot and Ridleys Rumpus, sensible prices, big barn of a place with alcoves around the sides, separate no smoking areas, open all day *(Robert Lester)*

Pied Bull [Bullsmoor Lane (A1055); handy for M25 junction 25, by A10]: Rustic red-tiled 17th-c pub with local prints on boarded walls, low beam-and-plank ceilings, lots of comfortable and friendly little rooms and extensions, turkey rugs on bare boards, well kept Adnams, Flowers Original, Fullers London Pride and Marstons Pedigree, wide choice of well priced food; conservatory, pleasant garden *(Ian Phillips)*

GREEN STREET GREEN TQ4563

Rose & Crown [Farnborough Way (A21)]: Newly refurbished civilised family-run pub with simple choice of good value bar food, good friendly service, several real ales inc Courage Best and Shepherd Neame Spitfire, restaurant; big child-friendly garden *(Tony Brace, Mike Buckingham)*

HARROW TQ1587

Castle [West St]: Fullers local in picturesque part, fine range of their ales with a guest such as St Austell, decent food from generous baguettes and baked potatoes to steaks, daily papers, several rooms inc classic lively traditional bar, sedate back lounge with sofas, prints and log-effect fires, rather austere dining room; steep steps from street; nice garden *(Ian Phillips)*

ILFORD TQ4386

Great Spoon of Ilford [Cranbrook Rd]: Friendly and relaxing large Wetherspoons, real ales such as Courage Best and Directors and Greene King Abbot, good mix of ages, good value food all day *(Robert Lester)*

Beehive [Beehive Lane (B192), Gants Hill]: Large Harvester restaurant with varied menu and separate bar, Fullers; bedrooms in adjoining Travelodge *(David Edwards, Robert Lester)*

Red House [Redbridge Lane E]: Large recently refurbished multi-level Beefeater with good value food; bedrooms in adjoining Travelodge *(Robert Lester)*

KEW TQ1977

Coach & Horses [Kew Green]: Neatly kept Youngs pub, their full beer range kept well, range of coffees, good value thick sandwiches, good ploughman's, enterprising snacks, main dishes esp fish and good steaks, no smoking restaurant area; tables on front terrace, nice setting *(LM, P R Morgan)*

Station [Station Parade]: Appealing pub with Ind Coope Burton, Tetleys and Charles Wells Bombardier, smart and efficient friendly staff, attractively priced food from sandwiches to steak and roast, Edwardian-style conservatory *(Ian Phillips)*

KINGSTON TQ1769

Bishop out of Residence [Bishops Hall, off Thames St – down alley by Superdrug]: Riverside Youngs pub with pleasant Thames views, big modern bar and eating area, impressive service, lunchtime emphasis on wide range of good value quick food, well kept ales, decent house wines; pleasant balcony tables *(Dave Braisted, R T and J C Moggridge)*

MALDEN RUSHETT TQ1763

☆ ***Star*** [Kingston Rd (A243 just N of M25 junction 9)]: Enjoyable family dining pub right on Surrey border, consistently good food from baguettes and baked potatoes to a good range of attractively priced hot dishes; several areas, good log fire, good friendly service and atmosphere; quiet piped music *(DWAJ)*

ORPINGTON TQ4963

Rock & Fountain [Rock Hill, past Chelsfield Park Hospital]: Partly rebuilt and comfortably extended, with large dining bar and side dining room, good value food from sandwiches and ploughman's through usual main dishes to steak, two or three real ales, friendly prompt service, quiz night; picnic-sets out on terrace, quiet country lane *(Alan M Pring, Tony Brace)*

RICHMOND TQ1772

Britannia [Brewers Lane]: Open-plan pub with big Georgian windows overlooking the passers-by, welcoming helpful staff, good value food inc some generous modern dishes, real ales such as Charles Wells Bombardier, heroic pictures; nice upstairs room, tables in small back courtyard *(R T and J C Moggridge, Mayur Shah)*

Dukes Head [The Vineyard]: Good choice of well kept beers such as Elgoods Black Dog, enjoyable food inc good value specials and Irish landlord, cheerful public bar and quiet lounge *(R T and J C Moggridge)*

New Inn [Petersham Rd (A307, Ham Common)]: Attractive and comfortable Georgian pub in good spot on Ham Common, comfortable banquettes and stools, brown décor, good home-made food from ciabattas and other snacks up, pleasant dining area, well kept Adnams Broadside, Courage Best and Youngs Special, quick service, big log fire one side, coal the other; disabled facilities, neat picnic-sets out in front and on back garden terrace *(Sarah Davis, Rod Lambert, LM, Mary Ellen Cummings)*

Rose of York [Petersham Rd]: Comfortable seats inc leather chesterfields, Turner prints on stripped pine panelling, old photographs, attractive layout inc no smoking area, cheap Sam Smiths, pleasant helpful service, open fire; high chairs, bar billiards, fruit machines, TV, piped pop music; lots of tables outside, some with Thames views, bedrooms, open all day *(R T and J C Moggridge)*

Victoria [Hill Rise]: Small, cosy and chatty local, well kept beers inc Youngs, low-priced bar food; sports TV *(Martin Brunt, R T and J C Moggridge)*

White Horse [Worple Way, off Sheen Rd]: Large and popular open-plan bare-boards Fullers pub with most tables reserved for eating (but leather settees at one end), imaginative modern food from upmarket sandwiches to restauranty meals with a mediterranean slant, good cheeseboard, friendly helpful service, well kept London Pride and ESB and good choice of wines from long aluminium bar; may be piped music; small terrace backing on to residential area and playground *(Marie Woods)*

Old Ship [King St]: Youngs pub close to centre and river, their beers kept well, welcoming service, food inc good Sun roast, three bustling communicating bars, fine panelling in refurbished upper floor; parking almost impossible; open all day *(the Didler)*

Orange Tree [Kew Rd]: Big open-plan room with well kept Youngs from central bar, good food, prompt friendly service; piped music may obtrude, sports TV; open all day, lots of tables out in front, small back covered terrace *(LYM, Mayur Shah, R T and J C Moggridge)*

Racing Page [Duke St]: Well done open-plan racing décor, neat attentive service, decent wines, well kept Courage-related ales, wide choice of reasonably priced generous thai food; big-screen sports TV; nice spot nr theatre and green *(anon)*

Watermans Arms [Water Lane]: Friendly atmosphere and helpful licensees in small two-bar local with Youngs beer, pub games; handy for Thames, nearby parking unlikely *(the Didler)*

ROMFORD TQ4889

Moby Dick [A1112/A12 (Whalebone Lane N)]: Large main-road pub/restaurant with carvery; good value food, John Smiths *(Robert Lester)*

TEDDINGTON TQ1671

Adelaide [Park Rd]: Good friendly corner local with pews around tables, red paintwork, well kept Shepherd Neame ales, wines on show, coffee machine, home-made slightly upmarket food inc good filled baguettes and sandwiches, welcoming young staff; attractive tables and seats in pretty honeysuckle-clad back yard with barbecue counter *(LM)*

TWICKENHAM TQ1673

☆ ***White Swan*** [Riverside; [BR] Twickenham]: Unpretentious take-us-as-you-find-us 17th-c Thames-side house up steep anti-flood steps, little riverside lawn across quiet lane, traditional bare-boards, bar with big rustic tables and blazing fires, back room full of rugby memorabilia, well kept Courage Directors, Greene King IPA and Shepherd Neame Spitfire, good choice of wines by the glass, winter mulled wine, sandwiches and one or two blackboard hot dishes, summer wkdy lunchtime buffet; backgammon, cribbage, piped blues or jazz, winter Weds folk night; children welcome, open all day summer *(LYM, Ian Phillips)*

UXBRIDGE TQ0582

☆ ***Load of Hay*** [Villier St, off Cleveland Rd opp Brunel University]: Warm and friendly local, with rambling main area and smaller front bar, reliably good value freshly made generous food inc popular Sun roast, good long-serving landlady, four well kept rotating beers, thoughtful choice of teas, impressive fireplace in no smoking back part used by diners, more public-bar atmosphere nearer serving bar, local paintings; dogs welcome, flower-filled back garden, pergola with mature vine *(Anthony Longden, Dr B and Mrs P B Baker)*

WALLINGTON TQ2864

Dukes Head [Manor Rd]: Youngs pub/hotel, bars divided into several rooms, log fire, decent food from nice sandwiches and interesting baguettes to chargrills, well kept Bitter and Special, friendly helpful staff; air-conditioned bedrooms, views over pleasant green *(Jenny and Brian Seller)*

Several well known guide books make establishments pay for entry, either directly or as a fee for inspection. These fees can run to many hundreds of pounds. We do not. Unlike other guides, we never take payment for entries. We never accept a free meal, free drink, or any other freebie from a pub. We do not accept any sponsorship – let alone from commercial schemes linked to the pub trade. All our entries depend solely on merit. And we are the only guide in which virtually all the main entries have been gained by a unique two-stage sifting process: first, a build-up of favourable reports from our thousands of reader-reporters; then anonymous vetting by one of the senior editorial staff.

Scotland

Away from Scotland's big cities, hotels often play the role that in England is played by pubs. Their bars have always attracted local people who want a drink and a chat, and in recent years have taken on the extra function of fuelling visitors with decent bar food. So you will find quite a few such places among the main entries. Pubs and inns which have recently been drawing particularly enthusiastic reports from readers include the remote Applecross Inn (good seafood, lovely setting, nice bedrooms – it gains a Star this year for its all-round appeal), the cheerful Fishermans Tavern in Broughty Ferry (good real ales, a pleasant place to stay), the chatty traditional Bow Bar in Edinburgh (lots of well kept beers, great whisky collection), Kays Bar there (bigger inside than it looks, but still a cosy place for all those real ales and fine malt whiskies), the Starbank more towards the outskirts of Edinburgh (good atmosphere, fine choice of drinks, great views), the Old Inn at Gairloch (back in these pages after quite a break, on great form all round), the Bon Accord in Glasgow (also new to this edition – splendid changing choice of real ales and malt whiskies in this lively bar), the well run Swan in its quiet spot at Kingholm Quay (a friendly all-rounder), the interesting Four Marys opposite the Palace in Linlithgow (also good all round), the beautifully placed Plockton Hotel (a lovely place to stay in or eat at, with particularly friendly staff), the Stein Inn in a wonderful position on Skye (great character, good all round), the Wheatsheaf at Swinton (a very good civilised dining pub), and the Ailean Chraggan at Weem (popular food, good bedrooms, fine whisky choice). All this shows that Scotland has plenty of fine pubs and inns for a special meal out. The award of Scotland Dining Pub of the Year goes to the Plockton Hotel – well worth the trip, and once you are there why not stay the night. We have divided the Lucky Dip section at the end of the chapter into the counties used as postal addresses (putting Glasgow under Lanarkshire, and Edinburgh under Midlothian). In this section, pubs and inns currently showing particularly well are the Loch Melfort Hotel at Arduaine (Argyll), Black Bull in Moffat (Dumfriesshire),. Village Inn at Arrochar (Dunbartonshire), Masonic Arms in Gatehouse of Fleet (Kirkcudbrightshire), Horseshoe in Glasgow (Lanarkshire), Canny Man's in Edinburgh (Midlothian), Cawdor Tavern (Nairnshire), Gordon Arms at Mountbenger (Selkirkshire), and on the islands the Port Charlotte Hotel (Islay), Mishnish in Tobermory (Mull) and Ardvasar Hotel and Sligachan Hotel (Skye). Many Scottish pubs and bars close at midnight, or even later at weekends; we have not mentioned this in the Lucky Dip entries. Drinks prices here tend to be higher than in England and Wales. However, Scotland now has some 30 small breweries of its own. The ones whose beers you are most likely to come across in Scotland's better pubs are (in a rough order of frequency) Caledonian, Orkney, Belhaven, Houston, Isle of Skye, Atlas, Harviestoun, Cairngorm, Moulin, Fyne, Isle of Arran and Traquair.

Places with gardens or terraces usually let children sit there – we note in the text the very few exceptions that don't.

ABERDEEN NJ9305 Map 11

Prince of Wales £

St Nicholas Lane

This cheerful city centre pub is a popular retreat from the surrounding shopping centre, and at lunchtime a busy mix of locals and visitors often makes for standing room only. Screened booths are furnished with pews and other wooden furniture, while a smarter main lounge has some panelling and a fruit machine; some say the counter in the middle cosy flagstoned area is the longest in Scotland. A good range of eight real ales includes Caledonian 80/-, Theakstons Old Peculier, and a beer named for the pub from Inveralmond, along with guests from brewers such as Atlas, Isle of Skye and Orkney. Friendly staff serve generous helpings of good value bar food such as sandwiches (from £1.30), filled baguettes or baked potatoes (£3.50), macaroni cheese (£4), steak pie (£4.50), and breaded haddock or beef stroganoff (£4.80), with a puddings such as chocolate fudge cake (£1.50). *(Recommended by Mark Walker, the Didler, David and Betty Gittins, Joe Green, Pete Walker)*

Free house ~ Licensee Kenny Gordon ~ Real ale ~ Bar food (11.30(12 Sun)-2.30 (4 Sat-Sun)) ~ (01224) 640597 ~ Children allowed in eating area of bar at lunchtime ~ Traditional folk music Sun evening, pop quiz Mon ~ Open 10-12

ABOYNE NO5298 Map 11

Boat

Charlestown Road (B968, just off A93)

They serve well kept Bass along with a couple of real ales from brewers such as Caledonian and Houston at this welcoming country inn. The fresh battered haddock (£7.95) is very popular, and other reasonably priced bar food includes soup (£2.50), lunchtime sandwiches (from £3.50), mince and tatties (£6.50), beef steak pie (£6.95), and lasagne (£7.25), while in the evening (when the same dishes cost a bit more) there are also a few more elaborate choices such as curried chicken (£9.25), pork and vegetable kebabs (£9.50), and chargrilled tuna steak (£9.95), with puddings such as sticky toffee pudding or lemon syllabub (£3.75). They use plenty of fresh local produce, and are happy to accommodate special requests. As you step inside, the first thing you'll notice is the model train, often chugging around just below the ceiling, making appropriate noises. There are also Scottish pictures and brasses in the two areas downstairs, and a bar counter that runs down the narrower linking section, and games along in the public-bar end. Spiral stairs take you up to a roomy additional dining area, which is no smoking. The atmosphere is relaxed and pubby, with an openable woodburning stove, and friendly service. Right by the River Dee, the pub used to serve the ferry that it's named for; there are tables outside, and they have a self-catering flat. *(Recommended by Sue and Andy Waters, Mike and Shelley Woodroffe, Callum and Letitia Smith-Burnett, David and Betty Gittins)*

Free house ~ Licensee Wilson Forbes ~ Real ale ~ Bar food (12-2(2.30 Sat-Sun), 5.30-9(9.30 Fri-Sat)) ~ Restaurant ~ (01339) 886137 ~ Children welcome ~ Dogs allowed in bar and bedrooms ~ Open 11-2.30, 5-11(12 Fri-Sat); 11-11 Sun; closed 25-26 Dec and 1-2 Jan

APPLECROSS NG7144 Map 11

Applecross Inn ★

Off A896 S of Shieldaig

Beautifully cooked food and a marvellous waterside setting, looking across to Skye's Cuillin Hills, make this remote pub a real hit with readers, and this year it gains a Star. The fresh seafood is a big draw, and most of the ingredients they use are local. Up on chalkboards, the menu might include local prawn cocktail (£6.95), battered haddock (£7.95), and seared halibut with lemon and herbs (£10.95), with non-fishy dishes such as garlic mushrooms in cream sauce (£4.95), home-made veggie sausages with spicy beans and mashed potatoes (£7.95), and venison casserole with mustard mash (£10.95), with home-made puddings such as rich chocolate mousse or fruit crumble (£3.50); they also do very good sandwiches. You must book for the small no smoking restaurant. With a friendly mix of locals and visitors, the no-nonsense bar has a woodburning stove, exposed stone walls, and upholstered pine furnishings on the stone floor; well kept Isle of Skye Red Cuillin, and around 50 malt whiskies. There's also a no smoking dining area, with lavatories for the disabled and baby changing facilities; pool (winter only), dominoes, and juke box (musicians may take over instead). Outside, you'll find tables in the nice shoreside garden. The drive to the inn over the pass of the cattle (Beallach na Ba) is one of the highest in Britain, and a truly exhilarating experience. The alternative route, along the single-track lane winding round the coast from just south of Shieldaig, has equally glorious sea loch and then sea views nearly all the way. *(Recommended by Brian and Anita Randall, Earl and Chris Pick, Neil Rose, Sarah and Peter Gooderham, Lesley Bass, Anthony Longden, Jeff and Wendy Williams, Dr D J and Mrs S C Walker, GSB, John and Claire Pettifer, Tim Maddison, JDM, KM, Dr D E Granger)*

Free house ~ Licensee Judith Fish ~ Real ale ~ Bar food (12-9; not 25 Dec, 1 Jan) ~ Restaurant ~ (01520) 744262 ~ Children welcome ~ Dogs welcome ~ Open 11-11.30 (11.45 Sat); 12.30-11 Sun; closed 25 Dec, 1 Jan ~ Bedrooms: £27.50/£60(£70B)

BADACHRO NG7773 Map 11

Badachro Inn

2½ miles S of Gairloch village turn off A832 on to B8056, then after another 3¼ miles turn right in Badachro to the quay and inn

This convivial black and white painted cottagey pub has a terrace which virtually overhangs the water (there are more seats on an attractively planted lochside lawn); inside too you can make the most of the lovely setting, as the dining conservatory overlooks the bay. There's an appealing local atmosphere in the bar, and gentle eavesdropping suggests that some of the yachtsmen have been calling in here annually for decades – the talk is still very much of fishing and boats. There are some interesting photographs and collages on the walls, and they put out the Sunday newspapers. The quieter dining area on the left has big tables by a huge log fire. Friendly staff serve a couple of well kept changing ales from brewers such as Caledonian and Isle of Skye on handpump, and they've around 50 malt whiskies, and a changing wine list; piped music, cribbage, shove-ha'penny and dominoes. Look out for the sociable pub spaniel Casper. Enjoyable food (with good fresh fish) includes snacks such as sandwiches (from £3.65), beef and spring onion burger (£3.95), baked potatoes (from £3.35), and ploughman's (£6.75), and changing specials such as home-smoked meats with lemon and ginger chilli chutney (£4.95), spaghetti with mushroom and basil sauce (£7.95), roast beef (£8.50), baked salmon with herb potato mash (£11.95), and local scallops with orange, ginger and garlic dressing (£14.40), with puddings such as hot chocolate fudge cake (£3.25). The pub is in a tiny village, and the quiet road comes to a dead end a few miles further on at the lovely Redpoint beach. The bay is very sheltered, virtually landlocked by Eilean Horrisdale just opposite. There are two pub moorings (free for visitors), and showers are available at a small charge. *(Recommended by Neil Rose, Peter F Marshall, Paul and Ursula Randall, Brian and Anita Randall, P R Morley, Tim Maddison)*

Free house ~ Licensee Martyn Pearson ~ Real ale ~ Bar food (12(12.30 Sun)-3, 6-9; not 25 Dec) ~ Restaurant ~ (01445) 741255 ~ Children welcome ~ Dogs allowed in bar ~ Open 12-12; 12.30-11 Sun; closed 25 Dec

BROUGHTY FERRY NO4630 Map 11

Fishermans Tavern

Fort Street; turning off shore road

Most attractive from the outside, this welcoming town pub has extended into the adjacent cottages. It's just yards from the seafront, where there are good views of the two long, low Tay bridges; on summer evenings, you can sit at tables on the front pavement, and they might have barbecues in the secluded walled garden (where they hold an annual beer festival on the last weekend in May). Their half a dozen real ales change every day, but might typically include Belhaven 80/-, Inveralmond Lia Fail, Timothy Taylors Landlord and guests from brewers such as Adnams, Marstons and Orkney, on handpump or tall fount air pressure. They also have a dozen wines by the glass, some local country wines, draught wheat beer, and a good range of malt whiskies. There's an enjoyable atmosphere, and the staff and locals are friendly. A little brown carpeted snug on the right has nautical tables, light pink soft fabric seating, basket-weave wall panels and beige lamps, and is the more lively bar; on the left is a secluded lounge area with an open coal fire. The carpeted back bar (popular with diners) has a Victorian fireplace; dominoes, TV and fruit machine, and a coal fire. The family and breakfast rooms are no smoking. Enjoyable, good value lunchtime bar food includes soup (£1.85), filled rolls (£2.25, toasties £1.75), steak and gravy pie (£2.40), haddock and cod fishcakes (£6.25), fried lambs liver, back bacon and onions (£6.55), and seafood crêpes (£6.95), with puddings such as home-made bread and butter pudding (£2.50); children's meals (£3.90). They have disabled lavatories, and baby changing facilities. The landlord also runs the well preserved Speedwell Bar in Dundee. *(Recommended by Alistair and Kay Butler, Callum and Letitia Smith-Burnett, Jo Lilley, Simon Calvert)*

Free house ~ Licensee Jonathan Stewart ~ Real ale ~ Bar food (12-2.30(3.30 Sat-Sun) only) ~ (01382) 775941 ~ Children in family room ~ Dogs allowed in bar ~ Folk music Thurs night ~ Open 11-12 (1am Sat) ~ Bedrooms: £39B/£62B

EAST LINTON NT5977 Map 11

Drovers

Bridge Street (B1407), just off A1 Haddington—Dunbar

The main bar of this pleasant old inn (now with a new landlady) feels a bit like a cosy living room, with wooden flooring, a basket of logs in front of the woodburning stove, and comfortable armchairs. There's a goat's head on a pillar in the middle of the room, fresh flowers and newspapers, and a mix of prints and pictures on the half panelled, half red-painted walls; piped music. A similar room leads off, and a door opens out on to a walled lawn with tables. Enjoyable home-made dishes might be nachos (from £3.95), spanish baguettes (£5.95), steak and ale pie (£9.95), cajun salmon (£10.50), lamb shank (£10.95), bass with green pesto (£11.25), and steaks (from £12.95), with puddings such as banoffi pie (£4.75); no chips. On Saturday evenings, the menu is more elaborate. Part of the upstairs restaurant is no smoking. Adnams Broadside, Belhaven Best and Caledonian Deuchars IPA are well kept on handpump, and they've a couple of weekly changing guests such as Hook Norton Old Hooky and Young's Waggle Dance. The pub is on a pretty village street. *(Recommended by Robert and Susan Whitehead, Pat and Sam Roberts, Dr and Mrs Guy Cocker, Christine and Malcolm Ingram)*

London and Edinburgh Inns~ Manager Sue Campbell ~ Real ale ~ Restaurant ~ (01620) 860298 ~ Children welcome ~ Dogs allowed in bar ~ Open 11-11(12 Thurs); 11-1 Fri-Sat; 12.30-12 Sun

EDINBURGH NT2574 Map 11

Abbotsford

Rose Street; E end, beside South St David Street

They now have over 72 different sorts of whisky at this single-bar pub, originally built for Jenners department store. With an old-fashioned atmosphere, the refreshingly uncluttered interior is traditional with dark wooden half-panelled walls, an impressive highly polished Victorian island bar counter, long wooden tables and leatherette benches, and a welcoming log-effect gas fire; there are prints on the walls, and a rather handsome plaster-moulded high ceiling; fruit machine, and TV. Served in the true Scottish fashion from a set of air pressure tall founts Caledonian Deuchars IPA and 80/- and Greene King IPA are well kept alongside a couple of changing guests from brewers such as Atlas, and Crouch Vale. Enjoyable and reasonably priced, lunchtime bar food includes sandwiches (from £1.25), all-day breakfast (£5.50), steak and kidney pie, roast of the day or haggis, neeps and tatties (£6.75), and scampi (£6.95), with puddings such as coconut-battered ice-cream with butterscotch sauce (£3.50). Efficient service from dark-uniformed or white-shirted staff; be warned that they close quite promptly after last orders. *(Recommended by C J Fletcher, Joel Dobris, the Didler, Joe Green, Ian and Nita Cooper, Patrick Hancock, Paul Hopton, R M Corlett)*

Free house ~ Licensee Colin Grant ~ Real ale ~ Bar food (12-3) ~ Restaurant ~ (0131) 225 5276 ~ Children welcome ~ Open 11-11; closed 25 Dec, 1 Jan

Bow Bar ★

West Bow

The eight superbly kept beers at this cheerfully traditional alehouse are served from impressive antique founts made by Aitkens, Mackie & Carnegie: a typical selection might include Belhaven 80/-, Caledonian Deuchars IPA, Timothy Taylors Landlord, and various changing guests from a whole range of brewers such as Atlas, Bath, Coniston, Goose Eye, and Harviestoun. But that's not the only draw – the grand carved mahogany gantry has a massive array of over 140 malts, including cask strength whiskies, and there's a good choice of rums and gins too. Busy and friendly with a good chatty atmosphere, the simple, neatly kept rectangular bar has a fine collection of appropriate enamel advertising signs and handsome antique trade mirrors, sturdy leatherette wall seats and heavy narrow tables on its wooden floor, and café-style bar seats. The only food they serve is tasty pies (from £1.30), and toasties (from £1.50). It's tucked away just below the castle. *(Recommended by Mark Walker, Joel Dobris, the Didler, Simon and Amanda Southwell, Joe Green, Patrick Hancock, Paul Hopton, R M Corlett, David Crook)*

Free house ~ Licensee Helen McLoughlin ~ Real ale ~ Bar food (12-2.30, not Sun) ~ (0131) 226 7667 ~ Dogs allowed in bar ~ Open 12-11.30; 12.30-11 Sun; closed 25-26 Dec, 1-2 Jan

Café Royal

West Register Street

Readers continue to be dazzled by the ornate Victorian interior of this vibrant city pub: the floor and stairway are laid with marble, chandeliers hang from the magnificent ceilings, and the big island bar is graced by a carefully recreated gantry. The pub was built in the 19th c as a flagship for the latest in gas and plumbing fittings, and the high-ceilinged café rooms have a series of highly detailed Doulton tilework portraits of historical innovators Watt, Faraday, Stephenson, Caxton, Benjamin Franklin and Robert Peel (forget police – his importance here is as the introducer of calico printing). There are some fine original fittings in the downstairs gents', and the stained-glass well in the seafood and game restaurant is well worth a look. Alongside a decent choice of wines, with ten by the glass, they've 25 malt whiskies, and well kept Caledonian Deuchars IPA and McEwans 80/-, with maybe a couple of guests such as Jennings Cumberland and Orkney Dark Island on handpump; there's a TV, fruit machine and piped music. Besides sandwiches (from £3.25), the tempting bar menu includes nachos (£3.95), mussels (£5.95; £9.95 large), oysters (from £6.95), cajun chicken breast (£5.75), and braised lamb shank (£7.25), with specials such as grilled perch with red pepper sauce and spinach (£6.25), and pudding such as sticky toffee pudding (£2.95). It can get very busy, and the décor is perhaps best appreciated on quiet afternoons. *(Recommended by C J Fletcher, the Didler, Joel Dobris, Ian and Nita Cooper, Patrick Hancock, Theocsbrian, Michael Butler, Joe Green, R M Corlett, David Crook)*

Scottish Courage ~ Manager Dave Allan ~ Real ale ~ Bar food (11(12.30 Sun)-10) ~ Restaurant ~ (0131) 556 1884 ~ Children in restaurant ~ Open 11(12.30 Sun)-11 (12 Thurs, 1 Fri-Sat); closed 25 Dec

Guildford Arms

West Register Street

With a splendid Victorian décor, this bustling pub serves 16 wines (and champagne) by the glass, and as many as a dozen beers on handpump. The main bar has lots of mahogany, glorious colourfully painted plasterwork and ceilings, big original advertising mirrors, and heavy swagged velvet curtains at the arched windows. The snug little upstairs gallery restaurant gives a dress-circle view of the main bar (notice the lovely old mirror decorated with two tigers on the way up). There's a TV, fruit machine, and piped music; it can get smoky. Well kept real ales include Caledonian Deuchars IPA and 80/-, Harviestoun Bitter & Twisted, Orkney Dark Island, and guests from brewers such as Atlas, Timothy Taylors, Fullers, Hop Back, Traquair and Yates on handpump; there's also a good choice of malt whiskies. Besides filled rolls (£2.30, served till they run out), home-made bar food might include haggis, neeps and tatties (£4.95), garlic prawns (£5.25), sausages with mustard mash and gravy (£6.85), steak and ale pie (£6.95), salmon fillet with lemon and lime dressing (£7.95), and rib-eye steak (£9.95), with home-made puddings (£3.50); in the evenings they serve food only in the galley restaurant. *(Recommended by the Didler, Simon and Amanda Southwell, Joel Dobris, C J Fletcher, Mark Walker, Joe Green, Patrick Hancock, Michael Butler, Paul Hopton, R M Corlett, David Crook)*

Free house ~ Licensee Scott Wilkinson ~ Real ale ~ Bar food (12-2.30; 12-8 during the festival) ~ Restaurant (12(12.30 Sun)-2.30, 6-9.30(10 Fri-Sat)) ~ (0131) 556 4312 ~ Open 11(12.30 Sun)-(12 Sat)11

Kays Bar £

Jamaica Street W; off India Street

Bigger than you might think from the outside, the cosy interior of this busy backstreet pub is decked out with various casks and vats, old wine and spirits merchant notices, gas-type lamps, well worn red plush wall banquettes and stools around cast-iron tables, and red pillars supporting a red ceiling. A quiet panelled back room leads off, with a narrow plank-panelled pitched ceiling and a collection of books ranging from dictionaries to ancient steam-train books for boys; lovely warming coal fire in winter. In days past, the pub was owned by John Kay, a whisky and wine merchant; wine barrels were hoisted up to the first floor and dispensed through pipes attached to nipples which can still be seen around the light rose. Nowadays, there's an interesting range of up to eight superbly kept real ales on handpump, including Belhaven 80/-, McEwans 80/-, Theakstons Best, and five guests from brewers such as Isle of Arran, Orkney and Timothy Taylors. The choice of whiskies is impressive too, with around 70 malts between eight and 50 years old, and ten blended whiskies. Service is friendly and obliging; TV, dominoes and cribbage, Scrabble and backgammon. Hearty lunchtime bar food includes soup (£1.25), haggis and neeps or mince and tatties, steak pie and filled baked potatoes (£3.25), and lasagne, beefburger and chips or chicken balti (£3.70). *(Recommended by W A Evershed, the Didler, Patrick Hancock, R T and J C Moggridge, R M Corlett)*

Free house ~ Licensee David Mackenzie ~ Real ale ~ Bar food (12-2.30; not on rugby international days) ~ (0131) 225 1858 ~ Dogs welcome ~ Open 11-12(1 Fri-Sat); 12.30-11 Sun

Starbank £

Laverockbank Road, off Starbank Road, just off A901 Granton—Leith

Locals and visitors mix happily at this stylish but friendly and relaxed pub, which boasts a great range of drinks and marvellous views over the Firth of Forth from the long light and airy bare-boarded bar. Around eight well kept real ales include Belhaven 80/- and Sandy Hunters, Caledonian Deuchars IPA, Timothy Taylors Landlord and guests from breweries all over Britain such as Badger, Broughton, Charles Wells and Houston. Nearly all of their wines are served by the glass, and there's a tempting selection of malt whiskies; cheerful service from the helpful staff. Tasty bar food (with prices unchanged since last year) includes soup (£1.50), herring rollmop salad (£2.50), a daily vegetarian dish (£4.50), ploughman's (£5), seafood salad (£5.50), haddock mornay or chicken supreme with cranberry sauce (£6), and poached salmon with lemon butter or minute steak with pepper sauce (£6.50), and puddings (£2.50). The conservatory restaurant is no smoking, and there's a sheltered back terrace. Parking on the adjacent hilly street. *(Recommended by Peter Burton, Ian and Nita Cooper, Paul and Ursula Randall, R T and J C Moggridge, Callum and Letitia Smith-Burnett, R M Corlett, Ken Richards)*

Free house ~ Licensee Valerie West ~ Real ale ~ Bar food (12-2.30, 6-9; 12(12.30 Sun)-9 wknds) ~ Restaurant ~ (0131) 552 4141 ~ Children welcome till 9pm ~ Dogs allowed in bar ~ Open 11-11(12 Thurs-Sat); 12.30-11 Sun

ELIE NO4900 Map 11

Ship

The Toft, off A917 (High Street) towards harbour

The unspoilt, villagey beamed bar of this harbourside pub has a buoyant nautical feel, with friendly locals and staff, warming winter coal fires, and partly panelled walls studded with old prints and maps. There's also simple carpeted back room; cribbage, dominoes, and shut the box. Tables on the terrace, and in the upstairs restaurant, enjoy shorefront views across Elie's broad sands and along the bay; on summer Sundays you can keep an eye on the progress of the pub's cricket team. Besides lunchtime haggis, neeps and tatties (£3.95), and club or steak sandwich (£7.50), enjoyable bar food includes haddock and chips or grilled vegetable platter (£7.50), steak and ale pie (£8), with evening dishes such as cantonese chicken stir fry (£9.95), rack of lamb with black pudding, sweet mash and rosemary sauce (£11.50), and thai-style bass (£14.95), with puddings such as lemon custard tart (£4); they do a good Sunday lunch. Well kept Caledonian Deuchars IPA, several wines by the glass, and half a dozen malt whiskies. In summer they hold regular barbecues, and serve food in the garden. The fairly simple bedrooms are in a neighbouring guesthouse, and an unmanned tourist booth in the garden has leaflets on the local area. More reports please. *(Recommended by Kay Wheat, Paul and Ursula Randall)*

Free house ~ Licensees Richard and Jill Philip ~ Real ale ~ Bar food (12-2.30, 6-9.30; 12.30-3, 6-9) ~ Restaurant ~ (01333) 330246 ~ Children in eating area of bar and restaurant ~ Dogs allowed in bar ~ Open 11-12(1 Fri-Sat); 12.30-12 Sun; closed 25 Dec ~ Bedrooms: £45B/£70B

GAIRLOCH NG8077 Map 11

Old Inn

Just off A832/B8021

It's not just the freshly cooked food or the great choice of beers that makes this 18th-c inn such a lovely place to visit – as one couple commented 'the staff could not have more helpful and friendly, it seemed that they took a real pleasure in making our stay enjoyable'. Nicely placed at the bottom of Flowerdale Glen, the pub is tucked comfortably away from the modern waterside road, but only yards away from the little fishing harbour, and handy for pleasant beaches. Picnic-sets are prettily placed outside by the trees that line the stream as it flows past under the old stone bridge, and on the opposite side are more trees with high crags above (look out for eagles). There are pleasant wooded walks up the glen, the ancestral home of Clan MacKenzie, to the Flowerdale waterfall. The well kept changing beers are a big draw, with anything from three to a dozen on offer: favourites include Adnams Broadside, Houston Peterswell, and Isle of Skye Red Cuillin and Blind Piper (the hotel's own blend of Isle of Skye ales rather in the way that Broadside was originally a blend of other Adnams ales, and named after a famed local 17th-c piper), with guests from brewers such as Atlas, Caledonian, Orkney. They have a lot of enjoyable fairly priced wines by the glass, a decent collection of malt whiskies, and you can get speciality coffees. The good food is popular, and fresh locally landed fish is a speciality, with bouillabaisse, seared scallops with lime, garlic and ginger butter, and home-made langoustine ravioli commonly on the board, and mussels, crabs, lobster, skate, haddock and hake often cropping up too. The regular bar menu includes soup (£2.85), wild venison sausages (£6.95), venison burger (£5.45), fish pie (£8.45), fresh pasta with smoked salmon, vodka and pink peppercorns (£7.50), seafood grill (£10.50), with puddings such as clootie dumpling and custard (£3.75); they also do lunchtime open sandwiches. The landlady makes her own chutneys and preserves – and grows many of the herbs they use (they also track down organic vegetables). It's nicely decorated with paintings and murals on exposed stone walls, and the cheerfully relaxed public bar has chatty locals; darts, TV, pool, fruit machine and juke box. The restaurant is no smoking. *(Recommended by Mike and Lynn Robinson, Paul and Ursula Randall, Paul and Penny Rampton, Brian and Anita Randall, Roger and Anne Newbury, Nelly Flowers)*

Free house ~ Licensees Alastair and Ute Pearson ~ Real ale ~ Bar food (12-2, 7-9; 12-9.30 in summer) ~ Restaurant ~ (01445) 712006 ~ Children welcome ~ Dogs allowed in bar and bedrooms ~ Scottish music most Thurs-Sat evenings ~ Open 11-1(12 Sat); 12.30-11.30 Sun ~ Bedrooms: £37.50B/£69B

GIFFORD NT5368 Map 11

Tweeddale Arms

S of Haddington; High Street (B6355)

Popular for its well cooked food, this comfortable white-painted hotel is probably the oldest building in this appealing Borders village. Freshly cooked with high quality ingredients, dishes might include soup (£2.50), deep-fried mushrooms with garlic dip (£4.75), vegetable crumble, roasted salmon supreme with tomato and basil or breaded pork escalope with mushroom cream sauce (£8.75), and aberdeen angus sirloin steak (£14.50), with puddings from a display cabinet such as raspberry pavlova (£3.75); efficient service. The modernised lounge bar is usually busy with customers; fruit machine, TV, dominoes and piped music. Two changing real ales might include Greene King Abbot and Orkney Dark Island, and they've quite a few malt whiskies, including the local Glenkinchie. If you're staying, the tranquil hotel lounge is particularly relaxing, with antique tables and paintings, chinoiserie chairs and chintzy easy chairs, an oriental rug on one wall, a splendid corner sofa and magazines on a table. The pub looks across the green to a 300-year-old avenue of lime trees leading to the former home of the Marquesses of Tweeddale. *(Recommended by Peter Burton, Richard J Holloway, Dr and Mrs R G J Telfer, Archie and Margaret Mackenzie)*

Free house ~ Licensees George, Colin, Yvonne and Linda Jarrin ~ Real ale ~ Bar food ~ Restaurant ~ (01620) 810240 ~ Children in eating area of bar and restaurant ~ Dogs allowed in bar and bedrooms ~ Open 11-11 ~ Bedrooms: £60B/£75B

GLASGOW NS5965 Map 11

Auctioneers £

North Court, St Vincent Place

Not the kind of place you'd come to for a quiet drink, this cheerful former auction house is now filled with a lively crowd. The main high-ceilinged flagstoned room has snug little areas around the edges, made out of the original valuation booths. Plenty of eye-catching antiques are dotted about as if they were for sale, with lot numbers clearly displayed. You'd probably be most tempted to bid for the goods in the smarter red-painted side room, which rather than the old lamps, radios, furnishings and golf clubs elsewhere has framed paintings, statues, and even an old rocking horse, as well as comfortable leather sofas, unusual lamp fittings, a big fireplace, and an elegant old dresser with incongruous china figures. The piped music is very audible in the bar (which has lots of old sporting photos, programmes and shirts along one of the panelled walls), and there are fruit machines, video games, a juke box and two TVs; the four big screens tend to dominate when sporting fixtures are being shown. Caledonian Deuchars IPA, Orkney Dark Island and perhaps a guest such as Cairngorm Wild Cat are well kept on handpump, and they've 25 malt whiskies, and very reasonably priced wines. Good value bar food includes soup (£2.75), sandwiches (from £4.50), haggis, neeps and tatties (£5.25), ploughman's or sausage and mash (£5.50), and specials such as giant filled yorkshire puddings (£5.75), and beef wellington (£6.25); friendly service. *(Recommended by Christine and Neil Townend, Ian Baillie)*

Mitchells & Butlers ~ Manager Michael Rogerson ~ Real ale ~ Bar food (12-8.45; 12.30-6.45 Sun) ~ Restaurant ~ (0141) 229 5851 ~ Children welcome 12-5 if eating ~ Open 12-11(12 Thurs-Fri); 11-12 Sat; 12.30-11 Sun

Babbity Bowster

Blackfriars Street

With something of the feel of a continental café-bar, this lively and stylish 18th-c town house is very popular, especially on Saturday when there's live music. The simply decorated light interior has fine tall windows, well lit photographs and big pen-and-wash drawings of Glasgow, its people and musicians, dark grey stools and wall seats around dark grey tables on the stripped wooden boards, and a peat fire. The bar opens on to a terrace with tables under cocktail parasols, trellised vines and shrubs, and adjacent boules; they may have barbecues out here in summer. You'll find well kept Caledonian Deuchars and a guest on air pressure tall fount, and a remarkably sound collection of wines, malt whiskies, and farm cider; good tea and coffee too. A short choice of interesting well cooked bar food might include hearty home-made soup (£2.75), croques monsieur or haggis, neeps and tatties (£4.95; they also do a vegetarian version), stovies (£5.75), panini (£5.95), mussels (£6.25), and cumberland sausage (£6.95), with puddings such as clootie dumpling (£2.95). The airy upstairs restaurant has more elaborate meals. A big ceramic of a kilted dancer and piper in the bar illustrates the mildly cheeky 18th-c Lowland wedding pipe tune (Bab at the Bowster) from which the pub takes its name – the friendly landlord or his staff will be happy to explain further. *(Recommended by Richard Lewis, Joe Green, Mark and Ruth Brock)*

Free house ~ Licensee Fraser Laurie ~ Real ale ~ Bar food (12-10) ~ Restaurant ~ (0141) 552 5055 ~ Children in restaurant ~ Dogs allowed in bar ~ Live music on Sat ~ Open 11(12.30 Sun)-12 ~ Bedrooms: £35S/£50S

Bon Accord £

North Street

Changing all the time (they have around 500 different kinds a year), the ten well kept beers at this friendly alehouse come from all over Britain, and are often from smaller brewers. A typical selection might include real ales from Brakspears, Broughton, Caledonian, Hop Back, Fullers, Harviestoun, Houston, Kelham Island, and Marstons. Whisky drinkers have lots to keep them happy too, with over 100 malts to choose from, and all 13 of their wines are available by the glass. There's a friendly atmosphere, and you'll find a good mix of customers (women find it welcoming here). The interior is neatly kept, partly polished bare-boards and partly carpeted, with a mix of tables and chairs, terracotta walls, and pot plants throughout; TV, fruit machine, cribbage, chess, and background music. Reasonably priced bar food includes baked potatoes or baguettes (£2.95), lasagne (£4.65), scampi (£4.80), and steak (£8.95); they do a two-course special (£3.95). It's open mike night on Tuesday, there's a quiz on Wednesday and a band on Saturday. *(Recommended by Richard Lewis, Ian Baillie, Patrick Hancock, Nelly Flowers)*

Scottish Courage ~ Lease Paul McDonagh ~ Real ale ~ Bar food (12-7) ~ (0141) 248 4427 ~ Open 11-12; 12.30-11 Sun

Pubs with outstanding views are listed at the back of the book.

Counting House £

St Vincent Place/George Square

The stunningly roomy and imposing interior of this busy Wetherspoons conversion (once a branch of the Royal Bank of Scotland) rises into a lofty, richly decorated coffered ceiling which culminates in a great central dome, with well lit nubile caryatids doing a fine supporting job in the corners. You'll also find the sort of decorative glasswork that nowadays seems more appropriate to a landmark pub than to a bank, as well as wall-safes, plenty of prints and local history, and big windows overlooking George Square. Away from the bar, several areas (some no smoking) have solidly comfortable seating, while a series of smaller rooms – once the managers' offices – leads around the perimeter of the building. Some of these are surprisingly cosy, one is like a well stocked library, and a few are themed with pictures and prints of historical characters such as Walter Scott or Mary, Queen of Scots. The central island servery has fairly priced Caledonian 80/- and Deuchars IPA, Courage Directors and Cairngorm Wildcat, along with well kept guests such as Batemans XXXB, Cairngorm Stag, Orkney Dark Island, and Timothy Taylors Landlord on handpump. They also do a good choice of bottled beers and malt whiskies, and a dozen wines by the glass; fruit machines. Friendly efficient staff serve the usual Wetherspoons menu which includes breakfasts (from £1.99, available till midday), sandwiches (from £2.25), wraps (from £3.55), chilli con carne, vegetarian moussaka or breaded scampi (£5.25), chicken balti (£5.75), and steaks (from £7.35), with puddings such as treacle sponge (£2.65); they offer two meals for £6.50. *(Recommended by Hugh A MacLean, Richard Lewis, Patrick Hancock, Nick Holding, Dave Braisted)*

Wetherspoons ~ Manager Stuart Coxshall ~ Real ale ~ Bar food (opening-10) ~ (0141) 225 0160 ~ Children in eating area of bar till 8pm ~ Open 7.30(10 Sat-Sun)-12

GLENELG NG8119 Map 11

Glenelg Inn

Unmarked road from Shiel Bridge (A87) towards Skye

Glenelg is the closest place on the mainland to Skye (there's a little car ferry across in summer), and on a sunny day tables in the beautifully kept garden of this charming inn have lovely views across the water. Feeling a bit like a mountain cabin (and still decidedly pubby given the smartness of the rest of the place), the unpretentious green-carpeted bar gives an overwhelming impression of dark wood, with lots of logs dotted about, a big fireplace, and only a very few tables and well worn cushioned wall benches – when necessary crates and fish boxes may be pressed into service as extra seating. Black and white photographs line the walls at the far end around the pool table, and there are various jokey articles and local information elsewhere; fruit machine, darts, winter pool, and piped music (usually Scottish). The don't have real ales, but there's a good collection of malt and cask strength whiskies; the locals are wecloming. At lunchtime they only do snacks such as soup (£3) or filled ciabatta and granary rolls (£5), while in the evening you can choose from dishes such as battered haddock, chicken, ham and mushroom pie, goats cheese and courgette tortilla, chicken kiev or toad in the hole (all £9), with puddings such as cheesecake (£3). They also do an outstanding four-course evening meal in the no smoking dining room (£29). The friendly staff or forthright landlord can organise local activities, and there are plenty of enjoyable walks nearby. Some of the bedrooms have great views. Getting here is an experience, with the single-track road climbing dramatically past heather-blanketed slopes and mountains with spectacular views to the lochs below. *(Recommended by Walter and Susan Rinaldi-Butcher, Lesley Bass, Di and Mike Gillam, John Ballard, JDM, KM; also in the* Good Hotel Guide*)*

Free house ~ Licensee Christopher Main ~ Bar food (12-2, 6-9; not Sun evening; not winter lunchtimes exc Sat) ~ Restaurant ~ (01599) 522273 ~ Children in eating area of bar and family room ~ Dogs allowed in bar ~ Ceilidh Sat evening ~ Open 12-2.30, 5-11; 12-2.30 Sun; cl lunchtime (exc Sat), and all Sun in winter ~ Bedrooms: /£80B

HOUSTON NS4166 Map 11

Fox & Hounds

South Street at junction with Main Street (B789, off B790 at Langbank signpost E of Bridge of Weir)

Home to the Houston Brewery, this enjoyable village pub has been in the same family for more than 25 years. Barochan, Killellan, and Peters Well are kept in top condition alongside a couple of seasonal brews, and a changing guest such as Timothy Taylors Landlord on handpump, and you'll also find half a dozen wines by the glass, and around 100 malt whiskies; friendly service. The clean plush hunting-theme lounge has comfortable seats by a fire and polished brass and copper; piped music. Popular with a younger crowd, the lively downstairs bar has a TV, pool and fruit machines. Served upstairs (downstairs they only do sandwiches; £2.95), a good choice of enjoyable bar food might include soup (£2.50), home-made fishcakes or prawn and smoked salmon salad (£4.50), steak and ale casserole or warm potato dumplings with spicy tomato sauce (£6.95), slow-braised lamb shank with creamy mash or beer-battered scampi (£8.95), and steaks (from £11.50), with puddings such as warm clootie dumpling with sweet brandy custard (£3.50); they do children's meals (from £1.95), and the restaurant has a more elaborate menu. There are no smoking areas in the lounge and restaurant. In summer they host a beer festival, and in winter there's a music festival.
(Recommended by Graham and Lynn Mason, Jean and Douglas Troup, Mike and Shelley Woodroffe)

Own brew ~ Licensee Jonathan Wengel ~ Real ale ~ Bar food (12-2.30, 5.30-10; 12-10 Sat-Sun) ~ Restaurant ~ (01505) 612448 ~ Children welcome till 8pm ~ Dogs allowed in bar ~ Open 11-12(1am Fri-Sat); 12.30-12 Sun

INVERARAY NN0908 Map 11

George

Main Street E

The bustling flagstoned bar of this comfortably modernised inn (run by the same family since 1860) shows plenty of age in its exposed joists, old tiles and bared stone walls. You'll find antique settles, cushioned stone slabs along the walls, carved wooden benches, nicely grained wooden-topped cast-iron tables, lots of curling club and ships' badges, and a cosy log fire in winter. Swiftly served by friendly staff (you order at the table), generously served enjoyable bar food includes soup (£2.20), fried mushrooms with smoky bacon, garlic and stilton (£4.25), good scampi and chips (£6.50), gammon and pineapple with cumberland sauce (£7.25), and salmon grilled with lemon and parsley butter or scottish lamb chop with parsnip crumble, caramelised baby onion and red wine sauce (£7.95). They are currently building a new conservatory restaurant with salvaged red pine beams and sandstone pillars. Two well kept changing beers include one from Fyne along with a guest such as Caledonian Deuchars IPA on handpump, and they've over 100 malt whiskies; darts, dominoes, pool and TV, but no bar games in summer. Nicely placed in the centre of this little Georgian town, stretching along Loch Fyne in front of Inveraray Castle, the pub is well placed for the great Argyll woodland gardens, best for their rhododendrons in May and early June; there are good nearby walks – you may spot seals or even a basking shark or whale. Some of the individually decorated bedrooms (reached by a grand wooden staircase) have jacuzzis and four-poster beds. *(Recommended by Philip and June Caunt, Charles and Pauline Stride, A H C Rainier, Patrick Hancock, Jenny and Brian Seller, Mrs B M Hill)*

Free house ~ Licensee Donald Clark ~ Real ale ~ Bar food (12-9.30) ~ Restaurant ~ (01499) 302111 ~ Children welcome ~ Dogs welcome ~ Open 11(12 Sun)-12 ~ Bedrooms: £35B/£60S(£120B)

If we know a pub has a no smoking area, we say so.

ISLE OF WHITHORN NX4736 Map 9

Steam Packet

Harbour Row

There's usually quite a bustle of yachts and inshore fishing boats in the picturesque working harbour – and you can watch it all from the large picture windows of this friendly inn. Swiftly served by helpful staff, the food is good, with changing evening specials such as steamed roast vegetable tartlet with three-cheese sauce (£6.95), asparagus with smoked salmon and hollandaise sauce (£7.95), and roast duck breast with root vegetable mash and cassis, anise and blackcurrant sauce (£10.95). Other well cooked dishes might include filled rolls (from £1.95, hot rolls from £2.50), glamorgan sausages or prawn cocktail (£5.95), gammon steak with honey and mustard cream sauce (£6.95), steamed mussels with tomato and pesto sauce (£10.50), and steaks (from £12.50), and puddings such as chocolate terrine with mixed fruits or rhubarb tartlet with stem ginger cream (£3.50); they do children's meals too (£1.95). The comfortable low-ceilinged bar is split into two: on the right, plush button-back banquettes and boat pictures, and on the left, green leatherette stools around cast-iron-framed tables on big stone tiles, and a woodburning stove in the bare stone wall. Bar food can be served in the lower-beamed dining room, which has excellent colour wildlife photographs, rugs on its wooden floor, and a solid fuel stove, and there's also a small eating area off the lounge bar. The conservatory is no smoking. Theakstons XB is well kept on handpump, along with a guest such as Houston Killellan, and they've two dozen malt whiskies, and a good wine list, with half a dozen by the glass; pool and dominoes. There are white tables and chairs in the garden. Several of the bedrooms have good views. Boat trips leave from the harbour; you can walk up to the remains of St Ninian's Kirk, on a headland behind the village. *(Recommended by Darly Graton, Graeme Gulibert, Pat and Tony Hinkins, Stan and Hazel Allen, Pam Hall, JWAC, Mike and Lynn Robinson, Richard J Holloway)*

Free house ~ Licensee John Scoular ~ Real ale ~ Bar food (12-2, 6.30-9) ~ Restaurant ~ (01988) 500334 ~ Children welcome away from bar ~ Dogs allowed in bar and bedrooms ~ Open 11(12 Sun)-11(12 Sat); closed Mon-Thurs 2.30-6 in winter; closed 25 Dec ~ Bedrooms: £25B/£50B

KILBERRY NR7164 Map 11

Kilberry Inn

B8024

Run by welcoming licensees, this homely whitewashed inn is entirely no smoking. Getting here is quite an adventure – it's so remote that local produce often arrives on the school bus. A very leisurely drive along the single-track road lets you make the most of the breathtaking views over rich coastal pastures to the sea and the island of Gigha beyond (readers recommend coming in the twilight when you'll see more wildlife). You'll know you've arrived when you spot the old-fashioned red telephone box outside, which was inherited from the pub's days as a post office. The small beamed and quarry-tiled dining bar, tastefully and simply furnished, is relaxed and warmly sociable, with a good log fire; piped music. Enjoyable home-made bar food (they appreciate booking if you want a meal) might include lunchtime salmon mousse or pork terrine (£2.95), and local sausage pie or spinach ricotta pasta (£5.95), with evening dishes such as warm goats cheese salad or local smoked salmon (£3.25), and wild mushroom risotto or medallions of pork in prune and armagnac sauce (£7.95); puddings could include good sticky toffee pudding with arran ice-cream or coffee and walnut cake (£3.50). There's no real ale, but they do a good range of bottled beers, and over 40 malt whiskies (with quite a few local ones). Please note the limited opening hours. *(Recommended by Mrs J Poole, Ian Ness, Patrick Hancock, John and Ann Carter, Les and Sandra Brown)*

Free house ~ Licensees Mr and Mrs George Primrose ~ Bar food (12-2, 7-9; see above) ~ Restaurant ~ (01880) 770223 ~ Children in restaurant and family room ~ Dogs allowed in bedrooms ~ Open 11-4, 6.30-10.30; 12.30-3 Sun; closed Sun evening, Mon except bank hols and Nov-Mar ~ Bedrooms: £39.50S/£85S

KINGHOLM QUAY NX9773 Map 9

Swan

B726 just S of Dumfries; or signposted off B725

Readers enjoy coming to this well run little pub, and the friendly staff are kind to families. The neat and comfortable public bar has well kept Theakstons Best on handpump, and good house wines; TV and quiet piped music. A short (but temptingly reasonably priced) selection of pubby food is served in the well ordered lounge or at busy times in the restaurant. Enjoyable dishes might include soup (£2.50), haggis with melted cheese (£3.50), liver and bacon (£5.95), steak pie or chicken with leeks and white wine (£6.25), spinach and ricotta cannelloni or chilli (£6.70), and battered haddock (£6.80), with evening specials such as rack of ribs or seafood risotto (£8.25), and steaks (from £8.50); puddings might include sticky toffee pudding (£3.20). Half the food service area is no smoking. The small garden has tables and a play area. In a quiet spot overlooking the old fishing jetty on the River Nith, the pub is handy for the Caerlaverock nature reserve with its multitude of geese. *(Recommended by Michael and Marion Buchanan, Malcolm Taylor, Richard J Holloway, Lucien Perring, Christine and Malcolm Ingram, David A Hammond, Nick Holding, Nick and Meriel Cox)*

Free house ~ Licensees Billy Houliston, Tracy Rogan and Alan Austin ~ Real ale ~ Bar food (12-2, 5-9) ~ (01387) 253756 ~ Children welcome ~ Dogs allowed in bar ~ Open 11.30-2.30, 5-10(11 Fri); 11.30-11 Sun

KIPPEN NS6594 Map 11

Cross Keys

Main Street; village signposted off A811 W of Stirling

Tables in the garden of this unpretentious and cosily comfortable 18th-c inn have good views towards the Trossachs. Popular with locals, the lounge is straightforward but welcoming with a good log fire; there's a coal fire too in the attractive no smoking family dining room. The menu changes every day, and enjoyable dishes are made using lots of fresh local produce; you can get smaller helpings for children. Generously served by friendly staff, bar food might include soup (£2.35), smoked salmon and prawn marie rose parcel (£4.65), home-made lasagne or gammon and pineapple (£6.95), and steak and mushroom pie or lamb casserole (£7.45), with puddings such as home-made sticky toffee pudding (£4.25); they also do sandwiches (from £2.60). Belhaven 80/- and maybe Harviestoun Bitter & Twisted are well kept on handpump, and they've more than 30 malt whiskies; piped music, and dominoes and TV in the separate public bar. The brightly lit exterior is a cheering sight on a cold winter night. *(Recommended by Sherrie Glass, Sandra and Dave Chadwick, Neil and Jean Spink, Nick Holding, Alistair and Kay Butler)*

Free house ~ Licensees Mr and Mrs Scott ~ Real ale ~ Bar food (12-2, 5.30-9; 12.30-9 Sun) ~ Restaurant ~ (01786) 870293 ~ Children welcome ~ Dogs allowed in bar and bedrooms ~ Open 12-2.30, 5.30-11; 12-12 Sat; 12.30-11 Sun; closed 25 Dec, 1 Jan ~ Bedrooms: /£60S(£50B)

KIRKTON OF GLENISLA NO2160 Map 11

Glenisla Hotel

B951 N of Kirriemuir and Alyth

Worth a detour, this welcoming 17th-c former coaching inn is set in one of the prettiest Angus Glens, and there are some good walks nearby. With a strong local feel (there'll probably be crowds of chatting regulars), the simple but cosy carpeted pubby bar has beams and ceiling joists, a roaring log fire (sometimes even in summer), wooden tables and chairs, and decent prints; a garden opens off it. The lounge is comfortable and sunny, and the elegant high-ceilinged dining room has rugs on the wooden floor, pretty curtains, candles and fresh flowers, and crisp cream tablecloths; piped music. A converted stable block has darts, dominoes, cribbage, pool and a fruit machine. As the pleasant licensees are keen to promote local produce, the beers, wines and cheeses all come from nearby suppliers; on handpump you might find a couple of well kept real ales from brewers such as Houston and Inveralmond, and they've fruit wines and a collection of malt whiskies. Delicious, regularly changing bar food in huge helpings might include soup, trio of scottish puddings with whisky cream sauce, cullen skink or warm goats cheese and vegetable tower, thai fishcakes with sweet ginger sauce, chicken breast in tarragon sauce, filo pastry filled with turkey and ham escalopes stuffed with lanark blue cheese, and fried duck breast with orange and Cointreau sauce. Staff can arrange fishing in local lochs. *(Recommended by Susan and John Douglas, Alistair and Kay Butler, Carol and Richard Glover)*

Free house ~ Licensees Steve and Susie Drysdale ~ Real ale ~ Bar food (12-2.30, 6.30-9.30) ~ Restaurant ~ (01575) 582223 ~ Children in eating area of bar and restaurant ~ Dogs allowed in bar and bedrooms ~ Live music last Sat in month ~ Open 11-11(1 Sat); 12.30-12 Sun; closed 3-5 on wkdys Nov-Easter ~ Bedrooms: £33S/£60B

LINLITHGOW NS9976 Map 11

Four Marys £

High Street; 2 miles from M9 junction 3 (and little further from junction 4) – town signposted

A fine selection of beers, reasonably priced bar food and friendly service make this bustling pub well worth popping into – and the building is interesting too. Dating from the 16th c, it takes its name from the four ladies-in-waiting of Mary, Queen of Scots, who was born at nearby Linlithgow Palace. Inside are masses of mementoes of the ill-fated queen, such as pictures and written records, a piece of bed curtain said to be hers, part of a 16th-c cloth and swansdown vest of the type she's likely to have worn, and a facsimile of her death-mask. The L-shaped bar also has mahogany dining chairs around stripped period and antique tables, a couple of attractive antique corner cupboards, and an elaborate Victorian dresser serving as a bar gantry. The walls are mainly stripped stone, including some remarkable masonry in the inner area; piped music. The atmosphere is a lot livelier now than during its days as an apothecary's shop, where David Waldie experimented with chloroform – its first use as an anaesthetic. Readers recommend the haggis, neeps and tatties (£5.35), while other simple generous bar food includes sandwiches (£2.95, baguettes from £3.75), mushroom hotpot (£3.25), burgers (from £4.95), macaroni cheese (£5.35), and home-made curry, lambs liver and bacon or scampi and chips (£5.95). The restaurant is no smoking. Swiftly changing guests such as Arran Blonde, Fullers London Pride, Greene King Old Speckled Hen, and Houston Texas are well kept alongside Belhaven 80/- and St Andrews, and Caledonian Deuchars IPA on handpump. During their May and October beer festivals they have 20 real ale pumps and live entertainment. Parking can be difficult. *(Recommended by Pete Yearsley, Christine and Neil Townend, Peter F Marshall, Nick Holding, Callum and Letitia Smith-Burnett, Pete Walker)*

Belhaven ~ Manager Eve Forrest ~ Real ale ~ Bar food (12-3, 5-9; 12(12.30 Sun)-9 in summer) ~ Restaurant ~ (01506) 842171 ~ Children in restaurant ~ Open 12(12.30 Sun)-11(12 Sat)

LYBSTER ND2436 Map 11

Portland Arms

A9 S of Wick

One area of this big welcoming hotel has been attractively laid out as a cosy country kitchen room with an Aga, pine furnishings and farmhouse crockery; the smart bar-bistro has warm colours and fabrics, solid dark wood furnishings, softly upholstered chairs and a cosy fire. Big helpings of enjoyable bar food include interesting (but not cheap) specials such as salmon terrine with herb and caper salad (£4.75), pork medallions with lemon and garlic rice and red pepper coulis or half a roast pheasant with winter fruit sauce and garlic mash (£14), along with other dishes such as sandwiches (£3; £3.50 toasted), roll mop herring (£3.50), bean and vegetable burger (£6.50), home-made steak pie or scampi and chips (£8), and steaks (from £12.50), with home-made puddings such as oaty, fruity crumble (£4.50). They serve a good selection of malt whiskies (the beers are keg); dominoes, trivia, piped music. The hotel was built as a staging post on the early 19th-c Parliamentary Road, and is a great base for exploring the spectacular cliffs and stacks of the nearby coastline; the friendly staff can arrange fishing and so forth. This is our most northerly main entry. *(Recommended by Dr D G Twyman, Robert F Smith; also in the* Good Hotel Guide*)*

Free house ~ Licensee Robert Reynolds ~ Bar food (12-3, 5-9; 12-10 in summer) ~ Restaurant ~ (01593) 721721 ~ Children in eating area of bar and restaurant ~ Open 12-12; 12-3, 5-11 in winter ~ Bedrooms: £55B/£80B

MELROSE NT5434 Map 9

Burts Hotel

B6374, Market Square

In summer you can sit out in the well tended garden of this comfortably sophisticated hotel, which is always busy and cheerful. The inviting L-shaped lounge bar has lots of cushioned wall seats and windsor armchairs, and Scottish prints on the walls. There are 80 malt whiskies to choose from, and Caledonian Deuchars IPA and 80/- and a guest such as Fullers London Pride are well kept on handpump; there's a good wine list too, with half a dozen by the glass. Enjoyable, swiftly served dishes might include soup (£2.75), grilled sardines with garlic butter (£4.50), braised rump of local lamb with creamy mash and rosemary and thyme jus or bass fillets with stir-fried noodles and prawns (£8.25), and aberdeen angus fillet steak (£13.75), with puddings such as lemon curd tartlets with citrus coulis (£4.50); good friendly service. The restaurant is no smoking. Melrose is perhaps the most villagey of the Border towns, and this is an ideal place to stay while you explore the area. *(Recommended by A K and J M Hill, David and Betty Gittins, Peter Burton, Keith and Janet Morris, Mark Walker, Mike and Lynn Robinson, Edward Perrott)*

Free house ~ Licensees Graham and Anne Henderson ~ Real ale ~ Bar food (12-2, 6-9.30, not 25-26 Dec) ~ Restaurant ~ (01896) 822285 ~ Children welcome in eating area of bar and family room; must be over 10 in restaurant ~ Dogs welcome ~ Open 11-2.30, 5-11; 12-2.30, 6-11 Sun; closed 26 Dec ~ Bedrooms: £54B/£98B

PITLOCHRY NN9459 Map 11

Moulin

Kirkmichael Road, Moulin; A924 NE of Pitlochry centre

A real bonus at this imposing 17th-c white-painted inn is the real ales, which are brewed in the little stables across the street: Ale of Atholl, Braveheart, Moulin Light, and the stronger Old Remedial are superbly kept on handpump (they do group brewery tours by arrangement). They also have around 40 malt whiskies. Although it has been much extended over the years, the bar, in the oldest part of the building, still seems an entity in itself. Above the fireplace in the smaller room is an interesting painting of the village before the road was built (Moulin used to be a bustling market town, far busier than upstart Pitlochry), while the bigger carpeted area has a good few tables and cushioned banquettes in little booths divided by stained-glass country scenes, another big fireplace, some exposed stonework, fresh flowers, and local prints and golf clubs around the walls; bar billiards, shove ha'penny, cribbage, dominoes and an old-fashioned fruit machine. The extensive bar menu includes soup (£2.50), mussels with garlic and cream (£5.25; £8.25 main), haggis, neeps and tatties (£5.95), macaroni cheese (£6.25), game casserole or lamb shank (£7.50), and salmon goujons (£7.50), and puddings such as sticky whisky fudge cake or honey sponge and custard (from £2.75); from 12 till 6pm they also serve baked potatoes and sandwiches (from £3.95). In the evening, readers enjoy eating in the restaurant. Surrounded by tubs of flowers, picnic-sets outside look across to the village kirk; there are rewarding walks nearby. The rooms are comfortable and breakfasts are good; they offer good value three-night breaks out of season. *(Recommended by David and Heather Stephenson, G Dobson, Paul and Ursula Randall)*

Own brew ~ Licensee Heather Reeves ~ Real ale ~ Bar food (12-9.30; not 25 Dec) ~ Restaurant ~ (01796) 472196 ~ Children in eating area of bar and restaurant ~ Dogs allowed in bar ~ Open 12-11(11.45 Sat) ~ Bedrooms: £50B/£65S(£75B)

PLOCKTON NG8033 Map 11

Plockton Hotel ★

Village signposted from A87 near Kyle of Lochalsh

Scotland Dining Pub of the Year

The very friendly staff help make a visit to this bewitching little hotel special; the food is very good too, and this is a charmingly relaxed place to stay (readers rave about the breakfasts). Forming part of a long, low terrace of stone-built houses, the inn is set in a lovely National Trust for Scotland village. Tables in the front garden look out past the village's trademark palm trees and colourfully flowering shrub-lined shore, and across the sheltered anchorage to the rugged mountainous surrounds of Loch Carron; a stream runs down the hill into a pond in the landscaped back garden. With a buoyant bustling atmosphere, the welcoming comfortably furnished lounge bar has window seats looking out to the boats on the water, as well as antiqued dark red leather seating around neat Regency-style tables on a tartan carpet, three model ships set into the woodwork, and partly panelled stone walls. The separate public bar has darts, pool, shove-ha'penny, dominoes, TV and piped music. The food is popular, so it is a good idea to book at busy times if you want a table. Well cooked, using lots of fresh local ingredients, dishes might include lunchtime filled baps (from £2.95), herring in oatmeal or skye mussels (£6.25), fish and chips (£6.50), and highland venison casserole (£7.75), with other dishes such as home-made soup (£2.50, with their own bread), haggis and whisky (£3.95), home-made lasagne (£7.25), local prawns (£8.75; £16.50 large), salmon poached with lime leaves and peppercorns (£9.25), braised lamb shank with red wine and rosemary (£10.95), and steaks (from £11.25); they also do children's meals (from £3.25), and from 9 till 10 you can get basket meals (from £4.75). The snug and Courtyard restaurant are no smoking. Well kept Caledonian Deuchars IPA and Isle of Skye Hebridean Gold on handpump, and bottled beers from the Isle of Skye brewery, along with a good collection of malt whiskies, and a short wine list. More than half of the no smoking bedrooms in the adjacent building have sea views – one even has a balcony and woodburning stove. A hotel nearby changed its name a few years ago to the Plockton Inn, so don't get the two confused. *(Recommended by G A Hemingway, Peter F Marshall, Douglas Keith, Michael and Marion Buchanan, Olive and Ray Hebson, Brian and Anita Randall, Neil Rose, Anthony Longden, Jeff and Wendy Williams, Bruce and Penny Wilkie, Patrick Hancock, GSB, Dr and Mrs M W A Haward, John and Claire Pettifer, Les and Sandra Brown, JDM, KM, Joan and Tony Walker)*

Free house ~ Licensee Tom Pearson ~ Real ale ~ Bar food (12(12.30 Sun)-2.15, 6-9; basket meals till 10) ~ Restaurant ~ (01599) 544274 ~ Children in eating area of bar and restaurant ~ Dogs allowed in bar ~ Live music summer Weds evenings ~ Open 11-12(11.45 Sat); 12.30-11 Sun; closed 25 Dec ~ Bedrooms: £55S(£45B)/£90B

SHIELDAIG NG8154 Map 11

Tigh an Eilean Hotel

Village signposted just off A896 Lochcarron—Gairloch

By summer 2005, the licensees hope to have added a new bar extension to this civilised hotel. They have told us their plans in some detail, and it sounds as if the changes will be a considerable boost to the appeal of the bar side – obviously, we are very much looking forward to seeing readers' reactions. In keeping with the rest of the conservation village, with a slate roof and wooden cladding, the airy new bar will have a pool table, and a no smoking upstairs dining area with a balcony (food will be served all day here), to make the most of the lovely sea views. Enjoyable food includes specials (with local fish and seafood, all hand-dived or reel-caught by local fishermen) such as seafood platter (£5.45), scallop mornay (£8.25), lamb shank hotpot or steak and mushroom pie (£7.25), and sirloin steak with mushroom and brandy sauce (£12.95), with other dishes such as soup (£2.35), smoked salmon with home-made bread (£5.50; £8.95 large), scampi and chips (£7.50), and seafood stew (£10.50), while puddings might include apricot crumble (£3); you can also get sandwiches all day (from £2.25). They now serve Isle of Skye Red Cuillin from handpump (and plan to introduce a guest or two), and they've six wines by the glass, and a dozen malt whiskies; winter darts, dominoes and background music. A sheltered front courtyard has five picnic-sets and wall benches. The pub is in a beautiful position looking over the forested Shieldaig Island to Loch Torridon and then out to the sea beyond; the National Trust Torridon estate and the Beinn Eighe nature reserve aren't too far away. *(Recommended by Dave Braisted, Mrs J Ekins-Daukes, Neil Rose, Peter F Marshall, Dr D J and Mrs S C Walker, Tim Maddison; also in the* Good Hotel Guide*)*

Free house ~ Licensees Cathryn and Christopher Field ~ Real ale ~ Bar food (12(12.30 Sun)-2.30, 6-8.30) ~ Restaurant ~ (01520) 755251 ~ Children welcome in restaurant, and in eating area of bar till 9pm ~ Dogs allowed in bedrooms ~ Trad music sessions Fri in July-Aug ~ Open 11-11; 12.30-10 Sun; closed 2.30-5 Mon-Fri Nov-March; 25, 31 Dec ~ Bedrooms: £55B/£120B

SKEABOST NG4148 Map 11

Skeabost House Hotel ★

A850 NW of Portree, 1½ miles past junction with A856

The new owner of this splendidly grand-looking hotel, developed from a Victorian hunting lodge, plans to hold regular concerts on the lawn, and on Saturday nights, there's live music in the bar. She's also redecorated the high-ceilinged bar (which is now more for residents), added a new restaurant and extended some of the bedrooms; a fine panelled billiards room leads off the stately hall. The wholly separate public bar has darts, pool, TV, juke box and even its own car park. Isle of Skye Red Cuillin is well kept on handpump, and they've over 100 malt whiskies, including their own and some rare single-year bottlings. Enjoyable food (which you can eat in the bar) might include soup (£3.50), mussels (£6), popular burger (£7.25), lamb hotpot (£8.25), wild mushroom and asparagus risotto (£8.50), oysters (£9), steaks (from £12), and langoustines (£14.50), with puddings such as banana cheesecake (£4.25); they also do bar snacks on Saturday, and three-course meals on Sunday. All the eating areas are no smoking. The hotel has 12 acres of secluded woodland and gardens, with glorious views over Loch Snizort; it's said to have some of the best salmon fishing on the island, and there's a golf course too. The price we show for bedrooms is for the cheapest room, prices can be much higher. *(Recommended by Dr Peter D Smart, Joan and Tony Walker)*

Free house ~ Licensee Helen Myers ~ Real ale ~ Bar food (10-11) ~ Restaurant ~ (01470) 532202 ~ Children in eating area of bar and family room ~ Dogs allowed in bar ~ Open 11-2, 5-11; 11-12.30 Sat; 12-11 Sun ~ Bedrooms: /£90S(£90B)

STEIN NG2656 Map 11

Stein Inn

End of B886 N of Dunvegan in Waternish, off A850 Dunvegan—Portree; OS Sheet 23 map reference 263564

With views over the sea to the Hebrides, tables outside this 18th-c inn are an ideal place to sit with a whisky (they've over 100 to choose from), and watch the sunset. Inside the original public bar has great character, with its sturdy country furnishings, flagstone floor, beam and plank ceiling, partly panelled stripped-stone walls and peat fire, and there is a comfortable no smoking lounge and no smoking dining area. The games area has a pool table, and darts, dominoes and cribbage; there may be piped radio. The evening crowd of local regulars (where do they all appear from?) and the owners are welcoming; good service from the smartly uniformed staff. Isle of Skye Red Cuillin or (brewed by Isle of Skye for the pub) Reeling Deck is well kept on handpump, along with a couple of guests from brewers such as Cairngorm and Orkney. Using local fish and highland meat, the very short bar food menu might include sandwiches (from £1.60), good ploughman's (£5.50), tuna salad (£5.95), breaded haddock (£6.25), and 8oz sirloin steak (£10.95), with specials such as home-made soup (£2.30), lamb hotpot (£6.25), and lemon chicken (£6.55); puddings might include home-made sticky toffee pudding (£3.95). There's a lively children's inside play area, and showers for yachtsmen. The pub is tranquilly set in a small untouched village just above a quiet sea inlet. Some of the bedrooms have sea views; readers tell us it's well worth pre-ordering the tasty smoked kippers if you stay here. *(Recommended by Richard and Karen Holt, Mike and Kathryn Budd, Walter and Susan Rinaldi-Butcher, Jeff and Wendy Williams, Charles and Pauline Stride, Patrick Hancock, Emma and Will, Joan and Tony Walker)*

Free house ~ Licensees Angus and Teresa Mcghie ~ Real ale ~ Bar food (12-4, 6-9.30 (9 Sun); not Mon exc bank and summer hols) ~ (01470) 592362 ~ Children in eating area of bar, family room and restaurant till 8.30pm ~ Dogs welcome ~ Open 11-12(12.30 Sat); 12.30-11 Sun; 4-12 wkdays, 12-12 Sat, 12.30-11 Sun in winter; closed 25 Dec, 1 Jan ~ Bedrooms: £24.50S/£64S

SWINTON NT8448 Map 10

Wheatsheaf

A6112 N of Coldstream

A great place for a meal, this civilised inn is nicely set in a pretty village surrounded by rolling countryside, just a few miles away from the River Tweed. There's plenty of choice on the imaginative changing menu: skilfully cooked with fresh local ingredients, lunchtime dishes might include soup (£3.50), pesto and goats cheese bruschetta (£4.95), chicken and pork terrine with vanilla and apple jelly (£5.65), organic pork and leek meatballs in cider and sage gravy with champ (£7.45), and baked salmon with pea purée and lemon (£9.95), with evening dishes such as black pudding fritters with stewed apple and redcurrant sauce (£5.45), caramelised pork with buttered spinach and sweet and sour sauce (£13.95), and roast rack of lamb with a mustard crust, butternut squash and rosemary (£15.75), with puddings such as sticky ginger and pear pudding with hot fudge sauce (£4.95); they also do lunchtime ciabattas. It's a good idea to book, particularly from Thursday to Saturday evening. Carefully thought-out, the main bar area has an attractive long oak settle and comfortable armchairs, and sporting prints and plates on the bottle-green wall covering; a small lower-ceilinged part by the counter has pubbier furnishings, and small agricultural prints on the walls, especially sheep. A further lounge area has a fishing-theme décor (with a detailed fishing map of the River Tweed). The front conservatory has a vaulted pine ceiling and walls of local stone; all the dining areas are no smoking. Caledonian Deuchars IPA and a guest such as Broughton Greenmantle are well kept on handpump, and they've three dozen malt whiskies and brandies, and a fine choice of wines (with eight by the glass), and cocktails; organic fruit juices too. Service is helpful and welcoming, and if you stay here, you'll get a good breakfast, with freshly squeezed orange juice. The friendly licensees have brightened up the exterior with new window boxes and hanging baskets. *(Recommended by Carolyn Dixon)*

Free house ~ Licensees Chris and Jan Winson ~ Real ale ~ Bar food (12-2, 6-9; not Sun evening Dec-Jan, 24-26 Dec) ~ Restaurant ~ (01890) 860257 ~ Children welcome ~ Dogs allowed in bedrooms ~ Open 11-2.30, 6-11.30(10.30 Sun); closed Sun evening in Dec-Jan; 24-26 Dec ~ Bedrooms: £62B/£95B

Stars after the name of a pub show exceptional character and appeal. They don't mean extra comfort. And they are nothing to do with food quality, for which there's a separate knife-and-fork symbol. Even quite a basic pub can win stars, if it's individual enough.

TAYVALLICH NR7386 Map 11

Tayvallich Inn

B8025, off A816 1 mile S of Kilmartin; or take B841 turn-off from A816 2 miles N of Lochgilphead

Great for sunny days, the terrace of this simply furnished bar/restaurant has lovely views over the yacht anchorage and water, and there's a garden too. Service is friendly, and people with children are made to feel welcome. One little room has local nautical charts on the cream walls, exposed ceiling joists, and pale pine upright chairs, benches and tables on its quarry-tiled floor; piped music. It leads into a no smoking dining conservatory, from where sliding glass doors open on to the terrace. With seafood freshly brought in by local fishermen from the bay of Loch Sween just across the lane, the short but enticing menu might include deep-fried whitebait or mussels steamed in white wine, garlic and thyme (£4.95), burger (£6.75), tagliatelle with porcini mushrooms, truffle oil and parmesan (£7.50), home-made fish pie (£8.25), scottish rib-eye steak (£14.25), and local langoustines grilled with olive oil and cayenne pepper (£14.95), with puddings such as crème brûlée (£3.95); they serve fresh milk shakes. There are twenty malt whiskies including a full range of Islay malts, and Caledonian 80/- on handpump.
(Recommended by Mrs B M Hill, Richard J Holloway, Ken Richards)

Free house ~ Licensee Roddy Anderson ~ Bar food (12-2, 6-10; 12-10 wknds, see below in winter) ~ Restaurant ~ (01546) 870282 ~ Children in eating area of bar and restaurant ~ Dogs allowed in bar ~ Live music two Sats a month ~ Open 11-12(1 Sat); 12-12 Sun; 5-11(12 Fri), Weds-Fri in winter; closed Mon-Tues, and lunchtime Weds-Fri in winter

THORNHILL NS6699 Map 11

Lion & Unicorn

A873

With a pleasant atmosphere and warming winter fire, the open-plan front room of this attractive partly 17th-c pub has beams and stone walls, and comfortable seats on the wooden floors. Friendly obliging staff serve a well kept real ale such as Caledonian Deuchars IPA or Timothy Taylors Landlord on handpump, and in the beamed public bar (with stone walls and floors) you'll find a juke box, pool, fruit machine, TV, darts, cribbage, dominoes, and piped music. Served all day, enjoyable bar food includes a couple of vegetarian dishes such as vegetable lasagne or mushroom, spinach, brie and cranberry wellington (£7.50), as well as soup (£2.50), baked potatoes (from £4.75), steak pie (£6.50), battered haddock (£6.75), and scampi (£6.95), with puddings such as apple pie and sticky toffee pudding (from £3.95). In the restaurant (half no smoking) you can see the original massive fireplace, almost big enough to drive a car into. There's a play area in the garden.
(Recommended by Rosemary and Tom Hall, Nick Holding, Ian Baillie)

Free house ~ Licensees Fiona and Bobby Stevenson ~ Real ale ~ Bar food (12-9) ~ Restaurant ~ (01786) 850204 ~ Children welcome away from bar ~ Open 11-12(1 Sat); 12.30-12 Sun ~ Bedrooms: £45B/£70B

ULLAPOOL NH1294 Map 11

Ferry Boat

Shore Street; coming from the S, keep straight ahead when main A835 turns right into Mill Street

You can get cakes and scones at this friendly inn, which is popular with locals as well as tourists. The unassuming two-roomed pubby bar has big windows with nice views, yellow walls, brocade-cushioned seats around plain wooden tables, quarry tiles by the corner serving counter and patterned carpet elsewhere, a stained-glass door hanging from the ceiling and a fruit machine; cribbage, dominoes and piped music. The more peaceful inner room has a coal fire, and a delft shelf of copper measures and willow-pattern plates. Hearty lunchtime bar food includes soup (£2.25), sandwiches (from £2.60), cheese platter (£4.25), haggis, neeps and tatties or venison sausages (£5.95), and gammon and egg or local haddock (£7.25), with puddings such as chocolate and ginger cheesecake (£3.10); in the evening (when dogs are allowed in the bar) food is served in the restaurant. They serve three changing real ales such as Cairngorm Highland IPA, Flowers IPA, and Wadworths 6X well kept on handpump. In summer you can sit on the wall across the road and take in the fine views to the tall hills beyond the attractive fishing port, with its bustle of yachts, ferry boats, fishing boats and tour boats for the Summer Isles. *(Recommended by Mr and Mrs M Stratton, Alistair and Kay Butler)*

Free house ~ Licensee Richard Smith ~ Real ale ~ Bar food (12-3 only) ~ Restaurant ~ (01854) 612366 ~ Children in eating area of bar and restaurant till 8pm ~ Dogs allowed in bedrooms ~ Thurs evening folk music ~ Open 11(12.30 Sun)-11; closed 25 Dec ~ Bedrooms: £36S/£72S

WEEM NN8449 Map 11

Ailean Chraggan

B846

Readers think very highly of this welcoming little family-run hotel, a lovely place to stay or come to for a meal. You can eat in either the comfortably carpeted modern lounge or the mainly no smoking dining room, and good changing dishes might include soup (£2.95), sandwiches (from £2.60), warm broccoli and cheese tart (£4.95), half a dozen oysters (£6), roast pheasant salad (£8.25), tomato, chick pea and kidney bean curry (£9.25), steamed salmon with watercress sauce (£10.65), and venison steak with red wine jus (£12.45), with puddings such as hot chocolate pudding (£4.95); they do children's meals too (£3.95). It's a good idea to book at busy times. They've a very good wine list, and there are around 100 malt whiskies; winter darts and dominoes. The atmosphere is friendly, and you're likely to find chatty locals in the bar. Two terraces outside give lovely views to the mountains beyond the Tay, sweeping up to Ben Lawers (the highest in this part of Scotland). *(Recommended by Paul and Ursula Randall, Mr and Mrs M Stratton, John Ballard, Dr and Mrs M W A Haward, Mark Flynn)*

Free house ~ Licensee Alastair Gillespie ~ Bar food ~ Restaurant ~ (01887) 820346 ~ Children welcome ~ Dogs allowed in bar and bedrooms ~ Open 11(12.30 Sun)-11; closed 25-26 Dec, 1-2 Jan ~ Bedrooms: £45B/£90B

LUCKY DIP

Besides the fully inspected pubs, you might like to try these Lucky Dips recommended to us and described by readers (if you do, please send us reports: www.goodguides.co.uk).

ABERDEENSHIRE

ABERDEEN NJ9306

Globe [N Silver St]: Extended old pub decorated with musical memorabilia (posters, sheet music, instruments), well kept real ales such as Isle of Skye Red Cuillin, enjoyable food lunchtime and evening, live music most nights; bedrooms *(Julian Templeman)*

Grill [Union St]: Spotless and old-fashioned, with polished dark panelling, attractive traditional features, well kept Boddingtons, Caledonian 80/-, Courage, Isle of Skye Red Cuillin and McEwans 80/-, enormous range of malt whiskies, match-strike metal strip under bar counter, basic snacks; open all day *(the Didler, Joe Green)*

GARLOGIE NJ7905

Garlogie Inn: Well run dining pub in pleasant setting overlooking Deeside, generous varied food inc good fish, decent wine, reasonable prices, friendly homely atmosphere, attentive staff *(Mrs Jane Kingsbury, Callum and Letitia Smith-Burnett)*

MUIR OF FOWLIS NJ5612

Muggarthaugh [Tough, just off A980]: Good friendly service, generous helpings of good value fresh food inc some imaginative dishes, nice wine choice; bedrooms, open for most of day at least in summer, handy for Craigievar *(David and Betty Gittins)*

OLDMELDRUM NJ8128

☆ *Redgarth* [Kirk Brae]: Good-sized comfortable lounge, traditional décor and subdued lighting, well kept changing ales such as Bass, Castle Eden and Isle of Skye, good range of malt whiskies, nicely presented satisfying food inc some interesting dishes and good puddings, more intimate restaurant, cheerful and attentive landlord and staff; gorgeous views to Bennachie, immaculate bedrooms *(David and Betty Gittins, Callum and Letitia Smith-Burnett)*

ANGUS

FINAVON NO4957

Finavon Hotel [off A90 northbound from Forfar]: Friendly prompt service, good range of home-made food, two guest ales, daily papers, restaurant; comfortable bedrooms with own bathrooms *(Callum and Letitia Smith-Burnett)*

INVERBERVIE NO8378

Cutty Sark [King St]: Newly refurbished, with wide food choice inc good fresh fish, good range of well kept beers inc guests, friendly efficient staff, comfortable restaurant *(Pat and Sam Roberts)*

ST CYRUS NO7464

St Cyrus Hotel [A92]: Good range of enjoyable inventive food in welcoming bar and large adjacent dining room, modern décor though old hotel, plenty of locals, old-fashioned village; bedrooms *(anon)*

ARGYLL

ARDFERN NM8004

Galley of Lorne [B8002; village and inn signposted off A816 Lochgilphead—Oban]: Cosy bar with warming log fire, big navigation lamps by counter, unfussy assortment of furniture, Caledonian Deuchars IPA and a local guest beer, about 50 malt whiskies, home-made bar food, darts, dominoes and board games, spacious no smoking restaurant (children welcome here); fruit machine, TV, piped music; good sea and loch views from sheltered terrace, comfortable bedrooms, open all day *(LYM)*

ARDUAINE NM7910

☆ *Loch Melfort Hotel* [A816 S of Oban]: Gorgeous view of sea and islands from front terrace and picture windows in comfortable hotel's airy modern nautical bar, good bar food all day from soup and sandwiches to aberdeen angus steak and lots of fresh local seafood, children's menu, no smoking restaurant with good wine list, perhaps a real ale in season – if not, try the Argyll bottled beers; children and dogs welcome, good sea-view bedrooms, by Arduaine woodland gardens (at best late Apr to early Jun, but lovely any time – fun for children, too), open all day *(Mark and Belinda Halton, LYM, Mark o'Sullivan, Jenny and Brian Seller)*

CLACHAN SEIL NM7819

☆ *Tigh an Truish* [linked by bridge via B844, off A816 S of Oban]: Friendly and interesting unsmart 18th-c local nr lovely anchorage, pine-clad walls and ceiling, bay windows overlooking inlet, prints and oil paintings, woodburner in one room, open fires in others; home-made bar food inc good fresh seafood (all day in summer), no smoking dining room, well kept McEwans 80/- and a local summer guest beer, good choice of malt whiskies; darts, dominoes, TV, piped music; children in restaurant, plenty of tables outside inc some in small suntrap side garden, good value bedrooms, open all day summer *(LYM, Nick Holding, Jenny and Brian Seller)*

CRINAN NR7894

☆ *Crinan Hotel* [B841, off A816]: Elegant hotel by Crinan Canal's entrance basin, picture-window views of fishing boats and yachts wandering out towards the Hebrides, smart nautical cocktail bar, simple public bar opening on to side terrace, coffee shop with sandwiches etc, good if pricey restaurant food, good wines, whiskies and soft drinks (keg beer); children and dogs welcome, open all day, comfortable bedrooms, outstanding breakfast *(Nick Holding, LYM, Jenny and Brian Seller)*

GLENCOE NN1058

☆ *Clachaig* [old Glencoe rd, behind NTS Visitor Centre]: Extended inn doubling as mountain rescue post and cheerfully crowded with outdoors people in season, with mountain photographs in flagstoned walkers' bar (two woodburners and pool), pine-panelled snug, big modern-feeling dining lounge; hearty snacks all day, wider evening choice, lots of malt whiskies, well kept real ales, unusual bottled beers, annual beer festival; children in no smoking restaurant; live music Sat; simple bedrooms, nourishing breakfast, spectacular setting surrounded by soaring mountains *(LYM, Mr and Mrs Maurice Thompson, Richard and Anne Ansell)*

KILCHRENAN NN0323

Kilchrenan Inn [B845]: Simple pub fitted out in local pine, window seat and rustic furniture, interesting old photographs, sandwiches and limited blackboard choice of good food here or in separate dining room, quiet and relaxed atmosphere, friendly staff, good malt whiskies, perhaps a real ale; dogs welcome, garden tables, lovely drive along Loch Awe to the pub and beyond to Ardanaiseig gardens *(Mr and Mrs J Curtis, Dave Braisted, Nick Holding)*

OBAN NM8630

☆ *Oban Inn* [Stafford Street, near North Pier]: Cheerful 18th-c harbour-town local, pubby beamed and slate-floored downstairs bar, partly panelled upstairs bar with button-back banquettes around cast-iron-framed tables, coffered woodwork ceiling and little stained-glass false windows, no smoking children's area, well kept McEwans 80/-, 45 malt whiskies, good value bar food served all day; fruit machine, juke box, piped music; dogs allowed in bar, open all day *(Mrs B M Hill, Dave Braisted, LYM)*

PORT APPIN NM9045

☆ *Pier House*: Beautiful location, pleasantly refurbished small bar with attractive terrace, very good picture-window seafood restaurant looking across to Lismore and beyond, helpful friendly staff, games room with pool; comfortable bedrooms, good breakfast *(Jenny and Brian Seller)*

STRONTIAN NM8161

Strontian Hotel: Pub/hotel with locally sourced home cooking (only a few tables, so worth booking), friendly helpful service; comfortable bedrooms overlooking Loch Sunart *(MJVK)*

TARBERT NR8768

Columba [Pier Rd]: Civilised and well preserved 1900s pub named for the then daily ferry from Glasgow, attractive and congenial bar, enjoyable food using local fish and fresh produce here and in charming restaurant; seven bedrooms being refurbished in Edwardian style, with own bathrooms *(Richard J Holloway)*

AYRSHIRE

AYR NS3320

Abbotsford [Corsehill Rd, just off B7024]: Small family-run hotel with cosy and comfortable bar, enjoyable sensibly priced bar food, friendly helpful service *(Mr and Mrs Colin Roberts)*

DALMELLINGTON NS4707

Craigmark [Burnton]: Former company store for iron works, alongside steam railway centre; bar food, Belhaven, great painting of the store and cottages in the works' heyday – landlord a mine of information on the area's industrial history *(Dave Braisted)*

KILMARNOCK NS4237

Clansman [John Finnie St]: Large friendly bar, good helpful service inc drinks to your table, bargain food from big baked potatoes up *(Mr and Mrs Colin Roberts)*

Cotton Mill [Annandale]: Useful suburban Brewers Fayre, clean and comfortable, usual food, cheerful helpful staff; bedrooms in attached Travel Inn *(Mr and Mrs Colin Roberts)*

LARGS NS2058

Queens [Brisbane St]: Good value bar diner with good choice of malt whiskies *(Dave Braisted)*

SORN NS5526

Sorn Inn [Main St]: New chef doing enjoyable food from bar food to set meals, smart restaurant; comfortable bedrooms, conservation village *(Roy Bromell)*

SYMINGTON NS3831

Wheatsheaf [just off A77 Ayr—Kilmarnock; Main St]: Busy rambling 17th-c pub in quiet pretty village, charming and cosy, two dining rooms with wide blackboard choice of consistently good original food served all day esp fish and local produce, Belhaven beers, friendly quick service, racehorse décor; must book wknd, can be seething with customers lunchtime; attractively set tables outside *(Gordon Scarlett, Nick Holding, Christine and Malcolm Ingram, Mrs Edna M Jones)*

BANFFSHIRE

GLENLIVET NJ2129

Croft: Former almshouse, small, intimate and cosy, with very welcoming atmosphere, interesting choice of good home-cooked food, Cairngorm real ale, dozens of malt whiskies, conservatory restaurant; open all day in summer *(Ian Smith)*

PORTSOY NJ5866

Shore [Church St]: Small harbourside pub, bare-boards L-shaped bar with dark bentwood seats, masses of nautical and other bric-a-brac, prints and pictures, good value straightforward food, Bass and Cairngorm Smugglers, cheerful chatty regulars, darts; subdued piped music, small TV *(Paul and Ursula Randall)*

BERWICKSHIRE

DUNS NT7853

White Swan [Market Sq]: Pleasant local atmosphere, well kept Belhaven beers, generous usual food (good home-made soups), nice service; bedrooms *(R T and J C Moggridge)*

LAUDER NT5347

Black Bull [Market Pl]: 17th-c inn reopened after refurbishment, already popular for good choice of interesting food from NZ chef; children welcome, open all day, bedrooms *(LYM, Dr and Mrs S Donald)*

Eagle [A68]: Dark wood and beams, pictures, plates, brass, plants, remarkably ornate bar counter, stone fireplace, smiling service and lively atmosphere, well kept changing real ales, decent bar food, games in public bar; children welcome, summer barbecues in old stableyard, bedrooms, open all day *(LYM, Jeff and Wendy Williams)*

CAITHNESS

MELVICH NC8864

Melvich Hotel [A836]: Britain's most northerly brewpub, friendly public bar, civilised back bar emphasising food from simple sandwiches to fresh wild salmon, relaxed atmosphere and friendly service, peat or log fire; lovely spot, beautiful sea and coast views, bedrooms *(Richard Houghton)*

DUMFRIESSHIRE

CANONBIE NY3976

Cross Keys: Attractive 17th-c coaching inn with River Esk fishing, wide choice of enjoyable and generous straightforward food using local produce from sandwiches to salmon in spacious and comfortably worn in lounge bar, good carvery Fri-Sun, friendly helpful staff even when very busy; spacious well equipped bedrooms, good breakfast *(J A Hooker, Canon David Baxter, Dr and Mrs S Donald)*

CARSETHORN NX9959

Steamboat [off A170 at Kirkbean]: Decent generous home-made food, good service, estuary views from front dining room, seafaring items in adjoining little bar *(Stan and Hazel Allen)*

CROCKETFORD NX8372

Galloway Arms: Well refurbished inn with well prepared reasonably priced food, attentive staff; comfortable bedrooms, own bathrooms *(Stan and Hazel Allen)*

DUMFRIES NX9776

Cavens Arms [Buccleuch St]: Former Rat & Carrot back to its original name, two regular real ales and up to four guests at attractive prices, decent food, no smoking area *(Joe Green)*

New Bazaar [Whitesands]: Traditional bar with up to five changing real ales inc rarities, lots of malt whiskies, helpful informative landlord, small lounge, inner snug; tables in small yard, open all day *(Eric Larkham, Joe Green, Nick Holding)*
Tam o' Shanter [Queensberry St]: Backstreet local with good choice of quickly changing unusual beers, two sitting rooms (one no smoking) off bar, lunchtime soup and rolls; tables in former coachyard, open all day *(Eric Larkham, Nick Holding)*

GLENCAPLE NX9968

Nith: Pleasant hotel bar, garden tables and picture-window dining room looking over river towards Criffel's hoary top, quickly served reasonably priced food inc good smoked salmon and wild salmon; spacious bedrooms with own bathrooms, good breakfast *(Dr Michael Denton, Nick and Meriel Cox)*

MOFFAT NT0805

☆ *Black Bull* [Churchgate]: Attractive and well kept small hotel, plush softly lit bar with Burns memorabilia, welcoming attentive service, enjoyable unpretentious generous food served quickly, from sandwiches to local ingredients cooked imaginatively, well kept McEwans 80/-, Theakstons XB and a guest such as Old Mill, several dozen malt whiskies, friendly public bar across courtyard with railway memorabilia and good open fire, simply furnished tiled-floor dining room; piped music a decidedly cut above the norm, side games bar with juke box, big-screen TV for golf; children welcome, tables in courtyard, 12 comfortable good value bedrooms, open all day *(LYM, Keith Moss, Nick Holding, Gwyn and Anne Wake, George Atkinson, Lee Potter)*
Moffat House [High St]: Large comfortably plush bar of Best Western hotel, relaxed and quiet, with coal fire, welcoming helpful service, usual bar food, conservatory coffee lounge, restaurant; comfortable bedrooms, good breakfast *(Christine and Neil Townend, Mr and Mrs Staples)*

NEW ABBEY NX9666

Abbey Arms [The Square]: Friendliness of the staff lifts this out of the ordinary; wide choice of freshly cooked food, a real ale such as Greene King Abbot *(Stan and Hazel Allen, Andy and Ali)*

THORNHILL NX8795

☆ *Buccleuch & Queensberry* [Drumlanrig St (A76)]: Substantial red sandstone Georgian former coaching inn with comfortable banquettes and coal fire in traditional main beamed bar, friendly service, food from interesting sandwiches and baked potatoes to some good value main dishes, well kept Caledonian 80/- and a changing guest beer; access to three miles of fishing on the River Nith; children welcome, comfortable bedrooms with good breakfast, attractive small town *(LYM, JWAC, Nick Holding)*

DUNBARTONSHIRE

ARROCHAR NN2903

☆ *Village Inn* [A814, just off A83 W of Loch Lomond]: Fine sea and hill views from informal candlelit all-day dining area with heavy beams, bare boards and big open fire, steps down to bar with generous and enjoyable lunchtime bar food from sandwiches up, well kept changing real ales such as Orkney Dark Island, several dozen malt whiskies, good coffee, cheerful attentive staff; piped music, juke box, can be loudly busy Sat in summer; children welcome in eating areas till 8, tables out on deck and lawn, comfortable bedrooms with own bathrooms, good breakfast, open all day *(LYM, Ian Baillie, A H C Rainier, Peter and Pat Frogley)*

BALLOCH NS3982

Balloch Hotel [just N of A811]: Vintage Inn dining pub in superb spot by River Leven's exit from Loch Lomond, good atmosphere in several seating areas, helpful young staff, good range of wines by the glass, well kept Bass and Caledonian Deuchars IPA, decent reasonably priced food all day; children welcome, bedrooms, open all day *(Ian Baillie)*
Meson del Lago [Loch Lomond Shores development, Old Luss Rd]: Superb loch and mountain view from minimalist modern bar and balcony tables, tapas and sandwiches all day, lagers and keg beers, restaurant with low-priced menu till 5 then more expensive meals *(Ian Baillie)*

EAST LOTHIAN

GIFFORD NT5368

Goblin Ha' [Main St]: Neatly kept village pub, welcoming and pretty, with varied food from simple bar lunches to more exotic or elaborate things, well kept Bass and a Scottish Courage beer such as Theakstons, long plainly furnished bar with jolly atmosphere and roomy dining area, quick friendly service, restaurant with large airy back conservatory; tables and chairs in good big garden with small play area; bedrooms *(Dr Peter D Smart)*

HADDINGTON NT5173

☆ *Waterside* [Waterside; just off A6093, over pedestrian bridge at E end of Town]: Attractively set riverside dining pub with plush bar, long cushioned benches and bigger tables in second room, more formal stripped-stone dining conservatory, popular food from sandwiches up, Greene King Abbot, Marstons Pedigree, Timothy Taylors Landlord and a guest beer, good range of wines; children welcome, no dogs, tables out overlooking the water, open all day wknds *(LYM, Nick Holding)*

FIFE

ANSTRUTHER NO5603

☆ *Craws Nest* [Bankwell Rd]: Well run and handsomely placed family-owned hotel, very popular lunchtime with older people for enjoyable bar meals (available early evening too); light long lounge with 1970s echoes, comfortable banquettes, photographs, paintings for sale, prompt courteous and helpful staff, restaurant; keg beer; comfortable bedrooms in modern wing *(Paul and Ursula Randall)*

CERES NO3911

Meldrums [Main St]: Small hotel with well run cottagey parlour bar, pleasant atmosphere, clean and attractive beamed dining lounge with good choice of enjoyable reasonably priced bar lunches, helpful friendly service even when busy; well appointed bedrooms, charming village nr Wemyss Pottery *(Peter and Jean Hoare, Clifford Payton)*

CRAIGROTHIE NO3710

Kingarroch [Main St]: Small 18th-c dining pub, enjoyable imaginative food in bar and evening restaurant with log fire, great choice of well priced wines, good service, Belhaven ale *(Ken Richards)*

CRAIL NO6107

Golf [High St S]: Welcoming service and hearty standard food inc high teas in airily refurbished dining rooms, small and basic beamed locals' bar (can be crowded and smoky), usually a real ale such as Atlas, good range of malt whiskies, coal fire; simple comfortable bedrooms, good breakfast *(Paul and Ursula Randall)*

LIMEKILNS NT0783

Ship [Halketts Hall, towards Charlestown; off A985]: Small blue and yellow lounge, friendly and comfortable, with good views over the Forth, mainly nautical décor, good value sandwiches and bar snacks, well kept Belhaven 80/- and perhaps other real ales, no smoking area; piped music (occasional live); children and dogs welcome, open all day, pavement seats, interesting waterside conservation area *(Comus and Sarah Elliott, Nick Holding, Mike Bell)*

INVERNESS-SHIRE

AVIEMORE NH8612

Cairngorm [Grampian Rd (A9)]: Warm friendly bar, pleasant helpful waiting service in eating area and restaurant, good choice of drinks and of well prepared food; children welcome *(Christine and Phil Young)*

Old Bridge [Dalfaber Rd, southern outskirts off B970]: Well kept inn with stripped stone and wood, local books and memorabilia, roaring open fire, good value food from sandwiches to carvery in bar (short but enterprising lunchtime choice) or large dining extension, good cheerful staff, well kept changing ales such as Caledonian and Orkney Dark Island; quiet piped music, Tues ceilidh; pleasant surroundings *(R T and J C Moggridge)*

CANNICH NH3331

Slaters Arms: Former single-storey building with dining extension, friendly landlord, reasonably priced food cooked by landlady *(Malcolm Thomas)*

CARRBRIDGE NH9022

☆ *Cairn* [Main Rd]: Friendly tartan-carpeted bar with charming Australian landlord and polite attentive staff, sensible all-day low-priced bar food inc children's dishes, all home-made as are evening meals, two well kept real ales such as Cairngorm and Isle of Skye Red Cuillin, log fire, no smoking eating area, old local pictures; comfortable bedrooms with own bathrooms, open all day till late *(Dr D E Granger)*

DRUMNADROCHIT NH5029

Blarmor Bar [Blairbeg]: Enjoyable food, hospitable service *(John Smith)*

Fiddlers Elbow: Good real ale choice, enjoyable food inc good value sandwiches (served through the afternoon, at least in summer), friendly atmosphere, pleasant service; original little girl effigy at entrance; handy for Urquhart Castle *(Dr Peter D Smart, R T and J C Moggridge)*

FORT WILLIAM NN1073

Ben Nevis Bar [High St]: Roomy beamed bar with decent standard food, McEwans 80/-, good cheery service, Loch Linnhe views from back windows, upstairs restaurant; TV, games, may be live music *(Sarah and Peter Gooderham, George Atkinson)*

INVERGARRY NH3001

Invergarry Hotel: Comfortably worn-in, with two well kept real ales (at least in summer), enjoyable food inc good soups and home-made gravadlax *(Dr D J and Mrs S C Walker)*

INVERNESS NH6645

Blackfriars [Academy St]: Good choice of particularly well kept real ales such as Black Isle, Broughton and Cairngorm Trade Winds, good value food from baguettes up, friendly service; popular with young people, can be noisy at night with live music *(R T and J C Moggridge)*

Clachnaharry Inn [A862 NW of city]: Cosily dim beamed bar, simple top lounge, more comfortable bottom lounge with picture windows looking over Beauly Firth, great atmosphere, good service, bargain freshly cooked food from big baked potatoes up, half a dozen well kept ales from Caledonian, Cairngorm and Skye breweries, some tapped from the cask; tables out by single-track railway, lovely walks by big flight of Caledonian Canal locks *(Richard Houghton)*

Palace [Ness Walk]: Civilised lounge in tourist hotel overlooking River Ness and castle, neat and comfortable, with smart staff, bar food from sandwiches to steaks, usually a real ale such as Black Island Red Kite; bedrooms *(Paul and Ursula Randall)*

Phoenix [Academy St]: Several well kept changing ales such as Caledonian Deuchars IPA and 80/- and Orkney Dark Island in unchanging bare-boards 1890s bar with much dark brown varnish and granite trough at foot of island servery, neat adjoining dining room with some booth seating; three TVs for sports *(Paul and Ursula Randall)*

☆ *Snow Goose* [Stoneyfield, about ¼ mile E of A9/A96 roundabout]: Well run Vintage Inn dining pub, the most northerly of this chain, with good imaginative well presented bar food at attractive prices in comfortable and relaxing informal country-feel room areas, beams and flagstones, several log fires, soft lighting, interesting décor, friendly helpful staff, good wine choice; comfortable bedrooms in adjacent Travelodge *(Rod Stoneman, Dr D G Twyman, Walter and Susan Rinaldi-Butcher, John and Claire Pettifer)*

MALLAIG NM6797

Marine Hotel [Station Rd]: Comfortable hotel lounge bar (up steep stairs) overlooking fishing harbour and beyond to Small Isles and Skye, good lunchtime bar food from sandwiches and baguettes to local seafood, courteous service, no smoking dining room, basic public bar downstairs (notable for its stuffed gannet in full flight) with games room; keg beers, piped music; bedrooms, in centre of fishing village *(Christine and Neil Townend, Olive and Ray Hebson)*

ONICH NN0263

Nether Lochaber Hotel [A82]: Sensibly priced bar food in small 18th-c hotel's typically unassuming side bar (from outside looks like a shed), friendly landlady and dog, bright cheerful dining room; bedrooms with own bathrooms, good breakfast *(Mr and Mrs M Stratton)*

TORLUNDY NN1477

Factors Inn [A82 NE of Fort William]: Newly refurbished, with good choice of wine, local real ale, friendly staff, small but imaginative choice of good food; children welcome, pleasant surroundings *(Christine and Phil Young)*

KINCARDINESHIRE

CATTERLINE NO8778

☆ *Creel*: Good generous imaginative food esp soups and local fish and seafood in big but cosy lounge with woodburner, plenty of tables, well kept ales such as Caledonian Deuchars IPA and Maclays 70/-, welcoming landladies, friendly cat, small second bar, compact no smoking seaview restaurant (same menu, booking advised); bedrooms, old fishing village, cl Tues *(Brenda and Rob Fincham)*

KIRKCUDBRIGHTSHIRE

AUCHENCAIRN NX8249

☆ *Balcary Bay Hotel* [about 2½ miles off A711]: Beautifully placed hotel with reasonably priced food from soup and open sandwiches to ambitious dishes (huge child's helpings) in civilised but friendly bar and in small conservatory with idyllic views over Solway Firth, prompt friendly service even when busy; tables on terrace and in gardens in peaceful seaside surroundings, comfortable bedrooms *(Richard Tosswill)*

COLVEND NX8555

Clonyard House: Attractive small hotel nr Solway coast, said to have enchanted tree; three bar rooms well used by locals, good value food inc enjoyable specials and puddings here and in conservatory and separate no smoking restaurant, half price for children for most dishes, three-course bargains, Sulwath real ales, decent wines, whiskies and coffee, charming helpful staff; dogs welcome, bedrooms and cosy log-cabin chalets *(Stan and Hazel Allen, Karen Eliot)*

DALRY NX6281

☆ *Clachan* [A713 Castle Douglas—Ayr]: Attractively refurbished yet pleasantly traditional and hospitable, two log fires, good inexpensive wine list, fine selection of malts, enjoyable food using local meat, game and fish, from good sandwiches and toasties up, good service, interesting fishing and shooting frieze; bedrooms with own bathrooms *(Dave Braisted)*

GATEHOUSE OF FLEET NX6056

☆ *Masonic Arms* [Ann St]: Welcoming and comfortable two-room bar, friendly staff, cheerful atmosphere, good choice of enjoyable generous fresh food served quickly even when busy, well kept Courage Directors, good choice of wines and whiskies, newly refurbished dining room with no smoking conservatory; children and dogs welcome, garden, has been cl Mon-Tues in winter *(Stan and Hazel Allen, Mrs Veronica Mellor, JWAC)*

KIPPFORD NX8355

Anchor [off A710 S of Dalbeattie]: Busy down-to-earth waterfront inn in lovely spot overlooking big natural harbour and peaceful hills, coal fire in traditional back bar, no smoking lounge bar, generous usual food from lunchtime sandwiches up, OAP bargain lunches, well kept local Sulwath beers, lots of malt whiskies, upstairs summer dining room; piped music, games room with table football and board games, also juke box, TV and machines; children welcome, tables outside (shouted order numbers), good walks and birdwatching, open all day in summer *(Darly Graton, Graeme Gulibert, LYM, JWAC, Michael Doswell)*

KIRKCUDBRIGHT NX6851

Royal [St Cuthbert St]: mall choice of good food in welcoming bar (dogs allowed here); restaurant *(Stan and Hazel Allen)*

NEW GALLOWAY NX6377

Cross Keys [High St]: 18th-c, with beams and stripped stone, lots of whiskies, main bar with log fire and adjoining dining area, separate clown-theme restaurant with plenty of fresh fish; terrace tables, seven newly refurbished bedrooms with own bathrooms *(anon)*

LANARKSHIRE

GLASGOW NS5861

Clockwork Beer Co [1153 Cathcart Rd]: Comfortable brightly decorated two-level café-bar in unappealing area, microbrewery on view brewing interestingly flavoured beers, also six or more weekly-changing guest beers on tall fount air pressure, good range of continental beers, farm cider, dozens of malt whiskies, speciality fruit schnapps, scottish and other country wines, good conventional wines, unusual fruit juices; good reasonably priced food all day, half helpings for children, good vegetarian choice, friendly service, daily papers, spiral stairs to gallery with TV, piano, games tables, books, toys and no smoking area; jazz Tues, disabled facilities and baby-changing, open all day *(Richard Lewis, Nick Holding, Richard Houghton)*

Drum & Monkey [St Vincent St]: Former bank, with good plasterwork and lots of carved mahogany, great atmosphere esp lunchtime with cheap quickly served filling snacks, friendly helpful staff, decent wines *(Ian Baillie)*

☆ ***Horseshoe*** [Drury St, nr Central Stn]: Classic high-ceilinged pub with enormous island bar, gleaming mahogany and mirrors, snob screens, other high Victorian features and interesting music-hall era memorabilia; friendly jovial staff and atmosphere, well kept Caledonian Deuchars IPA and 80/- and Orkney Red MacGregor, lots of malt whiskies, amazingly cheap food in plainer upstairs bar, no smoking restaurant (where children allowed); games machine, piped music; open all day *(Ian Baillie, Richard Lewis, LYM, Joe Green, Patrick Hancock, Pete Walker)*

Phoenix [West George St/Dundas St, outside Queen St station]: Light and airy two-floor former Hogshead, refurbished, renamed and now entirely no smoking; lots of light wood, three well kept real ales, friendly staff; nice on warm days, as whole front folds open; open all day *(Nick Holding)*

Scotia [Stockwell St]: Genuinely old, given attractive mock Tudor low beams and panelling in 1929, old Glasgow prints, cosy seating around island bar, service friendly even when very busy, low-priced lunchtime food, well kept Caledonian Deuchars IPA; piped music, folk nights; open all day *(Richard Lewis, Nick Holding)*

State [Holland St]: Handsome oak island servery in high-ceilinged bar with marble pillars, good changing choice of well kept real ales, very cheap enjoyable basic lunchtime food from sandwiches up, friendly staff, armchair among other comfortable seats, coal-effect gas fire in big wooden fireplace, lots of old prints and theatrical posters; piped music, games machine, wknd live music *(Nick Holding, Richard Lewis, Patrick Hancock)*

MIDLOTHIAN

BALERNO NT1666

Johnsburn House [Johnsburn Rd]: Lovely old-fashioned beamed bar in former mansion with masterpiece 1911 ceiling by Robert Lorimer; four well kept interesting changing ales, coal fire, panelled dining lounge with good food inc shellfish and game, more formal evening dining rooms; children welcome, open all day wknds, cl Mon *(the Didler)*

CRAMOND NT1876

Cramond Inn [Cramond Glebe Rd (off A90 W of Edinburgh)]: Softly lit smallish rooms nicely refurbished by Sam Smiths in old-fashioned style, wide range of popular usual food inc some local dishes such as haggis and bashed neeps, two good coal and log fires; picturesque Firth of Forth village at mouth of River Almond, delightful views from tables out on grass by car park *(J F M and M West, Michael and Marion Buchanan, LYM, Michael Butler)*

EDINBURGH NT2573

☆ ***Bannermans*** [Cowgate]: Friendly subterranean warren of simple flagstoned rooms with barrel-vaulted ceilings, bare stone walls, wood panelling and pillars at front, medley of interesting old furnishings; well kept Caledonian 80/-, Deuchars IPA and guests in one room, good bottled beer choice, around 30 malts; lively enough during the day, with fruit machine, piped music and perhaps big-screen sports TV; younger crowd in evenings, with DJs, discos, live music and karaoke; children allowed till 6, bar snacks 12-5, open all day till 1am *(LYM, Patrick Hancock)*

☆ ***Bennets*** [Leven St]: Ornate Victorian bar with original glass, mirrors, arcades, panelling and tiles, friendly service, well kept ales inc Belhaven 70/- and 80/- from tall founts, over a hundred malt whiskies, bar snacks and bargain homely lunchtime hot dishes (children allowed in eating area then), second bar with counter salvaged from old ship; can get smoky; open all day, cl Sun *(LYM, the Didler)*

Berts Bar [William St]: Well done up in traditional style, with well kept Caledonian Deuchars IPA and other ales such as two from Arran, good range of tasty straightforward food, long narrow bar, room off with lovely tiled fireplace and rugby shirt collection *(C J Fletcher, Patrick Hancock, R M Corlett)*

Caledonian Ale House [Haymarket Terr, by Stn]: Long convivial simply furnished bare-boards room with good range of food, good service, well kept Caledonian and scottish guest beers such as Arran Gold, imported beers on tap and in bottle; sports TVs *(Andrew York, Michael Butler)*

☆ ***Canny Man's*** [Morningside Rd]: Great bustling atmosphere, all sorts of interesting bric-a-brac, ceiling papered with sheet music, good bar food inc formidable open sandwiches and smorgasbord served with panache, huge choice of whiskies, well kept scottish beer, cheap children's drinks, very friendly staff *(Marianne and Peter Stevens, Dr and Mrs S Donald)*

Cask & Barrel [Broughton St]: Bare-boards traditional drinkers' pub, half a dozen well kept mainly scottish beers inc Caledonian Deuchars IPA from U-shaped bar, helpful service, good value bar food esp stovies Mon-Fri; several sports TVs *(BB, R M Corlett)*

Cloisters [Brougham St]: Friendly and interesting ex-parsonage alehouse mixing church pews and gantry recycled from redundant church with bare boards and lots of brewery mirrors; Caledonian Deuchars and 80/-, half a dozen or so interesting guest beers, friendly atmosphere, food till 3 (4 Sat) inc breakfasts and lunchtime toasties; lavatories down spiral stairs; open all day, folk music Fri-Sat *(the Didler, Eric Larkham, Patrick Hancock)*

Crown & Cushion [Jocks Lodge]: Newly refurbished bar with enjoyable food and wine, good service; live music, karaoke, quiz nights and other lively events *(Debbie Johnston)*
Cumberland [Cumberland St]: Classic unpretentious old-fashioned bar, several well kept ales such as Broughton, Caledonian and guests from England, lots of malt whiskies, busy chatty feel, good service, daily papers, lunchtime food; leather seating, panelling with brewery memorabilia and period advertisements, cosy side room, bright lighting, plain modern back extension; front terrace tables *(BB, R M Corlett)*
☆ *Dome* [St Georges Sq/George St]: Opulent italianate former bank, huge main bar with magnificent dome, elaborate plasterwork and stained-glass; central servery, pillars, lots of greenery, mix of wood and cushioned wicker chairs, Caledonian Deuchars IPA and 80/-, interesting if pricey food from generous sandwiches up, friendly efficient service, smart dining area; smaller and quieter art deco Frasers bar (may be cl some afternoons and evenings early in week) has atmospheric period feel, striking woodwork, unusual lights, red curtains, lots of good period advertisements, piped jazz, daily papers, same beers – also wines and cocktails; complex includes hotel bedrooms *(BB, R T and J C Moggridge)*
Doric [Market St]: Bar with plenty of atmosphere and well kept Caledonian Deuchars IPA and Maclays 70/-, decent wines and good mix of customers; wide range of enjoyable food in relaxing upstairs bistro *(Janet and Peter Race)*
Harbour Inn [Fishmarket Sq, off Newhaven Rd]: Old village pub with two well kept Atlas real ales, bar food; Weds folk night *(R M Corlett)*
☆ *Kenilworth* [Rose St]: Welcoming Edwardian pub with ornate high ceiling, carved woodwork and tiles, huge etched brewery mirrors and windows, red leather seating around tiled wall; central bar with well kept ales such as Caledonian Deuchars IPA, hot drinks inc espresso, good generous bar food lunchtime and evening, quick friendly attentive service, back family room; piped music, discreetly placed games machines, TV, may be live music Sat; space outside in summer, open all day *(the Didler, BB, R T and J C Moggridge, Janet and Peter Race, Michael Butler)*
Malt Shovel [Cockburn St]: Three levels, lots of panelling, soft leather sofas in top room, changing real ales from long serving bar; piped music, TV; open all day *(R M Corlett)*
☆ *Milnes* [Rose St/Hanover St]: Well reworked traditional city pub rambling down to several areas below street level and even in yard; busy old-fashioned bare-boards feel, dark wood furnishings and panelling, cask tables, lots of old photographs and mementoes of poets who used the 'Little Kremlin' room here, wide choice of well kept real ales, open fire, reasonably priced lunches inc various pies charged by size *(C J Fletcher, BB, the Didler, Janet and Peter Race, Edward Mirzoeff)*
Oxford [Young St]: Friendly unspoilt pub with two built-in wall settles in tiny bustling front bar, quieter back room, lino floor, well kept Belhaven and scottish guest ales, old-fashioned snacks; lavatories up a few steps *(C J Fletcher, Joe Green)*
☆ *Sheep Heid* [The Causeway, Duddingston]: Friendly former coaching inn in lovely spot nr King Arthur's Seat, relaxed pubby atmosphere, interesting pictures and fine rounded bar counter in main room, well kept ales inc Caledonian 80/-, daily papers, decent food in bar and restaurant, children allowed; piped music; pretty garden with summer barbecues, skittle alley; open all day, can get crowded *(LYM, T H Little, Malcolm M Stewart)*
Shore Bar [The Shore, Leith]: Cosy little dark-beamed bar with coal fire, candles and huge mirrors, Caledonian Deuchars IPA and 80/-, attentive staff, restaurant with some emphasis on good if pricey fish and seafood (best to book); children welcome, open all day, seats outside and on dock opposite overlooking Water of Leith *(Di and Mike Gillam)*
☆ *Standing Order* [George St]: Grand Wetherspoons conversion of former bank in three elegant Georgian houses, imposing columns, enormous main room with elaborate colourful high ceiling, lots of tables, smaller side booths, other rooms inc two no smoking rooms with floor-to-ceiling bookshelves, comfortable green sofa and chairs, Adam fireplace and portraits; civilised atmosphere, friendly helpful staff, good value food (inc Sun evening), coffee and pastries, real ales inc interesting guest beers from very long counter; wknd live music, extremely popular Sat night; disabled facilities, open all day *(Simon and Amanda Southwell, BB, Joe Green, Patrick Hancock)*
Thomsons [Morrison St]: Sensitively and simply refurbished, with fine woodwork behind bar, interesting glass and bar fittings, eight well kept beers inc some not often seen here, lunchtime food; open all day, cl Sun *(Eric Larkham, C J Fletcher, R M Corlett)*

MUSSELBURGH NT3472

Volunteer Arms [N High St; aka Staggs]: Same family since 1858, unspoilt busy bar, dark panelling, old brewery mirrors, great gantry with ancient casks, Caledonian Deuchars IPA, 60/- and 80/- and wknd guest beers; open all day (not Tues-Weds, cl Sun) *(the Didler, Joe Green)*

NAIRNSHIRE

CAWDOR NH8450

☆ *Cawdor Tavern* [just off B9090]: Elegant panelled lounge, nice features in public bar, good lunchtime bar food from sandwiches to seasonally changing hot food with local influences, more restauranty in evening with some stylish upmarket cooking and partly no smoking restaurant, great choice of malt whiskies, well kept Cairngorm Stag, pleasant attentive staff; pub games, also piped music and TV; children in eating areas, dogs allowed in bar, tables on attractive front terrace, open all day wknds and summer *(Dr D G Twyman, LYM, Mrs J Ekins-Daukes, Mary and David Richards, Sherrie Glass, Paul and Penny Rampton, R T and J C Moggridge, Ken Millar)*

PEEBLESSHIRE

INNERLEITHEN NT3336
Traquair Arms [B709, just off A72 Peebles—Galashiels]: Well worn in bar with warm fire, wide choice of bar food all day, another open fire in spacious dining room (all dining areas are no smoking), three real ales inc one from nearby Traquair House; piped music; children and dogs welcome, bedrooms, open all day *(Kevin Flack, LYM, Christine and Malcolm Ingram, JWAC)*

WEST LINTON NT1451
Gordon Arms [Dolphinton Rd]: Friendly and unpretentious L-shaped bar with a couple of leather chesterfields and more usual pub furniture, log fire, decent quickly served food from massive open sandwiches to sizzling steaks, well kept Caledonian Deuchars IPA and a guest beer such as Atlas Three Sisters, dining room; children welcome, dogs on leads too (biscuits for them), tables outside, bedrooms *(BB)*

PERTHSHIRE

ABERNETHY NO1916
☆ *Cree's* [Main St]: Friendly and comfortable, with open fire in snug, four changing well kept ales, good line-up of whiskies, good home-made pub lunches and evening meals; monthly folk music, handy for Irish Celtic tower with Pictish stone nearby *(Nick Holding)*

BLAIR ATHOLL NN8765
Atholl Arms: Sizeable hotel, with well priced good food all day from sandwiches to interesting dishes and local seafood and meat, helpful friendly staff, full range of Moulin real ales (same ownership) – and the singing gets better as the beers go down; 31 recently refurbished bedrooms, open all day *(Brian and Anita Randall)*

BRIDGE OF CALLY NO1451
Bridge of Cally Hotel [A93 Perth—Braemar]: Snug hotel in lovely wooded riverside spot overlooking bridge, homely bar with sofas, club fender around nice stone fireplace, old photographs, cheap food, friendly service, well kept Belhaven and John Smiths, enjoyable food from bar snacks to restaurant, decent house wines; tables in peaceful garden stepped down to river (private estate covering over two square miles of highland scenery – shooting, fishing etc), bedrooms *(J F M and M West)*

BRIG O' TURK NN5306
☆ *Byre* [A821 Callander—Trossachs, just outside village]: Beautifully placed high-raftered byre conversion with good interesting cooking (sensible-sized rather than over-large helpings), welcoming service; bar could sometimes do with more heating in winter; three bedrooms, good walks, cl Thurs in winter *(LYM, Rosemary and Tom Hall, Nick Holding)*

DUNBLANE NN7801
Tappit Hen [Kirk St]: Across close from cathedral, with interesting changing choice of four or so well kept real ales, both english and scottish; can get noisy and smoky when crowded *(Ian and Sue Wells)*

KENMORE NN7745
☆ *Kenmore Hotel* [A827 W of Aberfeldy]: Civilised small hotel in pretty 18th-c village by Loch Tay, comfortable traditional front lounge with warm log fire and long poem pencilled by Burns himself on the chimney-breast, bar food from sandwiches and baguettes up in light and airy back bar with pool and winter darts (also juke box, TV, fruit machine) and terrace overlooking River Tay, dozens of malt whiskies, polite uniformed staff, restaurant; children and dogs welcome, entertainment Weds and Sun, good bedrooms, open all day *(LYM, Susan and John Douglas, GSB)*

LOCH TUMMEL NN8160
☆ *Loch Tummel Inn* [B8019 4 miles E of Tummel Bridge]: Lochside former coaching inn with great views over water to Schiehallion, lots of local wildlife, big woodburner in cosy recently refurbished partly stripped stone bar, well kept local Moulin ales, good choice of wines and whiskies, good food inc home-smoked salmon, welcoming service, no music or machines; attractive loch-view bedrooms with log fires, even an open fire in one bathroom, good breakfast, fishing free for residents; has been cl winter *(LYM, Jane Holden, Kevin Fagan, Paul and Ursula Randall)*

LOCHEARNHEAD NN5923
Lochearnhead Hotel: Small hotel with lounge bar, terrace and restaurant overlooking Loch Earn, decent food, keg beer; bedrooms *(Paul and Penny Rampton)*

MEIKLEOUR NO1539
☆ *Meikleour Hotel* [A984 W of Coupar Angus]: Two quietly well furnished lounges, one with stripped stone and flagstones, another more chintzy, both with open fires, welcoming landlord, polite helpful staff, three well kept ales such as Fyne Maverick and Inveralmond Pale and Brown, local bottled water, good reasonably priced bar food inc fine sandwiches, back public bar; understated pretty building, picnic-sets in pleasant garden with tall pines and distant Highland view, comfortable bedrooms, good breakfast *(Stamford J Cartwright, GSB, Lee Potter)*

MUTHILL NN8617
☆ *Village Inn* [Drummond St]: Attractively modernised former coaching inn, cosy old-world bar with good choice of well kept real ales and of enjoyable bar food, friendly staff and locals, good traditional restaurant with central log fire, charming setting; spacious bedrooms with own bathrooms, generous breakfast *(P R Morley)*

PERTH NO1223
Capital Asset [Tay St]: Conversion of 1876 Perth Savings Bank HQ over rd from river, appealing family area with booth seating, usual

Wetherspoons menu, pleasant staff, real ales *(Nick Holding)*

☆ *Greyfriars* [South St]: Small, comfortable and very friendly, with pretty décor, good value lunchtime food from baguettes and baked potatoes up, four well kept changing ales inc good Friars Tipple brewed for them by local Inveralmond, friendly staff and core of local regulars; small restaurant upstairs *(R T and J C Moggridge, Richard Houghton, Peter Bell, Nick Holding, Christine and Neil Townend)*

Old Ship [High St]: Compact and neatly refurbished, with well kept Belhaven Sandy Hunters, Orkney Dark Island and a guest such as Greene King Abbot, good coffee and tea, lunchtime soup, baguettes and quiche (plans for upstairs dining room), comfortable banquettes and chairs, landlord's geological samples and his father's interesting World War II merchant seaman's history alongside the usual prints and photographs, handsome preserved former inn sign; no children *(Paul and Ursula Randall)*

PITLOCHRY NN9163

☆ *Killiecrankie Hotel* [Killiecrankie, off A9 N]: Comfortable and splendidly placed country hotel with extensive peaceful grounds and dramatic views, attractive panelled bar (may have piped music), airy conservatory extension, food here and in rather formal restaurant, friendly efficient service, extensive wine list; all no smoking exc bar; children in bar eating area, bedrooms, open all day in summer *(M Whitfield, Sherrie Glass, Hugh A MacLean, LYM, Dr and Mrs R G J Telfer, Joan and Tony Walker)*

TYNDRUM NN3230

Inververy [A82]: Two bars, jazz photographs and instruments, well kept ales such as Caledonian Deuchars IPA, enjoyable sensibly priced food, friendly staff, conservatory with great Trossachs views; bedrooms *(Jenny and Brian Seller)*

RENFREWSHIRE

UPLAWMOOR NS4355

Uplawmoor Hotel [A736 (Neilston Rd) SW of Neilston]: 18th-c coaching inn with comfortable village-inn atmosphere, friendly helpful staff and owners, good well priced bar food using local ingredients, good stock of whiskies, well kept changing real ales inc ones from Barrhead, Houston and Kelburn, separate cocktail bar and attractive restaurant; tables out on terrace, 14 bedrooms, open all day *(Graham and Lynn Mason, Dudley and Moira Cockroft)*

ROSS-SHIRE

CROMARTY NH7867

Royal [Marine Terrace]: Small old-fashioned harbourside hotel under cheerful and helpful newish owners, sleepy sea views across Cromarty Firth to Ben Wyvis, lounge bar, sensibly priced food, games etc in separate locals' bar; children and dogs welcome, comfortable newly refurbished bedrooms, good breakfast, open all day *(LYM, Paul and Ursula Randall, Walter and Susan Rinaldi-Butcher)*

GAIRLOCH NG8174

Creag Mor: Pleasantly placed comfortable family hotel, nicely furnished bar, inviting restaurant, friendly helpful staff; keg beer *(Paul and Ursula Randall)*

ROSEMARKIE NH7357

Plough [High St]: Cosy old-fashioned 17th-c pub with interesting organic Black Isle beers kept well, good range of malt whiskies, log fire in small panelled bar, cheerful helpful staff, restaurant with linking lounge, enjoyable sensibly priced food from wkdy lunchtime standards to interesting blackboard dishes; small garden *(Di and Mike Gillam, Paul and Ursula Randall)*

TORRIDON NG8854

Ben Damph Lodge [A896]: Large bar with mountain maps, ice axes etc, darts, pool table; bedrooms – and only petrol station for ten miles *(Tim Maddison)*

ULLAPOOL NH1294

Morefield Motel [A835 N edge of town]: Cheerful mainly no smoking L-shaped lounge bar with good generous local fish and seafood, well kept changing real ales, decent wines, plenty of malt whiskies; piped music, pool and darts; children welcome, terrace tables, simple bedrooms, open all day *(LYM, Walter and Susan Rinaldi-Butcher)*

ROXBURGHSHIRE

NEWCASTLETON NY4887

Grapes [B6357 N of Canonbie; Douglas Sq]: Recently refurbished small hotel with public bar/games room, friendly staff, enjoyable restaurant food in upstairs gabled and timbered extension; keg beers; bedrooms *(Maurice and Gill McMahon)*

ST BOSWELLS NT5930

☆ *Buccleuch Arms* [A68 just S of Newtown St Boswells]: Civilised sandstone hotel with pleasantly calm retro feel, wide choice of imaginative well prepared bar food (inc Sun), sandwiches all day, well kept Greenmantle, efficient uniformed staff, Georgian-style no smoking plush bar with light oak panelling, restaurant; children welcome, tables in garden behind, bedrooms *(LYM, GSB)*

SELKIRKSHIRE

ETTRICKBRIDGE NT3824

Cross Keys: Good atmosphere, enjoyable pub food, friendly efficient new management; bedrooms *(Bob Ellis)*

MOUNTBENGER NT3324

☆ *Gordon Arms* [A708/B709]: Welcoming oasis in these empty moorlands for over 160 years, friendly public bar with interesting 19th-c letters, poems and photographs, winter fire, well kept Courage Directors, lots of malt whiskies, enjoyable bar food from toasties to local trout and wknd barbecue; beware, the petrol pump outside no longer works; children welcome, bedrooms and cheap bunkhouse accommodation, open all day, in winter cl Sun evening and Mon-Tues *(LYM, Christine and Malcolm Ingram)*

TUSHIELAW NT3018

Tushielaw Inn [Ettrick Valley, B709/B7009 Lockerbie—Selkirk]: Former coaching inn with unpretentiously comfortable little bar attracting an interesting mix of customers, open fire, local prints and photographs, home-made bar food, decent house wines, a good few malt whiskies, darts, cribbage, dominoes, shove-ha'penny and liar dice, partly no smoking dining room; children and dogs welcome, terrace tables, bedrooms, open all day Sat in summer, cl Sun night and in winter all day Mon *(LYM)*

STIRLINGSHIRE

BALMAHA NS4290

Oak Tree: On Loch Lomond's quiet side, named for the 300-year-old oak cut for its bar counter; enterprising choice of enjoyable food, perhaps a real ale such as Caledonian Deuchars IPA, log fire, pleasant tartan décor, restaurant; plenty of tables outside, children welcome, bedrooms, bunkhouse *(Jim and Maggie Cowell, Ian Baillie)*

DRYMEN NS4788

Winnock [The Square]: Big Best Western hotel's modern stripped-stone lounge bar unusual for having well kept real ales; blazing coal or wood fire, friendly staff, good choice of malt whiskies; ceilidh Sun, big garden with picnic-sets, 48 bedrooms *(Mr and Mrs Maurice Thompson, Ian Baillie)*

FALKIRK NS8880

Behind the Wall [opp Grahamston Stn]: Lively bar brewing its own Falkirk 400 and a seasonal beer, several interesting guest beers, belgian bottled beers, efficient friendly service, bare-boards and brick top area, TV in sports-oriented side area, popular lower eating area, daily papers and large conservatory allowing children *(Richard Lewis, Richard Houghton)*

STIRLING NS7993

Portcullis [Castle Wynd]: Former 18th-c school below castle, overlooking town and surroundings, entry through high-walled courtyard, spacious high-ceilinged stripped-stone bar with friendly service, pleasant atmosphere, nice choice of sandwiches and enjoyable hot dishes (not Mon evening), well kept ales such as Isle of Skye Red Cuillin and Orkney Dark Island, good choice of whiskies, log fire; good bedrooms *(Nick Holding)*

SUTHERLAND

GOLSPIE NC8300

Ben Bhraggie [Old Bank Rd (A9)]: Friendly helpful staff, lively public bar, good value food in pleasant conservatory; pipe band practises outside Weds; handy for Dunrobin Castle *(Kay Hodge, Dr D G Twyman)*

KYLESKU NC2333

☆ *Kylesku Hotel* [A894, S side of former ferry crossing]: Useful for this remote NW coast (but in winter open only wknds, just for drinks), rather spartan but pleasant local bar facing the glorious mountain and sea view, with seals and red-throated divers often in sight (tables outside too); friendly helpful staff, short choice of reasonably priced wonderfully fresh local seafood, also sandwiches and soup, three dozen malt whiskies; sea-view restaurant extension, five comfortable and peaceful if basic bedrooms, good breakfast, boatman does good loch trips *(Peter F Marshall, Walter and Susan Rinaldi-Butcher)*

WIGTOWNSHIRE

NEWTON STEWART NX4165

Black Horse [Queen St]: Cheerful inn with substantial well prepared bar food; tables in sheltered courtyard, bedrooms, open all day at least in summer *(BB, Stan and Hazel Allen)*

PORTPATRICK NW9954

Crown [North Crescent]: Waterside hotel, the focal point of this delightful harbourside village, with tables in front (can watch the fishing fleet on Thurs), good atmosphere in rambling old-fashioned bar with cosy nooks and crannies, good bar food all day, over 70 malt whiskies, attractively decorated early 20th-c dining room (half no smoking) opening through quiet no smoking conservatory into sheltered back garden, carefully chosen wine list; TV, fruit machine, piped music; children and dogs welcome, bedrooms, open all day *(Stan and Hazel Allen, LYM, David A Hammond)*

Harbour House [Main St]: Seafront hotel's cheery and airily simple modern bar with well kept changing real ales, good value food, hands-on landlord and friendly efficient staff; dogs welcome, winter Weds quiz night; good-sized simple bedrooms overlooking harbour *(Darly Graton, Graeme Gulibert, David Heath, Stan and Hazel Allen)*

WIGTOWN NX4355

Ploughman [Bank St]: New chef doing enjoyable interesting food, real ales such as Houston, decent wines, pleasant staff, simple café-style surroundings; bedrooms in Wigtown House Hotel, handy for Scotland's book town *(Pete Yearsley, Stan and Hazel Allen)*

SCOTTISH ISLANDS

ARRAN

BRODICK NS0136

Brodick Bar [Alma Rd]: Simple refurbished bar and attached restaurant area tucked away off seafront, remarkably wide choice of enjoyable if not cheap food, friendly attentive service, Isle of Arran and McEwans real ale *(Ken Richards, Caroline and Gavin Callow)*

KILMORY NR9521

Lagg: Relaxing streamside inn dating from 18th c, enjoyable bar food, no smoking area, good value evening meals for residents; bedrooms, hearty breakfast, delightful view *(John Leslie)*

BUTE

PORT BANNATYNE NS0767

Port Royal [Marine Rd]: Stone-built inn looking across sea to Argyll, reworked with bare boards and timbers to evoke pre-revolution Russian tavern (think black and white film versions of *Boris Godunov*), all-day russian food inc good beef stroganoff and chocolate torte, also local fish and seafood, choice of russian vodkas as well as real ales such as Loch Fyne Maverick and Highlander tapped from casks on the bar, Weston's farm cider, good value house wine, cheerful atmosphere and landlord prepared to chat at length about Old Russia, occasional visiting Russian folk musicians; right by beach, deer on golf course behind, open 8am-midnight, four bedrooms *(Dave Braisted)*

ROTHESAY NS0864

Black Bull [W Princes St]: Enjoyable quickly served food, nice no smoking room *(anon)*

HARRIS

TARBERT NB1500

☆ *Harris Hotel* [Scott Rd]: Large hotel with small panelled bar, local Skye and (from Stornoway) Hebridean real ales, lots of malt whiskies, enjoyable bar lunches from good choice of sandwiches through some interesting light dishes to steak, good choice of evening restaurant meals; comfortable bedrooms *(Alistair and Kay Butler, BB)*

ISLAY

PORT CHARLOTTE NR2558

☆ *Port Charlotte Hotel* [Main St]: Doing well under new owners, with roaring log or peat fire and lovely sea loch views in charming smallish traditional bar, lots of wood, piano and charcoal prints, nicely furnished back lounge with books on the area, dozens of rare Islay malts and real ales such as Adnams, Black Sheep and Houston as well as the new local brew, wide choice of bar food lunchtime and evening esp good local seafood, good welcoming service, local art and sailing ship prints in comfortable restaurant, good wines; folk nights; good bedrooms *(A H C Rainier, John Knighton)*

LEWIS

STORNOWAY NB4233

County [Francis St]: Hotel with locally popular public bar, well worth knowing as one of the few local places where you can get decent food (from soup and sandwiches to full meals) and drink on a Sunday; cheerful helpful staff, bedrooms, close to harbour *(BB, Jane Taylor, David Dutton, George Atkinson)*

MULL

CRAIGNURE NM7236

Craignure Inn: Small stone-built 18th-c inn overlooking Sound of Mull, cheerful friendly bar with several dozen malt whiskies, limited range of decent pub food, friendly staff; open all day in summer, good-sized bedrooms with own bathrooms, good breakfast, handy for Oban car ferry *(Mike Dean)*

McGregors Roadhouse: No smoking café/bar by ferry terminal, open all day and useful for food, inc interesting pizzas and pastas to eat in or take away; good value wines, cheerful friendly service *(Paul and Ursula Randall)*

TOBERMORY NM5055

McGochans [Ledaig]: Modernised harbourside bar next to Tobermory Distillery, modestly priced usual food all day, cheerful friendly service, perhaps a guest cask beer (may be regular, when a planned microbrewery outside the town opens); popular with young people – pool, games machines, piped music or juke box, quiz night; picnic-sets under cocktail parasols out on terrace *(Tom McLean, Paul and Ursula Randall)*

☆ *Mishnish* [Main St – the yellow building]: Right on the bay and the first of these now-colourful buildings to paint itself brightly, very friendly with dim lighting and plenty of atmosphere, long lively heavily beamed bar with cask tables, little snugs, lots of old photographs and nautical/fishing bric-a-brac, open woodburner, basic good value food, perhaps a real ale such as Fyne Vital Spark, pool room; piped music may be obtrusive, big-screen TV at the back, quiz, disco and karaoke nights; tables outside, some barbecues, seaview bedrooms, good breakfast *(Tom McLean, Paul and Ursula Randall, Andy and Ali, Dave Braisted)*

SKYE

ARDVASAR NG6303

☆ *Ardvasar Hotel* [A851 at S of island, nr Armadale pier]: Comfortably modernised white stone inn with lovely sea and mountain views, helpful owner and staff, enjoyable home-made food inc good fish (children welcome in eating areas), prompt service, lots of malt whiskies, well kept beer, two bars and games room; TV, piped music; bedrooms, open all day *(Walter and Susan Rinaldi-Butcher, Richard and Karen Holt, LYM)*

CARBOST NG3731

Old Inn [B8009]: Unpretentious bare-boards bar close to Talisker distillery, friendly staff, perhaps a real ale such as Isle of Skye Hebridean Gold, simple furnishings, peat fire, darts, pool, cribbage and dominoes, limited bar food; TV, piped traditional music; children welcome, terrace with fine Loch Harport and Cuillin views (bar's at the back though), sea-view bedrooms in annexe (breakfast for non-residents too if you book the night before), bunkhouse and showers for yachtsmen, open all day, cl afternoons in midwinter *(Tom McLean, LYM, Mike and Kathryn Budd)*

FLODIGARRY NG4671

☆ *Flodigarry Hotel* [nr Staffin]: 1895 turreted former mansion with stunning views of sea and highlands, open all day for wide range of reasonably priced good enterprising food in warm and welcoming family bar (Moorish former billiard room), separate more spartan public bar, elegant and comfortable conservatory, or out on terrace; Theakstons, coffee and afternoon teas, very cheerful helpful staff; some live music, good bedrooms, Flora MacDonald connections – you can stay in her cottage *(Walter and Susan Rinaldi-Butcher)*

ISLE ORNSAY NG7012

Eilean Iarmain [off A851 Broadford—Armadale]: Bar is sideline for smart hotel (charming sea-view restaurant and very comfortable bedrooms), good choice of vatted (blended) malt whiskies inc its own Te Bheag, limited bar food, open fire *(Walter and Susan Rinaldi-Butcher, LYM)*

SLIGACHAN NG4930

☆ *Sligachan Hotel* [A87 Broadford—Portree, junction with A863]: Remote inn with almost a monopoly on the Cuillins, capacious and comfortable, with well laid-out huge modern pine-clad bar (children's play area, games room) separating the original basic climbers' and walkers' bar from the plusher more sedate hotel side; up to half a dozen real ales inc local brews, dozens of malt whiskies on optic, quickly served food all day from home-made cakes with tea or coffee through decent straightforward bar food to fresh local seafood; fine log or coal fire, welcoming staff, good meals in hotel restaurant; very lively some nights, with summer live music and big campsite opp; children welcome, tables outside, bedrooms good value, open all day *(BB, Tom Espley, Roger and Anne Newbury)*

UIG NG3964

Pier Inn [ferry terminal, A87]: Old pub right on pier, decent reasonably priced food in modern café-style eating extension overlooking water, Isle of Skye Red Cuillin ale, efficient service, friendly cream labrador *(Michael and Marion Buchanan, George Atkinson)*

SOUTH UIST

DALIBURGH NF7521

Borrodale: Simply furnished and straightforward, with a warm welcome, helpful service, decent food *(George Atkinson)*

ST KILDA

ST KILDA NF0999

Puff Inn [Village Bay, Hirta]: Britain's most remote pub, in effect a friendly and vibrant working men's club manned by volunteers among the 35 or so people stationed out here (£1 for a month's membership – quite a few people off visiting boats); puffins prominent in the décor, cheap bottled and canned beers and good choice of whiskies, pool room (the wall and ceiling graffiti are all part of the fun); memorable bay view from end of deserted village street, open 5-6, then 9-11 or later *(Tom McLean)*

Real ale may be served from handpumps, electric pumps (not just the on-off switches used for keg beer) or – common in Scotland – tall taps called founts (pronounced 'fonts') where a separate pump pushes the beer up under air pressure. The landlord can adjust the force of the flow – a tight spigot gives the good creamy head that Yorkshire lads like.

Wales

Recent editions have shown several new ventures refreshing the pub scene in Wales, offering a warmly inclusive atmosphere, contemporary food and a good choice of drinks in comfortable and relaxing surroundings – a far cry from the bloke-oriented taverns which tended to dominate just a few years ago. Three interesting new entries here this year confirm the trend: the very smartly reorganised and civilised Harbourmaster overlooking the water in Aberaeron, enjoyable food, stylish up-to-date bar and good bedrooms; the Bryn Tyrch near Capel Curig in Snowdonia, perfectly placed for walkers, with generous rather different food and a distinctive character; and the Griffin at Felinfach, another place updated in contemporary mode, with good enterprising food. Other pubs and inns which are currently giving our readers particular pleasure are the Penhelig Arms in Aberdovey (top-class service, good food, a great wine choice and comfortable bedrooms), the Bear in Crickhowell (a fine old coaching inn with plenty of individuality, good all round), the upmarket Pant-yr-Ochain in Gresford (good food and drink in handsome surroundings), the Queens Head tucked away near Llandudno Junction (consistently good food using local produce, good wines by the glass), the Clytha Arms near Raglan (splendid bar menu, good contemporary restaurant, well kept beer, lovely building), the ancient Groes at Ty'n-y-groes (a good dining pub in a charming spot), and the charming old Nags Head in Usk (a fine all-rounder with very friendly service). Food is a strong point in all of these top pubs, and all are rewarding for a special meal out. It is the Clytha Arms near Raglan which is awarded the title of Wales Dining Pub of the Year. The Lucky Dip section at the end of the chapter has a good many other recommendations – including some 95 pubs new to it this year. We have divided this section into the major areas, Clwyd, Gwent and so forth – more useful divisions for finding pubs than the new unitary authorities. Pubs in this section which have been showing well in recent months, and one or two good more hotelish or restauranty places which we know appeal to pub-lovers, include the West Arms at Llanarmon Dyffryn Ceiriog, White Lion at Llanelian-yn-Rhos, White Horse at Llangynhafal, Sun at Rhewl (Clwyd), Druidstone Hotel near Broad Haven, Dyffryn Arms at Cwm Gwaun, Georges in Haverfordwest, St Brides Hotel in Little Haven, Trewern Arms at Nevern, Plantagenet House in Tenby, Wolfe at Wolfs Castle (Dyfed), Raglan Arms at Llandenny, Greyhound at Llantrisant Fawr, Bell at Skenfrith, Fountain at Trelleck Grange (Gwent), Ty Gwyn in Betws-y-Coed, Lord Newborough at Dolgarrog, Ty Coch at Porth Dinllaen (Gwynedd), Prince of Wales at Kenfig (Mid Glamorgan), Llew Coch at Dinas Mawddwy, Crown and Triangle both in Rhayader (Powys), and Bear in Cowbridge (South Glamorgan). Also in South Glamorgan, the Blue Anchor at East Aberthaw, a splendid main entry until now, should reopen shortly after recent fire damage repairs. Pub drinks tend to cost rather less in Wales than in England (and interestingly, much less than in Scotland). The main independent welsh brewer is Brains; others you are likely to come across are Felinfoel, Tomos Watkins, Plassey and Breconshire, and there are a dozen or so other local brewers.

ABERAERON SN4562 Map 6

Harbourmaster

Harbour Lane

Painted a striking blue, and much changed since it last appeared in the *Guide* many years ago, this refurbished hotel restaurant is well placed by the water's edge, and in fine weather you can sit on the harbour wall and look across moored yachts and boats to a neat row of colourfully painted houses opposite – bedrooms have the same charming view. It's a splendidly civilised alternative to the area's true pubs. Buzzing with locals and visitors, and modern rustic in style, the wine bar (one reader found it a bit smoky in here) has dark wood panelling, sofas, and chunky blocks of wood as low tables or stools on dark wood floors. Tapas dishes served in here might include grilled mackerel or grilled aubergines with pesto (£5.50), grilled crevettes in chilli butter (£7.50) and mixed tapas (£9.50); well kept Brains SA and Buckleys Best on handpump, and a good wine list. The owners are chatty and welcoming, and service is good. In the restaurant, new light wood furniture looks stylishly modern on light wood floors against light and dark blue walls. Here, the imaginative menu might include lemon sole with sweet potato chips and red pepper coulis (£14.50), chargrilled welsh black beef fillet (£15.50), and blueberry and brazil nut brûlée with hazelnut ice-cream (£4) – a place for a special occasion. *(Recommended by John Hale, V Brogden, Pamela and Merlyn Horswell, Ron and Sheila Corbett)*

Free house ~ Licensees Glyn and Menna Heulyn ~ Real ale ~ Bar food (12-2, 6.30-9) ~ Restaurant ~ (01545) 570755 ~ Children welcome ~ Open 11-11; 12-3 Sun; closed Sun evening, Mon lunchtime ~ Bedrooms: £55S(£85B)/£95B

ABERCYCH SN2441 Map 6

Nags Head

Off B4332 Cenarth—Boncath

Very popular locally, the dimly lit beamed and flagstoned bar at this traditional ivy-covered pub attracts a lively mix of ages and accents. There's a comfortable old sofa in front of the big fireplace, clocks showing the time around the world, stripped wood tables, a piano, photographs and postcards of locals, and hundreds of bottles of beer displayed around the brick and stone walls – look out for the big stuffed rat. A plainer small room leads down to a couple of big dining areas (one of which is no smoking), and there's another little room behind the bar. Besides the good value beer brewed on the premises (named Old Emrys after one of the regulars), they serve a couple of well kept guests from brewers such as Greene King and Wadworths; piped music and TV. Popular bar food served in huge helpings includes soup (£3.25), breaded brie wedges with home-made pear and ginger chutney (£4.25), vegetable chilli (£6.95), battered cod or lasagne (£7.25), steak and kidney pudding (£7.50), and daily specials such as thai green vegetable curry (£8.95) and rosemary and redcurrant lamb steak (£9.95); they do smaller helpings of some dishes (from £4.95) and children's meals. Service is pleasant and efficient. Lit by fairy lights in the evening, the pub is tucked away in a little village and beautifully set next to a river. Tables under cocktail parasols across the quiet road look over the water, and there are nicely arranged benches, and a children's play area; they sometimes have barbecues out here in summer. *(Recommended by R Michael Richards, Alec and Barbara Jones, Colin Moore, Gene and Kitty Rankin)*

Own brew ~ Licensee Steven Jamieson ~ Real ale ~ Bar food (12-2, 6-9) ~ Restaurant ~ (01239) 841200 ~ Children welcome ~ Dogs allowed in bar ~ Open 11.30-3, 6-11.30; 12-10.30 Sun; closed Mon lunchtime

Post Office address codings confusingly give the impression that some pubs are in Gwent or Powys when they're really in Gloucestershire or Shropshire (which is where we list them).

ABERDOVEY SN6296 Map 6

Penhelig Arms

Opposite Penhelig railway station

'Made us wish we were staying here rather than further down the coast' is the sort of thing readers say once they've experienced this fabulous 18th-c hotel. In summer you can sit out by the harbour wall or on your bedroom balcony (some rooms) and soak up picturesque views across the Dyfi estuary, while good log fires in the small original beamed bar make it especially cosy in winter. Service is first-class, and there's a good welcoming atmosphere. Delivered daily by the local fish merchant, a highlight here is the fresh fish. There are usually around ten beautifully cooked dishes to choose from such as grilled cornish mullet fillets with thai noodle salad (£4.95), grilled plaice with lime and fresh herbs (£10.50), grilled tuna with olive salad and aïoli (£10.75) and fish stew (£13.95). As well as lunchtime sandwiches (from £2.95), other interesting dishes from the frequently changing menu (which they serve in the bar and restaurant) might include cream of onion soup (£2.95), duck and orange salad with lime and ginger (£4.95), warm goats cheese with roasted butternut squash or faggots with potato, swede and carrot mash (£7.95), fried pork with pancetta, olives and sun-dried tomato pesto (£10.50) and puddings such as banoffi pie or caramelised lemon and lime tart (£3.50). You do need to book. An excellent thoughtfully annotated wine list includes around 40 half bottles and 30 wines by the glass. Also well kept Brains SA and Buckleys Best on handpump, two dozen malt whiskies, fruit and peppermint teas, and various coffees; dominoes. The separate restaurant is no smoking. Bedrooms are very comfortable, and the breakfasts varied and good. *(Recommended by Dr and Mrs P Truelove, John and Brenda Bensted, S D and J L Cooke, DHV, V Brogden, E G Parish, Revd D Glover, Peter Meister, David Glynne-Jones, Gerry and Rosemary Dobson, E M Probyn, Prof Keith and Mrs Jane Barber)*

Free house ~ Licensees Robert and Sally Hughes ~ Real ale ~ Bar food ~ Restaurant ~ (01654) 767215 ~ Children in eating area of bar and restaurant ~ Dogs allowed in bar ~ Open 11-4, 5-11; 11-11 Sat; 12-10.30 Sun ~ Bedrooms: £49S/£78B

ABERGORLECH SN5833 Map 6

Black Lion

B4310 (a pretty road roughly NE of Carmarthen)

Well worth a detour, this welcoming little 17th-c coaching inn is delightfully placed in the beautiful Cothi Valley (lots of good walks nearby), with the Brechfa Forest around it. The plain but comfortably cosy stripped-stone bar is traditionally furnished with plain oak tables and chairs, high-backed black settles facing each other across the flagstones by the gas-effect log fire, and has horsebrasses and copper pans on the black beams, old jugs on shelves and fresh flowers and paintings by a local artist. The dining extension (candlelit at night) has french windows opening on to a newly landscaped enclosed garden. Reasonably priced bar food includes sandwiches (from £2.75), fried trout or steak, mushroom and ale pie (£6.95), local salmon steak (£8.95) and 8oz sirloin steak (£9.25), with puddings such as sherry trifle and home-made bread and butter pudding (£3.50); on Sunday you can also get roasts (£5.95), and in summer they do afternoon teas. Brains SA and Buckleys Best are well kept alongside a guest such as Youngs on handpump; daily papers, sensibly placed darts, chess, dominoes, draughts, and piped music. There are lovely views from picnic-sets, wooden seats and benches across the quiet road, and the garden slopes down towards the River Cothi where there's a Roman triple-arched bridge. More reports please. *(Recommended by Richard Siebert, Norman and June Williams)*

Free house ~ Licensees Michelle and Guy Richardson ~ Real ale ~ Bar food (12-2, 7-8.30) ~ Restaurant ~ (01558) 685271 ~ Children in eating area of bar and restaurant ~ Dogs allowed in bar ~ Open 12-3, 7-11; 12-11(10 Sun) Sat; closed Mon exc bank hols

BEAUMARIS SH6076 Map 6

Olde Bulls Head ♀ 🛏

Castle Street

The old-fashioned rambling low-beamed bar at this big 15th-c inn is genuinely pubby, with just the right atmosphere for a drink and a chat – they don't serve food in here. A rare 17th-c brass water clock, a bloodthirsty crew of cutlasses and even an oak ducking stool are tucked among the snug alcoves, and are interesting reminders of the town's past. Also lots of copper and china jugs, comfortable low-seated settles, leather-cushioned window seats, and a good log fire; piped music. Quite a contrast, the popular partly no smoking brasserie behind is lively and contemporary with a menu that includes enjoyable dishes such as home-made soup (£3.20), sandwiches (from £4.20), smoked tuna carpaccio, soused fennel salad and gremolata (£5.95), nut risotto with roast mediterranean vegetables (£6.50), cassoulet (£6.95), grilled hake with pea purée with pancetta and oyster mushroom and cream sauce (£7.25), grilled 10oz rib-eye steak with bacon and endive mash and chasseur sauce (£12.50), and puddings such as rhubarb, raspberry and meringue sundae or ginger and lemon syrup sponge (from £3.95); vegetable side dishes (from £1.50). They don't take bookings in here, but do for the smart no smoking restaurant upstairs. As well as an extensive wine list you'll find ten wines by the glass, Bass and Worthington Best, which are well kept alongside a guest such as Coors Hancocks HB on handpump, and freshly squeezed orange juice. The entrance to the pretty courtyard is closed by what is said to be the biggest simple-hinged door in Britain. Named after characters in Dickens's novels (both Charles Dickens and Samuel Johnson came here), the bedrooms are very well equipped. *(Recommended by David Crook, Richard Harris, Alison Hayes, Pete Hanlon, John and Tania Wood, Revd D Glover, Gordon Prince; also in the* Good Hotel Guide*)*

Free house ~ Licensee David Robertson ~ Real ale ~ Bar food (12-2, 6-9) ~ Restaurant ~ (01248) 810329 ~ Children in brasserie ~ Open 11-11; 12-10.30 Sun ~ Bedrooms: /£95B

BERRIEW SJ1801 Map 6

Lion 🛏

B4390; village signposted off A483 Welshpool—Newtown

Since the last edition of the *Guide* very friendly new licensees have taken over this characterful black and white country inn which is in a pretty village not far from Powis Castle. The black-beamed public bar is thoroughly old-fashioned, with a big woodburning stove in its inglenook, sturdy little plush-cushioned settles and copper-topped tables on its lino. The separate carpeted lounge bar, also beamed, has paintings and old brass between the timbers above its red and gold wall banquettes, and an open fire in one stripped stone wall. Served in the bar or the restaurant, home-made food might include sandwiches (from £3.25, baguettes from £4.50), soup (£3.25), ploughman's or crevettes in garlic butter (£5.25), steak, mushroom and ale pie or mushroom stroganoff (£8.25), salmon fillet with dill and hollandaise sauce (£8.95), delicious duck breast in red wine, orange and ginger casserole (£10.95), and 8oz fillet steak (£13.95), with home-made puddings (£3.95); roasts only on Sunday. Friendly, efficient staff serve Banks's Original and Marstons Old Empire and Pedigree on handpump, and they have decent house wines; piped music, TV, cribbage and dominoes. There's a lively modern sculpture gallery on the far side of the bridge over the River Rhiew rapids. *(Recommended by Paul and Margaret Baker, Rodney and Norma Stubington, DC, Di and Mike Gillam, John Hale, David Glynne-Jones, Mr and Mrs John Taylor, Gerry and Rosemary Dobson, Pamela and Merlyn Horswell, Simon Lawson, Geoffrey and Penny Hughes)*

Union Pub Company ~ Lease Marilyn and Patrick O'Keefe ~ Real ale ~ Bar food (not Sun evening) ~ Restaurant ~ (01686) 640452 ~ Children in eating area of bar and restaurant ~ Dogs welcome ~ Open 12-3, 6-11; 12-11 Sat; 12-3, 7-10.30 Sun ~ Bedrooms: £55B/£70B

It is illegal for bar staff to smoke while handling your drink.

CAIO SN6739 Map 6

Brunant Arms

Village signposted off A482 Llanwrda—Lampeter

Five frequently changing well kept real ales on handpump at this unpretentious village pub represent terrific changing choice (as shown by the proliferation of pumpclips), coming from brewers such as Bass, Cottage, Enville, Oakham and Wye Valley. They also have decent house wines and 25cl mini-bottles, and two farm ciders. Bar food is served in the smallish blue-carpeted lounge bar, where locals gather for a chatty drink around at the back on the right, and the atmosphere is convivial and relaxed. High-backed winged settles form booths around some tables, while others have studded leather chairs and dining chairs. A good log fire burns in the stone fireplace under a big mirror (and an array of china on the mantelpiece, including some interesting egg cups), house plants line the window, and shelves on the orange-painted walls hold a few books – and more bagatelle boards than we have ever seen in one place. The separate stripped stone public bar on the left has darts, board games, pool, fruit machine, juke box, shove-ha'penny, table skittles, cribbage, dominoes and a TV. The lounge leads out into a small Perspex-roofed verandah with three old-fashioned garden benches, and a lower terrace has picnic-sets. Judging by the amount of use the long hitching rail gets, this must be on a pony-trekking route. As there are so few tables, it may be best to book, and it's not a place for a hurried meal, as everything is cooked fresh to order: sandwiches (from £2.95), ploughman's (from £4.45), sausage and mash or chick peas and vegetable couscous (£5.95), battered cod (£6.25), and daily specials such as ciabatta with ratatouille and camembert or honey chilli prawns on naan bread (£3.95), tagliatelle with creamy roast pepper and tomato sauce (£6.95), chicken with apricots and almonds (£8.25), pork hock in cider apple gravy (£8.75) and puddings such as banana and mandarin pancakes with sticky toffee sauce or spotted dick (£3.25); they also do a roast on Sunday, and breakfasts. Service is friendly and efficient. The big church above is the resting place of welsh wizard Dr John Harries, and the Dolaucothi gold mines are only a mile up the road; there are good walks all around. *(Recommended by M and D Toms, Hilda and Jim Childs, Anne Morris, Neil and Anita Christopher, Richard Siebert, Gene and Kitty Rankin)*

Free house ~ Licensees Justin and Jane Jacobi ~ Real ale ~ Bar food (12-2, 6.30-9) ~ (01558) 650483 ~ Children welcome ~ Dogs allowed in bar ~ Open 12-3, 6-11; 12-11(10.30 Sun) Sat ~ Bedrooms: £25B/£45B

CAPEL CURIG SH7258 Map 6

Bryn Tyrch

A5 W of village

In the heart of Snowdonia, this remote but welcoming country inn is popular with walkers and climbers. Big picture windows run the length of one wall, with views across the road to picnic-sets on a floodlit patch of grass by a stream running down to a couple of lakes, and the Snowdon Horseshoe in the distance. Comfortably relaxed, the bar has several easy chairs round low tables, some by a coal fire with magazines and outdoor equipment catalogues piled to one side, and a pool table in the plainer hikers' bar. Wholesome food, with an emphasis on vegetarian and vegan dishes, is generously served to meet the healthy appetite of anyone participating in the local outdoor attractions – very much what this place is about. With more vegetarian dishes than you'd find on most menus, bar food includes soup (£3.80), yellow pepper, onion and tomato salad or chorizo with strips of mixed peppers and grated caerphilly cheese (£4.25), courgette and feta filo pie or sun-dried tomatoes, spinach and pesto with tagliatelle (£8.95), grilled trout with creamy chestnut and bacon white wine sauce or poached chicken with stilton sauce (£10.50) and puddings such as apple crumble or mocha meringue sundae (from £4.25). You can also pop in here for a cup of one of the many coffee blends or Twinings teas that are listed on a blackboard, and served with a piece of vegan cake. Well kept Bass, Flowers IPA and Whitbreads Castle Eden on handpump, and quite a few malt whiskies; shove-ha'penny and dominoes. There are tables on a steep little garden at the side. More reports on the refurbished bedrooms (some have views, £10 cleaning charge for dogs) please. *(Recommended by David and Higgs Wood, John and Tania Wood, John and Joan Nash, Richard and Anne Ansell, KC)*

Free house ~ Licensee Rita Davis ~ Real ale ~ Bar food ~ Restaurant ~ (01690) 720223 ~ Children welcome ~ Dogs allowed in bedrooms ~ Open 12-11(10.30 Sun); closed Mon, Tues Nov-Feb (but open school and bank hols) ~ Bedrooms: £39(£45B)/£52(£59B)

CAREW SN0403 Map 6

Carew Inn

A4075, just off A477

Seats in the prettily flowered little front garden of this cheerful old inn look down to the river, where a tidal watermill is open for afternoon summer visits. Also pleasant, the back garden overlooks the imposing ruins of Carew Castle, beyond a remarkable 9th-c celtic cross nearby. There's a wheelchair ramp and outdoor heating in summer, and it's safely enclosed for children to play, with a wendy house, climbing frame, slide and other toys. Inside, the pub is homely and unpretentious, there's a welcoming bustling atmosphere, and the landlady is chatty and attentive. The little panelled public bar and comfortable lounge have old-fashioned settles, scrubbed pine furniture, interesting prints and decorative china hanging from the beams. The no smoking upstairs dining room has an elegant china cabinet, a mirror over the tiled fireplace and sturdy chairs around well spaced tables. Well kept real ales include Brains Reverend James and Worthington and perhaps a third beer during the summer on handpump; sensibly placed darts, dominoes, cribbage and piped music. Generously served by friendly staff, reasonably priced bar food includes soup (£2.95), chicken liver and tarragon pâté (£3.95), goats cheese and red pepper quiche (£6.95), thai red chicken curry (£7.50), creamy seafood pasta (£7.95), steak and kidney pie (£8.50), fillet steak with mushroom and marsala sauce (£14.95), with puddings such as chocolate pudding or cheesecake of the day (from £3.25). *(Recommended by the Didler, Jane and Graham Rooth, P Price, Mr and Mrs A H Young, Sheila and Robert Robinson, Brian and Jacky Wilson)*

Free house ~ Licensee Mandy Hinchliffe ~ Real ale ~ Bar food (12-2.30, 5.30-9.30) ~ Restaurant ~ (01646) 651267 ~ Children in eating area of bar and restaurant ~ Dogs allowed in bar ~ Live music Thurs evening and summer Sun evening ~ Open 11-11; 12-10.30 Sun; 11-2.30, 4.30-11wkdys in winter

COLWYN BAY SH8478 Map 6

Pen-y-Bryn 🍷

B5113 Llanwrst Road, on S outskirts; when you see the pub turn off into Wentworth Avenue for its car park

Big windows have unbeatable views over the sea (there's a telescope too) and surrounding landscape, and let plenty of light into the spacious open plan interior of this modern pub. Working around the three long sides of the bar counter, the mix of seating and well spaced tables, oriental rugs on pale stripped boards, shelves of books, welcoming coal fires, profusion of pictures, big pot plants, careful lighting and dark green school radiators are all typical of the pubs in this small chain. Besides well kept Flowers Original, Thwaites and up to three guests such as Butcombe Gold, Phoenix White Monk and Timothy Taylor Landlord on handpump, they have well chosen good value wines including just over a dozen by the glass, proper coffee and freshly squeezed orange juice; cribbage, dominoes, faint piped music. Friendly efficient staff serve bar food which might include courgette and rosemary soup (£3.45), sandwiches (from £3.75), crispy duck and vegetable salad with black bean dressing (£5.45), steak sandwich (£5.95), ploughman's (£6.45), pork-and-leek sausages with cheddar cheese mash (£7.95), roast vegetable and chick pea curry (£8.25), fried salmon fillet on curried sweet potato risotto (£8.95), braised shoulder of lamb with garlic and rosemary roast potatoes, root vegetable purée and redcurrant and rosemary sauce (£11.75), and puddings such as steamed syrup sponge pudding or white chocolate and coconut tart (from £3.95). Outside there are sturdy tables and chairs on a side terrace and a lower one, by a lawn with picnic-sets. *(Recommended by W K Wood, Joan E Hilditch, E G Parish, Gwyn and Anne Wake, Paul Boot)*

Brunning & Price ~ Managers Graham Arathoon and Graham Price ~ Real ale ~ Bar food (12-9.30(9 Sun)) ~ Restaurant ~ (01492) 533360 ~ Children allowed till 7.30pm ~ Open 11.30-11; 12-10.30 Sun

CRESSWELL QUAY SN0406 Map 6

Cresselly Arms

Village signposted from A4075

Nothing changes from one year to the next at this traditional creeper-covered local, and although the pub seems an interesting throwback to some period early last century, it's very much alive with a thriving atmosphere. There's a relaxed and jaunty air in the two simple comfortably unchanging communicating rooms, which have red and black floor tiles, built-in wall benches, kitchen chairs and plain tables, an open fire in one room, a working Aga in the other, and a high beam-and-plank ceiling hung with lots of pictorial china. A third red-carpeted room is more conventionally furnished, with red-cushioned mate's chairs around neat tables. Well kept Worthington BB and a winter guest beer are tapped straight from the cask into glass jugs by the landlord, whose presence is a key ingredient of the atmosphere; fruit machine. The pub faces the tidal creek of the Cresswell River, with seats out by the water, and if the tides are right, you can get here by boat. *(Recommended by the Didler, Pete Baker)*

Free house ~ Licensees Maurice and Janet Cole ~ Real ale ~ No credit cards ~ (01646) 651210 ~ Open 12-3, 5-11; 11-11 Sat; 12-3, 6(7 winter)-10.30 Sun

CRICKHOWELL SO2118 Map 6

Bear ★

Brecon Road; A40

This charming old coaching inn is a delight from the moment you catch your first glimpse of its aged flower bedecked white frontage, which seems to sit so comfortably in its corner of this nice old town. It's well run and spotlessly kept, with a calmly civilised atmosphere in the comfortably decorated, heavily beamed lounge, which has fresh flowers on tables, lots of little plush-seated bentwood armchairs and handsome cushioned antique settles, and a window seat looking down on the market square. Up by the great roaring log fire, a big sofa and leather easy chairs are spread among rugs on the oak parquet floor. Other good antiques include a fine oak dresser filled with pewter and brass, a longcase clock, and interesting prints. Well kept Bass, Brains Rev James, Hancocks HB and Greene King Old Speckled Hen on handpump, as well as malt whiskies, vintage and late-bottled ports, unusual wines (with about a dozen by the glass) and liqueurs (with some hops tucked in among the bottles) and local apple juice; the family bar is partly no smoking. Friendly helpful staff serve bar food which includes sandwiches (from £2.50), soup (£3.50), chicken liver parfait with cumberland sauce and toasted brioche (£5.25), faggots with chips and peas (£6.95), lasagne, leek and ham pie or sausage and mash (£7.95), aubergine and gruyère torte with tomato and olive sauce (£8.95), braised hock of welsh lamb (£13.95) and puddings such as dark chocolate and orange mousse or sticky toffee pudding (£4.25); the more elaborate restaurant menu is pricier, and their Sunday lunch is very popular. You can eat in the garden in summer; disabled lavatories. *(Recommended by Alec and Barbara Jones, A S and M E Marriott, David Carr, Pamela and Merlyn Horswell, Dr T E Hothersall, Chris Smith, Graham Holden, Julie Lee, Keith Barker, Colette Annesley-Gamester, Jonathan Harding, David Jeffreys, JWAC, R Michael Richards, Mark and Ruth Brock, Patrick Hancock, Andrew Shore, Maria Williams, Ann and Colin Hunt, Steve Cawthray, Joyce and Maurice Cottrell, John Urquhart, Susie Symes, David and Nina Pugsley, Dr and Mrs*

C W Thomas, Alan Strong, Nigel Howard, Terry and Linda Moseley, Alan and Paula McCully, Charles Cooper, J C Poley, Norman and Sarah Keeping, Julia and Richard Tredgett, Brian and Jacky Wilson)

Free house ~ Licensee Judy Hindmarsh ~ Real ale ~ Bar food (12-2, 6-10) ~ Restaurant ~ (01873) 810408 ~ Children in eating area of bar and family room ~ Dogs welcome ~ Open 11-3, 6-11; 12-3, 7-11 Sun ~ Bedrooms: £57(£57S)(£77B)/£75(£75S)(£95B)

Nantyffin Cider Mill 🍷

1½ miles NW, by junction A40/A479

Smartly civilised, this very restauranty pink-washed place is decorated in brasserie style, with warm grey stonework, fresh and dried flowers, good solid comfortable tables and chairs and a woodburner in a fine broad fireplace. The counter at one end of the main open-plan area might have Fullers London Pride and Wadworths Henrys IPA on handpump, as well as thoughtfully chosen New World wines (a few by the glass or half bottle), Pimms in summer, hot punch and mulled wine in winter and home-made lemonade. A raftered barn with a big cider press has been converted into quite a striking no smoking restaurant. From a changing menu, not cheap restauranty food could include soup (£3.50), crispy moroccan spiced lamb and spinach filo parcels (£5.25), vegetarian risotto cake (£10.95), confit of lamb with rosemary garlic sauce (£11.95), loin of monkfish with braised chick peas, chorizo and confit red onions and saffron (£14.50), grilled rib of beef with roast tomatoes and mushrooms (£14.95), vegetable side dishes (£2.50), and puddings such as poached pears in red wine or treacle tart (£6.50). The River Usk is on the other side of a fairly busy road, and there are charming views from the tables out on the lawn above the pub's neat car park; a ramp makes disabled access easy; more reports please. *(Recommended by David Carr, Bernard Stradling, Terry and Linda Moseley)*

Free house ~ Licensees Glyn Bridgeman and Sean Gerrard ~ Real ale ~ Bar food (12-2.30, 6.30-9.30) ~ Restaurant ~ (01873) 810775 ~ Children welcome ~ Dogs allowed in bar ~ Open 12-2.30, 6.30-10; closed Sun evening, Mon except six weeks in summer

FELINFACH SO0933 Map 6

Griffin 🍷

A470 NE of Brecon

From the main road you can't miss this restauranty pub, with its bright orangey-red external paintwork. Inside, the back bar is quite pubby in an up-to-date way, with three leather sofas around a low table on pitted quarry tiles, by a high slate hearth with a log fire, and behind them mixed stripped seats around scrubbed kitchen tables on bare boards, and a bright blue-and-ochre colour scheme. It has a few modern prints, and some nice photoprints of a livestock market by Victoria Upton. An upright piano stands against one wall – the acoustics are pretty lively, with so much bare flooring and uncurtained windows. The two smallish no smoking front dining rooms, linking through to the back bar, are attractive: on the left, mixed dining chairs around mainly stripped tables on flagstones, and white-painted rough stone walls, with a cream-coloured Aga cooker in a big stripped-stone embrasure; on the right, similar furniture on bare boards, with big modern prints on terracotta walls, and good dark curtains. Table settings are classy, service is charming, and the good food (they are proud of never sourcing anything from further away than 15 miles) might include lunchtime dishes such as roast butternut soup (£4.50), open sandwiches (£5.95), sausage and mash (£7.95) and braised leg of rabbit with haricot beams and chorizo stew (£9.95). A pricier evening menu includes dishes such as roasted tomato soup (£4.50), wild mushroom tagliatelle (£6.50), pea and mushroom risotto (£13.95), calves liver and mash (£14.50) and rump of lamb or john dory with ragoût of wild asparagus and mushrooms (£15.95). They have a good choice of wines by the glass (in three sizes), and Tomos Watkin OSB and one of their seasonal beers on handpump. There may be piped Radio Wales in the bar. We have not yet heard from any readers who have stayed here, but would expect

…od news about their white bedrooms. Wheelchair access is good, and there are …ables outside. *(Recommended by Pamela and Merlyn Horswell, Rodney and Norma Stubington, Leo Horton, John Holroyd)*

Free house ~ Licensee Charles Inken ~ Real ale ~ Bar food (lunchtime only) ~ Restaurant ~ (01874) 620111 ~ Children welcome ~ Dogs welcome ~ Open 12-3.30, 6-11; 12-11(10.30 Sun) Sat; closed Mon lunchtime ~ Bedrooms: £67.50B/£92.50B

GRESFORD SJ3555 Map 6

Pant-yr-Ochain

Off A483 on N edge of Wrexham: at roundabout take A5156 (A534) towards Nantwich, then first left towards the Flash

An absolute delight to visit and doing very well at the moment, this gently upmarket place is set in its own attractive grounds with lovely trees and a small lake, and has the feel of a country house. Thoughtfully refurbished, the light and airy rooms are stylishly decorated, with a wide range of interesting prints and bric-a-brac on walls and on shelves, and a good mix of individually chosen country furnishings, including comfortable seats for relaxing as well as more upright ones for eating. There are good open fires, and the big dining area is set out as a library, with floor to ceiling bookshelves. Excellent food, from a well balanced daily changing menu, might typically include mushroom and spinach soup (£3.75), imaginative combination sandwiches (from £3.95), an interesting pâté such as shropshire blue and caramelised apple with red onion marmalade and crostini (£4.95), excellent chicken caesar salad (£5.75), smoked haddock and salmon fishcakes (£7.75), a burger such as minted lamb topped with feta cheese (£8.25), grilled sardines on ciabatta with roasted lemon fennel and gazpacho or thai green chicken and shi-itake mushroom curry with lemon grass rice (£9.95), braised boneless blade of pork with mustard lentils and cider sauce (£11.25), and puddings such as warmed waffle with chocolate fudge sauce and rum and raisin ice-cream or treacle tart with butterscotch sauce (£4.45); arrive early if you want a seat in the conservatory. Well kept real ales might include Flowers Original, Thwaites, Timothy Taylors Landlord, locally brewed Plassey Bitter and Weetwood Old Dog, and they have a good range of decent wines (strong on up-front New World ones), and more than 60 malt whiskies. Service is friendly and professional; two rooms are no smoking and one reader tells us there is good disabled access. *(Recommended by Roger and Anne Newbury, Mrs P J Carroll, Chris Flynn, Wendy Jones, MLR, Oliver and Sue Rowell, Maurice and Della Andrew, Revd D Glover, John Hendy, Brenda and Rob Fincham, Paul Boot)*

Brunning & Price ~ Licensee Lynsey Prole ~ Real ale ~ Bar food (12-9.30(9 Sun)) ~ (01978) 853525 ~ Children welcome away from bar till 6pm ~ Open 12-11(10.30 Sun)

HAY-ON-WYE SO2342 Map 6

Kilverts

Bullring

It's the enjoyably relaxed atmosphere that makes this friendly informal hotel such a pleasure for locals and visitors alike. Calm and understated, with no piped music or machines, the airy high-beamed bar has some stripped stone walls, *Vanity Fair* caricatures, a couple of standing timbers, candles on well spaced mixed old and new tables, and a pleasant variety of seating. You can watch the world go by from tables in a small front flagstoned courtyard (with outdoor heaters) or while away the hours by the fountain in a pretty terraced back garden. Enjoyable bar food from a sensibly balanced menu is served in generous helpings, and includes lunchtime filled baguettes or sandwiches (from £3.10), home-made soup (£3.95), about a dozen pizzas (£5.20–£6.95), thai-style fishcakes (£5.50), spaghetti napoli (£6.75), beer battered haddock and chips (£8.50), beef and ale pie (£9.95), grilled bass with fennel, lime and tarragon glaze (£10.25), spinach and mushroom roulade filled with mint and cream cheese on mediterranean vegetables (£10.95) and 12oz rump steak (£12.95); welcoming service; no smoking restaurant. They've an extensive wine list with about a dozen by the glass, as well as three real ales such as Brains Rev James, Hancocks HB and Wye Valley Butty Bach on handpump, farm cider and good coffees; piped music. There's a £5.50 cleaning charge for dogs in the comfortable bedrooms. *(Recommended by Steve and Liz Tilley, Brian Brooks, Ann and Colin Hunt, Andy and Jill Kassube, George Atkinson, Martin Grosberg, Sue Demont, Tim Barrow, Mike Pugh, Peter and Jean Hoare)*

Free house ~ Licensee Colin Thomson ~ Real ale ~ Bar food (12-2, 7-9.30) ~ Restaurant ~ (01497) 821042 ~ Children in eating area of bar and restaurant ~ Dogs welcome ~ Open 9-11(10.30 Sun); may close earlier in winter ~ Bedrooms: £50S/£70S(£80B)

Old Black Lion

Lion Street

The food at this civilised, well run and welcoming inn is good (if not cheap), and the restaurant menu can be eaten in the bar too. Examples given are a selection from the bar and restaurant menus: lunchtime sandwiches (£4.95), blue cheese and white onion soup with garlic croûtons (£4.95), smoked halibut, salmon and trout with citrus dressing (£6.50), beef and ale pie (£9.95), moroccan lamb with date and apricot compote and couscous (£10.50), grilled plaice with herb butter (£10.95), wild mushroom and leek crêpes with cheese sauce (£11.50), sirloin steak with brandy and peppercorn sauce (£14), duck breast with honey and five spice glaze on braised red cabbage with apples and sultanas (£16.50), fried venison on parsnip purée with blackberry and gin sauce (£17.50), puddings such as sticky toffee pudding or ginger crème brûlée (£4.25) and a cheese board (£5.50); Sunday lunch (£8); no smoking restaurant. With plenty of clues to its venerable age, the building dates back in part to the 13th c and is near the site of the former town wall – the gate in this part used to be called the Lion Gate. Peaceful and spotlessly kept, and with a snugly enveloping atmosphere, the comfortable low-beamed bar has crimson and yellow walls, nice old pine tables, and an original fireplace. As well as Old Black Lion (a good beer brewed for them by Wye Valley) on handpump, they serve a changing Wye Valley real ale, and good value wines; service is very friendly and enthusiastic. There are tables out behind on a sheltered terrace. Comfortably creaky bedrooms make this an atmospheric place to stay, and they can arrange pony trekking and golf, and trout and salmon fishing on the Wye. *(Recommended by Bruce Bird, Pam and David Bailey, Ann and Colin Hunt, Michael and Ann Cole, Andy and Jill Kassube, David Field, Mike and Mary Carter, Keith Symons, Kerry Law, Simon Smith, Sue Demont, Tim Barrow)*

Free house ~ Licensee Vanessa King ~ Real ale ~ Bar food (12-2.30, 6.30-9.30) ~ Restaurant ~ (01497) 820841 ~ Children over 5 away from main bar ~ Open 11-11; 12-10.30 Sun; closed two wks in Jan ~ Bedrooms: £50S(£42.50B)/£80B

LITTLE HAVEN SM8512 Map 6

Swan

Point Road; village signposted off B4341 W of Haverfordwest

Quaint and unchanging, this little pub, nestling in one of the prettiest coastal villages in west Wales, is a nice place to come for a quiet drink. Seats in the bay window, or on the terrace outside, give good views across a broad and sandy hill-sheltered cove to the sea, and it's right on the coastal path (though no dirty boots). Two communicating rooms have quite a cosily intimate feel, comfortable high-backed settles and windsor chairs, a winter open fire in one and a cast-iron woodburning stove in the other, and old prints on walls that are partly stripped back to the original stonework; look out for the huge ashtray. Well kept Brains Rev James, Worthington Best and a guest such as Hook Norton Old Hooky on handpump, as well as a good range of wines and whiskies from the heavily panelled bar counter; the landlord is friendly. A short choice of tasty lunchtime bar food includes sandwiches (from £2.50), home-made cawl – traditional welsh lamb and vegetable soup – (£4.25; £4.75 with cheese), garlic mushrooms (£4.95), crab bake (£5.25), chicken korma (£6.50) and smoked salmon or local crab salad (£8.50), with puddings (from £2.75); you need to book if you want to eat in the Victorian-style restaurant. Parking can be a problem in summer, when you may have to use the public car park at the other end of the village. One reader felt disabled access wasn't possible. More reports please. *(Recommended by Mike Pugh, John and Enid Morris, M C and S Jeanes, Mr and Mrs A H Young)*

Celtic Inns ~ Tenants Glyn and Beryl Davies ~ Real ale ~ Bar food (lunchtime only) ~ Restaurant (Thurs-Sat evenings, also Weds evening in summer) ~ No credit cards ~ (01437) 781256 ~ Open 11.30-3, 6(7 in winter)-11; 12-3, 7-10.30 Sun

LLANBERIS SH6655 Map 6

Pen-y-Gwryd £

Nant Gwynant; at junction of A498 and A4086, ie across mountains from Llanberis – OS Sheet 115 map reference 660558

Unique and interesting, this hospitable old inn, high in the mountains of Snowdonia, has been in the same family for years, and a great favourite with mountaineers for generations. The team that first climbed Everest in 1953 used it as a training base, leaving their fading signatures scrawled on the ceiling, and even today, it doubles up as a mountain rescue post. One snug little room in the homely slate-floored log cabin bar has built-in wall benches and sturdy country chairs to let you gaze at the surrounding mountain landscapes – like precipitous Moel-siabod beyond the lake opposite. A smaller room has a worthy collection of illustrious boots from famous climbs, and a cosy panelled smoke room has more fascinating climbing mementoes and equipment. There's a sociable atmosphere, and the landlady is chattily helpful. Alongside well kept Bass, they've home-made lemonade in summer, mulled wine in winter, and sherry from their own solera in Puerto Santa Maria. Simple home-made lunchtime bar food (you order it from a hatch) from a short menu could include soup (£2.50), rollmop herring with gherkins and capers or filled rolls (£3.50), ploughman's (£5) and welsh lamb and vegetable casserole (£5.50). Comfortable but basic bedrooms, excellent traditional breakfasts, dogs £2 a night. *(Recommended by Prof and Mrs Tony Palmer, Dr Emma Disley, Gill and Tony Morriss, Tim Maddison, R Michael Richards, Peter Meister; also in the* Good Hotel Guide*)*

Free house ~ Licensee Jane Pullee ~ Real ale ~ Bar food (lunchtime only) ~ Restaurant (evening) ~ No credit cards ~ (01286) 870211 ~ Children in eating area of bar and restaurant ~ Dogs allowed in bar and bedrooms ~ Open 11-11(10.30 Sun); closed Nov-Dec, Mon-Thurs Jan-Feb ~ Bedrooms: £28/£56(£68B)

LLANDDAROG SN5016 Map 6

White Hart

Just off A48 E of Carmarthen, via B4310; aka Yr Hydd Gwyn

This lovely old thatched pub is packed with bric-a-brac, lots of 17th-c welsh oak carving, a tall grandfather clock, stained-glass, a collection of hats and riding boots, china, brass and copper on walls and dark beams, antique prints and even a suit of armour. The heavily carved fireside settles by the huge crackling log fire are the best place to sit. There are steps down to the high-raftered dining room, also interestingly furnished; table skittles, shove-ha'penny, cribbage, dominoes and piped music. The five tasty Coles beers on handpump are brewed here using water from their own bore-hole. Generous helpings of food from the servery include sandwiches (from £3), toasties and baked potatoes (from £3.25), pizza (from £4.95), faggots, peas and gravy (£5.25), ploughman's (from £5.50) and home-made pie (£6.50). The restaurant menu (which you can also eat from in the bar) includes smoked mackerel (£3.50), salmon in spanish sauce or chicken chasseur (£11.95), roast duck (£13.50), steaks (from £12) and puddings (£3.50); 5% surcharge on credit cards. There are picnic-sets out on a terrace, and they can put a ramp in place for disabled access. Look out for Homer the great dane. *(Recommended by James Morrell, Mike Pugh, Michael and Alison Sandy, Emma Kingdon, Dr and Mrs A K Clarke, Don and Thelma Anderson, David and Nina Pugsley, P Price)*

Own brew ~ Licensees Marcus and Cain Coles ~ Real ale ~ Bar food (11.30-2, 6.30-10(9.30 Sun)) ~ Restaurant ~ (01267) 275395 ~ Children in eating area of bar and restaurant ~ Open 11.30-3, 6.30-11; 12-3, 7-10.30 Sun

LLANDEILO SN6222 Map 6

Castle

Rhosmaen Street (A483)

Considerably neatened up since the last edition of the *Guide*, the emphasis at this pleasant town pub has shifted marginally from the beers to a more all-round approach. There's still a good range of seven real ales including Greene King Abbot and Old Speckled Hen, Tomos Watkins Best and OSB and Worthingtons alongside a couple of guests such as Hancocks and a Tomos Watkins seasonal beer, and bar food is still pubby but it's now fresher and home-cooked where possible: sandwiches (from £2.50), provençale vegetable tart (£4.95), battered cod and chips, lasagne or steak and stout pie (£6.95), a couple of daily specials might be curry (£6.95) and lamb shank (£8.95), and puddings such as lemon brûlée and chocolate tart (£3.95). If there's any space left, the little tiled and partly green-painted back bar is perhaps the most interesting room, with a big fireplace and friendly locals sat in pews around the edge chatting. Freshly painted green, the front bar now has stripped bare-board floors, and a red painted side area has lots of earthenware pots and pews; courtyard area. *(Recommended by Anne Morris, Chris and Martin Taylor, R T and J C Moggridge, the Didler, Dr and Mrs A K Clarke, Mike Pugh)*

Enterprise ~ Lease Nigel and Kay Carpanini ~ Real ale ~ Bar food (12-3, 6-9.30(8 Sun); not winter Sun evening) ~ Restaurant ~ (01558) 823446 ~ Children in restaurant and family room ~ Dogs allowed in bar ~ Live music alt Fri, Sat evenings in the courtyard and subject to weather ~ Open 11.30-11; 12-10.30 Sun

LLANDUDNO JUNCTION SH8180 Map 6

Queens Head

Glanwydden; heading towards Llandudno on B5115 from Colwyn Bay, turn left into Llanrhos Road at roundabout as you enter the Penrhyn Bay speed limit; Glanwydden is signposted as the first left turn off this

This modest-looking pub, tucked away in an isolated village, has very good food that is a real treat. They use lots of fresh local produce and the menu changes every week. Well presented dishes could include soup (£3.75, tasty fish soup £4.25), open sandwiches (from £5.95), gravadlax (£6.50), mediterranean prawns in garlic butter or a generous seafood platter (£7.50; £16.50 main), home-made lasagne or jamaican chicken curry (£8.95), roast pork or chicken breast wrapped in smoked bacon with bread sauce and gravy (£8.25), and roast duck breast with mashed potatoes and black cherry and cinnamon sauce (£10.95); efficient service; no smoking eating area. Despite the emphasis on dining, locals do pop in for a drink, and you'll find well kept Ind Coope Burton, Tetleys and a weekly guest beer on handpump, as well as decent wines (including some unusual ones and eight by the glass), 20 malt whiskies and good coffee. The spaciously comfortable modern lounge bar – partly divided by a white wall of broad arches – has brown plush wall banquettes and windsor chairs around neat black tables, and there's a little public bar; unobtrusive piped music. There are some tables out by the car park. You can now rent the stone cottage across the road. *(Recommended by KC, Mr and Mrs Colin Roberts, John Lunt, Trevor and Sylvia Millum, Mike and Wendy Proctor, John and Tania Wood, Revd D Glover, Yvonne and Mike Meadley)*

Free house ~ Licensees Robert and Sally Cureton ~ Real ale ~ Bar food (12-2.15, 6-9; 12-9 Sun) ~ Restaurant ~ (01492) 546570 ~ Children over 7 in restaurant and eating area of bar ~ Open 12-3, 6-11(10.30 winter Mon); 12-10.30 Sun

Waterside pubs are listed at the back of the book.

LLANGEDWYN SJ1924 Map 6

Green Inn

B4396 ¾ m E of Llangedwyn

This neatly kept country dining pub is nicely laid out with various snug alcoves, nooks and crannies, a good mix of furnishings including oak settles and attractively patterned fabrics, and a blazing log fire in winter. Besides well kept Tetleys, they've three or four changing guests such as Charles Wells Bombardier, Greene King Abbot and Hook Norton Old Hooky as well as somerset farm cider in summer and a decent wine list; darts, dominoes, cribbage, fruit machine and piped music. Bar food includes soup (£2.75), lunchtime sandwiches (£3.25), ploughman's (£4.25), steak and kidney pie, breaded plaice or chilli con carne (£6.95), and daily specials such as plaice with parsley butter (£8.45), duck breast with orange and rosemary glaze (£9.95) and 20oz rump steak (£14.95); Sunday roast (£6.95). A no smoking restaurant upstairs opens in the evening. As it's on a well used scenic run from the Midlands to the coast, the pub can get busy in summer, when the attractive garden over the road comes into its own, with lots of picnic-sets down towards the river. The pub has some fishing available to customers – day permit £4. *(Recommended by Derek and Sylvia Stephenson, Mr and Mrs A Swainson, David and Judith Stewart, John and Tania Wood, Dave Braisted, Ian Phillips)*

Free house ~ Licensees Emma Richards and Scott Currie ~ Real ale ~ Bar food (12-2, 6.30-9) ~ Restaurant ~ (01691) 828234 ~ Children in eating area of bar and restaurant ~ Dogs allowed in bar ~ Open 12-3, 6-11; 11-11 Sat; 12-10.30 Sun

LLANGOLLEN SJ2142 Map 6

Corn Mill ♀

Dee Lane, off Castle Street (A539) just S of bridge

Well worth a visit just to see the building, this is a remarkable conversion of a big watermill, handsomely refitted inside with several uncluttered levels of new pale pine flooring on stout beams, a striking open stairway with gleaming timber and tensioned steel rails, mainly stripped stone walls, and quite a bit of the old mill machinery, pulleys and so forth. A great waterwheel turns between the building and external decking cantilevered over the River Dee, rushing broadly over rocks below. This terrace, running along the building and beyond, is a big plus, with lots of good teak tables and chairs, and a superb view over the river to the steam railway station and the embankment of the Llangollen Canal (you may see horse-drawn trip barges). Inside, there is a lively bustling chatty feel, with quick service from plenty of neat young staff, good-sized dining tables, big rugs, nicely chosen pictures (many to do with water) and lots of pot plants; the loft and conservatory are no smoking. Good changing food could include sandwiches (from £3.95), excellent ploughman's (£6.75), salmon and chive fishcakes with capers and lemon (£7.45), bacon chop with herb mashed potatoes and parsley sauce (£7.95), southern-style fried chicken with baked potato, corn and a blue cheese dip (£9.25), grilled local trout with lemon and herb butter (£9.75), and braised lamb shoulder with herb gravy (£11.95), with puddings such as bara brith bread and butter pudding with apricot sauce (from £4.50). One of the two serving bars, away from the water, has a much more local feel, with pews on dark slate flagstones, daily papers, and regulars on the bar stools; piped music. Well kept Boddingtons, Plassey and a couple of guests such as Bass, Oakham JHB and Timothy Taylor Landlord on handpump, and a good wine choice that includes pudding wines. *(Recommended by Mike Schofield, MLR, Mike and Mary Carter, Pamela and Merlyn Horswell)*

Brunning & Price ~ Manager Andrew Barker ~ Real ale ~ Bar food ~ (01978) 869555 ~ Open 12-11(10.30 Sun)

Ring the bull is an ancient pub game – you try to lob a ring on a piece of string over a hook (occasionally a bull's horn) on wall or ceiling.

LLWYNDAFYDD SN3755 Map 6

Crown

Coming S from Newquay on A486, both the first two right turns lead eventually to the village; the side roads N from A487 between junctions with B4321 and A486 also come within signpost distance; OS Sheet 145 map reference 371555

Bustling with happy customers, and quite often every stool taken in the evening, the friendly, partly stripped-stone bar at this attractive white painted 18th-c pub has red plush button-back banquettes around its copper-topped tables, and a big woodburning stove; piped music and winter darts. Tasty bar food (there may be quite a wait at peak times) includes soup (£3.55), garlic mushrooms (£4.25), pizzas (from £6.75), spinach, mushroom and cheese lasagne, grilled local rainbow trout, chicken curry or steak and kidney pie (£7.95), steaks (from £12.55), with daily specials such as duck breast with honey and apricot sauce (£9.85), glazed lamb shank with garlic mash (£9.75), fried black bream with soy sauce (£10.35), and puddings such as blackcurrant sundae or fresh cream gateau (from £4.45). The friendly landlady serves well kept Flowers IPA and Original from handpump, along with one or two guests such as Enville and Greene King Abbot, a decent range of wines and malt whiskies, and a good choice of liqueur coffees. A lane by the side of the pub leads down to a cove with caves by National Trust cliffs – well worth a walk if you're here in time for sunset; there are picnic-sets in a pretty tree-sheltered garden with carefully chosen shrubs and flowers, and on a covered terrace above a small pond, from where you can keep an eye on children playing in the good play area. More reports please. *(Recommended by Liz and Tony Colman, Brian Mills, Gene and Kitty Rankin, Mr and Mrs W E Cross)*

Free house ~ Licensee Ian Green ~ Real ale ~ Bar food (12-2, 6-9) ~ Restaurant ~ (01545) 560396 ~ Children in family room ~ Open 12-3, 6-11; 12-4, 6-10.30 Sun; closed Sun evening mid Nov-Sun before Easter

MOLD SJ2465 Map 6

Glasfryn

Raikes Lane, Sychdyn (the old main road N to Northop, now bypassed by and just off the A5119)

The lively buzz of evening theatre-goers (Theatr Clwyd is just over the road), happy families during the day, and the cheery bustle of enthusiastic young staff brightens up the spacious rooms of this bistro-style dining pub (a former farmhouse). There's plenty on offer here, from interesting well prepared food through to a great choice of drinks. Besides a good variety of around a dozen wines by the glass and around 100 whiskies, they've well kept Flowers, Plassey Bitter, Thwaites, Timothy Taylors Landlord and a couple of guests such as Greene King IPA and Shepherd Neame Spitfire on handpump. An inviting range of interesting reasonably priced bar food could include carrot and coriander soup (£3.50), sandwiches (from £4.25), minted lamb samosa with mango chutney (£4.35), ploughman's (£6.95), linguini with asparagus, peas, pesto and feta (£7.75), pork-and-leek sausage with vegetable mash and onion gravy (£7.95), grilled sardines on tomato and rocket salad with paprika butter (£9.25) and braised lamb rump with bubble and squeak mash with mustard and onion gravy (£11.50), with puddings such as chocolate jaffa orange torte with chocolate ice-cream (from £4.25). Open plan rooms have both spaciousness and nice quiet corners, with an informal and attractive mix of country furnishings, and interesting decorations; about half the pub is no smoking. Outside, sturdy timber tables on a big terrace give superb views to the Clwydian Hills – idyllic on a warm summer's evening. *(Recommended by Chris Flynn, Wendy Jones, John Lunt, Maurice and Della Andrew, Oliver and Sue Rowell, John Wooll, Brenda and Rob Fincham)*

Brunning & Price ~ Manager James Meakin ~ Real ale ~ Bar food (12-9.30(9 Sun)) ~ (01352) 750500 ~ Children welcome away from bar till 6pm ~ Open 11.30-11; 12-10.30 Sun

MONKNASH SS9270 Map 6

Plough & Harrow

Signposted Marcross, Broughton off B4265 St Brides Major—Llantwit Major – turn left at end of Water Street; OS Sheet 170 map reference 920706

Dating back to the early 12th c, this evocative country pub was originally part of a monastic grange. It's solidly built with massively thick stone walls. The dimly lit unspoilt but welcoming main bar (which used to be the scriptures room and mortuary) seems hardly changed over the last 70 years. There's a log fire in a huge fireplace with a side bread oven large enough to feed a village, as well as a woodburning stove with polished copper hot water pipes. The heavily black-beamed ceiling has ancient ham hooks, an intriguing arched doorway to the back, and a comfortably informal mix of furnishings that includes three fine stripped pine settles on the broad flagstones. The room on the left has lots of Wick rugby club memorabilia (it's their club room); daily papers, darts, dominoes, cribbage and piped music. Around seven well kept real ales on handpump or tapped from the cask might include Shepherd Neame Spitfire, Tomos Watkin Crw Haf, Worthingtons and Wye Valley Hereford Pale along with a couple of frequently changing guest beers from thoughtfully sourced brewers such as Breconshire or Cottage. Bar food could include soup (£2.95), filled baguettes (from £4.95), three-cheese ploughman's or spaghetti bolognese (£5.95), beef cooked in Guinness or liver, bacon and mash (£6.95), cod and chips (£7.95) and puddings such as rhubarb crumble (£3.95). Staff are friendly, and it can get crowded at weekends, when it's popular with families. In a peaceful spot not far from the coast near Nash Point, it's an enjoyable walk from here down to the sea, where you can pick up a fine stretch of the coastal path. There are picnic-sets in the front garden, which has a boules pitch, and they hold barbecues out here in summer; more reports please.
(Recommended by David Jeffreys, David and Nina Pugsley, Anthony Lee)

Free house ~ Licensee Lynne Moffat ~ Real ale ~ Bar food (12-2, 6-9) ~ Restaurant ~ (01656) 890209 ~ Children in eating area of bar ~ Dogs welcome ~ Live music Sun evening and some Sats ~ Open 11-11; 12-10.30 Sun

MONTGOMERY SO2296 Map 6

Brickys

Chirbury Road (B4386)

Don't be discouraged by the undistinguished exterior of this town pub. Inside is cosy with beams and standing timbers, red walls, a shiny red tiled floor throughout, cushioned pews by a woodburning stove in a big inglenook, and one or two bar stools by the little corner serving counter. The food here is the special thing. A short but interesting choice, using carefully chosen ingredients cooked and served attractively on big plates, might include home-made soup (£3.80), ricotta and sage tartlets with red onion and redcurrant chutney (£4.95), fishcakes on stir-fried leeks (£10.25), spinach, chicken and crème fraîche wrapped in filo pastry (£10.85), fried gressingham duck on raw shredded vegetables with hoi sin sauce (£13.95), and daily specials such as tomato, mozzarella and basil balsamic dressing (£4.95), poached smoked haddock fillets with butter and spring onions (£9.99) and braised lamb in red wine with tomatoes and peppers (£11.45); no smoking restaurant. Well kept Brains Rev James and Youngs on handpump, and a short but interesting choice of wines, including good ones by the glass, various whiskies and organic cider; piped music. Service is friendly and quietly helpful. There are picnic-sets out in front. *(Recommended by Brian and Jacky Wilson)*

Free house ~ Licensee Beverly Legge ~ Real ale ~ Bar food ~ Restaurant ~ (01686) 668177 ~ Children in restaurant ~ Open 12-2.30(3 Sun), 6.30-11.30; cl wkday lunchtimes winter; closed Sun evening, Mon-Tues

If you stay overnight in an inn or hotel, they are allowed to serve you an alcoholic drink at any hour of the day or night.

OLD RADNOR SO2559 Map 6

Harp 🛏

Village signposted off A44 Kington—New Radnor in Walton

Run by a friendly couple, this fabulous old pub has bundles of character and gets surprisingly busy given its peaceful village location. The village itself consists almost entirely of just the inn and its neighbour, a 15th-c turreted church – perhaps explaining why they don't open weekday lunchtimes. In the evening and at weekends chatty locals gather in the old-fashioned brownstone public bar, which has high-backed settles, an antique reader's chair and other elderly chairs around a log fire; cribbage, dominoes. The snug slate-floored lounge has a handsome curved antique settle and another log fire in a fine inglenook, and there are lots of local books and guides for residents. You'll find two well kept real ales on handpump from brewers such as Bishops Castle and Timothy Taylor; friendly, helpful service. Fairly simple bar food might include soup (£3.25), filled baguettes (from £4.95), ploughman's, home-made faggots or pork-and-herb sausages and mash (£5.95), lasagne or pasta and stilton bake (£6.50), cod and chips (£7.95), chicken wrapped in bacon with stilton sauce (£8.95) and rump steak (£10.50), with puddings such as home-made sticky toffee pudding (£3.25); on busy evenings, they sometimes don't serve food at all, so best to book. Outside, there's plenty of seating – either under the big sycamore tree, or on the side grass, where there's a play area, and there are lovely views over the Marches. The church is worth a look for its interesting early organ screen, and there are good nearby walks. *(Recommended by Nick and Meriel Cox, the Didler, Alan and Jill Bull, Helen Pickering, James Owen, MLR, Mr and Mrs M B Dalling, Peter Cole)*

Free house ~ Licensees Erfyl Protheroe and Heather Price ~ Real ale ~ Bar food (12-2, 7-9) ~ Restaurant ~ (01544) 350655 ~ Children in eating area of bar and restaurant ~ Dogs allowed in bar ~ Open 6-11; 12-3, 6-11(10.30 Sun) Sat; 7pm evening opening winter; closed lunchtimes and Mon ~ Bedrooms: £35(£35S)/£55(£58B)

OVERTON BRIDGE SJ3542 Map 6

Cross Foxes 🍴 🍷

A539 W of Overton, near Erbistock

The River Dee sweeps past below this substantial 18th-c coaching inn, and the end room on the left (with big windows all round its yellow walls) and picnic-sets out on a crazy-paved terrace give a great view of it. A grassy bank spreads down from the terrace, with a swing and slide – all safely fenced off from the water. The building is leased from Marstons (Wolverhampton & Dudley) by Brunning & Price, and has several linked but distinct areas, each with its own character, and all having framed pictures in abundance. Throughout is a good mix of individual tables in varying sizes, with big candles at night, grey carpet here, bare boards there, oriental rugs on quarry tiles elsewhere, mixed dining chairs in some places and built-in padded banquettes in others. They have good log fires, and the lighting is carefully thought out. As well as sandwiches (from £4.75) and ploughman's (£6.95), a big blackboard by the entrance shows a wide choice of consistently good food such as soup (£3.75), grilled black pudding with apple mash and red wine gravy (£4.75), smoked salmon roulade (£4.95), goats cheese and red onion tartlet with rocket and parmesan salad (£6.75), beef and wild mushroom suet pudding (£9.50), braised half a shoulder of lamb (£11.95), trout and prawn risotto with saffron and lemon (£12.50) and puddings such as mango and passion fruit cheesecake with mango coulis or cherry bakewell with raspberry sauce (£4.50). They have well kept Banks's, Mansfield Riding, Marstons Pedigree and a guest such as Caledonian Deuchars IPA on handpump, a good changing choice of wines by the glass, and good coffee. Service is kind and efficient; more reports please. *(Recommended by Mrs P J Carroll, Paul and Margaret Baker)*

Brunning & Price ~ Manager Paul Fletcher ~ Real ale ~ Bar food (12-9.30(9 Sun)) ~ Restaurant ~ (01978) 780380 ~ Children in restaurant ~ Dogs allowed in bar ~ Open 12-11(10.30 Sun)

PEMBROKE FERRY SM9603 Map 6

Ferry Inn

Nestled below A477 toll bridge, N of Pembroke

A new landlady since the last edition of the *Guide* has opened up the interior of this welcoming old sailors' haunt by knocking the bar and restaurant into one. There's quite a nautical feel, with lots of seafaring pictures and memorabilia, a lovely open fire and good views over the water. Some comfortable seating areas are now painted a cosy red. Bass, Felinfoel Double Dragon and a guest such as Coors Hancocks HB are well kept on handpump; fruit machine, board games and unobtrusive piped music. As well as a handful of fish specials such as plaice (£10), local black sea bream (£12) and dover sole (£18), other generously served bar food (from a shortish menu) could include chicken liver pâté (£4.25), gammon and pineapple (£7.50), curry (£7.25), mushroom, cranberry and brie wellington (£8.75), seafood pasta (£8.95), stuffed fillet of lamb (£9.95) and puddings such as belgian chocolate tart or gooseberry and apple treacle crunch (£3.50). The pub is in an appealing spot overlooking the Cleddau estuary, and in warm weather it's nice to sit out on the terrace by the water. Note that the all day opening hours are limited to the summer holiday. More reports please. *(Recommended by George Atkinson, Charles and Pauline Stride, Keith Barker, Don and Thelma Anderson)*

Free house ~ Licensee Jane Surtees ~ Real ale ~ Bar food (12-9.45(9 Sun); 12-2, 7-9.45 (9 Sun) in winter) ~ (01646) 682947 ~ Children in eating area of bar ~ Open 11.30-11; 12-10.30 Sun; 11.30-3, 6.30(7 Mon)-11; 12-2.30, 7-10.30 Sun winter

PONTYPOOL ST2998 Map 6

Open Hearth ¶

The Wern, Griffithstown; Griffithstown signposted off A4051 S – opposite main works entrance turn up hill, then first right

As well as Caledonian Deuchars IPA and Greene King Abbott, they may serve a surprising range of up to seven weekly changing guest beers from brewers such as Banks, Fullers, Elgood, Hook Norton, Highgate, Orkney and Wyre Piddle (with even more during their biennial beer festivals) at this pleasant local. They also have lots of malt whiskies and a decent choice of wines. The comfortably modernised smallish lounge bar has a turkey carpet and big stone fireplace, and a back bar. Seats outside overlook a shallow stretch of the Monmouthshire & Brecon Canal (the ducks out here like being fed), and there's an adventure play area. An astonishing choice of bar food means you can have your meat or fish cooked in quite a variety of ways. The menu includes soup (£2.15), welsh rarebit (£2.99), breaded camembert (£4.50), ploughman's (£4.50), steak and ale pie (£5.95), chicken and vegetable risotto (£6.50), fried lambs liver with onions, garlic, sherry and soy sauce (£6.90), garlic, lime and coriander chicken (£7.25), trout baked in garlic butter (£7.90), pork with honey and mustard (£8.50) and sirloin steak topped with stilton and flamed in whisky (£11.50); downstairs no smoking restaurant. TV, cribbage. *(Recommended by Terry and Linda Moseley, Emma Kingdon, Mike Pugh, Gwyneth and Salvo Spadaro-Dutturi)*

Enterprise ~ Lease Emma Bennett ~ Real ale ~ Bar food (12-2, 7-10) ~ Restaurant ~ (01495) 763752 ~ Children in eating area of bar and restaurant ~ Dogs allowed in bar ~ Open 11.30-11; 12-10.30 Sun

PORTHGAIN SM8132 Map 6

Sloop

Off A487 St Davids—Fishguard

This white-painted old pub is hugely popular in summer when you can sit at tables on the terrace overlooking the harbour (with outdoor heaters for cooler weather), and there are good nearby coastal walks. Inside, the walls of the plank-ceilinged bar are hung with quite a bit of interesting seafaring memorabilia from lobster pots and fishing nets, through ships' clocks and lanterns, to relics from wrecks along this stretch of the coast. Down a step, another room leads round to a decent-sized eating area, with simple wooden chairs and tables, cushioned wall seats, and a freezer with ice-creams for children; well kept Brains Rev James, Felinfoel Double Dragon and Worthingtons, and perhaps a changing guest beer such as Bass on handpump during busy months. Rather than having a number for food service, many of the tables are named after a wrecked ship. Breakfast is served first thing (£6.50); at other times dishes could include soup (£3.50), lunchtime baguettes (from £3), moules marinière (£4.95), fried cod (£6.50), home-made steak, kidney and mushroom pie (£7.45), crab salad (£10.90), steak (£13.50), and daily specials such as roast cod stuffed with salmon mousse with white wine and dijon cream sauce (£16.50); the lower dining area is no smoking. There's a well segregated games room (used mainly by children) which has a fruit machine, juke box, winter darts, pool, dominoes, Scrabble; TV for important sports events. It can get very busy here in summer, when they may extend food serving times. *(Recommended by Ian and Deborah Carrington, Mike Pugh, George Atkinson, John and Enid Morris, R Michael Richards, B and F A Hannam, Mrs Julie Thomas, R E Greenhalgh, Tony and Betty Parker)*

Free house ~ Licensee Matthew Blakiston ~ Real ale ~ Bar food (9.30-11.30, 12-2.30, 6-9.30) ~ (01348) 831449 ~ Children in games room, eating area of bar and restaurant ~ Open 9.30-11; 9.30-10.30 Sun

PRESTEIGNE SO3265 Map 6

Radnorshire Arms

High Street; B4355 N of centre

This fine black beamed Elizabethan house was the country retreat of Christopher Hatton, one of Elizabeth I's favourite courtiers. Past renovations have revealed secret passages and priest's holes, with one priest's diary showing he was walled up here for two years. Although it's now part of a small chain of hotels, it's full of individuality and historical charm – a great place for morning coffee or afternoon tea. Discreet well worn-in modern furnishings blend in well with venerable dark oak panelling, latticed windows, and elegantly moulded black oak beams (some decorated with horsebrasses); piped music. You'll find well kept Cains, Ruddles County and Shepherd Neame Spitfire on handpump, and they've several malt whiskies, and local wine. Friendly staff serve dishes from a bar menu which includes soup (from £3.55), sandwiches (£3.95), cold platter (£5.95), carvery (£7.45), 12oz T-bone (£11.95) and toffee apple crumble (£3.25). There are lots of tables on an elegant sheltered flower-bordered lawn, which used to be a bowling green. *(Recommended by Pam and David Bailey, J R Ringrose)*

Free house ~ Licensee Philip Smart ~ Real ale ~ Bar food ~ (01544) 267406 ~ Children in eating area of bar and restaurant ~ Dogs allowed in bedrooms ~ Open 11-3, 5-11; 11-11 Sat; 12-10.30 Sun ~ Bedrooms: £62.50S/£98.50B

RAGLAN SO3608 Map 6

Clytha Arms

Clytha, off Abergavenny road – former A40, now declassified

Wales Dining Pub of the Year

Doing very well at the moment, this beautifully positioned old white house with its long verandahs and diamond paned windows is a great all-rounder that delights reader after reader. It stands in its own extensive well cared-for grounds – a mass of colour in spring – on the edge of Clytha Park. Inside is comfortable, light and airy with scrubbed wood floors, pine settles, big faux fur cushions on the window seats by big windows, a good mix of old country furniture and a warming coal fire. Don't miss the murals in the lavatories. Run by charming licensees, it's the sort of relaxed place where everyone feels welcome, from locals who've walked here for a pint in the spotlessly kept bar (solidly comfortable furnishings and a couple of good fires), to diners in the contemporary linen-set restaurant. The very reasonably priced bar menu is well balanced with soundly imaginative rustic dishes: sandwiches (from £3.95), soup (£5.25), spaghetti with tomato and basil sauce

(£5.95), half a dozen oysters, charcuterie with catalan tomato bread or cider baked ham with parsley sauce (£6.95), ploughman's (£7.50), wild boar sausages with potato pancakes (£7.95), wild mushroom omelette with garlic and rosemary potatoes, crab and avocado salad, chicken breast with parmesan crust and pasta or smoked salmon with poached or scrambled eggs or grilled queen scallops (£8.50) and mixed grill of shellfish (£9.25). The restaurant menu is pricier and more elaborate. An impressive choice of drinks includes Bass, Felinfoel Double Dragon and Hook Norton, three interesting changing guest beers (around 300 different ones a year) from brewers such as Brains, Caledonian and Fullers, an extensive wine list with about a dozen or so by the glass, Weston's farm cider and a changing guest cider – even home-made perry. The restaurant and lounge are no smoking; darts, shove-ha'penny, boules, table skittles, cribbage, dominoes, draughts and chess. The two friendly labradors are Beamish and Stowford and there's an english setter. *(Recommended by Terry and Linda Moseley, JCW, the Didler, Mike Pugh, Guy Vowles, Ann and Colin Hunt, Richard Haw, Ian Phillips, Mike and Mary Carter, Lynda Payton, Sam Samuells, Nigel and Karen Smith, James Morrell, Alan and Paula McCully, Steve Whalley, M and J Lindsay, William Orchard)*

Free house ~ Licensees Andrew and Beverley Canning ~ Real ale ~ Bar food (12.30-2.15, 7-9.30; not Sun evening or Mon) ~ Restaurant ~ (01873) 840206 ~ Children welcome ~ Dogs allowed in bar ~ Open 12-3, 6-11; 12-11 Sat; 12-10.30 Sun; closed Mon lunchtime ~ Bedrooms: £50B/£70B

RED WHARF BAY SH5281 Map 6

Ship 🍷

Village signposted off B5025 N of Pentraeth

Tables on the front terrace of this 18th-c inn (run by the same family for over 30 years) are ideally placed to enjoy views along ten square miles of treacherous tidal cockle-sands and sea, with low wooded hills sloping down to the broad bay. Inside is old-fashioned and interesting, with lots of nautical bric-a-brac in big welcoming rooms on each side of the busy stone-built bar counter, both with long cushioned varnished pews built around the walls, glossily varnished cast-iron-framed tables and roaring fires. The restaurant and two bars are no smoking; piped music and dominoes. They have more than 50 malt whiskies, as well as three changing well kept real ales such as Adnams, Greene King IPA and Marstons Pedigree on handpump, and there's a wider choice of wines than is usual for the area (with about ten by the glass) and about 50 malt whiskies. The interesting menu (which includes quite a few seafood dishes) includes lunchtime sandwiches (from £2.95), soup (£2.95), filo basket of local mussels with leeks and local cheese (£4.95), roast vegetable and mozzarella timbale (£6.95), braised lamb shank on crushed celeriac and black pudding with mint pesto (£9.15), roast cod with pancetta on cherry tomato and feta mash with chorizo oil (£8.75), half a dozen daily specials such as poached skate on chive mash with black caper butter (£8.50), beef and kidney pudding (£8.95), platter of local seafood (£12.50) and puddings such as rhubarb crumble with white chocolate sauce or sticky toffee pudding with caramel ice-cream and treacle sauce (£3.95). You'll need to arrive early for a table at the weekend when it can get quite crowded, and they will probably ask to keep your credit card behind the bar if you want to run a tab. *(Recommended by J Roy Smylie, Michael Lamm, W K Wood, Gill and Tony Morriss, John and Tania Wood, Revd D Glover, Yvonne and Mike Meadley)*

Free house ~ Licensee Andrew Kenneally ~ Real ale ~ Bar food (12-2.30, 6-9; 12-8.30 Sun) ~ Restaurant ~ (01248) 852568 ~ Open 11-11; 12-10.30 Sun

The letters and figures after the name of each town are its Ordnance Survey map reference. *Using the Guide* at the beginning of the book explains how it helps you find a pub, in road atlases or large-scale maps as well as in our own maps.

RHYD-Y-MEIRCH SO2907 Map 6

Goose & Cuckoo £

Upper Llanover signposted up narrow track off A4042 S of Abergavenny; after ½ mile take first left, then keep on up (watch for hand-written Goose signs at the forks)

Getting to this remote unspoilt hillside pub – particularly if you come on foot, as many do – is part of its pleasure, and once here a small picture-window extension makes the most of the gorgeous view down the valley. It's basically one small simply furnished room with a woodburner in an arched stone fireplace, but what makes it special, apart from the setting, is the warmth of welcome you get from the friendly licensees. They have well kept Brains Rev James and Breconshire Ramblers Ruin and a guest such as Bullmastiff Best on handpump, and more than 75 whiskies, and good coffees; daily papers, cribbage, darts, dominoes, draughts, shove-ha'penny, quoits and boules. A fairly short choice of enjoyably simple home-made food includes home-baked rolls (from £1.70), good hearty 13-bean soup (£2.40), a variety of ploughman's (£5.50), baked potatoes or lasagne (£5.50), turkey and ham pie, liver and bacon casserole, spaghetti bolognese or chilli con carne (all £6), and home-made puddings (£2.50). There are a variety of rather ad hoc picnic-sets out on the gravel below, and the licensees keep sheep, geese and chickens. The bedroom has two single beds. More reports please. *(Recommended by Charles and Pauline Stride, Bruce Bird, Terry and Linda Moseley, Guy Vowles)*

Free house ~ Licensees Michael and Carol Langley ~ Real ale ~ Bar food ~ No credit cards ~ (01873) 880277 ~ Children welcome ~ Dogs allowed in bar ~ Open 11.30-3, 7-11; 11.30-11 Sat; 12-10.30 Sun; closed Mon exc bank hols ~ Bedroom: £25S/£50S

ROSEBUSH SN0729 Map 6

Tafarn Sinc

B4329 Haverfordwest—Cardigan

It's not just the sawdust on the floor that marks this eccentric place out as anything but your normal day to day pub. Left behind when a loop of railway closed over 70 years ago, this big dark maroon-painted corrugated iron shed used to be a railway halt. It's been more or less re-created, even down to life-size dummy passengers waiting out on the platform, and the sizeable garden is periodically enlivened by the sounds of steam trains chuffing through – actually broadcast from a replica signal box. Though not exactly elegant, inside is really interesting, almost a museum of local history. With an appealingly buoyant atmosphere, the bar has plank panelling, an informal mix of chairs and pews, woodburners, and well kept Cwrw Tafarn Sinc (brewed specially for the pub), Worthingtons and a weekly changing guest such as Brains Rev James on handpump; the Welsh-speaking staff and locals are welcoming; piped music, darts. Basic food includes home-made faggots with onion gravy, glamorgan sausages and chutney, breaded plaice or chicken breast (all £7.50), steaks (from £9.50), and puddings such as rice pudding (£3.50). There's a no smoking dining room. *(Recommended by Gwyneth and Salvo Spadaro-Dutturi, the Didler, John and Enid Morris, Sheila and Robert Robinson)*

Free house ~ Licensee Brian Llewelyn ~ Real ale ~ Bar food ~ Restaurant ~ (01437) 532214 ~ Children in eating area of bar and restaurant ~ Open 12-11(10.30 Sun); closed Mon in winter

SAUNDERSFOOT SN1304 Map 6

Royal Oak

Wogan Terrace (B4316)

It's a good idea to book if you're after a table at this well managed village pub during the holiday season, and being well placed above the harbour, tables outside (under outdoor heaters) get snapped up pretty quickly too. The main draw is the range of about ten fresh fish dishes a day that are served with a good range of sauces, and with prices varying depending on the catch: pint of prawns (£6.25), beer-battered haddock (£8.25), tuna steak topped with garlic prawns (£13.95), hake (£13.95) and grilled whole bass (£16.95). Other dishes include lunchtime sandwiches (from £3.25), local pork and garlic sausages or boeuf bourgignon (£7.95), sizzling platter of chicken and ribs (£10.95), cutlets of lamb with garlic, honey and rosemary or 8oz fillet steak (£15.95), with puddings such as cheesecake of the day or lemon mousse (from £3.95); two-course Sunday lunch (£7.95, three courses £9.95). Service is pleasant and attentive. There's a cheerful atmosphere in the no smoking dining area and carpeted lounge bar, which has captain's chairs and wall banquettes. Frequented by chatty locals, the small public bar has a TV and dominoes; piped music. Around five well kept real ales on handpump include Ansells, Greene King Abbot, Ind Coope Burton, Worthington, and a guest such as Greene King Old Speckled Hen. They've also over 30 malt whiskies and an interesting choice of wines (lots of New World ones), with about a dozen by the glass. *(Recommended by the Didler, Jane Blethyn, Keith Barker)*

Free house ~ Licensees T S and T L Suter ~ Real ale ~ Bar food (12-2.30, 6-9.30(10 Fri); 12-10 Sat; 12-9 Sun) ~ Restaurant ~ (01834) 812546 ~ Children in eating area of bar and restaurant ~ Dogs allowed in bar ~ Open 11-11; 12-10.30 Sun

SHIRENEWTON ST4894 Map 6

Carpenters Arms

Mynydd-bach; B4235 Chepstow—Usk, about ½ mile N

New licensees taking over just as we went to press weren't planning any big changes at this former country smithy – indeed we hope not as its main appeal is its proper pubby atmosphere. The series of small interconnecting rooms has lots to look at, from chamber-pots and a blacksmith's bellows hanging from the planked ceiling of one lower room, which has an attractive Victorian tiled fireplace, to a collection of chromolithographs of antique Royal occasions under another room's pitched ceiling (more chamber-pots here). Furnishings run the gamut too, from one very high-backed ancient settle to pews, kitchen chairs, a nice elm table, several sewing-machine trestle tables and so forth; it's popular with locals (especially for Sunday lunch); shove-ha'penny, cribbage, dominoes, table skittles, backgammon, bar billiards, and piped pop music. Beers now come from the Punch list so the range has changed a little: Bass, Flowers IPA, Fullers London Pride, Shepherd Neame Spitfire and Wadworths 6X on handpump. Bar food is likely to be straightforward. The pub is handy for Chepstow. *(Recommended by BOB)*

Punch ~ Tenants Sue and Terry Thomas ~ Real ale ~ Bar food (not Sun evening) ~ No credit cards ~ (01291) 641231 ~ Children in family room ~ Dogs welcome ~ Open 11-2.30, 6-11; 12-3, 7-11 Sun

ST HILARY ST0173 Map 6

Bush £

Village signposted from A48 E of Cowbridge

In a delightful spot not too far from Cardiff, this lovely old 16th-c thatched pub is cosily comfortable with a welcoming log fire, stripped old stone walls, and windsor chairs around copper-topped tables in the low-beamed carpeted lounge bar, and pubbier in the bar with old settles and pews on aged flagstones, and a pleasant mix of locals and visitors. Bass, Greene King Old Speckled Hen, Hancocks HB and a guest such as Greene King Abbot are well kept on hand or electric pump; darts, TV, shove-ha'penny, cribbage, dominoes and subdued piped music. Good value enjoyable bar food includes sandwiches (from £2.25), soup (£2.95), laverbread and bacon (£3.95), trout fillet grilled with bacon (£5.50), tagliatelle provençale or baked ham and parsley sauce (£5.95), chicken curry (£6.25), steak and ale pie (£6.50) and sirloin steak (£9.95). The restaurant and lounge bar are no smoking during food service. There are tables and chairs in front, and more in the back garden; reasonable disabled access. *(Recommended by David and Ruth Shillitoe, Ian Phillips, David Jeffreys, David and Nina Pugsley)*

Punch ~ Lease Sylvia Murphy ~ Real ale ~ Bar food (12-2.30, 7-9.30; 12-3, 6-8 Sun) ~ Restaurant ~ (01446) 772745 ~ Children welcome ~ Open 11.30-11; 12-10.30 Sun

TALYLLYN SH7209 Map 6

Tynycornel

B4405, off A487 S of Dolgellau

Idyllically peaceful, this comfortably civilised hotel is in a delightful position nestling peacefully below high mountains – Cadair Idris opposite (splendid walks) and Graig Goch behind – overlooking a charming lake. Though not at all pubby, it's relaxed and friendly, and in summer, the attractively planted side courtyard is a pleasant place for afternoon tea. It's immaculately kept, with deep armchairs and enveloping sofas around low tables, a central log fire, and big picture windows looking out over the water, as well as big bird prints, local watercolours, and a good range of malt whiskies (the serving bar, with keg beer, is tucked away behind). Enjoyable lunchtime bar food might include good sandwiches (from £3.20), courgette and tomato soup (£3.50), ploughman's (£6.95), courgette and hazelnut loaf with tomato sauce (£7.95), thai green vegetable curry (£8.50), steamed salmon fillet with hollandaise sauce or burgundy beef casserole in a yorkshire pudding (£8.95), and puddings such as tangy lemon tart (£3.95); courteous service from the uniformed staff. There's a no smoking restaurant and conservatory. Guests have the use of a sauna and fishing facilities, and can hire boats on the lake. More reports please. *(Recommended by Diane Bullock, Peter and Anne Hollindale, J C Poley, Jacquie and Jim Jones)*

Free house ~ Licensee Thomas Rowlands ~ Bar food (lunchtime only) ~ Restaurant ~ (01654) 782282 ~ Children welcome ~ Dogs allowed in bedrooms ~ Open 11-11; 12-10.30 Sun ~ Bedrooms: £50S/£100B

TINTERN SO5200 Map 6

Cherry Tree

Pub signed up narrow Raglan road off A446, beside Royal George; parking very limited

A new bar at this white-painted late 16th-c stone cottage (delightfully approached across a little stone slab bridge over a tiny stream) has been built using reclaimed materials to blend with the traditional character of the original building – now with slate floors throughout. The new area has dark wood furniture, and leads into the original beamed and lime-washed bar, which has a plain serving counter in one area and a good open fire in another; cribbage, darts, cards, dominoes and piped music. Look out for Guinness the dog. Generous good value food, made using lots of fresh local ingredients, might include sandwiches (from £2), soup (£3.50), ham and eggs, mushroom and ricotta tortellini, vegetarian lasagne or spicy meat balls with couscous (£5.95), beef and ale pie (£7.95) as well as quickly changing daily specials such as sizzling crevettes, grilled red snapper or talapia with garlic butter (£9.95) and their famous paella (£19.95 for two). Tapped straight from the cask, Hancocks HB is well kept alongside changing guests from brewers such as Felinfoel, Timothy Taylor and Wye Valley. They also serve farm cider, just over a dozen wines by the glass and milk shakes. It's in a quiet and attractive spot, yet only half a mile or so from the honey-pot centre of Tintern, and there are tables out in a charming garden, and on a green patio; disabled access is difficult. *(Recommended by the Didler, Tim and Ann Newell, LM, Emma Kingdon, Pete Baker, Kerry Law, Simon Smith)*

Free house ~ Licensees Jill and Steve Pocock ~ Real ale ~ Bar food (12-3, 6-9; 12-9 wknds) ~ Restaurant ~ (01291) 689292 ~ Children in eating area of bar ~ Dogs allowed in bar ~ Open 12-11(10.30 Sun); 12-3, 5-11 winter ~ Bedrooms: /£50B

TRELLECK SO5005 Map 6

Lion

B4293 6 miles S of Monmouth

The landlord's father is Hungarian and brings in some of the ingredients that are used in the interesting authentic hungarian specialities at this smallish stone-built pub. A blackboard hung with dried peppers above one fireplace lists a choice of these dishes, such as peppers filled with minced pork and rice with sweet tomato sauce (£9.75), hungarian sausage and egg baked with sour cream and cheese (£10.25) and fried pork steak with cream cheese and walnuts with leeks, cream and cheese (£12.75). Other food includes baguettes (from £2.75), filled baked potatoes (from £3.95), roasted chicken or scampi and chips (£5.75), home-made vegetarian hotpot (£7.30), grilled salmon steak (£7.75) and home-made cottage pie or chicken kiev (£8.25). There's a step up to the no smoking dining area. The unpretentious open-plan bar has one or two black beams in its low ochre ceiling, a mix of furnishings including some comfortable brocaded wall seats and tub chairs, old red plush dining chairs, a hop-hung window seat, varying-sized tables, and log fires in two fireplaces opposite each other. There's a small fish tank in a wall recess, and another bigger one in the lobby by the lavatories; piped music. A colourful galaxy of pumpclips in the porch and on a wall show the splendid range of quickly changing guest beers (though when one reader visited they only had one beer on offer) from brewers such as Archers and Milton, which are well kept alongside Bath SPA and Wye Valley Butty Bach, and they've around 30 malt whiskies. There are some picnic-sets and an aviary out on the grass. The pub is opposite the church, and handy for the standing stones; bedrooms in a nearby cottage. *(Recommended by Charles and Pauline Stride, S H Godsell, Mike Pugh)*

Free house ~ Licensees Tom and Debbie Zsigo ~ Real ale ~ Bar food (12-2, 7-9) ~ Restaurant ~ (01600) 860322 ~ Children welcome ~ Dogs allowed in bar ~ Open 12-3, 6(7 Mon)-11; 12-3, 6.30-11 Sat; 12-3 Sun; closed Sun evening ~ Bedrooms: /£65S

TY'N-Y-GROES SH7672 Map 6

Groes

B5106 N of village

The food at this attractive old hotel is good (if not cheap) and it's in a charming spot, making it a nice place to stay. Past the hot stove in the entrance area, the spotlessly kept homely series of rambling, low-beamed and thick-walled rooms is nicely decorated with antique settles and an old sofa, old clocks, portraits, hats and tins hanging from the walls, and fresh flowers. A fine antique fireback is built into one wall, perhaps originally from the formidable fireplace in the back bar, which houses a collection of stone cats as well as cheerful winter log fires; one area is no smoking. There's also an airy verdant no smoking conservatory. Ind Coope Burton and Tetleys are well kept on handpump, and they've a good few malt whiskies, kir, and a fruity Pimms in summer; light classical piped music at lunchtimes, nostalgic light music at other times, and a live harpist a couple of times a month. Well presented dishes might include soup (£3.95), sandwiches (from £4.75), grilled mushrooms with stilton, garlic and lemon (£6.50), chicken curry with saffron rice or home-made lasagne (£8.50), poached salmon and grilled plaice with hollandaise sauce (£13.50), and steaks (from £13.95), with daily specials such as game casserole (£9.50), local lamb steak (£11.75) and bass (£12.50). As well as puddings such as pecan and syrup tart (£4.65), they do delicious home-made ice-creams, with a few unusual flavours such as ginger, fragrant rose or honey and lemon. Run by the same family for the last 19 years, and said to have been the first Welsh pub to be properly licensed – in 1573 – it enjoys magnificent views over the Vale of Conwy and the distant mountains. The neatly kept, well equipped bedrooms (some have terraces or balconies) also have views, and in summer it's a pleasure to sit outside in the pretty back garden with its flower-filled hayricks, and there are also some seats on the flower-decked roadside. *(Recommended by KC, Maurice and Della Andrew, Alison Hayes, Pete Hanlon, Jarrod and Wendy Hopkinson, John and Tania Wood, Brian and Janet Ainscough, Mike and Jayne Bastin, Dennis Jenkin, A J Bowen, Dr Pete Crawshaw, Brenda and Rob Fincham, Sarah and Peter Gooderham, J C Poley, Tony and Betty Parker, Terry and Linda Moseley, Jacquie and Jim Jones; also in the* Good Hotel Guide*)*

Free house ~ Licensee Dawn Humphreys ~ Real ale ~ Bar food (12-2.15, 6.30-9) ~ Restaurant ~ (01492) 650545 ~ Children in family room till 7pm; must be over 10 in restaurant ~ Dogs allowed in bedrooms ~ Open 12-3, 6.30(6 Sat)-11(10.30 Sun) ~ Bedrooms: £79B/£95B

USK SO3801 Map 6

Nags Head

The Square

Readers are full of enthusiastic praise for this charming old coaching inn. Though doing well in all respects, it's the really friendly welcome (it's been in the same family for over 35 years) and the tasty food that really seem to hit the mark. Generously served well presented dishes (concentrating on local produce) could include home-made soup (£3.90), frogs legs in hot provençale sauce (£5.75), grilled sardines (£6), sausages (£6.50), home-made steak pie (£6.95), vegetable pancakes filled with mushrooms, broccoli and leeks (£7.75), and delicious rabbit pie (£7.75), and interesting specials including seasonal game dishes (lovely on a cold winter evening), such as wild boar steak in apricot and brandy sauce (£12.50), pheasant in port (£13) and stuffed partridge (£13.50). You can book tables, some of which may be candlelit at night; nice proper linen napkins. With a friendly chatty atmosphere, the beautifully kept traditional main bar has lots of well polished tables and chairs packed under its beams (some with farming tools), lanterns or horsebrasses and harness attached, as well as leatherette wall benches, and various sets of sporting prints and local pictures – look out for the original deeds to the pub. Tucked away at the front is an intimate little corner with some African masks, while on the other side of the room a passageway leads to the pub's own busy coffee bar (open between Easter and autumn). Built in the old entrance to the courtyard, it sells snacks, teas, cakes and ice-cream, and tables spill out from here on to the front pavement. A simpler room behind the bar has prints for sale, and perhaps a knot of sociable locals. They do 15 wines by the glass (nice glasses), along with well kept Brains SA, Buckleys Best and Rev James on handpump, 12 malt whiskies and a farm cider; quiet piped music. The centre of Usk is full of pretty hanging baskets and flowers in summer, and the church is well worth a look. *(Recommended by Peter and Audrey Dowsett, Eryl and Keith Dykes, Neville and Anne Morley, Sue and Ken Le Prevost, Mike and Mary Carter, Dr and Mrs C W Thomas, Terry and Linda Moseley, Dr Oscar Puls, Mike Pugh, Bernard Stradling, Brian Brooks, Ann and Colin Hunt, Ian Phillips, Joyce and Maurice Cottrell, Prof Keith and Mrs Jane Barber, Roy and Lindsey Fentiman)*

Free house ~ Licensees the Key family ~ Real ale ~ Bar food (11.30-1, 6-10) ~ Restaurant ~ (01291) 672820 ~ Children welcome ~ Dogs allowed in bar ~ Open 11-3(3.30 Sun), 5.30-11(10.30 Sun)

LUCKY DIP

Besides the fully inspected pubs, you might like to try these Lucky Dips recommended to us and described by readers (if you do, please send us reports: www.goodguides.co.uk).

ANGLESEY

BEAUMARIS SH6076

☆ *Sailors Return* [Church St]: Bright cheery partly divided open-plan bar with comfortable banquettes and open fire, some emphasis on popular usual food from sandwiches and baguettes up, smiling helpful service, well kept Bass and Hancocks HB, decent wines, bookable tables in no smoking dining area; unobtrusive piped music; children welcome in eating area, dogs in bar, bedrooms *(Keith and Chris O'Neill, LYM, Paul Humphreys, Terry and Linda Moseley, Michael and Alison Sandy)*

CLWYD

BODFARI SJ0970

Dinorben Arms [off A541 towards Tremeirchion]: Attractive black and white hillside pub nr Offa's Dyke, three well worn beamed and flagstoned rooms, old-fashioned settles, three open fires, a glassed-over old well, over 260 malt whiskies, well kept Banks's, Marstons Pedigree and a guest such as Batemans XB, good wines, straightforward bar food, darts and pool; fruit machine, TV, piped classical music; light and airy garden room and grassy play area; children welcome, charming views from pretty brick terraces, open all day wknds *(LYM, Michael Lamm, Mrs Jane Kingsbury)*

CARROG SJ1143

Grouse [B5436, signed off A5 Llangollen—Corwen]: Small unpretentious local with friendly regulars, local pictures, reasonably priced food all day from good sandwiches and hearty soup up, Lees Bitter, polite service, splendid River Dee view from bay window and tables on sunny terrace with pretty walled garden; pool in games room, piped music, narrow turn into car park; wheelchair access, handy for Llangollen steam railway, bedrooms *(Gill and Tony Morriss, Michael and Jenny Back)*

CILCAIN SJ1765

☆ *White Horse* [signed from A494 W of Mold; The Square]: Friendly and homely unchanging country local, several rooms, low joists, mahogany and oak settles, roaring inglenook log or coal fire, quarry-tiled back bar allowing dogs and muddy boots, two reliably well kept changing ales, pub games, home-made food (pickled eggs too if the long-serving landlord has left some); no children inside, picnic-sets outside, delightful village *(LYM, MLR, Peter Brooks, Deirdre Vereker)*

COLWYN BAY SH8278

Mountain View [Mochdre, S off A55—A470 link rd]: Roomy big-windowed modern pub with pine tables and chairs in divided bar, usual food, full Burtonwood beer range kept well, children in no smoking eating area, darts, dominoes, table football, pool; piped music may be obtrusive, fruit machine, juke box; tables on front terrace, bright window boxes *(LYM, KC)*

FFRITH SJ2855

Poachers Cottage [Cymau Rd (B5101, just off A541 Wrexham—Mold)]: Traditional 18th-c country pub, two bars and restaurant, good reasonably priced home-cooked food, warm friendly atmosphere, helpful service, real ales, extensive wine list *(W M Turner)*

GWAENYSGOR SJ0781

☆ *Eagle & Child* [off A5151 NE of Dyserth]: Large spotless open-plan pub, early 19th-c, with generous freshly cooked good value food from sandwiches up, well kept Theakstons Bitter, good service, shining brasses and plates, exemplary lavatories; children welcome, attractive floodlit gardens, in hilltop village with fine views nr Offa's Dyke Path *(MLR)*

GWYDDELWERN SJ0746

Ty Mawr: Medieval half-timbered stone-built inn with mix of traditional and sympathetic modern furnishings, lots of bottled traditional and belgian beers, wide choice of tasty reasonably priced food, good friendly service, erratic sloping floor upstairs; children welcome *(Emma and Will, Amanda Greenwood)*

HALKYN SJ2171

☆ *Britannia* [Britannia Pentre Rd, off A55 for Rhosesmor]: Star is for great views over Dee estuary from terrace and no smoking restaurant – on a clear day you may even be able to pick out Blackpool Tower; well worn in lounge bar with heavy beams, china and other bric-a-brac, well kept Lees, good value food inc children's helpings, games room with darts, pool, TV, juke box and board games, perhaps fresh eggs to buy; children in eating areas, open all day *(Mr and Mrs B Hobden, LYM)*

HOLYWELL SJ1876

Calcot Arms [A5026]: Wide choice of reasonably priced well presented food, pleasant staff, Thwaites real ale; views across River Dee *(KC)*

LLANARMON DYFFRYN CEIRIOG SJ1532

☆ *West Arms* [end of B4500 W of Chirk]: 16th-c beamed and timbered inn in lovely surroundings, picturesque upmarket lounge bar full of antique settles, sofas, even an elaborately carved confessional stall, good original bar food strong on local produce, friendly service, well kept Adnams, good range of wines and malt whiskies, Stowford Press cider, more sofas in old-fashioned entrance hall, comfortable back bar too, roaring log fires, good if pricey restaurant; piped music may obtrude in public bar, can be very busy; children welcome, pretty lawn running down to River Ceiriog (fishing for residents), comfortable character bedrooms, good walks *(LYM, Mr and Mrs John Taylor, Andrew York)*

LLANDEGLA SJ1952

Crown [Ruthin Rd (A525)]: Quickly served good value food in comfortable bright bar with good set of Hogarth prints, well kept Lees, good helpful service, popular restaurant; on Offa's Dyke Path *(KC)*

Plough [Ruthin Rd]: Cosy and popular upmarket dining pub, wide choice of enjoyable food all day, concerned staff, well kept Robinsons, large dining room, no smoking area; unobtrusive piped music; nr Offa's Dyke Path *(KC)*

LLANELIAN-YN-RHOS SH8676

☆ *White Lion* [signed off A5830 (shown as B5383 on some maps) and B5381, S of Colwyn Bay]: Family-run 16th-c inn, traditional flagstoned snug bar with antique settles and big fire, dining area on left with jugs hanging from beams, teapots above window, further comfortable more spacious no smoking dining area up broad steps, huge choice of good reasonably priced bar food from sandwiches and big tureen of home-made soup through to delicious puddings, good friendly staff, well kept Marstons Bitter, Pedigree and a seasonal beer, good range of wines, lots of malt whiskies, grotto filled with lion models; dominoes, cribbage, piped music; children in eating areas, rustic tables outside, good walking nearby, comfortable bedrooms *(Michael and Jenny Back, LYM)*

LLANFERRES SJ1860

☆ *Druid* [A494 Mold—Ruthin]: Valley and mountain views from extended 17th-c inn, civilised plush lounge and larger beamed back bar with log fire, attractive no smoking dining area, wide range of generous changing bar food, well kept Burtonwood Top Hat and a guest beer, good malt whisky choice, well equipped games room; TV, piped music may obtrude; children welcome, tables outside, bedrooms (good breakfast), open for food all day wknds and bank hols *(Chris Flynn, Wendy Jones, LYM, Mr and Mrs John Taylor, Alan Cole, Kirstie Bruce, KC)*

LLANGERNYW SH8767

Stag: 17th-c timbered and beamed pub with three linked areas, open fire, small nooks and settles, interesting collection of pottery jugs, mugs and other bric-a-brac, popular good value food inc generous puddings, Ansells Best and Greene King Old Speckled Hen, friendly staff *(Peter Meister)*

LLANGYNHAFAL SJ1263

☆ *White Horse* [Hendrerwydd, off B5429 SE of Denbigh]: Quietly set village pub with armchairs, open fire and interesting bric-a-brac in small old-fashioned rustic bar, opening into three smartly mediterranean-style bare-boards eating areas with good unusual changing fresh food from lunchtime sandwiches up; two well kept real ales, good range of wines, great collection of spirits, relaxed atmosphere, friendly attentive service, daily papers *(Steve Cawthray, Alan Cole, Kirstie Bruce, MLR, Pat and Sam Roberts)*

LLOC SJ1476

Rock [St Asaph Rd (A5151)]: Bright décor, interesting choice of enjoyable food in busy bar or (if you have a main dish) dining room *(KC)*

MOLD SJ2464

Bryn Awel [A541 Denbigh rd nr Bailey Hill]: Pleasant dining pub, welcoming attentive service, reliable choice of satisfying good value food, big helpings, sensibly priced wines, cheerful bustling atmosphere, pleasant décor, good no smoking area; may be piped music *(KC)*

PONTBLYDDYN SJ2761

New Inn [A5104, just S of A541 3 miles SE of Mold]: Unassuming building, interesting choice of enjoyable food in attractive upstairs dining room, pleasant staff, attention to detail *(KC)*

RHEWL SJ1744

☆ *Sun* [off A5 or A542 NW of Llangollen]: Unpretentious cottagey local with simple consistently good value generous food from sandwiches and bargain light lunches up, good Sun lunch, a well kept changing real ale, chatty landlord and friendly staff, old-fashioned hatch service to back room, dark little lounge, no piped music; outside lavatories, portakabin games room – children allowed here and in eating area; lovely peaceful spot, good walking country just off Horseshoe Pass, relaxing valley views from terrace and small pretty garden, cl Mon, open all day wknds *(LYM, MLR, Peter Brooks, Deirdre Vereker)*

RUTHIN SJ1258

Castle Hotel [St Peters Sq]: Small town hotel with several bars, interesting foreign beers and cocktails in back one, notable cooking at attractive prices, pleasant small restaurant *(John Wooll)*

ST GEORGE SH9775

Kinmel Arms [off A55 nr Abergele]: Newly refurbished 17th-c former posting inn in attractive village, interesting building with several rooms, nice mix of tables and chairs, rugs on stripped wood, wide range of reasonably priced interesting modern food from lunchtime baguettes and dutch-style open sandwiches up, changing ales such as Greene King Old Speckled Hen, Brains Rev James and Wychwood Shires, good choice of wines by the glass, friendly staff, conservatory; cl Mon *(Joan E Hilditch, H Bramwell)*

TAL-Y-CAFN SH7871

☆ *Tal-y-Cafn Hotel* [A470 Conway—Llanwrst]: Cheerful bustle in comfortable lounge bar with jugs hanging from ceiling and log fire in big inglenook, wide choice of good value satisfying home cooking (may be a wait when packed for a bargain offer), Bass, Boddingtons and Tetleys; children welcome, seats in spacious garden, pleasant surroundings, handy for Bodnant Gardens *(LYM, KC)*

DYFED

ABERGWILI SN4321

Black Ox [just off A40 E of Carmarthen; High St]: Welcoming 18th-c pub, two weekly changing guest beers, good spirits range, wide choice of enjoyable fresh food inc some interesting dishes and popular self-service salad bar, two dining rooms, darts (and HQ of local ladies' football team); monthly quiz night *(Neville Francis)*

ABERYSTWYTH SN6777

Yr Hen Orsaf [Alexandra Rd]: Wetherspoons in concourse of Cambrian Railways station, meeting place for students and profs – happy atmosphere, several different areas, enjoyable food and drink at appealing prices; terrace tables by the buffer stops, open all day *(Joan and Michel Hooper-Immins, C J Fletcher)*

ANGLE SM8703

☆ *Old Point House* [signed off B4320 in village; East Angle Bay]: Idyllic spot overlooking Milford Haven, dating from 14th c, unspoilt but comfortable, flagstoned bar with open fire, small lounge bar, well kept Felinfoel, basic food strong on good interestingly cooked local seafood; run by local lifeboat coxswain, many photographs; plenty of tables and ancient slate seats out by the seashore *(RWC, D and G Alderman, Stephen and Jean Curtis, Maurice and Della Andrew)*

BONCATH SN2038

Boncath Inn [B4332 Cenarth—Eglwyswrw]: Large village pub, attractive traditional décor with farm tools and photographs of former railway, real ales, reasonably priced food; open all day *(Colin Moore)*

BOSHERSTON SR9694

☆ *St Govans Country Inn* [off B4319 S of Pembroke]: Comfortably modernised spacious bar with good climbing photographs and murals of local beauty spots, log fire in big stone fireplace, helpful friendly service, well kept Adnams, Fullers London Pride, Ind Coope Burton, Tetleys and perhaps a guest beer, usual food, no smoking dining area, dominoes, board games, pool (winter only); piped music, TV, fruit machine; children and dogs welcome, picnic-sets on front terrace, good value spotless bedrooms, good breakfast, handy for water-lily lakes, beach and cliffy coast *(LYM, George Atkinson, P F Dakin, Peter Davey, Matthew Lidbury, Mike Pugh)*

BROAD HAVEN SM8614

☆ *Druidstone Hotel* [N of village on coast rd, bear left for about 1½ miles then follow sign left to Druidstone Haven – inn a sharp left turn after another ½ mile; OS Sheet 157 map ref 862168, marked as Druidston Villa]: Its club licence rules it out of the main entries (you can't go for just a drink and have to book to eat or stay there); inventively individual home cooking, with fresh ingredients and a leaning towards the organic; happily informal converted country house in a grand spot above the sea, terrific views, folksy cellar bar, well kept Worthington BB tapped from the cask, good wines, country wines and other drinks, ceilidhs and folk jamborees, chummy dogs (dogs welcomed), all sorts of sporting activities from boules to sand-yachting; cl Nov and Jan, restaurant cl Sun evening; spacious homely bedrooms, erratic plumbing *(LYM, John and Enid Morris, Mike Pugh, Robert Wivell)*

Galleon [Enfield Rd]: Popular and friendly seafront pub with softly lit small bar, rooms and alcoves leading off, mainstream real ales, good range of food, good service, upstairs dining room; children welcome *(P Price)*

CENARTH SN2641

White Hart [A484 Cardigan—Newcastle Emlyn]: Attractive 16th-c pub by famous River Teifi waterfalls, central bar and two separate rooms, simple pleasant furnishings, reasonably priced food in bar and restaurant, a couple of real ales; outside tables *(Colin Moore)*

CILGERRAN SN1943

Pendre Inn [High Street, off A478 2¼ miles S of Cardigan]: Friendly local with massive medieval stone walls and broad flagstones, good atmosphere, well kept Tomos Watkins OSB, pleasant newish licensees, plain food; cl Tues *(LYM, John and Enid Morris, Neil F Mason, David and Nina Pugsley, Colin Moore)*

CILYCWM SN7540

☆ *Neuadd Fawr Arms*: Welcoming Welsh-speaking traditional village local in interesting building with simple old-world furnishings, good range of real ales, reasonably priced homely food, friendly staff and cheerful atmosphere; good spot by churchyard above river Gwenlas, among lanes to Llyn Brianne *(BB, Geoff Palmer)*

CROESGOCH SM8430

Artramont Arms [A487 Fishguard—St David's, by Porthgain turn]: Welcoming landlady and well trained young staff in light bright village pub handy for camp site, well kept ales inc Brains Buckleys and Felinfoel Double Dragon, sensible choice of good value freshly made food inc good local lamb, fish and seafood, daily papers, pool, charming conservatory; dogs welcome, good enclosed garden for children *(Mike Pugh)*

CWM GWAUN SN0035

☆ *Dyffryn Arms* [Cwn Gwaun and Pontfaen signed off B4313 E of Fishguard]: Classic unspoilt country tavern, very relaxed, basic and idiosyncratic, with veteran landlady (her farming family have run it since 1840); 1920s front parlour with plain deal furniture inc rocking chair and draughts-boards inlaid into tables, coal fire, well kept Bass and Ind Coope Burton served by jug through a hatch, pickled eggs, time-warp prices, Great War prints and posters, darts; pretty countryside, open more or less all day (may close if no customers) *(the Didler, LYM, RWC, Colin Moore)*

FELINDRE FARCHOG SN0939

Olde Salutation [A487 Newport—Cardigan]: Smart, friendly and spacious antiqued pub with well kept local James Williams and guest beers, good value food from toasties and baguettes to bass, local beef and seasonal local sea trout, children's meals, good landlord, comfortable matching seats and tables, separate dining area; bedrooms, fishing and good walks by nearby River Nevern *(Blaise Vyner, R Michael Richards)*

FISHGUARD SM9537

☆ *Fishguard Arms* [Main St (A487)]: Tiny front bar with a couple of well kept changing real ales served by jug at unusually high counter, very friendly staff, open fire, rugby photographs, traditional games in back room; has been open all day Sun, cl Mon *(LYM, the Didler)*

Royal Oak [Market Sq, Upper Town]: Well worn in beamed front bar leading through panelled room to big no smoking picture-window dining extension; stone walls, cushioned wooden wall seats, woodburner, welsh dragon carved on bar counter, three well kept real ales inc Brains Buckley, plenty of hot drinks, well priced generous food inc several welsh dishes and children's things; bar billiards, fruit machine; pictures and mementoes commemorate defeat here of bizarre French raid in 1797 *(BB, the Didler, Mike Pugh)*

FRESHWATER EAST SS0298

Freshwater Inn: Village pub with lovely bay views from lounge, welcoming staff, two or three real ales, dining room, pool in public bar; well behaved children welcome, tables in nice garden, open all day summer (busy evenings then) *(Angie Coles)*

GOGINAN SN6881

Druid [A44 E of Aberystwyth]: Well kept Brains and food from good value sandwiches up in friendly roadside pub, interesting landlord happy to talk about area's silver/lead mining *(Pat and Robert Watt)*

HAVERFORDWEST SM9515

☆ *Georges* [Market St]: Behind front eclectibles shop and small coffee bar/teashop area is long narrow celtic-theme bar with small stable-like booths, three well kept ales such as Brains SA and Rev James and St Austell, good wine list (esp New World), quick friendly service even when busy, informal and relaxed rather whimsical atmosphere; larger upstairs restaurant, generous interesting home-made food using good meat, fresh veg and good fish and vegetarian ranges; back crafts shop/showroom, lovely walled garden, no dogs *(David and Nina Pugsley, Mike Pugh)*

HERBRANDSTON SM8607

Taberna: Well kept beer, friendly people, enjoyable food in bar and restaurant *(Tracey King, Stephen and Jean Curtis)*

HUNDLETON SR9499
Speculation [off B4320 W, towards Castlemartin]: Small refreshingly different local with old-fashioned Irish feel, gently updated 1920s ambiance, toys, books and old furniture, limited good value home-made food, friendly courteous service; children welcome *(Martyn Habberley)*

LITTLE HAVEN SM8512
☆ *Castle*: Good value open-plan pub well placed by green looking over sandy bay (lovely sunsets), good reasonably priced food in bare-boards bar and carpeted dining area inc local fish, well kept Brains, quick friendly attentive service, beams and stripped stone, big oak tables, castle prints, pool; children welcome, tables outside *(Robert Wivell)*

☆ *St Brides Hotel* [in village itself, not St Brides hamlet further W]: Compact and unassuming stripped-stone bar, communicating dining area allowing children, good value generous food from baked potatoes up, well kept Brains Rev James and Worthington, good wine choice, friendly locals and staff, cushioned pews, open fire, no piped music, interesting well in back corner grotto may be partly Roman; Pay & Display parking; big good value bedrooms, some in annexe over road by sheltered sunny terraced garden, short stroll from the sea *(George Atkinson, LYM, John and Enid Morris, Tim and Liz Sherbourne, Mr and Mrs A H Young)*

LLANDDAROG SN5016
☆ *Butchers Arms*: Cheery heavily black-beamed local with three smallish eating areas rambling off central bar, good low-priced generous home cooking from sandwiches through hearty country dishes to some interesting specials and good profiteroles (menu willingly adapted for children), friendly helpful staff, well kept Felinfoel Best and Double Dragon tapped from the cask, decent wines, conventional pub furniture, fairy lights and candles in bottles, woodburner in biggish fireplace; piped pop music; tables outside, delightful window boxes *(Emma Kingdon, Carol Mills, Tom Evans, BB, Dr and Mrs A K Clarke, B and F A Hannam)*

LLANDEILO SN5923
☆ *Cottage* [Pentrefelin (A40 towards Carmarthen)]: Roomily refurbished open-plan beamed dining pub, huge log fire and lots of horsey prints, plates and brasses, good generous food from sandwiches and baked potatoes through homely favourites to some interesting dishes, local fish and welsh black beef, well kept ales such as Boddingtons, Flowers IPA and Wadworths 6X, decent house wines, particularly kind friendly service, well appointed back dining room; piped music *(Tom Evans, Norman and Sarah Keeping)*

White Horse [Rhosmaen St]: Friendly 16th-c local popular for its particularly well kept changing real ales; occasional live music, tables outside front and back *(the Didler)*

LLANDOVERY SN7634
Red Lion [Market Sq]: One basic welcoming room with no bar, well kept Brains Buckleys and guest beers tapped from the cask, friendly landlord; cl Sun, may cl early evening if no customers *(BB, the Didler, RWC)*

LLANEGWAD SN5321
Halfway [A40 Llandeilo—Carmarthen]: Enterprising elegantly presented cooking, two large dining areas but still wise to book in season; cl Sun evening and Mon *(Dr and Mrs R E S Tanner)*

MATHRY SM8732
☆ *Farmers Arms* [Brynamlwg, off A487 Fishguard—St David's]: Carefully renovated homely bar with beams, flagstones and dark woodwork, wide food choice from good crab sandwiches to reasonably priced hot dishes esp fish, well kept ales such as Blackawton Headstrong, Brains Rev James and Felinfoel, fair range of reasonably priced wines, quick friendly and attentive service, children welcome in large no smoking dining conservatory; piped music; tables in small walled garden, open all day in summer, cl till 4 Mon-Weds in winter *(George Atkinson, David Field, Robert Wivell)*

NARBERTH SN1114
Angel [High St]: Good choice of fairly priced usual food inc lots of fresh local fish and good value Sun lunch, well kept Brains beers, pleasant relaxed surroundings with almost a hotel feel in lounge bar; pub pianist, fairly handy for Oakwood theme park and other attractions *(Mike Pugh)*

NEVERN SN0840
☆ *Trewern Arms*: Extended welcoming inn in delightful peaceful setting nr notable church and medieval bridge over River Nyfer, lively family area merging into appealing dark stripped-stone slate-floored bar, rafters hung with rural bric-a-brac, high-backed settles, plush banquettes, Wadworths 6X, quick friendly obliging service, enjoyable bar food from sandwiches up prepared in open servery, good value attractive Thurs-Sat restaurant; TV in bar, games room, no dogs; tables in pretty garden, bright comfortable bedrooms, big breakfast *(LYM, Maurice and Della Andrew, George Atkinson, T Gripper, Alec and Barbara Jones)*

PENALLY SS1199
Cross [Strawberry Lane]: Small friendly village pub with reasonably priced food in raised dining area, good choice of beers; terrace tables with stunning views of Caldy Island *(David and Nina Pugsley)*

PENTREGAT SN3352
New Inn [A487 W]: Big main-road family pub, ancient beams, two dining areas and public bar, friendly atmosphere, plenty of staff, wide choice of well kept beers, popular carvery Sun *(Angela Lawley)*

RHANDIRMWYN SN7843
Royal Oak: 17th-c stone inn in remote and peaceful walking country, plenty of hanging baskets and flowering tubs, good views from front garden, comfortable bar with log fire, up to six changing well kept ales, enjoyable reasonably priced food inc welsh black beef, big dining area (can book); 60s music on free juke box; dogs and children welcome, good big bedrooms with hill views, handy for Brecon

Beacons *(BB, JWAC, Geoff Palmer, Chris Power)*

SOLVA SM8024

☆ ***Cambrian*** [Lower Solva; off A487 Haverfordwest—St Davids]: Attractive neatly kept civilised dining pub much enjoyed by older people; clean and warm, food inc authentic pasta, fresh fish (good crispy chips) and popular Sun lunch in bar and restaurant, decent italian wines, real ales such as Brains Revd James and local Ceredigion Red Kite, courteous efficient service, log fires; piped music, no dogs or children; nice spot nr harbour and art and crafts shops *(George Atkinson, Neil Skidmore, Mrs Julie Thomas)*

Harbour Inn [Main St]: Basic three-bar beamed pub in delightful setting by small sailing harbour, splendid views, wide choice of reasonably priced food from quickly served sandwiches up, Greene King Old Speckled Hen, lots of local pictures, staff helpful to families; piped music, children's area with pool table; plenty of tables on suntrap terrace, bedrooms, open all day *(Mike Pugh, George Atkinson, B and F A Hannam, David Field)*

ST DAVID'S SM7525

☆ ***Farmers Arms*** [Goat St]: Bustling low-ceilinged pub by cathedral gate, cheerful and properly pubby, with cosy separate areas, wide choice of good value straightforward food from sandwiches to steaks, well kept Brains Rev James, Flowers IPA and Original, Wadworths 6X and Worthington, chatty landlord and locals; pool room, TV for rugby; cathedral view from tables in suntrap back garden, and lack of car park means no tour bus groups *(J Taylor, Simon Watkins, David Field)*

ST DOGMAELS SN1646

Ferry: Old stone building with modern additions overlooking Teifi estuary, character bar, pine tables, nice clutter of bric-a-brac inc many old advertising signs; well kept Marstons Pedigree and Wadworths 6X, generous bar food inc crab sandwiches and enjoyable baked welsh goats cheese (pay with your order), restaurant; take the ex-RN landlord with a pinch of salt; children welcome, tables out on terrace *(LYM, Gene and Kitty Rankin)*

STACKPOLE SR9896

Stackpole Inn [off B4319 S of Pembroke]: Relaxing refurbished L-shaped dining pub on four levels, partly no smoking, with good modern cooking, well kept Brains Rev James, Felinfoel Double Dragon and Worthington, neat light oak furnishings, ash beams in low ceilings, shove-ha'penny and dominoes; piped music; children welcome, disabled access and facilities, tables out in attractive gardens, good woodland and coastal walks in the Stackpole estate, open all day (Sun afternoon break) *(Mrs J Bairstow, LYM, Geoff Palmer)*

TENBY SN1300

☆ ***Plantagenet House*** [Quay Hill]: Well renovated and civilised early medieval building on two levels, marvellous old chimney, stripped stonework, tile and board floors; downstairs bar with well kept Boddingtons, Flowers IPA and Wadworths 6X; upstairs restaurant with interesting low-priced food inc fine soups, good baguettes, fresh local crab and fish, welsh cheeses, friendly service, cane furniture, candles on tables; piped music, fine Victorian lavatories; open all day in season, cl lunchtime out of season *(Jane and Graham Rooth, David and Nina Pugsley)*

TRESAITH SN2751

☆ ***Ship***: Tastefully decorated bistro-style pub on Cardigan Bay with magnificent views of sea, beach, famous waterfall, perhaps even dolphins; good generous home-made food from ploughman's with local cheeses to local fish, two weekly changing guest beers, good photographs, no smoking dining area *(Helene and Richard Lay, David and Nina Pugsley)*

WOLFS CASTLE SM9526

☆ ***Wolfe*** [A40 Haverfordwest—Fishguard]: Good fresh home-made food (not Sun or Mon evenings in winter) from reasonably priced bar lunches to more upmarket restaurant dishes inc authentic italian cooking and lovely lobster, comfortable brasserie dining lounge, garden room and conservatory, carefully chosen wines, two real ales, log fire, board games; pub dog, children welcome, attractively laid-out garden, bedrooms *(V Brogden, Mike Pugh, LYM, Janet Walters)*

GWENT

ABERGAVENNY SO2914

Angel [Cross St, by Town Hall]: Civilised well restored bar with thriving atmosphere, some big comfortable settees, lovely bevelled glass behind servery, good service, popular restaurant and adjacent lounge areas *(Pamela and Merlyn Horswell)*

Coliseum [Lion St/Frogmore St]: Steps up to modest Wetherspoons cinema conversion, very light and spacious, with lots of panelling, raised areas one end, their usual good value food, beers and wines with a couple of guest ales, friendly staff; wheelchair lift *(Mike Pugh)*

Hen & Chickens [Flannel St]: Unpretentious and relaxed traditional local, well kept Bass and Brains from bar unusually set against street windows, basic wholesome cheap lunchtime food (not Sun), mugs of tea and coffee, friendly efficient staff, interesting side areas, popular darts, cards and dominoes; TV, very busy on market day *(the Didler, MP, Pete Baker)*

Lamb & Flag [Llanwenarth; A40, 2 miles NW]: Brightly refurbished open-plan linked areas with light oak furniture, pottery, modern art and picture-window hill views, good range of enjoyable food (all day in summer), well kept Brains Bitter, SA and Rev James, conservatory; children welcome (high chairs), tables on terrace with play area, comfortable bedrooms with own bathrooms, open all day in summer *(Joan and Michel Hooper-Immins)*

BASSALEG ST2787

Tredegar Arms [handy for M4 junction 28; A468 towards Caerphilly]: Wide range of well cooked food inc interesting dishes, up to half a dozen or more well kept ales, enthusiastic landlord, pleasant eating area, family and outdoor areas (no dogs allowed in garden) *(Mike Pugh)*

BRYNGWYN SO4008

☆ *Cripple Creek* [off old A40 W of Raglan]: Smartly extended and civilised old country dining pub with wide range of good reasonably priced food from simple things to more elaborate meals inc fresh fish and choice of four Sun roasts, friendly prompt service, well kept ales such as Adnams Broadside, Brains and Tetleys, decent wines, teas and coffees, pleasant no smoking dining room; country views from small terrace, play area, open all day *(Eryl and Keith Dykes, Guy Vowles, Ann and Colin Hunt)*

BRYNMAWR SO1912

Bridgend [King St (A467, nr A465 junction)]: Similar style to Coach & Horses at Llangynidr (see Powys Lucky Dips), Bass, Bulmer's Original cider, good changing blackboard food at fair prices, friendly service *(John Brockington)*

CHEPSTOW ST5394

Castle View [Bridge St]: Hotel bar with white-painted walls and some exposed stonework, plush chairs and stools, good value bar food inc good sandwich range, well kept Wye Valley Hereford PA from small bar counter, daily papers; opp castle and its car park, tables in pretty back garden with fountain, 13 bedrooms with own bathrooms *(BB, Ian Phillips)*

Coach & Horses [Welsh St, just outside Town Arch]: Comfortable local with well appointed split-level rooms, fine old etched windows, open fire, prints, good helpings of reasonably priced pub food, well kept ales *(Pamela and Merlyn Horswell)*

GROSMONT SO4024

Angel: 17th-c friendly village local on attractive steep single street within sight of castle, seats out by ancient market cross beside surprisingly modern little town hall; several changing well kept ales from Tomos Watkins and (brewed for the pub) Wye Valley, farm cider, bar food (not Thurs pm); TV, separate room with pool and darts, a couple of tables and boules pitch behind *(BB, Mike Pugh)*

GWEHELOG SO3903

☆ *Hall* [old rd Usk—Raglan, S of village]: Neatly kept small former coaching inn, olde-worlde décor with beams and log fire, very friendly landlord, good choice of unusual fresh food using local ingredients, Bass and Hancocks HB, separate dining and games areas *(Gwyneth and Salvo Spadaro-Dutturi)*

KEMEYS COMMANDER SO3405

Chainbridge [B4598 Usk—Abergavenny]: Splendid riverside setting by historic Chain Bridge, several real ales, good range of food, spacious bar area with open fire at top level and views of river and hills from lower level; plenty of tables on verandah and waterside grass *(Richard Fendick)*

LLANDENNY SO4103

☆ *Raglan Arms*: Sturdily furnished linked rooms of extensive dining area leading through to conservatory, with relaxed atmosphere, good fresh food esp fish and seafood cooked to order, pleasant efficient service and good wine choice (booking advised Fri-Sat evenings and Sun lunchtime); terracotta-walled flagstoned bar with leather sofas around low table on oriental rug, broadsheet papers, big log fire in handsome stone fireplace, well kept Felinfoel Double Dragon and a Wye Valley seasonal beer, neat separate public bar with pool and wide-screen TV; garden tables *(Mervyn and Susan Underhill, BB, Colin Mansell, Pamela and Merlyn Horswell)*

LLANDEWI SKIRRID SO3416

☆ *Walnut Tree* [B4521]: Restaurant rather than pub, though it does have a nice small flagstoned bar with fireside seats as well as the airy main dining room; enjoyable inventive food at a price, very good wines (good cider, but no real ale), nice coffee and pleasantly relaxed and individual service; children welcome, cl Sun evening and Mon *(Anthony Rickards Collinson, Pamela and Merlyn Horswell, LYM, Stephen, Julie and Hayley Brown, Bernard Stradling, JHW, Duncan Cloud)*

LLANFIHANGEL CRUCORNEY SO3220

☆ *Skirrid* [signed off A465]: One of Britain's oldest pubs, dating partly from 1110; ancient studded door to high-ceilinged main bar, stone, flagstones and panelling, dark feel accentuated by furniture inc pews (some padded), huge log fire, separate dining room; well kept Marstons Pedigree and Ushers Founders and Best, helpful welcoming staff, good generous bar food using fresh local ingredients from big sandwiches up, reasonable prices; open all day summer, children welcome, tables on attractive terrace and small sloping back lawn, well equipped bedrooms *(LYM, Richard Fendick)*

LLANGATTOCK LINGOED SO3620

☆ *Hunters Moon* [off B4521 just E of Llanvetherine]: Attractive and tranquil tucked-away pub dating from 13th c, nicely refurbished keeping beams, dark stripped stone and flagstones; has had good unpretentious country cooking and well kept Wye Valley Cwrw Dewi Sant tapped from the cask, but new owners spring 2004 – no firm news yet on how they will be running it; dogs and children welcome, tables out on deck and in charming dell, comfortable bedrooms with own bathrooms, glorious country nr Offa's Dyke, has been cl Mon-Weds lunchtimes and Sun evening, at least in winter *(LYM, Terry and Linda Moseley)*

LLANTHONY SO2928

☆ *Abbey Hotel* [Llanthony Priory; off A465, back rd Llanvihangel Crucorney—Hay]: Terrific setting for plain bar in dim-lit vaulted flagstoned crypt of graceful ruined Norman abbey, with lawns around and the peaceful border hills beyond; well kept Brains and perhaps a guest beer, farm cider in summer, simple lunchtime bar food, no children;

occasional live music, open all day Sat (and Sun in summer – much its best time of year); cl Mon-Thurs, Sun evenings in winter; evening restaurant, bedrooms in restored parts of abbey walls, great walks all around *(LYM, the Didler)*

Half Moon: Basic dog-friendly country inn with decent plain food, well kept Bull Mastiff beers inc power-packed Son-of-a-Bitch, bar billiards; big back paddock (on the pony treks), gorgeous views from nice back garden, bedrooms not luxurious but clean and comfortable, unspoilt valley with great walks *(Eddie Edwards, Ian Phillips)*

LLANTRISANT FAWR ST3997

☆ ***Greyhound*** [off A449 nr Usk]: Prettily set 17th-c country inn with relaxed homely feel in three linked bar rooms of varying sizes, steps between two, nice mix of furnishings and rustic decorations, wide choice of consistently good home cooking at sensible prices, well kept Bass, Flowers Original, Greene King Abbot and a weekly guest beer, friendly helpful staff, log fires, colourful prints in pleasant grey-panelled dining room; picnic-sets in attractively laid-out garden with big fountain, hill views, adjoining pine shop, good bedrooms in small attached motel *(BB, Andy Sinden, Louise Harrington, M Joyner)*

MAMHILAD SO3003

Star: Comfortably worn in quiet local with coal fire in one bar, woodburner in another, well kept Bass, decent food, welcoming staff, a couple of basset hounds; not far from canal *(Pamela and Merlyn Horswell)*

MATHERN ST5291

Millers Arms [off A48 W of Chepstow]: Pleasant local with well kept changing beers such as Greene King IPA, enjoyable food cooked to order (so will be a wait), good service *(R T and J C Moggridge)*

MONMOUTH SO5012

Kings Head [Agincourt Sq]: Well run Wetherspoons in former period hotel, plenty of well spaced seating, their usual good deals on food and drink *(Ann and Colin Hunt, Geoff Pidoux)*

Punch House [Agincourt Sq]: 17th-c former gaol, relaxed and chatty open-plan beamed bar, red leatherette settles, old bound *Punch* volumes, big fireplace, no smoking area; generous food, prompt friendly service, three or four well kept ales inc Brains, decent wines, restaurant; discreet piped music; children in eating areas, tables out on cobbles overlooking square, open all day (cl Sun afternoon) *(Duncan Cloud, LYM)*

NEWBRIDGE ON USK ST3894

Newbridge Inn: Good enterprising reasonably priced food in bar and rather smart ground-floor and upstairs dining rooms, two real ales, good wines by the glass, sofas and easy chairs in relaxing area down steps from entrance; fine spot by bridge with view over Usk valley, comfortable bedrooms *(Guy Vowles)*

NEWPORT ST3189

Lyceum [A4051 just off M4 junction 26, towards centre; Malpas Rd]: Friendly and tastefully modernised Victorian local, several distinct areas around horseshoe bar, popular good value straightforward bar lunches, well kept Courage Best, Greene King Old Speckled Hen and perhaps a guest beer; several quiz nights, Thurs folk club, live music Sat *(Pete Baker)*

PANDY SO3322

Lancaster Arms [A465]: Well worn-in local right by Offa's Dyke path, welcoming landlady and staff, good cheerful service, enjoyable sensibly priced food, small range of well kept beers; dogs welcome, two tidy bedrooms, good breakfast *(Eddie Edwards, Joyce and Maurice Cottrell, Nigel Howard)*

Pandy Inn [A465 Abergavenny—Hereford]: Welcoming old slate-built family pub, good reasonably priced bar food inc huge steak pie, friendly staff, changing ales such as Fullers London Pride, comfortable modern settles, 3D Brecons maps, good Sun night nostalgic pianist; adjacent walkers' bunkhouse *(Bob Scott, Nigel Howard)*

Park Hotel: Hotel rather than pub, but well worth knowing for reasonably priced enjoyable food inc authentic austrian and hungarian dishes, decent low-priced wine, a well kept real ale and exotic lager; relaxed atmosphere and service, bedrooms *(Mike Pugh)*

PENHOW ST4191

Rock & Fountain [Llanvaches Rd]: Big 16th-c roadside pub with low-beamed main bar, comfortable window seats, two log fires, no smoking eating area, enjoyable food from sandwiches, baked potatoes and modern snacks to steak and Sun lunch, 2-for-1 bargains, real ales, house wine deals, Fri medieval banquets; children welcome *(BB, Andy Sinden, Louise Harrington)*

PONTYPOOL ST3398

Carpenters Arms [Coedypaen, just SE of Llandegfedd reservoir]: Pretty country pub reopened under welcoming new landlord, well kept Bass, good wine range, imaginative food with plenty for vegetarians; well behaved dogs and children welcome, pleasant seating outside *(Gwyneth and Salvo Spadaro-Dutturi)*

RAGLAN SO4107

Beaufort Arms [High St]: Former coaching inn with comfortable and roomy character beamed bars, well kept changing guest beers, log fire, good food choice in bar and restaurant from breakfast on, enthusiastic newish owners and friendly service; piped music; children welcome, 15 bedrooms with own bathrooms *(David Heath)*

ROGERSTONE ST2788

Tredegar Arms [Cefn Rd (A467 nr M4 junction 27)]: Family-run low-beamed suburban pub, cosy and friendly public bar, bigger comfortable lounge, wide blackboard food choice from baguettes and baked potatoes up, good value pies and Sun lunch, well kept Bass, Courage Best and a guest beer, welcoming licensees *(Pete Baker)*

SKENFRITH SO4520

☆ ***Bell***: Beautiful setting by bridge over River Monnow, modern light and airy linked areas with flagstones and canary walls, settees, pews and carved settles among more conventional pub furniture, church candles on tables, log fire in big fireplace, welcoming enthusiastic owners, charming staff, good wines by the glass, Freeminer and Hook Norton Best, interesting if not cheap meals inc welsh black beef and entirely using named local suppliers, extensive bare-boards restaurant, games room; piped nostalgic pop music; children very welcome, picnic-sets out on terrace, steps up to sloping lawn, bedrooms *(BB, Anthony Rickards Collinson, Pamela and Merlyn Horswell, Theocsbrian, Mrs Kitty Lloyd, Duncan Cloud, Alec and Barbara Jones)*

TINTERN SO5301

☆ ***Moon & Sixpence*** [A466 Chepstow—Monmouth]: Flower-decked small pub, attractively furnished and largely smoke-free, with lots of beams and steps, one room with sofas and wicker armchairs, natural spring feeding indoor goldfish pool, good choice of good value food, well kept ales such as Greene King Abbot, Hook Norton Best and Wye Valley Butty Bach from back bar, friendly helpful service; quiet piped music; children welcome, terrace tables under arbour look along River Wye to abbey, good walks *(A H C Rainier, BB, Di and Mike Gillam)*

TRELLECK GRANGE SO5001

☆ ***Fountain*** [minor rd Tintern—Llanishen, SE of village]: Peaceful spot on back country road, dark-beamed bar, roomy and comfortable dining room, wide range of good value food from good fresh sandwiches to carefully prepared interesting dishes and popular Sun lunch, cheerful patient staff, well kept ales such as Wye Valley Butty Bach, good value house wines, decent malt whiskies, darts; may be nostalgic piped pop music; children allowed away from bar, small sheltered garden with summer kids' bar; bedrooms, camping available *(BB, Joyce and Maurice Cottrell)*

USK SO3801

☆ ***Castle Inn*** [Twyn Sq]: Relaxed and jaunty front bar with sofas, locals reading newspapers, interesting carved chair and comfortable window seats, big mirrors, lots of dried hops, generous well served food all day (part of pub now functioning as good chinese restaurant), well organised quick service, changing ales such as Hancocks HB and Wadworths 6X, freshly squeezed orange juice, a couple of cosy little alcoves off back dining room; piped music may be loud; pavement tables, garden behind with parakeets and lop-eared rabbits *(BB, Peter and Audrey Dowsett, Ian Phillips, Mike Pugh)*

Cross Keys [Bridge St]: Small friendly two-bar pub dating from 14th c, oak beams, interesting Last Supper tapestry, log fire, popular food, good range of drinks *(Ann and Colin Hunt)*

Kings Head [Old Market St]: Busy pub with fine choice of well kept real ales inc Fullers London Pride, enjoyable food, welcoming staff, huge log fire in superb fireplace; open all day, bedrooms *(Mike Pugh, Gwyneth and Salvo Spadaro-Dutturi)*

☆ ***Royal Hotel*** [New Market St]: Traditional fixtures and fittings, old china and pictures, old-fashioned fireplaces, comfortable wooden chairs and tables, filling food inc wider evening choice (not Sun; worth booking Sat and Sun lunch), well kept Bass, Hancocks HB and Felinfoel Double Dragon from deep cellar, friendly service; piped music; well behaved children welcome, has been cl Mon lunchtime *(LYM, Chris Flynn, Wendy Jones, Peter and Audrey Dowsett, Mike Pugh)*

Three Salmons [Porthycarne St/Bridge St]: Impeccable service, enjoyable if not cheap food, thriving atmosphere; good disabled access *(Pamela and Merlyn Horswell)*

GWYNEDD

BETWS-Y-COED SH7956

Pont y Pair: Welcoming mix of diners and local drinkers, reasonably priced food from good lunchtime baked potatoes up in small cosy bar (can get a bit smoky) and restaurant, separate no smoking room, Tetleys, decent wine, no piped music *(KC)*

Swallow Falls [A5 W]: Bar in hotel/youth hostel/camping complex, good value bistro meals such as lamb shank in mint gravy, Ansells Best and Tetleys *(Dave Braisted)*

☆ ***Ty Gwyn*** [A5 just S of bridge to village]: Restaurant-with-rooms rather than pub (you must eat or stay overnight to be served alcohol), but pubby feel in beamed lounge bar with ancient cooking range, easy chairs, antique prints and interesting bric-a-brac, friendly staff, interesting meals (they do sandwiches too), well kept ales such as Brains and Youngs, partly no smoking restaurant; piped music; children welcome (high chair and toys), cl Mon-Weds in Jan *(Paul A Moore, Alison Hayes, Pete Hanlon, Jarrod and Wendy Hopkinson, Keith and Chris O'Neill, LYM, J C Poley, Revd D Glover)*

BLAENAU FFESTINIOG SH7046

Queens [High St]: Small hotel with decent food from fresh cheap sandwiches up in smart comfortable lounge bar and dining room, well kept Bass, Greene King Abbot and Tetleys; may be sports TV *(Mr and Mrs Colin Roberts, Mike and Mary Carter)*

CAERNARFON SH4762

Black Boy [Northgate St]: Bustling pub by castle walls, beams from ships wrecked here in 16th c, bare floors, cheery fire, homely and cosy lounge bar with interesting variety of dark wood furniture and cheery fire, good value food all day from filled baguettes and huge doorstep sandwiches up, prompt pleasant service, Bass and Hancocks HB, restaurant, public bar with TV; a couple of pavement picnic-sets, bedrooms *(Michael and Alison Sandy)*

Palace Vaults [Palace St, opp castle]: Flower-decked pub with old-fashioned bar fittings, well kept Banks's and Camerons Strongarm, low-priced basic food till 4 (later in season), good mix of locals and visitors, family dining area; open all day, nr castle entrance and

Welsh Highland Railway *(Dave Braisted)*

CONWY SH7878

Bridge Hotel [Rose Hill St]: Polished boards in large neat bar, Burtonwood ales and a guest beer, reasonably priced lunchtime food and more restauranty evening choices, no smoking dining area; bedrooms *(Michael and Alison Sandy)*

☆ ***Castle Hotel*** [High St]: Plenty of tables in cosy bars, enjoyable food here and in restaurant, decent wines, friendly atmosphere and good service; interesting old building – with own car parks, which helps here; 30 bedrooms *(E G Parish)*

DOLGARROG SH7766

☆ ***Lord Newborough*** [Conwy Rd (B5106 just S)]: Black-beamed carpeted bar with lots of hanging jugs and other china, Boddingtons and good wines by the glass, big log fire, welcoming landlord and staff, linen-set dining rooms each side with good food esp fish; tables out on two terraces and small lawn with copsey woodland rising steeply behind, cl Tues lunchtime and Sun-Mon *(BB, John Hillmer)*

LLANBEDR-Y-CENNIN SH7669

Olde Bull [off B5106]: Neatly kept low-beamed hillside pub with good open fires and some antique settles among more usual furnishings in its knocked-through rooms, Lees Bitter and a seasonal guest beer, decent straightforward food (may take a while; not Sun night or Mon in winter) from sandwiches and baguettes up, restaurant (children allowed), darts, dominoes, and chess; outside lavatories; Vale of Conwy views from garden with wild area, waterfall and orchard, good walks, open all day *(LYM, Bruce Bird, Alison Hayes, Pete Hanlon)*

LLANDUDNO SH7882

Cottage Loaf [Market St]: Pleasant atmosphere in friendly former bakery with big log fire, flagstones, bare boards and salvaged ship's timbers, mix of individual tables and chairs, small choice of good value food inc good lunchtime baguettes, several well kept real ales; good piped music, some live *(Mike and Lynn Robinson)*

☆ ***Kings Head*** [Old Rd, behind tram station]: Rambling and pretty, much extended around 16th-c flagstoned core, spaciously open-plan, bright and clean but with plenty of interesting corners and comfortable traditional furnishings, old local tramway photographs, red wallpaper, dark pine, well kept ales inc a house beer from Phoenix, eclectic choice of wines in friendly-sized glasses, quick friendly service, huge log fire, smart back dining room up a few steps, wide range of generous food (busy at night, so get there early); children welcome, seats on front terrace overlooking quaint Victorian cable tramway's station (water for dogs here), open all day in summer *(LYM, Kevin Blake, MLR, Mike and Lynn Robinson)*

Olde Victoria [Church Walks]: Victorian splendour away from the high street bustle, coloured glass panels, Queen Victoria pictures, interesting old fireplace, well kept Banks's, Marstons Pedigree and guest beers, generous good value food, pleasant clean dining area with high chair (families welcome), upstairs restaurant *(E G Parish, Mike and Lynn Robinson)*

Palladium [Gloddaeth St]: Wetherspoons in beautifully converted former theatre, boxes and seats intact, spectacular ceilings, good value food and drinks inc bargain Shepherd Neame Spitfire, plenty of seating *(Kevin Blake, Keith and Chris O'Neill, E G Parish, Mike and Lynn Robinson)*

Parade [Church Walks]: Friendly young licensees, decent food, quiz night; good value bedrooms *(Keith and Chris O'Neill)*

LLANFROTHEN SH6141

Brondanw Arms [aka Y Ring; B4410]: Clean and friendly Welsh-speaking pub (Welsh piped music too), popular for food from good bacon baps to full meals inc Sun lunch, well kept beers such as Black Sheep and Marstons Pedigree, plenty of room; folk night alternate Sats; picnic-sets and play area outside, good walking area *(Steve Jennings, A J Bowen)*

LLANRWST SH7865

☆ ***Maenan Abbey Hotel*** [Maenan, A470 N]: Substantial steep-gabled Victorian hotel with battlemented tower, attentive new management and good service, bar food from sandwiches up, small comfortable front bar with well kept Tetleys, elegant and airy back dining lounge, log fires, partly no smoking restaurant; children welcome, lots of tables out in charming stately grounds, good play area, 14 comfortable bedrooms *(LYM, B and M Kendall, MLR)*

LLANUWCHLLYN SH8730

☆ ***Eagles*** [aka Eryrod; A494/B4403]: New licensees doing well, with good reasonably priced food from sandwiches to traditional and more enterprising dishes, young friendly efficient staff, thriving atmosphere in small front bar and plush back lounge, neat décor with beams and some stripped stone, no smoking dining area, back picture-window view of mountains with Lake Bala in distance, limited wine list, strong coffee, no music; disabled access, picnic-sets under cocktail parasols on flower-filled back terrace *(Michael and Jenny Back, Mike and Mary Carter)*

MAENTWROG SH6741

☆ ***Grapes*** [A496; village signed from A470]: Rambling old stripped stone inn, very popular with families in summer, with very wide choice of reasonably priced generous food inc good fish, well kept Greene King Old Speckled Hen and two or three changing guest beers, over 30 malt whiskies and decent wine choice, lots of stripped pine (pews, settles, panelling, pillars and carvings), good log fires, intriguing collection of brass blowlamps, lovely views from conservatory dining extension, pleasant back terrace and walled garden; they may try to keep your credit card while you eat, juke box in public bar; disabled lavatories, dogs welcome, open all day *(David Crook, Bruce Bird, Dr and Mrs P Truelove, GSB,*

LYM, John and Tania Wood, A J Bowen, Phil and Heidi Cook)

NANT PERIS SH6058

Vaynol Arms: Friendly and simple walkers' and climbers' Snowdonia pub, Robinsons beers, good value food; opens 7 *(Gill and Tony Morriss)*

PENMAENPOOL SH6918

George III [just off A493, nr Dolgellau]: Lovely views over Mawddach estuary from attractive inn with extended bottom public bar (children allowed and no smoking till 9.30), beams, flagstones and stripped stone, well kept ales such as Greene King Ruddles, good choice of wines by the glass; also civilised partly panelled upstairs bar opening into cosy inglenook lounge, with same food, and separate restaurant; open all day, sheltered terrace, good walks, good bedrooms inc some (allowing dogs) in quiet and interesting conversion of former station on disused line now a walkway *(Dr and Mrs Rod Holcombe, Nick and Meriel Cox, Dr and Mrs P Truelove, LYM, John and Tania Wood, Dennis Jenkin)*

PENTREFOELAS SH8950

Giler Arms [Rhydlydan, just off A5 SE of Betws-y-Coed]: Peaceful pleasantly worn in country hotel with well kept low-priced Bathams Bitter and Mild, good value food from sandwiches up inc good range of curries, locals' bar with pool, lounge with open woodburner, dining room; terrace tables, lake in streamside grounds, bedrooms with super views, open all day Sat and summer Sun *(Gill and Tony Morriss)*

PORTH DINLLAEN SH2741

☆ *Ty Coch* [beach car park signed from Morfa Nefyn, then 15-min walk]: Stunning spot on curving beach, far from the roads (and quite a long walk from the nearest car park), with great view along coast to mountains; pub itself full of attractive salvage, RNLI memorabilia, lamps and mugs, good prawn and crab salads and other usual lunchtime food, decent coffee; keg beer (and plastic beakers if you drink outside); cl winter exc Sat lunchtimes, but open all day summer and very popular then – idyllic on a hot still day *(LYM, John and Wendy Allin, Jason Caulkin)*

PORTHMADOG SH5639

Spooners [Harbour Station]: Decent pub lunches inc good filled baguettes and Fri-Sat evening meals at reasonable prices, lots of railway memorabilia, particularly well kept Banks's Original, Marstons Pedigree and interesting guest beers such as Spinning Dog Mutleys Pit Stop and Chase Your Tail and Wye Valley Battle; tables out on platform *(Keith and Chris O'Neill)*

RHYD DDU SH5753

Cwellyn Arms [A4085 N of Beddgelert]: Comfortably basic 18th-c pub with wide choice of good value straightforward food from baked potatoes up, up to nine changing ales such as Spinning Dog and Wye Valley; flagstones, log fire in huge ancient fireplace, pleasant restaurant area, small games bar with pool, darts and TV; children and walkers welcome, spectacular Snowdon views from garden tables with barbecue, babbling stream just over wall, big adventure playground; bedrooms, usually open all day, not far from Welsh Highland Railway top terminus *(KC, Bruce Bird, Dr and Mrs P Truelove, Michael and Alison Sandy)*

TREMADOG SH5640

☆ *Golden Fleece* [off A487 just N of Porthmadog; Market Sq]: Neat stone-built inn on attractive square, quick friendly service, well kept Worthington and a guest such as Enville, decent wines, partly partitioned rambling dark-beamed lounge with open fire, nice little snug (reserved seats for regulars Fri-Sat night), intriguing barrel-vaulted cellar bar, good value generous home-made bar food inc fish (ordered from back bistro, off sheltered inner courtyard with more tables), games room; children welcome in bistro and small family room, bedrooms and flats *(LYM, Tony Hobden)*

TUDWEILIOG SH2336

☆ *Lion* [Nefyn Rd (B4417), Lleyn Peninsula]: Cheerfully busy village inn with wide choice of good value straightforward food and some nice specials in bar and no smoking family dining conservatory (small helpings for children, who have a pretty free rein here), quick friendly service, well kept Boddingtons, Marstons Pedigree and Theakstons Best and Mild, dozens of malt whiskies, decent wines, games in lively public bar; pleasant front garden, good value bedrooms with own bathrooms *(LYM, Revd D Glover)*

WAUNFAWR SH5359

Snowdonia Parc [A4085 Caernarfon—Beddgelert]: Straightforward pub food inc enormous hot beef baguettes, brews its own strong Welsh Highland Bitter, family room with playthings; overlooks and really part of Welsh Highland Railway terminus, camping facilities *(Tony Hobden)*

Y FELINHELI SH5267

Gardd Fôn [Beach Rd, off A487 SW of Bangor]: Nautical-theme pub by Menai Straits, enjoyable food in bar or bistro restaurant, Burtonwood and a guest beer; great views from tables out on grass *(Maurice and Gill McMahon)*

MID GLAMORGAN

BRYNCETHIN SS9184

Masons Arms: Welcoming village inn with roomy lounge bar and local's bar with pool, good choice of well kept real ales, decent wines, enjoyable generous food inc some interesting dishes in bar and restaurant, good service; nine bedrooms *(Andy Sinden, Louise Harrington)*

CAERPHILLY ST1586

☆ *Courthouse* [Cardiff Rd]: 14th-c pub with splendid views of nearby moated castle from light and airy modern back café/bar and picnic-sets on grassy terrace; character original core has rugs on ancient flagstones, stripped stone walls, raftered gallery, enormous chimney breast, real ales such as Brains SA and Marstons Pedigree, good coffee, low-priced food all day (not Sun evening, not after 5.30 Mon, Fri or Sat) from baguettes up, partly no smoking restaurant; pub games, piped pop music, virtually no nearby parking; children welcome in eating areas, open all day *(LYM, Ian Phillips)*

KENFIG SS8383

☆ *Prince of Wales* [2¼ miles from M4 junction 37; A4229 towards Porthcawl, then right when dual carriageway narrows on bend, signed Maudlam and Kenfig]: Interesting ancient pub among sand dunes (nature reserve awash with orchids in Jun), well kept Bass, Worthington and wknd guest beers tapped from the cask, friendly landlord, wife does good food inc much enjoyed fish specials, good choice of malt whiskies and decent wines, stripped stone and log fires, lots of wreck pictures, traditional games, small upstairs dining room for summer and busy wknds; children and (in non-carpet areas) dogs welcome, handy for walks *(the Didler, Ian Phillips, John and Joan Nash, LYM, Phil and Sally Gorton)*

LLANGYNWYD SS8588

☆ *Old House* [off A4063 S of Maesteg; pub behind church, nearly a mile W of modern village]: Pretty thatched dining pub, much modernised inside and largely no smoking, with friendly efficient staff, more than 350 whiskies, well kept Brains, Worthington and a couple of guest beers, lots of brass and china especially around the huge fireplace and on the beams, usual food all day from filled rolls up, attractive conservatory extension leading to garden with good play area; piped music; children welcome, open all day, nearby huge churchyard and valley views worth a look *(Tom Evans, LYM, R Michael Richards)*

LLWYDCOED SN9905

Red Cow [Merthyr Rd (B4276 N of Aberdare)]: Friendly neatly kept traditional local, cosy and comfortable, large bar and restaurant, with well kept Brains SA and Hancocks HB, good value generous food inc Fri-Sun carvery, helpful landlord, no juke box or machines; large pleasant back garden *(John and Joan Nash)*

MACHEN ST2288

White Hart [White Hart Lane, off A468 towards Bedwas]: Welcoming bar and lounge full of salvaged ship memorabilia, restored ceiling painting, log fire, wide choice of reasonably priced generous wholesome bar meals (Sun lunches only, but a bargain); usually brewing its own beers, with guest beers too from small servery down panelled corridor, and annual beer festival; garden with play area, bedrooms *(Emma Kingdon, Mike Pugh)*

MISKIN ST0480

Miskin Arms [handy for M4 junction 34, via A4119 and B4264]: Friendly and roomy village pub with well kept Everards Tiger, Hancocks HB and guest beers, good value bar food, popular restaurant Sun lunch and Tues-Sat evenings *(Colin Moore)*

NANT DDU SO0015

Nant Ddu Lodge [Cwmtaf; A470 Merthyr Tydfil—Brecon]: Hotel with popular adjacent brasserie and bar, wide range of enjoyable and imaginative reasonably priced food, good atmosphere, real ale, no smoking lounge, large evening dining room; good bright well equipped bedrooms (some in separate block), good walking country by Taff Valley reservoirs *(Pamela and Merlyn Horswell, V Brogden)*

OGMORE SS8876

Pelican: Friendly and comfortably unpretentious old country pub in nice spot above ruined castle, attractive bar leading back to snug, cosy side area and pretty restaurant, well kept ales such as Bass, Greene King Abbot and Charles Wells Bombardier, enjoyable food from enterprising big rolls to interesting main dishes, smiling staff; tables on side terrace, quite handy for the beaches *(LYM, Christopher and Jo Barton, David and Nina Pugsley)*

PONTYPRIDD ST07690

Market Tavern [Market St]: Victorian pub in heart of market, good cheap lunches, thriving atmosphere *(Norman Lewis)*

PORTHCAWL SS7277

Porthcawl Hotel [John St]: Promptly served generous bargain food in bar or simple restaurant, friendly staff; sports TV in both areas *(R C Vincent)*

RUDRY ST2087

Maenllwyd [off A468 Newport—Caerphilly in Lower Machen, halfway towards Caerphilly on minor rd]: Comfortably extended Tudor Chef & Brewer, olde-worlde feel with interesting rambling layout, steps up and down, low beams, panelling, and logs burning in the lounge bar's huge fireplace; decent food all day, good choice of well kept real ales and of wines, good-sized family dining room; fruit machine, piped music, can be very busy Fri-Sat; nice spot on the edge of Rudry Common, open all day from noon *(LYM, Ian Phillips, Dr and Mrs A K Clarke, R Michael Richards)*

THORNHILL ST1484

☆ *Travellers Rest* [A469 S of Caerphilly]: Thatched stone-built Vintage Inn dining pub with well kept Bass, Hancocks HB and Tetleys, good sensibly priced wine choice, winter mulled wine, prompt friendly service, daily papers and magazines, reasonably priced food all day, huge fireplace and nooks and crannies in low-beamed bar on right, no smoking extension; piped music, separate food and drinks queues when they're busy, no bookings; children welcome lunchtimes, open all day, tables out on grass, good walks *(Ian Phillips, David Jeffreys, Mr and Mrs M Dalby, David and Nina Pugsley, R Michael Richards)*

TREOES SS9478

Star [off A48 Cardiff—Bridgend]: Thriving atmosphere, enjoyable food inc welsh black beef in bar and stripped stone dining room, well kept Brains, wide range of wines, friendly helpful service; lovely quiet village (beyond large industrial estate) *(David and Nina Pugsley)*

POWYS

ABERCRAVE SN8212
Abercrave Inn [Heol Tawe (A4067 NE of Ystradgynlais)]: Enjoyable generous reasonably priced food, good wine choice, quick friendly service and good local atmosphere; handy for Dan-yr-Ogof caves *(Isobel Carter)*

BETTWS CEDEWAIN SO1296
New Inn: Good popular local, long open-plan bar, welcoming helpful landlord, small choice of sensibly priced food from substantial well presented sandwiches up, real ales such as Boddingtons, Tetleys and Worthington, central fire, beams thickly hung with mugs, darts; games end with pool and TV; disabled access, tables outside *(Michael and Jenny Back)*

BRECON SO0428
Camden Arms [Watton]: Quiet unpretentious pub, sofa and dresser with books off main bar, friendly service, generous food inc good value ploughman's, good range of beers, decent house wines, games room; children welcome *(Piotr Chodzko-Zajko)*
George [George St]: Spacious town pub with attractive back courtyard bar (lovely floral displays) and dining conservatory, well kept changing ales such as Adnams, Cains Dr Duncans and Robert Cain and Ind Coope Burton, good blackboard choice of reasonably priced food all day from sandwiches and other snacks up, attentive service, log-effect gas fires; very busy Sat night; interesting cheeses etc from Welsh Food Centre in yard behind *(Ian Phillips)*
Three Horseshoes [Groesffford, off A40 E]: Charming small bar with log fire, good choice of enjoyable food, friendly attentive service, well kept Brains Rev James, sparkling new restaurant area, Brecon Beacons view; children welcome *(Phill Johnson, Martin Jeeves)*

BUILTH WELLS SO0451
Lion [Broad St]: Roomy hotel bar with wide range of good value home-made bar food, good service; newly refurbished traditional bedrooms *(Shirley and Clive Pickerill)*

CARNO SN9697
Aleppo Merchant [A470 Newtown—Machynlleth]: Very popular for decent reasonably priced food from good sandwiches to steaks, friendly helpful landlord, Boddingtons, occasional guest beer, tapestries in plushly modernised stripped stone bar, small peaceful lounge with open fire, no smoking area, restaurant (well behaved children allowed here), back games room; piped music; tables in good-sized garden, bedrooms, nice countryside *(LYM, Michael and Jenny Back, John and Tania Wood)*

CLYRO SO2143
Baskerville Arms: Long comfortable lounge with hops over panelled bar counter, small log fire one end, bigger one up stone steps the other, welcoming landlord and Rocky the dog, well kept Bass, Wye Valley and a guest beer, good choice of other drinks, enjoyable generous food, friendly service, fresh flowers, cartoons of well known phrases; TV; picnic-sets under cocktail parasols in good-sized garden, good bedrooms *(CMW, JJW, Bruce Bird)*

CRICKHOWELL SO2119
White Hart [Brecon Rd (A40 W)]: Stripped stone, beams and flagstones, well kept Brains Bitter, Buckleys Best and Rev James, usual food from lunchtime sandwiches up in eating area (with TV) off one end, or sizeable no smoking restaurant; pub games, may be piped classical music, quiz night Mon; children in eating areas, open all day Sat, some tables outside *(David Carr, LYM, Ann and Colin Hunt)*

DINAS MAWDDWY SH8514
☆ *Llew Coch* [aka Red Lion; just off A470 E of Dolgellau]: Genuine country local surrounded by steep fir forests (good walks), charming timbered front bar sparkling with countless brasses, well kept Bass, quick friendly service, cheap cheerful food from good sandwiches to trout or salmon from River Dovey just behind; inner family room lively with video games, pool and Sat evening live music, dining extension (popular for Sun lunch); dogs on leads welcome, good wheelchair access, tables out on quiet lane *(LYM, Dennis Jenkin)*

GLADESTRY SO2355
Royal Oak [B4594 W of Kington]: Relaxing two-bar beamed and flagstoned walkers' and locals' pub under new licensees, well kept Bass and Hancocks HB, decent food from sandwiches up; picnic-sets in lovely secluded garden behind, safe for children, good value bedrooms (talk of improving these), quiet village handy for Offa's Dyke Path *(Helen Pickering, James Owen, LYM, R B Berry)*

GLASBURY SO1739
Maesllwch Arms [B4350, just off A438]: Susbtantial building with cheerfully pubby panelled bar and roomy partly stripped stone dining room, wide choice of enjoyable food, well kept real ales, good friendly service; picnic-sets in good-sized garden, comfortable bedrooms *(LYM, R B Berry)*

HAY-ON-WYE SO2242
☆ *Blue Boar* [Castle St/Oxford Rd]: Good choice of generous straightforward home cooking (not Sun evening) in light and airy long no smoking dining room with food counter, lots of pictures for sale, bright tablecloths and cheery décor, big sash windows, good coffees and teas, also breakfasts; relaxed candlelit panelled medieval bar with pews and country chairs, well kept ales such as Brains SA and Flowers IPA, interesting bottled ciders inc organic, decent wines, friendly if not always speedy service, log fire; children welcome, may be quiet piped classical music *(BB, CMW, JJW, John Whitehead, Sue Demont, Tim Barrow)*
Three Tuns [Broad St]: One of Hay's oldest buildings, uniquely British; fireside settle and a few old tables and chairs in tiny dark basic quarry-tiled bar, charming veteran landlady knowledgeable about local history (her parents ran the pub before), ciders from barrels on the counter, local apple juice, perhaps a polypin of Wye Valley real ale, Edwardian bar fittings,

lots of bric-a-brac, daily papers, interesting old stove, some fresh flowers; no food *(the Didler, Bruce Bird, Pete Baker, RWC)*

LIBANUS SN9926

☆ ***Tai'r Bull*** [A470 SW of Brecon]: Friendly old well run pub, good helpings of enjoyable food from large ciabattas to smart restaurant dishes such as springbok fillet, real ales such as Brains SA and Charles Wells Bombardier, attentive young licensees, woodburner, light and airy no smoking restaurant, great views of Pen-y-Fan out in front; bedrooms well appointed and comfortable, good breakfast – good base for walking *(David Landey, Michael and Alison Sandy, Miss Joanne Mortimer, Mr and Mrs L J Morgan-Hayes)*

LLANAFAN FAWR SN9655

Red Lion [B4358 SW of Llandrindod Wells]: Attractive and ancient whitewashed pub in interesting small village, front bar, tables in two rooms off and extra dining area, cheerful friendly landlord, good freshly prepared generous food at reasonable prices, evocative atmosphere, real ales such as Merlins Oak and Worthington, farm cider; interesting gents', tables by roadside, three bedrooms and adjoining holiday cottage *(E J C and J M Parker, Mr and Mrs M B Dalling)*

LLANDRINDOD WELLS SO0561

☆ ***Llanerch*** [High St/Waterloo Rd; pub signed from station]: Cheerful rambling 16th-c inn, nice old-fashioned main bar with big inglenook fireplace and more up-to-date lounges off (one no smoking till 8), well kept ales such as Greene King Abbot, Marstons Bitter and Charles Wells Bombardier, inexpensive food from filled baps and baked potatoes up inc Sun roast; piped music, big-screen sports TV, games room with pool; children welcome, pleasant terrace and orchard garden with play area and boules, 12 bedrooms with own bathrooms, good breakfast, open all day *(LYM, E J C and J M Parker, John Urquhart, MLR)*

Metropole [Temple St (A483)]: Big Edwardian hotel's plush front bar with sunny streetside conservatory, well kept Brains SA and Felinfoel Double Dragon, simple bar food all day, imposing dining room; bedrooms with own bathrooms *(Joan and Michel Hooper-Immins)*

LLANFAIR CAEREINION SJ1006

Goat: Relaxed thriving local with settees and easy chairs in inglenook lounge, welcoming informal atmosphere, back dining area with good home cooking, well kept ales inc Worthington, games room; garden *(Geoffrey and Penny Hughes, Andrew York)*

LLANFIHANGEL-NANT-MELAN SO1958

☆ ***Red Lion*** [A44 10 miles W of Kington]: Warm and friendly stripped-stone 16th-c roadside dining pub with good if not cheap fresh food in roomy main area beyond standing timbers on right, smaller room with small pews around tables, well kept changing ale such as Wye Valley, nice wine choice, sensible prices, good service, some tables in front sun porch, back bar with pool; comfortable simple chalet bedrooms, handy for Radnor Forest walks, nr impressive waterfall, cl Tues-Thurs lunchtime, Tues evening *(BB, Christopher J Darwent)*

LLANFRYNACH SO0725

White Swan [off B4558, E of Brecon]: Rambling dining pub with stripped stone and flagstones, sturdy oak tables, leather sofas and armchairs at low tables, imaginative changing lunchtime bar food, well kept Hancocks and Robinsons Unicorn, good wines and coffees, more modern high-ceilinged bare-boards extension, heavily beamed partly no smoking restaurant with modern prints; piped music, and may not serve food at wknds if a function on; children welcome, charming secluded back terrace, cl Tues lunchtime and Mon *(LYM, David Jeffreys, Colette Annesley-Gamester, Jonathan Harding, Mrs M E Mills, David and Nina Pugsley)*

LLANGYNIDR SO1519

☆ ***Coach & Horses*** [Cwm Crawnon Rd (B4558 W of Crickhowell)]: Tidy and roomy flower-decked dining pub, chef now taking over as landlord, wide choice of generous enjoyable food from sandwiches and baguettes up, well kept Bass, Hancocks HB and a guest beer, comfortable banquettes and stripped stone, nice big open fire, large restaurant with no smoking area; pub games, piped music, TV; children welcome in eating areas, dogs allowed in bar, picnic-sets across road in safely fenced pretty sloping garden by lock of Newport & Brecon Canal; three good value comfortable bedrooms, good breakfast, lovely views and walks, open all day *(Steve and Liz Tilley, Revd John E Cooper, Theocsbrian, LYM, Norman Lewis, Neville and Anne Morley, Ann and Colin Hunt, David and Nina Pugsley, Andy and Yvonne Cunningham, M and J Lindsay)*

LLANWDDYN SJ0219

Lake Vyrnwy Hotel: Comfortable pub extension, well done in old tavern style, behind smart late 19th-c country hotel in remote beautiful spot with abundant fresh air, lake view from big-windowed blue-carpeted lounge and balcony, well kept Brains, good house wines, wide range of food worth the wait at busy times, friendly staff, darts, quiet piped music; bedrooms *(Simon Lawson)*

LLANWENARTH SO2516

Llanwenarth Hotel: Under new management, popular for food lunchtime and evening, good welcoming service in bar and dining room; bedrooms *(Pamela and Merlyn Horswell)*

LLANWRTYD WELLS SN8746

☆ ***Neuadd Arms*** [The Square]: Comfortably well worn in lounge with leather settees, big log fire and local pictures, separate small tiled public bar with craft tools and splendid row of old service bells, reasonably priced Felinfoel Double Dragon and guest beers, welcoming helpful staff, laid-back atmosphere, popular bar food inc homely favourites and hot curries, restaurant; beer festivals, various other events; tables out on front terrace, bedrooms pleasant and well equipped, engaging very small town – good walking area, mountain bike hire *(BB, Joan and Michel Hooper-Immins)*

LLOWES SO1941

Radnor Arms [A438 Brecon—Hereford]: Attractive country dining pub with very wide choice of good food served in local pottery (for sale here) from good filled rolls and inventive soups to fine restaurant-style dishes, dozens of puddings; cottagey bar with lots of knick-knacks, stuffed toys and so forth, beams and stripped stone, with well kept Felinfoel, good coffee, log fire and two small dining rooms; tables in imaginatively planted garden looking out over fields towards the Wye; cl Sun pm, Mon (exc bank hols) *(Rodney and Norma Stubington, Keith Symons)*

LLYSWEN SO1238

Bridge End: Friendly compact village pub with enjoyable food inc delicious puddings, good caring service, real ale, decent house wine, good coffee, coal fire; lovely flower tubs and window boxes, nr high Wye bridge with pleasant views *(Mrs June Wilmers)*

MACHYNLLETH SH7400

Skinners Arms [Penrallt St]: Well run community local with well kept ale, smoke-free areas *(A Boss)*

Wynnstay Arms [Maengwyn St]: Old market-town hotel with good sandwiches and interesting snacks in busy and welcoming pubby annexe bar with hospitable polite staff, three real ales, courtyard tables; good meals in main part's comfortable relaxed lounge and restaurant, good italian-based wine list, bedrooms *(Dennis Jenkin)*

NEW RADNOR SO2160

Radnor Arms [Broad St]: Unpretentious pub with enjoyable reasonably priced home cooking from baked potatoes up, children's dishes, two real ales, choice of ciders, friendly staff *(Christopher J Darwent)*

PENYBONT SO0561

Severn Arms [A44/A488, NE of Llandrindod Wells]: Welcoming hotel with real ales inc Brains Rev James, tempting menu, friendly helpful landlady, sizeable bar with games area, secluded lounge, restaurant; plenty of tables in sizeable garden by little River Ithon, bedrooms, own fishing *(George Atkinson)*

RHAYADER SN9768

Crown [North St]: Rambling 17th-c timbered inn with comfortable beamed bar partitioned for eating areas, good helpings of reasonably priced sensible food from snacks to steaks, well kept Brains SA, Arms Park and Rev James, reasonable prices, very friendly landlord and helpful staff, nice nooks and crannies, lots of interesting photographs and fish-related mottoes and witty notices; soft piped music, games machine; disabled access, small garden behind, open all day (cl Sun afternoon) *(Michael and Jenny Back, George Atkinson, Joan and Michel Hooper-Immins)*

☆ *Triangle* [Cwmdauddwr; B4518 by bridge over Wye, SW of centre]: Interesting mainly 16th-c pub, small and spotless, with enjoyable reasonably priced home-made food from good toasties and ploughman's up lunchtime and early evening, well kept Greene King IPA and Abbot and Hancocks HB, decent wines, sensible prices, quick friendly helpful service, separate dining area with view over park to Wye, darts and quiz nights; three tables on small front terrace *(Dennis Jenkin, J A Ellis, Christopher J Darwent, Lucien Perring)*

TALYBONT-ON-USK SO1122

Star [B4558]: Old-fashioned canalside local with several well kept changing real ales and Weston's Old Rosie farm cider, three bustling plain rooms off central servery inc brightly lit games area, lots of beermats, bank notes and coins on beams; cheering winter fires, basic food from sandwiches up, live band Weds, winter quiz Mon; dogs and children welcome, picnic-sets in sizeable tree-ringed garden below Monmouth & Brecon Canal, bedrooms, open all day Sat *(LYM, Pete Baker, the Didler, Neil and Anita Christopher)*

TRECASTLE SN8729

☆ *Castle Hotel*: Pleasantly decorated Georgian inn, neatly kept lounge and dining room up a few stairs from tiled floor bar, enjoyable food from good ploughman's and bar snacks to imaginative restaurant dishes, well kept Greene King Old Speckled Hen and a choice of coffees, friendly service, roaring fire; unobtrusive piped music; terrace tables, comfortable bedrooms *(George Atkinson, Richard and Anne Norris)*

SOUTH GLAMORGAN

CARDIFF ST1776

Cayo Arms [Cathedral Rd]: Friendly pub with well kept ales such as Brains Rev James, Thwaites Lancaster Bomber, Tomos Watkins and Worthington, two areas separated by ironwork, comfortable seats inc fine old wooden armchairs, lots of prints, well priced food all day inc good range of sandwiches, a few hot dishes and Sun lunch, quick service, daily papers; piped music, very busy wknds; tables out in front, more in yard behind (with parking), open all day *(Meg and Colin Hamilton, Mr and Mrs M Dalby, Ian Phillips)*

Conway [Conway Rd/Mortimer Rd, Pontcanno]: Jolly corner local with sports SkyTV in small traditional front bar, drinking corridor to large comfortable back lounge/dining area, well kept ales such as Bass, Greene King Abbot and Tomos Watkins Old Style and Whoosh, usual food at low prices, plenty of daily papers; pavement picnic-sets *(Mr and Mrs M Dalby, Ian Phillips)*

COWBRIDGE SS9974

☆ *Bear* [High St, with car park behind off North St; signed off A48]: Neatly kept old coaching inn with well kept Brains Bitter, SA and Revs Charger, Hancocks HB and Wye Valley Butty Bach, decent house wines, friendly efficient young staff, three bars with flagstones, bare boards or carpet, some stripped stone and panelling, big open fires, enjoyable usual bar food from sandwiches up, barrel-vaulted cellar restaurant; children welcome, CCTV in car park, bedrooms quiet and comfortable *(LYM, David and Nina Pugsley, V Brogden)*

EAST ABERTHAW ST0367

☆ *Blue Anchor* [B4265]: This charming ancient thatched pub, a popular starred main entry for its good beers, enjoyable food and splendid atmosphere, was badly damaged by fire in Feb 2004; as we went to press restoration was under way (even routine rethatching here takes four months), and it is hoped that the pub will be up and running again in late 2004; news please *(LYM)*

LLANCARFAN ST0570

☆ *Fox & Hounds* [signed off A4226; can also be reached from A48 from Bonvilston or B4265 via Llancadle]: Village pub doing well under current management, freshly cooked food and a couple of real ales in neat comfortably modernised open-plan bar rambling through arches, traditional settles and plush banquettes, coal fire, candlelit bistro, more sparely furnished end family room; children welcome, unobtrusive piped music; pretty streamside setting by interesting church, tables out behind, has been open all day wknds *(BB, R Michael Richards)*

LLANDAFF ST1577

Churchills [Llandaff Pl/Cardiff Rd]: Recently refurbished, with good pre-match atmosphere on rugby international days; good value well equipped bedrooms *(Ian Arthur)*

MICHAELSTON-Y-FEDW ST2484

Cefn Mably Arms [a mile off A48 at Castleton]: Brightly furnished country local with very friendly service, well kept Bass and Hancocks HB, enjoyable fresh food inc fish and imaginative dishes in bar and pleasant dining room; soft piped music; garden tables *(Richard Fendick)*

SIGINGSTONE SS9771

☆ *Victoria* [off B4270 S of Cowbridge]: Spotlessly well kept neo-Victorian dining pub, light airy paintwork, antique furniture and interesting bric-a-brac, emphasis on good value quickly served food from simple bar meals to more elaborate dishes, thriving bar area and popular upstairs restaurant, well kept Tomos Watkins ales, cheerful helpful service; pretty hanging baskets, picturesque village *(Alec and Barbara Jones, John and Joan Nash)*

ST FAGANS ST1277

☆ *Plymouth Arms*: Stately Victorian pub reworked as Vintage Inn with plenty of nice touches in bustling linked areas inc log fires, good range of generous food, Bass and Hancocks, decent wines by the glass at reasonable prices, prompt friendly service; water-bowls outside for dogs, handy for Museum of Welsh Life *(Pamela and Merlyn Horswell)*

WEST GLAMORGAN

BISHOPSTON SS5789

☆ *Joiners Arms* [Bishopston Rd, just off B4436 SW of Swansea]: Thriving local brewing their own good value Swansea beers, also well kept guests such as Charles Wells Bombardier and Marstons Pedigree, decent wines; clean and welcoming, with quarry-tiled floor, old-fashioned décor and furnishings, local paintings and massive solid fuel stove, good generous food, cheap and simple, lunchtime and early evening inc big triangular sandwiches, chilli, curries, sizzler dishes and OAP lunches Sat; big-screen TV for rugby – it's the club's local on Sat nights; late May bank hol beer and music festival; children welcome, open all day Thurs-Sat; parking can be difficult *(Michael and Alison Sandy, LYM, Anne Morris, Chris and Martin Taylor)*

BLACK PILL SS6190

Woodman [A4067 Swansea—Mumbles]: Good Chef & Brewer attractively renovated with lots of wood, several sensibly furnished areas opening out of bar, hundreds of wine bottles above panelled dado, airy restaurant and conservatory, good value blackboard food all day from sandwiches and baguettes to fresh local fish, well kept Courage Directors and guests such as Brains SA and Fullers London Pride, good choice of wines by the glass, friendly young staff; next to beautiful Clyne Gardens *(John and Vivienne Rice, John and Joan Nash, Alan Davies)*

OLDWALLS SS4891

Greyhound: New kitchen extension doing good value food inc thai curries, local fish and some interesting blackboard specials, busy but spacious beamed and dark-panelled plush lounge bar, well kept Bass, Flowers Original and guest beers such as Wadworths 6X, good coffee inc decaf, decent wine, roaring coal fires, friendly service; back bar with display cases; restaurant popular at wknds, folk club Sun; big tree-shaded garden with new terrace, play area and good views *(Guy Vowles, Michael and Alison Sandy)*

PONTLLIW SN6002

☆ *Glamorgan Arms* [Bryntirion Rd]: Nicely set country pub with cheerful and helpful Italian/Welsh licensees, good fresh food inc pasta and great chargrilled welsh black steaks, attractive homely décor, good log fires and housekeeping; very child-friendly, with huge play area in grounds *(Andrew Wood, Michael Dugdale, B Harrison)*

SWANSEA SS6592

No Sign Wine Bar [Wind St, 200 yds below Castle]: Four narrow old-fashioned rooms, first parlourish and welcoming, with mahogany cabinets and other fittings, large portrait in oils, cellars under bar; second more of an alcove, third full of church pews, fourth flagstoned and rather bare; some emphasis on decent fairly priced food (can get crowded lunchtimes), good wines, two glass sizes, also three real ales *(Guy Vowles, Patrick Hancock)*

THREE CROSSES SS5694

Poundffald Inn [Tirmynydd Rd, NW end]: 17th-c beamed and timbered pub popular for generous good value food all day (children's last orders 6.30) inc tasty welsh black curry, well kept changing ales such as Greene King Abbot and Old Speckled Hen, Marstons Pedigree and Worthington, cheerful friendly landlord, prompt service, good coal fires, stuffed birds and animals; sports TV in separate public bar; smart tables on attractively spruced up side terrace, pretty hanging baskets and raised beds *(Michael and Alison Sandy)*

WEST CROSS SS6189

West Cross Inn [A4067 Mumbles—Swansea]: Great view over Mumbles Bay from beach-side balcony and popular glassed back dining extension upstairs, good choice of reasonably priced usual food inc excellent fresh fish and chips, comfortably refurbished bar with well kept ales such as Greene King Old Speckled Hen and Worthington, decent wines, friendly quick service; just above beach, garden below by shoreside ex-railway pedestrian/cycle way *(Ian Phillips)*

'Children welcome' means the pub says it lets children inside without any special restriction. If it allows them in, but to restricted areas such as an eating area or family room, we specify this. Places with separate restaurants often let children use them, hotels usually let them into public areas such as lounges. Some pubs impose an evening time limit – let us know if you find this.

Channel Islands

Over the years, we ourselves or our trusty band of peripatetic reporters have checked out over 150 pubs and bars on the islands, so our listing in this chapter is the distillation of really rather a lot of discriminating pub-hunting. On Guernsey, the current favourite is the Fleur du Jardin at King's Mills (a peaceful small hotel with good interesting food and a nice bar). On Jersey, the Old Portelet in a good spot above the beach at St Brelade is great for families; the Old Court House Inn in St Aubin is a charming hotel with a good pubby bar; the little Rozel Bay Hotel combines an enjoyable fish restaurant with a welcoming traditional bar; and La Pulente on St Ouens Bay is notable for its great seaside position and sweeping views. We are also fond of the tucked-away back bar of Les Fontaines at St John – at quiet times, a glimpse of how the islands used to be a few decades ago. A pub which emerged in our last edition as quite a favourite with readers – the Moulin de Lecq at Greve de Lecq – was due to close while this new edition was printing. It's sad to lose this converted former mill, so we are rather hoping that it will find a new owner who sees its potential as a good family pub. In the Lucky Dip section at the end of the chapter, the Auberge Divette at St Martin on Guernsey has been winning warm approval recently; another place to note is the Original Wine Bar in St Helier on Jersey. Drinks prices on the islands, once so attractive to UK visitors, have in the last few years been rapidly catching up on the mainland. This year for the first time we found that on average beer here now costs more than it does in Lancashire and Nottinghamshire, the two cheapest mainland areas. Part of the problem is that so many pubs rely on high-priced mainland brewers for their supplies; it makes sense to look out for the local brews, Guernsey and Tipsy Toad (both actually brewed on Jersey) and Randalls (Guernsey), which can be a lot cheaper.

KING'S MILLS Map 1

Fleur du Jardin

King's Mills Road

Making a nice place to stay on the island, this peacefully set attractive old hotel is aptly named, with its good-sized gardens, and picnic-sets among colourful borders, shrubs, bright hanging baskets and flower barrels (they do not serve meals outside). Inside, the cosy relaxing rooms have low beams and thick granite walls, a good log fire in the public bar (popular with locals), and individual country furnishings in the lounge bar on the hotel side. Good interesting bar food includes soup (from £2.75), sandwiches (from £2.95), gravadlax of tuna with beetroot carpaccio (£4.25), 8oz home-made beef burger (£5.95), linguini with porcini mushrooms, tomatoes, spinach and garlic (£7.50), fish and chips (£8.25), steak, kidney and ale pudding (£8.95), bass fillet on honey roasted apple and lemon balm (£13.75), 8oz fillet steak (£14.95) and puddings such as fruit crumble or cold lemon soufflé with hazelnut brittle (from £3.75); meals in the restaurant (partly no smoking) include some bar menu items and some pricier more elaborate dishes. Well kept Bass and Tipsy Toad Sunbeam on handpump, and a good wine list with around 15 by the glass (most by small or large glass); friendly efficient service; unobtrusive piped music. They have a large car park and there is a swimming pool for residents. *(Recommended by Phil and Sally Gorton, Stephen R Holman, Sue Demont, Tim Barrow)*

Free house ~ Licensee Keith Read ~ Real ale ~ Bar food (12-2, 6-9.30) ~ Restaurant ~ (01481) 257996 ~ Children in eating area of bar and restaurant ~ Open 11(12 Sun)-11.45 ~ Bedrooms: £65B/£92B

ROZEL Map 1

Rozel Bay Hotel

Tucked away at the edge of a sleepy little fishing village, this friendly inn is just out of sight of the sea. The bar counter (Bass, Charles Wells Bombardier and Courage Directors under light blanket pressure) and tables in the traditional-feeling and cosy little dark-beamed back bar are stripped to their original light wood finish, and there are dark plush wall seats and stools, an open granite fireplace, and old prints and local pictures on the cream walls. Leading off is a carpeted area with flowers on big solid square tables. Piped music, and TV, darts, pool, cribbage and dominoes in the games room. The good value short pubby menu includes big helpings of dishes such as soup (£2.95), sandwiches (from £3.95), fish and chips, bangers and mash (£5.95), beef and ale pie (£6.90) and puddings such as white chocolate panna cotta (£3.95). The upstairs restaurant now concentrates on fresh fish in a relaxed rustic French atmosphere, with up to ten fish dishes a day and good value specials. The pub has an attractive steeply terraced, partly covered, hillside garden. *(Recommended by Mrs Romey Heaton, Dr and Mrs A K Clarke)*

Randalls ~ Lease Ian King ~ Real ale ~ Bar food (12-2(3 Sun), 6-8.30) ~ Restaurant (not Sun evening) ~ (01534) 863438 ~ Children welcome ~ Dogs allowed in bar ~ Open 11-11

ST AUBIN Map 1

Old Court House Inn 🛏

Harbour Boulevard

This charming 15th-c hotel has an interesting past. The front rooms were once the home of a wealthy merchant, whose cellars stored privateers' plunder alongside more legitimate cargo, and the upstairs restaurant still shows signs of its time as a courtroom. The pubby downstairs bar has cushioned wooden seats built against its stripped granite walls, low black beams, joists in a white ceiling, a turkey carpet and an open fire. A dimly lantern-lit inner room has an illuminated rather brackish-looking deep well, and beyond that the spacious cellar room which is open in summer. The conservatory enjoys delightful views over the tranquil harbour and on past St Aubin's fort right across the bay to St Helier. The Westward Bar is elegantly constructed from the actual gig of a schooner and offers a restauranty menu with prices to match. Enjoyable food (you can eat from the bar or restaurant menu downstairs) includes soup (£2.75), baguettes (from £4.75), vegetable lasagne (£4.95), moules marinière (£5.75), fish and chips or wild mushroom and asparagus risotto (£8.95), fruits de mer cocktail (£9.95), local plaice (£10.50), fresh crab (£12.50), fried duck breast with plum sauce (£13.95), local lobster (from £25). Two well kept beers might be Courage Directors and Theakstons Old Peculier on handpump; TV and piped music. It can be difficult to park near the hotel. *(Recommended by Ian Phillips, Mrs Ann Gray, Patrick Hancock)*

Free house ~ Licensee Jonty Sharp ~ Real ale ~ Bar food (12.30-2.30, 7-10) ~ Restaurant ~ (01534) 746433 ~ Children welcome ~ Open 11-11.30 ~ Bedrooms: £60B/£120B

> Bedroom prices are for high summer. Even then you may get reductions for more than one night, or (outside tourist areas) weekends. Winter special rates are common, and many inns cut bedroom prices if you have a full evening meal.

ST BRELADE Map 1

Old Portelet Inn

Portelet Bay

This popular 17th-c farmhouse is often busy, particularly with families and visitors to the island. It's well placed at the head of a long flight of granite steps, giving views across Portelet (Jersey's most southerly bay) as you go down to a sheltered cove. Children will be happily occupied in either the supervised indoor play area (entrance 60p) or another one outside, watching the kiddies' entertainment they sometimes put on during the summer, or with board games in the wooden-floored loft bar. The picnic-sets on the partly covered flower-bower terrace by a wishing well are a good place to relax, and there are more seats in the sizeable landscaped garden with lots of scented stocks and other flowers. Generous helpings of bar food, served by neatly dressed friendly staff, include sandwiches (from £2.10), soup (£2.75), filled baked potatoes (from £5.15), chilli nachos (£4.75), ploughman's (£5.20), ratatouille and goats cheese pancake (£5.25), moules marinière (£6.95), steak and mushroom pie (£6.50) and sirloin steak (£9.95) and puddings such as chocolate fudge cake (from £2.95). The low-beamed downstairs bar has a stone bar counter (well kept Bass and Courage Directors kept under light blanket pressure and reasonably priced house wine), a huge open fire, gas lamps, old pictures, etched glass panels from France and a nice mixture of old wooden chairs on bare oak boards and quarry tiles. It opens into the big timber-ceilinged no smoking family dining area, with standing timbers and plenty of highchairs; TV, cribbage, dominoes, and very audible piped music; disabled and baby-changing facilities. *(Recommended by Ian Phillips, Mrs Catherine Draper, Emma Kingdon, Kevin Blake, Kevin Flack, Roger and Jenny Huggins, Alistair and Kay Butler, John Evans, Patrick Hancock)*

Randalls ~ Manager Stephen Jones ~ Real ale ~ Bar food (12-9) ~ (01534) 741899 ~ Children welcome ~ Dogs allowed in bar ~ Live music 2 or 3 nights a week in the summer, 1 in winter ~ Open 9-11

Old Smugglers

Ouaisne Bay; OS map reference 595476

The welcoming bar at this straightforward pub has thick walls, black beams, log fires, and cosy black built-in settles, also well kept Bass and two guests from brewers such as Greene King and Ringwood on handpump; sensibly placed darts as well as cribbage. Bar food includes soup (£2.95), vegetarian spring roll with sweet chilli dip (£4.75), prawn cocktail (£4.95), burgers (from £5.25), filled baked potatoes (from £5.25), lasagne (£6.25), steak and Guinness pie (£6.50), battered cod (£6.75), duck breast with orange and brandy sauce (£7.50), king prawns with garlic butter or black bean sauce (£8.95) and steaks (from £9.25). A room in the restaurant (the only area with piped music) is no smoking. The building is a conversion of a row of old fishermen's cottages, and is picturesquely set on a lane just above the beach with interesting views over one of the island's many defence towers from a weatherproof porch. *(Recommended by Emma Kingdon, Darren Le Poidevin, Patrick Hancock)*

Free house ~ Licensee Nigel Godfrey ~ Real ale ~ Bar food (12-2, 6-9; not Sun evening Nov-Mar) ~ Restaurant ~ (01534) 741510 ~ Children welcome ~ Dogs allowed in bar ~ Open 11-11.30

ST HELIER Map 1

Town House

New Street

Fairly unassuming in appearance, the exterior of this 1930s pub is reminiscent of a converted cinema. More attractive inside, its two main bars are divided by heavy but airy glass and brass doors. The sports bar on the left has two giant TV screens, darts and pool. To the right, the lounge area has parquet flooring, some attractive panelling and stained-glass and solid furnishings. Well kept Tipsy Toad Jimmys, and sound house wines; piped music. Bar food includes sandwiches (from £3.55), burgers (from £4.25), fish and chips (£5.25), steak and Guinness pie (£5.55), fettuccine with salmon and cream or goats cheese crumble (£7.25), duck stir fry (£9.25) and puddings such as Baileys bread and butter pudding (£3.95). *(Recommended by Ian Phillips, Roger and Jenny Huggins, Patrick Hancock)*

Jersey ~ Managers Jackie and Martin Kelly ~ Real ale ~ Bar food (12-2, 6.30-9(not Mon evening or Sun)) ~ Restaurant ~ (01534) 615000 ~ Open 11-11

ST JOHN Map 1

Les Fontaines

Le Grand Mourier, Route du Nord

In a pretty spot on the north coast and a nice place for a pint after a walk (well kept Bass and Charles Wells Bombardier), this former farmhouse is a popular local haunt. The best part is the public bar where you're likely to hear the true Jersey patois – look out for a worn, unmarked door at the side of the building, or as you go down the main entry lobby towards the bigger main bar go through the tiny narrow door on your right. In here you'll find very heavy beams in the low dark ochre ceiling, massively thick irregular red granite walls, cushioned settles on the quarry-tiled floor and antique prints. The big granite-columned fireplace with a log fire warming its unusual inglenook seats may date back to the 14th c, and (a rarity these days) has kept its old smoking chains and side oven. The carpeted main bar is a marked contrast, with plenty of wheelback chairs around neat dark tables, and a spiral staircase leading up to a wooden gallery under the high pine-raftered plank ceiling; one large area is no smoking; piped music. A bonus for families is Pirate Pete's, a supervised play area for children (entry 50p for half an hour), though children are also welcome in the other rooms. Bar food includes soup (£2.65), sandwiches (from £2.45), ploughman's (from £5.25), battered cod (£6.50), sweet and sour chicken (£6.85) cumberland sausage (£6.75), and specials such as baked lamb shank with mash (£8.35), grilled local plaice (£8.80), lobster or crab salad (from £12) and whole bass (£11). Seats on a terrace outside have good views, although lorries from the nearby quarry can mar the atmosphere. *(Recommended by BOB, Alistair and Kay Butler, Darren Le Poidevin, Dr and Mrs A K Clarke)*

Randalls ~ Manager Hazel O'Gorman ~ Real ale ~ Bar food (12-2.15(2.45 Sun), 6-9(8.30) Sun) ~ (01534) 862707 ~ Children in eating area of bar and restaurant ~ Dogs allowed in bar ~ Open 11-11

ST OUENS BAY Map 1

La Pulente

Start of Five Mile Road; OS map reference 562488

It's the impressive location that makes this civilised pub special. There are sweeping views across the endless extent of Jersey's longest beach from the terrace, lounge (no smoking) and conservatory. The carpeted eating area upstairs has ragged walls and scrubbed wood tables, and leads off on to the terrace; piped music. Cheerful and busy, the public bar has a surfing theme, with photographs and prints on the walls, well kept Bass and Courage Directors on handpump, and a juke box, darts, pool, fruit machine and TV. Very enjoyable bar food, served by friendly staff, includes sandwiches (from £2.50), baked potatoes (from £3.50), ploughman's (from £5), beer-battered cod (£6.75), fried chicken breast with asparagus and leek tart and chive mash (£8.95), and daily specials such as spaghetti with feta and mushrooms, bass fillet with scallops (£15.95) and fruits de mer (£30 for two, 24 hours' notice required). *(Recommended by Kevin Flack, Ian Phillips, Dr and Mrs A K Clarke)*

Randalls ~ Manager Julia Wallace ~ Real ale ~ Bar food (12-2.15 6-9; not Sun evening) ~ Restaurant ~ (01534) 744487 ~ Children welcome in lounge area ~ Dogs allowed in bar ~ Open 11-11

LUCKY DIP

Besides the fully inspected pubs, you might like to try these Lucky Dips recommended to us and described by readers (if you do, please send us reports: www.goodguides.co.uk).

ALDERNEY

LONGIS BAY

Old Barn [Venelle Jeanette]: Tucked-away restaurant rather than pub, but well worth knowing for its good value food, good range of wines and wonderful gardens *(Geoff Pidoux)*

NEWTOWN

☆ *Harbour Lights*: Welcoming, clean and well run pub adjoining family-run hotel in a quieter part of this quiet island, comfortably refurbished bar with limited choice of good well presented bar food (not Sun nor wkdy lunchtime) from ploughman's with home-baked bread and home-made pickles to carefully prepared fresh local fish and seafood, attractive prices, well kept real ales such as Courage Directors and a guest from Badger, reasonably priced wines; caters well for families, terrace in pleasant garden, bedrooms *(Donald Godden)*

ST ANNE

Marais Hall [Marais Sq]: Traditional pub with good range of real ales, long list of pub food, friendly staff *(Geoff Pidoux)*

Rose & Crown [Le Huret]: Well kept pub/hotel, good real ales, lunchtime sandwiches, neat gardens; bedrooms *(Geoff Pidoux)*

GUERNSEY

CASTEL

Vazon Bay Hotel [Vazon Coast Rd]: Hotel on stunning beach, pleasant bar with dozens of whiskies, Randalls and Sam Smiths beers, enjoyable food in sensibly priced restaurant; 25 bedrooms *(Geoff Pidoux)*

ST MARTIN

Ambassador [Sausmarez Rd]: Good sensibly priced food inc good fresh fish, well kept John Smiths, pleasant surroundings; gets busy evenings; pretty garden, bedrooms *(J S Rutter)*

☆ *Auberge Divette* [Jerbourg Rd]: Glorious view of coast and Herm from pub/restaurant's fairy-lit garden high above sea, smartly refurbished picture-window lounge and dining room, good food, good range of wines by the glass, helpful staff; spectacular cliff walk to St Peter Port *(LYM, Geoff Pidoux)*

Bella Luce [La Fosse]: Dark and pretty 14th-c bar, enjoyable food, reasonably priced wines, attentive service; lovely garden with superb tulip tree *(J S Rutter)*

Captains Hotel [La Fosse]: Has a proper pubby bar with well kept ales such as Adnams Broadside and Fullers London Pride; bedrooms *(Phil and Sally Gorton)*

La Trelade [Forest Rd]: Smart, quiet and civilised, with good waiter service in bar, John Smiths *(Michael and Deirdre Ellis)*

Saints Bay [Icart Rd]: Hotel on headland with lovely views, good range of beers, cider and wines, good service in pleasant restaurant; swimming pool, bedrooms *(Geoff Pidoux)*

ST PETER PORT

Ship & Crown [opp Crown Pier, Esplanade]: Bustling town pub with bay windows overlooking harbour, very popular with yachting people and smarter locals, sharing building with Royal Guernsey Yacht Club; interesting photographs (esp concerning World War II German Occupation, also boats and ships), good value food from sandwiches through fast foods to steak, well kept real ale such as local Tipsy Toad Sunbeam, welcoming prompt service even when busy; TVs rather detract from the atmosphere; open all day from 10am *(Phil and Sally Gorton, LYM, Geoff Pidoux)*

TORTEVAL

☆ *Imperial* [Pleinmont (coast rd, nr Pleinmont Point)]: Good choice of meals inc good seafood in seaview dining room overlooking the sea, Randalls beers; tables in suntrap garden, bedrooms in hotel part separate from the pub, handy for good beach *(Mrs Romey Heaton)*

HERM

HERM

☆ *Mermaid* [linked to White House Hotel]: Lovely spot on idyllic island, exceptionally friendly service, big nautical-theme panelled bar with nice coal fire, snack bar (with cream teas), children's games area, large conservatory; Randalls Patois, bar food from bacon rolls up, restaurant dishes running up to duck, fish and seafood, also good barbecues; pleasant bedrooms, ranks of picnic-sets in spacious courtyard – best at peaceful times, can be busy on fine days *(Phil and Sally Gorton)*

JERSEY

GOREY

Village Pub [Gorey Common]: Friendly and comfortably refurbished, light and cheerful, with well kept real ales, good value straightforward food (not Sun) all day inc good fresh fish, no smoking room *(Ian and Lin Gill, Darren Le Poidevin)*

GREVE DE LECQ

Moulin de Lecq: Black-shuttered mill in lovely location, which has been a popular family pub, but closing as we went to press; news please *(LYM)*

ST HELIER

Bonds [Bond St]: Warm inviting bar with charming landlady, local Tipsy Toad Jimmys real ale, decent wines by the glass, sandwiches, paninis and lunchtime bar food, comfortable sofas, darts; sports TV *(Peter Hopkins)*

☆ *Original Wine Bar* [Bath St]: Welcoming, informal and relaxed, with comfortable sofas and armchairs and great character, good choice of interesting lunchtime food (not Sun), five real ales from island and mainland, dutch lager on tap, very good choice of wines by the glass, coffees and teas, friendly knowledgeable staff, relaxing cheerful atmosphere, no smoking area; good wheelchair access *(BB, Peter Hopkins)*

SARK

SARK

Bel Air: First tourist stop (where the tractors climb to from the jetty): big woodburner in friendly and comfortable Boat Bar with plank ceiling, easy chairs and settees, model ship, boat-shaped counter; old boat pictures in simpler Pirate Bar, sandwiches and other snacks, darts; piped music; tables on terrace outside this pretty cottage *(BB, Richard and Anne Norris)*

Several well known guide books make establishments pay for entry, either directly or as a fee for inspection. These fees can run to many hundreds of pounds. We do not. Unlike other guides, we never take payment for entries. We never accept a free meal, free drink, or any other freebie from a pub. We do not accept any sponsorship – let alone from commercial schemes linked to the pub trade. All our entries depend solely on merit.

Overseas Lucky Dip

We're always interested to hear of good bars and pubs overseas – preferably really good examples of bars that visitors would find memorable, rather than transplanted 'British pubs'. A star marks places we would be confident would deserve a main entry. It's common for good bars overseas, if they serve food, to serve it all day (a pleasant contrast to the UK, where most pubs outside big cities actually close for much of the day, let alone serve food all day). In many foreign bars, partly thanks to the fairly strong £, drinks are relatively cheap – note that this is not the case in Hong Kong, nor (surprisingly) in Dublin. On the other hand, the Republic of Ireland's new ban on smoking in pubs is now having a real effect. For this reason, we have this year separated the Ireland pubs listed into Republic (smoking ban) and Northern (no ban yet).

AUSTRALIA

CAIRNS

Barristers [38 Abbot St; Queensland]: Former courthouse, big lively central bar with local beers and two TVs, separate eating area (order from kitchen) with tempting choice from sandwiches to barramundi fish and great steaks, very friendly staff *(Roger and Jenny Huggins)*

MELBOURNE

James Squire Brewhouse [Russell St/Little Collins St; Victoria]: Visibly brewing its own Pilsner, Original Amber Ale, Porter, IPA, Portland Pale, Craic and Highwayman, bare boards and simple furnishings inc a couple of nice window seats, also chesterfields by the fireplace, silenced TV, daily papers; a second bigger more comfortable room *(Roger and Jenny Huggins)*

SYDNEY

Fortune of War [George St, The Rocks]: Sydney's oldest pub, used to film the fight scene in *A Town Like Alice*, and good for a lunchtime swifty – good choice of local beers on tap (along with Guinness); no air-conditioning, just ceiling fans, unobtrusive corner TV, fruit machines in back room; impressive beer garden, evening crowds spill out into the street *(Roger and Jenny Huggins)*

Molly Malones [part of Mercantile Hotel, George St, The Rocks]: Almost under S end of Harbour Bridge; green tiles outside, ornate ceiling, smoked glass, walling tiles and panelling in, with comfortably unpretentious atmosphere, good value food in room off, several local beers (and Guinness of course), some Irish staff, Irish bands most nights; TV, unobtrusive piped music; bedrooms *(Roger and Jenny Huggins)*

AUSTRIA

WÖRGL

Euroton [Augasse 220]: Highly modernistic bar in small Tyrolean market town, bar with snacks, local Zipfer beer and good coffee, stylish and comfortable almost palatial upper floor, wonderful roof terrace with stunning mountain views on all sides *(Ian Phillips)*

BELGIUM

BRUGES

☆ ***Brugs Beertje*** [Kemelstraat, off Steenstr nr cathedral]: Small friendly bar known as the Beer Academy, serving 350 of the country's bottled beers, most of them strong ones, in each beer's distinctive glass, as well as several on tap; vibrant atmosphere, especially in the two front rooms, table menus, helpful English-speaking staff (and customers), good basic bar food; open from 4, can get a bit smoky later, very popular with tourists *(Mike and Wendy Proctor, Jo Lilley, Simon Calvert)*

Craenenburg [Markt]: Large bar with own little turret, quiet and refined, Leffe, Hoegaarden and Jupiter, coffee, cakes and good waffles, daily papers, leather walls, stained-glass window medallions; pavement tables *(Mike and Wendy Proctor, Jo Lilley)*

Erasmus [Wollestraat 35]: Bustling and welcoming modernish hotel bar enlivened by character landlord's interest in his 300-plus helpfully described beers, enjoyable food *(Mike and Wendy Proctor)*

☆ ***Garre*** [1 de Garre, off Breidelstraat]: Attractive and welcoming little bar in 16th-c timbered building, stripped brickwork, upper gallery, elegant and civilised but very relaxed and unstuffy, well over 100 mainly local beers inc five Trappists and its own draught beer – each well served in its own glass with cheese nibbles; sensible prices, knowledgeable helpful staff,

sandwiches, unobtrusive piped classical music; children welcome *(MP, Jo Lilley, Simon Calvert)*
Passage [Dweersstr 26]: Dim candlelight and oak panelling, several beers on tap inc local Brugse Tripel, more by the bottle, friendly staff, some bar seats, emphasis on table meals; popular hostel upstairs *(anon)*

BRUSSELS

Bécasse [11 rue de Tabora]: Rather genteel brown café, ornate scrolled metal lamps showing its dark panelling and beams well, wide range of beers inc unblended Lambic (young and old) as well as Kriek served at the table in jugs, good snacks such as croustades made with beer and asparagus; open all day *(Tracey and Stephen Groves)*
Poechenellekeller [rue de Chêne]: Eccentric three-level bar, dark, cosy and cavern-like, welcoming and civilised; about 45 beers mainly from smaller breweries, strange puppetry collectibles (name means Mannequin Cellar – it's opposite the Mannekin Pis) *(Tracey and Stephen Groves)*

BRITISH VIRGIN ISLANDS

WEST END

Pussers Landing [Sopers Hole; Tortola]: Haven of Britishness at waterside of major marina, Newcastle Brown on tap, some heady concoctions with Pussers Naval Rum, good value food with some interesting things as well as fish and chips, friendly attentive staff *(Paul Coleman)*

CYPRUS

AGHIOS THEODOROS

Limni [Ag Theodoros beach, Mazotos—Zighi rd, off A5/A1 Larnaca—Limassol; aka The Lake]: Fresh fish and usual beers in family bar/restaurant, modern concrete building softened by big terrace overlooking small harbour where children can paddle or swim, buoyant mix of local and visiting families *(Ian Phillips)*

PAPHOS

Friends [9 Contandias St, Kato Paphos]: Reasonably priced central pub with snacky menu, Carlsberg Export as well as Keo on tap, friendly owners, darts and pool; big-screen sports TVs, video games *(Jeff and Sue Evans)*

POTAMOS CREEK

Demetrion [W of Aghia Napa]: Beach bar and restaurant, basic décor, fantastic view across to Cape Greco, very fresh fish and octopus (creek is home to colourful fishing fleet), also lamb, pork etc, usual lagers, drinkable local wine *(Ian Phillips)*

CZECH REPUBLIC

PRAGUE

Cerneho Vola [Loretanske Namesti 1]: Up steps above castle, still unspoilt, friendly and jolly, with beams, leaded lights, long dark benches or small stand-up entrance bar, good Kozel Pale and Dark 12 black beer, and Velkopopovicky Korel lager, local snacks; can get very busy (though rarely too touristy), cl 9 *(the Didler)*
☆ ***Fleku*** [Kremencova 11, Nove Mesto]: Brewing its own strong flavoursome black Flekovsky Dark 13 since 1843 (some say 1499); waiters will try to sell you a schnapps with it – say Ne firmly; huge, with benches and big refectory tables in two big dark-beamed rooms – tourists on right with 10-piece oompah band, more local on left (music here too), also courtyard after courtyard; good basic food – sausages, pork, goulash with dumplings; open early morning to late night, very popular with tourists wknds *(the Didler)*
Klasterni [Strahovske Nadvori 302]: Brewpub with good food such as goulash soup in a cottage loaf, big restaurant and lovely summer courtyard; good strong dark St Norbert beer, brass band and folk dancing at night, next to wonderful 12th-c Strahov monastery *(Mrs Jane Kingsbury)*
Medvidku [Na Perstyne 5, Stare Mesto]: Superb old building in red light district, namesake bears etched in stone over entry, lots of copper in left bar, bigger right room more for eating (low-priced food inc lots of czech specialities), Budvar Budweiser on tap *(the Didler, Myke and Nicky Crombleholme)*
Radegast Pivnice [Templova, Stare Mesto]: Low narrow beer hall, cheap Radegast Pale 10 and 12, excellent value food all day, service quick even when very busy; open all day *(the Didler)*
Vejvodu [Jilska 4]: Carefully rebuilt and extended next door, with thriving atmosphere, good service, well presented food, good value Pilsner Urquell; roomy but can get busy, handy for old town square *(the Didler, Myke and Nicky Crombleholme)*
☆ ***Zlateho Tygra*** [Husova 17, Stare Mesto]: 13th-c cellars with superb Pilsner Urquell 12 and eponymous Golden Tiger served by white-coated waiters; sometimes a queue of locals even before 3pm opening, and no standing allowed, but worth the wait (don't be put off by Reserved signs as the seats, mainly long wooden benches, aren't usually being used till later – and they do make tourists feel welcome) *(the Didler)*

FRANCE

GRIGNOLS

Relais du Château [Dordogne]: Bar unusual for its interesting belgian beers (Belgian owner); great value daily set menu, pleasant staff *(Ann and Max Cross)*

PARIS

Grand Carnot [32 Avenue Carnot]: Good value convivial brasserie, friendly efficient service, reasonably priced beers, good choice of wines by the glass (best buys are beaujolais crus and lesser clarets), robust food inc good steaks *(Steve Whalley)*

ST-PAUL-LIZONNE

Gouillat [aka St Paul's Pub; 8km N of Ribérac]: Small range of french beers in pub part, great value restaurant – good generous lunch and very good range of evening food; pleasant staff *(Ann and Max Cross)*

GIBRALTAR

IRISH TOWN

Clipper: So British (like other pubs here), with usual pub food such as fish and chips, chilli con carne and good steak and ale pie, bar stools, nautical prints, vibrant local atmosphere, good service; keg beers, UK football on TV, games machines *(David Crook)*

HONG KONG

QUARRY BAY

East End Brewery [23-27 Tong Chung St]: Very pub-like (apart from huge windows), with over 30 mainly bottled beers, two local microbrews on tap, old photographs of English pubs; open all day from 10am *(Martin Grosberg)*

WANCHAI

Horse & Groom [161 Lockhart R]: Pleasant and fairly quiet (despite video karaoke), with San Miguel on tap, reasonably priced lunch; open till late *(Martin Grosberg)*

IRELAND (NORTHERN)

ANNALONG

Harbour [Harbour Dr; Co Down]: Good if not cheap food, particularly fish, plenty of menu choice, good service *(Betty Laker)*

BANGOR

Jenny Watts [High St; Co Down]: A pub since 1780, open-plan with lots of woodwork, enjoyable food, 1920s/30s advertisement and *Titanic* drawings *(Dave Braisted)*

BELFAST

☆ *Crown* [Gt Victoria St, opp Europa Hotel]: Well preserved bustling 19th-c National Trust gin palace with pillared entrance, opulent tiles outside and in, elaborately coloured windows, almost church-like ceiling, handsome mirrors, lots of individual snug booths with little doors and bells for waiter service (some graffiti too now, alas), gas lighting, mosaic floor, Whitewater real ale, good lunchtime meals till 5 upstairs inc oysters; very wide and sometimes noisy range of customers (can take their toll on the downstairs gents'), and shame about the TV; open all day *(Joe Green, Patrick Hancock, GLD, J M Tansey)*

Nicholl Bar [Church Lane]: Named for 19th-c artist Andrew Nicholl born next door, brasserie food (not Sun to Weds evenings), changing art shows, live music most nights *(anon)*

COLERAINE

Old Courthouse [Castlerock Rd (A2); Co Londonderry]: Well designed Wetherspoons conversion, usual solid furnishings and well priced food and beer *(J M Tansey)*

IRELAND (REPUBLIC OF)

AVOCA

Fitzgeralds [just off R752; Co Wicklow]: Coach trips come to this small ordinary village to see this, the pub in TV's *Ballykissangel*; lots of souvenirs, reasonable drinks prices *(Keith and Chris O'Neill)*

BALLYVAUGHAN

Monks [Co Clare]: Traditional village pub with bay view close to quay, seafood specials and other food all day, peat fire in bar, woodburners in other rooms; TV or piped music may be loud, traditional live music wknds; children welcome, disabled facilities (but steps in pub), courtyard picnic-sets *(CMW, JJW)*

BANSHA

O'Henrys [Main St (N27); Co Tipperary]: Unpretentious, two bar areas, restaurant up steps, enjoyable fresh food (breakfast too); piped music, wknd live music *(CMW, JJW)*

BRITTAS

Blue Gardenia [N81; Co Dublin]: Large bar/diner with lots of wood and bric-a-brac, unlit kitchen range, decent food all day till 8 inc snacks and children's, obliging service, usual drinks, restaurant and smaller bar too; can get noisy in bar, piped music, live traditional music Mon *(CMW, JJW)*

CAHERDANIEL

Scariff [N70 towards Ardkearagh]: Decent food, usual drinks; main draw is the staggering view down to the sea with a picturesque scattering of islands (extensions cope with the coach parties) *(Ian Phillips)*

CLOGHROE

Blairs [Co Cork]: Welcoming, with enjoyable food from interesting sandwiches to restaurant dishes, attractive dining room; handy for Blarney Castle *(M and R Thomas)*

DINGLE

Dick Macks [opp church; Co Kerry]: Great atmosphere in former old-fashioned haberdasher's, charming exterior and delightful inside, good stouts, many whiskeys, friendly staff; little entrance snug with off-sales hatch, mainly standing room in bar on right with singing, whistle-playing, story-telling etc, counter for continuing boot and shoe business on left *(M G Hart)*

DOOLIN

Gus O'Connors [Co Clare]: Large yet cosy, with several areas, real fire, good choice of generous food all day inc lots of fish at reasonable prices, one own brew as well as usual drinks; TV, games machines in back lobby, live Irish music nightly; children and dogs welcome, disabled access *(CMW, JJW)*

Macdermotts [off R478/479; Co Clare]: Three rooms with real fire, reasonably priced food all day in dining area; piped music, several TVs, very busy, esp for live traditional music late evening; children welcome *(CMW, JJW)*

McGanns [Co Clare]: Usual food and drink, very busy for late evening live traditional music (get there much earlier for a table); TV; children welcome till 8pm, bedrooms *(CMW, JJW)*

DRINAGH

Farmers Kitchen [aka Irene Scallans, just off N25; Co Wexford]: Friendly bar and lounge, woodburner, enjoyable reasonably priced generous food all day, speedy pleasant service; quiet piped music (live wknds and bank hols); picnic-sets out among flower tubs, adjacent hotel bedrooms *(CMW, JJW)*

DUBLIN

Arlington [Bachelor's Walk, O'Connell St]: Huge open-plan bar by River Liffey, several areas, enjoyable food, efficient service, great atmosphere, nightly live folk music and dancing – several TVs show this live, then in repeats next day *(Keith and Chris O'Neill)*

Auld Dubliner [Anglesea St, Temple Bar]: Crowded typical Irish pub, friendly staff, enjoyable food from sandwiches up, usual drinks, very laid-back atmosphere, good live music daily *(Chris Raisin)*

Brazen Head [Lower Bridge St]: Charming bar, said to be oldest here, maze of dimly lit cosy unspoilt rooms off attractive red and white tiled passage, with old beams, mirrors, old settles inc one given by Thin Lizzy's Phil Lynnot, open fires; lunchtime bar food from filled cobs to carvery, evening restaurant, well served Guinness; peaceful front courtyard, traditional music each night, main bar very busy Sun lunchtime with music too *(Keith and Chris O'Neill)*

Doheny & Nesbitt [Lower Baggot St, by the Shelburne just below St Stephens Green]: Friendly traditional pub, originally a grocer's, close to Parliament; sensitively extended from original core, with Victorian bar fittings, marble-topped tables, wooden screens, old whiskey mirrors etc; mainly drink (inc good Guinness) and conversation, but has good value toasties, panini, irish stew and so forth; live music, can get very busy but worth the wait *(Joe Green, Jo Lilley, Simon Calvert)*

Gravity Bar [St James Gate Guinness Brewery]: Great views from huge round glass-walled tasting bar on top floor, and Guinness at its best; culmination of up-to-date exhibition on firm's history, brewing and advertising campaigns, also lower Storehouse bar with lunchtime food and gift shop *(Keith and Chris O'Neill)*

Madigans [O'Connell St]: Plenty of atmosphere in relaxed traditional pub very near the historic GPO of the 1916 Easter Rising; good choice of snacks and light meals at a fair price, friendly people, usual drinks, good tea; may be piped pop music *(Keith and Chris O'Neill)*

Messrs Maguires [O'Connell Bridge, S side]: Well restored early 19th-c splendour, four floors with huge staircase, superb woodwork and ceilings, flame-effect gas fires, tasteful décor inc contemporary irish prints and functioning library; good own-brewed beers inc Stout, Extra Stout, Red Ale, Rusty Ale and lager, good coffee, enjoyable reasonably priced food from interesting sandwiches through very popular lunchtime carvery to top-floor gourmet restaurant; two TVs; Irish music Sun-Tues from 9.30 *(CMW, JJW)*

O'Neills [Suffolk St]: Spreading early Victorian pub with lots of dark panelling and cubby-holes off big lively bar, more rooms upstairs, good lunchtime carvery (go around 2 to avoid the crush; it's on all day Sun), good value doorstep sandwiches and home-made soup, quick efficient service, good Guinness *(Janet and Peter Race, Keith and Chris O'Neill, Simon Calvert, Jo Lilley)*

Oliver St John Gogarty [Anglesea St, Temple Bar]: Large bustling bare-boards bars, bric-a-brac inc bicycle above counter, good Guinness, generous, good if not cheap food in fairly small cosy upper-floor restaurant (former bank, interesting preserved features) and at lunchtime in main bar, very friendly efficient service; rambles through into adjoining Left Bank bar which has integral heated terrace tables; live music upstairs *(Keith and Chris O'Neill)*

Palace [Fleet St, Temple Bar]: Splendidly unspoilt Victorian bar standing out from the ersatz 'craic' elsewhere in Temple Bar, with snob screens, rooms through etched-glass doors, tiny snug, plainer back room with interesting well preserved cupola; good Guinness *(Joe Green, Jo Lilley)*

Porterhouse [Parliament St, nr Wellington Quay]: Vibrant three-storey modern pub, lots of pine and brass for café-bar feel, brewing half a dozen good beers inc several Porters (particularly good) and usually a cask-conditioned real ale, guest beers such as Shepherd Neame, dozens of foreign bottled beers, friendly efficient service, lots of anti-Guinness propaganda; high tables and equally high seats, good food from ciabatta sandwiches to steaks, upstairs restaurant; piped music, nightly live music, can be standing room only wknds; see Central London Lucky Dip under WC2 for an offshoot there *(Janet and Peter Race, Emma and Will, Keith and Chris O'Neill, Jo Lilley, Simon Calvert)*

Temple Bar [Temple Bar]: Rambling multi-levelled, many-roomed pub, much extended at back; rather bohemian, usually crowded; tables out in big yard, good live music from 4pm *(Keith and Chris O'Neill)*

GOWRAN

Paddy's [Flagmount, N10 Kilkenny—Carlow; Co Kilkenny]: Handy creeper-covered stop, enjoyable food, usual drinks; piped local radio *(CMW, JJW)*

INAGH

Biddy Early [Co Clare]: Good lager, ale and stout from next-door brewery (tours available), chatty friendly landlord, darts and pool in second room; TV *(CMW, JJW)*

KILLARNEY

Laurels [High St; Co Kerry]: Renamed for top-notch greyhound race won by landlord's dog in the 1930s; shop window full of beer bottles, usual beers on tap, friendly local bar, folk music virtually every night in season, separate dining area *(Ian Phillips)*

KILMORE QUAY

Kehoes [R739; Co Wexford]: Interesting L-shaped bar, friendly and bustling, with lots of nautical equipment, ship models and pictures, ship's doors as tables, usual drinks plus Bulmer's cider, good helpings of enjoyable reasonably priced food all day from sandwiches up; no prams or buggies, tables on terrace with more boat bits *(CMW, JJW)*

LISDOONVARNA

Roadside Tavern [Co Clare]: Three linked recently refurbished rooms with pine tables, fish-oriented food all day, two real fires, usual drinks; TV; good nightly traditional music *(CMW, JJW)*

Royal Spa [N67; Co Clare]: Food all day, pizzas till midnight, usual drinks (tea, coffee and milk popular too); unobtrusive piped traditional music; live music nightly at least in summer *(CMW, JJW)*

MURRISK

Tavern [R335 W of Westport]: At the foot of Croagh Patrick, good interesting up-to-date lunches with plenty of local fish, Guinness and decent wine *(Joyce and Maurice Cottrell)*

RATHCOOLE

An Poitin Stil [N7 Dublin—Naas; Co Dublin]: Big busy rambling main-road pub, bar, lounge with carvery food servery, generous reasonably priced food until 10pm, usual drinks, downstairs restaurant with aquarium; piped music; children welcome, picnic-sets outside *(CMW, JJW)*

ISLE OF MAN

DOUGLAS [SC3876]

Cornerhouse [Ridgeway St, between Lord St bus station and Peel Rd railway station]: Open-plan brasserie feel, lots of little nooks and crannies as well as larger areas, lunchtime food, good atmosphere and friendly staff, decent wines in baby bottles, pool and darts; live music; open all day *(Dr J Barrie Jones)*

PORT ST MARY [SC2167]

Station Hotel [Station Rd]: Two friendly interconnecting bars with good value food and bottle or carafe wines, separate restaurant; handy for steam railway, picnic-sets outside, bedrooms *(Dr J Barrie Jones)*

ITALY

GENOA

Britannia [Vico Casana 76]: Long-standing (since 1977) approximation of a British pub, with 1970s brewery advertisements in alcoves around long main bar, masses of bank notes behind it, Guinness and Smithwicks Kilkenny on tap, some continental and local beers, simple food such as burgers, lasagne and spaghetti, lower seating areas with waitress service, model British cars, even a replica telephone box *(Martin Grosberg)*

LATVIA

RIGA

Alus Seta [6 Tirgonu Iela, by Dome Sq]: Beams, timbers and panelling, sliding windows to pavement tables, cheap Lido (brewed at another establishment in this Lido chain – most of which are more restauranty), Aldaris and excellent Uzavas, also tea and coffee, all-day self-service food bar inc shashliks and local specialities as well as lasagne and steaks, narrow passage to back drinking hall with own bar, décor of old prints, Latvian sayings, bric-a-brac and a constellation of small lights; tables outside (where you can hear bands playing for the nearby more expensive Dome beer gardens), open all day, very wide range of customers – they may give children balloons *(Martin Grosberg)*

MADEIRA

FUNCHAL

Prince Albert [off Avenida do Infante, nr Savoy Hotel]: Refuge for homesick Brits, owned by ex-pats, with Victorian-style dark panelling, dark wood furniture inc cast-iron-framed tables on tiled floor, old-fashioned curved bar, lots of advertising mirrors and colonial prints, good value sandwich snacks with chips until midnight, a dozen unusual though pricey british bottled beers as well as local lagers and keg beers; darts, TV football, quiz nights, piped local and 60s music; open all day *(Kevin Thorpe)*

NAMIBIA

WINDHOEK

Joe's Pub: Bierkeller meets african village, german and local Windhoek beers, amazing germano-african food choice from bratwürst and grillhäxi to bushman game kebabs and springbok stir-fries; cheap Sun buffet – eat as much as you like *(Richard Lippiett, Joe Green)*

NETHERLANDS

AMSTERDAM

Arendsnest [Herengracht]: Neatly kept appealing bar, good civilised atmosphere, long row of bentwood high stools by mahogany counter with plenty of other drinks besides the comprehensive range of dutch beers (a dozen on tap, over a hundred by the bottle); open 4pm till late *(Kerry Law, Simon Smith)*

Café Dulac [Haarlemmer Str]: Grand café-bar quirkily mixing art deco style with gothic/kitsch fixtures, mainly dutch beers with some notable belgian ones, good food worth waiting for *(C J Fletcher)*

Prins [Prinsengracht 124]: Friendly and appealing brown café on one of the most picturesque canals, well prepared generous food from good lunchtime sandwiches and fashionable snacks to steaks, wider evening choice (can be hard to get a table then), mainly dutch beers with one or two belgians such as La Chouffe, nice local atmosphere; handy for Anne Frank Museum *(Michael Doswell, Christine and Neil Townend)*

NEW ZEALAND

AUCKLAND

Loaded Hog: Very popular brewpub, friendly and lively, part of a chain of this name, in excellent spot overlooking yacht basin, spacious bare-boards room with central bar open to street, balcony, Loaded Hog, Red Dog and other cold beers in chilled glasses, good quick food in good-sized helpings inc prime burgers, good cheerful service, wide choice of wine by the glass – all cheaper than UK *(Dr and Mrs M E Wilson, Alan Sutton)*

Occidental Belgian Beer Café [6-8 Vulcan Lane]: Large town-centre pub with Edwardian-feel woodwork and mirrors, authentic belgian food (delicious mussels) and beer, in the appropriate glasses and (unusually for NZ) at the right temperature, friendly efficient young staff (as elsewhere in NZ); tables and chairs flowing out into the quiet narrow street *(Dr and Mrs M E Wilson, Ian Runcie)*

RENWICK

Cork & Keg [nr Blenheim]: Brews own english-style beer, served at room temperature, ex-pat landlord and anglophile locals, usual pub food *(Ian Runcie)*

POLAND

KRAKÓW

Singer: Smoky bo-ho place, strong on atmosphere rather than mod cons, old sewing machine tables (hence the name?); piped music to suit, such as old jazz, blues, French songs *(Kerry Law, Simon Smith)*

SINGAPORE

SINGAPORE

☆ *Raffles* [Beach Rd]: Magnificent national monument, lavishly restored: Long Bar well worth a visit for its atmosphere, Singapore slings, waving 'leaf' fans overhead, and underfoot peanut shells (they're said to polish the floor); also sedate Billiards Bar, Tiffin Room with elaborate changing buffets, more expensive meals in the Writer's Room, and five other food outlets each with its own style of cooking; cultural and Raffles displays; even with the strong pound prices can be daunting if you stay *(Roger and Jenny Huggins)*

SWITZERLAND

BERNE

Old Tramdepot [next to Bear Pits]: Brews its own good beers, great views over river and city from terrace; food too, and they make and sell nice beer glasses *(Mrs Jane Kingsbury)*

USA

CAMDEN

Cappys Chowder House [Main St; Maine]: Cosy pub overlooking attractive harbour, good food, local Shipyard ales and Sam Adams, good bustling atmosphere, attentive friendly staff; adjoining shop selling their own canned clam chowder with other food, papers etc *(Comus and Sarah Elliott)*

COLUMBUS

Barleys Brewing Co [North High St]: Enjoyable meals in brewpub with a weekly special brew on Fri – perhaps an english-style Pale Ale; delightful market just outside, trendy part of town *(Tom McLean)*

LUDLOW

Pot Bellys [Main St; Vermont]: Like a busy english town pub (except for the baseball on TVs all round main bar), with good modestly priced food, good friendly service, enjoyable beers – Samuel Adams and Otter Creek Red and Dark; occasional music nights *(Comus and Sarah Elliott)*

NEW YORK

Spotted Pig [314 West 11th St]: Outstanding food in London-style gastropub, chef from River Café; british beer, too *(Jan Dobris)*

SAN FRANCISCO

Magnolia Brewpub [Haight St]: Good place to sample their own and other SF beers *(Giles and Annie Francis)*

SEDONA

Oak Creek Brewery [Highway 89A W; Arizona]: Microbrewery in tourist hot-spot, excellent choice of beers, owner's German wife does good german cooking; spacious pleasant terrace; also a separate restaurant/bar at Tlaquepaque Village, smart and upmarket, with pleasant atmosphere and good food *(Mike Gorton)*

WASHINGTON

Capitol City [1100 New York Ave, DC]: Big beer hall in office building, brewing its own very wide range of beers in various mainly british and european styles, friendly staff, good US-style bar food, reasonable prices; branches on Capitol Hill and in Arlington (S Quincy St) and Baltimore (Harborplace) *(Simon and Tannahill Keymer)*

WISCASSET

Schooners [Maine]: Friendly bustling pub/restaurant/shop, enjoyable food, wide choice of New England beers on tap inc Sam Adams and Otter Creek, balcony overlooking river; in what is said to be Maine's prettiest village *(Comus and Sarah Elliott)*

Please keep sending us reports. We rely on readers for news of new discoveries, and particularly for news of changes – however slight – at the fully described pubs.
No stamp needed: *The Good Pub Guide*, FREEPOST TN1569, Wadhurst, E Sussex TN5 7BR or send your report through our web site: www.goodguides.co.uk

Special Interest Lists

PUBS WITH GOOD GARDENS

The pubs listed here have bigger or more beautiful gardens, grounds or terraces than are usual for their areas. Note that in a town or city this might be very much more modest than the sort of garden that would deserve a listing in the countryside.

BEDFORDSHIRE
Northill, Crown
Old Warden, Hare & Hounds
Pegsdon, Live & Let Live
Riseley, Fox & Hounds

BERKSHIRE
Aldworth, Bell
Ashmore Green, Sun in the Wood
Crazies Hill, Horns
Frilsham, Pot Kiln
Inkpen, Crown & Garter
Marsh Benham, Red House
Shinfield, Magpie & Parrot
Winterbourne, Winterbourne Arms

BUCKINGHAMSHIRE
Bovingdon Green, Royal Oak
Denham, Swan
Ford, Dinton Hermit
Hambleden, Stag & Huntsman
Hawridge Common, Full Moon
Hedgerley, White Horse
Mentmore, Stag
Penn, Crown
Skirmett, Frog

CAMBRIDGESHIRE
Elton, Black Horse
Fowlmere, Chequers
Heydon, King William IV
Madingley, Three Horseshoes

CHESHIRE
Aldford, Grosvenor Arms
Bunbury, Dysart Arms
Haughton Moss, Nags Head
Lower Peover, Bells of Peover
Macclesfield, Sutton Hall Hotel

CORNWALL
Helford, Shipwrights Arms
Mousehole, Old Coastguard
Philleigh, Roseland
St Agnes, Turks Head
St Kew, St Kew Inn
St Mawgan, Falcon
Trematon, Crooked Inn
Tresco, New Inn

CUMBRIA
Ambleside, Wateredge
Barbon, Barbon Inn
Bassenthwaite Lake, Pheasant
Bouth, White Hart
Staveley, Eagle & Child

DERBYSHIRE
Birch Vale, Waltzing Weasel
Buxton, Bull i' th' Thorn
Hathersage, Plough
Melbourne, John Thompson
Woolley Moor, White Horse

DEVON
Berrynarbor, Olde Globe
Broadhembury, Drewe Arms
Clayhidon, Merry Harriers
Clyst Hydon, Five Bells
Cornworthy, Hunters Lodge
Exeter, Imperial
Exminster, Turf Hotel
Haytor Vale, Rock
Lower Ashton, Manor Inn
Lydford, Castle Inn
Newton Abbot, Two Mile Oak
Newton Ferrers, Dolphin
Poundsgate, Tavistock Inn
Sidbury, Hare & Hounds
Sidford, Blue Ball
South Zeal, Oxenham Arms
Torbryan, Old Church House

DORSET
Cerne Abbas, Royal Oak
Chideock, George
Corfe Castle, Fox
Osmington Mills, Smugglers
Shroton, Cricketers
Sturminster Newton, Swan
Tarrant Monkton, Langton Arms
West Bexington, Manor Hotel

ESSEX
Castle Hedingham, Bell
Chappel, Swan
Fyfield, Queens Head
Great Yeldham, White Hart
Hastingwood, Rainbow & Dove
Mill Green, Viper
Stock, Hoop
Wendens Ambo, Bell

GLOUCESTERSHIRE
Blaisdon, Red Hart
Ewen, Wild Duck
Kingscote, Hunters Hall
Nailsworth, Egypt Mill
North Nibley, New Inn
Northleach, Wheatsheaf
Old Sodbury, Dog
Upper Oddington, Horse & Groom

HAMPSHIRE
Bramdean, Fox
Minstead, Trusty Servant
North Gorley, Royal Oak
Ovington, Bush
Steep, Harrow
Stockbridge, Grosvenor
Tichborne, Tichborne Arms

HEREFORDSHIRE
Aymestrey, Riverside Inn
Sellack, Lough Pool
Ullingswick, Three Crowns

HERTFORDSHIRE
Ashwell, Three Tuns
Chapmore End, Woodman
Potters Crouch, Holly Bush
Sarratt, Boot, Cock

ISLE OF WIGHT
Shorwell, Crown

KENT
Biddenden, Three Chimneys
Bough Beech, Wheatsheaf
Boyden Gate, Gate Inn
Brookland, Woolpack
Chiddingstone, Castle Inn
Dargate, Dove
Fordcombe, Chafford Arms
Groombridge, Crown
Hucking, Hook & Hatchet
Ickham, Duke William
Newnham, George
Penshurst, Bottle House
Selling, Rose & Crown
Ulcombe, Pepper Box

LANCASHIRE
Newton, Parkers Arms
Whitewell, Inn at Whitewell

LEICESTERSHIRE AND RUTLAND
Barrowden, Exeter Arms
Exton, Fox & Hounds
Lyddington, Old White Hart
Medbourne, Nevill Arms
Old Dalby, Crown
Stathern, Red Lion

LINCOLNSHIRE
Billingborough, Fortescue Arms
Coningsby, Lea Gate Inn
Lincoln, Victoria
Newton, Red Lion
Stamford, George of Stamford

NORFOLK
Burnham Thorpe, Lord Nelson
Cley next the Sea, Three Swallows
Great Cressingham, Windmill
Letheringsett, Kings Head
Ringstead, Gin Trap
Snettisham, Rose & Crown
Stanhoe, Crown
Stow Bardolph, Hare Arms
Woodbastwick, Fur & Feather

NORTHAMPTONSHIRE
Bulwick, Queens Head
East Haddon, Red Lion
Farthingstone, Kings Arms

NORTHUMBRIA
Anick, Rat
Blanchland, Lord Crewe Arms
Diptonmill, Dipton Mill Inn
Greta Bridge, Morritt Arms
Newburn, Keelman
Thropton, Three Wheat Heads
Weldon Bridge, Anglers Arms

NOTTINGHAMSHIRE
Caunton, Caunton Beck
Colston Bassett, Martins Arms
Kimberley, Nelson & Railway
Walkeringham, Three Horse Shoes

OXFORDSHIRE
Burford, Lamb
Clifton, Duke of Cumberlands Head
Highmoor, Rising Sun
Hook Norton, Gate Hangs High, Pear Tree
Kelmscott, Plough
Maidensgrove, Five Horseshoes
Sibford Gower, Bishop Blaize
Stanton St John, Star
Stoke Row, Grouse & Claret
Swalcliffe, Stags Head
Tadpole Bridge, Trout

SHROPSHIRE
Bishop's Castle, Castle Hotel, Three Tuns
Hopton Wafers, Crown
Norton, Hundred House

SOMERSET
Axbridge, Lamb
Chiselborough, Cat Head
Compton Martin, Ring o' Bells
Exford, Crown
Freshford, Inn at Freshford
Monksilver, Notley Arms
Rowberrow, Swan
Shepton Montague, Montague Inn

STAFFORDSHIRE
Salt, Holly Bush
Stourton, Fox

SUFFOLK
Brome, Cornwallis
Dennington, Queens Head
Hundon, Plough
Lavenham, Angel
Laxfield, Kings Head
Long Melford, Black Lion
Rede, Plough
Stoke-by-Nayland, Crown
Walberswick, Bell
Waldringfield, Maybush

SURREY
Charleshill, Donkey
Coldharbour, Plough
Compton, Withies
Eashing, Stag
Laleham, Three Horseshoes
Lingfield, Hare & Hounds
Mickleham, King William IV
Newdigate, Surrey Oaks
Ockley, Kings Arms
Ottershaw, Castle
West End, Inn at West End

SUSSEX
Alfriston, George
Amberley, Black Horse
Balls Cross, Stag
Berwick, Cricketers Arms
Blackboys, Blackboys Inn
Byworth, Black Horse
Danehill, Coach & Horses
Elsted, Three Horseshoes
Fittleworth, Swan
Fletching, Griffin
Heathfield, Star
Henley, Duke of Cumberland Arms
Oving, Gribble Inn
Rushlake Green, Horse & Groom
Rye, Ypres Castle
Singleton, Fox & Hounds
Wineham, Royal Oak

WARWICKSHIRE
Edge Hill, Castle
Farnborough, Inn at Farnborough
Ilmington, Howard Arms
Priors Marston, Holly Bush
Wharf, Wharf Inn

WILTSHIRE
Berwick St James, Boot
Brinkworth, Three Crowns
Chicksgrove, Compasses
Ebbesbourne Wake, Horseshoe
Great Durnford, Black Horse
Kilmington, Red Lion
Lacock, George, Rising Sun
Norton, Vine Tree
Seend, Barge
Whitley, Pear Tree
Woodborough, Seven Stars

WORCESTERSHIRE
Welland, Anchor

YORKSHIRE
East Witton, Blue Lion
Egton Bridge, Horse Shoe
Halifax, Shibden Mill
Heath, Kings Arms
Scawton, Hare
Sutton upon Derwent, St Vincent Arms

LONDON
Central London, Cross Keys
East London, Prospect of Whitby
North London, Spaniards Inn
South London, Crown & Greyhound, Founders Arms, Ship
West London, Colton Arms, Dove, Windsor Castle

SCOTLAND
Badachro, Badachro Inn
Edinburgh, Starbank
Gairloch, Old Inn
Gifford, Tweeddale Arms
Glenelg, Glenelg Inn
Skeabost, Skeabost House Hotel
Thornhill, Lion & Unicorn

WALES
Colwyn Bay, Pen-y-Bryn
Crickhowell, Bear, Nantyffin Cider Mill
Gresford, Pant-yr-Ochain
Llangedwyn, Green Inn
Llangollen, Corn Mill
Llwyndafydd, Crown
Mold, Glasfryn
Old Radnor, Harp
Presteigne, Radnorshire Arms
Raglan, Clytha Arms
Rosebush, Tafarn Sinc
St Hilary, Bush
Tintern, Cherry Tree
Ty'n-y-groes, Groes

CHANNEL ISLANDS
King's Mills, Fleur du Jardin
Rozel, Rozel Bay Hotel

WATERSIDE PUBS

The pubs listed here are right beside the sea, a sizeable river, canal, lake or loch that contributes significantly to their attraction.

BERKSHIRE
Kintbury, Dundas Arms

CAMBRIDGESHIRE
Sutton Gault, Anchor

CHESHIRE
Chester, Old Harkers Arms
Wrenbury, Dusty Miller

CORNWALL
Bodinnick, Old Ferry
Helford, Shipwrights Arms
Malpas, Heron
Mousehole, Old Coastguard
Mylor Bridge, Pandora
Polkerris, Rashleigh
Port Isaac, Port Gaverne Inn, Slipway
Porthleven, Ship
Sennen Cove, Old Success
St Agnes, Turks Head
Tresco, New Inn

CUMBRIA
Ambleside, Wateredge
Staveley, Eagle & Child
Ulverston, Bay Horse

DERBYSHIRE
Hathersage, Plough
Shardlow, Old Crown

DEVON
Culmstock, Culm Valley
Exminster, Turf Hotel
Newton Ferrers, Dolphin
Noss Mayo, Ship
Torcross, Start Bay

DORSET
Chideock, Anchor

ESSEX
Burnham-on-Crouch, White Harte
Chappel, Swan
Fyfield, Queens Head

GLOUCESTERSHIRE
Ashleworth Quay, Boat

HAMPSHIRE
Ovington, Bush
Portsmouth, Still & West

HEREFORDSHIRE
Aymestrey, Riverside Inn

ISLE OF WIGHT
Bembridge, Crab & Lobster
Seaview, Seaview Hotel
Ventnor, Spyglass

KENT
Deal, Kings Head
Oare, Shipwrights Arms

LANCASHIRE
Little Eccleston, Cartford
Liverpool, Baltic Fleet
Manchester, Dukes 92
Whitewell, Inn at Whitewell

LINCOLNSHIRE
Brandy Wharf, Cider Centre

NORFOLK
Brancaster Staithe, White Horse

NORTHUMBRIA
Newcastle upon Tyne, Head of Steam @ The Cluny
Newton-by-the-Sea, Ship

OXFORDSHIRE
Tadpole Bridge, Trout

SHROPSHIRE
Ludlow, Unicorn
Shrewsbury, Armoury

SOMERSET
Churchill, Crown
Compton Martin, Ring o' Bells
Portishead, Windmill

SUFFOLK
Chelmondiston, Butt & Oyster
Nayland, Anchor
Southwold, Harbour Inn
Waldringfield, Maybush

SURREY
Eashing, Stag

WARWICKSHIRE
Lapworth, Navigation
Wharf, Wharf Inn

WILTSHIRE
Great Durnford, Black Horse
Seend, Barge

WORCESTERSHIRE
Knightwick, Talbot
Wyre Piddle, Anchor

YORKSHIRE
Hull, Minerva
Whitby, Duke of York

LONDON
East London, Grapes, Prospect of Whitby
North London, Waterside
South London, Cutty Sark, Founders Arms, Ship
West London, Bulls Head, Dove

SCOTLAND
Aboyne, Boat
Badachro, Badachro Inn
Edinburgh, Starbank
Elie, Ship
Gairloch, Old Inn
Glenelg, Glenelg Inn
Isle of Whithorn, Steam Packet
Kingholm Quay, Swan
Plockton, Plockton Hotel
Shieldaig, Tigh an Eilean Hotel
Skeabost, Skeabost House Hotel
Stein, Stein Inn
Tayvallich, Tayvallich Inn
Ullapool, Ferry Boat

WALES
Aberaeron, Harbourmaster
Aberdovey, Penhelig Arms
Abergorlech, Black Lion
Cresswell Quay, Cresselly Arms
Little Haven, Swan
Llangedwyn, Green Inn
Llangollen, Corn Mill
Overton Bridge, Cross Foxes
Pembroke Ferry, Ferry Inn
Pontypool, Open Hearth
Red Wharf Bay, Ship
Talyllyn, Tynycornel

CHANNEL ISLANDS
St Aubin, Old Court House Inn
St Ouens Bay, La Pulente

PUBS IN ATTRACTIVE SURROUNDINGS

These pubs are in unusually attractive or interesting places – lovely countryside, charming villages, occasionally notable town surroundings. Waterside pubs are listed again here only if their other surroundings are special, too.

BEDFORDSHIRE
Old Warden, Hare & Hounds
Pegsdon, Live & Let Live

BERKSHIRE
Aldworth, Bell
Frilsham, Pot Kiln

BUCKINGHAMSHIRE
Bovingdon Green, Royal Oak
Hambleden, Stag & Huntsman
Hawridge Common, Full Moon
Skirmett, Frog
Turville, Bull & Butcher

CAMBRIDGESHIRE
Elton, Black Horse
Reach, Dyke's End

CHESHIRE
Barthomley, White Lion
Bunbury, Dysart Arms
Lower Peover, Bells of Peover

CORNWALL
Altarnun, Rising Sun
Blisland, Blisland Inn
Helston, Halzephron
St Agnes, Turks Head
St Breward, Old Inn
St Kew, St Kew Inn
St Mawgan, Falcon
Tresco, New Inn

CUMBRIA
Bassenthwaite Lake, Pheasant
Bouth, White Hart
Broughton Mills, Blacksmiths Arms
Buttermere, Bridge Hotel
Crosthwaite, Punch Bowl
Elterwater, Britannia
Ennerdale Bridge, Shepherds Arms

Hawkshead, Drunken Duck, Kings Arms
Hesket Newmarket, Old Crown
Ings, Watermill
Langdale, Old Dungeon Ghyll
Little Langdale, Three Shires
Loweswater, Kirkstile Inn
Mungrisdale, Mill Inn
Santon Bridge, Bridge Inn
Seathwaite, Newfield Inn
Stonethwaite, Langstrath
Troutbeck, Queens Head
Ulverston, Bay Horse

DERBYSHIRE
Alderwasley, Bear
Brassington, Olde Gate
Foolow, Bulls Head
Froggatt Edge, Chequers
Hardwick Hall, Hardwick Inn
Hathersage, Plough, Scotsmans Pack
Kirk Ireton, Barley Mow
Ladybower Reservoir, Yorkshire Bridge
Litton, Red Lion
Monsal Head, Monsal Head Hotel
Over Haddon, Lathkil
Sheldon, Cock & Pullet
Woolley Moor, White Horse

DEVON
Branscombe, Fountain Head
Buckland Monachorum, Drake Manor
Culmstock, Culm Valley
East Budleigh, Sir Walter Raleigh
Exminster, Turf Hotel
Haytor Vale, Rock
Holbeton, Mildmay Colours
Holne, Church House
Horndon, Elephants Nest
Iddesleigh, Duke of York
Kingston, Dolphin
Lower Ashton, Manor Inn
Lustleigh, Cleave
Lydford, Castle Inn, Dartmoor Inn
Meavy, Royal Oak
Molland, London
Parracombe, Fox & Goose
Peter Tavy, Peter Tavy Inn
Postbridge, Warren House
Rattery, Church House
Slapton, Tower
Widecombe, Rugglestone
Wonson, Northmore Arms

DORSET
Corfe Castle, Fox
Corscombe, Fox
East Chaldon, Sailors Return
Osmington Mills, Smugglers
Pamphill, Vine
Worth Matravers, Square & Compass

ESSEX
Fuller Street, Square & Compasses
Mill Green, Viper

GLOUCESTERSHIRE
Ashleworth Quay, Boat
Bisley, Bear
Bledington, Kings Head
Chedworth, Seven Tuns
Chipping Campden, Eight Bells
Coln St Aldwyns, New Inn
Eastleach Turville, Victoria
Glasshouse, Glasshouse Inn
Guiting Power, Hollow Bottom
Miserden, Carpenters Arms
Nailsworth, Weighbridge
Newland, Ostrich
North Nibley, New Inn
Northleach, Wheatsheaf
Sapperton, Bell
St Briavels, George
Stow-on-the-Wold, Eagle & Child

HAMPSHIRE
East Tytherley, Star
Fritham, Royal Oak
Hawkley, Hawkley Inn
Lymington, Kings Head
Micheldever, Half Moon & Spread Eagle
Minstead, Trusty Servant
North Gorley, Royal Oak
Ovington, Bush
Tichborne, Tichborne Arms

HEREFORDSHIRE
Aymestrey, Riverside Inn
Dorstone, Pandy
Sellack, Lough Pool
Titley, Stagg
Walterstone, Carpenters Arms
Weobley, Salutation

HERTFORDSHIRE
Aldbury, Greyhound
Frithsden, Alford Arms
Sarratt, Cock

KENT
Brookland, Woolpack
Chiddingstone, Castle Inn
Elham, Rose & Crown
Groombridge, Crown
Hucking, Hook & Hatchet
Newnham, George
Selling, Rose & Crown

LANCASHIRE
Blackstone Edge, White House
Bury, Lord Raglan
Little Eccleston, Cartford
Newton, Parkers Arms
Sawley, Spread Eagle
Tunstall, Lunesdale Arms
Uppermill, Church Inn
Whitewell, Inn at Whitewell

LEICESTERSHIRE AND RUTLAND
Barrowden, Exeter Arms
Exton, Fox & Hounds
Upper Hambleton, Finches Arms

NORFOLK
Blakeney, White Horse
Burnham Market, Hoste Arms
Cley next the Sea, Three Swallows
Horsey, Nelson Head
Thornham, Lifeboat
Woodbastwick, Fur & Feather

NORTHAMPTONSHIRE
Harringworth, White Swan

NORTHUMBRIA
Allenheads, Allenheads Inn
Blanchland, Lord Crewe Arms
Diptonmill, Dipton Mill Inn
Great Whittington, Queens Head
Haltwhistle, Milecastle Inn
Langley on Tyne, Carts Bog Inn
Newton-by-the-Sea, Ship
Romaldkirk, Rose & Crown
Stannersburn, Pheasant

NOTTINGHAMSHIRE
Laxton, Dovecote

OXFORDSHIRE
Checkendon, Black Horse
Great Tew, Falkland Arms
Kelmscott, Plough
Maidensgrove, Five Horseshoes
Oxford, Kings Arms, Turf Tavern
Stoke Row, Grouse & Claret
Swalcliffe, Stags Head
Swinbrook, Swan

SHROPSHIRE
Bridges, Horseshoe
Cardington, Royal Oak
Picklescott, Bottle & Glass

SOMERSET
Appley, Globe
Axbridge, Lamb
Batcombe, Three Horseshoes
Crowcombe, Carew Arms
Exford, White Horse
Luxborough, Royal Oak
Triscombe, Blue Ball
Wells, City Arms
Winsford, Royal Oak

STAFFORDSHIRE
Alstonefield, George
Stourton, Fox

SUFFOLK
Dennington, Queens Head
Dunwich, Ship
Lavenham, Angel

Levington, Ship
Walberswick, Bell

SURREY
Blackbrook, Plough
Cobham, Cricketers
Esher, Marneys
Lingfield, Hare & Hounds
Mickleham, King William IV
Reigate Heath, Skimmington Castle

SUSSEX
Alfriston, George
Amberley, Black Horse
Burpham, George & Dragon
Chilgrove, White Horse
East Dean, Tiger
Fletching, Griffin
Heathfield, Star
Henley, Duke of Cumberland Arms
Lurgashall, Noahs Ark
Rye, Mermaid, Ypres Castle
Wineham, Royal Oak

WARWICKSHIRE
Edge Hill, Castle
Himley, Crooked House
Priors Marston, Holly Bush

WILTSHIRE
Axford, Red Lion
Donhead St Andrew, Forester
Ebbesbourne Wake, Horseshoe
Lacock, Rising Sun
Newton Tony, Malet Arms
Stourton, Spread Eagle

WORCESTERSHIRE
Berrow Green, Admiral Rodney
Broadway, Crown & Trumpet
Kidderminster, King & Castle
Knightwick, Talbot
Pensax, Bell

YORKSHIRE
Beck Hole, Birch Hall
Blakey Ridge, Lion
Bradfield, Strines Inn
Byland Abbey, Abbey Inn
Chapel le Dale, Hill Inn
Cray, White Lion
East Witton, Blue Lion
Halifax, Shibden Mill
Heath, Kings Arms
Hubberholme, George
Langthwaite, Charles Bathurst
Lastingham, Blacksmiths Arms
Linton in Craven, Fountaine
Litton, Queens Arms
Lund, Wellington
Masham, Kings Head
Osmotherley, Golden Lion
Ripley, Boars Head
Robin Hood's Bay, Laurel
Shelley, Three Acres
Thornton in Lonsdale, Marton Arms
Thornton Watlass, Buck
Wath in Nidderdale, Sportsmans Arms
Widdop, Pack Horse

LONDON
Central London, Olde Mitre
North London, Spaniards Inn
South London, Crown & Greyhound

SCOTLAND
Applecross, Applecross Inn
Gairloch, Old Inn
Kilberry, Kilberry Inn
Kingholm Quay, Swan
Stein, Stein Inn

WALES
Abergorlech, Black Lion
Berriew, Lion
Caio, Brunant Arms
Capel Curig, Bryn Tyrch
Carew, Carew Inn
Crickhowell, Nantyffin Cider Mill
Llanberis, Pen-y-Gwryd
Llangedwyn, Green Inn
Old Radnor, Harp
Red Wharf Bay, Ship
Rhyd-y-Meirch, Goose & Cuckoo
Talyllyn, Tynycornel
Tintern, Cherry Tree

CHANNEL ISLANDS
St Brelade, Old Portelet Inn, Old Smugglers
St John, Les Fontaines

PUBS WITH GOOD VIEWS

These pubs are listed for their particularly good views, either from inside or from a garden or terrace. Waterside pubs are listed again here only if their view is exceptional in its own right – not just a straightforward sea view for example.

BUCKINGHAMSHIRE
Penn, Crown

CHESHIRE
Higher Burwardsley, Pheasant
Langley, Hanging Gate

CORNWALL
Sennen Cove, Old Success
St Agnes, Turks Head
St Anns Chapel, Rifle Volunteer

CUMBRIA
Cartmel Fell, Masons Arms
Hawkshead, Drunken Duck
Keswick, Swinside Inn
Langdale, Old Dungeon Ghyll
Loweswater, Kirkstile Inn
Mungrisdale, Mill Inn
Stonethwaite, Langstrath
Troutbeck, Queens Head
Ulverston, Bay Horse

DERBYSHIRE
Alderwasley, Bear
Foolow, Barrel, Bulls Head
Idridgehay, Black Swan
Monsal Head, Monsal Head Hotel
Over Haddon, Lathkil

DEVON
Newton Ferrers, Dolphin
Postbridge, Warren House
Sidbury, Hare & Hounds

DORSET
West Bexington, Manor Hotel
Worth Matravers, Square & Compass

GLOUCESTERSHIRE
Sheepscombe, Butchers Arms

ISLE OF WIGHT
Bembridge, Crab & Lobster
Ventnor, Spyglass

KENT
Tunbridge Wells, Beacon
Ulcombe, Pepper Box

LANCASHIRE
Blackstone Edge, White House
Bury, Lord Raglan
Newton, Parkers Arms
Sawley, Spread Eagle
Uppermill, Church Inn

NORFOLK
Brancaster Staithe, White Horse

NORTHUMBRIA
Anick, Rat
Newfield, Fox & Hounds
Seahouses, Olde Ship
Thropton, Three Wheat Heads

OXFORDSHIRE
Sibford Gower, Bishop Blaize

SOMERSET
Portishead, Windmill
Shepton Montague, Montague Inn

SUFFOLK
Erwarton, Queens Head
Hundon, Plough
Levington, Ship

SURREY
Mickleham, King William IV

SUSSEX
Byworth, Black Horse
Elsted, Three Horseshoes
Fletching, Griffin
Henley, Duke of Cumberland Arms

Icklesham, Queens Head
Rye, Ypres Castle

WILTSHIRE
Axford, Red Lion
Box, Quarrymans Arms
Donhead St Andrew, Forester
Lacock, Rising Sun

WORCESTERSHIRE
Malvern, Nags Head
Pensax, Bell
Wyre Piddle, Anchor

YORKSHIRE
Blakey Ridge, Lion
Bradfield, Strines Inn
Kirkham, Stone Trough
Langthwaite, Charles Bathurst
Litton, Queens Arms
Shelley, Three Acres
Whitby, Duke of York

LONDON
South London, Founders Arms

SCOTLAND
Applecross, Applecross Inn
Badachro, Badachro Inn
Edinburgh, Starbank
Glenelg, Glenelg Inn
Kilberry, Kilberry Inn
Shieldaig, Tigh an Eilean Hotel
Stein, Stein Inn
Ullapool, Ferry Boat
Weem, Ailean Chraggan

WALES
Aberdovey, Penhelig Arms
Capel Curig, Bryn Tyrch
Colwyn Bay, Pen-y-Bryn
Llanberis, Pen-y-Gwryd
Llangollen, Corn Mill
Mold, Glasfryn
Old Radnor, Harp
Overton Bridge, Cross Foxes
Rhyd-y-Meirch, Goose & Cuckoo
Talyllyn, Tynycornel
Ty'n-y-groes, Groes

CHANNEL ISLANDS
St Aubin, Old Court House Inn

PUBS IN INTERESTING BUILDINGS

Pubs and inns are listed here for the particular interest of their building – something really out of the ordinary to look at, or occasionally a building that has an outstandingly interesting historical background.

BUCKINGHAMSHIRE
Forty Green, Royal Standard of England

DERBYSHIRE
Buxton, Bull i' th' Thorn

DEVON
Dartmouth, Cherub
Harberton, Church House
Rattery, Church House
South Zeal, Oxenham Arms

ESSEX
Great Yeldham, White Hart

LANCASHIRE
Liverpool, Philharmonic Dining Rooms

LINCOLNSHIRE
Grantham, Angel & Royal
Stamford, George of Stamford

NORTHUMBRIA
Blanchland, Lord Crewe Arms

NOTTINGHAMSHIRE
Nottingham, Olde Trip to Jerusalem

OXFORDSHIRE
Banbury, Reindeer

SUFFOLK
Laxfield, Kings Head

SUSSEX
Rye, Mermaid

WARWICKSHIRE
Himley, Crooked House

WILTSHIRE
Salisbury, Haunch of Venison

YORKSHIRE
Hull, Olde White Harte

LONDON
Central London, Black Friar, Cittie of Yorke
South London, George

SCOTLAND
Edinburgh, Café Royal, Guildford Arms

PUBS THAT BREW THEIR OWN BEER

The pubs listed here brew their own beer on the premises; many others not listed have beers brewed for them specially, sometimes an individual recipe (but by a separate brewer). We mention these in the text.

BERKSHIRE
Frilsham, Pot Kiln

CAMBRIDGESHIRE
Peterborough, Brewery Tap

CUMBRIA
Cockermouth, Bitter End
Hawkshead, Drunken Duck
Hesket Newmarket, Old Crown
Loweswater, Kirkstile Inn
Tirril, Queens Head

DERBYSHIRE
Derby, Brunswick
Fenny Bentley, Bentley Brook
Melbourne, John Thompson

DEVON
Branscombe, Fountain Head

HAMPSHIRE
Cheriton, Flower Pots

HEREFORDSHIRE
Hereford, Victory

KENT
West Peckham, Swan on the Green

LANCASHIRE
Bury, Lord Raglan
Little Eccleston, Cartford
Liverpool, Baltic Fleet
Manchester, Marble Arch
Uppermill, Church Inn
Wheelton, Dressers Arms

LEICESTERSHIRE AND RUTLAND
Barrowden, Exeter Arms
East Langton, Bell
Oakham, Grainstore

LINCOLNSHIRE
South Witham, Blue Cow

NORTHUMBRIA
Diptonmill, Dipton Mill Inn
Newburn, Keelman

NOTTINGHAMSHIRE
Caythorpe, Black Horse
Nottingham, Fellows Morton & Clayton

SHROPSHIRE
Bishop's Castle, Six Bells, Three Tuns
Wistanstow, Plough

STAFFORDSHIRE
Burton upon Trent, Burton Bridge Inn

SUFFOLK
South Elmham, St Peters Brewery

SURREY
Coldharbour, Plough

WARWICKSHIRE
Sedgley, Beacon

WORCESTERSHIRE
Knightwick, Talbot

YORKSHIRE
Cropton, New Inn
Goose Eye, Turkey
Linthwaite, Sair
Sheffield, Fat Cat

SCOTLAND
Houston, Fox & Hounds
Pitlochry, Moulin

WALES
Abercych, Nags Head
Llanddarog, White Hart

OPEN ALL DAY (at least in summer)

We list here all the pubs that have told us they plan to stay open all day, even if it's only Saturday. We've included the few pubs which close just for half an hour to an hour, and the many more, chiefly in holiday areas, which open all day only in summer. The individual entries for the pubs themselves show the actual details.

BEDFORDSHIRE
Old Warden, Hare & Hounds
Pegsdon, Live & Let Live
Stanbridge, Five Bells
Turvey, Three Cranes

BERKSHIRE
Boxford, Bell
Marsh Benham, Red House
Reading, Hobgoblin, Sweeney & Todd
Windsor, Two Brewers
Woodside, Rose & Crown

BUCKINGHAMSHIRE
Bennett End, Three Horseshoes
Bovingdon Green, Royal Oak
Denham, Swan
Easington, Mole & Chicken
Ford, Dinton Hermit
Hedgerley, White Horse
Ley Hill, Swan
Mentmore, Stag
Penn, Crown
Soulbury, Boot
Turville, Bull & Butcher
Wooburn Common, Chequers

CAMBRIDGESHIRE
Cambridge, Eagle
Elton, Black Horse
Fen Drayton, Three Tuns
Godmanchester, Exhibition
Helpston, Blue Bell
Huntingdon, Old Bridge Hotel
Kimbolton, New Sun
Longstowe, Red House
Peterborough, Brewery Tap, Charters

CHESHIRE
Aldford, Grosvenor Arms
Astbury, Egerton Arms
Barthomley, White Lion
Bunbury, Dysart Arms
Chester, Old Harkers Arms
Cotebrook, Fox & Barrel
Daresbury, Ring o' Bells
Eaton, Plough
Haughton Moss, Nags Head
Higher Burwardsley, Pheasant
Lower Peover, Bells of Peover
Macclesfield, Sutton Hall Hotel
Plumley, Smoker
Prestbury, Legh Arms
Tarporley, Rising Sun
Wettenhall, Boot & Slipper
Wybunbury, Swan

CORNWALL
Altarnun, Rising Sun
Blisland, Blisland Inn
Bodinnick, Old Ferry
Lostwithiel, Royal Oak
Mitchell, Plume of Feathers
Mousehole, Old Coastguard
Mylor Bridge, Pandora
Polkerris, Rashleigh
Port Isaac, Golden Lion, Port Gaverne Inn, Slipway
Porthleven, Ship
Sennen Cove, Old Success
St Agnes, Turks Head
Tregadillett, Eliot Arms
Trematon, Crooked Inn
Tresco, New Inn
Truro, Old Ale House

CUMBRIA
Ambleside, Golden Rule, Wateredge
Armathwaite, Dukes Head
Bouth, White Hart
Broughton Mills, Blacksmiths Arms
Buttermere, Bridge Hotel
Cartmel Fell, Masons Arms
Cockermouth, Bitter End
Crosthwaite, Punch Bowl
Dalton-in-Furness, Black Dog
Elterwater, Britannia
Ennerdale Bridge, Shepherds Arms
Hawkshead, Kings Arms, Queens Head
Ings, Watermill
Langdale, Old Dungeon Ghyll
Little Langdale, Three Shires
Loweswater, Kirkstile Inn
Mungrisdale, Mill Inn
Santon Bridge, Bridge Inn
Seathwaite, Newfield Inn
Sedbergh, Dalesman
Stonethwaite, Langstrath
Tirril, Queens Head
Troutbeck, Queens Head
Ulverston, Bay Horse, Farmers Arms

DERBYSHIRE
Alderwasley, Bear
Beeley, Devonshire Arms
Buxton, Bull i' th' Thorn
Castleton, Castle Hotel
Derby, Alexandra, Brunswick, Olde Dolphin
Eyam, Miners Arms
Fenny Bentley, Bentley Brook, Coach & Horses
Foolow, Barrel, Bulls Head
Froggatt Edge, Chequers
Hardwick Hall, Hardwick Inn
Hathersage, Plough, Scotsmans Pack
Hayfield, Royal
Holbrook, Dead Poets
Idridgehay, Black Swan
Ladybower Reservoir, Yorkshire Bridge
Litton, Red Lion
Monsal Head, Monsal Head Hotel
Over Haddon, Lathkil
Shardlow, Old Crown
Wardlow, Three Stags Heads
Woolley Moor, White Horse

DEVON
Branscombe, Masons Arms
Cockwood, Anchor
Culmstock, Culm Valley
Dartmouth, Cherub
Dolton, Union
Exeter, Imperial
Exminster, Turf Hotel
Haytor Vale, Rock
Horns Cross, Hoops
Iddesleigh, Duke of York
Lydford, Castle Inn
Marldon, Church House
Newton Abbot, Two Mile Oak
Nomansland, Mount Pleasant
Noss Mayo, Ship
Postbridge, Warren House
Rockbeare, Jack in the Green
Sidbury, Hare & Hounds
Sidford, Blue Ball
Stoke Gabriel, Church House
Torcross, Start Bay
Widecombe, Rugglestone
Winkleigh, Kings Arms
Wonson, Northmore Arms
Woodbury Salterton, Diggers Rest
Woodland, Rising Sun

DORSET
Burton Bradstock, Anchor
Chideock, Anchor
East Chaldon, Sailors Return
Farnham, Museum
Mudeford, Ship in Distress
Osmington Mills, Smugglers
Sturminster Newton, Swan
Tarrant Monkton, Langton Arms
West Bexington, Manor Hotel
Worth Matravers, Square & Compass

ESSEX
Burnham-on-Crouch, White Harte
Chappel, Swan
Chelmsford, Alma
Clavering, Cricketers
Fingringhoe, Whalebone
Little Braxted, Green Man
Little Walden, Crown
Stock, Hoop
Stow Maries, Prince of Wales
Wendens Ambo, Bell
Youngs End, Green Dragon

GLOUCESTERSHIRE
Almondsbury, Bowl
Barnsley, Village Pub
Brimpsfield, Golden Heart
Broad Campden, Bakers Arms
Chedworth, Seven Tuns
Chipping Campden, Eight Bells
Coln St Aldwyns, New Inn
Cowley, Green Dragon
Didmarton, Kings Arms
Dursley, Old Spot
Ewen, Wild Duck
Ford, Plough
Guiting Power, Hollow Bottom
Kingscote, Hunters Hall
Nailsworth, Egypt Mill, Weighbridge
North Nibley, New Inn
Northleach, Wheatsheaf
Old Sodbury, Dog
Oldbury-on-Severn, Anchor
Sheepscombe, Butchers Arms
Stow-on-the-Wold, Eagle & Child
Upper Oddington, Horse & Groom
Winchcombe, White Hart

HAMPSHIRE
Axford, Crown
Bank, Oak
Bentworth, Sun
Boldre, Red Lion
Easton, Chestnut Horse
Fritham, Royal Oak
Lymington, Kings Head
Monxton, Black Swan
North Gorley, Royal Oak
Portsmouth, Still & West
Rotherwick, Falcon
Rowland's Castle, Castle Inn
Southsea, Wine Vaults
Stockbridge, Grosvenor
Well, Chequers
Winchester, Wykeham Arms

HEREFORDSHIRE
Aymestrey, Riverside Inn
Bodenham, Englands Gate
Dorstone, Pandy
Hereford, Victory
Ledbury, Feathers
Lugwardine, Crown & Anchor
Weobley, Salutation

HERTFORDSHIRE
Aldbury, Greyhound, Valiant Trooper
Ashwell, Three Tuns
Batford, Gibraltar Castle
Frithsden, Alford Arms
Hertford, White Horse
Royston, Old Bull
Sarratt, Boot, Cock

ISLE OF WIGHT
Arreton, White Lion
Bembridge, Crab & Lobster
Rookley, Chequers
Shorwell, Crown
Ventnor, Spyglass

KENT
Bough Beech, Wheatsheaf
Brookland, Woolpack
Chiddingstone, Castle Inn
Deal, Kings Head
Fordcombe, Chafford Arms
Groombridge, Crown
Hawkhurst, Queens
Hodsoll Street, Green Man
Hollingbourne, Windmill
Hucking, Hook & Hatchet
Iden Green, Woodcock
Ightham Common, Harrow
Langton Green, Hare
Penshurst, Bottle House
Smarden, Chequers
Stodmarsh, Red Lion
Tunbridge Wells, Beacon, Sankeys
West Peckham, Swan on the Green

LANCASHIRE
Barnston, Fox & Hounds
Belmont, Black Dog
Bispham Green, Eagle & Child
Blackstone Edge, White House
Bury, Lord Raglan
Goosnargh, Horns
Little Eccleston, Cartford
Liverpool, Baltic Fleet, Philharmonic Dining Rooms
Longridge, Derby Arms
Lydgate, White Hart
Lytham, Taps
Manchester, Britons Protection, Dukes 92, Lass o' Gowrie, Marble Arch
Newton, Parkers Arms
Ribchester, White Bull
Stalybridge, Station Buffet
Uppermill, Church Inn
Wheelton, Dressers Arms
Yealand Conyers, New Inn

LEICESTERSHIRE AND RUTLAND
Belmesthorpe, Blue Bell
Clipsham, Olive Branch
Empingham, White Horse
Mowsley, Staff of Life
Newton Burgoland, Belper Arms
Oadby, Cow & Plough
Oakham, Grainstore
Somerby, Three Crowns
Stathern, Red Lion
Stretton, Ram Jam Inn
Upper Hambleton, Finches Arms
Wing, Kings Arms

LINCOLNSHIRE
Brandy Wharf, Cider Centre
Dyke, Wishing Well
Grantham, Angel & Royal
Lincoln, Victoria, Wig & Mitre
South Witham, Blue Cow
Stamford, George of Stamford
Surfleet, Mermaid

NORFOLK
Blakeney, Kings Arms
Brancaster Staithe, White Horse
Burnham Market, Hoste Arms
Cawston, Ratcatchers
Cley next the Sea, Three Swallows
Larling, Angel
Letheringsett, Kings Head
Norwich, Adam & Eve, Fat Cat
Snettisham, Rose & Crown
Swanton Morley, Darbys
Thornham, Lifeboat
Tivetshall St Mary, Old Ram
Upper Sheringham, Red Lion
Wells-next-the-Sea, Crown
Winterton-on-Sea, Fishermans Return
Woodbastwick, Fur & Feather

NORTHAMPTONSHIRE
Badby, Windmill
Kilsby, George
Oundle, Ship
Woodnewton, White Swan

NORTHUMBRIA
Allenheads, Allenheads Inn
Blanchland, Lord Crewe Arms
Carterway Heads, Manor House Inn
Greta Bridge, Morritt Arms
Newburn, Keelman
Newcastle upon Tyne, Crown Posada
Newton-by-the-Sea, Ship
Rennington, Masons Arms
Seahouses, Olde Ship
Stannington, Ridley Arms

Thropton, Three Wheat Heads

NOTTINGHAMSHIRE
Beeston, Victoria
Caunton, Caunton Beck
Halam, Waggon & Horses
Kimberley, Nelson & Railway
Nottingham, Bell, Fellows Morton & Clayton, Lincolnshire Poacher, Olde Trip to Jerusalem, Pit & Pendulum, Vat & Fiddle

OXFORDSHIRE
Banbury, Reindeer
Buckland, Lamb
Burford, Lamb
Chipping Norton, Chequers
Churchill, Chequers
Great Tew, Falkland Arms
Henley, Anchor
Highmoor, Rising Sun
Hook Norton, Pear Tree
Kelmscott, Plough
Oxford, Kings Arms, Turf Tavern
Thame, Swan
Wootton, Kings Head

SHROPSHIRE
Bishop's Castle, Six Bells, Three Tuns
Bridges, Horseshoe
Bromfield, Cookhouse Café Bar
Hopton Wafers, Crown
Ironbridge, Malthouse
Ludlow, Church Inn
Much Wenlock, Talbot
Shrewsbury, Armoury, Three Fishes
Wentnor, Crown

SOMERSET
Axbridge, Lamb
Bath, Old Green Tree, Star
Bleadon, Queens Arms
Cheddar, Gardeners Arms
Chew Magna, Bear & Swan
Churchill, Crown
Clapton-in-Gordano, Black Horse
Crowcombe, Carew Arms
Exford, Crown, White Horse
Holcombe, Ring o' Roses
Huish Episcopi, Rose & Crown
Stanton Wick, Carpenters Arms
Taunton, Masons Arms
Triscombe, Blue Ball
Wells, City Arms, Crown

STAFFORDSHIRE
Alstonefield, George
Lichfield, Boat
Salt, Holly Bush
Stourton, Fox
Warslow, Greyhound

SUFFOLK
Brome, Cornwallis
Bury St Edmunds, Nutshell
Chelmondiston, Butt & Oyster
Cotton, Trowel & Hammer
Dennington, Queens Head
Dunwich, Ship
Lavenham, Angel
Long Melford, Black Lion
South Elmham, St Peters Brewery
Southwold, Crown, Harbour Inn
Stoke-by-Nayland, Angel, Crown
Walberswick, Bell
Waldringfield, Maybush

SURREY
Betchworth, Dolphin
Bletchingley, Prince Albert
Charleshill, Donkey
Cobham, Cricketers
Coldharbour, Plough
Eashing, Stag
Esher, Marneys
Laleham, Three Horseshoes
Leigh, Plough
Lingfield, Hare & Hounds
Mickleham, King William IV, Running Horses
Ottershaw, Castle
Reigate Heath, Skimmington Castle
West End, Inn at West End

SUSSEX
Alfriston, George
Amberley, Black Horse
Arlington, Old Oak
Berwick, Cricketers Arms
Charlton, Fox Goes Free
Chiddingly, Six Bells
Donnington, Blacksmiths Arms
Duncton, Cricketers
East Dean, Star & Garter, Tiger
East Hoathly, Foresters Arms
Fittleworth, Swan
Fletching, Griffin
Henley, Duke of Cumberland Arms
Horsham, Black Jug
Icklesham, Queens Head
Lewes, Snowdrop
Oving, Gribble Inn
Rye, Mermaid, Ypres Castle
Singleton, Fox & Hounds
Wilmington, Giants Rest

WARWICKSHIRE
Aston Cantlow, Kings Head
Birmingham, Old Joint Stock
Brierley Hill, Vine
Coventry, Old Windmill
Dunchurch, Dun Cow
Easenhall, Golden Lion
Edge Hill, Castle
Farnborough, Inn at Farnborough
Gaydon, Malt Shovel
Himley, Crooked House
Lapworth, Navigation
Long Itchington, Duck on the Pond
Shipston-on-Stour, White Bear
Stratford-upon-Avon, Garrick
Wharf, Wharf Inn

WILTSHIRE
Box, Quarrymans Arms
Devizes, Bear
Heytesbury, Angel
Hindon, Lamb
Lacock, George, Red Lion, Rising Sun
Malmesbury, Smoking Dog
Norton, Vine Tree
Salisbury, Haunch of Venison
Seend, Barge
Stourton, Spread Eagle

WORCESTERSHIRE
Berrow Green, Admiral Rodney
Bewdley, Little Pack Horse
Broadway, Crown & Trumpet
Childswickham, Childswickham Inn
Clent, Fountain
Flyford Flavell, Boot
Kempsey, Walter de Cantelupe
Kidderminster, King & Castle
Knightwick, Talbot
Malvern, Nags Head
Pensax, Bell
Welland, Anchor
Wyre Piddle, Anchor

YORKSHIRE
Aldborough, Ship
Asenby, Crab & Lobster
Beck Hole, Birch Hall
Beverley, White Horse
Blakey Ridge, Lion
Boroughbridge, Black Bull
Bradfield, Strines Inn
Cray, White Lion
Cropton, New Inn
East Witton, Blue Lion
Elslack, Tempest Arms
Ferrensby, General Tarleton
Goose Eye, Turkey
Halifax, Shibden Mill
Harome, Star
Heath, Kings Arms
Heckmondwike, Old Hall
Hubberholme, George
Hull, Minerva, Olde White Harte
Kettlesing, Queens Head
Kirkbymoorside, George & Dragon
Langthwaite, Charles Bathurst

Lastingham, Blacksmiths Arms
Ledsham, Chequers
Leeds, Whitelocks
Linthwaite, Sair
Linton, Windmill
Linton in Craven, Fountaine
Low Catton, Gold Cup
Masham, Kings Head
Osmotherley, Golden Lion
Pickering, White Swan
Pickhill, Nags Head
Ripley, Boars Head
Robin Hood's Bay, Laurel
Scarborough, Hole in the Wall
Scawton, Hare
Sheffield, Fat Cat, New Barrack
Thornton in Lonsdale, Marton Arms
Thornton Watlass, Buck
Whitby, Duke of York
Widdop, Pack Horse

LONDON

Central London, Admiral Codrington, Albert, Archery Tavern, Argyll Arms, Black Friar, Cittie of Yorke, Coopers Arms, Cross Keys, Dog & Duck, Eagle, Grapes, Grenadier, Guinea, Jerusalem Tavern, Lamb, Lamb & Flag, Lord Moon of the Mall, Nags Head, Old Bank of England, Olde Cheshire Cheese, Olde Mitre Red Lion, Seven Stars, Star, Westminster Arms
East London, Crown, Grapes, Prospect of Whitby
North London, Chapel, Compton Arms, Drapers Arms, Duke of Cambridge, Flask, Holly Bush, Olde White Bear, Spaniards Inn, Waterside
South London, Alma, Boathouse, Crown & Greyhound, Cutty Sark, Fire Station, Founders Arms, Fox & Hounds, George, Market Porter, Ship, White Cross
West London, Anglesea Arms (both pubs), Atlas, Bulls Head, Churchill Arms, Dove, Havelock Tavern, Portobello Gold, White Horse, Windsor Castle

SCOTLAND

Aberdeen, Prince of Wales
Aboyne, Boat
Applecross, Applecross Inn
Badachro, Badachro Inn
Broughty Ferry, Fishermans Tavern
East Linton, Drovers
Edinburgh, Abbotsford, Bow Bar, Café Royal, Guildford Arms, Kays Bar, Starbank
Elie, Ship
Gairloch, Old Inn
Gifford, Tweeddale Arms
Glasgow, Auctioneers, Babbity Bowster, Bon Accord, Counting House
Houston, Fox & Hounds
Inveraray, George
Isle of Whithorn, Steam Packet
Kilberry, Kilberry Inn
Kingholm Quay, Swan
Kippen, Cross Keys
Kirkton of Glenisla, Glenisla Hotel
Linlithgow, Four Marys
Lybster, Portland Arms
Pitlochry, Moulin
Plockton, Plockton Hotel
Shieldaig, Tigh an Eilean Hotel
Skeabost, Skeabost House Hotel
Stein, Stein Inn
Swinton, Wheatsheaf
Tayvallich, Tayvallich Inn
Thornhill, Lion & Unicorn
Ullapool, Ferry Boat
Weem, Ailean Chraggan

WALES

Aberaeron, Harbourmaster
Abercych, Nags Head
Aberdovey, Penhelig Arms
Abergorlech, Black Lion
Beaumaris, Olde Bulls Head
Berriew, Lion
Caio, Brunant Arms
Capel Curig, Bryn Tyrch
Carew, Carew Inn
Colwyn Bay, Pen-y-Bryn
Cresswell Quay, Cresselly Arms
Felinfach, Griffin
Gresford, Pant-yr-Ochain
Hay-on-Wye, Kilverts, Old Black Lion
Llanberis, Pen-y-Gwryd
Llandeilo, Castle
Llandudno Junction, Queens Head
Llangedwyn, Green Inn
Llangollen, Corn Mill
Mold, Glasfryn
Monknash, Plough & Harrow
Overton Bridge, Cross Foxes
Pembroke Ferry, Ferry Inn
Pontypool, Open Hearth
Porthgain, Sloop
Presteigne, Radnorshire Arms
Raglan, Clytha Arms
Red Wharf Bay, Ship
Rhyd-y-Meirch, Goose & Cuckoo
Rosebush, Tafarn Sinc
Saundersfoot, Royal Oak
St Hilary, Bush
Talyllyn, Tynycornel
Tintern, Cherry Tree

CHANNEL ISLANDS

King's Mills, Fleur du Jardin
Rozel, Rozel Bay Hotel
St Aubin, Old Court House Inn
St Brelade, Old Portelet Inn, Old Smugglers
St Helier, Town House
St John, Les Fontaines
St Ouens Bay, La Pulente

PUBS WITH NO SMOKING AREAS

We have listed all the pubs which have told us they do set aside at least some part of the pub as a no smoking area. Look at the individual entries for the pubs themselves to see just what they do: provision is much more generous in some pubs than in others.

BEDFORDSHIRE

Biddenham, Three Tuns
Broom, Cock
Houghton Conquest, Knife & Cleaver
Northill, Crown
Old Warden, Hare & Hounds
Pegsdon, Live & Let Live
Stanbridge, Five Bells

BERKSHIRE

Ashmore Green, Sun in the Wood
Boxford, Bell
Crazies Hill, Horns
Frilsham, Pot Kiln
Inkpen, Crown & Garter
Kintbury, Dundas Arms
Marsh Benham, Red House
Ruscombe, Royal Oak
Stanford Dingley, Bull, Old Boot
Winterbourne, Winterbourne Arms
Woodside, Rose & Crown
Yattendon, Royal Oak

BUCKINGHAMSHIRE

Chalfont St Giles, White Hart
Chenies, Red Lion
Ford, Dinton Hermit
Forty Green, Royal Standard of England
Great Hampden, Hampden Arms
Haddenham, Green Dragon
Hawridge Common, Full Moon
Ley Hill, Swan
Mentmore, Stag

Newton Longville, Crooked Billet
Penn, Crown
Prestwood, Polecat
Skirmett, Frog
Soulbury, Boot
Turville, Bull & Butcher
Wooburn Common, Chequers

CAMBRIDGESHIRE

Cambridge, Cambridge Blue, Eagle, Free Press, Live & Let Live
Elton, Black Horse
Fen Ditton, Ancient Shepherds
Fen Drayton, Three Tuns
Fordham, White Pheasant
Fowlmere, Chequers
Godmanchester, Exhibition
Helpston, Blue Bell
Heydon, King William IV
Hinxton, Red Lion
Huntingdon, Old Bridge Hotel
Keyston, Pheasant
Longstowe, Red House
Newton, Queens Head
Peterborough, Brewery Tap, Charters
Reach, Dyke's End
Stilton, Bell
Sutton Gault, Anchor
Thriplow, Green Man

CHESHIRE

Aldford, Grosvenor Arms
Astbury, Egerton Arms
Aston, Bhurtpore
Bunbury, Dysart Arms
Chester, Albion, Old Harkers Arms
Cotebrook, Fox & Barrel
Daresbury, Ring o' Bells
Haughton Moss, Nags Head
Higher Burwardsley, Pheasant
Langley, Hanging Gate
Lower Peover, Bells of Peover
Peover Heath, Dog
Plumley, Smoker
Wettenhall, Boot & Slipper
Wincle, Ship
Wrenbury, Dusty Miller
Wybunbury, Swan

CORNWALL

Blisland, Blisland Inn
Cadgwith, Cadgwith Cove Inn
Constantine, Trengilly Wartha
Duloe, Olde Plough House
Egloshayle, Earl of St Vincent
Helston, Halzephron
Kingsand, Halfway House
Lanlivery, Crown
Lostwithiel, Royal Oak
Malpas, Heron
Mitchell, Plume of Feathers
Mithian, Miners Arms
Mousehole, Old Coastguard
Mylor Bridge, Pandora
Penzance, Turks Head
Perranwell, Royal Oak
Philleigh, Roseland
Polkerris, Rashleigh
Port Isaac, Golden Lion, Port Gaverne Inn, Slipway
Porthleven, Ship
Sennen Cove, Old Success
St Agnes, Turks Head
St Breward, Old Inn
St Mawgan, Falcon
Treburley, Springer Spaniel
Tresco, New Inn

CUMBRIA

Ambleside, Golden Rule
Appleby, Royal Oak
Armathwaite, Dukes Head
Barbon, Barbon Inn
Bassenthwaite Lake, Pheasant
Beetham, Wheatsheaf
Bouth, White Hart
Broughton Mills, Blacksmiths Arms
Buttermere, Bridge Hotel
Cartmel Fell, Masons Arms
Casterton, Pheasant
Cockermouth, Bitter End
Crosthwaite, Punch Bowl
Dalton-in-Furness, Black Dog
Elterwater, Britannia
Ennerdale Bridge, Shepherds Arms
Hawkshead, Drunken Duck, Kings Arms, Queens Head
Hesket Newmarket, Old Crown
Ings, Watermill
Keswick, Swinside Inn
Langdale, Old Dungeon Ghyll
Little Langdale, Three Shires
Loweswater, Kirkstile Inn
Mungrisdale, Mill Inn
Penruddock, Herdwick
Sandford, Sandford Arms
Santon Bridge, Bridge Inn
Seathwaite, Newfield Inn
Sedbergh, Dalesman
Stonethwaite, Langstrath
Talkin, Blacksmiths Arms
Tirril, Queens Head
Troutbeck, Queens Head
Ulverston, Bay Horse, Farmers Arms

DERBYSHIRE

Beeley, Devonshire Arms
Birch Vale, Waltzing Weasel
Buxton, Bull i' th' Thorn
Castleton, Castle Hotel
Derby, Alexandra, Brunswick, Olde Dolphin
Eyam, Miners Arms
Fenny Bentley, Bentley Brook
Foolow, Bulls Head
Froggatt Edge, Chequers
Hardwick Hall, Hardwick Inn
Hassop, Eyre Arms
Hathersage, Plough
Hognaston, Red Lion
Idridgehay, Black Swan
Kirk Ireton, Barley Mow
Ladybower Reservoir, Yorkshire Bridge
Litton, Red Lion
Milltown, Miners Arms
Monsal Head, Monsal Head Hotel
Over Haddon, Lathkil
Woolley Moor, White Horse

DEVON

Berrynarbor, Olde Globe
Branscombe, Fountain Head
Broadhembury, Drewe Arms
Buckland Brewer, Coach & Horses
Buckland Monachorum, Drake Manor
Butterleigh, Butterleigh Inn
Cheriton Bishop, Old Thatch Inn
Clayhidon, Merry Harriers
Clyst Hydon, Five Bells
Cockwood, Anchor
Coleford, New Inn
Dalwood, Tuckers Arms
Dartmouth, Cherub
Doddiscombsleigh, Nobody Inn
Dolton, Union
Drewsteignton, Drewe Arms
East Budleigh, Sir Walter Raleigh
Exminster, Turf Hotel
Harberton, Church House
Haytor Vale, Rock
Holbeton, Mildmay Colours
Holne, Church House
Horndon, Elephants Nest
Horns Cross, Hoops
Kingston, Dolphin
Lustleigh, Cleave
Lydford, Castle Inn, Dartmoor Inn
Marldon, Church House
Meavy, Royal Oak
Molland, London
Newton Abbot, Two Mile Oak
Newton Ferrers, Dolphin
Nomansland, Mount Pleasant
Noss Mayo, Ship
Parracombe, Fox & Goose
Peter Tavy, Peter Tavy Inn
Postbridge, Warren House
Rattery, Church House
Rockbeare, Jack in the Green
Sidford, Blue Ball
Slapton, Tower
South Zeal, Oxenham Arms
Staverton, Sea Trout
Stockland, Kings Arms
Stoke Fleming, Green Dragon
Topsham, Bridge
Torbryan, Old Church House
Torcross, Start Bay

Widecombe, Rugglestone
Winkleigh, Kings Arms
Woodbury Salterton, Diggers Rest
Woodland, Rising Sun

DORSET

Burton Bradstock, Anchor
Cerne Abbas, Royal Oak
Chideock, Anchor, George
Church Knowle, New Inn
Corscombe, Fox
East Chaldon, Sailors Return
East Knighton, Countryman
East Morden, Cock & Bottle
Farnham, Museum
Mudeford, Ship in Distress
Osmington Mills, Smugglers
Pamphill, Vine
Sherborne, Skippers
Shroton, Cricketers
Sturminster Newton, Swan
Tarrant Monkton, Langton Arms
West Bay, West Bay
West Bexington, Manor Hotel

ESSEX

Arkesden, Axe & Compasses
Birchanger, Three Willows
Burnham-on-Crouch, White Harte
Castle Hedingham, Bell
Chappel, Swan
Chelmsford, Alma
Clavering, Cricketers
Fingringhoe, Whalebone
Gosfield, Green Man
Great Yeldham, White Hart
Hastingwood, Rainbow & Dove
Horndon-on-the-Hill, Bell
Little Braxted, Green Man
Paglesham, Punchbowl
Pleshey, White Horse
Stow Maries, Prince of Wales
Wendens Ambo, Bell
Youngs End, Green Dragon

GLOUCESTERSHIRE

Almondsbury, Bowl
Ashleworth, Queens Arms
Ashleworth Quay, Boat
Awre, Red Hart
Barnsley, Village Pub
Bisley, Bear
Blaisdon, Red Hart
Bledington, Kings Head
Brimpsfield, Golden Heart
Broad Campden, Bakers Arms
Chedworth, Seven Tuns
Chipping Campden, Eight Bells
Coln St Aldwyns, New Inn
Cowley, Green Dragon
Didmarton, Kings Arms
Duntisbourne Abbots, Five Mile House
Dursley, Old Spot
Eastleach Turville, Victoria
Ford, Plough
Kingscote, Hunters Hall
Meysey Hampton, Masons Arms
Miserden, Carpenters Arms
Nailsworth, Egypt Mill, Weighbridge
Newland, Ostrich
North Cerney, Bathurst Arms
Northleach, Wheatsheaf
Old Sodbury, Dog
Oldbury-on-Severn, Anchor
Sapperton, Bell
Sheepscombe, Butchers Arms
St Briavels, George
Stow-on-the-Wold, Eagle & Child
Tetbury, Trouble House
Todenham, Farriers Arms
Upper Oddington, Horse & Groom
Winchcombe, White Hart

HAMPSHIRE

Axford, Crown
Bank, Oak
Boldre, Red Lion
Bramdean, Fox
Chalton, Red Lion
East Tytherley, Star
Easton, Chestnut Horse
Hambledon, Vine
Hawkley, Hawkley Inn
Longstock, Peat Spade
Lymington, Kings Head
Micheldever, Half Moon & Spread Eagle
Minstead, Trusty Servant
Monxton, Black Swan
North Gorley, Royal Oak
Ovington, Bush
Petersfield, Trooper
Portsmouth, Still & West
Rotherwick, Falcon
Rowland's Castle, Castle Inn
Southsea, Wine Vaults
Sparsholt, Plough
Stockbridge, Three Cups
Well, Chequers
Wherwell, White Lion
Winchester, Wykeham Arms

HEREFORDSHIRE

Aymestrey, Riverside Inn
Bodenham, Englands Gate
Brimfield, Roebuck Inn
Little Cowarne, Three Horseshoes
Lugwardine, Crown & Anchor
Orleton, Boot
Pembridge, New Inn
Sellack, Lough Pool
St Owen's Cross, New Inn
Stockton Cross, Stockton Cross Inn
Titley, Stagg
Ullingswick, Three Crowns
Upton Bishop, Moody Cow
Walterstone, Carpenters Arms
Wellington, Wellington
Weobley, Salutation
Whitney-on-Wye, Rhydspence

HERTFORDSHIRE

Aldbury, Greyhound, Valiant Trooper
Ardeley, Jolly Waggoner
Ashwell, Three Tuns
Cottered, Bull
Hertford, White Horse
Royston, Old Bull
Sarratt, Boot, Cock

ISLE OF WIGHT

Arreton, White Lion
Bembridge, Crab & Lobster
Bonchurch, Bonchurch Inn
Rookley, Chequers
Seaview, Seaview Hotel
Shalfleet, New Inn
Shorwell, Crown
Ventnor, Spyglass

KENT

Bekesbourne, Unicorn
Boyden Gate, Gate Inn
Chiddingstone, Castle Inn
Elham, Rose & Crown
Groombridge, Crown
Hawkhurst, Queens
Hodsoll Street, Green Man
Hollingbourne, Windmill
Hucking, Hook & Hatchet
Ickham, Duke William
Ightham Common, Harrow
Newnham, George
Oare, Shipwrights Arms
Penshurst, Bottle House
Pluckley, Rose & Crown
Selling, Rose & Crown
Smarden, Chequers
Tunbridge Wells, Sankeys
Ulcombe, Pepper Box

LANCASHIRE

Bay Horse, Bay Horse
Belmont, Black Dog
Bispham Green, Eagle & Child
Blackstone Edge, White House
Goosnargh, Horns
Liverpool, Baltic Fleet, Philharmonic Dining Rooms
Longridge, Derby Arms
Lydgate, White Hart
Manchester, Britons Protection, Dukes 92, Lass o' Gowrie
Mellor, Oddfellows Arms
Newton, Parkers Arms
Ribchester, White Bull
Rimington, Black Bull
Sawley, Spread Eagle
Wheelton, Dressers Arms
Yealand Conyers, New Inn

LEICESTERSHIRE AND RUTLAND

Barrowden, Exeter Arms
Castle Donington, Nags Head
Clipsham, Olive Branch
Cottesmore, Sun
East Langton, Bell
Empingham, White Horse
Gumley, Bell
Lyddington, Old White Hart
Market Overton, Black Bull
Mowsley, Staff of Life
Oadby, Cow & Plough
Old Dalby, Crown
Somerby, Stilton Cheese, Three Crowns
Stathern, Red Lion
Stretton, Jackson Stops, Ram Jam Inn
Thorpe Langton, Bakers Arms
Wing, Kings Arms

LINCOLNSHIRE

Allington, Welby Arms
Barnoldby le Beck, Ship
Belchford, Blue Bell
Brandy Wharf, Cider Centre
Coningsby, Lea Gate Inn
Dyke, Wishing Well
Gedney Dyke, Chequers
Grantham, Angel & Royal
Lincoln, Victoria, Wig & Mitre
Newton, Red Lion
South Witham, Blue Cow
Stamford, George of Stamford
Surfleet, Mermaid
Woolsthorpe, Chequers

NORFOLK

Blakeney, Kings Arms, White Horse
Brancaster Staithe, White Horse
Burnham Market, Hoste Arms
Burnham Thorpe, Lord Nelson
Cawston, Ratcatchers
Cley next the Sea, Three Swallows
Great Cressingham, Windmill
Horsey, Nelson Head
Itteringham, Walpole Arms
Larling, Angel
Letheringsett, Kings Head
Norwich, Adam & Eve
Ringstead, Gin Trap
Snettisham, Rose & Crown
Stiffkey, Red Lion
Stow Bardolph, Hare Arms
Swanton Morley, Darbys
Terrington St John, Woolpack
Thornham, Lifeboat
Tivetshall St Mary, Old Ram
Upper Sheringham, Red Lion
Warham, Three Horseshoes
Wells-next-the-Sea, Crown
West Beckham, Wheatsheaf
Winterton-on-Sea, Fishermans Return
Woodbastwick, Fur & Feather

NORTHAMPTONSHIRE

Aynho, Great Western Arms
Bulwick, Queens Head
Crick, Red Lion
East Haddon, Red Lion
Fotheringhay, Falcon
Great Oxendon, George
Harringworth, White Swan
Kilsby, George
Nether Heyford, Old Sun
Oundle, Ship
Sulgrave, Star
Woodnewton, White Swan

NORTHUMBRIA

Allenheads, Allenheads Inn
Anick, Rat
Aycliffe, County
Carterway Heads, Manor House Inn
Corbridge, Errington Arms
Cotherstone, Fox & Hounds
Eglingham, Tankerville Arms
Great Whittington, Queens Head
Greta Bridge, Morritt Arms
Langley on Tyne, Carts Bog Inn
Newburn, Keelman
Newcastle upon Tyne, Head of Steam @ The Cluny
Newfield, Fox & Hounds
Newton-on-the-Moor, Cook & Barker Arms
Rennington, Masons Arms
Romaldkirk, Rose & Crown
Seahouses, Olde Ship
Stannersburn, Pheasant
Stannington, Ridley Arms
Thropton, Three Wheat Heads
Weldon Bridge, Anglers Arms

NOTTINGHAMSHIRE

Caunton, Caunton Beck
Colston Bassett, Martins Arms
Elkesley, Robin Hood
Halam, Waggon & Horses
Kimberley, Nelson & Railway
Laxton, Dovecote
Morton, Full Moon
Nottingham, Fellows Morton & Clayton, Lincolnshire Poacher

OXFORDSHIRE

Alvescot, Plough
Banbury, Reindeer
Buckland, Lamb
Burford, Lamb
Caulcott, Horse & Groom
Chipping Norton, Chequers
Churchill, Chequers
Clifton, Duke of Cumberlands Head
East Hendred, Eyston Arms
Great Tew, Falkland Arms
Henley, Anchor
Highmoor, Rising Sun
Hook Norton, Gate Hangs High, Pear Tree, Sun
Kelmscott, Plough
Lewknor, Olde Leathern Bottel
Maidensgrove, Five Horseshoes
Oxford, Kings Arms, Rose & Crown
Ramsden, Royal Oak
Roke, Home Sweet Home
Stanton St John, Star
Steeple Aston, Red Lion
Swalcliffe, Stags Head
Tadpole Bridge, Trout
Wootton, Kings Head

SHROPSHIRE

Bishop's Castle, Castle Hotel, Six Bells, Three Tuns
Bromfield, Cookhouse Café Bar
Burlton, Burlton Inn
Cardington, Royal Oak
Hopton Wafers, Crown
Longville, Longville Arms
Ludlow, Church Inn, Unicorn
Much Wenlock, Talbot
Norbury, Sun
Norton, Hundred House
Picklescott, Bottle & Glass
Shrewsbury, Armoury, Three Fishes
Wentnor, Crown
Wistanstow, Plough

SOMERSET

Appley, Globe
Axbridge, Lamb
Batcombe, Three Horseshoes
Bath, Old Green Tree
Bleadon, Queens Arms
Cheddar, Gardeners Arms
Chew Magna, Bear & Swan
Chiselborough, Cat Head
Compton Martin, Ring o' Bells
Congresbury, White Hart
Doulting, Waggon & Horses
East Lyng, Rose & Crown
Exford, Crown, White Horse
Freshford, Inn at Freshford
Holcombe, Ring o' Roses
Huish Episcopi, Rose & Crown
Ilminster, George
Kingsdon, Kingsdon Inn
Langley Marsh, Three Horseshoes
Lovington, Pilgrims Rest
Luxborough, Royal Oak
Mells, Talbot
Monksilver, Notley Arms
North Curry, Bird in Hand
Oake, Royal Oak

Portishead, Windmill
Shepton Montague, Montague Inn
Stanton Wick, Carpenters Arms
Stoke St Gregory, Rose & Crown
Triscombe, Blue Ball
Wells, City Arms, Crown
Winsford, Royal Oak
Withypool, Royal Oak
Wookey, Burcott

STAFFORDSHIRE

Abbots Bromley, Goats Head
Alstonefield, George, Watts Russell Arms
Burton upon Trent, Burton Bridge Inn
Lichfield, Boat
Stourton, Fox
Warslow, Greyhound
Wetton, Olde Royal Oak

SUFFOLK

Bramfield, Queens Head
Brome, Cornwallis
Buxhall, Crown
Chelmondiston, Butt & Oyster
Cretingham, Bell
Dennington, Queens Head
Dunwich, Ship
Erwarton, Queens Head
Hundon, Plough
Lavenham, Angel
Levington, Ship
Lidgate, Star
Long Melford, Black Lion
Nayland, Anchor
Rattlesden, Brewers Arms
Rede, Plough
Snape, Crown
South Elmham, St Peters Brewery
Southwold, Crown
Stoke-by-Nayland, Angel, Crown
Swilland, Moon & Mushroom
Walberswick, Bell
Waldringfield, Maybush

SURREY

Blackbrook, Plough
Bletchingley, Prince Albert
Charleshill, Donkey
Cobham, Cricketers
Coldharbour, Plough
Compton, Withies
Eashing, Stag
Laleham, Three Horseshoes
Lingfield, Hare & Hounds
Newdigate, Surrey Oaks
Ockley, Kings Arms
Ottershaw, Castle
West End, Inn at West End

SUSSEX

Alciston, Rose Cottage
Alfriston, George
Amberley, Black Horse
Arlington, Old Oak
Balls Cross, Stag
Berwick, Cricketers Arms
Blackboys, Blackboys Inn
Bodiam, Curlew
Chilgrove, White Horse
Cowbeech, Merrie Harriers
Danehill, Coach & Horses
Donnington, Blacksmiths Arms
Duncton, Cricketers
East Ashling, Horse & Groom
East Chiltington, Jolly Sportsman
East Dean, Star & Garter
East Hoathly, Foresters Arms
Elsted, Three Horseshoes
Fernhurst, Kings Arms
Fittleworth, Swan
Fletching, Griffin
Horsham, Black Jug
Icklesham, Queens Head
Lewes, Snowdrop
Lodsworth, Halfway Bridge Inn
Lurgashall, Noahs Ark
Oving, Gribble Inn
Rye, Mermaid, Ypres Castle
Salehurst, Salehurst Halt
Singleton, Fox & Hounds
Trotton, Keepers Arms
Wartling, Lamb
Wilmington, Giants Rest

WARWICKSHIRE

Alderminster, Bell
Armscote, Fox & Goose
Aston Cantlow, Kings Head
Dunchurch, Dun Cow
Easenhall, Golden Lion
Edge Hill, Castle
Farnborough, Inn at Farnborough
Gaydon, Malt Shovel
Great Wolford, Fox & Hounds
Himley, Crooked House
Ilmington, Howard Arms
Lapworth, Navigation
Little Compton, Red Lion
Long Itchington, Duck on the Pond
Priors Marston, Holly Bush
Shipston-on-Stour, White Bear
Stratford-upon-Avon, Garrick
Welford-on-Avon, Bell
Wharf, Wharf Inn

WILTSHIRE

Axford, Red Lion
Beckhampton, Waggon & Horses
Berwick St John, Talbot
Box, Quarrymans Arms
Bradford-on-Avon, Dandy Lion
Brinkworth, Three Crowns
Chicksgrove, Compasses
Devizes, Bear
Donhead St Andrew, Forester
Ebbesbourne Wake, Horseshoe
Great Durnford, Black Horse
Great Hinton, Linnet
Grittleton, Neeld Arms
Heytesbury, Angel
Hindon, Lamb
Holt, Toll Gate
Kilmington, Red Lion
Lacock, George, Red Lion
Lower Chute, Hatchet
Malmesbury, Smoking Dog
Newton Tony, Malet Arms
Norton, Vine Tree
Ogbourne St Andrew, Wheatsheaf
Pitton, Silver Plough
Poulshot, Raven
Ramsbury, Bell
Rowde, George & Dragon
Salisbury, Haunch of Venison
Seend, Barge
Stourton, Spread Eagle
Whitley, Pear Tree
Woodborough, Seven Stars

WORCESTERSHIRE

Baughton, Jockey
Berrow Green, Admiral Rodney
Bewdley, Little Pack Horse
Birtsmorton, Farmers Arms
Bransford, Bear & Ragged Staff
Bredon, Fox & Hounds
Childswickham, Childswickham Inn
Clent, Fountain
Crowle, Old Chequers
Flyford Flavell, Boot
Holy Cross, Bell & Cross
Kempsey, Walter de Cantelupe
Malvern, Nags Head
Pensax, Bell
Welland, Anchor
Wyre Piddle, Anchor

YORKSHIRE

Aldborough, Ship
Appleton-le-Moors, Moors
Beverley, White Horse
Blakey Ridge, Lion
Boroughbridge, Black Bull
Bradfield, Strines Inn
Brearton, Malt Shovel
Burton Leonard, Hare & Hounds
Byland Abbey, Abbey Inn
Carthorpe, Fox & Hounds
Chapel le Dale, Hill Inn
Constable Burton, Wyvill Arms
Cray, White Lion
Crayke, Durham Ox
Cropton, New Inn

Egton Bridge, Horse Shoe
Elslack, Tempest Arms
Fadmoor, Plough
Felixkirk, Carpenters Arms
Ferrensby, General Tarleton
Flamborough, Seabirds
Goose Eye, Turkey
Harome, Star
Heckmondwike, Old Hall
Hetton, Angel
Hull, Minerva, Olde White Harte
Ingleton, Wheatsheaf
Kettlesing, Queens Head
Kirkbymoorside, George & Dragon
Kirkham, Stone Trough
Langthwaite, Charles Bathurst
Lastingham, Blacksmiths Arms
Leyburn, Sandpiper
Linthwaite, Sair
Linton, Windmill
Linton in Craven, Fountaine
Litton, Queens Arms
Low Catton, Gold Cup
Lund, Wellington
Marton, Appletree
Masham, Kings Head
Middleham, White Swan
Mill Bank, Millbank
Nosterfield, Freemasons Arms
Nunnington, Royal Oak
Osmotherley, Golden Lion
Pickering, White Swan
Pickhill, Nags Head
Ripley, Boars Head
Robin Hood's Bay, Laurel
Sawley, Sawley Arms
Scawton, Hare
Sheffield, Fat Cat, New Barrack
Sinnington, Fox & Hounds
Sutton upon Derwent, St Vincent Arms
Thorganby, Jefferson Arms
Thornton in Lonsdale, Marton Arms
Thornton Watlass, Buck
Wass, Wombwell Arms
Wath in Nidderdale, Sportsmans Arms

LONDON

Central London, Albert, Black Friar, Grapes, Lamb, Lord Moon of the Mall, Olde Cheshire Cheese, Star, Westminster Arms
East London, Crown
North London, Duke of Cambridge, Holly Bush, Spaniards Inn, Waterside
South London, Boathouse, Crown & Greyhound, Founders Arms, George, Market Porter
West London, Bulls Head, Churchill Arms, Portobello Gold, White Horse, Windsor Castle

SCOTLAND

Aboyne, Boat
Applecross, Applecross Inn
Badachro, Badachro Inn
Broughty Ferry, Fishermans Tavern
East Linton, Drovers
Edinburgh, Abbotsford, Café Royal, Starbank
Gairloch, Old Inn
Gifford, Tweeddale Arms
Glasgow, Auctioneers, Counting House
Houston, Fox & Hounds
Isle of Whithorn, Steam Packet
Kilberry, Kilberry Inn
Kingholm Quay, Swan
Kippen, Cross Keys
Linlithgow, Four Marys
Lybster, Portland Arms
Melrose, Burts Hotel
Plockton, Plockton Hotel
Stein, Stein Inn
Swinton, Wheatsheaf
Tayvallich, Tayvallich Inn
Thornhill, Lion & Unicorn
Ullapool, Ferry Boat
Weem, Ailean Chraggan

WALES

Aberaeron, Harbourmaster
Abercych, Nags Head
Abergorlech, Black Lion
Beaumaris, Olde Bulls Head
Berriew, Lion
Carew, Carew Inn
Colwyn Bay, Pen-y-Bryn
Crickhowell, Bear, Nantyffin Cider Mill
Felinfach, Griffin
Gresford, Pant-yr-Ochain
Hay-on-Wye, Kilverts, Old Black Lion
Little Haven, Swan
Llanberis, Pen-y-Gwryd
Llandeilo, Castle
Llandudno Junction, Queens Head
Llangedwyn, Green Inn
Llangollen, Corn Mill
Llwyndafydd, Crown
Mold, Glasfryn
Montgomery, Brickys
Pembroke Ferry, Ferry Inn
Pontypool, Open Hearth
Porthgain, Sloop
Raglan, Clytha Arms
Red Wharf Bay, Ship
Rosebush, Tafarn Sinc
Saundersfoot, Royal Oak
Shirenewton, Carpenters Arms
St Hilary, Bush
Talyllyn, Tynycornel
Tintern, Cherry Tree
Trelleck, Lion
Ty'n-y-groes, Groes

CHANNEL ISLANDS

King's Mills, Fleur du Jardin
Rozel, Rozel Bay Hotel
St Brelade, Old Portelet Inn, Old Smugglers
St John, Les Fontaines
St Ouens Bay, La Pulente

PUBS CLOSE TO MOTORWAY JUNCTIONS

The number at the start of each line is the number of the junction. Detailed directions are given in the main entry for each pub. In this section, to help you find the pubs quickly before you're past the junction, we give the name of the chapter where you'll find the text.

M1

16: Nether Heyford, Old Sun (Northants) 1.8 miles
18: Crick, Red Lion (Northants) 1 mile; Kilsby, George (Northants) 2.6 miles
24: Kegworth, Cap & Stocking (Leics and Rutland) 1 mile; Shardlow, Old Crown (Derbys) 3 miles
26: Kimberley, Nelson & Railway (Notts) 1.7 miles
29: Hardwick Hall, Hardwick Inn (Derbys) 4 miles

M2

5: Hucking, Hook & Hatchet (Kent) 3.5 miles

M3

3: West End, Inn at West End (Surrey) 2.4 miles
5: Rotherwick, Falcon (Hants) 4 miles
10: Winchester, Black Boy (Hants) 1 mile

M4

9: Bray, Crown (Berks) 1.75 miles
11: Shinfield, Magpie & Parrot (Berks) 2.6 miles
12: Stanford Dingley, Bull (Berks) 4 miles
13: Winterbourne, Winterbourne Arms (Berks) 3.7 miles
17: Norton, Vine Tree (Wilts) 4 miles
18: Old Sodbury, Dog (Gloucs) 2 miles

M5

4: Holy Cross, Bell & Cross (Worcs) 4 miles
6: Crowle, Old Chequers (Worcs) 2 miles
7: Kempsey, Walter de Cantelupe (Worcs) 3.75 miles
9: Bredon, Fox & Hounds (Worcs) 4.5 miles
16: Almondsbury, Bowl (Gloucs) 1.25 miles
19: Portishead, Windmill (Somerset) 3.7 miles; Clapton-in-Gordano, Black Horse (Somerset) 4 miles
26: Clayhidon, Merry Harriers (Devon) 3.1 miles
28: Broadhembury, Drewe Arms (Devon) 5 miles
30: Topsham, Bridge (Devon) 2.25 miles; Woodbury Salterton, Diggers Rest (Devon) 3.5 miles

M6

4: Shustoke, Griffin (Warwicks) 5 miles
16: Barthomley, White Lion (Cheshire) 1 mile
19: Plumley, Smoker (Cheshire) 2.5 miles
33: Bay Horse, Bay Horse (Lancs) 1.2 miles
35: Yealand Conyers, New Inn (Lancs) 3 miles
40: Tirril, Queens Head (Cumbria) 3.5 miles

M9

3: Linlithgow, Four Marys (Scotland) 2 miles

M11

7: Hastingwood, Rainbow & Dove (Essex) .25 mile
8: Birchanger, Three Willows (Essex) 0.8 mile
10: Hinxton, Red Lion (Cambs) 2 miles; Thriplow, Green Man (Cambs) 3 miles

M20

8: Hollingbourne, Windmill (Kent) 1 mile

M25

8: Reigate Heath, Skimmington Castle (Surrey) 3 miles
10: Cobham, Cricketers (Surrey) 3.75 miles
11: Ottershaw, Castle (Surrey) 2.6 miles
13: Laleham, Three Horseshoes (Surrey) 5 miles
16: Denham, Swan (Bucks) 0.75 mile
18: Chenies, Red Lion (Bucks) 2 miles
21A: Potters Crouch, Holly Bush (Herts) 2.3 miles

M27

1: Minstead, Trusty Servant (Hants) 2.2 miles; Fritham, Royal Oak (Hants) 4 miles

M40

2: Hedgerley, White Horse (Bucks) 2.4 miles; Forty Green, Royal Standard of England (Bucks) 3.5 miles
6: Lewknor, Olde Leathern Bottel (Oxon) .5 mile
12: Gaydon, Malt Shovel (Warwicks) 0.9 mile

M45

1: Dunchurch, Dun Cow (Warwicks) 1.3 miles

M48

1: Littleton-upon-Severn, White Hart (Gloucs) 3.5 miles

M50

1: Baughton, Jockey (Worcs) 4 miles
3: Upton Bishop, Moody Cow (Herefs) 2 miles

M53

3: Barnston, Fox & Hounds (Lancs) 3 miles

M56

11: Daresbury, Ring o' Bells (Cheshire) 1.5 miles

M61

8: Wheelton, Dressers Arms (Lancs) 2.1 miles

M66

1: Bury, Lord Raglan (Lancs) 0.75 miles

REPORT FORMS

REPORT FORMS

Please report to us: you can use the tear-out forms on the following pages, the card in the middle of the book, or just plain paper – whichever's easiest for you, or you can report to our website, **www.goodguides.co.uk**. We need to know what you think of the pubs in this edition. We need to know about other pubs worthy of inclusion. We need to know about ones that should not be included.

The atmosphere and character of the pub are the most important features – why it would, or would not, appeal to strangers, so please try to describe what is special about it. In particular, we can't consider including a pub in the Lucky Dip section unless we know something about what it looks like inside, so that we can describe it to other readers. And obviously with existing entries, we need to know about any changes in décor and furnishings, too. But the bar food and the drink are also important – please tell us about them.

If the food is really quite outstanding, tick the FOOD AWARD box on the form, and tell us about the special quality that makes it stand out – the more detail, the better. And if you have stayed there, tell us about the standard of accommodation – whether it was comfortable, pleasant, good value for money. Again, if the pub or inn is worth special attention as a place to stay, tick the PLACE-TO-STAY AWARD box.

If you're in a position to gauge a pub's suitability or otherwise for **disabled people**, do please tell us about that.

Please try to gauge whether a pub should be a main entry, or is best as a Lucky Dip (and tick the relevant box). In general, main entries need qualities that would make it worth other readers' while to travel some distance to them; Lucky Dips are the pubs that are worth knowing about if you are nearby. But if a pub is an entirely new recommendation, the Lucky Dip may be the best place for it to start its career in the *Guide* – to encourage other readers to report on it.

The more detail you can put into your description of a Lucky Dip pub that's only scantily described in the current edition (or not in at all), the better. A description of its character and even furnishings is a tremendous boon.

It helps enormously if you can give the full address for any new pub – one not yet a main entry, or without a full address in the Lucky Dip sections. In a town, we need the street name; in the country, if it's hard to find, we need directions. Even better for us is the post code. If we can't find out a pub's post code, we no longer include it in the *Guide* – and the Post Office directories we use will not yet have caught up with new pubs, or ones which have changed their names. With any pub, it always helps to let us know about prices of food (and bedrooms, if there are any), and about any lunchtimes or evenings when food is not served. We'd also like to have your views on drinks quality – beer, wine, cider and so forth, even coffee and tea; and do let us know about bedrooms.

If you know that a Lucky Dip pub is open all day (or even late into the afternoon), please tell us – preferably saying which days.

When you go to a pub, don't tell them you're a reporter for the *Good Pub Guide*; we do make clear that all inspections are anonymous, and if you declare yourself as a reporter you risk getting special treatment – for better or for worse!

Sometimes pubs are dropped from the main entries simply because very few readers have written to us about them – and of course there's a risk that people may not write if they find the pub exactly as described in the entry. You can use the forms at the front of the batch of report forms just to list pubs you've been to, found as described, and can recommend.

When you write to The Good Pub Guide, FREEPOST TN1569, WADHURST, East Sussex TN5 7BR, you don't need a stamp in the UK. We'll gladly send you more forms (free) if you wish.

Though we try to answer letters, please understand if there's a delay. And from June till September, when we are fully extended getting the next edition to the printers, we put all letters and reports aside, not answering them until the rush is over (and after our post-press-day late summer holiday). The end of May is the cut-off date for reports for the next edition, and we can still cope with reports to our web site during the following weeks. But it is much more helpful if you can send reports earlier, rather than storing them up till then.

We'll assume we can print your name or initials as a recommender unless you tell us otherwise.

I have been to the following pubs in *The Good Pub Guide 2005* in the last few months, found them as described, and confirm that they deserve continued inclusion:

Continued overleaf

PLEASE GIVE YOUR NAME AND ADDRESS ON THE BACK OF THIS FORM

Pubs visited continued...

By returning this form, you consent to the collection, recording and use of the information you submit, by The Random House Group Ltd. Any personal details which you provide from which we can identify you are held and processed in accordance with the Data Protection Act 1998 and will not be passed on to any third parties.

The Random House Group Ltd may wish to send you further information on their associated products. Please tick box if you do not wish to receive any such information. ☐

Your own name and address ***(block capitals please)***

Postcode

In returning this form I confirm my agreement that the information I provide may be used by The Random House Group Ltd, its assignees and/or licensees in any media or medium whatsoever.

Please return to
The Good Pub Guide,
FREEPOST TN1569,
WADHURST,
East Sussex
TN5 7BR

IF YOU PREFER, YOU CAN SEND US REPORTS THROUGH OUR WEB SITE:
www.goodguides.co.uk

I have been to the following pubs in *The Good Pub Guide 2005* in the last few months, found them as described, and confirm that they deserve continued inclusion:

Continued overleaf

PLEASE GIVE YOUR NAME AND ADDRESS ON THE BACK OF THIS FORM

Pubs visited continued...

By returning this form, you consent to the collection, recording and use of the information you submit, by The Random House Group Ltd. Any personal details which you provide from which we can identify you are held and processed in accordance with the Data Protection Act 1998 and will not be passed on to any third parties.

The Random House Group Ltd may wish to send you further information on their associated products. Please tick box if you do not wish to receive any such information. ☐

Your own name and address *(block capitals please)*

Postcode

In returning this form I confirm my agreement that the information I provide may be used by The Random House Group Ltd, its assignees and/or licensees in any media or medium whatsoever.

Please return to
The Good Pub Guide,
FREEPOST TN1569,
WADHURST,
East Sussex
TN5 7BR

IF YOU PREFER, YOU CAN SEND US REPORTS THROUGH OUR WEB SITE:
www.goodguides.co.uk

REPORT ON (PUB'S NAME)

Pub's address

☐ **YES** MAIN ENTRY ☐ **YES** LUCKY DIP ☐ **NO** DON'T INCLUDE

Please tick one of these boxes to show your verdict, and give reasons and descriptive comments, prices etc

☐ DESERVES **FOOD award** ☐ DESERVES **PLACE-TO-STAY award** 2005:1

PLEASE GIVE YOUR NAME AND ADDRESS ON THE BACK OF THIS FORM

REPORT ON (PUB'S NAME)

Pub's address

☐ **YES** MAIN ENTRY ☐ **YES** LUCKY DIP ☐ **NO** DON'T INCLUDE

Please tick one of these boxes to show your verdict, and give reasons and descriptive comments, prices etc

☐ DESERVES **FOOD award** ☐ DESERVES **PLACE-TO-STAY award** 2005:2

PLEASE GIVE YOUR NAME AND ADDRESS ON THE BACK OF THIS FORM

Your own name and address *(block capitals please)*

In returning this form I confirm my agreement that the information I provide may be used by The Random House Group Ltd, its assignees and/or licensees in any media or medium whatsoever.

DO NOT USE THIS SIDE OF THE PAGE FOR WRITING ABOUT PUBS

By returning this form, you consent to the collection, recording and use of the information you submit, by The Random House Group Ltd. Any personal details which you provide from which we can identify you are held and processed in accordance with the Data Protection Act 1998 and will not be passed on to any third parties. The Random House Group Ltd may wish to send you further information on their associated products. Please tick box if you do not wish to receive any such information. ☐

Your own name and address *(block capitals please)*

In returning this form I confirm my agreement that the information I provide may be used by The Random House Group Ltd, its assignees and/or licensees in any media or medium whatsoever.

DO NOT USE THIS SIDE OF THE PAGE FOR WRITING ABOUT PUBS

By returning this form, you consent to the collection, recording and use of the information you submit, by The Random House Group Ltd. Any personal details which you provide from which we can identify you are held and processed in accordance with the Data Protection Act 1998 and will not be passed on to any third parties. The Random House Group Ltd may wish to send you further information on their associated products. Please tick box if you do not wish to receive any such information. ☐

IF YOU PREFER, YOU CAN SEND US REPORTS THROUGH OUR WEB SITE:

www.goodguides.co.uk

REPORT ON (PUB'S NAME)

Pub's address

☐ **YES** MAIN ENTRY ☐ **YES** LUCKY DIP ☐ **NO** DON'T INCLUDE

Please tick one of these boxes to show your verdict, and give reasons and descriptive comments, prices etc

☐ DESERVES **FOOD award** ☐ DESERVES **PLACE-TO-STAY award** 2005:3

PLEASE GIVE YOUR NAME AND ADDRESS ON THE BACK OF THIS FORM

REPORT ON (PUB'S NAME)

Pub's address

☐ **YES** MAIN ENTRY ☐ **YES** LUCKY DIP ☐ **NO** DON'T INCLUDE

Please tick one of these boxes to show your verdict, and give reasons and descriptive comments, prices etc

☐ DESERVES **FOOD award** ☐ DESERVES **PLACE-TO-STAY award** 2005:4

PLEASE GIVE YOUR NAME AND ADDRESS ON THE BACK OF THIS FORM

Your own name and address *(block capitals please)*

In returning this form I confirm my agreement that the information I provide may be used by The Random House Group Ltd, its assignees and/or licensees in any media or medium whatsoever.

DO NOT USE THIS SIDE OF THE PAGE FOR WRITING ABOUT PUBS

By returning this form, you consent to the collection, recording and use of the information you submit, by The Random House Group Ltd. Any personal details which you provide from which we can identify you are held and processed in accordance with the Data Protection Act 1998 and will not be passed on to any third parties. The Random House Group Ltd may wish to send you further information on their associated products. Please tick box if you do not wish to receive any such information. ☐

Your own name and address *(block capitals please)*

In returning this form I confirm my agreement that the information I provide may be used by The Random House Group Ltd, its assignees and/or licensees in any media or medium whatsoever.

DO NOT USE THIS SIDE OF THE PAGE FOR WRITING ABOUT PUBS

By returning this form, you consent to the collection, recording and use of the information you submit, by The Random House Group Ltd. Any personal details which you provide from which we can identify you are held and processed in accordance with the Data Protection Act 1998 and will not be passed on to any third parties. The Random House Group Ltd may wish to send you further information on their associated products. Please tick box if you do not wish to receive any such information. ☐

IF YOU PREFER, YOU CAN SEND US REPORTS THROUGH OUR WEB SITE:

www.goodguides.co.uk

REPORT ON (PUB'S NAME)

Pub's address

☐ **YES** MAIN ENTRY ☐ **YES** LUCKY DIP ☐ **NO** DON'T INCLUDE

Please tick one of these boxes to show your verdict, and give reasons and descriptive comments, prices etc

☐ DESERVES **FOOD award** ☐ DESERVES **PLACE-TO-STAY award** 2005:5

PLEASE GIVE YOUR NAME AND ADDRESS ON THE BACK OF THIS FORM

REPORT ON (PUB'S NAME)

Pub's address

☐ **YES** MAIN ENTRY ☐ **YES** LUCKY DIP ☐ **NO** DON'T INCLUDE

Please tick one of these boxes to show your verdict, and give reasons and descriptive comments, prices etc

☐ DESERVES **FOOD award** ☐ DESERVES **PLACE-TO-STAY award** 2005:6

PLEASE GIVE YOUR NAME AND ADDRESS ON THE BACK OF THIS FORM

Your own name and address ***(block capitals please)***

In returning this form I confirm my agreement that the information I provide may be used by The Random House Group Ltd, its assignees and/or licensees in any media or medium whatsoever.

DO NOT USE THIS SIDE OF THE PAGE FOR WRITING ABOUT PUBS

By returning this form, you consent to the collection, recording and use of the information you submit, by The Random House Group Ltd. Any personal details which you provide from which we can identify you are held and processed in accordance with the Data Protection Act 1998 and will not be passed on to any third parties. The Random House Group Ltd may wish to send you further information on their associated products. Please tick box if you do not wish to receive any such information. ☐

Your own name and address ***(block capitals please)***

In returning this form I confirm my agreement that the information I provide may be used by The Random House Group Ltd, its assignees and/or licensees in any media or medium whatsoever.

DO NOT USE THIS SIDE OF THE PAGE FOR WRITING ABOUT PUBS

By returning this form, you consent to the collection, recording and use of the information you submit, by The Random House Group Ltd. Any personal details which you provide from which we can identify you are held and processed in accordance with the Data Protection Act 1998 and will not be passed on to any third parties. The Random House Group Ltd may wish to send you further information on their associated products. Please tick box if you do not wish to receive any such information. ☐

IF YOU PREFER, YOU CAN SEND US REPORTS THROUGH OUR WEB SITE:

www.goodguides.co.uk

REPORT ON (PUB'S NAME)

Pub's address

☐ **YES** MAIN ENTRY ☐ **YES** LUCKY DIP ☐ **NO** DON'T INCLUDE

Please tick one of these boxes to show your verdict, and give reasons and descriptive comments, prices etc

☐ DESERVES **FOOD award** ☐ DESERVES **PLACE-TO-STAY award** 2005:9

PLEASE GIVE YOUR NAME AND ADDRESS ON THE BACK OF THIS FORM

REPORT ON (PUB'S NAME)

Pub's address

☐ **YES** MAIN ENTRY ☐ **YES** LUCKY DIP ☐ **NO** DON'T INCLUDE

Please tick one of these boxes to show your verdict, and give reasons and descriptive comments, prices etc

☐ DESERVES **FOOD award** ☐ DESERVES **PLACE-TO-STAY award** 2005:10

PLEASE GIVE YOUR NAME AND ADDRESS ON THE BACK OF THIS FORM

Your own name and address *(block capitals please)*

In returning this form I confirm my agreement that the information I provide may be used by The Random House Group Ltd, its assignees and/or licensees in any media or medium whatsoever.

DO NOT USE THIS SIDE OF THE PAGE FOR WRITING ABOUT PUBS

By returning this form, you consent to the collection, recording and use of the information you submit, by The Random House Group Ltd. Any personal details which you provide from which we can identify you are held and processed in accordance with the Data Protection Act 1998 and will not be passed on to any third parties. The Random House Group Ltd may wish to send you further information on their associated products. Please tick box if you do not wish to receive any such information. ☐

Your own name and address *(block capitals please)*

In returning this form I confirm my agreement that the information I provide may be used by The Random House Group Ltd, its assignees and/or licensees in any media or medium whatsoever.

DO NOT USE THIS SIDE OF THE PAGE FOR WRITING ABOUT PUBS

By returning this form, you consent to the collection, recording and use of the information you submit, by The Random House Group Ltd. Any personal details which you provide from which we can identify you are held and processed in accordance with the Data Protection Act 1998 and will not be passed on to any third parties. The Random House Group Ltd may wish to send you further information on their associated products. Please tick box if you do not wish to receive any such information. ☐

IF YOU PREFER, YOU CAN SEND US REPORTS THROUGH OUR WEB SITE:

www.goodguides.co.uk